99TH ANNUAL EDITION

WRITER'S MARKET

2020

Robert Lee Brewer, Editor

www.penguinrandomhouse.com

Library of Congress Catalog Number 31-20772
ISSN: 0084-2729
ISBN-13: 978-1-44030-122-3
ISBN-10: 1-44030-122-0

Edited by: Robert Lee Brewer
Designed by: Wendy Dunning

CONTENTS

MARKETS

RESOURCES

INDEXES

FROM THE EDITOR

Believe it or not, this is my 20th edition working on *Writer's Market*, which seems kind of impossible since it feels like just yesterday that I purchased my first copy of the book...in 1996! But I guess that's how time works.

So much has changed in the publishing industry over the past two decades, but so much has also stayed the same. For instance, *Writer's Market* is still devoted to the same goal it had when I started: Help writers get published and get paid for their writing. That's what this book has always been about, and this edition is no different.

Inside this book, you'll find the ever popular "How Much Should I Charge?" freelance pay rate chart. You'll also find a brand new list of "20 Literary Agents" actively searching for writers and their writing. But most importantly, you'll find thousands of listings for literary agents, consumer magazines, trade journals, book publishers, contests, and more!

Our goal has remained the same, because we know your goal has remained the same, even if the platforms, the submission methods, trends, and fads have all evolved: It's always been about getting published and getting paid for what you write. So let's keep changing and staying the same.

Until next we meet, keep writing and marketing what you write.

Robert Lee Brewer
Senior Editor
Writer's Market and WritersMarket.com
http://writersdigest.com/publishing-insights
http://twitter.com/robertleebrewer

HOW TO USE WRITER'S MARKET

Writer's Market is here to help you decide where and how to submit your writing to appropriate markets. Each listing contains information about the editorial focus of the market, how it prefers material to be submitted, payment information, and other helpful tips.

WHAT'S INSIDE?

Since 1921, *Writer's Market* has been giving you the information you need to knowledgeably approach a market. We've continued to develop improvements to help you access that information more efficiently.

NAVIGATIONAL TOOLS. We've designed the pages of *Writer's Market* with you, the writer, in mind. Within the pages you will find **readable market listings** and **accessible charts and graphs.** One such chart can be found in the ever-popular "How Much Should I Charge?" article.

We've taken all of the updated information in this feature and put it into an easy-to-read-and-navigate chart, making it convenient for you to find the rates that accompany the freelance jobs you're seeking.

ICONS. There are a variety of icons that appear before each listing. A complete Key to Icons & Abbreviations appears on the right. Icons let you know whether a book publisher accepts only agented writers (Ⓐ), comparative pay rates for a magazine ($-$$$$), and more.

CONTACT NAMES, ROYALTY RATES AND ADVANCES. In every section, we identify key contact people with the boldface word **Contact** to help you get your manuscript to the right person.

EDITORS, PAY RATES, ROYALTIES, ADVANCES, AND PERCENTAGE OF MATERIAL WRITTEN BY FREELANCE WRITERS. For Book Publishers, royalty rates and advances are highlighted in boldface, as is other important information on the percentage of first-time writers and unagented writers the company publishes, the number of books published, and the number of manuscripts received each year. In the Consumer Magazines and Trade Journals sections, we identify the amount (percentage) of material accepted from freelance writers, and the pay rates for features, columns and departments, and fillers in boldface to help you quickly identify the information you need to know when considering whether to submit your work.

QUERY FORMATS. We asked editors how they prefer to receive queries and have indicated in the listings whether they prefer them by mail, e-mail, fax or phone. Be sure to check an editor's individual preference before sending your query.

ARTICLES. Writers who want to improve their submission techniques should read the articles in the **Finding Work** section. The **Managing Work** section is geared more toward post-acceptance topics, such as contract negotiation, organization, and self-promotion.

IF THIS BOOK IS NEW TO YOU . . .

Look at the **Contents** pages to familiarize yourself with the arrangement of *Writer's Market*. The three largest sections of the book are the market listings of Book Publishers; Consumer Magazines; and Trade Journals. You will also find other sections of market listings for Literary Agents and Contests & Awards.

KEY TO ICONS & ABBREVIATIONS

- Ⓐ market accepts agented submissions only
- ⊘ market does not accept unsolicited submissions
- (maple leaf icon) Canadian market
- (arrow icon) market located outside of the U.S. and Canada
- $ market pays 0-9¢/word or $0-$150/article
- $$ market pays 10-49¢/word or $151-$750/article
- $$$ market pays 50-99¢/word or $751-$1,500/article
- $$$$ market pays $1/word or over $1,500/article
- (speech bubble icon) comment from the editor of Writer's Market
- (key icon) tips to break into a specific market
- **MS, MSS** manuscript(s)
- **B&W** black & white (photo)
- **SASE** self-addressed, stamped envelope
- **SAE** self-addressed envelope
- **IRC** International Reply Coupon, for use when mailing to countries other than your own

IMPORTANT LISTING INFORMATION

1. Listings are based on editorial questionnaires and interviews. They are not advertisements; publishers do not pay for their listings. The markets are not endorsed by *Writer's Market* editors. Writer's Digest Books and its employees go to great effort to ascertain the validity of information in this book. However, transactions between users of the information and individuals and/or companies are strictly between those parties.
2. All listings have been verified before publication of this book. If a listing has not changed from last year, then the editor said the market's needs have not changed and the previous listing continues to accurately reflect its policies.
3. *Writer's Market* reserves the right to exclude any listing.
4. When looking for a specific market, check the index. A market may not be listed for one of these reasons:
   - It doesn't solicit freelance material.
   - It doesn't pay for material.
   - It has gone out of business.
   - It has failed to verify or update its listing for this edition.
   - It hasn't answered *Writer's Market* inquiries satisfactorily.

Narrowing your search

After you've identified the market categories that interest you, you can begin researching specific markets within each section.

Consumer Magazines and Trade Journals are categorized by subject within their respective sections to make it easier for you to identify markets for your work.

There is a subject index available for Book Publishers in the back of the book. It is broken into fiction and nonfiction categories and subcategories.

Contests & Awards are categorized by genre of writing. If you want to find journalism contests, you would search the Journalism category; if you have an unpublished novel, check the Fiction category.

Interpreting the markets

Once you've identified companies or publications that cover the subjects in which you're interested, you can begin evaluating specific listings to pinpoint the markets most receptive to your work and most beneficial to you.

In evaluating individual listings, check the location of the company, the types of material it is interested in seeing, submission requirements, and rights and payment policies. Depending on your personal concerns, any of these items could be a deciding factor as you determine which markets you plan to approach. Many listings also include a reporting time.

Whenever possible, obtain submission guidelines before submitting material. You can usually obtain guidelines by sending a SASE to the address in the listing or by checking online. Many of the listings contain instructions on how to obtain sample copies, catalogs or market lists. The more research you do upfront, the better your chances of acceptance, publication and payment.

BEFORE YOUR FIRST SALE

Everything in life has to start somewhere and that somewhere is always at the beginning. Stephen King, Stephenie Meyer, Jeff Kinney, Nora Roberts—they all had to start at the beginning. It would be great to say becoming a writer is as easy as waving a magic wand over your manuscript and "Poof!" you're published, but that's not how it happens. While there's no one true "key" to becoming successful, a long, well-paid writing career *can* happen when you combine four elements:

- Good writing
- Knowledge of writing markets
- Professionalism
- Persistence

Good writing is useless if you don't know which markets will buy your work or how to pitch and sell your writing. If you aren't professional and persistent in your contact with editors, your writing is just that—your writing. But if you are a writer who embraces the above four elements, you have a good chance at becoming a paid, published writer who will reap the benefits of a long and successful career.

As you become more involved with writing, you may read articles or talk to editors and authors with conflicting opinions about the right way to submit your work. The truth is, there are many different routes a writer can follow to get published, but no matter which route you choose, the end is always the same—becoming a published writer.

The following advice on submissions has worked for many writers, but it is by no means the be-all-end-all of proper submission guidelines. It's very easy to get wrapped up in the specifics of submitting (Should I put my last name on every page of my manuscript?) and ignore the more important issues (Will this idea on ice fishing in Alaska be appropriate for a regional magazine in Seattle?). Don't allow yourself to become so blinded by submission procedures that you forget common sense. If you use your common sense and develop professional, courteous relations with editors, you will eventually find your own submission style.

DEVELOP YOUR IDEAS, THEN TARGET THE MARKETS

Writers often think of an interesting story, complete the manuscript, and then begin the search for a suitable publisher or magazine. While this approach is common for fiction, poetry and screenwriting, it reduces your chances of success in many nonfiction writing areas. Instead, choose categories that interest you and study those sections in *Writer's Market*. Select several listings you consider good prospects for your type of writing. Sometimes the individual listings will even help you generate ideas.

Next, make a list of the potential markets for each idea. Make the initial contact with markets using the method stated in the market listings. If you exhaust your list of possibilities, don't give up. Instead, reevaluate the idea or try another angle. Continue developing ideas and approaching markets. Identify and rank potential markets for an idea and continue the process.

As you submit to the various publications listed in *Writer's Market*, it's important to remember that every magazine is published with a particular audience and slant in mind. Probably the number one complaint we receive from editors is the submissions they receive are completely wrong for their magazines or book line. The first mark of professionalism is to know your market well. Gaining that knowledge starts with *Writer's Market*, but you should also do your own detective work. Search out back issues of the magazines you wish to write for, pick up recent issues at your local newsstand, or visit magazines' websites—anything that will help you figure out what subjects specific magazines publish. This research is also helpful in learning what topics have been covered ad nauseum—the topics you should stay away from or approach in a fresh way. Magazines' websites are invaluable as most post the current issue of the magazine, as well as back issues, and most offer writer's guidelines.

The same advice is true for submitting to book publishers. Research publisher websites for their submission guidelines, recently published titles and their backlist. You can use this information to target your book proposal in a way that fits with a publisher's other titles while not directly competing for sales.

Prepare for rejection and the sometimes lengthy wait. When a submission is returned, check your file folder of potential markets for that idea. Cross off the market that rejected the idea. If the editor has given you suggestions or reasons why the manuscript was not accepted, you might want to incorporate these suggestions when revising your manuscript.

After revising your manuscript mail it to the next market on your list.

Take rejection with a grain of salt

Rejection is a way of life in the publishing world. It's inevitable in a business that deals with such an overwhelming number of applicants for such a limited number of positions. Anyone who has published has lived through many rejections, and writers with thin skin are at a distinct disadvantage. A rejection letter is not a personal attack. It simply indicates your submission is not appropriate for that market. Writers who let rejection dissuade them from pursuing their dream or who react to an editor's "No" with indignation or fury do themselves a disservice. Writers who let rejection stop them do not get published. Resign yourself to facing rejection now. You will live through it, and you'll eventually overcome it.

QUERY AND COVER LETTERS

A query letter is a brief, one-page letter used as a tool to hook an editor and get him interested in your idea. When you send a query letter to a magazine, you are trying to get an editor to buy your idea or article. When you query a book publisher, you are attempting to get an editor interested enough in your idea to request your book proposal or your entire manuscript. (Note: Some book editors prefer to receive book proposals on first contact. Check individual listings for which method editors prefer.)

Here are some basic guidelines to help you create a query that's polished and well-organized. For more tips see "Query Letter Clinic" article.

- **LIMIT IT TO ONE PAGE, SINGLE-SPACED**, and address the editor by name (Mr. or Ms. and the surname). *Note*: Do not assume that a person is a Mr. or Ms. unless it is obvious from the name listed. For example, if you are contacting a D.J. Smith, do not assume that D.J. should be preceded by Mr. or Ms. Instead, address the letter to D.J. Smith.
- **GRAB THE EDITOR'S ATTENTION WITH A STRONG OPENING.** Some magazine queries, for example, begin with a paragraph meant to approximate the lead of the intended article.
- **INDICATE HOW YOU INTEND TO DEVELOP THE ARTICLE OR BOOK.** Give the editor some idea of the work's structure and content.
- **LET THE EDITOR KNOW IF YOU HAVE PHOTOS** or illustrations available to accompany your magazine article.
- **MENTION ANY EXPERTISE OR TRAINING THAT QUALIFIES YOU** to write the article or book. If you've been published before, mention it; if not, don't.
- **END WITH A DIRECT REQUEST TO WRITE THE ARTICLE.** Or, if you're pitching a book, ask for the go-ahead to send in a full proposal or the entire manuscript. Give the editor an idea of the expected length and delivery date of your manuscript.

A common question that arises is: If I don't hear from an editor in the reported response time, how do I know when I can safely send the query to another market? Many writers find it helpful to indicate in their queries that if they don't receive a response from the editor (slightly after the listed reporting time), they will assume the editor is not interested. It's best to take this approach, particularly if your topic is timely.

QUERY LETTER RESOURCES

The following list of books provides you with more detailed information on writing query letters, cover letters, and book proposals. All titles are published by Writer's Digest Books.

- *Formatting & Submitting Your Manuscript*, 3rd Edition, by Chuck Sambuchino
- *How to Write Attention-Grabbing Query & Cover Letters*, by John Wood
- *How to Write a Book Proposal*, 5th Edition, by Michael Larsen
- *Writer's Market Companion*, 2nd Edition, by Joe Feiertag and Mary Cupito

A brief, single-spaced cover letter is helpful when sending a manuscript as it helps personalize the submission. However, if you have previously queried the editor, use the cover letter to politely and briefly remind the editor of that query—when it was sent, what it contained, etc. "Here is the piece on low-fat cooking that I queried you about on December 12. I look forward to hearing from you at your earliest convenience." Do not use the cover letter as a sales pitch.

If you are submitting to a market that accepts unsolicited manuscripts, a cover letter is useful because it personalizes your submission. You can, and should, include information about the manuscript, yourself, your publishing history, and your qualifications.

In addition to tips on writing queries, the "Query Letter Clinic" article offers eight example query letters, some that work and some that don't, as well as comments on why the letters were either successful or failed to garner an assignment or contract.

Querying for fiction

Fiction is sometimes queried, but more often editors prefer receiving material. Many fiction editors won't decide on a submission until they have seen the complete manuscript. When submitting a fiction book idea, most editors prefer to see at least a synopsis and sample chapters (usually the first three). For fiction published in magazines, most editors want to see the complete short story manuscript. If an editor does request a query for fiction, it should include a description of the main theme and story line, including the conflict and resolution. Take a look at individual listings to see what editors prefer to receive.

THE SYNOPSIS

Most fiction books are sold by a complete manuscript, but most editors and agents don't have the time to read a complete manuscript of every wannabe writer. As a result, publishing decision-makers use the synopsis and sample chapters to help the screening process of fiction. The synopsis, on its most basic level, communicates what the book is about.

The length and depth of a synopsis can change from agent to agent or publisher to publisher. Some will want a synopsis that is one to two single-spaced pages; others will want a synopsis that can run up to 25 double-spaced pages. Checking your listings in *Writer's Market*, as well as double-checking with the listing's website, will help guide you in this respect.

The content should cover all the essential points of the novel from beginning to end and in the correct order. The essential points include main characters, main plot points, and, yes, the ending. Of course, your essential points will vary from the editor who wants a one-page synopsis to the editor who wants a 25-page synopsis.

NONFICTION PROPOSALS

Most nonfiction books are sold by a book proposal—a package of materials that details what your book is about, who its intended audience is, and how you intend to write the book. It includes some combination of a cover or query letter, an overview, an outline, author's information sheet, and sample chapters. Editors also want to see information about the audience for your book and about titles that compete with your proposed book.

Submitting nonfiction proposals

A proposal package should include the following items:

- **A COVER OR QUERY LETTER.** This letter should be a short introduction to the material you include in the proposal.
- **AN OVERVIEW.** This is a brief summary of your book. It should detail your book's subject and give an idea of how that subject will be developed.
- **AN OUTLINE.** The outline covers your book chapter by chapter and should include all major points covered in each chapter. Some outlines are done in traditional outline form, but most are written in paragraph form.
- **AN AUTHOR'S INFORMATION SHEET.** This information should acquaint the editor with your writing background and convince her of your qualifications regarding the subject of your book.
- **SAMPLE CHAPTERS.** Many editors like to see sample chapters, especially for a first book. Sample chapters show the editor how you write and develop ideas from your outline.
- **MARKETING INFORMATION.** Facts about how and to whom your book can be successfully marketed are now expected to accompany every book proposal. If you can

provide information about the audience for your book and suggest ways the book publisher can reach those people, you will increase your chances of acceptance.

- **COMPETITIVE TITLE ANALYSIS.** Check the *Subject Guide to Books in Print* for other titles on your topic. Write a one- or two-sentence synopsis of each. Point out how your book differs and improves upon existing topics.

For more information on nonfiction book proposals, read Michael Larsen's *How to Write a Book Proposal* (Writer's Digest Books).

A WORD ABOUT AGENTS

An agent represents a writer's work to publishers, negotiates contracts, follows up to see that contracts are fulfilled, and generally handles a writer's business affairs, leaving the writer free to write. Effective agents are valued for their contacts in the publishing industry, their knowledge about who to approach with certain ideas, their ability to guide an author's career, and their business sense.

While most book publishers listed in *Writer's Market* publish books by unagented writers, some of the larger houses are reluctant to consider submissions that have not reached them through a literary agent. Companies with such a policy are noted by an (Ⓐ) icon at the beginning of the listing, as well as in the submission information within the listing.

Writer's Market includes a list of literary agents who are all members of the Association of Authors' Representatives and who are also actively seeking new and established writers.

MANUSCRIPT FORMAT

You can increase your chances of publication by following a few standard guidelines regarding the physical format of your manuscript. It should be your goal to make your manuscript readable. Follow these suggestions as you would any other suggestions: Use what works for you and discard what doesn't.

In general, when submitting a manuscript, you should use white, 8½×11, 20 lb. paper, and you should also choose a legible, professional looking font (i.e., Times New Roman)—no all-italic or artsy fonts. Your entire manuscript should be double-spaced with a 1½-inch margin on all sides of the page. Once you are ready to print your manuscript, you should print either on a laser printer or an ink-jet printer.

ESTIMATING WORD COUNT

All computers provide you with a word count of your manuscript. Your editor will count again after editing the manuscript. Although your computer is counting characters, an editor or production editor is more concerned about the amount of space the text will

MANUSCRIPT FORMATTING SAMPLE

❶ Your Name   50,000 Words ❸
Your Street Address
City State ZIP Code
Day and Evening Phone Numbers
E-mail Address
Website (if applicable)

❷

TITLE

by

❹ Your Name

❺ You can increase your chances of publication by following a few standard guidelines regarding the physical format of your article or manuscript. It should be your goal to make your manuscript readable. Use these suggestions as you would any other suggestions: Use what works for you and discard what doesn't.

In general, when submitting a manuscript, you should use white, 8½×11, 20-lb. bond paper, and you should also choose a legible, professional-looking font (i.e., Times New Roman)—no all-italic or artsy fonts. Your entire manuscript should be double-spaced with a 1½-inch margin on all sides of the page. Once you are ready to print your article or manuscript, you should print either on a laser printer or an ink-jet printer.

Remember, articles should be written after you send a one-page query letter to an editor, and the editor then asks you to write the article. If, however, you are sending an article "on spec" to an editor, you should send both a query letter and the complete article.

Fiction and poetry is a little different from nonfiction articles, in that it is rarely queried. More often than not, poetry and fiction editors want to review the complete manuscript before making a final decision.

① Type your real name (even if you use a pseudonym) and contact information ② Double-space twice ③ Estimated word count ④ Type your title in capital letters, double-space and type "by," double-space again, and type your name (or pseudonym if you're using one) ⑤ Double-space twice, then indent first paragraph and start text of your manuscript ⑥ On subsequent pages, type your name, a dash, and the page number in the upper left or right corner occupy on a page. Several small headlines or subheads, for instance, will be counted the same by your computer as any other word of text. However, headlines and subheads usually employ a different font size than the body text, so an editor may count them differently to be sure enough space has been estimated for larger type.

For short manuscripts, it's often quickest to count each word on a representative page and multiply by the number of pages. You can get a very rough count by multiplying the number of pages in your manuscript by 250 (the average number of words on a double-spaced typewritten page).

PHOTOGRAPHS AND SLIDES

In some cases, the availability of photographs and slides can be the deciding factor as to whether an editor will accept your submission. This is especially true when querying a publication that relies heavily on photographs, illustrations or artwork to enhance the article (e.g., craft magazines, hobby magazines, etc.). In some instances, the publication may offer additional payment for photographs or illustrations.

Check the individual listings to find out which magazines review photographs and what their submission guidelines are. Most publications prefer you do not send photographs with your submission. However, if photographs or illustrations are available, you should indicate that in your query. As with manuscripts, never send the originals of your photographs or illustrations. Instead, send digital images, which is what most magazine and book publishers prefer to use.

SEND PHOTOCOPIES

If there is one hard-and-fast rule in publishing, it's this: *Never* send the original (or only) copy of your manuscript. Most editors cringe when they find out a writer has sent the only copy of their manuscript. You should always send copies of your manuscript.

Some writers choose to send a self-addressed, stamped postcard with a photocopied submission. In their cover letter they suggest if the editor is not interested in their manuscript, it may be tossed out and a reply sent on the postcard. This method is particularly helpful when sending your submissions to international markets.

MAILING SUBMISSIONS

No matter what size manuscript you're mailing, always include a self-addressed, stamped envelope (SASE) with sufficient return postage. The website for the U.S. Postal Service (www.usps.com) and the website for the Canadian Post (www.canadapost.ca) both have postage calculators if you are unsure how much postage to affix.

A book manuscript should be mailed in a sturdy, well-wrapped box. Enclose a self-addressed mailing label and paper clip your return postage to the label. However, be aware that some book publishers do not return unsolicited manuscripts, so make sure you know the practice of the publisher before sending any unsolicited material.

Types of mail service

There are many different mailing service options available to you whether you are sending a query letter or a complete manuscript. You can work with the U.S. Postal Service, United Parcel Service, Federal Express, or any number of private mailing companies. The following are the five most common types of mailing services offered by the U.S. Postal Service.

- **FIRST CLASS** is a fairly expensive way to mail a manuscript, but many writers prefer it. First-Class mail generally receives better handling and is delivered more quickly than Standard mail.
- **PRIORITY MAIL** reaches its destination within two or three days.
- **STANDARD MAIL** rates are available for packages, but be sure to pack your materials carefully because they will be handled roughly. To make sure your package will be returned to you if it is undeliverable, print "Return Postage Guaranteed" under your address.
- **CERTIFIED MAIL** must be signed for when it reaches its destination.
- **REGISTERED MAIL** is a high-security method of mailing where the contents are insured. The package is signed in and out of every office it passes through, and a receipt is returned to the sender when the package reaches its destination.

MAILING MANUSCRIPTS

- Fold manuscripts under five pages into thirds, and send in a #10 SASE.
- Mail manuscripts five pages or more unfolded in a 9×12 or 10×13 SASE.
- For return envelope, fold the envelope in half, address it to yourself, and add a stamp, or, if going to Canada or another international destination, International Reply Coupons (available at most post office branches).
- Don't send by Certified Mail—this is a sign of an amateur.

QUERY LETTER CLINIC

Many great writers ask year after year, "Why is it so hard to get published?" In many cases, these writers have spent years developing their craft. They submit to the appropriate markets, yet rejection is always the end result. The culprit? A weak query letter.

The query letter is often the most important piece of the publishing puzzle. In many cases, it determines whether editors or agents will even read your manuscript. A good query makes a good first impression; a bad query earns a swift rejection.

ELEMENTS OF A QUERY

A query letter should sell editors or agents on your idea or convince them to request your finished manuscript. The most effective query letters get into the specifics from the very first line. It's important to remember that the query is a call to action, not a listing of features and benefits.

In addition to selling your idea or manuscript, a query can include information on the availability of photographs or artwork. You can include a working title and projected word count. Depending on the piece, you might also mention whether a sidebar might be appropriate and the type of research you plan to conduct. If appropriate, include a tentative deadline and indicate whether the query is being simultaneously submitted.

Biographical information should be included as well, but don't overdo it unless your background actually helps sell the article or proves that you're the only person who could write your proposed piece.

THINGS TO AVOID IN QUERY

The query is not a place to discuss pay rates. This step comes after an editor has agreed to take on your article or book. Besides making an unprofessional impression, it can also work to your disadvantage in negotiating your fee. If you ask too much, an editor may not even contact you to see if a lower rate works. If you ask for too little, you may start an editorial relationship where you make less than the normal rate.

You should also avoid rookie mistakes, such as mentioning your work is copyrighted or including the copyright symbol on your work. While you want to make it clear that you've researched the market, avoid using flattery as a technique for selling your work. It often has the opposite effect of what you intend. In addition, don't hint that you can re-write the piece, as this only leads the editor to think there will be a lot of work involved in shaping up your writing.

Also, never admit several other editors or agents have rejected the query. Always treat your new audience as if they are the first place on your list.

HOW TO FORMAT A QUERY

It's OK to break writing rules in a short story or article, but you should follow the rules when it comes to crafting an effective query. Here are guidelines for query writing.

- Use a normal font and typeface, such as Courier and 10- or 12-point type.
- Include your name, address, phone number, e-mail address and website.
- Use one-inch margin on paper queries.
- Address a specific editor or agent. (Note: It's wise to double-check contact names online or by calling.)
- Limit query to one single-spaced page.
- Include self-addressed, stamped envelope or postcard for response with post submissions.

HOW TO FOLLOW UP

Accidents do happen. Queries may not reach your intended reader. Staff changes or interoffice mail snafus may end up with your query letter thrown away. Or the editor may have set your query off to the side for further consideration and forgotten it. Whatever the case may be, there are some basic guidelines you should use for your follow-up communication.

Most importantly, wait until the reported response time, as indicated in *Writer's Market* or their submission guidelines, has elapsed before contacting an editor or agent. Then, you should send a short and polite e-mail describing the original query sent, the date it was sent, and asking if they received it or made a decision regarding its fate.

The importance of remaining polite and businesslike when following up cannot be stressed enough. Making a bad impression on an editor can often have a ripple effect—as that editor may share his or her bad experience with other editors at the magazine or publishing company. Also, don't call.

HOW THE CLINIC WORKS

As mentioned earlier, the query letter is the most important weapon for getting an assignment or a request for your full manuscript. Published writers know how to craft a well-written, hard-hitting query. What follows are eight queries: four are strong; four are not. Detailed comments show what worked and what did not. As you'll see, there is no cut-and-dried "good" query format; every strong query works on its own merit.

GOOD NONFICTION MAGAZINE QUERY

Jimmy Boaz, editor
American Organic Farmer's Digest
8336 Old Dirt Road
Macon GA 00000

Dear Mr. Boaz, (1)

There are 87 varieties of organic crops grown in the United States, but there's only one farm producing 12 of these—Morganic Corporation.

Located in the heart of Arkansas, this company spent the past decade providing great organic crops at a competitive price helping them grow into the ninth leading organic farming operation in the country. Along the way, they developed the most unique organic offering in North America.

As a seasoned writer with access to Richard Banks, the founder and president of Morganic, I propose writing a profile piece on Banks for your Organic Shakers department. After years of reading this riveting column, I believe the time has come to cover Morganic's rise in the organic farming industry. (3)

This piece would run in the normal 800-1,200 word range with photographs available of Banks and Morganic's operation.

I've been published in *Arkansas Farmer's Deluxe, Organic Farming Today* and in several newspapers. (4)

Thank you for your consideration of this article. I hope to hear from you soon.

Sincerely,

Jackie Service
34 Good St.
Little Rock AR 00000
jackie.service9867@email.com

(1) My name is only available on our magazine's website and on the masthead. This writer has done her research. (2) Here's a story that hasn't been pitched before. I didn't know Morganic was so unique in the market. I want to know more. (3) The writer has access to her interview subject, and she displays knowledge of the magazine by pointing out the correct section in which her piece would run. (4) While I probably would've assigned this article based on the idea alone, her past credits do help solidify my decision.

BAD NONFICTION MAGAZINE QUERY

Dear Gentlemen, (1)

I'd like to write the next great article you'll ever publish. My writing credits include amazing pieces I've done for local and community newspapers and for my college English classes. I've been writing for years and years. (2)

Your magazine may not be a big one like *Rolling Stone* or *Sports Illustrated*, but I'm willing to write an interview for you anyway. I know you need material, and I need money. (Don't worry. I won't charge you too much.) (3)

Just give me some people to interview, and I'll do the best job you've ever read. It will be amazing, and I can re-write the piece for you if you don't agree. I'm willing to re-write 20 times if needed. (4)

You better hurry up and assign me an article though, because I've sent out letters to lots of other magazines, and I'm sure to be filled up to capacity very soon. (5)

Later gents,

Carl Bighead
76 Bad Query Lane
Big City NY 00000

(1) This is sexist, and it doesn't address any contact specifically. (2) An over-the-top claim by a writer who does not impress me with his publishing background. (3) Insults the magazine and then reassures me he won't charge too much? (4) While I do assign material from time to time, I prefer writers pitch me their own ideas after studying the magazine. (5) I'm sure people aren't going to be knocking down his door anytime soon.

GOOD FICTION MAGAZINE QUERY

Marcus West
88 Piano Drive
Lexington KY 00000

August 8, 2011 ❶

Jeanette Curic, editor
Wonder Stories
45 Noodle Street
Portland OR 00000

Dear Ms. Curic,

Please consider the following 1,200-word story, "Turning to the Melon," a quirky coming-of-age story with a little magical realism thrown in the mix. ❷

After reading *Wonder Stories* for years, I think I've finally written something that would fit with your audience. My previous short story credits include *Stunned Fiction Quarterly* and *Faulty Mindbomb.* ❸

Thank you in advance for considering "Turning to Melon."

Sincerely,

Marcus West
(123) 456-7890
marcusw87452@email.com

Encl: Manuscript and SASE ❹

❶ Follows the format we established in our guidelines. Being able to follow directions is more important than many writers realize. ❷ Story is in our word count, and the description sounds like the type of story we would consider publishing. It's flattering to know he reads our magazine. While it won't guarantee publication, it does make me a little more hopeful that the story I'm reading will be a good fit. Also, good to know he's been published before. ❹ I can figure it out, but it's nice to know what other materials were included in the envelope. This letter is not flashy, but it gives me the basics and puts me in the right frame of mind to read the actual story.

BAD FICTION MAGAZINE QUERY

To: curic@wonderstories808.com (1)
Subject: A Towering Epic Fantasy

Hello there. (2)

I've written a great fantasy epic novel short story of about 25,000 words that may be included in your magazine if you so desire. (3)

More than 20 years, I've spent chained to my desk in a basement writing out the greatest story of our modern time. And it can be yours if you so desire to have it. (4)

Just say the word, and I'll ship it over to you. We can talk money and movie rights after your acceptance. I have big plans for this story, and you can be part of that success. (5)

Yours forever (if you so desire), (6)

Harold
(or Harry for friends)

(1) We do not consider e-mail queries or submissions. (2) This is a little too informal. (3) First off, what did he write? An epic novel or short story? Second, 25,000 words is way over our 1,500-word max. (4) I'm lost for words. (5) Money and movie rights? We pay moderate rates and definitely don't get involved in movies. (6) I'm sure the writer was just trying to be nice, but this is a little bizarre and kind of creepy. I do not so desire more contact with "Harry."

GOOD NONFICTION BOOK QUERY

To: corey@bigbookspublishing.com
Subject: Query: Become a Better Parent in 30 Days (1)

Dear Mr. Corey,

(2) As a parent of six and a high school teacher for more than 20 years, I know first hand that being a parent is difficult work. Even harder is being a good parent. My proposed title, (3) *Taking Care of Yourself and Your Kids: A 30-day Program to Become a Better Parent While Still Living Your Life*, would show how to handle real-life situations and still be a good parent.

This book has been years in the making, as it follows the outline I've used successfully in my summer seminars I give on the topic to thousands of parents every year. It really works, because past participants contact me constantly to let me know what a difference my classes have made in their lives. (4)

In addition to marketing and selling *Taking Care of Yourself and Your Kids* at my summer seminars, I would also be able to sell it through my website and promote it through my weekly e-newsletter with over 25,000 subscribers. Of course, it would also make a very nice trade title that I think would sell well in bookstores and possibly retail outlets, such as Wal-Mart and Target. (5)

Please contact me for a copy of my full book proposal today. (6)

Thank you for your consideration.

Marilyn Parent
8647 Query St.
Norman OK 00000
mparent8647@email.com
www.marilynsbetterparents.com

(1) Effective subject line. Lets me know exactly what to expect when I open the e-mail. (2) Good lead. Six kids and teaches high school. I already trust her as an expert. (3) Nice title that would fit well with others we currently offer. (4) Her platform as a speaker definitely gets my attention. (5) 25,000 e-mail subscribers? She must have a very good voice to gather that many readers. (6) I was interested after the first paragraph, but every paragraph after made it impossible to not request her proposal.

BAD NONFICTION BOOK QUERY

To: info@bigbookspublishing.com
Subject: a question for you (1)

I really liked this book by Mega Book Publishers called *Build Better Trains in Your Own Backyard.* It was a great book that covered all the basics of model train building. My father and I would read from it together and assemble all the pieces, and it was magical like Christmas all through the year. Why wouldn't you want to publish such a book? (2)

Well, here it is. I've already copyrighted the material for 2006 and can help you promote it if you want to send me on a worldwide book tour. As you can see from my attached digital photo, I'm not the prettiest person, but I am passionate. (3)

There are at least 1,000 model train builders in the United States alone, and there might be even more than that. I haven't done enough research yet, because I don't know if this is an idea that appeals to you. If you give me maybe $500, I could do that research in a day and get back to you on it. (4)

Anyway, this idea is a good one that brings back lots of memories for me.

Jacob (5)

(1) The subject line is so vague I almost deleted this e-mail as spam without even opening it. (2) The reason we don't publish such a book is easy—we don't do hobby titles. (3) I'm not going to open an attachment from an unknown sender via e-mail. Also, copyrighting your work years before pitching is the sign of an amateur. (4) 1,000 possible buyers is a small market, and I'm not going to pay a writer to do research on a proposal. (5) Not even a last name? Or contact information? At least I won't feel guilty for not responding.

GOOD FICTION BOOK QUERY

Jeremy Mansfield, editor
Novels R Us Publishing
8787 Big Time Street
New York NY 00000

Dear Mr. Mansfield,

My 62,000-word novel, *The Cat Walk*, is a psychologically complex thriller in the same mold as James Patterson's Alex Cross novels, but with a touch of the supernatural a la Stephenie Meyer. ❶

Rebecca Frank is at the top of the modeling world, posing for magazines in exotic locales all over the world and living life to its fullest. Despite all her success, she feels something is missing in her life. Then she runs into Marcus Hunt, a wealthy bachelor with cold blue eyes and an ambiguous past.

Within 24 hours of meeting Marcus, Rebecca's understanding of the world turns upside down, and she finds herself fighting for her life and the love of a man who may not have the ability to return her the favor.

Filled with demons, serial killers, trolls, maniacal clowns and more, *The Cat Walk* follows Rebecca through a gauntlet of trouble and turmoil, leading up to a final climactic realization that may lead to her own unraveling. ❷

The Cat Walk should fit in well with your other titles, such as *Bone Dead* and *Carry Me Home*, though it is a unique story. Your website mentioned supernatural suspense as a current interest, so I hope this is a good match. ❸

My short fiction has appeared in many mystery magazines, including a prize-winning story in *The Mysterious Oregon Quarterly*. This novel is the first in a series that I'm working on (already half-way through the second). ❹

As stated in your guidelines, I've included the first 30 pages. Thank you for considering *The Cat Walk*.

Sincerely,

Merry Plentiful
54 Willow Road
East Lansing MI 00000
merry865423@email.com

❶ Novel is correct length and has the suspense and supernatural elements we're seeking. ❷ The quick summary sounds like something we would write on the back cover of our paperbacks. That's a good thing, because it identifies the triggers that draw a response out of our readers. ❸ She mentions similar titles we've done and that she's done research on our website. She's not afraid to put in a little extra effort. ❹ At the moment, I'm not terribly concerned that this book could become a series, but it is something good to file away in the back of my mind for future use.

BAD FICTION BOOK QUERY

Jeremy Mansfield
Novels R Us Publishing
8787 Big Time Street
New York NY 00000

Dear Editor,

My novel has an amazing twist ending that could make it a worldwide phenomenon overnight while you are sleeping. It has spectacular special effects that will probably lead to a multi-million dollar movie deal that will also spawn action figures, lunch boxes, and several other crazy subsidiary rights. I mean, we're talking big-time money here. (1)

I'm not going to share the twist until I have a signed contract that authorizes me to a big bank account, because I don't want to have my idea stolen and used to promote whatever new initiative "The Man" has in mind for media nowadays. Let it be known that you will be rewarded handsomely for taking a chance on me. (2)

Did you know that George Lucas once took a chance on an actor named Harrison Ford by casting him as Han Solo in Star Wars? Look at how that panned out. Ford went on to become a big actor in the Indiana Jones series, *The Fugitive, Blade Runner*, and more. It's obvious that you taking a risk on me could play out in the same dramatic way. (3)

I realize that you've got to make money, and guess what? I want to make money too. So we're on the same page, you and I. We both want to make money, and we'll stop at nothing to do so.

If you want me to start work on this amazing novel with an incredible twist ending, just send a one-page contract agreeing to pay me a lot of money if we hit it big. No other obligations will apply. If it's a bust, I won't sue you for millions. (4)

Sincerely,

Kenzel Pain
92 Bad Writer Road
Austin TX 00000

(1) While I love to hear enthusiasm from a writer about his or her work, this kind of unchecked excitement is worrisome for an editor. (2) I need to know the twist to make a decision on whether to accept the manuscript. Plus, I'm troubled by the paranoia and emphasis on making a lot of money. (3) I'm confused. Does he think he's Harrison Ford? (4) So that's the twist: He hasn't even written the novel yet. There's no way I'm going to offer a contract for a novel that hasn't been written by someone with no experience or idea of how the publishing industry works.

WRITE BETTER QUERIES AND SELL MORE ARTICLES

by Krissy Brady

The steps to scoring a byline in your favorite publication are straightforward enough: Come up with a mind-blowing article idea for your target market. Write an attention-grabbing query letter. Submit it to the appropriate editor. Rinse. Repeat. But there's one aspect of the pitching process new writers tend to ignore that could spell disaster for them down the line.

Once you've got the nuts-and-bolts of query writing on lockdown, your primary goal as a writer needs to shift from learning how to write quality pitches to learning how to write them more efficiently. As assignments start rolling in (and they will), you'll inevitably have less time to dedicate to pitches—and the last thing you want is your income stream slowing to a trickle.

By making the following tiny changes now, you'll not only avoid the whole assignments vs. pitches tug-of-war as your portfolio grows, but churn out top notch query letters in a fraction of the time. (This is not a drill.)

1. ESTABLISH YOUR EXACT MISSION

Make sure the focus of your primary writing goal is laser sharp. Don't just decide the category of magazine you want to write for: Pinpoint your exact target demographic within that category, the exact magazines that cater to that demographic, and the exact section you want to break into. Focus your attention on the bullseye, not the entire dartboard. It will make the process of breaking in much less overwhelming—and once you've built a solid relationship with the editor of one department, you'll have an automatic referral once you're ready to branch out into others.

2. KEEP TABS ON YOUR MARKETS

Know your markets better than you know yourself. Keep files on each market you'd like to write for, and track everything you learn about them along the way. Include submission guidelines (which you score by signing up for a Mediabistro.com premium membership), the name of the section you want to break into, as well as the name and e-mail address of the editor who runs that department. If they also accept pitches for their website, add their web editor's info to your roster as well.

For unlimited access to your target markets (not to mention years worth of back issues!), sign up for a Texture.com account. Keep track of the articles that are being published in your section: List each headline and sub-headline in your file, along with a brief description of how each article was packaged (feature with sidebars, list post, as told to, etc.). As each new issue launches, update your file. Finally, visit their website on a daily or weekly basis and track what they're publishing online.

Sure, it's a little cyber-stalkerish, but studying your markets on a regular basis takes the guesswork out of what to pitch, who to pitch to, and how to package your ideas, putting you miles ahead of the competition. Over time, your files will become a treasure trove of information that other writers would hand over a kidney for.

3. FIND THE DIAMONDS IN THE ROUGH

While it's important to subscribe to sites like ScienceDaily and EurekAlert! for the latest news on studies and scientific breakthroughs, they're not the best places for new writers to find interesting stories—especially if you don't already have a relationship with the editor you're pitching the story to. More often than not, a staff writer or regular contributor will have written the story before you've so much as decided on a lede.

Instead, visit sites like Google Scholar (scholar.google.com), PubMed (www.ncbi.nlm.nih.gov/pubmed), and ScienceDirect (www.sciencedirect.com). Search for interesting studies that haven't hit the mainstream using keywords that best describe the topics you're most interested in writing about. Best of all, all three sites let you create alerts based on your fave keywords, so you can have the latest studies sent directly to your inbox on a daily or weekly basis. Not sure if a study is worth writing about? Grab a copy of *Basics for Evaluating Medical Research Studies: A Simplified Approach*, by Sheri Ann Strite and Michael E. Stuart, M.D. (Delfini Group, 2013) to help you wade through the medical jargon.

4. LET THE INFORMATION COME TO YOU

Set up an e-mail address specifically for subscribing to scholarly journals, press release websites, and newsletters by the top experts in your field. Each time you read a new article in your niche, look into the studies that were mentioned, where they were published, and subscribe to notifications from those journals. Add the experts that were quoted to your contact list for future reference, and follow them on social media. If applicable, introduce yourself to the PR people who represent these experts and let them know you'd like to be kept in the loop on interesting developments. Use digital doo-dads like Flipboard (flipboard.com) and Nuzzel (nuzzel.com) to streamline your news hunting experience. Instead of scouring the Internet for new material (which almost always leads to hours of unnecessary Facebook and IMDB creeping), all you'll have to do is check your e-mail and voila—so many ideas, so little time.

5. PITCH LESS

No, but seriously. Focus on the quality of your pitches, not on how fast you can send them out. Once the process of building a solid query is second nature to you, the speed at which you write them will increase naturally. In the meantime, think each of your ideas through from head(line) to toe, and thoughtfully decide which markets you're going to submit them to. I now send one-quarter of the pitches that I used to, but receive (way) more acceptances than rejections—which is the only statistic that matters.

6. BE A PERSONAL PROFESSIONAL

Ditch the business speak and write your pitches like you're writing an e-mail to a friend. Allow the editor to hear your voice as they read your words. I've built an entire writing career using my emotional baggage as bait, and you can too. Define what makes you quirky, and run with it.

7. HONE YOUR PACKAGING SKILLS

Once you've worked with the same editor a few times, you don't have to be as formal with your query letters since they already know you've got the goods. But your pitches still need to pack a punch, and this is where the art of packaging comes in handy. Each time you come up with a new idea, search articles that have been written on the topic in the past and brainstorm ways to package your idea to make it stand out. Consistently putting this habit into practice means the next time a breaking story hits your radar, you'll be able to send your editor an insta-packaged idea that just might lead to an insta-assignment.

8. DON'T LET ANYTHING SLIP THROUGH THE CRACKS

Eventually, you're not only going to have multiple assignments on the go at various stages of completion, but multiple pitches circulating that will need to be followed up on at specific times. Use a program or app like Story Tracker (andrewnicolle.com) to remind yourself of when to touch base with an editor—and when to send your pitch elsewhere.

9. DEVELOP BACKUP ANGLES AND PITCHES

Like you, I was told the odds are slim-to-none that two editors will show interest in the same pitch. And then it happened. Twice. In a row. Naturally, I wasn't prepared, and didn't know whether to do a happy dance or throw up. Save yourself the panic attack by developing 1-2 backup angles for each pitch that can be offered to the second editor if they work for a non-competing market, and a backup pitch that's of equal or higher value if they work for a direct competitor.

10. CREATE YOUR OWN LEARNING EXPERIENCE

Typically, editors only respond to the ideas they're interested in publishing, which means it's on you to determine why your rejected queries were... well, rejected. We've all sent out pitches that were slightly off or "almost" worthy of a sale, and it's important to take stock of what went wrong to refine your process. Compare them to pitches you've nailed in the past, and you'll find the answers are right in front of you: Maybe your intro wasn't catchy enough or your angle was too vague. Maybe your headline was a snore or you sent the pitch from a place of impatience instead of finality. You don't need an editor to write back and confirm your suspicions, because deep down you already know what you need to improve on.

11. PITCH FOR THE RIGHT REASONS

Pitch stories you're drawn to and have a legit interest in covering; don't just pitch an idea because you think it'll sell. If you come across a study that'd make an excellent front-of-book piece for your target market du jour, but you find the subject matter blasé, your query will reflect that. Editors can tell the difference between your heart calling the shots—and your empty wallet.

KRISSY BRADY is so out of shape, it's like she has the innards of an 80-year-old—so naturally, she became a women's health + wellness writer. Since turning her emotional baggage into a writing career, she's been published in magazines like *Cosmopolitan* and *Women's Health*, as well as on websites like Prevention.com and Shape.com. You can follow her shenanigans at writtenbykrissy.com (you know, if you want).

LANDING THE SIX-FIGURE DEAL

What Makes Your Proposal Hot

by SJ Hodges

It's the question every first-time author wants to ask:

"If I sell my book, will the advance even cover my rent?"

Authors, I am happy to tell you that, yes, the six-figure book deal for a newbie still exists—even if you're not a celebrity with your own television show! As a ghostwriter, I work with numerous authors and personalities to develop both nonfiction and fiction proposals, and I've seen unknown first-timers land life-changing deals even in a down economy. Is platform the ultimate key to their success? You better believe it's a huge consideration for publishers, but here's the good news: Having a killer platform is only one element that transforms a "nice deal" into a "major deal."

You still have to ensure the eight additional elements of your proposal qualify as major attractions. Daniela Rapp, editor at St. Martin's Press explains, "In addition to platform, authors need to have a fantastic, original idea. They have to truly be an expert in their field and they must be able to write." So how do you craft a proposal that conveys your brilliance, your credentials, your talent and puts a couple extra zeroes on your check?

ONE: NARRATIVE OVERVIEW

Before you've even written word one of your manuscript, you are expected to, miraculously, summarize the entirety of your book in such a compelling and visceral way that a publisher or agent will feel as if they are reading *The New York Times* review. Sound impossible? That's because it is.

That's why I'm going to offer two unorthodox suggestions. First, consider writing the first draft of your overview after you've created your table of contents and your chapter outlines. You'll know much more about the content and scope of your material even if you're not 100 percent certain about the voice and tone. That's why you'll take another pass after you complete your sample chapters. Because then you'll be better acquainted with the voice of your book which brings me to unorthodox suggestion number two... treat your overview as literature.

I believe every proposal component needs to be written "in voice" especially because your overview is the first page the editor sees after the title page. By establishing your voice on the page immediately, your proposal becomes less of a sales document and more of a page-turner. Remember, not everyone deciding your fate works in marketing and sales. Editors still have some buying power and they are readers, first and foremost.

TWO: TABLE OF CONTENTS AND CHAPTER OUTLINES

Television writers call this "breaking" a script. This is where you break your book or it breaks you. This is where you discover if what you plan to share with the world actually merits 80,000 words and international distribution.

Regardless of whether you're writing fiction or nonfiction, this element of your proposal must take your buyer on a journey (especially if it's nonfiction) and once more, I'm a big fan of approaching this component with creativity particularly if you're exploring a specific historical time period, plan to write using a regional dialect, rely heavily on "slanguage," and especially if the material is highly technical and dry.

This means you'll need to style your chapter summaries and your chapter titles as a form of dramatic writing. Think about the arc of the chapters, illuminating the escalating conflict, the progression towards a resolution, in a cinematic fashion. Each chapter summary should end with an "emotional bumper," a statement that simultaneously summarizes and entices in the same way a television show punches you in the gut before they cut to a commercial.

Is it risky to commit to a more creative approach? Absolutely. Will it be perfect the first time you write it? No. The fifth time you write it? No. The tenth time? Maybe. But the contents and chapter summary portion of your proposal is where you really get a chance to show off your skills as an architect of plot and structure and how you make an editor's job much, much easier. According to Lara Asher, acquisitions editor at Globe Pequot Press, it is the single most important component of your proposal. "If I can't easily understand what a book is trying to achieve then I can't present it to my colleagues," Asher says. "It won't make it through the acquisitions process."

THREE: YOUR AUTHOR BIO

Your author bio page must prove that you are more than just a pro, that you are recognized by the world at large as "the definitive expert" on your topic, that you have firsthand experience tackling the problems and implementing your solutions, and that you've seen positive results not only in your personal life but in the lives of others. You have to have walked the walk and talked the talk. You come equipped with a built-in audience, mass media attention, and a strong social network. Your bio assures your buyer that you are the right writer exploring the right topic at the right time.

FOUR: YOUR PLATFORM

Platform, platform, platform. Sit through any writing conference, query any agent, lunch with any editor and you'll hear the "P" word over and over again. What you won't hear is hard-and-fast numbers about just how large this platform has to be in order to secure a serious offer. Is there an audience-to-dollar-amount ratio that seems to be in play? Are publishers paying per head?

"I haven't found this to be the case," says Julia Pastore, former editor for Random House. "It's easier to compel someone to 'Like' you on Facebook or follow you on Twitter than it is to compel them to plunk down money to buy your book. Audience engagement is more important than the sheer number of social media followers."

With that said, if you're shooting for six-figures, publishers expect you'll have big numbers and big plans. Your platform will need to include:

Cross-promotional partnerships

These are organizations or individuals that already support you, are already promoting your brand, your products or your persona. If you host a show on HGTV or Nike designed a tennis racket in your honor, they definitely qualify. If, however, you're not rolling like an A-lister just yet, you need to brainstorm any and every possible connection you have to organizations with reach in the 20,000+ range. Maybe your home church is only 200 people but the larger association serves 40,000 and you often write for their newsletter. Think big. Then think bigger.

Specific, verifiable numbers proving the loyalty of your audience

"Publishers want to see that you have direct contact with a loyal audience," says Maura Teitelbaum, an agent at Folio Literary Management. This means having a calendar full of face-to-face speaking engagements, a personal mailing list, extensive database and verifiable traffic to your author website.

But how much traffic does there need to be? How many public appearances? How many e-mails in your Constant Contact newsletter? Publishers are loathe to quote concrete numbers for "Likes" and "Followers" so I'll stick my neck out and do it instead. At a minimum, to land a basic book deal, meaning a low five-figure sum, you'll need to prove that you've got 15,000-20,000 fans willing to follow you into hell and through high water.

For a big six-figure deal, you'll need a solid base of 100,000 rabid fans plus access to hundreds of thousands more. If not millions. Depressed yet? Don't be. Because we live in a time when things as trivial as Angry Oranges or as important as scientific TED talks can go viral and propel a writer out of obscurity in a matter of seconds. It is only your job to become part of the conversation. And once your foot is in the door, you'll be able to gather…

Considerable media exposure

Publishers are risk averse. They want to see that you're a media darling achieving pundit status. Organize and present all your clips, put together a DVD demo reel of your on-air appearances and be able to quote subscriber numbers and demographics about the publications running your articles or features about you.

Advance praise from people who matter

Will blurbs really make a difference in the size of your check? "I would include as many in a proposal as possible," says Teitelbaum. "Especially if those people are willing to write letters of commitment saying they will promote the book via their platform. That shows your efforts will grow exponentially."

FIVE: PROMOTIONAL PLANS

So what is the difference between your platform and your promotional plan? Your promotional plan must demonstrate specifically how you will activate your current platform and the expected sales results of that activation. These are projections starting three to six months before your book release date and continuing for one year after its hardcover publication. They want your guarantee to sell 15,000 books within that first year.

In addition, your promotional plan also issues promises about the commitments you are willing to make in order to promote the book to an even wider market. This is your expansion plan. How will you broaden your reach and who will help you do it? Publishers want to see that your goals are ambitious but doable.

Think about it this way. If you own a nail salon and you apply for a loan to shoot a movie, you're likely to be rejected. But ask for a loan to open your second salon and your odds get much better. In other words, keep your promotional plans in your wheelhouse while still managing to include:

- Television and radio appearances
- Access to print media
- A massive social media campaign

- Direct e-mail solicitations
- E-commerce and back-of-room merchandising
- New joint partnerships
- Your upcoming touring and speaking schedule with expected audience

You'll notice that I did not include hiring a book publicist as a requirement. Gone are the days when an advance-sucking, three-month contract with a book publicist makes any difference. For a six-figure author, publishers expect there is a team in place: a powerful agent, a herd of assistants and a more generalized media publicist already managing the day-to-day affairs of building your brand, growing your audience. Hiring a book publicist at the last minute is useless.

SIX: YOUR MARKET ANALYSIS

It would seem the odds against a first-time author hitting the jackpot are slim but that's where market analysis provides a glimmer of hope. There are actually markets considered more desirable to publishers. "Broader is generally better for us," says Rapp. "Niche generally implies small. Not something we [St. Martin's Press] can afford to do these days. Current affairs books, if they are explosive and timely, can work. Neuroscience is hot. Animal books (not so much animal memoirs) still work. Military books sell."

"The health and diet category will always be huge," says Asher. "But in a category like parenting which is so crowded, we look for an author tackling a niche topic that hasn't yet been covered."

Niche or broad, your market analysis must position your book within a larger context, addressing the needs of the publishing industry, the relevant cultural conversations happening in the zeitgeist, your potential audience and their buying power, and the potential for both domestic and international sales.

SEVEN: YOUR C.T.A.

Choose the books for your Competitive Title Analysis not only for their topical similarities but also because the author has a comparable profile and platform to your own. Says Pastore, "It can be editorially helpful to compare your book to *Unbroken* by Hillenbrand, but unless your previous book was also a bestseller, this comparison won't be helpful to our sales force."

Limit your C.T.A. to five or six solid offerings then get on BookScan and make sure none of the books sold fewer than 10,000 copies. "Higher sales are preferable," says Rapp. "And you should leave it to the publisher to decide if the market can hold one more title or not. We always do our own research anyway, so just because the book is not mentioned in your line-up doesn't mean we won't know about it."

EIGHT: SAMPLE CHAPTERS

Finally, you have to/get to prove you can … write. Oh yeah, that!

This is the fun part, the pages of your proposal where you really get to shine. It is of upmost importance that these chapters, in harmony with your overview and chapter summaries, allow the beauty, wisdom and/or quirkiness of your voice to be heard. Loud and clear.

"Writing absolutely matters and strong sample chapters are crucial." Pastore explains, "An author must be able to turn their brilliant idea into engaging prose on the page."

Approach the presentation of these chapters creatively. Consider including excerpts from several different chapters and not just offering the standard Introduction, Chapter One and Two. Consider the inclusion of photographs to support the narrative, helping your editor put faces to names. Consider using sidebars or box quotes from the narrative throughout your proposal to build anticipation for the actual read.

NINE: YOUR ONE-PAGER

Lastly, you'll need a one-pager, which is a relatively new addition to the book proposal format. Publishers now expect an author to squeeze a 50- or 60-page proposal down to a one-page summary they can hand to their marketing and sales teams. In its brevity, the one-pager must provide your buyer with "a clear vision of what the book is, why it's unique, why you are the best person to write it, and how we can reach the audience," says Pastore. And it must do that in fewer than 1,000 words. There is no room to be anything but impressive.

And if you're shooting for that six-figure deal, impressive is what each component of your book proposal must be. Easy? No. But still possible? Yes.

SJ HODGES is an 11-time published playwright, ghostwriter and editor. Her most recent book, a memoir co-authored with Animal Planet's "Pit Boss" Shorty Rossi was purchased by Random House/Crown, hit #36 on the Amazon bestseller list and went into its 3rd printing less than six weeks after its release date. As a developmental editor, SJ has worked on books published by Vanguard Press, Perseus Book Group and St. Martin's Press. SJ is a tireless advocate for artists offering a free listing for jobs, grants and fellowships at her Facebook page: facebook.com/constantcreator. She can be reached through her website: sjhodges.com.

20 LITERARY AGENTS

Actively Seeking Writers and Their Writing

by Robert Lee Brewer

Literary agents are the gatekeepers of the publishing industry for most of the larger book publishers, including many medium-sized presses. As such, they're the only vehicle available for writers to get their writing in front of editors at many houses. However, there are hundreds of literary agents—and not all of them are open to new writers.

That's why I've put together this list of 20 literary agents who are actively seeking writers and their writing. Many of these agents are relatively new to agenting and working hard to build their client lists. Others are established, but they're still looking for the right projects.

In this list, there are agents who represent picture books, middle grade, young adult, and adult fiction and nonfiction in a variety of genres. If you're working on a book project, there's likely one or more fits in this list.

KEELY BOEVING OF WORDSERVE LITERARY

Keely Boeving is an agent with WordServe Literary. After receiving her B.A. in English from the University of Virginia, she attended the Denver Publishing Institute and then began her career in New York working in the editorial departments of Bloomsbury and then Oxford University Press, where she acquired books for the trade history list.

She moved back to her home state of Colorado in 2014 and began her own freelance editorial company before joining WordServe the following year. She lives in Denver with her husband and their twins.

Seeking: Keely represents projects in both the general and Christian markets. She is actively seeking nonfiction and memoir as well as select adult and middle grade fiction. She is particularly interested in well-researched nonfiction books in the areas of parenting and family life; health and wellness; the intersection of faith and culture; business (especially books targeting women in the workplace); social justice; and religious studies; as well as projects from diverse and under-represented voices.

For the Christian market, she seeks books in the areas of Christian living, spiritual transformation, devotion and worship, and women's topics including motherhood, relationships and marriage, and calling.

How to Submit: Please send a query letter to admin@wordserveliterary.com, with "Query Attn: Keely Boeving" in the subject line. Additionally, please include five sample pages in the body of your e-mail (not as an attachment). You can see more about what to include in your query by visiting the WordServe Submission Guidelines page (https://www.wordserveliterary.com/submission-guidlines/).

JEVON BOLDEN OF EMBOLDEN MEDIA GROUP

Editor, writer, writing coach, and now literary agent, Jevon Bolden moved into her latest role as literary agent out of necessity to more effectively serve her existing network of authors and has opened her transom to other authors needing the right representation and publishing home for their most treasured messages and stories. She operates under her own boutique consulting firm, Embolden Media Group.

Starting her 15-year career in traditional book publishing as a copy editor, she moved quickly into senior editor and acquisitions roles with publishers for both adult Christian nonfiction and children's nonfiction titles. The books Jevon has written as other people or edited as herself have appeared on national best-seller lists and have sold millions of copies around the world.

Jevon has a bachelor's degree in English, with a minor in sociology, from the University of Alabama in Huntsville and lives in sunny Central Florida with her family and Cocker Spaniel, Langston Hughes.

Seeking: Jevon is seeking to acquire adult Christian nonfiction in the following categories: Christian living, spiritual growth, personal growth, women's issues, prayer, faith, select spirit-filled/charismatic topics, and select topics on race and diversity. Jevon will also consider some devotionals; some children's books—picture, middle grade, or young adult—Christian or mainstream; and some fiction. Authors must have a well-honed concept and well-established or actively growing platform. She is not accepting Bible studies or personal testimonies/memoirs at this time.

How to Submit: Submit queries at https://www.jevonbolden.com/representation-request-form/. Or e-mail her at info@jevonbolden.com with the word "QUERY" in the subject line, along with a query letter, author bio with socials, book summary, annotated table of contents, and one sample chapter (full manuscript for children's and fiction).

JOSEPH PERRY OF PERRY LITERARY, INC.

Joseph Perry is a new agent at Perry Literary, Inc. Before founding Perry Literary, Joseph began his book publishing career when he attended the New York University Summer Publishing Institute in 2010. After interning at FinePrint Literary Management, Joseph enrolled at St. John's University School of Law to learn about the legal aspects of publishing and graduated with a juris doctor in 2015.

During law school, Joseph interned in the legal departments at Hachette Book Group; Rodale, Inc.; and William Morris Endeavor, as well as the subsidiary rights department at Columbia University Press. Joseph also holds a B.A. and M.A. in English from St. Bonaventure University.

Seeking: Joseph is actively acquiring nonfiction and fiction. Within nonfiction, he has a particular interest in music and sports. Specifically, he's interested in music books about the 1950s, 1960s, and 1970s, as well as sports books about football, basketball, baseball, running, and golf.

He is also interested in trade and academic books about film; pop culture; biography; politics; current affairs; law; medicine; journalism; history (in particular 20th Century US history and US legal history); business books (biography, history, technology, and economics); cookbooks; food and wine; parenting; philosophy; photography; psychology; science and technology; and social sciences.

Within fiction, he is acquiring literary fiction, historical fiction, graphic novels, legal thrillers, and picture books. He does not acquire fantasy, science fiction, romance, and middle grade or young adult fiction.

How to Submit: Queries should be sent to jperry@perryliterary.com with the words "QUERY (the title of the manuscript)" in the subject line. Please submit a query letter and the first 10 pages of your manuscript within the body of the e-mail (not as an attachment, please). If submitting a picture book, please include the entire manuscript.

MELISSA RICHESON OF THE APOKEDAK LITERARY AGENCY

Melissa Richeson recently moved into the role of associate agent at Apokedak Literary Agency, where she is building her list of children's book authors. Melissa joined ALA in the spring of 2018 as an intern, which allowed her to learn the nuances of children's book publishing firsthand before being promoted into her current role. With a unique background in both marketing and elementary literature education, she's able to serve clients well while also keeping readers in mind. Melissa has also been working as a writer for years, in both the content and creative realms. She had a children's fiction serial run in an online magazine for over a year, is a current staff columnist, and is a represented young adult and picture book author.

Seeking: In picture books, Melissa appreciates stories with funny characters or heartfelt themes, ones that make her laugh or cry. Well-done rhymes will always catch her eye, and she finds nonfiction stories about little-known subjects fascinating. In middle grade, she loves to see magic, humor, and a sense of imagination. A great hook and quick pacing are keys to her heart.

In young adult, she's typically drawn to contemporary and historical, but fantasy intrigues her sometimes as well. Subtle wit and intelligent wordplay make for a fabulous read, in Melissa's opinion, but she's not a fit for horror, paranormal, or graphic violence.
How to Submit: Queries can be sent to melissa.richeson@apokedakliterary.com. For young adult and middle grade, please send a query letter with the first 10 pages of the manuscript pasted below and include the full manuscript and synopsis as attachments. For picture books, please send a query letter with the full manuscript pasted below and include links to any portfolio art or dummies.

MARLO BERLINER OF THE JENNIFER DE CHIARA LITERARY AGENCY

Marlo Berliner is an award-winning young adult author, freelance editor, and bookseller. She joined The Jennifer De Chiara Literary Agency in March 2018 as an editorial intern after having completed a previous internship with The Bent Agency. Now, she is actively building her list as an associate agent. She is a member of SCBWI, RWA, NJ-RWA, and YA-RWA. Prior to her career in the publishing world, Marlo was an accounting manager for a Fortune 500 company. She holds B.S. degrees in Economics and Industrial Management from Carnegie Mellon University.
Seeking: For middle grade and young adult, she's interested in all genres of fiction, with particular emphasis on adventure, psychological thriller, suspense, mystery, paranormal, urban fantasy, horror, speculative, and romance. She enjoys magic, magical realism, unusual settings, pirates, dark elements, gothic tone, secrets or secretive characters, treasure hunts, and unreliable narrators. Also, if you can take a story or intellectual property (in TV or books) that is popular with the adult crowd and give her it's middle grade or young adult version, then she'll give it a look because she believes these types of stories may have strong potential for the market. Stories told by #ownvoices, and stories with diverse characters of all kinds, including neuro-diverse and LGBTQIA+ are all welcomed. She is also open to coming-of-age stories set in college that walk the line between upper young adult and new adult.

While she likes contemporary tales, she may not be the best fit for 'issue' books where the central conflict revolves primarily around rape/rape-culture, drugs, or illness. She will also consider some select nonfiction projects in middle grade and young adult, particularly if they involve pop-culture or current events.

For adults, she's interested in all genres of romance, except inspirational, historical and erotic. She's also open to women's fiction, mystery, thriller, and suspense.
How to Submit: Please submit your query and first 20 manuscript pages via my Query Manager: http://QueryMe.Online/marloberliner. You will receive an automatic response from Query Manager that lets you know your submission is in her inbox, and you can track your query's progress. She'll respond within 6 weeks, but only to projects that interest her. Any queries sent by e-mail or regular mail will not be considered.

MAUREEN MORETTI OF P.S. LITERARY

Maureen Moretti began her publishing career as an intern with several prestigious literary agencies before joining P.S. Literary as an associate agent. She holds a B.A. from Saint Mary's College of California and attended the Columbia Publishing Course.
Seeking: Maureen is actively acquiring both nonfiction and fiction. Within nonfiction she is searching for narrative nonfiction, culture, history, biography, LGBTQ+, cookbooks, and lifestyle. Within fiction, she is looking for women's fiction, thrillers, LGBTQ+, romance, select science fiction, literary fiction and genre-bending unique voices.
How to Submit: Send query to query@psliterary.com with the word "query," the genre and the agent's name in the subject line. Please limit your submission to just a query letter that consists of the following: Paragraph one—introduction, including the title and category of your work (i.e., fiction or nonfiction and topic), an estimated word count, and a brief, general introduction; paragraph two—brief overview that should read similar to back cover copy; and paragraph three—writer's bio that tells a little bit about yourself and your background (awards and affiliations, etc.).

NICOLE BEZANSON OF METAMORPHOSIS LITERARY AGENCY

Nicole Bezanson is a junior agent with Metamorphosis Literary Agency, having honed her skills for writing and editing through a wide variety of educational programs. She received her B.A. in Sociology with a double minor in Anthropology and Environmental Science from Saint Mary's University in 2010, her paralegal diploma with honors in 2011, and between 2013 and present has completed courses and certificate programs in transcription, cultural competence, technical writing, management, and communications. She most recently finished her agency internship with Metamorphosis in November of 2018 and in addition to working as a literary agent and writing contemporary young adult fiction, Nicole is also a technical writer for a global manufacturer of CPAP masks, machines, and other products that manage sleep-disordered breathing.

When she isn't busy updating her manuscript portfolio or responding to queries, she can usually be found reading, horseback riding, or pursuing her new hobby of learning to cook. She and her husband share their home in Eastern Canada with a collection of disabled cats and a lifetime's worth of books.

Seeking: Middle grade and young adult fiction in all forms and genres, new adult/college-aged novels, and adult contemporary, romance, horror, and psychological thrillers. Manuscripts featuring animal appearances are always appreciated, cats and horses in particular, as are stories taking place in Canada or 'up north.' Nicole loves to read about small towns, cowboys, social and mental health issues, protagonists with pets, and romantic and mysterious subplots, but is not a great fit for historical fiction, nonfiction, or memoirs at this time. She requests to only be forwarded fantasy novels focusing on mythical creatures—mermaids, unicorns, centaurs, and the like.

How to Submit: Submit queries at http://QueryMe.Online/nicolebezanson or e-mail her at: nbezanson@metamorphosisliteraryagency.com.

CLAIRE HARRIS OF FOUNDRY LITERARY + MEDIA

Claire received her B.A. in English from The University of Texas at Austin and attended the NYU Summer Publishing Institute before joining Foundry Literary + Media. She enjoys the creative process of working with writers and collaborating closely with them throughout all stages of their careers. Claire is a thriller fanatic, candy addict, and a lover of all things creepy. Her favorite place to curl up with a good book is on a screened porch during a thunderstorm. She's been on more ghost tours than she can count.

Seeking: In fiction projects, Claire looks for psychological and commercial thrillers, serial detective stories, works of fiction inspired by actual crimes, mystery, suspense, cozies, anything involving serial killers, and contemporary family dramas. She is a lover of the dark and twisted, and she's happiest when reading manuscripts with unexpected endings, especially those that stay with you for days. Having grown up in Wisconsin, Claire has a special love of stories set in the Midwest.

For nonfiction, Claire looks for a range of projects, including humor, celebrity memoir, lifestyle guides, pop culture celebrations, and illustrated books for adults. While she is interested in a variety of nonfiction projects, those who have read this bio from the first line will not be surprised to learn that her passion lies in true crime.

How to Submit: Claire only accepts e-mail submissions. You can query her at chsubmissions@foundrymedia.com. For fiction, please send query letter, synopsis, first three chapters of manuscript, and author bio. For nonfiction, please send query letter, sample chapters, table of contents, and author bio.

CECILIA LYRA OF THE RIGHTS FACTORY

Cecilia Lyra holds a Master's Degree in Banking and Financial Law from Boston University and is completing a graduate certificate in publishing. In 2016, she bid adieu to her life as lawyer and professor of law to become a writer and literary agent. She blames this heretical career move on her nine-year-old-self, who was bitten by the reading bug and began to dream of the day when she would work with books. When she isn't devouring novels—or dessert—Cecilia can be found drinking wine, writing her own novels, and snuggling with Babaganoush, her adorable English bulldog.

Seeking: Cecilia is actively seeking literary and commercial adult fiction that feature diverse, layered characters and unexpected plot twists. As a feminist, Cecilia loathes the term *women's fiction*—it's just *fiction*—but, for the purposes of clarity, that is her favorite genre. Cecilia is also looking for unique and compelling narrative nonfiction and memoirs (think: nonfiction that would be perfect for book clubs). She is particularly passionate about representing under- or misrepresented voices and stories that contribute to a larger cultural conversation. Do not send a manuscript where the dog dies—Cecilia can't handle it.

How to Submit: Submissions can be e-mailed to cecilia@therightsfactory.com. Please include (in the body of the e-mail): a pitch; a bio (including a summary of your writing credentials and platform, if applicable); and the first 10 pages of your work. Preferred format: Times, 12-size font, justified paragraphs, 1.5 spacing. Attachments will not be opened. Because Cecilia understands writers' anxiety, she will respond to each and every query within six weeks.

ANNE TIBBETS OF D4EO

Anne Tibbets began her career as a screenwriter, author, and literary agency intern at D4EO, becoming a full-time agent in 2018 at Red Sofa Literary. Anne joined D4EO Literary in 2019.

Seeking: She's seeking adult and young adult science fiction, horror, historical, mystery, and young adult thrillers. No middle grade, chapter, or picture books. No nonfiction, scripts, or self-published works.

How to Submit: E-mail Anne at anne@d4eo.com. Include category and genre (Adult or YA: SFF, Thriller, Horror, etc.), word count, a one to three paragraph pitch, short author bio, and previously published titles (self-published counts), 10-page writing sample within the body of the e-mail—double-spaced, 12-point font. Unrequested attachments will be deleted. Please allow Anne up to six weeks to respond to queries before nudging. She reads every query. If you don't hear back from her in six weeks, please nudge. Responds to partial requests in four to six weeks; full requests in six to eight weeks.

SAVANNAH BROOKS OF THE JENNIFER DE CHIARA LITERARY AGENCY

Savannah Brooks joined the Jennifer De Chiara team in 2018, after interning for a year and a half. She's an MFA candidate at Hamline University focusing in creative nonfiction as well as an editor at Red Bird Chapbooks, a teaching artist at the Loft Literary Center, and a reader for multiple literary magazines. Her own creative work has been publishing in *Barely South Review*, *Hobart*, *Lime Hawk*, and *Every Writer's Resource*, among others. When not immersed in the world of words, she can be found on her bike, at a dive bar, or lounging at one of Minnesota's 10,000 lakes. She lives in the most beautiful literary capital: Saint Paul.

Seeking: Currently, she's most focused on young adult. She's especially interested in books that bring to light the challenges teens face in their day-to-day (uncertainty about the future, friendship tension, mental health, etc.), but she'd like to read a work where the protagonist actually enjoys high school (or at least doesn't dread it). She's always drawn in by a protagonist venturing into a realm where society says they don't belong (think swapping gender norms), and characters with weird obsessions are a weird obsession of hers—teach her strange new things, and she's yours. She's all about magical realism, mythology, and modern retellings, but she's not the best fit for high fantasy or science fiction. Mostly, she's invested in representing the diverse world in which we live and would like to see that reflected in a cast of characters. Show her variations in race, sexuality, gender, dis/ability, and ethnicity without that difference being a point of contention, and she'll be thrilled.

And, of course, she still loves a chewy piece of adult contemporary fiction and would like to find more works that center around women and their careers. She recently finished Liane Moriarty's *Nine Perfect Strangers* and was just captured by her characters. She'd love a cast equally as meaty.

How to Submit: Submit your query and the first 20 pages of your manuscript via QueryMe.Online/SavannahBrooks. Queries sent by any other medium will not be considered. For non-query related matters, e-mail her at savannahlbrooks91@gmail.com.

ANN TANENBAUM OF TANENBAUM INTERNATIONAL LITERARY AGENCY

Ann Tanenbaum is a veteran of the publishing industry with 50 years of experience. Over the course of her career, she has held editorial and marketing positions at The Viking Press and Random House as well as executive positions at Harry N. Abrams Inc., Doubleday International, and Newsweek. In addition to representing books on seasoned gallery artists and museums, the theatre, and many children's books, Ann has a commitment to nurturing projects on current affairs, politics, and history.

Seeking: Ann is always looking for new authors and artists to represent. For nonfiction, she is currently accepting submissions in the areas of current affairs, cultural criticism, and narrative journalism, as well as some memoirs. Ann also has experience in collaborating with non-profits who wish to promote their message through a serious full-length book project. For fiction submissions, she is looking for literary fiction, upmarket fiction, and young adult fiction that is off the beaten track.
How to Submit: Submissions can be e-mailed to hello@tanenbauminternational.com. Please submit a one-page query that includes: A brief synopsis of your book; a short description of what makes your book compelling in today's market; a summary of your writing credentials and platform (if applicable); and a sample chapter in the body of your e-mail.

AMY STAPP OF WOLFSON LITERARY AGENCY

Amy Stapp received her B.A. from Samford University and M.A. from Georgia State University before beginning her publishing career at Macmillan, where she was an editor for seven years and had the privilege of working with bestselling authors such as Katie McGarry, Shelley Noble, and Amber Lynn Natusch, among others. Amy joined Wolfson Literary in 2018 and is actively building her list.
Seeking: Amy is interested in women's fiction, mystery, suspense, historical fiction, young adult, and select narrative nonfiction. She is particularly drawn to well-paced prose and smart, multidimensional characters. Other authors she admires include Megan Abbott, Sarah Addison Allen, and Karen McManus.
How to Submit: Please e-mail a query letter and the first five pages to amy@wolfsonliterary.com.

NATALIE GRAZIEN OF MARTIN LITERARY & MEDIA MANAGEMENT

Natalie has a B.A. in English and Minor in Spanish from Santa Clara University. Upon graduating, she worked as a sales representative for W. W. Norton and interned for two literary agencies: Kimberley Cameron & Associates and Martin Literary Management. For two years, Natalie was the Fiction Editor of *The Santa Clara Review*, the oldest literary magazine on the West Coast. Natalie is happiest outside, with (you guessed it) a book. She is distrustful of any purse that can't fit a slim paperback.
Seeking: Dark psychological thrillers and mysteries, witty rom-coms, historical settings, and bookclub-worthy women's fiction are right up her alley. For sci-fi and fantasy, she prefers subtle, surreal twists in contemporary stories and feminist retellings of legends and fairytales. More than anything, she looks for assured prose, a strong sense of place,

finely-tuned plots, and smart, distinctive characters who make the unrelatable relatable. If those elements are present, any genre is welcome.

How to Submit: Queries sent to her e-mail will not receive a response. Please submit through QueryManager: http://QueryMe.Online/1429. Please include a query letter in the body of your e-mail and attach the first 10 pages of your manuscript, preferably as a Word doc.

DEVIN ROSS OF NEW LEAF LITERARY & MEDIA

Devin earned her B.A. in English from Lawrence University and her Publishing Certificate at the Denver Publishing Institute. She began her publishing carreer as an author's assistant, helping authors grow their platforms and meet their deadlines. Her next career move landed her in the Subsidiary Rights department at Crown Publishing Group before she found her home at New Leaf Literary & Media.

Seeking: In adult, Devin is looking for peculiar, eccentric, character-driven, commercial or upmarket fiction that is conceptually unique. She loves all types of science fiction and fantasy and is drawn to stories with magical realism.

In nonfiction she's looking books about pop science, pop culture, feminism and social justice.

In young adult, she's looking for commercial fiction; coming of age, plot-driven books with strong voices and crossover appeal that break the status quo. She is drawn to fantasy, science fiction, and thrillers that suck you in from the very first page.

How to Submit: Send query to query@newleafliterary.com. The word "Query" must be in the subject line, plus the agent's name (e.g., Subject: Query, Devin Ross). Please also include the category (e.g., picture book, chapter book, middle grade, young adult, adult fiction, adult nonfiction, etc.). You may include up to five double-spaced sample pages within the body of the e-mail, please no attachments. Include all necessary contact information. You will receive an auto-response confirming receipt of your query.

ALEXANDRA LEVICK OF WRITERS HOUSE

Alexandra Levick has worked with a wide range of established *New York Times* bestsellers, national award winners, and debut clients. After graduating from the University of Rochester with a degree in English focused on Creative Writing, Alexandra attended New York University where she received her Masters of Science in Publishing with a specialization in Content Development. Prior to Writers House, she spent time at Sterling Lord Literistic, in publicity at Bloomsbury, and as a bookseller for Barnes and Noble. Today, she is building a broad list and works on everything from picture books to speculative adult fiction.

Seeking: Picture book author-illustrators, a wide range of middle grade and young adult, and more speculative-leaning or genre-bent upmarket adult works. She's committed to working with writers from diverse backgrounds and looking to put forth an intersectional list of outstanding creators who will be able to provide both windows and mirrors into all kinds of experiences. She's particularly looking for own-voices stories about historically underrepresented characters and cultures.

No matter the genre or age-range, she craves a distinctive voice and strong thematic meaning behind the work—she wants to run screaming to her friends and family about your book because there is so much to discuss. She loves character-driven stories that revolve around BIG topics (discussing things like mortality or grief in a new and hopefully somewhat uplifting way is always an instant lightbulb!). One might say that she has a great affinity for what used to be known as 'issue books,' however, she'd argue that she likes to represent authors and stories that stand for more than just a good yarn; she'd like to represent authors that provoke conversations around important topics in our world today. And she doesn't just want contemporary versions of these stories, either. Send her your fantasy, your sci-fi, your genre-bender! Please send your horizon-expanding work. She can't wait to give it a read.

How to Submit: Please send your personalized query letter along with your first 10 pages (pasted into the body of the e-mail) to alevick@writershouse.com.

JENNIFER GRIMALDI OF CHALBERG & SUSSMAN

Prior to joining Chalberg & Sussman as an agent, Jennifer Grimaldi worked at St. Martin's Press/Thomas Dunne, where she edited and acquired S. Jae-Jones' *New York Times* bestseller *Wintersong*—a Labyrinth-inspired gothic young adult—and worked with numerous bestselling and award-winning authors. Jennifer's broad exposure to the domestic and foreign publishing markets as a scout with Barbara Tolley & Associates further shaped her taste for the eclectic. On those rare occasions without a book or Kindle in hand, Jennifer can be found replaying Dragon Age Origins, adding to her collection of increasingly elaborate board games (current favorite: Through The Ages), and entertaining friends and strangers alike with NYC trivia.

Seeking: Science fiction and fantasy in both adult and young adult, historical fiction, romance and horror. She is particularly intrigued by strong world-building and sense of place, and would love to see a wide variety of diversity in the gender, sexuality, presentation, race, and mental/physical abilities of characters. She also loves stories inspired by true events or myths and fairy tales, and deconstructed tropes. More than any of the above, however, she looks for genre books supported by a strong emotional core. While she is not interested in issue books, she is interested in character studies in trauma, whether that be a mysterious disappearance, extraterrestrial abduction, or emotional abuse.

She is also enormously fond of rakes and scoundrels in all varieties (thieves, pirates, spies), multi-dimensional villains, atmospheric creepiness, and longing glances.

How to Submit: To query Jennifer, please e-mail jennifer@chalbergsussman.com and include the first five pages of your manuscript in the body of an e-mail. Jennifer accepts queries by e-mail only. Please note that per agency policy, replies will be sent only for submissions being actively considered.

BRITT SIESS OF MARTIN LITERARY & MEDIA MANAGEMENT

Britt has a strong background in publishing. She has interned with the Taryn Fagerness Agency, Wales Literary Agency, and Martin Literary & Media Management. She joined Martin Literary & Media Management in July 2018 as an Associate Literary Manager. Prior to becoming an agent, she worked in the sales division of The Quarto Group where she worked in domestic and foreign book sales. Britt has a B.A. in English Literature and Cinema and Media Studies from the University of Washington.

Seeking: On the adult side, she's looking for SF/Fantasy novels that feature elaborately built worlds and realistically flawed characters. She's especially interested in retellings of fairy-tales or stories that are based on myths and legends by #ownvoices authors. She loves a like-able villain and is a sucker for speculative fiction that makes us confront the choices we've made. She'd also like to see a bit more horror in her inbox, but think more Gothic than gore.

For middle grade submissions, she's looking for anything magical or spooky. She loves witches, fairies, and evil queens (she's a huge fan of Holly Black). She's definitely looking for flawed main characters and kids who can learn from their own mistakes.

How to Submit: For all queries, please include a query letter, a detailed synopsis of your story, and the first chapter of your work pasted into the body of your e-mail. Please also include a link to your blog, website, Instagram, and/or Twitter account. Please send your queries to britt@martinlit.com.

SARAH GERTON OF CURTIS BROWN, LTD.

Sarah grew up in small-town Minnesota amidst several siblings, many pets, and even more books; then headed east to study English and political science at Wesleyan University. She earned a certificate in publishing at the Columbia Publishing Course, and started at Curtis Brown, Ltd., in 2015 as assistant to Elizabeth Harding and Katherine Fausset. She's excited every day for the chance to bring great new books to the world.

Seeking: Sarah is looking for fiction and select narrative nonfiction for young adult and middle grade audiences. While fantasy is her first love, she's eager to read anything for teens and tweens—from literary to commercial, horror to memoir, as long as it has distinctive writing and unforgettable characters.

How to Submit: Please e-mail query letters to sg@cbltd.com, with the first 10 pages pasted in the body of the e-mail.

TESS CALLERO OF CURTIS BROWN, LTD.

After graduating with a dual degree in Marketing and English from Indiana University, Tess moved to New York City to pursue a career in publishing. She has been with Curtis Brown since 2015, building her list in both the adult and young adult space. She also serves as the Social Media Director for the agency and is a member of the Digital Innovations and the Contracts committees of the AAR.

Seeking: Contemporary young adult across genres, but she's especially looking for a good romance or suspense. She'd love a heartfelt friendship story, or a coming-of-age that makes her ugly cry. She's also interested in accessible young adult fantasy and magical realism. Some recent favorites include *One of Us Is Lying, They Both Die at the End,* and *Dear Martin.*

On the adult side, she's looking for mystery/thriller/suspense, upmarket women's fiction, and #ownvoices romance, both historical and contemporary. She especially appreciates a smart, young, self-aware female narrator. Think *Sweetbitter, The Assistants,* or *Luckiest Girl Alive* in these categories.

For nonfiction, she's on the hunt for food narrative, cookbooks, pop culture, science, business, history/biography, women's issues, humor, and true crime. Recent favorites include *American Fire, Cork Dork,* and *Bachelor Nation.*

How to Submit: Query her at tc@cbltd.com. No attachments please. She will respond if interested.

FUNDS FOR WRITERS 101

Find Money You Didn't Know Existed

by C. Hope Clark

When I completed writing my novel over a decade ago, I imagined the next step was simply to find a publisher and watch the book sell. Like most writers, my goal was to earn a living doing what I loved so I could walk away from the day job. No such luck. Between rejection and newfound knowledge that a novel can take years to sell enough for a single house payment, I opened my mind to other writing avenues. I learned that there's no *one* way to find funds to support your writing; instead there are *many*. So many, in fact, that I felt the need to share the volume of knowledge I collected, and I called it FundsforWriters.com.

Funds are money. But obtaining those funds isn't necessarily a linear process, or a one-dimensional path. As a serious writer, you study all options at your fingertips, entertaining financial resources that initially don't make sense as well as the obvious.

GRANTS

Grants come from government agencies, nonprofits, businesses and even generous individuals. They do not have to be repaid, as long as you use the grant as intended. No two are alike. Therefore, you must do your homework to find the right match between your grant need and the grant provider's mission. Grantors like being successful at their mission just as you like excelling at yours. So they screen applicants, ensuring they fit the rules and show promise to follow through.

Don't fear grants. Sure, you're judged by a panel, and rejection is part of the game, but you already know that as a writer. Gigi Rosenberg, author of *The Artist's Guide to Grant Writing*, states, "If one funder doesn't want to invest in your project, find another who does. And if nobody does, then begin it any way you can. Once you've started, that momentum will help your project find its audience and its financial support."

TYPES OF GRANTS

Grants can send you to retreats, handle emergencies, provide mentors, pay for conferences, or cover travel. They also can be called awards, fellowships, residencies, or scholarships. But like any aspect of your writing journey, define how any tool, even a grant, fits into your plans. Your mission must parallel a grantor's mission.

The cream-of-the-crop grants have no strings attached. Winning recipients are based upon portfolios and an application that defines a work-in-progress. You don't have to be a Pulitzer winner, but you must prove your establishment as a writer.

You find most of these opportunities in state arts commissions. Find them at www.nasaa-arts.org or as a partner listed at the National Endowment for the Arts website, www.nea.gov. Not only does your state's arts commission provide funding, but the players can direct you to other grant opportunities, as well as to artists who've gone before you. Speaking to grant winners gives you a wealth of information and a leg up in designing the best application.

Foundations and nonprofits fund the majority of grants. Most writers' organizations are nonprofits. Both the Mystery Writers of America (www.mysterywriters.org) and Society of Children's Book Writers and Illustrators (www.scbwi.org) offer scholarships and grants.

Many retreats are nonprofits. Journalist and freelancer Alexis Grant (http://alexisgrant.com/) tries to attend a retreat a year. Some ask her to pay, usually on a sliding scale based upon income, and others provide scholarships. Each time, she applies with a clear definition of what she hopes to gain from the two to five-week trips. "It's a great way to get away from the noise of everyday responsibilities, focus on writing well and meet other people who prioritize writing. I always return home with a new perspective." One resource to find writing retreats is the Alliance of Artists Communities (www.artistcommunities.org/).

Laura Lee Perkins won four artist-in-residence slots with the National Park Service (www.nps.gov). The federal agency has 43 locations throughout the United States where writers and artists live for two to four weeks. From Acadia National Park in Maine to Sleeping Bear Dunes National Lakeshore in Michigan, Perkins spoke to tourists about her goals to write a book about Native American music. "Memories of the US National Parks' beauty and profound serenity will continue to enrich my work. Writers find unparalleled inspiration, quietude, housing, interesting staff, and a feeling of being in the root of your artistic desires."

Don't forget writers' conferences. While they may not advertise financial aid, many have funds available in times of need. Always ask as to the availability of a scholarship or work-share program that might enable your attendance.

Grants come in all sizes. FundsforWriters posts emergency grants on its grants page (www.fundsforwriters.com) as well as new grant opportunities such as the Sustainable Arts Foundation (www.sustainableartsfoundation.org) that offers grants to writers and artists with children under the age of 18, or the Awesome Foundation (www.awecomefoundation.org), which gives $1,000 grants to creative projects.

Novelist Joan Dempsey won an Elizabeth George Foundation grant (http://www.elizabethgeorgeonline.com/foundation/index.htm) in early 2012. "I applied to the Foundation for a research grant that included three trips to places relevant to my novel-in-progress, trips I otherwise could not have afforded. Not only does the grant provide travel funds, but it also provides validation that I'm a serious writer worthy of investment, which is great for my psyche and my résumé."

FISCAL SPONSORSHIP

Nonprofits have access to an incredibly large number of grants that individuals do not, and have the ability to offer their tax-exempt status to groups and individuals involved in activities related to their mission. By allowing a nonprofit to serve as your grant overseer, you may acquire funds for your project.

Deborah Marshall is President of the Missouri Writers Guild (www.missouriwritersguild.org) and founder of the Missouri Warrior Writers Project, with ample experience with grants in the arts. "Although grant dollars are available for individual writers, writing the grant proposal becomes difficult without significant publication credits. Partnering with a nonprofit organization, whether it is a writing group, service, community organization, or any 501(c)3, can fill in those gaps to make a grant application competitive. Partnering not only helps a writer's name become known, but it also assists in building that all-important platform."

Two excellent groups that offer fiscal sponsorship for writers are The Fractured Atlas (www.fracturedatlas.org) and Artspire (www.artspire.org), sponsored by the New York Foundation for the Arts and open to all US citizens. Visit The Foundation Center (www.foundationcenter.org) for an excellent tutorial guide to fiscal sponsorship.

CROWD SOURCING

Crowd sourcing is a co-op arrangement where people support artists directly, much like the agricultural co-op movement where individuals fund farming operations in exchange for fresh food. Kickstarter (www.kickstarter.com) has made this funding method successful in the arts.

Basically, the writer proposes his project, and for a financial endorsement as low as $1, donors receive some token in return, like an autographed book, artwork, or bookmark. The higher the donation, the bigger the *wow* factor in the gift. Donors do not receive ownership in the project.

Meagan Adele Lopez (www.ladywholunches.net) presented her debut self-published book *Three Questions* to Kickstarter readers, requesting $4,400 to take her book on tour, create a book trailer, pre-order books, and redesign the cover. Eighty-eight backers pledged a total of $5,202. She was able to hire an editor and a company that designed film trailers. For every $750 she received over her plan, she added a new city to her book tour.

Other up-and-coming crowd sourcing companies include Culture 360 (www.culture360.org) that serves Asia and Europe, and Indiegogo (www.indiegogo.com), as well as Rocket Hub (www.rockethub.com). And nothing stops you from simply asking those you know to support your project. The concept is elementary.

CONTESTS

Contests offer financial opportunity, too. Of course you must win, place or show, but many writers overlook the importance that contests have on a career. These days, contests not only open doors to publishing, name recognition, and money, but listing such achievements in a query letter might make an agent or publisher take a second glance. Noting your wins on a magazine pitch might land a feature assignment. Mentioning your accolades to potential clients could clinch a freelance deal.

I used contests as a barometer when fleshing out my first mystery novel, *A Lowcountry Bribe* (Bell Bridge Books). After I placed in several contests, earned a total of $750, and reached the semi-finals of the Amazon Breakthrough Novel Award (www.createspace.com/abna), my confidence grew strong enough to pitch agents. My current agent admits that the contest wins drew her in.

Contests can assist in sales of existing books, not only aiding sales but also enticing more deals for future books . . . or the rest of your writing profession.

Whether writing short stories, poetry, novels, or nonfiction, contests abound. As with any call for submission, study the rules. Double checking with entities that screen, like FundsforWriters.com and WinningWriters.com, will help alleviate concerns when selecting where to enter.

FREELANCING

A thick collection of freelancing clips can make an editor sit up and take notice. You've been vetted and accepted by others in the business, and possibly established a following. The more well known the publications, the brighter your aura.

Sooner or later in your career, you'll write an article. In the beginning, articles are a great way to gain your footing. As your career develops, you become more of an expert, and are expected to enlighten and educate about your journey and the knowledge you've acquired. Articles are, arguably, one of the best means to income and branding for writers.

Trade magazines, national periodicals, literary journals, newsletters, newspapers and blogs all offer you a chance to present yourself, earn money, and gain readers for a platform. Do not discount them as income earners.

Linda Formichelli, of Renegade Writer fame (www.therenegadewriter.com) leaped into freelance magazine writing because she simply loved to write, and that love turned her into an expert. "I never loved working to line someone else's pockets." A full-time freelancer since 1997, with credits like *Family Circle*, *Redbook*, and *Writer's Digest*, she also writes articles, books, e-courses, and e-books about her profession as a magazine writer.

JOBS

Part-time, full-time, temporary or permanent, writing jobs hone your skills, pad your resume, and present avenues to movers and shakers you wouldn't necessarily meet on your own. Government and corporate managers hire writers under all sorts of guises like Social Media Specialist and Communications Specialist, as well as the expected Reporter and Copywriter.

Alexis Grant considers her prior jobs as catapults. "Working at a newspaper (*Houston Chronicle*) and a news magazine (*US News & World Report*) for six years provided the foundation for what I'm doing now as a freelancer. Producing stories regularly on tight deadlines will always make you a better writer."

Joan Dempsey chose to return to full-time work and write her novel on the side, removing worries about her livelihood. "My creative writing was suffering trying to freelance. So, I have a day job that supports me now." She still maintains her Facebook presence to continue building her platform for her pending novel.

DIVERSIFICATION

Most importantly, however, is learning how to collect all your funding options and incorporate them into your plan. The successful writer doesn't perform in one arena. Instead, he thrives in more of a three-ring circus.

Grant states it well: "For a long while I thought of myself as only a journalist, but there are so many other ways to use my skills. Today my income comes from three streams: helping small companies with social media and blogging (the biggest source), writing and selling e-guides and courses (my favorite), and taking freelance writing or editing assignments."

Formichelli is proud of being flexible. "When I've had it with magazine writing, I put more energy into my e-courses, and vice versa. Heck, I'm even a certified personal trainer, so if I get really sick of writing I can work out. But a definite side benefit to diversifying is that I'm more protected from the feast-or-famine nature of writing."

Sometimes pursuing the more common sense or lucrative income opportunity can open doors for the dream. When my novel didn't sell, I began writing freelance articles. Then I established FundsforWriters, using all the grant, contest, publisher and market research I did for myself. A decade later, once the site thrived with over 45,000 readers, I used the very research I'd gleaned for my readers to find an agent and sign a publishing contract . . . for the original novel started so long ago.

You can fight to fund one project or study all resources and fund a career. Opportunity is there. Just don't get so wrapped up in one angle that you miss the chance to invest more fully in your future.

C. HOPE CLARK manages FundsForWriters.com and is the author of several books, including *Lowcountry Bribe* and *Palmetto Poison*. Learn more at http://chopeclark.com.

WHY EVERY WRITER NEEDS A BUSINESS PLAN

And Why Writing One Is Easy

by Sophia McDonald Bennett

When I transitioned from being a part-time to full-time writer, I was lucky enough to pick up a full roster of clients quickly. But after my first year I was seriously questioning my decision to become a freelancer. In my rush to build a business, I'd taken on every project I could find regardless of how much it paid, whether it was a good fit with my skills, or whether I really had time for it. The result? I was exhausted, uninspired and had no time to tackle the projects I'd dreamed of doing when I quit my day job.

One evening I sat down with a notepad and started making lists. What did I want to accomplish over the next six months? How much income did I want to report at the end of the year? What did I need to do—and stop doing—in order to meet my goals?

Those lists eventually turned into a rudimentary business plan that guided me through the next six months. I let go of a few poorly-paying clients that weren't helping me build my clip file. Instead of pursuing blogging jobs when I had spare time, I refocused on pitching national magazines. And when I considered new projects, I asked myself if they fit within my plan. If they didn't, it was magically easier to say no.

Since then I've engaged in business planning twice a year. It gives me a chance to reflect on what I've learned about myself and my profession over the preceding months, consider what opportunities are and aren't worth pursuing, and determine if I'm on track toward meeting my professional aspirations. I also use this time to consider how I'm doing at finding that tricky work/life balance. One of the best things about this process is that it's helped me grow my income by 25 percent annually over the last two years.

BUSINESS PLANNING VS. A BUSINESS PLAN

There are a few reason I refer to this process as "business planning" rather than "writing a business plan." It's been my experience that people start shaking in their socks as soon as you utter the words "business plan." That seems to be true even of writers, who I would argue are uniquely positioned to succeed at this particular task.

Why? "When you write a business plan, you're telling your story," says Doug Wilson, MBA, a senior instructor of marketing at the University of Oregon's Lundquist College of Business. "What you want to do is tell it in the most compelling way possible for yourself and your potential customers." Since most writers don't need to apply for bank loans or approach investors to support their business, no one else ever needs to see their business plan. And since we're natural storytellers, I find this approach heartening.

In addition, the document that results from my planning process isn't nearly as extensive as a traditional business plan. It's typically a one- to two-page framework that outlines my goals and tasks for the next six months. Sometimes it's a series of lists or charts. One year, when I was eager to dig into the adult coloring book I'd received for Christmas, I turned my business plan into an art project.

Here, again, Wilson has some sage advice. "Don't be intimidated by the structure or the format," he says. "The real value in the business planning process is not in producing a document, but in having to think through all of the elements a business requires before you start making commitments or signing contracts."

While content matters more than form, there is some value in considering the sections typically included in a business plan. The following five subjects can be quite applicable to writers.

MISSION, VISION AND VALUES STATEMENTS

Most businesses have a set of guiding principles that govern the way they work and serve their clients. Your writing practice is no different. Creating a set of simple statements can serve as a powerful framework for everything you do.

A mission statement broadly describes what you do and what you hope to accomplish. My most recent mission statement reads: "To support myself as a writer, editor and communications consultant who specializes in writing for and about food/beverage and other lifestyle topics, sustainability, business and nonprofits."

A vision statement shares where you envision yourself and your practice in the future. In that sense it's the most goal-oriented of these sections. My vision statement includes things such as writing for more national magazines, doing more work as an editor and engaging in more public speaking.

A values statement often reflects why you do the things you do, but can also encompass the morals or standards you hold yourself to as a professional. My values include providing outstanding customer service, meeting deadlines and working with companies whose belief systems are a good match with mine.

If you don't have one already, this may be a good time to develop a professional bio. Summarize your relevant experience with an eye toward what you can offer a company or publisher. Why should they hire you over someone else?

PRODUCTS AND SERVICES

You're in the business of producing writing. But what kind of writing can you do? Especially if you're just starting your career as a freelancer, it's a good idea to write down the types of services you can provide clients. Are you a technical writer or a news writer? Do you have experience penning articles about business and financial trends or covering lifestyle topics?

After that, think about the types of writing you want to do. Do you want to do less corporate copywriting and more long-form nonfiction or personal essays? Do you want to ditch your focus on covering the healthcare industry from a business perspective and focus on writing about the human impacts of disease and medicine?

Clearly identifying your products and services will help you set goals for your business. To stay focused on my yearly plans, I create a list of both the subjects I want to write about and the kinds of clients I want to work with. I've also found it helpful to create a grid with the different types of services I offer and list my clients under each heading. It's a quick way to assess whether my focus is falling more heavily in areas I want to pursue or those I'm trying to move away from.

The best goals are ambitious but realistic, measureable, and time-bound. You don't want to get your first big byline or earn six figures a year by the time you retire. Presumably you want to do it in the next year, two years or five years. You can write down the details of how you'll reach your goals here or in the timeline section.

FINANCIAL PLAN

While most writers don't need a balance sheet or profile/loss statement, doing some financial planning can be quite beneficial. If you're new to freelancing and are trying to set your rates, consider making a spreadsheet that shows all of your expenses. From there you can determine how much you need to earn per hour to cover them. Keep in mind that you will now have to pay self-employment tax on your earnings. Also, remember that all of the time you spend on business development is unpaid and must be accounted for in your hourly rate.

When I was considering the move to full-time freelancing, I set up an income calculator to estimate how much money I could realistically earn every month. I plugged in the amount I was earning from my existing clients (many of whom paid per piece, not by the hour) and then started playing with the numbers. If I could double the volume of blog posts I produced, would that give me a solid income? Or would I be better off picking up more regional magazines that paid about the same as the other publications I wrote for?

My income calculator is often accompanied by a time calculator that helps me estimate how much time it takes to write certain types of content (articles vs. blog posts vs. press releases) and how many more pieces I can realistically create every month. Figuring out how much time is dedicated to certain projects – including new business development – keeps me from getting too overloaded.

A basic budget that tracks spending on necessities such as office supplies, subscriptions, travel, conference fees and marketing expenses can also be quite helpful. Set projections for the time period of your business plan and track actual expenses so you can make adjustments in future budgets.

MARKETING PLAN

If you've gotten this far into the planning process, you already have answers to some of the hard questions you need to address before creating a bare-bones marketing plan. Now it's about getting down to details.

Start by looking back at the types of writing you want to do. That will help you identify who is in your target market. The next thing you need to do is determine where to find those people. If you want to offer copywriting services to businesses, a Chamber of Commerce, professional association or your personal network are good places to start mining contacts. If you want to write for magazines or author a nonfiction book, you're in luck—you're already in the best place to find people who need writers.

Next, determine how you'll reach out to potential clients. For copywriting, it may be a letter of introduction. For magazines, you'll need to write query letters. For books, start learning how to create a book proposal.

A marketing budget may be useful in years when you plan to shell out cash for promotions. Digital advertising (such as a website, LinkedIn Premium subscription, or paid ads on Google or Facebook) can be an affordable and highly targeted way to reach decision-makers depending on what your professional goals are. Before you invest in advertising, make sure you put some real time into honing your message and understanding your audience.

TIMELINE/WORKPLAN

Now that you have a list of goals and some ideas for marketing your services, list the steps you'll take each month to grow or change your business. You can also place them on your calendar if that makes them easier to remember. Having a plan for how you'll accomplish your goals will keep you moving forward. Setting deadlines will also keep you accountable (even if the only person making sure you check off each item is you).

Once you've wrapped up your business planning process, don't put the resulting document away in a drawer. Revisit it on a regular basis to remind yourself of your vision and goals and revel in your progress. That's another reason to make the document brief, well-organized and even attractive. You'll be much more likely to review a short and sweet pathway to your dreams than one that seems like a long and winding road.

Sophia McDonald Bennett is a freelance writer, editor, communications consultant and marketing instructor in Eugene, Oregon.

HOW TO DEVELOP AN EFFECTIVE AUTHOR BRAND

by Leslie Lee Sanders

An author's brand isn't just the specific colors of your website, a catchy tagline, or a recognizable face. Branding is delivering on a promise after setting an expectation. Determining how you want to be perceived and what sets you apart is essential when organizing an author's image, but that is only the tip of the iceberg when it comes to branding. Diving deeper when creating an author brand is a must.

Following is an in-depth look at how to build a successful author brand and become a fierce competitor in the publishing business.

ESTABLISH AN IMAGE

When establishing your image, think beyond color scheme and website layout. Humans are unique for their feeling capabilities, and the way we feel about something usually stays with us longer than any color or image. If applied properly, certain phrases, images, and colors trigger emotions, and this is your main goal when establishing your image. However, you must recognize the emotion you want to convey and how it links people to your brand.

For example, you might want to convey love, calm, excitement, wonder, intrigue, nostalgia, or even hilarity, but deep down the feeling should be universal enough to be relatable.

This is how branding works. A brand effectively engages emotion. Remember the Geico commercial where the massive camel awkwardly strolls through a busy office during the middle of the day asking the workers what day it is? Sure, it is a funny ad, but what is that commercial doing on a deeper level? The commercial is selling a service using a situation most people relate to by making you laugh. Actually, Geico's history of running funny ads have become their brand, from the gecko, the cavemen, Maxwell the Pig, and now the "Hump Day" camel.

Most people relate to the situation of working a demanding nine-to-five and counting the days until the weekend. Most people are probably familiar with a co-worker who, much like the camel, points out the middle of the week in the same tedious way, prompting tired sighs and eye rolls. The commercial triggers something most people "get" and therefore it sticks with them. This is what your brand should do too.

What you do for your readers through your website, blogs, videos, and podcasts is your "service." The books and stories you sell is your "product." How you manage it is your "business." Connect to your audience using emotion to form your reputation and establish your image.

What feelings do you want to trigger?

List the emotions you want others to feel when visiting your website or when reading your books. An easy way to accomplish this is by asking yourself what words you want to associate with your image. Take the third party route, step outside of yourself, and look at what you offer through an objective view. If someone were to describe you and your brand, what words or emotion would you like them to use? Trigger those emotions by using specific words in your content, books, blog posts, and author bio. Use images and colors on your website and book covers to convey your overall message.

What emotion or message do you want to resonate?

Triggering feelings and having them resonate are two different things. The former is what sucks you into the brand. The latter is what you take from it, what you're left with, or what stays with you. What would you like readers to take away from your book after reading it? After visiting your website, what message will they remember you by? Make your mission clear in your work.

What promises do you want to communicate?

By communicating a promise, and most importantly, delivering on that promise, you establish trust that produces satisfied readers, which not only translates into repeat service from avid fans, but generates new readers through word-of-mouth marketing. People will seek you out because you've become the go-to person for your particular service and product. Think Starbucks and coffee. When you've become the go-to person, you have successfully built a brand. Your brand's promise is what your audience comes to expect from your business.

To further expand or maintain your brand requires consistency.

CREATE CONSISTENCY

Being consistent falls under the tier of delivering on your promises. There's a cycle when building a brand; make a promise, deliver, build trust, and repeat. By performing this cycle, you are practicing consistency, which is the reason people come to you instead of your competitor. Take away one of the components and you break the cycle. Break the cycle and your brand might suffer.

You might think to get ahead or to produce sales requires you to beat your competitors, and to be on top means to flaunt what makes you unique. Today, in the writing business, this kind of thinking is retroactive because with so many books and authors flooding the market, being unique is a one in a million chance. The truth is, establishing a brand, building an audience, and keeping your audience satisfied is the trick to success in most businesses. Do this and in return your readers will help you expand your audience by advertising your products and services through recommendations (i.e., word of mouth, social media sharing, and book reviews). This is the tried-and-true formula of every successful brand.

How do you satisfy your audience? Consistency.

Consistency with book releases, series, and the production and design of content

Whatever your service, provide it regularly. Readers expect a new book from you once a year? Meet or exceed that expectation and release a new book every year or sooner. If your newsletter subscribers expect a monthly newsletter and your YouTube videos to highlight important writing techniques for novelist, continue giving them what they come for or give them what they want and more.

Establishing your place within your genre

Sure, you write in a specific genre with no plans of crossing genres anytime soon. Still there are other ways to stay consistent. Do your novels end with happily ever after? Don't try experimenting with the latest story now. You may lose some readers if they're convinced their favorite author or series is becoming something other than what they've grown to love.

Cultivating an overall tone and a distinct voice

Your voice and style, the words you use, and the way you piece them together in your writing is unique to you and your personality. Your audience will grow familiar with your writing mechanics and may even recognize your style in your speaking voice. Keep it consistent. You may have read a book by an author whose writing style reminded you of another author. For example, you may believe the book you are currently hooked on reads like a Stephen King or J.K. Rowling novel. If you're consistent, your style can become recognizable and be a distinctive part of your brand too.

BUILD TRUST

Establishing your image, being consistent, and building trust are some of what it takes to build an effective brand. Let's talk coffee. When mentioning coffee, which establishment do you think of first, Starbucks or McDonalds? Most would say Starbucks. Why? Because Starbucks successfully built their coffeehouse brand.

Starbucks is one of the largest and most successful coffeehouses for many reasons, but one reason is they are consistent with their products, using the same ingredients and measurements to make each coffee the same as the one before. You know exactly how your favorite latte should taste, and they meet that expectation each time. Your brand should build a similar kind of trust with your audience.

Image familiarity, logos, and other insignia

When mentioning branding your business, the next thought might be logos. Your logo is not your brand but the visual symbol of your brand. Your logo is a way to identify your brand in its simplest form, a visual representation of your business.

Here are the best ways to use your logo to maximize your brand's exposure:

- **BOOK SERIES COVER.** A perfect way to use a logo is on the cover of your books in a particular series. It's a recognizable insignia that communicates the promise and trust exchange between you and your readers. When they see that logo on the cover they know each book contains your familiar voice and writing style, and they will know what to expect of the books in that series.
- **STATIONARY, BUSINESS CARDS, BOOKMARKS, LETTERHEAD, ETC.** Office supplies are probably the most obvious place to add your logo. Also make sure your logo appears on business forms like invoices, packing slips, and receipts.
- **ONLINE USE.** Use your logo in place of your profile picture on Twitter and Facebook. Add it to your website header and favicon. Use it in your e-mail signature, in your guest posts, or in your Gravitar (Globally Recognized Avatar) in conjunction with guest posting to get your logo in front of new audiences when commenting on other people's blogs.
- **CUSTOM GOODS.** Add your logo to custom-made apparel, mugs, water bottles, chocolates, pens, totes, etc. Make sure the logo is large enough to be discernable at a distance, and use colors and fonts that can be easily read.

REPUTATION

Overall, your brand, brand identity, logo, content, message, storytelling, and reader experience is your reputation. Your reputation is built from the general feelings, opinions, and

beliefs of the majority of people who encounter your brand. And to be just as successful in your niche as Starbucks is to coffee, remember these steps to building your author brand:

1. **Establish your image by creating a specific emotion to trigger; message to resonate; and promise to communicate.**
2. **The following should stay consistent in your brand: identity; voice and style; and production.**
3. **Build trust by staying consistent; delivering on promises; and creating a visual representation of your business.**

LESLIE LEE SANDERS is a published author with over ten years of fiction writing and book publishing experience. She teaches the art and craft of blogging, writing, and publishing on her blog at leslieleesanders.com. Her work has been included in the following Writer's Market books: 2016 Writer's Market, 2016 Novel and Short Story Writer's Market, the 2014 and 2015 editions of Guide to Self-Publishing. She's currently writing the fifth installment of her post-apocalyptic and dystopian book series, Refuge Inc.

BLOGGING BASICS

by Robert Lee Brewer

In these days of publishing and media change, writers have to build platforms and learn how to connect to audiences if they want to improve their chances of publication and overall success. There are many methods of audience connection available to writers, but one of the most important is through blogging.

Since I've spent several years successfully blogging—both personally and professionally—I figure I've got a few nuggets of wisdom to pass on to writers who are curious about blogging or who already are.

Here's my quick list of tips:

1. **START BLOGGING TODAY.** If you don't have a blog, use Blogger, WordPress, or some other blogging software to start your blog today. It's free, and you can start off with your very personal "Here I am, world" post.
2. **START SMALL.** Blogs are essentially simple, but they can get complicated (for people who like complications). However, I advise bloggers start small and evolve over time.
3. **USE YOUR NAME IN YOUR URL.** This will make it easier for search engines to find you when your audience eventually starts seeking you out by name. For instance, my url is http://robertleebrewer.blogspot.com. If you try Googling "Robert Lee Brewer," you'll notice that My Name Is Not Bob is one of the top five search results (behind my other blog: Poetic Asides).
4. **UNLESS YOU HAVE A REASON, USE YOUR NAME AS THE TITLE OF YOUR BLOG.** Again, this helps with search engine results. My Poetic Asides blog includes my name in the title, and it ranks higher than My Name Is Not Bob. However, I felt the play on my name was worth the trade off.

5. **FIGURE OUT YOUR BLOGGING GOALS.** You should return to this step every couple months, because it's natural for your blogging goals to evolve over time. Initially, your blogging goals may be to make a post a week about what you have written, submitted, etc. Over time, you may incorporate guests posts, contests, tips, etc.
6. **BE YOURSELF.** I'm a big supporter of the idea that your image should match your identity. It gets too confusing trying to maintain a million personas. Know who you are and be that on your blog, whether that means you're sincere, funny, sarcastic, etc.
7. **POST AT LEAST ONCE A WEEK.** This is for starters. Eventually, you may find it better to post once a day or multiple times per day. But remember: Start small and evolve over time.
8. **POST RELEVANT CONTENT.** This means that you post things that your readers might actually care to know.
9. **USEFUL AND HELPFUL POSTS WILL ATTRACT MORE VISITORS.** Talking about yourself is all fine and great. I do it myself. But if you share truly helpful advice, your readers will share it with others, and visitors will find you on search engines.
10. **TITLE YOUR POSTS IN A WAY THAT GETS YOU FOUND IN SEARCH ENGINES.** The more specific you can get the better. For instance, the title "Blogging Tips" will most likely get lost in search results. However, the title "Blogging Tips for Writers" specifies which audience I'm targeting and increases the chances of being found on the first page of search results.
11. **LINK TO POSTS IN OTHER MEDIA.** If you have an e-mail newsletter, link to your blog posts in your newsletter. If you have social media accounts, link to your blog posts there. If you have a helpful post, link to it in relevant forums and on message boards.
12. **WRITE WELL, BUT BE CONCISE.** At the end of the day, you're writing blog posts, not literary manifestos. Don't spend a week writing each post. Try to keep it to an hour or two tops and then post. Make sure your spelling and grammar are good, but don't stress yourself out too much.
13. **FIND LIKE-MINDED BLOGGERS.** Comment on their blogs regularly and link to them from yours. Eventually, they may do the same. Keep in mind that blogging is a form of social media, so the more you communicate with your peers the more you'll get out of the process.
14. **RESPOND TO COMMENTS ON YOUR BLOG.** Even if it's just a simple "Thanks," respond to your readers if they comment on your blog. After all, you want your readers to be engaged with your blog, and you want them to know that you care they took time to comment.
15. **EXPERIMENT.** Start small, but don't get complacent. Every so often, try something new. For instance, the biggest draw to my Poetic Asides blog are the poetry prompts and challenges I issue to poets. Initially, that was an experiment—one that worked

very well. I've tried other experiments that haven't panned out, and that's fine. It's all part of a process.

SEO TIPS FOR WRITERS

Most writers may already know what SEO is. If not, SEO stands for *search engine optimization*. Basically, a site or blog that practices good SEO habits should improve its rankings in search engines, such as Google and Bing. Most huge corporations have realized the importance of SEO and spend enormous sums of time, energy and money on perfecting their SEO practices. However, writers can improve their SEO without going to those same extremes.

In this section, I will use the terms of *site pages* and *blog posts* interchangeably. In both cases, you should be practicing the same SEO strategies (when it makes sense).

Here are my top tips on ways to improve your SEO starting today:

16. **USE APPROPRIATE KEYWORDS.** Make sure that your page displays your main keyword(s) in the page title, content, URL, title tags, page header, image names and tags (if you're including images). All of this is easy to do, but if you feel overwhelmed, just remember to use your keyword(s) in your page title and content (especially in the first and last 50 words of your page).
17. **USE KEYWORDS NATURALLY.** Don't kill your content and make yourself look like a spammer to search engines by overloading your page with your keyword(s). You don't get SEO points for quantity but for quality. Plus, one of the main ways to improve your page rankings is when you...
18. **DELIVER QUALITY CONTENT.** The best way to improve your SEO is by providing content that readers want to share with others by linking to your pages. Some of the top results in search engines can be years old, because the content is so good that people keep coming back. So, incorporate your keywords in a smart way, but make sure it works organically with your content.
19. **UPDATE CONTENT REGULARLY.** If your site looks dead to visitors, then it'll appear that way to search engines too. So update your content regularly. This should be very easy for writers who have blogs. For writers who have sites, incorporate your blog into your site. This will make it easier for visitors to find your blog to discover more about you on your site (through your site navigation tools).
20. **LINK BACK TO YOUR OWN CONTENT.** If I have a post on Blogging Tips for Writers, for instance, I'll link back to it if I have a Platform Building post, because the two complement each other. This also helps clicks on my blog, which helps SEO. The one caveat is that you don't go crazy with your linking and that you make sure your links are relevant. Otherwise, you'll kill your traffic, which is not good for your page rankings.

21. **LINK TO OTHERS YOU CONSIDER HELPFUL.** Back in 2000, I remember being ordered by my boss at the time (who didn't last too much longer afterward) to ignore any competitive or complementary websites—no matter how helpful their content—because they were our competitors. You can try basing your online strategy on these principles, but I'm nearly 100 percent confident you'll fail. It's helpful for other sites and your own to link to other great resources. I shine a light on others to help them out (if I find their content truly helpful) in the hopes that they'll do the same if ever they find my content truly helpful for their audience.
22. **GET SPECIFIC WITH YOUR HEADLINES.** If you interview someone on your blog, don't title your post with an interesting quotation. While that strategy may help get readers in the print world, it doesn't help with SEO at all. Instead, title your post as "Interview With (insert name here)." If you have a way to identify the person further, include that in the title too. For instance, when I interview poets on my Poetic Asides blog, I'll title those posts like this: Interview With Poet Erika Meitner. Erika's name is a keyword, but so are the terms *poet* and *interview*.
23. **USE IMAGES.** Many expert sources state that the use of images can improve SEO, because it shows search engines that the person creating the page is spending a little extra time and effort on the page than a common spammer. However, I'd caution anyone using images to make sure those images are somehow complementary to the content. Don't just throw up a lot of images that have no relevance to anything. At the same time...
24. **OPTIMIZE IMAGES THROUGH STRATEGIC LABELING.** Writers can do this by making sure the image file is labeled using your keyword(s) for the post. Using the Erika Meitner example above (which does include images), I would label the file "Erika Meitner headshot.jpg"—or whatever the image file type happens to be. Writers can also improve image SEO through the use of captions and ALT tagging. Of course, at the same time, writers should always ask themselves if it's worth going through all that trouble for each image or not. Each writer has to answer that question for him (or her) self.
25. **USE YOUR SOCIAL MEDIA PLATFORM TO SPREAD THE WORD.** Whenever you do something new on your site or blog, you should share that information on your other social media sites, such as Twitter, Facebook, LinkedIn, online forums, etc. This lets your social media connections know that something new is on your site/blog. If it's relevant and/or valuable, they'll let others know. And that's a great way to build your SEO.

Programmers and marketers could get even more involved in the dynamics of SEO optimization, but I think these tips will help most writers out immediately and effectively while still allowing plenty of time and energy for the actual work of writing.

BLOG DESIGN TIPS FOR WRITERS

Design is an important element to any blog's success. But how can you improve your blog's design if you're not a designer? I'm just an editor with an English Lit degree and no formal training in design. However, I've worked in media for more than a decade now and can share some very fundamental and easy tricks to improve the design of your blog.

Here are my seven blog design tips for writers:

26. **USE LISTS.** Whether they're numbered or bullet points, use lists when possible. Lists break up the text and make it easy for readers to follow what you're blogging.
27. **BOLD MAIN POINTS IN LISTS.** Again, this helps break up the text while also highlighting the important points of your post.
28. **USE HEADINGS.** If your posts are longer than 300 words and you don't use lists, then please break up the text by using basic headings.
29. **USE A READABLE FONT.** Avoid using fonts that are too large or too small. Avoid using cursive or weird fonts. Times New Roman or Arial works, but if you want to get "creative," use something similar to those.
30. **LEFT ALIGN.** English-speaking readers are trained to read left to right. If you want to make your blog easier to read, avoid centering or right aligning your text (unless you're purposefully calling out the text).
31. **USE SMALL PARAGRAPHS.** A good rule of thumb is to try and avoid paragraphs that drone on longer than five sentences. I usually try to keep paragraphs to around three sentences myself.
32. **ADD RELEVANT IMAGES.** Personally, I shy away from using too many images. My reason is that I only like to use them if they're relevant. However, images are very powerful on blogs, so please use them—just make sure they're relevant to your blog post.

If you're already doing everything on my list, keep it up! If you're not, then you might want to re-think your design strategy on your blog. Simply adding a header here and a list there can easily improve the design of a blog post.

GUEST POSTING TIPS FOR WRITERS

Recently, I've broken into guest posting as both a guest poster and as a host of guest posts (over at my Poetic Asides blog). So far, I'm pretty pleased with both sides of the guest posting process. As a writer, it gives me access to an engaged audience I may not usually reach. As a blogger, it provides me with fresh and valuable content I don't have to create. Guest blogging is a rare win-win scenario.

That said, writers could benefit from a few tips on the process of guest posting:

33. **PITCH GUEST POSTS LIKE ONE WOULD PITCH ARTICLES TO A MAGAZINE.** Include

what your hook is for the post, what you plan to cover, and a little about who you are. Remember: Your post should somehow benefit the audience of the blog you'd like to guest post.

34. **OFFER PROMOTIONAL COPY OF YOUR BOOK (OR OTHER GIVEAWAYS) AS PART OF YOUR GUEST POST.** Having a random giveaway for people who comment on a blog post can help spur conversation and interest in your guest post, which is a great way to get the most mileage out of your guest appearance.
35. **CATER POSTS TO AUDIENCE.** As the editor of *Writer's Market* and *Poet's Market*, I have great range in the topics I can cover. However, if I'm writing a guest post for a fiction blog, I'll write about things of interest to a novelist—not a poet.
36. **MAKE IT PERSONAL, BUT PROVIDE NUGGET.** Guest posts are a great opportunity for you to really show your stuff to a new audience. You could write a very helpful and impersonal post, but that won't connect with readers the same way as if you write a very helpful and personal post that makes them want to learn more about you (and your blog, your book, your Twitter account, etc.). Speaking of which...
37. **SHARE LINKS TO YOUR WEBSITE, BLOG, SOCIAL NETWORKS, ETC.** After all, you need to make it easy for readers who enjoyed your guest post to learn more about you and your projects. Start the conversation in your guest post and keep it going on your own sites, profiles, etc. And related to that...
38. **PROMOTE YOUR GUEST POST THROUGH YOUR NORMAL CHANNELS ONCE THE POST GOES LIVE.** Your normal audience will want to know where you've been and what you've been doing. Plus, guest posts lend a little extra "street cred" to your projects. But don't stop there...
39. **CHECK FOR COMMENTS ON YOUR GUEST POST AND RESPOND IN A TIMELY MANNER.** Sometimes the comments are the most interesting part of a guest post (no offense). This is where readers can ask more in-depth or related questions, and it's also where you can show your expertise on the subject by being as helpful as possible. And guiding all seven of these tips is this one:
40. **PUT SOME EFFORT INTO YOUR GUEST POST.** Part of the benefit to guest posting is the opportunity to connect with a new audience. Make sure you bring your A-game, because you need to make a good impression if you want this exposure to actually help grow your audience. Don't stress yourself out, but put a little thought into what you submit.

ONE ADDITIONAL TIP: Have fun with it. Passion is what really drives the popularity of blogs. Share your passion and enthusiasm, and readers are sure to be impressed.

ROBERT LEE BREWER is an editor with the Writer's Digest Writing Community and author of *Solving the World's Problems* (Press 53). Follow him on Twitter @robertleebrewer.

CONTRACTS 101

by Cindy Ferraino

After you do a victory dance about getting the book deal you always dreamed about or your article hitting the top of the content list of a popular magazine, the celebration quickly comes to a halt when you realize you are not at the finish line yet. Your heart begins to beat faster because you know the next possible hurdle is just around the corner—the contract. For many, the idea of reviewing a contract is like being back in first grade. You know you have to listen to the teacher when you could be playing outside. You know you have to read this contract but why because there are terms in there that look like an excerpt from a foreign language syllabus.

Before I changed my status to self-employed writer, I was working as a grants and contracts administrator at a large medical university in Philadelphia. I helped shepherd the M.D. and Ph.D. researchers through the channels of grants and contracts administration. While the researchers provided the technical and scientific pieces that could potentially be the next cure for diabetes, heart disease, or cancer, I was there to make sure they did their magic within the confines of a budget and imposed contractual regulations. The budget process was easy but when it came to contract regulations—oh well, that was a different story. I became familiar with the terms such as indemnifications, property and intellectual rights, and conditions of payments. I was an integral part of reviewing and negotiating a grant or contract that had the best interests for every party involved.

After my son was born, I left the university and my contracts background went on a brief hiatus. Once my son went off to school, I began freelance writing. After a few writing gigs sprinkled with a few too many rejection slips, I landed an assignment for *Dog Fancy* magazine. I was thrilled and eagerly anticipated the arrival of a contract in my inbox. As I opened the document, the hiatus had lifted. I read through the contract and was able to send it back within a few hours.

For many new freelancers or writers who have been around the block, contract administration is not something that they can list as a perk on their resume. Instead of searching through the Yellow Pages for a contract lawyer or trying to call in a special favor to a writer friend, there are some easy ways for a newbie writer or even a seasoned writer to review a contract before putting a smiley face next to the dotted line.

TAKE A DEEP BREATH, THEN READ ON

Remember breaking those seals on test booklets and the voice in the background telling you, "Please read the directions slowly." As you tried to drown out the voice because your stomach was in knots, little did you know that those imparting words of wisdom would come in handy as you perspired profusely over the legal jargon that unfolded before your eyes. The same words go for contracts.

Many writers, including myself, are anxious to get an assignment underway, but the contract carrot continues to loom over our creative minds. "I'm surprised by writers who just skim a contract and then sign it without understanding what it means," says Kelly James-Enger, author of books including *Six Figure Freelancing: The Writer's Guide to Making More* (Random House) and the blog Dollarsanddeadlines.blogspot.com. "Most of the language in magazine contracts isn't that complicated, but it can be confusing when you're new to the business."

When I receive a contract from a new publisher or editor, I make a second copy. My children call it "my sloppy copy." I take out a highlighter and begin to mark up the key points of the contract: beginning and end date, conditions of payment, how my relationship is defined by the publisher, and what the outline of the article should look like.

The beginning and end date of a contract is crucial. After I recently negotiated a contract, the editor changed the due date of the article in an e-mail. I made sure the contract was changed to reflect the new due date. The conditions of the payments are important because it will describe when the writer will be paid and by what method. Most publishers have turned to incremental payment schedules or payments to be made online like PayPal. How the publisher considers your contractor status is important. If you're a freelance contract writer, the contract should reflect that as well as identify you as an independent contractor for IRS tax purposes. Finally, the contract will highlight an outline of what your article or proposal should look like.

As you slowly digest the terms you are about to agree to for your assignment or book project, you gain a better understanding of what an editor or publisher expects from you and when.

PAYMENT TYPES

There are any number of different arrangements for publishers to pay writers. However, here are three of the most common and what they mean.

- Pays on acceptance. This means a publisher pays (or cuts a check) for the writer upon acceptance of the manuscript. This is usually the best deal a writer can hope to receive.
- Pays on publication. In these cases, a publisher pays (or cuts a check) for the writer by the publication date of the manuscript. For magazines, this could mean several months after the manuscript was accepted and approved. For books, this could mean more than a year.
- Pays after publication. Sometimes contracts will specify exactly how long after publication. Be wary of contracts that leave it open-ended.

CUTTING TO THE LEGAL CHASE

Once you have had a chance to review a contract, you may be scratching your head and saying, "Okay, now what does this all mean to me as a writer?" James-Enger describes three key areas where writers should keep sharp on when it comes to contracts—indemnification, pay and exclusivity provisions.

INDEMNIFICATION is a publisher's way of saying if something goes wrong, we are not responsible. If a claim is brought against another writer's work, a publisher does not want to be responsible for the legal aftermath but you could be the one receiving a notice in the mail. James-Enger warns writers to be on the lookout for indemnification clauses. "In the U.S., anyone can sue anyone over just about anything," she says; "I'm okay with agreeing to indemnification clauses that specify breaches of contract because I know I'm not going to plagiarize, libel or misquote anyone. But I can't promise that the publication will never be sued by anyone whether or not I actually breached the contract."

PAY is where you want the publisher "to show you the money." Writers need to be aware of how publishers will discuss the terms of payment in the contract. James-Enger advises to have "payment on acceptance." This means you will be paid when the editor agrees to accept your manuscript or article. If there is "no payment on acceptance," some publishers will pay when the article is published. "Push for payment whenever you can," she says.

EXCLUSIVITY PROVISIONS are where a particular publisher will not allow the writer to publish an article or manuscript that is "about the same or similar subject" during the time the publisher runs the piece. Because of the nature of the writing business, James-Enger feels writers need to negotiate this part of the contract. "I specialize in health, fitness and nutrition, and I'm always writing about a similar subject," she says.

CONTRACT TIPS

Even seasoned freelancers can find themselves intimidated by contracts. Here are a few things to consider with your contract:

- **KEEP COPY ON RECORD.** If the contract is sent via e-mail, keep a digital copy, but also print up a hard copy and keep it in an easy-to-find file folder.
- **CHECK FOR RIGHTS.** It's almost never a good idea to sell all rights. But you should also pay attention to whether you're selling any subsidiary or reprint rights. The more rights you release the more payment you should expect (and demand).
- **WHEN PAYMENT.** Make sure you understand when you are to be paid and have it specified in your contract. You may think that payment will come when the article is accepted or published, but different publishers have different policies. Get it in writing.
- **HOW MUCH PAYMENT.** The contract should specify exactly how much you are going to be paid. If there is no payment listed on the contract, the publisher could use your work for free.
- **TURN IN CONTRACT BEFORE ASSIGNMENT.** Don't start working until the contract is signed, and everything is official. As a freelancer, time is as important as money. Don't waste any of your time and effort on any project that is not yet contracted.

WHEN TO HEAD TO THE BARGAINING TABLE

Recently, I became an independent contractor for the American Composites Manufacturing Association (ACMA). When I reviewed the terms of the contract, I was concerned how my independent contractor status was identified. Although I am not an ACMA employee, I wanted to know if I could include my ACMA publications on my resume. Before I signed the contract, I questioned this issue with my editor. My editor told me I may use this opportunity to put on my resume. I signed the contract and finished my assignment.

Writers should be able to talk to an editor or a publisher if there is a question about a term or clause in a contract. "Don't be afraid to talk to the editor about the changes you'd like to make to a contract," James-Enger says; "You don't know what you'll get or if an editor is willing to negotiate it, until you ask."

When writers have to approach an editor for changes to a contract, James-Enger advises writers to act professionally when it comes to the negotiations. "I start out with saying—I am really excited to be working with you on this story and I appreciate the assignment, but I have a couple of issues with the contract that I'd like to talk to you about," she says. "Sure I want a better contract but I also want to maintain a good working relationship with my editor. A scorched-earth policy doesn't benefit any freelancer in the long run."

Negotiating payment terms is a tricky subject for some writers. Writers want to get the most bang for their buck but they don't want to lose a great writing assignment. Do your research first before you decide to ask an editor for more money to complete the assignment. Double check the publisher's website or look to see if the pay scale is equivalent to other publishers in the particular industry. Some publishers have a set publishing fee whereas others may have a little more wiggle room depending on the type of the assignment given. In today's economy, writers are a little more reluctant to ask for a higher rate for an article. If the publisher seems to be open to discussion about the pay scale, just make sure you approach the situation in a professional manner so as to not turn the publisher away from giving you another assignment.

WHO OWNS YOUR WRITING?

Besides payment terms, another area that writers may find themselves on the other end of the negotiation table is with ownership rights. We all want to take credit for the work that we have poured our heart and soul into. Unfortunately, the business of publishing has different ways of saying how a writer can classify their work. Ownership rights vary, but the biggest one that writers have a hard time trying to build up a good case against is "all rights." "All rights" is exactly what it means: *hope you are not in love with what you have just written because you will not be able to use it again.*

In recent months, I have written for two publications that I had given "all rights" to the company. My rationale is that I knew I would never need to use those articles again but I did make sure I was able to include those articles for my byline to show that I have publishing experience.

If you feel that you want to reuse or recycle an article that you had written a few years ago, you might want to consider negotiating an "all rights" clause or maybe going to another publisher. "We don't take all rights so there is no reason for authors to request we change the rights clause," says Angela Hoy, author and owner of WritersWeekly.com and Booklocker.com. "Our contracts were rated 'Outstanding' by Mark Levine (author of *The Fine Print of Self-Publishing*) and has also been called the clearest and fairest in the industry."

James-Enger is also an advocate of negotiating against contracts with an "all rights" clause. "I hate 'all rights' contracts, and try to avoid signing them as they preclude me from ever reselling the piece as a reprint to other markets," she says. "I explain that to editors, and I have been able to get editors to agree to let me retain nonexclusive reprint rights even when they buy all rights—which still lets me market the piece as a reprint." James-Enger also advises that "if the publisher demands all rights, then negotiate if the payment is sub-standard."

So if you are just receiving a contract in the mail for the first time or you are working with a new publisher, you should not be afraid of the legal lingo that blankets the message "we want to work with you." Contracts are meant to protect both the interests of the publishers and writers. Publishers want the commitment from writers that he or she will provide their best work and writers want to be recognized for their best work. But between those contracts lines, the legal lingo can cause writers to feel they need a law degree to review the contract. No, just sit back and relax and enjoy the prose that will take your writing to the next level.

RIGHTS AND WHAT THEY MEAN

A creative work can be used in many different ways. As the author of the work, you hold all rights to the work in question. When you agree to have your work published, you are granting a publisher the right to use your work in any number of ways. Whether that right is to publish the manuscript for the first time in a publication, or to publish it as many times and in as many ways as a publisher wishes, is up to you—it all depends on the agreed-upon terms. As a general rule, the more rights you license away, the less control you have over your work and the money you're paid. You should strive to keep as many rights to your work as you can.

Writers and editors sometimes define rights in a number of different ways. Below you will find a classification of terms as they relate to rights.

- **FIRST SERIAL RIGHTS.** Rights that the writer offers a newspaper or magazine to publish the manuscript for the first time in any periodical. All other rights remain with the writer. Sometimes the qualifier "North American" is added to these rights to specify a geographical limitation to the license. When content is excerpted from a book scheduled to be published, and it appears in a magazine or newspaper prior to book publication, this is also called first serial rights.
- **ONE-TIME RIGHTS.** Nonexclusive rights (rights that can be licensed to more than one market) purchased by a periodical to publish the work once (also known as simultaneous rights). That is, there is nothing to stop the author from selling the work to other publications at the same time.
- **SECOND SERIAL (REPRINT) RIGHTS.** Nonexclusive rights given to a newspaper or magazine to publish a manuscript after it has already appeared in another newspaper or magazine.
- **ALL RIGHTS.** This is exactly what it sounds like. "All rights" means an author is selling every right he has to a work. If you license all rights to your work, you forfeit the right to ever use the work again. If you think you may want to use the article again, you should avoid submitting to such markets or refuse payment and withdraw your material.
- **ELECTRONIC RIGHTS.** Rights that cover a broad range of electronic media, including websites, CD/DVDs, video games, smart phone apps, and more. The contract should

specify if—and which—electronic rights are included. The presumption is unspecified rights remain with the writer.

- **SUBSIDIARY RIGHTS.** Rights, other than book publication rights, that should be covered in a book contract. These may include various serial rights; movie, TV, audio, and other electronic rights; translation rights, etc. The book contract should specify who controls the rights (author or publisher) and what percentage of sales from the licensing of these rights goes to the author.
- **DRAMATIC, TV, AND MOTION PICTURE RIGHTS.** Rights for use of material on the stage, on TV, or in the movies. Often a one-year option to buy such rights is offered (generally for 10 percent of the total price). The party interested in the rights then tries to sell the idea to other people—actors, directors, studios, or TV networks. Some properties are optioned numerous times, but most fail to become full productions. In those cases, the writer can sell the rights again and again.

Sometimes editors don't take the time to specify the rights they are buying. If you sense that an editor is interested in getting stories, but doesn't seem to know what his and the writer's responsibilities are, be wary. In such a case, you'll want to explain what rights you're offering (preferably one-time or first serial rights only) and that you expect additional payment for subsequent use of your work.

The Copyright Law that went into effect January 1, 1978, states writers are primarily selling one-time rights to their work unless they—and the publisher—agree otherwise in writing. Book rights are covered fully by contract between the writer and the book publisher.

CINDY FERRAINO has been blessed with a variety of assignments, including newspaper articles, magazine articles, ghost-written articles, stories for books, and most recently authoring a book on accounting and bookkeeping terminology, *The Complete Dictionary of Accounting & Bookkeeping Terms Explained Simply* (Atlantic Publishing Group).

HOW MUCH SHOULD I CHARGE?

by Aaron Belz

The first question most aspiring freelance writers ask themselves is, "Where do I find paying gigs?" But once a writer finds that first freelance gig, they often ask, "How much should I charge?"

They ask this question, because often their clients ask them. In the beginning, this can be one of the most stressful parts of the freelancing process: Trying to set rates that don't scare away clients, but that also help put dinner on the table.

Maybe that's why the "How Much Should I Charge?" pay rate chart is one of the most popular and useful pieces of the *Writer's Market*. Freelancers use the rates to justify their worth on the market to potential clients, and clients use the chart as an objective third party authority on what the current market is paying.

Use the following chart to help you get started in figuring out your freelance rates. If you're a beginner, it makes sense to price yourself closer to the lower end of the spectrum, but always use your gut in negotiating rates. The rate on that first assignment often helps set the expectations for future rates.

As you find success in securing work, your rates should naturally increase. If not, consider whether you're building relationships with clients that lead to multiple assignments. Also, take into account whether you're negotiating for higher rates on new assignments with familiar and newer clients.

Remember that smarter freelancers work toward the goal of higher rates, because better rates mean one of two things for writers: Either they're able to earn money, or they're able to earn the same money in less time. For some freelancers, having that extra time is worth more than anything money can buy.

Use the listings in *Writer's Market* to find freelance work for magazines, book publishers, and other traditional publishing markets. But don't restrict your search to the traditional markets if you want to make a serious living as a freelance writer.

As the pay rate chart shows, there are an incredible number of opportunities for writers to make a living doing what they love: writing. Maybe that means writing critiques, editing anthologies, blogging, or something else entirely.

While this pay rate chart covers a wide variety of freelance writing gigs, there are some that are just too unique to get a going rate. If you can't find a specific job listed here, try to find something that is similar to use as a guide for figuring out a rate. There are times when you just have to create the going rate yourself.

Thank you, Aaron Belz, for assembling this pay rate chart and sharing your sources in the sidebar below. I know it will help more than one freelance writer negotiate the freelance rates they deserve.

—Robert Lee Brewer

PARTICIPATING ORGANIZATIONS

Here are the organizations surveyed to compile the "How Much Should I Charge?" pay rate chart. You can also find Professional Organizations in the Resources.

- American Medical Writers Association (AMWA), www.amwa.org
- American Society of Journalists & Authors (ASJA), www.asja.org
- American Society of Media Photographers (ASMP), www.asmp.org
- American Society of Picture Professionals (ASPP), www.aspp.com
- American Translators Association (ATA), www.atanet.org
- Association of Independents in Radio (AIR), www.airmedia.org
- Editorial Freelancers Association (EFA), www.the-efa.org
- Freelance Success (FLX), www.freelancesucess.com
- Investigative Reporters & Editors (IRE), www.ire.org
- Media Communicators Association International (MCA-I), www.mca-i.org
- National Cartoonists Society (NCS), www.reuben.org/main.asp
- National Writers Union (NWU), www.nwu.org
- National Association of Science Writers (NASW), www.nasw.org
- Society of Professional Journalists (SPJ), www.spj.org
- Women in Film (WIF), www.wif.org
- Writer's Guild of America East (WGAE), www.wgaeast.org
- Writer's Guild of America West (WGA), www.wga.org

AARON BELZ is the author of *The Bird Hoverer* (BlazeVOX), *Lovely, Raspberry* (Persea), and *Glitter Bomb* (Persea). A St. Louis native, he now lives and works in Hillsborough, North Carolina. Visit him online at belz.net or follow him on Twitter @aaronbelz.

	PER HOUR			PER PROJECT			OTHER		
	HIGH	LOW	AVG	HIGH	LOW	AVG	HIGH	LOW	AVG
ADVERTISING & PUBLIC RELATIONS									
Advertising copywriting	$156	$36	$84	$9,000	$160	$2,760	$3/word	30¢/word	$1.57/word
Advertising editing	$125	$20	$65	n/a	n/a	n/a	$1/word	30¢/word	66¢/word
Advertorials	$182	$51	$93	$1,890	$205	$285	$3/word	85¢/word	$1.58/word
Business public relations	$182	$30	$85	n/a	n/a	n/a	$500/day	$200/day	$356/day
Campaign development or product launch	$156	$36	$100	$8,755	$1,550	$4,545	n/a	n/a	n/a
Catalog copywriting	$156	$25	$71	n/a	n/a	n/a	$350/item	$30/item	$116/item
Corporate spokesperson role	$182	$72	$107	n/a	n/a	n/a	$1,200/day	$500/day	$740/day
Direct-mail copywriting	$156	$36	$85	$8,248	$500	$2,839	$4/word $400/page	$1/word $200/page	$2.17/word $315/page
Event promotions/publicity	$126	$30	$76	n/a	n/a	n/a	n/a	n/a	$500/day
Press kits	$182	$31	$81	n/a	n/a	n/a	$850/60sec	$120/60sec	$458/60sec
Press/news release	$182	$30	$80	$1,500	$125	$700	$2/word $750/page	50¢/word $150/page	$1.20/word $348/page

	PER HOUR			PER PROJECT			OTHER		
	HIGH	LOW	AVG	HIGH	LOW	AVG	HIGH	LOW	AVG
Radio commercials	$102	$30	$74	n/a	n/a	n/a	$850/60sec	$120/60sec	$456/60sec
Speech writing/editing for individuals or corporations	$168	$36	$92	$10,000	$2,700	$5,036	$355/minute	$105/minute	$208/minute
BOOK PUBLISHING									
Abstracting and abridging	$125	$30	$74	n/a	n/a	n/a	$2/word	$1/word	$1.48/word
Anthology editing	$80	$23	$51	$7,900	$1,200	$4,588	n/a	n/a	n/a
Book chapter	$100	$35	$60	$2,500	$1,200	$1,758	20¢/word	8¢/word	14¢/word
Book production for clients	$100	$40	$67	n/a	n/a	n/a	$17.50/page	$5/page	$10/page
Book proposal consultation	$125	$25	$66	$1,500	$250	$788	n/a	n/a	n/a
Book publicity for clients	n/a	n/a	n/a	$10,000	$500	$2,000	n/a	n/a	n/a
Book query critique	$100	$50	$72	$500	$75	$202	n/a	n/a	n/a
Children's book writing	$75	$35	$50	n/a	n/a	n/a	$5/word $5,000/adv	$1/word $450/adv	$2.75/word $2,286/adv
Content editing (scholarly/textbook)	$125	$20	$51	$15,000	$500	$4,477	$20/page	$3/page	$6.89/page

	PER HOUR			PER PROJECT			OTHER		
	HIGH	LOW	AVG	HIGH	LOW	AVG	HIGH	LOW	AVG
Content editing (trade)	$125	$19	$54	$20,000	$1,000	$6,538	$20/page	$3.75/page	$8/page
Copyediting (trade)	$100	$16	$46	$5,500	$2,000	$2,892	$6/page	$1/page	$4.22/page
Encyclopedia articles	n/a	n/a	n/a	n/a	n/a	n/a	50¢/word $3,000/item	15¢/word $50/item	35¢/word $933/item
Fiction book writing (own)	n/a	n/a	n/a	n/a	n/a	n/a	$40,000/adv	$525/adv	$14,193/adv
Ghostwriting, as told to	$125	$35	$67	$47,000	$5,500	$22,892	$100/page	$50/page	$87/page
Ghostwriting, no credit	$125	$30	$73	n/a	n/a	n/a	$3/word $500/page	50¢/word $50/page	$1.79/word $206/page
Guidebook writing/editing	n/a	n/a	n/a	n/a	n/a	n/a	$14,000/adv	$10,000/adv	$12,000/adv
Indexing	$60	$22	$35	n/a	n/a	n/a	$12/page	$2/page	$4.72/page
Manuscript evaluation and critique	$150	$23	$66	$2,000	$150	$663	n/a	n/a	n/a
Manuscript typing	n/a	n/a	$20	n/a	n/a	n/a	$3/page	95¢/page	$1.67/page
Movie novelizations	n/a	n/a	n/a	$15,000	$5,000	$9,159	n/a	n/a	n/a

	PER HOUR			PER PROJECT			OTHER		
	HIGH	LOW	AVG	HIGH	LOW	AVG	HIGH	LOW	AVG
Nonfiction book writing (collaborative)	$125	$40	$80	n/a	n/a	n/a	$110/page $75,000/adv	$50/page $1,300/adv	$80/page $22,684/adv
Nonfiction book writing (own)	$125	$40	$72	n/a	n/a	n/a	$110/page $50,000/adv	$50/page $1,300/adv	$80/page $14,057/adv
Novel synopsis (general)	$60	$30	$45	$450	$150	$292	$100/page	$10/page	$37/page
Personal history writing/editing (for clients)	$125	$30	$60	$40,000	$750	$15,038	n/a	n/a	n/a
Proofreading	$75	$15	$31	n/a	n/a	n/a	$5/page	$2/page	$3.26/page
Research for writers or book publishers	$150	$15	$52	n/a	n/a	n/a	$600/day	$400/day	$525/day
Rewriting/structural editing	$120	$25	$67	$50,000	$2,500	$13,929	14¢/word	5¢/word	10¢/word
Translation—literary	n/a	n/a	n/a	$95,000	$6,500	$8,000	17¢/target word	4¢/target word	8¢/target word
Translation—nonfiction/technical	n/a	n/a	n/a	n/a	n/a	n/a	30¢/target word	5¢/target word	12¢/target word

	PER HOUR			PER PROJECT			OTHER		
	HIGH	LOW	AVG	HIGH	LOW	AVG	HIGH	LOW	AVG
Annual reports	$185	$60	$102	$15,000	$500	$5,850	$600	$100	$349
Brochures, booklets, flyers	$150	$45	$91	$15,000	$300	$4,230	$2.50/word $800/page	35¢/word $50/page	$1.21/word $341/page
Business editing (general)	$155	$40	$80	n/a	n/a	n/a	n/a	n/a	n/a
Business letters	$155	$40	$79	n/a	n/a	n/a	$2/word	$1/word	$1.47/word
Business plan	$155	$40	$87	$15,000	$200	$4,115	n/a	n/a	n/a
Business writing seminars	$155	$70	$112	$8,600	$550	$2,919	n/a	n/a	n/a
Consultation on communications	$155	$50	$80	n/a	n/a	n/a	$1,300/day	$530/day	$830/day
Copyediting for business	$155	$35	$65	n/a	n/a	n/a	$4/page	$2/page	$3/page
Corporate histories	$155	$45	$91	160,000	$5,000	$54,525	$2/word	$1/word	$1.50/word
Corporate periodicals, editing	$155	$45	$74	n/a	n/a	n/a	$2.50/word	75¢/word	$1.42/word
Corporate periodicals, writing	$155	$45	$83	n/a	n/a	$1,880	$3/word	$1/word	$1.71/word
Corporate profiles	$155	$45	$93	n/a	n/a	$3,000	$2/word	$1/word	$1.50/word

	PER HOUR			PER PROJECT			OTHER		
	HIGH	LOW	AVG	HIGH	LOW	AVG	HIGH	LOW	AVG
Ghostwriting for business execs	$155	$45	$89	$3,000	$500	$1,400	$2.50/word	50¢/word	$2/word
Ghostwriting for businesses	$155	$45	$114	$3,000	$500	$1,790	n/a	n/a	n/a
Newsletters, desktop publishing/production	$155	$45	$75	$6,600	$1,000	$3,490	$750/page	$150/page	$429/page
Newsletters, editing	$155	$35	$72	n/a	n/a	$3,615	$230/page	$150/page	$185/page
Newsletters, writing	$155	$35	$82	$6,600	$800	$3,581	$5/word	$1/word	$2.31/word
							$1,250/page	$150/page	$514/page
Translation services for business use	$80	$45	$57	n/a	n/a	n/a	$35/ target word	7¢/ target word	$2.31/ target word
							$1.41/ target line	$1/ target line	$1.21/ target line
Resume writing	$105	$70	$77	$500	$150	$295	n/a	n/a	n/a
COMPUTER, INTERNET & TECHNICAL									
Blogging—paid	$150	$35	$100	$2,000	$500	$1,250	$500/post	$6/post	$49/post
E-mail copywriting	$135	$30	$85	n/a	n/a	$300	$2/word	30¢/word	91¢/word

	PER HOUR			PER PROJECT			OTHER		
	HIGH	LOW	AVG	HIGH	LOW	AVG	HIGH	LOW	AVG
Educational webinars	$500	$0	$195	n/a	n/a	n/a	n/a	n/a	n/a
Hardware/Software help screen writing	$95	$60	$81	$6,000	$1,000	$4,000	n/a	n/a	n/a
Hardware/Software manual writing	$165	$30	$80	$23,500	$5,000	$11,500	n/a	n/a	n/a
Internet research	$95	$25	$55	n/a	n/a	n/a	n/a	n/a	n/a
Keyword descriptions	n/a	n/a	n/a	n/a	n/a	n/a	$200/page	$130/page	$165/page
Online videos for clients	$95	$60	$76	n/a	n/a	n/a	n/a	n/a	n/a
Social media postings for cli-ents	$95	$25	$62	n/a	n/a	$500	n/a	n/a	$10/word
Technical editing	$150	$30	$65	n/a	n/a	n/a	n/a	n/a	n/a
Technical writing	$160	$30	$80	n/a	n/a	n/a	n/a	n/a	n/a
Web editing	$100	$25	$57	n/a	n/a	n/a	$10/page	$4/page	$5.67/page
Webpage design	$150	$25	$80	$4,000	$200	$1,278	n/a	n/a	n/a
Website or blog promotion	n/a	$30	n/a	$650	$195	$335	n/a	n/a	n/a

	PER HOUR			PER PROJECT			OTHER		
	HIGH	LOW	AVG	HIGH	LOW	AVG	HIGH	LOW	AVG
Website reviews	n/a	$30	n/a	$900	$50	$300	n/a	n/a	n/a
Website search engine optimization	$89	$30	$76	$50,000	$8,000	$12,000	n/a	n/a	n/a
White papers	$135	$30	$82	$10,000	$2,500	$4,927	n/a	n/a	n/a
EDITORIAL/DESIGN PACKAGES									
Desktop publishing	$150	$18	$67	n/a	n/a	n/a	$750/page	$30/page	$202/page
Photo brochures	$125	$60	$87	$15,000	$400	$3,869	$65/picture	$30/picture	$48/picture
Photography	$100	$45	$71	$10,500	$50	$2,100	$2,500/day	$500/day	$1,340/day
Photo research	$75	$45	$49	n/a	n/a	n/a	n/a	n/a	n/a
Picture editing	$100	$45	$64	n/a	n/a	n/a	$65/picture	$30/picture	$53/picture
EDUCATIONAL & LITERARY SERVICES									
Author appearances at national events	n/a	n/a	n/a	n/a	n/a	n/a	$500/hour $30,000/event	$100/hour $500/event	$285/hour $5,000/event

	PER HOUR			PER PROJECT			OTHER		
	HIGH	LOW	AVG	HIGH	LOW	AVG	HIGH	LOW	AVG
Author appearances at regional events	n/a	n/a	n/a	n/a	n/a	n/a	$1,500/event	$50/event	$615/event
Author appearances at local groups	$63	$40	$47	n/a	n/a	n/a	$400/event	$75/event	$219/event
Authors presenting in schools	$125	$25	$78	n/a	n/a	n/a	$350/class	$50/class	$183/class
Educational grant and proposal writing	$100	$35	$67	n/a	n/a	n/a	n/a	n/a	n/a
Manuscript evaluation for theses/dissertations	$100	$15	$53	$1,550	$200	$783	n/a	n/a	n/a
Poetry manuscript critique	$100	$25	$62	n/a	n/a	n/a	n/a	n/a	n/a
Private writing instruction	$60	$50	$57	n/a	n/a	n/a	n/a	n/a	n/a
Readings by poets, fiction writers	n/a	n/a	n/a	n/a	n/a	n/a	$3,000/event	$50/event	$225/event
Short story manuscript critique	$150	$30	$75	$175	$50	$112	n/a	n/a	n/a
Teaching adult writing classes	$125	$30	$82	n/a	n/a	n/a	$800/class $5,000/course	$115/class $500/course	$450/class $2,667/course

	PER HOUR			PER PROJECT			OTHER		
	HIGH	LOW	AVG	HIGH	LOW	AVG	HIGH	LOW	AVG
TV scripts (teleplay/MOW)	$70,000/120 min								
MAGAZINES & TRADE JOURNALS									
Article manuscript critique	$130	$25	$69	n/a	n/a	n/a	n/a	n/a	n/a
Arts query critique	$105	$50	$80	n/a	n/a	n/a	n/a	n/a	n/a
Arts reviewing	$100	$65	$84	$335	$95	$194	$1.25/word	12¢/word	63¢/word
Book reviews	n/a	n/a	n/a	$900	$12	$348	$1.50/word	20¢/word	73¢/word
City magazine calendar	n/a	n/a	n/a	$250	$45	$135	$1/word	35¢/word	75¢/word
Comic book/strip writing	$225 original story, $525 existing story, $50 short script.								
Consultation on magazine editorial	$155	$35	$86	n/a	n/a	n/a	n/a	n/a	$100/page
Consumer magazine column	n/a	n/a	n/a	$2,500	$70	$898	$2.50/word	37¢/word	$1.13/word
Consumer front-of-book	n/a	n/a	n/a	$850	$320	$550	n/a	n/a	n/a
Content editing	$130	$30	$62	$6,500	$2,000	$3,700	15¢/word	6¢/word	11¢/word
Contributing editor	n/a	n/a	n/a	n/a	n/a	n/a	$160,000/ contract	$22,000/ contract	$53,000/ contract

	PER HOUR			PER PROJECT			OTHER		
	HIGH	LOW	AVG	HIGH	LOW	AVG	HIGH	LOW	AVG
Copyediting magazines	$105	$18	$55	n/a	n/a	n/a	$10/page	$2.90/page	$5.78/page
Fact checking	$130	$15	$46	n/a	n/a	n/a	n/a	n/a	n/a
Gag writing for cartoonists	$35/gag; 25% sale on spec.								
Ghostwriting articles (general)	$225	$30	$107	$3,500	$1,100	$2,200	$10/word	65¢/word	$2.50/word
Magazine research	$125	$20	$53	n/a	n/a	n/a	$500/item	$100/item	$200/item
Proofreading	$80	$20	$40	n/a	n/a	n/a	n/a	n/a	n/a
Reprint fees	n/a	n/a	n/a	$1,500	$20	$439	$1.50/word	10¢/word	76¢/word
Rewriting	$130	$25	$74	n/a	n/a	n/a	n/a	n/a	$50/page
Trade journal feature article	$128	$45	$80	$4,950	$150	$1,412	$3/word	20¢/word	$1.20/word
Transcribing interviews	$185	$95	$55	n/a	n/a	n/a	$3/min	$1/min	$2/min
MEDICAL/SCIENCE									
Medical/scientific conference coverage	$125	$50	$85	n/a	n/a	n/a	$800/day	$300/day	$600/day
Medical/scientific editing	$96	$15	$33	n/a	n/a	n/a	$12.50/page $600/day	$3/page $500/day	$4.40/page $550/day

	PER HOUR			PER PROJECT			OTHER		
	HIGH	LOW	AVG	HIGH	LOW	AVG	HIGH	LOW	AVG
Medical/scientific writing	$91	$20	$46	$4,000	$500	$2,500	$2/word	25¢/word	$1.12/word
Medical/scientific multimedia presentations	$100	$50	$75	n/a	n/a	n/a	$100/slide	$50/slide	$77/slide
Medical/scientific proofreading	$80	$18	$50	n/a	n/a	$500	$3/page	$2.50/page	$2.75/page
Pharmaceutical writing	$125	$100	$50	n/a	n/a	n/a	n/a	n/a	n/a
NEWSPAPERS									
Arts reviewing	$69	$30	$53	$200	$15	$101	60¢/word	6¢/word	36¢/word
Book reviews	$69	$45	$58	$350	$15	$140	60¢/word	25¢/word	44¢/word
Column, local	n/a	n/a	n/a	$600	$25	$206	$1/word	38¢/word	50¢/word
Column, self-syndicated	n/a	n/a	n/a	n/a	n/a	n/a	$35/insertion	$4/insertion	$16/insertion
Copyediting	$35	$15	$27	n/a	n/a	n/a	n/a	n/a	n/a
Editing/manuscript evaluation	$75	$25	$35	n/a	n/a	n/a	n/a	n/a	n/a
Feature writing	$79	$40	$63	$1,040	$85	$478	$1.60/word	10¢/word	59¢/word
Investigative reporting	n/a	n/a	n/a	n/a	n/a	n/a	$10,000/grant	$250/grant	$2,250/grant

	PER HOUR			PER PROJECT			OTHER		
	HIGH	LOW	AVG	HIGH	LOW	AVG	HIGH	LOW	AVG
Obituary copy	n/a	n/a	n/a	$225	$35	$124	n/a	n/a	n/a
Proofreading	$45	$15	$23	n/a	n/a	n/a	n/a	n/a	n/a
Stringing	n/a	n/a	n/a	$2,400	$40	$525	n/a	n/a	n/a
NONPROFIT									
Grant writing for nonprofits	$150	$12	$75	$3,000	$400	$1,852	n/a	n/a	n/a
Nonprofit annual reports	$100	$28	$60	n/a	n/a	n/a	n/a	n/a	n/a
Nonprofit writing	$150	$17	$65	$17,600	$100	$4,706	n/a	n/a	n/a
Nonprofit editing	$125	$16	$50	n/a	n/a	n/a	n/a	n/a	n/a
Nonprofit fundraising literature	$110	$35	$74	$3,500	$200	$1,597	$1,000/day	$300/day	$767/day
Nonprofit presentations	$100	$40	$73	n/a	n/a	n/a	n/a	n/a	n/a
Nonprofit public relations	$100	$30	$60	n/a	n/a	n/a	n/a	n/a	n/a
POLITICS/GOVERNMENT									
Government agency writing/editing	$110	$25	$64	n/a	n/a	n/a	$1.25/word	25¢/word	75¢/word

	PER HOUR			PER PROJECT			OTHER		
	HIGH	LOW	AVG	HIGH	LOW	AVG	HIGH	LOW	AVG
Government grant writing/ editing	$150	$19	$72	n/a	n/a	n/a	n/a	n/a	n/a
Government-sponsored research	$110	$35	$66	n/a	n/a	n/a	n/a	n/a	$600/day
Public relations for political campaigns	$150	$40	$86	n/a	n/a	n/a	n/a	n/a	n/a
Speechwriting for government officials	$200	$40	$96	$4,550	$1,015	$2,755	$200/run min	$110/run min	$155/run min
Speechwriting for political campaigns	$155	$65	$101	n/a	n/a	n/a	$200/run min	$100/run min	$162/run min

MAKING THE MOST OF THE MONEY YOU EARN

by Sage Cohen

Writers who manage money well can establish a prosperous writing life that meets their short-term needs and long-term goals. This article will introduce the key financial systems, strategies, attitudes, and practices that will help you cultivate a writing life that makes the most of your resources and sustains you over time.

DIVIDING BUSINESS AND PERSONAL EXPENSES

If you are reporting your writing business to the IRS, it is important that you keep the money that flows from this source entirely separate from your personal finances. Here's what you'll need to accomplish this:

- **BUSINESS CHECKING ACCOUNT:** Only two types of money go into this account: money you have been paid for your writing and/or "capital investments" you make by depositing your own money to invest in the business. And only two types of payments are made from this account: business-related expenses (such as: subscriptions, marketing and advertisement, professional development, fax or phone service, postage, computer software and supplies), and "capital draws" which you make to pay yourself.
- **BUSINESS SAVINGS ACCOUNT OR MONEY MARKET ACCOUNT:** This account is the holding pen where your quarterly tax payments will accumulate and earn interest. Money put aside for your retirement account(s) can also be held here.
- **BUSINESS CREDIT CARD:** It's a good idea to have a credit card for your business as a means of emergency preparedness. Pay off the card responsibly every month and this will help you establish a good business credit record, which can be useful down the line should you need a loan for any reason.

When establishing your business banking and credit, shop around for the best deals, such as highest interest rates, lowest (or no) monthly service fees, and free checking. Mint.com is a good source for researching your options.

EXPENSE TRACKING AND RECONCILING

Once your bank accounts are set up, it's time to start tracking and categorizing what you earn and spend. This will ensure that you can accurately report your income and itemize your deductions when tax time rolls around every quarter. Whether you intend to prepare your taxes yourself or have an accountant help you, immaculate financial records will be the key to speed and success in filing your taxes.

For the most effective and consistent expense tracking, I highly recommend that you use a computer program such as QuickBooks. While it may seem simpler to do accounting by hand, I assure you that it isn't. Even a luddite such as I, who can't comprehend the most basic principles of accounting, can use QuickBooks with great aplomb to plug in the proper categories for income and expenses, easily reconcile bank statements, and with a few clicks prepare all of the requisite reports that make it easy to prepare taxes.

PAYING BILLS ONLINE

While it's certainly not imperative, you might want to check out your bank's online bill pay option if you're not using this already. Once you've set up the payee list, you can make payments in a few seconds every month or set up auto payments for expenses that are recurring. Having a digital history of bills paid can also come in handy with your accounting.

MANAGING TAXES

Self-employed people need to pay quarterly taxes. A quick, online search will reveal a variety of tax calculators and other online tools that can help you estimate what your payments should be. Programs such as TurboTax are popular and useful tools for automating and guiding you step-by-step through tax preparation. An accountant can also be helpful in understanding your unique tax picture, identifying and saving the right amount for taxes each quarter, and even determining SEP IRA contribution amounts (described later in this article). The more complex your finances (or antediluvian your accounting skills), the more likely that you'll benefit from this kind of personalized expertise.

Once you have forecasted your taxes either with the help of a specialized, tax-planning program or an accountant, you can establish a plan toward saving the right amount for quarterly payments. For example, once I figured out what my tax bracket was and the approximate percentage of income that needed to be set aside as taxes, I would immediately transfer a percentage of every deposit to my savings account, where it would sit and grow a little interest until quarterly tax time came around. When I could afford to do so, I would also set aside the appropriate percentage of SEP IRA contribution from each deposit so that I'd be ready at end-of-year to deposit as much as I possibly could for retirement.

THE PRINCIPLE TO COMMIT TO IS THIS: Get that tax-earmarked cash out of your hot little hands (i.e., checking account) as soon as you can, and create whatever deterrents you need to leave the money in savings so you'll have it when you need it.

INTELLIGENT INVESTING FOR YOUR CAREER

Your writing business will require not only the investment of your time but also the investment of money. When deciding what to spend and how, consider your values and your budget in the three, key areas in the chart below: education, marketing and promotion, and keeping the wheels turning.

This is not an absolute formula for spending—just a snapshot of the types of expenses you may be considering and negotiating over time. My general rule would be: start small and modest with the one or two most urgent and/or inexpensive items in each list, and grow slowly over time as your income grows.

The good news is that these legitimate business expenses may all be deducted from your income—making your net income and tax burden less. Please keep in mind that the IRS allows losses as long as you make a profit for at least three of the first five years you are in business. Otherwise, the IRS will consider your writing a non-deductible hobby.

EDUCATION	MARKETING AND PROMOTION	KEEPING THE WHEELS TURNING
Subscriptions to publications in your field	URL registration and hosting for blogs and websites	Technology and application purchase, servicing and back-up
Memberships to organizations in your field	Contact database subscription (such as Constant Contact) for communicating with your audiences	Office supplies and furniture
Books: on topics you want to learn, or in genres you are cultivating	Business cards and stationery	Insurance for you and/or your business

Conferences and seminars	Print promotions (such as direct mail), giveaways and schwag	Travel, gas, parking
Classes and workshops	Online or print ad placement costs	Phone, fax and e-mail

PREPARATION AND PROTECTION FOR THE FUTURE

As a self-employed writer, in many ways your future is in your hands. Following are some of the health and financial investments that I'd recommend you consider as you build and nurture The Enterprise of You. Please understand that these are a layperson's suggestions. I am by no means an accountant, tax advisor, or financial planning guru. I am simply a person who has educated herself on these topics for the sake of her own writing business, made the choices I am recommending, and benefited from them. I'd like you to benefit from them, too.

SEP IRAS

Individual Retirement Accounts (IRAs) are investment accounts designed to help individuals save for retirement. But I do recommend that you educate yourself about the Simplified Employee Pension Individual Retirement Account (SEP IRA) and consider opening one if you don't have one already.

A SEP IRA is a special type of IRA that is particularly beneficial to self-employed people. Whereas a Roth IRA has a contribution cap of $5,000 or $6,000, depending on your age, the contribution limit for self-employed people in 2011 is approximately 20% of adjusted earned income, with a maximum contribution of $49,000. Contributions for a SEP IRA are generally 100% tax deductible and investments grow tax deferred. Let's say your adjusted earned income this year is $50,000. This means you'd be able to contribute $10,000 to your retirement account. I encourage you to do some research online or ask your accountant if a SEP IRA makes sense for you.

CREATING A 9-MONTH SAVINGS BUFFER

When you're living month-to-month, you are extremely vulnerable to fluctuation in the economy, client budget changes, life emergencies and every other wrench that could turn a good working groove into a frightening financial rut. The best way to prepare for the unexpected is to start (or continue) developing a savings buffer. The experts these days are suggesting that we accumulate nine months of living expenses to help us navigate transition in a way that we feel empowered rather than scared and desperate to take the next thing that comes along.

I started creating my savings buffer by opening the highest-interest money market account I could find and setting up a modest, monthly automatic transfer from my checking account. Then, when I paid off my car after five years of monthly payments, I added my car payment amount to the monthly transfer. (I'd been paying that amount for five years, so I was pretty sure I could continue to pay it to myself.) When I paid off one of my credit cards in full, I added that monthly payment to the monthly savings transfer. Within a year, I had a hefty sum going to savings every month before I had time to think about it, all based on expenses I was accustomed to paying, with money that had never been anticipated in the monthly cash flow.

What can you do today—and tomorrow—to put your money to work for your life, and start being as creative with your savings as you are with language?

DISABILITY INSURANCE

If writing is your livelihood, what happens if you become unable to write? I have writing friends who have become incapacitated and unable to work due to injuries to their brains, backs, hands and eyes. Disability insurance is one way to protect against such emergencies and ensure that you have an income in the unlikely event that you're not physically able to earn one yourself.

Depending on your health, age, and budget, monthly disability insurance payments may or may not be within your means or priorities. But you won't know until you learn more about your coverage options. I encourage you to investigate this possibility with several highly rated insurance companies to get the lay of the land for your unique, personal profile and make an informed decision.

HEALTH INSURANCE

Self-employed writers face tough decisions about health insurance. If you're lucky, there's someone in your family with health coverage also available to you. Without the benefit of group health insurance, chances are that self-costs are high and coverage is low. As in disability insurance, age and health status are significant variables in costs and availability.

Ideally, of course, you'll have reasonably-priced health insurance that helps make preventive care and health maintenance more accessible and protects you in case of a major medical emergency. The following are a few possibilities to check out that could reduce costs and improve access to health coverage:

- Join a group that aggregates its members for group coverage, such as a Chamber of Commerce or AARP. Ask an insurance agent in your area if there are any other group coverage options available to you.

- Consider a high-deductible health plan paired with a Health Savings Account (HSA). Because the deductible is so high, these plans are generally thought to be most useful for a major medical emergency. But an HSA paired with such a plan allows you to put aside a chunk of pre-tax change every year that can be spent on medical expenses or remain in the account where it can be invested and grow.

Establishing effective financial systems for your writing business will take some time and energy at the front end. I suggest that you pace yourself by taking an achievable step or two each week until you have a baseline of financial management that works for you. Then, you can start moving toward some of your bigger, longer-term goals. Once it's established, your solid financial foundation will pay you in dividends of greater efficiency, insight, and peace of mind for the rest of your writing career.

SAGE COHEN is the author of *The Productive Writer* and *Writing the Life Poetic*, both from Writer's Digest Books. She's been nominated for a Pushcart Prize, won first prize in the Ghost Road Press Poetry contest and published dozens of poems, essays and articles on the writing life. Sage holds an MFA in creative writing from New York University and a BA from Brown University. Since 1997, she has been a freelance writer serving clients including Intuit, Blue Shield, Adobe, and Kaiser Permanente.

LITERARY AGENTS

The literary agencies listed in this section are open to new clients and are members of the Association of Authors' Representatives (AAR), which means they do not charge for reading, critiquing, or editing. Some agents in this section may charge clients for office expenses such as photocopying, foreign postage, long-distance phone calls, or express mail services. Make sure you have a clear understanding of what these expenses are before signing any agency agreement.

FOR MORE...

The *2020 Guide to Literary Agents* (Writer's Digest Books) offers more than 600 literary agents, as well as information on writers' conferences. It also offers a wealth of information on the author/agent relationship and other related topics.

SUBHEADS

Each listing is broken down into subheads to make locating specific information easier. In the first section, you'll find contact information for each agency. Further information is provided which indicates an agency's size, its willingness to work with a new or previously unpublished writer, and its general areas of interest.

ADAMS LITERARY

7845 Colony Rd., C4 #215, Charlotte NC 28226. (704)542-1440. **Fax:** (704)542-1450. **E-mail:** info@adamsliterary.com. **Website:** www.adamsliterary.com. **Contact:** Tracey Adams, Josh Adams. Estab. 2004. Member of AAR. Other memberships include SCBWI and WNBA.

MEMBER AGENTS Tracey Adams, Josh Adams, Lorin Oberweger.

REPRESENTS Considers these fiction areas: middle grade, picture books, young adult.

Represents "the finest children's book and young adult authors and artists."

HOW TO CONTACT Submit through online form on website only. Send e-mail if that is not operating correctly. All submissions and queries should first be made through the online form on website. Will not review—and will promptly recycle—any unsolicited submissions or queries received by mail. Before submitting work for consideration, review complete guidelines online, as the agency sometimes shuts off to new submissions. Accepts simultaneous submissions. Responds in 6 weeks if interested. "While we have an established client list, we do seek new talent—and we accept submissions from both published and aspiring authors and artists."

TERMS Agent receives 15% commission on domestic sales; 20% on foreign sales. Offers written contract.

RECENT SALES *The Cruelty*, by Scott Bergstrom (Feiwel & Friends); *The Little Fire Truck*, by Margery Cuyler (Christy Ottaviano); *Unearthed*, by Amie Kaufman and Meagan Spooner (Disney-Hyperion); *A Handful of Stars*, by Cynthia Lord (Scholastic); *Under Their Skin*, by Margaret Peterson Haddix (Simon & Schuster); *The Secret Horses of Briar Hill*, by Megan Shepherd (Delacorte); *The Secret Subway*, by Shana Corey (Schwartz & Wade); *Impyrium*, by Henry Neff (HarperCollins).

TIPS "Guidelines are posted (and frequently updated) on our website."

BRET ADAMS LTD. AGENCY

Bret Adams, Ltd., 448 W. 44th St., New York NY 10036. (212)765-5630. **Fax:** (212)265-2212. **Website:** bretadamsltd.net. Member of AAR.

MEMBER AGENTS Bruce Ostler; Mark Orsini; Alexis Williams.

REPRESENTS Theatrical stage play, stage plays. **Considers these script areas:** stage plays, theatrical stage play.

Handles theatre projects. No books or screenplays. Cannot accept unsolicited material.

HOW TO CONTACT Use the online submission form. Because of this agency's submission policy and interests, it's best to approach with a professional recommendation from a client. Accepts simultaneous submissions.

AEVITAS CREATIVE MANAGEMENT

19 W. 21st St., Suite 501, New York NY 10010. (212)765-6900. **Website:** aevitascreative.com. Member of AAR. Signatory of WGA.

MEMBER AGENTS Esmond Harmsworth, managing partner; David Kuhn, managing partner; Todd Shuster, managing partner; Jennifer Gates, senior partner; Laura Nolan, senior partner; Janet Silver, senior partner; Lane Zachary, senior partner; Bridget Wagner Matzie, partner; Rick Richter, partner; Jane von Mehren, partner; Rob Arnold, agent; Sarah Bowlin, agent; Michelle Brower, agent; Nick Chiles, agent; Lori Galvin, agent; David Granger, agent; Jim Kelly, agent; Sarah Lazin, agent; Sarah Levitt, agent; Will Lippincott, agent; Jen Marshall, agent; Penny Moore, agent; Lauren Sharp, agent; Becky Sweren, agent; Nan Thornton, agent; Susan Zanger, agent; Erica Bauman, associate agent; Justin Brouckaert, associate agent; Kate Mack, associate agent; Nate Muscato, associate agent.

REPRESENTS Nonfiction, fiction.

HOW TO CONTACT Find specific agents on the Aevitas website to see their specific interests and guidelines. Accepts simultaneous submissions.

BETSY AMSTER LITERARY ENTERPRISES

607 Foothill Blvd. #1061, La Cañada Flintridge CA 91012. **E-mail:** b.amster.assistant@gmail.com (for adult titles); b.amster.kidsbooks@gmail.com (for children's and young adult). **Website:** www.amsterlit.com; www.cummingskidlit.com. **Contact:** Betsy Amster (adult); Mary Cummings (children's and young adult). Estab. 1992. Member of AAR. PEN America (Amster); Society of Children's Books Writers and Illustrators (Cummings). Represents more than 75 clients.

Prior to opening her agency, Ms. Amster was an editor at Pantheon and Vintage for 10 years and served as editorial director for the Globe Pequot Press for 2 years. Prior to joining the agency, Mary Cummings served as education director at the Loft Literary Center in Minneapolis for 14 years, overseeing classes, workshops, and conferences. She curated the annual Festival of Children's Literature and selected judges for the McKnight Award in Children's Literature.

REPRESENTS Nonfiction, novels, juvenile books. **Considers these nonfiction areas:** autobiography, biography, business, child guidance, cooking, creative nonfiction, cultural interests, decorating, design, foods, gardening, health, history, horticulture, how-to, interior design, investigative, medicine, memoirs, money, multicultural, parenting, popular culture, psychology, science, self-help, sociology, travel, women's issues, young adult. **Considers these fiction areas:** crime, detective, family saga, juvenile, literary, middle grade, multicultural, mystery, picture books, police, suspense, thriller, women's, young adult.

"Betsy Amster is actively seeking strong narrative nonfiction, particularly by journalists; outstanding literary fiction; witty, intelligent commercial women's fiction; character-driven mysteries and thrillers that open new worlds to us; high-profile self-help, psychology, and health, preferably research-based; and cookbooks and food narratives by West Coast–based chefs and food writers with an original viewpoint and national exposure. Does not want to receive poetry, romances, western, science fiction, action/adventure, screenplays, fantasy, technothrillers, spy capers, apocalyptic scenarios, or political or religious arguments. Mary Cummings is actively seeking great read-aloud picture books and middle-grade novels with strong story arcs, a spunky central character, and warmth, humor, or quirky charm as well as picture-book biographies and lyrically written children's nonfiction on science, nature, mindfulness, and social awareness."

HOW TO CONTACT "For adult fiction or memoirs, please embed the first 3 pages in the body of your e-mail. For nonfiction, please embed the overview of your proposal. For children's picture books, please embed the entire text in the body of your e-mail. For longer middle-grade and YA fiction and nonfiction, please embed the first 3 pages." Accepts simultaneous submissions. Responds in 1 month to queries; 2 months to mss. Obtains most new clients through recommendations from others, solicitations, and conferences.

TERMS Agent receives 15% commission on domestic sales; 20% commission on foreign sales. Offers written contract, binding for 1 year; three-month notice must be given to terminate contract. Charges for photocopying, postage, messengers, galleys/books used in submissions to foreign and film agents and to magazines for first serial rights. (Please note that it is rare to incur much in the way of expenses now that most submissions are made by e-mail.)

RECENT SALES **Betsy Amster**: *Sugarproof: How Sugar Puts Your Kid at Risk—and What You Can Do About It*, by Michael I. Goran, Ph.D. and Emily Ventura, Ph.D., M.P.H. (Avery); *What Makes a Wine Worth Drinking: In Praise of the Sublime*, by Terry Theise (Houghton Mifflin Harcourt); *Good Trouble: Lessons from the Civil Rights Playbook*, by Christopher Noxon (Abrams); *The Lost Gutenberg: The Astounding Story of One Book's Five-Hundred-Year Odyssey*, by Margaret Leslie Davis (TarcherPerigee). **Mary Cummings**: *Counting Elephants*, by Dawn Young (Running Press Kids); *Those Are Not My Underpants!*, by Melissa Martin (Random House Childrens); *We Love Fishing!*, by Ariel Bernstein (Paula Wiseman Books/Simon & Schuster); *Little Things*, by Nick Dyer (Peter Pauper Press);*Small Walt to the Rescue*, by Elizabeth Verdick (Paula Wiseman Books/Simon & Schuster).

WRITERS CONFERENCES SDSU (Amster); Minnesota Writing Workshop and regional SCBWI (Cummings).

APONTE LITERARY AGENCY

E-mail: agents@aponteliterary.com. **Website:** aponteliterary.com. **Contact:** Natalia Aponte. Member of AAR. Signatory of WGA.

MEMBER AGENTS Natalia Aponte (any genre of mainstream fiction and nonfiction, but she is especially seeking women's novels, historical novels, supernatural and paranormal fiction, fantasy novels, political and science thrillers); Victoria Lea (any category, especially interested in women's fiction, science fiction and speculative fiction).

REPRESENTS Novels. **Considers these fiction areas:** fantasy, historical, paranormal, science fiction, supernatural, thriller, women's.

Actively seeking women's novels, historical novels, supernatural and paranormal fiction, fantasy novels, political and science thrillers, science fiction and speculative fiction. In nonfiction, will look at any genre with commercial potential.

HOW TO CONTACT E-query. Accepts simultaneous submissions. Responds in 6 weeks if interested.

RECENT SALES *The Nightingale Bones*, by Ariel Swan; *An Irish Doctor in Peace and At War*, by Patrick Taylor; *Siren's Treasure*, by Debbie Herbert.

THE AXELROD AGENCY

55 Main St., P.O. Box 357, Chatham NY 12037. (518)392-2100. **E-mail:** steve@axelrodagency.com. **Website:** www.axelrodagency.com. **Contact:** Steven Axelrod. Member of AAR. Represents 15-20 clients.

Prior to becoming an agent, Mr. Axelrod was a book club editor.

MEMBER AGENTS Steven Axelrod, representation; Lori Antonson, subsidiary rights.

REPRESENTS Novels. **Considers these fiction areas:** crime, mystery, new adult, romance, women's.

This agency specializes in women's fiction and romance.

HOW TO CONTACT Query via e-mail. Accepts simultaneous submissions. Obtains most new clients through recommendations from others.

TERMS Agent receives 15% commission on domestic sales; 20% commission on foreign sales. No written contract.

WRITERS CONFERENCES RWA National Conference.

BARONE LITERARY AGENCY

385 North St., Batavia OH 45103. (513)732-6740. **Fax:** (513)297-7208. **E-mail:** baronelit@outlook.com. **Website:** www.baroneliteraryagency.com. **Contact:** Denise Barone. Estab. 2010. Member of AAR. Signatory of WGA. Member of RWA. Represents 14 clients.

REPRESENTS Fiction, novels. **Considers these nonfiction areas:** memoirs, theater, young adult. **Considers these fiction areas:** action, adventure, cartoon, comic books, commercial, confession, contemporary issues, crime, detective, erotica, ethnic, experimental, family saga, fantasy, feminist, frontier, gay, glitz, hi-lo, historical, horror, humor, inspirational, juvenile, lesbian, literary, mainstream, metaphysical, military, multicultural, multimedia, mystery, new adult, New Age, occult, paranormal, plays, police, psychic, regional, religious, romance, satire, science fiction, spiritual, sports, supernatural, suspense, thriller, translation, urban fantasy, war, westerns, women's, young adult.

Actively seeking adult contemporary romance. Does not want textbooks.

HOW TO CONTACT "Do not send anything through the mail. I accept only email queries. If I like your query letter, I will ask for the first 3 chapters and a synopsis as attachments." Accepts simultaneous submissions. "I make every effort to respond within 4 months." Obtains new clients by queries/submissions via e-mail only.

TERMS Agency receives 15% commission on domestic sales; 20% on foreign sales. Offers written contract.

RECENT SALES *Haunting You*, by Molly Zenk (Intrigue Publishing); *The Beekeeper*, by Robert E. Hoxie (Six Gun Pictures); *All The Glittering Bones*, by Anna Snow (Entangled Publishing); *Devon's Choice*, by Cathy Bennett (Clean Reads); *Molly's Folly*, by Denise Gwen (Clean Reads); *In Deep*, by Laurie Albano (Solstice Publishing); *The Trouble with Charlie*, by Cathy Bennett (Clean Reads); *The Fairy Godmother Files: Cinderella Complex*, by Rebekah L. Purdy (Clean Reads).

WRITERS CONFERENCES The Sell More Books Show, Chicago, Illinois, 2018; Annual Conference of Romance Writers of America, Orlando, Florida, 2017; Lori Foster's Readers and Authors' Get-Together, West Chester, Ohio; A Weekend with the Authors, Nashville, Tennessee; Willamette Writers' Conference, Portland, Oregon.

TIPS "The best writing advice I ever got came from a fellow writer, who wrote, 'Learn how to edit yourself,' when signing her book to me."

THE BENT AGENCY

19 W. 21st St., #201, New York NY 10010. **E-mail:** info@thebentagency.com. **E-mail:** Please see website. **Website:** www.thebentagency.com. **Contact:** Jenny Bent. Estab. 2009. Member of AAR.

Prior to forming her own agency, Ms. Bent was an agent and vice president at Trident Media Group.

MEMBER AGENTS Jenny Bent (adult fiction, including women's fiction, romance, and crime/suspense; she particularly likes novels with magical or fantasy elements that fall outside of genre fiction; young adult and middle-grade fiction; memoir; humor); Nicola Barr (literary and commercial fiction for adults and children, and nonfiction in the areas of sports, popular science, popular culture, and social and cultural history); Molly Ker Hawn (young adult and middle-grade books, including contemporary, historical, fantasy, science fiction, thrillers, and mystery); Gemma Cooper (all ages of children's and young adult books, including picture books; likes historical, contemporary, thrillers, mystery, humor, and science fiction); Louise Fury (children's fiction: picture books, literary middle-grade, and all young adult; adult fiction: speculative fiction, suspense/thriller, commercial fiction, and all subgenres of romance including erotic; nonfiction: cookbooks and pop culture); Sarah Manning (commercial and accessible literary adult fiction and nonfiction in the area of memoir, lifestyle, and narrative nonfiction); Beth Phelan (young adult, thrillers, suspense and mystery, romance and women's fiction, literary and general fiction, cookbooks, lifestyle, and pets/animals); Victoria Cappello (commercial and literary adult fiction as well as narrative nonfiction); Heather Flaherty (young adult and middle-grade fiction: all genres; select adult fiction: upmarket fiction, women's fiction, and female-centric thrillers; select nonfiction: pop culture, humorous, and social media–based projects, as well as teen memoir).

REPRESENTS Nonfiction, novels, short story collections, juvenile books. **Considers these nonfiction areas:** animals, cooking, creative nonfiction, foods, juvenile nonfiction, popular culture, women's issues, young adult. **Considers these fiction areas:** adventure, commercial, crime, erotica, fantasy, feminist, historical, horror, humor, juvenile, literary, mainstream, middle grade, multicultural, mystery, new adult, picture books, romance, short story collections, suspense, thriller, women's, young adult.

HOW TO CONTACT "Tell us briefly who you are, what your book is, and why you're the one to write it. Then include the first 10 pages of your material in the body of your e-mail. We respond to all queries; please resend your query if you haven't had a response within 4 weeks." Accepts simultaneous submissions.

RECENT SALES *Caraval*, by Stephanie Garber (Flatiron); *Rebel of the Sands*, by Alwyn Hamilton (Viking Children's/Penguin BFYR); *The Square Root of Summer*, by Harriet Reuter Hapgood (Roaring Brook/Macmillan); *Dirty Money*, by Lisa Renee Jones (Simon & Schuster); *True North*, by Liora Blake (Pocket Star).

VICKY BIJUR LITERARY AGENCY

27 W. 20th St., Suite 1003, New York NY 10011. **E-mail:** queries@vickybijuragency.com. **Website:** www.vickybijuragency.com. Estab. 1988. Member of AAR.

Vicky Bijur worked at Oxford University Press and with the Charlotte Sheedy Literary Agency. Books she represents have appeared on *the New York Times Bestseller List*, in the *New York Times* Notable Books of the Year, *Los Angeles Times* Best Fiction of the Year, *Washington Post* Book World Rave Reviews of the Year.

MEMBER AGENTS Vicky Bijur; Alexandra Franklin.

REPRESENTS Nonfiction, novels. **Considers these nonfiction areas:** memoirs. **Considers these fiction areas:** commercial, literary, mystery, new adult, thriller, women's, young adult, Campus novels, coming-of-age.

"We are not the right agency for screenplays, picture books, poetry, self-help, science fiction, fantasy, horror, or romance."

HOW TO CONTACT "Please send a query letter of no more than 3 paragraphs on what makes your book special and unique, a very brief synopsis, its length and genre, and your biographical information, along with the first 10 pages of your manuscript. Please let us know in your query letter if it is a multiple submission, and kindly keep us informed of other agents' interest and offers of representation. If sending electronically, paste the pages in an e-mail as we don't open attachments from unfamiliar senders. If sending by hard copy, please include an SASE for our response. If you want your material returned, include an SASE large enough to contain pages and enough postage to send back to you." Accepts simultaneous submissions. "We generally respond to all queries within 8 weeks of receipt."

RECENT SALES *That Darkness*, by Lisa Black; *Long Upon the Land*, by Margaret Maron; *Daughter of Ashes*, by Marcia Talley.

DAVID BLACK LITERARY AGENCY

335 Adams St., Suite 2707, Brooklyn NY 11201. (718)-852-5500. **Fax:** (718)852-5539. **Website:** www.davidblackagency.com. **Contact:** David Black, owner. Estab. 1989. Member of AAR. Represents 150 clients.

MEMBER AGENTS David Black; Jenny Herrera; Gary Morris; Joy E. Tutela (narrative nonfiction, memoir, history, politics, self-help, investment, business, science, women's issues, GLBT issues, parenting, health and fitness, humor, craft, cooking and wine, lifestyle and entertainment, commercial fiction, literary fiction, MG, YA); Susan Raihofer (commercial fiction and nonfiction, memoir, pop culture, music, inspirational, thrillers, literary fiction); Sarah Smith (memoir, biography, food, music, narrative history, social studies, literary fiction).

REPRESENTS Nonfiction, novels. **Considers these nonfiction areas:** biography, business, cooking, crafts, gay/lesbian, health, history, humor, inspirational, memoirs, music, parenting, popular culture, politics, science, self-help, sociology, sports, women's issues. **Considers these fiction areas:** commercial, literary, middle grade, thriller, young adult.

HOW TO CONTACT "To query an individual agent, please follow the specific query guidelines outlined in the agent's profile on our website. Not all agents are currently accepting unsolicited queries. To query the agency, please send a 1-2 page query letter describing your book, and include information about any previously published works, your audience, and your platform." Do not e-mail your query unless an agent specifically asks for an e-mail. Accepts simultaneous submissions. Responds in 2 months to queries.

RECENT SALES Some of the agency's best-selling authors include: Erik Larson, Stuart Scott, Jeff Hobbs, Mitch Albom, Gregg Olsen, Jim Abbott, and John Bacon.

BOOK CENTS LITERARY AGENCY, LLC

121 Black Rock Turnpike, Suite #499, Redding Ridge CT 06876. **E-mail:** cw@bookcentsliteraryagency.com. **Website:** www.bookcentsliteraryagency.com. **Contact:** Christine Witthohn. Estab. 2005. Member of AAR. RWA, MWA, SinC, KOD.

REPRESENTS Novels. **Considers these nonfiction areas:** cooking, gardening, travel, women's issues. **Considers these fiction areas:** commercial, mainstream, multicultural, mystery, paranormal, romance, suspense, thriller, women's, young adult.

⊶ Actively seeking upmarket fiction, commercial fiction (particularly if it has crossover appeal), women's fiction (emotional and layered), romance (single title or category), mainstream mystery/suspense, thrillers (particularly psychological), and young adult. For a detailed list of what this agency is currently searching for, visit the website. Does not want to receive third party submissions, previously published titles, short stories/novellas, erotica, inspirational, historical, science fiction/fantasy, horror/pulp/slasher thrillers, middle-grade, children's picture books, poetry, or screenplays. Does not want stories with priests/nuns, religion, abuse of children/animals/elderly, rape, or serial killers.

HOW TO CONTACT Submit via agency website. Does not accept mail or e-mail submissions.

TIPS Sponsors the International Women's Fiction Festival in Matera, Italy. See www.womensfictionfestival.com for more information. Ms. Witthohn is also the U.S. rights and licensing agent for leading French publisher Bragelonne, German publisher Egmont, and Spanish publisher Edebe.

BOOKENDS LITERARY AGENCY

Website: www.bookendsliterary.com. **Contact:** Jessica Faust, Kim Lionetti, Jessica Alvarez, Moe Ferrara, Tracy Marchini, Rachel Brooks, Natascha Morris, Naomi Davis, Amanda Jain, James McGowan. Estab. 1999. Member of AAR. RWA, MWA, SCBWI, SFWA. Represents 50+ clients.

MEMBER AGENTS Jessica Faust (women's fiction, mysteries, thrillers, suspense); Kim Lionetti (romance, women's fiction, young adult); Jessica Alvarez (romance, women's fiction, mystery, suspense, thrillers, and nonfiction); Moe Ferrara (middle-grade, young adult, and adult: romance, science fiction, fantasy, horror); Tracy Marchini (picture book, middle-grade, and young adult: fiction and nonfiction); Rachel Brooks (young adult, romance, women's fiction, cozy mysteries); Natascha Morris (young adult, middle grade, picture book); Naomi Davis (science fiction, fantasy, young adult, middle grade, picture books); Amanda Jain (mystery, romance, women's fiction, upmarket, historical fiction); James McGowan (literary, upmarket, mystery, suspense, thrillers, young adult).

REPRESENTS Nonfiction, novels, juvenile books. **Considers these nonfiction areas:** art, business, creative nonfiction, ethnic, how-to, inspirational, juvenile nonfiction, money, self-help, women's issues, young adult, picture book, middle grade. **Considers these fiction areas:** adventure, comic books, commercial, crime, detective, erotica, family saga, fantasy, gay, historical, horror, juvenile, lesbian, mainstream, middle grade, multicultural, mystery, paranormal, picture books, police, romance, science fiction, supernatural, suspense, thriller, urban fantasy, women's, young adult.

- "BookEnds is currently accepting queries from published and unpublished writers in the areas of romance, mystery, suspense, science fiction and fantasy, horror, women's fiction, picture books, middle-grade, and young adult. In nonfiction we represent titles in the following areas: current affairs, reference, business and career, parenting, pop culture, coloring books, general nonfiction, and nonfiction for children and teens." BookEnds does not represent short fiction, poetry, screenplays, or techno-thrillers.

HOW TO CONTACT Visit website for the most up-to-date guidelines and current preferences. BookEnds agents accept all submissions through their personal Query Manager forms. These forms are accessible on the agency website under Submissions. Accepts simultaneous submissions. "Our response time goals are 6 weeks for queries and 12 weeks on requested partials and fulls."

THE BOOK GROUP

20 W. 20th St., Suite 601, New York NY 10011. (212)803-3360. **E-mail:** submissions@thebookgroup.com. **Website:** www.thebookgroup.com. Estab. 2015. Member of AAR. Signatory of WGA.

MEMBER AGENTS Julie Barer; Faye Bender; Brettne Bloom (fiction: literary and commercial fiction, select young adult; nonfiction, including cookbooks, lifestyle, investigative journalism, history, biography, memoir, and psychology); Elisabeth Weed (upmarket fiction, especially plot-driven novels with a sense of place); Rebecca Stead (innovative forms, diverse voices, and open-hearted fiction for children, young adults, and adults); Dana Murphy (story-driven fiction with a strong sense of place, narrative nonfiction/essays with a pop-culture lean, and YA with an honest voice).

REPRESENTS Considers these nonfiction areas: biography, cooking, history, investigative, memoirs, psychology. **Considers these fiction areas:** commercial, literary, mainstream, women's, young adult.

- Please do not send poetry or screenplays.

HOW TO CONTACT Send a query letter and 10 sample pages to submissions@thebookgroup.com, with the first and last name of the agent you are querying in the subject line. All material must be in the body of the e-mail, as the agents do not open attachments. "If we are interested in reading more, we will get in touch with you as soon as possible." Accepts simultaneous submissions.

RECENT SALES *This Is Not Over*, by Holly Brown; *Perfect Little World*, by Kevin Wilson; *City of Saints & Thieves*, by Natalie C. Anderson; *The Runaway Midwife*, by Patricia Harman; *Always*, by Sarah Jio; *The Young Widower's Handbook*, by Tom McAllister.

BRADFORD LITERARY AGENCY

5694 Mission Center Rd., #347, San Diego CA 92108. (619)521-1201. **E-mail:** queries@bradfordlit.com. **Website:** www.bradfordlit.com. **Contact:** Laura Bradford, Natalie Lakosil, Sarah LaPolla, Kari Sutherland, Jennifer Chen Tran. Estab. 2001. Member of AAR. RWA, SCBWI, ALA Represents 130 clients.

MEMBER AGENTS Laura Bradford (romance [historical, romantic suspense, paranormal, category, contemporary, erotic], mystery, women's fiction, thrillers/suspense, middle grade & YA); Natalie Lakosil (children's literature [from picture book through teen and New Adult], romance [contemporary and historical], cozy mystery/crime, upmarket women's/general fiction and select children's nonfiction); Sarah LaPolla (YA, middle grade, literary fiction, science fiction, magical realism, dark/psychological mystery, literary horror, and upmarket contemporary fiction); Kari Sutherland (children's literature, middle grade, YA, upmarket women's fiction, magical realism, historical dramas, light-hearted contemporary fiction, biography, humor, and parenting); Jennifer Chen Tran (women's fiction, YA, middle grade, graphic novels, narrative nonfiction, parenting, culinary, lifestyle, business, memoir, parenting, psychology).

REPRESENTS Nonfiction, fiction, novels, juvenile books. **Considers these nonfiction areas:** biography, cooking, creative nonfiction, cultural interests, foods, history, humor, juvenile nonfiction, memoirs, parenting, popular culture, politics, psychology, self-help, women's issues, women's studies, young adult. **Considers these fiction areas:** commercial, crime, ethnic, gay, historical, juvenile, lesbian, literary, mainstream, middle grade, multicultural, mystery, new adult, paranormal, picture books, romance, science fiction, thriller, women's, young adult.

- Laura Bradford does not want to receive poetry, screenplays, short stories, westerns, horror, new age, religion, crafts, cookbooks, gift books. Natalie Lakosil does not want to receive inspirational novels, memoir, romantic suspense, adult thrillers, poetry, screenplays. Sarah LaPolla does not want to receive nonfiction, picture books, inspirational/spiritual novels, romance, or erotica. Kari Sutherland does not want to receive horror, romance, erotica, memoir, adult sci-fi/fantasy, thrillers, cookbooks, business, spiritual/religious, poetry, or screenplays. Jennifer Chen Tran does not want to receive picture books, sci-fi/fantasy, urban fantasy, westerns, erotica, poetry, or screenplays.

HOW TO CONTACT Accepts e-mail queries only; For submissions to Laura Bradford, send to queries@bradfordlit.com. For submissions to Natalie Lakosil, use the form listed on the website under the "How to Submit" page. For submissions to Sarah LaPolla, send to sarah@bradfordlit.com. For submissions to Kari Sutherland, send to kari@bradfordlit.com. For submissions to Jennifer Chen Tran, send to jen@bradfordlit.com. The entire submission must appear in the body of the e-mail and not as an attachment. The subject line should begin as follows: "QUERY: (the title of the ms or any short message that is important should follow)." For fiction: e-mail a query letter along with the first chapter of ms and a synopsis. Include the genre and word count in your query letter. Nonfiction: e-mail full nonfiction proposal including a query letter and a sample chapter. Accepts simultaneous submissions. Responds in 4 weeks to queries; 10 weeks to mss. Obtains most new clients through queries.

TERMS Agent receives 15% commission on domestic sales; 25% commission on foreign sales. Offers written contract. Charges for extra copies of books for foreign submissions.

RECENT SALES Sold 80 titles in the last year, including Vox by Christina Dalcher (Berkley); *The Last 8*, by Laura Pohl (Sourcebooks Fire); *You'll Miss Me When I'm Gone*, by Rachel Solomon (Simon Pulse); *Monday's Not Coming*, by Tiffany Jackson (Harper Collins); *Where She Fell*, by Kaitlin Ward (Adaptive); *Into the Nightfell Wood*, by Kristin Bailey (Katherine Tegen Books); *Yasmin the Explorer*, by Saadia Faruqi (Capstone); *Fix Her Up*, by Tessa Bailey (Entangled); *The Protector*, by HelenKay Dimon (Avon); *The Spitfire Girls*, by Soraya Lane (St. Martins); *Highland Wrath*, by Madeline Martin (Diversion); *Everybody's Favorite Book*, by Mike Allegra (Macmillan); *The Hook Up*, by Erin McCarthy (PRH); *Next Girl to Die*, by Dea Poirier (Thomas & Mercer); *The Fearless King*, by Katee Robert (Entangled); *Noble Hops*, by Layla Reyne (Carina Press); *The Rogue on Fifth Avenue*, by Joanna Shupe (Kensington).

WRITERS CONFERENCES RWA National Conference, Romantic Times Booklovers Convention.

BRANDT & HOCHMAN LITERARY AGENTS, INC.

1501 Broadway, Suite 2310, New York NY 10036. (212)840-5760. **Fax:** (212)840-5776. **Website:** brandthochman.com. **Contact:** Gail Hochman or individual agent best suited for the submission. Estab. over a century ago. Member of AAR. Represents 200 clients.

MEMBER AGENTS Gail Hochman (works of literary fiction, idea-driven nonfiction, literary memoir and children's books); Marianne Merola (fiction, nonfiction and children's books with strong and unique narrative voices); Bill Contardi (voice-driven young adult and middle grade fiction, commercial thrillers, psychological suspense, quirky mysteries, high fantasy, commercial fiction and memoir); Emily Forland (voice-driven literary fiction and nonfiction, memoir, narrative nonfiction, history, biography, food writing, cultural criticism, graphic novels, and young adult fiction); Emma Patterson (fiction from dark, literary novels to upmarket women's and historical fiction; narrative nonfiction that includes memoir, investigative journalism, and popular history; young adult fiction); Jody Kahn (literary and upmarket fiction; narrative nonfiction, particularly books related to sports, food, history, science and pop culture—including cookbooks, and literary memoir and journalism); Henry Thayer (nonfiction on a wide variety of subjects and fiction that inclines toward the literary). The e-mail addresses and specific likes of each of these agents is listed on the agency website.

REPRESENTS Nonfiction, novels. **Considers these nonfiction areas:** biography, cooking, current affairs, foods, health, history, memoirs, music, popular culture, science, sports, narrative nonfiction, journalism. **Considers these fiction areas:** fantasy, historical, literary, middle grade, mystery, suspense, thriller, women's, young adult.

⊶ No screenplays or textbooks.

HOW TO CONTACT "We accept queries by e-mail and regular mail; however, we cannot guarantee a response to e-mailed queries. For queries via regular mail, be sure to include a SASE for our reply. Query letters should be no more than 2 pages and should include a convincing overview of the book project and information about the author and his or her writing credits. Address queries to the specific Brandt & Hochman agent whom you would like to consider your work. Agent e-mail addresses and query preferences may be found at the end of each agent profile on the 'Agents' page of our website." Accepts simultaneous submissions. Obtains most new clients through recommendations from others.

TERMS Agent receives 15% commission on domestic sales; 20% commission on foreign sales.

RECENT SALES This agency sells 40-60 new titles each year. A full list of their hundreds of clients is on the agency website.

TIPS "Write a letter which will give the agent a sense of you as a professional writer—your long-term interests as well as a short description of the work at hand."

THE BRATTLE AGENCY

P.O. Box 380537, Cambridge MA 02238. (617)721-5375. **E-mail:** christopher.vyce@thebrattleagency.com. **E-mail:** submissions@thebrattleagency.com. **Website:** thebrattleagency.com. **Contact:** Christopher Vyce. Member of AAR. Signatory of WGA.

Prior to being an agent, Mr. Vyce worked for the Beacon Press in Boston as an acquisitions editor.

REPRESENTS Nonfiction, novels. **Considers these nonfiction areas:** art, biography, creative nonfiction, cultural interests, film, history, literature, music, popular culture, politics, regional, sports, race studies, American studies. **Considers these fiction areas:** literary.

HOW TO CONTACT Query by e-mail. Include cover letter, brief synopsis, brief CV. Accepts simultaneous submissions. Responds to queries in 72 hours. Responds to approved submissions in 6-8 weeks.

BARBARA BRAUN ASSOCIATES, INC.

7 E. 14th St., #19F, New York NY 10003. **Fax:** (212)604-9023. **E-mail:** bbasubmissions@gmail.com. **Website:** www.barbarabraunagency.com. **Contact:** Barbara Braun. Member of AAR. Authors Guild, PEN Center USA

REPRESENTS Nonfiction, novels. **Considers these nonfiction areas:** architecture, art, biography, design, film, history, photography, politics, psychology, women's issues, social issues, cultural criticism, fashion, narrative nonfiction. **Considers these fiction areas:** commercial, historical, literary, multicultural, mystery, thriller, women's, young adult, Art-related fiction.

"Our fiction is strong on stories for women, art-related fiction, historical and multicultural stories, and to a lesser extent mysteries and thrillers. We are interested in narrative nonfiction and current affairs books by journalists, as well as YA literature." Does not represent poetry, science fiction, fantasy, horror, or screenplays.

HOW TO CONTACT "We no longer accept submissions by regular mail. Please send all queries via e-mail, marked 'Query' in the subject line. Your query should include: a brief summary of your book, word count, genre, any relevant publishing experience, and the first 5 pages of your manuscript pasted into the body of the e-mail. (No attachments—we will not open these.)" Accepts simultaneous submissions.

TERMS Agent receives 15% commission on domestic sales; 20% commission on foreign sales. No reading fees.

TIPS "Our clients' books are represented throughout Europe, Asia, and Latin America by various subagents. We are also active in selling motion picture rights to the books we represent, and work with various Hollywood agencies."

CURTIS BROWN, LTD.

10 Astor Place, New York NY 10003. (212)473-5400. **Fax:** (212)598-0917. **Website:** www.curtisbrown.com. Member of AAR. Signatory of WGA.

MEMBER AGENTS Noah Ballard (literary debuts, upmarket thrillers, narrative nonfiction, always looking for honest and provocative new writers); Tess Callero (young adult, upmarket commercial women's fiction, mysteries/ thrillers, romance, nonfiction: pop culture, business, cookbooks, humor, biography, self-help, and food narrative projects); Ginger Clark (science fiction, fantasy, paranormal romance, literary horror, and young adult and middle grade fiction); Kerry D'Agostino (literary and commercial fiction, as well as narrative nonfiction and memoir); Katherine Fausset (literary fiction, upmarket commercial fiction, journalism, memoir, popular science, and narrative nonfiction); Holly Frederick; Peter Ginsberg, president; Elizabeth Harding, vice president (represents authors and illustrators of juvenile, middle-grade and young adult fiction); Ginger Knowlton, executive vice president (authors and illustrators of children's books in all genres—picture book, middle grade, young adult fiction and nonfiction); Timothy Knowlton, CEO; Jonathan Lyons (biographies, history, science, pop culture, sports, general narrative nonfiction, mysteries, thrillers, science fiction and fantasy, and young adult fiction); Sarah Perillo (middle grade fiction and commercial fiction for adults, nonfiction:history, politics, science, pop culture, and humor, and is especially fond of anything involving animals or food); Laura Blake Peterson, vice president (memoir and biography, natural history, literary fiction, mystery, suspense, women's fiction, health and fitness, children's and young adult, faith issues and popular culture); Steven Salpeter (literary fiction, fantasy, graphic novels, historical fiction, mysteries, thrillers, young adult, narrative nonfiction, gift books, history, humor, and popular science); Maureen Walters, senior vice president (working primarily in women's fiction and nonfiction projects on subjects as eclectic as parenting & child care, popular psychology, inspirational/motivational volumes as well as a few medical/nutritional books); Mitchell Waters (literary and commercial fiction and nonfiction, including mystery, history, biography, memoir, young adult, cookbooks, self-help and popular culture); Monika Woods (plot-driven literary novels, non-fiction that is creatively critical, unique perspectives, a great cookbook, and above all, original prose).

REPRESENTS Nonfiction, fiction, novels, short story collections, juvenile books. **Considers these nonfiction areas:** animals, biography, computers, cooking, creative nonfiction, current affairs, ethnic, gardening, health, history, humor, juvenile nonfiction, memoirs, money, popular culture, psychology, religious, science, self-help, spirituality, sports, young adult. **Considers these fiction areas:** contemporary issues, ethnic, fantasy, feminist, historical, horror, humor, juvenile, literary, mainstream, middle grade, mystery, paranormal, picture books, religious, romance, spiritual, sports, suspense, thriller, women's, young adult.

HOW TO CONTACT Please refer to the "Agents" page on the website for each agent's submission guidelines. Accepts simultaneous submissions. Responds in 4 weeks to queries; 6 weeks to mss. (but do see Agent page on website for more information) Obtains most new clients through recommendations from others, solicitations, conferences.

TERMS Agent receives 15% commission on domestic sales; 20% on foreign sales. Offers written contract. 75-day notice must be given to terminate contract. Charges for some postage (overseas, etc.).

RECENT SALES This agency prefers not to share information on specific sales.

BROWNE & MILLER LITERARY ASSOCIATES

52 Village Place, Hinsdale IL 60521. (312)922-3063. **E-mail:** mail@browneandmiller.com. **Website:** www.browneandmiller.com. **Contact:** Danielle Egan-Miller, president. Estab. 1971. Member of AAR. RWA, MWA, Authors Guild.

Prior to joining the agency as Jane Jordan Browne's partner, Danielle Egan-Miller worked as an editor.

REPRESENTS Nonfiction, fiction.

Browne & Miller is most interested in literary and commercial fiction, women's fiction, women's historical fiction, literary-leaning crime fiction, dark suspense/domestic suspense,romance, and Christian/inspirational fiction by established authors, and a wide range of platform-driven nonfiction by nationally-recognized author-experts. "We do not represent children's books of any kind or Young Adult; no adult Memoirs; we do not represent horror, science fiction or fantasy, short stories, poetry, original screenplays,or articles."

HOW TO CONTACT Query via e-mail only; no attachments. Do not send unsolicited mss. Accepts simultaneous submissions.

ANDREA BROWN LITERARY AGENCY, INC.

E-mail: andrea@andreabrownlit.com; caryn@andreabrownlit.com; lauraqueries@gmail.com; jennifer@andreabrownlit.com; kelly@andreabrownlit.com; jennL@andreabrownlit.com; jamie@andreabrownlit.com; jmatt@andreabrownlit.com; kathleen@andreabrownlit.com; lara@andreabrownlit.com; soloway@andreabrownlit.com. **Website:** www.andreabrownlit.com. Estab. 1981. Member of AAR.

Prior to opening her agency, Ms. Brown served as an editorial assistant at Random House and Dell Publishing and as an editor with Knopf.

MEMBER AGENTS Andrea Brown (president); Laura Rennert (executive agent); Caryn Wiseman (senior agent); Jennifer Laughran (senior agent); Jennifer Rofé (senior agent); Kelly Sonnack (senior agent); Jamie Weiss Chilton (senior agent); Jennifer Mattson (agent); Kathleen Rushall (agent); Lara Perkins (agent, digital manager); Jennifer March Soloway (associate agent).

REPRESENTS Juvenile books. **Considers these nonfiction areas:** juvenile nonfiction, young adult, narrative. **Considers these fiction areas:** juvenile, middle grade, picture books, young adult, middle-grade, all juvenile genres.

⊶ Specializes in all kinds of children's books—illustrators and authors. 98% juvenile books. Considers: nonfiction, fiction, picture books, young adult.

HOW TO CONTACT Writers should review the large agent bios on the agency website to determine which agent to contact. Please choose only one agent to query. The agents share queries, so a no from one agent at Andrea Brown Literary Agency is a no from all. (Note that Jennifer Laughran and Kelly Sonnack only receive queries by querymanager - please visit the agency's website for information.) For picture books, submit a query letter and complete ms in the body of the e-mail. For fiction, submit a query letter and the first 10 pages in the body of the e-mail. For nonfiction, submit proposal, first 10 pages in the body of the e-mail. Illustrators: submit a query letter and 2-3 illustration samples (in jpeg format), link to online portfolio, and text of picture book, if applicable. "We only accept queries via e-mail. No attachments, with the exception of jpeg illustrations from illustrators." Visit the agents' bios on our website and choose only one agent to whom you will submit your e-query. Send a short e-mail query letter to that agent with "QUERY" in the subject field. Accepts simultaneous submissions. If we are interested in your work, we will certainly follow up by e-mail or by phone. However, if you haven't heard from us within 6-8 weeks, please assume that we are passing on your project. Obtains most new clients through queries and referrals from editors, clients and agents. Check website for guidelines and information.

TERMS Agent receives 15% commission on domestic sales; 25% commission on foreign sales. Offers written contract. No fees.

RECENT SALES Supriya Kelkar's middle grade novel *American As Paneer Pie* to Jennifer Ung at Aladdin, at auction, for publication in summer 2020, by Kathleen Rushall. Mitali Perkins's *You Bring the Distant Near*sold at auction, in a two-book deal, to Grace Kendall at Farrar, Straus Children's, by Laura Rennert. Cynthia Salaysay's YA novel *Private Lessons* to Kate Fletcher at Candlewick, for publication in the spring of 2020, by Jennifer March Soloway. Dev Petty's picture book text, *The Bear Must Go On* to Talia Benamy at Philomel, for publication in spring 2021, by Jennifer Rofe. Carrie Pearson's nonfiction picture book text *A Girl Who Leaped, A Woman Who Soared* to Simon Boughton at Norton Children's by Kelly Sonnack. K. C. Johnson's YA novel, *This is My America* to Chelsea Eberly at Random House Children's in a two-book deal by Jennifer March Soloway. Nancy Castaldo's nonfiction YA, *Water* to Elise Howard at Algonquin Young Readers, by Jennifer Laughran. Kate Messner's picture book text, *The Next President* to Melissa Manlove at Chronicle Children's, in a two book deal, by Jennifer Laughran. Amber Lough's YA novel, *Summer of War* to Amy Fitzgerald at Carolrhoda Lab by Laura Rennert and Jennifer March Soloway. Andrea Zimmerman and David Clemesha's picture book *All Buckled Up!* to Jeffrey Salane at Little Simon, in a two-book deal by Jamie Weiss Chilton. Jennifer Berne's picture book *Dinosaur Doomsday* to Melissa Manlove at Chronicle Children's by Caryn Wiseman. Tami Charles's *Serena Williams—G.O.A.T.: Making the Case for the Greatest of All Time*, a sports biography of Serena Williams to Ada Zhang at Sterling Children's by Lara Perkins. Katy Loutzenhiser's YA *If You're Out There* to Donna Bray at Balzer & Bray in a two-book deal by Jennifer Mattson. Barry Eisler's *The Killer Collective*, as well as a John Rain prequel, and two more in the Livia Lone series, to Gracie Doyle at Thomas & Mercer, in a major deal by Laura Rennert. Maggie Stiefvater's The Raven Cycle series to Universal Cable Productions by Laura Rennert.

WRITERS CONFERENCES SCBWI, Asilomar; Maui Writers' Conference, Southwest Writers' Conference, San Diego State University Writers' Conference, Big Sur Children's Writing Workshop, William Saroyan Writers' Conference, Columbus Writers' Conference, Willamette Writers' Conference, La Jolla Writers' Conference, San Francisco Writers' Conference, Hilton Head Writers' Conference, Pacific Northwest Conference, Pikes Peak Conference.

SHEREE BYKOFSKY ASSOCIATES, INC.

P.O. Box 706, Brigantine NJ 08203. **E-mail:** shereebee@aol.com. **Website:** www.shereebee.com. **Contact:** Sheree Bykofsky. Estab. 1991. Member of AAR.

Author's Guild, Atlantic City Chamber of Commerce, PRC Council. Represents 1,000+ clients.

Prior to opening her agency, Sheree Bykofsky served as executive editor of the Stonesong Press and managing editor of Chiron Press. Janet Rosen worked as associate book editor at *Glamour* and as the senior books and fiction editor at *Woman* before turning to agenting at Sheree Bykofsky Associates, where she represents a range of nonfiction and a limited amount of fiction.

MEMBER AGENTS Sheree Bykofsky, Janet Rosen.

REPRESENTS Nonfiction, novels. **Considers these nonfiction areas:** Americana, animals, anthropology, architecture, art, autobiography, biography, business, child guidance, cooking, crafts, creative nonfiction, cultural interests, current affairs, dance, decorating, diet/nutrition, design, economics, education, environment, ethnic, film, foods, gardening, gay/lesbian, government, health, history, hobbies, how-to, humor, inspirational, interior design, investigative, language, law, literature, medicine, memoirs, metaphysics, military, money, multicultural, music, New Age, parenting, philosophy, photography, popular culture, politics, psychology, recreation, regional, religious, science, self-help, sex, sociology, software, spirituality, sports, technology, theater, translation, travel, true crime, war, women's issues, creative nonfiction. **Considers these fiction areas:** commercial, contemporary issues, crime, detective, literary, mainstream, mystery, suspense, women's. **Considers these script areas:**Dramatic rights represented by Joel Gotler.

This agency is seeking nonfiction, both prescriptive and narrative, and some fiction. Prescriptive nonfiction: primarily health and business. Narrative nonfiction: pop culture, biography, history, popular and social science, language, music, cities, medicine, fashion, military, and espionage. Fiction: women's commercial fiction (with a literary quality) and mysteries. Does not want to receive poetry, children's, screenplays, westerns, science fiction, or horror.

HOW TO CONTACT Query via e-mail to submitbee@aol.com. "We only accept e-queries. We respond only to those queries in which we are interested. No attachments, snail mail, or phone calls, please. We do not open attachments." Fiction: one-page query, one-page synopsis, and first three pages of ms in body of the e-mail. Nonfiction: one-page query in the body of the e-mail. Currently we are focusing much more on our nonfiction portfolio, especially business, prescriptive nonfiction, and popular culture. Accepts simultaneous submissions. Responds in 1 month to requested mss. Obtains most new clients through referrals but still reads all submissions closely.

TERMS Agent receives 15% commission on domestic sales. Agent receives 15% commission on foreign sales, plus international co-agent receives another 10%. Offers written contract, binding for 1 year. Charges for international postage.

RECENT SALES *That Thin, Wild Mercury Sound: Dylan, Nashville, and the Making of Blonde on Blonde* by Daryl Sanders (Chicago Review Press), A Tangled Web by Leslie Rule (Kensington), Sneaky Uses for Everyday Things, 2nd Edition by Cy Tymony (Andrews McMeel), Don't Believe Everything you Think by Rod Evans (Sterling), Gamer Nation by Eric Geissinger (Prometheus Books), *Virtual Billions: The Genius, the Drug Lord, and the Ivy League Twins Behind the Rise of Bitcoin* by Eric Geissinger (Prometheus Books), *Thank You, Teacher: Grateful Students Tell the Stories of the Teachers Who Changed Their Lives* by Holly and Bruce Holbert (New World Library), *The Type B Manager: Leading Successfully in a Type A World* by Victor Lipman (Prentice Hall), *Let the Story Do the Work: The Art of Storytelling for Business Success* by Esther Choy (Amacom), *Convicting Avery: The Bizarre Laws and Broken System Behind "Making a Murderer"* by Michael D. Cicchini (Prometheus Books), *The Curious Case of Kiryas Joel: The Rise of a Village Theocracy and the Battle to Defend the Separation of Church and State* by Louis Grumet with John Caher (Chicago Review Press), *Cells are the New Cure* by Robin L. Smith, M.D. and Max Gomez, Ph.D.; dozens of international sales.

WRITERS CONFERENCES Truckee Meadow Community College Keynote, Southwest Florida Writers Conference, Philadelphia Writer's Conference, Push to Publish, Lewes Writers Conference, Pennwriters, League of Vermont Writers, Asilomar, Florida Suncoast Writers' Conference, Whidbey Island Writers' Conference, Florida First Coast Writers' Festival, Agents and Editors Conference, Columbus Writers' Conference, Southwest Writers' Conference, Willamette Writers' Conference, Dorothy Canfield Fisher Conference, Maui Writers' Conference, Pacific Northwest Writers' Conference, IWWG.

KIMBERLEY CAMERON & ASSOCIATES

1550 Tiburon Blvd., #704, Tiburon CA 94920. (415)789-9191. **Website:** www.kimberleycameron.com. **Contact:** Kimberley Cameron. Member of AAR. Signatory of WGA.

Kimberley Cameron & Associates (formerly The Reece Halsey Agency) has had an illustrious client list of established writers, including Aldous Huxley, Upton Sinclair, William Faulkner, and Henry Miller.

MEMBER AGENTS Kimberley Cameron; Elizabeth Kracht (nonfiction: memoir, self-help, spiritual, investigative, creative / fiction: women's, literary, historical, mysteries, thrillers); Amy Cloughley (literary and upmarket fiction, women's, historical, narrative nonfiction, travel or adventure memoir); Mary C. Moore (fantasy, science fiction, upmarket "book club," genre romance, thrillers with female protagonists, and stories from marginalized voices); Lisa Abellera (currently closed to unsolicited submissions); Pooja Menon; Dorian Maffei (only open to submissions requested through Twitter pitch parties, conferences, or #MSWL).

REPRESENTS Nonfiction, fiction, novels. **Considers these nonfiction areas:** animals, creative nonfiction, cultural interests, current affairs, environment, ethnic, gay/lesbian, health, history, how-to, humor, investigative, literature, memoirs, metaphysics, psychology, science, self-help, sex, spirituality, travel, true crime, women's issues, women's studies, narrative non-fiction. **Considers these fiction areas:** action, adventure, commercial, confession, crime, detective, gay, historical, literary, mainstream, military, mystery, police, romance, science fiction, spiritual, thriller, women's, young adult, LGBTQ.

"We are looking for a unique and heartfelt voice that conveys a universal truth."

HOW TO CONTACT Prefers queries via site. Only query one agent at a time. For fiction, fill out the correct submissions form for the individual agent and attach the first 50 pages and a synopsis (if requested) as a Word doc or PDF. For nonfiction, fill out the correct submission form of the individual agent and attach a full book proposal and sample chapters (includes the first chapter and no more than 50 pages) as a Word doc or PDF. Accepts simultaneous submissions. Obtains new clients through recommendations from others, solicitations.

CYNTHIA CANNELL LITERARY AGENCY

54 W. 40th St., New York NY 10018. (212)396-9595. **E-mail:** info@cannellagency.com. **Website:** www.cannellagency.com. **Contact:** Cynthia Cannell. Estab. 1997. Member of AAR. Women's Media Group and the Authors Guild

Prior to forming the Cynthia Cannell Literary Agency, Ms. Cannell was the vice president of Janklow & Nesbit Associates for 12 years.

REPRESENTS Nonfiction, fiction. **Considers these nonfiction areas:** biography, current affairs, memoirs, self-help, spirituality.

Does not represent screenplays, children's books, illustrated books, cookbooks, romance, category mystery, or science fiction.

HOW TO CONTACT "Please query us with an e-mail or letter. If querying by e-mail, send a brief description of your project with relevant biographical information including publishing credits (if any) to info@cannellagency.com. Do not send attachments. If querying by conventional mail, enclose an SASE." Responds if interested. Accepts simultaneous submissions.

RECENT SALES Check the website for an updated list of authors and sales.

CAPITAL TALENT AGENCY

419 S. Washington St., Alexandria VA 22314. (703)349-1649. **E-mail:** literary.submissions@capitaltalentagency.com. **Website:** capitaltalentagency.com/html/literary.shtml. **Contact:** Cynthia Kane. Estab. 2014. Member of AAR. Signatory of WGA.

Prior to joining CTA, Ms. Kane was involved in the publishing industry for more than 10 years. She has worked as a development editor for different publishing houses and individual authors and has seen more than 100 titles to market.

MEMBER AGENTS Cynthia Kane; Shaheen Qureshi.

REPRESENTS Nonfiction, fiction, movie scripts, stage plays.

HOW TO CONTACT "We accept submissions only by e-mail. We do not accept queries via postal mail or fax. For fiction and nonfiction submissions, send a query letter in the body of your e-mail. Please note that while we consider each query seriously, we are unable to respond to all of them. We endeavor to respond within 6 weeks to projects that interest us." Accepts simultaneous submissions. 6 weeks

CHALBERG & SUSSMAN

115 W. 29th St., Third Floor, New York NY 10001. (917)261-7550. **Website:** www.chalbergsussman.com. Member of AAR. Signatory of WGA.

Prior to her current position, Ms. Chalberg held a variety of editorial positions, and was an agent with The Susan Golomb Literary Agency. Ms. Sussman was an agent with Zachary Shuster Harmsworth. Ms. James was with The Aaron Priest Literary Agency.

MEMBER AGENTS Terra Chalberg; Rachel Sussman (narrative journalism, memoir, psychology, history, humor, pop culture, literary fiction); Nicole James (plot-driven fiction, psychological suspense, uplifting female-driven memoir, upmarket self-help, and lifestyle books); Lana Popovic (young adult, middle grade, contemporary realism, speculative fiction, fantasy, horror, sophisticated erotica, romance, select nonfiction, international stories).

REPRESENTS Nonfiction, fiction, novels. **Considers these nonfiction areas:** history, humor, memoirs, popular culture, psychology, self-help, narrative journalism. **Considers these fiction areas:** erotica, fantasy, horror, literary, middle grade, romance, science fiction, suspense, young adult, contemporary realism, speculative fiction.

HOW TO CONTACT To query by e-mail, please contact one of the following: terra@chalbergsussman.com, rachel@chalbergsussman.com, nicole@chalbergsussman.com, lana@chalbergsussman.com. To query by regular mail, please address your letter to one agent and include SASE. Accepts simultaneous submissions.

RECENT SALES The agents' sales and clients are listed on their website.

WM CLARK ASSOCIATES

54 W. 21st St., Suite 809, New York NY 10010. (212)675-2784. **E-mail:** general@wmclark.com. **Website:** www.wmclark.com. **Contact:** William Clark. Estab. 1997. Member of AAR. Member, Board of Directors, Association of Authors Representatives.

Prior to opening WCA, Mr. Clark was an agent at the William Morris Agency.

REPRESENTS Nonfiction, novels. **Considers these nonfiction areas:** architecture, art, autobiography, biography, creative nonfiction, cultural interests, current affairs, dance, design, economics, ethnic, film, foods, history, inspirational, interior design, literature, memoirs, music, popular culture, politics, religious, science, sociology, technology, theater, translation, travel. **Considers these fiction areas:** historical, literary.

Agency does not represent screenplays or respond to screenplay pitches. "It is advised that before querying you become familiar with the kinds of books we handle by browsing our Book List, which is available on our website."

HOW TO CONTACT Accepts queries via online query form only. "We will endeavor to respond as soon as possible as to whether or not we'd like to see a proposal or sample chapters from your manuscript." Responds in 1-2 months to queries.

TERMS Agent receives 15% commission on domestic sales; 20% commission on foreign sales. Offers written contract.

WRITERS CONFERENCES London Book Fair, Frankfurt Book Fair.

TIPS "Translation rights are sold directly in the German, Italian, Spanish, Portuguese, Latin American, French, Dutch, and Scandinavian territories; and through corresponding agents in China, Bulgaria, Czech Republic, Latvia, Poland, Hungary, Russia, Japan, Greece, Israel, Turkey, Korea, Taiwan, Vietnam, and Thailand."

FRANCES COLLIN, LITERARY AGENT

Sarah Yake, Literary Agent, P.O. Box 33, Wayne PA 19087-0033. **E-mail:** queries@francescollin.com. **Website:** www.francescollin.com. Estab. 1948. Member of AAR. Represents 50 clients.

Sarah Yake has been with the agency since 2005 and handles foreign and subsidiary rights as well as her own client list. She holds an M.A. in English Literature and has been a sales rep for a major publisher and a bookstore manager. She currently teaches in the Rosemont College Graduate Publishing Program.

MEMBER AGENTS Frances Collin; Sarah Yake.

REPRESENTS Nonfiction, fiction, novels, short story collections. **Considers these nonfiction areas:** architecture, art, autobiography, biography, creative nonfiction, cultural interests, dance, environment, history, literature, memoirs, popular culture, science, sociology, travel, women's issues, women's studies. **Considers these fiction areas:** adventure, commercial, experimental, feminist, gay, historical, juvenile, literary, middle grade, multicultural, science fiction, short story collections, women's, young adult.

- Actively seeking authors who are invested in their unique visions and who want to set trends not chase them. "I'd like to think that my authors are unplagiarizable by virtue of their distinct voices and styles." Does not want previously self-published work. Query with new mss only, please.

HOW TO CONTACT "We periodically close to queries, so please check our Publishers Marketplace account or other social media accounts before querying. When we are open to queries, we ask that writers send a traditional query e-mail describing the project and copy and paste the first 5 pages of the manuscript into the body of the e-mail. We look forward to hearing from you at queries@francescollin.com. Please send queries to that e-mail address. Any queries sent to another e-mail address within the agency will be deleted unread." Accepts simultaneous submissions. Responds in 1-4 weeks for initial queries, longer for full mss.

DON CONGDON ASSOCIATES INC.

110 William St., Suite 2202, New York NY 10038. (212)645-1229. **Fax:** (212)727-2688. **E-mail:** dca@doncongdon.com. **Website:** doncongdon.com. Estab. 1983. Member of AAR.

MEMBER AGENTS Cristina Concepcion (crime fiction, narrative nonfiction, political science, journalism, history, books on cities, classical music, biography, science for a popular audience, philosophy, food and wine, iconoclastic books on health and human relationships, essays, and arts criticism); Michael Congdon (commercial and literary fiction, suspense, mystery, thriller, history, military history, biography, memoir, current affairs, and narrative nonfiction [adventure, medicine, science, and nature]); Katie Grimm (literary fiction, historical, women's fiction, short story collections, graphic novels, mysteries, young adult, middle-grade, memoir, science, academic); Katie Kotchman (business [all areas], narrative nonfiction [particularly popular science and social/cultural issues], self-help, success, motivation, psychology, pop culture, women's fiction, realistic young adult, literary fiction, and psychological thrillers); Maura Kye-Casella (narrative nonfiction, cookbooks, women's fiction, young adult, self-help, and parenting); Susan Ramer (literary fiction, upmarket commercial fiction [contemporary and historical], narrative nonfiction, social history, cultural history, smart pop culture [music, film, food, art], women's issues, psychology and mental health, and memoir).

REPRESENTS Nonfiction, novels, short story collections. **Considers these nonfiction areas:** art, biography, business, cooking, creative nonfiction, cultural interests, current affairs, film, foods, history, humor, literature, medicine, memoirs, military, multicultural, music, parenting, philosophy, popular culture, politics, psychology, science, self-help, sociology, sports, women's issues, young adult. **Considers these fiction areas:** crime, hi-lo, historical, literary, middle grade, mystery, short story collections, suspense, thriller, women's, young adult.

- Susan Ramer: "Not looking for romance, science fiction, fantasy, espionage, mysteries, politics, health/diet/fitness, self-help, or sports." Katie Kotchman: "Please do not send her screenplays or poetry."

HOW TO CONTACT "For queries via e-mail, you must include the word 'query' and the agent's full name in your subject heading. Please also include your query and sample chapter in the body of the e-mail, as we do not open attachments for security reasons. Please query only one agent within the agency at a time. If you are sending your query via regular mail, please enclose a SASE for our reply. If you would like us to return your materials, please make sure your postage will cover their return." Accepts simultaneous submissions.

RECENT SALES This agency represents many bestselling clients such as David Sedaris and Kathryn Stockett.

CREATIVE MEDIA AGENCY, INC.

(212)812-1494. **E-mail:** paige@cmalit.com. **Website:** www.cmalit.com. **Contact:** Paige Wheeler. Estab. 1997. Member of AAR. WMG, RWA, MWA, Authors Guild. Represents about 30 clients.

- After starting out as an editor for Harlequin Books in NY and Euromoney Publications in London, Paige repped writers, producers, and celebrities as an agent with Artists Agency, until she formed Creative Media Agency in 1997. In 2006 she co-created Folio Literary Management and grew that company for 8 years into a successful mid-sized agency. In 2014 she decided to once again pursue a boutique approach, and she relaunched CMA.

REPRESENTS Nonfiction, fiction, novels. **Considers these nonfiction areas:** biography, business, creative nonfiction, diet/nutrition, health, inspirational, memoirs, money, parenting, popular culture, self-help, travel, women's issues, prescriptive nonfiction, narrative nonfiction. **Considers these fiction areas:** commercial, crime, detective, historical, inspirational, mainstream, middle grade, mystery, new adult, romance, suspense, thriller, women's, young adult, general fiction.

Fiction: All commercial and upscale (think book club) fiction, as well as women's fiction, romance (all types), mystery, thrillers, inspirational/Christian and psychological suspense. I enjoy both historical fiction as well as contemporary fiction, so do keep that in mind. I seem to be especially drawn to a story if it has a high concept and a fresh, unique voice. Nonfiction: I'm looking for both narrative nonfiction and prescriptive nonfiction. I'm looking for books where the author has a huge platform and something new to say in a particular area. Some of the areas that I like are lifestyle, relationship, parenting, business/entrepreneurship, food-subsistence-homesteading topics, popular/trendy reference projects and women's issues. I'd like books that would be a good fit on the *Today* show. Does not want to receive children's books, science fiction, fantasy, or academic nonfiction.

HOW TO CONTACT E-query. Write "query" in your e-mail subject line. For fiction, paste in the first 5 pages of the ms after the query. For nonfiction, paste in an extended author bio as well as the marketing section of your book proposal after the query. Accepts simultaneous submissions. Responds in 4-6 weeks.

LAURA DAIL LITERARY AGENCY, INC.

121 W. 27th St., Suite 1201, New York NY 10001. (212)239-7477. **E-mail:** literary@ldlainc.com. **E-mail:** queries@ldlainc.com. **Website:** www.ldlainc.com. Member of AAR.

MEMBER AGENTS Laura Dail; Tamar Rydzinski; Elana Roth Parker.

REPRESENTS Nonfiction, fiction, novels, juvenile books. **Considers these nonfiction areas:** biography, cooking, creative nonfiction, current affairs, government, history, investigative, juvenile nonfiction, memoirs, multicultural, popular culture, politics, psychology, sociology, true crime, war, women's studies, young adult. **Considers these fiction areas:** commercial, contemporary issues, crime, detective, ethnic, fantasy, feminist, gay, historical, juvenile, lesbian, mainstream, middle grade, multicultural, mystery, picture books, thriller, women's, young adult.

Specializes in women's fiction, literary fiction, young adult fiction, as well as both practical and idea-driven nonfiction. "Due to the volume of queries and mss received, we apologize for not answering every e-mail and letter. None of us handles children's picture books or chapter books. No New Age. We do not handle screenplays or poetry."

HOW TO CONTACT "If you would like, you may include a synopsis and no more than 10 pages. If you are mailing your query, please be sure to include a self-addressed, stamped envelope; without it, you may not hear back from us. To save money, time and trees, we prefer queries by e-mail to queries@ldlainc.com. We get a lot of spam and are wary of computer viruses, so please use the word 'Query' in the subject line and include your detailed materials in the body of your message, not as an attachment." Accepts simultaneous submissions. Responds in 2-4 weeks.

DARHANSOFF & VERRILL LITERARY AGENTS

133 W. 72nd St., Room 304, New York NY 10023. (917)305-1300. **E-mail:** submissions@dvagency.com. **Website:** www.dvagency.com. Member of AAR.

MEMBER AGENTS Liz Darhansoff; Chuck Verrill; Michele Mortimer; Eric Amling.

REPRESENTS Nonfiction, novels. **Considers these nonfiction areas:** creative nonfiction, juvenile nonfiction, memoirs, young adult. **Considers these fiction areas:** literary, middle grade, suspense, young adult.

HOW TO CONTACT Send queries via e-mail. Accepts simultaneous submissions.

RECENT SALES A full list of clients is available on their website.

LIZA DAWSON ASSOCIATES

121 W. 27th St., Suite 1201, New York NY 10001. (212)465-9071. **Website:** www.lizadawsonassociates.com. **Contact:** Caitie Flum. Member of AAR. MWA, Women's Media Group. Represents 50+ clients.

Prior to becoming an agent, Ms. Dawson was an editor for 20 years, spending 11 years at William Morrow as vice president and 2 years at Putnam as executive editor. Ms. Blasdell was a senior editor at HarperCollins and Avon. Ms. Johnson-Blalock was an assistant at Trident Media Group. Ms. Flum was the coordinator for the Children's Book of the Month club.

MEMBER AGENTS Liza Dawson, queryliza@lizadawsonassociates.com (plot-driven literary and popular fiction, historical, thrillers, suspense, history, psychology [both popular and clinical], politics, narrative nonfiction, and memoirs); Caitlin Blasdell, querycaitlin@lizadawsonassociates.com (science fiction, fantasy [both adult and young adult], parenting, business, thrillers, and women's fiction); Hannah Bowman, queryhannah@lizadawsonassociates.com (commercial fiction [especially science fiction and fantasy, young adult] and nonfiction in the areas of mathematics, science, and spirituality); Monica Odom, querymonica@lizadawsonassociates.com (nonfiction in the areas of Social Studies, including topics of: identity, race, gender, sexual orientation, socioeconomics, civil rights and social justice, advice/relationships, self-help/self-reflection, how-to, crafting/creativity, food and cooking, humor, pop culture, lifestyle, fashion & beauty, biography, memoir, narrative, business, politics and current affairs, history, science and literary fiction and upmarket fiction, Illustrators with demonstrable platforms, preferably author/illustrators, working on nonfiction, graphic memoirs or graphic novels); Caitie Flum, querycaitie@lizadawsonassociates.com (commercial fiction, especially historical, women's fiction, mysteries, crossover fantasy, young adult, and middle-grade; nonfiction in the areas of theater, current affairs, and pop culture).

REPRESENTS Nonfiction, novels. **Considers these nonfiction areas:** agriculture, Americana, animals, anthropology, archeology, architecture, art, autobiography, biography, business, computers, cooking, creative nonfiction, cultural interests, current affairs, environment, ethnic, film, gardening, gay/lesbian, history, humor, investigative, juvenile nonfiction, memoirs, multicultural, parenting, popular culture, politics, psychology, religious, science, sex, sociology, spirituality, theater, travel, true crime, women's issues, women's studies, young adult. **Considers these fiction areas:** action, adventure, commercial, contemporary issues, crime, detective, ethnic, family saga, fantasy, feminist, gay, historical, horror, humor, juvenile, lesbian, mainstream, middle grade, multicultural, mystery, new adult, police, romance, science fiction, supernatural, suspense, thriller, urban fantasy, women's, young adult.

This agency specializes in readable literary fiction, thrillers, mainstream historicals, women's fiction, young adult, middle-grade, academics, historians, journalists, and psychology.

HOW TO CONTACT Query by e-mail only. No phone calls. Each of these agents has their own specific submission requirements, which you can find online at the agency's website. Obtains most new clients through recommendations from others, conferences, and queries.

TERMS Agent receives 15% commission on domestic sales; 20% commission on foreign sales. Offers written contract.

DEFIORE & COMPANY

47 E. 19th St., 3rd Floor, New York NY 10003. (212)925-7744. **Fax:** (212)925-9803. **E-mail:** info@defliterary.com, submissions@defliterary.com. **Website:** www.defliterary.com. Member of AAR. Signatory of WGA.

Prior to becoming an agent, Mr. DeFiore was publisher of Villard Books (1997-1998), editor-in-chief of Hyperion (1992-1997), editorial director of Delacorte Press (1988-1992), and an editor at St. Martin's Press (1984-88).

MEMBER AGENTS Brian DeFiore (popular nonfiction, business, pop culture, parenting, commercial fiction); Laurie Abkemeier (memoir, parenting, business, how-to/self-help, popular science); Matthew Elblonk (young adult, popular culture, narrative nonfiction); Caryn Karmatz-Rudy (popular fiction, self-help, narrative nonfiction); Adam Schear (commercial fiction, humor, young adult, smart thrillers, historical fiction, quirky debut literary novels, popular science, politics, popular culture, current events); Meredith Kaffel Simonoff (smart upmarket women's fiction, literary fiction [especially debut], literary thrillers, narrative nonfiction, nonfiction about science and tech, sophisticated pop culture/humor books); Rebecca Strauss (literary and commercial fiction, women's fiction, urban fantasy, romance, mystery, young adult, memoir, pop culture, select nonfiction); Lisa Gallagher (fiction and nonfiction); Nicole Tourtelot (narrative and prescriptive nonfiction, food, lifestyle, wellness, pop culture, history, humor, memoir, select young adult and adult fiction); Ashely Collom (women's fiction, children's and young adult, psychological thrillers, memoir, politics, photography, cooking, narrative nonfiction, LGBT issues, feminism, occult); Miriam Altshuler (adult literary and commercial fiction, narrative nonfiction, middle-grade, young adult, memoir, narrative nonfiction, self-help, family sagas, historical novels); Reiko Davis (adult literary and upmarket fiction, narrative nonfiction, young adult, middle-grade, memoir).

REPRESENTS Nonfiction, novels, short story collections, juvenile books, poetry books. **Considers these nonfiction areas:** autobiography, biography, business, child guidance, cooking, economics, foods, gay/lesbian, how-to, inspirational, money, multicultural, parenting, photography, popular culture, politics, psychology, religious, science, self-help, sex, sports, technology, travel, women's issues, young adult. **Considers these fiction areas:** comic books, commercial, ethnic, feminist, gay, lesbian, literary, mainstream, middle grade, mystery, paranormal, picture books, poetry, romance, short story collections, suspense, thriller, urban fantasy, women's, young adult.

"Please be advised that we are not considering dramatic projects at this time."

HOW TO CONTACT Query with SASE or e-mail to submissions@defliterary.com. "Please include the word 'query' in the subject line. All attachments will be deleted; please insert all text in the body of the e-mail. For more information about our agents, their individual interests, and their query guidelines, please visit our 'About Us' page on our website." Accepts simultaneous submissions. Obtains most new clients through recommendations from others.

TERMS Agent receives 15% commission on domestic sales; 20% commission on foreign sales. Offers written contract; 10-day notice must be given to terminate contract. Charges clients for photocopying and overnight delivery (deducted only after a sale is made).

JOELLE DELBOURGO ASSOCIATES, INC.

101 Park St., Montclair NJ 07042. (973)773-0836. **E-mail:** joelle@delbourgo.com. **E-mail:** submissions@delbourgo.com. **Website:** www.delbourgo.com. **Contact:** Joelle Delbourgo. Estab. 1999. Member of AAR. Represents more than 500 clients.

Prior to becoming an agent, Ms. Delbourgo was an editor and senior publishing executive at HarperCollins and Random House. She began her editorial career at Bantam Books where she discovered the Choose Your Own Adventure series. Joelle Delbourgo brings more than three decades of experience as an editor and agent. Prior to joining the agency, Jacqueline Flynn was Executive Editor at Amacom for more than 15 years.

MEMBER AGENTS Joelle Delbourgo; Jacqueline Flynn.

REPRESENTS Nonfiction, fiction, novels. **Considers these nonfiction areas:** Americana, animals, anthropology, archeology, autobiography, biography, business, child guidance, cooking, creative nonfiction, current affairs, dance, decorating, diet/nutrition, design, economics, education, environment, film, gardening, gay/lesbian, government, health, history, how-to, humor, inspirational, interior design, investigative, juvenile nonfiction, literature, medicine, memoirs, military, money, multicultural, music, parenting, philosophy, popular culture, politics, psychology, science, self-help, sex, sociology, spirituality, sports, translation, travel, true crime, war, women's issues, women's studies, young adult. **Considers these fiction areas:** adventure, commercial, contemporary issues, crime, detective, fantasy, feminist, juvenile, literary, mainstream, middle grade, military, mystery, new adult, New Age, romance, science fiction, thriller, urban fantasy, women's, young adult.

"We are former publishers and editors with deep knowledge and an insider perspective. We have a reputation for individualized attention to clients, strategic management of authors' careers, and creating strong partnerships with publishers for our clients." We are looking for strong narrative and prescriptive nonfiction including science, history, health and medicine, business and finance, sociology, parenting, women's issues. We prefer books by credentialed experts and seasoned journalists, especially ones that are research-based. We are taking on very few memoir projects. In fiction, you can send mystery and thriller, commercial women's fiction, book club fiction and literary fiction. Do not send scripts, picture books, poetry.

HOW TO CONTACT E-mail queries only are accepted. Query one agent directly, not multiple agents at our agency. No attachments. Put the word "Query" in the subject line. If you have not received a response in 60 days you may consider that a pass. Do not send us copies of self-published books. Let us know if you are sending your query to us exclusively or if this is a multiple submission. For nonfiction, wait to send your query when you have a completed proposal. For fiction and memoir, embed the first 10 pages of ms into the e-mail after your query letter. Please no attachments. If we like your first pages, we may ask to see your synopsis and more manuscript. Please do not cold call us or make a follow-up call unless we call you. Accepts simultaneous submissions. Our clients come via referral, and occasionally over the transom.

TERMS Agent receives 15% commission on domestic sales and 20% commission on foreign sales as well as television/film adaptation when a co-agent is involved. Offers written contract. Standard industry commissions. Charges clients for postage and photocopying.

RECENT SALES *The Rule of St. Benedict*, translated by Philip Freeman (St. Martins Essentials); *Holly Banks Full of Angst* & Untitled Novel 2, Julie Valerie (Lake Union); *Flat, Fluid & Fast*, Brynne S. Kennedy (McGraw-Hill); *The Dog Went Over the Mountain*, Peter Zheutlin (Pegasus), *The Remarriage Manual*, Terry Gaspard (Sounds True); *The Narcissistic Family*, Julie Hall (Da Capo Lifelong/Hachette); *Queen of the West*, Theresa Kaminski (Rowman & Littlefield); *The Wealth Creator's Playbook*, John C. Christianson (Praeger).

WRITERS CONFERENCES Jewish Writer's Conference (sponsored by the Jewish Book Council).

TIPS "Do your homework. Do not cold call. Read and follow submission guidelines before contacting us. Do not call to find out if we received your material. No e-mail queries. Treat agents with respect, as you would any other professional, such as a doctor, lawyer or financial advisor."

SANDRA DIJKSTRA LITERARY AGENCY

1155 Camino del Mar, PMB 515, Del Mar CA 92014. **E-mail:** queries@dijkstraagency.com. **Website:** www.dijkstraagency.com. Member of AAR. Authors Guild, Organization of American Historians, RWA. Represents 200+ clients.

MEMBER AGENTS President: Sandra Dijkstra (adult only). Acquiring Associate agents: Elise Capron (adult only); Jill Marr (adult only); Thao Le (adult and YA); Roz Foster (adult and YA); Jessica Watterson (subgenres of adult romance, and women's fiction); Suzy Evans (adult and YA); Jennifer Kim (adult and YA).

REPRESENTS Nonfiction, fiction, novels, short story collections, juvenile books, scholarly books. **Considers these nonfiction areas:** Americana, animals, anthropology, art, biography, business, creative nonfiction, cultural interests, current affairs, design, economics, environment, ethnic, gardening, government, health, history, juvenile nonfiction, literature, memoirs, multicultural, parenting, popular culture, politics, psychology, science, self-help, sports, true crime, women's issues, women's studies, young adult, narrative. **Considers these fiction areas:** commercial, contemporary issues, detective, family saga, fantasy, feminist, historical, horror, juvenile, literary, mainstream, middle grade, multicultural, mystery, new adult, romance, science fiction, short story collections, sports, suspense, thriller, urban fantasy, women's, young adult.

HOW TO CONTACT "Please see guidelines on our website, www.dijkstraagency.com. Please note that we only accept e-mail submissions. Due to the large number of unsolicited submissions we receive, we are only able to respond those submissions in which we are interested." Accepts simultaneous submissions. Responds to queries of interest within 6 weeks.

TERMS Works in conjunction with foreign and film agents. Agent receives 15% commission on domestic sales and 20% commission on foreign sales. Offers written contract. No reading fee.

TIPS "Remember that publishing is a business. Do your research and present your project in as professional a way as possible. Only submit your work when you are confident that it is polished and ready for prime-time. Make yourself a part of the active writing community by getting stories and articles published, networking with other writers, and getting a good sense of where your work fits in the market."

DUNHAM LITERARY, INC.

110 William St., Suite 2202, New York NY 10038. (212)929-0994. **E-mail:** query@dunhamlit.com. **Website:** www.dunhamlit.com. **Contact:** Jennie Dunham. Estab. 2000. Member of AAR. SCBWI Represents 50 clients.

Prior to opening her agency, Ms. Dunham worked as a literary agent for Russell & Volkening. The Rhoda Weyr Agency is now a division of Dunham Literary, Inc.

MEMBER AGENTS Jennie Dunham, Bridget Smith, Leslie Zampetti.

REPRESENTS Nonfiction, fiction, novels, short story collections, juvenile books. **Considers these nonfiction areas:** anthropology, archeology, art, biography, creative nonfiction, cultural interests, environment, gay/lesbian, health, history, language, literature, medicine, memoirs, multicultural, parenting, popular culture, politics, psychology, science, sociology, technology, women's issues, women's studies, young adult. **Considers these fiction areas:** family saga, fantasy, feminist, gay, historical, humor, juvenile, lesbian, literary, mainstream, middle grade, multicultural, mystery, picture books, science fiction, short story collections, sports, urban fantasy, women's, young adult.

"We are not looking for Westerns, genre romance, poetry, or individual short stories."

HOW TO CONTACT E-mail queries preferred, with all materials pasted in the body of the e-mail. Attachments will not be opened. Paper queries are also accepted. Please include a SASE for response and return of materials. Please include the first 5 pages with the query. Accepts simultaneous submissions. Responds in 4 weeks to queries; 2 months to mss. Obtains most new clients through recommendations from others.

TERMS Agent receives 15% commission on domestic sales; 20% commission on foreign sales.

RECENT SALES *The Bad Kitty Series*, by Nick Bruel (Macmillan); *Believe*, by Robert Sabuda (Candlewick); *The Gollywhopper Games* and Sequels, by Jody Feldman (HarperCollins); *Foolish Hearts*, by Emma Mills (Macmillan); *Gangster Nation*, by Tod Goldberg (Counterpoint); *A Shadow All of Light*, by Fred Chappell (Tor).

DUNOW, CARLSON, & LERNER AGENCY

27 W. 20th St., Suite 1107, New York NY 10011. (212)645-7606. **E-mail:** mail@dclagency.com. **Website:** www.dclagency.com. Member of AAR.

MEMBER AGENTS Jennifer Carlson (narrative nonfiction writers and journalists covering current events and ideas and cultural history, as well as literary and upmarket commercial novelists); Henry Dunow (quality fiction–literary, historical, strongly written commercial–and with voice-driven nonfiction across a range of areas–narrative history, biography, memoir, current affairs, cultural trends and criticism, science, sports); Erin Hosier (nonfiction: popular culture, music, sociology and memoir); Betsy Lerner (nonfiction writers in the areas of psychology, history, cultural studies, biography, current events, business; fiction: literary, dark, funny, voice driven); Yishai Seidman (broad range of fiction: literary, postmodern, and thrillers; nonfiction: sports, music, and pop culture); Amy Hughes (nonfiction in the areas of history, cultural studies, memoir, current events, wellness, health, food, pop culture, and biography; also literary fiction); Eleanor Jackson (literary, commercial, memoir, art, food, science and history); Julia Kenny (fiction—adult, middle grade and YA—and is especially interested in dark, literary thrillers and suspense); Edward Necarsulmer IV (strong new voices in teen & middle grade as well as picture books); Stacia Decker; Rachel Vogel (nonfiction, including photography, humor, pop culture, history, memoir, investigative journalism, current events, science, and more); Arielle Datz (fiction—adult, YA, or middle-grade—literary and commercial, nonfiction—essays, unconventional memoir, pop culture, and sociology).

REPRESENTS Nonfiction, fiction, novels, short story collections. **Considers these nonfiction areas:** art, biography, creative nonfiction, cultural interests, current affairs, foods, health, history, memoirs, music, popular culture, psychology, science, sociology, sports. **Considers these fiction areas:** commercial, literary, mainstream, middle grade, mystery, picture books, thriller, young adult.

HOW TO CONTACT Query via snail mail with SASE, or by e-mail. E-mail preferred, paste 10 sample pages below query letter. No attachments. Will respond only if interested. Accepts simultaneous submissions. Responds in 4-6 weeks if interested.

RECENT SALES A full list of agency clients is on the website.

DYSTEL, GODERICH & BOURRET LLC

1 Union Square W., Suite 904, New York NY 10003. (212)627-9100. **Fax:** (212)627-9313. **Website:** www.dystel.com. Estab. 1994. Member of AAR. Other membership includes SCBWI. Represents 600+ clients.

MEMBER AGENTS Jane Dystel; Miriam Goderich, miriam@dystel.com (literary and commercial fiction as well as some genre fiction, narrative nonfiction, pop culture, psychology, history, science, art, business books, and biography/memoir); Stacey Glick, sglick@dystel.com (adult narrative nonfiction including memoir, parenting, cooking and food, psychology, science, health and wellness, lifestyle, current events, pop culture, YA, middle grade, children's nonfiction, and select adult contemporary fiction); Michael Bourret, mbourret@dystel.com (middle grade and young adult fiction, commercial adult fiction, and all sorts of nonfiction, from practical to narrative; he's especially interested in food and cocktail related books, memoir, popular history, politics, religion (though not spirituality), popular science, and current events); Jim McCarthy, jmccarthy@dystel.com (literary women's fiction, underrepresented voices, mysteries, romance, paranormal fiction, narrative nonfiction, memoir, and paranormal nonfiction); Jessica Papin, jpapin@dystel.com (plot-driven literary and smart commercial fiction, and narrative non-fiction across a range of subjects, including history, medicine, science, economics and women's issues); Lauren Abramo, labramo@dystel.com (humorous middle grade and contemporary YA on the children's side, and upmarket commercial fiction and well-paced literary fiction on the adult side; adult narrative nonfiction, especially pop culture, psychology, pop science, reportage, media, and contemporary culture; in nonfiction, has a strong preference for interdisciplinary approaches, and in all categories she's especially interested in underrepresented voices); John Rudolph, jrudolph@dystel.com (picture book author/illustrators, middle grade, YA, select commercial fiction, and narrative nonfiction—especially in music, sports, history, popular science, "big think", performing arts, health, business, memoir, military history, and humor); Sharon Pelletier, spelletier@dystel.com (smart commercial fiction, from upmarket women's fiction to domestic suspense to literary thrillers, and strong contemporary romance novels; compelling nonfiction projects, especially feminism and religion); Michael Hoogland, mhoogland@dystel.com (thriller, SFF, YA, upmarket women's fiction, and narrative nonfiction); Amy Bishop, abishop@dystel.com (commercial and literary women's fiction, fiction from diverse authors, historical fiction, YA, personal narratives, and biographies); Kemi Faderin, kfaderin@dystel.com (smart, plot-driven YA, historical fiction/non-fiction, contemporary women's fiction, and literary fiction); Ann Leslie Tuttle, atuttle@dystel.com (romance); Kieryn Ziegler, kziegler@dystel.com (books about exciting new worlds, found families, fantastic female characters, and stories with diverse POVs, especially YA and MG).

REPRESENTS Considers these nonfiction areas: animals, art, autobiography, biography, business, cooking, cultural interests, current affairs, ethnic, foods, gay/lesbian, health, history, humor, inspirational, investigative, medicine, memoirs, metaphysics, military, New Age, parenting, popular culture, politics, psychology, religious, science, sports, women's issues, women's studies. **Considers these fiction areas:** commercial, ethnic, gay, lesbian, literary, mainstream, middle grade, mystery, paranormal, romance, suspense, thriller, women's, young adult.

⊶ "We are actively seeking fiction for all ages, in all genres." No plays, screenplays, or poetry.

HOW TO CONTACT Query via e-mail and put "Query" in the subject line. "Synopses, outlines or sample chapters (say, one chapter or the first 25 pages of your manuscript) should either be included below the cover letter or attached as a separate document. We won't open attachments if they come with a blank e-mail." Accepts simultaneous submissions. Responds in 6 to 8 weeks to queries; within 8 weeks to mss. Obtains most new clients through recommendations from others, solicitations, conferences.

TERMS Agent receives 15% commission on domestic sales; 19% commission on foreign sales. Offers written contract.

WRITERS CONFERENCES Backspace Writers' Conference, Pacific Northwest Writers' Association, Pike's Peak Writers' Conference, Writers League of Texas, Love Is Murder, Surrey International Writers Conference, Society of Children's Book Writers and Illustrators, International Thriller Writers, Willamette Writers Conference, The South Carolina Writers Workshop Conference, Las Vegas Writers Conference, Writer's Digest, Seton Hill Popular Fiction, Romance Writers of America, Geneva Writers Conference.

TIPS "DGLM prides itself on being a full-service agency. We're involved in every stage of the publishing process, from offering substantial editing on mss and proposals, to coming up with book ideas for authors looking for their next project, negotiating contracts and collecting monies for our clients. We follow a book from its inception through its sale to a publisher, its publication, and beyond. Our commitment to our writers does not, by any means, end when we have collected our commission. This is one of the many things that makes us unique in a very competitive business."

EDEN STREET LITERARY

P.O. Box 30, Billings NY 12510. **E-mail:** info@edenstreetlit.com. **E-mail:** submissions@edenstreetlit.com. **Website:** www.edenstreetlit.com. **Contact:** Liza Voges. Member of AAR. Signatory of WGA. Represents over 40 clients.

REPRESENTS Nonfiction, fiction, novels, juvenile books. **Considers these fiction areas:** juvenile, middle grade, picture books, young adult.

HOW TO CONTACT E-mail a picture book ms or dummy; a synopsis and 3 chapters of a MG or YA novel; a proposal and 3 sample chapters for nonfiction. Accepts simultaneous submissions. Responds only to submissions of interest.

RECENT SALES *Dream Dog*, by Lou Berger; *Biscuit Loves the Library*, by Alyssa Capucilli; *The Scraps Book*, by Lois Ehlert; *Two Bunny Buddies*, by Kathryn O. Galbraith; *Between Two Worlds*, by Katherine Kirkpatrick.

EINSTEIN LITERARY MANAGEMENT

27 W. 20th St., No. 1003, New York NY 10011. (212)221-8797. **E-mail:** info@einsteinliterary.com. **E-mail:** submissions@einsteinliterary.com. **Website:** http://einsteinliterary.com. **Contact:** Susanna Einstein. Estab. 2015. Member of AAR. Signatory of WGA.

Prior to her current position, Ms. Einstein was with LJK Literary Management and the Einstein Thompson Agency.

MEMBER AGENTS Susanna Einstein, Susan Graham, Shana Kelly.

REPRESENTS Nonfiction, fiction, novels, short story collections, juvenile books. **Considers these nonfiction areas:** cooking, creative nonfiction, memoirs, blog-to-book projects. **Considers these fiction areas:** comic books, commercial, crime, fantasy, historical, juvenile, literary, middle grade, mystery, picture books, romance, science fiction, suspense, thriller, women's, young adult.

"As an agency we represent a broad range of literary and commercial fiction, including upmarket women's fiction, crime fiction, historical fiction, romance, and books for middle-grade children and young adults, including picture books and graphic novels. We also handle non-fiction including cookbooks, memoir and narrative, and blog-to-book projects. Please see agent bios on the website for specific information about what each of ELM's agents represents." Does not want poetry, textbooks, or screenplays.

HOW TO CONTACT Please submit a query letter and the first 10 double-spaced pages of your manuscript in the body of the e-mail (no attachments). Does not respond to mail queries or telephone queries or queries that are not specifically addressed to this agency. Accepts simultaneous submissions. Responds in 6 weeks if interested.

THE LISA EKUS GROUP, LLC

57 North St., Hatfield MA 01038. (413)247-9325. **Fax:** (413)247-9873. **E-mail:** info@lisaekus.com. **Website:** www.lisaekus.com. **Contact:** Sally Ekus. Estab. 1982. Member of AAR.

MEMBER AGENTS Lisa Ekus; Sally Ekus.

REPRESENTS Nonfiction. **Considers these nonfiction areas:** cooking, diet/nutrition, foods, health, how-to, humor, women's issues, occasionally health/well-being and women's issues; humor; lifestyle.

"Please note that we do not handle fiction, poetry, or children's books. If we receive a query for titles in these categories, please understand that we do not have the time or resources to respond."

HOW TO CONTACT "For more information about our literary services, visit http://lisaekus.com/services/literary-agency. Submit a query via e-mail or through our contact form on the website. You can also submit complete hard copy proposal with title page, proposal contents, concept, bio, marketing, TOC, etc. Include SASE for the return of materials." Accepts simultaneous submissions. Responds in 4-6 weeks.

RECENT SALES "Please see the regularly updated client listing on our website."

TIPS "Please do not call. No phone queries."

EMPIRE LITERARY

115 W. 29th St., 3rd Floor, New York NY 10001. (917)213-7082. **E-mail:** abarzvi@empireliterary.com. **E-mail:** queries@empireliterary.com. **Website:** www.empireliterary.com. Estab. 2013. Member of AAR. Signatory of WGA.

MEMBER AGENTS Andrea Barzvi; Carrie Howland; Kathleen Schmidt; Penny Moore.

REPRESENTS Nonfiction, novels. **Considers these nonfiction areas:** diet/nutrition, health, memoirs, popular culture. **Considers these fiction areas:** literary, middle grade, women's, young adult.

HOW TO CONTACT Please only query one agent at a time. "If we are interested in reading more we will get in touch with you as soon as possible." Accepts simultaneous submissions.

FELICIA ETH LITERARY REPRESENTATION

555 Bryant St., Suite 350, Palo Alto CA 94301-1700. **E-mail:** feliciaeth.literary@gmail.com. **Website:** eth-literary.com. **Contact:** Felicia Eth. Member of AAR.

Worked as agent in NY at Writers House Inc. Prior to that worked in the movie business, Warner Bros NY. and Palomar Pictures for Story Dept.

REPRESENTS Nonfiction, fiction, novels. **Considers these nonfiction areas:** animals, creative nonfiction, cultural interests, current affairs, foods, history, investigative, memoirs, parenting, popular culture, psychology, science, sociology, travel, women's issues. **Considers these fiction areas:** contemporary issues, historical, literary, mainstream, suspense.

This agency specializes in high-quality fiction (preferably mainstream/contemporary) and provocative, intelligent, and thoughtful nonfiction on a wide array of commercial subjects. "The agency does not represent genre ficiton, including romance novels, sci fi and fantasy, westerns, anime and graphic novels, mysteries."

HOW TO CONTACT For fiction: Please write a query letter introducing yourself, your book, your writing background. Don't forget to include degrees you may have, publishing credits, awards and endorsements. Please wait for a response before including sample pages. "We only consider material where the manuscript for which you are querying is complete, unless you have previously published." For nonfiction: A query letter is best, introducing idea and what you have written already (proposal, manuscript?). "For writerly nonficiton (narratives, bio, memoir) please let us know if you have a finished manuscript. Also it's important you include information about yourself, your background and expertise, your platform and notoriety, if any. We do not ask for exclusivity in most instances but do ask that you inform us if other agents are considering the same material." Accepts simultaneous submissions. Responds in ideally 2 weeks for query, a month if more.

TERMS Agent receives 15% commission on domestic sales; 20% commission on foreign and film sales. Charges clients for photocopying and express mail service

RECENT SALES *Bumper Sticker Philosophy*, by Jack Bowen (Random House); *Boys Adrift*, by Leonard Sax (Basic Books); *The Memory Thief*, by Emily Colin (Ballantine Books); *The World is a Carpet*, by Anna Badkhen (Riverhead).

WRITERS CONFERENCES "Wide array—from Squaw Valley to Mills College."

MARY EVANS INC.

242 E. Fifth St., New York NY 10003. (212)979-0880. **Fax:** (212)979-5344. **E-mail:** info@maryevansinc.com. **Website:** maryevansinc.com. Member of AAR.

MEMBER AGENTS Mary Evans (progressive politics, alternative medicine, science and technology, social commentary, American history and culture); Julia Kardon (literary and upmarket fiction, narrative nonfiction, journalism, and history); Tom Mackay (nonfiction that uses sport as a platform to explore other issues and playful literary fiction).

REPRESENTS Nonfiction, novels. **Considers these nonfiction areas:** creative nonfiction, cultural interests, history, medicine, politics, science, technology, social commentary, journalism. **Considers these fiction areas:** literary, upmarket.

No screenplays or stage plays.

HOW TO CONTACT Query by mail or e-mail. If querying by mail, include a SASE. If querying by e-mail, put "Query" in the subject line. For fiction: Include the first few pages, or opening chapter of your novel as a single Word attachment. For nonfiction: Include your book proposal as a single Word attachment. Accepts simultaneous submissions. Responds within 4-8 weeks.

FAIRBANK LITERARY REPRESENTATION

Post Office Box Six, Hudson NY 12534-0006. (617)576-0030. **E-mail:** queries@fairbankliterary.com. **Website:** www.fairbankliterary.com; www.publishersmarketplace.com/members/SorcheFairbank/. **Contact:** Sorche Elizabeth Fairbank. Estab. 2002. Member of AAR. Author's Guild, the Agents Round Table, and Grub Street's Literary Advisory Council.

MEMBER AGENTS Sorche Fairbank (narrative nonfiction, commercial and literary fiction, memoir, food and wine); Matthew Frederick, matt@fairbankliterary.com (scout for sports nonfiction, architecture, design).

REPRESENTS Nonfiction, fiction, novels, short story collections, juvenile books. **Considers these nonfiction areas:** agriculture, animals, architecture, art, autobiography, biography, cooking, crafts, creative nonfiction, cultural interests, current affairs, decorating, diet/nutrition, design, environment, ethnic, foods, gardening, gay/lesbian, government, history, hobbies, horticulture, how-to, humor, interior design, investigative, juvenile nonfiction, law, literature, memoirs, photography, popular culture, politics, science, sociology, sports, technology, true crime, women's issues, women's studies. **Considers these fiction areas:** commercial, ethnic, feminist, juvenile, literary, mainstream, middle grade, mystery, new adult, picture books, short story collections, suspense, thriller, women's, young adult, International voices. Southern voices.

"I tend to gravitate toward literary fiction and narrative nonfiction, with a strong interest in women's issues and women's voices, international voices, class and race issues, and projects that simply teach me something new about the greater world and society around us. We have a good reputation for working closely and developmentally with our authors, and love what we do." Actively seeking literary fiction, international and culturally diverse voices, narrative nonfiction, topical subjects (politics, current affairs), history, sports, humor, architecture/design and humor/pop culture. Also looking for picture books by artist authors only. Does not want to receive romance, screenplays, poetry, science fiction or fantasy, or children's works unless by an artist-author.

HOW TO CONTACT Query by e-mail queries@fairbankliterary.com or by mail with SASE. Accepts simultaneous submissions. Obtains most new clients through recommendations from others, solicitations, conferences, ideas generated in-house.

TERMS Agent receives 15% commission on domestic sales; 20% commission on foreign sales. Offers written contract, binding for 12 months; 60-day notice must be given to terminate contract.

RECENT SALES 3-book deal for Terry Border for picture books to Philomel; 2-book deal for Lisa Currie, *Surprise Yourself* and *Notes to Self* to Marian Lizzi at Tarcher Perigee; scratch & sniff spin-off and an early reader adaptation of Terry Border's best-selling *Peanut Butter & Cupcake* to Grosset and Dunlap/Penguin; 10-book deal for Matthew Frederick for his best-selling *101 Things I Learned Series* moving to Crown.

TIPS "Show me that you know your audience—and your competition. Have the writing and/or proposal at the very, very best it can be before starting the querying process. Don't assume that if someone likes it enough they'll 'fix' it. The biggest mistake new writers make is starting the querying process before they—and the work—are ready. Take your time and do it right."

LEIGH FELDMAN LITERARY

E-mail: assistant@lfliterary.com. **E-mail:** query@lfliterary.com. **Website:** http://lfliterary.com. **Contact:** Leigh Feldman. Estab. 2014. Member of AAR. Signatory of WGA.

During her 25 years as a literary agent based in New York City, Leigh Feldman has established herself as an invaluable partner to the writers she represents, and is highly respected by her peers in the industry. Her agency, Leigh Feldman Literary, is the culmination of experiences and lessons learned from her 20-plus years at Darhansoff, Verrill, Feldman Literary Agency and Writer's House. In that time, Feldman has represented National Book Award winners and bestsellers of literary fiction, historical fiction, memoir, middle grade, and young adult. No matter the writer or the category, Feldman only represents books she believes in, that captivate her, and that she can best serve with her passion and tenacity. Leigh Feldman Literary is a full service literary agency.

REPRESENTS Nonfiction, fiction, novels, short story collections. **Considers these nonfiction areas:** creative nonfiction, memoirs. **Considers these fiction areas:** commercial, contemporary issues, family saga, feminist, gay, historical, lesbian, literary, mainstream, multicultural, short story collections, women's, young adult.

Does not want mystery, thriller, romance, paranormal, sci-fi.

HOW TO CONTACT E-query. "Please include 'query' in the subject line. Due to large volume of submissions, we regret that we can not respond to all queries individually. Please include the first chapter or the first 10 pages of your manuscript (or proposal) pasted after your query letter. I'd love to know what led you to query me in particular, and please let me know if you are querying other agents as well." Accepts simultaneous submissions.

RECENT SALES List of recent sales and best known sales are available on the agency website.

DIANA FINCH LITERARY AGENCY

116 W. 23rd St., Suite 500, New York NY 10011. (917)544-4470. **E-mail:** diana.finch@verizon.net. **Website:** dianafinchliteraryagency.blogspot.com. **Contact:** Diana Finch. Estab. 2003. Member of AAR. Represents approximately 40 active clients clients.

Seeking to represent books that change lives. Prior to opening her own agency in 2003, Ms. Finch worked at Ellen Levine Literary Agency for 18 years. She started her publishing career in the editorial department at St. Martin's Press.

REPRESENTS Nonfiction, fiction, novels, scholarly books. **Considers these nonfiction areas:** autobiography, biography, business, child guidance, computers, cultural interests, current affairs, dance, diet/nutrition, economics, environment, ethnic, film, government, health, history, how-to, humor, investigative, juvenile nonfiction, law, medicine, memoirs, military, money, music, parenting, photography, popular culture, politics, psychology, satire, science, self-help, sex, sports, technology, theater, translation, true crime, war, women's issues, women's studies, young adult. **Considers these fiction areas:** action, adventure, contemporary issues, crime, detective, ethnic, fantasy, historical, literary, mainstream, middle grade, multicultural, new adult, police, science fiction, sports, thriller, urban fantasy, young adult.

For news about the agency and agency clients, see the agency Facebook page at https://www.facebook.com/DianaFinchLitAg/.

"Does not want romance or children's picture books."

HOW TO CONTACT This agency prefers submissions via its online form. Accepts simultaneous submissions. Obtains most new clients through recommendations from others.

TERMS Agent receives 15% commission on domestic sales; 20% commission on foreign sales. Offers written contract. "I charge for overseas postage, galleys, and books purchased, and try to recoup these costs from earnings received for a client, rather than charging outright."

RECENT SALES *The Journeys of the Trees*, by Zach St George (W. W. Norton); *Owls of the Eastern Ice*, by Jonathan Slaght (FSG/Scientific American); *Uncolor: on toxins in personal products*, by Ronnie Citron-Fink (Island Press); *Cutting School*by Professor Noliwe Rooks (The New Press); *Merchants of Men*, by Loretta Napoleoni (Seven Stories Press); *Beyond $15*, by Jonathan Rosenblum (Beacon Press); *The Age of Inequality*, by the Editors of In These Times (Verso Books); *Seeds of Resistance*, by Mark Schapiro (Hot Books/Skyhorse).

WRITERS CONFERENCES Washington Writers Conference; Writers Digest NYC Conference; CLMP/New School conference, and others on an individual basis.

TIPS "Do as much research as you can on agents before you query. Have someone critique your query letter before you send it. It should be only 1 page and describe your book clearly—and why you are writing it—but also demonstrate creativity and a sense of your writing style."

FINEPRINT LITERARY MANAGEMENT

207 W. 106th St., Suite 1D, New York NY 10025. (212)279-1412. **E-mail:** info@fineprintlit.com. **Website:** www.fineprintlit.com. **Contact:** Peter Rubie. Estab. 2007. Member of AAR.

MEMBER AGENTS Peter Rubie, CEO, peter@fineprintlit.com (nonfiction interests include narrative nonfiction, popular science, spirituality, history, biography, pop culture, business, technology, parenting, health, self help, music, and food; fiction interests include literate thrillers, crime fiction, science fiction and fantasy, military fiction and literary fiction, middle grade and boy-oriented YA fiction); Laura Wood, laura@fineprintlit.com (serious nonfiction, especially in the areas of science and nature, along with substantial titles in business, history, religion, and other areas by academics, experienced professionals, and journalists; select genre fiction only (no poetry, literary fiction or memoir) in the categories of science fiction & fantasy and mystery); June Clark, june@fineprintlit.com (nonfiction projects in the areas of entertainment, self-help, parenting, reference/how-to books, food and wine, style/beauty, and prescriptive business titles); Lauren Bieker, lauren@fineprintlit.com (commercial and upmarket women's fiction and differentiated YA novels).

REPRESENTS Nonfiction, fiction, novels, short story collections. **Considers these nonfiction areas:** biography, business, cooking, cultural interests, current affairs, diet/nutrition, environment, foods, health, history, how-to, humor, investigative, medicine, memoirs, music, parenting, popular culture, psychology, science, self-help, spirituality, technology, travel, women's issues, fitness, lifestyle. **Considers these fiction areas:** action, adventure, commercial, crime, detective, fantasy, feminist, frontier, historical, literary, mainstream, middle grade, military, multicultural, multimedia, mystery, police, romance, science fiction, suspense, thriller, translation, urban fantasy, war, women's, young adult.

HOW TO CONTACT E-query. For fiction, send a query, synopsis, bio, and 30 pages pasted into the e-mail. No attachments. For nonfiction, send a query only; proposal requested later if the agent is interested. Accepts simultaneous submissions. Obtains most new clients through recommendations from others, solicitations.

TERMS Agent receives 15% commission on domestic sales; 20% commission on foreign sales.

FLETCHER & COMPANY

78 Fifth Ave., 3rd Floor, New York NY 10011. **E-mail:** info@fletcherandco.com. **Website:** www.fletcherandco.com. **Contact:** Christy Fletcher. Estab. 2003. Member of AAR.

MEMBER AGENTS Christy Fletcher (referrals only); Melissa Chinchillo (select list of her own authors); Rebecca Gradinger (literary fiction, up-market commercial fiction, narrative nonfiction, self-help, memoir, Women's studies, humor, and pop culture); Gráinne Fox (literary fiction and quality commercial authors, award-winning journalists and food writers, American voices, international, literary crime, upmarket fiction, narrative nonfiction); Lisa Grubka (fiction—literary, upmarket women's, and young adult; and nonfiction—narrative, food, science, and more); Sylvie Greenberg (literary fiction, business, sports, science, memoir and history); Donald Lamm (history, biography, investigative journalism, politics, current affairs, and business); Todd Sattersten (business books); Eric Lupfer; Sarah Fuentes; Veronica Goldstein; Alyssa Taylor; Erin McFadden.

REPRESENTS Nonfiction, novels. **Considers these nonfiction areas:** biography, business, creative nonfiction, current affairs, foods, history, humor, investigative, memoirs, popular culture, politics, science, self-help, sports, women's studies. **Considers these fiction areas:** commercial, crime, literary, women's, young adult.

HOW TO CONTACT Send queries to info@fletcherandco.com. Please do not include e-mail attachments with your initial query, as they will be deleted. Address your query to a specific agent. No snail mail queries. Accepts simultaneous submissions.

RECENT SALES *The Profiteers*, by Sally Denton; *The Longest Night*, by Andrea Williams; *Disrupted: My Misadventure in the Start-Up Bubble*, by Dan Lyons; *Free Re-Fills: A Doctor Confronts His Addiction*, by Peter Grinspoon, M.D.; *Black Man in a White Coat: A Doctor's Reflections on Race and Medicine*, by Damon Tweedy, M.D.

FOLIO LITERARY MANAGEMENT, LLC

The Film Center Building, 630 Ninth Ave., Suite 1101, New York NY 10036. (212)400-1494. **Fax:** (212)967-0977. **Website:** www.foliolit.com. Member of AAR. Represents 100+ clients.

Prior to creating Folio Literary Management, Mr. Hoffman worked for several years at another agency; Mr. Kleinman was an agent at Graybill & English.

MEMBER AGENTS Claudia Cross (romance novels, commercial women's fiction, cooking and food writing, serious nonfiction on religious and spiritual topics); Scott Hoffman (literary and commercial fiction, journalistic or academic nonfiction, narrative nonfiction, pop culture books, business, history, politics, spiritual or religious-themed fiction and nonfiction, sci-fi/fantasy literary fiction, heartbreaking memoirs, humorous nonfiction); Jeff Kleinman (bookclub fiction (not genre commercial, like mysteries or romances), literary fiction, thrillers and suspense novels, narrative nonfiction, memoir); Dado Derviskadic (nonfiction: cultural history, biography, memoir, pop science, motivational self-help, health/nutrition, pop culture, cookbooks; fiction that's gritty, introspective, or serious); Frank Weimann (biography, business/investing/finance, history, religious, mind/body/spirit, health, lifestyle, cookbooks, sports, African-

American, science, memoir, special forces/CIA/FBI/ mafia, military, prescriptive nonfiction, humor, celebrity; adult and children's fiction); Michael Harriot (commercial nonfiction (both narrative and prescriptive) and fantasy/science fiction); Erin Harris (book club, historical fiction, literary, narrative nonfiction, psychological suspense, young adult); Katherine Latshaw (blogs-to-books, food/cooking, middle grade, narrative and prescriptive nonfiction); Annie Hwang (literary and upmarket fiction with commercial appeal; select nonfiction: popular science, diet/health/ fitness, lifestyle, narrative nonfiction, pop culture, and humor); Erin Niumata (fiction: commercial women's fiction, romance, historical fiction, mysteries, psychological thrillers, suspense, humor; nonfiction: self-help, women's issues, pop culture and humor, pet care/ pets, memoirs, and anything blogger); Ruth Pomerance (narrative nonfiction and commercial fiction); Marcy Posner (adult: commercial women's fiction, historical fiction, mystery, biography, history, health, and lifestyle, commercial novels, thrillers, narrative nonfiction; children's: contemporary YA and MG, mystery series for boys, select historical fiction and fantasy); Jeff Silberman (narrative nonfiction, biography, history, politics, current affairs, health, lifestyle, humor, food/cookbook, memoir, pop culture, sports, science, technology; commercial, literary, and book club fiction); Steve Troha; Emily van Beek (YA, MG, picture books), Melissa White (general nonfiction, literary and commercial fiction, MG, YA); John Cusick (middle grade, picture books, YA); Jamie Chambliss.

REPRESENTS Nonfiction, novels. **Considers these nonfiction areas:** animals, art, biography, business, cooking, creative nonfiction, economics, environment, foods, health, history, how-to, humor, inspirational, memoirs, military, parenting, popular culture, politics, psychology, religious, satire, science, self-help, technology, war, women's issues, women's studies. **Considers these fiction areas:** commercial, fantasy, horror, literary, middle grade, mystery, picture books, religious, romance, thriller, women's, young adult.

No poetry, stage plays, or screenplays.

HOW TO CONTACT Query via e-mail only (no attachments). Read agent bios online for specific submission guidelines and e-mail addresses, and to check if someone is closed to queries. "All agents respond to queries as soon as possible, whether interested or not. If you haven't heard back from the individual agent within the time period that they specify on their bio page, it's possible that something has gone wrong, and your query has been lost–in that case, please e-mail a follow-up."

TIPS "Please do not submit simultaneously to more than one agent at Folio. If you're not sure which of us is exactly right for your book, don't worry. We work closely as a team, and if one of our agents gets a query that might be more appropriate for someone else, we'll always pass it along. It's important that you check each agent's bio page for clear directions as to how to submit, as well as when to expect feedback."

JEANNE FREDERICKS LITERARY AGENCY, INC.

221 Benedict Hill Rd., New Canaan CT 06840. (203)972-3011. **Fax:** (203)972-3011. **E-mail:** jeanne.fredericks@gmail.com. **Website:** www.jeannefredericks.com. **Contact:** Jeanne Fredericks. Estab. 1997. Member of AAR. Other memberships include Authors Guild. Represents 100+ clients.

Prior to opening her agency in 1997, Ms. Fredericks was an agent and acting director with the Susan P. Urstadt, Inc. Agency. Previously she was the editorial director of Ziff-Davis Books and managing editor and acquisitions editor at Macmillan Publishing Company.

REPRESENTS Nonfiction. **Considers these nonfiction areas:** Americana, animals, autobiography, biography, child guidance, cooking, decorating, diet/ nutrition, environment, foods, gardening, health, history, how-to, interior design, medicine, parenting, photography, psychology, self-help, women's issues.

This agency specializes in quality adult nonfiction by authorities in their fields. "We do not handle: fiction, true crime, juvenile, textbooks, poetry, essays, screenplays, short stories, science fiction, pop culture, guides to computers and software, politics, horror, pornography, books on overly depressing or violent topics, romance, teacher's manuals, or memoirs."

HOW TO CONTACT Query first by e-mail, then send outline/proposal, 1-2 sample chapters, if requested and after you have consulted the submission guidelines on the agency website. If you do send requested submission materials, include the word "Requested" in the subject line. Accepts simultaneous submissions. Responds in 3-5 weeks to queries; 2-4 months to mss. Obtains most new clients through recommendations from others, solicitations, conferences.

TERMS Agent receives 15% commission on domestic sales; 25% commission on foreign sales with co-agent. Offers written contract, binding for 9 months; 2-month notice must be given to terminate contract. Charges client for photocopying of whole proposals and mss, overseas postage, expedited mail services. Almost all submissions are made electronically so these charges rarely apply.

RECENT SALES *Between Grit and Grace*, by Sasha Shillcutt, M.D. (Health Communications); *Coming to Our Senses About Concussion*, by Elizabeth Sandel, M.D. (Harvard University Press); *The Autoimmune Disease Handbook*, by Julius Birnbaum, M.D. (Johns Hopkins University Press); *The Secret Language of Cells*, by Jonathan Lieff, M.D. (BenBella Books); *How to Build Your Own Tiny Home*, by Roger Marshall (Taunton Press); *Yoga Therapy*, by Larry Payne, PH.D.,Terra Gold, D.O.M., and Eden Goldman, D.C. (Basic Health/Turner); *The Creativity Cure*, by Carrie Alton, M.D. and Alton Barron, M.D. (Scribner); *Storm of the Century*, by Willie Drye (Lyons); *Lilias! Yoga*, by Lilias Folan (Skyhorse); *Horse Stories*, by Sharon Smith (Lyons).

WRITERS CONFERENCES Harvard Medical School CME Course in Publishing, Connecticut Authors and Publishers Association-University Conference, ASJA Writers' Conference, BookExpo America, Garden Writers' Association Annual Symposium.

TIPS "Be sure to research competition for your work and be able to justify why there's a need for your book. I enjoy building an author's career, particularly if he/she is professional, hardworking, and courteous, and actively involved in establishing a marketing platform. Aside from 25 years of agenting experience, I've had 10 years of editorial experience in adult trade book publishing that enable me to help an author polish a proposal so that it's more appealing to prospective editors. My MBA in marketing also distinguishes me from other agents."

REBECCA FRIEDMAN LITERARY AGENCY

E-mail: queries@rfliterary.com. **Website:** www.rfliterary.com. Estab. 2013. Member of AAR. Signatory of WGA.

Prior to opening her own agency in 2013, Ms. Friedman was with Sterling Lord Literistic from 2006 to 2011, then with Hill Nadell Agency.

MEMBER AGENTS Rebecca Friedman (commercial and literary fiction with a focus on literary novels of suspense, women's fiction, contemporary romance, and young adult, as well as journalistic nonfiction and memoir); Susan Finesman, susan@rfliterary.com (fiction, cookbooks, and lifestyle); Abby Schulman, abby@rfliterary.com (YA and nonfiction related to health, wellness, and personal development).

REPRESENTS Nonfiction, fiction, novels. **Considers these nonfiction areas:** cooking, crafts, creative nonfiction, cultural interests, decorating, foods, health, humor, interior design, investigative, memoirs, parenting, women's issues, young adult, journalistic nonfiction. **Considers these fiction areas:** commercial, family saga, fantasy, feminist, gay, historical, juvenile, lesbian, literary, mystery, science fiction, suspense, thriller, women's, young adult.

HOW TO CONTACT Please submit your brief query letter and first chapter (no more than 15 pages, double-spaced). No attachments. Accepts simultaneous submissions. Tries to respond in 6-8 weeks.

RECENT SALES A complete list of agency authors is available online.

THE FRIEDRICH AGENCY

19 W. 21st St., Suite 201, New York NY 10010. (212)317-8810. **E-mail:** mfriedrich@friedrichagency.com; lcarson@friedrichagency.com; kwolf@friedrichagency.com. **Website:** www.friedrichagency.com. **Contact:** Molly Friedrich; Lucy Carson; Kent D. Wolf. Estab. 2006. Member of AAR. Signatory of WGA. Represents 50+ clients.

Prior to her current position, Ms. Friedrich was an agent at the Aaron Priest Literary Agency.

MEMBER AGENTS Molly Friedrich, founder and agent (open to queries); Lucy Carson, TV/film rights director and agent (open to queries); Kent D. Wolf, foreign rights director and agent (open to queries).

REPRESENTS Nonfiction, fiction, novels, short story collections. **Considers these nonfiction areas:** autobiography, biography, creative nonfiction, memoirs, true crime, young adult. **Considers these fiction areas:** commercial, detective, family saga, feminist, gay, lesbian, literary, multicultural, mystery, science fiction, short story collections, suspense, thriller, women's, young adult.

HOW TO CONTACT Query by e-mail only. Please query only 1 agent at this agency. Accepts simultaneous submissions. Responds in 2-4 weeks.

RECENT SALES *W is For Wasted*, by Sue Grafton; *Olive Kitteridge*, by Elizabeth Strout. Other clients include Frank McCourt, Jane Smiley, Esmeralda Santiago, Terry McMillan, Cathy Schine, Ruth Ozeki, Karen Joy Fowler, and more.

FULL CIRCLE LITERARY, LLC

San Diego CA **Website:** www.fullcircleliterary.com. **Contact:** Stefanie Von Borstel. Estab. 2005. Member of AAR. Society of Children's Books Writers & Illustrators, Authors Guild. Represents 100+ clients.

MEMBER AGENTS Stefanie Sanchez Von Borstel; Adriana Dominguez; Taylor Martindale Kean; Lilly Ghahremani.

REPRESENTS Considers these nonfiction areas: how-to, multicultural, women's issues, young adult. **Considers these fiction areas:** literary, middle grade, multicultural, young adult.

- Actively seeking nonfiction and fiction projects that offer new and diverse viewpoints, and literature with a global or multicultural perspective. "We are particularly interested in books with a Latino or Middle Eastern angle."

HOW TO CONTACT Online submissions only via submissions form online. Please complete the form and submit cover letter, author information and sample writing. For sample writing: fiction please include the first 10 ms pages. For nonfiction, include a proposal with 1 sample chapter. Accepts simultaneous submissions. "Due to the high volume of submissions, please keep in mind we are no longer able to personally respond to every submission. However, we read every submission with care and often share for a second read within the office. If we are interested, we will contact you by email to request additional materials (such as a complete manuscript or additional manuscripts). Please keep us updated if there is a change in the status of your project, such as an offer of representation or book contract." If you have not heard from us in 6-8 weeks, your project is not right for our agency at the current time and we wish you all the best with your writing. Thank you for considering Full Circle Literary, we look forward to reading! Obtains most new clients through recommendations from others and conferences.

TERMS Agent receives 15% commission on domestic sales; 25% commission on foreign sales. Offers written contract which outlines responsibilities of the author and the agent.

THE G AGENCY, LLC

P.O. Box 374, Bronx NY 10471. **E-mail:** gagencyquery@gmail.com. **Website:** www.publishersmarketplace.com/members/jeffg/. **Contact:** Jeff Gerecke. Estab. 2012. Member of AAR.

MEMBER AGENTS Jeff Gerecke.

REPRESENTS Nonfiction, fiction. **Considers these nonfiction areas:** biography, business, computers, history, military, money, popular culture, technology. **Considers these fiction areas:** historical, mainstream, military, mystery, suspense, thriller, war.

- Does not want screenplays, sci-fi/fantasy or romance.

HOW TO CONTACT E-mail submissions required. Please do attach sample chapters or proposal. Enter "QUERY" along with the title in the subject line of e-mails. "I cannot guarantee replies to every submission. If you do not hear from me the first time, you may send me one reminder. I encourage you to make multiple submissions but want to know that is the case if I ask for a manuscript to read." Accepts simultaneous submissions.

RECENT SALES *The Race for Paradise*, by Paul Cobb (Oxford UP); *Barles Story*, by Else Poulsen (Greystone); *Weed Land*, by Peter Hecht (Univ of Calif Press); *Nothin' But Blue Skies*, by Edward McClelland (Bloomsbury); *Tear Down*, by Gordon Young (Univ of Calif Press).

TIPS "I am interested in commercial and literary fiction, as well as serious nonfiction and pop culture. My focus as an agent has always been on working with writers to shape their work for its greatest commercial potential. I provide lots of editorial advice in sharpening manuscripts and proposals before submission. I've been a member of the Royalty Committee of the Association of Authors Representatives since its founding and am always keen to challenge publishers for their willfully obscure royalty reporting. Also I have recently taken over the position of Treasurer of the A.A.R. My publishing background includes working at the University of California Press so I am always intrigued by academic subjects which are given a commercial spin to reach an audience outside academia. I've also worked as a foreign scout for publishers like Hodder & Stoughton in England and Wilhelm Heyne in Germany, which gives me a good sense of how American books can be successfully translated overseas."

GELFMAN SCHNEIDER/ICM PARTNERS

850 7th Ave., Suite 903, New York NY 10019. **E-mail:** mail@gelfmanschneider.com. **Website:** www.gelfmanschneider.com. **Contact:** Jane Gelfman, Deborah Schneider. Member of AAR. Represents 300+ clients.

MEMBER AGENTS Deborah Schneider (all categories of literary and commercial fiction and nonfiction); Jane Gelfman; Heather Mitchell (particularly interested in narrative nonfiction, historical fiction and young debut authors with strong voices); Penelope Burns, penelope.gsliterary@gmail.com (literary and commercial fiction and nonfiction, as well as a variety of young adult and middle grade).

REPRESENTS Nonfiction, fiction, juvenile books. **Considers these nonfiction areas:** creative nonfiction, popular culture. **Considers these fiction areas:** commercial, fantasy, historical, literary, mainstream, middle grade, mystery, science fiction, suspense, women's, young adult.

"Among our diverse list of clients are novelists, journalists, playwrights, scientists, activists & humorists writing narrative nonfiction, memoir, political & current affairs, popular science and popular culture nonfiction, as well as literary & commercial fiction, women's fiction, and historical fiction." Does not currently accept screenplays or scripts, poetry, or picture book queries.

HOW TO CONTACT Query. Check Submissions page of website to see which agents are open to queries and further instructions. Accepts simultaneous submissions.

TERMS Agent receives 15% commission on domestic sales; 20% commission on foreign sales; 15% commission on film sales. Offers written contract. Charges clients for photocopying and messengers/couriers.

GHOSH LITERARY

E-mail: submissions@ghoshliterary.com. **Website:** www.ghoshliterary.com. **Contact:** Anna Ghosh. Member of AAR. Signatory of WGA.

Prior to opening her own agency, Ms. Ghosh was previously a partner at Scovil Galen Ghosh.

REPRESENTS Nonfiction, fiction.

"Anna's literary interests are wide and eclectic and she is known for discovering and developing writers. She is particularly interested in literary narratives and books that illuminate some aspect of human endeavor or the natural world. Anna does not typically represent genre fiction but is drawn to compelling storytelling in most guises."

HOW TO CONTACT E-query. Please send an e-mail briefly introducing yourself and your work. Although no specific format is required, it is helpful to know the following: your qualifications for writing your book, including any publications and recognition for your work; who you expect to buy and read your book; similar books and authors. Accepts simultaneous submissions.

GLASS LITERARY MANAGEMENT

138 W. 25th St., 10th Floor, New York NY 10001. (646)237-4881. **E-mail:** alex@glassliterary.com; rick@glassliterary.com. **Website:** www.glassliterary.com. **Contact:** Alex Glass or Rick Pascocello. Estab. 2014. Member of AAR. Signatory of WGA.

MEMBER AGENTS Alex Glass; Rick Pascocello.

REPRESENTS Nonfiction, novels.

Represents general fiction, mystery, suspense/thriller, juvenile fiction, biography, history, mind/body/spirit, health, lifestyle, cookbooks, sports, literary fiction, memoir, narrative nonfiction, pop culture. "We do not represent picture books for children."

HOW TO CONTACT "Please send your query letter in the body of an e-mail and if we are interested, we will respond and ask for the complete manuscript or proposal. No attachments." Accepts simultaneous submissions.

RECENT SALES *100 Days of Cake*, by Shari Goldhagen; *The Red Car*, by Marcy Dermansky; *The Overnight Solution*, by Dr. Michael Breus; *So That Happened: A Memoir*, by Jon Cryer; *Bad Kid*, by David Crabb; *Finding Mr. Brightside*, by Jay Clark; *Strange Animals*, by Chad Kultgen.

BARRY GOLDBLATT LITERARY LLC

320 7th Ave. #266, Brooklyn NY 11215. **E-mail:** query@bgliterary.com. **Website:** www.bgliterary.com. **Contact:** Barry Goldblatt; Jennifer Udden. Estab. 2000. Member of AAR. Signatory of WGA.

MEMBER AGENTS Barry Goldblatt; Jennifer Udden, query.judden@gmail.com (speculative fiction of all stripes, especially innovative science fiction or fantasy; contemporary/erotic/LGBT/paranormal/historical romance; contemporary or speculative YA; select mysteries, thrillers, and urban fantasies).

REPRESENTS Fiction. **Considers these fiction areas:** fantasy, middle grade, mystery, romance, science fiction, thriller, young adult.

- "Please see our website for specific submission guidelines and information on our particular tastes."

HOW TO CONTACT "E-mail queries can be sent to query@bgliterary.com and should include the word 'query' in the subject line. To query Jen Udden specifically, e-mail queries can be sent to query.judden@gmail.com. Please know that we will read and respond to every e-query that we receive, provided it is properly addressed and follows the submission guidelines below. We will not respond to e-queries that are addressed to no one, or to multiple recipients. Your e-mail query should include the following within the body of the e-mail: your query letter, a synopsis of the book, and the first 5 pages of your manuscript. We will not open or respond to any e-mails that have attachments. If we like the sound of your work, we will request more from you. Our response time is 4 weeks on queries, 6-8 weeks on full manuscripts. If you haven't heard from us within that time, feel free to check in via e-mail." Accepts simultaneous submissions. Obtains clients through referrals, queries, and conferences.

TERMS Agent receives 15% commission on domestic sales; 20% on foreign and dramatic sales. Offers written contract. 60 days notice must be given to terminate contract.

RECENT SALES *Trolled*, by Bruce Coville; *Grim Tidings*, by Caitlin Kittridge; *Max at Night*, by Ed Vere.

TIPS "We're a hands-on agency, focused on building an author's career, not just making an initial sale. We don't care about trends or what's hot; we just want to sign great writers."

FRANCES GOLDIN LITERARY AGENCY, INC.

214 W. 29th St., Suite 410, New York NY 10001. (212)777-0047. **Fax:** (212)228-1660. **Website:** www.goldinlit.com. Estab. 1977. Member of AAR.

MEMBER AGENTS Frances Goldin, founder/president; Ellen Geiger, vice president/principal (nonfiction: history, biography, progressive politics, photography, science and medicine, women, religion and serious investigative journalism; fiction: literary thriller, and novels in general that provoke and challenge the status quo, as well as historical and multicultural works. Please no New Age, romance, how-to or right-wing politics); Matt McGowan, agent/rights director, mm@goldinlit.com, (literary fiction, essays, history, memoir, journalism, biography, music, popular culture & science, sports [particularly soccer], narrative nonfiction, cultural studies, as well as literary travel, crime, food, suspense and sci-fi); Sam Stoloff, vice president/principal, (literary fiction, memoir, history, accessible sociology and philosophy, cultural studies, serious journalism, narrative and topical nonfiction with a progressive orientation); Ria Julien, agent/counsel; Caroline Eisenmann, associate agent.

REPRESENTS Nonfiction, novels. **Considers these nonfiction areas:** biography, creative nonfiction, cultural interests, foods, history, investigative, medicine, memoirs, music, philosophy, photography, popular culture, politics, science, sociology, sports, travel, women's issues, crime. **Considers these fiction areas:** historical, literary, mainstream, multicultural, suspense, thriller.

- "We are hands on and we work intensively with clients on proposal and manuscript development." "Please note that we do not handle screenplays, romances or most other genre fiction, and hardly any poetry. We do not handle work that is racist, sexist, ageist, homophobic, or pornographic."

HOW TO CONTACT There is an online submission process you can find online. Responds in 4-6 weeks to queries.

IRENE GOODMAN LITERARY AGENCY

27 W. 24th St., Suite 700B, New York NY 10010. **E-mail:** miriam.queries@irenegoodman.com, barbara.queries@irenegoodman.com, rachel.queries@irenegoodman.com, kim.queries@irenegoodman.com, victoria.queries@irenegoodman.com, irene.queries@irenegoodman.com, brita.queries@irenegoodman.com. **E-mail:** submissions@irenegoodman.com. **Website:** www.irenegoodman.com. **Contact:** Brita Lundberg. Estab. 1978. Member of AAR. Represents 150 clients.

MEMBER AGENTS Irene Goodman, Miriam Kriss, Barbara Poelle, Rachel Ekstrom, Kim Perel, Brita Lundberg, Victoria Marini.

REPRESENTS Nonfiction, fiction, novels, juvenile books. **Considers these nonfiction areas:** animals, autobiography, cooking, creative nonfiction, cultural interests, current affairs, decorating, diet/nutrition, design, foods, health, history, how-to, humor, interior design, juvenile nonfiction, memoirs, parenting, politics, science, self-help, women's issues, young adult, parenting, social issues, francophilia, anglophilia, Judaica, lifestyles, cooking, memoir. **Considers these fiction areas:** action, crime, detective, family saga, historical, horror, middle grade, mystery, romance, science fiction, suspense, thriller, urban fantasy, women's, young adult.

Commercial and literary fiction and nonfiction. No screenplays, poetry, or inspirational fiction.

HOW TO CONTACT Query. Submit synopsis, first 10 pages pasted into the body of the email. E-mail queries only! See the website submission page. No e-mail attachments. Query 1 agent only. Accepts simultaneous submissions. Responds in 2 months to queries. Consult website for each agent's submission guidelines.

TERMS 15% commission.

TIPS "We are receiving an unprecedented amount of e-mail queries. If you find that the mailbox is full, please try again in two weeks. E-mail queries to our personal addresses will not be answered. E-mails to our personal inboxes will be deleted."

DOUG GRAD LITERARY AGENCY, INC.

156 Prospect Park West, #3L, Brooklyn NY 11215. **E-mail:** query@dgliterary.com. **Website:** www.dgliterary.com. **Contact:** Doug Grad. Estab. 2008. Represents 50+ clients.

Prior to being an agent, Doug Grad spent 22 years as an editor at imprint at 4 major publishing houses—Simon & Schuster, Random House, Penguin, and HarperCollins.

MEMBER AGENTS Doug Grad (narrative nonfiction, military, sports, celebrity memoir, thrillers, mysteries, cozies, historical fiction, music, style, business, home improvement, food, science and theater).

REPRESENTS Nonfiction, fiction, novels. **Considers these nonfiction areas:** Americana, autobiography, biography, business, cooking, creative nonfiction, current affairs, diet/nutrition, design, film, government, history, humor, investigative, language, military, music, popular culture, politics, science, sports, technology, theater, travel, true crime, war. **Considers these fiction areas:** action, adventure, commercial, crime, detective, historical, horror, literary, mainstream, military, mystery, police, romance, science fiction, suspense, thriller, war, young adult.

Does not want fantasy, young adult, or children's picture books.

HOW TO CONTACT Query by e-mail first. No sample material unless requested; no printed submissions by mail. Accepts simultaneous submissions. Due to the volume of queries, it's impossible to give a response time.

RECENT SALES *Net Force* series created by Tom Clancy and Steve Pieczenik, written by Jerome Preisler (Hanover Square); *A Serial Killer's Daughter* by Kerri Rawson (Thomas Nelson); *The Next Greatest Generation*, by Joseph L. Galloway and Marvin J. Wolf (Thomas Nelson); *All Available Boats* by L. Douglas Keeney (Lyons Press); *Here Comes the Body*, Book 1 in the Catering Hall mystery series, by Agatha Award-winner Ellen Byron writing as Maria DiRico (Kensington); *Please Don't Feed the Mayor* and *Alaskan Catch*, by Sue Pethick (Kensington).

SANFORD J. GREENBURGER ASSOCIATES, INC.

55 Fifth Ave., New York NY 10003. (212)206-5600. **Fax:** (212)463-8718. **Website:** www.greenburger.com. Member of AAR. Represents 500 clients.

MEMBER AGENTS Matt Bialer, querymb@sjga.com (fantasy, science fiction, thrillers, and mysteries as well as a select group of literary writers, and also loves smart narrative nonfiction including books about current events, popular culture, biography, history, music, race, and sports); Brenda Bowen, querybb@sjga.com (literary fiction, writers and illustrators of picture books, chapter books, and middle-grade and teen fiction); Faith Hamlin, fhamlin@sjga.com (receives submissions by referral); Heide Lange, queryhl@sjga.com (receives submissions by referral); Daniel Mandel, querydm@sjga.com (literary and commercial fiction, as well as memoirs and nonfiction about business, art, history, politics, sports, and popular culture); Rachael Dillon Fried, rfried@sjga.com (both fiction and nonfiction authors, with a keen interest in unique literary voices, women's fiction, narrative nonfiction, memoir, and comedy); Stephanie Delman, sdelman@sjga.com (literary/upmarket contemporary fiction, psychological thrillers/suspense, and atmospheric, near-historical fiction); Ed Maxwell, emaxwell@sjga.com (expert and narrative nonfiction authors, novelists and graphic novelists, as well as children's book authors and illustrators).

REPRESENTS Nonfiction, fiction, novels, juvenile books. **Considers these nonfiction areas:** art, biography, business, creative nonfiction, current affairs, ethnic, history, humor, memoirs, music, popular culture, politics, sports. **Considers these fiction areas:** commercial, crime, family saga, fantasy, feminist, historical, literary, middle grade, multicultural, mystery, picture books, romance, science fiction, thriller, women's, young adult.

No screenplays.

HOW TO CONTACT E-query. "Please look at each agent's profile page for current information about what each agent is looking for and for the correct email address to use for queries to that agent. Please be sure to use the correct query e-mail address for each agent." Agents may not respond to all queries; will respond within 6-8 weeks if interested. Obtains most new clients through recommendations from others.

TERMS Agent receives 15% commission on domestic sales; 20% commission on foreign sales. Charges for photocopying and books for foreign and subsidiary rights submissions.

RECENT SALES *Origin*, by Dan Brown; *Sweet Pea and Friends: A Sheepover*, by

JOHN CHURCHMAN and Jennifer Churchman; *Code of Conduct*, by Brad Thor.

THE GREENHOUSE LITERARY AGENCY

E-mail: submissions@greenhouseliterary.com. **Website:** www.greenhouseliterary.com. **Contact:** Sarah Davies. Estab. 2008. Member of AAR. Other memberships include SCBWI. Represents 70 clients.

Before launching Greenhouse, Sarah Davies had an editorial and management career in children's publishing spanning 25 years; for 5 years prior to launching the Greenhouse she was Publishing Director of Macmillan Children's Books in London, and published leading authors from both sides of the Atlantic.

MEMBER AGENTS Sarah Davies, vice president (fiction and nonfiction by North American authors, chapter books through to middle grade and young adult); Polly Nolan, agent (fiction by North American, UK, Irish, Commonwealth–including Australia, NZ and India–authors, plus European authors writing in English, young fiction series, through middle grade and young adult).

REPRESENTS Juvenile books. **Considers these nonfiction areas:** juvenile nonfiction, young adult. **Considers these fiction areas:** juvenile, young adult.

"We represent authors writing fiction and nonfiction for children and teens. The agency has offices in both the US and UK, and the agency's commission structure reflects this—taking 15% for sales to both US and UK, thus treating both as 'domestic' market." All genres of children's and YA fiction. Occasionally, a nonfiction proposal will be considered. Does not want to receive picture books texts (ie, written by writers who aren't also illustrators) or short stories, educational or religious/inspirational work, pre-school/novelty material, screenplays. Represents novels and some nonfiction. Considers these fiction areas: juvenile, chapter book series, middle grade, young adult. Does not want to receive poetry, picture book texts (unless by author/illustrators) or work aimed at adults; short stories, educational or religious/inspirational work, pre-school/novelty material, or screenplays.

HOW TO CONTACT Query 1 agent only. Put the target agent's name in the subject line. Paste the first 5 pages of your story after the query. Please see our website for up-to-date information as occasionally we close to queries for short periods of time. Accepts simultaneous submissions.

TERMS Agent receives 15% commission on domestic sales; 25% commission on foreign sales. Offers written contract. This agency occasionally charges for submission copies to film agents or foreign publishers.

RECENT SALES *Agents of the Wild*, by Jennifer Bell & Alice Lickens (Walker UK); *Bookshop Girl in Paris*, by Chloe Coles (Hot Key); *Votes for Women*, by Winifred Conkling (Algonquin); *The Monster Catchers*, by George Brewington (Holt); *City of the Plague God*, by Sarwat Chadda (Disney-Hyperion); *Whiteout*, by Gabriel Dylan (Stripes); *The Lying Woods*, by Ashley Elston (Disney-Hyperion); *When You Trap a Tiger*, by Tae Keller (Random House); *We Speak in Storms*, by Natalie Lund (Philomel); *When We Wake*, by Elle Cosimano (HarperCollins); *Carpa Fortuna*, by Lindsay Eagar (Candlewick); *Instructions Not Included*, by Tami Lewis Brown & Debbie Loren Dunn (Disney-Hyperion); *Fake*, by Donna Cooner (Scholastic); *Unicorn Academy*, by Julie Sykes (Nosy Crow); *The Girl*

Who Sailed the Stars, by Matilda Woods (Scholastic UK/Philomel US).

WRITERS CONFERENCES Bologna Children's Book Fair, ALA and SCBWI conferences, BookExpo America.

TIPS "Before submitting material, authors should visit the Greenhouse Literary Agency website and carefully read all submission guidelines."

GREYHAUS LITERARY

3021 20th St., Pl. SW, Puyallup WA 98373. **E-mail:** scott@greyhausagency.com. **E-mail:** submissions@greyhausagency.com. **Website:** www.greyhausagency.com. **Contact:** Scott Eagan, member RWA. Estab. 2003. Member of AAR. Signatory of WGA.

REPRESENTS Novels. **Considers these fiction areas:** new adult, romance, women's.

Greyhaus only focuses on romance and women's fiction. Please review submission information found on the website to know exactly what Greyhaus is looking for. Stories should be 75,000-120,000 words in length or meet the word count requirements for Harlequin found on its website. Greyhaus does not deviate from these genres. Does not want fantasy, single title inspirational, young adult or middle grade, picture books, memoirs, biographies, erotica, urban fantasy, science fiction, screenplays, poetry, authors interested in only e-publishing or self-publishing.

HOW TO CONTACT Submissions to Greyhaus can be done in one of three ways: 1) A standard query letter via e-mail. If using this method, do not attach documents or send anything else other than a query letter. 2) Use the Submission Form found on the website on the Contact page. Or 3) send a query, the first 3 pages and a synopsis of no more than 3-5 pages (and a SASE), using a snail mail submission. Do not submit anything more than asked. Please also understand Greyhaus does not consider queries through social media sites. Accepts simultaneous submissions. Responds in up to 3 months.

TERMS 15%

WRITERS CONFERENCES Scott Eagan is available to assist writing chapters and organizations through conference attendance, teaching workshops, guest blogging, judging contest final rounds, online workshops and certainly listening to pitches. The agency does not make it a practice of just showing up. If you want the Scott to help out, please reach out to the agency.

JILL GRINBERG LITERARY MANAGEMENT, LLC

392 Vanderbilt Ave., Brooklyn NY 11238. (212)620-5883. **E-mail:** info@jillgrinbergliterary.com. **Website:** www.jillgrinbergliterary.com. Estab. 1999. Member of AAR.

Prior to her current position, Ms. Grinberg was at Anderson Grinberg Literary Management.

MEMBER AGENTS Jill Grinberg; Cheryl Pientka; Katelyn Detweiler; Sophia Seidner.

REPRESENTS Nonfiction, fiction, novels. **Considers these nonfiction areas:** biography, creative nonfiction, current affairs, ethnic, history, language, literature, memoirs, parenting, popular culture, politics, science, sociology, spirituality, sports, travel, women's issues, young adult. **Considers these fiction areas:** fantasy, historical, juvenile, literary, mainstream, middle grade, multicultural, picture books, romance, science fiction, women's, young adult.

"We do not accept unsolicited queries for screenplays."

HOW TO CONTACT "Please send queries via e-mail to info@jillgrinbergliterary.com–include your query letter, addressed to the agent of your choice, along with the first 50 pages of your ms pasted into the body of the e-mail or attached as a doc. or docx. file. We also accept queries via mail, though e-mail is much preferred. Please send your query letter and the first 50 pages of your ms by mail, along with a SASE, to the attention of your agent of choice. Please note that unless a SASE with sufficient postage is provided, your materials will not be returned. As submissions are shared within the office, please only query one agent with your project." Accepts simultaneous submissions.

TIPS "We prefer submissions by electronic mail."

THE JOY HARRIS LITERARY AGENCY, INC.

1501 Broadway, Suite 2310, New York NY 10036. (212)924-6269. **Fax:** (212)540-5776. **E-mail:** contact@joyharrisliterary.com. **E-mail:** submissions@joyharrisliterary.com. **Website:** joyharrisliterary.com. **Contact:** Joy Harris. Estab. 1990. Member of AAR. Represents 100+ clients.

MEMBER AGENTS Joy Harris (literary fiction, strongly-written commercial fiction, narrative nonfiction across a broad range of topics, memoir and biography); Adam Reed (literary fiction, science and technology, and pop culture); Olivia Nathan.

REPRESENTS Nonfiction, fiction. **Considers these nonfiction areas:** art, biography, creative nonfiction, memoirs, popular culture, science, technology. **Considers these fiction areas:** commercial, literary.

"We are not accepting poetry, screenplays, genre fiction, or self-help submissions at this time."

HOW TO CONTACT Please e-mail all submissions, comprised of a query letter, outline or sample chapter, to submissions@joyharrisliterary.com. Accepts simultaneous submissions. Obtains most new clients through recommendations from clients and editors.

TERMS Agent receives 15% commission on domestic sales; 20% commission on foreign sales. Charges clients for some office expenses.

RECENT SALES *Smash Cut*, by Brad Gooch; *The Other Paris*, by Luc Sante; *The Past*, by Tessa Hadley; *In A Dark Wood*, by Joseph Luzzi.

JOHN HAWKINS & ASSOCIATES, INC.

80 Maiden Ln., Suite 1503, New York NY 10038. (212)807-7040. **E-mail:** jha@jhalit.com. **Website:** www.jhalit.com. **Contact:** Moses Cardona (rights and translations); Annie Kronenberg (permissions); Warren Frazier, literary agent; Anne Hawkins, literary agent; William Reiss, literary agent. Estab. 1893. Member of AAR. The Author Guild Represents 100+ clients.

MEMBER AGENTS Moses Cardona, moses@jhalit.com (commercial fiction, suspense, business, science, and multicultural fiction); Warren Frazier, frazier@jhalit.com (fiction; nonfiction, specifically technology, history, world affairs and foreign policy); Anne Hawkins, ahawkins@jhalit.com (thrillers to literary fiction to serious nonfiction; interested in science, history, public policy, medicine and women's issues).

REPRESENTS Nonfiction, fiction, novels, short story collections, novellas, juvenile books. **Considers these nonfiction areas:** biography, business, history, medicine, politics, science, technology, women's issues. **Considers these fiction areas:** commercial, historical, literary, multicultural, suspense, thriller.

HOW TO CONTACT Query. Include the word "Query" in the subject line. For fiction, include 1-3 chapters of your book as a single Word attachment. For nonfiction, include your proposal as a single attachment. E-mail a particular agent directly if you are targeting one. Accepts simultaneous submissions. Responds in 1 month to queries. Obtains most new clients through recommendations from others.

TERMS Agent receives 15% commission on domestic sales; 20% commission on foreign sales. Charges clients for photocopying.

RECENT SALES *Forty Rooms*, by Olga Grushin; *A Book of American Martyrs*, by Joyce Carol Oates; *City on Edge*, by Stefanie Pintoff; *Cold Earth*, by Ann Cleeves; *The Good Lieutenant*, by Whitney Terrell; *Grief Cottage*, by Gail Godwin.

HOLLOWAY LITERARY

P.O. Box 771, Cary NC 27512. **E-mail:** submissions@hollowayliteraryagency.com. **Website:** hollowayliteraryagency.com. **Contact:** Nikki Terpilowski. Estab. 2011. Member of AAR. Signatory of WGA. International Thriller Writers and Romance Writers of America Represents 26 clients.

MEMBER AGENTS Nikki Terpilowski (romance, women's fiction, Southern fiction, historical fiction, cozy mysteries, lifestyle no-fiction (minimalism, homesteading, southern, etc.) commercial, upmarket/book club fiction, African-American fiction of all types, literary); Rachel Burkot (young adult contemporary, women's fiction, upmarket/book club fiction, contemporary romance, Southern fiction, nonfiction).

REPRESENTS Nonfiction, fiction, movie scripts, feature film. **Considers these nonfiction areas:** Americana, environment, humor, narrative nonfiction, New Journalism, essays. **Considers these fiction areas:** action, adventure, commercial, contemporary issues, crime, detective, ethnic, family saga, fantasy, glitz, historical, inspirational, literary, mainstream, metaphysical, middle grade, military, multicultural, mystery, new adult, New Age, regional, romance, short story collections, spiritual, suspense, thriller, urban fantasy, war, women's, young adult. **Considers these script areas:** action, adventure, biography, contemporary issues, ethnic, romantic comedy, romantic drama, teen, thriller, TV movie of the week.

"Note to self-published authors: While we are happy to receive submissions from authors who have previously self-published novels, we do not represent self-published works. Send us your unpublished manuscripts only." Nikki is open to submissions and is selectively reviewing queries for cozy mysteries with culinary, historical or book/publishing industry themes written in the vein of Jaclyn Brady, Laura Childs, Julie Hyzy and Lucy Arlington; women's fiction with strong magical realism similar to Meena van Praag's *The Dress Shop of Dreams*, Sarah Addison Allen's *Garden Spells*, *Season of the Dragonflies* by Sarah Creech and Mary Robinette Kowal's Glamourist Series. She would love to find a wine-themed mystery series similar to Nadia Gordon's Sunny McCoskey series or Ellen Crosby's Wine County Mysteries that combine culinary themes with lots of great Southern history. Nikki is also interested in seeing contemporary romance set in the southern US or any wine county or featuring a culinary theme, dark, edgy historical romance, gritty military romance or romantic suspense with sexy Alpha heroes and lots of technical detail. She is also interested in acquiring historical fiction written in the vein of Alice Hoffman, Lalita Tademy and Isabel Allende. Nikki is also interested in espionage, military, political and AI thrillers similar to Tom Clancy, Robert Ludlum, Steve Berry, Vince Flynn, Brad Thor and Daniel Silva. Nikki has a special interest in non-fiction subjects related to governance, politics, military strategy and foreign relations; food and beverage, mindfulness, southern living and lifestyle. Does not want horror, true crime or novellas.

HOW TO CONTACT Send query and first 15 pages of ms pasted into the body of e-mail to submissions@hollowayliteraryagency.com. In the subject header write: (Insert Agent's Name)/Title/Genre. Holloway Literary does accept submissions via mail (query letter and first 50 pages). Expect a response time of at least 3 months. Include e-mail address, phone number, social media accounts, and mailing address on your query letter. Accepts simultaneous submissions. Responds in 6-8 weeks. If the agent is interested, he/she'll respond with a request for more material.

RECENT SALES A list of recent sales are listed on the agency website's "news" page.

HSG AGENCY

37 W. 28th St., 8th Floor, New York NY 10001. **E-mail:** channigan@hsgagency.com; jsalky@hsgagency.com; jgetzler@hsgagency.com; sroberts@hsgagency.com; leigh@hsgagency.com. **Website:** hsgagency.com. **Contact:** Carrie Hannigan; Jesseca Salky; Josh Getzler; Soumeya Roberts; Julia Kardon; Rhea Lyons. Estab. 2011. Member of AAR. Signatory of WGA.

Prior to opening HSG Agency, Ms. Hannigan, Ms. Salky. and Mr. Getzler were agents at Russell & Volkening.

MEMBER AGENTS Carrie Hannigan (children's books, illustrators, YA and MG); Jesseca Salky (literary and mainstream fiction); Josh Getzler (foreign and historical fiction; both women's fiction, straight-ahead historical fiction, and thrillers and mysteries); Soumeya Roberts (literary fiction and narrative non-fiction); Julia Kardon (literary fiction, memoir, essays, narrative non-fiction); Rhea Lyons (commercial fiction, pop-culture, health and wellness, science fiction/fantasy).

REPRESENTS Nonfiction, fiction, novels, short story collections, juvenile books. **Considers these nonfiction areas:** animals, business, cooking, creative nonfiction, cultural interests, current affairs, diet/nutrition, education, environment, foods, gardening, health, history, hobbies, humor, literature, memoirs, money, multicultural, music, parenting, photography, popular culture, politics, psychology, science, self-help, sports, women's issues, women's studies, young adult. **Considers these fiction areas:** adventure, commercial, contemporary issues, crime, detective, ethnic, experimental, family saga, fantasy, feminist, historical, humor, juvenile, literary, mainstream, middle grade, multicultural, mystery, picture books, science fiction, suspense, thriller, translation, women's, young adult.

Carrie Hannigan: In the kidlit world, right now Carrie is looking for humorous books and books with warmth, heart and a great voice in both contemporary and fantasy. She is also open to graphic novels and nonfiction. Jesseca Salky: Jesseca is looking for literary fiction submissions that are family stories (she loves a good mother/daughter tale), have a strong sense of place (where the setting feels like its own character), or a daring or unique voice (think Jamie Quatro), as well as upmarket fiction that can appeal to men and women and has that Tropper/Hornby/Matt Norman quality to it. Josh Getzler: Josh is particularly into foreign and historical fiction; both women's fiction (your Downton Abbey/Philippa Gregory Mashups), straight ahead historical fiction (think Wolf Hall or The Road to Wellville); and thrillers and mysteries (The Alienist, say; or Donna Leon or Arianna Franklin). He'd love a strong French Revolution novel. In nonfiction, he's very interested in increasing his list in history (including micro-histories), business, and political thought–but not screeds. Soumeya Roberts: In fiction, Soumeya is seeking literary and upmarket novels and collections, and also represents realistic young-adult and middle-grade. She likes books with vivid voices and compelling, well-developed story-telling, and is particularly interested in fiction that reflects on the post-colonial world and narratives by people of color. In nonfiction, she is primarily looking for idea-driven or voice-forward memoirs, personal essay collections, and approachable narrative nonfiction of all stripes. Leigh Eisenman: Leigh seeks submissions in the areas of literary and upmarket commercial fiction for adults, and is particularly drawn to: flawed protagonists she can't help but fall in love with (Holden Caulfield was her first crush); stories that take place in contemporary New York, but also any well-defined, vivid setting; explorations of relationships (including journeys of self-discovery); and of course, excellent writing. On the nonfiction side, Leigh is interested in cookbooks, food/travel-related works, health and fitness, lifestyle, humor/gift, and select narrative nonfiction. Please note that we do not represent screenplays, romance fiction, or religious fiction.

HOW TO CONTACT Please send a query letter and the first 5 pages of your ms (within the e-mail–no attachments please) to the appropriate agent for your book. If it is a picture book, please include the entire ms. If you were referred to us, please mention it in the first line of your query. Please note that we do not represent screenplays, romance fiction, or religious fiction. If Carrie and Jesseca have not responded to your query within 10 weeks of submission, please consider this a pass. All agents are open to new clients.

RECENT SALES *A Spool of Blue Thread*, by Anne Tyler (Knopf); *Blue Sea Burning*, by Geoff Rodkey (Putnam); *The Partner Track*, by Helen Wan (St. Martin's Press); *The Thrill of the Haunt*, by E.J. Copperman (Berkley); *Aces Wild*, by Erica Perl (Knopf Books for Young Readers); *Steve & Wessley: The Sea Monster*, by Jennifer Morris (Scholastic); *Infinite Worlds*, by Michael Soluri (Simon & Schuster).

HARVEY KLINGER, INC.

300 W. 55th St., Suite 11V, New York NY 10019. (212)581-7068. **E-mail:** queries@harveyklinger.com. **Website:** www.harveyklinger.com. **Contact:** Harvey Klinger. Estab. 1977. Member of AAR. PEN Represents 100 clients.

MEMBER AGENTS Harvey Klinger, harvey@harveyklinger.com; David Dunton, david@harveyklinger.com (popular culture, music-related books, literary fiction, young adult, fiction, and memoirs); Andrea Somberg, andrea@harveyklinger.com (literary fiction, commercial fiction, romance, sci-fi/fantasy, mysteries/thrillers, young adult, middle grade, quality narrative nonfiction, popular culture, how-to, self-help, humor, interior design, cookbooks, health/fitness); Wendy Silbert Levinson, wendy@harveyklinger.com (literary and commercial fiction, occasional children's YA or MG, wide variety of nonfiction); Rachel Ridout, rachel@harveyklinger.com (children's MG and YA).

REPRESENTS Nonfiction, fiction, novels, juvenile books. **Considers these nonfiction areas:** anthropology, autobiography, biography, business, child guidance, cooking, crafts, creative nonfiction, cultural interests, current affairs, diet/nutrition, foods, gay/lesbian, health, history, how-to, investigative, juvenile nonfiction, literature, medicine, memoirs, money, music, popular culture, psychology, science, self-help, sociology, spirituality, sports, technology, true crime, women's issues, women's studies, young adult. **Considers these fiction areas:** action, adventure, commercial, contemporary issues, crime, detective, erotica, family saga, fantasy, gay, glitz, historical, horror, juvenile, lesbian, literary, mainstream, middle grade, mystery, new adult, police, romance, suspense, thriller, women's, young adult.

This agency specializes in big, mainstream, contemporary fiction and nonfiction. Great debut or established novelists and in nonfiction, authors with great ideas and a national platform already in place to help promote one's book. No screenplays, poetry, textbooks or anything too technical.

HOW TO CONTACT Use online e-mail submission form on the website, or query with SASE via snail mail. No phone or fax queries. Don't send unsolicited mss or e-mail attachments. Make submission letter to the point and as brief as possible. A bit of biographical information is always welcome, particularly with non-fiction submissions where one's national platform is vitally important. Accepts simultaneous submissions. Responds in 2-4 weeks to queries, if interested. Obtains most new clients through recommendations from others.

TERMS Agent receives 15% commission on domestic sales; 25% commission on foreign sales. Offers written contract. Charges for photocopying mss and overseas postage for mss.

RECENT SALES *The Far River*, by Barbara Wood; *I Am Not a Serial Killer*, by Dan Wells; *Me, Myself and Us*, by Brian Little; *The Secret of Magic*, by Deborah Johnson; *Children of the Mist*, by Paula Quinn. Other clients include George Taber, Terry Kay, Scott Mebus, Jacqueline Kolosov, Jonathan Maberry, Tara Altebrando, Alex McAuley, Eva Nagorski, Greg Kot, Justine Musk, Michael Northrup, Nina LaCour, Ashley Kahn, Barbara De Angelis, Robert Patton, Augusta Trobaugh, Deborah Blum, Jonathan Skariton.

THE KNIGHT AGENCY

232 W. Washington St., Madison GA 30650. **E-mail:** deidre.knight@knightagency.net. **E-mail:** submissions@knightagency.net. **Website:** http://knightagency.net/. **Contact:** Deidre Knight. Estab. 1996. Member of AAR. SCWBI, WFA, SFWA, RWA Represents 200+ clients.

MEMBER AGENTS Deidre Knight (romance, women's fiction, erotica, commercial fiction, inspirational, m/m fiction, memoir and nonfiction narrative, personal finance, true crime, business, popular culture, self-help, religion, and health); Pamela Harty (romance, women's fiction, young adult, business, motivational, diet and health, memoir, parenting, pop culture, and true crime); Elaine Spencer (romance (single title and category), women's fiction, commercial "book-club" fiction, cozy mysteries, young adult and middle grade material); Lucienne Diver (fantasy, science fiction, romance, suspense and young adult); Nephele Tempest (literary/commercial fiction, women's fiction, fantasy, science fiction, romantic suspense, paranormal romance, contemporary romance, historical fiction, young adult and middle grade fiction); Melissa Jeglinski (romance [contemporary, category, historical, inspirational], young adult, middle grade, women's fiction and mystery); Kristy Hunter (romance, women's fiction, commercial fiction, young adult and middle grade material), Travis Pennington (young adult, middle grade, mysteries, thrillers, commercial fiction, and romance [nothing paranormal/fantasy in any genre for now]); Janna Bonikowski (romance, women's fiction, young adult, cozy mystery, upmarket fiction).

REPRESENTS Nonfiction, fiction, novels. **Considers these nonfiction areas:** autobiography, business, creative nonfiction, cultural interests, current affairs, diet/nutrition, design, economics, ethnic, film, foods, gay/lesbian, health, history, how-to, inspirational, interior design, investigative, juvenile nonfiction, literature, memoirs, military, money, multicultural, parenting, popular culture, politics, psychology, self-help, sociology, technology, travel, true crime, women's issues, young adult. **Considers these fiction areas:** commercial, crime, erotica, fantasy, gay, historical, juvenile, lesbian, literary, mainstream, middle grade, multicultural, mystery, new adult, paranormal, psychic, romance, science fiction, thriller, urban fantasy, women's, young adult.

⊶ Actively seeking Romance in all subgenres, including romantic suspense, paranormal romance, historical romance (a particular love of mine), LGBT, contemporary, and also category romance. Occasionally I represent new adult. I'm also seeking women's fiction with vivid voices, and strong concepts (think me before you). Further seeking YA and MG, and select nonfiction in the categories of personal development, self-help, finance/business, memoir, parenting and health. Does not want to receive screenplays, short stories, poetry, essays, or children's picture books.

HOW TO CONTACT E-queries only. "Your submission should include a one page query letter and the first five pages of your manuscript. All text must be contained in the body of your e-mail. Attachments will not be opened nor included in the consideration of your work. Queries must be addressed to a specific agent. Please do not query multiple agents." Accepts simultaneous submissions. Responds in 1-2 weeks on queries, 6-8 weeks on submissions.

TERMS 15% Simple agency agreement with open-ended commitment. 15% commission on all domestic sales, 20% on foreign and film.

LINDA KONNER LITERARY AGENCY

10 W. 15th St., Suite 1918, New York NY 10011. **E-mail:** ldkonner@cs.com. **Website:** www.lindakonnerliteraryagency.com. **Contact:** Linda Konner. Estab. 1996. Member of AAR. Other memberships include ASJA and Authors Guild. Represents 50 clients.

REPRESENTS Nonfiction. **Considers these nonfiction areas:** business, child guidance, cooking, diet/nutrition, foods, health, how-to, inspirational, investigative, medicine, money, parenting, popular culture, psychology, science, self-help, true crime, women's issues, celebrity memoir, African American and Latino issues, relationships, popular science.

This agency specializes in health, self-help, and how-to books. Authors/co-authors must be top experts in their field with a substantial media and/ or social media platform. Prescriptive (self-help) books written by recognized experts in their field with a large social media following and/or national profile via traditional media and large/frequent speaking engagements. Does not want fiction, children's, YA, religious.

HOW TO CONTACT Query by e-mail with synopsis and author bio, including size of social media following, size of website following (your own and bigger ones you blog for regularly), appearances in traditional media (print/TV/radio), podcasts and frequency/size of speaking engagements. Prefers to read materials exclusively for 2 weeks. Accepts simultaneous submissions. Responds within 2 weeks. Obtains most new clients through recommendations from others, occasional solicitation among established authors/journalists.

TERMS Agent receives 15% commission on domestic sales; 25% commission on foreign sales. Offers written contract. Charges one-time fee for domestic expenses; additional expenses may be incurred for foreign sales.

RECENT SALES Nincompoopery: Why your customers hate you & how to fix it, by John R. Brandt (Harper Leadership); In This Together: How successful women support each other in work and life, by Nancy D. O'Reilly, PsyD (Adams/ Simon & Schuster); Never Too Old to Get Rich: The entrepreneur's guide to starting a business mid-life, by Kerry Hannon with Next Avenue (Wiley); Become Your Child's Sleep Coach: The Bedtime Doctor's 5-step guide, by Lynelle Schneeberg, PsyD (Da Capo Lifelong/ Hachette).

WRITERS CONFERENCES ASJA Writers Conference, Harvard Medical School's "Publishing Books, Memoirs, and Other Creative Nonfiction" Annual Conference.

STUART KRICHEVSKY LITERARY AGENCY, INC.

6 E. 39th St., Suite 500, New York NY 10016. (212)725-5288. **Fax:** (212)725-5275. **Website:** www.skagency.com. Member of AAR.

MEMBER AGENTS Stuart Krichevsky, query@skagency.com (emphasis on narrative nonfiction, literary journalism and literary and commercial fiction); Ross Harris, rhquery@skagency.com (voice-driven humor and memoir, books on popular culture and our society, narrative nonfiction and literary fiction); David Patterson, dpquery@skagency.com (writers of upmarket narrative nonfiction and literary fiction, historians, journalists and thought leaders); Mackenzie Brady Watson, mbwquery@skagency.com (narrative nonfiction, science, history, sociology, investigative journalism, food, business, memoir, and select upmarket and literary YA fiction); Hannah Schwartz, hsquery@skagency; Laura Usselman, luquery@skagency.com; Melissa Danaczko; Laura Usselman; Aemilia Phillips.

REPRESENTS Nonfiction, novels. **Considers these nonfiction areas:** business, creative nonfiction, foods, history, humor, investigative, memoirs, popular culture, science, sociology, memoir. **Considers these fiction areas:** commercial, contemporary issues, literary, young adult.

HOW TO CONTACT Please send a query letter and the first few (up to 10) pages of your ms or proposal in the body of an e-mail (not an attachment) to one of the e-mail addresses. No attachments. Responds if interested. Accepts simultaneous submissions. Obtains most new clients through recommendations from others, solicitations.

KT LITERARY, LLC

9249 S. Broadway, #200-543, Highlands Ranch CO 80129. **E-mail:** contact@ktliterary.com. **E-mail:** katequery@ktliterary.com, saraquery@ktliterary.com, reneequery@ktliterary.com, hannahquery@ktliterary.com, hilaryquery@ktliterary.com. **Website:** www.ktliterary.com. **Contact:** Kate Schafer Testerman, Sara Megibow, Renee Nyen, Hannah Fergesen, Hilary Harwell. Estab. 2008. Member of AAR. Other agency memberships include SCBWI, YALSA, ALA, SFWA and RWA. Represents 75 clients.

MEMBER AGENTS Kate Testerman (middle grade and young adult); Renee Nyen (middle grade and young adult); Sara Megibow (middle grade, young adult, romance, science fiction and fantasy); Hannah Fergesen (middle grade, young adult and speculative fiction); and Hilary Harwell (middle grade and young adult). Always LGBTQ and diversity friendly!.

REPRESENTS Fiction. **Considers these fiction areas:** fantasy, middle grade, romance, science fiction, young adult.

Kate is looking only at young adult and middle grade fiction, especially #OwnVoices, and selective nonfiction for teens and tweens. Sara seeks authors in middle grade, young adult, romance, science fiction, and fantasy. Renee is looking for young adult and middle grade fiction only. Hannah is interested in speculative fiction in young adult, middle grade, and adult. Hilary is looking for young adult and middle grade fiction only. "We're thrilled to be actively seeking new clients with great writing, unique stories, and complex characters, for middle grade, young adult, and adult fiction. We are especially interested in diverse voices." Does not want adult mystery, thrillers, or adult literary fiction.

HOW TO CONTACT "To query us, please select one of the agents at kt literary at a time. If we pass, you can feel free to submit to another. Please e-mail your query letter and the first 3 pages of your manuscript in the body of the e-mail to either Kate at katequery@ktliterary.com, Sara at saraquery@ktliterary.com, Renee at reneequery@ktliterary.com, Hannah at hannahquery@ktliterary.com, or Hilary at hilaryquery@ktliterary.com. The subject line of your e-mail should include the word 'Query' along with the title of your manuscript. Queries should not contain attachments. Attachments will not be read, and queries containing attachments will be deleted unread. We aim to reply to all queries within 4 weeks of receipt. For examples of query letters, please feel free to browse the About My Query archives on the KT Literary website. In addition, if you're an author who is sending a new query, but who previously submitted a novel to us for which we requested chapters but ultimately declined, please do say so in your query letter. If we like your query, we'll ask for the first 5 chapters and a complete synopsis. For our purposes, the synopsis should include the full plot of the book including the conclusion. Don't tease us. Thanks! We are not accepting snail mail queries or queries by phone at this time. We also do not accept pitches on social media." Accepts simultaneous submissions. Responds in 2-4 weeks to queries; 2 months to mss. Obtains most new clients through query slush pile.

TERMS Agent receives 15% commission on domestic sales; 20% commission on foreign sales. Offers written contract; 30-day notice must be given to terminate contract.

RECENT SALES *Most Likely*, by Sarah Watson, *All of Us With Wings*, by Michelle Ruiz Keil, *Postcards for a Songbird*, by Rebekah Crane, *The Tourist Trap*, by Sarah Morgenthaler, *The Last Year of James and Kat*, by Amy Spalding, and many more. A full list of clients and most recent sales are available on the agency website and some recent sales are available on Publishers Marketplace.

WRITERS CONFERENCES Various SCBWI conferences, ALA, BookExpo, Bologna, RWA, WonderCon, ComicCon.

THE LESHNE AGENCY

New York NY **E-mail:** info@leshneagency.com. **E-mail:** submissions@leshneagency.com. **Website:** www.leshneagency.com. **Contact:** Lisa Leshne, agent and owner. Estab. 2011. Member of AAR. Women's Media Group

Lisa Leshne has been in the media and entertainment business for over 25 years. Lisa's experience spans the broadest range of the industry. In 1991, she co-founded The Prague Post, the largest English-language newspaper in Central Europe, along with its book division and website, PraguePost.com. Lisa worked in Prague as the newspaper's Publisher for almost a decade. In 1999, she moved to Manhattan to work for Accenture as a Senior Consultant in the Entertainment & Media Group. She later worked in strategy and business development for Dow Jones, and was Executive Director, International, for WSJ.com, the Wall Street Journal Online, responsible for digital business operations in Europe and Asia, where she oversaw advertising, marketing and circulation. Lisa also served as VP, Strategy and Business Development, for Ink2, an industry leader in the print-on-demand industry and the owner of Cardstore.com. Lisa worked for a year after

9/11 at the Partnership for New York City's Financial Recovery Fund, evaluating grant applications and providing strategic advice to small businesses destroyed in the World Trade Center attacks. Prior to founding The Leshne Agency in 2011, she was a literary agent at LJK Literary.

MEMBER AGENTS Lisa Leshne, agent and owner; Sandy Hodgman, director of foreign rights.

REPRESENTS Nonfiction, fiction, novels. **Considers these nonfiction areas:** business, creative nonfiction, cultural interests, health, how-to, humor, inspirational, memoirs, parenting, politics, science, self-help, sports, women's issues. **Considers these fiction areas:** commercial, middle grade, young adult.

An avid reader of blogs, newspapers and magazines in addition to books, Lisa is most interested in narrative and prescriptive nonfiction, especially on social justice, sports, health, wellness, business, political and parenting topics. She loves memoirs that transport the reader into another person's head and give a voyeuristic view of someone else's extraordinary experiences. Lisa also enjoys literary and commercial fiction and some young adult and middle-grade books that take the reader on a journey and are just plain fun to read. Wants "authors across all genres. We are interested in narrative, memoir, and prescriptive nonfiction, with a particular interest in sports, wellness, business, political and parenting topics. We will also look at truly terrific commercial fiction and young adult and middle grade books."

HOW TO CONTACT The Leshne Agency is seeking new and existing authors across all genres. "We are especially interested in narrative; memoir; prescriptive nonfiction, with a particular interest in sports, health, wellness, business, political and parenting topics; and truly terrific commercial fiction, young adult and middle-grade books. We are not interested in screenplays; scripts; poetry; and picture books. If your submission is in a genre not specifically listed here, we are still open to considering it, but if your submission is for a genre we've mentioned as not being interested in, please don't bother sending it to us. All submissions should be made through the Authors.me portal by clicking on this link: https://app.authors.me/#submit/the-leshne-agency." Accepts simultaneous submissions.

LEVINE GREENBERG ROSTAN LITERARY AGENCY, INC.

307 Seventh Ave., Suite 2407, New York NY 10001. (212)337-0934. **Fax:** (212)337-0948. **E-mail:** submit@lgrliterary.com. **Website:** www.lgrliterary.com. Member of AAR. Represents 250 clients.

Prior to opening his agency, Mr. Levine served as vice president of the Bank Street College of Education.

MEMBER AGENTS Jim Levine (nonfiction, including business, science, narrative nonfiction, social and political issues, psychology, health, spirituality, parenting); Stephanie Rostan (adult and YA fiction; nonfiction, including parenting, health & wellness, sports, memoir); Melissa Rowland; Daniel Greenberg (nonfiction: popular culture, narrative nonfiction, memoir, and humor; literary fiction); Victoria Skurnick; Danielle Svetcov (nonfiction); Lindsay Edgecombe (narrative nonfiction, memoir, lifestyle and health, illustrated books, as well as literary fiction); Monika Verma (nonfiction: humor, pop culture, memoir, narrative nonfiction and style and fashion titles; some young adult fiction (paranormal, historical, contemporary)); Kerry Sparks (young adult and middle grade; select adult fiction and occasional nonfiction); Tim Wojcik (nonfiction, including food narratives, humor, pop culture, popular history and science; literary fiction); Arielle Eckstut (no queries); Sarah Bedingfield (literary and upmarket commercial fiction, Epic family dramas, literary novels with notes of magical realism, darkly gothic stories, psychological suspense).

REPRESENTS Nonfiction, novels. **Considers these nonfiction areas:** business, creative nonfiction, health, history, humor, memoirs, parenting, popular culture, science, spirituality, sports. **Considers these fiction areas:** commercial, literary, mainstream, middle grade, suspense, young adult.

HOW TO CONTACT E-query to submit@lgrliterary.com, or online submission form. "If you would like to direct your query to one of our agents specifically, please feel free to name them in the online form or in the email you send." Cannot respond to submissions by mail. Do not attach more than 50 pages. "Due to the volume of submissions we receive, we are unable to respond to each individually. If we would like more information about your project, we'll contact you within 3 weeks (though we do get backed up on occasion!)." Accepts simultaneous submissions.

Obtains most new clients through recommendations from others.

TERMS Agent receives 15% commission on domestic sales; 20% commission on foreign sales. Offers written contract. Charges clients for out-of-pocket expenses—telephone, fax, postage, photocopying—directly connected to the project.

RECENT SALES **Notorious RBG**, by Irin Carmon and Shana Knizhnik; **Pogue's Basics: Life**, by David Pogue; **Invisible City**, by Julia Dahl; **Gumption**, by Nick Offerman; **All the Bright Places**, by Jennifer Niven.

WRITERS CONFERENCES ASJA Writers' Conference.

TIPS "We focus on editorial development, business representation, and publicity and marketing strategy."

STERLING LORD LITERISTIC, INC.

115 Broadway, New York NY 10006. (212)780-6050. **Fax:** (212)780-6095. **E-mail:** info@sll.com. **Website:** www.sll.com. Estab. 1987. Member of AAR. Signatory of WGA.

MEMBER AGENTS Philippa Brophy (represents journalists, nonfiction writers and novelists, and is most interested in current events, memoir, science, politics, biography, and women's issues); Laurie Liss (represents authors of commercial and literary fiction and nonfiction whose perspectives are well developed and unique); Sterling Lord; Peter Matson (abiding interest in storytelling, whether in the service of history, fiction, the sciences); Douglas Stewart (primarily fiction for all ages, from the innovatively literary to the unabashedly commercial); Neeti Madan (memoir, journalism, popular culture, lifestyle, women's issues, multicultural books and virtually any intelligent writing on intriguing topics); Robert Guinsler (literary and commercial fiction (including YA), journalism, narrative nonfiction with an emphasis on pop culture, science and current events, memoirs and biographies); Jim Rutman; Celeste Fine (expert, celebrity, and corporate clients with strong national and international platforms, particularly in the health, science, self-help, food, business, and lifestyle fields); Martha Millard (fiction and nonfiction, including well-written science fiction and young adult); Mary Krienke (literary fiction, memoir, and narrative nonfiction, including psychology, popular science, and cultural commentary); Jenny Stephens (nonfiction: cookbooks, practical lifestyle projects, transportive travel and nature writing, and creative nonfiction; fiction: contemporary literary narratives strongly rooted in place); Alison MacKeen (idea-driven research books: social scientific, scientific, historical, relationships/parenting, learning and education, sexuality, technology, the life-cycle, health, the environment, politics, economics, psychology, geography, and culture; literary fiction, literary nonfiction, memoirs, essays, and travel writing); John Maas (serious nonfiction, specifically business, personal development, science, self-help, health, fitness, and lifestyle); Sarah Passick (commercial nonfiction in the celebrity, food, blogger, lifestyle, health, diet, fitness and fashion categories).

REPRESENTS Nonfiction, fiction. **Considers these nonfiction areas:** biography, business, cooking, creative nonfiction, current affairs, economics, education, foods, gay/lesbian, history, humor, memoirs, multicultural, parenting, popular culture, politics, psychology, science, technology, travel, women's issues, fitness. **Considers these fiction areas:** commercial, juvenile, literary, middle grade, picture books, science fiction, young adult.

HOW TO CONTACT Query via snail mail. "Please submit a query letter, a synopsis of the work, a brief proposal or the first 3 chapters of the manuscript, a brief bio or resume, and SASE for reply. Original artwork is not accepted. Enclose sufficient postage if you wish to have your materials returned to you. We do not respond to unsolicited e-mail inquiries." Accepts simultaneous submissions.

TERMS Agent receives 15% commission on domestic sales; 20% commission on foreign sales. Offers written contract.

LOWENSTEIN ASSOCIATES INC.

115 E. 23rd St., Floor 4, New York NY 10010. (212)206-1630. **E-mail:** assistant@bookhaven.com. **Website:** www.lowensteinassociates.com. **Contact:** Barbara Lowenstein. Member of AAR.

MEMBER AGENTS Barbara Lowenstein, president (nonfiction interests include narrative nonfiction, health, money, finance, travel, multicultural, popular culture, and memoir; fiction interests include literary fiction and women's fiction); Mary South (literary fiction and nonfiction on subjects such as neuroscience, bioengineering, women's rights, design, and digital humanities, as well as investigative journalism, essays, and memoir).

REPRESENTS Nonfiction, fiction, novels, short story collections. **Considers these nonfiction areas:** autobiography, biography, business, creative nonfiction, cultural interests, health, humor, literature, memoirs, money, multicultural, popular culture, science, technology, travel, women's issues. **Considers these fiction areas:** commercial, literary, middle grade, science fiction, women's, young adult.

Barbara Lowenstein is currently looking for writers who have a platform and are leading experts in their field, including business, women's issues, psychology, health, science and social issues, and is particularly interested in strong new voices in fiction and narrative nonfiction. Does not want westerns, textbooks, children's picture books and books in need of translation.

HOW TO CONTACT "For fiction, please send us a 1-page query letter, along with the first 10 pages pasted in the body of the message by e-mail to assistant@bookhaven.com. If nonfiction, please send a 1-page query letter, a table of contents, and, if available, a proposal pasted into the body of the e-mail. Please put the word 'QUERY' and the title of your project in the subject field of your e-mail and address it to the agent of your choice. Please do not send an attachment as the message will be deleted without being read and no reply will be sent." Accepts simultaneous submissions. Will respond if interested. Obtains most new clients through recommendations from others, solicitations, conferences.

TERMS Agent receives 15% commission on domestic sales; 20% commission on foreign sales. Offers written contract. Charges for large photocopy batches, messenger service, international postage.

TIPS "Know the genre you are working in and read!"

DONALD MAASS LITERARY AGENCY

1000 Dean St., Suite 252, Brooklyn NY 11238. (212)727-8383. **E-mail:** query.dmaass@maassagency.com. **Website:** www.maassagency.com. Estab. 1980. Member of AAR. Other memberships include SFWA, MWA, RWA. Represents more than 200 clients.

Prior to opening his agency, Mr. Maass worked as an editor at Dell Publishing (New York) and as a reader at Gollancz (London). He is a past president of the Association of Authors' Representatives, Inc. (AAR).

MEMBER AGENTS Donald Maass (mainstream, literary, mystery/suspense, science fiction, romance, women's fiction); Jennifer Jackson (science fiction and fantasy for both adult and YA markets, thrillers that mine popular and controversial issues, YA that challenges traditional thinking); Cameron McClure (literary, mystery/suspense, urban, fantasy, narrative nonfiction and projects with multicultural, international, and environmental themes, gay/lesbian); Katie Shea Boutillier (women's fiction/book club, edgy/dark, realistic/contemporary YA, commercial-scale literary fiction, and celebrity memoir); Paul Stevens (science fiction, fantasy, horror, mystery, suspense, and humorous fiction, LBGT a plus); Jennie Goloboy (fun, innovative, diverse, and progressive science fiction and fantasy for adults); Caitlin McDonald (SF/F - YA/MG/Adult, genre-bending/cross-genre fiction, diversity); Michael Curry (science fiction and fantasy, near future thrillers).

REPRESENTS Nonfiction, fiction, novels, short story collections, novellas, juvenile books. **Considers these nonfiction areas:** autobiography, biography, creative nonfiction, memoirs, popular culture, science. **Considers these fiction areas:** commercial, contemporary issues, crime, detective, ethnic, family saga, fantasy, feminist, frontier, gay, historical, horror, humor, juvenile, lesbian, literary, mainstream, middle grade, military, multicultural, mystery, new adult, occult, paranormal, police, psychic, regional, religious, romance, satire, science fiction, short story collections, spiritual, supernatural, suspense, thriller, urban fantasy, war, westerns, women's, young adult.

This agency specializes in commercial fiction, especially science fiction, fantasy, thrillers, suspense, women's fiction—for both the adult and YA markets. All types of fiction, including YA and MG. Does not want poetry, screenplays, picture books.

HOW TO CONTACT Query via e-mail only. All the agents have different submission addresses and instructions. See the website and each agent's online profile for exact submission instructions. Accepts simultaneous submissions.

TERMS Agency receives 15% commission on domestic sales; 20% commission on foreign sales.

RECENT SALES *The Aeronaut's Windlass*, by Jim Butcher (Penguin Random House); *City of Blades*, by Robert Jackson Bennett (Crown); *I am Princess X*, by Cherie Priest (Scholastic); *Treachery at Lancaster Gate*, by Anne Perry (Random House); *Marked in Flesh*, by Anne Bishop (Penguin Random House); *We Are the Ants*, by Shaun David Hutchinson (Simon & Schuster); *Binti*, by Nnedi Okorafor (DAW); *Ninefox Gambit*, by Yoon Ha Lee (Solaris); *The Far End of Happy*, by Kathryn Craft (Sourcebooks); *The Traitor Baru Cormorant*, by Seth Dickinson (Tor).

WRITERS CONFERENCES See each agent's profile page at the agency website for conference schedules.

TIPS "We are fiction specialists, also noted for our innovative approach to career planning. We are always open to submissions from new writers." Works with subagents in all principle foreign countries and for film and television.

GINA MACCOBY LITERARY AGENCY

P.O. Box 60, Chappaqua NY 10514. (914)238-5630. **E-mail:** query@maccobylit.com. **Website:** www.publishersmarketplace.com/members/ginamaccoby/. **Contact:** Gina Maccoby. Estab. 1986. Member of AAR. AAR Board of Directors; Royalties and Ethics and Contracts subcommittees; Authors Guild, SCBWI.

REPRESENTS Nonfiction, fiction, novels, juvenile books. **Considers these nonfiction areas:** autobiography, biography, cultural interests, current affairs, ethnic, history, juvenile nonfiction, literature, popular culture, women's issues, women's studies, young adult. **Considers these fiction areas:** crime, detective, family saga, historical, juvenile, literary, mainstream, middle grade, multicultural, mystery, new adult, suspense, thriller, women's, young adult.

HOW TO CONTACT Query by e-mail only. Accepts simultaneous submissions. Owing to volume of submissions, may not respond to queries unless interested. Obtains most new clients through recommendations.

TERMS Agent receives 15% commission on domestic sales; 20-25% commission on foreign sales, which includes subagents commissions. May recover certain costs, such as purchasing books, shipping books overseas by airmail, legal fees for vetting motion picture contracts, bank fees for electronic funds transfers, overnight delivery services.

WRITERS CONFERENCES ThrillerFest PitchFest, Washington Independent Writers Conference, New England Crime Bake, Ridgefield Writers Conference, CLMP Literary Writers Conference.

CAROL MANN AGENCY

55 Fifth Ave., 18th Floor, New York NY 10003. (212)206-5635. **Fax:** (212)675-4809. **E-mail:** submissions@carolmannagency.com. **Website:** www.carolmannagency.com. **Contact:** Agnes Carlowicz. Member of AAR. Represents Roughly 200 clients.

MEMBER AGENTS Carol Mann (health/medical, religion, spirituality, self-help, parenting, narrative nonfiction, current affairs); Laura Yorke; Gareth Esersky; Myrsini Stephanides (nonfiction areas of interest: pop culture and music, humor, narrative nonfiction and memoir, cookbooks; fiction areas of interest: offbeat literary fiction, graphic works, and edgy YA fiction); Joanne Wyckoff (nonfiction areas of interest: memoir, narrative nonfiction,personal narrative, psychology, women's issues, education, health and wellness, parenting, serious self-help, natural history; also accepts fiction); Lydia Shamah (edgy, modern fiction and timely nonfiction in the areas of business, self-improvement, relationship and gift books, particularly interested in female voices and experiences); Tom Miller (narrative nonfiction, self-help/psychology, popular culture, body-mind-spirit, wellness, business, and literary fiction).

REPRESENTS Nonfiction, fiction, novels. **Considers these nonfiction areas:** anthropology, archeology, architecture, art, autobiography, biography, business, child guidance, cultural interests, current affairs, design, ethnic, government, health, history, humor, law, medicine, memoirs, money, music, parenting, popular culture, politics, psychology, self-help, sociology, sports, women's issues, women's studies. **Considers these fiction areas:** commercial, literary, young adult, graphic works. **Considers these script areas:** romantic drama.

⊶ Does not want to receive genre fiction (romance, mystery, etc.).

HOW TO CONTACT Please see website for submission guidelines. Accepts simultaneous submissions. Responds in 4 weeks to queries.

TERMS Agent receives 15% commission on domestic sales; 20% commission on foreign sales. Offers written contract.

MANUS & ASSOCIATES LITERARY AGENCY, INC.

425 Sherman Ave., Suite 200, Palo Alto CA 94306. (650)470-5151. **Fax:** (650)470-5159. **E-mail:** manuslit@manuslit.com. **Website:** www.manuslit.com.

Contact: Jillian Manus, Jandy Nelson, Penny Nelson. NYC address: 444 Madison Ave., 39th Floor, New York NY 10022. Member of AAR.

Prior to becoming an agent, Ms. Manus was associate publisher of two national magazines and director of development at Warner Bros. and Universal Studios; she has been a literary agent for 20 years.

MEMBER AGENTS Jandy Nelson (currently not taking on new clients); Jillian Manus, jillian@manuslit.com (political, memoirs, self-help, history, sports, women's issues, thrillers); Penny Nelson, penny@manuslit.com (memoirs, self-help, sports, nonfiction).

REPRESENTS Nonfiction, novels. **Considers these nonfiction areas:** cooking, history, inspirational, memoirs, politics, psychology, religious, self-help, sports, women's issues. **Considers these fiction areas:** thriller.

"Our agency is unique in the way that we not only sell the material, but we edit, develop concepts, and participate in the marketing effort. We specialize in large, conceptual fiction and nonfiction, and always value a project that can be sold in the TV/feature film market." Actively seeking high-concept thrillers, commercial literary fiction, women's fiction, celebrity biographies, memoirs, multicultural fiction, popular health, women's empowerment and mysteries. No horror, romance, science fiction, fantasy, western, young adult, children's, poetry, cookbooks, or magazine articles.

HOW TO CONTACT Snail mail submissions welcome. E-queries also accepted. For nonfiction, send a full proposal via snail mail. For fiction, send a query letter and 30 pages (unbound) if submitting via snail mail. Send only an e-query if submitting fiction via e-mail. If querying by e-mail, submit directly to one of the agents. Accepts simultaneous submissions. Responds in 3 months. Obtains most new clients through recommendations from others, solicitations, conferences.

TERMS Agent receives 15% commission on domestic sales; 20-25% commission on foreign sales. Offers written contract, binding for 2 years; 60-day notice must be given to terminate contract. Charges for photocopying and postage/UPS.

RECENT SALES *Nothing Down for the 2000s* and *Multiple Streams of Income for the 2000s*, by Robert Allen; *Missed Fortune 101*, by Doug Andrew; *Cracking the Millionaire Code*, by Mark Victor Hansen and Robert Allen; *Stress Free for Good*, by Dr. Fred Luskin and Dr. Ken Pelletier; *The Mercy of Thin Air*, by Ronlyn Domangue; *The Fine Art of Small Talk*, by Debra Fine; *Bone Men of Bonares*, by Terry Tamoff.

WRITERS CONFERENCES Maui Writers' Conference; San Diego State University Writers' Conference; Willamette Writers' Conference; BookExpo America; MEGA Book Marketing University.

TIPS "Research agents using a variety of sources."

DENISE MARCIL LITERARY AGENCY, LLC

483 Westover Rd., Stamford CT 06902. (203)327-9970. **E-mail:** dmla@denisemarcilagency.com; annemarie@denisemarcilagency.com. **E-mail:** dmla@denisemacilagency.com. **Website:** www.denisemarcilagency.com. **Contact:** Denise Marcil, Anne Marie O'Farrell. Address for Anne Marie O'Farrell: 86 Dennis St., Manhasset, NY 11030. Estab. 1977. Member of AAR. Women's Media Group

Prior to opening her agency, Ms. Marcil served as an editorial assistant with Avon Books and as an assistant editor with Simon & Schuster.

MEMBER AGENTS Denise Marcil (self-help and popular reference books such as wellness, health, women's issues); Anne Marie O'Farrell (books that convey and promote innovative, practical and cutting edge information and ideas which help people increase their self-awareness and fulfillment and maximize their potential in whatever area they choose; she is dying to represent a great basketball book).

REPRESENTS Nonfiction. **Considers these nonfiction areas:** business, cooking, diet/nutrition, education, health, how-to, New Age, psychology, self-help, spirituality, women's issues. **Considers these fiction areas:** commercial, suspense, thriller, women's.

"In nonfiction we are looking for self-help, personal growth, popular psychology, how-to, business, and popular reference; we want to represent books that help people's lives." Does not want fiction.

HOW TO CONTACT E-query. Accepts simultaneous submissions.

TERMS Agent receives 15% commission on domestic sales; 20% commission on foreign sales and film sales. Offers written contract, binding for 2 years.

RECENT SALES *Lilac Lane*, by Sherryl Woods; *Dr. Knox*, by Peter Spiegelman; *The Baby Book*, by William Sears, M.D. and Martha Sears, R.N.; Dr. Sears T5 Wellness Plan,by William Sears, M.D. and Erin Sears Basile; *The Allergy Book*, by Robert W. Sears, M.D. and William Sears, M.D.; Work that Works, by Geil Browning, Ph.D.; *Exponential Living*, by Sheri Riley;*The Girls of Ennismore and The Yellow House*, by Patricia Falvey; *Irresistible Force* and *Force Of Attraction*, by D.D. Ayres; *The Soldier's Forever Family*, by Gina Wilkins.

THE EVAN MARSHALL AGENCY

1 Pacio Ct., Roseland NJ 07068-1121. (973)287-6216. **E-mail:** evan@evanmarshallagency.com. **Website:** www.evanmarshallagency.com. **Contact:** Evan Marshall. Estab. 1987. Member of AAR. Novelists, Inc. Represents 50+ clients.

Prior to becoming an agent, Evan Marshall held senior editorial positions at Houghton Mifflin, Ariel Books, New American Library, Everest House and Dodd, Mead, where he acquired national and international bestsellers.

REPRESENTS Fiction, novels. **Considers these fiction areas:** action, adventure, crime, detective, erotica, ethnic, family saga, fantasy, feminist, frontier, gay, glitz, historical, horror, humor, inspirational, lesbian, literary, mainstream, military, multicultural, multimedia, mystery, new adult, New Age, occult, paranormal, police, psychic, regional, religious, romance, satire, science fiction, spiritual, sports, supernatural, suspense, thriller, translation, urban fantasy, war, westerns, women's, young adult, romance (contemporary, gothic, historical, regency).

"We represent all genres of adult and young-adult full-length fiction." Represent all genres of adult and young-adult full-length fiction. Does not want articles, children's books, essays, memoirs, nonfiction, novellas, poetry, screenplays, short stories, stage plays.

HOW TO CONTACT "We consider new clients by referral only." Accepts simultaneous submissions. Responds in 1 week to queries if interested; 2 months to mss. Considers new clients by referral only.

TERMS Agent receives 15% commission on domestic sales; 20% commission on foreign and film/TV sales. Offers written contract.

RECENT SALES *The Taster*, by V. S. Alexander (Kensington); *A Man for Honor*, by Emma Miller (Love Inspired); *The Devil's Wind*, by Steve Goble (Seventh Street); *The Maverick's Holiday Surprise*, by Karen Rose Smith (Harlequin); *Nemesis*, by Joe Yogerst (Blank Slate Press); *Echoes of the Haight*, by Max Tomlinson (Oceanview).

MARGRET MCBRIDE LITERARY AGENCY

P.O. Box 9128, La Jolla CA 92038. (858)454-1550. **E-mail:** staff@mcbridelit.com. **Website:** www.mcbrideliterary.com. Estab. 1981. Member of AAR. Other memberships include Authors Guild.

Prior to opening her agency, Ms. McBride worked at Random House and Ballantine Books. Later, she became the Director of Publicity at Warner Books, and Director of Publicity, Promotions and Advertising for Pinnacle Books.

MEMBER AGENTS Margret McBride; Faye Atchison.

REPRESENTS Nonfiction, fiction, novels. **Considers these nonfiction areas:** autobiography, biography, business, cooking, creative nonfiction, cultural interests, current affairs, diet/nutrition, ethnic, foods, gay/lesbian, health, history, hobbies, how-to, inspirational, investigative, juvenile nonfiction, medicine, memoirs, money, multicultural, music, popular culture, psychology, science, self-help, sex, sociology, theater, travel, true crime, women's issues, young adult. **Considers these fiction areas:** action, adventure, comic books, commercial, confession, contemporary issues, crime, detective, family saga, feminist, historical, horror, juvenile, mainstream, multicultural, multimedia, mystery, new adult, paranormal, police, psychic, regional, supernatural, suspense, thriller, young adult.

This agency specializes in mainstream nonfiction and some commercial fiction. Actively seeking commercial nonfiction, business, health, self-help. Does not want screenplays, romance, poetry, or children's.

HOW TO CONTACT Please check our website, as instructions are subject to change. Only e-mail queries are accepted: staff@mcbridelit.com. In your query letter, provide a brief synopsis of your work, as well as any pertinent information about yourself. We recommend that authors look at book jacket copy of professionally published books to get an idea of the style and content that should be included in a query letter. Essentially, you are marketing yourself and your work to us, so that we can determine whether we feel we can market you and your work to publishers. There are detailed nonfiction proposal guidelines on our website, but we recommend author's get a copy of How to Write a Book Proposal by Michael Larsen for further instruction. **Please note: The McBride Agency will not respond to queries sent by mail, and will not be responsible for the return of any material submitted by mail.** Accepts simultaneous submissions. Responds within 8 weeks to queries; 6-8 weeks to requested mss. "You are welcome to follow up by phone or e-mail after 6 weeks if you have not yet received a response."

TERMS Agent receives 15% commission on domestic sales; 25% commission on translation rights sales (15% to agency, 10% to sub-agent). Charges for overnight delivery and photocopying.

RECENT SALES *Millennial Money*, by Grant Sabatier (Atria/Penguin Random House); *Nimble*, by Baba Prasad (Perigee/Penguin Random House—US and World rights excluding India); *Carefrontation*, by Dr. Arlene Drake (Regan Arts/Phaidon); *There Are No Overachievers*, by Brian Biro (Crown Business/Penguin Random House); *Cheech Is Not My Real Name*, by Richard Marin (Grand Central Books/Hachette); *Killing It!*, by Sheryl O'Loughlin (Harper Business/HarperCollins); *Scrappy*, by Terri Sjodin (Portfolio/Penguin Random House).

TIPS "E-mail queries only. Please don't call to pitch your work by phone."

MCCORMICK LITERARY

37 W. 20th St., New York NY 10011. (212)691-9726. **E-mail:** queries@mccormicklit.com. **Website:** mccormicklit.com. Member of AAR. Signatory of WGA.

MEMBER AGENTS David McCormick; Pilar Queen (narrative nonfiction, practical nonfiction, and commercial women's fiction); Bridget McCarthy (literary and commercial fiction, narrative nonfiction, memoir, and cookbooks); Alia Hanna Habib (literary fiction, narrative nonfiction, memoir and cookbooks); Edward Orloff (literary fiction and narrative nonfiction, especially cultural history, politics, biography, and the arts); Daniel Menaker; Leslie Falk; Emma Borges-Scott.

REPRESENTS Nonfiction, novels. **Considers these nonfiction areas:** biography, cooking, history, memoirs, politics. **Considers these fiction areas:** literary, women's.

HOW TO CONTACT Snail mail queries only. Send an SASE. Accepts simultaneous submissions.

MCINTOSH & OTIS, INC.

353 Lexington Ave., New York NY 10016. (212)687-7400. **Fax:** (212)687-6894. **E-mail:** info@mcintoshandotis.com. **Website:** www.mcintoshandotis.com. **Contact:** Elizabeth Winick Rubinstein. Estab. 1928. Member of AAR. Signatory of WGA. SCBWI

MEMBER AGENTS Elizabeth Winick Rubinstein, ewrquery@mcintoshandotis.com (literary fiction, women's fiction, historical fiction, and mystery/suspense, along with narrative nonfiction, spiritual/self-help, history and current affairs); Christa Heschke, chquery@mcintoshandotis.com (picture books, middle grade, young adult and new adult projects); Adam Muhlig, amquery@mcintoshandotis.com (music–from jazz to classical to punk–popular culture, natural history, travel and adventure, and sports).

REPRESENTS Nonfiction, fiction, novels, juvenile books. **Considers these nonfiction areas:** creative nonfiction, current affairs, history, popular culture, self-help, spirituality, sports, travel. **Considers these fiction areas:** fantasy, historical, horror, literary, middle grade, mystery, new adult, paranormal, picture books, romance, science fiction, suspense, urban fantasy, women's, young adult.

⊶ Actively seeking "books with memorable characters, distinctive voices, and great plots."

HOW TO CONTACT E-mail submissions only. Each agent has their own e-mail address for subs. For fiction: Please send a query letter, synopsis, author bio, and the first 3 consecutive chapters (no more than 30 pages) of your novel. For nonfiction: Please send a query letter, proposal, outline, author bio, and 3 sample chapters (no more than 30 pages) of the ms. For children's & young adult: Please send a query letter, synopsis and the first 3 consecutive chapters (not to exceed 25 pages) of the ms. Accepts simultaneous submissions. Obtains clients through recommendations from others, editors, conferences and queries.

TERMS Agent receives 15% commission on domestic sales; 20% on foreign sales.

WRITERS CONFERENCES Attends Bologna Book Fair, in Bologna Italy in April, SCBWI Conference in New York in February, and regularly attends other conferences and industry conventions.

MENDEL MEDIA GROUP, LLC

115 W. 30th St., Suite 209, New York NY 10001. (646)239-9896. **E-mail:** query@mendelmedia.com.

Website: www.mendelmedia.com. Estab. 2002. Member of AAR.

Prior to becoming an agent, Mr. Mendel was an academic. "I taught American literature, Yiddish, Jewish studies, and literary theory at the University of Chicago and the University of Illinois at Chicago while working on my PhD in English. I also worked as a freelance technical writer and as the managing editor of a healthcare magazine. In 1998, I began working for the late Jane Jordan Browne, a long-time agent in the book publishing world."

REPRESENTS Nonfiction, fiction, novels. **Considers these nonfiction areas:** Americana, animals, anthropology, architecture, art, biography, business, child guidance, cooking, current affairs, dance, education, environment, ethnic, foods, gardening, gay/lesbian, government, health, history, how-to, humor, investigative, language, medicine, memoirs, military, money, multicultural, music, parenting, philosophy, popular culture, psychology, recreation, regional, religious, science, self-help, sex, sociology, software, spirituality, sports, travel, true crime, war, women's issues, women's studies, all narrative projects, and creative nonfiction. **Considers these fiction areas:** action, adventure, contemporary issues, crime, detective, erotica, ethnic, feminist, gay, glitz, historical, humor, inspirational, juvenile, lesbian, literary, mainstream, mystery, picture books, police, religious, romance, satire, sports, thriller, young adult, commercial and literary fiction.

"I am interested in major works of history, current affairs, biography, business, politics, economics, science, major memoirs, narrative nonfiction, and other sorts of general nonfiction." Actively seeking new, major or definitive work on a subject of broad interest, or a controversial, but authoritative, new book on a subject that affects many people's lives. "I also represent more light-hearted nonfiction projects, such as gift or novelty books, when they suit the market particularly well." Does not want "queries about projects written years ago that were unsuccessfully shopped to a long list of trade publishers by either the author or another agent. I am specifically not interested in considering serious poetry, original plays, or original film scripts."

HOW TO CONTACT You should e-mail your work to query@mendelmedia.com. We no longer accept or read submissions sent by mail, so please do not send inquiries by any other method. If we want to read more or discuss your work, we will respond to you by e-mail or phone. Fiction queries: If you have a novel you would like to submit, please paste a synopsis and the first twenty pages into the body of your email, below a detailed letter about your publication history and the history of the project, if it has been submitted previously to publishers or other agents. Please do not use attachments, as we will not open them. Nonfiction queries: If you have a completed nonfiction book proposal and sample chapters, you should paste those into the body of an e-mail, below a detailed letter about your publication history and the history of the project, if it has been submitted previously to any publishers or other agents. Please do not use attachments, as we will not open them. If we want to read more or discuss your work, we will call or e-mail you directly. If you do not receive a personal response within a few weeks, we are not going to offer representation. In any case, however, please do not call or email to inquire about your query. Accepts simultaneous submissions. Responds within a few weeks, if interested. Obtains most new clients through referrals.

TERMS Agent receives 15% commission on domestic sales; 20% commission on foreign sales.

WRITERS CONFERENCES BookExpo America; Frankfurt Book Fair; London Book Fair; RWA National Conference; Modern Language Association Convention; Jerusalem Book Fair.

TIPS "While I am not interested in being flattered by a prospective client, it does matter to me that she knows why she is writing to me in the first place. Is one of my clients a colleague of hers? Has she read a book by one of my clients that led her to believe I might be interested in her work? Authors of descriptive nonfiction should have real credentials and expertise in their subject areas, either as academics, journalists, or policy experts, and authors of prescriptive nonfiction should have legitimate expertise and considerable experience communicating their ideas in seminars and workshops, in a successful business, through the media, etc."

HOWARD MORHAIM LITERARY AGENCY

30 Pierrepont St., Brooklyn NY 11201. (718)222-8400. **Fax:** (718)222-5056. **E-mail:** info@morhaimliterary.com. **Website:** www.morhaimliterary.com. Member of AAR.

MEMBER AGENTS Howard Morhaim, howard@morhaimliterary.com; Kate McKean, kmckean@morhaimliterary.com; DongWon Song, dongwon@morhaimliterary.com; Kim-Mei Kirtland, kimmei@morhaimliterary.com.

REPRESENTS **Considers these nonfiction areas:** biography, business, cooking, crafts, creative nonfiction, design, economics, foods, health, humor, memoirs, parenting, self-help, sports. **Considers these fiction areas:** fantasy, historical, literary, middle grade, new adult, romance, science fiction, women's, young adult, LGBTQ young adult, magical realism, fantasy should be high fantasy, historical fiction should be no earlier than the 20th century.

⊶ Kate McKean is open to many subgenres and categories of YA and MG fiction. Check the website for the most details. Actively seeking fiction, nonfiction, and young adult novels.

HOW TO CONTACT Query via e-mail with cover letter and 3 sample chapters. See each agent's listing for specifics. Accepts simultaneous submissions.

JEAN V. NAGGAR LITERARY AGENCY, INC.

JVNLA, Inc., 216 E. 75th St., Suite 1E, New York NY 10021. (212)794-1082. **Website:** www.jvnla.com. **Contact:** Jennifer Weltz. Estab. 1978. Member of AAR. Other memberships include Women's Media Group, SCBWI, Pace University's Masters in Publishing Board Member. Represents 450 clients.

MEMBER AGENTS Jennifer Weltz (well-researched and original historicals, thrillers with a unique voice, wry dark humor, and magical realism; enthralling narrative nonfiction; voice driven young adult, middle grade); Alice Tasman (literary, commercial, YA, middle grade, and nonfiction in the categories of narrative, biography, music or pop culture); Ariana Philips (nonfiction both prescriptive and narrative); Alicia Brooks (fiction, non-fiction and YA).

REPRESENTS Nonfiction, fiction, novels, short story collections, novellas, juvenile books, scholarly books, poetry books. **Considers these nonfiction areas:** animals, child guidance, cooking, creative nonfiction, economics, education, environment, ethnic, foods, gardening, gay/lesbian, how-to, humor, literature, medicine, memoirs, multicultural, parenting, popular culture, politics, psychology, satire, science, self-help, sex, travel, true crime, women's issues, women's studies, young adult. **Considers these fiction areas:** action, adventure, cartoon, comic books, commercial, contemporary issues, crime, detective, ethnic, family saga, fantasy, feminist, gay, historical, humor, inspirational, juvenile, lesbian, literary, mainstream, middle grade, multicultural, mystery, picture books, romance, satire, science fiction, suspense, thriller, women's, young adult.

⊶ This agency specializes in mainstream fiction and nonfiction and literary fiction with commercial potential as well as young adult, middle grade, and picture books. Does not want to receive screenplays.

HOW TO CONTACT "Visit our website to send submissions and see what our individual agents are looking for. No snail mail submissions please!" Accepts simultaneous submissions. Depends on the agent. No responses for queries unless the agent is interested.

TERMS Agent receives 15% commission on domestic sales; 20% commission on foreign and film sales. Offers written contract. Charges for overseas mailing, messenger services, book purchases, photocopying—all deductible from royalties received.

RECENT SALES *Mort(e)*, by Robert Repino; *The Paying Guests*, by Sarah Waters; *The Third Victim*, by Phillip Margolin; *Every Kind of Wanting*, by Gina Frangello; *The Lies They Tell*, by Gillian French; *Dietland*, by Sarai Walker; *Mr. Rochester*, by Sarah Shoemaker; *Not If I See You First*, by Eric Lindstrom.

TIPS "We recommend courage, fortitude, and patience: the courage to be true to your own vision, the fortitude to finish a novel and polish it again and again before sending it out, and the patience to accept rejection gracefully and wait for the stars to align themselves appropriately for success."

NELSON LITERARY AGENCY

1732 Wazee St., Suite 207, Denver CO 80202. (303)292-2805. **E-mail:** query@nelsonagency.com. **E-mail:** querykristin@nelsonagency.com; querydanielle@nelsonagency.com; queryjoanna@nelsonagency.com; queryqurессa@nelsonagency.com. **Website:** www.nelsonagency.com. **Contact:** Kristin Nelson, President. Estab. 2002. Member of AAR. RWA, SCBWI, SFWA. Represents 95 clients.

MEMBER AGENTS Danielle Burby; Joanna MacKenzie; Quressa Robinson.

REPRESENTS Fiction, novels.young adult, middle grade, literary commercial, upmarket women's fiction, single-title romance, science fiction, fantasy. **Considers these fiction areas:** commercial, family saga, fantasy, gay, historical, horror, literary, mainstream, middle grade, multicultural, mystery, romance, science fiction, suspense, thriller, urban fantasy, women's, young adult.

NLA specializes in representing commercial fiction and high-caliber literary fiction. "We represent many popular genre categories, including historical romance, steampunk, and all subgenres of YA." Regardless of genre, "we are actively seeking good stories well told." Does not want nonfiction, memoir, stage plays, screenplays, short story collections, poetry, children's picture books, early reader chapter books, or material for the Christian/inspirational market.

HOW TO CONTACT "Please visit our website and carefully read our submission guidelines. We do not accept any queries on Facebook or Twitter." Accepts simultaneous submissions. Makes best efforts to respond to all queries within 3 weeks. Response to full mss requested can take up to 3 months.

TERMS Agent charges industry standard commission.

TIPS "If you would like to learn how to write an awesome pitch paragraph for your query letter or would like any info on how publishing contracts work, please visit Kristin's popular industry blog Pub Rants: http://nelsonagency.com/pub-rants/."

NEW LEAF LITERARY & MEDIA, INC.

110 W. 40th St., Suite 2201, New York NY 10018. (646)248-7989. **Fax:** (646)861-4654. **E-mail:** query@newleafliterary.com. **Website:** www.newleafliterary.com. Estab. 2012. Member of AAR.

MEMBER AGENTS Joanna Volpe (women's fiction, thriller, horror, speculative fiction, literary fiction and historical fiction, young adult, middle grade, art-focused picture books); Kathleen Ortiz, Director of Subsidiary Rights and literary agent (new voices in YA and animator/illustrator talent); Suzie Townsend (new adult, young adult, middle grade, romance [all subgenres], fantasy [urban fantasy, science fiction, steampunk, epic fantasy] and crime fiction [mysteries, thrillers]); Pouya Shahbazian, Director of Film and Television (no unsolicited queries); Janet Reid, janet@newleafliterary.com; JL Stermer (nonfiction, smart pop culture, comedy/satire, fashion, health & wellness, self-help, and memoir).

REPRESENTS Nonfiction, fiction, novels, novellas, juvenile books, poetry books. **Considers these nonfiction areas:** cooking, crafts, creative nonfiction, science, technology, women's issues, young adult. **Considers these fiction areas:** crime, fantasy, historical, horror, literary, mainstream, middle grade, mystery, new adult, paranormal, picture books, romance, thriller, women's, young adult.

HOW TO CONTACT Send query via e-mail. Please do not query via phone. The word "Query" must be in the subject line, plus the agent's name, i.e.–Subject: Query, Suzie Townsend. You may include up to 5 double-spaced sample pages within the body of the e-mail. No attachments, unless specifically requested. Include all necessary contact information. You will receive an auto-response confirming receipt of your query. "We only respond if we are interested in seeing your work." Responds only if interested. All queries read within 1 month.

RECENT SALES *Carve the Mark*, by Veronica Roth (HarperCollins); *Red Queen*, by Victoria Aveyard (HarperCollins); *Lobster is the Best Medicine*, by Liz Climo (Running Press); *Ninth House*, by Leigh Bardugo (Henry Holt); *A Snicker of Magic*, by Natalie Lloyd (Scholastic).

DANA NEWMAN LITERARY

1800 Avenue of the Stars, 12th Floor, Los Angeles CA 90067. **E-mail:** dananewmanliterary@gmail.com. **Website:** dananewman.com. **Contact:** Dana Newman. Estab. 2009. Member of AAR. California State Bar. Represents 30 clients.

Prior to becoming an agent, Ms. Newman was an attorney in the entertainment industry for 14 years.

MEMBER AGENTS Dana Newman (narrative nonfiction, business, lifestyle, current affairs, parenting, memoir, pop culture, sports, health, literary and upmarket fiction).

REPRESENTS Nonfiction, fiction, novels. **Considers these nonfiction areas:** architecture, art, autobiography, biography, business, child guidance, cooking, creative nonfiction, cultural interests, current affairs, diet/nutrition, design, education, ethnic, film, foods, gay/lesbian, government, health, history, how-to, inspirational, interior design, investigative, language, law, literature, medicine, memoirs, money, multicultural, music, New Age, parenting, popular culture, politics, psychology, science, self-help, sociology, sports, technology, theater, travel, true crime, women's issues, women's studies. **Considers these**

fiction areas: commercial, contemporary issues, family saga, feminist, historical, literary, multicultural, sports, women's.

Ms. Newman has a background as an attorney in contracts, licensing, publishing and intellectual property law. She is experienced in digital content creation and distribution. "We are interested in practical nonfiction (business, health and wellness, psychology, parenting, technology) by authors with smart, unique perspectives and established platforms who are committed to actively marketing and promoting their books. We love compelling, inspiring narrative nonfiction in the areas of memoir, biography, history, pop culture, current affairs/women's interest, sports, and social trends. On the fiction side, we consider a very selective amount of literary fiction and women's upmarket fiction." Does not want religious, children's, poetry, horror, mystery, thriller, romance, or science fiction. Does not represent screenplays.

HOW TO CONTACT E-mail queries only. For both nonfiction and fiction, please submit a query letter including a description of your project and a brief biography. "If we are interested in your project, we will contact you and request a full book proposal (nonfiction) or a synopsis and the first 25 pages (fiction)." Accepts simultaneous submissions. "If we have requested your materials after receiving your query, we will use our best efforts to respond within 4 weeks although response time may vary." Obtains new clients through recommendations from others, queries, and submissions.

TERMS Obtains 15% commission on domestic sales; 20% on foreign sales. Offers 1 year written contract. Notice must be given 1 month prior to terminate a contract.

RECENT SALES *Eat Like a Local: France*, by Lynne Martin and Deborah Scarborough (Countryman Press); *Climbing the Hill*, by Jaime Harrison and Amos Snead (Ten Speed Press); *Nora Murphy's Country House Style*, by Nora Murphy (Vendome Press); *Crawl of Fame*, by Julie Moss and Robert Yehling (Pegasus Books); *Into the Abyss*, by Ginger Lerner-Wren (Beacon Press); *Native Advertising*, by Mike Smith (McGraw-Hill); *Breakthrough: The Making of America's First Woman President*, by Nancy L. Cohen (Counterpoint); *Just Add Water*, by Clay Marzo and Robert Yehling (Houghton Mifflin Harcourt); *A Stray Cat Struts*, by Slim Jim Phantom (St. Martin's Press); *Tuff Juice*, by Caron Butler and Steve Springer (Lyons Press).

HAROLD OBER ASSOCIATES

425 Madison Ave., New York NY 10017. (212)759-8600. **Fax:** (212)759-9428. **Website:** www.haroldober.com. **Contact:** Appropriate agent. Member of AAR. Represents 250 clients.

MEMBER AGENTS Phyllis Westberg; Craig Tenney (few new clients, mostly Ober backlist and foreign rights).

HOW TO CONTACT Submit concise query letter addressed to a specific agent with the first 5 pages of the ms or proposal and SASE. No fax or e-mail. Does not handle filmscripts or plays. Responds as promptly as possible. Obtains most new clients through recommendations from others.

TERMS Agent receives 15% commission on domestic sales; 20% commission on foreign sales. Charges clients for express mail/package services.

ALLEN O'SHEA LITERARY AGENCY

Weston CT 06883. (203)222-9004; (203)359-9965. **E-mail:** coleen@allenoshea.com; marilyn@allenoshea.com. **Website:** www.allenoshea.com. Riverside, CT 06878 Member of AAR. Women's Media Group.

Prior to becoming agents, both Ms. O'Shea and Ms. Allen held senior positions in publishing.

MEMBER AGENTS Coleen O'Shea; Marilyn Allen.

REPRESENTS Nonfiction. **Considers these nonfiction areas:** animals, autobiography, biography, business, cooking, crafts, creative nonfiction, cultural interests, current affairs, decorating, diet/nutrition, design, environment, film, foods, gardening, gay/lesbian, health, history, horticulture, how-to, humor, inspirational, interior design, medicine, memoirs, military, money, multicultural, New Age, parenting, popular culture, psychology, regional, science, self-help, spirituality, sports, true crime, women's issues, women's studies.

This agency specializes in practical nonfiction, including health, cooking and cocktails, business, and pop culture. Looks for passionate clients with strong marketing platforms and new ideas coupled with writing talent. Actively seeking narrative nonfiction, health, mind, body spirit, popular science, cookbooks, food narrative, and history writers; very interested in writers who have large media platforms and interesting topics. Does not want to receive fiction, poetry, textbooks or children's books.

HOW TO CONTACT Query via e-mail or mail with SASE. Submit book proposal with sample chapters, competitive analysis, outline, author bio, and marketing page. No phone or fax queries. Accepts simultaneous submissions. Obtains most new clients through recommendations from others; conferences.

TERMS Agent receives 15% commission on domestic sales. Offers written contract, binding for 2 years; one-month notice must be given to terminate contract.

TIPS "Prepare a strong book proposal that includes an overview, table of contents, sample chapter, author bio and platform, a well-thought out marketing plan, a competitive analysis. We will consider your project when your proposal is ready. Thanks for the opportunity to review your work."

L. PERKINS AGENCY

5800 Arlington Ave., Riverdale NY 10471. (718)543-5344. **E-mail:** submissions@lperkinsagency.com. **Website:** lperkinsagency.com. Estab. 1987. Member of AAR. Represents 150 clients.

Ms. Perkins has been an agent for 25 years. She is also the author of *The Insider's Guide to Getting an Agent* (Writer's Digest Books), as well as 3 other nonfiction books. She has edited 25 erotic anthologies, and is also the founder and publisher of Riverdale Avenue Books, an award-winning hybrid publisher with 9 imprints.

MEMBER AGENTS Tish Beaty, ePub agent (erotic romance–including paranormal, historical, gay/lesbian/bisexual, and light-BDSM fiction; also, she seeks new adult and YA); Sandy Lu, sandy@lperkinsagency.com (fiction: she is looking for dark literary and commercial fiction, mystery, thriller, psychological horror, paranormal/urban fantasy, historical fiction, YA, historical thrillers or mysteries set in Victorian times; nonfiction: narrative nonfiction, history, biography, pop science, pop psychology, pop culture [music/theatre/film], humor, and food writing); Lori Perkins (not currently taking new clients); Leon Husock (science fiction & fantasy, as well as young adult and middle-grade); Rachel Brooks (picture books, all genres of young adult and new adult fiction, as well as adult romance—especially romantic suspense [NOTE: Rachel is currently closed to unsolicited submissions]); Maximilian Ximinez (fiction: science fiction, fantasy, horror, thrillers; nonfiction: popular science, true crime, arts and trends in developing fields and cultures).

REPRESENTS Nonfiction, fiction, novels, short story collections. **Considers these nonfiction areas:** autobiography, biography, business, creative nonfiction, cultural interests, current affairs, film, foods, gay/lesbian, history, how-to, humor, literature, memoirs, music, popular culture, psychology, science, sex, theater, true crime, women's issues, women's studies, young adult. **Considers these fiction areas:** commercial, crime, detective, erotica, fantasy, feminist, gay, historical, horror, lesbian, literary, middle grade, mystery, new adult, paranormal, picture books, romance, science fiction, short story collections, supernatural, thriller, urban fantasy, women's, young adult.

"Most of our clients write both fiction and nonfiction. This combination keeps our clients publishing for years. The founder of the agency is also a published author, so we know what it takes to write a good book." Actively seeking erotic romance, romance, young adult, middle grade, science fiction, fantasy, memoir, pop culture, thrillers. Does not want poetry, stand alone short stories or novellas, scripts, plays, westerns, textbooks.

HOW TO CONTACT E-queries only. Include your query, a 1-page synopsis, and the first 5 pages from your novel pasted into the e-mail, or your proposal. No attachments. Submit to only 1 agent at the agency. No snail mail queries. "If you are submitting to one of our agents, please be sure to check the submission status of the agent by visiting their social media accounts listed [on the agency website]." Accepts simultaneous submissions. Obtains most new clients through recommendations from others, solicitations, conferences.

TERMS Agent receives 15% commission on domestic sales; 20% commission on foreign sales. No written contract. Charges clients for photocopying.

RECENT SALES *Arena*, by Holly Jennings; *Taking the Lead*, by Cecilia Tan; *The Girl with Ghost Eyes*, by M. H. Boroson; *Silent Attraction*, by Lauren Brown.

WRITERS CONFERENCES Romantic Times; Romance Writers of America nationals; Rainbow Book Fair; NECON; Killercon; BookExpo America; World Fantasy Convention.

TIPS "Research your field and contact professional writers' organizations to see who is looking for what.

Finish your novel before querying agents. Read my book, *An Insider's Guide to Getting an Agent*, to get a sense of how agents operate. Read agent blogs-agentinthemiddle.blogspot.com and ravenousromance.blogspot.com."

RUBIN PFEFFER CONTENT

648 Hammond St., Chestnut Hill MA 02467. **E-mail:** info@rpcontent.com. **Website:** www.rpcontent.com. **Contact:** Rubin Pfeffer. Estab. 2014. Member of AAR. Signatory of WGA.

Rubin has previously worked as the vice-president and publisher of Simon & Schuster Children's Books and as an independent agent at East West Literary Agency.

MEMBER AGENTS Melissa Nasson is an associate agent at Rubin Pfeffer Content and an attorney. She previously interned at Zachary Shuster Harmsworth, Perseus Books Group, and East-West Literary Agency before joining Rubin Pfeffer Content. Melissa also works as contracts director at Beacon Press.

REPRESENTS Considers these nonfiction areas: juvenile nonfiction, young adult. **Considers these fiction areas:** juvenile, middle grade, picture books, young adult.

High-quality children's fiction and nonfiction, including picture books, middle-grade, and young adult. No manuscripts intended for an adult audience.

HOW TO CONTACT Note: Rubin Pfeffer accepts submissions by referral only. Melissa Nasson is open to queries for picture books, middle-grade, and young adult fiction and nonfiction. To query Melissa, email her at melissa@rpcontent.com, include the query letter in the body of the email, and attach the first 50 pages as a Word doc or PDF. If you wish to query Rubin Pfeffer by referral only, specify the contact information of your reference when submitting. Authors/illustrators should send a query and a 1-3 chapter ms via e-mail (no postal submissions). The query, placed in the body of the e-mail, should include a synopsis of the piece, as well as any relevant information regarding previous publications, referrals, websites, and biographies. The ms may be attached as a .doc or a .pdf file. Specifically for illustrators, attach a PDF of the dummy or artwork to the e-mail. Accepts simultaneous submissions. Strives to respond within 6-8 weeks.

AARON M. PRIEST LITERARY AGENCY

200 W. 41st St., 21st Floor, New York NY 10036. (212)818-0344. **Fax:** (212)573-9417. **E-mail:** info@aaronpriest.com. **Website:** www.aaronpriest.com. Estab. 1974. Member of AAR.

MEMBER AGENTS Aaron Priest, querypriest@aaronpriest.com (thrillers, commercial fiction, biographies); Lisa Erbach Vance, queryvance@aaronpriest.com (contemporary fiction, thrillers/suspense, international fiction, narrative nonfiction); Lucy Childs, querychilds@aaronpriest.com (literary and commercial fiction, memoir, edgy women's fiction); Mitch Hoffman, queryhoffman@aaronpriest.com (thrillers, suspense, crime fiction, and literary fiction, as well as narrative nonfiction, politics, popular science, history, memoir, current events, and pop culture).

REPRESENTS Considers these nonfiction areas: biography, current affairs, history, memoirs, popular culture, politics, science. **Considers these fiction areas:** commercial, contemporary issues, crime, literary, middle grade, suspense, thriller, women's, young adult.

Does not want to receive poetry, screenplays, horror or sci-fi.

HOW TO CONTACT Query one of the agents using the appropriate e-mail listed on the website. "Please do not submit to more than 1 agent at this agency. We urge you to check our website and consider each agent's emphasis before submitting. Your query letter should be about one page long and describe your work as well as your background. You may also paste the first chapter of your work in the body of the e-mail. Do not send attachments." Accepts simultaneous submissions. Responds in 4 weeks, only if interested.

TERMS Agent receives 15% commission on domestic sales.

PROSPECT AGENCY

551 Valley Rd., PMB 377, Upper Montclair NJ 07043. (718)788-3217. **Fax:** (718)360-9582. **E-mail:** https://www.prospectagency.com/submit.html. **Website:** www.prospectagency.com. Estab. 2005. Member of AAR. Signatory of WGA. Represents 130+ clients.

MEMBER AGENTS Emily Sylvan Kim focuses on romance, women's, commercial, young adult, new adult, nonfiction and memoir. She is currently looking for commercial and upmarket women's fiction; self-published authors looking to explore a hybrid career; established and strong debut romance writing mainstream romance; memoir and high interest nonfiction; literary and commercial YA fiction; and select middle grade and early reader fiction with strong commercial appeal. Rachel Orr focuses on picture books, illustrators, middle grade and young adult. She is currently looking for short, punchy picture books (either in prose or rhyme) that are humorous and have a strong marketing hook; non-fiction picture books (especially biographies or stories with a historical angle); illustrators for the trade market; and literary and commercial middle-grade and YA (all time periods and genres.) Ann Rose focuses on middle grade, young adult and commercial adult fiction. She is currently seeking YA of all genres; MG of all genres, especially ones that push the boundaries of middle grade; Swoony romances; Light sci-fi or fantasy; Commercial fiction; Heartwarming (or heart wrenching) contemporaries; any stories with unique voices, diverse perspectives, vivid settings; stories that explore tough topics; and dark and edgy stories with unlikeable characters. Emma Sector focuses on picture books, illustrators, middle grade and young adult. She is currently seeking quirky, character driven chapter books; literary and commercial middle-grade and YA Novels; picture book authors and illustrators; middle-grade graphic novels; and nonfiction middle-grade. Please use the agency form to submit your query: https://www.prospectagency.com/submit.html.

REPRESENTS Nonfiction, fiction, novels, novellas, juvenile books, scholarly books, textbooks. **Considers these nonfiction areas:** biography, cooking, creative nonfiction, cultural interests, gardening, gay/lesbian, government, health, history, horticulture, inspirational, memoirs, parenting, popular culture, psychology, women's issues. **Considers these fiction areas:** commercial, contemporary issues, crime, ethnic, family saga, fantasy, feminist, gay, hi-lo, historical, horror, humor, juvenile, lesbian, literary, mainstream, middle grade, multicultural, mystery, new adult, picture books, romance, science fiction, suspense, thriller, urban fantasy, women's, young adult.

"We're looking for strong, unique voices and unforgettable stories and characters."

HOW TO CONTACT All submissions are electronic and must be submitted through the portal at prospectagency.com/submit.html. We do not accept any submissions through snail mail. Accepts simultaneous submissions. Obtains new clients through conferences, recommendations, queries, and some scouting.

TERMS Agent receives 15% on domestic sales, 20% on foreign sales sold directly and 25% on sales using a subagent. Offers written contract.

REES LITERARY AGENCY

14 Beacon St., Suite 710, Boston MA 02108. (617)227-9014. **E-mail:** lorin@reesagency.com. **Website:** reesagency.com. Estab. 1983. Member of AAR. Represents more than 100 clients.

MEMBER AGENTS Ann Collette, agent10702@aol.com (fiction: literary, upscale commercial women's, crime [including mystery, thriller and psychological suspense], upscale western, historical, military and war, and horror; nonfiction: narrative, military and war, books on race and class, works set in Southeast Asia, biography, pop culture, books on film and opera, humor, and memoir); Lorin Rees, lorin@reesagency.com (literary fiction, memoirs, business books, self-help, science, history, psychology, and narrative nonfiction); Rebecca Podos, rebecca@reesagency.com (young adult and middle grade fiction, particularly books about complex female relationships, beautifully written contemporary, genre novels with a strong focus on character, romance with more at stake than "will they/won't they," and LGBTQ books across all genres).

REPRESENTS Novels. **Considers these nonfiction areas:** biography, business, film, history, humor, memoirs, military, popular culture, psychology, science, war. **Considers these fiction areas:** commercial, crime, historical, horror, literary, middle grade, mystery, suspense, thriller, westerns, women's, young adult.

HOW TO CONTACT Consult website for each agent's submission guidelines and e-mail addresses, as they differ. Accepts simultaneous submissions. Obtains most new clients through recommendations from others, conferences, submissions.

TERMS Agent receives 15% commission on domestic sales; 20% commission on foreign sales.

REGAL HOFFMANN & ASSOCIATES LLC

143 West 29th St., Suite 901, New York NY 10001. (212)684-7900. **Website:** www.rhaliterary.com. Estab. 2002. Member of AAR. Represents 70 clients.

MEMBER AGENTS Claire Anderson-Wheeler (nonfiction: memoirs and biographies, narrative histories, popular science, popular psychology; adult fiction: primarily character-driven literary fiction, but open to genre fiction, high-concept fiction; all genres of young adult/middle grade fiction); Markus Hoffmann (international and literary fiction, crime, [pop] cultural studies, current affairs, economics, history, music, popular science, and travel literature); Stephanie Steiker (serious and narrative nonfiction, literary fiction, graphic novels, history, philosophy, current affairs, cultural studies, biography, music, international writing); Grace Ross (literary fiction, historical fiction, international narratives, narrative nonfiction, popular science, biography, cultural theory, memoir); Elianna Kan (Spanish-language fiction and non-fiction writers, literature in translation).

REPRESENTS Nonfiction, fiction, novels, short story collections, juvenile books, scholarly books. **Considers these nonfiction areas:** biography, creative nonfiction, cultural interests, current affairs, economics, ethnic, gay/lesbian, history, investigative, juvenile nonfiction, literature, memoirs, music, popular culture, psychology, science, translation, travel, women's issues, women's studies, young adult. **Considers these fiction areas:** literary, mainstream, middle grade, short story collections, thriller, women's, young adult.

We represent works in a wide range of categories, with an emphasis on literary fiction, outstanding thriller and crime fiction, and serious narrative nonfiction. Actively seeking literary fiction and narrative nonfiction. Does not want romance, science fiction, poetry, or screenplays.

HOW TO CONTACT Query with SASE or via Submittable (https://rhaliterary.submittable.com/submit). No phone calls. Submissions should consist of a 1-page query letter detailing the book in question, as well as the qualifications of the author. For fiction, submissions may also include the first 10 pages of the novel or one short story from a collection. Accepts simultaneous submissions. Responds in 4-8 weeks.

TERMS Agent receives 15% commission on domestic sales; 20% commission on foreign sales. We charge no reading fees.

RECENT SALES *Wily Snare*, by Adam Jay Epstein; *Perfectly Undone*, by Jamie Raintree; *A Sister in My House*, by Linda Olsson; *This Is How It Really Sounds*, by Stuart Archer Cohen; *Autofocus*, by Lauren Gibaldi; *We've Already Gone This Far*, by Patrick Dacey; *A Fierce and Subtle Poison*, by Samantha Mabry; *The Life of the World to Come*, by Dan Cluchey; *Willful Disregard*, by Lena Andersson; *The Sweetheart*, by Angelina Mirabella.

TIPS "We are deeply committed to every aspect of our clients' careers, and are engaged in everything from the editorial work of developing a great book proposal or line editing a fiction manuscript to negotiating state-of-the-art book deals and working to promote and publicize the book when it's published. We are at the forefront of the effort to increase authors' rights in publishing contracts in a rapidly changing commercial environment. We deal directly with co-agents and publishers in every foreign territory and also work directly and with co-agents for feature film and television rights, with extraordinary success in both arenas. Many of our clients' works have sold in dozens of translation markets, and a high proportion of our books have been sold in Hollywood. We have strong relationships with speaking agents, who can assist in arranging author tours and other corporate and college speaking opportunities when appropriate."

ANGELA RINALDI LITERARY AGENCY

P.O. Box 7875, Beverly Hills CA 90212-7875. (310)842-7665. **Fax:** (310)837-8143. **E-mail:** info@rinaldiliterary.com. **Website:** www.rinaldiliterary.com. **Contact:** Angela Rinaldi. Member of AAR.

Prior to opening her agency, Ms. Rinaldi was an editor at NAL/Signet, Pocket Books and Bantam, and the manager of book development for *The Los Angeles Times*.

REPRESENTS Nonfiction, novels.TV and motion picture rights (for clients only). **Considers these nonfiction areas:** biography, business, cooking, current affairs, health, memoirs, parenting, psychology, self-help, women's issues, women's studies, narrative nonfiction, food narratives, wine, lifestyle, relationships, wellness, personal finance. **Considers these fiction areas:** commercial, historical, literary, mainstream, mystery, suspense, thriller, women's, contemporary, gothic, women's book club fiction.

Actively seeking commercial and literary fiction, as well as nonfiction. For fiction, we do not want to receive humor, CIA espionage, drug thrillers, techno thrillers, category romances, science fiction, fantasy, horror/occult/paranormal, poetry, film scripts, magazine articles or religion. For nonfiction, please do not send us magazine articles, celebrity bios, or tell alls.

HOW TO CONTACT E-queries only. Include the word "Query" in the subject line. For fiction, please send a brief synopsis and paste the first 10 pages into an e-mail. Nonfiction queries should include a detailed cover letter, your credentials and platform information as well as any publishing history. Tell us if you have a completed proposal. Accepts simultaneous submissions. Responds in 2-4 weeks.

TERMS Agent receives 15% commission on domestic sales; 25% commission on foreign sales. Offers written contract.

ANN RITTENBERG LITERARY AGENCY, INC.

15 Maiden Lane, Suite 206, New York NY 10038. (212)684-6936. **E-mail:** info@rittlit.com. **Website:** www.rittlit.com. **Contact:** Ann Rittenberg, president. Estab. 1992. Member of AAR. Represents 30 clients.

MEMBER AGENTS Ann Rittenberg, Rosie Jonker.

REPRESENTS Nonfiction, fiction, novels, juvenile books. **Considers these nonfiction areas:** biography, history, literature, memoirs, popular culture, true crime. **Considers these fiction areas:** crime, detective, family saga, literary, mainstream, mystery, suspense, thriller, women's.

"We don't represent screenplays, poetry, plays, or self-help."

HOW TO CONTACT Query via e-mail or postal mail (with SASE). Submit query letter with 3 sample chapters pasted into the body of the e-mail. If you query by e-mail, we will only respond if interested. If you are making a simultaneous submission, you must tell us in your query. Accepts simultaneous submissions. Responds in 6-8 weeks. However, as noted above, if you don't receive a response to an emailed query, that means it was a pass. Obtains most new clients through referrals from established writers and editors.

TERMS Agent receives 15% commission on domestic sales, and 20% commission on foreign and film deals. This 20% is shared with co-agents. Offers written contract. No charges except for PDFs or finished books for foreign and film submissions.

RECENT SALES *Since We Fell*, by Dennis Lehane; *Your First Novel - Revised and Expanded Edition*, by Ann Rittenberg and Laura Whitcomb with Camille Goldin; *Paradise Valley*, by C.J. Box; *The Field Guide to Dumb Birds of North America*, by Matt Kracht; *Stay Hidden*, by Paul Doiron.

TIPS "Refrain from sending enormous bouquets of red roses. Elegant bouquets of peonies, tulips, ranunculus, calla lily, and white roses are acceptable."

RLR ASSOCIATES, LTD.

420 Lexington Ave., Suite 2532, New York NY 10170. (212)541-8641. **E-mail:** website.info@rlrassociates.net. **Website:** www.rlrassociates.net. **Contact:** Scott Gould. Member of AAR. Represents 50 clients.

REPRESENTS Nonfiction, novels. **Considers these nonfiction areas:** biography, creative nonfiction, foods, history, humor, popular culture, sports. **Considers these fiction areas:** commercial, literary, mainstream, middle grade, picture books, romance, women's, young adult, genre.

"We provide a lot of editorial assistance to our clients and have connections." Does not want to receive screenplays.

HOW TO CONTACT Query by snail mail. For fiction, send a query and 1-3 chapters (pasted). For nonfiction, send query or proposal. Accepts simultaneous submissions. "If you do not hear from us within 3 months, please assume that your work is out of active consideration." Obtains most new clients through recommendations from others.

TERMS Agent receives 15% commission on domestic sales; 20% commission on foreign sales. Offers written contract.

RECENT SALES Clients include Shelby Foote, The Grief Recovery Institute, Don Wade, David Plowden, Nina Planck, Karyn Bosnak, Gerald Carbone, Jason Lethcoe, Andy Crouch.

TIPS "Please check out our website for more details on our agency."

BJ ROBBINS LITERARY AGENCY

5130 Bellaire Ave., North Hollywood CA 91607-2908. **E-mail:** robbinsliterary@gmail.com. **Website:** www.bjrobbinsliterary.com. **Contact:** (Ms.) BJ Robbins. Estab. 1992. Member of AAR.

Prior to becoming an agent, Robbins spent 15 years in publishing, starting in publicity at Simon & Schuster and later as Marketing Director and Senior Editor at Harcourt.

REPRESENTS Nonfiction, fiction, novels. **Considers these nonfiction areas:** autobiography, biography, creative nonfiction, cultural interests, current affairs, ethnic, film, health, history, investigative, medicine, memoirs, multicultural, music, popular culture, psychology, science, sociology, sports, theater, travel, true crime, women's issues, women's studies. **Considers these fiction areas:** contemporary issues, crime, detective, ethnic, historical, literary, mainstream, multicultural, mystery, sports, suspense, thriller, women's.

"We do not represent screenplays, plays, poetry, science fiction, fantasy, westerns, romance, techno-thrillers, religious tracts, dating books or anything with the word 'unicorn' in the title."

HOW TO CONTACT E-query with no attachments. For fiction, okay to include first 10 pages in body of e-mail. Accepts simultaneous submissions. Only responds to projects if interested. Obtains most new clients through conferences, referrals.

TERMS Agent receives 15% commission on domestic sales; 20% commission on foreign sales. Offers written contract. No fees.

RECENT SALES *Shoot for the Moon: The Perilous Voyage of Apollo 11*, by James Donovan (Little, Brown); *Mongrels*, by Stephen Graham Jones (William Morrow); *Blood Brothers: The Story of the Strange Friendship between Sitting Bull and Buffalo Bill*, by Deanne Stillman (Simon & Schuster); *Reliance, Illinois*, by Mary Volmer (Soho Press), Mapping the Interior by Stephen Graham Jones (Tor).

RODEEN LITERARY MANAGEMENT

3501 N. Southport #497, Chicago IL 60657. **E-mail:** info@rodeenliterary.com. **E-mail:** submissions@rodeenliterary.com. **Website:** www.rodeenliterary.com. **Contact:** Paul Rodeen. Estab. 2009. Member of AAR. Signatory of WGA.

Paul Rodeen established Rodeen Literary Management in 2009 after 7 years of experience with the literary agency Sterling Lord Literistic, Inc.

REPRESENTS Nonfiction, novels, juvenile books. illustrations, graphic novels. **Considers these fiction areas:** juvenile, middle grade, picture books, young adult, graphic novels, comics.

Actively seeking "writers and illustrators of all genres of children's literature including picture books, early readers, middle-grade fiction and nonfiction, graphic novels and comic books, as well as young adult fiction and nonfiction." This is primarily an agency devoted to children's books.

HOW TO CONTACT Unsolicited submissions are accepted by e-mail only. Cover letters with synopsis and contact information should be included in the body of your e-mail. An initial submission of 50 pages from a novel or a longer work of nonfiction will suffice and should be pasted into the body of your e-mail. Accepts simultaneous submissions.

LINDA ROGHAAR LITERARY AGENCY, LLC

P.O. Box 3561, Amherst MA 01004. **E-mail:** contact@lindaroghaar.com. **Website:** www.lindaroghaar.com. **Contact:** Linda L. Roghaar. Member of AAR.

Prior to opening her agency, Ms. Roghaar worked in retail bookselling for 5 years and as a publishers' sales rep for 15 years.

REPRESENTS Nonfiction.

The Linda Roghaar Literary Agency represents authors with substantial messages and specializes in nonfiction. We sell to major, independent, and university presses. Does not want fiction.

HOW TO CONTACT We prefer e-queries. Please mention 'query' in the subject line, and do not include attachments. For queries by mail, please include an SASE. Accepts simultaneous submissions. Responds within 12 weeks if interested.

TERMS Agent receives 15% commission on domestic sales. Agent receives negotiable commission on foreign sales. Offers written contract.

THE ROSENBERG GROUP

23 Lincoln Ave., Marblehead MA 01945. (781)990-1341. **Fax:** (781)990-1344. **Website:** www.rosenberggroup.com. **Contact:** Barbara Collins Rosenberg. Estab. 1998. Member of AAR. Recognized agent of the RWA. Represents 25 clients.

Prior to becoming an agent, Ms. Rosenberg was a senior editor for Harcourt.

REPRESENTS Nonfiction, novels, textbooks.college textbooks only. **Considers these nonfiction areas:** biography, current affairs, foods, music, popular culture, psychology, science, self-help, sports, women's issues, women's studies, women's health, wine/beverages. **Considers these fiction areas:** romance, women's, chick lit.

Ms. Rosenberg is well-versed in the romance market (both category and single title). She is a frequent speaker at romance conferences. The Rosenberg Group is accepting new clients working in romance fiction (please see my Areas of Interest for specific romance subgenres); women's fiction and chick lit. Does not want to receive inspirational, time travel, futuristic or paranormal.

HOW TO CONTACT Query via snail mail. Your query letter should not exceed one page in length. It should include the title of your work, the genre and/or sub-genre; the manuscript's word count; and a brief description of the work. If you are writing category romance, please be certain to let her know the line for which your work is intended. Accepts simultaneous submissions. Obtains most new clients through recommendations from others, solicitations, conferences.

TERMS Agent receives 15% commission on domestic and foreign sales. Offers written contract; 1-month notice must be given to terminate contract. Charges maximum of $350/year for postage and photocopying.

RECENT SALES Sold 27 titles in the last year.

WRITERS CONFERENCES RWA National Conference; BookExpo America.

RITA ROSENKRANZ LITERARY AGENCY

440 West End Ave., #15D, New York NY 10024. (212)873-6333. **E-mail:** rrosenkranz@mindspring.com. **Website:** www.ritarosenkranzliteraryagency.com. **Contact:** Rita Rosenkranz. Member of AAR. Women's Media Group, Authors Guild. Represents 40 clients.

Prior to opening her agency, Ms. Rosenkranz worked as an editor at major New York publishing houses.

REPRESENTS Nonfiction. **Considers these nonfiction areas:** agriculture, Americana, animals, anthropology, archeology, architecture, art, autobiography, biography, business, child guidance, computers, cooking, crafts, creative nonfiction, cultural interests, current affairs, dance, decorating, diet/nutrition, design, economics, education, environment, ethnic, film, foods, gardening, gay/lesbian, government, health, history, hobbies, horticulture, how-to, humor, inspirational, interior design, investigative, language, law, literature, medicine, memoirs, military, money, multicultural, music, New Age, parenting, philosophy, photography, popular culture, politics, psychology, regional, religious, satire, science, self-help, sex, software, spirituality, sports, technology, theater, true crime, war, women's issues, women's studies.

"This agency focuses on adult nonfiction, stresses strong editorial development and refinement before submitting to publishers, and brainstorms ideas with authors." Actively seeks authors who are well paired with their subject, either for professional or personal reasons.

HOW TO CONTACT Send query letter only (no proposal) via regular mail or e-mail. Submit proposal package with SASE only on request. No fax queries. Accepts simultaneous submissions. Responds in 2 weeks to queries. Obtains most new clients through directory listings, solicitations, conferences, word of mouth.

TERMS Agent receives 15% commission on domestic sales; 20% commission on foreign sales. Offers written contract, binding for 3 years; 3-month written notice must be given to terminate contract. Charges clients for photocopying. Makes referrals to editing services.

RECENT SALES *Mindshift: How Ordinary and Extraordinary People Have Transformed Their Lives Through Learning—And You Can Too*, by Barbara A. Oakley (Tarcher); *On the Verge: Experience the Stillness of Presence, the Pulse of Potential, and the Power of Being Fully Alive*, by Cara Bradley (New World Library); *Lost Science*, by Kitty Ferguson (Sterling); *Get Lit Rising*, by Diane Luby Lane and the Get Lit Players (Beyond Words/Atria).

TIPS "Identify the current competition for your project to make sure the project is valid. A strong cover letter is very important to help get to the next step."

ANDY ROSS LITERARY AGENCY

767 Santa Ray Ave., Oakland CA 94610. (510)238-8965. **E-mail:** andyrossagency@hotmail.com. **Website:** www.andyrossagency.com. **Contact:** Andy Ross. Estab. 2008. Member of AAR. Represents See website for client list. clients.

I was the owner of Cody's Books in Berkeley California for 30 years.

REPRESENTS Nonfiction, fiction, novels, juvenile books, scholarly books. **Considers these nonfiction areas:** anthropology, autobiography, biography, child guidance, cooking, creative nonfiction, cultural interests, current affairs, economics, education, environment, ethnic, gay/lesbian, government, history, investigative, juvenile nonfiction, language, law, literature, memoirs, military, parenting, philosophy, popular culture, politics, psychology, science, sociology, technology, war, women's issues, women's studies, young adult. **Considers these fiction areas:** commercial, contemporary issues, historical, juvenile, literary, middle grade, picture books, young adult.

"This agency specializes in general nonfiction, politics and current events, history, biography, journalism and contemporary culture as well as literary, commercial, and YA fiction." Does not want to receive poetry.

HOW TO CONTACT Queries should be less than half page. Please put the word "query" in the title header of the e-mail. In the first sentence, state the category of the project. Give a short description of the book and your qualifications for writing. Accepts simultaneous submissions. Responds in 1 week to queries.

TERMS Agent receives 15% commission on domestic sales; 20% commission on foreign sales or other deals made through a sub-agent. Offers written contract.

RECENT SALES See my website.

JANE ROTROSEN AGENCY LLC

318 E. 51st St., New York NY 10022. (212)593-4330. **Fax:** (212)935-6985. **Website:** www.janerotrosen.com. Estab. 1974. Member of AAR. Other memberships include Authors Guild. Represents more than 100 clients.

MEMBER AGENTS Jane Rotrosen Berkey (not taking on clients); Andrea Cirillo, acirillo@janerotrosen.com (general fiction, suspense, and women's fiction); Annelise Robey, arobey@janerotrosen.com (women's fiction, suspense, mystery, literary fiction, and select nonfiction); Meg Ruley, mruley@janerotrosen.com (commercial fiction, including suspense, mysteries, romance, and general fiction); Christina Hogrebe, chogrebe@janerotrosen.com (young adult, new adult, book club fiction, romantic comedies, mystery, and suspense); Amy Tannenbaum, atannenbaum@janerotrosen.com (contemporary romance, psychological suspense, thrillers, and new adult, as well as women's fiction that falls into that sweet spot between literary and commercial, memoir, narrative and prescriptive non-fiction in the areas of health, business, pop culture, humor, and popular psychology); Rebecca Scherer rscherer@janerotrosen.com (women's fiction, mystery, suspense, thriller, romance, upmarket/literary-leaning fiction); Jessica Errera (assistant to Christina and Rebecca).

REPRESENTS Nonfiction, novels. **Considers these nonfiction areas:** business, health, humor, memoirs, popular culture, psychology, narrative nonfiction. **Considers these fiction areas:** commercial, literary, mainstream, mystery, new adult, romance, suspense, thriller, women's, young adult.

Jane Rotrosen Agency is best known for representing writers of commercial fiction: thrillers, mystery, suspense, women's fiction, romance, historical novels, mainstream fiction, young adult, etc. We also work with authors of memoirs, narrative and prescriptive nonfiction.

HOW TO CONTACT Check website for guidelines. Accepts simultaneous submissions. Obtains most new clients through recommendations from others.

TERMS Agent receives 15% commission on domestic sales; 20% commission on foreign sales. Offers written contract, binding for 3 years; 2-month notice must be given to terminate contract. Charges clients for photocopying, express mail, overseas postage, book purchase.

THE RUDY AGENCY

825 Wildlife Ln., Estes Park CO 80517. (970)577-8500. **E-mail:** mak@rudyagency.com; claggett@rudyagency.com; gstone@rudyagency.com. **Website:** www.rudyagency.com. **Contact:** Maryann Karinch. Estab. 2004. Adheres to AAR canon of ethics. Represents 30 clients.

Prior to becoming an agent, Ms. Karinch was, and continues to be, an author of nonfiction books—primarily covering the subjects of health/medicine and human behavior. Prior to that, she was in public relations and marketing: areas of expertise she also applies in her practice as an agent.

MEMBER AGENTS Maryann Karinch, Hilary Claggett, and Geoffrey Stone.

REPRESENTS Nonfiction, fiction, novels, scholarly books. **Considers these nonfiction areas:** Americana, anthropology, archeology, architecture, autobiography, biography, business, child guidance, computers, cooking, creative nonfiction, cultural interests, current affairs, diet/nutrition, design, economics, education, environment, gay/lesbian, government, health, history, how-to, inspirational, investigative, law, literature, medicine, memoirs, military, money, multicultural, parenting, popular culture, politics, psychology, science, self-help, sex, sociology, sports, technology, theater, true crime, war, women's issues, women's studies. **Considers these fiction areas:** action, adventure, commercial, contemporary issues, crime, erotica, gay, historical, lesbian, literary, military, multicultural, mystery, sports, thriller, women's.

"We support authors from the proposal stage through promotion of the published work. We work in partnership with publishers to promote the published work and coach authors in their role in the marketing and public relations campaigns for the book." Actively seeking projects with social value, projects that open minds to new ideas and interesting lives, and projects that entertain through good storytelling. Does not want to receive poetry, screenplays, novellas, religion books, children's lit, and joke books.

HOW TO CONTACT "Query us. If we like the query, we will invite a complete proposal (or complete ms if writing fiction). No phone queries, please. We won't hang up on you, but it makes it easier if you send us a note first." Accepts simultaneous submissions. Responds in under 3 weeks to non-fiction proposals and 12 weeks to invited manuscripts. Obtains most new clients through recommendations from others, solicitations.

TERMS Agent receives 15% commission on domestic sales. Offers written contract, binding for 1 year.

RECENT SALES *The Art of Creating Value*, by Jeffrey Ansell (Rowman & Littlefield); *Palace Coup*, by Max Frumes and Sujeet Indap (Diversion); *Get People to Do What You Want*, by Gregory Hartley (Red Wheel/Weiser).

TIPS "Present yourself professionally. Know what we need to see in a query and what a proposal for a work of non-fiction must contain before you contact us."

REGINA RYAN PUBLISHING ENTERPRISES, INC.

251 Central Park W., 7D, New York NY 10024. **E-mail:** https://app.authors.me/submit/regina-ryan-books. **Website:** www.reginaryanbooks.com. **Contact:** Regina Ryan. Estab. 1976. Member of AAR.

Prior to becoming an agent, Ms. Ryan was an editor at Alfred A. Knopf, editor-in-chief of Macmillan Adult Trade, and a book producer.

REPRESENTS Nonfiction. **Considers these nonfiction areas:** Americana, animals, anthropology, archeology, architecture, autobiography, biography, business, child guidance, cooking, cultural interests, diet/nutrition, environment, foods, gardening, health, history, horticulture, medicine, parenting, popular culture, politics, psychology, recreation, science, self-help, sex, sports, travel, true crime, women's issues, women's studies, adult and juvenile nonfiction: narrative nonfiction; natural history (especially birds and birding); popular science, lifestyle, sustainability, mind-body-spirit;.

"We are always looking for new and exciting books in our areas of interest, including well-written narrative nonfiction, architecture, history, politics, natural history (especially birds), science (especially the brain), the environment, women's issues, parenting, cooking, psychology, health, wellness, diet, lifestyle, sustainability, popular reference, and leisure activities including sports, narrative travel, and gardening. We represent books that have something new and fresh to say, are well-written and that will, if possible, make the world a better place." Actively seeking narrative nonfiction, food related travel projects, brain science.

HOW TO CONTACT All queries must come through the following site https://app.authors.me/submit/regina-ryan-books. Accepts simultaneous submissions. "We try to respond in 4-6 weeks but only if we are interested in pursuing the project. If you don't hear from us in that time frame, it means that we are not interested." Obtains most new clients through internet submissions.

TERMS Agent receives 15% commission on domestic and foreign sales. Offers written contract. Charges clients for all out-of-pocket expenses (e.g., long distance calls, messengers, freight, copying) if it's more than just a nominal amount.

RECENT SALES *The Friendly Orange Glow: The Untold Story of the PLATO Learning System and the Dawn of Cyberculture*, by Brian Dear; *What's Wrong With My Weed?*, by David Deardorff and Kathryn Wadsworth; *Itch! Everything You Didn't Want to Know about What Makes You Scratch*, by Anita Sanchez; *Craft Wines*, by Richard Bender; *Hair: A Human History*, by Kurt Stenn; *Wildlife Spectacles: Mass Migrations, Mating Rituals, and Other Fascinating Animal Behaviors*, by Vladimir Dinets; *Connecting in the Land of Dementia*, by Deborah Shouse; *The Backyard Birdsong Guide*, by Donald Kroodsma.

TIPS "It's important to include an analysis of comparable books that have had good sales, as well as an analysis of competitive books, that explains why your proposed book is different. Both are essential."

THE SAGALYN AGENCY / ICM PARTNERS

Chevy Chase MD **E-mail:** info@sagalyn.com. **E-mail:** query@sagalyn.com. **Website:** www.sagalyn.com. Estab. 1980. Member of AAR.

MEMBER AGENTS Raphael Sagalyn; Brandon Coward; Abby Serino.

REPRESENTS Nonfiction. **Considers these nonfiction areas:** biography, business, creative nonfiction, economics, popular culture, science, technology.

"Our list includes upmarket nonfiction books in these areas: narrative history, biography, business, economics, popular culture, science, technology."

HOW TO CONTACT Please send e-mail queries only. Accepts simultaneous submissions.

TIPS "We receive 1,000-1,200 queries a year, which in turn lead to 2 or 3 new clients. See our website for sales information and recent projects."

VICTORIA SANDERS & ASSOCIATES

440 Buck Rd., Stone Ridge NY 12484. (212)633-8811. **E-mail:** queriesvsa@gmail.com. **Website:** www.victoriasanders.com. **Contact:** Victoria Sanders. Estab. 1992. Member of AAR. Signatory of WGA. Represents 135 clients.

MEMBER AGENTS Victoria Sanders; Bernadette Baker-Baughman; Jessica Spivey.

REPRESENTS Nonfiction, fiction, novels, short story collections, juvenile books. **Considers these nonfiction areas:** autobiography, biography, cooking, cultural interests, current affairs, ethnic, film, foods, gay/lesbian, government, history, humor, law, literature, memoirs, music, parenting, popular culture, politics, psychology, satire, theater, translation, women's issues, women's studies. **Considers these fiction areas:** action, adventure, cartoon, comic books, contemporary issues, crime, detective, ethnic, family saga, feminist, gay, historical, humor, inspirational, juvenile, lesbian, literary, mainstream, middle grade, multicultural, multimedia, mystery, new adult, picture books, suspense, thriller, women's, young adult.

HOW TO CONTACT Authors who wish to contact us regarding potential representation should send a query letter with the first 3 chapters (or about 25 pages) pasted into the body of the message to queriesvsa@gmail.com. We will only accept queries via e-mail. Query letters should describe the project and the author in the body of a single, 1-page e-mail that does not contain any attached files. Important note: Please paste the first 3 chapters of your manuscript (or about 25 pages, and feel free to round up to a chapter break) into the body of your e-mail. Accepts simultaneous submissions. Responds in 1-4 weeks, although occasionally it will take longer. "We will not respond to e-mails with attachments or attached files."

TERMS Agent receives 15% commission on domestic sales; 20% commission on foreign/film sales. Offers written contract.

TIPS "Limit query to letter (no calls) and give it your best shot. A good query is going to get a good response."

WENDY SCHMALZ AGENCY

402 Union St., #831, Hudson NY 12534. (518)672-7697. **E-mail:** wendy@schmalzagency.com. **Website:** www.schmalzagency.com. **Contact:** Wendy Schmalz. Estab. 2002. Member of AAR.

REPRESENTS Juvenile books. **Considers these nonfiction areas:** young adult, Many nonfiction subjects are of interest to this agency. **Considers these fiction areas:** middle grade, young adult.

Not looking for picture books, science fiction or fantasy.

HOW TO CONTACT Accepts only e-mail queries. Paste synopsis into the e-mail. Do not attach the ms or sample chapters or synopsis. Replies to queries only if they want to read the ms. If you do not hear from this agency within 2 weeks, consider that a no. Accepts simultaneous submissions. I respond to queries within 2 weeks of receipt. If I don't respond within 2 weeks, it means I'm not interested in reading the ms. Obtains clients through recommendations from others.

TERMS Agent receives 15% commission on domestic sales; 20% on foreign sales; 25% for Asia.

SUSAN SCHULMAN LITERARY AGENCY LLC

454 W. 44th St., New York NY 10036. (212)713-1633. **E-mail:** susan@schulmanagency.com. **E-mail:** queries@schulmanagency.com. **Website:** www.publishersmarketplace.com/members/schulman/. **Contact:** Susan Schulman. Estab. 1980. Member of AAR. Signatory of WGA. Other memberships include Dramatists Guild, Writers Guild of America, East, New York Women in Film, Women's Media Group, Agents' Roundtable, League of New York Theater Women.

REPRESENTS Nonfiction, fiction, novels, juvenile books, feature film, TV scripts, theatrical stage play. **Considers these nonfiction areas:** anthropology, archeology, architecture, art, biography, business, child guidance, cooking, creative nonfiction, current affairs, economics, ethnic, government, health, history, juvenile nonfiction, law, money, popular culture, politics, psychology, religious, science, spirituality, women's issues, women's studies, young adult. **Considers these fiction areas:** commercial, contemporary issues, juvenile, literary, mainstream, new adult, religious, women's, young adult. **Considers these script areas:** theatrical stage play.

"We specialize in books for, by and about women and women's issues including nonfiction self-help books, fiction, and theater projects. We also handle the film, television. and allied rights for several agencies as well as foreign rights for several publishing houses." Actively seeking new nonfiction. Considers plays. Does not want to receive poetry, television scripts or concepts for television.

HOW TO CONTACT "For fiction: query letter with outline and three sample chapters, resume and SASE. For nonfiction: query letter with complete description of subject, at least one chapter, resume and SASE. Queries may be sent via regular mail or e-mail. Please do not submit queries via UPS or Federal Express. Please do not send attachments with e-mail queries Please incorporate the chapters into the body of the e-mail." Accepts simultaneous submissions. Responds in less than 1 week generally to a full query and 6 weeks to a full ms. Obtains most new clients through recommendations from others, solicitations, conferences.

TERMS Agent receives 15% commission on domestic sales; 20% commission on foreign sales. Offers written contract; 30-day notice must be given to terminate contract.

RECENT SALES Sold 70 titles in the last year; hundreds of subsidiary rights deals.

WRITERS CONFERENCES Geneva Writers' Conference (Switzerland); Columbus Writers' Conference; Skidmore Conference of the Independent Women's Writers Group. Attends Frankfurt Book Fair, London Book Fair, and BEA annually.

TIPS "Keep writing!" Schulman describes her agency as "professional boutique, long-standing, eclectic."

SERENDIPITY LITERARY AGENCY, LLC

305 Gates Ave., Brooklyn NY 11216. **E-mail:** rbrooks@serendipitylit.com; info@serendipitylit.com. **Website:** www.serendipitylit.com; facebook.com/serendipitylit. **Contact:** Regina Brooks. Estab. 2000. Member of AAR. Signatory of WGA. Represents 150 clients.

Prior to becoming an agent, Ms. Brooks was an acquisitions editor for John Wiley & Sons, Inc. and McGraw-Hill Companies.

MEMBER AGENTS Regina Brooks; Christina Morgan (literary fiction, crime fiction, and narrative nonfiction in the categories of pop culture, sports, current events and memoir); Jocquelle Caiby (literary fiction, horror, middle grade fiction, and children's books by authors who have been published in the adult market, athletes, actors, journalists, politicians, and musicians).

REPRESENTS Nonfiction, fiction, novels, juvenile books. **Considers these nonfiction areas:** Americana, anthropology, architecture, art, autobiography, biography, business, cooking, creative nonfiction, cultural interests, current affairs, ethnic, foods, inspirational, interior design, juvenile nonfiction, memoirs, metaphysics, multicultural, music, parenting, popular culture, politics, psychology, religious, science, self-help, spirituality, sports, travel, true crime, women's issues, women's studies, young adult. **Considers these fiction areas:** commercial, gay, historical, lesbian, literary, middle grade, mystery, romance, thriller, women's, young adult, Christian.

HOW TO CONTACT Check the website, as there are online submission forms for fiction, nonfiction and juvenile. Website will also state if we're temporarily closed to submissions to any areas. Accepts simultaneous submissions. Obtains most new clients through conferences, referrals and social media.

TERMS Agent receives 15% commission on domestic sales; 20% commission on foreign sales. Offers written contract; 2-month notice must be given to terminate contract. Charges clients for office fees, which are taken from any advance.

TIPS "See the books *Writing Great Books For Young Adults* and *You Should Really Write A Book: How To Write Sell And Market Your Memoir.* We are looking for high concept ideas with big hooks. If you get writer's block try possibiliteas.co, it's a muse in a cup."

THE SEYMOUR AGENCY

475 Miner St., Canton NY 13617. (239)398-8209. **E-mail:** nicole@theseymouragency.com; julie@theseymouragency.com. **Website:** www.theseymouragency.com. Member of AAR. Signatory of WGA. Other memberships include RWA, Authors Guild, RWA, ACFW, HWA, MWA, SCBWI.

MEMBER AGENTS Nicole Rescinti, nicole@theseymouragency.com; Julie Gwinn, julie@theseymouragency.com; Tina Wainscott, tina@theseymouragency.com; Jennifer Wills, jennifer@theseymouragency.com; Lesley Sabga, lesley@theseymouurageency.com.

REPRESENTS Nonfiction, fiction, novels, juvenile books. **Considers these nonfiction areas:** Americana, anthropology, business, child guidance, cooking, crafts, cultural interests, decorating, diet/nutrition, design, foods, gardening, gay/lesbian, health, history, hobbies, how-to, humor, inspirational, juvenile nonfiction, literature, memoirs, metaphysics, military, music, New Age, parenting, philosophy, photography, popular culture, politics, psychology, religious, self-help, sex, spirituality, sports, theater, travel, true crime, war, women's issues, women's studies, young adult, cookbooks; any well-written nonfiction that includes a proposal in standard format and 1 sample chapter. **Considers these fiction areas:** action, adventure, commercial, contemporary issues, crime, detective, erotica, ethnic, experimental, family saga, fantasy, feminist, frontier, gay, horror, humor, inspirational, lesbian, literary, mainstream, metaphysical, middle grade, military, multicultural, multimedia, mystery, new adult, New Age, occult, paranormal, picture books, police, religious, romance, science fiction, spiritual, sports, supernatural, suspense, thriller, translation, urban fantasy, war, westerns, women's, young adult.

HOW TO CONTACT Accepts e-mail queries. Check online for guidelines. Accepts simultaneous submissions. Responds in 1 month to queries; 3 months to mss.

TERMS Agent receives 12-15% commission on domestic sales.

DENISE SHANNON LITERARY AGENCY, INC.

121 W. 27th St., Suite 303, New York NY 10001. **E-mail:** info@deniseshannonagency.com. **E-mail:** submissions@deniseshannonagency.com. **Website:** www.deniseshannonagency.com. **Contact:** Denise Shannon. Estab. 2002. Member of AAR.

Prior to opening her agency, Ms. Shannon worked for 16 years with Georges Borchardt and International Creative Management.

REPRESENTS Nonfiction, novels. **Considers these nonfiction areas:** biography, business, health, narrative nonfiction, politics, journalism, social history. **Considers these fiction areas:** literary.

"We are a boutique agency with a distinguished list of fiction and nonfiction authors."

HOW TO CONTACT "Queries may be submitted by post, accompanied by a SASE, or by e-mail to submissions@deniseshannonagency.com. Please include a description of the available book project and a brief bio including details of any prior publications. We will reply and request more material if we are interested. We request that you inform us if you are submitting material simultaneously to other agencies." Accepts simultaneous submissions.

RECENT SALES *Mister Monkey*, by Francine Prose (Harper); *Hotel Solitaire*, by Gary Shteyngart (Random House); *White Flights*, by Jess Row (Graywolf Press); *The Underworld*, by Kevin Canty (Norton).

TIPS "Please do not send queries regarding fiction projects until a complete manuscript is available for review. We request that you inform us if you are submitting material simultaneously to other agencies."

WENDY SHERMAN ASSOCIATES, INC.

138 W. 25th St., Suite 1018, New York NY 10001. (212)279-9027. **E-mail:** submissions@wsherman.com. **Website:** www.wsherman.com. **Contact:** Wendy Sherman. Estab. 1999. Member of AAR.

Prior to opening the agency, Ms. Sherman held positions as vice president, executive director, associate publisher, subsidiary rights director, and sales and marketing director for major publishers including Simon & Schuster and Henry Holt.

MEMBER AGENTS Wendy Sherman (women's fiction that hits that sweet spot between literary and mainstream, Southern voices, suspense with a well-developed protagonist, anything related to food, dogs, mothers and daughters).

REPRESENTS Nonfiction, fiction, novels, juvenile books. **Considers these nonfiction areas:** creative nonfiction, foods, humor, memoirs, parenting, popular culture, psychology, self-help, narrative nonfiction.

Considers these fiction areas: mainstream, Mainstream fiction that hits the sweet spot between literary and commercial.

"We specialize in developing new writers, as well as working with more established writers. My experience as a publisher has proven to be a great asset to my clients." Does not want genre fiction, picture books.

HOW TO CONTACT Query via e-mail only. "We ask that you include your last name, title, and the name of the agent you are submitting to in the subject line. For fiction, please include a query letter and your first 10 pages copied and pasted in the body of the e-mail. We will not open attachments unless they have been requested. For nonfiction, please include your query letter and author bio. Due to the large number of e-mail submissions that we receive, we only reply to e-mail queries in the affirmative. We respectfully ask that you do not send queries to our individual e-mail addresses." Accepts simultaneous submissions. Obtains most new clients through recommendations from other writers.

TERMS Agent receives standard 15% commission. Offers written contract.

RECENT SALES *All is Not Forgotten*, by Wendy Walker; *Z, A Novel of Zelda Fitzgerald*, by Therese Anne Fowler; *The Charm Bracelet*, by Viola Shipman; *The Silence of Bonaventure Arrow*, by Rita Leganski; *Together Tea*, by Marjan Kamali; *A Long Long Time Ago and Essentially True*, by Brigid Pasulka; *Lunch in Paris*, by Elizabeth Bard; *The Rules of Inheritance*, by Claire Bidwell Smith; *Eight Flavors*, by Sarah Lohman; *How to Live a Good Life*, by Jonathan Fields; *The Essential Oil Hormone Solution*, by Dr. Mariza Snyder.

TIPS "The bottom line is: do your homework. Be as well prepared as possible. Read the books that will help you present yourself and your work with polish. You want your submission to stand out."

SPENCERHILL ASSOCIATES

8131 Lakewood Main St., Building M, Suite 205, Lakewood Ranch FL 34202. (941)907-3700. **E-mail:** submission@spencerhillassociates.com. **Website:** www.spencerhillassociates.com. **Contact:** Karen Solem, Nalini Akolekar, Amanda Leuck, Sandy Harding, and Ali Herring. Estab. 2001. Member of AAR.

Prior to becoming an agent, Ms. Solem was editor-in-chief at HarperCollins and an associate publisher.

MEMBER AGENTS Karen Solem; Nalini Akolekar; Amanda Leuck; Sandy Harding; Ali Herring.

REPRESENTS Fiction, novels, juvenile books. **Considers these fiction areas:** commercial, contemporary issues, crime, detective, erotica, ethnic, family saga, feminist, gay, historical, humor, inspirational, lesbian, literary, mainstream, middle grade, multicultural, mystery, new adult, paranormal, police, religious, romance, supernatural, suspense, thriller, urban fantasy, women's, young adult.

"We handle mostly commercial women's fiction, historical novels, romance (historical, contemporary, paranormal, urban fantasy), thrillers, and mysteries. We also represent Christian fiction only—no nonfiction." No nonfiction, poetry, children's picture books, or scripts.

HOW TO CONTACT "We accept electronic submissions only. Please send us a query letter in the body of an e-mail, pitch us your project and tell us about yourself: Do you have prior publishing credits? Attach the first three chapters and synopsis preferably in .doc, rtf or txt format to your email. Send all queries to submission@spencerhillassociates.com. Or submit through the QueryManager link on our website. We do not have a preference for exclusive submissions, but do appreciate knowing if the submission is simultaneous. We receive thousands of submissions a year and each query receives our attention. Unfortunately, we are unable to respond to each query individually. If we are interested in your work, we will contact you within 12 weeks." Accepts simultaneous submissions. Responds in approximately 12 weeks.

TERMS Agent receives 15% commission on domestic sales; 20% commission on foreign sales. Offers written contract; 3-month notice must be given to terminate contract.

RECENT SALES A full list of sales and clients is available on the agency website.

PHILIP G. SPITZER LITERARY AGENCY, INC

50 Talmage Farm Ln., East Hampton NY 11937. (631)329-3650. **E-mail:** lukas.ortiz@spitzeragency.com; annelise.spitzer@spitzeragency.com. **E-mail:** kim.lombardini@spitzeragency.com. **Website:** www.spitzeragency.com. **Contact:** Lukas Ortiz. Estab. 1969. Member of AAR.

Prior to opening his agency, Mr. Spitzer served at New York University Press,

McGraw-Hill, and the John Cushman Associates Literary Agency.

MEMBER AGENTS Philip G. Spitzer; Anne-Lise Spitzer; Lukas Ortiz.

REPRESENTS Novels. **Considers these nonfiction areas:** biography, current affairs, history, politics, sports. **Considers these fiction areas:** literary, mainstream, suspense, thriller.

This agency specializes in mystery/suspense, literary fiction, sports, and general nonfiction (no how-to).

HOW TO CONTACT E-mail query containing synopsis of work, brief biography, and a sample chapter (pasted into the e-mail). Be aware that this agency openly says their client list is quite full. Obtains most new clients through recommendations from others.

TERMS Agent receives 15% commission on domestic sales; 20% commission on foreign sales.

RECENT SALES *New Iberia Blues*, by James Lee Burke (Simon & Schuster); *The Better Sister*, by Alafair Burke (HarperCollins); *Gone So Long*, by Andre Dubus III (Norton); *Two Kinds of Truth*, by Michael Connelly (Little, Brown & Co); *The Emerald Lie*, Ken Bruen (Mysterious Press/Grove-Atlantic); *Terror in the City of Champions*, by Tom Stanton (Lyons Press); *The Brain Defense*, by Kevin Davis (Penguin Press); *The Names of Dead Girls*, by Eric Rickstad (HarperCollins); *Assume Nothing*, Gar Anthony Haywood (Severn House); *The Man on the Stair*, by Gary Inbinder (Norton); *Running in the Dark*, by Sam Reaves (Thomas & Mercer); *Green Sun*, by Kent Anderson (Mulholland Books).

WRITERS CONFERENCES London Bookfair, Frankfurt, BookExpo America, Bouchercon.

STIMOLA LITERARY STUDIO

308 Livingston Ct., Edgewater NJ 07020. **E-mail:** info@stimolaliterarystudio.com. **E-mail:** see submission page on website. **Website:** www.stimolaliterarystudio.com. **Contact:** Rosemary B. Stimola. Estab. 1997. Member of AAR. PEN, Authors Guild, ALA Represents 75 clients.

Prior to opening her agency, Rosemary Stimola was an independent children's bookseller. Erica Rand Silverman, Senior Agent, was a high school teacher and former senior agent at Sterling Lord Literistic. Allison Remcheck was an Assistant Editor at Feiwel & Friends/Macmillan, and then Editorial Assistant at the Stimola Literary Studio before acquiring for her own list. Adriana Stimola worked as Content Manager at Stone Barns, Food and Agricultural Institute. Peter Ryan continues to be the Director of Operations at the Stimola Literary Studio, and now represents graphic novels for all ages.

MEMBER AGENTS Rosemary B. Stimola; Erica Rand Silverman; Allison Remcheck; Adriana Stimola, Peter Ryan.

REPRESENTS Nonfiction, juvenile books. **Considers these nonfiction areas:** agriculture, cooking, foods, juvenile nonfiction, young adult. **Considers these fiction areas:** comic books, juvenile, middle grade, multicultural, mystery, picture books, suspense, thriller, young adult.

Actively seeking remarkable middle grade, young adult fiction, and debut picture book author/illustrators. Also seeking fresh graphic novels for juvenile and adult readers. No institutional books.

HOW TO CONTACT Query via e-mail as per submission guidelines on website. Author/illustrators of picture books may attach text and sample art. with query. A PDF dummy is preferred. Accepts simultaneous submissions. Responds in 3 weeks to queries "we wish to pursue further;" 2 months to requested mss. While unsolicited queries are welcome, most clients come through editor, agent, client referrals.

TERMS Agent receives 15% commission on domestic sales; 20% (if subagents are employed) commission on foreign sales. Offers written contract, binding for all children's projects. 60 days notice must be given to terminate contract.

RECENT SALES *King Alice*, by Matthew Cordell; *Snakes on a Train*, by Kathryn Dennis; *Mapping Sam*, by Joyce Hesselberth; *Butterfly Yellow*, by Thanhha Lai; *Killing November*, by Adriana Mather; *Two Can Keep a Secret*, by Karen M. McManus; *Monster Street*, by J.H. Reynolds; *Death Prefers Blondes*, by Caleb Roehrig; *Through the Window*, by Barb Rosenstock and Mary GrandPre; *I Am Human*, by Susan Verde.

TIPS Agent is hands-on, no-nonsense. May request revisions. Does not line edit but may offer suggestions for improvement before submission. Well-respected by clients and editors. "A firm but reasonable deal negotiator."

STONESONG

270 W. 39th St. #201, New York NY 10018. (212)929-4600. **E-mail:** editors@stonesong.com. **E-mail:** submissions@stonesong.com. **Website:** stonesong.com. Member of AAR. Signatory of WGA.

MEMBER AGENTS Alison Fargis; Ellen Scordato; Judy Linden; Emmanuelle Morgen; Leila Campoli (business, science, technology, and self improvement); Maria Ribas (cookbooks, self-help, health, diet, home, parenting, and humor, all from authors with demonstrable platforms; she's also interested in narrative nonfiction and select memoir); Melissa Edwards (children's fiction and adult commercial fiction, as well as select pop-culture nonfiction); Alyssa Jennette (children's and adult fiction and picture books, and has dabbled in humor and pop culture nonfiction); Madelyn Burt (adult and children's fiction, as well as select historical nonfiction).

REPRESENTS Nonfiction, fiction, novels, juvenile books. **Considers these nonfiction areas:** architecture, art, biography, business, cooking, crafts, creative nonfiction, cultural interests, current affairs, dance, decorating, diet/nutrition, design, economics, foods, gay/lesbian, health, history, hobbies, how-to, humor, interior design, investigative, literature, memoirs, money, music, New Age, parenting, photography, popular culture, politics, psychology, science, self-help, sociology, spirituality, sports, technology, women's issues, young adult. **Considers these fiction areas:** action, adventure, commercial, confession, contemporary issues, ethnic, experimental, family saga, fantasy, feminist, gay, historical, horror, humor, juvenile, lesbian, literary, mainstream, middle grade, military, multicultural, mystery, new adult, New Age, occult, paranormal, regional, romance, satire, science fiction, supernatural, suspense, thriller, urban fantasy, women's, young adult.

Does not represent plays, screenplays, picture books, or poetry.

HOW TO CONTACT Accepts electronic queries for fiction and nonfiction. Submit query addressed to a specific agent. Include first chapter or first 10 pages of ms. Accepts simultaneous submissions.

RECENT SALES *Sweet Laurel*, by Laurel Gallucci and Claire Thomas; *Terrain: A Seasonal Guide to Nature at Home*, by Terrain; *The Prince's Bane*, by Alexandra Christo; *Deep Listening*, by Jillian Pransky; *Change Resilience*, by Lior Arussy; *A Thousand Words*, by Brigit Young.

ROBIN STRAUS AGENCY, INC.

The Wallace Literary Agency, 229 E. 79th St., Suite 5A, New York NY 10075. (212)472-3282. **Fax:** (212)472-3833. **E-mail:** info@robinstrausagency.com. **Website:** www.robinstrausagency.com. **Contact:** Ms. Robin Straus. Estab. 1983. Member of AAR.

Prior to becoming an agent, Robin Straus served as a subsidiary rights manager at Random House and Doubleday. She began her career in the editorial department of Little, Brown.

REPRESENTS **Considers these nonfiction areas:** biography, cooking, creative nonfiction, current affairs, environment, foods, gay/lesbian, health, history, memoirs, multicultural, music, parenting, popular culture, politics, psychology, science, travel, women's issues, mainstream science. **Considers these fiction areas:** commercial, contemporary issues, fantasy, feminist, literary, mainstream, science fiction, translation, women's.

Does not represent juvenile, young adult, horror, romance, Westerns, poetry, or screenplays.

HOW TO CONTACT E-query only. No physical mail accepted. See our website for full submission instructions. Email us a query letter with contact information, an autobiographical summary, a brief synopsis or description of your book project, submission history, and information on competition. If you wish, you may also include the opening chapter of your manuscript (pasted). While we do our best to reply to all queries, you can assume that if you haven't heard from us after six weeks, we are not interested. Accepts simultaneous submissions.

TERMS Agent receives 15% commission on domestic sales; 20% commission on foreign sales. Offers written contract.

THE STRINGER LITERARY AGENCY LLC

P.O. Box 111255, Naples FL 34108. **E-mail:** mstringer@stringerlit.com. **Website:** www.stringerlit.com. **Contact:** Marlene Stringer. Estab. 2008. Member of AAR. RWA, MWA, ITW, SBCWI, The Writers Guild Represents 50 +/- clients.

REPRESENTS Fiction, novels. **Considers these fiction areas:** commercial, crime, detective, fantasy, historical, horror, mainstream, multicultural, mystery, new adult, paranormal, police, romance, science fiction, suspense, thriller, urban fantasy, women's, young adult, No space opera SF.

This agency specializes in fiction. "We are an editorial agency, and work with clients to make their manuscripts the best they can be in preparation for submission. We focus on career planning, and help our clients reach their publishing goals. We advise clients on marketing and promotional strategies to help them reach their target readership. Because we are so hands-on, we limit the size of our list; however, we are always looking for exceptional voices and stories that demand we read to the end. You never know where the next great story is coming from." This agency is seeking thrillers, crime fiction (not true crime), mystery, women's fiction, single title and category romance, fantasy (all subgenera), grounded science fiction (no space opera, aliens, etc.), and YA/teen. Does not want to receive picture books, MG, plays, short stories, or poetry. This is not the agency for inspirational romance or erotica. No space opera. The agency is not seeking nonfiction as of this time.

HOW TO CONTACT Electronic submissions through website only. Please make sure your ms is as good as it can be before you submit. Agents are not first readers. For specific information on what we like to see in query letters, refer to the information at www.stringerlit.com. Accepts simultaneous submissions. "We strive to respond quickly, but current clients' work always comes first." Obtains new clients through referrals, submissions, conferences.

TERMS Standard commission. "We do not charge fees."

RECENT SALES *Don't Believe It by Charlie Donlea; The Waiting Room*, by Emily Bleeker; *The Numina Trilogy*, by Charlie N. Holmberg; *Belle Chasse*, by Suzanne Johnson; *The Evermore Chronicles by Emily R. King; Wilds of the Bayou*, by Susannah Sandlin; Death In The Family by Tessa Wegert; *The Vine Witch by Luanne Smith; The Scottish Trilogy*, by Anna Bradley; *Fly By Night*, by Andrea Thalasinos; The Dragonsworn Series, by Caitlyn McFarland; *The Devious Dr. Jekyll*, by Viola Carr; *The Dragon's Price*, by Bethany Wiggins; The Hundredth Queen Series by Emily R. King; Film Rights to *The Paper Magician*, by Charlie N. Holmberg.

WRITERS CONFERENCES Various conferences each year.

TIPS "If your ms falls between categories, or you are not sure of the category, query and we'll let you know if we'd like to take a look. We strive to respond as quickly as possible. If you have not received a response in the time period indicated on website, please re-query."

THE STROTHMAN AGENCY, LLC

63 E. 9th St., 10X, New York NY 10003. **E-mail:** info@strothmanagency.com. **E-mail:** strothmanagency@gmail.com. **Website:** www.strothmanagency.com. **Contact:** Wendy Strothman, Lauren MacLeod. Estab. 2003. Member of AAR. Represents 100+ clients.

Prior to becoming an agent, Ms. Strothman was head of Beacon Press (1983-1995) and executive vice president of Houghton Mifflin's Trade & Reference Division (1996-2002).

MEMBER AGENTS Wendy Strothman (history, narrative nonfiction, narrative journalism, science and nature, and current affairs); Lauren MacLeod (young adult fiction and nonfiction, middle grade novels, as well as adult narrative nonfiction, particularly food writing, science, pop culture and history).

REPRESENTS Nonfiction, juvenile books. **Considers these nonfiction areas:** anthropology, archeology, business, cooking, cultural interests, current affairs, economics, environment, foods, government, history, investigative, juvenile nonfiction, language, law, literature, popular culture, politics, science, sociology, true crime, war, women's issues, women's studies, young adult. **Considers these fiction areas:** middle grade, young adult.

Specializes in history, science, biography, politics, narrative journalism, nature and the environment, current affairs, narrative nonfiction, business and economics, young adult fiction and nonfiction, and middle grade fiction and nonfiction. "The Strothman Agency seeks out scholars, journalists, and other acknowledged and emerging experts in their fields. We specialize in history, science, narrative journalism, nature and the environment, current affairs, narrative nonfiction, business and economics, young adult fiction and nonfiction, middle grade fiction and nonfiction. We are not signing up projects in romance, science fiction, picture books, or poetry."

HOW TO CONTACT Accepts queries only via e-mail. See submission guidelines online. Accepts simultaneous submissions. "All e-mails received will be responded to with an auto-reply. If we have not replied to your query within 6 weeks, we do not feel that it is right for us." Accepts simultaneous submissions. Obtains most new clients through recommendations from others.

TERMS Agent receives 15% commission on domestic sales; 20% commission on foreign sales. Offers written contract; 30-day notice must be given to terminate contract.

EMMA SWEENEY AGENCY, LLC

245 E 80th St., Suite 7E, New York NY 10075. **E-mail:** info@emmasweeneyagency.com. **E-mail:** queries@emmasweeneyagency.com. **Website:** www.emmasweeneyagency.com. Estab. 2006. Member of AAR. Other memberships include Women's Media Group. Represents 80 clients.

Prior to becoming an agent, Ms. Sweeney was director of subsidiary rights at Grove Press. Since 1990, she has been a literary agent. Ms. Sutherland Brown was an Associate Editor at St. Martin's Press/Thomas Dunne Books and a freelance editor. Ms. Watson attended Hunter College where she earned a BA in English (with a focus on Creative Writing) and a BA in Russian Language & Culture.

MEMBER AGENTS Emma Sweeney, president; Margaret Sutherland Brown (commercial and literary fiction, mysteries and thrillers, narrative nonfiction, lifestyle, and cookbook); Hannah Brattesani (poetry, and literary fiction).

REPRESENTS Nonfiction, fiction, novels, poetry books. **Considers these nonfiction areas:** biography, cooking, creative nonfiction, cultural interests, decorating, diet/nutrition, design, environment, foods, gardening, history, how-to, interior design, literature, memoirs, popular culture, psychology, religious, science, self-help, sex, sociology. **Considers these fiction areas:** commercial, contemporary issues, crime, historical, horror, literary, mainstream, mystery, poetry, spiritual, suspense, thriller, women's.

Does not want erotica.

HOW TO CONTACT "We accept only electronic queries, and ask that all queries be sent to queries@emmasweeneyagency.com rather than to any agent directly. Please begin your query with a succinct (and hopefully catchy) description of your plot or proposal. Always include a brief cover letter telling us how you heard about ESA, your previous writing credits, and a few lines about yourself. We cannot open any attachments unless specifically requested, and ask that you paste the first 10 pages of your proposal or novel into the text of your e-mail." Accepts simultaneous submissions.

TESSLER LITERARY AGENCY, LLC

27 W. 20th St., Suite 1003, New York NY 10011. (212)242-0466. **Website:** www.tessleragency.com. **Contact:** Michelle Tessler. Estab. 2004. Member of AAR. Women's Media Group.

Prior to forming her own agency, Ms. Tessler worked at the prestigious literary agency Carlisle & Company (now Inkwell Management) and at the William Morris Agency.

REPRESENTS Nonfiction, fiction, novels. **Considers these nonfiction areas:** animals, autobiography, biography, business, cooking, creative nonfiction, cultural interests, current affairs, diet/nutrition, economics, education, environment, ethnic, foods, gardening, health, history, how-to, humor, investigative, literature, medicine, memoirs, military, money, multicultural, parenting, philosophy, photography, popular culture, psychology, religious, science, self-help, spirituality, technology, travel, women's issues, women's studies. **Considers these fiction areas:** commercial, ethnic, family saga, historical, literary, multicultural, women's.

"Tessler Literary Agency represents a select number of best-selling and emerging authors. Based in the Flatiron District in Manhattan, we are dedicated to writers of high quality fiction and nonfiction. Our clients include accomplished journalists, scientists, academics, experts in their field, as well as novelists and debut authors with unique voices and stories to tell. We value fresh, original writing that has a compelling point of view. Our list is diverse and far-reaching. In nonfiction, it includes narrative, popular science, memoir, history, psychology, business, biography, food, and travel. In many cases, we sign authors who are especially adept at writing books that cross many of these categories at once. In fiction, we represent literary, women's, and commercial. If your project is in keeping with the kind of books we take on, we want to hear from you." Does not want genre fiction or children's books or anthologies.

HOW TO CONTACT Submit query through online query form only. Accepts simultaneous submissions. New clients by queries/submissions through the website and recommendations from others.

TERMS Receives 15% commission on domestic sales; 20% on foreign sales. Offers written contract.

THOMPSON LITERARY AGENCY

115 W. 29th St., Third Floor, New York NY 10001. (716)257-8149. **E-mail:** submissions@thompsonliterary.com. **Website:** thompsonliterary.com. **Contact:** Meg Thompson, founder. Estab. 2014. Member of AAR. Signatory of WGA.

Before her current position, Ms. Thompson was with LJK Literary and the Einstein Thompson Agency.

MEMBER AGENTS Cindy Uh, senior agent; Kiele Raymond, senior agent; Ashley Collom, Senior Agent; John Thorn, affiliate agent; Sandy Hodgman, director of foreign rights.

REPRESENTS Nonfiction, fiction, novels, juvenile books. **Considers these nonfiction areas:** autobiography, biography, business, cooking, crafts, creative nonfiction, current affairs, diet/nutrition, design, education, foods, health, history, how-to, humor, inspirational, interior design, juvenile nonfiction, memoirs, multicultural, popular culture, politics, science, self-help, sociology, sports, travel, women's issues, women's studies, young adult. **Considers these fiction areas:** commercial, contemporary issues, experimental, fantasy, feminist, historical, juvenile, literary, middle grade, multicultural, picture books, women's, young adult.

The agency is always on the lookout for both commercial and literary fiction, as well as young adult and children's books. "Nonfiction, however, is our specialty, and our interests include biography, memoir, music, popular science, politics, blog-to-book projects, cookbooks, sports, health and wellness, fashion, art, and popular culture." "Please note that we do not accept submissions for poetry collections or screenplays, and we only consider picture books by established illustrators."

HOW TO CONTACT "For fiction: Please send a query letter, including any salient biographical information or previous publications, and attach the first 25 pages of your manuscript. For nonfiction: Please send a query letter and a full proposal, including biographical information, previous publications, credentials that qualify you to write your book, marketing information, and sample material. You should address your query to whichever agent you think is best suited for your project." Accepts simultaneous submissions. Responds in 6 weeks if interested.

THREE SEAS LITERARY AGENCY

P.O. Box 444, Sun Prairie WI 53590. (608)834-9317. **E-mail:** threeseaslit@aol.com. **E-mail:** queries@threeseaslit.com. **Website:** threeseasagency.com. **Contact:** Michelle Grajkowski, Cori Deyoe. Estab. 2000. Member of AAR. Other memberships include RWA (Romance Writers of America), SCBWI Represents 55 clients.

Since its inception, 3 Seas has sold more than 500 titles worldwide. Ms. Grajkowski's authors have appeared on all the major lists including *The New York Times*, *USA Today* and *Publishers Weekly*. Prior to joining the agency in 2006, Ms. Deyoe was a multi-published author. She represents a wide range of authors and has sold many projects at auction.

MEMBER AGENTS Michelle Grajkowski (romance, women's fiction, young adult and middle grade fiction, select nonfiction projects); Cori Deyoe (all sub-genres of romance, women's fiction, young adult, middle grade, picture books, thrillers, mysteries and select nonfiction); Linda Scalissi (women's fiction, thrillers, young adult, mysteries and romance).

REPRESENTS Nonfiction, novels. **Considers these fiction areas:** middle grade, mystery, picture books, romance, thriller, women's, young adult.

"We represent more than 50 authors who write romance, women's fiction, science fiction/fantasy, thrillers, young adult and middle grade fiction, as well as select nonfiction titles. Currently, we are looking for fantastic authors with a voice of their own." 3 Seas does not represent poetry or screenplays.

HOW TO CONTACT E-mail queries only; no attachments, unless requested by agents. For fiction, please e-mail the first chapter and synopsis along with a cover letter. Also, be sure to include the genre and the number of words in your manuscript, as well as pertinent writing experience in your query letter.

For nonfiction, e-mail a complete proposal, including a query letter and your first chapter. For picture books, query with complete text. Accepts simultaneous submissions. Obtains most new clients through recommendations from others, conferences.

TERMS Agent receives 15% commission on domestic sales; 20% commission on foreign sales. Offers written contract.

RECENT SALES Bestselling authors, including Jennifer Brown, Katie MacAlister, Kerrelyn Sparks, and C.L. Wilson.

TRIADA US

P.O. Box 561, Sewickley PA 15143. (412)401-3376. **E-mail:** uwe@triadaus.com; brent@triadaus.com; laura@triadaus.com; lauren@triadaus.com; amelia@triadaus.com. **Website:** www.triadaus.com. **Contact:** Dr. Uwe Stender, President. Estab. 2004. Member of AAR.

MEMBER AGENTS Uwe Stender; Brent Taylor; Laura Crockett; Lauren Spieller; Amelia Appel.

REPRESENTS Nonfiction, fiction, novels, juvenile books. **Considers these nonfiction areas:** biography, business, cooking, crafts, creative nonfiction, cultural interests, current affairs, diet/nutrition, economics, education, environment, ethnic, foods, gardening, health, history, how-to, juvenile nonfiction, literature, memoirs, music, parenting, popular culture, politics, science, self-help, sports, true crime, women's issues, young adult. **Considers these fiction areas:** action, adventure, comic books, commercial, contemporary issues, crime, detective, ethnic, family saga, fantasy, feminist, gay, historical, horror, juvenile, lesbian, literary, mainstream, middle grade, multicultural, mystery, occult, picture books, police, suspense, thriller, urban fantasy, women's, young adult.

Actively seeking fiction and non-fiction across a broad range of categories of all age levels.

HOW TO CONTACT E-mail queries preferred. Please paste your query letter and the first 10 pages of your ms into the body of a message e-mailed to the agent of your choice. Do not simultaneously query multiple Triada agents. Please query one and wait for their response before moving onto another agent within our agency. Triada US agents personally respond to all queries and requested material and pride themselves on having some of the fastest response times in the industry. Obtains most new clients through submission inbox (query letters and requested mss), client referrals, and conferences.

TERMS Triada US retains 15% commission on domestic sales and 20% commission on foreign and translation sales. Offers written contract; 30-day notice must be given prior to termination.

RECENT SALES *Playing Back the 80s* by Jim Beviglia (Rowman & Littlefield), *Game of Stars* by Sayantani DasGupta (Scholastic), *The Voice in My Head* by Dana Davis (Inkyard), *The Sound of Stars* by Alechia Dow (Inkyard), *Fake Blood* by Whitney Gardner (Simon & Schuster), *Maiden & Princess* by Daniel Haack and Isabel Galupo (Little Bee), *Bear No Malice* by Clarissa Harwood (Pegasus), *The Last Chance Dance* by Kate Hattemer (Knopf), *Hunting Annabelle* by Wendy Heard (Mira), *Beside Herself* by Elizabeth LaBan (Lake Union), *Don't Date Rosa Santos* by Nina Moreno (Disney-Hyperion), *Don't Call the Wolf* by Aleksandra Ross (HarperTeen), *Empire of Sand* by Tasha Suri (Orbit), *Ghost Wood Song* by Erica Waters (HarperTeen), *The Light Between Worlds* by Laura Weymouth (HarperTeen), *Going Off-Script* by Jen Wilde (Swoon Reads).

TRIDENT MEDIA GROUP

41 Madison Ave., 36th Floor, New York NY 10010. (212)333-1511. **E-mail:** info@tridentmediagroup.com. **Website:** www.tridentmediagroup.com. **Contact:** Ellen Levine. Member of AAR.

MEMBER AGENTS Kimberly Whalen, ws.assistant@tridentmediagroup (commercial fiction and nonfiction, including women's fiction, romance, suspense, paranormal, and pop culture); Alyssa Eisner Henkin (picture books through young adult fiction, including mysteries, period pieces, contemporary school-settings, issues of social justice, family sagas, eerie magical realism, and retellings of classics; children's/YA nonfiction: history, STEM/STEAM themes, memoir) Scott Miller, smiller@tridentmediagroup.com (commercial fiction, including thrillers, crime fiction, women's, book club fiction, middle grade, young adult; nonfiction, including military, celebrity and pop culture, narrative, sports, prescriptive, and current events); Melissa Flashman, mflashman@tridentmediagroup.com (nonfiction: pop culture, memoir, wellness, popular science, business and economics, technology; fiction: adult and YA, literary and commercial); Don Fehr, dfehr@tridentmediagroup.com (literary and commercial fiction, young adult fiction, narrative nonfiction, memoirs, travel, science, and health); John Silbersack, silbersack.assistant@tridentmediagroup.com (fiction: literary fiction, crime fiction, science fiction and fantasy, children's, thrillers/suspense; nonfiction: narrative nonfiction, science, history, biography, current events, memoirs, finance, pop culture); Erica Spellman-Silverman; Ellen Levine, levine.assistant@tridentmediagroup.com (popular commercial fiction and compelling nonfiction, including memoir, popular culture, narrative nonfiction, history, politics, biography, science, and the odd quirky book); Mark Gottlieb (fiction: science fiction, fantasy, young adult, graphic novels, historical, middle grade, mystery, romance, suspense, thrillers; nonfiction: business, finance, history, religious, health, cookbooks, sports, African-American, biography, memoir, travel, mind/body/spirit, narrative nonfiction, science, technology); Alexander Slater, aslater@tridentmdiagroup.com (children's, middle grade, and young adult fiction); Amanda O'Connor, aoconnor@tridentmediagroup.com; Tara Carberry, tcarberry@tridentmediagroup.com (women's commercial fiction, romance, new adult, young adult, and select nonfiction); Alexa Stark, astark@tridentmediagroup.com (literary fiction, upmarket commercial fiction, young adult, memoir, narrative nonfiction, popular science, cultural criticism and women's issues).

REPRESENTS Considers these nonfiction areas: biography, business, cooking, creative nonfiction, current affairs, economics, health, history, memoirs, military, popular culture, politics, religious, science, sports, technology, travel, women's issues, young adult, middle grade. **Considers these fiction areas:** commercial, crime, fantasy, historical, juvenile, literary, middle grade, mystery, new adult, paranormal, picture books, romance, science fiction, suspense, thriller, women's, young adult.

Actively seeking new or established authors in a variety of fiction and nonfiction genres.

HOW TO CONTACT Submit through the agency's online submission form on the agency website. Query only one agent at a time. If you e-query, include no attachments. Accepts simultaneous submissions.

TIPS "If you have any questions, please check FAQ page before e-mailing us."

THE UNTER AGENCY

23 W. 73rd St., Suite 100, New York NY 10023. (212)401-4068. **E-mail:** jennifer@theunteragency.com. **Website:** www.theunteragency.com. **Contact:** Jennifer Unter. Estab. 2008. Member of AAR. Women Media Group

Ms. Unter began her book publishing career in the editorial department at Henry Holt & Co. She later worked at the Karpfinger Agency while she attended law school. She then became an associate at the entertainment firm of Cowan, DeBaets, Abrahams & Sheppard LLP where she practiced primarily in the areas of publishing and copyright law.

REPRESENTS Nonfiction, fiction, novels, short story collections, juvenile books. **Considers these nonfiction areas:** animals, art, autobiography, biography, cooking, creative nonfiction, current affairs, diet/nutrition, environment, foods, health, history, how-to, humor, juvenile nonfiction, law, memoirs, popular culture, politics, spirituality, sports, travel, true crime, women's issues, young adult, nature subjects. **Considers these fiction areas:** action, adventure, cartoon, commercial, family saga, inspirational, juvenile, mainstream, middle grade, mystery, paranormal, picture books, thriller, women's, young adult.

This agency specializes in children's, nonfiction, and quality fiction.

HOW TO CONTACT Send an e-query. There is also an online submission form. If you do not hear back from this agency within 3 months, consider that a no. Accepts simultaneous submissions. Responds in 3 months.

RECENT SALES A full list of recent sales/titles is available on the agency website.

UPSTART CROW LITERARY

244 Fifth Avenue, 11th Floor, New York NY 10001. **E-mail:** danielle.submission@gmail.com. **Website:** www.upstartcrowliterary.com. **Contact:** Danielle Chiotti, Alexandra Penfold. Estab. 2009. Member of AAR. Signatory of WGA.

MEMBER AGENTS Michael Stearns (not accepting submissions); Danielle Chiotti (all genres of young adult and middle grade fiction; adult upmarket commercial fiction [not considering romance, mystery/suspense/thriller, science fiction, horror, or erotica]; nonfiction in the areas of narrative/memoir, lifestyle, relationships, humor, current events, food, wine, and cooking); Ted Malawer (not accepting submissions); Alexandra Penfold (not accepting submissions); Susan Hawk (books for children and teens only).

REPRESENTS Considers these nonfiction areas: cooking, current affairs, foods, humor, memoirs.

Considers these fiction areas: commercial, mainstream, middle grade, picture books, young adult.

HOW TO CONTACT Submit a query and 20 pages pasted into an e-mail. Accepts simultaneous submissions.

VERITAS LITERARY AGENCY

601 Van Ness Ave., Opera Plaza, Suite E, San Francisco CA 94102. (415)647-6964. **Fax:** (415)647-6965. **E-mail:** submissions@veritasliterary.com. **Website:** www.veritasliterary.com. **Contact:** Katherine Boyle. Member of AAR. Other memberships include Author's Guild and SCBWI.

MEMBER AGENTS Katherine Boyle, kboyle@veritasliterary.com (literary fiction, middle grade, young adult, narrative nonfiction/memoir, historical fiction, crime/suspense, history, pop culture, popular science, business/career); Michael Carr, michael@veritasliterary.com (historical fiction, women's fiction, science fiction and fantasy, nonfiction); Chiara Rosati, literary scout.

REPRESENTS Nonfiction, novels. **Considers these nonfiction areas:** business, history, memoirs, popular culture, women's issues. **Considers these fiction areas:** commercial, crime, fantasy, historical, literary, middle grade, new adult, science fiction, suspense, women's, young adult.

HOW TO CONTACT This agency accepts short queries or proposals via e-mail only. "Fiction: Please include a cover letter listing previously published work, a one-page summary and the first 5 pages in the body of the e-mail (not as an attachment). Nonfiction: If you are sending a proposal, please include an author biography, an overview, a chapter-by-chapter summary, and an analysis of competitive titles. We do our best to review all queries within 4-6 weeks; however, if you have not heard from us in 12 weeks, consider that a no." Accepts simultaneous submissions. If you have not heard from this agency in 12 weeks, consider that a no.

WALES LITERARY AGENCY, INC.

1508 10th Ave. E. #401, Seattle WA 98102. (206)284-7114. **E-mail:** waleslit@waleslit.com. **Website:** www.waleslit.com. **Contact:** Elizabeth Wales; Neal Swain. Estab. 1990. Member of AAR. Other memberships include Authors Guild.

Prior to becoming an agent, Ms. Wales worked at Oxford University Press and Viking Penguin.

MEMBER AGENTS Elizabeth Wales; Neal Swain.

REPRESENTS Nonfiction, fiction, novels.

This agency specializes in quality mainstream fiction and narrative nonfiction. "We're looking for more narrative nonfiction writing about nature, science, and animals." Does not handle screenplays, children's picture books, genre fiction, or most category nonfiction (such as self-help or how-to books).

HOW TO CONTACT E-query with no attachments. Submission guidelines can be found at the agency website along with a list of current clients and titles. Accepts simultaneous submissions. Responds in 2 weeks to queries, 2 months to mss.

TERMS Agent receives 15% commission on domestic sales; 20% commission on foreign sales.

RECENT SALES *Half-broke*, by Ginger Gaffney (W.W. Norton); *What Your Food Ate*, by David Montgomery and Anne Bikle (W.W. Norton); *Edgar Martinez: My Life and Baseball* by Edgar Martinez and Larry Stone (Triumph Books); *Every Penguin in the World* by Charles Bergman (Sasquatch/Penguin Random).

TIPS "We are especially interested in work that espouses a progressive cultural or political view, projects a new voice, or simply shares an important, compelling story. We also encourage writers living in the Pacific Northwest, West Coast, Alaska, and Pacific Rim countries, and writers from historically underrepresented groups, such as gay and lesbian writers and writers of color, to submit work (but does not discourage writers outside these areas). Most importantly, whether in fiction or nonfiction, the agency is looking for talented storytellers."

WELLS ARMS LITERARY

In association with HSG Agency, New York NY **Website:** www.wellsarms.com. Estab. 2013. Member of AAR. SCBWI, Society of Illustrators. Represents 25 clients.

Victoria's career began as an editor at Dial Books for Young Readers, then G. P. Putnam's Sons and then as the founding editorial director and Associate Publisher of Bloomsbury USA's Children's Division. She opened the agency in 2013.

REPRESENTS Nonfiction, fiction, novels, juvenile books.children's book illustrators. **Considers these nonfiction areas:** juvenile nonfiction, young adult. **Considers these fiction areas:** juvenile, middle grade, new adult, picture books, young adult.

"We focus on books for young readers of all ages: board books, picture books, readers, chapter books, middle grade, and young adult fiction." Actively seeking middle grade, young adult, magical realism, contemporary, romance, fantasy. "We do not represent to the textbook, magazine, adult romance or fine art markets."

HOW TO CONTACT Wells Arms Literary is currently closed to queries or submissions "unless you've met me at a conference." Accepts simultaneous submissions. "We try to respond in a month's time." If no response, assume it's a no.

WERNICK & PRATT AGENCY

E-mail: submissions@wernickpratt.com. **Website:** www.wernickpratt.com. **Contact:** Marcia Wernick; Linda Pratt; Emily Mitchell. Member of AAR. Signatory of WGA. SCBWI

Prior to co-founding Wernick & Pratt Agency, Ms. Wernick worked at the Sheldon Fogelman Agency, in subsidiary rights, advancing to director of subsidiary rights; Ms. Pratt also worked at the Sheldon Fogelman Agency. Emily Mitchell began her publishing career at Sheldon Fogelman Agency and then spent eleven years as an editor at Charlesbridge Publishing.

MEMBER AGENTS Marcia Wernick, Linda Pratt, Emily Mitchell.

REPRESENTS Juvenile books. **Considers these fiction areas:** middle grade, young adult.

"Wernick & Pratt Agency specializes in children's books of all genres, from picture books through young adult literature and everything in between. We represent both authors and illustrators. We do not represent authors of adult books." Wants people who both write and illustrate in the picture book genre; humorous young chapter books with strong voice, and which are unique and compelling; middle grade/YA novels, both literary and commercial. No picture book mss of more than 750 words, or mood pieces; work specifically targeted to the educational market; fiction about the American Revolution, Civil War, or World War II unless it is told from a very unique perspective.

HOW TO CONTACT Submit via e-mail only to submissions@wernickpratt.com. "Please indicate to which agent you are submitting." Detailed submission guidelines available on website. "Submissions will only be responded to further if we are interested in them. If you do not hear from us within 6 weeks of your submission, it should be considered declined." Accepts simultaneous submissions. Responds in 6 weeks.

WOLFSON LITERARY AGENCY

P.O. Box 266, New York NY 10276. **E-mail:** query@wolfsonliterary.com. **Website:** www.wolfsonliterary.com. **Contact:** Michelle Wolfson. Estab. 2007. Adheres to AAR canon of ethics.

Prior to forming her own agency in December 2007, Ms. Wolfson spent 2 years with Artists & Artisans, Inc. and 2 years with Ralph Vicinanza, Ltd.

REPRESENTS Nonfiction, fiction. **Considers these fiction areas:** commercial, mainstream, new adult, romance, thriller, women's, young adult.

Actively seeking commercial fiction: young adult, mainstream, women's fiction, romance. "I am not taking on new nonfiction clients at this time."

HOW TO CONTACT E-queries only. Accepts simultaneous submissions. Responds only if interested. Positive response is generally given within 2-4 weeks. Responds in 3 months to mss. Obtains most new clients through queries or recommendations from others.

TERMS Agent receives 15% commission on domestic sales; 25% commission on foreign sales. Offers written contract; 30-day notice must be given to terminate contract.

TIPS "Be persistent."

WRITERS HOUSE

21 W. 26th St., New York NY 10010. (212)685-2400. **Fax:** (212)685-1781. **Website:** www.writershouse.com. Estab. 1973. Member of AAR.

MEMBER AGENTS Amy Berkower; Stephen Barr; Susan Cohen; Dan Conaway; Lisa DiMona; Susan Ginsburg; Susan Golomb; Merrilee Heifetz; Brianne Johnson; Daniel Lazar; Simon Lipskar; Steven Malk; Jodi Reamer, Esq.; Robin Rue; Rebecca Sherman; Geri Thoma; Albert Zuckerman; Alec Shane; Stacy Testa; Victoria Doherty-Munro; Beth Miller; Andrea Morrison; Soumeya Roberts.

REPRESENTS Nonfiction, novels. **Considers these nonfiction areas:** biography, business, cooking, economics, history, how-to, juvenile nonfiction, memoirs, parenting, psychology, science, self-help. **Considers these fiction areas:** commercial, fantasy, juvenile, literary, mainstream, middle grade, picture books, science fiction, women's, young adult.

This agency specializes in all types of popular fiction and nonfiction, for both adult and juvenile books as well as illustrators. Does not want to receive scholarly, professional, poetry, plays, or screenplays.

HOW TO CONTACT Individual agent email addresses are available on the website. "Please e-mail us a query letter, which includes your credentials, an explanation of what makes your book unique and special, and a synopsis. Some agents within our agency have different requirements. Please consult their individual Publisher's Marketplace (PM) profile for details. We respond to all queries, generally within six to eight weeks." If you prefer to submit my mail, address it to an individual agent, and please include SASE for our reply. (If submitting to Steven Malk: Writers House, 7660 Fay Ave., #338H, La Jolla, CA 92037.) Accepts simultaneous submissions. "We respond to all queries, generally within 6-8 weeks." Obtains most new clients through recommendations from authors and editors.

TERMS Agent receives 15% commission on domestic sales. Agent receives 20% commission on foreign sales. Offers written contract, binding for 1 year. Agency charges fees for copying mss/proposals and overseas airmail of books.

TIPS "Do not send mss. Write a compelling letter. If you do, we'll ask to see your work. Follow submission guidelines and please do not simultaneously submit your work to more than one Writers House agent."

JASON YARN LITERARY AGENCY

3544 Broadway, No. 68, New York NY 10031. **E-mail:** jason@jasonyarnliteraryagency.com. **Website:** www.jasonyarnliteraryagency.com. Member of AAR. Signatory of WGA.

REPRESENTS Nonfiction, fiction. **Considers these nonfiction areas:** creative nonfiction, current affairs, foods, history, science. **Considers these fiction areas:** commercial, fantasy, literary, middle grade, science fiction, suspense, thriller, young adult, graphic novels, comics.

HOW TO CONTACT Please e-mail your query to jason@jasonyarnliteraryagency.com with the word "Query" in the subject line, and please paste the first 10 pages of your manuscript or proposal into the text of your e-mail. Do not send any attachments. "Visit the About page for information on what we are interested in, and please note that JYLA does not accept queries for film, TV, or stage scripts." Accepts simultaneous submissions.

BOOK PUBLISHERS

The markets in this year's Book Publishers section offer opportunities in nearly every area of publishing. There are large, commercial houses and medium-sized presses. Smaller publishers can be found on WritersMarket.com.

The Book Publishers Subject Index is the best place to start your search. You'll find it in the back of the book, before the General Index. Subject areas for both fiction and nonfiction are broken out for all of the book publisher listings.

When you have compiled a list of publishers interested in books in your subject area, read the detailed listings. Pare down your list by cross-referencing two or three subject areas and eliminating the listings only marginally suited to your book. When you have a good list, send for those publishers' catalogs and manuscript guidelines, or check publishers' websites, which often contain catalog listings, manuscript preparation guidelines, current contact names, and other information helpful to prospective authors. You want to use this information to make sure your book idea is in line with a publisher's list but is not a duplicate of something already published.

You should also visit bookstores and libraries to see if the publisher's books are well represented. When you find a couple of books the house has published that are similar to yours, write or call the company to find out who edited those books. This extra bit of research could be the key to getting your proposal to precisely the right editor.

Publishers prefer different methods of submission on first contact. Most like to see a one-page query, especially for nonfiction. Others will accept a brief proposal package that might include an outline and/or a sample chapter. Some publishers will accept submissions from agents only. Each listing in the Book Publishers section includes specific submission methods, if provided by the publisher. Make sure you read each listing carefully to find out exactly what the publisher wants to receive.

When you write your one-page query, give an overview of your book, mention the intended audience, the competition for your book (check local bookstore shelves), and what sets your book apart from the competition. You should also include any previous publishing experience or special training relevant to the subject of your book. For more on queries, read "Query Letter Clinic."

Personalize your query by addressing the editor individually and mentioning what you know about the company from its catalog or books. Under the heading **Contact**, we list the names of editors who acquire new books for each company, along with the editors' specific areas of expertise. Try your best to send your query to the appropriate editor. Editors move around all the time, so it's in your best interest to look online or call the publishing house to make sure the editor you are addressing your query to is still employed by that publisher.

Author-subsidy publishers' not included

Writer's Market is a reference tool to help you sell your writing, and we encourage you to work with publishers that pay a royalty. Subsidy publishing involves paying money to a publishing house to publish a book. The source of the money could be a government, foundation or university grant, or it could be the author of the book. If one of the publishers listed in this book offers you an author-subsidy arrangement (sometimes called "cooperative publishing," "co-publishing," or "joint venture"); or asks you to pay for part or all of the cost of any aspect of publishing (editing services, manuscript critiques, printing, advertising, etc.); or asks you to guarantee the purchase of any number of the books yourself, we would like you to inform us of that company's practices immediately.

⊘ ABBEVILLE FAMILY

Abbeville Press, 116 W. 23rd St., New York NY 10011. (646)375-2136. **Fax:** (646)375-2359. **E-mail:** abbeville@abbeville.com. **Website:** www.abbeville.com. Estab. 1977. Our list is full for the next several seasons. *Not accepting unsolicited book proposals at this time.* **Publishes 8 titles/year. 10% of books from first-time authors.** Accepts simultaneous submissions.

FICTION Picture books: animal, anthology, concept, contemporary, fantasy, folktales, health, hi-lo, history, humor, multicultural, nature/environment, poetry, science fiction, special needs, sports, suspense. Average word length 300-1,000 words. Please refer to website for submission policy.

⊘ ABBEVILLE PRESS

655 3rd Avenue, Suite 2520, New York NY 10017. (646)375-5585. **Fax:** (646)375-2359. **E-mail:** abbeville@abbeville.com. **Website:** www.abbeville.com. Email: claroya@abbeville.com Estab. 1977. Mainstay in the art book publishing world. "Our list is full for the next several seasons." **10% of books from first-time authors.** Accepts simultaneous submissions.

NONFICTION Subjects include art. Not accepting unsolicited book proposals at this time.

FICTION Subjects include adventure. Picture books through imprint Abbeville Family. Not accepting unsolicited book proposals at this time.

ABC-CLIO/GREENWOOD

Acquisitions Department, P.O. Box 1911, Santa Barbara CA 93116. (805)968-1911. **E-mail:** acquisition_inquiries@abc-clio.com. **Website:** www.abc-clio.com. Estab. 1955. ABC-CLIO is an award-winning publisher of reference titles, academic and general interest books, electronic resources, and books for librarians and other professionals. **Publishes 600 titles/year. 20% of books from first-time authors. 90% from unagented writers. Pays variable royalty on net price.** Accepts simultaneous submissions. Catalog and guidelines online.

IMPRINTS ABC-CLIO; Greenwood Press; Praeger; Linworth and Libraries Unlimited.

NONFICTION Subjects include business, child guidance, education, government, history, humanities, language, music, psychology, religion, social sciences, sociology, sports. No memoirs, drama. Query with proposal package, including scope, organization, length of project, whether a complete ms is available or when it will be, CV, and SASE. Check guidelines online for each imprint.

TIPS "Looking for reference materials and materials for educated general readers. Many of our authors are college professors who have distinguished credentials and who have published research widely in their fields."

ABDO PUBLISHING CO.

8000 W. 78th St., Suite 310, Edina MN 55439. (800)800-1312. **Fax:** (952)831-1632. **E-mail:** nonfiction@abdopublishing.com. **E-mail:** fiction@abdopublishing.com; illustrations@abdopublishing.com. **Website:** www.abdopublishing.com. Estab. 1985. Publishes hardcover originals. ABDO publishes nonfiction children's books (pre-kindergarten to 8th grade) for school and public libraries—mainly history, sports, biography, geography, science, and social studies. "Please specify each submission as either nonfiction, fiction, or illustration. **Publishes 300 titles/year.** Accepts simultaneous submissions. Guidelines online.

NONFICTION Subjects include animals, history, science, sports, geography, social studies.

ABINGDON PRESS

Imprint of The United Methodist Publishing House, 201 Eighth Ave. S., P.O. Box 801, Nashville TN 37202. (615)749-6000. **Fax:** (615)749-6512. **E-mail:** submissions@umpublishing.org. **Website:** www.abingdonpress.com. Estab. 1789. Publishes hardcover and paperback originals. Abingdon Press, America's oldest theological publisher, provides an ecumenical publishing program dedicated to serving the Christian community—clergy, scholars, church leaders, musicians, and general readers—with quality resources in the areas of Bible study, the practice of ministry, theology, devotion, spirituality, inspiration, prayer, music and worship, reference, Christian education, and church supplies. **Publishes 120 titles/year. 3,000 queries; 250 mss received/year. 85% from unagented writers. Pays 7½% royalty on retail price.** Publishes ms 2 years after acceptance. Responds in 2 months to queries. Book catalog available free. Guidelines online.

NONFICTION Subjects include education, religion, theology. Query with outline and samples only. The author should retain a copy of any unsolicited material submitted.

FICTION Publishes stories of faith, hope, and love that encourage readers to explore life. Agented submissions only for fiction.

ABRAMS

115 W. 18th St., 6th Floor, New York NY 10011. (212)206-7715. **Fax:** (212)519-1210. **E-mail:** abrams@abramsbooks.com. **Website:** www.abramsbooks.com. **Contact:** Managing Editor. Estab. 1951. Publishes hardcover and a few paperback originals. **Publishes 250 titles/year.** Accepts simultaneous submissions.

IMPRINTS Stewart, Tabori & Chang: Abrams Appleseed; Abrams Books for Young Readers; Abrams Image; STC Craft; Amulet Books.

Does not accept unsolicited materials.

NONFICTION Subjects include recreation.

FICTION Subjects include young adult. Publishes hardcover and "a few" paperback originals. Averages 150 total titles/year.

TIPS "We are one of the few publishers who publish almost exclusively illustrated books. We consider ourselves the leading publishers of art books and high-quality artwork in the U.S. Once the author has signed a contract to write a book for our firm the author must finish the manuscript to agreed-upon high standards within the schedule agreed upon in the contract."

ABRAMS BOOKS FOR YOUNG READERS

195 Broadway, 9th floor, New York NY 10007. **Website:** www.abramsyoungreaders.com. Accepts simultaneous submissions.

Abrams no longer accepts unsolicted mss or queries.

ACADEMY CHICAGO PUBLISHERS

814 N. Franklin St., Chicago IL 60610. (312)337-0747. **Fax:** (312)337-5985. **Website:** www.chicagoreviewpress.com. **Contact:** Yuval Taylor, senior editor. Estab. 1975. Publishes hardcover and some paperback originals and trade paperback reprints. "We publish quality fiction and nonfiction. Our audience is literate and discriminating. No novelized biography, history, or science fiction. No electronic submissions." **Publishes 10 titles/year. Pays 7-10% royalty on wholesale price.** Publishes ms 18 months after acceptance. Accepts simultaneous submissions. Responds in 3 months. Book catalog online. Guidelines online.

NONFICTION Subjects include history, travel. No religion, cookbooks, or self-help. Submit proposal package, outline, bio, 3 sample chapters.

FICTION Subjects include historical, mystery. "We look for quality work, but we do not publish experimental, avant garde, horror, science fiction, thrillers novels." Submit proposal package, synopsis, 3 sample chapters, and short bio.

TIPS "At the moment, we are looking for good nonfiction; we certainly want excellent original fiction, but we are swamped. No fax queries, no disks. No electronic submissions. We are always interested in reprinting good out-of-print books."

ACE SCIENCE FICTION AND FANTASY

Imprint of the Berkley Publishing Group, Penguin Random House LLC., 1745 Broadway, New York NY 10019. (212)366-2000. **Website:** www.penguinrandomhouse.com. Estab. 1953. Publishes hardcover, paperback, and trade paperback originals and reprints. Ace publishes science fiction and fantasy exclusively. **Publishes 75 titles/year. Pays royalty. Pays advance.**

As imprint of Penguin, Ace is not open to unsolicited submissions.

FICTION Subjects include fantasy, science fiction. No other genre accepted. No short stories. Due to the high volume of manuscripts received, most Penguin Group (USA) Inc. imprints do not normally accept unsolicited mss.

ACTA PUBLICATIONS

4848 N. Clark St., Chicago IL 60640. **Website:** www.actapublications.com. **Contact:** Acquisitions Editor. Estab. 1958. Publishes trade paperback originals. ACTA publishes nonacademic, practical books aimed at the mainline religious market. **Publishes 12 titles/year. 100 queries received/year. 25 mss received/year. 50% of books from first-time authors. 90% from unagented writers. Pays 10-12% royalty on wholesale price.** Publishes book 1 year after acceptance of ms. Responds in 2-3 months to proposals. Book catalog and guidelines online.

"While some of ACTA's material is specifically Catholic in nature, most of the company's products are aimed at a broadly ecumenical audience."

NONFICTION Subjects include religion, spirituality. True Submit outline, 1 sample chapter. No e-mail submissions. Reviews artwork/photos. Send photocopies.

RECENT TITLE(S) *The Geography of God's Mercy*, by Patrick Hannon (spirituality/stories); *Portraits of Grace*, by James Stephen Behrens (spirituality/photography); *God's Word is Alive*, by Alice Camille (lectionary).

TIPS "Don't send a submission unless you have examined our catalog, website and several of our books."

ADAMS MEDIA

Division of Simon & Schuster, Inc., 57 Littlefield St., Avon MA 02322. (508)427-7100. **Fax:** (800)872-5628. **Website:** www.adamsmedia.com. **Contact:** Acquisitions Editor. Estab. 1980. Publishes hardcover originals, trade paperback, e-book originals, and reprints. Adams Media publishes commercial nonfiction, including self-help, women's issues, pop psychology, relationships, business, careers, pets, parenting, New Age, gift books, cookbooks, how-to, reference, and humor. Does not return unsolicited materials. **Publishes more than 250 titles/year. 5,000 queries received/year. 1,500 mss received/year. 40% of books from first-time authors. Pays standard royalty or makes outright purchase. Pays variable advance.** Publishes book 12-18 months after acceptance. Accepts simultaneous submissions. Responds in 3 months to queries. Guidelines online.

RECENT TITLE(S) *Oh Boy, You're Having a Girl*, by Brian A. Klems; *Graphic the Valley*, by Peter Hoffmeister.

ADDICUS BOOKS, INC.

P.O. Box 45327, Omaha NE 68145. (402)330-7493. **Fax:** (402)330-1707. **E-mail:** info@addicusbooks.com. **Website:** www.addicusbooks.com. **Contact:** Acquisitions Editor. Estab. 1994. Addicus Books, Inc. publishes nonfiction books. "Our focus is on consumer health topics and legal topics for consumers, but we will consider other topics. We publish every book in trade paperback and in two e-book formats. We partner with a master book distributor that sells books into the trade—bookstores and libraries; we continually seek other sales channels outside bookstores. We need at least one solid sales channel outside the bookstore market. To submit your book idea, first e-mail a short description of your book; tell us who the audience is and how they could be reached. If we need more info, we'll ask for it." **Publishes 15 titles/year. 90% of books from first-time authors. 95% from unagented writers. Standard contract—royalties, paid every 6 months, are based on a percentage of revenue.** Publishes ms 9 months after acceptance. Accepts simultaneous submissions. Responds in 1 month or less to inquiries. Catalog and submission guidelines online.

NONFICTION Subjects include business, economics, health, law, consumer health, consumer legal topics, economics, investment advice. "We are continuously expanding our line of consumer health and consumer legal titles." Submit inquiry in a brief e-mail. "If we are interested, we may ask for a proposal. See proposal guidelines on our Website. Do not send entire ms unless requested. Please do not mail submissions by certified mail."

RECENT TITLE(S) *Overcoming Postpartum Depression*, by Linda Sebastian, ARNP; *Divorce in North Carolina*, by Bill Trosch, Esq. and Eric Trosch.

TIPS "We focus heavily on the quality of editorial content. We strive for good organization, clarity, and appropriate tone in a manuscript. Our books are concise and reader-friendly."

⊘ ALADDIN

Simon & Schuster, 1230 Avenue of the Americas, 4th Floor, New York NY 10020. (212)698-7000. **Website:** www.simonandschuster.com. **Contact:** Acquisitions Editor. Publishes hardcover/paperback originals and imprints of Simon & Schuster Children's Publishing Children's Division. Aladdin publishes picture books, beginning readers, chapter books, middle grade and tween fiction and nonfiction, and graphic novels and nonfiction in hardcover and paperback, with an emphasis on commercial, kid-friendly titles. Accepts simultaneous submissions.

FICTION Simon & Schuster does not review, retain or return unsolicited materials or artwork. "We suggest prospective authors and illustrators submit their mss through a professional literary agent."

⊘ ALGONQUIN BOOKS OF CHAPEL HILL

Workman Publishing, P.O. Box 2225, Chapel Hill NC 27515-2225. (919)967-0108. **Website:** www.algonquin.com. **Contact:** Editorial Department. Publishes hardcover originals. Algonquin Books publishes quality literary fiction and literary nonfiction. **Publishes 24 titles/year.** Guidelines online.

IMPRINTS Algonquin Young Readers.

NONFICTION Does not accept unsolicited submissions at this time. "Visit our website for full submission policy to queries."

FICTION Subjects include literary. Does not accept unsolicited submissions at this time.

RECENT TITLE(S) *Descent*, by Tim Johnston.

ALGONQUIN YOUNG READERS

P.O. Box 2225, Chapel Hill NC 27515. **Website:** algonquinyoungreaders.com. Algonquin Young Readers is a new imprint that features books for readers 7-17. "From short illustrated novels for the youngest independent readers to timely and topical crossover young adult fiction, what ties our books together are unforgettable characters, absorbing stories, and superior writing. Accepts simultaneous submissions. Guidelines online.

FICTION Algonquin Young Readers publishes ficiton and a limited number of narrative nonfiction titles for middle grade and young adult readers. "We don't publish poetry, picture books, or genre fiction." Query with 15-20 sample pages and SASE.

RECENT TITLE(S) *The Walls Around Us*, by Nova Ren Suma; *Catch You Later, Traitor*, by Avi.

ALGORA PUBLISHING

222 Riverside Dr., 16th Floor, New York NY 10025-6809. (212)678-0232. **Fax:** (212)666-3682. **Website:** www.algora.com. Estab. 1992. Publishes hardcover and trade paperback originals and reprints. Algora Publishing is an academic-type press, focusing on works by North and South American, European, Asian, and African authors for the educated general reader. **Publishes 25 titles/year. 1,500 queries; 800 mss received/year. 20% of books from first-time authors. 85% from unagented writers. Pays $0-1,000 advance.** Publishes book 10-18 months after acceptance of ms. Accepts simultaneous submissions. Responds in 1 month to queries/proposals; 3 months to mss. Book catalog and guidelines online.

NONFICTION Subjects include anthropology, archeology, creative nonfiction, dance, education, environment, finance, government, history, language, literature, military, money, music, nature, philosophy, politics, psychology, religion, science, sociology, translation, war, womens issues, womens studies, economics. Algora Publishing welcomes proposals for original mss, but "we do not handle self-help, recovery, or children's books." Submit a query or ms by uploading file to our website.

RECENT TITLE(S) *A Guide to the Phantom Dark Age*, by Emmet Scott; *Against the Grain: Six Men Who Helped Shape America*, by Robert Underhill.

TIPS "We welcome first-time writers; we help craft an author's raw manuscript into a literary work."

ALLWORTH PRESS

An imprint of Skyhorse Publishing, 307 West 36th St., 11th Floor, New York NY 10018. (212)643-6816. **Fax:** (212)643-6819. **E-mail:** allworthsubmissions@skyhorsepublishing.com. **Website:** www.allworth.com. Estab. 1989. Publishes hardcover and trade paperback originals. Allworth Press publishes business and self-help information for artists, designers, photographers, authors and film and performing artists, as well as books about business, money and the law for the general public. The press also publishes the best of classic and contemporary writing in art and graphic design. Currently emphasizing photography, graphic and industrial design, performing arts, fine arts and crafts, et al. **Publishes 12-18 titles/year. Pays advance.** Responds in 4-6 weeks. Book catalog and ms guidelines free.

NONFICTION Subjects include photography, film, television, graphic design, performing arts, as well as business and legal guides for the public. "We are currently accepting query letters for practical, legal, and technique books targeted to professionals in the arts, including designers, graphic and fine artists, craftspeople, photographers, and those involved in film and the performing arts." Query with 1-2 page synopsis, chapter outline, market analysis, sample chapter, bio, SASE.

TIPS "We are helping creative people in the arts by giving them practical advice about business and success."

AMACOM BOOKS

American Management Association, 1601 Broadway, New York NY 10019. (212)586-8100. **E-mail:** ekadin@amanet.org; tburgard@amanet.org. **Website:** www.amacombooks.org. **Contact:** Ellen Kadin, executive editor (marketing, career, personal development); Tim Burgard, senior editor (sales, customer service, project management, finance, supply chain). Book proposals on general business, leadership, management, human resources, training, education, science & technology, popular psychology, parenting, or health & fitness topics may be submitted to any editor. Estab. 1923. Publishes nonfiction trade hardcover and paperback originals and e-books. AMACOM Books—the publishing arm of the American Management Association (AMA)—is a nonfiction publisher devoted to helping readers lead more satisfying lives by publishing works that enhance their personal and professional growth and success. "Our authors—practitioners, journalists, and world-class educators—are noted experts and leaders in their fields. At AMACOM we can give authors the individual attention of a small publisher as well as the advantage of distributing and selling their books in both print and digital form through multiple channels around the world. Our high standards for both editing and packaging mean authors will have book of which they can be proud. We partner with our authors on creating the most effective marketing copy for their books. AMACOM's publicity department generates thousands of reviews, articles, excerpts, and other media placements for our books each year—in addition to promoting our books through our blog, e-newsletter, and social media outreach. Of course our books are showcased at international book fairs. Through such meetings millions of copies of our authors' books have been translated into 40 languages. We make our authors' books available through myriad electronic databases and partnerships with aggregators of content sold throughout the world. And our authors of business and personal development books have the unique opportunity to have their books selected for promotion directly to AMA's audiences—through AMA's website, podcasts, webcasts, blog, social media, e-newsletters, conferences, workshops, seminar catalogs and offerings, in AMA's own bookstores, and other means. At AMACOM we believe in what we publish—especially because we work toward publishing books that can make a positive difference in people's lives. (And unlike some publishers, we do not require that authors purchase copies of their books in bulk as a condition of publishing.) AMACOMers enjoy working with each other, and with our authors. Our authors feel the personal attention and camaraderie that publishing with AMACOM affords. This, and all the reasons above, may be why so many of our authors have chosen to publish with us multiple times." **Publishes 35-50 titles/year. Receives 500-1,000 submissions/year. Pays advance.** Depends on the circumstances. Standard schedule is seven months to bound books. Accepts simultaneous submissions. Catalog available. Guidelines online.

NONFICTION Subjects include business, career guidance, child guidance, communications, counseling, economics, education, finance, government, health, nutrition, parenting, psychology, real estate, science, womens issues, personal development (business self-help); fitness. Publishes nonfiction books for consumer and professional markets, including all business topics, parenting, health & fitness, popular psychology, popular science and technology, real estate, and education Submit proposals including brief book description and rationale, TOC, author bio and platform, intended audience, competing books and sample chapters. Proposals returned with SASE only.

RECENT TITLE(S) *Start a Successful Business, Ask More, Einstein's Boss,Talking to "Crazy", Becoming Facebook, Fitter Faster, The Un-Prescription for Autism, No Sweat.*

TIPS "Platform info in proposal reflects author activities that demonstrate author's visibility, authority, and audience reach."

AMADEUS PRESS

Hal Leonard Publishing Group, 33 Plymouth St., Suite 302, Montclair NJ 07402. (973)337-5034. **Fax:** (973)337-5227. **E-mail:** submissions@halleonardbooks.com. **Website:** www.amadeuspress.com. **Contact:** Carol Flannery, editorial director. Publishes books on classical music and opera. **Publishes Publishes 8-10 titles/year. titles/year. 30% of books from first-time authors. 75% from unagented writers. Pays modest advance.** Publishes ms 18-24 months after acceptance. Accepts simultaneous submissions. Responds in 30-45 days. Guidelines online.

NONFICTION Subjects include education, entertainment, memoirs, music. "Amadeus Press welcomes submissions pertaining to opera and classical music. Send proposal including: a letter describing the purpose and audience for your book, along with your background and qualifications; please indicate which word-processing software you use as we ask that final ms be submitted on disk; an outline or table of contents and an estimate of the length of the completed ms in numbers of words or double-spaced pages; a sample chapter or two, printed out (no electronic file transfers, please); sample illustrations as well as an estimate of the total numbers and types (for example, pen-and-ink artwork for line drawings, black-and-white glossy photographic prints, camera-ready music examples) of illustrations planned for your book; your schedule to complete the book. Generally, we ask authors to submit book proposals early in the writing process as this allows us to give editorial advice during the development phase and cuts down the amount of revisions needed later. Due to the large volume of submissions, you may not receive a response from us. If you wish to have the materials you submit returned to you, please so indicate and include return postage."

AMBERJACK PUBLISHING

P.O. Box 4668 #89611, New York NY 10163. (888)959-3352. **Website:** www.amberjackpublishing.com. Amberjack Publishing offers authors the freedom to write without burdening them with having to promote the work themselves. They retain all rights. "You will have no rights left to exploit, so you cannot resell, republish or use your story again." Accepts simultaneous submissions.

FICTION Amberjack Publishing is always on the lookout for the next great story. "We are interested in fiction, children's books, graphic novels, science fiction, fantasy, humor, and everything in between." Submit via online query form with book proposal and first 10 pages of ms.

RECENT TITLE(S) *Forever*, by J. Channing.

AMERICAN CHEMICAL SOCIETY

Publications/Books Division, 1155 16th St. NW, Washington DC 20036. (202)452-2120. **Fax:** (202)513-8819. **Website:** pubs.acs.org/books/. Estab. 1876. Publishes hardcover originals. American Chemical Society publishes symposium-based books for chemistry. **Publishes 35 titles/year. Pays royalty.** Accepts simultaneous submissions. Responds in 2 months to proposals. Book catalog available free. Guidelines online.

NONFICTION Subjects include science. Emphasis is on meeting-based books. Log in to submission site online.

AMERICAN CORRECTIONAL ASSOCIATION

206 N. Washington St., Suite 200, Alexandria VA 22314. (703)224-0000. **Fax:** (703)224-0179. **Website:** www.aca.org. Estab. 1870. Publishes trade paperback originals. American Correctional Association provides practical information on jails, prisons, boot camps, probation, parole, community corrections, juvenile facilities and rehabilitation programs, substance abuse programs, and other areas of corrections. **Publishes 18 titles/year. 90% of books from first-time authors. 100% from unagented writers.** Publishes ms 1 year after acceptance. Accepts simultaneous submissions. Responds in 4 months to queries. Book catalog available free. Guidelines online.

NONFICTION "We are looking for practical, how-to texts or training materials written for the corrections profession. We are especially interested in books on management, development of first-line supervisors, and security-threat group/management in prisons." No autobiographies or true-life accounts by current or former inmates or correctional officers, theses, or dissertations. No fiction or poetry. Query with SASE. Reviews artwork/photos.

TIPS "Authors are professionals in the field of corrections. Our audience is made up of corrections professionals and criminal justice students. No books by inmates or former inmates. This publisher advises out-of-town freelance editors, indexers, and proofreaders to refrain from requesting work from them."

AMERICAN COUNSELING ASSOCIATION

6101 Stevenson Ave., Suite 600, Alexandria VA 22304. (703)823-9800, x356. **Fax:** (703)823-4786. **E-mail:** cbaker@counseling.org. **Website:** www.counseling.org. **Contact:** Carolyn C. Baker, associate publisher. Estab. 1952. Publishes paperback originals. The American Counseling Association is a not-for-profit, professional and educational organization that is dedicated to the growth and enhancement of the counseling profession. Founded in 1952, ACA is the world's largest association exclusively representing professional counselors in various practice settings. ACA publishes textbooks and continuing education materials for professional counselors and not books written for the general public. **Publishes 8-10 titles/year. 1% of books from first-time authors. 90% from unagented writers.** Accepts simultaneous submissions. Responds in 1 month to queries. Guidelines and catalog online.

NONFICTION Subjects include career guidance, education, gay, lesbian, multicultural, psychology, religion, social sciences, spirituality, womens issues, womens studies, LGBTQ mental health, school counseling, marriage, family, couples counseling. ACA does not publish self-help books or autobiographies. Query with SASE. Submit proposal package, outline, 2 sample chapters, vitae.

RECENT TITLE(S) *Orientation to Professional Counseling; Assessment in Counseling, 6th Ed.; Counselor Self-Care.*

TIPS "Target your market. Your books will not be appropriate for everyone across all disciplines."

AMERICAN FEDERATION OF ASTROLOGERS

6535 S. Rural Rd., Tempe AZ 85283. (480)838-1751. **Fax:** (480)838-8293. **Website:** www.astrologers.com. Estab. 1938. Publishes trade paperback originals and reprints. American Federation of Astrologers publishes astrology books, calendars, charts, and related aids. **Publishes 10-15 titles/year. 10 queries; 20 mss received/year. 50% of books from first-time authors. 100% from unagented writers. Pays 10% royalty.** Publishes book 10 months after acceptance of ms. Accepts simultaneous submissions. Responds in 6 months to mss. Book catalog available free. Guidelines online.

NONFICTION "Our market for beginner books, Sun-sign guides, and similar material is limited and we thus publish very few of these. The ideal word count for a book-length manuscript published by AFA is about 40,000 words, although we will consider manuscripts from 20,000 to 60,000 words." Submit complete ms.

TIPS "AFA welcomes articles for *Today's Astrologer*, our monthly journal for members, on any astrological subject. Most articles are 1,500-3,000 words, but we do accept shorter and longer articles. Follow the guidelines online for book manuscripts. You also can e-mail your article to info@astrologers.com, but any charts or illustrations must be submitted as attachments and not embedded in the body of the e-mail or in an attached document."

AMERICAN QUILTER'S SOCIETY

5801 Kentucky Dam Rd., Paducah KY 42003. (270)898-7903. **Fax:** (270)898-1173. **Website:** www.americanquilter.com. Estab. 1984. Publishes trade paperbacks. American Quilter's Society publishes how-to and pattern books for quilters (beginners through intermediate skill level). We are not the publisher for non-quilters writing about quilts. We now publish quilt-related craft cozy romance and mystery titles, series only. Humor is good. Graphic depictions and curse words are bad. **Publishes 20-24 titles/year. 100 queries received/year. 60% of books from first-time authors. Pays 5% royalty on retail price for both nonfiction and fiction.** Publishes nonfiction ms 9-18 months after acceptance. Fiction published on a different schedule TBD. Responds in 2 months to proposals. Guidelines online.

Accepts simultaneous nonfiction submissions. Does not accept simultaneous fiction submissions.

NONFICTION No queries; proposals only. Note: 1 or 2 completed quilt projects must accompany proposal.

FICTION Submit a synopsis and 2 sample chapters, plus an outline of the next 2 books in the series.

RECENT TITLE(S) *Liberated Quiltmaking II*, by Gwen Marston; *T-Shirt Quilts Made Easy*, by Martha Deleonardis; *Decorate Your Shoes*, by Annemart Berendse.

AMERICAN WATER WORKS ASSOCIATION

6666 W. Quincy Ave., Denver CO 80235. (303)347-6260. **Fax:** (303)794-7310. **E-mail:** submissions@awwa.org. **Website:** www.awwa.org. **Contact:** Senior Manager, Acquisitions and Content. Estab. 1881. Publishes hardcover and trade paperback originals. AWWA strives to advance and promote the safety and knowledge of drinking water and related issues to all audiences—from kindergarten through post-doctorate. **Publishes 25 titles/year.** Responds in 4 months to queries. Book catalog and ms guidelines free.

NONFICTION Subjects include science, software, drinking water- and wastewater-related topics, operations, treatment, sustainability. Query with SASE. Submit outline, bio, 3 sample chapters. Reviews artwork/photos. Send photocopies.

TIPS "See website to download submission instructions."

AMG PUBLISHERS

AMG International, Inc., 6815 Shallowford Rd., Chattanooga TN 37421. (423)894-6060. **Fax:** (423)894-9511. **E-mail:** sales@amgpublishers.com. **Website:** www.amgpublishers.com. **Contact:** Amanda Jenkins, Sales Manager/Author Liaison. Estab. 1985. Publishes hardcover and trade paperback originals, electronic originals, and audio Bible and book originals. Publishing division of AMG International began in 1985 with release of the *Hebrew-Greek Key Word Study Bible* in the King James Version. This groundbreaking study Bible is now published in four other Bible translations. In-depth study and examination of original biblical languages provide some of our core Bible study and reference tools. In 1998, AMG launched the successful Following God Bible study series (primarily for women) that examine key characters of the Bible along with life application principles. AMG has also been publishing young adult inspirational fantasy fiction since 2005 but is not currently accepting fiction. "Profits from sales of our books and Bibles are funneled back into world missions and childcare efforts of parent organization, AMG Publishers." **Publishes 5-10 titles/year. 2,500 queries; 500 mss received/year. 25% of books from first-time authors. 35% from unagented writers. Pays 10-16% royalty on net sales. Advance negotiable.** Publishes book 12-18 months after acceptance of ms. Accepts simultaneous submissions. Responds in 2 month to queries, 5 months to proposals/mss. Book catalog and guidelines online.

IMPRINTS Living Ink Books; God and Country Press; AMG Bible Studies.

NONFICTION Subjects include Americana, education, history, military, parenting, religion, spirituality, war, womens issues, womens studies. Bibles, trade nonfiction books, and workbook Bible studies. Does not want self-help, memoir, autobiography, biography, fiction, New Age, prosperity gospel. Query with letter first, e-mail preferred.

FICTION "We are not presently acquiring fiction of any genre, though we continue to publish a number of titles in the young adult inspirational fantasy category."

RECENT TITLE(S) *Grin with Grace Bible Study*; *Rooted: Understanding God's Word*; *The Book of Ruth* (Key Word Bible Studies).

TIPS "AMG is open to well-written, niche Bible study, reference, and devotional books that meet immediate needs."

AMHERST MEDIA, INC.

P.O. Box 538, Buffalo NY 14213. (716)874-4450. **E-mail:** craigalesse@gmail.com. **E-mail:** submissions@amherstmedia.com. **Website:** www.amherstmedia.com. **Contact:** Craig Alesse, publisher. Associate Publisher: Kate Neaverth. Estab. 1974. Publishes trade paperback originals and reprints. Amherst Media publishes illustrated books on all subjects including photographic instruction. **Publishes 50 titles/year. 60% of books from first-time authors. 90% from unagented writers. Pays 12-18% royalty. Pays advance.** Publishes book 1 year after acceptance. Accepts simultaneous submissions. Responds in 2 weeks to queries. Book catalog online. Guidelines upon request.

NONFICTION Subjects include agriculture, animals, architecture, art, automotive, communications, contemporary culture, crafts, creative nonfiction, environment, gardening, hobbies, horticulture, house and home, marine subjects, medicine, nature, New Age, photography, pop culture, recreation, transportation, womens issues. Looking for author/photographers for illustrated books. 100-200 high quality photographs around a theme. Reviews artwork/photos.

RECENT TITLE(S) *Extreme Weather*; *Dog Photography*; *Painting with Light*.

TIPS "Our audience is made up of enthusiasts in all subject areas."

Ⓐ⊘ AMULET BOOKS

Imprint of Abrams, 115 W. 18th St., 6th Floor, New York NY 10001. **Website:** www.amuletbooks.com. Estab. 2004. *Does not accept unsolicited mss or queries.* **10% of books from first-time authors.** Accepts simultaneous submissions.

FICTION Middle readers: adventure, contemporary, fantasy, history, science fiction, sports. Young adults/teens: adventure, contemporary, fantasy, history, science fiction, sports, suspense.

ANDREWS MCMEEL UNIVERSAL

1130 Walnut St., Kansas City MO 64106. (816)581-7500. **Website:** www.andrewsmcmeel.com. **Contact:** Book Submissions. Estab. 1973. Publishes hardcover and paperback originals. Andrews McMeel publishes general trade books, humor books, miniature gift books, calendars, and stationery products. **Publishes 300 titles/year. Pays royalty on retail price or net receipts. Pays advance.** Accepts simultaneous submissions. Guidelines online.

NONFICTION Subjects include cooking, games, comics, puzzles. Submit proposal.

⊘ ANHINGA PRESS

P.O. Box 3665, Tallahassee FL 32315. **E-mail:** info@anhinga.org. **Website:** www.anhingapress.org. **Contact:** Kristine Snodgrass, co-director. Publishes hardcover and trade paperback originals. Publishes four full-length poetry collections and one chapbook per year. Also publishes anthologies, broadsides. **Publishes 5 titles/year. 600 Pays 10% royalty on retail**

price. Does not pay advance. Accepts simultaneous submissions. Responds in 3-5 months. Guidelines online.

POETRY Not accepting any unsolicited submissions at this time. Enter Anhinga- Robert Dana for Poetry and Rick Campbell Chapbook Prize. Details on website.

ANKERWYCKE

American Bar Association, 321 N. Clark St., Chicago IL 60654. **Website:** www.ababooks.org. Estab. 1878. Publishes hardcover and trade paperback originals. In 1215, the Magna Carta was signed underneath the ancient Ankerwycke Yew tree, starting the process which led to rule by constitutional law—in effect, giving rights and the law to the people. And today, the ABA's Ankerwycke line of books continues to bring the law to the people. With legal fiction, true crime books, popular legal histories, public policy handbooks, and prescriptive guides to current legal and business issues, Ankerwycke is a contemporary and innovative line of books for everyone from a trusted and vested authority. **Publishes 30-40 titles/year. 1,000's of queries received/year. 25% of books from first-time authors. 50% from unagented writers.** Publishes ms 12-18 months after acceptance. Accepts simultaneous submissions. Responds in 1 month to queries and proposals; 3 months to mss. Book catalog and ms guidelines online.

NONFICTION Subjects include business, consumer legal. "Extremely high quality nonfiction with a legal aspect; business books specifically for service professionals; consumer legal on a wide range of topics—we're actively acquiring in all these areas." Query with cover letter; outline or TOC; and CV/bio including other credits. Include e-mail address for response.

FICTION "We're actively acquiring legal fiction with extreme verisimilitude." Query with cover letter; outline or TOC; and CV/bio including other credits. Include e-mail address for response.

APA BOOKS

American Psychological Association, 750 First St. NE, Washington DC 20002. (202)336-5500. **Website:** www.apa.org/pubs/books/index.aspx. Publishes hardcover and trade paperback originals. Accepts simultaneous submissions. Book catalog online. Guidelines online.

IMPRINTS Magination Press (children's books).

NONFICTION Subjects include education, multicultural, psychology, science, social sciences, sociology. Submit cv and prospectus with TOC, intended audience, selling points, and outside competition.

TIPS "Our press features scholarly books on empirically supported topics for professionals and students in all areas of psychology."

APPALACHIAN MOUNTAIN CLUB BOOKS

5 Joy St., Boston MA 02138. (617)523-0636. **Fax:** (617)523-0722. **E-mail:** amcbooks@outdoors.org. **Website:** www.outdoors.org. Estab. 1876. Publishes hardcover, trade paperback, and digital originals. AMC Books are written and published by the experts in the Northeast outdoors. "Our mission is to publish authoritative, accurate, and easy-to-use books and maps based on AMC's expertise in outdoor recreation, education, and conservation. We are committed to producing books and maps that appeal to novices and day visitors as well as outdoor enthusiasts in our core activity areas of hiking and paddling. By advancing the interest of the public in outdoor recreation and helping our readers to access back country trails and waterways, and by using our books to educate the public about safety, conservation, and stewardship, we support AMC's mission of promoting the protection, enjoyment, and wise use of the Northeast outdoors. We work with the best professional writers possible and draw upon the experience of our programs staff and chapter leaders from Maine to Washington, DC. **Publishes 8-12 titles/year. 1% of books from first-time authors. 98% from unagented writers. Pays advance.** Publishes ms 1-2 years after acceptance. Responds in 4 weeks. Catalog online. Guidelines online.

NONFICTION Subjects include creative nonfiction, environment, nature, recreation, regional, Maps that are based on our direct work with land managers and our on-the-ground collection of data on trails, natural features, and points of interest. Appalachian Mountain Club publishes hiking, paddling, nature, conservation, and mountain-subject guides for America's Northeast. "We also publish narrative titles related to outdoor recreation, mountaineering, and adventure, often with a historical perspective, and always with a deep connection to our region (from Maine to Washington, D.C.). We connect recreation to conservation and education." Please no Appalachian Trail memoirs. Send a query letter and the first three chapters of your ms to the publications department via e-mail. Your query letter should explain the subject of your book and why it would be appropriate for AMC Books to publish. Include information about word count (our guidebooks are typically between 80,000 and 100,000 words) and any special art or graphic treatment that you envision. Tell us how the book would be distinctive by comparing it to similar titles that are already on the market. Also explain the intended audience for your book and why you think your book would generate interest. Present some ideas of how you would help us market the book and reach readers. Conclude with a summary of your relevant experience and credentials, including previously published writing on related topics. Allow us four weeks to respond to your query.

TIPS "Our audience is outdoor recreationists, conservation-minded hikers and canoeists, family outdoor lovers, armchair enthusiasts. Visit our website for proposal submission guidelines and more information. Please no fiction, children's books, or poetry."

ARBORDALE PUBLISHING

612 Johnnie Dodds, Suite A2, Mt. Pleasant SC 29464. (843)971-6722. **Fax:** (843)216-3804. **E-mail:** submissions@arbordalepublishing.com. **Website:** www.arbordalepublishing.com. **Contact:** Acquisitions Editor. Estab. 2004. Publishes hardcover, trade paperback, and electronic originals. "The picture books we publish are usually, but not always, fictional stories with nonfiction woven into the story that relate to science or math. All books should subtly convey an educational theme through a warm story that is fun to read and that will grab a child's attention. Each book has a 4-page '*For Creative Minds*' section to reinforce the educational component. This section will have a craft and/or game as well as 'fun facts' to be shared by the parent, teacher, or other adult. Authors do not need to supply this information with their submission, but if their ms is accepted, they may be asked to provide additional information for this section. Mss should be less than 1,000 words and meet all of the following 4 criteria: fun to read—mostly fiction with nonfiction facts woven into the story; national or regional in scope; must tie into early elementary school curriculum; must be marketable through a niche market such as a zoo, aquarium, or museum gift shop." **Publishes 12 titles/year. 1,000 mss received/year. 50% of books from first-time authors. 99% from unagented writers. Pays 6-8% royalty on wholesale price. Pays small advance.** Publishes book 18 months after acceptance. May hold onto mss of interest for 1 year until acceptance. Accepts simultaneous submissions. Accepts electronic submissions only. Snail mail submissions are discarded without being opened. Acknowledges receipt of ms submission within 1 month. Book catalog and guidelines online.

NONFICTION Subjects include animals, creative nonfiction, environment, ethnic, marine subjects, multicultural, science. Prefer fiction, but will consider nonfiction as well. All mss should be submitted via e-mail. Mss should be less than 1,000 words. Reviews artwork/photos. Send 1-2 JPEGS and link to online portfolio

FICTION Subjects include picture books. Picture books: animal, folktales, nature/environment, science- or math-related. No more than 1,000 words. Holiday-specific, cats or dogs All mss should be submitted via e-mail to Acquisitions Editor. Mss should be less than 1,000 words.

POETRY "We do not accept books of poetry. Will consider mss written in rhyming verse, but prefer prose."

RECENT TITLE(S) *Bat Count*, by Anna Forrester, illustrated by Susan Detwiler; *Moonlight Crab Count*, by Dr. Neeti Bathala and Jennifer Keats Curtis, illustrated by Veronica Jones; *Vivian and the Legend of the Hoodoos*, by Terry Catasus Jennings, illustrated by Phyllis Saroff.

TIPS "Please make sure that you have looked at our website to read our complete submission guidelines and to see if we are looking for a particular subject. Manuscripts must meet all four of our stated criteria. We look for fairly realistic, bright and colorful art-no cartoons. We want the children excited about the books. We envision the books being used at home and in the classroom."

ARCADE PUBLISHING

Skyhorse Publishing, 307 W. 36th St., 11th Floor, New York NY 10018. (212)643-6816. **Fax:** (212)643-6819. **E-mail:** arcadesubmissions@skyhorsepublishing.com. **Website:** www.arcadepub.com. **Contact:** Acquisitions Editor. Estab. 1988. Publishes hardcover originals, trade paperback reprints. Arcade prides itself on publishing top-notch literary nonfiction and fiction, with a significant proportion of foreign writers. **Publishes 35 titles/year. 5% of books from first-time**

authors. Pays royalty on retail price and 10 author's copies. Pays advance. Publishes book 18 months after acceptance. Accepts simultaneous submissions. Responds in 2 months if interested. Book catalog and ms guidelines for #10 SASE.

NONFICTION Subjects include history, memoirs, travel, popular science, current events. Submit proposal with brief query, 1-2 page synopsis, chapter outline, market analysis, sample chapter, bio.

FICTION Subjects include literary, short story collections, translation. No romance, historical, science fiction. Submit proposal with brief query, 1-2 page synopsis, chapter outline, market analysis, sample chapter, bio.

ARCADIA PUBLISHING

420 Wando Park Blvd., Mt. Pleasant SC 29464. (843)853-2070. **Fax:** (843)853-0044. **Website:** www.arcadiapublishing.com. Estab. 1993. Publishes trade paperback originals. Arcadia publishes photographic vintage regional histories. "We have more than 3,000 Images of America series in print. We have expanded our California program." **Publishes 600 titles/year. Pays 8% royalty on retail price.** Publishes book 9 months after acceptance. Accepts simultaneous submissions. Book catalog online. Guidelines available free.

NONFICTION Subjects include history. "Arcadia accepts submissions year-round. Our editors seek proposals on local history topics and are able to provide authors with detailed information about our publishing program as well as book proposal submission guidelines. Due to the great demand for titles on local and regional history, we are currently searching for authors to work with us on new photographic history projects. Please contact one of our regional publishing teams if you are interested in submitting a proposal." Specific proposal form to be completed.

TIPS "Writers should know that we only publish history titles. The majority of our books are on a city or region, and contain vintage images with limited text."

ARCHAIA

Imprint of Boom! Studios, 5670 Wilshire Blvd., Suite 450, Los Angeles CA 90036. **Website:** www.archaia.com. Use online submission form. Accepts simultaneous submissions.

FICTION Subjects include adventure, fantasy, horror, mystery, science fiction. Looking for graphic novel submissions that include finished art. "Archaia is a multi-award-winning graphic novel publisher with more than 75 renowned publishing brands, including such domestic and international hits as *Artesia, Mouse Guard*, and a line of Jim Henson graphic novels including *Fraggle Rock* and *The Dark Crystal*. Publishes creator-shared comic books and graphic novels in the adventure, fantasy, horror, pulp noir, and science fiction genres that contain idiosyncratic and atypical writing and art. *Archaia does not generally hire freelancers or arrange for freelance work, so submissions should only be for completed book and series proposals.*"

A-R EDITIONS, INC.

1600 Aspen Commons, Suite 100, Middleton WI 53562. (608)836-9000. **E-mail:** info@areditions.com. **Website:** www.areditions.com. Estab. 1962. A-R Editions publishes modern critical editions of music based on current musicological research. Each edition is devoted to works by a single composer or to a single genre of composition. The contents are chosen for their potential interest to scholars and performers, then prepared for publication according to the standards that govern the making of all reliable, historical editions. **Publishes 30 titles/year. 40 queries; 30 mss received/year. 75% of books from first-time authors. 100% from unagented writers. Pays royalty or honoraria.** Book catalog online. Guidelines online.

NONFICTION Subjects includehistorical music editions; computer music and digital audio topics. Computer Music and Digital Audio Series titles deal with issues tied to digital and electronic media, and include both textbooks and handbooks in this area.

ARROW PUBLICATIONS, LLC

7716 Bells Mill Rd., Bethesda MD 20817. (301)299-9422. **E-mail:** arrow_info@arrowpub.com. **Website:** www.arrowpub.com. **Contact:** Tom King, managing editor. Estab. 1987. No graphic novels until further notice. **Publishes Publishes 50 e-book titles/year. Paperback version launched in 2009 with 12 English and 12 Spanish titles/year. titles/year. 150 queries; 100 mss received/year. 80% of books from first-time authors. 100% from unagented writers. Makes outright purchase of accepted completed scripts.** Publishes book 4-6 months after acceptance of ms. Accepts simultaneous submissions. Responds in 2 month to queries; 1 month to mss sent upon request. Guidelines online.

NONFICTION Subjects include business, womens issues.

FICTION Subjects include comic books, ethnic, historical, mainstream, romance. "We are looking for outlines of stories heavy on romance with elements of adventure/intrigue/mystery. We will consider other romance genres such as fantasy, western, inspirational, and historical as long as the romance element is strong." Query with outline first with SASE. Consult submission guidelines online before submitting.

TIPS "Our audience is primarily women 18 and older. Send query with outline only."

ARTE PUBLICO PRESS

University of Houston, 4902 Gulf Fwy, Bldg 19, Rm 100, Houston TX 77204-2004. **Fax:** (713)743-2847. **E-mail:** submapp@uh.edu. **Website:** artepublicopress.com. Estab. 1979. Publishes hardcover originals, trade paperback originals and reprints. Arte Publico Press is the oldest and largest publisher of Hispanic literature for children and adults in the United States. "We are a showcase for Hispanic literary creativity, arts and culture. Our endeavor is to provide a national forum for U.S.-Hispanic literature." **Publishes 25-30 titles/year. 1,000 queries; 2,000 mss received/year. 50% of books from first-time authors. 80% from unagented writers. Pays 10% royalty on wholesale price. Provides 20 author's copies; 40% discount on subsequent copies. Pays $1,000-3,000 advance.** Publishes book 2 years after acceptance of ms. Accepts simultaneous submissions. Responds in 1 month to queries and proposals; 4 months to mss. Book catalog available free. Guidelines online.

NONFICTION Subjects include ethnic, regional, translation. Hispanic civil rights issues for new series: The Hispanic Civil Rights Series. Submissions made through online submission form.

FICTION Subjects include contemporary, ethnic, literary, mainstream. "Written by U.S.-Hispanics." Submissions made through online submission form.

POETRY Submissions made through online submission form.

TIPS "Include cover letter in which you 'sell' your book—why should we publish the book, who will want to read it, why does it matter, etc. Use our ms submission online form. Format files accepted are: Word, plain/text, rich/text files. Other formats will not be accepted. Manuscript files cannot be larger than 5MB. Once editors review your ms, you will receive an e-mail with the decision. Revision process could take up to 4 months."

ASA, AVIATION SUPPLIES & ACADEMICS

7005 132 Place SE, Newcastle WA 98059. (425)235-1500. **E-mail:** feedback@asa2fly.com. **Website:** www.asa2fly.com. ASA is an industry leader in the development and sales of aviation supplies, publications, and software for pilots, flight instructors, flight engineers and aviation technicians. All ASA products are developed by a team of researchers, authors and editors. Book catalog available free.

NONFICTION Subjects include education. "We are primarily an aviation publisher. Educational books in this area are our specialty; other aviation books will be considered." All subjects must be related to aviation education and training. Query with outline. Send photocopies or MS Word files.

RECENT TITLE(S) *Managing Risk: Best Practices for Pilots*, by Dale Wilson and Gerald Binnema; *Practical Aviation Law, 5th Edition*, by J. Scott Hamilton; *Pilots in Command: Your Best Trip, Every Trip*, by Kristofer Pierson.

TIPS "Two of our specialty series include ASA's *Focus Series*, and ASA *Aviator's Library*. Books in our *Focus Series* concentrate on single-subject areas of aviation knowledge, curriculum and practice. The *Aviator's Library* is comprised of titles of known and/or classic aviation authors or established instructor/authors in the industry, and other aviation specialty titles."

ASABI PUBLISHING

Asabi Publishing, **E-mail:** submissions@asabipublishing.com. **Website:** https://asabipublishing.com. **Contact:** Tressa Sanders, publisher. Estab. 2004. Publishes hardcover, mass market and trade paperback originals. **Publishes 5 titles/year. Accepts professional queries only. 30% of books from first-time authors. 30% from unagented writers. Pays 40% royalty on wholesale or list price. Pays up to $500 advance.** Publishes ms 2 years after acceptance. Responds in 1 month to queries and proposals, 2-6 months to mss. Book catalog online. Guidelines online.

IMPRINTS Solomon Publishing Group-Sweden.

NONFICTION Subjects include business, ethnic, gay, lesbian, nature, nutrition, photography, psychology, sex, travel, true crime. Does not want anything religious or spiritual, astrology. Submit professional query letter only. "We do not publish poetry or titles containing religious or spiritual content of any kind." Reviews artwork/photos. Writers should send photocopies.

FICTION Subjects include confession, erotica, ethnic, horror, lesbian, mystery, romance, science fiction, suspense, classic noir. "We will only consider publishing a fiction title if it is a part of a series." The series should not already exist (except for the first unpublished title). There should be a plan/outline for at least two more titles in the series beyond the initial title. Does not want anything religious or spiritual, astrology, ghosts, aliens, vampires or werewolves. Submit professional query letter.

RECENT TITLE(S) *A Peek Inside the Goo: Depression & the Borderline Personality*, by Njemile Zakiya; *God Free: Black Critical Thinking & Disbelief*, by Shamakani Bahiya; *Sizzle and Drop*, by Isis Jones.

ASCEND BOOKS

7221 W. 79th St., Suite 206, Overland Park KS 66204. (913)948-5500. **E-mail:** bsnodgrass@ascendbooks.com. **Website:** ascendbooks.com. **Contact:** Robert Snodgrass. Estab. 2008. Ascend Books is positioned to acquire and execute publishing projects written by national and regional sports celebrities and educators. Our authors include athletes, coaches, and the teams themselves. Ascend Books also works with celebrities and educators in the fields of entertainment and children's books. Ascend Books is a highly specialized publishing company with a burgeoning presence in the sports, entertainment, and children's books. Ascend Books is positioned to acquire and execute publishing projects in a tightly defined market–that of sports celebrities, including athletes, coaches, and teams, and of significant anniversary celebrations of sports institutions, such as football bowl games, franchises, and halls of fame. Ascend Books also works with celebrities and educators in the fields of entertainment and children's books. Ascend Books differentiates itself from traditional publishers by extending the intellectual property of a book and its author into professional speaking and educational avenues. Currently Ascend Books publishes a variety of formats each year—in a variety of subject areas. Our Publishing Initiative can provide a multi-dimensional approach for a select number of titles. The Ascend Books distribution team shepherds thousands of books from press to audience each month. Ascend employs professionals in editorial, sales, production, and distribution roles. Our stringent publishing criteria however, limits the number of books we publish each year. When we accept and initiate a book publishing project we put our full resources of talented editors, collaborators, photographers, artists and sales professionals behind each project. The Ascend Books Team works with setting goals, then establishing defined objectives to maximize the sales opportunities for each title on our list. When the decision is made to proceed on a book, we put the full strength of our sales, editorial, production and distribution resources to work. **Publishes 12-15 titles/year. 50% of books from first-time authors. 75% from unagented writers. Pays advance.** Accepts simultaneous submissions. Responds in 4-6 weeks. Catalog online.

NONFICTION Subjects include child guidance, entertainment, memoirs, sports.

FICTION Subjects include picture books, sports.

RECENT TITLE(S) *Mommy Please Don't Go to Work*, by Rhiannon Ally; *Merry Menagerie*, by Angie Pickman; *Mayor Sly and the Magic Bow Tie*, by Aja James, Audrey Masoner and Sly James; *Let's Go Yankees*, by Scott Pitoniak; *It's A Sunny Life*, by Gary Lezak; *Go Cubs Go*, by Marv Levy; *Dickie V's ABCs and 1-2-3s*, by Dick VItale.

ASCE PRESS

American Society of Civil Engineers, 1801 Alexander Bell Dr., Reston VA 20191. (703)295-6275. **E-mail:** ascepress@asce.org. **Website:** www.asce.org/bookstore. Estab. 1989. "ASCE Press publishes technical volumes that are useful to practicing civil engineers and civil engineering students, as well as allied professionals. We publish books by individual authors and editors to advance the civil engineering profession. Currently emphasizing geotechnical, structural engineering, sustainable engineering and engineering history. De-emphasizing highly specialized areas with narrow scope." **Publishes 5-10 titles/year. 20% of books from first-time authors. 100% from unagented writers.** Guidelines online.

NONFICTION Subjects includecivil engineering. "We are looking for topics that are useful and instructive to the engineering practitioner." No children's books. No memoirs. Query with proposal, sample chapters, CV, TOC, and target audience.

TIPS "As a traditional publisher of scientific and technical materials, ASCE Press applies rigorous standards to the expertise, scholarship, readability and attractiveness of its books."

ASM PRESS

Book division for the American Society for Microbiology, 1752 N St., NW, Washington DC 20036. (202)737-3600. **Fax:** (202)942-9342. **E-mail:** books@asmusa.org. **Website:** www.asmscience.org. Estab. 1899. Publishes hardcover, trade paperback and electronic originals. **Publishes 30 titles/year. 40% of books from first-time authors. 95% from unagented writers. Pays 5-15% royalty on wholesale price. Pays $1,000-10,000 advance.** Publishes book 6-9 months after acceptance. Accepts simultaneous submissions. Responds in 2 months. Book catalog online. Guidelines online.

NONFICTION Subjects include agriculture, animals, education, history, horticulture, science, microbiology and related sciences. "Must have bona fide academic credentials in which they are writing." Query with SASE or by e-mail. Submit proposal package, outline, prospectus. Reviews artwork/photos. Send photocopies.

TIPS "Credentials are most important."

ASSOCIATION FOR SUPERVISION AND CURRICULUM DEVELOPMENT

ASCD, 1703 N. Beauregard St., Alexandria VA 22311-1714. (703)578-9600. **Fax:** (703)575-5400. **E-mail:** acquisitions@ascd.org. **Website:** www.ascd.org. **Contact:** Genny Ostertag, director, content acquisitions. Estab. 1943. Publishes trade paperback originals. ASCD publishes high-quality professional books for educators. **Publishes 30 titles/year. Receives approximately 200 proposals/year. 30% of books from first-time authors. 95% from unagented writers. Pays negotiable royalty on actual monies received.** Publishes ms 1 year after acceptance. Accepts simultaneous submissions. Responds in 2-3 months to proposals. Book catalog and guidelines online.

NONFICTION Subjects include education. Submit full proposal, 2 sample chapters. Reviews artwork/photos. Send photocopies.

RECENT TITLE(S) *Fostering Resilient Learners: Strategies for Creating a Trauma-Sensitive Classroom* by Kristin Souers with Pete Hall; *Leading with Focus: Elevating the Essentials for School and District Improvement* by Mike Schmoker; *The Teacher 50: Critical Questions for Inspiring Classroom Excellence* by Baruti Kafele.

Ⓐ⊘ ATHENEUM BOOKS FOR YOUNG READERS

Simon & Schuster, 1230 Avenue of the Americas, New York NY 10020. **Website:** kids.simonandschuster.com. Estab. 1961. Publishes hardcover originals. Accepts simultaneous submissions. Guidelines for #10 SASE.

NONFICTION Subjects include Americana, animals, history, photography, psychology, recreation, religion, science, sociology, sports, travel. Publishes hardcover originals, picture books for young kids, nonfiction for ages 8-12 and novels for middle-grade and young adults. 100% require freelance illustration. Agented submissions only.

FICTION Subjects include adventure, ethnic, experimental, fantasy, gothic, historical, horror, humor, mystery, science fiction, sports, suspense, western, Animal. All in juvenile versions. "We have few specific needs except for books that are fresh, interesting and well written. Fad topics are dangerous, as are works you haven't polished to the best of your ability. We also don't need safety pamphlets, ABC books, coloring books and board books. In writing picture book texts, avoid the coy and 'cutesy,' such as stories about characters with alliterative names." Agented submissions only. No paperback romance-type fiction.

TIPS "Study our titles."

A.T. PUBLISHING

23 Lily Lake Rd., Highland NY 12528. (845)691-2021. **E-mail:** tjp2@optonline.net. **Contact:** Anthony Prizzia, publisher (education). Estab. 2001. Publishes trade paperback originals. **Publishes 1-3 titles/year. 5-10 queries received/year. 100% of books from first-time authors. 100% from unagented writers. Pays 15% royalty on retail price. Makes outright purchase of $500-1,500.** Accepts simultaneous submissions. Responds in 1 month to queries; 2 months to proposals; 4 months to mss.

NONFICTION Subjects include education, recreation. Query with SASE. Submit complete ms. Reviews artwork/photos. Send photocopies.

RECENT TITLE(S) *The Portion Principle*, by Kaitlin Louie; *Itchin' for a Snitchin'*, by Michael Spatafore; *Had To Take Another Break*, written by Clayton Dorn Coburn, illustrated by Sharon Dorn Gill.

TIPS "Audience is people interested in a variety of topics, general. Submit typed manuscript for consideration, including a SASE for return of ms."

AUTUMN HOUSE PRESS

5530 Penn Ave., Pittsburgh PA 15206. (412)362-2665. **E-mail:** info@autumnhouse.org. **Website:** www.autumnhouse.org. **Contact:** Christine Stroud, editor-in-chief. Managing Editor: Mike Good. Assistant Editor: Shelby Newsom. Estab. 1998. Publishes trade paperback and electronic originals. Format: acid-free paper; offset printing. A nonprofit literary publisher, Autumn House Press was launched in 1998 when prominent American publishers, driven by economic concerns, dramatically reduced their poetry lists. Since our launch, Autumn House has expanded to publish fiction (2008) and nonfiction titles (2010). These books receive the same attention to design and manufacturing as our award-winning poetry titles. Autumn House publications have received a great deal of recognition and acclaim. In 2011, we earned a Certificate of Appreciation from the Pennsylvania legislature recognizing our contribution to the arts. Our books are regularly reviewed in *Ploughshares, Brevity, London Grip Review, The Women's Review of Books, The Jewish Review of Books*, and *Poets Quarterly*. Many of our poems have been featured in *The New York Times Magazine*, on *The Writer's Almanac*, and Ted Kooser's *American Life in Poetry*. Our titles also circulate within the local Pittsburgh community, with reviews in *The Pittsburgh City Paper* and *The Pittsburgh Post-Gazette*. Our books have won numerous awards over the years, such as *Love for Sale and Other Essays* by Clifford Thompson, which won the 2013 Whiting Award. **Publishes 8 titles/year. Receives 1,800 mss/year. 30-50% of books from first-time authors. 100% from unagented writers. Pays 8% royalty on wholesale price. Pays $0-2,500 advance.** Publishes twelve months after acceptance. Accepts simultaneous submissions. Responds in 1-3 days on queries and proposals; 3 months on mss. Catalog online. Guidelines online.

IMPRINTS Coal Hill Review.

NONFICTION Subjects include computers, creative nonfiction, gay, literary criticism, literature, memoirs, multicultural, nature, spirituality. Submit through our annual contest or open-call period. See guidelines online.

FICTION Subjects include contemporary, experimental, literary, poetry, spiritual. Submit through our annual contest or open-call period. See guidelines online.

POETRY Submit through our annual contest or open-call period. See guidelines online.

RECENT TITLE(S) *Thank Your Lucky Stars*, by Sherrie Flick; *Blue Mistaken for Sky*, by Andrea Hollander; *Carry You*, by Glori Simmons; *Darling Nova*, by Melissa Cundieff; *Paper Sons*, by Dickson Lam.

TIPS "Though we are open to all styles of poetry, fiction, and nonfiction, we suggest you familiarize yourself with previous Autumn House publications before submitting. We are committed not just to publishing the prominent voices of our age, but also to publishing first books and lesser-known authors who will become the important writers of their generation. Many of our past winners have been first-book authors. We encourage writers from all backgrounds to submit; it is our goal at Autumn House to develop a rich and varied literary tradition."

AVALON TRAVEL PUBLISHING

Avalon Publishing Group, 1700 4th St., Berkeley CA 94710. (510)595-3664. **Fax:** (510)595-4228. **E-mail:** avalon.acquisitions@perseusbooks.com. **Website:** www.avalontravelbooks.com. Estab. 1973. Publishes trade paperback originals. Avalon travel guides feature practicality and spirit, offering a traveler-to-traveler perspective perfect for planning an afternoon hike, around-the-world journey, or anything in between. ATP publishes 7 major series. Each one has a different emphasis and a different geographic coverage. "We have expanded our coverage, with a focus on European and Asian destinations. Our main areas of interest are North America, Central America, South America, the Caribbean, and the Pacific. We are seeking only a few titles in each of our major series. Check online guidelines for our current needs. Follow guidelines closely." **Publishes 100 titles/year. 5,000 queries received/year. 25% of books from first-time authors. 95% from unagented writers. Pays up to $17,000 advance.** Publishes ms an average of 9 months after acceptance. Accepts simultaneous submissions. Responds in 4 months. Guidelines online.

NONFICTION Subjects include regional, travel. "We are not interested in fiction, children's books, and travelogues/travel diaries." Submit cover letter, resume, and up to 5 relevant clips.

AVON ROMANCE

Harper Collins Publishers, 10 E. 53 St., New York NY 10022. **E-mail:** info@avonromance.com. **Website:** www.avonromance.com. Estab. 1941. Publishes paperback and digital originals and reprints. Avon has been publishing award-winning books since 1941. It is recognized for having pioneered the historical romance category and continues to bring the best of commercial literature to the broadest possible audience. **Publishes 400 titles/year.** Accepts simultaneous submissions.

FICTION Subjects include historical, literary, mystery, romance, science fiction, young adult. Submit a query and ms via the online submission form.

BACKBEAT BOOKS

Hal Leonard Publishing Group, 33 Plymouth St., Suite 302, Montclair NJ 07042. (973)337-5034. **E-mail:** bmalavarca@halleonard.com. **Website:** www.backbeatbooks.com. **Contact:** Bernadette Malavarca, senior editor. Publishes hardcover and trade paperback originals; trade paperback reprints. **Publishes 30 titles/year. 30% of books from first-time authors. 60% from unagented writers. Pays modest advance.** Publishes ms 18-24 months after acceptance. Accepts simultaneous submissions. Guidelines online.

NONFICTION Subjects include music, pop culture. Query with TOC, sample chapter, sample illustrations.

THE BACKWATERS PRESS

1124 Pacific St., #8392, Omaha NE 68108-3265. **E-mail:** thebackwaterspress@gmail.com. **Website:** www.thebackwaterspress.org. **Contact:** Michael Catherwood, editor. Editor Emeritus: Greg Kosmicki. Estab. 1998. Publishes poetry in English; no children's poetry. The Backwaters Press is a 501-(C)-3 non-profit literary press that publishes poetry and poetry-related books, including anthologies. The press sponsors an annual book award prize, The Backwaters Prize, which includes a cash prize and publication. **Publishes 2-5 titles/year. 300-400 50% of books from first-time authors. 100% from unagented writers. Pays in copies, publication. Contest winner receives $2,500 and copies. Does not pay advance.** Publishes ms 6-12 months after acceptance. Accepts simultaneous submissions. Responds to contest: 2-3 months. All others, up to 6 months. Catalog online. Guidelines online.

POETRY Only considers submissions to Backwaters Prize. More details on website. Open to all styles and forms. Complete book mss only.

BAEN BOOKS

P.O. Box 1188, Wake Forest NC 27588. (919)570-1640. **E-mail:** info@baen.com. **Website:** www.baen.com. Estab. 1983. "We publish only science fiction and fantasy. Writers familiar with what we have published in the past will know what sort of material we are most likely to publish in the future: powerful plots with solid scientific and philosophical underpinnings are the sine qua non for consideration for science fiction submissions. As for fantasy, any magical system must be both rigorously coherent and integral to the plot, and overall the work must at least strive for originality." Accepts simultaneous submissions. Responds to mss within 12-18 months.

FICTION "Style: Simple is generally better; in our opinion good style, like good breeding, never calls attention to itself. Length: 100,000-130,000 words Generally we are uncomfortable with manuscripts under 100,000 words, but if your novel is really wonderful send it along regardless of length." "Query letters are not necessary. We prefer to see complete manuscripts accompanied by a synopsis. We prefer not to see simultaneous submissions. Electronic submissions are strongly preferred. *We no longer accept submissions by e-mail.* Send ms by using the submission form at: http://ftp.baen.com/Slush/submit.aspx. No disks unless requested. Attach ms as a Rich Text Format (.rtf) file. Any other format will not be considered."

BAEN PUBLISHING ENTERPRISES

P.O. Box 1188, Wake Forest NC 27588. (919)570-1640. **E-mail:** info@baen.com; toni@baen.com. **Website:** www.baen.com. Contact: Jim Minz, Tony Daniel. Estab. 1983. Publishes hardcover, trade paperback and mass market paperback originals and reprints. Accepts simultaneous submissions. Responds in 9-12 months to mss. Book catalog available free. Guidelines online.

FICTION Subjects include adventure, fantasy, historical, military, science fiction, young adult. Submit synopsis and complete ms. "Electronic submissions are strongly preferred. Attach manuscript as a Rich Text Format (.rtf) file. Any other format will not be considered." Additional submission guidelines online. Include estimated word count, brief bio. Send SASE or IRC. Responds in 9-12 months. No simultaneous submissions. Sometimes comments on rejected mss.

TIPS "Keep an eye and a firm hand on the overall story you are telling. Style is important but less important than plot. Good style, like good breeding, never calls attention to itself. Read *Writing to the Point*, by Algis Budrys. We like to maintain long-term relationships with authors."

BAILIWICK PRESS

309 East Mulberry St., Fort Collins CO 80524. (970)672-4878. **Fax:** (970)672-4731. **E-mail:** info@bailiwickpress.com. **E-mail:** aldozelnick@gmail.com. **Website:** www.bailiwickpress.com. "We're a micro-press that produces books and other products that inspire and tell great stories. Our motto is 'books with something to say.' We are now considering submissions, agented and unagented, for children's and young adult fiction. We're looking for smart, funny, and layered writing that kids will clamor for. Authors who already have a following have a leg up. We are only looking for humorous children's fiction. Please do not submit work for adults. Illustrated fiction is desired but not required. (Illustrators are also invited to send samples.) Make us laugh out loud, ooh and aah, and cry, 'Eureka!'" Accepts simultaneous submissions. Responds in 6 months.

FICTION "Please read the Aldo Zelnick series to determine if we might be on the same page, then fill out our submission form. Please do not send submissions via snail mail or phone calls. You must complete the online submission form to be considered. If, after completing and submitting the form, you also need to send us an e-mail attachment (such as sample illustrations or excerpts of graphics), you may e-mail them to aldozelnick@gmail.com."

BAKER ACADEMIC/BRAZOS PRESS

Division of Baker Publishing Group, 6030 E. Fulton Rd., Ada MI 49301. (616)676-9185. **E-mail:** submissions@bakeracademic.com. **Website:** bakerpublishinggroup.com/bakeracademic. Estab. 1939. "We produce primary and supplementary textbooks, reference works, and scholarly monographs that extend the academic conversation to a range of readers, from students to experts on the cutting edge of research. Our main areas of focus include biblical studies, theology, ethics, cultural studies, and church history. We also publish textbooks on Christian education, mission, and ministry as well as integrative works in a variety of liberal arts disciplines, such as literature, communication, philosophy, and psychology.". Baker Academic serves the academy and the church by publishing works that further the pursuit of knowledge and understanding within the context of Christian faith. "Building on our Reformed and evangelical heritage, we connect authors and readers across the broader academic community by publishing books that reflect historic Christianity and its contemporary expressions. Our authors are scholars who are leaders in their fields, write irenically, and display a healthy respect for other perspectives and traditions. Our goal is to publish books that are notable for their inherent quality and deemed essential reading by students and scholars. Brazos Press publishes books that foster faithful cultural engagement, creatively bringing the riches of our catholic Christian heritage to bear on the complexity and wonder of life. Brazos is animated by a vision of God reaching out to embrace all of humanity with a love as wide and deep as God's creation. Our books inspire faithful interaction with issues of importance to the church and the world." **Publishes 50 titles/year. Pays advance.** Publishes book 1 year after ms turned in. Accepts simultaneous submissions. Responds in approximately 2 weeks. Guidelines online.

NONFICTION Subjects include education, psychology, religion, Biblical studies, Christian doctrine, books for pastors and church leaders, contemporary issues.

BAKER BOOKS

Division of Baker Publishing Group, 6030 E. Fulton Rd., Ada MI 49301. (616)676-9185. **Website:** bakerpublishinggroup.com/bakerbooks. Estab. 1939. Publishes in hardcover and trade paperback originals, and trade paperback reprints. "We will consider unsolicited work only through one of the following avenues. Materials sent through a literary agent will be considered. In addition, our staff attends various writers' conferences at which prospective authors can develop relationships with those in the publishing industry." Accepts simultaneous submissions. Book catalog for 9½×12½ envelope and 3 first-class stamps. Guidelines online.

"Baker Books publishes popular religious nonfiction reference books and professional books for church leaders. Most of our authors and readers are evangelical Christians, and our books are purchased from Christian bookstores, mail-order retailers, and school bookstores. Does not accept unsolicited queries."

NONFICTION Subjects includeChristian doctrines.

TIPS "We are not interested in historical fiction, romances, science fiction, biblical narratives or spiritual warfare novels. Do not call to 'pass by' your idea."

BAKER PUBLISHING GROUP

6030 E. Fulton Rd., Ada MI 49301. (616)676-9185. **Fax:** (616)676-9573. **Website:** www.bakerpublishinggroup.com. Accepts simultaneous submissions.

IMPRINTS Baker Academic; Baker Books; Bethany House; Brazos Press; Chosen; Fleming H. Revell.

Does not accept unsolicited queries.

BALLANTINE BOOKS

Imprint of Penguin Random House, Inc., 1745 Broadway, 18th Floor, New York NY 10019. (212)782-9000. **Website:** www.penguinrandomhouse.com. Estab. 1952. Publishes hardcover, trade paperback, mass market paperback originals. Ballantine Bantam Dell publishes a wide variety of nonfiction and fiction. Accepts simultaneous submissions. Guidelines online.

NONFICTION Subjects include animals, child guidance, community, creative nonfiction, education, history, memoirs, recreation, religion, sex, spirituality, travel, true crime. Agented submissions only. Reviews artwork/photos. Send photocopies.

FICTION Subjects include confession, ethnic, fantasy, feminist, historical, humor, literary, multicultural, mystery, romance, short story collections, spiritual, suspense, translation, general fiction. Agented submissions only.

BALZER & BRAY

HarperCollins Children's Books, 10 E. 53rd St., New York NY 10022. **Website:** www.harpercollinschildrens.com. Estab. 2008. "We publish bold, creative, groundbreaking picture books and novels that appeal directly to kids in a fresh way." **Publishes 10 titles/year. Offers advances. Pays illustrators by the project.** Publishes book 18 months after acceptance. Accepts simultaneous submissions.

NONFICTION Subjects include animals, cooking, dance, environment, history, multicultural, music, nature, science, social sciences, sports. "We will publish very few nonfiction titles, maybe 1-2 per year." Agented submissions only.

FICTION Picture Books, Young Readers: adventure, animal, anthology, concept, contemporary, fantasy, history, humor, multicultural, nature/environment, poetry, science fiction, special needs, sports, suspense. Middle readers, young adults/teens: adventure, animal, anthology, contemporary, fantasy, history, humor, multicultural, nature/environment, poetry, science fiction, special needs, sports, suspense. Agented submissions only.

BANTAM BOOKS

Imprint of Penguin Random House, Inc., 1745 Broadway, New York NY 10019. (212)782-9000. **Website:** www.randomhousebooks.com. *Not seeking mss at this time.* Accepts simultaneous submissions.

BARBOUR PUBLISHING, INC.

P.O. Box 719, Urichsville OH 44683. **E-mail:** submissions@barbourbooks.com. **Website:** www.barbourbooks.com. Estab. 1981. "Barbour Books publishes inspirational/devotional material that is nondenominational and evangelical in nature. We're a Christian evangelical publisher." Specializes in short, easy-to-read Christian bargain books. "Faithfulness to the Bible and Jesus Christ are the bedrock values behind every book Barbour's staff produces."

"We no longer accept unsolicited submissions unless they are submitted through professional literary agencies. For more information, we encourage new fiction authors to join a professional writers organization like American Christian Fiction Writers."

BAREFOOT BOOKS

2067 Massachusettes Ave., 5th Floor, Cambridge MA 02140. (617)576-0660. **Fax:** (617)576-0049. **E-mail:** help@barefootbooks.com. **Website:** www.barefootbooks.com. **Contact:** Acquisitions Editor. Publishes hardcover and trade paperback originals. "We are a small, independent publishing company that publishes high-quality picture books for children of all ages and specializes in the work of artists and writers from many cultures. We focus on themes that support independence of spirit, encourage openness to others, and foster a life-long love of learning. Prefers full manuscript." **Publishes 30 titles/year. 2,000 queries received/year. 3,000 mss received/year. 35% of books from first-time authors. 60% from unagented writers. Pays advance.** Accepts simultaneous submissions. Book catalog for 9x12 SAE stamped with $1.80 postage.

FICTION Subjects include juvenile. "Barefoot Books only publishes children's picture books and anthologies of folktales. We do not publish novels." Barefoot Books is not currently accepting ms queries or submissions.

BARRICADE BOOKS, INC.

2037 Lemoine Ave., Suite 362, Fort Lee NJ 07024. (201)944-7600. **Fax:** (201)917-4951. **Website:** www.barricadebooks.com. **Contact:** Carole Stuart, publisher. Estab. 1991. Publishes hardcover and trade paperback originals, trade paperback reprints. "Barricade Books publishes nonfiction, mostly of the controversial type, and books we can promote with authors who can talk about their topics on radio and television and to the press." **Publishes 12 titles/year. 200 queries received/year. 100 mss received/year. 80% of books from first-time authors. 50% from unagented writers. Pays 10-12% royalty on retail price for hardcover. Pays advance.** Publishes book 18 months after acceptance. Accepts simultaneous submissions. Responds in 1 month to queries.

NONFICTION Subjects include ethnic, history, psychology, sociology, true crime. "We look for quality nonfiction mss—preferably with a controversial lean." Query with SASE. Submit outline, 1-2 sample chapters. Material will not be returned or responded to without SASE. "We do not accept proposals on disk or via e-mail." Reviews artwork/photos. Send photocopies.

TIPS "Do your homework. Visit bookshops to find publishers who are doing the kinds of books you want to write. Always submit to a person—not just 'Editor.'"

BARRONS EDUCATIONAL SERIES

250 Wireless Blvd., Hauppauge NY 11788. **Fax:** (631)434-3723. **Website:** www.barronseduc.com. **Contact:** Wayne R. Barr, manuscript acquisitions. Estab. 1945. **Pays authors royalty of 10-12% based on net price or buys ms outright for $2,000 minimum. Pays illustrators by the project based on retail price.** Publishes book 1 year after acceptance. Accepts simultaneous submissions. Due to the large volume of unsolicited submissions received, a complete evaluation of a proposal may take 4-6 weeks. Please do not call about the status of individual submissions. Catalog available for 9x12 SASE. Guidelines available on website.

NONFICTION Picture books: concept, reference. Young readers: biography, how-to, reference, self-help, social issues. Middle readers: hi-lo, how-to, reference, self-help, social issues. Young adults: reference, self-help, social issues, sports. Submit outline/synopsis and sample chapters. "Nonfiction submissions must be accompanied by SASE for response."

FICTION Picture books: animal, concept, multicultural, nature/environment. Young readers: adventure, multicultural, nature/environment, fantasy, suspense/mystery. Middle readers: adventure, fantasy, multicultural, nature/environment, problem novels, suspense/mystery. Young adults: problem novels. "Stories with an educational element are appealing." Query via e-mail with no attached files. Full guidelines are listed on the website.

TIPS Writers: "We publish pre-school storybooks, concept books and middle grade and YA chapter books. No romance novels. Those with an educational element." Illustrators: "We are happy to receive a sample illustration to keep on file for future consideration. Periodic notes reminding us of your work are acceptable." Children's book themes "are becoming much more contemporary and relevant to a child's day-to-day activities, fewer talking animals. We are interested in fiction (ages 7-11 and ages 12-16) dealing with modern problems."

Ⓐ⊘ BASIC BOOKS

Hachette Book Group, 1290 Avenue of the Americas, Suite 1500, New York NY 10104. **Website:** www.basicbooks.com. **Contact:** Editor. Estab. 1952. Publishes hardcover and trade paperback originals and reprints. Accepts simultaneous submissions. Responds in at least 3 months to queries. Book catalog available free. Guidelines online.

NONFICTION Subjects include history, psychology, sociology, politics, current affairs.

BAYLOR UNIVERSITY PRESS

One Bear Place 97363, Waco TX 76798. (254)710-3164. **Fax:** (254)710-3440. **E-mail:** carey_newman@baylor.edu. **Website:** www.baylorpress.com. **Contact:** Dr. Carey C. Newman, director. Estab. 1897. Publishes hardcover and trade paperback originals. "We publish contemporary and historical scholarly works about culture, religion, politics, science, and the arts." **Publishes 30 titles/year. Pays 10% royalty on wholesale price.** Publishes ms 1 year after acceptance. Accepts simultaneous submissions. Responds in 2 months to proposals. Guidelines online.

NONFICTION Submit outline, 1-3 sample chapters via e-mail.

RECENT TITLE(S) *Decreation*, by Paul J. Griffiths; *Galatians*, by David A. deSilva.

BEACON PRESS

24 Farnsworth St., Boston MA 02210. **E-mail:** editorial@beacon.org. **Website:** www.beacon.org. Estab. 1854. Publishes hardcover originals and paperback reprints. Beacon Press publishes general interest books that promote the following values: the inherent worth and dignity of every person; justice, equity, and compassion in human relations; acceptance of one another; a free and responsible search for truth and meaning; the goal of world community with peace, liberty, and justice for all; respect for the interdependent web of all existence. Currently emphasizing innovative nonfiction writing by people of all colors. De-emphasizing poetry, children's stories, art books, self-help. **Publishes 60 titles/year. 10% of books from first-time authors. Pays royalty. Pays advance.** Accepts simultaneous submissions. Responds in 3 months to queries.

NONFICTION Subjects include child guidance, education, ethnic, philosophy, religion, world affairs. *Strongly prefers agented submissions.* Query by e-mail only. *Strongly prefers referred submissions, on exclusive.*

TIPS "We probably accept only 1 or 2 manuscripts from an unpublished pool of 4,000 submissions/year. No fiction, children's books, or poetry submissions invited. An academic affiliation is helpful."

BEARMANOR MEDIA

P.O. Box 71426, Albany GA 31708. **E-mail:** books@benohmart.com. **Website:** www.bearmanormedia.com. **Contact:** Ben Ohmart, publisher. Estab. 2000. Publishes trade paperback originals, hardbacks, e-books, and audio books. "We specialize in entertainment biographies, and books on radio, TV and stage projects, as well as film scripts." **Publishes 70 titles/year. 90% of books from first-time authors. 90% from unagented writers. Negotiable per project. Pays upon acceptance. Occasionally pays advance.** Accepts simultaneous submissions. Responds within a few days. Book catalog online, or free upon request.

IMPRINTS BearManor Bare, MagicImage, BearManor Media, Needed Books.

NONFICTION Subjects include cinema, dance, entertainment, film, memoirs, pop culture, stage. Only entertainment-related books please. Query with SASE. E-mail queries preferred. Submit proposal package, outline, list of credits on the subject. No.

RECENT TITLE(S) Richard Pryor Jr. autobiography, Buck Privates film script, Jaws 2: The Making of the Hollywood Sequel, Mel Blanc biography, The Gilmore Girls, The Charlie Chan Films, Dracula's Daughter film script, Sydney Greenstreet biography, Jan Michael-Vincent biography, The Making of Stephen King's Cujo, and more.

TIPS "My readers love the past. Radio, old movies, old television. My own tastes include voice actors and scripts, especially of radio and television no longer available. I prefer books on subjects that haven't previously been covered as full books. It doesn't matter to me if you're a first-time author or have a track record. Just know your subject and know how to write a sentence!"

BEHRMAN HOUSE INC.

11 Edison Place, Springfield NJ 07081. (973)379-7200. **Fax:** (973)379-7280. **E-mail:** customersupport@behrmanhouse.com. **Website:** www.behrmanhouse.com. **Contact:** Editorial Committee. Estab. 1921. Publishes books on all aspects of Judaism: history, cultural, textbooks, holidays. "Behrman House publishes quality books of Jewish content—history, Bible, philosophy, holidays, ethics—for children and adults." **12% of books from first-time authors. Pays authors royalty of 3-10% based on retail price or buys ms outright for $1,000-5,000. Offers advance. Pays illustrators by the project (range: $500-5,000).** Publishes book 18 months after acceptance. Accepts simultaneous submissions. Responds in 1 month to queries; 2 months to mss. Book catalog free on request. Guidelines online.

NONFICTION All levels: Judaism, Jewish educational textbooks. Average word length: young reader—1,200; middle reader—2,000; young adult—4,000. Submit outline/synopsis and sample chapters.

FREDERIC C. BEIL, PUBLISHER, INC.

609 Whitaker St., Savannah GA 31401. (912)233-2446. **E-mail:** fcb@beil.com. **Website:** www.beil.com. **Contact:** Frederic Beil. Estab. 1982. Publishes original titles in hardcover, softcover, and e-book. Beil publishes books in the fields of biography, history, and fiction. While under way, Beil has published authors of meaningful works and adhered to high standards in bookmaking craftsmanship. **Publishes 6 titles/**

year. 300 queries; 6 mss received/year. 60% of books from first-time authors. 100% from unagented writers. Pays 7.5% royalty on retail price. Does not pay advance. Publishes ms 15-18 months after acceptance. Accepts simultaneous submissions. Responds in 1 week to queries received via postal mail. Catalog online. Upon agreement with author, Beil will provide guidelines to author.

IMPRINTS The Sandstone Press.

NONFICTION Subjects include history, humanities, literature, memoirs, philosophy, regional. Query with SASE.

FICTION Subjects include historical, literary. Query with SASE.

TIPS "Our objectives are to offer carefully selected texts; to adhere to high standards in the choice of materials and in bookmaking craftsmanship; to produce books that exemplify good taste in format and design; and to maintain the lowest cost consistent with quality."

BELLEBOOKS

P.O. Box 300921, Memphis TN 38130. (901)344-9024. **Fax:** (901)344-9068. **E-mail:** bellebooks@bellebooks.com. **Website:** www.bellebooks.com. Estab. 1999. BelleBooks began by publishing Southern fiction. It has become a "second home" for many established authors, who also continue to publish with major publishing houses. **Publishes 30-40 titles/year.** Accepts simultaneous submissions. Guidelines online.

FICTION Subjects include juvenile, young adult. "Yes, we'd love to find the next Harry Potter, but our primary focus for the moment is publishing for the teen market." Query e-mail with brief synopsis and credentials/credits with full ms attached (RTF format preferred).

RECENT TITLE(S) *Alias Dragonfly*, by Jane Singer; *Crossroads Cafe*, by Deborah Smith.

TIPS "Our list aims for the teen reader and the crossover market. If you're a 'Southern Louise Rennison,' that would catch our attention. Humor is always a plus. We'd love to see books featuring teen boys as protagonists. We're happy to see dark edgy books on serious subjects."

BELLEVUE LITERARY PRESS

Website: https://blpress.org/. Estab. 2005. Bellevue Literary Press is devoted to publishing literary fiction and nonfiction at the intersection of the arts and sciences because we believe that science and the humanities are natural companions for understanding the human experience. With each book we publish, our goal is to foster a rich, interdisciplinary dialogue that will forge new tools for thinking and engaging with the world. Accepts simultaneous submissions. Guidelines online.

NONFICTION We publish narrative nonfiction at the intersection of the arts and sciences for a general adult audience. Please see our nonfiction catalog for examples of the books we're looking for on our website. We do not publish books for children or young adults, memoirs, or self-help. Please submit the complete manuscript (preferred) or a detailed proposal including sample chapters during one of our open reading periods.

FICTION Subjects include literary. We publish literary fiction at the intersection of the arts and sciences, or in other words, excellently written books of ideas. We do not publish books for children or young adults, poetry, single short stories, or commercial fiction (such as thrillers or romances). Please see our fiction catalog for examples of the books we're looking for on our website. Please submit the complete manuscript during one of our open reading periods.

RECENT TITLE(S) *Tinkers*, by Paul Harding; *A Wilder Time: Notes from a Geologist at the Edge of the Greenland Ice*, by William E. Glassley.

BENBELLA BOOKS

10300 N. Central Expressway, Suite 530, Dallas TX 75231. (214)750-3600. **E-mail:** glenn@benbellabooks.com. **Website:** www.benbellabooks.com. **Contact:** Glenn Yeffeth, publisher. Estab. 2001. Publishes hardcover and trade paperback originals. **Publishes 30-40 titles/year. Pays 6-15% royalty on retail price.** Publishes ms 10 months after acceptance. Accepts simultaneous submissions. Guidelines online.

NONFICTION Subjects include literary criticism, science. Submit proposal package, including: outline, 2 sample chapters (via e-mail).

BENTLEY PUBLISHERS

1734 Massachusetts Ave., Cambridge MA 02138. (617)547-4170. **Fax:** (617)876-9235. **Website:** www.bentleypublishers.com. Estab. 1950. Publishes hardcover and trade paperback originals and reprints. "Bentley Publishers publishes books for automotive enthusiasts. We are interested in books that showcase good research, strong illustrations, and valuable technical information." Automotive subjects only. Query with SASE. Submit sample chapters, bio, synopsis, target market. Reviews artwork/photos. Book catalog and ms guidelines online.

NONFICTION Query with SASE. Submit sample chapters, bio, synopsis, target market. Rreviews artwork/photos.

TIPS "Our audience is composed of serious, intelligent automobile, sports car, and racing enthusiasts, automotive technicians and high-performance tuners."

BERGLI BOOKS

Schwabe Verlag, Steinentorstrasse 11, Basel CH-4010, Switzerland. **E-mail:** info@bergli.ch. **Website:** www.bergli.ch. **Contact:** Richard Harvell, executive editor. Estab. 1991. Bergli Books publishes books in Switzerland that bridge intercultural gaps. "It's mostly English list has included many Swiss-interest bestsellers of the past two decades, including the *Ticking Along* Series, Margaret Oertig's *Beyond Chocolate*, and Sergio Lievano and Nicole Egger's *Hoi* books—the best-selling Swiss German guides of all time. An imprint of Schwabe since 2013, Bergli is unique in Switzerland—connecting English readers to Swiss culture and tradition." **Publishes 3-4 titles/year. Receives 50 queries/year. 50% of books from first-time authors. Pays 7-12% royalties on retail price. Pays $1,000-5,000 advance.** Publishes ms 12 months after acceptance. Accepts simultaneous submissions. Responds in 1 month to queries, proposals, and mss. Catalog available online. Guidelines available for SASE.

NONFICTION Subjects include travel, Swiss culture, Switzerland for expats. "Our chief market is among English speakers in Switzerland." Submit proposal package, outline, and 1 sample chapter. Reviews artwork, submit photocopies.

RECENT TITLE(S) *Swiss Democracy in a Nutshell* by Gregoire Nappey; *Hoi: Your New Swiss German Survival Guide* by Sergio Lievano.

TIPS "We like illustrated books, show us something that has been done elsewhere but not in Switzerland."

BERKLEY

An Imprint of Penguin Random House LLC, 1745 Broadway, New York NY 10019. **Website:** penguinrandomhouse.com. President: Ivan Held. Estab. 1955. Publishes paperback and mass market originals and reprints. The Berkley Publishing Group publishes a variety of general nonfiction and fiction including the traditional categories of romance, mystery and science fiction. **Publishes 700 titles/year.**

IMPRINTS Ace; Jove; Heat; Sensation; Berkley Prime Crime; Berkley Caliber.

"Due to the high volume of manuscripts received, most Penguin Group (USA) Inc. imprints do not normally accept unsolicited mss. The preferred and standard method for having mss considered for publication by a major publisher is to submit them through an established literary agent."

NONFICTION Subjects include child guidance, creative nonfiction, history, New Age, psychology, true crime, job-seeking communication. No memoirs or personal stories. Prefers agented submissions.

FICTION Subjects include adventure, historical, literary, mystery, romance, spiritual, suspense, western, young adult. No occult fiction. Prefers agented submissions.

BERRETT-KOEHLER PUBLISHERS, INC.

1333 Broadway, Suite #1000, Oakland CA 94612. **E-mail:** bkpub@bkpub.com. **E-mail:** submissions@bkpub.com. **Website:** www.bkconnection.com. **Contact:** Anna Leinberger, associate editor. Publishes hardcover and trade paperback originals, mass market paperback originals, hardcover and trade paperback reprints. "Berrett-Koehler Publishers' mission is to publish books that support the movement toward a world that works for all. Our titles promote positive change at personal, organizational and societal levels." Please see proposal guidelines online. **Publishes 40 titles/year. 1,300 queries received/year. 800 mss received/year. 20-30% of books from first-time authors. 70% from unagented writers. Pays 10-20% royalty.** Publishes book 10 months after acceptance. Accepts simultaneous submissions. Responds in 1 month. Book catalog online.

NONFICTION Subjects include community, New Age, spirituality. Submit proposal package, outline, bio, 1-2 sample chapters. Hard-copy proposals only. Do not e-mail, fax, or phone please. Reviews artwork/photos. Send photocopies or originals with SASE.

TIPS "Our audience is business leaders. Use common sense, do your research."

BESS PRESS

3565 Harding Ave., Honolulu HI 96816. (808)734-7159. **Fax:** (808)732-3627. **Website:** www.besspress.com. Estab. 1979. Bess Press is a family-owned independent book publishing company based in Honolulu. For over 30 years, Bess Press has been producing both educational and popular general interest titles about Hawai'i and the Pacific. Accepts simultaneous submissions. Responds in 4 months. Catalog online. Guidelines online.

NONFICTION "We are constantly seeking to work with authors, artists, photographers, and organizations that are developing works concentrating on Hawai'i and the Pacific. Our goal is to regularly provide customers with new, creative, informative, educational, and entertaining publications that are directly connected to or flowing from Hawai'i and other islands in the Pacific region." Not interested in material that is unassociated with Hawai'i or the greater Pacific in theme. Please do not submit works if it does not fall into this regional category. Submit your name, contact information, working title, genre, target audience, short (4-6 sentences) description of your work, identifies target audience(s), explains how your work differs from other books already publishing on the same subject, includes discussion of any additional material with samples. All submissions via e-mail.

TIPS "As a regional publisher, we are looking for material specific to the region (Hawaii and Micronesia), preferably from writers and illustrators living within (or very familiar with) the region.", "As a regional publisher, we are looking for material specific to the region (Hawaii and Micronesia), preferably from writers and illustrators living within (or very familiar with) the region."

⊘ BETHANY HOUSE PUBLISHERS

Division of Baker Publishing Group, 6030 E. Fulton Rd., Ada MI 49301. (616)676-9185. **Fax:** (616)676-9573. **Website:** bakerpublishinggroup.com/bethanyhouse. Estab. 1956. Publishes hardcover and trade paperback originals, mass market paperback reprints. Bethany House Publishers specializes in books that communicate Biblical truth and assist people in both spiritual and practical areas of life. Considers unsolicited work only through a professional literary agent or through manuscript submission services, Authonomy or Christian Manuscript Submissions. Guidelines online. *All unsolicited mss returned unopened.* **Publishes 90-100 titles/year. 2% of books from first-time authors. 50% from unagented writers. Pays royalty on net price. Pays advance.** Publishes a book 1 year after acceptance. Accepts simultaneous submissions. Responds in 3 months to queries. Book catalog for 9 x 12 envelope and 5 first-class stamps.

NONFICTION Subjects include child guidance, Biblical disciplines, personal and corporate renewal, emerging generations, devotional, marriage and family, applied theology, inspirational.

FICTION Subjects include historical, young adult, contemporary.

TIPS "Bethany House Publishers' publishing program relates Biblical truth to all areas of life—whether in the framework of a well-told story, of a challenging book for spiritual growth, or of a Bible reference work. We are seeking high-quality fiction and nonfiction that will inspire and challenge our audience."

Ⓐ⊘ BEYOND WORDS PUBLISHING, INC.

20827 NW Cornell Rd., Suite 500, Hillsboro OR 97124. (503)531-8700. **Fax:** (503)531-8773. **E-mail:** info@beyondword.com. **Website:** www.beyondword.com. **Contact:** Submissions Department (for agents only). Estab. 1984. Publishes hardcover and trade paperback originals and paperback reprints. "At this time, we are not accepting any unsolicited queries or proposals, and recommend that all authors work with a literary agent in submitting their work." **Publishes 10-15 titles/year.** Accepts simultaneous submissions.

NONFICTION Subjects include health, young adult. For adult nonfiction, wants whole body health, the evolving human, and transformation. For children and YA, wants health, titles that inspire kids' power to incite change, and titles that allow young readers to explore and/or question traditional wisdom and spiritual practices. Does not want children's picture books, adult fiction, cookbooks, textbooks, reference books, photography books, or illustrated coffee table books. Agent should submit query letter with proposal, including author bio, 5 sample chapters, complete synopsis of book, market analysis, SASE.

FICTION Subjects include juvenile, young adult. Agent should submit query letter with proposal, including author bio, 5 sample chapters, complete synopsis of book, market analysis, SASE.

⊘ BIRCH BOOK PRESS

Birch Brook Impressions, P.O. Box 81, Delhi NY 13753. **Fax:** (607)746-7453. **E-mail:** birchbrook@copper.net. **Website:** www.birchbrookpress.info. **Contact:** Tom Tolnay, editor/publisher; Leigh Eckmair, art &

research editor; Joyce Tolnay, account services. Estab. 1982. Occasionally publishes trade paperback originals. Birch Brook Press "is a book printer/typesetter/designer that uses monies from these activities to publish several titles of its own each year with cultural and literary interest." Specializes in literary work, flyfishing, baseball, outdoors, themed short fiction anthologies, and books about books. *Not considering any new mss in the foreseeable future.* **Publishes 2 titles/year. 200+ queries; 200+ mss received/year. 95% from unagented writers. Pays modest royalty on acceptance.** Publishes ms 10-18 months after acceptance. Accepts simultaneous submissions. Responds in 3-6 months. Book catalog online.

FICTION "Mostly we do anthologies around a particular theme generated inhouse. We make specific calls for fiction when we are doing an anthology." Currently, BBP is not seeking manuscripts on any subject. Overstocked. *Not currently accepting any submissions.*

POETRY *Not currently seeking any poetry submissions.*

RECENT TITLE(S) *Graceful Ghost*, by Gwendolyn Jensen; *Weathering Wilderness*, by Richard B. Hoffman; *Homecomings*, by Lance Lee.

BLACK LAWRENCE PRESS

E-mail: editors@blacklawrencepress.com. **Website:** www.blacklawrencepress.com. **Contact:** Diane Goettel, executive editor. Estab. 2003. Black Lawrence press seeks to publish intriguing books of literature—novels, short story collections, poetry collections, chapbooks, anthologies, and creative nonfiction. Will also publish the occasional translation from German. Publishes 22-24 books/year, mostly poetry and fiction. Mss are selected through open submission and competition. Books are 20-400 pages, offset-printed or high-quality POD, perfect-bound, with 4-color cover. **Accepts submissions during the months of June and November. Pays royalties.** Accepts simultaneous submissions. Responds in 6 months to mss. Catalog online.

NONFICTION Subjects include creative nonfiction, gay, humanities, language, lesbian, literary criticism, literature, memoirs, multicultural, translation, womens issues, womens studies.

FICTION Subjects include contemporary, experimental, fantasy, feminist, gay, lesbian, literary, poetry, poetry in translation, short story collections, translation. Submit complete ms.

POETRY Submit complete ms.

⊘ BLACK LYON PUBLISHING, LLC

P.O. Box 567, Baker City OR 97814. **E-mail:** info@blacklyonpublishing.com. **E-mail:** queries@blacklyonpublishing.com. **Website:** www.blacklyonpublishing.com. **Contact:** The Editors. Estab. 2007. Publishes paperback and e-book originals. "Black Lyon Publishing is a small, independent publisher. We are currently closed to all except existing Black Lyon authors through 2017." **Publishes 15-20 titles/year.** Guidelines online.

FICTION Subjects include gothic, historical, romance.

BLACK OCEAN

P.O. Box 52030, Boston MA 02205. **E-mail:** carrie@blackocean.org. **Website:** www.blackocean.org. **Contact:** Carrie Olivia Adams, poetry editor. Estab. 2006. Publishes poetry, literary nonfiction, and translations. Black Ocean is an award-winning independent publisher based out of Boston, with satellites in Detroit and Chicago. From early silent films to early punk rock, Black Ocean brings together a spectrum of influences to produce books of exceptional quality and content. In conjunction with our book releases we manifest our aesthetic in celebrations around the country. We believe in the fissures art can create in consciousness when, even if just for a moment, we experience a more vital way of operating in the world—and through that moment then seek out more extreme and enlightened modes of existence. We believe in the freedom we find through enlightened modes of existence, and we are committed to promoting artists we firmly believe in by sharing our enthusiasm for their work with a global audience. **Publishes 6 titles/year.** Accepts simultaneous submissions. Catalog online. Guidelines online.

POETRY Wants poetry that is well-considered, risks itself, and by its beauty and/or bravery disturbs a tiny corner of the universe. Mss are selected through open submission. Books are 60+ pages. Book/chapbook mss may include previously published poems. We only accept unsolicited submissions during our open reading periods, and specific guidelines are updated and posted on our website.

RECENT TITLE(S) Published books by Zachary Schomburg, Kristin George Bagdanov, Tomaz Salamun, Joe Hall, Zach Savich, Rauan Klassnik, Aase Berg, Feng Sun Chen.

TIPS "Before you submit, read our books."

BLACK ROSE WRITING

P.O. Box 1540, Castroville TX 78009. **E-mail:** creator@blackrosewriting.com. **Website:** www.blackrosewriting.com/home. **Contact:** Reagan Rothe. Estab. 2006. Publishes fiction, nonfiction, and illustrated children's books. Black Rose Writing is an independent publishing house that strongly believes in developing a personal relationship with their authors. The Texas-based publishing company doesn't see authors as clients or just another number on a page, but rather as individual people. people who deserve an honest review of their material and to be paid traditional royalties without ever paying any fees to be published. Black Rose Writing, established in 2006, features books from an array of fiction, nonfiction, and children's book genres, all having one thing in common, an individual's originality and hardship. It can take endless hours to finish a deserving manuscript, and Black Rose Writing applauds each and every author, giving them a chance at their dream. Because Black Rose Writing takes full advantage of modern printing technology, the company has an infinite print run via print-on-demand services. Black Rose Writing's success with their authors is due mainly to their many lines of promotion, (examples: showcasing book titles at festivals, scheduling book events, flexible marketing programs, and sending out press releases and review copies, etc.) and they provide a broad distribution (Ingram, Baker & Taylor, Amazon, Barnes & Noble, and more.) that larger book publishers also reach. We are proud members of IBPA (Independent Book Publishers Association), a recognized ITW (International Thriller Writers) publisher, members of Publishers Marketplace, and currently serving on the Ingram Publisher Advisory Board. **Publishes 150+ titles/year. 3,500 submissions received/year. 75% of books from first-time authors. 80% from unagented writers. Royalties start at 20%, e-book royalties 25%** Publishes ms 4-6 months after acceptance. Accepts simultaneous submissions. Responds in 3-6 weeks on queries; 3-6 months on mss. Catalog online. Guidelines online.

IMPRINTS DigiTerra Publishing, Bookend Design.

NONFICTION Subjects include animals, anthropology, archeology, art, business, creative nonfiction, economics, education, ethnic, health, history, medicine, memoirs, military, politics, psychology, science, sociology, sports, transportation, travel, true crime, war. "Our preferred submission method is via Authors.me, please click 'Submit Here' on our website." Reviews artwork.

FICTION Subjects include adventure, fantasy, historical, horror, humor, juvenile, literary, mainstream, military, mystery, occult, picture books, regional, romance, science fiction, sports, suspense, war, western, young adult. "Our preferred submission method is via Authors.me, please click 'Submit Here' on our website."

RECENT TITLE(S) *Eyes Pried Open*, by Vincent Sellers (crime fiction); *One Creepy Street: The Spider on the Web*, by Lee Jordan (children's); *If Jack Had*, by Steve Rappaport (literary/humor).

BLACK VELVET SEDUCTIONS PUBLISHING

E-mail: ric@blackvelvetseductions.com. **E-mail:** submissions@blackvelvetseductions.com. **Website:** www.blackvelvetseductions.com. **Contact:** Richard Savage, CEO. Estab. 2005. Publishes trade paperback and electronic originals and reprints. "We publish across a wide range of romance sub-genres, from soft sweet romance to supernatural romance, domestic discipline to highly erotic romance stories containing D/s and BDSM relationships. We are looking for authors who take something ordinary and make it extraordinary. We want stories with well-developed multi-dimensional characters with back-stories, a high degree of emotional impact, with strong sexual tension between the heroine and hero, and stories that contain strong internal conflict. We prefer stories told in the third person viewpoint, but will consider first person narratives. We put the emphasis on romance, rather than just the erotic. Although we will consider a high level of erotic content, it needs to be in the context of a romance story line. The plots may twist and turn and be full of passion, but please remember that our audience likes a happy ending. Do not be afraid to approach us with a non-traditional character or plot." **Publishes 25 titles/year. 500 queries; 1,000 mss received/year. 75% of books from first-time authors. 100% from unagented writers. Pays 10% royalty for paperbacks; 50% royalty for electronic books.** Publishes ms 6-12 months after acceptance. Accepts simultaneous submissions. Responds as swiftly as possible. Catalog free or online. Guidelines online.

FICTION Subjects include contemporary, erotica, fantasy, gay, historical, lesbian, romance, short story collections, erotic romance, historical romance, multicultural romance, romance, short story collections romantic stories, romantic suspense, western romance. All stories must have a strong romance element. "There are very few sexual taboos in our erotic line. We tend to give our authors the widest latitude. If it is safe, sane, and consensual we will allow our authors latitude to show us the eroticism. However, we will not consider manuscripts with any of the following: bestiality (sex with animals), necrophilia (sex with dead people), pedophillia (sex with children)." Only accepts electronic submissions.

TIPS "We publish romance and erotic romance. We look for books written in very deep point of view. Shallow point of view remains the number one reason we reject manuscripts in which the storyline generally works."

BLAZEVOX [BOOKS]

131 Euclid Ave., Kenmore NY 14217. **E-mail:** editor@blazevox.org. **Website:** www.blazevox.org. **Contact:** Geoffrey Gatza, editor/publisher. Estab. 2005. "We are a major publishing presence specializing in innovative fictions and wide-ranging fields of innovative forms of poetry and prose. Our goal is to publish works that are challenging, creative, attractive, and yet affordable to individual readers. Articles of submission depend on many criteria, but overall items submitted must conform to one ethereal trait, your work must not suck. This put plainly, bad art should be punished; we will not promote it. However, all submissions will be reviewed and the author will receive feedback. We are human too." **65% of books from first-time authors. 100% from unagented writers. Pays 10% royalties on fiction and poetry books, based on net receipts. This amount may be split across multiple contributors. "We do not pay advances."** Accepts simultaneous submissions. Guidelines online.

FICTION Subjects include contemporary, experimental, lesbian, literary, poetry, poetry in translation, short story collections. Submit complete ms via e-mail.

POETRY Submit complete ms via e-mail.

TIPS "We actively contract and support authors who tour, read and perform their work, play an active part of the contemporary literary scene, and seek a readership."

BLIND EYE BOOKS

1141 Grant St., Bellingham WA 98225. **E-mail:** editor@blindeyebooks.com. **Website:** www.blindeyebooks.com. **Contact:** Nicole Kimberling, editor. Estab. 2007. "Blind Eye Books publishes science fiction, fantasy and paranormal romance novels featuring gay or lesbian protagonists. We do not publish short story collections, poetry, erotica, horror or nonfiction. We would hesitate to publish any manuscript that is less than 70,000 or over 150,000 words." Accepts simultaneous submissions. Guidelines online.

FICTION Subjects include fantasy, gay, lesbian, science fiction, paranormal romance. Submit complete ms with cover letter. Accepts queries by snail mail. Send disposable copy of ms and SASE for reply only. Does not return rejected mss. Authors living outside the U.S. can e-mail the editor for submission guidelines.

BLOOMBERG PRESS

Imprint of John Wiley & Sons, Professional Development, 111 River St., Hoboken NJ 07030. **E-mail:** info@wiley.com. **Website:** www.wiley.com. Estab. 1995. Publishes hardcover and trade paperback originals. Bloomberg Press publishes professional books for practitioners in the financial markets. "We publish commercially successful, very high-quality books that stand out clearly from the competition by their brevity, ease of use, sophistication, and abundance of practical tips and strategies; books readers need, will use, and appreciate." **Publishes 18-22 titles/year. 200 queries; 20 mss received/year. 45% from unagented writers. Pays negotiable, competitive royalty. Pays negotiable advance for trade books.** Publishes book 9 months after acceptance. Accepts simultaneous submissions. Responds in 1 month to queries.

NONFICTION Subjects include professional books on finance, investment and financial services, and books for financial advisors. "We are looking for authorities and for experienced service journalists. Do not send us unfocused books containing general information already covered by books in the marketplace. We do not publish business, management, leadership, or career books." Submit outline, sample chapters, SAE with sufficient postage. Submit complete ms.

ⒶⓄ BLOOMSBURY CHILDREN'S BOOKS

Imprint of Bloomsbury USA, 1385 Broadway, 5th Floor, New York NY 10018. **Website:** www.bloomsbury.com/us/childrens. No phone calls or e-mails.

Agented submissions only. **Publishes 60 titles/year. 25% of books from first-time authors. Pays royalty. Pays advance.** Accepts simultaneous submissions. Responds in 6 months. Book catalog online. Guidelines online.

FICTION Subjects include adventure, fantasy, historical, humor, juvenile, multicultural, mystery, picture books, poetry, science fiction, sports, suspense, young adult, animal, anthology, concept, contemporary, folktales, problem novels. *Agented submissions only.*

Ⓐ⊘ BLOOMSBURY CONTINUUM

Imprint of Bloomsbury Group, 1385 Broadway, 5th Floor, New York NY 10018. (212)419-5300. **Website:** www.bloomsbury.com/us/bloomsbury/bloomsbury-continuum. Continuum publishes textbooks, monographs, and reference works in religious studies, the humanities, arts, and social sciences for students, teachers, and professionals worldwide. *Does not accept unsolicited submissions.* Book catalog online.

NONFICTION Subjects include education, history, philosophy, religion, sociology, linguistics.

BLUEBRIDGE

Imprint of United Tribes Media, Inc., (914)301-5901. **E-mail:** janguerth@bluebridgebooks.com. **Website:** www.bluebridgebooks.com. **Contact:** Jan-Erik Guerth, publisher (general nonfiction). Estab. 2004. Publishes hardcover and trade paperbacks. BlueBridge is an independent publisher of international nonfiction based near New York City. BlueBridge book subjects include Culture, History, Biography; Nature and Science; Inspiration and Self-Help. BlueBridge is an imprint of United Tribes Media Inc. **Publishes 3-6 titles/year. Pays variable advance.** Accepts simultaneous submissions.

NONFICTION Subjects include alternative lifestyles, Americana, animals, anthropology, archeology, architecture, art, community, contemporary culture, creative nonfiction, economics, environment, ethnic, gardening, history, humanities, literary criticism, multicultural, nature, philosophy, politics, psychology, public affairs, religion, science, social sciences, sociology, spirituality, travel, womens issues, womens studies, world affairs. BlueBridge only accepts submission queries per e-mail, without any attachments to the e-mail, and only for nonfiction.

RECENT TITLE(S) *Two Dogs and a Parrot*, by Joan Chittister; *How Should We Live?*, by Roman Krznaric; *Herzl's Vision*, by Shlomo Avineri; *The Wisdom of the Beguines*, by Laura Swan; *Embracing the Seasons*, by Gunilla Norris; *Island*, by J. Edward Chamberlin; *Mr. Langshaw's Square Piano*, by Madeline Goold; *Queen Elizabeth in the Garden*, by Trea Martyn; *The Gift of Years*, by Joan Chittister.

TIPS "We target a broad general nonfiction audience."

BLUE LIGHT PRESS

P.O. Box 150300, San Rafael CA 94915. **E-mail:** bluelightpress@aol.com. **Website:** www.bluelightpress.com. **Contact:** Diane Frank, chief editor. Estab. 1988. "We like poems that are imagistic, emotionally honest, and push the edge—where the writer pushes through the imagery to a deeper level of insight and understanding. No rhymed poetry." Has published poetry by Stephen Dunn, Kim Addonizio, Jane Hirshfield, Rustin Larson, Mary Kay Rummel, Thomas Centolella,, Loretta Walker, Prartho Sereno, and K.B. Ballentine. "Books are elegantly designed and artistic. Our books are professionally printed, with original cover art, and we publish full-length books of poetry and chapbooks." **Publishes 5-8 titles/year. 400 50% of books from first-time authors. 90% from unagented writers. Poetry books retail at 15.95. Authors receive a 30% royalty of profits (not of cover price). Author copies are available at close to a 50% discount, for sale at readings and book events. Does not pay advance.** Publishes ms 2-8 months after acceptance. Accepts simultaneous submissions. Catalog online. Guidelines by e-mail.

NONFICTION Subjects include literature.

FICTION Subjects include poetry, poetry in translation, short story collections, flash fiction, micro fiction. We have published flash fiction and micro fiction.

POETRY Blue Light Press is dedicated to the publication of poetry that is imagistic, inventive, emotionally honest, and pushes the language to a deeper level of insight. "We are a collective of poets based in San Francisco, and our books are artistically designed. We also have an online poetry workshop with a wonderful group of American and international poets—open to new members 3 times/year. Send an e-mail for info — bluelightpress@aol.com." No rhymed poetry. For guidelines, send an e-mail to bluelightpress@aol.com. "Let us know if you want guidelines for a chapbook or full-length ms."

RECENT TITLE(S) *River of Earth and Sky: Poems for the 21st Century*, selected by Diane Frank; *Word Ghetto*, by Loretta Diane Walker; *Indian Rope Trick*, by

Prartho Sereno; *The Book of Cold Mountain*, by Cameron Keller Scott; *The Return of the Bees*, by Marianne Betterly; *The Perfume of Leaving*, by KB Ballentine; *Pavement*, by Rustin Larson; *Lyrics for a Low Noon*, by James Ralston.

TIPS "To see more than 100 poets we love, get a copy of *River of Earth and Sky: Poems for the Twenty-First Century*. It is full of examples of poems we like to publish. It's like a box of chocolates for poets."

BLUE MOUNTAIN PRESS

Blue Mountain Arts, Inc., P.O. Box 4219, Boulder CO 80306. (800)525-0642. **E-mail:** bmpbooks@sps.com. **Website:** www.sps.com. **Contact:** Patti Wayant, director. Estab. 1971. Publishes hardcover originals, trade paperback originals, electronic originals. We are the book division of Blue Mountain Arts, a leading publisher of greeting cards, calendars, and gift books. The books we publish inspire hope, encourage confidence, bolster dreams, convey comfort, and/or express heartfelt feelings for friends, family, significant others, and other important people in life. They may be given as a gift to someone special or purchased for personal inspiration. **Pays royalty on wholesale price. Pays royalty advance.** Publishes ms 12-16 months after acceptance. Accepts simultaneous submissions. Responds in 2-4 months. E-mail to request submission guidelines.

We are open to receiving new book proposals that have a highly original and positive message. We publish in these categories: self-help, personal growth, inspirational but not religious, teen/tween, family, and relationships. We do not publish fiction, memoir/biographies, narrative nonfiction, chapbooks, literary poetry, or children's books, nor do we wish to receive poetry compilations or writings gathered from the public domain.

NONFICTION Subjects includepersonal growth, teens/tweens, family, relationships, motivational, and inspirational but not religious. Query with SASE. Submit proposal package including outline and 3-5 sample chapters.

POETRY We publish poetry appropriate for gift books, self-help books, and personal growth books. We do not publish chapbooks or literary poetry. We do not accept rhyming poetry. Query. Submit 10+ sample poems.

BLUE RIVER PRESS

Cardinal Publishers Group, 2402 N. Shadeland Ave., Suite A, Indianapolis IN 46219. (317)352-8200. **Fax:** (317)352-8202. **E-mail:** dmccormick@cardinalpub.com; tdoherty@cardinalpub.com. **Website:** www.brpressbooks.com; www.cardinalpub.com. **Contact:** Dani McCormick, editor; Tom Doherty, president (adult nonfiction). Estab. 2000. Publishes hardcover, trade paperback, and electronic originals and reprints. Blue River Press released its first book in the spring of 2004. "Today we have more than 100 books and e-books in print on the subjects of sports, health, fitness, games, popular culture, travel and our All About. series for early readers. Our books have been recognized with awards and national and regional review attention. We have had many titles reach Nielsen BookScan category top 50 status in retail sales; illustrating that readers have responded by purchasing Blue River Press titles. Our distributor, Cardinal Publishers Group, has placed our books in chain and independent book retailers, libraries of all sorts, mass-merchant retailers, gift shops, and many specialty retail and wholesale channels. Our authors, editors and designers always keep the reader in mind when creating and developing the content and designing attractive books that are competitively priced. At Blue River Press our mission is to produce and market books that present the reader with good educational and entertaining information at a value." **Publishes 8-12 titles/year. 200 queries received/year. 25% of books from first-time authors. 80% from unagented writers. Pays 10-15% on wholesale price. Outright purchase of $500-5,000. Offers advance up to $5,000.** Publishes ms 6-12 months after acceptance. Accepts simultaneous submissions. Responds to queries in 2 months. Book catalog for #10 SASE or online. Guidelines available by e-mail.

NONFICTION Subjects include Americana, business, career guidance, education, entertainment, environment, games, health, history, recreation, regional, sports, travel. "Most non-religious adult nonfiction subjects are of interest. We like concepts that can develop into series products. Most of our books are paperback or hardcover in the categories of sport, business, health, fitness, lifestyle, yoga, and educational books for teachers and students."

BNA BOOKS

P.O. Box 7814, Edison NJ 08818. (800)960-1220. **Fax:** (723)346-1624. **Website:** www.bnabooks.com. Estab. 1929. Publishes hardcover and softcover originals. BNA Books publishes professional reference books written by lawyers, for lawyers. Accepts simultaneous submissions. Book catalog online. Guidelines online.

NONFICTION No fiction, biographies, bibliographies, cookbooks, religion books, humor, or trade books. Submit detailed TOC or outline, CV, intended market, estimated word length.

TIPS "Our audience is made up of practicing lawyers and law librarians. We look for authoritative and comprehensive treatises that can be supplemented or revised every year or 2 on legal subjects of interest to those audiences."

BOA EDITIONS, LTD.

250 N. Goodman St., Suite 306, Rochester NY 14607. (585)546-3410. **Fax:** (585)546-3913. **E-mail:** contact@boaeditions.org. **Website:** www.boaeditions.org. **Contact:** Ron Martin-Dent, director of publicity and production; Peter Conners, publisher. Director of Development and Operations: Kelly Hatton. Estab. 1976. Publishes hardcover, trade paperback, and digital e-book originals. BOA Editions, Ltd., a not-for-profit publisher of poetry, short fiction, and poetry-in-translation, fosters readership and appreciation of contemporary literature. By identifying, cultivating, and publishing both new and established poets and selecting authors of unique literary talent, BOA brings high quality literature to the public. **Publishes 10-12 titles/year. 1,000-2,000 queries and mss received/year. 15% of books from first-time authors. 90% from unagented writers. Negotiates royalties. Pays variable advance.** Publishes ms 18-24 months after acceptance. Accepts simultaneous submissions. Responds in 1 week to queries; 5 months to mss. Book catalog online. Guidelines online.

FICTION Subjects include literary, poetry, short story collections. BOA publishes literary fiction through its American Reader Series. While aesthetic quality is subjective, our fiction will be by authors more concerned with the artfulness of their writing than the twists and turns of plot. Our strongest current interest is in short story collections (and short-short story collections). We strongly advise you to read our published fiction collections. *BOA does not accept novel submissions.* Check BOA's website for reading periods for the American Reader Series and the BOA Short Fiction Prize. Please adhere to the general submission guidelines for each series. Guidelines online.

POETRY Readers who, like Whitman, expect the poet to 'indicate more than the beauty and dignity which always attach to dumb real objects . . They expect him to indicate the path between reality and their souls,' are the audience of BOA's books. BOA Editions, a Pulitzer Prize and National Book Award-winning not-for-profit publishing house, acclaimed for its work, reads poetry manuscripts for the American Poets Continuum Series (new poetry by distinguished poets in mid-to-late career), the New Poets of America Series (publication of a poet's first book, selected through the A. Poulin, Jr. Poetry Prize), and the America Reader Series (short fiction and prose on poetics). Check BOA's website for reading periods for the American Poets Continuum Series and the A. Poulin, Jr. Poetry Prize. Please adhere to the general submission guidelines for each series. Guidelines online.

RECENT TITLE(S) *The Black Maria*, by Aracelis Girmay; *The Trembling Answers*, by Craig Morgan Teicher; *When I Grow Up I Want to Be a List of Further Possibilities*, by Chen Chen; *Sky Country*, by Christine Kitano; *Cenzontle*, by Marcelo Hernandez Castillo; *Rail*, by Kai Carlson-Wee; *Holy Moly Carry Me*, by Erika Meitner; *Permanent Exhibit*, by Matthew Vollmer.

TIPS "Please adhere to the general submission guidelines on BOA's website for each series. BOA cannot accept unsolicited manuscript submissions outside of contests or open-reading periods."

BOLD STROKES BOOKS, INC.

P.O. Box 249, Valley Falls NY 12094. (518)677-5127. **Fax:** (518)677-5291. **E-mail:** sandy@boldstrokesbooks.com. **E-mail:** submissions@boldstrokesbooks.com. **Website:** www.boldstrokesbooks.com. **Contact:** Sandy Lowe, senior editor. Estab. 2004. Publishes trade paperback originals and reprints; electronic originals and reprints. **Publishes 120+ titles/year. 300 queries/year; 300 mss/year. 10-20% of books from first-time authors. 95% from unagented writers. Sliding scale based on sales volume and format. Pays advance.** Publishes ms 6-16 months after acceptance. Responds in 1 month to queries; 2 months to proposals; 4 months to mss. Guidelines online.

IMPRINTS BSB Fiction; Victory Editions Lesbian Fiction; Liberty Editions Gay Fiction; Soliloquy Young Adult; Heat Stroke Erotica.

NONFICTION Subjects include gay, lesbian, memoirs, young adult. Submit completed ms with bio, cover letter, and synopsis electronically only. Does not review artwork.

FICTION Subjects include adventure, erotica, fantasy, gay, gothic, historical, horror, lesbian, literary, mainstream, mystery, romance, science fiction, suspense, western, young adult. "Submissions should have a gay, lesbian, transgendered, or bisexual focus and should be positive and life-affirming." We do not publish any non-lgbtqi focused works. Submit completed ms with bio, cover letter, and synopsis—electronically only.

TIPS "We are particularly interested in authors who are interested in craft enhancement, technical development, and exploring and expanding traditional genre definitions and boundaries and are looking for a long-term publishing relationship. LGBTQ-focused works only."

BOOKFISH BOOKS

E-mail: bookfishbooks@gmail.com. **Website:** bookfishbooks.com. **Contact:** Tammy Mckee, acquisitions editor. BookFish Books is looking for novel lengthed young adult, new adult, and middle grade works in all subgenres. Both published and unpublished, agented or unagented authors are welcome to submit. "Sorry, but we do not publish novellas, picture books, early reader/chapter books or adult novels." Responds to every query. Accepts simultaneous submissions. Guidelines online.

FICTION Query via e-mail with a brief synopsis and first 3 chapters of ms.

RECENT TITLE(S) *This Is Sarah*, by Ally Malinenko; *The Prophecy*, by Erin Rhew.

TIPS "We only accept complete manuscripts. Please do not query us with partial manuscripts or proposals."

BOTTOM DOG PRESS, INC.

P.O. Box 425, Huron OH 44839. (419)602-1556. **E-mail:** lsmithdog@smithdocs.net. **Website:** smithdocs.net. **Contact:** Larry Smith, director; Susanna Sharp-Schwacke, associate editor. Estab. 1985. Publishes fiction, poetry, and memoirs. Bottom Dog Press, Inc., "is a nonprofit literary and educational organization dedicated to publishing the best writing and art from the Midwest and Appalachia. Query via e-mail first with 2 paragraphs on book and author." **Publishes 8 titles/year. 200 4% of books from first-time authors. 8% from unagented writers. Pays 10 copies and 15% royalty. Does not pay advance.** Publishes ms 4 months after acceptance. Accepts simultaneous submissions.

NONFICTION Subjects include alternative lifestyles, contemporary culture, creative nonfiction, humanities, lesbian, literature, memoirs, multicultural, New Age, regional, social sciences, spirituality, womens issues, sense of place, memoir.

FICTION Subjects include contemporary, ethnic, gay, historical, literary, poetry, short story collections, Appalachian, working-class.

RECENT TITLE(S) Has published poetry by Jeff Gundy, Jim Daniels, Maj Ragain, Diane di Prima, and Kenneth Patchen. Publishes the Midwest Series, Working Lives Series, Harmony Series, Memoir Series, Appalachian Writing Series, and Laughing Buddha Series (190 books to date).

BOYDS MILLS PRESS

Highlights for Children, Inc., 815 Church St., Honesdale PA 18431. (570)253-1164. **Website:** www.boydsmillspress.com. Estab. 1990. Boyds Mills Press publishes picture books, nonfiction, activity books, and paperback reprints. Their titles have been named notable books by the International Reading Association, the American Library Association, and the National Council of Teachers of English. They've earned numerous awards, including the National Jewish Book Award, the Christopher Medal, the NCTE Orbis Pictus Honor, and the Golden Kite Honor. Boyds Mills Press welcomes unsolicited submissions from published and unpublished writers and artists. Submit a ms with a cover letter of relevant information, including experience with writing and publishing. Label the package "Manuscript Submission" and include an SASE. For art samples, label the package "Art Sample Submission." All submissions will be evaluated for all imprints. Responds to mss within 3 months. Catalog online. Guidelines online.

POETRY Send a book-length collection of poems. Do not send an initial query. Keep in mind that the strongest collections demonstrate a facility with multiple poetic forms.

GEORGE BRAZILLER, INC.

277 Broadway, Suite 708, New York NY 10007. **Website:** www.georgebraziller.com. Publishes hardcover and trade paperback originals and reprints. Accepts simultaneous submissions.

FICTION Subjects include ethnic, gay, lesbian, literary. "We rarely do fiction but when we have published novels, they have mostly been literary novels." Submit 4-6 sample chapter(s), SASE. Agented fiction 20%. Responds in 3 months to proposals.

NICHOLAS BREALEY PUBLISHING

53 State St., 9th Floor, Boston MA 02109. (617)523-3801. **Fax:** (617)523-3708. **Website:** www.nicholasbrealey.com. **Contact:** Aquisitions Editor. Estab. 1992. "Nicholas Brealey Publishing has a reputation for publishing high-quality and thought-provoking business books with international appeal. Over time our list has grown to focus also on careers, professional and personal development, travel narratives and crossing cultures. We welcome fresh ideas and new insights in all of these subject areas." Submit via e-mail and follow the guidelines on the website. Accepts simultaneous submissions.

BREWERS PUBLICATIONS

Imprint of Brewers Association, 1327 Spruce St., Boulder CO 80302. **E-mail:** kristi@brewersassociation.org. **Website:** www.brewerspublications.com. **Contact:** Kristi Switzer, publisher. Estab. 1986. Publishes trade paperback originals. "BP is the largest publisher of contemporary and relevant brewing literature for today's craft brewers and homebrewers." **Publishes 2 titles/year. 50% of books from first-time authors. 100% from unagented writers. Pays advance.** Publishes book 9 months after acceptance. Accepts simultaneous submissions. Responds in 3 months to relevant queries. "Only those submissions relevant to our needs will receive a response to queries.". Guidelines online.

NONFICTION Subjects includeprofessional brewing, homebrewing, technical brewing, craft beer consumer. "We seek to do this in a positive atmosphere, create lasting relationships and shared pride in our contributions to the brewing and beer community. The books we select to carry out this mission include titles relevant to homebrewing, professional brewing, starting a brewery, books on particular styles of beer, industry trends, ingredients, processes and the occasional broader interest title on cooking or the history/impact of beer in our society." Query first with proposal and sample chapter.

RECENT TITLE(S) *How To Brew: Everything You Need to Know to Brew Great Beer Every Time*, by John J Palmer; *Session Beers: Brewing for Flavor and Balance*, by Jennifer Talley; *Brewing Eclectic IPA: Pushing the Boundaries of India Pale Ale*, by Dick Cantwell; *Gose: Brewing a Classic German Beer for the Modern Era*, by Fal Allen.

BRICK ROAD POETRY PRESS, INC.

513 Broadway, Columbus GA 31901. (706)221-4370. **Fax:** (706)649-3094. **E-mail:** kbadowski@brickroadpoetrypress.com. **Website:** www.brickroadpoetrypress.com. **Contact:** Ron Self and Keith Badowski, co-editors/founders. Estab. 2009. Publishes poetry only: books (single author collections). The mission of Brick Road Poetry Press is to publish and promote poetry that entertains, amuses, edifies, and surprises a wide audience of appreciative readers. "We concentrate on publishing what we enjoy. Our preference is for poetry geared toward dramatizing the human experience in language rich with sensory image and metaphor, recognizing that poetry can be, at one and the same time, both familiar as the perspiration of daily labor and as outrageous as a carnival sideshow. We prefer poetry that offers a coherent human voice, a sense of humor, attentiveness to words and language, narratives with surprise twists, persona poems, and/or philosophical or spiritual themes explored through the concrete scenes and images." Does not want intentional obscurity or riddling, highfalutin vocabulary, greeting card verse, and/or abstractions. **Publishes 3-6 titles/year. 500 submissions received/year. 40% of books from first-time authors. 100% from unagented writers. Pays royalties and 15 author copies. Initial print run of 150, print-on-demand thereafter. Does not pay advance.** Publishes 18 months after acceptance. Accepts simultaneous submissions. Responds in 3-9 months. Guidelines online.

POETRY Publishes poetry only: book-length, single author collections. Does not want intentional obscurity or riddling, highfalutin vocabulary, greeting card verse, and/or abstractions. Open general submissions are accepted annually December 1-January 15. "We are moving toward blind reading of submissions. While there is always a chance we might recognize the work of a poet, we would like as much is humanly possible to read manuscripts without knowing the name of the author. To that end we request all submission documents omit the author's name from the cover page, the headings, and the content of the poetry. If you include a cover letter, omit your name there as well please. We accept .doc, .rtf, or .pdf file formats. We prefer electronic submissions via the submission manager on our website but will consider hard copy submissions by mail if USPS Flat Rate Mailing Envelope is used and with the stipulation that, should the author's work be chosen for publication, an electronic version (.doc or .rtf) must be prepared in a timely manner and at the poet's expense. Please omit the author's name from the cover letter and the manuscript. For hard copy submissions only, do include basic contact info on a separate sheet, including the name of the manuscript."

RECENT TITLE(S) *Ultra Deep Field*, by Ace Boggess; *Lauren Bacall Shares a Limousine*, by Susan J. Erickson; *Having and Keeping*, by David Watts; *Ambushing Water*, by Danielle Hanson; *Battle Sleep*, by Shannon Tate Jonas; *Cracker Sonnets*, by Amy Wright; *Things Seen*, by Joseph Stanton.

TIPS "We want to publish poets who are engaged in the literary community, including regular submission of work to various publications and participation in poetry readings, workshops, and writers' groups. That said, we would never rule out an emerging poet who demonstrates ability and motivation to move in that direction. The best way to discover all that poetry can be and to expand the limits of your own craft is to expansively read poetry, both classic and contemporary . We recommend the following poets: Kim Addonizio, Ken Babstock, Coleman Barks, David Bottoms, Billy Collins, Morri Creech, Cynthia Cruz, Stephen Dunn, Alice Friman, Hannah Gamble, John Glenday, Beth A. Gylys, Jane Hirshfield, Jane Kenyon, Ted Kooser, Stanley Kunitz, Thomas Lux, Barry Marks, Michael Meyerhofer, Linda Pastan, Mark Strand, and Natasha D. Trethewey. Support your fellow poets and poetry in general by buying and reading lots of poetry books!"

Ⓐ⊘ BROADWAY BOOKS

Penguin Random House, 1745 Broadway, New York NY 10019. (212)782-9000. **Fax:** (212)782-9411. **Website:** crownpublishing.com/imprint/broadway-books. Estab. 1995. Publishes hardcover and trade paperback books. "Broadway publishes high quality general interest nonfiction and fiction for adults." **Receives thousands of mss/year. Pays royalty on retail price. Pays advance.** Accepts simultaneous submissions.

IMPRINTS Broadway Books; Broadway Business; Doubleday; Doubleday Image; Doubleday Religious Publishing; Main Street Books; Nan A. Talese.

NONFICTION Subjects include child guidance, contemporary culture, history, memoirs, multicultural, New Age, psychology, sex, spirituality, sports, travel, current affairs, motivational/inspirational, popular culture, consumer reference. *Agented submissions only.*

FICTION *Agented submissions only.*

BRONZE MAN BOOKS

Millikin University, 1184 W. Main, Decatur IL 62522. (217)424-6264. **E-mail:** sfrech@millikin.edu. **Website:** www.bronzemanbooks.com. **Contact:** Dr. Randy Brooks, publisher; Stephen Frech, editorial board, Edwin Walker, editorial board. Estab. 2006. Publishes hardcover, trade paperback, literary chapbooks and mass market paperback originals. A student-owned and operated press located on Millikin University's campus in Decatur, Ill., Bronze Man Books is dedicated to integrating quality design and meaningful content. The company exposes undergraduate students to the process of publishing by combining the theory of writing, publishing, editing and designing with the practice of running a book publishing company. This emphasis on performance learning is a hallmark of Millikin's brand of education. **Publishes 2-3 titles/year. 80% of books from first-time authors. 100% from unagented writers. Outright purchase based on wholesale value of 10% of a press run.** Publishes book 6-12 months after acceptance. Accepts simultaneous submissions. Responds in 1-3 months.

NONFICTION Subjects include architecture, art, child guidance, literature, parenting. Only e-mail inquiries are welcome.

FICTION Subjects include picture books, poetry. Subjects include art, graphic design, exhibits, general. Submit completed ms.

POETRY Submit completed ms.

TIPS "The art books are intended for serious collectors and scholars of contemporary art, especially of artists from the Midwestern US. These books are published in conjunction with art exhibitions at Millikin University or the Decatur Area Arts Council. The children's books have our broadest audience, and the literary chapbooks are intended for readers of contemporary fiction, drama, and poetry."

BUCKNELL UNIVERSITY PRESS

Bucknell University, 1 Dent Dr., Lewisburg PA 17837. (570)577-3674. **E-mail:** universitypress@bucknell.edu. **Website:** www.bucknell.edu/universitypress. **Contact:** Greg Clingham, director. Estab. 1968. Publishes hardcover, paperback, and e-books on various platforms. "In all fields, our criteria are scholarly excellence, critical originality, and interdisciplinary and theoretical expertise and sensitivity." **Publishes 35-40 titles/year.** Book catalog available free. Guidelines online.

NONFICTION Subjects include environment, ethnic, history, law, literary criticism, multicultural, philosophy, psychology, sociology, Luso-Hispanic studies, Latin American studies, 18-century studies, ecocriticism, African studies, Irish literature, cultural studies, historiography, legal theory. Series: Transits: Literature, Thought & Culture 1650-1850; Bucknell Series in Latin American Literature and Theory; Eighteenth-Century Scotland; New Studies in the Age of Goethe; Contemporary Irish Writers; Griot Project Book Series; Apercus: Histories Texts Cultures. Submit full proposal and CV by Word attachment.

BULLITT PUBLISHING

P.O. Box, Austin TX 78729. **E-mail:** bullittpublishing@yahoo.com. **E-mail:** submissions@bullittpublishing.com. **Website:** bullittpublishing.com. **Contact:** Pat Williams, editor. Estab. 2012. Publishes trade paperback and electronic originals. "Bullitt Publishing is a royalty-offering publishing house specializing in smart, contemporary romance. We are proud to provide print on demand distribution through the world's most comprehensive distribution channels. Whether this is your first novel or your 101st novel, Bullitt Publishing will treat you with the same amount of professionalism and respect. While we expect well-written entertaining manuscripts from all of our authors, we promise to provide high quality, professional product in return." **Publishes 12 titles/year.** Accepts simultaneous submissions.

IMPRINTS Tempo Romance.

FICTION Subjects include romance.

BURFORD BOOKS

101 E. State St., #301, Ithaca NY 14850. (607)319-4373. **E-mail:** info@burfordbooks.com. **Website:** www.burfordbooks.com. **Contact:** Burford Books Editorial Department. Estab. 1997. Publishes hardcover originals, trade paperback originals and reprints. Burford Books publishes books on all aspects of the outdoors, from backpacking to sports, practical and literary, as well as books on food & wine, military history, and the Finger Lakes region of New York State. **Publishes 12 titles/year. 300 queries; 200 mss received/year. 30% of books from first-time authors. 60% from unagented writers. Pays royalty on wholesale price.** Publishes book 18 months after acceptance. Accepts simultaneous submissions. Responds in 1 week to queries; 1 month to proposals; 2 months to mss. Book catalog and ms guidelines online.

NONFICTION Subjects include Americana, animals, cooking, foods, gardening, history, hobbies, military, recreation, sports, travel, war, fitness. "Burford Books welcomes proposals on new projects, especially in the subject areas in which we specialize: sports, the outdoors, golf, nature, gardening, food and wine, travel, and military history. We are not currently considering fiction or children's books. In general it's sufficient to send a brief proposal letter that outlines your idea, which should be e-mailed to info@burfordbooks.com with the word 'query' in the subject line." Reviews artwork/photos. Send digital images.

RECENT TITLE(S) *Complete Guide to Surfcasting*, by Joe Cermele; *Timeless Bounty: Food and Wine in New York's Finger Lakes*, by Thomas Pellechia.

BUTTE PUBLICATIONS, INC.

P.O. Box 1328, Hillsboro OR 97123-1328. (503)648-9791. **E-mail:** service@buttepublications.com. **Website:** www.buttepublications.com. Estab. 1992. Butte Publications, Inc., publishes classroom books related to deafness and language. **Publishes several titles/year.** Accepts simultaneous submissions. Responds in 6 months to mss. Book catalog and ms guidelines for #10 SASE or online.

NONFICTION Subjects include education. Not seeking autobiographies or novels. Submit proposal package, including author bio, synopsis, market survey, 2-3 sample chapters, SASE and ms (if completed). Reviews artwork/photos. Send photocopies.

TIPS "Audience is students, teachers, parents, and professionals in the arena dealing with deafness and hearing loss."

BY LIGHT UNSEEN MEDIA

325 Lakeview Dr., Winchendon MA 01475. (978)433-8866. **Fax:** (978)433-8866. **E-mail:** vyrdolak@bylightunseenmedia.com. **Website:** bylightunseenmedia.com. **Contact:** Inanna Arthen, owner/editor-in-chief. Estab. 2006. Publishes hardcover, paperback and electronic originals. The only small press owned and operated by a recognized expert in vampire folklore, media and culture, By Light Unseen Media was founded in 2006. "Our mission is to explore and celebrate the variety, imagination and ambiguities of the vampire theme in fiction, history and the human psyche." No other mythic trope remotely approaches the vampire as an ever-changing and evolving mirror of the zeitgeist, deepest fears and most fervent fantasies of each successive generation—and none ever will. Particular trends and treatments rise and fall in popularity, but the vampire will never go out of style. By Light Unseen Media offers fiction and non-fiction that transcends the popular cliches of the day and demonstrates the creative variety and infinite potential of the vampire motif. **Publishes 5 titles/year. 5 mss; 50 queries received/year. 80% of books from first-time authors. 100% from unagented writers. Pays royalty of 50-70% on net as explicitly defined in contract. Payment quarterly. No advance.** Publishes book 4 months after acceptance. Accepts simultaneous submissions. Responds in 3 months. Catalog online. Ms guidelines online.

NONFICTION Subjects include creative nonfiction, vampire-related. "We are a niche small press that will *only* consider nonfiction on the theme of vampires (vampire folklore, movies, television, literature, vampires in culture, etc.). We're especially interested in academic or other well-researched material, but will consider self-help/New Age types of books (e.g. the kind of material published by Llewellyn). We use digital printing so all interiors would need to be black and white, including illustrations." Does not want anything that does not focus on vampires! Submit proposal package including outline, 3 sample chapters, brief author bio. *No unsolicited mss will be considered.* Reviews artwork. Send photocopies/scanned PDF/jpeg.

FICTION Subjects include contemporary, fantasy, feminist, gay, gothic, horror, lesbian, mystery, occult, science fiction, suspense, western, young adult, magical realism, thriller. "We are a niche small press that *only* publishes fiction relating in some way to vampires. Within that guideline, we're interested in almost any genre that includes a vampire trope, the more creative and innovative, the better. Restrictions are noted in the submission guidelines (no derivative fiction based on other works, such as Dracula, no gore-for-gore's-sake 'splatter' horror, etc.) We do not publish anthologies." Does not want anything that does not focus on vampires as the major theme. Submit proposal package including synopsis, 3 sample chapters, brief author bio. "We encourage electronic submissions." *Unsolicited mss will not be considered.*

RECENT TITLE(S) *Blood on the Water*, by David Burton; *A Most Malignant Spirit*, by Zvi Zaks.

TIPS "We strongly urge authors to familiarize themselves with the vampire genre and not imagine that they're doing something new and amazingly different just because they're not imitating the current fad."

C&T PUBLISHING

1651 Challenge Dr., Concord CA 94520-5206. (925)677-0377. **Fax:** (925)677-0373. **E-mail:** roxanec@ctpub.com. **E-mail:** support@ctpub.com. **Website:** www.ctpub.com. **Contact:** Roxane Cerda. Estab. 1983. Publishes hardcover and trade paperback originals. "C&T publishes well-written, beautifully designed books on quilting, sewing, fiber crafts, embroidery, dollmaking, mixed media and crafting for children." **Publishes 50 titles/year. 300 50% of books from first-time authors. 90% from unagented writers. Pays royalty.** Accepts simultaneous submissions. Responds in 2 months to queries. Book catalog free; guidelines online.

IMPRINTS Stash Books, Fun Stitch Studio, and Kansas City Star Quilts.

NONFICTION Subjects include art, crafts, hobbies, quilting books, occasional quilt picture books, quilt-related crafts, wearable art, needlework, fiber and surface embellishments, other books relating to fabric crafting and paper crafting. Extensive proposal guidelines are available on the company's website.

FICTION Subjects includenovels and cozy mysteries aimed at a quilting audience.

TIPS "In our industry, we find that how-to books have the longest selling life. Quiltmakers, sewing enthusiasts, needle artists, fiber artists and young crafters are our audience. We like to see new concepts or techniques. Include some great samples, and you'll get our attention quickly. Dynamic design is hard to resist, and if that's your forte, show us what you've done."

CALAMARI PRESS

Via Titta Scarpetta #28, Rome 153, Italy. **E-mail:** derek@calamaripress.com. **Website:** www.calamaripress.com. **Contact:** Derek White. Publishes paperback originals. Calamari Press publishes books of literary text and art. Mss are selected by invitation. Occasionally has open submission period—check website. Helps to be published in *SleepingFish* first. **Publishes 1-2 titles/year. Pays in author's copies.** Ms published 2-6 months after acceptance. Accepts simultaneous submissions. Responds to mss in 2 weeks. Guidelines online.

FICTION Query with outline/synopsis and 3 sample chapters. Accepts queries by e-mail only. Include brief bio. Send SASE or IRC for return of ms.

CALKINS CREEK

Boyds Mills Press, 815 Church St., Honesdale PA 18431. **Website:** www.boydsmillspress.com. Estab. 2004. "We aim to publish books that are a well-written blend of creative writing and extensive research, which emphasize important events, people, and places in U.S. history." **Pays authors royalty or work purchased outright.** Accepts simultaneous submissions. Guidelines online.

NONFICTION Subjects include history. Submit outline/synopsis and 3 sample chapters.

FICTION Subjects include historical. Submit outline/synopsis and 3 sample chapters.

TIPS "Read through our recently published titles and review our catalog. When selecting titles to publish, our emphasis will be on important events, people, and places in U.S. history. Writers are encouraged to submit a detailed bibliography, including secondary and primary sources, and expert reviews with their submissions."

CALYX BOOKS

P.O. Box B, Corvallis OR 97339-0539. (541)753-9384. **Fax:** (541)753-0515. **E-mail:** info@calyxpress.org. **E-mail:** editor@calyxpress.org. **Website:** www.calyxpress.org. **Contact:** The Editor. A. Bublitz Estab. 1986. Accepts simultaneous submissions.

"Due to the high volume of book manuscripts received, CALYX Books is currently closed for manuscript submissions until further notice except for the Sarah Lantz Poetry Book Prize."

FICTION Closed to submissions until further notice.

CANDLEWICK PRESS

99 Dover St., Somerville MA 02144. (617) 661-3330. **Fax:** (617) 661-0565. **E-mail:** bigbear@candlewick.com. **Website:** www.candlewick.com. Estab. 1991. Publishes hardcover and trade paperback originals, and reprints. "Candlewick Press publishes high-quality, illustrated children's books for ages infant through young adult. We are a truly child-centered publisher." **Publishes 200 titles/year. 5% of books from first-time authors. Pays authors royalty of 2½-10% based on retail price. Offers advance.** Accepts simultaneous submissions.

IMPRINTS Big Picture Press, Candlewick Entertainment, Candlewick Studio, Nosy Crow, Templar Books.

Candlewick Press is not accepting queries or unsolicited mss at this time.

NONFICTION Picture books: concept, biography, geography, nature/environment. Young readers: biography, geography, nature/environment.

FICTION Subjects include juvenile, picture books, young adult. Picture books: animal, concept, contemporary, fantasy, history, humor, multicultural, nature/environment, poetry. Middle readers, young adults: contemporary, fantasy, history, humor, multicultural, poetry, science fiction, sports, suspense/mystery. "We currently do not accept unsolicited editorial queries or submissions. If you are an author or illustrator and would like us to consider your work, please read our submissions policy (online) to learn more."

TIPS *"We no longer accept unsolicited mss.* See our website for further information about us."

CANTERBURY HOUSE PUBLISHING, LTD.

4535 Ottawa Trail, Sarasota FL 34233. (941)312-6912. **Website:** www.canterburyhousepublishing.com. **Contact:** Sandra Horton, editor. Estab. 2009. Publishes hardcover, trade paperback, and electronic originals. "Our audience is made up of readers looking for wholesome fiction with good southern stories, with elements of mystery, romance, and inspiration and/or are looking for true stories of achievement and triumph over challenging circumstances. We are very strict on our submission guidelines due to our small staff, and our target market of Southern regional settings." **Publishes 3-6 titles/year. 35% of books from first-time authors. 100% from unagented writers. Pays 10-15% royalty on wholesale price.** Publishes ms 9-12 months after acceptance. Accepts simultaneous submissions.

Responds in 1 month to queries; 3 months to mss. Book catalog online. Guidelines online.

NONFICTION Subjects include memoirs, regional. Query with SASE and through website e-mail upon request. Reviews artwork. Send photocopies.

FICTION Subjects include contemporary, historical, literary, mainstream, mystery, regional, romance, suspense. Query with SASE and through website.

TIPS "Because of our limited staff, we prefer authors who have good writing credentials and submit edited manuscripts. We also look at authors who are business and marketing savvy and willing to help promote their books."

CAPSTONE PRESS

Capstone Young Readers, 1710 Roe Crest Dr., North Mankato MN 56003. **E-mail:** author.sub@capstonepub.com; il.sub@capstonepub.com. **Website:** www.capstonepub.com. Estab. 1991. The Capstone Press imprint publishes nonfiction with accessible text on topics kids love to capture interest and build confidence and skill in beginning, struggling, and reluctant readers, grades pre-K-9. Responds only if submissions fit needs. Mss and writing samples will not be returned. "If you receive no reply within 6 months, you should assume the editors are not interested.". Catalog available upon request. Guidelines online.

RECENT TITLE(S) *All About Science*, by Angela Royston; *The Amazing Adventures of Superman!*, by Benjamin Bird.

THE CAREER PRESS, INC.

12 Parish Dr., Wayne NJ 07470. **Website:** www.careerpress.com. Estab. 1985. Publishes hardcover and paperback originals. Career Press publishes books for adult readers seeking practical information to improve themselves in careers, business, HR, sales, entrepreneurship, and other related topics, as well as titles on supervision, management and CEOs. New Page Books publishes in the areas of New Age, new science, paranormal, the unexplained, alternative history, spirituality. Accepts simultaneous submissions. Guidelines online.

NONFICTION Subjects include recreation, nutrition. Look through our catalog; become familiar with our publications. "We like to select authors who are specialists on their topic." Submit outline, bio, TOC, 2-3 sample chapters, marketing plan, SASE. Or, send complete ms (preferred).

CAROLINA WREN PRESS

120 Morris St., Durham NC 27701. (919)560-2738. **E-mail:** carolinawrenpress@earthlink.net. **Website:** www.carolinawrenpress.org. **Contact:** Robin Miura, Editor & Director. Estab. 1976. "We publish poetry, fiction, and memoirs by or about people of color, women, gay/lesbian issues, and work by writers from, living in, or writing about the U.S. South." Accepts simultaneous submissions, but "let us know if work has been accepted elsewhere." **We pay our a uthors an honorarium.** Publishes ms 2 year after acceptance. Accepts simultaneous submissions. Responds in 3 months to queries; 6 months to mss. Guidelines online.

NONFICTION Subjects include ethnic, gay, lesbian, literature, multicultural, womens issues.

FICTION Subjects include ethnic, experimental, feminist, literary, poetry, short story collections. "We are no longer publishing children's literature of any topic." Books: 6×9 paper; typeset; various bindings; illustrations. Distributes titles through John F. Blair, Amazon.com, Barnes & Noble, Baker & Taylor, and on their website. "We very rarely accept any unsolicited manuscripts, but we accept submissions for the Doris Bakwin Award for Writing by a Woman in Jan-June of even-numbered years and submissions for the Lee Smith Novel Prize in Jan-June of odd-numbered years." "We will accept e-mailed queries—a letter in the body of the e-mail describing your project—but please do not send large attachments." All other submissions are accepted via Submittable as part of our annual contests.

POETRY Publishes 2 poetry books/year, "usually through the Carolina Wren Press Poetry Series Contest. Otherwise we primarily publish women, minorities, and authors from, living in, or writing about the U.S. South." Not accepting unsolicited submissions except through Poetry Series Contest. Accepts e-mail queries, but send only letter and description of work, no large files. Carolina Wren Press Poetry Contest for a First or Second Book takes submissions, electronically, from January to June of odd-numbered years.

RECENT TITLE(S) *Hola and Goodbye*, by Donna Miscolta; *Midnight Bowling*, by Quinn Dalton; *What Else Could It Be*, by Ravi Shankar; *Goldberg—Variations*, by Charles Wyatt; *Mulberry*, by Paulette Boudreaux.

TIPS "Best way to get read is to submit to a contest."

CAROLRHODA BOOKS, INC.

1251 Washington Ave. N., Minneapolis MN 55401. **Website:** www.lernerbooks.com. Editorial Director: Alix Reid. Estab. 1959. "We will continue to seek targeted solicitations at specific reading levels and in specific subject areas. The company will list these targeted solicitations on our website and in national newsletters, such as the SCBWI Bulletin." Interested in "boundary-pushing" teen fiction. *Lerner Publishing Group no longer accepts submissions to any of their imprints except for Kar-Ben Publishing.* Accepts simultaneous submissions.

CARSON-DELLOSA PUBLISHING CO., INC.

P.O. Box 35665, Greensboro NC 27425. (336)632-0084. **E-mail:** freelancesamples@carsondellosa.com. **Website:** www.carsondellosa.com. Does not accept unsolicited product ideas or book proposals at this time. **Publishes 80-90 titles/year. 15-20% of books from first-time authors. 95% from unagented writers. Makes outright purchase.** Book catalog online. Guidelines available free.

NONFICTION Subjects include education. "We publish supplementary educational materials, such as teacher resource books, workbooks, and activity books." No textbooks or trade children's books, please.

CARTWHEEL BOOKS

Imprint of Scholastic Trade Division, 557 Broadway, New York NY 10012. (212)343-6100. **Website:** www.scholastic.com. Estab. 1991. Publishes novelty books, easy readers, board books, hardcover and trade paperback originals. Cartwheel Books publishes innovative books for children, up to age 8. "We are looking for 'novelties' that are books first, play objects second. Even without its gimmick, a Cartwheel Book should stand alone as a valid piece of children's literature." Accepts simultaneous submissions. Guidelines available free.

NONFICTION Subjects include animals, history, recreation, science, sports. Cartwheel Books publishes for the very young, therefore nonfiction should be written in a manner that is accessible to preschoolers through 2nd grade. Often writers choose topics that are too narrow or "special" and do not appeal to the mass market. Also, the text and vocabulary are frequently too difficult for our young audience. *Accepts mss from agents only.* Reviews artwork/photos. Send Please do not send original artwork.

FICTION Subjects include humor, juvenile, mystery, picture books. Again, the subject should have mass market appeal for very young children. Humor can be helpful, but not necessary. Mistakes writers make are a reading level that is too difficult, a topic of no interest or too narrow, or mss that are too long. *Accepts mss from agents only.*

CATHOLIC UNIVERSITY OF AMERICA PRESS

620 Michigan Ave. NE, Washington DC 20064. (202)319-5052. **E-mail:** cua-press@cua.edu. **Website:** cuapress.org. Estab. 1939. The Catholic University of America Press publishes in the fields of history (ecclesiastical and secular), literature and languages, philosophy, political theory, social studies, and theology. "We have interdisciplinary emphasis on patristics, and medieval studies. We publish works of original scholarship intended for academic libraries, scholars and other professionals and works that offer a synthesis of knowledge of the subject of interest to a general audience or suitable for use in college and university classrooms." **Publishes 30-35 titles/year. 50% of books from first-time authors. 100% from unagented writers. Pays variable royalty on net receipts.** Publishes book 18 months after acceptance. Accepts simultaneous submissions. Responds in 5 days to queries. Book catalog on request. Guidelines online.

NONFICTION Subjects include history, philosophy, religion, Church-state relations. No unrevised doctoral dissertations. Length: 40,000-120,000 words. Query with outline, sample chapter, CV, and list of previous publications.

RECENT TITLE(S) *St. Augustine's Interpretation of the Psalms of Ascent*, by Gerard McLarney.

TIPS "Scholarly monographs and works suitable for adoption as supplementary reading material in courses have the best chance."

CATO INSTITUTE

1000 Massachusetts Ave. NW, Washington DC 20001. (202)842-0200. **Website:** www.cato.org. **Contact:** Submissions Editor. Estab. 1977. Publishes hardcover originals, trade paperback originals and reprints. Cato Institute publishes books on public policy issues from a free-market or libertarian perspective. **Publishes 12 titles/year. 25% of books from first-time authors. 90% from unagented writers. Makes outright purchase of $1,000-10,000. Pays advance.** Publishes ms 9 months after acceptance.

Accepts simultaneous submissions. Responds in 3 months to queries. Book catalog online.

NONFICTION Subjects include education, sociology, public policy. Query with SASE.

CAVE HOLLOW PRESS

P.O. Drawer J, Warrensburg MO 64093. **E-mail:** gbcrump@cavehollowpress.com. **Website:** www.cavehollowpress.com. **Contact:** G.B. Crump, editor. Estab. 2001. Publishes trade paperback originals. **Publishes 1 titles/year. 85 queries; 6 mss received/year. 80% of books from first-time authors. 100% from unagented writers. Pays 7-12% royalty on wholesale price. Pays negotiable amount in advance.** Publishes ms 1 year after acceptance. Accepts simultaneous submissions. Responds in 1-2 months to queries and proposals; 3-6 months to mss. Catalog online. Guidelines available free.

FICTION Subjects include contemporary, literary, mainstream, mystery, suspense. "We publish fiction by Midwestern authors and/or with Midwestern themes and/or settings. Our website is updated frequently to reflect the current type of fiction Cave Hollow Press is seeking." Query with SASE.

RECENT TITLE(S) *The Poe Codec*, by Michael Crandell; *Around Centralia Square*, by Dennis Vannatta; *Show Me the Sinister Snowman*, by Carolyn Mulford.

TIPS "Our audience varies based on the type of book we are publishing. We specialize in Missouri and Midwest regional fiction. We are interested in talented writers from Missouri and the surrounding Midwest. Check our submission guidelines on the website for what type of fiction we are interested in currently."

CEDAR FORT, INC.

2373 W. 700 S, Springville UT 84663. (801)489-4084. **Website:** www.cedarfort.com. Estab. 1986. Publishes hardcover, trade paperback originals and reprints, mass market paperback and electronic reprints. "Each year we publish well over 100 books, and many of those are by first-time authors. At the same time, we love to see books from established authors. As one of the largest book publishers in Utah, we have the capability and enthusiasm to make your book a success, whether you are a new author or a returning one. We want to publish uplifting and edifying books that help people think about what is important in life, books people enjoy reading to relax and feel better about themselves, and books to help improve lives. Although we do put out several children's books each year, we are extremely selective. Our children's books must have strong religious or moral values, and must contain outstanding writing and an excellent storyline." **Publishes 150 titles/year. Receives 200 queries/year; 600 mss/year. 60% of books from first-time authors. 95% from unagented writers. Pays 10-12% royalty on wholesale price. Pays $2,000-50,000 advance.** Publishes book 10-14 months after acceptance. Accepts simultaneous submissions. Responds in 1 month on queries; 2 months on proposals; 4 months on mss. Catalog and guidelines online.

IMPRINTS Council Press, Sweetwater Books, Bonneville Books, Front Table Books, Hobble Creek Press, CFI, Plain Sight Publishing, Horizon Publishers, Pioneer Plus.

NONFICTION Subjects include agriculture, Americana, animals, anthropology, archeology, business, child guidance, communications, cooking, crafts, creative nonfiction, economics, education, foods, gardening, health, history, hobbies, horticulture, house and home, military, nature, recreation, regional, religion, social sciences, spirituality, war, womens issues, young adult. Query with SASE; submit proposal package, including outline, 2 sample chapters; or submit completed ms. Reviews artwork as part of the ms package. Send photocopies.

FICTION Subjects include adventure, contemporary, fantasy, historical, humor, juvenile, literary, mainstream, military, multicultural, mystery, regional, religious, romance, science fiction, spiritual, sports, suspense, war, western, young adult. Submit completed ms.

TIPS "Our audience is rural, conservative, mainstream. The first page of your ms is very important because we start reading every submission, but good-writing and plot keep us reading."

CENTERSTREAM PUBLISHING

P.O. Box 17878, Anaheim Hills CA 92817. (714)779-9390. **Fax:** (714)779-9390. **E-mail:** centerstrm@aol.com. **Website:** www.centerstream-usa.com. **Contact:** Ron Middlebrook. Estab. 1980. Publishes music hardcover and mass market paperback originals, trade paperback and mass market paperback reprints. Cedmterstream is known for its unique publications for a variety of instruments. From instructional and reference books and biographies,.to fun song collections and more, All created by experts who offer insight and invalu7aqboe information to players and collectors. **Publishes 12-15 titles/year. 15 queries; 15 mss received/year. 80% of books from first-time authors. 100% from unagented writers. Pays 10-15% royalty on wholesale price. Pays advance.** Publishes ms 8 months after acceptance. Accepts simultaneous submissions. Responds in 3 months to queries. Book catalog and ms guidelines for #10 SASE.

NONFICTION Subjects include film, music. Query with SASE.

CHALICE PRESS

CBP Books, Christian Board of Publication, 483 E. Lockwood Ave., Suite 100, St. Louis MO 63119. (314)231-8500. **E-mail:** submissions@chalicepress.com. **Website:** www.chalicepress.com. **Contact:** Brad Lyons, president and publisher. Estab. 1911. Publishes hardcover and trade paperback originals. The mission of CBP/Chalice Press is to publish resources inviting all people into deeper relationship with God, equipping them as disciples of Jesus Christ, and sending them into ministries as the Holy Spirit calls them. CBP is a 501(c)3 not-for-profit organization. **Publishes 20 titles/year. 300 queries; 50 mss received/year. 10% of books from first-time authors. 95% from unagented writers. Pays negotiable advance.** Publishes ms 12-24 months after manuscript submission. Accepts simultaneous submissions. Responds in 2 months to queries; 3 months to proposals and mss. Book catalog online. Guidelines online.

IMPRINTS Chalice Press, TCP Books, CBP, Inside-Out Church Camp Curriculum.

NONFICTION Subjects include community, multicultural, public affairs, religion, social sciences, spirituality, womens issues, Christian spirituality, social justice. Submit query as directed on www.chalicepress.com.

RECENT TITLE(S) Find complete listing online.

TIPS "We publish for lay Christian readers, church ministers, and educators."

S. CHAND & COMPANY LTD.

7361 Ram Nagar, Qutab Rd., New Delhi 110055, India. (91)(11)2367-2080. **Fax:** (91)(11)2367-7446. **Website:** www.schandpublishing.com. Accepts simultaneous submissions. Guidelines online.

NONFICTION Subjects include history, botany, chemistry, engineering, technical, English, mathematics, physics, political science, zoology. Query through website.

CHANGELING PRESS LLC

Website: changelingpress.com/submissions.php. **Contact:** Margaret Riley, publisher. Estab. 2004. Publishes e-books. "We publish sci-fi/futuristic, dark and urban fantasy, paranormal, action/adventure, BDSM, and guilty pleasures (contemporary) women's erotic romance. All submissions must be targeted for at least one of these genres and must be women's erotic romance. We accept submissions from 12 to 30 thousand words for single titles. Serials from unsigned authors must be submitted as a completed set." **Publishes 165 titles/year. 400+ 5% of books from first-time authors. 100% from unagented writers. Pays 35% gross royalties on site, 50% gross off site monthly. Does not pay advance.** Publishes ms 60-90 days after acceptance. Responds in 1 week to queries. Catalog online. Guidelines online.

NONFICTION Subjects include alternative lifestyles.

FICTION Subjects include adventure, contemporary, fantasy, gay, gothic, horror, humor, military, multicultural, romance, science fiction, suspense, young adult. Electronic submissions only. No lesbian fiction submissions without prior approval, please. Absolutely no lesbian fiction written by men. Child pornography will be reported to local authorities and the FBI. Please read and follow our submissions guidelines online. All submissions which do not follow the submissions guidelines will be rejected unread.

CHARLESBRIDGE PUBLISHING

85 Main St., Watertown MA 02472. (617)926-0329. **Fax:** (617)926-5720. **E-mail:** tradeeditorial@charlesbridge.com. **E-mail:** yasubs@charlesbridge.com. **Website:** www.charlesbridge.com. Estab. 1980. Publishes hardcover and trade paperback nonfiction and fiction, children's books for the trade and library markets. "Charlesbridge publishes high-quality books for children, with a goal of creating lifelong readers and lifelong learners. Our books encourage reading and discovery in the classroom, library, and home. We believe that books for children should offer accurate information, promote a positive worldview, and embrace a child's innate sense of wonder and fun. To this end, we continually strive to seek new voices, new visions, and new directions in children's literature. We are now accepting young adult novels for consideration." **Publishes 50 titles/year. 4,000**

submissions/year. 10-20% of books from first-time authors. 40% from unagented writers. Pays royalty. Pays advance. Publishes 2-4 years after acceptance. Responds in 3 months. Guidelines online. https://charlesbridge.com/pages/submissions.

IMPRINTS Charlesbridge Teen: Charlesbridge Teen features storytelling that presents new ideas and an evolving world. Our carefully curated stories give voice to unforgettable characters with unique perspectives. We publish books that inspire teens to cheer or sigh, laugh or reflect, reread or share with a friend, and ultimately, pick up another book. Our mission—to make reading irresistible!

NONFICTION Subjects include animals, creative nonfiction, history, multicultural, science, social science. Strong interest in nature, environment, social studies, and other topics for trade and library markets. Follow guidelines online. https://charlesbridge.com/pages/submissions

FICTION Subjects include young adult. Strong stories with enduring themes. Charlesbridge publishes both picture books and transitional bridge books (books ranging from early readers to middle-grade chapter books). Our fiction titles include lively, plot-driven stories with strong, engaging characters. No alphabet books, board books, coloring books, activity books, or books with audiotapes or CD-ROMs. Please submit only 1 ms at a time. For picture books and shorter bridge books, please send a complete ms. For fiction books longer than 30 ms pages, please send a detailed plot synopsis, a chapter outline, and 3 chapters of text. If sending a young adult novel, mark the front of the envelope with "YA novel enclosed." Please note, for YA, e-mail submissions are preferred to the following address; yasubs@charlesbridge.com. Only responds if interested. Full guidelines on site. https://charlesbridge.com/pages/submissions

TIPS "To become acquainted with our publishing program, we encourage you to review our books and visit our website where you will find our catalog."

CHARLES PRESS PUBLISHERS

230 North 21st St., Ste. 312, Philadelphia PA 19103. (215)470-5977. **E-mail:** mail@charlespresspub.com. **E-mail:** submissions@charlespresspub.com. **Website:** www.charlespresspub.com. **Contact:** Lauren Meltzer, Publisher. Estab. 1982. Publishes hardcover, trade paperback, and ebooks. Small independent press. Currently emphasizing mental and physical health, psychology, animals/pets/veterinary medicine, how-to (especially relating to health and wellness), aging/eldercare/geriatrics, medical and nursing books. **Publishes 7-9 titles/year. 600 40% of books from first-time authors. 90% from unagented writers. Royalties paid twice a year. Does not usually pay advance for scholarly books, but possibly for other types.** Publishes ms 10 months after acceptance. Accepts simultaneous submissions. Responds within 2 months. Book catalog on website. Guidelines on website.

NONFICTION Subjects include animals, art, beauty, business, child guidance, cooking, counseling, creative nonfiction, education, ethnic, fashion, foods, gardening, health, history, house and home, humanities, literature, medicine, memoirs, nutrition, parenting, philosophy, psychology, religion, science, sex, social sciences, sociology, spirituality, stage, true crime, womens studies, Medical nursing healthcare aging/eldercare wellness nutrition food nutrition cookbooks animals veterinary parenting. No poetry. Query first, then submit proposal package that includes a description of the book, a few representative sample chapters, intended audience, competing titles, author's qualifications/background. Reviews artwork/photos. Send photocopies or transparencies.

CHELSEA GREEN PUBLISHING CO.

85 N. Main St., Suite 120, White River Junction VT 05001. (802)295-6300. **Fax:** (802)295-6444. **E-mail:** web@chelseagreen.com. **E-mail:** submissions@chelseagreen.com. **Website:** www.chelseagreen.com. Estab. 1984. Publishes hardcover and trade paperback originals and reprints. "Since 1984, Chelsea Green has been the publishing leader for books on the politics and practice of sustainable living." **Publishes 18-25 titles/year. 600-800 queries; 200-300 mss received/year. 30% of books from first-time authors. 80% from unagented writers. Pays royalty on publisher's net. Pays advance.** Publishes book 18 months after acceptance. Accepts simultaneous submissions. Responds in 2 weeks to queries; 1 month to proposals/mss. Book catalog online. Guidelines online.

NONFICTION Subjects include agriculture, alternative lifestyles, animals, business, community, cooking, creative nonfiction, economics, environment, foods, gardening, government, health, horticulture, humanities, medicine, nature, nutrition, politics, science, social sciences, simple living, renewable energy, and other sustainability topics. Does not want academic, self-help, spiritual. Prefers electronic queries and proposals via e-mail (as a single attachment). If sending via snail mail, submissions will only be returned with SASE. Please review our guidelines on our website carefully before submitting. Reviews artwork/photos.

RECENT TITLE(S) *Pawpaw*, by Andrew Moore; *The Essential Bernie Sanders and His Vision for America*, by Jonathan Tasini; *The Carbon Farming Solution*, by Eric Toensmeier; *The New Wildcrafted Cuisine*, by Pascal Baudar; *The Lean Farm*, by Ben Hartman.

TIPS "Our readers and our authors are passionate about finding sustainable and viable solutions to contemporary challenges in the fields of energy, food production, economics, and building. It would be helpful for prospective authors to have a look at several of our current books, as well as our website."

CHICAGO REVIEW PRESS

814 N. Franklin St., Chicago IL 60610. (312)337-0747. **Fax:** (312)337-5110. **E-mail:** csherry@chicagoreviewpress.com; jpohlen@chicagoreviewpress.com; lreardon@chicagoreviewpress.com; ytaylor@chicagoreviewpress.com. **Website:** www.chicagoreviewpress.com. **Contact:** Cynthia Sherry, publisher; Yuval Taylor, senior editor; Jerome Pohlen, senior editor; Lisa Reardon, senior editor. Estab. 1973. "Chicago Review Press publishes high-quality, nonfiction, educational activity books that extend the learning process through hands-on projects and accurate and interesting text. We look for activity books that are as much fun as they are constructive and informative." **Pays authors royalty of 7.5-12.5% based on retail price. Offers advances of $3,000-6,000. Pays illustrators and photographers by the project (range varies considerably).** Publishes a book 1-2 years after acceptance. Accepts simultaneous submissions. Responds in 2 months. Book catalog available for $3. Ms guidelines available for $3.

IMPRINTS Academy Chicago; Ball Publishing; Chicago Review Press; Lawrence Hill Books; Zephyr Press.

NONFICTION Young readers, middle readers and young adults: activity books, arts/crafts, multicultural, history, nature/environment, science. "We're interested in hands-on, educational books; anything else probably will be rejected." Average length: young readers and young adults—144-160 pages. Enclose cover letter and a brief synopsis of book in 1-2 paragraphs, table of contents and first 3 sample chapters; prefers not to receive e-mail queries. For children's activity books include a few sample activities with a list of the others. Full guidelines available on site.

FICTION Guidelines now available on website.

TIPS "We're looking for original activity books for small children and the adults caring for them—new themes and enticing projects to occupy kids' imaginations and promote their sense of personal creativity. We like activity books that are as much fun as they are constructive. Please write for guidelines so you'll know what we're looking for."

⊘ CHILDREN'S BRAINS ARE YUMMY (CBAY) BOOKS

Children's Brains are Yummy Productions, LLC, P.O. Box 670296, Dallas TX 75367. **E-mail:** submissions@cbaybooks.com. **Website:** www.cbaybooks.blog. **Contact:** Madeline Smoot, publisher. Estab. 2008. "CBAY Books currently focuses on quality fantasy and science fiction books for the middle grade and teen markets. We are not currently accepting unsolicited submissions. We do not publish picture books." **Publishes 3-6 titles/year. 30% of books from first-time authors. 80% from unagented writers. Pays authors royalty 10-15% based on wholesale price. Offers advances against royalties. Average amount $500. Pays advance.** Publishes ms 24 months after acceptance. Accepts simultaneous submissions. Responds in 2 months. "We are distributed by IPG. Our books can be found in their catalog at www.ipgbooks.com.". Brochure and guidelines online.

FICTION Subjects include adventure, fantasy, juvenile, mystery, science fiction, short story collections, suspense, young adult, folktales.

CHRONICLE BOOKS

680 Second St., San Francisco CA 94107. **E-mail:** submissions@chroniclebooks.com. **Website:** www.chroniclebooks.com. "We publish an exciting range of books, stationery, kits, calendars, and novelty formats. Our list includes children's books and interactive formats; young adult books; cookbooks; fine art, design, and photography; pop culture; craft, fashion, beauty, and home decor; relationships, mind-body-spirit; innovative formats such as interactive journals, kits, decks, and stationery; and much, much more." **Publishes 90 titles/year. Generally pays authors in royalties based on retail price,**

"though we do occasionally work on a flat fee basis." Advance varies. Illustrators paid royalty based on retail price or flat fee. Publishes a book 1-3 years after acceptance. Accepts simultaneous submissions. Responds to queries in 1 month. Book catalog for 9x12 SAE and 8 first-class stamps. Ms guidelines for #10 SASE.

NONFICTION Subjects include art, beauty, cooking, crafts, house and home, New Age, pop culture. "We're always looking for the new and unusual. We do accept unsolicited manuscripts and we review all proposals. However, given the volume of proposals we receive, we are not able to personally respond to unsolicited proposals unless we are interested in pursuing the project." Submit via mail or e-mail (prefers e-mail for adult submissions; only by mail for children's submissions). Submit proposal (guidelines online) and allow 3 months for editors to review and for children's submissions, allow 6 months. If submitting by mail, do not include SASE since our staff will not return materials.

FICTION Only interested in fiction for children and young adults. No adult fiction. Submit complete ms (picture books); submit outline/synopsis and 3 sample chapters (for older readers). Will not respond to submissions unless interested. Will not consider submissions by fax, e-mail or disk. Do not include SASE; do not send original materials. No submissions will be returned.

POETRY Submit via mail only. Children's submissions only. Submit proposal (guidelines online) and allow up to 3 months for editors to review. If submitting by mail, do not include SASE since our staff will not return materials.

CHRONICLE BOOKS FOR CHILDREN

680 Second St., San Francisco CA 94107. (415)537-4200. **Fax:** (415)537-4460. **Website:** www.chroniclekids.com. Publishes hardcover and trade paperback originals. "Chronicle Books for Children publishes an eclectic mixture of traditional and innovative children's books. Our aim is to publish books that inspire young readers to learn and grow creatively while helping them discover the joy of reading. We're looking for quirky, bold artwork and subject matter." **Publishes 100-110 titles/year. 30,000 queries received/year. 6% of books from first-time authors. 25% from unagented writers. Pays variable advance.** Publishes a book 18-24 months after acceptance. Accepts simultaneous submissions. Responds in 2-4 weeks to queries; 6 months to mss. Book catalog for 9x12 envelope and 3 first-class stamps. Guidelines online.

NONFICTION Subjects include animals, multicultural, science. Query with synopsis. Reviews artwork/photos.

FICTION Subjects include multicultural, young adult, picture books. Does not accept proposals by fax, via e-mail, or on disk. When submitting artwork, either as a part of a project or as samples for review, do not send original art.

TIPS "We are interested in projects that have a unique bent to them—be it in subject matter, writing style, or illustrative technique. As a small list, we are looking for books that will lend our list a distinctive flavor. Primarily we are interested in fiction and nonfiction picture books for children ages up to 8 years, and nonfiction books for children ages up to 12 years. We publish board, pop-up, and other novelty formats as well as picture books. We are also interested in early chapter books, middle grade fiction, and young adult projects."

CHURCH PUBLISHING INC.

19 E. 34th St., New York NY 10016. (800)223-6602. **Fax:** (212)779-3392. **E-mail:** nabryan@cpg.org. **Website:** www.churchpublishing.org. **Contact:** Nancy Bryan, VP editorial. Estab. 1884. "With a religious publishing heritage dating back to 1918 and headquartered today in New York City, CPI is an official publisher of worship materials and resources for The Episcopal Church, plus a multi-faceted publisher and supplier to the broader ecumenical marketplace. In the nearly 100 years since its first publication, Church Publishing has emerged as a principal provider of liturgical and musical resources for The Episcopal Church, along with works on church leadership, pastoral care and Christian formation. With its growing portfolio of professional books and resources, Church Publishing was recognized in 1997 as the official publisher for the General Convention of the Episcopal Church in the United States. Simultaneously through the years, Church Publishing has consciously broadened its program, reach, and service to the church by publishing books for and about the worldwide Anglican Communion." Accepts simultaneous submissions.

IMPRINTS Church Publishing, Morehouse Publishing, Seabury Books.

TIPS "Prefer using freelancers who are located in central Pennsylvania and are available for meetings when necessary."

CITY LIGHTS BOOKS

261 Columbus Ave., San Francisco CA 94133. (415)362-8193. **Fax:** (415)362-4921. **Website:** www.citylights.com. Estab. 1953. Accepts simultaneous submissions.

CLARION BOOKS

Houghton Mifflin Co., 215 Park Ave. S., New York NY 10003. **Website:** www.hmhco.com. Estab. 1965. Publishes hardcover originals for children. "Clarion Books publishes picture books, nonfiction, and fiction for infants through grade 12. Avoid telling your stories in verse unless you are a professional poet. *We are no longer responding to your unsolicited submission unless we are interested in publishing it. Please do not include a SASE. Submissions will be recycled, and you will not hear from us regarding the status of your submission unless we are interested. We regret that we cannot respond personally to each submission, but we do consider each and every submission we receive.*" **Publishes 50 titles/year. Pays 5-10% royalty on retail price. Pays minimum of $4,000 advance.** Publishes a book 2 years after acceptance. Accepts simultaneous submissions. Responds in 2 months to queries. Guidelines online.

NONFICTION Subjects include Americana, history, photography, holiday. No unsolicited mss. Query with SASE. Submit proposal package, sample chapters, SASE. Reviews artwork/photos. Send photocopies.

FICTION Subjects include adventure, historical, humor, mystery, suspense, strong character studies, contemporary. "Clarion is highly selective in the areas of historical fiction, fantasy, and science fiction. A novel must be superlatively written in order to find a place on the list. Mss that arrive without an SASE of adequate size will *not* be responded to or returned. Accepts fiction translations." Submit complete ms. No queries, please. Send to only *one* Clarion editor.

TIPS "Looks for freshness, enthusiasm—in short, life."

CLARITY PRESS, INC.

2625 Piedmont Rd. NE, Suite 56, Atlanta GA 30324. (404)647-6501. **E-mail:** claritypress@usa.net. **Website:** www.claritypress.com. **Contact:** Diana G. Collier, editorial director (contemporary foreign policy /social justice issues). Estab. 1984. Publishes hardcover and trade paperback originals and e-books. **Publishes 8 titles/year. 20% of books from first-time authors. 100% from unagented writers.** Accepts simultaneous submissions. Responds to queries only if interested. Please no SASE. Guidelines available.

IMPRINTS Clear Day Books.

NONFICTION Subjects include contemporary culture, economics, environment, ethnic, government, history, labor, law, military, multicultural, politics, public affairs, world affairs, human rights/socioeconomic and minority issues, globalization, social justice. Publishes books on contemporary global issues in U.S., Middle East and Africa, on US public and foreign policy. No fiction. Query by e-mail only with synopsis, TOC, résumé, publishing history.

RECENT TITLE(S) *Central Bankers at the End of Their Rope?*, by Jack Rasmus; *The Neoconservative Threat to World Order*, by Paul Craig Roberts; *Unprecedented Crime: Climate Science Denial & Game Changers for Survival*, by Dr. Peter D. Carter and Elizabeth Woodworth.

TIPS "Check our titles on the website."

Ⓐ CLARKSON POTTER

Penguin Random House, 1745 Broadway, New York NY 10019. (212)782-9000. **Website:** www.clarksonpotter.com. Estab. 1959. Publishes hardcover and trade paperback originals. Accepts agented submissions only. Clarkson Potter specializes in publishing cooking books, decorating and other around-the-house how-to subjects.

NONFICTION Subjects include child guidance, memoirs, photography, psychology, translation. Agented submissions only.

CLEIS PRESS

101 Hudson St., 37th Floor, Suite 3705, Jersey City NJ 07302. **Fax:** (510)845-8001. **Website:** www.cleispress.com. Estab. 1980. Publishes books that inform, enlighten, and entertain. Areas of interest include gift, inspiration, health, family and childcare, self-help, women's issues, reference, cooking. "We do our best to bring readers quality books that celebrate life, inspire the mind, revive the spirit, and enhance lives all around. Our authors are practical visionaries; people who offer deep wisdom in a hopeful and helpful manner.". Cleis Press publishes provocative, intelligent books in the areas of sexuality, gay and lesbian studies, erotica, fiction, gender studies, and human rights. **Publishes 45 titles/year. 10% of books from first-time authors. 40% from unagented writers.**

Publishes ms 2 years after acceptance. Accepts simultaneous submissions. Responds in 2 month to queries.

NONFICTION Subjects include sexual politics. "Cleis Press is interested in books on topics of sexuality, human rights and women's and gay and lesbian literature. Please consult our website first to be certain that your book fits our list." Query or submit outline and sample chapters.

FICTION Subjects include feminist, literary. "We are looking for high quality fiction and nonfiction." Submit complete ms. Include brief bio, list of publishing credits. Send SASE for return of ms or send a disposable ms and SASE for reply only.

TIPS "Be familiar with publishers' catalogs; be absolutely aware of your audience; research potential markets; present fresh new ways of looking at your topic; avoid 'PR' language and include publishing history in query letter."

CLEVELAND STATE UNIVERSITY POETRY CENTER

2121 Euclid Ave., RT 1841, Cleveland OH 44115. (216)687-3986. **Fax:** (216)687-6943. **E-mail:** poetrycenter@csuohio.edu. **Website:** www.csupoetrycenter.com. **Contact:** Dan Dorman, managing editor. Estab. 1962. The Cleveland State University Poetry Center was established in 1962 at the former Fenn College of Engineering to promote poetry through readings and community outreach. In 1971, it expanded its mission to become a national non-profit independent press under the auspices of the Cleveland State University Department of English, and has since published nearly 200 rangy, joyful, profound, astonishing, complicated, surprising, and aesthetically diverse collections of contemporary poetry and prose by established and emerging authors. The Cleveland State University Poetry Center publishes between three and five collections of contemporary poetry and prose a year, with a national distribution and reach. The Poetry Center currently acquires manuscripts through three annual contests (one dedicated to publishing and promoting first books of poetry, one to supporting an established poet's career, and one to publishing collections of literary essays). **Publishes 3-5 titles/year. 500-1,200 submissions received/year. 50% of books from first-time authors. 100% from unagented writers. Pays $1,000 for competition winners.** Publishes ms 1-2 years after acceptance. Accepts simultaneous submissions. Responds in less than a year. Catalog online. Guidelines online.

POETRY Most mss are accepted through the competitions. All mss sent for competitions are considered for publication. Outside of competitions, mss are accepted by solicitation only.

COACHES CHOICE

P.O. Box 1828, Monterey CA 93942. (888)229-5745. **E-mail:** info@coacheschoice.com. **Website:** www.coacheschoice.com. Publishes trade paperback originals and reprints. "We publish books for anyone who coaches a sport or has an interest in coaching a sport—all levels of competition." Detailed descriptions, step-by-step instructions, and easy-to-follow diagrams set our books apart. Accepts simultaneous submissions. Book catalog available free.

NONFICTION Subjects include sports, sports specific training. Submit proposal package, outline, resume, 2 sample chapters. Reviews artwork/photos. Send photocopies and diagrams.

COFFEE HOUSE PRESS

79 13th Ave. NE, Suite 110, Minneapolis MN 55413. (612)338-0125. **Fax:** (612)338-4004. **Website:** www.coffeehousepress.org. Estab. 1984. Publishes hardcover and trade paperback originals. This successful nonprofit small press has received numerous grants from various organizations including the NEA, the McKnight Foundation and Target. Books published by Coffee House Press have won numerous honors and awards. Example: *The Book of Medicines*, by Linda Hogan won the Colorado Book Award for Poetry and the Lannan Foundation Literary Fellowship. **Publishes 16-18 titles/year.** Accepts simultaneous submissions. Responds in 4-6 weeks to queries; up to 6 months to mss. Book catalog and ms guidelines online.

NONFICTION Subjects include creative nonfiction, memoirs, book-length essays, collections of essays. Query with outline and sample pages during annual reading periods (March 1-31 and September 1-30).

FICTION Seeks literary novels, short story collections and poetry. Query first with outline and samples (20-30 pages) during annual reading periods (March 1-31 and September 1-30).

POETRY Coffee House Press will not accept unsolicited poetry submissions. Please check our web page periodically for future updates to this policy.

RECENT TITLE(S) *A Girl is a Half-formed Thing*, by Eimear McBride; *Prelude to a Bruise*, by Saeed Jones; *Faces in the Crowd*, by Valeria Luiselli.

TIPS "Look for our books at stores and libraries to get a feel for what we like to publish. No phone calls, e-mails, or faxes."

COLLEGE PRESS PUBLISHING CO.

P.O. Box 1132, 2111 N. Main St., Suite C, Joplin MO 64801. (800)289-3300. **Fax:** (417)623-1929. **E-mail:** collpressbooks@gmail.com. **Website:** www.college-press.com. **Contact:** Acquisitions Editor. Estab. 1959. Publishes hardcover and trade paperback originals and reprints. College Press is a traditional Christian publishing house. Seeks proposals for Bible studies, topical studies (biblically based), apologetic studies. Accepts simultaneous submissions. Responds in 3 months to proposals; 2 months to mss. Guidelines online.

NONFICTION Seeks Bible studies, topical studies, apologetic studies. No poetry, games/puzzles, books on prophecy from a premillennial or dispensational viewpoint, or any book without a Christian message. Query with SASE.

TIPS "Our core market is Christian Churches/Churches of Christ and conservative evangelical Christians. Have your material critically reviewed prior to sending it. Make sure that it is non-Calvinistic and that it leans more amillennial (if it is apocalyptic writing)."

CONARI PRESS

Red Wheel/Weiser, LLC., 665 Third Street Suite 400, San Fransisco CA 94107. **E-mail:** submissions@rwwbooks.com: info@rwwbooks.com. **Website:** www.redwheelweiser.com. Estab. 1987. "Conari Press, an imprint of Red Wheel/Weiser, publishes books on topics ranging from spirituality, personal growth, and relationships to women's issues, parenting, and social issues. Our mission is to publish quality books that will make a difference in people's lives—how we feel about ourselves and how we relate to one another. We value integrity, compassion, and receptivity, both in the books we publish and in the way we do business." Accepts simultaneous submissions.

NONFICTION Subjects include foods, health, parenting, spirituality, womens issues, womens studies. "Inspire, literally to breathe life into. That's what Conari Press books aim to do—inspire all walks of life, mind, body, and spirit; inspire creativity, laughter, gratitude, good food, good health, and all good things in life." Guidelines online.

TIPS "Review our website to make sure your work is appropriate."

CONCORDIA PUBLISHING HOUSE

3558 S. Jefferson Ave., St. Louis MO 63118. (314)268-1187. **Fax:** (314)268-1329. **E-mail:** editorial.concordia@cph.org. **Website:** www.cph.org. Estab. 1869. Publishes hardcover and trade paperback originals. Concordia Publishing House is the publishing arm of The Lutheran Church—Missouri Synod. "We develop, produce, and distribute (1) resources that support pastoral and congregational ministry, and (2) scholary and professional books in exegetical, historical, dogmatic, and practical theology." Accepts simultaneous submissions.

Ⓐ CONSTABLE & ROBINSON, LTD.

50 Victoria Embankment, London EC4Y 0DZ, United Kingdom. **E-mail:** info@littlebrown.co.uk. **Website:** https://www.littlebrown.co.uk/ConstableRobinson/about-constable-publisher.page. Publishes hardcover and trade paperback originals. **Publishes 60 titles/year. 3,000 queries/year; 1,000 mss/year. Pays royalty. Pays advance.** Publishes book 1 year after acceptance. Accepts simultaneous submissions. Responds in 1-3 months. Book catalog available free.

NONFICTION Subjects include health, history, medicine, military, photography, politics, psychology, science, travel, war. Query with SASE. Submit synopsis. Reviews artwork/photos. Send photocopies.

FICTION Subjects include historical, mystery. Publishes "crime fiction (mysteries) and historical crime fiction." Length 80,000 words minimum; 130,000 words maximum. *Agented submissions only.*

COPPER CANYON PRESS

P.O. Box 271, Port Townsend WA 98368. (360)385-4925. **Fax:** (360)385-4985. **E-mail:** poetry@coppercanyonpress.org. **Website:** www.coppercanyonpress.org. **Contact:** Joseph Bednarik and George Knotek, co-publishers. Managing Editor: Tonaya Craft. Estab. 1972. Copper Canyon Press is a nonprofit publisher that believes poetry is vital to language and living. Since 1972, the press has published poetry exclusively and has established an international reputation for its commitment to authors, editorial acumen, and dedication to the poetry audience. Accepts simultaneous submissions. Catalog online. Guidelines online.

POETRY Has open submission periods throughout the year; see website for details. Charges $35 fee for each submission, which entitles poets to select 2 Copper Canyon Press titles from a list. Submit complete ms via Submittable.

RECENT TITLE(S) *Night Sky With Exit Wounds*, by Ocean Vuong; *Like a Beggar*, by Ellen Bass.

TIPS "Please familiarize yourself with our mission, catalog, and submissions FAQ before submitting a manuscript."

CORNELL UNIVERSITY PRESS

Sage House, 512 E. State St., Ithaca NY 14850. (607)277-2338. **Fax:** (607)277-2374. **Website:** www.cornellpress.cornell.edu. **Contact:** Mahinder Kingra, editor-in-chief; Roger Haydon, executive editor; Emily Andrew, senior editor; James Lance, senior editor; Michael J. McGandy, senior editor. Estab. 1869. Publishes hardcover and paperback originals. "Cornell Press is an academic publisher of nonfiction with particular strengths in anthropology, Asian studies, biological sciences, classics, history, labor and business, literary criticism, politics and international relations, women's studies, Slavic studies, philosophy, urban studies, health care work, regional titles, and security studies. Currently emphasizing sound scholarship that appeals beyond the academic community." **Publishes 150 titles/year. Pays royalty. Pays $0-5,000 advance.** Publishes ms 1 year after acceptance. Accepts simultaneous submissions. Book catalog and guidelines online.

NONFICTION Subjects include agriculture, ethnic, history, philosophy, regional, sociology, translation, classics, life sciences. Submit résumé, cover letter, and prospectus.

CORWIN PRESS, INC.

2455 Teller Rd., Thousand Oaks CA 91320. (800)818-7243. **Fax:** (805)499-2692. **E-mail:** ariel.bartlett@corwin.com; erin.null@corwin.com; jessica.allan@corwin.com. **Website:** www.corwinpress.com. **Contact:** Ariel Bartlett, acquisitions editor; Erin Null, acquisitions editor; Jessica Allan, senior acquisitions editor. Estab. 1990. Publishes paperback originals. **Publishes 150 titles/year.** Publishes ms 7 months after acceptance. Accepts simultaneous submissions. Responds in 1-2 months to queries. Guidelines online.

"Corwin Press, Inc., publishes leading-edge, user-friendly publications for education professionals."

NONFICTION Subjects include education. Seeking fresh insights, conclusions, and recommendations for action. Prefers theory or research-based books that provide real-world examples and practical, hands-on strategies to help busy educators be successful. Professional-level publications for administrators, teachers, school specialists, policymakers, researchers and others involved with Pre K-12 education. No textbooks that simply summarize existing knowledge or mass-market books. Query with SASE.

COVENANT COMMUNICATIONS, INC.

Deseret Book Company, 1226 South 630 East Suite #4, P.O. Box 416, American Fork UT 84003. (801)756-1041. **Fax:** (801)756-1049. **E-mail:** samantham@covenant-lds.com. **E-mail:** submissionsdesk@covenant-lds.com. **Website:** www.covenant-lds.com. **Contact:** Samantha Millburn, managing editor. Estab. 1958. "Currently emphasizing inspirational, doctrinal, historical, biography, and fiction." **Publishes 80-100 titles/year. Receives 400 mss/year. 30% of books from first-time authors. 99% from unagented writers. Pays 6-15% royalty on retail price.** Publishes book 6-12 months after acceptance. Responds in 1 month on queries; 2-6 months on mss. Guidelines online.

NONFICTION Subjects include cooking, history, parenting, religion, spirituality. "We target an audience of members of The Church of Jesus Christ of Latter-day Saints, LDS, or Mormon. All mss must be acceptable to that audience." We do not accept anything dealing with the occult or alternative lifestyles. Submit complete ms. Reviews artwork. Send photocopies.

FICTION Subjects include adventure, historical, mystery, picture books, regional, religious, romance, short story collections, spiritual, suspense. "Manuscripts do not necessarily have to include LDS/Mormon characters or themes, but cannot contain profanity, sexual content, gratuitous violence, witchcraft, vampires, and other such material." We do not accept nor publish young adult, middle grade, science fiction, fantasy, occult, steampunk, or gay/lesbian/bisexual/transgender themes. Submit complete ms.

POETRY We do not publish poetry.

RECENT TITLE(S) *The Shipbuilder's Wife*, by Jennifer Moore; *Butch Cassidy and Other Mormon Outlaws of the Old West*, by Kathryn Gordon; *Proximity*, by Traci Hunter Abramson.

TIPS "We are actively looking for new, fresh Regency romance authors."

CQ PRESS

2455 Teller Rd., Thousand Oaks CA 91320. (805)410-7582. **Website:** www.cqpress.com. Estab. 1945. Publishes hardcover and online paperback titles. CQ Press seeks to educate the public by publishing authoritative works on American and international politics, policy, and people. Accepts simultaneous submissions. Book catalog available free.

NONFICTION Subjects include history. "We are interested in American government, public administration, comparative government, and international relations." Submit proposal package, including prospectus, TOC, 1-2 sample chapters.

TIPS "Our books present important information on American government and politics, and related issues, with careful attention to accuracy, thoroughness, and readability."

⊘ CRABTREE PUBLISHING COMPANY

350 Fifth Ave., 59th Floor, New York NY 10118. (212)496-5040; (800)387-7650. **Fax:** (800)355-7166. **Website:** www.crabtreebooks.com. Estab. 1978. Crabtree Publishing Company is dedicated to producing high-quality books and educational products for K-8+. Each resource blends accuracy, immediacy, and eye-catching illustration with the goal of inspiring nothing less than a life-long interest in reading and learning in children. The company began building its reputation in 1978 as a quality children's nonfiction book publisher with acclaimed author Bobbie Kalman's first series about the early pioneers. The Early Settler Life Series became a mainstay in schools as well as historic sites and museums across North America. Accepts simultaneous submissions.

"Crabtree does not accept unsolicited manuscripts. Crabtree Publishing has an editorial team in-house that creates curriculum-specific book series."

TIPS "Since our books are for younger readers, lively photos of children and animals are always excellent." Portfolio should be diverse and encompass several subjects rather than just 1 or 2; depth of coverage of subject should be intense so that any publishing company could, conceivably, use all or many of a photographer's photos in a book on a particular subject."

CRAFTSMAN BOOK CO.

6058 Corte Del Cedro, Carlsbad CA 92011. (760)438-7828 or (800)829-8123. **Fax:** (760)438-0398. **E-mail:** jacobs@costbook.com. **Website:** www.craftsman-book.com. **Contact:** Laurence D. Jacobs, editorial manager. Estab. 1957. Publishes paperback originals. Publishes how-to manuals for professional builders. Currently emphasizing construction software for cost estimating, insurance replacement costs, contract and lien writing software and construction forms. **Publishes 9 titles/year. 1 85% of books from first-time authors. 99% from unagented writers. Pays 7-12% royalty on wholesale price and 12-1/2% on retail price. Does not pay advance.** Publishes ms 2 years after acceptance. Accepts simultaneous submissions. Responds in 2 months to queries. Book catalog and ms guidelines free.

NONFICTION Subjects include business, software. All titles are related to construction for professional builders. Reviews artwork/photos.

TIPS "The book submission should be loaded with step-by-step instructions, illustrations, charts, reference data, forms, samples, cost estimates, rules of thumb, and examples that solve actual problems in the builder's office and in the field. It must cover the subject completely, become the owner's primary reference on the subject, have a high utility-to-cost ratio, and help the owner make a better living in his chosen field."

CRAIGMORE CREATIONS

PMB 114, 4110 SE Hawthorne Blvd., Portland OR 97124. (503)477-9562. **E-mail:** info@craigmorecreations.com. **Website:** www.craigmorecreations.com. Estab. 2009. Accepts simultaneous submissions.

NONFICTION Subjects include animals, anthropology, archeology, creative nonfiction, environment, multicultural, nature, regional, science, young adult, Earth sciences, natural history. "We publish books that make time travel seem possible: nonfiction that explores pre-history and Earth sciences for children." Submit proposal package. See website for detailed submission guidelines. Send photocopies.

FICTION Subjects include juvenile, picture books, young adult. Submit proposal package. See website for detailed submission guidelines.

RECENT TITLE(S) *Terra Tempo; Letters of the West: An ABC Book of the Many Plants, Animals, and Other*

Curious Features of the West, by Michelle Walch and John Maddin; *Tracks Count: A Guide to Counting Animal Prints*, by Steve Engel.

THE CREATIVE COMPANY

P.O. Box 227, Mankato MN 56002. (800)445-6209. **Fax:** (507)388-2746. **E-mail:** info@thecreativecompany.us. **Website:** www.thecreativecompany.us. Estab. 1932. "We are currently not accepting fiction submissions." **Publishes 140 titles/year.** Publishes a book 2 years after acceptance. Accepts simultaneous submissions. Responds in 3-6 months. Guidelines available for SAE.

IMPRINTS Creative Editions (picture books); Creative Education (nonfiction).

NONFICTION Picture books, young readers, young adults: animal, arts/crafts, biography, careers, geography, health, history, hobbies, multicultural, music/dance, nature/environment, religion, science, social issues, special needs, sports. Average word length: young readers—500; young adults—6,000. Submit outline/synopsis and 2 sample chapters, along with division of titles within the series.

TIPS "We are accepting nonfiction, series submissions only. Fiction submissions will not be reviewed or returned. Nonfiction submissions should be presented in series (4, 6, or 8) rather than single."

CRESTON BOOKS

P.O. Box 9369, Berkeley CA 94709. **E-mail:** submissions@crestonbooks.co. **Website:** crestonbooks.co. Estab. 2013. Creston Books is author-illustrator driven, with talented, award-winning creators given more editorial freedom and control than in a typical New York house. **50% of books from first-time authors. 50% from unagented writers. Pays advance.** Accepts simultaneous submissions. Catalog online. Guidelines online.

FICTION Subjects include juvenile, multicultural, picture books, young adult. Please paste text of picture books or first chapters of novels in the body of e-mail. Words of Advice for submitting authors listed on the site.

RECENT TITLE(S) *Minnie & Moo: Hooves of Fire*, by Denys Cazet; *Blood Diaries: Tales of a 6th-Grade Vampire*, by Marissa Moss.

CRIMSON ROMANCE

Simon & Schuster, Inc., 57 Littlefield St., Avon MA 02322. **E-mail:** crimsonsubmissions@simonandschuster.com. **Website:** crimsonromance.com. **Contact:** Tara Gelsomino, Executive Editor. Estab. 2012. Publishes electronic originals and print-on-demand copies. Direct to e-book romance imprint of Simon & Schuster, Inc. **20% of books from first-time authors. 80% from unagented writers. Does not pay advance.** Accepts simultaneous submissions. Guidelines online.

FICTION Subjects include romance. Crimson seeks submissions featuring strong characters, smart stories, and satisfying romance in five popular subgenres: contemporary, historical, paranormal, romantic suspense, and spicy. We're looking for previously unpublished novellas (between 20,000 – 50,000 words) and full-length novels (between 50,000 – 90,000 words). All authors—agented or unagented, beginner or veteran writers—are welcome to submit any works that have not been previously published in whole or in part in any media, including self-publishing (Kindle, CreateSpace, etc.). While your work can include other genre elements, Crimson Romances must focus first and foremost on a couple's emotional journey together towards love. Romances, by nature, must be between consenting adults of any gender, race, creed, etc., and have a happily-ever-after or at least happy-for-now ending. We are strictly a romance publisher and will not look at manuscripts for memoirs or other non-fiction, women's fiction or chick lit, young adult, mysteries and thrillers, horror, or general fiction. We're specifically seeking diverse romances (own voices preferred). Please see current submission guidelines online.

CROSS-CULTURAL COMMUNICATIONS

Cross-Cultural Literary Editions, 239 Wynsum Ave., Merrick NY 11566-4725. (516)869-5635. **Fax:** (516)379-1901. **E-mail:** info@cross-culturalcommunications.com; cccpoetry@aol.com. **Website:** www.cross-culturalcommunications.com. **Contact:** Stanley H. Barkan; Bebe Barkan. Estab. 1971. Publishes hardcover and trade paperback originals. **Publishes 10 titles/year. 200 queries; 50 mss received/year. 10-25% of books from first-time authors. 100% from unagented writers.** Publishes book 1 year after acceptance. Responds in 1 month to proposals; 2 months to mss. Book catalog (sample flyers) for #10 SASE. Inquire for specifics. Prefer submissions with a query letter including full contact data and brief bio. Focus on bilingual poetry: include original and translations, 3-6 samples.

IMPRINTS Ostrich editions. Cooperative editions with The Seventh Quarry and the Feral and the New Feral Press.

Focua on bilingual poetry.

NONFICTION Subjects include Americana, art, contemporary culture, fashion, language, literature, memoirs, multicultural, photography, translation. "Query first; we basically do not want the focus on nonfiction." Query with SASE. Reviews artwork/photos. Send photocopies.

FICTION Subjects include ethnic, historical, literary, multicultural, poetry, poetry in translation, translation, bilingual poetry. Query with SASE.

POETRY For bilingual poetry submit 3-6 short poems in original language with English translation, a brief (3-5 lines) bio of the author and translator(s).

TIPS "Best chance: poetry from a translation."

THE CROSSROAD PUBLISHING COMPANY

83 Chestnut Ridge Rd., Chestnut Ridge NY 10977. **Fax:** (845)517-0181. **E-mail:** submissions@crossroadpublishing.com. **Website:** www.crossroadpublishing.com. Estab. 1980. Publishes hardcover and trade paperback originals and reprints. **Publishes 45 titles/year. 1,000 queries received/year. 200 mss received/year. 10% of books from first-time authors. 75% from unagented writers. Pays 6-14% royalty on wholesale price.** Publishes ms 14 months after acceptance. Accepts simultaneous submissions. Responds in 6 weeks to queries and proposals; 12 weeks to mss. Book catalog available free. Guidelines online.

IMPRINTS Crossroad (trade); Herder (classroom/academic).

NONFICTION Subjects include creative nonfiction, ethnic, religion, spirituality, leadership, Catholicism. "We want hopeful, well-written books on religion and spirituality." Query with SASE.

TIPS "Refer to our website and catalog for a sense of the range and kinds of books we offer. Follow our application guidelines as posted on our website."

CROSSWAY

A publishing ministry of Good News Publishing, 1300 Crescent St., Wheaton IL 60187. (630)682-4300. **Fax:** (630)682-4785. **E-mail:** info@crossway.org. **E-mail:** submissions@crossway.org. **Website:** www.crossway.org. **Contact:** Jill Carter, editorial administrator. Estab. 1938. "'Making a difference in people's lives for Christ' as its maxim, Crossway Books lists titles written from an evangelical Christian perspective." Member ECPA. Distributes titles through Christian bookstores and catalogs. Promotes titles through magazine ads, catalogs. *Does not accept unsolicited mss.* "Please check our website for the types of books we publish. Submission guidelines are posted." **Publishes 85 titles/year. Pays negotiable royalty.** Publishes ms 18 months after acceptance. Accepts simultaneous submissions.

NONFICTION "Send us an e-mail query and, if your idea fits within our acquisitions guidelines, we'll invite a proposal."

FICTION Not accepted at this time.

TIPS "Please check website for the type of books we publish. Our submission guidelines are posted."

CROWN BUSINESS

Penguin Random House, 1745 Broadway, New York NY 10019. (212)572-2275. **Website:** crownpublishing.com. Estab. 1995. Publishes hardcover and trade paperback originals. *Agented submissions only.* Accepts simultaneous submissions. Book catalog online.

CROWN PUBLISHING GROUP

Penguin Random House, 1745 Broadway, New York NY 10019. (212)782-9000. **Website:** crownpublishing.com. Estab. 1933. Publishes popular fiction and nonfiction hardcover originals. Accepts simultaneous submissions. *Agented submissions only.* See website for more details.

IMPRINTS Amphoto Books; Back Stage Books; Billboard Books; Broadway Books; Clarkson Potter; Crown; Crown Archetype; Crown Business; Crown Forum; Harmony Books; Image Books; Potter Craft; Potter Style; Ten Speed Press; Three Rivers Press; Waterbrook Multnomah; Watson-Guptill.

CRYSTAL SPIRIT PUBLISHING, INC.

P.O. Box 12506, Durham NC 27709. **E-mail:** crystalspiritinc@gmail.com. **Website:** www.crystalspiritinc.com. **Contact:** V. S. O'Neal, Senior Managing Editor. Estab. 2004. Publishes hardcover, trade paperback, mass market paperback, and electronic originals. "Our readers are lovers of high-quality books that are sold as direct sales, in bookstores, gift shops and placed in libraries and schools. They support independent authors and they expect works that will provide them with entertainment, inspiration, romance, and education. Our audience loves to read and will embrace niche authors that love to write." **Publishes 3-5 titles/year. Receives 1,100 mss/year. 80% of books from first-time authors. 100% from unagented writers. Pays 20-45% royalty on retail price.** Publishes ms 3-6 months after acceptance. Accepts simultaneous submissions. Responds in 15-30 days. Book catalog and ms guidelines online. Submissions are only accepted via the website. Please see guidelines as stated on the website. Postal mail submissions are not allowed and will not be reviewed. We do not acknowledge or respond to queries.

NONFICTION Subjects include alternative lifestyles, business, career guidance, child guidance, community, contemporary culture, cooking, counseling, creative nonfiction, economics, entertainment, ethnic, fashion, film, finance, foods, gay, health, house and home, humanities, language, law, lesbian, literary criticism, literature, medicine, memoirs, money, multicultural, music, New Age, nutrition, parenting, philosophy, pop culture, public affairs, real estate, recreation, religion, sex, social sciences, sociology, spirituality, sports, travel, womens issues, womens studies, world affairs, young adult, inspirational, Christian romance. Submissions are only accepted via the website. Please see guidelines as stated on the website. Postal mail submissions are not allowed and will not be reviewed. We do not acknowledge or respond to queries.

FICTION Subjects include confession, contemporary, erotica, ethnic, feminist, gay, humor, juvenile, literary, mainstream, multicultural, religious, romance, short story collections, spiritual, young adult, inspirational, Christian romance. Submissions are only accepted via the website. Please see guidelines as stated on the website. Postal mail submissions are not allowed and will not be reviewed. We do not acknowledge or respond to queries.

RECENT TITLE(S) *Love Your Jiggle: The Girl's Guide To Being Marvelous*, by Shanterra McBride; *The Chysalis Diaries*, by Traci Marie Brower; *Touched by the Power of God's Love*, by L.D. Schumacher; *A Branch of Ivy: The Timeless Service of Sigma Tau Omega.*

TIPS "Submissions are accepted for publication throughout the year. Works should be positive and non-threatening. All submissions are accepted via the website only! Ensure that all contact information is correct, abide by the submission guidelines and do not send follow-up e-mails or calls." Do not send queries as they will not be acknowledged or receive a response.

CSLI PUBLICATIONS

Condura Hall, Stanford University, 210 Panama St., Stanford CA 94305. (650)723-1839. **Fax:** (650)725-2166. **E-mail:** pubs@csli.stanford.edu. **Website:** csli-publications.stanford.edu. Publishes hardcover and scholarly paperback originals. CSLI Publications, part of the Center for the Study of Language and Information, specializes in books in the study of language, information, logic, and computation. Book catalog available free. Guidelines online.

NONFICTION Subjects include science, logic, cognitive science. "We do not accept unsolicited mss."

CURIOSITY QUILLS

Whampa, LLC, P.O. Box 2160, Reston VA 20195. (800)998-2509. **Fax:** (800)998-2509. **E-mail:** editor@curiosityquills.com. **E-mail:** acquisitions@curiosityquills.com. **Website:** curiosityquills.com. **Contact:** Alisa Gus. Additional Contacts: Eugene Teplitsky, Nikki Tetreault. Estab. 2011. Firm publishes sci-fi, speculative fiction, steampunk, paranormal and urban fantasy, and corresponding romance titles under its new Rebel Romance imprint. Curiosity Quills is a publisher of hard-hitting dark sci-fi, speculative fiction, and paranormal works aimed at adults, young adults, and new adults. **Publishes 75 titles/year. 1,000 submissions/year. 60% of books from first-time authors. 65% from unagented writers. Pays variable royalty. Does not pay advance.** Publishes ms 9-12 months after acceptance. Accepts simultaneous submissions. Responds in 1-6 weeks. Catalog available. Guidelines online.

IMPRINTS Curiosity Quills Press, Rebel Romance.

NONFICTION Writer's guides, on a strictly limited basis.

FICTION Subjects include adventure, contemporary, erotica, fantasy, gay, gothic, hi-lo, historical, horror, humor, juvenile, lesbian, literary, mainstream, multicultural, multimedia, mystery, romance, science fiction, suspense, young adult, steampunk, dieselpunk, space opera. Looking for "thought-provoking, mind-twisting rollercoasters—challenge our mind, turn our world upside down, and make us question. Those are the makings of a true literary marauder." Submit ms using online submission form or e-mail to acquisitions@curiosityquills.com.

RECENT TITLE(S) *Please Don't Tell My Parents I'm A Supervillain*, by Richard Roberts; *Deathsniffer's Assistant*by Kate McIntyre; Kiya trilogy, by Katie Hamstead; *Krampus: Three Sisters*, by Sonia Halbach.

CYCLE PUBLICATIONS, INC.

Van der Plas Publications, 1282 Seventh Ave., San Francisco CA 94112. (415)665-8214. **Fax:** (415)753-8572. **Website:** www.cyclepublishing.com. Estab. 1985. "Van der Plas Publications/Cycle Publishing was started in 1997 with 4 books. Since then, we have introduced about 4 new books each year, and in addition to our 'mainstay' of cycling books, we now also have books on manufactured housing, golf, baseball, and strength training. Our offices are located in San Francisco, where we do editorial work, as well as administration, publicity, and design. Our books are warehoused in Kimball, Michigan, which is close to the companies that print most of our books and is conveniently located to supply our book trade distributors and the major book wholesalers." Accepts simultaneous submissions.

DA CAPO PRESS

Perseus Books Group, 44 Farnsworth St., 3rd Floor, Boston MA 02210. (617)252-5200. **Website:** www.dacapopress.com. Estab. 1975. Publishes hardcover originals and trade paperback originals and reprints. **Publishes 115 titles/year. 500 queries; 300 mss received/year. 25% of books from first-time authors. 1% from unagented writers. Pays 7-15% royalty. Pays $1,000-225,000 advance.** Publishes book 1 year after acceptance. Accepts simultaneous submissions. Book catalog and guidelines online.

NONFICTION Subjects include contemporary culture, creative nonfiction, history, memoirs, social sciences, sports, translation, travel, world affairs. No unsolicited mss or proposals. Agented submissions only.

DARBY CREEK PUBLISHING

Lerner Publishing Group, 1251 Washington Ave. N., Minneapolis MN 55401. (612)332-3344. **Fax:** (612)332-7615. **Website:** www.lernerbooks.com. "Darby Creek publishes series fiction titles for emerging, striving and reluctant readers ages 7 to 18 (grades 2-12). From beginning chapter books to intermediate fiction and page-turning YA titles, Darby Creek books engage readers with strong characters and formats they'll want to pursue." Darby Creek does not publish picture books. Publishes children's chapter books, middle readers, young adult. Mostly series. **Publishes 25 titles/year. Offers advance-against-royalty contracts.** Accepts simultaneous submissions.

"We are currently not accepting any submissions. If that changes, we will provide all children's writing publications with our new info."

NONFICTION Middle readers: biography, history, science, sports. Recently published *Albino Animals*, by Kelly Milner Halls, illustrated by Rick Spears; *Miracle: The True Story of the Wreck of the Sea Venture*, by Gail Karwoski.

FICTION Middle readers, young adult. Recently published: *The Surviving Southside* series, by various authors; *The Agent Amelia* series, by Michael Broad; *The Mallory McDonald* series, by Laurie B. Friedman; and *The Alien Agent* series, by Pam Service.

DARK HORSE COMICS, INC.

10956 SE Main St., Milwaukie OR 97222. (503)652-8815. **Fax:** (503)654-9440. **E-mail:** dhcomics@darkhorse.com. **E-mail:** dhsubsproposals@darkhouse.com. **Website:** www.darkhorse.com. "In addition to publishing comics from top talent like Frank Miller, Mike Mignola, Stan Sakai and internationally-renowned humorist Sergio Aragonés, Dark Horse is recognized as the world's leading publisher of licensed comics." Accepts simultaneous submissions.

FICTION Subjects include comic books. Comic books, graphic novels. Published *Astro Boy Volume 10 TPB*, by Osamu Tezuka and Reid Fleming; *Flaming Carrot Crossover #1* by Bob Burden and David Boswell. Submit synopsis to dhcomics@darkhorse.com. See website (www.darkhorse.com) for detailed submission guidelines and submission agreement, which must be signed. Include a full script for any short story or single-issue submission, or the first eight pages of the first issue of any series. Submissions can no longer be mailed back to the sender.

TIPS "If you're looking for constructive criticism, show your work to industry professionals at conventions."

JONATHAN DAVID PUBLISHERS, INC.

68-22 Eliot Ave., Middle Village NY 11379. (718)456-8611. **Fax:** (718)894-2818. **Website:** www.jdbooks.com. **Contact:** David Kolatch, editorial director. Estab. 1948. Publishes hardcover and trade paperback originals and reprints. Jonathan David publishes popular Judaica. **Publishes 20-25 titles/year. 50% of books**

from first-time authors. 90% from unagented writers. Pays royalty, or makes outright purchase. Publishes ms 18 months after acceptance. Accepts simultaneous submissions. Responds in 1-2 months. Book catalog and guidelines online.

NONFICTION Subjects include creative nonfiction, ethnic, multicultural, religion, sports. Unsolicited mss are not being accepted at this time.

DAW BOOKS, INC.

Penguin Random House, 375 Hudson St., New York NY 10014. (212)366-2096. **Fax:** (212)366-2090. **E-mail:** daw@penguinrandomhouse.com. **Website:** www.dawbooks.com. **Contact:** Peter Stampfel, submissions editor. Estab. 1971. Publishes hardcover and paperback originals and reprints. DAW Books publishes science fiction and fantasy. **Publishes 50-60 titles/year. Pays in royalties with an advance negotiable on a book-by-book basis.** Responds in 3 months. Guidelines online.

FICTION Subjects include fantasy, science fiction. "Currently seeking modern urban fantasy and paranormals. We like character-driven books with appealing protagonists, engaging plots, and well-constructed worlds. We accept both agented and unagented manuscripts." Submit entire ms, cover letter, SASE. "Do not submit your only copy of anything. The average length of the novels we publish varies but is almost never less than 80,000 words."

KATHY DAWSON BOOKS

Penguin Random House, 1745 Broadway, New York NY 10019. (212)782-9000. **Website:** penguinrandomhouse.com. **Contact:** Kathy Dawson, vice-president and publisher. Estab. 2014. Mission statement: Publish stellar novels with unforgettable characters for children and teens that expand their vision of the world, sneakily explore the meaning of life, celebrate the written word, and last for generations. The imprint strives to publish tomorrow's award contenders: quality books with strong hooks in a variety of genres with universal themes and compelling voices—books that break the mold and the heart. Responds only if interested. Guidelines online.

FICTION Accepts fiction queries via snail mail only. Include cover sheet with one-sentence elevator pitch, main themes, author version of catalog copy for book, first 10 pages of ms (double-spaced, Times Roman, 12 point type), and publishing history. No SASE needed. Responds only if interested.

⊘ DC UNIVERSE

1700 Broadway, New York NY 10019. **Website:** www.dccomics.com. Accepts simultaneous submissions.

Ⓐ⊘ DELACORTE PRESS

an imprint of Random House Children's Books, a division of Penguin Random House LLC, New York, 1745 Broadway, New York NY 10019. (212)782-9000. **Website:** randomhousekids.com; randomhouseteens.com. Publishes middle grade and young adult fiction in hard cover, trade paperback, mass market and digest formats. Accepts simultaneous submissions.

All query letters and manuscript submissions must be submitted through an agent or at the request of an editor.

Ⓐ⊘ DEL REY BOOKS

Penguin Random House, 1745 Broadway, 18th Floor, New York NY 10019. (212)782-9000. **Website:** www.penguinrandomhouse.com. Estab. 1977. Publishes hardcover, trade paperback, and mass market originals and mass market paperback reprints. Del Rey publishes top level fantasy, alternate history, and science fiction. **Pays royalty on retail price. Pays competitive advance.**

IMPRINTS Del Rey/Manga, Del Rey/Lucas Books.

FICTION Subjects include fantasy, science fiction, alternate history. *Agented submissions only.*

TIPS "Del Rey is a reader's house. Pay particular attention to plotting, strong characters, and dramatic, satisfactory conclusions. It must be/feel believable. That's what the readers like. In terms of mass market, we basically created the field of fantasy bestsellers. Not that it didn't exist before, but we put the mass into mass market."

DIAL BOOKS FOR YOUNG READERS

Imprint of Penguin Random House LLC, 1745 Broadway, New York NY 10019. (212)782-9000. **Website:** www.penguinrandomhouse.com. Estab. 1961. Publishes hardcover originals. "Dial Books for Young Readers publishes quality picture books for ages 18 months-6 years; lively, believable novels for middle readers and young adults; and occasional nonfiction for middle readers and young adults." **Publishes 50 titles/year. 5,000 queries received/year. 20% of books from first-time authors. Pays royalty. Pays varies advance.** Responds in 4-6 months to queries. Book catalog and guidelines online.

NONFICTION Only responds if interested. "We accept entire picture book manuscripts and a maximum of 10 pages for longer works (novels, easy-to-reads). When submitting a portion of a longer work, please provide an accompanying cover letter that briefly describes your manuscript's plot, genre (i.e. easy-to-read, middle grade or YA novel), the intended age group, and your publishing credits, if any."

FICTION Subjects include adventure, fantasy, juvenile, picture books, young adult. Especially looking for lively and well-written novels for middle grade and young adult children involving a convincing plot and believable characters. The subject matter or theme should not already be overworked in previously published books. The approach must not be demeaning to any minority group, nor should the roles of female characters (or others) be stereotyped, though we don't think books should be didactic, or in any way message-y. No topics inappropriate for the juvenile, young adult, and middle grade audiences. No plays. Accepts unsolicited queries and up to 10 pages for longer works and unsolicited mss for picture books. Will only respond if interested.

TIPS "Our readers are anywhere from preschool age to teenage. Picture books must have strong plots, lots of action, unusual premises, or universal themes treated with freshness and originality. Humor works well in these books. A very well-thought-out and intelligently presented book has the best chance of being taken on. Genre isn't as much of a factor as presentation."

DIAL PRESS

1745 Broadway, New York NY 10019. **Website:** www.penguinrandomhouse.com. Estab. 1924. Accepts simultaneous submissions.

FICTION Subjects include literary. *Agented submissions only.*

DIVERTIR

P.O. Box 232, North Salem NH 03073. **E-mail:** info@divertirpublishing.com. **E-mail:** query@divertirpublishing.com. **Website:** www.divertirpublishing.com. **Contact:** Kenneth Tupper, publisher. Estab. 2009. Publishes trade paperback and electronic originals. Divertir Publishing is an independent publisher located in Salem, NH. "Our goal is to provide interesting and entertaining books to our readers, as well as to offer new and exciting voices in the writing community the opportunity to publish their work. We seek to combine an understanding of traditional publishing with a unique understanding of the modern market to best serve both our authors and readers." **Publishes 6-12 titles/year. 1,000 submissions received/year. 70% of books from first-time authors. 100% from unagented writers. Pays 10-15% royalty on wholesale price (for novels and nonfiction). Does not pay advance.** Publishes ms 9-12 months after acceptance. Accepts simultaneous submissions. Responds in 1-3 months on queries; 3-4 months on proposals and mss. Catalog online. Guidelines online.

NONFICTION Subjects include contemporary culture, government, politics, public affairs, world affairs, young adult. "We are particularly interested in the following: political/social commentary, current events, and humor/satire." "We currently do not publish memoirs." Reviews artwork/photos as part of the ms package. Submit electronically.

FICTION Subjects include adventure, contemporary, fantasy, gothic, horror, humor, mainstream, mystery, science fiction, suspense, young adult. "We are particularly interested in the following: science fiction, fantasy, historical, alternate history, contemporary mythology, mystery and suspense, paranormal, and urban fantasy." Does not consider erotica or mss with excessive violence. Electronically submit proposal package, including synopsis and query letter with author's bio.

RECENT TITLE(S) *Bonebelly*, by Christine Lajewski; *The Entropy of Knowledge*, by Mark Dellandre and Britton Learnard; *Guardian's Return*, by Darren Simon; *The Seven Sorrows*, by Gregg Kuehn.

TIPS "Please see our Author Info page (online) for more information."

DK PUBLISHING

Penguin Random House, 1450 Broadway, Suite 801, New York NY 10018. **Website:** www.dk.com. "DK publishes photographically illustrated nonfiction for children of all ages." *DK Publishing does not accept unagented mss or proposals.* Accepts simultaneous submissions.

DOUBLEDAY CANADA

1 Toronto St., Suite 300, Toronto ON M5C 2V6, Canada. **Website:** www.randomhouse.ca. Accepts simultaneous submissions.

DOVER PUBLICATIONS, INC.

31 E. Second St., Mineola NY 11501. (516)294-7000. **Fax:** (516)873-1401. **Website:** www.doverpublications.com. Estab. 1941. Publishes trade paperback originals and reprints. **Publishes 660 titles/year. Makes outright purchase.** Accepts simultaneous submissions. Book catalog online.

NONFICTION Subjects include agriculture, Americana, animals, history, hobbies, philosophy, photography, religion, science, sports, translation, travel. Publishes mostly reprints. Accepts original paper doll collections, game books, coloring books (juvenile). Query with SASE. Reviews artwork/photos.

DREAM OF THINGS

P.O. Box 872, Downers Grove IL 60515. **Website:** dreamofthings.com. Estab. 2009. Publishes trade paperback originals and reprints, electronic originals and reprints. Publishes memoirs, essay collections, and creative nonfiction. **Publishes 3-4 titles/year. 90% of books from first-time authors. 90% from unagented writers. Pays 10% royalties on retail price. No advance.** Accept to publish time is 6 months. Accepts simultaneous submissions. Catalog online. Guidelines online.

NONFICTION Subjects include creative nonfiction, memoirs, essay collections. Submit via online form. For memoirs, submit 1 sample chapter. For essay collections, submit 2-3 essays. Does not review artwork.

DUFOUR EDITIONS

P.O. Box 7, 124 Byers Rd., Chester Springs PA 19425. (610)458-5005. **Website:** www.dufoureditions.com. Estab. 1948. Publishes hardcover originals, trade paperback originals and reprints. **Publishes 1-2 titles/year. 200 queries; 15 mss received/year. 20-30% of books from first-time authors. 80% from unagented writers. Pays $100-500 advance.** Publishes ms 18 months after acceptance. Responds in 3-6 months. Book catalog available free.

NONFICTION Subjects include history, literary criticism, translation. Query with SASE. Reviews artwork/photos. Send photocopies.

FICTION Subjects include literary, short story collections, translation. "We like books that are slightly offbeat, different and well-written." Query with SASE.

POETRY Query.

THE DUNDURN GROUP

3 Church St., Suite 500, Toronto ON M5E 1M2, Canada. **Website:** www.dundurn.com. Estab. 1972. Dundurn prefers work by Canadian authors. First-time authors are welcome. Publishes hardcover and trade paperback originals and reprints. Accepts simultaneous submissions.

FICTION Subjects include literary, mystery, young adult. Query with SASE or submit 3 sample chapter(s), synopsis. Accepts queries by mail. Include estimated word count. Responds in 3-4 months to queries. Accepts simultaneous submissions. No electronic submissions.

DUNEDIN ACADEMIC PRESS LTD

Hudson House, 8 Albany St., Edinburgh EH1 3QB, United Kingdom. (44)(131)473-2397. **E-mail:** mail@dunedinacademicpress.co.uk. **Website:** www.dunedinacademicpress.co.uk. **Contact:** Anthony Kinahan, director. Estab. 2001. Dunedin Academic Press Ltd is a lively small independent academic publishing house. **Publishes 10-15 titles/year. 5% of books from first-time authors. 100% from unagented writers. Pays royalty.** Book catalog and proposal guidelines online.

"Read and respond to the proposal guidelines on our website before submitting. Do not send mss unless requested to do so. Do not send hard copy proposals. Approach first by e-mail, outlining your proposal, telling us why you are well-positioned to write on the subject and identifying the market for your proposed book. We will not respond to proposals outside our principal subject area of earth and environmental sciences. We do not publish non-academic books"

NONFICTION Subjects includeearth and environmental sciences only. Reviews artwork/photos.

TIPS "Dunedin's list contains authors and subjects from across the international the academic world. DAP's horizons are far broader than our immediate Scottish environment. One of the strengths of Dunedin is that we are able to offer our authors that individual support that comes from dealing with a small independent publisher committed to growth through careful treatment of its authors. Most of our publishing is commissioned from the academic authors who write in the narrow subject areas in which the company publishes"

THOMAS DUNNE BOOKS

Imprint of St. Martin's Press, 175 Fifth Ave., New York NY 10010. (212)674-5151. **E-mail:** thomasdunnebooks@stmartins.com. **Website:** www.thomasdunnebooks.com. Estab. 1986. Publishes hardcover and trade paperback originals, and reprints. "Thomas Dunne Books publishes popular trade fiction and nonfiction. His group covers a range of genres including commercial and literary fiction, thrillers, biography, politics, sports, popular science, and more. The list is intentionally eclectic and includes a wide range of fiction and nonfiction, from first books to international bestsellers." Accepts simultaneous submissions. Book catalog and ms guidelines free.

NONFICTION Subjects include history, science, true crime, political commentary. *Accepts agented submissions only.*

FICTION Subjects include mystery, suspense, thrillers, women's. *Accepts agented submissions only.*

DUTTON ADULT TRADE

Penguin Random House, 1745 Broadway, New York NY 10019. (212)782-9000. **Website:** penguinrandomhouse.com. Estab. 1852. Publishes hardcover originals. "Dutton currently publishes 45 hardcovers a year, roughly half fiction and half nonfiction." **Pays royalty. Pays negotiable advance.** Book catalog online.

NONFICTION Agented submissions only. *No unsolicited mss.*

FICTION Subjects include adventure, historical, literary, mystery, short story collections, suspense. Agented submissions only. *No unsolicited mss.*

TIPS "Write the complete ms and submit it to an agent or agents. They will know exactly which editor will be interested in a project."

DUTTON CHILDREN'S BOOKS

Penguin Random House, 1745 Broadway, New York NY 10019. **Website:** www.penguinrandomhouse.com. Estab. 1852. Publishes hardcover originals as well as novelty formats. Dutton Children's Books publishes high-quality fiction and nonfiction for readers ranging from preschoolers to young adults on a variety of subjects. Currently emphasizing middle grade and young adult novels that offer a fresh perspective. Deemphasizing photographic nonfiction and picture books that teach a lesson. **Publishes 100 titles/year. 15% of books from first-time authors. Pays royalty on retail price. Pays advance.** Accepts simultaneous submissions.

"Cultivating the creative talents of authors and illustrators and publishing books with purpose and heart continue to be the mission and joy at Dutton."

NONFICTION Subjects include animals, history, science. Query. Only responds if interested.

FICTION Subjects include juvenile, young adult. Dutton Children's Books has a diverse, general interest list that includes picture books; easy-to-read books; and fiction for all ages, from first chapter books to young adult readers. Query. Responds only if interested.

RECENT TITLE(S) *The Fault in Our Stars*, by John Green (young adult novel).

DYNAMITE ENTERTAINMENT

113 Gaither Dr., Suite 205, Mt. Laurel NJ 8054. **E-mail:** submissions@dynamite.com. **Website:** www.dynamiteentertainment.com. Accepts simultaneous submissions.

FICTION Query first. Does not accept unsolicited submissions. Include brief bio, list of publishing credits.

DZANC BOOKS

Dzanc Books, Inc., 2702 Lillian, Ann Arbor MI 48104. **Website:** www.dzancbooks.org. Accepts simultaneous submissions.

FICTION Subjects include literary. "We're an independent non-profit publishing literary fiction. We also set up writer-in-residence programs and help literary journals develop their subscription bases." Publishes paperback originals. Query with outline/synopsis and 35 sample pages. Accepts queries by e-mail. Include brief bio. Agented fiction: 3%. Accepts unsolicited mss. Considers simultaneous submissions, submissions on CD or disk. Rarely critiques/comments on rejected mss. Responds to mss in 5 months.

TIPS "Every word counts—it's amazing how many submissions have poor first sentences or paragraphs and that first impression is hard to shake when it's a bad one."

EASTLAND PRESS

P.O. Box 99749, Seattle WA 98139. (206)931-6957. **Fax:** (206)283-7084. **E-mail:** info@eastlandpress.com. **Website:** www.eastlandpress.com. **Contact:** John O'Connor, managing editor. Estab. 1981. Publishes hardcover and trade paperback originals. "Eastland Press publishes textbooks for practitioners of alternative medical therapies, primarily Chinese and physical therapies, and related bodywork." **Publishes 3-4 titles/year. 25 queries received/year. 30% of books from first-time authors. 90% from unagented writers. Pays 12-15% royalty on receipts, more for e-book receipts.** Publishes ms 1-2 years after acceptance. Accepts simultaneous submissions. Responds in 1 month to queries. Catalog online.

NONFICTION Subjects include health, medicine. "We prefer that a ms be completed or close to completion before we will consider publication. Proposals are rarely considered, unless submitted by a published author or teaching institution." Submit TOC and 2-3 sample chapters. Reviews artwork/photos.

RECENT TITLE(S) *Anatomy of Breathing*, by Blandine Calais-Germain; *The Fasciae: Anatomy, Dysfunction & Treatment*, by Serge Paoletti; *Chinese Herbal Medicine*, by Dan Bensky; *Clinical Handbook of Internal Medicine*, by William Maclean.

EDGE SCIENCE FICTION AND FANTASY PUBLISHING

Hades Publications, Box 1414, Calgary AB T2P 2L7, Canada. (403)254-0160. **E-mail:** publisher@hadespublications.com. **Website:** www.edgewebsite.com. **Contact:** Editorial Manager. Estab. 1996. Publishes trade paperback and e-book originals. EDGE publishes thought-provoking full length novels and anthologies of Science Fiction, Fantasy and Horror. Featuring works by established authors and emerging new voices, EDGE is pleased to provide quality literary entertainment in both print and pixels. **Publishes 12+ titles/year. 300-400 30% of books from first-time authors. 90% from unagented writers. Pays royalty on net price for distributed printed and eBook editions. Negotiable advance.** Publishes ms 18-20 months after acceptance. Responds in 4-5 months to mss. Catalog online. Guidelines online.

IMPRINTS EDGE, EDGE-Lite, Tesseracts Books, Absolute XPress.

NONFICTION Does not want erotica, juvenile.

FICTION Subjects include contemporary, fantasy, horror, mystery, occult, science fiction. "We are looking for all types of fantasy, science fiction, and horror - except juvenile, erotica, and religious fiction. Short stories and poetry are only required for announced anthologies." Length: 75,000-100,000/words. Does not want juvenile, erotica, and religious fiction. Submit first 3 chapters and synopsis. Check website for guidelines. Include estimated word count.

RECENT TITLE(S) *Dreamers*, by Donna Glee Williams; *nEvermore!* (Tales of Murder, Mystery, and the Macabre), edited by Nancy Kilpatrick & Caro Soles, *The Triforium: The Haunting of Westminster Abbey*, by Mark Patton; *Professor Challenger New Worlds, Lost Places*, edited by J. R. Campbell and Charles Prepolec.

EDUPRESS, INC.

Teacher Created Resources, 12621 Western Ave., Garden Grove CA 92841. (800)662-4321. **Fax:** (800)525-1254. **Website:** www.edupress.com. **Contact:** Editor-in-Chief. Estab. 1979. Edupress, Inc., publishes supplemental curriculum resources for PK-6th grade. Currently emphasizing Common Core reading and math games and materials. **Work purchased outright from authors.** Publishes ms 1-2 years after acceptance. Accepts simultaneous submissions. Responds in 2-4 months. Catalog online.

"Our mission is to create products that make kids want to go to school."

NONFICTION Submit complete ms via mail or e-mail with "Manuscript Submission" as the subject line.

TIPS "We are looking for unique, research-based, quality supplemental materials for Pre-K through 6th grade. We publish mainly reading and math materials in many different formats, including games. Our materials are intended for classroom and home schooling use. We do not publish picture books."

WILLIAM B. EERDMANS PUBLISHING CO.

2140 Oak Industrial Dr. NE, Grand Rapids MI 49505. (616)459-4591. **Fax:** (616)459-6540. **E-mail:** info@eerdmans.com. **E-mail:** submissions@eerdmans.com. **Website:** www.eerdmans.com. Estab. 1911. Publishes hardcover and paperback originals and reprints. "The majority of our adult publications are religious and most of these are academic or semi-academic in character (as opposed to inspirational or celebrity books), though we also publish general trade books on the Christian life. Our nonreligious titles, most of them in regional history or on social issues, aim, similarly, at an educated audience." Accepts simultaneous submissions. Responds in 4 weeks. Book catalog and ms guidelines free.

NONFICTION Subjects include history, philosophy, psychology, regional, religion, sociology, translation, Biblical studies. "We prefer that writers take the time to notice if we have published anything at all in the same category as their manuscript before sending it to us." Query with TOC, 2-3 sample chapters, and SASE for return of ms. Reviews artwork/photos.

FICTION Subjects include religious. Query with SASE.

EDWARD ELGAR PUBLISHING, INC.

The William Pratt House, 9 Dewey Ct., Northampton MA 01060. (413)584-5551. **Fax:** (413)584-9933. **E-mail:** info@e-elgar.com. **Website:** www.e-elgar.com. Estab. 1986. "Specializing in research monographs, reference books and upper-level textbooks in highly focused areas, we are able to offer a unique service in terms of editorial, production and worldwide marketing. We have three offices, Cheltenham and Camberley in the UK and Northampton, MA, US. We are actively commissioning new titles and are happy to consider and advise on ideas for monograph books, textbooks, professional law books and academic journals at any stage. Please complete a proposal form in as much detail as possible. We review all prososals with our academic advisors." Accepts simultaneous submissions.

ELLYSIAN PRESS

E-mail: publisher@ellysianpress.com. **E-mail:** submissions@ellysianpress.com. **Website:** www.ellysianpress.com. **Contact:** Maer Wilson. David A. Gray Estab. 2014. Publishes fantasy, science fiction, paranormal, paranormal romance, horror, and young/new adult in these genres. "Ellysian Press is a speculative fiction house. We seek to create a sense of home for our authors, a place where they can find fulfillment as artists. Just as exceptional mortals once sought a place in the Elysian Fields, now exceptional authors can find a place here at Ellysian Press. We are accepting submissions in the following genres only: Fantasy, Science Fiction, Paranormal, Paranormal Romance, Horror, along with Young/New Adult in these genres. Please submit polished manuscripts. It's best to have work read by critique groups or beta readers prior to submission. PLEASE NOTE: We do not publish children's books, picture books, or Middle Grade books. We do not publish books outside the genres listed above." **25% of books from first-time authors. 90% from unagented writers. Pays quarterly. Does not pay advance.** Publishes ms 12+ months after acceptance. Accepts simultaneous submissions. Responds in 1 week for queries; 4-6 weeks for partials and fulls. Catalog online. Guidelines online.

FICTION Subjects include fantasy, horror, occult, science fiction, young adult, paranormal, paranormal romance, new adult. "We accept online submissions only. Please submit a query letter, a synopsis and the first ten pages of your manuscript in the body of your e-mail. The subject line should be as follows: QUERY - Your Last Name, TITLE, Genre." If we choose to request more, we will request the full manuscript in standard format. This means your manuscript should be formatted as per the guidelines on our website. Please do not submit queries for any genres not listed above. Please do not submit children's books, picture books or Middle Grade books. You may email queries to submissions(at)ellysianpress(dot)com.

ELM BOOKS

1175 Hwy. 130, Laramie WY 82070. (610)529-0460. **E-mail:** leila.elmbooks@gmail.com. **Website:** www.elm-books.com. **Contact:** Leila Monaghan, publisher. "Follow us on Facebook to learn about our latest calls for science fiction, mystery and romance stories. We also welcome submissions of middle grade fiction featuring diverse children. No picture book submissions." **Pays royalties.** Accepts simultaneous submissions.

NONFICTION Subjects include young adult.

FICTION "Follow us on Facebook to learn about our latest calls for science fiction, mystery and romance stories. We also welcome submissions of middle grade fiction featuring diverse children. No picture book submissions." Send inquiries for middle grade fiction featuring diverse children via e-mail to Leila.elmbooks@gmail.com. No mail inquiries.

RECENT TITLE(S) *I am Jamal* by Lee Mullins, illustrated by Lottie Patterson;
Superbeetle, by S. Michel Chen, illustrated by Leda Chung;
The Death Series, edited by Jess Faraday.

Ⓐ⊘ ENCOUNTER BOOKS

900 Broadway, Suite 601, New York NY 10003. (212)871-6310. **Fax:** (212)871-6311. **Website:** www.encounterbooks.com. **Contact:** Acquisitions. Publisher/President: Roger Kimball. Publishes hardcover, trade paperback, and e-book originals and trade paperback reprints. Encounter Books publishes serious nonfiction—books that can alter our society, challenge our morality, stimulate our imaginations—in the areas of history, politics, religion, biography,

education, public policy, current affairs, and social sciences. Encounter Books is an activity of Encounter for Culture and Education, a tax-exempt, non profit corporation dedicated to strengthening the marketplace of ideas and engaging in educational activities to help preserve democratic culture. Accepts simultaneous submissions. Book catalog online. Guidelines online.

NONFICTION Subjects include child guidance, education, ethnic, history, memoirs, multicultural, philosophy, psychology, religion, science, sociology, gender studies. Only considers agented submissions.

ENETE ENTERPRISES

1321 Upland Dr. #6536, Houston TX 77043. **E-mail:** eneteenterprises@gmail.com. **Website:** www.eneteenterprises.com. **Contact:** Shannon Enete, editor. Estab. 2011. Publishes trade paperback originals, mass market paperback originals, electronic originals. **Publishes 6 titles/year. 290 queries received/year. 95% of books from first-time authors. 100% from unagented writers. Pays royalties of 10-20%.** Publishes book 3-6 months after acceptance. Accepts simultaneous submissions. Responds to queries/proposals in 1 month; mss in 1-3 months. Guidelines online.

NONFICTION Subjects include education, health, memoirs, travel, travel guides, travel memoirs, life abroad, retired living abroad. Submit query, proposal, or ms with marketing plan by e-mail.

TIPS "Send me your best work. Do not rush a draft. If you don't follow the submission guidelines your work will not be reviewed. A marketing plan is required."

ENSLOW PUBLISHERS, INC.

101 W. 23rd St., Suite 240, New York NY 10011. (973)771-9400. **Fax:** (877)980-4454. **E-mail:** customerservice@enslow.com. **Website:** www.enslow.com. Estab. 1977. Publishes hardcover originals. 10% require freelance illustration. Enslow publishes nonfiction and fiction series books for young adults and school-age children. **Publishes 250 titles/year. Pays royalty on net price with advance or flat fee. Pays advance.** Publishes ms 1 year after acceptance. Accepts simultaneous submissions. Responds in 1 month to queries. Guidelines via e-mail.

NONFICTION Subjects include history, recreation, science, sociology, sports. "Interested in new ideas for series of books for young people." No fiction, fictionalized history, or dialogue.

TIPS "We love to receive resumes from experienced writers with good research skills who can think like young people."

ENTANGLED TEEN

Website: www.entangledteen.com. "Entangled Teen and Entangled digiTeen, our young adult imprints publish the swoonworthy young adult romances readers crave. Whether they're dark and angsty or fun and sassy, contemporary, fantastical, or futuristic. We are seeking fresh voices with interesting twists on popular genres." **Pays royalty.** Accepts simultaneous submissions.

IMPRINTS Teen Crush; Teen Crave.

FICTION "We are seeking novels in the subgenres of romantic fiction for contemporary, upper young adult with crossover appeal." E-mail using site. "All submissions must have strong romantic elements. YA novels should be 50K to 100K in length. Revised backlist titles will be considered on a case by case basis." Agented and unagented considered.

RECENT TITLE(S) *Paper or Plastic*, by Vivi Barnes; *The Girl and the Clockwork Cat*, by Nikki McCormack.

ENTREPRENEUR PRESS

Entrepreneur Media Inc., 18061 Fitch, Irvine CA 92614. (949)261-2325. **Fax:** (949)622-7106. **E-mail:** books@entrepreneur.com. **E-mail:** submissions@entrepreneur.com. **Website:** http://entrepreneurmedia.com/books/. **Contact:** Vanessa Campos, sales & marketing director. Editorial Director: Jen Dorsey. Entrepreneur Press specializes in quality paperbacks and e-books that focus on the entrepreneur in us all. Addressing the diverse challenges at all stages of business, each Entrepreneur Press book aims to provide actionable solutions to help entrepreneurs excel in all ventures they take on. **Publishes 18+ titles/year. Pays competitive net royalty. Yes** Accepts simultaneous submissions. Catalog online. Guidelines online.

NONFICTION Subjects include business, career guidance, business start-up, small business management, business planning, marketing, finance, careers, personal finance, accounting, motivation, leadership, legal advise, management. When submitting work to us, please send as much of the proposed book as possible. Proposal should include: cover letter, preface, marketing plan, analysis of competition and comparative titles, author bio, TOC, 2 sample chapters. Go to website for more details. Reviews artwork/photos.

Send transparencies and all other applicable information.

RECENT TITLE(S) *Simplify* by Richard Koch; *The Hero Factor* by Jeffrey Hayzlett; *80/20 Sales and Marketing*, by Perry Marshall; *No B.S. Time Management, Second Edition*, by Dan S. Kennedy; *Market Like You Mean It*, by Al Lautenslager.

TIPS "We are currently seeking proposals covering sales, small business, startup, online businesses, marketing, etc."

EPICENTER PRESS, INC.

Aftershocks Media, 6524 NE 181st St. #2, Kenmore WA 98028. (425)485-6822. **Fax:** (425)481-8253. **E-mail:** info@epicenterpress.com. **Website:** www.epicenterpress.com. **Contact:** Lael Morgan, acquisitions editor. Estab. 1987. Publishes hardcover and trade paperback originals. "We are a regional press founded in Alaska whose interests include but are not limited to the arts, history, environment, and diverse cultures and lifestyles of the North Pacific and high latitudes. Our affiliated company, Aftershocks Media, provides a range of services to self-publisher industry distributors." **Publishes 4-8 titles/year. 200 queries; 100 mss received/year. 75% of books from first-time authors. 90% from unagented writers.** Publishes book 1-2 years after acceptance. Accepts simultaneous submissions. Responds in 6 months to queries. Book catalog and guidelines online.

NONFICTION Subjects include animals, ethnic, history, recreation, regional. "Our focus is Alaska and the Pacific Northwest. We do not encourage nonfiction titles from outside this region." Submit outline and 3 sample chapters. Reviews artwork/photos. Send photocopies.

RECENT TITLE(S) *Bering Sea Blues*, by Joe Upton; *Surviving the Island of Grace*, by Leslie Leyland Fields.

FACTS ON FILE, INC.

Infobase Learning, 132 W. 31st St., 16th Floor, New York NY 10001. (800)322-8755. **Fax:** (800)678-3633. **E-mail:** llikoff@infobaselearning.com; custserv@infobaselearning.com. **Website:** www.infobaselearning.com. **Contact:** Laurie Likoff. Estab. 1941. Publishes hardcover originals and reprints and e-books as well as reference databases. Facts On File produces high-quality reference materials in print and digital format on a broad range of subjects for the school and public library market and the general nonfiction trade. **Publishes 150-200 titles/year. 10% of books from first-time authors. 45% from unagented writers. Pays 10% royalty on retail price. Pays $3-5,000 advance.** Responds in 6 months to 1 year. Accepts simultaneous submissions. Responds in 2 months to queries. Reference catalog available free. Guidelines online.

IMPRINTS Bloom's Literature; Ferguson's; Chelsea House; World Almanac.

NONFICTION Subjects include career guidance, contemporary culture, education, environment, government, history, literary criticism, multicultural, nutrition, politics, religion, sports, womens studies, young adult, careers, entertainment, natural history, popular culture. "We publish serious, informational e-books for a targeted audience. All our books must have strong library interest, but we also distribute books effectively to the trade. Our library books fit the junior and senior high school curriculum." No computer books, technical books, cookbooks, biographies (except YA), pop psychology, humor, fiction or poetry. Query or submit outline and sample chapter with SASE. No submissions returned without SASE.

TIPS "Our audience is school and public libraries for our more reference-oriented books and libraries, schools and bookstores for our less reference-oriented informational titles."

FAMILIUS

1254 Commerce Way, Sanger CA 93657. (559)876-2170. **Fax:** (559)876-2180. **E-mail:** bookideas@familius.com. **Website:** familius.com. **Contact:** Acquisitions. Design & Digital: Derek George. Managing Editor: Brooke Jorden. Marketing & Publicity: Kate Faller. Sales: Ashley Mireles. Estab. 2012. Publishes hardcover, trade paperback, and electronic originals and reprints. Familius is a value's driven trade publishing house, publishing in children's, parenting, relationships, cooking, health and wellness, and education. The company's mission is to help families be happy. **Publishes 60 titles/year. 200 queries; 100 mss received/year. 30% of books from first-time authors. 70% from unagented writers. Authors are paid 10-30% royalty on wholesale price. Advances periodically paid to participating illustrators.** Publishes book 12 months after acceptance. Accepts simultaneous submissions. Responds in 1 month to queries and proposals; 2 months to mss. Catalog online and print. Guidelines online.

NONFICTION Subjects include Americana, beauty, child guidance, cooking, counseling, crafts, finance, foods, games, gardening, health, hobbies, medicine, memoirs, military, nutrition, parenting. All mss must align with Familius mission statement to help families succeed. Submit a proposal package, including an outline, 1 sample chapter, competition evaluation, and your author platform. Reviews JPEGS and PDFs if sent as part of the submission package.

FICTION Subjects include picture books. All picture books must align with Familius values statement listed on the website footer. Submit a proposal package, including a synopsis, 3 sample chapters, and your author platform.

RECENT TITLE(S) *Book*, by David Miles; *Coconut Kitchen*, by Meredith Baird; *Fairy House*, by Mike and Debbie Schramer, *The Half-Diet Diet*, by Richard and Linda Eyre.

FANTAGRAPHICS BOOKS, INC.

7563 Lake City Way NE, Seattle WA 98115. (206)524-1967. **Fax:** (206)524-2104. **Website:** www.fantagraphics.com. **Contact:** Submissions Editor. Estab. 1976. Publishes original trade paperbacks. Publishes comics for thinking readers. Does not want mainstream genres of superhero, vigilante, horror, fantasy, or science fiction. Accepts simultaneous submissions. Responds in 2-3 months to queries. Book catalog online. Guidelines online.

FICTION Subjects include comic books. "Fantagraphics is an independent company with a modus operandi different from larger, factory-like corporate comics publishers. If your talents are limited to a specific area of expertise (i.e. inking, writing, etc.), then you will need to develop your own team before submitting a project to us. We want to see an idea that is fully fleshed-out in your mind, at least, if not on paper. Submit a minimum of 5 fully-inked pages of art, a synopsis, SASE, and a brief note stating approximately how many issues you have in mind."

TIPS "Take note of the originality and diversity of the themes and approaches to drawing in such Fantagraphics titles as *Love & Rockets* (stories of life in Latin America and Chicano L.A.), *Palestine* (journalistic autobiography in the Middle East), *Eightball* (surrealism mixed with kitsch culture in stories alternately humorous and painfully personal), and *Naughty Bits* (feminist humor and short stories which both attack and commiserate). Try to develop your own, equally individual voice; originality, aesthetic maturity, and graphic storytelling skill are the signs by which Fantagraphics judges whether or not your submission is ripe for publication."

FARCOUNTRY PRESS

P.O. Box 5630, Helena MT 59604. (800)821-3874. **Fax:** (406)443-5480. **E-mail:** will@farcountrypress.com. **Website:** www.farcountrypress.com. **Contact:** Will Harmon, Sr. Editor. Estab. 1980. Award-winning publisher Farcountry Press specializes in softcover and hardcover color photography books showcasing the nation's cities, states, national parks, and wildlife. Farcountry also publishes several children's series, as well as guidebooks, cookbooks, and regional history titles nationwide. **Publishes The staff produces about 30 books annually; the backlist has grown to more than 400 titles. titles/year.** Accepts simultaneous submissions. Guidelines online.

NONFICTION Subjects include agriculture, Americana, animals, community, cooking, environment, foods, history, memoirs, nature, photography, regional, travel.

RECENT TITLE(S) *Georgia Unforgettable*; *Portrait of Houston*; *Bad Girls of the Midwest*; *Field Guide to Yellowstone*; *Tasting Colorado*; *Fish do WHAT In the Water?*.

FARRAR, STRAUS & GIROUX

18 W. 18th St., New York NY 10011. (646)307-5151. **Website:** us.macmillan.com/fsg. **Contact:** Editorial Department. Estab. 1946. Publishes hardcover originals and trade paperback reprints. "We publish original and well-written material for all ages." **Publishes 75 titles/year. 6,000 queries and mss received/year. 5% of books from first-time authors. 50% from unagented writers. Pays 2-6% royalty on retail price for paperbacks, 3-10% for hardcovers. Pays $3,000-25,000 advance.** Publishes ms 18 months after acceptance. Accepts simultaneous submissions. Responds in 2-3 months. Catalog available by request. Guidelines online.

NONFICTION All levels. Send cover letter describing submission with first 50 pages.

FICTION Subjects include juvenile, picture books, young adult. Do not query picture books; just send ms. Do not fax or e-mail queries or mss. Send cover letter describing submission with first 50 pages.

POETRY Send cover letter describing submission with 3-4 poems. By mail only.

FARRAR, STRAUS & GIROUX FOR YOUNG READERS

Macmillan Children's Publishing Group, 175 Fifth Ave., New York NY 10010. (212)741-6900. **Fax:** (212)633-2427. **E-mail:** childrens.editorial@fsgbooks.com. **Website:** www.fsgkidsbooks.com. Estab. 1946. Accepts simultaneous submissions. Book catalog available by request. Ms guidelines online.

NONFICTION All levels: all categories. "We publish only literary nonfiction." Submit cover letter, first 50 pages by mail only.

FICTION All levels: all categories. "Original and well-written material for all ages." Submit cover letter, first 50 pages by mail only.

POETRY Submit cover letter, 3-4 poems by mail only.

TIPS "Study our catalog before submitting. We will see illustrators' portfolios by appointment. Don't ask for criticism and/or advice—due to the volume of submissions we receive, it's just not possible. Never send originals. Always enclose SASE."

FEIWEL AND FRIENDS

Macmillan Children's Publishing Group, 175 Fifth Ave., New York NY 10010. (646)307-5151. **Website:** us.macmillan.com. Feiwel and Friends is a publisher of innovative children's fiction and nonfiction literature, including hardcover, paperback series, and individual titles. The list is eclectic and combines quality and commercial appeal for readers ages 0-16. The imprint is dedicated to "book by book" publishing, bringing the work of distinctive and oustanding authors, illustrators, and ideas to the marketplace. This market does not accept unsolicited mss due to the volume of submissions; they also do not accept unsolicited queries for interior art. The best way to submit a ms is through an agent. Catalog online.

FENCE BOOKS

Science Library 320, Univ. of Albany, 1400 Washington Ave., Albany NY 12222. (518)591-8162. **E-mail:** jessp.fence@gmail.com. **Website:** www.fenceportal.org. **Contact:** Submissions Manager. Publishes hardcover originals. "Fence Books publishes poetry, fiction, and critical texts and anthologies, and prioritizes sustained support for its authors, many of whom come to us through our book contests and then go on to publish second, third, fourth books." Accepts simultaneous submissions. Guidelines online.

FICTION Subjects include literary, poetry. Submit via contests and occasional open reading periods.

POETRY Submit via contests and occasional open reading periods.

FERGUSON PUBLISHING CO.

Infobase Publishing, 132 W. 31st St., 17th Floor, New York NY 10001. (800)322-8755. **E-mail:** editorial@factsonfile.com. **Website:** www.infobasepublishing.com. Estab. 1940. Publishes hardcover and trade paperback originals. "We are primarily a career education publisher that publishes for schools and libraries. We need writers who have expertise in a particular career or career field (for possible full-length books on a specific career or field)." **Publishes 50 titles/year. Pays by project.** Accepts simultaneous submissions. Responds in 6 months to queries. Guidelines online.

NONFICTION "We publish work specifically for the elementary/junior high/high school/college library reference market. Works are generally encyclopedic in nature. Our current focus is career encyclopedias and young adult career sets and series. We consider manuscripts that cross over into the trade market." No mass market, poetry, scholarly, or juvenile books, please. Query or submit an outline and 1 sample chapter.

TIPS "We like writers who know the market—former or current librarians or teachers or guidance counselors."

FILBERT PUBLISHING

Box 326, Kandiyohi MN 56251-0326. **E-mail:** filbertpublishing@filbertpublishing.com. **Website:** filbertpublishing.com. **Contact:** Maurice Erickson, acquisitions. Estab. 2001. Publishes trade paperback and electronic originals and reprints. "We really like to publish books that creative entrepreneurs can use to help them make a living following their dream. This includes books on marketing, anything that encourages living a full life, freelancing, self-help, we'll consider a fairly wide range of subjects under this umbrella. The people who purchase our titles (and visit our website) tend to be in their fifties, female, well-educated; many are freelancers who want to make a living writing. Any well-written manuscript that would appeal to that audience is nearly a slam dunk to get reviewed." **Publishes 6-12 titles/year. 85% of books from first-time authors. 99% from unagented writers. Paperback authors receive 10% royalty on retail price. E-books receive 50% net. Does not pay advance.** Publishes book 6-9 months after acceptance. Accepts simultaneous submissions. Responds in 1-2 months. Sometimes we get really behind on this. If after a couple months you haven't heard from us, feel free to resend. Catalog online. Guidelines online.

NONFICTION Subjects include business, communications, creative nonfiction, spirituality, reference books for freelancers and creative entrepreneurs with an emphasis on marketing. "Our projects tend to be evergreen. If you've got a great project that's as relevant today as it will be 10 years from now, something that you're passionate about (within our guidelines), query." Submit a query, SASE with a proposal package. Include an outline and 2 sample chapters. You can also query via e-mail. However, sometimes legit queries get lost because we get a ton of e-mail. If you haven't received a reply within a couple weeks, don't hesitate to resend. Will review artwork. Writers should send photocopies or send electronically. "We like to publish books that creative entrepreneurs can use to help them make a living following their dream. This includes books on marketing, anything that encourage living a full life, freelancing, self-help, we'll consider a fairly wide range of subjects under this umbrella. The people who purchase our titles (and visit our website) tend to be in their fifties, female, well-educated; many are freelancers who want to make a living writing. Any well-written manuscript that would appeal to that audience is nearly a slam dunk to get reviewed."

FICTION Subjects include contemporary, mainstream, mystery, short story collections, suspense. "We're thrilled when we find a story that sweeps us off our feet. Good fiction queries have been sparse the last couple of years, and we're keen on expanding our current mystery/suspense line in the coming year." Query, include SASE with a proposal package, including a synopsis, 5 sample chapters, information regarding your web platform, and a brief mention of your current marketing plan. "If you'd like to submit a query via e-mail, that's fine. However, we get a lot of e-mail and if you don't receive a reply within a couple weeks, don't hesitate to resend."

RECENT TITLE(S) The Pocket Power series, by Rudie Jakerson and L.J. Fringe; The Consecrated Journal Series; The Reclaimed Series, by B.A. Erickson.

TIPS "Get to know us. Subscribe to Writing Etc./The Creative Entrepreneur to capture our preferred tone. Dig through our website, you'll get many ideas of what we're looking for. We enjoy nurturing new talent and most of our authors have stuck with us since our humble beginning. All new authors begin their journey with us with e-book publication. If that goes well, we move on to print. We love words. We enjoy marketing. We really love the publishing business. If you share those passions, feel free to query."

FINISHING LINE PRESS

P.O. Box 1626, Georgetown KY 40324. **E-mail:** finishingbooks@aol.com. **E-mail:** http://finishinglinepress.submittable.com/submit. **Website:** www.finishinglinepress.com. **Contact:** Christen Kincaid, director. Estab. 1998. Finishing Line Press seeks to "discover new talent" and hopes to publish chapbooks by both men and women poets who have not previously published a book or chapbook of poetry. Has published *Parables and Revelations* by T. Crunk, *Family Business* by Paula Sergi, *Putting in a Window* by John Brantingham, and *Dusting the Piano* by Abigail Gramig. Publishes 100+ poetry chapbooks/year. Chapbooks are usually 16-35 pages,and perfect bound. Publishes 50+ full-length books per year. Submit poetry with cover letter, bio, acknowledgments, and **no reading fee in November**. Responds to queries and mss in up to 3 months. Pay varies; pays in author's copies. "Sales profits, if any, go to publish the next new poet." Sample chapbooks available by sending $6 to Finishing Line Press or through website. See The Finishing Line Press Open Chapbook Competition and the New Women's Voices Chapbook Competition. Member of CLMP. **Publishes 100+ titles/year. 2,500 50% of books from first-time authors. 98% from unagented writers. Pays in copies, or standard royalties contract. Pays advance against royalties for fiction and nonfiction.** Accepts simultaneous submissions. Responds in 3-6 months. Catalog online. Guidelines online.

NONFICTION Subjects include alternative lifestyles, Americana, animals, art, creative nonfiction, entertainment, history, humanities, language, lesbian, literary criticism, literature, memoirs, religion, spirituality, travel, womens issues, womens studies, art history, craft of writing, biography.

FICTION Subjects include comic books, contemporary, ethnic, experimental, feminist, gay, historical, literary, mainstream, multicultural, plays, poetry,

poetry in translation, religious, short story collections, spiritual, translation.

POETRY "We read manuscripts in November. There is no fee for manuscripts submitted via regular post during the month of November. If you would like to submit outside of the month of November, please see guidelines below: We read general submissions year round. Please include a $3 reading fee with your manuscript. Submit 16-35 pages of poetry, plus bio, acknowledgments, SASE and cover letter (you can pay by check or money order) or submit online using our online submissions manager."

RECENT TITLE(S) *Voluptuous Bristle*, chapbook by Ravi Shankar.

FINNEY COMPANY, INC.

5995 149th St. W., Suite 105, Apple Valley MN 55124. **E-mail:** info@finneyco.com. **Website:** www.finneyco.com. **Contact:** Acquisitions. Publishes trade paperback originals. **Publishes 2 titles/year. Pays 10% royalty on wholesale price. Does not pay advance.** Publishes ms 1 year after acceptance. Accepts simultaneous submissions. Responds in 2-3 months to queries.

NONFICTION Subjects include education, career exploration/development. Finney publishes career development educational materials. Query with SASE. Reviews artwork/photos.

Ⓐ⊘ FIRST SECOND

Macmillan Children's Publishing Group, 175 5th Ave., New York NY 10010. **E-mail:** mail@firstsecondbooks.com. **Website:** www.firstsecondbooks.com. First Second is a publisher of graphic novels and an imprint of Macmillan Children's Publishing Group. First Second does not accept unsolicited submissions. Responds in about 6 weeks. Catalog online.

FLOATING BRIDGE PRESS

Pontoon Poetry, 909 NE 43rd St., #205, Seattle WA 98105. **E-mail:** editor@floatingbridgepress.org. **Website:** www.floatingbridgepress.org. **Contact:** John Pierce or Meghan McClure. Estab. 1994. Chapbooks of poetry and poems at our review, *Pontoon Poetry*. Floating Bridge Press is a 501(c)(3) nonprofit literary arts organization, founded in 1994. Floating Bridge Press promotes the diverse voices of Washington State poets through an annual poetry chapbook competition, archival-quality books, online publishing, broadsides, and community readings. Floating Bridge Press publishes Washington State poets whose writing engages individuals, enriches communities, and enlivens the arts. "We believe that poets are leaders and poetry enriches the community; diverse voices enrich poetry; poetry deserves the highest editorial attention; poetry deserves promotion and increased attention in our community." **150-200 The winning poet receives a minimum of $500, 15 copies of a perfect-bound, archival-quality chapbook, local promotion, distribution of the chapbook, and a featured reading in the Seattle area. Three or four finalists receive $50 each and are also featured at the winner's reading. In 2015 and 2016 we published 2 finalist's chapbooks along with the winning chapbook.** Publishes ms 6 months after acceptance. Accepts simultaneous submissions. Responds in 3-6 months.

POETRY Floating Bridge Press publishes chapbooks and anthologies by Washington State poets, selected through an annual competition. Floating Bridge Press reads manuscripts for our Chapbook Competition from November 1st to March 15th. Submit through Submittable: https://floatingbridgepress.submittable.com/submit

The winning poet receives a minimum of $500, 15 copies of a perfect-bound, archival-quality chapbook, local promotion, distribution of the chapbook, and a featured reading in the Seattle area. Three or four finalists receive $50 each and are also featured at the winner's reading. In 2015 and 2016 we published 2 finalist's chapbooks along with the winning chapbook. Every poem will be considered for inclusion in our sister publication Pontoon Poetry and for the Paula Jones Gardiner Memorial Award.

FOCAL PRESS

Imprint of Elsevier (USA), Inc., 711 3rd Ave., 8th Floor, New York NY 10017. **Website:** routledge.com/focalpress. Estab. US, 1981; UK, 1938. Publishes hardcover and paperback originals and reprints. "Focal Press provides excellent books for students, advanced amateurs, and working professionals involved in all areas of media technology. Topics of interest include photography (digital and traditional techniques), film/video, audio, broadcasting, and cinematography, through to journalism, radio, television, video, and writing. Currently emphasizing graphics, gaming, animation, and multimedia." **Publishes 80-120 UK-US titles/year; entire firm publishes over 1,000 titles/year. 25% of books from first-time authors.**

90% from unagented writers. Publishes ms 6 months after acceptance. Accepts simultaneous submissions. Responds in 2 months to queries. Guidelines online.

NONFICTION Subjects include photography, film, cinematography, broadcasting, theater and performing arts, audio, sound and media technology. Does not publish collections of photographs or books composed primarily of photographs. To submit a proposal for consideration by Elsevier, complete the proposal form online. "Once we have had a chance to review your proposal in line with our publishing plan and budget, we will contact you to discuss the next steps." Reviews artwork/photos.

FODOR'S TRAVEL PUBLICATIONS, INC.

Imprint of Penguin Random House LLC., 1745 Broadway, 15th Floor, New York NY 10019. **E-mail:** editors@fodors.com. **Website:** www.fodors.com. Estab. 1936. Publishes trade paperback originals. Fodor's publishes travel books on many regions and countries. "Remember that most Fodor's writers live in the areas they cover. Note that we do not accept unsolicited mss." **Most titles are collective works, with contributions as works for hire. Most contributions are updates of previously published volumes.** Accepts simultaneous submissions. Responds in 2 months to queries. Book catalog available free.

NONFICTION Subjects include travel. "We are interested in unique approaches to favorite destinations. Writers seldom review our catalog or our list and often query about books on topics that we're already covering. Beyond that, it's important to review competition and to say what the proposed book will add. Do not send originals without first querying as to our interest in the project. We're not interested in travel literature or in proposals for general travel guidebooks." Submit writing clips and résumé via mail or e-mail. In cover letter, explain qualifications and areas of expertise.

TIPS "In preparing your query or proposal, remember that it's the only argument Fodor's will hear about why your book will be a good one, and why you think it will sell; and it's also best evidence of your ability to create the book you propose. Craft your proposal well and carefully so that it puts your best foot forward."

FORDHAM UNIVERSITY PRESS

2546 Belmont Ave., University Box L, Bronx NY 10458. (718)817-4795. **Fax:** (718)817-4785. **Website:** www.fordhampress.com. **Contact:** Tom Lay, acquisitions editor. Editorial Director: Richard W. Morrison. Publishes hardcover and trade paperback originals and reprints. "We are a publisher in humanities, accepting scholarly monographs, collections, occasional reprints and general interest titles for consideration. No fiction." Accepts simultaneous submissions. Book catalog and ms guidelines free.

NONFICTION Subjects include education, history, philosophy, regional, religion, science, sociology, translation, business, Jewish studies, media, music. Submit query letter, CV, SASE.

RECENT TITLE(S) *Strut: The Peacock and Beauty in Art*, edited by Bartholomew F. Bland and Laura L. Vookles; *Walking New York*, by Stephen Miller; *From a Nickel to a Token*, by Andrew J. Sparberg.

TIPS "We have an academic and general audience."

FORTRESS PRESS

P.O. Box 1209, Minneapolis MN 55440. (612)330-3300. **Website:** www.fortresspress.com. Publishes hardcover and trade paperback originals. "Fortress Press publishes academic books in Biblical studies, theology, Christian ethics, church history, and professional books in pastoral care and counseling." **Pays royalty on retail price.** Accepts simultaneous submissions. Book catalog free. Guidelines online.

NONFICTION Subjects include religion, church history, African-American studies. Use online form. Please study guidelines before submitting.

FORWARD MOVEMENT

412 Sycamore St., Cincinnati OH 45202. (513)721-6659; (800)543-1813. **Fax:** (513)721-0729. **E-mail:** editorialstaff@forwardmovement.org. **Website:** www.forwardmovement.org. Estab. 1934. "Forward Movement was established to help reinvigorate the life of the church. Many titles focus on the life of prayer, where our relationship with God is centered, death, marriage, baptism, recovery, joy, the Episcopal Church and more. Currently emphasizing prayer/spirituality." **Publishes 30 titles/year.** Accepts simultaneous submissions. Responds in 1 month. Book catalog free. Guidelines online.

NONFICTION Subjects include religion. "We are an agency of the Episcopal Church. There is a special need for tracts of under 8 pages. (A page usually runs about 200 words.) On rare occasions, we publish a full-length book." Query with SASE or by e-mail with complete ms attached.

FICTION Subjects include juvenile.

TIPS "Audience is primarily Episcopalians and other Christians."

WALTER FOSTER PUBLISHING

Quarto Publishing Group, 26391 Crown Valley Parkway, Suite 220, Mission Viejo CA 92691. (949)380-7510. **E-mail:** rebecca.razo@quarto.com. **Website:** www.quartoknows.com. **Contact:** Publisher. Estab. 1922. Publishes trade paperback originals, some hardcover and flexi formats, and art/craft kits. Walter Foster publishes instructional/how-to books in the fine art, craft, and hobby categories. **60% of books from first-time authors. 80% from unagented writers. Competitive for category. Determined on a case-by-case basis.** 12-14 months between acceptance and publication. Accepts simultaneous submissions. Responds in 6-8 weeks. Prefer digital submissions. No phone calls. Guidelines online. Pitches that do not adhere to guidelines will not be reviewed.

IMPRINTS Walter Foster Publishing, Walter Foster Jr.

Looking for both evergreen and on-trend subject matter.

NONFICTION Subjects include art, crafts, hobbies, ART Techniques, all categories. Art, craft, activity books. Submit proposal package.

THE FOUNDRY PUBLISHING

P.O. Box 419527, Kansas City MO 64141. (816)931-1900. **Fax:** (816)412-8306. **E-mail:** rmcfarland@thefoundrypublishing.com. **Website:** thefoundrypublishing.com. Publishes hardcover and paperback originals. "Beacon Hill Press is a Christ-centered publisher that provides authentically Christian resources faithful to God's word and relevant to life." **Publishes 15 titles/year. Pays royalty.** Publishes ms 2 years after acceptance. Accepts simultaneous submissions. Responds in 3 months to queries.

NONFICTION "Accent on holy living; encouragement in daily Christian life." No felt needs, fiction, autobiography, poetry, short stories, or children's picture books. Query or submit proposal electronically.

RECENT TITLE(S) *Manna*, by Kevin Stirratt; *So Long, Status Quo*, by Susy Flory.

FOUR WAY BOOKS

Box 535, Village Station, New York NY 10014. (212)334-5430. **E-mail:** editors@fourwaybooks.com. **Website:** www.fourwaybooks.com. Estab. 1993. "Four Way Books is a not-for-profit literary press dedicated to publishing poetry and short fiction by emerging and established writers. Each year, Four Way Books publishes the winners of its national poetry competitions, as well as collections accepted through general submission, panel selection, and solicitation by the editors." Accepts simultaneous submissions.

NONFICTION Subjects include literature.

FICTION Subjects include contemporary, poetry, short story collections. Open reading period: June 1-30. Book-length story collections and novellas. Submission guidelines will be posted online at end of May. Does not want novels or translations.

POETRY Four Way Books publishes poetry and short fiction. Considers full-length poetry and story and novella mss only. Books are about 70-2-300 pages, digital printing, perfect-bound, with paperback binding, art/graphics on covers. Does not want individual poems or poetry intended for children/young readers. See website for complete submission guidelines and open reading period in June. Book mss may include previously published poems. Responds to submissions in 4 months. Payment varies. Order sample books from Four Way Books online or through bookstores.

FOX CHAPEL PUBLISHING

1970 Broad St., East Petersburg PA 17520. (800)457-9112. **Fax:** (717)560-4702. **Website:** www.foxchapelpublishing.com. Publishes hardcover and trade paperback originals and trade paperback reprints. Fox Chapel publishes craft, lifestyle, and woodworking titles for professionals and hobbyists. **Publishes 90-150 titles/year. 30% of books from first-time authors. 100% from unagented writers. Pays royalty or makes outright purchase. Pays variable advance.** Accepts simultaneous submissions. Submission guidelines online.

NONFICTION Subjects include cooking, crafts, creative nonfiction.

RECENT TITLE(S) *Creative Coloring Inspirations; Zen Drawing for a Calm and Focused Mind; Zenspirations;.*

TIPS "We're looking for knowledgeable artists, craftspeople and woodworkers, all experts in their fields, to write books of lasting value."

FRANCISCAN MEDIA PRESS

28 W. Liberty St., Cincinnati OH 45202-6498. (513)241-5615. **Fax:** (513)241-0399. **E-mail:** info@franciscanmedia.org. **Website:** www.americancatholic.org. Estab. 1970. Publishes trade paperback

originals. "St. Anthony Messenger Press/Franciscan Communications seeks to communicate the word that is Jesus Christ in the styles of Saints Francis and Anthony. Through print and electronic media marketed in North America and worldwide, we endeavor to evangelize, inspire, and inform those who search for God and seek a richer Catholic, Christian, human life. Our efforts help support the life, ministry, and charities of the Franciscan Friars of St. John the Baptist Province, who sponsor our work. Currently emphasizing prayer/spirituality." **Publishes 20-25 titles/year. 300 queries received/year. 50 mss received/year. 5% of books from first-time authors. 99% from unagented writers. Pays $1,000 average advance.** Publishes ms 18 months after acceptance. Accepts simultaneous submissions. Responds in 2 months. Guidelines online.

IMPRINTS Servant Books.

NONFICTION Query with SASE. Submit outline. Reviews artwork/photos.

FREEBIRD PUBLISHERS

221 Pearl St., P.O. Box 541, North Dighton MA 02764. (774)406-8682. **E-mail:** diane@freebirdpublishers.com. **Website:** www.freebirdpublishers.com. **Contact:** Diane E. Schindelwig. Estab. 2013. Prisoner Publications. Freebird Publishers specializes in prisoner publications. Our books help prisoners keep in contact with the outside world. In addition, we assist prisoners get their books published. Freebird Publishers offers prisoner publications like resource books, reentry books, legal books and guides, how-to books, entertainment photo books, and other niche items created for and by incarcerated individuals. Our goals are to help prisoners allowing them to better ready themselves and their families upon release and become a stronger person getting ready for reentry. We work with all inmates within all the levels Federal BOP, state prisons and county jails in the country. Freebird Publishers can professionally handle all your publishing needs. We can assist you in every step of publishing your words into a printed or eBooks. We offer our self-publishing services to everyone but especially the incarcerated prisoners and inmates throughout the USA. **Hundreds 90% of books from first-time authors. 100% from unagented writers.** Responds in 60-90 days.

NONFICTION Subjects include business, career guidance, cooking, creative nonfiction, education, entertainment, law, money.

FICTION Subjects include adventure, comic books, confession, contemporary, fantasy, feminist, gay, gothic, juvenile, lesbian, mainstream, mystery, picture books, poetry, romance, science fiction, short story collections, spiritual, suspense, western, young adult.

FREE SPIRIT PUBLISHING, INC.

6325 Sandburg Rd., Suite 100, Minneapolis MN 55427-3674. (612)338-2068. **Fax:** (612)337-5050. **E-mail:** acquisitions@freespirit.com. **Website:** www.freespirit.com. Estab. 1983. Publishes trade paperback originals and reprints. "Free Spirit is the leading publisher of learning tools that support young people's social-emotional health and educational needs. We help children and teens think for themselves, overcome challenges, and make a difference in the world." Free Spirit does not accept general fiction, poetry or storybook submissions. **Publishes 25-30 titles/year.** Accepts simultaneous submissions. Responds to proposals within 6 months. Book catalog and guidelines online.

NONFICTION Subjects include child guidance, counseling, education, educator resources; early childhood education. "Many of our authors are educators, mental health professionals, and youth workers involved in helping kids and teens." No general fiction or picture storybooks, poetry, single biographies or autobiographies, books with mythical or animal characters, or books with religious or New Age content. We are not looking for academic or religious materials, or books that analyze problems with the nation's school systems. Query with cover letter stating qualifications, intent, and intended audience and market analysis (comprehensive list of similar titles and detailed explanation of how your book stands out from the field), along with your promotional plan, outline, 2 sample chapters (note: for early childhood submissions, the entire text is required for evaluation), resume, SASE. Do not send original copies of work.

FICTION Subjects include juvenile, picture books. "Please review catalog and author guidelines (both available online) for details before submitting proposal. If you'd like material returned, enclose a SASE with sufficient postage."

RECENT TITLE(S) *The 6Rs of Bullying Prevention; The Survival Guide for Money Smarts; I Like Being Me; Real Kids, Real Stories, Real Character; Differentiation for Gifted Learners; Being the Best Me Series.*

TIPS "Our books are issue-oriented, jargon-free, and solution-focused. Our audience is children, teens, teachers, parents and youth counselors. We are especially concerned with kids' social and emotional well-being and look for books with ready-to-use strategies for coping with today's issues at home or in school—written in everyday language. We are not looking for academic or religious materials, or books that analyze problems with the nation's school systems. Instead, we want books that offer practical, positive advice so kids can help themselves, and parents and teachers can help kids succeed."

FULCRUM PUBLISHING

4690 Table Mountain Dr., Suite 100, Golden CO 80403. **E-mail:** acquisitions@fulcrumbooks.com. **Website:** www.fulcrum-books.com. **Contact:** T. Baker, acquisitions editor. Estab. 1984. In physics, the word fulcrum denotes the point at which motion begins. We strive to create books that will inspire you to move forward in your life or to take action. Whether it's exploring the world around you or discussing the ideas and issues that shape that world, our books provide the tools to create forward motion in your life. Our mission is simple, yet profound: Publish books that inspire readers to live life to the fullest and to learn something new every day. More than thirty years ago, when Bob Baron started Fulcrum Publishing, his goal was to publish high-quality books from extraordinary authors. Fulcrum recognizes that good books can't exist without the best authors. To that end, we have published books from prominent politicians (Governors Richard Lamm and Bill Ritter, Jr., Senators Gary Hart and Eugene McCarthy), influential Native Americans (Wilma Mankiller, Vine Deloria Jr., and Joseph Bruchac), master gardeners (Lauren Springer, Tom Peace, and Richard Hartlage), and important organizations in the environmental community (Campaign for America's Wilderness, World Wilderness Congress, Defenders of Wildlife). Our books have received accolades from the likes of Tom Brokaw, Elizabeth Dole, Nelson Mandela, Paul Newman, William Sears, MD, Gloria Steinem, Dr. Henry Louis Gates, Jr., and Kurt Vonnegut. In addition, Fulcrum authors have received awards from prestigious organizations such as the American Booksellers Association, American Library Association, Colorado Center for the Book, ForeWord magazine, National Book Foundation, National Parenting Publications, New York Public Library, PEN USA Literary Awards, Smithsonian National Museum of the American Indian, Teacher's Choice, Harvey Awards, and more. **200 40% of books from first-time authors. 90% from unagented writers. Pays authors royalty based on wholesale price. Offers advances.** Ms published 18-24 months after acceptance. Accepts simultaneous submissions. Because of the volume of submissions we receive, we can only reply to submissions we are interested in pursuing, and it may take up to three months for a reply. No editorial remarks will be supplied. We do not provide consulting services for authors on the suitability of their mss. Catalog for SASE. Your submission must include: A proposal of your work, including a brief synopsis; 2-3 sample chapters; a brief biography of yourself; a description of your audience; your assessment of the market for the book; a list of competing titles; what you can do to help market your book.

NONFICTION Subjects include Americana, anthropology, contemporary culture, history, literature, nature, parenting, politics, recreation, regional, science, travel, true crime, young adult. Looking for nonfiction-based graphic novels and comics, U.S. history and culture, Native American history or culture studies, conservation-oriented materials. "We do not accept memoir or fiction manuscripts." "Your submission must include: a proposal of your work, including a brief synopsis, 2-3 sample chapters, brief biography of yourself, description of your audience, your assessment of the market for the book, list of competing titles, and what you can do to help market your book. We are a green company and therefore only accept e-mailed submissions. Paper queries submitted via US Mail or any other means (including fax, FedEx/UPS, and even door-to-door delivery) will not be reviewed or returned. Please help us support the preservation of the environment by e-mailing your query to acquisitions@fulcrumbooks.com."

TIPS "Research our line first. We look for books that appeal to the school market and trade."

FUTURE HORIZONS

721 W. Abram St., Arlington TX 76013. (817)277-0727. **Fax:** (817)277-2270. **Website:** www.fhautism.

com. **Contact:** Jennifer Gilpin-Yacio, editorial director. Publishes hardcover originals, trade paperback originals and reprints. **Publishes 10 titles/year. 250 queries received/year. 125 mss received/year. 75% of books from first-time authors. 95% from unagented writers. Pays 10% royalty. Makes outright purchase.** Publishes book 2 months after acceptance of ms. Accepts simultaneous submissions. Responds in 1 month to queries; 2 months to proposals. Book catalog available free. Guidelines online.

NONFICTION Subjects include education, autism. Submit proposal package, outline by mail (no e-mail). Reviews artwork/photos. Send photocopies.

RECENT TITLE(S) *Unwritten Rules of Social Relationships*, by Dr. Temple Grandin and Sean Barron; *Ten Things Every Child With Autism Wishes You Knew*, by Ellen Notbohm.

TIPS "Audience is parents, teachers."

GENEALOGICAL PUBLISHING CO., INC

Genealogical.com, 3600 Clipper Mill Rd., Suite 229, Baltimore MD 21211. (410)837-8271. **Fax:** (410)752-8492. **E-mail:** iwebsite@genealogical.com. **E-mail:** jgaronzi@genealogical.com. **Website:** www.genealogical.com. **Contact:** Joe Garonzik, marketing director. Production Manager: Eileen Perkins. Estab. 1959. Publishes hardcover and trade paperback originals and reprints. Genealogical Publishing Company, and its affiliate Clearfield Company, are the leading publishers of how-to books, reference books, and source materials in the fields of genealogy and family history. **Publishes 50 titles/year. Receives 100 queries/year; 20 mss/year. 10% of books from first-time authors. 99% from unagented writers. Pays 10% royalty on selling price. Does not pay advance.** Publishes book 6 months after acceptance. Accepts simultaneous submissions. Responds in 1 month. Catalog free on request.

IMPRINTS Clearfield Company.

NONFICTION Subjects include Americana, ethnic, history, hobbies. Submit outline, 1 sample chapter. Reviews artwork/photos as part of the mss package.

RECENT TITLE(S) *International Vital Records Handbook (6th Ed.)*, by Thomas J. Kemp (directory); *Sustainable Genealogy: Separating Fact From Fiction in Family Legends*, by Richard Hite (how-to).

TIPS "Our audience is genealogy hobbyists."

GIBBS SMITH

P.O. Box 667, Layton UT 84041. (801)544-9800. **Fax:** (801)544-8853. **E-mail:** debbie.uribe@gibbs-smith.com. **Website:** www.gibbs-smith.com. Estab. 1969. **Publishes 3 titles/year. 50% of books from first-time authors. 50% from unagented writers. Pays authors royalty of 2% based on retail price or work purchased outright ($500 minimum). Offers advances (average amount: $2,000).** Publishes ms 1-2 years after acceptance. Accepts simultaneous submissions. Responds in 2 months. Book catalog available for 9×12 SAE and $2.30 postage. Ms guidelines available by e-mail.

NONFICTION Middle readers: activity, arts/crafts, cooking, how-to, nature/environment, science. Average word length: picture books—under 1,000 words; activity books—under 15,000 words. Submit an outline and writing samples for activity books; query for other types of books.

TIPS "We target ages 5-11. We do not publish young adult novels or chapter books."

GLENBRIDGE PUBLISHING, LTD.

19923 E. Long Ave., Centennial CO 80016. (800)986-4135. **Fax:** (720)230-1209. **E-mail:** glenbridge10@gmail.com. **Website:** www.glenbridgepublishing.com. Estab. 1986. Publishes hardcover originals and reprints, trade paperback originals. "Glenbridge has an eclectic approach to publishing. We look for titles that have long-term capabilities." **Publishes 6-8 titles/year. Pays 10% royalty.** Publishes ms 1 year after acceptance. Accepts simultaneous submissions. Responds in 2 months to queries. Book catalog online. Guidelines for #10 SASE.

NONFICTION Subjects include Americana, history, philosophy, sociology. Send e-mail on website. Query with outline/synopsis, sample chapters.

THE GLENCANNON PRESS

P.O. Box 1428, El Cerrito CA 94530. (510)455-9027. **E-mail:** merships@yahoo.com. **Website:** www.glencannon.com. **Contact:** Bill Harris (maritime, maritime children's). Estab. 1993. Publishes hardcover and paperback originals and hardcover reprints. "We publish quality books about ships and the sea." Average print order: 300. Member PMA, BAIPA. Promotes titles through direct mail, magazine advertising and word of mouth. Accepts unsolicited mss. Often comments on rejected mss. **Publishes 3-4 titles/year. 20 25% of books from first-time authors. 100% from unagented writers. Pays 10-20% royalty. Does not**

pay advance. Publishes ms 6-24 months after acceptance. Accepts simultaneous submissions. Responds in 1 month to queries; 2 months to mss. Available on request. Submit complete paper ms with SASE. "We do not look at electronic submissions due to the danger of computer viruses.".

IMPRINTS Smyth: perfect binding; illustrations.

NONFICTION Subjects include history, marine subjects, transportation, travel, war. "We specialize on books about ships and the sea, with an emphasis on the U.S. merchant marine and navy."

FICTION Subjects include adventure, historical, mainstream, military, multicultural, mystery, war, western. Submit complete ms. Include brief bio, list of publishing credits. Send SASE for return of ms or send a disposable ms and SASE for reply only.

RECENT TITLE(S) *Bay Pilot: A History of the Association of Maryland Pilots*, by Captain Brian Hope; *Blue Water Beat: The Two Lives of the Battleship USS California*, by George F. Gruner.

TIPS "Write a good story in a compelling style."

Ⓐ⊘ DAVID R. GODINE, PUBLISHER

15 Court Square, Suite 320, Boston MA 02108. (617)451-9600. **Fax:** (617)350-0250. **E-mail:** info@godine.com. **Website:** www.godine.com. Estab. 1970. "We publish books that matter for people who care." This publisher is no longer considering unsolicited mss of any type. Only interested in agented material. Accepts simultaneous submissions.

IMPRINTS Black Sparrow Books, Verba Mundi, Nonpareil.

NONFICTION Subjects include Americana, art, creative nonfiction, gardening, history, language, law, literary criticism, literature, photography, young adult, typography.

FICTION Subjects include literary, multicultural, poetry, poetry in translation, translation, young adult.

RECENT TITLE(S) *A Million Windows*, US edition by Gerald Murnane, *The Knack of Doing* by Jeremy Davies, *Farnsworth's Classical English Metaphor* by Ward Farnsworth, *The House Tells the Story* by Adam Van Doren with foreward by David McCullough, *Suspended Worlds* by Christine Hadsel.

Ⓐ⊘ GOLDEN BOOKS FOR YOUNG READERS GROUP

An Imprint of Penguin Random House LLC. 1745 Broadway, New York NY 10019. **Website:** www.penguinrandomhouse.com. Estab. 1935. "Random House Books aims to create books that nurture the hearts and minds of children, providing and promoting quality books and a rich variety of media that entertain and educate readers from 6 months to 12 years." *Random House-Golden Books does not accept unsolicited mss, only agented material.* They reserve the right not to return unsolicited material. **2% of books from first-time authors. Pays authors in royalties; sometimes buys mss outright.** Accepts simultaneous submissions. Book catalog free on request.

GOLD WAKE PRESS

E-mail: gwakepress@gmail.com. **Website:** goldwake.com. Estab. 2008. Gold Wake Press is an independent literary house founded in the suburbs of Boston by Jared Michael Wahlgren, who ran the press until 2014. Accepts simultaneous submissions. Guidelines online.

POETRY Check website for open submission periods.

RECENT TITLE(S) *In the Kettle, the Shriek*, by Hannah Stephenson; *Aerialist*, by Mary Buchinger.

TIPS "The press seeks to bring voices to the spotlight who combine daring content with meticulous attention to form."

⊘ GOOSEBOTTOM BOOKS

POB 150764, San Rafael CA 94915. **E-mail:** submissions@goosebottombooks.com. **Website:** goosebottombooks.com. **Contact:** Pamela Livingston. Estab. 2010. Middle grade nonfiction and fiction. Goosebottom Books is a small press dedicated to "fun non-fiction"representing the histories of underrepresented voices. Founded by Shirin Yim Bridges, author of *Ruby's Wish*. *The Thinking Girl's Treasury of Dastardly Dames* was named by *Booklist* as one of the Top 10 Nonfiction Series for Youth. *Horrible Hauntings* made the IRA Children's Choices list with a mention that it "motivated even the most reluctant reader." And *Call Me Ixchel, Goddess of the Moon* was named one of the Top 10 Middle Grade Novels 2013 by Foreword Reviews. The Last Celt, by A.E. Conran, has been awarded First Place for Middle Grade Fiction and Charity/Making a Difference Categories in the Purple Dragonfly Awards 2018; Finalist in three categories, Children's Fiction, First Novel and War/Military (Fiction and Non-Fiction) of the Independent Author Network Book of the Year Awards, 2018; 2016 Gold Medal Winner for Children's Chapter Books from The Military Writers Society of America; and listed as a Top 100 Notable Book: Shelf Unbound

Magazine Best in Independent Publishing Competition, 2018. **Publishes less than 6 titles/year. 1,000 submissions received/year. 50% of books from first-time authors. 75% from unagented writers. Goosebottom Books: Pays work-for-hire only at this time; Gosling Press: Pays royalties only.** Publishes ms 18-36 months after acceptance. Accepts simultaneous submissions. We are not currently accepting submissions. Catalog online. Goosebottom Books is not accepting submissions at this time. Goosebottom Books never accepts hard copy submissions. "We like trees.".

IMPRINTS Goosebottom Books, Gosling Press.

NONFICTION Subjects include creative nonfiction, education, gay, history, multicultural, social sciences, womens studies, young adult.

FICTION Subjects include adventure, ethnic, fantasy, feminist, gay, gothic, historical, horror, humor, juvenile, literary, mainstream, multicultural, mystery, picture books, suspense, young adult, A historical presentation of an under-represented population must be integrated within the story line. Gosling Press is a new partnership publishing imprint for children's middle grade fiction. Any fiction for adults.

RECENT TITLE(S) *Horrible Hauntings*, by Shirin Yim Bridges, illustrated by William Maughan; The Thinking Girl's Treasury to Dastardly Dames series.

GRAYWOLF PRESS

250 Third Ave. N., Suite 600, Minneapolis MN 55401. (651)641-0077. **Fax:** (651)641-0036. **Website:** www.graywolfpress.org. Estab. 1974. Publishes trade cloth and paperback originals. "Graywolf Press is an independent, nonprofit publisher dedicated to the creation and promotion of thoughtful and imaginative contemporary literature essential to a vital and diverse culture." **Publishes 30 titles/year. Pays royalty on retail price. Pays $1,000-25,000 advance.** Publishes 18 months after acceptance. Accepts simultaneous submissions. Responds in 3 months to queries. Book catalog free. Guidelines online.

NONFICTION Subjects include contemporary culture, culture. Agented submissions only.

FICTION Subjects include short story collections, literary novels. "Familiarize yourself with our list first." No genre books (romance, western, science fiction, suspense) Agented submissions only.

POETRY "We are interested in linguistically challenging work." Agented submissions only.

RECENT TITLE(S) *Duplex* by Kathryn Davis, *On Sal Mal Lane* by Ru Freeman, *Song of the Shank* by Jeffery Renard Allen, *I Curse the River of Time* by Per Petterson.

GREENHAVEN PRESS

27500 Drake Rd., Farmington Hills MI 48331. (800)877-4523. **Website:** www.gale.com/greenhaven. Estab. 1970. Publishes 220 young adult academic reference titles/year. 50% of books by first-time authors. Greenhaven continues to print quality nonfiction anthologies for libraries and classrooms. "Our well-known Opposing Viewpoints series is highly respected by students and librarians in need of material on controversial social issues." Greenhaven accepts no unsolicited mss. Send query, resume, and list of published works by e-mail. Work purchased outright from authors; write-for-hire, flat fee. Accepts simultaneous submissions.

NONFICTION Young adults (high school): controversial issues, social issues, history, literature, science, environment, health.

GREENWILLOW BOOKS

HarperCollins Publishers, 10 E. 53rd St., New York NY 10022. (212)207-7000. **Website:** www.greenwillowblog.com. Estab. 1974. Publishes hardcover originals, paperbacks, e-books, and reprints. *Does not accept unsolicited mss.* "Unsolicited mail will not be opened and will not be returned." **Publishes 40-50 titles/year. Pays 10% royalty on wholesale price for first-time authors. Offers variable advance.** Publishes ms 2 years after acceptance. Accepts simultaneous submissions.

FICTION Subjects include fantasy, humor, literary, mystery, picture books. *Agented submissions only.*

GREY GECKO PRESS

38 S. Blue Angel Parkway, Suite 312, Pensacola FL 32506. **E-mail:** info@greygeckopress.com. **E-mail:** submissions@greygeckopress.com. **Website:** www.greygeckopress.com. **Contact:** Submissions Coordinator. Estab. 2011. Publishes hardcover, trade paperback, audiobook, and electronic originals. Not open for submissions; check website for updates. Grey Gecko focuses on new and emerging authors and great books that might not otherwise get a chance to see the light of day. "We publish all our titles in hardcover, trade paperback, and e-book formats, as well as audiobook and foreign-language editions. Our books

are available worldwide, for readers of all types, kinds, and interests." **Publishes 5 titles/year. 200+ queries; 30-40 mss received/year. 79% of books from first-time authors. 100% from unagented writers. Pays 50-75% royalties on net revenue. Does not pay advance.** Publishes ms 18-24 months after acceptance. Accepts simultaneous submissions. Responds in 6-12 months. Catalog online. Guidelines online.

NONFICTION Subjects include architecture, art, contemporary culture, cooking, creative nonfiction, environment, foods, history, marine subjects, military, nature, photography, travel, war. Not accepting submissions.

FICTION Subjects include adventure, contemporary, ethnic, experimental, fantasy, feminist, gay, historical, horror, humor, juvenile, lesbian, literary, mainstream, military, multicultural, mystery, occult, regional, romance, science fiction, short story collections, sports, suspense, war, western, young adult. Not accepting submissions. "We do not publish extreme horror, erotica, or religious fiction. New and interesting stories by unpublished authors will always get our attention. Innovation is a core value of our company." Does not want extreme horror (e.g. *Saw* or *Hostel*), religious, or erotica. Not currently accepting submissions. When open, use online submission page.

RECENT TITLE(S) *The Omega Chronicles #1: Invasion at Miratev, The John Morano Eco-adventure Series #3: Out There, Somewhere, Death by Harmony, Addleton Heights,Tai Chi: Moving at the Speed of Truth.*

TIPS "Be willing to be a part of the Grey Gecko family. Publishing with us is a partnership, not indentured servitude. Authors are expected and encouraged to be proactive and contribute to their book's success."

GROSSET & DUNLAP PUBLISHERS

Penguin Random House, 1745 Broadway, New York NY 10019. **Website:** www.penguinrandomhouse.com. Estab. 1898. Publishes hardcover (few) and mass market paperback originals. Grosset & Dunlap publishes children's books that show children that reading is fun, with books that speak to their interests, and that are affordable so that children can build a home library of their own. Focus on licensed properties, series and readers. "Grosset & Dunlap publishes high-interest, affordable books for children ages 0-10 years. We focus on original series, licensed properties, readers and novelty books." **Publishes 140 titles/year. Pays royalty. Pays advance.**

NONFICTION Subjects include science. *Agented submissions only.*

FICTION Subjects include juvenile. *Agented submissions only.*

GROUP PUBLISHING, INC.

1515 Cascade Ave., Loveland CO 80539. **E-mail:** info@group.com. **Website:** www.group.com. Estab. 1974. Publishes trade paperback originals. "Our mission is to equip churches to help children, youth, and adults grow in their relationship with Jesus." **Publishes 65 titles/year. 500 queries; 500 mss received/year. 40% of books from first-time authors. 95% from unagented writers. Pays up to 10% royalty on wholesale price or makes outright purchase or work for hire. Pays up to $1,000 advance.** Publishes ms 18 months after acceptance. Accepts simultaneous submissions. Responds in 1 month to queries; 6 months to proposals and mss. Book catalog for 9x12 envelope and 2 first-class stamps.

NONFICTION Subjects include education, religion. "We're an interdenominational publisher of resource materials for people who work with adults, youth or children in a Christian church setting. We also publish materials for use directly by youth or children (such as devotional books, workbooks or Bibles stories). Everything we do is based on concepts of active and interactive learning as described in *Why Nobody Learns Much of Anything at Church: And How to Fix It*, by Thom and Joani Schultz. We need new, practical, hands-on, innovative, out-of-the-box ideas—things that no one's doing, yet." Query with SASE. Submit proposal package, outline, 3 sample chapters, cover letter, introduction to book, and sample activities if appropriate.

RECENT TITLE(S) *Outflow*, by Steve Sjogren and Dave Ping; *Dare to Be Uncommon*, by Tony Dungy and Karl Leuthauser; *Hope Lives*, by Amber Van Schooneveld.

TIPS "Our audience consists of pastors, Christian education directors, youth leaders, and Sunday school teachers."

GROVE/ATLANTIC, INC.

154 W. 14th St., 12th Floor, New York NY 10011. **E-mail:** info@groveatlantic.com. **Website:** www.groveatlantic.com. Estab. 1917. Publishes hardcover and trade paperback originals, and reprints. "Due to limited resources of time and staffing, Grove/Atlantic cannot accept manuscripts that do not come through

a literary agent. In today's publishing world, agents are more important than ever, helping writers shape their work and navigate the main publishing houses to find the most appropriate outlet for a project." **Publishes 100 titles/year. 1,000+ queries; 1,000+ mss received/year. 10% of books from first-time authors. Pays 7 ½-12 ½% royalty. Makes outright purchase of $5-500,000.** Book published 9 months after acceptance of ms. Accepts simultaneous submissions. Responds in 1 month to queries; 2 months to proposals; 4 months to mss. Book catalog available online.

IMPRINTS Black Cat, Atlantic Monthly Press, Grove Press.

NONFICTION Subjects include creative nonfiction, education, memoirs, philosophy, psychology, science, social sciences, sports, translation. Agented submissions only.

FICTION Subjects include erotica, horror, literary, science fiction, short story collections, suspense, western. Agented submissions only.

POETRY Agented submissions only.

GRYPHON HOUSE, INC.

P.O. Box 10, 6848 Leon's Way, Lewisville NC 27023. (800)638-0928. **E-mail:** info@ghbooks.com. **Website:** www.gryphonhouse.com. Estab. 1981. Publishes trade paperback originals. "At Gryphon House, our goal is to publish books that help teachers and parents enrich the lives of children from birth through age 8. We strive to make our books useful for teachers at all levels of experience, as well as for parents, caregivers, and anyone interested in working with children." Query. Submit outline/synopsis and 2 sample chapters. Responds to queries/mss in 6 months. Publishes a book 18 months after acceptance. Will consider simultaneous submissions, e-mail submissions. Book catalog and ms guidelines available via website or with SASE. **Publishes 12-15 titles/year. Pays royalty on wholesale price.** Responds in 3-6 months to queries. Guidelines available online.

NONFICTION Subjects include child guidance, education. Currently emphasizing social-emotional intelligence and classroom management; de-emphasizing literacy after-school activities. "We prefer to receive a letter of inquiry and/or a proposal, rather than the entire manuscript. Please include: the proposed title, the purpose of the book, table of contents, introductory material, 20-40 sample pages of the actual book. In addition, please describe the book, including the intended audience, why teachers will want to buy it, how it is different from other similar books already published, and what qualifications you possess that make you the appropriate person to write the book. If you have a writing sample that demonstrates that you write clear, compelling prose, please include it with your letter."

RECENT TITLE(S) *Baby Smarts*, by Jackie Silberg; *Art With Anything*, by Maryann Kohl; *Primary Art*, by Mary Ann Kohl; *Seven Skills for School Success*, by Pam Schillder; *Preschool Math*, by Robert Williams, Debra Cunningham and Joy Lubawy.

TIPS "We are looking for books of creative, participatory learning experiences that have a common conceptual theme to tie them together. The books should be on subjects that parents or teachers want to do on a daily basis."

GUERNICA EDITIONS

1569 Heritage Way, Oakville ON L6M 2Z7, Canada. (905)599-5304. **E-mail:** michaelmirolla@guernicaeditions.com. **Website:** www.guernicaeditions.com. **Contact:** Michael Mirolla, editor/publisher (poetry, nonfiction, short stories, novels). Associate Publisher/Publicist: Anna Geisler (annageisler@guernicaeditions.com). Estab. 1978. Publishes trade paperback originals and reprints. Guernica Editions is a literary press that produces works of poetry, fiction and nonfiction often by writers who are ignored by the mainstream. "We feature an imprint (MiroLand) which accepts memoirs, how-to books, graphic novels, genre fiction with the possibility of children's and cook books." A new imprint, Guernica World Editions, features writers who are non-Canadian. **Publishes 25-30 titles/year. Several hundred mss received/year. 20% of books from first-time authors. 99% from unagented writers. Pays 10% royalty on either cover or retail price. Pays $450-750 advance.** Publishes 24-36 months after acceptance. Accepts simultaneous submissions. Responds in 1 month to queries; 6 months to proposals; 1 year to mss. Book catalog online. Queries and submissions accepted via e-mail January 1-April 30.

IMPRINTS MiroLand, Guernica World Editions.

NONFICTION Subjects include contemporary culture, creative nonfiction, ethnic, gay, history, lesbian, literary criticism, literature, memoirs, multicultural, philosophy, politics, pop culture, psychology, regional, social sciences, translation, womens issues, womens studies. Query by e-mail only. Reviews artwork/photos. Send photocopies.

FICTION Subjects include comic books, contemporary, ethnic, experimental, feminist, gay, historical, lesbian, literary, multicultural, mystery, plays, poetry, poetry in translation, science fiction, short story collections, translation. "We wish to open up into the literary fiction world and focus less on poetry." Does not want fantasy, YA. E-mail queries only.

POETRY Feminist, gay/lesbian, literary, multicultural, poetry in translation. Full books only. Query.

RECENT TITLE(S) *Notes of a Mediocre Man*, by Bipin Aurora; *Cadillac Road*, by Kristin Andrychuk; *Through the Sad Wood Our Corpses Will Hang*, by Ava Farmehri; *Faithful & Other Stories*, by Daniel Karasik.

GULF PUBLISHING COMPANY

P.O. Box 2608, Houston TX 77252. (713)529-4301. **Fax:** (713)520-4433. **Website:** www.gulfpub.com. Estab. 1916. Publishes hardcover originals and reprints; electronic originals and reprints. "Gulf Publishing Company is the leading publisher to the oil and gas industry. Our specialized publications reach over 100,000 people involved in energy industries worldwide. Our magazines and catalogs help readers keep current with information important to their field and allow advertisers to reach their customers in all segments of petroleum operations. More than half our editorial staff have engineering degrees. The others are thoroughly trained and experienced business journalists and editors." **Publishes 12-15 titles/year. 3-5 queries and mss received in a year. 30% of books from first-time authors. 80% from unagented writers. Royalties on retail price. Pays $1,000-$1,500 advance.** Publishes ms 8-9 months after acceptance. Accepts simultaneous submissions. Responds in 2 months to queries; 1 month to proposals and mss. Catalog free on request. Guidelines available by e-mail.

NONFICTION Subjects includeEngineering. "We don't publish a lot in the year, therefore we are able to focus more on marketing and sales—we are hoping to grow in the future." Submit outline, 1-2 sample chapters, completed ms. Reviews artwork. Send high res file formats with high dpi in b&w.

RECENT TITLE(S) *Gulf Drilling Series: Managed Pressure Drilling*, by Bill Rehm, Jerome Schubert, Arash Haghshenas, Amir Paknejad, Jim Hughes; *Well Productivity*, by Boyun Guo, Kai Sun, Ali Ghalambor; *Advanced Piping Design*, Rutger Botermans, Peter Smith.

TIPS "Our audience would be engineers, engineering students, academia, professors, well managers, construction engineers. We recommend getting contributors to help with the writing process—this provides a more comprehensive overview for technical and scientific books. Work harder on artwork. It's expensive and time-consuming for a publisher to redraw a lot of the figures."

Ⓐ GUN DIGEST BOOKS

P.O.Box 7772, Appleton WI 54913 **E-mail:** info@gundigest.com. **Website:** www.gundigest.com. Estab. 1944. Hardcover, trade paperback, mass market paperback, and electronic originals (all). **Publishes 25 titles/year. 75 submissions received/year. 30% of books from first-time authors. 80% from unagented writers. 10-20% royalty on wholesale price. Pays advance between $2,800-5,000.** Publishes book 7 months after acceptance. Accepts simultaneous submissions. Responds immediately to queries; 2 months to proposals/ms. Catalog online. Guidelines available.

IMPRINTS Gun Digest Books, Krause Publications.

NONFICTION Subjects includeFirearms, hunting-related titles only. "Must have mainstream appeal and not be too narrowly focused." Submit proposal package, including outline, 2 sample chapters, and author bio; submit completed ms. Review artwork/photos (required); high-res digital only (.jpg, .tif).

TIPS "Our audience is shooters, collectors, hunters, outdoors enthusiasts. We prefer not to work through agents."

HACHAI PUBLISHING

527 Empire Blvd., Brooklyn NY 11225. (718)633-0100. **Fax:** (718)633-0103. **E-mail:** info@hachai.com; dlr@hachai.com. **Website:** www.hachai.com. **Contact:** Devorah Leah Rosenfeld, editor. Estab. 1988. Publishes hardcover originals. Hachai is dedicated to producing high quality Jewish children's literature, ages 2-10. Story should promote universal values such as sharing, kindness, etc. **Publishes 5 titles/year. 75% of books from first-time authors. Work purchased outright from authors for $800-1,000.** Accepts simultaneous submissions. Responds in 2 months to mss. Guidelines online.

"All books have spiritual/religious themes, specifically traditional Jewish content. We're seeking books about morals and values; the Jewish experience in current and Biblical times; and Jewish observance, Sabbath and holidays."

NONFICTION Subjects include ethnic, religion. Submit complete ms. Reviews artwork/photos. Send photocopies.

FICTION Subjects include juvenile. Picture books and young readers: contemporary, historical fiction, religion. Middle readers: adventure, contemporary, problem novels, religion. Does not want to see fantasy, animal stories, romance, problem novels depicting drug use or violence. Submit complete ms.

RECENT TITLE(S) *The Creation Book*, by Chani Gansburg; *We Can Find a Way*, by Dina Rosenfeld; *My Sometimes Feelings*, by Leah Rubabshi.

TIPS "We are looking for books that convey the traditional Jewish experience in modern times or long ago; traditional Jewish observance such as Sabbath and holidays and mitzvos such as mezuzah, blessings etc.; positive character traits (middos) such as honesty, charity, respect, sharing, etc. We are also interested in historical fiction for young readers (7-10) written with a traditional Jewish perspective and highlighting the relevance of Torah in making important choices. Please, no animal stories, romance, violence, preachy sermonizing. Write a story that incorporates a moral, not a preachy morality tale. Originality is the key. We feel Hachai publications will appeal to a wider readership as parents become more interested in positive values for their children."

HADLEY RILLE BOOKS

P.O. Box 25466, Overland Park KS 66225. **E-mail:** contact@hadleyrillebooks.com. **E-mail:** subs@hadleyrillebooks.com. **Website:** https://hadleyrillebks.wordpress.com. **Contact:** Eric T. Reynolds, editor/publisher. Estab. 2005. Currently closed to submissions. Check website for future reading periods. Accepts simultaneous submissions.

FICTION Subjects include fantasy, science fiction, short story collections.

TIPS "We aim to produce books that are aligned with current interest in the genres. Anthology markets are somewhat rare in SF these days, we feel there aren't enough good anthologies being published each year and part of our goal is to present the best that we can. We like stories that fit well within the guidelines of the particular anthology for which we are soliciting manuscripts. Aside from that, we want stories with strong characters (not necessarily characters with strong personalities, flawed characters are welcome). We want a sense of wonder and awe. We want to feel the world around the character and so scene description is important (however, this doesn't always require a lot of text, just set the scene well so we don't wonder where the character is). We strongly recommend workshopping the story or having it critiqued in some way by readers familiar with the genre. We prefer clichés be kept to a bare minimum in the prose and avoid re-working old story lines."

HAMPTON ROADS PUBLISHING CO., INC.

65 Parker St, Suite 7, Newburyport MA 01950. **E-mail:** submissions@rwwbooks.com. **Website:** www.redwheelweiser.com. Estab. 1989. Publishes and distributes hardcover and trade paperback originals on subjects including metaphysics, health, complementary medicine, and other related topics. "Our reason for being is to impact, uplift, and contribute to positive change in the world. We publish books that will enrich and empower the evolving consciousness of mankind. Though we are not necessarily limited in scope, we are most interested in manuscripts on the following subjects: Body/Mind/Spirit, Health and Healing, Self-Help. Please be advised that at the moment we are not accepting fiction or novelized material that does not pertain to body/mind/spirit, channeled writing." **Publishes 35-40 titles/year. 1,000 queries; 1,500 mss received/year. 50% of books from first-time authors. 70% from unagented writers. Pays royalty. Pays $1,000-50,000 advance.** Publishes ms 1 year after acceptance. Accepts simultaneous submissions. Responds in 2-4 months to queries; 1 month to proposals; 6-12 months to mss. Guidelines online.

NONFICTION Subjects include New Age, spirituality. Submit by e-mail.

HANCOCK HOUSE PUBLISHERS

Unit 104, 4550 Birch Bay-Lynden Rd., Blaine WA 98230. (800)938-1114. **Fax:** (604)538-2262. **E-mail:** submissions@hancockhouse.com. **Website:** www.hancockhouse.com. Estab. 1971. Publishes hardcover, trade paperback, and e-book originals and reprints. "Hancock House Publishers is the largest North American publisher of wildlife and Native Indian titles. We also cover Pacific Northwest, fishing, history, Canadiana, biographies. We are seeking agriculture, natural history, and popular science titles with a regional (Pacific Northwest), national, or international focus.

Currently emphasizing nonfiction wildlife, cryptozoology, guide books, native history, biography, fishing." **Publishes 12-20 titles/year. 50% of books from first-time authors. 90% from unagented writers. Pays 10% royalty.** Publishes book 1 year after acceptance. Accepts simultaneous submissions. Responds to proposals in 3-6 months. Book catalog available free. Guidelines online.

NONFICTION Subjects include agriculture, animals, ethnic, history, horticulture, regional. Centered around Pacific Northwest, local history, nature guide books, international ornithology, and Native Americans. Query via e-mail, including outline with word count, a short author bio, table of contents, 3 sample chapters. Accepts double-spaced word .docs or PDFs. Reviews artwork/photos. Send photocopies.

RECENT TITLE(S) *The Man Who Filmed Nessie; Wrong Highway; Asian Wild Man.*

HANSER PUBLICATIONS

6915 Valley Ave., Cincinnati OH 45244. (800)950-8977. **Fax:** (513)527-8801. **E-mail:** info@hanserpublications.com. **Website:** www.hanserpublications.com. **Contact:** Development Editor. Estab. 1993. Publishes hardcover and paperback originals, and digital educational and training programs. "Hanser Publications publishes books and electronic media for the manufacturing (both metalworking and plastics) industries. Publications range from basic training materials to advanced reference books." **Publishes 10-15 titles/year. 100 queries received/year. 10-20 mss received/year. 50% of books from first-time authors. 100% from unagented writers.** Publishes ms 10 months after acceptance. Accepts simultaneous submissions. Responds in 2 weeks to queries; 1 month to proposals/mss. Book catalog available free. Guidelines available online.

"Hanser Publications is currently seeking technical experts with strong writing skills to author training and reference books and related products focused on various aspects of the manufacturing industry. Our goal is to provide manufacturing professionals with insightful, easy-to-reference information, and to educate and prepare students for technical careers through accessible, concise training manuals. Do your publishing ideas match this goal? If so, we'd like to hear from you. Submit your detailed product proposals, resume of credentials, and a brief writing sample to: Development Editor, Prospective Authors."

NONFICTION "We publish how-to texts, references, technical books, and computer-based learning materials for the manufacturing industries. Titles include award-winning management books, encyclopedic references, and leading references." Submit outline, sample chapters, resume, preface, and comparison to competing or similar titles.

RECENT TITLE(S) *Engineered Rubber Products*, by J.G. Sommer; *Mixing and Compounding*, 2nd edition, by Kamel.

TIPS "E-mail submissions speed up response time."

HARLEQUIN BLAZE

225 Duncan Mill Rd., Don Mills ON M3B 3K9, Canada. (416)445-5860. **Website:** www.harlequin.com. **Contact:** Kathleen Scheibling, senior editor. Publishes paperback originals. "Harlequin Blaze is a red-hot series. It is a vehicle to build and promote new authors who have a strong sexual edge to their stories. It is also the place to be for seasoned authors who want to create a sexy, sizzling, longer contemporary story." Accepts simultaneous submissions. Guidelines online.

FICTION Subjects include romance. "Sensuous, highly romantic, innovative plots that are sexy in premise and execution. The tone of the books can run from fun and flirtatious to dark and sensual. Submissions should have a very contemporary feel—what it's like to be young and single today. We are looking for heroes and heroines in their early 20s and up. There should be a a strong emphasis on the physical relationship between the couples. Fully described love scenes along with a high level of fantasy and playfulness." Length: 55,000-60,000 words.

TIPS "Are you a *Cosmo* girl at heart? A fan of *Sex and the City*? Or maybe you have a sexually adventurous spirit. If so, then Blaze is the series for you!"

HARLEQUIN DESIRE

233 Broadway, Suite 1001, New York NY 10279. (212)553-4200. **Website:** www.harlequin.com. **Contact:** Stacy Boyd, senior editor. Publishes paperback originals and reprints. Always powerful, passionate, and provocative. "Desire novels are sensual reads and a love scene or scenes are still needed. But there is no set number of pages that needs to be fulfilled. Rather, the level of sensuality must be appropriate to the storyline. Above all, every Silhouette Desire novel must fulfill the promise of a powerful, passionate

and provocative read." **Pays royalty. Offers advance.** Accepts simultaneous submissions. Guidelines online.

FICTION Subjects include romance. Looking for novels in which "the conflict is an emotional one, springing naturally from the unique characters you've chosen. The focus is on the developing relationship, set in a believable plot. Sensuality is key, but lovemaking is never taken lightly. Secondary characters and subplots need to blend with the core story. Innovative new directions in storytelling and fresh approaches to classic romantic plots are welcome." Manuscripts must be 50,000-55,000 words.

HARLEQUIN INTRIGUE

225 Duncan Mill Rd., Don Mills ON M3B 3K9, Canada. **Website:** www.harlequin.com. **Contact:** Denise Zaza, senior editor. Wants crime stories tailored to the series romance market packed with a variety of thrilling suspense and whodunit mystery. Word count: 55,000-60,000. Accepts simultaneous submissions. Guidelines online.

FICTION Subjects include mystery, romance, suspense. Submit online.

HARLEQUIN SUPERROMANCE

225 Duncan Mill Rd., Don Mills ON M3B 3K9, Canada. **Website:** www.harlequin.com. **Contact:** Victoria Curran, senior editor. Publishes paperback originals. "The Harlequin Superromance line focuses on believable characters triumphing over true-to-life drama and conflict. At the heart of these contemporary stories should be a compelling romance that brings the reader along with the hero and heroine on their journey of overcoming the obstacles in their way and falling in love. Because of the longer length relevant subplots and secondary characters are welcome but not required. This series publishes a variety of story types—family sagas, romantic suspense, Westerns, to name a few—and tones from light to dramatic, emotional to suspenseful. Settings also vary from vibrant urban neighborhoods to charming small towns. The unifying element of Harlequin Superromance stories is the realistic treatment of character and plot. The characters should seem familiar to readers—similar to people they know in their own lives—and the circumstances within the realm of possibility. The stories should be layered and complex in that the conflicts should not be easily resolved. The best way to get an idea of we're looking for is to read what we're currently publishing. The aim of Superromance novels is to produce a contemporary, involving read with a mainstream tone in its situations and characters, using romance as the major theme. To achieve this, emphasis should be placed on individual writing styles and unique and topical ideas." **Pays royalties. Pays advance.** Accepts simultaneous submissions. Guidelines online.

FICTION Subjects include romance. "The criteria for Superromance books are flexible. Aside from length (80,000 words), the determining factor for publication will always be quality. Authors should strive to break free of stereotypes, clichés and worn-out plot devices to create strong, believable stories with depth and emotional intensity. Superromance novels are intended to appeal to a wide range of romance readers." Submit online.

TIPS "A general familiarity with current Superromance books is advisable to keep abreast of ever-changing trends and overall scope, but we don't want imitations. We look for sincere, heartfelt writing based on true-to-life experiences the reader can identify with. We are interested in innovation."

HARMONY INK PRESS

Dreamspinner Press, 5032 Capital Circle SW, Suite 2 PMB 279, Tallahassee FL 32305. (850)632-4648. **Fax:** (888)308-3739. **E-mail:** submissions@harmonyinkpress.com. **Website:** harmonyinkpress.com. **Contact:** Anne Regan. Estab. 2010. Teen and new adult fiction featuring at least 1 strong LGBTQ+ main character who shows significant personal growth through the course of the story. **Publishes 26 titles/year. Pays royalty. Pays $500-1,000 advance.** Accepts simultaneous submissions.

FICTION "We are looking for stories in all subgenres, featuring primary characters across the whole LGBTQ+ spectrum between the ages of 14 and 21 that explore all the facets of young adult, teen, and new adult life. Sexual content should be appropriate for the characters and the story." Submit complete ms.

RECENT TITLE(S) *An Unexpected Summer*, by Kate Sands; *Always Leaving*, by Gene Grant.

HARPERBUSINESS

Imprint of HarperCollins General Books Group, 195 Broadway, New York NY 10007. (212)207-7000. **Website:** www.harpercollins.com. Estab. 1991. Publishes hardcover, trade paperback originals and reprints. HarperBusiness publishes the inside story on ideas that will shape business practices with cutting-edge information and visionary concepts. **Pays royalty on retail price. Pays advance.** Accepts simultaneous submissions.

"The gold standard of business book publishing for 50 years, Harper Business brings you innovative, authoritative, and creative works from world-class thinkers. Building upon this rich legacy of paradigm-shifting books, Harper Business authors continue to help readers see the future and to lead and live successfully."

NONFICTION Subjects includemarketing subjects. "We don't publish how-to, textbooks or things for academic market; no reference (tax or mortgage guides), our reference department does that. Proposals need to be top notch. We tend not to publish people who have no business standing. Must have business credentials." Agented submissions only.

RECENT TITLE(S) *The Flight of the Creative Class*, by Richard Florida; *Fortune Favors the Bold*, by Lester C. Thurow; *Reinventing the Wheel*, by Steve Kemper.

HARPERCOLLINS

195 Broadway, New York NY 10007. (212)207-7000. **Website:** www.harpercollins.com. Publishes hardcover and paperback originals and paperback reprints. HarperCollins, one of the largest English language publishers in the world, is a broad-based publisher with strengths in academic, business and professional, children's, educational, general interest, and religious and spiritual books, as well as multimedia titles. **Pays royalty. Pays negotiable advance.** Accepts simultaneous submissions.

NONFICTION Agented submissions only. Unsolicited mss returned unopened.

FICTION Subjects include adventure, fantasy, gothic, historical, literary, mystery, science fiction, suspense, western. "We look for a strong story line and exceptional literary talent." Agented submissions only. *All unsolicited mss returned.*

TIPS "We do not accept any unsolicited material."

HARPERCOLLINS CHILDREN'S BOOKS/ HARPERCOLLINS PUBLISHERS

195 Broadway, New York NY 10007. (212)207-7000. **Website:** www.harpercollins.com. Publishes hardcover and paperback originals and paperback reprints. HarperCollins, one of the largest English language publishers in the world, is a broad-based publisher with strengths in academic, business and professional, children's, educational, general interest, and religious and spiritual books, as well as multimedia titles. **Publishes 500 titles/year. Negotiates payment upon acceptance.** Accepts simultaneous submissions. Responds in 1 month, will contact only if interested. Does not accept any unsolicted texts. Catalog online.

IMPRINTS HarperCollins Australia/New Zealand: Angus & Robertson, Fourth Estate, HarperBusiness, HarperCollins, HarperPerenniel, HarperReligious, HarperSports, Voyager; **HarperCollins Canada**: HarperFlamingoCanada, PerennialCanada; **HarperCollins Children's Books Group:** Amistad, Julie Andrews Collection, Avon, Joanna Cotler Books, Eos, Laura Geringer Books, Greenwillow Books, HarperAudio, HarperCollins Children's Books, HarperFestival, HarperTempest, HarperTrophy, Rayo, Katherine Tegen Books; **HarperCollins General Books Group:** Access, Amistad, Avon, Caedmon, Ecco, Eos, Fourth Estate, HarperAudio, HarperBusiness, HarperCollins, HarperEntertainment, HarperLargePrint, HarperResource, HarperSanFrancisco, HarperTorch, Harper Design International, Perennial, PerfectBound, Quill, Rayo, ReganBooks, William Morrow, William Morrow Cookbooks; **HarperCollins UK:** Collins Bartholomew, Collins, HarperCollins Crime & Thrillers, Collins Freedom to Teach, HarperCollins Children's Books, Thorsons/Element, Voyager Books; **Zondervan:** Inspirio, Vida, Zonderkidz, Zondervan.

NONFICTION *No unsolicited mss or queries.* Agented submissions only. Unsolicited mss returned unopened.

FICTION Subjects include picture books, young adult, chapter books, middle grade, early readers. "We look for a strong story line and exceptional literary talent." Agented submissions only. *All unsolicited mss returned.*

TIPS "We do not accept any unsolicited material."

HARPER PERENNIAL

10 E. 53rd St., New York NY 10022. **E-mail:** harperperennial@harpercollins.com. **Website:** harperperennial.tumblr.com. Harper Perennial is one of the paperback imprints of HarperCollins. "We publish paperback originals and reprints of authors like Ann Patchett, Justin Taylor, Barbara Kingsolver, and Blake Butler. Accepts simultaneous submissions.

HARPER VOYAGER

Imprint of HarperCollins General Books Group, 195 Broadway, New York NY 10007. (212)207-7000. **Website:** www.harpercollins.com. Estab. 1998. Publishes hardcover originals, trade and mass market paperback originals, and reprints. Eos publishes quality science fiction/fantasy with broad appeal. **Pays royalty on retail price. Pays variable advance.** Accepts simultaneous submissions. Guidelines online.

FICTION Subjects include fantasy, science fiction. No horror or juvenile. Agented submissions only. *All unsolicited mss returned.*

THE HARVARD COMMON PRESS

100 Cummings Center, Suite 406-L, Beverly MA 01915. (978)282-9590. **Fax:** (978)282-7765. **E-mail:** info@harvardcommonpress.com. **E-mail:** editorial@harvardcommonpress.com. **Website:** https://www.quartoknows.com/Harvard-Common-Press. **Contact:** Submissions. Estab. 1976. Publishes hardcover and trade paperback originals and reprints. "We want strong, practical books that help people gain control over a particular area of their lives. Currently emphasizing cooking, child care/parenting, health. De-emphasizing general instructional books, travel." **Publishes 16 titles/year. 20% of books from first-time authors. 40% from unagented writers. Pays royalty. Pays average $2,500-10,000 advance.** Publishes ms 1 year after acceptance. Accepts simultaneous submissions. Responds in 2 months to queries. Guidelines online.

NONFICTION Subjects include child guidance. "A large percentage of our list is made up of books about cooking, child care, and parenting; in these areas we are looking for authors who are knowledgeable, if not experts, and who can offer a different approach to the subject. We are open to good nonfiction proposals that show evidence of strong organization and writing, and clearly demonstrate a need in the marketplace. First-time authors are welcome." Submit outline. Potential authors may also submit a query letter or e-mail of no more than 300 words, rather than a full proposal; if interested, will ask to see a proposal. Queries and questions may be sent via e-mail. "We will not consider e-mail attachments containing proposals. No phone calls, please."

TIPS "We are demanding about the quality of proposals; in addition to strong writing skills and thorough knowledge of the subject matter, we require a detailed analysis of the competition."

Ⓐ⊘ HARVEST HOUSE PUBLISHERS

990 Owen Loop, Eugene OR 97402. (541)343-0123. **Fax:** (541)302-0731. **Website:** www.harvesthousepublishers.com. Estab. 1974. Publishes hardcover, trade paperback, and mass market paperback originals and reprints. **Publishes 160 titles/year. 1,500 queries; 1,000 mss received/year. 1% of books from first-time authors. Pays royalty.** Accepts simultaneous submissions.

NONFICTION Subjects include child guidance, religion, Bible studies. *No unsolicited mss.*

FICTION *No unsolicited mss, proposals, or artwork.* Agented submissions only.

TIPS "For first time/nonpublished authors we suggest building their literary résumé by submitting to magazines, or perhaps accruing book contributions."

Ⓐ HAY HOUSE, INC.

P.O. Box 5100, Carlsbad CA 92018. (760)431-7695. **Fax:** (760)431-6948. **E-mail:** editorial@hayhouse.com. **Website:** www.hayhouse.com. Estab. 1985. Publishes hardcover, trade paperback and e-book/POD originals. "We publish books, audios, and videos that help heal the planet." **Publishes 50 titles/year. Pays standard royalty.** Accepts simultaneous submissions. Guidelines online.

IMPRINTS Hay House Lifestyles; Hay House Insights; Hay House Visions; SmileyBooks.

NONFICTION Subjects include alternative lifestyles, astrology, cooking, education, foods, health, New Age, nutrition, philosophy, psychic, psychology, sociology, spirituality, womens issues, mind/body/spirit. "Hay House is interested in a variety of subjects as long as they have a positive self-help slant to them. No poetry, children's books, or negative concepts that are not conducive to helping/healing ourselves or our planet." Accepts e-mail submissions from agents.

TIPS "Our audience is concerned with our planet, the healing properties of love, and general self-help principles. If I were a writer trying to market a book today, I would research the market thoroughly to make sure there weren't already too many books on the subject I was interested in writing about. Then I would make sure I had a unique slant on my idea. Simultaneous submissions from agents must include SASEs."

HEALTH COMMUNICATIONS, INC.

3201 SW 15th St., Deerfield Beach FL 33442. (954)360-0909, ext. 232. **Fax:** (954)360-0034. **E-mail:** editorial@hcibooks.com. **Website:** www.hcibooks.com. **Contact:** Editorial Committee. Estab. 1976. Publishes hardcover and trade paperback nonfiction only. "While HCI is a best known for recovery publishing, today recovery is only one part of a publishing program that includes titles in self-help and psychology, health and wellness, spirituality, inspiration, women's and men's issues, relationships, family, teens and children, memoirs, mind/body/spirit integration, and gift books." **Publishes 60 titles/year.** Accepts simultaneous submissions. Responds in 3-6 months. Guidelines online.

NONFICTION Subjects include child guidance, health, parenting, psychology, young adult, self-help.

TIPS "Due to the volume of submissions, Health Communications cannot guarantee response times or personalize responses to individual proposals. Under no circumstances do we accept phone calls or e-mails pitching submissions."

WILLIAM S. HEIN & CO., INC.

2350 N. Forest Rd., Getzville NY 14068. (716)882-2600. **Fax:** (716)883-8100. **E-mail:** mail@wshein.com. **Website:** www.wshein.com. Estab. 1961. "William S. Hein & Co. publishes reference books for law librarians, legal researchers, and those interested in legal writing. Currently emphasizing legal research, legal writing, and legal education." **Publishes 18 titles/year. 30 queries received/year. 15 mss received/year. 30% of books from first-time authors. 99% from unagented writers. Pays 10-20% royalty on net price for print; higher royalties if published as an e-book.** Publishes book 9 months after acceptance. Accepts simultaneous submissions. Responds in 6 weeks to queries. Book catalog online. Guidelines by e-mail.

NONFICTION Subjects include education, law, world affairs, legislative histories.

RECENT TITLE(S) *A Bibliographical Catalog of William Blackstone*, by Ann Jordan Laeuchli; *Mark Twain vs. Lawyers, Lawmakers and Lawbreakers*, by Kenneth Bresler; *Environmental Justice: A Legal Research Guide*, by Lauren M. Collins.

HELLGATE PRESS

L&R Publishing, LLC, P.O. Box 3531, Ashland OR 97520. (541)973-5154. **E-mail:** sales@hellgatepress.com. **Website:** www.hellgatepress.com. **Contact:** Harley B. Patrick. Estab. 1996. "Hellgate Press specializes in military history, veteran memoirs, other military topics, travel adventure, and historical/adventure fiction." **Publishes 15-25 titles/year. 85% of books from first-time authors. 95% from unagented writers. Pays royalty.** Publishes ms 4-6 months after acceptance. Accepts simultaneous submissions. Responds in 1-2 month to queries.

NONFICTION Subjects include history, memoirs, military, travel, war, womens issues, world affairs, young adult. Query/proposal by e-mail only. No phone queries, please. *Do not send mss.*

FICTION Subjects include historical, military, war, young adult.

RECENT TITLE(S) *Nam '68*, by James Hogan; *An American Soldier in the Great War*, by John DelaGiustina, *Tower 13*, by Nathan Ritzo, *Sailor Man*, by Del Stacker, *Everyone Will Hate You for This*, by James Pirtle.

⊘ HENDRICKSON PUBLISHERS, INC.

P.O. Box 3473, Peabody MA 01961. **Fax:** (978)573-8276. **E-mail:** editorial@hendrickson.com. **Website:** www.hendrickson.com. Estab. 1981. Publishes trade reprints, bibles, and scholarly material in the areas of New Testament; Hebrew Bible; religion and culture; patristics; Judaism; and practical, historical, and Biblical theology. "Hendrickson is an academic publisher of Biblical scholarship and trade books that encourage spiritual growth. Currently emphasizing Biblical language and reference, pastoral resources, and Biblical studies." **Publishes 35 titles/year. 800 queries received/year. 10% of books from first-time authors. 90% from unagented writers.** Publishes ms 1 year after acceptance. Guidelines online.

NONFICTION Subjects include contemporary culture, creative nonfiction, education, entertainment, film, history, humanities, language, literature, religion, social sciences, spirituality. "We cannot accept unsolicited mss or book proposals except through one of the 2 following avenues: Materials sent to our editorial staff through a professional literary agent will be considered; Our staff would be happy to discuss book ideas at the various conferences we attend throughout the year (most notably, the AAR/SBL annual meeting)."

HERITAGE BOOKS, INC.

5810 Ruatan St., Berwyn Heights MD 20740. (800)876-6103. **Fax:** (800)876-6103. **E-mail:** info@heritagebooks.com. **E-mail:** submissions@heritagebooks.com. **Website:** www.heritagebooks.com. Estab. 1978. Publishes hardcover and paperback originals and reprints. "Our goal is to celebrate life by exploring all aspects of American life: settlement, development, wars, and other significant events, including family histories, memoirs, etc. Currently emphasizing early American life, early wars and conflicts, ethnic studies." **Publishes 200 titles/year. 25% of books from first-time authors. Pays 10% royalty on list price. Does not pay advance.** Ms published 1-3 months after acceptance. Responds in 3 months to queries. Book catalog and ms guidelines free.

NONFICTION Subjects include Americana, ethnic, history, memoirs, military, regional, war. Military memoirs. Query with SASE. Submit outline via e-mail. Reviews artwork/photos.

TIPS "The quality of the book is of prime importance; next is its relevance to our fields of interest."

HEYDAY

c/o Acquisitions Editor, Box 9145, Berkeley CA 94709. **E-mail:** editor@heydaybooks.com. **Website:** www.heydaybooks.com. **Contact:** Marthine Satris, acquisitions editor. Estab. 1974. Publishes hardcover originals, trade paperback originals and reprints. Heyday is an independent, nonprofit publisher with a focus on California and the American West. We publish nonfiction books that explore history, celebrate Native cultural renewal, fight injustice, and honor nature. **Publishes 15-20 titles/year. 50% of books from first-time authors. 90% from unagented writers.** Publishes book ~18 months after acceptance. Accepts simultaneous submissions. Responds in 3 months. Book catalog online. If you think that Heyday would be an appropriate publisher for your manuscript, send us a query or proposal by email to editor (at) heydaybooks (dot) com (please include "Heyday" in your subject line, or your proposal may be discarded), or by post to Heyday, P.O. Box 9145, Berkeley, CA 94709 (please include a self-addressed stamped envelope if you would like your submission materials returned). Please include the following: A cover letter introducing yourself and your qualifications. A brief description of your project. An annotated table of contents and list of illustrations (if any). Notes on the audiences you are trying to reach and why your book will appeal to them. A list of comparable titles and a brief description of the ways your book adds to the existing literature. Estimates of your book's expected length and your timeline for completing the writing. A sample chapter. We will do our best to respond to your query within twelve weeks of receiving it. No follow-up calls, please.

NONFICTION Subjects include Americana, contemporary culture, creative nonfiction, ethnic, film, gardening, history, marine subjects, multicultural, music, nature, recreation, regional, science. Books about California only.

HIGH PLAINS PRESS

P.O. Box 123, 403 Cassa Rd., Glendo WY 82213. (307)735-4370. **Fax:** (307)735-4590. **E-mail:** editor@highplainspress.com. **Website:** www.highplainspress.com. **Contact:** Nancy Curtis, publisher. Estab. 1984. Publishes hardcover and trade paperback originals. High Plains Press is a regional book publishing company specializing in books about the American West, with special interest in things relating to Wyoming. **Publishes 3 titles/year. 50 queries; 75 mss received/year. 75% of books from first-time authors. 100% from unagented writers. Pays 10% royalty on wholesale price. Pays $200-2,000 advance.** Publishes book 2 years after acceptance of ms. Accepts simultaneous submissions. Responds in 1 month to queries and proposals; 6 months on mss. Book catalog and guidelines online.

NONFICTION Subjects include agriculture, Americana, environment, history, horticulture, memoirs, nature, regional, womens studies. "We consider only books with strong connection to the West." Does not want art books, children's books. Query with SASE. Reviews artwork/photos. Send photocopies.

POETRY "We publish 1 poetry volume a year. Sometimes we skip a year. Require connection to West. Consider poetry in August." Submit 5 sample poems.

RECENT TITLE(S) *Gathering from the Grassland: A Plains Journal* by Linda M. Hasselstrom;*Reshaw: The Life & Times of John Baptiste Reshaw*, by Jefferson Glass (history); *Soap Suds Row: The Bold Lives of Army Laundresses, 1802-1876*, by Jennifer J. Lawrence (history); *Wilderness Fever: A Family's Adventures Homesteading in Early Jackson Hole*, by Linda Preston McKinstry with Harold Cole McKinstry (memoir); *Married Into It*, by Patricia Frolander (poetry).

TIPS "Our audience comprises general readers interested in history and culture of the Rockies."

Ⓐ⊘ HILL AND WANG

Farrar Straus & Giroux, Inc., 18 W. 18th St., New York NY 10011. (212)741-6900. **Fax:** (212)633-9385. **Website:** www.fsgbooks.com. Estab. 1956. Publishes hardcover and trade paperbacks. "Hill and Wang publishes serious nonfiction books, primarily in history, science, mathematics and the social sciences. We are not considering new fiction, drama, or poetry." **Publishes 12 titles/year. 1,500 queries received/year. 50% of books from first-time authors. 50% from unagented writers.** Publishes ms 1 year after acceptance. Accepts simultaneous submissions. Book catalog available free.

NONFICTION Subjects include history. *Agented submissions only.*

HIPPOCRENE BOOKS, INC.

171 Madison Ave., Suite 1605, New York NY 10016. 212-685-4371. **E-mail:** info@hippocrenebooks.com. **Website:** www.hippocrenebooks.com. Estab. 1971. *Mastering Arabic 1 and 2, Beginner's Russian with Interactive Online Workbook, Farsi Concise Dictionary, Tagalog Standard Dictionary, The Ghana Cookbook, Muy Bueno, Latin Twist, Healthy South Indian Cooking.* "Over the last forty years, Hippocrene Books has become one of America's foremost publishers of foreign language reference books and ethnic cookbooks. As a small publishing house in a marketplace dominated by conglomerates, Hippocrene has succeeded by continually reinventing its list while maintaining a strong international and ethnic orientation." Accepts simultaneous submissions. Please include summary, author background/resume including ability to promote book, sample chapter, table of contents, and audience. Do not send entire manuscript (hard copy or document file).

Hippocrene Books offers guides to over 120 languages and cookbooks in 80 inernational cuisines. We're seeking new languages not a part of our catalog, or additional titles in top-selling languages. Our cookbooks highlight a specific region or country, and stay clear of trends or fads.

FICTION No fiction is accepted.

POETRY Not seeking new poetry submissions.

HOLIDAY HOUSE, INC.

425 Madison Ave., New York NY 10017. (212)688-0085. **Fax:** (212)421-6134. **E-mail:** info@holidayhouse.com. **Website:** holidayhouse.com. Estab. 1935. Publishes hardcover originals and paperback reprints. "Holiday House publishes children's and young adult books for the school and library markets. We have a commitment to publishing first-time authors and illustrators. We specialize in quality hardcovers from picture books to young adult, both fiction and nonfiction, primarily for the school and library market." **Publishes 50 titles/year. 5% of books from first-time authors. 50% from unagented writers. Pays royalty on list price, range varies.** Publishes 1-2 years after acceptance. Responds in 4 months. Guidelines for #10 SASE.

NONFICTION Subjects include Americana, history, science, Judaica. Please send the entire ms, whether submitting a picture book or novel. "All submissions should be directed to the Editorial Department, Holiday House. We do not accept certified or registered mail. There is no need to include a SASE. We do not consider submissions by e-mail or fax. Please note that you do not have to supply illustrations. However, if you have illustrations you would like to include with your submission, you may send detailed sketches or photocopies of the original art. Do not send original art." Reviews artwork/photos. Send photocopies-no originals.

FICTION Subjects include adventure, historical, humor, literary, Judaica and holiday, animal stories for young readers. Children's books only. Query with SASE. No phone calls, please.

TIPS "We need manuscripts with strong stories and writing."

HENRY HOLT

175 Fifth Ave., New York NY 10011. (646)307-5095. **Fax:** (212)633-0748. **Website:** www.henryholt.com. *Agented submissions only.* Accepts simultaneous submissions.

HOLY CROSS ORTHODOX PRESS

Hellenic College, Inc., 50 Goddard Ave., Brookline MA 02445. (617)850-1321. **Fax:** (617)850-1457. **E-mail:** press@hchc.edu. **Website:** www.hchc.edu/community/administrative_offices/holy.cross.orthodox.press/. **Contact:** Mrs. Sarah Parro, production manager. Managing Director: Kevin Kovalycsik (kkovalycsik@hchc.edu). Estab. 1974. Publishes trade paperback originals. "Holy Cross publishes titles that are rooted in the tradition of the Eastern Orthodox Church." **Publishes 8 titles/year. 10-15 queries; 10-15 mss received/year. 85% of books from first-time authors. 100% from unagented writers. Pays 10% royalty on net revenue from retail sales.** Publishes ms 2 years after acceptance. Accepts simultaneous submissions. Responds in 6 months to mss. Guidelines online.

NONFICTION Subjects include ethnic, religion. Holy Cross Orthodox Press publishes scholarly and popular literature in the areas of Orthodox Christian theology and Greek letters. Submissions are often far too technical usually with very limited audiences. Submit outline. Submit complete ms. Reviews artwork/photos. Digital formats preferred.

RECENT TITLE(S) *The Schism in Philosophy*, by Christos Yannaras; *In Africa: Orthodox Christian Witness and Service*, by Archbishop Anastasios (Yannoulatos).

HOPEWELL PUBLICATIONS

P.O. Box 11, Titusville NJ 08560. **Website:** www.hopepubs.com. **Contact:** E. Martin, publisher. Estab. 2002. Format publishes in hardcover, trade paperback, and electronic originals; trade paperback and electronic reprints. "Hopewell Publications specializes in classic reprints—books with proven sales records that have gone out of print—and new titles of interest. Our catalog spans from 1 to 60 years of publication history. We print fiction and nonfiction, and we accept agented and unagented materials. Submissions are accepted online only." **Publishes 20-30 titles/year. Receives 2,000 queries/year; 500 mss/year. 25% of books from first-time authors. 75% from unagented writers. Pays royalty on retail price.** Publishes ms 6-12 months after acceptance. Accepts simultaneous submissions. Responds in 3 months to queries; 6 months to proposals; 9 months to mss. Catalog online. Guidelines online.

IMPRINTS Hopewell Publications, Egress Books, Legacy Classics.

NONFICTION Subjects includeAll nonfiction subjects acceptable. Query online using online guidelines.

FICTION Subjects include adventure, confession, contemporary, experimental, fantasy, feminist, gay, historical, humor, juvenile, literary, mainstream, mystery, plays, science fiction, short story collections, spiritual, suspense, young adult, All fiction subjects acceptable. Query online using our online guidelines.

RECENT TITLE(S) *The Syndicated News Articles*, by Eric Hoffer; *Writers on the Job*, by Thomas Kennedy, *Time & Money*, by Robert Gover; *True Surrealism*, by Christopher Klim; *Two Brothers*, by Robert Gover; *Read this Book or You Are Dead to Me*, by Matt Ryan.

HOUGHTON MIFFLIN HARCOURT BOOKS FOR CHILDREN

Imprint of Houghton Mifflin Trade & Reference Division, 222 Berkeley St., Boston MA 02116. (617)351-5000. **Fax:** (617)351-1111. **Website:** www.houghtonmifflinbooks.com. Publishes hardcover originals and trade paperback originals and reprints. Houghton Mifflin Harcourt gives shape to ideas that educate, inform, and above all, delight. *Does not respond to or return mss unless interested.* **Publishes 100 titles/year. 5,000 queries received/year. 14,000 mss received/year. 10% of books from first-time authors. 60% from unagented writers. Pays 5-10% royalty on retail price. Pays variable advance.** Publishes ms 2 years after acceptance. Accepts simultaneous submissions. Responds in 4-6 months to queries. Guidelines online.

NONFICTION Subjects include animals, ethnic, history, science, sports. Interested in innovative books and subjects about which the author is passionate. Query with SASE. Submit sample chapters, synopsis. Reviews artwork/photos. Send photocopies.

FICTION Subjects include adventure, ethnic, historical, humor, juvenile, literary, mystery, picture books, suspense, young adult, board books. Submit complete ms.

Ⓐ⊘ HOUGHTON MIFFLIN HARCOURT CO.

222 Berkeley St., Boston MA 02116. (617)351-5000. **Website:** www.hmhco.com. Estab. 1832. Publishes hardcover originals and trade paperback originals and reprints. "Houghton Mifflin Harcourt gives shape to ideas that educate, inform and delight. In a new era of publishing, our legacy of quality thrives as we combine imagination with technology, bringing you new ways to know." Accepts simultaneous submissions.

NONFICTION "We are not a mass market publisher. Our main focus is serious nonfiction. We do practical self-help but not pop psychology self-help." *Agented submissions only. Unsolicited mss returned unopened.*

HUMAN KINETICS PUBLISHERS, INC.

P.O. Box 5076, Champaign IL 61825-5076. (800)747-4457. **Fax:** (217)351-1549. **E-mail:** acquisitions@hkusa.com. **Website:** www.humankinetics.com. Estab. 1974. Publishes hardcover, ebooks, and paperback text and reference books, trade paperback originals, course software and audiovisual. "*Human Kinetics* publishes books which provide expert knowledge in sport and fitness training and techniques, physical education, sports sciences and sports medicine for coaches, athletes and fitness enthusiasts and professionals in the physical action field." **Publishes 160 titles/year. Pays 10-15% royalty on net income.** Publishes ms up to 18 months after acceptance. Accepts simultaneous submissions. Responds in 2 months to queries. Book catalog available free. Guidelines online.

NONFICTION Subjects include education, psychology, recreation, sports. "Here is a current listing of our divisions: Amer. Sport Education; Aquatics Edu.; Professional Edu.; HPERD Div., Journal Div.; STM Div., Trade Div." Submit outline, sample chapters. Reviews artwork/photos.

IBEX PUBLISHERS

P.O. Box 30087, Bethesda MD 20824. (301)718-8188. **Fax:** (301)907-8707. **E-mail:** info@ibexpub.com. **Website:** www.ibexpublishers.com. Estab. 1979. Publishes hardcover and trade paperback originals and reprints. "Ibex publishes books about Iran and the Middle East and about Persian culture and literature." **Publishes 10-12 titles/year. Payment varies.** Accepts simultaneous submissions. Book catalog available free.

IMPRINTS Iranbooks Press.

NONFICTION Subjects include cooking, history, humanities, language, literary criticism, literature, spirituality, translation. Query with SASE, or submit proposal package, including outline and 2 sample chapters.

POETRY "Translations of Persian poets will be considered."

ICONOGRAFIX/ENTHUSIAST BOOKS

2017 O'Neil Rd., Hudson WI 54016. (715)381-9755. **Website:** www.enthusiastbooks.com. Estab. 1992. Publishes trade paperback originals. "Iconografix publishes special, historical-interest photographic books for transportation equipment enthusiasts. Currently emphasizing emergency vehicles, buses, trucks, railroads, automobiles, auto racing, construction equipment, snowmobiles." **Publishes 6-10 titles/year. 50 queries received/year. 20 mss received/year. 50% of books from first-time authors. 100% from unagented writers. Pays 8-12% royalty on wholesale price. Pays $1,000-3,000 advance.** Publishes book 1 year after acceptance. Accepts simultaneous submissions. Responds in 1 month to queries; 3 months to proposals and mss. Book catalog and ms guidelines free.

NONFICTION Subjects include Americana, history, hobbies, transportation (older photos of specific vehicles). Interested in photo archives. Query with SASE, or submit proposal package, including outline. Reviews artwork/photos. Send photocopies.

RECENT TITLE(S) *Trolley Buses Around the World*, by William A. Luke; *Vintage Snowmobilia*, by Jon D. Bertolinol.

ICS PUBLICATIONS

Institute of Carmelite Studies, 2131 Lincoln Rd. NE, Washington DC 20002-1199. (202)832-8489. **Fax:** (202)832-8967. **E-mail:** editor@icspublications.org. **Website:** www.icspublications.org. **Contact:** Patricia Lynn Morrison, editorial director. Business Manager: Clair Jerge. Marketing Manager: Pier-Giorgio Pacelli, OCD. Estab. 1973. Publishes hardcover and trade paperback originals and reprints. ICS Publications is the publishing ministry of the Washington Province of Discalced Carmelite Friars. We are a small independent non-profit niche publisher specializing in the critical editions of the works of Carmelite saints (Teresa of Avila, John of the Cross, Therese of Lisieux, Edith Stein, etc.) as well as in commentary and scholarship on them, and general Carmelite spirituality for the average reader as well as the specialist/academic. **Publishes 4-6 titles/year. 20-40 queries; 15 mss received/year. 50% of books from first-time authors. 90-100% from unagented writers. Pays 10% royalty after 1st year of publication; paid annual on minimum. Pays $500 advance on acceptance; additional $500 on publication; advance paid against royalties.** Publishes ms usually 3 years after acceptance. Responds in 3-6 months to proposals. Publishes one general catalog annually, several themed/seasonal catalogs; mail and online. Guidelines online.

NONFICTION Subjects include religion, spirituality, spirituality, Carmelite and general. Does not want accounts of personal religious experiences/conversion; children's books; poetry; books that we deem too specialized in content/style for the general reader.

IDW PUBLISHING

2765 Truxtun Rd., San Diego CA 92106. **E-mail:** letters@idwpublishing.com. **Website:** www.idwpublishing.com. Estab. 1999. Publishes hardcover, mass market and trade paperback originals. IDW Publishing currently publishes a wide range of comic books and graphic novels including titles based on GI Joe, Star Trek, Terminator: Salvation, and Transformers. Creator-driven titles include Fallen Angel by Peter David and JK Woodward, Locke & Key by Joe Hill and Gabriel Rodriguez, and a variety of titles by writer Steve Niles including Wake the Dead, Epilogue, and Dead, She Said. Accepts simultaneous submissions.

IDYLL ARBOR, INC.

39129 264th Ave. SE, Enumclaw WA 98022. (360)825-7797. **Fax:** (360)825-5670. **E-mail:** editors@idyllarbor.com. **Website:** www.idyllarbor.com. **Contact:** Tom Blaschko. Estab. 1984. Publishes hardcover and trade paperback originals. "Idyll Arbor publishes practical information on the current state and art of healthcare practice. Currently emphasizing therapies (recreational, horticultural), and activity directors in long-term care facilities. Issues Press looks at problems in society from video games to returning veterans and their problems reintegrating into the civilian world. Pine Winds Press publishes books about strange phenomena such as souls, life force, the Sidhe, and Bigfoot." **Publishes 6 titles/year. 40% of books from first-time authors. 100% from unagented writers. Pays 8-15% royalty on wholesale price or retail price.** Publishes book 1 year after acceptance. Accepts simultaneous submissions. Responds in 1 month; 2 months to proposals; 6 months to mss. Book catalog and ms guidelines free.

IMPRINTS Issues Press; Pine Winds Press.

NONFICTION Subjects include health, medicine, New Age, psychic, psychology, recreation, religion, science, spirituality. "Idyll Arbor is publishing a line of books under the Pine Winds Press imprint that is based on the theme that We All Have Souls. It looks at ways to bring experiences of realities outside of physical reality back into Western culture in ways that are not tied to religion." Query preferred with outline and 1 sample chapter. Reviews artwork/photos. Send photocopies.

RECENT TITLE(S) *We All Have Souls and I Think We Can Prove It*; *Witnessing Bigfoot*; *Boomerstress*; *Long-Term Care for Activity Professionals, Social Services Professionals, and Recreational Therapists.*

TIPS "The books must be useful for the health practitioner who meets face to face with patients or the books must be useful for teaching undergraduate and graduate level classes. Pine Winds Press books should be compatible with the model of the soul found on weallhavesouls.com."

ILIUM PRESS

2407 S. Sonora Dr., Spokane WA 99037. (509)701-8866. **E-mail:** iliumpress@outlook.com. **Contact:** John Lemon, owner/editor. Estab. 2010. Publishes trade paperback originals and reprints, electronic originals and reprints. "Ilium Press is a small, 1-person press that I created to cultivate and promote the relevance of epic poetry in today's world. My focus is book-length narrative poems in blank (non-rhyming) metered verse, such as iambic parameter or sprung verse. I am very selective about my projects, but I provide extensive editorial care to those projects I take on." **Publishes 1-3 titles/year. 25% of books from first-time authors. Pays 20-50% royalties on receipts. Does not pay advance.** Publishes ms up to 1 year after acceptance. Accepts simultaneous submissions. Responds in 6 months.

POETRY Ilium Press specializes in original, book-length narrative epic poems written in blank (non-rhyming) metered verse (such as iambic pentameter or sprung verse) in contemporary language. "I'm looking for original work that shows how epic poetry is still relevant in today's world. Please query via e-mail if you have questions." Submit via e-mail (preferred) or via mail with first 20 pages. Don't forget to include your contact information!

RECENT TITLE(S) *The New World, Genesis,* and *Apocalypse*, by Fredrick Turner; *The Epic of Clair*, by E.C. Hansen; and *The Turner Erotica*, by Robert Begiebing.

ILR PRESS

Cornell University Press, Sage House, 512 E. State St., Ithaca NY 14850. (607)277-2338. **Fax:** (607)277-2374. **E-mail:** fgb2@cornell.edu. **Website:** www.cornellpress.cornell.edu. **Contact:** Frances Benson, editorial director. Estab. 1945. Publishes hardcover and trade paperback originals and reprints. "We are interested in manuscripts with innovative perspectives on current workplace issues that concern both academics and the general public." **Publishes 10-15 titles/year. Pays royalty.** Responds in 2 months to queries. Book catalog available online. Guidelines online.

NONFICTION Subjects include history, sociology. All titles relate to labor relations and/or workplace issues including relevant work in the fields of history, sociology, political science, economics, human resources, and organizational behavior. Special series: culture and politics of health care work. Query with SASE. Submit outline, sample chapters, CV.

TIPS "Manuscripts must be well documented to pass our editorial evaluation, which includes review by academics in related fields."

IMAGE COMICS

2701 NW Vaughn St., Suite 780, Portland OR 97210. **E-mail:** submissions@imagecomics.com. **Website:** www.imagecomics.com. Estab. 1992. Publishes creator-owned comic books, graphic novels. See this company's website for detailed guidelines. Does not accept writing samples without art. Accepts simultaneous submissions.

FICTION Query with 1-page synopsis and 5 pages or more of samples. "We do not accept writing (that is plots, scripts, whatever) samples! If you're an established pro, we might be able to find somebody willing to work with you but it would be nearly impossible for us to read through every script that might find its way our direction. Do not send your script or your plot unaccompanied by art—it will be discarded, unread."

TIPS "We are not looking for any specific genre or type of comic book. We are looking for comics that are well written and well drawn, by people who are dedicated and can meet deadlines."

IMBRIFEX BOOKS

Flattop Productions, Inc., 8275 S. Eastern Ave., Suite 200, Las Vegas NV 89123. (702)309-0130. **E-mail:** acquisitions@imbrifex.com. **Website:** https://imbrifex.com. **Contact:** Mark Sedenquist. Estab. 2016. Based in Las Vegas, Nevada, Imbrifex Books publishes both fiction and nonfiction, with a particular interest in books for road trip aficionados and books that have a connection with Las Vegas and the desert Southwest. Titles are distributed world-wide through Pacific Group West, (PGW), and Audible.com. **Publishes 6-8 titles/year. 70% of books from first-time authors. 60% from unagented writers. Pays advance.** Accepts simultaneous submissions. Responds in 2 months. Guidelines online.

NONFICTION Subjects include community, marine subjects, multicultural, travel, true crime, womens issues, young adult.

FICTION Subjects include adventure, experimental, feminist, gay, humor, lesbian, literary, mainstream, multicultural, mystery, poetry, short story collections, suspense.

IMPACT BOOKS

An Imprint of Penguin Random House LLC. 1745 Broadway, New York NY 10019 **Website:** www.penguinrandomhouse.com. Estab. 2004. Publishes trade paperback originals. IMPACT Books publishes titles that emphasize illustrated how-to-draw-manga, science- fiction, fantasy and comics art instruction. Currently emphasizing manga and anime art, science fiction, traditional American comics styles, including humor, and pop art. Looking for good science fiction art instruction. This market is for experienced artists who are willing to work with an IMPACT editor to produce a step-by-step how-to book about how to create the art and the artist's creative process. **Publishes 9 titles/year. 50 queries; 10-12 mss received/year. 70% of books from first-time authors. 80% from unagented writers. Pays advance.** Publishes ms 11 months after acceptance. Accepts simultaneous submissions. Responds in 4 months. Visit website for booklist. Guidelines available online.

NONFICTION Subjects include art, contemporary culture, creative nonfiction, hobbies. Submit via e-mail only. Submit proposal package, outline, 1 sample chapter, at least 20 examples of sample art. Reviews artwork/photos. Send digital art.

TIPS "Audience comprised primarily of 12- to 18-year-old beginners along the lines of comic buyers, in general—mostly teenagers—but also appealing to a broader audience of young adults 19-30 who need basic techniques. Art must appeal to teenagers and be submitted in a form that will reproduce well. Authors need to know how to teach beginners step-by-step. A sample step-by-step demonstration is important."

IMPACT PUBLISHERS, INC.

5674 Shattuck Ave., Oakland CA 94609. **E-mail:** proposals@newharbinger.com. **Website:** www.newharbinger.com/imprint/impact-publishers. **Contact:** Acquisitions Department. Estab. 1970. "Our purpose is to make the best human services expertise available to the widest possible audience. We publish only popular psychology and self-help materials written in everyday language by professionals with advanced degrees and significant experience in the human services." **Publishes 3-5 titles/year. 20% of books from first-time authors. Pays authors royalty of 10-12%. Offers advances.** Accepts simultaneous submissions. Responds in 3 months. Book catalog for #10 SASE with 2 first-class stamps. Guidelines for SASE.

IMPRINTS Little Imp Books, Rebuilding Books, The Practical Therapist Series.

NONFICTION Young readers, middle readers, young adults: self-help. Query or submit complete ms, cover letter, résumé.

RECENT TITLE(S) *Finding Meaning*, Facing Fears, by Jerry Shapiro; *Teen Esteem*, by Pat Palmer and Melissa Alberti Froehner.

TIPS "Please do not submit fiction, poetry or narratives."

INCENTIVE PUBLICATIONS, INC.

233 N. Michigan Ave., Suite 2000, Chicago IL 60601. **E-mail:** incentive@worldbook.com. **Website:** www.incentivepublications.com. Estab. 1970. Publishes paperback originals. "Incentive publishes developmentally appropriate teacher/school administrator/parent resource materials and supplementary instructional materials for children in grades K-12. Actively seeking proposals for student workbooks, all grades/all subjects, and professional development resources for pre K-12 classroom teachers and school administrators." **Publishes 10-15 titles/year. 25% of books from first-time authors. 100, but agent proposals welcome% from unagented writers. Pays royalty, or makes outright purchase.** an average of 1 year Accepts simultaneous submissions. Responds in 1 month to queries.

NONFICTION Subjects include education. Instructional, teacher/administrator professional development books in pre-K through 12th grade. Query with synopsis and detailed outline.

RECENT TITLE(S) *Taming of the Team*, by Jack Berckemeyer; The Ready to Learn Book Series, by Imogene Forte (Grades pre K-K); *Drumming to the Beat of a Different Marcher*, by Debbie Silver; *As Reading Programs Come and Go, This Is What You Need to Know*, by Judith Cochran.

INDIANA HISTORICAL SOCIETY PRESS

450 W. Ohio St., Indianapolis IN 46202. (317)233-6073. **Fax:** (317)233-0857. **E-mail:** ihspress@indianahistory.org. **Website:** www.indianahistory.org. **Contact:** Submissions Editor. Estab. 1830. Publishes hardcover and paperback originals. **Publishes 10 titles/year.** Accepts simultaneous submissions. Responds in 1 month to queries.

NONFICTION Subjects include agriculture, ethnic, history, sports, family history, children's books. All topics must relate to Indiana. "We seek book-length manuscripts that are solidly researched and engagingly written on topics related to Indiana: biography, history, literature, music, politics, transportation, sports, agriculture, architecture, and children's books." Query with SASE.

INFORMATION TODAY, INC.

143 Old Marlton Pike, Medford NJ 08055. (609)654-6266. **Fax:** (609)654-4309. **E-mail:** rcolding@infotoday.com. **Website:** www.infotoday.com. **Contact:** Rob Colding, Book Marketing Manager. Publishes hardcover and trade paperback originals. "We look for highly-focused coverage of cutting-edge technology topics. Written by established experts and targeted to a tech-savvy readership. Virtually all our titles focus on how information is accessed, used, shared, and transformed into knowledge that can benefit people, business, and society. Currently emphasizing Web 2.0, customer experience (CX), user experience (UX), content marketing, AI, streaming media, internet/online technologies, including their social significance: biography, how-to, technical, reference, scholarly. De-emphasizing fiction." **Publishes 15-20 titles/year. 200 queries; 30 mss received/year. 30% of books from first-time authors. 90% from unagented writers. Pays 10-15% royalty on wholesale price. Pays $500-2,500 advance.** Publishes book 9 months after acceptance. Accepts simultaneous submissions. Responds in 1 month to queries; 2 months to proposals; 3 months to mss. Book catalog free or on website. Proposal guidelines free or via e-mail as attachment.

IMPRINTS ITI (academic, scholarly, library science); CyberAge Books (high-end consumer and business technology books-emphasis on Internet/WWW topics including online research).

NONFICTION Subjects include business, computers, education, science, Internet and cyberculture. Query with SASE. Reviews artwork/photos. Send photocopies.

RECENT TITLE(S) *Deep Text: Using Text Analytics to Conquer Information Overload, Get Real Value from Social Media, and Add Big(ger) Text to Big Data*, by Tom Reamy; *The Future Scholar: Researching and Teaching the Frameworks for Writing and Information Literacy*, edited by James P. Purdy and Randall McClure; *Editing Research: The Author Editing Approach to Providing Effective Support to Writers of Research Papers*, by Valerie Matarese; *The Accidental Taxonomist*, Second Edition, by Heather Hedden; *Online Teaching in K-12: Models, Methods, and Best Practices for Teachers and Administrators*, edited by Sarah Bryans-Bongey and Kevin J. Graziano; *Inside Content Marketing: EContent; Magazine's Guide to*

Roles, Tools, and Strategies for Thriving in the Age of Brand Journalism, by Theresa Cramer.

TIPS "Our readers include scholars, academics, educators, indexers, librarians, information professionals (ITI imprint), as well as high-end consumer and business users of Internet/WWW/online technologies, and people interested in the marriage of technology with issues of social significance (i.e., Web 2.0 relevance)."

INTERLINK PUBLISHING GROUP, INC.

46 Crosby St., Northampton MA 01060. (413)582-7054. **E-mail:** info@interlinkbooks.com. **E-mail:** submissions@interlinkbooks.com. **Website:** www.interlinkbooks.com. Estab. 1987. Publishes hardcover and trade paperback originals. Interlink is an independent publisher of general trade adult fiction and nonfiction with an emphasis on books that have a wide appeal while also meeting high intellectual and literary standards. "Our list is devoted to works of literature, history, contemporary politics, travel, art, and cuisine from around the world, often from areas underrepresented in Western media." **Publishes 50 titles/year. 30% of books from first-time authors. 50% from unagented writers. Pays 6-8% royalty on retail price. Pays small advance.** Publishes ms 18 months after acceptance. Accepts simultaneous submissions. Responds in 3-6 months to queries. Book catalog and guidelines online.

IMPRINTS Olive Branch Press; Crocodile Books; Interlink Books.

NONFICTION Subjects include contemporary culture, creative nonfiction, ethnic, foods, history, humanities, literary criticism, literature, multicultural, politics, regional, translation, war, womens issues, world affairs. Submit outline and sample chapters via e-mail.

FICTION Subjects include ethnic, feminist, literary, multicultural, translation, international. "We are looking for translated works relating to the Middle East, Africa or Latin America. The only fiction we publish falls into our 'Interlink World Fiction' series. Most of these books, as you can see in our catalog, are translated fiction from around the world. The series aims to bring fiction from other countries to a North American audience. In short, unless you were born outside the United States, your novel will not fit into the series." No science fiction, romance, plays, erotica, fantasy, horror. Query by e-mail. Submit outline, sample chapters.

RECENT TITLE(S) *Soup for Syria*, by Barbara Abdeni Massad; *The Aleppo Cookbook*, by Marlene Matar; *Man Enough?* by Jackson Katz; *The Shell* by Mustafa Khalifa; *The Ninety-Ninth Floor*, by Jana Fawaz Elhassan; *Kahlil Gibran: Beyond Borders*, by Jean and Kahlil G. Gibran.

TIPS "Any submissions that fit well in our publishing program will receive careful attention. A visit to our website, your local bookstore, or library to look at some of our books before you send in your submission is recommended."

INTERNATIONAL FOUNDATION OF EMPLOYEE BENEFIT PLANS

18700 W. Bluemound Rd., Brookfield WI 53045. (262)786-6700. **Fax:** (262)786-8780. **Website:** www.ifebp.org. Estab. 1954. Publishes trade paperback originals. IFEBP publishes general and technical monographs on all aspects of employee benefits—pension plans, health insurance, etc. **Publishes 6 titles/year. 15% of books from first-time authors. 80% from unagented writers. Pays 5-15% royalty on wholesale and retail price.** Publishes ms 1 year after acceptance. Accepts simultaneous submissions. Responds in 3 months to queries. Book catalog online. Guidelines online.

NONFICTION Subjects limited to health care, pensions, retirement planning and employee benefits and compensation. Query with outline.

RECENT TITLE(S) *Multiemployer Plans*, by Joseph A. Brislin; *Trustee Handbook: A Guide to Labor-Management Employee Benefit Plans*, Claude L. Kordus, editor and contributor.

TIPS "Be aware of interests of employers and the marketplace in benefits topics, for example, pension plan changes, healthcare cost containment."

INTERNATIONAL MARINE

The McGraw-Hill Companies, 90 Mechanic St., Camden ME 04843. (207)236-4838. **Fax:** (207)236-6314. **E-mail:** christopher.brown@mheducation.com. **Website:** www.internationalmarine.com. **Contact:** Acquisitions Editor. Estab. 1969. Publishes hardcover and paperback originals. International Marine publishes the best books about boats. **Publishes 50 titles/year. 500-700 mss received/year. 30% of books from first-time authors. 60% from unagented writers. Pays standard royalties based on net price. Pays advance.** Publishes ms 1 year after acceptance. Accepts simultaneous submissions. Responds in 2 months to queries. Guidelines online.

IMPRINTS Ragged Mountain Press (sports and outdoor books that take you off the beaten path).

NONFICTION All books are illustrated. Material in all stages welcome. Publishes a wide range of subjects include: sea stories, seamanship, boat maintenance, etc. Query first with outline and 2-3 sample chapters. Reviews artwork/photos.

TIPS "Writers should be aware of the need for clarity, accuracy and interest. Many progress too far in the actual writing."

INTERNATIONAL PRESS

P.O. Box 502, Somerville MA 02143. (617)623-3855. **Fax:** (617)623-3101. **E-mail:** ipb-mgmt@intlpress.com. **Website:** www.intlpress.com. **Contact:** Brian Bianchini. Estab. 1992. Publishes hardcover originals and reprints. International Press of Boston, Inc. is an academic publishing company that welcomes book publication inquiries from prospective authors on all topics in Mathematics and Physics. International Press also publishes high-level mathematics and mathematical physics book titles and textbooks. **Publishes 12 titles/year. 200 queries received/year. 500 mss received/year. 10% of books from first-time authors. 100% from unagented writers. Pays 3-10% royalty.** Publishes ms 6 months after acceptance. Responds in 5 months to queries and proposals; 1 year to mss. Book catalog available free. Guidelines online.

NONFICTION Subjects include science. All our books will be in research mathematics. Authors need to provide ready to print latex files. Submit complete ms. Reviews artwork/photos. Send EPS files.

TIPS "Audience is PhD mathematicians, researchers and students."

INTERNATIONAL SOCIETY FOR TECHNOLOGY IN EDUCATION (ISTE)

1530 Wilson Blvd., Suite 730, Arlington VA 22209. (703)348-4784. **E-mail:** iste@iste.org. **Website:** www.iste.org. Publishes trade paperback originals. "Currently emphasizing books on educational technology standards, curriculum integration, professional development, and assessment. De-emphasizing software how-to books." **Publishes 10 titles/year. 100 queries received/year. 40 mss received/year. 75% of books from first-time authors. 95% from unagented writers. Pays 10% royalty on retail price.** Publishes ms 6-9 months after acceptance. Accepts simultaneous submissions. Responds in 2 weeks to queries; 1 month to proposals and mss. Book catalog and guidelines online.

NONFICTION Submit proposal package, outline, sample chapters, TOC, vita. Reviews artwork/photos. Send photocopies.

TIPS "Our audience is K-12 teachers, teacher educators, technology coordinators, and school and district administrators."

INTERNATIONAL WEALTH SUCCESS INC.

IWS Inc., P.O. Box 186, Merrick NY 11570. (516)766-5850. **Fax:** (516)766-5919. **E-mail:** admin@iwsmoney.com. **Website:** www.iwsmoney.com. **Contact:** Tyler G. Hicks, president. Estab. 1966. International Wealth Success Inc. (IWS) is a full-service newsletter, book and self-study course publisher of print and digital media on small business and income real estate. The company's mission is to help beginning and experienced business people choose, start, finance, and succeed in their own small businesses. Topics include real estate investment, import-export, mail order, home-based business, marketing, fundraising, and financing. **Publishes 10 titles/year. Pays 10% royalty on wholesale or retail price.** Publishes ms 4 months after acceptance. Accepts simultaneous submissions. Responds within 1 month to queries. Catalog online.

NONFICTION Subjects include business, career guidance, finance, real estate, private money, financial institutions, homebased business, marketing, export-import, grants and fundraising. Techniques, methods, sources for building wealth. Personal, how-to-do-it with case histories and examples. Publications are aimed at aspiring wealth builders and are sympathetic to their problems and challenges. Publications present a wide range of business opportunities while providing practical, hands-on, step-by-step instructions aimed at helping readers achieve their personal goals in as short a time as possible while adhering to ethical and professional business standards. Length: 60,000-70,000 words. Does not want anything that doesn't pertain to small business, entrepreneurism, business opportunities, or real estate. Query. Reviews artwork/photos.

INTERVARSITY PRESS

P.O. Box 1400, Downers Grove IL 60515. **E-mail:** email@ivpress.com. **Website:** www.ivpress.com/submissions. Estab. 1947. Publishes hardcover originals, trade paperback and mass market paperback originals. "InterVarsity Press publishes a full line of books from an explicitly Christian perspective targeted to an open-minded audience. We serve those in the university, the academy, the church, and the world." **Publishes 110 titles/year. 1,000 queries; 900 mss received/year. 13% of books from first-time authors. 80% from unagented writers. Payment policy varies. Pays negotiable advance.** Publishes book 18 months after acceptance. Accepts simultaneous submissions. "We are unable to provide updates on the review process or personalized responses to unsolicited proposals. We regret that submissions will not be returned.". Book catalog online. Guidelines online.

IMPRINTS IVP Academic; IVP Books.

NONFICTION Subjects include business, child guidance, contemporary culture, economics, ethnic, history, multicultural, philosophy, psychology, religion, science, social sciences, sociology, spirituality. "InterVarsity Press publishes a full line of books from an explicitly Christian perspective targeted to an open-minded audience. We serve those in the university, the church, and the world." "We review The Writer's Edge at writersedgeservice.com." Does not review artwork.

RECENT TITLE(S) *Brave Souls*, by Belinda Bauman; *The Common Rule*, by Justin Whitmel Earley.

TIPS "The best way to submit to us is to go to a conference where one of our editors is attending. Networking is key. We are seeking writers who have good ideas and a presence/platform where they have been testing out their ideas (a church, university, on a prominent blog). We need authors who will bring resources to the table for helping to publicize and sell their books (speaking at seminars and conferences, writing for national magazines or newspapers, etc.)."

INTERWEAVE PRESS

An Imprint of Penguin Random House. 1745 Broadway, New York NY 10019. (212)782-9000. **Website:** www.penguinrandomhouse.com. Estab. 1975. Publishes hardcover and trade paperback originals. Interweave Press publishes instructive titles relating to the fiber arts and beadwork topics. **Publishes 20-25 titles/year. 60% of books from first-time authors. 90% from unagented writers.** Publishes ms 6-18 months after acceptance. Accepts simultaneous submissions. Responds in 2 months to queries. Book catalog and guidelines online.

NONFICTION Subjects include crafts, hobbies. Subjects limited to fiber arts (spinning, knitting, dyeing, weaving) and jewelry making (beadwork, stringing, wireworking, metalsmithing). Submit outline, sample chapters. Accepts simultaneous submissions if informed of non-exclusivity. Reviews artwork/photos.

RECENT TITLE(S) *AlterKnit Stitch Dictionary*, by Andrea Rangel; *Woven in Wire*, by Sarah Thompson.

TIPS "We are looking for very clear, informally written, technically correct manuscripts, generally of a how-to nature, in our specific fiber and beadwork fields only. Our audience includes a variety of creative self-starters who appreciate inspiration and clear instruction. They are often well educated and skillful in many areas."

INVERTED-A

P.O. Box 267, Licking MO 65542. **E-mail:** katzaya@gmail.com. **Website:** inverteda.com. **Contact:** Aya Katz, chief editor (poetry, novels, political); Nets Katz, science editor (scientific, academic). Estab. 1985. Publishes paperback originals. Books: POD. Distributes through Amazon, Bowker, Barnes Noble. **Pays 10 author's copies.** Publishes ms 1 year after acceptance. Accepts simultaneous submissions. Responds in 1 month to queries; 3 months to mss. Guidelines for SASE.

NONFICTION Subjects include Americana, history, literature, politics, stage, translation, libertarian.

FICTION Subjects include historical, picture books, science fiction, translation, war, young adult, utopian, political. Does not accept unsolicited mss. Query with SASE. Reading period open from January 2 to March 15. Accepts queries by e-mail. Include estimated word count.

TIPS "Read our books. Read the *Inverted-A Horn*. We are different. We do not follow industry trends."

IRON GATE PUBLISHING

P.O. Box 999, Niwot CO 80544. **E-mail:** editor@irongate.com. **Website:** www.irongate.com. **Contact:** Dina C. Carson, publisher (how-to, genealogy, local history). Publishes hardcover and trade paperback originals. "Our readers are people who are looking for solid, how-to advice on self-publishing a family or local history, or who are conducting genealogical or local history research in Colorado." **Publishes 20-30 titles/year. 100 queries; 20 mss received/year. 30% of books from first-time authors. 10% from unagented writers. Pays royalty on a case-by-case basis.** Publishes book 6 months after acceptance. Accepts simultaneous submissions. Responds in 2 months to proposals. Book catalog and writer's guidelines free or online.

NONFICTION Subjects include history, genealogy, local history. Query with SASE, or submit proposal package, including outline, 2 sample chapters, and marketing summary. Reviews artwork/photos. Send photocopies.

TIPS "Please look at the other books we publish and tell us in your query letter why your book would fit into our line of books."

ITALICA PRESS

99 Wall St., Suite 650, New York NY 10005. (917)371-0563. **E-mail:** inquiries@italicapress.com. **Website:** www.italicapress.com. Estab. 1985. Publishes hardcover and trade paperback originals. "Italica Press publishes English translations of modern Italian fiction and medieval and Renaissance nonfiction." **Publishes 6 titles/year. 600 queries; 60 mss received/year. 5% of books from first-time authors. 100% from unagented writers. Pays 7-15% royalty on wholesale price; author's copies.** Publishes ms 1 year after acceptance. Accepts simultaneous submissions. Responds in 1 month to queries; 4 months to mss. Book catalog and guidelines online.

NONFICTION Subjects include history, literature, translation. "We publish English translations of medieval and Renaissance source materials and English translations of modern Italian fiction." Query via e-mail. Reviews artwork/photos.

FICTION Subjects include poetry in translation, translation. "First-time translators published. We would like to see translations of Italian writers who are well-known in Italy who are not yet translated for an American audience." Query via e-mail.

POETRY Poetry titles are always translations and generally dual language. Query with 10 sample translations of medieval and Renaissance Italian poets. Include cover letter, bio, and list of publications.

TIPS "We are interested in considering a wide variety of medieval and Renaissance topics (not historical fiction), and for modern works we are only interested in translations from Italian fiction by well-known Italian authors. Only fiction that has been previously published in Italian. A brief e-mail saves a lot of time. 90% of proposals we receive are completely off base—but we are very interested in things that are right on target."

JAIN PUBLISHING CO.

P.O. Box 3523, Fremont CA 94539. (510)659-8272. **Fax:** (510)659-0501. **E-mail:** mail@jainpub.com. **Website:** www.jainpub.com. **Contact:** Mukesh Jain, editor-in-chief. Estab. 1989. Publishes hardcover and paperback originals and reprints. Jain Publishing Co. is a humanities and social sciences publisher that publishes academic and scholarly references, as well as books for the general reader in both print and electronic formats. A substantial part of its publishing program pertains to books dealing with Asia, commonly categorized as "Asian Studies." **Publishes 6-8 titles/year. 300 queries received/year. 100% from unagented writers. Pays 5-10% royalty on net sales.** Publishes ms 1-2 years after acceptance. Accepts simultaneous submissions. Responds in 3 months to mss. Book catalog and ms guidelines online.

NONFICTION Subjects include environment, humanities, multicultural, nature, philosophy, religion, social sciences, spirituality, Asian studies. Submit proposal package, publishing history. Reviews artwork/photos. Send photocopies.

RECENT TITLE(S) *Strange Tales From Liaozhai*, by Peter Songling, English translation Sidney L. Sondergard.

ALICE JAMES BOOKS

114 Prescott St., Farmington ME 04938. (207)778-7071. **Fax:** (207)778-7766. **Website:** www.alicejamesbooks.org. Estab. 1973. Publishes trade paperback originals. "Alice James Books is a nonprofit cooperative poetry press. The founders' objectives were to give women access to publishing and to involve authors in the publishing process. The cooperative selects mss for publication through both regional and national competitions." **Publishes 6 titles/year. Approximately 1,000 mss received/year. 50% of books from first-time authors. 100% from unagented writers. Pays through competition awards.** Publishes ms 1 year after acceptance. Accepts simultaneous submissions. Responds promptly to queries; 4 months to mss. Book catalog online. Guidelines online.

POETRY "Alice James Books is a nonprofit cooperative poetry press. The founders' objectives were to give women access to publishing and to involve authors in the publishing process. The cooperative selects mss for publication through both regional and national competitions." Does not want children's poetry or light verse.

RECENT TITLE(S) *Hum*, by Jamaal May; *Viral*, by Suzanne Parker; *We Come Elemental*, by Tamiko Beyer.

TIPS "Send SASE for contest guidelines or check website. Do not send work without consulting current guidelines."

JEWISH LIGHTS PUBLISHING

LongHill Partners, Inc., Sunset Farm Offices, Rt. 4, P.O. Box 237, Woodstock VT 05091. (802)457-4000. **Fax:** (802)457-4004. **E-mail:** submissions@turner-publishing.com. **Website:** www.jewishlights.com. Estab. 1990. Publishes hardcover and trade paperback originals, trade paperback reprints. "Jewish Lights publishes books for people of all faiths and all backgrounds who yearn for books that attract, engage, educate and spiritually inspire. Our authors are at the forefront of spiritual thought and deal with the quest for the self and for meaning in life by drawing on the Jewish wisdom tradition. Our books cover topics including history, spirituality, life cycle, children, self-help, recovery, theology and philosophy. We do not publish autobiography, biography, fiction, haggadot, poetry or cookbooks. At this point we plan to do only two books for children annually, and one will be for younger children (ages 4-10)." **Publishes 30 titles/year. 50% of books from first-time authors. 75% from unagented writers. Pays authors royalty of 10% of revenue received; 15% royalty for subsequent printings.** Publishes ms 1 year after acceptance. Accepts simultaneous submissions. Responds in 6 months to queries. Book catalog and guidelines online.

NONFICTION Subjects include history, philosophy, religion, spirituality. Picture book, young readers, middle readers: activity books, spirituality. "We do *not* publish haggadot, biography, poetry, memoirs, or cookbooks." Query. Reviews artwork/photos. Send photocopies.

FICTION Picture books, young readers, middle readers: spirituality. "We are not interested in anything other than spirituality." Query with outline/synopsis and 2 sample chapters; submit complete ms for picture books.

TIPS "We publish books for all faiths and backgrounds that also reflect the Jewish wisdom tradition. Explain in your cover letter why you're submitting your project to us in particular. Make sure you know what we publish."

THE JOHNS HOPKINS UNIVERSITY PRESS

2715 N. Charles St., Baltimore MD 21218. (410)516-6900. **Fax:** (410)516-6968. **Website:** www.press.jhu.edu. Estab. 1878. Publishes hardcover originals and reprints, and trade paperback reprints. **Publishes 140 titles/year. Pays royalty.** Publishes ms 1 year after acceptance. Accepts simultaneous submissions.

NONFICTION Subjects include history, humanities, literary criticism, regional, religion, science. Submit proposal package, outline, 1 sample chapter, CV. Reviews artwork/photos. Send photocopies.

POETRY "One of the largest American university presses, Johns Hopkins publishes primarily scholarly books and journals. We do, however, publish short fiction and poetry in the series Johns Hopkins: Poetry and Fiction, edited by John Irwin."

JOHNSON BOOKS

Imprint of Big Earth Publishing, 3005 Center Green Dr., Suite 225, Boulder CO 80301. (303)443-9766. **Fax:** (303)443-9687. **E-mail:** books@bigearthpublishing.com. **Website:** bigearthpublishing.com/johnson-books. Estab. 1979. Publishes hardcover and paperback originals and reprints. Johnson Books specializes in books on the American West, primarily outdoor, useful titles that will have strong national appeal. **Publishes 20-25 titles/year. 30% of books from first-time authors. 90% from unagented writers. Royalties vary.** Publishes ms 1 year after acceptance. Accepts simultaneous submissions. Responds in 4 months to queries. Book catalog for 9 x 12 SAE with 5 first-class stamps. Guidelines available.

NONFICTION Subjects include history, recreation, regional, science, travel, general nonfiction. "We are primarily interested in books for the informed popular market, though we will consider vividly written scholarly works. Looks for good writing, thorough research, professional presentation, and appropriate style. Marketing suggestions from writers are helpful." Submit outline/synopsis, 3 sample chapters and a author bio.

JOSSEY-BASS

John Wiley & Sons, Inc., One Montgomery St., Suite 1000, San Francisco CA 94104. **Website:** www.wiley.com. Jossey-Bass is an imprint of Wiley, specializing in books and periodicals for thoughtful professionals and researchers in the areas of business and management, leadership, human resource development, education, health, psychology, religion, and the public and nonprofit sectors. **Publishes 250 titles/year. Pays variable royalties. Pays occasional advance.** Publishes ms 1 year after acceptance. Accepts simultaneous submissions. Responds in 2-3 months to queries. Guidelines online.

NONFICTION Subjects include education, psychology, religion. Jossey-Bass publishes first-time and unagented authors. Publishes books on topics of interest to a wide range of readers: business and management, conflict resolution, mediation and negotiation, K-12 education, higher and adult education, healthcare management, psychology/behavioral healthcare, nonprofit and public management, religion, human resources and training. Also publishes 25 periodicals. See guidelines online.

JOURNEYFORTH

Imprint of BJU Press, 1430 Wade Hampton Blvd., Greenville SC 29609. **E-mail:** journeyforth@bjupress.com. **Website:** www.journeyforth.com. **Contact:** Nancy Lohr. Estab. 1974. Publishes paperback originals. JourneyForth Books publishes fiction and nonfiction that reflects a worldview based solidly on the Bible and that encourages Christians to live out their faith. JourneyForth is an imprint of BJU Press. **Publishes 6-8 titles/year. 300+ 30% of books from first-time authors. 80% from unagented writers. Pays royalty. Pays advance.** Publishes book 12-18 months after acceptance. Accepts simultaneous submissions. Responds in 1 month to queries; 3 months to mss. Book catalog available free in SASE or online. Guidelines online—https://www.bjupress.com/books/freelance.php.

NONFICTION Subjects include parenting, religion, spirituality, young adult, Bible studies, Christian living, Christian apologetics. Christian living, Bible studies, church and ministry, church history. "We produce books for the adult Christian market that are from a conservative Christian worldview."

FICTION Subjects include adventure, hi-lo, historical, juvenile, mystery, sports, western, young adult. "Our fiction is for the youth market only and is based on a Christian worldview. Our catalog ranges from first chapter books to YA titles." Does not want picture books, short stories, romance, speculative fiction, poetry, or fiction for the adult market. Submit proposal with synopsis, market analysis of competing works, and first 5 chapters. Will look at simultaneous submissions, but not multiple submissions.

TIPS "Study the publisher's guidelines. We are looking for engaging text and a biblical worldview. Will read hard copy submissions, but prefer e-mail queries/proposals/submissions."

JUDAICA PRESS

123 Ditmas Ave., Brooklyn NY 11218. (718)972-6200. **Fax:** (718)972-6204. **E-mail:** submissions@judaicapress.com. **Website:** www.judaicapress.com. Estab. 1963. Publishes hardcover and trade paperback originals and reprints. "We cater to the Orthodox Jewish market." **Publishes 12 titles/year.** Accepts simultaneous submissions. Responds in 3 months to queries. Book catalog in print and online.

NONFICTION Subjects include religion, prayer, holidays, life cycle. Looking for Orthodox Judaica in all genres. Submit ms with SASE.

JUDSON PRESS

1075 First Ave., King of Prussia PA 19406. (610)768-2127. **Fax:** (610)768-2441. **E-mail:** acquisitions@judsonpress.com. **Website:** www.judsonpress.com. **Contact:** Acquisitions Editor. Estab. 1824. Publishes hardcover and paperback originals. "Our audience is comprised primarily of pastors, leaders, and Christians who seek a more fulfilling personal spiritual life and want to serve God in their churches, communities, and relationships. We have a large African American and multicultural readership. Currently emphasizing Baptist identity and small group resources. Not accepting biography, memoir, children's books, poetry." **Publishes 10-12 titles/year. 500 queries received/year. 50% of books from first-time authors. 85% from unagented writers. Pays royalty or makes outright purchase.** Publishes ms 12-18 months after acceptance. Accepts simultaneous submissions. Responds in 3-6 months to queries. Catalog online. Guidelines online.

NONFICTION Subjects include community, multicultural, parenting, religion, spirituality, womens issues. Adult religious nonfiction of 30,000-80,000 words. Does not want biography, autobiography, memoir. Query by e-mail or mail. Submit annotated outline, sample chapters, CV, competing titles, marketing plan.

TIPS "Writers have the best chance selling us practical books assisting clergy or laypersons in their ministry and personal lives. Our audience consists of Protestant church leaders and members. Be informed about the market's needs and related titles. Be clear about your audience, and be practical in your focus. Books on multicultural issues are very welcome. Also seeking books that respond to real (felt) needs of pastors and churches."

JUST US BOOKS, INC.

P.O. Box 5306, East Orange NJ 07019. (973)672-7701. **Fax:** (973)677-7570. **Website:** justusbooks.com. Estab. 1988. "Just Us Books is the nation's premier independent publisher of Black-interest books for young people. Our books focus primarily on the culture, history, and contemporary experiences of African Americans." Accepts simultaneous submissions. Guidelines online.

IMPRINTS Marimba Books.

NONFICTION Query with synopsis and 3-5 sample pages.

FICTION Subjects include juvenile. Just Us Books is currently accepting queries for chapter books and middle reader titles only. "We are not considering any other works at this time."

RECENT TITLE(S) *The President Looks Like Me*, by Tony Medina; *One Million Men and Me*, by Kelly Starling Lyons, illustrated by Peter Ambush.

TIPS "We are looking for realistic, contemporary characters; stories and interesting plots that introduce both conflict and resolution. We will consider various themes and story-lines, but before an author submits a query we urge them to become familiar with our books."

KALMBACH PUBLISHING CO.

21027 Crossroads Circle, P.O. Box 1612, Waukesha WI 53186. (262)796-8776. **Fax:** (262)798-6468. **Website:** www.kalmbach.com. Estab. 1934. Publishes paperback originals and reprints. **Publishes 40-50 titles/year. 50% of books from first-time authors. 99% from unagented writers. Pays 7% royalty on net receipts. Pays $1,500 advance.** Publishes ms 18 months after acceptance. Accepts simultaneous submissions. Responds in 2 months to queries.

NONFICTION "Focus on beading, wirework, and one-of-a-kind artisan creations for jewelry-making and crafts and in the railfan, model railroading, plastic modeling and toy train collecting/operating hobbies. Kalmbach publishes reference materials and how-to publications for hobbyists, jewelry-makers, and crafters." Query with 2-3 page detailed outline, sample chapter with photos, drawings, and how-to text. Reviews artwork/photos.

TIPS "Our how-to books are highly visual in their presentation. Any author who wants to publish with us must be able to furnish good photographs and rough drawings before we'll consider his or her book."

Ⓐ KANE/MILLER BOOK PUBLISHERS

4901 Morena Blvd., Suite 213, San Diego CA 92117. (858)456-0540. **Fax:** (858)456-9641. **E-mail:** submissions@kanemiller.com. **Website:** www.kanemiller.com. **Contact:** Editorial Department. Estab. 1985. "Kane/Miller Book Publishers is a division of EDC Publishing, specializing in award-winning children's books from around the world. Our books bring the children of the world closer to each other, sharing stories and ideas, while exploring cultural differences and similarities. Although we continue to look for books from other countries, we are now actively seeking works that convey cultures and communities within the US. We are committed to expanding our picture book list and are interested in great stories with engaging characters, especially those with particularly American subjects. When writing about the experiences of a particular community, we will express a preference for stories written from a firsthand experience." Submission guidelines on site. Accepts simultaneous submissions. If interested, responds in 90 days to queries.

NONFICTION Subjects include Americana, history, sports, young adult.

FICTION Subjects include adventure, fantasy, historical, juvenile, multicultural, mystery, picture books. Picture Books: concept, contemporary, health, humor, multicultural. Young Readers: contemporary, multicultural, suspense. Middle Readers: contemporary, humor, multicultural, suspense. "At this time, we are not considering holiday stories (in any age range) or self-published works."

TIPS "We like to think that a child reading a Kane/Miller book will see parallels between his own life and what might be the unfamiliar setting and characters of the story. And that by seeing how a character who is somehow or in some way dissimilar—an outsider—finds a way to fit comfortably into a culture or community or situation while maintaining a healthy sense of self and self-dignity, she might be empowered to do the same."

KAR-BEN PUBLISHING

Lerner Publishing Group, 241 North First St., Minneapolis MN 55401. **E-mail:** editorial@karben.com. **Website:** www.karben.com. **Contact:** Joni Sussman.

Estab. 1974. Publishes hardcover, trade paperback, board books and e-books. Kar-Ben publishes exclusively Jewish-themed children's books. **Publishes 25 titles/year. 800 mss received/year. 20% of books from first-time authors. 70% from unagented writers. Pays 5% royalty on NET sale. Pays $500-2,500 advance.** Most mss published within 2 years. Accepts simultaneous submissions. Only responds if interested. Book catalog online; free upon request. Guidelines online.

NONFICTION Subjects include religion. "In addition to traditional Jewish-themed stories about Jewish holidays, history, folktales and other subjects, we especially seek stories that reflect the rich diversity of the contemporary Jewish community." Picture books, young readers; Jewish history, Israel, Holocaust, folktales, religion, social issues, special needs; must be of Jewish interest. No textbooks, games, or educational materials. Submit completed ms. Reviews artwork separately. Works with 15-20 illustrators/year. Final art must be submitted digitally. Reviews illustration packages from artists. Submit sample of art or link to online portfolio.

FICTION "We seek picture book mss 800-1,000 words on Jewish-themed topics for children." Picture books: Adventure, concept, folktales, history, humor, multicultural, religion, special needs; must be on a Jewish theme. Average word length: picture books–1,000. Recently published titles: *The Count's Hanukkah Countdown*, *Sammy Spider's First Book of Jewish Holidays*, *The Cats of Ben Yehuda Street*. Submit full ms. Picture books only.

TIPS "Authors: Do a literature search to make sure similar title doesn't already exist. Illustrators: Look at our online catalog for a sense of what we like—bright colors and lively composition."

KAYA PRESS

c/o USC ASE, 3620 S. Vermont Ave. KAP 462, Los Angeles CA 90089. (213) 740-2285. **E-mail:** info@kaya.com. **E-mail:** acquisitions@kaya.com. **Website:** www.kaya.com. Estab. 1994. Publishes hardcover originals and trade paperback originals and reprints. Kaya is an independent literary press dedicated to the publication of innovative literature from the Asian Pacific diaspora. Accepts simultaneous submissions. Responds in 6 months to mss. Book catalog available free. Guidelines online.

NONFICTION Subjects include multicultural. Submit proposal package, outline, sample chapters, previous publications, SASE. Reviews artwork/photos. Send photocopies.

FICTION Submit 2-4 sample chapters, clips, SASE.

POETRY Submit complete ms.

TIPS "Audience is people interested in a high standard of literature and who are interested in breaking down easy approaches to multicultural literature."

KENSINGTON PUBLISHING CORP.

119 W. 40th St., New York NY 10018. (212)407-1500. **Fax:** (212)935-0699. **E-mail:** jscognamiglio@kensingtonbooks.com. **Website:** www.kensingtonbooks.com. **Contact:** John Scognamiglio, editorial director, fiction (historical romance, Regency romance, women's contemporary fiction, gay and lesbian fiction and nonfiction, mysteries, suspense, mainstream fiction); Michaela Hamilton, editor-in-chief, Citadel Press (thrillers, mysteries, mainstream fiction, true crime, current events); Selena James, executive editor, Dafina Books (African American fiction and nonfiction, inspirational, young adult, romance); Peter Senftleben, assistant editor (mainstream fiction, women's contemporary fiction, gay and lesbian fiction, mysteries, suspense, thrillers, romantic suspense, paranormal romance). Estab. 1975. Publishes hardcover and trade paperback originals, mass market paperback originals and reprints. "Kensington focuses on profitable niches and uses aggressive marketing techniques to support its books." **Publishes over 500 titles/year. 5,000 queries received/year. 2,000 mss received/year. 10% of books from first-time authors. Pays 6-15% royalty on retail price. Makes outright purchase. Pays $2,000 and up advance.** Publishes ms 9-12 months after acceptance. Accepts simultaneous submissions. Responds in 1 month to queries and proposals; 4 months to mss. Book catalog and guidelines online.

NONFICTION Subjects include Americana, animals, child guidance, contemporary culture, history, hobbies, memoirs, multicultural, philosophy, psychology, recreation, regional, sex, sports, travel, true crime, pop culture. Query.

FICTION Subjects include ethnic, historical, horror, mainstream, multicultural, mystery, occult, romance, suspense, western, thrillers, women's. No science fiction/fantasy, experimental fiction, business texts or children's titles. Query.

TIPS "Agented submissions only, except for submissions to romance lines. For those lines, query with

SASE or submit proposal package including 3 sample chapters, synopsis."

KENT STATE UNIVERSITY PRESS

P.O. Box 5190, 1118 University Library, Kent OH 44242. **Fax:** (330)672-3104. **E-mail:** ksupress@kent.edu. **Website:** www.kentstateuniversitypress.com. **Contact:** Will Underwood, acquiring editor. Estab. 1965. Publishes hardcover and paperback originals and some reprints. "Kent State publishes primarily scholarly works and titles of regional interest. Currently emphasizing US history, US literary criticism." **Publishes 30-35 titles/year. Non-author subsidy publishes 20% of books. Standard minimum book contract on net sales.** Accepts simultaneous submissions. Responds in 4 months to queries. Book catalog available free.

NONFICTION Subjects include history, literary criticism, regional, true crime, literary criticism, material culture, textile/fashion studies, US foreign relations. "Especially interested in scholarly works in history (US and world) and US literary studies of high quality, any titles of regional interest for Ohio, scholarly biographies and general nonfiction. Send a letter of inquiry before submitting mss. Decisions based on in-house readings and 2 by outside scholars in the field of study." Please, no faxes, phone calls, or e-mail submissions.

KIRKBRIDE BIBLE CO., INC.

1102 Deloss St., Indianapolis IN 46203. (800)428-4385. **Fax:** (317)633-1444. **E-mail:** info@kirkbride.com. **Website:** www.kirkbride.com. **Contact:** Paula Haggard, David Gage, Bill Cross. Estab. 1915. Publishes Thompson Chain-Reference Bible hardcover originals and quality leather bindings styles and translations of the Bible. Types of books include reference and religious. Specializes in reference and study material. Accepts simultaneous submissions.

KNOPF

Imprint of Random House, 1745 Broadway, New York NY 10019. **Fax:** (212)940-7390. **Website:** knopfdoubleday.com/imprint/knopf. Estab. 1915. Publishes hardcover and paperback originals. **Publishes 200 titles/year. Royalties vary. Offers advance.** Publishes ms 1 year after acceptance. Accepts simultaneous submissions. Responds in 2-6 months to queries.

NONFICTION Usually only accepts mss submitted by agents. However, writers may submit sample 25-50 pages with SASE.

FICTION Publishes book-length fiction of literary merit by known or unknown writers. Length: 40,000-150,000 words. Usually only accepts mss submitted by agents. However, writers may submit sample 25-50 pages with SASE.

KRAUSE PUBLICATIONS

An Imprint of Penguin Random House LLC. 1745 Broadway, New York NY 10019. (212)782-9000. **Website:** www.penguinrandomhouse.com. Estab. 1952. Publishes hardcover and trade paperback originals. "We are the world's largest hobby and collectibles publisher." **Publishes 20 titles/year. 100 queries received/year. 25% of books from first-time authors. 99% from unagented writers. Pays advance. Photo budget.** Publishes ms 18 months after acceptance. Accepts simultaneous submissions. Responds in 1 month.

NONFICTION Subjects include automotive, entertainment, games, music, pop culture, sports, transportation. Submit proposal package, including outline, TOC, a sample chapter, and letter explaining your project's unique contributions. Reviews artwork/photos. Accepts only digital photography. Send sample photos.

RECENT TITLE(S) *Antique Trader Antiques & Collectibles 2018*; *Pokemon Cards: The Unofficial Ultimate Collector's Guide*, by Ryan Majeskei; *Standard Catalog of World Coins*;*Collecting Rocks, Gems & Minerals*, by Patti Polk.

TIPS Audience consists of serious hobbyists. "Your work should provide a unique contribution to the special interest."

⊘ KREGEL PUBLICATIONS

2450 Oak Industrial Dr. NE, Grand Rapids MI 49505. (616)451-4775. **Fax:** (616)451-9330. **E-mail:** kregelbooks@kregel.com. **Website:** www.kregelpublications.com. Estab. 1949. Publishes hardcover and trade paperback originals and reprints. "Our mission as an evangelical Christian publisher is to provide—with integrity and excellence—trusted, Biblically based resources that challenge and encourage individuals in their Christian lives. Works in theology and Biblical studies should reflect the historic, orthodox Protestant tradition." **Publishes 90 titles/year. 20% of books from first-time authors. 10% from unagented writers. Pays royalty on wholesale price. Pays negotiable advance.** Publishes ms 12-16 months after acceptance. Accepts simultaneous submissions. Responds in 2-3 months. Guidelines online.

IMPRINTS Kregel Publications, Kregel Academic, Kregel Childrens, Kregel Classics.

NONFICTION Subjects include history, religion. "We serve evangelical Christian readers and those in career Christian service." Finds works through The Writer's Edge and Christian Manuscript Submissions ms screening services.

FICTION Subjects include religious, young adult. Fiction should be geared toward the evangelical Christian market. Wants books with fast-paced, contemporary storylines presenting a strong Christian message in an engaging, entertaining style. Finds works through The Writer's Edge and Christian Manuscript Submissions ms screening services.

TIPS "Our audience consists of conservative, evangelical Christians, including pastors and ministry students."

KRIEGER PUBLISHING CO.

1725 Krieger Ln., Malabar FL 32950. (321)724-9542. **Fax:** (321)951-3671. **E-mail:** info@krieger-publishing.com. **Website:** www.krieger-publishing.com. **Contact:** Sharan B. Merriam and Ronald M. Cervero, series editor (adult education); David E. Kyvig, series director (local history); James B. Gardner, series editor (public history). Also publishes in the fields of natural sciences, history and space sciences. Estab. 1969. Publishes hardcover and paperback originals and reprints. "We are a short-run niche publisher providing accurate and well-documented scientific and technical titles for text and reference use, college level and higher." **Publishes 30 titles/year. 30% of books from first-time authors. 100% from unagented writers. Pays royalty on net price.** Publishes ms 9-18 months after acceptance. Accepts simultaneous submissions. Responds in 3 months to queries. Book catalog online.

IMPRINTS Anvil Series; Orbit Series; Public History; Professional Practices in Adult Education and Lifelong Learning Series.

NONFICTION Subjects include agriculture, animals, education, history, horticulture, science, herpetology. Query with SASE. Reviews artwork/photos.

RECENT TITLE(S) *Children of Divorce*, by William Bernet & Don Ash; *Classic Irises and the Men and Women Who Created Them*, by Clarence E. Mahan.

LANGMARC PUBLISHING

P.O. Box 90488, Austin TX 78709-0488. (512)394-0989. **E-mail:** langmarc@booksails.com. **Website:** www.langmarc.com. **Contact:** Lois Qualben. Estab. 1982. Publishes trade paperback originals. **"We are cutting back in accepting new work." 60% of books from first-time authors. 80% from unagented writers. Pays 14% royalty on sales price.** Accepts simultaneous submissions. Responds in one month. Book catalog online. Guidelines online.

NONFICTION Subjects include counseling, creative nonfiction, military, music, parenting, psychology, religion, spirituality. Query with SASE.

LANTANA PUBLISHING

London, United Kingdom. **E-mail:** info@lantanapublishing.com. **E-mail:** submissions@lantanapublishing.com. **Website:** www.lantanapublishing.com. Estab. 2014. Lantana Publishing is a young, independent publishing house producing inclusive picture books for children. "Our mission is to publish outstanding writing for young readers by giving new and aspiring BAME authors and illustrators a platform to publish in the UK and by working with much-loved authors and illustrators from around the world. Lantana's award-winning titles have so far received high praise, described as 'dazzling', 'delectable', 'enchanting' and 'exquisite' by bloggers and reviewers. They have been nominated for a Kate Greenaway Medal (three times), received starred Kirkus reviews (three times), been shortlisted for the Teach Early Years Awards, the North Somerset Teachers' Book Awards, and the Sheffield Children's Books Awards, and won the Children's Africana Best Book Award. Lantana's founder, Alice Curry, is the recipient of the 2017 Kim Scott Walwyn Prize for women in publishing." **Pays royalty. Pays advance.** Accepts simultaneous submissions. Responds in 6 weeks. Guidelines online.

NONFICTION "We accept some nonfiction content for the 7-11 range if it is international in scope."

FICTION Subjects include picture books. "We primarily publish picture books for 4-8 year-olds with text no longer than 500 words (and we prefer 200-400 words). We love writing that is contemporary and fun. We particularly like stories with modern-day settings in the UK or around the world, especially if they feature BAME families, and stories that lend themselves to great illustration."

POETRY "We are interested in receiving poetry submissions for young readers."

LEAPFROG PRESS

Box 505, Fredonia NY 14063. **E-mail:** leapfrog@leapfrogpress.com. **Website:** www.leapfrogpress.com. **Contact:** Nathan Carter, acquisitions editor; Lisa Graziano, publicity. Estab. 1996. **Publishes 4-6 titles/year. 2,000 submissions received/year. 50% of books from first-time authors. 75% from unagented writers. Pays 10% royalty on net receipts. Average advance: negotiable.** Publishes ms approximately 1 year after acceptance. Accepts simultaneous submissions. Response time varies. One week to several months. Guidelines online. Submissions through Submittable only.

NONFICTION Subjects include creative nonfiction.

FICTION Subjects include adventure, contemporary, ethnic, experimental, feminist, gay, historical, juvenile, lesbian, literary, mainstream, military, multicultural, mystery, poetry, regional, science fiction, short story collections, suspense, war, young adult. "We search for beautifully written literary titles and market them aggressively to national trade and library accounts. We also sell film, translation, foreign, and book club rights." Publishes paperback originals. Books: acid-free paper; sewn binding. Print runs range from about 1,000 to 4,000. Distributes titles through Consortium Book Sales and Distribution, St. Paul, MN. Promotes titles through all national review media, bookstore readings, author tours, website, radio shows, chain store promotions, advertisements, book fairs. "Genres often blur; look for good writing. We are most interested in works that are quirky, that fall outside of any known genre,and of course well written and finely crafted. We are most interested in literary fiction." Genre romance, fantasy, and Western. Religious. Occult. Picture books. Query with several chapters or stories through Submittable.

RECENT TITLE(S) *The Quality of Mercy*, by Katayoun Medhat; *And Yet They Were Happy*, by Helen Phillips; *Trip Wires by Sandra Hunter, Kiska*, by John Smelcer; *The Subway Stops at Bryant Park*, by N. West Moss; *Greenhorns*, by Richard Slotkin (fall 2018); *Among the Dead and Dreaming*, by Samuel Ligon; *The Solace of Monsters*, by Laurie Blauner. See website for other titles.

TIPS "We like anything that is superbly written and genuinely original. We like the idiosyncratic and the peculiar. We rarely publish nonfiction. Send only your best work, and send only completed work that is ready. That means the completed ms has already been through extensive editing and is ready to be judged. We consider submissions from both previously published and unpublished writers, and both agented and unagented submissions. We do not accept submissions through postal mail and cannot return physical letters or manuscripts."

LEE & LOW BOOKS

95 Madison Ave., #1205, New York NY 10016. (212)779-4400. **E-mail:** general@leeandlow.com. **Website:** www.leeandlow.com. Estab. 1991. Publishes hardcover originals and trade paperback reprints. "Our goals are to meet a growing need for books that address children of color, and to present literature that all children can identify with. We only consider multicultural children's books. Sponsors a yearly New Voices Award for first-time picture book authors of color. Contest rules online at website or for SASE." **Publishes 12-14 titles/year. Receives 100 queries/year; 1,200 mss/year. 20% of books from first-time authors. 50% from unagented writers. Pays net royalty. Pays authors advances against royalty. Pays illustrators advance against royalty. Photographers paid advance against royalty.** Publishes book 2 years after acceptance. Responds in 6 months to mss if interested. Book catalog available online. Guidelines available online or by written request with SASE.

NONFICTION Picture books: concept. Picture books, middle readers: biography, history, multicultural, science and sports. Average word length: picture books-1,500-3,000. Submit complete ms. Reviews artwork/photos only if writer is also a professional illustrator or photographer. Send photocopies and nonreturnable art samples only.

FICTION Picture books, young readers: anthology, contemporary, history, multicultural, poetry. Picture book, middle reader: contemporary, history, multicultural, nature/environment, poetry, sports. Average word length: picture books—1,000-1,500 words. "We do not publish folklore or animal stories." Submit complete ms.

POETRY Submit complete ms.

RECENT TITLE(S) *Parrots Over Puerto Rico*, by Cindy Trumbore and Susan L. Roth; *The Hula-Hoopin' Queen*, by Thelma Lynne Godin (illustrated picture book); *Little Melba and Her Big Trombone*, by Katheryn Russell-Brown (illustrated picture book).

TIPS "Check our website to see the kinds of books we publish. Do not send mss that don't fit our mission."

LEHIGH UNIVERSITY PRESS

B040 Christmas-Saucon Hall, 14 E. Packer Ave., Bethlehem PA 18015. (610)758-3933. **Fax:** (610)758-6331. **E-mail:** inlup@lehigh.edu. **Website:** https://lupress.cas2.lehigh.edu. **Contact:** Kate Crassons. Estab. 1985. Publishes nonfiction hardcover originals. Currently emphasizing works on 18th-century studies, history of technology, literary criticism, and topics involving Asian Studies. **Publishes 10 titles/year. 90-100 queries; 50-60 mss received/year. 70% of books from first-time authors. 100% from unagented writers. Pays royalty.** Publishes ms 18 months after acceptance. Responds in 3 months to queries. Book catalog available free. Guidelines online.

NONFICTION Subjects include Americana, history, science. Lehigh University Press is a conduit for nonfiction works of scholarly interest to the academic community. Submit proposal package with cover letter, several sample chapters, current CV and SASE.

HAL LEONARD BOOKS

Hal Leonard Publishing Group, 33 Plymouth St., Suite 302, Montclair NJ 07042. (973)337-5034. **Website:** www.halleonardbooks.com. **Contact:** John Cerullo, publisher. **Publishes 30 titles/year.** Accepts simultaneous submissions.

NONFICTION Subjects include music. Query with SASE.

⊘ LES FIGUES PRESS

P.O. Box 7736, Los Angeles CA 90007. **E-mail:** info@lesfigues.com. **Website:** www.lesfigues.com. **Contact:** Teresa Carmody, director. Estab. 2005. Les Figues Press is an independent, nonprofit publisher of poetry, prose, visual art, conceptual writing, and translation. With amission is to create aesthetic conversations between readers, writers, and artists, Les Figues Press favors projects which push the boundaries of genre, form, and general acceptability. "We are currently closed to all submissions." Accepts simultaneous submissions.

LETHE PRESS

118 Heritage Ave., Maple Shade NJ 8052. (609)410-7391. **Website:** www.lethepressbooks.com. Estab. 2001. "Welcomes submissions from authors of any sexual or gender identity." Accepts simultaneous submissions. Guidelines online.

NONFICTION Query via e-mail.

FICTION Subjects include gay, lesbian, occult, science fiction. "Named after the Greek river of memory and forgetfulness (and pronounced Lee-Thee), Lethe Press is a small press devoted to ideas that are often neglected or forgotten by mainstream, profit-oriented publishers." Distributes/promotes titles. Lethe Books are distributed by Ingram Publications and Bookazine, and are available at all major bookstores, as well as the major online retailers. Query via e-mail.

POETRY "Lethe Press is a small press seeking gay and lesbian themed poetry collections." Lethe Books are distributed by Ingram Publications and Bookazine, and are available at all major bookstores, as well as the major online retailers. Query with 7-10 poems, list of publications.

ARTHUR A. LEVINE BOOKS

Scholastic, Inc., 557 Broadway, New York NY 10012. (212)343-4436. **Fax:** (212)343-6143. **Website:** www.arthuralevinebooks.com. Estab. 1996. Publishes hardcover, paperback, and e-book editions. Publishes a book 18 months after acceptance. Accepts simultaneous submissions. Responds in 1 month to queries; 5 months to mss. Picture Books: Query letter and full text of pb. Novels: Send Query letter, first 2 chapters and synopsis. Other: Query letter, 10-page sample and synopsis/proposal.

NONFICTION Please follow submission guidelines. Works with 8 illustrators/year. Will review ms/illustration packages from artists. Query first. Illustrations only: Send postcard sample with tearsheets. Samples not returned.

FICTION Subjects include juvenile, picture books, young adult. "Arthur A. Levine is looking for distinctive literature, for children and young adults, for whatever's extraordinary." Averages 18-20 total titles/year. Query.

LIGUORI PUBLICATIONS

One Liguori Dr., Liguori MO 63057. (636)464-2500. **Fax:** (636)464-8449. **Website:** www.liguori.org. Estab. 1947. Publishes paperback originals and reprints under the Ligouri and Libros Ligouri imprints. Liguori Publications, faithful to the charism of St. Alphonsus, is an apostolate within the mission of the Denver Province. Its mission, a collaborative effort of Redemptorists and laity, is to spread the gospel of Jesus Christ primarily through the print and electronic media. It shares in the Redemptorist priority of giving special attention to the poor and the most abandoned. Currently emphasizing practical spirituality, prayers and devotions, how-to spirituality. **Publishes 20-25 titles/year. Pays royalty. Makes outright purchase. Pays varied advance.** Publishes ms 2 years after acceptance. Responds in 2-3 months. Guidelines online.

NONFICTION Subjects include religion, spirituality. Mostly adult audience; limited children/juvenile. Mss with Catholic sensibility. Query with SASE. Submit outline, 1 sample chapter.

TIPS "As a rule, Liguori Publications does not accept unsolicited fiction, poetry, art books, biography, autobiography, private revelations."

LILLENAS PUBLISHING CO.

Imprint of Lillenas Drama Resources, P.O. Box 419527, Kansas City MO 64141. (800)877-0700. **Fax:** (816)412-8390. **E-mail:** drama@lillenas.com. **Website:** www.lillenasdrama.com. Publishes mass market paperback and electronic originals. "We purchase only original, previously unpublished materials. Also, we require that all scripts be performed at least once before it is submitted for consideration. We do not accept scripts that are sent via fax or e-mail. Direct all manuscripts to the Drama Resources Editor." **Publishes 50+ titles/year. Pays royalty on net price. Makes outright purchase.** Responds in 4-6 months to material. Guidelines online.

NONFICTION No musicals. Query with SASE. Submit complete ms.

FICTION "Looking for sketch and monologue collections for all ages – adults, children and youth. For these collections, we request 12 - 15 scripts to be submitted at one time. Unique treatments of spiritual themes, relevant issues and biblical messages are of interest. Contemporary full-length and one-act plays that have conflict, characterization, and a spiritual context that is neither a sermon nor an apologetic for youth and adults. We also need wholesome so-called secular full-length scripts for dinner theatres and schools." No musicals.

TIPS "We never receive too many manuscripts."

LINDEN PUBLISHING, INC.

2006 S. Mary, Fresno CA 93721. (559)233-6633. **Fax:** (559)233-6933. **E-mail:** richard@lindenpub.com. **Website:** www.lindenpub.com; www.quilldriverbooks.com. **Contact:** Richard Sorsky, president; Kent Sorsky, vice president. Estab. 1976. Publishes hardcover and trade paperback originals; hardcover and trade paperback reprints. **Publishes 10-12 titles/year. 100+ queries; 25+ mss received/year. 40% of books from first-time authors. 50% from unagented writers. Pays 7½ -12% royalty on wholesale price. Pays $500-6,000 advance.** Publishes ms 18 months after acceptance. Responds in 1 month. Book catalog online. Guidelines available via e-mail.

IMPRINTS Quill Driver Books, Craven Street Books. Pace Press.

NONFICTION Subjects include crafts, health, history, hobbies, regional, true crime, Regional California history. Submit proposal package, outline, 3 sample chapters, bio. Reviews artwork/photos. Send electronic files, if available.

FICTION Subjects include adventure, fantasy, gothic, historical, horror, mystery, occult, science fiction, suspense.

RECENT TITLE(S) *Passion Projects for Smart People*; *The Edge*; *Handmade*; *400 Things Cops Know*; *Harvest Your Own Lumber*; *Sitting Kills.*

LISTEN & LIVE AUDIO

1700 Manhattan Ave., Union City NJ 07087. (201)558-9000. **Website:** www.listenandlive.com. **Contact:** Alfred C. Martino, president. Independent audiobook publisher. "We also license audiobooks for the download market. We specialize in the following genres: fiction, mystery, nonfiction, self-help, business, children's, and teen." **Publishes 10+ titles/year.** Accepts simultaneous submissions. Catalog online.

RECENT TITLE(S) *Unleashed*, by David Rosenfelt (mystery audio); *Boston Jacky*, by LA Meyer (teen audio); *How to Talk to Anyone*, by Leil Lowndes (self-help audio).

Ⓐ⊘ LITTLE, BROWN AND CO. ADULT TRADE BOOKS

1290 Avenue of the Americas, New York NY 10104. **Website:** www.littlebrown.com. Estab. 1837. Publishes hardcover originals and paperback originals and reprints. "The general editorial philosophy for all divisions continues to be broad and flexible, with high quality and the promise of commercial success as always the first considerations." **Publishes 100 titles/year. Pays royalty. Offer advance.** Accepts simultaneous submissions. Guidelines online.

NONFICTION *Agented submissions only.*

FICTION Subjects include contemporary, literary, mainstream. *Agented submissions only.*

Ⓐ⊘ LITTLE, BROWN BOOKS FOR YOUNG READERS

Hachette Book Group USA, 1290 Avenue of the Americas, New York NY 10104. (212)364-1100. **Fax:** (212)364-0925. **Website:** littlebrown.com. Estab. 1837. "Little, Brown and Co. Children's Publishing publishes all formats including board books, picture books, middle grade fiction, and nonfiction YA titles. We are looking for strong writing and presentation, but no predetermined topics." *Only interested in solicited agented material.* **Publishes 100-150 titles/year. Pays authors royalties based on retail price. Pays illustrators and photographers by the project or royalty based on retail price. Sends galleys to authors; dummies to illustrators. Pays negotiable advance.** Publishes ms 2 years after acceptance. Accepts simultaneous submissions. Responds in 1-2 months.

NONFICTION Subjects include animals, ethnic, history, hobbies, recreation, science, sports. "Writers should avoid looking for the 'issue' they think publishers want to see, choosing instead topics they know best and are most enthusiastic about/inspired by." *Agented submissions only.*

FICTION Subjects include adventure, fantasy, feminist, historical, humor, mystery, science fiction, suspense, chick lit, multicultural. Average word length: picture books—1,000; young readers—6,000; middle readers—15,000- 50,000; young adults—50,000 and up. *Agented submissions only.*

TIPS "In order to break into the field, authors and illustrators should research their competition and try to come up with something outstandingly different."

LITTLE PICKLE PRESS

3701 Sacramento St., #494, San Francisco CA 94118. (415)340-3344. **Fax:** (415)366-1520. **E-mail:** info@march4thinc.com. **Website:** www.littlepicklepress.com. Little Pickle Press is a 21st Century publisher dedicated to helping parents and educators cultivate conscious, responsible little people by stimulating explorations of the meaningful topics of their generation through a variety of media, technologies, and techniques. Submit through submission link on site. Includes YA imprint Relish Media. Accepts simultaneous submissions. Uses Author.me for submissions for Little Pickle and YA imprint Relish Media. Guidelines available on site.

RECENT TITLE(S) *A Bird on Water Street*, by Elizabeth O. Dulemba; *Ripple's Effect*, by Amy Blankson, illustrated by Shawn Achor.

TIPS "We have lots of manuscripts to consider, so it will take up to 8 weeks before we get back to you."

Ⓐ⊘ LITTLE SIMON

Imprint of Simon & Schuster, 1230 Avenue of the Americas, New York NY 10020. (212)698-1295. **Fax:** (212)698-2794. **Website:** www.simonandschuster.com/kids. Publishes novelty and branded books only. "Our goal is to provide fresh material in an innovative format for preschool to age 8. Our books are often, if not exclusively, format driven." **Offers advance and royalties.** Accepts simultaneous submissions.

NONFICTION "We publish very few nonfiction titles." No picture books. *Currently not accepting unsolicited mss.*

FICTION Novelty books include many things that do not fit in the traditional hardcover or paperback format, such as pop-up, board book, scratch and sniff, glow in the dark, lift the flap, etc. Children's/juvenile. No picture books. Large part of the list is holiday-themed. *Currently not accepting unsolicited mss.*

LIVINGSTON PRESS

University of West Alabama, 100 N. Washington St., Station 22, University of West Alabama, Livingston AL 35470. **Fax:** (205)652-3717. **E-mail:** jwt@uwa.edu. **Website:** https://livingstonpress.uwa.edu. **Contact:** Joe Taylor, director. Estab. 1974. Publishes hardcover and trade paperback originals, plus Kindle. "Livingston Press, as do all literary presses, looks for authorial excellence in style. Currently emphasizing novels." Reading year around. We do recommend simultaneous submissions, since we can publish only eight or so titles per year. **Publishes 7-10 titles/year. 50% of books from first-time authors. 100% from unagented writers. Pays 80 contributor's copies, after sales of 1,000, standard royalty.** Publishes ms 18 months after acceptance. Accepts simultaneous submissions. Responds in 4 months to queries; 6-12 months to mss. Book catalog online. Guidelines online.

IMPRINTS Swallow's Tale Press.

FICTION Subjects include contemporary, experimental, literary, off-beat or Southern. "We are interested in form and, of course, style." No genre or children's fiction, please.

RECENT TITLE(S) *Pretend I Am Someone You Like*, by Shome Dasgupta; *The Land of Grace*, by Mike Burrell.

TIPS "Our readers are interested in literature, often quirky literature that emphasizes form and style. Please visit our website for current needs."

LLEWELLYN PUBLICATIONS

Imprint of Llewellyn Worldwide, Ltd., 2143 Wooddale Dr., Woodbury MN 55125. (651)291-1970. **Fax:** (651)291-1908. **E-mail:** submissions@llewellyn.com. **Website:** www.llewellyn.com. Estab. 1901. Publishes trade and mass market paperback originals. "Llewellyn publishes New Age fiction and nonfiction exploring new worlds of mind and spirit. Currently emphasizing astrology, alternative health and healing, tarot. De-emphasizing fiction, channeling." **Publishes 100+ titles/year. 30% of books from first-time authors. 50% from unagented writers. Pays 10% royalty on wholesale or retail price.** Accepts simultaneous submissions. Responds in 3 months to queries. Book catalog online.

NONFICTION Subjects include New Age, psychology. Submit outline, sample chapters. Reviews artwork/photos.

LONELY PLANET PUBLICATIONS

124 Linden St., Oakland CA 94607. (510)250-6400. **Fax:** (510)893-8572. **Website:** www.lonelyplanet.com. Estab. 1973. Publishes trade paperback originals. "Lonely Planet publishes travel guides, atlases, travel literature, phrasebooks, condensed pocket guides, diving and snorkeling guides." **Work-for-hire: on contract, 1/3 on submission, 1/3 on approval. Pays advance.** Accepts simultaneous submissions. Responds in 3 months to queries. Book catalog online. Guidelines online.

NONFICTION Subjects include travel. "We only work with contract writers on book ideas that we originate. We do not accept original proposals. Request our writer's guidelines. Send resume and clips of travel writing." Query with SASE.

LOOSE ID

P.O. Box 806, San Francisco CA 94104. **E-mail:** submissions@loose-id.com. **Website:** www.loose-id.com. **Contact:** Treva Harte, editor-in-chief. Estab. 2004. "*Loose Id* is love unleashed. We're taking romance to the edge." Publishes e-books and some print books. Distributes/promotes titles. "The company promotes itself through web and print advertising wherever readers of erotic romance may be found, creating a recognizable brand identity as the place to let your id run free and the people who unleash your fantasies. It is currently pursuing licensing agreements for foreign translations, and has a print program of 2 to 5 titles per month." **Pays e-book royalties of 40%.** Publishes ms within 1 year after acceptance. Accepts simultaneous submissions. Responds to queries in 1 month. Guidelines online.

"Loose Id is actively acquiring stories from both aspiring and established authors."

FICTION Subjects include erotica, romance. Wants nontraditional erotic romance stories, including gay, lesbian, heroes and heroines, multi-culturalism, cross-genre, fantasy, and science fiction, straight contemporary or historical romances. Query with outline/synopsis and 3 sample chapters. Accepts queries by e-mail. Include estimated word count, list of publishing credits, and why your submission is love unleashed. "Before submitting a query or proposal, please read the guidelines on our website. Please don't hesitate to contact us by e-mail for any information you don't see there."

LOST HORSE PRESS

105 Lost Horse Lane, Sandpoint ID 83864, US. (208)255-4410. **E-mail:** losthorsepress@mindspring.com. **Website:** www.losthorsepress.org. **Contact:** Christine Holbert, publisher. Estab. 1998. Publishes hardcover and paperback poetry titles. Established in 1998, Lost Horse Press—a nonprofit independent press—publishes poetry titles by emerging as well as established poets, and makes available other fine contemporary literature through cultural, educational and publishing programs and activities. Lost Horse Press is dedicated to works—often ignored by conglomerate publishers—which are so much in danger of vanishing into obscurity in what has become the age of chain stores and mass appeal food, movies, art and books. Distributed by University of Washington Press. "*Does not accept unsolicited mss.* However, we welcome submissions for the Idaho Prize for Poetry, a national competition offering $1,000 prize money plus publication for a book-length ms. Please check the submission guidelines for the Idaho Prize for Poetry on our website." **Publishes 4-12 titles/year.** *500-600* **50% of books from first-time authors. 140% from unagented writers. 10% royalties Occasion-**

ally pays advance. Publishes ms 3-12 months after acceptance. Accepts simultaneous submissions. Book catalog may be viewed online at www.losthorsepress.org, plus the University of Washington Press, our distributor, offers both online and print catalogs. Please check the Lost Horse Press website or the Submittable.com website for Submission Guidelines.

FICTION Subjects include literary, poetry, poetry in translation.

POETRY Does not want language-based, rhyming, cowboy. Submit poetry via Submittable.com: The Idaho Prize for Poetry

RECENT TITLE(S) *Habitation: Collected Poems*, by Sam Hamill; *Whelm*, by dawn lonsinger; *Detroit as Barn*, by Crystal Williams.

LOYOLA PRESS

3441 N. Ashland Ave., Chicago IL 60657. (773)281-1818. **Fax:** (773)281-0152. **E-mail:** durepos@loyolapress.com. **Website:** www.loyolapress.org. **Contact:** Joseph Durepos, acquisitions editor. Estab. 1912. Publishes hardcover and trade paperback. **Publishes 20-30 titles/year. 500 queries received/year. Pays standard royalties. Offers reasonable advance.** Accepts simultaneous submissions. Book catalog online. Guidelines online.

NONFICTION Subjects include memoirs, religion, spirituality, inspirational, prayer, Catholic life, parish and adult faith formation resources with a special focus on Ignatian spirituality and Jesuit history. E-mail query, or snail mail query with SASE.

RECENT TITLE(S) *The Church of Mercy*, by Pope Francis; *Mercy in the City*, by Kerry Weber; *Sacred Space*, by the Irish Jesuits; *The Ignatian Book of Days*, by Jim Manney.

TIPS "Check our submission guidelines."

LRP PUBLICATIONS, INC.

360 Hiatt Dr., Palm Beach Gardens FL 33418. **Website:** www.lrp.com. Estab. 1977. Publishes hardcover and trade paperback originals. "LRP publishes two industry-leading magazines, *Human Resource Executive*® and *Risk & Insurance*®, as well as hundreds of newsletters, books, videos and case reporters in the fields of: human resources, federal employment, workers' compensation, public employment law, disability, bankruptcy, education administration and law." **Pays royalty.** Book catalog free. Guidelines free.

NONFICTION Subjects include education. Submit proposal package, outline.

LSU PRESS

338 Johnston Hall, Baton Rouge LA 70803. (225)578-6294. **Website:** lsupress.org. Estab. 1935. LSU Press has established itself as one of the nation's outstanding scholarly presses and garners national and international accolades, including 4 Pulitzer Prizes. Accepts simultaneous submissions. Responds in 4-6 months. Catalog online. Guidelines online.

POETRY Poetry proposals should include a cover letter, 4-5 sample pages from the ms, and a current resume.

RECENT TITLE(S) *Get Up, Please*, by David Kirby; *Black Aperture*, by Matt Rasmussen.

⊘ LUNA BISONTE PRODS

137 Leland Ave., Columbus OH 43214-7505. **E-mail:** bennettjohnm@gmail.com. **Website:** www.johnmbennett.net. **Contact:** John M. Bennett, editor/publisher. Estab. 1967. Avant-garde literature and poetry only. Please look at our titles before querying. **Publishes 5 titles/year. Pays copy or copies of book; further copies at cost. Does not pay advance.** Not considering unsolicited submissions at this time.

NONFICTION Subjects include language, literature, poetry, visual poetry.

FICTION Subjects include poetry.

POETRY "Interested in avant-garde and highly experimental work only." Has published poetry by Jim Leftwich, Sheila E. Murphy, Al Ackerman, Richard Kostelanetz, Carla Bertola, Olchar Lindsann, and many others. See http://www.lulu.com/spotlight/lunabisonteprods Query first, with a few sample poems and cover letter with brief bio and publication credits. "Keep it brief. Chapbook publishing usually depends on grants or other subsidies, and is usually by solicitation. **Will also consider subsidy arrangements on negotiable terms.**" A sampling of various Luna Bisonte Prods products is available for $20.

⊘ THE LYONS PRESS

The Globe Pequot Press, Inc., Box 480, 246 Goose Ln., Guilford CT 6437. (203)458-4500. **Fax:** (203)458-4668. **Website:** www.lyonspress.com. Estab. 1984 (Lyons & Burford), 1997 (The Lyons Press). Publishes hardcover and trade paperback originals and reprints. The Lyons Press publishes practical and literary books, chiefly centered on outdoor subjects—natural history, all sports, gardening, horses, fishing, hunting, survival, self-reliant living, plus cooking, memoir, bio, nonfiction. "At this time, we are not accepting unsolicited mss or proposals." Check back for updates. **Pays $3,000-25,000 advance.** Book catalog online. Guidelines online.

NONFICTION Subjects include agriculture, Americana, animals, history, recreation, sports, adventure, fitness, the sea, woodworking.

MAGENTA FOUNDATION

151 Winchester St., Toronto ON M4X 1B5, Canada. **E-mail:** info@magentafoundation.org. **Website:** www.magentafoundation.org. **Contact:** Submissions. Estab. 2004. "Established in 2004, The Magenta Foundation is Canada's pioneering non-profit, charitable arts publishing house. Magenta was created to organize promotional opportunities for artists, in an international context, through circulated exhibitions and publications. Projects mounted by Magenta are supported by credible international media coverage and critical reviews in all mainstream-media formats (radio, television and print). Magenta works with respected individuals and international organizations to help increase recognition for artists while uniting the global photography community." Accepts simultaneous submissions.

MAGINATION PRESS

750 First St. NE, Washington DC 20002. (202)336-5618. **Fax:** (202)336-5624. **E-mail:** magination@apa.org. **Website:** www.apa.org. Estab. 1988. Magination Press is an imprint of the American Psychological Association. "We publish books dealing with the psycho/therapeutic resolution of children's problems and psychological issues with a strong self-help component." Submit complete ms. Full guidelines available on site. Materials returned only with SASE. **Publishes 12 titles/year. 75% of books from first-time authors.** Publishes a book 18-24 months after acceptance. Accepts simultaneous submissions. Responds to queries in 1-2 months; mss in 2-6 months.

NONFICTION All levels: psychological and social issues, self-help, health, multicultural, special needs.

FICTION All levels: psychological and social issues, self-help, health, parenting concerns and, special needs. Picture books, middle school readers.

MANDALA PUBLISHING

Mandala Publishing and Earth Aware Editions, 800 A St., San Rafael CA 94901. **E-mail:** info@mandalapublishing.com. **Website:** www.mandalaeartheditions.com. Estab. 1989. Publishes hardcover, trade paperback, and electronic originals. "In the traditions of the East, wisdom, truth, and beauty go hand in- hand. This is reflected in the great arts, music, yoga, and philosophy of India. Mandala Publishing strives to bring to its readers authentic and accessible renderings of thousands of years of wisdom and philosophy from this unique culture-timeless treasures that are our inspirations and guides. At Mandala, we believe that the arts, health, ecology, and spirituality of the great Vedic traditions are as relevant today as they were in sacred India thousands of years ago. As a distinguished publisher in the world of Vedic literature, lifestyle, and interests today, Mandala strives to provide accessible and meaningful works for the modern reader." **Publishes 12 titles/year. 200 queries received/year. 100 mss received/year. 40% of books from first-time authors. 100% from unagented writers. Pays 3-15% royalty on retail price.** Publishes ms 8 months after acceptance. Accepts simultaneous submissions. Responds in 6 months. Book catalog online.

NONFICTION Subjects include education, philosophy, photography, religion, spirituality. Query with SASE. Reviews artwork/photos. Send photocopies and thumbnails.

FICTION Subjects include juvenile, religious, spiritual. Query with SASE.

RECENT TITLE(S) *Prince of Dharma*, by Ranchor Prinie (illustrated biography); *The Gita Deck*, by Mandala Publishing (inspirational card deck).

MARINER BOOKS

222 Berkeley St., Boston MA 2116. (617)351-5000. **Website:** www.hmco.com. Estab. 1997. Accepts simultaneous submissions.

Mariner Books' *Interpreter of Maladies*, by debut author Jhumpa Lahiri, won the 2000 Pulitzer Prize for fiction and *The Caprices*, by Sabina Murray, received the 2003 PEN/Faulkner Award. Mariner Books' *Interpreter of Maladies*, by debut author Jhumpa Lahiri, won the 2000 Pulitzer Prize for fiction and *The Caprices*, by Sabina Murray, received the 2003 PEN/Faulkner Award.

POETRY Has published poetry by Thomas Lux, Linda Gregerson, and Keith Leonard. Agented submissions only.

MARVEL COMICS

135 W. 50th St., 7th Floor, New York NY 10020. **Website:** www.marvel.com. Publishes hardcover originals and reprints, trade paperback reprints, mass market comic book originals, electronic reprints. **Pays on a per page work for hire basis or creator-owned which is then contracted. Pays negotiable advance.** Responds in 3-5 weeks to queries. Guidelines online.

FICTION Subjects include adventure, comic books, fantasy, horror, humor, science fiction, young adult. Our shared universe needs new heroes and villains; books for younger readers and teens needed. Submit inquiry letter, idea submission form (download from website), SASE.

MASTER BOOKS

P.O. Box 726, Green Forest AR 72638. **E-mail:** submissions@newleafpress.net. **Website:** www.masterbooks.com. **Contact:** Craig Froman, acquisitions editor. Estab. 1975. Publishes 3 middle readers/year; 2 young adult nonfiction titles/year; 10 homeschool curriculum titles; 20 adult trade books/year. **500 5% of books from first-time authors. 99% from unagented writers. Pays authors royalty of 3-15% based on wholesale price.** Publishes book 1 year after acceptance. Accepts simultaneous submissions. We are no longer able to respond to every query. If you have not heard from us within 90 days, it means we are unable to partner with you on that particular project. Book catalog available upon request. Guidelines online.

NONFICTION Subjects include archeology, religion, science, womens issues, world affairs. Picture books: activity books, animal, nature/environment, creation. Young readers, middle readers, young adults: activity books, animal, biography Christian, nature/environment, science, creation. Submission guidelines on website. http://www.nlpg.com/submissions

TIPS "All of our children's books are creation-based, including topics from the Book of Genesis. We look also for home school educational material as we are expanding our home school curriculum resources."

MAVEN HOUSE PRESS

4 Snead Ct., Palmyra VA 22963. (610)883-7988. **E-mail:** jim@mavenhousepress.com. **Website:** www.mavenhousepress.com. **Contact:** Jim Pennypacker, publisher. Estab. 2012. Publishes trade paperback, and electronic originals. Maven House is an independent publisher of books that inspire people to use business as a force for good, books that challenge conventional thinking, introduce new ideas, offer practical advice, and illuminate paths to greatness. **Publishes 4 titles/year. 50% of books from first-time authors. 50% from unagented writers. Pays 10-50% royalty based on wholesale price. Does not pay advance.** Publishes ms 12 months after acceptance. Accepts simultaneous submissions. If interested in publishing the manuscript, we respond within 1 month.

NONFICTION Subjects include business, career guidance, communications, economics, environment, finance, sustainable development, corporate social responsibility, social entrepreneurship, servant leadership, climate change, triple bottom line, green business, diversity and inclusion, transparency, social impact, workplace culture, corporate social responsibility, social entrepreneurship, climate change. Submit proposal package including: outline, 1-2 sample chapters. See submission form online.

⊘ MAVERICK DUCK PRESS

E-mail: maverickduckpress@yahoo.com. **Website:** www.maverickduckpress.com. **Contact:** Kendall A. Bell, editor. Assistant Editor: Brielle Kelton. Estab. 2005. Maverick Duck Press is a "publisher of chapbooks from undiscovered talent. We are looking for fresh and powerful work that shows a sense of innovation or a new take on passion or emotion. Previous publication in print or online journals could increase your chances of us accepting your manuscript." Does not want "unedited work." **Pays 20 author's copies.**

POETRY Send ms in Microsoft Word format with a cover letter with brief bio and publication credits. Chapbook mss may include previously published poems. "Previous publication is always a plus, as we may be more familiar with your work. Chapbook mss should have 16-24 poems, but no more than 24 poems."

RECENT TITLE(S) *Harlem Mestiza*, by Christine Stoddard; *Until The Light*, by Kendall A. Bell; *How The Blessed Travel*, by Devon Balwit; *Cliche Buddhist White Girl*, by Schuyler Peck; *Pink Plastic House*, by Kristin Garth.

⊘ MCBOOKS PRESS

ID Booth Building, 520 N. Meadow St., Ithaca NY 14850. (607)272-2114. **E-mail:** mcbooks@mcbooks.com. **E-mail:** alex@mcbooks.com. **Website:** www.mcbooks.com. **Contact:** Alexander G. Skutt, publisher. Art Director & Associate Publisher: Panda Musgrove. Estab. 1979. Publishes trade paperback and hardcover originals and reprints. McBooks Press has been publishing books independently for over 30 years in Ithaca, New York. McBooks' extensive list of publications features works of historical fiction—including naval and military fiction in series. We continue to seek excellent historical naval adventures that are suitable for publication in series. In the past, we have also published nonfiction, including books on boxing, food and health, and the Finger Lakes Region of New York State. **Publishes 5 titles/year. 15% of books from first-time authors. 30% from unagented writers. Pays a percentage of cover price for physical books plus a percentage of net income for e-books. Pays advance.** Publishes ms over 1 year after acceptance. Accepts simultaneous submissions. Responds in 2 months. Guidelines online.

"Currently not accepting submissions or queries for fiction or nonfiction." The only exceptions that we would look at are: 1) well-written nautical historical fiction that could grow into a series 2) great books about the Finger Lakes or adjacent regions of Upstate New York.

NONFICTION Subjects include history, marine subjects.

FICTION Subjects include adventure, military, war. Publishes Julian Stockwin, John Biggins, Colin Sargent, and Douglas W. Jacobson. Distributes titles through Independent Publishers Group.

TIPS "We are currently only publishing authors with whom we have a pre-existing relationship. If this policy changes, we will announce the change on our website."

MARGARET K. MCELDERRY BOOKS

Imprint of Simon & Schuster Children's Publishing Division, 1230 Sixth Ave., New York NY 10020. (212)698-7200. **Website:** imprints.simonandschuster.biz/margaret-k-mcelderry-books. VP/Publisher: Justin Chanda. Estab. 1971. "Margaret K. McElderry Books publishes hardcover and paperback trade books for children from pre-school age through young adult. This list includes picture books, middle grade and teen fiction, poetry, and fantasy. The style and subject matter of the books we publish is almost unlimited. We do not publish textbooks, coloring and activity books, greeting cards, magazines, pamphlets, or religious publications." **Publishes 30 titles/year. 15% of books from first-time authors. 50% from unagented writers. Pays authors royalty based on retail price. Pays illustrator royalty of by the project. Pays photographers by the project. Original artwork returned at job's completion. Offers $5,000-8,000 advance for new authors.** Accepts simultaneous submissions. Guidelines for #10 SASE.

NONFICTION Subjects include history, adventure. *No unsolicited mss. Agented submissions only.*

FICTION Subjects include adventure, fantasy, historical, mystery, picture books, young adult. *No unsolicited mss. Agented submissions only.*

TIPS "Read! The children's book field is competitive. See what's been done and what's out there before submitting. We look for high quality: an originality of ideas, clarity and felicity of expression, a well organized plot, and strong character-driven stories. We're looking for strong, original fiction, especially mysteries and middle grade humor. We are always interested in picture books for the youngest age reader. Study our titles."

MCFARLAND & CO., INC., PUBLISHERS

Box 611, Jefferson NC 28640. (336)246-4460. **Fax:** (336)246-5018. **E-mail:** info@mcfarlandpub.com. **Website:** www.mcfarlandpub.com. **Contact:** Editorial Department. Estab. 1979. Publishes hardcover and quality paperback originals. "McFarland publishes serious nonfiction in a variety of fields, including general reference, performing arts, popular culture, sports (particularly baseball); women's studies, librarianship, literature, Civil War, history and international studies. Currently emphasizing medieval history, automotive history. De-emphasizing memoirs." **Publishes 350 titles/year. 50% of books from first-time authors. 95% from unagented writers.** Publishes book 10 months after acceptance. Accepts simultaneous submissions. Responds in 1 month to queries. Guidelines online.

NONFICTION Subjects include history, recreation, sociology, African-American studies (very strong). Reference books are particularly wanted—fresh material (i.e., not in head-to-head competition with an established title). "We prefer manuscripts of 250 or more double-spaced pages or at least 75,000 words." No fiction, New Age, exposes, poetry, children's books, devotional/inspirational works, Bible studies, or personal essays. Query with SASE. Submit outline, sample chapters. Reviews artwork/photos.

TIPS "We want well-organized knowledge of an area in which there is not information coverage at present, plus reliability so we don't feel we have to check absolutely everything. Our market is worldwide and libraries are an important part."

MCGRAW-HILL PROFESSIONAL BUSINESS

Imprint of The McGraw-Hill Companies, 2 Penn Plaza, New York NY 10121. (212)438-1000. **Website:** www.mcgraw-hill.com. McGraw Hill Professional is a publishing leader in business/investing, management, careers, self-help, consumer health, language reference, test preparation, sports/recreation, and general interest titles. Publisher not responsible for returning mss or proposals. Accepts simultaneous submissions. Guidelines online.

NONFICTION Subjects include child guidance, education, sports, management, consumer reference, English and foreign language reference. Current, up-to-date, original ideas are needed. Good self-promotion is key. Submit proposal package, outline, concept of book, competition and market info, CV.

MC PRESS

3695 W. Quail Heights Ct., Boise ID 83703. (208)629-7275. **Fax:** (208)639-1231. **E-mail:** duptmor@mcpressonline.com. **Website:** www.mc-store.com. **Contact:** David Uptmor, publisher. Editor: Anne Grubb. Estab. 2001. Publishes trade paperback originals. **Publishes 12 titles/year. 50 queries received/year. 15 mss received/year. 50% of books from first-time authors. 100% from unagented writers. Pays 10-16% royalty on wholesale price.** Publishes book 5 months after acceptance. Accepts simultaneous submissions. Responds in 1 month. Book catalog and ms guidelines free.

IMPRINTS MC Press, IBM Press.

NONFICTION "We specialize in computer titles targeted at IBM technologies." Submit proposal package, outline, 2 sample chapters, abstract. Reviews artwork/photos. Send photocopies.

RECENT TITLE(S) *Flexible Input, Dazzling Output with IBM i*, by Rafael Victoria-Pereia (computer); *Advanced Guide to PHP on IBM i*, by Kevin Schroeder (computer).

MCSWEENEY'S POETRY SERIES

San Francisco CA **E-mail:** poetry@mcsweeneys.net. **Website:** mcsweeneys.net. McSweeney's regularly publishes poetry collections, as part of the McSweeney's Poetry Series. Accepts simultaneous submissions. Catalog online. Guidelines online.

POETRY The McSweeney's Poetry Series publishes new collections of poetry. "We are open to all styles. Book-length mss should be sent as PDF to poetry@mcsweeneys.net. In the cover letter, include your name, phone number, and e-mail address.

RECENT TITLE(S) *Tradition*, by Daniel Khalastchi; *The Boss*, by Victoria Chang; *TOMBO*, by W.S. Di Piero.

TIPS "We're a very small operation, and we may not be able to get back to you about the manuscript. We will do our very best."

MEDIA LAB BOOKS

Topix Media Lab, 14 Wall St., Suite 4B, New York NY 10005. **E-mail:** phil@topixmedia.com. **Website:** onnewsstandsnow.com. **Contact:** Phil Sexton, vice president and publisher. Estab. 2015. Publishes cooking, children's books, games, puzzles, reference, humor, biography, history. Media Lab Books is a premier imprint that partners with industry leaders to publish branded titles designed to inform, educate and entertain readers around the world. "With brand partners that run the gamut, our books are widely variable in category and topic. From John Wayne to Disney and every brand in between, our partners have loyal followings, strong media presences and amazing stories to tell. While leveraging the platforms of our brand partners, we publish highly visual, illustrated books that surprise and delight readers of all ages. From *Jack Hanna's Big Book of Why* to *The John Wayne Code*, we truly have something for everyone. In the end, our aim is to match great ideas with amazing brands. We're looking for creative nonfiction ideas from authors with a voice (and a platform). Though we specialize in creating visually dynamic books built around big brands, we're also interested in original works focusing on popular or trending topics in most nonfiction categories, but given a unique, one-of-a-kind spin that demands publication. For example, *I'm Just Here for the Drinks*, by Sother Teague." **Publishes 20 titles/year. 20% of books from first-time authors. 20% from unagented writers.** Publishes ms 12-18 months after acceptance. Accepts simultaneous submissions. Responds in 30 days. Catalog available. Electronic submissions only. On the first page of the document, please include author's name and contact information. Please send full submission packet, including overview, USP (unique selling proposition), comparable titles, proposed TOC, and 1-3 sample chapters (no more than 50 pages).

IMPRINTS Media Lab Books, Media Lab Kids.

NONFICTION Subjects include Americana, animals, art, astrology, cinema, communications, contemporary culture, cooking, crafts, education, entertainment, environment, film, finance, foods, games, gardening, hobbies, house and home, memoirs, New Age, nutrition, photography, politics, pop culture, sex.

RECENT TITLE(S) *John Wayne: Made in America*; *I'm Just Here for the Drinks*; *Get Crocked Fast & Easy Slow Cooker Recipes*.

TIPS "Be sure to check out the kind of books we've already published. You'll see that most of them are brand-driven. The ones that are author-driven address popular topics with a unique approach. More general books are of no interest unless the topic in question is trending and there's minimal competition in the market."

MELANGE BOOKS, LLC

White Bear Lake MN 55110-5538. **E-mail:** melangebooks@melange-books.com. **E-mail:** submissions@melange-books.com. **Website:** www.melange-books.com. **Contact:** Nancy Schumacher, publisher and acquiring editor for Melange and Satin Romance; Caroline Andrus, acquiring editor for Fire and Ice for Young Adult. Estab. 2011. Publishes trade paperback originals and electronic originals. Melange is a royalty-paying company publishing e-books and print books. **Publishes 62 titles/year. Receives 1,000 queries/year; 700 mss/year. 65% of books from first-time authors. 75% from unagented writers. Authors receive a minimum of 20% royalty on print sales, 40% on electronic book sales. Does not offer an advance.** Publishes book 12-15 months after acceptance. Accepts simultaneous submissions. Responds in 1 month on queries; 2 months on proposals; 4-6 months on mss. Send SASE for book catalog. Guidelines online.

IMPRINTS Fire and Ice (young and new adult) www.fireandiceya.com; Satin Romance www.satinromance.com.

FICTION Subjects include adventure, contemporary, erotica, fantasy, gay, gothic, historical, lesbian, mainstream, multicultural, mystery, romance, science fiction, suspense, western, young adult. Submit a clean mss by following guidelines on website. Query electronically by clicking on "submissions" on website. Include a synopsis and 4 chapters.

MENASHA RIDGE PRESS

AdventureKEEN, 2204 First Ave. S., Suite 102, Birmingham AL 35233. (205)322-0439. **E-mail:** tim@adventurewithkeen.com. **Website:** www.menasharidge.com. **Contact:** Tim Jackson, acquisitions editor. Publishes hardcover and trade paperback originals. Menasha Ridge Press publishes distinctive books in the areas of outdoor sports, recreation, and travel. We are primarily looking for outdoors guidebooks. "Our authors are among the best in their fields." **Publishes 20 titles/year. 30% of books from first-time authors. 90% from unagented writers. Pays varying royalty. Pays varying advance.** Publishes ms 1 year after acceptance. Accepts simultaneous submissions. Responds in 2 months to queries.

NONFICTION Subjects include nature, recreation, sports, travel, outdoors. Most concepts are generated in-house, but a few come from outside submissions. Submit proposal package, resume, clips. Reviews artwork/photos.

MERRIAM PRESS

489 South St., Hoosick Falls NY 12090. **E-mail:** ray@merriam-press.com. **Website:** www.merriam-press.com. **Contact:** Ray Merriam, owner. Estab. 1988. Publishes hardcover and softcover trade paperback original works and reprints. Titles are also made available in e-book editions. Merriam Press specializes in military history, particularly World War II history. We are also branching out into other genres, including fiction, historical fiction, poetry, children. Provide brief synopsis of ms. Never send any files in body of e-mail. Send manuscript as attachment to email. Publisher will ask for full ms for review. Publisher requires unformatted mss. Mss must be thoroughly edited and error-free. **Publishes 12+ titles/year. 70-90% of books from first-time authors. 100% from unagented writers. Pays 10% royalty for printed editions and 50% royalty for e-book editions. Royalty payment is based on the amount paid to the publisher, not the retail or list prices. Does not pay advance.** Publishes ms 6 months or less after acceptance. Responds quickly (e-mail preferred) to queries. Book catalog available in print and PDF editions. Author guidelines and additional information are available on publisher's website.

NONFICTION Subjects include Americana, creative nonfiction, history, memoirs, military, war. Especially but not limited to military history. Query with SASE or by e-mail first. Do not send ms (in whole or in part) unless requested to do so. When asked to submit ms, include all artwork, photos and other materials.

FICTION Subjects include historical, military, poetry, war. Especially but not limited to military history. Query with SASE or by e-mail first. Do not send ms (in whole or in part) unless requested to do so.

POETRY Especially but not limited to military topics. Query with SASE or by e-mail first. Do not send ms (in whole or in part) unless requested to do so.

RECENT TITLE(S) *The 13 Dog Days of Christmas*; *Cries In the Wind*; *An Ocean Apart: A War Bride's Tale*; *A Concise History of the Second World War*; *A Dangerous Assignment: An Artillery Forward Observer In World War 2*; *A Dishonorable Discharge: A Novel of Love and War*; *A Song in the Night: Story of a War Bride*; *A World At Risk*.

TIPS "Our military history books are geared for military historians, collectors, model kit builders, wargamers, veterans, general enthusiasts. We now publish some historical fiction and poetry and will consider well-written books on a variety of non-military topics."

METAL POWDER INDUSTRIES FEDERATION

105 College Rd. E., Princeton NJ 08540. (609)452-7700. **Fax:** (609)987-8523. **Website:** www.mpif.org. Estab. 1946. Publishes hardcover originals. "Metal Powder Industries publishes monographs, textbooks, handbooks, design guides, conference proceedings, standards, and general titles in the field of powder metallurgy or particulate materials." **Publishes 10 titles/year. Pays 3-12% royalty on wholesale or retail price. Pays $3,000-5,000 advance.** Accepts simultaneous submissions. Responds in 1 month to queries.

NONFICTION Work must relate to powder metallurgy or particulate materials.

⊘ MIAMI UNIVERSITY PRESS

301 S. Patterson Ave., 356 Bachelor Hall, Miami University, Oxford OH 45056. **E-mail:** mupress@miamioh.edu. **Website:** www.miamioh.edu/mupress. **Contact:** Keith Tuma, editor; Amy Toland, managing editor. Estab. 1992. Publishes 1-2 books of poetry and/or poetry in translation per year and 1 novella, in paperback editions. Accepts simultaneous submissions.

NONFICTION Subjects include literature.

FICTION Subjects include contemporary, experimental, feminist, gay, literary, multicultural, poetry, poetry in translation, translation.

POETRY Miami University Press is unable to respond to unsolicited mss and queries.

RECENT TITLE(S) *Scorpio*, by Katy Bohinc; *Temper CA*, by Paul Skenazy; *Day of All Saints*, by Patricia Grace King; *Fastness*, by Trevor Joyce; *Leaving CLE*, by Janice Lowe.

MICHIGAN STATE UNIVERSITY PRESS

1405 S. Harrison Rd., Suite 25, East Lansing MI 48823. (517)355-9543. **Fax:** (517)432-2611. **E-mail:** msupress@msu.edu. **Website:** msupress.org. **Contact:** Alex Schwartz and Julie Loehr, acquisitions. Estab. 1947. Publishes hardcover and softcover originals. Michigan State University Press has notably represented both scholarly publishing and the mission of Michigan State University with the publication of numerous award-winning books and scholarly journals. In addition, they publish nonfiction that addresses, in a more contemporary way, social concerns, such as diversity and civil rights. They also publish literary fiction and poetry. **Pays variable royalty.** Book catalog and ms guidelines online.

NONFICTION Distributes books for: University of Calgary Press, University of Alberta Press, and University of Manitoba Press. Submit proposal/outline and sample chapter. Hard copy is preferred but email proposals are also accepted. Initial submissions to MSU Press should be in the form of a short letter of inquiry and a sample chapter(s), as well as our preliminary Marketing Questionnaire, which can be downloaded from their website. We do not accept: Festschrifts, conference papers, or unrevised dissertations. Reviews artwork/photos.

FICTION Subjects include literary. Publishes literary fiction. Submit proposal.

POETRY Publishes poetry collections. Submit proposal with sample poems.

MICROSOFT PRESS

E-mail: 4bkideas@microsoft.com. **Website:** www.microsoft.com/learning/en/us/microsoft-press-books.aspx. **Publishes 80 titles/year. 25% of books from first-time authors. 90% from unagented writers.** Accepts simultaneous submissions. Book proposal guidelines online.

NONFICTION Subjects include software. A book proposal should consist of the following information: TOC, a resume with author biography, a writing sample, and a questionnaire. "We place a great deal of emphasis on your proposal. A proposal provides us with a basis for evaluating the idea of the book and how fully your book fulfills its purpose."

MILKWEED EDITIONS

1011 Washington Ave. S., Suite 300, Minneapolis MN 55415. (612)332-3192. **Fax:** (612)215-2550. **Website:** www.milkweed.org. Estab. 1979. Publishes hardcover, trade paperback, and electronic originals; trade paperback and electronic reprints. "Milkweed Editions publishes with the intention of making a humane impact on society, in the belief that literature is a transformative art uniquely able to convey the essential experiences of the human heart and spirit. To that end, Milkweed Editions publishes distinctive voices of literary merit in handsomely designed, visually dynamic books, exploring the ethical, cultural, and esthetic issues that free societies need continually to address." **Publishes 15-20 titles/year. 25% of books from first-time authors. 75% from unagented writers. Pays authors variable royalty based on retail price. Offers advance against royalties. Pays varied advance from $500-10,000.** Publishes book in 18 months. Accepts simultaneous submissions. Responds in 6 months. Book catalog online. Only accepts submissions during open submission periods. See website for guidelines.

NONFICTION Subjects include agriculture, animals, art, contemporary culture, creative nonfiction, environment, gardening, gay, government, history, humanities, language, literature, multicultural, nature, politics, translation, world affairs. Does not review artwork.

FICTION Subjects include experimental, short story collections, translation, young adult. Novels for adults and for readers 8-13. High literary quality. For adult readers: literary fiction, nonfiction, poetry, essays. Middle readers: adventure, contemporary, fantasy, multicultural, nature/environment, suspense/mystery. Average length: middle readers—90-200 pages. No romance, mysteries, science fiction. "Please submit a query letter with three opening chapters (of a novel) or three representative stories (of a collection). Publishes YR."

POETRY Milkweed Editions is "looking for poetry manuscripts of high quality that embody humane values and contribute to cultural understanding." Not limited in subject matter. Open to writers with previously published books of poetry or a minimum of 6 poems published in nationally distributed commercial or literary journals. Considers translations and bilingual mss. Query with SASE; submit completed ms.

TIPS "We are looking for excellent writing with the intent of making a humane impact on society. Please read submission guidelines before submitting and acquaint yourself with our books in terms of style and quality before submitting. Many factors influence our selection process, so don't get discouraged. Nonfiction is focused on literary writing about the natural world, including living well in urban environments."

⊘ THE MILLBROOK PRESS

Lerner Publishing Group, 1251 Washington Ave N, Minneapolis MN 55401. **E-mail:** info@lernerbooks.com. **Website:** www.lernerbooks.com. **Contact:** Carol Hinz, editorial director. "Millbrook Press publishes informative picture books, illustrated nonfiction titles, and inspiring photo-driven titles for grades K–5. Our authors approach curricular topics with a fresh point of view. Our fact-filled books engage readers with fun yet accessible writing, high-quality photographs, and a wide variety of illustration styles. We cover subjects ranging from the parts of speech and other language arts skills; to history, science, and math; to art, sports, crafts, and other interests. Millbrook Press is the home of the bestselling Words Are CATegorical® series and Bob Raczka's Art Adventures. We do not accept unsolicited manuscripts from authors. Occasionally, we may put out a call for submissions, which will be announced on our website." Accepts simultaneous submissions.

MINNESOTA HISTORICAL SOCIETY PRESS

Minnesota Historical Society, 345 Kellogg Blvd. W., St. Paul MN 55102. (651)259-3200. **Fax:** (651)297-1345. **E-mail:** ann.regan@mnhs.org. **Website:** www.mnhspress.org. **Contact:** Ann Regan, editor-in-chief. Estab. 1852. Publishes hardcover, trade paperback and electronic originals; trade paperback and electronic reprints. The Minnesota Historical Society Press is a leading publisher of the history and culture of Minnesota and the Upper Midwest. The Minnesota Historical Society Press seeks proposals for book manuscripts relating to the history and culture of Minnesota and the Upper Midwest. We are especially interested in excellent works of history and in well-researched and well-written manuscripts that use the best tools of narrative journalism to tell history for general audiences. Successful manuscripts will address themes or issues that are important to understanding life in this region and will reveal a strong sense of place. Preferred topics include Native

American studies, Scandinavian studies, nature and environment, women's history, popular culture, food, adventure and travel, true crime, war and conflict, and the histories of Minnesota's diverse peoples. **Publishes 20 titles/year. 300 queries; 150 mss received/year. 60% of books from first-time authors. 95% from unagented writers. Royalties are negotiated; 5-10% on wholesale price. Pays $1,000 and up.** Publishes ms 16 months after acceptance. Accepts simultaneous submissions. Responds in 1-4 months. Book catalog online. Guidelines online.

NONFICTION Subjects include Americana, community, contemporary culture, cooking, creative nonfiction, ethnic, history, memoirs, multicultural, music, photography, politics, pop culture, regional, Native American studies. Books must have a connection to the Midwest. Regional works only. Submit proposal package, outline, 1 sample chapter and other materials listed in our online website in author guidelines: CV, brief description, intended audience, readership, length of ms, schedule. Reviews artwork/photos. Send photocopies.

MISSOURI HISTORY MUSEUM PRESS

The Missouri Historical Society, P.O. Box 11940, St. Louis MO 63112. (314)746-4559. **Fax:** (314)746-4548. **E-mail:** lmitchell@mohistory.org. **Website:** www.mohistory.org. **Contact:** Lauren Mitchell. Estab. 1992. Publishes hardcover and trade paperback books on the history of Missouri. "Our mission is to expose our readers—through the books we publish, our magazine, Gateway, and our online publications, History Happens Here and Voices—to perspectives of St. Louis and Missouri not usually introduced in simple history lessons. Mining both the historical and contemporary cultural, social, and political issues of our region, we strive to publish stories that resonate with our community and highlight the common heritage we all share." **Publishes 2-3 titles/year. 30 queries; 20 mss received/year. 10% of books from first-time authors. 80% from unagented writers. Pays 8-10% royalty.** Ms published 15 months after acceptance. Accepts simultaneous submissions. Responds in 3-4 months. Guidelines available.

NONFICTION Subjects include history, multicultural, regional, sports, popular culture, photography, children's nonfiction. Query with SASE and request author-proposal form.

TIPS "We're looking for new perspectives, even if the topics are familiar. You'll get our attention with nontraditional voices and views."

MITCHELL LANE PUBLISHERS

2001 S.W. 31st Ave., Hallandale FL 33009. (954)985-9400. **Fax:** (800)223-3251. **E-mail:** phil@mitchelllane.com; customerservice@mitchelllane.com. **Website:** www.mitchelllane.com. **Contact:** Phil Comer. Estab. 1993. Publishes hardcover and library bound originals and has it's own eBook platform and delivery system. **Publishes 80 titles/year. 100 queries/year; 5 mss received/year. 90% from unagented writers. Work purchased outright from authors (range: $350-2,000). Pays illustrators by the project (range: $40-400).** Publishes ms 1 year after acceptance. Responds only if interested to queries. Book catalog available free.

NONFICTION Subjects include ethnic, multicultural. Young readers, middle readers, young adults: biography, nonfiction, and curriculum-related subjects. Average word length: 4,000-50,000 words. Recently published: *My Guide to US Citizenship*, *Rivers of the World* and *Vote America*. Query with SASE. *All unsolicited mss discarded.*

RECENT TITLE(S) *Lionel Messi*, *LL Cool J*, *Mike Trout*, *A Teen Guide to Investing*, *Practical Economics for Teens* and *American Jazz*.

TIPS "We hire writers on a 'work-for-hire' basis to complete book projects we assign. Send résumé and writing samples that do not need to be returned."

MONDIAL

203 W. 107th St., Suite 6C, New York NY 10025. 212-864-7095. **Fax:** (208)361-2863. **E-mail:** contact@mondialbooks.com. **Website:** www.mondialbooks.com; www.librejo.com. **Contact:** Andrew Moore, editor. Estab. 1996. Publishes hard cover, trade paperback originals and reprints. Mondial publishes fiction and non-fiction in English, Esperanto, and Hebrew: novels, short stories, poetry, textbooks, dictionaries, books about history, linguistics, and psychology, among others. Since 2007, it has been publishing a literary magazine in Esperanto. **Publishes 20 titles/year. 2,000 queries; 500 mss received/year. 20% of books from first-time authors. 100% from unagented writers. Pays 10% royalty on wholesale price. Does not pay advance.** Publishes ms 4 months after acceptance. Accepts simultaneous submissions. Responds to queries in 3 months, only if interested. Guidelines online.

NONFICTION Subjects include ethnic, history, literary criticism, memoirs, multicultural, philosophy, psychology, sex, sociology, translation. Submit proposal package, outline, 1 sample chapters. Send only electronically by e-mail.

FICTION Subjects include adventure, erotica, ethnic, historical, literary, multicultural, mystery, poetry, romance, short story collections, translation. Query through online submission form.

RECENT TITLE(S) *The Great Bordello: A Story of the Theatre*, by Avery Hopwood (novel); *The Honesties of Love* by Bruce Kellner (novel); *The Fire at the Core: Discourses on African Aesthetics, Music, Jurisprudence, Ethno-Politics and Good Governance*, by Malama Katulwende (essays); *Reluctant Messiah*, by Trevor Steele (historical novel); *Facing Forward: A Life Reclaimed*, by Reba D (domestic violence-a personal story); *Caruso's Mustache Off and Other Writings About Music and Musicians*, by Carl Van Vechten (essays).

Ⓐ⊘ MOODY PUBLISHERS

Moody Bible Institute, 820 N. LaSalle Blvd., Chicago IL 60610. (800)678-8812. **Fax:** (312)329-4157. **Website:** www.moodypublishers.org. **Contact:** Acquisitions Coordinator. Estab. 1894. Publishes hardcover, trade, and mass market paperback originals. "The mission of Moody Publishers is to educate and edify the Christian and to evangelize the non-Christian by ethically publishing conservative, evangelical Christian literature and other media for all ages around the world, and to help provide resources for Moody Bible Institute in its training of future Christian leaders." **Publishes 60 titles/year. 1,500 queries received/year. 2,000 mss received/year. 1% of books from first-time authors. 80% from unagented writers. Royalty varies.** Publishes book 1 year after acceptance. Responds in 2-3 months to queries. Book catalog for 9×12 envelope and 4 first-class stamps. Guidelines online.

NONFICTION Subjects include child guidance, religion, spirituality. "We are no longer reviewing queries or unsolicited manuscripts unless they come to us through an agent,are from an author who has published with us, an associate from a Moody Bible Institute ministry or a personal contact at a writer's conference. Unsolicited proposals will be returned only if proper postage is included. We are not able to acknowledge the receipt of your unsolicited proposal." Does not accept unsolicited nonfiction submissions.

FICTION Subjects include fantasy, historical, mystery, religious, science fiction, young adult. *Agented submissions only.*

TIPS "In our fiction list, we're looking for Christian storytellers rather than teachers trying to present a message. Your motivation should be to delight the reader. Using your skills to create beautiful works is glorifying to God."

MOTORBOOKS

Quarto Publishing Group, 401 2nd Ave. N., Suite 310, Minneapolis MN 55401. (612)344-8100. **Fax:** (612)344-8691. **E-mail:** zack.miller@quarto.com. **Website:** https://www.quartoknows.com/Motorbooks. **Contact:** Zack Miller. Estab. 1973. Publishes hardcover and paperback originals. "Motorbooks is one of the world's leading transportation publishers, covering subjects from classic motorcycles to heavy equipment to today's latest automotive technology. We satisfy our customers' high expectations by hiring top writers and photographers and presenting their work in handsomely designed books that work hard in the shop and look good on the coffee table." **Publishes 200 titles/year. 300 queries; 50 mss received/year. 95% from unagented writers. Pays $5,000 average advance.** Publishes ms 1 year after acceptance. Accepts simultaneous submissions. Responds in 6-8 months to proposals. Book catalog available free. Guidelines online.

NONFICTION Subjects include Americana, history, hobbies, photography, recreation, transportation. Query with SASE. Reviews artwork/photos. Send photocopies.

MOUNTAINEERS BOOKS

The Mountaineers, 1001 SW Klickitat Way, Suite 201, Seattle WA 98134. (206)223-6303. **Fax:** (206)223-6306. **E-mail:** submissions@mountaineersbooks.org. **Website:** www.mountaineersbooks.org. Estab. 1961. Publishes trade hardcover, paperback, and e-book originals and reprints. "Mountaineers Books publishes nonfiction books on outdoor recreation, lifestyle, and conservation topics. The sports in its recreation line are all muscle-powered activities, including climbing, hiking, biking, and others. The lifestyle imprint, Skipstone, focuses on sustainable-living topics, such as cooking and gardening. The conservation titles are published in the Braided River imprint, and are uniquely used in partnership with other conservation organizations to highlight, educate, and advocate for specific environmental concerns. Mountaineers Books is an independent nonprofit publisher." **Publishes 40 titles/year. 25% of books from first-time authors. 98% from unagented writers. Pays advance.** Publishes ms 1 year after acceptance. Responds in 3 months to queries. Guidelines online.

IMPRINTS Skipstone, Braided River.

NONFICTION Subjects include cooking, environment, gardening, horticulture, memoirs, nature, nutrition, recreation, regional, sports, translation, travel, natural history, conservation. Accepts nonfiction translations. Looks for expert knowledge, good organization. Also interested in nonfiction adventure narratives. Does not want to see anything dealing with hunting, fishing, or motorized travel. Submit outline, 2 sample chapters, bio.

TIPS "The type of book the writer has the best chance of selling to our firm is an authoritative guidebook (*in our field*) to a specific area not otherwise covered; or a how-to that is better than existing competition (again, *in our field*)."

MOUNTAIN PRESS PUBLISHING CO.

P.O. Box 2399, Missoula MT 59806. (406)728-1900 or (800)234-5308. **Fax:** (406)728-1635. **E-mail:** info@mtnpress.com. **Website:** www.mountain-press.com. **Contact:** Jennifer Carey, editor. Estab. 1948. Publishes hardcover and trade paperback originals. "We are expanding our Roadside Geology, Geology Underfoot, and Roadside History series (done on a state-by-state basis). We are interested in well-written regional field guides—plants and flowers—and readable history and natural history." **Publishes 15 titles/year. 50% of books from first-time authors. 90% from unagented writers. Pays 7-12% royalty on wholesale price.** Publishes ms 2 years after acceptance. Accepts simultaneous submissions. Responds in 3 months to queries. Book catalog online.

Expanding children's/juvenile nonfiction titles.

NONFICTION Subjects include animals, history, regional, science. No personal histories or journals, poetry or fiction. Query with SASE. Submit outline, sample chapters. Reviews artwork/photos.

RECENT TITLE(S) *Roadside Geology of Oregon, Ohio Rocks, Outlaw Weeds of the West, Roadside History of Illinois.*

TIPS "Find out what kind of books a publisher is interested in and tailor your writing to them; research markets and target your audience. Research other books on the same subjects. Make yours different. Don't present your manuscript to a publisher—sell it. Give the information needed to make a decision on a title. Please learn what we publish before sending your proposal. We are a 'niche' publisher."

MOVING PARTS PRESS

10699 Empire Grade, Santa Cruz CA 95060. (831)427-2271. **E-mail:** frice@movingpartspress.com. **Website:** www.movingpartspress.com. **Contact:** Felicia Rice, poetry editor. Estab. 1977. Moving Part Press publishes handsome, innovative books, broadsides, and prints that "explore the relationship of word and image, typography and the visual arts, the fine arts and popular culture." Accepts simultaneous submissions.

POETRY *Does not accept unsolicited mss.*

MSI PRESS LLC

1760-F Airline Hwy, #203, Hollister CA 95023. **Fax:** (831)886-2486. **E-mail:** editor@msipress.com. **Website:** www.msipress.com. **Contact:** Betty Lou Leaver, managing editor (self-help, spirituality, religion, memoir, mind/body/spirit, some humor, popular psychology, foreign language & culture, parenting). Estab. 2003. Publishes trade paperback originals and corresponding e-books. "We are a small press that specializes in award-winning quality publications, refined through strong personal interactions and productive working relationships between our editors and our authors. A small advance may be offered to previously published authors with a strong book, strong platform, and solid sales numbers. We will accept first-time authors with credibility in their fields and a strong platform, but we do not offer advances to first-time authors. We may refer authors with a good book but little experience or lacking a strong platform to San Juan Books, our hybrid publishing venture." **Publishes 10-15 titles/year. 100-200 50% of books from first-time authors. 100% from unagented writers. Pays 10% royalty on retail price for paperbacks and hard cover books; pays 50% royalty on net for e-books. By exception, pays small advance to previously published authors with good sales history.** Publishes ms 6-10 months after acceptance. Accepts simultaneous submissions. Responds in 2 weeks to queries sent by e-mail and to proposals submitted via the template on our website. If response not received in 2 weeks, okay to query. Catalog online. Guidelines online.

IMPRINTS MSI Press, LLC; San Juan Books.

NONFICTION Subjects include animals, child guidance, counseling, creative nonfiction, education, ethnic, health, humanities, labor, language, memoirs, multicultural, parenting, philosophy, psychology, regional, religion, spirituality, travel, womens issues, Ask; we are open to new ideas. "We continue to expand our spirituality, psychology, and self-help lines and are interested in adding to our collection of books in Spanish. We do not do or publish translations." Does not want erotica. Submit proposal package, including: annotated outline, 1 sample chapter, professional resume, platform information. Electronic submissions preferred. We are open to foreign writers (non-native speakers of English), but please have an English editor proofread the submission prior to sending; if the query letter or proposal is written in poor English, we will not take a chance on a manuscript. Reviews artwork/photos; send e-file or use dropbox.

RECENT TITLE(S) *Road Map to Power* (Husain and Husain); *Living Well with Chronic Illness* (Charnas); *Healing from Incest* (Henderson & Emerton); *It Only Hurts When I Can't Run* (Parker); *Anxiety Anonymous* (Ortman); *The Subversive Utopia* (Sakr).

TIPS "Learn the mechanics of writing. Too many submissions are full of grammar and punctuation errors and poorly worded with trite expressions. Read to write; observe and analyze how the great authors of all time use language to good avail. Capture our attention with active verbs, not bland description. Before writing your book, determine its audience, write to that audience, and go about developing your credibility with that audience—and then tell us what you have done and are doing in your proposal."

Ⓐ⊘ NATIONAL GEOGRAPHIC CHILDREN'S BOOKS

1145 17th St. NW, Washington DC 20090-8199. (800)647-5463. **Website:** kids.nationalgeographic.com. National Geographic CHildren's Books provides quality nonfiction for children and young adults by award-winning authors. *This market does not currently accept unsolicited mss.*

NATUREGRAPH PUBLISHERS, INC.

P.O. Box 1047, 3543 Indian Creek Rd., Happy Camp CA 96039. (530)493-5353. **Fax:** (530)493-5240. **E-mail:** nature@sisqtel.net. **Website:** www.naturegraph.com. **Contact:** Barbara Brown, owner. Estab. 1946. Publishes trade paperback originals. **Publishes 2 titles/year. 100 queries; 6 mss received/year. 80% of books from first-time authors. 90% from unagented writers. Pays royalties. Does not pay advance.** Publishes ms 2 years after acceptance. Accepts simultaneous submissions. Responds in 1 month to queries; 2 months to mss. Book catalog for #10 SASE.

NONFICTION Subjects include crafts, ethnic, nature, science, crafts.

RECENT TITLE(S) *Dear Mad'm, Who Was She?; Springer's Quest, Life of a Pacific Chinook Salmon; Where the Wild Things Live; Wildlife Watching Techniques, Packing with Burros, Grover Ladd A New River Packer, Linda Lookout, IVAN, The Forest Service Pack Mule, Letitia, She's Iron, Stone and Beautiful Flowers, Colorado Homesteading, 1916 to 1950.*

TIPS "Please-always send a stamped reply envelope. Publishers get hundreds of manuscripts yearly."

NAVAL INSTITUTE PRESS

US Naval Institute, 291 Wood Rd., Annapolis MD 21402. (410)268-6110. **Fax:** (410)295-1084. **Website:** www.usni.org. Estab. 1873. "The Naval Institute Press publishes trade and scholarly nonfiction. We are interested in national and international security, naval, military, military jointness, intelligence, and special warfare, both current and historical." **Publishes 80-90 titles/year. 50% of books from first-time authors. 90% from unagented writers.** Accepts simultaneous submissions. Guidelines online.

NONFICTION Submit proposal package with outline, author bio, TOC, description/synopsis, sample chapter(s), page/word count, number of illustrations, ms completion date, intended market; or submit complete ms. Send SASE with sufficient postage for return of ms. Send by postal mail only. No e-mail submissions, please.

⊘ NAVPRESS

3820 N. 30th St., Colorado Springs CO 80904. **Website:** www.navpress.com. Estab. 1975. Publishes hardcover, trade paperback, direct and mass market paperback originals and reprints; electronic books and Bible studies. **Pays royalty. Pays low or no advances.** Accepts simultaneous submissions. Book catalog available free.

NONFICTION Subjects include child guidance.

NBM PUBLISHING

160 Broadway, Suite 700, East Bldg., New York NY 10038. **E-mail:** nbmgn@nbmpub.com. **Website:** nbmpub.com. **Contact:** Terry Nantier, editor. Estab. 1976. Publishes graphic novels for an audience of YA/adults. Types of books include fiction, mystery, biographies and social parodies. **Publishes 16 titles/**

year. 5% of books from first-time authors. 90% from unagented writers. Advance negotiable. Publishes ms 1 year after acceptance. Accepts simultaneous submissions. Responds to e-mail 1-2 days; mail 1 week. Catalog online.

NONFICTION Subjects includebiographies.

FICTION Subjects include comic books, contemporary, gay, humor, lesbian, literary, multicultural, mystery, translation, young adult.

THOMAS NELSON, INC.

HarperCollins Christian Publishing, Box 141000, Nashville TN 37214. (615)889-9000. **Website:** www.thomasnelson.com. Publishes hardcover and paperback orginals. Thomas Nelson publishes Christian lifestyle nonfiction and fiction, and general nonfiction. **Publishes 100-150 titles/year. Rates negotiated for each project. Pays advance.** Publishes ms 1-2 years after acceptance. Accepts simultaneous submissions.

NONFICTION Subjects include gardening, religion, spirituality, adult inspirational, motivational, devotional, Christian living, prayer and evangelism, Bible study, personal development, political, biography/autobiography. *Does not accept unsolicited mss.* No phone queries.

FICTION Publishes authors of commercial fiction who write for adults from a Christian perspective. *Does not accept unsolicited mss.* No phone queries.

TOMMY NELSON

Imprint of Thomas Nelson, Inc., P.O. Box 141000, Nashville TN 37214-1000. (615)889-9000. **Fax:** (615)902-2219. **Website:** www.tommynelson.com. Publishes hardcover and trade paperback originals. "Tommy Nelson publishes children's Christian nonfiction and fiction for boys and girls up to age 14. We honor God and serve people through books, videos, software and Bibles for children that improve the lives of our customers." **Publishes 50-75 titles/year.** Guidelines online.

NONFICTION Subjects include religion. *Does not accept unsolicited mss.*

FICTION Subjects include adventure, juvenile, mystery, picture books, religious. No stereotypical characters. *Does not accept unsolicited mss.*

TIPS "Know the Christian Booksellers Association market. Check out the Christian bookstores to see what sells and what is needed."

NEW DIRECTIONS

80 Eighth Ave., New York NY 10011. **Fax:** (212)255-0231. **E-mail:** editorial@ndbooks.com. **Website:** www.ndbooks.com. **Contact:** Editorial Assistant. Estab. 1936. Hardcover and trade paperback originals. "Currently, New Directions focuses primarily on fiction in translation, avant garde American fiction, and experimental poetry by American and foreign authors. If your work does not fall into one of those categories, you would probably do best to submit your work elsewhere." **Publishes 30 titles/year.** Responds in 3-4 months to queries. Book catalog and guidelines online.

FICTION Subjects include ethnic, experimental, historical, humor, literary, poetry, poetry in translation, regional, short story collections, suspense, translation. No juvenile or young adult, occult or paranormal, genre fiction (formula romances, sci-fi or westerns), arts & crafts, and inspirational poetry. Brief query only.

POETRY Query.

TIPS "Our books serve the academic community."

NEW FORUMS PRESS

New Forums, 1018 S. Lewis St., Stillwater OK 74074. (405)372-6158. **Fax:** (405)377-2237. **E-mail:** contact@newforums.com. **E-mail:** submissions@newforums.com. **Website:** www.newforums.com. **Contact:** Doug Dollar, president (interests: higher education, Oklahoma-Regional, US military). Estab. 1981. Hardcover and trade paperback originals. "New Forums Press is an independent publisher offering works devoted to various aspects of professional development in higher education, home and office aides, US military, and various titles of a regional interest. We welcome suggestions for thematic series of books and thematic issues of our academic journals—addressing a single issue, problem, or theory." **50 60% of books from first-time authors. 100% from unagented writers. 10% of Gross Sales paid as royalty. Does not pay advance.** Publishes ms 4 months after acceptance. Accepts simultaneous submissions. Responds in 1-2 weeks. Guidelines online.

NONFICTION Subjects include business, education, history, literature, military, regional, sociology, war. "We are actively seeking new authors—send for review copies and author guidelines, and visit our website." Mss should be submitted as a Microsoft Word document, or a similar standard word processor document (saved in RTF rich text), as an attachment to an e-mail sent to submissions@newforums.com. Otherwise, submit your ms on 8 ½ x 11 inch white bond paper (one original). The name and complete address, telephone, fax number, and e-mail address of each author should appear on a separate cover page, so it can be removed for the blind review process.

RECENT TITLE(S) *It Works For Me as a Scholar-Teacher: Shared Tips for the Classroom*, by Hal Blythe & Charlie Sweet; *Dollars & Sense: A Guide to Financial Security*, by Sherry Raines & William Austin; *Stillwater: A Cradle of Oklahoma History*, by D. Earl Newsom.

NEW HARBINGER PUBLICATIONS

5674 Shattuck Ave., Oakland CA 94609. (510)652-0215. **Fax:** (510)652-5472. **E-mail:** proposals@newharbinger.com. **Website:** www.newharbinger.com. Estab. 1973. "We look for psychology and health self-help books that teach readers how to master essential life skills. Mental health professionals who want simple, clear explanations or important psychological techniques and health issues also read our books. Thus, our books must be simple ane easy to understand but also complete and authoritative. Most of our authors are therapists or other helping professionals." **Publishes 55 titles/year. 1,000 queries received/year. 300 mss received/year. 60% of books from first-time authors. 75% from unagented writers.** Publishes ms 1 year after acceptance. Accepts simultaneous submissions. Responds in 2 weeks to queries; 1 month to proposals; 2 months to mss. Book catalog free. Guidelines online.

NONFICTION Subjects include psychology, psycho spirituality, anger management, anxiety, coping, mindfulness skills. Authors need to be qualified psychotherapists or health practitioners to publish with us. Submit proposal package, outline, 2 sample chapters, TOC, competing titles, and a compelling, supported reason why the book is unique.

TIPS "Audience includes psychotherapists and lay readers wanting step-by-step strategies to solve specific problems. Our definition of a self-help psychology or health book is one that teaches essential life skills. The primary goal is to train the reader so that, after reading the book, he or she can deal more effectively with health and/or psychological challenges."

⊘ NEW HOPE PUBLISHERS

Iron Stream Media, 100 Missionary Ridge Dr., Birmingham AL 35242. (888)811-9934. **E-mail:** info@newhopepublishers.com. **E-mail:** proposals@newhopepublishers.com. **Website:** www.newhopepublishers.com. **Contact:** Ramona Richards, associate publisher. Iron Stream Media/New Hope Publishers is a Christian media company providing resources to advance the Gospel of Jesus Christ, making disciples as we go. **Publishes 20-30 titles/year. Receives 50-100 mss per year. 40% of books from first-time authors. 50% from unagented writers. Royalty-based payment. Pays occasional advance; established authors only.** Publishes ms within 2 years after acceptance. Accepts simultaneous submissions. Responds in 3-6 months. Catalog online. Guidelines online.

IMPRINTS Ascender Books, New Hope Kids.

NONFICTION Subjects include religion, Church leadership, Christian living; spiritual growth. "We publish books dealing with all facets of Christian life for women and families, including health, discipleship, missions, ministry, Bible studies, spiritual development, parenting, and marriage. We are particularly interested in niche categories and books on lifestyle development and change." We do not currently publish works without a strong Christian worldview or reader takeaway. We do not accept queries. Proposals only, following our online guidelines and submissions e-mail.

FICTION Subjects include religious, Romantic Suspense, Cozies, Visionary, Women's Fiction from a Christian perspective. Please follow our online submission guidelines.

NEW HORIZON PRESS

P.O. Box 669, Far Hills NJ 07931. (908)604-6311. **Fax:** (908)604-6330. **Website:** www.newhorizonpressbooks.com. **Contact:** Acquisitions Editor. Estab. 1983. Publishes hardcover and trade paperback originals. "New Horizon publishes adult nonfiction featuring true stories of uncommon heroes, true crime, social issues, and self help." **Publishes 12 titles/year. 90% of books from first-time authors. 50% from unagented writers. Pays standard royalty on net receipts. Pays advance.** Publishes book within 2 years of acceptance. Accepts simultaneous submissions. Book catalog available free. Guidelines online.

IMPRINTS Small Horizons.

NONFICTION Subjects include child guidance, creative nonfiction, psychology, true crime. Submit proposal package, outline, résumé, bio, 3 sample chapters, photo, marketing information.

RECENT TITLE(S) *Murder in Mayberry*, by Mary and Jack Branson; *Thrill Killers*, by Raymond Pingitore and Paul Lonardo; *Boot Camp for the Broken Hearted*, by Audrey Valeriani.

TIPS "We are a small publisher, thus it is important that the author/publisher have a good working relationship. The author must be willing to promote his book."

NEW ISSUES POETRY & PROSE

Western Michigan University, 1903 W. Michigan Ave., Kalamazoo MI 49008-5463. (269)387-8185. **E-mail:** new-issues@wmich.edu. **Website:** newissuespress.com. **Contact:** Managing Editor. Estab. 1996. **50% of books from first-time authors. 95% from unagented writers.** Publishes 18 months after acceptance. Accepts simultaneous submissions. Guidelines online.

FICTION Subjects include poetry. Only considers submissions to book contests.

POETRY New Issues Poetry & Prose offers two contests annually. The Green Rose Prize is awarded to an author who has previously published at least one full-length book of poems. The New Issues Poetry Prize, an award for a first book of poems, is chosen by a guest judge. Past judges have included Philip Levine, C.K. Williams, C.D. Wright, and Campbell McGrath. New Issues does not read mss outside our contests. Graduate students in the Ph.D. and M.F.A. programs of Western Michigan Univ. often volunteer their time reading mss. Finalists are chosen by the editors. New Issues often publishes 1-2 additional mss selected from the finalists.

NEW LIBRI PRESS

4907 Meridian Ave. N., Seattle WA 98103. **E-mail:** query@newlibri.com. **Website:** www.newlibri.com. **Contact:** Michael Muller, editor; Stanislav Fritz, editor. Estab. 2011. Publishes trade paperback, electronic original, electronic reprints. "We only accept e-mail submissions, not USPS. We have recently changed our publishing model to a HYBRID model. This means a shared risk model on expenses. Do not submit if you are uncomfortable with this model. We still curate submissions in this model, which means we still reject more than we accept. We are very small and eclectic. We tend to like slightly 'quirky' stuff. While we have only published a bit of non-fiction, we are open to more, but (as a reminder) we are a HYBRID publisher and thus there are no advances of any kind and the author shares the financial risks." **Publishes 5 titles/year. Receives over 100 submissions/year. 90% of books from first-time authors. 100% from unagented writers. Pays 20-35% royalty on wholesale price. No advance.** Publishes ms 9-12 months after acceptance. Accepts simultaneous submissions. Responds in 3 months to mss. Catalog online. Guidelines online. Electronic submissions only. "We are a hybrid publisher. Don't submit if you are not comfortable with that model.".

NONFICTION Subjects include agriculture, automotive, business, child guidance, computers, cooking, creative nonfiction, economics, electronics, environment, gardening, hobbies, house and home, nature, parenting, recreation, science, sex, software, translation, travel. "Writers should know we embrace e-books. This means that some formats and types of books work well and others don't." Does not want religious. Prefers e-mail. Submit proposal package, including outline, 2 sample chapters, and summary of market from author's perspective. Prefers complete ms.

FICTION Subjects include adventure, experimental, fantasy, historical, horror, humor, literary, mainstream, military, multicultural, mystery, science fiction, translation, war, western, young adult. "Open to most ideas right now; this will change as we mature as a press. As a new press, we are more open than most and time will probably shape the direction. That said, trite as it is, we want good writing that is fun to read. While we currently are not looking for some sub-genres, if it is well written and a bit off the beaten path, submit to us. We are now a hybrid publisher, which means shared financial risk. Don't submit if you are uncomfortable with that model." Submit query, synopsis, and full manuscript (so we don't have to ask for it later if we like it. We will read about 50 pages to start).

RECENT TITLE(S) *This is What it Smells Like*, by Cathy Adams; *Inheritors*, by Judith Kirscht.

TIPS "Our audience is someone who is comfortable reading an e-book,or someone who is tired of the recycled authors of mainstream publishing, but still wants a good, relatively fast, reading experience. The industry is changing, while we accept for the traditional model, we are searching for writers who are interested in sharing the risk and controlling their own destiny. We embrace writers with no agent."

NEW RIVERS PRESS

1104 Seventh Ave. S., Moorhead MN 56563. **Website:** www.newriverspress.com. **Contact:** Nayt Rundquist, managing editor. Estab. 1968. New Rivers Press publishes collections of poetry, novels, nonfiction, translations of contemporary literature, and collections of short fiction and nonfiction. "We continue to publish books regularly by new and emerging writers, but we also welcome the opportunity to read work of every character and to publish the best literature available nationwide. Each fall through the Many Voices Project competition, we choose 2 books: 1 poetry and 1 prose." Accepts simultaneous submissions.

FICTION Sponsors American Fiction Prize to find best unpublished short stories by American writers.

POETRY The Many Voices Project awards $1,000, a standard book contract, publication of a book-length ms by New Rivers Press, and national distribution. All previously published poems must be acknowledged. "We will consider simultaneous submissions if noted as such. If your manuscript is accepted elsewhere during the judging, you must notify New Rivers Press immediately. If you do not give such notification and your manuscript is selected, your entry gives New Rivers Press permission to go ahead with publication." Guidelines online.

NEW WORLD LIBRARY

14 Pamaron Way, Novato CA 94949. (415)884-2100. **Fax:** (415)884-2199. **E-mail:** submit@newworldlibrary.com. **Website:** www.newworldlibrary.com. **Contact:** Joel Prins, submissions editor. Estab. 1977. Publishes nonfiction hardcover and trade paperback originals and reprints and e-books. "NWL is dedicated to publishing books that inspire and challenge us to improve the quality of our lives and our world." Prefers e-mail submissions. No longer accepting children's mss. **Publishes 30-35 titles/year. 10% of books from first-time authors. 25% from unagented writers. Pays advance.** Publishes ms 12 months after acceptance. Accepts simultaneous submissions. Responds in 3 months to queries if interested. Reviews all queries. Book catalog free. Guidelines online.

NONFICTION Subjects include alternative lifestyles, animals, astrology, business, career guidance, child guidance, contemporary culture, counseling, education, environment, health, literary criticism, medicine, nature, New Age, parenting, philosophy, psychic, psychology, religion, spirituality, translation, womens issues. Submit outline, overview, bio, 2-3 sample chapters via e-mail. Does not review artwork.

NEW YORK UNIVERSITY PRESS

838 Broadway, 3rd Floor, New York NY 10003. (212)998-2575. **Fax:** (212)995-3833. **E-mail:** nyupressinfo@nyu.edu. **Website:** www.nyupress.org. **Contact:** Ellen Chodosh, director. Estab. 1916. Hardcover and trade paperback originals. "New York University Press embraces ideological diversity. We often publish books on the same issue from different poles to generate dialogue, engender and resist pat categorizations." **Publishes 100 titles/year. 800-1,000 queries received/year. 30% of books from first-time authors. 90% from unagented writers.** Publishes ms 9-11 months after acceptance. Accepts simultaneous submissions. Responds in 1-4 months (peer reviewed) to proposals. Guidelines online.

NONFICTION Subjects include ethnic, psychology, regional, religion, sociology, American history, anthropology. New York University Press is a publisher primarily of academic books and is a department of the New York University Division of Libraries. NYU Press publishes in the humanities and social sciences, with emphasis on sociology, law, cultural and American studies, religion, American history, anthropology, politics, criminology, media and film, and psychology. The Press also publishes books on New York regional history, politics, and culture. Query with SASE. Submit proposal package, outline, 1 sample chapter. Reviews artwork/photos. Send photocopies.

NIGHTBOAT BOOKS

P.O. Box 10, Callicoon NY 12723. **Fax:** (603)448-9429. **Website:** nightboat.org. Estab. 2003. Nightboat Books, a nonprofit organization, seeks to develop audiences for writers whose work resists convention and transcends boundaries, by publishing books rich with poignancy, intelligence and risk. Accepts simultaneous submissions. Catalog online. Guidelines online.

POETRY Considers poetry submitted to its poetry prize. More information online.

RECENT TITLE(S) *The Old Philosopher*, by Vi Khi Nao; *The Consequences of My Body*, by Maged Zaher.

TIPS "The name Nightboat signifies travel, passage, and possibility—of mind and body, and of language. The night boat maneuvers in darkness at the mercy of changing currents and weather, always immersed in forces beyond itself."

NIGHTSCAPE PRESS

P.O. Box 1948, Smyrna TN 37167. **E-mail:** info@nightscapepress.com. **E-mail:** submissions@nightscapepress.com. **Website:** www.nightscapepress.

com. Estab. 2012. Nightscape Press is seeking quality book-length words of at least 50,000 words (40,000 for young adult). **Pays monthly royalties. Offers advance.** Accepts simultaneous submissions. Guidelines online. Currently closed to submissions. Will announce on site when they re-open to submissions.

FICTION Subjects include experimental, fantasy, horror, science fiction, short story collections, suspense, young adult. "We are not interested in erotica or graphic novels." Query.

RECENT TITLE(S) *The Patchwork House*, by Richard Salter. *Release*, by Amelia Mangan. *Darkling Incidence: Obscure Reflections*, by K. M. Tonso.

⊘ NINETY-SIX PRESS

Special Collections, James B. Duke Library, 3300 Poinsett Hwy., Greenville SC 29613. (864)294-2194. **Website:** library.furman.edu/specialcollections/96Press/index.htm. Estab. 1991. For a sample, send $10.

TIPS "Between 1991 and 2015, the Ninety-Six Press published only poetry by South Carolina authors. The Press is not considering new publishing projects at this time. Check our website for up-to-date information."

NOLO

950 Parker St., Berkeley CA 94710. (510)549-1976. **Fax:** (510)859-0025. **Website:** www.nolo.com. **Contact:** Editorial Department. Estab. 1971. Publishes trade paperback originals. "We publish practical, do-it-yourself books, software and various electronic products on financial and legal issues that affect individuals, small business, and nonprofit organizations. We specialize in helping people handle their own legal tasks; i.e., write a will, file a small claims lawsuit, start a small business or nonprofit, or apply for a patent." **Publishes 75 new editions and 15 new titles/year. 20% of books from first-time authors. Pays advance.** Accepts simultaneous submissions. Responds in 3 weeks to queries. Responds in 5 weeks to proposals. Guidelines online.

NONFICTION Subjects includelegal guides in various topics including employment, small business, intellectual property, parenting and education, finance and investment, landlord/tenant, real estate, and estate planning. Query with SASE. Submit outline, 1 sample chapter.

NOMAD PRESS

2456 Christain St., White River Junction VT 05001. (802)649-1995. **E-mail:** info@nomadpress.net. **Website:** www.nomadpress.net. **Contact:** Acquisitions Editor. Estab. 2001. "We produce nonfiction children's activity books that bring a particular science or cultural topic into sharp focus. Nomad Press does not accept unsolicited manuscripts. If authors are interested in contributing to our children's series, please send a writing resume that includes relevant experience/expertise and publishing credits." **Pays authors royalty based on retail price or work purchased outright. Offers advance against royalties.** Publishes book 1 year after acceptance. Accepts simultaneous submissions. Responds to queries in 3-4 weeks. Catalog online.

Nomad Press does not accept picture books, fiction, or cookbooks.

NONFICTION Middle readers: activity books, history, science. Average word length: middle readers—30,000.

TIPS "We publish a very specific kind of nonfiction children's activity book. Please keep this in mind when querying or submitting."

NORTH ATLANTIC BOOKS

2526 Martin Luther King Jr. Way, Berkeley CA 94704. **E-mail:** submissions@northatlanticbooks.com. **Website:** www.northatlanticbooks.com. **Contact:** Acquisitions Board. Estab. 1974. Publishes hardcover, trade paperback, and electronic originals; trade paperback and electronic reprints. **Publishes 60 titles/year. Receives 200 mss/year. 50% of books from first-time authors. 75% from unagented writers. Pays royalty percentage on wholesale price.** Publishes ms 14 months after acceptance. Accepts simultaneous submissions. Responds in 3-6 months. Book catalog free on request (if available). Guidelines online.

IMPRINTS Evolver Editions, Blue Snake Books.

NONFICTION Subjects include agriculture, anthropology, archeology, architecture, art, astrology, business, child guidance, community, contemporary culture, cooking, economics, electronics, environment, finance, foods, gardening, gay, health, horticulture, lesbian, medicine, memoirs, money, multicultural, nature, New Age, nutrition, philosophy, politics, psychic, psychology, public affairs, religion, science, social sciences, sociology, spirituality, sports, travel, womens issues, womens studies, world affairs. Submit proposal package including an outline, 3-4 sample chapters, and "a 75-word statement about the book, your qualifications as an author, marketing plan/audience, for the book, and comparable titles." Reviews artwork with ms package.

FICTION Subjects include adventure, literary, multicultural, mystery, regional, science fiction, spiritual. "We only publish fiction on rare occasions." Submit proposal package including an outline, 3-4 sample chapters, and "a 75-word statement about the book, your qualifications as an author, marketing plan/a udience, for the book, and comparable titles."

POETRY Submit 15-20 sample poems.

NORTH LIGHT BOOKS

An Imprint of Penguin Random House LLC. 1745 Broadway, New York NY 10019. **Website:** www.penguinrandomhouse.com. Publishes hardcover and trade paperback how-to books. "North Light Books publishes art books, including watercolor, drawing, mixed media, acrylic that emphasize illustrated how-to art instruction. Currently emphasizing drawing including traditional, activity books and creativity and inspiration." **Publishes 50 titles/year. 50% of books from first-time authors. 80% from unagented writers. Pays 8% royalty on net receipts and $3,000 advance. Pays advance.** Publishes ms 10-24 months after acceptance. Accepts simultaneous submissions. Responds in 3 months to queries. Book catalog online. Does not return submissions.

This market is mainly for experienced fine artists and workshop instructors who are willing to work with an North Light editor to produce a step-by-step how-to book that teaches readers how to accomplish art techniques.

NONFICTION Subjects include art, watercolor, oil painting, acrylic painting realistic drawing, creativity, decorative painting, paper arts, collage and other craft instruction books. Interested in books on acrylic painting, basic drawing and sketching, journaling, pen and ink, colored pencil, decorative painting, art and how-to. Do not submit coffee table art books without how-to art instruction. Query via e-mail only. Submit outline with JPEG low-resolution images. Submissions via snail mail will not be returned.

NORTHSOUTH BOOKS

600 Third Ave., 2nd Floor, New York NY 10016. **E-mail:** submissionsb@gmail.com. **Website:** www.northsouth.com. **Contact:** Beth Terrill. Accepts simultaneous submissions. Guidelines online.

FICTION Looking for fresh, original fiction with universal themes that could appeal to children ages 3-8. "We typically do not acquire rhyming texts, since our books must also be translated into German." Submit picture book mss (1,000 words or less) via e-mail.

RECENT TITLE(S) *Surf's Up*, by Kwame Alexander and Daniel Miyares; *Lindbergh: Tale of a Flying Mouse*, by Torben Kuhlmann.

W.W. NORTON & COMPANY, INC.

500 Fifth Ave., New York NY 10110. (212)354-5500. **Fax:** (212)869-0856. **Website:** www.wwnorton.com. Estab. 1923. "W. W. Norton & Company, the oldest and largest publishing house owned wholly by its employees, strives to carry out the imperative of its founder to 'publish books not for a single season, but for the years' in fiction, nonfiction, poetry, college textbooks, cookbooks, art books and professional books. Due to the workload of our editorial staff and the large volume of materials we receive, *Norton is no longer able to accept unsolicited submissions.* If you are seeking publication, we suggest working with a literary agent who will represent you to the house." Accepts simultaneous submissions.

NO STARCH PRESS, INC.

245 8th St., San Francisco CA 94103. (415)863-9900. **Fax:** (415)863-9950. **E-mail:** editors@nostarch.com. **Website:** www.nostarch.com. **Contact:** William Pollock, publisher. Estab. 1994. Publishes trade paperback originals. "No Starch Press publishes the finest in geek entertainment—unique books on technology, with a focus on open source, security, hacking, programming, alternative operating systems, LEGO, science, and math. Our titles have personality, our authors are passionate, and our books tackle topics that people care about." **Publishes 25-30 titles/year. 300 queries; 50 mss received/year. 80% of books from first-time authors. 90% from unagented writers. Pays 10-15% royalty on wholesale price. Pays advance.** Publishes ms 4-6 months after acceptance. Accepts simultaneous submissions. Responds in 1-2 weeks. Book catalog online. Guidelines online.

NONFICTION Subjects include computers, electronics, science, software, technology, computing, mathematics, science, STEM, LEGO. Submit outline, bio, 1 sample chapter, market rationale. Reviews artwork/photos. Send digitally please.

TIPS "Books must be relevant to tech-savvy, geeky readers."

NOSY CROW PUBLISHING

The Crow's Nest, 10a Lant St., London SE1 1QR, United Kingdom. (44)(0)207-089-7575. **Fax:** (44)(0)207-089-7576. **E-mail:** hello@nosycrow.com. **E-mail:** submissions@nosycrow.com. **Website:** nosycrow.com. "We publish books for children 0-14. We're looking for 'parent-friendly' books, and we don't publish books with explicit sex, drug use or serious violence, so no edgy YA or edgy cross-over. And whatever New Adult is, we don't do it. We also publish apps for children from 2-7, and may publish apps for older children if the idea feels right." Accepts simultaneous submissions. Guidelines online.

NONFICTION Prefers submissions by e-mail, but post works if absolutely necessary.

FICTION "As a rule, we don't like books with 'issues' that are in any way overly didactic." Prefers submissions by e-mail, but post works if absolutely necessary.

RECENT TITLE(S) *Tiger Thief*, by Michaela Clarke; *Dinosaur Dig!*, by Penny Dale.

TIPS "Please don't be too disappointed if we reject your work! We're a small company and can only publish a few new books and apps each year, so do try other publishers and agents: publishing is necessarily a hugely subjective business. We wish you luck!"

NURSESBOOKS.ORG

American Nurses Association, 8515 Georgia Ave., Suite 400, Silver Spring MD 20901. (800)274-4ANA. **Fax:** (301)628-5003. **E-mail:** anp@ana.org. **Website:** www.nursesbooks.org. Publishes professional paperback originals and reprints. "Nursebooks.org publishes books designed to help professional nurses in their work and careers. Through the publishing program, Nursebooks.org provides nurses in all practice settings with publications that address cutting edge issues and form a basis for debate and exploration of this century's most critical health care trends." **Publishes 10 titles/year. 50 queries received/year. 8-10 mss received/year. 75% of books from first-time authors. 100% from unagented writers.** Publishes ms 4 months after acceptance. Responds in 3 months. Book catalog online. Guidelines available free.

NONFICTION Subjects include advanced practice, computers, continuing education, ethics, health care policy, nursing administration, psychiatric and mental health, quality, nursing history, workplace issues, key clinical topics, such as geriatrics, pain management, public health, spirituality and home health. Submit outline, 1 sample chapter, CV, list of 3 reviewers and paragraph on audience and how to reach them. Reviews artwork/photos. Send photocopies.

OAK KNOLL PRESS

310 Delaware St., New Castle DE 19720. (302)328-7232. **Fax:** (302)328-7274. **E-mail:** publishing@oakknoll.com. **Website:** www.oakknoll.com. **Contact:** Robert D. Fleck III, president. Estab. 1976. Publishes hardcover and trade paperback originals and reprints. "Oak Knoll specializes in books about books and manuals on the book arts: preserving the art and lore of the printed word." **Publishes 40 titles/year. 250 queries; 100 mss received/year. 50% of books from first-time authors. 100% from unagented writers.** Publishes ms 1 year after acceptance. Accepts simultaneous submissions. Guidelines online.

NONFICTION Reviews artwork/photos. Send photocopies.

RECENT TITLE(S) *ABC for Book Collectors, 8th Ed.*, by John Carter and Nicolas Barker; *A History of Chromolithography*, by Michael Twyman; *Greek Library*, by Konstantinos Staikos.

OCEANVIEW PUBLISHING

595 Bay Isles Rd., Suite 120-G, Longboat Key FL 34228. **E-mail:** mail@oceanviewpub.com. **E-mail:** submissions@oceanviewpub.com. **Website:** www.oceanviewpub.com. Estab. 2006. Publishes hardcover and electronic originals. "Independent publisher of nonfiction and fiction, with primary interest in original mystery, thriller and suspense titles. Accepts new and established writers." Accepts simultaneous submissions. Responds in 3 months on mss. Catalog and guidelines online.

FICTION Subjects include mystery, suspense, thriller. Accepting adult mss with a primary interest in the mystery, thriller and suspense genres—from new and established writers. No children's or YA literature, poetry, cookbooks, technical manuals or short stories. Within body of e-mail only, include author's name and brief bio (Indicate if this is an agent submission), ms title and word count, author's mailing address, phone number and e-mail address. Attached to the e-mail should be the following: A synopsis of 750 words or fewer. The first 30 pages of the ms. Please note that we accept only Word documents as attachments to the submission e-mail. Do not send query letters or proposals.

RECENT TITLE(S) *After the Fall*, by Patricia Gussin; *Elective Procedures*, by Merry Jones; *Shark Fin Soup*, by Susan Klaus.

OHIO STATE UNIVERSITY PRESS

1070 Carmack Rd., 180 Pressey Hall, Columbus OH 43210-1002. (614)292-6930. **Fax:** (614)292-2065. **E-mail:** eugene@osupress.org. **E-mail:** lindsay@osupress.org. **Website:** www.ohiostatepress.org. **Contact:** Eugene O'Connor, acquisitions editor (medieval studies and classics); Lindsay Martin, acquisitions editor (literary studies). Estab. 1957. The Ohio State University Press publishes scholarly nonfiction, and offers short fiction and short poetry prizes. Currently emphasizing history, literary studies, political science, women's health, classics, Victoria studies. **Publishes 30 titles/year. Pays royalty. Pays advance.** Accepts simultaneous submissions. Responds in 3 months to queries. Guidelines online.

NONFICTION Subjects include education, history, literary criticism, multicultural, regional, sociology, criminology, literary criticism, women's health. Query.

POETRY Offers poetry competition through *The Journal*.

OHIO UNIVERSITY PRESS

30 Park Place, Suite 101, Athens OH 45701. **Fax:** (740)593-4536. **E-mail:** huard@ohio.edu. **Website:** www.ohioswallow.com. **Contact:** Gillian Berchowitz, director. Estab. 1947. Publishes hardcover and trade paperback originals and reprints. "In addition to scholarly works in African studies, Appalachian studies, US history, and other areas, Ohio University Press publishes a wide range of creative works as part of its Hollis Summers Poetry Prize (yearly deadline in December), its Modern African Writing series, and under its trade imprint, Swallow Press." **Publishes 45-50 titles/year. 20% of books from first-time authors. 95% from unagented writers. Sometimes pays advance.** Publishes ms 1 year after acceptance. Accepts simultaneous submissions. Responds in 1-3 months. Catalog online. Guidelines online.

IMPRINTS Swallow Press.

NONFICTION Subjects include Americana, anthropology, contemporary culture, creative nonfiction, environment, gardening, government, history, horticulture, humanities, language, literature, memoirs, military, multicultural, nature, politics, pop culture, regional, social sciences, sociology, travel, womens studies, world affairs, young adult, African studies, Appalachian studies, US history, Midwestern studies, regional interest, guidebooks, military history, sustainability, middle-grade biographies. "We prefer queries or detailed proposals, rather than manuscripts. Editors will request the complete manuscript if it is of interest." Query via e-mail or with SASE; or online. Reviews artwork/photos. Send photocopies.

FICTION Subjects include contemporary, literary, multicultural, short story collections, translation.

RECENT TITLE(S) *Doubtful Harbor*, by Idris Anderson; *Penumbra*, by Michael Shewmaker; *Animal Purpose*, by Michelle Y. Burke; *Maggie Boylan*, by Michael Henson; *Weedeater*, by Robert Gipe; *In the House of Wilderness*, by Charles Dodd White; *The Extinction of Menai*, by Chuma Nwokolo.

TIPS "Rather than trying to hook the editor on your work, let the material be compelling enough and well-presented enough to do it for you."

OMNIDAWN PUBLISHING

2200 Adeline St., Suite 150, Oakland CA 94607. **Website:** www.omnidawn.com. Estab. 1999. Publishes ms 6-12 months after acceptance. Accepts simultaneous submissions. Guidelines online.

TIPS "Check our website for latest information."

ONSTAGE PUBLISHING

927 Highland Dr., Madison AL 35758. (256)542-3213. **E-mail:** submissions@onstagepublishing.com. **Website:** www.onstagepublishing.com. **Contact:** Dianne Hamilton, senior editor. Estab. 1999. "At this time, we only produce fiction books for ages 8-18. We have added an e-book only side of the house for mysteries for grades 6-12. See our website for more information. We will not do anthologies of any kind. Query first for nonfiction projects as nonfiction projects must spark our interest. We no longer are accepting written submissions. We want e-mail queries and submissions. For submissions: Put the first 3 chapters in the body of the e-mail. Do not use attachments! We will delete any submission with an attachment without acknowledgment." Suggested ms lengths: Chapter books: 3,000-9,000 words, Middle Grade novels: 10,000-40,000 words, Young adult novels: 40,000-60,000 words. **Publishes 1-5 titles/year. 500 + 80% of books from first-time authors. 95% from unagented writers. Pays authors/illustrators/photographers advance plus royalties. Pays advance.** Accepts simul-

taneous submissions. Responds in 1-6 months. Guidelines online.

NONFICTION Subjects include young adult.

FICTION Subjects include adventure, historical, mystery, young adult. Middle readers: adventure, contemporary, fantasy, history, nature/environment, science fiction, suspense/mystery. Young adults: adventure, contemporary, fantasy, history, humor, science fiction, suspense/mystery. Average word length: chapter books—4,000-6,000 words; middle readers—5,000 words and up; young adults—25,000 and up. Recently published *Mission: Shanghai* by Jamie Dodson (an adventure for boys ages 12+); *Birmingham, 1933: Alice* (a chapter book for grades 3-5). "We do not produce picture books."

TIPS "Study our titles and get a sense of the kind of books we publish, so that you know whether your project is likely to be right for us."

ON THE MARK PRESS

15 Dairy Ave., Napanee ON K7R 1M4, Canada. (800)463-6367. **Fax:** (800)290-3631. **E-mail:** lisa@onthemarkpress.com. **Website:** www.onthemarkpress.com. Estab. 1986. Publishes books for the Canadian curriculum. **15% of books from first-time authors.** Accepts simultaneous submissions.

OOLIGAN PRESS

369 Neuberger Hall, 724 SW Harrison St., Portland OR 97201. (503)725-9410. **E-mail:** acquisitions@ooliganpress.pdx.edu. **Website:** ooligan.pdx.edu. **Contact:** Acquisitions Co-Managers. Estab. 2001. Publishes trade paperbacks, electronic originals, and reprints. "We seek to publish regionally significant works of literary, historical, and social value.
We define the Pacific Northwest as Northern California, Oregon, Idaho, Washington, British Columbia, and Alaska. We recognize the importance of diversity, particularly within the publishing industry, and are committed to building a literary community that includes traditionally underrepresented voices; therefore, we are interested in works originating from, or focusing on, marginalized communities of the Pacific Northwest." **Publishes 3-4 titles/year. 250-500 queries; 50-75 mss received/year. 90% of books from first-time authors. 90% from unagented writers. Pays negotiable royalty on retail price.** Publishes ms 12-18 months after acceptance. Accepts simultaneous submissions. Responds in 3 weeks for queries; 3 months for proposals. Catalog online. Guidelines online.

NONFICTION Subjects include alternative lifestyles, Americana, community, contemporary culture, creative nonfiction, education, environment, ethnic, gay, history, humanities, lesbian, literary criticism, literature, memoirs, multicultural, philosophy, regional, social sciences, sociology, translation, travel, womens issues, womens studies, young adult. Cookbooks, self-help books, how-to manuals. Submit a query through Submittable. If accepted, then submit proposal package, outline, 4 sample chapters, projected page count, audience, marketing ideas, and a list of similar titles.

FICTION Subjects include adventure, contemporary, ethnic, experimental, fantasy, feminist, gay, historical, humor, lesbian, literary, mainstream, multicultural, mystery, plays, poetry, poetry in translation, regional, science fiction, short story collections, suspense, young adult, Middle grade. "We seek to publish regionally significant works of literary, historical, and social value. We define the Pacific Northwest as Northern California, Oregon, Idaho, Washington, British Columbia, and Alaska." We recognize the importance of diversity, particularly within the publishing industry, and are committed to building a literary community that includes traditionally underrepresented voices; therefore, we are interested in works originating from, or focusing on, marginalized communities of the Pacific Northwest. Does not want romance, horror, westerns, incomplete mss. Query with SASE. *"At this time we cannot accept science fiction or fantasy submissions."*

POETRY Ooligan is a not-for-profit general trade press that publishes books honoring the cultural and natural diversity of the Pacific Northwest. "We are limited in the number of poetry titles that we publish as poetry represents only a small percentage of our overall acquisitions. We are open to all forms of style and verse; however, we give special preference to prose poetry and traditional verse. Although spoken word, slam, and rap poetry are of interest to the press, we will consider such work if it does not translate well to the written page. Ooligan does not publish chapbooks." Query first through e-mail or Submittable.

RECENT TITLE(S) *Forgive Me If I've Told You This Before*, by Karelia Stetz-Waters; *The Wax Bullet War*, by Sean Davis; *Untangling the Knot: Queer Voices on Marriage, Relationships, and Identity*, edited by Carter

Sickels; *The Ghosts Who Travel with Me*, by Allison Green; *A Series of Small Maneuvers*, by Eliot Treichel.

TIPS "Search the blog for tips."

OPEN COURT PUBLISHING CO.

70 E. Lake St., Suite 800, Chicago IL 60601. **E-mail:** opencourt@cricketmedia.com. **Website:** www.opencourtbooks.com. **Contact:** Acquisitions Editor. Estab. 1887. Publishes hardcover and trade paperback originals. "Regrettably, now, and for the forseeable future, Open Court can consider no new unsolicited manuscripts for publication, with the exception of works suitable for our Popular Culture and Philosophy series." **Publishes 20 titles/year. Pays 5-15% royalty on wholesale price.** Publishes ms 2 years after acceptance. Book catalog online. Guidelines online.

NONFICTION Subjects include philosophy, Asian thought, religious studies and popular culture. Query with SASE. Submit proposal package, outline, 1 sample chapter, TOC, author's cover letter, intended audience.

TIPS "Audience consists of philosophers and intelligent general readers. Only accepting submissions to Popular Culture and Philosophy series."

ORCHARD BOOKS (US)

557 Broadway, New York NY 10012. **Website:** www.scholastic.com. *Orchard is not accepting unsolicited mss.* **Publishes 20 titles/year. 10% of books from first-time authors. Most commonly offers an advance against list royalties.** Accepts simultaneous submissions.

FICTION Picture books, early readers, and novelty: animal, contemporary, history, humor, multicultural, poetry.

OREGON STATE UNIVERSITY PRESS

121 The Valley Library, Corvallis OR 97331. (541)737-3873. **Fax:** (541)737-3170. **E-mail:** mary.braun@oregonstate.edu. **Website:** osupress.oregonstate.edu. **Contact:** Mary Elizabeth Braun, acquisitions editor. Estab. 1962. Publishes hardcover, paperback, and e-book originals. **Publishes 20-25 titles/year. 40% of books from first-time authors.** Publishes book 1 year after acceptance. Responds in 3 months to queries. Book catalog for 6x9 SAE with 2 first-class stamps. Guidelines online.

NONFICTION Subjects include regional, science. Publishes scholarly books in history, biography, geography, literature, natural resource management, with strong emphasis on Pacific or Northwestern topics and Native American and indigenous studies. Submit outline, sample chapters.

RECENT TITLE(S) *Diary of a Citizen Scientist*, by Sharman Apt Russell; *The Next Tsunami*, by Bonnie Henderson; *To Win the Indian Heart: Music at the Chemawa Indian School*, by Melissa Parkhurst.

O'REILLY MEDIA

1005 Gravenstein Highway N., Sebastopol CA 95472. (707)827-7000. **Fax:** (707)829-0104. **E-mail:** workwithus@oreilly.com. **Website:** www.oreilly.com. **Contact:** Acquisitions Editor. "We're always looking for new authors and new book ideas. Our ideal author has real technical competence and a passion for explaining things clearly." Accepts simultaneous submissions. Guidelines online.

NONFICTION "At the same time as you might say that our books are written 'by and for smart people,' they also have a down to earth quality. We like straight talk that goes right to the heart of what people need to know." Submit proposal package, outline, publishing history, bio.

TIPS "It helps if you know that we tend to publish 'high end' books rather than books for dummies, and generally don't want yet another book on a topic that's already well covered."

OUR SUNDAY VISITOR, INC.

200 Noll Plaza, Huntington IN 46750. **E-mail:** jlindsey@osv.com. **Website:** www.osv.com. Publishes paperback and hardbound originals. "We are a Catholic publishing company seeking to educate and deepen our readers in their faith. Currently emphasizing devotional, inspirational, Catholic identity, apologetics, and catechetics." **Publishes 40-50 titles/year. Pays authors royalty of 10-12% net. Pays illustrators by the project (range: $25-1,500).** Publishes ms 1-2 years after acceptance. Accepts simultaneous submissions. Responds in 2 months. Book catalog for 9×12 envelope and first-class stamps; ms guidelines available online.

Our Sunday Visitor, Inc. is publishing only those children's books that are specifically Catholic. See website for submission guidelines.

NONFICTION Prefers to see well-developed proposals as first submission with annotated outline and definition of intended market; Catholic viewpoints on family, prayer, and devotional books, and Catholic heritage books. Picture books, middle readers, young readers, young adults. Query, submit complete ms, or submit outline/synopsis and 2-3 sample chapters. Reviews artwork/photos.

TIPS "Stay in accordance with our guidelines."

RICHARD C. OWEN PUBLISHERS, INC.

P.O. Box 585, Katonah NY 10536. (914)232-3903; (800)262-0787. **E-mail:** richardowen@rcowen.com. **Website:** www.rcowen.com. **Contact:** Richard Owen, publisher. Estab. 1982. "We publish child-focused books, with inherent instructional value, about characters and situations with which 5, 6, and 7-year-old children can identify—books that can be read for meaning, entertainment, enjoyment and information. We include multicultural stories that present minorities in a positive and natural way. Our stories show the diversity in America." Not interested in lesson plans, or books of activities for literature studies or other content areas. Submit complete ms and cover letter. **Pays authors royalty of 5% based on net price or outright purchase (range: $25-500). Offers no advances. Pays illustrators by the project (range: $100-2,000) or per photo (range: $50-150).** Publishes book 2-3 years after acceptance. Accepts simultaneous submissions. Responds to mss in 1 year. Book catalog available with SASE. Ms guidelines with SASE or online.

"Due to high volume and long production time, we are currently limiting to nonfiction submissions only."

NONFICTION Subjects include history, recreation, science, sports, music, diverse culture, nature. "Our books are for kindergarten, first- and second-grade children to read on their own. The stories are very brief—up to 2,000 words—yet well structured and crafted with memorable characters, language, and plots. Picture books, young readers: animals, careers, history, how-to, music/dance, geography, multicultural, nature/environment, science, sports. Multicultural needs include: Good stories respectful of all heritages, races, cultural—African-American, Hispanic, American Indian, Asian, European, Middle Eastern." Wants lively stories. No "encyclopedic" type of information stories. Average word length: under 500 words.

OXFORD UNIVERSITY PRESS

198 Madison Ave., New York NY 10016. (212)726-6000. **E-mail:** custserv.us@oup.com. **Website:** www.oup.com/us. World's largest university press with the widest global audience. Accepts simultaneous submissions. Guidelines online.

NONFICTION Query with outline, proposal, sample chapters.

OXFORD UNIVERSITY PRESS: SOUTHERN AFRICA

P.O. Box 12119, NI City Cape Town 7463, South Africa. (27)(21)596-2300. **Fax:** (27)(21)596-1234. **E-mail:** oxford.za@oup.com. **Website:** www.oxford.co.za. Academic publisher known for its educational books for southern African schools. Also publishes general and reference titles. **Publishes 150 titles/year.** Accepts simultaneous submissions. Book catalog online. Guidelines online.

NONFICTION Submit cover letter, synopsis, first few chapters, and submission form (available online) via mail.

FICTION Submit cover letter, synopsis.

OZARK MOUNTAIN PUBLISHING, INC.

Cannon Holdings, LLC, P.O. Box 754, Huntsville AR 72740. (479)738-2348. **Fax:** (479)738-2448. **E-mail:** brandy@ozarkmt.com. **Website:** www.ozarkmt.com. **Contact:** Nancy Vernon, general manager. Estab. 1992. Publishes trade paperback originals. "We publish new age/metaphysical, spiritual nonfiction books." **Publishes 8-10 titles/year. 50-75 queries; 150-200 mss received/year. 50% of books from first-time authors. 95% from unagented writers. Pays 10-15% royalty on retail or wholesale price. Pays $250-500 advance.** Publishes ms within 18 months after acceptance. Accepts simultaneous submissions. Responds in 6 months to queries; 8 months to mss. Book catalog online. Guidelines online. Include postcard for notification of receipt. No phone call please. Payment required for unaccepted mss to be returned—all other unaccepted mss will be destroyed.

NONFICTION Subjects include astrology, New Age, philosophy, psychic, spirituality, metaphysical. No phone calls please. Query with SASE. Submit completed manuscripts. Guidelines online. No phone calls please.

RECENT TITLE(S) *The Convoluted Universe Book 5*, by Dolores Cannon; *Druidic Soul Star Astrology*, by Maria Wheatley; *Not Your Average Angel Book*, by Andy Myers; *The Alien Handbook*, by Patrick De Haan; *Spiritual Gold*, by Paulinne Delcour-Min; *The Old is New*, by L.R. Sumpter.

TIPS "We envision our audience to be open minded, spiritually expanding. Please do not call to check on submissions. Do not submit electronically. Send hard copy only."

P & R PUBLISHING CO.

P.O. Box 817, Phillipsburg NJ 08865. **Fax:** (908)859-2390. **E-mail:** editorial@prpbooks.com. **Website:** www.prpbooks.com. Estab. 1930. Publishes hardcover originals and trade paperback originals and reprints. **Publishes 40 titles/year. Up to 300 queries; 100 mss received/year. 5% of books from first-time authors. 95% from unagented writers. Pays 10-16% royalty on wholesale price.** Accepts simultaneous submissions. Responds in 3 months to proposals. Guidelines online.

NONFICTION Subjects include history, religion, spirituality, translation. Only accepts electronic submission with completion of online Author Guidelines. Hard copy mss will not be returned.

RECENT TITLE(S) *Life Everlasting: The Unfolding Story of Heaven*, by Dan C. Barber and Robert Peterson (theology/doctrine); *1 Samuel*, by Richard D. Phillips (theology/doctrine); *Gospel Treason*, by Brad Bigney (Christian living).

TIPS "Our audience is evangelical Christians and seekers. All of our publications are consistent with Biblical teaching, as summarized in the Westminster Standards."

PACIFIC PRESS PUBLISHING ASSOCIATION

Trade Book Division, 1350 N. Kings Rd., Nampa ID 83687. (208)465-2500. **Fax:** (208)465-2531. **Website:** www.pacificpress.com. Estab. 1874. Publishes hardcover and trade paperback originals and reprints. "We publish books that fit Seventh-day Adventist beliefs only. All titles are Christian and religious. For guidance, see www.adventist.org/beliefs/index.html. Our books fit into the categories of this retail site: www.adventistbookcenter.com." **Publishes 35 titles/year. 35% of books from first-time authors. 100% from unagented writers. Pays 8-16% royalty on wholesale price.** Publishes book 2 years after acceptance. Responds in 3 months to queries. Guidelines online.

NONFICTION Subjects include child guidance, philosophy, religion, spirituality, family living, Christian lifestyle, Bible study, Christian doctrine, prophecy. Query with SASE or e-mail, or submit 3 sample chapters, cover letter with overview of book. Electronic submissions accepted. Reviews artwork/photos.

FICTION Subjects include religious. "Pacific Press rarely publishes fiction, but we're interested in developing a line of Seventh-day Adventist fiction in the future. Only proposals accepted; no full manuscripts."

RECENT TITLE(S) *Grounds for Belief*, by Ed Dickerson (doctrine); *Chosen by Grace*, by Stuart Tyner (doctrine); *Peter: Fisher of Men*, by Noni Beth Gibbs (Biblical fiction); *Shepherd Warrior*, by Bradley Booth (children's).

TIPS "Our primary audience is members of the Seventh-day Adventist denomination. Almost all are written by Seventh-day Adventists. Books that do well for us relate the Biblical message to practical human concerns and focus more on the experiential rather than theoretical aspects of Christianity. We are assigning more titles, using less unsolicited material—although we still publish manuscripts from freelance submissions and proposals."

PAGESPRING PUBLISHING

P.O. Box 2113, Columbus OH 43221. **E-mail:** sales@pagespringpublishing.com. **E-mail:** submissions@pagespringpublishing.com. **Website:** www.pagespringpublishing.com. **Contact:** Lucky Marble Books Editor or Cup of Tea Books Editor. Estab. 2012. Publishes trade paperback and electronic originals. PageSpring Publishing publishes women's fiction under the Cup of Tea Books imprint and YA/middle grade titles under the Lucky Marble Books imprint. Visit the PageSpring Publishing website for submission details. **Publishes 4-7 titles/year. 50% of books from first-time authors. 90% from unagented writers. Pays royalty on wholesale price.** Publishes ms 9-12 months after acceptance. Accepts simultaneous submissions. Endeavors to respond to queries within 3 months. Catalog online. Guidelines online.

IMPRINTS Cup of Tea Books, Lucky Marble Books.

FICTION Subjects include adventure, contemporary, gothic, historical, humor, juvenile, mainstream, mystery, regional, romance, suspense, young adult. Cup of Tea Books publishes women's fiction. Lucky Marble Books specializes in middle grade and young adult fiction. Send submissions for both Cup of Tea Books and Lucky Marble Books to submissions@pagespringpublishing.com. Send a query, synopsis, and the first 30 pages of the manuscript in the body of the email. please. NO attachments.

RECENT TITLE(S) Cup of Tea Books: Hide Nor Hair, Dust Bunnies and Dead Bodies, More Tales from Suburbia.

TIPS Cup of Tea Books would love to see more cozy mysteries and humor. Lucky Marble Books is looking for humor and engaging contemporary stories for middle grade and young adult readers.

PAGESPRING PUBLISHING

PageSpring Publishing, P.O. Box 21133, Columbus OH 43221. **E-mail:** submissions@pagespringpublishing.com. **Website:** www.pagespringpublishing.com. Estab. 2012. Publishes trade paperback and electronic originals. PageSpring Publishing is a small independent publisher with two imprints: Cup of Tea Books and Lucky Marble Books. Cup of Tea Books publishes women's fiction, with particular emphasis on mystery and humor. Lucky Marble Books publishes young adult and middle grade fiction. "We are looking for engaging characters and well-crafted plots that keep our readers turning the page. We accept e-mail queries only; see our website for details." **Publishes 4-5 titles/year. 75% of books from first-time authors. 100% from unagented writers. Pays royalty.** Publishes ms 12 months after acceptance. Accepts simultaneous submissions. Responds in 3 months. Guidelines online.

IMPRINTS Cup of Tea Books and Lucky Marble Books.

FICTION Subjects include adventure, contemporary, fantasy, feminist, hi-lo, historical, humor, juvenile, literary, mainstream, multicultural, mystery, regional, romance, science fiction, sports, suspense, young adult. Cup of Tea Books publishes women's fiction. Lucky Marble Books publishes middle grade and young adult novels. No children's picture books. Submit proposal package via e-mail only. Include synopsis and 30 sample pages.

TIPS "Cup of Tea Books is particularly interested in cozy mystery novels. Lucky Marble Books is looking for funny, age-appropriate tales for middle grade and young adult readers."

PALADIN PRESS

5540 Central Ave., Suite 200, Boulder CO 80301. (303)443-7250. **Fax:** (303)442-8741. **E-mail:** editorial@paladin-press.com. **Website:** www.paladin-press.com. Estab. 1970. Publishes hardcover originals and paperback originals and reprints, videos. "Paladin Press publishes the action library of nonfiction in military science, police science, weapons, combat, personal freedom, self-defense, survival." **Publishes 50 titles/year. 50% of books from first-time authors. 95% from unagented writers. "We pay royalties in full and on time." Pays advance.** Publishes ms 1 year after acceptance. Accepts simultaneous submissions. Responds in 2 months to proposals. Book catalog available free.

IMPRINTS Sycamore Island Books; Flying Machines Press; Outer Limits Press; Romance Book Classics.

NONFICTION If applicable, send sample photographs and line drawings with complete outline and sample chapters. Paladin Press primarily publishes original manuscripts on military science, weaponry, self-defense, personal privacy, financial freedom, espionage, police science, action careers, guerrilla warfare, and fieldcraft. To submit a book proposal to Paladin Press, send an outline or chapter description along with 1-2 sample chapters (or the entire ms) to the address below. If applicable, samples of illustrations or photographs are also useful. Do not send a computer disk at this point, and be sure keep a copy of everything you send us. We are not accepting mss as electronic submissions at this time. Please allow 2-6 weeks for a reply. If you would like your sample material returned, a SASE with proper postage is required. Editorial Department, Paladin Press Gunbarrel Tech Center, 5540 Central Ave., Boulder, CO 80301, or e-mail us at: editorial@paladin-press.com. Query with SASE. Submitting a proposal for a video project is not much different than a book proposal. See guidelines online and send to: All materials related to video proposals should be addressed directly to: David Dubrow, Video Production Manager.

RECENT TITLE(S) *Surviving Workplace Violence: What to Do Before a Violent Incident; What to Do When the Violence Explodes*, by Loren W. Christensen.

TIPS "We need lucid, instructive material aimed at our market and accompanied by sharp, relevant illustrations and photos. As we are primarily a publisher of 'how-to' books, a manuscript that has step-by-step instructions, written in a clear and concise manner (but not strictly outline form) is desirable. No fiction, first-person accounts, children's, religious, or joke books. We are also interested in serious, professional videos and video ideas (contact Michael Rigg)."

PALETTES & QUILLS

1935 Penfield Rd., Penfield NY 14526. (585)383-0812. **E-mail:** palettesnquills@gmail.com. **Website:** http://palettesandquills.simplesite.com/. **Contact:** Donna M. Marbach, publisher/owner. Estab. 2002. Publishes chapbooks, broadsides, e-newsletter. Palettes

& Quills is devoted to the celebration and expansion of the literary and visual arts, offering both commissioned and consulting services. It works to support beginning and emerging writers and artists to expand their knowledge, improve their skills, and connect to other resources in the community. Further, Palettes & Quills seeks to increase the public's awareness and appreciation of these arts through education, advocacy, hands-on program assistance, and functioning as a small literary press. "We publish a chapbook every other year in a contest judged by a well-known poet. We also publish a monthly e-newsletter, and chapbooks/anthologies/ and broadsides on an irregular schedule. Reprints accepted only for our e-newsletter." **Contest winner gets $200 and 50 books. Others are paid copies.** Publishes ms 12 months after acceptance. Accepts simultaneous submissions. Response time varies. "We try to respond as quick as we can.". Guidelines online.

NONFICTION Subjects include art, crafts, creative nonfiction, entertainment, literary criticism, literature, music, photography. Does not want political and religious diatribes. Our preference is for book reviews, how to for literature and the arts, interviews with artists/authors/essay of interest for writing style or art and literature interest. Artwork can be photos, copies of paintings, collages, photos of sculptures. Photos can be on any subject but should be of interest to literary and visual artists. Reviews art work and photos for covers.

FICTION "We prefer short-shorts and stories. We might consider a novella, but we are too small for long epic novels. Encourage short essays, short stories, reviews for our monthy newsletter."

POETRY Palettes & Quills "is at this point is only considering chapbooks that are poetry, creative nonfiction, or fiction, a poetry press only, and produces only a handful of publications each year, specializing in anthologies, individual chapbooks, and broadsides." Wants "work that should appeal to a wide audience." Does not want "poems that are sold blocks of text, long-lined and without stanza breaks. Wildly elaborate free-verse would be difficult and in all likelihood fight with art background, amateurish rhyming poem, overly sentimental poems, poems that use excessive profanity, or which denigrate other people, or political and religious diatribes." Query first with 3-5 poems and a cover letter with brief bio and publication credits for individual unsolicited chapbooks. May include previously published poems. Chapbook poets would get 20 copies of a run; broadside poets and artists get 5-10 copies and occasionally paid $10 for reproduction rights. Anthology poets get 1 copy of the anthology. All poets and artists get a discount on purchases that include their work.

TIPS "We are very small and the best bet with us with our monthly e-newsletter Pencil Marks."

PALGRAVE MACMILLAN

St. Martin's Press, 175 Fifth Ave., New York NY 10010. (212)982-3900. **Fax:** (212)777-6359. **E-mail:** proposals@palgrave.com. **Website:** www.palgrave.com. Publishes hardcover and trade paperback originals. "Palgrave wishes to expand on our already successful academic, trade, and reference programs so that we will remain at the forefront of publishing in the global information economy of the 21st century. We publish high-quality academic works and a distinguished range of reference titles, and we expect to see many of our works available in electronic form. We do not accept fiction or poetry." Accepts simultaneous submissions. Book catalog and ms guidelines online.

Palgrave Macmillan is a cross-market publisher specializing in cutting edge academic and trade non-fiction titles. Our list consists of top authors ranging from academics making original contributions in their disciplines to trade authors, including journalists and experts, writing news-making books for a broad, educated readership.

NONFICTION Subjects include creative nonfiction, education, ethnic, history, multicultural, philosophy, regional, religion, sociology, spirituality, translation, humanities. We are looking for good solid scholarship. Query with proposal package including outline, 3-4 sample chapters, prospectus, cv and SASE. Reviews artwork/photos.

RECENT TITLE(S) *The Holocaust By Bullets*, by Father Patrick Desbois; *Engaging the Muslim World* by Juan Cole; *Future Jihad*, by Walid Phares; *Billions*, by Tom Doctoroff; *AIDS in Asia*, by Susan Houter.

PANTHEON BOOKS

Penguin Random House, 1745 Broadway, New York NY 10019. **Website:** www.pantheonbooks.com. Estab. 1942. Publishes hardcover and trade paperback originals and trade paperback reprints. Accepts simultaneous submissions.

Pantheon Books publishes both Western and non-Western authors of literary fiction and important nonfiction. "We only accept mss submitted by an agent."

NONFICTION *Does not accept unsolicited mss.* Agented submissions only.

FICTION *Does not accept unsolicited mss.* Agented submissions only.

PANTS ON FIRE PRESS

2062 Harbor Cove Way, Winter Garden FL 34787. (863)546-0760. **E-mail:** submission@pantsonfirepress.com. **Website:** www.pantsonfirepress.com. **Contact:** Becca Goldman, senior editor; Emily Gerety, editor. Estab. 2012. Publishes hardcover originals and reprints, trade paperback originals and reprints, and electronic originals and reprints. Pants On Fire Press is an award-winning book publisher of picture, middle-grade, young adult, and adult books. **Publishes 10 titles/year. Receives 36,300 queries and mss per year. 50% of books from first-time authors. 80% from unagented writers. Pays 10-50% royalties on wholesale price.** Publishes ms approximately 7 months after acceptance. Accepts simultaneous submissions. Responds in 3 months. Catalog online. Guidelines online.

Pants On Fire Press is an award-winning boutique book publisher of middle-grade, young adult and fictional books for adults. We publish in both print and e-book format. We love big story ideas and meaty characters. We are always on the lookout for the following subjects: Action, Adventure, Christian, Detective, Drama, Dystopian, Fantasy, Historical Fiction, Horror, Humor, Jewish, Love, Mystery, Paranormal, Romance, Science Fiction, Supernatural, Suspense and Thriller stories.

FICTION Subjects include adventure, ethnic, fantasy, gothic, historical, horror, humor, juvenile, mainstream, military, multicultural, mystery, picture books, regional, religious, romance, science fiction, spiritual, sports, suspense, war, young adult. Publishes big story ideas with high concepts, new worlds, and meaty characters for children, teens, and discerning adults. Submit a proposal package including a synopsis, 3 sample chapters, and a query letter via e-mail.

PAPERCUTZ

160 Broadway, Suite 700E, New York NY 10038. (646)559-4681. **Fax:** (212)643-1545. **E-mail:** papercutz@papercutz.com. **Website:** www.papercutz.com. Estab. 2004. Publishes major licenses and author created comics. Publisher of graphic novels for kids and teens. **Publishes 40 titles/year. 5% of books from first-time authors. 90% from unagented writers. Pays advance.** Publishes ms 1 year after acceptance. Accepts simultaneous submissions. Responds in 2-4 weeks.

IMPRINTS SuperGenius, Charmz.

NONFICTION Subjects include literature, pop culture, translation, young adult.

FICTION Subjects include comic books, fantasy, historical, horror, humor, juvenile, literary, mainstream, translation, young adult. "Independent publisher of graphic novels including popular existing properties aimed at the teen and tween market."

TIPS "Be familiar with our titles—that's the best way to know what we're interested in publishing. If you are somehow attached to a successful tween or teen property and would like to adapt it into a graphic novel, we may be interested. We also take submissions for new series preferably that have already a following online."

PARACLETE PRESS

P.O. Box 1568, Orleans MA 02653. (508)255-4685. **Fax:** (508)255-5705. **E-mail:** phil@paracletepress.com. **Website:** www.paracletepress.com. **Contact:** Phil Fox Rose. Estab. 1981. Publishes hardcover and trade paperback originals. Publisher of books on prayer, Christian living, spirituality, fiction, devotionals, new editions of classics. Also publishes audio and video. **Publishes 40 titles/year. 250 mss received/year.** Publishes ms up to 2 years after acceptance.

Does not accept unsolicited submissions of poetry, memoirs, or children's books.

NONFICTION Subjects include art, religion, spirituality. E-mail. Submit proposal, with intro plus 2-3 sample chapters, TOC, chapter summaries.

PARAGON HOUSE PUBLISHERS

3600 Labore Rd., Suite 1, St. Paul MN 55110. (651)644-3087. **Fax:** (651)644-0997. **E-mail:** paragon@paragonhouse.com. **Website:** www.paragonhouse.com. **Contact:** Gordon Anderson, acquisitions editor. Estab. 1962. Publishes hardcover and trade paperback originals and trade paperback reprints and e-books. "We publish general-interest titles and textbooks that provide the readers greater understanding of society and the world. Currently emphasizing philosophy, spirituality, economics, society, and governance." **Publishes**

5-10 titles/year. 1,500 queries; 150 mss received/ year. 7% of books from first-time authors. 90% from unagented writers. 10% of publisher's sales receipts for print books, 25% for e-books Does not generally pay advance. Royalties paid as-earned. Publishes ms 1 year after acceptance. Accepts simultaneous submissions. Guidelines online.

IMPRINTS Omega Books.

NONFICTION Subjects include anthropology, creative nonfiction, economics, environment, government, history, military, New Age, parenting, philosophy, politics, psychology, religion, social sciences, sociology, spirituality, world affairs, integral studies. Submit proposal package, outline, 2 sample chapters, market breakdown, SASE.

RECENT TITLE(S) *Bully Nation: What America's Approach to Childhood Aggression is Bad for Everyone, Plague in Paradise: The Black Death in Los Angeles. 1924, Tarot of the Future, Philosophical Imagination and the Evolution of Modern Philosophy, Rethinking the Oceans, Is Your God Big Enough, Close Enough, You Enough?, Understanding Scientific Progress, Your Behavior: Understanding and Changing the Things You Do,Heav'nly Tidings from the Afric Muse: The Grace and Genius of Phyllis Wheatly.*

PASSKEY CONSOLIDATED PUBLISHING NEVADA

5438 Vegas Dr., PMB 1670, Las Vegas NV 89108. (702)418-3326. **Fax:** (702)418-3326. **E-mail:** admin@passkeypublications.com. **Website:** www.passkeypublications.com. Estab. 2007. Publishes trade paperback originals. Publishes hardcover textbooks. PassKey Publications is an established financial textbook publisher that occasionally publishes other genres. **Publishes 15 titles/year. Receives 375 queries/year; 120 mss/ year. 15% of books from first-time authors. 90% from unagented writers. Pay varies. Pays advance.** Publishes ms 6 months after acceptance. Accepts simultaneous submissions. Responds in 1 month. Catalog and guidelines online. Submit query and/or partial manuscript in Word or pdf format to the e-mail address listed.

IMPRINTS Passkey Publications, PassKey EA Review.

NONFICTION Subjects include business, finance, accounting, taxation, financial topics. Accepting accounting, finance, taxation nonfiction. No self-help or memoirs. Submit query and partial ms.

TIPS "Accepting nonfiction (accounting, tax, finance and related subjects)."

⊘ PAUL DRY BOOKS

1700 Sansom St., Suite 700, Philadelphia PA 19103. (215)231-9939. **Fax:** (215)231-9942. **E-mail:** editor@pauldrybooks.com. **E-mail:** pdry@pauldrybooks.com. **Website:** pauldrybooks.com. Hardcover and trade paperback originals, trade paperback reprints. "We publish fiction, both novels and short stories, and nonfiction, biography, memoirs, history, and essays, covering subjects from Homer to Chekhov, bird watching to jazz music, New York City to shogunate Japan." Accepts simultaneous submissions. Book catalog online.

NONFICTION Subjects include agriculture, architecture, contemporary culture, education, history, language, literary criticism, literature, memoirs, multicultural, philosophy, religion, science, translation, travel, young adult, popular mathematics. "We do not accept unsolicited manuscripts."

FICTION Subjects include literary, short story collections, translation, young adult, novels. "We do not accept unsolicited manuscripts."

RECENT TITLE(S) *The Book Shopper*, by Murray Browne; *Philadelphia Architecture* by John Andrew Gallery; *Bombay Smiles*, by Jaune Sanllorente; *American Places*, by William Zinsser (treasured historic sites); *One is One*, by Barbara Leonie Picard (fiction).

TIPS "Our aim is to publish lively books 'to awaken, delight, and educate'—to spark conversation. We publish fiction and nonfiction, and essays covering subjects from Homer to Chekhov, bird watching to jazz music, New York City to shogunate Japan."

PAULINE BOOKS & MEDIA

50 St. Paul's Ave., Boston MA 02130. (617)522-8911. **Fax:** (617)541-9805. **E-mail:** design@paulinemedia.com; editorial@paulinemedia.com. **Website:** www.pauline.org. Estab. 1932. Publishes trade paperback originals and reprints. "Submissions are evaluated on adherence to Gospel values, harmony with the Catholic faith tradition, relevance of topic, and quality of writing." For board books and picture books, the entire manuscript should be submitted. For easy-to-read, young readers, and middle reader books and teen books, please send a cover letter accompanied by a synopsis and two sample chapters. "Electronic submissions are encouraged. We make every effort to respond to unsolicited submissions within 2 months." **Publishes 40 titles/year. 5% from unagented writers. Varies by project, but generally are royalties with**

advance. Flat fees sometimes considered for smaller works. Publishes a book approximately 11-18 months after acceptance. Responds in 2 months. Book catalog online. Guidelines online.

NONFICTION Subjects include child guidance, religion, spirituality, young adult. Picture books, young readers, middle readers, teen: religion and fiction. Average word length: picture books—500-1,000; young readers—8,000-10,000; middle readers—15,000-25,000; teen—30,000-50,000. Recently published children's titles: *Bible Stores for Little Ones* by Genny Monchapm; *I Forgive You: Love We Can Hear, Ask For and Give* by Nicole Lataif; *Shepherds To the Rescue* (first place Catholic Book Award Winner) by Maria Grace Dateno; *FSP*; *Jorge from Argentina*; *Prayers for Young Catholics.* Teen Titles: *Teens Share the Mission* by Teens; *Martyred: The Story of Saint Lorenzo Ruiz*; *Ten Commandmenst for Kissing Gloria Jean* by Britt Leigh; *A.K.A. Genius* (2nd Place Catholic Book Award Winner) by Marilee Haynes; *Tackling Tough Topics* with Faith and Fiction by Diana Jenkins. No memoir/autobiography, poetry, or strictly nonreligious works currently considered. Submit proposal package, including outline, 1-2 sample chapters, cover letter, synopsis, intended audience and proposed length.

FICTION Subjects include adventure, comic books, contemporary, juvenile, picture books, religious, romance, spiritual, young adult. Children's and teen fiction only. "We are now accepting submissions for easy-to-read and middle reader chapter, and teen well documented historical fiction. We would also consider well-written fantasy, fairy tales, myths, science fiction, mysteries, or romance if approached from a Catholic perspective and consistent with church teaching. Please see our writer's guidelines." "Submit proposal package, including synopsis, 2 sample chapters, and cover letter; complete ms."

RECENT TITLE(S) *Navigating the New Evangelization; When Faith Feels Fragile; Prayer and You; Saints Alive! the Faith Proclaimed; Understanding Love and Responsibility.*

TIPS "Manuscripts may or may not be explicitly catechetical, but we seek those that reflect a positive worldview, good moral values, awareness and appreciation of diversity, and respect for all people. All material must be relevant to the lives of readers and must conform to Catholic teaching and practice."

PAULIST PRESS

997 Macarthur Blvd., Mahwah NJ 07430. (201)825-7300. **Fax:** (201)825-8345. **E-mail:** submissions@paulistpress.com. **Website:** www.paulistpress.com. **Contact:** Trace Murphy, Editorial Director. Estab. 1865. Paulist Press publishes ecumenical theology, Roman Catholic studies, and books on scripture, liturgy, spirituality, church history, and philosophy, as well as works on faith and culture. Also publishes 2-3 children's titles a year. **Receives 400 submissions/year. 10% of books from first-time authors. 95% from unagented writers. Royalties and advances are negotiable. Pays negotiable advance.** Publishes a book 12-18 months after receipt of final, edited ms. Responds in 3 months to queries and proposals; 3-4 months on mss. Book catalog online. Guidelines online.

NONFICTION Subjects include religion. Accepts submissions via e-mail.

PAYCOCK PRESS

3819 N. 13th St., Arlington VA 22201. (703)525-9296. **E-mail:** rchrdpeabody9@gmail.com. **E-mail:** gargoyle@gargoylemagazine.com. **Website:** www.gargoylemagazine.com. **Contact:** Richard Peabody. Estab. 1976. "Too academic for the underground, too outlaw for the academic world. We tend to be edgy and look for ultra-literary work." Publishes paperback originals. Books: POD printing. Average print order: 500. Averages 1 total title/year. Member CLMP. Distributes through Amazon and website. Publishes ms 1 year after acceptance. Accepts simultaneous submissions. Responds to queries in 1 month; mss in 4 months.

FICTION Subjects include experimental, literary, poetry, short story collections. Accepts unsolicited mss. Accepts queries by e-mail. Include brief bio. Send SASE for return of ms or send a disposable ms and SASE for reply only.

POETRY Considers experimental, edgy poetry collections. Accepts unsolicited mss. Accepts queries by e-mail. Include brief bio. Send SASE for return of ms or send a disposable ms and SASE for reply only.

TIPS "Check out our website. Two of our favorite writers are Paul Bowles and Jeanette Winterson."

PEACHTREE PUBLISHING COMPANY INC.

Peachtree Publishing Company Inc., 1700 Chattahoochee Ave., Atlanta GA 30318. (404)876-8761. **Fax:** (404)875-2578. **E-mail:** hello@peachtree-online.com. **Website:** www.peachtree-online.com. **Contact:** Helen

Harriss, submissions editor. Publishes hardcover and trade paperback originals. "We publish a broad range of subjects and perspectives, with emphasis on innovative plots and strong writing." **Publishes 30 titles/year. 25% of books from first-time authors. 25% from unagented writers. Pays royalty on retail price.** Publishes ms 1 year after acceptance. Accepts simultaneous submissions. Responds in 6 months and mss. Book catalog for 6 first-class stamps. Guidelines online.

NONFICTION Subjects include animals, child guidance, creative nonfiction, education, ethnic, gardening, history, literary criticism, multicultural, recreation, regional, science, social sciences, sports, travel, young adult. No e-mail or fax queries of mss. Submit complete ms with SASE, or summary and 3 sample chapters with SASE.

FICTION Subjects include juvenile, picture books, young adult. Looking for very well-written middle grade and young adult novels. No adult fiction. No collections of poetry or short stories; no romance or science fiction. Submit complete ms with SASE.

PEACHTREE PUBLISHING COMPANY INC.

1700 Chattahoochee Ave., Atlanta GA 30318. (404)876-8761. **Fax:** (404)875-2578. **E-mail:** hello@peachtree-online.com. **Website:** www.peachtree-online.com. Estab. 1977. **Publishes 30-35 titles/year.** Publishes book 1-2 years after acceptance. Accepts simultaneous submissions. Responds in 6-9 months.

NONFICTION Picture books: animal, history, nature/environment. Young readers, middle readers, young adults: animal, biography, nature/environment. Does not want to see religion. Submit complete ms by postal mail only.

FICTION Picture books, young readers: adventure, animal, concept, history, nature/environment. Middle readers: adventure, animal, history, nature/environment, sports. Young adults: fiction, mystery, adventure. Does not want to see science fiction, romance. Submit complete manuscript by postal mail only.

PELICAN PUBLISHING COMPANY

1000 Burmaster St., Gretna LA 70053. (504)368-1175. **Fax:** (504)368-1195. **E-mail:** editorial@pelicanpub.com. **Website:** www.pelicanpub.com. Estab. 1926. Publishes hardcover, trade paperback and mass market paperback originals and reprints. "We believe ideas have consequences. One of the consequences is that they lead to a best-selling book. We publish books to improve and uplift the reader. Currently emphasizing business and history titles." Publishes 20 young readers/year; 1 middle reader/year. "Our children's books (illustrated and otherwise) include history, biography, holiday, and regional. Pelican's mission is to publish books of quality and permanence that enrich the lives of those who read them." **Pays authors in royalties; buys ms outright "rarely." Illustrators paid by "various arrangements." Advance considered.** Publishes a book 9-18 months after acceptance. Responds in 1 month to queries; 3 months to mss. Requires exclusive submission. Book catalog and ms guidelines online.

NONFICTION Subjects include Americana, ethnic, history, multicultural, regional, religion, sports, motivational (with business slant). "We look for authors who can promote successfully. We require that a query be made first. This greatly expedites the review process and can save the writer additional postage expenses." Young readers: biography, history, holiday, multicultural. Middle readers: Louisiana history, holiday, regional. No multiple queries or submissions. Reviews artwork/photos.

FICTION Subjects include historical, juvenile. We publish no adult fiction. Young readers: history, holiday, science, multicultural and regional. Middle readers: Louisiana History. Multicultural needs include stories about African-Americans, Irish-Americans, Jews, Asian-Americans, and Hispanics. Does not want animal stories, general Christmas stories, "day at school" or "accept yourself" stories. Maximum word length: young readers—1,100; middle readers—40,000. No young adult, romance, science fiction, fantasy, gothic, mystery, erotica, confession, horror, sex, or violence. Also no psychological novels. Submit outline, clips, 2 sample chapters, SASE. Full guidelines on website.

POETRY Considers poetry for "hardcover children's books only (1,100 words maximum), preferably with a regional focus. However, our needs for this are very limited; we publish 20 juvenile titles per year, and most of these are prose, not poetry." Books are 32 pages, magazine-sized, include illustrations.

TIPS "We do extremely well with cookbooks, popular histories, and business. We will continue to build in these areas. The writer must have a clear sense of the market and knowledge of the competition. A query letter should describe the project briefly, give the author's writing and professional credentials, and promotional ideas."

PENGUIN GROUP: SOUTH AFRICA

P.O. Box 9, Parklands 2121, South Africa. (27)(11)327-3550. **Fax:** (27)(11)327-3660. **E-mail:** fiction@penguinrandomhouse.co.za. **E-mail:** nonfiction@penguinrandomhouse.co.za. **Website:** www.penguinbooks.co.za. Seeks adult fiction (literary and mass market titles) and adult nonfiction (travel, sports, politics, current affairs, business). No children's, young adult, poetry, or short stories. **Publishes 20 titles/year. Pays royalty.** Accepts simultaneous submissions.

NONFICTION Subjects include history, sports, travel, health/fitness, politics/current affairs. Submit info letter, synopsis, SASE. No e-mail/fax queries.

FICTION Subjects include literary, mass market. Submit intro letter, 3 sample chapters.

PENGUIN GROUP USA

Penguin Random House LLC. 1745 Broadway, New York NY 10019. (212)782-9000. **Website:** www.penguinrandomhouse.com. General interest publisher of both fiction and nonfiction. *No unsolicited mss.* Submit work through a literary agent. DAW Books is the lone exception. Guidelines online.

PENGUIN POETS

An Imprint of Penguin Random House LLC. 1745 Broadway, New York NY 10019. **Website:** www.penguinrandomhouse.com. Agented submissions only. Accepts simultaneous submissions. Catalog online.

RECENT TITLE(S) *How to Be Drawn*, by Terrance Hayes; *Certain Magical Acts*, by Alice Notley.

PENGUIN RANDOM HOUSE, LLC

Division of Bertelsmann Book Group, 1745 Broadway, New York NY 10019. (212)782-9000. **Website:** www.penguinrandomhouse.com. Estab. 1925. Penguin Random House LLC is the world's largest English-language general trade book publisher. *Agented submissions only. No unsolicited mss.* Accepts simultaneous submissions.

IMPRINTS Crown Publishing Group; Knopf Doubleday Publishing Group; Random House Publishing Group; Random House Children's Books; RH Digital Publishing Group; RH International.

THE PERMANENT PRESS

Second Chance Press, Attn: Judith Shepard, 4170 Noyac Rd., Sag Harbor NY 11963. (631)725-1101. **E-mail:** judith@thepermanentpress.com; shepard@thepermanentpress.com. **Website:** www.thepermanentpress.com. **Contact:** Judith and Martin Shepard, acquisitions/co-publishers. Estab. 1978. Publishes hardcover originals. Mid-size, independent publisher of literary fiction. "We keep titles in print and are active in selling subsidiary rights." Average print order: 1,000-2,500. Averages 16 total titles. Accepts unsolicited mss. Pays 10-15% royalty on wholesale price. Offers $1,000 advance. *Will not accept simultaneous submissions.* **20% of books from first-time authors. 45% from unagented writers. Pays 10-15% royalty on wholesale price. Offers $1,000 advance.** Publishes ms within 18 months after acceptance. Responds in weeks or months. Catalog available.

NONFICTION Subjects include literature, memoirs, sex, true crime.

FICTION Subjects include adventure, contemporary, erotica, experimental, historical, literary, mainstream, mystery, science fiction, suspense, translation. Promotes titles through reviews. Literary, mainstream/contemporary, mystery. Especially looking for high-line literary fiction, "artful, original and arresting." Accepts any fiction category as long as it is a "well-written, original full-length novel."

RECENT TITLE(S) *Nakamura reality Alex Austin Do Not Find Me*, by Kathleen Novak; *The Good Life*, by Marian Thurm Hitler; *Mussolini and Me*, by Charles Davis; *Backlash*, by Chris Knopf; *Guy Novel*, by Michael Ryan; *Hot Start*, by David Freed; *Concrete Carnival*, by Danner Darclight; *Grace*, by Howard Owen.

TIPS "We are looking for good books—be they 10th novels or first ones, it makes little difference. The fiction is more important than the track record. Send us the first 25 pages; it's impossible to judge something that begins on page 302. Also, no outlines—let the writing present itself."

PERSEA BOOKS

277 Broadway, Suite 708, New York NY 10007. (212)260-9256. **Fax:** (212)267-3165. **E-mail:** info@perseabooks.com. **Website:** www.perseabooks.com. Estab. 1975. The aim of Persea is to publish works that endure by meeting high standards of literary merit and relevance. "We have often taken on important

books other publishers have overlooked, or have made significant discoveries and rediscoveries, whether of a single work or writer's entire oeuvre. Our books cover a wide range of themes, styles, and genres. We have published poetry, fiction, essays, memoir, biography, titles of Jewish and Middle Eastern interest, women's studies, American Indian folklore, and revived classics, as well as a notable selection of works in translation." Accepts simultaneous submissions. Responds in 8 weeks to proposals; 10 weeks to mss. Guidelines online.

NONFICTION Subjects include contemporary culture, literary criticism, literature, memoirs, translation, travel, young adult.

FICTION Subjects include contemporary, literary, short story collections, translation, young adult. Queries should include a cover letter, author background and publication history, a detailed synopsis of the proposed work, and a sample chapter. Please indicate if the work is simultaneously submitted.

POETRY "We have a longstanding commitment to publishing extraordinary contemporary poetry and maintain an active poetry program. At this time, due to our commitment to the poets we already publish, we are limited in our ability to add new collections." Send an e-mail to poetry@perseabooks.com describing current project and publication history, attaching a pdf or Word document with up to 12 sample pages of poetry. "If the timing is right and we are interested in seeing more work, we will contact you."

⊘ PERUGIA PRESS

P.O. Box 60364, Florence MA 01062. **E-mail:** editor@perugiapress.com. **Website:** www.perugiapress.com. **Contact:** Rebecca Olander, editor/director. Estab. 1997. Since 1997, Perugia Press has been publishing first and second books of poetry by women. "We publish one book a year, the winner of the Perugia Press Prize. Our mission is to help right gender inequity in publishing by launching women's voices into the world, one excellent book at a time." **Publishes 1 titles/year.** Publishes ms less than a year after acceptance. Accepts simultaneous submissions. See website.

NONFICTION Subjects include literature.

PETER PAUPER PRESS, INC.

202 Mamaroneck Ave., 4th Floor, White Plains NY 10601. **Website:** www.peterpauper.com. Estab. 1928. Publishes hardcover originals. "PPP publishes small and medium format, illustrated gift books for occasions and in celebration of specific relationships such as mom, sister, friend, teacher, grandmother, granddaughter. PPP has expanded into the following areas: books for teens and tweens, activity books for children, organizers, books on popular topics of nonfiction for adults and licensed books by best-selling authors." **Publishes 40-50 titles/year. 100 queries received/year. 150 mss received/year. 5% from unagented writers. Makes outright purchase only. Pays advance.** Publishes ms 1 year after acceptance. Responds in 2 months to queries.

NONFICTION "We do not publish fiction or poetry. We publish brief, original quotes, aphorisms, and wise sayings. Please do not send us other people's quotes." Submit cover letter and hard copy ms.

TIPS "Our readers are primarily female, age 10 and over, who are likely to buy a 'gift' book or gift book set in a stationery, gift, book, or boutique store or national book chain. Writers should become familiar with our previously published work. We publish only small- and medium-format, illustrated, hardcover gift books and sets of between 1,000-4,000 words. We have much less interest in work aimed at men."

PETERSON'S

121 S. 13 St., Lincoln NE 68508. **E-mail:** support@petersons.com. **Website:** www.petersons.com. Estab. 1966. Publishes trade and reference books. Peterson's publishes guides to graduate and professional programs, colleges and universities, financial aid, distance learning, private schools, summer programs, international study, executive education, job hunting and career opportunities, educational and career test prep, as well as online products and services offering educational and career guidance and information for adult learners and workplace solutions for education professionals. **Pays royalty. Pays advance.** Book catalog available free.

NONFICTION Subjects include education, careers. Looks for appropriateness of contents to our markets, author's credentials, and writing style suitable for audience.

PFEIFFER

John Wiley & Sons, Inc., 989 Market St., San Francisco CA 94103. **Website:** www.wiley.com. Pfeiffer is an imprint of Wiley. **Publishes 250 titles/year. Pays variable royalties. Pays occasional advance.** Publishes ms 1 year after acceptance. Accepts simultaneous submissions. Responds in 2-3 months to queries. Guidelines online.

NONFICTION Subjects include education, psychology, religion. See proposal guidelines online.

PFLAUM PUBLISHING GROUP

3055 Kettering Blvd., Suite 100, Dayton OH 45439. (800)543-4383. **Website:** www.pflaum.com. "Pflaum Publishing Group, a division of Peter Li, Inc., serves the specialized market of religious education, primarily Roman Catholic. We provide high quality, theologically sound, practical, and affordable resources that assist religious educators of and ministers to children from preschool through senior high school." **Publishes 20 titles/year. Payment by outright purchase.** Accepts simultaneous submissions. Book catalog and ms guidelines free.

NONFICTION Query with SASE.

PHAIDON PRESS

65 Bleecker St., 8th Floor, New York NY 10012. (212)652-5400. **Fax:** (212)652-5410. **E-mail:** submissions@phaidon.com. **Website:** www.phaidon.com. Estab. 1923. Publishes hardcover and trade paperback originals and reprints. Phaidon Press is the world's leading publisher of books on the visual arts, with offices in London, Paris, Berlin, Barcelona, Milan, New York and Tokyo. Their books are recognized worldwide for the highest quality of content, design, and production. They cover everything from art, architecture, photography, design, performing arts, decorative arts, contemporary culture, fashion, film, travel, cookery and children's books. **Publishes 100 titles/year. 500 mss received/year. 40% of books from first-time authors. 90% from unagented writers. Pays royalty on wholesale price, if appropriate. Offers advance, if appropriate.** Publishes ms 1 year after acceptance. Accepts simultaneous submissions. Responds in 3 months to proposals. Book catalog available free. Guidelines online.

NONFICTION Subjects include photography, design. Submit proposal package and outline, or submit complete ms. Submissions by e-mail or fax will not be accepted. Reviews artwork/photos. Send photocopies.

TIPS "Please do not contact us to obtain an update on the status of your submission until we have had your submission for at least three months, as we will not provide updates before this period of time has elapsed. Phaidon does not assume any responsibility for any unsolicited submissions, or any materials included with a submission."

Ⓐ⊘ PHILOMEL BOOKS

Imprint of Penguin Random House, 1745 Broadway, New York NY 10019. (212)782-9000. **Website:** www.penguinrandomhouse.com. **Contact:** Michael Green, president/publisher. Estab. 1980. Publishes hardcover originals. "We look for beautifully written, engaging manuscripts for children and young adults." **Publishes 8-10 titles/year. 5% of books from first-time authors. 20% from unagented writers. Pays authors in royalties. Average advance payment "varies." Illustrators paid by advance and in royalties. Pays negotiable advance.** Accepts simultaneous submissions.

NONFICTION Picture books. *Agented submissions only.*

FICTION Subjects include adventure, ethnic, fantasy, historical, juvenile, literary, picture books, regional, short story collections, translation, western, young adult. *No unsolicited mss.*

PHILOSOPHY DOCUMENTATION CENTER

P.O. Box 7147, Charlottesville VA 22906-7147. (434)220-3300. **Fax:** (434)220-3301. **E-mail:** leaman@pdcnet.org. **Website:** www.pdcnet.org. **Contact:** Dr. George Leaman, director. Estab. 1966. The Philosophy Documentation Center specializes in the publication of scholarly journals, book series, conference proceedings, and reference works. It has a unique commitment to support teaching, research, and professional activities in philosophy and related fields. **Publishes 20 titles/year. 20 queries; 4-6 mss received/year. 20% of books from first-time authors.** Publishes ms 1 year after acceptance. Responds in 1 week to queries.

NONFICTION Subjects include philosophy, social sciences, software. "We want to increase the range of philosophical titles that are available online, and we support online publication of philosophical work in multiple languages." Query with SASE. Submit outline.

PIANO PRESS

P.O. Box 85, Del Mar CA 92014. (619)884-1401. **Fax:** (858)755-1104. **E-mail:** pianopress@pianopress.com. **Website:** www.pianopress.com. **Contact:** Elizabeth C. Axford, editor. Estab. 1984. "We publish music-related books, either fiction or nonfiction, music-related coloring books, songbooks, sheet music, CDs, and music-related poetry." **Pays authors, illustra-**

tors, and photographers royalties based on the retail price. Publishes book 1 year after acceptance. Accepts simultaneous submissions. Responds if interested. Book catalog online.

NONFICTION Subjects include music. Picture books, young readers, middle readers, young adults: multicultural, music/dance. Average word length: picture books—1,500-2,000.

FICTION Subjects include multicultural, multimedia, picture books. Picture books, young readers, middle readers, young adults: folktales, multicultural, poetry, music. Average word length: picture books—1,500-2,000.

TIPS "We are looking for music-related material only for the juvenile market. Please do not send non-music-related materials. Query by e-mail first before submitting anything."

PICADOR USA

MacMillan, 175 Fifth Ave., New York NY 10010. (212)674-5151. **Website:** us.macmillan.com/picador. Estab. 1994. Picador publishes high-quality literary fiction and nonfiction. "We are open to a broad range of subjects, well written by authoritative authors." Publishes hardcover and trade paperback originals and reprints. Does not accept unsolicited mss. *Agented submissions only.* **Publishes 70-80 titles/year. Pays 7-15% on royalty. Advance varies.** Publishes ms 18 months after acceptance. Accepts simultaneous submissions.

PICCADILLY BOOKS, LTD.

P.O. Box 25203, Colorado Springs CO 80936. (719)550-9887. **Fax:** (719)550-8810. **E-mail:** info@piccadillybooks.com. **Website:** www.piccadillybooks.com. Estab. 1985. Publishes hardcover originals and trade paperback originals and reprints. "Picadilly publishes nonfiction, diet, nutrition, and health-related books with a focus on alternative and natural medicine." **Publishes 5-8 titles/year. 70% of books from first-time authors. 95% from unagented writers. Pays 6-10% royalty on retail price.** Publishes ms 1 year after acceptance. Responds only to assigned projects. We no longer accept unsolicited submissions.

NONFICTION Subjects include health, medicine, nutrition, health, nutrition, diet, and physical fitness. "Do your research. Let us know why there is a need for your book, how it differs from other books on the market, and how you will promote the book. No phone calls. We prefer to see the entire ms, but will accept a minimum of 3 sample chapters on your first inquiry. A cover letter is also required; please provide a brief overview of the book, information about similar books already in print and explain why yours is different or better. Tell us the prime market for your book and what you can do to help market it. Also, provide us with background information on yourself and explain what qualifies you to write this book."

RECENT TITLE(S) *Ketone Therapy: The Ketogenic Cleanse and Anti-Aging Diet*, by Bruce Fife, ND.

TIPS "We publish nonfiction, general interest, self-help books currently emphasizing alternative health."

THE PILGRIM PRESS

700 Prospect Ave. E., Cleveland OH 44115-1100. (216)736-3755. **Fax:** (216)736-2207. **Website:** www.thepilgrimpress.com. Publishes hardcover and trade paperback originals. No longer accepting unsolicited ms proposals. **Publishes 25 titles/year. 60% of books from first-time authors. 80% from unagented writers. Pays standard royalties. Pays advance.** Publishes ms an average of 18 months after acceptance. Responds in 3 months to queries. Book catalog and ms guidelines online.

NONFICTION Subjects include religion, ethics, social issues with a strong commitment to justice—addressing such topics as public policy, sexuality and gender, human rights and minority liberation—primarily in a Christian context, but not exclusively.

PIÑATA BOOKS

Imprint of Arte Publico Press, University of Houston, 4902 Gulf Fwy., Bldg. 19, Room 100, Houston TX 77204-2004. (713)743-2845. **Fax:** (713)743-3080. **E-mail:** submapp@uh.edu. **Website:** www.artepublicopress.com. Estab. 1994. Publishes hardcover and trade paperback originals. "Piñata Books is dedicated to the publication of children's and young adult literature focusing on U.S. Hispanic culture by U.S. Hispanic authors. Arte Publico's mission is the publication, promotion and dissemination of Latino literature for a variety of national and regional audiences, from early childhood to adult, through the complete gamut of delivery systems, including personal performance as well as print and electronic media." **Publishes 10-15 titles/year. 80% of books from first-time authors. Pays 10% royalty on wholesale price. Pays $1,000-3,000 advance.** Publishes book 2 years after acceptance. Accepts simultaneous submissions. Responds in 2-3 months to queries; 4-6 months to mss. Book catalog and guidelines online.

NONFICTION Subjects include ethnic. Piñata Books specializes in publication of children's and young adult literature that authentically portrays themes, characters and customs unique to U.S. Hispanic culture. Submissions made through online submission form.

FICTION Subjects include adventure, juvenile, picture books, young adult. Submissions made through online submission form.

POETRY Appropriate to Hispanic theme. Submissions made through online submission form.

TIPS "Include cover letter with submission explaining why your manuscript is unique and important, why we should publish it, who will buy it, etc."

PINEAPPLE PRESS, INC.

P.O. Box 3889, Sarasota FL 34230. (941)706-2507. **Fax:** (800)746-3275. **Website:** www.pineapplepress.com. **Contact:** June Cussen, executive editor. Estab. 1982. Publishes hardcover and trade paperback originals. "We are seeking quality nonfiction on diverse topics for the library and book trade markets. Our mission is to publish good books about Florida." **Publishes 21 titles/year. 1,000 queries; 500 mss received/year. 50% of books from first-time authors. 95% from unagented writers. Pays authors royalty of 10-15%.** Publishes a book 1 year after acceptance. Accepts simultaneous submissions. Responds in 2 months. Book catalog for 9×12 SAE with $1.32 postage. Guidelines online.

NONFICTION Subjects include regional, Florida. Picture books: animal, history, nature/environmental, science. Young readers, middle readers, young adults: animal, biography, geography, history, nature/environment, science. Query or submit outline/synopsis and intro and 3 sample chapters. Reviews artwork/photos. Send photocopies.

FICTION Subjects include regional. Picture books, young readers, middle readers, young adults: animal, folktales, history, nature/environment. Query or submit outline/synopsis and 3 sample chapters.

TIPS "Quality first novels will be published, though we usually only do one or two novels per year and they must be set in Florida. We regard the author/editor relationship as a trusting relationship with communication open both ways. Learn all you can about the publishing process and about how to promote your book once it is published. A query on a novel without a brief sample seems useless."

Ⓐ⊘ POCKET BOOKS

Simon & Schuster, 1230 Avenue of the Americas, New York NY 10020. (212)698-7000. **Website:** www.simonandschuster.com. Estab. 1939. Publishes paperback originals and reprints, mass market and trade paperbacks. Pocket Books publishes commercial fiction and genre fiction (WWE, Downtown Press, Star Trek). Book catalog available free. Guidelines online.

NONFICTION *Agented submissions only.*

FICTION Subjects include mystery, romance, suspense, western. *Agented submissions only.*

POCOL PRESS

3911 Prosperity Ave., Fairfax VA 22031. (703)870-9611. **E-mail:** info@pocolpress.com. **Website:** www.pocolpress.com. **Contact:** J. Thomas Hetrick, editor. Estab. 1999. Publishes trade paperback originals. "Pocol Press is dedicated to producing high-quality print books and e-books from first-time, non-agented authors. However, all submissions are welcome. We're dedicated to good storytellers and to the written word, specializing in short fiction and baseball. Several of our books have been used as literary texts at universities and in book group discussions around the nation. Pocol Press does not publish children's books, romance novels, or graphic novels. Our authors are comprised of veteran writers and emerging talents." **Publishes 6 titles/year. 90 queries; 20 mss received/year. 90% of books from first-time authors. 100% from unagented writers. Pays 10-12% royalty on wholesale price. Does not pay advance.** Publishes book less than 1 year after acceptance. Responds in 1 month to queries; 2 months to mss. Book catalog and guidelines online.

NONFICTION Subjects include computers, history, literature, medicine, memoirs, military, music, religion, spirituality, sports, war, womens studies.

FICTION Subjects include adventure, historical, horror, literary, mainstream, military, mystery, regional, religious, short story collections, spiritual, sports, suspense, war, western, baseball fiction. "We specialize in thematic short fiction collections by a single author, westerns, war stories, and baseball fiction. Expert storytellers welcome." Does not accept or return unsolicited mss. Query with SASE through US Mail or submit 1 sample chapter. No email queries accepted.

RECENT TITLE(S) *Some of Doc's Blues*, by Steve Hallock; *A Friendship, A Dime, and a Dream: The Biography of Willie Lee Buffington*, by Thomas K. Perry;

Between Mountain and River, by Thomas F. Sheehan; *All the Wrong Places*, by Elaine Pinkerton; *Because of You, We Live! The Untold Story of George & Simone Stalnaker*, by Len Sandler.

TIPS "Our audience is aged 18 and over. Pocol Press is unique; we publish good writing and great storytelling. Write the best stories you can. Read them to you friends/peers. Note their reaction. Publishes some of the finest fiction by a small press."

POISONED PEN PRESS

4014 N. Goldwater Blvd., Suite 201, Scottsdale AZ 85251. **E-mail:** submissions@poisonedpenpress.com. **Website:** www.poisonedpenpress.com. **Contact:** Diane DiBiase, Assistant Publisher. Estab. 1997. Publishes hardcover and trade paperback originals, and hardcover and trade paperback reprints. "Our publishing goal is to offer well-written mystery novels of crime and/or detection where the puzzle and its resolution are the main forces that move the story forward." *Not currently accepting submissions. Check website.* **Publishes 60 titles/year. 1,000 queries; 300 mss received/year. 35% of books from first-time authors. 65% from unagented writers. Pays 9-15% royalty on retail price.** Publishes book 10-12 months after acceptance. Responds in 2-3 months to queries and proposals; 6 months to mss. Book catalog and guidelines online.

FICTION Subjects include mystery. Mss should generally be longer than 65,000 words and shorter than 100,000 words. Member Publishers Marketing Associations, Arizona Book Publishers Associations, Publishers Association of West. Distributes through Ingram, Baker & Taylor, Brodart. Does not want novels centered on serial killers, spousal or child abuse, drugs, or extremist groups, although we do not entirely rule such works out. Accepts unsolicited mss. Electronic queries only. "Submit clips, first 3 pages. We must receive both the synopsis and ms pages electronically as separate attachments to an e-mail message."

RECENT TITLE(S) *Head Wounds*, by Dennis Palumbo; *Missing Persons*, by Michael Brandman; *Random Road*, by Thomas Kies, *Too Lucky to Live* by Annie Hogsett.

TIPS "Audience is adult readers of mystery fiction."

POLIS BOOKS

E-mail: info@polisbooks.com. **E-mail:** submissions@polisbooks.com. **Website:** www.polisbooks.com. Estab. 2013. "Polis Books is an independent publishing company actively seeking new and established authors for our growing list. We are actively acquiring titles in mystery, thriller, suspense, procedural, traditional crime, science fiction, fantasy, horror, supernatural, urban fantasy, romance, erotica, commercial women's fiction, commercial literary fiction, young adult and middle grade books." **Publishes 40 titles/year. 500+ 33% of books from first-time authors. 10% from unagented writers. Offers advance against royalties.** For e-book originals, ms published 6-9 months after acceptance. For front list print titles, 9-15 months. Accepts simultaneous submissions. Only responds to submissions if interested. Guidelines online.

FICTION Query with 3 sample chapters and bio via e-mail.

RECENT TITLE(S) *Ash*, by Shani Petroff and Darci Manley.

POPULAR WOODWORKING BOOKS

An Imprint of Penguin Random House LLC. 1745 Broadway, New York NY 10019. (212) 782-9000. **Website:** www.penguinrandomhouse.com. Publishes trade paperback and hardcover originals and reprints. "Popular Woodworking Books is one of the largest publishers of woodworking books in the world. From perfecting a furniture design to putting on the final coat of finish, our books provide step-by-step instructions and trusted advice from the pros that make them valuable tools for both beginning and advanced woodworkers. Currently emphasizing woodworking jigs and fixtures, woodworking techniques, furniture and cabinet projects, smaller finely crafted boxes, all styles of furniture. We are also looking for DIY-style maker projects for clever furniture projects or home decor created using wood and woodworking techiniques; techniques creating space-saving, modular furniture." **Publishes 8-10 titles/year. 20 queries; 10 mss received/year. 20% of books from first-time authors. 95% from unagented writers.** Accepts simultaneous submissions. Responds in 1 month to queries.

NONFICTION "We publish heavily illustrated how-to woodworking books that show, rather than tell, our readers how to accomplish their woodworking goals." Query with SASE, or electronic query. Proposal package should include an outline and digital photos.

RECENT TITLE(S) *Alan Lacer's Woodturning Projects & Techniques*, by Alan Lacer; *The Homemade Workshop*, by James Hamilton; *Workbenches, Revised Edition*, by Christopher Schwarz; *SketchUp: A Design*

Guide for Woodworkers, by Joe Zeh; *Mid-Century Modern Furniture*, by Michael Crow.

TIPS "Our books are for beginning to advanced woodworking enthusiasts."

PPI (PROFESSIONAL PUBLICATIONS, INC.)

1250 Fifth Ave., Belmont CA 94002. (650)593-9119. **Fax:** (650)592-4519. **E-mail:** info@ppi2pass.com. **E-mail:** acquisitions@ppi2pass.com. **Website:** www.ppi2pass.com. Estab. 1975. Publishes hardcover, paperback, and electronic products, CD-ROMs and DVDs. "PPI publishes professional, reference, and licensing preparation materials. PPI wants submissions from both professionals practicing in the field and from experienced instructors. Currently emphasizing engineering, interior design, architecture, landscape architecture and LEED exam review." **Publishes 10 titles/year. 5% of books from first-time authors. 100% from unagented writers.** Publishes ms 4-18 months after acceptance. Accepts simultaneous submissions. Responds in 1 month to queries. Book catalog and ms guidelines free.

NONFICTION Subjects include architecture, science, landscape architecture, engineering mathematics, engineering, surveying, interior design, greenbuilding, sustainable development, and other professional licensure subjects. Especially needs review and reference books for all professional licensing examinations. Please submit ms and proposal outlining market potential, etc. Proposal template available upon request. Reviews artwork/photos.

TIPS "We specialize in books for those people who want to become licensed and/or accredited professionals: engineers, architects, surveyors, interior designers, LEED APs, etc. Demonstrating your understanding of the market, competition, appropriate delivery methods, and marketing ideas will help sell us on your proposal."

PRESS 53

560 N. Trade St., Suite 103, Winston-Salem NC 27101. (336)770-5353. **E-mail:** editor@press53.com. **Website:** www.press53.com. **Contact:** Kevin Morgan Watson, Publisher and Editor in Chief. Estab. 2005. Poetry and short fiction collections only. "Press 53 was founded in October 2005 and quickly earned a reputation for publishing quality short fiction and poetry collections." **Publishes 14-15 titles/year. Finds mss through contests, referrals, and scouting journals, magazines, and other contests. 60% of books from first-time authors. 90% from unagented writers. Pays 10% royalty on gross sales. Pays advance only for contest winners.** Publishes ms 1 year after acceptance. Accepts simultaneous submissions. Catalog online. Guidelines online.

FICTION Subjects include literary, short story collections. "We publish roughly 4-5 short fiction collections each year by writers who are active and earning recognition through publication and awards, plus the winner of our Press 53 Award for Short Fiction." Collections should be between 100 and 250 pages (give or take). Including a novella is fine, but only one. Does not want novels or novellas. Finds mss through contests, referrals, and scouting magazines, journals, and other contests.

POETRY "We love working with poets who have been widely published and are active in the poetry community. We publish roughly 8-10 full-length poetry collections of around 70 pages or more each year, plus the winner of our Press 53 Award for Poetry." Does not want experimental, overtly political or religious. Finds mss through contests, referrals, and scouting magazines, journals, and other contests.

TIPS "We are looking for writers who are actively involved in the writing community, writers who are submitting their work to journals, magazines and contests, and who are getting published, building readership, and earning a reputation for their work."

PRESS HERE

22230 NE 28th Place, Sammamish WA 98074-6408. **Website:** www.gracecuts.com/press-here. **Contact:** Michael Dylan Welch, editor/publisher. Estab. 1989. Press Here publishes award-winning books of haiku, tanka, and related poetry by the leading poets of these genres, as well as essays, criticism, and interviews about these genres. "We publish work only by those poets who are already frequently published in the leading haiku and tanka journals." Publishes 1-2 poetry books/year, plus occasional books of essays or interviews. Mss are selected nearly always by invitation. Press Here publications have won the 1st-place Merit Book Award and other awards from the Haiku Society of America. **Pays a negotiated percentage of author's copies (out of a press run of 200-1,000).** Accepts simultaneous submissions. Responds to queries in up to 1 month; to mss in up to 2 months. Catalog online.

POETRY Does not want any poetry other than haiku, tanka, and related genres. Has published poetry by Lee Gurga, paul m., Paul O. Williams, Adele Kenny, Pat Shelley, Cor van den Heuvel, and William J. Higginson. Query first, with a few sample poems and a cover letter with brief bio and publication credits. Book mss may include previously published poems ("previous publication strongly preferred"). "All proposals must be by well-established haiku or tanka poets, and must be for haiku or tanka poetry, or criticism/discussion of these genres. If the editor does not already know your work well from leading haiku and tanka publications, then he is not likely to be interested in your manuscript."

PRESTWICK HOUSE, INC.

P.O. Box 658, Clayton DE 19938. **E-mail:** info@prestwickhouse.com. **Website:** www.prestwickhouse.com. Estab. 1980. Accepts simultaneous submissions.

NONFICTION Submit proposal package, outline, resume, 1 sample chapter, TOC.

TIPS "We market our books primarily for middle and high school English teachers. Submissions should address a direct need of grades 7-12 language arts teachers. Current and former English teachers are encouraged to submit materials developed and used by them successfully in the classroom."

PRICE STERN SLOAN, INC.

Penguin Random House LLC., 1745 Broadway, New York NY 10019. (212)782-9000. **Website:** www.penguinrandomhouse.com. Estab. 1963. "Price Stern Sloan publishes quirky mass market novelty series for childrens as well as licensed movie tie-in books." Price Stern Sloan only responds to submissions it's interested in publishing. Accepts simultaneous submissions. Book catalog online.

FICTION Publishes picture books and novelty/board books. *Agented submissions only.*

TIPS "Price Stern Sloan publishes unique, fun titles."

PRINCETON ARCHITECTURAL PRESS

202 Warren St., Hudson NY 12534. (518)671-6100. **E-mail:** submissions@papress.com. **Website:** www.papress.com. Estab. 1981. Publishes hardcover and trade paperback originals. **Publishes 50 titles/year. 300 queries; 150 mss received/year. 65% of books from first-time authors. 95% from unagented writers. Pays royalty on wholesale price.** Publishes book 1 year after acceptance. Accepts simultaneous submissions. Responds in 2 months. Catalog available in print and online. Princeton Architectural Press accepts proposals concerning architecture, landscape architecture, graphic design, and visual culture. Submissions of illustrated children's books are also welcome. Electronic submissions only. See website for detailed submission guidelines.

Princeton Architectural Press is a leading publisher in architecture, landscape architecture, design, and visual culture, as well as illustrated children's books.

NONFICTION Subjects include agriculture, animals, architecture, art, communications, community, contemporary culture, crafts, environment, gardening, history, house and home, humanities, nature, photography, politics, pop culture. Does not publish highly technical or purely academic titles.

PRINCETON UNIVERSITY PRESS

41 William St., Princeton NJ 08540. (609)258-4900. **Fax:** (609)258-6305. **Website:** press.princeton.edu. **Contact:** Susan Stewart, editor. "The Lockert Library of Poetry in Translation embraces a wide geographic and temporal range, from Scandinavia to Latin America to the subcontinent of India, from the Tang Dynasty to Europe of the modern day. It especially emphasizes poets who are established in their native lands and who are being introduced to an English-speaking audience. Manuscripts are judged with several criteria in mind: the ability of the translation to stand on its own as poetry in English; fidelity to the tone and spirit of the original, rather than literal accuracy; and the importance of the translated poet to the literature of his or her time and country." Accepts simultaneous submissions. Responds in 3-4 months. Guidelines online.

NONFICTION Query with SASE.

POETRY Submit hard copy of proposal with sample poems or full ms. Cover letter is required. Reads submissions year round. Mss will not be returned. Comments on finalists only.

PRINTING INDUSTRIES OF AMERICA

301 Brush Creek Rd., Warrendale PA 15086. (412)741-6860. **Fax:** (412)741-2311. **E-mail:** printing@printing.org. **Website:** www.printing.org. Estab. 1921. Publishes trade paperback originals and reference texts. "Printing Industries of America, along with its affiliates, delivers products and services that enhance the growth and profitability of its members and the

industry through advocacy, education, research, and technical information." Printing Industries of America's mission is to serve the graphic communications community as the major resource for technical information and services through research and education. **Publishes 8-10 titles/year. 20 mss; 30 queries received/year. 50% of books from first-time authors. 100% from unagented writers. Pays 15% royalty on wholesale price.** Publishes ms 18 months after acceptance. Accepts simultaneous submissions. Responds in 1 month to queries.

NONFICTION Subjects include business, communications, economics, education, printing and graphic arts reference, technical, textbook. Currently emphasizing technical textbooks as well as career guides for graphic communications and turnkey training curricula. Query with SASE, or submit outline, sample chapters, and SASE. Reviews artwork. Send photocopies.

RECENT TITLE(S) *Color Management Handbook*, by Richard Adams et al. (color handbook); *Printing Estimating, 5th Ed.*, by Philip K. Ruggles (textbook).

PROMETHEUS BOOKS

59 John Glenn Dr., Amherst NY 14228. (800)421-0351. **Fax:** (716)564-2711. **Website:** www.prometheusbooks.com. Estab. 1969. Publishes hardcover originals, trade paperback originals and reprints. "Prometheus Books is a leading independent publisher in philosophy, social science, popular science, and critical thinking. We publish authoritative and thoughtful books by distinguished authors in many categories. Currently emphasizing popular science, health, psychology, social science, current events, business and economics, atheism and critiques of religion." **Publishes 90-100 titles/year. 30% of books from first-time authors. 40% from unagented writers.** Accepts simultaneous submissions. Responds in 2 months to queries; 3 months to proposals; 4 months to mss. Book catalog and guidelines online.

NONFICTION Subjects include education, history, New Age, philosophy, psychology, religion, contemporary issues. Ask for a catalog, go to the library or our website, look at our books and others like them to get an idea of what our focus is. Submit proposal package including outline, synopsis, potential market, tentative ms length, résumé, and a well-developed query letter with SASE, two or three of author's best chapters. Reviews artwork/photos. Send photocopies.

TIPS "Audience is highly literate with multiple degrees; an audience that is intellectually mature and knows what it wants. They are aware, and we try to provide them with new information on topics of interest to them in mainstream and related areas."

Ⓐ⊘ PUFFIN BOOKS

Imprint of Penguin Random House LLC., 1745 Broadway, New York NY 10019. (212)782-9000. **Website:** www.penguinrandomhouse.com. Publishes trade paperback originals and reprints. "Puffin Books publishes high-end trade paperbacks and paperback reprints for preschool children, beginning and middle readers, and young adults." **Publishes 175-200 titles/year.** Publishes book 1 year after acceptance.

NONFICTION Subjects include education, history, womens issues, womens studies. "Women in history books interest us." *No unsolicited mss. Agented submissions only.*

FICTION Subjects include fantasy, picture books, science fiction, young adult, middle grade, easy-to-read grades 1-3, graphic novels, classics. *No unsolicited mss. Agented submissions only.*

TIPS "Our audience ranges from little children 'first books' to young adult (ages 14-16). An original idea has the best luck."

PURDUE UNIVERSITY PRESS

504 West State St., West Lafayette IN 47907-2058. (765)494-2038. **E-mail:** pupress@purdue.edu. **E-mail:** lpennywa@purdue.edu. **Website:** www.thepress.purdue.edu. **Contact:** Leah Pennywark, acquisitions assistant. Estab. 1960. Purdue University Press is administratively a unit of Purdue University Libraries and its Director reports to the Dean of Libraries. There are 3 full-time staff and 2 part-time staff, as well as student assistants. Dedicated to the dissemination of scholarly and professional information, the Press provides quality resources in several key subject areas including business, technology, health, veterinary sciences, and other selected disciplines in the humanities and sciences. As well as publishing 30 books a year, and 5 subscription-based journals, the Press is committed to broadening access to scholarly information using digital technology. As part of this initiative, the Press distributes a number of Open Access electronic-only journals. An editorial board of 9 Purdue faculty members is responsible for the imprint of the Press and meets twice a semester to consider mss and propos-

als, and guide the editorial program. A management advisory board advises the Director on strategy, and meets twice a year. Purdue University Press is a member of the Association of American University Presses.

G.P. PUTNAM'S SONS, PENGUIN YOUNG READERS GROUP

345 Hudson St., 14th Floor, New York NY 10014. (212)366-2000. **Website:** www.penguin.com. **Contact:** Dave Kopka, Junior Designer. Accepts simultaneous submissions.

G.P. PUTNAM'S SONS HARDCOVER

Imprint of Penguin Random House LLC, 1745 Broadway, New York NY 10019. (212)782-9000. **Website:** www.penguinrandomhouse.com. Publishes hardcover originals. **Pays variable royalties on retail price. Pays varies advance.** Accepts simultaneous submissions. Request book catalog through mail order department.

NONFICTION Subjects include animals, child guidance, contemporary culture, religion, science, sports, travel, celebrity-related topics. *Agented submissions only. No unsolicited mss.*

FICTION Subjects include adventure, literary, suspense, women's. *Agented submissions only.*

QUE

Pearson Education, 800 E. 96th St., Indianapolis IN 46240. (317)581-3500. **E-mail:** greg.wiegand@pearson.com. **Website:** www.quepublishing.com. **Contact:** Greg Wiegand, associate publisher. Estab. 1981. Publishes hardcover, trade paperback and mass market paperback originals and reprints. **Publishes 100 titles/year. 80% from unagented writers. Pays variable royalty on wholesale price or makes work-for-hire arrangements. Pays varying advance.** Accepts simultaneous submissions. Book catalog and guidelines online.

NONFICTION Subjects includetechnology, certification. Submit proposal package, resume, TOC, writing sample, competing titles.

QUILL DRIVER BOOKS

Linden Publishing, 2006 S. Mary St., Fresno CA 93721. (559)233-6633. **E-mail:** kent@lindenpub.com. **E-mail:** kent@lindenpub.com. **Website:** www.quilldriverbooks.com. **Contact:** Kent Sorsky. Publishes hardcover and trade paperback originals and reprints. Quill Driver Books publishes a mix of nonfiction titles, with an emphasis on how-to and self-help books. Our books, we hope, make a worthwhile contribution to the human community, and we have a little fun along the way. **Publishes 10-12 titles/year. 50% of books from first-time authors. 75% from unagented writers. Pays 8-12% royalty on net receipts. Pays $500-5,000 advance.** Publishes ms 12 months after acceptance. Accepts simultaneous submissions. Responds in 1 month to queries and proposals; 3 months to mss. Book catalog for #10 SASE. Guidelines online.

IMPRINTS Pace Press (genre fiction) and Craven Street Books (books about California).

NONFICTION Subjects include regional, writing, aging. Query with SASE. Submit proposal package. Reviews artwork/photos. Send photocopies.

QUITE SPECIFIC MEDIA GROUP, LTD.

7373 Pyramid Place, Hollywood CA 90046. **E-mail:** info@quitespecificmedia.com; info@silmanjamespress.com. **Website:** www.quitespecificmedia.com. Estab. 1967. Publishes hardcover originals, trade paperback originals and reprints. "Quite Specific Media Group is an umbrella company of 5 imprints specializing in costume and fashion, theater and design." **Publishes 12 titles/year. 75 queries; 30 mss received/year. 75% of books from first-time authors. 85% from unagented writers. Pays royalty on wholesale price. Pays varies advance.** Publishes ms 18 months after acceptance. Accepts simultaneous submissions. Responds to queries. Book catalog online.

NONFICTION Subjects include fashion, history, literary criticism, translation. Query by e-mail please. Reviews artwork/photos.

RAGGED SKY PRESS

270 Griggs Dr., Princeton NJ 08540. **E-mail:** raggedskyanthology@gmail.com. **Website:** www.raggedsky.com. **Contact:** Ellen Foos, publisher; Arlene Weiner, editor. Produces poetry anthologies and single-author poetry collections along with occasional inspired prose. Ragged Sky is a small, highly selective cooperative press. "We work with our authors closely." Individual poetry collections currently by invitation only. Learn more online. **Publishes 5 titles/year. 25 50% of books from first-time authors. 100% from unagented writers.** Publishes ms 1 year after acceptance. Accepts simultaneous submissions. Responds in 3 weeks.

NONFICTION Subjects include literature, poetry.

FICTION Subjects include literary.

RANDOM HOUSE CHILDREN'S BOOKS

1745 Broadway, New York NY 10019. (212)782-9000. **Website:** www.penguinrandomhouse.com. Estab. 1925. "Producing books for preschool children through young adult readers, in all formats from board to activity books to picture books and novels, Random House Children's Books brings together world-famous franchise characters, multimillion-copy series and top-flight, award-winning authors, and illustrators." Submit mss through a literary agent. Accepts simultaneous submissions.

IMPRINTS Kids@Random; Golden Books; Princeton Review; Sylvan Learning.

FICTION "Random House publishes a select list of first chapter books and novels, with an emphasis on fantasy and historical fiction." Chapter books, middle-grade readers, young adult. *Does not accept unsolicited mss.*

TIPS "We look for original, unique stories. Do something that hasn't been done before."

RANDOM HOUSE CHILDREN'S PUBLISHERS UK

20 Vauxhall Bridge Rd., London SW1V 2SA, United Kingdom. **Website:** www.randomhousechildrens.co.uk. *Only interested in agented material.* **Publishes 250 titles/year. Pays authors royalty. Offers advances.** Accepts simultaneous submissions.

IMPRINTS Bantam, Doubleday, Corgi, Johnathan Cape, Hutchinson, Bodley Head, Red Fox, Tamarind Books.

FICTION Picture books: adventure, animal, anthology, contemporary, fantasy, folktales, humor, multicultural, nature/environment, poetry, suspense/mystery. Young readers: adventure, animal, anthology, contemporary, fantasy, folktales, humor, multicultural, nature/environment, poetry, sports, suspense/mystery. Middle readers: adventure, animal, anthology, contemporary, fantasy, folktales, humor, multicultural, nature/environment, problem novels, romance, sports, suspense/mystery. Young adults: adventure, contemporary, fantasy, humor, multicultural, nature/environment, problem novels, romance, science fiction, suspense/mystery. Average word length: picture books—800; young readers—1,500-6,000; middle readers—10,000-15,000; young adults—20,000-45,000.

TIPS "Although Random House is a big publisher, each imprint only publishes a small number of books each year. Our lists for the next few years are already full. Any book we take on from a previously unpublished author has to be truly exceptional. Manuscripts should be sent to us via literary agents."

RANDOM HOUSE PUBLISHING GROUP

Division of Random House, Inc., 1745 Broadway, New York NY 10019. (212)782-9000. **Website:** www.penguinrandomhouse.com. Estab. 1925. Publishes hardcover and paperback trade books. Random House is the world's largest English-language general trade book publisher. It includes an array of prestigious imprints that publish some of the foremost writers of our time. **Publishes 120 titles/year.** Accepts simultaneous submissions.

IMPRINTS Ballantine Books; Bantam; Delacorte; Dell; Del Rey; Modern Library; One World; Presidio Press; Random House Trade Group; Random House Trade Paperbacks; Spectra; Spiegel & Grau; Triumph Books; Villard.

NONFICTION *Agented submissions only.*

FICTION *Agented submissions only.*

RATTAPALLAX PRESS

217 Thompson St., Suite 353, New York NY 10012. **Website:** www.rattapallax.com. **Contact:** Ram Devineni, founder/president; Flavia Rocha, editor-in-chief. Estab. 1998. Rattapallax Press publishes "contemporary poets and writers with unique, powerful voices." Publishes 5 paperbacks and 3 chapbooks/year. Books are usually 64 pages, digest-sized, offset-printed, perfect-bound, with 12-pt. CS1 covers. Accepts simultaneous submissions.

POETRY Query first, with a few sample poems and cover letter with brief bio and publication credits. Include SASE. Requires authors to first be published in *Rattapallax*. Responds to queries in 1 month; to mss in 2 months. Pays royalties of 10-25%. Order sample books from website.

RAZORBILL

Penguin Young Readers Group, 1745 Broadway, New York NY 10019. (212)782-9000. **E-mail:** asanchez@penguinrandomhouse.com; bschrank@penguinrandomhouse.com; jharriton@penguinrandomhouse.

com. **Website:** www.razorbillbooks.com. **Contact:** Jessica Almon, executive editor; Casey McIntyre, associate publisher; Deborah Kaplan, vice president and executive art director, Marissa Grossman; assistant editor, Tiffany Liao; associate editor. Estab. 2003. "This division of Penguin Young Readers is looking for the best and the most original of commercial contemporary fiction titles for middle grade and YA readers. A select quantity of nonfiction titles will also be considered." **Publishes 30 titles/year. Offers advance against royalties.** Publishes book 1-2 after acceptance. Accepts simultaneous submissions. Responds in 1-3 months.

NONFICTION Middle readers and young adults/teens: concept. Submit cover letter with up to 30 sample pages.

FICTION Middle Readers: adventure, contemporary, graphic novels, fantasy, humor, problem novels. Young adults/teens: adventure, contemporary, fantasy, graphic novels, humor, multicultural, suspense, paranormal, science fiction, dystopian, literary, romance. Average word length: middle readers—40,000; young adult—60,000. Submit cover letter with up to 30 sample pages.

TIPS "New writers will have the best chance of acceptance and publication with original, contemporary material that boasts a distinctive voice and well-articulated world. Check out website to get a better idea of what we're looking for."

REBELIGHT PUBLISHING, INC.

23-845 Dakota St., Suite 314, Winnipeg Manitoba R2M 5M3, Canada. **Website:** www.rebelight.com. **Contact:** Editor. Estab. 2014. Publishes paperback and electronic originals. Rebelight Publishing is interested in "crack the spine, blow your mind" manuscripts for middle grade, young adult and new adult novels. *Only considers submissions from Canadian writers.* **Publishes 6-10 titles/year. Receive about 500 submissions/year. 25-50% of books from first-time authors. 100% from unagented writers. Pays 12-22% royalties on retail price. Does not offer an advance.** Publishes ms 12-18 months after acceptance. Accepts simultaneous submissions. Responds in 3 months to queries and mss. Submissions accepted via email only. Catalog online or PDF available via e-mail request. Guidelines online.

FICTION Subjects include adventure, contemporary, fantasy, historical, horror, humor, juvenile, mainstream, multicultural, mystery, romance, science fiction, sports, suspense, young adult. All genres are considered, provided they are for a middle grade, young adult, or new adult audience. "Become familiar with our books. Study our website. Stick within the guidelines. Our tag line is 'crack the spine, blow your mind'—we are looking for well-written, powerful, fresh, fast-paced fiction. Keep us turning the pages. Give us something we just have to spread the word about." Submit proposal package, including a synopsis and 3 sample chapters. Read guidelines carefully.

RECENT TITLE(S) *Hannah Both Ways*, by Rosie Greenway; *Red Stone* and *Broken Stone*, by Gabriele Goldstone; *To Catch a Cat Thief*, by Sean Cummings; *Wonder Horse*, by Anita Daher; *One Bright Future: Enslavement*, by Melinda Friesen; *Missing in Paradise*, by Larry Verstraete; and *Empty Cup*, by Suzanne Costigan.

TIPS "Review your manuscript for passive voice prior to submitting! (And that means get rid of it.)"

RED DEER PRESS

195 Allstate Pkwy., Markham ON L3R 4TB, Canada. (905)477-9700. **Fax:** (905)477-9179. **E-mail:** rdp@reddeerpress.com. **Website:** www.reddeerpress.com. **Contact:** Richard Dionne, publisher. Estab. 1975. **Pays 8-10% royalty.** Publishes ms 18 months after acceptance. Book catalog for 9 x 12 SASE.

Red Deer Press is an award-winning publisher of children's and young adult literary titles.

FICTION Publishes young adult, adult science fiction, fantasy, and paperback originals "focusing on books by, about, or of interest to Canadians." Books: offset paper; offset printing; hardcover/perfect-bound. Average print order: 5,000. First novel print order: 2,500. Distributes titles in Canada and the US, the UK, Australia and New Zealand. Young adult (juvenile and early reader), contemporary. No romance or horror.

TIPS "We're very interested in young adult and children's fiction from Canadian writers with a proven track record (either published books or widely published in established magazines or journals) and for manuscripts with regional themes and/or a distinctive voice. We publish Canadian authors exclusively."

RED HEN PRESS

P.O. Box 40820, Pasadena CA 91114. (626)356-4760. **Fax:** (626)356-9974. **Website:** www.redhen.org. **Contact:** Mark E. Cull, publisher/executive director. Managing Editor: Kate Gale. Estab. 1993. Publishes trade paperback originals. "At this time, the best opportunity to be published by Red Hen is by entering one of our contests. Please find more information in our award submission guidelines." **Publishes 22 titles/year. 2,000 queries; 500 mss received/year. 10% of books from first-time authors. 90% from unagented writers.** Publishes ms 1 year after acceptance. Accepts simultaneous submissions. Responds in 1-2 months. Book catalog available free. Guidelines online.

NONFICTION Subjects include ethnic, memoirs, political/social interest. Query with synopsis and either 20-30 sample pages or complete ms using online submission manager.

FICTION Subjects include ethnic, experimental, feminist, historical, literary, poetry, poetry in translation, short story collections. Query with synopsis and either 20-30 sample pages or complete ms using online submission manager.

POETRY Submit to Benjamin Saltman Poetry Award.

TIPS "Audience reads poetry, literary fiction, intelligent nonfiction. If you have an agent, we may be too small since we don't pay advances. Write well. Send queries first. Be willing to help promote your own book."

REDLEAF LANE

Redleaf Press, 10 Yorkton Ct., St. Paul MN 55117. (800)423-8309. **E-mail:** info@redleafpress.org. **E-mail:** acquisitions@redleafpress.org. **Website:** www.redleafpress.org. **Contact:** David Heath, director. Redleaf Lane publishes engaging, high-quality picture books for children. "Our books are unique because they take place in group-care settings and reflect developmentally appropriate practices and research-based standards." Accepts simultaneous submissions. Guidelines online.

NONFICTION Subjects include child guidance, education.

RECENT TITLE(S) *Mama's Gloves*, by Mike Huber, illustrated by Joseph Cowman.

⊘ RED MOON PRESS

P.O. Box 2461, Winchester VA 22604. (540)722-2156. **E-mail:** jim.kacian@redmoonpress.com. **Website:** www.redmoonpress.com. **Contact:** Jim Kacian, editor/publisher. Estab. 1993. English-language haiku, contemporary haiku in other languages in English translation, haiku anthologies, books of haiku theory and criticism, books on related genres (tanka, haibun, haiga, renga, renku, etc.). Red Moon Press "is the largest and most prestigious publisher of English-language haiku and related work in the world." Publishes 10-15 volumes/year, usually 2-3 anthologies, 8-12 individual collections of English-language haiku, and 1-3 books of essays, translations, or criticism of haiku. Under other imprints, the press also publishes chapbooks of various sizes and formats. **Publishes 10-15 titles/year. 100+ 75% of books from first-time authors. 100% from unagented writers. Every book is a separate consideration.** Publishes 1-2 months after acceptance. Accepts simultaneous submissions. Catalog online. Guidelines available.

NONFICTION Subjects include alternative lifestyles, art, contemporary culture, education, environment, ethnic, history, hobbies, humanities, language, literary criticism, literature, memoirs, multicultural, music, nature, New Age, philosophy, photography, pop culture, psychology, recreation, spirituality, translation, travel.

POETRY Query first with book concept (not just "I've written a few haiku . ."); if interested we'll ask for samples. "Each contract separately negotiated."

RED WHEEL/WEISER

65 Parker St., Suite 7, Newburyport MA 01950. (978)465-0504. **Fax:** (978)465-0504. **E-mail:** submissions@rwwbooks.com. **Website:** www.redwheelweiser.com. **Contact:** Pat Bryce, acquisitions editor. Estab. 1956. Publishes hardcover and trade paperback originals and reprints. **Publishes 60-75 titles/year. 2,000 queries; 2,000 mss received/year. 20% of books from first-time authors. 50% from unagented writers. Pays royalty.** Publishes ms 1 year after accceptance. Accepts simultaneous submissions. Responds in 3-6 months. Book catalog available free. Guidelines online.

NONFICTION Subjects include New Age, spirituality, parenting. Guidelines online.

ROBERT D. REED PUBLISHERS

P.O. Box 1992, Bandon OR 97411. (541)347-9882. **Fax:** (541)347-9883. **E-mail:** cleone@rdrpublishers.com; bob@rdrpublishers.com. **Website:** www.rdrpublishers.com. **Contact:** Robert D. Reed, Cleone L. Reed. Estab. 1991. Publishes hardcover and trade paperback originals and e-books. **75% of books from first-time authors. 90% from unagented writers. Pays 12-35% royalty on wholesale price. Does not pay advance.** Publishes ms within 5 months after acceptance. Accepts simultaneous submissions. Responds in 1 month. Catalog and guidelines online.

NONFICTION Subjects include alternative lifestyles, business, career guidance, child guidance, communications, community, contemporary culture, counseling, education, entertainment, environment, ethnic, gay, health, history, humanities, language, lesbian, literature, memoirs, military, money, multicultural, nature, New Age, nutrition, parenting, philosophy, psychology, social sciences, sociology, spirituality, travel, true crime, womens issues, womens studies, world affairs. "We want titles that have a large audience with at least 10-year sales potential, and author's workshop, speaking and seminar participation. We like titles that are part of author's career." Submit proposal package with outline. Reviews artwork.

TIPS "We publish books to make this a better world. Nonfiction only."

REFERENCE SERVICE PRESS

1945 Golden Way, Mountain View CA 94040. **Website:** www.rspfunding.com. Estab. 1977. Publishes hardcover originals. "Reference Service Press focuses on the development and publication of financial aid resources in any format (print, electronic, e-book, etc.). We are interested in financial aid publications aimed at specific groups (e.g., minorities, women, veterans, the disabled, undergraduates majoring in specific subject areas, specific types of financial aid, etc.)." **Publishes 10-20 titles/year. 100% from unagented writers. Pays 10% royalty. Pays advance.** Publishes book 6 months after acceptance. Responds in 2 months to queries. Book catalog for #10 SASE.

NONFICTION Subjects include history, disabled. Submit outline, sample chapters.

RECENT TITLE(S) *Financial Aid for Veterans, Military Personnel, and Their Families; Directory of Financial Aid for Hispanic Americans; How to Pay for Your Degree in Engineering.*

TIPS "Our audience consists of librarians, counselors, researchers, students, re-entry women, scholars, and other fundseekers."

REVELL

Division of Baker Publishing Group, 6030 E. Fulton Rd., Ada MI 49301. (616)676-9185. **Fax:** (616)676-9573. **Website:** www.bakerbooks.com. Estab. 1870. Publishes hardcover, trade paperback and mass market paperback originals. "Revell publishes to the heart (rather than to the head). For 125 years, Revell has been publishing evangelical books for the personal enrichment and spiritual growth of general Christian readers." Accepts simultaneous submissions. Book catalog and ms guidelines online.

No longer accepts unsolicited mss.

NONFICTION Subjects include child guidance, religion, Christian living, marriage.

FICTION Subjects include historical, religious, suspense, contemporary.

RIO NUEVO PUBLISHERS

Imprint of Treasure Chest Books, P.O. Box 5250, Tucson AZ 85703. **Fax:** (520)624-5888. **E-mail:** info@rionuevo.com. **Website:** www.rionuevo.com. Estab. 1975. Publishes hardcover and trade paperback originals and reprints. **Publishes 12-20 titles/year. 30 queries received/year. 10 mss received/year. 30% of books from first-time authors. 100% from unagented writers. Pays $1,000-4,000 advance.** Publishes book 1 year after acceptance. Accepts simultaneous submissions. Responds in 6 months. Book catalog online. Guidelines online.

NONFICTION Subjects include animals, gardening, history, regional, religion, spirituality, travel. "We cover the Southwest but prefer titles that are not too narrow in their focus. We want our books to be of broad enough interest that people from other places will also want to read them." Query with SASE or via e-mail. Submit proposal package, outline, 2 sample chapters. Reviews artwork/photos. Send photocopies.

RECENT TITLE(S) *Boots and Burgers: An Arizona Handbook for Hungry Hikers; Ghost Riders in the Sky: The Life of Stan Jones, the Singing Ranger; Death Valley: Hottest Place on Earth.*

TIPS "We have a general audience of intelligent people interested in the Southwest-nature, history, culture. Many of our books are sold in gift shops throughout the region. Look at our books and website for inspiration and to see what we do."

RIPPLE GROVE PRESS

P.O. Box 910, Shelburne VT 05482. **E-mail:** submit@ripplegrovepress.com. **Website:** www.ripplegrovepress.com. **Contact:** Robert Broder. Estab. 2013. Publishes hardcover originals. Ripple Grove Press is an independent, family-run children's book publisher. "We started Ripple Grove Press because we have a passion for well-told and beautifully illustrated stories for children. Our mission is to bring together great writers and talented illustrators to make the most wonderful books possible. We hope our books find their way to the cozy spot in your home." **Publishes 3-6 titles/year. 3,000 submissions/year. Authors and illustrators receive royalties on net receipts. Pays negotiable advance.** Average length of time between acceptance of a book-length ms and publication is 12-18 months. Accepts simultaneous submissions. "Given the volume of submissions we receive we are no longer able to individually respond to each. Please allow 5 months for us to review your submission. If we are interested in your story, you can expect to hear from us within that time. If you do not hear from us after that time, we are not interested in publishing your story. It's not you, it's us! We receive thousands of submissions and only publish a few books each year. Don't give up!". Catalog online. Guidelines online.

NONFICTION We do review artwork. Illustrators should send samples or links to their website and online portfolio.

FICTION Subjects include adventure, contemporary, fantasy, humor, juvenile, literary, mainstream, multicultural, picture books. We are looking for something unique, that has not been done before; an interesting story that captures a moment with a timeless feel. We are looking for picture driven stories for children ages 2-6. Please do not send early readers, middle grade, or YA mss. No religious stories. Please do not submit your story with page breaks or illustration notes. Do not submit a story with doodles or personal photographs. Do not send your "idea" for a story, send your story in manuscript form. Submit completed mss. Accepts submissions by mail and e-mail. E-mail preferred. Please submit a cover letter including a summary of your story, the age range of the story, a brief biography of yourself, and contact information.

TIPS "Please read children's picture books. Please read our books to see what we look for in a story and in art. We create books that capture a moment, so that a child can create their own."

RIVER CITY PUBLISHING

1719 Mulberry St., Montgomery AL 36106. **E-mail:** fnorris@rivercitypublishing.com. **Website:** www.rivercitypublishing.com. **Contact:** Fran Norris, editor. Estab. 1989. Publishes hardcover and trade paperback originals. Midsize independent publisher. River City publishes literary fiction, regional, short story collections. No poetry, memoir, or children's books. We also consider narrative histories, sociological accounts, and travel; however, only biographies and memoirs from noted persons will be considered. **Publishes 6 titles/year.** Accepts simultaneous submissions. Responds within 9 months.

NONFICTION "We do not publish self-help, how-to, business, medicine, religion, education, or psychology." Accepts unsolicited submissions and submissions from unagented authors, as well as those from established and agented writers. Submit 5 consecutive sample chapters or entire ms for review. "Please include a short biography that highlights any previous writing and publishing experience, sales opportunities the author could provide, ideas for marketing the book, and why you think the work would be appropriate for River City." Send appropriate-sized SASE or IRC, "otherwise, the material will be recycled." Also accepts queries by e-mail.

FICTION Subjects include literary, regional, short story collections. No poetry, memoir, or children's books. Send appropriate-sized SASE or IRC, "otherwise, the material will be recycled." Also accepts queries by e-mail. "Please include your electronic query letter as inline text and not an as attachment; we do not open unsolicited attachments of any kind." No multiple submissions. Rarely comments on rejected mss.

RECENT TITLE(S) *Raising Aphrodite*, by Kirk Curnutt; *Captain Tom and Franny*, by Jennifer McGraw Micelli; *Once a Fighter Pilot: The Story of Korean War Ace Lt. Gen. Charles G. "Chick" Cleveland*, by Warren A. Trest; *Tell Him You Saw Me*, by Stephen March; *The Disappointment Room*, by Dee Phelps.

TIPS "Only send your best work after you have received outside opinions. From approximately 1,000 submissions each year, we publish no more than 8 books and few of those come from unsolicited material. Competition is fierce, so follow the guidelines exactly. First-time novelists are also encouraged to send work."

Ⓐ⊘ RIVERHEAD BOOKS

Penguin Random House, 1745 Broadway, New York NY 10019. **Website:** www.penguinrandomhouse.com. Accepts simultaneous submissions.

FICTION Subjects include contemporary, literary, mainstream. *Submit through agent only. No unsolicited mss.*

ROARING BROOK PRESS

Macmillan Children's Publishing Group, 175 Fifth Ave., New York NY 10010. (646)307-5151. **Website:** us.macmillan.com. Estab. 2000. Roaring Brook Press is an imprint of MacMillan, a group of companies that includes Henry Holt and Farrar, Straus & Giroux. *Roaring Brook is not accepting unsolicited mss.* **Pays authors royalty based on retail price.** Accepts simultaneous submissions.

NONFICTION Picture books, young readers, middle readers, young adults: adventure, animal, contemporary, fantasy, history, humor, multicultural, nature/environment, poetry, religion, science fiction, sports, suspense/mystery. *Not accepting unsolicited mss or queries.*

FICTION Picture books, young readers, middle readers, young adults: adventure, animal, contemporary, fantasy, history, humor, multicultural, nature/environment, poetry, religion, science fiction, sports, suspense/mystery. *Not accepting unsolicited mss or queries.*

TIPS "You should find a reputable agent and have him/her submit your work."

RODALE BOOKS

400 S. Tenth St., Emmaus PA 18098. (610)967-5171. **Fax:** (610)967-8961. **Website:** www.rodaleinc.com. Estab. 1932. "Rodale Books publishes adult trade titles in categories such health & fitness, cooking, spirituality, and pet care." Accepts simultaneous submissions.

ROSE ALLEY PRESS

4203 Brooklyn Ave. NE, #103A, Seattle WA 98105-5911. (206)633-2725. **E-mail:** rosealleypress@juno.com. **Website:** www.rosealleypress.com. **Contact:** David D. Horowitz. Estab. 1995. "Rose Alley Press primarily publishes books featuring rhymed metrical poetry and an annually updated booklet about writing and publication. We do not read or consider unsolicited manuscripts."

NONFICTION Subjects include literature.

POETRY Our focus is contemporary Pacific Northwest rhymed metrical poetry. We contact poets whose work we wish to publish. Please note we do not accept or consider unsolicited manuscripts. We wish all of our poet friends the very best, but given limitations of time and money, we can do only so much.

RECENT TITLE(S) *Footbridge Above the Falls: Poems by Forty-Six Northwest Poets*, edited by David D. Horowitz.

ROSEN PUBLISHING

29 E. 21st St., New York NY 10010. (800)237-9932. **Fax:** (888)436-4643. **Website:** www.rosenpublishing.com. Estab. 1950. Rosen Publishing is an independent educational publishing house, established to serve the needs of students in grades Pre-K-12 with high interest, curriculum-correlated materials. Rosen publishes more than 700 new books each year and has a backlist of more than 7,000.

ROTOVISION

Fourth Floor, Ovest House, 58 West St., Brighton BN1 2RA, United Kingdom. (44)(127)371-6000. **Website:** https://www.quartoknows.com/RotoVision. **Contact:** Isheeta Mustafi. Publishes hardcover and trade paperback originals, and trade paperback reprints. Accepts simultaneous submissions. Book catalog available free. Guidelines available free.

"RotoVision books showcase the works of top writers and designers reflecting excellence and innovation in the visual arts. If you wish to submit a book proposal, in the first instance please familiarise yourself with our publishing portfolio to ensure your proposal fits into our focus area."

NONFICTION Subjects include art, creative nonfiction. "Our books are aimed at keen amateurs and professionals who want to improve their skills." Submit an e-mail with "Book Proposal" in the subject line. Reviews artwork/photos. Send transparencies and PDFs.

RECENT TITLE(S) *Art Directors Annual 83*; *Motion Design*, by Matt Woolman; *Underwater Photography*, by Larry and Denise Tackett.

TIPS "Our audience includes professionals, keen amateurs, and students of visual arts including graphic design, general design, advertising, and photography. Make your approach international in scope. Content not to be less than 35% US."

ROWMAN & LITTLEFIELD PUBLISHING GROUP

4501 Forbes Blvd., Suite 200, Lanham MD 20706. (301)459-3366. **Fax:** (301)429-5748. **Website:** www.rowmanlittlefield.com. **Contact:** Linda Ganster. Estab. 1949. Textbooks, nonfiction general interest titles, professional development works,references, and select trade in hardcover and paperback. "We are an independent press devoted to publishing social science and humanities titles that engage, inform and educate: innovative, thought-provoking texts for college courses; research-based titles for professionals eager to remain abreast of developments within their domains; and general interest books intended to convey important trends to an educated readership. Our approach emphasizes thought leadership balanced with a deep understanding of the areas in which we publish. We offer a forum for responsible voices representing the diversity of opinion on college campuses, and take special pride in our commitment to covering critical societal issues." **Pays advance.** Book catalog online. Guidelines online. Please submit to only one R&L editor at a time. Multiple submissions slows down the process, and editors are very good about sharing proposals.

NONFICTION Subjects include alternative lifestyles, Americana, anthropology, archeology, architecture, art, career guidance, child guidance, cinema, communications, community, contemporary culture, counseling, education, environment, ethnic, fashion, film, foods, gay, government, health, history, humanities, lesbian, literary criticism, military, multicultural, music, nutrition, parenting, philosophy, politics, pop culture, psychology, public affairs, religion, sex, sociology, sports, stage, war, womens issues, world affairs, young adult. "Rowman & Littlefield is seeking proposals in the serious nonfiction areas of history, politics, current events, religion, sociology, criminal justice, social work, philosophy, communication and education. All proposal inquiries can be e-mailed or mailed to the respective acquisitions editor listed on the contacts page on our website. "

RUKA PRESS

P.O. Box 1409, Washington DC 20013. **E-mail:** contact@rukapress.com. **E-mail:** submissions@rukapress.com. **Website:** www.rukapress.com. **Contact:** Daniel Kohan, owner. Estab. 2010. Publishes in trade paperback originals, electronic. "We publish nonfiction books with a strong environmental component for a general audience. We are looking for books that explain things, that make an argument, that demystify. We are interested in economics, science, nature, climate change, and sustainability. We like building charts and graphs, tables and timelines. Our politics are progressive, but our books need not be political." **Publishes 0-1 titles/year. 40% of books from first-time authors. 80% from unagented writers. Pays advance. Royalties are 10-25% on wholesale price.** Publishes book an average of 9-12 months after acceptance of ms. Accepts simultaneous submissions. Responds in 1 month. Book catalog online. Guidelines online.

NONFICTION Subjects include environment, nature, science. Submit proposal package, including outline; marketing and promotion plans; resume, bio, or CV; and 1 sample chapter.

TIPS "We appeal to an audience of intelligent, educated readers with broad interests. Be sure to tell us why your proposal is unique, and why you are especially qualified to write this book. We are looking for originality and expertise."

RUTGERS UNIVERSITY PRESS

106 Somerset St., 3rd Floor, New Brunswick NJ 08901. **E-mail:** kimberly.guinta@rutgers.edu. **Website:** rutgersuniversitypress.org. **Contact:** Kimberly Guinta, editorial director, Caribbean/Latin American Studies, Women's Studies, Anthropology; Peter Micklaus, executive editor, Sociology, History, and Regional Interest; Nicole Solano, executive editor, Film and Media Studies; Elisabeth Maselli, assistant editor (Jewish studies), Lisa Banning, Editor, Education, Asian American Studies, Human Rights. Estab. 1936. Publishes hardcover and trade paperback originals and reprints. "Our press aims to reach audiences beyond the academic community with accessible scholarly and regional books." **Publishes 120 titles/year. 1,500 queries; 300 mss received/year. 40% of books from first-time authors. 80% from unagented writers. Pays 7 1/2-15% royalty. Pays $1,000-10,000 advance.** Publishes ms 1 year after acceptance. Accepts simultaneous submissions. Responds in 1 month to proposals. Book catalog online. Guidelines online.

NONFICTION Subjects include anthropology, cinema, communications, contemporary culture, education, ethnic, film, history, humanities, labor, lesbian, military, multicultural, politics, pop culture, public affairs, regional, religion, sex, social sciences, sociology, sports, war, womens issues, womens studies, world affairs, African-American studies. Books for use in undergraduate courses. Does not want memoirs, self-help/psychology. Submit book proposal (see website for guidelines), 2-3 sample chapters, resume or CV. Reviews artwork/photos. Send photocopies.

RECENT TITLE(S) *Beautiful Terrible Ruins*, by Dora Apel; *On Racial Icons*, by Nicole R. Fleetwood; *This Is Our Land*, by Cody Ferguson.

TIPS "Both academic and general audiences. Many of our books have potential for undergraduate course use. We are looking for intelligent, well-written, and accessible books. Avoid overly narrow topics."

SADDLEBACK EDUCATIONAL PUBLISHING

3120-A Pullman St., Costa Mesa CA 92626. (888)735-2225. **E-mail:** contact@sdlback.com. **Website:** www.sdlback.com. Saddleback is always looking for fresh, new talent. "Please note that we primarily publish books for kids ages 12-18." Accepts simultaneous submissions.

FICTION "We look for diversity for our characters and content." Mail typed submission along with a query letter describing the work simply and where it fits in with other titles.

RECENT TITLE(S) *A Heart Like Ringo Starr*, by Linda Oatman High; *Clan Castles*, by Evan Jacobs.

SAE INTERNATIONAL

400 Commonwealth Dr., Warrendale PA 15096-0001. (724)776-4841. **Website:** www.sae.org/writeabook. Estab. 1905. Publishes hardcover and trade paperback originals, e-books. Automotive means anything self-propelled. "We are a professional society serving engineers, scientists, and researchers in the automobile, aerospace, and off-highway industries." **Publishes approximately 10 titles/year. 50 queries received/year. 20 mss received/year. 70% of books from first-time authors. 100% from unagented writers. Pays royalty. Pays possible advance.** Publishes ms 9-10 months after acceptance. Accepts simultaneous submissions. Responds in 4 months to queries. Book catalog free. Guidelines online.

NONFICTION Query with proposal.

TIPS "Audience is automotive and aerospace engineers and managers, automotive safety and biomechanics professionals, students, educators, enthusiasts, and historians."

SAGUARO BOOKS, LLC

16845 E. Ave. of the Fountains, Ste. 325, Fountain Hills AZ 85268. **E-mail:** mjnickum@saguarobooks.com. **Website:** www.saguarobooks.com. **Contact:** Mary Nickum, CEO. Estab. 2012. Publishes trade paperback and electronic originals. Saguaro Books, LLC is a publishing company specializing in middle grade and young adult ficiton by first-time authors. **Publishes 4-6 titles/year. Receives 60-80 queries/year, 8-10 mss/year. 100% of books from first-time authors. 100% from unagented writers. Pays 20% royalties after taxes and publication costs. Does not offer advance.** Publishes ms 18-24 months after acceptance. Responds within 3 months only if we're interested. Catalog online. Guidelines by e-mail.

Only first-time authors (previously unpublished) authors will be considered. No Agents, please.

NONFICTION Subjects includeWe do not publish nonfiction.

FICTION Subjects include adventure, fantasy, historical, juvenile, military, multicultural, mystery, occult, science fiction, sports, suspense, war, western, young adult. Ms should be well-written; signed letter by a professional editor is required. Does not want agented work. Query via e-mail before submitting work. Any material sent before requested will be ignored.

RECENT TITLE(S) *Snow Moon*, by Tonya Coffey; *The Gardenia Curse*, by Carolyn Savage; *The Last 18*, by Travis Mewhirter.

TIPS "Visit our website before sending us a query. Pay special attention to the For Authors Only page."

ST. JOHANN PRESS

P.O. Box 241, Haworth NJ 07641. (201)387-1529. **E-mail:** d.biesel@verizon.net. **Website:** www.stjohannpress.com. Estab. 1991. Publishes hardcover originals, trade paperback originals and reprints. **Publishes 6-8 titles/year. Receives 30-50 submissions/year. 35% of books from first-time authors. 95% from unagented writers. Pays 10-15% royalty on wholesale price.** Publishes book 15 months after acceptance. Accepts simultaneous submissions. Responds in 1 month on queries. Catalog online. Guidelines free on request.

NONFICTION Subjects include cooking, crafts, foods, history, hobbies, marine subjects, military, nutrition, religion, spirituality, sports, Black history in sports. "We are a niche publisher with interests in titles that will sell over a long period of time. For example, the World Football League Encyclopedia, Chicago Showcase of Basketball, will not need to be redone. We do baseball but prefer soccer, hockey, etc." Query with SASE. Reviews artwork/photos as part of the ms package. Send photocopies.

TIPS "Our readership is libraries, individuals with special interests, (e.g. sports historians); we also do specialized reference."

ST. MARTIN'S PRESS, LLC

Holtzbrinck Publishers, 175 Fifth Ave., New York NY 10010. (212)674-5151. **Fax:** (212)420-9314. **Website:** www.stmartins.com. Estab. 1952. Publishes hardcover, trade paperback and mass market originals. General interest publisher of both fiction and nonfiction. **Publishes 1,500 titles/year. Pays royalty. Pays advance.** Accepts simultaneous submissions.

NONFICTION Subjects include sports, general nonfiction. *Agented submissions only. No unsolicited mss.*

FICTION Subjects include contemporary, fantasy, historical, horror, literary, mystery, science fiction, suspense, western, general fiction. *Agented submissions only. No unsolicited mss.*

SAINT MARY'S PRESS

702 Terrace Heights, Winona MN 55987. (800)533-8095. **Fax:** (800)344-9225. **E-mail:** submissions@smp.org. **Website:** www.smp.org. Accepts simultaneous submissions. Ms guidelines online or by e-mail.

NONFICTION Subjects include religion. Titles for Catholic youth and their parents, teachers, and youth ministers. High school Catholic religious education textbooks and primary source readings. Query with SASE. Submit proposal package, outline, 1 sample chapter, SASE. Brief author biography.

TIPS "Request product catalog and/or do research online of Saint Mary Press book lists before submitting proposal."

ST PAULS

Society of St. Paul, 2187 Victory Blvd., Staten Island NY 10314. (718)761-0047. **Fax:** (718)761-0057. **E-mail:** edmund_lane@juno.com. **Website:** www.stpauls.us. **Contact:** Edmund C. Lane, SSP, acquisitions editor. Estab. 1957. Publishes trade paperback and mass market paperback originals and reprints. **Publishes 22 titles/year. 250 queries; 150 mss received/year. 10% of books from first-time authors. 100% from unagented writers. Pays 5-10% royalty.** Publishes ms 10 months after acceptance. Responds in 1 month to queries and proposals; 2 months to mss. Book catalog and ms guidelines free.

NONFICTION Subjects include philosophy, religion, spirituality. Alba House is the North American publishing division of the Society of St. Paul, an International Roman Catholic Missionary Religious Congregation dedicated to spreading the Gospel message via the media of communications. Does not want fiction, children's books, poetry, personal testimonies, or autobiographies. Submit complete ms. Reviews artwork/photos. Send photocopies.

RECENT TITLE(S) *I Believe in One God*, by Pope Benedict XVI; *The Story of Friendship*, by Robert Nugent; *Everything Has Been Loaned to You*, by J. Robert Ouimet.

TIPS "Our audience is educated Roman Catholic readers interested in matters related to the Church, spirituality, Biblical and theological topics, moral concerns, lives of the saints, etc."

SAKURA PUBLISHING & TECHNOLOGIES

805 Lindaraxa Park North, Alhambra CA 91801. (330)360-5131. **E-mail:** skpublishing124@gmail.com. **Website:** www.sakura-publishing.com. **Contact:** Derek Vasconi, submissions coordinator. Estab. 2007. Publishes trade paperback, mass market paperback and electronic originals and reprints. Currently accepts only the following genres: Asian fiction, Japanese fiction (in English), and Japanese non-fiction (stories about living in Japan in particular are of interest). Please do not send queries for any other genres. Visit our website for query guidelines. Mss that don't follow guidelines will not be considered. Sakura Publishing is a traditional, independent book publishing company that seeks to publish Asian-themed books, particularly Asian-Horror, or anything dealing with Japan, Japanese culture, and Japanese horror. **Publishes 1-3 titles/year. 90% of books from first-time authors. 80% from unagented writers. Royalty payments on paperback, e-book, wholesale, and merchandise Does not pay advance.** Publishes ms 6 months after acceptance. Accepts simultaneous submissions. Responds in 1 week. Book catalog available for #10 SASE. Guidelines online.

NONFICTION Subjects include contemporary culture, creative nonfiction, entertainment, ethnic, film, games, history, hobbies, humanities, literature, memoirs, military, music, philosophy, pop culture, psychology, regional, religion, sex, travel, true crime, world affairs. Looking for memoirs by Asians, or any nonfiction that deals with Asia, especially Japan, or American experiences while living in Japan. No memoirs other than what we have listed above, cookbooks, humor, textbooks, technical, and definitely no books about suffering from diseases and overcoming them. Follow guidelines online.

FICTION Subjects include contemporary, erotica, ethnic, historical, horror, multicultural, occult, Asian, horror, occult. Only looking for Asian horror, with preference given to Japanese horror, as well as Japanese fiction, Japanese erotica, Asian erotica. Will consider other types of Asian-centered fiction, but top preference will be on fiction centered in or dealing with Japan or Japanese people living in America. Follow guidelines online.

POETRY Follow guidelines online.

TIPS "When submitting, only include a short query letter, the first three chapters of your manuscript included in the body of the email (no attachments will be opened), and your marketing plan. If you do not include these things, your manuscript will not be considered for publication. Also, please note we are looking only for Asian themed horror, Asian themed fiction, Japanese nonfiction and in particular, anything that has to deal with Japan. If you have a Japanese horror manuscript, or you have a nonfiction book about living in Japan or dating in Japan, your manuscript will be given the highest preference and priority."

SALEM PRESS, INC.

P.O. Box 56, 4919 Rt. 22, Amenia NY 12501. **E-mail:** lmars@greyhouse.com. **Website:** www.salempress.com. **Contact:** Laura Mars, editorial director. **Publishes 20-22 titles/year. 15 queries received/year. Work-for-hire pays 5-15¢/word.** Accepts simultaneous submissions. Responds in 3 months to queries; 1 month to proposals. Book catalog online.

NONFICTION Subjects include ethnic, history, philosophy, psychology, science, sociology. "We accept vitas for writers interested in supplying articles/entries for encyclopedia-type entries in library reference books. Will also accept multi-volume book ideas from people interested in being a general editor." Query with SASE.

SALMON POETRY

Knockeven, Cliffs of Moher, County ClareIreland. 353(0)852318909. **E-mail:** info@salmonpoetry.com. **E-mail:** jessie@salmonpoetry.com. **Website:** www.salmonpoetry.com. **Contact:** Jessie Lendennie, editor. Estab. 1981. Publishes contemporary poetry and literary nonfiction. **Publishes 30 titles/year. 300+ 5% of books from first-time authors. 100% from unagented writers. Pays advance.** Publishes ms 2 years after acceptance. Responds in 3 months. Guidelines available.

NONFICTION Subjects include literature, marine subjects.

POETRY "Salmon Press is one of the most important publishers in the Irish literary world; specializing in the promotion of new poets, particularly women. Established in 1981 as an alternative voice in Irish literature, Salmon is known for its international list and over the years has developed a cross-cultural literary dialog, broadening Irish Literature and urging new perspectives on established traditions." E-mail query with short biographical note and 5-10 sample poems.

TIPS "Read as much poetry as you can, and always research the publisher before submitting!"

SALVO PRESS

An imprint of Start Publishing, 101 Hudson St., 37th Floor, Suite 3705, Jersey City NJ 07302. **E-mail:** info@salvopress.com. **Website:** www.salvopress.com. Estab. 1998. Salvo Press proudly publishes mysteries, thrillers, and literary books in e-book and audiobook formats. **Publishes 6-12 titles/year. 75% from unagented writers. Pays 10% royalty.** Publishes ms 9-12 months after acceptance. Responds in 5 minutes to 1 month to queries; 2 months to mss. Book catalog and ms guidelines online.

FICTION Subjects include adventure, literary, mystery, science fiction, suspense, thriller/espionage. "We are a small press specializing in mystery, suspense, espionage and thriller fiction. Our press publishes in trade paperback and most e-book formats." Query by e-mail.

SANTA MONICA PRESS

P.O. Box 850, Solana Beach CA 92075. (858)793-1890. **E-mail:** books@santamonicapress.com. **E-mail:** acquisitions@santamonicapress.com. **Website:** www.santamonicapress.com. Estab. 1994. Publishes hardcover and trade paperback originals. Santa Monica Press has been publishing an eclectic line of books since 1994. "Our critically acclaimed titles are sold in chain, independent, online, and university bookstores around the world, as well as in some of the most popular retail outlets in North America. Our authors are recognized experts who are sought after by the media and receive newspaper, magazine, radio, and television coverage both nationally and internationally. At Santa Monica Press, we're not afraid to cast a wide editorial net. Our list of lively and modern non-fiction titles includes books in such categories as popular culture, film history, photography, humor, biography, travel, and reference." **Publishes 12 titles/year. 25% of books from first-time authors. 75% from unagented writers. Pays 6-10% royalty on net price. Pays $500-10,000+ advance.** Publishes book 1 year after acceptance. Accepts simultaneous submissions. Responds in 1-2 months to proposals. Guidelines available.

NONFICTION Subjects include Americana, art, cinema, contemporary culture, creative nonfiction, education, entertainment, film, history, humanities, language, literature, memoirs, music, parenting, photography, pop culture, regional, social sciences, sports, stage, travel. Submit proposal package, including outline, 2-3 sample chapters, biography, marketing and publicity plans, analysis of competitive titles, SASE with appropriate postage. Reviews artwork/photos. Send photocopies.

RECENT TITLE(S) *Turn Up the Radio! Rock, Pop, and Roll in Los Angeles 1956-1972*, by Harvey Kubernik with a foreword by Tom Petty; *L.A.'s Legendary Restaurants: Celebrating the Famous Places Where Hollywood Ate, Drank, and Played*, by George Geary; *We Were Going to Change the World: Interviews with Women from the 1970s and 1980s Southern California Punk Rock Scene*, by Stacy Russo, Foreword by Mike Watt; *Route 66 Adventure Handbook: High-Octane 5th Edition*, by Drew Knowles; *The Disneyland Encyclopedia: 3rd Edition*, by Chris Strodder; *Secret Walks: A Walking Guide to the Hidden Trails of Los Angeles*, by Charles Fleming.

TIPS "Visit our website before submitting to view our author guidelines and to get a clear idea of the types of books we publish. Carefully analyze your book's competition and tell us what makes your book different—and what makes it better. Also let us know what promotional and marketing opportunities you, as the author, bring to the project."

SARABANDE BOOKS, INC.

822 E. Market St., Louisville KY 40206. (502)458-4028. **E-mail:** info@sarabandebooks.org. **Website:** www.sarabandebooks.org. **Contact:** Sarah Gorham, editor-in-chief. Estab. 1994. Publishes trade paperback originals. "Sarabande Books was founded to publish poetry, short fiction, and creative nonfiction. We look for works of lasting literary value. Please see our titles to get an idea of our taste. Accepts submissions through contests and open submissions." **Publishes 10 titles/year. 1,500 queries; 3,000 mss received/year. 35% of books from first-time authors. 75% from unagented writers. Pays royalty. 10% on actual income received. Also pays in author's copies. Pays $500-3,000 advance.** Publishes ms 18 months after acceptance. Accepts simultaneous submissions. Responds within 8 months. Book catalog available free. Contest guidelines for #10 SASE or on website.

FICTION Subjects include literary, short story collections, novellas, short novels (300 pages maximum, 150 pages minimum). "We consider novels and nonfiction in a wide variety of genres. We do not consider genre fiction such as science fiction, fantasy, or horror. Our target length is 70,000-90,000 words." Queries can be sent via e-mail, fax, or regular post.

POETRY Poetry of superior artistic quality; otherwise no restraints or specifications. Sarabande Books publishes books of poetry of 48 pages minimum. Wants "poetry that offers originality of voice and subject matter, uniqueness of vision, and a language that startles because of the careful attention paid to it—language that goes beyond the merely competent or functional." Mss selected through literary contests, invitation, and recommendation by a well-established writer.

RECENT TITLE(S) *Portrait of My Mother Who Posed Nude in Wartime*, by Marjorie Sandor; *October*, by Louise Glück.

TIPS "Sarabande publishes for a general literary audience. Know your market. Read-and buy-books of literature. Sponsors contests for poetry and fiction. Make sure you're not writing in a vacuum, that you've read and are conscious of contemporary literature. Have someone read your manuscript, checking it for ordering, coherence. Better a lean, consistently strong manuscript than one that is long and uneven. We like a story to have good narrative, and we like to be engaged by language."

SAS PUBLISHING

100 SAS Campus Dr., Cary NC 27513. (919)677-8000. **Fax:** (919)677-4444. **E-mail:** saspress@sas.com. **Website:** support.sas.com/saspress. Estab. 1976. Publishes hardcover and trade paperback originals. "SAS publishes books for SAS and JMP software users, both new and experienced." **Publishes 40 titles/year. 50% of books from first-time authors. 100% from unagented writers. Payment negotiable. Pays nego-**

tiable advance. Responds in 2 weeks to queries. Book catalog and ms guidelines online.

NONFICTION Subjects include software, statistics. SAS Publishing jointly Wiley and SAS Business Series titles. "Through SAS, we also publish books by SAS users on a variety of topics relating to SAS software. SAS titles enhance users' abilities to use SAS effectively. We're interested in publishing manuscripts that describe or illustrate using any of SAS products, including JMP software. Books must be aimed at SAS or JMP users, either new or experienced." Mss must reflect current or upcoming software releases, and the author's writing should indicate an understanding of SAS and the technical aspects covered in the ms. Query with SASE. Submit outline, sample chapters. Reviews artwork/photos.

SASQUATCH BOOKS

1904 Third Ave., Suite 710, Seattle WA 98101. (206)467-4300. **Fax:** (206)467-4301. **E-mail:** custserv@sasquatchbooks.com. **Website:** www.sasquatchbooks.com. Estab. 1986. Publishes regional hardcover and trade paperback originals. "Sasquatch Books publishes books for and from the Pacific Northwest, Alaska, and California is the nation's premier regional press. Sasquatch Books' publishing program is a veritable celebration of regionally written words. Undeterred by political or geographical borders, Sasquatch defines its region as the magnificent area that stretches from the Brooks Range to the Gulf of California and from the Rocky Mountains to the Pacific Ocean. Our top-selling Best Places® travel guides serve the most popular destinations and locations of the West. We also publish widely in the areas of food and wine, gardening, nature, photography, children's books, and regional history, all facets of the literature of place. With more than 200 books brimming with insider information on the West, we offer an energetic eye on the lifestyle, landscape, and worldview of our region. Considers queries and proposals from authors and agents for new projects that fit into our West Coast regional publishing program. We can evaluate query letters, proposals, and complete mss." **Publishes 30 titles/year. 20% of books from first-time authors. 75% from unagented writers. Pays royalty on cover price. Pays wide range advance.** Publishes book 6-9 months after acceptance. Accepts simultaneous submissions. Responds to queries in 3 months. Guidelines online.

NONFICTION Subjects include animals, gardening, history, recreation, regional, sports, travel, outdoors. "We are seeking quality nonfiction works about the Pacific Northwest and West Coast regions (including Alaska to California). The literature of place includes how-to and where-to as well as history and narrative nonfiction." Picture books: activity books, animal, concept, nature/environment. "We publish a variety of nonfiction books, as well as children's books under our Little Bigfoot imprint." Query first, then submit outline and sample chapters with SASE. Send submissions to The Editors. E-mailed submissions and queries are not recommended. Please include return postage if you want your materials back.

FICTION Young readers: adventure, animal, concept, contemporary, humor, nature/environment.

TIPS "We sell books through a range of channels in addition to the book trade. Our primary audience consists of active, literate residents of the West Coast."

SATURNALIA BOOKS

105 Woodside Rd., Ardmore PA 19003. (267)278-9541. **E-mail:** info@saturnaliabooks.com. **Website:** www.saturnaliabooks.org. **Contact:** Henry Israeli, publisher. Estab. 2002. Publishes trade paperback originals and digital versions for e-readers. "We do not accept unsolicited submissions. We hold a contest, the Saturnalia Books Poetry Prize, annually in which 1 anonymously submitted title is chosen by a poet with a national reputation for publication. The editors then select an Editors Prize for publication. Submissions are accepted during the month of March. The submission fee is $30, and the prize is $1,500 and 20 copies of the book for the Saturnalia Books Poetry Prize and $500 plus 20 free books for the Saturnalia Books Editors Award. See website for details." **Publishes 5 titles/year. Receives 600 mss/year. 33% of books from first-time authors. 100% from unagented writers. Pays authors 4-6% royalty on retail price. Pays $400-1,500 advance.** Accepts simultaneous submissions. Responds in 4 months on mss. Catalog online. No unsolicited submissions. Contest guidelines online.

POETRY "Saturnalia Books has no bias against any school of poetry, but we do tend to publish writers who take chances and push against convention in some way, whether it's in form, language, content, or musicality." Submit complete ms to contest only.

RECENT TITLE(S) *Steal It Back*, by Sandra Simonds; *The Girls of Peculiar*, by Catherine Pierce; *In Memory of Brilliance & Balue*, by Michael Robins; *Telepathologies*, by Cortney Lamar Charleston.

TIPS "Our audience tend to be young avid readers of contemporary poetry. Read a few sample books first."

SCARECROW PRESS, INC.

Imprint of Rowman & Littlefield Publishing Group, 4501 Forbes Blvd., Suite 200, Lanham MD 20706. (301)459-3366. **Fax:** (301)429-5748. **Website:** www.scarecrowpress.com. Estab. 1955. Publishes hardcover originals. Scarecrow Press publishes several series: Historical Dictionaries (includes countries, religions, international organizations, and area studies); Studies and Documentaries on the History of Popular Entertainment (forthcoming); Society, Culture and Libraries. Emphasis is on any title likely to appeal to libraries. Currently emphasizing jazz, Africana, and educational issues of contemporary interest. **Publishes 165 titles/year. 70% of books from first-time authors. 99% from unagented writers. Pays 8% royalty on net of first 1,000 copies; 10% of net price thereafter.** Publishes ms 18 months after acceptance. Responds in 2 months to queries. Catalog and ms guidelines online.

NONFICTION Subjects include religion, sports, annotated bibliographies, handbooks and biographical dictionaries in the areas of women's studies and ethnic studies, parapsychology, fine arts and handicrafts, genealogy, sports history, music, movies, stage, library and information science. Query with SASE.

SCHIFFER PUBLISHING, LTD.

4880 Lower Valley Rd., Atglen PA 19310. (610)593-1777. **Fax:** (610)593-2002. **E-mail:** info@schifferbooks.com. **Website:** www.schifferbooks.com. Estab. 1975. **Publishes 10-20 titles/year. Pays royalty on wholesale price.** Accepts simultaneous submissions. Responds in 2 weeks to queries. Book catalog available free. Guidelines online.

NONFICTION Art-quality illustrated regional histories. Looking for informed, entertaining writing and lots of subject areas to provide points of entry into the text for non-history buffs who buy a beautiful book because they are from, or love, an area. Full color possible in the case of historic postcards. Fax or e-mail outline, photos, and book proposal.

TIPS "We want to publish books for towns or cities with relevant population or active tourism to support book sales. A list of potential town vendors is a helpful start toward selling us on your book idea."

Ⓐ⊘ SCHOCKEN BOOKS

Imprint of Knopf Publishing Group, Division of Random House, Inc., 1745 Broadway, New York NY 10019. (212)572-9000. **Fax:** (212)572-6030. **Website:** www.schocken.com. Estab. 1945. Publishes hardcover and trade paperback originals and reprints. "Schocken publishes quality Judaica in all areas-fiction, history, biography, current affairs, spirituality and religious practices, popular culture, and cultural studies." *Does not accept unsolicited mss. Agented submissions only.* **Publishes 9-12 titles/year. Pays varied advance.** Accepts simultaneous submissions.

SCHOLASTIC, INC.

557 Broadway, New York NY 10012. (212)343-6100. **Website:** www.scholastic.com. Accepts simultaneous submissions.

IMPRINTS Arthur A. Levine Books, Cartwheel Books®, Chicken House®, David Fickling Books, Graphix™, Little Shepherd™, Orchard Books®, Point™, PUSH, Scholastic en Español, Scholastic Licensed Publishing, Scholastic Nonfiction, Scholastic Paperbacks, Scholastic Press, Scholastic Reference™, and The Blue Sky Press® are imprints of the Scholastic Trade Books Division. In addition, Scholastic Trade Books included Klutz®, a highly innovative publisher and creator of "books plus" for children.

Scholastic Trade Books is an award-winning publisher of original children's books. Scholastic publishes approximately 600 new hardcover, paperback and novelty books each year. The list includes the phenomenally successful publishing properties Harry Potter, Goosebumps, Captain Underpants, Dog Man, and The Hunger Games; best-selling and award-winning authors and illustrators, including Suzanne Collins, Christopher Paul Curtis, Ann M. Martin, Dav Pilkey, J.K. Rowling, Pam Muñoz Ryan, Lauren Tarshis, Brian Selznick, David Shannon, Mark Teague, and Walter Wick, among others; as well as licensed properties such as Star Wars and Rainbow Magic.

SCHOLASTIC CHILDREN'S BOOKS UK

Euston House, 24 Eversholt St., London VI NW1 1DB, United Kingdom. **E-mail:** contactus@scholastic.co.uk. **Website:** www.scholastic.co.uk. Accepts simultaneous submissions.

Scholastic UK does not accept unsolicited submissions. Unsolicited illustrations are accepted, but please do not send any original artwork as it will not be returned.

RECENT TITLE(S) *The Hunger Games*, by Suzanne Collins; *Captain Underpants*, by Dav Pilkey; *Horrible Histories*, by Terry Deary and Martin Brown.

TIPS "Getting work published can be a frustrating process, and it's often best to be prepared for disappointment, but don't give up."

SCHOLASTIC LIBRARY PUBLISHING

90 Old Sherman Turnpike, Danbury CT 6816. (203)797-3500. **Fax:** (203)797-3197. **E-mail:** slpservice@scholastic.com. **Website:** www.scholastic.com/librarypublishing. **Contact:** Phil Friedman, vice president/publisher; Kate Nunn, editor-in-chief; Marie O'Neil, art director. Estab. 1895. Publishes hardcover and trade paperback originals. "Scholastic Library is a leading publisher of reference, educational, and children's books. We provide parents, teachers, and librarians with the tools they need to enlighten children to the pleasure of learning and prepare them for the road ahead. Publishes informational (nonfiction) for K-12; picture books for young readers, grades 1-3." **Pays authors royalty based on net or work purchased outright. Pays illustrators at competitive rates.**

IMPRINTS Grolier; Children's Press; Franklin Watts; Grolier Online.

Accepts agented submissions only.

NONFICTION Photo-illustrated books for all levels: animal, arts/crafts, biography, careers, concept, geography, health, history, hobbies, how-to, multicultural, nature/environment, science, social issues, special needs, sports. Average word length: young readers—2,000; middle readers—8,000; young adult—15,000. Query; submit outline/synopsis, resume, and/or list of publications, and writing sample. SASE required for response.

FICTION Publishes 1 picture book series, Rookie Readers, for grades 1-2. Does not accept unsolicited mss. *Does not accept fiction proposals.*

SCHOLASTIC PRESS

Imprint of Scholastic, Inc., 557 Broadway, New York NY 10012. (212)343-6100. **Fax:** (212)343-4713. **Website:** www.scholastic.com. Publishes hardcover originals. Scholastic Press publishes fresh, literary picture book fiction and nonfiction; fresh, literary nonseries or nongenre-oriented middle grade and young adult fiction. Currently emphasizing subtly handled treatments of key relationships in children's lives; unusual approaches to commonly dry subjects, such as biography, math, history, or science. De-emphasizing fairy tales (or retellings), board books, genre, or series fiction (mystery, fantasy, etc.). **Publishes 60 titles/year. 2,500 queries received/year. 1% of books from first-time authors. Pays royalty on retail price. Pays variable advance.** Publishes book 2 years after acceptance. Responds in 3 months to queries; 6-8 months to mss.

NONFICTION Agented submissions and previously published authors only.

FICTION Subjects include juvenile, picture books, novels. Looking for strong picture books, young chapter books, appealing middle grade novels (ages 8-11) and interesting and well-written young adult novels. Wants fresh, exciting picture books and novels—inspiring, new talent. *Agented submissions only.*

TIPS "Read *currently* published children's books. Revise, rewrite, rework and find your own voice, style and subject. We are looking for authors with a strong and unique voice who can tell a great story and have the ability to evoke genuine emotion. Children's publishers are becoming more selective, looking for irresistible talent and fairly broad appeal, yet still very willing to take risks, just to keep the game interesting."

SCHWARTZ & WADE BOOKS

Random House Children's Books, 1745 Broadway, New York NY 10019. **Website:** www.randomhousekids.com. Estab. 2006. Schwartz & Wade Books is an imprint of Random House Children's Books, co-directed by Anne Schwartz and Lee Wade, who take a unique approach to the creative process and believe that the best books for children grow from a seamless collaboration between editorial and design.

This market does not accept unsolicited submissions, proposals, mss, or submission queries. Recommends that authors work with an established literary agent.

RECENT TITLE(S) Recent titles: *Dream Dog*, by Lou Berger and illustrated by David Catrow; *Where's Mommy?*, by Beverly Donofrio and illustrated by Barbara McClintock; *The Dandelion's Tale*, by Kevin Sheehan and illustrated by Rob Dunlavey; *Poemmobiles*, by J. Patrick Lewis and Douglas Florian and illustrated by Jeremy Holmes.

SCRIBNER

Imprint of Simon & Schuster Adult Publishing Group, 1230 Avenue of the Americas, 12th Floor, New York NY 10020. (212)698-7000. **Website:** www.simonsays.com. Publishes hardcover originals. **Publishes 70-75 titles/year. Thousands queries received/year. 20% of books from first-time authors. Pays 7-15% royalty. Pays variable advance.** Publishes ms 9 months after acceptance. Accepts simultaneous submissions. Responds in 3 months to queries.

NONFICTION Subjects include education, ethnic, history, philosophy, psychology, religion, science, criticism. *Agented submissions only.*

FICTION Subjects include literary, mystery, suspense. *Agented submissions only.*

SEAL PRESS

Perseus Books Group, 1700 4th St., Berkeley CA 94710. (510)595-3664. **E-mail:** seal.press@perseusbooks.com. **E-mail:** emma.rose@perseusbooks.com. **Website:** www.sealpress.com. Estab. 1976. Publishes hardcover and trade paperback originals. "Seal Press is an imprint of the Perseus Book Group, a feminist book publisher interested in original, lively, radical, empowering and culturally diverse nonfiction by women addressing contemporary issues with the goal of informing women's lives. Currently emphasizing women outdoor adventurists, young feminists, political issues, health and fitness, parenting, personal finance, sex and relationships, and LGBT and gender topics. *Not accepting fiction at this time.*" **Publishes 30 titles/year. 1,000 queries received/year. 750 mss received/year. 25% of books from first-time authors. 50% from unagented writers. Pays 7-10% royalty on retail price. Pays variable royalty on retail price. Pays wide ranging advance.** Publishes ms 1 year after acceptance. Accepts simultaneous submissions. Responds in 2 months to queries. Book catalog and ms guidelines for SASE or online.

NONFICTION Subjects include alternative lifestyles, Americana, child guidance, contemporary culture, creative nonfiction, ethnic, gay, health, lesbian, memoirs, multicultural, parenting, politics, pop culture, sex, travel, womens issues, womens studies, popular culture, politics, domestic violence, sexual abuse. Query with SASE. Reviews artwork/photos. Send photocopies. No original art or photos accepted.

RECENT TITLE(S) *Better Than Perfect*, by Elizabeth Lombardo; *Yogalosophy*, by Mandy Ingber; *Goodbye to All That*, by Sari Botton.

TIPS "Seeking empowering and progressive nonfiction that can impact a woman's life across categories."

SEARCH INSTITUTE PRESS

Search Institute, 615 First Ave. NE, Suite 125, Minneapolis MN 55413. (612)376-8955. **Fax:** (612)692-5553. **E-mail:** si@search-institute.org. **Website:** www.search-institute.org. Estab. 1958. Publishes trade paperback originals. **Publishes 12-15 titles/year. Pays royalty.** Publishes book 1 year after acceptance. Accepts simultaneous submissions. Responds in 6 months. Catalog and guidelines online.

NONFICTION Subjects include career guidance, child guidance, community, counseling, education, entertainment, games, parenting, public affairs, social sciences, youth leadership, prevention, activities. Does not want children's picture books, poetry, New Age and religious-themes, memoirs, biographies, and autobiographies. Query with SASE. Does not review artwork/photos.

TIPS "Our audience is educators, youth program leaders, mentors, parents."

SEAWORTHY PUBLICATIONS, INC.

6300 N Wickham Rd, Unit # 130 - 416, Melbourne FL 32940. (321)610-3634. **Fax:** (321)259-6872. **E-mail:** queries@seaworthy.com. **Website:** www.seaworthy.com. **Contact:** Joseph F. Janson, publisher. Estab. 1992. Publishes trade paperback originals, hardcover originals, and reprints. "Seaworthy Publications is a nautical book publisher that primarily publishes books of interest to recreational boaters and bluewater cruisers, including cruising guides, and how-to books about boating. We will also consider first-person adventure and nautical fiction. Currently emphasizing cruising guides." **Publishes 10 titles/year. 50 queries; 30 mss received/year. 60% of books from first-time authors. 100% from unagented writers. Pays flat rate per copy sold, based on retail price. No advance.** Publishes ms 9 months after acceptance.

Responds in 1 month to queries. Book catalog and guidelines online.

IMPRINTS Tablet Publications, Island Hopping Digital Guides.

NONFICTION Subjects include environment, marine subjects, regional, sports, travel, sailing, boating, regional, boating guide books, boating how-to, Bahamas, Caribbean, travel, nautical adventure, nautical fiction. Regional guide books, first-person adventure, reference, how-to, technical—all dealing with boating. Query with SASE. Submit TOC and 3 sample chapters. Prefers electronic query via e-mail. Reviews artwork/photos. Send photocopies, color prints, or jpeg files.

RECENT TITLE(S) *The Captain's Guide to Hurricane Holes - The Bahamas and Caribbean*, by Capt. David Underill and Stephen J. Pavlidis.

TIPS "Our audience consists of sailors, boaters, and those interested in the sea, sailing, or long-distance cruising."

SEEDLING CONTINENTAL PRESS

520 E. Bainbridge St., Elizabethtown PA 17022. (800)233-0759. **Website:** www.continentalpress.com. "Continental publishes educational materials for grades K-12, specializing in reading, mathematics, and test preparation materials. We are not currently accepting submissions for Seedling leveled readers or instructional materials." **Work purchased outright from authors.** Publishes book 1-2 years after acceptance. Accepts simultaneous submissions. Responds to mss in 6 months.

NONFICTION Young readers: animal, arts/crafts, biography, careers, concept, multicultural, nature/environment, science. Does not accept texts longer than 12 pages or over 300 words. Average word length: young readers—100.

FICTION Young readers: adventure, animal, folktales, humor, multicultural, nature/environment. Does not accept texts longer than 12 pages or over 300 words. Average word length: young readers—100. Submit complete ms.

TIPS "See our website. Follow writers' guidelines carefully and test your story with children and educators."

SELF-COUNSEL PRESS

1481 Charlotte Rd., North Vancouver BC V7J 1H1, Canada. **E-mail:** editor@self-counsel.com. **Website:** www.self-counsel.com. **Contact:** Tyler Douglas. Estab. 1971. Publishes trade paperback originals. Self-Counsel Press publishes a range of quality self-help books written in practical, nontechnical style by recognized experts in the fields of business, financial, or legal guidance for people who want to help themselves. **Publishes 20 titles/year. 1,500 queries received/year. 50% of books from first-time authors. 95% from unagented writers. Pays rare advance.** Publishes ms 8-10 months after acceptance. Accepts simultaneous submissions. Responds in 2 months to queries. Book catalog online. Guidelines online.

NONFICTION Subjects includelegal and business issues for lay people. Submit proposal package, outline, resume, 2 sample chapters.

SENTIENT PUBLICATIONS

P.O. Box 7204, Boulder CO 80306. **Website:** www.sentientpublications.com. Estab. 2001. Publishes hardcover and trade paperback originals; trade paperback reprints. "We are not currently accepting submissions." **Publishes 4 titles/year. 200 queries; 100 mss received/year. 70% of books from first-time authors. 50% from unagented writers. Pays royalty on wholesale price. Sometimes pays advance.** Publishes ms 10 months after acceptance. Responds in 1 month to queries; 2 months to proposals and mss. Book catalog online.

NONFICTION Subjects include child guidance, contemporary culture, creative nonfiction, education, environment, gardening, history, philosophy, photography, psychology, science, social sciences, sociology, spirituality, travel. Does not review artwork/photos.

RECENT TITLE(S) *The Essence of Enlightenment*, by James Swartz (spirituality); *The Alchemy of Teaching*, by Jeremiah Conway (alternative education); *The Open Path*, by Elias Amidon (spirituality).

SEVEN STORIES PRESS

140 Watts St., New York NY 10013. (212)226-8760. **Fax:** (212)226-1411. **E-mail:** info@sevenstories.com. **Website:** www.sevenstories.com. **Contact:** Acquisitions. Estab. 1995. Publishes hardcover and trade paperback originals. Founded in 1995 in New York City, and named for the seven authors who committed to a home with a fiercely independent spirit, Seven Stories Press publishes works of the imagination and political titles by voices of conscience. While most widely known for its books on politics, human rights, and social and economic justice, Seven Stories

continues to champion literature, with a list encompassing both innovative debut novels and National Book Award–winning poetry collections, as well as prose and poetry translations from the French, Spanish, German, Swedish, Italian, Greek, Polish, Korean, Vietnamese, Russian, and Arabic. **Publishes 40-50 titles/year. 15% of books from first-time authors. 50% from unagented writers. Pays 7-15% royalty on retail price. Pays advance.** Publishes ms 1-3 years after acceptance. Accepts simultaneous submissions. Responds in 1 month. Book catalog and ms guidelines free.

NONFICTION Responds only if interested. Submit cover letter with 2 sample chapters.

FICTION Subjects include literary. Submit cover letter with 2 sample chapters.

SHAMBHALA PUBLICATIONS, INC.

4720 Walnut St., Boulder CO 80304. **E-mail:** submissions@shambhala.com. **Website:** www.shambhala.com. Estab. 1969. Publishes hardcover and trade paperback originals and reprints. **Publishes 90-100 titles/year. 500 queries; 1,200 mss/proposals received/year. 30% of books from first-time authors. 70% from unagented writers. Pays 8% royalty on retail price.** Publishes ms 1 year after acceptance. Accepts simultaneous submissions. Responds in 4 months. Book catalog free. Guidelines online.

IMPRINTS Roost Books; Snow Lion.

NONFICTION Subjects include cooking, crafts, parenting, Buddhism, martial arts, yoga, natural health, Eastern philosophy, creativity, green living, nature writing. To send a book proposal, include a synopsis of the book, see the submissions guidelines online. "We strongly prefer electronic submissions and do not take phone calls regarding book ideas or proposals."

SHEARSMAN BOOKS, LTD

50 Westons Hills Dr., Emersons Green, Bristol BS16 7DF, United Kingdom. **E-mail:** editor@shearsman.com. **Website:** www.shearsman.com. **Contact:** Tony Frazer, editor. Estab. 1981. Publishes trade paperback originals. **Publishes 45-60 titles/year. Receives 2,000 submissions/year. 10% of books from first-time authors. 95% from unagented writers. Pays 10% royalty on retail price after 150 copies have sold; authors also receive 10 free copies of their books. Does not pay advance.** Publishes ms 9-18 months after acceptance. Accepts simultaneous submissions. Responds in 3 months to mss. Book catalog online. Print copies available on request. Guidelines online.

NONFICTION Subjects include translation. All nonfiction has to do with poetry in some way. "We don't publish nonfiction unless it's related to poetry."

POETRY "Shearsman only publishes poetry, poetry collections, and poetry in translation (from any language but with an emphasis on work in Spanish & in German). Some critical work on poetry and also memoirs and essays by poets. Mainly poetry by British, Irish, North American, and Australian poets." No poetry by or for children. No devotional or religious verse.

RECENT TITLE(S) *The Bridge*, by Mary Austin Speaker; *Strange Country*, by Jon Thompson.

TIPS "Book ms submission: most of the ms must have already appeared in the UK or USA magazines of some repute, and it has to fill 70-72 pages of half letter or A5 pages. You must have sufficient return postage, or permit email responses. Submissions can also be made by email. It is unlikely that a poet with no track record will be accepted for publication as there is no obvious audience for the work. Try to develop some exposure to UK and US magazines and try to assemble a MS only later."

SHIPWRECKT BOOKS PUBLISHING COMPANY LLC

309 W. Stevens Ave., Rushford MN 55971. **E-mail:** contact@shipwrecktbooks.com. **Website:** www.shipwrecktbooks.press. **Contact:** Tom Driscoll, managing editor. Publishes trade paperback originals, mass market paperback originals, and electronic originals. **Publishes 6-10 titles/year. Receives 1,000 submissions/year. 60% of books from first-time authors. 80% from unagented writers. Authors receive 35% royalties unless otherwise negotiated.** Average length of time between acceptance of a book-length ms and publication is 6-18 months. Accepts simultaneous submissions. Responds to queries within 6 months. Catalog and guidelines online.

IMPRINTS Rocket Science Press (literary); Up On Big Rock Poetry Series; Lost Lake Folk Art (memoir, biography, essays, fiction and nonfiction).

NONFICTION Subjects include agriculture, alternative lifestyles, Americana, animals, anthropology, architecture, art, contemporary culture, creative nonfiction, environment, ethnic, film, foods, gardening, gay, government, health, history, hobbies, horticulture, house and home, humanities, language, lesbian, literary criticism, literature, medicine, memoirs, military, multicultural, music, nature, nutrition, politics, public affairs, recreation, regional, spirituality, sports, stage, true crime, war, womens issues, world affairs, young adult. Does not want religious. Use submissions portal at www.shipwrecktbooks.press; follow guidelines. Paper submissions are no longer accepted. Does not publish artwork books.

FICTION Subjects include adventure, comic books, contemporary, erotica, ethnic, experimental, fantasy, feminist, gay, historical, humor, lesbian, literary, mainstream, military, multicultural, mystery, poetry, poetry in translation, regional, science fiction, short story collections, sports, suspense, war, young adult. Use submissions portal at www.shipwrecktbooks.press; follow guidelines. Paper submissions are no longer accepted.

POETRY Poetry bar is very high. High-quality contemporary poetry. No religious or holiday verse. We do not publish chapbooks. Use submissions portal at www.shipwrecktbooks.press; follow guidelines. Paper submissions are no longer accepted.

TIPS "Quality writing. Please follow our guidelines. Manuscript development and full editorial services available."

SIBLING RIVALRY PRESS

P.O. Box 26147, Little Rock AR 72221. **E-mail:** info@siblingrivalrypress.com. **Website:** siblingrivalrypress.com. **Contact:** Bryan Borland, publisher; Seth Pennington, editor. Estab. 2010. While we champion our LGBTIQ authors and artists, and while we've been very fortunate in our successes in LGBTIQ publishing, we are an inclusive publishing house and welcome all authors, artists, and readers regardless of sexual orientation or identity. We publish work we love. Merit trumps category. SRP was the first press to ever win Lambda Literary Awards in both gay poetry and lesbian poetry. All SRP titles are housed permanently in the Library of Congress Rare Book and Special Collections Vault. **50% of books from first-time authors. 95% from unagented writers. Pays 30% royalties for print. Does not pay advance.** Publishes ms 1.5 years after acceptance (on average). Accepts simultaneous submissions. Catalog online. Guidelines online (changes each year).

POETRY Opening reading period: March 1-June 1. Submit complete ms.

RECENT TITLE(S) *Portrait of the Alcoholic*, by Kaveh Akbar; *All the Rage*, by Sam Sax; *Death by Sex Machine*, by Franny Choi.

TIPS "In lieu of a traditional cover letter, SRP asks authors to answer specific questions when submitting. Make sure you answer these questions."

SILMAN-JAMES PRESS

3624 Shannon Rd., Los Angeles CA 90027. (323)661-9922. **Fax:** (323)661-9933. **Website:** www.silmanjamespress.com. Publishes trade paperback originals and reprints. **Pays variable royalty on retail price.** Accepts simultaneous submissions. Book catalog available free.

NONFICTION Pertaining to film, theatre, music, performing arts. Submit proposal package, outline, 1+ sample chapters. Will accept phone queries. Reviews artwork/photos. Send photocopies.

TIPS "Our audience ranges from people with a general interest in film (fans, etc.) to students of film and performing arts to industry professionals. We will accept 'query' phone calls."

SILVER DOLPHIN BOOKS

(858)457-2500. **E-mail:** infosilverdolphin@readerlink.com. **Website:** www.silverdolphinbooks.com. Silver Dolphin Books publishes activity, novelty, and educational nonfiction books for preschoolers to 12-year-olds. Highly interactive formats such as the Field Guides and Uncover series both educate and entertain older children. "We will consider submissions only from authors with previously published works." Accepts simultaneous submissions.

FICTION Submit cover letter with full proposal and SASE.

RECENT TITLE(S) *Cuddly Koala*, by Emma Goldhawk, illustrated by Jonathan Lambert; *I Love Ponies*, by Annabel Savery.

SILVERFISH REVIEW PRESS

P.O. Box 3541, Eugene OR 97403. (541)344-5060. **E-mail:** sfrpress@earthlink.net. **Website:** www.silverfishreviewpress.com. Estab. 1978. Publishes trade paperback originals. "Sponsors the Gerald Cable Book Award. This prize is awarded annually to a book length manuscript of original poetry by an author who has not yet published a full-length collection. There are no restrictions on the kind of poetry or subject matter; translations are not acceptable. Winners will receive $1,000, publication, and 25 copies of the book. Entries must be postmarked by October 15. See website for instructions." **Publishes 2-3 titles/year. 50% of books from first-time authors. 100% from unagented writers.** Accepts simultaneous submissions. Guidelines online.

TIPS "Read recent Silverfish titles."

SILVER LAKE PUBLISHING

P.O. Box 173, Aberdeen WA 98520. (360)532-5758. **Fax:** (360)532-5728. **E-mail:** publisher@silverlakepub.com. **Website:** www.silverlakepub.com. Estab. 1998. Publishes hardcover and trade paperback originals and reprints. **Pays royalty.** Accepts simultaneous submissions. Responds in 6-8 weeks to proposals. Book catalog available free. Guidelines available free.

NONFICTION No fiction or poetry. Submit outline, resume, 2 sample chapters, cover letter, synopsis. Submit via mail only.

SIMON & SCHUSTER

1230 Avenue of the Americas, New York NY 10020. (212)698-7000. **Website:** www.simonandschuster.com. *Accepts agented submissions only.* Accepts simultaneous submissions.

IMPRINTS Aladdin; Atheneum Books for Young Readers; Atria; Beach Lane Books; Folger Shakespeare Library; Free Press; Gallery Books; Howard Books; Little Simon; Margaret K. McElderry Books; Pocket; Scribner; Simon & Schuster; Simon & Schuster Books for Young Readers; Simon Pulse; Simon Spotlight; Threshold; Touchstone; Paula Wiseman Books.

SIMON & SCHUSTER BOOKS FOR YOUNG READERS

Imprint of Simon & Schuster Children's Publishing, 1230 Avenue of the Americas, New York NY 10020. (212)698-7000. **Fax:** (212)698-2796. **Website:** www.simonsayskids.com. Publishes hardcover originals. "Simon and Schuster Books For Young Readers is the Flagship imprint of the S&S Children's Division. We are committed to publishing a wide range of contemporary, commercial, award-winning fiction and nonfiction that spans every age of children's publishing. BFYR is constantly looking to the future, supporting our foundation authors and franchises, but always with an eye for breaking new ground with every publication. We publish high-quality fiction and nonfiction for a variety of age groups and a variety of markets. Above all, we strive to publish books that we are passionate about." *No unsolicited mss.* All unsolicited mss returned unopened. **Publishes 75 titles/year. Pays variable royalty on retail price.** Publishes ms 2-4 years after acceptance. Accepts simultaneous submissions. Guidelines online.

NONFICTION Subjects include history, biography. Picture books: concept. All levels: narrative, current events, biography, history. "We're looking for picture books or middle grade nonfiction that have a retail potential. No photo essays." *Agented submissions only.*

FICTION Subjects include fantasy, historical, humor, juvenile, mystery, picture books, science fiction, young adult. *Agented submissions only.*

TIPS "We're looking for picture books centered on a strong, fully-developed protagonist who grows or changes during the course of the story; YA novels that are challenging and psychologically complex; also imaginative and humorous middle-grade fiction. And we want nonfiction that is as engaging as fiction. Our imprint's slogan is 'Reading You'll Remember.' We aim to publish books that are fresh, accessible and family-oriented; we want them to have an impact on the reader."

SKINNER HOUSE BOOKS

The Unitarian Universalist Association, 24 Farnsworth St., Boston MA 02210. (617)742-2100, ext. 603. **Fax:** (617)948-6466. **E-mail:** bookproposals@uua.org. **Website:** www.uua.org/publications/skinnerhouse. **Contact:** Betsy Martin. Estab. 1975. Publishes trade paperback originals and reprints. "We publish titles in Unitarian Universalist faith, liberal religion, history, biography, worship, and issues of social justice. Most of our children's titles are intended for religious education or worship use. They reflect Unitarian Universalist values. We also publish inspirational titles of poetic prose and meditations. Writers should know that Unitarian Universalism is a liberal religious denomination committed to progressive ideals. Currently emphasizing social justice concerns." **Publishes 10-20 titles/year. 30% of books from first-time authors. 100% from unagented writers.** Publishes book 1 year after acceptance. Accepts simultaneous submissions. Responds to queries in 1 month. Book catalog for 6×9 SAE with 3 first-class stamps. Guidelines online.

NONFICTION Subjects include religion, inspirational, church leadership. All levels: activity books, multicultural, music/dance, nature/environment, religion. Query or submit proposal with cover letter,

TOC, 2 sample chapters. Reviews artwork/photos. Send photocopies.

FICTION Only publishes fiction for children's titles for religious instruction. Query.

RECENT TITLE(S) *Testimony: The Transformative Power of Unitarian Universalism*, edited by Meg Riley; *The Call to Care: Essays by Unitarian Universalist Chaplains*, edited by Karen L. Hutt; *Living Revision: A Writer's Craft as Spiritual Practice*, by Elizabeth Jarrett Andrew.

TIPS "From outside our denomination, we are interested in manuscripts that will be of help or interest to liberal churches, Sunday School classes, parents, ministers, and volunteers. Inspirational/spiritual and children's titles must reflect liberal Unitarian Universalist values."

LIZZIE SKURNICK BOOKS

Ig Publishing, (718)797-0676. **Website:** lizzieskurnickbooks.com. Estab. 2013. Lizzie Skurnick Books, an imprint of Ig Publishing, is devoted to reissuing the very best in young adult literature, from the classics of the 1930s and 1940s to the social novels of the 1970s and 1980s. Ig does not accept unsolicited mss, either by e-mail or regular mail. If you have a ms that you would like Ig to take a look at, send a query through online contact form. If interested, they will contact. All unsolicited mss will be discarded. Accepts simultaneous submissions.

SKY PONY PRESS

307 W. 36th St., 11th Floor, New York NY 10018. (212)643-6816. **Fax:** (212)643-6819. **Website:** skyponypress.com. Estab. 2011. Sky Pony Press is the children's book imprint of Skyhorse Publishing. "Following in the footsteps of our parent company, our goal is to provide books for readers with a wide variety of interests." Accepts simultaneous submissions. Guidelines online.

NONFICTION "Our parent company publishes many excellent books in the fields of ecology, independent living, farm living, wilderness living, recycling, and other green topics, and this will be a theme in our children's books. We are also searching for books that have strong educational themes and that help inform children of the world in which they live." Submit proposal via e-mail.

FICTION "We will consider picture books, early readers, midgrade novels, novelties, and informational books for all ages." Submit ms or proposal.

RECENT TITLE(S) *Letters From an Alien Schoolboy*, by Ros Asquith; *Meet the McKaws*, by Ged Adamson.

SLEEPING BEAR PRESS

2395 South Huron Parkway #200, Ann Arbor MI 48104. (800)487-2323. **Fax:** (734)794-0004. **E-mail:** submissions@sleepingbearpress.com. **Website:** www.sleepingbearpress.com. **Contact:** Manuscript Submissions. Estab. 1998. Accepts simultaneous submissions. Book catalog available via e-mail.

FICTION Picture books: adventure, animal, concept, folktales, history, multicultural, nature/environment, religion, sports. Young readers: adventure, animal, concept, folktales, history, humor, multicultural, nature/environment, religion, sports. Average word length: picture books—1,800. Accepts unsolicited queries 3 times per year. See website for details. Query with sample of work (up to 15 pages) and SASE. Please address packages to Manuscript Submissions.

SMALL BEER PRESS

150 Pleasant St., #306, Easthampton MA 01027. (413)203-1636. **Fax:** (413)203-1636. **E-mail:** info@smallbeerpress.com. **Website:** www.smallbeerpress.com. Estab. 2000. Small Beer Press also publishes the zine *Lady Churchill's Rosebud Wristlet*. "SBP's books have recently received the Tiptree and Crawford Awards." **Publishes 6-10 titles/year. Advance and standard royalties.**

FICTION Subjects include experimental, literary, short story collections, speculative. Does not accept unsolicited novel or short story collection mss. Send queries with first 10-20 pages and SASE.

TIPS "Please be familiar with our books first to avoid wasting your time and ours, thank you. E-mail queries will be deleted. Really."

SMITH AND KRAUS PUBLISHERS, INC.

177 Lyme Rd., Hanover NH 03755. (603)643-6431. **E-mail:** editor@smithandkraus.com. **E-mail:** carolb@smithandkraus.com. **Website:** smithandkraus.com. Estab. 1990. Publishes hardcover and trade paperback originals. **Publishes 35-40 titles/year. 10% of books from first-time authors. 10-20% from unagented writers. Pays 7% royalty on retail price. Pays $500-2,000 advance.** Publishes ms 1 year after acceptance. Responds in 1 month to queries; 2 months

to proposals; 4 months to mss. Book catalog available free.

NONFICTION Subjects includedrama. Does not return submissions. Query with SASE.

FICTION Does not return submissions. Query with SASE.

GIBBS SMITH, PUBLISHER

P.O. Box 667, Layton UT 84041. (801)544-9800. **Fax:** (801)546-8853. **Website:** www.gibbs-smith.com. Estab. 1969. Publishes hardcover and trade paperback originals. "We publish books that enrich and inspire humankind. Currently emphasizing interior decorating and design, home reference. De-emphasizing novels and short stories." **Publishes 80 titles/year. 3,000-4,000 queries received/year. 50% of books from first-time authors. 75% from unagented writers. Pays 8-14% royalty on gross receipts. Offers advance based on first year saleability projections.** Publishes ms 1-2 years after acceptance. Accepts simultaneous submissions. Responds in 1 month to queries; 10 weeks to proposals and mss. Guidelines online.

NONFICTION Subjects include regional, interior design, cooking, business, western, outdoor/sports/ recreation. Query by e-mail only.

SOFT SKULL PRESS INC.

Counterpoint, 2650 Ninth St., Suite 318, Berkeley CA 94710. (510)704-0230. **Fax:** (510)704-0268. **E-mail:** info@counterpointpress.com. **Website:** www.softskull.com. Publishes hardcover and trade paperback originals. "Here at Soft Skull we love books that are new, fun, smart, revelatory, quirky, groundbreaking, cage-rattling and/or/otherwise unusual." **Publishes 40 titles/year. Pays 7-10% royalty. Average advance: $100-15,000.** Publishes ms 6 months after acceptance. Accepts simultaneous submissions. Responds in 2 months to proposals; 3 months to mss. Book catalog and guidelines online.

NONFICTION Subjects include contemporary culture, creative nonfiction, entertainment, literature, pop culture. Send a cover letter describing your project and a full proposal along with 2 sample chapters.

FICTION Subjects include comic books, confession, contemporary, erotica, experimental, gay, lesbian, literary, mainstream, multicultural, short story collections. Does not consider poetry. Soft Skull Press no longer accepts digital submissions. Send a cover letter describing your project in detail and a completed ms. For graphic novels, send a minimum of five fully inked pages of art, along with a synopsis of your storyline. "Please do not send original material, as it will not be returned."

TIPS "See our website for updated submission guidelines."

SOHO PRESS, INC.

853 Broadway, New York NY 10003. (212)260-1900. **E-mail:** soho@sohopress.com. **Website:** www.sohopress.com. **Contact:** Bronwen Hruska, publisher; Mark Doten, senior editor. Estab. 1986. Publishes hardcover and trade paperback originals; trade paperback reprints. Soho Press publishes primarily fiction, as well as some narrative literary nonfiction and mysteries set abroad. No electronic submissions, only queries by e-mail. **Publishes 60-70 titles/ year. 15-25% of books from first-time authors. 10% from unagented writers. Pays 10-15% royalty on retail price (varies under certain circumstances).** Publishes ms 18 months after acceptance. Accepts simultaneous submissions. Responds in 3 months. Guidelines online.

NONFICTION Subjects include creative nonfiction, ethnic, memoirs. "Independent publisher known for sophisticated fiction, mysteries set abroad, women's interest (no genre) novels and multicultural novels." Publishes hardcover and trade paperback originals and reprint editions. Books: perfect binding; halftone illustrations. First novel print order varies. We do not buy books on proposal. We always need to see a complete ms before we buy a book, though we prefer an initial submission of 3 sample chapters. We do not publish books with color art or photographs or a lot of graphical material." No self-help, how-to, or cookbooks. Submit 3 sample chapters and a cover letter with a synopsis and author bio; SASE. Send photocopies.

FICTION Subjects include ethnic, historical, humor, literary, mystery, In mysteries, we only publish series with foreign or exotic settings, usually procedurals. Adventure, ethnic, feminist, historical, literary, mainstream/contemporary, mystery (police procedural), suspense, multicultural. Submit 3 sample chapters and cover letter with synopsis, author bio, SASE. *No e-mailed submissions.*

TIPS "Soho Press publishes discerning authors for discriminating readers, finding the strongest possible writers and publishing them. Before submitting, look at our website for an idea of the types of books we publish, and read our submission guidelines."

SOURCEBOOKS, INC.

1935 Brookdale Rd., Suite 139, Naperville IL 60563. (630)961-3900. **Fax:** (630)961-2168. **E-mail:** editorialsubmissions@sourcebooks.com. **Website:** www.sourcebooks.com. Estab. 1987. Publishes hardcover and trade paperback originals. "Sourcebooks publishes many forms of fiction and nonfiction titles, including books on parenting, self-help/psychology, business, and health. Focus is on practical, useful information and skills. It also continues to publish in the reference, New Age, history, current affairs, and humor categories. Currently emphasizing gift, women's interest, history, reference, historical fiction, romance genre, and children's." **Publishes 300 titles/year. 30% of books from first-time authors. 25% from unagented writers. Pays royalty on wholesale or list price. Pays advance.** Publishes ms 1 year after acceptance. Accepts simultaneous submissions. Responds in 3 months to queries. Book catalog online. Guidelines online.

NONFICTION Subjects include child guidance, history, psychology, science, sports, contemporary culture. Books for small business owners, entrepreneurs, and students. A key to submitting books to us is to explain how your book helps the reader, why it is different from the books already out there (please do your homework), and the author's credentials for writing this book. Books likely to succeed with us are self-help, parenting and childcare, psychology, women's issues, how-to, history, reference, biography, humor, gift books, or books with strong artwork. "We seek unique books on traditional subjects and authors who are smart and aggressive." Query with SASE, 2-3 sample chapters (not the first). *No complete mss.* Reviews artwork/photos.

TIPS "Our market is a decidedly trade-oriented bookstore audience. We also have very strong penetration into the gift-store market. Books which cross over between these 2 very different markets do extremely well with us. Our list is a solid mix of unique and general audience titles and series-oriented projects. We are looking for products that break new ground either in their own areas or within the framework of our series of imprints."

SOURCEBOOKS CASABLANCA

Sourcebooks, Inc., 232 Madison Ave., Suite 1100, New York NY 10016. **E-mail:** romance@sourcebooks.com. **Website:** www.sourcebooks.com. **Contact:** Deb Werksman (deb.werksman@sourcebooks.com). "Our romance imprint, Sourcebooks Casablanca, publishes single title romance in all subgenres." Accepts simultaneous submissions. Responds in 2-3 months. Guidelines online.

FICTION "Our editorial criteria call for: a heroine the reader can relate to, a hero she can fall in love with, a world gets created that the reader can escape into, there's a hook that we can sell within 2-3 sentences, and the author is out to build a career with us."

TIPS "We are actively acquiring single-title and single-title series romance fiction (90,000-100,000 words) for our Casablanca imprint. We are looking for strong writers who are excited about marketing their books and building their community of readers, and whose books have something fresh to offer in the genre of romance."

SOURCEBOOKS FIRE

1935 Brookdale Rd., Suite 139, Naperville IL 60563. (630)961-3900. **Fax:** (630)961-2168. **E-mail:** submissions@sourcebooks.com. **Website:** www.sourcebooks.com. "We're actively acquiring knockout books for our YA imprint. We are particularly looking for strong writers who are excited about promoting and building their community of readers, and whose books have something fresh to offer the ever-growing young adult audience. We are not accepting any unsolicited or unagented manuscripts at this time. Unfortunately, our staff can no longer handle the large volume of manuscripts that we receive on a daily basis. We will continue to consider agented manuscripts." See website for details. Accepts simultaneous submissions.

FICTION Query with the full ms attached in Word doc.

SOURCEBOOKS LANDMARK

Sourcebooks, Inc., Sourcebooks, Inc., 232 Madison Ave., Suite 1100, New York NY 10016. **E-mail:** editorialsubmissions@sourcebooks.com. **Website:** www.sourcebooks.com. "Our fiction imprint, Sourcebooks Landmark, publishes a variety of commercial fiction, including specialties in historical fiction and Austenalia. We are interested first and foremost in books that have a story to tell." Accepts simultaneous submissions. Responds in 2-3 months.

FICTION "We are actively acquiring contemporary, book club, and historical fiction for our Landmark imprint. We are looking for strong writers who are excited about marketing their books and building their community of readers." Submit synopsis and full ms preferred. Receipt of e-mail submissions acknowledged within 3 weeks of e-mail.

SOUTHERN ILLINOIS UNIVERSITY PRESS

1915 University Press Dr., SIUC Mail Code 6806, Carbondale IL 62901. (618)453-2281. **Fax:** (618)453-1221. **E-mail:** mkpriddy@siu.edu. **Website:** www.siupress.com. **Contact:** Kristine Priddy, Acquisitions Editor. Estab. 1956. Publishes hardcover and trade paperback originals and reprints. Scholarly press specializes in theater studies, rhetoric and composition studies, American history, Civil War, regional and nonfiction trade, poetry. No fiction. Currently emphasizing theater and American history, especially Civil War. **Publishes 25-30 titles/year. 300 queries; 80 mss received/year. 40% of books from first-time authors. 99% from unagented writers. Pays 5-10% royalty on wholesale price. Rarely offers advance.** Publishes ms 1 year after acceptance. Responds in 2 months to queries. Book catalog and ms guidelines free.

NONFICTION Subjects include archeology, history, language, military, regional, stage, transportation, war, womens studies.

POETRY Crab Orchard Series in Poetry. Guidelines online.

SPENCER HILL PRESS

27 W. 20th St., Suite 1102, New York NY 10011. **Website:** www.spencerhillpress.com. Spencer Hill Press is an independent publishing house specializing in sci-fi, urban fantasy, and paranormal romance for young adult readers. "Our books have that 'I couldn't put it down!' quality." Accepts simultaneous submissions. Guidelines online.

FICTION "We are interested in young adult, new adult, and middle grade sci-fi, psych-fi, paranormal, or urban fantasy, particularly those with a strong and interesting voice." Check website for open submission periods.

RECENT TITLE(S) *Elixir*, by Jennifer L. Armentrout; *Betrayed*, by Ednah Walters.

SPINNER BOOKS

University Games, 2030 Harrison St., San Francisco CA 94110. (415)503-1600. **Fax:** (415)503-0085. **E-mail:** info@ugames.com. **Website:** www.ugames.com. Estab. 1985. "Spinners Books publishes books of puzzles, games and trivia." Publishes book 6 months after acceptance. Accepts simultaneous submissions. Responds to queries in 3 months; mss in 2 months only if interested.

NONFICTION Picture books: games and puzzles. Query.

SPLASHING COW BOOKS

P.O. Box 867, Manchester VT 05254. **Website:** www.splashingcowbooks.com. **Contact:** Gordon McClellan, publisher. Estab. 2014. Publishes mass market paperback and hardcover books. We do not publish digital books. Splashing Cow Books publishes books under three imprints: Splashing Cow (children), Blue Boot (women) and Yellow Dot (family). **Publishes 10 titles/year. 100% of books from first-time authors. 100% from unagented writers. Pays royalties on retail price. Does not offer an advance.** Accepts simultaneous submissions. We try to reply as soon as possible, but may take up to 3 months. Catalog online. Guidelines online.

IMPRINTS Blue Boot Books imprint publishes books for women. Yellow Dot publishes general interest topics.

NONFICTION Open to any topic that would be of interest to children, women or families.

FICTION Subjects include adventure, comic books, contemporary, ethnic, fantasy, historical, humor, juvenile, literary, mainstream, multicultural, mystery, picture books, romance, science fiction, short story collections, spiritual, sports, suspense, western, young adult. Interested in a wide range of subject matter for children, women and families. Please check our website for submission guidelines.

RECENT TITLE(S) *The Riddlers*, by Nancy Kelly Allen; *Isabella and the Wishing Machine*, by Sian Mole; *Tackling Tires*, by Joe Lawson; *Paddling Days*, by Lisa Schoener.

SQUARE ONE PUBLISHERS, INC.

115 Herricks Rd., Garden City Park NY 11040. (516)535-2010. **Fax:** (516)535-2014. **Website:** www.squareonepublishers.com. **Contact:** Acquisitions Editor. Publishes trade paperback originals. **Publishes 20 titles/year. 500 queries; 100 mss received/year. 95% of books from first-time authors. 95% from unagented writers. Pays 10-15% royalty on wholesale price. Pays variable advance.** Publishes ms 10 months after acceptance. Accepts simultaneous sub-

missions. Responds in 1 month. Book catalog and ms guidelines online.

NONFICTION Subjects include child guidance, cooking, health, hobbies, nutrition, psychology, religion, spirituality, sports, travel, writers' guides, cooking/foods, gaming/gambling. Query with SASE. Submit proposal package, outline, bio, introduction, synopsis, SASE. Reviews artwork/photos. Send photocopies.

TIPS "We focus on making our books accessible, accurate, and interesting. They are written for people who are looking for the best place to start, and who don't appreciate the terms 'dummy,' 'idiot,' or 'fool,' on the cover of their books. We look for smartly written, informative books that have a strong point of view, and that are authored by people who know their subjects well."

STANDARD PUBLISHING

Standex International Corp., 4050 Lee Vance View, Colorado Springs CO 80918. (800)323-7543. **Fax:** (800)323-0726. **Website:** www.standardpub.com. Estab. 1866. Publishes resources that meet church and family needs in the area of children's ministry. Guidelines online.

STANFORD UNIVERSITY PRESS

500 Broadway St., Redwood City CA 94063. (650)723-9434. **Fax:** (650)725-3457. **Website:** www.sup.org. Estab. 1925. "Stanford University Press publishes scholarly books in the humanities and social sciences, along with professional books in business, economics and management science; also high-level textbooks and some books for a more general audience." *Submit to specific editor.* **Pays variable royalty (sometimes none). Pays occasional advance.** Guidelines online.

NONFICTION Subjects include ethnic, history, humanities, literary criticism, philosophy, psychology, religion, science, social sciences, sociology, political science, law, education, history and culture of China, Japan and Latin America, European history, linguistics, geology, medieval and classical studies. Query with prospectus and an outline. Reviews artwork/photos.

TIPS "The writer's best chance is a work of original scholarship with an argument of some importance."

STAR BRIGHT BOOKS

13 Landsdowne St., Cambridge MA 02139. (617)354-1300. **Fax:** (617)354-1399. **E-mail:** lolabush@starbrightbooks.com. **Website:** www.starbrightbooks.com. **Contact:** Lola Bush. Estab. 1994. Star Bright Books accepts unsolicited mss and art submissions. "We welcome submissions for picture books and longer works, both fiction and particularly nonfiction." Also beginner readers and chapter books. Currently seeking bios, math infused books. **Publishes 12 titles/year. 75% of books from first-time authors. 99% from unagented writers. Pays advance. as well as flat fee** Publishes ms 1-3 years after acceptance. Accepts simultaneous submissions. Responds in several months. Catalog online.

NONFICTION Subjects include animals, ethnic, marine subjects, young adult. Almost anything of interest to children. Very keen on Biographies and any thing of interest to children. How things work, how things are made, nature. history, multi-ethnic.

RECENT TITLE(S) *Grandma is a Slow Poke*; *Questions and Answers about Blood.*

ST. AUGUSTINE'S PRESS

17917 Killington Way, South Bend IN 46614-9773. (574)291-3500. **Fax:** (574)291-3700. **E-mail:** bruce@staugustine.net. **Website:** www.staugustine.net. **Contact:** Bruce Fingerhut, president. Estab. 1996. Publishes hardcover originals and trade paperback originals and reprints. "Our market is scholarly in the humanities. We publish in philosophy, religion, cultural history, and history of ideas only." **Publishes 30+ titles/year. 350 queries; 300 mss received/year. 2% of books from first-time authors. 95% from unagented writers. Pays 6-15% royalty. Pays $500-5,000 advance.** Publishes book 8-18 months after acceptance. Accepts simultaneous submissions. Responds in 2-6 months to queries; 3-8 months to proposals; 4-8 months to mss. Book catalog available free.

IMPRINTS Carthage Reprints.

NONFICTION Subjects include humanities, philosophy, religion. Query with SASE. Reviews artwork/photos. Send photocopies.

RECENT TITLE(S) *Seeing Things Politically*, by Pierre Manent; *Plato's Bedroom*, by David O'Connor; *Christian Persecutions in the Middle East* by George Marlin; *Neo-Scholastic Essays*, by Edward Feser.

TIPS "Scholarly and college student audience."

STC CRAFT

Imprint of Abrams, 115 W. 18th St., 6th Floor, New York NY 10011. **Website:** abramscraft.com. Publishes a vibrant collection of exciting and visually stunning craft books specializing in knitting, sewing, quilting, felting, and other popular craft genres. Accepts simultaneous submissions. Guidelines online.

NONFICTION Subjects include crafts. Please submit via e-mail.

STEEL TOE BOOKS

Department of English, Western Kentucky University, 1906 College Heights Blvd. #11086, Bowling Green KY 42101. (270)745-5769. **E-mail:** tom.hunley@wku.edu. **Website:** www.steeltoebooks.com. **Contact:** Dr. Tom C. Hunley, director. Estab. 2003. Steel Toe Books publishes "full-length, single-author poetry collections. Our books are professionally designed and printed. We look for workmanship (economical use of language, high-energy verbs, precise literal descriptions, original figurative language, poems carefully arranged as a book); a unique style and/or a distinctive voice; clarity; emotional impact; humor (word plays, hyperbole, comic timing); performability (a Steel Toe poet is at home on the stage as well as on the page)." Does not want "dry verse, purposely obscure language, poetry by people who are so wary of being called 'sentimental' they steer away from any recognizable human emotions, poetry that takes itself so seriously that it's unintentionally funny." Has published poetry by Allison Joseph, Susan Browne, James Doyle, Martha Silano, Mary Biddinger, John Guzlowski, Jeannine Hall Gailey, and others. Publishes 1-3 poetry books/year. Mss are normally selected through open submission. Accepts simultaneous submissions.

POETRY "Check the website for news about our next open reading period." Book mss may include previously published poems. Responds to mss in 3 months. Pays $500 advance on 10% royalties and 10 author's copies. Order sample books by sending $12 to Steel Toe Books. *Must purchase a ms in order to submit.* See website for submission guidelines.

STENHOUSE PUBLISHERS

P.O. Box 11020, Portland ME 04104. **E-mail:** editors@stenhouse.com. **Website:** www.stenhouse.com. **Contact:** Philippa Stratton, editorial director. Estab. 1993. Publishes paperback originals. Stenhouse publishes exclusively professional books for teachers, K-12. **Publishes 15 titles/year. 300 queries received/year. 30% of books from first-time authors. 99% from unagented writers. Pays royalty on wholesale price.** Accepts simultaneous submissions. Responds in 2 weeks to queries; 1 month to mss. Book catalog free or online. Guidelines online.

NONFICTION Subjects include education, specializing in literary with offerings in elementary and middle level math and science. All of our books are a combination of theory and practice. No children's books or student texts. Query by e-mail (preferred) or SASE. Reviews artwork/photos. Send photocopies.

STERLING PUBLISHING CO., INC.

1166 Avenue of the Americas, 17th Floor, New York NY 10036. (212)532-7160. **Website:** www.sterlingpublishing.com. Publishes hardcover and paperback originals and reprints. "Sterling publishes highly illustrated, accessible, hands-on, practical books for adults and children. Our mission is to publish high-quality books that educate, entertain, and enrich the lives of our readers." **15% of books from first-time authors. Pays royalty or work purchased outright. Offers advances (average amount: $2,000).** Accepts simultaneous submissions. Catalog online. Guidelines online.

NONFICTION Subjects include animals, ethnic, gardening, hobbies, New Age, recreation, science, sports, fiber arts, games and puzzles, children's humor, children's science, nature and activities, pets, wine, home decorating, dolls and puppets, ghosts, UFOs, woodworking, crafts, medieval, Celtic subjects, alternative health and healing, new consciousness. Proposals on subjects such as crafting, decorating, outdoor living, and photography should be sent directly to Lark Books at their Asheville, North Carolina offices. Complete guidelines can be found on the Lark site: www.larkbooks.com/submissions. Publishes nonfiction only. Submit outline, publishing history, 1 sample chapter (typed and double-spaced), SASE. "Explain your idea. Send sample illustrations where applicable. For children's books, please submit full mss. We do not accept electronic (e-mail) submissions. Be sure to include information about yourself with particular regard to your skills and qualifications in the subject area of your submission. It is helpful for us to know your publishing history—whether or not you've written other books and, if so, the name of the publisher and whether those books are currently in print." Reviews artwork/photocopies.

FICTION Publishes fiction for children. Submit to attention of "Children's Book Editor."

TIPS "We are primarily a nonfiction activities-based publisher. We have a picture book list, but we do not publish chapter books or novels. Our list is not trend-driven. We focus on titles that will backlist well. "

STIPES PUBLISHING LLC

P.O. Box 526, Champaign IL 61824. (217)356-8391. **Fax:** (217)356-5753. **E-mail:** stipes01@sbcglobal.net. **Website:** www.stipes.com. Estab. 1925. Publishes hardcover and paperback originals. "Stipes Publishing is oriented towards the education market and educational books with some emphasis in the trade market." **Publishes 15-30 titles/year. 50% of books from first-time authors. 95% from unagented writers. Pays 15% maximum royalty on retail price.** Publishes ms 4 months after acceptance. Responds in 2 months to queries. Guidelines online.

NONFICTION Subjects include agriculture, recreation, science. "All of our books in the trade area are books that also have a college text market. No books unrelated to educational fields taught at the college level." Submit outline, 1 sample chapter.

STONE ARCH BOOKS

1710 Roe Crest Rd., North Mankato MN 56003. **Website:** www.stonearchbooks.com. **Work purchased outright from authors.** Accepts simultaneous submissions. Catalog online.

FICTION Imprint of Capstone Publishers.Young readers, middle readers, young adults: adventure, contemporary, fantasy, humor, light humor, mystery, science fiction, sports, suspense. Average word length: young readers—1,000-3,000; middle readers and early young adults—5,000-10,000. Submit outline/synopsis and 3 sample chapters. Electronic submissions preferred. Full guidelines available on website.

TIPS "A high-interest topic or activity is one that a young person would spend their free time on without adult direction or suggestion."

STONE BRIDGE PRESS

P.O. Box 8208, Berkeley CA 94707. **E-mail:** sbp@stonebridge.com. **Website:** www.stonebridge.com. **Contact:** Peter Goodman, publisher. Estab. 1989. "Independent press focusing on books about Asia, primarily Japan and China, in English (business, language, culture, literature, animation)." Publishes hardcover and trade paperback originals. Books: 60-70 lb. offset paper; web and sheet paper; perfect bound; some illustrations. Distributes titles through Consortium. Promotes titles through social media and Internet announcements, blogs, special-interest magazines and niche tie-ins to associations. **Publishes 6 titles/year. 90% from unagented writers. Pays royalty on wholesale price.** Publishes ms 2 years after acceptance. Responds to queries in 4 months; mss in 8 months. Catalog online. Do not send children's books. Do not send proposals that are outside our key Asia-related subject areas. No poetry.

NONFICTION Subjects include business, cinema, crafts, creative nonfiction, ethnic, film, house and home, language, literature, memoirs, nature, philosophy, pop culture, sex, spirituality, travel, womens issues. Query with e-mail first.

FICTION Subjects include comic books, contemporary, erotica, literary, translation. Experimental, gay/lesbian, literary, Asia-themed. "Primarily looking at material relating to Asia, especially Japan and China. " Does not accept unsolicited mss. Accepts queries by e-mail.

TIPS "Query first before submitting. Research us first and avoid sending mss not in our subject area. Generic and bulk submissions will be ignored. No poetry. Looking also for graphic novels, not manga or serializations."

STONESLIDE BOOKS

Stoneslide Media LLC, P.O. Box 8331, New Haven CT 06530. **Website:** www.stoneslidecorrective.com. Estab. 2012. Publishes trade paperback and electronic originals. "We like novels with strong character development and narrative thrust, brought out with writing that's clear and expressive." **Publishes 3-5 titles/year. Receives 300 queries/year; 150 mss/year. 100% of books from first-time authors. 100% from unagented writers. Pays 20-80% royalty.** Publishes book 8 months after acceptance. Responds in 1-2 months. Book catalog and guidelines online.

FICTION Subjects include adventure, contemporary, experimental, fantasy, gothic, historical, humor, literary, mainstream, mystery, science fiction, short story collections, suspense. "We will look at any genre. The important factor for us is that the story use plot, characters, emotions, and other elements of storytelling to think and move the mind forward." Submit proposal package via online submission form including: synopsis and 3 sample chapters.

RECENT TITLE(S) *Shock to Equilibrium*, by Jonathan T.F. Weisberg (thriller); *Red Mask Stories*, by B. Clim (fantasy); *Gracious Living Without Servants*, by Brenda Cronin (contemporary).

TIPS "Read the Stoneslide Corrective to see if your work fits with our approach."

STOREY PUBLISHING

210 MASS MoCA Way, North Adams MA 01247. (800)793-9396. **Fax:** (413)346-2199. **E-mail:** feedback@storey.com. **Website:** www.storey.com. Estab. 1983. Publishes hardcover and trade paperback originals and reprints. "The mission of Storey Publishing is to serve our customers by publishing practical information that encourages personal independence in harmony with the environment. We seek to do this in a positive atmosphere that promotes editorial quality, team spirit, and profitability. The books we select to carry out this mission include titles on gardening, small-scale farming, building, cooking, home brewing, crafts, part-time business, home improvement, woodworking, animals, nature, natural living, personal care, and country living. We are always pleased to review new proposals, which we try to process expeditiously. We offer both work-for-hire and standard royalty contracts." **Publishes 40 titles/year. 600 queries received/year. 150 mss received/year. 25% of books from first-time authors. 60% from unagented writers. We offer both work-for-hire and standard royalty contracts. Pays advance.** Publishes book 2 years after acceptance. Accepts simultaneous submissions. Responds in 1-3 months. Book catalog available free. Guidelines online.

NONFICTION Subjects include animals, gardening, home, mind/body/spirit, birds, beer and wine, crafts, building, cooking. Submit a proposal. Reviews artwork/photos.

STRATEGIC MEDIA BOOKS

782 Wofford St., Rock Hill SC 29730. (803)366-5440. **E-mail:** contact@strategicmediabooks.com. **Website:** strategicmediabooks.com. Estab. 2010. Publishes trade paperback, and electronic originals. "Strategic Media Books, LLC is an independent U.S. publisher that aims to bring extraordinary true-life stories to the widest possible audience. Founded in 2010, Strategic Media Books specializes in nonfiction/true crime books." **Publishes 5-10 titles/year. 200 queries received/year. 30-35 mss received/year. 40% of books from first-time authors. 75% from unagented writers. Authors receive 10% royalty on retail price for paperback; 25% royalty on e-book.** Publishes book 9 months after acceptance. Accepts simultaneous submissions. Responds in 1-2 months. Catalog online. Guidelines online.

NONFICTION Subjects include government, history, politics, true crime, world affairs, true crime. Query to contact@strategicmediabooks.com. Will review artwork as part of manuscript. Writers should send photocopies.

STYLUS PUBLISHING, LLC

22883 Quicksilver Dr., Sterling VA 20166. **E-mail:** sylusinfo@styluspub.com. **Website:** styluspub.com. Estab. 1996. Publishes hardcover and trade paperback originals. "We publish in higher education (diversity, professional development, distance education, teaching, administration)." **Publishes 10-15 titles/year. 50 queries received/year. 6 mss received/year. 50% of books from first-time authors. 100% from unagented writers. Pays 5-10% royalty on wholesale price. Pays advance.** Publishes ms 6 months after acceptance. Responds in 1 month to queries. Book catalog available free. Guidelines online.

NONFICTION Query or submit outline, 1 sample chapter with SASE. Reviews artwork/photos. Send photocopies.

SUN BOOKS / SUN PUBLISHING

P.O. Box 5588, Santa Fe NM 87502. (505)471-5177. **E-mail:** info@sunbooks.com. **Website:** www.sunbooks.com. Estab. 1973. Publishes trade paperback originals and reprints. Not accepting new mss at this time. **Publishes 10-15 titles/year. 5% of books from first-time authors. 90% from unagented writers. Pays 5% royalty on retail price. Occasionally makes outright purchase.** Publishes ms 16-18 months after acceptance. Accepts simultaneous submissions. "Will respond within 2 months, via e-mail, to queries if interested.". Book catalog online. Queries via e-mail only, please.

NONFICTION Subjects include agriculture, alternative lifestyles, Americana, astrology, career guidance, environment, history, New Age, regional, self-help, leadership, motivational, recovery, inspirational.

RECENT TITLE(S) *Eight Pillars of Prosperity*, by James Allen; *Ambition and Success*, by Orson Swett Marden; *Cheerfulness as a Life Power*, by Orson Swett Marden.

SUNBURY PRESS, INC.

PO Box 548, Boiling Springs PA 17007. **E-mail:** info@sunburypress.com. **E-mail:** proposals@sunburypress.

com. **Website:** www.sunburypress.com. Estab. 2004. Publishes trade paperback and hardcover originals and reprints; electronic originals and reprints. Sunbury Press, Inc., headquartered in Mechanicsburg, PA is a publisher of trade paperback, hard cover and digital books featuring established and emerging authors in many fiction and non-fiction categories. Sunbury's books are printed in the USA and sold through leading booksellers worldwide. "Please use our online submission form." **Publishes 60 titles/year. Receives 1,000 queries/year; 500 mss/year. 40% of books from first-time authors. 95% from unagented writers. Pays 10% royalty on wholesale price.** Publishes ms 6 months after acceptance. Accepts simultaneous submissions. Responds in 3 months. Catalog and guidelines online. Online submission form.

IMPRINTS Sunbury Press (history and nonfiction); Milford House Press (murder mysteries, historical fiction, young adult fiction); Hellbender Books (horror, thrillers); Brown Posey Press (literary fiction, art); Ars Metaphysica (religion, spiritual, metaphysical, visionary fiction); Speckled Egg Press (juvenile fiction/nonfiction).

NONFICTION Subjects include agriculture, Americana, animals, anthropology, archeology, architecture, art, astrology, business, career guidance, child guidance, cinema, communications, community, computers, contemporary culture, cooking, counseling, crafts, creative nonfiction, economics, education, electronics, entertainment, environment, ethnic, film, finance, government, health, history, hobbies, house and home, humanities, labor, language, law, literature, marine subjects, medicine, memoirs, military, money, multicultural, music, nature, New Age, nutrition, parenting, philosophy, politics, pop culture, psychic, psychology, public affairs, real estate, recreation, regional, religion, science, sex, social sciences, sociology, spirituality, sports, transportation, travel, true crime, war, womens issues, womens studies, world affairs, young adult. "We are currently seeking war memoirs of all kinds and local / regional histories and biographies. We are also looking for American Revolution manuscripts." Please use our online submission service. Reviews artwork.

FICTION Subjects include adventure, confession, contemporary, ethnic, experimental, fantasy, gothic, historical, horror, humor, juvenile, literary, mainstream, military, multicultural, mystery, occult, regional, religious, romance, science fiction, short story collections, spiritual, sports, suspense, war, western, young adult. "We are seeking manuscripts for our three fiction imprints: Milford House Press, Brown Posey Press, and Hellbender Books." Does not want vampires, zombies, erotica. Please use our online submission service.

POETRY Submit complete ms.

TIPS "We are a rapidly growing small press with six diverse imprints. We currently have over 250 authors and 500 works under management."

SUNRISE RIVER PRESS

838 Lake St. S., Forest Lake MN 55025. (800)895-4585. **Fax:** (651)277-1203. **E-mail:** info@sunriseriverpress.com. **E-mail:** submissions@sunriseriverpress.com. **Website:** www.sunriseriverpress.com. Estab. 1992. "E-mail is preferred method of contact." Sunrise River Press is currently seeking book proposals from health/medical writers or experts who are interested in authoring consumer-geared trade paperbacks on healthcare, fitness, and nutrition topics. **Publishes 30 titles/year. Pays advance.** Accepts simultaneous submissions. Guidelines online.

NONFICTION Subjects include health, genetics, immune system maintenance, fitness; also some professional healthcare titles. Check website for submission guidelines. No phone calls, please; no originals.

SUNSTONE PRESS

Box 2321, Santa Fe NM 87504. (800)243-5644. **Website:** www.sunstonepress.com. **Contact:** Submissions Editor. Sunstone's original focus was on nonfiction subjects that preserved and highlighted the richness of the American Southwest but it has expanded its view over the years to include mainstream themes and categories—both nonfiction and fiction—that have a more general appeal. Accepts simultaneous submissions. Guidelines online.

NONFICTION Query with 1 sample chapter.

FICTION Query with 1 sample chapter.

RECENT TITLE(S) *Santa Fe With Kids From A to Z: An Illustrated Guide*, by Mary Catherine Mathews and Kelsy Daly; *Done in the Sun: Solar Projects for Children*, by Anne Hillerman.

SUPERCOLLEGE

3286 Oak Ct., Belmont CA 94002. (650)618-2221. **Website:** www.supercollege.com. Estab. 1998. Publishes trade paperback originals. "We only publish books on admission, financial aid, scholarships, test preparation, student life, and career preparation for college and graduate students." **Publishes 8-10 titles/year. 50% of books from first-time authors. 70% from unagented writers. Pays royalty on wholesale price or makes outright purchase.** Publishes ms 7-9 months after acceptance. Accepts simultaneous submissions. Book catalog and writers guidelines online.

NONFICTION Subjects include education. Submit complete ms. Reviews artwork/photos. Send photocopies.

RECENT TITLE(S) *The Ultimate Scholarship Book*; *How to Write a Winning Scholarship Essay*.

TIPS "We want titles that are student and parent friendly, and that are different from other titles in this category. We also seek authors who want to work with a small but dynamic and ambitious publishing company."

SWAN SCYTHE PRESS

1468 Mallard Way, Sunnyvale CA 94087. **E-mail:** robert.pesich@gmail.com. **Website:** www.swanscythepress.com. **Contact:** Robert Pesich, editor. Estab. 1999. Accepts simultaneous submissions.

POETRY "Swan Scythe Press, a publishing group located in Northern California, is committed to discovering and publishing the best new poets in America today. Its authors have won many national and local grants, awards and fellowships, and have distinguished themselves as artists and educators throughout the U.S. and in foreign countries. Founding Editor and Publisher Sandra McPherson, a widely-known and honored poet, along with the present Editor, James DenBoer, have now turned over the editorial functions of the press to Robert Pesich." Query first before submitting a ms via e-mail or through website.

RECENT TITLE(S) *Mata Hari Blows a Kiss*, by Lisa Dominguez Abraham; *How to Build a House*, by Kyle Liang.

SYRACUSE UNIVERSITY PRESS

621 Skytop Rd., Suite 110, Syracuse NY 13244. (315)443-5534. **Fax:** (315)443-5545. **E-mail:** seguiod@syr.edu; dmmanion@syr.edu. **Website:** syracuseuniversitypress.syr.edu. **Contact:** Suzanne Guiod, editor-in-chief; Deborah Manion, acquisitions editor. Estab. 1943. "Currently emphasizing Middle East studies, Jewish studies, Irish studies, peace studies, disability studies, television and popular culture, sports and entertainment, Native American studies, gender and ethnic studies, New York State." **Publishes 50 titles/year. 25% of books from first-time authors. 95% from unagented writers.** Publishes book 15 months after acceptance. Book catalog online. Guidelines online.

NONFICTION Subjects include anthropology, history, humanities, literature, politics, pop culture, regional, religion, sociology, sports, translation, womens studies. "Special opportunity in our nonfiction program for books on New York state, sports history, Jewish studies, Irish studies, the Middle East, religion and politics, television and popular culture, disability studies, peace studies, Native American studies. Provide precise descriptions of subjects, along with background description of project. The author must make a case for the importance of his or her subject." Submit query via e-mail with the book proposal form found on our website and a copy of your CV. Reviews artwork/photos.

RECENT TITLE(S) *In the Wake of the Poetic: Palestinian Artists after Darwish* by Najat Rahman; *Market Orientalism: Cultural Economy and the Arab Gulf States* by Benjamin Smith; *Syria from Reform to Revolt, Volume 2: Culture, Society, and Religion* edited by Christa Salamandra and Leif Stenberg; *Postcolonial Overtures: The Politics of Sound in Contemporary Northern Irish Poetry* by Julia Obert; *Israelites in Erin: Exodus, Revolution, and the Irish Revival* by Abby Bender; *The African Burial Ground in New York City: Memory, Spirituality, and Space* by Andrea Frohne.

TIPS "We're seeking well-written and thoroughly researched books that will make a significant contribution to the subject areas listed above and will be favorably received in the marketplace."

Ⓐ⊘ NAN A. TALESE

Imprint of Doubleday, Random House, 1745 Broadway, New York NY 10019. (212)782-8918. **Fax:** (212)782-8448. **Website:** www.nanatalese.com. Publishes hardcover originals. Nan A. Talese publishes nonfiction with a powerful guiding narrative and relevance to larger cultural interests, and literary fiction of the highest quality. **Publishes 15 titles/year. 400 queries received/year. 400 mss received/year. Pays variable royalty on retail price. Pays varying advance.** Accepts simultaneous submissions.

NONFICTION Subjects include contemporary culture, history, philosophy, sociology. *Agented submissions only.*

FICTION Subjects include literary. Well-written narratives with a compelling story line, good characterization and use of language. We like stories with an edge. *Agented submissions only.*

TIPS "Audience is highly literate people interested in story, information and insight. We want well-written material submitted by agents only. See our website."

TANTOR MEDIA

Recorded Books, 6 Business Park Rd., Old Saybrook CT 06475. (860)395-1155. **Fax:** (860)395-1154. **E-mail:** rightsemail@tantor.com. **Website:** www.tantor.com. **Contact:** Ron Formica, director of acquisitions. Estab. 2001. Publishes audiobooks only. Tantor Media, a division of Recorded Books, is a leading audiobook publisher, producing more than 100 new titles every month. We do not publish print or e-books. **Publishes 1,500 titles/year.** Accepts simultaneous submissions. Responds in 2 months. Catalog online. Not accepting print or e-book queries. We only publish audiobooks.

We are not publishing print/e-book titles.

NONFICTION Subjects include agriculture, alternative lifestyles, Americana, animals, anthropology, astrology, business, child guidance, communications, contemporary culture, cooking, creative nonfiction, economics, education, entertainment, foods, games, gay, government, health, history, horticulture, law, lesbian, literary criticism, marine subjects, memoirs, military, money, multicultural, music, New Age, philosophy, psychology, religion, science, sex, social sciences, sociology, spirituality, sports, womens issues, womens studies, world affairs, young adult. Not accepting print submissions.

FICTION Subjects include adventure, contemporary, erotica, experimental, fantasy, feminist, gay, gothic, historical, horror, humor, juvenile, lesbian, literary, mainstream, military, multicultural, multimedia, mystery, occult, religious, romance, science fiction, short story collections, spiritual, sports, suspense, western, young adult.

TARPAULIN SKY PRESS

P.O. Box 189, Grafton VT 05146. **Website:** www.tarpaulinsky.com. Estab. 2006. Tarpaulin Sky Press publishes cross- and trans-genre works as well as innovative poetry and prose. Produces full-length books and chapbooks, hand-bound books and trade paperbacks, and offers both hand-bound and perfect-bound paperback editions of full-length books. "We're a small, author-centered press endeavoring to create books that, as objects, please our authors as much their texts please us." Accepts simultaneous submissions.

POETRY Writers whose work has appeared in or been accepted for publication in *Tarpaulin Sky* may submit chapbook or full-length mss at any time, with no reading fee. Tarpaulin Sky Press also considers chapbook and full-length mss from writers whose work has not appeared in the journal, but **asks for a $20 reading fee**. Make checks/money orders to Tarpaulin Sky Press. Cover letter is preferred. Reading periods may be found on the website.

TEACHERS COLLEGE PRESS

1234 Amsterdam Ave., New York NY 10027. (212)678-3929. **Fax:** (212)678-4149. **E-mail:** tcp.cs@aidcvt.com. **Website:** www.teacherscollegepress.com. Estab. 1904. Publishes hardcover and paperback originals and reprints. "Teachers College Press publishes a wide range of educational titles for all levels of students: early childhood to higher education. Publishing books that respond to, examine, and confront issues pertaining to education, teacher training, and school reform." **Publishes 60 titles/year. Pays industry standard royalty. Pays advance.** Publishes ms 1 year after acceptance. Responds in 2 months to queries. Book catalog available free. Guidelines online.

NONFICTION Subjects include education, history, philosophy, sociology. This university press concentrates on books in the field of education in the broadest sense, from early childhood to higher education: good classroom practices, teacher training, special education, innovative trends and issues, administration and supervision, film, continuing and adult education, all areas of the curriculum, computers, guidance and counseling, and the politics, economics, philosophy, sociology, and history of education. We have recently added women's studies to our list. The Press also issues classroom materials for students at all levels, with a strong emphasis on reading and writing and social studies. Submit outline, sample chapters.

TEBOT BACH

P.O. Box 7887, Huntington Beach CA 92615. (714)968-0905. **Fax:** (714)968-0905. **E-mail:** info@tebotbach.org. **Website:** www.tebotbach.org. **Contact:** Mifanwy

Kaiser, editor/publisher. Estab. 1999. Publishes mss 6 months-1 year after acceptance. Accepts simultaneous submissions. Responds in 3 months.

POETRY Offers 2 contests per year. The Patricia Bibby First Book Contest and The Clockwise Chapbook contest. Go online for more information. Query first via e-mail, with a few sample poems and cover letter with brief bio.

Ⓐ⊘ KATHERINE TEGEN BOOKS

HarperCollins, 10 E. 53rd St., New York NY 10022. **Website:** www.harpercollins.com. Estab. 2003. Katherine Tegen Books publishes high-quality, commercial literature for children of all ages, including teens. Talented authors and illustrators who offer powerful narratives that are thought-provoking, well-written, and entertaining are the core of the Katherine Tegen Books imprint. *Katherine Tegen Books accepts agented work only.*

TEMPLE UNIVERSITY PRESS

1852 N. 10th St., Philadelphia PA 19122. (215)926-2140. **Fax:** (215)926-2141. **Website:** www.temple.edu/tempress/. Estab. 1969. "Temple University Press has been publishing path-breaking books on Asian-Americans, law, gender issues, film, women's studies and other interesting areas for nearly 40 years." **Publishes 60 titles/year. Pays advance.** Publishes ms 10 months after acceptance. Responds in 2 months to queries. Book catalog available free. Guidelines online.

NONFICTION Subjects include ethnic, history, photography, regional, sociology, labor studies, urban studies, Latin American/Latino, Asian American, African American studies, public policy, women's studies. No memoirs, fiction or poetry. Query with SASE. Reviews artwork/photos.

Ⓐ⊘ TEN SPEED PRESS

Penguin Random House, The Crown Publishing Group, Attn: Acquisitions, 2625 Alcatraz Ave. #505, Berkeley CA 94705. (510)559-1600. **Fax:** (510)524-1052. **Website:** crownpublishing.com/imprint/ten-speed-press. Estab. 1971. Publishes trade paperback originals and reprints. "Ten Speed Press publishes authoritative books for an audience interested in innovative ideas. Currently emphasizing cookbooks, career, business, alternative education, and offbeat general nonfiction gift books." **Publishes 120 titles/year. 40% of books from first-time authors. 40% from unagented writers. Pays $2,500 average advance.** Publishes ms 1 year after acceptance. Accepts simultaneous submissions. Responds in 3 months to queries; 6-8 weeks to proposals. Book catalog for 9×12 envelope and 6 first-class stamps. Guidelines online.

NONFICTION Subjects include business, career guidance, cooking, crafts, relationships, how-to, humor, and pop culture. *Agented submissions only.*

TIPS "We like books from people who really know their subject, rather than people who think they've spotted a trend to capitalize on. We like books that will sell for a long time, rather than 9-day wonders. Our audience consists of a well-educated, slightly weird group of people who like food, the outdoors, and take a light, but serious, approach to business and careers. Study the backlist of each publisher you're submitting to and tailor your proposal to what you perceive as their needs. Nothing gets a publisher's attention like someone who knows what he or she is talking about, and nothing falls flat like someone who obviously has no idea who he or she is submitting to."

TEXAS TECH UNIVERSITY PRESS

1120 Main St., Second Floor, Box 41037, Lubbock TX 79415. (806)742-2982. **Fax:** (806)742-2979. **E-mail:** ttup@ttu.edu. **Website:** www.ttupress.org. Estab. 1971. Texas Tech University Press, the book publishing office of the university since 1971 and an AAUP member since 1986, publishes nonfiction titles in the areas of natural history and the natural sciences; 18th century and Joseph Conrad studies; studies of modern Southeast Asia, particularly the Vietnam War; costume and textile history; Latin American literature and culture; and all aspects of the Great Plains and the American West, especially history, biography, memoir, sports history, and travel. In addition, the Press publishes several scholarly journals, acclaimed series for young readers, an annual invited poetry collection, and literary fiction of Texas and the West. Accepts simultaneous submissions. Guidelines online.

NONFICTION Subjects include environment, ethnic, history, law, literary criticism, literature, regional, sports. Submit proposal that includes introduction, 2 sample chapters, cover letter, working title, anticipated ms length, description of audience, comparison of book to others published on the subject, brief bio or CV.

FICTION Subjects include ethnic, multicultural, religious, western. Fiction rooted in the American West and Southwest, Jewish literature, Latin American and Latino fiction (in translation or English).

POETRY "TTUP publishes an annual invited first-book poetry manuscript (please note that we cannot entertain unsolicited poetry submissions)."

THUNDERSTONE BOOKS

6575 Horse Dr., Las Vegas NV 89131. **E-mail:** info@thunderstonebooks.com. **Website:** www.thunderstonebooks.com. **Contact:** Rachel Noorda, editorial director. Estab. 2014. Publishes hardcover, trade paperback, mass market paperback, and electronic originals. "At ThunderStone Books, we aim to publish children's books that have an educational aspect. We are not looking for curriculum for learning certain subjects, but rather stories that encourage learning for children, whether that be learning about a new language/culture or learning more about science and math in a fun, fictional format. We want to help children to gain a love for other languages and subjects so that they are curious about the world around them. We are currently accepting fiction and nonfiction submissions. Picture books without accompanying illustration will not be accepted." **Publishes 2-5 titles/year. Receives 30 queries and mss/year. 100% of books from first-time authors. 100% from unagented writers. Pays 5-15% royalties on retail price. Pays $300-1,000 advance.** Publishes ms 6 months after acceptance. Accepts simultaneous submissions. Responds in 3 months. Catalog available for SASE. Guidelines available.

NONFICTION Subjects include creative nonfiction, education, language, literature, multicultural, regional, science, translation. Looking for engaging educational materials, not a set curriculum, but books that teach as well as have some fun. Open to a variety of educational subjects, but specialty and main interest lies in language exposure/learning, science, math, and history. Reviews photocopies of artwork.

FICTION Subjects include multicultural, picture books, regional. Interested in multicultural stories with an emphasis on authentic culture and language (these may include mythology). "If you think your book is right for us, send a query letter with a word attachment of the first 50 pages to info@thunderstonebooks.com. If it is a picture book or chapter book for young readers that is shorter than 50 pages send the entire manuscript."

RECENT TITLE(S) *Picturing Chinese*, by Thunder-Stone Books and illustrated by Bennet Noorda; *Elements of Evil*, by Brooke Maxwell; *Monkey Gains His Powers*, by Will Strong.

TIGHTROPE BOOKS

Toronto ONCanada. **E-mail:** tightropeasst@gmail.com. **Website:** www.tightropebooks.com. Estab. 2005. Publishes trade paperback originals. **Publishes 12 titles/year. 60% of books from first-time authors. 90% from unagented writers.**

Press is going out of business and not accepting new manuscripts.

NONFICTION Subjects include alternative lifestyles, art, contemporary culture, creative nonfiction, ethnic, gay, language, lesbian, literary criticism, literature, memoirs, multicultural, womens issues, womens studies.

FICTION Subjects include contemporary, ethnic, experimental, feminist, gay, lesbian, literary, multicultural, poetry, poetry in translation, short story collections, young adult.

TILBURY HOUSE PUBLISHERS

WordSplice Studio, Inc., 12 Starr St., Thomaston ME 04861. (207)582-1899. **Fax:** (207)582-8772. **E-mail:** info@tilburyhouse.com. **Website:** www.tilburyhouse.com. Estab. 1990. **Publishes 24 titles/year. Pays royalty based on wholesale price.** Publishes ms 1.5 years after acceptance. Accepts simultaneous submissions. Responds to mss in 6 months. Guidelines and catalog online.

NONFICTION Regional history/maritime/nature, and children's picture books that deal with issues, such as bullying, multiculturalism, etc. science/nature. Submit complete ms for picture books or outline/synopsis for longer works. Now uses online submission form. Reviews artwork/photos. Send URL.

FICTION Picture books: multicultural, nature/environment. Special needs include books that teach children about and honoring diversity. Send art/photography samples and/or complete ms to info@tilburyhouse.com.

TIPS "We are always interested in stories that will encourage children to understand the natural world and the environment, as well as stories with social justice themes. We really like stories that engage children to become problem solvers as well as those that promote respect, tolerance and compassion."

Ⓐ TIN HOUSE BOOKS

2617 NW Thurman St., Portland OR 97210. (503)473-8663. **Fax:** (503)473-8957. **E-mail:** masie@tinhouse.com. **Website:** www.tinhouse.com. **Contact:** Masie Cochran, editor; Tony Perez, editor. Publishes hardcover originals, paperback originals, paperback reprints. "We are a small independent publisher dedicated to nurturing new, promising talent as well as showcasing the work of established writers." Distributes/promotes titles through W. W. Norton. **Publishes 10-12 titles/year.** Publishes ms 1 year after acceptance. Accepts simultaneous submissions. Responds to queries in 2-3 weeks; mss in 2-3 months. Guidelines online.

NONFICTION *Agented mss only.* "We no longer read unsolicited submissions by authors with no representation. We will continue to accept submissions from agents."

FICTION *Agented mss only.* "We no longer read unsolicited submissions by authors with no representation. We will continue to accept submissions from agents."

RECENT TITLE(S) *Loitering*, by Charles D'Ambrosio; *Our Endless Numbered Days*, by Claire Fuller; *Trompe l'Oeil*, by Nancy Reisman.

TITAN PRESS

2150 Pickwick Dr. #455, Camarillo CA 93011. **E-mail:** titan91416@yahoo.com. **Website:** https://www.facebook.com/RVClef. **Contact:** Romana Von Clef, editor. Estab. 1981. Publishes hardcover and paperback originals. Little literary publisher. **Publishes 12 titles/year. Receives 100-200 submissions/year. 5% of books from first-time authors. 50% from unagented writers. Pays 20-40% royalty.** Publishes ms 1 year after acceptance. Accepts simultaneous submissions. Responds to queries in 3 months.

NONFICTION Subjects include creative nonfiction, entertainment, literary criticism, literature.

FICTION Subjects include contemporary, literary, mainstream, short story collections. Does not accept unsolicited mss. Query with SASE. Include brief bio, list of publishing credits.

POETRY Literary, not MFA banality.

TIPS "Look, act, sound, and *be* professional."

TOR BOOKS

Tom Doherty Associates, 175 Fifth Ave., New York NY 10010. **Website:** www.tor-forge.com. Tor Books is the "world's largest publisher of science fiction and fantasy, with strong category publishing in historical fiction, mystery, western/Americana, thriller, YA." **Publishes 10-20 titles/year. Pays author royalty. Pays illustrators by the project.** Accepts simultaneous submissions. Book catalog available. Guidelines online.

FICTION Subjects include adventure, fantasy, historical, humor, mystery, picture books, science fiction, suspense, young adult. Submit first 3 chapters, 3-10 page synopsis, dated cover letter, SASE.

TOWER PUBLISHING

588 Saco Rd., Standish ME 04084. (207)642-5400. **Fax:** (207)642-5463. **E-mail:** info@towerpub.com. **E-mail:** michaell@towerpub.com. **Website:** www.towerpub.com. **Contact:** Michael Lyons, president. Estab. 1772. Publishes hardcover originals and reprints, trade paperback originals. Tower Publishing specializes in legal publications. **Publishes 22 titles/year. 60 queries; 30 mss received/year. 10% of books from first-time authors. 90% from unagented writers.** Publishes ms 6 months after acceptance. Accepts simultaneous submissions. Responds in 1 month to queries; 2 months to proposals and mss. Book catalog and ms guidelines online.

NONFICTION Subjects include law. Looking for legal books of a national stature. Query with SASE. Submit outline.

TRAFALGAR SQUARE BOOKS

388 Howe Hill Rd., P.O. Box 257, North Pomfret VT 05053. (802)457-1911. **Website:** www.horseandriderbooks.com. **Contact:** Rebecca Didier. Estab. 1985. Publishes hardcover and trade paperback originals. "We publish high-quality instructional books for horsemen and horsewomen, always with the horse's welfare in mind." **Publishes 12 titles/year. 50% of books from first-time authors. 80% from unagented writers. Pays royalty. Pays advance.** Publishes ms 18 months after acceptance. Responds in 1 month to queries; 2 months to proposals; 2-3 months to mss. Catalog free on request and by e-mail.

NONFICTION Subjects include animals. "We rarely consider books for complete novices." Query with SASE. Submit proposal package including outline, 1-3 sample chapters, letter of introduction including qualifications for writing on the subject and why the proposed book is an essential addition to existing publications. Reviews artwork/photos as part of the ms package. We prefer color laser thumbnail sheets or duplicate prints (do not send original photos or art!).

RECENT TITLE(S) *The Art of Liberty Training for Horses*, by Jonathan Field; *When Two Spines Align: Dressage Dynamics*, by Beth Baumert.

TIPS "Our audience is comprised of horse lovers and riders interested in pursuing their passion and/or sport while doing what is best for horses."

TRAVELERS' TALES

Solas House, Inc., 2320 Bowdoin St., Palo Alto CA 94306. (650)462-2110. **Fax:** (650)462-6305. **Website:** www.travelerstales.com. Estab. 1993. Publishes inspirational travel books, mostly anthologies and travel advice books. "Due to the volume of submissions, we do not respond unless the material submitted meets our immediate editorial needs. All stories are read and filed for future use contingent upon meeting editorial guidelines." **Publishes 4-6 titles/year. Receives hundreds of submissions/year. 30% of books from first-time authors. 80% from unagented writers. Pays $100 honorarium for anthology pieces. Does not pay advance.** Accepts simultaneous submissions. "We contact you if we'd like to publish your work.". Guidelines online.

NONFICTION Subjects include creative nonfiction, literature, memoirs, spirituality, travel, womens issues, world affairs. Subjects include all aspects of travel.

TIPS "We publish personal nonfiction stories and anecdotes—funny, illuminating, adventurous, frightening, or grim. Stories should reflect that unique alchemy that occurs when you enter unfamiliar territory and begin to see the world differently as a result. Stories that have already been published, including book excerpts, are welcome as long as the authors retain the copyright or can obtain permission from the copyright holder to reprint the material."

TRIANGLE SQUARE

Seven Stories Press, 140 Watts St., New York NY 10013. (212)226-8760. **Fax:** (212)226-1411. **E-mail:** info@sevenstories.com. **Website:** https://www.sevenstories.com/imprints/triangle-square. Triangle Square is a children's and young adult imprint of Seven Story Press. Accepts simultaneous submissions.

FICTION Send a cover letter with 2 sample chapters and SASE. Send c/o Acquisitions.

RECENT TITLE(S) *A is for Activist*, by Innosanto Nagara; *Lizzie*, by Maxine W. Kumin.

THE TRINITY FOUNDATION

P.O. Box 68, Unicoi TN 37692. (423)743-0199. **Fax:** (423)743-2005. **E-mail:** tjtrinityfound@aol.com. **Website:** www.trinityfoundation.org. **Contact:** Thomas W. Juodaitis, editor. Publishes hardcover and paperback originals and reprints. **Publishes 1-3 titles/year.** Publishes ms 9 months after acceptance. Accepts simultaneous submissions. Responds in 1 month to queries and proposals; 3 months to mss. Book catalog online.

NONFICTION Subjects include economics, education, philosophy, religion. Only books that conform to the philosophy and theology of the Westminster Confession of Faith. Textbooks subjects include business/economics, education, government/politics, history, philosophy, religion, science. Query with SASE.

TRIUMPH BOOKS

814 N. Franklin St., Chicago IL 60610. (312)337-0747. **Fax:** (312)280-5470. **Website:** www.triumphbooks.com. Estab. 1990. Publishes hardcover originals and trade paperback originals and reprints. Accepts simultaneous submissions. Book catalog available free.

NONFICTION Subjects include recreation, sports, health, sports business/motivation. Query with SASE. Reviews artwork/photos. Send photocopies.

TRUMAN STATE UNIVERSITY PRESS

100 E. Normal Ave., Kirksville MO 63501. (660)785-7336. **E-mail:** tsup@truman.edu. **E-mail:** bsm@truman.edu. **Website:** tsup.truman.edu. **Contact:** Barbara Smith-Mandell, editor-in-chief. Estab. 1986.

TU BOOKS

Lee & Low Books, 95 Madison Ave., Suite #1205, New York NY 10016. **Website:** www.leeandlow.com/imprints/3. **Contact:** Stacy Whitman, publisher. Estab. 2010. Publishes young adult and middle grade novels and graphic novels: science fiction, fantasy, contemporary realism, mystery, historical fiction, and more, with particular interest in books with strong literary hooks. Also seeking middle grade and young adult nonfiction. The Tu Books imprint spans many genres: science fiction, fantasy, mystery, contemporary, and more. We don't believe in labels or limits, just great stories. Join us at the crossroads where fantasy and real life collide. You'll be glad you did. **Pub-**

lishes 6-8 titles/year. 40% of books from first-time authors. Advance against royalties. Pays advance. Accepts simultaneous submissions. Responds only if interested. Catalog available online. Please see our full submissions guidelines online.

For new writers of color, please be aware of the New Visions Award writing contest, which runs every year from May-August. Previously unpublished writers of color and Native American writers may submit their middle grade and young adult novels and graphic novels. See submission guidelines for the contest online.

NONFICTION Graphic novel manuscripts for author/illustrators as well as portfolios of illustrators for cover art/spot art in illustrated novels.

FICTION Subjects include adventure, comic books, contemporary, ethnic, fantasy, feminist, gay, hi-lo, historical, horror, humor, juvenile, lesbian, literary, mainstream, multicultural, mystery, poetry, poetry in translation, regional, romance, science fiction, short story collections, sports, suspense, translation, war, western, young adult, Middle grade. "Our focus is on fiction and narrative nonfiction centering people of color or Native people. We are interested in both middle grade stories for ages 8 to 12 and young adult stories for ages 12 to 18. Occasionally a manuscript might fall between these two categories; if your manuscript does, let us know. We look for fantasy set in worlds inspired by non-Western folklore or culture, contemporary mystery and fantasy set all over the world, and science fiction that centers the possibilities for people of color or Native people in the future. We also selectively publish realism and narrative nonfiction that explores the contemporary and historical experiences of people of color or Native people. We welcome intersectional narratives that feature LGBTQIA and disabled people as heroes in their own stories. Stacy Whitman and Cheryl Klein both acquire titles for Tu Books, and we ask that you identify which of them you wish to consider your submission. As loose rules of thumb, Cheryl has a more literary bent and does not acquire graphic novels, while Stacy has a more commercial focus and does not acquire narrative nonfiction." Not seeking picture books or chapter books. Please include a synopsis and first three chapters of the novel. Do not send the complete ms. Mss should be typed doubled-spaced. Mss should be accompanied by a cover letter that includes a brief biography of the author, including publishing history. The letter should be addressed to either Stacy Whitman or Cheryl Klein, and should also state if the ms is a simultaneous or an exclusive submission. "We're looking for middle grade (ages 8-12) and young adult (ages 12 and up) books. We are not looking for chapter books (ages 6 to 9) at this time. Be sure to include full contact information on the cover letter and first page of the manuscript. Page numbers and your last name/title of the book should appear on subsequent pages."

RECENT TITLE(S) *There's No Base Like Home*, by Jessica Mendoza and Alana Mendoza Dusan, illustrated by Ruth McNally Barshaw; *Rebel Seoul*, by Axie Oh; *I Am Alfonso Jones*, by Tony Medina, illustrated by Stacey Robinson & John Jennings; *Ahimsa*, by Supriya Kelkar.

TUMBLEHOME LEARNING

P.O. Box 71386, Boston MA 02117. **E-mail:** info@tumblehomelearning.com. **E-mail:** submissions@tumblehomelearning.com. **Website:** www.tumblehomelearning.com. **Contact:** Pendred Noyce, editor. Estab. 2011. Publishes hardcover, trade paperback, and electronic originals. Tumblehome Learning helps kids imagine themselves as young scientists or engineeers and encourages them to experience science through adventure and discovery. "We do this with exciting mystery and adventure tales as well as experiments carefully designed to engage students from ages 8 and up." **Publishes 8-10 titles/year. Receives 20 queries and 20 mss/year. 50% of books from first-time authors. 100% from unagented writers. Pays authors 8-12% royalties on retail price. Pays $500 advance.** Publishes ms 8 months after acceptance. Accepts simultaneous submissions. Responds in 1 month to queries and proposals, and 2 months to mss. Catalog available online. Guideliens available on request for SASE.

NONFICTION Subjects include science. Rarely publishes nonfiction. Book would need to be sold to trade, not just the school market.

FICTION Subjects include adventure, juvenile. "All our fiction has science at its heart. This can include using science to solve a mystery (see *The Walking Fish* by Rachelle Burk or *Something Stinks!* by Gail Hedrick), realistic science fiction, books in our Galactic Academy of Science series, science-based adventure tales, and the occasional picture book with a science theme, such as appreciation of the stars and constellations in *Elizabeth's Constellation Quilt* by Olivia Fu. A graphic novel about science would also be welcome." Submit completed ms electronically.

RECENT TITLE(S) Recent titles: *Magnificent Minds: Sixteen Women Pioneers of Science and Medicine* by Pendred Noyce; *Dinosaur Eggs and Blue Ribbons: Science Fairs, Inside and Out* by Barnas Monteith; *The Confounding Case of the Climate Crisis* by Owen Liu.

TIPS "Please don't submit to us if your book is not about science. We don't accept generic books about animals or books with glaring scientific errors in the first chapter. That said, the book should be fun to read and the science content can be subtle. We work closely with authors, including first-time authors, to edit and improve their books. As a small publisher, the greatest benefit we can offer is this friendly and respectful partnership with authors."

TURNING POINT

WordTech Communications LLC, P.O. Box 541106, Cincinnati OH 45254. **E-mail:** connect@wordtechcommunications.com. **Website:** www.turningpointbooks.com. **Pays in royalties.** Accepts simultaneous submissions. Catalog and guidelines online.

POETRY "Dedicated to the art of story in poetry. We seek to publish collections of narrative poetry that tell the essential human stories of our times." No e-mail submissions. No calls for book-length poetry right now.

TUTTLE PUBLISHING

364 Innovation Dr., North Clarendon VT 05759. (802)773-8930. **Fax:** (802)773-6993. **E-mail:** submissions@tuttlepublishing.com. **Website:** www.tuttlepublishing.com. Estab. 1832. Publishes hardcover and trade paperback originals and reprints. Tuttle is America's leading publisher of books on Japan and Asia. "Familiarize yourself with our catalog and/or similar books we publish. Send complete book proposal with cover letter, table of contents, 1-2 sample chapters, target audience description, SASE. No e-mail submissions." **Publishes 125 titles/year. 1,000 queries received/year. 20% of books from first-time authors. 40% from unagented writers. Pays 5-10% royalty on net or retail price, depending on format and kind of book. Pays advance.** Publishes book 18 months after acceptance. Accepts simultaneous submissions. Responds in 2-3 months to proposals. Tuttle accepts submissions by mail or e-mail. In the interest of environmental responsibility, we prefer digital submissions. (See below for more detail on where to send). Please allow three months for the editors to review a proposal. Please review the category section of our site carefully to help determine if your submission is a fit for Tuttle.

NONFICTION Publishes Asian cultures, language, martial arts, textbooks, art and design, craft books and kits, cookbooks, religion, philosophy, and more. Query with SASE.

TWILIGHT TIMES BOOKS

P.O. Box 3340, Kingsport TN 37664. **E-mail:** publisher@twilighttimesbooks.com. **Website:** www.twilighttimesbooks.com. **Contact:** Andy M. Scott, managing editor. Estab. 1999. "We publish compelling literary fiction by authors with a distinctive voice." Published 5 debut authors within the last year. Averages 120 total titles; 15 fiction titles/year. Member: AAP, IBPA, PAS, SPAN, SLF. **85% from unagented writers. Pays 8-15% royalty.** Accepts simultaneous submissions. Responds in 4 weeks to queries; 2 months to mss. Guidelines online.

NONFICTION Subjects include creative nonfiction, literary criticism, memoirs, military, nature, New Age, womens studies, young adult.

FICTION Subjects include fantasy, historical, humor, juvenile, literary, mainstream, military, mystery, regional, science fiction, suspense, war, young adult. Accepts unsolicited mss. Do not send complete mss. Queries via e-mail only. Include estimated word count, brief bio, list of publishing credits, marketing plan.

RECENT TITLE(S) *Equity of Life*, by Rudy Mazzocchi; *Death by Opera*, by Erica Miner; *Frozen: a Paranormal mystery*, by Christine Amsden; *The Coravian Conflict*, by Loren K. Jones; *The Gordian Knot*, by Christopher Nuttall; *Under Strange Suns*, by Ken Lizzi.

TIPS "The only requirement for consideration at Twilight Times Books is that your novel must be entertaining and professionally written."

TWO DOLLAR RADIO

Website: www.twodollarradio.com. **Contact:** Eric Obenauf, editorial director. Estab. 2005. Two Dollar Radio is a boutique family-run press, publishing bold works of literary merit, each book, individually and collectively, providing a sonic progression that "we believe to be too loud to ignore." Targets readers who admire ambition and creativity. Range of print runs:

2,000-7,500 copies. **Publishes 5-6 (plus a biannual journal of nonfiction essays,** ***Frequencies*****) titles/year. Advance: $500-1,000.**

FICTION Submit entire, completed ms with a brief cover letter, via Submittable. No previously published work. No proposals. No excerpts. There is a $2 reading fee per submission. Accepts submissions every other month (January, March, May, July, September, November).

TIPS "We want writers who show an authority over language and the world that is being created, from the very first sentence on."

TWO SYLVIAS PRESS

P.O. Box 1524, Kingston WA 98346. **E-mail:** twosylviaspress@gmail.com. **Website:** twosylviaspress.com. **Contact:** Kelli Russell Agodon and Annette Spaulding-Convy. Estab. 2010. Two Sylvias Press is an independent press located in the Seattle area. "We publish poetry, memoir, essays, books on the craft of writing, and creativity tools, such as The Poet Tarot and The Daily Poet. The press draws its inspiration from the poetic literary talent of Sylvia Plath and the editorial business sense of Sylvia Beach." Two Sylvias Press values inclusiveness, diversity, respect, creativity, and freedom of expression. "We welcome all readers and writers." **100% from unagented writers.** Publishes ms 12-18 months after acceptance. Accepts simultaneous submissions. Catalog online. "We currently only have two calls for submissions of poetry books: our Poetry Chapbook Prize (in the spring & open to all poets) and our Wilder Full-Length Poetry Prize (in autumn & open to women over 50). Currently, we are not accepting any unsolicited work.".

NONFICTION Subjects includeBooks on Creativity & Writing Craft. Two Sylvias Press focuses on books of creativity and writing craft/writing prompt books, but also publishes memoir/essay.

POETRY Chapbook & Full Length Poetry Book Prizes. Occasional calls for submissions for specific poetry anthologies. Subscribe to the Two Sylvias Press newsletter (www.tinyletter.com/twosylviaspress) for updates on submission periods.

RECENT TITLE(S) *PR for Poets: A Guidebook for Publicity and Marketing* by Jeannine Hall Gailey, *Appalachians Run Amok*, by Adrian Blevins; *Blood Song*, by Michael Schmeltzer; *Killing Marias: A Poem for Multiple Voices*, by Claudia Castro Luna.

TIPS "Created with the belief that great writing is good for the world, Two Sylvias Press mixes modern technology, classic style, and literary intellect with an eco-friendly heart. We are an indie press in the Seattle area that publishes books, offers online poetry writing retreats, writing prompts, and other creative tools for poets and writers. While we currently aren't accepting unsolicited manuscripts except for our poetry chapbook prize and a full-length poetry prize for women over 50, we recommend poets and writers interested in Two Sylvias Press subscribe to our newsletter to be the first to know when we are accepting new work. Many thanks to all the poets, writers, and readers who continue to support us and make art in challenging times."

Ⓐ⊘ TYNDALE HOUSE PUBLISHERS, INC.

351 Executive Dr., Carol Stream IL 60188. (800)323-9400. **Fax:** (800)684-0247. **Website:** www.tyndale.com. Estab. 1962. Publishes hardcover and trade paperback originals and mass paperback reprints. "Tyndale House publishes practical, user-friendly Christian books for the home and family." **Publishes 15 titles/year. Pays negotiable royalty. Pays negotiable advance.** Accepts simultaneous submissions. Guidelines online.

NONFICTION Subjects include child guidance, religion, devotional/inspirational. *Agented submissions only. No unsolicited mss.*

FICTION Subjects include juvenile, romance, Christian (children's, general, inspirational, mystery/suspense, thriller, romance). "Christian truths must be woven into the story organically. No short story collections. Youth books: character building stories with Christian perspective. Especially interested in ages 10-14. We primarily publish Christian historical romances, with occasional contemporary, suspense, or standalones." *Agented submissions only. No unsolicited mss.*

TIPS "All accepted manuscripts will appeal to Evangelical Christian children and parents."

FICTION Subjects include literary, mystery. Submissions currently closed; check website for updates.

UNBRIDLED BOOKS

8201 E. Highway WW, Columbia MO 65201. **E-mail:** michalsong@unbridledbooks.com. **Website:** unbridledbooks.com. **Contact:** Greg Michalson. Estab. 2004. "Unbridled Books is a premier publisher of works of rich literary quality that appeal to a broad audience." Accepts simultaneous submissions.

FICTION Please query first by e-mail. "Due to the heavy volume of submissions, we regret that at this time we are not able to consider uninvited mss."

TIPS "We try to read each ms that arrives, so please be patient."

⊘ UNITY HOUSE

1901 N.W. Blue Pkwy., Unity Village MO 64065. (816)524-3550. **Fax:** (816)347-5518. **E-mail:** unity@unityonline.org. **Website:** www.unityonline.org. Estab. 1889. Publishes hardcover, trade paperback, and electronic originals. Unity House publishes metaphysical Christian books based on Unity principles, as well as inspirational books on metaphysics and practical spirituality. All manuscripts must reflect a spiritual foundation and express the Unity philosophy, practical Christianity, universal principles, and/or metaphysics. **Publishes 5-7 titles/year. 50 queries received/year. 5% of books from first-time authors. 95% from unagented writers. Pays 10-15% royalty on retail price. Pays advance.** Publishes ms 13 months after acceptance. Responds in 6-8 months. Catalog and guidelines online.

NONFICTION Subjects include religion. "Writers should be familiar with principles of metaphysical Christianity but not feel bound by them. We are interested in works in the related fields of holistic health, spiritual psychology, and the philosophy of other world religions." *Not accepting mss for new books at this time.* Reviews artwork/photos. Writers should send photocopies.

FICTION Subjects include spiritual, inspirational, metaphysical, visionary fiction. "We are a bridge between traditional Christianity and New Age spirituality. Unity is based on metaphysical Christian principles, spiritual values and the healing power of prayer as a resource for daily living." *Not accepting mss for new books at this time.*

TIPS "We target an audience of spiritual seekers."

THE UNIVERSITY OF AKRON PRESS

120 E. Mill St., Suite 415, Akron OH 44308. **E-mail:** uapress@uakron.edu. **Website:** www.uakron.edu/uapress. **Contact:** Dr. Jon Miller, director and acquisitions. Estab. 1988. Publishes paperback and hardcover originals. The University of Akron Press is the publishing arm of The University of Akron and is dedicated to the dissemination of scholarly, professional, and regional books and other content. **Publishes 10-12 titles/year. 100 queries; 50-75 mss received/year. 40% of books from first-time authors. 80% from unagented writers. Pays 7-15% royalty.** Publishes book 9-12 months after acceptance. Accepts simultaneous submissions. Responds in 4 weeks to queries/proposals; 3-4 months to solicited mss. Query prior to submitting. Guidelines online.

NONFICTION Subjects include agriculture, Americana, anthropology, archeology, creative nonfiction, environment, foods, history, humanities, labor, law, literary criticism, literature, memoirs, multicultural, politics, pop culture, psychology, regional. For our readers in and of Northeast Ohio, we are always looking for new books on our history and culture. We've published books on our people and neighborhoods, our institutions, our sports teams, our parks, and through our cookbooks, on our food. For readers all over the world, we publish peer-reviewed books and collections on the history and culture of Akron and Ohio. In our Bliss Institute series, we publish scholarship on applied politics. With the Drs. Nicholas and Dorothy Cummings Center for the History of Psychology, we publish books and textbooks on the history of psychology. Query by e-mail. Mss cannot be returned unless SASE is included.

POETRY Follow the guidelines and submit mss only for the contest: www.uakron.edu/uapress/poetry.html. The Akron Series in Poetry brings forth at least 2 new books of poetry every year, mainly through our prestigious and long-running Akron Poetry Prize. We also publish scholarship on poetics.

RECENT TITLE(S) *The Book of Endings*, by Leslie Harrison; *River, Reaper, Rail: Agriculture and Identity in Ohio's Mad River Valley, 1795–1885*, by Timothy H. H. Thoresen; *Empty Clip*, by Emilia Phillips; *Brazen Creature*, by Anne Barngrover; *Doe*, by Aimee Baker; *Weather Inventions*, by Emily Rosko.

THE UNIVERSITY OF ALABAMA PRESS

200 Hackberry Lane, 2nd Floor, Tuscaloosa AL 35487. (205)348-5180 or (205)348-1571. **Fax:** (205)348-9201. **E-mail:** waterman@uapress.ua.edu. **Website:** www.uapress.ua.edu. **Contact:** Daniel Waterman, editor-in-chief. Publishes nonfiction hardcover and paperbound originals. **Publishes 70-75 titles/year. 70% of books from first-time authors. 95% from unagented writers. Pays advance in very limited number of circumstances.** Accepts simultaneous submissions. Responds in 2-3 weeks to queries. Book catalog available free.

NONFICTION Subjects include history, literary criticism, politics, religion. Considers upon merit almost any subject of scholarly interest, but specializes in communications, military history, public administration, literary criticism and biography, history, Judaic studies, and American archaeology. Accepts nonfiction translations. Query with SASE.

TIPS "Please direct inquiry to appropriate acquisitions editor. University of Alabama Press responds to an author within 2-3 weeks upon receiving the ms or proposal. If they think it is unsuitable for Alabama's program, they tell the author as soon as possible. If the ms warrants it, they begin the peer-review process, which may take 2-4 months to complete. During that process, they keep the author fully informed."

UNIVERSITY OF ALASKA PRESS

P.O. Box 756240, Fairbanks AK 99775-6240. (907)474-5831 or (888)252-6657. **Fax:** (907)474-5502. **Website:** www.uaf.edu/uapress. Estab. 1967. Publishes hardcover originals, trade paperback originals and reprints. "The mission of the University of Alaska Press is to encourage, publish, and disseminate works of scholarship that will enhance the store of knowledge about Alaska and the North Pacific Rim, with a special emphasis on the circumpolar regions." **Publishes 10 titles/year.** Publishes ms within 2 years of acceptance. Accepts simultaneous submissions. Responds in 2 months to queries. Book catalog available free. Guidelines online.

NONFICTION Subjects include Americana, animals, education, ethnic, history, regional, science, translation. Northern or circumpolar only. Query with SASE and proposal. Reviews artwork/photos.

FICTION Subjects include literary. Alaska literary series with Peggy Shumaker as series editor. Publishes 1-3 works of fiction/year. Submit proposal.

TIPS "Writers have the best chance with scholarly nonfiction relating to Alaska, the circumpolar regions and North Pacific Rim. Our audience is made up of scholars, historians, students, libraries, universities, individuals, and the general Alaskan public."

UNIVERSITY OF ARIZONA PRESS

Main Library Building, 5th Floor, 1510 E. University Blvd., Tucson AZ 85721. (520)621-1441. **Fax:** (520)621-8899. **E-mail:** kbuckles@uapress.arizona.edu. **Website:** www.uapress.arizona.edu. **Contact:** Kristen Buckles, acquiring editor. Estab. 1959. Publishes hardcover and paperback originals and reprints. "University of Arizona is a publisher of scholarly books and books of the Southwest." **Royalty terms vary; usual starting point for scholarly monography is after sale of first 1,000 copies. Pays advance.** Responds in 3 months to queries. Book catalog online. Guidelines online.

NONFICTION Subjects include Americana, ethnic, regional, environmental studies, western, and environmental history. Scholarly books about anthropology, Arizona, American West, archeology, Native American studies, Latino studies, environmental science, global change, Latin America, Native Americans, natural history, space sciences, and women's studies. Submit sample chapters, resume, TOC, ms length, audience, comparable books. Reviews artwork/photos.

TIPS "Perhaps the most common mistake a writer might make is to offer a book manuscript or proposal to a house whose list he or she has not studied carefully. Editors rejoice in receiving material that is clearly targeted to the house's list ('I have approached your firm because my books complement your past publications in') and presented in a straightforward, businesslike manner."

THE UNIVERSITY OF ARKANSAS PRESS

McIlroy House, 105 N. McIlroy Ave., Fayetteville AR 72701. (479)575-3246. **Fax:** (479)575-6044. **E-mail:** mbieker@uark.edu. **Website:** uapress.com. **Contact:** Mike Bieker, director. Estab. 1980. Publishes hardcover and trade paperback originals and reprints. "The University of Arkansas Press publishes series on Ozark studies, the Civil War in the West, poetry and poetics, food studies, and sport and society." **Publishes 22 titles/year. 30% of books from first-time authors. 95% from unagented writers.** Publishes book 1 year after acceptance. Accepts simultaneous submissions. Responds in 3 months to proposals. Book catalog and ms guidelines online.

NONFICTION Subjects include architecture, foods, history, humanities, literary criticism, regional, Arkansas. Accepted mss must be submitted electronically. Query with SASE. Submit outline, sample chapters, resume.

FICTION Subjects include historical, regional.

POETRY University of Arkansas Press publishes 4 poetry books per year through the Miller Williams Poetry Prize.

UNIVERSITY OF CALIFORNIA PRESS

155 Grand Ave., Suite 400, Oakland CA 94612. **Website:** www.ucpress.edu. **Contact:** Kate Marshall, acquisitions editor. Estab. 1893. Publishes hardcover and paperback originals and reprints. "University of California Press publishes mostly nonfiction written by scholars." **Pays advance.** Accepts simultaneous submissions. Response time varies, depending on the subject. Enclose return postage to queries. Guidelines online.

NONFICTION Subjects include history, translation, art, literature, natural sciences, some high-level popularizations. No length preference. Submit proposal package.

FICTION Publishes fiction only in translation.

⊘ THE UNIVERSITY OF CHICAGO PRESS

1427 E. 60th St., Chicago IL 60637. (773)702-7700. **Fax:** (773)702-9756. **E-mail:** rpetilos@uchicago.edu. **Website:** www.press.uchicago.edu. **Contact:** Randolph Petilos, Poetry and Medieval Studies Editor. Estab. 1891. Accepts simultaneous submissions.

The University of Chicago Press, publisher of scholarly books and journals since 1891, on average publishes four books in our Phoenix Poets series annually, and two books of poetry in translation, also the occasional book of poems outside the series or as a paperback reprint from another publisher. Recently, our list of poets includes Ahmad Almallah, Charles Bernstein, Michael Collier, David Gewanter, Mark Halliday, Alan Shapiro, Bruce Smith, and Connie Voisine.

NONFICTION Subjects include software.

UNIVERSITY OF GEORGIA PRESS

Main Library, Third Floor, 320 S. Jackson St., Athens GA 30602. (706)369-6130. **Fax:** (706)369-6131. **Website:** www.ugapress.org. **Contact:** Mick Gusinde-Duffy, executive editor; Walter Biggins, executive editor; Pat Allen, acquisitions editor; Beth Snead, assistant acquisitions editor. Estab. 1938. Publishes hardcover originals, trade paperback originals, and reprints. University of Georgia Press is a midsized press that publishes fiction only through the Flannery O'Connor Award for Short Fiction competition. **Publishes 85 titles/year. Pays 7-10% royalty on net receipts. Pays rare, varying advance.** Publishes book 1 year after acceptance. Responds in 2 months to queries. Book catalog and guidelines online.

NONFICTION Subjects include history, regional, environmental studies, literary nonfiction. Query with SASE. Submit bio, 1 sample chapter. Reviews artwork/photos. Send if essential to book.

FICTION Short story collections published in Flannery O'Connor Award Competition.

TIPS "Please visit our website to view our book catalogs and for all manuscript submission guidelines."

UNIVERSITY OF ILLINOIS PRESS

1325 S. Oak St., Champaign IL 61820-6903. (217)333-0950. **Fax:** (217)244-8082. **E-mail:** uipress@uillinois.edu. **Website:** www.press.uillinois.edu. **Contact:** Laurie Matheson, director; Daniel Nasset, acquisitions editor; Dawn Durante, acquisitions editor; James Engelhardt, acquisitions editor. Estab. 1918. Publishes hardcover and trade paperback originals and reprints. University of Illinois Press publishes scholarly books and serious nonfiction with a wide range of study interests. Currently emphasizing American history, especially immigration, labor, African-American, and military; American religion, music, women's studies, and film. **Publishes 150 titles/year. 35% of books from first-time authors. 95% from unagented writers. Pays $1,000-1,500 (rarely) advance.** Publishes ms 1 year after acceptance. Accepts simultaneous submissions. Responds in 1 month to queries. Guidelines online.

NONFICTION Subjects include Americana, animals, communications, ethnic, history, philosophy, regional, sociology, sports, translation, film/cinema/stage. "Always looking for solid, scholarly books in American history, especially social history; books on American popular music, and books in the broad area of American studies." Query with SASE. Submit outline.

TIPS "As a university press, we are required to submit all mss to rigorous scholarly review. Mss need to be clearly original, well written, and based on solid and thorough research. We cannot encourage memoirs or autobiographies."

UNIVERSITY OF IOWA PRESS

100 Kuhl House, 119 W. Park Rd., Iowa City IA 52242. (319)335-2000. **Fax:** (319)335-2055. **E-mail:** james-mccoy@uiowa.edu. **Website:** www.uiowapress.org. **Contact:** James McCoy, director. Estab. 1969. Publishes hardcover and paperback originals. The University of Iowa Press publishes both trade and academic work in a variety of fields. **Publishes 35 titles/year. 30% of books from first-time authors. 95% from unagented writers.** Accepts simultaneous submissions. Book catalog available free. Guidelines online.

NONFICTION Subjects include agriculture, contemporary culture, creative nonfiction, environment, history, humanities, literary criticism, multicultural, nature, pop culture, regional, travel, true crime, womens studies. "Looks for evidence of original research, reliable sources, clarity of organization, complete development of theme with documentation, supportive footnotes and/or bibliography, and a substantive contribution to knowledge in the field treated. Use *Chicago Manual of Style*." Query with SASE. Submit outline. Reviews artwork/photos.

FICTION Currently publishes the Iowa Short Fiction Award selections. "We do not accept any fiction submissions outside of the Iowa Short Fiction Award. See www.uiowapress.org for contest details."

POETRY Currently publishes winners of the Iowa Poetry Prize Competition and Kuhl House Poets (by invitation only). Competition guidelines available on website.

UNIVERSITY OF MICHIGAN PRESS

839 Greene St., Ann Arbor MI 48106. (734)764-4388. **Fax:** (734)615-1540. **Website:** www.press.umich.edu. **Contact:** Mary Francis, editorial director. "In partnership with our authors and series editors, we publish in a wide range of humanities and social sciences disciplines." Accepts simultaneous submissions. Guidelines online.

NONFICTION Submit proposal.

FICTION Subjects include literary, regional. In addition to the annual Michigan Literary Fiction Awards, this publishes literary fiction linked to the Great Lakes region. Submit cover letter and first 30 pages.

UNIVERSITY OF NEVADA PRESS

Mail Stop 0166, Reno NV 89557. (775)784-6573. **Fax:** (775)784-6200. **Website:** www.unpress.nevada.edu. **Contact:** Justin Race, director. Estab. 1961. Publishes hardcover and paperback originals and reprints. "University Press specializing in regional titles, fiction and memoir, and books in the fields of environmental studies, Basque studies, mining studies, nature, and the American West." **Publishes 25 titles/year.** Publishes ms 18 months after acceptance. Responds in 3-5 weeks. Guidelines online.

NONFICTION Subjects include agriculture, animals, archeology, architecture, creative nonfiction, environment, history, memoirs, nature, regional, western literature, gambling and gaming, Basque studies. No juvenile books. Submit electronically, instructions on website. Reviews artwork/photos. Send electronically.

FICTION Fiction should have some connection to the American West, whether in setting or theme. We do not publish historical fiction.

UNIVERSITY OF NEW MEXICO PRESS

1717 Roma Ave. NE, Albuquerque NM 87106. (505)277-3495 or (800)249-7737. **Fax:** (505)277-3343. **Website:** www.unmpress.com. **Contact:** John W. Byram, Director. Estab. 1929. Publishes hardcover originals and trade paperback originals and reprints. "The Press is well known as a publisher in the fields of anthropology, archeology, Latin American studies, art and photography, architecture and the history and culture of the American West, fiction, some poetry, Chicano/a studies and works by and about American Indians. We focus on American West, Southwest and Latin American regions." **Publishes 75 titles/year. 1,500 submissions received/year. 20% of books from first-time authors. 80% from unagented writers. Pays variable royalty. May pay advance.** Publishes ms 10 months after acceptance. Responds in 6 weeks. Book catalog available free. Guidelines online.

NONFICTION Subjects include Americana, anthropology, archeology, architecture, art, cooking, environment, ethnic, foods, gardening, history, humanities, literary criticism, literature, memoirs, military, multicultural, music, nature, photography, politics, pop culture, public affairs, regional, religion, science, social sciences, sports, translation, travel, true crime, womens issues, womens studies, world affairs, contemporary culture, cinema/stage, true crime, general nonfiction. No how-to, humor, juvenile, self-help, software, technical or textbooks. Query with SASE. Reviews artwork/photos. Send photocopies.

FICTION Subjects include ethnic, literary, multicultural, regional, translation.

THE UNIVERSITY OF NORTH CAROLINA PRESS

116 S. Boundary St., Chapel Hill NC 27514. (919)966-3561. **Fax:** (919)966-3829. **E-mail:** mark_simpson-vos@unc.edu. **Website:** www.uncpress.unc.edu. **Contact:** Mark Simpson-Vos, editorial director. Publishes hardcover originals, trade paperback originals and reprints. "UNC Press publishes nonfiction books for academic and general audiences. We have a special interest in trade and scholarly titles about our region. We do not, however, publish original fiction, drama, or poetry, memoirs of living persons, or festshriften." **Publishes 90 titles/year. 500 queries received/year. 200 mss received/year. 50% of books from first-time authors. 90% from unagented writers. Pays variable royalty on wholesale price. Offers variable advance.** Publishes ms 1 year after acceptance. Accepts simultaneous submissions. Responds in 3-4 weeks. Book catalog and guidelines online.

NONFICTION Subjects include Americana, gardening, history, multicultural, philosophy, photography, regional, religion, translation, African-American studies, American studies, cultural studies, Latin-American studies, American-Indian studies, media studies, gender studies, social medicine, Appalachian studies. Submit proposal package, outline, CV, cover letter, abstract, and TOC. Reviews artwork/photos. Send photocopies.

UNIVERSITY OF NORTH TEXAS PRESS

1155 Union Circle, #311336, Denton TX 76203. (940)565-2142. **Fax:** (940)565-4590. **E-mail:** karen.devinney@unt.edu. **Website:** untpress.unt.edu. **Contact:** Ronald Chrisman, director; Karen De Vinney, assistant director. Estab. 1987. Publishes hardcover and trade paperback originals and reprints. "We are dedicated to producing the highest quality scholarly, academic, and general interest books. We are committed to serving all peoples by publishing stories of their cultures and experiences that have been overlooked. Currently emphasizing military history, Texas history, music, Mexican-American studies." **Publishes 14-16 titles/year. 500 queries received/year. 50% of books from first-time authors. 95% from unagented writers.** Publishes ms 1-2 years after acceptance. Responds in 1 month to queries. Book catalog for 8 ½×11 SASE. Guidelines online.

NONFICTION Subjects include Americana, art, cooking, creative nonfiction, ethnic, government, history, humanities, military, multicultural, music, nature, photography, politics, regional, social sciences, war, womens issues, womens studies. Query by e-mail. Reviews artwork/photos. Send photocopies.

FICTION Subjects include short story collections. "The only fiction we publish is the winner of the Katherine Anne Porter Prize in Short Fiction, an annual, national competition with a $1,000 prize, and publication of the winning ms each Fall."

POETRY "The only poetry we publish is the winner of the Vassar Miller Prize in Poetry, an annual, national competition with a $1,000 prize and publication of the winning ms each Spring." Query.

TIPS "We publish series called War and the Southwest; Texas Folklore Society Publications; the Western Life Series; Practical Guide Series; Al-Filo: Mexican-American studies; North Texas Crime and Criminal Justice; Katherine Anne Porter Prize in Short Fiction; and the North Texas Lives of Musicians Series."

UNIVERSITY OF OKLAHOMA PRESS

2800 Venture Dr., Norman OK 73069. (405)325-5609. **E-mail:** adam.kane@ou.edu. **Website:** www.oupress.com. **Contact:** Adam C. Kane, editor-in-chief. Estab. 1928. Publishes hardcover and paperback originals and reprints. University of Oklahoma Press publishes books for both scholarly and nonspecialist readers. **Publishes 90 titles/year. Pays standard royalty.** Responds promptly to queries. Book catalog online.

IMPRINTS Plains Reprints.

NONFICTION Subjects include political science (Congressional, area and security studies), history (regional, military, natural), language/literature (American Indian, US West), American Indian studies, classical studies. Query with SASE or by e-mail. Submit outline, resume, 1-2 sample chapters. Use *Chicago Manual of Style* for ms guidelines. Reviews artwork/photos.

RECENT TITLE(S) *American Carnage: Wounded Knife, 1890*, by Jerome A. Greene; *Ethnic Cleansing and the Indian: The Crime That Should Haunt America*, by Gary Clayton Anderson; *Karl Bodmer's Amer-*

ica Revisited: Landscape Views Across Time, by Robert Lindholm and W. Raymond Wood.

UNIVERSITY OF PENNSYLVANIA PRESS

3905 Spruce St., Philadelphia PA 19104. (215)898-6261. **Fax:** (215)898-0404. **E-mail:** agree@upenn.edu. **Website:** www.pennpress.org. **Contact:** Peter Agree, editor-in-chief. Estab. 1890. Publishes hardcover and paperback originals, and reprints. "Manuscript submissions are welcome in fields appropriate for Penn Press's editorial program. The Press's acquiring editors, and their fields of responsibility, are listed in the Contact Us section of our Web site. Although we have no formal policies regarding manuscript proposals and submissions, what we need minimally, in order to gauge our degree of interest, is a brief statement describing the manuscript, a copy of the contents page, and a reasonably current vita. Initial inquiries are best sent by letter, in paper form, to the appropriate acquiring editor." **Publishes 100+ titles/year. 20-30% of books from first-time authors. 95% from unagented writers. Royalty determined on book-by-book basis. Pays advance.** Publishes ms 10 months after acceptance. Responds in 3 months to queries. Book catalog online. Guidelines online.

NONFICTION Subjects include Americana, history, literary criticism, sociology, anthropology, literary criticism, cultural studies, ancient studies, medieval studies, urban studies, human rights. Follow the *Chicago Manual of Style*. "Serious books that serve the scholar and the professional, student and general reader." Query with SASE. Submit outline, resume.

UNIVERSITY OF PITTSBURGH PRESS

7500 Thomas Blvd., Pittsburgh PA 15260. (412)383-2456. **Fax:** (412)383-2466. **E-mail:** info@upress.pitt.edu. **Website:** www.upress.pitt.edu. **Contact:** Sandy Crooms, editorial director. Estab. 1936. The University of Pittsburgh Press is a scholary publisher with distinguished books in several academic areas and in poetry and short fiction, as well as books about Pittsburgh and western Pennsylvania for general readers, scholars, and students. "Our mission is to extend the reach and reputation of the university through the publication of scholarly, artistic, and educational books that advance learning and knowledge and through the publication of regional books that contribute to an understanding of and are of special benefit to western Pennsylvania and the Upper Ohio Valley region. Accepts simultaneous submissions. Book catalog online. Guidelines online.

POETRY Publishes at least 4 books by poets who have previously published full-length collections of poetry. Submit complete ms in September and October only.

RECENT TITLE(S) *Catalog of Unabashed Gratitude*, by Ross Gay; *For Dear Life*, by Ronald Wallace; *Brain Camp*, by Charles Harper Webb.

TIPS "We pride ourselves on the eclectic nature of our list. We are not tied to any particular style or school of writing, but we do demand that any book we publish be of exceptional merit."

UNIVERSITY OF SOUTH CAROLINA PRESS

1600 Hampton St., 5th Floor, Columbia SC 29208. (803)777-5243. **Fax:** (803)777-0160. **E-mail:** batesvc@mailbox.sc.edu. **Website:** www.sc.edu/uscpress. **Contact:** Jonathan Haupt, director. Estab. 1944. Publishes hardcover originals, trade paperback originals and reprints. "We focus on scholarly monographs and regional trade books of lasting merit." **Publishes 50 titles/year. 500 queries received/year. 150 mss received/year. 30% of books from first-time authors. 95% from unagented writers.** Publishes ms 1 year after acceptance. Accepts simultaneous submissions. Responds in 3 months to mss. Book catalog available free. Guidelines online.

NONFICTION Subjects include history, regional, religion, rhetoric, communication. Query with SASE, or submit proposal package and outline, and 1 sample chapter and resume with SASE Reviews artwork/photos. Send photocopies.

POETRY Palmetto Poetry Series, a South Carolina-based original poetry series edited by Nikky Finney. Director: Jonathan Haupt, director (jhaupt@mailbox.sc.edu).

UNIVERSITY OF TAMPA PRESS

The University of Tampa, 401 W. Kennedy Blvd., Tampa FL 33606. (813)253-6266. **E-mail:** utpress@ut.edu. **Website:** www.ut.edu/tampapress. **Contact:** Richard Mathews, editor. Estab. 1952. Publishes hardcover originals and reprints; trade paperback originals and reprints. "We are a small university press publishing a limited number of titles each year, primarily in the areas of local and regional history, poetry, and printing history. We do not accept e-mail submissions." **Publishes 4-6 titles/year. Does not pay advance.** Publishes ms 6 months-2 years after acceptance. Responds in 3-4 months to queries. Book catalog online.

NONFICTION Subjects includeFlorida history. Does not consider unsolicited mss.

FICTION Subjects include literary, poetry.

POETRY "We consider original poetry collections through the annual Tampa Review Prize for Poetry competition, with a deadline of December 31 each year." Submit to the Tampa Review Prize for Poetry.

THE UNIVERSITY OF TENNESSEE PRESS

The University of Tennessee, 110 Conference Center, 600 Henley St., Knoxville TN 37996. (865)974-3321. **Fax:** (865)974-3724. **E-mail:** twells@utk.edu. **Website:** www.utpress.org. **Contact:** Thomas Wells, acquisitions editor. Estab. 1940. "Our mission is to stimulate scientific and scholarly research in all fields; to channel such studies, either in scholarly or popular form, to a larger number of people; and to extend the regional leadership of the University of Tennessee by stimulating research projects within the South and by nonuniversity authors." **Publishes 35 titles/year. 35% of books from first-time authors. 99% from unagented writers. Pays negotiable royalty on net receipts. Rarely offers advance.** Publishes ms 18 months after acceptance. Accepts simultaneous submissions. Guidelines online.

NONFICTION Subjects include Americana, archeology, architecture, history, literary criticism, military, music, regional, religion, war, African-American studies, Appalachian studies, folklore/folklife, material culture. Prefers scholarly treatment and a readable style. Authors usually have advanced degrees. Submissions in other fields, fiction or poetry, textbooks, and plays and translations are not invited Submit cover letter, outline, bio or CV, and sample chapters. Reviews artwork/photos.

FICTION The press no longer publishes works of fiction.

UNIVERSITY OF TEXAS PRESS

3001 Lake Austin Blvd., 2.200, Stop E4800, Austin TX 78703. **Fax:** (512)232-7178. **Website:** www.utexaspress.com. Estab. 1952. "In addition to publishing the results of advanced research for scholars worldwide, UT Press has a special obligation to the people of its state to publish authoritative books on Texas. We do not publish fiction or poetry, except as invited by a series editor, and some Latin American and Middle Eastern literature in translation." **Publishes 90 titles/year. 50% of books from first-time authors. 99% from unagented writers. Pays occasional advance.** Publishes ms 18-24 months after acceptance. Responds in 3 months to queries. Guidelines online.

NONFICTION Subjects include ethnic, history, literary criticism, regional, science, translation, natural history, American, Latin American, Native American, Latino, and Middle Eastern studies; classics and the ancient world, film, contemporary regional architecture, geography, ornithology, biology. Also uses specialty titles related to Texas and the Southwest, national trade titles and regional trade titles. Submit cover letter, TOC, CV, sample chapter.

UNIVERSITY OF WASHINGTON PRESS

P.O. Box 359570, Seattle WA 98195. (206)543-4050. **Fax:** (206)543-3932. **E-mail:** uwapress@uw.edu. **E-mail:** lmclaugh@uw.edu. **Website:** www.washington.edu/uwpress/. **Contact:** Laurin McLaughlin, editor-in-chief. Publishes in hardcover originals. **Publishes 70 titles/year.** Accepts simultaneous submissions. Book catalog guidelines online.

NONFICTION Subjects include ethnic, history, multicultural, photography, regional, social sciences. Go to our Book Search page for complete subject listing. We publish academic and general books, especially in anthropology, Asian studies, art, environmental studies, Middle Eastern Studies & regional interests. International Studies with focus on Asia; Jewish Studies; Art & Culture of the Northwest coast; Indians & Alaskan Eskimos; The Asian-American Experience; Southeast Asian Studies; Korean and Slavic Studies; Studies in Modernity & National Identity; Scandinavian Studies. Query with SASE. Submit proposal package, outline, sample chapters.

UNIVERSITY OF WISCONSIN PRESS

1930 Monroe St., 3rd Floor, Madison WI 53711. **E-mail:** kadushin@wisc.edu; gcwalker@wisc.edu. **Website:** uwpress.wisc.edu. **Contact:** Gwen Walker, executive editor (gcwalker@wisc.edu); Dennis Lloyd, director (dlloyd2@wisc.edu). Estab. 1937. **Publishes 50 titles/year. Pays royalty.** Publishes 10-14 months after acceptance of final ms. Accepts simultaneous submissions. Responds in 1-3 weeks to queries; 3-6 weeks to proposals. Rarely comments on rejected work. See submission guidelines on our website.

NONFICTION Subjects include cinema, contemporary culture, creative nonfiction, environment, film, gay, history, humanities, labor, lesbian, social sciences, travel, African Studies, classical studies, human rights, Irish studies, Jewish studies, Latin American studies, Latino/a memoirs, modern Western European history, Slavic studies, Southeast Asian studies. Does not accept unsolicited mss. See website for submission guidelines.

FICTION Subjects include gay, lesbian, mystery, regional. Query with SASE or submit outline, 1-2 sample chapter(s), synopsis.

POETRY The University of Wisconsin Press Awards the Brittingham Prize in Poetry and Felix Pollack Prize in Poetry. More details online.

TIPS "Make sure the query letter and sample text are well-written, and read guidelines carefully to make sure we accept the genre you are submitting."

UNIVERSITY PRESS OF KANSAS

2502 Westbrooke Circle, Lawrence KS 66045. (785)864-4154. **Fax:** (785)864-4586. **E-mail:** upress@ku.edu. **Website:** www.kansaspress.ku.edu. **Contact:** Conrad Roberts, interim director & business manager; Joyce Harrison, editor in chief; Kim Hogeland, acquisitions editor; David Congdon, acquisitions editor. Estab. 1946. Publishes hardcover originals, trade paperback originals and reprints. "The University Press of Kansas publishes scholarly books that advance knowledge and regional books that contribute to the understanding of Kansas, the Great Plains, and the Midwest." **Publishes 55 titles/year. 600 queries received/year. 20% of books from first-time authors. 98% from unagented writers. Pays selective advance.** Publishes book 10 months after acceptance. Responds in 1 month to proposals. Book catalog and ms guidelines free.

NONFICTION Subjects include Americana, archeology, environment, government, military, nature, politics, regional, war, American history, native studies, American cultural studies. "We are looking for books on topics of wide interest based on solid scholarship and written for both specialists and informed general readers. Do not send unsolicited, complete manuscripts." Submit outline, sample chapters, cover letter, CV, prospectus. Reviews artwork/photos. Send photocopies.

RECENT TITLE(S) *Hoover's War on Gays; American Organic; When Titans Clashed, revised and expanded.*

UNIVERSITY PRESS OF KENTUCKY

663 S. Limestone St., Lexington KY 40508. (859)257-8434. **Fax:** (859)323-1873. **E-mail:** adwatk0@email.uky.edu. **Website:** www.kentuckypress.com. **Contact:** Anne Dean Dotson, senior acquisitions editor. Estab. 1943. Publishes hardcover and paperback originals and reprints. "We are a scholarly publisher, publishing chiefly for an academic and professional audience, as well as books about Kentucky, the upper South, Appalachia, and the Ohio Valley." **Publishes 60 titles/year. Royalty varies.** Publishes ms 1 year after accceptance. Accepts simultaneous submissions. Responds in 2 months to queries. Book catalog available free. Guidelines online.

NONFICTION Subjects include history, regional, political science. No textbooks, genealogical material, lightweight popular treatments, how-to books, or books unrelated to our major areas of interest. The Press does not consider original works of fiction or poetry. Query with SASE.

UNIVERSITY PRESS OF MISSISSIPPI

3825 Ridgewood Rd., Jackson MS 39211. (601)432-6205. **Fax:** (601)432-6217. **E-mail:** press@mississippi.edu. **Website:** www.upress.state.ms.us. **Contact:** Craig W. Gill, Director. Estab. 1970. Publishes hardcover and paperback originals and reprints and e-books. "University Press of Mississippi publishes scholarly and trade titles, as well as special series, including: American Made Music; Conversations with Comics Artists; Conversations with Filmmakers; Faulkner and Yoknapatawpha; Great Comic Artists; Literary Conversations; Hollywood Legends; Caribbean Studies, Willie Morris Books in Memoir and Biography." **Publishes 80 titles/year. 80% of books from first-time authors. 90% from unagented writers. Pays competitive royalties and terms. Pays advance.** Publishes ms 1 year after acceptance. Responds in 3 months to queries.

NONFICTION Subjects include Americana, art, ethnic, history, literary criticism, regional, sports, womens studies, African American studies, comics studies, film studies, folklife, popular culture with scholarly emphasis, literary studies. "We prefer a proposal that describes the significance of the work and a chapter outline." Submit outline, sample chapters, CV.

UTAH STATE UNIVERSITY PRESS

3078 Old Main Hill, Logan UT 84322. **Website:** www.usu.edu/usupress. Estab. 1972. Publishes hardcover and trade paperback originals and reprints. Utah State University Press publishes scholarly works in the academic areas noted below. Currently interested in book-length scholarly mss dealing with folklore studies, composition studies, Native American studies, and history. **Publishes 18 titles/year. 8% of books from first-time authors.** Publishes ms 18 months after acceptance. Responds in 1 month to queries. Book catalog available free. Guidelines online.

NONFICTION Subjects include history, regional, folklore, the West, Native-American studies, studies in composition and rhetoric. Query via online submission form. Reviews artwork/photos. Send photocopies.

TIPS "Utah State University Press also sponsors the annual May Swenson Poetry Award."

VANDERBILT UNIVERSITY PRESS

PMB 351813, 2301 Vanderbilt Place, Nashville TN 37235. (615)322-3585. **Fax:** (615)343-8823. **E-mail:** vupress@vanderbilt.edu. **E-mail:** beth.itkin@vanderbilt.edu. **Website:** www.vanderbiltuniversitypress.com. Publishes hardcover originals and trade paperback originals and reprints. "Vanderbilt University Press publishes books on healthcare, social sciences, education, and regional studies, for both academic and general audiences that are intellectually significant, socially relevant, and of practical importance." **Publishes 20-25 titles/year. 500 queries received/year. 25% of books from first-time authors. 90% from unagented writers. Pays rare advance.** Publishes ms 10 months after acceptance. Accepts simultaneous submissions. Responds in 2 weeks to proposals. Book catalog online. Guidelines online.

NONFICTION Subjects include Americana, education, ethnic, history, multicultural, philosophy. Submit cover letter, TOC, CV, 1-2 sample chapters.

TIPS "Our audience consists of scholars and educated, general readers."

VAN SCHAIK PUBLISHERS

1059 Francis Baard St., Hatfield 0028, South Africa. **E-mail:** vanschaik@vanschaiknet.com. **Website:** www.vanschaiknet.com. **Contact:** Julia Read. Accepts simultaneous submissions. Guidelines online.

NONFICTION Subjects include education, social sciences, nursing/medicine, language, accounting, public administration. Submit proposal package, outline, sample text.

VENTURE PUBLISHING, INC.

1807 N. Federal Dr., Urbana IL 61801. (217)359-5940. **Website:** www.sagamorepub.com. Estab. 1978. Publishes hardcover and paperback originals and reprints. "Venture Publishing produces quality educational publications, also workbooks for professionals, educators, and students in the fields of recreation, parks, leisure studies, therapeutic recreation and long term care." **Pays royalty on wholesale price. Pays advance.** Book catalog and ms guidelines online.

NONFICTION Subjects include recreation, sociology, long-term care nursing homes, therapeutic recreation. Textbooks and books for recreation activity leaders high priority. Submit 1 sample chapter, book proposal, competing titles.

VERSO

20 Jay St., 10th Floor, Brooklyn NY 11201. (718)246-8160. **Fax:** (718)246-8165. **E-mail:** verso@versobooks.com. **E-mail:** submissions@versobooks.com. **Website:** www.versobooks.com. **Contact:** Editorial Department. Estab. 1970. Publishes hardcover and trade paperback originals. "Our books cover economics, politics, cinema studies, and history (among other topics), but all come from a critical, Leftist viewpoint, on the border between trade and academic." **Publishes 100 titles/year. Pays royalty. Pays advance.** Accepts simultaneous submissions. Book catalog available free. Guidelines online.

NONFICTION Subjects include history, philosophy, sociology. Submit proposal package.

⊘ VERTIGO

DC Universe, Vertigo-DC Comics, 1700 Broadway, New York NY 10019. **Website:** www.vertigocomics.com. At this time, DC Entertainment does not accept unsolicited artwork or writing submissions. Accepts simultaneous submissions.

Ⓐ⊘ VIKING

Imprint of Penguin Random House LLC, 1745 Broadway, New York NY 10019. (212)782-9000. **Website:** www.penguinrandomhouse.com. Estab. 1925. Publishes hardcover and originals. Viking publishes a mix of academic and popular fiction and nonfiction. **Publishes 100 titles/year. Pays 10-15% royalty on retail price.** Publishes ms 18 months after acceptance. Accepts simultaneous submissions.

NONFICTION Subjects include child guidance, history, philosophy. *Agented submissions only.*

FICTION Subjects include literary, mystery, suspense. *Agented submissions only.*

Ⓐ⊘ VIKING CHILDREN'S BOOKS

An Imprint of Penguin Random House LLC, 1745 Broadway, New York NY 10019. **Website:** www.penguinrandomhouse.com. Publishes hardcover originals. "Viking Children's Books is known for humorous, quirky picture books, in addition to more traditional fiction. We publish the highest quality fiction, nonfiction, and picture books for pre-schoolers through young adults." *Does not accept unsolicited submissions.* **Publishes 70 titles/year. Pays 2-10% royalty on retail price or flat fee. Pays negotiable advance.** Publishes book 1-2 years after acceptance. Accepts simultaneous submissions. Responds in 6 months.

NONFICTION All levels: biography, concept, history, multicultural, music/dance, nature/environment, science, and sports. *Agented submissions only.*

FICTION All levels: adventure, animal, contemporary, fantasy, history, humor, multicultural, nature/environment, poetry, problem novels, romance, science fiction, sports, suspense/mystery. *Accepts agented mss only.*

TIPS "No 'cartoony' or mass-market submissions for picture books."

Ⓐ⊘ VILLARD BOOKS

Penguin Random House, 1745 Broadway, New York NY 10019. (212)572-2600. **Website:** www.penguinrandomhouse.com. Estab. 1983. "Villard Books is the publisher of savvy and sometimes quirky, best-selling hardcovers and trade paperbacks." **Pays negotiable royalty. Pays negotiable advance.**

NONFICTION *Agented submissions only.*

FICTION Commercial fiction. *Agented submissions only.*

Ⓐ⊘ VINTAGE ANCHOR PUBLISHING

Penguin Random House, 1745 Broadway, New York NY 10019. **Website:** www.penguinrandomhouse.com. **Pays 4-8% royalty on retail price. Average advance: $2,500 and up.** Publishes ms 1 year after acceptance. Accepts simultaneous submissions.

FICTION Subjects include contemporary, literary, mainstream, short story collections. *Agented submissions only.*

VIVISPHERE PUBLISHING

675 Dutchess Turnpike, Poughkeepsie NY 12603. (845)463-1100, ext. 314. **Fax:** (845)463-0018. **E-mail:** cs@vivisphere.com. **Website:** www.vivisphere.com. **Contact:** Submissions. Estab. 1995. Publishes trade paperback originals and reprints and e-books. Vivisphere Publishing is now considering new submissions from any genre as follows: game of bridge (cards), nonfiction, history, military, new age, fiction, feminist/gay/lesbian, horror, contemporary, self-help, science fiction and cookbooks. **Pays royalty.** Publishes ms 6 months-2 years after acceptance. Accepts simultaneous submissions. Responds in 6-24 months. Book catalog and ms guidelines online.

"Cookbooks should have a particular slant or appeal to a certain niche. Also publish out-of-print books."

NONFICTION Subjects includegame of bridge. Query with SASE. Please submit a proposal package (printed paper copy) including: outline and 1st chapter along with your contact information. If submitting, please use above guidelines and e-mail cs@vivisphere.com.

FICTION Query with SASE.

⊘ VIZ MEDIA LLC

P.O. Box 77010, San Francisco CA 94107. (415)546-7073. **Website:** www.viz.com. "VIZ Media, LLC is one of the most comprehensive and innovative companies in the field of manga (graphic novel) publishing, animation and entertainment licensing of Japanese content. Owned by three of Japan's largest creators and licensors of manga and animation, Shueisha Inc., Shogakukan Inc., and Shogakukan-Shueisha Productions, Co., Ltd., VIZ Media is a leader in the publishing and distribution of Japanese manga for English speaking audiences in North America, the United Kingdom, Ireland, and South Africa and is a global ex-Asia licensor of Japanese manga and animation. The company offers an integrated product line including magazines such as *Shonen Jump* and *Shojo Beat*, graphic novels, and DVDs, and develops, markets, licenses, and distributes animated entertainment for audiences and consumers of all ages." Accepts simultaneous submissions.

FICTION "At the present, all of the manga that appears in our magazines come directly from manga that has been serialized and published in Japan."

VOYAGEUR PRESS

401 Second Ave. N., Suite 310, Minneapolis MN 55401. (800)458-0454. **Fax:** (612)344-8691. **Website:** https://www.quartoknows.com/Voyageur-Press. Publisher: Jeff Serena. Estab. 1972. Publishes hardcover and trade paperback originals. "Voyageur Press (and its sports imprint MVP Books) is internationally known as a leading publisher of quality music, sports, country living, crafts, natural history, and regional books. No children's or poetry books." **Publishes 80 titles/year. 1,200 queries received/year. 500 mss received/year. 10% of books from first-time authors. 90% from unagented writers. Pays royalty. Pays advance.** Publishes ms 1 year after acceptance. Accepts simultaneous submissions. Responds in 3 months to queries.

NONFICTION Subjects include Americana, cooking, environment, history, hobbies, music, nature, regional, sports, collectibles, country living, knitting and quilting, outdoor recreation. Query with SASE. Submit outline. Send sample digital images or transparencies (duplicates and tearsheets only).

TIPS "We publish books for an audience interested in regional, natural, and cultural history on a wide variety of subjects. We seek authors strongly committed to helping us promote and sell their books. Please present as focused an idea as possible in a brief submission (1-page cover letter; 2-page outline or proposal). Note your credentials for writing the book. Tell all you know about the market niche and marketing possibilities for proposed book. We use more book designers than artists or illustrators, since most of our books are illustrated with photographs."

VOYAGEUR PRESS

Quarto Publishing Group, 400 First Ave. N., Suite 400, Minneapolis MN 55401. (612)344-8100; (800)328-0590. **E-mail:** quartoexploressubmissions@quarto.com. **Website:** quartoknows.com. **Contact:** Jeff Serena, Voyageur Press, Publisher. Senior Acquisitions Editor: Dennis Pernu. Estab. 2004. Publishes hardcover and trade paperback originals, electronic originals, and reprints, hardcover and trade paperback reprints. Robert DuBois founded Voyageur Press and began publishing books in 1977, with a strong emphasis on nature and the wilderness, as well as books about Minnesota and the Upper Midwest. The company was sold to Motorbooks International in 2005 and acquired by the Quarto Group in 2007. Today, Voyageur Press publishes books that illuminate, inform, and instruct on self-sufficiency, country life, American food and drink, popular science, regional travel, and music and popular culture. **Publishes 210 titles/year. Receives 250 queries/year; 100 mss/year. 25% of books from first-time authors. 50% from unagented writers. Pays authors 6-8% royalty on wholesale price. Sometimes pays advance.** Publishes ms 1 year after acceptance. Accepts simultaneous submissions. Responds in 1 month. Catalog and guidelines online.

NONFICTION Subjects include Americana, animals, cooking, entertainment, foods, history, horticulture, house and home, music, pop culture, science. Book proposals must contain, at minimum, the items listed below. Remember to include a signed submission agreement with your proposal. When complete, email your submission to the appropriate submission email address above.

WALCH PUBLISHING

40 Walch Dr., Portland ME 04103. (207)772-3105. **Fax:** (207)774-7167. **Website:** www.walch.com. Estab. 1927. "We focus on English/language arts, math, social studies and science teaching resources for middle school through adult assessment titles." **Publishes 100 titles/year. 10% of books from first-time authors. 95% from unagented writers. Pays 5-8% royalty on flat rate.** Publishes ms 6 months after acceptance. Accepts simultaneous submissions. Responds in 2 months to queries.

NONFICTION Subjects include education, history, science, technology. "Most titles are assigned by us, though we occasionally accept an author's unsolicited submission. We have a great need for author/artist teams and for authors who can write at third- to seventh-grade levels." Looks for sense of organization, writing ability, knowledge of subject, skill of communicating with intended audience. Formats include teacher resources, reproducibles. "We do *not* want textbooks or anthologies. All authors should have educational writing experience." Query first.

WASHINGTON STATE UNIVERSITY PRESS

P.O. Box 645910, Pullman WA 99164-5910. (800)354-7360. **E-mail:** wsupress@wsu.edu. **E-mail:** robert.clark@wsu.edu. **Website:** wsupress.wsu.edu. **Contact:** Robert A. Clark, editor-in-chief. Beth DeWeese (beth.deweese@wsu.edu) Estab. 1928. Publishes hardcover originals, trade paperback originals, and reprints. WSU Press publishes scholarly nonfiction books on the history, pre-history, culture, and politics of the West, particularly the Pacific Northwest. **Publishes 8-10 titles/year. 40% of books from first-time authors. 95% from unagented writers. Pays 5% royalty graduated according to sales.** Publishes ms 18 months after acceptance. Accepts simultaneous submissions. Responds in 1 month to queries. Guidelines online.

NONFICTION Subjects include agriculture, anthropology, archeology, architecture, art, contemporary culture, cooking, environment, ethnic, foods, government, health, history, humanities, labor, marine subjects, military, multicultural, nature, politics, public affairs, regional, science, social sciences, sociology, womens studies, essays. "We welcome engaging and thought-provoking mss that focus on the greater Pacific Northwest (primarily Washington, Oregon, Idaho, British Columbia, western Montana, and southeastern Alaska). Currently we are not accepting how-to books, literary criticism, memoirs, novels, or poetry." We are not looking for memoirs or mss where photography is the primary element. Submit outline, sample chapters. See instructions on our website. Reviews artwork/photos.

RECENT TITLE(S) *Monumental Seattle: The Stories Behind the City's Statues, Memorials, and Markers*; *Protest on Trial: The Seattle 7 Conspiracy*; *Nowhere to Remember: Hanford, White Bluffs, and Richland to 1943*; *Hardship to Homeland: Pacific Northwest Volga Germans*; *Wheat Country Railroad: The Northern Pacific's Spokane & Palouse and Competitors*; *Low Dose Radiation: The History of the U.S. Department of Energy Research Program*; *Spirit in the Rock: The Fierce Battle for Modoc Homelands*; *On the Arctic Frontier: Ernest Leffingwell's Polar Explorations and Legacy*; *Crown Jewel Wilderness: Creating North Cascades National Park*; *Complexity in a Ditch: Bringing Water to the Idaho Desert*; *Protest on Trial: the Seattle 7 Conspiracy*; *Captain Cook's Final Voyage: the Untold Story from the Journals of James Burney and Henry Roberts*; *Governing the Evergreen State: Political Life in Washington*; *Hop King: Ezra Meeker's Boom Years*.

TIPS "We have developed our marketing in the direction of regional and local history, and use this as the base upon which to expand our publishing program. For history, the secret is to write strong narratives on significant topics or events. Stories should be told in imaginative, clever ways and be substantiated factually. Have visuals (photos, maps, etc.) available to help the reader envision what has happened. Explain stories in ways that tie them to wider-ranging regional, national—or even international—events. Weave them into the large pattern of history."

WASHINGTON WRITERS' PUBLISHING HOUSE

P.O. Box 15271, Washington DC 20003. **Website:** www.washingtonwriters.org. Estab. 1975. **Offers $1,000 and 50 copies of published book plus additional copies for publicity use.** Accepts simultaneous submissions. Guidelines online.

FICTION Washington Writers' Publishing House considers book-length mss for publication by fiction writers living within 75 driving miles of the U.S. Capitol, Baltimore area included, through competition only. Mss may include previously published stories and excerpts. "Author should indicate where they heard about WWPH." Submit an electronic copy by e-mail (use PDF, .doc, or rich text format) or 2 hard copies by snail mail of a short story collection or novel (no more than 350 pages, double or 1-1/2 spaced; author's name should not appear on any ms pages). Include separate page of publication acknowledgments plus 2 cover sheets: one with ms title, poet's name, address, telephone number, and e-mail address, the other with ms title only. Include SASE for results only; mss will not be returned (will be recycled).

POETRY Washington Writers' Publishing House considers book-length mss for publication by poets living within 75 driving miles of the U.S. Capitol (Baltimore area included) through competition only. Publishes 1-2 poetry books/year. "No specific criteria, except literary excellence."

RECENT TITLE(S) Has published books by Christopher Ankney, Robert Herschbach, Kathleen Hellen, and Holly Karapetkova.

Ⓐ⊘ WATERBROOK MULTNOMAH PUBLISHING GROUP

10807 New Allegiance Dr., Suite 500, Colorado Springs CO 80921. (719)590-4999. **Fax:** (719)590-8977. **Website:** www.waterbrookmultnomah.com. Estab. 1996. Publishes hardcover and trade paperback originals. **Publishes 70 titles/year. 2,000 queries received/year. 15% of books from first-time authors. Pays royalty.** Publishes book 1 year after acceptance. Accepts simultaneous submissions. Responds in 2-3 months. Book catalog online.

NONFICTION Subjects include child guidance, religion, spirituality, marriage, Christian living. "We publish books on unique topics with a Christian perspective." *Agented submissions only.*

FICTION Subjects include adventure, historical, literary, mystery, religious, romance, science fiction, spiritual, suspense. *Agented submissions only.*

WAVE BOOKS

1938 Fairview Ave. E., Suite 201, Seattle WA 98102. (206)676-5337. **E-mail:** info@wavepoetry.com. **Website:** www.wavepoetry.com. Estab. 2005. Publishes hardcover and trade paperback originals. "Wave Books is an independent poetry press based in Seattle, Washington, dedicated to publishing the best in contemporary American poetry, poetry in translation, and writing by poets. The Press was founded in 2005, merging with established publisher Verse Press. By publishing strong innovative work in finely crafted trade editions and handmade ephemera, we hope to continue to challenge the values and practices of readers and add to the collective sense of what's possible in contemporary poetry." Accepts simultaneous submissions. Catalog online.

POETRY "Please no unsolicited mss or queries. We will post calls for submissions on our website."

WAVELAND PRESS, INC.

4180 Illinois Rt. 83, Suite 101, Long Grove IL 60047. (847)634-0081. **Fax:** (847)634-9501. **E-mail:** info@waveland.com. **Website:** www.waveland.com. Estab. 1975. Waveland Press, Inc. is a publisher of college textbooks and supplements. "We are committed to providing reasonably priced teaching materials for the classroom and actively seek to add new titles to our growing lists in a variety of academic disciplines. If you are currently working on a project you feel serves a need and would have promise as an adopted text in the college market, we would like to hear from you." Accepts simultaneous submissions.

THE WAYWISER PRESS

P.O. Box 6205, Baltimore MD 21206. **E-mail:** info@waywiser-press.com. **Website:** waywiser-press.com. **Contact:** Philip Hoy. Estab. 2001. The Waywiser Press is a small independent company, with its main office in the UK, and a subsidiary in the USA. It publishes literary works of all kinds, but has a special interest in contemporary poetry in English. **Publishes 4-5 titles/year. 400-500 Royalties paid. Does not pay advance.** Ms published 9-18 months after acceptance. Accepts simultaneous submissions. Responds in 3-6 months. Catalog online. Guidelines online.

IMPRINTS Between The LInes.

NONFICTION Subjects include literary criticism, literature, memoirs, Letters, Memoirs.

POETRY Poets who've published one or no collections should submit to the Anthony Hecht Poetry Prize, open for submissions between August 1st and December 1st annually. Submit complete ms by post (if prospective author has already published 2 or more collections).

RECENT TITLE(S) *Plundered Hearts: New and Selected Poems*, by J. D. McClatchy; *Pleasures of the Game*, by Austin Allen; *Stone Fruit*, by Stephen Yenser.

TIPS "We are keen to promote the work of new as well as established authors, and would like to rescue still others from undeserved neglect."

WESLEYAN PUBLISHING HOUSE

P.O. Box 50434, Indianapolis IN 46250. (800)493-7539. **E-mail:** submissions@wesleyan.org. **Website:** www.wesleyan.org/wg. **Contact:** Katie Long, Communications Coordinator. Estab. 1843. Publishes hardcover and trade paperback originals. **100 submissions received/year. Pays royalty on wholesale price. Pays advance occasionally.** Publishes book 11 months after acceptance. Responds within 2 months to proposals. Catalog online. Guidelines online.

NONFICTION Subjects include religion, Christianity. Does not want biographies, memoirs, children's products, plays, poems, art work. Not accepting unsolicited proposals. Does not review artwork.

RECENT TITLE(S) *The Way of Hope*, by Beth and Dave Weikel; *Finding Your Way*, by Jane Rubietta; *Real Mercy*, by Thaddeus Barnum.

TIPS "Our books help evangelical Christians learn about the faith or grow in their relationship with God."

⊘ WESLEYAN UNIVERSITY PRESS

215 Long Ln., Middletown CT 06459. (860)685-7711. **Fax:** (860)685-7712. **E-mail:** stamminen@wesleyan.edu. **Website:** www.wesleyan.edu/wespress. **Contact:** Suzanna Tamminen, director and editor-in-chief. Estab. 1959. Publishes hardcover originals and paperbacks. "Wesleyan University Press is a scholarly press with a focus on poetry, music, dance and cultural studies." Wesleyan University Press is one of the major publishers of poetry in the nation. Poetry publications from Wesleyan tend to get widely (and

respectfully) reviewed. **"We are accepting manuscripts by invitation only until further notice." Pays royalties, plus 10 author's copies.** Accepts simultaneous submissions. Responds to queries in 2 months; to mss in 4 months. Book catalog available free. Guidelines online.

NONFICTION Subjects includefilm/TV & media studies, science fiction studies, dance and poetry. *Does not accept unsolicited mss.*

POETRY *Does not accept unsolicited mss.*

WESTMINSTER JOHN KNOX PRESS

Flyaway Books, Division of Presbyterian Publishing Corp., 100 Witherspoon St., Louisville KY 40202. **Fax:** (502)569-5113. **E-mail:** submissions@wjkbooks.com. **Website:** www.wjkbooks.com. Publishes hardcover and paperback originals. "All WJK books have a religious/spiritual angle, but are written for various markets-scholarly, professional, and the general reader. Flyaway Books is a new children's picture book imprint that is intentionally diverse in content and authorship.

Email submissions only. No submissions by mail. No phone queries. We do not publish fiction, poetry, or dissertations. We do not return or respond to submissions received by mail and do not respond to unsolicited phone messages. Westminster John Knox is affiliated with the Presbyterian Church (U.S.A.). " **Publishes 60 titles/year. 1,000 submissions received/ year. 10% of books from first-time authors. 75% from unagented writers. Pays royalty on net price. Pays advance.** Accepts simultaneous submissions. Responds in 2-3 months. Catalog online. Proposal guidelines online.

IMPRINTS Westminster John Knox Press, Flyaway Books.

Looking for fresh and challenging voices writing about social justice issues (race, LGBTQI, immigration, women's rights, economic justice, etc.) from a religious, spiritual, or humanitarian perspective. Looking for biblical studies and theology texts for graduate and seminary students and core textbooks in Bible for undergraduates. See more at www.wjkbooks.com. Flyaway Books is looking for picture books for a trade, school, and progressive church audience. See more at www.flyawaybooks.com.

NONFICTION Subjects include multicultural, religion, social sciences, spirituality, womens issues. No dissertations. Submit proposal package according to the WJK book proposal guidelines found online. Reviews artwork, but only for children's picture books.

RECENT TITLE(S) *No One Else Like You*, by Siska Goeminne (childrens); *Who Counts?*, by Amy-Jill Levine and Sandy Sasso (childrens); *A Bigger Table*, by John Pavlovitz (general reader); *Sabbath as Resistance*, by Walter Brueggemann (religious); *Still Christian*, by David Gushee (general reader); *Rise Up, Shepherd*, by Luke Powery (religious); *No Innocent Bystanders*, by Shannon Craigo-Snell and Christopher Doucot (general reader); *Fearless Dialogues*, by Gregory Ellison (general reader); *Pro-Choice and Christian*, by Kira Schlesinger (general reader).

WHITAKER HOUSE

1030 Hunt Valley Circle, New Kensington PA 15068. **E-mail:** publisher@whitakerhouse.com. **Website:** www.whitakerhouse.com. **Contact:** Editorial Department. Estab. 1970. Publishes hardcover, trade paperback, and mass market originals. **Publishes 70 titles/ year. 600 queries; 200 mss received/year. 15% of books from first-time authors. 60% from unagented writers. Pays 5-15% royalty on wholesale price.** Publishes ms 9 months after acceptance. Accepts simultaneous submissions. Responds in 3 months. Book catalog online. Guidelines online.

IMPRINTS Whitaker Espanol, SmartKidz.

NONFICTION Subjects include religion, science. Accepts submissions on topics with a Christian perspective. Query with SASE. Does not review artwork/photos.

FICTION Subjects include religious. All fiction must have a Christian perspective. Query with SASE.

RECENT TITLE(S) *Defining Moments*, by Bill Johnson; *Divine Dance*, by Richard Rohr Warfare, by Tom Brown; *Passionate Pursuit*, by James Goll.

TIPS "Audience includes those seeking uplifting and inspirational fiction and nonfiction."

WHITE MANE KIDS

73 W. Burd St., Shippensburg PA 17257. (717)532-2237. **Fax:** (717)532-6110. **E-mail:** marketing@whitemane.com. **Website:** www.whitemane.com. **Contact:** Harold Collier, acquisitions editor. Estab. 1987. **Pays authors royalty of 7-10%. Pays illustrators and photographers by the project.** Publishes book 18 months after acceptance. Accepts simultaneous submissions. Responds to queries in 1 month, mss in 6-9 months.

Book catalog and writer's guidelines available for SASE.

IMPRINTS White Mane Books, Burd Street Press, White Mane Kids, Ragged Edge Press.

NONFICTION Middle readers, young adults: history. Average word length: middle readers—30,000. Does not publish picture books. Submit outline/synopsis and 2-3 sample chapters. Book proposal form on website.

FICTION Middle readers, young adults: history (primarily American Civil War). Average word length: middle readers—30,000. Does not publish picture books. Query.

TIPS "Make your work historically accurate. We are interested in historically accurate fiction for middle and young adult readers. We do *not* publish picture books. Our primary focus is the American Civil War and some America Revolution topics."

WHITE PINE PRESS

P.O. Box 236, Buffalo NY 14201. **E-mail:** wpine@whitepine.org. **Website:** www.whitepine.org. **Contact:** Dennis Maloney, editor. Estab. 1973. Publishes trade paperback originals. White Pine Press is a nonprofit literary publisher of literature in translation and poetry. **Publishes 8-10 titles/year. Receives 500 queries/year. 1% of books from first-time authors. 100% from unagented writers. Pays contributor's copies.** Publishes ms 18 months after acceptance. Accepts simultaneous submissions. Responds in 1 month to queries and proposals; 4 months to mss. Catalog online. Guidelines online.

Due to a large backlog we are not currently reading manuscripts outside of our annual poetry contest.

NONFICTION Subjects include language, literature, multicultural, translation, poetry. *"We are currently not considering nonfiction mss."*

POETRY "Only considering submissions for our annual poetry contest."

ALBERT WHITMAN & COMPANY

250 S. Northwest Hwy., Suite 320, Park Ridge IL 60068. (800)255-7675. **Fax:** (847)581-0039. **E-mail:** submissions@albertwhitman.com. **Website:** www.albertwhitman.com. Estab. 1919. Publishes in original hardcover, paperback, boardbooks. Albert Whitman & Company publishes books for the trade, library, and school library market. Interested in reviewing the following types of projects: Picture book manuscripts for ages 2-8; novels and chapter books for ages 8-12; young adult novels; nonfiction for ages 3-12 and YA; art samples showing pictures of children. Best known for the classic series The Boxcar Children® Mysteries. "We are no longer reading unsolicited queries and manuscripts sent through the US mail. We now require these submissions to be sent by e-mail. You must visit our website for our guidelines, which include instructions for formatting your e-mail. E-mails that do not follow this format may not be read. We read every submission within 4 months of receipt, but we can no longer respond to every one. If you do not receive a response from us after four months, we have declined to publish your submission." **Publishes 60 titles/year. 10% of books from first-time authors. 50% from unagented writers.** Accepts simultaneous submissions. Guidelines online.

NONFICTION Picture books up to 1,000 words. Submit cover letter, brief description.

FICTION Picture books (up to 1,000 words); middle grade (up to 35,000 words); young adult (up to 70,000 words). For picture books, submit cover letter and brief description. For middle grade and young adult, send query, synopsis, and first 3 chapters.

WILDERNESS PRESS

2204 First Ave. S., Suite 102, Birmingham AL 35233. (800)443-7227. **Fax:** (205)326-1012. **Website:** www.wildernesspress.com. Estab. 1967. Publishes paperback originals. "Wilderness Press has a long tradition of publishing the highest quality, most accurate hiking and other outdoor activity guidebooks." **Publishes 12 titles/year.** Publishes ms 8-12 months after acceptance. Accepts simultaneous submissions. Responds in 2 months to queries. Book catalog and ms guidelines online.

NONFICTION Subjects include recreation, trail guides for hikers and backpackers. "We publish books about the outdoors and some general travel guides. Many are trail guides for hikers and backpackers, but we also publish climbing, kayaking, and other outdoor activity guides, how-to books about the outdoors and urban walking books. The manuscript must be accurate. The author must research an area in person. If writing a trail guide, you must walk all the trails in the area your book is about. Outlook must be strongly conservationist. Style must be appropriate for a highly literate audience." Download proposal guidelines from website.

THE WILD ROSE PRESS

P.O. Box 708, Adams Basin NY 14410-0708. (585)752-8770. **E-mail:** queryus@thewildrosepress.com. **Website:** www.thewildrosepress.com. **Contact:** Rhonda Penders, editor-in-chief. Estab. 2006. Publishes paperback originals, reprints, and e-books in a POD format. **Publishes approx. 60 fiction titles/year. Pays royalty of 7% minimum; 40% maximum. Sends prepublication galleys to author.** Publishes ms 1 year after acceptance. Responds to queries in 4 weeks; mss in 12 weeks. Guidelines online.

FICTION Subjects include adventure, contemporary, erotica, fantasy, gay, gothic, historical, horror, humor, lesbian, mainstream, multicultural, mystery, romance, science fiction, short story collections, suspense, western, young adult, We accept all genre of fiction and romance including young adult. *Does not accept unsolicited mss.* Send query letter with outline and synopsis of up to 5 pages. Accepts all queries by e-mail. Include estimated word count, brief bio, and list of publishing credits. Agented fiction less than 1%. Always comments on rejected mss.

TIPS "Polish your manuscript, make it as error free as possible, and follow our submission guidelines."

JOHN WILEY & SONS, INC.

111 River St., Hoboken NJ 07030. (201)748-6000. **Fax:** (201)748-6088. **Website:** www.wiley.com. Estab. 1807. Publishes hardcover originals, trade paperback originals and reprints. **Pays competitive rates.** Accepts simultaneous submissions. Book catalog online. Guidelines online.

NONFICTION Subjects include business, communications, computers, economics, education, finance, health, psychology, science. Wiley is a global publisher of print and electronic products—including scientific, scholarly, professional, consumer, and educational content. "Please visit our website to review our submissions guidelines for Books and Journals authors."

Ⓐ⊘ WILLIAM MORROW

HarperCollins, 195 Broadway, New York NY 10007. (212)207-7000. **Fax:** (212)207-7145. **Website:** www.harpercollins.com. Estab. 1926. "William Morrow publishes a wide range of titles that receive much recognition and prestige—a most selective house." **Pays standard royalty on retail price. Pays varying advance.** Accepts simultaneous submissions. Book catalog available free.

NONFICTION Subjects include history. Length 50,000-100,000 words. *No unsolicited mss or proposals. Agented submissions only.*

FICTION Publishes adult fiction. Morrow accepts only the highest quality submissions in adult fiction. *No unsolicited mss or proposals. Agented submissions only.*

WILLOW CREEK PRESS

P.O. Box 147, Minocqua WI 54548. (715)358-7010. **Fax:** (715)358-2807. **Website:** www.willowcreekpress.com. **Contact:** Sara R.W. Olson. Estab. 1986. Publishes hardcover and trade paperback, originals, and reprints. "We specialize in nature, outdoor, and sporting topics, including gardening, wildlife, and animal books. Pets, cookbooks, and a few humor books and essays round out our titles. Currently emphasizing pets (mainly dogs and cats), wildlife, outdoor sports (hunting, fishing). De-emphasizing essays, fiction." **Publishes 25 titles/year. 400 queries; 150 mss received/year. 15% of books from first-time authors. 50% from unagented writers. Pays 6-15% royalty on wholesale price. Pays $2,000-5,000 advance.** Publishes ms 18 months after acceptance. Accepts simultaneous submissions. Responds in 2 months to queries. Guidelines online.

NONFICTION Subjects include animals, gardening, recreation, sports, travel, wildlife, pets. Submit cover letter, chapter outline, 1-2 sample chapters, brief bio, SASE. Reviews artwork/photos.

WISCONSIN HISTORICAL SOCIETY PRESS

816 State St., Madison WI 53706. (608)264-6465. **Fax:** (608)264-6486. **Website:** www.wisconsinhistory.org/whspress/. Estab. 1855. Publishes hardcover and trade paperback originals; trade paperback reprints. **Publishes 12-14 titles/year. 60-75 queries received/year. 20% of books from first-time authors. 90% from unagented writers. Pays royalty on wholesale price.** Publishes ms 2 years after acceptance. Accepts simultaneous submissions. Book catalog available free. Guidelines online.

NONFICTION Subjects include history. Submit book proposal, form from website. Reviews artwork/photos. Send photocopies.

TIPS "Our audience reads about Wisconsin. Carefully review the book."

WISDOM PUBLICATIONS

199 Elm St., Somerville MA 02144. (617)776-7416, ext. 28. **Fax:** (617)776-7841. **E-mail:** editors@wisdompubs.org. **Website:** www.wisdompubs.org. **Contact:** David Kittelstrom, senior editor. Estab. 1976. Publishes hardcover originals and trade paperback originals and reprints. "Wisdom Publications is dedicated to making available authentic Buddhist works for the benefit of all. We publish translations, commentaries, and teachings of past and contemporary Buddhist masters and original works by leading Buddhist scholars. Currently emphasizing popular applied Buddhism, scholarly titles." **Publishes 30-35 titles/year. 300 queries received/year. 50% of books from first-time authors. 95% from unagented writers. Pays 8% royalty on wholesale price. Sometimes pays advance.** Publishes ms within 2 years of acceptance. Book catalog and ms guidelines online.

NONFICTION Subjects include philosophy, psychology, religion, spirituality, Buddhism, Tibet, Mindfulness. Submissions should be made electronically.

RECENT TITLE(S) *Interconnected: Embracing Life in Our Global Society; Coloring for Meditation: With Tibetan Buddhist Art.*

TIPS "Wisdom Publications is the leading publisher of contemporary and classic Buddhist books and practical works on mindfulness. Please see our catalog or our website before you send anything to us to get a sense of what we publish."

Ⓐ⊘ PAULA WISEMAN BOOKS

1230 Sixth Ave., New York NY 10020. (212)698-7000. **Fax:** (212)698-2796. **Website:** kids.simonandschuster.com. Estab. 2003. Paula Wiseman Books is an imprint of Simon & Schuster Children's Publishing that launched in 2003. It has since gone on to publish over 70 award-winning and bestselling books, including picture books, novelty books, and novels. The imprint focuses on stories and art that are childlike, timeless, innovative, and centered in emotion. "We strive to publish books that entertain while expanding the experience of the children who read them, as well as stories that will endure, including those based in other cultures. We are committed to publishing new talent in both picture books and novels. We are actively seeking submissions from new and published authors and artists through agents and from SCBWI conferences." **Publishes 30 titles/year. 15% of books from first-time authors.** Accepts simultaneous submissions.

NONFICTION Picture books: animal, biography, concept, history, nature/environment. Young readers: animal, biography, history, multicultural, nature/environment, sports. Average word length: picture books—500; others standard length. Does not accept unsolicited or unagented mss. By mail preferably.

FICTION Considers all categories. Average word length: picture books—500; others standard length.

Ⓐ WORDSONG

815 Church St., Honesdale PA 18431. **Fax:** (570)253-0179. **Website:** www.wordsongpoetry.com. Estab. 1990. "We publish fresh voices in contemporary poetry." **Pays authors royalty or work purchased outright.** Accepts simultaneous submissions. Responds to mss in 3 months.

POETRY *Agented submissions only.*

TIPS "Collections of original poetry, not anthologies, are our biggest need at this time. Keep in mind that the strongest collections demonstrate a facility with multiple poetic forms and offer fresh images and insights. Check to see what's already on the market and on our website before submitting."

WORKMAN PUBLISHING CO.

225 Varick St., New York NY 10014. **E-mail:** info@workman.com. **Website:** www.workman.com. Estab. 1967. Publishes hardcover and trade paperback originals, as well as calendars. "We are a trade paperback house specializing in a wide range of popular nonfiction. We publish no adult fiction and very little children's fiction. We also publish a full range of full-color wall and Page-A-Day calendars." **Publishes 40 titles/year. thousands of queries received/year. Open to first-time authors. Pays variable royalty on retail price. Pays variable advance.** Publishes ms approximately 1 year after acceptance. Accepts simultaneous submissions. Responds in 5 months to queries. Guidelines online.

NONFICTION Subjects include child guidance, gardening, sports, travel. Query.

TIPS "We prefer electronic submissions."

WORLD BOOK, INC.

180 N. LaSalle St., Suite 900, Chicago IL 60601. (312)729-5800. **Fax:** (312)729-5600. **E-mail:** service@worldbook.com. **Website:** www.worldbook.com. World Book, Inc. (publisher of

The World Book Encyclopedia), publishes reference sources and nonfiction series for children and young adults in the areas of science, mathematics, English-language skills, basic academic and social skills, social studies, history, and health and fitness. "We publish print and non-print material appropriate for children ages 3-14. WB does not publish fiction, poetry, or wordless picture books." **Payment negotiated on project-by-project basis.** Publishes book 18 months after acceptance. Accepts simultaneous submissions. Responds to queries in 2 months.

NONFICTION Young readers: animal, arts/crafts, careers, concept, geography, health, reference. Middle readers: animal, arts/crafts, careers, geography, health, history, hobbies, how-to, nature/environment, reference, science. Young adult: arts/crafts, careers, geography, health, history, hobbies, how-to, nature/environment, reference, science. Query.

WORLD WEAVER PRESS

Albuquerque NM 87154. **Website:** www.worldweaverpress.com. **Contact:** WWP Editors. Estab. 2012. World Weaver Press publishes digital and print editions of speculative fiction at various lengths for adult, young adult, and new adult audiences. "We believe in great storytelling." **Publishes 6-9 titles/year. 95% from unagented writers. Average royalty rate of 39% net on all editions. No advance.** Publishes ms 6-24 months after acceptance. Accepts simultaneous submissions. Responds to query letters within 3 weeks. Responses to mss requests take longer. Catalog online. Guidelines on website.

FICTION Subjects include adventure, erotica, fantasy, feminist, gay, lesbian, multicultural, romance, science fiction, young adult. "We believe that publishing speculative fiction isn't just printing words on the page — it's the act of weaving brand new worlds. Seeking speculative fiction in many varieties: protagonists who have strength, not fainting spells; intriguing worlds with well-developed settings; characters that are to die for (we'd rather find ourselves in love than just in lust)." Full list of interests on website. Not currently open to full-length fiction. Check anthology submission guidelines for short fiction calls. Not currently open for queries. Full guidelines will be updated approximately one month before queries reopen. Frequently open for submissions for themed short story anthologies. Check website for details.

RECENT TITLE(S) *He Sees You When He's Creepin': Tales of Krampus*, anthology edited by Kate Wolford; *The Falling of the Moon*, by A. E. Decker; *The Naughty List*, by Tiffany Reisz, et. al.; *Bite Somebody*, by Sara Dobie Bauer.

WORTHYKIDS

Hachette Book Group, 6100 Tower Circle, Suite 210, Franklin TN 37067. (615)932-7600. **E-mail:** idealsinfo@worthypublishing.com. **Website:** www.worthypublishing.com. Estab. 1944. "WorthyKids is an imprint of Hachette Book Group and publishes 20-30 new children's titles a year, primarily for 2-8 year-olds. Our backlist includes more than 400 titles, including The Berenstain Bears, VeggieTales, and Frosty the Snowman. We publish picture books, activity books, board books, and novelty/sound books covering a wide array of topics, such as Bible stories, holidays, early learning, history, family relationships, and values. Our bestselling titles include *The Story of Christmas, The Story of Easter, The Sparkle Box, Seaman's Journal, How Do I Love You?, God Made You Special, The Berenstain Bears' Please and Thank You Book*, and *My Daddy and I*. Through our dedication to publishing high-quality and engaging books, we never forget our obligation to our littlest readers to help create those special moments with books." Accepts simultaneous submissions. Due to the high volume of submissions, we are only able to respond to unsolicited manuscripts of interest to our publishing program. We cannot discuss submissions by telephone or in person and we cannot provide detailed editorial feedback.

FICTION Subjects include juvenile, religious. WorthyKids/Ideals publishes fiction and nonfiction picture books for children ages 2 to 8. Subjects include holiday, faith/inspirational, family values, and patriotic themes; relationships and values; and general fiction. Picture book mss should be no longer than 800 words. Board book mss should be no longer than 250 words. Editors will review complete mss only; please do not send query letters or proposals. Previous publications, relevant qualifications or background, and a brief synopsis of your manuscript may be included in a cover letter. Please send copies only—we cannot be responsible for an original ms. Include your name, address, and phone number or e-mail address on every page. Do not include original art or photographs. We do not accept digital submissions via e-mail or other electronic means. Send complete mss to: WorthyKids, Attn: SUBMISSIONS, 6100 Tower Circle, Suite 210, Franklin TN 37067.

WORTHY KIDS/IDEALS BOOKS

6100 Tower Circle, Suite 210, Franklin TN 37067. **Website:** www.idealsbooks.com. Estab. 1944. Accepts simultaneous submissions.

NONFICTION Worthy Kids/Ideals publishes for ages birth to 8, no longer than 800 words. Submit complete ms.

FICTION Subjects include juvenile. Picture books: animal, concept, history, religion. Board books: animal, history, nature/environment, religion. Worthy Kids/Ideals publishes for ages birth to 8, no longer than 800 words. Submit complete ms.

WRITE BLOODY PUBLISHING

Austin TX **Website:** writebloody.com. **Contact:** Derrick Brown, president. We publish and promote great books of poetry every year. We are a small press with a snappy look, dedicated to quality literature that is proud to be printed in the USA. We are not a printer. We are a sweet publishing house located on the outskirts of Austin, Texas. Accepts simultaneous submissions. Catalog online. Guidelines online.

POETRY Reading period August 1-31. Check online for details.

RECENT TITLE(S) *Said the Manic to the Muse*, by Jeanann Verlee; *Bouquet of Red Flags*, by Taylor Mali.

TIPS "You must tour if you are part of our family. At least 20 shows a year. Just like a band."

WRITER'S DIGEST BOOKS

Imprint of Penguin Random House LLC, 1745 Broadway, New York NY 10019. **Website:** www.penguinrandomhouse.com. Estab. 1920. Publishes hardcover originals and trade paperbacks. "Writer's Digest Books is the premiere source for instructional books on writing and publishing for an audience of aspirational writers. Typical mss are 80,000 words. E-mail queries strongly preferred; no phone calls please." **Publishes 18-20 titles/year. 300 queries; 50 mss received/year. 30% from unagented writers. Pays average $3,000 advance.** Publishes book 1 year after acceptance. Accepts simultaneous submissions. Responds in 3 months to queries. "Our catalog of titles is available to view online at www.Writers-DigestShop.com.".

Writer's Digest Books accepts query letters and complete proposals via e-mail at writersdigest@fwcommunity.com.

NONFICTION "Our instruction books stress results and how to achieve them. Should be well-researched, yet lively and readable. We do not want to see books telling readers how to crack specific nonfiction markets: *Writing for the Computer Market* or *Writing for Trade Publications*, for instance. We are most in need of fiction-technique books written by published authors. Be prepared to explain how the proposed book differs from existing books on the subject." No fiction or poetry. Query with SASE. Submit outline, sample chapters, SASE.

RECENT TITLE(S) *The Irresistible Novel*, by Jeff Gerke; *A Writer's Guide to Persistence*, by Jordan Rosenfeld; *The Truth of Memoir*, by Kerry Cohen; *Get a Literary Agent*, by Chuck Sambuchino.

TIPS "Most queries we receive are either too broad (how to write fiction) or too niche (how to write erotic horror), and don't reflect a knowledge of our large backlist of 150 titles. We rarely publish new books on journalism, freelancing, magazine article writing or marketing/promotion. We are actively seeking fiction and nonfiction writing technique books with fresh perspectives, interactive and visual writing instruction books, similar to *The Pocket Muse* by Monica Wood, and general reference works that appeal to an audience beyond writers."

YALE UNIVERSITY PRESS

P.O. Box 209040, New Haven CT 06520. (203)432-0960. **Fax:** (203)432-0948. **E-mail:** Contact specific editor (see website). **Website:** yalebooks.com. Estab. 1908. Publishes hardcover and trade paperback originals. "Yale University Press publishes scholarly and general interest books." Accepts simultaneous submissions. Book catalog and ms guidelines online.

NONFICTION Subjects include Americana, education, history, philosophy, psychology, religion, science, sociology. "Our nonfiction has to be at a very high level. Most of our books are written by professors or journalists, with a high level of expertise. *Submit proposals only.* We'll ask if we want to see more. *No unsolicited mss.* We won't return them." Submit sample chapters, cover letter, prospectus, CV, TOC, SASE. Reviews artwork/photos. Send photocopies.

POETRY Submit to Yale Series of Younger Poets Competition. Guidelines online.

TIPS "Audience is scholars, students and general readers."

YELLOW SHOE FICTION SERIES

LSU Press, P.O. Box 25053, Baton Rouge LA 70894. **Website:** www.lsu.edu/lsupress. **Contact:** Michael Griffith, editor. Estab. 2004. **Publishes 2 titles/year. Pays royalty. Offers advance.** Accepts simultaneous submissions.

"Looking first and foremost for literary excellence, especially good manuscripts that have fallen through the cracks at the big commercial presses. I'll cast a wide net."

FICTION Does not accept unsolicited mss. Accepts queries by mail, Attn: James W. Long.

RECENT TITLE(S) *Abbott Awaits*, by Chris Bachelder; *The Tree of Forgetfulness*, by Pam Durban.

ZEBRA BOOKS

Kensington, 119 W. 40th St., New York NY 10018. (212)407-1500. **E-mail:** esogah@kensingtonbooks.com. **Website:** www.kensingtonbooks.com. **Contact:** Esi Sogah, senior editor. Publishes hardcover originals, trade paperback and mass market paperback originals and reprints. Zebra Books is dedicated to women's fiction, which includes, but is not limited to romance. Publishes ms 12-18 months after acceptance. Accepts simultaneous submissions. Book catalog online.

FICTION Query.

ZEST BOOKS

2443 Fillmore St., Suite 340, San Francisco CA 94115. (415)777-8654. **Fax:** (415)777-8653. **E-mail:** info@zestbooks.net. **Website:** zestbooks.net. **Contact:** Dan Harmon, publishing director. Zest Books is a leader in young adult nonfiction, publishing books on entertainment, history, science, health, fashion, and lifestyle advice since 2006. Zest Books is distributed by Houghton Mifflin Harcourt. Accepts simultaneous submissions. Guidelines online.

NONFICTION Submit proposal.

RECENT TITLE(S) *Been There, Survived That: Getting Through Freshman Year of High School*, edited by Karen Macklin; *Uncool: A Girl's Guide to Misfitting In*, by Erin Elisabeth Conley.

TIPS "If you're interested in becoming a member of our author pool, send a cover letter stating why you are interested in young adult nonfiction, plus your specific areas of interest and specialties, your resume, 3-5 writing samples."

ZUMAYA PUBLICATIONS, LLC

3209 S. Interstate 35, Austin TX 78741. (512)333-4055. **Fax:** (512)276-6745. **E-mail:** business@zumayapublishing.com. **E-mail:** acquisitions@zumayapublications.com. **Website:** www.zumayapublications.com. **Contact:** Elizabeth K. Burton. Estab. 1999. Publishes trade paperback and electronic originals. Zumaya Publications is a digitally-based micro-press publishing mainly in on-demand trade paperback and e-book formats in an effort to reduce environmental impact. "We currently offer approximately 190 fiction titles in the mystery, SF/F, historical, romance, LGBTQ, horror, and occult genres in adult, young adult, and middle reader categories. In 2016, we plan to officially launch our graphic and illustrated novel imprint, Zumaya Fabled Ink. We publish approximately 10-15 new titles annually, at least five of which are from new authors. We do *not* publish erotica or graphic erotic romance at this time. We accept only electronic queries; all others will be discarded unread. A working knowledge of computers and relevant software is a necessity, as our production process is completely digital." **Publishes 10-15 titles/year. 1,000 queries; 50 mss requested/year. 5% of books from first-time authors. 100% from unagented writers. Pay 20% of net on paperbacks, net defined as cover price less printing and other associated costs; 50% of net on all e-books. Does not pay advance.** Publishes book 2 years after acceptance. Responds in 3 months to queries and proposals; 6 months to mss. Catalog online. Guidelines online. "We do not accept hard-copy queries or submissions.".

IMPRINTS Zumaya Arcane (New Age, inspirational fiction & nonfiction), Zumaya Boundless (GLBTQ); Zumaya Embraces (romance/women's fiction); Zumaya Enigma (mystery/suspense/thriller); Zumaya Thresholds (YA/middle grade); Zumaya Otherworlds (SF/F/H), Zumaya Yesterdays (memoirs, historical fiction, fiction, western fiction); Zumaya Fabled Ink (graphic and illustrated novels).

Zumaya was publishing diversity before it became a thing, and is always looking for fiction that presents the wonderful multiplicity of cultures in the world in ways that can lower the divisions that are too often keeping us from understanding one another. We also love books about people who are often either overlooked altogether or presented in clichéd ways. A romance between two 80-year-olds?

Bring it on. A police procedural where the officers have happy home lives? Yes, please. We like the idea of having fiction that reflects the manifold realities of people everywhere, even if the world they inhabit resides only in the author's imagination.

NONFICTION Subjects include creative nonfiction, memoirs, New Age, psychic, spirituality, true crime, true ghost stories. "The easiest way to figure out what we're looking for is to look at what we've already done. Our main nonfiction interests are in collections of true ghost stories, ones that have been investigated or thoroughly documented, memoirs that address specific regions and eras from a 'normal person' viewpoint and books on the craft of writing. That doesn't mean we won't consider something else." Electronic query only. Reviews artwork/photos. Send digital format.

FICTION Subjects include adventure, contemporary, ethnic, fantasy, feminist, gay, gothic, historical, horror, humor, juvenile, lesbian, literary, military, multicultural, mystery, occult, romance, science fiction, short story collections, spiritual, suspense, war, western, young adult, graphic novels. "We are open to all genres, particularly GLBT and YA/middle grade, historical and western, New Age/inspirational (no overtly Christian materials, please), non-category romance, thrillers. We encourage people to review what we've already published so as to avoid sending us more of the same, at least, insofar as the plot is concerned. While we're always looking for good mysteries, especially cozies, mysteries with historical settings, and police procedurals, we want original concepts rather than slightly altered versions of what we've already published. We do not publish erotica or graphically erotic romance at this time." Does not want erotica, graphically erotic romance, experimental, literary (unless it fits into one of our established imprints). A copy of our rules of submission is posted on our website and can be downloaded. They are rules rather than guidelines and should be read carefully before submitting. It will save everyone time and frustration.

RECENT TITLE(S) *Wars & Peaces*, by Chester Aaron; *Menace in Manatas*, by Roberta Rogow; *A Time for Us*, by Linda Andrews; *Goddesses Can Wait*, by Kim Baccellia; *Synergy*, by M.D. Benoit; *A Quilt in Time*, by Arlene Sachitano; *The Black Nebula*, by Robert E. Vardeman; *Megge of Bury Down*, by Rebecca Kightlinger; *The End of the Tether*, by Harold R. Thompson.

TIPS "We're catering to readers who may have loved last year's best seller but not enough to want to read 10 more just like it. Have something different. If it does not fit standard pigeonholes, that's a plus. On the other hand, it has to have an audience. And if you're not prepared to work with us on promotion and marketing, particularly via social media, it would be better to look elsewhere."

CONSUMER MAGAZINES

Selling your writing to consumer magazines is as much an exercise of your marketing skills as it is of your writing abilities. Editors of consumer magazines are looking for good writing which communicates pertinent information to their readers.

Marketing skills will help you successfully discern a magazine's editorial slant, and write queries and articles that prove your knowledge of the magazine's readership. You can gather clues about a magazine's readership—and establish your credibility with the editor—in a number of ways: Read the listing in *Writer's Market*; study a magazine's writer's guidelines; check a magazine's website; and read current issues of the magazine.

Writers who can correctly and consistently discern a publication's audience and deliver stories that speak to that target readership will win out every time over writers who submit haphazardly.

In nonfiction, editors continue to look for short feature articles covering specialized topics. Editors want crisp writing and expertise. If you are not an expert in the area about which you are writing, make yourself one through research. Always query before sending your manuscript.

Fiction editors prefer to receive complete manuscripts. Writers must keep in mind that fiction is competitive, and editors receive far more material than they can publish. For this reason, they often do not respond to submissions unless they are interested in using the story.

Most magazines listed here have indicated pay rates; some give very specific payment-per-word rates, while others state a range. Any agreement you come to with a magazine, whether verbal or written, should specify the payment you are to receive and when you are to receive it.

ANIMAL

$$ AKC GAZETTE

American Kennel Club, 260 Madison Ave., New York NY 10016. (212)696-8200. **Website:** www.akc.org/pubs/gazette. **85% freelance written.** Monthly magazine. "Geared to interests of fanciers of purebred dogs as opposed to commercial interests or pet owners. We require solid expertise from our contributors—we are *not* a pet magazine." Estab. 1889. Circ. 60,000. Byline given. Pays on publication. Offers 10% kill fee. Publishes ms an average of 6 months after acceptance. Submit seasonal material 6 months in advance. Accepts queries by mail. Accepts simultaneous submissions. Responds in 2 months to queries. Guidelines for #10 SASE.

NONFICTION Needs general interest, how-to, humor, interview, photo feature, travel, dog art, training and canine performance sports. No poetry, tributes to individual dogs, or fiction. **Buys 30-40 mss/year.** Length: 1,000-3,000 words. **Pays $300-500.** Pays expenses of writers on assignment.

PHOTOS Photo contest guidelines for #10 SASE. State availability. Captions, identification of subjects, model releases required. Reviews color transparencies, prints. Pays $50-200/photo. Buys one-time rights.

FICTION Annual short fiction contest only. Guidelines for #10 SASE. Send entries to AKC Publications Fiction Contest.

TIPS "Contributors should be involved in the dog fancy or be an expert in the area they write about (veterinary, showing, field trialing, obedience training, dogs in legislation, dog art or history or literature). All submissions are welcome but author must be a credible expert or be able to interview and quote the experts. Veterinary articles must be written by or with veterinarians. Humorous features or personal experiences relative to purebred dogs should have broader applications. For features, know the subject thoroughly and be conversant with jargon peculiar to the sport of dogs."

$$$$ THE AMERICAN QUARTER HORSE JOURNAL

AQHA, 1600 Quarter Horse Dr., Amarillo TX 79104. (806)376-4811. **Website:** www.aqha.com. Editor-in-Chief: Becky Newell. **30% freelance written. Prefers to work with published/established writers.** Monthly official publication of the american quarter horse association. covering American Quarter Horses/horse activities/western lifestyle. "Covers the American Wuarter Horse breed and more than 30 disciplines in which Quarter Horses compete. Business stories, lifestyles stories, how-to stories and others related to the breed and horse activities." Estab. 1948. Circ. 60,000. Byline given. Pays on acceptance. Offers 60% kill fee. Publishes ms an average of 3 months after acceptance. Editorial lead time 3 months. Submit seasonal material 3 months in advance. Accepts queries by mail, e-mail. Accepts simultaneous submissions. Responds in 1 week to queries. Responds in 1 month to mss. Sample copy free. Guidelines free.

NONFICTION Needs book excerpts, essays, general interest, historical, how-to, humor, inspirational, interview, "Must be about established horses or people who have made a contribution to the business, new prod, opinion, personal exp, photo, technical, equine updates, new surgery procedures, etc." Special issues: Annual stallion issue dedicated to the breeding of horses. **Buys 10 mss/year.** Query with published clips. Length: 700-3,000 words. **Pays $250-1,500 for assigned articles. Pays $250-1,500 for unsolicited articles.** Pays expenses of writers on assignment.

PHOTOS State availability. Captions, identification of subjects required. Reviews GIF/JPEG files. Buys all rights.

COLUMNS/DEPARTMENTS Quarter's Worth (Industry news); Horse Health (health items), 750 words. **Buys 6 mss/yr. mss/year.** Query with published clips. **Pays $100-$400.**

TIPS "Writers must have a knowledge of the horse business."

$$ APPALOOSA JOURNAL

2720 W. Pullman Rd., Moscow ID 83843. (208)882-5578. **Fax:** (208)882-8150. **E-mail:** editor@appaloosajournal.com; designer2@appaloosajournal.com. **Website:** www.appaloosajournal.com. **Contact:** Dana Russell, editor; John Langston, art director. **40% freelance written.** Monthly magazine covering Appaloosa horses. "*Appaloosa Journal* is the authoritative, association-based source for information about the Appaloosa Horse Club, the Appaloosa breed and the Appaloosa industry. Our mission is to cultivate a broader membership base and instill enthusiasm for the breed by recognizing the needs and achievements of the Appaloosa, ApHC members, enthusiasts and our readers. The Appaloosa Horse

Club is a not-for-profit organization. Serious inquiries within specified budget only." Estab. 1946. Circ. 25,000. Byline given. Pays on publication. Publishes ms an average of 3 months after acceptance. Accepts simultaneous submissions. Responds in 1 month to queries. Responds in 2 months to mss. Sample copy free. Guidelines available online.

Appaloosa Journal no longer accepts material for columns.

NONFICTION Needs historical, interview. **Buys 15-20 mss/year.** Send complete ms. *Appaloosa Journal* is not responsible for unsolicited materials. All freelance correspondence should be directed to editor Dana Russell via e-mail, with the subject line "'Freelance.' Article-length reports of timely and newsworthy events, such as shows, races, and overseas competition, are welcome but must be pre-approved by the editor. Mss exceeding the preferred word length will be evaluated according to relevance and content matter. Lengthy stories, opinion pieces, or poorly written pieces will be rejected. Mss may be sent on a CD or via e-mail in Microsoft Word or text-only format. If sent via CD, an accompanying hard copy should be printed, double spaced, following the guidelines." Length: 1,500-1,800 words (features); 600-800 words (article-length). **Pays $200-400.** Pays expenses of writers on assignment.

PHOTOS In photographer's samples, wants to see "high-quality color photos of world-class, characteristic (coat patterned) Appaloosa horses in appealing, picturesque outdoor environments." Send photos. Captions, identification of subjects required. Payment varies. Pays $200 for color cover; $25 minimum for color inside. Pays on publication. Credit line given. Buys first rights.

TIPS "Articles by writers with horse knowledge, news sense, and photography skills are in great demand. If it's a strong article about an Appaloosa, the writer has a pretty good chance of publication. A good understanding of the breed and the industry, breeders, and owners is helpful. Make sure there's some substance and a unique twist."

$$ THE CHRONICLE OF THE HORSE

P.O. Box 46, Middleburg VA 20118. (540)687-6341. **Fax:** (540)687-3937. **E-mail:** brasin@coth.com. **Website:** www.chronofhorse.com. **Contact:** Beth Rasin, executive editor. **40% freelance written.** Biweekly magazine covering horse sport. "We cover English riding sports, including horse showing, grand prix jumping competitions, steeplechase racing, foxhunting, dressage, endurance riding, para-dressage, and eventing. We feature news, profiles, how-to articles on equitation and horse care and interviews with leaders in the various fields." Estab. 1937. Byline given. Pays for features, news and other items on publication. Publishes an average of 4 months after acceptance. Submit seasonal material 3 months in advance. Accepts queries by mail, e-mail. Accepts simultaneous submissions. Responds in 5-6 weeks to queries. Guidelines online.

NONFICTION Needs essays, expose, general interest, historical, how-to, humor, interview, opinion, profile, technical, travel. No poetry, clinic reports, Western riding articles, personal experience or wild horses. **Buys 300 mss/year.** Send complete ms. Length: 1,500-2,500 words. **Pays $150-400.** Pays expenses of writers on assignment.

PHOTOS State availability. Identification of subjects required. Photo captions required with every subject identified. Reviews e-mailed image, prints or color slides; accepts color for color reproduction. Pays $30-50 base rate. Pays on publication. Buys one-time rights. Credit line given. Prefers first North American rights. Buys one-time rights.

COLUMNS/DEPARTMENTS Dressage, Eventing, Horse Shows, Horse Care, Racing over Fences, Young Entry (about young riders, geared for youth), Horses and Humanities, Hunting, Vaulting, Para-dressage, Endurance,1,500-2500 words. Query with published clips or send complete ms. **Pays $25-200.**

TIPS "Get our guidelines. Our readers are sophisticated, competitive horsemen. Articles need to go beyond common knowledge. Freelancers often attempt too broad or too basic a subject. We welcome well-written news stories on major events, but clear the assignment with us. Know horse sports."

$$ HORSE ILLUSTRATED

I-5 Publishing, 470 Conway Ct., Suite b-6, Lexington KY 40511. (800)546-7730. **E-mail:** horseillustrated@luminamedia.com. **Website:** www.horseillustrated.com. **Contact:** Elizabeth Moyer, editor. **90% freelance written. Prefers to work with published/established writers, but will work with new/unpublished writers.** Monthly magazine covering all aspects of horse ownership. "Our readers are adults, mostly women, between the ages of 18 and 40; stories should be geared to that age group and reflect responsible horse care." Estab. 1976. Circ. 160,660. Byline given. Pays on publication. Publishes ms an average of 8 months after acceptance. Submit seasonal material 6 months in advance. Accepts queries by mail. Accepts simultaneous submissions. Responds in 3 months to queries. Guidelines available at www.horsechannel.com/horse-magazines/horse-illustrated/submission-guidelines.aspx.

NONFICTION Needs general interest, how-to, inspirational, photo feature. "No little girl horse stories, cowboy and Indian stories, or anything not directly relating to horses." Buys 20 mss/year. Query or send complete ms. Length: 1,000-2,000 words. **Pays $200-475.** Pays expenses of writers on assignment.

PHOTOS Send high-res digital images on a CD with thumbnails.

TIPS "Freelancers can break in at this publication with feature articles on Western and English training methods; veterinary and general care how-to articles; and horse sports articles. We rarely use personal experience articles. Submit photos with training and how-to articles whenever possible. We have a very good record of developing new freelancers into regular contributors/columnists. We are always looking for fresh talent, but certainly enjoy working with established writers who know the ropes as well. We are accepting less unsolicited freelance work—much is now assigned and contracted."

$ MINIATURE DONKEY TALK

Miniature Donkey Talk, Inc., P.O. Box 982, Cripple Creek CO 80813. (719)689-2904. **E-mail:** mike@donkeytalk.com. **Website:** www.web-donkeys.com. **Contact:** Mike Gross. **65% freelance written.** Quarterly magazine covering donkeys, with articles on healthcare, promotion, and management of donkeys for owners, breeders, and donkey lovers. Estab. 1987. Circ. 4,925. Byline given. Pays on acceptance. Publishes ms an average of 4 months after acceptance. Editorial lead time 2 months. Submit seasonal material 3 months in advance. Accepts queries by mail, e-mail. Accepts simultaneous submissions. Responds in 2 weeks to queries; 1 month to mss. Sample copy for $5. Guidelines free.

NONFICTION Needs book excerpts, humor, interview, personal experience. **Buys 6 mss/year.** Query with published clips. Length: 700-5,000 words. **Pays $25-150.**

PHOTOS State availability. Identification of subjects required. Reviews 3x5 prints. Offers no additional payment for photos accepted with ms. Buys one-time rights.

COLUMNS/DEPARTMENTS Columns: Humor: 2,000 words; Healthcare: 2,000-5,000 words; Management: 2,000 words. **Buys 50 mss/year.** Query. **Pays $25-100.**

TIPS "Simply send your ms. If on topic and appropriate, good possibility it will be published. No fiction or poetry."

$$ MUSHING MAGAZINE

2300 Black Spruce Ct., Fairbanks AK 99709. (907)495-2468. **E-mail:** editor@mushing.com; jake@mushing.com. **Website:** www.mushing.com. **Contact:** Greg Sellentin, publisher and executive editor. Bimonthly magazine covering "all aspects of the growing sports of dogsledding, skijoring, carting, dog packing, and weight pulling. *Mushing* promotes responsible dog care through feature articles and updates on working animal health care, safety, nutrition, and training." Estab. 1987. Circ. 10,000. Byline given. Pays within 3 months of publication. No kill fee. Publishes ms an average of 4 months after acceptance. Submit seasonal material 4 months in advance. Accepts queries by mail, e-mail, fax, phone. Accepts simultaneous submissions. Responds in 8 months to queries. Sample copy: $5 ($6 U.S. to Canada). Guidelines online.

NONFICTION Needs historical, how-to. Special issues: Iditarod (January/February); Skijor/Sprint/Peak of Season (March/April); Health and Nutrition (May/June); Meet the Mushers/Tour Business Directory (July/August); Equipment (September/October); Races and Places/Sled Dog Events Calendar (November/December). See website for current editorial calendar. Query with or without published clips. "We prefer detailed queries but also consider unsolicited mss. Please make proposals informative yet to the point. Spell out your qualifications for handling the topic. We like to see clips of previously published material but are eager to work with new and unpublished authors, too." Considers complete ms by postal mail (with SASE) or e-mail (as attachment or part of message). Also accepts disk submissions. Length: 1,000-2,500 words. **Pays $50-250.** Pays expenses of writers on assignment.

PHOTOS "We look for good-quality color for covers and specials." Send photos. Captions, identification of subjects. Reviews digital images only. Pays $20-165/photo. Buys one-time and second reprint rights.

COLUMNS/DEPARTMENTS Query with or without published clips or send complete ms. Length: 150-500 words.

FILLERS Needs anecdotes, facts, newsbreaks, short humor, cartoons, puzzles. Length: 100-250 words. **Pays $20-35.**

TIPS "Read our magazine. Know something about dog-driven, dog-powered sports."

$$ PAINT HORSE JOURNAL

American Paint Horse Association, P.O. Box 961023, Ft. Worth TX 76161-0023. (817)834-2742. **Fax:** (817)834-3152. **E-mail:** jhein@apha.com. **Website:** apha.com/phj. **Contact:** Jessica Hein, editor. **10% freelance written. Works with a small number of new/unpublished writers each year.** Monthly magazine for people who raise, breed, and show Paint Horses. Estab. 1966. Circ. 12,000. Byline given. Pays on acceptance. Offers negotiable kill fee. Submit seasonal material 3 months in advance. Accepts queries by mail, e-mail, fax. Accepts simultaneous submissions. Guidelines online.

NONFICTION Needs general interest, historical, how-to. **Buys 4-5 mss/year.** Query. Length: 1,000-2,000 words. **Pays $100-500.** Pays expenses of writers on assignment.

PHOTOS Photos must illustrate article and must include registered Paint Horses. Send photos. Captions required. Offers no additional payment for photos accepted with accompanying ms.

TIPS "Well-written articles are welcomed. Submit items that show a definite understanding of the horse business. Be sure you understand precisely what a Paint Horse is as defined by the American Paint Horse Association. Use proper equine terminology. Photos with copy are almost always essential."

$$ USDF CONNECTION

United States Dressage Federation, 4051 Iron Works Pkwy., Lexington KY 40511. **E-mail:** connection@usdf.org. **E-mail:** editorial@usdf.org. **Website:** www.usdf.org. **Contact:** Jennifer Bryant. **40% freelance written.** Magazine published 6 times/year covering dressage (an equestrian sport). All material must relate to the sport of dressage in the U.S. Estab. 2000. Circ. 30,000. Byline given. Pays on acceptance. Offers 50% kill fee. Publishes ms an average of 6 months after acceptance. Editorial lead time: 3 months. Submit seasonal material 6 months in advance. Accepts queries by e-mail. Responds in 1 month to queries; 1-2 months to mss. Sample copy: $5. Guidelines online.

NONFICTION Needs book excerpts, essays, how-to, interview, opinion, personal experience, profile. Does not want general-interest equine material or stories that lack a U.S. dressage angle. **Buys 18 mss/year.** Query. Length: 500-2,000 words. **Pays $100-450 for assigned articles. Pays $100-300 for unsolicited articles. Byline only for "The Tail End," a one-page personal or op/ed column pertaining to USDF members' dressage experiences.**

PHOTOS State availability. Captions, identification of subjects required. Reviews JPEG files. Negotiates payment individually. Buys one-time rights.

COLUMNS/DEPARTMENTS Profiles of noteworthy USDF members, particularly adult amateur and youth members, and their dressage journeys. **Buys 6 mss/year.** Query with published clips. **Pays $150-300.**

TIPS "Know the organization and the sport. Most successful contributors are active in the horse industry and bring valuable perspectives and insights to their stories and images."

$$ YOUNG RIDER

2030 Main Street, Irvine CA 92614. (949) 855-8822. **Fax:** (949) 855-3045. **E-mail:** yreditor@i5publishing.com. **Website:** www.youngrider.com. "*Young Rider* magazine teaches young people, in an easy-to-read and entertaining way, how to look after their horses properly, and how to improve their riding skills safely." Byline given. Accepts simultaneous submissions. Guidelines available online.

NONFICTIONyoung adults: animal, careers, famous equestrians, health (horse), horse celebrities, riding. Special issues: Wants "'horsey-interest type stories. Stories or events that will interest kids ALL over the country that the editor is not able to personally attend. We need 4-5 good color photos with stories like this; the pictures must be color and tack sharp." Query with published clips. Length: 800-1,000 words. **Pays $200/story.** Pays expenses of writers on assignment.

FICTIONyoung adults: adventure, animal, horses. "We would prefer funny stories, with a bit of conflict, which will appeal to the 13-year-old age group. They should be written in the third person, and about kids." Query. Length: 800-1,000 words. **Pays $150.**

TIPS "Fiction must be in third person. Read magazine before sending in a query. No 'true story from when I was a youngster.' No moralistic stories. Fiction must be up-to-date and humorous, teen-oriented. No practical or how-to articles—all done in-house."

ART & ARCHITECTURE

ARTLINK

Artlink Australia, P.O. Box 182, Fullarton SA 5063 Australia. (61)(8)8271-6228. **E-mail:** info@artlink.com.au. **Website:** www.artlink.com.au. **Contact:** Eve Sullivan, executive editor. Quarterly magazine covering contemporary art in Australia. Estab. 1981. Accepts simultaneous submissions. Guidelines available online.

NONFICTION Needs general interest. Special issues: "*Artlink* welcomes proposals for writing and information on associated projects and exhibition programs that relate to forthcoming themed issues." See website for upcoming themes. Write or e-mail the editor with your CV and 2-3 examples of previously published writing. **Pays $300/1,000 words.** Pays expenses of writers on assignment.

TIPS "Because *Artlink* is a themed magazine which tries to make art relevant across society, we often need to find contributors who have expert knowledge of subjects outside of the art area who can put the work of artists in a broader context."

AZURE (ARCHITECTURE, DESIGN, INTERIORS, CURIOSITY)

213 Sterling Rd., Suite 206, Toronto ON M6R 2B2 Canada. 416-203-9674. **E-mail:** editorial@azureonline.com; azure@azureonline.com. **Website:** www.azuremagazine.com. **Contact:** David Dick-Agnew, senior editor. **75% freelance written.** Magazine covering design and architecture. "*AZURE* is an award-winning magazine with a focus on contemporary architecture and design. In 8 visually stunning issues per year, *AZURE* explores inventive projects, emerging trends, and design issues that relate to our changing society. In recent years, *AZURE* has evolved into a media brand offering digital editions, weekly e-newsletters featuring the latest design news, an interactive website updated daily, and an international awards program celebrating excellence in design." Estab. 1985. Byline given. Pays on publication. Offers variable kill fee. Publishes ms an average of 1 month after acceptance. Editorial lead time up to 45 days. Accepts queries by e-mail. Accepts simultaneous submissions. Responds in 6 weeks to queries.

NONFICTION Needs new product, profile, technical, travel. Special issues: January/February: Houses; March/April: Iconic Buildings; June: Office Spaces; July/August: AZ Awards Annual; October: Trends; December: Interiors and Higher Ed. Does not want "anything other than architecture, design, urbanism and landscape, and tangentially related topics." **Buys 25-30 mss/year.** Length: 300-1,500 words. **Pays $1/word (Canadian).** Pays expenses of writers on assignment.

COLUMNS/DEPARTMENTS Groundbreaker (profiles of new, large architectural projects) 350 words; book and documentary reviews, 300 words; Field Trip (profiles of hospitality/travel spaces with design angle), 800 words; Trailer (idiosyncratic design stories) 300 words. **Buys 30 mss/year.** Query. **Pays $1/word (Canadian).**

TIPS "Try to understand what the magazine is about. Writers must be well versed in the field of architecture and design. It's very unusual to get something from someone I haven't worked quite closely with and gotten a sense of who the writer is. The best way to introduce yourself is by sending clips or writing samples and describing what your background is in the field."

ESPACE

Le Centre de Diffusion 3D, 423-5445 Avenue De Gaspé, Montreal QC H2J 3B2 Canada. (514)907-6147. **E-mail:** info@espaceartactuel.com. **Website:** www.espaceartactuel.com. **Contact:** Serge Fisette, editor. **95% freelance written.** Quarterly magazine covering sculpture events. Estab. 1987. Circ. 1,400. Byline given. Pays on publication. No kill fee. Publishes ms an average of 3 months after acceptance. Editorial lead time 5 months. Submit seasonal material 3 months in advance. Accepts queries by e-mail. Accepts simultaneous submissions. Sample copy free. Guidelines online.

"Texts are published in both French and English. *ESPACE*'s objective is to serve the artistic community across Canada, while engaging with the international scene."

NONFICTION Needs interview, reviews, sculpture events. **Buys 60 mss/year.** Send complete ms. Length: up to 1,000 words for reviews; 1,500-2,000 words for interviews, events. **Pays $65/page.** Pays expenses of writers on assignment.

PHOTOS Send photos. Reviews transparencies, prints. Offers no additional payment for photos accepted with ms.

ASSOCIATIONS

$$$ AMERICAN EDUCATOR

American Federation of Teachers, 555 New Jersey Ave. NW, Washington DC 20001. **E-mail:** ae@aft.org. **Website:** www.aft.org/ae. **Contact:** Amy Hightower, editor. **5% freelance written.** Quarterly magazine covering education, condition of children, and labor issues. *American Educator,* the quaterly magazine of the American Federation of Teachers, reaches over 900,000 public school teachers, higher education faculty, and education researchers and policymakers. The magazine concentrates on significant ideas and practices in education, civics, and the condition of children in America and around the world. Estab. 1977. Circ. 900,000. Byline given. Pays on publication. Offers 50% kill fee. Publishes ms an average of 2-6 months after acceptance. Editorial lead time 1 year. Submit seasonal material 6 months in advance. Accepts queries by mail, e-mail. Accepts simultaneous submissions. Responds in 2 months to queries. Responds in 6 months to mss. Sample copy and guidelines online.

"We prefer queries to mss. When sending a ms, please keep at least 1 copy of your article on file, as we cannot be responsible for unsolicited mss. Be sure to include your contact information in the event we need to reach you. Payment varies according to length and topic. The minimum payment for an article is $300."

NONFICTION Needs book excerpts, essays, historical, interview, discussions of educational research. No pieces that are not supportive of the public schools. **Buys 8 mss/year.** Query with published clips. Length: 1,000-7,000 words. **Pays $750-3,000 for assigned articles. Pays $300-1,000 for unsolicited articles.** Pays expenses of writers on assignment.

PHOTOS State availability. Captions, identification of subjects, model releases required. Reviews contact sheets, negatives, transparencies, 8x10 prints, GIF/JPEG files. Negotiates payment individually. Buys one-time rights.

$$ BUGLE

Rocky Mountain Elk Foundation, 5705 Grant Creek, Missoula MT 59808. (406)523-4500. **Fax:** (800)225-5355. **E-mail:** bugle@rmef.org. **E-mail:** conservationeditor@rmef.org; huntingeditor@rmef.org; assistanteditor@rmef.org; photos@rmef.org. **Website:** www.rmef.org. **50% freelance.** *Bugle* is the membership publication of the Rocky Mountain Elk Foundation, a nonprofit wildlife conservation group. "Our readers are predominantly hunters, many of them conservationists who care deeply about protecting wildlife habitat." Bimonthly. Magazine: 114-212 pages; 55 lb. Escanaba paper; 80 lb. Steriling cover, b&w, 4-color illustrations; photos. Estab. 1984. Circ. 225,000. Byline given. Pays on acceptance. Kill fee. 3-9 months between acceptance and publication. Accepts queries by mail, e-mail. Accepts simultaneous submissions. Responds in 1 month to queries; 3 months to mss. Sample copy for $5. Guidelines online.

NONFICTION Needs essays, personal experience. Special issues: July/August Bowhunting section. Query or submit complete ms to appropriate e-mail address; see website for guidelines. Length: 750-5,000 words, depending on type of piece. **Pays 30¢/word and 3 contributor's copies.**

PHOTOS Digital files only unless specified. Reviews low-res digital photos, CDs. Pays $600 for cover, $250 for full-page spread, $200 for full page, $150 for half-page, $100 for third-page or smaller. Busy one-time North American rights.

FICTION "We accept fiction and nonfiction stories pertaining in some way to elk, other wildlife, hunting, habitat conservation, and related issues. We would like to see more humor." Needs adventure, historical, humorous, novel excerpts, slice-of-life vignettes, western, children's/juvenile, satire, human interest, natural history, conservation—as long as they related to elk. Query or submit complete ms to appropriate e-mail address; see website for guidelines. Length: 1,500-5,000 words; average length: 2,500 words. **Pays 30¢/word and 3 contributor's copies.**

TIPS "Hunting stories and essays should celebrate the hunting experience, demonstrating respect for wildlife, the land, and the hunt. Articles on elk behavior or elk habitat should include personal observations and should entertain as well as educate. No freelance product reviews or formulaic how-to articles accepted. Straight action-adventure hunting stories are in short supply, as are 'Situation Ethics' mss."

$$ HUMANITIES

National Endowment for the Humanities, 1100 Pennsylvania Ave. NW, Washington DC 20506. (202)606-8435. **Fax:** (202)606-8451. **E-mail:** dskinner@neh.gov; info@neh.gov. **Website:** www.neh.gov/humanities. **Contact:** David Skinner, editor. **50% freelance**

written. Bimonthly magazine covering news in the humanities focused on projects that receive financial support from the agency. Estab. 1980. Circ. 7,500. Byline given. Pays on publication. Publishes ms 3 to 6 months after acceptance. Editorial lead time 3 months. Submit seasonal material 4 months in advance. Accepts queries by mail, e-mail, fax, phone. Accepts simultaneous submissions. Sample copy available online. We are especially interested in hearing from writers outside of the big cities. Major areas of interest include humanities programs relating to veterans, endangered language projects, and humanities projects relating to Native American communities.

NONFICTION Needs book excerpts, essays, historical, interview, photo feature. **Buys 25 mss/year.** Query with published clips. Length: 400-2,500 words. **Pays $300-600.** Pays expenses of writers on assignment.

PHOTOS Contact: Contact mbiernik@neh.gov. Identification of subjects, model releases required. Offers no additional payment for photos accepted with ms; negotiates payment individually. Buys one-time rights.

COLUMNS/DEPARTMENTS In Focus (directors of state humanities councils), 700 words; Breakout (special activities of state humanities councils), 750 words. **Buys 12 mss/year.** Query with published clips. **Pays $300.**

$$ NEW MOBILITY

United Spinal Association, 120-34 Queens Blvd., #320, Kew Gardens NY 11415. (718)803-3782. **E-mail:** iruder@unitedspinal.org; jbyzek@unitedspinal.org. **Website:** www.newmobility.com. **Contact:** Josie Byzek, executive editor; Ian Ruder, editor. **50% freelance written.** Bimonthly magazine covering living with spinal cord injury/disorder (SCI/D). The monthly membership magazine for the National Spinal Cord Injury Association, a program of United Spinal Association. Members include people with spinal cord injury or disorder, as well as caregivers, parents, and some spinal cord injury/disorder professionals. All articles should reflect this common interest of the audience. Assume that your audience is better educated in the subject of spinal cord injury than average, but be careful not to be too technical. Each issue has a theme (available from editor) that unites features in addition to a series of departments focused on building community and providing solutions for the SCI/D community. Articles that feature members, chapters or the organization are preferred, but any article that deals with issue pertinent to SCI/D community will be considered. Estab. 2011. Circ. 35,000. Byline given. Pays on publication. No kill fee. Publishes ms an average of 1-2 months after acceptance. Accepts queries by e-mail. Accepts simultaneous submissions. Sample copy and guidelines available on website.

NONFICTION Needs essays, general interest, how-to, humor, interview, new product, personal experience, photo feature, travel, medical research. Does not want "articles that treat disabilities as an affliction or cause for pity, or that show the writer does not get that people with disabilities are people like anyone else. We aren't interested in 'courageous' or 'inspiring' tales of 'overcoming disability.'" **Buys 36 mss/year.** Query. Length: 800-1,600 words. Pays expenses of writers on assignment.

PHOTOS Send photos. Identification of subjects required. Reviews high-quality GIF/JPEG files. Offers no additional payment for photos accepted with ms.

COLUMNS/DEPARTMENTS Travel (report on access of a single travel destination based on conversations with disabled travelers), Access (hands-on look at how to improve access for a specific type of area), Ask Anything (tap members and experts to answer community question relating to life w/SCI/D), Advocacy (investigation of ongoing advocacy issue related to SCI/D). **Buys 40 mss/year.** Length: 800 words. Query with published clips. **Pays 15¢/word for new writers.**

TIPS "It helps (though is not necessary) if you have a disability, or if you are comfortable with people with disabilities; they are the subjects of most of our articles as well as the bulk of our readership. Our readers are looking for tips on how to live well with mobility impairment. They're concerned with access to jobs, travel, recreation, education, etc. They like to read about how others deal with like situations and hear about resources or ideas that will help them in their daily lives. They are sophisticated about spinal cord injuries and don't need to be 'inspired' by the typical stories about people with disabilities that appear in the human interest section of most newspapers."

$$$ TEXAS CO-OP POWER

Texas Electric Cooperatives, Inc., 1122 Colorado St., 24th Floor, Austin TX 78701. (512)486-6243. **E-mail:** clohrmann@texas-ec.org; twidlowski@texas-ec.org. **Website:** www.texascooppower.com. **Contact:** Charles Lohrmann, editor; Tom Widlowski, associate editor. **75% freelance written.** Monthly magazine covering Texas life, travel destinations, people, history and general culture as well as some issue-oriented content both in print and online. *Texas Co-op*

Power delivers top-notch writing and photography in features on Texas travel, history, food and culture to more than 1.5 million households and businesses. *Texas Co-op Power* enhances the quality of life of electric co-op member-customers in a well-designed and engaging format, both in print and online. Estab. 1948. Circ. 1.54 million. Byline given. Pays upon final acceptance. Kill fee is negotiated separately. Publishes ms an average of 6 months after acceptance. Editorial lead time 6-12 months. Submit seasonal material 6 months in advance. Accepts queries by e-mail, online submission form. Accepts simultaneous submissions. Responds in 1 month to queries. Responds in 3 months to mss. Magazine content is available online. No sample copies mailed. Guidelines online.

NONFICTION Needs book excerpts, essays, general interest, historical, how-to, humor, inspirational, interview, memoir, personal experience, profile, travel. **Buys 30 mss/year.** Read and review magazine content online at texascooppower.com. Query via e-mail with published clips.Do not query if unfamiliar with magazine content, Texas topics or if seeking general assignments. Length: 800-1,400 words. **Pays $300-1,200.**

PHOTOS State availability. Detailed identification of subjects, caption information, and model releases required. Typically review digital galleries online. Negotiates payment individually. Buys one-time rights.

TIPS "It is essential that all queries reflect a detailed understanding of the magazine's content and online archives. No random suggestions that do not relate to the magazine's established style of presenting history, travel, food and general-interest content."

ASTROLOGY, METAPHYSICAL & NEW AGE

$ FATE MAGAZINE

Fate Magazine, Inc., P.O. Box 460, Lakeville MN 55044. (952)431-2050. **E-mail:** fate@fatemag.com. **Website:** www.fatemag.com. **Contact:** Phyllis Galde, editor in chief. **75% freelance written.** Covers the paranormal, ghosts, UFOs, strange science. "Reports a wide variety of strange and unknown phenomena. We are open to receiving any well-written, well-documented article. Our readers especially like reports of current investigations, experiments, theories, and experiences." Estab. 1948. Circ. 15,000. Byline given. Pays after publication. Publishes ms 3-6 months after acceptance. Editorial lead time 3-6 months. Accepts queries by mail, e-mail. Accepts simultaneous submissions. Responds in 1-3 months to queries. Sample copy available for free online, by e-mail. Guidelines available online.

"*Fate* prefers first-person accounts and investigations of the topics we cover. We do not publish fiction or opinion pieces or book-length mss."

NONFICTION Needs general interest, historical, how-to, personal experience, photo feature, technical. "We do not publish poetry, fiction, editorial/opinion pieces, or book-length mss." **Buys 100 mss/year.** Submit complete ms by e-mail or on CD accompanied by hard copy. Length: 1,500-3,000 words. **Pays $50.** Pays expenses of writers on assignment. Pays with merchandise or ad space if requested.

PHOTOS Buys slides, prints, or digital photos/illustrations with ms. Send photos with submission. Reviews hi-res (300 dpi) GIF/JPEG files, 4x6 prints.

COLUMNS/DEPARTMENTS True Mystic Experiences (short reader-submitted stories of strange experiences); My Proof of Survival (short reader-submitted stories of proof of life after death), up to 500 words. Submit complete ms by e-mail or on CD accompanied by hard copy. **Pays $10.**

FILLERS Fillers are especially welcomed and must be fully authenticated. Needs anecdotes and facts. Length: 150-500 words. **Pays $10.**

TIPS "*Fate* is looking for exciting, first-hand accounts of UFO and paranormal experiences and investigations."

AUTOMOTIVE & MOTORCYCLE

$ AMERICAN MOTORCYCLIST

American Motorcyclist Association, 13515 Yarmouth Dr., Pickerington OH 43147. (614)856-1900. **E-mail:** submissions@ama-cycle.org. **Website:** www.americanmotorcyclist.com. **Contact:** Grant Parsons, director of communications; James Holter, managing editor. **25% freelance written.** Monthly magazine for enthusiastic motorcyclists investing considerable time and money in the sport, emphasizing the motorcyclist, not the vehicle. Monthly magazine of the American Motorcyclist Association. Emphasizes people involved in, and events dealing with, all aspects of motorcycling. Readers are "enthusiastic motorcyclists, investing considerable time in road riding or all aspects of the sport." Estab. 1947. Circ. 200,000.

Byline given. Pays on publication. No kill fee. Editorial lead time 3 months. Submit seasonal material 4 months in advance. Accepts queries by mail, e-mail. Accepts simultaneous submissions. Responds in 5 weeks to queries. Responds in 6 weeks to mss. Sample copy for $1.50. Guidelines free.

NONFICTION Needs interview, personal experience, travel. **Buys 8 mss/year.** Send complete ms. Length: 1,000-2,500 words. **Pays minimum $8/published column inch.** Pays expenses of writers on assignment.

PHOTOS Buys 10-20 photos/issue. Subjects include: travel, technical, sports, humorous, photo essay/feature and celebrity/personality. Photo captions preferred. Send photos. Captions, identification of subjects required. Reviews transparencies, prints. Pays $50/photo minimum. Pays $50-150/photo; $250 minimum for cover. Also buys photos in photo/text packages according to same rate; pays $8/column inch minimum for story. Pays on publication. Buys one-time rights, First North American serial rights.

TIPS "Our major category of freelance stories concerns motorcycling trips to interesting North American destinations. Prefers stories of a timeless nature."

$$$$ AUTOWEEK

Crain Communications, Inc., 1155 Gratiot Ave., Detroit MI 48207. (313)446-6000. **Fax:** (313)446-1027. **E-mail:** awletter@autoweek.com. **Website:** www.autoweek.com. Editor: Wes Raynal. **5% freelance written, most by regular contributors.** *AutoWeek* is a biweekly magazine for auto enthusiasts. Estab. 1958. Circ. 300,000. Byline given. Pays on publication. Publishes ms an average of 1 month after acceptance. Accepts queries by e-mail. Accepts simultaneous submissions.

NONFICTION Needs historical, interview. **Buys 5 mss/year.** Query. Length: 100-400 words. **Pays $1/word.** Pays expenses of writers on assignment.

$$$ CANADIAN BIKER MAGAZINE

108-2220 Sooke Rd., Victoria BC V9B 0G9 Canada. (250)384-0333. **Website:** www.canadianbiker.com. **Contact:** John Campbell, editor. **65% freelance written.** Magazine covering motorcycling. Estab. 1980. Circ. 20,000. Byline given. Publishes ms an average of 1 year after acceptance. Editorial lead time 3 months. Accepts queries by mail. Accepts simultaneous submissions. Responds in 6 weeks to queries; in 6 months to mss.

"A family-oriented motorcycle magazine whose purpose is to unite Canadian motorcyclists from coast to coast through the dissemination of information in a nonbiased, open forum. The magazine reports on new products, events, touring, racing, vintage and custom motorcycling, as well as new industry information."

NONFICTION Needs general interest, historical, how-to, interview, new product, technical, travel. **Buys 12 mss/year.** Query. Length: 500-1,500 words. **Pays $100-200 for assigned articles. Pays $80-150 for unsolicited articles.** Pays expenses of writers on assignment.

PHOTOS State availability of or send photos. Captions, identification of subjects, model releases required. Reviews 4×4 transparencies, 3×5 prints. Negotiates payment individually. Buys one-time rights.

TIPS "We're looking for more racing features, rider profiles, custom sport bikes, quality touring stories, 'extreme' riding articles. Contact editor first before writing anything. Have original ideas, an ability to write from an authoritative point of view, and an ability to supply quality photos to accompany text. Writers should be involved in the motorcycle industry and be intimately familiar with some aspect of the industry which would be of interest to readers. Observations of the industry should be current, timely, and informative."

AVIATION

$$ FLIGHT JOURNAL

Air Age Media, 88 Danbury Rd., Wilton CT 06897. (203)431-9000. **E-mail:** flight@airage.com. **Website:** www.flightjournal.com. Bimonthly magazine covering aviation-oriented material, for the most part with a historical overtone, but also with some modern history in the making reporting. "*Flight Journal* is like no other aviation magazine in the world, covering the world of flight from its simple beginnings to its high-tech, no-holds-barred future. We put readers in the cockpit and let them live the thrill and adventure of the aviation experience, narrated by those who know the technology and made the history. Each issue brings the stories of flight—past, present and future—to life." No kill fee. Accepts queries by mail, e-mail. Accepts simultaneous submissions.

NONFICTION Needs historical, humor, interview, new product, personal experience, photo feature, technical. "We do not want any general aviation articles as in 'My Flight to Baja in my 172,' nor detailed recitations of the technical capabilities of an aircraft. Avoid historically accurate but bland chronologies of events." Send a single page outline of your idea. Provide 1 or more samples of prior articles, if practical. Length: 2,500-3,000 words. Lengthier pieces should be discussed in advance with the editors. **Pays $600.**

PHOTOS See submission guidelines. Reviews 5x7 prints. Negotiates payment individually.

TIPS "Use an unusual slant that makes your story idea unique; unusual pictures for an exciting presentation; fantastic but true accounts; lots of human interest. The designers, builders, pilots, and mechanics are what aviation is all about. We like an upbeat style, with humor, where it fits. Use sidebars to divide content of technically dense subjects. If you have a good personal story but aren't a professional-quality writer, we'll help with the writing."

$$ FLYING ADVENTURES

Aviation Publishing Corporation, El Monte Airport (EMT), P.O. Box 93613, Pasadena CA 91109-3613. (626)618-4000. **E-mail:** editor@flyingadventures.com. **Website:** www.flyingadventures.com. **Contact:** Lyn Freeman, editor-in-chief. **20% freelance written.** Bimonthly magazine covering lifestyle travel for owners and passengers of private aircraft. Articles cover upscale travelers. Estab. 1994. Circ. 135,000. Byline given for features. Pays on acceptance. No kill fee. Editorial lead time 2-8 weeks. Accepts queries by e-mail. Accepts simultaneous submissions. Responds immediately.

NONFICTION "Nothing nonrelevant or not our style. See magazine." Query with published clips. Length: 500-1,500 words. **Pays $150-300 for assigned and unsolicited articles.** Pays expenses of writers on assignment.

PHOTOS State availability. Captions, identification of subjects, model releases required. Reviews GIF/JPEG files. Negotiates payment individually. Buys all rights.

COLUMNS/DEPARTMENTS Publication has numerous departments; see magazine. **Buys 100+ mss/year.** Query with published clips. **Pays up to $150.**

TIPS "Send clip that fits our content and style. Must fit our style!"

$$$ KITPLANES

P.O. Box 1295, Dayton NV 89403. **E-mail:** editorial@kitplanes.com. **Website:** www.kitplanes.com. **Contact:** Paul Dye, editor in chief; Mark Schrimmer, managing editor. **50% freelance written. Eager to work with new/unpublished writers.** Monthly magazine covering self-construction of private aircraft for pilots and builders. Estab. 1984. Circ. 72,000. Byline given. Pays on publication. Publishes ms an average of 3 months after acceptance. Submit seasonal material 6 months in advance. Accepts queries by mail, e-mail. Accepts simultaneous submissions. Responds in 1 month to queries; in 6 weeks to mss. Sample copy: $6. Guidelines available online.

NONFICTION Needs general interest, how-to, interview, new product, personal experience, photo feature, technical. No general-interest aviation articles, or "My First Solo" type of articles. **Buys 80 mss/year.** Query. Interested in articles on all phases of aircraft construction, from basic design to flight trials to construction technique in wood, metal, and composite. Length: varies, but feature articles average about 2,000 words. **Pays $250-1,000, including story photos.** Pays expenses of writers on assignment.

PHOTOS State availability of or send photos. Captions, identification of subjects required. Pays $300 for cover photos. Buys one-time rights.

TIPS "*Kitplanes* contains very specific information—a writer must be extremely knowledgeable in the field. Major features are entrusted only to known writers. We cannot emphasize enough that articles must be directed at the individual aircraft builder. We need more 'how-to' photo features in all areas of home-built aircraft."

BUSINESS & FINANCE

$$ ALASKA BUSINESS MAGAZINE

Alaska Business Publishing Company, Inc., 501 W. Northern Lights Blvd., Ste. 100, Anchorage AK 99503-2577. (907)276-4373; (800)770-4373. **Fax:** (907)279-2900. **E-mail:** editor@akbizmag.com. **Website:** www.akbizmag.com. **Contact:** Kathryn Mackenzie, managing editor. **80% freelance written.** *Alaska Business*, produced in Alaska for Alaskans and other U.S. and international audiences interested in the business affairs of the 49th state, provides thorough and objective analysis of issues and trends of interest to the Alaska business community. Story queries and pitches should be focused on special sections and topics listed on the editorial calendar, located on the editorial page of the website: www.akbizmag.com/editorial. "We are an Alaska-centric publication and typically feature Alaskan writers. However, we are interested in talented writers from throughout the US with interest in commodities markets, financial writing, and the ability to write about highly-technical subjects." The magazine features stories about individuals, organizations, and companies shaping the Alaska economy. *Alaska Business* emphasizes the importance of enterprise and strives for statewide business coverage. Basic industry sectors are highlighted. Estab. 1985. Circ. 13,000-15,000. Byline given. Pays in month of publication. Offers $50 kill fee. Publishes ms an average of 2 months after acceptance. Assignments are due 2 months before date published. Editorial lead time 2-6 months. Deadlines are 2 months prior to month published. Ideas generally need to be submitted 4-6 months in advance for approval and assignment. Accepts queries by e-mail, online submission form. Responds immediately to queries. Past issues available online. Send to editor@akbizmag.com as inline text of an e-mail.

NONFICTION Needs interview, new product, opinion, photo feature, profile, technical, travel, engineering, architecture, construction, conventions & meetings, oil & gas, transportation, Pacific Northwest, telecom & technology, international trade, environmental services, energy & power, Alaska native corporations, mining, healthcare, resource development, employee relations, small business tips, entrepreneur advice. Special issues: "A different industry is featured each month in a special section. Read our magazine and editorial calendar for an idea of the material we assign." No fiction, poetry, or anything not pertinent to Alaska business. Rarely uses any unsolicited or unassigned articles. **Buys 200 mss/year.** Send query and 3 clips of previously published articles. Do not send complete mss. Does not republish blog posts. Length: 500-2,500 words. **Pays $150-500 for assigned articles.** Does not pay expenses.

REPRINTS Rarely publishes reprints from other publications. Reprint payment varies.

PHOTOS Contact: Kathryn Mackenzie, Managing Editor. State availability. Captions, identification of subjects, model releases required. Reviews high-res JPEG files. Pays $25-50/photo. Buys all rights.

TIPS "Always query the pro-Alaska business angle. Read our magazine for ideas on style and content. Send a well-written query on a subject of importance to Alaska businesses that is on the editorial calendar. We seek informative, entertaining articles on everything from entrepreneurs to heavy industry. We cover all sectors of Alaska business and industry. Read the magazine and study the website before submitting anything."

$$$$ ALBERTA VENTURE

Venture Publishing Inc., 10339-124 St., #300, Edmonton AB T5N 3W1 Canada. (780)990-0839. **E-mail:** admin@albertaventure.com. **Website:** www.albertaventure.com. **70% freelance written.** Monthly magazine covering business in Alberta. "Our readers are mostly business owners and managers in Alberta who read the magazine to keep up with trends and run their businesses better." Estab. 1997. Circ. 35,000. Byline given. Pays on publication. Offers 30% kill fee. Publishes ms an average of 2 months after acceptance. Editorial lead time 3 months. Submit seasonal material 3 months in advance. Accepts queries by e-mail. Accepts simultaneous submissions. Responds in 2 weeks to queries. Sample copy available online. Guidelines by e-mail.

NONFICTION Does not want company or product profiles. **Buys 75 mss/year.** Query. Length: 1,000-3,000 words. **Pays $300-2,000 (Canadian).** Pays expenses of writers on assignment.

PHOTOS Contact: Contact Kim Larson, art director. State availability. Identification of subjects required. Reviews GIF/JPEG files. Negotiates payment individually. Buys one-time rights.

$$ ATLANTIC BUSINESS MAGAZINE

Communications Ten, Ltd., P.O. Box 2356, Station C, St. John's NL A1C 6E7 Canada. (709)726-9300. **Fax:** (709)726-3013. **E-mail:** dchafe@atlanticbusinessmagazine.com. **Website:** www.atlanticbusinessmagazine.net. **Contact:** Dawn Chafe, executive editor. **80% freelance written.** Bimonthly magazine covering business in Atlantic Canada. "We discuss positive business developments, emphasizing that the 4 Atlantic provinces are a great place to do business." Estab. 1989. Circ. 30,000. Byline given. Pays within 30 days of publication. No kill fee. Publishes ms an average of 2 months after acceptance. Editorial lead time 6 months. Accepts queries by e-mail. Accepts simultaneous submissions. Sample copy free. Guidelines online.

NONFICTION Needs general interest, interview, new product. "We don't want religious, technical, or scholarly material. We are not an academic magazine. We are interested only in stories concerning business topics specific to the 4 Canadian provinces of Nova

Scotia, New Brunswick, Prince Edward Island, and Newfoundland and Labrador." **Buys 36 mss/year.** Query with published clips. Length: 1,000-1,200 words for features; 3,500-4,000 for cover stories. **Pays 40¢/word.** Pays expenses of writers on assignment.

PHOTOS Send photos. Captions, identification of subjects required. Reviews contact sheets, transparencies, prints. Negotiates payment individually. Buys one-time rights.

COLUMNS/DEPARTMENTS Query with published clips.

TIPS "Writers should submit their areas of interest as well as samples of their work and, if possible, suggested story ideas."

$$ CORPORATE CONNECTICUT MAGAZINE

Corporate World LLC, P.O. Box 290724, Wethersfield CT 06129. **E-mail:** editor@corpct.com. **Website:** www.corpct.com. **50% freelance written.** Business magazine. Corporate/business leaders, entrepreneurs, technology, innovation. *Corporate Connecticut* is devoted to people who make business happen in the private sector and who create innovative change across public arenas. Centered in the Northeast between New York and Boston, Connecticut is positioned in a coastal corridor with a dense affluent population who are highly mobile, accomplished and educated. Estab. 2001. Byline given. Pays on publication. Offers 25% kill fee. Publishes ms an average of 2-3 months after acceptance. Editorial lead time 3-6 months. Submit seasonal material 10-12 months in advance. Accepts queries by mail, e-mail. Responds in 2 weeks to queries. Sample copy for #10 SASE.

NONFICTION Query with published clips. **Varying fees; excellence.** Pays expenses of writers on assignment.

PHOTOS State availability.

TIPS "Review our online content to get a general feel for the publication. Aim high, do the research, pitch with C-level perspective for business, technology, people."

$$ DOLLARS & SENSE

Real World Economics, Economic Affairs Bureau, Inc., 89 South St., LL02, Boston MA 02111. (617)447-2177. **Fax:** (617)477-2179. **E-mail:** dollars@dollarsandsense.org. **Website:** www.dollarsandsense.org. **Contact:** Alejandro Reuss and Chris Sturr, co-editors. **10% freelance written.** Bimonthly magazine covering economic, environmental, and social justice. "*Dollars & Sense* publishes economic news and analysis, reports on economic justice activism, primers on economic topics, and critiques of the mainstream media's coverage of the economy. Our readers include professors, students, and activists who value our smart and accessible economic coverage. We explain the workings of the U.S. and international economics and provide left perspectives on current economic affairs." Estab. 1974. Circ. 8,000. Byline given. Pays on publication. No kill fee. Publishes ms an average of 4 months after acceptance. Editorial lead time 3 months. Submit seasonal material 2 months in advance. Accepts queries by mail, e-mail. Accepts simultaneous submissions. Sample copy: $5 or on website. Guidelines online.

NONFICTION Special issues: Wants in-depth articles on a broad range of topics. **Buys 6 mss/year.** Query with published clips. Length: 1,500-3,000 words. **Pays up to $200.** Pays expenses of writers on assignment.

PHOTOS State availability. Captions, identification of subjects required. Negotiates payment individually. Buys one-time rights.

COLUMNS/DEPARTMENTS Active Culture (briefs on activism), 250-400 words; Reviews (coverage of recent books, movies, and other media), 700 words. Query with published clips.

TIPS "Be familiar with our magazine and the types of communities interested in reading us. *Dollars & Sense* is a progressive economics magazine that explains in a popular way both the workings of the economy and struggles to change it. Articles may be on the environment, the World Bank, community organizing, urban conflict, inflation, unemployment, union reform, welfare, changes in government regulation—a broad range of topics that have an economic theme. Find samples of our latest issue on our homepage."

$$ ELLIOTT WAVE INTERNATIONAL PUBLICATIONS

Elliott Wave International, P.O. Box 1618, Gainesville GA 30503. (770)536-0309. **E-mail:** customercare@elliottwave.com. **Website:** www.elliottwave.com. **10% freelance written.** Our publications are weekly to monthly in print and online formats covering investment markets. An understanding of technical market analysis is indispensible, knowledge of Elliott wave analysis even better. Clear, conversational prose is mandatory. Estab. 1979. Circ. 80,000. Byline sometimes given. Pays on publication. Publishes ms an average of 1 month after acceptance. Editorial lead time 1 month. Accepts queries by e-mail. Accepts simultaneous submissions.

NONFICTION Needs essays, how-to, technical. **Buys 12 mss/year.** Query with published clips. Length: 500-800 words. **Pays $100-200.**

COLUMNS/DEPARTMENTS Pop culture and the stock market, 500-800 words. **Buys 12 mss/year.** Query with published clips. **Pays $100-200.**

$$ THE LANE REPORT

Lane Communications Group, 201 E. Main St., 14th Floor, Lexington KY 40507. (859)244-3500. **E-mail:** markgreen@lanereport.com. **Website:** www.lanereport.com. **Contact:** Mark Green, managing editor. **60% freelance written.** Monthly magazine covering statewide business. *The Lane Report* is an intelligent, enterprising magazine that informs readers and drives a statewide dialogue by highlighting important business stories in Kentucky. Estab. 1985. Circ. 15,000. Byline given. Pays on publication. No kill fee. Editorial lead time 6 weeks. Submit seasonal material 3 months in advance. Accepts queries by mail, e-mail. Accepts simultaneous submissions. Responds in 1 month to queries. Sample copy and writer's guidelines free.

NONFICTION Needs essays, interview, new product, photo feature. **Buys 30-40 mss/year.** Query with published clips. Do not send unsolicited mss. Looking for major trends shaping the state, noteworthy business and practices, and stories with sweeping implications across industry sectors and state regions. Length: 750-3,000 words. **Pays $150-375.** Pays expenses of writers on assignment.

PHOTOS State availability. Identification of subjects required. Reviews contact sheets, negatives, transparencies, prints, digital images. Negotiates payment individually. Buys one-time rights.

COLUMNS/DEPARTMENTS Fast Lane Briefs (recent news and trends and how they might shape the future), 100-400 words; Opinion (opinion on a business or economic issue about which you, the writer, feel passionate and qualified to write), 750 words; Entrepreneurs (profile of a particularly interesting or quirky member of the business community), 750-1,400 words. Query.

TIPS "As Kentucky's only statewide business and economics publication, we look for stories that incorporate perspectives from the Commonwealth's various regions and prominent industries—tying it into the national picture when appropriate. We also look for insightful profiles and interviews of Kentucky's entrepreneurs and business leaders."

$$ THE NETWORK JOURNAL

The Network Journal Communication, 39 Broadway, Suite 2430, New York NY 10006. (212)962-3791. **Fax:** (212)962-3537. **E-mail:** tnjeditors@tnj.com. **Website:** www.tnj.com. **25% freelance written.** Monthly magazine covering business and career articles. *The Network Journal* caters to black professionals and small-business owners, providing quality coverage on business, financial, technology, and career news germane to the black community. Estab. 1993. Circ. 25,000. Byline given. Pays on publication. Editorial lead time 2 months. Submit seasonal material 3 months in advance. Accepts queries by mail, e-mail, fax, phone. Accepts simultaneous submissions. Sample copy for $1 or online. Writer's guidelines for SASE.

NONFICTION Needs how-to, interview. Send complete ms. Length: 1,200-1,500 words. **Pays $150-200.** Pays expenses of writers on assignment.

PHOTOS Send photos. Identification of subjects required. Offers $25/photo. Buys one time rights.

COLUMNS/DEPARTMENTS Book reviews, 700-800 words; career management and small business development, 800 words. **Pays $100.**

TIPS We are looking for vigorous writing and reporting for our cover stories and feature articles. Pieces should have gripping leads, quotes that actually say something and that come from several sources. Unless it is a column, please do not submit a 1-source story. Always remember that your article must contain a nutgraph—that's usually the third paragraph telling the reader what the story is about and why you are telling it now. Editorializing should be kept to a minimum. If you're writing a column, make sure your opinions are well-supported.

CAREER, COLLEGE & ALUMNI

$$ AFRICAN-AMERICAN CAREER WORLD

Equal Opportunity Publications, Inc., 445 Broad Hollow Rd., Suite 425, Melville NY 11747. (631)421-9421. **E-mail:** bloehr@eop.com. **Website:** www.eop.com. **Contact:** Barbara Capella Loehr, editor. **60%**

freelance written. Semiannual magazine focused on African-American students and professionals in all disciplines. Estab. 1969. Byline given. Pays on publication. No kill fee. Publishes ms an average of 3 months after acceptance. Editorial lead time 3 months. Accepts queries by mail, e-mail. Accepts simultaneous submissions. Sample copy free. Guidelines free.

NONFICTION Needs how-to, interview, personal experience. "We do not want articles that are too general." Query. Length: 1,500-2,500 words. **Pays $350 for assigned articles.** Pays expenses of writers on assignment.

TIPS "Gear articles to our audience."

$$$$ HARVARD MAGAZINE

7 Ware St., Cambridge MA 02138. (617)495-5746. **Fax:** (617)495-0324. **E-mail:** john_rosenberg@harvard.edu. **Website:** www.harvardmagazine.com. **Contact:** John S. Rosenberg, editor. **35-50% freelance written.** Bimonthly magazine for Harvard University faculty, alumni, and students. Estab. 1898. Circ. 245,000. Byline given. Pays on publication. No kill fee. Publishes ms an average of 4 months after acceptance. Editorial lead time 1 year. Accepts queries by mail, e-mail. Accepts simultaneous submissions. Responds in 1 month to queries and mss. Sample copy online.

NONFICTION Needs book excerpts, essays, interview, journalism on Harvard-related intellectual subjects. **Buys 20-30 mss/year.** Query with published clips. Length: 800-10,000 words. **Pays $400-3,000.** Pays expenses of writers on assignment.

$$ HISPANIC CAREER WORLD

Equal Opportunity Publications, Inc., 445 Broad Hollow Rd., Suite 425, Melville NY 11747. (631)421-9421, ext. 12. **Fax:** (631)421-1352. **E-mail:** bloehr@eop.com. **Website:** www.eop.com. **Contact:** Barbara Capella Loehr, editor. **60% freelance written.** Semiannual magazine aimed at Hispanic students and professionals in all disciplines. Estab. 1969. Byline given. Pays on publication. No kill fee. Publishes ms an average of 3 months after acceptance. Editorial lead time 3 months. Accepts queries by mail, e-mail, fax, phone. Accepts simultaneous submissions. Responds in 2 weeks to queries; 2 months to mss. Sample copy free. Guidelines free.

NONFICTION Needs how-to, interview, personal experience. Query. Length: 1,500-2,500 words. **Pays $350 for assigned articles.**

TIPS "Gear articles to our audience."

$$$$ NOTRE DAME MAGAZINE

University of Notre Dame, 500 Grace Hall, Notre Dame IN 46556-5612. (574)631-5335. **Fax:** (574)631-6767. **E-mail:** ndmag@nd.edu. **Website:** magazine.nd.edu. **Contact:** Kerry Temple, editor; Kerry Prugh, art director. **50% freelance written.** "We are a university magazine with a scope as broad as that found at a university, but we place our discussion in a moral, ethical and spiritual context reflecting our Catholic heritage." Estab. 1972. Circ. 150,000. Byline given. Pays on acceptance. No kill fee. Publishes ms an average of 1 year after acceptance. Accepts queries by mail, e-mail. Accepts simultaneous submissions. Responds in 2 months to queries. Sample copy available online and by request. Guidelines online.

NONFICTION Needs essays, general interest, personal experience, profile. **Buys 35 mss/year.** Query with published clips. Length: 600-3,000 words. **Pays $250-3,000.** Pays expenses of writers on assignment.

PHOTOS State availability. Identification of subjects, model releases required. Buys one-time, first and electronic rights.

COLUMNS/DEPARTMENTS CrossCurrents (essays, deal with a wide array of issues—some topical, some personal, some serious, some light). Query with or without published clips or send complete ms.

TIPS "The editors are always looking for new writers and fresh ideas. However, the caliber of the magazine and frequency of its publication dictate that the writing meet very high standards. The editors value articles strong in storytelling quality, journalistic technique, and substance. They do not encourage promotional or nostalgia pieces, stories on sports, or essays that are sentimentally religious."

$$ RIPON MAGAZINE

P.O. Box 248, 300 Seward St., Ripon WI 54971-0248. (920)748-8322. **Fax:** (920)748-9262. **Website:** www.ripon.edu/magazine. **15% freelance written.** Quarterly magazine that contains information relating to Ripon College and is mailed to alumni and friends of the college. Estab. 1851. Circ. 14,000. Byline given. Pays on publication. Publishes ms an average of 3 months after acceptance. Accepts queries by mail, e-mail, fax, phone. Accepts simultaneous submissions. Responds in 2 weeks to queries.

NONFICTION Needs historical, interview. **Buys 4 mss/year.** Send complete ms. Length: 250-1,000 words. **Pays $25-350.**

PHOTOS State availability. Captions, model releases required. Reviews contact sheets. Offers additional payment for photos accepted with ms. Buys one time rights.

TIPS Story ideas must have a direct connection to Ripon College.

$$ WORKFORCE DIVERSITY FOR ENGINEERING & IT PROFESSIONALS

Equal Opportunity Publications, Inc., 445 Broad Hollow Rd., Suite 425, Melville NY 11747. (631)421-9421. **Fax:** (631)421-1352. **E-mail:** info@eop.com; bloehr@eop.com. **Website:** www.eop.com. **Contact:** Barbara Capella Loehr, editor. **60% freelance written.** Quarterly magazine addressing workplace issues affecting technical professional women, members of minority groups, and people with disabilities. Estab. 1969. Byline given. Pays on publication. No kill fee. Publishes ms an average of 3 months after acceptance. Editorial lead time 3 months. Accepts queries by mail, e-mail, fax, phone. Accepts simultaneous submissions. Responds in 2 weeks to queries. Responds in 2 months to mss. Sample copy free. Guidelines free.

NONFICTION Needs how-to, interview, personal experience. We do not want articles that are too general. Query. Length: 1,500-2,500 words. **Pays $350 for assigned articles.** Pays expenses of writers on assignment.

TIPS "Gear articles to our audience."

CHILD CARE & PARENTAL GUIDANCE

$ ATLANTA PARENT

2346 Perimeter Park Dr., Atlanta GA 30341. (770)454-7599. **E-mail:** editor@atlantaparent.com; atlantaparent@atlantaparent.com. **Website:** www.atlantaparent.com. **Contact:** Editor. **50% freelance written.** Monthly magazine for parents in the Atlanta metro area with children from birth to 18 years old. "*Atlanta Parent* magazine has been a valuable resource for Atlanta families since 1983. It is the only magazine in the Atlanta area providing pertinent, local, and award-winning family-oriented articles and information. Atlanta parents rely on us for features that are timely, informative, and reader-friendly on important issues such as childcare, family life, education, adolescence, motherhood, health, and teens. Fun, easy, and inexpensive family activities and crafts as well as the humorous side of parenting are also important to our readers." Estab. 1983. Byline given. Pays on publication. Publishes ms an average of 3 months after acceptance. Submit seasonal material 6 months in advance. Accepts queries by mail, e-mail. Accepts simultaneous submissions. Responds in 4 months to queries. Sample copy: $3.

NONFICTION Needs general interest, how-to, humor, interview, travel. No religious or philosophical discussions. **Buys 60 mss/year.** Send complete ms by mail or e-mail. Length: 800-1,200 words. **Pays $5-50.** Pays expenses of writers on assignment.

REPRINTS Send tearsheet or photocopy with rights for sale noted and information about when and where the material previously appeared. Pays $30-50.

PHOTOS State availability of or send photos. Reviews 3x5 photos. Offers $10/photo. Buys one-time rights.

TIPS "Articles should be geared to problems or situations of families and parents. Should include down-to-earth tips and be clearly written. No philosophical discussions. We're also looking for well-written humor."

$$ BIRMINGHAM PARENT

Evans Publishing LLC, 3590-B Hwy 31S. #289, Pelham AL 35124. (205)987-7700. **Fax:** (205)987-7600. **E-mail:** carol@biringhamparent.com. **Website:** www.birminghamparent.com. **Contact:** Carol Evans, publisher/editor. **75% freelance written.** Monthly magazine covering family issues, parenting, education, babies to teens, health care, anything involving parents raising children. "We are a free, local parenting publication in central Alabama. All of our stories carry some type of local slant. Parenting magazines abound: we are the source for the local market." Estab. 2004. Circ. 30,000. Byline given. Pays within 30 days of publication. Offers 20% kill fee. Publishes ms an average of 3-4 months after acceptance. Editorial lead time 3-4 months. Submit seasonal material 4 months in advance. Accepts queries by e-mail. Accepts simultaneous submissions. Responds in 2-3 weeks to queries. Responds in 2-3 months to mss. Sample copy for $3. Guidelines available online.

NONFICTION Needs book excerpts, general interest, how-to, interview, parenting. Does not want first person pieces. "Our pieces educate and inform; we don't take stories without sources." **Buys 24 mss/year.** Send complete ms. Length: 350-2,500 words. **Pays $50-350 for assigned articles. Pays $35-200 for unsolicited articles.** Pays expenses of writers on assignment.

PHOTOS State availability. Captions, identification of subjects, model releases required. Reviews GIF/JPEG files. Negotiates payment individually; offers no additional payment for photos accepted with ms. Buys one-time rights.

COLUMNS/DEPARTMENTS Parenting Solo (single parenting), 650 words; Baby & Me (dealing with newborns or pregnancy), 650 words; Teens (raising teenagers), 650-1,500 words. **Buys 36 mss/year.** Query with published clips or send complete ms. **Pays $35-200.**

TIPS "Present your story so that you can add local slant to it, or suggest to us how to do so. Please no first person opinion pieces—no '10 great gifts for teachers,' for example, without sources. We expect some sources for our informative stories."

$ CHESAPEAKE FAMILY LIFE

Jefferson Communications, 121 Cathedral Street, Third Floor, Annapolis MD 21401. (410) 263-1641. **Fax:** (410) 280-0255. **E-mail:** editor@chesapeakefamily.com; calendar@jecoannapolis.com. **Website:** www.chesapeakefamily.com. **Contact:** Betsy Stein, editor. **80% freelance written.** Monthly magazine, website and e-mail newsletters covering parenting and other topics of interest to parents in Maryland. *Chesapeake Family LIFE* publishes a free, regional parenting publication, annual publications and e-mail newsletters serving readers in the Anne Arundel, Calvert, Prince George's and Queen Anne's counties of Maryland. Our goal is to identify tips, resources, and products that will make our readers' lives easier. "We answer the questions they don't have time to ask, doing the research for them so they have the information they need to make better decisions for their families' health, education, and well-being." Articles must have local angle and resources. Estab. 1990. Circ. 34,000. Byline given. Publishes ms an average of 2 months after acceptance. Editorial lead time 3-6 months. Submit seasonal material 4 months in advance. Accepts queries by mail, e-mail, fax. Accepts simultaneous submissions. Guidelines available online.

NONFICTION Needs how-to, interview, profile, travel. No general personal essays (however, personal anecdotes leading into a story with general applicability is fine). **Buys 25 mss/year.** Send complete ms. Length: 800-1,200 words. **Pays $75-150. Pays $35-50 for unsolicited articles.**

PHOTOS State availability. Model releases required. Reviews prints, GIF/JPEG files. Offers no additional payment for photos accepted with ms, unless original, assigned photo is selected for the cover.

COLUMNS/DEPARTMENTS Buys 25 mss/year. Pays $35-50.

TIPS "A writer's best chance is to know the issues specific to our local readers. Know how to research the issues well, answer the questions our readers need to know, and give them information they can act on—and present it in a friendly, conversational tone."

$ HUDSON VALLEY PARENT

The Professional Image, 174 South St., Newburgh NY 12550. (845)562-3606. **E-mail:** editor@excitingread.com. **Website:** www.hvparent.com. **Contact:** Sara Dunn. **95% freelance written.** Monthly magazine covering local parents and families. Estab. 1994. Circ. 80,000. Byline given. Pays on publication. No kill fee. Publishes ms an average of 3 months after acceptance. Editorial lead time 4 months. Submit seasonal material 4 months in advance. Accepts queries by e-mail. Accepts simultaneous submissions. Responds in 2-4 weeks to mss. Sample copy free. Guidelines available online.

NONFICTION Needs expose, general interest, humor, interview, personal experience. **Buys 20 mss/year.** Query. Length: 700-1,200 words. **Pays $80-120 for assigned articles. Pays $25-35 for unsolicited articles.** Pays expenses of writers on assignment.

REPRINTS Pays $25-35 for reprints.

$ MEDIA FOR LIVING, VALLEY LIVING MAGAZINE

Shalom Foundation, P.O. Box 1501, Harrisonburg VA 22803. (540)433-5351. **E-mail:** info@valleyliving.org. **E-mail:** melodie@valleyliving.org. **Website:** www.valleyliving.org. Lindsey Shantz. **80% freelance written.** Quarterly magazine covering family living. Articles focus on giving general encouragement for families of all ages and stages. "Our bias is to use articles *showing* rather than telling readers how to raise families (stories rather than how-to). We aim for articles that are well written, understandable, challenging (not the same old thing you've read elsewhere); they should stimulate readers to dig a little deeper, but not too deep with academic or technical language; that are interesting and fit our theological perspective (Christian) but are not preachy or overly patriotic. No favorable mentions of smoking, drinking, cursing, etc. We want our stories and articles to be very practical and upbeat. We do not assume a Christian audience. Writers need to take this into account. Personal-experience stories are welcome but are not the only approach. Our audience? Children, teenagers, singles, married couples, right on through to retired persons. We cover the wide variety of subjects that people face in the home and workplace. (See theme list in our guidelines online.)" Estab. 1990. Circ. 11,000. Byline given. Pays on publication. No kill fee. Publishes ms an average of 6-12 months after acceptance. Editorial lead time 4-6 months. Submit seasonal material 6 months in advance. Accepts queries by mail, e-mail, online submission form. Accepts simultaneous submissions. Responds in 2 months to queries; 2-4 months to mss. Sample copy for SAE with 9x12 envelope and 4 first-class stamps.

NONFICTION Needs general interest, how-to, humor, inspirational, personal experience. "We do not use devotional materials intended for Christian audiences. We seldom use pet stories and receive way too many grief/death/dealing-with-serious-illness stories. We publish in March, June, September, and December, so holidays that occur in other months are not usually the subject of articles." **Buys 48-52 mss/year.** Query. Length: 500-1,200 words. **Pays $35-60.**

PHOTOS Contact: Lindsey Shantz. State availability. Captions, identification of subjects, model releases required. Reviews 4x6 prints, GIF/JPEG files. Offers $15-25/photo. Buys one-time rights.

TIPS "We prefer 'good news' stories that are uplifting and noncontroversial in nature. We want articles that tell stories of people solving problems and dealing with personal issues rather than essays or 'preaching.' If you submit electronically, it is very helpful if you put the specific title of the submission in the subject line, and please include your e-mail address in the body of the e-mail or on your ms. Also, always include your address and phone number."

$ SAN DIEGO FAMILY MAGAZINE

Special Needs Resource Foundation of San Diego (non-profit), 1475 6th Ave., 5th Floor, San Diego CA 92101-3200. (619)685-6970. **Fax:** (619)685-6978. **E-mail:** family@sandiegofamily.com. **E-mail:** editor@sandiegofamily.com. **Website:** www.sandiegofamily.com; www.SNRFSD.org. **100% freelance written.** "*San Diego Family Magazine* is a regional monthly family publication. We focus on providing current, informative and interesting editorial about parenting and family life that educates and entertains." Estab. 1982. Circ. 100,000. Byline given. Pays on publication. No kill fee. Publishes an 1-6 months after acceptance. Editorial lead time 4 months. Submit seasonal material 2-6 months in advance. Accepts queries by e-mail. Accepts simultaneous submissions. Responds in 1 week-1 month to queries of interest. Sometimes no response if e-mail is "lost" in inbox. Sample copy for $4.50 to P.O. Box 23960, San Diego CA 92193. Guidelines online.

NONFICTION Needs general interest, how-to, interview, personal experience, technical, informational articles. Special issues: Summer camps: March through June *Flourishing Families*, a guide for families with special needs (annual); *Out and About*, an adventure guide for local and visiting families (annual). Does not want personal essays, opinion pieces. **Buys 350-500 mss/year.** Query. Length: 500-950 words. **Pays $35-120.**

REPRINTS E-mail with rights for sale, ted and information about when and where the material previously appeared.

FILLERS Buys 0-6 mss/year. Send complete ms. Length: 200-600 words.

TIPS "We publish short, informational articles. We give preference to stories about San Diego County personalities/events/etc., and stories that include regional resources for our readers. This is a local publication; don't address a national audience."

$$$$$ TODAY'S PARENT

Rogers Media, Inc., 1 Mt. Pleasant Rd., 8th Floor, Toronto Ontario M4Y 2Y5 Canada. (416)764-2883. **Fax:** (416)764-2894. **E-mail:** editors@todaysparent.com. **Website:** www.todaysparent.com. **Contact:** Alicia Kowalewski, art director. Monthly magazine for parents with children up to the age of 12. Circ. 2 million. No kill fee. Editorial lead time 5 months. Accepts simultaneous submissions.

NONFICTION Length: 1,800-2,500 words. **Pays $1,500-2,200.** Pays expenses of writers on assignment.

COLUMNS/DEPARTMENTS What's New (games/apps/movies/toys); Health (parents and children); Behaviour; Relationships; Steps and Stages; How Does He/She Do It; Bright Idea; Food/In the Kitchen.

TIPS "Because we promote ourselves as a Canadian magazine, we try to use only Canadian writers and focus on Canadian content."

$$ TWINS™ MAGAZINE

30799 Pinetree Rd., #256, Cleveland OH 44124. **E-mail:** twinseditor@twinsmagazine.com. **Website:** www.twinsmagazine.com. **Contact:** Keith Shirley, editor. **50% freelance written.** "We now publish 8 issues/year—4 print/4 digital covering all aspects of parenting twins/multiples. *Twins* is a national/international publication that provides informational and educational articles regarding the parenting of twins, triplets, and more. All articles must be multiple specific and have an upbeat, hopeful, and/or positive ending." Estab. 1984. Circ. 35,000. Byline given. Pays on publication. Editorial lead time 4 months. Submit seasonal material 6 months in advance. Accepts queries by e-mail, online submission form. Response time varies. Sample copy for $5 or on website. Guidelines online.

NONFICTION Needs personal experience, professional experience as it relates to multiples. Nothing on cloning, pregnancy reduction, or fertility issues. **Buys 12 mss/year.** Send complete ms. Length: 650-1,100 words. **Pays $25-250 for assigned articles. Pays $25-125 for unsolicited articles.** Pays expenses of writers on assignment.

PHOTOS State availability. Identification of subjects required. Offers no additional payment for photos accepted with ms.

COLUMNS/DEPARTMENTS A Word From Dad; Double Takes; Mom-2-Mom; LOL: Laugh Out Loud; Family Health; Resource Round Up; Tales From Twins; Twins in the News; Twin Start Spotlight; & Research. Pays $25-75. **Buys 8-10 mss/year.** Query with or without published clips or send complete ms. **Pays $40-75.**

TIPS "All department articles must have helpful information for parents of multiples."

COMIC BOOKS

$ THE COMICS JOURNAL

Fantagraphics Books, 7563 Lake City Way NE, Seattle WA 98115. (206)524-1967. **Fax:** (206)524-2104. **E-mail:** editorial@tcj.com. **Website:** www.tcj.com. Editorial Coordinator: Kristy Valenti. Magazine covering the comics medium from an arts-first perspective on a six-week schedule. "*The Comics Journal* is one of the nation's most respected single-arts magazines, providing its readers with an eclectic mix of industry news, professional interviews, and reviews of current work. Due to its reputation as the American magazine with an interest in comics as an art form, the *Journal* has subscribers worldwide, and in this country serves as an important window into the world of comics for several general arts and news magazines." Byline given. Accepts queries by mail, e-mail. Accepts simultaneous submissions. Guidelines available online.

NONFICTION Needs essays, interview, opinion, reviews. Send complete ms. Length: 2,000-3,000 words. **Pays 4¢/word, and 1 contributor's copy.** Pays expenses of writers on assignment.

COLUMNS/DEPARTMENTS On Theory, Art and Craft (2,000-3,000 words); Firing Line (reviews 1,000-5,000 words); Bullets (reviews 400 words or less). Send inquiries, samples **Pays 4¢/word, and 1 contributor's copy.**

TIPS "Like most magazines, the best writers guideline is to look at the material within the magazine and give something that approximates that material in terms of approach and sophistication. Anything else is a waste of time."

CONSUMER SERVICE & BUSINESS OPPORTUNITY

$$$$ CONSUMERS DIGEST

Consumers Digest Communications LLC, 520 Lake-Cook Rd., Suite 500, Deerfield IL 60015. (847)607-3000. **Fax:** (847)607-3009. **E-mail:** editor@consumersdigest.com. **Website:** www.consumersdigest.com. **95% freelance written.** Bimonthly magazine covering consumer matters, new products/services. *Consumers' Digest* is designed to provide opinions and recommendations in regard to consumer issues. Estab. 1959. Byline given. Pays on acceptance. Offers 50% kill fee. Publishes ms an average of 2 months after acceptance. Editorial lead time 3-4 months. Submit seasonal material 8 months in advance. Accepts queries by mail, e-mail. Accepts simultaneous submissions.

NONFICTION Needs expose, general interest, new product. **Buys 70 mss/year.** Query. Length: 1,300-3,500 words. **Pays 75¢-$1/word.** Pays expenses of writers on assignment.

$$ HOME BUSINESS MAGAZINE

20664 Jutland Place, Lakeville MN 55044. **E-mail:** editor@homebusinessmag.com. **Website:** www.homebusinessmag.com. **Contact:** Sherilyn Colleen. **75% freelance written.** Covers every angle of the home-based business market including: cutting edge editorial by well-known authorities on sales and marketing, business operations, the home office, franchising, business opportunities, network marketing, mail order, and other subjects to help readers choose, manage, and prosper in a home-based business; display advertising, classified ads and a directory of home-based businesses; technology, the Internet, computers, and the future of home-based business; home-office editorial including management advice, office set-up, and product descriptions; business opportunities, franchising and work-from-home success stories. Estab. 1993. Circ. 105,000. No kill fee. Publishes ms an average of 6 months after acceptance. Editorial lead time 6 months. Submit seasonal material 6 months in advance. Accepts queries by e-mail. Accepts simultaneous submissions. Sample copy for sae with 9x12 envelope and 8 first-class stamps. Guidelines for #10 SASE.

NONFICTION Needs book excerpts, general interest, how-to, inspirational, interview, new product, personal experience, photo feature. No non-home business related topics. **Buys 40 mss/year.** Send complete ms. "Send complete information by e-mail. We encourage writers to submit feature articles (2-3 pages) and departmental articles (1 page). Please submit polished, well-written, organized material. It helps to provide subheadings within the article. Boxes, lists, and bullets are encouraged because they make your article easier to read, use, and reference by the reader. A primary problem in the past is that articles do not stick to the subject of the title. Please pay attention to the focus of your article and to your title. Please don't call to get the status of your submission. We will call if we're interested in publishing the submission." Length: 200-1,000 words. **Pays 20¢/published word for work-for-hire assignments; 50-word byline for unsolicited articles.** Pays expenses of writers on assignment.

PHOTOS Identification of subjects required. Offers no additional payment for photos accepted with ms.

COLUMNS/DEPARTMENTS Marketing & Sales; Money Corner; Home Office; Management; Technology; Working Smarter; Franchising; Network Marketing, all 650 words. Send complete ms.

CONTEMPORARY CULTURE

$$ A&U

America's AIDS Magazine, Art & Understanding, Inc., 25 Monroe St., Suite 205, Albany NY 12210-2729. (518)426-9010. **Fax:** (518)436-5354. **E-mail:** chaelneedle@mac.com. **Website:** www.aumag.org. Poetry Editor: Noah Stetzer. Fiction Editor: Raymond Luczak. **Contact:** Chael Needle, managing editor. **50% freelance written.** Monthly national nonprofit print magazine covering cultural, political, and medical responses to HIV/AIDS, including poetry, fiction and drama. Estab. 1991. Circ. 135,000. Byline given. Pays 1-3 months after publication. Publishes ms an average of 1-3 months after acceptance. Editorial lead time 6 months. Accepts queries by e-mail. Accepts simultaneous submissions. Responds in 1 month to queries; in 2 months to mss. Sample copy: $5. Guidelines online.

NONFICTION Needs book excerpts, essays, general interest, humor, interview, opinion, personal experience, photo feature, profile. **Buys 6 mss/year.** Query with published clips. Length: 800-1,200 words. **Pays $150-300 for assigned articles.**

COLUMNS/DEPARTMENTS The Culture of AIDS (reviews of books, music, film), 300 words; Viewpoint (personal opinion), 750 words. **Buys 8 mss/year.** Send complete ms. **Pays $175.**

FICTION **Contact:** Raymond Luczak. Literary electronic submissions, as Word attachments, may be mailed to Brent Calderwood, literary editor, at aumaglit@gmail.com. Pay rate schedule available upon request. Send complete ms. Length: up to 1,500 words. **Pays $50.**

POETRY **Contact:** Noah Stetzer. Accepts any length/style (shorter works preferred). Buys 8-10 poems/year. **Pays $50.**

TIPS "We're looking for more articles on youth and HIV/AIDS; more international coverage; celebrity interviews; more coverage of how the pandemic is affecting historically underrepresented communities. We are also looking for literary submissions that address the past and present AIDS epidemic in fresh ways. Each year, we sponsor the Christopher Hewitt Award, given to the best poem, short story, creative nonfiction piece, and drama submitted."

$$O ADBUSTERS

Adbusters Media Foundation, 1243 W. Seventh Ave., Vancouver BC V6H 1B7 Canada. (604)736-9401. **E-mail:** editor@adbusters.org. **Website:** www.adbusters.org. **50% freelance written.** Bimonthly magazine on consumerism. "Based in Vancouver, British Columbia, Canada, *Adbusters* is a not-for-profit, reader-supported magazine concerned with the erosion of our physical and cultural environments by commercial forces. Since 1989, the magazine has been featured in hundreds of alternative and mainstream newspapers, magazines, television, and radio shows. Known worldwide for sparking Occupy Wall

Street, *Adbusters* is also responsible for social media campaigns such as Buy Nothing Day and Digital Detox Week. Included in the magazine are incisive philosophical articles and activist commentary, coupled with impact design that seeks to unbound the traditional magazine format. Issues relevant to our contemporary moment, such as media concentration, climate change, and genetically modified foods, are regularly featured. We seek out a world where economy and ecology exist in harmony. By challenging people to become participants as opposed to spectators, *Adbusters* takes aim at corporate disinformation, global injustice, and the industries and governments who actively pollute and destroy our physical and mental commons." Estab. 1989. Circ. 90,000. Byline given. Pays 1 month after publication. Accepts queries by mail, e-mail, fax. Accepts simultaneous submissions. Guidelines available online.

NONFICTION Needs essays, expose, interview, opinion. **Buys variable mss/year.** Query. Length: 250-3,000 words. **Pays $100/page for unsolicited articles; 50¢/word for solicited articles.** Pays expenses of writers on assignment.

FICTION Inquire about themes.

POETRY Inquire about themes.

$$$ FLAUNT

1422 N. Highland Ave., Los Angeles CA 90028. (323)836-1000. **E-mail:** info@flauntmagazine.com. **Website:** www.flaunt.com. **Contact:** Luis Barajas, editor in chief. **40% freelance written.** Monthly magazine covering culture, arts, entertainment, music, fashion, and film. "*Flaunt* features the bold work of emerging photographers, writers, artists, and musicians. The quality of the content is mirrored in the sophisticated, interactive format of the magazine, using advanced printing techniques, fold-out articles, beautiful papers, and inserts to create a visually stimulating, surprisingly readable, and intelligent book that pushes the magazine into the realm of art-object. *Flaunt* has, since 1998, made it a point to break new ground, earning itself a reputation as an engine of the avant-garde and an outlet for the culture of the cutting edge. *Flaunt* takes pride in reinventing itself each month, while consistently representing a hybrid of all that is interesting in entertaiment, fashion, music, design, film, art, and literature." Estab. 1998. Circ. 100,000. Byline given. No kill fee. Publishes ms an average of 3 months after acceptance. Editorial lead time 3 months. Submit seasonal material 3 months in advance. Accepts queries by mail, e-mail. Accepts simultaneous submissions. Responds in 2 weeks to queries; in 1 month to mss.

NONFICTION Needs book excerpts, essays, general interest, historical, humor, interview, new product, opinion, personal experience, photo feature, travel. Special issues: Special issues: September and March (fashion issues); February (men's issue); May (music issue). **Buys 20 mss/year.** Query with published clips. Length: 500-5,000 words. **Pays up to $500.** Pays expenses of writers on assignment.

PHOTOS State availability. Identification of subjects, model releases required. Reviews contact sheets, transparencies, prints, GIF/JPEG files. Buys one-time rights.

GOOD MAGAZINE

601 West 26th Street, Suite 235, New York NY 10001. (323)556-6780. **E-mail:** submissions@goodinc.com. **Website:** www.goodmagazine.com. *GOOD* is the integrated media platform for people who want to live well and do good. Has themed issues. Estab. 2006. Accepts simultaneous submissions.

NONFICTION Pays expenses of writers on assignment.

$$$$ MOTHER JONES

Foundation for National Progress, 222 Sutter St., Suite 600, San Francisco CA 94108. (415)321-1700. **E-mail:** query@motherjones.com. **Website:** www.motherjones.com. **Contact:** Mark Murrmann, photo editor; Ivylise Simones, creative director; Monika Bauerlein and Clara Jeffery, editors. **80% freelance written.** Bimonthly magazine covering politics, investigative reporting, social issues, and pop culture. "*Mother Jones* is a 'progressive' magazine—but the core of its editorial well is reporting (i.e., fact-based). No slant required. Estab. 1976. Circ. 240,000. Byline given. Pays on publication. Offers 33% kill fee. Publishes ms an average of 4 months after acceptance. Editorial lead time 4 months. Submit seasonal material 6 months in advance. Accepts simultaneous submissions. Responds in 2 months to queries. Sample copy for $6 and 9x12 SASE. Guidelines available online.

"*Mother Jones* magazine and *MotherJones.com* will consider solidly reported, hard-hitting, groundbreaking news stories. We're also open to thought-provoking, timely opinion and analysis pieces on important current issues. We're interested in just about anything that will raise our readers' eyebrows, but we focus especially on these areas: national politics, environmental issues, corporate wrongdoing, human rights, and political influence in all spheres.

NONFICTION Needs interview, photo feature, current issues, policy, investigative reporting. **Buys 70-100 mss/year.** Query with published clips. "Please also include your rèsumè and two or three of your most relevant clips. If the clips are online, please provide the complete URLs. Web pieces are generally less than 1,500 words. Because we have staff reporters it is extremely rare that we will pay for a piece whose timeliness or other qualities work for the Web only. Magazine pieces can range up to 5,000 words. There is at least a two-month lead time. No phone calls please." Length: 2,000-5,000 words. **Pays $1/word.** Pays expenses of writers on assignment.

PHOTOS Contact: Mark Murrmann.

COLUMNS/DEPARTMENTS Outfront (short, newsy and/or outrageous and/or humorous items), 200-800 words; Profiles of Hellraisers, 500 words. **Pays $1/word.**

TIPS "We're looking for hard-hitting, investigative reports exposing government cover-ups, corporate malfeasance, scientific myopia, institutional fraud or hypocrisy; thoughtful, provocative articles which challenge the conventional wisdom (on the right or the left) concerning issues of national importance; and timely, people-oriented stories on issues such as the environment, labor, the media, healthcare, consumer protection, and cultural trends. Send a great, short query and establish your credibility as a reporter. Explain what you plan to cover and how you will proceed with the reporting. The query should convey your approach, tone and style, and should answer the following: What are your specific qualifications to write on this topic? What 'ins' do you have with your sources? Can you provide full documentation so that your story can be fact-checked?"

$$$$ THE SUN

107 N. Roberson St., Chapel Hill NC 27516. (919)942-5282. **Fax:** (919)932-3101. **Website:** www.thesunmagazine.org. **Contact:** Sy Safransky, editor. **90% freelance written.** *The Sun* publishes essays, interviews, fiction, and poetry. "We are open to all kinds of writing, though we favor work of a personal nature." Estab. 1974. Circ. 72,000. Byline given. Pays on publication. Publishes ms an average of 6-12 months after acceptance. Accepts queries by mail. Responds in 3-6 months. Sample copy online. Guidelines online.

NONFICTION Needs essays, interview, memoir, personal experience, Also needs spiritual fields; in-depth philosophical; thoughtful essays on political, cultural, and philosophical themes. **Buys 50 mss/year.** Send complete ms. No fax or e-mail submissions. Length: up to 7,000 words. **Pays $300-2,000 and 1-year subscription.** Pays expenses of writers on assignment.

REPRINTS For reprints, send photocopy and information about when and where the material previously appeared. Pays 50% of standard pay.

PHOTOS Model releases required. Offers $100-500/photo. Buys one-time rights.

FICTION Open to all fiction. Receives 800 unsolicited mss/month. Accepts 20 short stories/year. Recently published work by Sigrid Nunez, Susan Straight, Lydia Peelle, Stephen Elliott, David James Duncan, Linda McCullough Moore, and Brenda Miller. No science fiction, horror, fantasy, or other genre fiction. "Read an issue before submitting." **Buys 20 mss/year.** Send complete ms. Accepts reprint submissions. Length: up to 7,000 words. **Pays $300-1,500 and 1-year subscription.**

POETRY Needs free verse. Submit up to 6 poems at a time. Considers previously published poems but strongly prefers unpublished work. "Poems should be typed and accompanied by a cover letter and SASE." Recently published poems by Tony Hoagland, Ellen Bass, Steve Kowit, Brian Doyle, and Alison Luterman. Rarely publishes poems that rhyme. **Pays $100-200 and 1-year subscription.**

TIPS "Do not send queries except for interviews. We're open to unusual work. Read the magazine to get a sense of what we're about. Our submission rate is extremely high. Please be patient after sending us your work and include return postage."

DISABILITIES

$$ ABILITIES

Canadian Abilities Foundation, 225 Duncan Mill Road, Suite 803, Toronto ON M3B 3H9 Canada. (416)421-7944. **Fax:** (416)421-8418. **E-mail:** abilities@bcsgroup.com. **Website:** www.abilities.ca. **Contact:** Caroline Tapp-McDougall, managing editor. **50% freelance written.** Quarterly magazine covering disability issues. "*Abilities* is Canada's foremost cross-disability lifestyle magazine. The mission of the magazine is to provide **information** about lifestyle topics, including travel, health, careers, education, relationships, parenting, new products, social policy and much more; **inspiration** to participate in organizations, events, and activities and pursue opportunities in sports, education, careers, and more; and **opportunity** to learn about a wealth of Canadian resources that facilitate self empowerment of people with disabilities." Estab. 1987. Circ. 20,000. Byline given. Pays on publication. Offers 50% kill fee. Publishes ms an average of 3 months after acceptance. Editorial lead time 3 months. Submit seasonal material 4 months in advance. Accepts queries by mail, e-mail. Responds in 3 months to queries. Sample copy free. Writer's guidelines for #10 SASE, online, or by e-mail.

NONFICTION Needs general interest, how-to, humor, inspirational, interview, new product, personal experience, photo feature, travel. Does not want articles that 'preach to the converted'—this means info that people with disabilities likely already know, such as what it's like to have a disability. **Buys 30-40 mss/year.** Query or send complete ms. Length: 500-2,000 words. **Pays $50-325 (Canadian) for assigned articles.** Pays expenses of writers on assignment.

REPRINTS Sometimes accepts previously published submissions (if stated as such).

PHOTOS State availability.

COLUMNS/DEPARTMENTS The Lighter Side (humor), 700 words; Profile, 1,200 words.

TIPS "We strongly prefer e-mail queries. When developing story ideas, keep in mind that our readers are in Canada."

$$$$ ARTHRITIS TODAY

Arthritis Foundation, 1355 Peachtree St. NE, 6th Floor, Atlanta GA 30309. **Website:** www.arthritistoday.org. **50% freelance written.** Bimonthly magazine covering living with arthritis and the latest in research/treatment. *Arthritis Today* is a consumer health magazine and is written for the more than 70 million Americans who have arthritis and for the millions of others whose lives are touched by an arthritis-related disease. The editorial content is designed to help the person with arthritis live a more productive, independent, and pain-free life. The articles are upbeat and provide practical advice, information, and inspiration. Estab. 1987. Circ. 650,000. Byline given. Pays on acceptance. Offers kill fee. Offers kill fee. Editorial lead time 6 months. Submit seasonal material 6 months in advance. Accepts queries by mail, online submission form. Accepts simultaneous submissions. Responds in 2 months to queries. Sample copy for 9x11 SAE with 4 first-class stamps.

NONFICTION Needs general interest, how-to, inspirational, new product, opinion, personal experience, photo feature, technical, travel. **Buys 12 unsolicited mss/year.** Query with published clips. Length: 150-2,500 words. **Pays $100-2,500.** Pays expenses of writers on assignment.

PHOTOS Send photos. Identification of subjects required. Reviews prints. Negotiates payment individually. Buys one-time rights.

COLUMNS/DEPARTMENTS Nutrition, 100-600 words; Fitness, 100-600 words; Balance (emotional coping), 100-600 words; MedWatch, 100-800 words; Solutions, 100-600 words; Life Makeover, 400-600 words.

FILLERS Needs facts, gags, short humor. **Buys 2 mss/year.** Length: 40-100 words. **Pays $80-150.**

TIPS "Our readers are already well informed. We need ideas and writers that give in-depth, fresh, interesting information that truly adds to their understanding of their condition and their quality of life. Quality writers are more important than good ideas. The staff generates many of our ideas but needs experienced, talented writers who are good reporters to execute them. Please provide published clips. In addition to articles specifically about living with arthritis, we look for articles to appeal to an older audience on subjects such as hobbies, general health, lifestyle, etc."

$$ CAREERS & THE DISABLED

Equal Opportunity Publications, 445 Broad Hollow Rd., Suite 425, Melville NY 11747. (631)421-9421, ext. 12. **E-mail:** bloehr@eop.com. **Website:** www.eop.com. **Contact:** Barbara Capella Loehr, editor. **60% freelance written.** Magazine published 6 times/year, with Fall, Winter, Spring, Summer, Expo and Veterans' editions, offering role-model profiles and career guidance articles geared toward disabled college students and professionals, and promoting personal and professional growth. Estab. 1968: EOP; 1986: CAREERS & the disABLED magazine. Circ. 10,000. Byline given. Pays on publication. Publishes ms an average of 6 months after acceptance. Editorial lead time 6 months. Submit seasonal material 6 months in advance. Accepts queries by mail, e-mail, phone. Accepts simultaneous submissions. Responds in 3 weeks to queries. Sample copy for 9x12 SAE with 5 first-class stamps. Guidelines free.

NONFICTION Needs essays, general interest, how-to, interview, new product, opinion, personal experience.

Buys 30 mss/year. Query. Length: 1,000-2,500 words. **Pays 10¢/word.** Pays expenses of writers on assignment.

PHOTOS Captions, identification of subjects, model releases required. Reviews transparencies, prints. Buys one-time rights.

TIPS "Be as targeted as possible. Role-model profiles and specific career guidance strategies that offer advice to disabled college students are most needed."

$$ DIABETES HEALTH

P.O. Box 1199, Woodacre CA 94973. **E-mail:** editor@diabeteshealth.com. **Website:** www.diabeteshealth.com. **Contact:** Nadia Al-Samarrie, editor in chief. **60% freelance written.** Monthly tabloid covering diabetes care. *Diabetes Health* covers the latest in diabetes care, medications, and patient advocacy. Personal accounts are welcome as well as medical-oriented articles by MDs, RNs, and CDEs (certified diabetes educators). Estab. 1991. Circ. 150,000. Byline given. Pays on publication. No kill fee. Publishes ms an average of 2 months after acceptance. Editorial lead time 2 months. Submit seasonal material 2 months in advance. Accepts queries by e-mail. Accepts simultaneous submissions. Sample copy available online. Guidelines free.

Accepts solicited submissions from contributing writers for feature-length stories.

NONFICTION Needs book excerpts, essays, how-to, humor, inspirational, interview, memoir, new product, nostalgic, opinion, personal experience, photo feature, reviews, technical, travel. *Diabetes Health* does not accept mss that promote a product, philosophy, or personal view. **Buys 25 mss/year.** Send complete ms. Length: 400-1,500 words. **Pays 10¢/word.**

POETRY Needs Personal poetry from people living with diabetes.

TIPS "Be actively involved in the diabetes community, or have diabetes. Writers need not have diabetes to write an article, but it must be diabetes-related."

$ DIALOGUE

Blindskills, Inc., P.O. Box 5181, Salem OR 97304. **E-mail:** blindskills@gmail.com. **Website:** www.blindskills.com. **60% freelance written.** Quarterly journal covering visually impaired people. Estab. 1962. Circ. 1,100. Byline given. Pays on publication. Publishes ms an average of 6 months after acceptance. Editorial lead time 3 months. Accepts queries by e-mail. Accepts simultaneous submissions. Sample copy: 1 free copy on request. Available in large print, Braille, digital audio Cartridge, and e-mail. Guidelines online.

NONFICTION Needs essays, general interest, historical, how-to, humor, interview, new product, opinion, personal experience, profile. No controversial, explicit sex, religious, or political topics. **Buys 50-60 mss/year.** Send complete ms. Length: 400-1,200 words. **Pays $15-35 for assigned articles; $15-25 for unsolicited articles.** Pays expenses of writers on assignment.

COLUMNS/DEPARTMENTS All material should be relative to blind and visually impaired readers. Living with Low Vision, 1,000 words; Hear's How (dealing with sight loss), 1,000 words; Technology Answer Book, 1,000 words. **Buys 80 mss/year.** Send complete ms. **Pays $25-50.**

$ KALEIDOSCOPE

United Disability Services, 701 S. Main St., Akron OH 44311-1019. (330)762-9755. **Fax:** (330)762-0912. **E-mail:** kaleidoscope@udsakron.org. **Website:** www.kaleidoscopeonline.org. **Contact:** Editor. **90% freelance written. Eager to work with new/unpublished writers.** Semiannual free online magazine. Kaleidoscope magazine creatively focuses on the experiences of disability through literature and the fine arts. As a pioneering literary resource for the field of disability studies, this award-winning publication expresses the diversity of the disability experience from a variety of perspectives including: individuals, families, friends, caregivers, educators, and healthcare professionals, among others." Estab. 1979. Byline given. Pays on publication. No kill fee. Publishes ms 1-3 years after acceptance. 3 months prior to publication Accepts queries by mail, e-mail, fax, phone, online submission form. Accepts simultaneous submissions. Responds in 6-9 months. Guidelines available online. Submissions and queries electronically via website and e-mail.

Kaleidoscope has received awards from the Great Lakes Awards Competition and Ohio Public Images; received the Ohioana Award of Editorial Excellence.

NONFICTION Needs essays, interview, personal experience, reviews, articles relating to both literary and visual arts. For book reviews: "Reviews that are substantive, timely, powerful works about publications in the field of disability and/or the arts. The writer's opinion of the work being reviewed should be clear. The review should be a literary work in its own right." **Buys 40-50 mss/year.** Submit complete ms by website or e-mail. Include cover letter. Length: up to 5,000 words. **Pays $25.**

REPRINTS Send double-spaced, typed ms with complete author's/artist's contact information, rights for sale noted, and information about when and where the material previously appeared. Reprints permitted with credit given to original publication. All rights revert to author upon publication

PHOTOS Send digital images.

FICTION Wants short stories with a well-crafted plot and engaging characters. Needs historical, humorous, mainstream, short stories, slice-of-life vignettes. No fiction that is stereotypical, patronizing, sentimental, erotic, or maudlin. No romance, religious or dogmatic fiction; no children's literature. Submit complete ms by website or e-mail. Include cover letter. Length: up to 5,000 words. **Pays $25.**

POETRY Wants poems that have strong imagery, evocative language. Submit up to 5 poems by website or e-mail. Include cover letter. Do not get caught up in rhyme scheme. Reviews any style. **$10 per poem.**

TIPS "The material chosen for Kaleidoscope challenges and overcomes stereotypical, patronizing, and sentimental attitudes about disability. We accept the work of writers with and without disabilities; however the work of a writer without a disability must focus on some aspect of disability. The criteria for good writing apply: effective technique, thought-provoking subject matter, and, in general, a mature grasp of the art of storytelling. Writers should avoid using offensive language and always put the person before the disability."

$$ SPORTS 'N SPOKES

The Magazine for Wheelchair Sports and Recreation, Paralyzed Veterans of America / PVA Publications, 2111 E. Highland Ave., Suite 180, Phoenix AZ 85016-4702. (602)224-0500. **Fax:** (602)224-0507. **E-mail:** brittany@pvamag.com; john@pvamag.com; andy@pvamag.com; anngarvey@pvamag.com; kerry@pvamag.com. **Website:** www.pvamag.com. **Contact:** Tom Fjerstad, editor; Andy Nemann, assistant editor; John Groth and Brittany Martin, editorial coordinators; Ann Garvey and Kerry Randolph (cartoon and photo submissions). Bimonthly magazine covering wheelchair sports and recreation. Writing must pertain to wheelchair sports and recreation. "*SPORTS 'N SPOKES* is committed to providing a voice for the wheelchair sporting and recreation community." Estab. 1974. Circ. 25,000. Byline given. Pays on publication. Publishes ms an average of 2-3 months after acceptance. Editorial lead time 2-3 months. Submit seasonal material 2-3 months in advance. Accepts queries by mail, e-mail. Accepts simultaneous submissions. Sample copy and guidelines free.

NONFICTION Needs general interest, interview, new product. **Buys 5-6 mss/year.** Query before submitting. Length: 1,200-2,500 words. **Pays $20-250.** Pays expenses of writers on assignment.

ENTERTAINMENT

$ IN TOUCH WEEKLY

270 Sylvan Ave., Englewood Cliffs NJ 07632. (201)569-6699. **E-mail:** contactus@intouchweekly.com. **Website:** www.intouchweekly.com. **10% freelance written.** Weekly magazine covering celebrity news and entertainment. Estab. 2002. Circ. 1,300,000. No byline given. Pays on publication. Editorial lead time 1 week. Accepts queries by mail, e-mail. Accepts simultaneous submissions.

NONFICTION Needs interview, gossip. **Buys 1,300 mss/year.** Query. Send a tip about a celebrity by e-mail. Length: 100-1,000 words. **Pays $50.** Pays expenses of writers on assignment.

$$ MOVIEMAKER MAGAZINE

MovieMaker Media LLC, 2525 Michigan Ave., Building I, Santa Monica CA 90404. (310)828-8388. **E-mail:** tim@moviemaker.com. **Website:** www.moviemaker.com. **Contact:** Timothy Rhys, editor in chief. **75% freelance written.** Bimonthly magazine covering film, independent cinema, and Hollywood. "*MovieMaker*'s editorial is a progressive mix of in-depth interviews and criticism, combined with practical techniques and advice on financing, distribution, and production strategies. Behind-the-scenes discussions with Hollywood's top moviemakers, as well as independents from around the globe, are routinely found in *MovieMaker*'s pages. E-mail is the preferred submission method, but we will accept queries via mail as well. Please, no telephone pitches. We want to read the idea with clips." Estab. 1993. Circ. 55,000. Byline given. Pays 30 days after newsstand publication. Offers variable kill fee. Publishes ms an average of 2 months after acceptance. Editorial lead time 3 months. Submit seasonal material 4 months in advance. Accepts queries by mail, e-mail. Accepts simultaneous submissions. Responds in 2-4 weeks to queries; in 4-6 weeks to mss. Sample copy available online. Guidelines by email.

NONFICTION Needs expose, general interest, historical, how-to, interview, new product, technical. **Buys 20 mss/year.** Query with published clips. Length: 800-3,000 words. **Pays $75-500 for assigned articles.**

PHOTOS State availability. Identification of subjects required. Payment varies for photos accepted with ms. Rights purchased negotiable.

COLUMNS/DEPARTMENTS Documentary; Home Cinema (home video/DVD reviews); How They Did It (first-person filmmaking experiences); Festival Beat (film festival reviews); World Cinema (current state of cinema from a particular country). Query with published clips **Pays $75-300.**

TIPS "The best way to begin working with *MovieMaker* is to send a list of 'pitches' along with your résumé and clips. As we receive a number of résumés each week, we want to get an early sense of not just your style of writing but the kinds of subjects that interest you most as they relate to film. We also want to know that you understand the magazine and our audience. The fastest way to have your story rejected (besides a typo in the pitch) is to clearly have never read a copy of the magazine. Please allow 1 month before following up on a query or résumé. All queries must be submitted in writing. No phone calls, please."

ETHNIC & MINORITY

$$ AMBASSADOR MAGAZINE

National Italian American Foundation, 1860 19th St. NW, Washington DC 20009. (202)939-3108. **E-mail:** don@niaf.org. **Website:** www.niaf.org. **Contact:** Don Oldenburg, director of publications and editor. **65% freelance written.** "We publish original nonfiction articles on the Italian American experience, culture, and traditions. We also publish profiles of Italian Americans (famous and not famous but doing something exceptional) and travel features, especially in Italy, but also relevant U.S. travel pieces. We rarely publish memoir-like pieces." *Ambassador* is a glossy, high-quality consumer magazine for Italian Americans, Italians, and Italophiles. Estab. 1989. Circ. 28,000. Byline given. Pays on publication. $50 kill fee for assigned stories. Time between acceptance and publication varies. Editorial lead time 2-4 months. Accepts queries by e-mail. Responds within 2 months to e-mailed queries. Sample copy online. Writer's guidelines available by e-mail.

NONFICTION Needs essays, general interest, interview, personal experience, photo feature, profile, reviews, travel. Query via e-mail before submitting ms. When submitting ms, send as a Word e-mail attachment. Phone and mailed queries and mss are discouraged. Length: 800-1,500 words. **Pays $300 for full feature or profile; $350 for full feature or profile with photos taken by writer.**

PHOTOS Photos must be high resolution (300 dpi) and relevant to an assigned story. Offers additional $50 total for original photos taken to support a story. Otherwise, for photography only, pay is negotiable. Buys one-time rights in magazine plus on the digital version of the magazine on NIAF website and archived through Proquest.

TIPS "Good photos, clear prose, and professional storytelling ability are all prerequisites."

$$$ B'NAI B'RITH MAGAZINE

1120 20th St. NW, Suite 300 N, Washington DC 20036. (202)857-6527. **E-mail:** bbmag@bnaibrith.org. **Website:** www.bnaibrith.org. **90% freelance written.** Quarterly magazine specializing in social, political, historical, religious, cultural, 'lifestyle,' and service articles relating chiefly to the Jewish communities of North America and Israel. Write for the American Jewish audience, i.e., write about topics from a Jewish perspective, highlighting creativity and innovation in Jewish life. Estab. 1886. Circ. 110,000. Byline given. Pays on publication. Publishes ms an average of 6 months after acceptance. Editorial lead time 3 months. Submit seasonal material 5 months in advance. Accepts queries by mail, e-mail. Accepts simultaneous submissions. Responds in 1 month to queries; 6 weeks to mss.

NONFICTION Needs interview, photo feature, religious, travel. No Holocaust memoirs, first-person essays/memoirs, fiction, or poetry. **Buys 14-20 mss/year.** Query with published clips. Length: 1,000-2,500 words. **Pays $300-800 for assigned articles; $300-700 for unsolicited articles.** Pays expenses of writers on assignment.

TIPS "Know what's going on in the Jewish world. Look at other Jewish publications also. Writers should submit clips with their queries. Read our guidelines carefully and present a good idea expressed well. Proofread your query letter."

$$ GERMAN LIFE

Zeitgeist Publishing, Inc., 1068 National Hwy., LaVale MD 21502. **E-mail:** editor@germanlife.com. **Website:** www.germanlife.com. **Contact:** Mark Slider. **80% freelance written.** Bimonthly magazine covering German-speaking Europe (Germany, Austria, Switzerland). "*German Life* is for all interested in the diversity of German-speaking culture—past and present—and in the various ways that the US (and North America in general) has been shaped by its German immigrants. The magazine is dedicated to solid reporting on travel, cultural, historical, social, genealogical, culinary and political topics." Estab. 1994. Circ. 40,000. Byline given. Pays on publication. Editorial lead time 4 months. Submit seasonal material 6-12 months in advance. Accepts queries by mail, e-mail. Responds in 2 months to queries; in 3 months to mss. Sample copy for $4.95 and SASE with 4 first-class stamps. Guidelines available online at www.germanlife.com.

NONFICTION Needs general interest, historical, interview, photo feature, reviews, travel. Special issues: February/March: Food, wine, beer; April/May: travel in Germany and other parts of German-speaking Europe; June/July: German-American travel destinations; August/September: Education; October/November: Oktoberfest;. December/January:Holiday Issue. **Buys 50 mss/year.** Query with published clips. Length: up to 1,200 words. **Pays $100-500.**

PHOTOS State availability. Identification of subjects required. High res digital images. Offers no additional payment for photos accepted with ms. Buys one-time rights.

COLUMNS/DEPARTMENTS German-Americana (regards specific German-American communities, organizations, and/or events past or present), 1,200 words; Profile (portrays prominent Germans, Americans, or German-Americans), 1,000 words; At Home (cuisine, etc. relating to German-speaking Europe), 800 words; Library (reviews of books, videos, CDs, etc.), 300 words. **Buys 30 mss/year.** Query with published clips. **Pays $100-130.**

FILLERS Needs facts, newsbreaks. Length: 100-300 words. **Pays $80.**

TIPS "The best queries include several informative proposals. Writers should avoid overemphasizing autobiographical experiences or stories. Please avoid 'superficial' travel articles. *GL* has been in publication for 20+ years and readers are savvy travelers, so we look for articles with substance."

$$ HADASSAH MAGAZINE

Hadassah, WZOA, 40 Wall St., Eighth Floor, New York NY 10005. **Fax:** (212)451-6257. **E-mail:** magazine@hadassah.org. **Website:** www.hadassahmagazine.org. **Contact:** Elizabeth Barnea. **90% freelance written.** Bimonthly magazine. Bimonthly publication of the Hadassah Women's Zionist Organization of America. Emphasizes Jewish life, Israel. Readers are 85% females who travel and are interested in Jewish affairs, average age 59. Circ. 255,000. Byline given. Pays on acceptance. Accepts simultaneous submissions. Responds in 4 months to mss. Sample copy and writer's guidelines with 9x12 SASE.

NONFICTION Needs historical. **Buys 10 unsolicited mss/year.** Query. Length: 1,500-2,000 words. Pays expenses of writers on assignment.

PHOTOS "We buy photos only to illustrate articles. Always interested in striking cover photos." Offers $50 for first photo, $35 for each additional photo.

COLUMNS/DEPARTMENTS "We have a family column and a travel column, but a query for topic or destination should be submitted first to make sure the area is of interest and the story follows our format."

FICTION Wants short stories with strong plots and positive Jewish values. Receives 20-25 unsolicited mss/month. Publishes some new writers/year. Needs ethnic. No personal memoirs, "schmaltzy" or shelter magazine fiction. Length: 1,500-2,000 words. **Pays $500 minimum.**

TIPS "Stories on a Jewish theme should be neither self-hating nor schmaltzy."

$ INTERNATIONAL EXAMINER

409 Maynard Ave. S., #203, Seattle WA 98104. (206)624-3925. **Fax:** (206)624-3046. **E-mail:** editor@iexaminer.org. **Website:** www.iexaminer.org. **Contact:** Travis Quezon, editor in chief. **75% freelance written.** Biweekly journal of Asian American news, politics, and arts. "*International Examiner* is about Asian American issues and things of interest to Asian

Americans. We do not want stuff about Asian things (stories on your trip to China, Japanese Tea Ceremony, etc. will be rejected). Yes, we are in English." Estab. 1974. Circ. 12,000. Pays on publication. No kill fee. Publishes ms an average of 1 month after acceptance. Editorial lead time 1 month. Submit seasonal material 2 months in advance. Accepts queries by mail, e-mail, fax. Accepts simultaneous submissions. Guidelines for #10 SASE.

NONFICTION Needs essays, general interest, historical, humor, interview, opinion, personal experience, photo feature. **Buys 100 mss/year.** Query with published clips. Length: 750-5,000 words, depending on subject. **Pays $25-100.** Pays expenses of writers on assignment.

REPRINTS Accepts previously published submissions (as long as published in same area). Send typed ms with rights for sale noted and information about when and where the material previously appeared. Payment negotiable.

PHOTOS State availability. Captions, identification of subjects required. Reviews contact sheets. Negotiates payment individually. Buys one-time rights.

FICTION Asian American authored fiction by or about Asian Americans only. **Buys 1-2 mss/year.** Query.

TIPS "Write decent, suitable material on a subject of interest to the Asian American community. All submissions are reviewed; all good ones are contacted. It helps to call and run an idea by the editor before or after sending submissions."

$$ ITALIAN AMERICA

219 E St. NE, Washington DC 20002. (202)547-2900. **Fax:** (202)546-8168. **E-mail:** ddesanctis@osia.org; mfisher@osia.org. **Website:** www.osia.org. **Contact:** Dona De Sanctis, editor; Miles Ryan Fisher, Editor-in-Chief. **20% freelance written.** Quarterly magazine. "*Italian America* provides timely information about OSIA, while reporting on individuals, institutions, issues, and events of current or historical significance in the Italian-American community." Estab. 1996. Circ. 65,000. Byline given. Pays on publication. Offers 50% kill fee. Publishes ms an average of 3 months after acceptance. Editorial lead time 3 months. Accepts queries by mail, e-mail, fax. Accepts simultaneous submissions. Sample copy free. Guidelines available online.

NONFICTION Needs historical, interview, opinion, current events. **Buys 8 mss/year.** Query with published clips. Length: 750-1,000 words. **Pays $50-250.** Pays expenses of writers on assignment.

TIPS "We pay particular attention to the quality of graphics that accompany the stories. We are interested in little known facts about historical/cultural Italian America."

$$ JEWISH CURRENTS

P.O. Box 111, Accord NY 12404. (845)626-2427. **E-mail:** editor@jewishcurrents.org. **Website:** jewishcurrents.org. **Contact:** Lawrence Bush, editor; Jacob Plitman, associate editor. *Jewish Currents*, published 4 times/year, is a progressive Jewish quarterly magazine that carries on the insurgent tradition of the Jewish left through independent journalism, political commentary, and a 'countercultural' approach to Jewish arts and literature. Our website is an active magazine in its own right, with new material published daily. *Jewish Currents* is 88 pages, magazine-sized, offset-printed, saddle-stapled with a full-color arts section, "JCultcha & Funny Pages." The Winter issue is a 12-month arts calendar. Estab. 1946. Circ. 5,000 print; 45,000 website. Publishes mss 1-4 months after acceptance. Accepts queries by mail, e-mail. Accepts simultaneous submissions. Responds in 1 month or less. Subscription: $30/year. First-year subscription: $18.

NONFICTION Submit complete ms with cover letter. "Writers should include brief biographical information." 2,000 words **$100 for website, $200+ for print** Pays expenses of writers on assignment.

FICTIONJewish, historical, multicultural, feminist, humor, satire, translations, contemporary. Send complete ms with cover letter. "Writers should include brief biographical information." **Pays contributor's copies or small honoraria.**

POETRY Submit 3 poems at a time with a cover letter. "Writers should include brief biographical information." Poems should be typed, double-spaced; include SASE. **Pays contributor's copies.**

$ KHABAR

3635 Savannah Place Dr., Suite 400, Duluth GA 30096. (770)451-3067, ext. 4. **E-mail:** editor@khabar.com. **Website:** www.khabar.com. **50% freelance written.** "*Khabar* is a monthly magazine for the Indian community, free in Georgia, Alabama, Tennessee, and South Carolina. Besides Indian-Americans, *Khabar* also reaches other South Asian immigrants in Georgia—those from countries such as Pakistan, Bangladesh, Nepal, and Sri Lanka who share common needs for good and services. 'Khabar' means 'news' or 'to know' in many Indian languages, but we are a features magazine rather than a news publication." Estab. 1992. Circ. 27,000. Pays on publication. Offers 25% kill fee. Publishes ms an average of 2 months after acceptance. Editorial lead time 2 months. Submit seasonal material 2 months in advance. Accepts queries by e-mail. Accepts simultaneous submissions. Sample copy free. Guidelines by e-mail.

NONFICTION Needs essays, interview, opinion, personal experience, travel. **Buys 5 mss/year.** Send complete ms. Length: 750-4,000 words. **Pays $100-300 for assigned articles. Pays $75 for unsolicited articles.** Pays expenses of writers on assignment.

PHOTOS State availability of or send photos. Captions, identification of subjects required. Negotiates payment individually.

COLUMNS/DEPARTMENTS Book Review, 1,200 words; Music Review, 800 words; Spotlight (profiles), 1,200-3,000 words. **Buys 5 mss/year.** Query with or without published clips or send complete ms. **Pays $75 minimum.**

FICTION Needs ethnic. **Buys 5 mss/year.** Query or send complete ms. **Pays $50-100.**

TIPS "Ask for our 'editorial guidelines' document by e-mail."

$$$ MOMENT

4115 Wisconsin Ave. NW, Suite LL10, Washington DC 20016. (202)363-6422. **Fax:** (202)362-2514. **E-mail:** editor@momentmag.com. **Website:** www.momentmag.com. **Contact:** Sarah Breger, deputy editor. **90% freelance written.** Bimonthly magazine on Judaism. *Moment* is committed to portraying intellectual, political, cultural, and religious debates within the community, and to educating readers about Judaism's rich history and contemporary movements, ranging from left to right, fundamentalist to secular. Estab. 1975. Circ. 65,000. Byline given. Pays on publication. Publishes ms an average of 6 months after acceptance. Editorial lead time 3 months. Submit seasonal material 6 months in advance. Accepts queries by mail, e-mail. Accepts simultaneous submissions. Responds in 1 month to queries; in 3 months to mss. Sample copy for $4.50 and SAE. Guidelines available online.

NONFICTION Buys 25-30 mss/year. Query with published clips. Length: 2,500-7,000 words. **Pays $200-1,200.**

PHOTOS State availability. Identification of subjects required. Negotiates payment individually. Buys one-time rights.

COLUMNS/DEPARTMENTS 5765 (snappy pieces about quirky events in Jewish communities, news and ideas to improve Jewish living), 250 words maximum; Olam (first-person pieces, humor, and colorful reportage), 600-1,500 words; book eviews (fiction and nonfiction) are accepted but generally assigned, 400-800 words. **Buys 30 mss/year.** Query with published clips. **Pays $50-250.**

TIPS "Successful features offer readers an in-depth journalistic treatment of an issue, phenomenon, institution, or individual. The more the writer can follow the principle of 'show, don't tell,' the better. The majority of the submissions we receive are about The Holocaust and Israel. A writer has a better chance of having an idea accepted if it is not on these subjects."

$$ NATIVE PEOPLES MAGAZINE

5333 N. Seventh St., Suite C-224, Phoenix AZ 85014. (602)265-4855. **Fax:** (602)265-3113. **E-mail:** sphillips@nativepeoples.com. **Website:** www.nativepeoples.com. **Contact:** Stephen Phillips, Publisher. Bimonthly magazine covering Native Americans. High-quality reproduction with full color throughout. The primary purpose of this magazine is to offer a sensitive portrayal of the arts and lifeways of native peoples of the Americas. Estab. 1987. Circ. 40,000. Byline given. Pays on publication. Accepts queries by mail, e-mail, fax. Accepts simultaneous submissions. Responds in 2 months to queries. Guidelines by request.

NONFICTION Needs personal experience. **Buys 35 mss/year.** Length: 1,000-2,500 words. **Pays 25¢/word.** Pays expenses of writers on assignment.

PHOTOS State availability. Identification of subjects required. Reviews transparencies, prefers high-res digital images and 35mm slides. Inquire for details. Offers $45-150/page rates, $250/cover photos. Buys one-time rights and nonexclusive web and reprint rights.

TIPS "We are focused upon authenticity and a positive portrayal of present-day Native American life and cultural practices. Our stories portray role models of Native people, young and old, with a sense of pride in their heritage and culture. Therefore, it is important that the Native American point of view be incorporated in each story."

FOOD & DRINK

$$ KASHRUS MAGAZINE

The Kashrus Institute, P.O. Box 204, Brooklyn NY 11204. (718)336-8544. **Fax:** (718)336-8550. **E-mail:** editorial@kashrusmagazine.com. **Website:** www.kashrusmagazine.com. **Contact:** Rabbi Yosef Wikler, editor. *Kashrus Magazine* is the kosher consumer's most established, authoritative, and independent source of news about kosher foods. Estab. 1981. Circ. 10,000. Byline given. Pays on publication. Offers 50% kill fee. Publishes ms an average of 2 months after acceptance. Submit seasonal material 2 months in advance. Accepts queries by mail, phone. Accepts simultaneous submissions. Responds in 2 weeks. Sample copy by e-mail.

NONFICTION Needs personal experience, photo feature, religious, technical. Special issues: International Kosher Travel (October); Passover Shopping Guide (March); Domestic Kosher Travel Guide (June). **Buys 8-12 mss/year.** Query with published clips. Length: 1,000-1,500 words. **Pays $100-250 for assigned articles. Pays up to $100 for unsolicited articles.** Pays expenses of writers on assignment.

REPRINTS Send tearsheet or photocopy and information about when and where the material previously appeared. Pays 25-50% of amount paid for an original article.

PHOTOS No guidelines; send samples or call. State availability. Offers no additional payment for photos accepted with ms. Buys one-time rights.

COLUMNS/DEPARTMENTS Health/Diet/Nutrition, 1,000-1,500 words; Book Review (cookbooks, food technology, kosher food), 250-500 words; People in the News (interviews with kosher personalities), 1,000-1,500 words; Regional Kosher Supervision (report on kosher supervision in a city or community), 1,000-1,500 words; Food Technology (new technology or current technology with accompanying pictures), 1,000-1,500 words; Kosher Travel (international, national—must include Kosher information and Jewish communities), 1,000-1,500 words; Regional Kosher Cooking, 1,000-1,500 words. **Buys 8-12 mss/year.** Query with published clips. **Pays $50-250.**

$$ VEGETARIAN JOURNAL

P.O. Box 1463, Baltimore MD 21203-1463. (410)366-8343. **E-mail:** vrg@vrg.org. **Website:** www.vrg.org. **Contact:** Debra Wasserman, editor. Quarterly non-profit vegan magazine that examines the health, environmental and ethical aspects of veganism. "Highly-educated audience including health professionals." Estab. 1982. Circ. 12,000. Accepts queries by mail, e-mail. Accepts simultaneous submissions. Sample copy: $4.

Vegetarian Journal is 36 pages, magazine-sized, professionally printed, saddle-stapled, with glossy card cover.

NONFICTION "The articles we publish are usually written by registered dietitians and individuals with a science background. We are open to non-paid articles by others, and possibly a paid feature for a super idea. If you have a great idea that you would like to be paid for, please send a query letter along with a resume, and indicate that you would like to be paid." **Pays $100-200/article.** Pays expenses of writers on assignment.

POETRY "Please, no submissions of poetry from adults; 18 and under only."

TIPS Areas most open to freelancers are recipe section and feature articles. "Review magazine first to learn our style. Send query letter with photocopy sample of line drawings of food."

$$$$ WINE ENTHUSIAST MAGAZINE

Wine Enthusiast Media, 200 Summit Lake Dr., Valhalla NY 10595. **E-mail:** editor@wineenthusiast.net. **E-mail:** jczerwin@wineenthusiast.net; jfink@wineenthusiast.net; lbortolot@wineenthusiast.net. **Website:** www.winemag.com. **Contact:** Lauren Buzzeo, managing editor; Jameson Fink, digital senior editor; Layla Schlack, senior editor. **25% freelance written.** Monthly magazine covering the lifestyle of wine. Demystifying wine without dumbing it down, and tapping into current trends of spirits, travel, entertaining and art through a savvy wine lovers' lens, Wine Enthusiast is the modern tome of popular wine culture—a magazine that provokes and drives global dialogue in one of the world's most vibrant and fast-paced lifestyle categories, educating and entertaining legions of smart and sophisticated consumers. Estab. 1988. Circ. 180,000. Byline given. Pays on acceptance. Offers 25% kill fee. Editorial lead time 4 months. Submit seasonal material 5 months in advance. Accepts queries by e-mail. Responds in 2 weeks to queries; 2 months to mss.

NONFICTION Needs essays, humor, interview, new product, nostalgic, personal experience, travel. **Buys 5 mss/year.** Submit a proposal (1 or 2 paragraphs) with clips and a resume. Submit short, web items to Jameson Fink; submit feature proposals to Lauren Buzzeo. Submit short, front-of-book items to Layla Schlack. **Pays $1/word.**

PHOTOS Send photos. Reviews GIF/JPEG files. Offers $135-400/photo.

GAMES & PUZZLES

$$ CHESS LIFE

P.O. Box 3967, Crossville TN 38557. (931)787-1234. **Fax:** (931)787-1200. **E-mail:** dlucas@uschess.org. **Website:** www.uschess.org. **Contact:** Daniel Lucas, editor. **15% freelance written. Works with a small number of new/unpublished writers/year.** Monthly magazine. "*Chess Life* is the official publication of the United States Chess Federation, covering news of most major chess events, both here and abroad, with special emphasis on the triumphs and exploits of American players." Estab. 1939. Circ. 85,000. Byline given. No kill fee. Publishes ms an average of 6 months after acceptance. Submit seasonal material 6 months in advance. Accepts simultaneous submissions. Responds in 3 months to mss. Sample copy via PDF is available.

NONFICTION Needs general interest, historical, humor, interview, photo feature, technical. No stories about personal experiences with chess. **Buys 30-40 mss/year.** Query with samples if new to publication. 3,000 words maximum. **Pays $100/page (800-1,000 words).** Pays expenses of writers on assignment.

PHOTOS Uses about 15 photos/issue; 7-8 supplied by freelancers. No answer. Captions, identification of subjects, model releases required. Reviews b&w contact sheets and prints, and color prints and slides. Pays $25-100 inside; covers negotiable. Pays $25-100 for b&w inside; cover payment negotiable. Pays on publication. Buys one-time rights; "we occasionally purchase all rights for stock mug shots." Credit line given. Buys all or negotiable rights.

FILLERS Submit with samples and clips. Buys first or negotiable rights to cartoons and puzzles. **Pays $25 upon acceptance.**

TIPS "Articles must be written from an informed point of view. Freelancers in major population areas (except NY and LA) who are interested in short personality profiles and perhaps news reporting have the best opportunities. We're looking for more personality pieces on chess players around the country; not just the stars, but local masters, talented youths, and dedicated volunteers. Freelancers interested in such pieces might let us know of their interest and their range. Could be we know of an interesting story in their territory that needs covering. Examples of published articles include a locally produced chess television program, a meeting of chess set collectors from around the world, chess in our prisons, and chess in the works of several famous writers."

$$$ GAMES WORLD OF PUZZLES

Kappa Publishing Group, Inc., 6198 Butler Pike, Suite 200, Blue Bell PA 19422. (215)643-6385. **Fax:** (215)628-3571. **E-mail:** games@kappapublishing.com. **Website:** www.gamesmagazine-online.com. **Contact:** Jennifer Orehowsky, senior editor. **50% freelance written.** *Games World of Puzzles*, published 10 times/year, features visual and verbal puzzles, quizzes, game reviews, contests, and feature articles. Estab. 1977. Circ. 75,000. Byline given. Pays on publication. Offers 25% kill fee. Publishes ms an average of 4 months after acceptance. Editorial lead time 3 months. Submit seasonal material 6 months in advance. Accepts queries by mail, e-mail. Accepts simultaneous submissions. Responds in 6-8 weeks to queries and mss. Sample copy: $5. Guidelines available online.

NONFICTION Needs humor, photo feature, game- and puzzle-related events or people, wordplay. Query or submit complete ms by e-mail. Length: 2,000-2,500 words. **Pays $500-1,000.** Pays expenses of writers on assignment.

PHOTOS State availability. Captions, identification of subjects, model releases required. Reviews contact sheets, negatives, transparencies, prints. Negotiates payment individually. Buys one-time rights.

COLUMNS/DEPARTMENTS Puzzles, tests, quizzes. **Buys 50 mss/year.** Query or send complete ms. **Payment varies.**

TIPS "We look for fresh, lively ideas, carefully worked out for solvability. Visual appeal, a sense of humor, and the incorporation of pictures/objects from popular culture and everyday life are big pluses. Novelty is essential."

GAY & LESBIAN INTEREST

$$ THE ADVOCATE

Here Media, Inc., 10990 Wilshire Blvd., Penthouse, Los Angeles CA 90024. (310)806-4288. **Fax:** (310)806-4268. **E-mail:** newsroom@advocate.com. **Website:** www.advocate.com. **Contact:** Matthew Breen, editor in chief; Meg Thomann, managing editor. Biweekly magazine covering national news events with a gay and lesbian perspective on the issues. Estab. 1967. Circ. 120,000. Byline given. Pays on publication. Accepts simultaneous submissions. Responds in 1 month to queries. Sample copy: $3.95. Guidelines on website.

NONFICTION Needs expose. Query. Length: 800 words. **Pays $550.** Pays expenses of writers on assignment.

COLUMNS/DEPARTMENTS Arts & Media (news and profiles of well-known gay or lesbians in entertainment); 750 words. Query. **Pays $100-500.**

TIPS "*The Advocate* is a unique newsmagazine. While we report on gay and lesbian issues and are published by one of the country's oldest and most established gay-owned companies, we also play by the rules of mainstream-not-gay-community journalism."

$$ CURVE MAGAZINE

E-mail: editor@curvemag.com; merryn@curvemag.com. **Website:** www.curvemag.com. **Contact:** Merryn Johns, editor-in-chief. **60% freelance written.** Magazine published 4 times/year covering lesbian entertainment, culture, and general interest categories. "We want dynamic and provocative articles that deal with issues, ideas, or cultural moments that are of interest or relevance to gay women." Does not publish fiction or poetry. Estab. 1990. Circ. 250,000. Byline given. Pays on publication. Offers 25% kill fee. Up to 3 months between acceptance and publication. Editorial lead time 6 months. Submit seasonal material 6 months in advance. Accepts queries by mail, e-mail, fax. Accepts simultaneous submissions. Sample copy for $4.95 with $2 postage. Guidelines online.

NONFICTION Needs general interest, interview, new product, photo feature, profile, reviews, travel, celebrity interview/profile. Special issues: See website for calendar. No fiction or poetry. **Buys 100 mss/year.** Query. Length: 200-2,000 words. **Pays 15¢/word.**

PHOTOS Send hi-res photos with submission. Captions, identification of subjects, model releases required. Offers $25-100/photo; negotiates payment individually. Buys one time rights.

TIPS "Feature articles generally fit into 1 of the following categories: Celebrity profiles (lesbian, bisexual, or straight women who are icons for the lesbian community or actively involved in coalition-building with the lesbian community); community segment profiles—i.e., lesbian firefighters, drag kings, sports teams (multiple interviews with a variety of women in different parts of the country representing a diversity of backgrounds); noncelebrity profiles (activities of unknown or low-profile lesbian and bisexual activists/political leaders, athletes, filmmakers, dancers, writers, musicians, etc.); controversial issues (spark a dialogue about issues that divide us as a community, and the ways in which lesbians of different backgrounds fail to understand and support one another). We are not interested in inflammatory articles that incite or enrage readers without offering a channel for action, but we do look for challenging, thought-provoking work. The easiest way to get published in *Curve* is with a front-of-the-book piece for our Curvatures section, topical/fun/newsy pop culture articles that are 100-350 words."

$ THE GAY & LESBIAN REVIEW

Gay & Lesbian Review, Inc., P.O. Box 16477, Hollywood CA 91615. (844)752-7829. **E-mail:** glreview@hubservice.com. **E-mail:** richard.schneider@glreview.org. **Website:** www.glreview.org. Stephen Hemrick, *Director of Advertising*
stephen.hemrick@glreview.org. **Contact:** Richard Schneider, Jr., editor. **100% freelance written.** "*The Gay & Lesbian Review* is a bimonthly magazine targeting an educated readership of gay, lesbian, bisexual, and transgendered (GLBT) men and women. Under the tagline 'a bimonthly journal of history, culture, and politics,' the *G&LR* publishes essays in a wide range of disciplines as well as reviews of books, movies, and plays." Estab. 1994. Circ. 12,000. A bimonthly magazine of history, culture, and politics. Pays on publication. No kill fee. Editorial lead time 2 months. Accepts simultaneous submissions. Sample copy free. Guidelines available online at http://www.glreview.org/writers-guidelines-for-submission/.

NONFICTION Needs book excerpts, essays, historical, humor, interview, memoir, opinion, photo feature, reviews, travel, book reviews. Special issues: See website: http://www.glreview.org/writers-guidelines-for-submission/. Query or send complete ms by e-mail. Length: 2,000-4,000 words for features; 600-1,200 words for book reviews. **Pays $50-100.** Pays expenses of writers on assignment.

COLUMNS/DEPARTMENTS Guest Opinion (op-ed pieces by GLBT writers and activists), 500-1,000 words; Artist's Profile (focuses on the creative output of a visual artist, musician, or writer), 1,000-1,500 words; Art Memo (reflections on a work or artist of the past who made a difference for gay culture), 1,000-1,500 words; International Spectrum (the state of GLBT rights or culture in city or region outside the U.S.), 1,000-1,500 words. Query or submit complete ms by e-mail.

POETRY Needs avant-garde, free verse, traditional. Submit poems by postal mail (no e-mail submissions) with SASE for reply. Submit maximum 3 poems. Length: "While there is no hard-and-fast limit on length, poems of over 50 lines become hard to accommodate."

TIPS "We prefer that a proposal be e-mailed before a completed draft is sent."

GENERAL INTEREST

$ THE ALMANAC FOR FARMERS & CITY FOLK

Greentree Publishing, Inc., Box 319, 840 S. Rancho Dr., Suite 4, Las Vegas NV 89106. (702)387-6777. **Fax:** (702)385-1370. **Website:** www.thealmanac.com. **30-40% freelance written.** Annual almanac of "down-home, folksy material pertaining to farming, gardening, homemaking, animals, etc." Estab. 1983. Circ. 300,000. Byline given. Pays on publication. No kill fee. Publishes ms an average of 6 months after acceptance. Accepts queries by mail. Accepts simultaneous submissions. Sample copy: $4.99.

NONFICTION Needs essays, general interest, historical, how-to, humor. "No fiction or controversial topics. Please, no first-person pieces!" **Buys 30-40 mss/year.** No queries, please. Editorial decisions made from mss only. Send complete ms by mail. Length: 350-1,400 words. **Pays $45/page.** Pays expenses of writers on assignment.

FILLERS Needs anecdotes, facts, short humor, gardening hints. Length: up to 125 words. **Pays $15 for short fillers or page rate for longer fillers.**

TIPS "Material should appeal to a wide range of people and should be on the 'folksy' side, preferably with a thread of humor woven in. No first-person pieces (using 'I' or 'my')."

$$ THE AMERICAN SCHOLAR

Phi Beta Kappa, 1606 New Hampshire Ave. NW, Washington DC 20009. (202)265-3808. **Fax:** (202)265-0083. **E-mail:** scholar@pbk.org. **E-mail:** theamericanscholar.submittable.org/submit. **Website:** www.theamericanscholar.org. **Contact:** Robert Wilson, editor. **100% freelance written.** Quarterly magazine dedicated to current events, politics, history, science, culture and the arts. "Our intent is to have articles written by scholars and experts but written in nontechnical language for an intelligent audience. Material covers a wide range in the arts, sciences, current affairs, history, and literature." Estab. 1932. Circ. 30,000. Byline given. Pays on publication. Offers 50% kill fee. Publishes ms an average of 1 year after acceptance. Editorial lead time 6 months. Submit seasonal material 6 months in advance. Accepts queries by online submission form. Accepts simultaneous submissions. Responds in 2 weeks to queries; 2 months to mss. Guidelines online.

NONFICTION Needs essays, general interest, historical, humor, memoir, reviews, travel. **Buys 40 mss/year.** Query. Length: 3,000-5,000 words. **Pays $500 maximum.**

POETRY **Contact:** Sandra Costich. "We're not considering any unsolicited poetry."

$ THE CHRISTIAN SCIENCE MONITOR

210 Massachussetts Ave., Boston MA 02115. **E-mail:** homeforum@csmonitor.com. **Website:** www.csmonitor.com. **Contact:** Editor, The Home Forum. **95% freelance written.** *The Christian Science Monitor Weekly* is the print product of *The Christian Science Monitor,* which also publishes a daily digital product. The Weekly publishes personal nonfiction essays and, occasionally, poetry in its Home Forum section. "We're looking for upbeat essays of 600-800 words and short (20 lines maximum) poems that explore and celebrate daily life." Estab. 1908. Circ. 36,000 print, 14,000 digital. Pays on publication. Offers 50% kill fee. Publishes MSS 1-8 months after acceptance. Editorial lead time 6-8 weeks. Accepts queries by

e-mail. Responds in 4 weeks to mss; only responds to accepted mss. Sample copy available online. Guidelines available online or by e-mail (send e-mail with "Submission" in "Subject" field to receive autoreply with link).

NONFICTION Needs essays, humor, personal experience. **Buys 1,500+ mss/year.** Length: 600-800 words. **Pays $175 on publication.**

POETRY Accepts submissions via email or Word attachment Does not want "work that presents people in helpless or hopeless states; poetry about death, aging, or illness; or dark, violent, sensual poems. No poems that are overtly religious or falsely sweet." Submit maximum 5 poems. Length: up to 20 lines/poem. **Pays $25/haiku; $75/poem.**

$$$$ TOWN & COUNTRY

The Hearst Corp., 300 W. 57th St., New York NY 10019-3794. **E-mail:** tnc@hearst.com. **Website:** www.townandcountrymag.com. **40% freelance written.** Monthly lifestyle magazine. "*Town & Country* is a lifestyle magazine for the affluent market. Features focus on fashion, beauty, travel, interior design, and the arts, as well as individuals' accomplishments and contributions to society.' Estab. 1846. Circ. 488,000. Byline given. Pays on acceptance. Offers 25% kill fee. Accepts queries by mail. Accepts simultaneous submissions. Responds in 2 months to queries.

NONFICTION Needs general interest, interview, travel. "Rarely publishes work not commissioned by the magazine. Does not publish poetry, short stories, or fiction." **Buys 25 mss/year.** Query by mail only with relevant clips before submitting. Column items, 100-300 words; feature stories, 800-2,000 words. **Pays $2/word.**

TIPS "We have served the affluent market for over 150 years, and our writers need to be expert in the needs and interests of that market. Most of our freelance writers start by doing short pieces for our front-of-book columns, then progress from there."

$$$ YES! MAGAZINE

284 Madrona Way NE, Suite 116, Bainbridge Island WA 98110. **E-mail:** editors@yesmagazine.org. **E-mail:** submissions@yesmagazine.org. **Website:** www.yesmagazine.org. **70% freelance written.** Quarterly magazine covering sustainability, social justice, grassroots activism, contemporary culture; nature, conservation, ecology, politics, and world affairs. "*YES! Magazine* documents how people are creating a more just, sustainable and compassionate world. Each issue includes articles focused on a theme—about solutions to a significant challenge facing our world—and a number of timely, non-theme articles. Our non-theme section provides ongoing coverage of issues like health, climate change, globalization, media reform, faith, democracy, economy and labor, social and racial justice and peace building. To inquire about upcoming themes, send an e-mail to submissions@yesmagazine.org; please be sure to type 'themes' as the subject line." Estab. 1997. Circ. 55,000. Byline given. Pays on publication. Rarely offers kill fee. Publishes ms an average of 1-6 months after acceptance. Editorial lead time 3-6 months. Submit seasonal material 2-6 months in advance. Accepts queries by e-mail. Accepts simultaneous submissions. Responds in 3 months. Sample copy and writer's guidelines online.

NONFICTION Needs book excerpts, opinion. "We don't want stories that are negative or too politically partisan." **Buys 30 mss/year mss/year.** Query with published clips. Length: 100-2,500 words. **Pays $50-1,250 for assigned articles. Pays $50-600 for unsolicited articles.** Pays expenses of writers on assignment.

REPRINTS Send photocopy or typed ms with rights for sale noted and information about when and where the material previously appeared.

PHOTOS Buys one time rights.

COLUMNS/DEPARTMENTS Signs of Life (positive news briefs), 100-250 words; Commentary (opinion from thinkers and experts), 500 words; Book and film reviews, 500-800 words. **Pays $20-300.**

TIPS "We practice positive, solution-oriented journalism. We're interested in articles that: 'Change the story' about what is possible; tell specific success stories of individuals, communities, movements,nations, or regions that are addressing society's challenges and problems; offer visions of a better world. Our material exemplifies our tagline: 'Powerful Ideas, Practical Actions.' We're less interested in articles that only describe or update a problem (unless there are dramatically new developments, reframings, or insights); primarily reinforce a sense of being a victim (and therefore powerless); are written in styles or about topics relevant or accessible only to narrow groups; lack grounding in research or reporting (except for occasional essays). Our readers are well-educated, well-informed, and politically and socially engaged. We seek to present complex topics in a way that is accessible to laypeople and is jargon-free. Our magazine content is available online at yesmagazine.org. We urge you to familiarize yourself with the content, tone, and angle of our material before you submit."

HEALTH & FITNESS

$$ AMERICAN FITNESS

1750 E. Northrop Blvd., Suite 200, Chandler AZ 85286. (800)446-2322, ext. 200. **E-mail:** americanfitness@afaa.com. **Website:** www.afaa.com. **Contact:** Meg Jordan, editor. **75% freelance written.** Bimonthly magazine covering exercise and fitness, health, and nutrition. "We need timely, in-depth, informative articles on health, fitness, aerobic exercise, sports nutrition, age-specific fitness, and outdoor activity. Absolutely no first-person accounts. Need well-researched articles for professional readers." Estab. 1983. Circ. 42,900. Byline given. Pays 30 days after publication. No kill fee. Publishes ms an average of 6 months after acceptance. Submit seasonal material 4 months in advance. Accepts queries by mail, fax. Accepts simultaneous submissions. Responds in 2 months to queries. Sample copy for $4.50 and SASE with 6 first-class stamps.

NONFICTION Needs historical, inspirational, interview, new product, personal experience, photo feature, travel. No articles on unsound nutritional practices, popular trends, or unsafe exercise gimmicks. **Buys 18-25 mss/year.** Send complete ms. Length: 800-1,200 words. **Pays $200 for features, $80 for news.** Pays expenses of writers on assignment.

PHOTOS Sports, action, fitness, aquatic aerobics competitions, and exercise class. We are especially interested in photos of high-adrenalin sports like rock climbing and mountain biking. No answer. Captions, identification of subjects, model releases required. Reviews transparencies, prints. Pays $35 for transparencies. Usually buys all rights; other rights purchased depend on use of photo.

COLUMNS/DEPARTMENTS Research (latest exercise and fitness findings); Alternative paths (nonmainstream approaches to health, wellness, and fitness); Strength (latest breakthroughs in weight training); Clubscene (profiles and highlights of fitness club industry); Adventure (treks, trails, and global challenges); Food (low-fat/nonfat, high-flavor dishes); Homescene (home-workout alternatives); Clip 'n' Post (concise exercise research to post in health clubs, offices or on refrigerators). Length: 800-1,000 words. Query with published clips or send complete ms. **Pays $100-200.**

TIPS "Make sure to quote scientific literature or good research studies and several experts with good credentials to validate exercise trend, technique, or issue. Cover a unique aerobics or fitness angle, provide accurate and interesting findings, and write in a lively, intelligent manner. Please, no first-person accounts of 'how I lost weight or discovered running.' *AF* is a good place for first-time authors or regularly published authors who want to sell spin-offs or reprints."

$$$ BETTER NUTRITION

Active Interest Media, 512 Main St., Suite 1, El Segundo CA 90245. (310)356-4100. **Fax:** (310)356-4110. **E-mail:** nbrechka@aimmedia.com. **Website:** www.betternutrition.com. **Contact:** Nicole Brechka, editor-in-chief. **57% freelance written.** Monthly magazine covering nutritional news and approaches to optimal health. "The new *Better Nutrition* helps people (men, women, families, old and young) integrate nutritious food, the latest and most effective dietary supplements, and exercise/personal care into healthy lifestyles." Estab. 1938. Circ. 460,000. Byline given. Pays on publication. No kill fee. Publishes ms an average of 2 months after acceptance. Editorial lead time 3 months. Accepts queries by mail, e-mail. Accepts simultaneous submissions. Sample copy free.

NONFICTION Buys 120-180 mss/year. Query. Length: 400-1,200 words. **Pays $400-1,000.**

PHOTOS State availability of photos. Captions, identification of subjects, model releases required. Reviews 4x5 transparencies, 3x5 prints. Negotiates payment individually. Buys one time rights or nonexclusive reprint rights.

TIPS "Be on top of what's newsbreaking in nutrition and supplementation. Interview experts. Fact-check, fact-check, fact-check. Send in a resume (including Social Security/IRS number), a couple of clips, and a list of article possibilities."

$$ THE HEALTH JOURNAL

Rian Enterprises, LLC, 4808 Courthouse St., Suite 204, Williamsburg VA 23188. (757)645-4475. **Fax:** (757)645-4473. **Website:** www.thehealthjournals.com. **70% freelance written.** Monthly tabloid covering consumer/family health and wellness in Virginia. "Articles accepted of local and national interest. Health-savvy, college educated audience of all gender, ages, and backgrounds." Estab. 2005. Circ.

81,000. Byline given on most pieces. Pays on publication. Publishes ms an average of 1-2 months after acceptance. Editorial lead time 4-6 months. Submit seasonal material 4-6 months in advance. Accepts queries by online submission form. Accepts simultaneous submissions. Only responds to mss of interest. Guidelines available by request only.

NONFICTION Needs book excerpts, essays, expose, general interest, historical, how-to, humor, inspirational, interview, new product, opinion, personal experience, photo feature, technical, travel. Does not want promotion of products, religious material, or anything over 1,000 words. **Buys 100 mss/year.** Query with published clips. Length: 400-1,000 words. **Pays 15¢/word (starting rate); $50/reprint.** Pays expenses of writers on assignment.

TIPS "Write for the consumer. Entertain and inform. If you are not a health expert on the topic, consult 1. Or 2. Or 3."

IMPACT MAGAZINE

IMPACT Productions, 2007 2nd St. SW, Calgary AB T2S 1S4 Canada. (403)228-0605. **E-mail:** editor@impactmagazine.ca. **Website:** www.impactmagazine.ca. **Contact:** Liane Angerman, editor-in-chief. **10% freelance written.** Bimonthly magazine covering fitness and sport performance. A leader in the industry, *IMPACT Magazine* is committed to publishing content provided by the best experts in their fields for those who aspire to higher levels of health, fitness, and sport performance. Estab. 1991. Circ. 90,000. Byline given. Pays 30 days after publication. Offers 25% kill fee. Publishes ms an average of 4-6 months after acceptance. Editorial lead time 6 months. Submit seasonal material 6 months in advance. Accepts queries by e-mail. Accepts simultaneous submissions. Responds in 4 weeks to queries. Sample copy and guidelines available online.

"Query first, outlining the parameters of the article, the length, sources, etc., before submitting a completed draft. We do not accept editorial articles that profile and promote a specific business or service. *IMPACT Magazine* is a bi-monthly publication; submission deadlines are16 weeks prior to the publishing date. E-mail the article in an MS Word or text format (Mac or PC format). *IMPACT Magazine* compensates writers whose qualifications and work meet our specific guidelines (available from the editor). We are happy to accept photos or illustrations and will give photos credit where due. Digital images must be a minimum of 300 dpi."

NONFICTION Needs general interest, how-to, interview, new product, opinion, technical. **Buys 4 mss/year.** Query before submitting. Length: 600-1,800 words. **Pays 25¢/word maximum.** Pays expenses of writers on assignment.

PHOTOS State availability. Identification of subjects, model releases required. Reviews contact sheets, GIF/JPEG files (300 dpi or greater). Negotiates payment individually. Acquires first-time print and all electronic rights.

ORGANIC LIFE

Rodale, 400 S. 10th St., Emmaus PA 18098-0099. **E-mail:** rolsubmissions@rodale.com. **Website:** www.organicgardening.com. **75% freelance written.** Bimonthly magazine covering living naturally in the modern world. "Pitches for the front-of-book Gather section, the Food, Home, Garden, or Wellbeing sections, or the back-of-book Almanac section should be succinct yet detailed." Estab. 1942. Circ. 300,000. Byline given. Pays between acceptance and publication. No kill fee. Accepts queries by mail. Accepts simultaneous submissions. Responds in 3 months to queries.

NONFICTION Query with published clips and outline. **Pays up to $1/word for experienced writers.** Pays expenses of writers on assignment.

TIPS "You should familiarize yourself thoroughly with the magazine before pitching so that you can suggest how the article might appear in the magazine and at what length it might run."

YOGA JOURNAL

Active Interest Media, Healthy Living Group, 475 Sansome St., Suite 850, San Francisco CA 94111. (415)591-0555. **Fax:** (415)591-0733. **E-mail:** queries@yjmag.com. **Website:** www.yogajournal.com. **Contact:** Kaitlin Quistgaard, editor in chief. **75% freelance written.** Magazine published 9 times a year covering the practice and philosophy of yoga. Estab. 1975. Circ. 300,000. Byline given. Pays within 90 days of acceptance. Offers kill fee. Offers kill fee on assigned articles. Publishes ms an average of 10 months after acceptance. Submit seasonal material 7 months in advance. Accepts queries by e-mail. Accepts simultaneous submissions. Responds in 6 weeks to queries if interested. Sample copy: $4.99. Guidelines on website.

NONFICTION Needs book excerpts, how-to, interview, opinion, photo feature, travel. Does not want unsolicited poetry or cartoons. "Please avoid New Age jargon and in-house buzz words as much as possible." **Buys 50-60 mss/year.** Query with SASE. Length: 3,000-5,000 words. **Pays $800-2,000.** Pays expenses of writers on assignment.

REPRINTS Send tearsheet or photocopy with rights for sale noted and information about when and where the material previously appeared.

COLUMNS/DEPARTMENTS Om: Covers myriad aspects of the yoga lifestyle (150-400 words). This department includes Yoga Diary, a 250-word story about a pivotal moment in your yoga practice. Eating Wisely: A popular, 1,400-word department about relationship to food. Most stories focus on vegetarian and whole-foods cooking, nutritional healing, and contemplative pieces about the relationship between yoga and food. Yoga Scene: Featured on the back page of the magazine, this photo depicts some expression of your yoga practice. Please tell us where the photo is from, what was going on during the moment the photo was taken, and any other information that will help put the photo into context. E-mail a well-written query.

TIPS "Please read several issues of *Yoga Journal* before submitting a query. Pitch your article idea to the appropriate department with the projected word count, and what sources you'd use. In your query letter, please indicate your writing credentials. If we are interested in your idea, we will require writing samples. Please note that we do not accept unsolicited mss for any departments except Yoga Diary, a first person, 250-word story that tells about a pivotal moment in the writer's yoga experience (diary@yjmag.com). Please read our writer's guidelines before submission. Do not e-mail or fax unsolicited mss."

HISTORY

$$ AMERICA'S CIVIL WAR

Weider History Group, 1600 Tysons Blvd., Suite 1140, Tysons VA 22102. **E-mail:** acw@historynet.com. **E-mail:** submissions@historynet.com. **Website:** www.historynet.com/americas-civil-war. **Contact:** editor. **60% freelance written.** Bimonthly magazine covering popular history and straight historical narrative for both the general reader and the American Civil War buff featuring firsthand accounts, remarkable photos, expert commentary, and maps in making the whole story of the most pivotal era in American history accessible and showing why it still matters in the 21st century. Estab. 1988. Circ. 78,000. Byline given. Pays on publication. No kill fee. Accepts queries by e-mail. Accepts simultaneous submissions. Guidelines online.

NONFICTION Buys 18 mss/year. "Query. Submit a page outlining the subject and your approach to it, and why you believe this would be an important article for the magazine. Briefly summarize your prior writing experience in a cover note." Length: 3,500 words; 250-word sidebar. **Pays $300 and up.** Pays expenses of writers on assignment.

PHOTOS Send photos with submission or cite sources. Captions, identification of subjects required.

TIPS "All stories must be true. We do not publish fiction or poetry. Write an entertaining, well-researched, informative and unusual story that grabs the reader's attention and holds it. Submit queries or mss by e-mail. All submissions are on speculation."

$ THE ARTILLERYMAN

Jack W. Melton Jr. LLC, 520 Folly Road, Suite P-379, Charleston SC 29412. (706)940-2673. **E-mail:** mail@artillerymanmagazine.com. **Website:** www.artillerymanmagazine.com. **Contact:** Jack Melton, Publisher. **60% freelance written.** Quarterly magazine covering antique artillery, fortifications, and crew-served weapons 1750-1900 for competition shooters, collectors, and living history reenactors using artillery. Estab. 1979. Circ. 1,200. Byline given. Pays on publication. Publishes ms an average of 6 months after acceptance. Accepts queries by mail, e-mail, fax. Accepts simultaneous submissions. Responds in 3 weeks to queries. Sample copy online.

NONFICTION Needs historical, how-to, interview, photo feature, technical, travel. **Buys 12 mss/year.** Send complete ms. Length: 300 words minimum. **Pays $40-60.**

PHOTOS Send photos. Captions, identification of subjects required.

TIPS "We regularly use freelance contributions for Places-to-Visit and Unit Profiles departments and welcome pieces on unusual cannon or cannon with a known and unique history. Writers should ask themselves if they could knowledgeably talk artillery with an expert."

AVIATION HISTORY

HistoryNet, LLC, 1919 Gallows Rd., Ste. 400, Vienna VA 22182. **E-mail:** aviationhistory@historynet.com. **Website:** www.historynet.com/aviation-history. **Contact:** Carl von Wodtke, editor. **95% freelance written.** Bimonthly magazine covering military and civilian aviation from first flight to the space age. "*Aviation History* aims to make aeronautical history not only factually accurate and complete but also enjoyable to a varied subscriber and newsstand audience." Estab. 1990. Circ. 50,000. Byline given. Pays on publication. 25% Publishes ms an average of 1-2 years after acceptance. Editorial lead time 6 months. Submit seasonal material 1 year in advance. Accepts queries by mail, e-mail. Accepts simultaneous submissions. Responds in 2 months to queries; 3 months to mss. Sample copy: $6. Guidelines with #10 SASE, or online.

NONFICTION Needs historical, interview, personal experience. **Buys 24 mss/year.** Query. Length: up to 3,000 words, with a 500-word sidebar where appropriate, author bio, and book suggestions for further reading. **Pays minimum $300 for features.** Pays expenses of writers on assignment.

COLUMNS/DEPARTMENTS Aviators; Restored; Extremes, all up to 1,100 words. **Pays minimum of $150. Book reviews, 300 words max, pays minimum of $75.**

TIPS "Choose stories with strong narrative and art possibilities. Write an entertaining, informative, and unusual story that grabs the reader's attention and holds it. All stories must be true. We do not publish fiction or poetry."

HISTORY MAGAZINE

Moorshead Magazines, 82 Church St. S., Suite 101, Ajax ON L1S 6B3 Canada. **E-mail:** edward@moorshead.com. **Website:** www.history-magazine.com. **Contact:** Edward Zapletal, publisher/editor. **99% freelance written.** Bimonthly magazine covering social history. A general interest history magazine, focusing on social history up to about 1960. Estab. 1999. Byline given. Pays on publication. See author notes. Publishes ms an average of 6 months after acceptance. Editorial lead time 6 months. Submit seasonal material 6 months in advance. Accepts queries by e-mail. Accepts simultaneous submissions. Responds in 1-2 months to queries. Sample PDF copy available on request. Guidelines online.

NONFICTION Needs book excerpts, historical. Does not want first-person narratives or revisionist history. **Buys 50 mss/year.** Query. Do not submit complete ms. "Please note: Submissions must be accompanied by the author's name, telephone number, postal address, and e-mail address. If not present in the ms, we will delay publication until we receive the necessary contact information." Length: 500-2,200 words. **Pays 8¢/word; $7/image submitted and used in the final layout.** Pays expenses of writers on assignment.

PHOTOS State availability. Captions required. Reviews JPEG files. See author guidelines. Prefers public domain images only. Buys one-time rights.

TIPS "A love of history helps a lot, as does a willingness to work with us to present interesting articles on the past to our readers."

TRACES OF INDIANA AND MIDWESTERN HISTORY

Indiana Historical Society, 450 W. Ohio St., Indianapolis IN 46202-3269. (317)232-1877. **Fax:** (317)233-0857. **E-mail:** rboomhower@indianahistory.org. **Website:** www.indianahistory.org. **Contact:** Ray E. Boomhower, senior editor. **80% freelance written.** Quarterly popular history magazine on Indiana history. "Conceived as a vehicle to bring to the public good narrative and analytical history about Indiana in its broader contexts of region and nation, *Traces* explores the lives of artists, writers, performers, soldiers, politicians, entrepreneurs, homemakers, reformers, and naturalists. It has traced the impact of Hoosiers on the nation and the world. In this vein, the editors seek nonfiction articles that are solidly researched, attractively written, and amenable to illustration, and they encourage scholars, journalists, and freelance writers to contribute to the magazine." Estab. 1989. Circ. 6,000. Byline given. No kill fee. Publishes ms an average of 10-12 months after acceptance. Submit seasonal material 1 year in advance. Accepts queries by mail, e-mail. Accepts simultaneous submissions. Responds in 3 months to mss. Guidelines online.

NONFICTION Needs historical. **Buys 20 mss/year.** Send complete ms. Length: 2,000-4,000 words. **Pays $100-500.**

PHOTOS Send photos. Captions, identification of subjects required. Reviews contact sheets, transparencies, photocopies, prints. Pays reasonable photographic expenses. Buys one-time rights.

TIPS "Freelancers should be aware of prerequisites for writing history for a broad audience. Writers should have some awareness of this magazine and other magazines of this type published by Midwestern historical societies. Preference is given to subjects with an Indiana connection and authors who are familiar with *Traces*. Quality of potential illustration is also important."

$$ TRAINS

Kalmbach Publishing Co., P.O. Box 1612, Waukesha WI 53187-1612. (262)796-8776. **Fax:** (262)796-1142. **E-mail:** editor@trainsmag.com; photoeditor@trainsmag.com. **Website:** www.trn.trains.com. **Contact:** Jim Wrinn, editor; Tom Danneman, art director. Monthly magazine covering railroading. "Appeals to consumers interested in learning about the function and history of the railroad industry." Estab. 1940. Circ. 92,419. No kill fee. Editorial lead time 2 months. Accepts simultaneous submissions.

Query before submitting.

NONFICTION *Trains* buys news stories and feature articles covering railroading's past and present, including first-person recollections. Before submitting a feature-length article, send a written query via e-mail. Send a brief paragraph explaining the story, its theme, and highlights. Queries should include a possible headline. **Payment: 10¢/word.** Pays expenses of writers on assignment.

HOBBY & CRAFT

$$$$ AMERICAN CRAFT

American Craft Council, 1224 Marshall St. NE, Suite 200, Minneapolis MN 55413. (612)206-3115. **E-mail:** mmoses@craftcouncil.org. **E-mail:** query@craftcouncil.org. **Website:** www.americancraftmag.org. **Contact:** Monica Moses, editor in chief. **75% freelance written.** Bimonthly magazine covering art, craft, design. "American Craft Council is a national nonprofit aimed at supporting artists and craft enthusiasts. We want to inspire people to live a creative life. *American Craft* magazine celebrates the age-old human impulse to make things by hand." Estab. 1941. Circ. 40,000. Byline given. Pays on acceptance. Offers 25% kill fee. Publishes ms an average of 2 months after acceptance. Editorial lead time 4-6 months. Submit seasonal material 4-6 months in advance. Accepts queries by mail, e-mail. Accepts simultaneous submissions. Responds in 1 month to queries; in 2 months to mss. See writer's guidelines online.

NONFICTION Needs essays, interview, profile, travel, craft artist profiles, art travel pieces, interviews with creative luminaries, essays on creativity. Query with images. Include medium (glass, clay, fiber, metal, wood, paper, etc.) and department in subject line. Length: 500-2,000 words. **Pays $1/word, according to assigned length.** Pays expenses of writers on assignment.

COLUMNS/DEPARTMENTS On Our Radar (profiles of emerging artists doing remarkable work); Product Placement (stylish, inventive, practical, and generally affordable goods in production and the people who design them); Shop Talk (Q&As with owners of galleries); Material Matters (an artist using unusual materials to make fine craft); Personal Paths (an artist doing very individual—even idiosyncratic—work from a personal motivation); Spirit of Craft (art forms that might not typically be considered fine craft but may entail the sort of devotion generally associated with craft); Craft in Action (artists or organizations using craft to make the world better); Crafted Lives (photo-driven Q&A with a person or people living in a particularly creative space); Ideas (Q&A with a thinker or practitioner whose views represent a challenge to the status quo); Wide World of Craft (foreign or U.S. travel destination for craft lovers). **Buys 10-12 mss/year.** Query with published clips.

TIPS "Keep pitches short and sweet, a paragraph or 2 at most. Please include visuals with any pitches."

$ ANTIQUE TRADER

Active Interest Media, 5225 Joerns Dr., Suite 2, Stevens Point WI 54481. (715)445-2214. **Fax:** (715)445-4087. **E-mail:** pkennedy@aimmedia.com or kmanty@aimmedia.com. **Website:** www.antiquetrader.com. **Contact:** Paul Kennedy and Kris Manty, editors. **60% freelance written.** Published 24 times per year. "We publish quote-heavy informational articles of timely interest in the antiques field. We also cover antiques shows, auctions, and antiques & collectibles-related news events." Estab. 1957. Byline given. Pays on publication. No kill fee. Publishes ms an average of 1-3 months after acceptance. Editorial lead time 2 months. Accepts queries by mail, e-mail, fax. Accepts simultaneous submissions. Responds in 1 week to queries;

2 months to mss. Sample copy for cover price, plus postage. No cost for digital (PDF) sample copy. Guidelines online.

NONFICTION Needs book excerpts, essays, general interest, historical, how-to, interview, nostalgic, personal experience, show and auction coverage. Does not want the same, dry textbook, historical stories on antiques that appear elsewhere. Our readers want personality and timeliness. Send complete ms. Length: 1,000-1,500 words. **Pays $50-150, plus contributor copy.**

PHOTOS State availability. Identification of subjects required. Reviews transparencies, prints, GIF/JPEG files. Offers no additional payment for photos accepted with ms.

COLUMNS/DEPARTMENTS Dealer Profile (interviews with interesting antiques dealers), 750-1,200 words; Collector Profile (interviews with interesting collectors), 750-1,000 words. **Buys 30-60 mss/year.** Query with or without published clips or send complete ms.

$ AUTOGRAPH MAGAZINE

P.O. Box 25559, Santa Ana CA 92799. (951)734-9636. **Fax:** (951)371-7139. **E-mail:** steve.cyrkin@autographmagazine.com. **Website:** autographmagazine.com. **Contact:** Steve Cyrkin, publisher. **80% freelance written.** Monthly magazine covering the autograph collecting hobby. The focus of *Autograph* is on documents, photographs, or any collectible item that has been signed by a famous person, whether a current celebrity or historical figure. Articles stress how and where to locate celebrities and autograph material, authenticity of signatures and what they are worth. Byline given. Offers negotiable kill fee. Editorial lead time 2 months. Submit seasonal material 3 months in advance. Accepts queries by mail, e-mail. Accepts simultaneous submissions. Responds in 2 weeks to queries.

NONFICTION Needs historical, how-to, interview, personal experience. **Buys 25-35 mss/year.** Query. Length: 1,600-2,000 words. **Pays 5¢/word.** Pays expenses of writers on assignment.

PHOTOS State availability. Captions, identification of subjects required. Reviews transparencies, prints. Offers $3/photo. Buys one-time rights.

COLUMNS/DEPARTMENTS *Autograph Collector* buys 8-10 columns per month written by regular contributors. **Buys 90-100 mss/year.** Query. **Pays $50 or as determined on a per case basis.**

FILLERS Needs anecdotes, facts. **Buys 20-25 mss/year.** Length: 200-300 words. **$15.**

TIPS "Ideally writers should be autograph collectors themselves and know their topics thoroughly. Articles must be well-researched and clearly written. Writers should remember that *Autograph Collector* is a celebrity-driven magazine and name recognition of the subject is important."

$$ BLADE MAGAZINE

F+W, A Content and Ecommerce Company, 700 E. State St., Iola WI 54990-0001. (715)445-2214. **Fax:** (715)445-4087. **E-mail:** steve.shackleford@fwmedia.com. **Website:** www.blademag.com. **Contact:** Steve Shackleford, editor. **5% freelance written.** Monthly magazine covering working and using collectible, popular knives. *Blade* prefers in-depth articles focusing on groups of knives, whether military, collectible, high-tech, pocket knives, or hunting knives, and how they perform. Estab. 1973. Circ. 39,000. Byline given. Pays on publication. No kill fee. Publishes ms an average of 9 months after acceptance. Editorial lead time 9 months. Submit seasonal material 9 months in advance. Accepts queries by e-mail. Accepts simultaneous submissions. Responds in 3 months to queries; in 6 months to mss. Guidelines online.

NONFICTION Needs general interest, historical, how-to, interview, new product, photo feature, technical. "We assign profiles, show stories, hammer-in stories, etc. We don't need those. If you've seen the story on the Internet or in another knife or knife/gun magazine, we don't need it. We don't do stories on knives used for self-defense." Send complete ms. Length: 700-1,400 words. **Pays $150-300.** Pays expenses of writers on assignment.

PHOTOS Send photos. Captions, identification of subjects required. Reviews transparencies, prints, digital images (300 dpi at 1200x1200 pixels). Offers no additional payment for photos accepted with ms. Buys all rights.

FILLERS Needs anecdotes, facts, newsbreaks. **Buys 1-2 mss/year.** Length: 50-200 words. **Pays $25-50.**

TIPS "We are always willing to read submissions from anyone who has read a few copies and studied the market. The ideal article for us is a piece bringing out the romance, legend, and love of man's oldest tool—the knife. We like articles that place knives in peoples' hands—in life-saving situations, adventure modes, etc. (Nothing gory or with the knife as the villain.) People and knives are good copy. We are getting more well-written articles from writers who are reading the publication beforehand. That makes for a harder sell for the quickie writer not willing to do his homework. Go to knife shows and talk to the makers and collectors. Visit knifemakers' shops and knife factories. Read anything and everything you can find on knives and knifemaking."

CANADIAN WOODWORKING AND HOME IMPROVEMENT

Sawdust Media, Inc., 51 Maple Ave. N., RR #3, Burford ON N0E 1A0 Canada. (519)449-2444. **Fax:** (519)449-2445. **E-mail:** pfulcher@canadianwoodworking.com. **E-mail:** rbrown@canadianwoodworking.com. **Website:** www.canadianwoodworking.com. **20% freelance written.** Bi-monthly magazine covering woodworking and home improvement; only accepts work from Canadian writers. Estab. 1999. Byline given. Pays on publication. Offers 50% kill fee. Accepts queries by e-mail. Accepts simultaneous submissions. Sample copy available online. Guidelines available by e-mail.

NONFICTION Needs how-to, humor, inspirational, new product, personal experience, photo feature, technical. Does not want profile on a woodworker. Query. Length: 500-4,000 words. **Pays $250-600 for assigned articles; $250-400 for unsolicited articles.** Pays expenses of writers on assignment.

PHOTOS State availability. Negotiates payment individually. Buys all rights.

CLASSIC TOY TRAINS

Kalmbach Media, P.O. Box 1612, 21027 Crossroads Circle, Waukesha WI 53187. (262)796-8776, ext. 524. **Fax:** (262)796-1142. **E-mail:** editor@classictoytrains.com. **Website:** www.classictoytrains.com. **Contact:** Carl Swanson, editor. **50% freelance written.** Magazine published 9 times/year covering collectible toy trains (O, S, Standard) like Lionel and American Flyer, etc. For the collector and operator of toy trains, *CTT* offers full-color photos of layouts and collections of toy trains, restoration tips, operating information, new product reviews and information, and insights into the history of toy trains. Estab. 1987. Circ. 32,000. Byline given. Pays on acceptance. Publishes ms an average of 1 year after acceptance. Editorial lead time 3 months. Submit seasonal material 6 months in advance. Accepts queries by mail, e-mail. Accepts simultaneous submissions. Responds in 3 weeks to queries; in 1 month to mss. Sample copy for $7.95, plus postage. Guidelines online.

NONFICTION Needs general interest, historical, how-to, interview, personal experience, photo feature, technical. **Buys 90 mss/year.** Query. Length: 500-2,000 words. **Pays $75-500.** Pays expenses of writers on assignment.

PHOTOS Send photos. Captions required. Reviews hi-res digital photos. Offers no additional payment for photos accepted with ms or $15-75/photo. Buys all rights.

TIPS "It's important to have a thorough understanding of the toy train hobby; most of our freelancers are hobbyists themselves. One-half to two-thirds of *CTT*'s editorial space is devoted to photographs; superior photography is critical."

CQ AMATEUR RADIO

CQ Communications, Inc., 17 W. John St., Hicksville NY 11801. (516)681-2922. **Fax:** (516)681-2926. **E-mail:** cq@cq-amateur-radio.com. **E-mail:** w2vu@cq-amateur-radio.com. **Website:** www.cq-amateur-radio.com. **Contact:** Richard Moseson, editor. **40% freelance written.** Monthly magazine covering amateur (ham) radio. "*CQ* is published for active ham radio operators and radio hobbyists. It is read by radio enthusiasts in over 100 countries. All articles must deal with amateur radio, shortwave listening or other types of personal two-way radio. Our focus is on operating and on practical projects. A thorough knowledge of amateur radio is required." Estab. 1945. Circ. 60,000. Byline given. Pays after publication. No kill fee. Publishes ms an average of 6 months after acceptance. Editorial lead time 4 months. Submit seasonal material 4 months in advance. Accepts queries by mail, e-mail, fax. Accepts simultaneous submissions. Responds in 3 weeks to queries; 3 months to mss. Sample copy free. Guidelines online.

NONFICTION Needs historical, how-to, interview, personal experience, technical, all related to amateur radio. Special issues: February: QRP (Low-Power operating); June: Take it to the Field (portable operating); October: Emergency Communications; December: Technology. **Buys 50-60 mss/year.** Query. Length: 2,000-4,000 words. **Pays $.05/published word, $5/published photo.**

PHOTOS State availability. Captions, identification of subjects, model releases required. Reviews contact sheets, 4x6 prints, TIFF or JPEG files with 300 dpi resolution. Digital photos preferred. Offers no additional payment for photos accepted with ms. Buys one-time rights.

TIPS "You must know and understand ham radio and ham radio operators. Most of our writers (95%) are licensed hams. Because our readers span a wide area of interests within amateur radio, don't assume they are already familiar with your topic. Explain. At the same time, don't write down to the readers. They are intelligent, well-educated people who will understand what you're saying when written and explained in plain English."

$$ DOLLHOUSE MINIATURES

P.O. Box 219, Kasson MN 55944. (507)634-3143. **E-mail:** usoffice@ashdown.co.uk. **Website:** www.dhminiatures.com. **70% freelance written.** Monthly magazine covering dollhouse scale miniatures. *Dollhouse Miniatures* is America's best-selling miniatures magazine and the definitive resource for artisans, collectors, and hobbyists. It promotes and supports the large national and international community of miniaturists through club columns, short reports, and by featuring reader projects and ideas. Estab. 1971. Circ. 25,000. Byline given. Pays on acceptance. Editorial lead time 6 months. Submit seasonal material 6 months in advance. Accepts queries by mail, e-mail. Accepts simultaneous submissions. Responds in 1 month to queries; 2 months to mss. Sample copy: $6.95, plus shipping. Guidelines by e-mail.

NONFICTION Needs how-to, interview, photo feature. No essays or articles on miniature shops. **Buys 50-60 mss/year.** Send complete ms. Length: 500-1,500 words. **Pays $30-250 for assigned articles and up to $150 for unsolicited articles.** Pays expenses of writers on assignment.

PHOTOS Send digital photos. Captions, identification of subjects required. Reviews 3x5 prints. Photos are paid for with ms. Seldom buys individual photos. Buys all rights.

TIPS "Familiarity with the miniatures hobby is very helpful. Accuracy to scale is extremely important to our readers. A complete digital package (ms/photos) has a better chance of publication."

$$ DOLLS

JP Media LLC, P.O. Box 5000, N7528 Aanstad Rd., Iola WI 54945. (715)445-5000. **Fax:** (715)445-4053. **E-mail:** editor@dollsmagazine.com. **Website:** www.dollsmagazine.com. **Contact:** Joyce Greenholdt, editor. **75% freelance written.** Magazine published 10 times/year covering dolls, doll artists, and related topics of interest to doll collectors and enthusiasts. "*Dolls* enhances the joy of collecting by introducing readers to the best new dolls from around the world, along with the artists and designers who create them. It keeps readers up to date on shows, sales, and special events in the doll world. With beautiful color photography, *Dolls* offers an array of easy-to-read, informative articles that help our collectors select the best buys." Estab. 1982. Circ. 100,000. Byline given. Pays on publication. No kill fee. Accepts queries by mail, e-mail. Accepts simultaneous submissions. Responds in 1 month to queries.

NONFICTION Needs historical, how-to, interview, new product, photo feature. **Buys 55 mss/year.** Send complete ms. Length: 750-1,200 words. **Pays $75-300.** Pays expenses of writers on assignment.

PHOTOS Send photos. Captions, identification of subjects, model releases required. Reviews transparencies. Offers no additional payment for photos accepted with ms. Buys all rights.

TIPS "Know the subject matter and artists. Having quality artwork and access to doll artists for interviews are big pluses. We need original ideas of interest to doll lovers."

$$$ FAMILY TREE MAGAZINE

Yankee Publishing, Inc., P.O. Box 520, Dublin NH 03444. **E-mail:** familytree@yankeepub.com. **Website:** www.familytreemagazine.com. **Contact:** Andrew Koch. **75% freelance written.** Magazine covering family history, heritage, and genealogy research. "*Family Tree Magazine* is a special-interest consumer magazine that helps readers discover, preserve, and celebrate their family's history. We cover genealogy, ethnic heritage, genealogy websites, and software, photography, and photo preservation, and other ways that families connect with their past." Please note that *Family Tree Magazine* does not cover general family or parenting topics. Estab. 1999. Circ. 75,000. Byline given. Pays on acceptance. Offers 25% kill fee. Publishes ms an average of 6 months after acceptance. Editorial lead time 8 months. Submit seasonal material 8 months in advance. Accepts queries by mail, e-mail. Responds in 6-8 weeks to queries. Sample copy: $8 from website. Guidelines online.

NONFICTION Needs book excerpts, historical, how-to, new product, technical. Does not publish personal experience stories (except brief stories in the Tree Talk column, which does not pay) or histories of specific families. Does not cover general family or parenting topics. **Buys 40 mss/year.** Query with a specific story idea and published clips. Length: 250-4,500 words. **Pays up to $800.**

PHOTOS State availability. Captions required. Reviews color transparencies. Negotiates payment individually. Buys all rights.

TIPS "Always query with a specific story idea. Look at sample issues before querying to get a feel for appropriate topics and angles. We see too many broad, general stories on genealogy or records and personal accounts of 'How I found great-aunt Sally' without how-to value."

FIBRE FOCUS

The Ontario Handweavers & Spinners, 1188 Walker Lake Dr., RR4, Huntsville ON P1H 2J6 Canada. **E-mail:** ffeditor@ohs.on.ca. **Website:** www.ohs.on.ca. **Contact:** Flannery Surette, editor. **75% freelance written.** Quarterly magazine covering handweaving, spinning, basketry, beading, and other fiber arts. "Our readers are weavers and spinners who also do dyeing, knitting, basketry, feltmaking, papermaking, sheep raising, and craft supply. All articles deal with some aspect of these crafts." Estab. 1957. Circ. 700. Byline given. Pays within 30 days after publication. Publishes ms 2-5 months after acceptance. Editorial lead time 3 months. Submit seasonal material 6 months in advance. Accepts simultaneous submissions. Responds in 1 month to queries. Sample copy: $8 (Canadian). Guidelines available online.

"Articles must reflect a true understanding of weaving, spinning, or fiber art you are writing about. Good-quality photographs and/or graphics are an essential part of any story. Travel articles focusing on fiber arts discovered in other countries are also considered."

NONFICTION Needs historical, how-to, interview, new product, opinion, personal experience, photo feature, profile, reviews, technical, travel. **Buys 40-60 mss/year.** Contact the *Fibre Focus* editor before undertaking a project or an article. Mss may be submitted c/o Flannery Surette by e-mail for anything you have to contribute for upcoming issues. Feature article deadlines: December 31, March 31, June 30, and September 15. Length: varies, but generally 600-1,800 words. **Pays $30 (Canadian)/published page.**

REPRINTS Pays $20 (Canadian) per published page.

PHOTOS Send photos. Captions, identification of subjects required. Payment is included as part of the article. Buys one-time rights.

TIPS "Visit the OHS website for current information."

FINESCALE MODELER

Kalmbach Publishing Co., 21027 Crossroads Circle, P.O. Box 1612, Waukesha WI 53187-1612. (414)796-8776. **Website:** www.finescale.com. **80% freelance written. Eager to work with new/unpublished writers.** Magazine published 10 times/year devoted to how-to-do-it modeling information for scale model builders who build non-operating aircraft, tanks, boats, automobiles, figures, dioramas, and science fiction and fantasy models. Circ. 60,000. Byline given. Pays on acceptance. No kill fee. Publishes ms an average of 14 months after acceptance. Accepts simultaneous submissions. Responds in 6 weeks to queries. Responds in 3 months to mss. Sample copy with 9x12 SASE and 3 first-class stamps. Guidelines available on website.

NONFICTION Needs how-to, technical. Query or send complete ms via www.contribute.kalmbach.com. Length: 750-3,000 words. **Pays $60/published page minimum.** Pays expenses of writers on assignment.

PHOTOS "Send original high-res digital images, slides, or prints with submission. You can submit digital images at www.contribute.kalmbach.com." Captions, identification of subjects required. Reviews transparencies, color prints. Pays $7.50 minimum for transparencies and $5 minimum for color prints. Buys one-time rights.

COLUMNS/DEPARTMENTS *FSM* Showcase (photos plus description of model); *FSM* Tips and Techniques (model building hints and tips). **Buys 25-50 mss/year.** Send complete ms. **Pays $25-50.**

TIPS "A freelancer can best break in first through hints and tips, then through feature articles. Most people who write for *FSM* are modelers first, writers second. This is a specialty magazine for a special, quite expert audience. Essentially, 99% of our writers will come from that audience."

$$ THE FINE TOOL JOURNAL LLC

P.O. Box 737, 9325 Dwight Boyer Rd., Watervliet MI 49098. (269)463-8255. **Fax:** (269)463-3767. **E-mail:** finetoolj@gmail.com; jim@finetooljournal.net. **Website:** www.finetooljournal.net. **Contact:** Jim Gehring. **90% freelance written.** "Quarterly magazine specializing in older or antique hand tools from all traditional trades. Readers are primarily interested in woodworking tools, but some subscribers have interests in such areas as leatherworking, wrenches, kitchen, and machinist tools. Readers range from beginners just getting into the hobby to advanced collectors and organizations." Estab. 1970. Circ. 2,500. Byline given. Pays on publication. Offers $50 kill fee. Publishes ms an average of 6 months after acceptance. Editorial lead time 9 months. Submit seasonal material 6 months in advance. Accepts queries by mail, online submission form. Accepts simultaneous submissions. Responds in 2 months to queries; 3 months to mss. Sample copy for $6. Guidelines for #10 SASE.

NONFICTION Needs general interest, historical, how-to, interview, personal experience, photo feature, technical. **Buys 24 mss/year.** Send complete ms. Length: 1,000-3,000 words. **Pays $50-200.** Pays expenses of writers on assignment.

PHOTOS Send photos. "Photographs and illustrations should be submitted in JPEG or PDF files—we can scan them if necessary, but this sometimes leads to loss of resolution. If you are writing about a patented tool and wish to illustrate it with the patent drawing, these can be downloaded as PDF files from Google Patents." Identification of subjects, model releases required. Reviews 4x5 prints. Negotiates payment individually. Buys all rights.

COLUMNS/DEPARTMENTS Stanley Tools (new finds and odd types), 300-400 words; Tips of the Trade (how to use tools), 100-200 words. **Buys 12 mss/year.** Send complete ms. **Pays $30-60.**

TIPS "The easiest way to get published in the *Journal* is to have personal experience or know someone who can supply the detailed information. We are seeking articles that go deeper than general interest, and that knowledge requires experience and/or research. Short of personal experience, find a subject that fits our needs and that interests you. Spend some time learning the ins and outs of the subject, and with hard work and a little luck you will earn the right to write about it."

$$ FINE WOODWORKING

The Taunton Press, Inc., 63 South Main St., P.O. Box 5506, Newtown CT 06470-5506. (203)426-8171. **Fax:** (203)426-3434. **E-mail:** fw@taunton.com. **Website:** www.finewoodworking.com. **Contact:** Tom McKenna, senior editor. Bimonthly magazine on woodworking in the small shop. Estab. 1975. Circ. 270,000. Byline given. Pays on acceptance. Offers variable kill fee. Submit seasonal material 6 months in advance. Accepts simultaneous submissions. Responds in 1 month to queries. Guidelines online at www.finewoodworking.com/pages/fw_authorguideline.asp.

NONFICTION Needs how-to. **Buys 120 mss/year.** Send article outline, helpful drawings or photos, and proposal letter. **Pays $150/magazine page.** Pays expenses of writers on assignment.

COLUMNS/DEPARTMENTS Fundamentals (basic how-to and concepts for beginning woodworkers); Master Class (advanced techniques); Finish Line (finishing techniques); Question & Answer (woodworking Q&A); Methods of Work (shop tips); Tools & Materials (short reviews of new tools). **Buys 400 mss/year. Pays $50-150/published page.**

TIPS "Look for authors guidelines and follow them. Stories about woodworking reported by non-woodworkers are *not* used. Our magazine is essentially reader-written by woodworkers."

$$ THE HOME SHOP MACHINIST

P.O. Box 629, Traverse City MI 49685. (231)946-3712. **Fax:** (231)946-6180. **E-mail:** gbulliss@villagepress.com; kellywagner@villagepress.com. **Website:** www.homeshopmachinist.net. **Contact:** George Bulliss, editor; Kelly Wagner, managing editor. **95% freelance written.** Bimonthly magazine covering machining and metalworking for the hobbyist. Circ. 34,000. Byline given. Pays on publication. Publishes ms an average of 2 years after acceptance. Accepts simultaneous submissions. Responds in 2 months to queries. Sample copy free. Guidelines for 9x12 SASE.

NONFICTION Needs how-to, technical. No fiction or people features. **Buys 40 mss/year.** Send complete ms. Length: open—"whatever it takes to do a thorough job." **Pays $40/published page, plus $9/published photo.**

PHOTOS Send photos. Captions, identification of subjects required. Pays $9-40 for 5x7 b&w prints; $70/page for camera-ready art; $40 for b&w cover photo.

COLUMNS/DEPARTMENTS "Become familiar with our magazine before submitting." Book Reviews; New Product Reviews; Micro-Machining; Foundry. Length: 600-1,500 words. **Buys 25-30 mss/year.** Query. **Pays $40-70.**

FILLERS **Buys 12-15 mss/year.** Length: 100-300 words. **Pays $30-48.**

TIPS "The writer should be experienced in the area of metalworking and machining; should be extremely thorough in explanations of methods and processes—always with an eye to safety; and should provide good quality b&w photos and/or clear dimensioned drawings to aid in description. Visuals are of increasing importance to our readers. Carefully planned photos, drawings and charts will carry a submission to our magazine much farther along the path to publication."

$ LOST TREASURE, INC.

P.O. Box 451589, Grove OK 74345. (866)469-6224. **Fax:** (918)786-2192. **E-mail:** managingeditor@losttreasure.com. **Website:** www.losttreasure.com. **Contact:** Carla Nielsen, Managing Editor. **75% freelance written.** Monthly and annual magazines covering lost treasure. Estab. 1966. Circ. 55,000. Byline given. Pays on publication. Approximately 2 months. Accepts queries by e-mail. Accepts simultaneous submissions. Responds within two weeks to queries via e-mail and website. For a sample copy send #10 SASE. Submission guidelines can be requested by e-mailing managingeditor@losttreasure.com.

NONFICTION Needs historical, how-to, personal experience, technical, All must be related to treasure hunting. **Buys 225 mss/year.** Query on Treasure Cache/Treasure Facts only. "Will buy articles, photographs, and cartoons that meet our editorial approval." Enclose SASE with all editorial submissions. Length: 1,000-2,000 words. **Pays 4¢/word.** Pays expenses of writers on assignment.

PHOTOS "Color or b&w prints, copied maps, art with source credit with mss will help sell your story. We are always looking for cover photos with or without accompanying ms. Pays $100/published cover photo. Must be vertical." High quality JPEG.Captions required. Pays $5/published photo.

TIPS "Queries welcome but not required. If you write about famous treasures and lost mines, be sure we haven't used your selected topic recently—the story must have a new slant or new information. Source documentation required. How-tos should cover some aspect of treasure hunting, and how-to steps should be clearly defined."

$ NATIONAL COMMUNICATIONS MAGAZINE

America's Hobby Radio Magazine, SCAN Services Co., P.O. Box 1, Aledo IL 61231-0001. (309)228-8000. **Fax:** (888)287-SCAN. **E-mail:** editor@natcommag.com. **Website:** www.natcommag.com. **Contact:** Chuck Gysi, editor and publisher. **50% freelance written.** Covers scanner radios and listening (VHF/UHF), citizens band (CB) radio, and other hobby two-way radio services such as the General Mobile Radio Service, the Family Radio Service and the Multi-Use Radio Service. *National Communications Magazine* was created for the hobby radio user. "Know our audience. Download a recent sample issue at www.nat-com.org/sample.pdf. We're only interested in scanner radios, citizens band radio, two-way radio, especially the hobby radio services such as GMRS, FRS. and MURS. We do not cover amateur radio, shortwave, broadcasting, etc. We're very focused." Estab. 1988. Circ. 5,000. Byline given. Pays *immediately* on publication. No kill fee. Publishes ms an average of 2 months after acceptance. Editorial lead time 2 months. Submit seasonal material 4 months in advance. Accepts queries by e-mail. Responds in 1 day-1 week. Current-issue sample copy: $6. Free recent PDF sample download at www.nat-com.org/sample.pdf. Contact the editor for any information.

NONFICTION **Contact:** Chuck Gysi, editor and publisher. Needs how-to, interview, new product, personal experience, photo feature, technical. Does not want articles off-topic of the publication's audience (radio hobbyists). "If you aren't writing about police scanners, CB radios, or two-way radios and don't know our audience, we're not interested in your article. It's essential to know your subject matter." **Buys 18 mss/year.** Query by e-mail only. "Inquire before writing with an outline of your proposed article. We're also interested in working with new authors, but we like to work with them in shaping articles before they are started. Photos and graphics are needed for all articles and must be provided by the author." Length:

2,500-3,000 words. **Pays $75 or more.** No expenses paid.

PHOTOS Attach photos and/or graphics with all submissions. Please avoid low-resolution photos. Captions, identification of subjects required. Photos must be author generated, or permission must be obtained for publication. Photos should be copyright-free. Reviews GIF/JPEG/TIF files. Offers no additional payment for photos accepted with ms. Buys all rights.

POETRY Does not accept any poetry whatsoever.

TIPS "If you don't know our subject matter well, which is the use and enjoyment of police scanners, citizens band radio, and two-way radios in the GMRS/FRS/MURS radio services, please do not waste our time and your time. We'll know instantly if you are a radio hobbyist or not. Make sure all submissions include artwork. Great artwork in a vertical format may be featured on our cover and help turn your article into a cover feature. The editor is a long-time journalist willing to work with new writers who are radio communications hobbyists."

$$ SEWNEWS

Peak Media Properties, 741 Corporate Circle, Golden CO 80401. **E-mail:** sewnews@sewnews.com. **Website:** www.sewnews.com. **Contact:** Amanda Carestio, editor-in-chief. **70% freelance written. Works with a small number of new/unpublished writers each year.** Monthly magazine covering fashion, gift, and home-dec sewing. "*Sew News* magazine is a monthly publication devoted to the enthusiastic and creative people who wants to sew. We provide them with accurate, helpful, step-by-step information for personalizing ready-to-wear and creating original fashions, accessories, gifts, and home décor that express her personal style." Estab. 1980. Circ. 185,000. Byline given. Pays on publication. No kill fee. Publishes ms an average of 6 months after acceptance. Submit seasonal material 6 months in advance. Accepts queries by mail, e-mail. Accepts simultaneous submissions. Responds in 2 months to mss. Sample copy: $5.99. Guidelines online.

NONFICTION Needs how-to, interview. **Buys 200-240 mss/year.** Query with published clips if available. Length: 500-2,000 words. **Pays $50-500.**

PHOTOS Prefers digital images, color photos, or slides. Send photos. Identification of subjects required. Payment included in ms price. Buys all rights.

TIPS "Query first with writing sample and outline of proposed story. Areas most open to freelancers are how-to and sewing techniques; give explicit, step-by-step instructions, plus rough art. We're using more home decorating and soft craft content."

$ SUNSHINE ARTIST

JP Media LLC, N7528 Aanstad Rd., PO Box 5000, Iola WI 54945. (800)597-2573. **Fax:** (715)445-4053. **E-mail:** editor@sunshineartist.com. **Website:** www.sunshineartist.com. Publisher: Diana Jones. Editor: Stephanie Hintz. Marketing Manager: Justin Van Slooten. Monthly magazine covering art shows in the US. "We are the premiere marketing/reference magazine for artists and crafts professionals who earn their living through art shows nationwide. We list more than 2,000 shows monthly, critique many of them, and publish articles on marketing, selling and other issues of concern to professional show circuit artists." Estab. 1972. Circ. 12,000. Byline given. Pays 60 days from publication date. Pays $50 kill fee. Publishes 1-3 months after acceptance. Accepts queries by e-mail. Accepts simultaneous submissions. Responds in 1 week to queries. Sample copy for $5.

NONFICTION Buys 5-10 freelance mss/year. Send complete ms. Length: 1,000-2,000 words. **Pays $30-250.**

REPRINTS Send photocopy and information about when and where the material previously appeared.

PHOTOS Send photos. Captions, identification of subjects, model releases, photo credits required. Offers no additional payment for photos accepted with ms.

$$ TEDDY BEAR & FRIENDS

JP Media LLC, P.O. Box 5000, Iola WI 54945-5000. 715-445-5000. **Fax:** 715-445-4053. **E-mail:** editor@teddybearandfriends.com. **Website:** www.teddybearandfriends.com. **Contact:** Joyce Greenholdt, editor. **65% freelance written. Works with a small number of new/unpublished writers each year.** Bimonthly magazine on teddy bears for collectors, enthusiasts, and bearmakers. Estab. 1985. Byline given. Payment upon publication on the last day of the month the issue is mailed. Submit seasonal material 6 months in advance. Accepts simultaneous submissions. Sample copy and writer's guidelines for $2 and 9x12 SAE.

NONFICTION Needs historical, how-to, interview. No articles from the bear's point of view. **Buys 30-40 mss/year.** Query with published clips. Length: 900-1,500 words. **Pays $100-350.** Pays expenses of writers on assignment.

PHOTOS Send photos. Captions required. Reviews transparencies, prints. Offers no additional payment for photos accepted with ms. Buys one-time rights.

TIPS "We are interested in good, professional writers around the country with a strong knowledge of teddy bears. Historical profile of bear companies, profiles of contemporary artists, and knowledgeable reports on museum collections are of interest."

$$ THREADS

Taunton Press, 63 South Main St., P.O. Box 5506, Newtown CT 06470. (203)426-8171. **Fax:** (203)426-3434. **E-mail:** th@taunton.com. **Website:** www.threadsmagazine.com. Bimonthly magazine covering garment sewing, garment design, and embellishments (including quilting and embroidery). Written by sewing experts; magazine is geared primarily to intermediate/advanced sewers. "We're seeking proposals from hands-on authors who first and foremost have a skill. Being an experienced writer is of secondary consideration." Estab. 1985. Circ. 129,000. Byline given. Offers $150 kill fee. Editorial lead time minimum 4 months. Accepts simultaneous submissions. Responds in 1-2 months to queries. Guidelines online.

NONFICTION Send proposal that includes: "a brief 1- or 2-paragraph summary; an outline of the ideas and points you'll cover; sample photographs of work illustrating the topic (quick snapshots are fine) or supporting fabric swatches if you have them. **Payment varies.** Pays expenses of writers on assignment.

COLUMNS/DEPARTMENTS Product reviews; book reviews; Tips; Closures (stories of a humorous nature). Query. **Closures pays $150/page. Each sewing tip printed pays $25.**

HOME & GARDEN

$$ THE AMERICAN GARDENER

American Horticultural Society, 7931 E. Boulevard Dr., Alexandria VA 22308-1300. (703)768-5700. **E-mail:** editor@ahsgardening.org. **Website:** www.ahsgardening.org. **Contact:** David J. Ellis, editor. **60% freelance written.** Bimonthly, 64-page, four-color magazine that addresses the intersection of gardening and environmental stewardship. "This is the official publication of the American Horticultural Society (AHS), a national, nonprofit, membership organization for gardeners, founded in 1922. The AHS mission is 'to open the eyes of all Americans to the vital connection between people and plants, and to inspire all Americans to become responsible caretakers of the earth, to celebrate America's diversity through the art and science of horticulture, and to lead this effort by sharing the society's unique national resources with all Americans.' All articles are also published in the digital edition." Estab. 1922. Circ. 20,000. Byline given. Pays on publication. Offers 25% kill fee. Publishes ms an average of 6 months after acceptance. Editorial lead time 6 months. Submit seasonal material at least 1 year in advance. Accepts queries by mail, e-mail. Responds in 3-4 months to queries. Sample copy: $8. Writer's guidelines by e-mail and online.

> "*The American Gardener* goes out bimonthly to about 20,000 members of the American Horticultural Society. *The American Gardener* is primarily freelance written, and its content differs considerably from that of other gardening publications. Articles are intended to bring this knowledgeable group new information, ranging from profiles of specific plant groups to advice on environmentally sustainable design and gardening techniques. We introduce readers to unusual plants, personalities, and issues that will enrich what we assume is already a passionate commitment to gardening and the natural world."

NONFICTION Needs book excerpts, general interest, how-to, personal experience, photo feature, profile, reviews. No poetry and no personal essays about your garden. **Buys 20 mss/year.** Query with published clips. Length: 1,500-2,000 words. **Pays $250-600, depending on complexity and author's experience.** Pays expenses of writers on assignment.

REPRINTS Rarely purchases second rights. Send PDF file of article with information about when and where the material previously appeared. Payment varies.

PHOTOS E-mail or check website for guidelines before submitting. It is very important to include some kind of plant list for your stock so we can determine if you specialize in the types of plants we cover. The list does not have to be comprehensive, but it should give some idea of the breadth of your photo archive. If, for instance, your list contains mostly tulips, pansies, roses, and other popular plants like these, your stock will not be a good match for our articles. Also, if your list does not include the botanical names for all plants, we will not be able to use the photos. Identification of subjects required. Photo captions required; include complete botanical names of plants including genus, species, and botanical variety or cultivar. Pays $350 maximum for color cover; $80-130 for color inside. Pays on publication. Credit line given. Buys one-time North American and nonexclusive rights. Buys one-time print rights, plus limited rights to run article on members-only website.

COLUMNS/DEPARTMENTS Natural Connections (explains a natural phenomenon—plant and pollinator relationships, plant and fungus relationships, parasites—that may be observed in nature or in the garden), 750-1,000 words; Homegrown Harvest (articles on edible plants delivered in a personal, reassuring voice. Each issue focuses on a single crop, such as carrots, blueberries, or parsley), 800-900 words; Plant in the Spotlight (profiles of a single plant species or cultivar, including a personal perspective on why it's a favored plant), 600 words. **Buys 3-5 mss/year.** Query with published clips. **Pays $150-250.**

TIPS "The majority of our readers are advanced, passionate amateur gardeners; about 20% are horticultural professionals. Most are interested in environmental stewardship and encouraging pollinators and other beneficial wildlife, so prefer to avoid the use of synthetic chemical pesticides."

$$ CALIFORNIA HOMES

McFadden-Bray Publishing Corp., P.O. Box 8655, Newport Beach CA 92658. **E-mail:** susan@calhomesmagazine.com. **Website:** www.calhomesmagazine.com. **Contact:** Susan McFadden, editor-in-chief. **80% freelance written.** Bimonthly magazine covering California interiors, architecture, some food, travel, history, and current events in the field. Estab. 1997. Circ. 80,000. Byline given. Pays on publication. Offers 50% kill fee. Publishes ms an average of 3 months after acceptance. Editorial lead time 3 months. Submit seasonal material 6 months in advance. Accepts queries by mail, e-mail. Accepts simultaneous submissions. Responds in 1 month to queries; in 2 months to mss. Sample copy: $7.50. Guidelines for #10 SASE.

NONFICTION Query. Length: 500-1,000 words. **Pays $250-750.** Pays expenses of writers on assignment.

PHOTOS State availability. Captions required. Negotiates payment individually. Buys one-time rights.

$$ CHARLESTON STYLE & DESIGN

P.O. Box 20098, Charleston SC 29413. **E-mail:** editor@charlestonstyleanddesign.com. **Website:** www.charlestonstyleanddesign.com. **Contact:** Mary K. Love, editor. **85% freelance written.** Quarterly magazine covering design (architecture and interior design) and lifestyle (wines, restaurants, fashion, local retailers, and travel). "*Charleston Style & Design* is a full-color magazine for discriminating readers eager to discover new horizons in Charleston and the world beyond. We offer vivid, well-researched articles on trends in home design, fashion, food and wine, health/fitness, antiques/collectibles, the arts, travel, and more. We also profile celebrities and opinion leaders who have a link with Charleston or the area." Need personal essays and local writers for assignments. Estab. 2008. Circ. 45,000. Byline given. Pays on publication. Pays 50% kill fee. Publishes ms 4 months after acceptance. Editorial lead time 3-6 months. Submit seasonal material 3 months in advance. Accepts queries by e-mail. Accepts simultaneous submissions. Responds in 2 weeks to queries; in 2 months to mss. Sample copy available online. Guidelines via e-mail.

NONFICTION Needs essays, general interest. Query with published clips. Length: 300-1,200 words. **Pays $120-500.** Pays expenses of writers on assignment. Sometimes pays expenses of writers on assignment.

PHOTOS State availability of photos with submission. Photos require captions, model releases, and identification of subjects. Reviews GIF/JPEG files. Offers no additional payment for photos accepted with ms.

COLUMNS/DEPARTMENTS Reflections (personal essays), 600 words. "Your essay should present an idea, concept, or experience that you think would be of interest to our readers. We believe that the best personal essays have all the characteristics of a good story, offering compelling descriptions, a narrative line, and, of course, a personal point of view. Beyond that, we look for essays that give readers a 'takeaway,' a thought or insight to which they can relate." Submit personal essay and short two-sentence bio via e-mail with the words "personal essay" in the subject line. **Pays $200.**

TIPS "Our magazine is looking for local reporters with a clear, vivid style and experience writing about design and lifestyle topics. The best way to break into our magazine is to submit strong clips that demonstrate your competence and versatility. Writers should be able to produce well-crafted articles on a tight deadline. References are required."

$$$$ COASTAL LIVING

Southern Progress Corp., 4100 Old Montgomery Hwy., Birmingham AL 35209. (205)445-6007. **E-mail:** letters@coastalliving.com. **E-mail:** ellen.mcgauley@timeinc.com; tracey.minkin@timeinc.com; chris.hughes@timeinc.com; katie_finley@timeinc.com. **Website:** www.coastalliving.com. **Contact:** Ellen McGauley, homes editor; Tracey Minkin, travel editor; Chris Hughes, food and wine editor; Katie Finley, deputy editor. "Bimonthly magazine for those who live or vacation along our nation's coasts. The magazine emphasizes home design and travel, but also covers a wide variety of other lifestyle topics and coastal concerns." Estab. 1997. Circ. 660,000. Pays on acceptance. Offers 25% kill fee. Accepts queries by e-mail. Accepts simultaneous submissions. Responds in 2 months to queries. Guidelines online.

NONFICTION Query with clips and SASE. **Pays $1/word.**

PHOTOS State availability.

TIPS "Query us with ideas that are very specifically targeted to the columns that are currently in the magazine."

$$ CONCRETE HOMES

Publications and Communications, Inc. (PCI), 13581 Pond Springs Rd., Suite 450, Austin TX 78729. (512)250-9023. **Fax:** (512)331-3950. **E-mail:** info@concretehomesmagazine.com. **Website:** concretehomesmagazine.com. **85% freelance written.** Bimonthly magazine covering homes built with concrete. *Concrete Homes* is a publication designed to be informative to consumers, builders, contractors, architects, etc., who are interested in concrete homes. The magazine profiles concrete home projects (they must be complete) and offers how-to and industry news articles. Estab. 1999. Circ. 25,000. Byline given. Pays on publication. Offers 100% kill fee. Publishes ms an average of 2 months after acceptance. Editorial lead time 2 months. Submit seasonal material 3-4 months in advance. Accepts queries by mail, e-mail. Accepts simultaneous submissions. Responds in 1 month.

NONFICTION Needs how-to, interview, new product, technical. **Buys 30-40 mss/year.** Query or query with published clips Length: 800-2,000 words. **Pays $200-250.** Pays expenses of writers on assignment.

PHOTOS State availability. Captions required. Reviews 8x10 transparencies, prints, GIF/JPEG files. Offers no additional payment for photos accepted with ms. Buys all rights.

TIPS Demonstrate awareness of concrete homes and some knowledge of the construction/building industry.

$$ EARLY AMERICAN LIFE

Firelands Media Group LLC, 16759 W Park Circle Dr, Chagrin Falls OH 44023. (440)543-8566. **E-mail:** queries@firelandsmedia.com. **Website:** www.earlyamericanlife.com. **Contact:** Jeanmarie Andrews, executive editor. **60% freelance written.** "Our readers are interested in America's founding heritage including antiques, traditional crafts, architecture, restoration, collecting, and re-enacting. We are particularly interested in using antiques and crafts in decorating, restoring old homes and building replicas of period examples, judging and making handcrafts of the period (including how-to's), and experiencing period lifestyles, be it though military re-enacting, playing old games and sports, or cooking on a hearth." *Early American Life* is a bimonthly magazine for people who are interested in experiencing the warmth and beauty of the 1600-1840 period in America, using period style in their homes and lives today, re-enacting past events and how people lived, and visiting historic sites and museums. Estab. 1970. Circ. 90,000. Byline given. Pays on acceptance. 25% kill fee. Publishes ms an average of 1 year after acceptance. For upcoming events, submit material at least four months before the event. We are geared to the seasons, so we prepare a year ahead. Accepts queries by mail, e-mail. Responds within 1 week to queries. Sample copy for 9x12 SAE with $2.50 postage. Guidelines online.

We do not assign stories to writers whose proficiency in history and written communication is unproven. We prefers to see samples both as submitted and after publication to distinguish a writer's skill from that of the editor. We offer regular assignments to freelance writers who have demonstrated the ability to deliver on-target work on-time.

NONFICTION Contact: Jeanmarie Andrews, executive editor. Needs book excerpts, historical, how-to, photo feature, travel, architecture and decorating, antiques, heritage studio crafts,historic destinations. Special issues: Christmas. No material outside our period (1600-1840). Must have some connection to

American history. **Buys 40 mss/year.** Query. Length: 750-2,500 words. **Pays $250-700; additional payment for photos.** Pays expenses of writers on assignment. For assigned stories.

PHOTOS Contact: Jeanmarie Andrews. In general, we uses photos to illustrate our stories, so we give photo assignments. We will consider unassigned photos that accompany a story or report an event, such as a re-enactment—but in such cases, the story is the key. Model releases required. Negotiated by assignment. Six months exclusive, later non-exclusive.

TIPS "Our readers are eager for ideas on how to bring early America into their lives. Conceive a new approach to satisfy their related interests in arts, crafts, travel to historic sites, and especially in houses decorated in the Early American style. Write to entertain and inform at the same time. We are visually oriented, so writers are asked to supply images or suggest sources for illustrations."

$$$ FINE GARDENING

Taunton Press, 63 S. Main St., P.O. Box 5506, Newtown CT 06470-5506. (800)309-9193. **Fax:** (203)426-3434. **E-mail:** fg@taunton.com. **Website:** www.finegardening.com. Bimonthly magazine covering gardening. High-value magazine on landscape and ornamental gardening. Articles written by avid gardeners—first person, handson gardening experiences. Estab. 1988. Circ. 200,000. Byline given. Pays on acceptance. No kill fee. Publishes an average of 6 months after acceptance. Editorial lead time 1 year. Submit seasonal material 1 year in advance. Accepts queries by mail. Accepts simultaneous submissions. Guidelines free.

NONFICTION Needs how-to, personal experience, photo feature. Pays expenses of writers on assignment.

PHOTOS Send photos. Reviews digital images. Buys serial rights.

TIPS "It's most important to have solid first-hand experience as a gardener. Tell us what you've done with your own landscape and plants."

$$ FINE HOMEBUILDING

The Taunton Press, Inc., 63 S. Main St., P.O. Box 5506, Newtown CT 06470-5506. (203)426-8171. **Fax:** (203)426-3434. **E-mail:** fh@taunton.com. **Website:** www.finehomebuilding.com. Bimonthly magazine for builders, architects, contractors, owner/builders and others who are seriously involved in building new houses or reviving old ones. Estab. 1981. Circ. 300,000. Byline given. Pays half on acceptance, half on publication. Offers kill fee. Offers on acceptance payment as kill fee. Publishes ms an average of 1 year after acceptance. Accepts simultaneous submissions. Responds in 1 month to queries. Guidelines online.

NONFICTION Query with outline, description, photographs, sketches and SASE. **Pays $150/published page.** Pays expenses of writers on assignment.

PHOTOS Take lots of work-in-progress photos. Color print film, ASA 400, from either Kodak or Fuji works best. If you prefer to use slide film, use ASA 100. Keep track of the negatives; we will need them for publication. If you're not sure what to use or how to go about it, feel free to call for advice.

COLUMNS/DEPARTMENTS Tools & Materials, Reviews, Questions & Answers, Tips & Techniques, Cross Section, What's the Difference?, Finishing Touches, Great Moments, Breaktime, Drawing Board (design column). Query with outline, description, photographs, sketches and SASE. **Payment varies**

TIPS "Our chief contributors are home builders, architects and other professionals. We're more interested in your point of view and technical expertise than your prose style. Adopt an easy, conversational style and define any obscure terms for non-specialists. We try to visit all our contributors and rarely publish building projects we haven't seen, or authors we haven't met."

$$ GREENPRINTS

P.O. Box 1355, Fairview NC 28730. (828)628-1902. **E-mail:** pat@greenprints.com. **Website:** www.greenprints.com. **Contact:** Pat Stone, managing editor. **90% freelance written.** "*GreenPrints* is the 'Weeder's Digest.' We share the human—*not* how-to—side of gardening. We publish true personal gardening stories and essays: humorous, heartfelt, insightful, inspiring. We love good, true, well-told personal *stories*—all must be about gardening!" Estab. 1990. Circ. 11,000. Byline given. No editorial lead time. Accepts queries by mail, e-mail. Accepts simultaneous submissions. Responds in 3 months to mss. Sample: $5. Guidelines available online (look under About Us).

NONFICTION Needs essays, general interest, historical, humor, inspirational, nostalgic, personal experience. Does not want how-to. **Buys 60 mss/year.** Submit complete ms by e-mail or snail. Please include your mailing address and a couple of interesting bio lies—I mean lines!—about yourself. Length: 250-2,500 words. **Pays $50-200 for unsolicited articles.** Pays expenses of writers on assignment.

COLUMNS/DEPARTMENTS Broken Trowel (the story of your funniest garden mistake), 300 words. **Buys 12 mss/year.** Submit complete ms. **Pays $50-75.**

FICTION "We run very little fiction." **Buys 2 mss/year.** Submit complete ms. **Pays $75-200.**

POETRY Needs free verse, light verse, traditional. "If it's not hands-on and gardening based, please don't send it." Buys 4 poems/year. Submit maximum 3 poems. **Pays $25.**

FILLERS Wants anecdotes, short humor. Length: 100-300 words. **Pays $50-75.**

TIPS Wants "a great, true, *unique* personal *story* with dialogue, a narrative, and something special that happens to make it truly stand out."

$$$$ HORTICULTURE

Active Interest Media, 5720 Flatiron Pwky., Boulder CO 80301. **E-mail:** edit@hortmag.com. **Website:** www.hortmag.com. Bimonthly magazine. *Horticulture*, the country's oldest gardening magazine, is designed for active home gardeners. Our goal is to offer a blend of text, photographs and illustrations that will both instruct and inspire readers. Circ. 160,000. Byline given. Offers kill fee. Submit seasonal material 10 months in advance. Accepts queries by mail, e-mail, fax. Accepts simultaneous submissions. Responds in 3 months to queries. Guidelines for SASE or by e-mail.

NONFICTION Buys 70 mss/year. Query with published clips, subject background material and SASE. Length: 800-1,000 words. **Pays $500.** Pays expenses of writers on assignment.

COLUMNS/DEPARTMENTS Length: 200-600 words. Query with published clips, subject background material and SASE. Include disk where possible. **Pays $250.**

TIPS "We believe every article must offer ideas or illustrate principles that our readers might apply on their own gardens. Our readers want to become better, more creative gardeners."

$$ MOUNTAIN LIVING

Wiesner Media Network Communications, Inc., 1780 S. Bellaire St., Suite 505, Denver CO 80222. (303)248-2060. **Fax:** (303)248-2066. **E-mail:** greatideas@mountainliving.com; hscott@mountainliving.com; cdeorio@mountainliving.com. **Website:** www.mountainliving.com. **Contact:** Holly Scott, publisher; Christine DeOrio, editor-in-chief. **50% freelance written.** Magazine published 7 times/year covering architecture, interior design, and lifestyle issues for people who live in, visit, or hope to live in the mountains. Estab. 1994. Circ. 40,000. Byline given. Pays on acceptance. Offers 15% kill fee. Publishes ms an average of 4 months after acceptance. Editorial lead time 6 months. Submit seasonal material 8-12 months in advance. Responds in 6-8 weeks to queries. Responds in 2 months to mss. Sample copy for $7. Guidelines by e-mail.

NONFICTION Needs photo feature, travel, home features. **Buys 30 mss/year.** Query with published clips. Length: 200-600 words. **Pays $250-600.** Pays expenses of writers on assignment.

PHOTOS Provide photos (digital files only, saved as JPEG or TIFF and at least 300 dpi). State availability. All features photography is assigned to photographers who specialize in architectural and interior photography. Negotiates payment individually. Buys one-time rights, plus rights to run photo on website.

COLUMNS/DEPARTMENTS ML Recommends; Short Travel Tips; New Product Information; Art; Insider's Guide; Entertaining. Length: 150-400 words.

TIPS "*Mountain Living* is an image-driven magazine and selects its featured homes for their exceptional architecture and interior design. The editorial staff will not consider queries that are not accompanied by professional or scouting photos. Story angles are determined by the editorial staff and assigned to freelance writers. To be considered for freelance assignments, please send your résumé and 4 published clips. Before you query, please read the magazine to get a sense of who we are and what we do."

$$$$ STYLE AT HOME

Transcontinental Media, G.P., 25 Sheppard Ave. W., Suite 100, Toronto ON M2N 6S7 Canada. (416)733-7600. **Fax:** (416)218-3632. **Website:** www.styleathome.com. **85% freelance written.** Magazine published 12 times/year. "The number one magazine choice of Canadian women aged 25 to 54 who have a serious interest in decorating. Provides an authoritative, stylish collection of inspiring and accessible Canadian interiors, decor projects; reports on style design trends." Estab. 1997. Circ. 235,000. Byline given. Pays on acceptance. Offers 50% kill fee. Editorial lead time 4 months. Submit seasonal material 6 months in advance. Accepts queries by online submission form. Accepts simultaneous submissions. Responds in 1 month to queries; 2 weeks to mss.

NONFICTION Needs interview, new product. No how-to; these are planned in-house. **Buys 80 mss/year.** Query with published clips; include scouting shots with interior story queries. Length: 300-700 words. **Pays $300-1,000.** Pays expenses of writers on assignment.

TIPS "Break in by familiarizing yourself with the type of interiors we show. Be very up-to-date with the design and home decor market in Canada. Provide a lead to a fabulous home or garden."

HUMOR

$ FUNNY TIMES

Funny Times, Inc., P.O. Box 18530, Cleveland Heights OH 44118. (216)371-8600. **E-mail:** info@funnytimes.com. **Website:** www.funnytimes.com. **Contact:** Ray Lesser and Susan Wolpert, publishers. **50% freelance written.** Monthly tabloid for humor. "*Funny Times* is a monthly review of America's funniest cartoonists and writers. We are a unique voice in modern American humor with a progressive/peace-oriented/environmental/politically activist slant." Estab. 1985. Circ. 58,000. Byline given. Pays on publication. Publishes ms an average of 6 months after acceptance. Editorial lead time 2 months. Accepts simultaneous submissions. Responds in 3 months to mss. Sample copy for $3 or 9x12 SAE with 3 first-class stamps ($1.61 postage). Guidelines online.

NONFICTION Needs essays, humor, interview, opinion, personal experience. **Buys 60 mss/year.** Send complete ms. Length: 600-800 words. **Pays $60 minimum.** Pays expenses of writers on assignment.

COLUMNS/DEPARTMENTS Query with published clips.

FICTION Wants anything funny. Needs humorous. **Buys 6 mss/year.** Query with published clips. Length: 600-800 words. **Pays $50-150.**

TIPS "Send us a small packet (1-3 items) of only your very funniest stuff. If this makes us laugh, we'll be glad to ask for more. We particularly welcome previously published material that has been well received elsewhere."

INFLIGHT

$$ HORIZON EDITION MAGAZINE

Paradigm Communications Group, 2701 First Ave., Suite 250, Seattle WA 98121. (206)441-5871. **Fax:** (206)448-6939. **E-mail:** info@paradigmcg.com. **Website:** www.alaskaairlinesmagazine.com/horizonedition. **Contact:** Michele Andrus Dill, editor. **90% freelance written.** Monthly inflight magazine covering travel, business, and leisure in the Pacific Northwest. "*Horizon Edition Magazine* is the monthly in-flight magazine for Horizon Air, reaching more than 574,000 travelers in Washington, Oregon, Idaho, Montana, California, Nevada, Western Canada and Baja, Mexico, each month." Estab. 1990. Byline given. Pays on publication. Offers 33% kill fee. Publishes ms an average of 1 year after acceptance. Editorial lead time 6 months. Submit seasonal material 6 months in advance. Accepts queries by mail, fax. Accepts simultaneous submissions. Sample copy for 9x12 SASE. Guidelines available online.

NONFICTION Needs essays, general interest, historical, how-to, humor, interview, personal experience, photo feature, travel, business. Special issues: Meeting planners' guide, golf, gift guide. No material unrelated to the Pacific Northwest. **Buys approximately 36 mss/year.** Query with published clips. Length: 2,000-2,500 words. **Pays $250 minimum.** Pays expenses of writers on assignment.

PHOTOS State availability. Captions, identification of subjects, model releases required. Reviews transparencies, prints. Negotiates payment individually. Buys one-time rights.

COLUMNS/DEPARTMENTS Region (Northwest news/profiles), 200-500 words. **Buys 15 mss/year.** Query with published clips. **Pays $100 minimum.**

INSURANCE

$$$$ ADVISOR TODAY

NAIFA, 2901 Telestar Court, Falls Church VA 22042. (703)770-8204. **E-mail:** amseka@naifa.org. **Website:** www.advisortoday.com. **Contact:** Ayo Mseka, editor in chief. **25% freelance written.** Monthly magazine covering life insurance and financial planning. "*Advisor Today* has the largest circulation among insurance and financial planning advising magazines. Founded in 1906 as *Life Association News*, *Advisor Today* is the official publication of the National Association of Insurance and Financial Advisors. Our mission is to provide practical information, sales ideas, resources, and business strategies to help insurance and financial advisors succeed." Estab. 1906. Circ. 110,000. Pays on acceptance or publication (by mutual agreement with editor). No kill fee. Publishes ms an average of 3 months after acceptance. Editorial lead time: 3 months. Submit seasonal material 6 months in advance. Accepts queries by mail, e-mail, fax, phone. Accepts simultaneous submissions. Sample copy free. Guidelines available online at www.advisortoday.com/about/contribute.cfm.

NONFICTION **Buys 8 mss/year.** "We prefer e-mail submissions in Microsoft Word format. For other formats and submission methods, please query first. For all articles and queries, contact Ayo Mseka. Web articles should cover the same subject matter covered in the magazine. The articles can be between 300-800 words and should be submitted to Ayo Mseka." Length: 2,300 words for cover articles; 1,000 words for feature articles; 650-700 words for columns and speciality articles; 300-800 words for Web articles. **Pays $800-2,000.** Pays expenses of writers on assignment.

JUVENILE

AQUILA

Studio 2 Willowfield Studios, 67a Willowfield Rd., Eastbourne BN22 8AP England. (44)(132)343-1313. **E-mail:** editor@aquila.co.uk. **Website:** www.aquila.co.uk. "*Aquila* is an educational magazine for readers ages 8-13 including factual articles (no pop/celebrity material), arts/crafts, and puzzles." Entire publication aimed at juvenile market. Estab. 1993. Circ. 40,000. Pays on publication. Accepts queries by mail, e-mail. Accepts simultaneous submissions. Sample copy: £5. Guidelines online.

NONFICTION Young Readers: animal, arts/crafts, concept, cooking, games/puzzles, health, history, how-to, interview/profile, math, nature/environment, science, sports. Middle Readers: animal, arts/crafts, concept, cooking, games/puzzles, health, history, interview/profile, math, nature/environment, science, sports. Query. Length: 600-800 words. **Pays £90.** Pays expenses of writers on assignment.

FICTION Young Readers: animal, contemporary, fantasy, folktales, health, history, humorous, multicultural, nature/environment, problem solving, religious, science fiction, sports, suspense/mystery. Middle Readers: animal, contemporary, fantasy, folktales, health, history, humorous, multicultural, nature/environment, problem solving, religious, romance, science fiction, sports, suspense/mystery. Length: 1,000-1,150 words. **Pays £90.**

TIPS "We only accept a high level of educational material for children ages 8-13 with a good standard of literacy and ability."

BABYBUG

Cricket Media, Inc., 7926 Jones Branch Dr., Suite 870, McLean VA 22102. (703)885-3400. **Website:** www.cricketmedia.com. **50% freelance written.** "*Babybug*, a look-and-listen magazine, presents simple poems, stories, nonfiction, and activities that reflect the natural playfulness and curiosity of babies and toddlers." Estab. 1994. Circ. 45,000. Byline given. Pays on publication. Accepts queries by online submission form. Accepts simultaneous submissions. Responds in 3-6 months to mss. Guidelines online.

NONFICTION "First Concepts," a playful take on a simple idea, expressed through very short nonfiction. See recent issues for examples. **Buys 10-20 mss/year.** Submit through online submissions manager: cricketmag.submittable.com/submit. Length: up to 6 sentences. **Pays up to 25¢/word.** Pays expenses of writers on assignment.

FICTION Wants very short, clear fiction.rhythmic, rhyming. **Buys 10-20 mss/year.** Submit complete ms via online submissions manager. Length: up to 6 sentences. **Pays up to 25¢/word.**

POETRY "We are especially interested in rhythmic and rhyming poetry. Poems may explore a baby's day, or they may be more whimsical." Submit via online submissions manager. **Pays up to $3/line; $25 minimum.**

TIPS "We are particularly interested in mss that explore simple concepts, encourage very young children's imaginative play, and provide opportunities for adult readers and babies to interact. We welcome work that reflects diverse family cultures and traditions."

BREAD FOR GOD'S CHILDREN

Bread Ministries, INC., P.O. Box 1017, Arcadia FL 34265. (863)494-6214. **E-mail:** bread@breadministries.org. **E-mail:** Do not accept. **Website:** www.breadministries.org. **Contact:** Judith M. Gibbs, editor. **10% freelance written.** An interdenominational Christian teaching publication published 4-6 times/year written to aid children and youth in leading a Christian life. Estab. 1972. Circ. 10,000 (U.S. and Canada). Byline given. Publication No kill fee. Publishes ms an average of 6 months after acceptance. Accepts queries by mail. Accepts simultaneous submissions. Responds in 6 months to mss. Sample copy for 9x12 SAE and 5 first-class stamps. Guidelines for #10 SASE.

NONFICTION Needs inspirational, All levels: how-to. "We do not want anything detrimental to solid family values. Most topics will fit if they are slanted to our basic needs." **Buys 3-4 mss/year.** Send complete ms. Length: 500-800 words **On publication**

REPRINTS Send tearsheet and information about when and where the material previously appeared.

COLUMNS/DEPARTMENTS Freelance columns: Let's Chat (children's Christian values), 500-700 words; Teen Page (youth Christian values), 600-800 words; Idea Page (games, crafts, Bible drills). **Buys 5-8 mss/year.** Send complete ms. **Pays $30.**

FICTION "We are looking for writers who have a solid knowledge of Biblical principles and are concerned for the youth of today living by those principles. Stories must be well written, with the story itself getting the message across—no preaching, moralizing, or tag endings." Needs historical, religious, Young readers, middle readers, young adult/teen: adventure, religious, problem-solving, sports. Looks for "teaching stories that portray Christian lifestyles without preaching." **Buys 10-15 mss/year.** Send complete ms. Length: 600-800 words for young children; 900-1,500 words for older children. **Pays $40-50.**

TIPS "We want stories or articles that illustrate overcoming obstacles by faith and living solid, Christian lives. Know our publication and what we have used in the past. Know the readership and publisher's guidelines. Stories should teach the value of morality and honesty without preaching. Edit carefully for content and grammar."

$ CADET QUEST MAGAZINE

Calvinist Cadet Corps, 1333 Alger St. SE, Grand Rapids MI 49507. (616)241-5616. **Fax:** (616)241-5558. **E-mail:** submissions@calvinistcadets.org. **Website:** www.calvinistcadets.org. **Contact:** Steve Bootsma, editor. Magazine published 7 times/year. *Cadet Quest Magazine* shows boys 9-14 how God is at work in their lives and in the world around them. Estab. 1958. Circ. 6,000. Byline given. Pays on acceptance. No kill fee. Publishes ms 4-11 months after acceptance. Accepts queries by mail, e-mail. Accepts simultaneous submissions. Responds in 2 months to mss. Sample copy for 9x12 SASE and $1.45 postage. Guidelines online.

NONFICTION Needs informational. Special issues: New themes list available online in January or for SASE. "Articles about Christian athletes, coaching tips, and developing Christian character through sports are appreciated. Photos of these sports or athletes are also welcomed. Be original in presenting these topics to boys. Articles about camping, nature, and survival should be practical—the 'how-to' approach is best. 'God in nature' articles, if done without being preachy, are appreciated." Send complete ms via postal mail or e-mail (in body of e-mail; no attachments). Length: up to 1,500 words. **Pays 5¢/word and 1 contributor's copy.**

REPRINTS For reprints, send typed ms with rights for sale noted or e-mail (in body of e-mail; no attachments). Payment varies.

PHOTOS Pays $5 each for photos purchased with ms.

COLUMNS/DEPARTMENTS Project/Hobby articles (simple projects boys 9-14 can do on their own, made with easily accessible materials; must provide clear, accurate instructions); Cartoons and Puzzles (wholesome and boy-oriented logic puzzles, crosswords, and hidden pictures).

TIPS "The best time to submit stories/articles is early in the year (January-April). Also remember readers are boys ages 9-14. Stories must reflect or add to the theme of the issue and be from a Christian perspective."

$$ CRICKET

Cricket Media, Inc., 7926 Jones Branch Dr., Suite 870, McLean VA 22102. (703)885-3400. **Website:** www.cricketmag.com. *Cricket* is a monthly literary magazine for ages 9-14. Publishes 9 issues/year. Estab. 1973. Circ. 73,000. Byline given. Pays on publication. Accepts queries by online submission form. Accepts simultaneous submissions. Responds in 3-6 months to mss. Sample copy available online. Guidelines available online.

NONFICTION *Cricket* publishes thought-provoking nonfiction articles on a wide range of subjects: history, biography, true adventure, science and technology, sports, inventors and explorers, architecture and engineering, archaeology, dance, music, theater, and art. Articles should be carefully researched and include a solid bibliography that shows that research has gone beyond reviewing websites. Submit via online submissions manager (cricketmag.submittable.com). Length: 1,200-1,800 words. **Pays up to 25¢/word.** Pays expenses of writers on assignment.

FICTIONrealistic, contemporary, historic, humor, mysteries, fantasy, science fiction, folk/fairy tales, legend, myth. No didactic, sex, religious, or horror stories. **Buys 75-100 mss/year.** Submit via online submissions manager (cricketmag.submittable.com). Length: 1,200-1,800 words. **Pays up to 25¢/word.**

POETRY *Cricket* publishes both serious and humorous poetry. Poems should be well-crafted, with precise and vivid language and images. Poems can explore a variety of themes, from nature, to family and friendships, to whatever you can imagine that will delight our readers and invite their wonder and emotional response. Buys 20-30 poems/year. Submit maximum 6 poems. Length: up to 35 lines/poem. Most poems run 8-15 lines. **Pays up to $3/line.**

FILLERS Crossword puzzles, logic puzzles, math puzzles, crafts, recipes, science experiments, games and activities from other countries, plays, music, art. **Pays $75.**

TIPS Writers: "Read copies of back issues and current issues. Adhere to specified word limits. *Please* do not query." Would currently like to see more fantasy and science fiction. Illustrators: "Send only your best work and be able to reproduce that quality in assignments. Put name and address on *all* samples. Know a publication before you submit."

$ THE FRIEND MAGAZINE

The Church of Jesus Christ of Latter-day Saints, 50 E. North Temple St., Salt Lake City UT 84150. (801)240-2210. **Fax:** (801)240-2270. **E-mail:** friend@ldschurch.org. **Website:** www.lds.org/friend. **Contact:** Paul B. Pieper, editor; Mark W. Robison, art director. Monthly magazine for 3-12 year olds. "The *Friend* is published by The Church of Jesus Christ of Latter-day Saints for boys and girls up to 3-12 years of age." Estab. 1971. Available online.

NONFICTION Needs historical, humor, inspirational. Pays expenses of writers on assignment.

FICTION Wants illustrated stories and "For Little Friends" stories. See guidelines online.

POETRY **Pays $30 for poems.**

$ FUN FOR KIDZ

P.O. Box 227, Bluffton OH 45817. 419-358-4610. **Website:** funforkidz.com. **Contact:** Marilyn Edwards, articles editor. "*Fun For Kidz* is an activity magazine that maintains the same wholesome values as the other publications. Each issue is also created around a theme. There is nothing in the magazine to make it out dated. *Fun For Kidz* offers creative activities for children with extra time on their hands." Estab. 2002. Byline given. Pays on acceptance. Accepts queries by mail. Accepts simultaneous submissions. Sample copy: $6 in U.S., $9 in Canada, and $12.25 internationally. Guidelines online.

NONFICTION Needs picture-oriented material, young readers, middle readers: animal, arts/crafts, cooking, games/puzzles, history, hobbies, how-to, humorous, problem-solving, sports, carpentry projects. Submit complete ms with SASE, contact info, and notation of which upcoming theme your content should be considered for. Length: 300-750 words. **Pays minimum 5¢/word for articles; variable rate for games and projects, etc.** Pays expenses of writers on assignment.

TIPS "Our point of view is that every child deserves the right to be a child for a number of years before he or she becomes a young adult. As a result, *Fun for Kidz* looks for activities that deal with timeless topics, such as pets, nature, hobbies, science, games, sports, careers, simple cooking, and anything else likely to interest a child."

$$ GIRLS' LIFE

3 S. Frederick St., Suite 806, Baltimore MD 21202. (410)426-9600. **Fax:** (866)793-1531. **E-mail:** writeforgl@girlslife.com. **Website:** www.girlslife.com. **Contact:** Karen Bokram, founding editor and publisher; Kelsey Haywood, senior editor; Chun Kim, art director. Bimonthly magazine covering girls ages 9-15. Estab. 1994. Circ. 2.16 million. Byline given. Pays on publication. Publishes an average of 3 months after acceptance. Editorial lead time 4 months. Submit seasonal material 5 months in advance. Accepts queries by mail, e-mail. Accepts simultaneous submissions. Responds in 1 month to queries. Sample copy for $5 or online. Guidelines online.

NONFICTION Needs book excerpts, essays, general interest, how-to, humor, inspirational, interview, new product, travel. Special issues: Special issues: Back to School (August/September); Fall, Halloween

(October/November); Holidays, Winter (December/January); Valentine's Day, Crushes (February/March); Spring, Mother's Day (April/May); and Summer, Father's Day (June/July). **Buys 40 mss/year.** Query by mail with published clips. Submit complete ms on spec only. "Features and articles should speak to young women ages 10-15 looking for new ideas about relationships, family, friends, school, etc. with fresh, savvy advice. Front-of-the-book columns and quizzes are a good place to start." Length: 700-2,000 words. **Pays $350/regular column; $500/feature.** Pays expenses of writers on assignment.

PHOTOS State availability. Captions, identification of subjects, model releases required. Reviews contact sheets, negatives, transparencies. Negotiates payment individually.

COLUMNS/DEPARTMENTS Buys 20 mss/year. Query with published clips. **Pays $150-450.**

FICTION "We accept short fiction. They should be stand-alone stories and are generally 2,500-3,500 words." Needs short stories.

TIPS "Send thought-out queries with published writing samples and detailed résumé. Have fresh ideas and a voice that speaks to our audience—not down to them. And check out a copy of the magazine or visit girlslife.com before submitting."

$$ HIGHLIGHTS FOR CHILDREN

803 Church St., Honesdale PA 18431. (570)253-1080. **Fax:** (570)251-7847. **E-mail:** eds@highlights.com (Do not send submissions to this address.). **E-mail:** Highlights.submittable.com. **Website:** www.highlights.com. **Contact:** Christine French Cully, editor-in-chief. **70% freelance written.** Monthly magazine for children ages 6-12. "This book of wholesome fun is dedicated to helping children grow in basic skills and knowledge, in creativeness, in ability to think and reason, in sensitivity to others, in high ideals, and worthy ways of living—for children are the world's most important people." We publish stories and articles for beginning and advanced readers. Up to 400 words for beginning readers, up to 750 words for advanced readers. Guidelines updated regularly at Highlights.submittable.com. Estab. 1946. Circ. Approximately 1 million. Byline given. Pays on acceptance. Accepts queries by online submission form. Accepts simultaneous submissions. Responds in 2 months. Guidelines online.

NONFICTION See guidelines online. Up to 400 words for beginning readers. Up to 750 words for advanced readers. **Pays $175 and up for articles; pays $40 and up for crafts, activities, and puzzles.**

FICTION Stories appealing to girls and boys ages 6-12. Vivid, full of action. Engaging plot, strong characterization, lively language. Prefers stories in which a child protagonist solves a dilemma through his or her own resources. No stories glorifying war, crime or violence. See Highlights.submittable.com. Up to 475 words for beginning readers. Up to 750 words for advanced readers. **Pays $175 and up.**

POETRY See Highlights.submittable.com. No previously published poetry. Buys all rights. 16 lines maximum. Pays $50 and up.

FILLERS Buys puzzles, crafts, and activities. See Highlights.submittable.com. Pays $40 and up.

TIPS "We update our guidelines and current needs regularly at Highlights.submittable.com. Read several recent issues of the magazine before submitting. In addition to fiction, nonfiction, and poetry, we purchase crafts, puzzles, and activities that will stimulate children mentally and creatively. We judge each submission on its own merits. Expert reviews and complete bibliography are required for nonfiction. Include special qualifications, if any, of author. Speak to today's kids. Avoid didactic, overt messages. Even though our general principles haven't changed over the years, we are contemporary in our approach to issues."

$ JACK AND JILL

U.S. Kids, P.O. Box 88928, Indianapolis IN 46208. (317)634-1100. **E-mail:** jackandjill@uskidsmags.com. **Website:** www.uskidsmags.com. **50% freelance written.** Bimonthly magazine published for children ages 6-12. *Jack and Jill* is an award-winning magazine for children ages 6-12. It promotes the healthy educational and creative growth of children through interactive activities and articles. The pages are designed to spark a child's curiosity in a wide range of topics through articles, games, and activities. Inside you will find: current real-world topics in articles in stories; challenging puzzles and games; and interactive entertainment through experimental crafts and recipes. Please do not send artwork. "We prefer to work with professional illustrators of our own choosing. Write entertaining and imaginative stories for kids, not just about them. Writers should understand what is funny to kids, what's important to them, what excites them. Don't write from an adult 'kids are so cute' perspective. We're also looking for health and healthful lifestyle stories and articles, but don't be preachy." Estab. 1938. Circ. 40,000. Byline given. Pays on publication. Publishes ms an average of 8 months after acceptance. Submit seasonal material 8 months in advance. Accepts queries by mail. Accepts simultaneous submissions. Responds to mss in 3 months. Guidelines online.

NONFICTION **Buys 8-10 mss/year.** Submit complete ms via postal mail; no e-mail submissions. Queries not accepted. We are especially interested in features or Q&As with regular kids (or groups of kids) in the *Jack and Jill* age group who are engaged in unusual, challenging, or interesting activities. No celebrity pieces, please. Length: up to 700 words. **Pays $25 minimum.** Pays expenses of writers on assignment.

FICTION Submit complete ms via postal mail; no e-mail submissions. The tone of the stories should be fun and engaging. Stories should hook readers right from the get-go and pull them through the story. Humor is very important! Dialogue should be witty instead of just furthering the plot. The story should convey some kind of positive message. Possible themes could include self-reliance, being kind to others, appreciating other cultures, and so on. There are a million positive messages, so get creative! Kids can see preachy coming from a mile away, though, so please focus on telling a good story over teaching a lesson. The message—if there is one—should come organically from the story and not feel tacked on. **Buys 30-35 mss/year.** Length: 600-800 words. **Pays $25 minimum.**

POETRY Submit via postal mail; no e-mail submissions. Wants light-hearted poetry appropriate for the age group. Mss must be typewritten with poet's contact information in upper-right corner of each poem's page. SASE required. Length: up to 30 lines/poem. **Pays $25-50.**

FILLERS Needs puzzles, activities, games. In general, we prefer to use in-house generated material for this category but on occasion we do receive unique and fun puzzles, games, or activities through submissions. Please make sure you are submitting a truly unique activity for our consideration. **Pays $25-40.**

TIPS "We are constantly looking for new writers who can tell good stories with interesting slants—stories that are not full of outdated and time-worn expressions. We like to see stories about kids who are smart and capable but not sarcastic or smug. Problem-solving skills, personal responsibility, and integrity are good topics for us. Obtain current issues of the magazine and study them to determine our present needs and editorial style."

$ KEYS FOR KIDS DEVOTIONAL

Keys for Kids Ministries, PO Box 1001, Grand Rapids MI 49501. **E-mail:** editorial@keysforkids.org. **Website:** www.keysforkids.org. **Contact:** Courtney Lasater, editor. **95% freelance.** Quarterly devotional featuring stories and Scripture verses for children ages 6-12 that help kids dig into God's Word and apply it to their lives. Please put your name and contact information on the first page of your submission. "We prefer to receive submissions via our website." Story length is typically 340-375 words. To see full guidelines or submit a story, please go to www.keysforkids.org/writersguidelines. Estab. 1982. Circ. 60,000 print (not including digital circulation). Byline given. Pays on acceptance. Typically publishes stories 6-9 months after acceptance. Editorial lead time 6-8 months. Accepts queries by e-mail, online submission form. Responds in 2-4 months. Sample copy online. Guidelines online.

FICTION Need short contemporary stories with spiritual applications for kids. Please suggest a key verse and an appropriate Scripture passage, generally 3-10 verses, to reinforce the theme of your story. (See guidelines for more details on our devotional format.) Length: Up to 375 words. **Pays $30.**

TIPS "We love devotional stories that use an everyday object/situation to illustrate a spiritual truth (especially in a fresh, unique way) with characters that pull the reader into the story."

$$$$ NATIONAL GEOGRAPHIC KIDS

National Geographic Society, 1145 17th St. NW, Washington DC 20036. **E-mail:** ashaw@ngs.org. **E-mail:** michelle.tyler@natgeo.com. **Website:** www.kids.nationalgeographic.com. **Contact:** Michelle Tyler, editorial assistant. **70% freelance written.** Magazine published 10 times/year. "It's our mission to find fresh ways to entertain children while educating and exciting them about their world." Estab. 1975. Circ. 1.3 million. Byline given. Pays on acceptance. Offers 10% kill fee. Publishes ms an average of 6 months after acceptance. Editorial lead time 6+ months. Submit seasonal material 6+ months in advance. Accepts queries by mail. Accepts simultaneous submissions. Sample copy for #10 SASE. Guidelines online.

"We do not want poetry, sports, fiction, or story ideas that are too young—our audience is between ages 6-14."

NONFICTION Needs general interest, humor, interview, technical. Query with published clips and résumé. Length: 100-1,000 words. **Pays $1/word for assigned articles.** Pays expenses of writers on assignment.

PHOTOS State availability. Captions, identification of subjects, model releases required. Reviews contact sheets, negatives, transparencies, prints. Negotiates payment individually.

COLUMNS/DEPARTMENTS Freelance columns: Amazing Animals (animal heroes, stories about animal rescues, interesting/funny animal tales), 100 words; Inside Scoop (fun, kid-friendly news items), 50-70 words. Query with published clips. **Pays $1/word.**

TIPS "Submit relevant clips. Writers must have demonstrated experience writing for kids. Read the magazine before submitting."

$$ POCKETS

The Upper Room, P.O. Box 340004, Nashville TN 37203. (615)340-7333. **E-mail:** pockets@upperroom.org. **Website:** pockets.upperroom.org. **Contact:** Lynn W. Gilliam, editor. **60% freelance written.** Magazine published 11 times/year. "*Pockets* is a Christian devotional magazine for children ages 6-12. All submissions should address the broad theme of the magazine. Each issue is built around a theme with material which can be used by children in a variety of ways. Scripture stories, fiction, poetry, prayers, art, graphics, puzzles and activities are included. Submissions do not need to be overtly religious. They should help children experience a Christian lifestyle that is not always a neatly wrapped moral package but is open to the continuing revelation of God's will. Seasonal material, both secular and liturgical, is desired." Estab. 1981. Byline given. Pays on acceptance. No kill fee. Publishes ms an average of 1 year after acceptance. Submit seasonal material 1 year in advance. Accepts simultaneous submissions. Responds in 8 weeks to mss. Each issue reflects a specific theme. Guidelines online.

Does not accept e-mail or fax submissions.

NONFICTION Picture-oriented, young readers, middle readers: cooking, games/puzzles. Special issues: "*Pockets* seeks biographical sketches of persons, famous or unknown, whose lives reflect their Christian commitment, written in a way that appeals to children." Does not accept how-to articles. "Nonfiction should read like a story." Multicultural needs include stories that feature children of various racial/ethnic groups and do so in a way that is true to those depicted. **Buys 10 mss/year.** Submit complete ms by mail. No e-mail submissions. Length: 400-1,000 words. **Pays 14¢/word.** Pays expenses of writers on assignment.

REPRINTS Accepts one-time previously published submissions. Send ms with rights for sale noted and information about when and where the material previously appeared.

PHOTOS Send 4-6 close-up photos of children actively involved in peacemakers at work activities. Send photos, contact sheets, prints, or digital images. Must be 300 dpi. Pays $25/photo. Buys one-time rights.

COLUMNS/DEPARTMENTS Family Time, 200-300 words; Peacemakers at Work (profiles of children working for peace, justice, and ecological concerns), 400-600 words. **Pays 14¢/word.** Activities/Games (related to themes). **Pays $25 and up.** Kids Cook (simple recipes children can make alone or with minimal help from an adult). **Pays $25.**

FICTION "Stories should contain lots of action, use believable dialogue, be simply written, and be relevant to the problems faced by this age group in everyday life." Submit complete ms by mail. No e-mail submissions. Length: 600-1,000 words.

POETRY Both seasonal and theme poems needed. Considers poetry by children. Buys 14 poems/year. Length: up to 20 lines. **Pays $25 minimum.**

TIPS "Theme stories, role models, and retold scripture stories are most open to freelancers. Poetry is also open. It is very helpful if writers read our writers' guidelines and themes on our website."

$ SHINE BRIGHTLY

GEMS Girls' Clubs, 1333 Alger St., SE, Grand Rapids MI 49507. (616)241-5616. **Fax:** (616)241-5558. **E-mail:** shinebrightly@gemsgc.org. **Website:** www.gemsgc.org. **Contact:** Kelli Gilmore, managing editor. **60% freelance written. Works with new and published/established writers.** Monthly magazine from September to May with a double issue for September/October. "Our purpose is to lead girls into a living relationship with Jesus Christ and to help them see how God is at work in their lives and the world around them. Puzzles, crafts, stories, and articles for girls ages 9-14." Estab. 1970. Circ. 13,000. Byline given. Pays on publication. No kill fee. Publishes ms an average of 4 months after acceptance. Submit seasonal material 1 year in advance. Accepts simultaneous submissions. Responds in 2 months to mss. Sample copy with 9x12 SASE with 3 first class stamps and $1. Guidelines online.

NONFICTION Needs humor, inspirational, interview, personal experience, photo feature, religious, travel. Avoid the testimony approach. **Buys 15 unsolicited mss/year.** Submit complete ms in body of e-mail. No attachments. Length: 100-800 words. **Pays up to $35, plus 2 copies.** Pays expenses of writers on assignment.

REPRINTS Send typed manuscript with rights for sale noted and information about when and where the material previously appeared.

PHOTOS Purchased with or without ms. Appreciate multicultural subjects. Reviews 5x7 or 8x10 clear color glossy prints. Pays $25-50 on publication.

COLUMNS/DEPARTMENTS How-to (crafts); puzzles and jokes; quizzes. Length: 200-400 words. Send complete ms. **Pay varies.**

FICTION Does not want "unrealistic stories and those with trite, easy endings. We are interested in manuscripts that show how real girls can change the world." Needs ethnic, historical, humorous, mystery, religious, slice-of-life vignettes. Believable only. Nothing too preachy. **Buys 30 mss/year.** Submit complete ms in body of e-mail. No attachments. Length: 700-900 words. **Pays up to $35, plus 2 copies.**

POETRY Needs free verse, haiku, light verse, traditional. **Limited need for poetry. Pays $5-15.**

TIPS Writers: "Please check our website before submitting. We have a specific style and theme that deals with how girls can impact the world. The stories should be current, deal with pre-adolescent problems and joys, and help girls see God at work in their lives through humor as well as problem-solving." Prefers not to see anything on the adult level, secular material, or violence. Writers frequently oversimplify the articles and often write with a Pollyanna attitude. An author should be able to see his/her writing style as exciting and appealing to girls ages 9-14. The style can be fun, but also teach a truth. Subjects should be current and important to *SHINE brightly* readers. Use our theme update as a guide. We would like to receive material with a multicultural slant."

LITERARY & LITTLE

AGNI

Boston University, 236 Bay State Rd., Boston MA 02215. **E-mail:** agni@bu.edu. **Website:** www.agnimagazine.org. **Contact:** Sven Birkerts, editor. **90% freelance written.** Eclectic literary magazine publishing first-rate poems, essays, translations, and stories. Estab. 1972. Circ. 3,000 in print, plus more than 60,000 distinct readers online per year. Byline given. Pays on publication. Publishes ms an average of 6 months after acceptance. Accepts queries by online submission form. Accepts simultaneous submissions. Responds in 4 months to mss. No queries please. Sample copy: $12 or online. Guidelines online.

Reading period is September 1-May 31 only. Online magazine carries original content not found in print edition. All submissions are considered for both. Founding editor Askold Melnyczuk won the PEN/Nora Magid Lifetime Achievement Award for Magazine Editing. Work from *AGNI* has been included and cited regularly in the *Pushcart Prize*, *O. Henry*, and *Best American* anthologies.

NONFICTION Contact: Nonfiction Editor. Needs essays, memoir, reviews. Literary only. "We do not publish journalism or academic work." **Buys 20+ mss/year.** Submit online or by regular mail, no more than one essay at a time. E-mailed submissions will not be considered. Include an SASE or your e-mail address if sending by mail. **Pays $20/page up to $300, plus a one-year subscription, and, for print publication, 2 contributor's copies and 4 gift copies.**

FICTION Contact: Fiction Editor. Needs short stories. No genre scifi, horror, mystery, or romance. **Buys 20+ mss/year.** Submit online or by regular mail, no more than 1 story at a time. E-mailed submissions will not be considered. Include a SASE or your e-mail address if sending by mail. **Pays $20/page up to $300, plus a one-year subscription, and, for print publication, 2 contributor's copies and 4 gift copies.**

POETRY Contact: Poetry Editor. Submit online or by regular mail, no more than 5 poems at a time. E-mailed submissions will not be considered. Include a SASE or your e-mail address if sending by mail. Buys 120+ poems/year. Submit maximum 5 poems. **Pays $20/page up to $300, plus a one-year subscription, and, for print publication, 2 contributor's copies and 4 gift copies.**

TIPS "We're also looking for extraordinary translations from little-translated languages. It is important to read work published in *AGNI* before submitting, to see if your own might be compatible."

$$ ALASKA QUARTERLY REVIEW

University of Alaska Anchorage, 3211 Providence Dr., Anchorage AK 99508. **E-mail:** uaa_aqr@uaa.alaska.edu. **Website:** www.uaa.alaska.edu/aqr. **Contact:** Ronald Spatz, editor in chief. **95% freelance written.** "*Alaska Quarterly Review* is a literary journal devoted to contemporary literary art, publishing fiction, short plays, poetry, photo essays, and literary nonfiction in traditional and experimental styles. The editors encourage new and emerging writers, while continuing to publish award-winning and established writers." Estab. 1982. Circ. 2,700. Byline given. Publishes ms an average of 6 months after acceptance. Accepts queries by mail. Accepts simultaneous submissions. Responds in 4 months to queries; in 6 weeks-4 months to mss. Sample copy: $6. Guidelines online.

Magazine: 6x9; 232-300 pages; 60 lb. Glatfelter paper; 12 pt. C15 black ink or 4-color; varnish cover stock; photos on cover and photo essays. Reads mss August 15-May 15.

NONFICTION Needs essays, literary nonfiction in traditional and experimental styles. Submit complete ms by mail. Include cover letter with contact information and SASE for return of ms. Length: up to 50 pages. **Pays contributor's copies and honoraria when funding is available.**

FICTION "Works in *AQR* have certain characteristics: freshness, honesty, and a compelling subject. The voice of the piece must be strong—idiosyncratic enough to create a unique persona. We look for craft, putting it in a form where it becomes emotionally and intellectually complex. Many pieces in *AQR* concern everyday life. We're not asking our writers to go outside themselves and their experiences to the absolute exotic to catch our interest. We look for the experiential and revelatory qualities of the work. We will champion a piece that may be less polished or stylistically sophisticated if it engages me, surprises me, and resonates for me. The joy in reading such a work is in discovering something true. Moreover, in keeping with our mission to publish new writers, we are looking for voices our readers do not know, voices that may not always be reflected in the dominant culture and that, in all instances, have something important to convey." Needs experimental, contemporary, prose poem, novel excerpts, drama: experimental and traditional one-acts. No romance, children's, or inspirational/religious. Submit complete ms by mail. Include cover letter with contact information and SASE for return of ms. Length: up to 50 pages. **Pays contributor's copies and honoraria when funding is available.**

POETRY Needs avant-garde, free verse, traditional. Submit poetry by mail. Include cover letter with contact information and SASE for return of ms. No light verse. Length: up to 20 pages. **Pays contributor's copies and honoraria when funding is available.**

TIPS "Although we respond to e-mail queries, we cannot review electronic submissions."

$ ALLEGORY

P.O. Box 2714, Cherry Hill NJ 08034. **E-mail:** submissions@allegoryezine.com. **Website:** www.allegoryezine.com. **Contact:** Ty Drago, publisher and managing editor. Biannual online magazine specializing in science fiction, fantasy, and horror. "We are an e-zine by writers for writers. Our articles focus on the art, craft, and business of writing. Our links and editorial policy all focus on the needs of fiction authors." *Allegory* (as Peridot Books) won the Page One Award for Literary Contribution. Estab. 1998. Circ. *Allegory* receives upwards of 250,000 hits per year. Pays on acceptance for one-time, electronic rights. Publishes in May and November. Accepts queries by e-mail. Accepts simultaneous submissions. Responds in 2 months to mss. Guidelines online.

NONFICTION Must be related to the craft or business of writing. Length: 1,500 words. **Pays $15/article.**

FICTION Receives 150 unsolicited mss/month. Accepts 12 mss/issue; 24 mss/year. Agented fiction 5%. Publishes 10 new writers/year. Also publishes literary essays, literary criticism. Often comments on rejected mss. "No media tie-ins (*Star Trek*, *Star Wars*, etc., or space opera, vampires)." "All submissions should be sent by e-mail (no letters or telephone calls) in either text or RTF format. Please place 'Submission [Title]-[first and last name]' in the subject line. Include the following in both the body of the e-mail and the attachment: your name, name to use on the story (byline) if different, your preferred e-mail address, your mailing address, the story's title, and the story's word count." Length: 1,500-7,500 words; average length: 2,500 words. **Pays $15/story.**

TIPS "Give us something original, preferably with a twist. Avoid gratuitous sex or violence. Funny always scores points. Be clever and imaginative, but be able to tell a story with proper mood and characterization. Put your name and e-mail address in the body of the story. Read the site and get a feel for it before submitting."

THE AMERICAN DISSIDENT

A Journal of Literature, Democracy & Dissidence, 217 Commerce Rd., Barnstable MA 02630. **E-mail:** todslone@hotmail.com. **E-mail:** Only subscribers can e-mail submit. **Website:** www.theamericandissident.org. **Contact:** G. Tod Slone, editor. *The American Dissident*, published 2 times/year, provides "a forum for, amongst other things, criticism of the academic/literary establishment, which clearly discourages vigorous debate, cornerstone of democracy, and especially vigorous criticism of its icons and institutions, to the evident detriment of American literature. Wants "poetry, reviews, artwork, and short (2-4pp) essays in English, French, or Spanish, written on the edge preferably with a dash of personal risk. and, if possible, stemming from personal experience and/or conflict with power." Submissions should be "iconoclastic and parrhesiastic in nature." Estab. 1998. Circ. 100. Publishes ms 2-6 months after acceptance. Accepts queries by mail, e-mail. Responds in a week or less. Almost always comments on rejected poems and essays. Single copy: $9; subscriptions: $18 for individuals; $20 for institutions. Guidelines available for SASE.

NONFICTION Needs essays, expose, interview, opinion, personal experience, reviews. Length: up to 1,000 words.

POETRY Submit 3 poems at a time. E-mail submissions from subscribers only. "Far too many poets submit without even reading the guidelines. Include SASE and cover letter containing not credits but rather personal dissident information, as well as incidents that provoked you to 'go upright and vital, and speak the rude truth in all ways' (Emerson)." **Pays 1 contributor's copy.**

TIPS "Every poet knows what he or she should not write about to avoid upsetting those in positions of literary, cultural, and/or academic power. *The American Dissident* seeks to publish those few poets who now and then break that taboo and thus raise truth-telling above getting published, funded, invited, tenured, nominated, and/or anointed. *The American Dissident* is a rare literary journal that not only brooks, but also encourages and publishes in each and every issue hardcore criticism regarding the editor and journal. In fact, I cannot think of another journal that will do that."

AMERICAN LITERARY REVIEW

University of North Texas, 1155 Union Circle #311307, Denton TX 76203. **E-mail:** americanliteraryreview@gmail.com. **Website:** www.americanliteraryreview.com. **Contact:** Bonnie Friedman, editor in chief. "*The American Literary Review* publishes "excellent poetry, fiction, and nonfiction by writers at all stages of their careers." Beginning in fall 2013, *ALR* became an online publication." Estab. 1990. Publishes ms within 2 years of acceptance. Accepts simultaneous submissions. Responds in 3-5 months to mss. Guidelines online.

Reading period is from October 1-May 1.

NONFICTION "We do not accept biographies, recipes, news articles. etc." Submit 1 complete ms through online submissions manager for a fee of $3. Does not accept submissions via e-mail or mail. Length: up to 6,500 words. Pays expenses of writers on assignment.

FICTION "We would like to see more short shorts and stylistically innovative and risk-taking fiction. We like to see stories that illuminate the various layers of characters and their situations with great artistry. Give us distinctive character-driven stories that explore the complexities of human existence." Looks for "the small moments that contain more than at first possible, that surprise us with more truth than we thought we had a right to expect." Has published work by Marylee MacDonald, Michael Isaac Shokrian, Arthur Brown, Roy Bentley, Julie Marie Wade, and Karin Forfota Poklen. No genre works. Submit 1 complete ms through online submissions manager for a fee of $3. Does not accept submissions via e-mail or mail. Length: up to 8,000 words.

POETRY "Poetry selections are made by a widely read group with eclectic tastes who look for the best poems, regardless of form or subject matter." Has published poetry by Kathleen Pierce, Mark Irwin, Stephen Dunn, William Olsen, David St. John, and Cate Marvin. Submit up to 5 poems through online submissions manager for a fee of $3. Does not accept submissions via e-mail or mail.

TIPS "We encourage writers and artists to examine our journal."

$ THE AMERICAN POETRY REVIEW

1906 Rittenhouse Square, Philadelphia PA 19103. **E-mail:** escanlon@aprweb.org. **Website:** www.aprweb.org. **Contact:** Elizabeth Scanlon, Editor-in-Chief. "*The American Poetry Review* is dedicated to reaching a worldwide audience with a diverse array of the best contemporary poetry and literary prose. *APR* also aims to expand the audience interested in poetry and literature, and to provide authors, especially poets, with a far-reaching forum in which to present their work." Estab. 1972. Circ. 8,000-10,000. Accepts queries by mail, online submission form. Accepts simultaneous submissions. Responds in 6 months. Sample: $5. Guidelines online.

NONFICTION Needs essays, interview, reviews. Submit complete ms via online submissions manager. Pays expenses of writers on assignment.

POETRY Submit up to 5 poems via online submissions manager. Has published poetry by John Murillo, Khadijah Queen, Brenda Shaughnessy, Kazim Ali, Gregory Pardlo, Deborah Landau, Sharon Olds, and many more. **Pays $1 per line.**

$$ AMERICAN SHORT FICTION

Badgerdog Literary Publishing, P.O. Box 301209, Austin TX 78703. **E-mail:** editors@americanshortfiction.org. **Website:** www.americanshortfiction.org. **Contact:** Rebecca Markovits and Adeena Reitberger, editors. "Issued triannually, *American Short Fiction* publishes work by emerging and established voices: stories that dive into the wreck, that stretch the reader between recognition and surprise, that conjure a particular world with delicate expertise—stories that take a different way home." Estab. 1991. Circ. 2,500. Byline given. Pays on publication. Publishes ms an average of 3 months after acceptance. Accepts queries by online submission form. Accepts simultaneous submissions. Responds in 2 weeks to queries; in 5 months to mss. "Sample copies are available for sale through our publisher's online store." Guidelines online.

Stories published by *American Short Fiction* are anthologized in *Best American Short Stories*, *Best American Non-Required Reading*, *The O. Henry Prize Stories*, *The Pushcart Prize: Best of the Small Presses*, and elsewhere.

FICTION "Open to publishing mystery or speculative fiction if we feel it has literary value." Does not want young adult or genre fiction. **Buys 20-25 mss/year.** *American Short Fiction* seeks "short fiction by some of the finest writers working in contemporary literature, whether they are established, new, or lesser-known authors." Also publishes stories under 2,000 words online. Submit 1 story at a time via online submissions manager ($3 fee). No paper submissions. Length: open. **Writers receive $250-500, 2 contributor's copies, free subscription to the magazine. Additional copies $5.**

TIPS "We publish fiction that speaks to us emotionally, uses evocative and precise language, and takes risks in subject matter and/or form. Try to read a few issues of *American Short Fiction* to get a sense of what we like. Also, to be concise is a great virtue."

$ ANCIENT PATHS

E-mail: skylarburris@yahoo.com. **Website:** www.editorskylar.com/magazine/table.html. **Contact:** Skylar H. Burris, editor. **100% freelance written.** *Ancient Paths* provides "a forum for quality spiritual poetry and short fiction. We consider works from writers of all religions, but poets and authors should be comfortable appearing in a predominantly Christian publication. Works published in *Ancient Paths* explore themes such as redemption, sin, forgiveness, doubt, faith, gratitude for the ordinary blessings of life, spiritual struggle, and spiritual growth. Please, no overly didactic works. Subtlety is preferred." Please send seasonally themed works for Lent and Advent at least 1 month prior to the start of each season. Works on other themes may be sent at any time. Estab. 1998. Byline given. Pays on publication. Time between acceptance and publication is 1-4 months. Accepts queries by e-mail. Accepts simultaneous submissions. Responds in 8 weeks, usually sooner. Sample copy of printed back issue: $9. Purchase online. Detailed guidelines are available on the website.

REPRINTS Buys reprints of short fiction and poetry at the regular rate of $1.25/piece.

PHOTOS "We accept submissions of photographs on Christian themes. Send as an attachment." Pays $1.25/published photo. Acquires electronic rights.

FICTION E-mail submissions only. Paste short fiction directly in the e-mail message. Use the subject heading "AP Online Submission (title of your work)." Include name and e-mail address at top of e-mail. Previously published works accepted, provided they are not currently available online. Please indicate if your work has been published elsewhere. Needs humorous, mainstream, novel excerpts, religious, short stories, slice-of-life vignettes, All fiction submissions should be under 2,000 words. Very short submission of under 800 words have a better chance of acceptance. Length: under 800 words preferred; up to 2,000 words. **Pays $1.25/work published. Published authors also receive discount code for $3 off 2 printed back issues.**

POETRY Needs formal verse or free verse on spiritual themes. E-mail all submissions. Paste poems in e-mail message. Use the subject heading "AP Online Submission (title of your work)." Include your name and e-mail address at the top of your e-mail. Poems may be rhymed, unrhymed, free verse, or formal and should have a spiritual theme, which may be explicit or implicit, but which should not be overly didactic. No "preachy" poetry; avoid inconsistent meter and forced rhyme; no stream-of-consciousness or avant-garde work; no esoteric academic poetry; no concrete (shape) poetry; no use of the lowercase *i* for the personal pronoun; do not center poetry. Buys 52 poems/year. Submit maximum 5 poems. Length: 8-60 lines. **Pays $1.25/poem. Published poets also receive discount code for $3 off 2 printed back issues.**

TIPS "Read the great religious poets: John Donne, George Herbert, T.S. Eliot, Lord Tennyson. Remember not to preach. This is a literary magazine, not a pulpit. This does not mean you do not communicate morals or celebrate God. It means you are not overbearing or simplistic when you do so."

ANOTHER CHICAGO MAGAZINE

P.O. Box 408439, Chicago IL 60640. **E-mail:** editors@anotherchicagomagazine.net. **Website:** www.anotherchicagomagazine.net. **Contact:** Caroline Eick Kasner, managing editor; Matt Rowan, fiction editor; David Welch, poetry editor; Colleen O'Connor, nonfiction editor. "*Another Chicago Magazine* is a biannual literary magazine that publishes work by both new and established writers. We look for work that goes beyond the artistic and academic to include and address the larger world. The editors read submissions in fiction, poetry, and creative nonfiction year round. The best way to know what we publish is to read what we publish. If you haven't read *ACM* before, order a sample copy to know if your work is appropriate." Sends prepublication galleys. Estab. 1977. Circ. 2,000. Byline given. Accepts simultaneous submissions. Responds in 3 months to queries; in 6 months to mss. Guidelines available online.

Work published in *ACM* has been included frequently in *The Best American Poetry* and *The Pushcart Prize* anthologies. **Charges $3 submissions fee.**

NONFICTIONcreative nonfiction. Submit complete ms via online submissions manager. Length: up to 25 pages. Pays expenses of writers on assignment.

FICTION Needs novel excerpts, short stories. Submit complete ms via online submissions manager. Length: up to 7,500 words.

POETRY Submit poems via online submissions manager in 1 document. Submit maximum 5 poems.

TIPS "Support literary publishing by subscribing to at least 1 literary journal—if not ours, another. Get used to rejection slips, and don't get discouraged. Keep introductory letters short. Make sure ms has name and address on every page, and that it is clean, neat, and proofread. We are looking for stories with freshness and originality in subject angle and style, and work that encounters the world."

THE ANTIGONISH REVIEW

St. Francis Xavier University, P.O. Box 5000, Immaculata Hall, Room 413, Antigonish NS B2G 2W5 Canada. (902)867-3962. **Fax:** (902)867-5563. **E-mail:** tar@stfx.ca. **Website:** www.antigonishreview.com. **Contact:** Gerald Trites, editor. **100% freelance written.** Quarterly literary magazine for thoughtful and creative readers. *The Antigonish Review*, published quarterly, features the writing of new and emerging writers as well as the ideas of established and innovative thinkers through poetry, stories, essays, book reviews and interviews." Estab. 1970. Circ. 650. Byline given. Pays on publication. Offers variable kill fee. Publishes ms an average of 8 months after acceptance. Editorial lead time 4 months. Submit seasonal material 8 months in advance. Accepts queries by mail, e-mail, fax, phone. Accepts simultaneous submissions. Responds in 1 month to queries; 6 months to mss. Guidelines online.

NONFICTION Needs essays, interview, memoir, reviews, book reviews/essays. No academic research. **Buys 15-20 mss/year.** Through website using Submittable. Length: 1,500-3,000 words **Pays $50, 1 print copy and 1 digital copy.**

FICTION Send complete ms only through Submittable on our website. Needs short stories. No erotica. **Buys 35-40 mss/year.** Send complete ms. Length: 500-5,000 words. **Pays $50, 1 print edition and 1 digital edition for stories.**

POETRY Open to poetry on any subject written from any point of view and in any form. However, writers should expect their work to be considered within the full context of old and new poetry in English and other languages. Has published poetry by Andy Wainwright, W.J. Keith, Michael Hulse, Jean McNeil, M. Travis Lane, and Douglas Lochhead. Buys 100-125 poems/year. Submit maximum 8 poems. Submit 6-8 poems at a time. A preferable submission would be 3-4 poems. Lines/poem: not over 80, i.e., 2 pages. **Pays $10/page to a maximum of $50 and 2 contributor's copies.**

TIPS Contact by e-mail (tar@stfx.ca) and submit through the website using Submittable. There is a submission fee.

$ ANTIOCH REVIEW

Antioch College, P.O. Box 148, Yellow Springs OH 45387-0148. (937)769-1365. **E-mail:** review@antiochcollege.edu. **Website:** www.antiochreview.org. **Contact:** Robert S. Fogarty, editor; Judith Hall, poetry editor. Quarterly magazine for general, literary, and academic audience. Literary and cultural review of contemporary issues and literature for general readership. *The Antioch Review* is an independent quarterly of critical and creative thought. We have a proud 75+ year history of publishing independent writers, exceptional poets, and brilliant thinkers—some only emerging upstarts when originally featured. *The Antioch Review*, founded in 1941, is one of the oldest, continuously publishing literary magazines in America. We publish fiction, essays, and poetry from prominent and promising poets, authors, and critics. Authors published in the *Review* are consistently included in Best American Anthologies and *Pushcart Prizes*. Our writers and poets are routinely recipients of prominent literary awards; and the *Review* has been the recipient of several prominent National Magazine Awards in essays and criticism and fiction. We have an international readership and reputation of publishing the "best words in the best order" for over 75 years. As a result, the competition is keen. We receive thousands of submissions each year from around the world. Form and content are so inseparable and reaction is so personal, it is difficult to state requirements or limitations. Studying prior issues of *The Antioch Review* and reviewing our "Writer's Guidelines" should be helpful. Estab. 1941. Circ. 3,000. Byline given. Pays on publication. Publishes ms an average of 10 months after acceptance. Accepts queries by mail, e-mail. Accepts simultaneous submissions. Responds varies on our workload. Generally, it is 3 to 6 months; however, could be longer. Sample copies may be purchased online. Guidelines online.

NONFICTION Needs essays, general interest, historical, humor, interview, memoir, reviews. Special issues: At times, we do publish special issues about topics, such as our Museum issue (http://review.antiochcollege.edu/spring-2016) or our all poetry or all fiction issues. Nonfiction submissions are not accepted between June 1-August 31. Length: 2,000-8,000 words. **Pays $20/printed page, plus 2 contributor's copies.**

FICTION Quality fiction only, distinctive in style with fresh insights into the human condition. Needs adventure, experimental, historical, humorous, religious, short stories, slice-of-life vignettes, suspense, contemporary. No science fiction, fantasy, or confessions. Send complete ms with SASE, preferably mailed flat. Fiction submissions are not accepted between June 1-August 31. **Pays $20/printed page, plus 2 contributor's copies.**

POETRY Has published poetry by Sylvia Plath, Mark Strand, Richard Howard, Jacqueline Osherow, Alice Fulton, Richard Kenney, and others. Receives thousands of submissions/year. No previously published poems or simultaneous submissions. Include SASE with all submissions. No light or inspirational verse. Poetry submissions are not accepted between between May 1-September 1. Submit maximum 6 poems. **Pays $20/printed page, plus 2 contributor's copies.**

$ ARC POETRY MAGAZINE

P.O. Box 81060, Ottawa Ontario K1P 1B1 Canada. **E-mail:** managingeditor@arcpoetry.ca. **Website:** www.arcpoetry.ca. **Contact:** Monty Reid, managing editor. *Arc Poetry Magazine* has been publishing the best in contemporary Canadian and international poetry and criticism for over 30 years. *Arc* is published 3 times/year, including an annual themed issue each fall. Canada's poetry magazine publishes poetry, poetry-related articles, interviews, and book reviews, and also publishes on its website; *Arc* also runs a Poet-in-Residence program. Estab. 1978. Accepts simultaneous submissions. Responds in 4-6 months. Subscriptions: 1 year: $35 CDN; 2 years: $60 CND (in Canada). U.S. subscriptions: 1 year: $45 CAD; 2 years: $80 CAD. International subscriptions: 1 year: $55 CDN; 2 year: $90 CDN. Online ordering available for subscriptions and single copies (with occasional promotions). Guidelines online.

Arc is 130-160 pages, perfect-bound, printed on matte white stock with a crisp, engaging design and a striking visual art portfolio in each issue. Receives over 2,500 submissions/year; accepts about 40-50 poems. Press run is 1,500.

NONFICTION Needs interview, reviews, articles related to poetry. Query first. Pays expenses of writers on assignment.

POETRY *Arc* accepts unsolicited submissions of previously unpublished poems from October 15-May 31; maximum of 3 poems, 1 submission per year per person. Use online submissions manager. Has published poetry by Don Coles, Karen Solie, Nicole Brossard, Christian Bok, Elizabeth Bachinsky, George Elliott Clarke, Ken Babstock, Michael Ondaatje, Stephanie Bolster, and Don Domanski. **Pays $50 CAD/page, plus 1 contributor's copy.**

ARC POETRY MAGAZINE

Arc Poetry Society, P.O. Box 81060, Ottawa ON K1P 1B1 Canada. **E-mail:** managingeditor@arcpoetry.ca; coordinatingeditor@arcpoetry.ca; arc@arcpoetry.ca. **Website:** www.arcpoetry.ca. **Contact:** Monty Reid, managing editor; Chris Johnson, coordinating editor. Semiannual magazine featuring poetry, poetry-related articles, and criticism. *Arc*'s focus is poetry, and particularly Canadian poetry, although it also publishes writers from elsewhere. Looking for the best poetry from new and established writers. Often publishes special issues. Send a SASE for upcoming special issues and contests. Estab. 1978. Circ. 1,500. Byline given. Pays on publication. Publishes mss an average of 6 months after acceptance. Accepts queries by online submission form. Accepts simultaneous submissions. Responds in 4-6 months. Guidelines available online.

Only accepts submissions via online submissions manager. Include a brief biographical note with submission. Accepts unsolicited mss each year from October 15, 2016 to May 31, 2017.

NONFICTION Needs essays, interview, reviews, poetry book reviews. Query first. Length: 500-4,000 words. **Pays $50/printed page (Canadian), and 2 copies.** Pays expenses of writers on assignment.

PHOTOS **Contact:** Kevin Matthews, the Art Editor; art@arcpoetry.ca. Query first. Pays $50/page upon publication, $100 for art featured on the front cover (CDN). Buys one-time rights.

POETRY Needs contemporary poetry. For over 30 years, *Arc* has been publishing the best in contemporary poetry. *Arc* invites submissions from emerging and established poets. Poets may only submit once each calendar year. Poetry submissions must not exceed 3 poems total. Submissions must be typed and single-spaced (double spaces will be interpreted as blank lines). Include your name, e-mail address, and mailing address on each page. Submit each poem in a separate document with bio. Your submission will be grouped in submission platform. Biographical statements should be 2-3 sentences or approximately 50 words. *Arc* can't promise to respond to inquiries regarding the status of submissions before the completion of an editorial cycle. Buys 60 poems/year. Submit maximum 3 poems. **Pays $50/printed page (Canadian).**

ARTS & LETTERS JOURNAL OF CONTEMPORARY CULTURE

Georgia College & State University, Milledgeville GA 31061. (478)445-1289. **Website:** al.gcsu.edu. **Contact:** Laura Newbern, editor; Faith Thompson, managing editor. *Arts & Letters Journal of Contemporary Culture*, published semiannually, is devoted to publishing contemporary work from established and emerging writers. Our editors seek work that doesn't try too hard to grab our attention, but rather guides it toward the human voice and its perpetual struggle into language. We're open to both formal and experimental fiction, nonfiction, and poetry; we're also open to work that defies classification. Above all, we look for work in which we can feel writers surprising themselves. Work published in *Arts & Letters Journal* has received the Pushcart Prize. Estab. 1999. Pays on publication. No kill fee. Accepts simultaneous submissions. Responds in 2-4 months. Guidelines online.

NONFICTION Submit complete ms via online submissions manager. Length: up to 25 pages typed and double-spaced. **Pays $10/printed page (minimum payment: $50) and 1 contributor's copy.** Pays expenses of writers on assignment.

FICTION Needs short stories. No genre fiction. Submit complete ms via online submissions manager. Length: up to 25 pages typed and double-spaced. **Pays $10/printed page (minimum payment: $50) and 1 contributor's copy.**

POETRY Submit via online submissions manager. Include cover letter. "Poems are screened, discussed by group of readers. If approved by group, poems are submitted to poetry editor for final approval." Has published poetry by Margaret Gibson, Marilyn Nelson, Stuart Lishan, R.T. Smith, Laurie Lamon, and Miller Williams. No light verse. Submit maximum 6 poems. **Pays $10/printed page (minimum payment: $50) and 1 contributor's copy.**

$ ART TIMES

arttimesjournal, P.O. Box 730, Mount Marion NY 12456. (845)246-6944. **Fax:** (845)246-6944. **E-mail:** info@arttimesjournal.com. **Website:** www.arttimesjournal.com. **Contact:** Raymond J. Steiner, editor. **80% freelance written.** "*Art Times*, now an online-only publication, covers the arts fields with essays about music, dance, theater, film, and art, and includes short fiction and poetry as well as editorials. Our readers are creatives looking for resources and people who appreciate good writing." Estab. 1984. Byline given. Pays on publication for short fiction, poetry and essays. No kill fee. Publishes within 4 months Accepts queries by mail, e-mail. Responds in 3 months Guidelines online.

NONFICTION Needs essays, opinion. **Buys 12+ mss/year.** Send complete ms via mail or e-mail. Length: up to 1,000 words. **Pays $25.**

COLUMNS/DEPARTMENTS Open to linking appropriate blogs to arttimesjournal.com **Buys 12 mss/year.** Columns appropriate to Creatives eg: tips for social media, marketing yourself as a creative, general essays about the arts. **Pays $25.**

FICTION Contact: Raymond J. Steiner. Looking for quality short fiction that aspires to be literary. Publishes up to 4 stories a month. Needs adventure, ethnic, fantasy, historical, humorous, mainstream, science fiction, contemporary. Nothing violent, sexist, erotic, juvenile, racist, romantic, political, off-beat, or related to sports or juvenile fiction. **Buys 25 mss/year.** Send complete ms. Length: up to 1,000 words. **Pays $25.**

POETRY Needs avant-garde, free verse, haiku, light verse, traditional. Send poems by mail or e-mail. Wants "poetry that strives to express genuine observation in unique language. All topics, all forms. We prefer well-crafted 'literary' poems. No excessively sentimental poetry." Publishes 2-3 poems each month. Nothing violent, sexist, erotic, juvenile, racist, romantic, political, off-beat, or related to sports or juvenile fiction. Buys 30-35 poems/year. Submit maximum 6 poems. Length: up to 20 lines. **Pays $5/poem.**

$ THE BALTIMORE REVIEW

6514 Maplewood Rd., Baltimore MD 21212. **E-mail:** editor@baltimorereview.org. **Website:** www.baltimorereview.org. **Contact:** Barbara Westwood Diehl, senior editor. **100% freelance written.** *The Baltimore Review* publishes poetry, fiction, and creative nonfiction from Baltimore and beyond. Submission periods are August 1-November 30 and February 1-May 31. Estab. 1996. Byline given. Pays on publication. No kill fee. Publishes ms 2-6 months after acceptance. Accepts simultaneous submissions. Responds in 4 months or less. Guidelines online. Can review work submitted through our website only. No e-mailed submissions.

NONFICTIONcreative nonfiction. Publishes 2-6 mss per online issue. Length: up to 5,000 words. **Pays $40.**

FICTION Needs short stories, literary fiction. Send complete ms using online submission form. Publishes 16-20 mss (combination of poetry, fiction, and creative nonfiction) per online issue. Work published online is also published in annual anthology. Length: 100-5,000 words. **Pays $40.**

POETRY Needs avant-garde, free verse, traditional. Submit 1-3 poems. See editor preferences on submission guidelines on website. **Pays $40.**

TIPS "See editor preferences on staff page of website."

BARRELHOUSE

E-mail: yobarrelhouse@gmail.com. **Website:** www.barrelhousemag.com. **Contact:** Dave Housley, Joe Killiany, and Matt Perez, fiction editors; Tom McAllister, nonfiction editor; Dan Brady, poetry editor. *Barrelhouse* is a biannual print journal featuring fiction, poetry, interviews, and essays about music, art, and the detritus of popular culture. Estab. 2004. Byline given. No kill fee. Accepts queries by online submission form. Accepts simultaneous submissions. Responds in 2-3 months to mss.

Stories originally published in *Barrelhouse* have been featured in *The Best American Nonrequired Reading, The Best American Science Fiction and Fantasy,* and the Million Writer's Award.

NONFICTION Needs essays. Submit via online submissions manager. DOC or RTF files only. Length: open, but prefers pieces under 8,000 words. **Pays $50 and 2 contributor copies.** Pays expenses of writers on assignment.

FICTION Needs experimental, humorous, mainstream. Submit complete ms via online submissions manager. DOC or RTF files only. Length: open, but prefers pieces under 8,000. **Pays $50 and 2 contributor copies.**

POETRY Submit up to 5 poems via online submissions manager. DOC or RTF files only. Submit maximum 5 poems. **Pays $50 and 2 contributor's copies.**

BEATDOM

Beatdom Books, 426 Blowrie St., Dundee Scotland DD3 1AH United Kingdom. **E-mail:** editor@beatdom.com. **Website:** www.beatdom.com. **Contact:** David Wills, editor. **75% freelance written.** Beatdom is a Beat Generation-themed literary journal that publishes essays, short stories, and poems related to the Beats. "We publish studies of Beat texts, figures, and legends; we look at writers and movements related to the Beats; we support writers of the present who take their influence from the Beats." Estab. 2007. Circ. 1,000. Byline given. Pays on publication. No kill fee. Publishes ms 6 months after acceptance. Accepts queries by e-mail. Accepts simultaneous submissions.

NONFICTION Needs essays, interview, profile, reviews. **Buys 10 mss/year.** Query. Length: 1,000-5,000 words. **Pays $50.** Pays expenses of writers on assignment.

FICTION Submit complete ms via e-mail. Length: up to 5,000 words. **Pays $50.**

POETRY Needs "Poems should ideally fit the theme of the issue, or display some sort of connection to the Beat Generation."

BELLINGHAM REVIEW

Mail Stop 9053, Western Washington University, Bellingham WA 98225. (360)650-4863. **E-mail:** bellingham.review@wwu.edu. **Website:** wwww.bhreview.org. **Contact:** Susanne Paola Antonetta, editor-in-chief; Bailey Cunningham, managing editor. **100% freelance written.** Annual small-press literary magazine covering poems, stories, and essays. No limitations on form or subject matter. Nonprofit magazine published once/year in the Spring. Seeks "literature of palpable quality: poems, stories, and essays so beguiling they invite us to touch their essence. *Bellingham Review* hungers for a kind of writing that nudges the limits of form or executes traditional forms exquisitely." The editors are actively seeking submissions of creative nonfiction, as well as stories that push the boundaries of the form. Open submission period is from September 15-December 1. Estab. 1977. Circ. 2,000. Pays on publication when funding allows. No kill fee. Publishes ms an average of 6 months after acceptance. Editorial lead time 6 months. Accepts simultaneous submissions. Responds in 1-4 months to mss. Sample copy: $12. Guidelines online.

NONFICTION Needs essays, personal experience. Does not want anything nonliterary. Submit complete ms via online submissions manager. Length: up to 6,000 words. For prose that is 1,500 words or fewer, submit up to three in one entry. **Pays as funds allow, plus contributor copies.** Pays expenses of writers on assignment.

FICTION Length: up to 6,000 words. For prose that is 1,500 words or fewer, submit up to three in one entry. Needs experimental, short stories. Does not want anything nonliterary. **Buys 4-6 mss/year.** Submit complete ms via online submissions manager. Length: up to 6,000 words. **Pays as funds allow, plus contributor's copies.**

POETRY Needs avant-garde, free verse, traditional. Wants "well-crafted poetry, but is open to all styles." Has published poetry by David Shields, Tess Gallagher, Gary Soto, Jane Hirshfield, Albert Goldbarth, and Rebecca McClanahan. Submit up to 3 poems via online submissions manager. Will not use light verse. Buys 10-30 poems/year. **Pays as funds allow, plus contributor's copies.**

TIPS "The *Bellingham Review* holds 3 annual contests: the 49th Parallel Award for poetry, the Annie Dillard Award for Nonfiction, and the Tobias Wolff Award for Fiction. See the individual listings for these contests under Contests & Awards for full details."

BIG PULP

Exter Press, P.O. Box 92, Cumberland MD 21501. **E-mail:** editors@bigpulp.com. **Website:** www.bigpulp.com. **Contact:** Bill Olver, editor. Quarterly literary magazine. Submissions accepted by e-mail only. *Big Pulp* defines "pulp fiction" very broadly: It's lively, challenging, thought provoking, thrilling, and fun, regardless of how many or how few genre elements are packed in. It doesn't subscribe to the theory that genre fiction is disposable; a great deal of literary fiction could easily fall under one of their general categories. Places a higher value on character and story than genre elements. Estab. 2008. Byline given. Pays on publication. Offers 100% kill fee. Publishes ms 1 year after acceptance. Accepts queries by e-mail. Accepts simultaneous submissions. Responds in 2 months to mss. Sample copy: $10; excerpts available online at no cost. Guidelines online.

"Submissions are only accepted during certain reading periods. Our website is updated to reflect when we are and are not reading, and what we are looking for."

FICTION Needs adventure, fantasy, horror, mystery, romance, science fiction, suspense, western, superhero. Does not want generic slice-of-life, memoirs, inspirational, political, pastoral odes. **Buys 70 mss/year.** Submit complete ms. Length: up to 2,500 words. **Pays $5-25.**

POETRY Needs avant-garde, free verse, haiku, light verse, traditional. All types of poetry are considered, but poems should have a genre connection. Buys 20 poems/year. Submit maximum 3 poems. **Pays $5/poem.**

TIPS "We like to be surprised, and we have few boundaries. Fantasy writers may focus on the mundane aspects of a fantastical creature's life or the magic that can happen in everyday life. Romances do not have to be requited or have happy endings, and the object of one's obsession may not be a person. Mysteries need not focus on 'whodunit?' We're always interested in science or speculative fiction focusing on societal issues, but writers should avoid being partisan or shrill. We also like fiction that crosses genre; for example, a science fiction romance or a fantasy crime story. We have an online archive for fiction and poetry and encourage writers to check it out. That said, *Big Pulp* has a strong editorial bias in favor of stories with monkeys. Especially talking monkeys."

BILINGUAL REVIEW

Arizona State University, Hispanic Research Center, P.O. Box 875303, Tempe AZ 85287-5303. (480)965-3867. **Fax:** (480)965-0315. **E-mail:** brp@asu.edu. **Website:** www.asu.edu/brp/submit. **Contact:** Gary Francisco Keller, publisher. Scholarly/literary journal focusing on the linguistics and literature of bilingualism and bilingual education. Publishes scholarly articles, literary criticism, and book reviews as well as creative literature: poetry, short stories, essays, and short theater. Accepts material in English or Spanish. U.S. Hispanic themes only. *Bilingual Review* is "committed to publishing high-quality writing by both established and emerging writers." Estab. 1974. Circ. 2,000. Publishes ms 1 year after acceptance. Accepts simultaneous submissions. Responds in 2-3 months. Often comments on rejected mss.

Magazine: 7x10; 96 pages; 55 lb. acid-free paper; coated cover stock.

NONFICTION Needs essays. Submit via mail. Send 2 copies of complete ms with SAE and loose stamps. **Pays 2 contributor's copies; 30% discount on additional copies.** Pays expenses of writers on assignment.

FICTION Receives 50 unsolicited mss/month. Accepts 3 mss/issue; 9 mss/year. Needs ethnic. "We do not publish literature about tourists in Latin America and their perceptions of the 'native culture.' We do not publish fiction about Latin America unless there is a clear tie to the U.S." Submit via mail. Send 2 copies of complete ms with SAE and loose stamps. Does not usually accept e-mail submissions except through special circumstance/prior arrangement. **Pays 2 contributor's copies; 30% discount for additional copies.**

POETRY Submit via mail. Send 2 copies of poetry with SAE and loose stamps. Does not usually accept e-mail submissions except through special circumstance/prior arrangement.

BLACK WARRIOR REVIEW

P.O. Box 862936, Tuscaloosa AL 35486. (205)348-4518. **E-mail:** interns.bwr@gmail.com. **Website:** www.bwr.ua.edu. **Contact:** Cat Ingrid Leeches, editor. **90% freelance written.** Semiannual magazine covering fiction, poetry, essays, art, comics, and reviews. "We publish contemporary fiction, poetry, reviews, essays, and art for a literary audience. We publish the freshest work we can find." Work that appeared in the *Black Warrior Review* has been included in the *Pushcart Prize* anthology, *Harper's Magazine, Best American Short Stories, Best American Poetry,* and *New Stories from the South.* Estab. 1974. Circ. 2,000. Byline given. Pays on publication. Publishes ms 6 months after acceptance. Accepts queries by online submission form.

Accepts simultaneous submissions. Responds in 3-6 months. Sample copy: $10. Guidelines online.

NONFICTION Needs essays, interview, "We are looking for essays that offer a new perspective, an unvoiced thought, an overlooked association—and we hope that you will send us pieces that not only challenge us with their content, but also with their form. We prize the lyric and the language driven, both the sparsely stated and the indulgently ruminative." **Buys 5 mss/year.** No queries; send complete ms. Length: up to 7,000 words. **Pays one-year subscription and nominal lump-sum fee.** Pays expenses of writers on assignment.

FICTION "We are open to good experimental writing and short-short fiction. No genre fiction please." Publishes novel excerpts if under contract to be published. Needs experimental, short stories. **Buys 10 mss/year.** One story/chapter per envelope. Wants work that is conscious of form and well-crafted. Length: up to 7,000 words. **Pays one-year subscription and nominal lump-sum fee.**

POETRY "We welcome most styles and forms, and we favor poems that take risks—whether they be quiet or audacious." Submit poems in 1 document. Submit maximum 5 poems. Length: up to 10 pages. **Pays one-year subscription and nominal lump-sum fee.**

TIPS "We look for attention to language, freshness, honesty, a convincing and sharp voice. Send us a clean, well-printed, proofread ms. Become familiar with the magazine prior to submission."

BLUE MESA REVIEW

Department of Language and Literature, Humanities Building, Second Floor, MSC03 2170, 1 University of New Mexico, Albuquerque NM 87131. **Website:** bluemesareview.org. **Contact:** Has rotating editorial board; see website for current masthead. "Originally founded by Rudolfo Anaya, Gene Frumkin, David Johnson, Patricia Clark Smith, and Lee Bartlette in 1989, the *Blue Mesa Review* emerged as a source of innovative writing produced in the Southwest. Over the years the magazine's nuance has changed, sometimes shifting towards more craft-oriented work, other times realigning with its original roots." Estab. 1989. Accepts queries by online submission form. Accepts simultaneous submissions. Responds in 2-6 months.

Open for submissions from September 30-March 31. Contest: June 1-August 31. Only accepts submissions through online submissions manager.

NONFICTION Submit via online submissions manager. Length: up to 6,000 words. Pays expenses of writers on assignment.

FICTION Submit via online submissions manager. Length: up to 6,000 words.

POETRY Submit 3-5 poems via online submissions manager.

TIPS "In general, we are seeking strong voices and lively, compelling narrative with a fine eye for craft. We look forward to reading your best work!"

BOMB MAGAZINE

80 Hanson Place, Ste. 703, Brooklyn NY 11217. (718)636-9100. **Fax:** (718)636-9200. **E-mail:** saul@bombsite.com. **Website:** www.bombmagazine.com. **Contact:** Saul Anton, senior editor. Quarterly magazine providing interviews between artists, writers, musicians, directors, and actors. "Written, edited, and produced by industry professionals and funded by those interested in the arts, *BOMB Magazine* publishes work which is unconventional and contains an edge, whether it be in style or subject matter." Estab. 1981. Circ. 36,000. Pays on publication. No kill fee. Publishes ms an average of 3-6 months after acceptance. Editorial lead time 3-4 months. Accepts queries by online submission form. Accepts simultaneous submissions. Responds in 3-5 months to mss. Sample copy: $10. Guidelines by e-mail.

FICTIONexperimental, novel concepts, contemporary. No genre fiction: romance, science fiction, horror, western. *BOMB Magazine* accepts unsolicited poetry and prose submissions for our literary supplement *First Proof* by online submission manager in January and August. Submissions sent outside these months will not be read. Submit complete ms via online submission manager. E-mailed submissions will not be considered. Length: up to 25 pages. **Pays $100 and contributor's copies.**

POETRY *BOMB Magazine* accepts unsolicited poetry and prose submissions for our literary supplement *First Proof* by online submission manager in January and August. Submissions sent outside these months will not be read. Submit 4-6 poems via online submission manager. E-mailed submissions will not be considered. **Pays $100 and contributor's copies.**

TIPS "Mss should be typed, double-spaced, and proofread, and should be final drafts. Purchase a sample issue before submitting work."

BOOK/MARK QUARTERLY REVIEW

P.O. Box 516, Miller Place NY 11764. (631)331-4118. **E-mail:** cyberpoet@optonline.net. **Contact:** Mindy Kronenberg, editor. **90% freelance written.** Quarterly newsletter. "*Book/Mark* is dedicated to publishing reviews of books and magazines by small and independent presses. We are eclectic and cover a wide variety of genres and topics, including literary subjects, the arts, popular culture, politics, history, and the sciences." Estab. 1994. Circ. 800. Byline given. No kill fee. Publishes ms an average of 3-6 months after acceptance. Editorial lead time 3 months. Submit seasonal material 3-6 months in advance. Accepts queries by mail, e-mail. Accepts simultaneous submissions. Responds in 1 week to queries; in 1 month to mss. Sample copy: $4 plus SASE with first-class stamp. Guidelines for #10 SASE.

NONFICTION Needs reviews, travel, We are interested in all genres of books coming from small, university, and independent presses. Does not want fiction or poetry. Query. Length: 600-950 words.

TIPS "We like reviews that zero in on the virtues and interesting aspects of books. Writers should be empathetic to the topics or close to the genre of each reviewed work."

BORDERLANDS: TEXAS POETRY REVIEW

P.O. Box 40876, Austin TX 78704. **E-mail:** borderlandspoetry@gmail.com. **Website:** www.borderlands.org. **Contact:** Ryan Sharp, editor. *Borderlands: Texas Poetry Review*, published semiannually, prints high-quality, outward-looking poetry by new and established poets, as well as brief reviews of poetry books and critical essays. Cosmopolitan in content, but particularly welcomes Texas and Southwest writers. Wants poems that exhibit social, political, geographical, historical, feminist, or spiritual awareness coupled with concise artistry. Does not want introspective work about the speaker's psyche, childhood, or intimate relationships. Has published poetry by Walter McDonald, Naomi Shihab Nye, Mario Susko, Wendy Barker, Larry D. Thomas, Reza Shirazi, and Scott Hightower. Estab. 1992. Sample copy: $12. Guidelines available online.

Borderlands is 100-150 pages, digest-sized, offset-printed, perfect-bound, with 4-color cover. Receives about 2,000 poems/year, accepts about 120. Press run is 1,000.

NONFICTION Needs essays, reviews. Include cover letter and SASE with submission. All essays and reviews must be germane to poetry and are accepted under the provision that the author be willing to work with the editors on recommended changes (length, punctuation, general editing, etc.). Length: up to 1,500 words for reviews; up to 2,500 words for essays. Pays expenses of writers on assignment.

POETRY Submit 5 typed poems at a time. Include cover letter and SASE with sufficient return postage. Open to traditional and experimental forms. **Pays 1 contributor's copy.**

TIPS "Editors read year round in 2 cycles. Submissions postmarked March 15-June 15 will be considered for the Fall/Winter issue, and submissions postmarked September 15-December 15 will be considered for the Spring/Summer issue. Occasionally, work may be held for publication in the following issue. Note that response times may be slower for work received immediately after a deadline. Do not submit work while we are considering a previous submission."

BOSTON COLLEGE MAGAZINE

140 Commonwealth Ave., Chestnut Hill MA 02467. (617)552-4820. **Fax:** (617)552-2441. **E-mail:** bcm@bc.edu. **Website:** bcm.bc.edu. **Contact:** Ben Birnbaum, editor. "*Boston College Magazine* presents the people, work, and spirit of a distinctive American university." Published quarterly and distributed free to the University's alumni, the parents of its undergraduate students, and its financial supporters. Accepts queries by e-mail. Accepts simultaneous submissions.

NONFICTION Query.

$$ BOULEVARD

Opojaz, Inc., 6614 Clayton Rd., Box 325, Richmond Heights MO 63117. **E-mail:** editors@boulevardmagazine.org. **Website:** www.boulevardmagazine.org; boulevard.submittable.com/submit. Managing Editor: Dusty Freund. **Contact:** Jessica Rogen, editor. **100% freelance written.** "*Boulevard* is a diverse literary magazine presenting original creative work by well-known authors as well as by writers of exciting promise." Triannual magazine featuring fiction, poetry, and essays. Sometimes comments on rejected mss. *Boulevard* has been called "one of the half-dozen best literary journals" by Poet Laureate Daniel Hoffman in *The Philadelphia Inquirer*. "We strive to publish the finest in poetry, fiction, and nonfiction. We frequently publish writers with previous credits, and we are very interested in publishing less experienced or unpublished writers with exceptional promise. We've published everything from John Ashbery to Donald Hall to a wide variety of styles from new or lesser known poets. We're eclectic. We are interested in original, moving poetry written from the head as well as the heart. It can be about any topic." *Boulevard* is 175-250 pages, digest-sized, flat-spined, with glossy card cover. Receives over 600 unsolicited mss/month. Accepts about 10 mss/issue. Publishes 10 new writers/year. Recently published work by Joyce Carol Oates, Floyd Skloot, John Barth, Stephen Dixon, David Guterson, Albert Goldbarth, Molly Peacock, Bob Hicok, Alice Friman, Dick Allen, and Tom Disch. Estab. 1985. Circ. 11,000. Byline given. Pays on publication. Offers no kill fee. Publishes ms an average of 9 months after acceptance. Accepts queries by mail, e-mail, online submission form. Accepts simultaneous submissions. Responds in 2 weeks to queries; 4-5 months to mss. Sample copy: $10. Subscription: $16 for 3 issues, $29 for 6 issues, $42 for 9 issues. Foreign subscribers, please add $10. Make checks payable to Opojaz, Inc. Subscriptions are available online at www.boulevardmagazine.org/subscribe.html. Guidelines online.

NONFICTION Needs book excerpts, essays, interview, opinion, photo feature. **Buys 10 mss/year.** Submit by mail or Submittable. Accepts multiple submissions. Does not accept mss May 1-October 1. Include SASE for reply. Length: up to 8,000 words. **Pays $100-300.**

FICTION Submit by mail or Submittable. Accepts multiple submissions. Does not accept mss May 1-October 1. SASE for reply. Needs ethnic, experimental, mainstream, novel excerpts, short stories, slice-of-life vignettes. "We do not want erotica, science fiction, romance, western, horror, or children's stories." **Buys 20 mss/year.** Length: up to 8,000 words. **Pays $50-500 (sometimes higher) for accepted work.**

POETRY Needs avant-garde, free verse, haiku, traditional. Submit by mail or Submittable. Accepts multiple submissions. Does not accept poems May 1-October 1. SASE for reply. Does not consider book reviews. "Do not send us light verse." Does not want "poetry that is uninspired, formulaic, self-conscious, unoriginal, insipid." Buys 80 poems/year. Submit maximum 5 poems. Length: up to 200 lines/poem. **Pays $25-250.**

TIPS "Read the magazine first. The work *Boulevard* publishes is generally recognized as among the finest in the country. We continue to seek more good literary or cultural essays. Send only your best work."

BRICK

Brick, P.O. Box 609, Station P, Toronto ON M5S 2Y4 Canada. **E-mail:** info@brickmag.com. **Website:** www.brickmag.com. **Contact:** Liz Johnston, managing editor. **90% freelance written.** Semiannual magazine covering literature and the arts. "We publish literary nonfiction of a very high quality on a range of arts and culture subjects." Estab. 1977. Circ. 3,000. Byline given. Pays on publication. No kill fee. Publishes ms 3-5 months after acceptance. Editorial lead time 5 months. Accepts simultaneous submissions. Responds in 6 months to mss. Sample copy: $16 plus shipping. Guidelines online.

NONFICTION Needs essays, interview, opinion, travel. No fiction, poetry, personal memoir, or art. **Buys 30-40 mss/year.** Send complete ms. Length: 1,000-5,000 words. **Pays $75-500 (Canadian).** Pays expenses of writers on assignment.

PHOTOS State availability. Reviews transparencies, prints, TIFF/JPEG files. Offers $25-50/photo. Buys one-time rights.

TIPS "*Brick* is interested in polished work by writers who are widely read and in touch with contemporary culture. The magazine is serious but not fusty. We like to feel the writer's personality in the piece, too."

BURNSIDE REVIEW

P.O. Box 1782, Portland OR 97207. **Website:** www.burnsidereview.org. **Contact:** Sid Miller, founder and editor; Dan Kaplan, managing editor. *Burnside Review*, published every 9 months, prints "the best poetry and short fiction we can get our hands on. We tend to publish writing that finds beauty in truly unexpected places; that combines urban and natural imagery; that breaks the heart." Estab. 2004. Pays on publication. Publishes ms 9 months after acceptance. Submit seasonal material 3-6 months in advance. Accepts queries by online submission form. Accepts simultaneous submissions. Responds in 1-6 months. Single copy: $8; subscription: $13.

Burnside Review is 80 pages, 6x6, professionally printed, perfect-bound. Charges a $3 submission fee to cover printing costs.

FICTION "We like bright, engaging fiction that works to surprise and captivate us." Needs experimental, short stories. Submit complete ms via online submissions manager. Length: up to 5,000 words. **Pays $25 and 1 contributor's copy.**

POETRY Needs avant-garde, free verse, traditional. Open to all forms. Translations are encouraged. "We like lyric. We like narrative. We like when the two merge. We like whiskey. We like hourglass figures. We like to be surprised. Surprise us." Has published poetry by Linda Bierds, Dorianne Laux, Ed Skoog, Campbell McGrath, Paul Guest, and Larissa Szporluk. Reads submissions year round. "Editors read all work submitted." Seldom comments on rejected work. Submit 3-5 poems via online submissions manager. **Pays $25 and 1 contributor's copy.**

BY&BY POETRY

Website: byandbylit.org. **Contact:** Jason Sears, editor. *By&By Poetry* aims to provide an eclectic online showcase for both established and up-and-coming poets. "We aspire to shape *By&By* into a celebration of poetry, a place where poets can congregate, read, and be heard. Join us." Estab. 2015. Accepts queries by online submission form. Accepts simultaneous submissions. Responds in 1 month. Sample copies online. Guidelines online.

NONFICTION Pays expenses of writers on assignment.

POETRY Submit up to 5 poems with a cover letter and short bio through online submissions manager.

TIPS "We welcome poems of any form, length, or style. Quite simply, we want your best."

THE CAFE IRREAL

E-mail: editors@cafeirreal.com. **Website:** www.cafeirreal.com. **Contact:** G.S. Evans and Alice Whittenburg, co-editors. **90% freelance written.** Quarterly webzine focusing on short stories and short shorts of an irreal nature. Also publishes literary essays, literary criticism. "Our audience is composed of people who read or write literary fiction with fantastic themes, similar to the work of Franz Kafka, Kobo Abe, or Ana María Shua. This is a type of fiction (irreal) that has difficulty finding its way into print in the English-speaking world and defies many of the conventions of American literature especially. As a result, ours is a fairly specialized literary publication, and we would strongly recommend that prospective writers look at our current issue and guidelines carefully." Recently published work by Tamara K. Walker, Jeff Friedman, Vanessa Gebbie, Viki Shock, JB Mulligan, Tess Gunty, Jiří Kratochvil, Ian Seed. Estab. 1998. Circ. 10,000. Byline given. Pays on publication for first electronic rights. Sends galleys to author. No kill fee. Accepts queries by e-mail. Responds in 2-4 months. Sometimes comments on rejected mss. Sample copy online. Guidelines online.

REPRINTS "We sometimes publish fiction that has previously appeared in print but not online."

FICTION Accepts submissions by e-mail. No attachments; include submission in body of e-mail. Include estimated word count. Accepts 6-8 mss/issue; 24-32 mss/year. Needs experimental, fantasy, science fiction. No horror or "slice-of-life" stories; no genre or mainstream science fiction or fantasy. Length: up to 2,000 words. **Pays 1¢/word, $2 minimum.**

TIPS "Forget formulas. Write about what you don't know, take me places I couldn't possibly go, don't try to make me care about the characters. Read short fiction by writers such as Franz Kafka, Jorge Luis Borges, Donald Barthelme, Leonora Carrington, Magnus Mills, and Stanislaw Lem. Also read our website and guidelines."

THE CAPILANO REVIEW

102-281 Industrial Ave., Vancouver BC V6A 2P2 Canada. **E-mail:** contact@thecapilanoreview.ca. **E-mail:** online through submittable. **Website:** www.thecapilanoreview.com. **Contact:** Matea Kulic, managing editor. **100% freelance written.** Triannual visual and literary arts magazine that "publishes only what the editors consider to be the very best fiction, poetry, drama, or visual art being produced. *TCR* editors are interested in fresh, original work that stimulates and challenges readers. Over the years, the magazine has developed a reputation for pushing beyond the boundaries of traditional art and writing. We are interested in work that is new in concept and in execution. We no longer accept submissions by mail. Please review our submission guidelines on our website and submit online through submittable." Estab. 1972. Circ. 800. Byline given. Pays on publication. Publishes work within 1 year after acceptance. Accepts queries by online submission form. Accepts simultaneous submissions. Responds in 4-6 months. Sample copy: $10 (outside of Canada, USD). Guidelines online.

NONFICTION Needs essays, interview, reviews. Pays expenses of writers on assignment.

PHOTOS Pays $50 for cover and $50/page to maximum of $200 Canadian. Additional payment for electronic rights; negotiable. Pays on publication. Credit line given. Buys first North American serial rights only.

FICTION Needs experimental, literary. No traditional, conventional fiction. Wants to see more innovative, genre-blurring work. **Buys 10-15 mss/year.** Length: up to 5,000 words. **Pays $50-150.**

POETRY Needs Experimental poetry. Submit up to 8 pages of poetry. Buys 40 poems/year. Submit maximum 8 poems. **Pays $50-150.**

THE CHARITON REVIEW

Truman State University Press, 100 E. Normal Ave., Kirksville MO 63501. (660)785-7336. **Fax:** (660)785-4480. **E-mail:** chariton@truman.edu. **Website:** tsup.truman.edu/product/chariton-review/. *The Chariton Review* is an international literary journal publishing the best in short fiction, essays, poetry, and translations in 2 issues each year. Estab. 1975. No kill fee. Accepts queries by online submission form. Accepts simultaneous submissions. Responds in 3 months. Guidelines available on website.

NONFICTION Submit through online submissions manager. English only. Length: up to 7,000 words.

FICTION No flash fiction. Submit 1 complete ms through online submissions manager. English only. Length: up to 7,000 words.

POETRY Submit 3-6 poems through online submissions manager. Include all poems in 1 file; start a new page for each poem. English only.

CHEST

CHEST Global Headquarters, 2595 Patriot Blvd., Glenview IL 60026. (800)343-2222. **E-mail:** poetrychest@aol.com. **Website:** www.chestjournal.org. **Contact:** Michael Zack, M.D., Poetry Editor. *CHEST*, published monthly, "is the official medical journal of the American College of Chest Physicians, the world's largest medical journal for pulmonologists, sleep, and critical care specialists, with over 30,000 subscribers." Wants "poetry with themes of medical relevance." Accepts simultaneous submissions. Responds in 2 months; always sends prepublication galleys. Subscription: $276. Make checks payable to American College Chest Physicians.

CHEST is approximately 300 pages, magazine-sized, perfect-bound, with a glossy cover, and includes ads. Press run is 22,000. Number of unique visitors: 400,000 to website.

NONFICTION Pays expenses of writers on assignment.

POETRY Only accepts e-mail submissions (as attachment or in body of e-mail); no fax or disk submissions. Brief cover letter preferred. Reads submissions year round. Poems are circulated to an editorial board. Sometimes comments on rejected poems. Never publishes theme issues. Guidelines available in magazine and on website. Submit no more than two poems. Submit maximum 2 poems. Length: up to 350 words.

CHICAGO QUARTERLY REVIEW

517 Sherman Ave., Evanston IL 60202. **E-mail:** cqr@icogitate.com. **Website:** www.chicagoquarterlyreview.com. **Contact:** S. Afzal Haider and Elizabeth McKenzie, senior editors. "The *Chicago Quarterly Review* is a nonprofit, independent literary journal publishing the finest short stories, poems, translations, and essays by both emerging and established writers. We hope to stimulate, entertain, and inspire." Estab. 1994. Circ. 500-1,000. Publishes ms 6 months-1 year after acceptance. Accepts queries by online submission form. Accepts simultaneous submissions. Responds in 6-8 months to mss. Sometimes comments on rejected mss. Sample copy: $15. Guidelines available online.

The *Chicago Quarterly Review* is 6x9; 225 pages; illustrations; photos. Receives 250 unsolicited mss/month. Accepts 10-15 mss/issue; 20-30 mss/year. Agented fiction 5%. **Publishes 8-10 new writers/year.**

NONFICTION Needs personal essays. Submit through online submissions manager only. Length: up to 5,000 words. **Pays 2 contributor's copies.** Pays expenses of writers on assignment.

FICTION Submit through online submissions manager only. Length: up to 5,000 words; average length: 2,500 words. **Pays 2 contributor's copies.**

POETRY Submit 3-5 poems through online submissions manager only. **Pays 2 contributor's copies.**

TIPS "The writer's voice ought to be clear and unique and should explain something of what it means to be human. We want well-written stories that reflect an appreciation for the rhythm and music of language, work that shows passion and commitment to the art of writing."

CHICAGO REVIEW

Taft House, 935 E. 60th St., Chicago IL 60637. **E-mail:** editors@chicagoreview.org. **Website:** chicagoreview.org. **Contact:** Gerónimo Sarmiento Cruz, managing editor. "Since 1946, *Chicago Review* has published a range of contemporary poetry, fiction, and criticism. Each year typically includes two single issues and a double issue with a special feature section." Estab. 1946. Accepts queries by online submission form. Accepts simultaneous submissions. Guidelines available on website.

NONFICTION Needs essays. *Chicago Review* publishes a wide range of critical essays but does not typically consider memoir nonfiction. Length: "*Chicago Review* publishes reviews of varying lengths: from notes (150-500 words) to regular book reviews (800-1,200 words) to review essays (1,200-6,000 words)."

FICTION "We will consider work in any literary style but are typically less interested in traditional narrative approaches." Needs experimental. Submit 1 short story or up to 5 short short stories submitted in 1 file. Submit via online submissions manager. Prefers electronic submissions. Length: up to 5,000 words. **Pays contributor's copies.**

POETRY Submit via online submission form, Submittable. Include cover letter. Length: no strict length requirements, but the poetry editors prefer to read at least 3 pages of work. **Pays contributor's copies.**

TIPS "We strongly recommend that authors familiarize themselves with recent issues of *Chicago Review* before submitting. Submissions that demonstrate familiarity with the journal tend to receive more attention than those that appear to be part of a carpet-bombing campaign."

$$ CHICKEN SOUP FOR THE SOUL PUBLISHING, LLC

Chicken Soup for the Soul Publishing, LLC, P.O. Box 700, Cos Cob CT 06807. **E-mail:** webmaster@chickensoupforthesoul.com (for all inquires). **Website:** www.chickensoup.com. **95% freelance written.** Paperback with 12 publications/year featuring inspirational, heartwarming, uplifting short stories. Estab. 1993. Circ. Over 200 titles; 100 million books in print. Byline given. Pays on publication. No kill fee. Accepts queries by online submission form. Accepts simultaneous submissions. Responds upon consideration. Guidelines available online.

"Stories must be written in the first person."

NONFICTION No sermon, essay, eulogy, term paper, journal entry, political, or controversial issues. **Buys 1,000 mss/year.** Send complete ms. Length: 300-1,200 words. **Pays $200.**

POETRY Needs traditional. No controversial poetry.

TIPS "We no longer accept submissions by mail or fax. Stories and poems can only be submitted on our website. Select the 'Submit Your Story' tab on the left toolbar. The submission form can be found there."

CHIRON REVIEW

Chiron, Inc., 522 E. South Ave., St. John KS 67576-2212. **E-mail:** editor@chironreview.com. **Website:** www.chironreview.com. **Contact:** Michael Hathaway, publisher. **90% freelance written.** *Chiron Review*, published quarterly, presents the widest possible range of contemporary creative writing—fiction and nonfiction, traditional and off-beat—in an attractive, perfect-bound digest, including artwork and photographs. No taboos. Estab. 1982 as *The Kindred Spirit*. Byline given. Pays on publication. No kill fee. Publishes ms 3-12 months after acceptance. "We accept simultaneous submissions but dislike them intensely." Accepts queries by e-mail. Accepts simultaneous submissions. Responds in 2-8 weeks. Subscription: $60, ppd/year (4 issues) and $100 ppd overseas. Single issue: $20 ppd and $34 ppd overseas. Guidelines available for SASE, or on website.

NONFICTION Needs essays, interview. Submit complete ms by mail with SASE, or by e-mail as DOC attachment. **Pays 1 contributor's copy.**

FICTION **Contact:** Rafael Zepeda, John Brantingham, Sarah Daugherty, fiction editors. Submit complete ms by mail with SASE, or by e-mail as DOC attachment. Length: up to 2,500 words. **Pays 1 contributor's copy.**

POETRY Submit up to 3 poems by mail with SASE, or by e-mail as DOC attachment. Has published poetry by Charles Bukowski, Charles Harper Webb, Edward Field, Wanda Coleman, Thich Nhat Hanh, and Marge Piercy. **Pays 1 contributor's copy.**

TIPS "Please check our website to see if we are open to submissions. When you do send submissions, please have mercy on the editors and follow the guidelines noted here and on our website."

$ THE CINCINNATI REVIEW

P.O. Box 210069, Cincinnati OH 45221-0069. **E-mail:** editors@cincinnatireview.com. **Website:** www.cincinnatireview.com. **Contact:** Michael Griffith, fiction editor; Rebecca Lindenberg, poetry editor; Kristen Iversen, literary nonfiction editor; Brant Russell, drama editor. **100% freelance written.** Semiannual magazine containing new literary fiction, creative nonfiction, poetry, drama, book reviews, essays, and interviews. A journal devoted to publishing the best new literary fiction, creative nonfiction, and poetry, as well as a short play, book reviews, essays, and occasional interviews. Estab. 2003. Byline given. Pays on publication. No kill fee. Publishes ms an average of 6 months after acceptance. Accepts queries by online submission form. Accepts simultaneous submissions. Responds in 4-10 months to mss. Always sends prepublication galleys. Sample copy: $7 (back issue). Single copy: $9 (current issue). Subscription: $15. Guidelines available on website.

The Cincinnati Review is 200-360 pages, digest-sized, perfect-bound, with matte paperback cover with full-color art. Press run is 1,500. Reads submissions September 1-March 1.

NONFICTION Submit complete ms via online submissions manager only. Length: up to 40 double-spaced pages. **Pays $25/page.**

FICTION Needs short stories. Does not want genre fiction. **Buys 13 mss/year.** Submit complete ms via online submissions manager only. Length: up to 40 double-spaced pages. **Pays $25/page.**

POETRY Needs avant-garde, free verse, traditional. Submit up to 5 poems (10 pages maximum) of poetry at a time via submission manager only. Buys 100 poems/year. **Pays $30/page.**

THE CLAREMONT REVIEW

1581-H Hillside Ave., Suite 101, Victoria BC V8T 2C1 Canada. **E-mail:** claremontreview@gmail.com. **Website:** www.theclaremontreview.ca. **Contact:** Ali Blythe, Editor-in-chief. The editors of *The Claremont Review* publish the best poetry, short stories, visual art and photography by youth ages 13-19, from anywhere in the English-speaking world. "We publish work in many styles that range from traditional to modern. We prefer edgy pieces that take chances, show your commitment to craft, explore real characters, and reveal authentic emotion. Read the samples in our resources or in past issues for a clearer understanding of what we accept. We strongly encourage readers to subscribe to our magazine, to read, connect with and support youth writing from all over the world." Estab. 1992. Pays on publication. Accepts queries by online submission form. Accepts simultaneous submissions. Responds in 3-6 months. Guidelines available.

FICTION Needs short stories. Only accepts submissions from writers ages 13-19. Length: up to 2,000 words. **Pays $10.**

POETRY Rarely publishes rhyming poetry. Only accepts submissions from writers ages 13-19. Submit maximum 3 poems. **Pays $10.**

TIPS "We love: Wild minds like yours.don't be afraid to try something new with form or thinking. Images, metaphor, leaps, research, specificity, images, sensory details, images. Writing that reveals YOUR artistic spirit.are you formal? Tricky? Elusive? Allusive? Quiet? Bold? Clean writing: read your piece word by word, then line by line, and fix spelling or grammatical errors. Entries that meet all our guidelines, read them."

CLOUDBANK

Journal of Contemporary Writing, P.O. Box 610, Corvallis OR 97339. (541)752-0075 or (877)782-6762. **E-mail:** cloudbank@cloudbankbooks.com. **Website:** www.cloudbankbooks.com. **Contact:** Michael Malan, editor. Journal of contemporary writing open to range of styles; never publishes theme issues. *Cloudbank* publishes poetry, short prose, and book reviews. Estab. 2009. Accepts queries by mail, online submission form. Accepts simultaneous submissions. Responds in 4 months. Single copy: $8. Subscription: $15. Make checks payable to *Cloudbank*. Guidelines available in magazine, for SASE, by e-mail, or on website.

Cloudbank is digest-sized, 96 pages of print, perfect-bound; color artwork on cover, includes ads. Press run is 400. Subscribers: 300; shelf sales: 100 distributed free. Prefers submissions from skilled, experienced poets; will consider work from beginning poets. Reviews books of poetry in 500 words.

FICTIONflash fiction. Submit flash fiction by mail with SASE. Length: up to 500 words. **Pays $200 prize for 1 poem or flash fiction piece per issue.**

POETRY Submit up to 5 poems by mail with SASE. Cover letter is preferred. Does not accept fax, e-mail, or disk submissions from U.S.; overseas e-mail submissions accepted. Reads year round. Rarely sends pre-publication galleys. Receives 1,600 poems/year; accepts about 8%. Has published poetry by Dennis Schmitz, Christopher Buckley, Stuart Friebert, Dore Kiesselbach, Karen Holmberg, and Vern Rutsala. Length: up to 150 lines/submission. **Pays $200 prize for 1 poem or flash fiction piece per issue.**

TIPS "Please consider reading a copy of *Cloudbank* before submitting."

CLOUD RODEO

E-mail: jakesyersak@gmail.com. **E-mail:** submit@cloudrodeo.org. **Website:** cloudrodeo.org. **Contact:** Jake Syersak, editor. "*Cloud Rodeo* is an irregularly published journal of the irregular. So let's get weird." Accepts queries by e-mail. Accepts simultaneous submissions. Guidelines available online.

NONFICTION Submit 1 prose piece via e-mail as a DOC or PDF attachment. Pays expenses of writers on assignment.

PHOTOS Submit up to 5 pieces of art.

FICTION Submit 1 prose piece via e-mail as a DOC or PDF attachment.

POETRY Submit up to 5 poems via e-mail as a DOC or PDF attachment.

COLD MOUNTAIN REVIEW

Department of English, Appalachian State University, ASU Box 32052, Boone NC 28608. (828)262-7687. **E-mail:** coldmountain@appstate.edu. **Website:** www.coldmountainreview.org. **Contact:** Mark Powell, editor; Katherine Abrams, managing editor; Rachel Sasser, assistant editor. *Cold Mountain Review*, published twice/year (in spring and fall), features fiction, nonfiction, poetry, and b&w art. "Themed fall issues rotate with general spring issues, but all work is considered beneath our broad social- and eco-justice umbrella." *Cold Mountain Review* is about 130 pages, digest-sized, perfect-bound, with light cardstock cover. Reading period is August and January. Estab. 1972. Accepts queries by online submission form. Accepts simultaneous submissions. Responds in 1-2 months.

NONFICTION Needs essays, interview, memoir, photo feature, narrative journalism, all subgenres of creative nonfiction. Submit 1 piece at a time through online submissions manager. Length: up to 6,000 words for creative nonfiction; up to 8 pages double-spaced for interviews. **Pays contributor's copies.** Pays expenses of writers on assignment.

FICTION Considers novel excerpts if the submissions is "an exemplary stand-alone piece." Needs experimental, novel excerpts, short stories. Submit 1 piece at a time through online submissions manager or by mail. Length: up to 6,000 words. **Pays contributor's copies.**

POETRY Publishes only 15-20 poems/issue. "We are extremely competitive: Send only your best." Submit up to 5 poems through online submissions manager or by mail. Poems should be single-spaced on one side of the page. When submitting online, submit a Word document rather than a PDF. **Pays contributor's copies.**

THE COLLAGIST

Dzanc Books, **E-mail:** editor@thecollagist.com; poetry@thecollagist.com; bookreviews@thecollagist.com. **Website:** thecollagist.com. **Contact:** Gabriel Blackwell, editor in chief; Marielle Prince, poetry editor; Michael Jauchen, book review editor. *The Collagist* is a monthly journal published on the 15th of each month, containing short fiction, poetry, essays, book reviews, and one of more excerpts from novels forthcoming from (mostly) independent presses. Estab. 2009. Accepts queries by online submission form. Accepts simultaneous submissions. Guidelines online.

NONFICTION Needs essays, reviews. Submit essays and book reviews through online submissions manager. Pays expenses of writers on assignment.

FICTION Submit short stories through online submissions manager.

POETRY Submit through online submission manager. Check site for reading periods.

$ COLORADO REVIEW

Center for Literary Publishing, Colorado State University, 9105 Campus Delivery, Fort Collins CO 80523. (970)491-5449. **E-mail:** creview@colostate.edu. **Website:** coloradoreview.colostate.edu. **Contact:** Stephanie G'Schwind, editor-in-chief and nonfiction editor; Steven Schwartz, fiction editor; Don Revell, Sasha Steensen, and Matthew Cooperman, poetry editors; Harrison Candelaria Fletcher, nonfiction editor; Dan Beachy-Quick, poetry book review editor; Jennifer Wisner Kelly, fiction and nonfiction book review editor. Literary magazine published 3 times/year. Work published in *Colorado Review* has been included in *Best American Essays, Best American Short Stories, Best American Poetry, Best New American Voices, Best Travel Writing, Best Food Writing,* and the *Pushcart Prize Anthology.* Estab. 1956. Circ. 1,000. Byline given. Pays on publication. No kill fee. Publishes ms an average of 6 months after acceptance. Editorial lead time 1 year. Accepts simultaneous submissions. Responds in 2 months to mss. Sample copy: $10. Guidelines online.

NONFICTION Needs essays, memoir, personal experience. **Buys 6-9 mss/year.** Mss for creative nonfiction are read year round. Send no more than 1 submission at a time. Length: up to 10,000 words. **Pays $200.** Pays expenses of writers on assignment.

FICTION Needs experimental, short stories, literary short fiction. No genre fiction. **Buys 12 mss/year.** Send complete ms. Fiction mss are read August 1-April 30. Mss received May 1-July 31 will be returned unread. Send no more than 1 story at a time. Length: up to 10,000 words. **Pays $200.**

POETRY Considers poetry of any style. Poetry mss are read August 1-April 30. Mss received May 1-July 31 will be returned unread. Has published poetry by Sherman Alexie, Laynie Browne, John Gallaher, Mathias Svalina, Craig Morgan Teicher, Pam Rehm, Elizabeth Robinson, Elizabeth Willis, and Rosmarie Waldrop. Buys 60-100 poems/year. Submit maximum 5 poems. **Pays $30 minimum or $10/page for poetry.**

COLUMBIA

A Journal of Literature and Art, Columbia University, New York NY 10027. **E-mail:** info@columbiajournal.org. **Website:** columbiajournal.org. **Contact:** Staff rotates each year. "*Columbia: A Journal of Literature and Art* is an annual publication that features the very best in poetry, fiction, nonfiction, and art. We were founded in 1977 and continue to be one of the few national literary journals entirely edited, designed, and produced by students. You'll find that our minds are open, our interests diverse. We solicit mss from writers we love and select the most exciting finds from our virtual submission box. Above all, our commitment is to our readers—to producing a collection that informs, surprises, challenges, and inspires." Estab. 1977. Accepts queries by online submission form. Accepts simultaneous submissions.

Reads submissions March 1-September 15.

NONFICTION Needs essays, memoir. Submit complete ms via online submissions manager. Include short bio. Length: up to 5,000 words. Pays expenses of writers on assignment.

FICTION Accepts all forms of short fiction: short stories, flash fiction, prose poetry. Needs short stories. Submit complete ms via online submissions manager. Include short bio. Length: up to 5,000 words.

POETRY Submit poetry via online submissions manager. Include short bio. Length: up to 5 pages.

COMMON THREADS

Ohio Poetry Association, 12886 Coventry Ave., Pickerington OH 43147. **E-mail:** team@ohiopoetryassn.org. **E-mail:** editor@ohiopoetryassn.org. **Website:** www.ohiopoetryassn.org. Common Threads Editor: Steve Abbott. **Contact:** Chuck Salmons, OPA president. *Common Threads*, published annually in autumn, is the Ohio Poetry Association's member journal. Submissions limited to OPA members and student and other contest winners. "We accept poems from both beginners and accomplished writers. We like poems to make us think as well as feel. We are uninterested in work that is highly sentimental, overly morbid, religiously coercive, or pornographic. Poetry by students will also be considered and prioritized if student is an OPA high school contest winner." While devoted primarily to members' poetry, *Common Threads* can include book reviews, essays on craft, interviews, and other articles related to poetry as an art. Estab. 1928. Circ. 200+. Accepts simultaneous submissions. Single copy: $10 back issues; $12 current issue. Subscription ($20; $15 for seniors 65+) in the form of annual OPA membership dues, which includes annual issue of *Common Threads*. Visit www.ohiopoetryassn.org for membership form and additional information on submissions.

POETRY Previously published poems are considered if first publisher is noted on submission. Submit up to 3 poems at a time to editor@ohiopoetryassociation.org (preferred) or as hard copies c/o 91 E. Duncan St., Columbus OH 43202 (with SASE or e-mail address) throughout the year, with August 31 deadline for consideration. Length: up to 50 lines/poem.

THE COMSTOCK REVIEW

4956 St. John Dr., Syracuse NY 13215. **E-mail:** poetry@comstockreview.org. **Website:** www.comstockreview.org. **Contact:** Betsy Anderson, managing editor. *The Comstock Review* accepts "poetry strictly on the basis of quality, not reputation. We publish both noted and mid-career poets as well as those who are new to publishing. It is the quality of the poem that is the decisive factor. We do not accept overly sexual material, sentimental or 'greeting card' verse, and very few haiku." Estab. 1986. Pays 1 copy except for contest winners. Accepts queries by mail, e-mail, online submission form. Responds in 2-3 months. Submit 4-5 poems, typed, by mail or on-line January 1-March 31 with SASE for mail. See website for details or Submittable link.

POETRY "We look for well-crafted poetry, either free or formal verse, with attention paid to the beauty of language, exceptional metaphor, unique voice, and fresh, vivid imagery. Poems may reflect any subject, although we have a slight bias toward poems dealing with the human condition in all its poignancy and humor." Accepts submissions of 4-5 poems by mail (include SASE) or online submissions manager during the Open Reading Period postmarked from January 1-March 31. Length: up to 38 lines/poem.

CONCHO RIVER REVIEW

Angelo State University, ASU Station #10894, San Angelo TX 76909. **E-mail:** ageyer@usca.edu; haleya@acu.edu; jerry.bradley@lamar.edu; roger.jackson@angelo.edu. **Website:** conchoriverreview.org. **Contact:** R. Mark Jackson, general editor and book review editor; Andrew Geyer, fiction editor; Albert Haley, nonfiction editor; Jerry Bradley, poetry editor. "*CRR* aims to provide its readers with escape, insight, laughter, and inspiration for many years to come. We urge authors to submit to the journal and readers to subscribe to our publication." Estab. 1987. Byline given. Accepts queries by mail, e-mail. Accepts simultaneous submissions. Responds in 1-2 months for poetry and in 2-6 months for fiction and nonfiction. Guidelines online.

NONFICTION Needs personal experience. Special issues: "Editors welcome submissions of creatively told personal narratives and innovative approaches to the essay form. We also consider thoughtful, researched articles; especially those that explore areas that are part of our southwestern landscape and heritage." Submit only 1 ms at a time with cover letter and brief bio. Electronic submissions are preferred. See website for appropriate section editor. Length: up to 6,000 words. **Pays 1 contributor's copy.** Pays expenses of writers on assignment.

FICTION "Editors tend to publish traditional stories with a strong sense of conflict, finely drawn characters, and crisp dialogue." Submit only 1 ms at a time. Electronic submissions preferred. See website for appropriate section editor. Length: 1,500-5,000 words. **Pays 1 contributor's copy.**

POETRY Welcomes original poetry submissions from all poets, established or emerging. Submit 3-5 poems at a time. Electronic submissions preferred. See website for appropriate section editor. "Length and form are open, but shorter poems (1 page or less) are preferred."

$$ CONFRONTATION

English Department, LIU Post, Brookville NY 11548. **E-mail:** confrontationmag@gmail.com. **Website:** www.confrontationmagazine.org. **Contact:** Jonna G. Semeiks, editor in chief; Belinda Kremer, poetry editor; Terry Kattleman, publicity director/production editor. **75% freelance written.** "*Confrontation* has been in continuous publication since 1968. Our taste and our magazine is eclectic, but we always look for excellence in style, an important theme, a memorable voice. We enjoy discovering and fostering new talent. Each issue contains work by both well-established and new writers. We read August 16-April 15. Do not send mss or e-mail submissions between April 16 and August 15." Estab. 1968. Circ. 2,000. Byline given. Pays on publication. Offers kill fee. Publishes work in the first or second issue after acceptance. Accepts queries by mail, e-mail. Accepts simultaneous submissions. Responds in 10 weeks to mss. "We prefer single submissions. Clear copy. **No e-mail submissions unless writer resides outside the U.S.** Mail submissions with a SASE."

Confrontation has garnered a long list of awards and honors, including the Editor's Award for Distinguished Achievement from CLMP (given to Martin Tucker, the founding editor of the magazine) and NEA grants. Work from the magazine has appeared in numerous anthologies, including the *Pushcart Prize*, *Best Short Stories*, and *The O. Henry Prize Stories*. "We also publish the work of 1 visual artist per issue, selected by the editors."

NONFICTION Needs essays, personal experience. Special issues: "We publish personal, cultural, political, and other kinds of essays as well as self-contained sections of memoirs." **Buys 5-10 mss/year.** Send complete ms. Length: 1,500-5,000 words. **Pays $100-150; more for commissioned work.**

FICTION "We judge on quality of writing and thought or imagination, so we will accept genre fiction. However, it must have literary merit or must transcend or challenge genre."experimental as well as more traditional fiction, self-contained novel excerpts, slice-of-life vignettes, lyrical or philosophical fiction. No "proselytizing" literature or conventional genre fiction. **Buys 10-15 mss/year.** Send complete ms. Length: up to 7,200 words. **Pays $175-250; more for commissioned work.**

POETRY Needs avant-garde or experimental as well as traditional poems (and forms), lyric poems, dramatic monologues, satiric or philosophical poems. In short, a wide range of verse. "*Confrontation* is interested in all poetic forms. Our only criterion is high literary merit. We think of our audience as an educated, lay group of intelligent readers." Has published poetry by David Ray, T. Alan Broughton, David Ignatow, Philip Appleman, Jane Mayhall, and Joseph Brodsky. Submit no more than 12 pages at a time (up to 6 poems). *Confrontation* also offers the annual Confrontation Poetry Prize. No sentimental verse. No previously published poems. Buys 20 poems/year. Length: up to 2 pages. **Pays $75-100; more for commissioned work.**

TIPS "We look for literary merit. Keep honing your skills, and keep trying."

CONJUNCTIONS

Bard College, 21 E. 10th St., #3E, New York NY 10003. (845)758-7054. **E-mail:** conjunctions@bard.edu. **Website:** www.conjunctions.com. Website covering innotive fiction, poetry, drama, criticism, interviews, art and other work by some of the leading literary lights of our time, both established and emerging. "We provide a forum for writers and artists whose work challenges accepted forms and modes of expression, experiments with language and thought, and is fully realized art." Unsolicited mss cannot be returned unless accompanied by SASE. Electronic and simultaneous submissions will not be considered. Estab. 1981. No kill fee. Accepts queries by mail.

NONFICTION Needs essays, interviews, art.

TIPS "Final selection of the material is made based on the literary excellence, originality, and vision of the writing. We have maintained a consistently high editorial and production quality with the intention of attracting a large and varied audience."

CONTEMPORARY HAIBUN

P.O. Box 2461, Winchester VA 22604-1661. **E-mail:** boblucky01@yahoo.com; ray@raysweb.net. **Website:** www.contemporaryhaibunonline.com; www.redmoonpress.com. **Contact:** Bob Lucky, editor/publisher; Ray Rasmussen, technical editor. *Contemporary Haibun Online* is a quarterly journal published in January, April, July, and October. It publishes haibun and tanka prose only. Time between acceptance and publication varies according to time of submission. Accepts simultaneous submissions. Sample available for SASE or by e-mail. Subscription: $17 plus $5 p&h.

Receives several hundred submissions/year, accepts about 5%. Print run is 1,000. Has published poetry by J. Zimmerman, Chen-ou Liu, Renée Owen, and Matthew Caretti.

NONFICTION Pays expenses of writers on assignment.

POETRY Needs haibun, tanka. Submit up to 3 poems at a time. Accepts e-mail submissions.

CONTEMPORARY VERSE 2

Contemporary Verse 2, Inc., 502-100 Arthur St., Winnipeg MB R3B 1H3 Canada. (204)949-1365. **Fax:** (204)942-5754. **E-mail:** submissions@contemporaryverse2.ca. **Website:** www.contemporaryverse2.ca. **75% freelance written.** Quarterly magazine covering poetry and critical writing about poetry. *CV2* publishes poetry of demonstrable quality as well as critical writing in the form of interviews, essays, articles, and reviews. With the critical writing we tend to create a discussion of poetry which will interest a broad range of readers, including those who might be skeptical about the value of poetry. Reading period: September 1-May 31. Estab. 1975. Circ. 600. Byline given. Pays on publication. Offers 50% kill fee. Editorial lead time 3-6 months. Submit seasonal material 3-6 months in advance. Accepts queries by online submission form. Accepts simultaneous submissions. Responds in 2-3 weeks to queries; 3-8 months to mss. Guidelines online.

NONFICTION Needs essays, interview, book reviews. No content that is not about poetry. **Buys 10-30 mss/year.** Query. Length: 800-3,000 words. **Pays $40-130 for assigned articles.**

POETRY Needs avant-garde, free verse. No rhyming verse, traditionally inspirational. Buys 110-120 poems/year. Submit maximum 6 poems. **Pays $20/poem.**

CONTRARY

The Journal of Unpopular Discontent, Chicago IL **E-mail:** chicago@contrarymagazine.com. **Website:** www.contrarymagazine.com. **Contact:** Jeff McMahon, editor; Frances Badgett, fiction editor; Shaindel Beers, poetry editor. **100% freelance written.** *Contrary* publishes fiction, poetry, and literary commentary, and prefers work that combines the virtues of all those categories. Founded at the University of Chicago, it now operates independently and not-for-profit on the South Side of Chicago. Quarterly. Member CLMP. "We like work that is not only contrary in content but contrary in its evasion of the expectations established by its genre. Our fiction defies traditional story form. For example, a story may bring us to closure without ever delivering an ending. We don't insist on the ending, but we do insist on the closure. And we value fiction as poetic as any poem." Estab. 2003. Circ. 38,000. Byline given. Pays on publication and receipt of invoice. Publishes ms 90 days after acceptance. Editorial lead time 3 months. Accepts queries by online submission form. Accepts simultaneous submissions. Responds in 2 weeks to queries; 3 months to mss. Rarely comments on/critiques rejected mss. Guidelines available online.

NONFICTION Needs book excerpts, essays, general interest, humor, memoir, opinion, personal experience, reviews, lyrical, literary nonfiction. Does not publish expository or argumentative nonfiction. **Buys 4-6 mss/year.** Accepts submissions through website only. Include estimated word count, brief bio, list of publications.

FICTION Receives 650 mss/month. Accepts 6 mss/issue; 24 mss/year. Publishes 14 new writers/year. Has published Sherman Alexie, Andrew Coburn, Amy Reed, Clare Kirwan, Stephanie Johnson, Laurence Davies, and Edward McWhinney. Needs experimental, mainstream, religious, short stories, slice-of-life vignettes, literary. **Buys 8-12 mss/year.** Accepts submissions through website only. Include estimated word count, brief bio, list of publications. Length: up to 2,000 words. Average length: 750 words. Publishes short shorts. Average length of short shorts: 750 words. **Pays $20-60.**

POETRY Accepts submissions through website only. Include estimated word count, brief bio, list of publications. Often comments on rejected poems. Submit maximum 3 poems. **Pays $20 per byline, $60 for featured work.**

TIPS "Beautiful writing catches our eye first. If we realize we're in the presence of unanticipated meaning, that's what clinches the deal. Also, we're not fond of expository fiction. We prefer to be seduced by beauty, profundity, and mystery than to be presented with the obvious. We look for fiction that entrances, that stays the reader's finger above the mouse button. That is, in part, why we favor microfiction, flash fiction, and short shorts. Also, we hope writers will remember that most editors are looking for very particular species of work. We try to describe our particular species in our mission statement and our submission guidelines, but those descriptions don't always convey nuance. That's why many editors urge writers to read the publication itself, in the hope that they will intuit an understanding of its particularities. If you happen to write that particular species of work we favor, your submission may find a happy home with us. If you don't, it does not necessarily reflect on your quality or your ability. It usually just means that your work has a happier home somewhere else."

THE COPPERFIELD REVIEW

A Journal for Readers and Writers of Historical Fiction, **E-mail:** copperfieldreview@gmail.com. **Website:** www.copperfieldreview.com. **Contact:** Meredith Allard, executive editor. **100%.** "We are an online literary journal that publishes historical fiction, reviews, and interviews related to historical fiction. We believe that by understanding the lessons of the past through historical fiction, we can gain better insight into the nature of our society today, as well as a better understanding of ourselves." Estab. 2000. Byline given. No kill fee. Accepts queries by e-mail. Accepts simultaneous submissions. Responds to mss 12-16 weeks after submission, sometimes sooner. Never comments on rejected mss. Sample copy online. Guidelines available online only.

"Remember that we are a journal for readers and writers of historical fiction. We only consider submissions that are historical in nature."

NONFICTION Needs book excerpts, essays, historical, interview, nostalgic, personal experience, reviews. We are a journal of historical fiction, so we are interested in nonfiction about history, interviews with historical authors, and book reviews of historical novels. We accept submissions of creative nonfiction if it is history based. We are also interested in tips for writing historical fiction. Please see our online guidelines for information on how to submit nonfiction. **Pays $25.**

FICTION "We will consider submissions in most fiction categories, but the setting must be historical in nature. We don't want to see anything not related to historical fiction." Receives 40 unsolicited mss/month. Publishes 80% new writers/year. Publishes short shorts. Needs historical, novel excerpts, short stories. **Buys 28-40 mss/year.** Send complete ms. Name and e-mail address should appear on the first page of the submission. Accepts submissions pasted into an e-mail only. "Do not query first. Send the complete ms according to our guidelines." Length: 500-3,000 words. **Pays $20.**

POETRY Contact: Paula Day. Needs All poems must be historical in nature. Accepts submissions pasted into an e-mail only. Anything not related to historical fiction. Buys 10-15 poems/year. Submit maximum Poets may submit one poem per month. poems. **Pays $15.**

TIPS "We wish to showcase the very best in historical fiction. Stories that use historical periods to illuminate universal truths will immediately stand out. We are thrilled to receive thoughtful work that is polished, poised, and written from the heart. Be professional, and only submit your very best work. Be certain to adhere to a publication's submission guidelines, and always treat your e-mail submissions with the same care you would use with a traditional publisher."

COPPER NICKEL

English Department, Campus Box 175, CU Denver, P.O. Box 173364, Denver CO 80217. (303)315-7358. **E-mail:** wayne.miller@ucdenver.edu. **Website:** copper-nickel.org. **Contact:** Wayne Miller, editor/managing editor; Brian Barker and Nicky Beer, poetry editors; Joanna Luloff, fiction and nonfiction editor; Teague Bohlen, fiction editor. *Copper Nickel*—the national literary journal housed at the University of Colorado Denver—was founded by poet Jake Adam York in 2002. Work published in *Copper Nickel* has appeared in *Best American Poetry*, *Best American Short Stories*, and *Pushcart Prize* anthologies. Contributors to *Copper Nickel* have received numerous honors for their work, including the National Book Critics Circle Award; the Kingsley Tufts Poetry Award; the American, California, Colorado, Minnesota, and Washington State Book Awards; the Georg Büchner Prize; the T.S. Eliot and Forward Poetry Prizes; the Anisfield-Wolf Book Award; the Whiting Writers Award; the Alice Fay Di Castagnola Award; the Lambda Literary Award; and fellowships from the National Endowment for the Arts; the MacArthur, Guggenheim, Ingram Merrill, Witter Bynner, Soros, Rona Jaffe, Bush, and Jerome Foundations; the Bunting Institute; Cave Canem; and the American Academy in Rome. Submission period: September 1 to December 15; January 15 to March 1. Estab. 2002. Pays on publication. Publishes ms 6 months-1 year. Accepts queries by online submission form. Accepts simultaneous submissions. Tries to respond in 2 months. Guidelines online.

NONFICTION Needs essays. Submit 1 essay at a time through submittable. **Pays $30/printed page, 2 contributor's copies, and a one-year subscription.**

FICTION Submit 1 story or 3 pieces of flash fiction at a time through submittable. **Pays $30/printed page, 2 contributor's copies, and a one-year subscription.**

POETRY Submit 4-6 poems through submittable. **Pays $30/printed page, 2 contributor's copies, and a one-year subscription.**

CRAB ORCHARD REVIEW

Southern Illinois University Carbondale, Department of English, Faner Hall 2380, Mail Code 4503, 1000 Faner Dr., Carbondale IL 62901. (618)453-6833. **Fax:** (618)453-8224. **E-mail:** jtribble@siu.edu. **Website:** www.craborchardreview.siu.edu. **Contact:** Allison Joseph, editor-in-chief and poetry editor; Carolyn Alessio, prose editor; Jon Tribble, managing editor. "We are a general-interest literary journal published twice/year. We strive to be a journal that writers admire and readers enjoy. We publish fiction, poetry, creative nonfiction, fiction translations, interviews, and reviews." Estab. 1995. Circ. 2,500. No kill fee. Publishes ms an average of 9-12 months after acceptance. Accepts queries by online submission form. Accepts simultaneous submissions. Responds in 3 weeks to queries; 9 months to mss. Sample copy online. Guidelines online.

NONFICTION Needs essays. Submit through online submissions manager. Length: up to 25 pages double-spaced. **No payment; publication only.**

FICTION Needs ethnic, novel excerpts. No science fiction, romance, western, horror, gothic, or children's. Wants more novel excerpts that also stand alone. Submit through online submissions manager. Length: up to 25 pages double-spaced. **Pays $25/published magazine page ($100 minimum), 2 contributor's copies, and one-year subscription.**

POETRY Wants all styles and forms from traditional to experimental. Does not want greeting card verse; literary poetry only. Has published poetry by Luisa A. Igloria, Erinn Batykefer, Jim Daniels, and Bryan Tso Jones. Submit through online submissions manager. Cover letter is preferred. "Indicate stanza breaks on poems of more than 1 page. Poems under serious consideration are discussed and decided on by the managing editor and poetry editor." **Pays $25/published magazine page ($100 minimum), 2 contributor's copies, and one-year subscription.**

CRAZYHORSE

College of Charleston, Department of English, 66 George St., Charleston SC 29424. (843)953-4470. **E-mail:** crazyhorse@cofc.edu. **Website:** crazyhorse.cofc.edu. **Contact:** Jonathan Bohr Heinen, managing editor; Emily Rosko, poetry editor; Anthony Varallo, fiction editor; Bret Lott, nonfiction editor. "We like to print a mix of writing regardless of its form, genre, school, or politics. We're especially on the lookout for original writing that doesn't fit the categories and that engages in the work of honest communication." Estab. 1960. Circ. 1,500. No kill fee. Publishes ms an average of 6-12 months after acceptance. Accepts queries by online submission form. Accepts simultaneous submissions. Responds in 1 week to queries; 3-4 months to mss. Sample copy: $5. Guidelines online.

Reads submissions September 1-May 31.

NONFICTION "*Crazyhorse* publishes 4-6 stories essays year, so we call for the very best writing, period. We believe literary nonfiction can take any form, from the letter to the list, from the biography to the memoir, from the journal to the obituary. All we call for is precision of word and vision, and that the truth of the matter be the flag of the day." Submit 1 essay through online submissions manager. Length: 2,500-8,500 words. **Pays $20/page ($200 maximum) and 2 contributor's copies.**

FICTION "We are open to all narrative styles and forms, and are always on the lookout for something we haven't seen before. Send a story we won't be able to forget." Submit 1 story through online submissions manager. **Buys 12-15 mss/year.** Length: 2,500-8,500 words. **Pays $20/page ($200 maximum) and 2 contributor's copies.**

POETRY "*Crazyhorse* aims to publish work that reflects the multiple poetries of the 21st century. While our taste represents a wide range of aesthetics, from poets at all stages of their writing careers, we read with a discerning eye for poems that demonstrate a rhetorical and formal intelligence—that is, poems that know why they are written in the manner that they are. We seek poems that exhibit how content works symbiotically with form, evidenced in an intentional art of the poetic line or in poems that employ or stretch lyric modes. Along with this, poems that capture our attention enact the lyric utterance through musical textures, tone of voice, vivid language, reticence, and skillful syntax. For us, overall, the best poems do not idly tell the reader how to feel or think, they engender feeling and thought in the reader. " Submit 3-5 poems at a time through online submissions manager. Buys 80 poems/year. Submit maximum 5 poems. **Pays $20/page ($200 maximum) and 2 contributor's copies.**

TIPS "Write to explore subjects you care about. The subject should be one in which something is at stake. Before sending, ask, 'What's reckoned with that's important for other people to read?'"

CRUCIBLE

Barton College, P.O. Box 5000, Wilson NC 27893. **E-mail:** crucible@barton.edu. **Website:** www.barton.edu/crucible. *Crucible*, published annually in the fall, publishes poetry and fiction as part of its Poetry and Fiction Contest run each year. Deadline for submissions is May 1. Estab. 1964. Circ. 500. Accepts queries by e-mail. Accepts simultaneous submissions. Notifies winners by October each year. Sample: $8. Guidelines online.

Crucible is under 100 pages, digest-sized, professionally printed on high-quality paper, with matte card cover. Press run is 500.

FICTION Needs ethnic. Submit ms by e-mail. Do not include name on ms. Include separate bio. Length: up to 8,000 words. **Pays $150 for first prize, $100 for second prize, contributor's copies.**

POETRY Submit "poetry that demonstrates originality and integrity of craftsmanship as well as thought. Traditional metrical and rhyming poems are difficult to bring off in modern poetry. The best poetry is written out of deeply felt experience which has been crafted into pleasing form." Wants "free verse with attention paid particularly to image, line, stanza, and voice." Does not want "very long narratives, poetry that is forced." Has published poetry by Robert Grey, R.T. Smith, and Anthony S. Abbott. Submit up to 5 poems by e-mail. Do not include name on poems. Include separate bio. **Pays $150 for first prize, $100 for second prize, contributor's copies.**

CUMBERLAND RIVER REVIEW

Trevecca Nazarene University, Department of English, 333 Murfreesboro Rd., Nashville TN 37210. **E-mail:** crr@trevecca.edu. **Website:** crr.trevecca.edu. **Contact:** Graham Hillard, editor; Torri Frye, managing editor. *The Cumberland River Review* is a quarterly online publication of new poetry, fiction, essays, and art. The journal is produced by the department of English at Trevecca Nazarene University and welcomes submissions from both national and international writers and artists. Reading period: September through April. Accepts queries by mail, online submission form. Accepts simultaneous submissions. Responds in 3 months. Guidelines online.

NONFICTION Submit 1 essay through online submissions manager or mail (include SASE). Length: up to 5,000 words.

FICTION Needs short stories. Submit 1 story through online submissions manager or mail (include SASE). Length: up to 5,000 words.

POETRY Submit 3-5 poems in a single document through online submissions manager or mail (include SASE).

DARKLING MAGAZINE

Darkling Publications, 28780 318th Ave., Colome SD 57528. **E-mail:** darkling@mitchelltelecom.net; jvanoort@darklingpublications.com. **Website:** darklingpublications.com. **Contact:** James C. Van Oort, editor in chief. *Darkling Magazine*, published annually in late summer, is "primarily interested in poetry. All submissions should be dark in nature and should help expose the darker side of man. Dark nature does not mean whiny or overly murderous, and being depressed does not make an artist's work dark." Has published poems by Robert Cooperman, Kenneth DiMaggio, Arthur Gottlieb, Simon Perchik, Cathy Porter, and Susanna Rich, among others. Estab. 2005. Accepts queries by mail, e-mail. Accepts simultaneous submissions.

Reading period: October 1-May 15.

NONFICTION Pays expenses of writers on assignment.

POETRY Submit by postal mail (with SASE) or e-mail (pasted into the body of message or as attachment). "Profanity should be used with extreme caution, and should be inherently necessary to the piece in order to be considered. Pornography of any sort will not be considered and will merit no response whatsoever." Submit maximum 8 poems. Length: any length is acceptable, but epic-length poetry must be of exceptional quality and content to be considered.

TIPS "Darkling Publications considers serious work from serious artists, and publishes only the best of the best alongside work from artists we feel show great promise but are early in their writing careers. Please submit only what you feel is your best work; darkness has many veins, sinews, and bloodlines, so show us the best of your dark art."

$$ DECEMBER

A Literary Legacy Since 1958, December Publishing, P.O. Box 16130, St. Louis MO 63105-0830. (314)301-9980. **E-mail:** editor@decembermag.org. **Website:** decembermag.org. **Contact:** Gianna Jacobson, editor; Jennifer Goldring, managing editor. Committed to distributing the work of emerging writers and artists, and celebrating more seasoned voices through a semiannual nonprofit literary magazine featuring fiction, poetry, creative nonfiction, and visual art. Estab. 1958. Circ. 1,500. Byline given. Pays on publication. Editorial lead time 5 months. Accepts queries by mail, e-mail. Responds in 2 months to mss. Sample copy: $12. Guidelines online.

NONFICTION Needs essays, general interest, humor, memoir, opinion, personal experience, literary journalism. Not interested in straight journalism (news or features). **Buys 4-10 mss/year.** Submit complete ms. Length: 25-6,000 words. **Pays $10/page (minimum $40; maximum $200).**

PHOTOS Photo and art submissions accepted. Send photos with submission. Reviews PNG/JPEG files. Negotiates payment individually. Purchases one-time rights on photos.

FICTION Needs experimental, humorous, novel excerpts, short stories, slice-of-life vignettes, literary fiction, flash fiction. Does not want genre fiction. **Buys 10-20 mss/year.** Send complete ms. Length: up to 10,000 words. **Pays $10/page (minimum $40; maximum $200).**

POETRY Needs avant-garde, free verse, traditional. Buys 100-150 poems/year. Submit maximum 5 poems. No length requirements. **Pays $10/page (minimum $40; maximum $200).**

DIAGRAM

Department of English, University of Arizona, P.O. Box 210067, ML 445, Tucson AZ 85721-0067. **E-mail:** editor@thediagram.com. **Website:** www.thediagram.com. **Contact:** Ander Monson, editor; T. Fleischmann and Nicole Walker, nonfiction editors; Sarah Blackman and Thomas Mira y Lopez, fiction editors; Heidi Gotz, Rafael Gonzalez, and Katie Jean Shinkle, poetry editors. Online journal covers poetry, fiction, nonfiction, and hybrid work. Sponsors a yearly chapbook competition. "*DIAGRAM* is an electronic journal of text and art, found and created. We're interested in representations, naming, indicating, schematics, labeling and taxonomy of things; in poems that masquerade as stories; in stories that disguise themselves as indices or obituaries. We specialize in work that pushes the boundaries of traditional genre or work that is in some way schematic. We do publish traditional fiction and poetry, too, but hybrid forms (short stories, prose poems, indexes, tables of contents, etc.) are particularly welcome! We also publish diagrams and schematics (original and found)." Publishes 15 new writers/year. Bimonthly. Member CLMP. "We cosponsor a yearly chapbook contest for prose, poetry, or hybrid work with New Michigan Press with a Spring deadline. Guidelines on website." Estab. 2000. Circ. 1,500 unique visitors/day online; 500,000+ hits/month. No kill fee. Publishes ms 6-9 months after acceptance. Accepts queries by e-mail. Accepts simultaneous submissions. Responds in 2 weeks to queries; in 2 months to mss. Sometimes comments on rejected mss. Sample copy: $12. Writer's guidelines online. Submit most work via submissions manager.

NONFICTION Needs essays, memoir, reviews. Send complete ms. Accepts submissions by online submissions manager; no e-mail. If sending by snail mail, send SASE for return of the ms or send disposable copy of the ms and #10 SASE for reply only.

PHOTOS Reviews prints, slides, zip disks, magnetic tapes, DCs, punch cards.

FICTION Receives 200 unsolicited mss/month. Accepts 3-4 mss/issue; 20 mss/year. Needs short stories. "We don't publish genre fiction unless it's exceptional and transcends the genre boundaries." Send complete ms. Accepts submissions by online submissions manager; no e-mail. If sending by snail mail, send SASE for return of the ms or send disposable copy of the ms and #10 SASE for reply only. Length: open.

POETRY Submit 3-6 poems. Electronic submissions accepted through submissions manager only; or send print. Electronic submissions much preferred; print submissions must include SASE if response is expected. Cover letter is preferred. Reads submissions year round. Poems are circulated to an editorial board. Sometimes comments on rejected poems. Sometimes publishes theme issues. Receives about 4,000 poems/year, accepts about 5%. Does not want light verse. No length limit.

TIPS "Submit interesting text, images, sound, and new media. We value the insides of things, vivisection, urgency, risk, elegance, flamboyance, work that moves us, language that does something new, or does something old—well. We like iteration and reiteration. Ruins and ghosts. Mechanical, moving parts, balloons, and frenzy. We want art and writing that demonstrates interaction; the processes of things; how functions are accomplished; how things become or expire, move or stand. We'll consider anything."

DIODE POETRY JOURNAL

E-mail: submit@diodepoetry.com. **Website:** www.diodepoetry.com. **Contact:** Patty Paine, editor. "We welcome all types of poetry (including, but not limited to, narrative experimental, visual, found and erasure poetry). We also accept poetry in translation, and collaborative poems. We accept submissions of book reviews, interviews, and essays on poetics. Submissions are accepted year-round, and we do not charge a reading fee. We publish three times a year, and we respond to submissions in 30 days, and often within 5 days. We do not accept work that has been previously published, in print or online. We accept simultaneous submissions, but please let us know immediately if your work is accepted elsewhere. Please submit 3–5 poems with a cover letter and contributor's bio. There are no length restrictions for submissions of reviews, interviews, or essays. Please submit a cover letter and bio, and send the review, interview or essay as a Word document." Estab. 2007. Time between acceptance and publication varies. Accepts queries by e-mail. Accepts simultaneous submissions. Responds in 1-2 months. Always sends prepublication galleys. Guidelines available on website.

Does not want "light verse, erotic." Receives about 12,000 poems/year; accepts about 2%.

POETRY Submit 3-5 poems at a time. Accepts submissions by e-mail. Cover letter is required. Reads submissions year round. Sometimes comments on rejected poems. Has published poetry by Bob Hicok, Beckian Fritz Golberg, G.C. Waldrep, sam sax, Kaveh Akbar, Dorianne Laux, David Wojahn, Tarfia Faizullah, and Rae Armantrout.

DMQ REVIEW

E-mail: editors@dmqreview.com. **Website:** www.dmqreview.com. **Contact:** Sally Ashton, editor in chief. Quarterly website covering poetry and artwork. *DMQ Review* seeks work that represents the diversity of contemporary poetry and demonstrates literary excellence, whether it be lyric, free verse, prose, or experimental form. Estab. 1999. No kill fee. Publishes ms 1-3 months after acceptance. Accepts queries by online submission form. Accepts simultaneous submissions. Responds in 3 months. Guidelines online.

POETRY Needs avant-garde, free verse, traditional. Submit up to 5 poems via online submissions manager. Has published poetry by David Lehman, Ellen Bass, Amy Gerstler, Bob Hicok, Ilya Kaminsky, and Jane Hirshfield. Receives about 3,000-5,000 poems/year, accepts about 1%.

TIPS "Check our current and past issues, and read and follow submission guidelines closely."

$ DUCTS

P.O. Box 3203, Grand Central Station, New York NY 10163. **E-mail:** vents@ducts.org. **Website:** www.ducts.org. **Contact:** Mary Cool, editor in chief; Tim Tomlinson, fiction editor; Lisa Kirchner, memoir editor; Amy Lemmon, poetry editor; Jacqueline Bishop, art editor. *Ducts* is a semiannual webzine of personal stories, fiction, essays, memoirs, poetry, humor, profiles, reviews, and art. "*Ducts* was founded in 1999 with the intent of giving emerging writers a venue to regularly publish their compelling, personal stories. The site has been expanded to include art and creative works of all genres. We believe that these genres must and do overlap. *Ducts* publishes the best, most compelling stories, and we hope to attract readers who are drawn to work that rises above." Estab. 1999. Circ. 12,000. Pays on publication. Accepts queries by e-mail. Accepts simultaneous submissions. Responds in 1-6 months. Guidelines available on website.

NONFICTION Needs essays, humor, memoir, profile. For essays: "We welcome new and established writers, fresh voices, and original perspectives on both common and uncommon topics. We do not publish research articles; however, we consider for publication essays that include research, as long as this research is connected to a personal narrative." For humor: "Both satire and humorous fiction pieces will be accepted." For memoir: "Please read through some issues to get an idea of what we like. Generally speaking, we're looking for a fresh take on personal experiences. We like quirky, edgy, witty, and smart. Also the heartfelt and moving. But mostly we like great writing." Submit by e-mail; see online guidelines for appropriate e-mail address. Length: up to 3,000 words for essays; 900-2,000 words for memoirs; 1,000-4,000 words for humor. **Pays $20.**

FICTION Needs experimental, mainstream, short stories. No novel excerpts. Submit by e-mail to julie@ducts.org. **Pays $20.**

POETRY Needs all forms and types. Submit 3-5 poems to poetry@ducts.org. Reads poetry January 1-August 31. **Pays $20.**

TIPS "We prefer writing that tells a compelling story with a strong narrative drive."

ECOTONE, REIMAGINING PLACE

University of North Carolina Wilmington, Department of Creative Writing, 601 S. College Rd., Wilmington NC 28403. **E-mail:** info@ecotonejournal.com. **Website:** www.ecotonemagazine.org. **Contact:** Anna Lena Phillips Bell, editor. "*Ecotone*'s mission is to publish and promote the best place-based work being written today. Founded at the University of North Carolina Wilmington in 2005, the award-winning magazine features writing and art that reimagine place, and our authors interpret this charge expansively. An ecotone is a transition zone between two adjacent ecological communities, containing the characteristic species of each. It is therefore a place of danger or opportunity, a testing ground. The magazine explores the ecotones between landscapes, literary genres, scientific and artistic disciplines, modes of thought. Semiannual. Estab. 2005. Circ. 1,500. Publishes mss 6-8 months after acceptance. Accepts queries by mail, online submission form. Accepts simultaneous submissions. Responds in 4-6 months to mss. Sample copy: $12.95. Guidelines online.

Literary magazine/journal: 6x9. For 2019–20, our windows are August 26–September 1, 2019, and January 26–February 1, 2020. *Ecotone* charges a small fee for electronic submissions. If you are unable to pay this fee, please submit by postal mail.

NONFICTION Submit via online submissions manager or postal mail with SASE. Include brief cover letter, listing both the title of the piece and the word count. Do not include identifying information on or within the ms itself. Length: up to 30 double-spaced pages.

FICTION Has published Kevin Brockmeier, Michael Branch, Brock Clarke, Daniel Orozco, Steve Almond, and Pattiann Rogers. Needs ethnic, experimental, historical, mainstream. Does not want genre (fantasy, horror, science fiction, etc.) or young adult fiction. Submit via online submissions manager or postal mail with SASE. Include brief cover letter, listing both the title of the piece and the word count. Do not include identifying information on or within the ms itself. Also publishes literary essays, poetry. Length: up to 30 pages. "We are now considering shorter prose works (under 2,500 words) as well."

POETRY Submit 3-5 poems via online submissions manager. Include brief cover letter. Do not include identifying information on or within the ms itself.

ELLIPSIS

Westminster College, 1840 S. 1300 E., Salt Lake City UT 84105. (801)832-2321. **E-mail:** ellipsis@westminstercollege.edu. **Website:** ellipsis.westminstercollege.edu. *Ellipsis*, published annually in April, needs good literary poetry, fiction, essays, plays, and visual art. Estab. 1965. Byline given. Pays on publication. No kill fee. Publishes ms an average of 3 months after acceptance. Accepts queries by online submission form. Accepts simultaneous submissions. Responds in 6 months to mss. Sample copy: $7.50. Guidelines available online.

Reads submissions August 1-November 1. Staff changes each year; check website for an updated list of editors. *Ellipsis* is 120 pages, digest-sized, perfect-bound, with color cover. Accepts about 5% of submissions received. Press run is 2,000; most distributed free through college.

NONFICTION Needs essays, creative nonfiction. Submit complete ms via online submissions manager. Include cover letter. **Pays $50 and 2 contributor's copies.**

FICTIONliterary fiction, plays. Submit complete ms via online submissions manager. Include cover letter. Length: up to 6,000 words. **Pays $50 and 2 contributor's copies.**

POETRY Submit poems via online submissions manager. Include cover letter. Has published poetry by Allison Joseph, Molly McQuade, Virgil Suaárez, Maurice Kilwein-Guevara, Richard Cecil, and Ron Carlson. Submit maximum 5 poems. **Pays $10/poem and 2 contributor's copies.**

EPOCH

251 Goldwin Smith Hall, Cornell University, Ithaca NY 14853-3201. (607)255-3385. **Website:** www.epoch.cornell.edu. **Contact:** Michael Koch, editor; Heidi E. Marschner, managing editor. **100% freelance written.** Literary magazine published 3 times/year. Looking for well-written literary fiction, poetry, personal essays. Newcomers welcome. Open to mainstream and avant-garde writing. Estab. 1947. Circ. 1,000. Byline given. Pays on publication. Offers 100% kill fee. Publishes ms an average of 6 months after acceptance. Editorial lead time 6 months. Submit seasonal material 8 months in advance. Accepts queries by mail. Responds in 2 weeks to queries; in 6 weeks to mss. Sometimes comments on rejected mss. Sample copy: $5. Guidelines online and for #10 SASE.

Magazine: 6×9; 128 pages; good quality paper; good cover stock. Receives 500 unsolicited mss/month. Accepts 15-20 mss/issue. Reads unsolicited submissions September 15-April 15. Publishes 3-4 new writers/year. Has published work by Antonya Nelson, Doris Betts, Heidi Jon Schmidt.

NONFICTION Needs essays, interview. No inspirational. **Buys 6-8 mss/year.** Send complete ms. **Pay varies; pays up to $150/unsolicited piece.** Pays expenses of writers on assignment.

PHOTOS Send photos. Reviews contact sheets, transparencies, any size prints. Negotiates payment individually. Buys one-time rights.

FICTION Needs ethnic, experimental, mainstream, literary short stories. No genre fiction. Would like to see more Southern fiction (Southern U.S.). **Buys 25-30 mss/year.** Send complete ms. Considers fiction in all forms, short short to novella length. **Pay varies; pays up to $150/unsolicited piece.**

POETRY Needs avant-garde, free verse, haiku, light verse, traditional. Mss not accompanied by SASE will be discarded unread. Occasionally provides criticism on poems. Considers poetry in all forms. Buys 30-75 poems/year. Submit maximum 5 poems. **Pay varies; pays $50 minimum/poem.**

TIPS "Tell your story, speak your poem, straight from the heart. We are attracted to language and to good writing, but we are most interested in what the good writing leads us to, or where."

EVENT

Douglas College, P.O. Box 2503, New Westminster British Columbia V3L 5B2 Canada. (604)527-5293. **Fax:** (604)527-5095. **E-mail:** event@douglascollege.ca. **Website:** www.eventmags.com. **100% freelance written.** Magazine published 3 times/year containing fiction, poetry, creative nonfiction, notes on writing, and reviews. "We are eclectic and always open to content that invites involvement. Generally, we like strong narrative." Estab. 1971. Circ. 1,000. Byline given. Pays on publication. Publishes ms an average of 8 months after acceptance. Accepts queries by mail. Accepts simultaneous submissions. Responds in 1 month to queries. Responds in 6 months to mss. Guidelines available online.

EVENT does not read mss in July, August, December, and January. No e-mail submissions. All submissions must include SASE (Canadian postage, or IRCs, or USD $1).

NONFICTION Pays expenses of writers on assignment.

FICTION "We look for readability, style, and writing that invites involvement." Submit maximum 2 stories.contemporary. No technically poor or unoriginal pieces. **Buys 12-15 mss/year.** Send complete ms. Length: 5,000 words maximum. **Pays $25/page up to $500.**

POETRY Needs free verse. "We tend to appreciate the narrative and sometimes the confessional modes." No light verse. Buys 30-40 poems/year. Submit maximum 10 poems. **Pays $25-500.**

TIPS "Write well and read some past issues of *EVENT*."

FICTION

Department of English, City College of New York, Convent Ave. & 138th St., New York NY 10031. **E-mail:** fictionmageditors@gmail.com. **Website:** www.fictioninc.com. **Contact:** Mark J. Mirsky, editor. "As the name implies, we publish only fiction; we are looking for the best new writing available, leaning toward the unconventional. *Fiction* has traditionally attempted to make accessible the inaccessible, to bring the experimental to a broader audience." Reading period for unsolicited mss is September 15-June 15. Estab. 1972. Circ. 4,000. No kill fee. Publishes ms an average of 1 year after acceptance. Accepts queries by mail, online submission form. Accepts simultaneous submissions. Responds in 3-6 months to mss. Sample copy: $7. Guidelines available online.

Stories first published in *Fiction* have been selected for the *Pushcart Prize: Best of the Small Presses, O. Henry Prize Stories,* and *Best American Short Stories.*

FICTION Needs experimental, short stories, contemporary, literary, translations. No romance, science fiction, etc. Submit complete ms via mail or online submissions manager. Length: reads any length, but encourages lengths under 5,000 words.

TIPS "The guiding principle of *Fiction* has always been to go to terra incognita in the writing of the imagination and to ask that modern fiction set itself serious questions, if often in absurd and comedic voices, interrogating the nature of the real and the fantastic. It represents no particular school of fiction, except the innovative. Its pages have often been a harbor for writers at odds with each other. As a result of its willingness to publish the difficult, experimental, and unusual, while not excluding the well known, *Fiction* has a unique reputation in the U.S. and abroad as a journal of future directions."

FICTION INTERNATIONAL

San Diego State University, San Diego State University, Department of English and Comp. Lit, 5500 Campanile Dr., San Diego CA 92182-6020. **E-mail:** fictioninternational@gmail.com. **E-mail:** https://fictioninternational.submittable.com/submit. **Website:** fictioninternational.sdsu.edu. **Contact:** Harold Jaffe, editor. **80% freelance written.** "*Fiction International* is the only literary journal in the United States emphasizing formal innovation and social activism. Each issue revolves around a theme and features a wide variety of fiction, nonfiction, indeterminate prose, and visuals by leading writers and artists from around the world." Has published works by William Burroughs, Clarice Lispector (Brazil), Robert Coover, Edmund White, Joyce Carol Oates, Walter Abish, and Kathy Acker. Estab. 1973. Byline given. No kill fee. Publishes ms an average of 1 year after acceptance. Editorial lead time 3 months. Accepts queries by mail, e-mail. Accepts simultaneous submissions. Responds in 1 week to queries; in 3 months to mss. Sample copy for #37 SASE. Guidelines online.

NONFICTION Needs essays. Special issues: Issues are themed; see website for details. **Buys 10 mss/year.** Submit complete ms via online submissions manager. Length: up to 5,500 words.

FICTION Each issue is themed; see website for details. Needs experimental, mainstream. No genre fiction. **Buys 20 mss/year.** Submit complete ms via online submissions manager. Length: up to 5,500 words.

THE FIDDLEHEAD

Campus House, 11 Garland Crt, PO Box 4400, University of New Brunswick, Fredericton NB E3B 5A3 Canada. (506)453-3501. **E-mail:** fiddlehd@unb.ca. **Website:** www.thefiddlehead.ca. Sue Sinclair, editor. **Contact:** Kathryn Taglia, managing editor or Ian LeTourneau, design & layout. The artwork on the covers of *The Fiddlehead* is drawn from the museums, galleries, and ateliers of Atlantic Canada and solicited from local artists; it is part of our mandate to showcase art from Atlantic Canada, especially New Brunswick art. *The Fiddlehead* is open to good writing in English or translations into English from all over the world and in a variety of styles, including experimental genres. Our editors are always happy to see new unsolicited works in fiction (including novel excerpts), creative nonfiction, and poetry. We also publish reviews, and occasionally other selected creative work such as excerpts from plays. Work is read on an ongoing basis; the acceptance rate is around 1-2% (we are, however, famous for our rejection notes!). We particularly welcome submissions from Indigenous writers, writers of colour, writers with disabilities, LGBTQQIA+ writers, and writers from other intersectional and under-represented communities. If you are comfortable identifying yourself as one or more of the above, please feel free to mention this in your cover letter. *The Fiddlehead*'s mandate is to publish accomplished poetry, short fiction, and Canadian literature reviews; to discover and promote new writing talent; to represent the Atlantic Canada's lively cultural and literary diversity; and to place the best of new and established Canadian writing in an international context. *The Fiddlehead* has published works from a long list of Canadian authors including Margaret Atwood, George Elliott Clarke, Kayla Czaga, Eden Robinson, Gregory Scofield, and Clea Young alongside international authors such as Jorie Graham, Jaki McCarrick, Thylias Moss, Les Murray, and Daniel Woodrell. *The Fiddlehead* also sponsors annual writing contests for creative nonfiction, poetry, and short fiction. Estab. 1945. Circ. 1,500. Pays on publication. Every attempt is made to publish work with 1-2 issues (3-8 months) of acceptance. If longer wait, editors will usually try to indicate this before final acceptance. Accepts simultaneous submissions. Responds in 3-9 months to mss. Occasionally comments on rejected mss. Sample copy: $15 U.S. Writer's guidelines online. Writers may only submit once per calendar year per genre. (This does not include submissions to *The Fiddlehead*'s contests. For that you may submit multiple times, so long as the work is not under consideration elsewhere.) For unsolicited submissions we only consider unpublished work. Please do not submit work that has been previously published or accepted for publication, including in anthologies, chapbooks, blogs, Facebook pages, or online journals.

NONFICTION Creative nonfiction only. No academic articles, general interest journal articles, interviews, political opinion pieces, new product reviews, reference articles, how-to or technical reviews, etc. Works such as these will simply be discarded without a response. Send SASE with **Canadian** postage for response or self-addressed envelope with cheque/money to cover postage (US or CA dollars). May request e-mail response if you do not want ms. returned. No e-mail or faxed submissions. Simultaneous submissions only if stated on cover letter; must contact immediately if accepted elsewhere. *The Fiddlehead* is now accepts online submissions via Submittable.com, please check website for details. 6,000 words maximum. 1 creative nonfiction work counts as one submission. **Pays up to $60 (Canadian)/published page plus 2 contributor's copies.**

FICTION A short fiction submission should be one story, double spaced. Unless a story is very, very short (under 1,000 words), please send only one story per submission. Please specify at the top of the first page the number of words in the story submitted. Needs experimental, mainstream, novel excerpts, short stories, Literary short fiction; literary novel and play excerpts. Experimental fiction welcome. No fiction aimed at children or teens. **Buys Receives 100-150 unsolicited mss/month. publishes 3-12 stories/issue; 15-30 stories/year. Publishes high percentage of new and emerging writers/year. mss/year.** Send SASE with Canadian postage for response or self-addressed envelope with cheque/money to cover postage (US or CA dollars). May request e-mail response if you do not want ms. returned. No e-mail or faxed submissions. Simultaneous submissions only if stated on cover letter; must contact immediately if accepted elsewhere.

The Fiddlehead is now accepts online submissions via Submittable.com, please check website for details. Length: up to 6,000 words. Rarely publishes flash fiction. **Pays up to $60 (Canadian)/published page and 2 contributor's copies.**

POETRY Needs All types of literary poetry considered, including experimental. Poetry series and longer poems are considered. Send SASE with Canadian postage for response or self-addressed envelope with cheque/money to cover postage (US or CA dollars). May request e-mail response if you do not want ms. returned. No e-mail or faxed submissions. Simultaneous submissions only if stated on cover letter; must contact immediately if accepted elsewhere. *The Fiddlehead* is now accepts online submissions via Submittable.com, please check website for details. No poetry aimed at children; no limericks, doggerel. Buys Receives 100-300 unsolicited mss/month. publishes 10-70 poems/issue; 30-100 poems/year. Publishes high percentage of new and emerging writers/year. poems/year. Submit maximum 6 poems per submission; *The Fiddlehead* prefers to accept several poems by the same author; please do not limit your submission to a single poem. poems. **Pays up to $60 (Canadian)/published page and 2 contributor's copies.**

TIPS "If you are serious about submitting to *The Fiddlehead*, you should subscribe or read several issues to get a sense of the journal. Contact us if you would like to order sample back issues."

FIELD

Contemporary Poetry & Poetics, Oberlin College Press, 50 N. Professor St., Oberlin OH 44074. (440)775-8408. **Fax:** (440)775-8124. **E-mail:** oc.press@oberlin.edu. **Website:** www.oberlin.edu/ocpress. **Contact:** Marco Wilkinson, managing editor. **60% freelance written.** Biannual magazine of poetry, poetry in translation, and essays on contemporary poetry by poets. *FIELD: Contemporary Poetry and Poetics*, published semiannually in April and October, is a literary journal with "emphasis on poetry, translations, and essays by poets. See electronic submission guidelines." Estab. 1969. Circ. 1,500. Byline given. Pays on publication. Editorial lead time 4 months. Accepts queries by online submission form. Responds in 6-8 weeks to mss. Sample copy: $8. Subscription: $16/year, $28 for 2 years. Guidelines available online and for #10 SASE.

FIELD is 100 pages, digest-sized, printed on rag stock, flat-spined, with glossy color card cover.

POETRY Needs contemporary, prose poems, free verse, traditional. Submissions are read August 1 through May 31. Submit 2-6 of your best poems through online submissions manager. No e-mail submissions. Has published poetry by Michelle Glazer, Tom Lux, Carl Phillips, Betsy Sholl, Charles Simic, Jean Valentine, and translations by Marilyn Hacker and Stuart Friebert. Buys 120 poems/year. **Pays $15/page and 2 contributor's copies.**

TIPS "Keep trying!"

FILLING STATION

P.O. Box 22135, Bankers Hall RPO, Calgary AB T2P 4J5 Canada. **E-mail:** mgmt@fillingstation.ca. **Website:** www.fillingstation.ca. **Contact:** Kyle Flemmer, managing editor. *filling Station*, published 3 times/year, prints contemporary poetry, fiction, visual art, interviews, reviews, and articles. "We are looking for all forms of contemporary writing, but especially that which is innovative and/or experimental." Estab. 1993. Publishes ms 3-4 months after acceptance. Accepts queries by online submission form. Accepts simultaneous submissions. Responds in 3-6 months. "After your work is reviewed by our Collective, you will receive an e-mail from an editor to let you know if your work has been selected for publication. If selected, you will later receive a second e-mail to let you know which issue your piece has been selected to appear in. Note that during the design phase, we sometimes discover the need to shuffle a piece to a future issue instead. In the event your piece is pushed back, we will inform you." Sample copy: $12. Subscription: $25 for 3 issues, $8 for 6. Guidelines online.

filling Station is 60 - 80 pages, 8.5x11, perfect-bound, with card cover, includes photos and artwork. Receives about 100 submissions for each issue, accepts approximately 10%. Press run is 500.

NONFICTION Needs essays, interview, reviews. "We encourage you to submit experimental interviews, articles, reviews, and creative nonfiction. Please note that *filling Station* will generally not accept reviews of nonexperimental literature unless the review itself is experimental. We are looking to engage with and draw attention to literature that pushes the boundaries of genre, form, methodology, style, etc. Submit any such kind via Submittable. If you have concerns about suitability, feel free to send a query to nonfiction@fillingstation.ca. **Pays $25 honorarium and three-issue subscription.**

FICTION Needs experimental, novel excerpts, short stories, flash fiction, postcard fiction. Submit fiction via Submittable. Length: up to 10 pages (submissions at the upper end of this length spectrum will need to be of exceptional quality to be considered). **Pays $25 honorarium and three-issue subscription.**

POETRY Submit up to 6 pages of poetry via Submittable. "If your poem is spaced in a particular way, please make sure to use spaces, never tabs, so we can accurately replicate your layout." Has published poetry by Fred Wah, Larissa Lai, Margaret Christakos, Robert Kroetsch, Ron Silliman, Susan Holbrook, and many more. **Pays $25 honorarium and three-issue subscription.**

TIPS "*filling Station* accepts singular or simultaneous submissions of previously unpublished poetry, fiction, creative nonfiction, nonfiction, or art. We are always on the hunt for great writing!"

THE FIRST LINE

Blue Cubicle Press, LLC, P.O. Box 250382, Plano TX 75025. (214)455-4324. **E-mail:** info@thefirstline.com. **E-mail:** submission@thefirstline.com. **Website:** www.thefirstline.com. Editor: David LaBounty. **Contact:** Robin LaBounty, manuscript coordinator. **100% freelance written.** "*The First Line* is an exercise in creativity for writers and a chance for readers to see how many different directions we can take when we start from the same place. The purpose of *The First Line* is to jump start the imagination—to help writers break through the block that is the blank page. Each issue contains short stories that stem from a common first line; it also provides a forum for discussing favorite first lines in literature." Estab. 1999. Circ. 2,000. Byline given. Pays on acceptance. Publishes ms 1 month after acceptance. Accepts queries by mail, e-mail. Responds 3 weeks after submission time closes. Sample copy and guidelines available online.

NONFICTION Contact: David LaBounty. Needs essays. **Buys 4 mss/year.** Submit complete ms. Length: 300-600 words. **Pays $25.**

FICTION "We only publish stories that start with the first line provided. We are a collection of tales—of different directions writers can take when they start from the same place." Needs adventure, ethnic, experimental, fantasy, historical, horror, humorous, mainstream, mystery, religious, romance, science fiction, short stories, suspense, western. "Stories that do not start with our first line." **Buys 35-50 mss/year.** Submit complete ms. Length: 300-5,000 words. **Pays $25-50.**

POETRY Buys 1-2 poems/year. Submit maximum 1 poems. **Payment varies.**

TIPS "Don't just write the first story that comes to mind after you read the sentence. If it is obvious, chances are other people are writing about the same thing. Don't try so hard. Be willing to accept criticism."

FIVE POINTS

Georgia State University, P.O. Box 3999, Atlanta GA 30302-3999. **Website:** www.fivepoints.gsu.edu. **Contact:** David Bottoms, co-editor. *Five Points*, published 3 times/year, is committed to publishing work that compels the imagination through the use of fresh and convincing language. Estab. 1996. Circ. 2,000. No kill fee. Publishes ms an average of 6 months after acceptance. Accepts queries by online submission form. Responds in 2 months. Sample copy: $10. Guidelines available on website.

Magazine: 6x9; 200 pages; cotton paper; glossy cover; photos. Has published Alice Hoffman, Natasha Tretheway, Pamela Painter, Billy Collins, Philip Levine, George Singleton, Hugh Sheehy, and others. All submissions received outside of our reading periods are returned unread.

NONFICTION Needs essays. Submit through online submissions manager. Include cover letter. Reading period: August 15-December 1 and January 11-March 31. Length: up to 7,500 words. **Pays $15/page ($250 maximum), plus free subscription to magazine and 2 contributor's copies; additional copies $4.**

FICTION Receives 250 unsolicited mss/month. Accepts 4 mss/issue; 15-20 mss/year. Reads fiction August 15-December 1 and January 3-March 31. Publishes 1 new writer/year. Sometimes comments on rejected mss. Sponsors awards/contests. Needs short stories. Submit through online submissions manager. Include cover letter. Length: up to 7,500 words. **Pays $15/page ($250 maximum), plus free subscription to magazine and 2 contributor's copies; additional copies $4.**

POETRY Reads poetry August 15-December 1 and January 3-March 31. Submit through online submissions manager. Include cover letter. Submit maximum 2 poems. Length: up to 50 lines/poem.

TIPS "We place no limitations on style or content. Our only criteria is excellence. If your writing has an original voice, substance, and significance, send it to us. We will publish distinctive, intelligent writing that has something to say and says it in a way that captures and maintains our attention."

THE FLORIDA REVIEW

Department of English, University of Central Florida, P.O. Box 161346, Orlando FL 32816-1346. **E-mail:** flreview@ucf.edu. **Website:** floridareview.cah.ucf.edu. **Contact:** Lisa Roney, editor. **95%.** "*The Florida Review* publishes exciting new work from around the world from writers both emerging and well known. We are not Florida-exclusive, though we acknowledge having a jungle mentality and a preference for grit, and we have provided and continue to offer a home for many Florida writers." Estab. 1972. Circ. 1,500. Byline given. Like most small literary magazines, we cannot pay all of our authors. We pay $1,000 to four prize-winners each year. In addition, we have a small $50 award for one author/artist per year in each genre that submits to us through our general submissions process. Publishes ms usually 3 months to 1 year after acceptance. Accepts queries by e-mail, online submission form. Accepts simultaneous submissions. Responds in 2-4 weeks to queries; in 3-8 months to mss. Sample copy: $10. Writer's guidelines online.

Has published work by Gerald Vizenor, Billy Collins, Sherwin Bitsui, Kelly Clancy, Denise Duhamel, Tony Hoagland, Baron Wormser, Marcia Aldrich, and Patricia Foster. Accepts mailed submissions only if author does not have regular access to the Internet.

NONFICTION Needs essays, interview, memoir, reviews. No literary criticism. No how-to or general readership articles. Literary nonfiction only. Submit complete ms via online submissions manager. Length: 3-20 pages.

PHOTOS We accept photos for possible publication online or as a cover as part of our Visual Arts category.

FICTION Needs ethnic, experimental, mainstream, novel excerpts, short stories, flash fiction, graphic narrative. No genre fiction. Submit complete ms via online submissions manager. Length: 3-20 pages.

POETRY "We look for clear, strong poems, filled with real people, emotions, and objects. Any style will be considered." Submit via online submissions manager. Submit maximum 5 poems.

TIPS "We're looking for writers with fresh voices and original stories. We like risk. Please visit our website and/or read a back issue of our magazine to understand what we seek."

FOGGED CLARITY

Fogged Clarity and Nicotine Heart Press, P.O. Box 1016, Muskegon MI 49443-1016. (231)670-7033. **E-mail:** editor@foggedclarity.com; submissions@foggedclarity.com. **Website:** www.foggedclarity.com. **Contact:** Editors. **90% freelance written.** A monthly comprehensive arts review. "*Fogged Clarity* is an arts review that accepts submissions of poetry, fiction, nonfiction, music, visual art, and reviews of work in all mediums. We seek art that is stabbingly eloquent. Our print edition is released once every year, while new issues of our online journal come out at the beginning of every month. Artists maintain the copyrights to their work until they are monetarily compensated for said work. If your work is selected for our print edition and you consent to its publication, you will be compensated." Estab. 2008. Circ. between 15,000 and 22,000 visitors per month. Byline given. Averages 1-2 months from acceptance to publishing. Accepts queries by e-mail only. Accepts simultaneous submissions. Responds in 3 months to mss. Sample copy online. Guidelines available at www.foggedclarity.com/submissions.

"By incorporating music and the visual arts and releasing a new issue monthly, *Fogged Clarity* aims to transcend the conventions of a typical literary journal. Our network is extensive, and our scope is as broad as thought itself; we are, you are, unconstrained. With that spirit in mind, *Fogged Clarity* examines the work of authors, artists, scholars, and musicians, providing a home for exceptional art and thought that warrants exposure."

NONFICTIONcreative nonfiction. Submit 1-2 complete ms by e-mail (submissions@foggedclarity.com) as attached .DOC or .DOCX file. Subject line should be formatted as: "Last Name: Medium of Submission." For example, "Evans: Creative Nonfiction." Include brief cover letter, complete contact information, and a third-person bio. Length: up to 8,000 words. Pays expenses of writers on assignment.

PHOTOS Send photos. Reviews GIF, JPEG, PNG, TIFF, PSD, AI, and PDF files, at least 700 pixels.

FICTIONliterary. Submit 1-2 complete ms by e-mail (submissions@foggedclarity.com) as attached .DOC or .DOCX file. Subject line should be formatted as: "Last Name: Medium of Submission." For example, "Evans: Fiction." Include brief cover letter, complete contact information, and a third-person bio. Length: up to 8,000 words.

POETRY Needs free verse, traditional. Submit up to 5 poems by e-mail (submissions@foggedclarity.com) as attached .DOC or .DOCX file. Subject line should be formatted as: "Last Name: Medium of Submission." For example, "Evans: Poetry." Include brief cover letter, complete contact information, and a third-person bio.

TIPS "The editors appreciate artists communicating the intention of their submitted work and the influences behind it in a brief cover letter. Any artists with proposals for features or special projects should feel free to contact Ben Evans directly at editor@foggedclarity.com."

FOLIATE OAK LITERARY MAGAZINE

University of Arkansas-Monticello, Arts & Humanities, 562 University Dr., Monticello AR 71656. (870)460-1247. **E-mail:** foliateoak@gmail.com. **Website:** www.foliateoak.com. **Contact:** Diane Payne, faculty advisor. **100% freelance written.** Monthly online magazine covering fiction, creative nonfiction, poetry, and art. The *Foliate Oak Literary Magazine* is an online student-run magazine accepting hybrid prose, poetry, fiction, flash, creative nonfiction, and artwork. "After you receive a rejection/acceptance notice, please wait 1 month before submitting new work. **Submission Period: August 1-April 24**. We do not read submissions during summer break. If you need to contact us for anything other than submitting your work, please write to foliateoak@gmail.com." No e-mail submissions. Estab. 1973. Circ. 4,000; 2,500 online monthly visitors. Byline given. No kill fee. Publishes ms an average of 1 month after acceptance. Editorial lead time: 1 month. Accepts queries by online submission form. Accepts simultaneous submissions. Responds in 1 week to queries; in 2 month to mss. Guidelines online.

NONFICTION Needs essays, humor, memoir, personal experience. Send complete ms through online submission manager. "Remember to include your brief third-person bio. We love lyrical and hybrid essays." Length: 200-3,500 words.

PHOTOS Reviews GIF/JPEG files. "We are always interested in publishing intriguing photography, artwork, and graphic (you know, comics) literature. If you are sending a one-page comic or excerpts from a graphic novel, use PDF or JPG format. Send all artwork as JPG or GIF. We like to have at least 3 images. Remember to include your brief third-person bio. Read guidelines before submitting."

FICTION Needs adventure, ethnic, experimental, historical, humorous, mainstream, short stories, slice-of-life vignettes, suspense. Does not want pornographic, racist, or homophobic content. We avoid genre fiction. Send complete ms through online submission manager. "Remember to include your brief third-person bio." Length: 200-2,500 words.

POETRY Needs avant-garde, free verse, haiku, traditional. Submit poems via online submission manager. "We enjoy poems that we understand, preferably not rhyming poems, unless you make the rhyme so fascinating we'll wonder why we ever said anything about avoiding rhymes. Give us something fresh, unexpected, and that will make us say, 'Wow!'" "No homophobic, religious rants, or pornographic, violent poems. Please avoid using offensive language. We tend to shy away from poems that rhyme." Submit maximum 5 poems.

TIPS "Please submit all material via our online submission manager. Read our guidelines before submitting. We are eager to include multimedia submissions of videos, music, and collages. Submit your best work."

FOOTHILL

A Journal of Poetry, 165 E. 10th St., Claremont CA 91711. **E-mail:** foothill@cgu.edu. **Website:** www.cgu.edu/foothill. **Contact:** Brock Rustin and Emily Schuck, co-editors-in-chief. Directed by students at Claremont Graduate University, *Foothill: A Journal of Poetry* is an annual journal devoted exclusively to poetry written by graduate students from around the world. Estab. 2011. Byline given. Accepts queries by e-mail. Accepts simultaneous submissions. Responds in 5 weeks. Sometimes comments on rejected poems. Subscription: $25. Make checks payable to CGU. Guidelines available in magazine, by e-mail, and on website.

Published online and in print annually. Digest-sized, 72 pages, digital press, perfect bound. Press run is 500. No ads. Never publishes theme issues.

POETRY Accepts any poetry by graduate students (currently enrolled or recently graduated) from anywhere in the world. Students do not need to be enrolled in an MFA or writing program. Welcomes poetry submissions from those in other disciplines. Submit via e-mail. Include document as attachment in e-mail. Cover letter preferred. Poems are circulated to an editorial board. Accepts submissions year round. Welcomes submissions from beginning poets. Does not consider poetry by children or teens. Submit maximum 6 poems. No limit for poem length.

THE FOURTH RIVER

Chatham University, Woodland Rd., Pittsburgh PA 15232. **E-mail:** 4thriver@gmail.com. **Website:** thefourthriver.com. **100% freelance written.** *The Fourth River*, an annual publication of Chatham University's MFA in Creative Writing Programs, features literature that engages and explores the relationship between humans and their environments. Wants writings that are richly situated at the confluence of place, space, and identity, or that reflect upon or make use of landscape and place in new ways. Estab. 2005. Byline given. Pays with contributor's copies only. No kill fee. Publishes mss in 5-8 months after acceptance. Accepts queries by online submission form. Accepts simultaneous submissions. Responds in 3-5 months to mss. Sample copy: $5 (back issue). Single copy: $10; subscription: $16 for 2 years. Guidelines available online.

The Fourth River is digest-sized, perfect-bound, with full-color cover by various artists. *The Fourth River*'s contributors have been published in *Glimmer Train, Alaska Quarterly Review, The Missouri Review, The Best American Short Stories, The O. Henry Prize Stories*, and *The Best American Travel Writing*. Reading periods: November 1-January 1 (fall online issue) and July 1-September 1 (spring print issue).

NONFICTION Needs book excerpts, essays, general interest, historical, humor, opinion, personal experience, travel. Submit complete ms via online submissions manager. Length: up to 7,000 words.

FICTION Needs adventure, condensed novels, ethnic, experimental, fantasy, historical, horror, humorous, mainstream, mystery, romance, science fiction, slice-of-life vignettes. Submit complete ms via online submissions manager. Length: up to 7,000 words.

POETRY Needs avant-garde, free verse, haiku, light verse, traditional. Submit 3-5 poems via online submissions manager.

FREEFALL MAGAZINE

FreeFall Literary Society of Calgary, 460, 1720 29th Ave. SW, Calgary AB T2T 6T7 Canada. **E-mail:** editors@freefallmagazine.ca. **Website:** www.freefallmagazine.ca. **Contact:** Ryan Stromquist, managing editor. **100% freelance written.** Magazine published triannually containing fiction, poetry, creative nonfiction, essays on writing, interviews, and reviews. "We are looking for exquisite writing with a strong narrative." Estab. 1990. Circ. 1,000. Pays on publication. Accepts queries by online submission form. Accepts simultaneous submissions. Guidelines and submission forms on website.

NONFICTION Needs essays, interview, creative nonfiction, writing-related and general-audience topics. Submit complete ms online submissions manager. Length: up to 4,000 words. **Pays $10/printed page in the magazine ($100 maximum) and 1 contributor's copy.**

FICTION Needs short stories, slice-of-life vignettes. Submit via online submissions manager. Length: up to 4,000 words. **Pays $10/printed page in the magazine ($100 maximum) and 1 contributor's copy.**

POETRY Submit 2-5 poems via online submissions manager. Accepts any style of poetry. Length: up to 6 pages. **Pays $25/poem and 1 contributor's copy.**

TIPS "Our mission is to encourage the voices of new, emerging, and experienced Canadian writers and provide a platform for their quality work."

FUGUE LITERARY JOURNAL

200 Brink Hall, University of Idaho, P.O. Box 44110, Moscow ID 83844. **E-mail:** fugue@uidaho.edu. **Website:** www.fuguejournal.com. **Contact:** Alexandra Teague, faculty advisor. "Begun in 1990 by the faculty in the Department of English at University of Idaho, *Fugue* has continuously published poetry, plays, fiction, essays, and interviews from established and emerging writers biannually. We take pride in the work we print, the writers we publish, and the presentation of each and every issue. Working in collaboration with local and national artists, our covers display some of the finest art from photography and digital art to ink drawings and oil paintings. We believe that each issue is a print and digital artifact of the deep-

est engagement with our culture, and we make it our personal goal that the writing we select and presentation of each issue reflect the reverence we have for art and letters." Work published in *Fugue* has won the Pushcart Prize and has been cited in *Best American Essays*. Submissions are accepted online only. Poetry, fiction, and nonfiction submissions are accepted September 1-May 1. All material received outside of this period will not be read. $3 submission fee per entry. See website for submission instructions. Estab. 1990. Circ. 500. Accepts queries by online submission form. Accepts simultaneous submissions. Responds in 3-6 months to mss. Sample copy: $10. Guidelines online.

NONFICTION Needs essays, historical, interview, memoir, travel. Submit 1 essay using online submissions manager. **Pays 1 contributor's copy and $15 per piece published.**

FICTION Needs ethnic, experimental, short stories. Submit complete ms via online submissions manager. "Please send no more than 2 short shorts or 1 story at a time. Submissions in more than 1 genre should be submitted separately. All multiple submissions will be returned unread. Once you have submitted a piece to us, wait for a response on this piece before submitting again." **Pays 1 contributor's copy and $15 per published piece.**

POETRY Submit up to 5 poems using online submissions manager. **Pays 1 contributor's copy and $15 per published piece.**

TIPS "The best way, of course, to determine what we're looking for is to read the journal. As the name *Fugue* indicates, our goal is to present a wide range of literary perspectives. We like stories that satisfy us both intellectually and emotionally, with fresh language and characters so captivating that they stick with us and invite a second reading. We are also seeking creative literary criticism which illuminates a piece of literature or a specific writer by examining that writer's personal experience."

GARGOYLE

Paycock Press, 3819 13th St. N, Arlington VA 22201. (703) 380-4893. **E-mail:** rchrdpeabody9@gmail.com. **Website:** www.gargoylemagazine.com. **Contact:** Richard Peabody, editor/publisher. **75% freelance written.** "*Gargoyle* has always been a scallywag magazine, a maverick magazine, a bit too academic for the underground and way too underground for the academics. We are a writer's magazine in that we are read by other writers and have never worried about reaching the masses." Annual. The submission window opens each year in August and remains open until full. Recently published works by: Jill Adams, Roberta Allen, Cathy Alter, Jacob Appel, Donna Baier Stein, Stacy Barton, C.L. Bledsoe, Caroline Bock, Jamie Brown, Grace Cavalieri, Laura Cesarco Eglin, Patrick Chapman, Juliet Cook, Rachel Dacus, Michael Dailey, Kristina Marie Darling, William Virgil Davis, Glenn Deutsch, Andrew Gifford, Sid Gold, Suzanne Feldman, Heather Fowler, Susan Gubernat, Myronn Hardy, Abhay K. George Kalamaras, Jesse Lee Kercheval, Leonard Kress, W. F. Lantry, Lyn Lifshin, Susan Neville, Kevin O'Cuinn, Donaji Olmedo, Frances Park, Pedro Ponce, Glen Pouricau, Melissa Reddish, Aria Riding, Bruce Sager, John Saul, Marija Stajic, Liza Nash Taylor, Susan Tepper, Sally Toner, Gretchen A. Van Lente, Idea Vilarino, Jesse Waters, Kathleen Wheaton, Andrea Wyatt, Katherine E. Young, and Bonnie ZoBell. Estab. 1976. Circ. 2,000. Publishes ms 1 year after acceptance. Accepts queries by mail, e-mail, online submission form. Accepts simultaneous submissions. Responds in 1 month. Sample copy: $12.95. Catalog available online at FAQ link. "We don't have guidelines; we have never believed in them." Query in an e-mail. "We prefer electronic submissions. Please use submission engine online." For snail mail, send SASE for reply and return of ms, or send a disposable copy of ms.

NONFICTION Needs book excerpts, essays, interview, memoir, photo feature, creative nonfiction, literary criticism. **Buys 5-10 mss/year. Pays 1 contributor's copy and offers 50% discount on additional copies.**

FICTION Wants "edgy realism or experimental works. We run both." Wants to see more Canadian, British, Australian, and Third World fiction. Receives 300 unsolicited mss/week during submission period. Accepts 20-50 mss/issue. Agented fiction 5%. **Publishes 2-3 new writers/year.** Publishes 1-2 titles/year. Format: trade paperback originals. Needs experimental, novel excerpts, short stories, literary, short story collections. No romance, horror, science fiction. **Buys 10-15 mss/year.** Length: up to 5,000 words. "We have run 2 novellas in the past 40 years." **Pays 1 contributor's copy and offers 50% discount on additional copies.**

POETRY Submit maximum 5 poems. **Pays 1 contributor's copy and offers 50% discount on additional copies.**

TIPS "We have to fall in love with a particular fiction."

$$ THE GEORGIA REVIEW

The University of Georgia, Main Library, Room 706A, 320 S. Jackson St., Athens GA 30602. (706)542-3481. **Fax:** (706)542-0047. **E-mail:** garev@uga.edu. **Website:** thegeorgiareview.com. **Contact:** Stephen Corey, editor. **99% freelance written.** Quarterly journal. "*The Georgia Review* is a literary quarterly committed to the art of editorial practice. We collaborate equally with established and emerging authors of essays, stories, poems, and reviews in the pursuit of extraordinary works that engage with the evolving concerns and interests of intellectually curious readers from around the world. Our aim in curating content is not only to elevate literature, publishing, and the arts, but also to help facilitate socially conscious partnerships in our surrounding communities." $3 online submission fee waived for subscribers. No fees for manuscripts submitted by post. Reading period: August 15-May 15. Estab. 1947. Circ. 3,500. Byline given. Pays on publication. No kill fee. Publishes ms an average of 6 months after acceptance. Accepts queries by mail. Accepts simultaneous submissions. Responds in 2 weeks to queries; in 2-3 months to mss. Sample copy: $15. Guidelines online.

NONFICTION Needs essays. **Buys 12-20 mss/year.** We generally avoid publishing scholarly articles that are narrow in focus and/or overly burdened with footnotes. *The Georgia Review* is interested in provocative, thesis-oriented essays that can engage both the intelligent general reader and the specialist, as well as those that are experimental or lyrical in approach but accessible to a range of readers. **Pays $50/published page.** Pays expenses of writers on assignment.

PHOTOS Send photos. Reviews 5x7 prints or larger. Offers no additional payment for photos accepted with ms. Buys one-time rights.

FICTION "We seek original, excellent short fiction not bound by type. Ordinarily we do not publish novel excerpts or works translated into English, and we discourage authors from submitting these." Needs short stories. **Buys 12-20 mss/year.** Send complete ms via online submissions manager or postal mail. **Pays $50/published page.**

POETRY We seek original, excellent poetry. Submit 3-5 poems at a time. Buys 60-75 poems/year. **Pays $4/line.**

$ THE GETTYSBURG REVIEW

Gettysburg College, Gettysburg College, 300 N. Washington St., Gettysburg PA 17325. (717)337-6770. **E-mail:** mdrew@gettysburg.edu. **Website:** www.gettysburgreview.com. **Contact:** Mark Drew, editor; Jess L. Bryant, managing editor. Published quarterly, *The Gettysburg Review* considers unsolicited submissions of poetry, fiction, and essays. "Our concern is quality. Mss submitted here should be extremely well written." Reading period September 1-May 31. Estab. 1988. Circ. 2,000. Byline given. Pays on publication. Publishes ms an average of 6 months after acceptance. Editorial lead time 1 year. Submit seasonal material 9 months in advance. Accepts queries by mail. Accepts simultaneous submissions. Responds in 1 month to queries; in 3-6 months to mss. Sample: $15. Guidelines online.

NONFICTION Needs book excerpts, essays, general interest, humor, memoir, personal experience, reviews, travel. **Buys 20 mss/year.** Send complete ms. Length: up to 25 pages. **Pays $25/printed page, a one-year subscription, and 1 contributor's copy.**

FICTION Wants high-quality literary fiction. Needs experimental, historical, humorous, mainstream, novel excerpts, short stories, slice-of-life vignettes, literary, contemporary. "We require that fiction be intelligent and aesthetically written." No genre fiction. **Buys 20 mss/year.** Send complete ms with SASE. Length: 2,000-7,000 words. **Pays $25/printed page, a one-year subscription, and 1 contributor's copy.**

POETRY Considers "well-written poems of all kinds on all subjects." Has published poetry by Rita Dove, Alice Friman, Philip Schultz, Michelle Boisseau, Bob Hicok, Linda Pastan, and G. C. Waldrep. Does not want sentimental, clichéd verse. Buys 50 poems/year. Submit maximum 5 poems. **Pays $2.50/line, a one-year subscription, and 1 contributor's copy.**

$ GRASSLIMB

P.O. Box 420816, San Diego CA 92142-0816. **E-mail:** editor@grasslimb.com. **Website:** www.grasslimb.com. **Contact:** Valerie Polichar, editor. **80% freelance.** *Grasslimb* publishes literary prose, poetry, and art. Fiction is best when it is short and avant-garde or otherwise experimental. Estab. 2002. Circ. 200. Pays on acceptance. $10 kill fee. Publishes ms 1-6 months after acceptance. Accepts simultaneous submissions.

Responds in 4-6 months to mss. Rarely comments on rejected mss. Sample copy: $3. Guidelines for SASE, e-mail, or on website.

Submit full mss—no queries. Although general topics are welcome, we're less likely to select work regarding romance, sex, aging, and children. Fiction in an experimental, avant-garde or surreal mode is often more interesting to us than a traditional story. When submitting poetry, 4-6 pieces are preferred; line count is not necessary. For artwork, please submit photocopies or electronic versions (if electronic, 600 dpi preferred) only. Prose must include a word count and should not exceed 2,500 words; 1,000-2,000 is best for us. Submissions over 3,000 words will be returned unread. Reviews of 500-1,000 words are preferred. Please do not submit work to us more often than once every six months unless you have had work accepted previously to our publication, in which case you are not subject to a limit.

NONFICTION Needs memoir, reviews. Pays expenses of writers on assignment.

PHOTOS "We are only able to print black-and-white or greyscale photos."

FICTION "Fiction in an experimental, avant-garde, or surreal mode is often more interesting to us than a traditional story." Needs experimental, short stories. "Although general topics are welcome, we're less likely to select work regarding romance, sex, aging, and children." Send complete ms via e-mail or postal mail with SASE. Length: up to 2,500 words; average length: 1,500 words. **Pays $10-70 and 2 contributor's copies.**

POETRY Submit poems via e-mail or postal mail with SASE. Submit maximum 5 poems. **Pays $5-20/poem.**

TIPS "We publish brief fiction work that can be read in a single sitting over a cup of coffee. Work is generally 'literary' in nature rather than mainstream. Experimental work welcome. Remember to have your work proofread and to send short work. We cannot read over 3,000 words and prefer under 2,000 words. Include word count."

GRIST: A JOURNAL OF THE LITERARY ARTS

English Dept., 301 McClung Tower, Univ. of Tennessee, Knoxville TN 37996-0430. **E-mail:** gristeditors@gmail.com. **Website:** www.gristjournal.com. Editor-in-Chief: Jeremy Michael Reed. Annual magazine featuring world class fiction, poetry and creative nonfiction, along with interviews with renowned writers and essays about craft. *Grist* is a nationally distributed journal of fiction, nonfiction, poetry, interviews, and craft essays. We seek work of high literary quality from both emerging and established writers, and we welcome all styles and aesthetic approaches. Each issue is accompanied by Grist Online, which features some of the best work we receive during our reading period. In addition to general submissions, *Grist* holds the ProForma Contest every spring, recognizing unpublished creative work that explores the relationship between content and form, whether in fiction, nonfiction, poetry, or a hybrid genre. Throughout the year, we publish interviews, craft essays, and reviews on our blog, The Writing Life. Estab. 2007. Byline given. Pays on publication. No kill fee. Accepts queries by online submission form. Accepts simultaneous submissions. See website for details.

NONFICTION Needs essays, how-to, interview, memoir. Send complete ms. **Pays 1 cent per word up to $50.**

FICTION Needs experimental, mainstream. Send complete ms. Length: 7,000 words. **Pays 1 cent per word up to $50.**

POETRY Needs avant-garde, free verse, traditional. Submit maximum 3-5 poems. **Pays $10/page.**

TIPS "*Grist* seeks work from both emerging and established writers, whose work is of high literary quality."

HANGING LOOSE

Hanging Loose Press, 231 Wyckoff St., Brooklyn NY 11217. (347)529-4738. **Fax:** (347)227-8215. **E-mail:** print225@aol.com. **Website:** www.hangingloosepress.com. **Contact:** Robert Hershon and Mark Pawlak, editors. *Hanging Loose*, published in April and October, concentrates on the work of new writers. Wants excellent, energetic poems and short stories. Estab. 1966. Accepts queries by mail. Responds in 3 months. Sample copy: $14. Guidelines available online.

Hanging Loose is 120 pages, offset-printed on heavy stock, flat-spined, with 4-color glossy card cover.

NONFICTION Rarely publishes nonfiction. **Pays small fee and 2 contributor's copies.** Pays expenses of writers on assignment.

FICTION Needs short stories. Submit 1 complete ms by postal mail with SASE. **Pays small fee and 2 contributor's copies.**

POETRY Submit up to 6 poems at a time by postal mail with SASE. "Would-be contributors should read the magazine first." Has published poetry by Sherman Alexie, Paul Violi, Donna Brook, Kimiko Hahn, Harvey Shapiro, and Ha Jin. Considers poetry by teens (1 section contains poems by high-school-age poets). **Pays small fee and 2 contributor's copies.**

HARVARD REVIEW

Harvard University, Lamont Library, Harvard University, Cambridge MA 02138. **E-mail:** info@harvardreview.org. **Website:** harvardreview.fas.harvard.edu. Chloe Garcia Roberts. **Contact:** Christina Thompson, editor; Suzanne Berne, fiction editor; Major Jackson, poetry editor; Chloe Garcia Roberts, managing editor. Semiannual magazine covering poetry, fiction, essays, drama, graphics, and reviews in the spring and fall by an eclectic range of international writers. "Previous contributors include John Updike, Alice Hoffman, Joyce Carol Oates, Miranda July, and Jim Crace. We also publish the work of emerging and previously unpublished writers." Does not accept e-mail submissions. Estab. 1992. No kill fee. Accepts queries by mail, online submission form. Accepts simultaneous submissions. Responds in 6 months to mss. Guidelines online.

NONFICTION Needs essays, reviews. Special issues: "If you are interested in reviewing for the *Harvard Review*, write to the editor and enclose 2 or more recent clips." No unsolicited book reviews. Submit by online submissions manager or mail (with SASE). Length: up to 7,000 words.

PHOTOS Contact: Judith Larsen, visual arts editor.

FICTION Needs mainstream, literary. No genre fiction (romance, horror, detective, etc.). Submit by online submissions manager or mail (with SASE). Length: up to 7,000 words.

POETRY Submit up to 5 poems via online submissions manager or postal mail. Submit maximum 5 poems.

TIPS "Writers at all stages of their careers are invited to apply; however, we can only publish a very small fraction of the material we receive. We recommend that you familiarize yourself with *Harvard Review* before you submit your work."

HAWAI'I PACIFIC REVIEW

1060 Bishop St., Honolulu HI 96813. **Website:** hawaiipacificreview.org. **Contact:** Tyler McMahon, editor; Christa Cushon, managing editor. "*Hawai'i Pacific Review* is the online literary magazine of Hawai'i Pacific University. It features poetry and prose by authors from Hawai'i, the mainland, and around the world. *HPR* was started as a print annual in 1987. In 2013, it began to publish exclusively online. *HPR* publishes work on a rolling basis. Poems, stories, and essays are posted 1 piece at a time, several times a month. All contents are archived on the site." Estab. 1987. Accepts queries by online submission form. Accepts simultaneous submissions.

NONFICTION Needs essays, memoir, flash nonfiction (up to 750 words). No journalism or academic work. Submit 1 ms via online submissions manager. Length: up to 4,000 words. Pays expenses of writers on assignment.

FICTIONliterary. Prefers literary work to genre work. Submit 1 ms via online submissions manager. Length: up to 4,000 words.

POETRY Submit up to 3 poems at a time via online submissions manager (each poem should be a separate submission). "Because we try to be readable on all sorts of screens and devices, we can't do justice to poems with unorthodox spacing. For this reason, we strongly prefer poetry that sticks to the left margin."

TIPS "We look for the unusual or original plot, and prose with the texture and nuance of poetry. Character development or portrayal must be unusual/original; humanity shown in an original, insightful way (or characters); sense of humor where applicable. Be sure it's a draft that has gone through substantial changes, with supervision from a more experienced writer, if you're a beginner. Write about intense emotion and feeling, not just about someone's divorce or shaky relationship. No soap-opera-like fiction."

HAWAI'I REVIEW

University of Hawaii Board of Publications, 2445 Campus Rd., Hemenway Hall 107, Honolulu HI 96822. (808)956-3030. **Fax:** (808)956-3083. **E-mail:** hawaiireview@gmail.com. **Website:** http://hawaiireview.org/. **100% freelance written.** *Hawai'i Review* is a student-run biannual literary and visual arts print journal featuring national and international writing and visual art, as well as regional literature and visual art of Hawai'i and the Pacific. Estab. 1973. Circ. 500. Byline given. Publishes ms an average of 3 months after acceptance. Accepts queries by online submission form. Accepts simultaneous submissions. Responds in 3 months to mss. Sample copy: free, plus $5 shipping (back issue). Single copy: $12.50. Guidelines available online.

Accepts submissions online through Submittable only. Offers yearly award with $500 prizes in poetry and fiction.

NONFICTION Needs essays. Send 1 complete ms via online submission manager. Length: up to 7,000 words. Pays expenses of writers on assignment.

FICTION Needs experimental, humorous, short shorts. Send 1 short story or 2 pieces of flash fiction via online submission manager. Length: up to 7,000 words for short stories, up to 2,500 words for flash fiction.

POETRY Needs avant-garde, free verse, haiku, traditional. Submit up to 6 poems via online submission manager. Length: up to 500 lines/poem (though space limitations are taken into account for longer poems).

TIPS "Make it new."

HAYDEN'S FERRY REVIEW

Arizona State University, c/o Dept. of English, Arizona State University, P.O. Box 871401, Tempe AZ 85287. **E-mail:** hfr@asu.edu. **Website:** haydensferryreview.com. **Contact:** Katie Berta. Semiannual magazine. "*Hayden's Ferry Review* publishes the best-quality fiction, poetry, and creative nonfiction from new, emerging, and established writers." Work from *Hayden's Ferry Review* has been selected for inclusion in *Pushcart Prize* anthologies and the *Best American* series. No longer accepts postal mail or e-mail submissions (except in the case of the incarcerated and the visually impaired). Estab. 1986. Circ. 1,000. Byline given. No kill fee. Publishes ms an average of 6 months after acceptance. Editorial lead time 5 months. Accepts queries by online submission form. Accepts simultaneous submissions. Responds in 6-7 months. Sample copy: $13. Back issues: $9. Guidelines online.

NONFICTION Needs book excerpts, essays, interview, memoir, personal experience. **Buys 2 mss/year.** Send complete manuscript via online submissions manager. Word length open, but typically does not accept submissions over 25 pages. **Pays 1 contributor's copy.** Pays expenses of writers on assignment.

PHOTOS Send photos. Reviews slides.

FICTION Needs ethnic, experimental, humorous, mainstream, short stories, Prefers literary fiction. Does not want genre fiction. Send complete ms via online submissions manager. Word length open, but typically does not accept submissions over 25 pages. **Pays 1 contributor's copy.**

POETRY Needs Avant-garde, free verse, haiku, light verse, traditional, experimental. Submit up to 5 poems via online submissions manager. Submit maximum 5 poems. **Pays 1 contributor's copy.**

THE HOLLINS CRITIC

P.O. Box 9538, Hollins University, Roanoke VA 24020-1538. **Website:** www.hollins.edu/who-we-are/news-media/hollins-critic. **100% freelance written.** Magazine published 5 times/year. *The Hollins Critic*, published 5 times/year, presents the first serious surveys of the whole bodies of contemporary writers' work, with complete checklists. In past issues, you'll find essays on such writers as Claudia Emerson (by Allison Seay), Wilma Dykeman (by Casey Clabough), Jerry Mirskin (by Howard Nelson), Sally Mann (by Martha Park), James Alan McPherson (by James Robert Saunders), Elise Partridge (by Nicholas Birns), and Ron Rash (by Jerry Wayne Wells). Estab. 1964. Circ. 400. Byline given. Pays on publication. No kill fee. Publishes ms an average of 1 year after acceptance. Accepts queries by online submission form. Accepts simultaneous submissions. Responds in 2 months to mss. Sample copy: $3. Guidelines for #10 SASE or online.

Uses a few short poems in each issue, interesting in form, content, or both. *The Hollins Critic* is 24 pages, magazine-sized. Press run is 500. Subscription: $12/year ($17 outside US). No postal or e-mail submissions. Has published poetry by Natasha Trethewey, Carol Moldaw, David Huddle, Margaret Gibson, and Julia Johnson.

POETRY Needs avant-garde, free verse, traditional. Submit up to 5 poems at a time using the online submission form at www.hollinscriticsubmissions.com, available September 15-December 1. Submissions received at other times will be returned unread. Publishes 16-20 poems/year. **Pays $25/poem plus 5 contributor's copies.**

TIPS "We accept unsolicited poetry submissions; all other content is by prearrangement."

HOOT

A Postcard Review of (Mini) Poetry and Prose, 4234 Chestnut St., Apt. 1 R, Philadelphia PA 19104. **E-mail:** info@hootreview.com. **Website:** www.hootreview.com. **Contact:** Jane-Rebecca Cannarella, editor in chief; Amanda Vacharat and Dorian Geisler, editors/co-founders. **100% freelance written.** *HOOT* publishes 1 piece of writing, designed with original art and/or photographs, on the front of a postcard every month, as well as 2-3 pieces online. The postcards are intended for sharing, to be hung on the wall, etc. Therefore, *HOOT* looks for very brief, surprising-yet-gimmick-free writing that can stand on its own, that also follows "The Refrigerator Rule"—something that you would hang on your refrigerator and would want to read and look at for a whole month. This rule applies to online content as well. Estab. 2011. Pays on publication. Publishes ms 2 months after acceptance. Accepts queries by mail, online submission form. Accepts simultaneous submissions. Sample copy: $2. Guidelines available online.

Costs $2 to submit up to 2 pieces of work. Submit through online submissions manager or postal mail.

NONFICTION Needs personal experience, creative nonfiction. **Buys 6 mss/year.** Submit complete ms. Length: up to 150 words. **Pays $10-100 for assigned and unsolicited pieces.** Pays expenses of writers on assignment.

PHOTOS Send photos (GIF/JPEG files) with submission. Buys one-time rights.

FICTIONliterary, flash/short short. **Buys 14 mss/year.** Submit complete ms. Length: up to 150 words. **Pays $10-100 for print publication.**

POETRY Needs avant-garde, free verse, haiku, light verse, traditional, prose. Buys 14 poems/year. Submit maximum 2 poems. Length: up to 10 lines. **Pays $10-100 for print publication.**

TIPS "We look for writing with audacity and zest from authors who are not afraid to take risks. We appreciate work that is able to go beyond mere description in its 150 words. We offer free online workshops every other Wednesday for authors who would like feedback on their work from the *HOOT* editors. We also often give feedback with our rejections. We publish roughly 6-10 new writers each year."

HOTEL AMERIKA

Columbia College Chicago, The Department of Creative Writing, 600 S. Michigan Ave., Chicago IL 60605. (312)369-8175. **Website:** www.hotelamerika.net. **Contact:** David Lazar, editor; Jenn Tatum, managing editor. *Hotel Amerika* is a venue for both well-known and emerging writers. Publishes exceptional writing in all forms. Strives to house the most unique and provocative poetry, fiction, and nonfiction available. Estab. 2002. No kill fee. Accepts queries by online submission form. Guidelines online.

Mss will be considered between September 1 and May 1. Materials received after May 1 and before September 1 will be returned unread. Work published in *Hotel Amerika* has been included in *The Pushcart Prize* and *The Best American Poetry*, and featured on *Poetry Daily*.

NONFICTION Needs essays. Submit complete ms through online submissions manager. Pays expenses of writers on assignment.

FICTION Welcomes submissions in all genres of creative writing, generously defined. Does not publish book reviews as such, although considers review-like essays that transcend the specific objects of consideration. Submit complete ms through online submissions manager.

POETRY Welcomes submissions in all genres.

$ HUBBUB

5344 SE 38th Ave., Portland OR 97202. **Website:** www.reed.edu/hubbub. **Contact:** J. Shugrue and Lisa M. Steinman, co-editors. *Hubbub*, published once/year, is designed "to feature a multitude of voices from interesting, contemporary American poets." Wants "poems that are well crafted, with something to say. We have no single style, subject, or length requirement and in particular will consider long poems." Estab. 1983. Pays on publication. Publishes poems 1-12 months (usually) after acceptance. Accepts queries by mail. Responds in 4 months. Sample: $3.35 (back issues), $7 (current issue). Subscription: $7/year. Guidelines for SASE or online.

Hubbub is 50-70 pages, digest-sized, offset-printed, perfect-bound, with cover art. Receives about 1,200 submissions/year, accepts up to 2%. Press run is 350.

POETRY Submit 3-6 typed poems at a time. Include SASE. "We review 2-4 poetry books/year in short (three-page) reviews; all reviews are solicited. We do, however, list books received/recommended." Send materials for review consideration. Has published poetry by Madeline DeFrees, Cecil Giscombe, Carolyn Kizer, Primus St. John, Shara McCallum, and Alice Fulton. Does not want light verse. Buys 40-50 poems/year. Submit maximum 6 poems. No length requirements. **Pays $20/poem.**

THE HUDSON REVIEW

33 W. 67th St., New York NY 10023. (212)650-0020. **E-mail:** info@hudsonreview.com. **Website:** hudsonreview.com. **Contact:** Paula Deitz, editor. **100% freelance written.** Since its beginning, the magazine has dealt with the area where literature bears on the intellectual life of the time and on diverse aspects of American culture. It has no university affiliation and is not committed to any narrow academic aim or to any particular political perspective. The magazine serves as a major forum for the work of new writers and for the exploration of new developments in literature and the arts. It has a distinguished record of publishing little-known or undiscovered writers, many of whom have become major literary figures. Each issue contains a wide range of material including poetry, fiction, essays on literary and cultural topics, book reviews, reports from abroad, and chronicles covering film, theater, dance, music, and art. *The Hudson Review* is distributed in 25 countries. Unsolicited mss are read according to the following schedule: April 1 through June 30 for poetry, September 1 through November 30 for fiction, and January 1 through March 31 for nonfiction. Estab. 1948. Circ. 2,000. Byline given. Pays on publication. No kill fee. Publishes ms an average of 6 months after acceptance. Editorial lead time 3 months. Accepts queries by mail, online submission form. Responds in 6 months to mss. Sample copy: $11. Guidelines online.

NONFICTION Needs essays, general interest, historical, memoir, reviews. **Buys 4-6 mss/year.** Send complete ms by mail from **January 1 through March 31** only. Length: up to 10,000 words. Pays expenses of writers on assignment.

FICTION If you go through our archives, most of the short stories fall into the nebulous category of "literary fiction." Many stories have elements of mystery, romance, historical fiction, science fiction/speculative fiction, etc. For novel excerpts, we ask that the work be able to stand on its own. For genre stories, we ask that the work go beyond its genre—a religious story would have to be more than a conversion narrative or cautionary tale; a comic story would ideally have a little pathos; a romance or mystery or sci-fi story would have some ambiguities or aesthetic concerns or experimentation. In general, we want stories that a writer has put a lot of thought into, and that readers will think about long after they've finished. Needs short stories. **Buys 3-8 mss/year.** Send complete ms by mail or online submissions manager from **September 1 through November 30** only. Length: up to 10,000 words.

POETRY Needs Anything goes. Formal, free verse, experimental, translations, prose poetry, etc. Submit up to 7 poems by mail from **April 1 through June 30** only. Buys 15-30 poems/year.

TIPS "We do not specialize in publishing any particular 'type' of writing; our sole criterion for accepting unsolicited work is literary quality. The best way for you to get an idea of the range of work we publish is to read a current issue. Unsolicited mss submitted outside of specified reading times will be returned unread. Do not send submissions via e-mail."

HUNGER MOUNTAIN

Vermont College of Fine Arts, 36 College St., Montpelier VT 05602. (802)828-8517. **E-mail:** hungermtn@vcfa.edu. **Website:** www.hungermtn.org. Editor: Erin Stalcup. **Contact:** Cameron Finch, managing editor. Annual perfect-bound journal covering high-quality fiction, poetry, creative nonfiction, craft essays, writing for children, and artwork. Four contests held annually, one in each genre. Accepts high-quality work from unknown, emerging, or successful writers. Publishing fiction, creative nonfiction, poetry, and young adult & children's writing. Four writing contests annually. *Hunger Mountain* is a print and online journal of the arts. The print journal is about 200 pages, 7x9, professionally printed, perfect-bound, with full-bleed color artwork on cover. Press run is 1,000. Over 10,000 visits online monthly. Uses online submissions manager (Submittable). Member: CLMP. Estab. 2002. Circ. 1,000. Byline given. Pays on publication. No kill fee. Publishes ms an average of 1 year after acceptance. General submissions between May 1-October 15. Accepts queries by online submission form. Accepts simultaneous submissions. Responds in 4-6 months to mss. Single issue: $12; subscription: $18 for 2 issues/2 years; back issue: $8. Checks payable to Vermont College of Fine Arts, or purchase online. Guidelines online.

NONFICTION "We welcome an array of traditional and experimental work, including, but not limited to, personal, lyrical, and meditative essays, memoirs, collages, rants, and humor. The only requirements are recognition of truth, a unique voice with a firm command of language, and an engaging story with multiple pressure points." No informative or instructive articles, no interviews, and no book reviews please. Payment varies. Submit complete ms using online submissions manager at Submittable. Length: up to 10,000 words. **Pays $50 for general fiction or creative nonfiction, for both children's lit and general adult lit.**

PHOTOS Send photos.

FICTION "We look for work that is beautifully crafted and tells a good story, with characters that are alive and kicking, storylines that stay with us long after we've finished reading, and sentences that slay us with their precision." Needs experimental, humorous, novel excerpts, short stories, slice-of-life vignettes. No genre fiction, meaning science fiction, fantasy, horror, detective, erotic, etc. Submit ms using online submissions manager: https://hungermtn.submittable.com/submit. Length: up to 10,000 words. **Pays $50 for general fiction.**

POETRY Needs avant-garde, free verse, traditional. Submit 1-5 poems at a time. "We are looking for truly original poems that run the aesthetic gamut: lively engagement with language in the act of pursuit. Some poems remind us in a fresh way of our own best thoughts; some poems bring us to a place beyond language for which there aren't quite words; some poems take us on a complicated language ride that is, itself, its own aim. Complex poem-architectures thrill us and still-points in the turning world do, too. Send us the best of what you have." Submit using online submissions manager. No light verse, humor/quirky/catchy verse, greeting card verse. Submit maximum 5 poems. **Pays $25 for poetry up to 2 poems (plus $5/poem for additional poems).**

TIPS "Mss must be typed, prose double-spaced. Poets submit poems as one document. No multiple genre submissions. Fresh viewpoints and human interest are very important, as is originality and diversity. We are committed to publishing an outstanding journal of the arts. Do not send entire novels, mss, or short story collections. Do not send previously published work."

$ ICONOCLAST

1675 Amazon Rd., Mohegan Lake NY 10547-1804. **Website:** www.iconoclastliterarymagazine.com. **Contact:** Phil Wagner, editor and publisher. *Iconoclast* seeks and chooses the best new writing and poetry available—of all genres and styles and entertainment levels. Its mission is to provide a serious publishing opportunity for unheralded, unknown, but deserving creators, whose work is often overlooked or trampled in the commercial, university, or Internet marketplace. Estab. 1992. Pays on publication. Accepts queries by mail. Responds in 6 weeks to mss. Sample copy: $4. Subscription: $20 for 6 issues.

FICTION "Subjects and styles are completely open (within the standards of generally accepted taste—though exceptions, as always, can be made for unique and visionary works)." Needs adventure, experimental, fantasy, mainstream, short stories. No slice-of-life stories, stories containing alcoholism, incest, and domestic or public violence. Accepts most genres, "with the exception of mysteries." Submit by mail; include SASE. Cover letter not necessary. **Pays 1¢/word and 2 contributor's copies. Contributors get 40% discount on extra copies.**

POETRY "Try for originality; if not in thought than expression. No greeting card verse or noble religious sentiments. Look for the unusual in the usual, parallels in opposites, the capturing of what is unique or often unnoticed in an ordinary or extraordinary moment. What makes us human—and the resultant glories and agonies. The universal usually wins out over the personal. Rhyme isn't as easy as it looks—especially for those unversed in its study." Submit by mail; include SASE. Cover letter not necessary. Length: up to 2 pages. **Pays $2-6/poem and 1 contributor's copy per page or work. Contributors get 40% discount on extra copies.**

TIPS "Please don't send preliminary drafts—rewriting is half the job. If you're not sure about the story, don't truly believe in it, or are unenthusiastic about the subject (we will not recycle your term papers or thesis), then don't send it. This is not a lottery (luck has nothing to do with it)."

$$ THE IDAHO REVIEW

Boise State University, 1910 University Dr., Boise ID 83725. **E-mail:** mwieland@boisestate.edu. **Website:**

idahoreview.org. **Contact:** Mitch Wieland, editor. *The Idaho Review* is the literary journal of Boise State University. Recent stories appearing in *The Idaho Review* have been reprinted in *The Best American Short Stories, The O. Henry Prize Stories, The Pushcart Prize,* and *New Stories from the South.* Recent contributors include Joyce Carol Oates, Rick Moody, Ann Beattie, T.C. Boyle, and Joy Williams. Reading period: September 15-March 15. Estab. 1998. Pays on publication. Publishes ms 1 year after acceptance. Accepts queries by online submission form. Accepts simultaneous submissions. Responds in 3-5 months. Guidelines online.

NONFICTION Needs book excerpts, essays, interview. Special issues: creative nonfiction. Submit through online submissions manager. Pays expenses of writers on assignment.

FICTION Needs experimental, novel excerpts, short stories, literary. No genre fiction of any type. Submit through online submissions manager. Length: up to 25 double-spaced pages. **Pays $300-$500/story and contributor's copies.**

POETRY Submit up to 5 poems using online submissions manager.

TIPS "We look for strongly crafted work that tells a story that needs to be told. We demand vision and intelligence and mystery in the fiction we publish."

IMAGE

3307 Third Ave. W., Seattle WA 98119. (206)281-2988. **Fax:** (206)281-2979. **E-mail:** image@imagejournal.org. **Website:** www.imagejournal.org. **Contact:** Gregory Wolfe, publisher and editor. **50% freelance written.** Quarterly magazine covering the intersection between art and faith. "*Image* is a unique forum for the best writing and artwork that is informed by—or grapples with—religious faith. We have never been interested in art that merely regurgitates dogma or falls back on easy answers or didacticism. Instead, our focus has been on writing and visual artwork that embody a spiritual struggle, that seek to strike a balance between tradition and a profound openness to the world. Each issue explores this relationship through outstanding fiction, poetry, painting, sculpture, architecture, film, music, interviews, and dance. *Image* also features 4-color reproductions of visual art." Magazine: 7×10; 136 pages; glossy cover stock; illustrations; photos. Estab. 1989. Circ. 4,500. Byline given. Pays on acceptance. No kill fee. Publishes ms an average of 8 months after acceptance. Accepts queries by mail, e-mail. Accepts simultaneous submissions. Responds in 1 month to queries; in 5 months to mss. Sample copy: $16 or available online. Guidelines online.

NONFICTION Needs essays, interview, profile, religious, reviews. No sentimental, preachy, moralistic, or obvious essays. **Buys 10 mss/year.** Send complete ms by postal mail (with SASE for reply or return of ms) or online submissions manager at www.imagejournal.org/journal/submit, or query Mary Mitchell (mkenagy@imagejournal.org). Does not accept e-mail submissions. Length: 3,000-6,000 words. **Pays $20/page and 4 contributor's copies.**

FICTION Needs religious, short stories. No sentimental, preachy, moralistic, obvious stories, or genre stories (unless they manage to transcend their genre). **Buys 8 mss/year.** Send complete ms by postal mail (with SASE for reply or return of ms) or online submissions manager at www.imagejournal.org/journal/submit. Does not accept e-mail submissions. Length: 3,000-6,000 words. **Pays $20/page and 4 contributor's copies.**

POETRY Wants poems that grapple with religious faith, usually Judeo-Christian. Send up to 5 poems by postal mail (with SASE for reply or return of ms) or online submissions manager. Does not accept e-mail submissions. Submit maximum 5 poems. Length: up to 10 pages. **Pays $2/line ($150 maximum) and 4 contributor's copies.**

TIPS "Fiction must grapple with religious faith, though subjects need not be overtly religious."

INDIANA REVIEW

Ballantine Hall 529, 1020 E. Kirkwood Ave., Indiana University, Bloomington IN 47405. **E-mail:** inreview@indiana.edu. **Website:** indianareview.org. **Contact:** See masthead for current editorial staff. **100% freelance written.** Biannual magazine. "*Indiana Review*, a nonprofit organization run by IU graduate students, is a journal of innovative fiction, nonfiction, and poetry. We're interested in energy, originality, and careful attention to craft. While we publish many well-known authors, we also welcome new and emerging poets and fiction writers." See website for open reading periods. Estab. 1976. Circ. 5,000. Byline given. Pays on publication. Publishes ms an average of 6-8 months after acceptance. Accepts queries by online submission form. Accepts simultaneous submissions. We make every effort to respond to work in four months. Back issues available for $10. Guidelines available online. We no longer accept hard-copy submissions. All submissions must be made online.

NONFICTION Needs essays. No coming-of-age/slice-of-life pieces or book reviews. **Buys 5-7 mss/year.** Submit complete ms through online submissions manager. Length: up to 8,000 words. **Pays $5/page ($10 minimum), plus 2 contributor's copies.** Pays expenses of writers on assignment.

FICTION "We look for daring stories which integrate theme, language, character, and form. We like polished writing, humor, and fiction which has consequence beyond the world of its narrator." Needs ethnic, experimental, mainstream, novel excerpts, short stories, literary, short fictions, translations. No genre fiction. **Buys 15-25 mss/year.** Submit via online submissions manager. Length: up to 8,000 words. **Pays $5/page ($10 minimum), plus 2 contributor's copies.**

POETRY "We look for poems that are skillful and bold, exhibiting an inventiveness of language with attention to voice and sonics." Wants experimental, free verse, prose poem, traditional form, lyrical, narrative. Submit poetry via online submissions manager. Buys 40-60 poems/year. Submit maximum 6 poems. **Pays $5/page ($10 minimum), plus 2 contributor's copies.**

TIPS "We're always looking for more nonfiction. We enjoy essays that go beyond merely autobiographical revelation and utilize sophisticated organization and slightly radical narrative strategies. We want essays that are both lyrical and analytical, where confession does not mean nostalgia. Read us before you submit. Back issues are available for $10. Our most recent issues have online previews available for free and accessible through the "Shop" page on our website. Often reading is slower in summer and holiday months. Submit work that 'stacks up' with the work we've published."

THE IOWA REVIEW

308 EPB, The University of Iowa, Iowa City IA 52242. (319)335-0462. **E-mail:** iowa-review@uiowa.edu. **Website:** www.iowareview.org. Lynne Nugent, managing editor. **Contact:** Harilaos Stecopoulos. Triannual magazine covering stories, essays, and poems for a general readership interested in contemporary literature. *The Iowa Review*, published 3 times/year, prints fiction, poetry, essays, reviews, and, occasionally, interviews. Receives about 5,000 submissions/year, accepts up to 100. Press run is 2,900; 1,500 distributed to stores. Estab. 1970. Circ. 3,500. Pays on publication. Publishes ms an average of 12-18 months after acceptance. Accepts queries by mail, online submission form. Accepts simultaneous submissions. Responds to mss in 4 months. Sample: $8.95 and online. Subscription: $20. Guidelines online.

This magazine uses the help of colleagues and graduate assistants. Its reading period for unsolicited work is September 1-December 1. From January through April, the editors read entries to the annual Iowa Review Awards competition. Check the website for further information.

NONFICTION Needs essays, interview. Send complete ms with cover letter. Don't bother with queries. SASE for return of ms. Accepts mss by snail mail (SASE required for response) and online submission form at iowareview.submittable.com/submit; no e-mail submissions. **Pays 8¢/word ($100 minimum), plus 2 contributor's copies.** Pays expenses of writers on assignment.

FICTION "We are open to a range of styles and voices and always hope to be surprised by work we then feel we need." Receives 600 unsolicited mss/month. Accepts 4-6 mss/issue; 12-18 mss/year. Does not read mss January-August. Publishes ms an average of 12-18 months after acceptance. Agented fiction less than 2%. **Publishes some new writers/year.** Recently published work by Johanna Hunting, Bennett Sims, and Pedro Mairal. Needs experimental, mainstream, novel excerpts, short stories. Send complete ms with cover letter. Don't bother with queries. SASE for return of ms. Accepts mss by snail mail (SASE required for response) and online submission form at iowareview.submittable.com/submit; no e-mail submissions. **Pays 8¢/word ($100 minimum), plus 2 contributor's copies.**

POETRY Submit up to 8 pages at a time. Online submissions accepted, but no e-mail submissions. Cover letter (with title of work and genre) is encouraged. SASE required. Reads submissions only during the fall semester, September through November, and then contest entries in the spring. Occasionally comments on rejected poems or offers suggestions on accepted poems. "We simply look for poems that, at the time we read and choose, we find we admire. No specifications as to form, length, style, subject matter, or purpose. Though we print work from established writers, we're always delighted when we discover new talent." **Pays $1.50/line, $40 minimum.**

TIPS "We publish essays, reviews, novel excerpts, stories, poems, and photography. We have no set guidelines regarding content but strongly recommend that writers read a sample issue before submitting."

IRIS

E-mail: submissions@creatingiris.org. **E-mail:** editorial@creatingiris.org. **Website:** www.creatingiris.org. "*Iris* seeks works of fiction and poetry that speak to LGBT young adults and their allies. We are interested in creative, thoughtful, original work that engages our young readers. We seek writing that challenges them and makes them think. We're looking for stories that capture their imaginations and characters that are relatable. We think there's a need in the young adult literary market for writing that speaks to the everyday experiences of LGBT adolescents: Themes of identity, friendship, coming out, families, etc., are especially welcome. The protagonist need not identify as LGBT, but we do ask that there be some kind of LGBT angle to your story. We welcome all genres of fiction and poetry!" Estab. 2014. Accepts queries by e-mail. Accepts simultaneous submissions. Sample copy online. Guidelines available online.

"Because we publish for a young demographic, work submitted to *Iris* may not include depictions of sex, drug use, and violence. They can certainly be discussed and referenced, but not directly portrayed."

NONFICTION Needs essays, reviews. Query with published clips. Pays expenses of writers on assignment.

FICTION Submit complete ms via e-mail as attachment. Include cover letter in text of e-mail. Length: up to 3,000 words.

POETRY Submit poems via e-mail as attachment. Include cover letter in text of e-mail.

ISLAND

Island Magazine, P.O. Box 4703, Hobart Tasmania 7000 Australia. (+61)(03)6234-1462. **E-mail:** admin@islandmag.com. **Website:** www.islandmag.com. **Contact:** Kate Harrison, general manager. Quarterly magazine. *Island* seeks quality fiction, poetry, and essays. It is "one of Australia's leading literary magazines, tracing the contours of our national, and international, culture while still retaining a uniquely Tasmanian perspective." Only publishes the work of subscribers; you can submit if you are not currently a subscriber, but if your piece is chosen, the subscription will be taken from the fee paid for the piece. Estab. 1979. Circ. 1,500. Accepts queries by online submission form. Accepts simultaneous submissions. Subscriptions and sample copies available for purchase online. Guidelines online.

NONFICTION Needs essays. Query with brief synopsis and at least the first 500 words of the article using online submissions manager. "We are not strict about word limits for nonfiction and consider all works on their merit." **Pay varies.**

FICTION Submit 1 piece via online submissions manager. "Although we are not strict about word limits, we tend not to publish flash fiction or microfiction at time. In terms of upper limits, we are less likely to publish works longer than 5,000 words. This is a general guideline: We do not have a formal cut-off for submissions. However, please be aware that if you submit a work longer than 4,000 words, we may not read beyond this length if we feel certain the work is not suited for publication with us." **Pay varies.**

POETRY Submit via online submissions manager. Submit maximum 3 poems. **Pay varies.**

THE JOURNAL

The Ohio State University, 164 Annie and John Glenn Ave., Columbus OH 43210. **E-mail:** managingeditor@thejournalmag.org. **Website:** thejournalmag.org. Quarterly magazine. "We are interested in quality fiction, poetry, nonfiction, art, and reviews of new books of poetry, fiction, and nonfiction. We impose no restrictions on category, type, or length of submission for fiction, poetry, and nonfiction. We are happy to consider long stories and self-contained excerpts of novels. Please double-space all prose submissions. Please send 3-5 poems in 1 submission. We only accept online submissions and will not respond to mailed submissions." Estab. 1973. Circ. 1,500. Byline given. Publishes ms an average of 1 year after acceptance. Accepts queries by online submission form. Accepts simultaneous submissions. Responds in 4-6 months to mss. Sample copy: $8 on Submittable, or free online. Guidelines available online.

"We're open to all forms; we tend to favor work that gives evidence of a mature and sophisticated sense of the language."

NONFICTION Needs essays, interview. **Buys 8 mss/year.** Does not accept queries. Send full ms via online submissions manager. Length: up to 6,000 words. **Pays 2 contributor's copies and one-year subscription.** Pays expenses of writers on assignment.

COLUMNS/DEPARTMENTS Publishes reviews of contemporary poetry, fiction, and nonfiction, up to 1,200 words. **Buys 12 mss/year.**

FICTIONliterary short stories, novel excerpts. No romance, science fiction, or religious/devotional. Send full ms via online submissions manager. "Mss are rejected because of lack of understanding of the short story form, shallow plots, undeveloped characters. Cure: Read as much well-written fiction as possible. Our readers prefer 'psychological' fiction rather than stories with intricate plots. Take care to present a clean, well-typed submission." Length: up to 10,000 words. **Pays 2 contributor's copies and one-year subscription.**

POETRY Needs avant-garde, free verse, traditional. "However else poets train or educate themselves, they must do what they can to know our language. Too much of the writing we see indicates poets do not, in many cases, develop a feel for the possibilities of language and do not pay attention to craft. Poets should not be in a rush to publish—until they are ready." Submit 3-5 poems via online submissions manager. Buys 100 poems/year. **Pays 2 contributor's copies and one-year subscription.**

KANSAS CITY VOICES

Whispering Prairie Press, P.O. Box 410661, Kansas City MO 64141. **E-mail:** info@wppress.org. **Website:** www.wppress.org. **Contact:** Tom Sullivan, managing editor. **100% freelance written.** *Kansas City Voices*, published annually, features an eclectic mix of fiction, poetry, and art. "We seek exceptional written and visual creations from established and emerging voices." Submission period: December 15 through March 15. Note: We will not be publishing KCV in 2018. Our next submission period begins December 15, 2018, for publication in 2019. Estab. 2003. Circ. 1,000. Byline given. Pays on publication. Publishes ms an average of 6 months after acceptance. Accepts queries by online submission form. Accepts simultaneous submissions. Sample copy online. Guidelines online.

FICTION Needs short stories. Submit up to 2 complete mss via online submissions manager. Length: up to 2,500 words. **Pays small honorarium and 1 contributor's copy.**

POETRY Needs avant-garde, free verse, light verse, traditional. Submit maximum 3 poems. Length: up to 35 lines/poem. **Pays small honorarium and 1 contributor's copy.**

TIPS "There is no 'type' of work we are looking for, and while we would love for you to read through our previous issues, it is not an indicator of what kind of work we actively seek. Our editors rotate, our tastes evolve, and good work is just *good work*. We want to feel something when we encounter a piece. We want to be excited, surprised, thoughtful, and interested. We want to have a reaction. We want to share the best voices we find. Send us that one."

$ THE KENYON REVIEW

Finn House, 102 W. Wiggin, Gambier OH 43022. (740)427-5208. **Fax:** (740)427-5417. **E-mail:** kenyonreview@kenyon.edu. **Website:** www.kenyonreview.org. **Contact:** Alicia Misarti. **100% freelance written.** Bimonthly magazine covering contemporary literature and criticism. "An international journal of literature, culture, and the arts, dedicated to an inclusive representation of the best in new writing (fiction, poetry, essays, interviews, criticism) from established and emerging writers." The *Kenyon Review* receives about 8,000 submissions/year. Also publishes KROnline, a separate and complementary online literary magazine. Estab. 1939. Circ. 6,000. Byline given. Pays on publication. No kill fee. Publishes ms an average of 1 year after acceptance. Editorial lead time 1 year. Submit seasonal material 1 year in advance. Accepts queries by online submission form. Accepts simultaneous submissions. Responds in 6 months to mss. Sample: $10; includes s&h. Call or e-mail to order. Guidelines online.

NONFICTION Needs essays, interview, criticism. Only accepts mss via online submissions manager; visit website for instructions. Do not submit via e-mail or mail. Receives 130 unsolicited mss/month. Unsolicited mss accepted September 15-November 1 only. Length: 3-15 typeset pages preferred. **Pays 8¢/published word of prose (minimum payment $80; maximum payment $450); word count does not include title, notes, or citations.**

FICTION Receives 800 unsolicited mss/month. Unsolicited mss accepted September 15-November 1 only. Recently published work by Leslie Blanco, Karl

Taro Greenfeld, Charles Johnson, Amit Majmudar, Joyce Carol Oates, and Rion Amilcar Scott. Needs condensed novels, ethnic, experimental, historical, humorous, mainstream, novel excerpts, short stories, contemporary, excerpts from novels, gay/lesbian, literary, translations. Only accepts mss via online submissions manager; visit website for instructions. Do not submit via e-mail or mail. Length: 3-15 typeset pages preferred. **Pays 8¢/published word of prose (minimum payment $80; maximum payment $450); word count does not include title, notes, or citations.**

POETRY Features all styles, forms, lengths, and subject matters. Considers translations. Submit up to 6 poems at a time. No previously published poems. Only accepts mss via online submissions program; visit website for instructions. Do not submit via e-mail or snail mail. Accepts submissions September 15-November 1. Has recently published work by Rae Armantrout, Stephen Burt, Meghan O'Rourke, Carl Phillips, Solmaz Sharif, and Arthur Sze. Submit maximum 6 poems. **Pays 16¢/published word of poetry (minimum payment $40; maximum payment $200); word count does not include title, notes, or citations.**

TIPS "We no longer accept mailed or e-mailed submissions. Work will only be read if it is submitted through our online program on our website. Reading period is September 15 through November 1. We look for strong voice, unusual perspective, and power in the writing."

LADY CHURCHILL'S ROSEBUD WRISTLET

Small Beer Press, 150 Pleasant St., #306, Easthampton MA 01027. **E-mail:** info@smallbeerpress.com. **Website:** www.smallbeerpress.com/lcrw. **Contact:** Gavin Grant, editor. **100%.** *Lady Churchill's Rosebud Wristlet* accepts fiction, nonfiction, poetry, and b&w art. "The fiction we publish tends toward, but is not limited to, the speculative. This does not mean only quietly desperate stories. We will consider items that fall out with regular categories. We do not accept multiple submissions." Semiannual. Estab. 1996. Circ. 1,000. Byline given. Pays on publication. Publishes ms 6-12 months after acceptance. Accepts queries by mail. Responds in 6 months to mss. Sometimes comments on rejected mss. Sample copy: $5. Guidelines online.

NONFICTION Needs essays. Send complete ms with a cover letter. Include estimated word count. Send SASE (or IRC) for return of ms, or send a disposable copy of ms and #10 SASE for reply only. **Pays $0.03 per word, $25 minimum.**

FICTION Receives 100 unsolicited mss/month. Accepts 4-6 mss/issue; 8-12 mss/year. Publishes 2-4 new writers/year. Also publishes literary essays, poetry. Has published work by Ted Chiang, Gwenda Bond, Alissa Nutting, and Charlie Anders. Needs experimental, fantasy, science fiction, short stories. "We do not publish gore, sword and sorcery, or pornography. We can discuss these terms if you like. There are places for them all; this is not one of them." Send complete ms with a cover letter. Include estimated word count. Send SASE (or IRC) for return of ms, or send a disposable copy of ms and #10 SASE for reply only. Length: 200-7,000 words. **Pays $0.03 per word, $25 minimum.**

POETRY Send submission with a cover letter. Include estimated word count. Send SASE (or IRC) for return of submission, or send a disposable copy of submission and #10 SASE for reply only. **Pays $10/poem.**

TIPS "We recommend you read *Lady Churchill's Rosebud Wristlet* before submitting. You can pick up a copy from our website or from assorted book shops."

LINE

6079 Academic Quadrangle, 8888 University Dr., Simon Fraser University, Burnaby BC V5A 1S6 Canada. **E-mail:** wcl@sfu.ca. **Website:** linejournal.tumblr.com/about. "*Line* (formerly *West Coast Line*) is a journal of poetry and critique." Estab. 1990. Circ. 500. Pays on publication. No kill fee. Editorial lead time 4 months. Accepts queries by mail, e-mail. Accepts simultaneous submissions. Responds in 6 months to queries and mss. Sample copy for $15 CAD, $20 U.S. Guidelines for SASE (U.S. must include IRC).

NONFICTION Needs essays, experimental prose. No journalistic articles or articles dealing with nonliterary material. **Buys 8-10 mss/year.** Send complete ms. Length: 1,000-5,000 words. **Pays $8/page, 2 contributor's copies, and a one-year subscription.** Pays expenses of writers on assignment.

FICTION Needs experimental. **Buys 3-6 mss/year.**

POETRY Needs avant-garde. No light verse, traditional. Buys 10-15 poems/year. Submit maximum 5-6 poems. **Pays $8/page.**

TIPS Submissions must be either scholarly or formally innovative. Contributors should be familiar with current literary trends in Canada and the U.S.

Scholars should be aware of current schools of theory. All submissions should be accompanied by a brief cover letter; essays should be formatted according to the MLA guide. The publication is not divided into departments. We accept innovative poetry, experimental prose, and scholarly essays.

LITERAL LATTÉ

200 E. 10th St., Ste. 240, New York NY 10003. (212)260-5532. **E-mail:** litlatte@aol.com. **Website:** www.literal-latte.com. **Contact:** Jenine Gordon Bockman and Jeffrey Michael Bockman, editors and publishers. **99% freelance written.** Bimonthly online publication. Print anthologies featuring the best of the website. "We want great writing in all styles and subjects. A feast is made of a variety of flavors." Estab. 1994. No kill fee. Publishes an average of 6 months after acceptance. Editorial lead time 3 months. Submit seasonal material 3 months in advance. Accepts queries by online submission form. Accepts simultaneous submissions. Responds in 6 months to mss. Guidelines online.

NONFICTION Needs essays, general interest, humor, memoir, opinion, personal experience, reviews, travel. Special issues: Special issues: food verse. No scholarly reviews or essays. They must be personal. **Buys 10 mss/year.** Submit via online submissions manager or postal mail. Length: up to 10,000 words. **Pays anthology copies. Cash prizes for contests.** Pays expenses of writers on assignment.

FICTION Accepts all styles and genres. Needs adventure, condensed novels, confessions, erotica, ethnic, experimental, fantasy, historical, horror, humorous, mainstream, mystery, novel excerpts, religious, romance, science fiction, serialized novels, short stories, slice-of-life vignettes, suspense, western. **Buys 20 mss/year.** Submit via online submissions manager or postal mail. Length: up to 10,000 words. **Pays anthology copies. Cash prizes for contests.**

POETRY "We want any poem that captures the magic of the form." Buys 20 poems/year. Submit maximum 6 poems. Length: up to 4,000 words.

TIPS "Keeping free thought free and challenging entertainment are not mutually exclusive. Words make a ms stand out, words beautifully woven together in striking and memorable patterns."

THE MALAHAT REVIEW

The University of Victoria, P.O. Box 1700, STN CSC, Victoria BC V8W 2Y2 Canada. (250)721-8524. **E-mail:** malahat@uvic.ca (for queries only). **Website:** www.malahatreview.ca. Rhonda Batchelor, assistant editor. **Contact:** Iain Higgins, editor. **100% freelance written. Eager to work with new/unpublished writers.** Quarterly magazine covering poetry, fiction, creative nonfiction, and reviews. "We try to achieve a balance of views and styles in each issue. We strive for a mix of the best writing by both established and new writers." Estab. 1967. Circ. 2,000. Byline given. Pays on acceptance. No kill fee. Publishes an average of 6 months after acceptance. Accepts queries by online submission form. Accepts simultaneous submissions. Responds in approximately 2 weeks to queries; 3-10 months to mss. Sample: $16.95 (U.S.). Guidelines online.

NONFICTION Needs essays, general interest, historical, memoir, personal experience, travel. Submit via Submittable link on Submissions page. Length: 1,000-3,500 words. **Pays $60/magazine page.** Pays expenses of writers on assignment.

FICTION Needs condensed novels, experimental, historical, mainstream, short stories, slice-of-life vignettes. **Buys 12-14 mss/year.** Submit via Submittable link on Submissions page. Length: up to 8,000 words. **Pays $60/magazine page.**

POETRY Needs avant-garde, free verse, traditional. Submit 3-6 poems via Submittable link on Submissions page. Buys 100 poems/year. Length: up to 6 pages. **Pays $60/magazine page.**

TIPS "Please do not send more than 1 submission at a time: 3-6 poems, 1 piece of creative nonfiction, or 1 short story (do not mix poetry and prose in the same submission). See *The Malahat Review*'s Contests section of our website for more info on our annual contests involving poetry, short fiction, creative nonfiction, long poems, and novellas."

MĀNOA

A Pacific Journal of International Writing, University of Hawaii at Mānoa, English Department, Honolulu HI 96822. **E-mail:** mjournal-l@lists.hawaii.edu. **Website:** manoajournal.hawaii.edu. **Contact:** Frank Stewart, editor. Semiannual magazine. *Mānoa* is seeking high-quality literary fiction, poetry, essays, and translations for an international audience. In general, each issue is devoted to new work from an area of the Asia-Pacific region. Because we feature different places and have guest editors, please contact us to see if your submission is appropriate for what we're working on. *Mānoa* has received numerous awards, and work published in the magazine has been selected for prize anthologies. Please see our website for recently published issues. Estab. 1989. Circ. 1,000 print, 10,000 digital. Byline given. Pays on publication. Editorial lead time 9 months. Accepts queries by e-mail. Accepts simultaneous submissions. Responds in 3 weeks to queries. Sample: $20. Guidelines online.

NONFICTION No Pacific exotica. Query first. Length: 1,000-5,000 words. **Pays $25/printed page.**

FICTION Query first. Needs mainstream, contemporary, excerpted novel. No Pacific exotica. **Buys 1-2 mss/year.** Send complete ms. Length: 1,000-7,500 words. **Pays $100-500 ($25/printed page).**

POETRY No light verse. Buys 10-20 poems/year. Submit maximum 6 poems. **Pays $25/poem.**

TIPS "Not accepting unsolicited mss at this time because of commitments to special projects. Please query before sending mss as e-mail attachments. If you would like to view a copy of the journal, you may do so at Project Muse or JSTOR, online archives available through universities, community libraries, and other institutions."

THE MASSACHUSETTS REVIEW

University of Massachusetts, Photo Lab 309, 211 Hicks Way, Amherst MA 01003. (413)545-2689. **E-mail:** massrev@external.umass.edu. **Website:** www.massreview.org. **Contact:** Emily Wojcik, managing editor. Quarterly magazine. Seeks a balance between established writers and promising new ones. Interested in material of variety and vitality relevant to the intellectual and aesthetic questions of our time. Aspire to have a broad appeal. Estab. 1959. Circ. 1,200. Pays on publication. Publishes ms an average of 18 months after acceptance. Accepts queries by mail. Responds in 2-6 months to mss. Sample copy: $8 for back issue, $10 for current issue. Guidelines available online.

Does not respond to mss without SASE.

NONFICTION No reviews of single books. Articles and essays of breadth and depth are considered, as well as discussions of leading writers; of art, music, and drama; analyses of trends in literature, science, philosophy, and public affairs. Include name and contact information on the first page. Encourages page numbers. Send complete ms or query with SASE. Length: up to 6,500 words. **Pays $50 and 2 contributor's copies.** Pays expenses of writers on assignment.

FICTION Wants short stories. Accepts 1 short story per submission. Include name and contact information on the first page. Encourages page numbers. Has published work by Ahdaf Soueif, Elizabeth Denton, and Nicholas Montemarano. **Buys 30-40 mss/year.** Send complete ms. Length: up to 30 pages or 8,000 words. **Pays $50 and 2 contributor's copies.**

POETRY Has published poetry by Catherine Barnett, Billy Collins, and Dara Wier. Include your name and contact on every page. Submit maximum 6 poems. Length: There are no restrictions for length, but generally poems are less than 100 lines. **Pays $50/publication and 2 contributor's copies.**

TIPS "No manuscripts are considered May-September. Electronic submission process can be found on website. No fax or e-mail submissions. Shorter rather than longer stories preferred (up to 28-30 pages)." Looks for works that "stop us in our tracks." Manuscripts that stand out use "unexpected language, idiosyncrasy of outlook, and are the opposite of ordinary."

MERIDIAN

University of Virginia, P.O. Box 400145, Charlottesville VA 22904-4145. **E-mail:** meridianuva@gmail.com; meridianpoetry@gmail.com; meridianfiction@gmail.com. **Website:** www.readmeridian.org. *Meridian*, published semiannually, prints poetry, fiction, nonfiction, interviews, and reviews. "*Meridian* is interested in writing that is vibrant, moving, and alive, and welcomes contributions from a variety of aesthetic approaches. Has published such poets as Alexandra Teague, Gregory Pardlo, Sandra Meek, and Bob Hicok, and such fiction writers as Matt Bell, Kate Milliken, and Ron Carlson. Has recently interviewed C. Michael Curtis, Ann Beatty, and Claire Messud, among other luminaries. Also publishes a recurring feature called 'Lost Classic,' which resurrects previously unpublished work by celebrated writers and which has included illustrations from the mss of Jorge Luis Borges, letters written by Elizabeth Bishop, Stephen Crane's deleted chapter from *The Red Badge of Courage*, and a letter written by Flannery O'Connor about her novel *Wise Blood*." Estab. 1998. Publishes ms 1-2 months after acceptance. Seldom comments on rejected poems and mss. Accepts queries by online submission form. Accepts simultaneous submissions. Responds in 1-4 months. Always sends prepublication galleys and author contracts. Sample copy: $6 (back issue). Single print copy: $7. Print subscription:

$12 for 1 year; $22 for 2 years. Single digital copy: $3. Digital subscription: $4 for 1 year; $7 for 2 years. Buy subscriptions online via credit card, or mail an order form with a check made out to *Meridian*. Guidelines online.

Meridian is 130 pages, digest-sized, offset-printed, perfect-bound, with color cover. Receives about 2,500 poems/year, accepts about 40 (less than 1%). Press run is 1,000 (750 subscribers, 15 libraries, 200 shelf sales); 150 distributed free to writing programs. Work published in *Meridian* has appeared in *The Best American Poetry* and *The Pushcart Prize Anthology*.

NONFICTION Needs essays. Submit complete ms via online submissions manager. Length: up to 7,000 words. **Pays 2 contributor's copies (additional copies available at discount).**

FICTION Submit complete ms via online submissions manager. Needs short stories. Length: up to 6,500 words. **Pays 2 contributor's copies (additional copies available at discount).**

POETRY Submit up to 5 poems via online submissions manager. Length: up to 10 pages total. **Pays 2 contributor's copies (additional copies available at discount).**

MICHIGAN QUARTERLY REVIEW

0576 Rackham Bldg., 915 E. Washington, Ann Arbor MI 48109-1070. (734)764-9265. **E-mail:** mqr@umich.edu. **Website:** www.michiganquarterlyreview.com. **Contact:** Jonathan Freedman, editor; Vicki Lawrence, managing editor. **75% freelance written.** Quarterly journal of literature and the humanities publishing literary essays, fiction, poetry, creative nonfiction, memoir, interviews, and book reviews. *Michigan Quarterly Review* is an eclectic interdisciplinary journal of arts and culture that seeks to combine the best of poetry, fiction, and creative nonfiction with outstanding critical essays on literary, cultural, social, and political matters. The flagship journal of the University of Michigan, *MQR* draws on lively minds here and elsewhere, seeking to present accessible work of all varieties for sophisticated readers from within and without the academy. Estab. 1962. Circ. 1,000. Byline given. Pays on publication. No kill fee. Publishes ms an average of 1 year after acceptance. Accepts queries by mail. Accepts simultaneous submissions. Responds in 2 months to queries and mss. Sample: $4. Guidelines available online.

The Laurence Goldstein Award is a $500 annual award to the best poem published in *MQR* during the previous year. The Lawrence Foundation Award is a $1,000 annual award to the best short story published in *MQR* during the previous year. The Page Davidson Clayton Award for Emerging Poets is a $500 annual award given to the best poet appearing in *MQR* during the previous year who has not yet published a book.

NONFICTION Needs essays. Special issues: Publishes theme issues. Upcoming themes available in magazine and on website. **Buys 35 mss/year.** Query. Length: 1,500-7,000 words, 5,000 words average. **Payment varies but is usually in the range of $50 -$150.** Pays expenses of writers on assignment.

FICTION Contact: Fiction editor. "No restrictions on subject matter or language. We are very selective. We like stories that are unusual in tone and structure, and innovative in language. No genre fiction written for a market. Would like to see more fiction about social, political, and cultural matters, not just centered on a love relationship or dysfunctional family." Receives 300 unsolicited mss/month. Accepts 3-4 mss/issue; 12-16 mss/year. Publishes 1-2 new writers/year. Has published work by Rebecca Makkai, Peter Ho Davies, Laura Kasischke, Gerald Shapiro, and Alan Cheuse. **Buys 10 mss/year.** Send complete ms. Length: 1,500-7,000 words; average length: 5,000 words. **Payment varies but is usually in the range of $50-$150.**

POETRY No previously published poems. No e-mail submissions. Cover letter is preferred. "It puts a human face on the ms. A few sentences of biography is all I want, nothing lengthy or defensive." Prefers typed mss. Reviews books of poetry. "All reviews are commissioned." Length: should not exceed 8-12 pages. **Pays $8-12/published page.**

TIPS "Read the journal and assess the range of contents and the level of writing. We have no guidelines to offer or set expectations; every ms is judged on its unique qualities. On essays, query with a very thorough description of the argument and a copy of the first page. Watch for announcements of special issues, which are usually expanded issues and draw upon a lot of freelance writing. Be aware that this is a university quarterly that publishes a limited amount of fiction and poetry and that it is directed at an educated audience, one that has done a great deal of reading in all types of literature."

$ MID-AMERICAN REVIEW

Bowling Green State University, Department of English, Bowling Green OH 43403. (419)372-2725. **E-mail:** mar@bgsu.edu. **E-mail:** marsubmissions.bgsu.edu. **Website:** www.bgsu.edu/midamericanreview. **Contact:** Abigail Cloud, editor-in-chief; Bridget Adams, fiction editor. Semiannual magazine of the highest-quality fiction, poetry, and translations of contemporary poetry and fiction. Also publishes creative nonfiction and book reviews of contemporary literature. Reads mss year round. Publishes new and established writers. "We aim to put the best possible work in front of the biggest possible audience. We publish contemporary fiction, poetry, creative nonfiction, translations, and book reviews." Contests: The Fineline Competition for Prose Poems, Short Shorts, and Everything In Between (June 1 deadline, $10 per 3 pieces, limit 500 words each); The Sherwood Anderson Fiction Award (November 1 deadline, $10 per piece); and the James Wright Poetry Award (November 1 deadline, $10 per 3 pieces). Estab. 1981. Circ. 1,500. Byline given. No kill fee. Publishes mss an average of 6 months after acceptance. Accepts queries by online submission form. Accepts simultaneous submissions. Responds in 5 months to mss. Sample copy: $9 (current issue), $5 (back issue), $10 (rare back issues). Guidelines online.

NONFICTION Submit ms by post with SASE, or through online submission manager. Pays expenses of writers on assignment.

FICTION Publishes traditional, character-oriented, literary, experimental, prose poem, and short-short stories. No genre fiction. Submit ms by mail with SASE, or through online submission manager. Agented fiction 5%. Recently published work by Mollie Ficek and J. David Stevens. Length: up to 6,000 words.

POETRY Submit by mail with SASE, or through online submission manager. Publishes poems with "textured, evocative images, an awareness of how words sound and mean, and a definite sense of voice. Each line should help carry the poem, and an individual vision must be evident." Recently published work by Mary Ann Samyn, G.C. Waldrep, and Daniel Bourne. Submit maximum 6 poems.

TIPS "We are seeking translations of contemporary authors from all languages into English; submissions must include the original and proof of permission to translate. We would also like to see more creative nonfiction."

THE MINNESOTA REVIEW

Virginia Tech, **E-mail:** editors@theminnesotareview.org. **E-mail:** submissions@theminnesotareview.org. **Website:** minnesotareview.wordpress.com. **Contact:** Janell Watson, editor. *The Minnesota Review*, published biannually, is a journal featuring creative and critical work from writers on the rise or who are already established. Each issue is about 200 pages, digest-sized, flat-spined, with glossy card cover. Press run is 1,000 (400 subscribers). Also available online. Subscription: $30 for 2 years for individuals, $60/year for institutions. Sample: $15. Estab. 1960. Accepts queries by e-mail, online submission form. Accepts simultaneous submissions. Guidelines available online.

Open to submissions August 1-November 1 and January 1-April 1.

NONFICTION critical essays, review essays, scholarly articles. Query at editors@theminnesotareview.org. Pays expenses of writers on assignment.

FICTION Submit up to 1 short story or 4 short shorts or flash fiction pieces per reading period via online submissions manager. Length: up to 5,000 words for short stories, up to 1,000 words for short shorts or flash fiction. **Pays 2 contributor's copies.**

POETRY Submit 3-5 poems per reading period as 1 document via online submissions manager **Pays 2 contributor's copies.**

$$$ THE MISSOURI REVIEW

357 McReynolds Hall, University of Missouri, Columbia MO 65211. (573)882-4474. **E-mail:** question@moreview.com. **Website:** www.missourireview.com. **Contact:** Kate McIntyre. **90% freelance written.** Quarterly magazine. Publishes contemporary fiction, poetry, interviews, personal essays, and special features—such as History as Literature series, Found Text series, and Curio Cabinet art features—for the literary and the general reader interested in a wide range of subjects. Estab. 1978. Circ. 6,500. Byline given. Pays on publication Editorial lead time 4-6 months. Accepts queries by mail, online submission

form. Accepts simultaneous submissions. Responds in 2 weeks to queries; in 10-12 weeks to mss. Sample copy: $10 or online. Guidelines online.

NONFICTION **Contact:** Evelyn Somers. Needs book excerpts, essays. No literary criticism. **Buys 10 mss/year.** Send complete ms. **Pays $40/printed page.**

FICTION Needs ethnic, humorous, mainstream, short stories, literary. **Buys 25 mss/year.** Send complete ms. Length: No restrictions, but longer mss (9,000-12,000 words) or flash fiction ms (up to 2,000 words) must be truly exceptional to be published. **Pays $40/printed page.**

POETRY *TMR* publishes poetry features only—6-14 pages of poems by each of 3-5 poets per issue. Keep in mind the length of features when submitting poems. Typically, successful submissions include 8-20 pages of unpublished poetry. (Note: Do not send complete mss—published or unpublished—for consideration.) No inspirational verse. **Pays $40/printed page and 3 contributor's copies.**

TIPS "Send your best work."

MODERN HAIKU

P.O. Box 930, Portsmouth RI 02871. **E-mail:** modernhaiku@gmail.com. **Website:** modernhaiku.org. **Contact:** Paul Miller, editor. **85% freelance written.** Magazine published 3 times/year in February, June, and October covering haiku poetry. *Modern Haiku* is the foremost international journal of English-language haiku and criticism and publishes high-quality material only. Haiku and related genres, articles on haiku, haiku book reviews, and translations comprise its contents. It has an international circulation; subscribers include many university, school, and public libraries. *Modern Haiku* is 140 pages (average), digest-sized, printed on heavy-quality stock, with full-color cover illustrations, 4-page full-color art sections. Receives about 15,000 submissions/year, accepts about 1,000. Estab. 1969. Byline given. No kill fee. Publishes ms an average of 6 months after acceptance. Editorial lead time 4 months. Accepts queries by mail, e-mail. Responds in 1 week to queries; in 6-8 weeks to mss. Sample copy: $15 in North America, $16 in Canada, $20 in Mexico, $22 overseas. Subscription: $35 ppd by regular mail in the U.S. Payment possible by PayPal on the *Modern Haiku* website. Guidelines available for SASE or on website.

NONFICTION Needs essays, general interest. Send complete ms. **Pays $5/page for essays.**

COLUMNS/DEPARTMENTS Haiku & Senryu; Haibun; Essays (on haiku and related genres); Reviews (books of haiku or related genres) are assigned. **Buys 40 mss/year.** Send complete ms. **Pays $5/page.**

POETRY Needs haiku, senryu, haibun, haiga. Postal submissions: "Send 5-15 haiku on 1 or 2 letter-sized sheets. Put name and address at the top of each sheet. Include SASE." E-mail submissions: "May be attachments (recommended) or pasted in body of message. Subject line must read: MH Submission. Adhere to guidelines on the website." Publishes 1000 poems/year. Has published haiku by Roberta Beary, Billy Collins, Lawrence Ferlinghetti, Carolyn Hall, Sharon Olds, Gary Snyder, John Stevenson, George Swede, and Cor van den Heuvel. Does not want "general poetry, tanka, renku, linked-verse forms. No special consideration given to work by children and teens." **Offers no payment.**

TIPS "Study the history of haiku, read books about haiku, learn the aesthetics of haiku and methods of composition. Write about your sense perceptions of the suchness of entities; avoid ego-centered interpretations. Be sure the work you send us conforms to the definitions on our website."

NARRATIVE MAGAZINE

2443 Fillmore St., #214, San Francisco CA 94115. **E-mail:** contact@narrativemagazine.com. **Website:** www.narrativemagazine.com. **Contact:** Michael Croft, senior editor; Mimi Kusch, managing editor; Michael Wiegers, poetry editor. **100% freelance written.** Online literary journal that publishes American and international literature 3 times/year. "*Narrative* publishes high-quality contemporary literature in a full range of styles, forms, and lengths. Submit poetry, fiction, and nonfiction, including stories, short shorts, novels, novel excerpts, novellas, personal essays, humor, sketches, memoirs, literary biographies, commentary, reportage, interviews, and short audio recordings of short-short stories and poems. We welcome submissions of previously unpublished mss of all lengths, ranging from short-short stories to complete book-length works for serialization. In addition to submissions for issues of *Narrative* itself, we also encourage submissions for our Story of the Week, Poem of the Week, literary contests, and Readers' Narratives. Please read our Submission Guidelines for all information on mss formatting, word lengths, author payment, and other policies. We accept submissions only through our electronic submission system. We do not accept submissions through postal services or e-mail. You may send us mss for the following submission categories: General Submissions, Narrative Prize, Story of the Week, Poem of the Week, Readers' Narrative, iPoem, iStory, Six-Word Story, or a specific Contest. Your mss must be in one of the following file forms: DOC, RTF, PDF, DOCX, TXT, WPD, ODF, MP3, MP4, MOV, or FLV." Estab. 2003. Circ. 250,000. Byline given. Accepts queries by e-mail. Accepts simultaneous submissions. Responds in 1 month-14 weeks to queries. Guidelines online. **Charges $25 reading fee except for 2 weeks in April.**

Narrative has received recognitions in *New Stories from the South, Best American Mystery Stories, O. Henry Prize Stories, Best American Short Stories, Best American Essays,* and the *Pushcart Prize Collection.* In an article on the business of books, the National Endowment for the Arts featured *Narrative* as the model for the evolution of both print and digital publishing.

NONFICTION Needs book excerpts, essays, general interest, humor, interview, memoir, personal experience, photo feature, travel. Send complete ms.

PHOTOS "We are always on the lookout for photography portfolios and photo essays of exceptional quality."

FICTION Has published work by Alice Munro, Tobias Wolff, Marvin Bell, Jane Smiley, Joyce Carol Oates, E.L. Doctorow, and Min Jin Lee. Publishes new and emerging writers.Fiction, cartoons, graphic art, and multimedia content "to entertain, inspire, and engage." Send complete ms. **Pays on publication between $150-1,000, $1,000-5,000 for book length, plus annual prizes of more than $28,000.**

POETRY Needs poetry of all forms.

TIPS "Log on and study our magazine online. Narrative fiction, graphic art, and multimedia are selected, first and foremost, for quality."

THE NATIONAL POETRY REVIEW

The University of Buffalo, P.O. Box 2080, Aptos CA 95001-2080. **Website:** www.nationalpoetryreview.com. **Contact:** Angela Vogel, editor in chief. *The National Poetry Review* seeks "distinction, innovation, and *joie de vivre.* We agree with Frost about delight and wisdom. We believe in rich sound. We believe in the beautiful—even if that beauty is not in the situation of the poem but simply the sounds of the poem, the images, or (ideally) the way the poem stays in the reader's mind long after it's been read." *TNPR* considers both experimental and 'mainstream' work." Does not want "overly self-centered or confessional poetry." Estab. 2003. Time between acceptance and publication is no more than 1 year. "The editor makes all publishing decisions." Sometimes comments on rejected poems. Accepts queries by online submission form. Accepts simultaneous submissions. Usually responds in 3-4 months. Guidelines available on website.

The National Poetry Review is an annual online journal that accepts less than 1% of submissions received. Poetry appearing in *The National Poetry Review* has also appeared in *The Pushcart Prize.* Has published poetry by Bob Hicok, Jennifer Michael Hecht, Larissa Szplorluk, Martha Zweig, Nance Van Winkel, William Waltz, and Ted Kooser.

NONFICTION Pays expenses of writers on assignment.

POETRY "Our reading period is January 1-April 1 annually. Please submit all poems in 1 file. Include a brief bio with previous publications."

THE NEW CRITERION

900 Broadway, Ste. 602, New York NY 10003. **Website:** www.newcriterion.com. **Contact:** Roger Kimball, editor and publisher; David Yezzi, poetry editor. "A monthly review of the arts and intellectual life, *The New Criterion* began as an experiment in critical audacity—a publication devoted to engaging, in Matthew Arnold's famous phrase, with 'the best that has been thought and said.' This also meant engaging with those forces dedicated to traducing genuine cultural and intellectual achievement, whether through obfuscation, politicization, or a commitment to nihilistic absurdity. We are proud that *The New Criterion* has been in the forefront both of championing what is best and most humanely vital in our cultural inheritance and in exposing what is mendacious, corrosive, and spurious. Published monthly from September through June, *The New Criterion* brings together a wide range of young and established critics whose common aim is to bring you the most incisive criticism being written today." Estab. 1982. Accepts queries by mail. Accepts simultaneous submissions.

The New Criterion is 90 pages, 7x10, flat-spined. Single copy: $12.

NONFICTION Pays expenses of writers on assignment.

POETRY Has published poetry by Donald Justice, Andrew Hudgins, Elizabeth Spires, and Herbert Morris.

NEW ENGLAND REVIEW

Middlebury College, Middlebury VT 05753. (802)443-5075. **E-mail:** nereview@middlebury.edu. **Website:** www.nereview.com. **Contact:** Marcia Pomerance, managing editor. Quarterly literary magazine. *New England Review* is a prestigious, nationally distributed literary journal. Reads September 1-May 31 (postmarked dates). *New England Review* is 200+ pages, 7x10, printed on heavy stock, flat-spined, with glossy cover with art. Receives 3,000-4,000 poetry submissions/year, accepts about 70-80 poems/year. Receives 550 unsolicited mss/month, accepts 6 mss/issue, 24 fiction mss/year. Does not accept mss June-August, December-January. Agented fiction less than 5%. Estab. 1978. Circ. 2,000. Byline given. Pays on publication. No kill fee. Publishes ms an average of 6 months after acceptance. Accepts simultaneous submissions. Responds in 2 weeks to queries; in 3 months to mss. Sometimes comments on rejected mss. Sample copy: $10 (add $5 for overseas). Subscription: $35. Overseas shipping fees add $25 for subscription, $12 for Canada. Guidelines online.

NONFICTION Buys 20-25 mss/year. Send complete ms via online submission manager. No e-mail submissions. Length: up to 7,500 words, though exceptions may be made. **Pays $20/page ($40 minimum) and 2 contributor's copies.** Pays expenses of writers on assignment.

FICTION Send 1 story at a time, unless it is very short. Wants only serious literary fiction and novel excerpts. Publishes approximately 10 new writers/year. Has published work by Steve Almond, Christine Sneed, Roy Kesey, Thomas Gough, Norman Lock, Brock Clarke, Carl Phillips, Lucia Perillo, Linda Gregerson, and Natasha Trethewey. **Buys 25 mss/year.** Send complete ms via online submission manager. No e-mail submissions. "Will consider simultaneous submissions, but it must be stated as such and you must notify us immediately if the ms is accepted for publication elsewhere." Length: not strict on word count. **Pays $20/page ($20 minimum), and 2 contributor's copies.**

POETRY Submit up to 6 poems at a time. No previously published or simultaneous submissions for poetry. Accepts submissions by online submission manager only; accepts questions by e-mail. "Cover letters are useful." Address submissions to "Poetry Editor." Buys 75-90 poems/year. Submit maximum 6 poems. **Pays $20/page ($20 minimum), and 2 contributor's copies.**

TIPS "We consider short fiction, including short shorts, novellas, and self-contained extracts from novels in both traditional and experimental forms. In nonfiction, we consider a variety of general and literary but not narrowly scholarly essays; we also publish long and short poems, screenplays, graphics, translations, critical reassessments, statements by artists working in various media, testimonies, and letters from abroad. We are committed to exploration of all forms of contemporary cultural expression in the U.S. and abroad. With few exceptions, we print only work not published previously elsewhere."

NEW LETTERS

University of Missouri-Kansas City, 5101 Rockhill Rd., Kansas City MO 64110. (816)235-1168. **Fax:** (816)235-2611. **E-mail:** newletters@umkc.edu. **Website:** www.newletters.org. **Contact:** Robert Stewart, editor-in-chief. **100% freelance written.** "*New Letters*, published quarterly, continues to seek the best new writing, whether from established writers or those ready and waiting to be discovered. In addition, it supports those writers, readers, and listeners who want to experience the joy of writing that can both surprise and inspire us all." Submissions are not read June 1st through July 30th. Estab. 1934. Circ. 3,000. Byline given. Pays on publication. No kill fee. Publishes ms an average of 6 months after acceptance. Editorial lead time 6 months. Submit seasonal material 6 months in advance. Accepts queries by mail. Accepts simultaneous submissions. Responds in 1 month to queries; 5 months to mss. Sample copy: $10; sample articles online. Guidelines online.

NONFICTION Needs essays. No self-help, how-to, or nonliterary work. **Buys 8-10 mss/year.** Send complete ms. Length: up to 5,000 words. **Pays $40-100.** Pays expenses of writers on assignment.

PHOTOS Send photos. Reviews contact sheets, 2x4 transparencies, prints. Pays $10-40/photo. Buys one-time rights.

FICTION Needs ethnic, experimental, humorous, mainstream, contemporary. No genre fiction. **Buys 15-20 mss/year.** Send complete ms. Length: up to 5,000 words. **Pays $30-75.**

POETRY Needs avant-garde, free verse, haiku, traditional. No light verse. Buys 40-50 poems/year. Submit maximum 6 poems. Length: open. **Pays $10-25.**

TIPS "We aren't interested in essays that are footnoted or essays usually described as scholarly or critical. Our preference is for creative nonfiction or personal essays. We prefer shorter stories and essays to longer ones (an average length is 3,500-4,000 words). We have no rigid preferences as to subject, style, or genre, although commercial efforts tend to put us off. Even so, our only fixed requirement is good writing."

NEW OHIO REVIEW

English Department, 201 Ellis Hall; 45 University Terrace, Ohio University, Athens OH 45701. **E-mail:** noreditors@ohio.edu. **Website:** www.ohiou.edu/nor. **Contact:** David Wanczyk, editor. *New Ohio Review*, published biannually in spring and fall, publishes fiction, nonfiction, and poetry. Member CLMP. Reading period is September 15-December 15 and January 15-April 15. Annual contests, Jan 15th-Apr 15th ($1,000 prizes). Estab. 2007. Byline given. No kill fee. Accepts queries by e-mail, online submission form. Accepts simultaneous submissions. Responds in 2-4 months. Single copy: $9. Subscription: $16. Guidelines online.

NONFICTION Needs essays, general interest, memoir. Submit complete ms. **Pays minimum of $30 in addition to 2 contributor's copies and one-year subscription.** Pays expenses of writers on assignment.

FICTION Considers literary short fiction; no novel excerpts. Send complete ms. **Pays $30 minimum in addition to 2 contributor's copies and one-year subscription.**

POETRY Needs quality free verse, formal, experimental. Please do not submit more than once every 6 months unless requested to do so. Submit maximum 6 poems.

NEW ORLEANS REVIEW

Box 195, Loyola University, New Orleans LA 70118. (504)865-2295. **E-mail:** noreview@loyno.edu. **Website:** neworleansreview.org. **Contact:** Heidi Braden, managing editor; Mark Yakich, Editor. *New Orleans Review* is an annual journal of contemporary literature and culture, publishing new poetry, fiction, nonfiction, art, photography, film, and book reviews. Estab. 1968. Circ. 1,500. Pays on publication. No kill fee. Accepts queries by online submission form. Accepts simultaneous submissions. Responds in 4 months to mss. Sample copy: $5.

The journal has published an eclectic variety of work by established and emerging writers, including Walker Percy, Pablo Neruda, Ellen Gilchrist, Nelson Algren, Hunter S. Thompson, John Kennedy Toole, Richard Brautigan, Barry Spacks, James Sallis, Jack Gilbert, Paul Hoover, Rodney Jones, Annie Dillard, Everette Maddox, Julio Cortazar, Gordon Lish, Robert Walser, Mark Halliday, Jack Butler, Robert Olen Butler, Michael Harper, Angela Ball, Joyce Carol Oates, Diane Wakoski, Dermot Bolger, Roddy Doyle, William Kotzwinkle, Alain Robbe-Grillet, Arnost Lustig, Raymond Queneau, Yusef Komunyakaa, Michael Martone, Tess Gallagher, Matthea Harvey, D. A. Powell, Rikki Ducornet, and Ed Skoog.

NONFICTION Pays expenses of writers on assignment.

FICTION Needs "good writing, from conventional to experimental." Submit complete ms using online submissions manager ($3 fee). Length: up to 6,500 words. **Pays 2 contributor's copies.**

POETRY Submit using online submissions manager ($3 fee). Submit maximum 6 poems.

TIPS "We're looking for dynamic writing that demonstrates attention to the language and a sense of the medium, writing that engages, surprises, moves us. We're not looking for genre fiction or academic articles. We subscribe to the belief that in order to truly write well, one must first master the rudiments: grammar and syntax, punctuation, the sentence, the paragraph, the line, the stanza. We receive about 3,000 mss a year and publish about 3% of them. Check out a recent issue, send us your best, proofread your work, be patient, be persistent."

THE NEW QUARTERLY

St. Jerome's University, 290 Westmount Rd. N., Waterloo ON N2L 3G3 Canada. (519)884-8111, ext. 28290. **E-mail:** editor@tnq.ca; info@tnq.ca. **Website:** www.tnq.ca. Sophie Blom. **95% freelance written.** Quarterly book covering Canadian fiction and poetry. "Emphasis on emerging writers and genres, but we publish more traditional work as well if the language and narrative structure are fresh." Open to Canadian writers only. Reading periods: March 1-August 31; September 1-February 28. Estab. 1981. Circ. 1,000. Byline given. Pays on publication. No kill fee. Editorial lead time 6 months. Accepts queries by mail. Accepts simultaneous submissions. Responds in early January to submissions received March 1-August 31; in early June to submissions received September 1-February 28. Sample copy: $16.95 (cover price, plus mailing). Guidelines online.

NONFICTION Needs essays. Query with a proposal.

FICTION "*Canadian work only.* We are not interested in genre fiction. We are looking for innovative, beautifully crafted, deeply felt literary fiction."literary. **Buys 20-25 mss/year.** Send complete ms with submission cover sheet and bio. Does not accept submissions by e-mail. Accepts simultaneoues submissions if indicated in cover letter. **Pays $250/story.**

POETRY Needs avant-garde, free verse, traditional. *Canadian work only.* Send with submission cover sheet and bio. Does not accept submissions by e-mail. Accepts simultaneoues submissions if indicated in cover letter. Submit maximum 3 poems. **Pays $40/poem.**

TIPS "Reading us is the best way to get our measure. We don't have preconceived ideas about what we're looking for other than that it must be Canadian work (Canadian writers, not necessarily Canadian content). We want something that's fresh, something that will repay a second reading, something in which the language soars and the feeling is complexly rendered."

NEW WELSH REVIEW

P.O. Box 170, Aberystwyth, Ceredigion SY23 1 WZ United Kingdom. 01970-628410. **E-mail:** editor@newwelshreview.com. **E-mail:** submissions@newwelshreview.com. **Website:** www.newwelshreview.com. **Contact:** Gwen Davies, editor. "*New Welsh Review*, a literary magazine published 3 times/year and ranked in the top 5 British literary magazines, publishes stories, poems, and critical essays. The best of Welsh writing in English, past and present, is celebrated, discussed, and debated. We seek poems, short stories, reviews, special features/articles, and commentary." Accepts queries by e-mail. Accepts simultaneous submissions.

NONFICTION Submit complete ms by e-mail. **Pays direct to account or sends check on publication and 1 copy at discounted contributor's rate of £5 inc p&p."** Pays expenses of writers on assignment.

FICTION Submit complete ms by e-mail. **Pays direct to account or sends check on publication and 1 copy at discounted contributor's rate of £5 inc p&p."**

POETRY Submit by e-mail. **Pays direct to account or sends check on publication and 1 copy at discounted contributor's rate of £5 inc p&p."**

NIMROD INTERNATIONAL JOURNAL

International Journal of Prose and Poetry, University of Tulsa, 800 S. Tucker Dr., Tulsa OK 74104-3189. (918)631-3080. **E-mail:** nimrod@utulsa.edu. **Website:** https://nimrod.utulsa.edu. **Contact:** Eilis O'Neal, editor-in-chief; Cassidy McCants, associate editor. Since its founding in 1956 at The University of Tulsa, *Nimrod International Journal of Prose and Poetry*'s mission has been the discovery, development, and promotion of new writing. On a national and international scale, *Nimrod* helps new writers find their audiences through publication in our semiannual journal. We offer new and promising work that may be unfamiliar to readers, such as writing from countries not well represented in the American mainstream, writing in translation, and writing from people of under-represented ages, races, and sexual identities. *Nimrod* supports and defends the literary tradition of small magazines, spotlighting lesser-known poets and writers and providing foundations for their literary careers. We promote a living literature, believing that it is possible to search for, recognize, and reward contemporary writing of imagination, substance, and skill. Semiannual magazine: 200 pages; perfect-bound; 4-color cover. Receives 300 unsolicited mss/month. **Publishes 50-120 new writers/year.** Reading period: January 1 through November 30. Online submissions accepted at nimrodjournal.submittable.com/submit. Does not accept submissions by email unless the writer is living outside the U.S. and cannot submit using the submissions manager. Estab. 1956. Circ. 3,000. Pays on publication. Accepts queries by mail, e-mail, phone, online submission form. Accepts simultaneous submissions. Responds in 3-5 months to mss. Sample copy: $11. Subscription: $18.50/year U.S., $25.00/year outside U.S. Guidelines online or for SASE.

NONFICTION Needs interview, memoir, creative nonfiction. Special issues: Upcoming themes available online or for SASE. Submit complete ms by mail or through the online submissions manager. Include

SASE for mss submitted by mail. Length: up to 7,500 words. **Pays $10/page and 2 contributor's copies.**

PHOTOS Pays $10/image and 2 contributor's copies.

FICTION Wants "vigorous writing, characters that are well developed, dialogue that is realistic without being banal." Needs ethnic, experimental, historical, mainstream, novel excerpts, short stories. Submit complete ms by mail or through the online submissions manager. Include SASE for work submitted by mail. Length: up to 7,500 words. **Pays $10/page and 2 contributor's copies.**

POETRY Needs Open to all styles and subjects. "We seek poems that go beyond 1 word or image, honor the impulse to reveal a truth about, or persuasive version of, the inner and outer worlds." Submit poems by mail or through the online submissions manager. Include SASE for work submitted by mail. Length: up to 7 pages. **Pays $10/page and 2 contributor's copies.**

NINTH LETTER

Department of English, University of Illinois, 608 S. Wright St., Urbana IL 61801. **E-mail:** info@ninthletter.com; editor@ninthletter.com; fiction@ninthletter.com; poetry@ninthletter.com; nonfiction@ninthletter.com. **Website:** www.ninthletter.com. **Contact:** Editorial staff rotates; contact genre-specific e-mail address with inquiries. "*Ninth Letter* accepts submissions of fiction, poetry, and essays from September 1-February 28 (postmark dates). *Ninth Letter* is published semiannually at the University of Illinois, Urbana-Champaign. We are interested in prose and poetry that experiment with form, narrative, and nontraditional subject matter, as well as more traditional literary work." Pays on publication. Accepts queries by mail, online submission form. Accepts simultaneous submissions.

Ninth Letter won Best New Literary Journal 2005 from the Council of Editors of Learned Journals (CELJ) and has had poetry selected for *Best American Poetry, The Pushcart Prize, Best New Poets,* and *The Year's Best Fantasy and Horror.*

NONFICTION "Please send only 1 essay at a time. All mailed submissions must include an SASE for reply." Length: up to 8,000 words. **Pays $25/printed page and 2 contributor's copies.**

FICTION "Please send only 1 story at a time. All mailed submissions must include an SASE for reply." Length: up to 8,000 words. **Pays $25/printed page and 2 contributor's copies.**

POETRY Submit 3-6 poems (no more than 10 pages) at a time. "All mailed submissions must include an SASE for reply." **Pays $25/printed page and 2 contributor's copies.**

NORTH AMERICAN REVIEW

University of Northern Iowa, 1200 W. 23th St., Cedar Falls IA 50614. (319)273-6455. **E-mail:** nar@uni.edu. **Website:** northamericanreview.org. **90% freelance written.** Published 4 times/year. "The *North American Review* is the oldest literary magazine in America and one of the most respected; though we have no prejudices about the subject matter of material sent to us, our first concern is quality." Estab. 1815. Circ. under 5,000. Byline given. No kill fee. Publishes ms an average of 1 year after acceptance. Accepts queries by mail. Accepts simultaneous submissions. Responds in 3 months to queries; 4 months to mss. Sample copy: $7. Guidelines online.

This is the oldest literary magazine in the country and one of the most prestigious. Also one of the most entertaining—and a tough market for the young writer.

NONFICTION Submit 1 ms via online submissions manager. Length: up to 30 pages.

FICTION Wants to see more "well-crafted literary stories that emphasize family concerns. We'd also like to see more stories engaged with environmental concerns." Reads fiction mss during academic year. **Publishes 2 new writers/year.** Recently published work by Lee Ann Roripaugh, Dick Allen, and Rita Welty Bourke. "No flat narrative stories where the inferiority of the character is the paramount concern." Submit ms via online submissions manager. Length: up to 30 pages.

POETRY Submit up to 5 poems via online submissions manager.

TIPS "We like stories that start quickly and have a strong narrative arc. Poems that are passionate about subject, language, and image are welcome, whether they are traditional or experimental, whether in formal or free verse (closed or open form). Nonfiction should combine art and fact with the finest writing."

NORTH CAROLINA LITERARY REVIEW

East Carolina University, Mailstop 555 English, Greenville NC 27858-4353. (252)328-1537. **Fax:** (252)328-4889. **E-mail:** bauerm@ecu.edu; nclruser@

ecu.edu. **E-mail:** nclrsubmissions@ecu.edu. **Website:** www.nclr.ecu.edu. **Contact:** Margaret Bauer. Biannual magazine published online in the winter and in print in the summer covering North Carolina writers, literature, culture, history. "Articles should have a North Carolina slant. Fiction, creative nonfiction, and poetry accepted through yearly contests. First consideration is always for quality of work. Although we treat academic and scholarly subjects, we do not wish to see jargon-laden prose; our readers, we hope, are found as often in bookstores and libraries as in academia. We seek to combine the best elements of a magazine for serious readers with the best of a scholarly journal." Accepts submissions through Submittable. Estab. 1992. Circ. 750. Byline given. No kill fee. Publishes ms an average of 1 year after acceptance. Editorial lead time 6 months. Accepts simultaneous submissions. Responds in 1 month to queries; in 3-6 months to mss. Sample copy: $5-25. Guidelines online.

NONFICTION Needs essays, interview, memoir, reviews. Submit creative nonfiction for Alex Albright Creative Nonfiction Prize competition via Submittable. A one-year subscription allows for 1 submission; a two-year subscription or membership in the NC Literary and Historical Association allows multiple submissions. Length: up to 7,500 words. **Published writers paid in copies of the journal. First-place winners of contests receive a prize of $250. Select finalists are published and receive a complimentary copy of the issue in which their work is published.** Pays expenses of writers on assignment.

PHOTOS State availability.

FICTION Submit fiction for the Doris Betts Fiction Prize competition via Submittable. Length: up to 6,000 words. **First-place winners of contests receive a prize of $250. Other writers whose stories are selected for publication receive contributor's copies.**

POETRY Submit poetry for the James Applewhite Poetry Prize competition via Submittable. Only subscribers can submit, and all poets must have a North Carolina connection. Submit up to 3 poems with a one-year subscription ($15), or up to 5 poems with a two-year subscription ($25). **First-place winners of contests receive a prize of $250. Other poets whose poems are selected for publication receive contributor's copies.**

TIPS "By far the easiest way to break in is with special issue sections. We are especially interested in reports on conferences, readings, meetings that involve North Carolina writers, and personal essays or short narratives with a strong sense of place. See back issues for other departments. Interviews are probably the other easiest place to break in; no discussions of poetics/theory, etc., except in reader-friendly (accessible) language. Interviews should be personal, more like conversations, and extensive, exploring connections between a writer's life and his or her work."

$ NOTRE DAME REVIEW

University of Notre Dame, B009C McKenna Hall, Notre Dame IN 46556. **Website:** ndreview.nd.edu. "The *Notre Dame Review* is an independent, noncommercial magazine of contemporary American and international fiction, poetry, criticism, and art. Especially interested in work that takes on big issues by making the invisible seen, that gives voice to the voiceless. In addition to showcasing celebrated authors like Seamus Heaney and Czelaw Milosz, the *Notre Dame Review* introduces readers to authors they may have never encountered before but who are doing innovative and important work. In conjunction with the *Notre Dame Review*, the online companion to the printed magazine, the *nd[re]view*, engages readers as a community centered in literary rather than commercial concerns, a community we reach out to through critique and commentary as well as aesthetic experience." Estab. 1995. Circ. 2,000. Pays on publication. Publishes ms an average of 6 months after acceptance. Accepts queries by online submission form. Accepts simultaneous submissions. Responds in 4 or more months to mss. Sample copy: $6. Guidelines online.

Does not accept e-mail submissions. Only reads hardcopy submissions September through November and January through March.

FICTION "We're eclectic. Upcoming theme issues planned. List of upcoming themes or editorial calendar available for SASE." No genre fiction. **Buys 10 mss/year.** Submit complete ms via online submissions manager. Length: up to 3,000 words. **Pays $5-25.**

POETRY Submit 3-5 poems via online submissions manager. Buys 90 poems/year.

TIPS "Excellence is our sole criteria for selection, although we are especially interested in fiction and poetry that take on big issues."

$ ONE STORY

232 3rd St., #A108, Brooklyn NY 11215. **Website:** www.one-story.com. **Contact:** Maribeth Batcha, publisher. **100% freelance written.** "*One Story* is a literary magazine that contains, simply, 1 story. Approximately every 3-4 weeks, subscribers are sent *One Story* in the mail. *One Story* is artfully designed, lightweight, easy to carry, and ready to entertain on buses, in bed, in subways, in cars, in the park, in the bath, in the waiting rooms of doctor's offices, on the couch, or in line at the supermarket. Subscribers also have access to a website where they can learn more about *One Story* authors and hear about *One Story* readings and events. There is always time to read *One Story*." Estab. 2002. Circ. 3,500. Byline given. Pays on publication. Publishes ms an average of 3-6 months after acceptance. Editorial lead time 3-4 months. Accepts queries by online submission form. Accepts simultaneous submissions. Responds in 2-4 months to mss. Sample copy: $2.50 (back issue). Guidelines available online.

Reading period: September 1-May 31.

FICTION Needs short stories. *One Story* only accepts short stories. Do not send excerpts. Do not send more than 1 story at a time. **Buys 18 mss/year.** Send complete ms using online submission form. Length: 3,000-8,000 words. **Pays $500 and 25 contributor's copies.**

TIPS "*One Story* is looking for stories that are strong enough to stand alone. Therefore they must be very good. We want the best you can give."

$ OVERTIME

Blue Cubicle Press, LLC, P.O. Box 250382, Plano TX 75025. **E-mail:** overtime@workerswritejournal.com. **Website:** www.workerswritejournal.com/overtime.htm. **Contact:** David LaBounty, editor. **100% freelance written.** Quarterly saddle-stitched chapbook covering working-class literature. Estab. 2006. Circ. 500. Byline given. Pays on acceptance of ms. Publishes ms 6 months after acceptance. Accepts queries by mail, e-mail. Accepts simultaneous submissions. Responds in 1 week to queries; 1 month to mss. Sample copy and writer's guidelines online.

FICTION Needs adventure, condensed novels, ethnic, experimental, historical, humorous, mainstream, novel excerpts, short stories, slice-of-life vignettes, working-class literature. **Buys 4 mss/year.** Query; send complete ms. Length: 5,000-12,000 words. **Pays $35-50 and one-year print subscription.**

POETRY Will accept working-class poetry collections.

THE OXFORD AMERICAN

P.O. BOX 3235, Little Rock AR 72205. (501)374-0000. **Fax:** (501)374-0001. **E-mail:** info@oxfordamerican.org. **Website:** www.oxfordamerican.org. **Contact:** Eliza Borne, editor. Quarterly literary magazine from the South with a national audience. Circ. 55,000. Pays on publication. Accepts queries by online submission form. Accepts simultaneous submissions. Responds in 2-3 months or sooner to mss. Guidelines online.

"*The Oxford American* will consider only unpublished mss that are from and/or about the South. Especially interested in nonfiction from diverse perspectives. Considers excerpts from forthcoming books."

NONFICTION Needs general interest, how-to, humor, personal experience, travel, reporting, business. Query with SASE or send complete ms. Pays expenses of writers on assignment.

PHOTOS Uses photos for the cover and throughout issue. Also uses illustration, original art, and comics. Send photos. Reviews contact sheets, GIF/JPEG files, slides.

COLUMNS/DEPARTMENTS Odes, Travel, Politics, Business, Writing on Writing, Southerner Abroad, Reports, Literature.

FICTION Stories should be from or about the South. Send complete ms.

POETRY Poems should be from or about the South. Submit maximum 3-5 poems.

OXFORD MAGAZINE

Miami University, Oxford OH 45056. **E-mail:** oxmag@miamioh.edu. **Website:** www.oxfordmagazine.org. *Oxford Magazine*, published annually online in May, is open in terms of form, content, and subject matter. "Since our premiere in 1984, our magazine has received Pushcart Prizes for both fiction and poetry and has published authors such as Charles Baxter, William Stafford, Robert Pinsky, Stephen Dixon, Helena Maria Viramontes, Andre Dubus, and Stuart Dybek." Estab. 1984. Accepts queries by online submission form. Accepts simultaneous submissions. Responds in 6 months, starting in September.

Work published in *Oxford Magazine* has been included in the *Pushcart Prize* anthology. Does not read submissions July through August.

NONFICTION Needs essays, memoir, personal experience. Submit complete ms via online submissions manager. Length: 3,000-5,000 words. Pays expenses of writers on assignment.

FICTION Needs short stories. Submit complete ms via online submissions manager. Length: up to 3,000 words.

POETRY Submit 3-5 poems via online submissions manager.

OYEZ REVIEW

Roosevelt University, Dept. of Literature & Languages, 430 S. Michigan Ave., Chicago IL 60605. **E-mail:** oyezreview@roosevelt.edu. **Website:** oyezreview.wordpress.com. **100% freelance written.** Annual magazine of the Creative Writing Program at Roosevelt University, publishing fiction, creative nonfiction, poetry, and art. There are no restrictions on style, theme, or subject matter. Estab. 1965. Circ. 600 with an e-book available. Byline given. Publishes ms an average of 2-3 months after acceptance. Accepts queries by mail, online submission form. Responds by mid-December each year. Sample copies available by request, or using e-book retailers. Guidelines online.

Reading period is August 1-October 1. Each issue has 104 pages: 92 pages of text and an 8-page spread of 1 artist's work (in color or b&w). Work by the issue's featured artist also appears on the front and back cover, totaling 10 pieces. The journal has featured work from such writers as Charles Bukowski, James McManus, Carla Panciera, Michael Onofrey, Tim Foley, John N. Miller, Gary Fincke, and Barry Silesky, and visual artists Vivian Nunley, C. Taylor, Jennifer Troyer, and Frank Spidale. Accepts queries by e-mail.

NONFICTION Needs essays. Send complete ms via online submissions manager or postal mail. Length: up to 5,000 words. Pays expenses of writers on assignment.

PHOTOS Accepts b&w and color artwork. Do not send originals. Porfolio not required. Submit at least 20 images (selecting 10 images from 1 artist each year requires several to choose from). Reviews prints and slides; strongly prefers digital files through submissions portal. Offers no additional payment for photos accepted with ms. Accepts first North American serial rights; will not negotiate if unwilling to provide all rights.

FICTION "We publish short stories and flash fiction on their merit as contemporary literature rather than the category within the genre." Send complete ms via online submissions manager or postal mail. Length: up to 5,000 words. **Pays 2 contributor's copies.**

POETRY Needs avant-garde, free verse, traditional. Send up to 5 poems via online submissions manager or postal mail. Length: up to 10 pages total.

PANK

PANK, Department of Humanities, 1400 Townsend Dr., Houghton MI 49931-1200. **Website:** www.pankmagazine.com. **100% freelance written.** Annual literary magazine. "*PANK* Magazine fosters access to emerging and experimental poetry and prose, publishing the brightest and most promising writers for the most adventurous readers. To the end of the road, up country, a far shore, the edge of things, to a place of amalgamation and unplumbed depths, where the known is made and unmade, and where unimagined futures are born, a place inhabited by contradictions, a place of quirk and startling anomaly. *PANK*, no soft pink hands allowed." Estab. 2006. Circ. 1,000/print; 18,000/online. Publishes ms an average of 3-12 months after acceptance. Accepts queries by online submission form. Accepts simultaneous submissions. Guidelines available on website.

NONFICTION Needs essays, general interest, historical, humor, nostalgic, opinion. Send complete ms through online submissions manager. **Pays $20, a one-year subscription, and a *PANK* t-shirt.** Pays expenses of writers on assignment.

FICTION "Bright, new, energetic, passionate writing, writing that pushes our tender little buttons and gets us excited. Push our tender buttons, excite us, and we'll publish you." Send complete ms through online submissions manager. **Pays $20, a one-year subscription, and a *PANK* t-shirt.**

POETRY Submit through online submissions manager. **Pays $20, a one-year subscription, and a *PANK* t-shirt.**

TIPS "To read *PANK* is to know *PANK*. Or, read a lot within the literary magazine and small-press universe—there's plenty to choose from. Unfortunately, we see a lot of submissions from writers who have clearly read neither *PANK* nor much else. Serious writers are serious readers. Read. Seriously."

$$$ THE PARIS REVIEW

544 West 27th St., New York NY 10001. (212)343-1333. **E-mail:** queries@theparisreview.org. **Website:** www.theparisreview.org. **Contact:** Lorin Stein, editor; Robyn Creswell, poetry editor. Quarterly magazine. *The Paris Review* publishes "fiction and poetry of superlative quality, whatever the genre, style, or mode. Our contributors include prominent, as well as less well-known and previously unpublished writers. The Writers at Work interview series includes important contemporary writers discussing their own work and the craft of writing." Pays on publication. No kill fee. Accepts queries by mail. Accepts simultaneous submissions. Responds in 4 months to mss. Guidelines available online.

Address submissions to proper department. Do not make submissions via e-mail.

NONFICTION Pays expenses of writers on assignment.

FICTION Study the publication. Annual Plimpton Prize award of $10,000 given to a new voice published in the magazine. Recently published work by Ottessa Moshfegh, John Jeremiah Sullivan, and Lydia Davis. Send complete ms. Length: no limit. **Pays $1,000-3,000.**

POETRY **Contact:** Robyn Creswell, poetry editor. Submit no more than 6 poems at a time. Poetry can be sent to the poetry editor (please include a self-addressed, stamped envelope). **Poets receive $100/poem.**

$$$ PARNASSUS

Poetry in Review, Poetry in Review Foundation, 205 W. 89th St., #8F, New York NY 10024. (212)787-3569. **E-mail:** info@parnassus.com. **Website:** www.parnassusreview.com. **Contact:** Herbert Leibowitz, editor and publisher. Annual magazine covering poetry and criticism. "We now publish 1 double issue/year." *Parnassus: Poetry in Review* provides "a forum where poets, novelists, and critics of all persuasions can gather to review new books of poetry, including translations—international poetries have occupied center stage from our very first issue—with an amplitude and reflectiveness that Sunday book supplements and even the literary quarterlies could not afford. Our editorial philosophy is based on the assumption that reviewing is a complex art. Like a poem or a short story, a review essay requires imagination; scrupulous attention to rhythm, pacing, and supple syntax; space in which to build a persuasive, detailed argument; analytical precision and intuitive gambits; verbal play, wit, and metaphor. We welcome and vigorously seek out voices that break aesthetic molds and disturb xenophobic habits." Estab. 1972. Circ. 1,800. Byline given. Pays on publication. No kill fee. Publishes ms an average of 12-14 months after acceptance. Accepts queries by mail. Accepts simultaneous submissions. Responds in 2 months to mss. Sample copy: $15.

NONFICTION Needs essays, reviews. **Buys 30 mss/year.** Query with published clips. Length: 1,500-7,500 words. **Pays $200-1,000.** Pays expenses of writers on assignment.

POETRY Needs avant garde, free verse, traditional. Accepts most types of poetry. Buys 3-4 unsolicited poems/year.

TIPS "Be certain you have read the magazine and are aware of the editor's taste. Blind submissions are a waste of everybody's time. We'd like to see more poems that display intellectual acumen and curiosity about history, science, music, etc., and fewer trivial lyrical poems about the self, or critical prose that's academic and dull. Prose should sing."

$ THE PEDESTAL MAGAZINE

6815 Honors Court, Charlotte NC 28210. **E-mail:** pedmagazine@carolina.rr.com. **Website:** www.thepedestalmagazine.com. **Contact:** John Amen, editor in chief. Committed to promoting diversity and celebrating the voice of the individual. Estab. 2000. No kill fee. Accepts queries by online submission form. Accepts simultaneous submissions. Responds in 1-2 months to mss. Guidelines available online.

See website for reading periods for different forms. Member: CLMP.

NONFICTION Needs essays, interview, reviews. **Pays $40.**

PHOTOS Reviews JPEG, GIF files.

FICTION "We are receptive to all sorts of high-quality literary fiction. Genre fiction is encouraged as long as it crosses or comments upon its genre and is both character-driven and psychologically acute. We encourage submissions of short fiction, no more than 3 flash fiction pieces at a time. There is no need to query prior to submitting; please submit via online submissions manager—no e-mail to the editor." Needs adventure, ethnic, experimental, historical, horror, humorous, mainstream, mystery, romance, science fiction, works that don't fit into a specific category. **Buys 10-25 mss/year.** Length: up to 4,000 words for short stories; up to 1,000 words for flash fiction. **Pays 3¢/word.**

POETRY Open to a wide variety of poetry, ranging from the highly experimental to the traditionally formal. Submit all poems in 1 form. No need to query before submitting. Submit maximum 5 poems. No length restriction.

TIPS "If you send us your work, please wait for a response to your first submission before you submit again."

PHILADELPHIA STORIES

Fiction/Nonfiction/Art/Poetry of the Delaware Valley, 93 Old York Rd., Suite 1/#1-753, Jenkintown PA 19046. **E-mail:** info@philadelphiastories.org. **Website:** www.philadelphiastories.org. Editorial Director/Co-Publisher: Carla Spataro. **Contact:** Christine Weiser, executive director/co-publisher. *Philadelphia Stories*, published quarterly, publishes "fiction, poetry, creative nonfiction, and art written by authors living in, or originally from, Pennsylvania, Delaware, or New Jersey. *Philadelphia Stories* also hosts 2 national writing contests: The Marguerite McGlinn Short Story Contest ($2,500 first-place prize; $750 second-place prize; $500 third-place prize) and the Sandy Crimmins National Poetry Contest ($1,000 first-place prize, 3 $100 runner-up prizes). Visit our website for details." Literary magazine/journal: 8.5x11; 32 pages; 70# matte text, all 4-color paper; 70# matte text cover. Contains illustrations, photographs. Subscription: "We offer $20 memberships that include home delivery." Make checks payable to *Philadelphia Stories*. Member: CLMP. Estab. 2004. Circ. 5,000. Publishes ms 1-2 months after acceptance. Accepts queries by online submission form. Accepts simultaneous submissions. Responds in 6 months. Rarely comments on/critiques rejected mss. Sample copy: $5 and on website. Guidelines online.

NONFICTION Send complete ms with cover letter via online submission form only. Include estimated word count, list of publications, and affiliation to the Philadelphia area. Has published work by Katherine Hill, Jenny Lentz, Liz Abrams-Morley, Randall Brown, Justin St. Germain, Rachel Paston, Allison Alsup, and Mitchell Sommers. Length: up to 2,500 words; 1,000 words average. **Pays $25 honorarium from the Conrad Weiser Author Fund and 2 contributor's copies.** Pays expenses of writers on assignment.

FICTION Receives 45-80 mss/month. Accepts 3-4 mss/issue for print, additional 1-2 online; 12-16 mss/year for print, 4-8 online. Publishes 50% new writers/year. Needs experimental, mainstream, literary. "We will consider anything that is well written but are most inclined to publish literary or mainstream fiction. We are *not* particularly interested in most genres (science fiction, fantasy, romance, etc.)." Length: up to 5,000 words; 4,000 words average. Also publishes short shorts; average length: 800 words. **Pays $25 honorarium from the Conrad Weiser Author Fund and 2 contributor's copies.**

POETRY Submit 3 poems at a time. No previously published poems. Cover letter is preferred. Reads submissions year round. "Each poem is reviewed by a preliminary board that decides on a final list; the entire board discusses this list and chooses the mutual favorites for print and Web. We send a layout proof to check for print poems." Receives about 600 poems/year, accepts about 15%. Considers poetry by teens. Wants "polished, well-crafted poems." Does not want "first drafts." Length: 36 lines/poem.

TIPS "We look for exceptional, polished prose, a controlled voice, strong characters and place, and interesting subjects. Follow guidelines. We cannot stress this enough. Read every guideline carefully and thoroughly before sending anything out. Send out only polished material. We reject many quality pieces for various reasons; try not to take rejection personally. Just because your piece isn't right for one publication doesn't mean it's bad. Selection is an extremely subjective process."

PLANET: THE WELSH INTERNATIONALIST

Berw Ltd., P.O. Box 44, Aberystwyth Ceredigion SY23 3ZZ United Kingdom. 01970 622408. **E-mail:** admin@planetmagazine.org.uk. **E-mail:** submissions@planetmagazine.org.uk. **Website:** www.planetmagazine.org.uk. Administrative and Marketing Assistant: Lowri Angharad Pearson. **Contact:** Emily Trahair, editor. Quarterly journal. A literary/cultural/political journal centered on Welsh affairs but with a strong interest in minority cultures in Europe and elsewhere. *Planet: The Welsh Internationalist*, published quarterly, is a cultural magazine centered on Wales, but with broader interests in arts, sociology, politics, history, and science. *Planet* is 96 pages, A5, professionally printed, perfect-bound, with glossy colour card cover. Receives about 500 submissions/year, accepts about 5%. Press run is 1,000 (800 subscribers, about 10% libraries, 200 shelf sales). Estab. 1970. Circ. 900. Publishes ms 4-6 months after acceptance. Accepts queries by mail, e-mail, phone. Responds in 3 months. Single copy: £6.75; subscription: £22 (£40 overseas). Sample copy: £5. Guidelines online.

NONFICTION Needs essays, general interest, historical, humor, interview, personal experience, reviews, travel. Query. Subscriptions.

FICTION Would like to see more inventive, imaginative fiction that pays attention to language and experiments with form. No magical realism, horror, science fiction. Submit complete ms via mail or e-mail (with attachment). For postal submissions, no submissions returned unless accompanied by an SASE. Writers submitting from abroad should send at least 3 IRCs for return of typescript; 1 IRC for reply only. Length: 1,500-2,750 words. **Pays £50/1,000 words.**

POETRY Wants good poetry in a wide variety of styles. No limitations as to subject matter; length can be a problem. Has published poetry by Nigel Jenkins, Anne Stevenson, and Les Murray. Submit 4-6 poems via mail or e-mail (with attachment). For postal submissions, no submissions returned unless accompanied by an SASE. Writers submitting from abroad should send at least 3 IRCs for return of typescript; 1 IRC for reply only. **Pays £30/poem.**

TIPS "We do not look for fiction that necessarily has a 'Welsh' connection, which some writers assume from our title. We try to publish a broad range of fiction, and our main criterion is quality. Try to read copies of any magazine you submit to. Don't write out of the blue to a magazine which might be completely inappropriate for your work. Recognize that you are likely to have a high rejection rate, as magazines tend to favor writers from their own countries."

$ PLEIADES

Literature in Context, University of Central Missouri, Department of English, Martin 336, 415 E. Clark St., Warrensburg MO 64093. (660)543-4268. **E-mail:** clintoncrockettp@gmail.com (nonfiction inquiries); pnguyen@ucmo.edu (fiction inquiries); pleiadespoetryeditor@gmail.com (poetry inquiries). **Website:** www.pleiadesmag.com. **Contact:** Clinton Crockett Peters, nonfiction editor; Phong Nguyen, fiction editor; and Jenny Molberg, poetry editor. **100% freelance written.** "We publish contemporary fiction, poetry, interviews, literary essays, special-interest personal essays, and reviews for a general and literary audience from authors from around the world." Reads in the months of July for the summer issue and December for the winter issue. Estab. 1991. Circ. 3,000. Byline given. Pays on publication. No kill fee. Publishes ms an average of 9 months after acceptance. Editorial lead time 9 months. Accepts queries by mail. Accepts simultaneous submissions. Responds in 2 months to queries; in 1-4 months to mss. Sample copy for $5 (back issue); $6 (current issue). Guidelines online.

NONFICTION Needs book excerpts, essays, interview, reviews. "Nothing pedantic, slick, or shallow." **Buys 4-6 mss/year.** Send complete ms via online submission manager. Length: 2,000-4,000 words. **Pays $10 and contributor's copies.**

FICTION Reads fiction year-round. Needs ethnic, experimental, humorous, mainstream, magic realism. No science fiction, fantasy, confession, erotica. **Buys 16-20 mss/year.** Send complete ms via online submission manager. Length: 2,000-6,000 words. **Pays $10 and contributor's copies.**

POETRY Needs Wants avant-garde, free verse, haiku, light verse, traditional. Submit 3-5 poems via online submission manager. "Nothing didactic, pretentious, or overly sentimental." Buys 40-50 poems/year. **Pays $3/poem and contributor copies.**

TIPS "Submit only 1 genre at a time to appropriate editors. Show care for your material and your readers—submit quality work in a professional format. Cover art is solicited directly from artists. We accept queries for book reviews."

$$ PLOUGHSHARES

Emerson College, 120 Boylston St., Boston MA 02116. (617)824-3757. **E-mail:** pshares@pshares.org. **Website:** www.pshares.org. **Contact:** Ladette Randolph, editor-in-chief/executive director; Ellen Duffer, managing editor. *Ploughshares* publishes issues four times a year. 2 of these issues are guest-edited by different, prominent authors. A third issue, a mix of both prose and poetry, is edited by our staff editors. The fourth issue is a collection of longform work edited by our Editor-in-chief, Ladette Randolph; these stories and essays are first published as e-books known as Ploughshares Solos. Translations are welcome if permission has been granted. We accept electronic submissions—there is a $3 fee per submission, which is waived if you are a subscriber. Ploughshares is 200 pages, digest-sized. Receives about 11,000 poetry, fiction, and essay submissions/year. Reads submissions June 1-January 15 (postmark); hosts the Emerging Writer's Contest, for writers who have yet to publish a book-length work, March 1-May 15; mss submitted at all other times will be returned unread. A competitive and highly prestigious market. Rotating and guest editors make cracking the line-up even tougher, since it's difficult to know what is appropriate to send. Estab. 1971. Circ. 6,000. Pays on publication. Publishes ms an average of 6 months after acceptance. Accepts queries by mail, online submission form. Accepts simultaneous submissions. Responds in 3-5 months to mss. Sample copy: $14 for current issue, $7 for back issue; please inquire for shipping rates. Subscription: $30 domestic, $30 plus shipping (see website) foreign. Guidelines online.

NONFICTION Needs essays. Submit complete ms via online submissions form or by mail. Length: up to 6,000 words. **Pays $45/printed page ($90 minimum, $450 maximum); 2 contributor's copies; and one-year subscription.** Pays expenses of writers on assignment.

FICTION Has published work by ZZ Packer, Antonya Nelson, and Stuart Dybek. Submit via online submissions form or by mail. Length: up to 6,000 words **Pays $45/printed page ($90 minimum, $450 maximum); 2 contributor's copies; and one-year subscription.**

POETRY Submit up to 5 poems via online submissions form or by mail. Has published poetry by Donald Hall, Li-Young Lee, Robert Pinsky, Brenda Hillman, and Thylias Moss. **Pays $45/printed page ($90 minimum, $450 maximum); 2 contributor's copies; and one-year subscription.**

$$ POETRY

The Poetry Foundation, 61 W. Superior St., Chicago IL 60654. (312)787-7070. **Fax:** (312)787-6650. **E-mail:** editors@poetrymagazine.org. **Website:** www.poetrymagazine.org. **Contact:** Don Share, editor. **100% freelance written.** Monthly magazine. *Poetry*, published monthly by The Poetry Foundation, "has no special ms needs and no special requirements as to form: We examine in turn all work received and accept that which seems best." Has published poetry by the major voices of our time as well as new talent. *Poetry's* website offers featured poems, letters, reviews, interviews, essays, and web-exclusive features. *Poetry* is elegantly printed, flat-spined. Receives 150,000 submissions/year, accepts about 300-350. Press run is 16,000. Estab. 1912. Circ. 30,000. Byline given. Pays on publication. No kill fee. Publishes ms an average of 9 months after acceptance. Accepts queries by e-mail. Accepts simultaneous submissions. Responds within 8 months to mss and queries. Guidelines online.

NONFICTION Buys 14 mss/year. Query. No length requirements. **Pays $150/page.**

POETRY Publishes poetry all styles and subject matter. Submit up to 4 poems via Submittable. Reviews books of poetry, most solicited. Buys 180-250 poems/year. Length: up to 10 pages total. **Pays $10 line (minimum payment of $300).**

POETRYBAY

P.O. Box 114, Northport NY 11768. **E-mail:** poetrybay@aol.com. **E-mail:** info@poetrybay.com. **Website:** www.poetrybay.com. **Contact:** George Wallace, editor and publisher. *Poetrybay*, published semiannually online, seeks "to add to the body of great contemporary American poetry by presenting the work of established and emerging writers. Also, we consider essays and reviews." Has published poetry by Robert Bly, Yevgeny Yevtushenko, Marvin Bell, Diane Wakoski, Cornelius Eady, and William Heyen. Estab. 2000. Accepts queries by mail, e-mail. Accepts simultaneous submissions. Guidelines available online.

NONFICTION Needs essays, reviews. Query by e-mail.

POETRY Open to format, length, and style. Works previously published in magazine or online publications will not be considered. Submit 3-5 poems in the body of an e-mail, with name, a brief bio, and address, or submit poems via snail mail with a cover letter and SASE for reply.

$$ POETRY IRELAND REVIEW

Poetry Ireland, 11 Parnell Square E., Dublin 1 Ireland. +353(0)16789815. **E-mail:** publications@poetryireland.ie. **Website:** www.poetryireland.ie. 3 times a year covers poetry, reviews, and essays in book form. Estab. 1981. Circ. 2,000. Pays on publication. No kill fee. Accepts queries by mail. Accepts simultaneous submissions. Responds in 1 week to queries; 3 months to mss. Guidelines online.

POETRY Needs contemporary, lyric, avant-garde, free verse, haiku. Buys 120 poems/year. Submit maximum 6 poems. **Pays €40-75/submission.**

THE PRAIRIE JOURNAL

A Magazine of Canadian Literature, P.O. Box 68073, 28 Crowfoot Terrace NW, Calgary AB T3G 3N8 Canada. **E-mail:** editor@prairiejournal.org (queries only); prairiejournal@yahoo.com. **Website:** www.prairiejournal.org. **Contact:** Anne Burke, literary editor. **100% freelance written.** Semiannual magazine publishing quality poetry, short fiction, drama, literary criticism, reviews, bibliography, interviews, profiles, and artwork. "The audience is literary, university, library, scholarly, and creative readers/writers. We welcome newcomers and unsolicited submission of writing and artwork. In addition to the print issues, we publish online long poems, fiction, interviews, drama, and reviews." Estab. 1983. Circ. 650-750. Byline given. Pays on publication. No kill fee. Publishes ms an average of 4-6 months after acceptance. Editorial lead time 2-6 months. Accepts queries by mail. Responds in 2 weeks to queries; 2-6 months to mss. Sample copy: $5. Guidelines online.

NONFICTION Needs essays, humor, interview, profile, reviews, literary. No inspirational, news, religious, or travel. **Buys 25-40 mss/year.** Query with published clips. Length: 100-3,000 words. **Pays $50-100, plus contributor's copy.** Pays expenses of writers on assignment.

PHOTOS State availability. Offers additional payment for photos accepted with ms. Rights purchased is negotiable.

COLUMNS/DEPARTMENTS Reviews (books from small presses publishing poetry, short fiction, essays, and criticism), 200-1,000 words. **Buys 5 mss/year.** Query with published clips. **Pays $10-50.**

FICTION Needs mainstream. No genre: romance, horror, western—sagebrush or cowboys—erotic, science fiction, or mystery. **Buys 6 mss/year.** Send complete ms. No e-mail submissions. Length: 100-3,000 words. **Pays $10-75.**

POETRY Needs avant-garde, free verse, haiku. Seeks poetry "of any length; free verse, contemporary themes (feminist, nature, urban, nonpolitical), aesthetic value, a poet's poetry." Does not want to see "most rhymed verse, sentimentality, egotistical ravings. No cowboys or sage brush." Has published poetry by Liliane Welch, Cornelia Hoogland, Sheila Hyland, Zoe Lendale, and Chad Norman. Receives about 1,000 poems/year, accepts 10%. No heroic couplets or greeting-card verse. Buys 25-35 poems/year. Submit maximum 6-8 poems. Length: 3-50 lines. **Pays $5-50.**

TIPS "We publish many, many new writers and are always open to unsolicited submissions because we are 100% freelance. Do not send U.S. stamps; always use IRCs. We have poems, interviews, stories, and reviews online (query first)."

PRISM INTERNATIONAL

Dept. of Creative Writing, Buch E462, 1866 Main Mall, University of British Columbia, Vancouver BC V6T 1Z1 Canada. (604)822-2514. **Fax:** (604)822-3616. **E-mail:** prismcirculation@gmail.com. **Website:** www.prismmagazine.ca. **100% freelance written. Works with new/unpublished writers.** A quarterly international journal of contemporary writing—fiction, poetry, drama, creative nonfiction and translation. *PRISM international* is digest-sized, elegantly printed, flat-spined, with original colour artwork on a nylon card cover. Readership: public and university libraries, individual subscriptions, bookstores—a world-wide audience concerned with the contemporary in literature. "We have no thematic or stylistic allegiances: Excellence is our main criterion for acceptance of manuscripts." Receives 1,000 submissions/year, accepts about 80. Circulation is for 1,200 subscribers. Subscription: $35/year for Canadian subscriptions, $40/year for US subscriptions, $45/year for international. Sample: $13. Estab. 1959. Circ. 1,200. Pays on publication. No kill fee. Publishes ms an average of 4 months after acceptance. Accepts queries by mail, e-mail, online submission form. Accepts simultaneous submissions. Responds in 4 months to queries; 3-6 months to mss. Sample copy for $13, more info online. Guidelines online.

NONFICTION No tracts, or scholarly essays. **Prose pays $30/printed page, and 2 copies of issue.** Pays expenses of writers on assignment.

PHOTOS PRISM international buys photography for covers only. Sample copies available for $13 each; art guidelines free for SASE with first-class Canadian postage. Portfolio review not required. Buys first rights. "Image may also be used for promotional purposes related to the magazine." Pays on publication: $300 Canadian and 2 copies of magazine. Portfolio review not required. Buys first rights. "Image may also be used for promotional purposes related to the magazine." Pays on publication: $300 Canadian and 2 copies of magazine.

FICTION For Drama: one-acts/excerpts of no more than 1,500 words preferred. Also interested in seeing dramatic monologues. Needs experimental, traditional. "New writing that is contemporary and literary. Short stories and self-contained novel excerpts. Works of translation are eagerly sought and should be accompanied by a copy of the original. Would like to see more translations. No gothic, confession, religious, romance, pornography, or science fiction." **Buys 12-16 mss/year.** Send complete ms. Length: 25 pages maximum. **Pays $30/printed page, and 2 copies of issue.**

POETRY Needs avant-garde, traditional. Wants "fresh, distinctive poetry that shows an awareness of traditions old and new. We read everything." Considers poetry by children and teens. "Excellence is the only criterion." Has published poetry by Margaret Avison, Elizabeth Bachinsky, John Pass, Warren Heiti, Don McKay, Bill Bissett, and Stephanie Bolster. Submit maximum up to 6 poems. **Pays $40/printed page, and 2 copies of issue.**

TIPS "We are looking for new and exciting fiction. Excellence is still our No. 1 criterion. As well as poetry, imaginative nonfiction and fiction, we are especially open to translations of all kinds, very short fiction pieces and drama which work well on the page. Translations must come with a copy of the original language work."

QUEEN'S QUARTERLY

402D - Douglas Library, 93 University Ave., Queen's University, Kingston ON K7L 5v4 Canada. (613)533-2667. **E-mail:** queens.quarterly@queensu.ca. **Website:** www.queensu.ca/quarterly. **Contact:** Dr. Boris Castel, editor; Joan Harcourt, literary editor. **95% freelance written.** Quarterly literary magazine. *Queen's Quarterly* is "a general-interest intellectual review featuring articles on science, politics, humanities, arts and letters, extensive book reviews, and some poetry and fiction." Has published work by Gail Anderson-Dargatz, Tim Bowling, Emma Donohue, Viktor Carr, Mark Jarman, Rick Bowers, and Dennis Bock. Estab. 1893. Circ. 3,000. Byline given. Pays on publication. Sends galleys to author. Publishes ms on average 6-12 months after acceptance. Accepts queries by mail, e-mail. Responds in 2-3 months to queries; 1-2 months to mss. Sample copy: $6.50. U.S. Subscription: $20 for Canada, $25 for U.S./Int'l. Guidelines online.

NONFICTION Needs essays, general interest, photo feature, reviews. Send complete ms with SASE and/or IRC. No reply with insufficient postage. Length: up to 2,500 words. **"Payment to new writers will be determined at time of acceptance."** Pays expenses of writers on assignment.

FICTION Send complete ms with SASE and/or IRC. No reply with insufficient postage. Accepts 2 mss/issue; 8 mss/year. Publishes 5 new writers/year. Length: up to 2,500 words. **"Payment to new writers will be determined at time of acceptance."**

POETRY Receives about 400 submissions of poetry/year; accepts 40. Submissions can be sent on hard copy with SASE (no replies/returns for foreign submissions unless accompanied by an IRC) or by e-mail, and will be responded to by same. "We are especially interested in poetry by Canadian writers. Shorter poems preferred." Has published poetry by Evelyn Lau, Sue Nevill, and Raymond Souster. Each issue contains about 12 pages of poetry. Buys 25 poems/year. Submit maximum 6 poems. **Usually pays $50 (Canadian)/poem (but it varies), plus 2 contributor's copies.**

THE RAG

P.O. Box 17463, Portland OR 97217. **E-mail:** submissions@raglitmag.com; seth@raglitmag.com. **Website:** raglitmag.com. **Contact:** Seth Porter, managing editor; Dan Reilly, editor. **90% freelance written.** *The Rag* focuses on the grittier genres that tend to fall by the wayside at more traditional literary magazines. *The Rag*'s ultimate goal is to put the literary magazine back into the entertainment market while rekindling the social and cultural value short fiction once held in North American literature. Estab. 2011. Byline given. Pays prior to publication. Editorial lead time 1-2 months. Accepts queries by e-mail. Accepts simultaneous submissions. Responds in 1 month or less for queries; in 1-2 months for mss. Guidelines available online.

Fee to submit online ($3) is waived if you subscribe or purchase a single issue.

NONFICTION Pays expenses of writers on assignment.

PHOTOS Reviews GIF/JPEG files. Negotiates payment individually. Purchases one-time rights.

FICTION Accepts all styles and themes. Needs humorous, transgressive. **Buys 12 mss/year.** Send complete ms. Length: up to 10,000 words. **Pays 5¢/word, $250 average/story.**

FILLERS Length: 150-1,000 words. **Pays $20-100.**

TIPS "We like gritty material: material that is psychologically believable and that has some humor in it, dark or otherwise. We like subtle themes, original characters, and sharp wit."

RALEIGH REVIEW LITERARY & ARTS MAGAZINE

Box 6725, Raleigh NC 27628-6725. **E-mail:** info@raleighreview.org. **Website:** www.raleighreview.org. **Contact:** Rob Greene, editor; Landon Houle, fiction editor; Bryce Emley, poetry editor. **90% freelance written.** Semiannual literary magazine. "*Raleigh Review* is a national nonprofit magazine of poetry, short fiction (including flash), and art. We believe that great literature inspires empathy by allowing us to see the world through the eyes of our neighbors, whether across the street or across the globe. Our mission is to foster the creation and availability of accessible yet provocative contemporary literature. We look for work that is emotionally and intellectually complex." Estab. 2010. Pays on publication. Publishes ms 3-6 months after acceptance. Accepts queries by online submission form. Accepts simultaneous submissions. Responds typically in 1-3 months, though sometimes up to 3-6 months. "Poetry and fiction submissions through Submittable; no prior query required." Sample copy: $15 hardcopy or $4.95 on Kindle. "Sample work also online at website." Guidelines online.

NONFICTION Pays expenses of writers on assignment.

FICTION Needs confessions, ethnic, humorous, mainstream, novel excerpts, slice-of-life vignettes. "We prefer work that is physically grounded and accessible, though complex and rich in emotional or intellectual power. We delight in stories from unique voices and perspectives. Any fiction that is born from a relatively unknown place grabs our attention. We are not opposed to genre fiction, so long as it has real, human characters and is executed artfully." **Buys 10-15 mss/year.** Submit complete ms. Length: 250-7,500 words. "While we accept fiction up to 7,500 words, we are more likely to publish work in the 4,500- to 5,000-word range." **Pays $15 per accepted title.**

POETRY Needs free verse, traditional, lyric, narrative poems of experience. Submit up to 5 poems. "If you think your poems will make a perfect stranger's toes tingle, heart leap, or brain sizzle, then send them our way. We typically do not publish avant garde, experimental, or language poetry. We *do* like a poem that causes—for a wide audience—a visceral reaction to intellectually and emotionally rich material." Buys 30-40 poems/year. Submit maximum 5 poems. Length: open. **Pays $15 per accepted title.**

TIPS "Please be sure to read the guidelines and look at sample work on our website. Every piece is read for its intrinsic value, so new/emerging voices are often published alongside nationally recognized, award-winning authors."

RATTLE

Rattle Foundation, 12411 Ventura Blvd., Studio City CA 91604. (818)505-6777. **E-mail:** tim@rattle.com. **Website:** www.rattle.com. **Contact:** Timothy Green, editor. *Rattle* publishes unsolicited poetry and translations of poetry, quarterly in print and daily online. Estab. 1994. Circ. 10,000. Publication Accepts queries by mail, e-mail, online submission form. Accepts simultaneous submissions. Responds in 1-6 months. Guidelines online.

At Rattle, anything always goes. If a poem is accessible, interesting, moving, and memorable, if it makes you laugh or cry, then it's the kind of poem that rattles around inside you for years, and it's our kind of poem.

POETRY "We're looking for poems that move us, that might make us laugh or cry, or teach us something new. We like both free verse and traditional forms—we try to publish a representative mix of what we receive. We read a lot of poems, and only those that are unique, insightful, and musical stand out—regardless of style." Submit up to 4 poems via online submissions manager or postal mail. Buys 300 poems/year. Submit maximum 4 poems. **Pays $100/poem and a one-year subscription for print contributors; $50/poem for online contributors.**

THE RIALTO

P.O. Box 309, Aylsham, Norwich NR11 6LN England. **E-mail:** info@therialto.co.uk. **Website:** www.therialto.co.uk. **Contact:** Michael Mackmin, editor. *The Rialto*, published 3 times/year, seeks to publish the best new poems by established and beginning poets. Seeks excellence and originality. Has published poetry by Alice Fulton, Jenny Joseph, Les Murray, George Szirtes, Philip Gross, and Ruth Padel. Estab. 1984. Pays on publication. Publishes ms 5 months after acceptance. Accepts queries by mail, online submission form. Accepts simultaneous submissions. Responds in 3-4 months. Guidelines available online.

The Rialto is 64 pages, A4, with full-color cover. Receives about 12,000 poems/year; accepts about 1%. Press run is 1,500. Single copy: £8.50; subscription: £24 (prices listed are U.K.: for U.S. and Canada add £12 shipping charge). Make checks payable to *The Rialto*. Checks in sterling only. Online payment also available on website.

POETRY Submit up to 6 poems at a time via postal mail (with SASE) or online submissions manager. **Pays £20/poem.**

TIPS *The Rialto* also publishes occasional books and pamphlets. Please do not send book-length mss. Query first. Details available in magazine and on website. Before submitting, "you will probably have read many poems by many poets, both living and dead. You will probably have put aside each poem you write for at least 3 weeks before considering it afresh. You will have asked yourself, 'Does it work technically?'; checked the rhythm, the rhymes (if used), and checked that each word is fresh and meaningful in its context, not jaded and tired. You will hopefully have read *The Rialto*."

RIBBONS

Tanka Society of America Journal, 1470 Keoncrest Dr., Berkeley CA 94702. **E-mail:** drice2@comcast.net. **Website:** sites.google.com/site/tankasocietyofamerica/home. **Contact:** David Rice, editor; Susan Weaver, tanka prose editor. Published 3 times/year, *Ribbons* seeks and regularly prints the best tanka poetry being written in English, together with reviews, critical and historical essays, commentaries, and translations. Wants poetry that exemplifies the very best in English-language tanka, having a significant contribution to make to the short poem in English. All schools and approaches are welcome. Tanka should reflect contemporary life, issues, values, and experience, in descriptive, narrative, and lyrical modes. Does not want work that merely imitates the Japanese masters. Considers poetry by teens. Estab. 2000. Publishes ms 2 months after acceptance. Accepts queries by mail, e-mail. Respond in 1-3 months. Guidelines online.

Ribbons is 90-120 pages, 6x9 perfect-bound, with color cover and art. Receives about 2,000 poems/year, accepts about 20%. Press run is 300; 15 distributed free. Single copy: $10; subscription: $30. Make checks payable to Tanka Society of America, and contact Kathabela Wilson, secretary (e-mail: poetsonsite@gmail.com; 439 S. Catalina Avenue, #306, Pasadena, CA 91106.

NONFICTION Pays expenses of writers on assignment.

POETRY "*Ribbons* seeks fresh material of the highest standard to present to our readers. Any tanka with a sensibility that distinguishes the form will be considered. Therefore, we welcome different syllable counts, varying individual styles and techniques, and we're open to diverse yet appropriate subject material." Submit up to 10 tanka or 2 tanka prose piece by e-mail or postal mail. Deadlines: April 30 (spring/summer issue), August 31 (fall issue), and December 31 (winter issue). Length: 5 lines. Sequences of up to 30 total lines considered.

TIPS "Work by beginning as well as established English-language tanka poets is welcome; first-time contributors are encouraged to study the tanka form and contemporary examples before submitting. No particular school or style of tanka is preferred over another; our publications seek to showcase the full range of English-language tanka expression and subject matter through the work of new and established poets in the genre from around the world."

ROOM

West Coast Feminist Literary Magazine Society, P.O. Box 46160, Station D, Vancouver BC V6J 5G5 Canada. **E-mail:** contactus@roommagazine.com. **Website:** www.roommagazine.com. "*Room* is Canada's oldest feminist literary journal. Published quarterly by a collective based in Vancouver, *Room* showcases fiction, poetry, reviews, artwork, interviews, and profiles by writers and artists who identify as women or genderqueer. Many of our contributors are at the beginning of their writing careers, looking for an opportunity to get published for the first time. Some later go on to great acclaim. *Room* is a space where women can speak, connect, and showcase their creativity. Each quarter we publish original, thought-provoking works that reflect women's strength, sensuality, vulnerability, and wit." Estab. 1975. Circ. 1,400. Byline given. Pays on publication. Offers kill fee if work is accepted but cannot be published. Accepts queries by online submission form. Accepts simultaneous submissions. Responds in 6 months. Sample copy: $12 or online at website.

Room is digest-sized; contains illustrations, photos. Press run is 1,600 (900 subscribers, 50-100 libraries, 100-350 shelf sales).

NONFICTION **Buys 1-2 mss/year.** Submit complete ms via online submissions manager. Length: up to 3,500 words. **Pays $50-120 CAD, 2 contributor's copies, and a one-year subscription.** Pays expenses of writers on assignment.

FICTION Accepts literature that illustrates the female experience—short stories, creative nonfiction, poetry—by, for, and about women. Submit complete ms via online submissions manager. **Pays $50-120 CAD, 2 contributor's copies, and a one-year subscription.**

POETRY *Room* uses "poetry by women, including trans and genderqueer writers, written from a feminist perspective. Nothing simplistic, clichéd. We prefer to receive up to 5 poems at a time, so we can select a pair or group." Submit via online submissions manager. Pays $50-120 CAD, 2 contributor's copies, and a one-year subscription.

THE SAINT ANN'S REVIEW

Saint Ann's School, 129 Pierrepont St., Brooklyn NY 11201. Best to email. **Fax:** (718)522-2599. **E-mail:** sareview@saintannsny.org. **Website:** www.saintannsreview.com. **100% freelance written.** Semiannual literary magazine. "*The Saint Ann's Review* publishes short fiction, poetry, essays, drama, novel excerpts, reviews, translations, interviews, and experimental works." Estab. 2000. Circ. 2,000. Byline given. Pays on publication. No kill fee. Publishes ms an average of 4 months after acceptance. Submit seasonal material 4 months in advance. Accepts queries by mail, e-mail. Responds up to 4-6 months to mss. Sample copy: $8. Guidelines online.

We seek honed work that conveys a sense of its necessity.

NONFICTION Needs book excerpts, essays, historical, humor, interview, memoir, personal experience, photo feature, reviews. **Buys 10 mss/year.** Send complete ms. Length: 6,000 words for short essays; up 25 pages for excerpts. **Pays $50 and 2 contributor copies.**

PHOTOS Send photos. Reviews transparencies, prints, GIF/JPEG files, b&w art. Offers $50/contributor and 2 contributor copies. Buys one time rights.

COLUMNS/DEPARTMENTS Book reviews, 1,500 words. **Buys 10 mss/year.** Send complete ms by mail or online submissions manager. **Pays $50/contributor plus 2 contributor copies.**

FICTION Needs ethnic, experimental, fantasy, historical, humorous, mainstream, novel excerpts, short stories, slice-of-life vignettes, translations. **Buys 40 mss/year.** Guidelines online. Length: up to 6,000 words for short stories; up to 25 pages for excerpts. **Pays $50/contributor and 2 contributor copies.**

POETRY Needs avant-garde, free verse, haiku, light verse, traditional. Guidelines available online. Buys 30 poems/year. Submit maximum 5 poems. Length: up to 10 pages. **Pays $50/contributor and 2 contributor copies.**

THE SARANAC REVIEW

Dept. of English, SUNY Plattsburgh, 101 Broad St., Plattsburgh NY 12901. (518)564-2241. **Fax:** (518)564-2140. **E-mail:** saranacreview@plattsburgh.edu. **Website:** www.saranacreview.com. **Contact:** Aimee Baker, executive editor. "*The Saranac Review* is committed to dissolving boundaries of all kinds, seeking to publish a diverse array of emerging and established writers from Canada and the U.S. *The Saranac Review* aims to be a textual clearing in which a space is opened for cross-pollination between American and Canadian writers. In this way the magazine reflects the expansive, bright spirit of the etymology of its name, Saranac, meaning 'cluster of stars.' *The Saranac Review* is digest-sized, with color photo or painting on cover. Publishes both digital and print-on-demand versions. Has published Lawrence Raab, Jacob M. Appel, Marilyn Nelson, Tom Wayman, Colette Inez, Louise Warren, Brian Campbell, Gregory Pardlo, Myfanwy Collins, William Giraldi, Xu Xi, Julia Alvarez, and other fine emerging and established writers." Published annually. Estab. 2004. Pays on publication. Publishes ms 8 months-1 year after acceptance. Accepts simultaneous submissions. Responds in 4-6 months to mss. Sample copy: $4.95. Guidelines online.

NONFICTION Needs creative nonfiction, excerpts from memoirs, intergenre pieces. Special issues: "We lean towards nonfiction that approaches any topic from a unique perspective and can deliver the reader fresh insights. We do not want informational prose but rather penetrating, literary writing that informs." No academic essays or reviews. Submit complete ms via online submissions manager. **Pays $5/printed page.**

FICTION "We're looking for well-crafted fiction that demonstrates respect for and love of language. Fiction that makes us feel and think, that edifies without being didactic or self-indulgent and ultimately connects us to our sense of humanity." Needs ethnic, historical, short stories, Also accepts short dramatic pieces, one-act plays, and flash drama. No genre material (fantasy, sci-fi, etc.) or light verse. Submit complete ms via online submissions manager (Submittable). Length: up to 7,000 words. **Pays $5/printed page.**

POETRY "We're open to most forms and styles. We want poetry that, to paragraph Dickinson, blows the top of your head off, and that, in Williams's view, prevents us from dying miserably every day." Submit 3-5 poems via online submissions manager. Length: up to 4 pages but typically 20-25 lines. **Pays $10/published page.**

THE SEATTLE REVIEW

Box 354330, University of Washington, Seattle WA 98195. (206)543-2302. **E-mail:** seattlereview@gmail.com. **Website:** www.seattlereview.org. **Contact:** Andrew Feld, editor in chief. Semiannual magazine. *The Seattle Review* includes poetry, fiction, and creative nonfiction. Estab. 1978. Circ. 1,000. Pays on publication. Responds in 2-4 months to mss. Subscriptions: $20 for 3 issues, $32 for 5 issues. Back issue: $6. Guidelines available online.

The Seattle Review will only publish long works. Poetry must be 10 pages or longer, and prose must be 40 pages or longer. *The Seattle Review* is 8x10; 175-250 pages. Receives 200 unsolicited mss/month. Accepts 10-15 mss/issue; 20-30 mss/year. Publishes ms 6 months-1 year after acceptance.

NONFICTION Submit via online submissions manager. Length: at least 40 double-spaced pages. **Pays 2 contributor's copies and 1-year subscription.**

FICTION Only publishes novellas.literary. "Currently, we do not consider, use, or have a place for genre fiction (sci-fi, detective, etc.) or visual art." **Buys 4-10 mss/year.** Send complete ms. Accepts electronic submissions only. Length: at least 40 double-spaced pages. **Pays 2 contributor's copies and 1-year subscription.**

POETRY "We are looking for exceptional, risk-taking, intellectual, and imaginative poems between 10 and 30 pages in length." *The Seattle Review* will publish, and will only publish, long poems and novellas. The long poem can be a single long poem in its entirety, a self-contained excerpt from a book-length poem, or a unified sequence or series of poems. Accepts electronic submissions only. **Pays 2 contributor's copies and 1-year subscription.**

TIPS "Know what we publish; no genre fiction. Look at our magazine and decide if your work might be appreciated. Beginners do well in our magazine if they send clean, well-written manuscripts. We've published a lot of 'first stories' from all over the country and take pleasure in discovery."

SEQUESTRUM

Sequestrum Publishing, 1023 Garfield Ave., Ames IA 50014. **E-mail:** sequr.info@gmail.com. **Website:** www.sequestrum.org. **Contact:** R.M. Cooper, managing editor. Biweekly literary magazine in tabloid and online formats. All publications are paired with a unique visual component. Regularly holds contests and features well-known authors, as well as promising new and emerging voices. Estab. 2014. Circ. 2,500 monthly. Byline given. Pays on acceptance. 100% kill fee. Publishes ms 2-6 months after acceptance. Editorial lead time: 3 months. Accepts queries by online submission form. Accepts simultaneous submissions. Sample copy available for free online. Guidelines online.

NONFICTION Needs book excerpts, essays, expose, general interest, humor, inspirational, memoir, opinion, personal experience, photo feature, religious, travel, narrative, experimental. Special issues: Two contests yearly: Editor's Reprint Award (for previously published material) and New Writer Awards (for writers yet to publish a book-length manuscript). **Buys 3-5 mss/year.** Submit complete ms via online submissions manager. Length: 500-12,000 words. **Pays $10/article.** Pays expenses of writers on assignment.

PHOTOS Send photos with submission (GIF/JPEG files). Pays $10/photo. Buys one-time rights.

FICTION Needs adventure, confessions, ethnic, experimental, fantasy, horror, humorous, mainstream, mystery, novel excerpts, science fiction, short stories, suspense, western, slipstream. **Buys 20-36 mss/year.** Submit complete ms via online submissions manager. Length: 12,000 words max. **Pays $10-15/story.**

POETRY Needs avant-garde, free verse, light verse, traditional, cross-genre. Buys 20 poems/year. Submit maximum 4 poems. Length: 40 lines. **Pays $10/set of poems.**

TIPS "Reading a past issue goes a long way; there's little excuse not to. Our entire archive is available online to preview, and subscription rates are variable. Send your best, most interesting work. General submissions are always open, and we regularly hold contests and offer awards which are themed."

$$ THE SEWANEE REVIEW

735 University Ave, Sewanee TN 37383. (931)598-1185. **E-mail:** sewaneereview@sewanee.edu. **Website:** thesewaneereview.com. **Contact:** Adam Ross, editor. *The Sewanee Review* is America's oldest continuously published literary quarterly. Publishes original fiction, poetry, essays, and interviews. Does not accept submissions June 1-Aug 31. Estab. 1892. Byline given. Pays on publication. Accepts queries by online submission form. Accepts simultaneous submissions. Responds in 10 weeks Sample copy: $12. Guidelines online.

NONFICTION Submit complete ms via online submissions manager. Queries accepted but not preferred. Rarely accepts unsolicited reviews. Length: up to 10,000 words. **Pays $25/page, $300 minimum.**

FICTIONliterary, contemporary. **Buys 10-15 mss/year.** Submit complete ms via online submissions manager. Length: up to 10,000 words. **Pays $25/page, $300 minimum.**

POETRY Submit up to 6 poems via online submissions manager. Buys 25-30 poems/year. **Pays $3.33/line, $100 minimum.**

$ SHENANDOAH

Washington and Lee University, Lexington VA 24450. (540)458-8908. **E-mail:** shenandoah@wlu.edu. **Website:** shenandoahliterary.org. **Contact:** Beth Staples, editor. Semiannual digital-only literary journal. For nearly 70 years,*Shenandoah* has been publishing poems, stories, essays, and reviews which display passionate understanding, formal accomplishment, and serious mischief. As of 2018, under new editor Beth Staples, *Shenandoah* aims to to showcase a wide variety of voices and perspectives in terms of gender identity, race, ethnicity, class, age, ability, nationality, regionality, sexuality, and educational background. We're excited to consider short stories, essays, excerpts of novels in progress, poems, comics, and translations of all the above. Estab. 1950. Circ. 2,000. Byline given. Pays on publication. No kill fee. Publishes ms an average of 10 months after acceptance. Accepts queries by online submission form. Accepts simultaneous submissions. Responds in 8 weeks to mss. Sample copy online. Guidelines online.

NONFICTION Needs essays, interview, memoir, personal experience, photo feature. **Buys 10 mss/year.** Send complete ms via online submissions manager. Query for interviews. Length: up to 8,000 words. **Pays $100 per 1,000 words up to $500.**

FICTION Needs experimental, mainstream, novel excerpts, short stories. **Buys 10 mss/year.** Send complete ms via online submissions manager. Length: Up to 8,000 words. **Pays $100 for every 1,000 words up to $500.**

POETRY Submit 3-7 poems via online submissions manager. Submit maximum 50 poems. **Pays $100/poem.**

$$ THE SOUTHERN REVIEW

338 Johnston Hall, Louisiana State University, Baton Rouge LA 70803. (225)578-6453. **Fax:** (225)578-6461. **E-mail:** southernreview@lsu.edu. **Website:** thesouthernreview.org. **Contact:** Jessica Faust, coeditor and poetry editor; Sacha Idell, coeditor and prose editor. **100% freelance written. Works with a moderate number of new/unpublished writers each year; reads unsolicited mss.** Quarterly magazine with emphasis on contemporary literature in the U.S. and abroad. "*The Southern Review* is one of the nation's premiere literary journals. Hailed by *Time* as 'superior to any other journal in the English language,' we have made literary history since our founding in 1935. We publish a diverse array of fiction, nonfiction, poetry, and translation by the country's—and the world's—most respected contemporary writers." Unsolicited submissions period: September 1 through December 1 (prose); September 1 through January 1 (poetry and translation). All mss submitted outside the reading period will be recycled. Estab. 1935. Circ. 2,900. Byline given. Pays on publication. No kill fee. Publishes ms an average of 7 months after acceptance. Accepts queries by online submission form. Accepts simultaneous submissions. Responds in 6-11 months. Sample copy: $12. Guidelines online.

NONFICTION Needs essays, general interest, memoir, personal experience, travel. **Buys 12 mss/year.** Submit ms through online submission form. Length: up to 8,000 words. **Pays $50 first page and $25 for each subsequent printed page (max $200), 2 contrib-**

utor's copies, and 1-year subscription. Pays expenses of writers on assignment.

FICTION Wants short stories of lasting literary merit, with emphasis on style and technique; novel excerpts. "We emphasize style and substantial content. No fantasy or religious mss." **Buys 30 mss/year.** Submit 1 ms at a time through online submission form. "We rarely publish work that is longer than 8,000 words. We consider novel excerpts if they stand alone." Length: up to 8,000 words. **Pays $50 for first pages and $25 for each subsequent printed page (max $200), 2 contributor's copies, and 1-year subscription.**

POETRY Submit poems through online submission form. Buys 128 poems/year. Submit maximum 5 poems. **Pays $50 for first page and $25 for each subsequent printed page (max $200); 2 contributor's copies, and 1-year subscription.**

TIPS "Careful attention to craftsmanship and technique combined with a developed sense of the creation of story will always make us pay attention."

STAND MAGAZINE

School of English, University of Leeds, Leeds LS2 9JT United Kingdom. (44)(113)343-4794. **E-mail:** editors@standmagazine.org. **Website:** www.standmagazine.org. North American submissions: David Latané, *Stand Magazine*, Department of English, Virginia Commonwealth University, Richmond VA 23284. **Contact:** Jon Glover, managing editor. *Stand Magazine* is concerned with what happens when cultures and literatures meet, with translation in its many guises, with the mechanics of language, with the processes by which the policy receives or disables its cultural makers. *Stand* promotes debate of issues that are of radical concern to the intellectual community worldwide. U.S. submissions can be made through the Virginia office (see separate listing). Does not accept e-mail submissions except from subscribers. Estab. 1952. Publishes ms an average of 1 year-18 months after acceptance. Accepts queries by mail, e-mail. Guidelines online.

NONFICTION Query.

FICTION Needs short stories. Does not want genre fiction. Submit ms by mail. Include SASE if from U.K; email address otherwise Length: up to 3,000 words.

POETRY Submit 4-6 poems by mail. Include SASE.

STIRRING

Sundress Publications, **E-mail:** stirring@sundresspublications.com. **E-mail:** stirring.nonfiction@gmail.com; reviews@sundresspublications.com; stirring.fiction@gmail.com; stirring.poetry@gmail.com; stirring.artphoto@gmail.com. **Website:** www.stirringlit.com. **Contact:** Luci Brown and Andrew Koch, managing editors and poetry editors; Shaun Turner, fiction editor; Donna Vorreyer, reviews writer; Katie Culligan, reviews editor; Gabe Montesanti, nonfiction editor. "*Stirring* is one of the oldest continually published literary journals on the Web. *Stirring* is a quarterly literary magazine that publishes poetry, short fiction, creative nonfiction, reviews and visual art by established and emerging writers and artists." Estab. 1999. Circ. 2,500/month. Publishes ms 1-2 weeks after acceptance. Accepts queries by e-mail. Accepts simultaneous submissions. Responds in 3-6 months. Visit our website for guidelines.

NONFICTION Needs essays, memoir, reviews. Submit complete ms by e-mail to stirring.nonfiction@gmail.com. Send book reviews to reviews@sundresspublications.com. Length: up to 5,000 words for nonfiction; up to 700 words for book reviews.

FICTION Needs literary. Submit complete ms by e-mail to stirring.fiction@gmail.com Length: up to 5,000 words.

POETRY Needs free verse, formal. Has published poetry by Dorianne Laux, Sharon Olds, Patricia Smith, Chad Davidson. Receives about 2,500 poems/year, accepts 45-60. Submit up to 5 poems by e-mail to stirring.poetry@gmail.com. Doesn't want religious verse, children's verse, or previously published work. Buys 45-60 poems/year. Submit maximum 5 poems. Length: 1-6 pages (most often accepts half- to full-page poems).

STORYSOUTH

3302 MHRA Building, UNCG, Greensboro NC 27412 USA. **E-mail:** terry@storysouth.com; fiction@storysouth.com; poetry@storysouth.com;. **Website:** www.storysouth.com. **Contact:** Terry Kennedy, editor; Cynthia Nearman, creative nonfiction editor; Drew Perry, fiction editor; Luke Johnson, poetry editor. Covers experimental, literary, regional (South), poetry, translations. "*storySouth* accepts unsolicited submissions of fiction, poetry, and creative nonfiction during 2 submission periods annually: May 15-July 1 and November 15-January 1. Long pieces are encouraged. Please make only 1 submission in a single genre per reading period." Estab. 2001. Publishes ms 1 month after acceptance. Accepts queries by online submission form. Accepts simultaneous submissions. Responds in 2-6 months to mss. Guidelines available online.

NONFICTIONtranslations. Submit 1 essay via online submissions manager. No word-count limit.

FICTION Submit 1 story via online submissions manager. No word-count limit.

POETRY Needs experimental, literary, regional (South), translations. Submit 3-5 poems via online submissions manager. No word-count or line limit.

TIPS "What really makes a story stand out is a strong voice and a sense of urgency—a need for the reader to keep reading the story and not put it down until it is finished."

THE STRAND MAGAZINE

P.O. Box 1418, Birmingham MI 48012-1418. (800)300-6652. **E-mail:** strandmag@strandmag.com. **Website:** www.strandmag.com. Quarterly magazine covering mysteries, short stories, essays, book reviews. "After an absence of nearly half a century, the magazine known to millions for bringing Sir Arthur Conan Doyle's ingenious detective, Sherlock Holmes, to the world has once again appeared on the literary scene. First launched in 1891, *The Strand* included in its pages the works of some of the greatest writers of the 20th century: Agatha Christie, Dorothy Sayers, Margery Allingham, W. Somerset Maugham, Graham Greene, P.G. Wodehouse, H.G. Wells, Aldous Huxley, and many others. In 1950, economic difficulties in England caused a drop in circulation, which forced the magazine to cease publication." Estab. 1998. Circ. 50,000. Byline given. Pays on acceptance. No kill fee. Publishes ms an average of 4 months after acceptance. Accepts queries by e-mail. Accepts simultaneous submissions. Responds in 1 month to queries; in 4-10 months to mss. Sample copy: $10. Guidelines online.

NONFICTION Query.

FICTION "We are interested in mysteries, detective stories, tales of terror and the supernatural as well as short stories. Stories can be set in any time or place, provided they are well written, the plots interesting and well thought." Occasionally accepts short shorts and short novellas. Needs horror, humorous, mystery, suspense. "We are not interested in submissions with any sexual content." Submit complete ms by postal mail. Include SASE. No e-mail submissions. Length: 2,000-6,000 words. **Pays $25-150.**

TIPS "No gratuitous violence, sexual content, or explicit language, please."

SUBTERRAIN

Strong Words for a Polite Nation, P.O. Box 3008, MPO, Vancouver BC V6B 3X5 Canada. (604)876-8710. **Fax:** (604)879-2667. **E-mail:** subter@portal.ca. **Website:** www.subterrain.ca. **Contact:** Brian Kaufman, editor-in-chief; Jessica Key, editorial and marketing assistant. "*subTerrain* magazine is published 3 times/year from modest offices just off of Main Street in Vancouver, BC. We strive to produce a stimulating fusion of fiction, poetry, photography, and graphic illustration from uprising Canadian, U.S., and international writers and artists." Estab. 1988. Circ. 3,500. Pays on publication for first North American serial rights. Publishes ms 4-9 months after acceptance. Accepts queries by mail, online submission form. Accepts simultaneous submissions. Responds in 6-9 months to mss. Rarely comments on rejected mss. Sample copy: $5 (subterrain.ca/subscriptions). Guidelines online.

Magazine: 8.5×11; 80 pages; colour matte stock paper; colour matte cover stock; illustrations; photos. "Strong words for a polite nation."

NONFICTION Needs book excerpts, essays, expose, general interest, humor, memoir, nostalgic, opinion, personal experience, travel, literary essays, literary criticism. Send complete ms. Include disposable copy of the ms and SASE for reply only. Accepts multiple submissions. Receives 100 unsolicited mss/month. Accepts 4 mss/issue; 10-15 mss/year. **Pays $50/page for prose and $50/poem.** Pays expenses of writers on assignment.

PHOTOS Uses colour and/or b&w prints. *No unsolicited material.* "We are now featuring 1 artist (illustration or photography) per issue and are generally soliciting that work."

FICTION Receives 100 unsolicited mss/month. Accepts 4 mss/issue; 10-15 mss/year. Recently published work by J.O. Bruday, Lisa Pike, and Peter Babiak. Needs confessions, erotica, ethnic, experimental, humorous, novel excerpts, short stories, slice-of-life vignettes. Does not want genre fiction or children's fiction. Send complete ms. Include disposable copy of the ms and SASE for reply only. Accepts multiple submissions. 3,000 words max. **Pays $50/page for prose.**

POETRY "We accept poetry, but we no longer accept unsolicited submissions, except when related to 1 of our theme issues." "We no longer accept unsolicited poetry submissions (unless specifically related to one of our theme issues)." Poems unrelated to any theme issues may be submitted to the annual "General" issue (usually the summer/fall issue). **Pays $50/poem.**

TIPS "Read the magazine first. Get to know what kind of work we publish."

$$$ SUBTROPICS

University of Florida, P.O. Box 112075, 4008 Turlington Hall, Gainesville FL 32611-2075. **E-mail:** subtropics@english.ufl.edu. **Website:** www.english.ufl.edu/subtropics. **Contact:** David Leavitt, editor. **100% freelance written.** Magazine published twice/year through the University of Florida's English department. *Subtropics* seeks to publish the best literary fiction, essays, and poetry being written today, both by established and emerging authors. Will consider works of fiction of any length, from short shorts to novellas and self-contained novel excerpts. Gives the same latitude to essays. Appreciates work in translation and, from time to time, republishes important and compelling stories, essays, and poems that have lapsed out of print by writers no longer living. Member: CLMP. Estab. 2005. Circ. 1,500. Byline given. Pays on acceptance for prose; pays on publication of the issue preceding the issue in which the author's work will appear for poetry. Publishes ms an average of 6 months after acceptance. Accepts simultaneous submissions. Responds in 1 month to queries and mss. Rarely comments on/critiques rejected mss Sample copy: $12.95. Guidelines online.

Literary magazine/journal: 9x6, 160 pages. Includes photographs. Submissions accepted from September 1-April 15.

NONFICTION No book reviews. **Buys 4-5 mss/year.** Send complete ms via online submissions manager. Length: up to 15,000 words. Average length: 5,000 words. **Pays $1,000.**

FICTION Does not read May 1-August 31. Agented fiction 33%. **Publishes 1-2 new writers/year.** Has published John Barth, Ariel Dorfman, Tony D'Souza, Allan Gurganus, Frances Hwang, Kuzhali Manickavel, Eileen Pollack, Padgett Powell, Nancy Reisman, Jarret Rosenblatt, Joanna Scott, and Olga Slavnikova. No genre fiction. **Buys 10-12 mss/year.** Submit complete ms via online submissions manager. Length: up to 15,000 words. Average length: 5,000 words. Average length of short shorts: 400 words. **Pays $500 for short shorts; $1,000 for full stories; 2 contributor's copies.**

POETRY Submit up to 4 poems via online submissions manager. Buys 50 poems/year. **Pays $100 per poem.**

TIPS "We publish longer works of fiction, including novellas and excerpts from forthcoming novels. Each issue includes a short-short story of about 250 words on the back cover. We are also interested in publishing works in translation for the magazine's English-speaking audience."

SYCAMORE REVIEW

Purdue University Department of English, 500 Oval Dr., West Lafayette IN 47907. (765) 494-3783. **Fax:** (765) 494-3780. **E-mail:** sycamore@purdue.edu. **Website:** www.sycamorereview.com. **Contact:** Anthony Sutton, editor in chief; Bess Cooley, managing editor. Semiannual magazine publishing poetry, fiction and nonfiction, books reviews, and art. *Sycamore Review* is Purdue University's internationally acclaimed literary journal, affiliated with Purdue's College of Liberal Arts and the Dept. of English. Strives to publish the best writing by new and established writers. Looks for well-crafted and engaging work, works that illuminate our lives in the collective human search for meaning. Would like to publish more work that takes a reflective look at national identity and how we are perceived by the world. Looks for diversity of voice, pluralistic worldviews, and political and social context. No kill fee. Accepts queries by online submission form. Accepts simultaneous submissions.

Reading period: September 1-March 31.

NONFICTION Needs essays, humor. No outside interviews, previously published work (except translations). No scholarly articles or journalistic pieces. Submit complete ms via online submissions manager. No mail or e-mail submissions. **Pays in contributor copies and $50/nonfiction piece.** Pays expenses of writers on assignment.

FICTION No genre fiction. Needs experimental, humorous, mainstream. Submit complete ms via online submissions manager. **Pays in contributor's copies and $50/short story.**

POETRY Submi via online submissions manager. Does not publish creative work by any student currently attending Purdue University. Former students should wait 1 year before submitting. **Pays $25/poem.**

TIPS "We look for originality, brevity, significance, strong dialogue, and vivid detail. We sponsor the Wabash Prize for Poetry (deadline: December 1) and Fiction (deadline: April 17), $1,000 award for each. All contest submissions will be considered for regular inclusion in the *Sycamore Review*."

TAKAHĒ

P.O. Box 13-335, Christchurch 8141 New Zealand. **E-mail:** admin@takahe.org.nz. **E-mail:** essays@takahe.org.nz; fiction@takahe.org.nz; poetry@takahe.org.nz. **Website:** www.takahe.org.nz. **Contact:** Jane Seaford and Rachel Smith, fiction editors. *Takahē* magazine is a New Zealand-based literary and arts magazine that appears 3 times/year with a mix of print and online issues. It publishes short stories, poetry, and art by established and emerging writers and artists as well as essays, interviews, and book reviews (by invitation) in these related areas. The Takahē Collective Trust is a nonprofit organization that aims to support emerging and published writers, poets, artists, and cultural commentators. Byline given. Pays on publication. Accepts queries by e-mail. Responds in 4 months. Guidelines online.

NONFICTION Needs essays, reviews, Preference will be given to essays, creative nonfiction, and works of cultural criticism that critically engage with or analyze culture or cultural practice in New Zealand and the South Pacific. E-mail submissions are preferred (essays@takahe.org.nz). Overseas submissions are only accepted by e-mail. Length: 1,000-2,500 words. **Pays small honorarium.**

FICTION "We look for stories that have something special about them: an original idea, a new perspective, an interesting narrative style or use of language, an ability to evoke character and/or atmosphere. Above all, we like some depth, an extra layer of meaning, an insight—something more than just an anecdote or a straightforward narration of events." Needs short stories. E-mail submissions are preferred (fiction@takahe.org.nz). Overseas submissions are only accepted by e-mail. Length: 1,500-3,000 words, "Stories up to 5,000 words may be considered for publication in the online magazine only." **Pays small honorarium.**

POETRY Email submissions preferred (poetry@takahe.org.nz). Overseas submissions are only accepted by e-mail. Accepts up to 4 poems per submission and no more than 3 submissions a year. "Please be aware that we publish only a handful of overseas poets each year." Long work (multiple pages) is unlikely to be accepted. **Pays small honorarium.**

TIPS "Editorials, book reviews, artwork, and literary commentaries are by invitation only."

TAMPA REVIEW

University of Tampa Press, 401 W. Kennedy Blvd., Tampa FL 33606. (813)253-6266. **Fax:** (813)258-7593. **E-mail:** utpress@ut.edu. **Website:** www.ut.edu/tampareview. **Contact:** Richard Mathews, editor; Daniel Dooghan, nonfiction editor; Shane Hinton and Yuly Restrepo, fiction editors; Geoff Bouvier and Elizabeth Winston, poetry editors. Semiannual magazine published in hardback format. An international literary journal publishing art and literature from Florida and Tampa Bay as well as new work and translations from throughout the world. "We no longer accept paper submissions. Please submit all work via the online submission manager. You will find it on our website under the link titled 'How to Submit.'" Estab. 1988. Circ. 700. Byline given. Pays on publication. No kill fee. Publishes ms an average of 10 months after acceptance. Editorial lead time 18 months. Accepts queries by mail, e-mail. Accepts simultaneous submissions. Responds in 3-4 months to mss. Sample copy: $12. Guidelines online.

NONFICTION Contact: Daniel Dooghan, nonfiction editor. Needs essays, general interest, personal experience, creative nonfiction. No how-to articles, fads, journalistic reprise, etc. **Buys 6 mss/year.** Send complete ms via online submissions manager. We no longer accept submissions by mail. Length: up to 5,000 words. **Pays $10/printed page, 1 contributor's copy, and offers 40% discount on additional copies.** Pays expenses of writers on assignment.

PHOTOS State availability. Captions, identification of subjects required. Reviews contact sheets, negatives, transparencies, prints, digital files. Offers $10/photo. Buys one-time rights.

FICTION Contact: Yuly Restrepo and Andrew Plattner, fiction editors. Needs ethnic, experimental, fantasy, historical, mainstream, Literary. "We are far more interested in quality than in genre. Nothing sentimental as opposed to genuinely moving, nor self-conscious style at the expense of human truth." **Buys 6 mss/year.** Send complete ms via online submissions manager. We no longer accept submissions by mail. Length: up to 5,000 words. **Pays $10/printed**

page, 1 contributor's copy, and offers 40% discount on additional copies.

POETRY Contact: Geoff Bouvier and Elizabeth Winston, poetry editors. Needs avant-garde, free verse, haiku, light verse, traditional. No greeting card verse, hackneyed, sing-song, rhyme-for-the-sake-of-rhyme. Buys 45 poems/year. Submit maximum 6 poems. Length: 2-225 lines. **Pays $10/printed page, 1 contributor's copy, and offers 40% discount on additional copies.**

TIPS "Send a clear cover letter stating previous experience or background. Our editorial staff considers submissions between September and December for publication in the following year."

TEXAS POETRY CALENDAR

Kallisto Gaia Press, Kallisto Gaia Press, PO Box 220, Davilla TX 76523-0220. (254)654-7205. **E-mail:** tony@kallistogaiapress.org. **E-mail:** kallistogaiapress.submittable.com/submit. **Website:** www.kallistogaiapress.org. **Contact:** Tony Burnett, managing editor. *Texas Poetry Calendar*, published annually in July, features a "week-by-week calendar side-by-side with poems with a Texas connection." Wants "a wide variety of styles, voices, and forms, including rhyme, though a Texas connection is preferred. Humor is welcome! Poetry only!" Does not want "children's poetry, erotic poetry, profanity, obscure poems, previously published work, or poems over 35 lines." *Texas Poetry Calendar* is about 144 pages, digest-sized, offset-printed, spiral-bound, with full-color cardstock cover. Receives about 600 poems/year, accepts about 80-85. Press run is around 600. Accepted work receives monetary compensation. Reads submissions December 1-February 20. Estab. 1998. Circ. 375+. Byline given. Pays on publication. Publishes 3-6 months after acceptance. Accepts queries by e-mail, online submission form. Sample copy: $14.95 plus $3 shipping. Make checks payable to Kallisto Gaia Press.

POETRY Contact: Tony Burnett. Submit 3 poems through Submittable: kallistogaiapress.submittable.com/submit. No fax, e-mail, or snail mail submissions; only electronic submissions via Submittable. Cover letter is required. "Include a short bio (less than100 words) and poem titles in cover letter. Also include e-mail address and phone number. Do not include poet's name on the poems themselves!" Never comments on rejected poems, but nominates poems for Pushcart Prizes each year. Deadline: January 15. Does not want children's, epic, erotica. Buys 85-90 poems/year. Submit maximum 3 poems. Length: up to 35 lines/poem, including spaces and title. **Pays $20 per acceptance.**

THEMA

Thema Literary Society, P.O. Box 8747, Metairie LA 70011-8747. **E-mail:** thema@cox.net. **E-mail:** For writers living outside the U.S. **Website:** thema literarysociety.com. **Contact:** Virginia Howard, editor; Gail Howard, poetry editor. **100% freelance written.** "*THEMA* is designed to stimulate creative thinking by challenging writers with unusual 'themes, such as "The Critter in the Attic' and 'Six before Eighty.' Appeals to writers, teachers of creative writing, artists, photographers, and general reading audience." *THEMA* is 100 pages, digest-sized professionally printed, with glossy card cover. Receives about 400 poems/year, accepts about 8%. Press run is 300 (180 subscribers, 30 libraries). Subscription: $30 U.S./$40 foreign. Has published poetry by Rosalie Calabrese, Deborah H. Doolittle, David Subacchi, and Wally Swist. Has published fiction/nonfiction by Virginia Butler, Madonna Dries Christensen, Tony Concannon, Diane Jackman, and Margaret Nelson. Has published photographs by Kathleen Gunton, Stanley Horowitz, and John McCluskey. Estab. 1988. Byline given. Pays on acceptance. No kill fee. Publishes ms, on average, within 6 months after acceptance. Accepts queries by mail, e-mail. Accepts simultaneous submissions. Responds in 1 week to queries; 5 months to mss (after deadline for submission on given theme). Sample $15 U.S./$25 foreign. Upcoming themes and guidelines available in magazine, for SASE, by e-mail, or on website.

NONFICTION Contact: Virginia Howard, editor. Needs book excerpts, essays, historical, humor, memoir, nostalgic, personal experience. Special issues: Nonfiction must relate to one of the upcoming themes. No salacious subject matter. Length: 300-6,000 words (1-20 double-spaced pages). **Pays $10 for under 1,000 words; $25 for articles over 1,000 words.**

PHOTOS Contact: Virginia Howard, editor. Submitted photograph must relate to one of the upcoming themes. high resolution; portrait orientation. Payment: $10 for interior black-and-white photo; $25 for full-color cover photo. Acquires one-time rights only.

FICTION Contact: Virginia Howard, editor. All stories must relate to one of *THEMA*'s upcoming themes (**indicate the target theme on submission of manuscript**). See website for themes. Needs adventure, ethnic, experimental, fantasy, historical, humorous, mainstream, mystery, religious, science fiction, short stories, slice-of-life vignettes, suspense, Fiction **must** relate to a target theme. No erotica. Send complete ms with SASE, cover letter; include "name and address, brief introduction, **specifying the intended target issue for the mss.**" SASE. Accepts simultaneous, multiple submissions, and reprints. Does not accept e-mailed submissions except from non-USA addresses. Length: 300-6,000 words (1-20 double-spaced pages). **Payment: $10 for under 1,000 words; $25 for stories over 1,000 words, plus one contributor copy.**

POETRY **Contact:** Gail Howard, poetry editor. Needs All poetry must relate to one of *THEMA*'s upcoming themes (**indicate the target theme on submission of manuscript**). See website for themes. Submit up to 3 poems at a time. Include SASE. All submissions should be typewritten on standard 8$^1{}_2$x11 paper. Submissions are accepted all year, but evaluated after specified deadlines. **Specify target theme.** Editor comments on submissions. Each issue is based on an unusual premise. Please send SASE for guidelines before submitting poetry to find out the upcoming themes. Does not want scatologic language or explicit love poetry. Buys 24 published out of 250 submitted poems/year. Submit maximum 3 poems. Length: 1-3 pages. **Payment: $10/poem and 1 contributor's copy.**

$$ THE THREEPENNY REVIEW

P.O. Box 9131, Berkeley CA 94709. (510)849-4545. **E-mail:** wlesser@threepennyreview.com. **Website:** www.threepennyreview.com. **Contact:** Wendy Lesser, editor. **100% freelance written. Works with small number of new/unpublished writers each year.** Quarterly tabloid. "We are a general-interest, national literary magazine with coverage of politics, the visual arts, and the performing arts." Reading period: January 1-June 30. Estab. 1980. Circ. 6,000-9,000. Byline given. Pays on acceptance. Publishes ms an average of 1 year after acceptance. Responds in 2 days to 2 months Sample copy: $12, or online. Guidelines online.

NONFICTION Needs essays, historical, memoir, personal experience, reviews, book, film, theater, dance, music, and art reviews. **Buys 40 mss/year.** Send complete ms. Length: 1,500-4,000 words. **Pays $400.**

FICTION No fragmentary, sentimental fiction. **Buys 8 mss/year.** Send complete ms. Length: 800-4,000 words. **Pays $400.**

POETRY Needs free verse, traditional. No poems without capital letters or poems without a discernible subject. Buys 30 poems/year. Submit maximum 5 poems. Length: up to 100 lines/poem. **Pays $200.**

TIPS "Nonfiction (political articles, memoirs, reviews) is most open to freelancers."

$$$ TIN HOUSE

McCormack Communications, P.O. Box 10500, Portland OR 97296. (503)219-0622. **E-mail:** info@tinhouse.com. **Website:** www.tinhouse.com. **Contact:** Cheston Knapp, managing editor; Holly MacArthur, founding editor. **90% freelance written.** "We are a general-interest literary quarterly. Our watchword is quality. Our audience includes people interested in literature in all its aspects, from the mundane to the exalted." Estab. 1999. Circ. 11,000. Byline given. Pays on publication. No kill fee. Publishes ms an average of 6 months after acceptance. Editorial lead time 6 months. Submit seasonal material 6 months in advance. Accepts queries by mail, online submission form. Accepts simultaneous submissions. Responds in 6 weeks to queries; in 4 months to mss. Sample copy: $15. Guidelines online.

Reading period: September 1-May 31.

NONFICTION Needs book excerpts, essays, interview, personal experience. Special issues: Check website for upcoming theme issues. Submit via online submissions manager or postal mail. Include cover letter with word count. Length: up to 10,000 words. **Pays $50-800 for assigned articles. Pays $50-500 for unsolicited articles.** Pays expenses of writers on assignment.

FICTION Needs experimental. Submit via online submissions manager or postal mail. Include cover letter with word count. Length up to 10,000 words. **Pays $200-800.**

POETRY Needs avant-garde, free verse, traditional. Submit via online submissions manager or postal mail. Include cover letter. Submit maximum 5 poems. **Pays $50-150.**

TRIQUARTERLY

School of Professional Studies, Northwestern University, 339 E. Chicago Ave., Chicago IL 60611. **E-mail:**

triquarterly@northwestern.edu. **Website:** www.triquarterly.org. **Contact:** Carrie Muehle, managing editor. "*TriQuarterly*, the literary magazine of Northwestern University, welcomes submissions of fiction, creative nonfiction, poetry, short drama, and hybrid work. We also welcome short-short prose pieces." Reading period: November 15-May 1. Estab. 1964. Accepts queries by online submission form. Accepts simultaneous submissions.

NONFICTION Submit complete ms via online submissions manager. Length: up to 5,000 words. **Pays honoraria.** Pays expenses of writers on assignment.

FICTION Submit complete ms via online submissions manager. Length: up to 5,000 words. **Pays honoraria.**

POETRY Submit up to 6 poems via online submissions manager. **Pays honoraria.**

TIPS "We are especially interested in work that embraces the world and continues, however subtly, the ongoing global conversation about culture and society that *TriQuarterly* pursued from its beginning in 1964."

TULANE REVIEW

Tulane University, Suite G08A Lavin-Bernick Center, Tulane University, New Orleans LA 70118. **E-mail:** litsoc@tulane.edu. **Website:** www.tulane.edu/~litsoc/index.html. *Tulane Review*, published biannually, is a national literary journal seeking quality submissions of prose, poetry, and art. Estab. 1988. Accepts simultaneous submissions. Single copy: $8; subscription: $15. Make checks payable to *Tulane Review*. Guidelines available online.

Tulane Review is the recipient of an AWP Literary Magazine Design Award. *Tulane Review* is 70 pages, 7x9, perfect-bound, with 100# cover with full-color artwork.

NONFICTION Submit via online submissions manager. Include a brief biography, an e-mail address, and a return address in cover letter. Length: up to 4,000 words. **Pays 2 contributor's copies.** Pays expenses of writers on assignment.

FICTION Submit via online submissions manager only. Include a brief biography, an e-mail address, and a return address in cover letter. Length: up to 4,000 words. **Pays 2 contributor's copies.**

POETRY Considers all types of poetry. Wants imaginative poems with bold, inventive images. Receives about 1,200 poems/year, accepts about 50 per issue. Has published poetry by Tom Chandler, Ace Boggess, Carol Hamilton, and Brady Rhoades. Submit up to 5 poems via online submissions manager. No longer accepts paper and e-mail submissions. Submit maximum 5 poems. **Pays 2 contributor's copies.**

UPSTREET

Ledgetop Publishing, P.O. Box 105, Richmond MA 01254-0105. (413)441-9702. **E-mail:** editor@upstreet-mag.org. **Website:** www.upstreet-mag.org. **Contact:** Vivian Dorsel, Founding Editor/Publisher. **95% freelance written.** Annual magazine covering literary fiction, nonfiction and poetry; author interview in each issue. Estab. 2005. Circ. 4,000. Byline given. Pays on publication. Publishes ms an average of 6 months after acceptance. Editorial lead time 6 months. Accepts queries by online submission form. Accepts simultaneous submissions. Responds in 2 weeks to queries; 6 months to mss. Sample copy for $12.00, plus shipping. Guidelines online and in each issue.

NONFICTION Contact: Richard Farrell, creative nonfiction editor. Needs book excerpts, essays, memoir, personal experience, literary, personal essay/memoir, lyric essay. Does not want journalism, religious, technical, anything but literary nonfiction. **Buys 8 mss/year.** Send complete ms. Length: 5,000 words. **Pays $50-250.**

FICTION Contact: Joyce A. Griffin, fiction editor. Needs experimental, mainstream, novel excerpts, short stories, quality literary fiction. Does not want run-of-the-mill genre, children's, anything but literary. **Buys 12 mss/year.** Send complete ms. Length: 5,000 words. **Pays $50-250.**

POETRY Contact: Frances Richey, poetry editor. Needs avant-garde, free verse, traditional. Quality is only criterion. Does not consider unsolicited poetry. Buys 20-25 poems/year. Submit maximum 3 poems. **Pays $50-150.**

TIPS "Get sample copy, submit electronically, and follow guidelines."

VALLUM: CONTEMPORARY POETRY

5038 Sherbrooke West, P.O. Box 23077, CP Vendome, Montreal QC H4A 1T0 Canada. **E-mail:** info@vallummag.com; editors@vallummag.com. **Website:** www.vallummag.com. **Contact:** Joshua Auerbach and Eleni Zisimatos, editors. Poetry/fine arts magazine published twice/year. Publishes exciting interplay of poets and artists. Content for magazine is selected according to themes listed on website. Material is not filed but is returned upon request by SASE. E-mail response is preferred. Seeking exciting, unpublished, traditional or avant-garde poetry that reflects contemporary experience. *Vallum* is 100 pages, digest sized (7x8½), digitally printed, perfect-bound, with color images on coated stock cover. Includes ads. Single copy: $12 CDN; subscription: $20/year CDN; $24 U.S. (shipping included). Make checks payable to *Vallum*. Estab. 2000. Pays on publication. Sample copy online. Guidelines online.

NONFICTIONAlso publishes reviews, interviews, essays and letters to the editor. Please send queries to editors@vallummag.com before submitting. **Pays $85 for accepted reviews or essays on poetry.** Pays expenses of writers on assignment.

POETRY **Pays honorarium for accepted poems.**

VERANDAH LITERARY & ART JOURNAL

Faculty of Arts, Deakin University, 221 Burwood Hwy., Burwood VIC 3125 Australia. (614)2381-1048. **E-mail:** verandah@deakin.edu.au. **Website:** verandahjournal.wordpress.com. **Contact:** Verandah 34. *Verandah*, published annually, is a high-quality literary and art journal edited by professional writing students. It aims to give voice to new and innovative writers and artists. Estab. 1985. Accepts queries by e-mail, phone. Accepts simultaneous submissions. Sample: $20 AUD. Guidelines online.

Submission period: April 1 through June 30. Has published work by Margaret Atwood, Christos Tsiolka, Dorothy Porter, Seamus Heaney, Les Murray, Ed Burger, and John Muk Muk Burke. *Verandah* is a print journal roughly pages, professionally printed often on glossy stock, flat-spined, with full-color glossy card cover.

NONFICTION Submit by e-mail. Do not submit work without the required submission form (available on website). Reads submissions by June 30 deadline. Maximum 2,500 words. **Pays 1 contributor's copy, "with prizes awarded accordingly." Aims to pay ~$30 per piece.** Pays expenses of writers on assignment.

FICTION Submit via Submittable, see our wordpress website for information www.verandahjournal.wordpress.com. Reads submissions by June 30 deadline. Maximum 2,500 words. **Pays 1 contributor's copy, "with prizes awarded accordingly." Aims to pay ~$30 per piece this year.**

POETRY Submit via Submittable, see website for instructions. Reads submissions by June 30 deadline. Length: 100 lines maximum. **Pays 1 contributor's copy, "with prizes awarded accordingly." Aims to pay ~$30 this year per piece.**

TIPS "Check our website!"

VERSE

English Department, University of Richmond, Richmond VA 23173. **Website:** versemag.blogspot.com. **Contact:** Brian Henry, co-editor; Andrew Zawacki, co-editor. *Verse*, published 3 times/year, is an international poetry journal which also publishes interviews with poets, essays on poetry, and book reviews. Wants no specific kind; looks for high-quality, innovative poetry. Focus is not only on American poetry, but on all poetry written in English, as well as translations. Has published poetry by James Tate, John Ashbery, Barbara Guest, Gustaf Sobin, and Rae Armantrout. Estab. 1984. Accepts simultaneous submissions. Guidelines available online.

Verse is 128-416 pages, digest-sized, professionally printed, perfect-bound, with card cover. Receives about 5,000 poems/year, accepts 10%. Press run is 1,000. Single copy: $10; subscription: $15 for individuals, $39 for institutions. Sample: $6. *Verse* has a $10 reading fee for the print edition. Note that *Verse* will sometimes publish individual pieces on the website if they decide not to publish the entire body of work.

NONFICTION Interested in any nonfiction, plus translations, criticisms, interviews, journals/notebooks, etc. Submissions should be chapbook-length (20-40 pages). **Pays $10/page, $250 minimum.** Pays expenses of writers on assignment.

FICTION Interested in any genre. Submissions should be chapbook-length (20-40 pages). **Pays $10/page, $250 minimum.**

POETRY Submissions should be chapbook-length (20-40 pages). **Pays $10/page, $250 minimum.**

TIPS "Read widely and deeply. Avoid inundating a magazine with submissions; constant exposure will not increase your chances of getting accepted."

VESTAL REVIEW

P.O. Box 35369, Brighton MA 02135. **E-mail:** submissions@vestalreview.net. **Website:** www.vestalreview.org. **Contact:** Mark Budman, editor. **100%.** Semiannual print magazine specializing in flash fiction. The oldest magazine of flash fiction. A paying market. Our reading periods are February-May and August-November. Estab. 2000. Circ. 1,500. Byline given. Pays on publication. No kill fee. Publishes ms an average of 6 months after acceptance. Accepts queries by online submission form. Accepts simultaneous submissions. Responds in 1 week to queries; in 6 months to mss. Guidelines online.

Please read our guidelines and send all submissions through the Submittable. Do not use our email address for submissions.

FICTION Only flash fiction under 500 words. Needs ethnic, experimental, fantasy, horror, humorous, mainstream, short stories, flash fiction. No porn, racial slurs, excessive gore, or obscenity. No children's or preachy stories. Nothing over 500 words. Publishes flash fiction. "We accept submissions only through our submission manager." Length: 50-500 words. **Pays $25 and 1 contributor's copy.**

POETRY Needs No poetry.

TIPS "We like literary fiction with a plot that doesn't waste words. Don't send jokes masked as stories."

THE VIRGINIA QUARTERLY REVIEW

VQR, P.O. Box 400223, Charlottesville VA 22904. **E-mail:** editors@vqronline.org. **Website:** www.vqronline.org. **Contact:** Allison Wright, executive editor. "*VQR*'s primary mission has been to sustain and strengthen Jefferson's bulwark, long describing itself as 'A National Journal of Literature and Discussion.' And for good reason. From its inception in prohibition, through depression and war, in prosperity and peace, *The Virginia Quarterly Review* has been a haven—and home—for the best essayists, fiction writers, and poets, seeking contributors from every section of the United States and abroad. It has not limited itself to any special field. No topic has been alien: literary, public affairs, the arts, history, the economy. If it could be approached through essay or discussion, poetry or prose, *VQR* has covered it." Press run is 4,000. Estab. 1925. Accepts queries by online submission form. Responds in 3 months to mss. Guidelines available on website.

NONFICTION "We publish literary, art, and cultural criticism; reportage; historical and political analysis; and travel essays. We publish few author interviews or memoirs. In general, we are looking for nonfiction that looks out on the world, rather than within the self." Accepts online submissions only at virginiaquarterlyreview.submittable.com/submit. You can also query via this site. Length: 3,500-10,000 words. **Pays $500 for book reviews; $1,000-3,000 for essays, memoir, criticism, and reportage.** Pays expenses of writers on assignment.

FICTION "We are generally not interested in genre fiction (such as romance, science fiction, or fantasy)." Accepts online submissions only at virginiaquarterlyreview.submittable.com/submit. Length: 2,000-10,000 words. **Pays $1,000-2,500 for short stories; $1,000-4,000 for novellas and novel excerpts.**

POETRY *The Virginia Quarterly Review* prints approximately 12 pages of poetry in each issue. No length or subject restrictions. Issues have largely included lyric and narrative free verse, most of which features a strong message or powerful voice. Accepts online submissions only at virginiaquarterlyreview.submittable.com/submit. Submit maximum 5 poems. **Pays $200/poem.**

WEST BRANCH

Stadler Center for Poetry, Bucknell University, Lewisburg PA 17837-2029. (570)577-1853. **Fax:** (570)577-1885. **E-mail:** westbranch@bucknell.edu. **Website:** www.bucknell.edu/westbranch. **Contact:** G.C. Waldrep, editor. Semiannual literary magazine. *West Branch* publishes poetry, fiction, and nonfiction in both traditional and innovative styles. Byline given. Pays on publication. No kill fee. Accepts queries by online submission form. Accepts simultaneous submissions. Sample copy for $3. Guidelines available online.

Reading period: August 15 through April 1. No more than 3 submissions from a single contributor in a given reading period.

NONFICTION Needs essays, general interest, literary. **Buys 4-5 mss/year.** Send complete ms. Length: no more than 30 pages. **Pays 5¢/word, with a maximum of $100.** Pays expenses of writers on assignment.

FICTION Needs novel excerpts, short stories. No genre fiction. **Buys 10-12 mss/year.** Send complete ms. Length: no more than 30 pages. **Pays 5¢/word, with a maximum of $100.**

POETRY Needs free and formal verse. Buys 30-40 poems/year. Submit maximum 6 poems. **Pays $50/ submission.**

TIPS "All submissions must be sent via our online submission manager. Please see website for guidelines. We recommend that you acquaint yourself with the magazine before submitting."

WESTERN HUMANITIES REVIEW

University of Utah, 3528 LNCO / English Department, 255 S. Central Campus Dr., Salt Lake City UT 84112-0494. (801)581-6168. **Fax:** (801)585-5167. **E-mail:** managingeditor.whr@gmail.com. **Website:** www.westernhumanitiesreview.com. **Contact:** Michael Mejia, editor; Emily Dyer Barker, managing editor. A tri-annual magazine for educated readers. *Western Humanities Review* is a journal of contemporary literature and culture housed in the University of Utah English Department. Publishes poetry, fiction, nonfiction essays, artwork, and work that resists categorization. Submissions are open year-round. All submissions must be sent through online submissions manager. Estab. 1947. Circ. 1,000. Pays in contributor copies. Publishes ms an average of 1 year after acceptance. Accepts simultaneous submissions. Responds in 3-6 months. Sample copy: $10. Guidelines online.

NONFICTION Buys 6-8 unsolicited mss/year. Send complete ms.

FICTION Contact: Michael Mejia, fiction editor. Needs experimental, innovative voices. Does not want genre (romance, science fiction, etc.). **Buys 5-8 mss/ year.** Send complete ms. Length: 5,000 words.

POETRY Contact: Poetry editors: Katharine Coles, Tom Stillinger. Considers simultaneous submissions but no more than 5 poems or 25 pages per reading period. No fax or e-mail submissions. Reads submissions year-round. Wants quality poetry of any form, including translations. Has published poetry by Charles Simic, Olena Kalytiak Davis, Ravi Shankar, Karen Volkman, Dan Beachy-Quick, Lucie Brock-Broido, Christine Hume, and Dan Chiasson. Innovative prose poems may be submitted as fiction or nonfiction to the appropriate editor. **Pays 2 contributor's copies.**

TIPS "Because of changes in our editorial staff, we urge familiarity with recent issues of the magazine. We do not publish writer's guidelines because we think that the magazine itself conveys an accurate picture of our requirements. Please, no e-mail submissions."

WILLOW SPRINGS

668 N. Riverpoint Blvd. #259, Spokane WA 99202. (509)828-1486. **E-mail:** willowspringsewu@gmail.com. **Website:** willowsprings.ewu.edu. **Contact:** Samuel Ligon, editor. **95% freelance written.** *Willow Springs* is a semiannual magazine covering poetry, fiction, literary nonfiction and interviews of notable writers. Published twice a year, in spring and fall. Reading period: September 1 through May 31 for fiction and poetry; year-round for nonfiction. Reading fee: $3/submission. Estab. 1977. Circ. 1,200. Byline given. Publishes ms an average of 3 months after acceptance. Accepts queries by e-mail, online submission form. Accepts simultaneous submissions. Sample copy: $10. Guidelines online.

NONFICTION Needs book excerpts, essays, general interest, humor, personal experience. **Buys 2-6 mss/ year.** Submit via online submissions manager. **Pays $100 and 2 contributor's copies.** Pays expenses of writers on assignment.

FICTION "We accept any good piece of literary fiction. Buy a sample copy." Needs adventure, ethnic, experimental, historical, mainstream, mystery, slice-of-life vignettes, suspense, western. Does not want to see genre fiction that does not transcend its subject matter. **Buys 10-15 mss/year.** Submit via online submissions manager. Length: open for short stories; up to 750 words for short shorts. **Pays $100 and 2 contributor's copies for short stories; $40 and 2 contributor's copies for short shorts.**

POETRY Needs avant-garde, free verse, haiku, traditional. "Buy a sample copy to learn our tastes. Our aesthetic is very open." Submit only 3-5 poems at a time. Buys 50-60 poems/year. **Pays $20/poem and 2 contributor's copies.**

TIPS "While we have no specific length restrictions, we generally publish fiction and nonfiction no longer than 10,000 words and poetry no longer than 120 lines, though those are not strict rules. *Willow Springs* values poems and essays that transcend the merely autobiographical and fiction that conveys a concern for language as well as story."

THE WORCESTER REVIEW

P.O. Box 804, Worcester MA 01613. **E-mail:** editor.worcreview@gmail.com. **Website:** www.theworcesterreview.org. **Contact:** Diane Vanaskie Mulligan, managing editor. Annual literary journal covering poetry and short fiction. *The Worcester Review*, published annually by the Worcester County Poetry Association, encourages "critical work with a New England connection; no geographic limitation on poetry and fiction." Wants "work that is crafted, intuitively honest and empathetic. We like high-quality, creative poetry, artwork, and fiction. Critical articles should be connected to New England." *The Worcester Review* is 160 pages, digest-sized, professionally printed in dark type on quality stock, perfect-bound, with matte card cover. Press run is 600. Estab. 1972. Circ. 500. Pays small honorarium upon publication. Publishes ms within 1 year of acceptance. Accepts queries by online submission form. Accepts simultaneous submissions. Responds in 1-3 months to mss. Sometimes comments on rejected mss. Guidelines online.

NONFICTIONcritical essays, literary essays, literary criticism. Send complete ms. Length: 1,000-4,000 words. Average length: 2,000 words. **Pays 2 contributor's copies and honorarium if possible.** Pays expenses of writers on assignment.

FICTION Accepts about 5% unsolicited mss. Needs short stories, literary fiction. Send complete ms via online submissions manager. "Send only 1 short story—reading editors do not like to read 2 by the same author at the same time. We will use only 1." Length: 1,000-4,000 words. Average length: 2,000 words. **Pays 2 contributor's copies and honorarium if possible.**

POETRY Submit up to 5 poems at a time via online submission manager. Cover letter is optional. Has published poetry by Kurt Brown, Cleopatra Mathis, and Theodore Deppe. **Pays 2 contributor's copies plus small honorarium.**

TIPS "We generally look for creative work with a blend of craftsmanship, insight, and empathy. This does not exclude humor. We won't print work that is shoddy in any of these areas."

$ WORKERS WRITE!

Blue Cubicle Press, LLC, P.O. Box 250382, Plano TX 75025. **E-mail:** info@workerswritejournal.com. **Website:** www.workerswritejournal.com. **Contact:** David LaBounty, managing editor. **100% freelance written.** Covers working-class literature. "*Workers Write!* is an annual print journal published by Blue Cubicle Press, an independent publisher dedicated to giving voice to writers trapped in the daily grind. Each issue focuses on a particular workplace; check website for details. Submit your stories via e-mail or send a hard copy." Estab. 2005. Circ. 500. Byline given. Pays on acceptance. Publishes mss 4-6 months after acceptance. Accepts queries by mail, e-mail. Accepts simultaneous submissions. Responds in 1 week to queries; in 3 months to mss. Sample copy available on website. Writer's guidelines free for #10 SASE and on website.

FICTION "We need your stories (5,000-12,000 words) about the workplace from our Overtime series. Every 3 months, we'll release a chapbook containing 1-2 related stories that center on work." Needs experimental, historical, humorous, mainstream, short stories, slice-of-life vignettes. **Buys Buys 10-12 mss/year mss/year.** Send complete ms. Length: 500-5,000 words. **Payment: $5-50 (depending on length and rights requested).**

POETRY Needs free verse and traditional. Buys 3-5 poems/year. **Pays $5-10.**

$$ THE YALE REVIEW

The Yale Review, P.O. Box 208243, New Haven CT 06520-8243. (203)432-0499. **Fax:** (203)432-0510. **Website:** www.yale.edu/yalereview. **Contact:** J.D. McClatchy, editor. **20% freelance written.** Quarterly magazine. "Like Yale's schools of music, drama, and architecture, like its libraries and art galleries, *The Yale Review* has helped give the University its leading place in American education. In a land of quick fixes and short view and in a time of increasingly commercial publishing, the journal has an authority that derives from its commitment to bold established writers and promising newcomers, to both challenging literary work and a range of essays and reviews that can explore the connections between academic disciplines and the broader movements in American society, thought, and culture. With independence and boldness, with a concern for issues and ideas, with a respect for the mind's capacity to be surprised by speculation and delighted by elegance, *The Yale Review* proudly continues into its third century." Estab. 1911. Circ. 7,000. Pays prior to publication. No kill fee. Publishes ms an average of 6 months after acceptance. Accepts simultaneous submissions. Responds in 1-3 months to mss. Sample copy online. Guidelines available online.

NONFICTION Send complete ms with cover letter and SASE. **Pays $400-500.** Pays expenses of writers on assignment.

FICTION Submit complete ms with SASE. All submissions should be sent to the editorial office. **Pays $400-500.**

POETRY Submit with SASE. All submissions should be sent to the editorial office. **Pays $100-250.**

$ THE YALOBUSHA REVIEW

University of Mississippi, **E-mail:** yreditors@gmail.com. **Website:** yr.olemiss.edu. Annual literary journal seeking quality submissions from around the globe. Estab. 1995. Circ. 500. Accepts queries by online submission form. Accepts simultaneous submissions. Responds in 2-4 months to mss.

NONFICTION Needs reviews.

FICTION Needs experimental. **Buys 3-6 mss/year.** Submit 1 short story or up to 3 pieces of flash fiction via online submissions manager. Length: up to 5,000 words for short stories; up to 1,000 words for flash fiction.

POETRY Needs experimental. Submit 3-5 poems via online submissions manager.

$$$ ZOETROPE: ALL-STORY

Zoetrope: All-Story, The Sentinel Bldg., 916 Kearny St., San Francisco CA 94133. **Website:** www.all-story.com. **Contact:** fiction editor. Quarterly magazine specializing in the best of contemporary short fiction. Winner of the National Magazine Award for Fiction as the finest literary publication in the United States. Estab. 1997. Circ. 20,000. Byline given. Publishes ms an average of 5 months after acceptance. Accepts simultaneous submissions. Responds in 8 months (if SASE included). Sample copy: $10 plus shipping. Guidelines online.

FICTION Buys 15-20 (of 10,000+ submissions annually) mss/year. Writers should submit only one story at a time. We do not accept artwork or design submissions. We do not accept unsolicited revisions nor respond to writers who don't include an SASE. Send complete ms by postal mail. Length: up to 7,000 words. Excerpts from larger works, screenplays, treatments, and poetry will be returned unread. **Pays $1,000.**

$ ZYZZYVA

57 Post St., Suite 604, San Francisco CA 94104. (415)757-0465. **E-mail:** editor@zyzzyva.org. **Website:** www.zyzzyva.org. **Contact:** Laura Cogan, editor; Oscar Villalon, managing editor. **100% freelance written. Works with a small number of new/unpublished writers each year.** "Every issue is a vibrant mix of established talents and new voices, providing an elegantly curated overview of contemporary arts and letters with a distinctly San Francisco perspective." Estab. 1985. Circ. 2,500. Byline given. Pays on acceptance. No kill fee. Publishes ms an average of 3 months after acceptance. Accepts queries by mail. Accepts simultaneous submissions. Responds in 1 week to queries; in 1 month to mss. Sample copy: $12. Guidelines available online.

Accepts submissions January 1-May 31 and August 1-November 30. Does not accept online submissions.

NONFICTION Needs book excerpts, general interest, historical, humor, personal experience. **Buys 50 mss/year.** Submit by mail. Include SASE and contact information. Length: no limit. **Pays $50.** Pays expenses of writers on assignment.

PHOTOS Reviews scans only at 300 dpi, 5.5.

FICTION Needs ethnic, experimental, humorous, mainstream. **Buys 60 mss/year.** Send complete ms by mail. Include SASE and contact information. Length: no limit. **Pays $50.**

POETRY Submit by mail. Include SASE and contact information. Buys 20 poems/year. Submit maximum 5 poems. Length: no limit. **Pays $50.**

MEN'S

$$$$ CIGAR AFICIONADO

M. Shanken Communications, Inc., 825 8th Ave., 33rd Floor, New York NY 10019. (212)684-4224. **Fax:** (212)684-5424. **E-mail:** dsavona@mshanken.com. **Website:** www.cigaraficionado.com. Senior Editor: Greg Mottola. **Contact:** David Savona, executive editor. **75% freelance written.** Bimonthly magazine for affluent men about the world of cigars. Estab. 1992. Circ. 275,000. Byline given. Pays on acceptance. Offers 25% kill fee. Publishes ms an average of 3-6 months after acceptance. Editorial lead time 6 months. Submit seasonal material 6 months in advance. Accepts queries by e-mail. Responds in 1 month to queries; 2 months to mss. Sample copy free.

NONFICTION Needs general interest. Query. Length: 1,500-3,000 words. **Pays variable amount.** Pays expenses of writers on assignment.

$$$$ ESQUIRE

Hearst Media, 300 W. 57th St., New York NY 10019. (212)649-4158. **E-mail:** editor@esquire.com. **Website:** www.esquire.com. Monthly magazine covering the ever-changing trends in American culture. *Esquire* is geared toward smart, well-off men. General readership is college educated and sophisticated, between ages 30 and 45. Written mostly by contributing editors on contract. Rarely accepts unsolicited mss. Estab. 1933. Circ. 720,000. Publishes ms an average of 2-6 months after acceptance. Editorial lead time at least 2 months. Accepts queries by mail, e-mail. Accepts simultaneous submissions. Guidelines on website.

NONFICTION Query. Length: 5,000 words average. **Payment varies.** Pays expenses of writers on assignment.

PHOTOS Uses mostly commissioned photography. Payment depends on size and number of photos.

TIPS "A writer has the best chance of breaking in at *Esquire* by querying with a specific idea that requires special contacts and expertise. Ideas must be timely and national in scope."

MILITARY

$$ AIR FORCE TIMES

Sightline Media Group, 1919 Gallows Road, 4th Floor, Vienna VA 22182. (703)750-8646. **Fax:** (703)750-8601. **Website:** www.airforcetimes.com. **Contact:** Michelle Tan, editor. "Weeklies edited separately for Army, Navy, Marine Corps, and Air Force military personnel and their families. They contain career information such as pay raises, promotions, news of legislation affecting the military, housing, base activities, and features of interest to military people." Estab. 1940. Byline given. Pays on acceptance. Offers kill fee. Accepts queries by mail, e-mail, phone. Accepts simultaneous submissions. Responds in 1 month to queries. Sample copy for #10 SASE. Guidelines for #10 SASE.

NONFICTION No advice pieces. **Buys 150-175 mss/year.** Query. Length: 750-2,000 words. **Pays $100-500.**

COLUMNS/DEPARTMENTS Length: 500-900 words. **Buys 75 mss/year. Pays $75-125.**

TIPS "Looking for stories on active duty, reserve and retired military personnel; stories on military matters and localized military issues; stories on successful civilian careers after military service."

$$ ARMY MAGAZINE

Association of the US Army, 2425 Wilson Blvd., Arlington VA 22201. (800)336-4570. **E-mail:** armymag@ausa.org. **Website:** www.ausa.org/publications/armymagazine. Managing Editor: Elizabeth Rathbun. **Contact:** Rick Maze, editor-in-chief. **70% freelance written. Prefers to work with published/established writers.** Monthly magazine emphasizing Army interests. Estab. 1950. Circ. 65,000. Byline given. Pays on publication. Publishes ms an average of 5 months after acceptance. Submit seasonal material 3 months in advance. Accepts queries by mail. Accepts simultaneous submissions. Responds to queries within a week.

NONFICTION Needs essays, historical, interview, photo feature, technical. Special issues: "We would like to see more pieces about little-known episodes involving interesting military personalities. We especially want material lending itself to heavy, contributor-supplied photographic treatment. The first thing a contributor should recognize is that our readership is very savvy militarily. 'Gee-whiz' personal reminiscences get short shrift, unless they hold their own in a company in which long military service, heroism, and unusual experiences are commonplace. At the same time, *ARMY* readers like a well-written story with a fresh slant, whether it is about an experience in a foxhole or the fortunes of a corps in battle." No rehashed history. No unsolicited book reviews. **Buys 40 mss/year.** Submit via e-mail to armymag@ausa.org. Length: 1,000-1,500 words for op-eds and opinion, 1,200-1,800 for features. **Pays 15-20¢/word for articles, more for cover stories.** Pays expenses of writers on assignment. Expenses paid only with prior approval.

PHOTOS Contact: armymag@ausa.org. Only high-resolution photos accepted. See our writer's guidelines for details. Send photos. Captions required. Reviews prints and high-resolution digital photos. Payment varies.

$$ ARMY TIMES

Sightline Media Group, 1919 Gallows Rd., 4th Floor, Vienna VA 22182. (703)750-9000. **Fax:** (703)750-8622. **E-mail:** tlombardo@armytimes.com. **Website:** www.armytimes.com. **Contact:** Tony Lombardo, editor. Weekly for Army military personnel and their families containing career information such as pay raises, promotions, news of legislation affecting the military, housing, base activities and features of interest to military people. Estab. 1940. Circ. 230,000. Byline given.

Pays on acceptance. Offers kill fee. Accepts queries by mail, e-mail. Accepts simultaneous submissions. Responds in 1 month to queries.

NONFICTION **Buys 150-175 mss/year.** Query. Length: 750-2,000 words. **Pays $100-500.** Pays expenses of writers on assignment.

COLUMNS/DEPARTMENTS Length: 500-900 words. **Buys 75 mss/year. Pays $75-125.**

TIPS "Looking for stories on active duty, reserve and retired military personnel; stories on military matters and localized military issues; stories on successful civilian careers after military service."

$ COMBAT HANDGUNS

Athlon Outdoors, **E-mail:** editdesk@athlonoutdoors.com. **Website:** www.personaldefenseworld.com/publications/combat-handguns. Magazine published 8 times/year covering combat handguns. Written for handgun owners and collectors. Circ. 126,498. No kill fee. Editorial lead time 2 months. Accepts queries by mail, e-mail. Accepts simultaneous submissions.

NONFICTION Query. Pays expenses of writers on assignment.

PHOTOS Send photos. Captions required. Reviews GIF/JPEG files.

$$$ MILITARY OFFICER

201 N. Washington St., Alexandria VA 22314-2539. **E-mail:** editor@moaa.org; msc@moaa.org. **Website:** www.moaa.org. **60% freelance written. Prefers to work with published/established writers.** Monthly magazine for officers of the 7 uniformed services and their families. Estab. 1945. Circ. 325,000. Byline given. Pays on acceptance. Publishes ms an average of 1 year after acceptance. Accepts queries by e-mail. Accepts simultaneous submissions. Responds in 3 months to queries. Sample copy and guidelines available online.

NONFICTION "We rarely accept unsolicited mss." **Buys 50 mss/year.** Query with résumé, sample clips. Length: 1,000-2,000 words (features). **Pays 80¢/word (features).**

PHOTOS Query with list of stock photo subjects. Images should be 300 dpi or higher. Pays $75-250 for inside color; $300 for cover.

$$ MILITARY TIMES

Sightline Media Group, 1919 Gallows Rd., 4th Floor, Vienna VA 22182. **Website:** www.militarytimes.com. **Contact:** Andrew Tilghman, editor. Bi-weekly magazines edited separately for Army, Navy, Marine Corps, and Air Force military personnel and their families. They contain career information such as pay raises, promotions, news of legislation affecting the military, housing, base activities and features of interest to military people. Estab. 1940. Circ. 230,000 (combined). Byline given. Pays on publication. Offers kill fee. Accepts simultaneous submissions. Responds in 1 month. Looking for stories between 600 and 2,000 words that are focused on the U.S. military and of interest to the U.S. military. Especially interested in stories from overseas military communities.

NONFICTION No advice pieces. **Buys 150-175 mss/year.** Query. Length: 750-2,000 words. **Pays $100-1,000.**

COLUMNS/DEPARTMENTS Length: 500-900 words. **Buys 75 mss/year. Pays $75-125.**

TIPS "Looking for stories on active duty, reserve and retired military personnel; stories on military matters and localized military issues; stories on successful civilian careers after military service."

$ PARAMETERS

U.S. Army War College, SSI, 47 Ashburn Dr., Carlisle PA 17013-5010. (717)245-4943. **E-mail:** usarmy.carlisle.awc.mbx.parameters@mail.mil. **Website:** http://ssi.armywarcollege.edu/pubs/parameters/index.cfm. **100% freelance written. Prefers to work with published/established writers or experts in the field.** Readership consists of senior leaders of US defense establishment, both uniformed and civilian, plus members of the media, government, industry and academia. Subjects include national and international security affairs, military strategy, military leadership and management, art and science of warfare, and military history with contemporary relevance. Estab. 1971. Circ. 13,500. Byline given. Pays on publication. No kill fee. Publishes ms an average of 6 months after acceptance. Accepts queries by mail, e-mail, phone. Responds to queries in 1-5 business days. Sample copy online. Guidelines online.

NONFICTION Needs historical. Send complete ms. Length: 4,500-5,000 words. Pays expenses of writers on assignment.

TIPS Submit scholarly journal articles on a contemporary topic with strategic implications to US policymakers and military practitioners. Clearly and concisely present your ideas. Get criticism from other experts, and revise your article to incorporate their feedback. Tackle a subject only if you are an authority. Review previous issues to learn more about our audience. Make your material interesting to both experts and practitioners. Conclude by summarizing the strategic implications of your topic and by providing actionable recommendations for the audience. E-mail submissions to usarmy.carlisle.awc.mbx.parameters@mail.mil.

MUSIC

AMERICAN SONGWRITER MAGAZINE

P.O. Box 330249, Nashville TN 37203. (615)321-6096. **Fax:** (615)321-6097. **E-mail:** info@americansongwriter.com. **Website:** www.americansongwriter.com. **90% freelance written.** Bimonthly magazine about songwriters and the craft of songwriting for many types of music, including pop, country, rock, metal, jazz, gospel, and r&b. Estab. 1984. Circ. 5,000. Pays on publication. Offers 25% kill fee. Publishes ms an average of 2 months after acceptance. Accepts simultaneous submissions. Responds in 2 months to queries. Sample copy for $4. Guidelines for #10 SASE or by e-mail.

NONFICTION Needs general interest, interview, new product, technical, home demo studios, movie and TV scores, performance rights organizations. **Buys 20 mss/year.** Query with published clips. Length: 300-1,200 words. **Pays $25-60.** Pays expenses of writers on assignment.

REPRINTS Send tearsheet or photocopy and information about when and where the material previously appeared. Pays same amount as paid for an original article

PHOTOS Send photos. Identification of subjects required. Reviews 3x5 prints. Offers no additional payment for photos accepeted with ms. Buys one time rights.

TIPS *American Songwriter* strives to present articles which can be read a year or 2 after they were written and still be pertinent to the songwriter reading them.

CHART ATTACK

Chart Communications, Inc., 41 Britain St., Suite 200, Toronto ON M5A 1R7 Canada. (416)363-3101. **Fax:** (416)363-3109. **E-mail:** richard@chartattack.com. **Website:** www.chartattack.com. **Contact:** Richard Trapunski, editor-in-chief. **90% freelance written.** *Chart Attack* is a guide to indie and alternative music. Estab. 1990. Circ. 40,000 (paid). Byline given. Pays on publication. No kill fee. Publishes ms an average of 3-6 months after acceptance. Editorial lead time 2 months. Submit seasonal material 3 months in advance. Accepts queries by e-mail. Responds in 4-6 weeks to queries; 2-3 months to mss. Guidelines free.

NONFICTION Needs book excerpts, essays, expose, humor, interview, personal experience, photo feature. Nothing that isn't related to popular music and pop culture (i.e., film, books, video games, fashion, etc., that would appeal to a hip youth demographic). Query with published clips and send complete ms. Length: varies. **Payment varies.** Pays expenses of writers on assignment.

PHOTOS Contact: Steven Balaban, art director. Send photos. Negotiates payment individually. Buys all rights.

GUITAR PLAYER

New Bay Media, LLC, 28 E. 28th St., 12th Floor, New York NY 10016. **E-mail:** etrabb@nbmedia.com. **Website:** www.guitarplayer.com. **50% freelance written.** Monthly magazine for persons interested in guitars, guitarists, manufacturers, guitar builders, equipment, careers, etc. Circ. 150,000. Byline given. Pays on acceptance. No kill fee. Publishes ms an average of 3 months after acceptance. Accepts simultaneous submissions. Responds in 6 weeks to queries.

NONFICTION Buys 30-40 mss/year. Query. Open **Pays $250-450.** Pays expenses of writers on assignment.

PHOTOS Reviews 35 mm color transparencies, b&w glossy prints. Payment varies. Buys one time rights.

MYSTERY

ALFRED HITCHCOCK'S MYSTERY MAGAZINE

Dell Magazines, 44 Wall St., Suite 904, New York NY 10005. **E-mail:** alfredhitchcockmm@dellmagazines.com. **Website:** www.themysteryplace.com/ahmm. **100% freelance written.** Monthly magazine featuring new mystery short stories. Estab. 1956. Circ. 90,000. Byline given. Pays on publication. No kill fee. Submit seasonal material 7 months in advance. Accepts queries by mail, online submission form. Responds in 3-5 months to mss. Sample copy: $5. Guidelines for SASE or on website.

NONFICTION Pays expenses of writers on assignment.

FICTION Wants "original and well-written mystery and crime fiction. Because this is a mystery magazine, the stories we buy must fall into that genre in some sense or another. We are interested in nearly every kind of mystery: stories of detection of the classic kind, police procedurals, private eye tales, suspense, courtroom dramas, stories of espionage, and so on. We ask only that the story be about crime (or the threat or fear of one). We sometimes accept ghost stories or supernatural tales, but those also should involve a crime." Needs mystery, suspense. No sensationalism. Send complete ms. Length: up to 12,000 words. **Payment varies.**

TIPS "No simultaneous submissions, please. Submissions sent to *Alfred Hitchcock's Mystery Magazine* are not considered for or read by *Ellery Queen's Mystery Magazine*, and vice versa."

$ ELLERY QUEEN'S MYSTERY MAGAZINE

44 Wall St., Suite 904, New York NY 10005-2401. **E-mail:** elleryqueenmm@dellmagazines.com. **Website:** www.themysteryplace.com/eqmm. **100% freelance written.** "*Ellery Queen's Mystery Magazine* welcomes submissions from both new and established writers. We publish every kind of mystery short story: the psychological suspense tale, the deductive puzzle, the private eye case—the gamut of crime and detection from the realistic (including the policeman's lot and stories of police procedure) to the more imaginative (including 'locked rooms' and 'impossible crimes'). We look for strong writing, an original and exciting plot, and professional craftsmanship. We encourage writers whose work meets these general criteria to read an issue of *EQMM* before making a submission." Estab. 1941. Circ. 100,000. Byline given. Pays on acceptance. No kill fee. Publishes ms an average of 6-12 months after acceptance. Accepts queries by online submission form. Accepts simultaneous submissions. Responds in 3 months to mss. Sample copy: $9.50. Make out check to *Ellery Queen Mystery Magazine*, and send to *Ellery Queen Mystery Magazine*, Attn: Sandy Marlowe, 6 Prowitt St., Norwalk CT 06855. Guidelines online.

PHOTOS Send photos.

FICTION "We always need detective stories. Special consideration given to anything timely and original." Publishes ms 6-12 months after acceptance. Agented fiction 50%. **Publishes 10 new writers/year.** Recently published work by Jeffery Deaver, Joyce Carol Oates, and Margaret Maron. Sometimes comments on rejected mss. Needs mystery, suspense. No explicit sex or violence, no gore or horror. Seldom publishes parodies or pastiches. "We do not want true detective or crime stories." **Buys up to 120 mss/year.** "*EQMM* uses an online submission system (eqmm.magazinesubmissions.com) that has been designed to streamline our process and improve communication with authors. We ask that all submissions be made electronically, using this system, rather than on paper. All stories should be in standard ms format and submitted in .DOC format. We cannot accept .DOCX, .RTF, or .TXT files at this time." Length: 2,500-8,000 words, but occasionally accepts longer and shorter submissions—including minute mysteries of 250 words, stories up to 12,000 words, and novellas of up to 20,000 words from established authors. **Pays 5-8¢/word; occasionally higher for established authors.**

TIPS "*EQMM*'s range in the mystery genre is extensive: Almost any story that involves crime or the threat of crime comes within our purview. However, like all magazines, *EQMM* has a distinctive tone and style, and you can only get a sense of whether your work will suit us by reading an issue."

NATURE, CONSERVATION & ECOLOGY

ALTERNATIVES JOURNAL

Alternatives Inc., 283 Duke St. W., Suite 204A, Kitchener ON N2H 3X7 Canada. (519)578-2327. **E-mail:** david@alternativesjournal.ca. **Website:** www.alternativesjournal.ca. **Contact:** David McConnachie, publisher. **90% freelance written.** Magazine published 4 times/year with special issue(s) covering international environmental issues. "*Alternatives Journal*, Canada's national environmental magazine, delivers thoughtful analysis and intelligent debate on Canadian and world environmental issues, the latest news and ideas, as well as profiles of environmental leaders who are making a difference. *A/J* is a quarterly+ magazine featuring bright, lively writing by the nation's foremost environmental thinkers and researchers. *A/J* offers a vision of a more sustainable future as well as the tools needed to take us there." Estab. 1971. Circ. 5,000. Byline given. Pays on publication. Offers 50% kill fee. Publishes ms an average of 5 months after acceptance. Editorial lead time 7 months. Submit seasonal material 5 months in advance. Accepts queries by e-mail, online submission form. Accepts simultaneous submissions. Sample copy free for Canadian writers only. Guidelines online.

NONFICTION Needs book excerpts, essays, expose, how-to, humor, interview, opinion, photo feature, profile, reviews, technical. **Buys 50 mss/year.** Query with published clips. Length: 800-3,000 words. **Pays 10¢/word (Canadian).** Pays expenses of writers on assignment.

PHOTOS State availability. Identification of subjects required. Pays $35-75/photo. Buys one-time rights.

FICTION Needs science fiction, short stories.

TIPS "Before responding to this call for submissions, please read several back issues of the magazine so that you understand the nature of our publication. We also suggest you go through our detailed submission procedures to understand the types and lengths of articles we accept. Queries should explain, in less than 300 words, the content and scope of your article, and should convey your intended approach, tone, and style. Please include a list of people you will interview, potential images or sources for images, and the number of words you propose to write. We would also like to receive a very short bio. And if you have not written for *Alternatives* before, please include other examples of your writing. Articles range from about 500-3,000 words in length. Keep in mind that our lead time is several months. Articles should not be so time-bound that they will seem dated once published. *Alternatives* has a limited budget of 10¢ per word for several articles. This stipend is available to professional and amateur writers and students only. Please indicate your interest in this funding in your submission."

$$$ ARIZONA WILDLIFE VIEWS

5000 W. Carefree Hwy., Phoenix AZ 85086. (800)777-0015. **E-mail:** awv@azgfd.gov; hrayment@azgfd.gov. **Website:** www.azgfd.gov/magazine. **Contact:** Heidi Rayment. **50% freelance written.** Bimonthly magazine covering Arizona wildlife, wildlife management, and outdoor recreation (specifically hunting, fishing, wildlife watching, boating and off-highway vehicle recreation). "*Arizona Wildlife Views* is a general interest magazine about Arizona wildlife, wildlife management and outdoor recreation. We publish material that conforms to the mission and policies of the Arizona Game and Fish Department. In addition to Arizona wildlife and wildlife management, topics include habitat issues, outdoor recreation involving wildlife, boating, fishing, hunting, bird-watching, animal observation, off-highway vehicle use, etc., and historical articles about wildlife and wildlife management." Circ. 22,000. Byline given. Pays on publication. No kill fee. Publishes ms an average of 10 months after acceptance. Editorial lead time 1 year. Submit seasonal material 2 months in advance. Accepts queries by mail. Accepts simultaneous submissions. Responds in 1 month to queries. Responds in 2 months to mss. Sample copy free. Guidelines available online.

NONFICTION Needs general interest, historical, how-to, interview, photo feature, technical. Does not want "Me and Joe" articles, anthropomorphism of wildlife, or opinionated pieces not based on confirmable facts. **Buys 20 mss/year.** Query. Length: 1,000-2,500 words. **Pays $450-800.** Pays expenses of writers on assignment.

TIPS "Unsolicited material without proper identification will be returned immediately."

$$ THE BEAR DELUXE MAGAZINE

Orlo, 240 N. Broadway, #112, Portland OR 97227. **E-mail:** beardeluxe@orlo.org. **Website:** www.orlo.org. **Contact:** Tom Webb, editor-in-chief; Kristin Rogers Brown, art director. **80% freelance written.** Covers fiction, essay, poetry, other. Do not combine submissions; rather submit poetry, fiction, and essay in separate packages. News essays, on occasion, are assigned if they have a strong element of reporting. Artists contribute to *The Bear Deluxe* in various ways, including: editorial illustration, editorial photography, spot illustration, independent art, cover art, graphic design, and cartoons. "*The Bear Deluxe Magazine* is a national independent environmental arts magazine publishing significant works of reporting, creative nonfiction, literature, visual art, and design. Based in the Pacific Northwest, it reaches across cultural and political divides to engage readers on vital issues effecting the environment. Published twice per year, *The Bear Deluxe* includes a wider array and a higher percentage of visual artwork and design than many other publications. Artwork is included both as editorial support and as standalone or independent art. It has included nationally recognized artists as well as emerging artists. As with any publication, artists are encouraged to review a sample copy for a clearer understanding of the magazine's approach. Unsolicited submissions and samples are accepted and encouraged." Estab. 1993. Circ. 19,000. Byline given. Pays on publication. Offers 25% kill fee. Publishes ms an average of 6 months after acceptance. Editorial lead time 6 months. Submit seasonal material 9 months in advance. Accepts queries by mail, e-mail. Accepts simultaneous submissions. Responds in 3-6 months to mail queries. Only responds to e-mail queries if interested. Sample copy: $5. Guidelines online.

NONFICTION Needs essays, general interest, interview, new product, opinion, personal experience, photo feature, travel. Special issues: Publishes 1 theme every 2 years. **Buys 40 mss/year.** Query with published clips. Length: 750-4,000 words. **Pays $25-400, depending on piece.** Pays expenses of writers on assignment. Sometimes pays expenses.

PHOTOS State availability. Identification of subjects, model releases required. Reviews contact sheets, transparencies, 8x10 prints. Offers $30/photo. Buys one-time rights.

COLUMNS/DEPARTMENTS Reviews (almost anything), 100-1,000 words; Front of the Book (mix of short news bits, found writing, quirky tidbits), 300-500 words; Portrait of an Artist (artist profiles), 1,200 words; Back of the Book (creative opinion pieces), 650 words. **Buys 16 mss/year.** Query with published clips. **Pays $25-400, depending on piece.**

FICTION "We are most excited by high-quality writing that furthers the magazine's goal of engaging new and divergent readers. We appreciate strong aspects of storytelling and are open to new formats, though we wouldn't call ourselves publishers of 'experimental fiction.'" Needs adventure, condensed novels, historical, horror, humorous, mystery, western. No traditional sci-fi, horror, romance, or crime/action. **Buys 8 mss/year.** Query or send complete ms. Prefers postal mail submissions. Length: up to 4,000 words. **Pays free subscription to the magazine, contributor's copies, and $25-400, depending on piece; additional copies for postage.**

POETRY Needs avant-garde, free verse, haiku, light verse, traditional. Submit 3-5 poems at a time. Poems are reviewed by a committee of 3-5 people. Publishes 1 theme issue per year. Buys 16-20 poems/year. Length: up to 50 lines/poem. **Pays $20, subscription, and contributor's copies.**

FILLERS Needs facts, newsbreaks, short humor. **Buys 10 mss/year.** Length: 100-750 words.

TIPS "Offer to be a stringer for future ideas. Get a copy of the magazine and guidelines, and query us with specific nonfiction ideas and clips. We're looking for original, magazine-style stories, not fluff or PR. Fiction, essay, and poetry writers should know we have an open and blind review policy and they should keep sending their best work even if rejected once. Be as specific as possible in queries."

$$ BIRD WATCHER'S DIGEST

P.O. Box 110, Marietta OH 45750. (740)373-5285; (800)879-2473. **E-mail:** submissions@birdwatchers-digest.com. **Website:** www.birdwatchersdigest.com. **Contact:** Bill Thompson III, editor; Dawn Hewitt, managing editor. **30% freelance written.** Bimonthly, digest-sized magazine covering birds, bird watching, travel for birding, and natural history, but not domesticated birds or pets. *Bird Watcher's Digest* is a nontechnical magazine interpreting ornithological material for amateur observers, including the knowledgeable birder, the serious novice, and the backyard bird watcher; strives to provide good reading and good ornithology. Works with a small number of new/unpublished writers each year. Estab. 1978. Circ. 42,000. Byline given. Pays after publication. Publishes ms an average of 2 years after acceptance. Submit seasonal material one year in advance or longer. Accepts queries by e-mail. Responds in 6 weeks to queries. Sample copy for $4.99 plus shipping, or access online. Guidelines online.

"We take pride in sharing wonderful stories about birds, bird watching, birders, and places to travel to enjoy birds. On rare occasion, we publish short poems; we do not publish fiction."

NONFICTION Needs book excerpts, essays, how-to, humor, new product, personal experience, reviews, travel, Only stories about wild birds, bird watching, bird watchers, birding gear, or birding hot spots are considered. No articles on domestic, pet or caged birds, or raising a baby bird. **Buys 30-40 mss/year.** "We gladly accept e-mail queries and ms submissions. When submitting by e-mail, please use the subject line 'Submission—[your topic].' Attach your submission to your e-mail in either MS Word (DOC) or RichText Format (RTF). Please include full contact information on every page." Length: 600-2,500 words. **Pays up to $200 for stories requiring specialized knowl-**

edge or training; complimentary subscription for anecdotes.

PHOTOS Reviews digital photos only. "Our payment schedule is $75 per image used, regardless of size. Images reused on our table of contents page or on our website will be paid an additional $25. There is no payment or contract for photos used in 'My Way,' or for photos that have been loaned for courtesy use." Buys one-time rights for simultaneous print and digital publication.

POETRY Prints short poems about birds or bird watching only on rare occasion. **Pays $10-25, or complimentary subscription.**

TIPS "Obtain a sample copy of *BWD* from us or at your local newsstand, bird store, or bookstore, and familiarize yourself with the type of material we regularly publish. We rarely repeat coverage of a topic within a period of 2-3 years. We aim at an audience ranging from the backyard bird watcher to the very knowledgeable birder; we include in each issue material that will appeal at various levels. We always strive for a good geographical spread, with material from every section of the country. We leave very technical matters to others, but we want facts and accuracy, depth and quality, directed at the veteran bird watcher and at the enthusiastic novice. We stress the joys and pleasures of bird watching, its environmental contribution, and its value for the individual and society."

$$ BIRDWATCHING

Madavor Media, LLC, BirdWatching Editorial Dept., 25 Braintree Hill Office Park, Suite 404, Braintree MA 02184. **E-mail:** mail@birdwatchingdaily.com. **Website:** www.birdwatchingdaily.com. Bimonthly magazine for birdwatchers who actively look for wild birds in the field. "*BirdWatching* concentrates on where to find, how to attract, and how to identify wild birds, and on how to understand what they do." Estab. 1987. Circ. 40,000. Byline given. Pays on publication. Accepts queries by mail, e-mail. Accepts simultaneous submissions. Guidelines online.

NONFICTION Needs book excerpts, essays, how-to, interview, personal experience, photo feature, travel. No poetry, fiction, or puzzles. **Buys 12 mss/year.** Query by mail or e-mail with published clips. Length: 500-2,400 words. **Pays $200-400.**

PHOTOS See photo guidelines online. State availability. Identification of subjects required. Buys one-time rights.

$$ EARTH ISLAND JOURNAL

Earth Island Institute, 2150 Allston Way, Suite 460, Berkeley CA 94704. **E-mail:** submissions@earthisland.org. **Website:** www.earthislandjournal.org. **80% freelance written.** Quarterly magazine covering the environment/ecology. *Earth Island Journal*, published quarterly, "combines investigative journalism and thought-provoking essays that make the subtle but profound connections between the environment and other contemporary issues." Does not publish poetry or fiction. Looking for in-depth, vigorously reported stories that reveal the connections between the environment and other contemporary issues. Audience, though modest, includes many of the leaders of the environmental movement. Article pitches should be geared toward this sophisticated audience. Estab. 1985. Circ. 10,000. Byline given. Pays on publication. Publishes ms an average of 4 months after acceptance. Editorial lead time 4 months. Submit seasonal material 4 months in advance. Accepts queries by mail, e-mail. Accepts simultaneous submissions. Responds in 1 month to queries and mss. Sample copy online. Guidelines online.

NONFICTION Needs book excerpts, essays, expose, general interest, interview, opinion, personal experience, photo feature. "We do not want product pitches, services, or company news." **Buys 20 mss/year.** Query with published clips. Length: 750-4,000 words. **Pays 25¢/word.** Pays expenses of writers on assignment.

PHOTOS Send photos. Reviews contact sheets, GIF/JPEG files. Negotiates payment individually.

COLUMNS/DEPARTMENTS Voices (first-person reflection about the environment in a person's life), 750 words. **Buys 4 mss/year.** Query. **Pays $50.**

TIPS "Given our audience, we are looking for stories that break new ground when it comes to environmental coverage. We are not going to publish a story 'about recycling.' We may, however, be interested in a story about, say, the waste manager in Kansas City, KS, who developed an innovative technology for sorting trash, and how his/her scheme is being copied around the world. In other words, we are looking for fresh angles on familiar stories, stories that so far have been overlooked by larger publications."

$$$$ HIGH COUNTRY NEWS

119 Grand Ave., P.O. Box 1090, Paonia CO 81428. (970)527-4898. **E-mail:** brianc@hcn.org; cindy@hcn.org. **E-mail:** editor@hcn.org; photos@hcn.org. **Web-**

site: www.hcn.org. **Contact:** Brian Calvert, editor-in-chief; Cindy Wehling, art director. **50% freelance written.** Biweekly nonprofit magazine covering environment, natural resources, and under-represented communities across 11 Western states and Alaska; for journalists, policymakers, environmentalists, conservationists, environmental justice advocates, politicians, companies, college classes, government agencies, grass roots activists, public land managers, and other people with a stake in the modern American West. *High Country News* will consider pitches for well-researched reportage, analysis, opinion, essay or criticism on issues vital to the West—especially under the broad frameworks of science and nature; conservation and preservation; food and agriculture; water; environmental justice and racism; climate change and energy; post-colonialism and the legacy of conquest; the rural-urban divide; environmental law and policy; public lands and resources (including water, mineral, timber, range, wildlife, recreation and preservation); military and nuclear legacies; and economics. We are especially interested in stories and perspectives from under-represented communities where they intersect with these issues. The magazine provides meaningful journalism and writing about the American West, not only as a geography, but also as an idea, part history, part mythology. We are looking for sophisticated storytelling that examines the varied landscapes and people across 11 states west of the 100th meridian—Arizona, California, Colorado, Idaho, Montana, New Mexico, Nevada, Oregon, Utah, Washington, Wyoming—and, because they face similar issues, Alaska and the High Plains. The writing in *High Country News* explores the region through unique stories that only the West can produce and that have broad significance beyond our borders. We emphasize intellectual honesty, clarity and nuance. Estab. 1970. Circ. 30,000. Byline given. Pays on publication. Offers kill fee of 1/4 of agreed rate. Publishes ms an average of 2-6 months after acceptance. Accepts queries by e-mail. Accepts simultaneous submissions. Responds in 2 weeks to queries. Sample copy online. Guidelines online.

NONFICTION Needs book excerpts, essays, expose, humor, personal experience, travel. **Buys 100 mss/year.** Query. Length: up to 4,900 words. **Pays 50¢-$1.50/word.** Pays expenses of writers on assignment.

PHOTOS Send photos. Captions, identification of subjects required. Reviews b&w or color prints.

COLUMNS/DEPARTMENTS Back-Page Essay, 700-900 words; Writers on the Range (taut and pithy opinion pieces). Submit back-page essay queries to Brian Calvert (brianc@hcn.org); submit Writers on the Range pieces to Betsy Marston (betsym@hsn.org).

TIPS "Familiarity with the newsmagazine is a must. Start by writing a brief, focused query letter. We are especially looking for stories from writers and communities of color, where they intersect with our core issues."

$$$ NATIONAL PARKS MAGAZINE

National Parks Conservation Association, 777 Sixth St. NW, Suite 700, Washington DC 20001. (202)223-6722; (800)628-7275. **Fax:** (202)454-3333. **E-mail:** npmag@npca.org. **Website:** www.npca.org/magazine. **Contact:** Scott Kirkwood, editor-in-chief. **60% freelance written. Prefers to work with published/established writers.** Quarterly magazine for a largely unscientific but highly educated audience interested in preservation of National Park System units, natural areas, and protection of wildlife habitat. "*National Parks* magazine publishes articles about areas in the National Park System, proposed new areas, threats to parks or park wildlife, scientific discoveries, legislative issues, and endangered species of plants or animals relevant to national parks. We do not publish articles on general environmental topics, nor do we print articles about land managed by the Fish and Wildlife Service, Bureau of Land Management, or other federal agencies." Estab. 1919. Circ. 340,000. Pays on acceptance. Offers 33% kill fee. Publishes ms an average of 2 months after acceptance. Accepts simultaneous submissions. Responds in 3-4 months to queries. Sample copy for $3 and 9x12 SASE or online. Guidelines available online.

NONFICTION Needs expose, descriptive articles about new or proposed national parks and wilderness parks. No poetry, philosophical essays, or first-person narratives. No unsolicited mss. Length: 1,500 words. **Pays $1,300 for 1,500-word features and travel articles.** Pays expenses of writers on assignment.

PHOTOS Not looking for new photographers. Send photos.

TIPS "Articles should have an original slant or news hook and cover a limited subject, rather than attempt to treat a broad subject superficially. Specific examples, descriptive details, and quotes are always preferable to generalized information. The writer must be able to document factual claims, and statements should be clearly substantiated with evidence within the article. *National Parks* does not publish fiction, poetry, personal essays, or 'My trip to .' stories."

$ NEW YORK STATE CONSERVATIONIST

New York State Department of Environmental Conservation, 625 Broadway, Albany NY 12233-4502. (518)402-8047. **Fax:** (518)402-8050. **E-mail:** magazine@dec.ny.gov. **Website:** www.dec.ny.gov/pubs/conservationist.html. **30% freelance written.** Bimonthly magazine covering outdoor education, environmental quality, hunting, fishing, wildlife profiles. Circ. 100,000. Byline given. Pays on publication. No kill fee. Publishes ms an average of 2 months-5 years after acceptance. Editorial lead time 6 months. Submit seasonal material 6-12 months in advance. Accepts queries by mail. Accepts simultaneous submissions. Responds in 2-4 weeks to queries; 2 months to mss. Sample copy online. Guidelines online.

NONFICTION Needs historical, personal experience, photo feature. **Buys 10 mss/year.** Query. **Pays $50-100.**

PHOTOS Send photos. Captions, identification of subjects, model releases required. Reviews transparencies. Offers $15-100/photo. Buys one time rights.

COLUMNS/DEPARTMENTS The Backpage (outdoor experiences, feel-good anectdotes), 700 words. **Buys 3 mss/year.** Query with published clips. **Pays $50.**

TIPS "The more organized a writer is, the more likely we are to use the piece. Captions, photos, and solid writing don't hurt, either. People doing things in the outdoors. Well-researched wildlife profiles."

$$$$ SIERRA

2101 Webster St., Suite 1300, Oakland CA 94612. **E-mail:** submissions.sierra@sierraclub.org. **Website:** www.sierraclub.org. Estab. 1893. Accepts queries by e-mail. Accepts simultaneous submissions. Responds in 6-8 weeks. Sample copy for $5 and SASE, or on. Guidelines available online.

The bimonthly magazine of the Sierra Club.

NONFICTION "*Sierra* is looking for strong, well-researched, literate nonfiction storytelling about significant environmental and conservation issues, adventure travel, nature, self-propelled sports, and trends in green living. Writers should look for ways to cast new light on well-established issues. We look for stories of national or international significance; local issues, while sometimes useful as examples of broader trends, are seldom of interest in themselves. We are always looking for adventure-travel pieces that weave events, discoveries, and environmental insights into the narrative. We are more interested in showcasing environmental solutions than adding to the list of environmental problems. We publish dramatic investigative stories that have the potential to reach a broad audience. Nonfiction essays on the natural world are welcome too. Features often focus on aspects of the Sierra Club's work, but few subjects are taboo. For more information about the Club's current campaigns, visit sierraclub.org." "We do not want descriptive wildlife articles unless larger conservation issues figure strongly in the story. We are not interested in editorials, general essays about environmentalism, or highly technical writing. We do not publish unsolicited cartoons, poetry, or fiction; please do not submit works in these genres." **Buys 30-36 mss/year.** Well-researched, tightly focused queries should be submitted to **Submissions.Sierra@sierraclub.org.** Phone calls are strongly discouraged. "Please do not send slides, prints, or other artwork. If photos or illustrations are required for your submission, we will request them when your work is accepted for publication." Length: 2,000-4,000 words. **Pays $1/word. More for "well-known writers with crackerjack credentials."** Pays expenses of writers on assignment. Expenses may be paid in some cases.

PHOTOS Publishes photographs pertaining to the natural world and the environment. "We use high-quality, mostly color photographs and prefer digital files. Photographers interested in submitting work to Sierra are encouraged to send a link to their website, along with a stock listing of regions and subjects of specialty for us to review. Please do not send unsolicited transparencies and prints. We review photographers' stock lists (subject matter and locations in photographs) and samples and keep the names of potential contributors on file. Photographers are contacted only when subjects they have in stock are needed. We typically do not post our photo-needs list online or elsewhere. Sierra does not accept responsibility for lost or damaged transparencies sent on spec or for portfolio review. Please e-mail Photo.Submissions@sierraclub.org." Send photos.

WOODS READER

P.O. Box 46, Warren MN 56762. **E-mail:** editor@woodsreader.com. **Website:** www.woodsreader.com. **Contact:** S Sedgwick. **60%.** A quarterly publication for those who love woodland areas: whether a public preserve, forest, tree farm, backyard woodlot or other patch of trees and wildlife. Will only consider articles based on woodlands. "We are looking for positive, whimsical, interesting articles. Our readers like to hear about others' experiences and insights. Please visit submissions page on website. We encourage stories of personal experience. We also buy forest ecology mss of general interest, DIY (photos must accompany), personal essays, book reviews (query first)." Estab. 2017. Byline given. Pays on acceptance or publication. Does not offer kill fee. Publishes ms 3-12 months after acceptance. Accepts queries by mail, e-mail. Accepts simultaneous submissions. Responds in 3 months or less. Sample copy available online for $8. Guidelines online or query.

NONFICTION Needs general interest, historical, how-to, humor, personal experience, photo feature, reviews, travel. No hunting, logging or political pieces. **Buys 12 mss/year.** Length: 500-700 words, will consider other lengths. **Pays $50-150.**

PHOTOS **Contact:** S Sedgwick. Pays $25 with article, $100 cover. First North American serial and reprint rights, digital and print.

FICTION Short fiction based on woodland setting. Will buy longer fiction for serialization over four issues. Needs short stories, slice-of-life vignettes. Length: 500-2,000 words. **Payment varies.**

POETRY Needs short poetry about woodland topics. Buys 4-8 poems/year. Submit maximum 2 poems. Length: 2-16 lines. **Pays $25.**

PERSONAL COMPUTERS

PC WORLD

IDG, One Letterman Dr., Bldg. D, Suite P100, San Francisco CA 94129. **Website:** www.pcworld.com. Monthly magazine covering personal computers. *PC World* was created to give PC-proficient managers advice on which technology products to buy, tips on how to use those products most efficiently, news about the latest technological developments, and alerts regarding current problems with products and manufacturers. Circ. 1,100,000. No kill fee. Editorial lead time 3 months. Accepts queries by mail. Accepts simultaneous submissions. Guidelines by e-mail.

We have very few opportunities for writers who are not already contributing to the magazine.

NONFICTION Needs how-to, reviews, news items, features. Query. **Payment varies**

TIPS "Once you're familiar with *PC World*, you can write us a query letter. Your letter should answer the following questions as specifically and consisely as possible. What is the problem, technique, or product you want to discuss? Why will *PC World* readers be interested in it? Which section of the magazine do you think it best fits? What is the specific audience for the piece (e.g., database or LAN users, desktop publishers, and so on)?"

PHOTOGRAPHY

APOGEE PHOTO MAGAZINE

24 Holborn Viaduct, City of London EC1A 2BN UK. (0)(333)360-1054. **E-mail:** editor.sales@apogeephoto.com. **Website:** apogeephoto.com. **Contact:** Marla Meier, owner. A free online magazine designed to inspire, educate and inform photographers of all ages and levels. Hundreds of articles, columns and tips covering a wide range of photo topics. Find listings of photo workshops and tours, camera clubs, and books. Submit your articles for publication." Accepts queries by e-mail. Accepts simultaneous submissions.

NONFICTION Needs essays, general interest, how-to, inspirational, interview, new product, photo feature, profile, reviews, technical, travel. Accepts well-written articles with 600-1,200 words on any photography related subject geared towards the beginner to advanced photographer. Articles must be accompanied by a minimum of 6 high quality photographs. Format and photo details will be given via email upon acceptance of terms.

PHOTOS "*Apogee Photo* is interested in providing an electronic forum for high quality work from photographic writers and photographers. We will accept articles up to 1,200 words on any photographic subject geared towards the beginning to advanced photographer. Articles must have a minimum of 4-6 photographs accompanying them. You must hold the copyright and/or have a copyright release from a 3rd party and you must have signed model releases where applicable for any identifiable person or persons which appear in your photographs." Accepts reviews of new products, 800/words max.

TIPS "Please do a search by subject before submitting your article to see if your article covers a new subject or brings a new perspective on a particular subject or theme."

POLITICS & WORLD AFFAIRS

COMMONWEAL

Commonweal Foundation, 475 Riverside Dr., Room 405, New York NY 10115. (212)662-4200. **Fax:** (212)662-4183. **E-mail:** editors@commonwealmagazine.org. **Website:** www.commonwealmagazine.org. **Contact:** Paul Baumann, editor; Tiina Aleman, production editor. Biweekly journal of opinion edited by Catholic lay people, dealing with topical issues of the day on public affairs, religion, literature, and the arts. Estab. 1924. Circ. 20,000. Byline given. Pays on publication. No kill fee. Submit seasonal material 4 months in advance. Accepts simultaneous submissions. Responds in 2 months to queries. Sample copy free. Guidelines available online.

NONFICTION Needs essays, general interest, interview, personal experience, religious. **Buys 30 mss/year.** Query with published clips. *Commonweal* welcomes original manuscripts dealing with topical issues of the day on public affairs, religion, literature, and the arts. Looks for articles that are timely, accurate, and well written. Length: 2,000-3,000 words for features. **Pays $200-300 for longer mss; $100-200 for shorter pieces.** Pays expenses of writers on assignment.

COLUMNS/DEPARTMENTS Upfronts: (750-1,000 words) brief, newsy reportorials, giving facts, information and some interpretation behind the headlines of the day; Last Word: (750 words) usually of a personal nature, on some aspect of the human condition: spiritual, individual, political, or social.

POETRY Needs free verse, traditional. *Commonweal*, published every 2 weeks, is a Catholic general interest magazine for college-educated readers. Does not publish inspirational poems. Buys 20 poems/year. Length: no more than 75 lines. **Pays 75¢/line plus 2 contributor's copies. Acquires all rights. Returns rights when requested by the author.**

TIPS "Articles should be written for a general but well-educated audience. While religious articles are always topical, we are less interested in devotional and churchy pieces than in articles which examine the links between 'worldly' concerns and religious beliefs."

THE FREEMAN: IDEAS ON LIBERTY

1819 Peachtree Road NE, Suite 300, Atlanta GA 30309 United States. (404)554-9980. **Fax:** (404)393-3142. **E-mail:** freeman@fee.org. **E-mail:** editor@fee.org. **Website:** fee.org. James Anderson, deputy publisher. **Contact:** Dan Sanchez, managing editor. **85% freelance written.** Monthly publication for the layman and fairly advanced students of liberty. Estab. 1946. Byline given. Pays on publication. No kill fee. Publishes online within weeks. Some online articles are also published in the quarterly print edition. Accepts queries by e-mail. Guidelines available on website.

Eager to work with new/unpublished writers.

NONFICTION Buys 100 mss/year. Query with SASE. Length: 3,500 words. **Pays 10¢/word.** Pays expenses of writers on assignment.

TIPS "It's most rewarding to find freelancers with new insights and fresh points of view. Facts, figures, and quotations cited should be fully documented, to their original source, if possible."

THE NATION

520 Eighth Avenue, 8th Flo, New York NY 10018. **E-mail:** submissions@thenation.com. **Website:** www.thenation.com. Steven Brower, art director. **Contact:** Roane Carey, managing editor; Ange Mlinko, poetry editor. *The Nation*, published weekly, is a journal of left/liberal opinion, with arts coverage that includes poetry. The only requirement for poetry is excellence. Estab. 1865. Circ. 100,000. Guidelines available online.

Poetry published by *The Nation* has been included in *The Best American Poetry*. Has published poetry by W.S. Merwin, Maxine Kumin, James Merrill, May Swenson, Edward Hirsch, and Charles Simic.

NONFICTION civil liberties, civil rights, labor, economics, environmental, feminist issues, politics, the arts. Queries accepted via online form. Length: 750-2,500 words. **Pays $150-500, depending on length.** Pays expenses of writers on assignment.

POETRY Contact: Ange Mliko, poetry editor. "Please email poems in a single PDF attachment to PoemNationSubmit@gmail.com. Submissions are not accepted from June 1-September 15." Buys 6 poems/year. Submit maximum 3 poems.

$$$ THE PROGRESSIVE

30 W. Mifflin St., Suite 703, Madison WI 53703. (608)257-4626. **E-mail:** normstoc@progressive.org. **E-mail:** editorial@progressive.org. **Website:** www.progressive.org. **Contact:** Norman Stockwell, publisher. **75% freelance written.** Bimonthly magazine of investigative reporting, political commentary, cultural coverage, activism, interviews, poetry, and humor. It steadfastly stands against militarism, the concentration of power in corporate hands, and the disenfranchisement of the citizenry. It champions peace, social and economic justice, civil rights, civil liberties, human rights, a preserved environment, and a reinvigorated democracy. Its bedrock values are nonviolence and freedom of speech. A voice for peace, justice, and the common good. Estab. 1909. Circ. 30,000. Byline given. Pays on publication. Publishes ms an average of 6 weeks after acceptance. Accepts queries by e-mail. Accepts simultaneous submissions. Responds in 1 month to queries. Sample copy for 9x12 SASE with 4 first-class stamps or sample articles online. Guidelines online.

NONFICTION Needs book excerpts, essays, historical, interview, opinion, photo feature, profile. Query. Length: 500-4,000 words. **Pays $100-1,000.** Pays expenses of writers on assignment. by prior arrangement only

POETRY Publishes 1 original poem a month. "We prefer poems that connect up—in 1 fashion or another, however obliquely—with political concerns." **Pays $150.**

TIPS Sought-after topics include electoral coverage, social movements, foreign policy, activism, and book reviews.

$ PROGRESSIVE POPULIST

Ampersand Publishing Co., P.O. Box 819, Manchaca TX 78652. (512)828-7245. **E-mail:** populist@usa.net. **Website:** www.populist.com. **90% freelance written.** Biweekly tabloid covering politics and economics. "We cover political and economic issues of interest to workers, small businesses, and family farmers and ranchers." Estab. 1994. Circ. 15,000. Byline given. Pays quarterly. No kill fee. Publishes ms an average of 1 month after acceptance. Editorial lead time 3 weeks. Submit seasonal material 1 month in advance. Accepts queries by mail, e-mail, fax, phone. Accepts simultaneous submissions. Sample copy and writer's guidelines free.

NONFICTION Needs essays, general interest, historical, humor, interview, opinion. "We are not much interested in 'sound-off' articles about state or national politics, although we accept letters to the editor. We prefer to see more 'journalistic' pieces in which the writer does enough footwork to advance a story beyond the easy realm of opinion." **Buys 400 mss/year.** Query. Length: 600-1,000 words. **Pays $15-50.** Pays expenses of writers on assignment. Pays writers with contributor copies or other premiums if preferred by writer.

REPRINTS Send photocopy with rights for sale noted and information about when and where the material previously appeared.

PHOTOS State availability. Identification of subjects required. Negotiates payment individually. Buys one-time rights.

TIPS "We do prefer submissions by e-mail. I find it's easier to work with e-mail, and for the writer it probably increases the chances of getting a response."

PSYCHOLOGY & SELF-IMPROVEMENT

$$$$ GRADPSYCH

American Psychological Association, 750 First St. NE, Washington DC 20009. **Fax:** (202)336-6103. **Website:** www.apa.org/gradpsych. **50% freelance written.** Quarterly magazine. "We cover issues of interest to psychology graduate students, including career outlook, tips for success in school, profiles of interesting students, and reports on student research. We aim for our articles to be readable, informative, and fun. Grad students have enough dry, technical reading to do at school; we don't want to add to it." Estab. 2003. Circ. 60,000. Byline given. Pays on acceptance. Offers $200 kill fee. Publishes ms an average of 4 months after acceptance. Editorial lead time 3-5 months. Submit seasonal material 4 months in advance. Accepts queries by e-mail. Accepts simultaneous submissions. Responds in 2 weeks to queries. Sample copy online.

NONFICTION Needs general interest, how-to, interview, journalism for grad students. **Buys 25 mss/year.** Query with published clips. Length: 300-2,000 words. **Pays $300-2,000 for assigned articles.**

PHOTOS State availability. Identification of subjects, model releases required. Reviews GIF/JPEG files. Negotiates payment individually. Buys one-time rights.

TIPS "Check out our website and pitch a story on a topic we haven't written on before or that gives an old topic a new spin. Also, have quality clips."

$$$$ PSYCHOLOGY TODAY

Sussex Publishers, Inc., 115 E. 23rd St., 9th Floor, New York NY 10010. (212)260-7210. **Fax:** (212)260-7445. **Website:** www.psychologytoday.com. Bimonthly magazine exploring every aspect of human behavior, from the cultural trends that shape the way we think and feel to the intricacies of modern neuroscience. "We're sort of a hybrid of a science magazine, a health magazine and a self-help magazine. While we're read by many psychologists, therapists and social workers, most of our readers are simply intelligent and curious people interested in the psyche and the self." Estab. 1967. Circ. 331,400. Byline given. Pays 30 days after publication. No kill fee. Publishes ms an average of 3 months after acceptance. Editorial lead time 5 months. Accepts queries by online submission form. Accepts simultaneous submissions. Responds in 1 month to queries. Guidelines online.

NONFICTION No fiction, poetry or first-person essays on How I Conquered Mental Disorder X. **Buys 20-25 mss/year.** Query with published clips. Length: 1,500-4,000 words. **Pays $1,000-2,500.**

COLUMNS/DEPARTMENTS Contact: News Editor. News & Trends, 150-300 words. Query with published clips. **Pays $150-300.**

TIPS "Send your query to one of the members of our staff."

$ SPOTLIGHT ON RECOVERY MAGAZINE

R. Graham Publishing Company, 9602 Glenwood Rd., #140, Brooklyn NY 11236. (347)831-9373. **E-mail:** rgraham_100@msn.com. **Website:** www.spotlightonrecovery.com. **Contact:** Robin Graham, publisher and editor-in-chief. **85% freelance written.** Quarterly magazine covering self-help, recovery, and empowerment. "This is the premiere outreach and resource magazine in New York. Its goal is to be the catalyst for which the human spirit could heal. Everybody knows somebody who has mental illness, substance abuse issues, parenting problems, educational issues, or someone who is homeless, unemployed, physically ill, or the victim of a crime. Many people suffer in silence. *Spotlight on Recovery* will provide a voice to those who suffer in silence and begin the dialogue of recovery." Estab. 2001. Circ. 3,000-6,000. Byline sometimes given. Pays on publication. No kill fee. Publishes ms an average of 6 months after acceptance. Editorial lead time 1 month. Submit seasonal material 1 month in advance. Accepts queries by mail, e-mail. Accepts simultaneous submissions. Responds in 2 weeks to queries; 1 month to mss. Sample copy and guidelines free.

NONFICTION Needs book excerpts, inspirational, interview, opinion, personal experience. **Buys 30-50 mss/year.** Query with published clips. Length: 150-1,500 words. **Pays 5¢/word or $75-80/article.**

PHOTOS State availability. Identification of subjects required. Reviews GIF/JPEG files. Pays $5-10/photo. Buys one-time rights.

COLUMNS/DEPARTMENTS Buys 4 mss/year. Query with published clips. **Pays 5¢/word or $75-80/column.**

FICTION Needs ethnic, mainstream, slice-of-life vignettes.

POETRY Contact: Robin Graham. Buys 10 poems/year. Submit maximum 2 poems. open **Pays 5 cents/word.**

FILLERS Needs facts, newsbreaks, short humor. **Buys 2 mss/year.**

REGIONAL

ALABAMA

$$ ALABAMA LIVING

Alabama Rural Electric Association, 340 Techna-Center Dr., Montgomery AL 36117. (800)410-2737. **E-mail:** agriffin@areapower.com. **Website:** http://www.areapower.coop. **Contact:** Allison Griffin, editor. **80% freelance written.** Monthly magazine covering topics of interest to rural and suburban Alabamians. "Our magazine is an editorially balanced, informational and educational service to members of rural electric cooperatives. Our mix regularly includes Alabama history, Alabama features, gardening, outdoor, and consumer pieces." Estab. 1948. Circ. 400,000. Byline given. Pays on acceptance. No kill fee. Editorial lead time 4 months. Submit seasonal material 4 months in advance. Accepts queries by mail, e-mail.

Accepts simultaneous submissions. Responds in 1 month to queries. Sample copy free.

NONFICTION Needs historical. Special issues: Gardening (March); Travel (April); Home Improvement (May); Holiday Recipes (December). **Buys 20 mss/year.** Send complete ms. Length: 500-750 words. **Pays $250 minimum for assigned articles. Pays $150 minimum for unsolicited articles.**

REPRINTS Send typed manuscript with rights for sale noted. Pays $100.

PHOTOS Buys 1-3 photos from freelancers/issue; 12-36 photos/year. Pays $100 for color cover; $50 for color inside; $60-75 for photo/text package. **Pays on acceptance.** Credit line given. Buys one-time rights for publication and website; negotiable.

TIPS "Preference given to submissions with accompanying art."

ARIZONA

$$ ARIZONA FOOTHILLS MAGAZINE

8132 N. 87th Place, Scottsdale AZ 85258. (480)460-5203. **Fax:** (480)443-1517. **Website:** www.azfoothillsmag.com. **10% freelance written.** Monthly magazine covering Arizona lifestyle. Estab. 1996. Circ. 60,000. Byline given. Pays on publication. No kill fee. Publishes ms an average of 6 months after acceptance. Editorial lead time 6 months. Submit seasonal material at least 4 months in advance. Accepts queries by mail, e-mail. Accepts simultaneous submissions. Responds in 1 month to queries. Sample copy for #10 SASE.

NONFICTION Needs general interest, photo feature, travel, fashion, decor, arts, interview. **Buys 10 mss/year.** Query with published clips. Length: 900-2,000 words. **Pays 35-40¢/word for assigned articles.**

PHOTOS Photos may be requested. Captions, identification of subjects, model releases required. Reviews contact sheets, transparencies. Negotiates payment individually. Occasionally buys one-time rights.

COLUMNS/DEPARTMENTS Travel, dining, fashion, home decor, design, architecture, wine, shopping, golf, performance & visual arts.

TIPS "We prefer stories that appeal to our affluent audience written with an upbeat, contemporary approach and reader service in mind."

$$$$ ARIZONA HIGHWAYS

2039 W. Lewis Ave., Phoenix AZ 85009. (602)712-2200. **Fax:** (602)254-4505. **E-mail:** kkramer@azdot.gov. **Website:** www.arizonahighways.com. **Contact:** Kelly Kramer, managing editor. **100% freelance written.** Magazine that is state-owned, designed to help attract tourists into and through Arizona. Estab. 1925. Circ. 425,000. Pays on acceptance. No kill fee. Accepts queries by mail, e-mail, fax. Accepts simultaneous submissions. Responds in 1 month. Guidelines online.

NONFICTION **Buys 50 mss/year.** Query with a lead paragraph and brief outline of story. Length: 600-1,800 words. **Pays up to $1/word.** Pays expenses of writers on assignment.

PHOTOS **Contact:** Peter Ensenberger, director of photography. For digital requirements, contact the photography department. Pays $125-600. Buys one-time rights.

COLUMNS/DEPARTMENTS Focus on Nature (short feature in first or third person dealing with the unique aspects of a single species of wildlife), 800 words; Along the Way (short essay dealing with life in Arizona, or a personal experience keyed to Arizona), 750 words; Back Road Adventure (personal back-road trips, preferably off the beaten path and outside major metro areas), 1,000 words; Hike of the Month (personal experiences on trails anywhere in Arizona), 500 words. **Pays $50-1,000, depending on department.**

TIPS "Writing must be of professional quality, warm, sincere, in-depth, well peopled, and accurate. Avoid themes that describe first trips to Arizona, the Grand Canyon, the desert, Colorado River running, etc. Emphasis is to be on Arizona adventure and romance as well as flora and fauna, when appropriate, and themes that can be photographed. Double check your manuscript for accuracy. Our typical reader is a 50-something person with the time, the inclination, and the means to travel."

$ PHOENIX MAGAZINE

Cities West Publishing, Inc., 15169 N. Scottsdale Rd., Suite C-310, Scottsdale AZ 85254. (866)481-6970. **Fax:** (602)604-0169. **Website:** www.phoenixmag.com. **70% freelance written.** Monthly magazine covering regional issues, personalities, events, neighborhoods, customs, and history of metro Phoenix. Estab. 1966. Circ. 60,000. Byline given. Pays on publication. No kill fee. Publishes ms an average of 3 months after acceptance. Submit seasonal material 1 year in advance. Accepts queries by online submission form. Responds in 2 months.

NONFICTION Needs general interest. "We do not publish fiction, poetry, personal essays, book reviews, music reviews, or product reviews, and our travel stories are staff written. With the exception of our travel stories, all of the content in *Phoenix* magazine is geographically specific to the Phoenix-metro region. We do not publish any non-travel news or feature stories that are outside the Phoenix area, and we prefer that our freelancers are located in the Phoenix metro area." **Buys 50 mss/year.** Query with published clips via e-mail. "Include a short summary, a list of sources, and an explanation of why you think your idea is right for the magazine and why you're qualified to write it." Length: 150-2,000 words.

TIPS "Stories must appeal to an educated Phoenix audience. We want solidly reported and diligently researched stories on key issues of public concern and the key players involved."

$$ TUCSON LIFESTYLE

Conley Publishing Group, Ltd., Suite 12, 7000 E. Tanque Verde Rd., Tucson AZ 85715-5318. (520)721-2929. **Fax:** (520)721-8665. **E-mail:** scott@tucsonlifestyle.com. **Website:** www.tucsonlifestyle.com. **Contact:** Scott Barker, executive editor. **90% freelance written. Prefers to work with published/established writers.** Monthly magazine covering Southern Arizona-related events and topics. No fiction, poetry, cartoons, or syndicated columns. Estab. 1982. Circ. 29,000. Byline given. Pays on acceptance. No kill fee. Publishes ms an average of 6 months after acceptance. Submit seasonal material 1 year in advance. Accepts queries by mail, e-mail. Accepts simultaneous submissions. Responds in 2 months to queries; in 3 months to mss. Sample copy: $3.99, plus $3 postage. Guidelines free.

NONFICTION "Avoid obvious tourist attractions and information that most residents of the Southwest are likely to know. No anecdotes masquerading as articles. Not interested in fish-out-of-water, Easterner-visiting-the-Old-West pieces." **Buys 20 mss/year. Pays $50-500.** Pays expenses of writers on assignment.

PHOTOS Query about photos before submitting anything.

TIPS "Read the magazine before submitting anything."

CALIFORNIA

$ JOURNAL PLUS

25 Johe Lane, San Luis Obispo CA 93405. (805) 546-0609. **E-mail:** info@slojournal.com. **Website:** slojournal.com. **Contact:** Tom Meinhold, publisher. **60% freelance written.** Monthly magazine that can be read online covering the 25-year old age group and up, but young-at-heart audience. "The *Journal Plus* is a combination of the *SLO County Journal* and *Plus Magazine.* It is the community magazine written for and by the local people of the Central Coast." Estab. 1981. Circ. 25,000. Byline given. Pays on publication. No kill fee. Publishes ms an average of 2 months after acceptance. Editorial lead time 2 months. Submit seasonal material 2 months in advance. Accepts queries by e-mail. Accepts simultaneous submissions. Responds in 2 weeks to queries; in 1 month to mss. Sample copy for 9x12 SAE with $2 postage. Guidelines online.

NONFICTION Needs historical, humor, interview, personal experience, profile, travel, book reviews, entertainment, health. Special issues: Christmas (December); Travel (October, April). No finance, heavy humor, poetry, or fiction. **Buys 60-70 mss/year.** Send complete ms. Length: 600-1,400 words. **Pays $50-75.** Pays expenses of writers on assignment.

PHOTOS Send photos. High resolution jpegs.

TIPS "Review an issue on the website before submitting."

$$ ORANGE COAST MAGAZINE

Orange Coast Kommunications, Inc., 3701 Birch St., Suite 100, Newport Beach CA 92660. (949)862-1133. **Fax:** (949)862-0133. **E-mail:** editorial@orangecoast.com; agibbons@orangecoastmagazine.com. **Website:** www.orangecoast.com. **Contact:** Martin J. Smith, editor-in-chief. **90% freelance written.** Monthly magazine designed to inform and enlighten the educated, upscale residents of Orange County, California; highly graphic and well researched. Estab. 1974. Circ. 52,000. Byline given. Pays on publication. Offers 20% kill fee. Publishes ms an average of 4 months after acceptance. Editorial lead time 5 months. Submit seasonal material 6 months in advance. Accepts queries by mail, e-mail. Accepts simultaneous submissions. Responds in 3 months to queries; 3 months to mss. Guidelines online.

NONFICTION Needs general interest, inspirational, interview, personal experience, celebrity profiles, guides to activities and services. Special issues: Health, Beauty, and Fitness (January); Dining (March and August); International Travel (April); Home Design (June); Arts (September); Local Travel (October). We do not accept stories that do not have specific Orange County angles. We want profiles on local people, stories on issues going on in our community, informational stories using Orange County-based sources. We cannot emphasize the local angle enough. **Buys up to 65 mss/year.** Query with published clips. Length: 1,000-2,000 words. **Negotiates payment individually.** Pays expenses of writers on assignment.

PHOTOS State availability. Captions, identification of subjects required. Negotiates payment individually. Buys one time rights.

COLUMNS/DEPARTMENTS Short Cuts (stories for the front of the book that focus on Orange County issues, people, and places), 150-250 words. **Buys up to 25 mss/year.** Query with published clips. **Negotiates payment individually.**

TIPS We're looking for more local personality profiles, analysis of current local issues, local takes on national issues. Most features are assigned to writers we've worked with before. Don't try to sell us 'generic' journalism. *Orange Coast* prefers articles with specific and unusual angles focused on Orange County. A lot of freelance writers ignore our Orange County focus. We get far too many generalized manuscripts.

$$$ SACRAMENTO MAGAZINE

Sacramento Magazines Corp., 231 Lathrop Way, Suite A, Sacramento CA 95815. (916)426-1720. **E-mail:** krista@sacmag.com. **Website:** www.sacmag.com. Publisher: Joe Chiodo. **Contact:** Krista Minard, editorial director. **80% freelance written. Works with a small number of new/unpublished writers each year.** Monthly magazine with a strictly local angle on local issues, human interest and consumer items for readers in the middle to high income brackets. Prefers to work with writers local to Sacramento area. Estab. 1975. Circ. 50,000. Pays on publication. No kill fee. Publishes ms an average of 3 months after acceptance. Accepts queries by mail. Accepts simultaneous submissions. Responds in 3 months.

NONFICTION Buys 5 unsolicited features mss/year. Query. 1,500-3,000 words, depending on author, subject matter and treatment. **Pays $400 and up.**

PHOTOS Send photos. Captions, identification of subjects required. Payment varies depending on photographer, subject matter and treatment. Buys one time rights.

COLUMNS/DEPARTMENTS Business, home and garden, first person essays, regional travel, gourmet, profile, sports, city arts, health, home and garden, profiles of local people (1,000-1,800 words); UpFront (250-300 words). **Pays $600-800.**

CANADIAN & INTERNATIONAL

$$$$ ALBERTA VIEWS

Alberta Views, Ltd., Suite 208, 320 23rd Ave. SW, Calgary AB T2S 0J2 Canada. (403)243-5334; (877)212-5334. **Fax:** (403)243-8599. **E-mail:** queries@albertaviews.ab.ca. **Website:** www.albertaviews.ab.ca. **Contact:** Evan Osenton, editor. **50% freelance written.** Bimonthly magazine covering Alberta culture: politics, economy, social issues, and art. "We are a regional magazine providing thoughtful commentary and background information on issues of concern to Albertans. Most of our writers are Albertans." Estab. 1997. Circ. 30,000. Byline given. Pays on publication. Offers 50% kill fee. Publishes ms an average of 3 months after acceptance. Editorial lead time 4 months. Submit seasonal material 3 months in advance. Accepts queries by e-mail. Accepts simultaneous submissions. Responds in 6 weeks to queries; 2 months to mss. Sample copy free. "If you are a writer, illustrator, or photographer interested in contributing to *Alberta Views*, please see our contributor's guidelines online."

No phone queries.

NONFICTION Needs essays. **Buys 18 mss/year.** "Query with written proposal of 300–500 words outlining your intended contribution to *Alberta Views*, why you are qualified to write about your subject, and what sources you intend to use; a résumé outlining your experience and education; recent examples of your published work (tear sheets)." Length: 3,000-5,000 words. **Pays $1,000-1,500 for assigned articles; $350-750 for unsolicited articles.**

PHOTOS State availability. Negotiates payment individually. Buys one-time rights, Web rights.

FICTION Only fiction by Alberta writers via the annual *Alberta Views* fiction contest. **Buys 6 mss/year.** Send complete ms. Length: 2,500-4,000 words. **Pays up to $1,000.**

POETRY Accepts unsolicited poetry. Submit complete ms.

CANADIAN GEOGRAPHIC

1155 Lola St., Suite 200, Ottawa ON K1K 4C1 Canada. (613)745-4629. **E-mail:** editor@canadiangeographic.ca. **Website:** www.canadiangeographic.ca. **90% freelance written. Works with a small number of new/unpublished writers each year.** Bimonthly magazine covering Canada. "*Canadian Geographic*'s colorful portraits of our ever-changing population show readers just how important the relationship between the people and the land really is." Estab. 1930. Circ. 240,000. Pays on acceptance. Publishes ms an average of 3 months after acceptance. Submit seasonal materials 1 year in advance. Accepts queries by e-mail. Accepts simultaneous submissions.

Canadian Geographic reports a need for more articles on earth sciences. Canadian writers only.

NONFICTION Needs photo feature, profile, travel. **Buys 30 mss/year.** Query. Length: 1,500-3,000 words. **Pays 80¢/word minimum.**

PHOTOS Pays $75-400 for color photos, depending on published size.

MONDAY MAGAZINE

Black Press Ltd., 818 Broughton St., Victoria British Columbia V8W 1E4 Canada. (250)382-6188. **E-mail:** editor@mondaymag.com. **Website:** www.mondaymag.com. **Contact:** Sarah Wilson, editor. **10% freelance written.** Weekly tabloid covering local news. "*Monday Magazine* is Victoria's only alternative newsweekly. For more than 35 years, we have published fresh, informative, and alternative perspectives on local events. We prefer lively, concise writing with a sense of humor and insight." Estab. 1975. Circ. 20,000. Byline given. **Currently not accepting freelance articles requiring payment.** Pays 1 month after publication. No kill fee. Publishes ms an average of 1 month after acceptance. Editorial lead time 1-2 months. Submit seasonal material 2 months in advance. Accepts queries by e-mail. Accepts simultaneous submissions. Responds in 6-8 weeks to queries; 3 months to mss. Guidelines online.

NONFICTION Needs expose, general interest, humor, interview, personal experience. Special issues: Body, Mind, Spirit (October); Student Survival Guide (August). Does not want fiction, poetry, or conspiracy theories. Send complete ms. Length: 300-1,000 words. **Pays $25-50. Currently not accepting freelance articles requiring payment.**

PHOTOS Send photos. Captions, identification of subjects required. Reviews GIF/JPEG files (300 dpi at 4x6). Offers no additional payment for photos accepted with ms. Buys one-time rights.

TIPS "Local writers tend to have an advantage, as they are familiar with the issues and concerns of interest to a Victoria audience."

RUSSIAN LIFE

RIS Publications, P.O. Box 567, Montpelier VT 05601. **Website:** russianlife.com. **75% freelance written.** Bimonthly magazine covering Russian culture, history, travel, and business. "Our readers are informed Russophiles with an avid interest in all things Russian. But we do not publish personal travel journals or the like." Estab. 1956. Circ. 15,000. Byline given. Pays on publication. Publishes ms an average of 3-6 months after acceptance. Editorial lead time 2 months. Submit seasonal material 3 months in advance. Accepts queries by mail, e-mail. Responds in 1 month to queries. Guidelines online.

NONFICTION Needs book excerpts, general interest, interview, photo feature, travel. No personal stories, i.e., How I came to love Russia. **Buys 15-20 mss/year.** Query. Length: 1,000-6,000 words. **Pays $100-300.**

REPRINTS Accepts previously published submissions rarely.

PHOTOS Send photos. Captions required. Model/property release preferred. Words with local freelancers only. Reviews contact sheets. Negotiates payment individually. Pays $20-50 (color photo with accompanying story), depending on placement in magazine. Pays on publication. Credit line given. Buys one-time rights.

DELAWARE

DELAWARE BEACH LIFE

Endeavours LLC, P.O. Box 417, Rehoboth Beach DE 19971. (302)227-9499. **E-mail:** info@delawarebeachlife.com. **Website:** www.delawarebeachlife.com. **Contact:** Terry Plowman, publisher/editor. Magazine published 8 times/year covering coastal Delaware. "*Delaware Beach Life* focuses on coastal Delaware: Fenwick to Lewes. You can go slightly inland as long as there's water and a natural connection to the coast, e.g., Angola or Long Neck." Estab. 2002. Circ. 15,000. Byline given. Pays on acceptance. 50% kill fee. Publishes ms 4 months after acceptance. Editorial lead time 6 months. Submit seasonal material 1 year in advance. Accepts queries by e-mail. Responds in 2 months to queries; in 6 months to mss. Sample copy available online at website. Guidelines free and by e-mail.

"*Delaware Beach Life* is the only full-color glossy magazine focused on coastal Delaware's culture and lifestyle. Created by a team of the best freelance writers, the magazine takes a deeper look at the wealth of topics that interest coastal residents. *Delaware Beach Life* features such top-notch writing and photography that it inspires 95% of its readers to save it as a 'coffee-table' magazine."

NONFICTION Needs book excerpts, essays, general interest, humor, interview, opinion, photo feature. Does not want anything not focused on coastal Delaware. Query with published clips. Length: 1,200-3,000 words. **Pays $400-1,000 for assigned articles.** Pays expenses of writers on assignment.

PHOTOS Send photos. Photos require captions, identification of subjects. Reviews GIF/JPEG files. Pays $25-100 per photo. Purchases one-time rights.

COLUMNS/DEPARTMENTS Profiles, History, Opinion (focused on coastal DE), all 1,200 words. **Buys 32 mss/year.** Query with published clips. **Pays $150-350.**

FICTION Needs adventure, condensed novels, historical, humorous, novel excerpts, Must have coastal theme. Does not want anything not coastal. **Buys 3 mss/year.** Query with published clips. Length: 1,000-2,000 words.

POETRY Needs avant-garde, free verse, haiku, light verse, traditional. Does not want anything not coastal. No erotic poetry. Buys 6 poems/year. Submit maximum 3 poems. Length: 6-15 lines/poem. **Pays up to $50.**

$$ DELAWARE TODAY

Today Media, 3301 Lancaster Pike, Suite 5C, Wilmington DE 19805. (302)656-1809. **Website:** www.delawaretoday.com. **Contact:** Drew Ostroski, managing editor. **50% freelance written.** Monthly magazine geared toward Delaware people, places, and issues. "For more than 50 years, *Delaware Today* has been the lifestyle authority in the First State. The publication boasts various awards for thoughtful commentary and stunning full-color design. As the state's premier magazine, *Delaware Today* helps readers make informed decisions to enhance their lives." Estab. 1962. Circ. 25,000. Byline given. Pays on publication. Offers 50% kill fee. Publishes ms an average of 4 months after acceptance. Editorial lead time 3 months. Submit seasonal material 6 months in advance. Accepts queries by online submission form. Accepts simultaneous submissions. Responds in 2 months to queries.

All stories must have Delaware slant. No pitches such as Delawareans will be interested in a national topic.

NONFICTION Needs historical, interview, photo feature, lifestyles, issues. Special issues: Newcomer's Guide to Delaware. **Buys 40 mss/year.** Query with published clips. Length: 100-3,000 words. **Pays $50-750.** Pays expenses of writers on assignment.

PHOTOS State availability. Identification of subjects required. Negotiates payment individually. Buys one-time rights.

COLUMNS/DEPARTMENTS Business, Health, History, People, all 1,500 words. **Buys 24 mss/year.** Query with published clips. **Pays $150-250.**

FILLERS Needs anecdotes, newsbreaks, short humor. **Buys 10 mss/year.** Length: 100-200 words. **Pays $50-75.**

TIPS "No story ideas that we would know about, i.e., a profile of the governor. Best bets are profiles of quirky/unique Delawareans whom we'd never know about or think of."

FLORIDA

$$$$ BOCA RATON MAGAZINE

JES Publishing, 1000 Clint Moore Rd., Suite 103, Boca Raton FL 33487. (561)997-8683. **Fax:** (561)997-8909. **E-mail:** magazine@bocamag.com. **Website:** www.

bocamag.com. Managing Editor: John Thomason. **30% freelance written.** Lifestyle and city/regional magazine devoted to the residents of South Florida, featuring fashion, interior design, food, people, places, and community issues that shape the affluent South Florida market. Estab. 1981. Circ. 25,000. Byline given. Pays 45 days after acceptance. No kill fee. Publishes ms an average of 3 months after acceptance. Submit seasonal material 7 months in advance. Accepts simultaneous submissions. Responds in 1 month to queries. Does not accept unsolicited queries. Guidelines for #10 SASE.

NONFICTION Needs general interest, historical, humor, interview, photo feature, travel. Send complete ms. Length: 800-2,500 words. **Pays $350-1,200.**

REPRINTS Send tearsheet. Payment varies.

PHOTOS Send photos.

COLUMNS/DEPARTMENTS Body & Soul (health, fitness and beauty column, general interest); Hitting Home (family and social interactions); History or Arts (relevant to South Florida); all 1,000 words. Query with published clips, or send complete ms. **Pays $350-400.**

TIPS "We prefer shorter ms, highly localized articles, and excellent art/photography."

$ FT. MYERS MAGAZINE

And Pat llc, 52 Park Ave. E., Merrick NY 11566. (516)652-6072. **E-mail:** ftmyers@optonline.net. **E-mail:** ftmyers2@optonline.net. **Website:** www.ftmyersmagazine.com. **Contact:** Andrew Elias. **90% freelance written.** Bimonthly magazine covering regional arts and living for educated, active, successful, and creative residents of Lee & Collier counties (FL) and people planning vacations, visits and moves to Southwest Florida. Content: Arts, entertainment, media and culture (fine arts, music, theater, film, literature, television) and living (health/fitness, travel/recreation, sports/recreation, home/garden, nutrition/dining, as well as history/environmental issues). Estab. 2001. Circ. 20,000. Byline given. 30 days after publication. No kill fee. Publishes ms an average of 2-6 months after acceptance. Editorial lead time 2-6 months. Submit seasonal material 2-6 months in advance. Accepts queries by e-mail. Accepts simultaneous submissions. Responds in 1-2 months to queries and to mss. Sample copy online. Guidelines online.

NONFICTION Needs book excerpts, essays, general interest, historical, how-to, humor, interview, personal experience, profile, reviews, travel, reviews, previews, news, informational. **Buys 10-25 mss/year.** Send complete ms. Length: 750-1,750 words. **Pays $75-175 or approximately 10¢/word.**

PHOTOS **Contact:** Andrew Elias. State availability of or send photos. Captions, identification of subjects required. Negotiates payment individually; generally offers $10-100/photo or art. Buys one-time rights.

$$ JACKSONVILLE

1261 King St., Jacksonville FL 32204. (904)389-3622. **Fax:** (904)389-3628. **E-mail:** jocelyn@jacksonvillemag.com. **Website:** www.jacksonvillemag.com. **Contact:** Jocelyn Tolbert, assistant editor. **50% freelance written.** Monthly magazine covering life and business in northeast Florida for upwardly mobile residents of Jacksonville and the Beaches, Orange Park, St. Augustine and Amelia Island, Florida. Estab. 1985. Circ. 25,000. Byline given. Pays on publication. Offers kill fee. Offers 25-33% kill fee to writers on assignment. Editorial lead time 3 months. Submit seasonal material 4 months in advance. Accepts queries by e-mail. Accepts simultaneous submissions. Responds in 6 weeks to queries; in 1 month to mss. Sample copy: $5 (includes postage). Guidelines online.

NONFICTION Needs book excerpts, expose, general interest, historical, how-to, humor, interview, personal experience, photo feature, travel, commentary. **Buys 50 mss/year.** Query with published clips. Length: 1,200-3,000 words. **Pays $50-500 for feature length pieces.**

REPRINTS Send photocopy. Payment varies.

PHOTOS State availability. Captions, model releases required. Negotiates payment individually. Buys one-time rights.

COLUMNS/DEPARTMENTS Business (trends, success stories, personalities), 1,000-1,200 words; Health (trends, emphasis on people, hopeful outlooks), 1,000-1,200 words; Money (practical personal financial advice using local people, anecdotes, and examples), 1,000-1,200 words; Real Estate/Home (service, trends, home photo features), 1,000-1,200 words; Travel (weekends, daytrips, excursions locally and regionally), 1,000-1,200 words; occasional departments and columns covering local history, sports, family issues, etc. **Buys 40 mss/year. Pays $150-250.**

TIPS "We are a writer's magazine and demand writing that tells a story with flair."

$$ PENSACOLA MAGAZINE

Ballinger Publishing, 314 N. Spring St., Suite A, Pensacola FL 32501. **E-mail:** kelly@ballingerpublishing.com. **Website:** www.ballingerpublishing.com. Executive Editor: Kelly Oden. **75% freelance written.** Monthly magazine. *Pensacola Magazine*'s articles are written in a casual, conversational tone. We cover a broad range of topics that citizens of Pensacola relate to. Most of our freelance work is assigned, so it is best to send a resume, cover letter and 3 clips to the above e-mail address. Estab. 1987. Circ. 10,000. Byline given. Pays at end of shelf life. Offers 20% kill fee. Editorial lead time 1 month. Submit seasonal material 6 months in advance. Accepts queries by e-mail. Accepts simultaneous submissions. Responds in 2 weeks to queries. Sample copy for $1, SASE and 1 First-Class stamp. Guidelines available online.

NONFICTION Special issues: Wedding (February); Home & Garden (May). Query with published clips. Length: 700-2,100 words. **Pays 10-15¢/word.** Pays expenses of writers on assignment.

PHOTOS State availability of or send photos. Captions, identification of subjects, model releases required. Reviews GIF/JPEG files. Offers $7/photo. Buys one time rights.

TIPS We accept submissions for *Pensacola Magazine*, *Northwest Florida's Business Climate*, and *Coming of Age*. Please query by topic via e-mail to shannon@ballingerpublishing.com. If you do not have a specific query topic, please send a resume and three clips via e-mail, and you will be given story assignments if your writing style is appropriate. You do not have to be locally or regionally located to write for us.

GENERAL

$$ A.T. JOURNEYS

Appalachian Trail Conservancy, P.O. Box 807, 799 Washington St., Harpers Ferry WV 25425-0807. (304)535-6331. **Fax:** (304)535-2667. **E-mail:** editor@appalachiantrail.org. **Website:** www.appalachiantrail.org. Estab. 1925. Accepts queries by mail, e-mail. Accepts simultaneous submissions. Responds in 2 months to queries. Guidelines available online.

NONFICTION Needs general interest, historical, how-to, interview, profile, travel. **Buys 5-10 mss/year.** Query with or without published clips, or send complete ms. Prefers e-mail queries. Length: 250-3,000 words. **Pays $25-300.**

REPRINTS Send photocopy with rights for sale noted and information about when and where the material previously appeared.

PHOTOS State availability. Identification of subjects, model releases required. Reviews contact sheets, 5x7 prints, slides, digital images. Offers $25-150/photo; $200/cover.

TIPS "Contributors should display a knowledge of or interest in the Appalachian Trail. Those who live in the vicinity of the Trail may opt for an assigned story and should present credentials and subject of interest to the editor."

$$ SOUTHERN EDITION

509 Old Wagon Rd., Walhalla SC 29691-5821. **E-mail:** southernedition@live.com. **Website:** southernedition.com. **Contact:** Greg Freeman, editor. **10% freelance written.** Dedicated to celebrating the beauty, character, culture, and heritage of the American South, *Southern Edition* brings to you the sights, sounds, tastes, and hospitality for which the region is known." New content is added consistently throughout the year. Past freelance articles include Dr. Ed Brotak's "Southern Live Oaks: Nature's Great Survivors," Debra Pamplin's travel piece "The Casa Marina Hotel and Jacksonville Beach," Tammy Blue's "The Immigrant Historian: British Expat Enjoys Exploring the South's Past" and Darrell Laurant's "Pierce Street: Lynchburg's Out-of-the-Way Connection with African American History." *Southern Edition* is an online magazine comprised of columns devoted to general interests, travel, food, gardening, history, books, and humor. Estab. 2006. Byline given. Typically pays 10-20 days upon publication. Publishes ms an average of 1 month after acceptance. Editorial lead time is 1-3 months. Submit seasonal material 1-2 months in advance. Accepts queries by mail, e-mail. Responds in 1-3 weeks to queries; 1 month to ms. Sample copies available online. Guidelines available online or via email. While freelance submissions are not actively

solicited, queries from writers, photographers, and visual artists are welcomed and entertained. All ideas must be related to the American South, and must be substantive and of educational value.

NONFICTION Needs essays, general interest, historical, interview, nostalgic, photo feature, profile, travel. Does not want to see any "romanticized" travel stories (think phrases like, "nestled in a quaint little village"), or notions that the Civil War is still ongoing. No content promoting bigotry or alt-right ideals. Query via e-mail. Minimum 350 words for nonfiction articles. Prefer articles in 1,200-word range. **Pays between $35-375 for assigned and unsolicited articles.** Pays expenses of writers on assignment.

PHOTOS Freelancers should state availability of photos with submission. Photos require captions and identification of subjects. Reviews GIF/JPEG files. Negotiates payment individually.

COLUMNS/DEPARTMENTS *Southern Edition* has 5 different, regular columns: Southern Exposure, which features interviews, history, music reviews, and other features (averages 500 words); Soul Food, which features cooking and Southern cuisine (averages 350 words); Magnolia Eden, which features gardening (averages 500 words); Sunbelt Excursions, which features travel (averages 750 words); and Southern Press, which features author interviews and book reviews (averages 500 words). Writer should query via e-mail. **Columns pay between $35-375.**

TIPS "Demonstrate an ability to write about the American South intelligently and concisely, always recognizing that fact-laden material should be palatable to a general audience."

GEORGIA

$ ATHENS MAGAZINE

One Press Place, Athens GA 30601. (706)208-2308. **Fax:** (706)208-2339. **Website:** www.athensmagazine.com. **70% freelance written.** Quarterly magazine focused on Athens, GA community and surrounding area (does not include Atlanta metro). Estab. 1989. Circ. 5,000. Byline given. Pays on publication. Offers 20% kill fee. Publishes ms an average of 6 months after acceptance. Editorial lead time 6-9 months. Submit seasonal material 12 months in advance. Accepts queries by mail, e-mail. Accepts simultaneous submissions. Responds in 6-8 weeks to queries. Sample copy free. Guidelines online.

PHOTOS State availability. Captions, identification of subjects required. Reviews GIF/JPEG files. Negotiates payment individually. Buys one time rights.

FILLERS Needs anecdotes, facts, short humor. Length: 25-150 words. **Pays $20-150.**

TIPS "I need freelancers who are well-acquainted with Athens area who can write to its unique audience of students, retirees, etc."

$$ ATLANTA TRIBUNE: THE MAGAZINE

875 Old Roswell Rd, Suite C-100, Roswell GA 30076. (770)587-0501. **Fax:** (770)642-6501. **E-mail:** info@atlantatribune.com. **Website:** www.atlantatribune.com. **30% freelance written.** Monthly magazine covering African-American business, careers, technology, wealth-building, politics, and education. The *Atlanta Tribune* is written for Atlanta's black executives, professionals and entrepreneurs with a primary focus of business, careers, technology, wealth-building, politics, and education. Our publication serves as an advisor that offers helpful information and direction to the black entrepreneur. Estab. 1987. Circ. 30,000. Byline given. Pays on publication. Offers 10% kill fee. Editorial lead time 3 months. Submit seasonal material 4 months in advance. Accepts queries by e-mail. Accepts simultaneous submissions. Responds in 6 weeks to queries. Sample copy online or mail a request. Guidelines available online.

NONFICTION Needs book excerpts, how-to, interview, new product, opinion, technical. **Buys 100 mss/year.** Query with published clips. Length: 1,400-2,500 words. **Pays $250-600.** Pays expenses of writers on assignment.

PHOTOS State availability. Identification of subjects, model releases required. Reviews 21/4x21/4 transparencies. Negotiates payment individually. Buys one time rights.

COLUMNS/DEPARTMENTS Business; Careers; Technology; Wealth-Building; Politics and Education; all 400-600 words. **Buys 100 mss/year.** Query with published clips. **Pays $100-200.**

TIPS Send a well-written, convincing query by e-mail that demonstrates that you have thoroughly read previous issues and reviewed our online writer's guidelines.

$ FLAGPOLE MAGAZINE

P.O. Box 1027, Athens GA 30603. (706)549-9523. **Fax:** (706)548-8981. **E-mail:** editor@flagpole.com. **Website:** www.flagpole.com. **Contact:** Pete McCommons, editor and publisher. **75% freelance written.** Local alternative weekly with a special emphasis on popular (and unpopular) music. Will consider stories on national, international musicians, authors, politicians, etc., even if they don't have a local or regional news peg. However, those stories should be original and irreverent enough to justify inclusion. Of course, local/Southern news/feature stories are best. We like reporting and storytelling more than opinion pieces. Estab. 1987. Circ. 16,000. Byline given. Pays on publication. No kill fee. Publishes ms an average of 1 month after acceptance. Editorial lead time 2 months. Submit seasonal material 2 months in advance. Accepts simultaneous submissions. Responds in 2 weeks to queries. Responds in 1 month to mss. Sample copy online.

NONFICTION Needs book excerpts, essays, expose, interview, new product, personal experience. **Buys 50 mss/year.** Query by e-mail Length: 600-2,000 words. Pays expenses of writers on assignment.

REPRINTS Send tearsheet, photocopy or typed ms with rights for sale noted and information about when and where the material previously appeared.

PHOTOS State availability. Captions required. Reviews prints. Negotiates payment individually. Buys one time rights.

TIPS "Read our publication online before querying, but don't feel limited by what you see. We can't afford to pay much, so we're open to young/inexperienced writer-journalists looking for clips. Fresh, funny/insightful voices make us happiest, as does reportage over opinion. If you've ever succumbed to the temptation to call a pop record 'ethereal' we probably won't bother with your music journalism. No faxed submissions, please."

$$ GEORGIA MAGAZINE

Georgia Electric Membership Corp., P.O. Box 1707, 2100 E. Exchange Place, Tucker GA 30085. (770)270-6500. **E-mail:** laurel.george@georgiaemc.com; magazine@georgiamc.com. **Website:** www.georgiamagazine.org. **Contact:** Laurel George, editor. **50% freelance written.** "We are a monthly magazine for and about Georgians, with a friendly, conversational tone and human interest topics." Estab. 1945. Circ. 500,000. Byline given. Pays on acceptance. No kill fee. Publishes ms an average of 6 months after acceptance. Editorial lead time 2 months. Submit seasonal material 6 months in advance. Accepts queries by mail, e-mail. Accepts simultaneous submissions. Responds in 1 month to subjects of interest. Sample copy: $2. Guidelines for #10 SASE, or by e-mail.

NONFICTION Needs general interest, historical, how-to, humor, inspirational, interview, photo feature, travel. Query with published clips. Length: 1,000-1,200 words; 800 words for smaller features and departments. **Pays $350-500.** Pays expenses of writers on assignment.

PHOTOS State availability. Identification of subjects, model releases required. Reviews digital images, websites, and prints. Negotiates payment individually. Buys one-time rights.

$$ KNOWATLANTA MAGAZINE

New South Publishing, Inc., 9040 Roswell Rd., Suite 210, Atlanta GA 30350. (770)650-1102. **Fax:** (770)650-2848. **E-mail:** lindsay@knowatlanta.com. **Website:** www.knowatlanta.com. **Contact:** Lindsay Penticuff, editor. **80% freelance written.** Quarterly magazine covering the Atlanta area. *KNOWAtlanta* is metro Atlanta's premier relocation guide. The magazine provides valuable information to people relocating to the area with articles on homes, healthcare, jobs, finances, temporary housing, apartments, education, county-by-county guides, and so much more. *KNOWAtlanta* puts Atlanta at its readers' fingertips. The magazine is used by executives relocating their companies, realtors working with future Atlantans, and individuals moving to the "capital of the Southeast." Estab. 1986. Circ. 192,000. Byline given. Pays on publication. Offers 100% kill fee. Editorial lead time 2 months. Submit seasonal material 2 months in advance. Accepts queries by e-mail. Accepts simultaneous submissions. Sample copy free.

NONFICTION Needs general interest, how-to, interview, personal experience, photo feature. No fiction. **Buys 20 mss/year.** Query with published clips. Length: 800-1,500 words. **Pays $100-500 for assigned articles. Pays $100-300 for unsolicited articles.** Pays expenses of writers on assignment.

PHOTOS Send photos with submission, if available. Captions, identification of subjects required. Reviews contact sheets. Negotiates payment individually. Buys one-time rights.

$$ SAVANNAH MAGAZINE

Morris Publishing Group, P.O. Box 1088, Savannah GA 31402. **Fax:** (912)525-0611. **E-mail:** editor@savannahmagazine.com. **Website:** www.savannahmagazine.com. **Contact:** Emily Testa, editor-in-chief. **95% freelance written.** Bimonthly magazine focusing on homes and entertaining covering coastal lifestyle of Savannah and South Carolina area. "*Savannah Magazine* publishes articles about people, places, and events of interest to the residents of the greater Savannah areas, as well as coastal Georgia and the South Carolina low country. We strive to provide our readers with information that is both useful and entertaining—written in a lively, readable style." Estab. 1990. Circ. 16,000. Byline given. Pays on publication. Offers 20% kill fee. Publishes ms an average of 2 months after acceptance. Editorial lead time 2 months. Submit seasonal material 4 months in advance. Accepts queries by mail, e-mail, fax. Accepts simultaneous submissions. Responds in 4 weeks to queries; 6 weeks to mss. Sample copy free. Guidelines by e-mail.

NONFICTION Needs general interest, historical, humor, interview, travel. Does not want fiction or poetry. Query with published clips. Length: 500-750 words. **Pays $250-450.** Pays expenses of writers on assignment.

PHOTOS **Contact:** Contact Michelle Karner, art director. State availability. Reviews GIF/JPEG files. Negotiates payment individually. Offers no additional payment for photos accepted with ms. Buys one-time rights.

HAWAII

$$$ HONOLULU MAGAZINE

PacificBasin Communications, 1000 Bishop Street, Suite 405, Honolulu HI 96813. (808)537-9500. **Fax:** (808)537-6455. **E-mail:** kristinl@honolulumagazine.com. **Website:** www.honolulumagazine.com. Michael Keany, managing editor. **Contact:** Kristin Lipman, creative director. Monthly magazine covering general-interest topics relating to Hawaii residents. Estab. 1888. Circ. 30,000. Byline given. Pays about 30 days after publication. Where appropriate, offers 50% kill fee. Prefers to work with published/established writers. Accepts queries by mail, e-mail. Accepts simultaneous submissions. Guidelines available online.

NONFICTION Needs historical, interview, sports, politics, lifestyle trends, all Hawaii-related. "We write for Hawaii residents, so travel articles about Hawaii are not appropriate." Send complete ms. Length determined when assignments discussed. **Pays $250-1,200.** Pays expenses of writers on assignment.

PHOTOS State availability. Captions, identification of subjects, model releases required. Pays $100 for stock, $200 for assigned shot. Package rates also negotiated.

COLUMNS/DEPARTMENTS Length determined when assignments discussed. Query with published clips or send complete ms. **Pays $100-300.**

ILLINOIS

$ ILLINOIS ENTERTAINER

4223 W. Lake St., Suite 490, Chicago IL 60624. (773)717-5665. **Fax:** (773)717-5666. **E-mail:** service@illinoisentertainer.com. **Website:** www.illinoisentertainer.com. **80% freelance written.** Monthly free magazine covering popular and alternative music, as well as other entertainment (film, media) in Illinois. Estab. 1974. Circ. 55,000. Byline given. Pays on publication. Offers 50% kill fee. Publishes ms an average of 2 months after acceptance. Editorial lead time 2 months. Submit seasonal material 2 months in advance. Accepts queries by mail. Accepts simultaneous submissions. Responds in 2 months to queries. Sample copy: $5.

NONFICTION Needs expose, how-to, humor, interview, new product, reviews. No personal, confessional, or inspirational articles. **Buys 75 mss/year.** Query with published clips. Length: 600-2,600 words. **Pays $15-160.** Pays expenses of writers on assignment.

REPRINTS Send typed ms with rights for sale noted and information about when and where the material previously appeared. Pays 100% of amount paid for an original article.

PHOTOS Send photos. Captions, identification of subjects, model releases required. Reviews contact sheets, transparencies, 5x7 prints. Offers $20-200/photo. Buys one-time rights.

COLUMNS/DEPARTMENTS Spins (LP reviews), 100-400 words. **Buys 200-300 mss/year.** Query with published clips. **Pays $8-25.**

TIPS "Send clips, résumé, etc. and be patient. Also, sending queries that show you've seen our magazine and have a feel for it greatly increases your publication chances. Don't send unsolicited material. No e-mail solicitations or queries of any kind."

$$ NORTHWEST QUARTERLY MAGAZINE

Hughes Media Corp., 222 Seventh St., Rockford IL 61104. (815)316-2300. **E-mail:** clinden@northwestquarterly.com. **Website:** www.northwestquarterly.com. **Contact:** Chris Linden, executive editor. **20% freelance written.** Quarterly magazine covering regional lifestyle of Northern Illinois and Southern Wisconsin, and also Kane and McHenry counties (Chicago collar counties), highlighting strengths of living and doing business in the area. Publishes information specifically related to its geographic territory. National stories without a local angle not accepted. Estab. 2004. Circ. 42,000. Byline given. Pays on publication. Publishes ms an average of 4-6 months after acceptance. Editorial lead time 6 months. Submit seasonal material 6 months in advance. Accepts queries by mail, e-mail. Accepts simultaneous submissions. Responds in 2 weeks to queries; in 2 months to mss. Sample copy and guidelines available by e-mail.

NONFICTION Needs historical, interview, photo feature, regional features. Does not want opinion, fiction, or "anything unrelated to our geographic region." **Buys 150 mss/year.** Query. Length: 700-2,500 words. **Pays $25-500.** Pays expenses of writers on assignment.

PHOTOS State availability. Captions required. Reviews GIF/JPEG files. Negotiates payment individually. Buys one-time rights.

COLUMNS/DEPARTMENTS Health & Fitness, 1,000-2,000 words; Home & Garden, 1,500 words; Destinations & Recreation, 1,000-2,000 words; Environment & Nature, 2,000-3,000 words. **Buys 120 mss/year.** Query. **Pays $100-500.**

FILLERS Needs short humor. **Buys 24 mss/year.** Length: 100-200 words. **Pays $30-50.**

TIPS "Any interesting, well-documented feature relating to the 16-county area we cover may be considered. Nature, history, geography, culture, and destinations are favorite themes."

$$ WEST SUBURBAN LIVING

C2 Publishing, Inc., P.O. Box 111, Elmhurst IL 60126. (630)834-4995. **Fax:** (630)834-4996. **E-mail:** wsl@westsuburbanliving.net. **Website:** www.westsuburbanliving.net. **80% freelance written.** Bimonthly magazine focusing on the western suburbs of Chicago. Estab. 1996. Circ. 25,000. Byline given. Pays on publication. Publishes ms an average of 2-4 months after acceptance. Accepts queries by mail, e-mail, fax. Sample copy available online.

NONFICTION Needs general interest, how-to, travel. "Does not want anything that does not have an angle or tie-in to the area we cover—Chicago's western suburbs." **Buys 15 mss/year. Pays $100-500.** Pays expenses of writers on assignment.

PHOTOS State availability. Model releases required. Offers $50-700/photo; negotiates payment individually.

INDIANA

$$ EVANSVILLE LIVING

Tucker Publishing Group, 223 NW Second St., Suite 200, Evansville IN 47708. (812)426-2115. **E-mail:** ktucker@evansvilleliving.com. **Website:** www.evansvilleliving.com. **Contact:** Kristen Tucker, publisher and editor. **80-100% freelance written.** Bimonthly magazine covering Evansville, Indiana, and the greater area. *Evansville Living* is the only full-color, glossy, 100+ page city magazine for the Evansville, Indiana, area. Regular departments include: Home Style, Garden Style, Day Tripping, Sporting Life, and Local Flavor (menus). Estab. 2000. Circ. 50,000. Byline given. Pays on acceptance. No kill fee. Publishes ms an average of 3 months after acceptance. Editorial lead time 6 months. Submit seasonal material 6 months in advance. Accepts queries by mail, e-mail. Accepts simultaneous submissions. Sample copy for $5 or online. Guidelines by e-mail.

NONFICTION Needs essays, general interest, historical, photo feature, travel. **Buys 60-80 mss/year.** Query with published clips. Length: 200-2,000 words. **Pays $100-300.** Pays expenses of writers on assignment.

PHOTOS State availability. Captions, identification of subjects required. Reviews contact sheets, negatives, transparencies, prints. Negotiates payment individually. Buys all rights.

COLUMNS/DEPARTMENTS Home Style (home); Garden Style (garden); Sporting Life (sports); Local

Flavor (menus), all 1,500 words. Query with published clips. **Pays $100-300.**

IOWA

$$ THE IOWAN

Pioneer Communications, Inc., 300 Walnut St., Suite 6, Des Moines IA 50309. (515)246-0402. **E-mail:** editor@iowan.com. **Website:** www.iowan.com. **Contact:** Erich Gaukel, editor. **75% freelance written.** Bimonthly magazine covering the state of Iowa. *The Iowan* is a bimonthly magazine exploring everything Iowa has to offer. Each issue travels into diverse pockets of the state to discover the sights, meet the people, learn the history, taste the cuisine, and experience the culture. Estab. 1952. Circ. 20,000. Byline given. Pays 60 days from invoice approval or publication date, whichever comes first. Offers $100 kill fee. Publishes ms an average of 3 months after acceptance. Editorial lead time 9-10 months. Submit seasonal material 6-12 months in advance. Accepts queries by mail, e-mail. Accepts simultaneous submissions. Sample copy for $4.95, plus s&h. Guidelines available online.

NONFICTION Needs essays, general interest, historical, interview, photo feature, travel. Special issues: Each issue offers readers a collection of "shorts" that cover timely issues, current trends, interesting people, noteworthy work, enticing food, historical and historic moments, captivating arts and culture, beckoning recreational opportunities, and more. Features cover every topic imaginable with only 2 primary rules: (1) solid storytelling and (2) great photography potential. **Buys 30 mss/year.** Query with published clips. Length: 500-750 words for "shorts"; 1,000-1,500 words for features. **Pays $150-450.** Pays expenses of writers on assignment.

PHOTOS Send photos. Captions, identification of subjects, model releases required. Reviews contact sheets, GIF/JPEG files (8x10 at 300 dpi minimum). Negotiates payment individually, according to space rates. Buys one-time rights.

COLUMNS/DEPARTMENTS Last Word (essay), 800 words. **Buys 6 mss/year.** Query with published clips. **Pays $100.**

TIPS "Must have submissions in writing, either via e-mail or snail mail. Submitting published clips is preferred."

KANSAS

$$ KANSAS!

1020 S. Kansas Ave., Suite 200, Topeka KS 66612-1354. (785)296-8478. **Fax:** (785)296-6988. **E-mail:** ksmagazine@sunflowerpub.com. **Website:** www.travelks.com/ks-mag. **Contact:** Andrea Etzel, editor. **90% freelance written.** Quarterly magazine emphasizing Kansas travel attractions and events. Estab. 1945. Circ. 45,000. Byline and courtesy bylines are given to all content. Pays on acceptance. No kill fee. Publishes ms an average of 1 year after acceptance. Submit seasonal material 8 months in advance. Accepts queries by mail, e-mail. Accepts simultaneous submissions. Responds in 2 months to queries. Guidelines available on website.

NONFICTION Needs general interest, photo feature, travel. Query. Length: 750-1,250 words. **Pays $200-350.** Pays expenses of writers on assignment. Mileage reimbursement is available for writers on assignment in the state of Kansas, TBD by assignment editor.

PHOTOS "We are a full-color photograph/ms publication. Send digital photos (original transparencies only or CD with images available in high resolution) with query." Captions and location of the image (county and city) are required. Pays $25-75 for gallery images, $150 for cover. Assignments also available, welcomes queries.

TIPS "History and nostalgia or essay stories do not fit into our format because they can't be illustrated well with color photos. Submit a query letter describing 1 appropriate idea with outline for possible article and suggestions for photos. Do not send unsolicited mss."

KENTUCKY

$$$ KENTUCKY LIVING

Kentucky Association of Electric Co-Ops, P.O. Box 32170, Louisville KY 40232. **Website:** www.kentuckyliving.com. **Contact:** Anita Travis Richter, editor. **Mostly freelance written. Prefers to work with published/established writers.** Monthly feature magazine primarily for Kentucky residents. Estab. 1948. Circ. 500,000. Byline given. Pays on acceptance. No kill fee. Publishes ms an average of 12 months after acceptance. Submit seasonal material at least 6 months in advance. Accepts queries by online submission form. Accepts simultaneous submissions. Responds in 1 month to queries. Sample copy with SASE (9x12 envelope and 4 first-class stamps). Guidelines online.

NONFICTION Special issues: Stories of interest include: Kentucky-related profiles (people, places, or events), business and social trends, history, biography, recreation, travel, leisure or lifestyle articles/book excerpts, articles on contemporary subjects of general public interest, and general consumer-related features. **Buys 18-24 mss/year.** Prefers queries rather than submissions. Length: 500-1,500 words. **Pays $75-935.** Pays expenses of writers on assignment.

PHOTOS State availability of or send photos. Identification of subjects required. Reviews photo e-files at online link or sent CD. Payment for photos included in payment for ms.

COLUMNS/DEPARTMENTS Accepts queries for Worth the Trip column. Other columns have established columnists.

TIPS "The quality of writing and reporting (factual, objective, thorough) is considered in setting payment price. We prefer general interest pieces filled with quotes and anecdotes. Avoid boosterism. Well-researched, well-written feature articles are preferred. All articles must have a strong Kentucky connection."

$$ KENTUCKY MONTHLY

Vested Interest Publications, P.O. Box 559, 100 Consumer Lane, Frankfort KY 40602-0559. (502)227-0053; (888)329-0053. **Fax:** (502)227-5009. **E-mail:** kymonthly@kentuckymonthly.com; steve@kentuckymonthly.com. **E-mail:** patty@kentuckymonthly.com. **Website:** www.kentuckymonthly.com. **Contact:** Stephen Vest, editor; Patricia Ranft, associate editor. **50% freelance written.** Monthly magazine. "We publish stories about Kentucky and by Kentuckians, including stories written by those who live elsewhere." Estab. 1998. Circ. 35,000. Byline given. Pays within 3 months of publication. Offers kill fee. Publishes ms an average of 3 months after acceptance. Editorial lead time 4-12 months. Submit seasonal material 4-10 months in advance. Accepts queries by e-mail. Accepts simultaneous submissions. Responds in 1-3 months to queries; in 1 month to mss. Sample copy and writer's guidelines online.

NONFICTION Needs book excerpts, essays, general interest, historical, humor, interview, personal experience, photo feature, profile, reviews, travel, All pieces should have a Kentucky angle. Special issues: Kentucky Derby Festival Guide (April); Kentucky Gift Guide (November). **Buys 50 mss/year.** Query. Length: 300-2,000 words. **Pays $45-300 for assigned articles; $50-200 for unsolicited articles.** Pays expenses of writers on assignment.

PHOTOS State availability. Captions required. Buys first rights and one-time rights.

FICTION We publish stories about Kentucky and by Kentuckians, including stories written by those who live elsewhere." Wants Kentucky-related stories. **Buys 30 mss/year.** Query with published clips. Accepts submissions by e-mail. Length: 1,000-5,000 words.

TIPS "Please read the magazine to get the flavor of what we're publishing each month. We accept articles via e-mail. Approximately 70% of articles are assigned."

MARYLAND

$$ BALTIMORE

1000 Lancaster St., Suite 400, Baltimore MD 21202. (443)873-3900. **Fax:** (410)625-0280. **E-mail:** wmax@baltimoremagazine.net; mjane@baltimoremagazine.net; blauren@balimoremagazine.net; iken@baltimoremagazine.net; cron@baltimoremagazine.net; wlydia@baltimoremagazine.net. **Website:** www.baltimoremagazine.net. **Contact:** Send correspondence to the appropriate editor: Max Weiss (lifestyle, film, pop culture, general inquiries); Jane Marion (food, travel); Lauren Bell (style, home, beauty, wellness); Ken Iglehart (business, special editions); Ron Cassie (politics, environment, health, sports); Lydia Woolever (calendar, events, party pages). **50-60% freelance written.** Monthly city magazine featuring news, profiles, and service articles. Estab. 1907. Circ. 70,000. Byline given. Pays within 1 month of publication. Offers kill fee in some cases. Submit seasonal material 4 months in advance. Accepts queries by mail, e-mail. Accepts simultaneous submissions. Guidelines online.

"Pieces must address an educated, active, affluent reader and must have a very strong Baltimore angle."

NONFICTION Needs book excerpts, essays, general interest, historical, humor, new product, personal experience, photo feature, travel. Does not want anything "that lacks a strong Baltimore focus or angle.

Unsolicited personal essays are almost never accepted. We've printed only 2 over the past few years; the last was by a 19-year veteran city judge reminiscing on his time on the bench and the odd stories and situations he encountered there. Unsolicited food and restaurant reviews, whether positive or negative, are likewise never accepted." Query appropriate subject editor by e-mail (preferred), or mail query with published clips. Length: 1,600-2,500 words. **Pays 30-40¢/word.** Pays expenses of writers on assignment. Sometimes pays expenses.

COLUMNS/DEPARTMENTS "The shorter pieces are the best places to break into the magazine." Up Front, 300-700 words; Hot Shots and Cameo, 800-2,000 words. Query with published clips.

TIPS "Too many writers send us newspaper-style articles. We are seeking: (1) *Human interest features*—strong, even dramatic profiles of Baltimoreans of interest to our readers; (2) *First-person accounts* of experience in Baltimore or experiences of a Baltimore resident; (3) *Consumer*—according to our editorial needs and with Baltimore sources. Writers should read/familiarize themselves with the style of *Baltimore* before submitting. You're most likely to impress us with writing that demonstrates how well you handle character, dramatic narrative, and factual analysis. We also admire inspired reporting and a clear, surprising style. We strongly prefer receiving queries via e-mail. If you use standard U.S. mail, your query should fit on 1 page."

MASSACHUSETTS

$$ CAPE COD LIFE

13 Steeple St., Suite 204, P.O. Box 1439, Mashpee MA 02649. (508)419-7381. **Fax:** (508)477-1225. **Website:** www.capecodlife.com. **Contact:** Jen Dow, Creative Director; Matthew Gill, *Cape Cod LIFE* Editor, Julie Wagner, *Cape Cod HOME* Editor. **80% freelance written.** Cape Cod LIFE Magazine published 7 times/year focusing on area lifestyle, history and culture, people and places, business and industry, and issues and answers for year-round and summer residents of Cape Cod, Nantucket, and Martha's Vineyard as well as nonresidents who spend their leisure time here. Cape Cod Life Magazine has become the premier lifestyle magazine for the Cape & Islands, featuring topics ranging from arts and events, history and heritage, beaches and boating as well as a comprehensive resource for planning the perfect vacation.

Cape Cod ART is published annually.

Cape Cod HOME is published 6 times per year. Estab. 1979. Circ. 45,000. Byline given. Pays 90 days after published. Submit seasonal material 6 months in advance. Accepts queries by mail, e-mail. Accepts simultaneous submissions. Responds in 3 months to queries. Responds in 3 months to mss. Sample copy for $5. Guidelines for #10 SASE.

NONFICTION Needs book excerpts, general interest, historical, interview, photo feature, travel, outdoors, gardening, nautical, nature, arts, antiques,history,housing. **Buys 20 mss/year.** Query. Length: 800-1,500 words. **Pays $200-400.** Pays expenses of writers on assignment.

PHOTOS Photo guidelines for #10 SASE. Captions, identification of subjects required. Pays $25-225. Buys first rights with right to reprint.

TIPS "Freelancers submitting *quality* spec articles with a Cape Cod and Islands angle have a good chance at publication. We like to see a wide selection of writer's clips before giving assignments. We also publish *Cape Cod HOME* covering architecture, landscape design, and interior design with a Cape and Islands focus. Also publish Cape Cod ART annually."

$$ WORCESTER MAGAZINE

72 Shrewbury St., Worcester MA 01604. (508)749-3166. **E-mail:** editor@worcestermag.com; wbird@worcestermag.com. **Website:** www.worcestermag.com. **Contact:** Walter Bird, Jr., editor; Kathy Real, publisher. **10% freelance written.** Weekly tabloid emphasizing the central Massachusetts region, especially the city of Worcester. Estab. 1976. Circ. 40,000. Byline given. Pays on publication. No kill fee. Publishes ms an average of 3 weeks after acceptance. Submit seasonal material 2 months in advance. Accepts queries by mail, e-mail, fax. Accepts simultaneous submissions.

Does not respond to unsolicited material.

NONFICTION Needs essays, expose, general interest, historical, humor, opinion, personal experience, photo feature. **Buys less than 75 mss/year.** Length: 500-1,500 words. **Pays 10¢/word.** Pays expenses of writers on assignment.

MICHIGAN

$$$ ANN ARBOR OBSERVER

Ann Arbor Observer Co., 2390 Winewood, Ann Arbor MI 48103. (734)769-3175. **Fax:** (734)769-3375. **E-mail:** editor@aaobserver.com. **Website:** www.annarborobserver.com. **Contact:** John Hilton, editor. **50% freelance written.** Monthly magazine devoted solely to life and work in Ann Arbor, Michigan. "We depend heavily on freelancers, and we're always glad to talk to new ones. We look for the intelligence and judgment to fully explore complex people and situations, and the ability to convey what makes them interesting." Estab. 1976. Circ. 60,000. Bylines in some sections. Pays on publication. No kill fee. Publishes ms an average of 2 months after acceptance. Accepts queries by mail, e-mail, phone. Responds in 3 weeks to queries; several months to mss. Sample copy for 12.5x15 SAE with $3 postage. Guidelines by e-mail or mail for #10 SASE.

NONFICTION **Buys 75 mss/year.** Length: 100-2,000 words. **Pays up to $1,000.** Pays expenses of writers on assignment.

COLUMNS/DEPARTMENTS Up Front (short, interesting tidbits), 150 words, pays $150; Inside Ann Arbor (concise stories), 300-500 words, pays $250; Around Town (unusual, compelling anecdotes), 750-1,500 words; pays $250-300.

TIPS "If you have an idea for a story, write a 100- to 200-word description telling us why the story is interesting. We are open most to intelligent, insightful features about interesting aspects of life in Ann Arbor—all stories must have a strong Ann Arbor tie."

$$ MICHIGAN HISTORY

Michigan History magazine, Historical Society of Michigan, 5815 Executive Dr., Lansing MI 48911. (517)332-1828. **Fax:** (517)324-4370. **E-mail:** hsm@hsmichigan.org. **E-mail:** editor@hsmichigan.org. **Website:** www.hsmichigan.org. Editorial Manager: Christopher N. Blaker. **Contact:** Nancy Feldbush, editor-in-chief. Each full-color, bimonthly issue of *Michigan History* magazine contains seven or more feature stories about Michigan's fascinating past, plus special sections that highlight historical sites to explore; spotlight the histories of communities, institutions, and businesses; feature individuals and groups who have left impressions upon our state; bring readers up to date on Michigan's history-related news; and more. The magazine is offered either as an individual subscription or as an enhancement to a Historical Society of Michigan membership. Bimonthly magazine, 68 colorful pages. "Since 1917, *Michigan History* magazine, published by the nonprofit Historical Society of Michigan, has celebrated the Great Lakes State's diverse history and cultures through intriguing stories and scores of photographs and images." Please query first. In addition to payment, authors receive 5 complimentary copies of issues in which their work appears. Estab. 1917. Circ. 22,000. Byline given. Pays 30 days after publication date. Publishes ms 6-18 months after acceptance. Editorial lead time 1 year. Accepts queries by mail, e-mail. Guidelines online.

NONFICTION "We are not a scholarly journal and do not accept academic papers." **Buys 40-50 mss/year.** "A manuscript submission must be accompanied by a list of sources for fact-checking purposes. Your article should draw upon multiple primary and secondary resources." Length: 1,500-2,500 words. **Pays $100-300.**

PHOTOS Include in your query if high-resolution photos are available to accompany your article. Authors are encouraged to provide illustrations or suggestions for image sources. Please note that the Society is unable to reimburse you for any expenses you incur in obtaining photographs.

TIPS "Articles should revolve around a Michigan history-related subject, and a significant amount of the article's content should take place within Michigan. Articles should approach a subject by finding an interesting angle to explore, rather than just listing its history."

MINNESOTA

$$ LAKE COUNTRY JOURNAL

1480 Northern Pacific Road, #2A, Brainerd MN 56401. (218)828-6424, ext. 14. **Fax:** (218)825-7816. **E-mail:** editor@lakecountryjournal.com; info@lakecountryjournal.com. **Website:** www.lakecountryjournal.com. **90% freelance written.** Bimonthly magazine covering central Minnesota's lake country. "Lake Country is one of the fastest-growing areas in the midwest. Each bimonthly issue of *Lake Country Journal* captures the essence of why we work, play, and live in this area. Through a diverse blend of articles from features and fiction, to recreation, recipes, gardening, and nature, this quality lifestyle magazine promotes positive family and business endeavors, showcases our natural and cultural resources, and highlights the best of our people, places, and events." Estab. 1996. Circ. 14,500. Byline given. Pays on publication. Offers 25% kill fee. Publishes ms an average of 6 months after acceptance. Submit seasonal material 1 year in advance. Accepts queries by mail, e-mail. Accepts simultaneous submissions. Responds in 2 months to queries. Responds in 3 months to mss. Sample copy for $6. Guidelines available online.

NONFICTION Needs essays, general interest, how-to, humor, interview, personal experience, photo feature. "No articles that come from writers who are not familiar with our target geographical location." **Buys 30 mss/year.** Query with or without published clips. Length: 1,000-1,500 words. **Pays $100-200.** Pays expenses of writers on assignment.

PHOTOS State availability. Identification of subjects, model releases required. Reviews transparencies. Negotiates payment individually. Buys one-time rights.

COLUMNS/DEPARTMENTS Profile-People from Lake Country, 800 words; Essay, 800 words; Health (topics pertinent to central Minnesota living), 500 words. **Buys 40 mss/year.** Query with published clips. **Pays $50-75.**

FICTION Needs adventure, humorous, mainstream. **Buys 6 mss/year.** Length: 1,500 words. **Pays $100-200.**

POETRY Needs free verse. "Never use rhyming verse, avant-garde, experimental, etc." Buys 6 poems/year. Submit maximum 4 poems. Length: 8-32 lines. **Pays $25.**

FILLERS Needs anecdotes, short humor. **Buys 20 mss/year.** Length: 100-300 words. **Pays $25/filler.**

TIPS "Most of the people who will read your articles live in the north central Minnesota lakes area. All have some significant attachment to the area. We have readers of various ages, backgrounds, and lifestyles. After reading your article, we hope to have a deeper understanding of some aspect of our community, our environment, ourselves, or humanity in general."

$$ LAKE SUPERIOR MAGAZINE

Lake Superior Port Cities, Inc., P.O. Box 16417, Duluth MN 55816-0417. (218)722-5002. **Fax:** (218)722-4096. **E-mail:** edit@lakesuperior.com. **Website:** www.lakesuperior.com. **Contact:** Konnie LeMay, editor. **40% freelance written. Works with a small number of new/unpublished writers each year. Please include phone number and address with e-mail queries.** Bimonthly magazine covering contemporary and historic people, places, and current events around Lake Superior. We are a family-owned business sustained with book and magazine publications as well as a Lake Superior Collection of retail items. Estab. 1979. Circ. 20,000. Byline given. Pays on publication. No kill fee. Publishes ms an average of 10 months after acceptance. Submit seasonal material 1 year in advance. Accepts queries by mail, e-mail. Accepts simultaneous submissions. Responds in 3 months to queries. Sample copy: $4.95 plus 6 first-class stamps. Guidelines online.

NONFICTION Needs book excerpts, essays, general interest, historical, how-to, humor, interview, memoir, nostalgic, personal experience, photo feature, profile, travel, city profiles, regional business, some investigative. **Buys 15 mss/year.** Prefers emailed queries or mss, but accepts mail submissions. Length: 1,600-2,000 words for features. **Pays $200-400.** Pays expenses of writers on assignment. Any expenses must be agreed upon before a story is assigned.

PHOTOS "Quality photography is our hallmark." Send photos. Captions, identification of subjects, model releases required. Reviews electronically only. Offers $50/image; $150 for covers.

COLUMNS/DEPARTMENTS Shorter articles on specific topics of interest: Homes, Health & Wellness, Lake Superior Journal, Wild Superior, Heritage, Destinations, Profile, all 800-1,200 words. **Buys 20 mss/year.** Query with published clips. **Pays $75-250.**

FICTION z

TIPS "Well-researched queries are attended to. We actively seek queries from writers in Lake Superior communities. We prefer queries. Provide enough information on why the subject is important to the region and our readers, or why and how something is unique. We want details. The writer must have a thorough knowledge of the subject and how it relates to our region. We prefer a fresh, unused approach to the subject that provides the reader with an emotional involvement. Almost all of our articles feature quality photography in color or b&w. It is a prerequisite of all nonfiction. All submissions should include a *short* biography of author/photographer; mug shot sometimes used. Blanket submissions need not apply."

$$$ MPLS. ST. PAUL MAGAZINE

MSP Communications, 220 S. Sixth St., Suite 500, Minneapolis MN 55402. **E-mail:** edit@mspmag.com. **Website:** www.mspmag.com. **Contact:** Kelly Ryan Kegans, executive editor. Monthly magazine covering the Minneapolis-St. Paul area. *Mpls. St. Paul Magazine* is a city magazine serving upscale readers in the Minneapolis-St. Paul metro area. Circ. 80,000. Pays on publication. Editorial lead time 3 months. Accepts queries by mail, e-mail. Accepts simultaneous submissions. Sample copy: $10.

NONFICTION Needs book excerpts, essays, general interest, historical, interview, personal experience, photo feature, travel. **Buys 150 mss/year.** Query with published clips. Length: 500-4,000 words. **Pays 50-75¢/word for assigned articles.** Pays expenses of writers on assignment.

MISSISSIPPI

$$ MISSISSIPPI MAGAZINE

Downhome Publications, 5 Lakeland Circle, Jackson MS 39216. (601)982-8418. **Fax:** (601)982-8447. **E-mail:** editor@mismag.com. **Website:** www.mississippimagazine.com. **Contact:** Melanie M. Ward, editor. **90% freelance written.** Bimonthly magazine covering Mississippi—the state and its lifestyles. "We are interested in positive stories reflecting Mississippi's rich traditions and heritage and focusing on the contributions the state and its natives have made to the arts, literature, and culture. In each issue we showcase homes and gardens, in-state travel, food, design, art, and more." Estab. 1982. Circ. 40,000. Byline given. Pays on publication. Offers 25% kill fee. Publishes ms an average of 6 months after acceptance. Editorial lead time 6 months. Submit seasonal material 1 year in advance. Accepts queries by mail, fax. Responds in 2 months to queries. Guidelines for #10 SASE or online.

NONFICTION Needs general interest, historical, how-to, interview, personal experience, travel. No opinion, political, sports, expose. **Buys 15 mss/year.** Query. Length: 100-1,200 words. **Pays $25-350.**

PHOTOS Send photos with query. Captions, identification of subjects, model releases required. Reviews transparencies, prints, digital images on CD. Negotiates payment individually. Buys one time rights.

COLUMNS/DEPARTMENTS Southern Scrapbook (see recent issues for example), 100-600 words; Gardening (short informative article on a specific plant or gardening technique), 800-1,200 words; Culture Center (story about an event or person relating to Mississippi's art, music, theatre, or literature), 800-1,200 words; On Being Southern (personal essay about life in Mississippi; only ms submissions accepted), 750 words. **Buys 6 mss/year.** Query. **Pays $25-250.**

MISSOURI

$$ 417 MAGAZINE

Whitaker Publishing, 2111 S. Eastgate Ave., Springfield MO 65809. (417)883-7417. **Fax:** (417)889-7417. **E-mail:** editor@417mag.com. **Website:** www.417mag.com. **Contact:** Katie Pollock Estes, editor. **50% freelance written.** Monthly magazine. "*417 Magazine* is a regional title serving southwest Missouri. Our editorial mix includes service journalism and lifestyle content on home, fashion and the arts; as well as narrative and issues pieces. The audience is affluent, educated, mostly female." Estab. 1998. Circ. 20,000. Byline given. Pays on acceptance. Publishes ms an average of 2-3 months after acceptance. Editorial lead time 6 months. Accepts queries by e-mail. Accepts simultaneous submissions. Responds in 1-2 months to queries. Sample copy by e-mail. Guidelines online.

NONFICTION Needs essays, expose, general interest, how-to, humor, inspirational, interview, new product, personal experience, photo feature, travel, local book reviews. "We are a local magazine, so anything not reflecting our local focus is something we have to pass on." **Buys 175 mss/year.** Query with published clips. Length: 300-3,500 words. **Pays $30-500, sometimes more.** Pays expenses of writers on assignment.

TIPS "Read the magazine before contacting us. Send specific ideas with your queries. Submit story ideas of local interest. Send published clips. Be a curious reporter, and ask probing questions."

NEVADA

$$ NEVADA MAGAZINE

401 N. Carson St., Carson City NV 89701. (775)687-0602. **Fax:** (775)687-6159. **E-mail:** editor@nevad-

amagazine.com. **Website:** www.nevadamagazine.com. **25% freelance written. Works with a small number of new/unpublished writers each year.** Bimonthly magazine published by the state of Nevada to promote tourism. Estab. 1936. Circ. 20,000. Byline given. Pays on publication. No kill fee. Publishes ms an average of 6 months after acceptance. Submit seasonal material 6 months in advance. Accepts simultaneous submissions. Responds in 1 month to queries. Sample copy available by request. Guidelines available online.

NONFICTION Prefers a well-written query or outline with specific story elements before receiving the actual story. Write, e-mail, or call if you have a story that might work. Length: 500-1,500 words. **Pays flat rate of $250 or less. For web stories, pays $100 or $200 depending on the assignment.** Pays expenses of writers on assignment.

PHOTOS Contact: Query art director Sean Nebeker (snebeker@nevadamagazine.com). Reviews digital images. Pays $25-250; cover, $250. Buys one-time rights.

COLUMNS/DEPARTMENTS Columns include: Up Front (the latest Nevada news), Visions (emphasizes outstanding photography with extended captions), City Limits (features destination stories for Nevada's larger cities), Wide Open (features destination stories for Nevada's rural towns and regions), Cravings (stories centered on food and drink), Travels (people traveling Nevada, sharing their adventures), History, and Events & Shows.

TIPS "Keep in mind the magazine's purpose is to promote Nevada tourism."

NEW HAMPSHIRE

$$ NEW HAMPSHIRE MAGAZINE

McLean Communications, Inc., 150 Dow St., Manchester NH 03101. (603)624-1442. **E-mail:** editor@nhmagazine.com. **Website:** www.nhmagazine.com. **Contact:** Rick Broussard, editor. **50% freelance written.** Monthly magazine devoted to New Hampshire. "We want stories written for, by, and about the people of New Hampshire with emphasis on qualities that set us apart from other states. We feature lifestyle, adventure, and home-related stories with a unique local angle." Estab. 1986. Circ. 32,000. Byline given. Pays on publication. Offers 40% kill fee. Editorial lead time 3 months. Submit seasonal material 1 year in advance. Accepts queries by mail, e-mail, fax. Accepts simultaneous submissions. Responds in 2 months to queries. Responds in 3 months to mss. Guidelines available online.

NONFICTION Needs essays, general interest, historical, photo feature, business. **Buys 30 mss/year.** Send ms or query via e-mail. Length: 300-2,000 words. **Payment varies.** Pays expenses of writers on assignment.

PHOTOS State availability. Captions, identification of subjects, model releases required. Possible additional payment for photos accepted with ms. Rights purchased vary.

FILLERS Length: 200-400 words.

NEW JERSEY

$$$$ NEW JERSEY MONTHLY

55 Park Place, P.O. Box 920, Morristown NJ 07963-0920. (973)539-8230. **Fax:** (973)538-2953. **E-mail:** kschlager@njmonthly.com. **Website:** www.njmonthly.com. **Contact:** Ken Schlager, editor. **75-80% freelance written.** Monthly magazine covering just about anything to do with New Jersey, from news, politics, and sports to decorating trends and lifestyle issues. Our readership is well-educated, affluent, and on average our readers have lived in New Jersey 20 years or more. Estab. 1976. Circ. 92,000. Byline given. Pays on completion of fact-checking. Offers 20% kill fee. Publishes ms an average of 3 months after acceptance. Editorial lead time 3 months. Submit seasonal material 6 months in advance. Accepts queries by mail, e-mail, fax, phone. Accepts simultaneous submissions. Responds in 2-3 months to queries. Guidelines available online.

This magazine continues to look for strong investigative reporters with novelistic style and solid knowledge of New Jersey issues.

NONFICTION Needs book excerpts, essays, expose, general interest, historical, humor, interview, personal experience, photo feature, travel, arts, sports, politics. No experience pieces from people who used to live in New Jersey or general pieces that have no New Jersey angle. **Buys 90-100 mss/year.** Query with published magazine clips via e-mail. Length: 250-3,000 words. **Payment varies.** Pays expenses of writers on assignment. Pays reasonable expenses of writers on assignment with prior approval.

PHOTOS Contact: Donna Panagakos, art director. State availability. Identification of subjects, model releases required. Reviews transparencies, prints. Payment negotiated. Buys one time rights.

COLUMNS/DEPARTMENTS Exit Ramp (back page essay usually originating from personal experience but written in a way that tells a broader story of statewide interest), 500 words; front-of-the-book Garden Variety (brief profiles or articles on local life, 250-350 words; restaurant reviews. **Buys 12 mss/year.** Query with published clips. **Payment varies.**

FILLERS Needs anecdotes, for front-of-book. **Buys 12-15 mss/year.** Length: 200-250 words. **Payment varies.**

TIPS "The best approach: Do your homework! Read the past year's issues to get an understanding of our well-written, well-researched articles that tell a tale from a well-established point of view."

$$ THE SANDPAPER

The SandPaper, Inc., 1816 Long Beach Blvd., Surf City NJ 08008. (609)494-5900. **Fax:** (609)494-1437. **E-mail:** jaymann@thesandpaper.net; letters@thesandpaper.net; photo@thesandpaper.net. **Website:** www.thesandpaper.net. **Contact:** Jay Mann, managing editor; Gail Travers, executive editor; Ryan Morrill, photography editor, Victoria Ford, entertainment editor, Pat Johnson, art editor. Weekly newspaper covering subjects of interest to Long Island Beach area residents and visitors. Each issue includes a mix of news, human interest features, opinion columns, and entertainment/calendar listings. Estab. 1976. Circ. 30,000. Byline given. Pays on publication. Offers 100% kill fee. Publishes ms an average of 1 month after acceptance. Submit seasonal material 3 months in advance. Accepts queries by mail, e-mail, fax, phone. Accepts simultaneous submissions. Responds in 1 month to queries.

"Contact the editorial department if you have breaking news or to suggest a story idea." Jay Mann, managing editor.

NONFICTION Pays expenses of writers on assignment.

COLUMNS/DEPARTMENTS Speakeasy (opinion and slice-of-life, often humorous); Commentary (forum for social science perspectives); both 1,000-1,500 words, preferably with local or Jersey Shore angle. **Buys 50 mss/year.** Send complete ms. **Pays $40.**

NEW MEXICO

$$ NEW MEXICO MAGAZINE

Lew Wallace Bldg., 495 Old Santa Fe Trail, Santa Fe NM 87501-2750. (505)827-7447. **E-mail:** artdirector@nmmagazine.com. **Website:** www.nmmagazine.com. **70% freelance written.** Covers areas throughout the state. "We want to publish a lively editorial mix, covering both the down-home (like a diner in Tucumcari) and the upscale (a new bistro in world-class Santa Fe)." Explore the gamut of the Old West and the New Age. "Our magazine is about the power of place—in particular more than 120,000 square miles of mountains, desert, grasslands, and forest inhabited by a culturally rich mix of individuals. It is an enterprise of the New Mexico Tourism Department, which strives to make potential visitors aware of our state's multicultural heritage, climate, environment, and uniqueness." Estab. 1923. Circ. 100,000. Pays on acceptance. 20% kill fee. Publishes ms an average of 3 months after acceptance. Submit seasonal material 1 year in advance. Accepts queries by mail. Accepts simultaneous submissions. Responds to queries if interested. Sample copy for $5. Guidelines available online.

Does not return unsolicited material.

NONFICTION Submit story idea along with a working head and subhead and a paragraph synopsis. Include published clips and a short sum-up about your strengths as a writer. Considers proposal as well as writer's potential to write the conceptualized stories. Pays expenses of writers on assignment.

REPRINTS Rarely publishes reprints, but sometimes publishes excerpts from novels and nonfiction books.

PHOTOS "Purchased as portfolio or on assignment. Photographers interested in photo assignments should reference submission guidelines on the contributors' page of our website."

NEW YORK

$$ ADIRONDACK LIFE

P.O. Box 410, Rt. 9N, Jay NY 12941-0410. (518)946-2191. **Fax:** (518)946-7461. **E-mail:** astoltie@adirondacklife.com; khofschneider@adirondacklife.com. **Website:** adirondacklifemag.com. **Contact:** Annie Stoltie, editor; Kelly Hofschneider, photo editor. **70% freelance written. Prefers to work with published/**

established writers. Magazine, published bimonthly, that emphasizes the Adirondack region and the North Country of New York State in articles covering outdoor activities, history, and natural history directly related to the Adirondacks. Estab. 1970. Circ. 50,000. Byline given. Pays 30 days after publication. No kill fee. Publishes ms an average of 10 months after acceptance. Submit seasonal material 1 year in advance. Accepts queries by mail, e-mail. Accepts simultaneous submissions. Responds in 1 month to queries. Sample copy for $3 and 9x12 SAE. Guidelines available online.

NONFICTION Special issues: Special issues: Annual Guide to the Great Outdoors (how-to and where-to articles that offer in-depth information about recreational offerings in the park); At Home in the Adirondacks (focuses on the region's signature style). Does not want poetry, fiction, or editorial cartoons. **Buys 20-25 unsolicited mss/year.** Query with published clips. Accepts queries, but not unsolicited mss, via e-mail. Length: 1,500-3,000 words. **Pays 30¢/word.** Pays expenses of writers on assignment.

PHOTOS "All photos must have been taken in the Adirondacks. Each issue contains a photo feature. Purchased with or without ms on assignment. All photos must be individually identified as to the subject or locale and must bear the photographer's name." Send photos. Reviews hi-res (300 dpi) TIFF/JPEG/PSD files via e-mail, or raw files on CD. Pays $150 for full page, b&w, or color; $400 for cover (color only,vertical in format). Credit line given.

COLUMNS/DEPARTMENTS Short Carries; Northern Lights; Special Places (unique spots in the Adirondack Park); Skills; Working (careers in the Adirondacks); The Scene; Back Page. Length: 1,000-1,800 words. Query with published clips. **Pays 30¢/word.**

FICTION Considers first-serial novel excerpts in its subject matter and region.

TIPS "Do not send a personal essay about your meaningful moment in the mountains. We need factual pieces about regional history, sports, culture, and business. We are looking for clear, concise, well-organized mss that are strictly Adirondack in subject. Check back issues to be sure we haven't already covered your topic. Check out our guidelines online."

$$$$ NEW YORK MAGAZINE

New York Media, Editorial Submissions, 75 Varick St., New York NY 10013. **E-mail:** comments@nymag.com. **E-mail:** editorialsubmissions@nymag.com. **Website:** nymag.com. **25% freelance written.** Weekly magazine focusing on current events in the New York metropolitan area. Circ. 405,149. Pays on acceptance. Offers 25% kill fee. Submit seasonal material 2 months in advance. Accepts queries by e-mail. Accepts simultaneous submissions. Responds in 1 month to queries. Guidelines online.

Does not accept unsolicited mss. Query first.

NONFICTION Query by e-mail or mail. **Pays $1/word.** Pays expenses of writers on assignment.

$$$ WESTCHESTER MAGAZINE

Today Media, 2 Clinton Ave., Rye NY 10580. (914)345-0601. **Website:** www.westchestermagazine.com. **40% freelance written.** Monthly magazine covering culture and lifestyle of Westchester County, New York. *Westchester Magazine* is an upscale, high-end regional lifestyle publication covering issues specific to Westchester County, New York. All stories must have a local slant. Estab. 2001. Circ. 60,475. Byline given. Pays on publication. Offers 20% kill fee. Publishes ms an average of 3 months after acceptance. Editorial lead time 3 months. Submit seasonal material 3 months in advance. Accepts queries by e-mail. Sample copy online.

NONFICTION Needs expose, general interest, historical, interview, photo feature, profile, local service. Does not want personal essays, reviews, stories not specific to Westchester. **Buys 36 mss/year.** Query with published clips. Length: 150-5,000 words. **Pays $50-1,000.** Pays expenses of writers on assignment.

PHOTOS Contact: Contact Aiko Masazumi, creative director. State availability. Captions, identification of subjects required. Reviews GIF/JPEG files. Negotiates payment individually. Negotiates rights individually.

COLUMNS/DEPARTMENTS Our Neighbor (profile of a local celebrity), 500 words; Westchester Chronicles (short items of local interest), 300 words; County Golf (articles about the local golf scene), 500 words. **Buys 36 mss/year.** Query with published clips. **Pays $30-200.**

TIPS "Be sure to query ideas applicable only to Westchester County that we have not written about before."

NORTH CAROLINA

$$ CHARLOTTE MAGAZINE

Morris Visitor Publications, 214 W. Tremont Ave., Suite 303, Charlotte NC 28203. (704)335-7181. **Fax:** (704)335-3757. **E-mail:** michael.graff@charlottemagazine.com. **Website:** www.charlottemagazine.com. **Contact:** Michael Graff, publisher. **75% freelance written.** Monthly magazine covering Charlotte life. This magazine tells its readers things they didn't know about Charlotte in an interesting, entertaining, and sometimes provocative style. Circ. 40,000. Byline given. Pays within 30 days of acceptance. Offers 25% kill fee. Publishes ms an average of 3 months after acceptance. Editorial lead time 3 months. Submit seasonal material 6 months in advance. Accepts queries by mail, e-mail. Accepts simultaneous submissions. Responds in 6 months to mss. Sample copy for $6.

NONFICTION Needs book excerpts, expose, general interest, interview, photo feature, travel. **Buys 35-50 mss/year.** Query with published clips. Length: 200-3,000 words. **Pays 20-40¢/word.** Pays expenses of writers on assignment.

PHOTOS State availability. Identification of subjects required. Negotiates payment individually. Buys one-time rights.

COLUMNS/DEPARTMENTS Buys 35-50 mss/year. Pays 20-40¢/word

TIPS "A story for *Charlotte* magazine could only appear in *Charlotte* magazine. That is, the story and its treatment are particularly germane to this area. Because of this, we rarely work with writers who live outside the Charlotte area."

$$ FIFTEEN 501

Weiss and Hughes Publishing, 189 Wind Chime Court, Suite 104, Raleigh NC 27615. (919)870-1722. **Fax:** (919)719-5260. **E-mail:** djackson@whmags.com. **Website:** www.fifteen501.com. **Contact:** Danielle Jackson, editor. **50% freelance written.** Quarterly magazine covering lifestyle issues relevant to residents in the U.S. 15/501 corridor of Durham, Orange, and Chatham counties in North Carolina. "We cover issues important to residents of Durham, Orange and Chatham counties. We're committed to improving our readers' overall quality of life and keeping them informed of the lifestyle amenities there." Estab. 2006. Circ. 30,000. Byline given. Pays within 30 days of publication. Offers 25% kill fee. Publishes ms an average of 2 months after acceptance. Editorial lead time 2-3 months. Submit seasonal material 6 months in advance. Accepts queries by mail, e-mail. Accepts simultaneous submissions. Responds in 2-4 weeks to queries. Sample copy available online. Guidelines by e-mail.

NONFICTION Needs general interest, historical, how-to, inspirational, interview, personal experience, photo feature, technical, travel. Does not want opinion pieces or political or religious topics. Query. Length: 600-1,200 words. **Pays 35¢/word.** Pays expenses of writers on assignment.

PHOTOS State availability. Captions, identification of subjects required. Reviews transparencies, GIF/JPEG files. Offers no additional payment for photos accepted with ms. Rights are negotiable.

COLUMNS/DEPARTMENTS Around Town (local lifestyle topics), 1,000 words; Hometown Stories, 600 words; Travel (around North Carolina), 1,000 words; Home Interiors/Landscaping (varies), 1,000 words; Restaurants (local, fine dining), 600-1,000 words. **Buys 20-25 mss/year.** Query. **Pays 35¢/word.**

TIPS "All queries must be focused on the issues that make Durham, Chapel Hill, Carrboro, Hillsborough, and Pittsboro unique and wonderful places to live."

$$ WAKE LIVING

Weiss and Hughes Publishing, 189 Wind Chime Ct., Suite 104, Raleigh NC 27615. (919)870-1722. **Fax:** (919)719-5260. **Website:** www.wakeliving.com. **Contact:** Janet Ladenburger, editor. **50% freelance written.** Quarterly magazine covering lifestyle issues in Wake County, North Carolina. "We cover issues important to residents of Wake County. We are committed to improving our readers' overall quality of life and keeping them informed of the lifestyle amenities here." Estab. 2003. Circ. 40,000. Byline given. Pays within 30 days of publication. Offers 25% kill fee. Publishes ms an average of 2 months after acceptance. Editorial lead time 2-3 months. Submit seasonal material 6 months in advance. Accepts queries by mail, e-mail. Accepts simultaneous submissions. Responds in 2-4 weeks to queries.

NONFICTION Needs general interest, historical, how-to, inspirational, interview, personal experience, photo feature, technical, travel. Does not want opinion pieces, political topics, religious articles. Query. Length: 600-1,200 words. **Pays 35¢/word. Pay is per**

article and varies by complexity of assignment. Pays expenses of writers on assignment.

PHOTOS State availability. Captions, identification of subjects required. Reviews transparencies, GIF/JPEG files. Offers no additional payment for photos accepted with ms.

COLUMNS/DEPARTMENTS Around Town (local lifestyle topics); Hometown Stories, 600 words; Travel (around North Carolina); Home Interiors/Landscaping, all 1,000 words. Restaurants (local restaurants, fine dining), 600-1,000 words. **Buys 20-25 mss/year.** Query. **Pays 35¢/word. Pay is per article and varies by complexity of assignment.**

TIPS "Articles must be specifically focused on Wake County/Raleigh metro issues. We like unusual angles about what makes living here unique from other areas."

NORTH DAKOTA

$$ NORTH DAKOTA LIVING MAGAZINE

North Dakota Association of Rural Electric Cooperatives, 3201 Nygren Dr. NW, P.O. Box 727, Mandan ND 58554. (701)663-6501. **Fax:** (701)663-3745. **Website:** www.ndliving.com. **20% freelance written.** Monthly magazine covering information of interest to memberships of electric cooperatives and telephone cooperatives. "We publish a general-interest magazine for North Dakotans. We treat subjects pertaining to living and working in the northern Great Plains. We provide progress reporting on electric cooperatives and telephone cooperatives." Estab. 1954. Circ. 70,000. Byline given. Pays on acceptance. No kill fee. Publishes ms an average of 6 months after acceptance. Editorial lead time 6 months. Submit seasonal material 6 months in advance. Accepts queries by mail, e-mail. Accepts simultaneous submissions.

NONFICTION Needs general interest, historical, how-to, humor, interview, new product, travel. **Buys 20 mss/year.** Query with published clips. Length: 1,500-2,000 words. **Pays $100-500 minimum for assigned articles. Pays $300-600 for unsolicited articles.** Pays expenses of writers on assignment.

PHOTOS State availability. Identification of subjects required. Reviews contact sheets. Negotiates payment individually. Buys one-time rights.

COLUMNS/DEPARTMENTS Energy Use and Financial Planning, both 750 words. **Buys 6 mss/year.** Query with published clips. **Pays $100-300.**

FICTION Needs historical, humorous, slice-of-life vignettes, western. **Buys 1 mss/year.** Query with published clips. Length: 1,000-2,500 words. **Pays $100-400.**

TIPS "Deal with what's real: real data, real people, real experiences, real history, etc."

OHIO

$$ AKRON LIFE

Baker Media Group, 1653 Merriman Rd., Suite 116, Akron OH 44313. (330)253-0056. **Fax:** (330)253-5868. **E-mail:** editor@bakermediagroup.com. **Website:** www.akronlife.com. **10% freelance written.** Monthly regional magazine covering Summit, Stark, Portage and Medina counties. "*Akron Life* is a monthly lifestyles publication committed to providing information that enhances and enriches the experience of living in or visiting Akron and the surrounding region of Summit, Portage, Medina and Stark counties. Each colorful, thoughtfully designed issue profiles, interesting places, personalities and events in the arts, sports, entertainment, business, politics and social scene. We cover issues important to the Greater Akron area and significant trends affecting the lives of those who live here." Estab. 2002. Circ. 15,000. Byline given. Pays on publication. Offers 50% kill fee. Publishes ms an average of 4-6 months after acceptance. Editorial lead time 2+ months. Submit seasonal material 6 months in advance. Accepts queries by mail, e-mail, fax. Accepts simultaneous submissions. Sample copy free. Guidelines free.

NONFICTION Needs essays, general interest, historical, how-to, humor, interview, photo feature, travel. Query with published clips. Length: 300-2,000 words. **Pays $0.10 max/word.** Pays expenses of writers on assignment.

PHOTOS State availability. Captions, identification of subjects, model releases required. Reviews GIF/JPEG files. Negotiates payment individually. Buys all rights.

TIPS "It's best to submit a detailed query along with samples of previously published works. Include why you think the story is of interest to our readers, and be sure to have a fresh approach."

$$$ OHIO MAGAZINE

Great Lakes Publishing Co., 1422 Euclid Ave., Suite 730, Cleveland OH 44115. (216)771-2833. **E-mail:** jvickers@ohiomagazine.com. **Website:** www.ohiomagazine.com. **Contact:** Jim Vickers, editor. **50% freelance written.** "*Ohio Magazine* serves energetic and involved Ohioans by providing award-winning stories and pictures of Ohio's most interesting people, arts, entertainment, history, homes, dining, family life, festivals, and regional travel. We capture the beauty, the adventure, and the fun of life in the Buckeye State." Estab. 1978. Circ. 40,000. Byline given. Pays on publication. 20% kill fee. Publishes ms an average of 6 months after acceptance. Submit seasonal material 6 months in advance. Accepts queries by mail, e-mail. Accepts simultaneous submissions. Responds in 3 months to queries; in 3 months to mss. Guidelines online.

NONFICTION Query with résumé and at least 3 published clips. Length: 1,000-3,000 words. **Pays $300-1,200.** Pays expenses of writers on assignment.

REPRINTS Contact Emily Vanuch, advertising coordinator. Pays 50% of amount paid for an original article.

PHOTOS Contact: Lesley Blake, art director (lblake@ohiomagazine.com). Rate negotiable.

COLUMNS/DEPARTMENTS Buys 5 unsolicited mss/year. Pays $100-600.

TIPS "Freelancers should send all queries in writing (either by mail or e-mail), not by telephone. Successful queries demonstrate an intimate knowledge of the publication. We are looking to increase our circle of writers who can write about the state in an informative and upbeat style. Strong reporting skills are highly valued."

OKLAHOMA

$$ INTERMISSION

Langdon Publishing, 110 E. 2nd St., Tulsa OK 74103. **E-mail:** nbizjack@cityoftulsa.org. **Website:** www.tulsapac.com. **Contact:** Nancy Bizjack, editor. **30% freelance written.** Monthly magazine covering events held at the Tulsa Performing Arts Center. "We feature profiles of entertainers appearing at our center, Q&As, stories on the events, and entertainers slated for the Tulsa PAC." Byline given. Pays on publication. Offers 50% kill fee. Publishes ms an average of 1 month after acceptance. Editorial lead time 2 months. Submit seasonal material 2 months in advance. Accepts queries by mail, e-mail. Accepts simultaneous submissions. Responds in 2 weeks to queries. Sample copy available online. Guidelines by e-mail.

NONFICTION Needs general interest, interview. Does not want personal experience articles. **Buys 35 mss/year.** Query with published clips. Length: 600-1,400 words. **Pays $100-200.**

COLUMNS/DEPARTMENTS Q&A (personalities and artists tied in to the events at the Tulsa PAC), 1,100 words. **Buys 12 mss/year.** Query with published clips. **Pays $100-150.**

TIPS "Look ahead at our upcoming events, and find an interesting slant on an event. Interview someone who would be of general interest."

OREGON

$$ OREGON COAST

P.O. Box 119, Florence OR 97439. (800)348-8401. **E-mail:** oregoncoasteditor@gmail.com. **Website:** www.oregoncoastmagazine.com. Editor: Rosemary Camozzi (oregoncoasteditor@gmail.com). **Contact:** Alicia Spooner. **65% freelance written.** Quarterly magazine covering the Oregon Coast. Celebrating the beautiful and bold Oregon Coast with stories about history, real estate, food, and happenings on the Coast. Editorial content limited to the Oregon Coast, Southwest Washington Coast, and Northern California Coast. Estab. 1982. Circ. 20000. Byline given. Pays after publication. Offers 25% (on assigned stories only, not on stories accepted on spec) kill fee. Publishes ms an average of up to 1 year after acceptance. Submit seasonal material 6 months in advance. Accepts queries by mail, e-mail. Accepts simultaneous submissions. Responds in 3 months to queries. Sample copy for $5.95. Guidelines available on website.

NONFICTION Needs book excerpts, historical, inspirational, memoir, nostalgic, personal experience, photo feature, profile, travel. **Buys 55 mss/year.** Query with published clips. Length: 500-1,500 words. **Pays $75-350, plus 2 contributor copies.**

REPRINTS Send tearsheet or photocopy and information about when and where the material previously appeared. Pays an average of 60% of the amount paid for an original article.

PHOTOS Photo submissions with no ms or stand alone or cover photos. Send photos. Captions, identification of subjects required. High-resolution digital. $100 full page, $400 cover, payment for smaller usage varies. Buys one time rights.

TIPS "Slant article for readers who do not live at the Oregon Coast. At least 1 historical article is used in each issue. Manuscript/photo packages are preferred over manuscripts with no photos. List photo credits and captions for each photo. Check all facts, proper names, and numbers carefully in photo/manuscript packages. Must pertain to Oregon Coast somehow."

PENNSYLVANIA

$$ BERKS COUNTY LIVING

201 Washington St., Suite 525, GoggleWorks Center for the Arts, Reading PA 19601. (610)763-7500. **Fax:** (610)898-1933. **E-mail:** nmurry@berkscountyliving.com. **Website:** www.berkscountyliving.com. **Contact:** Nikki M. Murry, editor in chief. **90% freelance written.** Bimonthly magazine covering topics of interest to people living in Berks County, Pennsylvania. Estab. 2000. Circ. 36,000. Byline given. Pays on publication. Offers 25% kill fee. Publishes ms an average of 4 months after acceptance. Editorial lead time 3 months. Submit seasonal material 4 months in advance. Accepts queries by mail, e-mail. Accepts simultaneous submissions. Responds in 1 week to queries; 1 month to mss.

NONFICTION Needs general interest, historical, how-to, humor, inspirational, interview, new product, photo feature. **Buys 25 mss/year.** Query. Length: 750-2,000 words. **Pays $150-400.** Pays expenses of writers on assignment.

PHOTOS State availability. Captions, identification of subjects, model releases required. Reviews 35mm or greater transparencies, any size prints. Negotiates payment individually. Buys one-time rights.

$$ PENNSYLVANIA MAGAZINE

Pennsylvania Magazine Co., P.O. Box 755, Camp Hill PA 17001-0755. (717)697-4660. **E-mail:** editor@pa-mag.com. **Website:** www.pa-mag.com. **Contact:** Matt Holliday, editor. **90% freelance written.** Bimonthly magazine covering people, places, events, and history in Pennsylvania. Estab. 1981. Circ. 30,000. Byline given. Usually pays on acceptance except for articles (by authors unknown to us) sent on speculation, then we pay on publication. Offers 25% kill fee for assigned articles. Publishes ms an average of 9 months after acceptance. Editorial lead time: a year or more. Submit seasonal material at least 9 months in advance. Accepts queries by mail, e-mail. Responds in 4-6 weeks to queries. Sample copy online. Guidelines online.

NONFICTION Needs essays, general interest, historical, personal experience, photo feature, profile, travel. Nothing on Amish topics, hunting, or skiing. **Buys 75-120 mss/year.** Query. Length: 750-2,500 words. **Pays 15-20¢/word. Sometimes more for exceptional work.**

REPRINTS For reprints, send photocopy with rights for sale noted and information about when and where the material previously appeared. Pays 10¢/word.

PHOTOS "Contact editor via e-mail for photography instructions. We work primarily with digital images and prefer raw when possible." Photography Essay (highlights annual photo essay contest entries and showcases individual photographers). Captions required. Digital photos (send images and CD or DVD or link to Dropbox folder access). Pays $35-40 for inside photos; $150 to 250 for covers. Buys one-time rights.

COLUMNS/DEPARTMENTS Round Up (short items about people, unusual events, museums, historical topics/events, family and individually owned consumer-related businesses), 250-1,300 words; Town and Country (items about people or events illustrated with photos or commissioned art), 500 words. Include SASE. Query. **Pays 15¢/word.**

TIPS "Our publication depends on freelance work—send queries. Remember that a subject isn't an idea. Send the topic and your approach when you query. Answer the question: Would this be interesting to someone across the state? Find things that interest you enough that you'd travel 30-50 miles in a car to see/do/explore it, and send a query on that."

$$ PHILADELPHIA STYLE

Philadelphia Style Magazine, LLC, 141 League St., Philadelphia PA 19147. (215)468-6670. **Fax:** (215)780-0003. **E-mail:** philadelphiastyle-editorial@greengale.com. **Website:** www.phillystylemag.com. **50% freelance written.** Bimonthly magazine covering upscale living in the Philadelphia region. Topics include: celebrity interviews, fashion (men's and women's), food, home and design, real estate, dining, beauty, travel, arts and entertainment, and more. "Our magazine is a positive look at the best ways to live in the Philadelphia region. Submitted articles should speak to an upscale, educated audience of professionals that live in the Delaware Valley." Estab. 1999. Circ. 60,000. Byline given. Pays on publication. Offers 25% kill fee. Publishes ms an average of 3 months after acceptance. Editorial lead time 2-4 months. Submit seasonal material 6 months in advance. Accepts queries by mail, e-mail. Accepts simultaneous submissions.

NONFICTION Needs general interest, interview, travel, region-specific articles. "We are not looking for articles that do not have a regional spin." **Buys 100+ mss/year.** Send complete ms. Length: 300-2,500 words. **Pays $50-500.**

COLUMNS/DEPARTMENTS Declarations (celebrity interviews and celebrity contributors); Currents (fashion news); Manor (home and design news); Liberties (beauty and travel news); Dish (dining news); Life in the City (fresh, quirky, regional reporting on books, real estate, art, retail, dining, events, and little-known stories/facts about the region), 100-500 words; Vanguard (people on the forefront of Philadelphia's arts, media, fashion, business, and social scene), 500-700 words; In the Neighborhood (reader-friendly reporting on up-and-coming areas of the region including dining, shopping, attractions, and recreation), 2,000-2,500 words. Query with published clips or send complete ms. **Pays $50-500.**

TIPS "Mail queries with clips or manuscripts. Articles should speak to a stylish, educated audience."

$$$$ PITTSBURGH MAGAZINE

WiesnerMedia, Washington's Landing, 600 Waterfront Dr., Suite 100, Pittsburgh PA 15222-4795. (412)304-0900. **Fax:** (412)304-0938. **E-mail:** editors@pittsburghmagazine.com. **Website:** www.pittsburghmagazine.com. **Contact:** Sean Collier, associate editor; Lauren Davidson, associate editor; Betsy Benson, publisher and vice president. **70% freelance written.** Monthly magazine covering the Pittsburgh metropolitan area. *Pittsburgh* presents issues, analyzes problems, and strives to encourage a better understanding of the community. Region is Western Pennsylvania, Eastern Ohio, Northern West Virginia, and Western Maryland. Estab. 1970. Circ. 75,000. Byline given. Pays on publication. Offers kill fee. Publishes ms an average of 2 months after acceptance. Submit seasonal material 6 months in advance. Accepts queries by mail, e-mail. Accepts simultaneous submissions. Responds in 2 months to queries. Guidelines online.

The editor reports a need for news, analysis, profiles with depth, and stories targeting readers in their 30s and 40s, especially those with young families. Prefers to work with published/established writers with knowledge of and contacts in Western Pennsylvania. The monthly magazine is purchased on newsstands and by subscription.

NONFICTION Needs expose, general interest, profile, sports, informational, service, business, medical, food, and lifestyle. "We do not publish fiction, poetry, advocacy, or personal reminiscence pieces." Query in writing with outline and clips. Length: 1,200-4,000 words. **Pays $300-1,500+.** Pays expenses of writers on assignment.

PHOTOS Query. Model releases required. Pays pre-negotiated expenses of writer on assignment.

TIPS "Best bet to break in is through a fresh take on news, sparkling writing, and a pitch with regional import or interest; also seeking fresh ideas for service pieces or profiles with a regional interest. We *never* consider any story without a strong regional focus or demonstrable relevance to our region."

$ SUSQUEHANNA LIFE MAGAZINE

217 Market St., Lewisburg PA 17837. (800)232-1670. **Fax:** (570)524-7796. **E-mail:** susquehannalife@gmail.com. **Website:** www.susquehannalife.com. **80% freelance written.** Quarterly magazine covering Central Pennsylvania lifestyle. Estab. 1993. Circ. 53,000. Byline given. Within two weeks after publication. Offers 50% kill fee. Publishes ms an average of 6-9 months after acceptance. Editorial lead time 3-6 months. Submit seasonal material 4-6 months in advance. Accepts queries by e-mail. Responds in 4-6 weeks to queries; 1-3 months to mss. Sample copy for $4.95, plus 5 first-class stamps. Guidelines available for #10 SASE.

NONFICTION Needs book excerpts, essays, general interest, historical, how-to, humor, inspirational, interview, memoir, nostalgic, personal experience, photo feature, profile, travel. Does not want fiction. **Buys 30-40 mss/year.** Query or send complete ms. Length: 850 words. **Pays $75-125.**

PHOTOS Send photos. High-resolution, high-quality jpgs. Captions, identification of subjects, model releases required. Reviews contact sheets, prints, GIF/JPEG files. Offers $20-25/photo; $100+ for cover photos. Buys one-time rights + use of photos on web site.

POETRY Must have a Central Pennsylvania angle.

TIPS "When you query, do not address letter to 'Dear Sir'; address the letter to the name of the publisher/editor. Demonstrate your ability to write. You need to be familiar with the type of articles we use and the particular flavor of the region. Only accepts submissions with a Central Pennsylvania angle."

SOUTH CAROLINA

$$ HILTON HEAD MONTHLY

Monthly Media LLC, P.O. Box 5926, Hilton Head Island SC 29938. (843)842-6988, ext. 230. **E-mail:** lance@hiltonheadmonthly.com. **Website:** www.hiltonheadmonthly.com. **Contact:** Lance Hanlin, editor in chief. **75% freelance written.** Monthly magazine covering the people, business, community, environment, and lifestyle of Hilton Head, SC, and the surrounding Lowcountry. "Our mission is to offer lively, fresh writing about Hilton Head Island, an upscale, environmentally conscious, and intensely proactive resort community on the coast of South Carolina." Circ. 35,000. Byline given. Pays on publication. Offers 50% kill fee. Publishes ms an average of 6 months after acceptance. Editorial lead time 3 months. Submit seasonal material 4 months in advance. Accepts queries by mail, e-mail. Accepts simultaneous submissions. Responds in 1 week to queries; in 4 months to mss. Sample copy: $3.

NONFICTION Needs general interest, how-to, humor, opinion, personal experience, travel. "Everything is local, local, local, so we're especially interested in profiles of notable residents (or those with Lowcountry ties) and original takes on home design/maintenance, environmental issues, entrepreneurship, health, sports, arts and entertainment, humor, travel, and volunteerism. We like to see how national trends/issues play out on a local level." **Buys 225-250 mss/year.** Query with published clips. Pays expenses of writers on assignment.

PHOTOS State availability. Reviews contact sheets, prints, digital samples. Negotiates payment individually. Buys one-time rights.

COLUMNS/DEPARTMENTS News; Business; Lifestyles (hobbies, health, sports, etc.); Home; Around Town (local events, charities, and personalities); People (profiles, weddings, etc.). Query with synopsis. **Pays 20¢/word.**

TIPS "Sure, Hilton Head is known primarily as an affluent resort island, but there's plenty more going on than just golf and tennis; this is a lively community with a strong sense of identity and decades-long tradition of community, volunteerism, and environmental preservation. We don't need any more tales of why you chose to retire here or how you fell in love with the beaches, herons, or salt marshes. Seek out lively, surprising characters—there are plenty—and offer fresh (but not trendy) takes on local personalities, Southern living, and green issues."

TENNESSEE

$$ MEMPHIS DOWNTOWNER MAGAZINE

Downtown Productions, Inc., 408 S. Front St., Suite 109, Memphis TN 38103. (901)525-7118. **Fax:** (901)525-7128. **E-mail:** editor@memphisdowntowner.com. **Website:** www.memphisdowntowner.com. **Contact:** Terre Gorham, editor. **50% freelance written.** Bi-monthly magazine covering features on positive aspects with a Memphis tie-in, especially to downtown. "We feature people, companies, nonprofits, and other issues that the general Memphis public would find interesting, entertaining, and informative. All editorial focuses on the positives Memphis has. No negative commentary or personal judgements. Controversial subjects should be treated fairly and balanced without bias." Estab. 1991. Circ. 30,000. Byline given. Pays on 15th of month in which assignment is published. Offers 25% kill fee. Publishes ms an average of 2-6 months after acceptance. Editorial lead time 3-6 months. Submit seasonal material 3-6 months in advance. Accepts queries by mail, e-mail. Responds in 2 weeks to queries. Sample copy free. Guidelines by e-mail.

NONFICTION Needs general interest, historical, how-to, humor, interview, personal experience, photo feature. **Buys 40-50 mss/year.** Query with published clips. Length: 600-2,000 words. **Pays scales vary depending on scope of assignment, but typically runs 15¢/word.** Pays expenses of writers on assignment.

PHOTOS State availability. Identification of subjects required. Reviews GIF/JPEG files (300 DPI). Negotiates payment individually.

COLUMNS/DEPARTMENTS So It Goes (G-rated humor), 600-800 words; Discovery 901 (Memphis one-of-a-kinds), 1,000-1,200 words. **Buys 6 mss/year.** Query with published clips. **Pays $100-150.**

FILLERS Unusual, interesting, or how-to or what to look for appealing to a large, general audience.

TIPS "Always pitch an actual story idea. E-mails that simply let us know you're a freelance writer mysteriously disappear from our inboxes. Actually read the magazine before you pitch. Get to know the regular columns and departments. In your pitch, explain where in the magazine you think your story idea would best fit. See website for magazine samples and past issues."

TEXAS

$ HILL COUNTRY SUN

TD Austin Lane, Inc., 100 Commons Rd., Suite 7, #319, Dripping Springs TX 78620. (512)484-9716. **E-mail:** melissa@hillcountrysun.com. **Website:** www.hillcountrysun.com. **Contact:** Melissa Maxwell Ball, editor. **75% freelance written.** Monthly tabloid covering traveling in the Central Texas Hill Country. Publishes stories of interesting people, places, and events in the Central Texas Hill Country. Estab. 1990. Circ. 34,000. Byline given. Pays on acceptance. Publishes ms an average of 2 months after acceptance. Editorial lead time 1 month. Submit seasonal material 2 months in advance. Accepts queries by e-mail. Accepts simultaneous submissions. Responds in 1 week to queries. Sample copy free. Guidelines available online.

NONFICTION Needs interview, travel. No first-person articles. **Buys 50 mss/year.** Query. Length: 600-800 words. **Pays $60 minimum.**

PHOTOS State availability of or send photos. Identification of subjects required. No additional payment for photos accepted with ms. Buys one-time rights.

TIPS "Writers must be familiar with both the magazine's style and the Texas Hill Country."

$$$$ TEXAS MONTHLY

Emmis Publishing LP, P.O. Box 1569, Austin TX 78767. (512)320-6900. **Fax:** (512)476-9007. **Website:** www.texasmonthly.com. **Contact:** Tim Taliaferro, editor-in-chief. **10% freelance written.** Monthly magazine covering Texas. Estab. 1973. Circ. 300,000. Byline given. Pays on acceptance, $1/word and writer's expenses. Publishes ms an average of 1-3 months after acceptance. Editorial lead time 2 months. Submit seasonal material 3 months in advance. Accepts queries by online submission form. Responds in 6-8 weeks to queries and mss. Guidelines available online.

NONFICTION Needs book excerpts, essays, expose, general interest, interview, personal experience, photo feature, travel. Does not want articles without a Texas connection. Query. Length: 2,000-5,000 words. Pays expenses of writers on assignment.

PHOTOS Contact: Leslie Baldwin (lbaldwin@texasmonthly.com).

TIPS "Stories must appeal to an educated Texas audience. *Texas Monthly* covers the state's politics, sports, business, culture and changing lifestyles. We like solidly researched reporting that uncovers issues of public concern, reveals offbeat and previously unreported topics, or uses a novel approach to familiar topics. It contains lengthly features, interviews, essays, book excerpts, and reviews of books and movies. Does not want articles without a Texas connection. Any issue of the magazine would be a helpful guide; sample copy for $7."

VIRGINIA

$$ THE ROANOKER

Leisure Media 360, 3424 Brambleton Ave., Roanoke VA 24018. (540)989-6138; (800)548-1672. **Fax:** (540)989-7603. **E-mail:** jwood@leisurepublishing.com; krheinheimer@leisurepublishing.com. **Website:** www.theroanoker.com. **Contact:** Liz Long, editor; **Patty Jackson, production director. 75% freelance written. Works with a small number of new/unpublished writers each year.** Magazine published 6 times/year. "*The Roanoker* is a general interest city magazine for the people of Roanoke, Virginia and the surrounding area. Our readers are primarily upper-income, well-educated professionals between the ages of 35 and 60. Coverage ranges from hard news and consumer information to restaurant reviews and local history." Estab. 1974. Circ. 10,000. Byline given. Pays on publication. No kill fee. Publishes ms an average of 4 months after acceptance. Submit seasonal material 4 months in advance. Accepts queries by mail, e-mail, fax. Accepts simultaneous submissions. Responds in 2 months to queries. Sample copy for $2 with 9x12 SASE and 5 first-class stamps or online.

NONFICTION Needs historical, how-to, interview, photo feature, travel, periodic special sections on fashion, real estate, media, banking, investing. **Buys 30 mss/year.** Send complete ms. 1,400 words maximum. **Pays $35-350.** Pays expenses of writers on assignment.

PHOTOS Send photos. Captions, model releases required. digital submissions. Pays $25-50/published photograph. Rights purchased vary.

COLUMNS/DEPARTMENTS Gist (shorts on people, Roanoke-related books, local issues, events, arts and culture).

TIPS "We're looking for more pieces on contemporary history (1930s-70s). It helps if freelancer lives in the area. The most frequent mistake made by writers in completing an article for us is not having enough Roanoke-area focus: use of area experts, sources, slants, etc."

WISCONSIN

WYOMING RURAL ELECTRIC NEWS (WREN)

2710 Thomas Ave., Cheyenne WY 82001. (307)772-1986. **Fax:** (307)634-0728. **E-mail:** wren@wyomingrea.org. **Website:** wyomingrea.org/community/wren-magazine. **40% freelance written.** Monthly magazine (except in January) for audience of rural residents, vacation-home owners, farmers, ranchers and business owners in Wyoming. Estab. 1954. Circ. 39,100. Byline given. Pays on publication. No kill fee. Publishes ms an average of 2 months after acceptance. At least 3 months. Submit seasonal material 2 months in advance. Accepts queries by mail, e-mail. Accepts simultaneous submissions. Responds in 1 month to queries. Sample copy for $2.50 and 9x12 SASE. Guidelines for #10 SASE.

NONFICTION No nostalgia, sarcasm, or tongue-in-cheek. **Buys 4-10 mss/year.** Send complete ms. Length: 600-800 words. **Pays up to $150, plus 3 copies.** Pays expenses of writers on assignment.

REPRINTS Send tearsheet or photocopy and information about when and where the material previously appeared.

PHOTOS Color only.

TIPS "Always looking for fresh, new writers. Submit entire ms. Don't submit a regionally set story from some other part of the country. Photos and illustrations (if appropriate) are always welcomed. We want factual articles that are to the point, accurate."

RELIGIOUS

ALIVE NOW

1908 Grand Ave., P.O. Box 340004, Nashville TN 37203. (615)340-7254. **E-mail:** alivenow@upperroom.org. **Website:** www.alivenow.org; alivenow.upperroom.org. **Contact:** Beth A. Richardson, editor. *Alive Now*, published bimonthly, is a devotional magazine that invites readers to enter an ever-deepening relationship with God. "*Alive Now* seeks to nourish people who are hungry for a sacred way of living. Submissions should invite readers to see God in the midst of daily life by exploring how contemporary issues impact their faith lives. Each word must be vivid and dynamic and contribute to the whole. We make selections based on a list of upcoming themes. Mss which do not fit a theme will be returned." Estab. 1971. Circ. 70,000. Pays on acceptance. Accepts queries by mail, e-mail. Accepts simultaneous submissions. Subscription: $17.95/year (6 issues); $26.95 for 2 years (12 issues). Additional subscription information, including foreign rates, available on website. Guidelines available online.

NONFICTION Needs meditations. Prefers electronic submissions attached as Word document. Postal submissions should include SASE. Include name, address, theme on each sheet. Length: 400-500 words. **Pays $35 minimum.** Pays expenses of writers on assignment.

FICTION Needs religious. Prefers electronic submissions attached as Word document. Postal submissions should include SASE. Include name, address, theme on each sheet. Length: 400-500 words. **Pays $35 minimum.**

POETRY Prefers electronic submissions attached as Word document. Postal submissions should include SASE. Include name, address, theme on each sheet. **Pays $35 minimum.**

BIBLE ADVOCATE

Church of God (Seventh Day), P.O. Box 33677, Denver CO 80233. **E-mail:** bibleadvocate@cog7.org. **Website:** baonline.org. **Contact:** Sherri Langton, associate editor. **35% freelance written.** Religious magazine published 6 times/year. "Our purpose is to advocate the Bible and represent the Church of God (Seventh Day) to a Christian audience." Estab. 1863. Circ. 13,500. Byline given. Pays on publication. No kill fee. Publishes ms an average of 3-9 months after acceptance. Editorial lead time 3 months. Submit seasonal material 6 months in advance. Accepts queries by e-mail. Accepts simultaneous submissions. Responds in 4-10 weeks to queries. Sample copy for SAE with 9x12 envelope and 3 first-class stamps. Guidelines online.

"Though the Church of God (Seventh Day) believes in the virgin birth and resurrection of Christ, we do not publish articles or poetry on celebrating a traditional Christmas or Easter. Please become familiar with our doctrines."

NONFICTION **Contact:** Sherri Langton, associate editor. Needs inspirational, personal experience, religious, Biblical studies. No articles on Christmas or Easter. **Buys 10-20 mss/year.** Send complete ms by e-mail, preferably. Length: 600-1,200 words. **Pays $25-65.**

REPRINTS E-mail ms with rights for sale noted. Same as for first rights.

POETRY **Contact:** Sherri Langton, associate editor. Needs Wants free verse, traditional, Christian/Bible themes. Seldom comments on rejected poems. No avant-garde. Buys 10-12 poems/year. Submit maximum 5 poems. Length: 5-20 lines. **Pays $20 and 2 contributor's copies.**

TIPS "Be fresh, not preachy! Articles must be in keeping with the doctrinal understanding of the Church of God (Seventh Day). Therefore, the writer should become familiar with what the Church generally accepts as truth as set forth in its doctrinal beliefs. We reserve the right to edit mss to fit our space requirements, doctrinal stands, and church terminology. Significant changes are referred to writers for approval. Accept email submissions only — no fax or snail mail."

THE CHRISTIAN CENTURY

104 S. Michigan Ave., Suite 1100, Chicago IL 60603-5901. (312)263-7510. **Fax:** (312)263-7540. **E-mail:** main@christiancentury.org. **E-mail:** submissions@christiancentury.org; poetry@christiancentury.org. **Website:** www.christiancentury.org. **Contact:** Jill Peláez Baumgaertner, poetry editor. **90% freelance written. Works with new/unpublished writers.** Biweekly magazine for ecumenically minded, progressive Protestants, both clergy and lay. "We seek mss that articulate the public meaning of faith, bringing the resources of religious tradition to bear on such topics as poverty, human rights, economic justice, international relations, national priorities, and popular culture. We are also interested in pieces that examine or critique the theology and ethos of individual religious communities. We welcome articles that find fresh meaning in old traditions and that adapt or apply religious traditions to new circumstances. Authors should assume that readers are familiar with main themes in Christian history and theology, are accustomed to the historical-critical study of the Bible and are already engaged in relating faith to social and political issues. Many of our readers are ministers or teachers of religion at the college level. Book reviews are solicited by our books editor. Please note that submissions via e-mail will not be considered. If you are interested in becoming a reviewer for *The Christian Century*, please send your résumé and a list of subjects of interest to "Attn: Book reviews." Authors must have a critical and analytical perspective on the church and be familiar with contemporary theological discussion." Estab. 1884. Circ. 37,000. Byline given. Pays on publication. No kill fee. Editorial lead time 1 month. Submit seasonal material 4 months in advance. Accepts queries by mail, e-mail. Accepts simultaneous submissions. Responds in 4-6 weeks to queries; in 2 months to mss. Sample copy: $3.50. Guidelines available online.

NONFICTION Needs essays, humor, interview, opinion, religious. Does not want inspirational. **Buys 150 mss/year.** Send complete ms; query appreciated but not essential. Length: 1,000-3,000 words. **Pays variable amount for assigned articles. Pays $100-300 for unsolicited articles.** Pays expenses of writers on assignment.

PHOTOS State availability. Reviews any size prints. Buys one-time rights.

COLUMNS/DEPARTMENTS "We do not accept unsolicited submissions for our regular columns."

POETRY **Contact:** Jill Pelàez Baumgaertner, poetry editor. Needs free verse, traditional. Wants "poems that are not statements but experiences, that do not talk about the world but show it. We want to publish poems that are grounded in images and that reveal an awareness of the sounds of language and the forms of poetry even when the poems are written in free verse."

Submissions without SASE (or SAE and IRCs) will not be returned. Submit poems typed, double-spaced, 1 poem/page. Include name, address, and phone number on each page. Please submit poetry to poetry@christiancentury.org. Has published poetry by Jeanne Murray Walker, Ida Fasel, Kathleen Norris, Luci Shaw, J. Barrie Shepherd, and Wendell Berry. Prefers shorter poems. Inquire about reprint permission. Does not want "pietistic or sentimental doggerel." Buys 50 poems/year. Length: up to 20 lines/poem. **Usually pays $50/poem plus 1 contributor's copy and discount on additional copies. Acquires all rights.**

TIPS "We suggest reading the poems in the past several issues to gain a clearer idea of the kinds of poetry we are seeking. We publish shorter poems that are grounded in images and that reveal an awareness of the sounds of language and the forms of poetry even when the poems are written in free verse."

$$ DECISION

Billy Graham Evangelistic Association, P.O. Box 668886, Charlotte NC 28266. (704)401-2432. **Fax:** (704)401-3009. **E-mail:** submissions@bgea.org. **Website:** www.decisionmag.org. **Contact:** Bob Paulson, editor. **5% freelance written. Works each year with small number of new/unpublished writers.** "Magazine published 11 times/year with a mission to communicate the Good News of Jesus Christ, to inform and challenge readers about key cultural and Biblical issues, and to extend the ministry of the Billy Graham Evangelistic Association." Include telephone number with submission. Estab. 1960. Circ. 400,000. Byline given. Pays on publication. Publishes ms up to 18 months after acceptance. Editorial lead time 6 months. Submit seasonal material 6 months in advance. Accepts queries by mail, e-mail. Sample copy for sae with 9x12 envelope and 4 first-class stamps. Guidelines online.

NONFICTION Needs personal experience, testimony. **Buys approximately 8 mss/year.** Send complete ms. Length: 400-1,000 words. **Pays $200-400.** Pays expenses of writers on assignment.

PHOTOS State availability. Captions, identification of subjects, model releases required. Reviews prints. Buys one time rights.

COLUMNS/DEPARTMENTS Finding Jesus (people who have become Christians through Billy Graham Ministries), 500-900 words. **Buys 11 mss/year.** Send complete ms. **Pays $200.**

TIPS "Articles should have some connection to the ministry of Billy Graham or Franklin Graham. For example, you may have volunteered in 1 of these ministries or been touched by them. The article does not need to be entirely about that connection, but it should at least mention the connection. Testimonies and personal experience articles should show how God intervened in your life and how you have been transformed by God. SASE required with submissions."

$ EVANGELICAL MISSIONS QUARTERLY

Billy Graham Center at Wheaton College, 500 College Ave., Wheaton IL 60187. (630)752-7158. **E-mail:** emq@wheaton.edu. **Website:** www.emqonline.com. **Contact:** Laurie Fortunak Nichols, managing editor; A. Scott Moreau, editor. **67% freelance written.** Quarterly magazine covering evangelical missions. *Evangelical Missions Quarterly* is a professional journal serving the worldwide missions community. *EMQ* articles reflect missionary life, thought, and practice. Each issue includes articles, book reviews, editorials, and letters. Subjects are related to worldwide mission and evangelism efforts and include successful ministries, practical ideas, new tactics and strategies, trends in world evangelization, church planting and discipleship, health and medicine, literature and media, education and training, relief and development, missionary family life, and much more. Estab. 1964. Circ. 7,000. Byline given. Pays on publication. Offers negotiable kill fee. Publishes ms an average of 18 months after acceptance. Editorial lead time 1 year. Accepts queries by e-mail. Accepts simultaneous submissions. Responds in 2 weeks to queries. Sample copy free. Guidelines available online.

NONFICTION Needs interview, opinion, personal experience, religious. No sermons, poetry, or straight news. **Buys 24 mss/year.** Query. Length: 3,000 words. **Pays $25-100.** Pays expenses of writers on assignment.

PHOTOS Send photos. Identification of subjects required. Offers no additional payment for photos accepted with ms. Buys first rights.

COLUMNS/DEPARTMENTS In the Workshop (practical how tos), 800-2,000 words; Perspectives (opinion), 800 words. **Buys 8 mss/year.** Query. **Pays $50-100.**

TIPS "We prefer articles about deeds done, showing the why and the how, not only claiming success but also admitting failure. Principles drawn from 1 example must be applicable to missions more generally. *EMQ* does not include articles which have been previously published in journals, books, websites, etc."

FAITH & FRIENDS

The Salvation Army, 2 Overlea Blvd., Toronto ON M4H 1P4 Canada. (416)422-6226. **Fax:** (416)422-6120. **E-mail:** faithandfriends@can.salvationarmy.org. **Website:** www.faithandfriends.ca. **25% freelance written.** Monthly magazine covering Christian living and religion. "*Faith & Friends*, a contemporary, full-color monthly magazine, is written and designed to show Jesus Christ at work in the lives of real people and to provide spiritual resources for those who are new to the Christian faith. Each issue contains stories about people whose lives have been changed through an encounter with Jesus." Estab. 1996. Circ. 50,000. Byline given. Pays on acceptance. Offers $50 kill fee. Publishes ms an average of 3 months after acceptance. Editorial lead time 3 months. Submit seasonal material 6 months in advance. Accepts queries by mail, e-mail, fax. Accepts simultaneous submissions. Usually responds in 10 days to queries and mss. Sample copy available online. Guidelines by e-mail.

NONFICTION Needs book excerpts, essays, general interest, historical, inspirational, interview, memoir, opinion, personal experience, photo feature, profile, religious, reviews, Testimonial (a first-person conversion testimony, conveying what Christ has done in your life, or the testimony of another, obtained through interview), 1,200 words; Personal Story (a concise narrative relating biblical principles to everyday living, using an anecdote or incident from your own or someone else's life), 750 words. "Articles should avoid references and concepts the unchurched would not understand and should focus on ideas and answers which are compatible with a Christian worldview. Take care not to submit an essay or preach at our readers." **Buys 12-24 mss/year.** Query or send complete ms. Approximately 250 words per page up to 1,000 words for a feature. **Pays approximately $50/page.** Pays expenses of writers on assignment.

PHOTOS Send photos. Captions required. Reviews prints, GIF/JPEG files. Negotiates payment individually. Buys one-time rights.

COLUMNS/DEPARTMENTS Faith Builders (reviews that explore the spiritual meaning be-hind popular movies or television shows); God in My Life (personal witness of the power of God in everyday life); Turning Point (how, with God's help, you faced a serious obstacle and got on with your life); Someone Cares (a profile or personal treatment of how you or someone you know was helped by The Salvation Army); Words to Live By (the Bible in action or a Bible message integrated into your life and presented in everyday terms); Big Questions (answers to difficult theological questions in terms that ordinary people can understand); Sacred Space (spiritual tools, exercises, disciplines and social justice issues that encourage new Christians to connect with God and reach out to others); Beyond Borders (inspirational stories of overseas missionaries or Christian workers who engage with the culture in innovative ways); The Bottom Line (Christian businesspeople who live out their be-liefs at work by establishing an ethical workplace with ethical practices); Love & Life (exploring the Christian dimension to spousal and family relationships); all 750 words. **Buys 12-18 mss/year.** Query or send complete ms.

FAITH TODAY

The Evangelical Fellowship of Canada, P.O. Box 5885, West Beaver Creek Post Office, Richmond Hill ON L4B 0B8 Canada. (905)479-5885. **Fax:** (905)479-4742. **E-mail:** editor@faithtoday.ca. **Website:** www.faithtoday.ca. **Contact:** Bill Fledderus and Karen Stiller, senior editors. **Over 80% freelance written.** Bimonthly magazine. *Faith Today* is the magazine of an association of more than 40 evangelical denominations in Canada but serves Evangelicals in all denominations. In 2016 it added a sister magazine for youth and young adults, called *Love Is Moving. Faith Today* focuses on church issues, social issues, and personal faith as they are tied to the Canadian context. Writing should explicitly acknowledge that Canadian evangelical context. Queries should have an explicit content connection to Canadian evangelical Christians. Estab. 1983. Circ. 20,000. Byline given. Pays on publication. Offers 30-50% kill fee. Publishes ms an average of 4 months after acceptance. Editorial lead time 4 months. Accepts queries by mail, e-mail. Accepts simultaneous submissions. Responds in 2 weeks to queries. Sample copy for SASE in Canadian postage or online. Guidelines online.

NONFICTION Needs book excerpts, essays, expose, general interest, historical, how-to, humor, inspirational, interview, opinion, profile, religious, reviews, news feature. Does not want Bible studies, poetry, serialized articles, seasonal material, generic or U.S.-focused Christian-living material. **Buys 75 mss/year.** Query. Length: 400-2,000 words. **Pays $100-500 Canadian.** Pays expenses of writers on assignment.

REPRINTS Pays 50% of amount paid for an original article.

PHOTOS State availability. Buys one-time rights.

TIPS "Query should include brief outline and names of the sources you plan to interview in your research. Use Canadian postage on SASE."

$$ HOPE FOR WOMEN

P.O. Box 3241, Muncie IN 47307. **E-mail:** hope@hopeforwomenmag.org. **Website:** www.hopeforwomenmag.com. **90% freelance written.** Bimonthly lifestyle magazine that offers faith, love, and virtue for the modern Christian Woman. *Hope for Women* presents refreshing, inspirational articles in an engaging and authentic tone to women from various walks of life. The magazine encourages readers and deals with real-world issues—all while adhering to Christian values and principles. Estab. 2005. Circ. 10,000. Byline given. Pays on publication. Publishes ms an average of 4-6 months after acceptance. Editorial lead time 4-6 months. Accepts queries by mail, e-mail. Accepts simultaneous submissions. Guidelines by email.

NONFICTION Needs book excerpts, essays, general interest, how-to, humor, inspirational, interview, new product, opinion, personal experience, photo feature, religious, travel. Query. Length: 500 words minimum. **Pays 10-20¢/word.** Pays expenses of writers on assignment.

COLUMNS/DEPARTMENTS Relationships (nurturing positive relationships—marriage, dating, divorce, single life), 800-1,200 words; Light (reports on issues such as infidelity, homosexuality, addiction, and domestic violence), 500-800 words; Journey (essays on finding your identity with Christ), 500-800 words; Marketplace (finance/money management), 800-1,200 words); E-Spot (book, music, TV, and film reviews), 500-800 words; Family First (parenting encouragement and instruction), 800-1,500 words; Health/Fitness (nutrition/exercise), 800-1,200 words; The Look (fashion/beauty tips), 500-800 words; Home Essentials (home/garden how-to), 500-800 words. Query. **Pays 10-20¢/word.**

TIPS "Our readers are a diverse group of women, ages 25-54. They want to read articles about real women dealing with real problems. Because our readers are balancing work and family, they want information presented in a no-nonsense fashion that is relevant and readable."

$ LIGHT + LIFE MAGAZINE

Free Methodist Church – USA, 770 N. High School Rd., Indianapolis IN 46214. (317)616-4776. **Fax:** (317)244-1247. **E-mail:** jeff.finley@fmcusa.org. **Website:** lightandlifemagazine.com. **Contact:** Jeff Finley, executive editor. **50% freelance written.** *Light + Life Magazine* is a monthly magazine published by Light + Life Communications, the publishing arm of the Free Methodist Church–USA. Each issue focuses on a specific theme with a cohesive approach in which the articles complement each other. The magazine has a flip format with articles in English and Spanish. Estab. 1868. Circ. 38,000. Byline given. Pays on publication. No kill fee. Accepts queries by e-mail. Accepts simultaneous submissions. Responds in 2 months. Guidelines online.

NONFICTION Needs religious. Query. Length: 2,100 words for feature articles, 800 words for print discipleship articles, 500-1,000 words for online discipleship articles, 500-1,000 words for online articles not published in the magazine. **Pays $50 per article.**

$ LIVE

Gospel Publishing House, 1445 N. Boonville Ave., Springfield MO 65802-1894. (417)862-1447. **E-mail:** rl-live@gph.org. **Website:** www.gospelpublishing.com. **100% freelance written.** Weekly magazine for weekly distribution covering practical Christian living. "*LIVE* is a take-home paper distributed weekly in young adult and adult Sunday school classes. We seek to encourage Christians in living for God through fiction and true stories which apply Biblical principles to everyday problems." Estab. 1928. Circ. 18,000. Byline given. Pays on acceptance. No kill fee. Publishes ms an average of 18 months after acceptance. Editorial lead time 12 months. Submit seasonal material 18 months in advance. Accepts queries by mail, e-mail. Accepts simultaneous submissions. Responds in 6 weeks to queries; in 8 weeks to mss. Sample copy for #10 SASE. Guidelines for #10 SASE or on website: www.gospelpublishing.com/store/startcat.cfm?cat=tWRITGUID.

NONFICTION Needs inspirational, religious. No preachy articles or stories that refer to religious myths (e.g., Santa Claus, Easter Bunny, etc.). **Buys 50-100 mss/year.** Send complete ms. Length: 550-1,100 words. **Pays 7-10¢/word.** Pays expenses of writers on assignment.

REPRINTS Send tearsheet, photocopy, or typed ms with rights for sale noted and information about when and where the material previously appeared. Pays 7¢/word.

PHOTOS Send photos. Identification of subjects required. Reviews 35mm transparencies and 3x4 prints or larger. Higher-resolution digital files also accepted. Offers $35-60/photo. Buys one-time rights.

FICTION Needs religious, inspirational, prose poem. No preachy fiction, fiction about Bible characters, or stories that refer to religious myths (e.g., Santa Claus, Easter Bunny, etc.). No science or Bible fiction. No controversial stories about such subjects as feminism, war, or capital punishment. **Buys 20-50 mss/year.** Send complete ms. Length: 800-1,200 words. **Pays 7-10¢/word.**

POETRY Needs free verse, haiku, light verse, traditional. Buys 15-24 poems/year. Submit maximum 3 poems. Length: 12-25 lines. **Pays $35-60.**

TIPS "Don't moralize or be preachy. Provide human interest articles with Biblical life application. Stories should consist of action, not just thought-life, interaction, or insight. Heroes and heroines should rise above failures, take risks for God, prove that scriptural principles meet their needs. Conflict and suspense should increase to a climax! Avoid pious conclusions. Characters should be interesting, believable, and realistic. Avoid stereotypes. Characters should be active, not just pawns to move the plot along. They should confront conflict and change in believable ways. Describe the character's looks and reveal his personality through his actions to such an extent that the reader feels he has met that person. Readers should care about the character enough to finish the story. Feature racial, ethnic, and regional characters in rural and urban settings."

LIVE

Canadian Baptist Women of Ontario and Quebec, 5 International Blvd., Etobicoke ON M9W 6H3 Canada. (416)651-8967. **Website:** www.baptistwomen.com. **Contact:** Renee James, editor/director of communications. **15% freelance written.** Magazine published 6 times/year designed to help women grow in their authentic experience of God and in their intimate connection to mission. Vision: evangelical, egalitarian, Canadian. Estab. 1878. Circ. 3,500. Byline given. Pays on publication. No kill fee. Publishes ms an average of 6 months after acceptance. Editorial lead time 2 months. Submit seasonal material 4 months in advance. Accepts simultaneous submissions. Sample copy for 9x12 SAE with 2 first-class Canadian stamps.

Canadian writers only.

NONFICTION Needs inspirational, interview, personal experience, religious. **Buys 15 mss/year.** Query first. Unsolicited mss not accepted. Length: 650-800 words. **Pays 10-12¢/word (Canadian).**

PHOTOS State availability. Captions required. Offers no additional payment for photos accepted with ms. Buys one-time rights.

TIPS "We cannot use unsolicited mss from non-Canadian writers. When submitting by e-mail, please send stories as messages, not as attachments."

THE LUTHERAN DIGEST

The Lutheran Digest, Inc., P.O. Box 100, Princeton MN 55371. **E-mail:** editor@lutherandigest.com. **Website:** www.lutherandigest.com. **Contact:** Nick Skapyak, editor. **95% freelance written.** Quarterly magazine covering Christianity from a Lutheran perspective. Publishes articles, humor, and poetry. Articles frequently reflect a Lutheran Christian perspective but are not intended to be sermonettes. Popular stories show how God has intervened in a person's life to help solve a problem. Estab. 1953. Circ. 20,000. No byline given. Pays on publication. No kill fee. Publishes ms an average of 6 months after acceptance. Editorial lead time 9 months. Submit seasonal material 9 months in advance. "No queries, please." Accepts simultaneous submissions. Responds in 4 months to mss. No response to e-mailed mss unless selected for publication. Sample copy: $3.50. Subscription: $16/year, $22 for 2 years. Guidelines online.

The Lutheran Digest is 64 pages, digest-sized, offset-printed, saddle-stapled, with 4-color paper cover, includes local ads. Press run is 20,000-30,000; most distributed free to Lutheran churches.

NONFICTION Needs general interest, historical, how-to, humor, inspirational, personal experience. Does not want to see personal tributes to deceased relatives or friends. These are seldom used unless the subject of the article is well known. Avoids articles about the moment a person finds Christ as his or her personal savior. **Buys 50-60 mss/year.** Send complete ms. Length: up to 1,500 words. **Pays $25-50.** Pays expenses of writers on assignment.

REPRINTS Accepts previously published submissions. "We prefer this as we are a digest and 70-80% of our articles are reprints."

PHOTOS "We never print photos from outside sources."

POETRY Submit up to 3 poems at a time. Prefers e-mail submissions but also accepts mailed submissions. Cover letter is preferred. Include SASE only if return is desired. Poems are selected by editor and reviewed by publication panel. Length: up to 25 lines/poem. **Pays 1 contributor's copy.**

TIPS "Reading our writers' guidelines and sample articles online is encouraged and is the best way to get a feel for the type of material we publish."

$$ MESSAGE MAGAZINE

North American Division of Seventh-day Adventists, 12501 Old Columbia Pike, Silver Spring MD 20904. (301)680-6598. **E-mail:** editor@messagemagazine.com; associateeditor@messagemagazine.com. **Website:** www.messagemagazine.com. **Contact:** Carmela Monk Crawford, editor. **10-20% freelance written.** Bimonthly magazine. "*Message* is the oldest religious journal addressing ethnic issues in the country. Our audience is predominantly Black and Seventh-day Adventist; however, *Message* is an outreach magazine for the churched and unchurched across cultural lines." Estab. 1898. Circ. 110,000. Byline given. Pays on acceptance. No kill fee. Publishes ms an average of 12 months after acceptance. Editorial lead time 6 months. Submit seasonal material 6 months in advance. Accepts simultaneous submissions. Responds in 9 months to queries. Sample copy by e-mail. Guidelines by e-mail and online.

"Our target reader is an 18- to 35-year-old urbanite who may not be religious but is seeking spiritual fulfillment and answers to life's dilemmas."

NONFICTION Send complete ms. Length: 300-900 words. **Pays $75-300 for features.** Pays expenses of writers on assignment.

PHOTOS State availability. Identification of subjects required. Buys one time rights.

COLUMNS/DEPARTMENTS Eye on the Times: religious liberty, public affairs, human rights, and news (300 words); Optimal Health: health news, how-tos, and healthy habits (550 words). **Pays $75-150.**

TIPS "Please look at the magazine before submitting mss. *Message* publishes a variety of writing styles as long as the writing style is easy to read and flows. Please avoid highly technical writing styles."

$$ ONE

1011 First Ave., New York NY 10022-4195. (212)826-1480. **Fax:** (212)838-1344. **E-mail:** cnewa@cnewa.org; editorial@cnewa.org. **Website:** www.cnewa.org. **Contact:** Deacon Greg Kandra, executive editor. **75% freelance written.** Bimonthly magazine for a Catholic audience with interest in the Near East, particularly its current religious, cultural, and political aspects. Estab. 1974. Circ. 100,000. Byline given. Pays on publication. No kill fee. Publishes ms an average of 6 months after acceptance. Accepts queries by mail, fax. Accepts simultaneous submissions. Responds in 1 month to queries. Sample copy and writer's guidelines for 7½×10½ SAE with 2 first-class stamps.

NONFICTION Query. Length: 1,200-1,800 words. **Pays 20¢/edited word.** Pays expenses of writers on assignment.

PHOTOS "Photographs to accompany ms are welcome; they should illustrate the people, places, ceremonies, etc. which are described in the article. We prefer color transparencies but occasionally use b&w." Pay varies depending on use—scale from $50-300.

TIPS "We are interested in current events in the Near East as they affect the cultural, political, and religious lives of the people."

$$ OUTREACH MAGAZINE

5550 Tech Center Dr., Colorado Springs CO 80919. (719)955-9600. **E-mail:** theeditors@outreachmagazine.com. **Website:** www.outreachmagazine.com. **80% freelance written.** Bimonthly magazine covering outreach in Christianity. *Outreach* magazine is the gathering place of ideas, insights and stories for Christian churches focused on reaching out to their community—locally and globally—with the love of Christ. Primary readers are pastors and other church leadership, as well as laity who are passionate about outreach. Practical outreach ideas; church profiles and best practices; essential perspectives for leadership; in-depth interviews with leading pastors; trend-oriented features. Estab. 2003. Circ. 32,000. Byline given. Pays on publication. Offers 10% kill fee. Publishes ms an average of 2-4 months after acceptance. Editorial lead time 6 months. Submit seasonal material 6 months in advance. Accepts queries by mail, e-mail. Accepts simultaneous submissions. Responds in 2 months to queries; 8 months to mss. Sample copy free. Guidelines online.

NONFICTION Needs how-to, inspirational, interview, personal experience, religious. Special issues: Small Church America / Church Planting; The American Megachurch Annual; Leadership; Outreach Resources of the Year; Evangelism, Discipleship, Service. Does not want fiction, poetry, non-outreach-related articles. **Buys 30 mss/year.** Query with published clips. Length: 1,500-2,500 words. Church Profiles/How-to: 300+ words. Interview sometimes run as long as 4,000 words (assignment only). **Pays approximately 35 cents/word.** Pays expenses of writers on assignment.

PHOTOS Send photos. Identification of subjects required. Reviews GIF/JPEG files. Negotiates payment individually. Buys all rights.

COLUMNS/DEPARTMENTS Ideas—For Any Church, Any Size (short stories about outreach-oriented churches and ministries), 250-350 words; Soulfires—Igniting Ministry (dramatic as-told-to features about average individuals (not paid clergy) who have become passionate about a need and established a ministry to meet it; Leadership—Essential Perspectives for Those Who Lead (assigned). Query with published clips. **Approximately 35 cents/per word.**

FILLERS Needs facts, gag.

TIPS "Study our magazine and writer's guidelines. Send published clips that showcase tight, bright writing as well as your ability to interview; research; and organize numerous sources into an article; and write a 100-word piece as well as a 1,600-word piece."

PRAIRIE MESSENGER

Benedictine Monks of St. Peter's Abbey, P.O. Box 190, 100 College Dr., Muenster Saskatchewan S0K 2Y0 Canada. (306)682-1772. **Fax:** (306)682-5285. **E-mail:** pm.canadian@stpeterspress.ca. **Website:** www.prairiemessenger.ca. **Contact:** Maureen Weber, associate editor. **30% freelance written.** Weekly Catholic publication published by the Benedictine Monks of St. Peter's Abbey. Has a strong focus on ecumenism, social justice, interfaith relations, aboriginal issues, arts, and culture. Estab. 1904. Circ. 4,000. Byline given. Pays on publication. No kill fee. Publishes ms an average of 4 months after acceptance. Submit seasonal material 3 months in advance. Accepts queries by mail, e-mail. Accepts simultaneous submissions. Responds only if interested; send nonreturnable samples. Sample copy for 9x12 SASE with $1 Canadian postage or IRCs. Guidelines available online. "Because of government subsidy regulations, we are no longer able to accept non-Canadian freelance material."

NONFICTION Needs book excerpts, essays, interview, opinion, religious. Special issues: Christmas, Easter. **Buys 15 mss/year.** Send complete ms. Length: 500-800 words. **Pays $70/article.**

PHOTOS Send photos. Captions required. Reviews 3x5 prints. Offers $25/photo. Buys all rights.

POETRY Needs Shorter poems preferred. Buys 45 poems/year. Length: up to 35 lines. **Pays $30/published poem.**

PURPOSE

MennoMedia, P.O. Box 866, 100 S. Mason St., Suite B, Harrisonburg VA 22801. **E-mail:** purposeeditor@mennomedia.org. **Website:** www.mennomedia.org/purpose. Publisher: Amy Gingerich. **Contact:** Melodie M. Davis. **80% freelance written.** Magazine focuses on Christian discipleship—how to be a faithful Christian in the midst of everyday life situations. Uses personal story form to present models and examples to encourage Christians in living a life of faithful discipleship. Each issue follows a designated theme. *Purpose* is published monthly by Mennomedia, the publisher for Mennonite Church Canada and Mennonite Church USA. It is a faith-based adult monthly magazine that focuses on every day inspiration, discipleship-living, simplicity, and the Christian faith. Check the theme list on the website. Estab. 1968. Circ. 4,400. Byline given. Pays upon publication. No kill fee. Publishes ms 6-9 months after acceptance. Editorial lead time: 9 months. Submit material according to writer guidelines and theme deadlines posted on the website. Accepts queries by e-mail. Responds in 1-3 months. Sample articles can be viewed on the website. Guidelines online.

NONFICTION **Buys 140 mss/year.** E-mail submissions preferred. Length: 500-700 words. **Pays $25-50/story.**

POETRY Needs free verse, light verse, traditional. Poetry must address monthly themes. and be of a spiritual nature. Buys 8-10 poems/year. Length: 12 lines maximum. **Pays $10-20/poem.**

TIPS "We seek true stories that follow monthly themes. Be sure to look at the website for the theme list and deadlines, as we only consider stories that are tied to the themes. Follow the writer guidelines on the website for the latest submission information."

THE SECRET PLACE

P.O. Box 851, Valley Forge PA 19482. (610)768-2434. **Fax:** (610)768-2441. **E-mail:** thesecretplace@abc-usa.org. **Website:** www.judsonpress.com/catalog_secret-place.cfm. **100% freelance written.** Quarterly devotional covering Christian daily devotions. Estab. 1937. Circ. 250,000. Byline given. Pays on acceptance. No kill fee. Editorial lead time 1 to 2 years. Submit seasonal material 9 months in advance. Guidelines online.

NONFICTION Needs inspirational, religious. **Buys 400 mss/year.** Send complete ms. Length: 100-200 words. **Pays $20.** Pays expenses of writers on assignment.

POETRY Needs avant-garde, free verse, light verse, traditional. Submit up to 6 poems by mail or e-mail. E-mail preferred. Buys 12-15 poems/year. Submit maximum 6 poems. Length: 4-30 lines/poem. **Pays $20.**

TIPS "Prefers submissions via e-mail."

U.S. CATHOLIC

Claretian Publications, 205 W. Monroe St., Chicago IL 60606. (312)236-7782. **Fax:** (312)236-8207. **E-mail:** literaryeditor@uscatholic.org. **E-mail:** submissions@claretians.org. **Website:** www.uscatholic.org. **Mostly freelance written.** Monthly magazine covering contemporary issues from a Catholic perspective. "*U.S. Catholic* puts faith in the context of everyday life. With a strong focus on social justice, we offer a fresh and balanced take on the issues that matter most in our world, adding a faith perspective to such challenges as poverty, education, family life, the environment, and even pop culture." Estab. 1935. Circ. 25,000. Byline given. Pays on acceptance. No kill fee. Publishes ms an average of 6 months after acceptance. Editorial lead time 8 months. Submit seasonal material 6 months in advance. Accepts queries by mail, e-mail. Responds in 1 month to queries; in 2 months to mss. Guidelines on website.

Please include SASE with written ms.

NONFICTION Needs essays, inspirational, opinion, personal experience, religious. **Buys 100 mss/year.** Send complete ms. Length: 700-1,400 words. **Pays minimum $200.**

PHOTOS State availability.

FICTION Accepts short stories. "Topics vary, but unpublished fiction should be no longer than 1,500 words and should include strong characters and cause readers to stop for a moment and consider their relationships with others, the world, and/or God. Specifically religious themes are not required; subject matter is not restricted. E-mail submissions@uscatholic.org." Needs ethnic, mainstream, religious, slice-of-life vignettes. **Buys 4-6 mss/year.** Send complete ms. Length: 700-1,500 words. **Pays minimum $200.**

POETRY Needs free verse. Submit 3-5 poems at a time. Accepts e-mail submissions (pasted into body of message or as attachments). Cover letter is preferred. No light verse. Buys 12 poems/year. Length: up to 50 lines/poem. **Pays $75.**

THE WAR CRY

The Salvation Army, 615 Slaters Lane, Alexandria VA 22314. (703)684-4128. **Fax:** (703)684-5539. **E-mail:** war_cry@usn.salvationarmy.org. **Website:** publications.salvationarmyusa.org. **10% freelance written.** "Inspirational magazine with evangelical emphasis and portrayals that express the mission of the Salvation Army. Twelve issues published per year, including special Easter and Christmas issues." Estab. 1881. Circ. 200,000 monthly; 1.7 million Christmas; 1.1 million Easter. Byline given. Pays on acceptance. No kill fee. Publishes ms an average of 2 months to 1 year after acceptance. Editorial lead time 2 months before issue date; Christmas and Easter issues 6 months before issue date. Submit Christmas and Easter material 6 months in advance. Accepts simultaneous submissions. Responds in 3-4 weeks to mss. Sample copy, theme list, and writer's guidelines free with #10 SASE or online.

Word limit for mss 800-1500 words.

NONFICTION "*The War Cry* represents The Salvation Army's mission through features, news, profiles, commentaries, and stories. It seeks to bring people to Christ, help believers grow in faith and character, and promote redemptive cultural practices from the perspective of The Salvation Army programs, minisitries, and doctrines." No missionary stories, confessions. **Buys 30 mss/year.** Complete mss and reprints accepted through website at publications.salvationarmyusa.org/writers-submissions. Submissions strengthened when photos included where appropriate. **Pays 35¢/word.** Pays expenses of writers on assignment.

REPRINTS Considers reprints.

PHOTOS Accepts submissions for the "In the Moment" feature appearing in each issue. High-resolution photos (600 dpi) with captions. Identification of subjects required. Pays $50. Buys one-time rights.

FICTIONShort stories that do not expound on dogma but depict how faith and life intersect.

POETRY Purchases limited poetry (10 per year maximum).

FILLERS Needs anecdotes, religious news, statistical analysis of trends, and vignettes. **Buys 10-20 mss/year.** Length: 100-400 words. **Pays 35¢/word.**

RETIREMENT

$ CHRISTIAN LIVING IN THE MATURE YEARS

The United Methodist Publishing House, 2222 Rosa L. Parks Blvd., Nashville TN 37228. **E-mail:** matureyears@umpublishing.org. **Website:** matureyears.submittable.com. **80% freelance written. Prefers to work with published/established writers.** Quarterly magazine designed to help persons in and nearing the retirement years understand and appropriate the resources of the Christian faith in dealing with specific problems and opportunities related to aging. Estab. 1954. Circ. 35,000. Byline given. Pays on acceptance. No kill fee. Publishes ms an average of 1 year after acceptance. Submit seasonal material 14 months in advance. Responds in 2-3 months to mss. Guidelines online.

NONFICTION Needs how-to, humor, inspirational, memoir, personal experience, religious, older adult health, life, faith, finance issues. **Buys 75-80 mss/year.** Send complete ms to matureyears.submittable.com. No longer accepts e-mailed or hard-copy submissions. Length: 300-2,000 words. **Pays 7¢/word.**

PHOTOS Send high-resolution photos. Captions, model releases required. Negotiates pay individually. Typically buys one-time rights.

○$ INSPIRED 55+ LIFESTYLE MAGAZINE

Stratis Publishing Ltd., 3354 Tennyson Ave, Victoria BC V8Z 3P6 Canada. (250)479-4705. **E-mail:** editor@seniorlivingmag.com. **Website:** www.seniorlivingmag.com. **Contact:** Bobbie Jo Reid, Managing Editor. **100% freelance written.** Magazine published 12 times/year covering active 55+ living. Inspiration for people over 55. Monthly magazine distributed throughout British Columbia, extensive website, 2 annual 55+ Lifestyle Shows. Estab. 2004. Circ. 35,000. Byline given. Pays quarterly. Pays kill fee. Publishes an average of 2-6 months after acceptance. Editorial lead time 6 months. Submit seasonal material 6 months in advance. Accepts queries by e-mail. Sample copy available online. Guidelines available.

NONFICTION Needs historical, how-to, humor, inspirational, interview, personal experience, travel, profiles of inspiring people age 55+ who live in British Columbia. Special issues: Special issues: housing, travel, charitable giving, fashion. Does not want politics; religion; promotion of business, service, or products; humor that demeans senior demographic or aging process. Query. Does not accept previously published material. Length: 500-1,200 words. **Pays $35-150 for assigned articles; $35-150 for unsolicited articles.** Pays expenses of writers on assignment. Sometimes pays expenses (limit agreed upon in advance).

PHOTOS Send photos. Identification of subjects, model releases required. Reviews GIF/JPEG files. Offers $10-75 per photo. Buys all rights.

COLUMNS/DEPARTMENTS Buys 5-6 mss/year. Query with published clips. **Pays $25-50.**

TIPS "Editorial must be about or reflect the lifestyles of people age 55+ living in British Columbia."

RURAL

$$ BACKWOODS HOME MAGAZINE

P.O. Box 712, Gold Beach OR 97444. (541)247-8900. **Fax:** (541)247-8600. **E-mail:** lisa@backwoodshome.com. **E-mail:** article-submission@backwoodshome.com. **Website:** www.backwoodshome.com. **Contact:** Lisa Nourse, editorial coordinator. **90% freelance written.** Bimonthly magazine covering self-reliance. *Backwoods Home Magazine* is written for people who have a desire to pursue personal independence, self-sufficiency, and their dreams. Offers how-to articles on self-reliance. Estab. 1989. Circ. 38,000. Byline given. Pays on acceptance. Editorial lead time 4-6 months. Submit seasonal material 4-6 months in advance. Accepts queries by mail, e-mail. Sample copy for 9x10 SAE and 6 first-class stamps. Guidelines available online.

NONFICTION Needs general interest, how-to, humor, personal experience, technical. **Buys 120 mss/year.** Send complete ms via e-mail (no attachments) or postal mail. Looking for straightforward, clear writing similar to what you would find in a good newspaper. Length: 500 words. **Pays $40-200.** Pays expenses of writers on assignment.

PHOTOS Send photos. Captions, identification of subjects, model releases required. Offers no additional payment for photos accepted with ms.

$$ COUNTRY

Trusted Media Brands, Inc., 1610 N. 2nd St., Suite 102, Milwaukee WI 53212. **Website:** www.countrymagazine.com. *Country* celebrates the breathtaking beauty, engaging people, enduring values, and spirutally rewarding lifestyle of the American countryside. Pays on acceptance. Accepts queries by online submission form. Accepts simultaneous submissions. Guidelines online.

NONFICTION All stories are considered on speculation, do not send a query. Submit via mail or e-mail. Photos and mss submitted through the mail will not be returned. E-mailed stories should be included in the body of an e-mail or in an attached .doc, .docx, .rtf, or .odt file. Word length usually runs 400-500 words for a 1-page story. **Pays $250 for story submissions that run a page or more.** Pays expenses of writers on assignment.

PHOTOS To e-mail photos, attach them as a high-res JPG file (at least 1800 x 1200 pixels or 1 MB file size). Requires caption information.

$$ FARM & RANCH LIVING

Trusted Media Brands, Inc., 1610 N. Second St., Suite 102, Milwaukee WI 53212-3906. (414)423-0100. **Fax:** (414)423-8463. **E-mail:** submissions@farmandranchliving.com. **Website:** farmandranchliving.com. **30% freelance written. Eager to work with new/unpublished writers.** Bimonthly magazine aimed at families that live on, work on, or have ties to a farm or ranch. FRL focuses on people who celebrate the pleasures of living off the land rather than production and profits. Estab. 1978. Byline given. Pays on publication. No kill fee. Publishes ms an average of 6 months after acceptance. Submit seasonal material 6 months in advance. Accepts queries by e-mail. Accepts simultaneous submissions. "We are unable to respond to queries." To purchase a single copy, contact customercare@farmandranchliving.com.

NONFICTION Needs humor, inspirational, interview, personal experience, photo feature, nostalgia, prettiest place in the country (photo/text tour of ranch or farm). No issue-oriented stories (pollution, animal rights, etc.). **Buys 30 mss/year.** Send complete ms. Length: 600-1,200 words. **Pays up to $400 for text/photo package.** Pays expenses of writers on assignment.

REPRINTS Send photocopy with rights for sale noted. Payment negotiable.

PHOTOS "We no longer accept slides. We look for photos of farm animals, people, and rural scenery." State availability. Buys one-time rights.

TIPS "Our readers enjoy stories and features that are upbeat and positive. A freelancer must see *F&RL* to fully appreciate how different it is from other farm publications—ordering a sample is strongly advised. Photo features (about interesting farm or ranch families) and personality profiles are most open to freelancers."

$$ HOBBY FARMS

I-5 Publishing, 470 Conway Court, Suite B6, Lexington KY 40511. **E-mail:** hobbyfarms@luminamedia.com. **Website:** www.hobbyfarms.com. **85% freelance written.** Bimonthly magazine covering small farms and rural lifestyle. "*Hobby Farms* is the magazine for rural enthusiasts. Whether you have a small garden or 100 acres, there is something in *Hobby Farms* to educate, enlighten, or inspire you." Estab. 2001. Circ. 252,801. Byline given. Pays on publication. Publishes ms an average of 6 months after acceptance. Editorial lead time 4 months. Submit seasonal material 6 months in advance. Accepts queries by mail, e-mail. Accepts simultaneous submissions. Responds in 2 months to queries and mss. Guidelines free.

"Writing tone should be conversational but authoritative."

NONFICTION Needs historical, how-to, interview, personal experience, technical, breed or crop profiles. **Buys 10 mss/year.** Send complete ms. Length: 1,000-1,500 words. Pays expenses of writers on assignment. Limit agreed upon in advance.

PHOTOS State availability of or send photos. Identification of subjects, model releases required. Reviews GIF/JPEG files. Negotiates payment individually. Buys one-time rights.

TIPS "Please state your specific experience with any aspect of farming (livestock, gardening, equipment, marketing, etc)."

$ THE LAND

Free Press Co., P.O. Box 3169, Mankato MN 56002-3169. (507)345-4523. **Fax:** (507)345-1027. **E-mail:** editor@thelandonline.com. **Website:** www.thelandonline.com. **40% freelance written.** Weekly tabloid covering farming and rural life in Minnesota and Northern Iowa. "Although we're not tightly focused on any one type of farming, our articles must be of interest to farmers. In other words, will your article topic have an impact on people who live and work in rural areas?" Prefers to work with Minnesota or Iowa writers. Estab. 1976. Circ. 27,000. Byline given. Pays on acceptance. No kill fee. Publishes ms an average of 2 months after acceptance. Editorial lead time 2 months. Submit seasonal material 2 months in advance. Accepts queries by mail, e-mail. Accepts simultaneous submissions. Responds in 3 weeks to queries; in 2 months to mss. Sample copy free. Guidelines with #10 SASE.

NONFICTION Needs general interest, how-to. **Buys 80 mss/year.** Query. Length:1000-1500 words. **Pays $50-70 for assigned articles.**

PHOTOS Send photos. Reviews contact sheets. Negotiates payment individually. Buys one-time rights.

COLUMNS/DEPARTMENTS Query. **Pays $10-50.**

TIPS "Be enthused about rural Minnesota and Iowa life and agriculture, and be willing to work with our editors. We try to stress relevance. When sending me a query, convince me the story belongs in a Minnesota farm publication."

MONADNOCK TABLE

The Guide to Our Region's Food, Farms & Community, 60 West St., Keene NH 03431. (603)369-2525. **E-mail:** marcia@monadnocktable.com. **Website:** www.monadnocktable.com. **Contact:** Marcia Passos-Duffy, editor. Quarterly magazine for local food/farms in the Monadnock Region of New Hampshire. Estab. 2010. Circ. 15,000. Byline given. Pays on publication. Offers 25% kill fee. Publishes ms 3 months after acceptance. Editorial lead time 3 months. Submit seasonal material 3 months in advance. Accepts queries by e-mail. Accepts simultaneous submissions. Responds in 1 month. Sample copy online. Guidelines online.

"Must be about trends, profiles, etc., of local food and farms in the Monadnock Region and the Upper Valley region of New Hampshire."

NONFICTION Needs book excerpts, essays, how-to, interview, opinion, personal experience. Query. Length: 500-1,200 words. **Pays $75-125.** Pays expenses of writers on assignment.

PHOTOS Freelancers should state availability of photos with submission. Captions required. Reviews GIF/JPEG files. Offers no additional payment for photos accepted with ms.

COLUMNS/DEPARTMENTS Local Farmer (profile of local farmer in Monadnock Region), up to 600 words; Local Eats (profile of local chef and/or restaurant using local food), up to 600 words; Feature (how-to or "think" piece about local foods), up to 1,000 words; Books/Opinion/Commentary (review of books, book excerpt, commentary, opinion pieces about local food), up to 500 words. **Buys 10 mss/year.** Query.

TIPS "Please query first with your qualifications. Please read magazine first for style (magazines available online). Must have a local (Monadnock Region/Upper Valley New Hampshire) angle."

MOTHER EARTH NEWS

Ogden Publications, 1503 SW 42nd St., Topeka KS 66609-1265. (785)274-4300. **E-mail:** letters@motherearthnews.com. **Website:** www.motherearthnews.com. **Contact:** Oscar "Hank" Will III, editor; Rebecca Martin, managing editor. **Mostly written by staff and team of established freelancers.** Bimonthly magazine emphasizing country living, country skills, natural health, and sustainable technologies for both long-time and would-be ruralists. "*Mother Earth News* promotes self-sufficient, financially independent, and environmentally aware lifestyles. Many of our feature articles are written by our Contributing Editors, but we also assign articles to freelance writers, particularly those who have experience with our subject matter (both firsthand and writing experience)." Circ. 350,000. Byline given. Pays on publication. No kill fee. Submit seasonal material 5 months in advance. Accepts queries by mail, e-mail. Accepts simultaneous submissions. Responds in 6 months to mss. Sample copy: $5. Guidelines available online.

NONFICTION Needs how-to, green building, do-it-yourself, organic gardening, whole foods and cooking, natural health, livestock and sustainable farming, renewable energy, 21st-century homesteading, nature-environment-community, green transportation. No fiction, please. **Buys 35-50 mss/year.** "Query. Please send a short synopsis of the idea, a one-page outline, and any relevant digital photos and samples. If available, please send us copies of 1 or 2 published articles, or tell us where to find them online." **Pays $25-150.**

PHOTOS "We welcome quality photographs for our 2 departments."

COLUMNS/DEPARTMENTS Country Lore (helpful how-to tips); 100-300 words; Firsthand Reports (first-person stories about sustainable lifestyles of all sorts), 1,500-2,000 words.

TIPS "Read our magazine, and take a close look at previous issues to learn more abut the various topics we cover. We assign articles about 6-8 months ahead of publication date, so keep in mind timing and the seasonality of some topics. Our articles provide hands-on, useful information for people who want a more fun, conscientious, sustainable, secure, and satisfying lifestyle. Practicality is critical; freelance articles must be informative, well-documented, and tightly written in an engaging and energetic voice. For how-to articles, complete, easy-to-understand instructions are essential."

$$ RANGE

Purple Coyote Corp., 106 E. Adams St., Suite 201, Carson City NV 89706. (775)884-2200. **Fax:** (775)884-2213. **E-mail:** edit@rangemagazine.com. **Website:** www.rangemagazine.com. **Contact:** C.J. Hadley, editor/publisher. **70% freelance written.** *RANGE* covers ranching, farming, and the issues that affect agriculture. Not interested in rodeo or travel stories. *RANGE* magazine is devoted to the issues that threaten the West, its people, lifestyles, lands, and wildlife. No stranger to controversy, *RANGE* is the leading forum for opposing viewpoints in the search for solutions that will halt the depletion of a national resource, the American rancher. Estab. 1991. Pays on publication. Publishes ms an average of 3-6 months after acceptance. Accepts queries by e-mail. Accepts simultaneous submissions. Responds in 1-2 months to queries; in 1-4 months to mss. Sample copy: $2. Guidelines online.

NONFICTION Needs expose, historical, humor, nostalgic, opinion, photo feature, profile. No sports or events. No book reviews. Writer must be familiar with *RANGE.* Query via e-mail. Length: 500-2,000 words. **Pays $50-500 for new writers. More for regulars.**

PHOTOS State availability of photography. Captions, photo credit, and contact information must be included with all photos. Reviews high-res digitals (JPEGS or TIFFS) via FTP site or on thumb drive with captions. Slides and prints also reviewed. Pays $25-75, $100 for cover. Buys one-time rights. First North American preferred.

SCIENCE

$$ AD ASTRA

National Space Society, P.O. Box 98106, Washington DC 20090. (202)429-1600. **Fax:** (703)435-4390. **E-mail:** adastra@nss.org. **Website:** www.nss.org/adastra. **Contact:** Rod Pyle, Editor-In-Chief. **80% freelance written.** *Ad Astra* ("to the stars") is the award-winning print and digital magazine of the National Space Society, featuring the latest news in space exploration and stunning full-color photography. Published in print and digital quarterly. "We publish nontechnical, lively articles about all aspects of NASA, private spaceflight, and international space programs, including robotic planetary science and occasionally light astronomy and astrophysics. NewSpace efforts are also of interest if written with editorial neutrality (e.g., no promotional articles accepted)." Estab. 1989. Circ. 10,000. Byline given. Pays on publication. No kill fee. Publishes ms 3-6 months after acceptance. Accepts queries by e-mail. Accepts simultaneous submissions. Responds only when interested. Sample copy for 9x12 SASE.

NONFICTION Needs book excerpts, essays, general interest, historical, interview, opinion, photo feature, technical. No fiction/science fiction or UFO stories, thanks. Query with published clips. Length: 1,200-2,500 words with 2-8 full-size (8.5x11) color images at 300 dpi; 100-600 words for sidebars; 600-750 words for book reviews. **Pays $250 for most articles.** Pays expenses of writers on assignment.

PHOTOS State availability. Identification of subjects required, with attribution credit for the image. Reviews color prints, digital, JPEG-IS, GISS. , Buys one-time rights.

TIPS "We require mss to be in MS Word or text file formats. Know the field of space technology, programs, and policy. Know the players. Look for fresh angles. Excellent writing skills are expected. We are NOT generally seeking highly technical or journal articles—this is a general interest space magazine."

$$$$ AMERICAN ARCHAEOLOGY

The Archaeological Conservancy, 1717 Girard Blvd. NE, Albuquerque NM 87106. (505)266-9668. **Fax:** (505)266-0311. **E-mail:** tacmag@nm.net. **Website:**

www.americanarchaeology.org. **Contact:** Michael Bawaya, editor; Vicki Singer, art director. **60% freelance written.** Quarterly magazine. "We're a popular archaeology magazine. Our readers are very interested in this science. Our features cover important digs, prominent archaeologists, and most any aspect of the science. We only cover North America." Estab. 1997. Circ. 35,000. Byline given. Pays on acceptance. Offers 20% kill fee. Publishes ms an average of 3 months after acceptance. Editorial lead time 3 months. Accepts queries by mail, e-mail, fax. Accepts simultaneous submissions. Responds in 3 weeks to queries; in 1 month to mss.

NONFICTION No fiction, poetry, humor. **Buys 15 mss/year.** Query with published clips. Length: 1,500-3,000 words. **Pays $1,000-2,000.** Pays expenses of writers on assignment.

PHOTOS State availability. Identification of subjects required. Reviews transparencies, prints. Pays $50 and up for occasional stock images; assigns work by project (pay varies); negotiable. **Pays on acceptance.** Credit line given. Buys one-time rights. Offers $400-600/photo shoot. Negotiates payment individually. Buys one-time rights.

TIPS "Read the magazine. Features must have a considerable amount of archaeological detail."

$$ ASTRONOMY

Kalmbach Publishing, 21027 Crossroads Circle, P.O. Box 1612, Waukesha WI 53187-1612. (800)533-6644. **Fax:** (262)798-6468. **Website:** www.astronomy.com. **Contact:** David J. Eicher, editor; LuAnn Williams Belter, art director (for art and photography). **50% of articles submitted and written by science writers; includes commissioned and unsolicited.** Monthly magazine covering the science and hobby of astronomy. "Half of our magazine is for hobbyists (who are active observers of the sky); the other half is directed toward armchair astronomers who are intrigued by the science." Estab. 1973. Circ. 108,000. Byline given. Pays on acceptance. Does pay a kill fee, although rarely used. Accepts simultaneous submissions. Responds in 1 month to queries. Responds in 3 months to mss. on website.

"We are governed by what is happening in astronomical research and space exploration. It can be up to a year before we publish a ms. Query for electronic submissions."

NONFICTION Needs book excerpts, new product, photo feature, technical, space, astronomy. **Buys 75 mss/year.** Please query on all article ideas Length: 500-3,000 words. **Pays $100-1,000.** Pays expenses of writers on assignment.

TIPS "Submitting to *Astronomy* could be tough—take a look at how technical astronomy is. But if someone is a physics teacher or an amateur astronomer, he or she might want to study the magazine for a year to see the sorts of subjects and approaches we use, and then submit a proposal. Submission guidelines available online."

$$$$ BIOSCIENCE

American Institute of Biological Sciences, 1900 Campus Commons Dr., Suite 200, Reston VA 20191. (202)628-1500. **Fax:** (202)628-1509. **Website:** www.aibs.org. **Contact:** Scott L. Collins, editor-in-chief. **5% freelance written.** Monthly peer-reviewed scientific journal covering organisms from molecules to the environment. "We contract professional science writers to write features on assigned topics, including organismal biology and ecology, but excluding biomedical topics." Estab. 1951. Byline given. Publishes ms an average of 3 months after acceptance. Editorial lead time 2 months. Accepts queries by e-mail. Accepts simultaneous submissions. Responds in 2-3 weeks to queries. Sample copy on website. Guidelines free.

NONFICTION Does not want biomedical topics. **Buys 10 mss/year.** Query. Length: 1,500-3,000 words. **Pays $1,500-3,000.** Pays expenses of writers on assignment.

TIPS "Queries can cover any area of biology. The story should appeal to a wide scientific audience, yet be accessible to the interested (and somewhat science-literate) layperson. *BioScience* tends to favor research and policy trend stories and avoids personality profiles."

$$$$ STARDATE

University of Texas, 2515 Speedway, Stop C1402, Austin TX 78712. (512)475-6763. **E-mail:** rjohnson@stardate.org. **Website:** stardate.org. **Contact:** Rebecca Johnson, editor. **80% freelance written.** Bimonthly magazine covering astronomy and skywatching. *StarDate* is written for people with an interest in astronomy and what they see in the night sky, but no special astronomy training or background. Query with published quips, by email or regular mail. No unsolicited mss. Estab. 1975. Circ. 10,000. Byline given. Pays on acceptance. Offers 25% kill fee. Publishes ms an average of 4 months after acceptance. Editorial lead time 6 months. Submit seasonal material 6 months in advance. Accepts queries by mail, e-mail, fax. Accepts simultaneous submissions. Responds in 6 weeks to queries. Sample copy and writer's guidelines free.

NONFICTION Needs general interest, historical, interview, photo feature, technical, travel. No first-person, first stargazing experiences, or paranormal. **Buys 8 mss/year.** Query with published clips. Length: 1,500-3,000 words. **Pays $800-1,700.** Pays expenses of writers on assignment.

PHOTOS Send photos. Identification of subjects required. Reviews transparencies, prints. Negotiates payment individually. Buys one time rights.

COLUMNS/DEPARTMENTS AstroNews (short astronomy news item), 250 words. **Buys 6 mss/year.** Query with published clips. **Pays $150-250.**

TIPS "Keep up to date with current astronomy news and space missions. No technical jargon."

SCIENCE FICTION, FANTASY & HORROR

ANALOG SCIENCE FICTION & FACT

Dell Magazines, 44 Wall St., Suite 904, New York NY 10005-2401. **E-mail:** analogsf@dellmagazines.com. **Website:** www.analogsf.com. **Contact:** Trevor Quachri, editor. **100% freelance written. Eager to work with new/unpublished writers.** *Analog* seeks "solidly entertaining stories exploring solidly thought-out speculative ideas. But the ideas, and consequently the stories, are always new. Real science and technology have always been important in *ASF*, not only as the foundation of its fiction but as the subject of articles about real research with big implications for the future." Estab. 1930. Circ. 50,000. Byline given. Pays on acceptance. No kill fee. Publishes ms an average of 10 months after acceptance. Accepts queries by mail, online submission form. Accepts simultaneous submissions. Responds in 2-3 months to mss. Sample copy: $5 and SASE. Guidelines online.

Fiction published in *Analog* has won numerous Nebula and Hugo Awards.

NONFICTION Special issues: Articles should deal with subjects of not only current but future interest, i.e., with topics at the present frontiers of research whose likely future developments have implications of wide interest. **Buys 11 mss/year.** Send complete ms via online submissions manager (preferred) or postal mail. Does not accept e-mail submissions. Length: up to 4,000 words. **Pays 9¢/word.**

FICTION "Basically, we publish science fiction stories. That is, stories in which some aspect of future science or technology is so integral to the plot that, if that aspect were removed, the story would collapse. The science can be physical, sociological, psychological. The technology can be anything from electronic engineering to biogenetic engineering. But the stories must be strong and realistic, with believable people (who needn't be human) doing believable things—no matter how fantastic the background might be." Needs science fiction. No fantasy or stories in which the scientific background is implausible or plays no essential role. Send complete ms via online submissions manager (preferred) or postal mail. Does not accept e-mail submissions. Length: 2,000-7,000 words for short stories, 10,000-20,000 words for novelettes and novellas, and 40,000-80,000 for serials. **Analog pays 8-10¢/word for short stories up to 7,500 words, 8-8.5¢ for longer material, 6¢/word for serials.**

POETRY Send poems via online submissions manager (preferred) or postal mail. Does not accept e-mail submissions. Length: up to 40 lines/poem. **Pays $1/line.**

TIPS "I'm looking for irresistibly entertaining stories that make me think about things in ways I've never done before. Read several issues to get a broad feel for our tastes, but don't try to imitate what you read."

APEX MAGAZINE

Apex Publications, LLC, P.O. Box 24323, Lexington KY 40524. **E-mail:** lesley@apex-magazine.com. **Website:** www.apex-magazine.com. **Contact:** Lesley Conner, managing editor. **100% freelance written.** Monthly e-zine publishing dark speculative fiction. "An elite repository for new and seasoned authors with an other-worldly interest in the unquestioned and slightly bizarre parts of the universe. We want science fiction, fantasy, horror, and mash-ups of all three of the dark, weird stuff down at the bottom of your little literary heart." Estab. 2004. Circ. 28,000 unique visits per month. Byline given. Pays 30 days after publication. Publishes mss an average of 6 months after acceptance. Editorial lead time 2 weeks. Submit seasonal material 6 months in advance. Accepts queries by e-mail. Responds in 20-30 days. Sample content online. Guidelines online.

NONFICTION **Buys 36 mss/year.** Send complete ms. Length: 100-7,500 words. **Pays $50 flat rate.**

REPRINTS Pays 1¢/word.

FICTION Needs fantasy, horror, science fiction, short stories. **Buys 36 mss/year.** Send complete ms. Length: 100-7,500 words. **Pays 6¢/word.**

ASIMOV'S SCIENCE FICTION

Dell Magazines, 44 Wall St., Suite 904, New York NY 10005. **E-mail:** asimovs@dellmagazines.com. **Website:** www.asimovs.com. **Contact:** Sheila Williams, editor; Victoria Green, senior art director. **98% freelance written. Works with a small number of new/unpublished writers each year.** *Asimov's*, published 10 times/year, including 2 double issues, is 5.875x8.625 (trim size); 112 pages; 30 lb. newspaper; 70 lb. to 8 pt. C1S cover stock; illustrations; rarely has photos. "Magazine consists of science fiction and fantasy stories for adults and young adults. Publishes the best short science fiction available." Estab. 1977. Circ. 50,000. Pays on acceptance. No kill fee. Publishes ms an average of 6-12 months after acceptance. Accepts queries by mail. Responds in 2 months to queries; in 3 months to mss. Sample copy: $5. Guidelines online or for #10 SASE.

NONFICTION Pays expenses of writers on assignment.

FICTION Wants "science fiction primarily. Some fantasy and humor. It is best to read a great deal of material in the genre to avoid the use of some very old ideas." Submit ms via online submissions manager or postal mail; no e-mail submissions. Needs fantasy, science fiction. No horror or psychic/supernatural, sword and sorcery, explicit sex or violence that isn't integral to the story. Would like to see more hard science fiction. Length: 750-15,000 words. **Pays 8-10¢/word for short stories up to 7,500 words; 8-8.5¢/word for longer material. Works between 7,500-10,000 words by authors who make more than 8¢/word for short stories will receive a flat rate that will be no less than the payment would be for a shorter story.**

TIPS "In general, we're looking for 'character-oriented' stories, those in which the characters, rather than the science, provide the main focus for the reader's interest. Serious, thoughtful, yet accessible fiction will constitute the majority of our purchases, but there's always room for the humorous as well."

BEYOND CENTAURI

White Cat Publications, LLC, 33080 Industrial Rd., Suite 101, Livonia MI 48150. (734)237-8522. **Fax:** (313)557-5162. **E-mail:** beyondcentauri@whitecatpublications.com. **Website:** www.whitecatpublications.com/guidelines/beyond-centauri. *Beyond Centauri*, published quarterly, contains fantasy, science fiction, sword and sorcery, very mild horror short stories, poetry, and illustrations for readers ages 10 and up. Estab. 2003. Publishes ms 1-2 months after acceptance. Accepts queries by e-mail. Accepts simultaneous submissions. Responds in 2-3 months. Single copy: $7.

Beyond Centauri is 44 pages, magazine-sized, offset printed, perfect-bound, with paper cover for color art, includes ads. Press run is 100; 5 distributed free to reviewers.

NONFICTION Needs opinion, reviews, short articles about space exploration, science, and technology. Send complete ms in the body of an e-mail, or as an RTF attachment. Length: up to 1,500 words. **Pays $7/piece and 1 contributor's copy.**

FICTION Looks for themes of science fiction or fantasy. "Science fiction and especially stories that take place in outer space will find great favor with us." Needs fantasy, horror, science fiction, short stories. Submit in the body of an e-mail, or as an RTF attachment. Length: up to 2,500 words. **Pays $6/story, $3/reprints, and $2/flash fiction (under 1,000 words), plus 1 contributor's copy.**

POETRY Wants fantasy, science fiction, spooky horror, and speculative poetry for younger readers. Considers poetry by children and teens. Has published poetry by Bruce Boston, Bobbi Sinha-Morey, Debbie Feo, Dorothy Imm, Cythera, and Terrie Leigh Relf. Looks for themes of science fiction and fantasy. Poetry should be submitted in the body of an e-mail, or as an RTF attachment. Does not want horror with excessive blood and gore. Length: up to 50 lines/poem. **Pays $2/original poem, $1/reprints, $1/scifaiku and related form, plus 1 contributor's copy.**

$ THE DARK

Prime Books, P.O. Box 1152, Germantown MD 20875. **E-mail:** thedarkmagazine@gmail.com. **Website:** www.thedarkmagazine.com. **Contact:** Silvia Moreno-Garcia and Sean Wallace, editors. **100% freelance written.** Monthly electronic magazine publishing horror and dark fantasy. Estab. 2013. Byline given. Pays on acceptance. No kill fee. Publishes ms an average of 2 months after acceptance. Editorial lead time 1 month. Accepts queries by e-mail. Responds in 1-2 days to mss. Always sends prepublication galleys. Sample: $2.99 (back issue). Guidelines online.

REPRINTS See submission guidelines. Pays 1¢/word.

FICTION Needs horror, suspense, strange, magic realism, dark fantasy. "Don't be afraid to experiment or to deviate from the ordinary; be different—try us with fiction that may fall out of 'regular' categories. However, it is also important to understand that despite the name, *The Dark* is not a market for graphic, violent horror." **Buys 24 mss/year.** Send complete ms by e-mail attached in Microsoft Word DOC only. No multiple submissions. Length: 2,000-6,000 words. **Pays 6¢/word.**

TIPS "All fiction must have a dark, surreal, fantastical bend to it. It should be out of the ordinary and/or experimental. Can also be contemporary."

$$ FANGORIA

The Brooklyn Company, 20 Railroad Ave., East Northport NY 11731. **E-mail:** musick@fangoria.com. **Website:** www.fangoria.com. **95% freelance written. Works with a small number of new/unpublished writers each year.** Magazine published 10 times/year covering horror films, TV projects, comics, videos, and literature, and those who create them. "We provide an assignment sheet (deadlines, info) to writers, thus authorizing queried stories that we're buying." Estab. 1979. Byline given. Pays 1-3 months after publication. Publishes ms an average of 3 months after acceptance. Submit seasonal material 4 months in advance. Accepts queries by mail. Accepts simultaneous submissions. Responds in 6 weeks to queries.

NONFICTION Avoids most articles on science-fiction films. **Buys 120 mss/year.** Query with published clips. Length: 1,000-3,500 words. **Pays $100-250.** Pays expenses of writers on assignment.

PHOTOS State availability. Captions, identification of subjects required. Reviews transparencies, prints (b&w, color) electronically.

COLUMNS/DEPARTMENTS Monster Invasion (exclusive, early information about new film productions; also mini-interviews with filmmakers and novelists). Query with published clips. **Pays $45-75.**

TIPS "Other than recommending that you study one or several copies of *Fangoria*, we can only describe it as a horror film magazine consisting primarily of interviews with technicians and filmmakers in the field. Be sure to stress the interview subjects' words—not your own opinions as much. We're very interested in small, independent filmmakers working outside of Hollywood. These people are usually more accessible to writers, and more cooperative. *Fangoria* is also sort of a de facto bible for youngsters interested in movie makeup careers and for young filmmakers. We are devoted only to reel horrors—the fakery of films, the imagery of the horror fiction of a Stephen King or a Clive Barker—we do not want nor would we ever publish articles on real-life horrors, murders, etc. A writer must enjoy horror films and horror fiction to work for us. If the photos in *Fangoria* disgust you, if the sight of (stage) blood repels you, if you feel 'superior' to horror (and its fans), you aren't a writer for us and we certainly aren't the market for you. We love giving new writers their first chance to break into print in a national magazine. We are currently looking for Louisiana- (New Orleans), New Mexico-, Arizona- and Las Vegas-based correspondents, as well as writers stationed in Spain (especially Barcelona), southern US cities, and Eastern Europe."

$$ HELIOTROPE

E-mail: heliotropeditor@gmail.com. **Website:** www.heliotropemag.com. *Heliotrope* is a quarterly e-zine that publishes fiction, articles, and poetry. Estab. 2006. Pays on publication. No kill fee. Accepts queries by e-mail. Responds in 1 month to mss. Guidelines available online.

NONFICTION Needs opinion. Submit complete ms via e-mail. Length: 2,000 words minimum. **Pays $90.**

FICTION "If your story is something we can't label, we're interested in that, too." Needs fantasy, horror, mystery, science fiction. Submit complete ms via e-mail. Length: up to 5,000 words. **Pays 10¢/word.**

POETRY Submit via e-mail. **Pays $50.**

KASMA MAGAZINE

E-mail: editors@kasmamagazine.com. **Website:** www.kasmamagazine.com. **Contact:** Alex Korovessis, editor. Online magazine. "We publish the best science fiction from promising new and established writers. Our aim is to provide stories that are well written, original, and thought provoking." Estab. 2009. Pays on publication. Publishes mss 2-3 months after acceptance. Editorial lead time 2 months. Submit seasonal material 1 month in advance. Accepts queries by e-mail. Accepts simultaneous submissions. Responds in 1 week to queries; in 3 months to mss. Sample copy online and by e-mail. Guidelines online.

NONFICTION Pays expenses of writers on assignment.

FICTION Needs science fiction. No erotica or excessive violence/language. Submit complete ms via e-mail. Length: 1,000-5,000 words. **Pays $25 CAD.**

TIPS "The type of stories I enjoy the most usually come as a surprise: I think I know what is happening, but the underlying reality is revealed to me as I read on. That said, I've accepted many stories that don't fit this model. Sometimes I'm introduced to a new story structure. Sometimes the story I like reminds me of another story, but it introduces a slightly different spin on it. Other times, the story introduces such interesting and original ideas that structure and style don't seem to matter as much."

LEADING EDGE MAGAZINE

Brigham Young University, 4087 JKB, Provo UT 84602. **E-mail:** editor@leadingedgemagazine.com; fiction@leadingedgemagazine.com; art@leadingedgemagazine.com; poetry@leadingedgemagazine.com; nonfiction@leadingedgemagazine.com. **Website:** www.leadingedgemagazine.com. **Contact:** Abigail Miner, editor-in-chief. **90% freelance written.** Semiannual magazine covering science fiction and fantasy. "*Leading Edge* is a magazine dedicated to new and upcoming talent in the fields of science fiction, fantasy, and horror. We strive to encourage developing and established talent and provide high-quality speculative fiction to our readers." Does not accept mss with sex, excessive violence, or profanity. Accepts unsolicited submissions. Estab. 1981. Circ. 200. Byline given. Pays on publication. No kill fee. Publishes ms an average of 2-4 months after acceptance. Accepts queries by mail, e-mail. Accepts simultaneous submissions. Responds within 12 months to mss. Single copy: $6.99. "We no longer provide subscriptions, but *Leading Edge* is now available on Amazon Kindle, as well as print-on-demand." Guidelines online.

NONFICTION Needs essays, expose, interview, personal experience, reviews. Special issues: Because we are a science fiction and fantasy journal, all nonfiction submissions should be related to a specific work or trend within the science fiction and fantasy genres. Send complete ms with cover letter and SASE. Include estimated word count. Send to nonfiction@leadingedgemagazine.com. Length: up to 15,000 words. **Pays 1¢/word; $50 maximum.** Pays expenses of writers on assignment.

FICTION Contact: Shelby Gardner, fiction@leadingedgemagazine.com. Needs fantasy, horror, science fiction. **Buys 14-16 mss/year.** Send complete ms with cover letter and SASE. Include estimated word count. Length: up to 15,000 words. **Pays 1¢/word; $50 maximum.**

POETRY Contact: Scott Darrington. Needs avant-garde, haiku, light verse, traditional. Publishes 2-4 poems per issue. Poetry should reflect both literary value and popular appeal and should deal with science fiction- or fantasy-related themes. Cover letter is preferred. Include name, address, phone number, length of poem, title, and type of poem at the top of each page. Please include SASE with every submission. Buys 4-8 poems/year. Submit maximum 10 poems. **Pays $10 for first 4 pages; $1.50/each subsequent page.**

TIPS "Buy a sample issue to know what is currently selling in our magazine. Also, make sure to follow the writer's guidelines when submitting."

ON SPEC

P.O. Box 4727, Station South, Edmonton AB T6E 5G6 Canada. (780)628-7121. **E-mail:** onspec@onspec.ca. **Website:** www.onspec.ca. **95% freelance written.** Quarterly magazine covering Canadian science fiction, fantasy, and horror. "We publish speculative fiction and poetry by new and established writers, with a strong preference for Canadian-authored works." Estab. 1989. Circ. 2,000. Byline given. Pays on acceptance. No kill fee. Publishes ms an average of 6-18 months after acceptance. Editorial lead time 6 months. Accepts queries by mail. Accepts simultaneous submissions. Responds in 2 weeks to queries; in 6 months after deadline to mss. Sample copy: $8. Guidelines on website.

See website guidelines for submission announcements. "Please refer to website for information regarding submissions, as we are not open year round."

NONFICTION Pays expenses of writers on assignment.

FICTION Needs fantasy, horror, science fiction, magic realism, ghost stories, fairy stories. No media tie-in or shaggy-alien stories. No condensed or excerpted novels, religious/inspirational stories, fairy tales. **Buys 50 mss/year.** Send complete ms. Electronic submissions preferred. Length: 1,000-6,000 words.

POETRY Needs avant-garde, free verse. No rhyming or religious material. Buys 6 poems/year. Submit maximum 10 poems. Length: 4-100 lines. **Pays $50 and 1 contributor's copy.**

TIPS "We want to see stories with plausible characters, a well-constructed, consistent, and vividly described setting, a strong plot, and believable emotions; characters must show us (not tell us) their emotional responses to each other and to the situation and/or challenge they face. Also: Don't send us stories written for television. We don't like media tie-ins, so don't watch TV for inspiration! Read instead! Strong preference given to submissions by Canadians."

SCIFAIKUEST

Alban Lake Publishing, P.O. Box 782, Cedar Rapids IA 52406. **E-mail:** gatrix65@yahoo.com. **Website:** https://www.albanlakepublishing.com/. **Contact:** Tyree Campbell, managing editor; Teri Santitoro, editor. *Scifaikuest*, published quarterly both online and in print, features "science fiction/fantasy/horror minimalist poetry, especially scifaiku, and related forms. We also publish articles about various poetic forms and reviews of poetry collections. The online and print versions of *Scifaikuest* are different." *Scifaikuest* (print edition) is 32 pages, digest-sized, offset-printed, perfect-bound, with color cardstock cover, includes ads. Receives about 500 poems/year, accepts about 160 (32%). Press run is 100/issue; 5 distributed free to reviewers. Member: The Speculative Literature Foundation. Estab. 2003. Time between acceptance and publication is 1-2 months. Submit seasonal poems 6 months in advance. Accepts queries by e-mail. Responds in 6-8 weeks. Single copy: $7; subscription: $20/year, $37 for 2 years. Make checks payable to Tyree Campbell/Alban Lake Publishing. Guidelines online.

NONFICTION "We're looking for articles related in some way to one or more of the poetry forms we publish, or related to similar forms such as sijo, cinquain, haibun and cherita." Length: under 1,000 words but considers longer essays. **Pays $6/article and 1 contributor's copy.** Pays expenses of writers on assignment.

POETRY Wants artwork, scifaiku, and speculative minimalist forms such as tanka, haibun, ghazals, senryu. Submit no more than 10 poems at a time. Accepts e-mail submissions (pasted into body of message). No disk submissions; artwork as e-mail attachment or inserted body of e-mail. Submission should include snail-mail address, email address, PayPal address and a short (1-2 lines) bio. Reads submissions year round. Editor Teri Santitoro makes all decisions regarding acceptances. Often comments on rejected poems. Has published poetry by Tom Brinck, Oino Sakai, Deborah P. Kolodji, Aurelio Rico Lopez III, Joanne Morcom, and John Dunphy. No 'traditional' poetry. Length: varies, depending on poem type. **Pays $1/poem, $6/review or article, and 1 contributor's copy.**

SPACE AND TIME

458 Elizabeth Ave., Somerset NJ 08873. **Website:** www.spaceandtimemagazine.com. **Contact:** Hildy Silverman, publisher. **100% freelance written.** *Space and Time* is the longest continually published small-press genre fiction magazine still in print. "We pride ourselves in having published the first stories of some of the great writers in science fiction, fantasy, and horror." Estab. 1966. Circ. 2,000. Byline given. Pays on publication. No kill fee. Publishes stories/poems 6-12 months after acceptance. Accepts queries by e-mail. Sample copy: $6. Guidelines online. Only opens periodically—announcements of open reading periods appear on Facebook page and website. No fiction or poetry considered outside of open reading periods.

"We love stories that blend elements—horror and science fiction, fantasy with science fiction elements, etc. We challenge writers to try something new and send us their hard to classify works-—what other publications reject because the work doesn't fit in their 'pigeonholes.'"

FICTION "We are looking for creative blends of science fiction, fantasy, and/or horror." Needs fantasy, horror, science fiction, short stories. "Do not send children's stories." Submit electronically as a Word doc or .rtf attachment only during open reading periods. Anything sent outside those period will be rejected out of hand. Length: 1,000-10,000 words. Average length: 6,500 words. Average length of short shorts: 1,000 words. **Pays 1¢/word.**

POETRY Contact: Linda Addison. Needs speculative nature—science fiction, fantasy, horror themes and imagery. "Multiple submissions are okay within reason (no more than 3 at a time). Submit embedded in an e-mail, a Word doc, or .rtf attachment. Only submit during open poetry reading periods, which are announced via the Facebook page and on the website. All other poetry submitted outside these reading periods will be rejected out of hand." Poetry without any sort of genre or speculative element. Buys average of 15 per year poems/year. Submit maximum 3 poems. No longer than a single standard page. **Pays $5/poem.**

$ STAR*LINE

Science Fiction and Fantasy Poetry Association, Languages and Literatures, University of Northern Iowa, Cedar Falls IA 50614-0502. **E-mail:** starlineeditor@gmail.com. **Website:** www.sfpoetry.com. **Contact:** Vince Gotera, editor. **All freelance.** *Star*Line*, published quarterly in print and .pdf format by the Science Fiction and Fantasy Poetry Association, is a speculative poetry magazine. "Open to all forms as long as your poetry uses speculative motifs: science fiction, fantasy, or horror." Estab. 1978. Circ. 300. Byline given. After publication. No kill fee. No more than 6 months. Accepts queries by e-mail. Accepts simultaneous submissions. Responds in 1 month. Guidelines online.

NONFICTION Needs reviews.

POETRY Submit 3-5 poems at a time. Accepts e-mail submissions (preferred; pasted into body of message, no attachments). Submit maximum 5 poems. **Pays 3¢/word rounded to the next dollar; minimum $3, maximum $25.**

$ STRANGE HORIZONS

Strange Horizons, Inc., P.O. Box 1693, Dubuque IA 52004-1693. **E-mail:** management@strangehorizons.com; fiction@strangehorizons.com. **Website:** strangehorizons.com. **Contact:** Jane Crowley and Kate Dollarhyde, editors-in-chief. "*Strange Horizons* is a magazine of and about speculative fiction and related nonfiction. Speculative fiction includes science fiction, fantasy, horror, slipstream, and other flavors of fantastica." Work published in *Strange Horizons* has been shortlisted for or won Hugo, Nebula, Rhysling, Theodore Sturgeon, James Tiptree Jr., and World Fantasy Awards. Estab. 2000. Accepts queries by online submission form. Responds in 90 days.

NONFICTION Contact: articles@strangehorizons.com. Needs essays. Special issues: "Nonfiction published in *Strange Horizons* should provide an original contribution to the field's discussion." Query (with the word "query" in subject line) or submit complete ms (with the word "sub" in subject line) by e-mail. Length: 3,000-5,000 words. **Pays $20-80.**

COLUMNS/DEPARTMENTS Contact: columns@strangehorizons.com. "We publish 1 column per week. Columns are standalone personal essays of 1,000-2,000 words on topics of interest to *Strange Horizons* readers. In the past we have published columns on SF in a wide range of media, from theatre to video games to comics to literature; debates within the SF community, and about the history of the community; and broader cultural, political, and technological issues of interest to the SF community." Submit complete ms (with the word SUB in subject line) by e-mail. **Pays $40.**

FICTION Contact: fiction@strangehorizons.com (questions only). "We love, or are interested in, fiction from or about diverse perspectives and traditionally under-represented groups, settings, and cultures, written from a nonexoticizing and well-researched position; unusual yet readable styles and inventive structures and narratives; stories that address political issues in complex and nuanced ways, resisting oversimplification; and hypertext fiction."speculative fiction, broadly defined. No excessive gore. Submit via online submissions manager; no e-mail or postal submission accepted. Length: up to 10,000 words (under 5,000 words preferred). **Pays 8¢/word, $50 minimum.**

POETRY Contact: poetry@strangehorizons.com. "We're looking for high-quality SF, fantasy, horror, and slipstream poetry. We're looking for modern, exciting poems that explore the possible and impossible: stories about human and nonhuman experiences, dreams and reality, past and future, the here-and-now and otherwhere-and-elsewhen. We want poems from imaginative and unconventional writers; we want voices from diverse perspectives and backgrounds." Submit up to 6 poems within 2 calendar months via e-mail; 1 poem per e-mail. Include "POETRY SUB: Your Poem Title" in subject line. **Pays $40 per poem.**

SEX

VANILLEROTICA LITERARY EZINE

Cleveland OH 44111. (216)203-4166. **E-mail:** talentdripseroticpublishing@yahoo.com. **Website:** eroticatalentdrips.wordpress.com. **Contact:** Kimberly Steele, founder. *Vanillerotica*, published bi-monthly online, focuses solely on showcasing new romantic erotic fiction. Estab. 2007. Time between acceptance and publication is 1 month. Accepts queries by e-mail. Accepts simultaneous submissions. Responds to general and submission queries within a week. Guidelines online.

NONFICTION Needs book excerpts, how-to, interview, reviews. Pays expenses of writers on assignment.

FICTION Needs erotica, romance, short stories. Submit short stories by e-mail to talentdripseroticpublishing@yahoo.com. Stories should be pasted into body of message. Reads submissions during publication months only. Length: 5,000-10,000 words. **Pays $15 for each accepted short story.**

POETRY Needs erotic. Submit poetry by e-mail to talentdripseroticpublishing@yahoo.com. Accepts e-mail pasted into body of message. Reads submissions during publication months only. Submit maximum 2-3 poems. Length: up to 30 lines/poem. **Pays $10 for each accepted poem.**

TIPS "Please read our take on the difference between *erotica* and *pornography* on the website. *Vanillerotica* does not accept pornography. And please keep poetry 30 lines or less."

SPORTS

ARCHERY & BOWHUNTING

PETERSEN'S BOWHUNTING

Outdoor Sportsman Group, 6385 Flank Dr., Ste. 800, Harrisburg PA 17112. (717)695-8085. **Fax:** (717)545-2527. **E-mail:** bowhunting@outdoorsg.com. **Website:** www.bowhuntingmag.com. **Contact:** Christian Berg, editor; Emily Kantner, associate editor; David Siegfried, art director. **70% freelance written.** Magazine published 9 times/year covering bowhunting. "Our readers are 'superenthusiasts,' therefore our writers must have an advanced knowledge of bowhunting." Estab. 1989. Circ. 126,000. Byline given. Pays on acceptance. No kill fee. Editorial lead time 6 months. Submit seasonal material 6 months in advance. Accepts queries by mail, e-mail. Accepts simultaneous submissions. Responds in 3 months to queries. Guidelines free.

NONFICTION Needs how-to, humor, interview, new product, opinion, personal experience, photo feature. **Buys 50 mss/year.** Query. Length: 1,500-2,000 words.

PHOTOS Send photos. Captions, model releases required. Digital submissions only. Buys one-time rights.

COLUMNS/DEPARTMENTS Query.

BASEBALL

BASEBALL AMERICA

Baseball America, Inc., P.O. Box 2089, Durham NC 27702. **Website:** www.baseballamerica.com. **10% freelance written.** Biweekly tabloid covering baseball. *Baseball America* is read by industry insiders and passionate, knowledgeable fans. Writing should go beyond routine baseball stories to include more depth or a unique angle. Estab. 1981. Circ. 80,000. Byline given. Pays on publication. No kill fee. Publishes ms an average of 2 months after acceptance. Editorial lead time 1 month. Submit seasonal material 2 months in advance. Accepts simultaneous submissions. Sample copy for $3.25.

NONFICTION Needs historical, interview, theme or issue-oriented baseball features. No major league player features that don't cover new ground or superficial treatments of baseball subjects. Send complete ms. Length: 100-2,000 words. Pays expenses of writers on assignment.

PHOTOS State availability. Identification of subjects required. Negotiates payment individually. Buys one time rights.

BICYCLING

$$ BIKE MAGAZINE

The Enthusiast Network, 2052 Corte Del Nogal, Suite 100, Carlsbad CA 92011. (949)325-6200. **Fax:** (949)325-6196. **E-mail:** nicole@bikemag.com. **Website:** www.bikemag.com. **Contact:** Nicole Formosa, managing editor. **35% freelance written.** Magazine publishes 8 times/year covering mountain biking. Estab. 1993. Circ. 170,000. Byline given. Pays on publication. Offers 25% kill fee. Publishes ms an average of 2 months after acceptance. Editorial lead time 4 months. Submit seasonal material 6 months in advance. Accepts queries by mail, e-mail. Accepts simultaneous submissions. Responds in 2 months to queries. Guidelines online.

"*Bike Magazine* showcases the sport of mountain biking like no other publication. It captures the sport's personalities, trends, and issues with a style all its own. Using insightful feature articles and the sport's best photography, *Bike* is sure to make you want to get outside and ride."

NONFICTION Needs humor, interview, personal experience, photo feature, travel. **Buys 20 mss/year.** Query. Length: 1,000-2,500 words. **Pays 50¢/word.** Pays expenses of writers on assignment. Sometimes pays expenses: $500 maximum.

PHOTOS Contact: Anthony Smith, photo editor (anthony@bikemag.com). Send photos. Captions, identification of subjects required. Reviews color transparencies, b&w prints. Negotiates payment individually. Buys one-time rights.

COLUMNS/DEPARTMENTS Splatter (news), 300 words; Urb (details a great ride within 1 hour of a major metropolitan area), 600-700 words. **Buys 20 mss/year.** Query. **Pays 50¢/word.**

TIPS "Remember that we focus on hardcore mountain biking, not beginners. We're looking for ideas that deliver the excitement and passion of the sport in ways that aren't common or predictable. Ideas should be vivid, unbiased, irreverent, probing, fun, humorous, funky, quirky, smart, good. Great feature ideas are always welcome, especially features on cultural matters or issues in the sport. However, you're much more likely to get published in *Bike* if you send us great ideas for short articles. In particular we need stories for our Splatter, a front-of-the-book section devoted to news, funny anecdotes, quotes, and odds and ends. We also need personality profiles of 600 words or so for our People Who Ride section. Racers are OK, but we're more interested in grassroots people with interesting personalities—it doesn't matter if they're Mother Theresas or scumbags, so long as they make mountain biking a little more interesting. Short descriptions of great rides are very welcome for our Urb column."

$ CYCLE CALIFORNIA! MAGAZINE

1702 Meridian Ave. Suite L, #289, San Jose CA 95125. (408)924-0270. **E-mail:** cycleca@cyclecalifornia.com. **E-mail:** tcorral@cyclecalifornia.com. **Website:** www.cyclecalifornia.com. **Contact:** Tracy L. Corral, publisher. **75% freelance written.** Magazine published 11 times/year covering Northern California bicycling events, races, people. Issues (topics) covered include bicycle commuting, bicycle politics, touring, racing, nostalgia, history—anything at all to do with riding a bike. Magazine published 11 times/year covering Northern California bicycling events, races, people. Issues (topics) covered include bicycle commuting, bicycle politics, touring, racing, nostalgia, history—anything at all to do with riding a bike. Use e-mail (tcorral@cyclecalifornia.com) or Twitter (@Tlynn48) to query editor. Estab. 1995. Circ. 30,000 print; 3,000 digital subscribers. Byline given. Pays on publication. No kill fee. Publishes ms an average of 3 months after acceptance. Editorial lead time 6 weeks. Submit seasonal material 3-6 months in advance. Accepts queries by e-mail. Accepts simultaneous submissions. Responds in 1 month to queries. Sample copy with 9x12 SASE and $1.75 first-class postage. Guidelines with #10 SASE.

NONFICTION Needs historical, how-to, humor, interview, memoir, opinion, personal experience, profile, technical, travel. Special issues: Bicycle Tour & Travel (January issue). No articles about any sport that doesn't relate to bicycling. No product reviews. **Buys 36 mss/year.** Query. Length: 500-1,000 words. **Pays 10-15¢/word.**

PHOTOS Send photos. Identification of subjects preferred. Identification of location or event required. Negotiates payment individually. Buys one-time rights.

COLUMNS/DEPARTMENTS Buys 2-3 mss/year. Query with links to published stories. **Pays 10-15¢/word.**

FICTION Needs adventure, humorous.

POETRY Needs Poetry as it relates to bike riding. Buys 1-2 poems/year.

TIPS "E-mail us with good ideas. While we don't exclude writers from other parts of the country, articles really should reflect a West Coast slant or be of general interest to bicyclists. We prefer stories written by people who like and use their bikes."

BOATING

$$$ BOATING

Bonnier Corporation, 460 N. Orlando Ave., Suite 200, Winter Park FL 32789. (407)628-4802. **Fax:** (407)628-7061. **E-mail:** editor@boatingmag.com. **Website:** www.boatingmag.com. **25% freelance written.** Magazine published 11 times/year covering performance boating. Estab. 1973. Circ. 175,000. Byline given. Pays on publication. Offers negotiable kill fee. Publishes ms an average of 3 months after acceptance. Editorial lead time 3 months. Submit seasonal material 4 months in advance. Accepts queries by e-mail. Accepts simultaneous submissions.

No unsolicited mss.

NONFICTION Needs how-to, interview, new product, photo feature. No general interest boating stories. **Buys numerous mss/year.** Query. Length: 300-2,000 words. **Pays $125-1,200.** Pays expenses of writers on assignment.

PHOTOS State availability. Captions required. Reviews negatives. Buys one-time rights.

$$ BOATING WORLD MAGAZINE

Duncan McIntosh Co., 18475 Bandilier, Fountain Valley CA 92708. (949)660-6150. **Fax:** (949)660-6172. **Website:** www.boatingworld.com. **60% freelance written.** Magazine published 8 times/year covering recreational trailer boats. "Typical reader owns a power boat between 14 and 32 feet long and has 3-9 years experience. Boat reports are mostly written by staff while features and most departments are provided by freelancers. We are looking for freelancers who can write well and who have at least a working knowledge of recreational power boating and the industry behind it." Estab. 1997. Circ. 100,000. Pays on publication. No kill fee. Publishes ms an average of 4 months after acceptance. Accepts simultaneous submissions. Responds in 3 months to queries. Sample copy free. Guidelines for #10 SASE.

NONFICTION Needs general interest, how-to, humor, new product, personal experience, travel. **Buys 20-25 mss/year.** Query. Length: 1,400-1,600 words. **Pays $150-450.** Pays expenses of writers on assignment.

PHOTOS State availability. Identification of subjects, model releases required. Reviews transparencies, prints, digital images. Offers $50-250/photo. Buys one-time rights.

FILLERS Needs anecdotes, facts, newsbreaks. Length: 250-500 words. **Pays $50-100.**

TIPS "We are looking for solid writers who are familiar with power boating and who can educate, entertain, and enlighten our readers with well-written and researched feature stories."

$$$ CANOE & KAYAK

GrindMedia, LLC, 2052 Corte del Nogal, Suite 100, Carlsbad CA 92011. (425)827-6363. **Website:** www.canoekayak.com. **75% freelance written.** Quarterly magazine covering paddlesports. "*Canoe & Kayak* is North America's No. 1 paddlesports resource. Our readers include flatwater and whitewater canoeists and kayakers of all skill levels. We provide comprehensive information on destinations, technique and equipment. Beyond that, we cover canoe and kayak camping, safety, the environment, and the history of boats and sport." Estab. 1972. Circ. 35,000. Byline given. Pays on or shortly after publication. No kill fee. Publishes ms an average of 6 months after acceptance. Editorial lead time 6 months. Submit seasonal material 8 months in advance. Accepts queries by online submission form. Accepts simultaneous submissions. Responds in 2 months to queries. Guidelines online.

NONFICTION Needs historical, how-to, personal experience, photo feature, technical, travel. Special issues: Kayak Fish. No cartoons, poems, stories in which bad judgement is portrayed or 'Me and Molly' articles. **Buys 25 mss/year.** Send complete ms. Length: 400-2,500 words. **Pays $100-800 for assigned articles; $100-500 for unsolicited articles.** Pays expenses of writers on assignment.

PHOTOS "Some activities we cover are canoeing, kayaking, canoe fishing, camping, canoe sailing or poling, backpacking (when compatible with the main activity) and occasionally inflatable boats. We are not interested in groups of people in rafts, photos showing disregard for the environment or personal safety, gasoline-powered engines unless appropriate to the discussion, or unskilled persons taking extraordinary risks." State availability. Captions, identification of subjects. Reviews 35mm transparencies, 4x6 prints, digital files preferred. Offers $75-500/photo. Buys one-time print and web rights.

COLUMNS/DEPARTMENTS Put In (environment, conservation, events), 500 words; Destinations (canoe and kayak destinations in US, Canada), 1,500 words; Essays, 750 words. **Buys 40 mss/year.** Send complete ms. **Pays $100-350.**

FILLERS Needs anecdotes, facts, newsbreaks. **Buys 20 mss/year.** Length: 200-500 words. **Pays $25-50.**

TIPS "Start with Put-In articles (short featurettes) or short, unique equipment reviews. Or give us the best, most exciting article we've ever seen—with great photos. Read the magazine before submitting."

$$$ CHESAPEAKE BAY MAGAZINE

601 Sixth St., Annapolis MD 21403. (410)263-2662. **Fax:** (410)267-6924. **E-mail:** joe@chesapeakebaymagazine.com. **E-mail:** editor@chesapeakebaymagazine.com. **Website:** www.chesapeakebaymagazine.com. **Contact:** Kate Livie, managing editor; Joe Evans, editor. **70% freelance written.** Monthly magazine covering boating and the Chesapeake Bay. "Our readers are boaters—sailors, paddlers, power boaters, anglers, conservationists, and foodies. Read the magazine before submitting." Estab. 1972. Circ. 25,000. Byline given. Pays on publication. No kill fee. Publishes ms an average of 6 months after acceptance. Editorial lead time 1 year. Submit seasonal material 1 year in advance. Accepts queries by mail, e-mail, fax, phone. Accepts simultaneous submissions. Responds in 2 months to queries; 3 months to mss. Sample copy for $5.19 prepaid and SASE.

NONFICTION Needs book excerpts, essays, historical, how-to, humor, interview, new product, nostalgic, photo feature, profile, technical, travel. **Buys 30 mss/year.** Query with published clips. Length: 300-3,000 words. **Pays $100-1,000.** Pays expenses of writers on assignment.

PHOTOS Captions, identification of subjects required. Offers $75-250/photo, $400/day rate for assignment photography. Pays $275 for color cover; $75-250 for color *stock* inside, depending on size; $200-1,200 for *assigned* photo package. Pays on publication. Credit line given. Buys one-time rights. Buys one-time rights.

TIPS "Send us unedited writing samples (not clips) that show the writer can write, not just string words together. We look for well-organized, lucid, lively, intelligent writing."

$$$$ CRUISING WORLD

The Sailing Co., 55 Hammarlund Way, Middletown RI 02842. (401)845-5100. **Fax:** (401)845-5180. **E-mail:** mark.pillsbury@cruisingworld.com. **E-mail:** editor@cruisingworld.com. **Website:** www.cruisingworld.com. **60% freelance written.** Monthly magazine covering sailing, cruising/adventuring, do-it-yourself boat improvements. "*Cruising World* is a publication by and for sailboat owners who spend time in home waters as well as voyaging the world. Its readership is extremely loyal, savvy, and driven by independent thinking." Estab. 1974. Circ. 91,244. Byline given. **Pays on acceptance for articles;** on publication for photography. No kill fee. Publishes ms an average of 18 months after acceptance. Editorial lead time 3 months. Submit seasonal material 1 year in advance. Accepts queries by mail. Accepts simultaneous submissions. Responds in 2 months to queries. Responds in 4 months to mss. Sample copy free. Guidelines available online.

NONFICTION Needs book excerpts, essays, expose, general interest, historical, how-to, humor, interview, new product, opinion, personal experience, photo feature, technical, travel. No travel articles that have nothing to do with cruising aboard sailboats from 20-50 feet in length. **Buys dozens mss/year.** Send complete ms. **Pays $50-1,500 for assigned articles. Pays $50-1,000 for unsolicited articles.** Pays expenses of writers on assignment.

PHOTOS Send high-res (minimum 300 DPI) images on CD. Send photos. Captions required. Payment upon publication. Also buys stand-alone photos. Buys first and one-time rights.

COLUMNS/DEPARTMENTS Underway Shoreline (sailing news, people, and short features; contact Elaine Lembo), 300 words maximum; Hands-on Sailor (refit, voyaging, seamanship, how-to), 1,000-1,500 words. **Buys dozens mss/year.** Query with or without published clips or send complete ms.

TIPS "*Cruising World's* readers know exactly what they want to read, so our best advice to freelancers is to carefully read the magazine and envision which exact section or department would be the appropriate place for proposed submissions."

$ GOOD OLD BOAT

The Sailing Magazine for the Rest of Us, Good Old Boat, Inc., 7340 Niagara Lane N., Maple Grove MN

55311-2655. (701)952-9433. **Fax:** (701)952-9434. **E-mail:** michael_r@goodoldboat.com. **Website:** www.goodoldboat.com. **Contact:** Michael Robertson, editor. **95% freelance written.** Bimonthly magazine covering DIY fiberglass sailboat maintenance, repair, and upgrade, as well as lessons-learned stories and love-of-sailing stories. Good photos are key. "We pay $100 for cover photos. Action photos are prized. In addition to sailing and anchored-boat shots, interested in good boat yard photos showing people working on their boats." *Good Old Boat* magazine focuses on maintaining, upgrading, and loving fiberglass cruising sailboats from the 1960s and well into the 2000s. Readers see themselves as part of a community of sailors who share similar maintenance and replacement concerns not generally addressed in the other sailing publications. Readers do much of the writing about projects they have done on their boats and the joy they receive from sailing them. Please send text files in .doc format. Please do not embed photos in text documents. In-depth submission guidelines, including payment info, on our website. Estab. 1998. Circ. 25,000. Byline given. Pays 2 months in advance of publication, occasionally upon submission. Rarely pays kill fee. Publishes ms an average of 12-18 months after acceptance, though occasionally sooner. Editorial lead time 4-6 months. Submit seasonal material 12-15 months in advance. Accepts queries by e-mail. Accepts simultaneous submissions. Responds in 1 week to queries; in 1 month to mss. Downloadable sample copy free. Guidelines online.

NONFICTION Needs general interest, historical, how-to, interview, personal experience, photo feature, profile, technical. Articles written by non-sailors. **Buys 150 mss/year.** Query or send complete ms. Length: up to 3,000 words. **Payment varies, info on our website.**

PHOTOS Contact: Michael Robertson. See our website for comprehensive guidelines. State availability of, or send photos. At least 300 dpi. "We do not pay additional fees for photos except when they run as covers, or are specifically requested to support an article." Retained by submitter.

TIPS "Our shorter pieces are the best way to break into our magazine. We publish many Simple Solutions and Quick & Easy pieces. These are how-to tips that have worked for sailors on their boats. In addition, our readers send lists of projects which they've done on their boats and which they could write for publication. We respond to these queries with a thumbs up or down by project. Articles are submitted on speculation, but they have a better chance of being accepted once we have approved of the suggested topic."

$$ HOUSEBOAT MAGAZINE

Harris Publishing, Inc., 360 B St., Idaho Falls ID 83402. 833-268-1039. **Fax:** (208)522-5241. **E-mail:** blk@houseboatmagazine.com. **Website:** www.houseboatmagazine.com. Heather Serrano, assistant editor (heather@houseboatmagazine.com). **Contact:** Brady L. Kay, executive editor. **15% freelance written.** Bimonthly magazine for houseboaters who enjoy reading everything that reflects the unique houseboating lifestyle. If it is not a houseboat-specific article, please do not query. Estab. 1990. Circ. 25,000. Byline given. Pays on acceptance. Offers 25% kill fee. Publishes ms an average of 3 months after acceptance. Editorial lead time 2 months. Submit seasonal material 6 months in advance. Accepts queries by mail, e-mail. Accepts simultaneous submissions. Responds in 1 week to queries. Sample copy for $5. Guidelines by e-mail.

No unsolicited mss. Accepts queries by mail and fax, but e-mail strongly preferred.

NONFICTION Needs how-to, interview, new product, personal experience, travel. **Buys 36 mss/year.** Query before submitting. Length: 1,500-2,200 words. **Pays $200-500.**

PHOTOS Often required as part of submission package. Color prints discouraged. Digital prints are unacceptable. Seldom purchases photos without ms, but occasionally buys cover photos. Captions, model releases required. Reviews transparencies, high-resolution electronic images. Offers no additional payment for photos accepted with ms. Buys one-time rights.

COLUMNS/DEPARTMENTS Pays $150-300.

TIPS "As a general rule, how-to articles are always in demand. So are stories on unique houseboats or houseboaters. You are less likely to break in with a travel piece that does not revolve around specific people or groups. Personality profile pieces with excellent supporting photography are your best bet."

$$ LAKELAND BOATING

O'Meara-Brown Publications, Inc., 630 Davis St., Suite 301, Evanston IL 60201. **E-mail:** info@lakelandboating.com. **Website:** www.lakelandboating.com. **50% freelance written.** Magazine covering Great

Lakes boating. Estab. 1946. Circ. 60,000. Byline given. Pays on publication. No kill fee. Accepts queries by e-mail. Accepts simultaneous submissions. Responds in 4 months to queries. Sample copy for $5.50 and 9x12 SAE with 6 first-class stamps. Guidelines free.

NONFICTION Needs book excerpts, historical, how-to, interview, personal experience, photo feature, technical, travel, must relate to boating in Great Lakes. No inspirational, religious, expose, or poetry. **Buys 20-30 mss/year.** Length: 300-1,500 words. **Pays $100-600.**

PHOTOS State availability. Captions required. Reviews prefers 35mm transparencies, high-res digital shots. Buys one time rights.

COLUMNS/DEPARTMENTS Bosun's Locker (technical or how-to pieces on boating), 100-1,000 words. **Buys 40 mss/year.** Query. **Pays $25-200.**

$$ PONTOON & DECK BOAT

PDB Magazine, Harris Publishing, Inc., 360 B. St., Idaho Falls ID 83402. (833)268-1039. **Fax:** (208)522-5241. **E-mail:** blk@pdbmagazine.com. **Website:** www.pdbmagazine.com. **Contact:** Brady L. Kay, executive editor. **15% freelance written.** Magazine published 11 times/year covering boating. A boating niche publication geared toward the pontoon and deck boating lifestyle and consumer market. Audience is comprised of people who utilize these boats for varied family activities and fishing. Magazine is promotional of the PDB industry and its major players. Seeks to give the reader a twofold reason to read publication: to celebrate the lifestyle, and to do it aboard a first-class craft. Estab. 1995. Circ. 84,000. Byline given. Pays on publication. No kill fee. Editorial lead time 2 months. Submit seasonal material 3 months in advance. Accepts queries by mail, e-mail. Accepts simultaneous submissions. Responds in 3 weeks to queries; 3 months to mss. Sample copy and writer's guidelines available.

NONFICTION Needs how-to, personal experience. "No general boating (must be pontoon or deck boat specific), no humor, fiction, or poetry." **Buys 15 mss/year.** Send complete ms. Length: 600-2,000 words. **Pays $50-300.**

PHOTOS State availability. Captions, model releases required. Reviews transparencies. Rights negotiable.

COLUMNS/DEPARTMENTS No Wake Zone (short, fun quips); Better Boater (how-to). **Buys 6-12 mss/year.** Query with published clips. **Pays $50-150.**

TIPS "Be specific to pontoon and deck boats. Any general boating material goes to the slush pile. The more you can tie together the lifestyle, attitudes, and the PDB industry, the more interest we'll take in what you send us."

$$ SOUTHERN BOATING

Southern Boating & Yachting, Inc., 330 N. Andrews Ave., Suite 200, Ft. Lauderdale FL 33301. (954)522-5515. **Fax:** (954)522-2260. **E-mail:** liz@southernboating.com. **Website:** www.southernboating.com. **Contact:** Liz Pasch, editorial director; Dan Brooks, art director. **75% freelance written.** Monthly boating magazine. Upscale monthly yachting magazine focusing on the Southeast US, Bahamas, Caribbean, and Gulf of Mexico. Estab. 1972. Circ. 40,000. Byline given Pays 30 days after publication. Publishes ms an average of 3 months after acceptance. Editorial lead time 3 months. Submit seasonal material 6 months in advance. Accepts queries by e-mail. Accepts simultaneous submissions.

NONFICTION Needs how-to, new product, profile, reviews, technical, travel. Query. Length: 900-1,200 words. **Pays $400-600 with art.**

PHOTOS State availability of hi-res digital photos. Captions, identification of subjects, model releases required. Reviews digital files. Buys one-time rights.

COLUMNS/DEPARTMENTS DIY (how-to/maintenance), 900 words; What's New in Electronics (electronics), 900 words; Engine Room (new developments), 900 words. **Buys 24 mss/year.** Query first; see media kit for special issue focus.

$$$ YACHTING

Bonnier Corporation, 55 Hammarlund Way, Middletown RI 02842. **Website:** www.yachtingmagazine.com. **30% freelance written.** Monthly magazine covering yachts, boats. Monthly magazine written and edited for experienced, knowledgeable yachtsmen. Estab. 1907. Circ. 132,000. Byline given. Pays on acceptance. No kill fee. Editorial lead time 2 months. Submit seasonal material 6 months in advance. Accepts queries by mail, e-mail, fax. Accepts simultaneous submissions. Responds in 1 month to queries. Responds in 3 months to mss. Sample copy free.

NONFICTION Needs personal experience, technical. **Buys 50 mss/year.** Query with published clips. Length: 750-800 words. **Pays $150-1,500.** Pays expenses of writers on assignment.

PHOTOS Send photos. Captions, identification of subjects, model releases required. Reviews transparencies. Negotiates payment individually.

GENERAL INTEREST

$$ FCA MAGAZINE

Fellowship of Christian Athletes, 8701 Leeds Rd., Kansas City MO 64129. (816)921-0909; (800)289-0909. **Fax:** (816)921-8755. **E-mail:** mag@fca.org. **Website:** www.fca.org/mag. **Contact:** Clay Meyer, editor; Matheau Casner, creative director. **50% freelance written. Prefers to work with published/established writers, but works with a growing number of new/unpublished writers each year.** Published 6 times/year. *FCA Magazine*'s mission is to serve as a ministry tool of the Fellowship of Christian Athletes by informing, inspiring and involving coaches, athletes and all whom they influence, that they may make an impact for Jesus Christ. Estab. 1959. Circ. 75,000. Byline given. Pays on publication. No kill fee. Publishes ms an average of 4 months after acceptance. Submit seasonal material 6 months in advance. Accepts simultaneous submissions. Responds to queries/mss in 3 months. Sample copy for $2 and 9x12 SASE with 3 first-class stamps. Guidelines available at www.fca.org/mag/media-kit.

NONFICTION Needs inspirational, personal experience, photo feature. **Buys 5-20 mss/year.** Articles should be accompanied by at least 3 quality photos. Query and submit via e-mail. Length: 1,000-2,000 words. **Pays $150-400 for assigned and unsolicited articles.** Pays expenses of writers on assignment.

PHOTOS State availability. Reviews contact sheets. Payment based on size of photo. Buys one-time rights.

TIPS "Profiles and interviews of particular interest to coed athlete, primarily high school and college age. Our graphics and editorial content appeal to youth. The area most open to freelancers is profiles on or interviews with well-known athletes or coaches (male, female, minorities) who have been or are involved in some capacity with FCA."

GOLF

$ AFRICAN AMERICAN GOLFER'S DIGEST

80 Wall St., Suite 720, New York NY 10005. (212)571-6559. **E-mail:** debertcook@aol.com. **Website:** www.africanamericangolfersdigest.com. **Contact:** Debert Cook, publisher. **100% freelance written.** Quarterly. Covering golf lifestyle, health, travel destinations and reviews, golf equipment, golfer profiles. "Editorial should focus on interests of our market demographic of African Americans with historical, artistic, musical, educational (higher learning), automotive, sports, fashion, entertainment, and other categories of high interest to them." Estab. 2003. Circ. 20,000. Byline given. No kill fee. Publishes ms an average of 3 months after acceptance. Editorial lead time 3-6 months. Submit seasonal material 3-6 months in advance. Accepts queries by e-mail. Accepts simultaneous submissions. Responds in 3 weeks to queries; 3 months to mss. Sample copy for $8. Guidelines by e-mail.

NONFICTION Needs how-to, interview, new product, opinion, personal experience, photo feature, reviews, technical, travel, golf-related. **Buys 3 mss/year.** Query. Length: 250-1,500 words. **Pays 0.03-0.5¢/word.** Pays expenses of writers on assignment.

PHOTOS State availability. Captions, identification of subjects, model releases required. Reviews GIF/JPEG files (300 dpi or higher at 4x6). Negotiates payment individually. Credit line given. Buys all rights.

COLUMNS/DEPARTMENTS Profiles (celebrities, national leaders, entertainers, corporate leaders, etc., who golf); Travel (destination/golf course reviews); Golf Fashion (jewelry, clothing, accessories). **Buys 3 mss/year.** Query. **Pays 10-50¢/word.**

FILLERS Needs anecdotes, facts, gags, newsbreaks, short humor. **Buys 3 mss/year. mss/year.** Length: 20-125 words. **Pays 10-50¢/word.**

TIPS "Emphasize golf and African American appeal."

$$ THE GOLFER

59 E. 72nd St., New York NY 10021. (212)867-7070. **Website:** www.thegolferinc.com. **40% freelance written.** Bimonthly magazine covering golf. A sophisticated tone for a lifestyle-oriented magazine. "The Golfer Inc. is an international luxury brand, a new media company that is a driving force in the game. Its website is the source for those who want the best the game has to offer—the classic courses, great destinations, finest accoutrements, most intriguing personalities, and latest trends on and off the course.The magazine has distinguished itself as the highest quality, most innovative in its field. It is written for the top of the market—those who live a lifestyle shaped by their passion for the game. With its stunning photogra-

phy, elegant design and evocative writing, *The Golfer* speaks to its affluent readers with a sense of style and sophistication—it is a world-class publication with an international flair, celebrating the lifestyle of the game." Estab. 1994. Circ. 253,000. Byline given. Pays on publication. Offers negotiable kill fee. Publishes ms an average of 2 months after acceptance. Editorial lead time 2 months. Submit seasonal material 4 months in advance. Accepts queries by mail. Accepts simultaneous submissions. Sample copy free.

NONFICTION Needs book excerpts, essays, general interest, historical, how-to, humor, inspirational, interview, new product, opinion, personal experience, photo feature, technical, travel. Send complete ms. Length: 300-2,000 words. **Pays $150-600.** Pays expenses of writers on assignment.

PHOTOS Send photos. Reviews any size digital files. Buys one-time rights.

$$$ GOLF TIPS

Madavor Media, 25 Braintree Hill Office Park, Suite 404, Braintree MA 02184. (617)706-9110. **Fax:** (617)536-0102. **E-mail:** editors@golftipsmag.com; vwilliams@madavor.com. **Website:** www.golftipsmag.com. **Contact:** Vic Williams, editor. **95% freelance written.** Magazine published 9 times/year covering golf instruction and equipment. "We provide mostly concise, very clear golf instruction pieces for the serious golfer." Estab. 1986. Circ. 300,000. Byline given. Pays on publication. Offers 33% kill fee. Publishes ms an average of 2 months after acceptance. Editorial lead time 3 months. Submit seasonal material 4 months in advance. Accepts queries by e-mail. Accepts simultaneous submissions. Responds in 1 month to queries. Sample copy free. Guidelines on website.

NONFICTION Needs book excerpts, how-to, interview, new product, photo feature, technical. "Generally, golf essays rarely make it." **Buys 125 mss/year.** Query. Length: 250-2,000 words. **Pays $300-1,000 for assigned articles. Pays $300-800 for unsolicited articles.** Pays expenses of writers on assignment.

PHOTOS State availability. Captions, identification of subjects required. Reviews 2¼×2¼, 4×5, or 35mm transparencies. Negotiates payment individually. Buys all rights.

COLUMNS/DEPARTMENTS Stroke Saver (very clear, concise instruction), 350 words; Lesson Library (book excerpts—usually in a series), 1,000 words; Travel Tips (formatted golf travel), 2,500 words. **Buys 40 mss/year.** Query. **Pays $300-850.**

TIPS "Contact a respected PGA professional and find out if they're interested in being published. A good writer can turn an interview into a decent instruction piece."

GUNS

$$ MUZZLE BLASTS

P.O. Box 67, Friendship IN 47021. (812)667-5131. **Fax:** (812)667-5136. **E-mail:** llarkin@nmlra.org. **Website:** www.nmlra.org. **Contact:** Lee A. Larkin, editor. **65% freelance written.** Monthly magazine. "Articles must relate to muzzleloading or the muzzleloading era of American history." Estab. 1939. Circ. 17,500. Byline given. Pays on publication. Offers $50 kill fee. Publishes ms an average of 6 months after acceptance. Editorial lead time 4 months. Submit seasonal material 6 months in advance. Accepts queries by mail, e-mail. Responds in 1 month to mss. Sample copy and writer's guidelines free.

NONFICTION Needs general interest, historical, how-to, humor, interview, new product, personal experience, photo feature, technical, travel. No subjects that do not pertain to muzzleloading. **Buys 80 mss/year.** Query. Length: 2,000-2,500 words. **Pays $150 minimum for assigned articles. Pays $50 minimum for unsolicited articles.**

PHOTOS Send photos. Captions, model releases required. Reviews prints and digital images. Negotiates payment individually. Buys one-time rights.

COLUMNS/DEPARTMENTS Buys 96 mss/year. Query. **Pays $50-200.**

FICTION Must pertain to muzzleloading. Needs adventure, historical, humorous. **Buys 6 mss/year.** Query. Length: 2,500 words. **Pays $50-300.**

FILLERS Needs facts. **Pays $50.**

HIKING & BACKPACKING

$$$$ BACKPACKER MAGAZINE

Cruz Bay Publishing, Inc., Active Interest Media Co., 5720 Flatiron Pkwy., Boulder CO 80301. **E-mail:** dlewon@backpacker.com; mhorjus@aimmedia.com; caseylyons@aimmedia.com; mleister@aimmedia.com. **Website:** www.backpacker.com. **Contact:** Dennis Lewon, editor-in-chief; Casey Lyons, deputy editor; Maren Horjus, destinations editor; Adam Roy, senior digital editor; Eli Bernstein, associate gear editor; Corey Buhay, assistant skills editor; Mike Leister, art director; Giovanni C. Leone, assistant art director; Louisa Albanese, photo assistant; Genny Fullerton, photography director. **50% freelance written.** Magazine published 9 times/year covering wilderness travel for backpackers. "*Backpacker* is the source for backpacking gear reviews, outdoor skills information and advice, and destinations for backpacking, camping, and hiking." E-mail the appropriate editor when querying; list can be found on website. Estab. 1973. Circ. 340,000. Byline given. Pays on acceptance. Offers 25% kill fee. Editorial lead time 6 months. Accepts queries by e-mail. Accepts simultaneous submissions. Responds in 2-4 weeks to queries. Guidelines online.

NONFICTION Needs essays, general interest, how-to, inspirational, interview, new product, opinion, personal experience, reviews, technical, "Features usually fall into a distinct category: destinations, personality, skills, or gear. Gear features are generally staff written. In order to make the grade, a potential feature needs an unusual hook, a compelling story, a passionate sense of place, or unique individuals finding unique ways to improve or enjoy the wilderness." Special issues: See website for upcoming issue themes. "Journal-style articles are generally unacceptable." Query with published clips before sending complete ms. Length: 1,500-5,000 words. **Pays 10¢-$1/word.** Pays expenses of writers on assignment.

PHOTOS **Contact:** Genny Fullerton, photo director: gfullerton@backpacker.com. Buys 80 photos from freelancers/issue; 720 photos/year. Needs transparencies or hi-res digital of people backpacking, camping, landscapes/scenics. Reviews photos with or without a ms. Model/property release required (if necessary). Accepts images in digital format. Send via ZIP; e-mail as JPEG files at 72 dpi for review (300 dpi needed to print). State availability. Payment varies. Buys one-time rights.

COLUMNS/DEPARTMENTS Life List (personal essay telling a story about a premier wilderness destination or experience), 300-400 words; Done in a Day (a hike that can be finished in a day), 500 words; Weekend (a trip of 1-2 nights, 6-10 miles/day, within striking distance of a major city, and seasonally appropriate for the month in which they run); Skills (the advice source for all essential hiking and adventure skills, with information targeted to help both beginners and experts); Gear (short reviews of gear that has been field-tested; unlike other departments, Gear is done by assignment only). **Buys 50-75 mss/year.** Query with published clips. **Pays 10¢-$1/word.**

HOCKEY

$$$ USA HOCKEY MAGAZINE

Touchpoint Sports, 1775 Bob Johnson Dr., Colorado Springs CO 80906. (719)576-8724. **Fax:** (763)538-1160. **E-mail:** usah@usahockey.org. **Website:** www.usahockeymagazine.com. **Contact:** Harry Thompson, editor-in-chief. **60% freelance written.** Magazine published 10 times/year covering amateur hockey in the U.S. The world's largest hockey magazine, *USA Hockey Magazine* is the official magazine of USA Hockey, Inc., the national governing body of hockey. Estab. 1980. Circ. 444,000. Byline given. Pays on acceptance or publication. No kill fee. Editorial lead time 6 months. Submit seasonal material 4 months in advance. Accepts simultaneous submissions. Sample copy and writer's guidelines free.

NONFICTION Needs essays, general interest, historical, how-to, humor, inspirational, interview, new product, opinion, personal experience, photo feature, hockey camps, pro hockey, juniors, college, NCAA hockey championships, Olympics, youth, etc. **Buys 20-30 mss/year.** Query. Length: 500-5,000 words. **Pays $50-750.** Pays expenses of writers on assignment.

PHOTOS State availability. Captions, identification of subjects required. Reviews contact sheets. Negotiates payment individually. Rights purchased varies.

COLUMNS/DEPARTMENTS Short Cuts (news and notes); Coaches' Corner (teaching tips); USA Hockey; Inline Notebook (news and notes). **Pays $150-250.**

FICTION Needs adventure, humorous, slice-of-life vignettes. **Buys 10-20 mss/year. Pays $150-1,000.**

FILLERS Needs anecdotes, facts, gags, newsbreaks, short humor. **Buys 20-30 mss/year.** Length: 10-100 words. **Pays $25-250.**

TIPS "Writers must have a general knowledge and enthusiasm for hockey, including ice, inline, street, and other. The primary audience is youth players in the U.S."

HORSE RACING

$$ AMERICAN TURF MONTHLY

747 Middle Neck Rd., Great Neck NY 11024. (516)773-4075. **Fax:** (516)773-2944. **E-mail:** jcorbett@americanturf.com; editor@americanturf.com. **Website:**

www.americanturf.com. **Contact:** Joe Girardi, editor. **90% freelance written.** Monthly magazine squarely focused on Thoroughbred racing, handicapping and wagering. *ATM* is a magazine for horseplayers, not owners, breeders, or 12-year-old girls enthralled with ponies. Estab. 1946. Circ. 30,000. Byline given. Pays on publication. No kill fee. Publishes ms an average of 4 months after acceptance. Editorial lead time 2 months. Submit seasonal material 2 months in advance. Accepts queries by mail, e-mail. Accepts simultaneous submissions. Responds in 1 month to queries. Sample copy and writer's guidelines free.

"*American Turf Monthly*, the only handicapping magazine sold on news stands within the U.S. and Canada, has been entertaining horse racing enthusiasts since 1946. Each issue draws the reader into the exhilarating world of horse racing with features written by premier handicapping authors in the sport. The photography and creative design capture the spellbinding highlights of the race tracks to satiate the thrill seeking desire of the wagering player."

NONFICTIONNo historical essays, bilious 'guest editorials,' saccharine poetry, fiction. Special issues: Triple Crown/Kentucky Derby (May); Saratoga/Del Mar (August); Breeder's Cup (November). **Buys Length: 800-2,000 words. Pays $75-300 for assigned articles. Pays $100-500 for unsolicited articles. mss/year.** Query. Length: 800-2,000 words. **Pays $75-300 for assigned articles. Pays $100-500 for unsolicited articles.** Pays expenses of writers on assignment. No.

PHOTOS Send photos. Identification of subjects required. Reviews 3 x 5 transparencies, prints, 300 dpi TIFF images on CD. Offers $25 for b&w or color interior; $150 min. for color cover. Pays on publication. Credit line given. Buys one-time rights.

FILLERS newsbreaks, short humor Needs newsbreaks, short humor. **Buys 5 mss/year.** Length: 400 words. **Pays $25.**

TIPS "Like horses and horse racing."

$$ HOOF BEATS

U.S. Trotting Association, 6130 S. Sunbury Rd., Westerville OH 43081-9309. **E-mail:** hoofbeats@ustrotting.com. **Website:** www.hoofbeatsmagazine.com. **Contact:** Kim French. **60% freelance written.** Monthly magazine covering harness racing and standardbred horses. "Articles and photos must relate to harness racing or Standardbreds. We do not accept any topics that do not touch on these subjects." Estab. 1933. Circ. 7,000. Byline given. Pays on publication. Offers 25% kill fee. Publishes ms an average of 2-4 months after acceptance. Editorial lead time 6 months. Submit seasonal material 6 months in advance. Accepts queries by mail, e-mail, fax. Accepts simultaneous submissions. Responds in 2 weeks to queries; 1 month to mss. Sample copy online. Guidelines free.

NONFICTION Needs general interest, how-to, interview, personal experience, photo feature, technical. "We do not want any fiction or poetry." **Buys 48-72 mss/year.** Query. Length: 750-2,000 words. **Pays $100-500.** Pays expenses of writers on assignment.

PHOTOS State availability. Identification of subjects required. Reviews contact sheets. We offer $25-100 per photo. Buys one-time rights.

COLUMNS/DEPARTMENTS Equine Clinic (Standardbreds who overcame major health issues), 900-1,200 words; Profiles (short profiles on people or horses in harness racing), 600-1,000 words; Industry Trends (issues impacting Standardbreds & harness racing), 1,000-2,000 words. **Buys 60 mss/year mss/year.** Query for column submissions. **Pays $100-500.**

TIPS "We welcome new writers who know about harness racing or are willing to learn about it. Make sure to read *Hoof Beats* before querying to see our slant & style. We look for informative/promotional stories on harness racing—not exposés on the sport."

HUNTING & FISHING

$$$ THE ATLANTIC SALMON JOURNAL

The Atlantic Salmon Federation, P.O. Box 5200, St. Andrews New Brunswick E5B 3S8 Canada. (514)457-8737. **Fax:** (506)529-1070. **E-mail:** savesalmon@asf.ca; martinsilverstone@videotron.ca. **Website:** www.asf.ca. **Contact:** Martin Silverstone, editor. **50-68% freelance written.** Quarterly magazine covering conservation efforts for the Atlantic salmon, catering to the dedicated angler and conservationist. Circ. 11,000. Byline given. Pays on publication. No kill fee. Publishes ms an average of 6 months after acceptance. Submit seasonal material 3 months in advance. Accepts simultaneous submissions. Responds in 2 months to queries. Sample copy for 9x12 SAE with $1 (Canadian), or IRC. Guidelines free.

NONFICTION Needs historical, how-to, humor, interview, new product, opinion, personal experience, photo feature, technical. **Buys 15-20 mss/year.** Query with published clips. Length: 2,000 words. **Pays $400-800 for articles with photos.** Pays expenses of writers on assignment.

PHOTOS State availability. Captions, identification of subjects required. Pays $50 minimum; $350-500 for covers; $300 for 2-page spread; $175 for full page photo; $100 for 1/2-page photo.

COLUMNS/DEPARTMENTS Fit To Be Tied (conservation issues and salmon research; the design, construction, and success of specific flies); interesting characters in the sport and opinion pieces by knowledgeable writers, 900 words; Casting Around (short, informative, entertaining reports, book reviews, and quotes from the world of Atlantic salmon angling and conservation). Query. **Pays $50-300.**

TIPS "Articles must reflect informed and up-to-date knowledge of Atlantic salmon. Writers need not be authorities, but research must be impeccable. Clear, concise writing is essential, and submissions must be typed."

$$ BASSMASTER MAGAZINE

B.A.S.S. Publications, 1170 Celebration Blvd., Suite 200, Celebration FL 32830. (407)566-2277. **Fax:** (407)566-2072. **Website:** www.bassmaster.com. **80% freelance written.** Magazine published 11 times/year about largemouth, smallmouth, and spotted bass, offering how-to articles for dedicated beginning and advanced bass fishermen, including destinations and new product reviews. Estab. 1968. Circ. 600,000. Byline given. Pays on acceptance. No kill fee. Publishes ms an average of less than 1 year after acceptance. Editorial lead time 2 months. Submit seasonal material 6 months in advance. Accepts queries by mail, e-mail. Accepts simultaneous submissions. Responds in 2 months to queries. Sample copy upon request. Guidelines for #10 SASE.

Needs destination stories (how to fish a certain area) for the Northwest and Northeast.

NONFICTION Needs historical, how-to, interview, new product, travel, conservation related to bass fishing. No first-person, personal experience-type articles. **Buys 100 mss/year.** Query. Length: 500-1,500 words. **Pays $100-300.**

PHOTOS Send photos. Captions, model releases required. Reviews transparencies. Offers no additional payment for photos accepted with ms, but pays $800 for color cover transparencies. Buys all rights.

COLUMNS/DEPARTMENTS Short Cast/News/Views/Notes/Briefs (upfront regular feature covering news-related events such as new state bass records, unusual bass fishing happenings, conservation, new products, and editorial viewpoints). Length: 250-400 words. **Pays $100-300.**

TIPS "Editorial direction continues in the short, more direct how-to article. Compact, easy-to-read information is our objective. Shorter articles with good graphics, such as how-to diagrams, step-by-step instruction, etc., will enhance a writer's articles submitted to *Bassmaster Magazine*. The most frequent mistakes made by writers in completing an article for us are poor grammar, poor writing, poor organization, and superficial research. Send in detailed queries outlining specific objectives of article, obtain writer's guidelines. Be as concise as possible."

$$ BC OUTDOORS HUNTING AND SHOOTING

Outdoor Group Media, 7261 River Place, 201a, Mission BC V4S 0A2 Canada. (604)820-3400; (800)898-8811. **Fax:** (604)820-3477. **E-mail:** mmitchell@outdoorgroupmedia.com. **Website:** www.bcoutdoorsmagazine.com. **Contact:** Mike Mitchell, editor. **80% freelance written.** Biannual magazine covering hunting, shooting, camping, and backroads in British Columbia, Canada. *BC Outdoors Magazine* publishes 7 sport fishing issues a year with 2 hunting and shooting supplement issues each summer and fall. "Our magazine is about the best outdoor experiences in BC. Whether you're camping on an ocean shore, hiking into your favorite lake, or learning how to fly-fish on your favourite river, we want to showcase what our province has to offer to sport fishing and outdoor enthusiasts. *BC Outdoors Hunting and Shooting* provides trusted editorial for trapping, deer hunting, big buck, bowhunting, bag limits, baitling, decoys, calling, camouflage, tracking, trophy hunting, pheasant hunting, goose hunting, hunting regulations, duck hunting, whitetail hunting, hunting regulations, hunting trips, and mule deer hunting." Estab. 1945. Circ. 30,000. Byline given. Pays on publication. Offers kill fee. Publishes ms an average of 3 months after acceptance. Accepts queries by e-mail. Accepts simultaneous submissions. Guidelines for 8x10 SASE with 7 Canadian first-class stamps.

NONFICTION Needs how-to, personal experience. **Buys 50 mss/year.** Query the publication before submitting. Do not send unsolicited mss or photos. Submit no more than 100-words outlining exactly what your story will be. "You should be able to encapsulate the essence of your story and show us why our readers would be interested in reading or knowing what you are writing about. Queries need to be clear, succinct and straight to the point. Show us why we should publish your article in 150 words or less." Length: 1,700-2,000 words. **Pays $300-500.** Pays expenses of writers on assignment.

PHOTOS Biannual magazine emphasizing hunting, RV camping, canoeing, wildlife and management issues in British Columbia only. Sample copy available for $4.95 Canadian. Family oriented. "By far, most photos accompany manuscripts. We are always on the lookout for good covers—wildlife, recreational activities, people in the outdoors—of British Columbia, vertical and square format. Photos with manuscripts must, of course, illustrate the story. There should, as far as possible, be something happening. Photos generally dominate lead spread of each story. They are used in everything from double-page bleeds to thumbnails." State availability. Model/property release preferred. Photo captions or at least full identification required. Buys one-time rights.

COLUMNS/DEPARTMENTS Column needs basically supplied in-house.

TIPS "Send us material on fishing and hunting. We generally just send back nonrelated work. We want in-depth information and professional writing only. Emphasis on environmental issues. Those pieces with a conservation component have a better chance of being published. Subject must be specific to British Columbia. We receive many mss written by people who obviously do not know the magazine or market. The writer has a better chance of breaking in with short, lesser-paying articles and fillers, because we have a stable of regular writers who produce most main features."

$$ THE BIG GAME FISHING JOURNAL

Open Ocean Publications, LLC, 308 S. Main St., Suite 2, Forked River NJ 08731. **E-mail:** info@biggamefishingjournal.com. **Website:** www.biggamefishingjournal.com. **90% freelance written.** Bimonthly magazine covering big game fishing. Estab. 1994. Circ. 45,000. Byline given. Pays on publication. Offers 50% kill fee. Editorial lead time 3 months. Submit seasonal material 3 months in advance. Accepts queries by mail. Accepts simultaneous submissions. Responds in 2 weeks to queries; in 1 month to mss. Guidelines free.

"We require highly instructional articles prepared by qualified writers/fishermen."

NONFICTION Needs how-to, interview, technical. **Buys 50-70 mss/year.** Send complete ms. Length: 2,000-3,000 words. Pays expenses of writers on assignment.

PHOTOS Send photos. Captions required. Reviews transparencies. Offers no additional payment for photos accepted with ms. Buys one-time rights.

TIPS "Our format is considerably different than most publications. We prefer to receive articles from qualified anglers on their expertise—if the author is an accomplished writer, all the better. We require highly instructional articles that teach both novice and expert readers."

$$ BOWHUNTER

InterMedia Outdoors, 6385 Flank Dr., Suite 800, Harrisburg PA 17112. (717)695-8085. **Fax:** (717)545-2527. **Website:** www.bowhunter.com. **50% freelance written.** Bimonthly magazine covering hunting big and small game with bow and arrow. "We are a special-interest publication, produced by bowhunters for bowhunters, covering all aspects of the sport. Material included in each issue is designed to entertain and inform readers, making them better bowhunters." Estab. 1971. Circ. 126,480. Byline given. Pays on acceptance. No kill fee. Submit seasonal material 8 months in advance. Accepts queries by mail. Accepts simultaneous submissions. Responds in 1 month to queries. Responds in 2 months to mss.

NONFICTION Needs general interest, how-to, interview, opinion, personal experience, photo feature. **Buys 60-plus mss/year.** Query. Length: 250-2,000 words. **Pays $500 maximum for assigned articles; $100-400 for unsolicited articles.** Pays expenses of writers on assignment.

PHOTOS Send photos. Captions required. Reviews high-res digital images. Reviews photos with or without a manuscript. Offers $50-300/photo. Pays $50-125 for b&w inside; $75-300 for color inside; $600 for cover, "occasionally more if photo warrants it." **Pays on acceptance.** Credit line given. Buys one-time publication rights. Buys one-time rights.

TIPS "A writer must know bowhunting and be willing to share that knowledge. Writers should anticipate *all* questions a reader might ask, then answer them in the article itself or in an appropriate sidebar. Articles should be written with the reader foremost in mind; we won't be impressed by writers seeking to prove how good they are—either as writers or bowhunters. We care about the reader and don't need writers with 'I' trouble. Features are a good bet because most of our material comes from freelancers. The best advice is: Be yourself. Tell your story the same as if sharing the experience around a campfire. Don't try to write like you think a writer writes."

$$ BOWHUNTING WORLD

Grand View Media Group, 200 Croft St., Suite 1, Birmingham AL 35242. (888)431-2877. **E-mail:** bowhunting@omedia.com. **Website:** www.bowhuntingworld.com. **50% freelance written.** Bimonthly magazine with 3 additional issues for bowhunting and archery enthusiasts who participate in the sport year-round. Estab. 1952. Circ. 95,000. Byline given. Pays on acceptance. No kill fee. Publishes ms an average of 5 months after acceptance. Accepts simultaneous submissions. Responds in 1 week to e-mail queries; 6 weeks to mss. Guidelines with #10 SASE.

Accepts queries by mail, but prefers e-mail.

NONFICTION **Buys 60 mss/year.** Send complete ms. Length: 1,500-2,500 words. **Pays $350-600.** Pays expenses of writers on assignment.

PHOTOS "We are seeking cover photos that depict specific behavioral traits of the more common big game animals (scraping whitetails, bugling elk, etc.) and well-equipped bowhunters in action. Must include return postage."

TIPS "Writers are strongly advised to adhere to guidelines and become familiar with our format, as our needs are very specific. Writers are urged to query by e-mail. We prefer detailed outlines of 6 or so article ideas/query. Assignments are made for the next 18 months."

$$ FUR-FISH-GAME

2878 E. Main St., Columbus OH 43209-9947. **E-mail:** ffgcox@ameritech.net; subs@furfishgame.com. **Website:** www.furfishgame.com. **Contact:** Mitch Cox, editor. **65% freelance written.** Monthly magazine for outdoorsmen of all ages who are interested in hunting, fishing, trapping, dogs, camping, conservation, and related topics. Estab. 1900. Circ. 118,000. Byline given. Pays on acceptance. No kill fee. Publishes ms an average of 4 months after acceptance. Accepts simultaneous submissions. Responds in 2 months to queries. Sample copy for $1 and 9x12 SASE. Guidelines with #10 SASE.

NONFICTION Query. Length: 500-3,000 words. **Pays $50-250 or more for features depending upon quality, photo support, and importance to magazine.** Pays expenses of writers on assignment.

PHOTOS Send photos. Captions, True required. Reviews transparencies, color 5×7 or 8×10 prints, digital photos on CD only with thumbnail sheet of small images and a numbered caption sheet. Pays $35 for separate freelance photos.

TIPS "We are always looking for quality how-to articles about fish, game animals, or birds that are popular with everyday outdoorsmen but often overlooked in other publications, such as catfish, bluegill, crappie, squirrel, rabbit, crows, etc. We also use articles on standard seasonal subjects such as deer and pheasant, but like to see a fresh approach or new technique. Instructional trapping articles are useful all year. Articles on gun dogs, ginseng, and do-it-yourself projects are also popular with our readers. An assortment of photos and/or sketches greatly enhances any manuscript, and sidebars, where applicable, can also help. No phone queries, please."

$$$ GRAY'S SPORTING JOURNAL

735 Broad St., Augusta GA 30901. **E-mail:** russ.lumpkin@morris.com; wayne.knight@morris.com. **Website:** www.grayssportingjournal.com. **Contact:** Russ Lumpkin, editor-in-chief; Wayne Knight, art director. **75% freelance written.** "*Gray's Hunting Journal* is published 7 times/year. Because 90% of our readers are bird hunters, 85% are fly fishers, and 67% hunt big game, we're always looking for good upland-bird-hunting, fly-fishing, and big-game mss throughout the year, but don't confine yourself to these themes. Other subjects of interest include waterfowl, turkeys, small game, unusual quarry (feral hogs, etc.), sporting adventures in exciting locales (foreign and domestic) and yarns (tall tales or true)." Estab. 1975. Circ. 32,000. Byline given. Pays on publication. No kill fee. Publishes ms an average of 1 year after acceptance. Editorial lead time 14 months. Submit seasonal material 16 months in advance. Accepts queries by e-mail. Accepts simultaneous submissions. Responds in 3 months to mss. Guidelines online.

NONFICTION Needs essays, historical, humor, personal experience, photo feature, travel. Special issues: Publishes 4 themed issues: the Fly Fishing Edition (March/April), the Upland Bird Hunting Edition (August), the Big Game Edition (September/October), and the Expeditions and Guides Annual (December). Does not want how-to articles. **Buys 20-30 mss/year.** Send complete ms via e-mail with "Gray's Manuscript" in subject line. Length: 1,500-12,000 words. **Pays $600-1,250 (based on quality, not length).** Pays expenses of writers on assignment.

PHOTOS State availability. Reviews GIF/JPEG files. Pays $50-300.

FICTION Accepts quality fiction with some aspect of hunting or fishing at the core. Needs adventure, experimental, historical, humorous, slice-of-life vignettes. If some aspect of hunting or fishing isn't at the core of the story, it has zero chance of interesting *Gray's*. **Buys 20 mss/year.** Send complete ms. Length: 750-1,500 words. **Pays $600.**

POETRY Needs avant-garde, haiku, light verse, traditional. Buys 7 poems/year. Submit maximum 1 poems. Length: up to 1,000 words. **Pays $100.**

TIPS "Write something different, write something well—fiction or nonfiction—write something that goes to the heart of hunting or fishing more elegantly, more inspirationally, than the 1,500 or so other unsolicited mss we review each year."

$$ THE MAINE SPORTSMAN

183 State St., Suite 101, Augusta ME 04330. (207)622-4242. **Fax:** (207)622-4255. **E-mail:** will.sportster@yahoo.com. **Website:** www.mainesportsman.com. **90% freelance written.** Monthly tabloid-size magazine covering Maine's outdoors, especially hunting, fishing, ATVs and snowmobiles. Willing to work with new/unpublished writers, but because we run over 30 regular columns, it's difficult to get into *The Maine Sportsman* as a beginner. Estab. 1972. Circ. 30,000. Byline given. Pays during month of publication. No kill fee. Publishes an average of 3 months after acceptance. Accepts queries by mail, e-mail. Responds in 2 weeks to queries.

NONFICTION Special issues: Biggest Bucks issue, ATVs, Snowmobiling, Spring trout fishing, moose season, whitetail season, blackpowder season. **Buys 25-40 mss/year.** Send complete ms via e-mail. Length: 200-1,200 words. **Pays $25-250.**

PHOTOS Send JPGs/TIFFs via e-mail. Pays $25-100.

TIPS "We publish numerous special sections each year and are eager to buy Maine-oriented articles on snowmobiling, ice fishing, boating, salt water and deer hunting. Send articles or queries."

$ MIDWEST OUTDOORS

MidWest Outdoors, Ltd., 111 Shore Dr., Burr Ridge IL 60527. (630)887-7722. **Fax:** (630)887-1958. **Website:** www.midwestoutdoors.com. **100% freelance written.** Monthly tabloid emphasizing fishing, hunting, camping, and boating. Estab. 1967. Byline given. Pays on publication. No kill fee. Publishes ms an average of 3 months after acceptance. Submit seasonal material 2 months in advance. Accepts simultaneous submissions. Responds in 3 weeks to queries. Sample copy for $1 or online. Guidelines available online.

NONFICTION Needs how-to. "We do not want to see any articles on 'my first fishing, hunting, or camping experiences,' 'cleaning my tackle box,' 'tackle tune-up,' 'making fishing fun for kids,' or 'catch and release.'" **Buys 1,800 unsolicited mss/year.** Send complete ms. Submissions should be submitted via website's online form as a Microsoft Word doc. Length: 600-1,500 words. **Pays $15-30.**

PHOTOS Captions required. Reviews slides and b&w prints. Offers no additional payment for photos accompanying ms. Buys all rights.

COLUMNS/DEPARTMENTS Fishing; Hunting. Send complete ms. **Pays $30.**

TIPS "Break in with a great unknown fishing hole or new technique within 500 miles of Chicago. Where, how, when, and why. Know the type of publication you are sending material to."

$$ MUSKY HUNTER MAGAZINE

P.O. Box 340, 7978 Hwy. 70 E., St. Germain WI 54558. (715)477-2178. **Fax:** (715)477-8858. **E-mail:** editor@muskyhunter.com. **Website:** www.muskyhunter.com. **Contact:** Jim Saric, editor. **90% freelance written.** Bimonthly magazine on musky fishing. Serves the vertical market of musky fishing enthusiasts. "We're interested in how-to, where-to articles." Estab. 1988. Circ. 37,000. Byline given. Pays on publication. No kill fee. Publishes ms an average of 4 months after acceptance. Submit seasonal material 4 months in advance. Accepts simultaneous submissions. Responds in 2 months to queries. Sample copy for 9x12 SASE and $2.79 postage. Guidelines for #10 SASE.

NONFICTION Needs historical, how-to, travel. **Buys 50 mss/year.** Send complete ms. Length: 1,000-2,500 words. **Pays $100-300 for assigned articles. Pays $50-300 for unsolicited articles.** Pays expenses of writers on assignment.

PHOTOS Send photos. Identification of subjects required. Reviews 35mm transparencies, 3x5 prints, high-res digital images preferred. Offers no additional payment for photos accepted with ms. Buys one-time rights.

OUTDOOR CANADA MAGAZINE

Outdoor Canada West Magazine, 130 Merton St., Suite 200, Toronto ON M4S 1A4 Canada. (416)599-2000. **E-mail:** editorial@outdoorcanada.ca. **Website:** www.outdoorcanada.ca. **60% freelance written. Works with a small number of new/unpublished writers each year.** Fishing, hunting and conservation in Canada. Estab. 1972. Circ. 110,000. Byline given. Pays on publication. 50% Publishes ms an average of 3 months after acceptance. Submit seasonal ideas 1 year in advance. Accepts queries by mail, e-mail. Accepts simultaneous submissions. Responds in 1 month to queries. Guidelines online.

NONFICTION Needs how-to, fishing, hunting, conservation, outdoor issues, outdoor destinations in Canada. **Buys 35-40 mss/year.** Does not accept unsolicited mss. Length: 1,000-2,500 words **Pays flat rate of $400-600 for a feature.**

PHOTOS Emphasize people in the Canadian outdoors. Captions, model releases required. Fees negotiable.

FILLERS Buys 30-40 mss/year. Length: 100-500 words.

PENNSYLVANIA ANGLER & BOATER

Pennsylvania Fish & Boat Commission, P.O. Box 67000, Harrisburg PA 17106-7000. (717)705-7835. **E-mail:** ra-pfbcmagazine@pa.gov. **Website:** www.fishandboat.com. **80% freelance written.** Bimonthly magazine covering fishing, boating, and related conservation topics in Pennsylvania. Circ. 28,000. Byline given. Pays 2 months after acceptance. Publishes ms an average of 8 months after acceptance. Submit seasonal material 8 months in advance. Accepts simultaneous submissions. Responds in 1 month to queries; 2 months to mss. Sample copy for 9x12 SAE with 9 first-class stamps. Guidelines online.

No unsolicited mss.

NONFICTION Needs how-to, technical. No saltwater or hunting material. **Buys 75 mss/year.** Query. Length: 600-2,500 words. **Payment varies.**

PHOTOS Send photos. Captions, identification of subjects, model releases required. Reviews 35mm and larger transparencies, hi-res digital submissions on CD (preferred). Offers no additional payment for photos accompanying mss. Rights purchased vary.

RACK MAGAZINE

Buckmasters, Ltd., 10350 U.S. Hwy. 80 E., P.O. Box 244022, Montgomery AL 36117. (334)215-3337. **Fax:** (334)215-3535. **E-mail:** mikehandley@mac.com. **Website:** www.buckmasters.com. **Contact:** Mike Handley, editor. **80% freelance written.** Magazine published 10 times/year (February, March, April/May, June, July, August, September, October, November and Winter). "All features are either first- or third-person narratives detailing the successful hunts for world-class, big game animals—mostly white-tailed deer and other North American species." Ask for writer's guidelines. Estab. 1998. Circ. 75,000. Byline given. Pays within one month of publication. No kill fee. Publishes ms an average of 9 months after acceptance. Editorial lead time 9-12 months. Submit seasonal material 9 months in advance. Accepts queries by mail, e-mail. Accepts simultaneous submissions. Responds to queries within a week. Guidelines available.

NONFICTION Needs personal experience. "We're interested only in articles chronicling successful hunts." **Buys 150 mss/year.** Query. Length: 1,000 words. **Pays $100-360.**

REPRINTS Pays 50% of first-time rate for reprints.

PHOTOS Send photos. Captions, identification of subjects required. Reviews transparencies, prints, JPEG files. Buys one-time rights.

SPORTS AFIELD

Field Sports Publishing, P.O. Box 271305, Fort Collins CO 80527. **Website:** www.sportsafield.com. **60% freelance written.** Magazine published 6 times/year covering big game hunting. "We cater to the upscale hunting market, especially hunters who travel to exotic destinations like Alaska and Africa. We are not a deer hunting magazine, and we do not cover fishing." Estab. 1887. Circ. 50,000. Byline given. Pays 1 month prior to publication. Publishes ms an average of 6 months after acceptance. Editorial lead time 4 months. Submit seasonal material 5 months in advance. Accepts queries by online submission form. Accepts simultaneous submissions. Responds in 2 months. Guidelines online.

NONFICTION Needs personal experience, travel. **Buys 6-8 mss/year.** Query. Length: 1,500-2,500 words. **Pays $500-800.** Pays expenses of writers on assignment.

PHOTOS State availability. Captions, model releases required. Reviews 35mm slides transparencies, TIFF/JPEG files. Offers no additional payment for photos accepted with ms. Buys first time rights.

FILLERS Needs newsbreaks. **Buys 30 mss/year.** Length: 200-500 words. **Pays $75-150.**

MARTIAL ARTS

$$ BLACK BELT

Black Belt Communications, LLC, 24900 Anza Dr., Unit E, Valencia CA 91355. **Fax:** (661)257-3028. **E-mail:** byoung@aimmedia.com. **Website:** www.blackbeltmag.com. **Contact:** Robert W. Young, executive editor. **80% freelance written. Works with a small number of new/unpublished writers each year.** Monthly magazine emphasizing martial arts for both experienced practitioner and layman. Estab. 1961. Circ. 100,000. Pays on publication. No kill fee. Publishes ms an average of 1 year after acceptance. Accepts queries by mail, e-mail. Accepts simultaneous submissions. Responds in 3 weeks to queries. Guidelines online.

NONFICTION Needs expose, how-to, interview, new product, personal experience, technical, travel, Informational. We never use personality profiles. **Buys 40-50 mss/year.** Query with outline 1,200 words minimum. **Pays $150-300 for feature articles with good photos.**

PHOTOS Very seldom buys photographs without accompanying ms. Captions, model releases required. Total purchase price for ms includes payment for photos.

$ KUNG FU TAI CHI

TC Media International, 40748 Encyclopedia Circle, Fremont CA 94538. (510)656-5100. **Fax:** (510)656-8844. **E-mail:** gene@kungfumagazine.com. **Website:** www.kungfumagazine.com. **Contact:** Gene Ching. **70% freelance written.** Quarterly magazine covering Chinese martial arts and culture. *Kung Fu Tai Chi* covers the full range of Kung Fu culture, including healing, philosophy, meditation, Fengshui, Buddhism, Taoism, history, and the latest events in art and culture, plus insightful features on the martial arts. Estab. 1992. Circ. 10,000. Byline given. Pays on publication. No kill fee. Publishes ms 3 or more months after acceptance. Editorial lead time 4 months. Submit seasonal material 4 months in advance. Accepts queries by e-mail. Responds in 2 months to queries; in 3 months to mss. Sample copy for $4.99 or online. Guidelines online.

NONFICTION Needs general interest, historical, interview, personal experience, religious, technical, travel, cultural perspectives. No poetry or fiction. **Buys 70 mss/year.** Query. Length: 500-2,500 words. **Pays $35-125.**

PHOTOS Send photos. Captions, identification of subjects required. Reviews 5x7 prints, GIF/JPEG files. Offers no additional payment for photos accepted with ms. Buys one-time rights.

TIPS "Check out our website and get an idea of past articles."

MISCELLANEOUS

$$ CLIMBING

Cruz Bay Publishing, Inc., 5720 Flatiron Pkwy., Boulder CO 80301. (303)625-1600. **Fax:** (303)440-3618. **E-mail:** queries@climbing.com. **Website:** www.climbing.com. Magazine published 9 times/year covering climbing and mountaineering. Provides features on rock climbing and mountaineering worldwide. Estab. 1970. Circ. 51,000. Pays on publication. No kill fee. Editorial lead time 6 weeks. Accepts queries by e-mail. Accepts simultaneous submissions. Guidelines online.

"We pride ourselves on running the best, most exciting, and most experimental climbing photography and writing in the world. We're glad that you are interested in helping us convey passion and creativity for the sport."

NONFICTION Needs interview, personal experience. Query. Length: 1,500-3,500 words. **Pays 35¢/word.** Pays expenses of writers on assignment.

PHOTOS State availability. Reviews negatives, 35mm transparencies, prints, digital submissions on CD. Pays $25-800.

COLUMNS/DEPARTMENTS Query. **Payment varies.**

MOTOR SPORTS

⊘ 4-WHEEL & OFF ROAD

The Enthusiast Network, 831 S. Douglas St., El Segundo CA 90245. (310)531-9900. **Website:** www.4wheeloffroad.com. Monthly magazine covering off road driving. Intended for the connoisseur of four wheel drive vehicles and their specific applications. Estab. 1977. Circ. 379,284. No kill fee. Accepts simultaneous submissions.

NONFICTION Needs how-to, new product, travel, legal issues.

RUNNING

$ INSIDE TEXAS RUNNING

P.O. Box 19909, Houston TX 77224. (713)935-0555. **Fax:** (713)935-0559. **Website:** www.insidetexasrunning.com. **Contact:** Lance Phegley, editor. **70% freelance written.** Monthly (except June and August) tabloid covering running and running-related events. "Our audience is made up of Texas runners who may also be interested in cross training." Estab. 1977. Circ. 10,000. Byline given. Pays on publication. No kill fee. Publishes ms an average of 2 months after acceptance. Submit seasonal material 2 months in advance. Accepts simultaneous submissions. Responds in 1 month to mss. Sample copy: $4.95. Guidelines for #10 SASE.

NONFICTION Special issues: Shoe Review (March); Fall Race Review (September); Marathon Focus (October); Resource Guide (December). **Buys 20 mss/year.** Send complete ms. Length: 500-1,500 words. **Pays $100 maximum for assigned articles. Pays $50 maximum for unsolicited articles.**

REPRINTS Send tearsheet, photocopy, or typed ms with rights for sale noted and information about when and where the material previously appeared.

PHOTOS Send photos. Captions required. Offers $25 maximum/photo. Buys one-time rights.

TIPS "Writers should be familiar with the sport and the publication."

$$$$ RUNNER'S WORLD

Rodale, 400 S. Tenth St., Emmaus PA 18098. (610)967-8441. **Fax:** (610)967-8883. **E-mail:** rwedit@rodale.com. **Website:** www.runnersworld.com. **Contact:** David Willey, editor-in-chief; Suzanne Perrault, senior managing editor; Benjamen Purvis, design director. **5% freelance written.** Monthly magazine on running—mainly long-distance running. *Runner's World* is the magazine for and about distance running, training, health and fitness, nutrition, motivation, injury prevention, race coverage, and personalities of the sport. Estab. 1966. Circ. 500,000. Byline given. Pays on publication. No kill fee. Publishes ms an average of 6 months after acceptance. Submit seasonal material 6 months in advance. Accepts queries by mail. Accepts simultaneous submissions. Responds in 2 months to queries. Guidelines online.

NONFICTION Needs how-to, interview, personal experience. No "my first marathon" stories. No poetry. **Buys 5-7 mss/year.** Query. **Pays $1,500-2,000.** Pays expenses of writers on assignment.

PHOTOS State availability. Identification of subjects required. Buys one-time rights.

COLUMNS/DEPARTMENTS Finish Line (back-of-the-magazine essay, personal experience, humor). **Buys 24 mss/year.** Send complete ms. **Pays $300.**

TIPS "We are always looking for 'Adventure Runs' from readers—runs in wild, remote, beautiful, and interesting places. These are rarely race stories but more like backtracking/running adventures. Great color slides are crucial; 2,000 words maximum."

$$ TRAIL RUNNER

Big Stone Publishing, 2567 Dolores Way, Carbondale CO 81623. (970)704-1442. **Fax:** (970)963-4965. **E-mail:** pcunobooth@bigstonepub; mbenge@bigstonepub.com. **Website:** www.trailrunnermag.com. **Contact:** Michael Benge, editor; Paul Cuno-Booth, associate editor. **80% freelance written.** Magazine published 8x year, covering trail runing, ultratanning, fastpacking, adventure racing, and snowshoeing. Covers all aspects of off-road running. "North America's only magazine dedicated to trail running. In-depth editorial and compelling photography informs, entertains and inspires readers of all ages and abilities to enjoy the outdoors and to improve their health and fitness through the sport of trail running." Estab. 1999. Circ. 31,000. Byline given. Pays 30 days post-publication Publishes ms an average of 2 months after acceptance. Editorial lead time is 3 months. Submit seasonal material 5 months in advance. Accepts queries by e-mail. Accepts simultaneous submissions. Responds in 4 weeks to queries. Sample copy for $5. Guidelines online.

"Your well-written query should present a clear, original and provocative story angle, not merely a topic or idea, and should reflect your thorough knowledge of the magazine's content, editorial style and tone."

NONFICTION Needs expose, historical, how-to, humor, inspirational, interview, personal experience, technical, travel, racing. Does not want "My first trail race." **Buys 30-40 mss/year.** Query with one or two writing samples (preferably previously published articles), including your name, phone number and email address. Identify which department your story would be best suited for. **Pays 25¢/word for assigned and unsolicited articles.** Pays expenses of writers on assignment.

PHOTOS "*Trail Runner* regularly features stunning photography of trail running destinations, races, adventures and faces of the sport." State availability of photos with submission. Captions, identification of subjects. Reviews GIF/JPEG files. Send low-res samples or lightbox to photos@bigstonepub.com. Offers $50-250/photo. Buys one-time rights.

COLUMNS/DEPARTMENTS Contact: Michael Benge, editor, or Yitka Winn, associate editor. Making Tracks (news, race reports, athlete Q&A), 300-800 words; Trail Tips, TrainingTrail Rx (injury prevention/treatment, recovery), Take Your Mark (race previews); Nutrition (sports nutrition, health news), 800-1,000 words; Adventure, Great Escapes (running destinations/trails), Faces (athlete profiles), 1,200 words **Buys 40 mss/year. mss/year.** Query with published clips. **Pays 25 cents/word.**

FILLERS Needs anecdotes, facts, newsbreaks, short humor. **Buys Buys 10 mss/year. mss/year.** Length: 75-400 words. **Pays 30 cents/word.**

TIPS "Demonstrate familiarity with the sport. Best way to break in is with interesting and unique news, stories, insights. Submit thoughtful, detailed queries, not just vague story ideas."

SKIING & SNOW SPORTS

AMERICAN SNOWMOBILER

Kalmbach Publishing Co., 21027 Crossroads Circle, P.O. Box 1612, Waukesha WI 53187-1612. **E-mail:** editor@amsnow.com. **Website:** www.amsnow.com. **Contact:** Mark Savage, executive editor. **30% freelance written.** Magazine published 6 times seasonally covering snowmobiling. Estab. 1985. Circ. 54,000. Byline given. Pays on acceptance. No kill fee. Publishes an average of 4 months after acceptance. Editorial lead time 4 months. Submit seasonal material 6 months in advance. Accepts queries by mail, e-mail, fax. Accepts simultaneous submissions. Responds in 1 month to queries. Responds in 2 months to mss. Guidelines available online.

NONFICTION Needs general interest, historical, how-to, interview, personal experience, photo feature, travel. **Buys 10 mss/year.** Query with published clips. Length: 500-1,200 words. **Pay varies for assigned articles. Pays $100 minimum for unsolicited articles.**

PHOTOS State availability. Captions, identification of subjects, model releases required. Offers no additional payment for photos accepted with ms. Buys all rights.

WATER SPORTS

SURFER MAGAZINE

The Enthusiast Network, 2052 Corte Del Nogal, Suite 100, Carlsbad CA 92011. (949)325-6212. **Website:** www.surfer.com. **Contact:** Todd Prodanovich, editor. Monthly magazine edited for the avid surfers and those who follow the beach, wave riding scene. Circ. 118,570. No kill fee. Editorial lead time 10 weeks. Accepts queries by online submission form. Accepts simultaneous submissions.

Query before submitting.

NONFICTION Pays expenses of writers on assignment.

TEEN & YOUNG ADULT

DEVOZINE

1908 Grand Ave., P.O. Box 340004, Nashville TN 37203-0004. **E-mail:** devozine@upperroom.org. **Website:** www.devozine.org. **Contact:** Sandy Miller, editor. *devozine*, published bimonthly, is a 64-page devotional magazine for youth (ages 14-19) and adults who care about youth. Offers meditations, scripture, prayers, poems, stories, songs, and feature articles to "aid youth in their prayer life, introduce them to spiritual disciplines, help them shape their concept of God, and encourage them in the life of discipleship." Accepts queries by mail, e-mail, online submission form. Accepts simultaneous submissions.

NONFICTION Special issues: Submit by postal mail with SASE, or by e-mail. Include name, age/birth date (if younger than 25), mailing address, e-mail address, phone number, and fax number (if available). Always publishes theme issues (available for SASE or online). Indicate theme you are writing for. Submit devotionals by mail or e-mail listed above. Submit feature article **queries** by e-mail to smiller@upperroom.org. Length: 150-250 words for devotionals; 500-600 words for feature articles. **Pays $25-100.**

POETRY Needs religious. Considers poetry by teens. Submit by postal mail with SASE, or by e-mail. Include name, age/birth date (if younger than 25), mailing address, e-mail address, phone number, and fax number (if available). Always publishes theme issues (available for SASE or online). Indicate theme you are writing for. Length: 10-20 lines/poem. **Pays $25.**

TRAVEL, CAMPING & TRAILER

$$ AAA MIDWEST TRAVELER

AAA Auto Club of Missouri, 12901 N. 40 Dr., St. Louis MO 63141. (314)523-7350, ext. 6301. **Fax:** (314)523-6982. **E-mail:** dreinhardt@aaamissouri.com. **Website:** services.autoclubmo.aaa.com/traveler/mid. **Contact:** Deborah Reinhardt, managing editor. **80% freelance written.** Bimonthly magazine covering travel and automotive safety and is sent to 560,000 AAA households in Missouri, southern Illinois, southern Indiana, and eastern Kansas. "We provide members with useful information on travel, auto safety and related topics." Estab. 1901. Circ. 500,000. Byline given. Pays on acceptance. Offers $50 kill fee. Editorial lead time 1 year. Best time to query is January through April. Submit seasonal material 6 months in advance. Accepts queries by mail, e-mail, fax. Accepts simultaneous submissions. Responds in 1 month. Sample copy with 10x13 SASE and 4 First-Class stamps. Guidelines with #10 SASE.

NONFICTION Needs travel. No humor, fiction, poetry or cartoons. **Buys 20-30 mss/year.** Query; query with published clips the first time. Length: 800-1,200 words. **Pays $400.** Pays expenses of writers on assignment.

PHOTOS State availability. Captions required. Reviews transparencies, prints. Offers no additional payment for photos accepted with ms. Buys one time and electronic rights.

TIPS "Send queries between December and February, as we plan our calendar for the following year. Request a copy. Serious writers ask for media kit to help them target their piece. Send a SASE or download online. Travel destinations and tips are most open to freelancers; all departments and auto-related news handled by staff. We see too many 'Here's a recount of our family vacation' manuscripts. Go easy on first-person accounts."

$ BACKROADS

P.O. Box 620, Augusta NJ 07822. (973)948-4176. **Fax:** (973)948-0823. **E-mail:** editor@backroadsusa.com. **Website:** www.backroadsusa.com. **50% freelance written.** Monthly tabloid covering motorcycle touring. "*Backroads* is a motorcycle tour magazine geared toward getting motorcyclists on the road and traveling. We provide interesting destinations, unique roadside attractions and eateries, plus Rip & Ride Route Sheets. We cater to all brands. Although *Backroads* is geared towards the motorcycling population, it is not by any means limited to just motorcycle riders. Non-motorcyclists enjoy great destinations, too. As time has gone by, *Backroads* has developed more and more into a cutting-edge touring publication. We like to see submissions that give the reader the distinct impression of being part of the ride they're reading. Words describing the feelings and emotions brought on by partaking in this great and exciting lifestyle are encouraged." All submissions must be motorcycle related article and stories with high res images to go with them. Estab. 1995. Circ. 40,000. Byline given. Pays 1-3 months after publication. Editorial lead time 1 month. Submit seasonal material 3 months in advance. Accepts queries by mail, e-mail. Responds in 1 month. Sample copy: $4. Guidelines online.

NONFICTION "What *Backroads* does not want is any 'us vs. them' submissions. We are decidedly nonpolitical and secular. *Backroads* is about getting out and riding, not getting down on any particular group, nor do we feel this paper should be a pulpit for a writer's beliefs . be they religious, political, or personal." Query. Needs travel features: "This type of story offers a good opportunity for prospective contributors. They must feature spectacular photography, color preferably, and may be used as a cover story, if of acceptable quality. All submissions must be accompanied by images, with an SASE of adequate size (10x13) to return all material sent, as well as a copy of the issue in which they were published, and a hard copy printout of the article, including your name, address, and phone number. If none is enclosed, the materials will not be returned. Text submissions are accepted via U.S. mail or e-mail. We can usually convert most file types, although it is easier to submit in plain text format, sometimes called ASCII." **Pays $75 and up; varies.** Pays expenses of writers on assignment.

PHOTOS Digital photos may be sent via U.S. mail on CD or via e-mail if they are in a stuffed file or Drop Box. All images must be no smaller then 300 dpi and at least 4x6. If you are sending images at 72 dpi, they must be no smaller than 20x30 for proper resizing. We do not accept photographs, slides, or negatives. Send photos. Offers no additional payment for photos accepted with ms.

COLUMNS/DEPARTMENTS We're Outta Here (weekend destinations), 500-750 words; Great All-American Diner Run (good eateries with great location), 500-750 words; Thoughts from the Road (personal opinion/insights), 400-600 words; Mysterious America (unique and obscure sights), 500-750 words; Big City Getaway (day trips), 500-750 words. **Buys 20-24 mss/year.** Query. **Pays $75/article.**

$$ ESCAPEES

Sharing the RV Lifestyle, Roving Press, 100 Rainbow Dr., Livingston TX 77351. (888)757-2582. **Fax:** (409)327-4388. **E-mail:** editor@escapees.com. **Website:** escapees.com. **Contact:** Kelly Evans-Hill, editorial assistant. *Escapees* magazine contributors are RVers interested in sharing the RV lifestyle. Our audience includes full- and part-time RVers, RVing snowbirds (those who travel south for the winter), and anyone considering extensive travel. Escapees members have varying levels of RVing experience; therefore, the magazine looks for a wide variety of material typically not found in conventional RV magazines. We welcome submissions on all phases of RV life and for all age demographics. Escapees RV Club members range in age from younger RVers, with or without children, who are working from the road, to retirees. A large majority of members live in their motorhomes, fifth-wheel trailers, or travel trailers, on a full-time basis. Popular topics are mechanical/technical, RV modifications and conversions, lifestyle issues and tips. A bimonthly magazine that provides a total support network to RVers and shares the RV lifestyle. Estab. 1979. Circ. 30,000. Byline given. Pays on publication. Publishes ms an average of 3-6 months after acceptance. Editorial lead time 3 months. Submit seasonal material 6 months in advance. Accepts queries by mail, e-mail. Accepts simultaneous submissions. Responds in 2 weeks to queries; in 3 months to mss. Sample copy available free online. Guidelines available online and by e-mail at departmentseditor@escapees.com. Editor does not accept articles based on queries alone. Decisions for use of material are based on the full article with any accompanying photos, graphics, or diagrams. Only complete articles are considered.

Submissions must be related to RVing. Travel destination locations should be RV-friendly and the focus of the story. Regions: U.S., Canada or Mexico.

NONFICTION Needs general interest, historical, how-to, humor, inspirational, new product, nostalgic, personal experience, photo feature, profile, technical, travel. Do not send anything religious, political, or unrelated to RVs. Submit complete ms. When submitting an article via e-mail as an attachment, please include the text in the body of the e-mail. Length: 300-1,500 words. Please include word count on first page of article. **Pays $25-$200 for unsolicited articles.** Pays expenses of writers on assignment.

PHOTOS **Contact:** Cole Carter, graphic artist. Freelancers should send photos with submissions. Captions, model releases, and identification of subjects required. Reviews GIF/JPEG files. Negotiates payment individually. Purchases one-time rights.

COLUMNS/DEPARTMENTS SKP Stops (short blurbs with photos on unique travel destination stops for RVers), 300-500 words. **Buys 10-15 mss/year.** Submit complete ms. **Pays $25-75.**

POETRY We do not accept poetry.

FILLERS Tips and DIY projects related to the RV lifestyle. 50-300 words.

TIPS "Use an engaging, conversational tone. Well-placed humor is refreshing. Eliminate any fluff and verbosity. Avoid colloquialisms."

$$ INTERNATIONAL LIVING

International Living Publishing, Ltd., Elysium House, Ballytruckle, Waterford Ireland (800)643-2479. **Fax:** 353-51-304-561. **E-mail:** submissions@internationalliving.com; editor@internationalliving.com. **Website:** www.internationalliving.com. **Contact:** Eoin

Bassett, editorial director. **50% freelance written.** "*International Living* magazine aims at providing a scope and depth of information about global travel, living, retiring, investing, and real estate that is not available anywhere else at any price." Estab. 1981. Circ. 500,000. Byline given. Pays on publication. Offers 25-50% kill fee. Publishes ms an average of 3 months after acceptance. Editorial lead time 2 months. Submit seasonal material 3 months in advance. Accepts queries by e-mail. Accepts simultaneous submissions. Responds in 2 months to mss. Sample copy available online. Guidelines available online.

NONFICTION Needs how-to, interview, new product, personal experience, travel, health care. No descriptive, run-of-the-mill travel articles. **Buys 100 mss/year.** Query. Length: 840-1,400 words. **Pays $250-400.**

PHOTOS State availability. Identification of subjects required. Reviews contact sheets, negatives, transparencies, prints. Offers $50/photo. Buys all rights.

TIPS "Make recommendations in your articles. We want first-hand accounts. Tell us how to do things: how to catch a cab, order a meal, buy a souvenir, buy property, start a business, etc. *International Living*'s philosophy is that the world is full of opportunities to do whatever you want, whenever you want. We will show you how."

$$$ MOTORHOME

2750 Park View Court, Suite 240, Oxnard CA 93036. **E-mail:** info@motorhomemagazine.com. **Website:** www.motorhome.com. **Contact:** Eileen Hubbard, editor. **60% freelance written.** Monthly magazine covering topics for RV enthusiasts. "*MotorHome* is a magazine for owners and prospective buyers of motorized recreational vehicles who are active outdoorsmen and wide-ranging travelers. We cover all aspects of the RV lifestyle; editorial material is both technical and nontechnical in nature. Regular features include tests and descriptions of various models of motorhomes, travel adventures, and hobbies pursued in such vehicles, objective analysis of equipment and supplies for such vehicles, and do-it-yourself articles. Guides within the magazine provide listings of manufacturers, rentals, and other sources of equipment and accessories of interest to enthusiasts. Articles must have an RV slant and excellent photography accompanying text." Estab. 1968. Circ. 150,000. Byline given. Pays on acceptance. Offers 30% kill fee. Publishes ms an average of 1 year after acceptance. Editorial lead time 4 months. Submit seasonal material 6 months in advance. Accepts queries by mail. Accepts simultaneous submissions. Responds in 1 month to queries; in 2 months to mss. Guidelines online.

NONFICTION Needs general interest, historical, how-to, humor, interview, new product, personal experience, photo feature, technical. No diaries of RV trips or negative RV experiences. **Buys 120 mss/year.** Query with published clips. Length: 800-2,500 words. **Pays $400-900.** Pays expenses of writers on assignment.

PHOTOS Digital photography accepted. Captions, identification of subjects, model releases required. Reviews hi-res photos at 300 dpi. Offers no additional payment for art accepted with ms. Pays $500 for covers. Buys first North American rights.

COLUMNS/DEPARTMENTS Crossroads (offbeat briefs of people, places, and events of interest to travelers), 100-200 words; Keepers (tips, resources). Query with published clips, or send complete ms. **Pays $100.**

TIPS "If a freelancer has an idea for a good article, it's best to send a query and include possible photo locations to illustrate the article. We prefer to assign articles and work with the author in developing a piece suitable to our audience. We are in a specialized field with very enthusiastic readers who appreciate articles by authors who actually enjoy motor homes."

$$$ PORTHOLE CRUISE MAGAZINE

Panoff Publishing / PPI Group, 6261 NW 6th Ave, Ft. Lauderdale FL 33309-3403. (954)377-7777. **Fax:** (954)377-7000. **E-mail:** publications@ppigroup.com. **Website:** www.porthole.com. Grant Balfour, managing editor. **Contact:** Bill Panoff, publisher/editor-in-chief. **70% freelance written.** Bimonthly magazine covering the cruise industry. *Porthole Cruise Magazine* entices its readers to take a cruise vacation by delivering information that is timely, accurate, colorful, and entertaining. We look at ocean-going ships, river ships, and destinations from Barbados to Bali, Budapest to Bangkok. Estab. 1992. Circ. 80,000. Byline given. Pays on publication. Offers 20% kill fee. Publishes ms an average of 6 months after acceptance. Editorial lead time 8 months. Submit seasonal material at least 5 months in advance. Accepts queries by e-mail. Accepts simultaneous submissions. Guidelines online.

Our ideal reader is an experienced cruiser - we are not a trade magazine, but a consumer-focused publication, opening a window on everything cruise.

NONFICTION Needs general interest, historical, how-to, humor, interview, new product, personal experience, photo feature, travel. No articles on destinations that can't be reached by ship. **Buys 60 mss/year.** Length: 1,000-1,200 words. **Pays $500-600 for assigned feature articles.** Pays expenses of writers on assignment.

PHOTOS **Contact:** Linda Douthat, creative director. State availability. Captions, identification of subjects, model releases required. Reviews digital images and original transparencies. Rates available upon request to ldouthat@ppigroup.com. Buys one-time rights.

$ RECREATION NEWS

Official Publication of the GovEmployee.com, 2699 Bay Dr., Sparrows Point MD 21219. (410)944-4852. **Fax:** (410)638-6902. **E-mail:** editor@recreationnews.com. **Website:** www.recreationnews.com. **Contact:** Marvin Bond, editor. **75% freelance written.** Monthly guide to leisure-time activities for federal and private industry workers covering Mid-Atlantic travel destinations, outdoor recreation, and cultural activities. Estab. 1982. Circ. 115,000. Byline given. Pays on publication. No kill fee. Publishes ms an average of 3 months after acceptance. Submit seasonal material 10 months in advance. Accepts queries by mail, e-mail, phone. Accepts simultaneous submissions. Responds in 2 months to queries. See sample copy and writer's guidelines online.

NONFICTION Needs travel. No reviews/critiques or material outside of Mid-Atlantic region. Query with published clips or links. Length: 600-1,000 words. **Pays $50-300.**

REPRINTS Send tearsheet or typed ms with rights for sale noted and information about when and where the material previously appeared. Pays $50.

TIPS "Our articles are lively and conversational and deal with specific travel destinations in the Mid-Atlantic. We do not buy international or Caribbean stories. Outdoor recreation of all kinds is good, but avoid first-person narrative. Stories need to include info on nearby places of interest, places to eat, and places to stay. Keep contact information in separate box at end of story."

$$ TRAILER LIFE

GS Media & Events, 2750 Park View Ct, Suite 240, Oxnard CA 93036. **E-mail:** info@trailerlife.com. **Website:** www.trailerlife.com. Managing Editor: Donya Carlson. **Contact:** Valerie Law, editor. **40% freelance written.** Monthly magazine, website and video channel covering the RV-camping lifestyle including recreational vehicles, RV travel, RV upgrades and maintenance, outdoor recreation and activities, and RV campgrounds. "*Trailer Life* is written for active people who enjoy travel and recreation with their RV. Every issue includes recreational vehicle and product tests, travel articles, and other features ranging from lifestyle to vehicle maintenance." Estab. 1941. Circ. 270,000. Byline given. Pays on acceptance. Offers kill fee. Offers 30% kill fee for assigned articles that are not acceptable. Publishes ms an average of 6 months after acceptance. Editorial lead time 4 months. Submit seasonal material 6 months in advance. Accepts queries by mail, e-mail, online submission form. Accepts simultaneous submissions. Responds in 2 months. Guidelines online.

NONFICTION Needs book excerpts, historical, how-to, humor, new product, opinion, personal experience, profile, technical, travel. "Nothing without an RV hook." **Buys 75 mss/year.** E-mail query. Length: Travel Features: 1,500-2,000 words; Technical Features: 1,000-2,000 words; Do-It-Yourself Features: 1,200 words. **Pays $100-700.** Pays expenses of writers on assignment.

PHOTOS Send photos. Identification of subjects, model releases required for covers. Negotiated upon assignment. Buys print and electronic rights.

COLUMNS/DEPARTMENTS Around the Bend (news, trends of interest to RVers), 75-100 words; 10-Minute Tech (technical RV tips) 50-200 words. **Buys 70 mss/year.** Email query or send complete ms **Pays $75-250.**

TIPS "Prerequisite: Articles must have an RV focus, and digital photos must be magazine quality. These are the two biggest reasons why articles are rejected. Readers are travel and outdoor enthusiasts who own RVs (primarily travel trailers, fifth-wheels, toy haulers, tent campers, teardrop trailers and truck campers) in which they explore North America and embrace the great outdoors in national and state parks and commercial RV campgrounds. They're are an active and adventurous community."

$ TRANSITIONS ABROAD PUBLISHING

P.O. Box 1369, Amherst MA 01004-1369. (413)992-6486. **E-mail:** webeditorial@transitionsabroad.com. **Website:** www.transitionsabroad.com. **Contact:**

Gregory Hubbs, editor-in-chief. **70-90% freelance written.** Online resource for educational travel with a strong work-teaching-intern-volunteer component. Long-term, independent, budget, and cultural immersion travel are also covered. The underlying focus is on enriching, informed, affordable, and transformational travel. For over 40 years, Transitions Abroad magazine has been the only travel publication and website dedicated to work, study, volunteering, and living abroad. Its purpose is the dissemination of practical information leading to a greater understanding of other cultures through direct participation in the daily life of the host community. Estab. 1977. Circ. 8,000,000 visitors per year. Byline given. Pays before publication. No kill fee. Accepts queries by e-mail. Accepts simultaneous submissions. Responds in 1-2 weeks to queries and mss if interested. Guidelines online.

NONFICTION Needs book excerpts, travel. **Buys 300-1,000 unsolicited mss/year.** "Submit online. Attach only Microsoft Word documents or Google docs. Send digital photos as attachments or ideally point to them on the Cloud. Include contact info." Length: 800-2,000 words. **Pays $50-150/piece. Average: $100. Regular columnist pay per negotiation. Contests: Hosts 3 different writing contests per year, with winner paid $500; 2nd Place, $150; 3rd Place, $100.**

PHOTOS Send photos with submission. Captions, identification of subjects preferred.

COLUMNS/DEPARTMENTS Working Traveler (how to find jobs and what to expect, including short-term jobs, teaching English, volunteering, internships, and international careers); Living Abroad (expatriate advice and participant reports); Worldwide Travel Bargains (destinations, activities, and accommodations for budget travelers); Study Abroad and Educational Travel (for teens to college through seniors); Activity Vacations (travel opportunities that involve action and learning, usually by direct involvement in host culture); Responsible Travel (information on community-organized tours). **Buys 100-200 mss/year mss/year.** Send complete ms. **Pays $50-150; negotiable up for very experienced published freelancers.**

TIPS "We like practical yet inspirational information, especially on how to work, live, study, travel and cut costs abroad in order to facilitate cultural immersion. Our readers want usable information on planning a travel itinerary as well as info on work, study, living, and volunteering abroad. Be specific with links to websites. We are very interested in educational, long-term travel, and study abroad for teens to college students to adults to senior citizens."

WESTERN JOURNEY MAGAZINE

AAA Washington, 3605 132nd Ave S.E.1745 114th Ave. SE, Bellevue WA 98004. **E-mail:** robbhatt@aaawa.com; sueboylan@aaawa.com. **Website:** www.wa.aaa.com/journey. Sue Boylan, art director. **Contact:** Rob Bhatt, editor. Bimonthly magazine. "The magazine for AAA members in Washington state and North Idaho combines regional and international travel coverage with articles on auto technology, traffic safety, insurance and other AAA-centric topics." Circ. 670,000. Pays on acceptance. Accepts queries by e-mail. Response time varies.

NONFICTION "We consider all pitches and assign stories based on need. We look for writers who combine sound research and reporting skills with a strong voice and excellent storytelling ability. We adhere to AP style. Each spring, we create our features calendar for the following calendar year. We encourage you to read several issues of the magazine to familiarize yourself with our publication before you submit article ideas. We run all articles with high-quality photographs and illustrations. If you are a published photographer, let us know—but please do not submit any photos unless requested. To be considered for an assignment, submit a query by e-mail with 3 samples of published work (or links to websites where your work can be found)." Length: 200-1,500 words. **Pay negotiable, based on experience.** Travel expenses must be approved ahead of time.

PHOTOS Contact: Sue Boylan, art director.

WOMEN'S

$ COUNTRY WOMAN

Trusted Media Brands, Inc., 1610 N. 2nd St., Suite 102, Milwaukee WI 53212. (414)423-0100. **E-mail:** submissions@countrywomanmagazine.com. **Website:** www.countrywomanmagazine.com. **75-85% freelance written.** Bimonthly magazine. *Country Woman* is for contemporary rural women of all ages and backgrounds and from all over the U.S. and Canada. It includes a sampling of the diversity that makes up rural women's lives—love of home, family, farm, ranch, community, hobbies, enduring values, humor, attaining new skills and appreciating present, past and future all within the context of the lifestyle that surrounds country living. Estab. 1970. Byline given. Pays on acceptance. No kill fee. Submit seasonal material 5 months in advance. Accepts queries by mail. Accepts simultaneous submissions. Responds in 2 months to queries; 3 months to mss.

NONFICTION Needs general interest, historical, how-to, humor, inspirational, interview, personal experience, photo feature. Query. Length: 1,000 words maximum. Pays expenses of writers on assignment.

REPRINTS Send typed ms with rights for sale noted and information about when and where the material previously appeared. Payment varies

PHOTOS Uses only excellent quality color photos. No b&w. We pay for photo/feature packages. State availability of or send photos. Captions, identification of subjects, model releases required. Reviews 35mm or 2.25 transparencies, excellent-quality color prints. Buys one-time rights.

COLUMNS/DEPARTMENTS Why Farm Wives Age Fast (humor), I Remember When (nostalgia), and Country Decorating. Length: 500-1,000 words. **Buys 10-12 mss/year.** Query or send ms.

FICTION Main character *must* be a country woman. All fiction must have a country setting. Fiction must have a positive, upbeat message. Includes fiction in every issue. Would buy more fiction if stories suitable for our audience were sent our way. No contemporary, urban pieces that deal with divorce, drugs, etc. Send complete ms. Length: 750-1,000 words.

POETRY Needs light verse, traditional. Poetry must have rhythm and rhyme. It must be country-related, positive, and upbeat. Always looking for seasonal poetry. Buys 6-12 poems/year. Submit maximum 6 poems. Length: 4-24 lines. **Pays $10-25/poem plus one contribtor's copy.**

TIPS "We have broadened our focus to include country women, not just women on farms and ranches but also women who live in a small town or country home and/or simply have an interest in country-oriented topics. This allows freelancers a wider scope in material. Write as clearly and with as much zest and enthusiasm as possible. We love good quotes, supporting materials (names, places, etc.) and strong leads and closings. Readers relate strongly to where they live and the lifestyle they've chosen. They want to be informed and entertained, and that's just exactly why they subscribe. Readers are busy—not too busy to read—but when they do sit down, they want good writing, reliable information and something that feels like a reward. How-to, humor, personal experience and nostalgia are areas most open to freelancers. Profiles, to a certain degree, are also open. Be accurate and fresh in approach."

$$$$ GLAMOUR

Condé Nast, 1 World Trade Center, New York NY 10007. (212)286-2860. **Fax:** (212)286-8336. **Website:** www.glamour.com. **Contact:** Cyndi Leive, editor-in-chief. Monthly magazine covering subjects ranging from fashion, beauty, health, personal relationships, career, travel, food, and entertainment. *Glamour* is edited for the contemporary woman. It informs her of current trends, recommends how she can adapt them to her needs, and motivates her to take action. Estab. 1939. Circ. 2.3 million. No kill fee. Accepts queries by mail. Accepts simultaneous submissions.

Query before submitting.

NONFICTION Needs personal experience, travel. Pays expenses of writers on assignment.

PHOTOS Only uses professional photographers.

$$$$ LADIES' HOME JOURNAL

Meredith Corp., P.O.Box 37508, Boone IA 50037. 212-499-2087. **E-mail:** lhjcustserv@cdsfulfillment.com. **Website:** www.divinecaroline.com/ladies-home-journal. **50% freelance written.** Monthly magazine focusing on issues of concern to women 30-45. *Ladies' Home Journal* is for active, empowered women who are evolving in new directions. It addresses informational needs with highly focused features and articles on a variety of topics: self, style, family, home, world, health, and food. Estab. 1882. Circ. 4.1 million. Pays on acceptance. Offers 25% kill fee. Publishes ms an average of 4-12 months after acceptance. Editorial lead time 4 months. Accepts queries by mail, e-mail. Accepts simultaneous submissions. Responds in 3 months to queries. Guidelines available online.

NONFICTION Send 1-2 page query, SASE, résumé, and clips via mail or e-mail (preferred). Length: 2,000-3,000 words. **Pays $2,000-4,000.** Pays expenses of writers on assignment.

PHOTOS *LHJ* arranges for its own photography almost all the time. State availability. Captions, identification of subjects, model releases required. Offers variable payment for photos accepted with ms. Rights bought vary with submission.

FICTION Only short stories and novels submitted by an agent or publisher will be considered. No poetry of any kind. **Buys 12 mss/year.** Send complete ms. Length: 2,000-2,500 words.

$$ LONG ISLAND WOMAN

P.O. Box 176, Malverne NY 11565. **E-mail:** editor@liwomanonline.com. **Website:** www.liwomanonline.com. **20% freelance written.** Monthly magazine covering issues of importance to women (age 45-69) in Nassau and Suffolk counties in New York—health, finance, arts, entertainment, fitness, travel, home. Estab. 2001. Circ. 30,000. Byline given. Pays within 1 month of publication. Offers 20% kill fee. Publishes an average of 3 months after acceptance. Editorial lead time 3 months. Submit seasonal material 3 months in advance. Accepts queries by e-mail. Accepts simultaneous submissions. Auto response and response when/if interested. Sample copy for $5. Guidelines online.

Responds if interested in using reprints that were submitted.

NONFICTION Needs essays, humor, interview, memoir, nostalgic, travel. **Buys 12-15 mss/year.** Send complete ms. Length: 600-2,250 words. **Pays $70-200.**

REPRINTS Length: 500-2,250 words. Pays $40-100.

PHOTOS State availability of or send photos. Captions, identification of subjects, model releases required.

COLUMNS/DEPARTMENTS Humor; Health Issues; Adult Family Issues; Financial and Business Issues; Book Reviews and Books; Arts and Entertainment; Travel and Leisure; Home and Garden; Fitness.

$$ NA'AMAT WOMAN

21515 Vanowen Street, Suite 102, Canoga Park CA 91303. (818)431-2200. **E-mail:** naamat@naamat.org; judith@naamat.org. **Website:** www.naamat.org. **Contact:** Judith Sokoloff, editor. **80% freelance written.** Published 3 times per year, covering Jewish issues/subjects. "Magazine covering a wide variety of subjects of interest to the Jewish community— including political and social issues, arts, profiles; many articles about Israel and women's issues. Fiction must have a Jewish theme. Readers are the American Jewish community." Estab. 1926. Circ. 10,000. Byline given. Pays on publication. No kill fee. Publishes ms an average of 6 months after acceptance. Submit seasonal material 6 months in advance. Accepts queries by e-mail. Accepts simultaneous submissions. Responds in 4 weeks to queries. Responds in 3 months to mss. Sample copy for $2. Guidelines by e-mail.

NONFICTION Needs book excerpts, essays, historical, interview, personal experience, photo feature, travel, Jewish topics & issues, political & social issues & women's issues. **Buys 16-20 mss/year.** Send complete ms. **Pays 10-20¢/word for assigned and unsolicited articles.** Pays expenses of writers on assignment.

PHOTOS State availability. Reviews GIF/JPEG files. Negotiates payment individually. Buys one-time rights.

FICTION "We want serious fiction, with insight, reflection and consciousness." Needs novel excerpts, literary with Jewish content. "We do not want fiction that is mostly dialogue. No corny Jewish humor. No Holocaust fiction." **Buys 1-2 mss/year. mss/year.** Query with published clips or send complete ms. Length: 2,000-3,000 words. **Pays 10-20¢/word for assigned articles and for unsolicited articles.**

TIPS "No maudlin nostalgia or romance; no hackneyed Jewish humor."

$$ SKIRT!

Morris Communications, 1 Henrietta St., First Floor, Charleston SC 29403. (843)958-0027. **Fax:** (843)958-0029. **E-mail:** submissions@skirt.com. **Website:** www.skirt.com. **Contact:** Shelley Young, editor. **10 percent freelance written.** Monthly magazine covering women's interest. *Skirt!* is all about women—their work, play, families, creativity, style, health, wealth, bodies, and souls. The magazine's attitude is spirited, independent, outspoken, serious, playful, irreverent, sometimes controversial, and always passionate. Estab. 1994. Circ. 285,000. Byline given. Pays on publication. No kill fee. Publishes ms an average of 2 months after acceptance. Editorial lead time 2 months. Submit seasonal material 2 months in advance. Accepts queries by e-mail. Accepts simultaneous submissions. Responds in 1-2 months. Guidelines online.

NONFICTION Needs essays, personal experience. "Do not send feature articles. We only accept submissions of completed personal essays that will work with our monthly themes available online." **Buys 100+ mss/year.** Send complete ms (preferably as a Rich Text Format attachment) via e-mail. Publishes personal essays on topics related to women and women's interests. Length: 800-1,100 words. **Pays $100-200.**

TIPS "Surprise and charm us. We look for fearless essays that take chances with content and subject. *Skirt!* is not your average women's magazine. We push the envelope and select content that makes our readers think. Please review guidelines and themes online before submitting."

TRADE JOURNALS

Many writers who pick up *Writer's Market* for the first time do so with the hope of selling an article to one of the popular, high-profile consumer magazines found on newsstands and in bookstores. Many of those writers are surprised to find an entire world of magazine publishing exists outside the realm of commercial magazines—trade journals. Writers who *have* discovered trade journals have found a market that offers the chance to publish regularly in subject areas they find interesting, editors who are typically more accessible than their commercial counterparts, and pay rates that rival those of the big-name magazines.

Trade journal is the general term for any publication focusing on a particular occupation or industry. Other terms used to describe the different types of trade publications are business, technical, and professional journals. They are read by truck drivers, bricklayers, farmers, fishermen, heart surgeons, and just about everyone else working in a trade or profession. Trade periodicals are sharply angled to the specifics of the professions on which they report. They offer business-related news, features, and service articles that will foster their readers' professional development.

Writers for trade journals have to either possess knowledge about the field in question or be able to report it accurately from interviews with those who do. Writers who have or can develop a good grasp of a specialized body of knowledge will find trade magazine editors who are eager to hear from them.

An ideal way to begin your foray into trade journals is to write for those that report on your present profession. If you don't have experience in a profession but can demonstrate an ability to understand (and write about) the intricacies and issues of a particular trade that interests you, editors will still be willing to hear from you.

ADVERTISING, MARKETING & PR

DECA DIRECT

1908 Association Dr., Reston VA 20191. (703)860-5000. **E-mail:** info@deca.org. **E-mail:** christopher_young@deca.org. **Website:** www.decadirect.org. **Contact:** Christopher Young, editor in chief. **30% freelance written.** Quarterly magazine covering marketing, professional development, business, and career training during school year (no issues published May-August). *DECA Direct* is the membership magazine for DECA—The Association of Marketing Students, primarily ages 15-19 in all 50 states, the U.S. territories, Germany, and Canada. The magazine is delivered through the classroom. Students are interested in developing professional, leadership, and career skills. Estab. 1947. Circ. 160,000. Byline given. Pays on publication. No kill fee. Editorial lead time 3 months. Submit seasonal material 4 months in advance. Accepts queries by e-mail. Accepts simultaneous submissions. Sample copy free online.

NONFICTION Needs essays, general interest, how-to, interview, personal experience. **Buys 10 mss/year.** Submit a paragraph description of your article by e-mail. Length: 500-1,000 words. **Pays $125 for assigned articles. Pays $100 for unsolicited articles.** Pays expenses of writers on assignment.

REPRINTS Send typed ms and information about when and where the material previously appeared. Pays 85% of amount paid for an original article.

COLUMNS/DEPARTMENTS Professional Development; Leadership, 500-1,000 words. **Buys 6 mss/year.** Send complete ms. **Pays $75-100.**

TIPS "Articles can be theme specific, but we accept a variety of articles that are appropriate for our readership on topics such as community service, leadership development, or professionalism. The primary readership of the magazine is compromised of high school students, and articles should be relevant to their needs and interests. In most cases, articles should not promote the products or services of a specific company or organization; however, you may use examples to convey concepts or principles."

FORMAT MAGAZINE

315 5th Ave. NW, St. Paul MN 55112. **Website:** www.formatmag.com. **90% freelance written.** Estab. 1954. Circ. 6,000. Byline given. Pays on publication. No kill fee. Editorial lead time 1 months. Accepts simultaneous submissions.

"*Format* Magazine is your source for the most current and compelling information relating to urban aesthetics. *Format* strives to maintain a broad scope, encompassing elements from every corner of the urban art world, including, but not limited to: design, electro, graffiti, hip hop, lowbrow, menswear, punk, skate, sneakers, street art, streetwear, tattoo, vinyl toys."

NONFICTION Needs general interest, historical, humor, interview, photo feature. **Buys 2 mss/year.** Length: 300-800 words. **Pays $25-50.**

PHOTOS Send photos. Identification of subjects required. Negotiates payment individually. Buys one-time rights.

COLUMNS/DEPARTMENTS Advertising (ad humor), 400 words. **Buys 12 mss/year. Pays $25-50.**

FILLERS Needs anecdotes, facts, gags, newsbreaks, short humor. **Buys 12 mss/year.** Length: 100-300 words. **Pays $10-25.**

INCENTIVE

Northstar Travel Media LLC, 100 Lighting Way, Secaucus NJ 07094. (646)380-6247; (646)380-6251. **E-mail:** valonzo@ntmllc.com; apalmer@successfulmeetings.com. **Website:** www.incentivemag.com. **Contact:** Vincent Alonzo, editor in chief; Alex Palmer, managing editor. Monthly magazine covering sales promotion and employee motivation: managing and marketing through motivation. Estab. 1905. Circ. 41,000. Byline given. Pays on acceptance. No kill fee. Publishes ms an average of 3 months after acceptance. Accepts queries by mail, e-mail. Accepts simultaneous submissions. Responds in 1 month to queries; in 2 months to mss. Sample copy for SAE with 9x12 envelope.

NONFICTION Needs general interest, how-to, interview, travel, corporate case studies. **Buys 48 mss/year.** Query with published clips. Length: 1,000-2,000 words. **Pays $250-700 for assigned articles. Does not pay for unsolicited articles.** Pays expenses of writers on assignment.

REPRINTS Send tearsheet and information about when and where the material previously appeared. Pays 50% of the amount paid for an original article.

PHOTOS Send photos. Identification of subjects required. Reviews contact sheets, transparencies. Offers some additional payment for photos accepted with ms.

TIPS "Read the publication, then query."

$$ MIDWEST MEETINGS®

Hennen Publishing, 302 Sixth St. W., Suite A, Brookings SD 57006. (605)692-9559. **Fax:** (605)692-9031. **E-mail:** info@midwestmeetings.com; editor@midwestmeetings.com. **Website:** www.midwestmeetings.com. **Contact:** Randy Hennen. **20% freelance written.** Quarterly magazine covering meetings/conventions industry. "We provide information and resources to meeting/convention planners with a Midwest focus." Estab. 1996. Circ. 28,500. Byline given. Pays on acceptance. Publishes ms an average of 5 months after acceptance. Editorial lead time 3 months. Submit seasonal material 3 months in advance. Accepts queries by e-mail. Accepts simultaneous submissions. Sample copy free. Guidelines by e-mail.

NONFICTION Needs essays, general interest, historical, how-to, humor, interview, personal experience, travel. Does not want marketing pieces related to specific hotels/meeting facilities. **Buys 15-20 mss/year.** Send complete ms. Length: 500-1,000 words. **Pays 5-50¢/word.** Pays expenses of writers on assignment.

PHOTOS Send photos. Captions, identification of subjects and permission statements/photo releases required. Reviews JPEG/EPS/TIF files (300 dpi). Offers no additional payment for photos accepted with ms. Buys one time rights.

TIPS "If you were a meeting/event planner, what information would help you perform your job better? We like lots of quotes from industry experts, insider tips, personal experience stories, etc. If you're not sure, e-mail the editor."

$$ O'DWYER'S PR REPORT

271 Madison Ave., #600, New York NY 10016. (212)679-2471; (866)395-7710. **Fax:** (212)683-2750. **E-mail:** john@odwyerpr.com. **Website:** www.odwyerpr.com. **Contact:** John O'Dwyer, associate publisher/editor. Monthly magazine providing PR articles. *O'Dwyer's* has been covering public relations, marketing communications, and related fields for over 40 years. The company provides the latest news and information about PR firms and professionals, the media, corporations, legal issues, jobs, technology, and much more through its website, weekly newsletter, monthly magazine, directories, and guides. Many of the contributors are PR people publicizing themselves while analyzing something. Byline given. No kill fee. Accepts queries by mail. Accepts simultaneous submissions.

NONFICTION Needs opinion. Query. **Pays $250.** Pays expenses of writers on assignment.

$$ PROMO MAGAZINE

Access Intelligence, 761 Main Avenue, Norwalk CT 06851. (203)899-8442. **E-mail:** podell@accessintel.com. **Website:** www.chiefmarketer.com/promotional-marketing. **Contact:** Patricia Odell, senior editor. **5% freelance written.** Monthly magazine covering promotion marketing. *Promo* serves marketers, and stories must be informative, well written, and familiar with the subject matter. Estab. 1987. Circ. 25,000. Byline given. Pays on publication. Offers 25% kill fee. Publishes ms an average of 2 months after acceptance. Editorial lead time 3 months. Submit seasonal material 3 months in advance. Accepts simultaneous submissions. Responds in 1 month to queries. Sample copy for $5.

NONFICTION Needs general interest, how-to, interview, new product. No general marketing stories not heavily involved in promotions. Generally does not accept unsolicited mss; query first. **Buys 6-10 mss/year.** Query with published clips. **Pays $1,000 maximum for assigned articles. Pays $500 maximum for unsolicited articles.** Pays expenses of writers on assignment.

PHOTOS State availability. Captions, identification of subjects, model releases required. Reviews contact sheets, negatives. Negotiates payment individually.

TIPS "Understand that our stories aim to teach marketing professionals about successful promotion strategies. Case studies or new promos have the best chance."

$$ SIGN BUILDER ILLUSTRATED

Simmons-Boardman Publishing Corp., 55 Broad St., 26th Floor, New York NY 10004. (212)620-7244. **E-mail:** jwooten@sbpub.com; abray@sbpub.com. **Website:** www.signshop.com. **Contact:** Jeff Wooten, editor; Ashley Bray, managing editor. **40% freelance written.** Monthly magazine covering sign and graphic industry. *Sign Builder Illustrated* targets sign professionals where they work: on the shop floor. Topics cover the broadest spectrum of the sign industry, from design to fabrication, installation, maintenance, and repair. Readers own a similarly wide range of shops, including commercial, vinyl, sign erection and maintenance, electrical and neon, architectural, and awnings. Estab. 1987. Circ. 19,000. Byline given. Pays on acceptance. Offers 10% kill fee. Publishes ms an average of 3 months after acceptance. Editorial lead time 3 months. Submit seasonal material 4 months in advance. Accepts queries by mail, e-mail, phone. Accepts simultaneous submissions. Responds in 1 month to queries. Sample copy and writer's guidelines free.

NONFICTION Needs how-to, interview, photo feature, technical. **Buys 50-60 mss/year.** Query. Length: 1,000-1,500 words. **Pays $250-400 for assigned articles.** Pays expenses of writers on assignment.

PHOTOS Send photos. Captions, identification of subjects required. Reviews 3x5 prints. Negotiates payment individually,. Buys all rights.

TIPS "Be very knowledgeable about a portion of the sign industry you are covering. We want our readers to come away from each article with at least 1 good idea, 1 new technique, or 1 more 'trick of the trade.' At the same time, we don't want a purely textbook listing of 'do this, do that.' Our readers enjoy *Sign Builder Illustrated* because the publication speaks to them in a clear and lively fashion, from 1 sign professional to another. We want to engage the reader who has been in the business for some time. While there might be a place for basic instruction in new techniques, our average paid subscriber has been in business over 20 years, employs over 7 people, and averages $800,000 in annual sales. These people aren't neophytes content with retread articles they can find anywhere. It's important for our writers to use anecdotes and examples drawn from the daily sign business."

$$$ SOCAL MEETINGS + EVENTS MAGAZINE

Tiger Oak Publications, One Tiger Oak Plaza, 900 S. Third St., Minneapolis MN 55415. **Fax:** (612)338-0532. **E-mail:** bobby.hart@tigeroak.com. **Website:** http://meetingsmags.com. **Contact:** Bobby Hart, managing editor. **80% freelance written.** Meetings + Events Media Group, including Minnesota Meetings + Events, Illinois Meetings + Events, Colorado Meetings & Events, Michigan Meetings + Events, California Meetings + Events, Texas Meetings + Events, Northwest Meetings + Events, Mountain Meetings, Pennsylvania Meetings + Evens and New Jersey Meetings + Events is a group of premier quarterly trade magazines for meetings planners and hospitality service providers throughout the US. Thesemagazines aim to report on and promote businesses involved in the meetings and events industry, covering current and emerging trends, people and venues in the meetings and events industry in their respective regions. Estab. 1993. Circ. approximately 20,000 per title. Byline given. Pays on acceptance. Offers 20% kill fee. Publishes ms an average of 4 months after acceptance. Editorial lead time 4-6 months. Submit seasonal material 6 months in advance. Accepts queries by mail. Accepts simultaneous submissions. Responds in 1-2 weeks to queries.

NONFICTION Needs general interest, historical, interview, new product, opinion, personal experience, photo feature, technical, travel. **Buys 30 mss/year.** "Each query should tell us: What the story will be about; how you will tell the story (what sources you will use, how you will conduct research, etc.); why is the story pertinent to the market audience. Please also attach PDFs of 3 published magazine articles." Length: 600-1,500 words. **The average department length story (4-700 words) pays about $2-300 and the average feature length story (1,000-1,200 words) pays up to $800, depending on the story. These rates are not guaranteed and vary.**

PHOTOS State availability. Identification of subjects, model releases required. Negotiates payment individually. Buys one-time rights.

COLUMNS/DEPARTMENTS Meet + Eat (restaurant reviews); Facility Focus (venue reviews); Regional Spotlight (city review), 1,000 words. **Buys 30 mss/year.** Query with published clips. **Pays $400-600.**

TIPS "Familiarization with the meetings and events industry is critical, as well as knowing how to write for a trade magazine. Writers experienced in writing for the trade magazine business industry are preferred."

$$$ TEXAS MEETINGS + EVENTS

Tiger Oak Publications, One Tiger Oak Plaza, 900 S. 3rd St., Minneapolis MN 55401. (612)548-3180. **Fax:** (612)548-3181. **E-mail:** bobby.hart@tigeroak.com. **Website:** http://tx.meetingsmags.com. **Contact:** Bobby Hart, managing editor. **80% freelance written.** Quarterly magazine covering meetings and events industry. *Texas Meetings & Events* magazine is the premier trade publication for meetings planners and hospitality service providers in the state. This magazine aims to report on and promote businesses involved in the meetings and events industry. The magazine covers current and emerging trends, people and venues in the meetings and events industry in the state. Estab. 1993. Circ. 20,000. Byline given. Pays on acceptance. Offers 20% kill fee. Publishes ms an average of 4 months after acceptance. Editorial lead time 4-6 months. Submit seasonal material 6 months in advance. Accepts queries by mail. Accepts simultaneous submissions. Responds in 1-2 weeks to queries. Guidelines online.

NONFICTION Needs general interest, historical, interview, new product, opinion, personal experience, photo feature, technical, travel. **Buys 30 mss/year.** Query with published clips of 3 magazine articles. Length: 600-1,500 words. **Pays $400-800.**

PHOTOS State availability. Identification of subjects, model releases required. Negotiates payment individually. Buys one-time rights.

COLUMNS/DEPARTMENTS Meet + Eat (restaurant reviews); Facility Focus (venue reviews); Regional Spotlight (city review), 1,000 words. **Buys 30 mss/year.** Query with published clips. **Pays $400-600.**

TIPS "Familiarization with the meetings and events industry is critical, as well as knowing how to write for a trade magazine. Writers experienced in writing for the trade magazine business industry are preferred."

ART, DESIGN & COLLECTIBLES

$$ AIRBRUSH ACTION MAGAZINE

Action, Inc., P.O. Box 438, Allenwood NJ 08720. (732)223-7878; (800)876-2472. **E-mail:** ceo@airbrushaction.com. **Website:** www.airbrushaction.com. **Contact:** Cliff Stieglitz, publisher. **80% freelance written.** Bimonthly magazine covering the spectrum of airbrush applications: automotive and custom paint applications, illustration, T-shirt airbrushing, fine art, automotive and sign painting, hobby/craft applications, wall murals, fingernails, temporary tattoos, artist profiles, reviews, and more. Estab. 1985. Circ. 35,000. Byline given. Pays 1 month after publication. Publishes ms an average of 6 months after acceptance. Editorial lead time 6 months. Submit seasonal material 6 months in advance. Accepts queries by mail, e-mail. Accepts simultaneous submissions.

NONFICTION Needs how-to, humor, inspirational, interview, new product, personal experience, technical. Doesn't want anything unrelated to airbrush. Query with published clips. **Pays 15¢/word.** Pays expenses of writers on assignment.

PHOTOS Digital images preferred. Send photos. Captions, identification of subjects, model releases required. Negotiates payment individually. Buys all rights.

COLUMNS/DEPARTMENTS Query with published clips.

TIPS "Send bio and writing samples. Send well-written technical information pertaining to airbrush art. We publish a lot of artist profiles—they all sound the same. Looking for new pizzazz!"

$$ ANTIQUEWEEK

MidCountry Media, 27 N. Jefferson St., P.O. Box 90, Knightstown IN 46148. (800)876-5133, ext. 131. **Fax:** (800)695-8153. **E-mail:** connie@antiqueweek.com. **Website:** www.antiqueweek.com. **Contact:** Connie Swaim, managing editor. **90% freelance written.** Weekly tabloid covering antiques and collectibles with 3 editions: Eastern, Central, and National, plus the monthly *AntiqueWest*. *AntiqueWeek* has a wide range of readership from dealers and auctioneers to collectors, both advanced and novice. Readers demand accurate information presented in an entertaining style. Estab. 1968. Circ. 50,000. Byline given. Pays the month after publication. Offers 10% kill fee or $25. Submit seasonal material 1 month in advance. Accepts queries by e-mail. Accepts simultaneous submissions. Sample copy free. Guidelines by e-mail.

NONFICTION Needs historical, how-to, interview, opinion, personal experience, antique show and auction reports, feature articles on particular types of antiques and collectibles. **Buys 400-500 mss/year.** Query. Length: 1,000-2,000 words. **Pays $50-250.** Pays expenses of writers on assignment.

REPRINTS Send electronic copy with rights for sale noted and information about when and where the material previously appeared.

PHOTOS All material must be submitted via e-mail. Send photos. Identification of subjects required.

TIPS "Writers should know their topics thoroughly. Feature articles must be well researched and clearly written. An interview and profile article with a knowledgeable collector might be the break for a first-time contributor. We seek a balanced mix of information on traditional antiques and 20th-century collectibles."

$ THE APPRAISERS STANDARD

New England Appraisers Association, 6973 Crestridge Dr., Memphis TN 38119. (901)758-2659. **E-mail:** etuten551@aol.com. **Website:** www.newenglandappraisers.org. **Contact:** Edward Tuten, editor. **50% freelance written. Works with a small number of**

new/unpublished writers each year. Quarterly publication covering the appraisals of antiques, art, collectibles, jewelry, coins, stamps, and real estate. Estab. 1980. Circ. 1,000. Short bio and byline given. Pays on publication. No kill fee. Publishes ms an average of 1 year after acceptance. Submit seasonal material 2 months in advance. Accepts queries by mail, e-mail. Accepts simultaneous submissions. Responds in 1 month to queries. Responds in 2 months to mss. Sample copy for 9x12 SAE with $1 postage. Guidelines for #10 SASE.

NONFICTION Needs interview, personal experience, technical, travel. Send complete ms. Length: 700 words. **Pays $60.**

REPRINTS "Send typed manuscript with rights for sale noted and information about when and where the material previously appeared."

PHOTOS Send photos. Identification of subjects required. Reviews negatives, prints. Offers no additional payment for photos accepted with ms. Buys one time rights.

TIPS "Interviewing members of the association for articles, reviewing, shows, and large auctions are all ways for writers who are not in the field to write articles for us. Articles should be geared to provide information which will help the appraisers with ascertaining value, detecting forgeries or reproductions, or simply providing advice on appraising the articles. I would like writers to focus on particular types of antiques: i.e. types of furniture, glass, artwork, etc., giving information on the history of this type of antique, good photos, recent sale prices, etc."

$ ART MATERIALS RETAILER

Fahy-Williams Publishing, Inc., 171 Reed St., P.O. Box 1080, Geneva NY 14456. (315)789-0458. **Fax:** (315)789-4263. **E-mail:** tmanzer@fwpi.com. **Website:** www.artmaterialsretailer.com. Publisher: J. Kevin Fahy (kfahy@fwpi.com). **Contact:** Tina Manzer, editorial director. **10% freelance written.** Quarterly magazine covering retail stores that sell art materials. Offers book reviews, retailer-recommended products, and profiles of stores from around the country. Estab. 1998. Byline given. Pays on publication. No kill fee. Editorial lead time 2 months. Submit seasonal material 3 months in advance. Accepts simultaneous submissions. Responds in 3 weeks to queries. Responds in 3 months to mss. Sample copy and writer's guidelines free.

NONFICTION Needs book excerpts, how-to, interview, personal experience. **Buys 2 mss/year.** Send complete ms. Length: 1,500-3,000 words. **Pays $50-250.** Pays expenses of writers on assignment.

PHOTOS State availability. Identification of subjects required. Reviews transparencies. Offers no additional payment for photos accepted with ms. Buys one-time rights.

FILLERS Needs anecdotes, facts, newsbreaks. **Buys 5 mss/year.** Length: 500-1,500 words. **Pays $50-125.**

TIPS "We like to review mss rather than queries. Artwork (photos, drawings, etc.) is a real plus. We (and our readers) enjoy practical, nuts-and-bolts, news-you-can-use articles."

$$$ HOW

F+W, a Content + eCommerce Company, 10151 Carver Rd., Suite 300, Blue Ash OH 45242. (513)531-2690. **Fax:** (513)531-2902. **E-mail:** editorial@howdesign.com. **Website:** www.howdesign.com. **75% freelance written.** Bi-monthly magazine covering graphic design profession. *HOW: Design Ideas at Work* strives to serve the business, technological and creative needs of graphic-design professionals. The magazine provides a practical mix of essential business information, up-to-date technological tips, the creative whys and hows behind noteworthy projects, and profiles of professionals who are impacting design. The ultimate goal of *HOW* is to help designers, whether they work for a design firm or for an inhouse design department, run successful, creative, profitable studios. Estab. 1985. Circ. 40,000. Byline given. Pays on acceptance. No kill fee. Accepts simultaneous submissions. Responds in 6 weeks to queries.

NONFICTION Special issues: Self-Promotion Annual (September/October); Business Annual (November/December); In-House Design Annual (January/February); International Annual of Design (March/April); Creativity/Paper/Stock Photography (May/June); Digital Design Annual (July/August). No how-to articles for beginning artists or fine-art-oriented articles. **Buys 40 mss/year.** Query with published clips and samples of subject's work, artwork, or design. Length: 1,500-2,000 words. **Pays $700-900.** Pays expenses of writers on assignment.

PHOTOS State availability. Captions required. Reviews information updated and verified. Buys one-time rights.

COLUMNS/DEPARTMENTS Creativity (focuses on creative exercises and inspiration) 1,200-1,500 words. In-House Issues (focuses on business and creativity issues for corporate design groups), 1,200-1,500 words. Business (focuses on business issue for design firm owners), 1,200-1, 500 words. **Buys Number of columns: 35. mss/year.** Query with published clips. **Pays $250-400.**

TIPS "We look for writers who can recognize graphic designers on the cutting-edge of their industry, both creatively and business-wise. Writers must have an eye for detail, and be able to relay *HOW*'s editorial style in an interesting, concise manner—without omitting any details. Showing you've done your homework on a subject—and that you can go beyond asking those same old questions—will give you a big advantage."

$$ THE PASTEL JOURNAL

Peak Media Properties, 9912 Carver Rd., Blue Ash OH 45242. **E-mail:** ahevener@peakmediaproperties.com. **Website:** www.pasteljournal.com. **Contact:** Anne Hevener, editor. Bimonthly magazine covering pastel art. *Pastel Journal* is the only national magazine devoted to the medium of pastel. Addressing the working professional as well as passionate amateurs, *Pastel Journal* offers inspiration, information, and instruction to our readers. Estab. 1999. Circ. 22,000. Byline given. Pays on acceptance. Offers 25% kill fee. Publishes ms an average of 3-6 months after acceptance. Editorial lead time 6 months. Submit seasonal material 6 months in advance. Accepts queries by mail, e-mail. Accepts simultaneous submissions. Responds in 4-6 weeks to queries. Guidelines online.

NONFICTION Needs how-to, interview, new product, profile. Does not want articles that aren't art-related. Review magazine before submitting. Query with or without published clips. Length: 500-2,000 words. **Payment does not exceed $600.**

PHOTOS State availability of or send photos. Captions required. Reviews transparencies, prints, GIF/JPEG files. Offers no additional payment for photos accepted with ms. Buys all rights.

$$ PRINT

F+W, a Content + eCommerce Company, 10151 Carver Rd., Suite 300, Blue Ash OH 45242. (513)531-2690. **E-mail:** info@printmag.com. **Website:** www.printmag.com. **75% freelance written.** Quarterly magazine covering graphic design and visual culture. *PRINT*'s articles, written by design specialists and cultural critics, focus on the social, political and historical context of graphic design, and on the places where consumer culture and popular culture meet. Aims to produce a general interest magazine for professionals with engagingly written text and lavish illustrations. By covering a broad spectrum of topics, both international and local, *Print* tries to demonstrate the significance of design in the world at large. Estab. 1940. Circ. 45,000. Byline given. Pays on acceptance. Offers 25% kill fee. Publishes ms an average of 2 months after acceptance. Editorial lead time 3 months. Submit seasonal material 3 months in advance. Accepts queries by e-mail. Accepts simultaneous submissions. Responds in 2 weeks to queries. Responds in 1 month to mss.

NONFICTION Needs book excerpts, essays, interview, opinion, photo feature, profile, reviews. **Buys 35-40 mss/year.** Query with published clips. Length: 500-3,500 words. **Pays 50¢/word.**

COLUMNS/DEPARTMENTS Query with published clips. **Pays 50¢/word.**

TIPS "Be well versed in issues related to the field of graphic design; don't submit ideas that are too general or geared to nonprofessionals."

$ PROFESSIONAL ARTIST

Turnstile Media Group, 1500 Park Center Dr., Orlando FL 32835. (407)563-7000. **Fax:** (407)563-7099. **E-mail:** nhassanein@professionalartistmag.com. **Website:** www.professionalartistmag.com. **Contact:** Nada Hassanein, associate editor. **75% freelance written.** Monthly magazine. *Professional Artist* is dedicated to providing independent visual artists from all backgrounds with the insights, encouragement and business strategies they need to make a living with their artwork. Estab. 1986. Circ. 20,000. Pays on publication. No kill fee. Accepts simultaneous submissions. Sample print copy for $5. Guidelines online.

Welcomes nuts-and-bolts, practical articles of interest to professional visual artists, emerging or professional. Examples: How-to's, first-person stories on how an artist has built his career or an aspect of it, interviews with artists (business/career-building emphasis), web strategies, and pieces on business practices and other topics of use to artists. The tone of magazine is practical, and uplifting.

NONFICTION Needs essays, how-to, interview, cartoons, art law, including pending legislation that affects artists (copyright law, Internet regulations, etc.). Does not run reviews or art historical pieces, nor writing characterized by "critic-speak," philosophical hyperbole, psychological arrogance, politics, or New Age religion. Also, does not condone a get-rich-quick attitude. Send complete ms. **Pays $150-350.**

REPRINTS Send photocopy or typed ms and information about when and where the material previously appeared. Pays $50.

COLUMNS/DEPARTMENTS "If an artist or freelancer sends us good articles regularly, and based on results we feel that he is able to produce a column at least 3 times per year, we will invite him to be a contributing writer. If a gifted artist-writer can commit to producing an article on a monthly basis, we will offer him a regular column and the title contributing editor." Send complete ms.

TIPS "We strongly suggest that you read a copy of the publication before submitting a proposal. Most queries are rejected because they are too general for our audience."

$$ WATERCOLOR ARTIST

Peak Media Properties, 9912 Carver Rd., Blue Ash OH 45242. **E-mail:** ahevener@peakmediaproperties.com. **Website:** www.watercolorartistmagazine.com. **Contact:** Anne Hevener, editor. Bimonthly magazine covering water media arts. Estab. 1984. Circ. 44,000. Byline given. Pays on acceptance. Publishes ms an average of 3-6 months after acceptance. Editorial lead time 6 months. Submit seasonal material 6 months in advance. Accepts queries by mail. Accepts simultaneous submissions. Writer's guidelines available at www.artistsnetwork.com/contactus.

"*Watercolor Artist* is the definitive source of how-to instruction and creative inspiration for artists working in water-based media."

NONFICTION Needs book excerpts, essays, how-to, inspirational, interview, new product, personal experience. Does not want articles that aren't art-related. Review magazine before submitting. **Buys 36 mss/year.** Send query letter with images. Length: 350-2,500 words. **Pays $150-600.** Pays expenses of writers on assignment.

PHOTOS State availability of or send photos. Captions required. Reviews transparencies, prints, slides, GIF/JPEG files. Buys one-time rights.

AUTO & TRUCK

$ AUTO RESTORER

i5 Publishing, Inc., 3 Burroughs, Irvine CA 92618. (213)385-2222. **Fax:** (213)385-8565. **E-mail:** tkade@i5publishing.com. **Website:** www.autorestorermagazine.com. **Contact:** Ted Kade, editor. **85% freelance written.** Monthly magazine covering auto restoration. "Our readers own old cars, and they work on them. We help our readers by providing as much practical, how-to information as we can about restoration and old cars." Estab. 1989. Circ. 60,000. Pays on publication. Publishes mss 3 months after acceptance. Submit seasonal material 4 months in advance. Accepts queries by mail, e-mail, fax. Accepts simultaneous submissions. Responds in 2 months to queries. Sample copy: $7. Guidelines free.

NONFICTION Needs how-to, new product, photo feature. **Buys 60 mss/year.** Query first. Length: 250-2,000 words. **Pays $150/published page, including photos and illustrations.** Pays expenses of writers on assignment.

PHOTOS Emphasizes restoration of collector cars and trucks. Readers are 98% male, professional/technical/managerial, ages 35-65. Buys 47 photos from freelancers/issue; 564 photos/year. Send photos. Model/property release preferred. Photo captions required; include year, make, and model of car; identification of people in photo. Reviews photos with accompanying ms only. Reviews contact sheets, transparencies, 5x7 prints. Looks for "technically proficient or dramatic photos of various automotive subjects, auto portraits, detail shots, action photos, good angles, composition, and lighting. We're also looking for photos to illustrate how-to articles such as how to repair a damaged fender or how to repair a carburetor.". Pays $50 for b&w cover; $35 for b&w inside. Pays on publication. Credit line given. Buys first North American serial rights.

TIPS "Interview the owner of a restored car. Present advice to others on how to do a similar restoration. Seek advice from experts. Go light on history and nonspecific details. Make it something that the magazine regularly uses. Do automotive how-tos."

$$ BUSINESS FLEET

Bobit Publishing, 3520 Challenger St., Torrance CA 90503. (310)533-2400. **E-mail:** chris.brown@bobit.

com. **Website:** www.businessfleet.com. **Contact:** Chris Brown, executive editor. **10% freelance written.** Bimonthly magazine covering businesses which operate 10-50 company vehicles. Estab. 2000. Circ. 100,000. Byline given. Pays on publication. Offers 25% kill fee. Publishes ms an average of 3 months after acceptance. Editorial lead time 2 months. Submit seasonal material 2 months in advance. Accepts queries by mail, e-mail, fax. Accepts simultaneous submissions. Responds in 3 weeks to queries; 2 months to mss. Sample copy and guidelines free.

While it is a trade publication aimed at a business audience, *Business Fleet* has a lively, conversational style. The best way to get a feel for their "slant" is to read the magazine.

NONFICTION Needs how-to, interview, new product, personal experience, photo feature, technical. **Buys 16 mss/year.** Query with published clips. Length: 500-2,000 words. **Pays $100-400.** Pays expenses of writers on assignment.

PHOTOS State availability. Captions required. Reviews 3x5 prints. Negotiates payment individually. Buys one-time, reprint, and electronic rights.

TIPS "Our mission is to educate our target audience on more economical and efficient ways of operating company vehicles, and to inform the audience of the latest vehicles, products, and services available to small commercial companies. Be knowledgeable about automotive and fleet-oriented subjects."

$$ FENDERBENDER

DeWitt Publishing, 571 Snelling Avenue North, St. Paul MN 55104. (651)224-6207. **Fax:** (651)224-6212. **E-mail:** news@fenderbender.com; jweyer@fenderbender.com. **Website:** www.fenderbender.com. **Contact:** Jake Weyer, editor. **50% freelance written.** Monthly magazine covering automotive collision repair. Estab. 1999. Circ. 58,000. Byline given. Pays on publication. Offers 20% kill fee. Publishes ms an average of 2 months after acceptance. Editorial lead time 3 months. Submit seasonal material 6 months in advance. Accepts queries by e-mail. Accepts simultaneous submissions. Responds in 1-2 months to queries; 2-3 months to mss. Sample copy for SAE with 10x13 envelope and 6 first-class stamps. Guidelines online.

NONFICTION Needs expose, how-to, inspirational, interview, technical. Does not want personal narratives or any other first-person stories. No poems or creative writing mss. Query with published clips. Length: 1,800-2,500 words. **Pays 25-60¢/word.** Pays expenses of writers on assignment.

PHOTOS Send photos. Captions, identification of subjects, model releases required. Reviews PDF, GIF/JPEG files. Offers no additional payment for photos accepted with ms. Buys one-time rights.

COLUMNS/DEPARTMENTS Q&A, 600 words; Shakes, Rattles & Rollovers; Rearview Mirror. Query with published clips. **Pays 25-35¢/word.**

TIPS "Potential writers need to be knowledgeable about the auto collision repair industry. They should also know standard business practices and be able to explain to shop owners how they can run their businesses better."

$$ FLEETSOLUTIONS

NAFA Fleet Management Association, 125 Village Blvd., Suite 200, Princeton NJ 08540. (609)986-1063; (609)720-0882. **Fax:** (609)452-8004. **E-mail:** publications@nafa.org; ddunphy@nafa.org. **Website:** www.nafa.org. **Contact:** Donald W. Dunphy, communications manager/editor. **10% freelance written.** Magazine published 6 times/year covering automotive fleet management. Generally focuses on car, van, and light-duty truck management in US and Canadian corporations, government agencies, and utilities. Editorial emphasis is on general automotive issues; improving jobs skills, productivity, and professionalism; legislation and regulation; alternative fuels; safety; interviews with prominent industry personalities; technology; association news; public service fleet management; and light-duty truck fleet management. Estab. 1957. Circ. 4,000. Bylines provided. Pays on publication. No kill fee. Publishes ms an average of 4 months after acceptance. Editorial lead time 2 months. Accepts queries by mail. Accepts simultaneous submissions. Responds in 1 month to queries. Sample copy online.

NONFICTION Needs interview, technical. **Buys 24 mss/year.** Query with published clips. Length: 500-3,000 words. **Pays $500 maximum.**

PHOTOS State availability. Reviews electronic images.

$$$$ OVERDRIVE

Randall-Reilly Publishing, 3200 Rice Mine Rd. NE, Tuscaloosa AL 35406. (205)349-2990. **Fax:** (205)750-8070. **E-mail:** mheine@rrpub.com. **Website:** www.etrucker.com. **Contact:** Max Heine, editorial director. **5% freelance written.** Monthly magazine for independent truckers. Estab. 1961. Circ. 100,000. Byline given. Pays on publication. Offers 10% kill fee. Publishes ms an average of 2 months after acceptance. Accepts simultaneous submissions. Responds in 2 months to queries. Sample copy for 9x12 SASE. Digital copy online.

NONFICTION Needs essays, expose, how-to, interview, personal experience, photo feature, technical. Send complete ms. Length: 500-2,500 words. **Pays $300-1,500 for assigned articles.**

PHOTOS Photo fees negotiable. Buys all rights.

TIPS "Talk to independent truckers. Develop a good knowledge of their concerns as small-business owners, truck drivers, and individuals. We prefer articles that quote experts, people in the industry, and truckers, to first-person expositions on a subject. Get straight facts. Look for good material on truck safety, on effects of government regulations, and on rates and business relationships between independent truckers, brokers, carriers, and shippers."

$ ROADKING MAGAZINE

28 White Bridge Rd., Suite 209, Nashville TN 37205. (615)627-2250. **Fax:** (615)690-3401. **Website:** www.roadking.com. **80% freelance written.** Bimonthly magazine. *Road King* is published bimonthly for long-haul truckers. It celebrates the lifestyle and work and profiles interesting and/or successful drivers. It also reports on subjects of interest to our audience, including outdoors, vehicles, music, and trade issues. Estab. 1963. Circ. 229,900. Byline given. Pays 3 weeks after acceptance. Offers negotiable kill fee. Publishes ms an average of 4 months after acceptance. Editorial lead time 4 months. Submit seasonal material 6 months in advance. Accepts queries by mail, e-mail. Accepts simultaneous submissions. Responds in 2 months to queries. Sample copy for sae with 9x12 envelope and 5 First-Class stamps. Guidelines online.

NONFICTION Needs how-to, interview, new product, photo feature, technical, travel. Special issues: Road Gear (the latest tools, techniques and industry developments to help truckers run a smarter, more efficient trucking business); At Home on the Road (creature comfort products, services, and information for the road life, including what's new, useful, interesting, or fun for cyber-trucking drivers). No fiction, poetry. **Buys 20 mss/year.** Query with published clips. Length: 850-2,000 words. **Payment negotiable.** Pays expenses of writers on assignment.

PHOTOS State availability. Identification of subjects, model releases required. Reviews contact sheets. Negotiates payment individually. Buys negotiable rights.

COLUMNS/DEPARTMENTS Lead Driver (profile of outstanding trucker), 250-500 words; Roadrunner (new products, services suited to the business of trucking or to truckers' lifestyles), 100-250 words. **Buys 6-10 mss/year.** Query. **Payment negotiable.**

FILLERS Needs anecdotes, facts, gags, short humor. Length: 100-250 words. **Pays $50.**

$ ✪ TIRE NEWS

Rousseau Automotive Communication, 455, Notre-Dame East, Suite 311, Montreal QC H2Y 1C9 Canada. (514)289-0888; 1-877-989-0888. **Fax:** (514)289-5151. **E-mail:** info@autosphere.ca. **E-mail:** news@autosphere.ca. **Website:** www.autosphere.ca. Bimonthly magazine covering the Canadian tire industry. *Tire News* focuses on education/training, industry image, management, new tires, new techniques, marketing, HR, etc. Estab. 2004. Circ. 18,725. Byline given. Pays on publication. Publishes ms an average of 2 months after acceptance. Editorial lead time 2 months. Submit seasonal material 2 months in advance. Accepts simultaneous submissions. Responds in 2 weeks to queries. Responds in 2 months to mss. Sample copy free. Guidelines by e-mail.

NONFICTION Needs general interest, how-to, inspirational, interview, new product, technical. Does not want opinion pieces. **Buys 5 mss/year.** Query with published clips. Length: 550-610 words. **Pays up to $200 (Canadian).**

PHOTOS Send photos. Captions required. Reviews GIF/JPEG files. Offers no additional payment for photos accepted with ms. Buys all rights.

FILLERS Needs facts. **Buys 2 mss/year.** Length: 550-610 words. **Pays $0-200.**

$$ ✪ WESTERN CANADA HIGHWAY NEWS

Craig Kelman & Associates, 2020 Portage Ave., 3rd Floor, Winnipeg MB R3J 0K4 Canada. (204)985-9785. **Fax:** (204)985-9795. **E-mail:** terry@kelman.ca. **Website:** highwaynews.ca. **Contact:** Terry Ross, editor. **30% freelance written.** Quarterly magazine covering trucking. The official magazine of the Alberta, Saskatchewan, and Manitoba trucking associations.

As the official magazine of the trucking associations in Alberta, Saskatchewan and Manitoba, *Western Canada Highway News* is committed to providing leading edge, timely information on business practices, technology, trends, new products/services, legal and legislative issues that affect professionals in Western Canada's trucking industry. Estab. 1995. Circ. 4,500. Byline given. Pays on publication. No kill fee. Publishes ms an average of 2 months after acceptance. Editorial lead time 3 months. Submit seasonal material 3 months in advance. Accepts simultaneous submissions. Responds in 1 month. Sample copy for 10x13 SAE with 1 IRC. Guidelines for #10 SASE.

NONFICTION Needs essays, general interest, how-to, interview, new product, opinion, personal experience, photo feature, technical, profiles in excellence (bios of trucking or associate firms enjoying success). **Buys 8-10 mss/year.** Query. Length: 500-3,000 words. **Pays 18-25¢/word.** Pays expenses of writers on assignment.

PHOTOS State availability. Identification of subjects required. Reviews 4x6 prints. Buys one-ime rights.

COLUMNS/DEPARTMENTS Safety (new safety innovation/products), 500 words; Trade Talk (new products), 300 words. Query. **Pays 18-25¢/word.**

TIPS "Our publication is fairly time sensitive regarding issues affecting the trucking industry in Western Canada. Current 'hot' topics are international trucking, security, driver fatigue, health and safety, emissions control, and national/international highway systems."

AVIATION & SPACE

$$$$ AEROSAFETY WORLD MAGAZINE

Flight Safety Foundation, 701 N. Fairfax St., Suite 4250, Alexandria VA 22314-2058. (703)739-6700. **Fax:** (703)739-6708. **E-mail:** jackman@flightsafety.org. **Website:** www.flightsafety.org. **Contact:** Frank Jackman, vice president of communications. Monthly newsletter covering safety aspects of airport operations. Full-color monthly magazine offers in-depth analysis of important safety issues facing the industry, with emphasis on timely news coverage in a convenient format and eye-catching contemporary design. Estab. 2006. Pays on publication. Accepts queries by mail, e-mail. Guidelines available online.

"*AeroSafety World* continues Flight Safety Foundation's tradition of excellence in aviation safety journalism that stretches back more than 50 years. The new full-color monthly magazine, initially called *Aviation Safety World*, offers in-depth analysis of important safety issues facing the industry, along with several new departments and a greater emphasis on timely news coverage—in a convenient format and eye-catching contemporary design. While *AeroSafety World* has taken the place of the 7 newsletters the Foundation used to produce, including *Airport Operations*, the archives remain active, and back issues of the newsletters are still available."

NONFICTION Needs technical. Query. **Pays $300-1,500.**

PHOTOS Pays $75 for each piece of original art.

TIPS "Few aviation topics are outside its scope."

$$ AVIATION INTERNATIONAL NEWS

AIN Publications, 214 Franklin Ave., Midland Park NJ 07432. (201)444-5075. **E-mail:** aineditor@ainonline.com. **Website:** www.ainonline.com. **Contact:** Mark Phelps, executive editor. **30% freelance written.** Monthly magazine covering business and commercial aviation with news features, special reports, aircraft evaluations and surveys on business aviation worldwide, written for business pilots and industry professionals. Sister print products include daily onsite issues published at 6 conventions and 4 international air shows. Electronic products include four-times-weekly AINalerts, once-weekly AIN Air Transport Perspective and AIN Defense Perspective, and AINonline website. "While the heartbeat of *AIN* is driven by the news it carries, the human touch is not neglected. We pride ourselves on our people stories about the industry's 'movers and shakers' and others in aviation who make a difference." Estab. 1972. Circ. 40,000. Byline given. Pays on acceptance and upon receipt of writer's invoice. Offers variable kill fee. Publishes ms an average of 2 months after acceptance. Editorial lead time 2 months. Submit seasonal material 3 months in advance. Accepts queries by mail, e-mail. Responds in 6 weeks to queries; 2 months to mss. Sample copy for $10.

NONFICTION Needs how-to, interview, new product, opinion, personal experience, photo feature, technical. No place for puff pieces. "Our readers expect serious, real news. We don't pull any punches. *AIN* is not a 'good news' publication; it tells the story, both good and bad." **Buys 150-200 mss/year.** Query with published clips or links to online material. Length: 200-3,000 words. **Pays 45¢/word to first timers, higher rates to proven *AIN* freelancers.** Pays expenses of writers on assignment.

PHOTOS Send photos. Captions required. Digital photos must be high-res (300 dpi). Reviews contact sheets, transparencies, prints, TIFF files (300 dpi). Negotiates payment individually. Buys one-time rights.

TIPS "Our core freelancers are professional pilots with good writing skills, or good journalists and reporters with an interest in aviation (some with pilot certificates) or technical experts in the aviation industry. The ideal *AIN* writer has an intense interest in and strong knowledge of aviation, a talent for writing news stories, and journalistic cussedness. Hit me with a strong news story relating to business aviation that takes me by surprise—something from your local area or area of expertise. Make it readable, fact-filled and in the inverted-pyramid style. Double-check facts and names. Interview the right people. Send me good, clear photos and illustrations. Send me well-written, logically ordered copy. Do this for me consistently and we may take you along on our staff to one of the conventions in the U.S. or an airshow in Paris, Singapore, London or Dubai."

$$$ PROFESSIONAL PILOT

Queensmith Communications Corp., 5290 Shawnee Road, Suite 201, Alexandria VA 22312. (703)370-0606. **Fax:** (703)370-7082. **E-mail:** editor@propilotmag.com; editorial@propilotmag.com. **E-mail:** rafael@propilotmag.com. **Website:** www.propilotmag.com. **Contact:** Murray Smith, editor/publisher; Rafael Henriquez, associate editor. **75% freelance written.** Monthly magazine covering corporate, noncombat government, law enforcement, and various other types of professional aviation. The typical reader of *Professional Pilot* has a sophisticated grasp of piloting/aviation knowledge and is interested in articles that help him/her do the job better or more efficiently. Estab. 1967. Circ. 40,000. Byline given. Pays on publication. Offers kill fee. Kill fee negotiable. Publishes ms an average of 2-3 months after acceptance. Accepts queries by mail, e-mail. Accepts simultaneous submissions.

NONFICTION **Buys 40 mss/year.** Query. Length: 750-2,500 words. **Pays $200-1,000, depending on length. A fee for the article will be established at the time of assignment.** Pays expenses of writers on assignment.

PHOTOS Prefers transparencies or high resolution 300 JPEG digital images. Send photos. Captions, identification of subjects required. Additional payment for photos negotiable. Buys all rights.

TIPS "Query first. Freelancer should be a professional pilot or have background in aviation. Authors should indicate relevant aviation experience and pilot credentials (certificates, ratings and hours). We place a greater emphasis on corporate operations and pilot concerns."

BEAUTY & SALON

$$ ASCP SKIN DEEP

Associated Skin Care Professionals, 25188 Genesee Trail Rd., Suite 200, Golden CO 80401. (800)789-0411. **E-mail:** editor@ascpskincare.com; getconnected@ascpskincare.com. **Website:** www.ascpskincare.com. **Contact:** Mary Abel, editor. **80% freelance written.** Bimonthly member magazine of Associated Skin Care Professionals (ASCP), covering technical, educational, and business information for estheticians with an emphasis on solo practitioners and spa/salon employees or independent contractors. Audience is the U.S. individual skin care practitioner who may work on her own and/or in a spa or salon setting. Magazine keeps her up to date on skin care trends and techniques and ways to earn more income doing waxing, facials, peels, microdermabrasion, body wraps, and other skin treatments. Product-neutral stories may include novel spa treatments within the esthetician scope of practice. Does not cover mass-market retail products, hair care, nail care, physician-only treatments/products, cosmetic surgery, or invasive treatments like colonics or ear candling. Successful stories have included how-tos on paraffin facials, aromatherapy body wraps, waxing tips, how to read ingredient labels, how to improve word-of-mouth advertising, and how to choose an online scheduling software package. Estab. 2003. Circ. 14,000+. Byline given. Pays on acceptance. No kill fee. Publishes ms an average of 4-6 months after acceptance. Editorial lead time 4-5 months. Submit seasonal material 7 months in advance. Accepts queries by e-mail. Accepts simultaneous submissions. Responds in 2-4 weeks to queries. Sample copy online at www.ascp-skindeepdigital.com.

NONFICTION Needs how-to. "We don't run general consumer beauty material or products, and very rarely run a new product that is available through retail outlets. 'New' products means introduced in the last 12 months. We do not run industry personnel announcements or stories on individual spas/salons or getaways. We don't cover hair or nails." **Buys 12 mss/year.** Query. Length: 1,200-1,600 words. **Pays $75-300 for assigned articles.** Pays expenses of writers on assignment.

TIPS "Visit website to read previous issues and learn about what we do. Submit a brief query with an idea to determine if you are on the right track. State specifically what value this has to estheticians and their work/income. Please note that we do not publish fashion, nails, hair, or consumer-focused articles."

$$ COSMETICS

Rogers Publishing Limited, 420 Britannia Road East, Suite 102, Mississauga ON L4Z 3L5 Canada. (905)890-5161. **E-mail:** jhicks@cctfa.com. **Website:** www.cosmeticsmag.com. **Contact:** Jim Hicks. **10% freelance written.** Bimonthly magazine covering cosmetics for industry professionals. Estab. 1972. Circ. 13,000. Byline given. Pays on acceptance. Offers 50% kill fee. Publishes ms an average of 3 months after acceptance. Editorial lead time 4 months. Submit seasonal material 4 months in advance. Accepts queries by mail. Accepts simultaneous submissions. Responds in 1 month to queries. Sample copy for $6 (Canadian) and 8% GST.

Main reader segment is the retail trade—department stores, drugstores, salons, estheticians—owners and cosmeticians/beauty advisors; plus manufacturers, distributors, agents, and suppliers to the industry.

NONFICTION Needs general interest, interview, photo feature. **Buys 1 mss/year.** Query. Length: 250-1,200 words. **Pays 25¢/word.** Pays expenses of writers on assignment.

PHOTOS Send photos. Captions, identification of subjects, model releases required. Reviews 2 1/2 up to 8x10 transparencies, 4x6 up to 8x10 prints, 35mm slides; e-mail pictures in 300 dpi JPEG format. Offers no additional payment for photos accepted with ms. Buys all rights.

COLUMNS/DEPARTMENTS "All articles assigned on a regular basis from correspondents and columnists that we know personally from the industry."

TIPS "Must have broad knowledge of the Canadian cosmetics, fragrance, and toiletries industry and retail business. 99.9% of freelance articles are assigned by the editor to writers involved with the Canadian cosmetics business."

$$ DAYSPA

Creative Age Publications, 7628 Densmore Ave., Van Nuys CA 91406. (818)782-7328, ext. 301. **Fax:** (818)782-7450. **Website:** www.dayspamagazine.com. **Contact:** Lesley McCave, executive editor. **50% freelance written.** Monthly magazine covering the business of day spas, multiservice/skincare salons, and resort/hotel spas. *Dayspa* includes only well-targeted business and trend articles directed at the owners and managers. It serves to enrich, enlighten, and empower spa/salon professionals. Estab. 1996. Circ. 31,000. Byline given. Pays on acceptance. No kill fee. Publishes ms an average of 4 months after acceptance. Editorial lead time 4 months. Submit seasonal material 4 months in advance. Accepts queries by online submission form. Accepts simultaneous submissions. Responds in 2 months to queries. Sample copy: $5.

NONFICTION Buys 40 mss/year. Query. Length: 1,500-1,800 words. **Pays $150-500.**

PHOTOS Send photos. Identification of subjects, model releases required. Negotiates payment individually. Buys one-time rights.

COLUMNS/DEPARTMENTS Legal Pad (legal issues affecting salons/spas); Money Matters (financial issues); Management Workshop (spa management issues); Health Wise (wellness trends), all 1,200-1,500 words. **Buys 20 mss/year.** Query. **Pays $150-400.**

$$ MASSAGE MAGAZINE

820 A1A N. Highway, Suite W18, Ponte Vedra Beach FL 32082. **E-mail:** kmenehan@massagemag.com. **Website:** www.massagemag.com. **Contact:** Karen Menehan, editor-in-chief. **50% freelance written.** Magazine about massage and other touch therapies published 12 times/year. Readers are professional massage therapists who have been in practice for several years. About 70% are self-employed; 95% live in the U.S. The techniques they practice include Swedish, sports, and geriatric massage and energy work. Readers work in settings ranging from home-based studios to spas to integrated clinics. Readers care deeply that

massage is portrayed in a professional manner. "We publish articles on self-care, news on integrative care and massage, business, marketing and techniques. Understand the profession of massage therapy." Estab. 1985. Circ. 50,000. Byline given. Pays the month of publication. Offers kill fee. Publishes ms an average of 1-3 months after submission. Editorial lead time 1 month. Advance time 1 month. Accepts queries by e-mail. Responds in 2 weeks to queries. Do not send ms without querying first. Sample copy: $6.95; however; sample articles available via e-mail. Guidelines available by request.

NONFICTION Needs general interest, how-to, interview, personal experience, profile, News: hard news, features and profiles. "We do not publish humorous travel pieces about unusual massage experiences. We do not publish cartoons." **Buys 200 mss/year.** Length: 700-1,500 words for news; 1,600 words for features. **Pays $80-200.**

PHOTOS Send photos with submission via e-mail. Buys one-time rights.

COLUMNS/DEPARTMENTS Profiles; News and Current Events; Practice Building (business); Technique; Mind/Body/Spirit. Length: 200-2,500 words. See website for details.

FILLERS Needs Facts, newsbreaks.

TIPS "Our readers seek practical information on how to help their clients and make their businesses more successful, as well as feature articles that place massage therapy in a positive or inspiring light. Since most of our readers are professional therapists, we do not publish articles on topics like 'How Massage Can Help You Relax'; nor do we publish humorous essays or travel essays. We do use freelancers to research and report hard news on the integrative health field."

NAILPRO

Creative Age Publications, 7628 Densmore Ave., Van Nuys CA 91406. (800)442-5667; (818)782-7328. **Fax:** (818)782-7450. **E-mail:** nailpro@creativeage.com. **Website:** www.nailpro.com. **Contact:** Stephanie Lavery, executive editor. **20% freelance written.** Monthly magazine written for manicurists and salon owners working as an independent contractor or in a full-service salon or nails-only salons. Estab. 1989. Circ. 65,000. Byline given. Pays on acceptance. 25% kill fee. Publishes ms an average of 6 months after acceptance. Editorial lead time 3 months. Submit seasonal material 3 months in advance. Accepts queries by e-mail. Accepts simultaneous submissions. Responds in 6 weeks to queries only if interested. Sample copy: $2 and 9x12 SASE.

"*Nailpro* is the premiere magazine for the professional nail industry. Content includes nail trends, products and techniques, from simple polishing to elaborate nail art, as well as tips and tricks for running a successful nail business."

NONFICTION Needs book excerpts, how-to, humor, inspirational, interview, personal experience, photo feature, profile, technical. No general interest articles or business articles not geared to the nail-care industry. **Buys 50 mss/year.** Query. Length: 1,000-3,000 words. **Pays $150-450.** Pays expenses of writers on assignment.

PHOTOS Send photos. Identification of subjects, model releases required. Reviews transparencies, prints. Negotiates payment individually. Pays on acceptance. Buys one-time rights for print and web.

COLUMNS/DEPARTMENTS Business (articles on building salon business, marketing and advertising, dealing with employees), 1,500-2,500 words; Attitudes (aspects of operating a nail salon and trends in the nail industry), 1,200-2,500 words. **Buys 50 mss/year.** Query. **Pays $250-350.**

NAILS

Bobit Business Media, 3520 Challenger St., Torrance CA 90503. (310)533-2457. **E-mail:** judy.lessin@bobit.com. **Website:** www.nailsmag.com. **Contact:** Judy Lessin, senior managing editor. **10% freelance written.** Monthly magazine. *NAILS* seeks to educate its readers on new techniques and products, nail anatomy and health, customer relations, working safely and ergonomically, salon sanitation, and the business aspects of running a salon. Estab. 1983. Circ. 55,000. Byline given. Pays on acceptance. No kill fee. Editorial lead time 3 months. Submit seasonal material 4 months in advance. Accepts queries by e-mail. Responds in 1 month to queries. Visit website to view past issues.

NONFICTION Needs how-to, inspirational, interview, personal experience, photo feature, profile, technical. No articles on one particular product, company profiles, or articles slanted toward a particular company or manufacturer. **Buys 20 mss/year.** Query with published clips. Length: 750-1,600 words. **Pays $100-350.** Pays expenses of writers on assignment.

PHOTOS State availability. Captions, identification of subjects, model releases required. Rarely buys unsolicited photos. Buys all rights.

TIPS "Send clips and query; *do not send unsolicited manuscripts.* We would like to see fresh and unique angles on business, health, or technical topics. Topics must be geared specifically to salon owners and nail technicians. Focus on an innovative business idea or unique point of view. Articles from experts on specific business issues—handling difficult employees, cultivating clients, navigating social media, technical troubleshooting, industry trends—are encouraged."

$$ PULSE MAGAZINE

HOST Communications Inc., 2365 Harrodsburg Rd., Suite A325, Lexington KY 40504. (859)226-4326. **Fax:** (859)226-4445. **E-mail:** mae.manacap-johnson@ispastaff.com. **Website:** www.experienceispa.com/media/pulse-magazine. **Contact:** Mae Manacap-Johnson, editor. **20% freelance written.** Magazine published 10 times/year covering spa industry. *Pulse* is the magazine for the spa professional. As the official publication of the International SPA Association, its purpose is to advance the business of the spa professionals by informing them of the latest trends and practices and promoting the wellness aspects of spa. *Pulse* connects people, nurtures their personal and professional growth, and enhances their ability to network and succeed in the spa industry. Estab. 1991. Circ. 5,300. Byline given. Pays on publication. Publishes ms an average of 1 month after acceptance. Editorial lead time 3 months. Submit seasonal material 4 months in advance. Accepts queries by e-mail. Accepts simultaneous submissions. Sample copy for #10 SASE. Guidelines by e-mail.

NONFICTION Needs general interest, how-to, interview, new product. Does not want articles focused on spas that are not members of ISPA, consumer-focused articles (market is the spa industry professional), or features on hot tubs ("not *that* spa industry"). **Buys 8-10 mss/year.** Query with published clips. Length: 800-2,000 words. **Pays $250-500.** Pays expenses of writers on assignment.

PHOTOS Send photos. Captions required. Reviews GIF/JPEG files. Negotiates payment individually. Buys one-time rights.

TIPS "Understand the nuances of association publishing (different than consumer and B2B). Send published clips, not Word documents. Experience in writing for health and wellness market is helpful. Only feature ISPA member companies in the magazine; visit our website to learn more about our industry and to see if your pitch includes member companies before making contact."

$$ SKIN INC. MAGAZINE

Allured Business Media, P.O. Box 3009, Northbrook IL 60065. (1-800)362-2192. **Fax:** (1-847)291-4816. **E-mail:** kanderson@allured.com. **Website:** www.skininc.com. **Contact:** Katie Anderson, managing editor. **30% freelance written.** Magazine published 12 times/year as an educational resource for skin care professionals interested in business solutions, treatment techniques, and skin science. Estab. 1988. Circ. 30,000. Byline given. Pays on publication. No kill fee. Publishes ms an average of 6 months after acceptance. Editorial lead time 6 months. Submit seasonal material 1 year in advance. Accepts queries by mail, e-mail, fax, phone. Accepts simultaneous submissions. Responds in 3 weeks to queries; 1 month to mss. Sample copy and guidelines free.

"Mss considered for publication that contain original and new information in the general fields of skin care and makeup, dermatological and esthetician-assisted surgical techniques. The subject may cover the science of skin, the business of skin care and makeup, and plastic surgeons on healthy (i.e., nondiseased) skin."

NONFICTION Needs general interest, how-to, interview, personal experience, technical. **Buys 6 mss/year.** Query with published clips. Length: 2,000 words. **Pays $100-300 for assigned articles. Pays $50-200 for unsolicited articles.**

PHOTOS State availability. Captions, identification of subjects, model releases required. Reviews 3x5 prints. Offers no additional payment for photos accepted with ms. Buys one-time rights.

COLUMNS/DEPARTMENTS Finance (tips and solutions for managing money), 2,000-2,500 words; Personnel (managing personnel), 2,000-2,500 words; Marketing (marketing tips for salon owners), 2,000-2,500 words; Retail (retailing products and services in the salon environment), 2,000-2,500 words. Query with published clips. **Pays $50-200.**

FILLERS Needs facts, newsbreaks. **Buys 6 mss/year. mss/year.** Length: 250-500 words. **Pays $50-100.**

TIPS "Have an understanding of the professional spa industry."

BEVERAGES & BOTTLING

$$ BAR & BEVERAGE BUSINESS MAGAZINE

Mercury Publications, 1313 Border St., Unit 16, Winnipeg MB R3H 0X4 Canada. (204)954-2085, ext. 213. **Fax:** (204)954-2057. **E-mail:** edufault@mercurypublications.ca. **Website:** www.barandbeverage.com. **Contact:** Elaine Dufault, associate publisher and national account manager. **33% freelance written.** Bimonthly magazine providing information on the latest trends, happenings, and buying/selling of beverages and product merchandising. Estab. 1998. Circ. 15,000+. Byline given. Pays 30-45 days from receipt of invoice. Offers 33% kill fee. Submit seasonal material 3 months in advance. Accepts simultaneous submissions. Sample copy and writer's guidelines free or by e-mail.

Does not accept queries for specific stories. Assigns stories to Canadian writers.

NONFICTION Needs how-to, interview. Does not want industry reports, profiles on companies. Query with published clips. Length: 500-9,000 words. **Pays 25-35¢/word.** Pays expenses of writers on assignment.

PHOTOS State availability. Captions required. Reviews negatives; transparencies; 3x5 prints; JPEG, EPS, or TIFF files. Negotiates payment individually. Buys all rights.

COLUMNS/DEPARTMENTS Out There (bar and beverage news in various parts of the country), 100-500 words. Query. **Pays up to $100.**

$$ BARTENDER® MAGAZINE

Foley Publishing, P.O. Box 691302, Vero Beach FL 32969. (772)999-3994. **E-mail:** info@bartender.com. **Website:** bartender.com/mixologist.com. **Contact:** Jackie Foley, editor. **75% freelance written. Prefers to work with published/established writers; eager to work with new/unpublished writers.** Quarterly publication for full-service on-premise establishments able to serve a mixed drink on-premise. Features bartenders, bars, creative cocktails, signature drinks, jokes, cartoons, wine, beer, liquor, new products and those products aligned to the field. Estab. 1979. Circ. 150,000. Byline given. Pays on publication. No kill fee. Publishes ms an average of 3 months after acceptance. Submit seasonal material 3 months in advance. Accepts queries by mail, e-mail. Accepts simultaneous submissions. Responds in 2 months to mss. Sample copy with 9x12 SAE and 4 first-class stamps.

NONFICTION Needs general interest, historical, how-to, humor, new product, opinion, personal experience, photo feature. Special issues: Special issues: Annual Calendar and Daily Cocktail Recipe Guide. Send complete ms and SASE. Length: 100-1,000 words. Pays expenses of writers on assignment.

REPRINTS Send tearsheet and information about when and where the material previously appeared. Pays 25% of amount paid for an original article.

PHOTOS Send photos. Captions, model releases required. Pays $7.50-50 for 8x10 b&w glossy prints; $10-75 for 8x10 color glossy prints.

COLUMNS/DEPARTMENTS Bar of the Month; Bartender of the Month; Creative Cocktails; Bar Sports; Quiz; Bar Art; Wine Cellar; Tips from the Top (from prominent figures in the liquor industry); One For the Road (travel); Collectors (bar or liquor-related items); Photo Essays. Length: 200-1,000 words. Query by mail only with SASE. **Pays $50-200.**

FILLERS Needs anecdotes, newsbreaks, short humor, clippings, jokes, gags. Length: 25-100 words. **Pays $5-25.**

TIPS "To break in, absolutely make sure your work will be of interest to all bartenders across the country. Your style of writing should reflect the audience you are addressing. The most frequent mistake made by writers in completing an article for us is using the wrong subject."

$$ MICHIGAN HOSPITALITY REVIEW

Michigan Licensed Beverage Association, 101 S. Washington Sq., Suite 800, Lansing MI 48933. (800)292-2896; (517)374-9611. **Fax:** (517)374-1165. **E-mail:** editor@mlba.org; mdoerr@mlba.org. **Website:** www.mlba.org. **Contact:** Mason Doerr, editor. **40-50% freelance written.** Monthly trade magazine devoted to the beer, wine, and spirits industry in Michigan. It is dedicated to serving those who make their living serving the public and the state through the orderly and responsible sale of beverages. Estab. 1983. Circ. 4,200. Pays on publication. No kill fee. Editorial lead time 3 months. Submit seasonal material 3 months in advance. Accepts queries by mail, e-mail. Accepts simultaneous submissions. Responds in 2 weeks to queries. Responds in 1 month to mss. Sample copy for $5 or online.

NONFICTION Needs essays, general interest, historical, how-to, humor, interview, new product, opinion, personal experience, photo feature, technical. **Buys 24 mss/year.** Send complete ms. Length: 1,000 words. **Pays $20-200.**

COLUMNS/DEPARTMENTS Open to essay content ideas. Interviews (legislators, others), 750-1,000 words; personal experience (waitstaff, customer, bartenders), 500 words. **Buys 12 mss/year.** Send complete ms. **Pays $25-100.**

TIPS "We are particularly interested in nonfiction concerning responsible consumption/serving of alcohol. We are looking for product reviews, company profiles, personal experiences, and news articles that would benefit our audience. Our audience is a busy group of business owners and hospitality professionals striving to obtain pertinent information that is not too wordy."

$ VINEYARD & WINERY MANAGEMENT

P.O. Box 14459, Santa Rosa CA 95402-6459. (707)577-7700. **Fax:** (707)577-7705. **E-mail:** jfpowers@vwmmedia.com. **Website:** www.vwmmedia.com. **Contact:** Julie Fadda Powers, editor in chief. **80% freelance written.** Bimonthly magazine of professional importance to grape growers, winemakers, and winery sales and business people. Headquartered in Sonoma County, California, *Vineyard & Winery Management* proudly remains a leading independent wine trade magazine serving all of North America. Estab. 1975. Circ. 6,500. Byline given. Pays on publication. 20% kill fee. Accepts queries by e-mail. Accepts simultaneous submissions. Responds in 3 weeks to queries. Responds in 1 month to mss. Sample copy free. Guidelines available by e-mail.

NONFICTION Needs how-to, interview, new product, technical. **Buys 30 mss/year.** Query. Length: 1,500-2,000 words. **Pays approximately $500/feature.** Pays expenses of writers on assignment.

PHOTOS State availability. Captions, identification of subjects required. Digital photos preferred, JPEG or TIFF files 300 pixels/inch resolution at print size. Pays $20/each photo published.

TIPS "We're looking for long-term relationships with authors who know the business and write well. Electronic submissions required; query for formats."

$$ WINES & VINES

Wine Communications Group, 65 Mitchell Blvd., Suite A, San Rafael CA 94903. (415)453-9700; (866)453-9701. **Fax:** (415)453-2517. **E-mail:** edit@winesandvines.com; info@winesandvines.com. **Website:** www.winesandvines.com. **Contact:** Jim Gordon, editor; Kate Lavin, managing editor. **50% freelance written.** Monthly magazine covering the North American winegrape and winemaking industry. "Since 1919, *Wines & Vines Magazine* has been the authoritative voice of the wine and grape industry—from prohibition to phylloxera, we have covered it all. Our paid circulation reaches all 50 states and many foreign countries. Because we are intended for the trade—including growers, winemakers, winery owners, wholesalers, restauranteurs, and serious amateurs—we accept more technical, informative articles. We do not accept wine reviews, wine country tours, or anything of a wine consumer nature." Estab. 1919. Circ. 5,000. Byline given. Pays 30 days after acceptance. No kill fee. Publishes ms an average of 3 months after acceptance. Editorial lead time 2 months. Submit seasonal material 4 months in advance. Accepts queries by e-mail. Accepts simultaneous submissions. Responds in 2-3 weeks to queries. Sample copy: $5. Guidelines free.

NONFICTION Needs interview, new product, technical. "No wine reviews, wine country travelogues, 'lifestyle' pieces, or anything aimed at wine consumers. Our readers are professionals in the field." **Buys 60 mss/year.** Query with published clips. Length: 1,000-2,000 words. **Pays flat fee of $500 for assigned articles.** Pays expenses of writers on assignment.

PHOTOS Prefers JPEG files (JPEG, 300 dpi minimum). Can use high-quality prints. State availability of or send photos. Captions, identification of subjects required. Does not pay for photos submitted by author, but will give photo credit.

BOOK & BOOKSTORE

AMERICAN BOOK REVIEW

The Writer's Review, Inc., School of Arts & Sciences, Univ. of Houston-Victoria, 3007 N. Ben Wilson, Victoria TX 77901. (361)570-4848. **E-mail:** americanbookreview@uhv.edu. **Website:** www.americanbookreview.org. Bimonthly magazine covering book reviews. "We specialize in reviewing books published by independent presses." Estab. 1977. Circ. 15,000. Byline given. Pays on publication. Offers $50 kill fee. Publishes ms an average of 2-4 months after acceptance. Editorial lead time 1 month. Accepts queries by mail, e-mail, fax, phone. Accepts simultaneous submissions. Responds in 2 weeks to queries; 1-2 months to mss. Sample copy for $4. Guidelines online.

NONFICTION Does not want fiction, poetry, or interviews. Query with published clips. Length: 750-1,250 words. **Pays $50.** Pays expenses of writers on assignment.

TIPS "Most of our reviews are assigned, but we occasionally accept unsolicited reviews. Send query and samples of published reviews."

$$ FOREWORD REVIEWS

FOREWORD MAGAZINE INC., 425 Boardman Ave., Traverse City MI 49684. (231)933-3699. **Fax:** (231)933-3899. **E-mail:** victoria@forewordreviews.com. **E-mail:** mschingler@forewordreviews.com. **Website:** www.forewordreviews.com. **Contact:** Michelle Anne Schingler, managing editor. **75% freelance written.** Quarterly magazine covering reviews of good books independently published. In each issue of the magazine, there are 3 to 4 feature *ForeSight* articles focusing on trends in popular categories. These are in addition to the 100 or more critical reviews of forthcoming titles from independent and university presses in the *Review* section. Look online for review submission guidelines or view editorial calendar. Estab. 1998. Circ. 10,000 (about 80% librarians, 10% bookstores, 10% publishing professionals). Byline given. Pays 1 month after submissions. $20 kill fee. Publishes ms an average of 2-3 months after acceptance. Editorial lead time 2-3 months. Submit seasonal material 5 months in advance. Accepts queries by mail, e-mail. Accepts simultaneous submissions. Responds in 1 month. Sample copy for $5.99 and 8 ½ x11 SASE with $1.50 postage.

NONFICTION Contact: Matt Sutherland. Needs book excerpts, interview, profile. **Buys 4 mss/year.** Query with published clips. All review submissions should be sent to the book review editor. Submissions should include a fact sheet or press release. Length: 400-1,500 words. **Pays $50-250 for assigned articles.**

TIPS "Be knowledgeable about the needs of booksellers and librarians—remember we are an industry trade journal, not a how-to or consumer publication. We review books prior to publication, so book reviews are always assigned—but send us a note telling subjects you wish to review, as well as a résumé."

$ VIDEO LIBRARIAN

9479 Bayshore Dr. NW, Suite 203, Silverdale WA 98383. (360)626-1259. **Fax:** (360)626-1260. **E-mail:** vidlib@videolibrarian.com. **Website:** www.videolibrarian.com. **75% freelance written.** Bimonthly magazine covering DVD/Blu-ray reviews for librarians. "*Video Librarian* reviews approximately 225 titles in each issue: children's, documentaries, how-to's, movies, TV, music and anime." Estab. 1986. Circ. 2,000. Byline given. Pays on publication. Publishes ms an average of 2 months after acceptance. Editorial lead time 2 months. Accepts queries by e-mail. Accepts simultaneous submissions. Responds in 1 week to queries. Sample copy: $11.

NONFICTION Buys 500+ mss/year. Query with published clips. Length: 200-300 words. **Pays $10-20/review.** Pays expenses of writers on assignment.

TIPS "We are looking for DVD/Blu-ray reviewers with a wide range of interests, good critical eye, and strong writing skills."

BRICK, GLASS & CERAMICS

$ STAINED GLASS

Stained Glass Association of America, 9313 East 63rd St., Raytown MO 64133. (800)438-9581. **Fax:** (816)737-2801. **E-mail:** webmaster@sgaaonline.com. **Website:** www.stainedglassquarterly.com. **Contact:** Richard Gross, editor and media director. **70% freelance written.** Quarterly magazine. *Stained Glass* is the official voice of the Stained Glass Association of America. As the oldest, most respected stained glass publication in North America, *Stained Glass* preserves the techniques of the past as well as illustrates the trends of the future. This vital information, of significant value to the professional stained glass studio, is also of interest to those for whom stained glass is an avocation or hobby. Estab. 1906. Circ. 8,000. Byline given. Pays on publication. No kill fee. Publishes ms an average of 1 year after acceptance. Editorial lead time 6 months. Submit seasonal material 8 months in advance. Accepts queries by mail, e-mail, fax. Accepts simultaneous submissions. Responds in 3 months to queries. Sample copy free. Guidelines on website.

NONFICTION Needs how-to, humor, interview, new product, opinion, photo feature, technical. **Buys 9 mss/year.** Query or send complete ms, but must include photos or slides—very heavy on photos. Length:

2,500-3,500 words. **Pays $125/illustrated article; $75/nonillustrated.**

REPRINTS Accepts previously published submissions from stained glass publications only. Send tearsheet of article. Payment negotiable.

PHOTOS Send photos. Identification of subjects required. Reviews 4x5 transparencies, send slides with submission. Pays $75 for non-illustrated. Pays $125, plus 3 copies for line art or photography. Buys one-time rights.

COLUMNS/DEPARTMENTS Columns must be illustrated. Teknixs (technical, how-to, stained and glass art), word length varies by subject. **Buys 4 mss/year.** Query or send complete ms, but must be illustrated.

TIPS "We need more technical articles. Writers should be extremely well versed in the glass arts. Photographs are extremely important and must be of very high quality. Submissions without photographs or illustrations are seldom considered unless something special and writer states that photos are available. However, prefer to see with submission."

$$ US GLASS, METAL & GLAZING

Key Communications, Inc., 20 PGA Dr., Suite 201, Stafford VA 22554. (540)720-5584, ext.118. **Fax:** (540)720-5687. **E-mail:** info@usglassmag.com. **E-mail:** erogers@glass.com. **Website:** www.usglassmag.com. **Contact:** Ellen Rogers, editor. **25% freelance written.** Monthly magazine for companies involved in the flat glass trades. Estab. 1966. Circ. 27,000. Byline given. Pays on publication. No kill fee. Publishes ms an average of 3 months after acceptance. Editorial lead time 3 months. Submit seasonal material 2 months in advance. Accepts queries by mail, e-mail. Accepts simultaneous submissions. Responds in 1 month to queries. Responds in 2 months to mss. Sample copy online.

NONFICTION Buys 12 mss/year. Query with published clips. **Pays $300-600 for assigned articles.** Pays expenses of writers on assignment.

PHOTOS State availability. Captions, identification of subjects required. Reviews contact sheets. Offers no additional payment for photos accepted with ms. Buys first North American rights.

BUILDING INTERIORS

$$ FABRICS + FURNISHINGS INTERNATIONAL

SIPCO Publications + Events, 3 Island Ave., Suite 6i, Miami Beach FL 33139. **E-mail:** eric@sipco.net. **Website:** www.fandfi.com. **Contact:** Eric Schneider, editor/publisher. **10% freelance written.** Bimonthly magazine covering commercial, hospitality interior design, and manufacturing. *F+FI* covers news from vendors who supply the hospitality interiors industry. Estab. 1990. Circ. 11,000+. Byline given. Pays on publication. Offers $100 kill fee. Editorial lead time 3 months. Submit seasonal material 3 months in advance. Accepts queries by e-mail. Accepts simultaneous submissions. Sample copy available online.

NONFICTION Needs interview, technical. Does not want opinion or consumer pieces. Readers must learn something from our stories. Query with published clips. Length: 500-1,000 words. **Pays $250-350.** Pays expenses of writers on assignment.

PHOTOS Send photos. Captions, identification of subjects required. Reviews GIF/JPEG files. Offers no additional payment for photos accepted with ms.

TIPS "Give us a lead on a new project that we haven't heard about. Have pictures of space and ability to interview designer on how they made it work."

$$ KITCHEN & BATH DESIGN NEWS

SOLA Group Inc., 724 12th St., Suite 1W, Wilmette IL 60091. (631)581-2029 or (516)605-1426. **E-mail:** anita@solabrands.com; janice@solabrands.com. **Website:** www.kitchenbathdesign.com. **15% freelance written.** Monthly tabloid for kitchen and bath dealers and design professionals, offering design, business, and marketing advice to help readers be more successful. It is not a consumer publication about design, a book for do-it-yourselfers, or a magazine created to showcase pretty pictures of kitchens and baths. Rather, the magazine covers the professional kitchen and bath design industry in depth, looking at the specific challenges facing these professionals, and how they address these challenges. Estab. 1983. Circ. 51,000. Byline given. Pays on publication. Publishes ms an average of 2-3 months after acceptance. Editorial lead time 2 months. Accepts queries by mail, e-mail. Accepts simultaneous submissions. Responds in 2-4 weeks to queries. Sample copy available online. Guidelines by e-mail.

NONFICTION Needs how-to, interview. Does not want consumer stories, generic business stories, or "I remodeled my kitchen and it's so beautiful" stories. This is a magazine for trade professionals, so stories need to be both slanted for these professionals, as well as sophisticated enough that people who have been working in the field 30 years can still learn something from them. **Buys 16 mss/year.** Query with published clips. Length: 1,100-3,000 words. **Pays $200-650.** Pays expenses of writers on assignment.

PHOTOS Send photos. Identification of subjects required. Offers no additional payment for photos accepted with ms.

TIPS "This is a trade magazine for kitchen and bath dealers and designers, so trade experience and knowledge of the industry are essential. We look for writers who already know the unique challenges facing this industry, as well as the major players, acronyms, etc. This is not a market for beginners, and the vast majority of our freelancers are either design professionals or experienced in the industry."

$$ QUALIFIED REMODELER

SOLA Group, Inc., 1880 Oak Ave., Suite 350, Evanston IL 60201. (847)920-9513. **Website:** www.forresidentialpros.com. Publisher/Editorial Director: Patrick L. O'Toole. **5% freelance written.** Monthly magazine covering residential remodeling. Estab. 1975. Circ. 83,500. Byline given. Pays on acceptance. No kill fee. Publishes ms an average of 1 month after acceptance. Editorial lead time 3 months. Submit seasonal material 2 months in advance. Accepts queries by mail, e-mail, fax, phone. Accepts simultaneous submissions. Sample copy available online.

NONFICTION Needs how-to, new product. **Buys 12 mss/year.** Query with published clips. Length: 1,200-2,500 words. **Pays $300-600 for assigned articles. Pays $200-400 for unsolicited articles.** Pays expenses of writers on assignment.

PHOTOS Send photos. Reviews negatives, transparencies. Negotiates payment individually. Buys one-time rights.

COLUMNS/DEPARTMENTS Query with published clips. **Pays $400**

TIPS "We focus on business management issues faced by remodeling contractors. For example, sales, marketing, liability, taxes, and just about any matter addressing small business operation."

$$$$ REMODELING

HanleyWood, LLC, One Thomas Circle NW, Suite 600, Washington DC 20005. (202)452-0800. **Fax:** (202)785-1974. **E-mail:** cwebb@hanleywood.com. **Website:** www.remodelingmagazine.com. **Contact:** Craig Webb, editor. **10% freelance written.** Monthly magazine covering residential and light commercial remodeling. "We cover the best new ideas in remodeling design, business, construction and products." Estab. 1985. Circ. 80,000. Byline given. Pays on publication. Offers 5¢/word kill fee. Publishes ms an average of 3 months after acceptance. Accepts queries by mail, e-mail, fax. Accepts simultaneous submissions. Sample copy free.

NONFICTION Needs interview, new product, technical, small business trends. **Buys 6 mss/year.** Query with published clips. Length: 250-1,000 words. **Pays $1/word.** Pays expenses of writers on assignment.

PHOTOS State availability. Captions, identification of subjects, model releases required. Reviews 4x5 transparencies, slides, 8x10 prints. Offers $25-125/photo. Buys one-time rights.

TIPS "We specialize in service journalism for remodeling contractors. Knowledge of the industry is essential."

$$ WALLS & CEILINGS

2401 W. Big Beaver Rd., Suite 700, Troy MI 48084. **Fax:** (248)362-5103. **E-mail:** wyattj@bnpmedia.com; mark@wwcca.org. **Website:** www.wconline.com. **Contact:** John Wyatt, editor; Mark Fowler, editorial director. **20% freelance written.** Monthly magazine for contractors involved in lathing and plastering, drywall, acoustics, fireproofing, curtain walls, and movable partitions, together with manufacturers, dealers, and architects. Estab. 1938. Circ. 30,000. Byline given. Pays on publication. No kill fee. Publishes ms an average of 6 months after acceptance. Submit seasonal material 4 months in advance. Accepts queries by mail, e-mail. Accepts simultaneous submissions. Responds in 6 months to queries. Sample copy for 9x12 SAE with $2 postage. Guidelines for #10 SASE.

NONFICTION Needs how-to, technical. **Buys 20 mss/year.** Query or send complete ms. Length: 1,000-1,500 words. **Pays $50-500.** Pays expenses of writers on assignment.

REPRINTS Send tearsheet or photocopy with rights for sale noted and information about when and where the material previously appeared. Pays 50% of the amount paid for an original article.

PHOTOS Send photos. Captions, identification of subjects required. Reviews contact sheets, negatives, transparencies, prints. Buys one-time rights.

BUSINESS MANAGEMENT

$$$$ BEDTIMES

International Sleep Products Association, 501 Wythe St., Alexandria VA 22314. (336)500-3816. **E-mail:** mbest@sleepproducts.org. **Website:** www.bedtimesmagazine.com. **Contact:** Mary Best, editorial director. **20-40% freelance written.** *BedTimes*, published monthly, focuses on news, trends, and issues of interest to mattress manufacturers and their suppliers, as well as more general business stories. Estab. 1917. Circ. 3,800. Byline given. Pays on acceptance. No kill fee. Publishes ms an average of 3 months after acceptance. Editorial lead time 2 months. Accepts queries by e-mail. Accepts simultaneous submissions. Responds in 1 month to queries. Sample copy: $4. Guidelines by e-mail or online.

"We are particularly interested in stories that show mattress manufacturers ways to reduce costs and operate more efficiently. *BedTimes* is not written for retailers or consumers: We do not run stories about how to shop for a mattress or how to lure customers into a bedding store."

NONFICTION **Buys 15-25 mss/year.** Query with published clips. Length: 500-2,500 words. **Pays 50-$1/word for short features; $2,000 for cover story.**

PHOTOS State availability. Identification of subjects required. Negotiates payment individually. Buys one-time rights.

TIPS "Cover topics have included annual industry forecast, e-commerce, flammability and home furnishings, the risks and rewards of marketing overseas, the evolving family business, the shifting workplace environment, and what do consumers really want? Our news and features are straightforward—we are not a lobbying vehicle for our association. No special slant."

$$ BUSINESS TRAVEL EXECUTIVE

5768 Remington Dr., Winston-Salem NC 27104. (336)766-1961. **E-mail:** dbooth@askbte.com. **Website:** www.askbte.com. **Contact:** Dan Booth, managing editor. **90% freelance written.** Monthly magazine covering corporate procurement of travel services. Byline given. Pays on publication. No kill fee. Publishes ms an average of 2 months after acceptance. Editorial lead time 0-3 months. Accepts queries by e-mail. Accepts simultaneous submissions.

NONFICTION Needs how-to, technical. **Buys 48 mss/year.** Please send unsolicited submissions, at your own risk. Please enclose a SASE for return of material. Submission of letters implies the right to edit and publish all or in part. Length: 800-2,000 words. **Pays $200-800.** Pays expenses of writers on assignment.

COLUMNS/DEPARTMENTS Meeting Place (meeting planning and management); Hotel Pulse (hotel negotiations, contracting and compliance); Security Watch (travel safety); all 1,000 words. **Buys 24 mss/year.** Query. **Pays $200-400.**

TIPS "We are not a travel magazine. We publish articles designed to help corporate purchasers of travel negotiate contracts, enforce policy, select automated services, track business travelers, and account for their safety and expenditures, understand changes in the various industries associated with travel. Do not submit mss without an assignment. Look at the website for an idea of what we publish."

$$ CHRISTIAN MARKET

CBA, the Association for Christian Retail, 1365 Garden of the Gods Rd., Suite 105, Colorado Springs CO 80907. **Fax:** (719)272-3510. **E-mail:** cellis@cbaonline.org; info@cbaonline.org. **Website:** www.cbaonline.org. **Contact:** Cathy Ellis. **80% freelance written.** Monthly trade magazine covering the Christian products industry. Writers must have knowledge of and direct experience in the Christian products industry. Subject matter must specifically pertain to the Christian products audience. Estab. 1968. Byline given. Pays on publication. No kill fee. Publishes ms an average of 3 months after acceptance. Editorial lead time 3 months. Submit seasonal material 6 months in advance. Accepts queries by e-mail. Accepts simultaneous submissions. Responds in 2 months to queries. Sample copy for $9.50 or online.

NONFICTION **Buys 24 mss/year.** Query. Length: 650-1,500 words. **Pays 25¢/word.**

TIPS "Only experts on Christian retail industry, completely familiar with supplier and retail audience and their needs and considerations, should submit a query. Do not submit articles unless requested."

$$ CONTRACTING PROFITS

Trade Press Publishing, 2100 W. Florist Ave., Milwaukee WI 53209. (414)228-7701; (800)727-7995. **Fax:** (414)228-1134. **E-mail:** dan.weltin@tradepress.com. **Website:** www.cleanlink.com/cp. **Contact:** Dan Weltin, editor-in-chief. **40% freelance written.** Magazine published 10 times/year covering building service contracting and business management advice. The pocket MBA for this industry—focusing not only on cleaning-specific topics, but also discussing how to run businesses better and increase profits through a variety of management articles. Estab. 1995. Circ. 32,000. Byline given. Pays within 30 days of acceptance. No kill fee. Editorial lead time 2 months. Submit seasonal material 3 months in advance. Accepts queries by mail, e-mail. Accepts simultaneous submissions. Responds in weeks to queries. Sample copy available online. Guidelines free.

NONFICTION Needs expose, how-to, interview, technical. No product-related reviews or testimonials. **Buys 30 mss/year.** Query with published clips. Length: 1,000-1,500 words. **Pays $100-500.** Pays expenses of writers on assignment.

COLUMNS/DEPARTMENTS Query with published clips.

TIPS "Read back issues on our website and be able to understand some of those topics prior to calling."

$$ CONTRACT MANAGEMENT

National Contract Management Association, 21740 Beaumeade Circle, Suite 125, Ashburn VA 20147. (571)382-0082. **Fax:** (703)448-0939. **E-mail:** khansen@ncmahq.org. **Website:** www.ncmahq.org. **Contact:** Kerry McKinnon Hansen, director of publications and editor-in-chief. **10% freelance written.** Monthly magazine covering contract and business management. Most of the articles published in *Contract Management (CM)* are written by NCMA members, although one does not have to be an NCMA member to be published in the magazine. Articles should concern some aspect of the contract management profession, whether at the level of a beginner or that of the advanced practitioner. Estab. 1960. Circ. 23,000. Byline given. Pays on publication. No kill fee. Publishes ms an average of 3 months after acceptance. Editorial lead time 10 weeks. Submit seasonal material 3 months in advance. Accepts queries by mail, e-mail, fax, phone. Accepts simultaneous submissions. Responds in 2 weeks to queries. Responds in 1 month to mss. Sample copy and writer's guidelines available online.

NONFICTION Needs essays, general interest, how-to, humor, inspirational, new product, opinion, technical. No company or CEO profiles. Read a copy of publication before submitting. **Buys 6-10 mss/year.** Query with published clips. Send an inquiry including a brief summary (150 words) of the proposed article to the managing editor before writing the article. Length: 1,800-4,000 words. **Pays $300.**

PHOTOS State availability. Captions, identification of subjects required. Offers no additional payment for photos accepted with ms. Buys one-time rights.

COLUMNS/DEPARTMENTS Professional Development (self-improvement in business), 1,000-1,500 words; Back to Basics (basic how-tos and discussions), 1,500-2,000 words. **Buys 2 mss/year.** Query with published clips. **Pays $300.**

TIPS "Query and read at least 1 issue. Visit website to better understand our audience."

$$ INTENTS

Industrial Fabrics Association International, 1801 County Rd. B W, Roseville MN 55113. (651)222-2508. **Fax:** (651)631-9334. **E-mail:** generalinfo@ifai.com. **Website:** intentsmag.com. **50% freelance written.** Bimonthly magazine covering tent-rental and special-event industries. *InTents* is the official publication of IFAI's Tent Rental Division, delivering "the total tent experience." *InTents* offers focused, credible information needed to stage and host safe, successful tented events. Issues of the magazine include news, trends and behind-the-scenes coverage of the latest events in tents. Estab. 1995. Circ. 12,000. Byline given. Pays on acceptance. No kill fee. Publishes ms an average of 2 months after acceptance. Editorial lead time 3 months. Accepts queries by mail, e-mail, fax. Accepts simultaneous submissions. Sample copy and writer's guidelines free.

NONFICTION Needs how-to, interview, new product, photo feature, technical. **Buys 12-18 mss/year.** Query. Length: 800-2,000 words. **Pays $300-500.** Pays expenses of writers on assignment.

PHOTOS State availability. Captions, identification of subjects, model releases required. Reviews contact sheets, negatives, prints, digital images. Negotiates payment individually.

TIPS "We look for lively, intelligent writing that makes technical subjects come alive."

$$ MAINEBIZ

Mainebiz Publications, Inc., 48 Free St., Portland ME 04101. (207)761-8379. **Fax:** (207)761-0732. **E-mail:** pvanallen@mainebiz.biz; editorial@mainebiz.biz. **Website:** www.mainebiz.biz. **Contact:** Peter Van Allen, editor. **25% freelance written.** Biweekly tabloid covering business in Maine. *Mainebiz* is read by business decision makers across the state. Readerslook to the publication for business news and analysis. Estab. 1994. Circ. 13,000. Byline given. Pays on publication. Offers 10% kill fee. Publishes ms an average of 1 month after acceptance. Editorial lead time 1 month. Submit seasonal material 2 months in advance. Accepts queries by mail, e-mail. Accepts simultaneous submissions. Responds in 3 weeks to queries. Sample copy online.

NONFICTION Needs essays, expose, interview, business trends. Special issues: See website for editorial calendar. **Buys 50+ mss/year.** Query with published clips. Length: 500-2,500 words. **Pays $75-350.** Pays expenses of writers on assignment.

PHOTOS State availability. Identification of subjects required. Reviews GIF/JPEG files. Negotiates payment individually. Buys one-time rights.

TIPS "If you wish to contribute, please spend some time familiarizing yourself with *Mainebiz*. Tell us a little about yourself, your experience and background as a writer and qualifications for writing a particular story. If you have clips you can send us via e-mail, or web addresses of pages that contain your work, please send us a representative sampling (no more than 3 or 4, please). Stories should be well thought out with specific relevance to Maine. Arts and culture-related queries are welcome, as long as there is a business angle. We appreciate unusual angles on business stories and regularly work with new freelancers. Send the text of your query or submission in plain text in the body of your e-mail, rather than as an attached file, as we may not be able to read the format of your file. We do our best to respond to all inquiries, but be aware that we are sometimes inundated."

$$$ RETAIL INFO SYSTEMS NEWS

Edgell Communications, 4 Middlebury Blvd., Randolph NJ 07869. (973)607-1300. **Fax:** (973)607-1395. **E-mail:** ablair@edgellmail.com; jskorupa@edgellmail.com. **Website:** www.risnews.com. **Contact:** Adam Blair, editor; Joe Skorupa, group editor-in-chief. **65% freelance written.** Monthly magazine covering retail technology. Estab. 1988. Circ. 22,000. Byline sometimes given. Pays on publication. No kill fee. Publishes ms an average of 2 months after acceptance. Editorial lead time 3 months. Submit seasonal material 3 months in advance. Accepts queries by mail. Accepts simultaneous submissions. Sample copy available online.

Readers are functional managers/executives in all types of retail and consumer goods firms. They are making major improvements in company operations and in alliances with customers/suppliers.

NONFICTION Needs essays, how-to, humor, interview, technical. **Buys 80 mss/year.** Query with published clips. Length: 700-1,900 words. **Pays $600-1,200 for assigned articles.** Pays expenses of writers on assignment.

PHOTOS State availability of or send photos. Identification of subjects required. Negotiates payment individually. Buys one-time rights plus reprint, if applicable.

COLUMNS/DEPARTMENTS News/trends (analysis of current events), 150-300 words. **Buys 4 articles/year mss/year.** Query with published clips. **Pays $100-300.**

TIPS "Case histories about companies achieving substantial results using advanced management practices and/or advanced technology are best."

$$ RTOHQ: THE MAGAZINE

1504 Robin Hood Trail, Austin TX 78703. (800)204-2776. **Fax:** (512)794-0097. **E-mail:** nferguson@rtohq.org; bkeese@rtohq.org. **Website:** www.rtohq.org. **Contact:** Neil Ferguson, art director; Bill Keese, executive editor. **50% freelance written.** Bimonthly magazine covering the rent-to-own industry. *RTOHQ: The Magazine* is the only publication representing the rent-to-own industry and members of APRO. The magazine covers timely news and features affecting the industry, association activities, and member profiles. Awarded best 4-color magazine by the American Society of Association Executives in 1999. Estab. 1980. Circ. 5,500. Byline given. Pays on acceptance. Offers 25% kill fee. Publishes ms an average of 2 months after acceptance. Editorial lead time 2 months. Submit seasonal material 4 months in advance. Accepts queries by mail, e-mail, fax, phone, online submission form. Accepts simultaneous submissions. Responds in 1 month to queries. Responds in 2 months to mss. Sample copy free.

NONFICTION Needs expose, general interest, how-to, inspirational, interview, technical, industry features. **Buys 12 mss/year.** Query with published clips. Length: 1,200-2,500 words. **Pays $150-700.** Pays expenses of writers on assignment.

SECURITY DEALER & INTEGRATOR

Southcomm, 12735 Morris Road Bldg. 200 Suite 180, Alpharetta GA 30004. (800)547-7377, ext 2226. **E-mail:** paul.rothman@cygnus.com. **Website:** www.securityinfowatch.com/magazine. **Contact:** Paul Rothman, editor-in-chief. **25% freelance written.** Circ. 25,000. Byline sometimes given. Pays 3 weeks after publication. No kill fee. Publishes ms an average of 3 months after acceptance. Accepts queries by e-mail. Accepts simultaneous submissions.

Security Dealer & Integrator (SD&I) magazine is The Path to Greater Profits for its audience of security professionals who own, manage or help maintain dealer, integrator, reseller and installation businesses. *SD&I* keeps you informed of the latest in security technology solutions, while always providing strategies to run a more effective and profitable security business.

NONFICTION Needs how-to, interview, technical. No consumer pieces. Query by e-mail. Length: 1,000-3,000 words. **Pays $250.** Pays expenses of writers on assignment.

PHOTOS State availability. Captions, identification of subjects required. Reviews contact sheets, transparencies. Offers $25 additional payment for photos accepted with ms.

COLUMNS/DEPARTMENTS Query by mail only.

TIPS "The areas of our publication most open to freelancers are technical innovations, trends in the alarm industry, and crime patterns as related to the business as well as business finance and management pieces."

SMART BUSINESS

Smart Business Network, Inc., 835 Sharon Dr., Suite 200, Cleveland OH 44145. (440)250-7000. **Fax:** (440)250-7001. **E-mail:** mscott@sbnonline.com. **Website:** www.sbnonline.com. **Contact:** Mark Scott, senior associate editor. **5% freelance written.** Monthly business magazine with an audience made up of business owners and top decision makers. *Smart Business* is one of the fastest growing national chains of regional management journals for corporate executives. Every issue delves into the minds of the most innovative executives in each of our regions to report on how market leaders got to the top and what strategies they use to stay there. Estab. 1989. Byline given. Pays on publication. Offers 50% kill fee. Publishes ms an average of 2 months after acceptance. Editorial lead time 3 months. Submit seasonal material 3 months in advance. Accepts queries by mail, e-mail. Accepts simultaneous submissions. Responds in 2 weeks to queries. Responds in 1 month to mss. Sample copy available online. Guidelines by e-mail.

Publishes local editions in Dallas, Houston, St. Louis, Northern California, San Diego, Orange County, Tampa Bay/St. Petersburg, Miami, Philadephia, Cincinnati, Detroit, Los Angeles, Broward/Palm Beach, Cleveland, Akron/Canton, Columbus, Pittsburgh, Atlanta, Chicago, and Indianapolis.

NONFICTION Needs how-to, interview. No breaking news or news features. **Buys 10-12 mss/year.** Query with published clips. Length: 1,150-2,000 words. **Pays $200-500.** Pays expenses of writers on assignment.

PHOTOS State availability. Identification of subjects required. Reviews negatives, prints. Offers no additional payment for photos accepted with ms. Buys one-time, reprint, and Web rights.

TIPS "The best way to submit to *Smart Business* is to read us—either online or in print. Remember, our audience is made up of top level business executives and owners."

STAMATS MEETINGS MEDIA

615 5th St. SE, Cedar Rapids IA 52401. **Fax:** (319)364-4278. **E-mail:** tyler.davidson@meetingsfocus.com. **Website:** www.meetingsfocus.com. **Contact:** Tyler Davidson, chief content director. **75% freelance written.** Monthly tabloid covering meeting, event, and conference planning. Estab. 1986. Circ. *Meetings East* and *Meetings South* 22,000; *Meetings West* 26,000. Byline given. Pays 1 month after publication. No kill fee. Publishes ms an average of 1 month after acceptance. Editorial lead time 3 months. Submit seasonal material 3 months in advance. Accepts queries by mail, e-mail, fax. Accepts simultaneous submissions. Responds in 3 weeks to queries. Sample copy for DSR with 9x13 envelope and 5 first-class stamps.

"*Meetings Focus* is the premier one-stop resource for meeting planning professionals who need information on destinations, meeting facilities, meeting room setup ideas, sustainable meetings, and other components of successful meetings, conventions, conferences, and events in the U.S., Mexico, Canada, and the Caribbean. Provides highly targeted audience marketing opportunities through online, live event, and print media branded products. Consistent high-quality audience qualification requirements and processes combined with award-winning staff-written content have kept Stamats Business Media at the forefront of each industry market it serves for over 80 years."

NONFICTION Needs how-to, travel. "No first-person fluff—this is a business magazine." **Buys 150 mss/year.** Query with published clips. Length: 1,200-2,000 words. **Pays $500 flat rate/package.**

PHOTOS State availability. Identification of subjects required. Offers no additional payment for photos accepted with ms. Buys one-time rights.

TIPS "We're always looking for freelance writers who are local to our destination stories. For Site Inspections, get in touch in late September or early October, when we usually have the following year's editorial calendar available."

$ SUPERVISION MAGAZINE

National Research Bureau, 320 Valley St., Burlington IA 52601. (319)752-5415. **E-mail:** articles@supervisionmagazine.com. **Website:** www.supervisionmagazine.com/. **Contact:** Todd Darnall. **80% freelance written.** Monthly magazine covering management and supervision. *Supervision Magazine* explains complex issues in a clear and understandable format. Articles written by both experts and scholars provide practical and concise answers to issues facing today's supervisors and managers. Estab. 1939. Circ. 500. Byline given. Pays on acceptance. Publishes ms an average of 1 month after acceptance. Editorial lead time 1 month. Submit seasonal material 2 months in advance. Accepts queries by e-mail. Accepts simultaneous submissions. Sample copy free. Guidelines available online.

NONFICTION Needs personal experience, "We can use articles dealing with motivation, leadership, human relations and communication.". Send complete ms. Length: 1,500-2,000 words. **Pays 4¢/word.** Pays expenses of writers on assignment.

CHURCH ADMINISTRATION & MINISTRY

$ CHRISTIAN COMMUNICATOR

American Christian Writers, 9118 W. Elmwood Dr., Suite 1G, Niles IL 60714-5820. (847)296-3964. **E-mail:** ljohnson@wordprocommunications.com. **E-mail:** submissions@wordprocommunications.com. **Website:** acwriters.com. **Contact:** Lin Johnson, managing editor; Sally Miller, poetry editor (sallymiller@ameritech.net). **50% freelance written.** Estab. 1988. Circ. 800. Byline given. Pays on publication. No kill fee. Publishes ms an average of 6-12 months after acceptance. Editorial lead time 3 months. Submit seasonal material 6 months in advance. Accepts queries by e-mail. Responds in 2-8 weeks to queries; in 3-12 weeks to mss. Sample copy online. Writers guidelines by e-mail or on website.

NONFICTION Needs essays, how-to, interview, reviews, "Articles on writing nonfiction, research, creativity.". **Buys 36-40 mss/year.** Query or send complete ms only by e-mail. Length: 750-1,000 words. **Pays $10. $5 for reviews and anecdotes.**

REPRINTS Same as first rights.

POETRY **Contact:** Sally Miller, sallymiller@ameritech.net. Needs free verse, light verse, traditional. Buys Publishes 12 poems/year. poems/year. Submit maximum 2 poems. Length: 4-20 lines. **Pays $5.**

FILLERS Needs anecdotes, short humor.

TIPS "Everything, including poetry, must be related to writing, publishing, or speaking. We primarily use how-to articles but are willing to look at other types of manuscripts."

$$ THE JOURNAL OF ADVENTIST EDUCATION

General Conference of SDA, 12501 Old Columbia Pike, Silver Spring MD 20904. (301)680-5069. **Fax:** (301)622-9627. **E-mail:** mcgarrellf@gc.adventist.org; goffc@gc.adventist.org. **Website:** jae.adventist.org. **Contact:** Faith-Ann McGarrell, editor; Chandra Goff, editorial assistant. A quarterly professional journal for Christian teachers, administrators, and stakeholders, with specific emphasis on educators in Seventh-day Adventist schools. Published 4 times per year in English, French, Spanish, and Portuguese. Emphasizes procedures, philosophy, and subject matter of

Christian education. Estab. 1939. Circ. 14,000 in English; 13,000 in other languages. Byline given. Pays on publication. No kill fee. Publishes ms an average of 1 year after acceptance. Editorial lead time 1 year. Accepts queries by mail, e-mail, fax, phone. Accepts simultaneous submissions. Responds in 6 weeks to queries; 4 months to mss. Sample copy for SAE with 10x12 envelope and 5 first-class stamps. Guidelines online.

NONFICTION Needs book excerpts, essays, how-to, personal experience, photo feature, religious. "No brief first-person stories about Sunday Schools." Query. All articles must be submitted in electronic format to http://www.editorialmanager.com/jae/default.aspx. Store in Word or .rtf format. If you submit a CD, include a printed copy of the article with the CD. Articles should be 6-8 pages long, with a max of 10 pages, including references. Two-part articles will be considered. Length: 1,500-2,500 words. **Pays $25-300.**

REPRINTS Send tearsheet or photocopy and information about when and where the material previously appeared.

PHOTOS Buys 5-15 photos from freelancers/issue; up to 75 photos/year. Photos of children/teens, multicultural, parents, education, religious, health/fitness, technology/computers with people, committees, offices, school photos of teachers, students, parents, activities at all levels, elementary though graduate school. Reviews photos with or without a ms. Model release preferred. Photo captions preferred. Uses mostly digital color images but also accepts color prints; 35mm, 21/4x21/4, 4x5 transparencies. Send digital photos via ZIP, CD, or DVD (preferred); e-mail as TIFF, GIF, JPEG files at 300 DPI. Do not send large numbers of photos as e-mail attachments, instead use file sharing products such as Dropbox or WeTransfer. Send query letter with prints, photocopies, transparencies. Provide self-promotion piece to be kept on file for possible future assignments. Responds in 1 month to queries. Simultaneous submissions and previously published work OK. State availability of or send photos. Pays $100-350 for color cover; $50-100 for color inside. Willing to negotiate on electronic usage of photos. Pays on publication. Credit line given. Buys one-time rights for use in magazine and on website.

TIPS "Articles may deal with educational theory or practice, although the *Journal* seeks to emphasize the practical. Articles dealing with the creative and effective use of methods to enhance teaching skills or learning in the classroom are especially welcome. Whether theoretical or practical, such essays should demonstrate the skillful integration of Seventh-day Adventist faith/values and learning."

$$ LEADERSHIP JOURNAL

Christianity Today International, 465 Gundersen Dr., Carol Stream IL 60188. (630)260-6200. **Fax:** (630)260-0114. **E-mail:** ljeditor@leadershipjournal.net. **Website:** www.christianitytoday.com/le. Skye Jethani, managing editor. **Contact:** Marshall Shelley, editor-in-chief. **75% freelance written. Works with a small number of new/unpublished writers each year.** Quarterly magazine. Writers must have a knowledge of and sympathy for the unique expectations placed on pastors and local church leaders. Each article must support points by illustrating from real life experiences in local churches. Estab. 1980. Circ. 48,000. Byline given. Pays on acceptance. Offers 33% kill fee. Publishes ms an average of 6 months after acceptance. Editorial lead time 6 months. Submit seasonal material 6 months in advance. Accepts queries by mail, e-mail, fax. Accepts simultaneous submissions. Responds in 2 weeks to queries. Responds in 2 months to mss. Sample copy for free or online.

NONFICTION Needs how-to, humor, interview, personal experience, sermon illustrations. No articles from writers who have never read our journal. No unsolicited ms. **Buys 60 mss/year.** Query with proposal. Send a brief query letter describing your idea and how you plan to develop it. Length: 300-3,000 words. **Pays $35-400.** Pays expenses of writers on assignment.

COLUMNS/DEPARTMENTS **Contact:** Skye Jethanis, managing editor. Toolkit (book/software reviews), 500 words. **Buys 8 mss/year. mss/year.** Query.

TIPS "Every article in *Leadership* must provide practical help for problems that church leaders face. *Leadership* articles are not essays expounding a topic or editorials arguing a position or homilies explaining Biblical principles. They are how-to articles, based on first-person accounts of real-life experiences in ministry. They allow our readers to see `over the shoulder' of a colleague in ministry who then reflects on those experiences and identifies the lessons learned. As you know, a magazine's slant is a specific personality that readers expect (and it's what they've sent us their subscription money to provide). Our style is that of friendly conversation rather than directive discourse—what I learned about local church ministry rather than what you need to do."

$ MOMENTUM

National Catholic Educational Association, 1005 N. Glebe Rd., Suite 525, Arlington VA 22201. (800)711-6232. **Fax:** (703)243-0025. **E-mail:** momentum@ncea.org. **Website:** www.ncea.org/publications/momentum. **Contact:** Gabrielle Gallagher, editor. **65% freelance written.** Quarterly educational journal covering educational issues in Catholic schools and parishes. *Momentum* is a membership journal of the National Catholic Educational Association. The audience is educators and administrators in Catholic schools K-12, and parish programs. Estab. 1970. Circ. 19,000. Byline given. Pays on publication. No kill fee. Publishes ms an average of 3 months after acceptance. Accepts queries by e-mail. Accepts simultaneous submissions. Sample copy for $5 SASE and 8 first-class stamps. Guidelines online.

NONFICTION No articles unrelated to educational and catechesis issues. **Buys 40-60 mss/year.** Query and send complete ms. Length: 1,500 words for feature articles; 700-1,000 words for columns, "From the Field," and opinion pieces or essays; 500-750 words for book reviews. **Pays $75 maximum.**

PHOTOS State availability of photos. Captions, identification of subjects required. Reviews prints. Offers no additional payment for photos accepted with ms.

$ RTJ'S CREATIVE CATECHIST

Twenty-Third Publications, P.O. Box 6015, New London CT 06320. (800)321-0411, ext. 188. **Fax:** (860)437-6246. **E-mail:** creativesubs@rtjscreativecatechist.com; editor@rtjscreativecatechist.com; pat.gohn@bayard-inc.com. **Website:** www.rtjscreativecatechist.com. **Contact:** Pat Gohn, editor. Monthly magazine for Catholic catechists and religion teachers. The mission of *RTJ's Creative Catechist* is to encourage and assist Catholic DREs and catechists in their vocation to proclaim the gospel message and lead others to the joy of following Jesus Christ. *RTJ* provides professional support, theological content, age appropriate methodology, and teaching tools. Estab. 1966. Circ. 30,000. Byline given. Pays on acceptance. Publishes ms an average of 3-20 months after acceptance. Editorial lead time 4 months. Submit seasonal material 6 months in advance. Accepts queries by mail, e-mail. Accepts simultaneous submissions. Responds in 1-2 weeks to queries. Responds in 1-2 months to mss. Sample copy for SAE with 9x12 envelope and 3 first-class stamps. Guidelines free.

NONFICTION Needs how-to, inspirational, personal experience, religious, articles on celebrating church seasons, sacraments, on morality, on prayer, on saints. Special issues: Sacraments; Prayer; Advent/Christmas; Lent/Easter. All should be written by people who have experience in religious education, or a good background in Catholic faith. Does not want fiction, poems, plays, articles written for Catholic school teachers (i.e., math, English, etc.), or articles that are academic rather than catechetical in nature. **Buys 35-40 mss/year.** Send complete ms. Length: 600-1,300 words. **Pays $100-125 for assigned articles. Pays $75-125 for unsolicited articles.**

COLUMNS/DEPARTMENTS Catechist to Catechist (brief articles on crafts, games, etc., for religion lessons); Faith and Fun (full-page religious word games, puzzles, mazes, etc., for children). **Buys 30 mss/year.** Send complete ms. **Pays $20-125.**

TIPS "We look for clear, concise articles written from experience. Articles should help readers move from theory/doctrine to concrete application. Unsolicited mss not returned without SASE. No fancy formatting; no handwritten mss. Author should be able to furnish article on disk or via e-mail if possible."

$$ TODAY'S CATHOLIC TEACHER

Peter Li Education Group, 3055 Kettering Blvd., Suite 100, Dayton OH 45439. (937)293-1415; (800)523-4625, x1139. **Fax:** (937)293-1310. **E-mail:** bshepard@peterli.com; danielle.bean@bayard-inc.com. **E-mail:** bshepard@peterli.com. **Website:** www.catholicteacher.com. **Contact:** Dr. Lisa D'Souza, editor; Danielle Bean, publisher. **60% freelance written.** Magazine published 6 times/year during school year covering Catholic education for grades K-12. Looks for topics of interest and practical help to teachers in Catholic elementary schools in all curriculum areas including religion technology, discipline, and motivation. Estab. 1972. Circ. 50,000. Byline given. Pays on publication. No kill fee. Publishes ms an average of 2 months after acceptance. Editorial lead time 3 months. Submit seasonal material 6 months in advance. Accepts queries by mail, e-mail, fax. Accepts simultaneous submissions. Responds in 1 month to queries. Responds in 3 months to mss. Sample copy for $3 or on website. Guidelines available online.

NONFICTION Needs essays, how-to, humor, interview, personal experience. No articles pertaining to public education. **Buys 15 mss/year.** Query or send complete ms. Query letters are encouraged. E-mail, write, call, or fax the editor for editorial calendar. Articles may be submitted as hard copy; submission by e-mail with accompanying hard copy is appreciated. Length: 600-1,500 words. **Pays $100-250.** Pays expenses of writers on assignment.

PHOTOS State availability. Captions, identification of subjects, model releases required. Reviews transparencies, prints. Offers $20-50/photo. Buys one-time rights.

TIPS "Although our readership is primarily classroom teachers, *Today's Catholic Teacher* is also read by principals, supervisors, superintendents, boards of education, pastors, and parents. *Today's Catholic Teacher* aims to be for Catholic educators a source of information not available elsewhere. The focus of articles should span the interests of teachers from early childhood through junior high. Articles may be directed to just 1 age group, yet have wider implications. Preference is given to material directed to teachers in grades 4-8. The desired magazine style is direct, concise, informative, and accurate. Writing should be enjoyable to read, informal rather than scholarly, lively, and free of educational jargon."

$$ YOUTHWORKER JOURNAL

Salem Publishing/CCM Communications, 402 BNA Dr., Suite 400, Nashville TN 37217-2509. **E-mail:** ALee@SalemPublishing.com. **Website:** www.youthworker.com. **Contact:** Steve Rabey, editor; Amy L. Lee, managing editor. **100% freelance written.** Website and bimonthly magazine covering professional youth ministry in the church and parachurch. Estab. 1984. Circ. 20,000. Byline given. Pays on publication. No kill fee. Publishes ms an average of 3 months after acceptance for print; immediately online. Editorial lead time 6 months for print; immediately online. Submit seasonal material 6 months in advance for print. Accepts queries by e-mail, online submission form. Accepts simultaneous submissions. Responds within 6 weeks to queries. Sample copy for $5. Guidelines available online.

NONFICTION Needs essays, new product, personal experience, photo feature, religious. Special issues: See website for themes in upcoming issues. Query. Length: 250-3,000 words. **Pays $15-200.**

PHOTOS Send photos. Reviews GIF/JPEG files. Negotiates payment individually.

TIPS "We exist to help meet the personal and professional needs of career, Christian youth workers in the church and parachurch. Proposals accepted on the posted theme, according to the writer's guidelines on our website. It's not enough to write well—you must know youth ministry."

CLOTHING

$$$ FOOTWEAR PLUS

9 Threads, 135 West 20th Street, 4th Floor, New York NY 10011. (646)278-1550. **Fax:** (646)278-1553. **E-mail:** editorialrequests@9threads.com. **Website:** www.footwearplusmagazine.com. **Contact:** Brittany Leitner, assistant editor. **20% freelance written.** Monthly magazine covering footwear fashion and business. A business-to-business publication targeted at footwear retailers. Covers all categories of footwear and age ranges with a focus on new trends, brands and consumer buying habits, as well as retailer advice on operating the store more effectively. Estab. 1990. Circ. 18,000. Byline given. Pays on publication. No kill fee. Publishes ms an average of 1-2 months after acceptance. Editorial lead time 1-2 months. Accepts simultaneous submissions. Sample copy for $5.

NONFICTION Needs interview, new product, technical. Does not want pieces unrelated to footwear/fashion industry. **Buys 10-20 mss/year.** Query. Length: 500-2,500 words. **Pays $1,000 maximum.** Pays expenses of writers on assignment.

$$ IMPRESSIONS

Emerald Expositions, 1145 Sanctuary Pkwy., Suite 355, Alpharetta GA 30009-4772. (770)291-5574. **E-mail:** mderryberry@impressionsmag.com; jlaster@impressionsmag.com; michelle.havich@emeraldexpo.com. **Website:** www.impressionsmag.com. **Contact:** Marcia Derryberry, editor-in-chief; Jamar Laster, executive editor; Dustin Shrader, managing editor. **50% freelance written.** Magazine, published 13 times/year, covering screen printing, computerized embroidery, digitizing, digital decorating technologies, including direct-to-garment printing, sublimation and heat-applied graphics. Features authoritative, up-to-date information on screen printing, embroidery, heat-applied graphics, and inkjet-to-garment printing. Readable, practical business and/or technical articles show readers how to succeed in their profession. Estab. 1994. Circ. 20,000. Byline given. Pays on publication.

No kill fee. Publishes ms an average of 3 months after acceptance. Editorial lead time 3 months. Submit seasonal material 6 months in advance. Accepts queries by mail, e-mail. Accepts simultaneous submissions. Sample copy: $10.

NONFICTION Needs how-to, interview, new product, photo feature, technical. **Buys 40 mss/year.** Query. Length: 800-2,000 words. **Pays $300 and up for assigned articles.** Pays expenses of writers on assignment.

PHOTOS Send photos. Reviews transparencies, prints. Negotiates payment individually.

TIPS "Show us you have specified knowledge, experience, or contacts in the embroidery industry or a related field."

$$ TEXTILE WORLD

Billian Publishing Co., P.O. Box 683155, Marietta GA 30068. (678)483-6102; (404)518-9599. **Fax:** (770)952-0669. **E-mail:** editor@textileworld.com; rsdavis@textileworld.com. **Website:** www.textileworld.com. **Contact:** editor. **5% freelance written.** Bimonthly magazine covering the business of textile, apparel, and fiber industries with considerable technical focus on products and processes. Estab. 1868. Byline given. Pays on publication. No kill fee. Accepts simultaneous submissions.

NONFICTION No puff pieces pushing a particular product. **Buys 10 mss/year.** Query. Length: 500 words minimum. **Pays $200/published page.**

PHOTOS Send photos. Captions required. Reviews prints. Offers no additional payment for photos accepted with ms. Buys one-time rights.

CONSTRUCTION & CONTRACTING

$$ AUTOMATED BUILDER

CMN Associates, Inc., 2401 Grapevine Dr., Oxnard CA 93036. (805)351-5931. **Fax:** (805)351-5755. **E-mail:** cms03@pacbell.net. **Website:** www.automatedbuilder.com. **Contact:** Don O. Carlson, editor/publisher. **5% freelance written.** "*Automated Builder* covers management, production and marketing information on all 7 segments of home, apartment and commercial construction. These include: (1) production (site) builders, (2) panelized home manufacturers, (3) HUD-code (mobile) home manufacturers, (4) modular home manufacturers, (5) component manufacturers, (6) special unit (commercial) manufacturers, and (7) all types of builders and builders/dealers. The in-plant material is technical in content and covers new machine technologies and improved methods for in-plant building and erecting. Home and commercial buyers will see the latest in homes and commercial structures." Estab. 1964. Circ. 75,000 when printed. Byline given if desired. Pays on acceptance. Publishes ms an average of 2 months after acceptance. Editorial lead time 2 months. Accepts queries by mail, e-mail, fax. Accepts simultaneous submissions. Responds in 2 weeks to queries.

NONFICTION "No fiction and no planned 'dreams.' Housing projects must be built or under construction. Same for commercial structures." **Buys 6-8 mss/year.** Phone queries OK. Length: 500-750 words. **Pays $250 for stories including photos.** Pays expenses of writers on assignment.

PHOTOS Captions are required for each photo. Offers no additional payment for photos accepted with ms. Payment is on acceptance.

TIPS "Stories often are too long, too loose; we prefer 500-750 words plus captions. We prefer a phone query on feature articles. If accepted on query, articles will rarely be rejected later. It is required that every story and photos are cleared with the source before sending to *Automated Builder*. At-Home segment will contain details and photos of newest residential and commercial buildings sold or ready for sale. At-Home segment also will welcome stories and photos of new units added to existing homes or commercial structures. Ideal layout would be one page of photos with exterior and/or interior photos of the structures and an adjoining page for text."

$$ CONCRETE CONSTRUCTION

Hanley Wood, 5600 N. River Rd., Suite 250, Rosemont IL 60018. (773)824-2400. **E-mail:** bpalmer@hanleywood.com. **Website:** www.concreteconstruction.net/magazine. **Contact:** William D. Palmer Jr., editor-in-chief. **20% freelance written.** Monthly magazine for concrete contractors, engineers, architects, specifiers, and others who design and build residential, commercial, industrial, and public works, cast-in-place concrete structures. It also covers job stories and new equipment in the industry. Estab. 1956. Circ. 80,000. Byline given. Pays on acceptance. No kill fee. Publishes ms an average of 4 months after acceptance. Editorial lead time 4 months. Submit seasonal material 4 months in advance. Accepts queries by mail, e-mail, fax. Accepts simultaneous submissions. Responds in 2 weeks to queries; 1 month to mss. Sample copy and writer's guidelines free.

NONFICTION Needs how-to, new product, personal experience, photo feature, technical, job stories. **Buys 7-10 mss/year.** Query with published clips. 2,000 words maximum **Pays $250 or more for assigned articles; $200 minimum for unsolicited articles.** Pays expenses of writers on assignment.

PHOTOS Send photos. Captions required. Reviews contact sheets, negatives, transparencies, prints. Offers no additional payment for photos accepted with ms. Buys one time rights.

TIPS "Have a good understanding of the concrete construction industry. How-to stories accepted only from industry experts. Job stories must cover procedures, materials, and equipment used as well as the project's scope."

$$$ THE CONCRETE PRODUCER

Hanley-Wood, LLC, 8725 W. Higgins Rd., Suite 600, Chicago IL 60631. (773)824-2400 or (773)824-2496. **E-mail:** tbagsarian@hanleywood.com; ryelton@hanleywood.com; tcpeditor@hanleywood.com. **Website:** www.theconcreteproducer.com. **Contact:** Tom Bagsarian, group managing editor; Richard Yelton, editor-at-large. **25% freelance written.** Monthly magazine covering concrete production. Audience consists of producers who have succeeded in making concrete the preferred building material through management, operating, quality control, use of the latest technology, or use of superior materials. Estab. 1982. Circ. 18,000. Byline given. Pays on acceptance. No kill fee. Publishes ms an average of 2 months after acceptance. Editorial lead time 4 months. Accepts queries by mail, e-mail, fax, phone. Accepts simultaneous submissions. Responds in 1 week to queries; in 2 months to mss. Sample copy: $4. Guidelines free.

NONFICTION Needs how-to, new product, technical. **Buys 10 mss/year.** Send complete ms. Length: 500-2,000 words. **Pays $200-1,000.** Pays expenses of writers on assignment.

PHOTOS Scan photos at 300 dpi. State availability. Captions, identification of subjects required. Reviews transparencies, prints. Offers no additional payment for photos accepted with ms.

$ HARD HAT NEWS

Lee Publications, Inc., 6113 State Highway 5, P.O. Box 121, Palatine Bridge NY 13428. (518)673-3763 or (800)218-5586. **Fax:** (518)673-2381. **E-mail:** jcasey@leepub.com. **Website:** www.hardhat.com. **Contact:** Jon Casey, editor. **50% freelance written.** Biweekly tabloid covering heavy construction, equipment, road, and bridge work. "Our readers are contractors and heavy construction workers involved in excavation, highways, bridges, utility construction, and underground construction." Estab. 1980. Circ. 15,000. Byline given. No kill fee. Editorial lead time 2 weeks. Submit seasonal material 2 weeks in advance. Accepts queries by mail, e-mail, fax, phone. Sample copy and writer's guidelines free.

NONFICTION Needs interview, new product, opinion, photo feature, technical. Send complete ms. Length: 800-2,000 words. **Pays $2.50/inch.** Pays expenses of writers on assignment.

PHOTOS Send photos. Captions, identification of subjects required. Reviews prints, digital preferred. Offers $15/photo.

COLUMNS/DEPARTMENTS Association News; Parts and Repairs; Attachments; Trucks and Trailers; People on the Move.

TIPS "Every issue has a focus—see our editorial calendar. Special consideration is given to a story that coincides with the focus. A color photo is necessary for the front page. Vertical shots work best. We need more writers in the metro New York area. Also, we are expanding our distribution into the Mid-Atlantic states and need writers in New York, Massachusetts, Vermont, Connecticut, and New Hampshire."

$$ HOME ENERGY MAGAZINE

Energy Auditor & Retrofitter, 1250 Addison St., Suite 211B, Berkeley CA 94702. (510) 524-5405. **Fax:** (510) 981-1406. **E-mail:** contact@homeenergy.org; jpgunshinan@homeenergy.org. **Website:** www.homeenergy.org. **Contact:** Jim Gunshinan, editor. **10% freelance written.** Quarterly print and digital magazine plus online articles and blog covering green home building and renovation. Readers are building contractors, energy auditors, and weatherization professionals. They expect technical detail, accuracy, and brevity. Estab. 1984. Circ. 5,000. Byline given. Pays on publication. Offers 10% kill fee. Publishes ms an average of 4 months after acceptance. Editorial lead time

4 months. Accepts queries by e-mail. Accepts simultaneous submissions. Responds in 2 weeks to queries; 2 months to mss. Guidelines online.

NONFICTION Needs interview, technical. Does not want articles for consumers/general public. **Buys 6 mss/year.** Query with published clips. Submit article via e-mail. Length: 400-2,500 words. **Pays 20¢/word; $400 maximum for both assigned and unsolicited articles.**

COLUMNS/DEPARTMENTS "Trends" are short stories explaining a single advance or research result (400-1,500 words). "Features" are longer pieces that provide more in-depth information (1,500-2,500 words). "Field Notes" provide readers with first-person testimonials (1,500-2,500 words). "Columns" provide readers with direct answers to their specific questions (400-1,500 words). Submit columns via e-mail. Accepts Word, RTF documents, Text documents, and other common formats.

$$ INTERIOR CONSTRUCTION

Ceilings & Interior Systems Construction Association, 1010 Jorie Blvd., Suite 30, Oak Brook IL 60523. (630)584-1919. **Fax:** (866)560-8537. **E-mail:** cisca@cisca.org; csmith@naylor.com. **E-mail:** csmith@naylor.com. **Website:** www.cisca.org. **Contact:** Cody Smith. Quarterly magazine on acoustics and commercial specialty ceiling construction. The resource for the Ceilings & Interior Systems Construction Industry. Features examine leading industry issues and trends like specialty ceilings, LEED, acoustics, and more. Each issue features industry news, new products, columns from industry experts, and CISCA news and initiatives. Estab. 1950. Circ. 3,000. Byline given. Pays on publication. No kill fee. Publishes ms an average of 1 1/2 months after acceptance. Editorial lead time 2-3 months. Accepts queries by e-mail. Accepts simultaneous submissions. Sample copy by e-mail. Guidelines available.

NONFICTION Needs new product, technical. Query with published clips. Publishes 1-2 features per issue. Length: 700-1,700 words. **Pays $400 minimum, $800 maximum for assigned articles.**

$$$ NETCOMPOSITES

4a Broom Business Park, Bridge Way Chesterfield S41 9QG UK. **E-mail:** info@netcomposites.com. **Website:** www.netcomposites.com. **1% freelance written.** Bimonthly newsletter covering advanced materials and fiber-reinforced polymer composites, plus a weekly electronic version called *Composite eNews. Advanced Materials & Composites News* covers markets, applications, materials, processes, and organizations for all sectors of the global hi-tech materials world. Audience is management, academics, researchers, government, suppliers, and fabricators. Focus on news about growth opportunities. Estab. 1978. Circ. 15,000+. Byline sometimes given. Pays on publication. No kill fee. Publishes ms an average of 1 month after acceptance. Editorial lead time 2 weeks. Submit seasonal material 1 month in advance. Accepts queries by e-mail. Accepts simultaneous submissions. Responds in 1 week to queries. Responds in 1 month to mss. Sample copy for #10 SASE.

NONFICTION Needs new product, technical, industry information. **Buys 4-6 mss/year.** Query. 300 words. **Pays $200/final printed page.**

PHOTOS State availability. Captions, identification of subjects, model releases required. Reviews 4x5 transparencies, prints, 35mm slides, JPEGs (much preferred). Offers no additional payment for photos accepted with ms. Buys all rights.

$$ POB MAGAZINE

BNP Media, 2401 W. Big Beaver Rd., Suite 700, Troy MI 48084. (248)362-3700. **E-mail:** trunickp@bnpmedia.com. **Website:** www.pobonline.com. **Contact:** Perry Trunick, editor. **5% freelance written,.** Monthly magazine covering surveying, mapping, and geomatics. Estab. 1975. Circ. 39,000. Byline given. Pays on publication. Publishes ms an average of 3 months after acceptance. Editorial lead time 3 months. Accepts queries by e-mail, phone. Accepts simultaneous submissions. Sample copy and guidelines available online.

NONFICTION Query. Document should be saved in Microsoft Word or text-only format. Also include an author byline and biography. Length: 1,700-2,200 words, with 2 graphics included. **Pays $400.**

PHOTOS State availability. Captions, identification of subjects required. Reviews GIF/JPEG files. Offers no additional payment for photos accepted with ms. Buys one-time rights.

TIPS "Authors must know our profession and industry."

$$$$ PRECAST INC.

National Precast Concrete Association, 1320 City Center Dr., Suite 200, Carmel IN 46032. (317)571-9500. **Fax:** (317)571-0041. **E-mail:** npca@precast.

org; sgeer@precast.org. **Website:** www.precast.org. **Contact:** Sara Geer, managing editor. **75% freelance written.** Bimonthly magazine covering manufactured concrete products. *Precast Inc.* is a publication for owners and managers of plant-produced concrete products used in construction. Publishes business articles, technical articles, company profiles, safety articles, and project profiles, with the intent of educating our readers in order to increase the quality and use of precast concrete. Estab. 1995. Circ. 4,500. Byline given. Pays on acceptance. No kill fee. Publishes ms an average of 6 months after acceptance. Editorial lead time 3 months. Accepts queries by mail, e-mail, fax. Accepts simultaneous submissions. Responds in 1 month to queries; 2 months to mss. Sample copy online. Guidelines online.

NONFICTION Needs how-to, interview, technical. No humor, essays, fiction, or fillers. **Buys 8-14 mss/year.** Query or send complete ms. Length: 1,500-2,500 words. **Pays $1/word.** Pays expenses of writers on assignment.

PHOTOS State availability. Captions required. Offers no additional payment for photos accepted with ms. Buys all rights.

$ TEXAS ARCHITECT

Texas Society of Architects, 500 Chicon St., Austin TX 78702. (512)478-7386. **Fax:** (512)478-0528. **Website:** www.texasarchitect.org. **Contact:** Aaron Seward, editor. **30% freelance written. Mostly written by unpaid members of the professional society.** Bimonthly journal covering architecture and architects of Texas. *Texas Architect* is a highly visually-oriented look at Texas architecture, design, and urban planning. Articles cover varied subtopics within architecture. Readers are mostly architects and related building professionals. Estab. 1951. Circ. 12,500. Byline given. Pays on publication. No kill fee. Publishes ms an average of 3 months after acceptance. Submit seasonal material 4 months in advance. Accepts queries by mail, e-mail. Accepts simultaneous submissions. Responds in 6 weeks to queries. Guidelines online.

NONFICTION Needs interview, photo feature, technical, book reviews. Query with published clips. Length: 100-2,000 words. **Pays $50-100 for assigned articles.**

PHOTOS Send photos. Identification of subjects required. Reviews contact sheets, 35mm or 4x5 transparencies, 4x5 prints. Offers no additional payment for photos accepted with ms. Buys one-time rights.

COLUMNS/DEPARTMENTS News (timely reports on architectural issues, projects, and people), 100-500 words. **Buys 10 articles/year mss/year.** Query with published clips. **Pays $50-100.**

$$$$ UNDERGROUND CONSTRUCTION

Gulf Energy Information, 2 Greenway Plaza, Suite 1020, Houston TX 77046. (713)520-4420. **Fax:** (281)558-7029. **E-mail:** robert.carpenter@ucononline.com. **Website:** www.ucononline.com. **Contact:** Robert Carpenter, editor-in-chief; Brian Nessen, publisher; Elizabeth Fitzpatrick, art director. **50% freelance written.** Monthly magazine covering underground utilities and pipeline construction and rehabilitation. Markets include: water and sewer pipelines, underground telecommunications, underground power. Content is for contractors, owners/municipalities, consulting engineers. Estab. 1945. Circ. 40,000. Byline given, if independent writer not affiliated with vendor/manufacturer. Roughly every 2 weeks No kill fee. Publishes ms an average of 6 months after acceptance. Editorial lead time 3 months. Accepts queries by mail, e-mail, phone. Accepts simultaneous submissions. Responds in 1 month to mss. Sample copy for SAE.

NONFICTION Needs historical, how-to, interview, new product, profile, technical, project stories and industry issues. Query with published clips. Length: 1,000-2,000 words. **Pays $400-1,500.** Pays expenses of writers on assignment.

PHOTOS Send photos. Captions required. Reviews high definition digitial. Buys one-time rights.

EDUCATION & COUNSELING

$ ARTS & ACTIVITIES

Publishers' Development Corp., 12345 World Trade Dr., San Diego CA 92128. (858)605-0242. **Fax:** (858)605-0247. **E-mail:** ed@artsandactivities.com. **Website:** www.artsandactivities.com. **Contact:** Maryellen Bridge, editor-in-chief. **95% freelance written. Eager to work with new/unpublished writers.** Monthly (except July and August) magazine covering art education at levels from preschool through college for educators and therapists engaged in arts and crafts education and training. Estab. 1932. Circ. 20,000. Byline given. Pays on publication. No kill fee. Publishes ms 6 months to 3 years after acceptance.

Submit seasonal material 6 months in advance. Accepts queries by mail, e-mail. Responds in 3 months to queries. Sample copy for SAE with 9x12 envelope and 8 first-class stamps. Guidelines available on website.

NONFICTION Needs historical, how-to. **Buys 80-100 mss/year.** Length: 500-1,500 words. **Pays $35-150.**

TIPS "Frequently in unsolicited mss, writers obviously have not studied the magazine to see what style of articles we publish. Send for a sample copy to familiarize yourself with our style and needs. The best way to find out if his/her writing style suits our needs is for the author to submit a ms on speculation. We prefer an anecdotal style of writing so that readers will feel as though they are there in the art room as the lesson/project is taking place. Also, good quality photographs of student artwork are important. We are a visual art magazine!"

THE ATA MAGAZINE

11010 142nd St. NW, Edmonton Alberta T5N 2R1 Canada. (780)447-9400. **Fax:** (780)455-6481. **E-mail:** government@teachers.ab.ca. **Website:** www.teachers.ab.ca. Quarterly magazine covering education. Estab. 1920. Circ. 42,100. Byline given. Pays on publication. No kill fee. Publishes ms an average of 4 months after acceptance. Editorial lead time 2 months. Submit seasonal material 2 months in advance. Accepts queries by mail, e-mail, fax, phone. Accepts simultaneous submissions. Responds in 2 months to queries. Previous articles available for viewing online. Guidelines available online.

NONFICTION Query with published clips. Length: 500-1,500 words. **Pays $100 (Canadian).** Pays expenses of writers on assignment.

PHOTOS Send photos. Captions required. Reviews 4x6 prints. Negotiates payment individually. Negotiates rights.

DANCE TEACHER

McFadden Performing Arts Media, 333 Seventh Ave., 11th Floor, New York NY 10001. **E-mail:** khildebrand@dancemedia.com; jsullivan@dancemedia.com. **Website:** www.dance-teacher.com. **Contact:** Karen Hildebrand, editor in chief; Joe Sullivan, managing editor. **60% freelance written.** Monthly magazine. Estab. 1979. Circ. 25,000. Byline given. Pays on publication. No kill fee. Publishes ms an average of 3 months after acceptance. Submit seasonal material 6 months in advance. Accepts queries by e-mail. Accepts simultaneous submissions. Responds in 3 months to mss. Sample copy for SAE with 9x12 envelope and 6 first-class stamps. Guidelines available for free.

"Our readers are professional dance educators, business persons, and related professionals in all forms of dance."

NONFICTION Needs how-to. Special issues: Summer Programs (January); Music & More (May); Costumes and Production Preview (November); College/Training Schools (December). No PR or puff pieces. All articles must be well researched. **Buys 50 mss/year.** Query. Length: 700-2,000 words. **Pays $100-300.** Pays expenses of writers on assignment.

PHOTOS Send photos. Reviews contact sheets, negatives, transparencies, prints. Limited photo budget.

TIPS "Read several issues—particularly seasonal. Stay within writer's guidelines."

THE FORENSIC TEACHER MAGAZINE

Wide Open Minds Educational Services, P.O. Box 5263, Wilmington DE 19808. **E-mail:** admin@theforensicteacher.com. **Website:** www.theforensicteacher.com. **Contact:** Dr. Mark R. Feil, editor. **70% freelance written.** Quarterly magazine covering forensic education. Readers are middle, high and post-secondary teachers who are looking for better, easier and more engaging ways to teach forensics as well as law enforcement and scientific forensic experts. Writers understand this and are writing from a forensic or educational background, or both. Prefers a first-person writing style. Estab. 2006. Circ. 16,000. Byline given. Pays 60 days after publication. No kill fee. Publishes ms an average of 6 months after acceptance. Editorial lead time 6 months. Submit seasonal material 6 months in advance. Accepts queries by e-mail. Accepts simultaneous submissions. Responds in 2 weeks to queries; 2 months to mss. Sample copy online. Guidelines online.

NONFICTION Needs general interest, historical, how-to, memoir, personal experience, photo feature, technical. Does not want poetry, fiction, or anything unrelated to medicine, law, forensics or teaching. **Buys 18 mss/year.** Send complete ms. Length: 400-3,000 words. **Pays 2¢/word.**

PHOTOS State availability. Captions required. Reviews GIF/JPEG files/pdf. Send photos separately in e-mail, not in the article. Negotiates payment individually. Buys electronic rights.

COLUMNS/DEPARTMENTS Needs lesson experiences or ideas, personal or professional experiences with a branch of forensics. "If you've done it in your classroom please share it with us. Also, if you're a professional, please tell our readers how they can duplicate the lesson/demo/experiment in their classrooms. Please share what you know."

FILLERS Needs facts, newsbreaks. **Buys 15 mss/year.** Length: 50-200 words. **Pays 2¢/word.**

TIPS "Your article will benefit forensics teachers and their students. It should inform, entertain and enlighten the teacher and the students. Would you read it if you were a busy forensics teacher? Also, don't send a rèsumè and tell us how much experience you have and ask for an assignment; query via e-mail with an outline of your proposed piece."

$$ THE HISPANIC OUTLOOK IN HIGHER EDUCATION

299 Market Street, Suite 145, Saddle Brook NJ 07663. (800)587-8800. **Fax:** (201)587-9105. **Website:** www.hispanicoutlook.com. **Contact:** Mary Ann Cooper, editor in chief. **50% freelance written.** Biweekly magazine (except during the summer) covering higher education of Hispanics. Looking for higher education story articles, with a focus on Hispanics and the advancements made by and for Hispanics in higher education. Circ. 28,000. Byline given. Pays on publication. No kill fee. Publishes ms an average of 2 months after acceptance. Editorial lead time 2 months. Submit seasonal material 3 months in advance. Accepts queries by mail, e-mail, fax. Accepts simultaneous submissions. Sample copy free.

NONFICTION Needs historical. **Buys 20-25 mss/year.** Query with published clips. Length: 1,800-2,200 words. **Pays $400 minimum for print articles, and $300 for online articles when accepted.** Pays expenses of writers on assignment.

PHOTOS Send photos. Reviews color or b&w prints, digital images must be 300 dpi (call for e-mail photo address). Offers no additional payment for photos accepted with ms.

TIPS "Articles explore the Hispanic experience in higher education. Special theme issues address sports, law, health, corporations, heritage, women, and a wide range of similar issues; however, articles need not fall under those umbrellas."

$$ PTO TODAY

School Family Media Inc., 100 Stonewall Blvd., Suite 3, Wrentham MA 02093. (800)644-3561. **E-mail:** queries@ptotoday.com. **Website:** www.ptotoday.com. **Contact:** Emily Graham, chief content editor. **30% freelance written.** Magazine published 6 times during the school year covering the work of school parent-teacher groups. Celebrates the work of school parent group volunteers and provide resources to help parent group leaders do that work more effectively. Estab. 1999. Circ. 80,000. Byline given. Pays on acceptance, net 30 days. Offers 30% kill fee. Publishes ms an average of 4-6 months after acceptance. Editorial lead time 4-6 months. Submit seasonal material 4-6 months in advance. Accepts queries by e-mail. Accepts simultaneous submissions. Sample copy by request. Guidelines by e-mail or online.

NONFICTION Needs general interest, how-to, interview, personal experience. **Buys 8-10 mss/year.** Query. "We review but do not encourage unsolicited submissions." Features are roughly 800-1,500 words. Average assignment is 1,000-1,200 words. Department pieces are 600-900 words. **Payment depends on the difficulty of the topic and the experience of the writer. "We pay by the assignment, not by the word; our pay scale ranges from $200 to $500 for features and $150 to $400 for departments. We occasionally pay more for high-impact stories and highly experienced writers. We buy all rights, and we pay on acceptance (within 30 days of invoice)."**

PHOTOS State availability. Identification of subjects required. Negotiates payment individually. Permission for publication in print, on website, and in marketing materials.

TIPS "It's difficult for us to find talented writers who have strong experience with parent groups. This experience is a big plus. Also, it helps to review our writer's guidelines before querying. All queries must have a strong parent group angle."

$ SCHOOLARTS MAGAZINE

Davis Art, 50 Portland St., Worcester MA 01608. **E-mail:** lmarkey@schoolartsmagazine.com. **E-mail:** sasubmissions@davisart.com. **Website:** schoolartsmagazine.com. **Contact:** Lorraine Markey. **85% freelance written.** Monthly magazine (September-July), serving arts and craft education profession, K-12, higher education, and museum education programs written by and for art teachers. Estab. 1901. Pays on publication (honorarium and 6 copies). No kill fee. Publishes ms an average of 24 months after acceptance. Accepts queries by mail. Responds in 2-4 months to queries. Yes. Guidelines available online.

Each issue of the volume year revolves around a theme that focuses on the human side of the studio art projects, i.e., story, play, meaning. The editor determines which issue/theme is the best fit for articles, so don't worry about fitting a theme. It is more important to be passionate about your lesson, idea, or concept. Look online for upcoming themes.

NONFICTION Query or send complete ms and SASE. E-mail submissions are also accepted. See website for details. Length: 800 words maximum. **Pays $30-150.** Pays expenses of writers on assignment.

TIPS "We prefer articles on actual art projects or techniques done by students in actual classroom situations. Philosophical and theoretical aspects of art and art education are usually handled by our contributing editors. Our articles are reviewed and accepted on merit and each is tailored to meet our needs. Keep in mind that art teachers want practical tips above all—more hands-on information than academic theory. Write your article with the accompanying photographs in hand. The most frequent mistakes made by writers are bad visual material (photographs, drawings) submitted with articles, a lack of complete descriptions of art processes, and no rationale behind programs or activities. Familiarity with the field of art education is essential. Review recent issues of *SchoolArts.*"

$ TEACHERS & WRITERS MAGAZINE

Teachers & Writers Collaborative, 540 President St., 3rd Floor, Brooklyn NY 11215. (212)691-6590. **Fax:** (212)675-0171. **E-mail:** editors@twc.org. **Website:** http://teachersandwritersmagazine.org/. **Contact:** Amy Swauger. **30% freelance written.** *Teachers & Writers Magazine* covers a cross-section of contemporary issues and innovations in education and writing, and engages writers, educators, critics, and students in a conversation on the nature of creativity and the imagination. Estab. 1967. Circ. 7,000. Byline given. Pays on publication. No kill fee. Publishes ms an average of 2-4 months after acceptance. Editorial lead time 2-4 months. Submit seasonal material 2-4 months in advance. Accepts queries by e-mail. Accepts simultaneous submissions. Responds in 1-2 months to queries and submissions. Guidelines online.

NONFICTION Needs book excerpts, essays, how-to, interview, opinion, personal experience, creative writing exercises. Length: 500-2,500 words. **Pays $50-150.**

$ TEACHERS OF VISION

A Publication of Christian Educators Association, P.O. Box 45610, Westlake OH 44145. (888)798-1124. **E-mail:** TOV@ceai.org. **Website:** www.ceai.org. **70% freelance written.** Magazine published 3 times/year for Christians in public education. *Teachers of Vision*'s articles inspire, inform, and equip teachers and administrators in the educational arena. Readers look for teacher tips, integrating faith and work, and general interest education articles. Topics include subject matter, religious expression and activity in public schools, and legal rights of Christian educators. Audience is primarily public school educators. Other readers include teachers in private schools, university professors, school administrators, parents, and school board members. Estab. 1953. Circ. 10,000. Byline given. Pays on publication. No kill fee. Publishes ms an average of 6 months after acceptance. Editorial lead time 4 months. Submit seasonal material 4 months in advance. Accepts queries by mail, e-mail. Accepts simultaneous submissions. Responds in 1 month to queries; 3-4 months to mss. Sample copy for SAE with 9x12 envelope and 4 first-class stamps. Guidelines available online.

NONFICTION Needs how-to, humor, inspirational, interview, opinion, personal experience, religious. No preaching. **Buys 30-50 mss/year.** Query or send complete ms if 2,000 words or less. Length: 1,500 words. **Pays $25-50.** Pays expenses of writers on assignment.

REPRINTS Buys reprints.

PHOTOS State availability of photos. Offers no additional payment for photos accepted with ms. Buys one-time, web, and reprint rights by members for educational purposes.

COLUMNS/DEPARTMENTS Query. **Pays $25-50.**

POETRY Will accept poetry if it pertains to education.

FILLERS Send with SASE—must relate to public education.

TIPS "We are looking for material on living out one's faith in appropriate, legal ways in the public school setting."

$$ TEACHING THEATRE

Educational Theatre Association, 2343 Auburn Ave., Cincinnati OH 45219-2815. (513)421-3900. **E-mail:**

gbossler@schooltheatre.org; publicationsdept@schooltheatre.org. **Website:** www.schooltheatre.org. **Contact:** Gregory Bossler, managing editor. **65% freelance written.** Quarterly magazine covering education theater K-12; primary emphasis on middle and secondary level education. Estab. 1989. Circ. 5,000. Byline given. Pays on acceptance. No kill fee. Publishes ms an average of 3 months after acceptance. Editorial lead time 2 months. Accepts queries by mail, e-mail. Accepts simultaneous submissions. Responds in 4-6 weeks to queries. Responds in 3 months to mss. Sample copy available online. Guidelines available online.

Teaching Theatre emphasizes the teaching, theory, philosophy issues that are of concern to teachers at the elementary, secondary, and—as they relate to teaching K-12 theater—college levels. A typical issue includes an article on acting, directing, playwriting, or technical theatre; a profile of an outstanding educational theatre program; a piece on curriculum design, assessment, or teaching methodology; and a report on current trends or issues in the field, such as funding, standards, or certification.

NONFICTION Needs book excerpts, essays, how-to, interview. **Buys 12-15 mss/year.** Query. A typical issue might include: an article on theatre curriculum development; a profile of an exemplary theatre education program; a how-to teach piece on acting, directing, or playwriting; and a news story or 2 about pertinent educational theatre issues and events. Once articles are accepted, authors are asked to supply their work electronically via e-mail. Length: 750-4,000 words. **Pays $150-500.** Pays expenses of writers on assignment.

PHOTOS State availability. Reviews digital images (300 dpi minimum), prints. Unless other arrangements are made, payment for articles includes payment for the photos and illustrations.

TIPS Wants "articles that address the needs of the busy but experienced high school theater educators. Fundamental pieces on the value of theater education are not of value to us—our readers already know that."

$$$$ TEACHING TOLERANCE

A Project of The Southern Poverty Law Center, 400 Washington Ave., Montgomery AL 36104. (334)956-8374. **Fax:** (334)956-8488. **E-mail:** editor@teachingtolerance.org. **Website:** www.teachingtolerance.org. **Contact:** Adrienne van der Valk, managing editor. **30% freelance written.** Semiannual magazine. Estab. 1991. Circ. 400,000. Byline given. Pays on acceptance. No kill fee. Editorial lead time 6 months. Submit seasonal material 6 months in advance. Accepts queries by mail, fax, online submission form. Accepts simultaneous submissions. Sample copy avialble online. Guidelines available online.

"*Teaching Tolerance* is dedicated to helping K-12 teachers promote tolerance and understanding between widely diverse groups of students. Includes articles, teaching ideas, and reviews of other resources available to educators."

NONFICTION Needs essays, how-to, personal experience, photo feature. No jargon, rhetoric or academic analysis. No theoretical discussions on the pros/cons of multicultural education. **Buys 2-4 mss/year.** Submit outlines or complete mss. Length: 400-1,600 words. **Pays $1/word.** Pays expenses of writers on assignment.

PHOTOS State availability. Captions, identification of subjects required. Reviews contact sheets, transparencies. Buys one-time rights.

COLUMNS/DEPARTMENTS Features (stories and issues related to anti-bias education), 800-1,600 words; Why I Teach (personal reflections about life in the classroom), 600 words or less; Story Corner (designed to be read by or to students and must cover topics that are appealing to children), 600 words; Activity Exchange (brief descriptions of classroom lesson plans, special projects or other school activities that can be used by others to promote tolerance), 400 words. **Buys 8-12 mss/year.** Query with published clips. Does not accept unsolicited mss. **Pays $1/ word.**

TIPS "We want lively, simple, concise writing. Be descriptive and reflective, showing the strength of programs dealing successfully with diversity by employing clear descriptions of real scenes and interactions, and by using quotes from teachers and students. Study previous issues of the magazine before submitting. Most open to articles that have a strong classroom focus. We are interested in approaches to teaching tolerance and promoting understanding that really work that we might not have heard of. We want to inform, inspire and encourage our readers. We know what's happening nationally; we want to know what's happening in your neighborhood classroom."

$ TECH DIRECTIONS

Prakken Publications, Inc., P.O. Box 8623, Ann Arbor MI 48107-8623. (734)975-2800. **Fax:** (734)975-2787. **E-mail:** vanessa@techdirections.com. **Website:** www.techdirections.com. **Contact:** Vanessa Revelli, managing editor. **100% freelance written. Eager to work with new/unpublished writers.** Monthly (except June and July) magazine covering issues, trends, and activities of interest to science, technical, and technology educators at the elementary through post-secondary school levels. Estab. 1934. Circ. 40,000. Byline given. Pays on publication. No kill fee. Publishes ms an average of 1 year after acceptance. Responds in 1 month to queries. Sample copy for $5. Guidelines available online.

NONFICTION Needs general interest, how-to, personal experience, technical, think pieces. **Buys 50 unsolicited mss/year.** Length: 2,000 words. **Pays $50-150.** Pays expenses of writers on assignment.

PHOTOS Send photos. Reviews color prints. Payment for photos included in payment for ms. Will accept electronic art as well.

COLUMNS/DEPARTMENTS Direct from Washington (education news from Washington, DC); Technology Today (new products under development); Technologies Past (profiles the inventors of last century); Mastering Computers, Technology Concepts (project orientation).

TIPS "We are mostly interested in articles written by technology and science educators about their class projects and their ideas about the field. We need more and more technology-related articles, especially written for the community college level."

ELECTRONICS & COMMUNICATION

$ THE ACUTA JOURNAL

Information Communications Technology in Higher Education, 152 W. Zandale Dr., Suite 200, Lexington KY 40503. (859)278-3338. **Fax:** (859)278-3268. **E-mail:** pscott@acuta.org. **Website:** www.acuta.org. **Contact:** Pat Scott, director of communications. **20% freelance written.** Quarterly professional association journal covering information communications technology (ICT) in higher education. Audience includes, primarily, middle to upper management in the IT/telecommunications department on college/university campuses. They are highly skilled, technology-oriented professionals who provide data, voice, and video communications services for residential and academic purposes. Estab. 1997. Circ. 2,200. Byline given. Pays on publication. No kill fee. Publishes ms an average of 6 months after acceptance. Editorial lead time 6 months. Accepts queries by mail, e-mail, fax, phone. Accepts simultaneous submissions. Responds in 2 weeks to queries. Request a sample copy by calling (859)721-1659. Guidelines online.

NONFICTION Needs how-to, technical, case study, college/university application of technology. **Buys 6-8 mss/year.** Query. Length: 1,200-4,000 words. **Pays 8-10¢/word.** Pays expenses of writers on assignment.

PHOTOS State availability. Captions, model releases required. Reviews prints. Offers no additional payment for photos accepted with ms.

TIPS "Our audience expects every article to be relevant to information communications technology on the college/university campus, whether it is related to technology, facilities, or management. Writers must read back issues to understand this focus and the level of technicality we expect."

$$ DIGITAL OUTPUT

Rockport Custom Publishing, LLC, 100 Cummings Center, Suite 321E, Beverly MA 01915. (978)921-7850, ext. 13. **E-mail:** mdonovan@rdigitaloutput.net; edit@rockportpubs.com. **Website:** www.digitaloutput.net. **Contact:** Melissa Donovan, editor. **70% freelance written.** Monthly magazine covering electronic prepress, desktop publishing, and digital imaging, with articles ranging from digital capture and design to electronic prepress and digital printing. *Digital Output* is a national business publication for electronic publishers and digital imagers, providing monthly articles which examine the latest technologies and digital methods and discuss how to profit from them. Readers include service bureaus, prepress and reprographic houses, designers, commercial printers, wide-format printers, ad agencies, corporate communications, sign shops, and others. Estab. 1994. Circ. 25,000. Byline given. Pays on publication. Offers 10-20% kill fee. Publishes ms an average of 2 months after acceptance. Editorial lead time 3 months. Submit seasonal material 3 months in advance. Accepts queries by mail, e-mail. Accepts simultaneous submissions. Responds in 3 weeks to queries. Responds in 1 month to mss. Sample copy for $4.50 or online.

NONFICTION Needs how-to, interview, technical, case studies. **Buys 36 mss/year.** Query with published clips or hyperlinks to posted clips. Length: 1,500-4,000 words. **Pays $250-600.**

PHOTOS Send photos.

TIPS "Our readers are graphic arts professionals. The freelance writers we use are deeply immersed in the technology of commercial printing, desktop publishing, digital imaging, color management, PDF workflow, inkjet printing, and similar topics."

$$ ELECTRICAL APPARATUS

Barks Publications, Inc., Suite 901, 500 N. Michigan Ave., Chicago IL 60611. (312)321-9440. **Fax:** (312)321-1288. **E-mail:** eamagazine@barks.com. **Website:** www.barks.com. **Contact:** Elizabeth Van Ness, publisher; Kevin N. Jones, senior editor. Monthly magazine for persons working in electrical and electronic maintenance, in industrial plants and service and sales centers, who install and service electric motors, transformers, generators, controls, and related equipment. Contact staff members by telephone for their preferred e-mail addresses. Estab. 1967. Circ. 16,000. Byline given. Pays on publication. No kill fee. Publishes ms an average of 1 month after acceptance. Accepts queries by mail, e-mail, fax. Accepts simultaneous submissions. Responds in 1 week to queries sent by US mail.

NONFICTION Needs technical. Length: 1,500-2,500 words. **Pays $250-500 for assigned articles.** Pays expenses of writers on assignment.

TIPS "We welcome queries re: technical columns on electro-mehanical subjects as pump repari, automation, drives, etc. All feature articles are assigned to staff and contributing editors and correspondents. Professionals interested in appointments as contributing editors and correspondents should submit résumé and article outlines, including illustration suggestions. Writers should be competent with a camera, which should be described in résumé. Technical expertise is absolutely necessary, preferably an E.E. degree, or practical experience. We are also book publishers and some of the material in *EA* is now in book form, bringing the authors royalties. Also publishes an annual directory, subtitled *ElectroMechanical Bench Reference*."

$$ SOUND & VIDEO CONTRACTOR

NewBay Media, LLC, 28 E. 28th St., 12th Floor, New York NY 10016. (818)236-3667. **Fax:** (913)514-3683. **E-mail:** cwisehart@nbmedia.com; jgutierrez@nbmedia.com. **Website:** www.svconline.com. Cynthia Wisehart, editor. **Contact:** Cynthia Wisehart, editor; Jessaca Gutierrez, managing and online editor. **60% freelance written.** Monthly magazine covering professional audio, video, security, acoustical design, sales, and marketing. Estab. 1983. Circ. 24,000. Byline given. Pays on acceptance. No kill fee. Publishes ms an average of 3 months after acceptance. Editorial lead time 3 months. Accepts queries by mail, e-mail, fax, phone. Accepts simultaneous submissions. Responds ASAP to queries. Sample copy and writer's guidelines free.

NONFICTION Needs historical, how-to, photo feature, technical, professional audio/video applications, installations, product reviews. No opinion pieces, advertorial, interview/profile, expose/gossip. **Buys 60 mss/year.** Query. Length: 1,000-2,500 words. **Pays $200-1,200 for assigned articles. Pays $200-650 for unsolicited articles.**

REPRINTS Accepts previously published submissions.

PHOTOS Send photos. Identification of subjects required. Reviews transparencies, prints. Offers no additional payment for photos accepted with ms.

COLUMNS/DEPARTMENTS Security Technology Review (technical install information); Sales & Marketing (techniques for installation industry); Video Happenings (Pro video/projection/storage technical info), all 1,500 words. **Buys 30 mss/year.** Query. **Pays $200-350.**

TIPS "We want materials and subject matter that would be of interest to audio/video/security/low-voltage product installers/contractors/designers professionals. If the piece allows our readers to save time, money and/or increases their revenues, then we have reached our goals. Highly technical is desirable."

$$ SQL SERVER MAGAZINE

Penton Media, 221 E. 29th St., Loveland CO 80538. (970)663-4700. **Fax:** (970)667-2321. **E-mail:** Debra.Donston-Miller@penton.com. **Website:** www.sqlmag.com. **Contact:** Deb Donston-Miller, editor. **35% freelance written.** Monthly magazine covering Microsoft SQL Server. *SQL Server Magazine* is the only magazine completely devoted to helping developers and DBAs master new and emerging SQL Server technologies and issues. It provides practical advice and lots of code examples for SQL Server developers and administrators, and includes how-to articles, tips, tricks, and programming techniques offered by SQL Server experts. Estab. 1999. Circ. 20,000. Byline given. "Penton Media pays for articles upon publication. Payment rates are based on the author's writing experience and the quality of the article submitted. We will discuss the payment rate for your article when we notify you of its acceptance." Offers $100 kill fee. Publishes ms an average of 6 months after acceptance. Editorial lead time 4+ months. Accepts queries by mail, e-mail. Accepts simultaneous submissions. Responds in 6 weeks to queries. Responds in 2-3 months to mss. Sample copy available online. Guidelines available online.

NONFICTION Needs how-to, technical, SQL Server administration and programming. Nothing promoting third-party products or companies. **Buys 25-35 mss/year.** Send complete ms. Length: 1,800-2,500 words. **Pays $200 for feature articles; $500 for Focus articles.**

COLUMNS/DEPARTMENTS **Contact:** R2R Editor. Reader to Reader (helpful SQL Server hints and tips from readers), 200-400 words. **Buys 6-12 mss/year.** Send complete ms. **Pays $50**

TIPS "Read back issues and make sure that your proposed article doesn't overlap previous coverage. When proposing articles, state specifically how your article would contain new information compared to previously published information, and what benefit your information would be to *SQL Server Magazine*'s readership."

ENERGY & UTILITIES

ELECTRICAL BUSINESS

CLB Media, Inc., 222 Edward St., Aurora ON L4G 1W6 Canada. (905)727-0077; (905)713-4391. **Fax:** (905)727-0017. **E-mail:** acapkun@annexweb.com. **Website:** www.ebmag.com. **Contact:** Anthony Capkun, editor. **35% freelance written.** Tabloid published 10 times/year covering the Canadian electrical industry. *Electrical Business* targets electrical contractors and electricians. It provides practical information readers can use right away in their work and for running their business and assets. Estab. 1964. Circ. 18,097. Byline given. Pays on acceptance. Offers 50% kill fee. Publishes ms an average of 1-2 months after acceptance. Editorial lead time 3 months. Submit seasonal material 6 months in advance. Accepts queries by e-mail, phone. Accepts simultaneous submissions. Responds in 1 month. Sample copy online. Guidelines online.

NONFICTION Needs how-to, technical. Special issues: Summer Blockbuster issue (June/July); Special Homebuilders' issue (November/December). **Buys 15 mss/year.** Query. Length: 800-1,200 words. **Pays 40¢/word.** Pays expenses of writers on assignment.

PHOTOS State availability. Captions, identification of subjects, model releases required. Reviews GIF/JPEG files. Negotiates payment individually. Buys simultaneous rights.

COLUMNS/DEPARTMENTS Atlantic Focus (stories from Atlantic Canada); Western Focus (stories from Western Canada, including Manitoba); Trucks for the Trade (articles pertaining to the vehicles used by electrical contractors); Tools for the Trade (articles pertaining to tools used by contractors); all 800 words. **Buys 6 mss/year.** Query. **Pays 40¢/word.**

TIPS "Call me, and we'll talk about what I need, and how you can provide it. Stories must have Canadian content."

PUBLIC POWER

2451 Crystal Dr., Suite 1000, Arlington VA 22202-4804. (202)467-2900. **Fax:** (202)467-2910. **E-mail:** news@publicpower.org; ldalessandro@publicpower.org; rthomas@publicpower.org. **Website:** www.publicpower.org. **Contact:** Laura D'Alessandro, editor; Robert Thomas, art director. **60% freelance written. Prefers to work with published/established writers.** Publication of the American Public Power Association, published 6 times a year. Emphasizes electric power provided by cities, towns, and utility districts. Estab. 1942. Circ. 14,000. Byline given. Pays on acceptance. No kill fee. Publishes ms an average of 3 months after acceptance. Accepts queries by mail, e-mail, fax. Accepts simultaneous submissions. Responds in 6 months to queries. Sample copy and writer's guidelines free.

NONFICTION **Pays $500 and up.** Pays expenses of writers on assignment.

PHOTOS Reviews electronic photos (minimum 300 dpi at reproduction size).

TIPS "We look for writers who are familiar with energy policy issues."

ENGINEERING & TECHNOLOGY

CANADIAN CONSULTING ENGINEER

Business Information Group, 80 Valleybrook Dr., Toronto ON M3B 2S9 Canada. (416)510-5119. **Fax:** (416)510-5134. **E-mail:** dpicklyk@ccemag.com. **Website:** www.canadianconsultingengineer.com. **Contact:** Doug Picklyk, editor. **20% freelance written.** Bimonthly magazine covering consulting engineering in private practice. Estab. 1958. Circ. 8,900. Byline given depending on length of story. Pays on publication. Offers 50% kill fee. Publishes ms an average of 4 months after acceptance. Editorial lead time 6 months. Accepts simultaneous submissions. Responds in 3 months to mss. Sample copy free.

Canadian content only. Impartial editorial required.

NONFICTION Needs historical, new product. **Buys 8-10 mss/year.** Query with published clips. Length: 300-1,500 words. **Pays $200-1,000 (Canadian).** Pays expenses of writers on assignment.

PHOTOS State availability. Negotiates payment individually. Buys one-time rights.

COLUMNS/DEPARTMENTS Export (selling consulting engineering services abroad); Management (managing consulting engineering businesses); On-Line (trends in CAD systems); Employment; Business; Construction and Environmental Law (Canada); all 800 words. **Buys 4 mss/year.** Query with published clips. **Pays $250-400.**

COMPOSITES MANUFACTURING MAGAZINE

(formerly *Composites Fabrication Magazine*), American Composites Manufacturers Association, 3033 Wilson Blvd., Suite 420, Arlington VA 22201. (703)525-0511. **E-mail:** communications@acmanet.org; info@acmanet.org. **Website:** www.acmanet.org. Monthly magazine covering any industry that uses reinforced composites: marine, aerospace, infrastructure, automotive, transportation, corrosion, architecture, tub and shower, sports, and recreation. Primarily publishes educational pieces, the how-to of the shop environment. Also publishes marketing, business trends, and economic forecasts relevant to the composites industry. Estab. 1979. Circ. 12,000. Byline given. Pays on acceptance. No kill fee. Publishes ms an average of 2-3 months after acceptance. Editorial lead time 2 months. Accepts queries by e-mail. Accepts simultaneous submissions. Responds in 1 week to queries. Responds in 1 month to mss. Sample copy free. Guidelines by e-mail and online. Specific details on submission types available online.

NONFICTION Needs how-to, new product, technical, marketing, related business trends and forecasts. Special issues: "Each January we publish a World Market Report where we cover all niche markets and all geographic areas relevant to the composites industry. Freelance material will be considered strongly for this issue.". No need to query company or personal profiles unless there is an extremely unique or novel angle. **Buys 5-10 mss/year.** Query. *Composites Manufacturing* invites freelance feature submissions, all of which should be sent via e-mail as a Microsoft Word attachment. A query letter is required. Length: 1,500-2,000 words. **Pays 20-40¢/word (negotiable).** Pays expenses of writers on assignment.

COLUMNS/DEPARTMENTS "We publish columns on HR, relevant government legislation, industry lessons learned, regulatory affairs, and technology. Average word length for columns is 500 words. We would entertain any new column idea that hits hard on industry matters." Query. **Pays $300-350.**

TIPS "The best way to break into the magazine is to empathize with the entrepreneurial and technical background of readership, and come up with an exclusive, original, creative story idea. We pride ourselves on not looking or acting like any other trade publication (composites industry or otherwise). Our editor is very open to suggestions, but they must be unique. Don't waste his time with canned articles dressed up to look exclusive. This is the best way to get on the 'immediate rejection list.'"

CONNECTIONS+

The Magazine for ICT Professionals, Business Information Group, 80 Valleybrook Dr., Toronto ON M3B 2S9 Canada. (416)510-6752. **Fax:** (416)510-5134. **E-mail:** pbarker@connectionsplus.ca. **Website:** www.connectionsplus.ca. **Contact:** Paul Barker, editor. **50% freelance written.** Magazine published 6 times/year covering the structured cabling/telecommunications industry. Estab. 1998. Circ. 15,000 print; 45,000 electronic. Byline given. Pays on publication. No kill fee. Publishes ms an average of 1 month after acceptance.

Editorial lead time 3 months. Submit seasonal material 1 month in advance. Accepts queries by mail, e-mail, phone. Accepts simultaneous submissions. Sample copy available online. Guidelines free.

Connections+ is written for engineers, designers, contractors, and end users who design, specify, purchase, install, test, and maintain structured cabling and telecommunications products and systems.

NONFICTION Needs technical. No reprints or previously written articles. All articles are assigned by editor based on query or need of publication. **Buys 12 mss/year.** Query with published clips. Length: 1,500-2,500 words. **Pays 40-50¢/word.** Pays expenses of writers on assignment.

PHOTOS State availability. Captions, identification of subjects required. Reviews contact sheets, prints. Negotiates payment individually.

COLUMNS/DEPARTMENTS Focus on Engineering/Design; Focus on Installation; Focus on Maintenance/Testing; all 1,500 words. **Buys 7 mss/year.** Query with published clips. **Pays 40-50¢/word.**

TIPS "Visit our website to see back issues, and visit links on our website for background."

$$$ ENTERPRISE MINNESOTA MAGAZINE

Enterprise Minnesota, Inc., 310 Fourth Ave. S., Suite 7050, Minneapolis MN 55415. (612)373-2900. **Fax:** (612)373-2901. **E-mail:** editor@enterpriseminnesota.org. **Website:** www.enterpriseminnesota.org. **90% freelance written.** Magazine published 5 times/year. *Enterprise Minnesota Magazine*is for the owners and top management of Minnesota's technology and manufacturing companies. The magazine covers technology trends and issues, global trade, management techniques, and finance. Profiles new and growing companies, new products, and the innovators and entrepreneurs of Minnesota's technology sector. Estab. 1991. Circ. 16,000. Byline given. Pays on publication. Offers 10% kill fee. Publishes ms an average of 3 months after acceptance. Editorial lead time 1 month. Submit seasonal material 1 year in advance. Accepts queries by mail, e-mail. Accepts simultaneous submissions. Guidelines free.

NONFICTION Needs general interest, how-to, interview. **Buys 60 mss/year.** Query with published clips. **Pays $150-1,000.** Pays expenses of writers on assignment.

COLUMNS/DEPARTMENTS Feature Well (Q&A format, provocative ideas from Minnesota business and industry leaders), 2,000 words; Up Front (mini profiles, anecdotal news items), 250-500 words. Query with published clips.

$$ MFRTECH EJOURNAL

Manufacturers Group Inc., P.O. Box 4310, Lexington KY 40544. **E-mail:** editor@mfrtech.com. **Website:** www.mfrtech.com. **40% freelance written.** Magazine published daily online covering manufacturing and technology from news throughout the U.S. Editorial includes anufacturing news, expansions, acquisition white papers, case histories, new product announcements, feature submissions, book synopsis. Estab. 1976 (print). Circ. 60,000+ weekly subscribers (e-mail); 750,000 monthly online visitors. Byline given. Pays 30 days following publication. Offers 25% kill fee. Publishes ms 3-4 days after acceptance. Editorial lead time 2 weeks. Submit seasonal material 2 weeks in advance. Accepts simultaneous submissions. Sample copy online. Guidelines by e-mail.

NONFICTION Needs new product, opinion, technical. Does not want general interest, inspirational, personal, travel, book excerpts. Length: 750-1,500 words; byline: 75 words. **Pays $0.20/word published (prior to approval from editor).**

PHOTOS Up to 3 photo or graphic images permitted; must come as an attachment to ms submissions via e-mail as JPEGs and no larger than 300x300 pixels each.

COLUMNS/DEPARTMENTS New Plant Announcement, Acquisitions, Expansions, New Technology, Federal, Case Histories, Human Resources, Marketing. Query. **Pays $0.20/word (prior to approval from editor).**

$$ MINORITY ENGINEER

Equal Opportunity Publications, Inc., 445 Broad Hollow Rd., Suite 425, Melville NY 11747. (631)421-9421. **Fax:** (516)421-0359. **E-mail:** bloehr@eop.com; info@eop.com. **Website:** www.eop.com. **Contact:** Barbara Capella Loehr, editor. **60% freelance written. Prefers to work with published/established writers.** Triannual magazine covering career guidance for minority engineering students and minority professional engineers. Estab. 1969. Circ. 15,000. Byline given. Pays on publication. No kill fee. Publishes ms an average of 3 months after acceptance. Editorial lead time 3 months. Accepts queries by mail, e-mail, fax, phone. Accepts simultaneous submissions. Responds in 2 weeks to queries. Responds in 2 months to mss. Sample copy and writer's guidelines for 9x12 SAE with 5 first-class stamps. Guidelines free.

NONFICTION Needs book excerpts, general interest, how-to, interview, opinion, personal experience, technical, articles on job search techniques, role models. No general information. Query. Length: 1,500-2,500 words. **Pays $350 for assigned articles.** Pays expenses of writers on assignment.

REPRINTS Send typed ms with rights for sale noted and information about when and where the material previously appeared. Pays 100% of amount paid for an original article.

PHOTOS State availability.

TIPS Articles should focus on career guidance, role model and industry prospects for minority engineers. Prefers articles related to careers, not politically or socially sensitive.

$$ WOMAN ENGINEER

Equal Opportunity Publications, Inc., 445 Broad Hollow Rd., Suite 425, Melville NY 11747. (631)421-9421. **Fax:** (631)421-1352. **E-mail:** info@eop.com; bloehr@eop.com. **Website:** www.eop.com. **Contact:** Barbara Capella Loehr, editor. **60% freelance written. Works with a small number of new/unpublished writers each year.** Triannual magazine aimed at advancing the careers of women engineering students and professional women engineers. Estab. 1968. Circ. 16,000. Byline given. Pays on publication. No kill fee. Publishes ms an average of 3 months after acceptance. Editorial lead time 3 months. Accepts queries by mail, e-mail, fax, phone. Accepts simultaneous submissions. Responds in 2 weeks to queries. Responds in 2 months to mss. Sample copy and writer's guidelines free.

NONFICTION Needs how-to, interview, personal experience. Query. Length: 1,500-2,500 words. **Pays $350 for assigned articles.** Pays expenses of writers on assignment.

PHOTOS Captions, identification of subjects required. Reviews color slides but will accept b&w. Buys all rights.

TIPS "We are looking for first-person 'As I See It' personal perspectives. Gear it to our audience."

ENTERTAINMENT & THE ARTS

$$$$ AMERICAN CINEMATOGRAPHER

American Society of Cinematographers, 1782 N. Orange Dr., Hollywood CA 90028. (800)448-0145; outside US: (323)969-4333. **Fax:** (323)876-4973. **E-mail:** stephen@ascmag.com. **E-mail:** jon@ascmag.com. **Website:** www.theasc.com. **Contact:** Stephen Pizzello, editor-in-chief and publisher; Jon Witmer, Jon Witmer, managing editor (jon@ascmag.com). **90% freelance written.** Monthly magazine covering cinematography (motion picture, TV, music video, commercial). "*American Cinematographer* is a trade publication devoted to the art and craft of cinematography. Our readers are predominantly film industry professionals." Estab. 1919. Circ. 33,000. Byline given. Pays on publication. Offers 50% kill fee. Publishes ms an average of 2-3 months after acceptance. Editorial lead time 2 months. Submit seasonal material 3 months in advance. Accepts queries by mail, e-mail, phone. Responds in 2 weeks to queries; 2 months to mss. Sample copy and guidelines free.

NONFICTION Needs interview, new product, technical. No reviews or opinion pieces. **Buys 20-25 mss/year.** Query with published clips. Length: 1,000-4,000 words. **Pays $400-1,500.** Pays expenses of writers on assignment.

TIPS "Familiarity with the technical side of film production and the ability to present that information in an articulate fashion to our audience are crucial."

$$ AMERICAN THEATRE

Theatre Communications Group, 520 Eighth Ave., 24th Floor, New York NY 10018. (212)609-5900. **Fax:** (212)609-5902. **E-mail:** rwkendt@tcg.org. **Website:** www.tcg.org. **Contact:** Rob Weinert-Kendt, editor-in-chief. **60% freelance written.** Monthly magazine covering theatre. Focus is on American regional nonprofit theatre. *American Theatre* typically publishes 2-3 features and 4-6 back-of-the-book articles covering trends and events in all types of theatre, as well as economic and legislative developments affecting the arts. *American Theatre* rarely publishes articles about commercial, amateur, or university theatre, nor about works that would widely be classified as dance or opera, except at the editors' discretion. While significant productions may be highlighted in the Critic's Notebook section, *American Theatre* does not review productions (but does review theatre-related books). Estab. 1982. Circ. 100,000. Byline given. Pays on publication. Editorial lead time 2 months. Submit seasonal material 3 months in advance. Accepts queries by mail, e-mail, online submission form. Accepts simultaneous submissions. Responds in 2 months to queries. Sample copy and guidelines available online.

NONFICTION Needs book excerpts, essays, general interest, historical, how-to, humor, inspirational, interview, opinion, personal experience, photo feature, travel. Special issues: Training (January); International (May/June); Season Preview (October). No unsolicited submissions (rarely accepted). No reviews. Writers wishing to submit articles to *American Theatre* should mail or e-mail a query to editor-in-chief Rob Weinert-Kendt outlining a particular proposal; unsolicited material is rarely accepted. Include a brief résumé and sample clips. Planning of major articles usually occurs at least 3 months in advance of publication. All mss are subject to editing. Length: 200-2,000 words. **"While fees are negotiated per ms, we pay an average of $350 for full-length (2,500-3,500 words) features, and less for shorter pieces."** Pays expenses of writers on assignment.

PHOTOS **Contact:** Kitty Suen, creative director: atphoto@tcg.com. Send photos. Captions required. Reviews JPEG files. Negotiates payment individually.

TIPS "The main focus is on professional American nonprofit theatre. Don't pitch music or film festivals. Must be about theatre."

$$ MAKE-UP ARTIST MAGAZINE

12808 NE 95th St., Vancouver WA 98682. (360)882-3488. **E-mail:** heatherw@kpgmedia.com. **Website:** www.makeupmag.com; www.makeup411.com; www.imats.net. **Contact:** Heather Wisner, managing editor. **90% freelance written.** Bimonthly magazine covering all types of professional make-up artistry. Audience is a mixture of high-level make-up artists, make-up students, fashion and movie buffs. Writers should be comfortable with technical writing, and should have substantial knowledge of at least one area of make-up, such as effects or fashion. This is an entertainment-industry magazine, so writing should have an element of fun and storytelling. Good interview skills required. Estab. 1996. Circ. 16,000. Byline given. Pays within 30 days of publication. No kill fee. Editorial lead time 6 weeks. Submit seasonal material 2 months in advance. Accepts queries by e-mail. Accepts simultaneous submissions. Sample copy for $7. Guidelines available via e-mail.

NONFICTION "Does not want fluff pieces about consumer beauty products." **Buys 20+ mss/year.** Query with published clips. Length: 500-3,000 words. **Pays 20-50¢/word.** Pays expenses of writers on assignment.

PHOTOS Send photos. Captions, identification of subjects required. Reviews prints, GIF/JPEG files. Negotiates payment individually. Buys all rights.

COLUMNS/DEPARTMENTS Lab Tech, how-to advice for effects artists, written by a current make-up artist working in a lab (700 words + photos); Backstage (behind the scenes info on a theatrical production's make-up (700 words + photos): Out of the Kit, written by make-up artists working on sets (700 words + photos); Industry Buzz (industry news), length varies. Query with published clips..

TIPS "Read books about professional make-up artistry (see http://makeupmag.com/shop). Read online interviews with make-up artists. Read make-up oriented mainstream magazines, such as *Allure*. Read *Cinefex* and other film-industry publications. Meet and talk to make-up artists and make-up students."

$ SCREEN MAGAZINE

Screen Enterprises, Inc., 676 N. LaSalle Blvd., #501, Chicago IL 60654. (312)640-0800. **Fax:** (312)640-1928. **E-mail:** editor@screenmag.com. **Website:** www.screenmag.com. **Contact:** Andrew Schneider, editor. **5% freelance written.** Biweekly Chicago-based trade magazine covering advertising and film production in the Midwest and national markets. *Screen* is written for Midwest producers (and other creatives involved) of commercials, AV, features, independent corporate, and multimedia. Estab. 1979. Circ. 15,000. Byline given. Pays on publication. No kill fee. Accepts queries by e-mail. Accepts simultaneous submissions. Responds in 3 weeks to queries. Sample copy available online.

NONFICTION Needs interview, new product, technical. No general AV; nothing specific to other markets; no no-brainers or opinion. **Buys 26 mss/year.** Query with published clips. Length: 750-1,500 words. **Pays $50.** Pays expenses of writers on assignment.

PHOTOS Send photos. Captions required. Reviews prints. Offers no additional payment for photos accepted with ms.

TIPS "Our readers want to know facts and figures. They want to know the news about a company or an individual. We provide exclusive news of this market, in as much depth as space allows without being boring, with lots of specific information and details. We write knowledgably about the market we serve. We recognize the film/video-making process is a difficult one because it 1) is often technical, 2) has implications not immediately discerned."

$ SOUTHERN THEATRE

Southeastern Theatre Conference, 1175 Revolution Mill Drive, Studio 14, Greensboro NC 27405. (336)272-3645. **E-mail:** kim@setc.org. **Website:** www.setc.org/southern-theatre. **Contact:** Kim Doty. **100% freelance written.** Quarterly magazine covering all aspects of theater in the Southeast, from innovative theater companies, to important trends, to people making a difference in the region. All stories must be written in a popular magazine style but with subject matter appropriate for theater professionals (not the general public). The audience includes members of the Southeastern Theatre Conference, founded in 1949 and the nation's largest regional theater organization. These members include individuals involved in professional, community, college/university, children's, and secondary school theater. The magazine also is purchased by more than 100 libraries. Estab. 1962. Circ. 4,200. Byline given. Pays on publication. No kill fee. Publishes ms an average of 3 months after acceptance. Editorial lead time 3 months. Submit seasonal material 6 months in advance. Accepts queries by mail, e-mail. Accepts simultaneous submissions. Responds in 3 months to queries. Responds in 6 months to mss. Sample copy for $10. Guidelines available online.

NONFICTION Needs general interest, interview. Special issues: Playwriting (Fall issue, all stories submitted by January 1). No scholarly articles. **Buys 15-20 mss/year.** Send complete ms. Length: 1,000-3,000 words. **Pays $50 for feature stories.** Pays expenses of writers on assignment.

PHOTOS State availability of or send photos. Captions, identification of subjects, model releases required. Reviews transparencies, prints. Offers no additional payment for photos accepted with ms.

COLUMNS/DEPARTMENTS *Outside the Box* (innovative solutions to problems faced by designers and technicians), 800-1,000 words; *400 Words* (column where the theater professionals can sound off on issues), 400 words; 800-1,000 words; *Words, Words, Words* (reviews of books on theater), 400 words. Query or send complete ms **No payment for columns.**

TIPS "Look for a theater or theater person in your area that is doing something different or innovative that would be of interest to others in the profession, then write about that theater or person in a compelling way. We also are looking for well-written trend stories (talk to theaters in your area about trends that are affecting them), and we especially like stories that help our readers do their jobs more effectively. Send an e-mail detailing a well-developed story idea, and ask if we're interested."

FARM

AGRICULTURAL EQUIPMENT

$ AG WEEKLY

Lee Agri-Media, P.O. Box 918, Bismarck ND 58501. (701)255-4905. **Fax:** (701)255-2312. **E-mail:** editor@theprairiestar.com. **Website:** www.agweekly.com. **40% freelance written.** *Ag Weekly* is an agricultural publication covering production, markets, regulation, politics. Writers need to be familiar with Idaho agricultural commodities. No printed component; website with 6,000 monthly unique visitors; weekly email newsletter with 3,000 subscribers. Byline given. Pays on publication. Publishes ms an average of 1 month after acceptance. Editorial lead time 1 month. Submit seasonal material 1 month in advance. Accepts queries by e-mail. Accepts simultaneous submissions. Responds in 2 weeks to queries. Responds in 1 month to mss. Sample copy available online. Guidelines with #10 SASE.

NONFICTION Needs interview, new product, opinion, travel, ag-related. Does not want anything other than local/regional ag-related articles. No cowboy poetry. **Buys 100 mss/year.** Query. Length: 250-700 words. **Pays $40-70.** Pays expenses of writers on assignment.

PHOTOS State availability. Captions required. Reviews GIF/JPEG files. Offers $10/photo. Buys one-time rights.

$$ FLORIDA GROWER

Meister Media Worldwide, 37733 Euclid Ave., Willoughby OH 44094. (440)942-2000. **E-mail:** fgiles@meistermedia.com; pprusnak@meistermedia.com.

Website: www.growingproduce.com/magazine/florida-grower; www.meistermedia.com/publications/florida-grower. **Contact:** Frank Giles, editor; Paul Rusnak, managing editor. **10% freelance written.** Monthly magazine edited for the Florida farmer with commercial production interest primarily in citrus, vegetables, and other ag endeavors. Goal is to provide articles that update and inform on such areas as production, ag financing, farm labor relations, technology, safety, education, and regulation. Estab. 1907. Circ. 12,200. Byline given. Pays on publication. No kill fee. Editorial lead time 2 months. Submit seasonal material 3 months in advance. Accepts queries by mail, e-mail, fax, phone. Accepts simultaneous submissions. Responds in 1 month to queries. Sample copy for SAE with 9x12 envelope and 5 First-Class stamps. Guidelines free.

NONFICTION Needs interview, photo feature, technical. Query with published clips. Length: 700-1,000 words. **Pays $150-250.**

PHOTOS Send photos.

CROPS & SOIL MANAGEMENT

$$ AMERICAN AGRICULTURIST

Farm Progress Company/Informa, 5227 Baltimore Pike, Littlestown PA 17340. (717)359-0150. **Fax:** (717)359-0250. **E-mail:** john.vogel@informa.com. **Website:** www.americanagriculturist.com. **Contact:** John Vogel, editor. **20% freelance written.** Monthly magazine covering cutting-edge technology and news to help farmers improve their operations. Publishes cutting-edge technology with ready on-farm application. Estab. 1842. Circ. 32,000. Pays on publication. No kill fee. Publishes ms an average of 3 months after acceptance. Editorial lead time 3 months. Submit seasonal material 3 months in advance. Accepts queries by e-mail, fax. Responds in 2 weeks to queries; in 1 month to mss. Guidelines for #10 SASE.

NONFICTION Needs how-to, interview, new product, technical. No stories without a strong tie to Northeast and Mid-Atlantic farming. **Buys 20 mss/year.** Query. Length: 500-1,000 words. **Pays $250-500.** Pays expenses of writers on assignment.

PHOTOS Send photos. Captions, identification of subjects, model releases required. Reviews transparencies, JPEG files. Offers $75-200/photo. Buys one-time rights.

AMERICAN FRUIT GROWER AND WESTERN FRUIT GROWER

Meister Media Worldwide, 37733 Euclid Ave., Willoughby OH 44094. (290)573-8740. **E-mail:** deddy@meistermedia.com. **Website:** www.fruitgrower.com. **Contact:** David Eddy, editor. **3% freelance written.** Annual magazines covering commercial fruit growing. "Founded in 1880, *American Fruit Grower* and *Western Fruit Grower* magazines reaches producers, shippers, and other influencers who serve the fresh and processing markets for deciduous fruits, citrus, grapes, berries, and nuts. *Western Fruit Grower* has additional reach to producers and others who work with unique varieties and climate and market conditions in the American West." Estab. 1880. Circ. 44,000. Byline given. Pays on publication. No kill fee. Publishes ms an average of 4 months after acceptance. Editorial lead time 2 months. Submit seasonal material 4 months in advance. Accepts queries by mail, e-mail, fax, phone. Accepts simultaneous submissions. Responds in 2 weeks to queries; in 2 months to mss. Sample copy and writer's guidelines free.

NONFICTION Needs how-to. **Buys 6-10 mss/year.** Send complete ms. Length: 800-1,200 words. **Pays $200-250.** Pays expenses of writers on assignment.

PHOTOS Send photos. Reviews prints, slides. Negotiates payment individually. Buys one-time rights.

TIPS "How-to articles are best."

$$ COTTON GROWER MAGAZINE

Meister Media Worldwide, Cotton Media Group, 8000 Centerview Pkwy., Suite 114, Cordova TN 38018-4246. (901)756-8822. **E-mail:** mccue@meistermedia.com. **Website:** www.cotton247.com. **Contact:** Mike McCue, editor. **5% freelance written.** Monthly magazine covering cotton production, cotton markets, and related subjects. Circ. 43,000. Byline given. Pays on acceptance. No kill fee. Publishes ms an average of 2 months after acceptance. Editorial lead time 2 months. Submit seasonal material 2 months in advance. Accepts queries by mail, e-mail, fax, phone. Accepts simultaneous submissions. Sample copy free.

Readers are mostly cotton producers who seek information on production practices, equipment, and products related to cotton.

NONFICTION Needs interview, new product, photo feature, technical. No fiction or humorous pieces. **Buys 5-10 mss/year.** Query with published clips. Length: 500-800 words. **Pays $200-400.** Pays expenses of writers on assignment.

PHOTOS State availability. Captions, identification of subjects required. Reviews transparencies. Offers no additional payment for photos accepted with ms. Buys all rights.

$$ DIGGER

Oregon Association of Nurseries, 29751 SW Town Center Loop W., Wilsonville OR 97070. (503)682-5089. **Fax:** (503)682-5099. **E-mail:** ckipp@oan.org; info@oan.org. **Website:** www.diggermagazine.com. **Contact:** Curt Kipp, editor. **50% freelance written.** Monthly magazine covering the nursery and greenhouse industry. *Digger* is a monthly magazine that focuses on industry trends, regulations, research, marketing, and membership activities. In August the magazine becomes *Digger Farwest Edition*, with all the features of *Digger* plus a complete guide to the annual Farwest Show, one of North America's top-attended nursery industry trade shows. Circ. 8,000. Byline given. Pays on receipt of copy. Offers 100% kill fee. Publishes ms an average of 2 months after acceptance. Editorial lead time 6 weeks. Submit seasonal material 2 months in advance. Accepts queries by mail, e-mail, fax, phone. Accepts simultaneous submissions. Sample copy and writer's guidelines free.

NONFICTION Needs general interest, how-to, interview, personal experience, technical. Special issues: Farwest Edition (August): "This is a triple-size issue that runs in tandem with our annual trade show (14,500 circulation for this issue).". No articles not related or pertinent to nursery and greenhouse industry. **Buys 20-30 mss/year.** Query. Length: 800-2,000 words. **Pays $125-400 for assigned articles. Pays $100-300 for unsolicited articles.** Pays expenses of writers on assignment.

PHOTOS State availability. Captions, identification of subjects required. Reviews high-res digital images sent by e-mail or on CD. Offers $25-150/photo. Buys one-time rights, which includes Web posting.

TIPS "Our best freelancers are familiar with or have experience in the horticultural industry. Some 'green' knowledge is a definite advantage. Our readers are mainly nursery and greenhouse operators and owners who propagate nursery stock/crops, so we write with them in mind."

$$ FRUIT GROWERS NEWS

Great American Publishing, P.O. Box 128, Sparta MI 49345. (616)887-9008. **Fax:** (616)887-2666. **E-mail:** fgnedit@fruitgrowersnews.com. **Website:** www.fruitgrowersnews.com. **Contact:** Matt Milkovich, managing editor; Lee Dean, editorial director. **10% freelance written.** Monthly tabloid covering agriculture. "Our objective is to provide commercial fruit growers of all sizes with information to help them succeed." Estab. 1961. Circ. 16,429. Pays on publication. No kill fee. Publishes ms an average of 2 months after acceptance. Editorial lead time 1-2 months. Submit seasonal material 3 months in advance. Accepts queries by mail, e-mail, fax. Accepts simultaneous submissions. Responds in 2 weeks to queries. Responds in 1 month to mss. Sample copy free.

NONFICTION Needs general interest, interview, new product. No advertorials or other puff pieces. **Buys 25 mss/year.** Query with published clips and résumé. Length: 600-1,000 words. **Pays $150-250.** Pays expenses of writers on assignment.

PHOTOS Send photos. Captions required. Reviews prints. Offers $15/photo. Buys one-time rights.

$ GRAIN JOURNAL

Country Journal Publishing Co., 3065 Pershing Court, Decatur IL 62526. (800)728-7511. **E-mail:** ed@grainnet.com. **Website:** www.grainnet.com. **Contact:** Ed Zdrojewski, editor. **5% freelance written.** Bimonthly magazine covering grain handling and merchandising. *Grain Journal* serves the North American grain industry, from the smallest country grain elevators and feed mills to major export terminals. Estab. 1972. Circ. 12,000. Byline sometimes given. Pays on publication. No kill fee. Publishes ms an average of 2 months after acceptance. Editorial lead time 2 months. Submit seasonal material 2 months in advance. Accepts simultaneous submissions. Sample copy free.

NONFICTION Needs how-to, interview, new product, technical. Query. 750 words maximum. **Pays $100.** Pays expenses of writers on assignment.

PHOTOS Send photos. Captions, identification of subjects required. Reviews contact sheets, negatives, transparencies, 3x5 prints, electronic files. Offers $50-100/photo. Buys one time rights.

TIPS "Call with your idea. We'll let you know if it is suitable for our publication."

$ ONION WORLD

Columbia Publishing, P.O. Box 333, Roberts ID 83444. (208)520-6461. **Fax:** (509)248-4056. **E-mail:** dkeller@columbiapublications.com. **Website:** www.onionworld.net. **Contact:** Denise Keller, editor. **25% freelance written.** Monthly magazine covering the world of onion production and marketing for onion growers and shippers. Estab. 1985. Circ. 5,500. Byline given. Pays on publication. No kill fee. Publishes ms an average of 1 month after acceptance. Submit seasonal material 1 month in advance. Accepts simultaneous submissions. Responds in 1 month to queries. Sample copy for SAE with 9x12 envelope and 5 first-class stamps.

Columbia Publishing also produces *The Tomato Magazine*, *Potato Country* and *Carrot Country*.

NONFICTION Needs general interest, historical, interview. Special issues: Editorial calendar available online. **Buys 30 mss/year.** Query. Length: 1,200-1,250 words. **Pays $100-250 per article, depending upon length. Mileage paid, but query first.**

REPRINTS Send photocopy and information about when and where the material previously appeared. Pays 50% of amount paid for an original article.

PHOTOS Send photos. Captions, identification of subjects required. Offers no additional payment for photos accepted with ms, unless it's a cover shot. Buys all rights.

TIPS "Writers should be familiar with growing and marketing onions. We use a lot of feature stories on growers, shippers, and others in the onion trade—what they are doing, varieties grown, their problems, solutions, marketing plans, etc."

$ THE VEGETABLE GROWERS NEWS

Great American Publishing, P.O. Box 128, Sparta MI 49345. (616)887-9008, ext. 102. **Fax:** (616)887-2666. **E-mail:** vgnedit@vegetablegrowersnews.com. **Website:** www.vegetablegrowersnews.com. **Contact:** Matt Milkovich, managing editor. **10% freelance written.** Monthly tabloid covering agriculture. Estab. 1970. Circ. 16,000. Pays on publication. No kill fee. Publishes ms an average of 2 months after acceptance. Editorial lead time 1-2 months. Submit seasonal material 3 months in advance. Accepts queries by mail, e-mail, fax. Accepts simultaneous submissions. Responds in 2 weeks to queries. Responds in 1 month to mss. Sample copy free.

"Our objective is to provide commercial vegetable growers of all sizes with information to help them succeed."

NONFICTION Needs general interest, interview, new product. No advertorials, other puff pieces. **Buys 25 mss/year.** Query with published clips and résumé. Length: 800-1,200 words. **Pays $100-125.** Pays expenses of writers on assignment.

PHOTOS Send photos. Captions required. Reviews prints. Offers $15/photo. Buys one-time rights.

LIVESTOCK

$$$ ANGUS JOURNAL

Angus Productions, Inc., 3201 Frederick Ave., St. Joseph MO 64506-2997. (816)383-5270. **E-mail:** shermel@angusjournal.com. **Website:** www.angusjournal.com. **40% freelance written.** Monthly magazine covering Angus cattle. *Angus Journal* is the official magazine of the American Angus Association. Its primary function as such is to report to the membership association activities and information pertinent to raising Angus cattle. Estab. 1919. Circ. 13,500. Byline given. Pays on publication. No kill fee. Publishes ms an average of 3 months after acceptance. Editorial lead time 2 months. Submit seasonal material 3 months in advance. Accepts queries by mail, e-mail. Accepts simultaneous submissions. Responds in 3 weeks to queries; in 2 months to mss. Sample copy: $5. Guidelines with #10 SASE.

NONFICTION Needs how-to, interview, technical. **Buys 20-30 mss/year.** Query with published clips. Length: 800-3,500 words. **Pays $50-1,000.** Pays expenses of writers on assignment.

PHOTOS Send photos. Identification of subjects required. Reviews 5×7 glossy prints. Offers $25-400/photo. Buys all rights.

TIPS "Have a firm grasp of the cattle industry."

$$ BEE CULTURE

623 W Liberty St., Medina OH 44256-0706 USA. (330)725-6677; (800)289-7668. **Fax:** (330)725-5624. **E-mail:** kim@beeculture.com; info@beeculture.com. **Website:** www.beeculture.com. **Contact:** Mr. Kim Flottum, editor. **50% freelance written.** Covers the natural science of honey bees, and honey bee management. "Monthly magazine for beekeepers and those interested in the natural science of honey bees, with

environmentally-oriented articles relating to honey bees or pollination." Estab. 1873. Pays on publication. No kill fee. Publishes ms an average of 4 months after acceptance. Accepts queries by mail, e-mail. Accepts simultaneous submissions. Responds in 1 month to mss. Sample copy with 9x12 SASE and 5 first-class stamps. Guidelines and sample copy available online.

NONFICTION Needs interview, personal experience, photo feature. No "How I Began Beekeeping" articles. Length: 2,000 words average. **Pays $200-250.**

REPRINTS Send photocopy and information about when and where the material previously appeared. Pays about the same as for an original article, on negotiation.

PHOTOS Electronic images encouraged. Digital JPEG, color only, at 300 dpi best,. Model release required. Photo captions preferred. Pays $50 for cover photos. Photos payment included with article payment. Buys first rights.

TIPS "Do an interview story on commercial beekeepers who are cooperative enough to furnish accurate, factual information on their operations. Frequent mistakes made by writers in completing articles are that they are too general in nature and lack management knowledge."

$$ THE BRAHMAN JOURNAL

Carl and Victoria Lambert, 915 12th St., Hempstead TX 77445. (979)826-4347. **Fax:** (979)826-2007. **E-mail:** info@brahmanjournal.com; vlambert@brahmanjournal.com. **Website:** www.brahmanjournal.com. **Contact:** Victoria Lambert, editor. **10% freelance written.** Monthly magazine promoting, supporting, and informing the owners and admirers of American Brahman Cattle through honest and forthright journalism. *The Brahman Journal* provides timely and useful information about one of the largest and most dynamic breeds of beef cattle in the world. In each issue, *The Brahman Journal* reports on Brahman shows, events, and sales as well as technical articles and the latest research as it pertains to the Brahman Breed. Estab. 1971. Circ. 4,000. Byline given. Pays on publication. No kill fee. Publishes ms an average of 2 months after acceptance. Submit seasonal material 3 months in advance. Accepts simultaneous submissions. Sample copy for SAE with 9x12 envelope and 5 first-class stamps.

NONFICTION Needs general interest, historical, interview. Special issues: See the Calendar online for special issues. **Buys 3-4 mss/year.** Query with published clips. Length: 1,200-3,000 words. **Pays $100-250.** Pays expenses of writers on assignment.

REPRINTS Send typed ms with rights for sale noted. Pays 50% of amount paid for an original article.

PHOTOS Photos needed for article purchase. Send photos. Captions required. Reviews 4x5 prints. Offers no additional payment for photos accepted with ms. Buys one-time rights.

TIPS "Since *The Brahman Journal* is read around the world, being sent to 48 different countries, it is important that the magazine contain a wide variety of information. *The Brahman Journal* is read by seed stock producers, show ring competitors, F-1 breeders and Brahman lovers from around the world."

$$ FEED LOT

Feed Lot Magazine, Inc., P.O. Box 850, Dighton KS 67839. (800)798-9515. **Fax:** (620)397-2839. **E-mail:** feedlot@st-tel.net. **Website:** www.feedlotmagazine.com. Annita Lorimor. **Contact:** Jill Dunkel, editor. **80% freelance written.** Published 8 times/year. Magazine provides readers with the most up-to-date information on the beef industry in concise, easy-to-read articles designed to increase overall awareness among the feedlot community. "The editorial information content fits a dual role: large feedlots and their related cow/calf operations, and large 500+ cow/calf, 100+ stocker operations. The information covers all phases of production from breeding, genetics, animal health, nutrition, equipment design, research through finishing fat cattle. *Feed Lot* publishes a mix of new information and timely articles which directly affect the cattle industry." Estab. 1992. Circ. 11,000. Byline given. Pays on publication. Offers 50% kill fee. Publishes ms an average of 2 months after acceptance. Editorial lead time 2 months. Submit seasonal material 6 months in advance. Accepts queries by mail, e-mail, fax. Accepts simultaneous submissions. Responds in 1 month to queries. Sample copy and guidelines by e-mail.

NONFICTION Needs interview, new product, photo feature. Send complete ms; original material only. Length: 100-700 words. **Pays 30¢/word.** Pays expenses of writers on assignment.

PHOTOS State availability or send photos. Captions, model releases required. Reviews contact sheets. Negotiates payment individually. Buys all rights.

TIPS "Know what you are writing about—have a good knowledge of the subject."

$ SHEEP! MAGAZINE

Countryside Publications, Ltd., 145 Industrial Dr., Medford WI 54451. (715)785-7979; (800)551-5691. **Fax:** (715)785-7414. **E-mail:** sheepmag@tds.net; singersol@countrysidemag.com. **Website:** www.sheepmagazine.com. **Contact:** Nathan Griffith, editor. **35% freelance written. Prefers to work with published/established writers.** Bimonthly magazine published in north-central Wisconsin. Estab. 1980. Circ. 11,000. Byline given. Pays on publication. Offers $30 kill fee. Submit seasonal material 3 months in advance. Accepts simultaneous submissions.

Looking for clear, concise, useful information for sheep raisers who have a few sheep to a 1,000 ewe flock.

NONFICTION Needs book excerpts, how-to, interview, new product, technical. **Buys 80 mss/year.** Send complete ms. Length: 750-2,500 words. **Pays $45-150.** Pays expenses of writers on assignment.

PHOTOS Color photos (vertical compositions of sheep and/or people) for cover. 35mm photos or other visuals improve chances of a sale. Identification of subjects required. Buys all rights.

TIPS "Send us your best ideas and photos! We love good writing!"

MANAGEMENT

$ AG JOURNAL

Gatehouse Media, Inc., 422 Colorado Ave., (P.O. Box 500), La Junta CO 81050. (719)384-1453. **E-mail:** publisher@ljtdmail.com; bcd@ljtdmail.com. **Website:** www.agjournalonline.com. **Contact:** Candi Hill, publisher/editor; Jennifer Justice, assistant editor. **20% freelance written.** Weekly journal covering agriculture. Estab. 1949. Circ. 11,000. Byline given. Pays on publication. No kill fee. Publishes ms an average of 2 weeks after acceptance. Editorial lead time 1 month. Submit seasonal material 1 month in advance. Accepts queries by e-mail. Accepts simultaneous submissions. Responds in 2 weeks to queries. Sample copy and writer's guidelines free.

The *Ag Journal* covers people, issues, and events relevant to agriculture producers in a seven-state region (Colorado, Kansas, Oklahoma, Texas, Wyoming, Nebraska, New Mexico).

NONFICTION Needs how-to, interview, new product, opinion, photo feature, technical. Query by e-mail only. **Pays 4¢/word.** Pays expenses of writers on assignment.

PHOTOS State availability. Captions, identification of subjects required. Offers $8/photo. Buys one-time rights.

$$$ PRODUCE BUSINESS

Phoenix Media Network Inc., P.O. Box 810425, Boca Raton FL 33481. (561)994-1118. **E-mail:** kwhitacre@phoenixmedianet.com; info@producebusiness.com. **Website:** www.producebusiness.com. **Contact:** Ken Whitacre, publisher/editorial director. **90% freelance written.** Monthly magazine covering produce and floral marketing. Addresses the buying end of the produce/floral industry, concentrating on supermarkets, chain restaurants, etc. Estab. 1985. Circ. 16,000. Byline given. Pays 30 days after publication. Offers $50 kill fee. Editorial lead time 2 months. Accepts queries by e-mail. Sample copy and guidelines free.

NONFICTION Does not want unsolicited articles. **Buys 150 mss/year.** Query with published clips. Length: 1,200-10,000 words. **Pays $240-1,200.** Pays expenses of writers on assignment.

$$ PRODUCE RETAILER

Vance Publishing Corp., 10901 W. 84th Ter., Suite 200, Lenexa KS 66214. (913)438-0603; (512)906-0733. **E-mail:** PamelaR@produceretailer.com; treyes@produceretailer.com. **Website:** produceretailer.com. **Contact:** Pamela Riemenschneider, editor; Tony Reyes, art director. **10% freelance written.** Monthly magazine. "*Produce Merchandising* is the only monthly journal on the market that is dedicated solely to produce merchandising information for retailers. Our purpose is to provide information about promotions, merchandising, and operations in the form of ideas and examples." Estab. 1988. Circ. 12,000. Byline given. Pays on acceptance. No kill fee. Publishes ms an average of 3 months after acceptance. Editorial lead time 3 months. Accepts queries by mail. Accepts simultaneous submissions. Responds in 2 weeks to queries. Sample copy free.

NONFICTION Needs how-to, interview, new product, photo feature, technical. **Buys 48 mss/year.** Query with published clips. Length: 1,000-1,500 words. **Pays $200-600.** Pays expenses of writers on assignment.

PHOTOS State availability of or send photos. Captions, identification of subjects, model releases required. Reviews color slides and 3x5 or larger prints. Offers no additional payment for photos accepted with ms. Buys all rights.

COLUMNS/DEPARTMENTS Contact: Contact editor for a specific assignment. **Buys 30 mss/year.** Query with published clips. **Pays $200-450.**

TIPS Send in clips and contact the editor with specific story ideas. Story topics are typically outlined up to a year in advance.

SMALLHOLDER MAGAZINE

Newsquest Media Group, 3 Falmouth Business Park, Bickland Water Rd., Falmouth Cornwall TR11 4SZ United Kingdom. (01)326-213338. **Fax:** (01)326-212084. **E-mail:** editorial@smallholder.co.uk. **Website:** www.smallholder.co.uk. **Contact:** Paul Armstrong, editor. *Smallholder* magazine is the leading monthly publication for the small producer and self-reliant household and has a publishing history spanning more than 100 years. The magazine has a reputation for quality and informed editorial content, and back issues are highly collectable. It is available nationally, through newsagent sales, specialist retail outlets and by subscription. No kill fee. Accepts queries by e-mail. Accepts simultaneous submissions. Sample copy available online. Guidelines by e-mail.

"Copy is required at least 2 months before publication, e.g. 1st April for June. News items may be accepted up until one month before publication. The editor's decision on copy is final and, although every effort will be made to return mss and photos, no responsibility can be accepted."

NONFICTION Length: 700-1,400 words. **Pays 4£/word.** Pays expenses of writers on assignment.

PHOTOS Send photos. Reviews 300 dpi digital images. Pays £5-50.

MISCELLANEOUS

ACRES U.S.A.

P.O. Box 1690, Greeley CO 80632. (800)355-5313. **E-mail:** editor@acresusa.com. **Website:** www.acresusa.com. **Contact:** Tara Maxwell. "Monthly trade journal written by people who have a sincere interest in the principles of organic and sustainable agriculture." Estab. 1971. Circ. 20,000. Byline given. Pays on publication. No kill fee. Editorial lead time 3 months. Submit seasonal material 6 months in advance. Accepts queries by mail, e-mail. Accepts simultaneous submissions. Sample copy and writer's guidelines free.

NONFICTION Needs book excerpts, expose, how-to, interview, new product, opinion, personal experience, photo feature, profile, technical. Special issues: Seeds (January), Poultry (March), Permaculture (May), Livestock (June), Homesteading (August), Soil Fertility & Testing (October). Does not want poetry, fillers, product profiles, or anything with an overly promotional tone. **Buys about 50 mss/year.** Send complete ms. Length: 500-3,000 words. **Pays 10¢/word.** Pays expenses of writers on assignment.

PHOTOS State availability of or send photos. Captions, identification of subjects required. Reviews JPEG/TIFF files. Negotiates payment individually. Buys one-time rights.

REGIONAL

MAINE ORGANIC FARMER & GARDENER

Maine Organic Farmers & Gardeners Association, P.O. Box 170, Unity ME 04988. (207)568-4142. **Fax:** (207)568-4141. **E-mail:** jenglish@tidewater.ne. **Website:** www.mofga.org. **40% freelance written. Prefers to work with published/established local writers.** Quarterly newspaper. "The *MOF&G* promotes and encourages sustainable agriculture and environmentally sound living. Our primary focus is organic farming, gardening, and forestry, but we also deal with local, national, and international agriculture, food, and environmental issues." Estab. 1976. Circ. 10,000. Byline and bio offered. Pays on publication. No kill fee. Publishes ms an average of 8 months after acceptance. Submit seasonal material 1 year in advance. Accepts queries by mail, e-mail. Accepts simultaneous submissions. Responds in 2 months to queries. Sample copy for $2 and SAE with 7 first-class stamps; from MOFGA, P.O. Box 170, Unity ME 04988. Guidelines available at www.mofga.org.

NONFICTION Buys 30 mss/year. Send complete ms. Length: 250-3,000 words. **Pays $25-300.** Pays expenses of writers on assignment.

REPRINTS E-mail manuscript with rights for sale noted and information about when and where the material previously appeared. Pays 50% of amount paid for an original article.

PHOTOS State availability of photos with query. Captions, identification of subjects, model releases required. Buys one time rights. We rarely buy photos without an accompanying article.

TIPS "We are a nonprofit organization. Our publication's primary mission is to inform and educate, but we also want readers to enjoy the articles. Most of our articles are written by our staff or by freelancers who have been associated with the publication for several years."

FINANCE

$$$$ ADVISOR'S EDGE

Rogers Media, Inc., 333 Bloor St. E., 6th Floor, Toronto ON M4W 1G6 Canada. **E-mail:** melissa.shin@rci.rogers.com. **Website:** www.advisor.ca. **Contact:** Melissa Shin, editor. Monthly magazine covering the financial industry (financial advisors and investment advisors). *Advisor's Edge* focuses on sales and marketing opportunities for the financial advisor (how they can build their business and improve relationships with clients). Estab. 1998. Circ. 36,000. Byline given. Pays on publication. Offers 25% kill fee. Publishes ms an average of 3 months after acceptance. Editorial lead time 3 months. Accepts queries by e-mail. Accepts simultaneous submissions. Sample copy available online.

NONFICTION Needs how-to, interview. No articles that aren't relevant to how a financial advisor does his/her job. **Buys 12 mss/year.** Query with published clips. Length: 1,500-2,000 words. **Pays $900 (Canadian).** Pays expenses of writers on assignment.

$$$$ AFP EXCHANGE

Association for Financial Professionals, 4520 East West Hwy., Suite 750, Bethesda MD 20814. (301)907-2862. **E-mail:** exchange@afponline.org. **Website:** www.afponline.org/exchange. **20% freelance written.** Monthly magazine covering corporate treasury, corporate finance, B2B payments issues, corporate risk management, accounting, and regulatory issues from the perspective of corporations. Welcomes interviews with CFOs and senior-level practitioners. Best practices and practical information for corporate CFOs and treasurers. Tone is professional, intended to appeal to financial professionals on the job. Most accepted articles are written by professional journalists and editors, many featuring high-level AFP members in profile and case studies. Estab. 1979. Circ. 25,000. Byline given. Pays on publication. Offers kill fee. Pays negotiable kill fee in advance. Editorial lead time 2 months. Submit seasonal material 3 months in advance. Accepts queries by e-mail. Accepts simultaneous submissions. Responds in 1 week to queries; in 1 month to mss.

NONFICTION Needs book excerpts, how-to, interview, personal experience, technical. No PR-type articles pointing to any type of product or solution. **Buys 3-4 mss/year.** Query. Length: 1,100-1,800 words. **Pays 75¢-$1/word for assigned articles.** Pays expenses of writers on assignment.

COLUMNS/DEPARTMENTS Cash Flow Forecasting (practical tips for treasurers, CFOs); Financial Reporting (insight, practical tips); Risk Management (practical tips for treasurers, CFOs); Corporate Payments (practical tips for treasurers), all 1,000-1,300 words. Professional Development (success stories, career related, about high-level financial professionals), 1,100 words. **Buys 10 mss/year.** Query. **Pays $75¢-$1/word.**

FILLERS Needs anecdotes. Length: 400-700 words. **Pays 75¢/word.**

TIPS "Accepted submissions deal with high-level issues relevant to today's corporate CFO or treasurer, including issues of global trade, global finance, accounting, M&A, risk management, corporate cash management, international regulatory issues, communications issues with corporate boards and shareholders, and especially new issues on the horizon. Preference given to articles by or about corporate practitioners in the finance function of mid- to large-size corporations in the U.S. or abroad. We also purchase articles by accomplished financial writers. We cannot accept content that points to any product, 'solution,' or that promotes any vendor. We should not be considered a PR outlet. Authors may be required to sign agreement."

$$$ CREDIT TODAY

P.O. Box 20091, Roanoke VA 24018. (540)343-7500. **E-mail:** robl@credittoday.net; editor@credittoday.net. **Website:** www.credittoday.net. **Contact:** Rob Lawson, publisher. **10% freelance written.** Web-based publication covering business or trade credit. Estab. 1997. No byline given. Pays on acceptance. Publishes ms an average of 1 week after acceptance. Editorial lead time

1-2 months. Accepts queries by e-mail. Sample copy free. Guidelines free.

NONFICTION Needs how-to, interview, technical. Does not want "puff" pieces promoting a particular product or vendor. **Buys 20 mss/year.** Send complete ms. Length: 700-1,800 words. **Pays $200-1,400.** Pays expenses of writers on assignment.

TIPS "Make pieces actionable, personable, and a quick read."

$$ CREDIT UNION MANAGEMENT

Credit Union Executives Society, 5710 Mineral Point Road, Madison WI 53705. (800)231-4211. **E-mail:** apeterson@cuna.com. **Website:** www.cuna.org. **Contact:** Ann Hayes Peterson, editor in chief. **44% freelance written.** Monthly magazine covering credit union, banking trends, management, HR, and marketing issues. "Our philosophy mirrors the credit union industry of cooperative financial services." Estab. 1978. Circ. 7,413. Pays on acceptance. No kill fee. Publishes ms an average of 2 months after acceptance. Editorial lead time 3 months. Submit seasonal material 4 months in advance. Accepts queries by mail. Accepts simultaneous submissions. Responds in 2 weeks to queries; 1 month to mss. Sample copy and writer's guidelines free.

NONFICTION Needs book excerpts, how-to, interview, technical. **Buys 74 mss/year.** Query with published clips. Length: 700-2,400 words. **$250-350 for assigned features.** Pays expenses of writers on assignment.

COLUMNS/DEPARTMENTS Management Network (book/Web reviews, briefs), 300 words; e-marketing, 700 words; Point of Law, 700 words; Best Practices (new technology/operations trends), 700 words. Query with published clips.

TIPS "The best way is to e-mail an editor; include rèsumè, cover letter and clips. Knowledge of financial services is very helpful."

$$$ THE FEDERAL CREDIT UNION

National Association of Federal Credit Unions, 3138 10th St. N., Arlington VA 22201. (703)522-4770; (800)336-4644. **Fax:** (703)524-1082. **E-mail:** msc@nafcu.org; sbroaddus@nafcu.org. **Website:** www.nafcu.org/tfcuonline. **Contact:** Susan Broaddus, managing editor. **30% freelance written.** Published bimonthly, *The Federal Credit Union* is the official publication of the National Association of Federal Credit Unions. The magazine is dedicated to providing credit union management, staff, and volunteers with in-depth information (HR, technology, security, board management, etc.) they can use to fulfill their duties and better serve their members. The editorial focus includes coverage of management issues, operations, and technology as well as volunteer-related issues. Looking for writers with financial, banking, or credit union experience, but will work with inexperienced (unpublished) writers based on writing skill. Estab. 1967. Circ. 8,000. Byline given. Pays on publication. No kill fee. Publishes ms an average of 3 months after acceptance. Submit seasonal material 5 months in advance. Accepts queries by mail, e-mail, fax. Accepts simultaneous submissions. Responds in 2 months to queries. Sample copy for SAE with 10x13 envelope and 5 first-class stamps. Guidelines for #10 SASE.

NONFICTION Needs humor, inspirational, interview. Query with published clips and SASE. Length: 1,200-2,000 words. **Pays $400-1,000.**

PHOTOS Send photos. Identification of subjects, model releases required. Reviews 35mm transparencies, 5x7 prints, high-resolution photos. Offers no additional payment for photos accepted with ms. Pays $50-500. Buys all rights.

TIPS "We would like more articles on how credit unions are using technology to serve their members and more articles on leading-edge technologies they can use in their operations. If you can write on current trends in technology, human resources, or strategic planning, you stand a better chance of being published than if you wrote on other topics."

FLORISTS, NURSERIES & LANDSCAPERS

$ GROWERTALKS

Ball Publishing, 622 Town Rd., P.O. Box 1660, West Chicago IL 60186. (630)231-3675; (630)588-3401. **Fax:** (630)231-5254. **E-mail:** info@ballpublishing.com. **E-mail:** cbeytes@ballpublishing.com. **Website:** www.growertalks.com. **Contact:** Chris Beytes, editor. **50% freelance written.** Monthly magazine covering horticulture. *GrowerTalks* serves the commercial greenhouse grower. Editorial emphasis is on floricultural crops: bedding plants, potted floral crops, foliage, and fresh cut flowers. Readers are growers, managers, and owners. Looking for writers who've had experience in the greenhouse industry. Estab. 1937. Circ. 9,500. Byline given. Pays on publication. No kill fee. Publishes ms an average of 3 months after acceptance. Editorial lead time 4 months. Submit seasonal material 3 months in advance. Accepts queries by mail, e-mail, fax. Accepts simultaneous submissions. Responds in 1 month to queries. Sample copy and writer's guidelines free.

NONFICTION Needs how-to, interview, personal experience, technical. No articles that promote only 1 product. **Buys 36 mss/year.** Query. Length: 1,200-1,600 words. **Pays $125 minimum for assigned articles. Pays $75 minimum for unsolicited articles.**

PHOTOS State availability. Captions, identification of subjects, model releases required. Reviews 2 1/2x2 1/2 slides and 3x5 prints. Negotiates payment individually. Buys one-time rights.

TIPS "Discuss magazine with ornamental horticulture growers to find out what topics that have or haven't appeared in the magazine interest them."

GOVERNMENT & PUBLIC SERVICE

$$ AMERICAN CITY & COUNTY

Penton Media, 6151 Powers Ferry Rd. NW, Suite 200, Atlanta GA 30339. (770)618-0401. **E-mail:** bill.wolpin@penton.com; derek.prall@penton.com. **Website:** www.americancityandcounty.com. **Contact:** Bill Wolpin, editorial director; Derek Prall, managing editor. **40% freelance written.** Monthly magazine covering local and state government in the U.S. Estab. 1909. Circ. 65,000. Byline given. Pays on publication. Offers 25% kill fee. Publishes ms an average of 2 months after acceptance. Editorial lead time 3 months. Accepts queries by e-mail. Accepts simultaneous submissions. Sample copy available online. Guidelines by e-mail.

American City & County is received by elected and appointed local and state government officials and public and private engineers. Included in the circulation list are administrators, supervisors, and department heads of municipal, county, township, state, and special district governments. The magazine maintains its leadership position by providing these readers with news, government trends, policy alternatives, and operational solutions.

NONFICTION Needs new product. **Buys 36 mss/year.** Query. Length: 600-2,000 words. **Pays 30¢/published word.** Pays expenses of writers on assignment.

PHOTOS State availability. Captions required. Reviews GIF/JPEG files. Negotiates payment individually. Buys all rights.

COLUMNS/DEPARTMENTS Issues & Trends (local and state government news analysis), 500-700 words. **Buys 24 mss/year.** Query. **Pays $150-250.**

TIPS "We use only third-person articles. We do not tell the reader what to do; we offer the facts and assume the reader will make his or her own informed decision. We cover city and county government and state highway departments. We do not cover state legislatures or the federal government, except as they affect local government."

$$ COUNTY

Texas Association of Counties, 1210 San Antonio St., Austin TX 78701. (512)478-8753. **Fax:** (512)481-1240. **E-mail:** marias@county.org. **Website:** www.county.org. **Contact:** Maria Sprow, managing editor. **15% freelance written.** Bimonthly magazine covering county and state government in Texas. Provides elected and appointed county officials with insights and information that help them do their jobs and enhances communications among the independent office-holders in the courthouse. Estab. 1988. Circ. 5,500. Byline given. Pays on acceptance. No kill fee. Publishes ms an average of 2 months after acceptance. Editorial lead time 2 months. Submit seasonal material 4 months in advance. Accepts queries by mail, e-mail, phone. Accepts simultaneous submissions. Responds in 2 weeks to queries. Responds in 1 month to mss. Sample copy and writer's guidelines for 8x10 SAE with 3 first-class stamps.

NONFICTION Needs historical. **Buys 5 mss/year.** Query with published clips. Length: 1,000-3,000 words. **Pays $500-700.** Pays expenses of writers on assignment.

PHOTOS State availability. Captions, identification of subjects, model releases required. Negotiates payment individually. Buys all rights.

COLUMNS/DEPARTMENTS Safety; Human Resources; Risk Management (all directed toward education of Texas county officials), maximum length 1,000 words. **Buys 2 mss/year. mss/year.** Query with published clips. **Pays $500.**

TIPS "Identify innovative practices or developing trends that affect Texas county officials, and have the basic journalism skills to write a multi-sourced, informative feature."

$$ FIRE CHIEF

Primedia Business, 330 N. Wabash Ave., Suite 2300, Chicago IL 60611. (312)595-1080. **Fax:** (312)595-0295. **E-mail:** Rick.Markley@praetoriangroup.com. **Website:** www.firechief.com. **Contact:** Rick Markley, editor in chief. **60% freelance written.** Monthly magazine covering the fire chief occupation. "*Fire Chief* is the management magazine of the fire service, addressing the administrative, personnel, training, prevention/education, professional development, and operational issues faced by chiefs and other fire officers, whether in paid, volunteer, or combination departments. We're potentially interested in any article that can help them do their jobs better, whether that's as incident commanders, financial managers, supervisors, leaders, trainers, planners, or ambassadors to municipal officials or the public." Estab. 1956. Circ. 53,000. Byline given. Pays on publication. Offers kill fee. Kill fee negotiable. Publishes ms an average of 6 months after acceptance. Editorial lead time 2 months. Submit seasonal material 4 months in advance. Accepts queries by mail, e-mail, fax. Responds in 1 month to queries. Responds in 2 months to mss. Sample copy and submission guidelines free.

NONFICTION Needs how-to, technical. "We do not publish fiction, poetry, or historical articles. We also aren't interested in straightforward accounts of fires or other incidents, unless there are one or more specific lessons to be drawn from a particular incident, especially lessons that are applicable to a large number of departments." **Buys 50-60 mss/year.** Query first with published clips. Length: 1,000-10,000 words. **Pays $50-400.** Pays expenses of writers on assignment.

PHOTOS State availability. Captions, identification of subjects required. Reviews transparencies, prints. Buys one-time or reprint rights.

COLUMNS/DEPARTMENTS Training Perspectives; EMS Viewpoints; Sound Off; Volunteer Voice; all 1,000-1,800 words.

TIPS "Writers who are unfamiliar with the fire service are very unlikely to place anything with us. Many pieces that we reject are either too unfocused or too abstract. We want articles that help keep fire chiefs well informed and effective at their jobs."

$$ FIREHOUSE MAGAZINE

Cygnus Business Media, 1233 Janesville Ave., Fort Atkinson WI 53538. (800)547-7377. **E-mail:** janelle@firehouse.com. **Website:** www.firehouse.com. **Contact:** Janelle Foskett, executive editor. **85% freelance written. Works with a small number of new/unpublished writers each year.** Monthly magazine. *Firehouse* covers major fires nationwide, controversial issues and trends in the fire service, the latest firefighting equipment and methods of firefighting, historical fires, firefighting history and memorabilia. Fire-related books, fire safety education, hazardous-materials incidents, and the emergency medical services are also covered. Estab. 1976. Circ. 83,538 (print). Byline given. Pays on publication. No kill fee. Accepts queries by mail, e-mail, fax, online submission form. Sample copy for SAE with 9x12 envelope and 8 first-class stamps.

"Our primary editorial objectives are to educate, inform and entertain our audience of 1.5 million career and volunteer firefighters and thousands of fire buffs."

NONFICTION Needs book excerpts, historical, how-to, trends in the fire service. No profiles of people or departments that are not unusual or innovative, reports of nonmajor fires, articles not slanted toward firefighters' interests. No poetry. **Buys 100 mss/year.** Query. "If you have any story ideas, questions, hints, tips, etc., please do not hesitate to call." Length: 500-3,000 words. The average length of each article is between 2-3 pages, including visuals. **Pays $50-400 for assigned articles.**

PHOTOS *Firehouse* is a visually-oriented publication. Please include photographs (color preferred) with captions (or a description of what is taking place in the photo), illustrations, charts or diagrams that support your ms. The highest priority is given to those submissions that are received as a complete package. Pays $25-200 for transparencies and color prints. Cannot accept negatives.

COLUMNS/DEPARTMENTS Training (effective methods); Book Reviews; Fire Safety (how departments teach fire safety to the public); Communicating (PR, dispatching); Arson (efforts to combat it). Length: 750-1,000 words. **Buys 50 mss/year.** Query or send complete ms. **Pays $100-300.**

TIPS "Have excellent fire service credentials and be able to offer our readers new information. Read the magazine to get a full understanding of the subject matter, the writing style, and the readers before sending a query or ms. Indicate sources for photos. Be sure to focus articles on firefighters."

$ FIRERESCUE

PennWell Corporation, 21-00 Route 208 South, Fair Lawn NJ 07410. (973)251-5055. **E-mail:** frm.editor@pennwell.com; dianer@pennwell.com. **Website:** www.firefighternation.com. **Contact:** Diane Rothschild, executive editor. "FireRescue covers the fire and rescue markets. Our 'Read It Today, Use It Tomorrow' mission weaves through every article and image we publish. Our readers consist of fire chiefs, company officers, training officers, firefighters, and technical rescue personnel." Estab. 1997. Circ. 50,000. Pays on publication. Accepts queries by mail, e-mail. Responds in 1 month to mss. Guidelines available online.

NONFICTION Needs general interest, how-to, interview, new product, technical. "All story ideas must be submitted with a cover letter that outlines your qualifications and includes your name, full address, phone, and e-mail address. We accept story submissions in 1 of the following 2 formats: query letters and mss." Length: 800-2,200 words. **Pays $100—$200 for features.** Pays expenses of writers on assignment.

PHOTOS Looks for "photographs that show firefighters in action, using proper techniques and wearing the proper equipment. Submit timely photographs that show the technical aspects of firefighting and rescue. ". Digital images in JPEG, TIFF, or EPS format at 72 dpi for initial review. We require 300 dpi resolution for publication. If you send images as attachments via e-mail, compress your files first.

TIPS "Read back issues of the magazine to learn our style. Research back issues to ensure we haven't covered your topic within the past three years. Read and follow the instructions on our guidelines page."

$$ LAW ENFORCEMENT TECHNOLOGY MAGAZINE

Cygnus Business Media, 1233 Janesville Ave., Fort Atkinson WI 53538. (800)547-7377. **Website:** www.officer.com. **40% freelance written.** Monthly magazine covering police management and technology. Estab. 1974. Circ. 30,000. Byline given. Pays on publication. No kill fee. Publishes ms an average of 4 months after acceptance. Editorial lead time 6 months. Accepts simultaneous submissions. Responds in 1 month to queries; 2 months to mss. Guidelines free.

NONFICTION Needs how-to, interview, photo feature, police management and training. **Buys 30 mss/year.** Query. Length: 1,200-2,000 words. **Pays $75-400 for assigned articles.**

REPRINTS Send typed ms with rights for sale noted and information about when and where the material previously appeared. Payment negotiable.

PHOTOS Send photos. Captions required. Reviews contact sheets, negatives, 5x7 or 8x10 prints. Offers no additional payment for photos accepted with ms. Buys one-time rights.

TIPS "Writer should have background in police work or currently work for a police agency. Most of our articles are technical or supervisory in nature. Please query first after looking at a sample copy. Prefers mss, queries, and images be submitted electronically."

$$$$ PLANNING

American Planning Association, 205 N. Michigan Ave., Suite 1200, Chicago IL 60601. (312)431-9100. **Fax:** (312)786-6700. **E-mail:** mstromberg@planning.org. **Website:** www.planning.org. **Contact:** Meghan Stromberg, executive editor; Sylvia Lewis, editor; Joan Cairney, art director. **30% freelance written.** Monthly magazine emphasizing urban planning for adult, college-educated readers who are regional and urban planners in city, state, or federal agencies or in private business, or university faculty or students. Estab. 1972. Circ. 44,000. Byline given. Pays on publication. No kill fee. Publishes ms an average of 2 months after acceptance. Accepts queries by mail, e-mail. Accepts simultaneous submissions. Responds in 5 weeks to queries. Guidelines available online.

NONFICTION Special issues: Transportation issue. Also needs news stories up to 500 words. **Buys 44 features and 33 news stories mss/year.** Length: 500-3,000 words. **Pays $150-1,500.** Pays expenses of writers on assignment.

PHOTOS "We prefer authors supply their own photos, but we sometimes take our own or arrange for them in other ways.". State availability. Captions required. Pays $100 minimum for photos used on inside pages and $300 for cover photos. Buys one-time rights.

$$ POLICE AND SECURITY NEWS

Performance Publishing, LLC, 15 S. Main St., PO Box 1185, Quakertown PA 18951-1520. (215)538-1240.

Fax: (215)538-1208. **E-mail:** jdevery@policeandsecuritynews.com. **E-mail:** amenear@policeandsecuritynews.com. **Website:** www.policeandsecuritynews.com. **Contact:** Al Menear, publisher. **40% freelance written.** A nationally circulated bimonthly magazine serving law enforcement and Homeland Security, reaching all levels: municipal/city; county; state and federal law enforcement personnel. Police and Security News edits its content for the expert–in a manner even the non-expert can understand and utilize. Every issue features useful, hard to find information which is, oftentimes, entertaining and always contemporary and relevant. Every edition provides in-depth articles by industry known writers; current news and information; useful tips and guidelines; and the latest innovations. P&SN is always looking for quality articles and information pertaining to all levels of law enforcement and Homeland Security. Estab. 1984. Circ. 21,000. Byline given. Pays on publication. Pays kill fee. Publishes ms an average of 2 months after acceptance. Editorial lead time: 4-6 weeks. Submit 4 weeks in advance. Accepts queries by mail, e-mail, fax, phone. Accepts simultaneous submissions. Responds immediately. Sample copy online.

NONFICTION Contact: James Devery, managing editor. Needs book excerpts, historical, how-to, humor, interview, new product, nostalgic, opinion, personal experience, photo feature, reviews, technical. **Buys 12 mss/year.** Query. Length: 200-2,500 words. **Pays 10¢/word. Sometimes pays in trade-out of services.** Pays expenses of writers on assignment.

REPRINTS Send tearsheet, photocopy or emailed manuscript with rights for sale noted and information about when and where the material previously appeared. Pays 10¢/word.

PHOTOS State availability. Reviews 3x5 or larger images. Offers $10-50/photo. Buys one-time rights.

FILLERS Contact: James Devery. Law Enforcement - related topics Needs facts, newsbreaks, short humor. **Buys 6 mss/year.** Length: 200-2,000 words. **10¢/word.**

$$$$ YOUTH TODAY

Kennesaw State University, 1000 Chastain Rd., MD 2212, Bldg. 22, Kennesaw GA 30144. (678)797-2899. **E-mail:** jfleming@youthtoday.org. **Website:** www.youthtoday.org. **Contact:** John Fleming, editor. **50% freelance written.** Bi-monthly newspaper covering businesses that provide services to youth. Audience is people who run youth programs—mostly nonprofits and government agencies—who want help in providing services and getting funding. Estab. 1994. Circ. 9,000. Byline given. Pays on publication. Offers $200 kill fee for features. Editorial lead time 2 months. Accepts queries by mail. Accepts simultaneous submissions. Responds in 2 weeks to queries. Responds in 1 month to mss. Sample copy for $5. Guidelines available on website.

"Our freelance writers work for or have worked for daily newspapers, or have extensive experience writing for newspapers and magazines."

NONFICTION Needs general interest, technical. "No feel-good stories about do-gooders. We examine the business of youth work." **Buys 5 mss/year.** Query. Send rèsumè, short cover letter, clips. Length: 600-2,500 words. **Pays $150-2,000 for assigned articles.** Pays expenses of writers on assignment.

PHOTOS Identification of subjects required. Offers no additional payment for photos accepted with ms. Buys one-time and Internet rights.

COLUMNS/DEPARTMENTS "*Youth Today* also publishes 750-word guest columns, called Viewpoints. These pieces can be based on the writer's own experiences or based on research, but they must deal with an issue of interest to our readership and must soundly argue an opinion, or advocate for a change in thinking or action within the youth field."

TIPS "Business writers have the best shot. Focus on evaluations of programs, or why a program succeeds or fails. Please visit online."

GROCERIES & FOOD PRODUCTS

$$ CONVENIENCE DISTRIBUTION

American Wholesale Marketers Association, 11311 Sunset Hills Road, Reston VA 20190. (703)208-3358. **Fax:** (703)573-5738. **E-mail:** info@awmanet.org; joanf@awmanet.org. **Website:** www.cdaweb.net. **Contact:** Joan Fay, associate publisher and editor. **70% freelance written.** Magazine published 10 times/year. See website for editorial calendar. Covers trends in candy, tobacco, groceries, beverages, snacks, and other product categories found in convenience stores, grocery stores, and drugstores, plus distribution topics. Contributors should have prior experience writing about the food, retail, and/or distribution industries. Editorial includes a mix of columns, departments, and features (2-6 pages). Also covers AWMA programs. Estab. 1948. Circ. 11,000. Byline given. Pays on acceptance. No kill fee. Publishes ms an average of 2 months after acceptance. Editorial lead time 3-4 months. Accepts simultaneous submissions. Guidelines available online.

NONFICTION Needs how-to, technical, industry trends, also profiles of distribution firms. No comics, jokes, poems, or other fillers. **Buys 40 mss/year.** Query with published clips. Length: 1,200-3,600 words. **Pays 50¢/word.** Pays expenses of writers on assignment.

PHOTOS Authors must provide artwork (with captions) with articles.

TIPS "We're looking for reliable, accurate freelancers with whom we can establish a long-term working relationship. We need writers who understand this industry. We accept very few articles on speculation. Most are assigned. To consider a new writer for an assignment, we must first receive his or her résuméat least 2 writing samples, and references."

$ FRESH CUT MAGAZINE

Great American Publishing, P.O. Box 128, 75 Applewood Dr., Suite A, Sparta MI 49345. (616)887-9008. **Fax:** (616)887-2666. **E-mail:** fcedit@freshcut.com. **Website:** www.freshcut.com. **Contact:** Lee Dean, editorial director. **20% freelance written.** Monthly magazine covering the value-added and pre-cut fruit and vegetable industry. Interested in articles that focus on what different fresh-cut processors are doing. Estab. 1993. Circ. 16,000. Byline given. Pays on publication. No kill fee. Publishes ms an average of 2 months after acceptance. Editorial lead time 2 months. Accepts queries by mail, e-mail, fax, phone, online submission form. Accepts simultaneous submissions. Responds in 1 month to queries. Responds in 2 months to mss. Sample copy for SAE with 9x12 envelope. Guidelines for #10 SASE.

NONFICTION Needs historical, new product, opinion, technical. **Buys 2-4 mss/year.** Query with published clips.

REPRINTS Send tearsheet with rights for sale noted and information about when and where the material previously appeared. Pays 50% of amount paid for an original article.

PHOTOS Send photos. Identification of subjects required. Reviews transparencies. Offers no additional payment for photos accepted with ms. Buys one-time rights.

COLUMNS/DEPARTMENTS Packaging; Food Safety; Processing/Engineering. **Buys 20 mss/year.** Query. **Pays $125-200.**

$ THE PRODUCE NEWS

800 Kinderkamack Rd., Suite 100, Oradell NJ 07649. (201)986-7990. **Fax:** (201)986-7996. **E-mail:** groh@theproducenews.com. **Website:** www.theproducenews.com. **Contact:** John Groh, editor/publisher. **10% freelance written. Works with a small number of new/unpublished writers each year.** Weekly magazine for commercial growers and shippers, receivers, and distributors of fresh fruits and vegetables, including chain store produce buyers and merchandisers. Estab. 1897. Pays on publication. No kill fee. Publishes ms an average of 2 weeks after acceptance. Accepts queries by mail, e-mail. Accepts simultaneous submissions. Responds in 1 month to queries. Sample copy and writer's guidelines for 10x13 SAE and 4 first-class stamps.

NONFICTION Query. **Pays $1/column inch minimum.** Pays expenses of writers on assignment.

PHOTOS B&W glossies or color prints. Pays $8-10/photo.

TIPS "Stories should be trade oriented, not consumer oriented. As our circulation grows, we are interested in stories and news articles from all fresh-fruit-growing areas of the country."

$$ WESTERN GROCER MAGAZINE

Mercury Publications Ltd., 1313 Border Ave., Unit 16, Winnipeg MB R3H 0X4 Canada. (204)954-2085, ext. 219; (800)337-6372. **Fax:** (204)954-2057. **E-mail:** rbradley@mercurypublications.ca. **Website:** www.westerngrocer.com. **Contact:** Robin Bradley, associate publisher and national account manager. **75% freelance written.** Bimonthly magazine covering the grocery industry. Reports for the Western Canadian grocery, allied non-food and institutional industries. Each issue features a selection of relevant trade news and event coverage from the West and around the world. Feature reports offer market analysis, trend views, and insightful interviews from a wide variety of industry leaders. *The Western Grocer* target audience is independent retail food stores, supermarkets, manufacturers and food brokers, distributors and wholesalers of food, and allied non-food products, as well as bakers, specialty and health food stores, and convenience outlets. Estab. 1916. Circ. 15,500. Byline given. Pays 30-45 days from receipt of invoice. Offers 33% kill fee. Submit seasonal material 3 months in advance. Sample copy and writer's guidelines free.

Assigns stories to Canadian writers based on editorial needs of publication.

NONFICTION Needs how-to, interview. Does not want industry reports and profiles on companies. Query with published clips. Length: 500-9,000 words. **Pays 25-35¢/word.** Pays expenses of writers on assignment.

PHOTOS State availability. Captions required. Reviews negatives, transparencies, 3x5 prints, JPEG, EPS, or TIF files. Negotiates payment individually. Buys all rights.

TIPS "E-mail, fax, or mail a query outlining your experience, interest, and pay expectations. Include clippings."

HOME FURNISHINGS & HOUSEHOLD GOODS

$$ HOME FURNISHINGS RETAILER

National Home Furnishings Association (NHFA), 500 Giuseppe Ct., Suite 6, Roseville CA 95678. (336)801-6156; (800)422-3778. **E-mail:** wynnryan@rcn.com. **Website:** www.nhfa.org. **Contact:** Mary Wynn Ryan, editor-in-chief. **75% freelance written.** Monthly magazine published by NHFA covering the home furnishings industry. "We hope home furnishings retailers view our magazine as a profitability tool. We want each issue to help them make or save money." Estab. 1927. Circ. 15,000. Byline given. Pays on acceptance. No kill fee. Publishes ms an average of 6 weeks after acceptance. Editorial lead time 3 months. Accepts queries by mail, e-mail. Accepts simultaneous submissions. Responds in 1 month to queries. Sample copy available with proper postage. Guidelines available.

Requires writers to have credentials that include specific knowledge of the industry and extensive experience in writing about it. "We rely heavily on home furnishings industry experts to author articles. Some freelance material is used. However, the NHFA Board of Directors, which provides direction for the publication, requires that writers have credentials that include specific knowledge of the industry and extensive experience in writing about it. Freelancers are compensated based on subject matter and the amount of research required. Suggestions for freelance articles relating to the business interests of retailers will be reviewed."

NONFICTION Query. "When submitting a query or requesting a writing assignment, include a résumé, writing samples, and credentials. When articles are assigned, *Home Furnishings Retailer* will provide general direction along with suggestions for appropriate artwork. The author is responsible for obtaining photographs or other illustrative material. Assigned articles should be submitted via e-mail or on disc along with a list of sources with telephone numbers, fax numbers, and e-mail addresses." Length: 3,000-5,000 words (features). **Pays $350-500.**

PHOTOS Author is responsible for obtaining photos or other illustrative material. State availability. Identification of subjects required. Reviews transparencies. Negotiates payment individually. Buys one-time rights.

COLUMNS/DEPARTMENTS Columns cover business and product trends that shape the home furnishings industry. Advertising and Marketing; Finance; Technology; Training; Creative Leadership; Law; Style and Operations. Length: 1,200-1,500 words. Query with published clips.

TIPS "Our readership includes owners of small 'ma and pa' furniture stores, executives of medium-sized chains (2-10 stores), and executives of big chains. Articles should be relevant to retailers and provide them with tangible information, ideas, and products to better their business."

$$ WINDOW FASHION VISION

Grace McNamara, Inc., 4756 Banning Ave., Suite 206, St. Paul MN 55110. **E-mail:** sophia@wf-vision.com. **Website:** www.wf-vision.com. **Contact:** Sophia Bennett, editor-in-chief. **30% freelance written.** Monthly magazine dedicated to the advancement of the window fashions industry, *Window Fashions* provides comprehensive information on design and business principles, window fashion aesthetics, and product applications. The magazine serves the window-treatment and wall-coverings industry, including designers, retailers, dealers, specialty stores, workrooms, manufacturers, fabricators, and others associated with the field of interior design. Writers should be thoroughly knowledgable on the subject, and submissions need to be comprehensive. Estab. 1981. Circ. 11,000. Byline given. Pays on publication. No kill fee. Publishes ms an average of 3 months after acceptance. Editorial lead time 3 months. Submit seasonal material 6 months in advance. Accepts queries by e-mail. Accepts simultaneous submissions. Sample copy available online.

NONFICTION Needs book excerpts, how-to, interview, new product, personal experience, photo feature, profile, technical, specific topics within the field. Special issues: Each issue has a different theme. Contact editor for more details. No broad topics not specific to the window fashions industry. **Buys 24 mss/year.** Query or send complete ms Length: 1,000-1,500 words. **Pays $300-500.**

TIPS "The most helpful experience is if a writer has knowledge of interior design or, specifically, window treatments. We already have a pool of generalists, although we welcome clips from writers who would like to be considered for assignments. Our style is professional business writing—no flowery prose. Articles tend to be to the point, as our readers are busy professionals who read for information, not for leisure. Most of all we need creative ideas and approaches to topics in the field of window treatments and interior design."

HOSPITALS, NURSING & NURSING HOMES

$$ CURRENT NURSING IN GERIATRIC CARE

Freiberg Press Inc., P.O. Box 612, Cedar Falls IA 50613. (319)553-0642; (800)354-3371. **Fax:** (319)553-0644. **E-mail:** bfreiberg@cfu.net. **Website:** www.care4elders.com. **Contact:** Bill Freiberg. **25% freelance written.** Bimonthly trade journal covering medical information and new developments in research for geriatric nurses and other practitioners. Estab. 2006. Byline sometimes given. Pays on acceptance. No kill fee. Accepts queries by e-mail. Accepts simultaneous submissions. Sample copy free; send e-mail to Kathy Freiderg at kfreiberg@cfu.net.

NONFICTION Query. Length: 500-1,500 words. **Pays 15¢/word for assigned articles.** Pays expenses of writers on assignment.

PHOTOS State availability.

$$$ NURSEWEEK

Gannett Healthcare Group, 1721 Moon Lake Blvd., Suite 540, Hoffman Estates IL 60169. **E-mail:** editor@nurse.com. **Website:** www.nurse.com. **Contact:** Nick Hut, editor. **98% freelance written.** Biweekly magazine covering nursing news. Covers nursing news about people, practice, and the profession. Review several issues for content and style. Also consider e-mailing your idea to the editorial director in your region (see list online). The editorial director can help you with the story's focus or angle, along with the organization and development of ideas. Estab. 1999. Circ. 155,000. Byline given. Pays on publication. Offers $200 kill fee. Publishes ms an average of 2 months after acceptance. Editorial lead time 2-3 months. Submit seasonal material 4 months in advance. Accepts queries by e-mail. Accepts simultaneous submissions. Sample copy free. Guidelines on website.

NONFICTION Needs interview, personal experience, articles on innovative approaches to clinical care and evidence-based nursing practice, health-related legislation and regulation, community health programs, healthcare delivery systems, and professional development and management, advances in nursing specialties such as critical care, geriatrics, perioperative care, women's health, home care, long-term care, emergency care, med/surg, pediatrics, advanced practice, education, and staff development. **Buys 20 mss/year mss/year.** Query with a 50-word summary of story and a list of RN experts you plan to interview. Length: 900 words. **Pays $200-800 for assigned or unsolicited articles.**

PHOTOS Send photos. Captions, model releases required. Reviews contact sheets, GIF/JPEG files. Offers no additional payment for photos accepted with ms. Buys all rights.

TIPS "Pitch us nursing news, AP style, minimum 3 sources, incorporate references. The stories we publish are short and written in a conversational, magazine-style rather than a scholarly tone. In keeping with any article appearing in a nursing publication, clinical accuracy is essential."

$$ NURSING

Lippincott Williams & Wilkins, 323 Norristown Rd., Suite 200, Ambler PA 19002-2758. (215)646-8700. **Fax:** (215)654-1328. **E-mail:** nursingeditor@wolterskluwer.com. **Website:** http://journals.lww.com/nursing/pages/default.aspx. **Contact:** Linda

Laskowski-Jones, RN, ACNS-BC, CCRN, CEN, MS, FAWM. **100% freelance written.** Monthly magazine written by nurses for nurses. Looks for practical advice for the direct caregiver that reflects the author's experience. Any form acceptable, but focus must be nursing. Published monthly, *Nursing2014* is widely regarded as offering current, practical contents to its readers, and has won many editorial awards testifying to the quality of its copy and graphics. The editorial and clinical staff, a 18-member editorial board of distinguished clinicians and practitioners, and over 100 invited reviewers help ensure the quality of this publication. Estab. 1971. Circ. over 300,000. Byline given. Pays on publication. Offers 50% kill fee. Publishes ms an average of 18 months after acceptance. Submit seasonal material 8 months in advance. Accepts simultaneous submissions. Responds in 2 weeks to queries. Responds in 3 months to mss. Sample copy for $5. Guidelines available online.

NONFICTION Needs book excerpts, how-to, inspirational, opinion, personal experience, photo feature. No articles from patients' point of view, poetry, etc. **Buys 100 mss/year.** Query. All mss can be submitted online through the journal's submission website. Using this process will expedite review and feedback, and allows the the author to see where the ms is in the editorial process at any time after it's accepted. Encourages authors to register there and follow the directions. Length: 3,500 words (continuing ed feature); 2,100 words (features); short features/departments, 700 words. **Pays $50-400 for assigned articles.** Pays expenses of writers on assignment.

REPRINTS Send photocopy and information about when and where the material previously appeared. Pays 50% of amount paid for an original articles.

PHOTOS State availability. Model releases required. Offers no additional payment for photos accepted with ms. Buys all rights.

TIPS "Basically, *Nursing2013* is a how-to journal, full of hands-on, practical articles. We look for the voice of experience from authors and for articles that help our readers deal with problems they face. We're always interested in taking a look at mss that fall into the following categories: clinical articles, drug articles, charting/documentation, emotional problems, legal problems, ethical dilemnas, and difficult or challenging cases."

$ SCHOOL NURSE NEWS

Franklin Communications, Inc., 767 Buena Vista Ave. W., #101, San Francisco CA 94117. (415)670-0436. **Fax:** (415)663-4768. **E-mail:** editor@schoolnursenews.org. **Website:** www.schoolnursenews.org. **Contact:** Deb Ilardi. **10% freelance written.** Magazine published 5 times/year covering school nursing. *School Nurse News* focuses on topics related to the health issues of school-aged children and adolescents (grades K-12), as well as the health and professional issues that concern school nurses. This is an excellent opportunity for both new and experienced writers. *School Nurse News* publishes feature articles as well as news articles and regular departments, such as Asthma & Allergy Watch, Career & Salary Survey, Oral Health, Nursing Currents, and Sights & Sounds. Estab. 1982. Circ. 7,500. Byline given. Pays on publication. Publishes ms an average of 3-6 months after acceptance. Editorial lead time 3-6 months. Submit seasonal material 6 months in advance. Accepts queries by e-mail, fax, phone. Accepts simultaneous submissions. Sample copy free. Guidelines available on website.

NONFICTION Needs how-to, interview, new product, personal experience. **Buys 1-2 mss/year.** Query. Send via e-mail or forward ms with disk. Mss can include case histories, scenarios of health office situations, updates on diseases, reporting of research, and discussion of procedures and techniques, among others. The author is responsible for the accuracy of content. References should be complete, accurate, and in APA format. Tables, charts and photographs are welcome. Authors are responsible for obtaining permission to reproduce any material that has a pre-existing copyright. The feature article, references, tables, and charts should total 8-10 typewritten pages, double-spaced. The author's name should be included only on the top sheet. The top sheet should also include the title of the article, the author's credentials, current position, address, and phone. **Pays $100.** Pays expenses of writers on assignment.

HOTELS, MOTELS, CLUBS, RESORTS & RESTAURANTS

$$ CRUISE INDUSTRY NEWS

441 Lexington Ave., Suite 809, New York NY 10017. (212)986-1025. **Fax:** (212)986-1033. **E-mail:** oivind@

cruiseindustrynews.com. **Website:** www.cruiseindustrynews.com. **Contact:** Oivind Mathisen, editor. **20% freelance written.** Quarterly magazine covering cruise shipping. Magazine about the business of cruise shipping for the industry, including cruise lines, shipyards, financial analysts, etc. Estab. 1991. Circ. 10,000. Byline given. Pays on acceptance or on publication. Offers 25% kill fee. Publishes ms an average of 4 months after acceptance. Editorial lead time 3 months. Accepts queries by mail. Accepts simultaneous submissions. Reponse time varies. Sample copy for $15. Guidelines for #10 SASE.

NONFICTION Needs interview, new product. No travel stories. **Buys more than 20 mss/year.** Query with published clips. Length: 500-1,500 words. **Pays $.50/word published.** Pays expenses of writers on assignment.

PHOTOS State availability. Pays $25-50/photo. Buys one-time rights.

$$ EL RESTAURANTE

P.O. Box 2249, Oak Park IL 60303-2249. (708)267-0023. **E-mail:** kfurore@comcast.net. **Website:** www.restmex.com. **Contact:** Kathleen Furore, editor. Bimonthly magazine covering Mexican and other Latin cuisines. "*el Restaurante* offers features and business-related articles that are geared specifically to owners and operators of Mexican, Tex-Mex, Southwestern, and Latin cuisine restaurants and other foodservice establishments that want to add that type of cuisine." Estab. 1997. Circ. 25,000. Byline given. Pays on publication. No kill fee. Publishes ms an average of 3 months after acceptance. Accepts simultaneous submissions. Responds in 2 months to queries. Sample copy free.

NONFICTION "No specific knowledge of food or restaurants is needed; the key qualification is to be a good reporter who knows how to slant a story toward the Mexican restaurant operator." **Buys 2-4 mss/year.** Query with published clips. Length: 800-1,200 words. **Pays $250-300.**

TIPS "Query with a story idea, and tell how it pertains to Mexican restaurants."

$$$$ HOSPITALITY TECHNOLOGY

EnsembleIQ, 1 Gateway Center, 11-43 Raymond PLZ Fl 16, Newark NJ 07102. (973)607-1300. **E-mail:** dcreamer@ensembleiq.com; mescobar@ensembleiq.com; jbinns@ensembleiq.com. **Website:** www.ht-magazine.com. **Contact:** Dorothy Creamer, editor; Jessica Binns, senior editor; Michal Christine Escobar, managing editor. **40% freelance written.** Magazine published 8 times/year covering restaurant and lodging executives who manage hotels, casinos, cruise lines, quick service restaurants, etc. Covers the technology used in restaurants and lodging. Readers are the operators, who have significant IT responsibilities. This publication will not respond to all inquiries, due to the number of submissions—only those that are of particular interest to the editor. Estab. 1996. Circ. 16,000. Byline given. Pays on acceptance. No kill fee. Publishes ms an average of 1 month after acceptance. Editorial lead time 2 months. Accepts queries by mail, e-mail. Accepts simultaneous submissions. Responds in 2 weeks to queries.

NONFICTION Needs how-to, interview, new product, technical. Special issues: Publishes 3 studies each year: the Restaurant Industry Technology Study; the Lodging Industry Technology Study and the Customer Engagement Technology Study. No unsolicited mss. **Buys 40 mss/year.** Query with published clips. Length: 800-1,200 words. **Pays $1/word.** Pays expenses of writers on assignment.

$$$ HOTELIER

Kostuch Media Ltd., 101-23 Lesmill Rd., Toronto ON M3B 3P6 Canada. (416)447-0888. **Fax:** (416)447-5333. **E-mail:** rcaira@foodservice.ca. **Website:** www.hoteliermagazine.com. **Contact:** Rosanna Caira, editor & publisher. **40% freelance written.** Magazine published 8 times/year covering the Canadian hotel industry. Canada's leading hotel publication. Provides comprehensive and insightful content focusing on business developments, trend analysis, and profiles of the industry's movers and shakers. Estab. 1989. Circ. 9,000. Byline given. Pays on publication. No kill fee. Editorial lead time 3 months. Submit seasonal material 2 months in advance. Accepts queries by mail, fax. Accepts simultaneous submissions. Query for free sample copy. Query for free guidelines.

NONFICTION Needs how-to, new product. No case studies. **Buys 30-50 mss/year.** Query. Length: 700-1,500 words. **Pays 35¢/word (Canadian) for assigned articles.** Pays expenses of writers on assignment.

PHOTOS Send photos. Offers $30-75/photo.

$$ PIZZA TODAY

Macfadden Protech, LLC, 908 S. 8th St., Suite 200, Louisville KY 40203. (502)736-9500. **Fax:** (502)736-9502. **E-mail:** jwhite@pizzatoday.com. **Website:**

www.pizzatoday.com. **Contact:** Jeremy White, editor-in-chief. **30% freelance written. Works with published/established writers; occasionally works with new writers.** Monthly magazine for the pizza industry, covering trends, features of successful pizza operators, business and management advice, etc. Estab. 1984. Circ. 44,000. Byline given. Pays on acceptance. No kill fee. Publishes ms an average of 2 months after acceptance. Submit seasonal material 3 months in advance. Accepts queries by mail, e-mail, fax. Accepts simultaneous submissions. Responds in 2 months to queries. Responds in 3 weeks to mss. Sample copy for sae with 10x13 envelope and 6 first-class stamps. Guidelines for #10 SASE and online.

Offer solid information and creative solutions to specific management problems. Strive to present an "insider's view." Every story published in *Pizza Today* should be crammed with tips for operating a better business. Complex or technical concepts should be presented in a manner that's clear to the lay reader contemplating entry into the pizza foodservice industry, but not so basic that experienced veterans are turned off.

NONFICTION Needs interview, entrepreneurial slants, pizza production and delivery, employee training, hiring, marketing, and business management. No fillers, humor, or poetry. **Buys 85 mss/year.** Length: 1,000 words. **Pays 50¢/word, occasionally more.** Pays expenses of writers on assignment.

PHOTOS Captions required. Reviews contact sheets, negatives, transparencies, color slides, 5x7 prints.

TIPS "Our most pressing need is for articles that would fall within our Front of the House section. Review the magazine before sending in your query."

$$$ SANTÉ MAGAZINE

On-Premise Communications, 160 Benmont Ave., Suite 92, Third Floor, West Wing, Bennington VT 05201. (802)442-6771. **Fax:** (802)442-6859. **E-mail:** mvaughan@santemagazine.com. **Website:** www.isantemagazine.com. **Contact:** Mark Vaughan, editor. **75% freelance written.** Four issues/year magazine covering food, wine, spirits, and management topics for restaurant professionals. Information and specific advice for restaurant professionals on operating a profitable food and beverage program. Writers should "speak" to readers on a professional-to-professional basis. Estab. 1996. Circ. 45,000. Byline given. Pays on publication. Offers 50% kill fee. Publishes ms an average of 2 months after acceptance. Editorial lead time 3 months. Submit seasonal material 6 months in advance. Accepts queries by e-mail. Accepts simultaneous submissions. Responds in 2 weeks to queries. Does not accept mss. Sample copy available. Guidelines by e-mail.

"Articles should be concise and to the point and should closely adhere to the assigned word count. Our readers will only read articles that provide useful information in a readily accessible format. Where possible, articles should be broken into stand-alone sections that can be boxed or otherwise highlighted."

NONFICTION Needs interview, restaurant business news. Does not want consumer-focused pieces. **Buys 20 mss/year.** Query with published clips. Length: 650-1,800 words. Pays expenses of writers on assignment.

PHOTOS State availability. Captions required. Reviews PDF/GIF/JPEG files 500kb-10mb. Offers no additional payment for photos accepted. Buys one-time rights.

COLUMNS/DEPARTMENTS Due to a Redesign, 650 words; Bar Tab (focuses on 1 bar's unique strategy for success), 1,000 words; Restaurant Profile (a business-related look at what qualities make 1 restaurant successful), 1,000 words; Maximizing Profits (covers 1 great profit-maximizing strategy per issue from several sources), Signature Dish (highlights 1 chef's background and favorite dish with recipe), Sommeliers Choice (6 top wine managers recommend favorite wines; with brief profiles of each manager), Distillations (6 bar professionals offer their favorite drink for a particular type of spirit; with brief profiles of each manager), 1,500 words; Provisions (like The Goods only longer; an in-depth look at a special ingredient), 1,500 words. **Buys 20 mss/year.** Query with published clips. **Pays $300-800.**

TIPS "Present 2 or 3 of your best ideas via e-mail. Include a brief statement of your qualifications. Attach your resumè and 3 electronic clips. The same format may be used to query via postal mail if necessary."

$$ WESTERN HOTELIER MAGAZINE

Mercury Publications, Ltd., 1313 Border St., Unit 16, Winnipeg MB R3H 0X4 Canada. (800)337-6372 ext. 221. **Fax:** (204)954-2057. **E-mail:** dbastable@mercurypublications.ca. **Website:** www.westernhotelier.com. **Contact:** David Bastable, associate publisher and national accounts manager. **33% freelance written.** Quarterly magazine covering the hotel industry. *Western Hotelier* is dedicated to the accommodation industry in Western Canada and U.S. western border states. *WH* offers the West's best mix of news and feature reports geared to hotel management. Feature reports are written on a sector basis and are created to help generate enhanced profitability and better understanding. Circ. 4,342. Byline given. Pays 30-45 days from receipt of invoice. Offers 33% kill fee. Submit seasonal material 3 months in advance. Accepts queries by mail, fax. Accepts simultaneous submissions. Responds in 2 weeks to queries. Sample copy and writer's guidelines free.

NONFICTION Needs how-to, interview. Industry reports and profiles on companies. Query with published clips. Length: 500-9,000 words. **Pays 25-35¢/word.** Pays expenses of writers on assignment.

PHOTOS State availability. Captions required. Reviews negatives, transparencies, 3x5 prints, JPEG, EPS, or TIF files. Negotiates payment individually. Buys all rights.

TIPS "E-mail, fax, or mail a query outlining your experience, interests, and pay expectations. Include clippings."

WESTERN RESTAURANT NEWS

Mercury Publications, Ltd., 1313 Border St., Unit 16, Winnipeg MB R3H 0X4 Canada. (800)337-6372 ext. 213. **Fax:** (204)954-2057. **E-mail:** editorial@mercury.mb.ca; edufault@mercurypublications.ca. **Website:** www.westernrestaurantnews.com; www.mercury.mb.ca. **Contact:** Elaine Dufault, associate publisher and national accounts manager. **20% freelance written.** Bimonthly magazine covering the restaurant trade in Western Canada. Reports profiles and industry reports on associations, regional business developments, etc. *Western Restaurant News* is the authoritative voice of the food service industry in Western Canada. Offering a total package to readers, *WRN* delivers concise news articles, new product news, and coverage of the leading trade events in the West, across the country, and around the world. Estab. 1994. Circ. 14,532. Byline given. Pays 30-45 days from receipt of invoice. Offers 33% kill fee. Submit seasonal material 3 months in advance. Accepts queries by mail, fax. Accepts simultaneous submissions. Sample copy and writer's guidelines free.

NONFICTION Needs how-to, interview. Industry reports and profiles on companies. Query with published clips. "E-mail, fax, or mail a query outlining your experience, interests, and pay expectations. Include clippings." Length: 500-9,000 words. **Pays 25-35¢/word.** Pays expenses of writers on assignment.

PHOTOS State availability. Captions required. Reviews negatives, transparencies, 3x5 prints, JPEG, EPS, or TIFF files. Negotiates payment individually. Buys all rights.

INDUSTRIAL OPERATIONS

COMMERCE & INDUSTRY

Mercury Publications, Ltd., 1313 Border Street, Unit 16, Winnipeg MB R3H 0X4 Canada. (204)954-2085. **Fax:** (204)954-2057. **E-mail:** editorial@mercury.mb.ca. **Website:** www.commerceindustry.ca. **Contact:** Nicole Sherwood, editorial coordinator. **75% freelance written.** Bimonthly magazine covering the business and industrial sectors. Offers new product news, industry event coverage, and breaking trade specific business stories. Industry reports and company profiles provide readers with an in-depth insight into key areas of interest in their profession. Estab. 1948. Circ. 18,876. Byline given. Pays 30-45 days from receipt of invoice. Offers 33% kill fee. Submit seasonal material 3 months in advance. Accepts queries by mail, e-mail, fax. Accepts simultaneous submissions. Responds in 2 weeks to queries. Sample copy and writer's guidelines free or by e-mail.

NONFICTION Needs how-to, interview. Industry reports and profiles on companies. Query with published clips. Length: 500-9,000 words. **Pays 25-35¢/word.** Pays expenses of writers on assignment.

PHOTOS State availability. Captions required. Reviews negatives, transparencies, 3x5 prints, JPEG, EPS or TIF files. Negotiates payment individually. Buys all rights.

TIPS "E-mail, fax, or mail a query outlining your experience, interests and pay expectations. Include clippings."

INDUSTRIAL WEIGH & MEASURE

WAM Publishing Company, Inc., P.O. Box 2247, Hendersonville TN 37077. (615)239-8087. **E-mail:** dave.mathieu@comcast.net. **Website:** www.weighproducts.

com. **Contact:** David M. Mathieu, publisher and editor. Bimonthly magazine for users of industrial scales; covers material handling and logistics industries. Estab. 1914. Circ. 13,900. Byline given. Pays on acceptance. Offers 20% kill fee. Accepts queries by mail, e-mail, phone. Accepts simultaneous submissions. Responds in 2 weeks to queries. Sample copy available online.

NONFICTION Needs general interest, technical. **Buys 15 mss/year.** Query on technical articles; submit complete ms for general interest material. Length: 1,000-2,500 words. **Pays $175-300.** Pays expenses of writers on assignment.

$$$$ MACHINERY & EQUIPMENT MRO

Annex Business Media, 111 Gordon Baker Rd., Suite 400, Toronto ON M2H 3R1 Canada. (416)510-6851. **Fax:** (416)510-5134. **E-mail:** rbegg@annexweb.com. **Website:** www.mromagazine.com. **Contact:** Rehana Begg, Editor. **30% freelance written.** Bimonthly magazine looking for informative articles on issues that affect plant floor operations and maintenance. Estab. 1985. Circ. 18,000. Byline given. Pays on publication. No kill fee. Publishes ms an average of 3 months after acceptance. Editorial lead time 4 months. Submit seasonal material 4 months in advance. Accepts simultaneous submissions. Responds in 3 weeks to queries; 1 month to mss. Sample copy free. Guidelines available.

NONFICTION Needs essays, how-to, interview, new product, profile, technical. **Buys 6 mss/year.** Query with published clips. Length: 750-4,000 words. **Pays $200-1,400 (Canadian).** Pays expenses of writers on assignment.

PHOTOS State availability. Captions required. Reviews transparencies, prints. Negotiates payment individually. Buys one-time rights.

TIPS "Information can be found at our website. Call us for sample issues, ideas, etc."

$$ MODERN MATERIALS HANDLING

Peerless Media, 111 Speen St., Suite 200, Framingham MA 01701. (508)663-1500. **E-mail:** mlevans@ehpub.com; robert.trebilcock@myfairpoint.net. **Website:** www.mmh.com. **Contact:** Michael Levans, editorial director. **40% freelance written.** Magazine published 13 times/year covering warehousing, distribution centers, and inventory. *Modern Materials Handling* is a national magazine read by managers of warehouses and distribution centers. Focuses on lively, well-written articles telling readers how they can achieve maximum facility productivity and efficiency. Covers technology, too. Estab. 1945. Circ. 81,000. Byline given. Pays on acceptance (allow 4-6 weeks for invoice processing). No kill fee. Publishes ms an average of 1 month after acceptance. Editorial lead time 3 months. Accepts queries by mail, e-mail, fax. Accepts simultaneous submissions. Sample copy and guidelines free.

NONFICTION Needs how-to, new product, technical. Special issues: State-of-the-Industry Report, Peak Performer, Salary and Wage survey, Warehouse of the Year. Doesn't want anything that doesn't deal with the topic of warehousing. No general-interest profiles or interviews. **Buys 25 mss/year.** Query with published clips. **Pays $300-650.**

PHOTOS State availability. Captions, identification of subjects required. Reviews negatives, transparencies, prints. Offers no additional payment for photos accepted with ms. Buys all rights.

TIPS "Learn a little about warehousing and distributors, and write well. We typically don't accept specific article queries, but welcome introductory letters from journalists to whom we can assign articles. But authors are welcome to request an editorial calendar and develop article queries from it."

INFORMATION SYSTEMS

$ JOURNAL OF INFORMATION ETHICS

McFarland & Co., Inc., Publishers, P.O. Box 611, Jefferson NC 28640. (336)246-4460. **E-mail:** hauptman@stcloudstate.edu. **90% freelance written.** Semiannual scholarly journal covering all of the information sciences. Addresses ethical issues in all of the information sciences with a deliberately interdisciplinary approach. Topics range from electronic mail monitoring to library acquisition of controversial material to archival ethics. The *Journal*'s aim is to present thoughtful considerations of ethical dilemmas that arise in a rapidly evolving system of information exchange and dissemination. Estab. 1992. Byline given. Pays on publication. No kill fee. Publishes ms an average of 2 years after acceptance. Submit seasonal material 8 months in advance. Accepts queries by mail, e-mail, phone. Accepts simultaneous submissions. Sample copy for $30. Guidelines free.

NONFICTION Needs essays, reviews. **Buys 10-12 mss/year.** Send complete ms. Length: 500-3,500 words. **Pays $25-50, depending on length.**

TIPS "Familiarize yourself with the many areas subsumed under the rubric of information ethics, e.g., privacy, scholarly communication, errors, peer review, confidentiality, e-mail, etc. Present a well-rounded discussion of any fresh, current, or evolving ethical topic within the information sciences or involving real-world information collection/exchange."

$$ SYSTEM INEWS

Penton Technology Media, 748 Whalers Way, Fort Collins CO 80525. (970)663-4700; (800)621-1544. **E-mail:** editors@iprodeveloper.com. **Website:** www.iprodeveloper.com. **40% freelance written.** Magazine, published 12 times/year, focused on programming, networking, IS management, and technology for users of IBM AS/400, iSERIES, SYSTEM i, AND IBM i platform. Estab. 1982. Circ. 30,000 (international). Byline given. Pays on publication. Offers 50% kill fee. Publishes ms an average of 3 months after acceptance. Editorial lead time 4 months. Submit seasonal material 4 months in advance. Accepts queries by e-mail. Accepts simultaneous submissions. Responds in 3 weeks to queries. Responds in 5 weeks to mss. Guidelines available online.

NONFICTION Needs technical. Query. Length: 1,500-2,500 words. **Pays $300/$500 flat fee for assigned articles, depending on article quality and technical depth.** Pays expenses of writers on assignment.

REPRINTS Send photocopy. Payment negotiable.

PHOTOS State availability. Offers no additional payment for photos accepted with ms.

COLUMNS/DEPARTMENTS Load'n'go (complete utility).

TIPS "Must have in-depth knowledge of IBM AS/400/ iSERIES/SYSTEM i/IBM i computer platform."

$$$$ TECHNOLOGY REVIEW

MIT, One Main St., 13th Floor, Cambridge MA 02142. (617)475-8000. **Fax:** (617)475-8042. **E-mail:** jason.pontin@technologyreview.com; david.rotman@technologyreview.com. **Website:** www.technologyreview.com. **Contact:** Jason Pontin, editor in chief; David Rotman, editor. Magazine published 10 times/year covering information technology, biotech, material science, and nanotechnology. *Technology Review* promotes the understanding of emerging technologies and their impact. Estab. 1899. Circ. 310,000. Byline given. Pays on acceptance. Accepts queries by mail, e-mail. Accepts simultaneous submissions.

NONFICTION Query with a pitch via online contact form. Length: 2,000-4,000 words. **Pays $1-3/word.** Pays expenses of writers on assignment.

FILLERS Short tidbits that relate laboratory prototypes on their way to market in 1-5 years. Length: 150-250 words. **Pays $1-3/word.**

JEWELRY

$ ADORNMENT

The Magazine of Jewelry & Related Arts, Association for the Study of Jewelry & Related Arts, 5070 Bonnie Branch Rd., Ellicott City MD 21043. **E-mail:** elyse@jewelryandrelatedarts.com. **Website:** www.jewelryandrelatedarts.com; www.asjra.net; www.jewelryconference.com. **50% freelance written.** Quarterly magazine covering jewelry, from antique to modern. "This magazine is a perk of membership in the Association for the Study of Jewelry & Related Arts. It is not sold as a stand-alone publication. It is delivered electronically. Readers are collectors, appraisers, antique jewelry dealers, gemologists, jewelry artists, museum curators—anyone with an interest in jewelry. You need to have a good working knowledge of jewelry subjects or we are not interested." Estab. 2002. Circ. 1,000+. Byline given. Pays on publication. No kill fee. Publishes ms an average of 3 months after acceptance. Editorial lead time 3 months. Accepts queries by mail, e-mail. Responds in 1-2 weeks to queries; 1 month to mss. Sample copy free as an e-mailed PDF. Guidelines free.

NONFICTION Needs book excerpts, historical, interview, exhibition reviews—in-depth articles on jewelry subjects. "We do not want articles about retail jewelry. We write about ancient, antique, period, and unique and studio jewelers." **Buys 12-15 mss/ year.** Query with published clips. Length: 1,000-3,000 words. **Pays up to $125 for assigned articles. Does not pay for unsolicited articles.**

PHOTOS "We only want photos that accompany articles. Quality must be professional. We pay $25 flat fee for them; we don't accept articles without accompanying photography. You must obtain permission for the use of photos. We won't publish without written approvals.".

TIPS "Know your subject, and provide applicable credentials."

$$ BEAD & BUTTON

Kalmbach Publishing, P.O. Box 1612, 21027 Crossroads Circle, Waukesha WI 53187-1612. **E-mail:** editor@beadandbutton.com. **Website:** www.beadandbutton.com. **Contact:** Julia Gerlach, editor. **50% freelance written.** "*Bead & Button* is a bimonthly magazine devoted to techniques, projects, designs, and materials relating to making beaded jewelry. Our readership includes both professional and amateur bead and button makers, hobbyists, and enthusiasts who find satisfaction in making beautiful things." Estab. 1994. Circ. 100,000. Byline given. Pays on acceptance. Offers $75 kill fee. Publishes ms an average of 4-12 months after acceptance. Editorial lead time 4-5 months. Accepts queries by e-mail. Accepts simultaneous submissions. Responds to queries in 4-6 weeks. Guidelines online.

NONFICTION Needs how-to, interview, profile. **Buys 20-25 mss/year.** Query. Length: 1,000-1,200 words. **Pays $75-400.**

PHOTOS Send photos. Identification of subjects required. Offers no additional payment for photos accepted with ms.

$$ THE ENGRAVERS JOURNAL

P.O. Box 318, Brighton MI 48116. (810)229-5725. **Fax:** (810)229-8320. **E-mail:** editor@engraversjournal.com. **Website:** www.engraversjournal.com. **Contact:** Senior editor. **70% freelance written.** Monthly magazine covering the recognition and personalization industry (engraving, sublimation, digital printing, sandcarving, personalized products, promotional products, awards and incentives, and signage). "We provide practical information for the education and advancement of our readers, mainly retail business owners." Estab. 1975. Byline given. Pays on acceptance. No kill fee. Publishes ms an average of 3-9 months after acceptance. Accepts queries by mail, e-mail, fax. Accepts simultaneous submissions. Responds in 2 weeks to mss. Sample copy free. Guidelines free.

NONFICTION Needs general interest, how-to, personal experience, technical. No general overviews of the industry. Length: 1,000-5,000 words. **Pays $200 and up.**

REPRINTS Send tearsheet, photocopy, or typed ms with rights for sale noted, and information about when and where the material previously appeared. Pays 50-100% of amount paid for original article.

PHOTOS Send photos. Captions, identification of subjects, model releases required. Pays variable rate.

TIPS "Articles should always be down to earth, practical, and thoroughly cover the subject with authority. We do not want the 'textbook' writing approach, vagueness, or theory—our readers look to us for sound, practical information. We use an educational slant, publishing both trade-oriented articles and general business topics of interest to a small retail-oriented readership."

JOURNALISM & WRITING

$$$$ AMERICAN JOURNALISM REVIEW

University of Maryland Foundation, Knight Hall, University of Maryland, College Park MD 20742. (301)405-8805. **E-mail:** editor@ajr.org. **Website:** www.ajr.org. **Contact:** Lucy Dalglish, dean and publisher. **80% freelance written.** Bimonthly magazine covering print, broadcast, and online journalism. *American Journalism Review* covers ethical issues, trends in the industry, and coverage that falls short. Circ. 25,000. Byline given. Pays 1 month after publication. Offers 25% kill fee. Publishes ms an average of 2 months after acceptance. Editorial lead time 1 month. Accepts queries by mail, e-mail. Responds in 1 month to queries and unsolicited mss. Sample copy: $4.95 prepaid or online. Guidelines available online.

NONFICTION Needs expose. Query or send complete ms. Length: 2,000-4,000 words. **Pays $1,500-2,000.** Pays expenses of writers on assignment.

FILLERS Needs anecdotes, facts, short humor, short pieces. Length: 150-1,000 words. **Pays $100-250.**

TIPS "Write a short story for the front-of-the-book section. We prefer queries to completed articles. Include in a page what you'd like to write about, who you'll interview, why it's important, and why you should write it."

$ AUTHORSHIP

National Writers Association, 10940 S. Parker Rd., #508, Parker CO 80134. **E-mail:** natlwritersassn@hotmail.com. **Website:** www.nationalwriters.com. Quarterly magazine covering writing articles only. "Association magazine targeted to beginning and professional writers. Covers how-to, humor, marketing issues. Disk and e-mail submissions preferred." Estab. 1950s. Circ. 4,000. Byline given. Pays on acceptance. No kill fee. Editorial lead time 3 months. Submit seasonal material 6 months in advance. Accepts queries by mail, e-mail. Accepts simultaneous submissions. Responds in 2 months to queries. Sample copy for stamped, self-addressed, 8½x11 envelope. Also available on our website.

NONFICTION **Buys 25 mss/year.** Query or send complete ms. Length: 1,200 words. **Pays $10, or discount on memberships and copies.** Pays expenses of writers on assignment.

PHOTOS State availability. Identification of subjects, model releases required. Reviews 5x7 prints. Offers no additional payment for photos accepted with ms. Buys one-time rights.

TIPS "Members of National Writers Association are given preference."

✪ $ $ $ $ CANADIAN SCREENWRITER

Writers Guild of Canada, 366 Adelaide St. W., Suite 401, Toronto ON M5V 1R9 Canada. (416)979-7907. **Fax:** (416)979-9273. **E-mail:** info@wgc.ca. **Website:** www.wgc.ca. **Contact:** Li Robbins, director of communications. **80% freelance written.** Magazine published 3 times/year covering Canadian screenwriting for television, film, and digital media. *Canadian Screenwriter* profiles Canadian screenwriters, provides industry news, and offers practical writing tips for screenwriters. Estab. 1998. Circ. 4,000. Byline given. Pays on acceptance. Offers 50% kill fee. Publishes ms an average of 1 month after acceptance. Editorial lead time 2 months. Submit seasonal material 2 months in advance. Accepts queries by e-mail. Accepts simultaneous submissions. Responds in 1 week to queries; in 1 month to mss. Sample copy free. Guidelines by e-mail.

NONFICTION Needs how-to, humor, interview. Does not want writing on foreign screenwriters; the focus is on Canadian-resident screenwriters. **Buys 12 mss/year.** Query with published clips. Length: 750-2,200 words. **Pays $1/word.** Pays expenses of writers on assignment.

PHOTOS State availability. Identification of subjects required. Reviews GIF/JPEG files. Negotiates payment individually. Buys one-time rights.

TIPS "Read other Canadian film and television publications."

$ $ ECONTENT MAGAZINE

Information Today, Inc., 143 Old Marlton Pike, Medford NJ 08055. **E-mail:** theresa.cramer@infotoday.com. **Website:** www.econtentmag.com. **Contact:** Theresa Cramer, editor. **90% freelance written.** Quarterly magazine covering digital content trends, strategies, etc. *EContent* is a leading authority on the businesses of digital publishing, media, and marketing, targeting executives and decision-makers in these fast-changing markets. By covering the latest tools, strategies, and thought-leaders in the digital content ecosystem, *EContent* magazine and EContentmag.com keep professionals ahead of the curve in order to maximize their investment in digital content strategies while building sustainable, profitable business models. Visit our About page for writer's guidelines and more information about what kinds of pitches we look for. Estab. 1979. Circ. 12,000. Byline given. Pays within 1 month of publication. No kill fee. Editorial lead time 3-4 months. Accepts simultaneous submissions. Responds in 3 weeks to queries; in 1 month to mss. Sample copy and writer's guidelines online.

NONFICTION Needs expose, how-to, interview, new product, opinion. No academic or straight Q&A. **Buys 48 mss/year.** Query with published clips. Submit electronically as e-mail attachment. Length: 1,000 words. Pays expenses of writers on assignment.

PHOTOS State availability. Captions required. Negotiates payment individually. Buys one-time rights.

COLUMNS/DEPARTMENTS Profiles (short profile of unique company, person or product), 1,200 words; New Features (breaking news of content-related topics), up to 500 words. **Buys 40 mss/year.** Query with published clips. **Pays 30-40¢/word.**

TIPS "Take a look at the website. Most of the time, an e-mail query with specific article ideas works well. A general outline of talking points is good, too. State prior experience."

FELLOWSCRIPT

InScribe Christian Writers' Fellowship, P.O. Box 99509, Edmonton AB T5B 0E1 Canada. **E-mail:** fellowscripteditor2@gmail.com. **Website:** https://inscribe.org/. Vice President: Charity Mongrain. **Contact:** Nina Faye Morey, editor. **100% freelance written.** Quarterly writers' magazine focused on Christian faith and writing. Most open to instructional articles on specific topics of interest to Christian writers. Readers are Christians with a commitment to writing. Among readership are best-selling authors and unpublished beginning writers. Submissions should include practical information, i.e., something the reader can immediately put into practice. Estab. 1983. Circ. 200. Byline given. Pays on publication. No kill fee. Publishes ms an average of 6-12 months after acceptance. Editorial lead time 3 months. Submit seasonal material 4 months in advance. Accepts queries by e-mail. Accepts simultaneous submissions. Responds in 1 month to queries and mss. Sample copy for $9.50, 9x12 SAE, and 3 first-class stamps (Canadian) or IRCs. Guidelines online.

NONFICTION Needs book excerpts, essays, how-to, humor, inspirational, interview, new product, opinion, personal experience, profile, religious, reviews, technical. Does not want memoir, autobiography, testimony, or scholarly articles. **Buys 30-45 mss/year.** Send complete ms attached in doc or rtf format. Length: 350-650 words. **Pays 3¢/word (first rights); 1 1/2¢/word reprints (Canadian funds).**

REPRINTS Pays 1 1/2¢/word reprints (Canadian funds).

COLUMNS/DEPARTMENTS Contact: Carol Schafer, Columns Editor, E: schaferc@telus.net. Columnists are contracted for four issues. Send a query about your proposed column to the columns editor. Regular Columns, 501-600 words; Mini-Columns, up to 300 words. **Buys 1-4. mss/year.** Send complete ms attached in doc format. **Pays $21 (Canadian) for regular columns; no payment for mini-columns; 1 contributor's copy.**

FICTION Contact: Nina Faye Morey, Editor, E: fellowscripteditor2@gmail.com. Christian short stories or book excerpts. Needs novel excerpts, short stories. **Buys 1-4 mss/year.** Send complete ms attached in doc format. Length: Maximum 650 words. **Pays 3¢/word (first rights); 1 1/2¢/word reprints (Canadian funds).**

POETRY Contact: Violet Nesdoly, Poetry Editor, E: fspoetryeditor@gmail.com. Poetry related to faith or writing; traditional or free-verse. Buys 8-12 poems/year. Submit maximum 3-6 poems. Length: 4-20 lines. **Pays $10 for original, unpublished; $5 for original, previously published (Canadian funds).**

FILLERS Contact: Nina Faye Morey, Editor, E: fellowscripteditor2@gmail.com. Book reviews (writing or faith related), members' profiles, members' books and book launches (150–300 words), writers' tips, anecdotes, market updates (50–300 words), quotes, humour. **Buys 5-10 mss/year.** Send complete ms attached in doc format. Length: 25-300 words. **Pays 1 contributor's copy.**

TIPS "Email your complete ms with the word count and a brief (50-word max.) bio. Write in a casual, first-person, anecdotal style. Be sure your article is full of practical information that the reader can apply. Most of our accepted freelance submissions fall into the instructional or 'how-to' category for Christian writers."

FREELANCE MARKET NEWS

The Writers Bureau Ltd., 8-10 Dutton St., Manchester M3 1LE England. (44)(161)819-9919. **Fax:** (44) (161)819-2842. **E-mail:** fmn@writersbureau.com. **Website:** www.freelancemarketnews.com. **15% freelance written.** Monthly newsletter covering freelance writing. For all writers, established and new, *Freelance Market News* is an excellent source of the most up-to-date information about the publishing world. It is packed with news, views and the latest advice about new publications, plus the trends and developments in established markets, in the UK and around the world. Informs readers about publications that are looking for new writers and even warn about those writers should avoid. Estab. 1968. Byline given. Pays on acceptance. No kill fee. Publishes ms an average of 3 months after acceptance. Editorial lead time 3 months. Submit seasonal material 3 months in advance. Accepts queries by mail, e-mail. Sample copy and guidelines available online.

Prefers to receive a complete ms rather than a query.

NONFICTION Buys 12 mss/year. Length: 1,00 words. **Pays £50/1,000 words.** Pays expenses of writers on assignment.

COLUMNS/DEPARTMENTS New Markets (magazines which have recently been published); Fillers & Letters; Overseas Markets (obviously only English-language publications); Market Notes (established publications accepting articles, fiction, reviews, or poetry). All should be between 40 and 200 words. **Pays £40/1,000 words.**

FREELANCE WRITER'S REPORT

CNW Publishing, Inc., 45 Main St., P.O. Box A, North Stratford NH 03590-0167. (603)922-8338. **E-mail:** fwrwm@writers-editors.com. **Website:** www.writers-editors.com. **10% freelance written.** Monthly newsletter covering the business of freelance writing. *FWR* covers the marketing and business/office management aspects of running a freelance writing business. Articles must be of value to the established freelancer; nothing basic. Estab. 1982. Byline given. Pays on publication. No kill fee. Publishes ms an average of 12 months after acceptance. Editorial lead time 2 months. Submit seasonal material 2 months in advance. Accepts simultaneous submissions. Responds in 1 week to queries; 2 weeks to mss. Sample copy for 6x9 SAE with 2 first-class stamps (for back copy); $4 for current copy. Guidelines and sample copy available online.

NONFICTION Needs book excerpts. Does not want articles about the basics of freelancing. **Buys 5 mss/year.** Send complete ms by e-mail. Length: up to 900 words. **Pays 10¢/word.**

TIPS "Write in a terse, newsletter style."

MSLEXIA

Mslexia Publications Ltd, P.O. Box 656, Newcastle upon Tyne NE99 1PZ United Kingdom. (+44) (191)204-8860. **E-mail:** postbag@mslexia.co.uk. **E-mail:** submissions@mslexia.co.uk. **Website:** www.mslexia.co.uk. **Contact:** Debbie Taylor, editorial director. **60% freelance written.** Quarterly magazine plus monthly email supplement offering advice and publishing opportunities for women writers, plus publication of poetry, fiction, memoir, reportage, journalism, reviews, etc. from open submissions and commissions. "*Mslexia* tells you all you need to know about exploring your creativity and getting into print. No other magazine provides *Mslexia*'s unique mix of advice and inspiration; news, reviews, interviews; competitions, events, grants; all served up with a challenging selection of new poetry and prose. *Mslexia* is read by authors and absolute beginners. A quarterly master class in the business and psychology of writing, it's the essential magazine for women who write. We accept submissions from any woman from any country writing in English. There are 14 ways of submitting to the magazine, for every kind of writing, and we pay for everything we publish. Submissions guidelines are on our website. We also run a series of women's fiction competitions with top cash prizes and career development opportunities for finalists." Estab. 1997. Circ. 8,000. Byline given. Pays on publication. Offers 50% kill fee. Publishes ms an average of 1 month after acceptance. Editorial lead time 12 weeks. Submit seasonal material 3 months in advance. Accepts queries by mail, e-mail, phone. Accepts simultaneous submissions. Responds in 12 weeks. Purchase of single issues via office or website. Writer's guidelines online or by e-mail.

NONFICTION Needs how-to, inspirational, interview, opinion, personal experience, profile, reviews. No general items about women or academic features. "We are only interested in features (for tertiary-educated readership) about women's writing and literature." **Buys 40 mss/year.** Query with published clips. Length: 500-3,000 words by commission only. **Pays $70-600 for assigned articles; $30-300 for unsolicited articles.** Pays expenses of writers on assignment.

COLUMNS/DEPARTMENTS "We are open to suggestions, but would only commission 1 new column/year, probably from a UK-based writer." **Buys 12 mss/year.** Query with published clips.

FICTION See guidelines on website. "Submissions not on 1 of our current themes will be returned (if submitted with a SASE) or destroyed." **Buys 30 mss/year.** Send complete ms. Length: 50-2,200 words. **Pays £15 per 1,000 words prose plus contributor's copies.**

POETRY Needs avant-garde, free verse, haiku, traditional. Buys 40 poems/year. Submit maximum 4 poems. **Pays £25 per poem plus contributor's copies.**

TIPS "Read the magazine; subscribe if you can afford it. *Mslexia* has a particular style and relationship with its readers which is hard to assess at a quick glance. The majority of our readers live in the UK, so feature pitches should be aware of this. We never commission work without seeing a written sample first. We rarely accept unsolicited manuscripts, but prefer a short letter suggesting a feature, plus a brief bio and writing sample."

POETS & WRITERS MAGAZINE

90 Broad St., Suite 2100, New York NY 10004. (212)226-3586. **E-mail:** editor@pw.org. **Website:** www.pw.org/magazine. **Contact:** Kevin Larimer,

editor. **95% freelance written.** Bimonthly professional trade journal for poets and fiction writers and creative nonfiction writers. Estab. 1987. Circ. 60,000. Byline given. Pays on publication. Offers 25% kill fee. Publishes ms an average of 4 months after acceptance. Submit seasonal material 4 months in advance. Accepts queries by mail, e-mail. Accepts simultaneous submissions. Responds in 2 months to mss. Sample copy: $5.95. Guidelines available online.

No poetry or fiction submissions.

NONFICTION Needs how-to. **Buys 35 mss/year.** Send complete ms. Length: 700-3,000 words (depending on topic). Pays expenses of writers on assignment.

PHOTOS State availability. Reviews color prints. Offers no additional payment for photos accepted with ms.

COLUMNS/DEPARTMENTS Literary and Publishing News, 700-1,000 words; Profiles of Emerging and Established Poets, Fiction Writers and Creative Nonfiction Writers, 2,000-3,000 words; Craft Essays and Publishing Advice, 2,000-2,500 words. Query with published clips or send complete ms. **Pays $225-500.**

TIPS "We typically assign profiles to coincide with an author's forthcoming book publication. We are not looking for the Get Rich Quick or 10 Easy Steps variety of writing and publishing advice."

$ QUILL & SCROLL MAGAZINE

Quill and Scroll International Honorary Society for High School Journalists, University of Iowa, School of Journalism and Mass Communication, 100 Adler Journalism Bldg., Iowa City IA 52242. (319)335-3457. **Fax:** (319)335-3989. **E-mail:** quill-scroll@uiowa.edu. **Website:** www.quillandscroll.org. **Contact:** Jeffrey Browne, executive director; Judy Hauge. **20% freelance written.** Fall and spring issues covering scholastic journalism-related topics during school year. Primary audience is high school journalism students working on and studying topics related to newspapers, yearbooks, radio, television, and online media; secondary audience is their teachers and others interested in this topic. Invites journalism students and advisers to submit mss about important lessons learned or obstacles overcome. Estab. 1926. Circ. 8000. Byline given. Pays on acceptance and publication. No kill fee. Publishes ms an average of 4 months after acceptance. Editorial lead time 2 months. Accepts queries by mail, e-mail. Accepts simultaneous submissions. Responds in 2 weeks to queries. Guidelines available.

NONFICTION Needs essays, how-to, humor, interview, new product, opinion, personal experience, photo feature, technical, travel, types on topic. Does not want articles not pertinent to high school student journalists. Query with your submission. Length: 600-1,000 words. **Pays $10-100 for assigned articles.** Pays expenses of writers on assignment.

PHOTOS State availability. Reviews GIF/JPEG files. Offers no additional payment for photos accepted with ms.

$$$ QUILL MAGAZINE

Society of Professional Journalists, 3909 N. Meridian St., Indianapolis IN 46208. (317)927-8000, ext. 211. **Fax:** (317)920-4789. **E-mail:** sleadingham@spj.org. **E-mail:** quill@spj.org. **Website:** www.spj.org/quill.asp. **Contact:** Scott Leadingham, editor. **75% freelance written.** Monthly magazine covering journalism and the media industry. *Quill* is a how-to magazine written by journalists. Focuses on the industry's biggest issues while providing tips on how to become better journalists. Estab. 1912. Circ. 10,000. Byline given. Pays on acceptance. Offers 25% kill fee. Publishes ms an average of 2 months after acceptance. Editorial lead time 2-3 months. Submit seasonal material 2-3 months in advance. Accepts queries by e-mail. Accepts simultaneous submissions. Sample copy available online.

NONFICTION Needs general interest, how-to, technical. Does not want personality profiles and straight research pieces. **Buys 12 mss/year.** Query. Length: 800-2,500 words. **Pays $150-800.**

$ THE WRITER'S CHRONICLE

Association of Writers & Writing Programs (AWP), 4400 University Drive, George Mason University, Fairfax VA 22030-4444. (703)993-4301. **Fax:** (703)993-4302. **E-mail:** chronicle@awpwriter.org. **Website:** www.awpwriter.org. **90% freelance written.** Published 6 times during the academic year; 3 times a semester. Magazine covering the art and craft of writing. "*Writer's Chronicle* strives to: present the best essays on the craft and art of writing poetry, fiction, and nonfiction; help overcome the over-specialization of the literary arts by presenting a public forum for the appreciation, debate, and analysis of contemporary literature; present the diversity of accomplishments and points of view within contemporary literature;

provide serious and committed writers and students of writing the best advice on how to manage their professional lives; provide writers who teach with new pedagogical approaches for their classrooms; provide the members and subscribers with a literary community as a compensation for a devotion to a difficult and lonely art; provide information on publishing opportunities, grants, and awards; and promote the good works of AWP, its programs, and its individual members." Estab. 1967. Circ. 35,000. Byline given. Pays on publication. No kill fee. Editorial lead time 3 months. Accepts simultaneous submissions. Responds in 2 weeks to queries. Sample copy free. Guidelines online. Reading period: February 1 through September 30.

NONFICTION Needs essays, interview, opinion. No personal essays. **Buys 15-20 mss/year.** Send complete ms. Length: 2,500-7,000 words. **Pays $18/100 words for assigned articles.**

TIPS "In general, the editors look for articles that demonstrate an excellent working knowledge of literary issues and a generosity of spirit that esteems the arguments of other writers on similar topics. When writing essays on craft, do not use your own work as an example. Keep in mind that 18,000 of our readers are students or just-emerging writers. They must become good readers before they can become good writers, so we expect essays on craft to show exemplary close readings of a variety of contemporary and older works. Essays must embody erudition, generosity, curiosity, and discernment rather than self-involvement. Writers may refer to their own travails and successes if they do so modestly, in small proportion to the other examples. We look for a generosity of spirit—a general love and command of literature as well as an expert, writerly viewpoint."

$$$ WRITER'S DIGEST

Active Interest Media, Inc., 5720 Flatiron Pkwy., Boulder CO 80301. **E-mail:** wdsubmissions@aimmedia.com. **Website:** www.writersdigest.com. **75% freelance written.** Magazine for those who want to write better, get published, and participate in the vibrant culture of writers. Readers look for specific ideas and tips that will help them succeed, whether success means getting into print, finding personal fulfillment through writing, or building and maintaining a thriving writing career and network. *Writer's Digest*, the No. 1 magazine for writers, celebrates the writing life and what it means to be a writer in today's publishing environment. Estab. 1920. Byline given. Pays on acceptance. Offers 25% kill fee. Publishes ms an average of 4 months after acceptance. Accepts simultaneous submissions. Responds in 1-4 months to queries and mss. Guidelines and editorial calendar available online (writersdigest.com/submission-guidelines).

The magazine does not accept or read e-queries with attachments.

NONFICTION essays; short front-of-book pieces; how-to (writing craft, business of publishing, etc.); humor; inspirational; interviews/profiles (rarely, as those are typically handled in house). Does not accept phone, snail mail, or fax queries, and queries of this nature will receive no response. Does not buy newspaper clippings or reprints of articles previously published in other mainstream media, whether in print or online. Product reviews are handled in-house. **Buys 80 mss/year.** A query should include a thorough outline that introduces your article proposal and highlights each of the points you intend to make. Your query should discuss how the article will benefit readers, why the topic is timely, and why you're the appropriate writer to discuss the topic. Please include your publishing credential related to your topic with your submission. Do not send attachments. Length: 800-2,400 words. **Pays 30-50¢/word.** Pays expenses of writers on assignment.

TIPS "*InkWell* is the best place for new writers to break in. We recommend you consult our editorial calendar before pitching feature-length articles. Check our writer's guidelines for more details."

$$$$ WRITTEN BY

7000 W. Third St., Los Angeles CA 90048. (323)782-4574. **Fax:** (323)782-4800. **Website:** www.writtenby.com. **40% freelance written.** Magazine published 9 times/year. *Written By* is the premier magazine written by and for America's screen and TV writers. Focuses on the craft of screenwriting and covers all aspects of the entertainment industry from the perspective of the writer. Audience is screenwriters and most entertainment executives. Estab. 1987. Circ. 12,000. Byline given. Pays on acceptance. Offers 10% kill fee. Publishes ms an average of 2 months after acceptance. Editorial lead time 4 months. Submit seasonal material 4 months in advance. Accepts queries by mail, e-mail, fax, phone, online submission form. Accepts simultaneous submissions. Guidelines for #10 SASE or online contact form.

Guidelines are currently being rewritten. Contact via phone or online contact form to pitch a story idea.

NONFICTION Needs book excerpts, essays, historical, humor, interview, opinion, personal experience, photo feature, technical. No beginner pieces on how to break into Hollywood or how to write scripts. **Buys 20 mss/year.** Query with published clips. Length: 500-3,500 words. **Pays $500-3,500 for assigned articles.** Pays expenses of writers on assignment.

PHOTOS State availability. Captions, identification of subjects, model releases required. Reviews transparencies. Offers no additional payment for photos accepted with ms. Buys one-time rights.

COLUMNS/DEPARTMENTS Pays $1,000 maximum.

TIPS "We are looking for more theoretical essays on screenwriting past and/or present. Also, the writer must always keep in mind that our audience is made up primarily of working writers who are inside the business; therefore all articles need to have an 'insider' feel and not be written for those who are still trying to break in to Hollywood. We prefer a hard copy of submission or e-mail."

LAW

$$$$ ABA JOURNAL

American Bar Association, 321 N. Clark St., 20th Floor, Chicago IL 60654. (312)988-6018. **Fax:** (312)988-6014. **E-mail:** releases@americanbar.org. **Website:** www.abajournal.com. **Contact:** Molly McDonough. **10% freelance written.** Monthly magazine covering the trends, people, and finances of the legal profession from Wall Street to Main Street to Pennsylvania Avenue. The *ABA Journal* is an independent, thoughtful, and inquiring observer of the law and the legal profession. The magazine is edited for members of the American Bar Association. Circ. 380,000. Byline given. Pays on acceptance. No kill fee. Accepts queries by e-mail, fax. Accepts simultaneous submissions. Sample copy free. Guidelines available online.

NONFICTION "We don't want anything that does not have a legal theme. No poetry or fiction." **Buys 5 mss/year.** "We use freelancers with experience reporting for legal or consumer publications; most have law degrees. If you are interested in freelancing for the *Journal*, we urge you to include your résumé and published clips when you contact us with story ideas." Length: 500-3,500 words. **Pays $300-2,000 for assigned articles.** Pays expenses of writers on assignment.

COLUMNS/DEPARTMENTS The National Pulse/Ideas from the Front (reports on legal news and trends), 650 words; eReport (reports on legal news and trends), 500-1,500 words. "The *ABA Journal eReport* is our weekly online newsletter sent out to members." **Buys 25 mss/year.** Query with published clips. **Pays $300, regardless of story length.**

$$$$ BENCH & BAR OF MINNESOTA

Minnesota State Bar Association, 600 Nicollet Mall #380, Minneapolis MN 55402. (612)333-1183; 800-882-6722. **Fax:** (612)333-4927. **E-mail:** jhaverkamp@mnbar.org. **Website:** www.mnbar.org. **Contact:** Judson Haverkamp, editor. **5% freelance written.** Magazine published 11 times/year. *Bench & Bar* seeks reportage, analysis, and commentary on changes in the law, trends and issues in the law and the legal profession, especially in Minnesota. Preference to items of practical/professional human interest to lawyers and judges. Audience is mostly Minnesota lawyers. Estab. 1931. Circ. 17,000. Byline given. Pays on acceptance. No kill fee. Publishes ms an average of 3 months after acceptance. Accepts simultaneous submissions. Responds in 1 month to queries. Guidelines for free online or by mail.

NONFICTION Does not want one-sided opinion pieces or advertorial. **Buys 2-3 mss/year.** Send query or complete ms. Length: 1,000-3,500 words. **Pays $500-1,500.** Pays expenses of writers on assignment.

PHOTOS State availability. Identification of subjects, model releases required. Reviews 5x7 prints. Pays $25-100 upon publication. Buys one-time rights.

$$$$ CALIFORNIA LAWYER

Daily Journal Corp., 44 Montgomery St., Suite 500, San Francisco CA 94104. (415)296-2400. **Fax:** (415)296-2440. **E-mail:** cl_contributingeditor@dailyjournal.com; bo_links@dailyjournal.com. **Website:** www.callawyer.com. **Contact:** Bo Links, legal editor; Marsha Sessa, art director. **30% freelance written.** Monthly magazine of law-related articles and general-interest subjects of appeal to lawyers and judges. Primary mission is to cover the news of the world as it affects the law and lawyers, helping readers better comprehend the issues of the day and to cover changes and trends in the legal profession. Readers are all California lawyers, plus judges, legislators, and corporate executives. Although the magazine focuses on California and the West, they have subscribers in every state. *California Lawyer* is a general interest magazine for people interested in law. Estab. 1981. Circ. 140,000. Byline given. Pays on acceptance. Offers 25% kill fee. Publishes ms an average of 3 months after acceptance. Editorial lead time 3 months. Accepts queries by e-mail. Accepts simultaneous submissions. Guidelines available online.

NONFICTION Needs essays, general interest, profile, "We will consider well-researched, in-depth stories on the law, including legal trends of statewide and national significance, thought-provoking legal issues, and profiles of lawyers doing groundbreaking work. We will consider local issues if they have statewide or national implications or if you have a new unique angle to the story.". **Buys 12 mss/year.** Query contributing editor: cl_contributingeditor@dailyjournal.com. Please do not send unsolicited mss. Length: 500-5,000 words. **Pays $50-2,000.** Pays expenses of writers on assignment.

PHOTOS Contact: Marsha Sessa, art director. State availability. Identification of subjects, model releases required. Reviews prints.

COLUMNS/DEPARTMENTS Expert Advice (specific, practical tips on an area of law or practice management), 650-750 words; Tech (lawyers and technology), up to 1,000 words; First Person (personal experience), 700 words; In House (working as corporate counsel in California), up to 1,000 words. Query appropriate editor (see website submission guidelines). **Pays $50-250.**

$$$$ INSIDECOUNSEL

ALM Media, LLC, 120 Broadway, 5th Floor, New York NY 10271. (212)457-9400. **E-mail:** apaonita@alm.com. **Website:** www.insidecounsel.com. **Contact:** Anthony Paonita, editor-in-chief. **50% freelance written.** Monthly tabloid covering legal information for attorneys. *InsideCounsel* is a monthly national magazine that gives general counsel and inhouse attorneys information on legal and business issues to help them better manage corporate law departments. It routinely addresses changes and trends in law departments, litigation management, legal technology, corporate governance and inhouse careers. Law areas covered monthly include: intellectual property, international, technology, project finance, e-commerce, and litigation. All articles need to be geared toward the inhouse attorney's perspective. Estab. 1991. Circ. 45,000. Byline given. Pays on publication. No kill fee. Publishes ms an average of 3 months after acceptance. Editorial lead time 3 months. Submit seasonal material 3 months in advance. Accepts queries by mail, e-mail. Accepts simultaneous submissions. Responds in 3 weeks to queries. Sample copy for $17. Guidelines available online.

NONFICTION Buys 12-25 mss/year. Query with published clips. Length: 500-3,000 words. **Pays $500-2,000.**

PHOTOS Freelancers should state availability of photos with submission. Identification of subjects required. Reviews color transparencies, b&w prints. Offers $25-150/photo. Buys all rights.

TIPS "Our publication targets general counsel and inhouse lawyers. All articles need to speak to them, not to the general attorney population. Query with clips and a list of potential in-house sources."

$$$$✪ NATIONAL

The Canadian Bar Association, 865 Carling Ave., Ottawa ON K1S 5S8 Canada. (613)237-2925. **Fax:** (613)237-0185. **E-mail:** beverleys@cba.org; national@cba.org. **Website:** www.nationalmagazine.ca. **Contact:** Beverley Spencer, editor in chief. **90% freelance written.** Magazine published 8 times/year covering practice trends and business developments in the law, with a focus on technology, innovation, practice management, and client relations. Estab. 1993. Circ. 37,000. Byline given. Pays on acceptance. Offers 50% kill fee. Publishes ms an average of 2 months after acceptance. Editorial lead time 2 months. Accepts queries by e-mail. Accepts simultaneous submissions. Sample copy free.

NONFICTION Buys 25 mss/year. Query with published clips. Length: 1,000-2,500 words. **Pays $1/word.** Pays expenses of writers on assignment.

$$ THE NATIONAL JURIST AND PRE LAW

Cypress Magazines, 7670 Opportunity Rd #105, San Diego CA 92111. (858)300-3201; (800)296-9656. **Fax:** (858)503-7588. **E-mail:** jack@cypressmagazines.com; callahan@cypressmagazines.com. **Website:** www.nationaljurist.com. **Contact:** Jack Crittenden, editor in chief. **25% freelance written.** Bimonthly magazine covering law students and issues of interest to law students. Estab. 1991. Circ. 145,000. Pays on publication.

No kill fee. Accepts queries by mail, e-mail. Accepts simultaneous submissions.

NONFICTION Needs general interest, how-to, humor, interview. **Buys 4 mss/year.** Query. Length: 750-3,000 words. **Pays $100-500.** Pays expenses of writers on assignment.

PHOTOS State availability. Reviews contact sheets. Negotiates payment individually.

COLUMNS/DEPARTMENTS **Pays $100-500.**

$$ PARALEGAL TODAY

Conexion International Media, Inc., 6030 Marshalee Dr., Suite 455, Elkridge MD 21075-5935. (443)445-3057. **Fax:** (443)445-3257. **E-mail:** pinfanti@connexionmedia.com. **Website:** www.paralegaltoday.com. **Contact:** Patricia E. Infanti, editor in chief; Charles Buckwalter, publisher. Quarterly magazine geared toward all legal assistants/paralegals throughout the U.S. and Canada, regardless of specialty (litigation, corporate, bankruptcy, environmental law, etc.). How-to articles to help paralegals perform their jobs more effectively are most in demand, as are career and salary information, technolgoy tips, and trends pieces. Estab. 1983. Circ. 8,000. Byline given. Pays on publication. Offers kill fee ($25-50 standard rate). Editorial lead time is 10 weeks. Submit seasonal material 3 months in advance. Accepts queries by mail, e-mail, fax, online submission form. Accepts simultaneous submissions. Responds in 2 months to mss. Sample copy available online. Guidelines available online.

NONFICTION Needs interview, news (brief, hard news topics regarding paralegals), features (present information to help paralegals advance their careers). Send query letter first; if electronic, send submission as attachment. **Pays $75-300.** Pays expenses of writers on assignment.

PHOTOS Send photos.

TIPS "Query editor first. Features run 1,500-2,500 words with sidebars. Writers must understand our audience. There is some opportunity for investigative journalism as well as the usual features, profiles, and columns. How-to articles are especially desired. If you are a great writer who can interview effectively and really dig into the topic to grab readers' attention, we need you."

$$ THE PENNSYLVANIA LAWYER

Pennsylvania Bar Association, 100 South St., P.O. Box 186, Harrisburg PA 17108. **E-mail:** editor@pabar.org. **Website:** www.pabar.org. **Contact:** Editor. **25% freelance written. Prefers to work with published/established writers.** Bimonthly magazine published as a service to the legal profession and the members of the Pennsylvania Bar Association. Estab. 1979. Circ. 26,000. Byline given. Pays on acceptance. No kill fee. Publishes ms an average of 6 months after acceptance. Submit seasonal material 6 months in advance. Accepts queries by mail, e-mail. Accepts simultaneous submissions. Responds in 2 months. Sample copy for $2. Writer's guidelines for #10 SASE or by e-mail.

NONFICTION Needs how-to, interview, law-practice management, technology. **Buys 8-10 mss/year.** Query. Length: 1,200-1,500 words. **Pays $50 for book reviews; $75-400 for assigned articles; $150 for unsolicited articles.** Pays expenses of writers on assignment.

PHOTOS State availability. Identification of subjects required. Reviews contact sheets. Negotiates payment individually. Buys one-time rights.

$$$$ SUPER LAWYERS

Thomson Reuters, 610 Opperman Dr., Eagan MN 55123. (877)787-5290. **Website:** www.superlawyers.com. **Contact:** Erik Lundegaard, editor. **100% freelance written.** Monthly magazine covering law and politics. Publishes glossy magazines in every region of the country; all serve a legal audience and have a storytelling sensibility. Writes profiles of interesting attorneys exclusively. Estab. 1990. Byline given. Pays on acceptance. Offers 25% kill fee. Publishes ms an average of 1 month after acceptance. Editorial lead time 6 months. Submit seasonal material 6 months in advance. Accepts queries by phone, online submission form. Accepts simultaneous submissions. Sample copy free. Guidelines free.

NONFICTION Needs general interest, historical. Query. Length: 500-2,000 words. **Pays 50¢-$1.50/word.** Pays expenses of writers on assignment.

LUMBER

$$ PALLET ENTERPRISE

Industrial Reporting, Inc., 10244 Timber Ridge Dr., Ashland VA 23005. (804)550-0323. **Fax:** (804)550-2181. **E-mail:** edb@ireporting.com; mbrindleypallet@gmail.com. **Website:** www.palletenterprise.com. **Contact:** Edward C. Brindley, Jr., Ph.D., publisher; Melissa Brindley, editor. **40% freelance writ-**

ten. Monthly magazine covering lumber and pallet operations. The *Pallet Enterprise* is a monthly trade magazine for the sawmill, pallet, remanufacturing, and wood processing industries. Articles should offer technical, solution-oriented information. Anti-forest articles are not accepted. Articles should focus on machinery and unique ways to improve profitability/make money. Estab. 1981. Circ. 14,500. Pays on publication. Editorial lead time 2 months. Submit seasonal material 2 months in advance. Accepts queries by mail, e-mail, fax, phone. Accepts simultaneous submissions. Sample copy available online. Guidelines free.

NONFICTION Needs interview, new product, opinion, technical, industry news, environmental, forests operation/plant features. No lifestyle, humor, general news, etc. **Buys 20 mss/year.** Query with published clips. Length: 1,000-3,000 words. **Pays $200-400 for assigned articles. Pays $100-400 for unsolicited articles.** Pays expenses of writers on assignment.

PHOTOS State availability. Captions, identification of subjects required. Reviews 3x5 prints. Negotiates payment individually. Buys one-time rights and Web rights.

COLUMNS/DEPARTMENTS Green Watch (environmental news/opinion affecting US forests), 1,500 words. **Buys 12 mss/year.** Query with published clips. **Pays $200-400.**

TIPS "Provide unique environmental or industry-oriented articles. Many of our freelance articles are company features of sawmills, pallet manufacturers, pallet recyclers, and wood waste processors."

$$ TIMBERWEST

TimberWest Publications, LLC, P.O. Box 610, Edmonds WA 98020. (425)778-3388. **Fax:** (425)771-3623. **E-mail:** timberwest@forestnet.com; diane@forestnet.com. **Website:** www.forestnet.com. **Contact:** Diane Mettler, managing editor. **75% freelance written.** Monthly magazine covering logging and lumber segment of the forestry industry in the Northwest. Primarily publishes profiles on loggers and their operations—with an emphasis on the machinery—in Washington, Oregon, Idaho, Montana, Northern California, and Alaska. Some timber issues are highly controversial, and although the magazine will report on the issues, this is a pro-logging publication. Does not publish articles with a negative slant on the timber industry. Estab. 1975. Circ. 10,000. Byline given. Pays on acceptance. No kill fee. Editorial lead time 2 months. Accepts queries by mail, fax. Accepts simultaneous submissions. Responds in 3 weeks to queries. Sample copy: $2. Guidelines for #10 SASE.

NONFICTION Needs historical, interview, new product. No articles that put the timber industry in a bad light, such as environmental articles against logging. **Buys 50 mss/year.** Query with published clips. Length: 1,100-1,500 words. **Pays $400.** Pays expenses of writers on assignment.

PHOTOS Send photos. Captions, identification of subjects required. Reviews contact sheets, transparencies, prints, GIF/JPEG files. Offers no additional payment for photos accepted with ms, but does pay $50 if shot is used on cover. Buys first rights.

FILLERS Needs facts, newsbreaks. **Buys 10 mss/year.** Length: 400-800 words. **Pays $100-250.**

TIPS "We are always interested in profiles of loggers and their operations in Alaska, Oregon, Washington, Montana, and Northern California. We also want articles pertaining to current industry topics, such as fire abatement, sustainable forests, or new technology. Read an issue to get a clear idea of the type of material *TimberWest* publishes. The audience is primarily loggers, and topics that focus on an 'evolving' timber industry versus a 'dying' industry will find a place in the magazine. When querying, a clear overview of the article will enhance acceptance."

MACHINERY & METAL

$$$ AMERICAN MACHINIST

Penton Media, 1300 E. 9th St., Cleveland OH 44114. (216)696-7000. **Fax:** (913)696-8208. **E-mail:** robert.brooks@penton.com. **Website:** www.americanmachinist.com. **Contact:** Robert Brooks, editor-in-chief. **10% freelance written.** Monthly online website covering all forms of metalworking covering all forms of metalworking. Accepts contributed features and articles. *American Machinist* is an essential online source dedicated to metalworking in the United States. Readers are the owners and managers of metalworking shops. Publishes articles that provide the managers and owners of job shops, contract shops, and captive shops the information they need to make their operations more efficient, more productive, and more profitable. Articles are technical in nature and must be focused on technology that will help these shops to become more competitive on a global basis. Readers are skilled machinists. This is not the place for lightweight items about manufacturing. Not interested in articles on management theories. Estab. 1877. Circ. 80,000. Byline sometimes given. Offers 20% kill fee. Publishes ms an average of 1-2 months after acceptance. Editorial lead time 3-6 months. Submit seasonal material 4-6 months in advance. Accepts queries by mail, e-mail, phone. Accepts simultaneous submissions. Responds in 1-2 weeks to queries; 1 month to mss. Sample copy online.

NONFICTION Needs general interest, how-to, new product, opinion, personal experience, photo feature, technical. Query with published clips. Length: 600-2,400 words. **Pays $300-1,200.** Pays expenses of writers on assignment.

PHOTOS State availability. Captions, identification of subjects, model releases required. Reviews GIF/JPEG files. Negotiates payment individually. Buys all rights.

FILLERS Needs anecdotes, facts, gags, newsbreaks, short humor. **Buys 12-18 mss/year. mss/year.** Length: 50-200 words. **Pays $25-100.**

TIPS "With our exacting audience, a writer would do well to have some background working with machine tools."

$$$ CUTTING TOOL ENGINEERING

CTE Publications, Inc., 1 Northfield Plaza, Suite 240, Northfield IL 60093. (847)714-0175. **Fax:** (847)559-4444. **E-mail:** alanr@ctemedia.com. **Website:** www.ctemag.com. **Contact:** Alan Richter, editor. **40% freelance written.** Monthly magazine covering industrial metal cutting tools and metal cutting and grinding operations. *Cutting Tool Engineering* serves owners, managers, and engineers who work in manufacturing, specifically manufacturing that involves cutting or grinding metal or other materials. Writing should be geared toward improving manufacturing processes. Estab. 1948. Circ. 60,000. Byline given. Pays on publication. Offers 50% kill fee. Publishes ms an average of 2 months after acceptance. Editorial lead time 2 months. Accepts queries by mail, e-mail, phone. Responds in 2 months to mss. Sample copy and guidelines free.

NONFICTION Needs how-to, opinion, personal experience, profile, technical. Does not want fiction or articles that don't relate to manufacturing. **Buys 10 mss/year.** Length: 1,500-2,000 words. **Pays $750-1,100.** Pays expenses of writers on assignment.

PHOTOS State availability. Captions required. Reviews transparencies, prints. Negotiates payment individually. Buys all rights.

TIPS "For queries, write 2 clear paragraphs about how the proposed article will play out. Include sources that would be in the article."

$$ EQUIPMENT JOURNAL

Pace Publishing, 5160 Explorer Dr., Unit 6, Mississauga ON L4W 4T7 Canada. (416)459-5163. **E-mail:** editor@equipmentjournal.com. **E-mail:** editor@equipmentjournal.com. **Website:** www.equipmentjournal.com. **Contact:** Nathan Medcalf. **5% freelance written.** Canada's national heavy equipment newspaper. Focuses on the construction, material handling, mining, forestry, and on-highway transportation industries. Estab. 1966. Circ. 22,000. Byline given. Pays on publication. Kill fee: $50. Publishes ms an average of 1-2 months after acceptance. Editorial lead time 2-3 months. Accepts queries by e-mail, phone. Accepts simultaneous submissions. Sample copy and guidelines free.

Looking for job stories, features, and tips.

NONFICTION Needs how-to, interview, new product, photo feature, technical. Does not want "material that falls outside of *Equipment Journal*'s mandate—the Canadian equipment industry." **Buys 15 mss/year.** Send complete ms. "We prefer electronic submissions." Length: 400-900 words. **Pays 40-50¢/word.** Pays expenses of writers on assignment.

REPRINTS Reprint payment negotiable.

PHOTOS Contact: Nathan Medcalf, editor. State availability. Identification of subjects required. Negotiates payment individually. Buys one-time rights.

COLUMNS/DEPARTMENTS Contact: Nathan Medcalf, editor. **Buys 2 mss/year.**

TIPS "Please pitch a story, instead of asking for an assignment. We are looking for stories of construction sites."

$$$ THE FABRICATOR

2135 Point Blvd., Elgin IL 60123. (815)399-8700. **E-mail:** timh@thefabricator.com. **Website:** www.thefabricator.com. **Contact:** Dan Davis, editor in chief; Tim Heston, senior editor. **15% freelance written.** Monthly magazine covering metal forming and fabricating. Purpose is to disseminate information about modern metal forming and fabricating techniques, machinery, tooling, and management concepts for the metal fabricator. Estab. 1971. Circ. 58,000. Byline given. Pays on publication. No kill fee. Editorial lead time 6 months. Accepts queries by mail, e-mail. Accepts simultaneous submissions. Responds in 2 weeks to queries; in 1 month to mss. Sample copy free.

NONFICTION Needs how-to, technical. Query with published clips. Length: 1,200-2,000 words. Pays expenses of writers on assignment.

PHOTOS Request guidelines for digital images. State availability. Captions, identification of subjects required. Reviews transparencies, prints. Negotiates payment individually. Rights purchased depends on photographer requirements.

$$ ORNAMENTAL & MISCELLANEOUS FABRICATOR

P. O. Box 492167, Lawrenceville GA 30049. (888)516-8585. **Fax:** (888)279-7994. **E-mail:** editor@nomma.org; todd@nomma.org. **Website:** www.nomma.org. **Contact:** Todd Daniel, editor. **20% freelance written.** "Bimonthly magazine to inform, educate, and inspire members of the ornamental and miscellaneous metalworking industry.". Estab. 1959. Circ. 9,000. Byline given. Pays on publication. No kill fee. Editorial lead time 1-2 months. Accepts queries by mail, e-mail, fax. Accepts simultaneous submissions. Responds by e-mail in 1 month (include e-mail address in query). Guidelines by email.

NONFICTION Needs book excerpts, essays, general interest, historical, how-to, humor, interview, opinion, personal experience, technical. **Buys 8-12 mss/year.** Query. Length: 1,200-2,000 words. **Pays $250-400.** Pays expenses of writers on assignment.

REPRINTS Send tearsheet, photocopy or typed ms with rights for sale noted and information about when and where the material previously appeared. Pays 100% of amount paid for an original article.

PHOTOS Artwork and sidebars preferred. State availability. Model releases required. Reviews contact sheets, negatives, transparencies, prints.

COLUMNS/DEPARTMENTS 700-900 words. **Pays $ 50-100.**

TIPS "Please request and review recent issues. Contacting the editor for guidance on article topics is welcome."

$$$ PRACTICAL WELDING TODAY

FMA Communications, Inc., 2135 Point Blvd., Elgin IL 60123. (815)399-8700. **E-mail:** amandac@thefabricator.com. **Website:** www.thefabricator.com. **Contact:** Amanda Carlson, editor. **15% freelance written.** Bimonthly magazine covering welding. "We generally publish how-to and educational articles that teach people about a process or how to do something better." Estab. 1997. Circ. 40,000. Byline given. Pays on publication. No kill fee. Editorial lead time 6 months. Accepts queries by mail, e-mail. Accepts simultaneous submissions. Responds in 2 weeks to queries; 2 months to mss. Sample copy free. Guidelines online.

NONFICTION Needs how-to, technical, company profiles. Special issues: Forecast issue on trends in welding (January/February). No promotional, one-sided, persuasive articles or unsolicited case studies. **Buys 5 mss/year.** Query with published clips. Length: 800-1,200 words. **Pays 40-80¢/word.** Pays expenses of writers on assignment.

PHOTOS State availability. Captions, identification of subjects required. Reviews contact sheets. Negotiates payment individually. Rights purchased depends on photographer requirements.

TIPS "Follow our author guidelines and editorial policies to write a how-to piece from which our readers can benefit."

$$ SNIPS MAGAZINE

BNP Media, 2401 W. Big Beaver Rd., Suite 700, Troy MI 48084. (248)244-6416. **Fax:** (248)362-0317. **E-mail:** mcconnellm@bnpmedia.com. **Website:** www.snipsmag.com. **Contact:** Michael McConnell, editor. **2% freelance written.** Monthly magazine for sheet metal, heating, ventilation, air conditioning, and metal roofing contractors. Estab. 1932. No kill fee. Publishes ms an average of 3 months after acceptance. Accepts queries by mail, e-mail, fax, phone. Accepts simultaneous submissions. Call for writer's guidelines.

NONFICTION Length: under 1,000 words unless on special assignment. **Pays $200-300.** Pays expenses of writers on assignment.

PHOTOS Negotiable.

$$ SPRINGS

Spring Manufacturers Institute, 2001 Midwest Rd., Suite 106, Oak Brook IL 60523-1335. (630)495-8588. **Fax:** (630)495-8595. **E-mail:** lynne@smihq.org. **Website:** www.smihq.org. **Contact:** Lynne Carr, general manager. **10% freelance written.** Quarterly magazine covering precision mechanical spring manufacture. Articles should be aimed at spring manufacturers. Estab. 1962. Circ. 10,800. Byline given. Pays on publication. No kill fee. Publishes ms an average of 3-6 months after acceptance. Editorial lead time 4 months. Accepts simultaneous submissions. Sample copy free. Guidelines available online.

NONFICTION Needs general interest, how-to, interview, opinion, personal experience, technical. **Buys 4-6 mss/year.** Length: 2,000-10,000 words. **Pays $100-600 for assigned articles.**

PHOTOS State availability. Captions required. Reviews prints, digital photos. Offers no additional payment for photos accepted with ms. Buys one-time rights.

TIPS "In analyzing all contributions, *Springs* looks for information that will help our readers run their businesses more effectively. We are far more interested in comprehensive detail than flashy writing. In fact, we like to develop a 'partnership in expertise' with our authors; you provide the technical knowledge and we assist you with communications and presentation skills. Thus, once your article is accepted for publication, you should expect the editor to be in touch regarding the edited version of your ms. All authors receive edited copy before publication so they can verify the factual accuracy of the reworked piece."

$$ STAMPING JOURNAL

Fabricators & Manufacturers Association (FMA), 2135 Point Blvd., Elgin IL 60123. (815)399-8700. **Fax:** (815)381-1370. **E-mail:** kateb@thefabricator.com. **Website:** www.thefabricator.com. **Contact:** Dan Davis, editor-in-chief; Kate Bachman, editor. **15% freelance written.** Bimonthly magazine covering metal stamping. Looks for how-to and educational articles—nonpromotional. Estab. 1989. Circ. 35,000. Byline given. Pays on publication. No kill fee. Editorial lead time 6 months. Accepts queries by mail, e-mail, phone. Accepts simultaneous submissions. Responds in 2 weeks to queries. Sample copy and writer's guidelines free.

NONFICTION **Pays 40-80¢/word.** Pays expenses of writers on assignment.

PHOTOS State availability. Captions, identification of subjects required. Negotiates payment individually. Rights purchased depends on photographer requirements.

TIPS "Articles should be impartial and should not describe the benefits of certain products available from certain companies. They should not be biased toward the author's or against a competitor's products or technologies. The publisher may refuse any article that does not conform to this guideline."

$$$ TPJ—THE TUBE & PIPE JOURNAL

Fabricators & Manufacturers Association (FMA), 2135 Point Blvd., Elgin IL 60123. (815)399-8700. **Fax:** (815)381-1370. **E-mail:** ericl@thefabricator.com. **Website:** www.thefabricator.com. **Contact:** Eric Lundin, editor. **15% freelance written.** Magazine published 8 times/year covering metal tube and pipe. Educational perspective—emphasis is on how-to articles to accomplish a particular task or improve on a process. New trends and technologies are also important topics. Estab. 1990. Circ. 30,000. Byline given. Pays on publication. No kill fee. Editorial lead time 6 months. Accepts queries by mail, e-mail. Accepts simultaneous submissions. Responds in 2 weeks to queries; 2 months to mss. Sample copy free. Guidelines online.

NONFICTION Needs how-to, technical. Special issues: Forecast issue (January). No unsolicited case studies. **Buys 5 mss/year.** Query with published clips. Length: 800-1,200 words. **Pays 40-80¢/word.** Pays expenses of writers on assignment.

PHOTOS State availability. Captions, identification of subjects required. Reviews contact sheets. Negotiates payment individually. Rights purchased depends on photographer requirements.

TIPS "Submit a detailed proposal, including an article outline, to the editor."

$$$ WELDING DESIGN & FABRICATION

Penton Media, 1300 E. 9th St., Cleveland OH 44114. (216)696-7000. **Fax:** (216)931-9524. **E-mail:** wdeditor@penton.com; robert.brooks@penton. **Website:** www.weldingdesign.com. **Contact:** Robert E. Brooks, editor. **10% freelance written.** Bimonthly magazine covering all facets of welding and running a welding business. *Welding Design & Fabrication* provides information to the owners and managers of welding shops, including business, technology and trends. We include information on engineering and technological developments that could change the business as it is currently known, and feature stories on how welders are doing business with the goal of helping our readers to be more productive, effecient, and competitive. Welding shops are very local in nature and need to be addressed as small businessmen in a field that is consolidating and becoming more challenging and more global. We do not write about business management theory as much as we write about putting into practice good management techniques that have proved to work at similar businesses. Estab. 1930. Circ. 40,000. Byline given. Pays on publication. Offers 20% kill fee. Publishes ms an average of 1-2 months after acceptance. Editorial lead time 3-6 months. Submit seasonal material 4-6 months in advance. Accepts queries by mail, e-mail, phone. Accepts simultaneous submissions. Responds in 1-2 weeks to queries. Responds in 1 month to mss. Sample copy available online.

NONFICTION Needs general interest, how-to, new product, opinion, personal experience, photo feature, technical. Query. Length: 600-2,400 words. **Pays $300-1,200.** Pays expenses of writers on assignment.

PHOTOS State availability. Captions, identification of subjects, model releases required. Reviews GIF/JPEG files (300 dpi). Negotiates payment individually. Buys all rights.

FILLERS Needs anecdotes, facts, gags, newsbreaks, short humor. **Buys 12-18 mss/year.** Length: 50-200 words. **Pays $25-100.**

TIPS Writers should be familiar with welding and/or metalworking and metal joining techniques. With that, calling or e-mailing me directly is the next best approach. We are interested in information that will help to make welding shops more competitive, and a writer should have a very specific idea before approaching me.

$$ WIRE ROPE NEWS & SLING TECHNOLOGY

Wire Rope News LLC, P.O. Box 871, Clark NJ 07066. (908)486-3221. **Fax:** (732)396-4215. **E-mail:** info@wireropenews.com. **Website:** www.wireropenews.com. **Contact:** Edward Bluvias III, publisher and editorial director. **100% freelance written.** Bimonthly magazine published for manufacturers and distributors of wire rope, chain, cordage, related hardware, and sling fabricators. Content includes technical articles, news and reports describing the manufacturing and use of wire rope and related products in marine, construction, mining, aircraft and offshore drilling operations. Estab. 1979. Circ. 4,300. Byline sometimes given. Pays on acceptance. No kill fee. Publishes ms an average of 6 months after acceptance. Editorial lead time 2 months. Submit seasonal material 2 months in advance. Accepts queries by mail, fax. Accepts simultaneous submissions.

NONFICTION Needs general interest, historical, interview, photo feature, technical. **Buys 30 mss/year.** Send complete ms. Length: 2,500-5,000 words. **Pays $300-500.** Pays expenses of writers on assignment.

PHOTOS Send photos. Identification of subjects required. Reviews contact sheets, 5x7 prints, digital. Offers no additional payment for photos accepted with ms. Buys all rights.

TIPS We are accepting more submissions and queries by e-mail.

MAINTENANCE & SAFETY

$$ AMERICAN WINDOW CLEANER MAGAZINE

12Twelve Publishing Corp., 750-B NW Broad St., Southern Pines NC 28387. (910)693-2644. **Fax:** (910)246-1681. **E-mail:** info@awcmag.com; karen@awcmag.com. **Website:** www.awcmag.com. **Contact:** Karen Grinter, creative director. **20% freelance written.** Bimonthly magazine on window cleaning. Produces articles to help window cleaners become more profitable, safe, professional, and feel good about what they do. Estab. 1986. Circ. 8,000. Byline given. Pays on acceptance. Offers 33% kill fee. Publishes ms an average of 4-8 months after acceptance. Editorial lead time 2 months. Submit seasonal material 3 months in advance. Accepts simultaneous submissions. Responds in 2 weeks to queries; in 1 month to mss. Sample copy free.

NONFICTION Needs how-to, humor, inspirational, interview, personal experience, photo feature. "We do not want PR-driven pieces. We want to educate—not push a particular product." **Buys 20 mss/year.** Query. Length: 500-5,000 words. **Pays $50-250.** Pays expenses of writers on assignment.

PHOTOS State availability. Captions required. Reviews contact sheets, transparencies, 4x6 prints. Offers $10 per photo. Buys one-time rights.

COLUMNS/DEPARTMENTS Window Cleaning Tips (tricks of the trade); 1,000-2,000 words; Humor-anecdotes-feel good-abouts (window cleaning industry); Computer High-Tech (tips on new technology), all 1,000 words. **Buys 12 mss/year.** Query. **Pays $50-100.**

TIPS "*American Window Cleaner Magazine* covers an unusual niche that gets people's curiosity. Articles that are technical in nature and emphasize practical tips or safety, and how to work more efficiently, have the best chances of being published. Articles include: window cleaning unusual buildings, landmarks; working for well-known people/celebrities; window cleaning in resorts/casinos/unusual cities; humor or satire about our industry or the public's perception of it. At some point, we make phone contact and chat to see if our interests are compatible."

$$ PEST MANAGEMENT PROFESSIONAL

North Coast Media, 1360 E. 9th St., Suite 1070, Cleveland OH 44114. (216)706-3754. **Fax:** (216)706-3711. **E-mail:** hgooch@northcoastmedia.net. **Website:** www.mypmp.net. **Contact:** Heather Gooch, editor. Monthly magazine for professional pest management professionals and sanitarians. Estab. 1933. Circ. 25,400. Pays on publication. No kill fee. Submit seasonal material 3 months in advance. Accepts queries by e-mail. Accepts simultaneous submissions. Responds in 1 month to mss.

Author must be in the professional pest management industry.

NONFICTION Needs how-to, humor, inspirational, interview, new product, personal experience, case histories, new technological breakthroughs. No general information type of articles desired. **Buys 3 mss/year.** Query. Length: 1,000-1,400 words. **Pays $150-400 minimum.**

PHOTOS Digital photos accepted; please query on specs. State availability. No additional payment for photos used with ms.

COLUMNS/DEPARTMENTS Regular columns use material oriented to this profession, 550 words.

MANAGEMENT & SUPERVISION

$$$ HUMAN RESOURCE EXECUTIVE

LRP Publications Magazine Group, P.O. Box 980, Horsham PA 19044-0980. (215)784-0910. **Fax:** (215)784-0275. **E-mail:** kfrasch@lrp.com. **E-mail:** tgarrison@lrp.com. **Website:** www.hronline.com. **Contact:** Kristen B. Frasch, managing editor; Terri Garrison, editorial assistant. **30% freelance written.** Magazine published 16 times/year serving the information needs of chief human resource professionals/executives in companies, government agencies, and nonprofit institutions with 500 or more employees. Estab. 1987. Circ. 75,000. Byline given. Pays on acceptance. Offers kill fee. Pays 50% kill fee on assigned stories. Publishes ms an average of 2 months after acceptance. Accepts queries by mail, e-mail, fax. Accepts simultaneous submissions. Responds in 1 month to mss. Guidelines available online.

NONFICTION Needs book excerpts, interview. **Buys 16 mss/year.** Query with published clips. Length: 1,800 words. **Pays $200-1,000.** Pays expenses of writers on assignment.

PHOTOS State availability. Identification of subjects required. Reviews contact sheets. Offers no additional payment for photos accepted with ms. Buys first and repeat rights.

$$ PLAYGROUND MAGAZINE

Harris Publishing, P.O. Box 595, Ashton ID 83420. (208)652-3683. **Fax:** (208)652-7856. **Website:** www.playgroundmag.com. **25% freelance written.** Magazine published quarterly covering playgrounds, play-related issues, equipment, and industry trends. *Playground Magazine* targets park and recreation management, elementary school teachers and administrators, child care facilities, and parent-group leader readership. Articles should focus on play and the playground market as a whole, including aquatic play and surfacing. Estab. 2000. Circ. 35,000. Byline given. Pays on publication. No kill fee. Publishes ms an average of 6 months after acceptance. Editorial lead time 2 months. Submit seasonal material 1 year in advance. Accepts queries by mail, e-mail. Accepts simultaneous submissions. Responds in 1 month to queries. Responds in 2 months to mss. Sample copy for $5. Guidelines for #10 SASE.

NONFICTION Needs how-to, interview, new product, opinion, personal experience, photo feature, technical, travel. *Playground Magazine* does not publish any articles that do not directly relate to play and the playground industry. **Buys 4-6 mss/year.** Query. Length: 800-1,500 words. **Pays $50-300 for assigned articles.** Pays expenses of writers on assignment.

PHOTOS State availability of or send photos. Captions, identification of subjects, model releases required. Reviews 35mm transparencies, GIF/JPEG files (350 dpi or better). Offers no additional payment for photos accepted with ms. Buys one-time rights.

COLUMNS/DEPARTMENTS Dream Spaces (an article that profiles a unique play area and focuses on community involvement, unique design, or human interest), 800-1,200 words. **Buys 2 mss/year.** Query. **Pays $100-300.**

TIPS "We are looking for articles that managers can use as a resource when considering playground construction, management, safety, installation, maintenance, etc. Writers should find unique angles to playground-related features such as current trends in the industry, the value of play, natural play, the need for recess, etc. We are a trade journal that offers up-to-date industry news and features that promote play and the playground industry."

MARINE & MARITIME INDUSTRIES

$$ CURRENTS

Marine Technology Society, 1100 H St. NW, Suite LL-100, Washington DC 20005. (202)717-8705. **Fax:** (202)347-4302. **E-mail:** morganteeditorial@verizon.net. **Website:** www.mtsociety.org. **Contact:** Amy Morgante, managing editor. Bimonthly newsletter covering commercial, academic, scientific marine technology. Readers are engineers and technologists who design, develop ,and maintain the equipment and instruments used to understand and explore the oceans. The newsletter covers society news, industry news, science and technology news, and similar news. Estab. 1963. Circ. 3,200. Byline given. Pays on acceptance. No kill fee. Editorial lead time 1-2 months. Accepts queries by e-mail. Accepts simultaneous submissions. Responds in 4 weeks to queries Sample copy free.

NONFICTION Needs interview, technical. **Buys 1-6 mss/year.** Query. Length: 250-500 words. **Pays $100-500 for assigned articles.** Pays expenses of writers on assignment.

$$ PROFESSIONAL MARINER

Navigator Publishing, P.O. Box 569, Portland ME 04112. (207)772-2466. **Fax:** (207)772-2879. **E-mail:** rmiller@professionalmariner.com. **Website:** www.professionalmariner.com. **Contact:** Rich Miller, editor. **75% freelance written.** Bimonthly magazine covering professional seamanship and maritime industry news. Estab. 1993. Circ. 29,000. Byline given. Pays on publication. No kill fee. Editorial lead time 3 months. Accepts queries by mail, e-mail. Accepts simultaneous submissions.

NONFICTION Buys 15 mss/year. Query. Length: varies; short clips to long profiles/features. **Pays 25¢/word.** Pays expenses of writers on assignment.

PHOTOS Send photos. Captions, identification of subjects required. Reviews prints, slides. Negotiates payment individually. Buys one-time rights.

TIPS "Remember that our audience comprises maritime industry professionals. Stories must be written at a level that will benefit this group."

MEDICAL

$$$$ ACP INTERNIST/ACP HOSPITALIST

American College of Physicians, 191 N. Independence Mall W., Philadelphia PA 19106-1572. (215)351-2400. **E-mail:** acpinternist@acponline.org. **E-mail:** acphospitalist@acponline.org. **Website:** www.acpinternist.org; www.acphospitalist.org. **Contact:** Jennifer Kearney-Strouse, executive editor. **40% freelance written.** Monthly magazine covering internal medicine/hospital medicine. Writes for specialists in internal medicine, not a consumer audience. Topics include clinical medicine, practice management, health information technology, and Medicare issues. Estab. 1981. Circ. 85,000 (*Internist*), 24,000 (*Hospitalist*). Byline given. Offers kill fee. Negotiable. Publishes ms an average of 2 months after acceptance. Editorial lead time 4 months. Submit seasonal material 6 months in advance. Accepts queries by e-mail. Accepts simultaneous submissions. Sample copy online. Guidelines online.

NONFICTION Needs interview. Query with published clips. Length: 700-2,000 words. **Pays $500-2,000 for assigned articles.** Pays expenses of writers on assignment.

PHOTOS Contact: Ryan Dubosar, senior editor. State availability. Reviews TIFF/JPEG files. Negotiates payment individually.

$$ AHIP COVERAGE

America's Health Insurance Plans, 601 Pennsylvania Ave. NW, South Bldg., Suite 500, Washington DC 20004. (202)778-3200. **Fax:** (202)331-7487. **E-mail:** ahip@ahip.org. **Website:** www.ahip.org. **75% freelance written.** Bimonthly magazine geared toward administrators in America's health insurance companies. Articles should inform and generate interest and discussion about topics on anything from patient care to regulatory issues. Estab. 1990. Circ. 12,000. Byline given. Pays within 30 days of acceptance of article in final form. Offers 30% kill fee. Publishes ms an average of 2 months after acceptance. Editorial lead time 2 months. Submit seasonal material 4 months in advance. Accepts queries by mail, e-mail, fax. Accepts simultaneous submissions. Sample copy free.

NONFICTION Needs book excerpts, how-to, opinion. "We do not accept stories that promote products." Send complete ms. Length: 1,800-2,500 words. **Pays 65¢/word minimum.** Pays expenses of writers on assignment. Pays phone expenses of writers on assignment.

PHOTOS Buys all rights.

TIPS "Look for health plan success stories in your community; we like to include case studies on a variety of topics—including patient care, provider relations, regulatory issues—so that our readers can learn from their colleagues. Our readers are members of our trade association and look for advice and news. Topics relating to the quality of health plans are the ones more frequently assigned to writers, whether a feature or department. We also welcome story ideas. Just send us a letter with the details."

$$ JEMS: JOURNAL OF EMERGENCY MEDICAL SERVICES

Clarion Events, 21-00 State 208, Vanguard Building, Fair Lawn NJ 07452. (678)285-3936. **E-mail:** ryan.kelley@clarionevents.com. **Website:** www.jems.com. Editor-in-Chief: A.J. Heightman. **Contact:** Ryan Kelley, managing editor. **95% freelance written.** Website directed to personnel who serve the pre-hospital emergency medicine industry: paramedics, EMTs, emergency physicians and nurses, administrators, EMS consultants, etc. *JEMS (Journal of Emergency Medical Services)* seeks to improve patient care in the prehospital setting and promote positive change in EMS by delivering information and education from industry leaders, change makers and emerging voices. With a rich tradition of editorial excellence and an unparalleled consortium of subject matter experts and state-of-the-science content, *JEMS* fulfills its commitment to EMS providers, instructors and administrators through all media channels including online and print. Estab. 1980. Byline given. Authors are typically not paid and are in the emergency medical services industry. No kill fee. Publishes ms an average of 6 months after acceptance. Submit seasonal material 6 months in advance. Accepts queries by e-mail. Responds in 1-2 months to queries. All articles are online. Guidelines online.

NONFICTION Needs general interest, how-to, interview, new product, personal experience, photo feature, profile, technical, All articles should be focused on emergency medical services and prehospital care. Does not want stories, poems, and personal stories. **Buys 100 mss/year.** Query Ryan Kelley with contact information, suggested title, ms document (can be an outline), a summary, a general ms classification, and photos or figures to be considered with the ms. Please also submit professional CV/resume. Length: 1,800-2,400 words, plus references. **Authors are typically not paid and are in the emergency medical services industry. Occasionally pays $100-200. (Authors should indicate they expect payment at the time of submission.**

PHOTOS **Contact:** Ryan Kelley, Managing Editor. State availability. Identification of subjects, model releases required (when necessary). Reviews digital images. Offers $25 per photo used online. No high-res photos needed. Buys one-time rights.

COLUMNS/DEPARTMENTS Length: up to 850 words. Query with or without published clips. **Authors of columns are not paid and must be in the emergency medical services industry.**

TIPS "Please submit an email along with your ms that answers these questions: (1) What specifically are you going to tell *JEMS* readers about pre-hospital medical care? (2) Why do *JEMS* readers need to know this? (3) How will you make your case (i.e., literature review, original research, interviews, personal experience, observation)? Your query should explain your qualifications, as well as include previous writing samples."

$$$ MANAGED CARE

780 Township Line Rd., Yardley PA 19067. (267)685-2788. **Fax:** (267)685-2966. **E-mail:** pwehrwein@medimedia.com. **Website:** www.managedcaremag.com. **Contact:** Peter Wehrwein, editor. **75% freelance written.** Monthly magazine that delivers high-interest, full-length articles and shorter features on clinical and business aspects of the health care industry. Emphasizes practical, usable information that helps HMO medical directors and pharmacy directors cope with the options, challenges, and hazards in the rapidly changing health care industry. Estab. 1992. Circ. 60,000. Byline given. Pays on acceptance. Offers 20%

kill fee. Publishes ms an average of 6 weeks after acceptance. Editorial lead time 3 months. Submit seasonal material 4 months in advance. Accepts queries by mail, e-mail, fax. Accepts simultaneous submissions. Responds in 3 weeks to queries. Responds in 2 months to mss. Sample copy free. Guidelines available online.

NONFICTION Needs book excerpts, general interest, how-to, original research and review articles that examine the relationship between health care delivery and financing. Also considered occasionally are personal experience, opinion, interview/profile, and humor pieces, but these must have a strong managed care angle and draw upon the insights of (if they are not written by) a knowledgeable managed care professional. **Buys 40 mss/year.** Query with published clips. Length: 1,000-3,000 words. **Pays 75¢/word.** Pays expenses of writers on assignment.

PHOTOS State availability. Reviews contact sheets, negatives, transparencies, prints. Negotiates payment individually. Buys first-time rights.

TIPS "Know our audience (health plan executives) and their needs. Study our website to see what we cover."

$$○ OPTICAL PRISM

250 The East Mall, Suite 1113, Toronto ON M9B 6L3 Canada. (416)233-2487. **Fax:** (416)233-1746. **E-mail:** info@opticalprism.ca. **Website:** www.opticalprism.ca. **30% freelance written.** Magazine published 10 times/year. Covers the health, fashion, and business aspects of the optical industry in Canada. Estab. 1982. Circ. 10,000. Byline given. Pays on publication. Publishes ms an average of 2 months after acceptance. Editorial lead time 3 months. Submit seasonal material 3 months in advance. Accepts queries by mail, e-mail. Accepts simultaneous submissions. Digital copy available online.

NONFICTION Needs interview, related to optical industry. Special issues: Editorial themes and feature topics available online in media kit. Query. Length: 1,000-1,600 words. **Pays 40¢/word (Canadian).** Pays expenses of writers on assignment.

COLUMNS/DEPARTMENTS Insight (profiles on people in the eyewear industry—also sometimes schools and businesses), 700-1,000 words. **Buys 5 mss/year.** Query. **Pays 40¢/word.**

TIPS "Please look at our editorial themes, which are on our website, and pitch articles that are related to the themes for each issue."

$$ PHYSICIAN MAGAZINE

Physicians News Network, 10755 Scripps Poway Parkway, Suite 615, San Diego CA 92131. (858)226-7647. **E-mail:** sheri@physiciansnetwork.com; editors@physiciansnewsnetwork.com. **Website:** www.physiciansnewsnetwork.com. **Contact:** Sheri Carr, COO/editor. **25% freelance written.** Monthly magazine covering non-technical articles of relevance to physicians. Estab. 1908. Circ. 18,000. Byline given. Pays on acceptance. Offers 10% kill fee. Publishes ms an average of 2-3 months after acceptance. Editorial lead time 2-3 months. Accepts queries by e-mail. Accepts simultaneous submissions. Responds in 4 weeks to queries. Responds in 2 months to mss. Sample copy available online.

NONFICTION Needs general interest. **Buys 12-24 mss/year.** Query with published clips. Length: 600-3,000 words. **Pays $200-600 for assigned articles.**

PHOTOS State availability.

COLUMNS/DEPARTMENTS Medical World (tips/how-to's), 800-900 words. Query with published clips. **Pays $200-600.**

TIPS "We want professional, well-researched articles covering policy, issues, and other concerns of physicians. No personal anecdotes or patient viewpoints."

$$ PODIATRY MANAGEMENT

Kane Communications, Inc., Rosemont Plaza, 1062 Lancaster Ave., Rosemont PA 19010. (718)897-9700. **Fax:** (718)896-5747. **E-mail:** bblock@podiatrym.com. **Website:** www.podiatrym.com. Magazine published 9 times/year for practicing podiatrists. Aims to help the doctor of podiatric medicine to build a bigger, more successful practice, to conserve and invest his money, to keep him posted on the economic, legal, and sociological changes that affect him. Estab. 1982. Circ. 16,500. Byline given. Pays on publication. $75 kill fee. Submit seasonal material 4 months in advance. Accepts queries by e-mail. Accepts simultaneous submissions. Responds in 2 weeks to queries. Sample copy for $5 and 9x12 SAE. Guidelines for #10 SASE.

NONFICTION Buys 35 mss/year. Length: 1,500-3,000 words. **Pays $350-600.** Pays expenses of writers on assignment.

REPRINTS Send photocopy. Pays 33% of amount paid for an original article.

PHOTOS State availability. Pays $15 for b&w contact sheet. Buys one-time rights.

TIPS "Articles should be tailored to podiatrists, and preferably should contain quotes from podiatrists."

$$ PRIMARY CARE OPTOMETRY NEWS

SLACK Inc., 6900 Grove Rd., Thorofare NJ 08086-9447. (856)848-1000. **Fax:** (856)848-5991. **E-mail:** editor@healio.com; optometry@healio.com. **Website:** www.healio.com/optometry. **Contact:** Michael D. DePaolis, editor. **5% freelance written.** Monthly tabloid covering optometry. *Primary Care Optometry News* strives to be the optometric professional's definitive information source by delivering timely, accurate, authoritative and balanced reports on clinical issues, socioeconomic and legislative affairs, ophthalmic industry, and research developments, as well as updates on diagnostic and thereapeutic regimens and techniques to enhance the quality of patient care. Estab. 1996. Circ. 39,000. Byline given. Pays on publication. Offers 50% kill fee. Publishes ms an average of 2 months after acceptance. Editorial lead time 2 months. Accepts queries by mail, e-mail, fax, phone. Accepts simultaneous submissions. Responds in 2 weeks to queries. Sample copy available online. Guidelines by e-mail.

NONFICTION Needs how-to, interview, new product, opinion, technical. **Buys 20 mss/year.** Query. Length: 800-1,000 words. **Pays $350-500.** Pays expenses of writers on assignment.

PHOTOS State availability. Captions, model releases required. Reviews GIF/JPEG files. Offers no additional payment for photos accepted with ms. Buys all rights.

COLUMNS/DEPARTMENTS What's Your Diagnosis (case presentation), 800 words. **Buys 40 mss/year.** Query. **Pays $100-500.**

TIPS "Either e-mail or call the editor with questions or story ideas."

$$ STRATEGIC HEALTH CARE MARKETING

Health Care Communications, 11 Heritage Ln., P.O. Box 594, Rye NY 10580. (914)967-6741; (866)641-4548. **Fax:** (914)967-3054. **E-mail:** mhumphrey@plaineng-lishmedia.com. **Website:** www.strategichealthcare.com. **Contact:** Matt Humphrey, publisher. **90% freelance written.** Monthly newsletter covering health care marketing and management in a wide range of settings, including hospitals, medical group practices, home health services, and managed care organizations. Emphasis is on strategies and techniques employed within the health care field and relevant applications from other service industries. Works with published/established writers only. *Strategic Health Care Marketing* is specifically seeking writers with expertise/contacts in managed care, patient satisfaction, and e-health. Estab. 1984. Byline given. Pays on publication. Offers 25% kill fee. Publishes ms an average of 2 months after acceptance. Accepts queries by mail, e-mail. Accepts simultaneous submissions. Responds in 1 month to queries. Sample copy for SAE with 9x12 envelope and 3 first-class stamps. Guidelines sent with sample copy only.

NONFICTION Needs how-to, interview, new product, technical. **Buys 50 mss/year.** Query. Length: 1,000-1,800 words. **Pays $100-500.** Pays expenses of writers on assignment. Sometimes pays expenses of writers on assignment with prior authorization.

PHOTOS Photos, unless necessary for subject explanation, are rarely used. State availability. Captions, model releases required. Reviews contact sheets. Offers $10-30/photo. Buys one-time rights.

TIPS "Writers with prior experience on the business beat for newspapers or newsletters will do well. We require a sophisticated, in-depth knowledge of health care and business. This is not a consumer publication—the writer with knowledge of both health care and marketing will excel. Absolutely no unsolicited mss; any received will be returned or discarded unread."

MUSIC

$ INTERNATIONAL BLUEGRASS

International Bluegrass Music Association, 4206 Gallatin Pk., Nashville TN 37216. (615)256-3222. **Fax:** (615)256-0450. **E-mail:** info@ibma.org. **Website:** www.ibma.org. **10% freelance written.** Bimonthly newsletter of the International Bluegrass Music Association. *International Bluegrass* is the business publication for the bluegrass music industry. Interested in hard news and features concerning how to reach that potential and how to conduct business more effectively. Estab. 1985. Circ. 4,500. Byline given. Pays on publication. No kill fee. Publishes ms an average of

2 months after acceptance. Submit seasonal material 4 months in advance. Accepts queries by mail, e-mail, phone. Accepts simultaneous submissions. Responds in 1 month to queries. Sample copy for SAE with 6x9 envelope and 2 first-class stamps.

NONFICTION Needs book excerpts, essays, how-to, new product, opinion. No interview/profiles/feature stories of performers (rare exceptions) or fans. **Buys 6 mss/year.** Query. Length: 1,000-1,200 words. **Pays up to $150/article for assigned articles.**

REPRINTS Send photocopy of article and information about when and where the article previously appeared. Does not pay for reprints.

PHOTOS Send photos. Captions, identification of subjects, True required. Offers no additional payment for photos accepted with ms. Buys one-time rights.

COLUMNS/DEPARTMENTS Staff written.

TIPS "We're interested in a slant strongly toward the business end of bluegrass music. We're especially looking for material dealing with audience development and how to book bluegrass bands outside of the existing market."

$$ THE MUSIC & SOUND RETAILER

Testa Communications, 25 Willowdale Ave., Port Washington NY 11050. (516)767-2500. **E-mail:** dferrisi@testa.com. **Website:** www.msretailer.com. **Contact:** Dan Ferrisi, editor. **10% freelance written.** Monthly magazine covering business to business publication for music instrument products. *The Music & Sound Retailer* covers the music instrument industry and is sent to all dealers of these products, including Guitar Center, Sam Ash, and all small independent stores. Estab. 1983. Circ. 11,700. Byline given. Pays on publication. Offers $100 kill fee. Editorial lead time 1 month. Submit seasonal material 2 months in advance. Accepts queries by e-mail. Accepts simultaneous submissions. Responds in 2 weeks to queries. Responds in 1 month to mss. Sample copy for #10 SASE. Guidelines free.

NONFICTION Needs how-to, new product, opinion, personal experience. Concert and CD reviews are never published; neiter are interviews with musicians. **Buys 25 mss/year.** Query with published clips. Length: 1,000-2,000 words. **Pays $300-400 for assigned and unsolicited articles.** Pays expenses of writers on assignment.

PHOTOS Send photos. Captions required. Reviews GIF/JPEG files. Offers no additional payment for photos accepted with ms. Buys one-time rights.

$$$ OPERA NEWS

Metropolitan Opera Guild, Inc., 70 Lincoln Center Plaza, 6th Floor, New York NY 10023. **E-mail:** info@operanews.com. **Website:** www.operanews.com. **Contact:** Kitty March. **75% freelance written.** Monthly magazine for people interested in opera—the opera professional as well as the opera audience. Estab. 1936. Circ. 105,000. Byline given. Pays on publication. No kill fee. Publishes ms an average of 4 months after acceptance. Editorial lead time 4 months. Accepts queries by e-mail. Accepts simultaneous submissions. Sample copy for $5.

NONFICTION Needs historical, interview, informational, think pieces, opera, and CD, DVD and book reviews. Does not accept works of fiction or personal remembrances. Send unsolicited mss, article proposals and queries, along with several published clips. Length: 1,500-2,800 words. **Pays $450-1,200.** Pays expenses of writers on assignment.

PHOTOS State availability. Buys one-time rights.

COLUMNS/DEPARTMENTS Buys 24 mss/year.

$ OVERTONES

Handbell Musicians of America, P.O. Box 1765, Findlay OH 45839-1765. **E-mail:** jrsmith@handbellmusicians.org. **Website:** http://handbellmusicians.org/music-resources/overtones. **Contact:** J.R. Smith, publications director. **80% freelance written.** Bimonthly magazine covering English handbell ringing and conducting. *Overtones* is a 48-page magazine with extensive educational articles, photos, advertisements, and graphic work. Handbell Musicians of America is dedicated to advancing the musical art of handbell/handchime ringing through education, community, and communication. The purpose of *Overtones* is to provide a printed resource to support that mission. Offers how-to articles, inspirational stories, and interviews with well-known people and unique ensembles. Estab. 1954. Circ. 8,000. Byline given. Pays on publication. No kill fee. Publishes ms an average of 4 months after acceptance. Editorial lead time 4 months. Submit seasonal material 4 months in advance. Accepts queries by mail, e-mail. Accepts simultaneous submissions. Responds in 1 month to queries and to mss. Sample copy available by e-mail. Guidelines available online. Style guideline should follow *The Chicago Manual of Style.*

NONFICTION Needs essays, general interest, historical, how-to, inspirational, interview, religious, technical. Does not want product news or promotional material. **Buys 8-12 mss/year.** Send complete ms via e-mail, CD, DVD, or hard copy. Length: 1,200-2,000 words. **Pays $120.** Pays expenses of writers on assignment.

PHOTOS State availability of or send photos. Captions required. Reviews 8x10 prints, JPEG/TIFF files. Offers no additional payment for photos accepted with ms. Buys one-time rights.

COLUMNS/DEPARTMENTS Handbells in Education (topics covering the use of handbells in school setting, teaching techniques, etc.); Handbells in Worship (topics and ideas for using handbells in a church setting); Tips & Tools (variety of topics from ringing and conducting techniques to score study to maintenance); Community Connections (topics covering issues relating to the operation/administration/techniques for community groups); Music Reviews (recommendations and descriptions of music following particular themes, i.e., youth music, difficult music, seasonal, etc.). Length should be 800-1,200 words. Query. **Pays $80.**

TIPS "When writing profiles/interviews, try to determine what is especially unique or inspiring about the individual or ensemble and write from that viewpoint. Please have some expertise in handbells, education, or church music to write department articles."

PAPER

$$ THE PAPER STOCK REPORT

McEntee Media Corp., 9815 Hazelwood Ave., Strongsville OH 44149. (440)238-6603. **Fax:** (440)238-6712. **E-mail:** ken@recycle.cc; psr@recycle.cc. **Website:** www.recycle.cc/psrpage.htm. **Contact:** Ken McEntee, editor/publisher. Bimonthly newsletter covering market trends and news in the paper recycling industry. Audience is interested in new innovative markets, applications for recovered scrap paper, as well as new laws and regulations impacting recycling. Estab. 1990. Circ. 2,000. Byline given. Pays on publication. No kill fee. Publishes ms an average of 1 month after acceptance. Editorial lead time 2 months. Submit seasonal material 2 months in advance. Accepts queries by mail, e-mail, fax, phone. Accepts simultaneous submissions. Responds in 1 month to queries. Sample copy for #10 SAE with 55¢ postage.

NONFICTION Needs book excerpts, essays, expose, general interest, historical, interview, new product, opinion, photo feature, technical, all related to paper recycling. **Buys 0-13 mss/year.** Send complete ms. Length: 250-1,000 words. **Pays $50-250 for assigned articles. Pays $25-250 for unsolicited articles.** Pays expenses of writers on assignment.

PHOTOS State availability. Identification of subjects required. Reviews contact sheets. Negotiates payment individually.

TIPS "Articles must be valuable to readers in terms of presenting new market opportunities or cost-saving measures."

$$ RECYCLED PAPER NEWS

McEntee Media Corp., 9815 Hazelwood Ave., Strongsville OH 44149. (440)238-6603. **Fax:** (440)238-6712. **E-mail:** ken@recycle.cc. **Website:** www.recycle.cc. **Contact:** Ken McEntee, owner. **10% freelance written.** Monthly newsletter covering the recycling and composting industries. Interested in any news impacting the paper recycling industry, as well as other environmental issues in the paper industry, i.e., water/air pollution, chlorine-free paper, forest conservation, etc., with special emphasis on new laws and regulations. Estab. 1990. Pays on publication. No kill fee. Publishes ms an average of 2 months after acceptance. Editorial lead time 1 month. Submit seasonal material 1 month in advance. Accepts queries by mail, e-mail, fax, phone. Accepts simultaneous submissions. Responds in 2 months to queries. Sample copy for 9x12 SAE and 55¢ postage. Guidelines for #10 SASE.

NONFICTION Needs book excerpts, essays, how-to, interview, new product, opinion, personal experience, photo feature. **Buys 0-5 mss/year.** Query with published clips. **Pays $10-500.** Pays expenses of writers on assignment.

COLUMNS/DEPARTMENTS Query with published clips. **Pays $10-500.**

TIPS "We appreciate leads on local news regarding recycling or composting, i.e., new facilities or businesses, new laws and regulations, unique programs, situations that impact supply and demand for recyclables, etc. International developments are also of interest."

PETS

$$ PET AGE

Journal Multimedia, 220 Davidson Ave., Suite 302, Somerset NJ 08873. (732)246-5734. **Website:** www.petage.com. **Contact:** Glen Polyn, editor-in-chief. **90% freelance written.** Monthly magazine for pet/

pet supplies retailers, covering the complete pet industry. Estab. 1971. Circ. 23,022. Byline given. Pays on acceptance. No kill fee. Publishes ms an average of 3 months after acceptance. Accepts simultaneous submissions. Sample copy and writer's guidelines available.

Prefers to work with published/established writers. Will consider new writers.

NONFICTION No profiles of industry members and/or retail establishments or consumer-oriented pet articles. **Buys 80 mss/year.** Query with published clips. Length: 1,500-2,200 words. **Pays 15¢/word for assigned articles.** Pays expenses of writers on assignment. Pays documented telephone expenses.

PHOTOS Captions, identification of subjects required. Reviews transparencies, slides, and 5x7 glossy prints. Buys one-time rights.

TIPS "This is a business publication for busy people, and must be very informative in easy-to-read, concise style. Articles about animal care or business practices should have the pet-retail angle or cover issues specific to this industry."

$$ PET PRODUCT NEWS INTERNATIONAL

I-5 Publishing, LLC, P.O. Box 6050, Mission Viejo CA 92690. (949)855-8822. **Fax:** (949)855-3045. **E-mail:** lwojcik@petproductnews.com. **Website:** www.petproductnews.com. **Contact:** Lindsey Wojcik, managing editor. **70% freelance written.** Monthly magazine. *Pet Product News* covers business/legal and economic issues of importance to pet product retailers, suppliers, and distributors, as well as product information and animal care issues. Looking for straightforward articles on the proper care of dogs, cats, birds, fish, and exotics (reptiles, hamsters, etc.) as information the retailers can pass on to new pet owners. Estab. 1947. Circ. 26,000. Byline given. Pays on publication. Offers $50 kill fee. Editorial lead time 3 months. Submit seasonal material 4 months in advance. Accepts queries by mail, fax. Accepts simultaneous submissions. Responds in 2 weeks to queries. Sample copy for $5.50. Guidelines for #10 SASE.

NONFICTION Needs general interest, interview, new product, photo feature, technical. No "cute" animal stories or those directed at the pet owner. **Buys 150 mss/year.** Query. Length: 500-1,500 words. **Pays $175-350.** Pays expenses of writers on assignment.

COLUMNS/DEPARTMENTS The Pet Dealer News™ (timely news stories about business issues affecting pet retailers), 800-1,000 words; Industry News (news articles representing coverage of pet product suppliers, manufacturers, distributors, and associations), 800-1,000 words; Pet Health News™ (pet health and articles relevant to pet retailers); Dog & Cat (products and care of), 1,000-1,500 words; Fish & Bird (products and care of), 1,000-1,500 words; Small Mammals (products and care of), 1,000-1,500 words; Pond/Water Garden (products and care of), 1,000-1,500 words. **Buys 120 mss/year.** Query. **Pays $150-300.**

TIPS "Be more than just an animal lover. You have to know about health, nutrition, and care. Product and business articles are told in both an informative and entertaining style. Talk to pet store owners and see what they need to know to be better business people in general, who have to deal with everything from balancing the books and free trade agreements to animal rights activists. All sections are open, but you have to be knowledgeable on the topic, be it taxes, management, profit building, products, nutrition, animal care, or marketing."

PLUMBING, HEATING, AIR CONDITIONING & REFRIGERATION

$$$ HPAC: HEATING PLUMBING AIR CONDITIONING

80 Valleybrook Dr., Toronto Ontario M3B 2S9 Canada. (416)510-5218. **Fax:** (416)510-5140. **E-mail:** smacisaac@hpacmag.com; kturner@hpacmag.com. **Website:** www.hpacmag.com. **Contact:** Sandy MacIsaac, art director; Kerry Turner, editor. **20% freelance written.** Monthly magazine. Estab. 1923. Circ. 19,500. Pays on publication. No kill fee. Publishes an average of 3 months after acceptance. Accepts queries by mail, e-mail. Accepts simultaneous submissions. Responds in 2 months to queries.

"We primarily want articles that show *HPAC* readers how they can increase their sales and business step-by-step based on specific examples of what others have done."

NONFICTION Needs how-to, technical. Length: 1,000-1,500 words. **Pays 50¢/word.** Pays expenses of writers on assignment.

REPRINTS Send tearsheet or photocopy with rights for sale noted and information about when and where the material previously appeared.

PHOTOS Prefers JPEGs or hi-res PDFs. Photos purchased with ms.

TIPS "Topics must relate directly to the day-to-day activities of *HPAC* readers in Canada. Must be detailed, with specific examples, quotes from specific people or authorities—show depth. We specifically want material from other parts of Canada besides southern Ontario. U.S. material must relate to Canadian readers' concerns."

PRINTING

$$ THE BIG PICTURE

ST Media Group International, 11262 Cornell Park Dr., Cincinnati OH 45242. (513)421-2050. **E-mail:** adrienne.palmer@stmediagroup.com. **Website:** www.bigpicture.net. **Contact:** Adrienne Palmer, editor-in-chief. **20% freelance written.** Magazine published 9 times/year covering wide-format digital printing. *The Big Picture* covers wide-format printing as well as digital workflow, finishing, display, capture, and other related topics. Readers include digital print providers, sign shops, commercial printers, in-house print operations, and other print providers across the country. Primarily interested in the technology and work processes behind wide-format printing, but also run trend features on segments of the industry (innovations in point-of-purchase displays, floor graphics, fine-art printing, vehicle wrapping, textile printing, etc.). Estab. 1996. Circ. 21,500 controlled. Byline given. Pays on publication. Offers 20% kill fee. Publishes ms an average of 2 months after acceptance. Editorial lead time 2 months. Accepts queries by e-mail. Accepts simultaneous submissions. Responds in 2 weeks to queries. Responds in 1 month to mss. Sample copy available online. Guidelines available.

NONFICTION Needs how-to, interview, new product, technical. Does not want broad consumer-oriented pieces that do not speak to the business and technical aspects of producing print for pay. **Buys 15-20 mss/year.** Query with published clips. Length: 1,500-2,500 words. **Pays $500-700 for assigned articles.** Pays expenses of writers on assignment.

PHOTOS Send photos. Reviews GIF/JPEG files hi-res. Offers no additonal payment for photos accepted with ms.

TIPS "Interest in and knowledge of the digital printing industry will position you well to break into this market. You have to be willing to drill down into the production aspects of digital printing to write for us."

$$ IN-PLANT GRAPHICS

NAPCO Media, 1500 Spring Garden St., 12th Floor, Philadelphia PA 19130. (215)238-5321. **Fax:** (215)238-5457. **E-mail:** bobneubauer@napco.com. **Website:** www.inplantgraphics.com. **Contact:** Bob Neubauer, editor. **20% freelance written.** *In-plant Graphics* features articles designed to help in-house printing departments increase productivity, save money, and stay competitive. *IPG* features advances in graphic arts technology and shows in-plants how to put this technology to use. Audience consists of print shop managers working for (nonprint related) corporations (i.e., hospitals, insurance companies, publishers, nonprofits), universities, and government departments. They often oversee graphic design, prepress, printing, bindery, and mailing departments. Estab. 1951. Circ. 23,100. Byline given. Pays on publication. No kill fee. Publishes ms an average of 3 months after acceptance. Editorial lead time 2 months. Submit seasonal material 3 months in advance. Accepts queries by e-mail. Accepts simultaneous submissions. Guidelines online.

NONFICTION Needs interview, new product, technical. Special issues: See editorial calendar online. No articles on desktop publishing software or design software. No Internet publishing articles. **Buys 5 mss/year.** Query with published clips. Length: 800-1,500 words. **Pays $350-500.** Pays expenses of writers on assignment.

PHOTOS Photos should be at least 266 dpi. State availability. Captions, identification of subjects required. Reviews transparencies, prints. Negotiates payment individually. Buys one-time rights.

COLUMNS/DEPARTMENTS Query with published clips.

TIPS "To get published in *IPG*, writers must contact the editor with an idea in the form of a query letter that includes published writing samples. Writers who have covered the graphic arts in the past may be assigned stories for an agreed-upon fee. We don't want stories that tout only 1 vendor's products and serve as glorified commercials. All profiles must be well balanced, covering a variety of issues. If you can tell us about an in-house printing operation doing innovative things, we will be interested."

$$ SCREEN PRINTING

ST Media Group International, 11262 Cornell Park Dr., Cincinnati OH 45242. (513)421-2050, ext. 331. **Fax:** (513)421-5144. **E-mail:** kiersten.wones@stmedia-group.com; ben.rosenfield@stmediagroup.com. **Website:** www.screenweb.com. **Contact:** Kiersten Wones, editorial assistant; Ben Rosenfield, managing editor. **30% freelance written.** Monthly magazine for the screen printing industry, including screen printers (commercial, industrial, and captive shops), suppliers and manufacturers, ad agencies, and allied profession. Estab. 1953. Circ. 17,500. Byline given. Pays on publication. No kill fee. Publishes ms an average of 3 months after acceptance. Accepts queries by mail, e-mail, fax. Accepts simultaneous submissions. Sample copy available. Guidelines for #10 SASE.

Works with a small number of new/unpublished writers each year.

NONFICTION **Buys 10-15 mss/year.** Query. Unsolicited mss not returned. Length: 2,000-3,000 words. **Pays $300-500 for major features.** Pays expenses of writers on assignment.

PHOTOS Cover photos negotiable; b&w or color. Published material becomes the property of the magazine.

TIPS "Be an expert in the screen-printing industry with supreme or special knowledge of a particular screen-printing process, or have special knowledge of a field or issue of particular interest to screen-printers. If the author has a working knowledge of screen printing, assignments are more readily available. General management articles are rarely used."

PROFESSIONAL PHOTOGRAPHY

$$ NEWS PHOTOGRAPHER

National Press Photographers Association, Inc., 6677 Whitemarsh Valley Walk, Austin TX 78746-6367. **E-mail:** magazine@nppa.org; tburton@nppa.org. **Website:** www.nppa.org. **Contact:** Tom Burton, editor. Magazine on photojournalism published 10 times/year. *News Photographer* magazine is dedicated to the advancement of still and television news photography. The magazine presents articles, interviews, profiles, history, new products, electronic imaging, and news related to the practice of photojournalism. Estab. 1946. Circ. 11,000. Byline given. Pays on acceptance. Offers 100% kill fee. Publishes ms an average of 4 months after acceptance. Editorial lead time 2 months. Submit seasonal material 2 months in advance. Accepts queries by mail, e-mail, fax, phone. Accepts simultaneous submissions. Responds in 1 month to queries. Sample copy for SAE with 9x12 envelope and 3 first-class stamps. Guidelines free.

NONFICTION Needs historical, how-to, interview, new product, opinion, personal experience, photo feature, technical. **Buys 10 mss/year.** Query. Length: 1,500 words. **Pays $300.** Pays expenses of writers on assignment.

PHOTOS State availability. Captions, identification of subjects required. Reviews high resolution, digital images only. Negotiates payment individually. Buys one-time rights.

COLUMNS/DEPARTMENTS Query.

$$ THE PHOTO REVIEW

200 East Maple Avenue, Suite 200, Langhorne PA 19047. (215)891-0214. **Fax:** (215)891-9358. **E-mail:** info@photoreview.org. **Website:** www.photoreview.org. **50% freelance written.** Biannual magazine covering art photography and criticism. "*The Photo Review* publishes critical reviews of photography exhibitions and books, critical essays, and interviews. We do not publish how-to or technical articles." Estab. 1976. Circ. 2,000. Byline given. Pays on publication. No kill fee. Publishes ms an average of 9-12 months after acceptance. Editorial lead time 3 months. Submit seasonal material 6 months in advance. Accepts queries by mail. Accepts simultaneous submissions. Responds in 2 months to queries. Responds in 3 months to mss. Sample copy for $7. Email for guidelines.

NONFICTION Needs essays, historical, interview, reviews. No how-to articles. **Buys 20 mss/year.** Send complete ms. Length: 2-20 typed pages by email. **Pays $10-250.** Pays expenses of writers on assignment.

REPRINTS Send tearsheet, photocopy, or typed ms with rights for sale noted and information about when and where the material previously appeared. Payment varies.

PHOTOS Send photos. Captions required. Reviews electronic images. Offers no additional payment for photos accepted with ms. Buys all rights.

REAL ESTATE

$$O CANADIAN PROPERTY MANAGEMENT

Media Edge, 5255 Yonge St., Suite 1000, Toronto ON M2N 2P4 Canada. (416)512-8186. **E-mail:** barbc@mediaedge.ca. **Website:** www.reminetwork.com/canadian-property-management/home/. **Contact:** Barbara Carss, editor in chief. **10% freelance written.** Magazine published 8 times/year covering Canadian commercial, industrial, institutional (medical and educational), and residential properties. *Canadian Property Management* is a trade journal supplying building owners and property managers with Canadian industry news, case law reviews, technical updates for building operations, and events listings. Building and professional profile articles are regular features. Estab. 1985. Circ. 12,500. Byline given. Pays on publication. No kill fee. Publishes ms an average of 3 months after acceptance. Editorial lead time 2 months. Submit seasonal material 2 months in advance. Accepts queries by mail, e-mail, phone. Accepts simultaneous submissions. Responds in 3 weeks to queries; in 2 months to mss. Sample copy: $5, subject to availability. Guidelines free.

NONFICTION Needs interview, technical. No promotional articles (i.e., marketing a product or service geared to this industry). Query with published clips. Length: 700-1,200 words. **Pays 35¢/word.** Pays expenses of writers on assignment.

PHOTOS State availability. Captions, identification of subjects, model releases required. Reviews transparencies, 3x5 prints, digital (at least 300 dpi). Offers no additional payment for photos accepted with ms.

TIPS "We do not accept promotional articles serving companies or their products. Freelance articles that are strong and information-based and that serve the interests and needs of property managers and building owners stand a better chance of being published. Proposals and inquiries with article ideas are appreciated the most. A good understanding of the real estate industry (management structure) is also helpful for the writer."

$$ THE COOPERATOR

Yale Robbins, Inc., 205 Lexington Ave., 12th Floor, New York NY 10016. (212)683-5700. **Fax:** (212)545-0764. **E-mail:** editorial@cooperator.com. **Website:** www.cooperator.com. **70% freelance written.** Monthly tabloid covering real estate in the New York City metro area. *The Cooperator* covers condominium and cooperative issues in New York and beyond. It is read by condo unit owners and co-op shareholders, real estate professionals, board members and managing agents, and other service professionals. Estab. 1980. Circ. 40,000. Byline given. Pays on publication. No kill fee. Publishes ms an average of 3 months after acceptance. Submit seasonal material 3 months in advance. Accepts queries by mail, e-mail, fax. Accepts simultaneous submissions. Responds in 1 month to queries. Sample copy and writer's guidelines free.

NONFICTION Needs interview, new product, personal experience. No submissions without queries. Query with published clips. Length: 1,500-2,000 words. **Pays $325-425.** Pays expenses of writers on assignment.

PHOTOS State availability.

COLUMNS/DEPARTMENTS Profiles of co-op/condo-related businesses with something unique; Building Finance (investment and financing issues); Buying and Selling (market issues, etc.); Design (architectural and interior/exterior design, lobby renovation, etc.); Building Maintenance (issues related to maintaining interior/exterior, facades, lobbies, elevators, etc.); Legal Issues Related to Co-Ops/Condos; Real Estate Trends, all 1,500 words. **Buys 100 mss/year.** Query with published clips.

TIPS "You must have experience in business, legal, or financial. Must have published clips to send in with rèsumè and query."

$$ FLORIDA REALTOR MAGAZINE

Florida Association of Realtors, 7025 Augusta National Dr., Orlando FL 32822. (407)438-1400. **Fax:** (407)438-1411. **E-mail:** flrealtor@floridarealtors.org. **Website:** www.floridarealtormagazine.com. **Contact:** Doug Damerst, editor-in-chief. **70% freelance written.** Journal published 10 times/year covering the Florida real estate profession. "As the official publication of the Florida Association of Realtors, we provide helpful articles for our 125,000 members. We report new practices that lead to successful real estate careers and stay up on the trends and issues that affect business in Florida's real estate market." Estab. 1925. Circ. 114,592. Byline given. Pays on publication. No kill fee. Publishes ms an average of 2 months after acceptance.

Editorial lead time 3 months. Accepts queries by mail, e-mail, fax. Sample copy available online.

NONFICTION No fiction or poetry. **Buys varying number of mss/year.** Query with published clips. Length: 800-1,500 words. **Pays $500-700.** Pays expenses of writers on assignment.

PHOTOS State availability of photos. Captions, identification of subjects, model releases required. Negotiates payment individually. Buys one-time print rights and Internet use rights.

COLUMNS/DEPARTMENTS Some written in-house: Law & Ethics, 900 words; Market It, 600 words; Technology & You, 800 words; ManageIt, 600 words. **Buys varying number of mss/year. Payment varies.**

TIPS "Build a solid reputation for specializing in real estate business writing in state/national publications. Read the magazine online at floridarealtors.org/magazine. Query with specific article ideas."

OFFICE BUILDINGS MAGAZINE

Yale Robbins, Inc., 205 Lexington Ave., 12th Fl., New York NY 10016. (212)683-5700. **Fax:** (212)497-0017. **E-mail:** mrosupport@mrofficespace.com. **Website:** marketing.yrpubs.com/officebuildings. **15% freelance written.** Annual magazine published in 12 separate editions covering market statistics, trends, and thinking of area professionals on the current and future state of the real estate market. Estab. 1987. Circ. 10,500. Byline sometimes given. Pays 1 month after publication. Offers kill fee. Editorial lead time 2 months. Accepts queries by mail, e-mail. Accepts simultaneous submissions. Sample copy and writer's guidelines free.

NONFICTION Buys 15-20 mss/year. Query with published clips. Length: 1,500-2,000 words. **Pays $600-700.** Pays expenses of writers on assignment.

PROPERTIES MAGAZINE

Properties Magazine, Inc., 3826 W. 158th St., Cleveland OH 44111. (216)251-2655. **Fax:** (216)251-0064. **E-mail:** mwatt@propertiesmag.com. **Website:** www.propertiesmag.com. **Contact:** Mark Watt, managing editor/art director. **25% freelance written.** Monthly magazine covering real estate, residential, commerical construction. *Properties Magazine* is published for executives in the real estate, building, banking, design, architectural, property management, tax, and law community—busy people who need the facts presented in an interesting and informative format. Estab. 1946. Circ. over 10,000. Byline given. Pays on publication. No kill fee. Publishes ms an average of 2 months after acceptance. Editorial lead time 2 months. Submit seasonal material 2 months in advance. Accepts queries by mail, fax. Accepts simultaneous submissions. Responds in 3 weeks to queries. Sample copy for $3.95.

NONFICTION Needs general interest, how-to, humor, new product. Special issues: Environmental issues (September); Security/Fire Protection (October); Tax Issues (November); Computers In Real Estate (December). **Buys 30 mss/year.** Send complete ms. Length: 500-2,000 words. **Pays 50¢/column line.** Pays expenses of writers on assignment.

PHOTOS Send photos. Captions required. Reviews prints. Offers no additional payment for photos accepted with ms. Negotiates payment individually. Buys one-time rights.

COLUMNS/DEPARTMENTS Buys 25 mss/year. Query or send complete ms. **Pays 50¢/column line.**

REM

Real Estate Magazine, 2255B Queen St. E., Suite #1178, Toronto ON M4E 1G3 Canada. (416)425-3504. **E-mail:** jim@remonline.com. **Website:** www.remonline.com. **Contact:** Jim Adair, managing editor. **35% freelance written.** Monthly Canadian trade journal covering real estate. "*REM* provides Canadian real estate agents and brokers with news and opinions they can't get anywhere else. It is an independent publication and not affiliated with any real estate board, association, or company." Estab. 1989. Circ. 20,000. Byline given. Pays on acceptance. Offers 25% kill fee. Publishes ms an average of 2 months after acceptance. Editorial lead time 3 months. Submit seasonal material 3 months in advance. Accepts queries by mail, e-mail. Accepts simultaneous submissions. Responds in 2 weeks. Sample copy free.

NONFICTION Needs book excerpts, expose, inspirational, interview, new product, personal experience. "No articles geared to consumers about market conditions or how to choose a realtor. Must have Canadian content." **Buys 60 mss/year.** Query. Length: 500-1,500 words. **Pays $100-300.**

PHOTOS Send photos. Captions, identification of subjects required. Reviews GIF/JPEG files. Offers $25/photo. Buys one-time rights plus rights to place on REM websites.

TIPS "Stories must be of interest or practical use for Canadian realtors. Check out our website to see the types of stories we require."

$ ZONING PRACTICE

American Planning Association, 205 N. Michigan Ave., Suite 1200, Chicago IL 60601. (312)431-9100; (312)786-6392. **Fax:** (312)786-6700. **E-mail:** zoningpractice@planning.org. **Website:** www.planning.org/zoningpractice/. **90% freelance written.** Monthly newsletter covering land-use regulations including zoning. Publication is aimed at practicing urban planners and those involved in land-use decisions, such as zoning administrators and officials, planning commissioners, zoning boards of adjustment, land-use attorneys, developers, and others interested in this field. The material published comes from writers knowledgeable about zoning and subdivision regulations, preferably with practical experience in the field. Anything published needs to be of practical value to our audience in their everyday work. Estab. 1984. Circ. 2,000. Byline given. Pays on publication. Offers 50% kill fee. Publishes ms an average of 3 months after acceptance. Editorial lead time 6 months. Accepts queries by mail, e-mail, fax, phone. Accepts simultaneous submissions. Responds in 2 weeks to queries. Responds in 1 month to mss. Single copy: $10. Guidelines available at www.planning.org/zoningpractice/guidelines.htm.

NONFICTION Needs technical. See description. We do not need general or consumer-interest articles about zoning because this publication is aimed at practitioners. **Buys 12 mss/year.** Query. Length: 3,000-5,000 words. **Pays $300 minimum for assigned articles.** Pays expenses of writers on assignment.

PHOTOS State availability. Captions required. Reviews GIF/JPEG files. Negotiates payment individually. Buys all rights.

TIPS "Breaking in is easy if you know the subject matter and can write in plain English for practicing planners. We are always interested in finding new authors. We generally expect authors will earn another $200 premium for participating in an online forum called Ask the Author, in which they respond to questions from readers about their article. This requires a deep practical sense of how to make things work with regard to your topic."

RESOURCES & WASTE REDUCTION

$$ COMPOSTING NEWS

McEntee Media Corp., 9815 Hazelwood Ave., Strongsville OH 44149. (440)238-6603. **Fax:** (440)238-6712. **E-mail:** ken@recycle.cc. **Website:** www.compostingnews.com. **Contact:** Ken McEntee, editor. **5% freelance written.** Monthly newsletter about the composting industry. *Composting News* features the latest news and vital issues of concern to the producers, marketers, and end-users of compost, mulch and other organic waste-based products. Estab. 1992. Circ. 1,000. Pays on publication. No kill fee. Publishes ms an average of 1 month after acceptance. Editorial lead time 1 month. Submit seasonal material 1 month in advance. Accepts queries by mail, e-mail, fax, phone. Accepts simultaneous submissions. Responds in 2 months to queries. Sample copy for 9x12 SAE and 55¢ postage. Guidelines for #10 SASE.

NONFICTION Needs book excerpts, essays, general interest, how-to, interview, new product, opinion, personal experience, photo feature. **Buys 0-5 mss/year.** Query with published clips. Length: 100-5,000 words. **Pays $10-500.**

COLUMNS/DEPARTMENTS Query with published clips. **Pays $10-500.**

TIPS "We appreciate leads on local news regarding composting, i.e., new facilities or business, new laws and regulations, unique programs, situations that impact supply and demand for composting. International developments are also of interest."

$$$ EROSION CONTROL

Forester Media Inc., P.O. Box 3100, Santa Barbara CA 93130. (805)679-7629. **E-mail:** asantiago@forester.net. **Website:** www.erosioncontrol.com. **Contact:** Arturo Santiago. **60% freelance written.** Magazine published 7 times/year covering all aspects of erosion prevention and sediment control. *Erosion Control* is a practical, hands-on, how-to professional journal. Readers are civil engineers, landscape architects, builders, developers, public works officials, road and highway construction officials and engineers, soils specialists, farmers, landscape contractors, and others involved with any activity that disturbs significant areas of surface vegetation. Estab. 1994. Circ. 23,000. Byline given. Pays 1 month after acceptance. No kill fee. Publishes ms an average of 3 months after acceptance. Editorial lead time 4 months. Submit seasonal material 4 months in advance. Accepts queries by e-mail, phone. Responds in 3 weeks to queries. Sample copy and writer's guidelines free.

NONFICTION Needs photo feature, technical. **Buys 15 mss/year.** Query with published clips. Length: 2,000-4,000 words. **Pays $700-850.** Pays expenses of writers on assignment.

PHOTOS Send photos. Captions, identification of subjects, model releases required. Reviews transparencies, prints. Offers no additional payment for photos accepted with ms. Buys all rights.

TIPS "Writers should have a good grasp of technology involved and good writing and communication skills. Most of our freelance articles include extensive interviews with engineers, contractors, developers, or project owners, and we often provide contact names for articles we assign."

$$ WATER WELL JOURNAL

National Ground Water Association, 601 Dempsey Rd., Westerville OH 43081. **Fax:** (614)898-7786. **E-mail:** tplumley@ngwa.org. **Website:** www.waterwelljournal.org. **Contact:** Thad Plumley, director of publications/editor; Mike Price, senior editor. Each month the *Water Well Journal* covers the topics of drilling, rigs and heavy equipment, pumping systems, water quality, business management, water supply, on-site waste water treatment, and diversification opportunities, including geothermal installations, environmental remediation, irrigation, dewatering, and foundation installation. It also offers updates on regulatory issues that impact the ground water industry. Circ. 24,000. Byline given. Pays on publication. Publishes ms an average of 3 months after acceptance. Editorial lead time 6 weeks. Submit seasonal material 3 months in advance. Accepts queries by mail. Accepts simultaneous submissions. Responds in 2 weeks to queries. Responds in 1 month to mss. Guidelines free.

NONFICTION Needs essays, historical, how-to, interview, new product, personal experience, photo feature, technical, business management. No company profiles or extended product releases. **Buys up to 30 mss/year.** Query with published clips. Length: 1,000-3,000 words. **Pays $150-400.** Pays expenses of writers on assignment.

PHOTOS State availability. Captions, identification of subjects required. Offers $50-250/photo.

TIPS "Some previous experience or knowledge in groundwater/drilling/construction industry helpful. Published clips are a must."

SELLING & MERCHANDISING

$ THE AMERICAN SALESMAN

National Research Bureau, 320 Valley St., Burlington IA 52601. (319)752-5415. **Fax:** (319)752-3421. **E-mail:** contact@salestrainingandtechniques.com. **E-mail:** articles@salestrainingandtechniques.com. **Website:** www.salestrainingandtechniques.com. **80% freelance written.** Monthly magazine covering sales and marketing. *The American Salesman Magazine* is designed for sales professionals. Its primary objective is to provide informative articles that develop the attitudes, skills, and personal and professional qualities of sales representatives, allowing them to use more of their potential to increase productivity and achieve goals. Byline given. Publishes ms an average of 1 month after acceptance. Editorial lead time 1 month. Submit seasonal material 2 months in advance. Accepts queries by e-mail. Accepts simultaneous submissions. Sample copy free. Guidelines by e-mail.

NONFICTION Needs personal experience. **Buys 24 mss/year.** Send complete ms. Length: 500-1,000 words. **Pays 4¢/word.** Pays expenses of writers on assignment.

$$ BALLOONS & PARTIES MAGAZINE

PartiLife Publications, LLC, 65 Sussex St., Hackensack NJ 07601. (201)441-4224. **Fax:** (201)342-8118. **E-mail:** info@balloonsandparties.com. **Website:** www.balloonsandparties.com. **Contact:** Mark Zettler, publisher. **10% freelance written.** International trade journal published bi-monthly for professional party decorators and gift delivery businesses. *BALLOONS & Parties Magazine* is published 6 times/year by PartiLife Publications, LLC, for the balloon, party, and event fields. New product data, letters, mss, and photographs should be sent as "Attention: Editor" and should include sender's full name, address, and telephone number. SASE required on all editorial submissions. All submissions considered for publication unless otherwise noted. Unsolicited materials are submitted at sender's risk and *BALLOONS & Parties*/PartiLife Publications, LLC, assumes no responsibility for unsolicited materials. Estab. 1986. Circ. 7,000. Byline given. Pays on publication. No kill fee. Publishes ms an average of 3 months after acceptance. Submit seasonal material 6 months in advance. Accepts queries by mail, e-mail, fax, phone. Accepts simultaneous submissions. Responds in 6 weeks to queries. Sample copy for SAE with 9x12 envelope.

NONFICTION Needs essays, how-to, interview, new product, personal experience, photo feature, technical. **Buys 12 mss/year.** Send complete ms. Length: 500-1,500 words. **Pays $100-300 for assigned articles. Pays $50-200 for unsolicited articles.** Pays expenses of writers on assignment.

REPRINTS Send typed ms with rights for sale noted and information about when and where the material previously appeared. Length: up to 2,500 words. Pays 10¢/word.

PHOTOS Send photos. Captions, identification of subjects, model releases required. Reviews 2x2 transparencies, 3x5 prints. Buys all rights.

COLUMNS/DEPARTMENTS Problem Solver (small business issues); Recipes That Cook (centerpiece ideas with detailed how-to); 400-1,000 words. Send complete ms with photos.

TIPS "Show unusual, lavish, and outstanding examples of balloon sculpture, design and decorating, and other craft projects. Offer specific how-to information. Be positive and motivational in style."

$$ BRAND PACKAGING

BNP Media, 2401 W. Big Beaver Rd., Suite 700, Troy MI 48084. (248)362-3700. **Fax:** (847)362-0317. **E-mail:** kalkowskij@bnpmedia.com. **Website:** www.brandpackaging.com. **Contact:** John Kalkowski, editor-in-chief. **15% freelance written.** Magazine published 10 times/year covering how packaging can be a marketing tool. Publishes strategies and tactics to make products stand out on the shelf. Market is brand managers who are marketers but need to know something about packaging. Estab. 1997. Circ. 33,000. Byline given. Pays on acceptance. Publishes ms an average of 2 months after acceptance. Editorial lead time 3 months. Submit seasonal material 3 months in advance. Accepts queries by mail, fax. Accepts simultaneous submissions. Sample copy free.

NONFICTION Needs how-to, interview, new product. **Buys 10 mss/year.** Send complete ms. Length: 600-2,400 words. **Pays 40-50¢/word.** Pays expenses of writers on assignment.

PHOTOS State availability. Identification of subjects required. Reviews contact sheets, 35mm transparencies, 4x5 prints. Negotiates payment individually. Buys one-time rights.

COLUMNS/DEPARTMENTS Emerging Technology (new packaging technology), 600 words. **Buys 10 mss/year.** Query. **Pays $150-300.**

TIPS "Be knowledgeable on marketing techniques and be able to grasp packaging techniques. Be sure you focus on packaging as a marketing tool. Use concrete examples. We are not seeking case histories at this time."

$$ CASUAL LIVING MAGAZINE

Progresive Business Media/Today Group, 7025 Albert Pick Rd., Suite 200, Greensboro NC 27409. (336)605-1122. **Fax:** (336)605-1143. **E-mail:** wgoodson@casualliving.com. **Website:** www.casualliving.com. **Contact:** Waynette Goodson, editorial director. **10% freelance written.** Monthly magazine covering outdoor furniture and accessories, barbecue grills, spas, and more. *Casual Living* is a trade only publication for the casual furnishings and related industries, published monthly. Writes about new products, trends, and casual furniture retailers, plus industry news. Estab. 1958. Circ. 10,000. Pays on publication. Publishes ms an average of 1-2 months after acceptance. Editorial lead time 1-2 months. Submit seasonal material 2 months in advance. Accepts queries by mail, e-mail. Accepts simultaneous submissions. Responds in 2 weeks to queries. Sample copy available online.

NONFICTION Needs how-to, interview. **Buys 20 mss/year.** Query with published clips. Length: 300-1,000 words. **Pays $300-700.** Pays expenses of writers on assignment.

PHOTOS Contact: Alexa Boschini, editorial assistant. Identification of subjects required. Reviews GIF/JPEG files. Negotiates payment individually. Buys all rights.

$$$ CONSUMER GOODS TECHNOLOGY

Edgell Communications, 4 Middlebury Blvd., Randolph NJ 07869. (973)607-1354. **Fax:** (973)607-1395. **E-mail:** arajagopal@edgellmail.com. **Website:** www.consumergoods.edgl.com. **Contact:** Alarice Rajagopal, editor. **40% freelance written.** Monthly tabloid benchmarking business technology performance. Estab. 1987. Circ. 25,000. Byline given. Pays on publication. No kill fee. Publishes ms an average of 2 months after acceptance. Editorial lead time 3 months. Accepts queries by e-mail. Accepts simultaneous submissions. Sample copy available online. Guidelines by e-mail.

NONFICTION Needs essays, expose, interview. **Buys 60 mss/year.** Query with published clips. Length: 700-1,900 words. **Pays $600-1,200.** Pays expenses of writers on assignment.

PHOTOS Identification of subjects, model releases required. Negotiates payment individually. Buys all rights.

COLUMNS/DEPARTMENTS Columns 400-750 words—featured columnists. **Buys 4 mss/year.** Query with published clips. **Pays 75¢-$1/word.**

TIPS "All stories in *Consumer Goods Technology* are told through the voice of the consumer goods executive. We only quote VP-level or C-level CG executives. No vendor quotes. We're always on the lookout for freelance talent. We look in particular for writers with an in-depth understanding of the business issues faced by consumer goods firms and the technologies that are used by the industry to address those issues successfully. 'Bits and bytes' tech writing is not sought; our focus is on benchmarketing the business technology performance of CG firms, CG executives, CG vendors, and CG vendor products. Our target reader is tech-savvy, CG C-level decision maker. We write to, and about, our target reader."

$$$$ DIRECT SELLING NEWS

Video Plus, 5800 Democracy Drive, Plano TX 75024. **E-mail:** tday@directsellingnews.com. **Website:** www.directsellingnews.com. **Contact:** Teresa Day, editorial director. **20% freelance written.** Monthly magazine covering direct selling/network marketing industry. Though we are a business publication, we prefer feature-style writing rather than a newsy approach. Circ. 6,000. Byline given. Pays 30 days after publication. Publishes ms an average of 1-2 months after acceptance. Editorial lead time 3 months. Submit seasonal material 3 months in advance. Accepts queries by e-mail. Accepts simultaneous submissions. Responds in 3 weeks to queries. Sample copy available online.

NONFICTION Needs general interest, how-to. Query. Length: 1,500-3,000 words. **Pays 50¢-$1/word.**

$$ GIFTWARE NEWS

704 N. Wells St., Chicago IL 60654. (312)849-2220. **Fax:** (312)849-2174. **E-mail:** giftwarenews@talcott.com. **E-mail:** dfields@talcott.com. **Website:** www.giftwarenews.com. **Contact:** Dayna Fields, managing editor. **20% freelance written.** Monthly magazine covering gifts, collectibles, and tabletops for giftware retailers. "*Giftware News* is designed and written for those professionals involved in the retail giftware industry. *Giftware News* serves gift stores, stationary stores, department stores, as well as other retail outlets selling giftware, stationary, party and paper, tabletop, and decorative accessories. *Giftware News* is unique in the industry with an abundance of information, a wealth of product photography, outstanding graphic design, and high-quality printing that all combine with *Giftware News*' digital products to result in a package that is unmatched by any other giftware publication." Estab. 1976. Circ. 21,000. Byline given. Pays on publication. No kill fee. Publishes ms an average of 2 months after acceptance. Submit seasonal material 6 months in advance. Accepts queries by mail, e-mail. Accepts simultaneous submissions. Responds in 2 months to mss. Sample copy: $8.

NONFICTION Needs how-to, new product. **Buys 20 mss/year.** Send complete ms. Length: 1,500-2,000 words. **Pays $400-500 for assigned articles. Pays $200-300 for unsolicited articles.** Pays expenses of writers on assignment.

PHOTOS Send photos. Identification of subjects required. Reviews 4x5 transparencies, 5x7 prints, electronic images. Offers no additional payment for photos accepted with ms.

COLUMNS/DEPARTMENTS Stationery, giftbaskets, collectibles, holiday, merchandise, tabletop, wedding market and display—all for the gift retailer. Length: 1,500-2,500 words. **Buys 10 mss/year.** Send complete ms. **Pays $100-250.**

TIPS "We are not looking so much for general journalists but rather experts in particular fields who can also write."

$$ NICHE

The Rosen Group, 3000 Chestnut Ave., Suite 112, Baltimore MD 21211. (410)889-3093, ext. 231. **Fax:** (410)243-7089. **E-mail:** hoped@rosengrp.com. **Website:** www.nichemagazine.com. **Contact:** Hope Daniels, editorial director. **50% freelance written.** Quarterly trade magazine for the progressive craft gallery retailer. Each issue includes retail gallery profiles, store design trends, management techniques, financial information, and merchandising strategies for small business owners, as well as articles about craft artists and craft mediums. Estab. 1988. Circ. 15,000. Byline given. Pays on publication. No kill fee. Publishes ms an average of 6-9 months after acceptance. Editorial lead time 9 months. Submit queries for seasonal material 1 year in advance. Accepts queries by e-mail. Accepts simultaneous submissions. Responds in 4-6 weeks to queries; 3 months to mss. Sample copy for $3.

NONFICTION Needs interview. **Buys 15-20 mss/year.** Query with published clips. **Pays $150-300.**

PHOTOS Send photos. Captions required. Reviews e-images only. Negotiates payment individually.

COLUMNS/DEPARTMENTS Retail Details (short items at the front of the book, general retail information); Artist Profiles (short biographies of American Craft Artists); Retail Resources (including book/video/seminar reviews and educational opportunities pertaining to retailers). Query with published clips. **Pays $25-100 per item.**

$ O&A MARKETING NEWS

KAL Publications, Inc., 559 S. Harbor Blvd., Suite A, Anaheim CA 92805-4525. (714)563-9300. **Fax:** (714)563-9310. **E-mail:** kathy@kalpub.com. **Website:** www.kalpub.com. **3% freelance written.** Bimonthly tabloid. *O&A Marketing News* is editorially directed to people engaged in the distribution, merchandising, installation, and servicing of gasoline, oil, TBA, quick lube, carwash, convenience store, alternative fuel, and automotive aftermarket products in the 13 Western states. Estab. 1966. Circ. 7,500. Byline sometimes given. Pays on publication. No kill fee. Publishes ms an average of 2 months after acceptance. Editorial lead time 1 month. Submit seasonal material 1 month in advance. Accepts queries by mail, e-mail, fax. Accepts simultaneous submissions. Responds in 2 months. Sample copy for SASE with 9x13 envelope and 10 first-class stamps.

NONFICTION Needs interview, photo feature, industry news. Does not want anything that doesn't pertain to the petroleum marketing industry in the 13 Western states. **Buys 35 mss/year.** Send complete ms. Length: 100-500 words. **Pays $1.25/column inch.**

PHOTOS State availability of or send photos. Captions, identification of subjects required. Reviews contact sheets, 4x6 prints, digital images. Offers $5/photo. Buys electronic rights.

COLUMNS/DEPARTMENTS Nevada News (petroleum marketing news in state of Nevada). **Buys 7 mss/year.** Send complete ms. **Pays $1.25/column inch.**

FILLERS Needs gags, short humor. **Buys 7 mss/year.** Length: 1-200 words. **Pays per column inch.**

TIPS "Seeking Western industry news pertaining to the petroleum marketing industry. It can be something simple—like a new gas station or quick lube opening. News from 'outlying' states such as Montana, Idaho, Wyoming, New Mexico, and Hawaii is always needed—but any timely, topical news-oriented stories will also be considered."

$$$$ OPERATIONS & FULFILLMENT

Primedia, Inc., 761 Main Ave, Second Floor, Norwalk CT 06851. (203)358-4106. **E-mail:** dforte@accessintel.com. **Website:** www.opsandfulfillment.com. **Contact:** Daniela Forte, content manager. **25% freelance written.** Monthly magazine covering catalog/direct mail operations. *Operations & Fulfillment (O&F)* is a monthly publication that offers practical solutions for catalog online, and direct response operations management. The magazine covers such critical areas as material handling, bar coding, facility planning, transportation, call centers, warehouse management, information systems, online fulfillment and human resources. Estab. 1993. Circ. 17,600. Pays on publication. No kill fee. Publishes ms an average of 2 months after acceptance. Editorial lead time 2 months. Accepts queries by mail, e-mail, phone. Accepts simultaneous submissions. Responds in 1 week to queries. Sample copy and writer's guidelines free.

NONFICTION Needs book excerpts, how-to, interview, new product, technical. **Buys 4-6 mss/year.** Query with published clips. Length: 2,500-3,000 words. **Pays $1,000-1,800.**

PHOTOS In addition to the main article, you must include at least one sidebar of about 400 words that contains a detailed example or case study of how a direct-to-customer catalog company implements or benefits from the process you're writing about; a check list or set of practical guidelines (i.e., Twelve Ways to Ship Smarter) that describe how to implement what you suggest in the article; supporting materials such as flow charts, graphs, diagrams, illustrations and photographs (these must be clearly labeled and footnoted); and an author biography of no more than 75 words. Send photos. Captions, identification of subjects required.

TIPS Writers need some knowledge of the direct-to-customer industry. They should be able to deal clearly with highly technical material and provide attention to detail and painstaking research.

$$ SMART RETAILER

JP Media, P.O. Box 5000, N7528 Aanstad Rd., Iola WI 54945. **Fax:** (715)445-4053. **E-mail:** danb@jonespublishing.com. **Website:** www.smart-retailer.com. **Contact:** Dan Brownell, editor. **50% freelance written.** Magazine published 8 times/year covering independent retail, gift, and home decor. *Smart Retailer* is a trade publication for independent retailers of gifts and home accents. Estab. 1993. Circ. 32,000. Byline given. Pays 3 months after acceptance of final ms. Offers $50 kill fee. Publishes ms an average of 3 months after acceptance. Editorial lead time 4-6 months. Submit seasonal material 6 months in advance. Accepts queries by mail, e-mail. Usually responds in 4-6 weeks (only if accepted). Sample articles are available on website. Guidelines by e-mail.

NONFICTION Needs how-to, interview, new product, finance, legal, marketing, small business, general merchandising, and visual merchandising. No fiction, poetry, fillers, photos, artwork, or profiles of businesses, unless queried and first assigned. **Buys 20 mss/year.** Send complete ms, with résumé and published clips to: Writers Query, *Smart Retailer*. Length: 1,000-1,500 words. **Pays $150-300 for assigned articles. Pays $150-300 for unsolicited articles.** Pays expenses of writers on assignment. Limit agreed upon in advance.

COLUMNS/DEPARTMENTS Display & Design (store design and product display), 1,500 words; Retailer Profile (profile of retailer, assigned only), 1,500 words; Vendor Profile (profile of manufacturer, assigned only), 1,200 words; Technology (Internet, computer-related articles as applies to small retailers), 1,500 words; Marketing (marketing ideas and advice as applies to small retailers), 1,500 words; Finance (financial tips and advice as applies to small retailers), 1,500 words; Legal (legal tips and advice as applies to small retailers), 1,500 words; Employees (tips and advice on hiring, firing, and working with employees as applies to small retailers), 1,500 words. **Buys 15 mss/year.** Query with published clips or send complete ms. **Pays $250-350.**

$$ TRAVEL GOODS SHOWCASE

Travel Goods Association, 301 North Harrison St., #412, Princeton NJ 08540. (877)842-1938. **Fax:** (877)842-1938. **E-mail:** info@travel-goods.org; cathy@travel-goods.org. **Website:** www.travel-goods.org. **Contact:** Cathy Hays. **5-10% freelance written.** Magazine published quarterly. *Travel Goods Showcase*, the largest trade magazine devoted to travel products, contains articles for retailers, dealers, manufacturers, and suppliers about luggage, business cases, personal leather goods, handbags, and accessories. Special articles report on trends in fashion, promotions, selling and marketing techniques, industry statistics, and other educational and promotional improvements and advancements. Estab. 1975. Circ. 21,000. Byline given. Pays on acceptance. Offers $50 kill fee. Publishes ms an average of 2 months after acceptance. Editorial lead time 3 months. Submit seasonal material 2 months in advance. Accepts queries by mail, e-mail. Accepts simultaneous submissions. Responds in 2 weeks to queries; 1 month to mss. Sample copy and writer's guidelines free.

NONFICTION Needs interview, new product, technical, travel, retailer profiles with photos. No manufacturer profiles. **Buys 3 mss/year.** Query with published clips. Length: 1,200-1,600 words. **Pays $200-400.** Pays expenses of writers on assignment.

$$ VENUES TODAY

4952 Warner Ave., Suite 201, Huntington Beach CA 92649. (714)378-5400. **Fax:** (714)378-0040. **E-mail:** linda@venuestoday.com; dave@venuestoday.com. **Website:** www.venuestoday.com. **Contact:** Linda Deckard, publisher and editor in chief. **70% freelance written.** Weekly magazine covering the live entertainment industry and the buildings that host shows and sports. Needs writers who can cover an exciting industry from the business side, not the consumer side. Readers are venue managers, concert promoters, those in the concert and sports business, not the audience for concerts and sports. Need business journalists who can cover the latest news and trends in the market. Estab. 2002. Byline given. Pays on publication. Publishes ms an average of 1 month after acceptance. Editorial lead time 1-2 months. Submit seasonal material 1-2 months in advance. Accepts queries by mail, e-mail, fax. Accepts simultaneous submissions. Responds in 1 week to queries. Sample copy available online. Guidelines free.

NONFICTION Needs interview, photo feature, technical, travel. Does not want customer slant, marketing pieces. Query with published clips. Length: 500-1,500 words. **Pays $100-250.** Pays expenses of writers on assignment.

PHOTOS State availability. Captions, identification of subjects required. Reviews GIF/JPEG files. Negotiates payment individually. Buys one-time rights.

COLUMNS/DEPARTMENTS Venue News (new buildings, trend features, etc.); Bookings (show tours, business side); Marketing (of shows, sports, convention centers); Concessions (food, drink, merchandise). Length: 500-1,200 words. **Buys 250 mss/year. mss/year.** Query with published clips. **Pays $100-250.**

FILLERS Needs gags. **Buys 6 mss/year. Pays $100-300.**

$$$ VMSD

VMSD magazine, ST Media Group International, 11262 Cornell Park Dr., Cincinnati OH 45242. (513)421-2050. **Fax:** (513)421-5144. **E-mail:** jennifer.acevedo@stmediagroup.com; carly.hagedon@stmediagroup.com. **Website:** www.vmsd.com. **Contact:** Jennifer Acevedo, editor-in-chief; Carly Hagedon, managing editor. **10% freelance written.** Monthly magazine covering retailing store design, store planning, visual merchandising, brand marketing. VMSD magazine (Visual Merchandising Store Design) is the leading resource for retail designers and store display professionals, serving the retail industry since its founding by L. Frank Baum in 1897 (then called The Show Window, and later Display World). Articles need to get behind the story, tell not only what retailers did when building a new store, renovating an existing store, mounting a new in-store merchandise campaign, but also why they did what they did: specific goals, objectives, strategic initiatives, problems to solve, target markets to reach, etc.

Available both in print and online, VMSD showcases the latest store designs and visual presentations, presents merchandising strategies and new products, and reports on industry news and events. Estab. 1897. Circ. 25,450+. Byline given. Pays on acceptance. Publishes ms an average of 1-2 months after acceptance. Editorial lead time 2-3 months. Submit seasonal material 3-4 months in advance. Accepts queries by e-mail. Accepts simultaneous submissions. Sample copy free. Guidelines available online and by e-mail.

NONFICTION Query with details of project, including a press release if available, high-resolution, professional photos, the date the store opened, and any other information available. Length: 500-1,000 words. **Pays $250-1,000.** Pays expenses of writers on assignment.

PHOTOS Send photos. Reviews GIF/JPEG files. Negotiates payment individually. Buys one-time rights.

COLUMNS/DEPARTMENTS Editorial calendar available online. **Buys 5-6 mss/year.** Query. **Pays $500-1000.**

TIPS "We need to see a demonstrated understanding of our industry, its issues and major players; strong reporting and interviewing skills are also important. Merely facile writing is not enough for us."

SPORT TRADE

$$ AQUATICS INTERNATIONAL

Hanley Wood, LLC, 6222 Wilshire Blvd., Suite 600, Los Angeles CA 90048. **Fax:** (323)801-4972. **E-mail:** jmcclain@hanleywood.com. **Website:** www.aquaticsintl.com. **Contact:** Joanne McClain, editor-in-chief. Magazine published 10 times/year covering public swimming pools and waterparks. Devoted to the commercial and public swimming pool industries. The magazine provides detailed information on designing, building, maintaining, promoting, managing, programming, and outfitting aquatics facilities. Estab. 1989. Circ. 30,000. Byline given. Pays on publication. No kill fee. Publishes ms an average of 3 months after acceptance. Editorial lead time 3 months. Accepts simultaneous submissions. Responds in 1 month to queries. Sample copy for $10.50.

NONFICTION Needs how-to, interview, technical. **Buys 6 mss/year.** Send query letter with published clips/samples. Length: 1,500-2,500 words. **Pays $525 for assigned articles.**

COLUMNS/DEPARTMENTS Pays $250.

$$ ARROWTRADE MAGAZINE

Arrow Trade Publishing Corp., 3479 409th Ave. NW, Braham MN 55006. (320)396-3473. **Fax:** (320)396-3206. **E-mail:** info@arrowtrademag.com. **Website:** www.arrowtrademag.com. **Contact:** Tim Dehn, editorial. **80% freelance written.** Bimonthly magazine covering the archery industry. Readers are interested in articles that help them operate their businesses better. They are primarily owners or managers of sporting goods stores and archery pro shops. Estab. 1996. Circ. 13,000. Byline given. Pays on publication. No kill fee. Publishes ms an average of 2 months after acceptance. Editorial lead time 2 months. Accepts queries by mail, e-mail, fax. Accepts simultaneous submissions. Responds in 2 weeks to queries. Responds in 2 weeks to mss. Sample copy for SAE with 9x12 envelope and 10 First-Class stamps.

NONFICTION Needs interview, new product. "Generic business articles won't work for our highly specialized audience." **Buys 24 mss/year.** Query with published clips. Length: 3,400-4,800 words. **Pays $350-550.** Pays expenses of writers on assignment.

PHOTOS Send photos. Captions required. Must provide digital photos on CD or DVD or sent to FTP site. Offers no additional payment for photos accepted with ms.

TIPS "Our readers are hungry for articles that help them decide what to stock and how to do a better job selling or servicing it. Articles needed typically fall into 1 of these categories: business profiles on outstanding retailers, manufacturers, or distributors; equipment articles that cover categories of gear, citing trends in the market, and detailing why products have been designed a certain way and what type of use they're best suited for; basic business articles that help dealers do a better job of promoting their business, managing their inventory, training their staff, etc. Good interviewing skills are a must, as especially in the equipment articles we like to see a minimum of 6 sources."

$$ BOATING INDUSTRY

EPG Media, 3300 Fernbrook Lane N., Suite 200, Plymouth MN 55447. (763)383-4400. **E-mail:** jonathan.sweet@boatingindustry.com. **Website:** www.boatingindustry.com. **Contact:** Jonathan Sweet, editor-in-chief. **Less than 10% freelance written.** Bimonthly magazine covering recreational marine industry management. "We write for those in the industry—not the consumer. Our subject is the business of boating. All of our articles must be analytical and predictive, telling our readers where the industry is going, rather than where it's been." Estab. 1929. Circ. 23,000. Byline given. Pays on publication. Offers 50% kill fee. Publishes ms an average of 2 months after acceptance. Editorial lead time 2 months. Submit seasonal material 2 months in advance. Accepts queries by mail, e-mail. Accepts simultaneous submissions. Responds in 1 month to queries. Sample copy available online. Guidelines free.

NONFICTION **Buys 30 mss/year.** Query with published clips. Length: 250-2,500 words. **Pays $25-250.** Pays expenses of writers on assignment.

PHOTOS State availability. Captions, identification of subjects required. Reviews 2x2 transparencies, 4x6 prints. Negotiates payment individually. Buys one-time rights.

$$ BOWLING CENTER MANAGEMENT

Luby Publishing, 122 S. Michigan Ave., Suite 1806, Chicago IL 60603. (312)341-1110. **Fax:** (312)341-1180. **E-mail:** mikem@lubypublishing.com. **Website:** www.bcmmag.com. **Contact:** Michael Mazek, editor. **50% freelance written.** Monthly magazine covering bowling centers, family entertainment. *Bowling Center Management* is the industry's leading business publication and offical trade magazien of the Bowling Proprietor's Association of America. Readers are looking for novel ways to draw more customers. Accordingly, the magazine looks for articles that effectively present such ideas. Estab. 1995. Circ. 12,000. Byline given. Pays on acceptance. Publishes ms an average of 3 months after acceptance. Editorial lead time 3 months. Submit seasonal material 6 months in advance. Accepts queries by e-mail. Accepts simultaneous submissions. Responds in 2-3 weeks to queries. Sample copy for $10.

NONFICTION Needs how-to, interview. **Buys 10-20 mss/year.** Query. Length: 750-1,500 words. **Pays $150-350.** Pays expenses of writers on assignment.

TIPS "Send a solid, clever query by e-mail with knowledge and interest in an industry trend."

$$ GOLF COURSE MANAGEMENT

Golf Course Superintendents Association of America (GCSAA), 1421 Research Park Dr., Lawrence KS 66049. (785)832-4456. **Fax:** (785)832-3665. **E-mail:** shollister@gcsaa.org; mhirt@gcsaa.org; tcarson@gcsaa.org. **Website:** www.gcsaa.org. **Contact:** Scott Hollister, editor in chief; Megan Hirt, managing editor; Teresa Carson, science editor. **50% freelance written.** Monthly magazine covering the golf course superintendent. *GCM* helps the golf course superintendent become more efficient in all aspects of their job. Estab. 1924. Circ. 40,000. Byline given. Pays on acceptance. No kill fee. Publishes ms an average of 6 months after acceptance. Editorial lead time 6 months. Submit seasonal material 6 months in advance. Accepts queries by e-mail. Accepts simultaneous submissions. Responds in 3 weeks to queries; in 1 month to mss. Sample copy free. Guidelines available online.

NONFICTION Needs how-to, interview. No articles about playing golf. **Buys 40 mss/year.** Query for either feature, research, or superintendent article. Submit electronically, preferably as e-mail attachment. Send one-page synopsis or query for feature article to Scott Hollister. For research articles, submit to Teresa Carson. If you are a superintendent, contact Megan Hirt. Length: 1,500-2,500 words. **Pays $400-600.** Pays expenses of writers on assignment.

PHOTOS Send photos. Identification of subjects required. Offers no additional payment for photos accepted with ms. Buys all rights.

TIPS "Writers should have prior knowledge of golf course maintenance, agronomy and turfgrass science, and the overall profession of the golf course superintendent."

$$ INTERNATIONAL BOWLING INDUSTRY

B2B Media, Inc., 12655 Ventura Blvd., Studio City CA 91604. (818)789-2695. **Fax:** (818)789-2812. **E-mail:** info@bowlingindustry.com. **Website:** www.bowlingindustry.com. **40% freelance written.** Online monthly magazine covering ownership and management of bowling centers (alleys) and pro shops. *IBI* publishes articles in all phases of bowling center and bowling pro shop ownership and management, among them finance, promotion, customer service, relevant technology, architecture, and capital improvement. The magazine also covers the operational areas of bowling centers and pro shops such as human resources, food and beverage, corporate and birthday parties, ancillary attractions (go-karts, gaming and the like), and retailing. Articles must have strong how-to emphasis. They must be written specifically in terms of the bowling industry, although content may be applicable more widely. Estab. 1993. Circ. 10,200. Byline given. Pays on acceptance. Offers $50 kill fee. Publishes ms an average of 3 months after acceptance. Submit seasonal material 3 months in advance. Accepts queries by mail, e-mail, fax. Accepts simultaneous submissions. Responds in 2 weeks to queries. Responds in 1 month to mss. Sample copy for #10 SASE. Guidelines free.

NONFICTION Needs how-to, interview, new product, technical. **Buys 40 mss/year.** Send complete ms. Length: 1,100-1,400 words. **Pays $250.** Pays expenses of writers on assignment.

PHOTOS State availability. Identification of subjects required. Reviews JPEG photos. Offers no additional payment for photos accepted with ms. Buys all rights.

TIPS "Please supply writing samples, applicable list of credits, and bio."

$$ NSGA NOW

National Sporting Goods Association, 1601 Feehanville Dr., Suite 300, Mt. Prospect IL 60056-6035. (847)296-6742. **Fax:** (847)391-9827. **E-mail:** info@nsga.org. **E-mail:** kbruce@nsga.org. **Website:** www.nsga.org. **Contact:** Katie Bruce. **5% freelance written. Works with a small number of new/unpublished writers each year.** Bimonthly magazine. *NSGA Now* serves as a bimonthly trade journal for sporting goods retailers who are members of the association. Estab. 1948. Circ. 2,000. Byline given. Pays on publication. Publishes ms an average of 1 month after acceptance. Submit seasonal material 6 months in advance. Accepts queries by e-mail. Accepts simultaneous submissions. Sample copy for sale with 9x12 envelope and 5 first-class stamps.

NONFICTION Needs interview. No articles written without sporting goods retail business people in mind as the audience. In other words, no generic articles sent to several industries. **Buys 12 mss/year.** Query with published clips. **Pays $150-300.** Pays expenses of writers on assignment.

PHOTOS State availability. Reviews high-resolution, digital images. Payment negotiable. Buys one-time rights.

COLUMNS/DEPARTMENTS Personnel Management (succinct tips on hiring, motivating, firing, etc.); Sales Management (in-depth tips to improve sales force performance); Retail Management (detailed explanation of merchandising/inventory control); Store Design; Visual Merchandising, all 1,500 words. **Buys 12 columns/year. mss/year.** Query. **Pays $150-300.**

$$ POOL & SPA NEWS

Hanley Wood, LLC, 6222 Wilshire Blvd., Suite 600, Los Angeles CA 90048. (323)801-4972. **Fax:** (323)801-4986. **E-mail:** jmcclain@hanleywood.com. **Website:** http://poolspanews.com. **Contact:** Joanne McClain, editor. **15% freelance written.** Semimonthly magazine covering the swimming pool and spa industry for builders, retail stores, and service firms. Estab. 1960. Circ. 16,300. Pays on publication. No kill fee. Publishes ms an average of 2 months after acceptance. Accepts queries by mail, e-mail. Accepts simultaneous submissions. Responds in 1 month to queries. Sample copy for $5 and 9x12 SAE and 11 first-class stamps.

NONFICTION Needs interview, technical. Send résumé with published clips. Length: 500-2,000 words. **Pays $150-550.** Pays expenses of writers on assignment.

REPRINTS Send typed ms with rights for sale noted and information about when and where the material previously appeared. Payment varies.

PHOTOS Payment varies.

COLUMNS/DEPARTMENTS **Payment varies.**

$$ REFEREE

Referee Enterprises, Inc., 2017 Lathrop Ave., Racine WI 53405. (262)632-8855. **Fax:** (262)632-5460. **E-mail:** submissions@referee.com. **Website:** www.referee.com. **Contact:** Brent Killackey, managing editor. **75% freelance written.** Monthly magazine covering sports officiating. *Referee* is a magazine for and read by sports officials of all kinds with a focus on baseball, basketball, football, softball, and soccer officiating. Estab. 1976. Circ. 40,000. Byline given. Pays on acceptance. Offers kill fee. Kill fee negotiable. Publishes ms an average of 6 months after acceptance. Editorial lead time 6 months. Accepts queries by mail, e-mail. Accepts simultaneous submissions. Responds in 2 weeks to queries; 1 month to mss. Sample copy with #10 SASE. Guidelines online.

NONFICTION Needs book excerpts, essays, historical, how-to, humor, interview, opinion, photo feature, technical. "We don't want to see articles with themes not relating to sport officiating. General sports articles, although of interest to us, will not be published." **Buys 40 mss/year.** Query with published clips. Length: 500-3,500 words. **Pays $50-400.** Pays expenses of writers on assignment.

PHOTOS State availability. Identification of subjects required. Reviews photos mailed on CD or DVD. Offers $40 per photo. Purchase of rights negotiable.

TIPS "Query first and be persistent. We may not like your idea, but that doesn't mean we won't like your next one. Professionalism pays off."

$$ SKI AREA MANAGEMENT

Beardsley Publications, SAM, P.O. Box 644, Woodbury CT 06798. (203)263-0888. **Fax:** (203)266-0452. **E-mail:** donna@saminfo.com; jenn@saminfo.com. **Website:** www.saminfo.com. **Contact:** Donna Jacobs. **85% freelance written.** Bimonthly magazine covering everything involving the management and development of ski resorts. Report on new ideas, developments, marketing, and regulations with regard to ski and snowboard resorts. Estab. 1962. Circ. 4,500. Byline given. Pays on publication. Offers kill fee. Offers kill fee. Editorial lead time 2 months. Submit seasonal material 3 months in advance. Accepts queries by mail, e-mail. Accepts simultaneous submissions. Responds in 2 weeks to queries. Sample copy for 9x12 SAE with $3 postage or online. Guidelines for #10 SASE.

NONFICTION Needs historical, how-to, interview, new product, opinion, personal experience, technical. Does not want anything that does not specifically pertain to resort operations, management, or financing. **Buys 25-40 mss/year.** Query. Length: 500-2,500 words. **Pays $50-400.**

PHOTOS Send photos. Identification of subjects required. Reviews transparencies, prints. Offers no additional payment for photos accepted with ms. Buys one-time rights or all rights.

TIPS "Know what you are writing about. We are read by people dedicated to skiing and snowboarding and to making the resort experience the best possible for their customers. It is a trade publication read by professionals."

$$ SKI PATROL MAGAZINE

National Ski Patrol, 133 S. Van Gordon St., Suite 100, Lakewood CO 80228. (303)988-1111, ext. 2625. **Fax:** (303)988-3005. **E-mail:** editor@nsp.org. **Website:** www.nsp.org. **Contact:** Candace Horgan, editor. **80% freelance written.** Covers the National Ski Patrol, skiing, snowboarding, backcountry travel and recreation, and snow sports safety. *Ski Patrol Magazine* is a triannual publication for the members and affiliates of the National Ski Patrol. Topics are related to patrolling, mountain rescue, and the ski industry. "We cannot consider your ms if it is being reviewed by other publishers or if it has already been published. You must guarantee the originality of your work. If you write about other people's ideas, be sure to credit them where appropriate." Estab. 1984. Circ. 33,000. Byline given. Pays on publication. No kill fee. Publishes ms 3-6 months after acceptance. Editorial lead time 3 months. Submit seasonal material 3 months in advance. Accepts queries by mail, e-mail. Reponds in 1-2 weeks to queries; in 2 months to mss. Sample copy available for SASE with $3 postage. Guidelines available for SASE with 1 first-class stamp.

NONFICTION Needs essays, expose, general interest, historical, how-to, humor, inspirational, interview, nostalgic, opinion, personal experience, photo feature, profile, reviews, technical, travel. Special issues: Fall Issue: Gear Guide. **Buys 10-15 mss/year.** Query with published clips. Length: 700-3,000 words. **Pays $300-400.**

PHOTOS "Feel free to submit high resolution digital prints to complement your ms. In a separate document, include descriptions of each image and photo credits. *SPM* prefers to publish action shots wherever possible, as long as the actions depicted are in compliance with the standards of care taught by the National Ski Patrol. Faces should be visible, but not looking directly at the camera if possible.". State availability of photos with submission. Photos require captions, model releases, identification of subjects. Review contact sheets, GIF/JPEG files. Negotiates payment individually. Acquires one-time rights.

COLUMNS/DEPARTMENTS Columns are on NSP education programs. Length: 1,000-1,500 words. **Buys 8-12 mss/year.** Query with published clips. **Pays $100-250.**

TIPS "Our target audience is ski patrollers and those working in the ski industry. A background in patrolling is helpful but not mandatory. Our readers are especially interested in articles on medical issues and treatment, ski and snowboard tips and tricks, and historical and personal profiles. Articles about rescues are of particular interest."

STONE, QUARRY & MINING

$ CONTEMPORARY STONE & TILE DESIGN

Business News Publishing Media, 210 Route 4 East, Suite 203, Paramus NJ 07652. (201)291-9001, ext. 8611. **Fax:** (201)291-9002. **E-mail:** jennifer@stoneworld.com. **Website:** www.stoneworld.com. **Contact:** Jennifer Richinelli, editor. Quarterly magazine covering the full range of stone and tile design and architecture—from classic and historic spaces to current projects. Estab. 1995. Circ. 21,000. Byline given. Pays on publication. No kill fee. Publishes ms an average of 3 months after acceptance. Submit seasonal material 6 months in advance. Accepts simultaneous submissions. Responds in 3 weeks to queries. Sample copy for $10.

NONFICTION Needs interview, photo feature. **Buys 8 mss/year.** Query with published clips. Length: 1,500-3,000 words. **Pays $6/column inch.** Pays expenses of writers on assignment.

PHOTOS State availability. Captions, identification of subjects required. Reviews transparencies, prints. Pays $10/photo accepted with ms. Buys one-time rights.

COLUMNS/DEPARTMENTS Upcoming Events (for the architecture and design community); Stone Classics (featuring historic architecture); question and answer session with a prominent architect or designer. Length: 1,500-2,000 words. **Pays $6/inch.**

TIPS "The visual aspect of the magazine is key, so architectural photography is a must for any story. Cover the entire project, but focus on the stonework or tile work and how it relates to the rest of the space. Architects are very helpful in describing their work and often provide excellent quotes. As a relatively new magazine, we are looking for freelance submissions and are open to new feature topics. This is a narrow subject, however, so it's a good idea to speak with an editor before submitting anything."

$$ MINING PEOPLE MAGAZINE

Al Skinner, Inc., 629 Virginia St. W, P.O. Box 6247, Charleston WV 25362 Kanawha. (304)342-4129. **Fax:** (304)343-3124. **E-mail:** alskinner@ntelos.net; cpm@ntelos.net. **Website:** www.miningpeople.org. **Contact:** Christina Karawan, managing editor; Al Skinner, editor. **50% freelance written.** Most stories are about people or historical—either narrative or biographical on all levels of coal and mining people, past and present—from mining execs down to grass roots miners. Most stories are upbeat—showing warmth of family or success from underground up! Estab. 1976. Circ. 12,300 hard copy, est. 26,000 digital. Byline given. Pays on publication. No kill fee. Publishes ms an average of 3 months after acceptance. Submit seasonal material 2 months in advance. Accepts queries by mail, e-mail, online submission form. Accepts simultaneous submissions. Responds in 3 months to mss. Sample copy for sae with 9x12 envelope and 10 first-class stamps.

NONFICTION Needs book excerpts, historical, humor, interview, personal experience, photo feature. Special issues: Calendar issue for more than 300 annual coal shows, association meetings, etc. (January); Surface Mining/Reclamation Award (July); Christmas in Coal Country (December). No poetry, fiction, or environmental attacks on the mining industry. **Buys 32 mss/year.** Query with published clips. Length: 750-2,500 words. **Pays $150-250.**

REPRINTS Send tearsheet and information about when and where the material previously appeared. Pays 50% of amount paid for an original article.

PHOTOS Send photos. Captions, identification of subjects required. Reviews contact sheets, transparencies, 5x7 prints. Buys one-time reprint rights.

COLUMNS/DEPARTMENTS Length: 300-500 words. Editorials—anything to do with current coal issues (nonpaid); Mine'ing Our Business (bull pen column—gossip—humorous anecdotes); Coal Show Coverage (freelance photojournalist coverage of any coal function across the US). **Buys 10 mss/year.** Query. **Pays $50.**

FILLERS Needs Filler needs: anecdotes. Length: 300 words. **Pays $35.**

TIPS "We are looking for good feature articles on coal professionals, companies—past and present, color slides (for possible cover use), and b&w photos to complement stories. Writers wanted to take photos and do journalistic coverage on coal events across the country. Slant stories more toward people and less on historical. More faces and names than old town, company store photos. Include more quotes from people who lived these moments! The following geographical areas are covered: North America and overseas."

$$ PIT & QUARRY

Questex Media Group, 1360 E. Ninth St., Suite 1070, Cleveland OH 44114. (216)706-3711; (216)706-3747. **Fax:** (216)706-3710. **E-mail:** info@pitandquarry.com; kyanik@northcoastmedia.net. **Website:** www.pitandquarry.com. **Contact:** Kevin Yanik, managing editor. **10-20% freelance written.** Monthly magazine covering nonmetallic minerals, mining, and crushed stone. Audience has knowledge of construction-related markets, mining, minerals processing, etc. Estab. 1916. Circ. 23,000. Byline given. Pays on acceptance. No kill fee. Publishes ms an average of 2 months after acceptance. Editorial lead time 2 months. Accepts queries by e-mail. Accepts simultaneous submissions. Responds in 1 month to queries. Responds in 4 months to mss.

NONFICTION Needs how-to, interview, new product, technical. No humor or inspirational articles. **Buys 3-4 mss/year.** Query. Length: 2,000-2,500 words. **Pays $250-500 for assigned articles. Does not pay for unsolicited articles.** Pays expenses of writers on assignment.

PHOTOS State availability. Identification of subjects, model releases required. Offers no additional payment for photos accepted with ms. Buys one-time rights.

COLUMNS/DEPARTMENTS Brand New; Techwatch; E-business; Software Corner; Equipment Showcase. Length: 250-750 words. **Buys 5-6 mss/year.** Query. **Pays $250-300.**

TIPS "Be familiar with quarry operations (crushed stone or sand and gravel), as opposed to coal or metallic minerals mining. Know construction markets. We always need equipment-focused features on specific quarry operations."

TRANSPORTATION

$$$ RAILWAY TRACK AND STRUCTURES

Simmons-Boardman Publishing, 55 Broad St., 26th Floor, New York NY 10004. (212)620-7200. **Fax:** (212)633-1165. **E-mail:** Mischa@sbpub-chicago.com; ksenese@sbpub.com. **Website:** www.rtands.com. **Contact:** Mischa Wanek-Libman, editor; Kyra Senese, assistant editor. **1% freelance written.** Monthly magazine covering railroad civil engineering. *RT&S* is a nuts-and-bolts journal to help railroad civil engineers do their jobs better. Estab. 1904. Circ. 9,500. Byline given. Pays on publication. Offers 90% kill fee. Publishes ms an average of 1 month after acceptance. Editorial lead time 2 months. Submit seasonal material 3 months in advance. Accepts queries by mail, fax, phone. Accepts simultaneous submissions. Responds in 1 month to queries and to mss. Sample copy available online.

NONFICTION Needs how-to, new product, technical. Does not want nostalgia or "railroadiana." **Buys 1 mss/year.** Query. Length: 900-2,000 words. **Pays $500-1,000.** Pays expenses of writers on assignment.

PHOTOS State availability. Captions, identification of subjects, model releases required. Reviews GIF/JPEG files. Negotiates payment individually. Buys one-time rights.

TIPS "We prefer writers with a civil engineering background and railroad experience."

$$ SCHOOL TRANSPORTATION NEWS

STN Media Co., P.O. Box 789, Redondo Beach CA 90277. (310)792-2226. **Fax:** (310)792-2231. **E-mail:** ryan@stnmedia.com; sean@stnmedia.com. **Website:** www.stnonline.com. **Contact:** Ryan Gray, editor in chief; Sean Gallagherean Gallagher, associate editor.

20% freelance written. Monthly magazine covering school bus and pupil transportation industries in North America. Contributors to *School Transportation News* must have a basic understanding of K-12 education and automotive fleets and specifically of school buses. Articles cover such topics as manufacturing, operations, maintenance and routing software, GPS, security and legislative affairs. A familiarity with these principles is preferred. Additional industry information is available on website. New writers must perform some research of the industry or exhibit core competencies in the subject matter. Estab. 1991. Circ. 24,000. Byline given. Pays on publication. No kill fee. Editorial lead time 1-2 months. Submit seasonal material 3 months in advance. Accepts queries by e-mail. Accepts simultaneous submissions. Sample copy free. Guidelines free.

NONFICTION Needs book excerpts, general interest, historical, humor, inspirational, interview, new product, personal experience, photo feature, technical. Does not want strictly localized editorial. Wants articles that put into perspective the issues of the day. Query with published clips. Length: 600-1,200 words. **Pays $150-300.** Pays expenses of writers on assignment.

PHOTOS **Contact:** Sylvia Arroyo, managing editor. No Answer. Captions, model releases required. Reviews GIF/JPEG files. Offers $150-200/photo. Buys all rights.

COLUMNS/DEPARTMENTS Creative Special Report, Cover Story, Top Story; Book/Video Reviews (new programs/publications/training for pupil transporters), both 600 words. **Buys 40 mss/year.** Query with published clips. **Pays $150.**

TIPS "Potential freelancers should exhibit a basic proficiency in understanding school bus issues and demonstrate the ability to report on education, legislative and business affairs, as well as a talent with feature writing. It would be helpful if the writer has previous contacts within the industry. Article pitches should be e-mailed only."

TRAVEL

$$$ RVBUSINESS

G&G Media Group, 2901 E. Bristol St., Suite B, Elkhart IN 46514. (574)266-7980, ext. 13. **Fax:** (574)266-7984. **E-mail:** bhampson@rvbusiness.com; bhampson@g-gmediagroup.com. **Website:** www.rvbusiness.com. **Contact:** Bruce Hampson, editor. **50% freelance written.** Bimonthly magazine. *RVBusiness* caters to a specific audience of people who manufacture, sell, market, insure, finance, service and supply, components for recreational vehicles. Estab. 1972. Circ. 21,000. Byline given. Pays on acceptance. Offers kill fee. Publishes ms an average of 2 months after acceptance. Editorial lead time 2 months. Accepts simultaneous submissions. Sample copy free.

NONFICTION Needs new product, photo feature, industry news and features. No general articles without specific application to market. **Buys 50 mss/year.** Query with published clips. Length: 125-2,200 words. **Pays $50-1,000.** Pays expenses of writers on assignment.

COLUMNS/DEPARTMENTS Top of the News (RV industry news), 75-400 words; Business Profiles, 400-500 words; Features (indepth industry features), 800-2,000 words. **Buys 50 mss/year.** Query. **Pays $50-1,000.**

TIPS "Query. Send 1 or several ideas and a few lines letting us know how you plan to treat it/them. We are always looking for good authors knowledgeable in the RV industry or related industries. We need more articles that are brief, factual, hard hitting, and business oriented. Review other publications in the field, including enthusiast magazines."

$$ SPECIALTY TRAVEL INDEX

Alpine Hansen, P.O. Box 458, San Anselmo CA 94979. (415)455-1643. **E-mail:** info@specialtytravel.com; aalpine@specialtytravel.com. **Website:** www.specialtytravel.com. **Contact:** Andy Alpine. **90% freelance written.** Semiannual magazine covering adventure and special interest travel. Estab. 1980. Circ. 35,000. Byline given. Pays on receipt and acceptance of all materials. No kill fee. Editorial lead time 3 month. Submit seasonal material 3 months in advance. Accepts queries by mail, e-mail. Accepts simultaneous submissions. Writer's guidelines on request.

NONFICTION Needs how-to, personal experience, photo feature, travel. **Buys 15 mss/year.** Query. Length: 1,250 words. **Pays $300 minimum.** Pays expenses of writers on assignment.

REPRINTS Send tearsheet. Pays 100% of amount paid for an original article.

PHOTOS State availability. Captions, identification of subjects required. Reviews EPS/TIFF files. Negotiates payment individually.

TIPS "Write about group travel and be both creative and factual. The articles should relate to both the travel agent booking the tour and the client who is traveling."

VETERINARY

$$ ANIMAL SHELTERING

The Humane Society of the United States, P.O. Box 15276, North Hollywood CA 91615. (800)565-9226. **E-mail:** asm@humanesociety.org. **Website:** www.animalsheltering.org. **Contact:** Shevaun Brannigan, production/marketing manager; Carrie Allan, editor. **20% freelance written.** Magazine for animal care professionals and volunteers, dealing with animal welfare issues faced by animal shelters, animal control agencies, and rescue groups. Emphasis on news for the field and professional, hands-on work. Readers are shelter and animal control directors, kennel staff, field officers, humane investigators, animal control officers, animal rescuers, foster care volunteers, general volunteers, shelter veterinarians, and anyone concerned with local animal welfare issues. Estab. 1978. Circ. 6,000. Accepts simultaneous submissions. Sample copies are free; contact Shevaun Brannigan at sbrannigan@hsus.org. Guidelines available by e-mail.

NONFICTION Approximately 6-10 submissions published each year from non-staff writers; of those submissions, 50% are from writers new to the publication. **"Payment varies depending on length and complexity of piece. Longer features generally $400–600; short news pieces generally $200. We rarely take unsolicited work, so it's best to contact the editor with story ideas."** Pays expenses of writers on assignment.

REPRINTS "Aquires first publication rights. We also grant permission, with a credit to the magazine and writer, to readers who want to use the materials to educate their supporters, staff and volunteers. Contact asm@humanesociety.org for writers' guidelines."

PHOTOS Pays $150 for cover; $75 for inside.

TIPS "We almost always need good photos of people working with animals in an animal shelter or in the field. We do not use photos of individual dogs, cats, and other companion animals as often as we use photos of people working to protect, rescue or care for dogs, cats, and other companion animals."

$$ VETERINARY ECONOMICS

8033 Flint St., Lenexa KS 66214. (800)255-6864. **Fax:** (913)871-3808. **E-mail:** dvmnews@advanstar.com. **Website:** veterinarybusiness.dvm360.com. **20% freelance written.** Monthly magazine covering veterinary practice management. "We address the business concerns and management needs of practicing veterinarians." Estab. 1960. Circ. 54,000. Byline given. Pays on publication. No kill fee. Publishes ms an average of 6 months after acceptance. Editorial lead time 3 months. Submit seasonal material 3 months in advance. Accepts queries by mail, e-mail. Accepts simultaneous submissions. Responds in 3 months to queries. Sample copy free. Guidelines available online.

NONFICTION Needs how-to, interview, personal experience. **Buys 24 mss/year.** Send complete ms. Length: 1,000-2,000 words. **Pays $40-350.** Pays expenses of writers on assignment.

PHOTOS Send photos. Captions, identification of subjects required. Reviews transparencies, prints. Offers no additional payment for photos accepted with ms. Buys one-time rights.

COLUMNS/DEPARTMENTS Practice Tips (easy, unique business tips), 250 words or fewer. Send complete ms. **Pays $40.**

TIPS "Among the topics we cover: veterinary hospital design, client relations, contractual and legal matters, investments, day-to-day management, marketing, personal finances, practice finances, personnel, collections, and taxes. We also cover news and issues within the veterinary profession; for example, articles might cover the effectiveness of Yellow Pages advertising, the growing number of women veterinarians, restrictive-covenant cases, and so on. Freelance writers are encouraged to submit proposals or outlines for articles on these topics. Most articles involve interviews with a nationwide sampling of veterinarians; we will provide the names and phone numbers if necessary. We accept only a small number of unsolicited mss each year; however, we do assign many articles to freelance writers. All material submitted by first-time contributors is read on speculation, and the review process usually takes 12-16 weeks. Our style is concise yet conversational, and all mss go through a fairly rigorous editing process. We encourage writers to provide specific examples to illustrate points made throughout their articles."

PLAYWRITING

For years, *Writer's Market* for has focused solely on the most traditional publishing formats, including getting published in consumer magazines and trade journals and by book publishers with the assistance of literary agents, as well as writing contests. Those markets aren't going away, but we can add in other venues, including playwriting and screenwriting.

Playwriting is a unique market in that writers have to create scripts that speak to live audiences with live actors. Plus, there are sets to consider, number of roles, and how to engage a captive audience.

⊘ ABINGDON THEATRE CO.

101 E. 15th St., 2nd Floor, New York NY 10003. (212)868-2055. **Fax:** (212)868-2056. **Website:** www.abingdontheatre.org. Artistic Director: Tony Speciale. Estab. 1993. Professional productions for a general audience. **Produces 2-3 Mainstage and 2-3 Studio productions/year. plays/year.** Buys variable rights. Submit full-length script in hard copy, cast breakdown, synopsis and development history, if any. No one-acts or musicals. Include SASE for return of manuscript. Payment is negotiated. Responds in 4 months. All scripts should be suitable for small stages.

TIPS "In an effort to make our development process as effective as possible with the resources we have available, Abingdon will no longer accept unsolicited scripts."

ACT II PLAYHOUSE

56 E. Butler Ave., Ambler PA 19002. (215)654-0200. **Website:** www.act2.org. Producing Artistic Director: Tony Braithwaite. Estab. 1998. **Produces 4 plays/year.** Submit query and synopsis. Include SASE for return of submission. Payment negotiable. Responds in 1 month. Contemporary comedy, drama, musicals. Full length. 6 character limitation; 1 set or unit set. Does not want period pieces. Limited number of scenes per act.

ACTORS THEATRE OF LOUISVILLE

316 W. Main St., Louisville KY 40202-4218. (502)584-1265. **Fax:** (502)561-3300. **E-mail:** awegener@actorstheatre.org. **Website:** www.actorstheatre.org. **Contact:** Amy Wegener, literary director. Estab. 1964. "Professional productions are performed for subscription audience from diverse backgrounds. Agented submissions only for full-length plays, will read 10-page samples of unagented full-length works. Open submissions to National Ten-Minute Play Contest (plays 10 pages or less) are due November 1." **Produces approximately 25 new plays of varying lengths/year. plays/year.** Buys variable rights. Offers variable royalty. Responds in 9-12 months to submissions, mostly in the fall/winter. Full-length and 10-minute plays and plays of ideas, language, humor, experiment and passion.

Ⓐ ACT THEATRE

A Contemporary Theatre, Kreielsheimer Place, 700 Union St., Seattle WA 98101. (206)292-7660. **Fax:** (206)292-7670. **E-mail:** artistic@acttheatre.org. **Website:** www.acttheatre.org. Artistic Director: Kurt Beattie. Estab. 1965. "ACT performs a subscription-based season on 3 stages: 2 main stages (a thrust and an arena) and a smaller, flexible 99-seat space. Although our focus is towards our local Seattle audience, some of our notable productions have gone on to other venues in other cities." **Produces 5-6 mainstage plays/year.** *Agented submissions only* or through theatre professional's recommendation. No unsolicited submissions. Query and synopsis only for Northwest playwrights. Pays 5-10% royalty. Responds in 6 months. ACT produces full-length contemporary scripts ranging from solo pieces to large ensemble works, with an emphasis on plays that embrace the contradictions and mysteries of our contemporary world and that resonate with audiences of all backgrounds through strong storytelling and compelling characters.

TIPS "ACT is looking for plays that offer strong narrative, exciting ideas, and well-drawn, dimensional characters that will engage an audience emotionally and intellectually. These may sound like obvious prerequisites for a play, but often it seems that playwrights are less concerned with the story they have to tell than with the way they're telling it, emphasizing flashy, self-conscious style over real substance and solid structure."

ALABAMA SHAKESPEARE FESTIVAL

#1 Festival Dr., Montgomery AL 36117. **Website:** www.asf.net. Estab. 1972. The Alabama Shakespeare Festival (ASF), the State's theater, builds community by engaging, entertaining, and inspiring people with transformative theatrical performances and compelling educational and outreach programs. Located in Montgomery, the state capital of Alabama, ASF is a LORT theatre that produces up to ten productions each season in association with Actors' Equity Association, The Stage Directors and Choreographers Society and United Scenic Artists union. Though productions of Shakespeare are at the artistic core of the company, the seasons offer a diverse selection of Broadway musicals, literary classics, children's productions and world premieres of new work developed through the Southern Writer's Project (SWP.) SWP focuses on the diverse, varied heritage of the South and explores who we are today. It offers emerging and established playwrights the opportunity to develop their stories through a collaborative workshop with actors, directors, dramaturgs and an audience. For more information go to http://southernwritersproject.net/.

ALLEYWAY THEATRE

One Curtain Up Alley, Buffalo NY 14202. (716)852-2600. **Fax:** (716)852-2266. **E-mail:** email@alleyway.com. **Website:** www.alleyway.com. **Contact:** Literary Manager. Estab. 1980. **Produces 4-5 full-length, 6-12 one-act plays/year.** Seeks first production rights. Submit complete script; include CD for musicals. Alleyway Theatre also sponsors the Maxim Mazumdar New Play Competition. Pays 7% royalty. Responds in 6 months. "Works written uniquely for the theatre. Theatricality, breaking the fourth wall, and unusual settings are of particular interest. We are less interested in plays which are likely to become TV or film scripts."

ALLIANCE THEATRE

1280 Peachtree St. NE, Atlanta GA 30309. (404)733-4650. **Fax:** (404)733-4625. **E-mail:** allianceinfo@alliancetheatre.org. **Website:** www.alliancetheatre.org. **Contact:** Literary Intern. Estab. 1969. Professional production for local audience. Only accepts agent submissions and unsolicited samples from Georgia residents only. Electronic correspondence preferred. **Produces 11 plays/year.** Query with synopsis and sample or submit through agent. Enclose SASE. Responds in 9 months. Full-length scripts and scripts for young audiences no longer than 60 minutes.

TIPS "As the premier theater of the southeast, the Alliance Theatre sets the highest artistic standards, creating the powerful experience of shared theater for diverse people."

⊘ AMERICAN CONSERVATORY THEATER

30 Grant Ave., 7th Floor, San Francisco CA 94108-5800. (415)834-3200. **Website:** www.act-sf.org. **Contact:** Andy Donald, associate artistic director. Dramaturg: Michael Paller. Estab. 1965. Plays are performed in Geary Theater, a 1,000-seat classic proscenium. **Produces 8 plays/year.** No unsolicited scripts.

AMERICAN STAGE

163 3rd St. N., St. Petersburg FL 33701. (727)823-1600. **Website:** www.americanstage.org. Producing Artistic Director: Stephanie Gularte. Development Director: Stephanie Snyder. Estab. 1977. Limited by "Small mainstage venue, 1 touring production conducive to small cast, light technical pieces." Subject matter: classics and original work for children (ages K-12) and families. Recently produced plays: *King Island Christmas for the Mainstage* and *Alexander and the Terrible, Horrible, No Good Very Bad Day* for the School Tour and Mainstage. Query with synopsis, character breakdown and set description. Will consider simultaneous submissions and previously performed work.

TIPS Sees a move in plays toward basic human values, relationships and multicultural communities.

ANCHORAGE PRESS PLAYS, INC.

Dramatic Publishing, 311 Washington St., Woodstock IL 60098. (800)448-7469. **Fax:** (800)334-5302. **Website:** www.applays.com. **Contact:** Kevin Wright, submissions coordinator. Estab. 1935. "We are an international agency for plays for young people. First in the field since 1935. We are primarily a publisher of theatrical plays with limited textbooks. "Publishes solicited hardcover and trade paperback originals. "Anchorage Press PLAYS, Inc serves a specialty field of TYA - Theatre for Young Audiences. We publish play scripts and license the performance rights for plays to be presented, by skilled performers, before audiences of children, youth, teens, and young adults or a family audience. Anchorage also has a limited number of plays of faith that are more suitable for a family audience or teen/adult audience in subject complexity. Representing the playwrights of these works, Anchorage serves as the licensing agency for the performance rights. We also publish and distribute a select number of books for the field." **Publishes 4-6 plays/year.** "A play manuscript must be computer-printed with dark ink. It should be submitted by mail to (Submissions, Anchorage Press Plays, Linda Habjan, Submissions Editor, 311 Washington St., Woodstock, IL 60098) and accompanied by a SASE. Manuscripts will not be accepted via fax or email. Please send a play script only after it has had staged productions, workshop readings, peer reviews, and rewrites. We cannot accept plays for publication that have not been produced. (Please send information about productions: programs, reviews, etc.) **Send your final version.** We will consider plays with 2 or more characters. See more guidelines online at website." Pays 10-15% royalty. Playwrights also receive 50-75% royalties. Responds in 1-2 years. drama, stage plays, for children and young people.

TIPS "The plays we publish are chosen for their suitability to be produced for a youth or family audience. We are less interested in classroom teaching aids."

Ⓐ ARENA STAGE

1101 6th St. SW, Washington DC 20024. (202)554-9066. **Fax:** (202)488-4056. **Website:** www.arenastage.org. Artistic Director: Molly Smith. Estab. 1950. **Produces 8 plays/year.** Only accepts scripts from writers with agent or theatrical representation. "Plays that illuminate the broad canvas of American work, with a commitment to aesthetic, cultural, and geographic diversity. Arena is committed to showcasing the past, present, and future of American theatre." Seeks only full-length plays and musicals in all genres.

ARIZONA THEATRE CO.

P.O. Box 1631, Tucson AZ 85702. (520)884-8210. **Fax:** (520)628-9129. **Website:** arizonatheatre.org. **Contact:** Literary Department. Artistic Director: David Ivers. Estab. 1966. "Arizona Theatre Company is the State Theatre of Arizona. Each season reflects the rich variety of world drama—from classics to contemporary plays, from musicals to new works—along with a wide array of outreach programs, educational opportunities, access initiatives, and new play programs." **Produces 6-8 plays/year.** Only Arizona writers may submit unsolicited scripts, along with production history (if any), brief bio, and SAE. Out-of-state writers can send a synopsis, 10-page sample dialogue, production history (if any), brief bio, and SAE. Payment negotiated. Responds in 4-6 months. Full length plays of a variety of genres and topics and full length musicals. No one-acts.

TIPS "Please include in the cover letter something about your current situation and goals."

ARTISTS REPERTORY THEATRE

Portland OR 97205. **Website:** www.artistsrep.org. Estab. 1982. Plays performed in professional theater with a subscriber-based audience. No unsolicited mss accepted. Pays royalty. No response to unsolicited scripts. Full-length, hard-hitting, emotional, intimate, actor-oriented shows with small casts (rarely exceeds 10-13, usually 2-7). Language and subject matter are not a problem. No one-acts or children's scripts.

ART STATION THEATRE

P.O. Box 1998, Stone Mountain GA 30083. (770)469-1105. **Website:** www.artstation.org. Co-founders/directors: David Thomas and Michael Hidalgo. Estab. 1986. ART Station Theatre is a professional theater located in a contemporary arts center in Stone Mountain, GA, which is part of Metro Atlanta. Audience consists of middle-aged to senior, suburban patrons. **Produces 3 plays/year.** Query with synopsis and writing samples. Pays 5-7% royalty. Responds in 1 year. Full length comedy, drama and musicals, preferably relating to the human condition in the contemporary South. Cast size no greater than 6.

⊘ ASOLO THEATRE CO.

5555 N. Tamiami Trail, Sarasota FL 34234. (941)351-9010. **Fax:** (941)351-5796. **E-mail:** asolo@asolo.org. **Website:** www.asolo.org. **Contact:** Michael Donald Edwards, producing artistic director. Estab. 1960. A LORT theater with 2 intimate performing spaces. **Produces 7-8 plays/year.** Negotiates rights and payment. Play must be full length. We operate with a resident company in rotating repertory.

BARTER THEATRE

127 W. Main St., Abingdon VA 24210. (276)628-3991. **E-mail:** dramaturge@bartertheatre.com. **Website:** www.bartertheatre.com. Estab. 1933. The Barter Players produces professional children's productions with 100% of roles written for adults. **Produces 17 plays/year.** Query with synopsis, character breakdown, set description, first 10 pages, SASE, and a sample CD with three songs if it is a musical. Will consider simultaneous submissions and previously performed work. Responds only if interested. Mail to Dramaturge, Barter Theatre, P.O. Box 867, Abingdon, VA 24212-0867. Pays $30-75 for performance. Responds in 9-12 months. "Creative, interesting material for children K-12. We are seeking shows for students that go hand in hand with school standards of learning that can be performed by 6 actors. We are also seeking summer shows for young children for casts of 12-15. Works that talk down to the audience will not be considered."

Does not accept unsolicited mss.

TIPS "We are looking for material that appeals to diverse, family audiences. We accept no one-act play queries."

BLOOMSBURG THEATRE ENSEMBLE

226 Center St., Bloomsburg PA 17815. (570)784-5530. **E-mail:** bte@bte.org. **Website:** www.bte.org. Estab. 1979. Professional productions for a non-urban audience. **Produces 9 plays/year.** Buys negotiable rights Submit query and synopsis. Pays 6-9% royalty. Pays $50-70/performance. Responds in 9 months. Because of our non-urban location, we strive to expose our audience to a broad range of theatre—both classical and contemporary. We are drawn to language and

ideas and to plays that resonate in our community. We are most in need of articulate comedies and cast sizes under 6.

TIPS Because of our non-urban setting we are less interested in plays that focus on dilemmas of city life in particular. Most of the comedies we read are cynical. Many plays we read would make better film scripts; static/relationship-heavy scripts that do not use the 'theatricality' of the theatre to an advantage.

CELEBRATION THEATRE

1049 Havenhurst Dr., #101-1, West Hollywood CA 90046. (323)957-1884. **Fax:** (323)957-1826. **E-mail:** info@celebrationtheatre.com. **Website:** www.celebrationtheatre.com. **Contact:** Literary Management Team. Co-Artistic Directors: Michael Matthews and Michael A. Shepperd. Estab. 1983. Performed in a small theatre in Los angeles. For all audiences, but with gay and lesbian characters at the center of the plays. **Produces 4 plays/year.** Submit query and synopsis. Pays 6-7% royalty. Responds in 5 months. Produce works with gay and lesbian characters at the center of the narrative. There aren't any limitations, but simple productions work best. Don't send coming-out plays/stories.

CHILDSPLAY, INC.

900 S. Mitchell Dr., Tempe AZ 85281. (480)921-5700. **Fax:** (480)921-5777. **E-mail:** info@childsplayaz.org. **Website:** childsplayaz.org. Estab. 1978. Professional touring and in-house productions for youth and family audiences. **Produces 5-6 plays/year.** Submit synopsis, character descriptions and 7- to 10-page dialogue sample. Pays royalty of $20-35/performance (touring) or pays $3,000-8,000 commission. Holds a small percentage of royalties on commissioned work for 3-5 years. Responds in 6 months. Seeking theatrical plays on a wide range of contemporary topics. Our biggest market is K-6. We need intelligent theatrical pieces for this age group that meet touring requirements and have the flexibility for in-house staging. The company has a reputation, built up over 30 years, of maintaining a strong aesthetic. We need scripts that respect the audience's intelligence and support their rights to dream and to have their concerns explored. Innovative, theatrical and small is a constant need. Touring shows limited to 5 actors; in-house shows limited to 6-10 actors.

TIPS No traditionally-handled fairy tales. Theater for young people is growing up and is able to speak to youth and adults. The material must respect the artistry of the theater and the intelligence of our audience. Our most important goal is to benefit children. If you wish your materials returned send SASE.

Ⓐ CLEVELAND PLAY HOUSE

8500 Euclid Ave., Cleveland OH 44106. **E-mail:** sgordon@clevelandplayhouse.com. **Website:** www.clevelandplayhouse.com. **Contact:** Seth Gordon, associate artistic director. Artistic Director: Michael Bloom. Estab. 1915. We have five theatres, 100-550 seats. **Produces 10 plays/year.** Submit 10-page sample with synopsis. Will return submissions if accompanied by SASE. Payment is negotiable. Responds in 6 months. All styles and topics of new plays.

COLONY THEATRE CO.

555 N. Third St., Burbank CA 91502. (818)558-7000. **Fax:** (818)558-7110. **E-mail:** colonytheatre@colonytheatre.org. **Website:** www.colonytheatre.org. **Contact:** Michael David Wadler, literary manager. Professional 276-seat theater with thrust stage. Casts from resident company of professional actors. **Produces 6 plays/year.** Negotiated rights. Submit query and synopsis. Pays royalty for each performance. Full length (90-120 minutes) with a cast of 4-12. Especially interested in small casts of 4 or fewer. No musicals or experimental works.

TIPS We seek works of theatrical imagination and emotional resonance on universal themes.

CREEDE REPERTORY THEATRE

P.O. Box 269, Creede CO 81130-0269. (719)658-2541. **E-mail:** litmgr@creederep.com. **Website:** www.creederep.org. **Contact:** Frank Kuhn, Literary Manager. Estab. 1966. Plays performed for a smaller audience. **Produces 6 plays/year.** Submit synopsis, 10-page dialogue sample, letter of inquiry, resume; electronic submissions only. Royalties negotiated with each author—paid on a per performance basis. Responds in 6 months. "Special consideration given to plays focusing on the cultures and history of the American West and Southwest."

TIPS "We seek new adaptations of classical or older works as well as original scripts."

DALLAS CHILDREN'S THEATER

Rosewood Center for Family Arts, 5938 Skillman, Dallas TX 75231. **E-mail:** artie.olaisen@dct.org. **Website:** www.dct.org. **Contact:** Artie Olaisen, associate artistic director. Estab. 1984. "Professional theater for family and student audiences." **Produces up to 6 youth/family plays/year. Produces 1-2 youth/family musicals/year. plays/year.** Rights negotiable. Query with synopsis, number of actors required, any material regarding previous productions of the work, and a demo tape or lead sheets (for musicals). No materials will be returned without a SASE included. All scripts should be sent to the attention of Artie Olaisen. Pays negotiable royalty. Responds in up to 8 months. "Seeking substantive material appropriate for youth and family audiences. Most consideration given to full-length, nonmusical works, especially classic and contemporary adaptations of literature. Also interested in social, topical, issue-oriented material. Very interested in scripts which enlighten diverse cultural experiences, particularly Hispanic and African-American experiences. Prefers scripts with no more than 15 cast members; 6-12 is ideal."

TIPS "No adult experience material. We are a family theater. Not interested in material intended for performance by children or in a classroom. Productions are performed by professional adults. Children are cast in child-appropriate roles. We receive far too much light musical material that plays down to children and totally lacks any substance. Be patient. We receive an enormous amount of submissions. Most of the material we have historically produced has had previous production. We are not against perusing non-produced material, but it has rarely gone into our season unless we have been involved in its development. No phone calls."

DIVERSIONARY THEATRE

4545 Park Blvd., Suite 101, San Diego CA 92116. (619)220-6830. **E-mail:** dkirsch@diversionary.org. **Website:** www.diversionary.org. **Contact:** Matt M. Morrow, executive artistic director. Estab. 1986. "Professional non-union full-length productions of gay, lesbian, bisexual and transgender content. Ideal cast size is 2-6." **Produces 5-6 plays/year.** Submit application and 10-15 pages of script. Responds in 6 months.

Ⓐ DORSET THEATRE FESTIVAL

Box 510, Dorset VT 05251-0510. (802)867-2223. **Website:** www.dorsettheatrefestival.org. Estab. 1976. Our plays will be performed in our Equity theater and are intended for a sophisticated community. **Produces 5 plays/year (1 a new work). plays/year.** Agented submissions only. Rights and compensation negotiated. Looking for full-length contemporary American comedy or drama. Limited to a cast of 6.

TIPS Language and subject matter must be appropriate to general audience.

DRAMATIC PUBLISHING, INC.

311 Washington St., Woodstock IL 60098. (800)448-7469. **E-mail:** submissionseditor@dpcplays.com. **Website:** www.dramaticpublishing.com. **Contact:** Linda Habjan, submissions editor. Estab. 1885. Recently published: *Redwall: The Legend of Redwall Abbey*, by Evelyn Swensson, based on the book by Brian Jacques. *Gooney Bird Green and Her True-Life Adventures*, adapted by Kent R. Brown from the book by Lois Lowry; *Anastasia Krupnik*, by Meryl Friedman, based on the book by Lois Lowry; *A Village Fable*, by James Still, adapted from *In the Suicide Mountain*, by John Gardner; *The Little Prince*, adapted by Rick Cummins and John Scoullar. See website for detailed submission guidelines. Accepts submissions by postal mail only. Include your contact information, a cast list with specific character descriptions and set/technical requirements, a synopsis of the play and its production history, and a CD with any written sheet music if it is a musical. Include an SASE for reply. Pays royalties.

TIPS "Original plays dealing with hopes, joys and fears of today's children are preferred to adaptations of old classics. No more adapted fairytales."

EAST WEST PLAYERS

120 N. Judge John Aiso St., Los Angeles CA 90012. (213)625-7000. **E-mail:** literary@eastwestplayers.org. **Website:** www.eastwestplayers.org. Producing Artistic Director: Snehal Desai. Estab. 1965. Professional 240-seat theater performing under LOA-BAT contract, presenting plays which explore the Asian Pacific American experience. **Produces 4 plays/year.** Scripts should be submitted in a PDF format and must include the following: 1. A cover sheet, including your name, address, telephone number, website, and e-mail address; 2. A theatrical resume (two pages max) listing major productions, workshops, readings, commissions, publications, awards, education, and training information; 3. A 100-word max synopsis of the play. "Our Literary Committee will read all scripts we deem to be in line with the mission of the theater. Due to the large volume of submissions, we will only reach out to playwrights whose work we are interested in." Pays royalty against percentage of box office. Responds in

9-12 months. "Whether dramas, comedies, or musicals, all plays must either address the Asian American experience or have a special resonance when cast with Asian American actors."

ELDRIDGE PUBLISHING CO. INC.

P.O. Box 4904, Lancaster PA 17604. (850)385-2463. **E-mail:** info@histage.com. **Website:** www.histage.com; www.95church.com. **Contact:** Meredith Edwards, acquisitions editor. Estab. 1906. Play publisher. Publishes new plays and musicals for junior and senior high school, community theater, and children's theater (adults performing for children), all genres; also religious plays. **Publishes 50 plays and 2-3 musicals a year. plays/year.** Buys all dramatic rights. "Submit complete ms to appropriate online portal; snail mail CD of songs or provide a web link to them." Will consider simultaneous submissions if noted. Pays 50% royalty and 10% copy sales. Responds in 2 months.

TIPS "Try to have your work performed, if at all possible, before submitting. We're always on the lookout for comedies which provide a lot of fun for our customers. But other more serious topics, as well as intriguing mysteries and children's theater programs, are of interest to us as well. We know there are many new talented playwrights out there, and we look forward to reading their fresh scripts."

THE ENSEMBLE STUDIO THEATRE

545 W. 52nd St., 2nd Floor, New York NY 10019. (212)247-4982. **Fax:** (212)664-0041. **E-mail:** firman@estnyc.org. **Website:** www.ensemblestudiotheatre.org. **Contact:** Linsay Firman, Director of Play Development. Artistic Director: William Carden. Estab. 1972. **Produces 250 projects, readings, workshops and productions/year for off-off Broadway developmental theater in a 100-seat house, 60-seat workshop space. plays/year.** Do not fax mss or resumes. Please check website for current submission guidelines and deadlines. Responds in 10 months. "Full-length plays with strong dramatic actions and situations and solid one-acts, humorous and dramatic, which can stand on their own. Special programs include Going to the River Series, which workshops new plays by African-American women, and the Sloan Project, which commissions new works on the topics of science and technology. Seeks original plays with strong dramatic action, believable characters and dynamic ideas. We are interested in writers who respect the power of language. No verse-dramas or elaborate costume dramas or musicals. Accepts new/unproduced work only."

ENSEMBLE THEATRE OF CINCINNATI

1127 Vine St., Cincinnati OH 45202. (513)421-3555. **Fax:** (513)562-4104. **E-mail:** script@ensemblecincinnati.org. **Website:** www.ensemblecincinnati.org. **Contact:** D. Lynn Meyers, producing artistic director. Estab. 1986. Professional year-round theater. **Produces 12 plays/year, including a staged reading series. plays/year.** Query with synopsis, submit complete ms or submit through agent. Pays 5-10% royalty. Responds in 6-9 months. Dedicated to good writing of any style for a small, contemporary cast (prefers a maximum of 8). Small technical needs, big ideas.

TIPS Looking for "creative, inventive, contemporary subjects or classic tales. If we ask you to send your script, please send materials as complete as possible, including a SASE."

Ⓐ FOUNTAIN THEATRE

5060 Fountain Ave., Los Angeles CA 90029. (323)663-1525. **E-mail:** info@fountaintheatre.com. **Website:** fountaintheatre.com. Estab. 1990. Produces both a theater and dance season. Produced at Fountain Theatre (99-seat equity contract). *Professional recommendation only.* **Produces 3-4 plays/year.** Rights acquired vary. Agent submissions only. Pays royalty.or standard per performance rate. Responds in 3-6 months. Original play and premieres; material that incorporates dance or language into text with unique use and vision; socially and politically-conscious work that reflects the various communities of Los Angeles and America.

SAMUEL FRENCH, INC.

235 Park Ave. S., 5th Floor, New York NY 10003. (866)598-8449. **Fax:** (212)206-1429. **E-mail:** publications@samuelfrench.com. **Website:** www.samuelfrench.com. Estab. 1830. Publishes paperback acting editions of plays. *Not currently accepting unsolicited submissions.* **Publishes 50-60 titles/year. plays/year.** Pays 10% royalty on retail price, plus amateur and stock royalties on productions. Comedies, mysteries, children's plays, high school plays.

WILL GEER THEATRICUM BOTANICUM

P.O. Box 1222, Topanga CA 90290. (310)455-2322. **Fax:** (310)455-3724. **E-mail:** egtree@theatricum.com. **Website:** www.theatricum.com. **Contact:** Ellen Geer, artistic director. Estab. 1973. Professional productions for summer theater. Botanicum Seedlings new plays selected for readings and one play each year developed. **Produces 4 classical and 1 new play if selected/year. plays/year.** Send synopsis, sample dialogue and tape if musical. Pays 6% royalty or $150 per show. Responds in 6 months. Socially relevant plays, musicals; all full-length. Cast size of 4-10 people. "We are a large outdoor theatre—small intimate works could be difficult."

TIPS "September submissions have best turn around for main season; year-round for 'Botanicum Seedlings.'"

⊘ GEORGE STREET PLAYHOUSE

P.O. Box 194, New Brunswick NJ 08903. (732)846-2895. **Website:** www.georgestplayhouse.org. **Contact:** Literary Associate. Artistic Director: David Saint. Professional regional theater (LORT C). Proscenium/thurst stage with 367 seats. **Produces 6 plays/year.** *No unsolicited scripts. Agent or professional recommendation only.*

TIPS "It is our firm belief that theater reaches the mind via the heart and the funny bone. Our work tells a compelling, personal, human story that entertains, challenges and stretches the imagination."

GEVA THEATRE CENTER

75 Woodbury Blvd., Rochester NY 14607. (585)232-1366. **Contact:** Marge Betley, literary manager. Professional and regional theater, modified thrust, 552 seats; second stage has 180 seats. Subscription and single-ticket sales. **Produces 7-11 plays/year.** Query with sample pages, synopsis, and resume. Responds in 3 months. Full-length plays, translations, and adaptations.

Ⓐ THE GOODMAN THEATRE

170 N. Dearborn St., Chicago IL 60601-3205. (312)443-3811. **Fax:** (312)443-3821. **E-mail:** artistic@goodmantheatre.org. **Website:** www.goodman-theatre.org. **Contact:** Tanya Palmer, literary manager. Estab. 1925. The Goodman is a professional, not-for-profit theater producing a series in both the Albert Theatre and the Owen Theatre, which includes an annual New Play Series. The Goodman does not accept unsolicited scripts, nor will it respond to synopsis of plays submitted by playwrights unless accompanied by a stamped, self-addressed postcard. The Goodman may request plays to be submitted for production consideration after receiving a letter of inquiry or telephone call from recognized literary agents or producing organizations. **Produces 9 plays/year.** Buys variable rights. Pays variable royalty. Responds in 6 months. Full-length plays, translations, musicals; special interest in social or political themes.

Ⓐ GRETNA THEATRE

P.O. Box 578, Mt. Gretna PA 17064. **Fax:** (717)964-2189. **E-mail:** larryfrenock@gretnatheatre.com. **Website:** www.gretnatheatre.com. **Contact:** Larry Frenock, producing artistic director. Estab. 1927. Musicals and plays are produced at a professional equity theater during summer. Rarely produce new work for mainstage; will consider small cast musicals for children of 1 hour or less duration. Will accept submissions from writers or agents. Pays negotiable royalty ($50-65/performance). Subject, language and content are important factors in this open-air theatre.

TIPS "Large cast shows or those with elaborate scenic/costume needs will not be considered as these children's shows are performed on whatever mainstage set is on deck at the time."

Ⓐ HARTFORD STAGE CO.

50 Church St., Hartford CT 06103. (860)525-5601. **Fax:** (860)525-4420. **Website:** www.hartfordstage.org. **Contact:** Scripts Manager. Estab. 1963. Regional theater productions with a wide range in audience. Hartford Stage accepts scripts by agent submission or professional recommendation. As a dedicated supporter of our community, we also accept scripts from Connecticut residents. (Please note, we do not accept one-act plays, or unsolicited material. **Produces 6 plays/year.** For questions, contact our scripts manager. If you qualify, we respond within 3-6 months. Classics, new plays, musicals.

HORIZON THEATRE CO.

P.O. Box 5376, Atlanta GA 31107. (404)523-1477. **Fax:** (404)584-8815. **Website:** www.horizontheatre.com. **Contact:** Literary Manager. Estab. 1983. Professional productions. **5+ plays/year, and workshops 6 plays as part of New South Playworks Festival plays/year.** Buys rights to produce in Atlanta area. Accepts unsolicited résumés, samples, treatments, and summaries with SASE. Responds in 1 year. "We produce contemporary plays that seek to bridge cultures and communities, utilizing a realistic base but with heightened visual or language elements. Particularly interested in comedy, satire, plays that are entertaining and topical, but thought provoking. Also particular interest in plays by women, African-Americans, or that concern the contemporary South. No more than 8 in cast."

ILLINOIS THEATRE CENTRE

371 Artists' Walk, P.O. Box 397, Park Forest IL 60466. (708)481-3510. **Fax:** (708)481-3693. **E-mail:** ilthctr@sbcglobal.net. **Website:** www.ilthctr.org. Estab. 1976. Professional Resident Theatre Company in our own space for a subscription-based audience. **Produces 8 plays/year.** Buys casting and directing and designer selection rights. Query with synopsis or agented submission. Pays 7-10% royalty. Responds in 2 months. All types of 2-act plays, musicals, dramas. Prefers cast size of 6-10.

TIPS Always looking for mysteries and comedies. Make sure your play arrives between November and January when play selections are made.

INDIANA REPERTORY THEATRE

140 W. Washington St., Indianapolis IN 46204. (317)635-5277. **E-mail:** rroberts@irtlive.com. **Website:** www.irtlive.com. **Contact:** Richard J Roberts, resident dramaturg. Executive Artistic Director: Janet Allen. Estab. 1972. "Modified proscenium stage with 600 seats; thrust stage with 300 seats." Send synopsis with résumé via e-mail to the dramaturg. No unsolicited scripts. Submit year-round (season chosen by January). Responds in 6 months. Full-length plays, translations, adaptations, solo pieces. Also interested in adaptations of classic literature and plays that explore cultural/ethnic issues with a midwestern voice. Special program: Discovery Series (plays for family audiences with a focus on youth). Cast size should be 6-8.

TIPS "The IRT employs a playwright-in-residence from whom the majority of our new work is commissioned. We occasionally place other subject-specific commissions."

INTERACT THEATRE CO.

The Adrienne, 2030 Sansom St., Philadelphia PA 19103. (215)568-8077. **Fax:** (215)568-8095. **E-mail:** pbonilla@interacttheatre.org. **Website:** www.interacttheatre.org. **Contact:** Peter Bonilla, literary associate. Estab. 1988. Produces professional productions for adult audience. **Produces 4 plays/year.** Query with synopsis and bio. No unsolicited scripts. Pays 2-8% royalty or $25-100/performance. Responds in 6 months. Contemporary dramas and comedies that explore issues of political, social, cultural or historical significance. Virtually all of our productions have political content in the foregound of the drama. Prefer plays that raise interesting questions without giving easy, predictable answers. We are interested in new plays. Limit cast to 8. No romantic comedies, family dramas, agit-prop.

Ⓐ INTIMAN THEATRE

201 Mercer St., Seattle WA 98109. (206)269-1901. **Fax:** (206)269-1928. **E-mail:** literary@intiman.org. **Website:** www.intiman.org. **Contact:** Sheila Daniels. Artistic Director: Bartlett Sher. Estab. 1972. LORT C Regional Theater in Seattle. Best submission time is October through March. **Produces 6 plays/year.** *Agented submissions only* or by professional recommendation. Responds in 8 months. Well-crafted dramas and comedies by playwrights who fully utilize the power of language and character relationships to explore enduring themes. Prefers nonnaturalistic plays and plays of dynamic theatricality.

JEWEL BOX THEATRE

3700 N. Walker, Oklahoma City OK 73118-7099. (405)521-7031. **Fax:** (405)525-6562. **Contact:** Charles Tweed, production director. Estab. 1956. Amateur productions. 3,000 season subscribers and general public. **Produces 6 plays/year.** Pays $500 contest prize. Annual Playwriting Competition: Send SASE in September-October. Deadline: mid-January.

JEWISH ENSEMBLE THEATRE

6600 W. Maple Rd., West Bloomfield MI 48322. (248)788-2900. **E-mail:** e.orbach@jettheatre.org. **Website:** www.jettheatre.org. **Contact:** Evelyn Orbach, artistic director. Estab. 1989. Professional productions at the Aaron DeRoy Theatre (season), The Detroit Institue of Arts Theatre, and Scottish Rite Cathedral Theatre (schools), as well as tours to schools. **Produces 4-6 plays/year.** Obtains rights for our season productions and staged readings for festival. Submit complete script. Pays 6-8% royalty for full production or honorarium for staged reading—$100/full-length play. Responds in 1 year. We do few children's plays except original commissions; we rarely do musicals. Cast limited to a maximum of 8 actors.

TIPS We are a theater of social conscience with the following mission: to produce work on the highest possible professional level; to deal with issues of community & humanity from a Jewish perspective; to provide a platform for new voices and a bridge for understanding to the larger community.

KUMU KAHUA

46 Merchant St., Honolulu HI 96813. (808)536-4222. **Fax:** (808)536-4226. **E-mail:** kumukahuatheatre@hawaiiantel.net. **Website:** kumukahua.org. Estab. 1971. Plays performed at new Kumu Kahua Theatre, flexible 120-seat theater, for community audiences. **Produces 5 productions, 3-4 public readings/year. plays/year.** Submit complete script. Pays royalty of $50/performance; usually 20 performances of each production. Responds in 4 months. Plays must have some interest for local Hawai'i audiences.

LONG WHARF THEATRE

222 Sargent Dr., New Haven CT 06511. (203)787-4284. **Fax:** (203)776-2287. **E-mail:** gordon.edelstein@longwharf.org. **Website:** www.longwharf.org. **Contact:** Gordon Edelstein, artistic dir. Estab. 1965. "Professional regional theatre has been and continues to be an incubator of new works, including last season's *A Civil War Christmas* by Paula Vogel and *Coming Home* by Athol Fugard. Long Wharf Theatre has received New York Drama Critics Awards, Obie Awards, the Margo Jefferson Award for Production of New Works and more." **Produces 6 plays/year on its 2 stages. plays/year.** *Agented submissions or professional recommendations only.* Full-length plays, translations, adaptations. Special interest: Dramatic plays and comedies about human relationships, social concerns, ethical and moral dilemmas.

TIPS "We no longer accept queries."

LOS ANGELES DESIGNERS' THEATRE

P.O. Box 1883, Studio City CA 91614-0883. **Contact:** Richard Niederberg, artistic dir. Estab. Established 1970. "Professional shows/industry audience." **Produces 8-20 plays/year.** Purchases rights by negotiation, first refusal for performance/synchronization rights only. Submit proposal only (i.e., 1 page in #10 SASE) We want highly commercial work without liens, 'understandings,' or promises to anyone. Does not return submissions accompanied by a SASE. Payment varies. Reports in 3 months (minimum) to submission. All types. "No limitations—We seek design challenges. No boring material. Shorter plays with musical underscores are desirable; nudity, street language, and political themes are OK."

MAGIC THEATRE

Fort Mason Center, Bldg. D, 3rd Floor, San Francisco CA 94123. (415)441-8001. **Fax:** (415)771-5505. **E-mail:** info@magictheatre.org. **Website:** www.magictheatre.org. **Contact:** Mark Routhier, director of artistic development. Artistic Director: Chris Smith. Estab. 1967. Regional theater. **Produces 6 mainstage plays/year, plus monthly reading series and several festivals each year which contain both staged readings and workshop productions. plays/year.** Bay area residents can send complete ms or query with cover letter, résumé, 1-page synopsis, SASE, dialogue sample (10-20 pages). Those outside the Bay area can query or submit through an agent. Pays royalty or per performance fee. Responds in 6-8 months. Plays that are innovative in theme and/or craft, cutting-edge sociopolitical concerns, intelligent comedy. Full-length only, strong commitment to multicultural work.

TIPS Not interested in classics, conventional approaches and cannot produce large-cast (over 10) plays. Send query to Mark Routhier, literary manager.

MALTHOUSE THEATRE

113 Sturt St., Southbank VIC 3006, Australia. (61)(3)9685-5100. **Fax:** (61)(3)9685-5111. **E-mail:** admin@malthousetheatre.com.au. **Website:** www.malthousetheatre.com.au. **Contact:** Michael Kantor, artistic director. We are dedicated to contemporary Australian theatre. Writers should have had at least 1 professional production of their work. Proposals are called for on March 1, July 1, and October 1. Mail 1-page synopsis, brief author bio, and 10-page sample. Responds in 3 months if interested.

MANHATTAN THEATRE CLUB

311 W. 43rd St., 8th Floor, New York NY 10036. (212)399-3000. **Fax:** (212)399-4329. **E-mail:** questions@mtc-nyc.org. **Website:** www.mtc-nyc.org. **Contact:** Raphael Martin, literary manager. Artistic Director: Director of Artistic Development: Paige Evans. 1 Broadway and 2 Off-Broadway theatres, using professional actors. **Produces 7 plays/year.** *Solicited and agented submissions only.* No queries. Responds within 6 months. We present a wide range of new work, from this country and abroad, to a subscription audience. We want plays about contemporary concerns and people. All genres are welcome. MTC also maintains an extensive play development program.

MCCARTER THEATRE

91 University Place, Princeton NJ 08540. **E-mail:** literary@mccarter.org. **Website:** www.mccarter.org. **Contact:** Literary Manager. Artistic Director: Emily Mann. Produces professional productions for a 1,077-seat and 360-seat theaters. **Produces 5 plays/year;**

1 second stage play/year. plays/year. Agented submissions only. Pays negotiable royalty. Responds in 4-6 months. Full length plays, musicals, translations.

MELBOURNE THEATRE COMPANY

129 Ferrars St., Southbank VIC 3006, Australia. (61)(3)9684-4500. **Fax:** (61)(3)9696-2627. **E-mail:** info@mtc.com.au. **Website:** www.mtc.com.au. **Contact:** Aiden Fennessey, associate director. "MTC produces classic plays, modern revivals and the best new plays from Australia and overseas. Victorian work is given emphasis. MTC does not accept unsolicited manuscripts and it is our strict policy to return them unread. MTC does not produce work from previously unproduced Australian playwrights. New Australian plays generally come from three sources: by the commissioning of established writers; by the invitation to submit work to emerging writers with a track record and the potential to write for a mainstream subscription audience; and through a recommendation from an industry body, such as the Australian Script Centre or any of the major playwriting competitions." Responds in 3 months.

METROSTAGE

1201 N. Royal St., Alexandria VA 22314. (703)548-9044. **Fax:** (703)548-9089. **E-mail:** info@metrostage.org. **Website:** www.metrostage.org. **Contact:** Carolyn Griffin, producing artistic director. Estab. 1984. Professional productions for 130-seat theatre, general audience. **Produces 5-6 plays/year.** Agented submissions only. Pays royalty. Responds in 3 months. Contemporary themes, small cast (up to 6 actors), unit set.

TIPS "Plays should have *already* had readings and workshops before being sent for our review. Do not send plays that have never had a staged reading."

MILWAUKEE CHAMBER THEATRE

158 N. Broadway, Milwaukee Chamber Theatre, Milwaukee WI 53202. (414)276-8842. **Fax:** (414)277-4477. **E-mail:** mail@chamber-theatre.com. **Website:** www.chamber-theatre.com. **Contact:** Jaque Troy, Education Director/Literary Manager. Estab. 1975. Plays produced for adult and student audience. **Produces 5 plays/year.** Submit query and synopsis. Submissions accompanied by a SASE will be returned. Pays royalty. Responds in 3 months. Produces literary, thought-provoking, biographical plays. Plays require small-unit settings. No plays for a large cast.

NATIONAL PLAYWRIGHTS CONFERENCE

305 Great Neck Rd., Waterford CT 06385. (860)443-5378, x227. **E-mail:** litoffice@theoneill.org. **Website:** www.theoneill.org/summer-conferences/npc/. **Contact:** Lexy Leuszler, literary manager. Estab. 1965. The National Playwrights Conference is hosted at the O'Neill Theater Center and operates under an Equity LORT contract. Please check online at www.theoneill.org for details. **Produces 7-8 plays/year.** Pays stipend plus room, board, and transportation.

NEBRASKA THEATRE CARAVAN

6915 Cass St., Omaha NE 68132. **Fax:** (402)553-6288. **E-mail:** info@omahaplayhouse.com. **Website:** www.omahaplayhouse.com. **Contact:** Alena Furlong, development director. Artistic Director: Carl Beck. Estab. 1976. Nebraska Theatre Caravan is a touring company which produces professional productions in schools, arts centers, and small and large theaters for elementary, middle, high school and family audiences. **Produces 4-5 plays/year.** Negotiates production rights unless the work is commissioned by us. Submit query and synopsis. Pays $20-50/performance. Responds in 3 weeks. All genres are acceptable bearing in mind the student audiences. We are truly an ensemble and like to see that in our choice of shows; curriculum ties are very important for elementary and hich school shows; 75 minutes for middle/high school shows. No sexually explicit material.

TIPS We tour eight months of the year to a variety of locations. Flexibility is important as we work in both beautiful performing arts facilities and school multipurpose rooms.

THE NEW GROUP

410 W. 42nd St., New York NY 10036. (212)244-3380. **Fax:** (212)244-3438. **E-mail:** info@thenewgroup.org. **Website:** www.thenewgroup.org. **Contact:** Ian Morgan, associate artistic director. Artistic Director: Scott Elliott. Estab. 1991. Off-Broadway theater. **Produces 4 plays/year.** Submit 10-page sample, cover letter, résumé, synopsis, and SASE. No submissions that have already been produced in NYC. Include SASE for return of script. Pays royalty. Makes outright purchase. Responds in 9 months to submissions. We produce challenging, character-based scripts with a contemporary sensibility. Does not want to receive musicals, historical scripts or science fiction.

NEW JERSEY REPERTORY COMPANY

179 Broadway, Long Branch NJ 07740. (732)229-3166. **E-mail:** njrep@njrep.org. **Website:** www.njrep.org. **Contact:** Joel Stone, literary manager (literary@njrep.org). Artistic Director: SuzAnne Barabas. Estab. 1997. Professional productions year-round. Previously unproduced plays and musicals only. **Produces 6 plays/year and 20 script-in-hand readings. plays/year.** Rights negotiable. Submit full script via e-mail with synopsis, cast breakdown, playwright bio to literary@njrep.org. For musicals, include mp3 of songs. Hard copies not accepted. Cast of 4 or fewer only, previously unproduced. Response time 12-18 months. For 2018 festival submissions visit http://www.njrep.org/plays/circus.htm. Responds in 12-18 months if interested. Full-length plays with a cast size no more than 4. Unit set.

TIPS "Annual Theatre Brut Festival of Short Plays. Previously unproduced. 1-4 actors; simple set, no more than 10-15 minutes in length. Themes vary for festival."

NEW REPERTORY THEATRE

200 Dexter Ave., Waterton MA 02472. (617)923-7060. **Fax:** (617)923-7625. **E-mail:** artistic@newrep.org. **Website:** www.newrep.org. **Contact:** Rick Lombardo, producing artistic director. Estab. 1984. Professional theater, general audience. **Produces 5 plays/year.** Buys production and subsidiary rights. Query with synopsis and dialogue sample. Pays 5-10% royalty. Idea laden, all styles, full-length only. New musicals.

TIPS No sitcom-like comedies. Incorporating and exploring styles other than naturalism.

NEW STAGE THEATRE

1100 Carlisle, Jackson MS 39202. (601)948-3533. **Fax:** (601)948-3538. **E-mail:** mail@newstagetheatre.com. **Website:** www.newstagetheatre.com. Estab. 1965. Professional productions, 8 mainstage, 3 in our 'second space.' We play to an audience comprised of Jackson, the state of Mississippi and the Southeast. **Produces 8 plays/year.** Exclusive premiere contract upon acceptance of play for mainstage production. Submit query and synopsis. Pays 5-8% royalty. Pays $25-60/performance. Southern themes, contemporary issues, small casts (5-8), single set plays.

TIPS Eudora Welty New Play Series - winners received staged readings of new plays and monetary award from $100 - $1000. Submissions are accepted from June 1st through December 31st.

NEW THEATRE

4120 Laguna St., Coral Gables FL 33146. (305)443-5373. **Fax:** (305)443-1642. **E-mail:** tvodihn@new-theatre.org. **Website:** www.new-theatre.org. **Contact:** Tara Vodihn, literary manager. Estab. 1986. Professional productions. **Produces 7 plays/year.** Rights subject to negotiation. Submit query and synopsis. Payment negotiable. Responds in 3-6 months. Interested in full-length, non-realistic, moving, intelligent, language-driven plays with a healthy dose of humor. No musicals or large casts.

TIPS No kitchen sink realism. Send a simple query with synopsis. Be mindful of social issues.

NEW YORK THEATRE WORKSHOP

83 E. 4th St., New York NY 10003. **Fax:** (212)460-8996. **E-mail:** litern@nytw.org. **Website:** nytw.org. **Contact:** Literary Department. Artistic Director: James C. Nicola. Estab. 1979. "NYTW is renowned for producing intelligent and complex plays that expand the boundaries of theatrical form and in some new and compelling way address issues that are critical to our times. Plays are performed off-Broadway. Audience is New York theater-going audience and theater professionals." **Produces four to five full productions and approximately 50 readings/year. plays/year.** Prefer email submissions. Type "synopsis submission." If mailing: Query with cover letter, synopsis, 10-page dialogue sample, 2 letters of recommendation; SASE if requesting return of materials. Include tape/CD/video where appropriate. Responds in 6-10 months. Full-length plays, translations/adaptations, music theater pieces; proposals for performance projects. Socially relevant issues, innovative form, and language.

TIPS "No overtly commercial and conventional musicals or plays."

NORTHLIGHT THEATRE

9501 Skokie Blvd., Skokie IL 60077. (847)679-9501. **Fax:** (847)679-1879. **E-mail:** kleahey@northlight.org. **Website:** www.northlight.org. **Contact:** Kristin Leahey, Dramaturg. Artistic Director: BJ Jones; Lynn Baber, Artistic Administrator, at lbaber@northlight.org. Estab. 1975. "We are a professional, equity theater, LORT C. We have a subscription base of over 8,000 and have a significant number of single ticket buyers." **Produces 5 plays/year.** Buys production rights, plus royalty on future mountings. Query with 10-page dialogue sample, synopsis, resume/bio, and SASE/SASPC for response. Pays royalty. Responds in 3-4 months.

Full-length plays, translations, adaptations, musicals. Interested in plays of 'ideas'; plays that are passionate and/or hilarious; accessible plays that challenge, incite, and reflect the beliefs of our society/community. Generally looking for cast size of 6 or fewer, but there are exceptions made for the right play.

TIPS As a mainstream regional theater, we are unlikely to consider anything overtly experimental or absurdist. We seek good stories, vivid language, rich characters, and strong understandings of theatricality.

ODYSSEY THEATRE ENSEMBLE

2055 S. Sepulveda Blvd., Los Angeles CA 90025-5621. (310)477-2055. **Fax:** (310)444-0455. **Website:** www.odysseytheatre.com. **Contact:** Sally Essex-Lopresti, director of literary programs. Artistic Director: Ron Sossi. Estab. 1969. Plays performed in a 3-theater facility. All 3 theaters are Equity 99-seat theater plan. We have a subscription audience of 4,000 for a 9-play main season. **Produces 9 plays/year.** Buys negotiable rights. No unsolicited material. Query with resume, synopsis, 10 pages of sample dialogue, and cassette if musical. Does not return scripts without SASE. Pays 5-7% royalty. Responds in 2 weeks. Full-length plays only with either an innovative form and/or provocative subject matter. We desire highly theatrical pieces that explore possibilities of the live theater experience. We are not reading one-act plays or light situation comedies.

"Our purpose is the creation of new work, the revitalization and re-exploration of classical material, experimentation with current developments at the forefront of the "state of the art" in the international theatre world. Ultimately, the institution moves toward the creation of a larger International Experimental Theatre Center, facilitating the crosspolination of artists from different countries, cultures and disciplines, and the exposure of this collaborative work to the Southern California audience."

OMAHA THEATER CO./ROSE THEATER

2001 Farnam St., Omaha NE 68102. (402)345-9718. **E-mail:** jlarsonotc@msn.com. **Website:** www.rosetheater.org. **Contact:** James Larson, artistic director. "Our target audience is children, preschool through high school, and their parents." **Produces 6-10 plays/year.** Submit query and synopsis. Send SASE. Pays royalty. Responds in 9 months. Plays must be geared to children and parents (PG rating). Titles recognized by the general public have a stronger chance of being produced. Cast limit: 25 (8-10 adults). No adult scripts.

TIPS "Unproduced plays may be accepted only after a letter of inquiry (familiar titles only!)."

ONE ACT PLAY DEPOT

Box 335, Spiritwood Saskatchewan S0J 2M0, Canada. **E-mail:** submissions@oneactplays.net. **Website:** http://oneactplays.net. "Accepts unsolicited submissions only in February of each year." Submit complete script by mail or e-mail. : one-act plays. Does not want musicals or farces. Do not mail originals. Plays should run between 10 and 60 minutes.

O'NEILL MUSIC THEATER CONFERENCE

Eugene O'Neill Theater Center, 305 Great Neck Rd., Waterford CT 06385. (860)443-5378. **Fax:** (860)443-9653. **E-mail:** theaterlives@theoneill.org. **Website:** www.theoneill.org. **Contact:** Jill A. Anderson, general manager. Estab. 1964. "At The Music Theater Conference, creative artists are in residence with artistic staff and an equity company of actors/singers. Public and private readings, script in hand, piano only." An open submission process begins in the fall of each year and concludes in May. The conference takes place in July and August at the O'Neill Theater Center. Works are accepted based on their readiness to be performed, but when there is still enough significant work to be accomplished that a fully staged production would be premature. For guidelines and application deadlines, send SASE or see guidelines online. Pays stipend, room and board.

OREGON SHAKESPEARE FESTIVAL

15 S. Pioneer St., Ashland OR 97520. **Fax:** (541)482-0446. **Website:** www.osfashland.org. **Contact:** Director of Literary Development and Dramaturgy. Bill Rauch, artistic director. Estab. 1935. **Produces 11 plays/year.** OSF directly solicits playwright or agent, and does not accept unsolicited submissions.

PHILADELPHIA THEATRE CO.

230 S. Broad St., Suite 1105, Philadelphia PA 19102. (215)985-1400. **Fax:** (215)985-5800. **Website:** www.philadelphiatheatrecompany.org. **Contact:** Literary Office. Estab. 1974. "Under the direction of Sara Garonzik since 1982, Philadelphia Theatre Company has introduced more than 140 new plays and musicals to audiences in Philadelphia, New York and around the country, establishing the Company's national reputation for artistic quality, risk-taking and diverse

programming." **Produces 4 plays/year.** No e-mail submissions, letter of inquiry, summaries or excerpts please. Agented submissions only. Responds in 6-12 months. Philadelphia Theatre Company produces contemporary American plays and musicals.

"We have introduced countless award-winning premieres. Rather than revisit old standards, we are committed to finding the classics of the future."

TIPS Our work is challenging and risky—look to our history for guidance.

PIONEER DRAMA SERVICE, INC.

P.O. Box 4267, Englewood CO 80155-4267. (303)779-4035. **Fax:** (303)779-4315. **E-mail:** editors@pioneerdrama.com. **Website:** www.pioneerdrama.com. **Contact:** Brian Taylor, Acquisitions Editor. Plays are performed for audiences of all ages. Playwrights paid 50% royalty (10% sales) split when there are multiple authors/composers. Publishes plays that are performed by schools, colleges, community theaters, recreation programs, churches, and professional children's theaters for audiences of all ages. For musicals, query with character breakdown, synopsis and set description or submit full ms and CD of music. Include SASE. Retains all rights. All submissions automatically entered in Shubert Fendrich Memorial Playwriting Contest. SASE for guidelines. Retains all rights. Responds in 6 months. "We seek full length children's musicals, high school musicals, and one-act children's musicals to be performed by children, secondary school students, and/or adults. We want musicals that are easy to perform, simple sets, many female roles, and very few solos. Must be appropriate for educational market. We are not interested in profanity, themes with exclusively adult interest, sex, drinking, smoking, etc."

TIPS "Check out our website to see what we carry and if your material would be appropriate for our market. Make sure to include proof of productions and a SASE if you want your material returned."

PITTSBURGH PUBLIC THEATER

621 Penn Ave., Pittsburgh PA 15222. (412)316-8200. **Fax:** (412)316-8216. **Website:** www.ppt.org. **Contact:** Dramaturg. Artistic Director: Ted Pappas. Estab. 1975. O'Reilly Theater, 650 seats, thrust seating. **Produces 7 plays/year.** Submit full script through agent, or query with synopsis, cover letter, 10-page dialogue sample, and SASE. Responds in 4 months. Full-length plays, adaptations and musicals.

"The mission of Pittsburgh Public Theater is to provide artistically diverse theatrical experiences of the highest quality."

PLAYSCRIPTS, INC.

450 7th Ave., Suite 809, New York NY 10023. Phone/**Fax:** (866)639-7529. **E-mail:** submissions@playscripts.com. **Website:** www.playscripts.com. Estab. 1998. Audience is professional, community, college, high school, middle school, and children's theaters worldwide. Contracts for exclusive publication and performance licensing rights. See website for complete submission guidelines. "Materials accompanied by SASE will be returned; however, submissions sent through our website at www.playscripts.com/submit are strongly preferred." Pays negotiated book and production royalties. Responds in 3-6 months. "We are open to a wide diversity of writing styles and content. Unsolicited musicals are not accepted."

TIPS "Playscripts, Inc. is a play publishing company dedicated to new work by established and emerging playwrights. We provide all of the same licensing and book production services as a traditional play publisher, along with unique promotional features that maximize the exposure of each dramatic work. Be sure to view our guidelines before submitting."

THE PLAYWRIGHTS' CENTER'S PLAYLABS

2301 Franklin Ave. E., Minneapolis MN 55406. (612)332-7481. **Fax:** (612)332-6037. **E-mail:** info@pwcenter.org. **Website:** www.pwcenter.org. Producing Artistic Director: Polly K. Carl. Estab. 1971. PlayLabs is a 2-week developmental workshop for new plays. The program is held in Minneapolis and is open by script competition. Up to 5 new plays are given reading performances and after the festival, a script sample and contact link are posted on the Center's website. Announcements of playwrights by May 1. Playwrights receive honoraria, travel expenses, room and board. We are interested in playwrights with ambitions for a sustained career in theater, and scripts that could benefit from development involving professional dramaturgs, directors, and actors. US citizens or permanent residents only. Participants must attend entire festival. Submission deadline in October; see website for application and exact deadline. No previously produced materials.

PLAYWRIGHTS HORIZONS

416 W. 42nd St., New York NY 10036. (212)564-1235. **Fax:** (212)594-0296. **E-mail:** lit@phnyc.org. **Website:** www.playwrightshorizons.org. **Contact:** Sarah Lunnie, literary manager. Estab. 1971. Plays performed off-Broadway for a literate, urban, subscription audience. **Produces 6 plays/year.** Negotiates for future rights. Submit complete ms with author bio and resume; include CD for musicals. Pays royalty. Makes outright purchase. Responds in 6-8 months. "We are looking for new, full-length plays and musicals by American authors."

TIPS "We do not accept one-acts, one-person shows, translations, children's shows, screenplays, or works by non-US writers. We dislike synopses because we accept unsolicited manuscripts. We look for plays with a strong sense of language and a clear dramatic action that truly use the resources of the theater."

PLAYWRIGHTS' PLATFORM

398 Columbus Ave., #604, Boston MA 02116. **Website:** www.playwrightsplatform.org. **Contact:** Regina Eliot-Ramsey, president. Estab. 1972. "Our website contains all information regarding The Platform. The Platform provides dues paying members with the opportunity to read their plays before an audience. Meetings are held at Rosen Auditorium, Brennan Library, Lasell College, Auburndale, MA 02466. Scripts should not be mailed. Readings must be requested through the calendar coordinator. Only dues paying members can submit scripts and are allowed to participate in Platform productions. The Platform produces a short play festival each year in June, held at the Boston Playwrights Theatre, Boston, MA. Only dues paying members can participate. Short one acts, and scenes from full-length plays can be read throughout the calendar year. The festival only produces plays with running times of 20 minutes or less. Members come from the northeast region and are not limited to Massachusetts. There are no restrictions on content." **Produces approximately 50 readings/year plays/year.** Submit script and SASE (or e-mail or hand deliver). Responds in 2 months. "Any types of plays. We will not accept scripts we think are sexist or racist. Massachusetts residents only. There are no restrictions on length or number of characters, but it's more difficult to schedule full-length pieces."

We do not want unsolicited scripts being mailed to our address.

PLAYWRIGHTS THEATRE OF NEW JERSEY

P.O. Box 1295, Madison NJ 07940-1295. (973)514-1787. **Fax:** (973)514-2060. **Website:** www.ptnj.org. **Contact:** Alysia Souder, director of program development. Artistic Director: John Pietrowski. Estab. 1986. We operate under a Small Professional Theatre Contract (SPT), a development theatre contract with Actors Equity Association. Readings are held under a staged reading code. **Produces 3 plays/year.** For productions we ask the playwright to sign an agreement that gives us exclusive rights to the play for the production period and for 30 days following. After the 30 days we give the rights back with no strings attached, except for commercial productions. We ask that our developmental work be acknowledged in any other professional productions. Makes outright purchase of 750. Responds in 1 year. Any style or length; full length, one acts, musicals.

TIPS We are looking for American plays in the early stages of development—plays of substance, passion, and light (comedies and dramas) that raise challenging questions about ourselves and our communities. We prefer plays *that can work only on the stage* in the most theatrical way possible—plays that are not necessarily 'straight-on' realistic, but rather ones that use imagery, metaphor, poetry and musicality in new and interesting ways. Plays can go through a 3-step development process: A roundtable, a concert reading, and then a workshop production.

PORTLAND STAGE CO.

P.O. Box 1458, Portland ME 04104. (207)774-1043. **Fax:** (207)774-0576. **E-mail:** literary@portlandstage.org. **Website:** www.portlandstage.org. **Contact:** Todd Brian Backus, literary manager. Artistic Director: Anita Stewart. Estab. 1974. Portland Stage, Maine's largest fully professional, non-profit theater, is committed to providing the finest productions for audiences in a broad region of Northern New England. Founded in 1974 as the Profile Theater, Portland Stage currently produces: A season of seven Mainstage shows that play to over 50,000 people annually. New and experimental work in our 75-seat Studio Theater. New Works Programs: From Away, Little Festival of the Unexpected, and the Clauder Competition. Education Programs: Play Me a Story, Classes, Vacation Camps, Summer Theater Camps, PlayNotes, Student Matinees, PLAY in Schools, Directors Lab, and Classroom Workshops. Affiliate Artists Events: Longfellow's Shorts and invited readings. **Produces 7 plays/year.** Buys 3- or 4-week run in Maine. The two primary ways playwrights can submit new plays for consideration at Portland Stage are through the Little Festival of the Unexpected (Portland Stage's annual new play development festival, open to all playwrights) and Clauder Competition (for New England-based Playwrights only). Specific submission guidelines for these opportunities can be found at portlandstage.org/script-submissions. In general: Literary Agents may submit complete full-length scripts on behalf of their clients. Playwrights from the U.S. or abroad who do not have agents may submit 10-page dialogue samples of new, full-length plays for consideration in Little Festivals. New England-based Playwrights may submit complete full-length scripts to the Clauder Competition. (The next round of the Clauder Competition will open for submissions in summer 2020.). Pays royalty for productions, Pays Stipend for Little Festival of the Unexpected, Pays Award for Clauder Competition. Little Festival of the Unexpected - Responds in 3-6 months from submissions opening. Clauder Competition - Responds in 18 months from submissions opening. Developmental Staged Readings: Little Festival of the Unexpected.

TIPS "Work developed in Little Festival generally will be more strongly considered for future production."

PRINCE MUSIC THEATER

1412 Chestnut St., Philadelphia PA 19102. **E-mail:** info@princemusictheater.org. **Website:** www.princemusictheater.org. Estab. 1984. "Professional musical productions. Drawing upon operatic and popular traditions as well as European, African, Asian, and South American forms, new work, and new voices take center stage." **Produces 4 musicals/year. plays/year.** Send synopsis and sample audio tape with no more than 4 songs. Pays royalty. Responds in 6 months. Song-driven music theater, varied musical styles. Nine-member orchestra, 10-14 cast, 36x60 stage.

TIPS "Innovative topics and use of media, music, technology a plus. Sees trends of arts in technology (interactive theater, virtual reality, sound design); works are shorter in length (1-1 and 1/2 hours with no intermissions or 2 hours with intermission)."

PRINCETON REP COMPANY

44 Nassau St., Suite 350, Princeton NJ 08542. **E-mail:** prcreprap@aol.com. **Website:** www.princetonrep.org. **Contact:** New Play Submissions. Estab. 1984. Plays are performed in site-specific venues, outdoor amphitheatres, and indoor theatres with approximately 199 seats. Princeton Rep Company works under Actors' Equity contracts, and its directors are members of the SSDC. Rights are negotiated on a play-by-play basis. Query with synopsis, SASE, résumé, and 10 pages of sample dialogue. Submissions accompanied by a SASE will be returned. Payment negotiated on a play-by-play basis. Responds in up to 2 years. Stories that investigate the lives of middle and working class people. Love stories of the rich, famous, and fatuous. If the play demands a cast of thousands, please don't waste your time and postage. No drama or comedy set in a prep school or ivy league college.

THE PUBLIC THEATER

425 Lafayette St., New York NY 10003. (212)539-8500. **Website:** www.publictheater.org. **Contact:** Literary Department. Artistic Director: Oskar Eustis. Estab. 1964. Professional productions. **Produces 6 plays/year.** Query with synopsis,10-page sample, letter of inquiry, cassette with 3-5 songs for musicals/operas. Responds in 3 months. Full-length plays, translations, adapatations, musicals, operas, and solo pieces. All genres, no one-acts.

⊘ PULSE ENSEMBLE THEATRE

248 W. 35th St., 15th Floor, New York NY 10001. (212)695-1596. **Fax:** (212)695-1596. **E-mail:** theatre@pulseensembletheatre.org. **Website:** www.pulseensembletheatre.org. **Contact:** Brian Richardson. Estab. 1989. **Produces 3 plays/year.** Buys variable rights. No unsolicited submissions. Only accepts new material through the Playwright's Lab. Include SASE for return of submission. Usually pays 2% of gross. meaningful theater. No production limitations.

THE PURPLE ROSE THEATRE CO.

137 Park St., Chelsea MI 48118. (734)433-7782. **Fax:** (734)475-0802. **Website:** www.purplerosetheatre.org. **Contact:** Guy Sanville, artistic director. Artistic Director: Guy Sanville. Estab. 1990. "PRTC is a regional theater with an S.P.T. equity contract which produces plays intended for Midwest/Middle American audience. It is dedicated to creating opportunities for Midwest theatre professionals." **Produces 4 plays/year.** Query with synopsis, character breakdown, and 10-page dialogue sample. Pays 5-10% royalty. Responds in 9 months. Modern, topical full length, 75-120 minutes. Prefers scripts that use comedy to deal with

serious subjects. 8 cast maximum. No fly space, unit set preferable. Intimate 168 seat 3/4 thrust house.

RED LADDER THEATRE CO.

3 St. Peter's Buildings, York St., Leeds LS9 1AJ, United Kingdom. (44)(113)245-5311. **E-mail:** rod@redladder.co.uk. **Website:** www.redladder.co.uk. **Contact:** Rod Dixon, artistic director. Estab. 1969. Our work tours nationally to young people, aged 13-25, in youth clubs, community venues and small scale theatres. **Produces 2 plays/year.** Submit query and synopsis. Offers ITC/Equity writers contract. Responds in 6 months. One hour in length for cast size no bigger than 5. Work that connects with a youth audience that both challenges them and offers them new insights. We consider a range of styles and are seeking originality. Small scale touring. Does not want to commission single issue drama. The uses of new technologies in production (DVD, video projection). Young audiences are sophisticated.

TIPS Please do not submit full length plays. Get in touch with us first. Tell us about yourself and why you would like to write for Red Ladder. We like to hear about ideas you may have in the first instance.

RESOURCE PUBLICATIONS

160 E. Virginia St., Suite 170, San Jose CA 95112-5176. (408)286-8505. **Fax:** (408)287-8748. **E-mail:** editor@rpinet.com. **Website:** www.resourcepublications.com. Estab. 1973. Audience includes laity and ordained seeking resources (books/periodicals/software) in Christian ministry, worship, faith formation, education, and counseling (primarily Roman Catholic, but not all). Submit query and synopsis via e-mail. Responds in 3 months. : materials for those in pastoral ministry, faith formation, youth ministry, and parish administration. No fiction, children's books, or music.

AWARD WINNING PUB ROUND HOUSE THEATRE

P.O. Box 30688, Bethesda MD 20824. (240)644-1099. **Fax:** (240)644-1090. **E-mail:** roundhouse@roundhousetheatre.org. **Website:** www.roundhousetheatre.org. **Contact:** Danisha Crosby, associate producer. Producing Artistic Director: Blake Robison. "Professional AEA Theatre that is recognized nationally as a center for the development of literary works for the stage. Our critically-acclaimed Literary Works Project features new adaptations of contemporary and classical novels, re-interpreted through a theatrical prism for today's audiences. We give these stories a fresh voice, a bold visual presence, and a new relevance in our ever-changing society. The project has garnered 10 Helen Hayes Award nominations and strong notices in the regional and national press." **Produces 5-7 plays/year.** Query with synopsis; no unsolicited scripts accepted. Pays negotiated percentage for productions. Responds in 2-12 months.

SALTWORKS THEATRE CO.

569 N. Neville St., Pittsburgh PA 15213. (412)621-6150. **Fax:** (412)621-6010. **E-mail:** nalrutz@saltworks.org. **Website:** www.saltworks.org. **Contact:** Norma Alrutz, executive director. Estab. 1981. **Produces 8-10 plays/year.** Obtains regional performance rights for educational grants. Submit query and synopsis. Pays $25/performance. Responds in 2 months. Wants plays for children, youth, and families that address social issues like violence prevention, sexual responsibility, peer pressures, tobacco use, bullying, racial issues/diversity, drug and alcohol abuse (grades 1-12). Limited to 5 member cast, 2 men/2 women/1 either.

TIPS Check website for current play contest rules and deadlines.

SEATTLE REPERTORY THEATRE

P.O. Box 900923, Seattle WA 98109. **E-mail:** bradena@seattlerep.org. **Website:** www.seattlerep.org. **Contact:** Braden Abraham, associate artistic director. Artistic Director: Jerry Manning. Estab. 1963. **Produces 8 plays/year.** Buys percentage of future royalties. Send query, resume, synopsis and 10 sample pages. Pays royalty. Responds in 6 months. "The Seattle Repertory Theatre produces eclectic programming. We welcome a wide variety of writing."

SECOND STAGE THEATRE

305 W. 43rd St., New York NY 10036. (212)246-4422. **Fax:** (212)399-4115. **E-mail:** cburney@2st.com. **Website:** www.2st.com. **Contact:** Christopher Burney, associate artistic director. Estab. 1979. "Second Stage Theatre gives new life to contemporary American plays through 'second stagings'; provides emerging authors with their Off-Broadway debuts; and produces world premieres by America's most respected playwrights. Adult and teen audiences." **Produces 6 plays/year.** Query with synopsis and 10-page writing sample or agented submission. Payment varies. Responds in 6 months. "We need socio-political plays, comedies, musicals, dramas—full lengths for full production."

TIPS "Submit through agent; have strong references; always submit the best of your material in small quantities: 5 outstanding songs are better than 10 mediocre ones. No biographical or historical dramas, or plays in verse. Writers are realizing that audiences can be entertained while being moved. Patience is a virtue but persistence is appreciated."

SHAW FESTIVAL THEATRE

P.O. Box 774, Niagara-on-the-Lake ON L0S 1J0, Canada. (905)468-2153. **Fax:** (905)468-7140. **Website:** www.shawfest.com. **Contact:** Jackie Maxwell, artistic director. Estab. 1962. Professional theater company operating 3 theaters (Festival: 869 seats; Court House: 327 seats; Royal George: 328 seats). Shaw Festival presents the work of George Bernard Shaw and his contemporaries written during his lifetime (1856-1950) and in 2000 expanded the mandate to include contemporary works written about the period of his lifetime. **Produces 12 plays/year.** We prefer to hold rights for Canada and northeastern US, also potential to tour. Query with SASE or SAE and IRC's, depending on country of origin. Pays 5-10% royalty. We operate an acting ensemble of up to 75 actors; and we have sophisticated production facilities. During the summer season (April-November) the Academy of the Shaw Festival organizes workshops of new plays commissioned for the company.

SOUTH COAST REPERTORY

P.O. Box 2197, Costa Mesa CA 92628-2197. (714)708-5500. **Fax:** (714)545-0391. **Website:** www.scr.org. **Contact:** Kelly Miller, Literary Manager. Artistic Directors: Martin Benson and David Emmes. Estab. 1964. Professional nonprofit theater; a member of LORT and TCG. "We operate in our own facility which houses the 507-seat Segerstrom stage and 336-seat Julianne Argyros stage. We have a combined subscription audience of 18,000. We commit ourselves to exploring the most urgent human and social issues of our time, and to merging literature, design and performance in ways that test the bounds of theatre's artistic possibilities." **Produces 14 plays/year.** Acquires negotiable rights. Query with synopsis and 10 sample pages of dialogue, and full list of characters. Pays royalty. Responds in 1-2 months on queries; 6-9 months on full scripts. "We produce full-length contemporary plays, as well as theatre for young audiences, scripts geared toward a 4th grade target audience with a running time of approximately 65 minutes. We prefer plays that address contemporary concerns and are dramaturgically innovative. A play whose cast is larger than 15-20 will need to be extremely compelling, and its cast size must be justifiable."

TIPS "We don't look for a writer to write for us—he or she should write for him or herself. We look for honesty and a fresh voice. We're not likely to be interested in writers who are mindful of any trends. Originality and craftsmanship are the most important qualities we look for."

SOUTHERN APPALACHIAN REPERTORY THEATRE (SART)

P.O. Box 1720, Mars Hill NC 28754. (828)689-1384. **E-mail:** sart@mhc.edu. **Contact:** Bill Gregg, producing artistic director; LoriLynn Mullett, business manager. Estab. 1975. Since 1975, the Southern Appalachian Repertory Theatre has produced over 50 world premieres in the 166-seat Owen Theater on the Mars Hill College campus. SART is a professional summer theatre company whose audiences range from students to senior citizens. SART also conducts an annual playwrights' conference called ScriptFEST in which 4-5 playwrights are invited for a weekend of public readings of their new scripts. The conference is held in the fall of each year. Submissions must be postmarked between August 1 and September 30. If a script read at the conference is selected for production, it will be given a fully-staged production in an upcoming SART summer season. Playwrights receive honorarium and housing. **Produces 5-6 plays/year.** "No film or television scripts, translations, or adaptations. Please send 2 hard copies of the script on white paper, standard 3-hole punched, or, better yet, in a binder. Must be full-length plays and musicals, synopsis, and a recording of at least 4 songs (for musicals). No one-acts or children's plays. Include name and contact information only on a separate cover sheet. New plays are defined as those that have not been published and have not received a fully-staged professional production. Workshops and other readings do not constitute a fully-staged production. Check website for detailed submission guidelines."

STAGE LEFT THEATRE

3408 N. Sheffield, Chicago IL 60657. (773)883-8830. **E-mail:** scripts@stagelefttheatre.com. **Website:** www.stagelefttheatre.com. **Contact:** Zev Valancy, literary manager. Estab. 1982. "Professional productions for all audiences." **Produces 2-3 mainstage productions**

and 1 new-play workshop festival per season. "There are also 2 playwright residencies per season, with applications accepted winter/spring. Please see website for details." plays/year. Submit script through an agent or query with cover letter, 10-page excerpt, 1-page synopsis, SASE, supporting material, and résumé. E-mail submissions preferred. Responds in 3 months. "any length, any genre, any style that fits the Stage Left mission—to produce plays that raise debate on political and social issues. We do have an emphasis on new work."

Ⓐ STAMFORD THEATRE WORKS

307 Atlantic St., Stamford CT 06901. (203)359-4414. **Fax:** (203)356-1846. **E-mail:** stwct@aol.com. **Website:** www.stamfordtheatreworks.org. **Contact:** Steve Karp, producing director. Estab. 1988. Professional productions for an adult audience. **Produces 4-6 plays/year.** *Agented submissions* or queries with a professional recommendation. Include SASE for return of submission. Pays 5-8% royalty. Responds in 3 months. Plays of social relevance; contemporary work. Limited to unit sets; maximum cast of about 8.

Ⓐ STEPPENWOLF THEATRE CO.

758 W. North Ave., 4th Floor, Chicago IL 60610. (312)335-1888. **Fax:** (312)335-0808. **Website:** www.steppenwolf.org. **Contact:** Joy Meads, literary manager. Artistic Director: Martha Lavey. Estab. 1976. "Steppenwolf Theatre Company's mission is to advance the vitality and diversity of American theater by nurturing artists, encouraging repeatable creative relationships and contributing new works to the national canon. 500-, 250- and 100-seat performance venues. Many plays produced at Steppenwolf have gone to Broadway. We currently have 20,000 savvy subscribers." **Produces 9 plays/year.** Buys commercial, film, television, and production rights. Agented submissions only with full scripts. Others please check our website for submission guidelines. Unrepresented writers may send a 10-page sample along with cover letter, bio, and synopsis. Pays 5% royalty. Responds in 6-8 months. Actor-driven works are crucial to us, plays that explore the human condition in our time. We max at around 10 characters.

TIPS No musicals, one-person shows, or romantic/light comedies. Plays get produced at STC based on ensemble member interest.

Ⓐ STUDIO ARENA THEATRE

710 Main St., Buffalo NY 14202. (716)856-8025. **E-mail:** jblaha@studioarena.com. **Website:** www.studioarena.org. **Contact:** Jana Blaha, executive assistant. Estab. 1965. Professional productions. **Produces 6-8 plays/year.** Agented submissions only. Full-length plays. No fly space.

TIPS Do not fax or send submissions via the Internet. Submissions should appeal to a diverse audience. We do not generally produce musicals. Please send a character breakdown and 1-page synopsis for a faster reply.

SUPERIOR PLAYS

200 Thrasher Way, Salisbury MD 21804-1987. (410)742-7168. **E-mail:** editor@superiorplays.com. **Website:** www.superiorplays.com. **Contact:** Gerard DiCairano, publisher/editor. Estab. 2013. "We aim to publish plays which have a little more 'meat' and substance to them than those found in many play catalogs. We like to think that our characters are more complex, that our plots are more interesting and unpredictable, and that our situations and conflicts give audiences something to ponder as they follow the action." Target audience: community theater, colleges, and churches/synagogues. **12 plays/year.** Query via e-mail. Guidelines available online. Writers receive 50% royalties, per performance, and up to 30% on scripts. Responds in 3 business days. one-act and full-length comedies and dramas.

TEATRO VISIÓN

1700 Alum Rock Ave., Suite 265, San José CA 95116. (408)272-9926. **Fax:** (408)928-5589. **E-mail:** elisamarina@teatrovision.org. **Website:** www.teatrovision.org. **Contact:** Elisa Marina Alvarado, artistic director. Estab. 1984. Professional productions for a Latino population. **Produces 3 plays/year.** Query with synopsis or submit complete ms. Responds in 6 months. We produce plays by Latino playwrights—plays that highlight the Chicano/Latino experience.

THE TEN-MINUTE MUSICALS PROJECT

P.O. Box 461194, West Hollywood CA 90046. **E-mail:** info@tenminutemusicals.org. **Website:** www.tenminutemusicals.org. **Contact:** Michael Koppy, producer. Estab. 1987. "Plays performed in Equity regional theaters in the US and Canada. Deadline August 31; notification by November 30." **Produces 1-10 plays/year.** Buys first performance rights. Complete guidelines and information at website. Pays $250 royalty advance upon selection, against equal share of performance royalties when produced. Looking for complete short stage musicals lasting 8-15 minutes. Limit cast to 9. "No parodies—original music only."

All pieces are new musicals. Submit complete ms, score, and CD or DVD of songs. Include SASE. Responds in 3 months.

TIPS "Start with a solid story—either an adaptation or an original idea—but with a solid beginning, middle and end (probably with a plot twist at the climax). We caution that it will surely take much time and effort to create a quality work. (Occasionally a clearly talented and capable writer and composer seem to have almost 'dashed' something off, under the misconception that inspiration can carry the day in this format. Works selected in previous rounds all clearly evince that considerable deliberation and craft were invested.) We're seeking short contemporary musical theater material, in the style of what might be found on Broadway, Off-Broadway or the West End. Think of shows like *Candide* or *Little Shop of Horrors*, pop operas like *Sweeney Todd* or *Chess*, or chamber musicals like *Once on this Island* or *Falsettos*. (Even small accessible operas like *The Telephone* or *Trouble in Tahiti* are possible models.) All have solid plots, and all rely on sung material to advance them. Of primary importance is to start with a strong story, even if it means postponing work on music and lyrics until the dramatic foundation is complete."

THEATER AT LIME KILN

P.O. Box 1244, Lexington VA 24450. **Website:** www.theateratlimekiln.com. Estab. 1984. Outdoor summer theater (May through October) and indoor space (October through May, 144 seats). **Produces 3 (1 new) plays/year.** Buys performance rights. Submit query and synopsis. Include SASE for return of submitted materials. Pays $25-75/performance. Responds in 3 months. Plays that explore the history and heritage of the Appalachian region. Minimum set required.

TIPS Searching for plays that can be performed in outdoor space. Prefer plays that explore the cultural and/or history of the Appalichian region.

THEATER BY THE BLIND

306 W. 18th St., New York NY 10011. (212)243-4337. **Fax:** (212)243-4337. **E-mail:** gar@nyc.rr.com. **Website:** www.tbtb.org. **Contact:** Ike Schambelan, artistic director. Estab. 1979. Off Broadway, Theater Row, general audiences, seniors, students, disabled. If play transfers, we'd like a piece. **Produces 2 plays/year.** Submit complete script. Pays $1,000-1,500/production. Responds in 3 months. Genres about blindness.

THEATRE BUILDING CHICAGO

1225 W. Belmont Ave., Chicago IL 60657. (773)929-7367 ext. 229. **Fax:** (773)327-1404. **E-mail:** allan@theatrebuildingchicago.org. **Website:** www.theatrebuildingchicago.org. **Contact:** Allan Chambers, artistic director. "Develops and produces readings of new musicals and Stages festival of new music, some works developed in our writers' workshop. Some scripts produced are unagented submissions. Developmental readings and workshops performed in 3 small off-Loop theaters are seating 148 for a general theater audience, urban/suburban mix." Submit synopsis, sample scene, CD or cassette tape and piano/vocal score of three songs, and author bios along with Stages Festival application, available on our website. Responds in 3 months. "Musicals *only*. We're interested in all forms of musical theater including more innovative styles. Our production capabilities are limited by the lack of space, but we're very creative and authors should submit anyway. The smaller the cast, the better. We are especially interested in scripts using a younger (35 and under) ensemble of actors. We mostly look for authors who are interested in developing their scripts through workshops, readings and production. We rarely work on one-man shows or 'single author' pieces."

TIPS "We would like to see the musical theater articulating something about the world around us, as well as diverting an audience's attention from that world. Offers Script Consultancy—A new program designed to assist authors and composers in developing new musicals through private feedback sessions with professional dramaturgs and musical directors. For further info contact Allan Chambers, (773)929-7367, ext. 229."

THEATRE IV

114 W. Broad St., Richmond VA 23220. (804)783-1688. **Fax:** (804)775-2325. **E-mail:** j.serresseque@theatreivrichmond.org. **Website:** www.theatreiv.org. **Contact:** Janine Serresseque. Estab. 1975. National tour of plays for young audiences—maximum cast of 5, maximum length of an hour. Mainstage plays for young audiences in 600 or 350 seat venues. **Produces approximately 20 plays/year.** Buys standard production rights. Submit query and synopsis. Include SASE for return of submission. Payment varies. Responds

in 1 month. Touring and mainstage plays for young audiences. Touring—maximum cast of 5, length of 60 minutes.

THEATRE THREE

P.O. Box 512, 412 Main St., Port Jefferson NY 11777-0512. (631)928-9202. **Fax:** (631)928-9120. **Website:** www.theatrethree.com. **Contact:** Jeffrey Sanzel, artistic director. Estab. 1969. "We produce an Annual Festival of One-Act Plays on our Second Stage. Deadline for submission is September 30. Send SASE for festival guidelines or visit website." We ask for exclusive rights up to and through the festival. Include SASE. No email submissions. Guidelines online. Pays $75 for the run of the festival. Responds in 6 months. One-act plays. Maximum length: 40 minutes. Any style, topic, etc. We require simple, suggested sets and a maximum cast of 6. No adaptations, musicals or children's works.

TIPS "Too many plays are monologue-dominant. Please—reveal your characters through action and dialogue."

Ⓐ THEATRE THREE

2800 Routh St., #168, Dallas TX 75201. (214)871-3300. **Fax:** (214)871-3139. **E-mail:** admin@theatre3dallas.com. **Website:** theater3dallas.com. **Contact:** Jac Alder, executive producer-director. Estab. 1961. Professional regional theatre, in-the-round. Audience is college age to senior citizens. **Produces 7 plays/year.** Query with synopsis; agented submissions only. Contractual agreements vary. Responds in 6 months. Musicals, dramas, comedies, bills of related one-acts. Modest production requirement; prefer casts no larger than 10. Theatre Three also produces in a studio theatre (its former rehearsal hall) called Theatre Too. The space is variously configured according to demands of the show. Shows in that space include cabaret type revues, experimental work, dramas with small casts and staged readings or concert versions of musicals.

TIPS No parodies or political commentary/comedy. Most produced playwrights at Theatre Three (to show taste of producer) are Moliere, Sondheim, Ayckbourne, Miller, Stoppard, Durang (moralists and irony-masters).

THEATRE WEST

3333 Cahuenga Blvd. W., Hollywood CA 90068-1365. (323)851-4839. **Fax:** (323)851-5286. **E-mail:** theatrewest@theatrewest.org. **Website:** www.theatrewest.org. **Contact:** Chris DiGiovanni and Doug Haverty, moderators of the Writers Workshop. Estab. 1962. "We operate a 168 seat theater under a letter of agreement with Actors Equity, including a TYA contract for young audiences. Audiences are primarily young urban professionals. Residence in Southern California is vital as it's a weekly workshop." Contracts a percentage of writer's share to other media if produced on MainStage by Theatre West. Submit script, résumé and letter requesting membership. Pays royalty based on gross box office. Responds in 4 months. Full-length plays only, no one-acts. Uses minimalistic scenery, no fly space.

TIPS "Theatre West is a dues-paying membership company. Only members can submit plays for production. So you must first seek membership to the Writers Workshop."

THEATREWORKS

P.O. Box 50458, Palo Alto CA 94303. (650)463-1950. **Fax:** (650)463-1963. **E-mail:** kent@theatreworks.org. **Website:** www.theatreworks.org. **Contact:** Kent Nicholson, new works director. Estab. 1970. Specializes in development of new musicals. Plays are professional productions intended for an adult audience. **Produces 8 plays/year.** Buys performance rights. Submit synopsis, 10 pages of sample dialogue, and SASE. Include SASE for return of submission. Payment varies per contract. Responds in 6-8 months. TheatreWorks has a high standard for excellence. We prefer well-written, well-constructed plays that celebrate the human spirit through innovative productions and programs inspired by our exceptionally diverse community. There is no limit on the number of characters, and we favor plays with multi-ethnic casting possibilities. We are a LORT C company. Plays are negotiated per playwright. Does not want one-acts, plays with togas. We are particularly interested in plays with musical elements.

TIPS Guidelines are online—check out our website for Submission Checklist Request and the New Works Program under New Works.

⊘ THEATREWORKS/USA

151 W. 26th St., 7th Floor, New York NY 10001. (212)647-1100. **Fax:** (212)924-5377. **Website:** www.twusa.org. Estab. 1961. "The theatre is an arena for previously unproduced plays, and works towards their future development. Professional equity productions for young audiences. Weekend series at

Equitable Towers, NYC. Also, national and regional tours of each show." **Produces 3-4 plays/year.** Obtains performing rights. Submit query and synopsis only. *No unsolicited submissions.* Pays 6% royalty. Responds in 1 month.

UNICORN THEATRE

3828 Main St., Kansas City MO 64111. (816)531-7529. **Fax:** (816)531-0421. **Website:** www.unicorntheatre.org. **Contact:** Herman Wilson, literary assistant. Producing Artistic Director: Cynthia Levin. "We are a professional Equity Theatre. Typically, we produce plays dealing with contemporary issues." **Produces 6-8 plays/year.** Send complete script (to Herman Wilson) with brief synopsis, cover letter, bio, character breakdown. Send #10 SASE for results. Does not return scripts. Responds in 4-8 months. Prefers contemporary (post-1950) scripts. Does not accept musicals, one-acts, or historical plays.

URBAN STAGES

555 8th Avenue #1800, New York NY 10018. (212)421-1380. **Fax:** (212)421-1387. **E-mail:** lschmiedel@urbanstages.org. **Website:** www.urbanstages.org. **Contact:** Lauren Schmiedel, managing director. Estab. 1986. Professional productions off Broadway—throughout the year. General audience. **Produces 2-4 plays/year.** If produced, option for 1 year. Submit complete script year-round, no submission fee. Enter Emerging Playwright Award competition. Prize is $500, plus NYC production. Pays royalty. Responds in 4 months. Full-length; generally 1 set or styled playing dual. Good imaginative, creative writing. Cast limited to 3-6.

TIPS "We tend to reject 'living-room' plays. We look for imaginative settings. Be creative and interesting. No one acts. No e-mail submissions, scripts are not returned."

WALNUT STREET THEATRE

Ninth and Walnut Streets, Philadelphia PA 19107. (215)574-3550. **Fax:** (215)574-3598. **Contact:** Literary Office. Producing Artistic Director: Bernard Havard. Estab. 1809. Our plays are performed in our own space. WST has 3 theaters—a proscenium (mainstage), 1,052 seats; and 2 studios, 79-99 seats. We have a subscription audience—the largest in the nation. **Produces 10 plays/year.** Rights negotiated per project. If you have written a play or musical that you feel is appropriate for the Walnut Street Theatre's Mainstage or Independence Studio on 3, please send the following: 1-2 page synopsis, 5-10 page excerpt from the scrip, a character breakdown, bios for the playwright, composer, lyricist, and any other artistic collaborators, Demo CD with tracks clearly labeled (musicals only). Include SASE for return of materials. Pays negotiable royalty or makes outright purchase. Responds in 5 months. Full-length dramas and comedies, musicals, translations, adaptations, and revues. The studio plays must have a cast of no more than 4 and use simple sets.

TIPS "Bear in mind that on the mainstage we look for plays with mass appeal, Broadway-style. The studio spaces are our off-Broadway. No children's plays. Our mainstage audience goes for work that is entertaining and light. Our studio season is where we look for plays that have bite and are more provocative."

WILLOWS THEATRE CO.

636 Ward St., Martinez CA 94553-1651. **Website:** www.willowstheatre.org. Artistic Director: Richard Elliott. Professional productions for a suburban audience. **Produces 6 plays/year.** Accepting only commercially viable, small-medium size comedies right now. Guidelines are online at website. Send synopsis, character breakdown, resume, SASE. Do not send full script unless invited to do so. Do not email submission or email the office for information on your submission. Pays standard royalty. Responds in 6 months to scripts. Commercially viable, small-medium size musicals or comedies that are popular, rarely produced, or new. Certain stylized plays or musicals with a contemporary edge to them (e.g., *Les Liasons Dangereuses, La Bete, Candide*). No more than 15 actors. Unit or simple sets with no fly space, no more than 7 pieces. We are not interested in 1-character pieces.

TIPS "Our audiences want light entertainment, comedies, and musicals. Also, have an interest in plays and musicals with a historical angle."

Ⓐ THE WILMA THEATER

265 S. Broad St., Philadelphia PA 19107. (215)893-9456. **Fax:** (215)893-0895. **E-mail:** wcb@wilmatheater.org. **Website:** www.wilmatheater.org. **Contact:** Walter Bilderback, dramaturg and literary manager. Estab. 1980. LORT-D 300-seat theater, 5,000 subscribers. **Produces 4 plays/year.** *Agented submissions only* for full mss. Accepts queries with cover letter, résumé, synopsis, and sample if recommended by a literary manager, dramaturg, or other theater professional. Electronic inquiries and submissions preferred. Will

not respond to mailed queries unless self-addressed stamp envelope or postcard is included. Responds in 6 months. Full-length plays, translations, adaptations, and musicals from an international repertoire with emphasis on innovative, bold staging; world premieres; works with poetic dimension; plays with music; multimedia works; social issues, particularly the role of science in our lives. Prefers maximum cast size of 12. Stage 44'x46'.

TIPS Before submitting any material to The Wilma Theater, please research our production history. Considering the types of plays we have produced in the past, honestly assess whether or not your play would suit us. In general, I believe researching the various theaters to which you send your play is important in the long and short run. Different theaters have different missions and therefore seek out material corresponding with those goals. In other words, think through what is the true potential of your play and this theater, and if it is a compatible relationship.

WOMEN'S PROJECT AND PRODUCTIONS

55 West End Ave., New York NY 10023. (212)765-1706. **Fax:** (212)765-2024. **Website:** www.womensproject.org. **Contact:** Megan E. Carter, Associate Artistic Director. Estab. 1978. Professional Off-Broadway productions. Agented submissions only. **Produces 3 plays/year.** Please see website for submission guidelines and details. "We are looking for full-length plays written by women."

Ⓐ WOOLLY MAMMOTH THEATRE CO.

641 D St. NW, Washington DC 20004. (202)289-2443. **E-mail:** elissa@woollymammoth.net. **Website:** www.woollymammoth.net. **Contact:** Elissa Goetschius, literary manager. Artistic Director: Howard Shalwitz. Estab. 1980. Produces professional productions for the general public. **Produces 5 plays/year.** Buys first- and second-class production rights. Solicited submissions only. Pays variable royalty. Responds in 6 months to scripts; very interesting scripts often take much longer. We look for plays with a distinctive authorial voice. Our work is word and actor driven. One-acts and issue-driven plays are not used. Cast limit of 5.

SCREENWRITING

For years, *Writer's Market* for has focused solely on the most traditional publishing formats, including getting published in consumer magazines and trade journals and by book publishers with the assistance of literary agents, as well as writing contests. Those markets aren't going away, but we can add in other venues, including playwriting and screenwriting.

Screenwriting is a unique market in that writers create scripts that are likely to be only the springboard to the collaborative effort involved with films. Whether writing full-length movies or shorter pieces, screenwriters are bound to have revisions to their scripts made by directors, actors, and producers. But that's okay.

What gets the whole process started is an amazing script that could last for two hours or two minutes...or, more likely, somewhere in between.

ALLIANCE FILMWORKS

9595 Wilshire Blvd., Suite 900, Beverly Hills CA 90212. **Website:** www.alliancefilmworks.com. Estab. 2001. Produces 3 movies/year. *Alliance is not accepting unsolicited TV or film submissions, screenplays, pitches, log lines or treatments at this time.* Pays option; makes outright purchase.

Produces all genres. Budgets are $1.5 million+.

ALLIED ARTISTS, INC.

2251 N. Rampart Blvd., 1479, Las Vegas NV 89128. (702)991-9011. **E-mail:** query@alliedartistsonline.com. **Website:** www.alliedartistsonline.com. Estab. 1990. Produces material for broadcast and cable television, home video, and film **Buys 3-5 scripts/year. Uses Works with 10-20 writers/year. writers/year.** Buys first or all rights. Submit synopsis, outline. Pays in accordance with writer's guild standards. Responds in 2 months to queries. Responds in 3 months to mss.

TIPS "We are looking for positive, uplifting dramatic stories involving 'real people' situations. Future trend is for more reality-based programming, as well as interactive television programs for viewer participation. Send brief e-mail query only. Do not send scripts or additional material until requested. No phone pitches accepted."

AMERICAN WORLD PICTURES, INC.

16027 Ventura Blvd., Suite 320, Encino CA 91436. (818)380-9100. **Fax:** (818)380-0050. **E-mail:** jason@americanworldpictures.com. **Website:** www.americanworldpictures.com. **Contact:** Jason Corey, acquisitions. **Buys 4 scripts/year. Uses Works with 5 writers/year. writers/year.** Buys all rights. Query. Pays only $15,000 for scripts. Do not contact if price is more than that. Responds in 2 months to queries. Responds in 3 months to mss.

Needs feature-length films. Send DVD/VHS to the Acquisitions Department.

TIPS "Use strong characters and strong dialogue."

AUTOMATIC PICTURES

5225 Wilshire Blvd., Ste. 525, Los Angeles CA 90036. (323)935-1800. **Fax:** (323)935-8040. **E-mail:** azentertainment@hotmail.com. **Website:** www.automaticpictures.net. **Contact:** Frank Beddor, producer. Credits include *There's Something About Mary* and *Wicked*.

Looking for comedy, horror, or romantic comedy.

BIG EVENT PICTURES

3940 Laurel Canyon Blvd., #1137, Studio City CA 91604. **E-mail:** bigevent1@bigeventpictures.com. **Contact:** Michael Cargile, president. "Produces G, PG, and R-rated feature films for theaters, cable TV, and home video." Query by e-mail. Producers will respond if interested.

TIPS "Interesting query letters intrigue us—and tell us something about the writer. Query letter should include a short log line or pitch encapsulating what this story is about and should be no more than 1 page in length. We look for unique stories with strong characters and would like to see more action and science fiction submissions. We make movies that we would want to see. Producers are known for encouraging new/unproduced screenwriters and giving real consideration to their scripts."

BIZAZZ MEDIA

3315 S. Bentley Ave., Los Angeles CA 90034. (424)325-3295. **E-mail:** rupert@bizazzmedia.com. **Website:** www.bizazzmedia.com. **Contact:** Rupert Hitzig. "Bizazz Media is a full service video production company, built around Emmy and Peabody Award winning Producer Rupert Hitzig and a diverse cast of creative professionals with experienced vision. We specialize in the production of documentaries, electronic press kits, marketing videos, corporate videos, industrial videos, and training films. Whether it's for broadcast, non- broadcast presentation, or the Internet, our productions are engaging, informative, and never dull!"

SAM BLATE ASSOCIATES, LLC

10331 Watkins Mill Dr., Montgomery Village MD 20886-3950. (301)840-2248. **Fax:** (301)990-0707. **E-mail:** info@writephotopro.com. **Website:** www.writephotopro.com. **Contact:** Sam Blate, CEO. Produces educational and multimedia for marine, fishing, boating, business, education, institutions and state and federal governments. **Uses Works with 2 local writers/year on a per-project basis—it varies as to business conditions and demand. writers/year.** Buys first rights when possible Query with writing samples and SASE for return. Payment depends on contact with client. Pays some expenses. Responds in 1 month to queries.

TIPS Writers must have a strong track record of technical and aesthetic excellence.

CHEYENNE ENTERPRISES

406 Wilshire Blvd., Santa Monica CA 90401. (310)455-5000. **Fax:** (310)688-8000. **E-mail:** info@rifkin-eberts.com. **Website:** www.rifkin-ebertsproductions.com. Production company of actor Bruce Willis; credits include *Bandits, Hart's War, Timber Falls.*

CONTEMPTIBLE ENTERTAINMENT

c/o USA Films, 9333 Wilshire Blvd., Beverly Hills CA 90210. (310)385-4183. **Fax:** (310)385-6633. Production company of actor/director Neil Labute. Credits include *Your Friends & Neighbors, In the Company of Men, Nurse Betty.*

LEE DANIELS ENTERTAINMENT

315 W. 36th St., Suite 1002, New York NY 10018. (212)334-8110. **Fax:** (212)334-8290. **E-mail:** info@leedanielsentertainment.com. **Website:** www.leedanielsentertainment.com. VP of Development We work in all aspects of entertainment, including film, television, and theater. All nonagency scripts must be accompanied by a signed copy of the submission release form, which can be downloaded from the website. All scripts should be registered or copyrighted for your protection. All scripts should be in standard screenplay format. Include a synopsis, logline, and character breakdown (including lead and supporting roles). Do not send any extraneous materials.

TIPS Lee Daniels produced *Monster's Ball* and *The Woodsman*, and produced/directed *Shadowboxer.* He is the first African-American sole producer of an Academy-Award-winning film.

ESCAPE ARTISTS

10202 W. Washington Blvd., Lean, No. 333, Culver City CA 90232. (310)244-8833. **Fax:** (310)244-2151. Lead developers and producers include Steve Tisch, Todd Black and Jason Blumenthal. Credits include *The Weather Man* (2005), *Alex & Emma* (2003) and *A Knight's Tale (2001).*

TIPS Escape Artists distributes its films domestically via Columbia Pictures and internationally via Summit Entertainment.

FAST CARRIER PICTURES, INC.

820 Majorca Place, Los Angeles CA 90049. (213)300-1896. **E-mail:** fastcarriervp@aol.com. **Website:** www.fastcarrier.com. **Contact:** Rory Aylward. Estab. 2000. Mass market motion picture/TV audience. **Buys 1-2 scripts/year. Uses Works with 1-2 writers/year. writers/year.** No options or cash up front. Query with synopsis. No teen sex comedies, large science fiction movies, historical epics, serial killer movies, or gross violence and humor at the expense of women, children, or minorities.

Our bread basket is cable, broadcast, and smaller theatrical films in the following genres: women in jeopardy, low-budget family movies tied to a holiday, low-budget westerns, horror, and romantic comedy.

GINTY FILMS

16255 Ventura Blvd., Suite 625, Encino CA 91436. (310)277-1408. **E-mail:** ginty@robertginty.com. **Website:** www.robertginty.com. **Contact:** Robert Ginty. Estab. 1989. Commercial audience. **Buys 12-15 scripts/year. Uses Works with 10-20 writers/year. writers/year.** Buys first rights, all rights. Query with synopsis. Pays in accordance with WGA standards. Responds in 1 month to queries. Responds in 1 month to mss.

GREY LINE ENTERTAINMENT

115 W. California Blvd., #310, Pasadena CA 91105-3005. (626)943-0950. **E-mail:** submissions@greyline.net. **Website:** www.greyline.net. **Contact:** Sara Miller, submissions coordinator. Grey Line Entertainment is a full-service motion picture production and literary management company. We offer direct management of all services associated with the exploitation of stories. When our clients' motion picture screenplays are ready for the marketplace, we place them directly with studios or with major co-producers who can assist in packaging cast and/or director before approaching financiers (Warner Bros., New Line, Fox, Disney, etc.), or broadcasters (HBO, Showtime, etc.). Query via e-mail only. No attachments. Review online submission guidelines before sending. Responds in 2 weeks to queries.

Queries for screenplays and treatments should consist of a compelling and business-like letter giving us a brief overview of your story and a 1-sentence pitch. Be sure to include your return address and a phone number. No multiple submissions. Treatments and screenplays submitted without a completed and signed Grey Line submission form will be discarded. Include SASE for reply. We recommend you register your screenplays/treatments with the copyright office or WGA before submitting.

TIPS Your work must be finished and properly edited before seeking our representation (meaning proofread, spell-checked, and rewritten until it's perfect).

BETH GROSSBARD PRODUCTIONS

9696 Culver Blvd., Suite 208, Culver City CA 90232. (310)841-2555. **Fax:** (310)841-5934 or (818)705-7366. **Contact:** Jessica Roach, development executive; Beth Grossbard, executive producer. Estab. 1994. Buys first rights and true-life story rights Query with synopsis, treatment/outline. Responds in 1 month to queries.

TIPS Company develops material for television and the feature film markets. Interested in women's stories/issues, compelling true stories, social issues, contemporary legal issues, literary material, including young adult, children's titles, and small press books. We are also interested in plays, short stories, and original ideas.

INTERNATIONAL HOME ENTERTAINMENT

1440 Veteran Ave., Suite 650, Los Angeles CA 90024. (323)663-6940. **Contact:** Jed Leland, Jr., assistant to the president. Estab. 1976. Buys first rights. Query. Pays in accordance with writer's guild standards. Responds in 2 months to queries.

Looking for material that is international in scope.

TIPS Our response time is faster on average now (3-6 weeks), but we do not reply without a SASE. No unsolicited mss. We do not respond to unsolicited phone calls or e-mail.

ARNOLD LEIBOVIT ENTERTAINMENT

P.O. Box 33544, Santa Fe NM 87594-3544. **Website:** www.scifistation.com. **Contact:** Barbara Schimpf, V.P., production; Arnold Leibovit, director/producer. Estab. 1988. "Produces material for motion pictures and television." **Uses Works with 1 writer/year. writers/year.** Query with log line and synopsis via e-mail. Do not send full script unless requested. A submission release must be included with all scripts. Pays in accordance with writer's guild standards. Responds in 2 months to queries. Does not want novels, plays, poems, treatments, or submissions on disk.

LEO FILMS

6548 Country Squire Ln., Omaha NE 68152. (323)459-5574. **E-mail:** lustgar@pacbell.net. **Website:** www.leofilms.com. **Contact:** Steve Lustgarten, president. Estab. 1989. Has released over 75 feature films. **Buys 5 scripts/year. Uses Works with 8 writers/year. writers/year.** Buys all rights. Query by e-mail with synopsis. Payment varies—options and sales. Responds in 1 week to queries. Responds in 2 months to mss.

TIPS "Will also consider novels, short stories, and treatments that have true movie potential."

THE MARSHAK/ZACHARY CO.

8840 Wilshire Blvd., 1st Floor, Beverly Hills CA 90211. **Fax:** (310)358-3192. **E-mail:** marshakzachary@aol.com; alan@themzco.com. **Contact:** Alan W. Mills, associate. Estab. 1981. "Audience is film goers of all ages and television viewers." **Buys 3-5 scripts/year. Uses Works with 10 writers/year. writers/year.** Rights purchased vary. Query with synopsis. Payment varies. Responds in 2 weeks to queries. Responds in 3 months to mss.

TIPS "Submit logline (1-line description), a short synopsis of storyline, and a short biographical profile (focus on professional background). SASE required for all mailed inquiries. If submissions are sent via e-mail, subject must include specific information or else run the risk of being deleted as junk mail. All genres accepted, but ideas must be commercially viable, high concept, original, and marketable."

MARULLUS PRODUCTIONS

PO Box 2435, Venice CA 90291. **E-mail:** info@marullus.com. **Website:** www.marullus.com. Gerhard Schwarz: gerhard@marullus.com; Fernando Ramiros: fernando@marullus.com; Development: development@marullus.com; Company Relations: info@marullus.com. The goal of Marullus Productions Inc. is nothing short of a revolution in independent film, providing both commercially viable and artistically polished films for both the art house and the local cinema around the block. From family films, mainstream feature films to surreal independent dramas and television series.

NITE OWL PRODUCTIONS

126 Hall Rd., Aliquippa PA 15001. (724)775-1993. **Fax:** (801)881-3017. **E-mail:** niteowlprods@aol.com; mark@niteowlproductionsltd.com. **Website:** www.niteowlproductionsltd.com. **Contact:** Bridget Petrella. Estab. 2001. Production credits include *Shopping Cart Commandos* and *American Playhouse: Three Sovereigns for Sarah*. Send a 1-page, single-spaced query letter via e-mail or mail.

We will be producing at least 5-10 feature films in the next 2-5 years. We are searching for polished, well-structured, well-written, and professional-looking screenplays that are ready for production. If your screenplay does not meet these standards, do not send us a query. All screenplays must be in English and be in standard industry format. Provide a working title for your screenplay.

TIPS All submissions must include a dated and signed Submission Release Form or they will be discarded immediately. All full-length feature film screenplays must be 80-130 pages in length. One-hour TV spec scripts must be 55-65 pages in length. Do not send us computer disks. One hardcopy of your screenplay will suffice. Do not cheat on your margins—we will notice. Proofread your screenplay thoroughly before submitting to avoid typos and punctuation and grammar mistakes. Copyright your script with the US Copyright Office and register it with the WGA. All screenplays must be firmly bound and include a cover page with the title of the work and your name, address, and contact information. Your materials will not be returned.

POP/ART FILM FACTORY

23679 Calabasas Rd., Suite 686, Calabasas CA 91302. **E-mail:** popartfilms@earthlink.net. **Website:** popartfilmfactory.com. **Contact:** Daniel Zirilli, CEO/director. Estab. 1990. Produces material for all audiences/feature films Query with synopsis. Pays on per project basis.

"We also have domestic and international distribution, and are always looking for finished films. We're producing 3 feature films/year and 15-20 music-oriented projects."

TIPS "Send a query/pitch letter and let me know if you are willing to write on spec (for the first job only; you will be paid if the project is produced). Be original. Do not play it safe. If you don't receive a response from anyone you have ever sent your ideas to, or you continually get rejected, don't give up if you believe in yourself. Good luck and keep writing!"

THE PUPPETOON STUDIOS

P.O. Box 33544, Santa Fe NM 87594-3544. **Website:** www.scifistation.com. **Contact:** Arnold Leibovit, director/producer. Estab. 1987. "Wants plays geared toward a broad audience." **Uses Works with 1 writer/year. writers/year.** Query with logline and synopsis via e-mail. Do not send script unless requested. Submission release required with all scripts. Pays in accordance with writer's guild standards. Responds in 2 month to queries. No novels, plays, poems, treatments, or submissions on disk.

SHORELINE ENTERTAINMENT, INC.

1875 Century Park E., Suite 600, Los Angeles CA 90067. (310)551-2060. **Fax:** (310)201-0729. **E-mail:** info@shorelineentertainment.com. **Website:** www.shorelineentertainment.com. Production credits include *Glengarry Glen Ross*, *The Visit*, *The Man From Elysian Fields*. Estab. 1993. Mass audience. **Buys 8 scripts/year. Uses Works with 8 writers/year. writers/year.** Buys all rights. Query. Responds in 1 week to queries.

TIPS Looking for character driven films that are commercial as well as independent. Completed screenplays only. Especially looking for big-budget action, thrillers. We accept submissions by mail, e-mail or fax. No unsolicited screenplays, please.

SPENCER PRODUCTIONS, INC.

P.O. Box 2247, Westport CT 06880. **E-mail:** spencerprods@yahoo.com. **Contact:** Bruce Spencer, general manager; Alan Abel, creative director. Produces material for high school students, college students and adults. Occasionally uses freelance writers with considerable talent Query. Payment negotiable. Responds in 1 month to queries.

TIPS "For a comprehensive view of our humor requirements, we suggest viewing our feature film productions, *Is There Sex After Death* (Rated R), starring Buck Henry. It is available at Netflix. Also, *Abel Raises Cain*. Or read *Don't Get Mad . Get Even* and *How to Thrive on Rejection* by Alan Abel (published by W.W. Norton), both available from Amazon.com. Send brief synopsis (one page) and outline (2-4 pages)."

TALCO PRODUCTIONS

279 E. 44th St., New York NY 10017-4354. (212)697-4015. **Fax:** (212)697-4827. **Contact:** Alan Lawrence, president; Marty Holberton, vice president. Estab. 1968. Produces variety of material for TV, radio, business, trade associations, nonprofit organizations, public relations (chiefly political and current events), etc. Audiences range from young children to senior citizens. **20-40% freelance written scripts/year. Uses Buys scripts from published/produced writers only writers/year.** Buys all rights. Submit resume. Makes outright purchase. Pays in accordance with WGA

standards. Sometimes pays the expenses of writers on assignment. Responds in 3 weeks to queries.

TIPS We maintain a file of writers and call on those with experience in the same general category as the project in production. *We do not accept unsolicited manuscripts.* We prefer to receive a writer's résumé listing credits. If his/her background merits, we will be in touch when a project seems right. We are doing more public relations-oriented work (print and DVD) and are concentrating on TV productions. Production budgets are tighter.

TNP AUDIOBOOKS

TNP, LLC, 911 Lakeville St., Suite 201, Petaluma CA 94952. (707)637-0027. **E-mail:** info@toonutsproductions.com. **Website:** toonutsproductions.com. **Contact:** Ralph Scott, executive producer. Estab. 1994. Produces audiobooks and audiobook demos that capture the intrigue of some of the largest publishers and distributors in the industry. **Buys 25-30 scripts/year. Uses Works with 25-30 writers/year. writers/year.** Buys both first rights and all rights. Query with synopsis. Submit resume. Submit writing samples. Submit production history. Creative but brief cover letter/e-mail. Works with 20% first time writers. Illustrators query with creative but brief cover letter, samples of work by e-mail or hyperlink to your online portfolio. Pays royalty and makes outright purchase. Responds in less than 3 months to queries; 6 months to mss. "Please do not submit anything with violence, chainsaws, axes, ice picks, and general blood and guts.".

Really good original—clean—content.

TIPS "Suggestion: Use the words 'Too Nuts' at least twice in your query. (Do the math.) If you don't know how to giggle all the way to the bank, you may want to try someone else. If you've already exorcised your inner child, lizard, monkey, etc., that's a 'no no.' Please visit our website before querying. We receive too many submissions about axe murderers and with clearly adult themes. Even if you're still searching for your inner child through your writing, those subjects are clearly not for our audiences. If you send us anything like this, expect a very 'spirited' response. Find your inner child on your own time!"

TREASURE ENTERTAINMENT

468 N. Camden Dr., Suite 200, Beverly Hills CA 90210. (310)860-7490. **Fax:** (310)943-1488. **E-mail:** info@treasureentertainment.net. **Website:** www.treasureentertainment.net. **Contact:** Mark Heidelberger, Treasure Entertainment co-chairman/chief executive officer. Estab. 2000. Management consideration given to writers with produced credits only. Intended audience is theatrical, festival, television, home video/DVD, Internet. **Buys 1-2 scripts/year. Uses Works with 8-10 writers/year. writers/year.** Query. Pays 1-10% royalty. Makes outright purchase of $1-100,000. Responds in up to 6 months to queries. Responds in up to 6 months to mss.

TIPS "We reserve the right to reject or return any unsolicited material. We also reserve the right not to purchase any material if we don't feel that any submissions are of sufficient merit. Our needs tend to change with the market and will vary from year to year. We are agreeing to look at writer's queries only. Queries should be sent by mail or e-mail only."

VALEO FILMS

P.O. Box 250, Orange Lake FL 32681. (352)591-4714. **E-mail:** screenplays@valeofilms.com. **Website:** www.valeofilms.com. Query by e-mail or mail.

Currently considering projects that contain one or more of the following: character or story driven, identifies moral values, romance/love story, educational/documentary, presents the human condition, strong visual imagery, coming of age/learning, or intellectual drama/mystery.

TIPS "We require that you provide your name, phone number, address, title of your work, and WGA registration or copyright number. We will send an Unsolicited Project Release letter for you to sign and return with a signed copy of your screenplay/treatment. We don't want projects that contain the following characteristics: one character saves the world, SFX based, highly action based, extreme/grotesque violence, high sexual content, or strong explicit language. Although we do have a vast array of production resources available to us, we are a relatively small production company who prefers to limit the number of projects we have in production. Consequently, we tend to be very selective when it comes to choosing new material."

CONTESTS & AWARDS

The contests and awards listed in this section are arranged by subject. Nonfiction writers can turn immediately to nonfiction awards listed alphabetically by the name of the contest or award. The same is true for fiction writers, poets, playwrights and screenwriters, journalists, children's writers, and translators. You'll also find general book awards, fellowships offered by arts councils and foundations, and multiple category contests.

New contests and awards are announced in various writer's publications nearly every day. However, many lose their funding or fold, and sponsoring magazines go out of business just as often. **Contact names, entry fees,** and **deadlines** have been highlighted and set in bold type for your convenience.

To make sure you have all the information you need about a particular contest, always send a SASE to the contact person in the listing before entering a contest or check their website. The listings in this section are brief, and many contests have lengthy, specific rules and requirements that we could not include in our limited space. Often a specific entry form must accompany your submission.

When you receive a set of guidelines, you'll see some contests are not applicable to all writers. The writer's age, previous publication, geographic location, and length of the work are common matters of eligibility. Read the requirements to ensure you don't enter a contest for which you're not qualified.

Winning a contest or award can launch a successful writing career. Take a professional approach by doing a little extra research. Find out who the previous winner of the award was by investing in a sample copy of the magazine in which the prize-winning article, poem, or short story appeared. Attend the staged reading of an award-winning play. Your extra effort will be to your advantage in competing with writers who simply submit blindly.

PLAYWRITING & SCREENWRITING

A+ PLAYWRITING CONTEST FOR TEACHERS

Pioneer Drama Service, Inc., P.O. Box 4267, Englewood CO 80155-4267. (303)779-4035. **Fax:** (303)779-4315. **E-mail:** editors@pioneerdrama.com. **E-mail:** submissions@pioneerdrama.com. **Website:** www.pioneerdrama.com. **Contact:** Brian Taylor, Acquisitions Editor. Playwright must be a current or retired faculty member at an accredited K-12 public or private school in the US or Canada. All plays submitted through this contest must have been produced within the last 2 years at the school where the playwright teaches. Rules and guidelines available online. Encourages the development of quality plays written specifically by teachers and other educators. All qualifying mss accepted for publication will be considered contest finalists. Deadline: Submissions will be accepted on an ongoing basis with a June 30 cutoff each year. Prize: $500 royalty advance and a one-time $500 donation to the school theatre program where the play was first produced. Judged by editors.

THE ACADEMY NICHOLL FELLOWSHIPS IN SCREENWRITING

1313 Vine St., Hollywood CA 90028-8107. (310)247-3010. **E-mail:** nicholl@oscars.org. **Website:** www.oscars.org/nicholl. An entrant's total earnings for motion picture and television writing may not exceed $25,000 before the end of the competition. This limit applies to compensation for motion picture and television writing services as well as for the sale of (or sale of an option on) screenplays, teleplays, stage plays, books, treatments, stories, premises and any other source material. Members and employees of the Academy of Motion Picture Arts and Sciences and their immediate families are not eligible, nor are competition judges and their immediate families. Deadline: May 1. The first and quarterfinal rounds are judged by industry professionals who are not members of the Academy. The semifinal round is judged by Academy members drawn from across the spectrum of the motion picture industry. The finalist scripts are judged by the Academy Nicholl Committee.

ADLER FEST

Stella Adler Academy of Acting And Theatre LA, 6773 Hollywood Blvd., 2nd floor, Hollywood CA 90028. (323)465-4446. **E-mail:** youth@stellaadler-la.com. **Website:** www.stellaadler.la. **Contact:** Kaz Matamura, festival director. Contest is offered twice a year for unpublished and unproduced plays. 1) Ten Minute Plays - 8-12 minutes long. 2) Short Plays - One Act plays under 75 min. 3) Full Length. Stella Adler Academy of Los Angeles is a nonprofit organizations that are committed to discovering new playwrights and giving them opportunities to work with directors and producers. Deadline: March 31. Prizes: 1) & 2) 1st Place: $200; 2nd Place: $100; 3) $500 professionally mounted production for winners and semi-finalists. Guest judges are entertainment professionals including writers, producers, directors, and agents. The members of the Academy will go through the first evaluation. Acquires right to produce and mount the plays if chosen as festival finalists or semi-finalists. No royalties are gathered for those performances.

AMERICAN ZOETROPE SCREENPLAY CONTEST

American Zoetrope, 916 Kearny St., San Francisco CA 94133. **E-mail:** contests@zoetrope.com. **Website:** www.zoetrope.com/contests. Scripts must be between 87 to 130 pages in standard screenplay format. The writer must own all rights to the work. The writer must be at least 18 years old and have never have made more than $5,000 as a screen- or television-writer. The contest's aim is to seek out and encourage compelling film narratives, and to introduce the next generation of great screenwriters to today's leading production companies and agencies. Deadline: August 1; September 2. The grand prize-winner receives $5,000. The winner and top-ten finalists will be considered for representation by icm, uta, paradigm, william morris independent, the gersh agency, caa, exile entertainment, the schiff company, and the firm. Their scripts will be considered for film option and development by leading production companies, including: american zoetrope, samuel goldwyn films, fox searchlight, sony pictures classics, ifc entertainment, paramount classics, icon pictures, working title, dimension films, antidote films, bull's eye entertainment, c/w productions, the film department, first look, frelaine, greenestreet films, matinee pictures, michael london productions, number 9 films, phoenix pictures, pretty pictures, this is that, roserock films, benderspink, room 9 entertainment, industry entertainment, ovie entertainment, nine yards entertainment, and ziskin productions.

ANNUAL NATIONAL PLAYWRITING COMPETITION

Wichita State University, School of Performing Arts, 1845 Fairmount, Box 153, Wichita KS 67260. (316)978-3646. **Fax:** (316)978-3202. **E-mail:** jeannine.russell@wichita.edu. **Contact:** Jeannine Russell, Theatre Instructor. The contest will be open to all undergraduate and graduate students enrolled at any college or university in the United States. Please indicate school affiliation. All submissions must be original, unpublished and unproduced. Both full-length and one-act plays may be submitted. Full-length plays in 1 or more acts should be a minimum of 90 minutes playing time. Two or 3 short plays on related themes by the same author will be judged as 1 entry. The total playing time should be a minimum of 90 minutes. One-act plays should be a minimum of 30 minutes playing time to a maximum of 60 minutes playing time. Musicals should be a minimum of 90 minutes playing time and must include a CD of the accompanying music. Scripts should contain no more than 4-6 characters and setting must be suitable for an 85-seat Black box theatre. Eligible playwrights may submit up to 2 entries per contest year. One typewritten, bound copy should be submitted. Scripts must be typed and arranged in professional play script format. See information provided in *The Dramatist's Sourcebook* or the following website (www.pubinfo.vcu.edu/artweb/playwriting/format.html) for instruction on use of professional format. Two title pages must be included: 1 bound and the other unbound. The unbound title page should display the author's name, address, telephone number, and e-mail address if applicable. The bound title page should only display the name of the script; do not include any personal identifying information on the bound title page. Scripts may be submitted via e-mail. Submit in PDF format. Include all information requested for mail in scripts with electronic submission. Deadline: January 16. Prize: Production or staged reading by the Wichita State University Theatre. Winner will be announced after March 15. No entry may be withdrawn after March 1. Judged by a panel of 3 or more selected from the school faculty. May also include up to 3 experienced, faculty approved WSU School of Performing Arts students.

APPALACHIAN FESTIVAL OF PLAYS & PLAYWRIGHTS

Barter Theatre, Appalachian Festival of Plays and Playwrights, c/o Barter Theatre, Box 867, Abingdon VA 24212-0867. (276)619-3316. **Fax:** (276)619-3335. **E-mail:** apfestival@bartertheatre.com. **E-mail:** apfestival@bartertheatre.com. **Website:** www.bartertheatre.com. **Contact:** Nick Piper, Associate Artistic Director/Director, New Play Development. With the annual Appalachian Festival of New Plays & Playwrights, Barter Theatre wishes to celebrate new, previously unpublished/unproduced plays by playwrights from the Appalachian region. If the playwrights are not from Appalachia, the plays themselves must be about the region. Deadline: March 31. Prize: $250, a staged reading performed at Barter's Stage II theater, and some transportation compensation and housing during the time of the festival.

ATLANTIS AWARD

The Poet's Billow, 6135 Avon, Portage MI 49024. **E-mail:** thepoetsbillow@gmail.com. **Website:** thepoetsbillow.org. **Contact:** Robert Evory. Annual award open to any writer to recognize one outstanding poem from its entries. Finalists with strong work will also be published. Submissions must be previously unpublished. Deadline: October 1. Submissions open July 1. Prize: $200 and winning poet will be featured in an interview on The Poet's Billow website. Poem will be published and displayed in The Poet's Billow Literary Art Gallery and nominated for a Pushcart Prize. If the poet qualifies, the poem will also be submitted to The Best New Poets anthology. Judged by the editors, and, occasionally, a guest judge.

THE BLANK THEATRE COMPANY YOUNG PLAYWRIGHTS FESTIVAL

P.O. Box 38756, Hollywood CA 90038. (323)662-7734. **Fax:** (323)661-3903. **E-mail:** info@theblank.com. **E-mail:** submissions@youngplaywrights.com. **Website:** ypf.theblank.com. To give young playwrights an opportunity to learn more about playwriting and to give them a chance to have their work mentored, developed, and presented by professional artists. Entries must be postmarked by March 15.

CALIFORNIA YOUNG PLAYWRIGHTS CONTEST

Playwrights Project, 3675 Ruffin Rd., Suite 330, San Diego CA 92123-1870. (858)384-2970. **Fax:** (858)384-2974. **E-mail:** write@playwrightsproject.org. **Website:** www.playwrightsproject.org/programs/contest/. **Contact:** Cecelia Kouma, Executive Director. The California Young Playwrights Contest is open to Californians under age 19. Every year, young playwrights submit original scripts to the contest. Every writer who requests feedback receives an individualized script critique. Selected writers win script readings or full professional productions in Plays by Young Writers festival. Distinguished artists from major theatres select festival scripts and write comments to the playwrights. Submissions are required to be unpublished and not produced professionally. Submissions made by the author. SASE for contest rules and entry form. Scripts must be a minimum of 10 standard typewritten pages. Scripts will *not* be returned. If requested, entrants receive detailed evaluation letter. Guidelines available online. Deadline: June 1. Prize: Scripts will be produced in spring at a professional theatre in San Diego. Writers submitting scripts of 10 or more pages receive a detailed script evaluation letter upon request. Judged by professionals in the theater community, a committee of 5-7; changes somewhat each year.

CANADIAN AUTHORS ASSOCIATION AWARD FOR FICTION

192 Spadina Avenue, Suite 107, Toronto ON M5T 2C2 Canada. **Website:** www.canadianauthors.org. **Contact:** Anita Purcell, executive director. Award for full-length, English language literature for adults by a Canadian author. Deadline: January 15. Prize: $1,000. Judging: Each year a trustee for each award appointed by the Canadian Authors Association selects up to 3 judges. Identities of the trustee and judges are confidential.

THE EMILY CONTEST

West Houston RWA, Houston TX **E-mail:** emily.contest@whrwa.com. **Website:** www.whrwa.com. Annual award to promote publication of previously unpublished writers of romance. Open to any writer who has not published in a given category within the past 3 years. Send up to first 5,600 words and end on a hook. Contest is open to published and unpublished writers. Unpublished authors may enter in any category not contracted in (book-length) by the deadline. Published authors may enter in a category not published (book-length) in the past three years. (Book-length: 40,000+ words.) See website for specific details. The mission of The Emily is to professionally support writers and guide them toward a path to publication. Deadline: October 2. Submission period begins September 1. Prize: $100. Final judging done by an editor and an agent.

ESSENTIAL THEATRE PLAYWRITING AWARD

The Essential Theatre, The Essential Theatre, 1414 Foxhall Lane, #10, Atlanta GA 30316. (404)212-0815. **E-mail:** pmhardy@aol.com. **Website:** www.essentialtheatre.com. **Contact:** Peter Hardy. Offered annually for unproduced, full-length plays by Georgia-resident writers. No limitations as to style or subject matter. Submissions can be e-mailed in PDF or Word Documents, or sent via postal mail. See website for full guidelines. Deadline: April 23. Prize: $750 and full production.

SHUBERT FENDRICH MEMORIAL PLAYWRITING CONTEST

Pioneer Drama Service, Inc., Pioneer Drama Service, Inc. - Att'n: Submissions Editor, P.O. Box 4267, Englewood CO 80155-4267. (303)779-4035. **Fax:** (303)779-4315. **E-mail:** editors@pioneerdrama.com. **E-mail:** submissions@pioneerdrama.com. **Website:** www.pioneerdrama.com. **Contact:** Brian Taylor, Acquisitions Editor. Annual competition that encourages the development of quality theatrical material for educational, community, and children's theatre markets. Previously unpublished submissions only. Only considers mss with a running time between 20-120 minutes. Open to all writers not currently published by Pioneer Drama Service. Guidelines available online. No entry fee. Cover letter, SASE for return of ms, and proof of production or staged reading must accompany all submissions. Deadline: Ongoing contest; a winner is selected by June 1 each year from all submissions received the previous year. Prize: $1,000 royalty advance in addition to publication. Judged by editors.

FILMMAKERS INTERNATIONAL SCREENWRITING AWARDS

Beverly Hills CA 90210 USA. **E-mail:** info@filmmakers.com. **Website:** www.filmmakers.com/screenplay/. Deadlines: Early: Feb. 28; Regular: May 31; Final: June 30; Extended Final: July 31. Prizes: Grand Prize: $2,500; Elite Prizes: $500 per category.

GARDEN STATE FILM FESTIVAL SCREENPLAY COMPETITION

Asbury Park NJ 07712. (877)908-7050. **E-mail:** info@gsff.org. **Website:** www.gsff.org. **Contact:** Diane Raver, founder. The artistic philosophy of the Garden State Film Festival is rooted in the celebration of the independent film genre and the creation of a forum where local and other independent filmmakers can exhibit their work. It was also created to pay tribute to New Jersey's legacy as the birthplace of the American filmmaking industry in Thomas Edison's Menlo Park laboratories where he invented the first film cameras and projectors, to Fort Lee, where the original studios were founded. Our event provides novice and aspiring filmmakers, writers, composers, actors, and others interested in careers in the film business, the opportunity to meet and network with industry professionals in an atmosphere conducive to learning and mentoring. Further, we are happy to present each spring in Asbury Park and to serve as an added engine for the city's vitality through arts, commerce and culture. See you at the movies! Entered screenplays must not have been previously optioned, sold, or produced. All screenplays should be registered with the WGA and/or a Library of Congress copyright. Screenplays must be the original work of the writer. If based on another person's life story, a statement attesting to the rights obtained must be attached. No adaptations of other written work will be accepted. Multiple entries are accepted. A separate entry form and fee must accompany each script. Screenplays containing multiple writers are also accepted. Include two cover pages with each screenplay. One that only contains the screenplay's title. A second one that contains all contact information (name, address, phone, and email and Withoutabox tracking number). The writer's name must not appear any where inside the body of the screenplay. All screenplays must abide by proper industry format. All screenplays must be in English, with numbered, plain-write pages. All screenplays MUST be uploaded as a PDF via withoutbox.com. No substitutions of new drafts, or corrected pages, for any screenplay, for any reason, will be accepted after the initial submission. Please enter the draft you are most confident about. No individual feedback or coverage will be made available pertaining to submitted screenplays. Deadline: November 1. Submissions are accepted beginning June 1 each year. The winner receives a live staged reading with a professional director and professional actors in a seated venue during the festival.

HRC SHOWCASE THEATRE PLAYWRITING CONTEST

P.O. Box 940, Hudson NY 12534. **E-mail:** hrcshowcaseplaycontest@gmail.com. **Website:** www.hrcshowcasetheatre.com. **Contact:** Jesse Waldinger, Chair Play Selection Committee. HRC Showcase Theatre invites submissions of full-length plays to its annual contest from new, aspiring, or established playwrights. Each submitted play should be previously unpublished, run no more than 90 minutes, require no more than 6 actors, and be suitable for presentation as a staged reading by Equity actors. No musicals or children's plays. Deadline: February 1. Prize: $500. Four runner-ups will receive $100 each.

L.A. DESIGNERS' THEATRE-COMMISSIONS

L.A. Designers' Theatre, P.O. Box 1883, Studio City CA 91614-0883. **E-mail:** ladesigners@gmail.com. **Contact:** Richard Niederberg, artistic director. "Quarterly contest to promote new work and push it through a Theatrical Production onto the conveyor belt to Filmed or Digital Origination entertainment. All submissions must be registered with the copyright office and be unpublished. Material will not be returned. Do not submit any proposal that will not fit in a #10 envelope. No rules, guidelines, fees, or entry forms. Just present an idea that can be commissioned into a full work. Proposals for as of yet uncompleted works are encouraged. Unpopular political, religious, social, or other themes are encouraged; 'street' language and nudity are acceptable. Open to any writer." Deadline: March 15, June 15, September 15, December 15. Prize: Production or publication of the work in the Los Angeles market. "We only want 'first refusal' for the Rights License that is clear of any legal, stated, unstated, or implied obligation to any other person or entity. You continue to *own* your work."

MCKNIGHT FELLOWSHIP IN PLAYWRITING

The Playwrights' Center, 2301 E. Franklin Ave., Minneapolis MN 55406-1099. (612)332-7481. **Fax:** (612)332-6037. **E-mail:** submissions@pwcenter.org. **Website:** www.pwcenter.org. **Contact:** Julia Brown, artistic programs administrator. The Playwrights' Center today serves more playwrights in more ways than any other organization in the country. Applications are screened for eligibility by the Playwrights' Center and evaluated by an initial select panel of professional theater artists; finalists are then evaluated by a second panel of national theater artists. Selection is based on artistic excellence and professional achievement, and is guided by the Playwrights' Center's mission statement. The McKnight Fellowships in Playwriting recognize playwrights whose work demonstrates exceptional artistic merit and excellence in the field, and whose primary residence is in the state of Minnesota. Deadline: January 17. Prize: 2 fellowships of $25,000 each will be awarded. Additional funds of $2,500 can be used to support a play development workshop and other professional expenses.

MOONDANCE INTERNATIONAL FILM FESTIVAL

970 Ninth St., Boulder CO 80302. (303)818-5771. **E-mail:** moondancefestival@gmail.com. **Website:** www.moondancefilmfestival.com; www.moondancefestival.com/blog. Written works submissions: feature screenplays, short screenplays, feature & short musical screenplays, feature & short screenplays for children, 1, 2 or 3-act stageplays, mini-series for TV, television movies of the week, television pilots, libretti, musical film scripts, short stories, radio plays & short stories for children. Submission service: www.withoutabox.com/login/1240. Accepts hard-copies of submissions, as well as digital submissions. Please include your full contact info on the cover page of your entry. Check out our submission guidelines on the website. Regular deadline: May 31; late deadline: June 30, extended deadline: July 15.

NASHVILLE FILM FESTIVAL SCREENWRITING COMPETITION

161 Rains Ave, Nashville TN 37203. (615)742-2500. **E-mail:** info@nashfilm.org. **E-mail:** 2019entries@nashfilm.org. **Website:** www.nashvillefilmfestival.org. **Contact:** Programming Team. This contest seeks film submissions less than 40 minutes in length, as well as full-length features and documentaries. Deadline: June-January. There are numerous awards: press/industry screenings, $1,000 and option of international representation for one year. Scripts are judged by a carefully curated jury of industry professionals and agents. Past and future juries have included representatives from CAA, Voltage Pictures (The Hurt Locker, Dallas Buyers Club), APA, and Mosaic (Bad Teacher, Step Brothers, The Other Guys).

NATIONAL ONE-ACT PLAYWRITING COMPETITION (CANADA)

Ottawa Little Theatre, Ottawa Little Theatre, 400 King Edward Ave., Ottawa ON K1N 7M7 Canada. (613)233-8948. **Fax:** (613)233-8027. **Website:** www.ottawalittletheatre.com. **Contact:** Geoff Gruson, Executive. Encourages literary and dramatic talent in Canada. Guidelines available online. Deadline: October 15. Prize: 1st Place: $1,000; 2nd Place: $750; 3rd Place: $500; Sybil Cooke Award for a Play Written for Children or Young People: $500. All winning plays will receive a public reading in April, and the winning playwrights will have a one-on-one meeting with a resident dramaturg. Judged by 3 adjudicators, including dramaturgs, directors who develop new work, and playwrights from across Canada.

NEW WORKS FOR THE STAGE

COE College Theatre Arts Department, 1220 First Ave. NE, Cedar Rapids IA 52402. (319)399-8624. **Fax:** (319)399-8557. **E-mail:** swolvert@coe.edu. **Website:** www.public.coe.edu/departments/theatre. **Contact:** Susan Wolverton. Offered in odd-numbered years to encourage new work, to provide an interdisciplinary forum for the discussion of issues found in new work, and to offer playwright contact with theater professionals who can provide response to new work. Full-length, original, unpublished and unproduced scripts only. No musicals, adaptations, translations, or collaborations. Submit 1-page synopsis, résumé, and SASE if the script is to be returned. Deadline: November 1 even years. Prize: $500, plus travel, room and board for residency at the college.

THE PAGE INTERNATIONAL SCREENWRITING AWARDS

7190 W. Sunset Blvd. #610, Hollywood CA 90046. **E-mail:** info@pageawards.com. **Website:** pageawards.com. **Contact:** Zoe Simmons, contest coordinator. Annual competition to discover the most talented new screenwriters from across the country and around the world. Each year, awards are presented to 31 screenwriters in 10 different genre categories: Action/Adventure, Comedy, Drama, Family Film, Historical Film, Science Fiction, Thriller/Horror, Short Film Script, TV Drama Pilot, and TV Comedy Pilot. The contest is open to all writers 18 years of age and older who have not previously earned more than $50,000 writing for film and/or television. (Please visit contest website for entry forms and a complete list of rules and regulations.)

Deadlines: January 15 (early), February 15 (regular), March 15 (late), April 15 (last minute). Each year the PAGE Judges present over $50,000 in cash and prizes, including a $25,000 Grand Prize, plus Gold, Silver & Bronze Prizes in 10 genre categories. Most importantly, the winning writers receive extensive publicity and industry exposure for their scripts. As a result of entering the contest, many PAGE Award Winners now have movies and television shows in production, on the air and in theaters. Judging is done entirely by working Hollywood professionals, including literary agents, managers, producers, script analysts, and development executives.

SCREENPLAY FESTIVAL

15021 Ventura Blvd., #523, Sherman Oaks CA 91403. (424)248-9221. **Fax:** (866)770-2994. **E-mail:** info@screenplayfestival.com. **Website:** www.screenplayfestival.com. This festival is an opportunity to give all scriptwriters a chance to be noticed and have their work read by the power players. Entries in the feature-length competition must be more than 60 pages; entries in the short screenplay contest must be fewer than 60 pages. The Screenplay Festival was established to solve two major problems. One, it is simply too difficult for talented writers who have no "connections" to gain recognition and get their material read by legitimate agents, producers, directors and investors. Two, agents, producers, directors, and investors complain that they cannot find any great material, but they will generally not accept "unsolicited material." This means that unless the script comes from a source that is known to them, they will not read it. Screenplay Festival was established to help eliminate this "chicken and egg" problem. By accepting all submitted screenplays and judging them based upon their quality—not their source or their standardized formatting or the quality of the brads holding them together—Screenplay Festival looks to give undiscovered screenwriters an opportunity to rise above the crowd. Deadline: September 9. Prize: $500 for feature film categories, $500 for television categories.

SCRIPTAPALOOZA SCREENPLAY & SHORTS COMPETITION

Endorsed by Write Brothers and Robert McKee, (310)594-5384. **E-mail:** info@scriptapalooza.com. **Website:** www.scriptapalooza.com. "From choosing our judges to creating opportunities, our top priority has always been the writer. We surround ourselves with reputable and successful companies, including many producers, literary agents, and managers who read your scripts. Our past winners have won Emmy's, been signed by agents, managers, had their scripts optioned, and even made into movies. Scriptapalooza will promote, pitch and push the semifinalists and higher for a full year." Deadline: January 7, February 4, March 4, April 15, and April 29. Prize: 1st Place: $10,000; over $50,00 in prizes for the entire competition. The top 100 scripts will be considered by over 95 production companies. Judged by over 90 producers.

SCRIPTAPALOOZA TELEVISION WRITING COMPETITION

(310)594-5384. **E-mail:** info@scriptapalooza.com. **Website:** www.scriptapaloozatv.com. Bi-annual competition accepting entries in 4 categories: Reality shows, sitcoms, original pilots, and 1-hour dramas. There are more than 30 producers, agents, and managers reading the winning scripts. Two past winners won Emmys because of Scriptapalooza and 1 past entrant now writes for Comedy Central. Winners announced February 15 and August 30. For contest results, visit website. Length: Standard television format whether 1 hour, 1-half hour, or pilot. Open to any writer 18 or older. Guidelines available on website. Accepts inquiries by e-mail or phone. Deadline: October 15 and April 15 of every year. Prizes: 1st Place: $500; 2nd Place: $200; 3rd Place: $100. Judged by over 25 producers.

SCRIPT PIPELINE SCREENWRITING COMPETITION

2633 Lincoln Blvd. #701, Santa Monica CA 90405. (323)424-4243. **E-mail:** entry@scriptpipeline.com. **Website:** scriptpipeline.com. **Contact:** Matt Misetich, senior executive. Now in its 16th year, the Script Pipeline Screenwriting Competition seeks talented writers to connect with production companies, agencies, and managers. As one of the longest-running screenplay contests, we focus specifically on finding writers representation, supporting diverse voices, championing marketable, unique storytelling, and pushing more original projects into production. The company's distinctive long-term facilitation process helps contest selections gain elite representation and crucial introductions to Hollywood, with $6 million in screenplays and pilots sold by competition finalists and "Recommend" writers since 2010 alone. To circulate exceptional material industry-wide, support our writers long-term, and launch careers. Early deadline: March 1. Regular deadline: May 1. Late Deadline: May 15. Screenwriting Contest: $25,000 awarded to winner.

SCRIPTWRITERS NETWORK

The Scriptwriters Network Foundation, Inc., P.O. Box 642806, Los Angeles CA 90064 USA. (888)796-9673. **E-mail:** info@scriptwritersnetwork.org. **Website:** www.scriptwritersnetwork.org. **Contact:** Melessa Y. Sargent, President. The Scriptwriters Network Foundation, Inc., aka Scriptwriters Network (SWN), founded in 1986, is an educational, tax-exempt 501(c)(3) Non-Profit, volunteer-driven organization created by writers for writers and industry professionals. The Network serves its members by providing educational programming, enhancing their awareness of the realities of the business, developing access and opportunity through alliances with industry professionals, and furthering the cause and quality of writing in the entertainment industry. We bring in entertainment professionals to speak and teach on the art, craft and business of script writing for TV, features and new media. Whether you are a filmmaker, a screenwriter, a television scriptwriter or involved in screenwriting for non-traditional media, we help take your writing to the next level.

REVA SHINER COMEDY AWARD

Bloomington Playwrights Project, 107 W. 9th St., Bloomington IN 47404. (812)334-1188. **E-mail:** literarymanager@newplays.org. **Website:** www.newplays.org. **Contact:** Susan Jones, literary manager. Annual award for unpublished/unproduced plays. The Bloomington Playwrights Project is a script-developing organization. Winning playwrights are expected to become part of the development process, working with the director in person or via long-distance. Check the website for more details. Deadline: October 31. Prize: $1,000, full production as a part of the Mainstage season. Judged by the literary committee of the BPP.

SHRIEKFEST HORROR/SCI-FI FILM FESTIVAL & SCREENPLAY COMPETITION

P.O. Box 950921, Lake Mary FL 32795. **E-mail:** shriekfest@aol.com. **Website:** www.shriekfest.com. **Contact:** Denise Gossett. Shriekfest, the Los Angeles Horror/SciFi Film Festival, continues its tradition as Los Angeles' premier horror film event, presenting an exciting program of films each fall with beautiful Los Angeles as its backdrop. Now in its 19th year, Shriekfest L.A takes place at the legendary Raleigh Studios, which is the largest independent studio operator in the country. Shriekfest Orlando takes place at the famous Wayne Densch Performing Arts Center, which was originally founded in 1923. We offer filmmakers and film fans alike an ideal setting in 2 world-famous cities. Both established and emerging filmmakers gain media exposure, connect with the region's diverse audiences, and participate in an acclaimed event attended by industry professionals, as well as horror and sci-fi fans. Every film accepted into Shriekfest has the opportunity to screen on both coasts for the price of one admission! Over the past 17 years, Shriekfest has welcomed numerous indie icons into its family, and we are always looking to add to the Shriekfest Family. We are looking for original films and screenplays. We are accepting films/screenplays in six categories: narrative feature, narrative short, narrative super-short, music video, feature screenplay, and short screenplay. And these genres: horror, comedy horror, thriller, sci-fi, and fantasy. We will be awarding prizes to the winning filmmaker or screenwriter in each category. Festival Founder and Director Denise Gossett says, "We are already planning some exciting things for our 18th year!" Last year's festival was a great success. We had our biggest audience yet, with more than 55 filmmakers/screenwriters in attendance. Plus we were able to introduce some amazing indie horror films to Los Angeles and Orlando. "We accept award-winning screenplays. No restrictions as long as it's in the horror/thriller or sci-fi/fantasy genres. We accept shorts and features. No specific lengths." Deadline: February 1, May 1, July 1, July 10. Prize: Trophies, product awards, usually cash. "Our awards are updated all year long as sponsors step onboard." Judged by at least 10-20 judges who are all in different aspects of the entertainment industry, such as producers, directors, writers, actors, and agents.

SKIPPING STONES YOUTH AWARDS

P.O. Box 3939, Eugene OR 97403-0939. (541)342-4956. **Fax:** (541)342-4956. **E-mail:** editor@skippingstones.org. **Website:** www.skippingstones.org. **Contact:** Arun N. Toké. Annual awards to promote creativity as well as multicultural and nature awareness in youth. Cover letter should include name, address, phone, and e-mail. Entries must be unpublished. Length: 1,000 words maximum; 30 lines maximum for poems. Open to any writer between 7 and 17 years old. Guidelines available by SASE, e-mail, or on website. Accepts inquiries by e-mail or phone. Results announced in the October-December issue of *Skipping Stones*. Winners notified by mail. For contest results, visit website. Everyone who enters receives the issue which features the award winners. Deadline: June 25. Prize: Publication in the autumn issue of *Skipping Stones*, honor certificate, subscription to magazine, plus 5 multicultural and/or nature books. Judged by editors and reviewers at *Skipping Stones* magazine.

SOUTHERN PLAYWRIGHTS COMPETITION

Jacksonville State University, Department of English, 700 Pelham Rd. N., Jacksonville AL 36265-1602. (256)782-5412. **Fax:** (256)782-5441. **E-mail:** jmaloney@jsu.edu. **E-mail:** jmaloney@jsu.edu. **Website:** www.jsu.edu/depart/english/southpla.htm. **Contact:** Joy Maloney. Competition for playwrights native to or a resident of Alabama, Arkansas, Florida, Georgia, Kentucky, Louisiana, Mississippi, North Carolina, South Carolina, Tennessee, Texas, Virginia, or West Virginia. Plays must deal with the Southern experience. Entries must be original, full-length plays. No musicals or adaptations will be accepted. The playwright may submit only one play. All entries must be typed, securely bound, and clearly identified. Synopsis of script must be included. No electronic entries accepted. Legal clearance of all materials not in the public domain will be the responsibility of the playwright. The Southern Playwrights Competition seeks to identify and encourage the best of Southern playwriting. Deadline: January 15. Prize: $1,000 and production of the play.

THEATRE CONSPIRACY ANNUAL NEW PLAY CONTEST

Theatre Conspiracy, 10091 McGregor Blvd., Ft. Myers FL 33919. (239)939-2787. **E-mail:** tcnewplaycontest@gmail.com. **Website:** artinlee.org. **Contact:** Bill Taylor, Producing Artistic Director. Offered annually for full-length plays that have had up to 3 previous productions. Work submitted to the contest must be a full length play with 7 actors or less and have simple to moderate technical demands. Plays having up to three previous productions are welcome. No musicals. Deadline: March 30. Prize: $700 and full production. Judged by a panel of qualified theatre teachers, directors, and performers.

THEATRE IN THE RAW BIENNIAL ONE-ACT PLAY WRITING CONTEST

Theatre In the Raw, 3521 Marshall St., Vancouver BC V5N 4S2 Canada. (604)708-5448. **E-mail:** theatreintheraw@telus.net. **Website:** www.theatreintheraw.ca. Biennial contest for an original one-act play, presented in proper stage-play format, that is unpublished and unproduced. The play (with no more than 6 characters) cannot be longer than 25 double-spaced, typed pages equal to 30 minutes. Scripts must have page numbers. Scripts are to be mailed only & will not be accepted by e-mail. Deadline: December 31. Prize: 1st Place: $200, at least 1 dramatic reading or staging of the play at a Theatre In the Raw Cafe/Venue, or as part of a mini-tour program for the One-Act Play Series Nights; 2nd Place: $100; 3rd Place: $75. Winners announced June 30.

JACKIE WHITE MEMORIAL NATIONAL CHILDREN'S PLAY WRITING CONTEST

1800 Nelwood Dr., Columbia MO 65202-1447. (573)874-5628. **E-mail:** jwmcontest@cectheatre.org. **Website:** www.cectheatre.org. **Contact:** Tom Phillips. Annual contest that encourages playwrights to write quality plays for family audiences. Previously unpublished submissions only. Submissions made by author. Play may be performed during the following season. All submissions will be read by at least 3 readers. Author will receive a written evaluation of the script. Guidelines available online. Deadline: June 1. Prize: $500 with production possible. Judging by current and past board members of CEC and by non-board members who direct plays at CEC.

WORLDFEST-HOUSTON INDEPENDENT INTERNATIONAL FILM FESTIVAL

52nd Annual WorldFest-Houston, April 5-14, 2019, 9898 Bissonnet St., Suite 650, Houston TX 77036. (713)965-9955. **Fax:** (713)965-9960. **E-mail:** info@worldfest.org. **Website:** www.worldfest.org. mixed media art **Contact:** Kelly Mann, entry coordinator. WorldFest discovered Steven Spielberg, George Lucas, Ang Lee, Ridley Scott, the Coen Brothers, Francis Ford Coppola, Randal Kleiser, John Lee Hancock, and David Lynch with their first awards. Screenplays must be submitted as actual printed scripts, 3-hole or some sort of binders, no online reading. Competition for all genres of screenplays, plus 10 other competition categories of films and videos. Deadline: December 31; Final deadline is January 15. Prize: Cash, options, production deals, workshops, master classes, and seminars. Judged by a jury whose members are credentialed, experienced, award-winning writers, producers, and directors. No production assistants.

WRITE NOW

Indiana Repertory Theatre, 140 W. Washington St., Indianapolis IN 46204. 480-921-5770. **E-mail:** info@writenow.co. **Website:** www.writenow.co. The purpose of this biennial workshop is to encourage writers to create strikingly original scripts for young audiences. It provides a forum through which each playwright receives constructive criticism and the support of a development team consisting of a professional director and dramaturg. Finalists will spend approximately one week in workshop with their development team. At the end of the week, each play will be read as a part of the Write Now convening. Guidelines available online. Deadline: August 15.

YEAR END SERIES (YES) FESTIVAL OF NEW PLAYS

Theatre and Dance Program, School of the Arts, Nunn Dr., Northern Kentucky University, Highland Heights KY 41099-1007. 859.572.5648. **Fax:** (859)572-6057. **E-mail:** daniellyc1@nku.edu, or mking@nku.edu. **Website:** http://artscience.nku.edu/departments/theatre.html, https://artscience.nku.edu/content/dam/artscience/theatre/docs/16755YesFestivalFlyer.pdf. **Contact:** Michael King, co-project director; Corrie Danieley, co-project director. Receives submissions until September 30 in even-numbered years for the festivals which occur in April of odd-numbered years. Open to all writers. Flyers with submission guidelines and entry forms available on the website, or via email. Deadline: September 30. Open to submissions on May 1. Prize: $250 and an expense-paid visit (travel and housing) to Northern Kentucky University to see the play produced.

ANNA ZORNIO MEMORIAL CHILDREN'S THEATRE PLAYWRITING COMPETITION

University of New Hampshire, Department of Theatre and Dance, PCAC, 30 Academic Way, Durham NH 03824. **E-mail:** mike.wood@unh.edu. **Website:** cola.unh.edu/theatre-dance/program/anna-zornio-childrens-theatre-playwriting-award. **Contact:** Michael Wood. Offered every 4 years for unpublished well-written plays or musicals appropriate for young audiences with a maximum length of 60 minutes. May submit more than 1 play, but not more than 3. Honors the late Anna Zornio, an alumna of The University of New Hampshire, for dedication to and inspiration of playwriting for young people, K-12th grade. Deadline: March 1, 2021. Prize: $500.

ARTS COUNCILS & FELLOWSHIPS

$50,000 GIFT OF FREEDOM

A Room of Her Own Foundation, P.O. Box 778, Placitas NM 87043. **E-mail:** awards@aroho.org. **Website:** www.aroomofherownfoundation.org. **Contact:** Tracey Cravens-Gras, Associate Director. The publicly funded award provides very practical help—both materially and in professional guidance and moral support with mentors and advisory council—to assist women in making their creative contribution to the world. The Gift of Freedom competition will determine superior finalists from each of 3 genres: Creative nonfiction, fiction, and poetry. Open to female residents of the US. Award-application cycle dates are yet to be determined. Visit website at www.aroho.org for more information about the next application window. Deadline: November 2. Prize: One genre finalist will be awarded the $50,000 Gift of Freedom grant, distributed over 2 years in support of the completion of a particular creative project. The 2 remaining genre finalists will each receive a $5,000 prize.

ALABAMA STATE COUNCIL ON THE ARTS FELLOWSHIP-LITERATURE

Alabama State Council on the Arts, 201 Monroe St., Montgomery AL 36130-1800. (334)242-4076, ext. 224. **Fax:** (334)240-3269. **Website:** www.arts.alabama.gov. **Contact:** Randy Shoults. "Literature fellowship offered every year (for previously published or unpublished work) to set aside time to create and improve skills. Two-year Alabama residency required. Guidelines available." Deadline: March 1. $10,000 or $5,000

ALABAMA STATE COUNCIL ON THE ARTS INDIVIDUAL ARTIST FELLOWSHIP

201 Monroe St., Suite 110, Montgomery AL 36130. (334)242-4076, ext. 236. **Fax:** (334)240-3269. **E-mail:** anne.kimzey@arts.alabama.gov. **Website:** www.arts.state.al.us. **Contact:** Anne Kimzey, Literary Arts Program Manager. Must be a legal resident of Alabama who has lived in the state for 2 years prior to application. Competition receives 30+ submissions annually. Accepts inquiries by e-mail and phone. The following

should be submitted: a résumé and a list of published works with reviews, if available; and a minimum of 10 pages of poetry or prose, with a maximum of 20 pages. Please label each page with title, artist's name, and date. If published, indicate where and the date of publication. Please do not submit bound material. Guidelines available in January on website. Recognizes the achievements and potential of Alabama writers. Deadline: March 1. Applications must be submitted online by eGRANT. Judged by independent peer panel. Fellowship recipients notified by mail and announced on website in June.

GEORGE BENNETT FELLOWSHIP

Phillips Exeter Academy, 20 Main Street, Exeter NH 03833-2460. **E-mail:** teaching_opportunities@exeter.edu. **Website:** www.exeter.edu/bennettfellowship. Annual award for fellow and family to provide time and freedom from material considerations to a person seriously contemplating or pursuing a career as a writer. Applicants should have a ms in progress that they intend to complete during the fellowship period. Ms should be fiction, nonfiction, novel, short stories, or poetry. Duties: To be in residency at the Academy for the academic year; to make oneself available informally to students interested in writing. Committee favors writers who have not yet published a book with a major publisher. Deadline: November 30. A choice will be made, and all entrants notified in mid-April. Cash stipend (currently $15,260), room and board. Judged by committee of the English Department.

DOBIE PAISANO WRITER'S FELLOWSHIP

The Graduate School, The University of Texas at Austin, Attn: Dobie Paisano Program, 110 Inner Campus Drive Stop G0400, Austin TX 78712-0531. (512)232-3612. **Fax:** (512)471-7620. **E-mail:** gbarton@austin.utexas.edu. **Website:** www.utexas.edu/ogs/Paisano. **Contact:** Gwen Barton. Sponsored by the Graduate School at The University of Texas at Austin and the Texas Institute of Letters, the Dobie Paisano Fellowship Program provides solitude, time, and a comfortable place for Texas writers or writers who have written significantly about Texas through fiction, nonfiction, poetry, plays, or other mediums. The Dobie Paisano Ranch is a very rural and rustic setting, and applicants should read the guidelines closely to ensure their ability to reside in this secluded environment. At the time of the application, the applicant must meet one of the following requirements: (1) be a native Texan, (2) have resided in Texas at least 3 years at some time, or (3) have published significant work with a Texas subject. Those who meet requirement 1 or 2 do not have to meet the Texas subject-matter restriction. Deadline: January 15. Applications are accepted beginning December 1 and must be post-marked no later than January 15. The Ralph A. Johnston memorial Fellowship is for a period of 4 months with a stipend of $6,250 per month. It is aimed at writers who have already demonstrated some publishing and critical success. The Jesse H. Jones Writing Fellowship is for a period of approximately 6 months with a stipend of $3,000 per month. It is aimed at, but not limited to, writers who are early in their careers.

FELLOWSHIPS FOR CREATIVE AND PERFORMING ARTISTS AND WRITERS

American Antiquarian Society, 185 Salisbury St., Worcester MA 01609-1634. (508)755-5221. **Fax:** (508)754-9069. **E-mail:** jmoran@mwa.org; library@americanantiquarian.org. **Website:** www.americanantiquarian.org. **Contact:** Cheryl McRell, Program Administrator. Annual fellowship for creative and performing artists, writers, filmmakers, journalists, and other persons whose goals are to produce imaginative, non-formulaic works dealing with pre-20th century American history. Application instructions available online. Website also lists potential fellowship projects. Deadline: October 5. Prize: For fellows who reside on campus in the Society's scholars' housing, located next to the main library building, the stipend will have the room fee deducted from the $1850 stipend. (Room fees range from $700 to $500 per month.) The stipend will be $1,850 for fellows residing off campus. Judged by AAS staff and outside reviewers.

GETTING IT WRITE

The Writers' Colony at Dairy Hollow, 515 Spring St., Eureka Springs AR 72632. (479)253-7444. **E-mail:** director@writerscolony.org. **Website:** www.writerscolony.org. **Contact:** Linda Caldwell, director. The Writers' Colony at Dairy Hollow would like to help a screenwriter or playwright produce a film or play that positively portrays LGBTQ life and the struggles faced by all members of that community. We are doing that by offering a two-week, all expenses paid fellowship: Getting it Write. This gift of time will allow the recipient to focus completely on their work. For information and to apply: https://www.writerscolony.org/fellowships. Deadline: January 31.

GUGGENHEIM FELLOWSHIPS

John Simon Guggenheim Memorial Foundation, John Simon Guggenheim Memorial Foundation, 90 Park Ave., New York NY 10016. (212)687-4470. **E-mail:** fellowships@gf.org. **Website:** www.gf.org. Often characterized as "midcareer" awards, Guggenheim Fellowships are intended for men and women who have already demonstrated exceptional capacity for productive scholarship or exceptional creative ability in the arts. Fellowships are awarded through two annual competitions: one open to citizens and permanent residents of the United States and Canada, and the other open to citizens and permanent residents of Latin America and the Caribbean. Candidates must apply to the Guggenheim Foundation in order to be considered in either of these competitions. The Foundation receives between 3,500 and 4,000 applications each year. Although no one who applies is guaranteed success in the competition, there is no prescreening: all applications are reviewed. Approximately 200 Fellowships are awarded each year. Deadline: September 17.

MARILYN HOLLINSHEAD VISITING SCHOLARS FELLOWSHIP

University of Minnesota, Marilyn Hollinshead Visiting Scholars Fellowship, 113 Anderson Library, 222 21st Ave. South, Minneapolis MN 55455. **Website:** http://www.lib.umn.edu/clrc/awards-grants-and-fellowships. Marilyn Hollinshead Visiting Scholars Fund for Travel to the Kerlan Collection is available for research study. Applicants may request up to $1,500. Send a letter with the proposed purpose, plan to use specific research materials (manuscripts and art), dates, and budget (including airfare and per diem). Travel and a written report on the project must be completed and submitted in the previous year. Deadline: January 30.

HENRY HOYNS & POE-FAULKNER FELLOWSHIPS

Creative Writing Program, 219 Bryan Hall, P.O. Box 400121, University of Virginia, Charlottesville VA 22904-4121. (434)924-6074. **Fax:** (434)924-1478. **E-mail:** creativewriting@virginia.edu. **Website:** creativewriting.virginia.edu. **Contact:** Barbara Moriarty, Administrative Assistant. Two-year MFA program in poetry and fiction; all students receive fellowships and teaching stipends that total $20,000 in both years of study. Sample poems/prose required with application. Optional third year with partial funding. Deadline: December 15.

MASS CULTURAL COUNCIL ARTIST FELLOWSHIP PROGRAM

Mass Cultural Council, Mass Cultural Council, 10 St. James Ave., #302, Boston MA 02116-3803. (617)727-3668. **Fax:** (617)727-0044. **E-mail:** mcc@art.state.ma.us. **Website:** www.massculturalcouncil.org; http://artsake.massculturalcouncil.org. **Contact:** Dan Blask, Program Officer. Awards in poetry, fiction/creative nonfiction, and dramatic writing (among other discipline categories) are given in recognition of exceptional original work (check website for award amount). Accepts inquiries by fax, e-mail, and phone. Must be 18 years or older and a legal residents of Massachusetts for the last 2 years and at time of award. This excludes students in directly related degree programs, and grant recipients within the last 3 years. Looking to award artistic excellence and creative ability, based on work submitted for review. Judged by independent peer panels composed of artists and arts professionals.

MCKNIGHT ARTIST FELLOWSHIPS FOR WRITERS, LOFT AWARD(S) IN CHILDREN'S LITERATURE/CREATIVE PROSE/POETRY

The Loft Literary Center, 1011 Washington Ave. S., Suite 200, Open Book, Minneapolis MN 55415. (612)215-2575. **Fax:** (612)215-2576. **E-mail:** loft@loft.org. **Website:** www.loft.org. **Contact:** Bao Phi. The Loft administers the McKnight Artists Fellowships for Writers. Five $25,000 awards are presented annually to accomplished Minnesota writers and spoken word artists. Four awards alternate annually between creative prose (fiction and creative nonfiction) and poetry/spoken word. The fifth award is presented in children's literature and alternates annually for writing for ages 8 and under and writing for children older than 8. The awards provide the writers the opportunity to focus on their craft for the course of the fellowship year. Prize: $25,000, plus up to $3,000 in reimbursement for a writer's retreat or conference. The judge is announced after selections are made.

JENNY MCKEAN MOORE VISITING WRITER

Department of English, George Washington University, Phillips Hall, 801 22nd St. NW, Suite 643, Washington DC 20052. (202)994-6180. **Fax:** (202)994-7915. **E-mail:** engldept@gwu.edu; lpageinc@gwu.edu.

Website: https://english.columbian.gwu.edu/activities-events. **Contact:** Lisa Page, Director of Creative Writing. The position is filled annually, bringing a visiting writer to The George Washington University. During each semester the Writer teaches 1 creative-writing course at the university as well as a community workshop. Seeks someone specializing in a different genre each year—fiction, poetry, creative nonfiction. Annual stipend between $50,000 and $60,000, plus reduced-rent townhouse on campus (not guaranteed). Application deadline: December 12. Annual stipend varies, depending on endowment performance; most recently, stipend was $60,000, plus reduced-rent townhouse (not guaranteed).

NORTH CAROLINA ARTS COUNCIL REGIONAL ARTIST PROJECT GRANTS

North Carolina Arts Council, Dept. of Natural and Cultural Resources, MSC #4632, Raleigh NC 27699-4634. (919)807-6512. **Fax:** (919)807-6532. **E-mail:** david.potorti@ncdcr.gov. **Website:** www.ncarts.org. **Contact:** David Potorti, literature and theater director. See website for contact information for the consortia of local arts councils that distribute these grants. Open to any writer living in North Carolina. Deadline: Dates vary in fall/spring. Prize: $500-3,000 awarded to writers to pursue projects that further their artistic development. These grants are awarded through consortia of local arts councils. See our website for details.

NORTH CAROLINA WRITERS' FELLOWSHIPS

North Carolina Arts Council, NC Department of Natural and Cultural Resources, North Carolina Arts Council, Mail Service Center #4632, Raleigh NC 27699-4632. (919)814-6512. **E-mail:** david.potorti@ncdcr.gov. **Website:** www.ncarts.org. **Contact:** David Potorti, literature and theater director. The North Carolina Arts Council offers fellowship grants to support writers of fiction, creative non-fiction, poetry, spoken word, playwrighting, screenwriting and literary translation. Artists must be N.C. residents for at least one year prior to the deadline, and at least 18 years old. They must be a U.S. citizen or holder of permanent resident alien status, remain a N.C. resident during the grant period, and be physically present in the state for the majority of that time. Artists who received the fellowship grant in the past five years or are enrolled in an academic or degree-granting program at the time of application or during the grant period are not eligible. Fellowships are offered to support writers in the development and creation of new work. See website for details. Offered every even-numbered year to support writers of fiction, creative nonfiction, poetry, spoken word, playwriting, screenwriting and literary translation. See website for guidelines and other eligibility requirements. Deadline: November 1 of even-numbered years. Next deadline is Nov. 1, 2020. Prize: $10,000 grant. Reviewed by a panel of literature professionals (writers and editors).

NYSCA/NYFA ARTIST FELLOWSHIP

New York Foundation for the Arts, 20 Jay St., 7th Floor, Brooklyn NY 11201. (212)366-6900. **E-mail:** fellowships@nyfa.org. **Website:** www.nyfa.org. **Contact:** NYFA Grants. NYSCA/NYFA Artist Fellowships, awarded in fifteen different disciplines over a three-year period, are $7,000 cash awards made to individual originating artists living and working in the state of New York for unrestricted use. These fellowships are not project grants but are intended to fund an artist's vision or voice, regardless of the level of his or her artistic development. Visit www.nyfa.org/fellowships for eligibility requirements and more information. Open to residents of New York State and/or Indian Nations located in New York State. End of January. Grants of $7,000. Judged by peer-reviewed panel.

OREGON LITERARY FELLOWSHIPS

925 S.W. Washington, Portland OR 97205. (503)227-2583. **E-mail:** susan@literary-arts.org. **Website:** www.literary-arts.org. **Contact:** Susan Moore, Director of programs and events. Oregon Literary Fellowships are intended to help Oregon writers initiate, develop, or complete literary projects in poetry, fiction, literary nonfiction, drama, and young readers literature. Writers in the early stages of their career are encouraged to apply. The awards are merit-based. Guidelines available in February for SASE. Accepts inquiries by e-mail, phone. Oregon residents only. Recipients announced in January. Deadline: Last Friday in June. Prize: $3,000 minimum award, for approximately 8 writers and 2 publishers. Judged by out-of-state writers

WALLACE E. STEGNER FELLOWSHIPS

Creative Writing Program, Stanford University, Stanford CA 94305-2087. (650)723-0011. **E-mail:** stegnerfellowship@stanford.edu. **Website:** https://creativewriting.stanford.edu/stegner-fellowship/overview.

Offers 5 fellowships in poetry and 5 in fiction for promising writers who can benefit from 2 years of instruction and participation in the program. Online application preferred. "We do not require a degree for admission. No school of writing is favored over any other. Chronological age is not a consideration." Deadline: December 1. Open to submissions on September 1. Prize: Fellowships of $37,500, plus tuition and health insurance.

TENNESSEE ARTS COMMISSION LITERARY FELLOWSHIP

Tennessee Arts Commission, 401 Charlotte Ave., Nashville TN 37243-0780. **Fax:** (615)741-8559. **E-mail:** lee.baird@state.tn.us. **Website:** tnartscommission.org. **Contact:** Lee Baird, director of literary programs. Awarded annually in recognition of professional Tennessee artists, i.e., individuals who have received financial compensation for their work as professional writers. Applicants must have a publication history other than vanity press. Three fellowships awarded annually to outstanding literary artists who live and work in Tennessee. Categories are in fiction, creative nonfiction, and poetry. Deadline: January 26. Prize: $5,000. Judged by an out-of-state adjudicator.

WISCONSIN INSTITUTE FOR CREATIVE WRITING FELLOWSHIP

6195B H.C. White Hall, 600 N. Park St., Madison WI 53706. **E-mail:** sbbishop@wisc.edu. **Website:** creativewriting.wisc.edu/fellowships.html. **Contact:** Sean Bishop, graduate coordinator. Fellowship provides time, space and an intellectual community for writers working on first books.Since 2012, we have also considered applicants who have published only one full-length collection of creative writing prior to the application deadline, although unpublished authors remain eligible, and quality of writing remains the near-exclusive criterion for selection. Receives approximately 300 applicants a year for each genre. Judged by English Department faculty and current fellows. Candidates can have up to one published book in the genre for which they are applying. Open to any writer with either an M.F.A. or Ph.D. in creative writing. Results announced on website by May 1. Applicants should submit up to 10 pages of poetry or one story or excerpt of up to 30 pages and a résumé or vita directly to the program during the month of February. See instructions on website for submitting online. An applicant's name must not appear on the writing sample (which must be in ms form) but rather on a separate sheet along with address, social security number, phone number, e-mail address and title(s) of submission(s). Candidates should also supply the names and phone numbers of two references. Accepts inquiries by e-mail and phone. Deadline: Last day of February. Open to submissions on February 1. Prize: $38,000 for a 9-month appointment.

FICTION

AEON AWARD

Albedo One/Aeon Press, Aeon Award, Albedo One & Yellow Brick Road, 8 Bachelor's Walk, Dublin D1 Ireland. (353)1-8730177. **E-mail:** fraslaw@yahoo.co.uk. **Website:** www.albedo1.com. **Contact:** Frank Ludlow, Event Coordinator. Prestigious fiction-writing competition for short stories in any speculative fiction genre such as fantasy, science fiction, horror, or anything in-between or unclassifiable. Submit your story (which must be less than 10,000 words in length and previously unpublished) in the body of an e-mail with contact details, and "Aeon Award Submission" as the subject. Annual Deadline: November 30. Contest begins January 1. Grand Prize: €1,000; 2nd Prize: €200; 3rd Prize: €100. The top 3 stories are guaranteed publication in *Albedo One*. Judged by Ian Watson, Priya Sharma, Juliet E. McKenna, and Michael Carroll.

AHWA FLASH & SHORT STORY COMPETITION

AHWA (Australian Horror Writers Association), **E-mail:** ahwacomps@australianhorror.com; ahwa@australianhorror.com. **Website:** www.australianhorror.com. **Contact:** Competitions Officer. Competition/award for short stories and flash fiction. There are 2 categories: short stories (1,001 to 8,000 words) and flash fiction (less than 1,000 words). Writers may submit to one or both categories, but entry is limited to 1 story per author per category. Send submission as an attached rtf or doc. Mail submissions accepted only as a last resort. No previously published entries will be accepted—all tales must be an original work by the author. Stories can be as violent or as bloody as the storyline dictates, but those containing gratuitous sex or violence will not be considered. Please check entries for spelling and grammar mistakes and follow standard submission guidelines (e.g., 12 point font, Ariel, Times New Roman, or Courier New, one and a half spacing between lines, with title and page number on each page). Looking for horror stories, tales that frighten, yarns that unsettle readers in their comfortable homes. All themes in this genre will be accepted, from the well-used (zombies, vampires, ghosts etc) to the highly original, so long as the story is professional and well written. Deadline: May 31. Prize: The authors of the winning Flash Fiction and Short Story entries will each receive paid publication in *Midnight Echo*, the Magazine of the AHWA, and an engraved plaque. Judged by previous winners.

SHERWOOD ANDERSON FICTION AWARD

Mid-American Review, Mid-American Review, Dept. of English, Box WM, BGSU, Bowling Green OH 43403. (419)372-2725. **Fax:** (419)372-4642. **E-mail:** mar@bgsu.edu. **Website:** www.bgsu.edu/midamericanreview. **Contact:** Abigail Cloud, Editor-in-Chief. Offered annually for unpublished mss (6,000 word limit). Contest is open to all writers not associated with a judge or *Mid-American Review*. Guidelines available online or for SASE. Deadline: December 15, 2019. Prize: $1,000, plus publication in the Spring issue of *Mid-American Review*. Four finalists: Notation, possible publication. Judged by editors and a well-known writer (Aimee Bender or Anthony Doerr). Judged by Charles Yu in 2017. 2017-2018 judges: Alexander Weinstein and Dara Wier.

AUTUMN HOUSE PRESS FULL-LENGTH FICTION PRIZE

Autumn House Press, 5530 Penn Ave., Pittsburgh PA 15206. **E-mail:** info@autumnhouse.org. **Website:** autumnhouse.org. Fiction submissions should be approximately 200-300 pages. All fiction sub-genres (short stories, short-shorts, novellas, or novels), or any combination of sub-genres, are eligible. All finalists will be considered for publication. Deadline: June 30. Prize: Winners will receive book publication, $1,000 advance against royalties, and a $1,500 travel grant. Judged by Aimee Bender (final judge).

BALCONES FICTION PRIZE

Austin Commmunity College, Department of Creative Writing c/o Joe O'Connell, 4400 College Park Dr,, Round Rock TX 78665. (512)584-5045. **E-mail:** joconne@austincc.edu. **Website:** www.austincc.edu/crw/html/balconescenter.html. **Contact:** Joe O'Connell. Awarded to the best book of literary fiction published the previous year. Books of prose may be submitted by publisher or author. Send three copies. Deadline: January 31. Prize: $1,500, winner is flown to Austin for a campus reading.

BARD FICTION PRIZE

Bard College, P.O. Box 5000, Annandale-on-Hudson NY 12504-5000. (845)758-7087. **Fax:** (845)758-7917. **E-mail:** bfp@bard.edu. **Website:** www.bard.edu/bfp. **Contact:** Irene Zedlacher. The Bard Fiction Prize is awarded to a promising, emerging writer who is an American citizen aged 39 years or younger at the time of application. Cover letter should include name, address, phone, e-mail, and name of publisher where book was previously published. Entries must be previously published. Open to U.S. citizens aged 39 and below. Guidelines available by SASE, fax, phone, e-mail, or on website. Results announced by October 15. Winners notified by phone. For contest results, e-mail, or visit website. The Bard Fiction Prize is intended to encourage and support young writers of fiction to pursue their creative goals and to provide an opportunity to work in a fertile and intellectual environment. Deadline: June 15. Prize: $30,000 and appointment as writer-in-residence at Bard College for 1 semester. Judged by a committee of 5 judges (authors associated with Bard College).

BELLEVUE LITERARY REVIEW GOLDENBERG PRIZE FOR FICTION

Bellevue Literary Review, NYU Dept of Medicine, 550 First Ave., OBV-A612, New York NY 10016. (212)263-3973. **E-mail:** info@blreview.org; stacy@blreview.org. **Website:** www.blreview.org. **Contact:** Stacy Bodziak, managing editor. The BLR prizes award outstanding writing related to themes of health, healing, illness, the mind and the body. Annual competition/award for short stories. Receives about 200-300 entries per category. Submit online. Guidelines available in February. Accepts inquiries by e-mail, phone, mail. Submissions open March 1st. Results announced in December and made available to entrants with SASE, by e-mail, on website. Winners notified by mail, by e-mail. Entries should be unpublished. Anyone may enter contest. Length: No minimum; maximum of 5,000 words. Writers may submit own work. Deadline: July 1. Prize: $1,000 and publication in *The Bellevue Literary Review*. Honorable mention winners receive $250 and publication. BLR editors select semi-finalists to be read by an independent judge who chooses the winner. Previous judges include Nathan

Englander, Jane Smiley, Francine Prose, Andre Dubus III, Ha Jin, and Geraldine Brooks.

BINGHAMTON UNIVERSITY JOHN GARDNER FICTION BOOK AWARD

Creative Writing Program, Binghamton University, Binghamton University, Department of English, General Literature, and Rhetoric, Library North Room 1149, P.O. Box 6000, Binghamton NY 13902-6000. (607)777-2713. **E-mail:** cwpro@binghamton.edu. **Website:** http://binghamton.edu/english/creative-writing/. **Contact:** Maria Mazziotti Gillan, Director. Contest offered annually for a novel or collection of fiction published in previous year in a press run of 500 copies or more. Each book submitted must be accompanied by an application form. Publisher may submit more than 1 book for prize consideration. Send 2 copies of each book. Guidelines available on website. Author or publisher may submit. Deadline: February 1. $1,000. Judged by a professional writer not on Binghamton University faculty.

JAMES TAIT BLACK MEMORIAL PRIZES

English Literature, University of Edinburgh, School of Literatures, Languages, and Cultures, 50 George Square, Edinburgh EH8 9LH Scotland. (44-13)1650-3619. **E-mail:** s.strathdee@ed.ac.uk. **Website:** https://www.ed.ac.uk/events/james-tait-black. Open to any writer. Entries must be previously published. Winners notified by phone, via publisher. Contact department of English Literature for list of winners or check website. Accepts inquiries by e-mail or phone. Eligible works must be written in English, and first published or co-published in Britain in the year of the award. Works should be submitted by publishers. Deadline: December 1. Two prizes each of £10,000 are awarded: one for the best work of fiction, one for the best biography or work of nature, published during the calendar year January 1 to December 31. Judged by professors of English Literature, with the assistance of teams of postgraduate readers.

BOULEVARD SHORT FICTION CONTEST FOR EMERGING WRITERS

Boulevard Magazine, Boulevard Emerging Writers Contest, PMB #325, 6614 Clayton Rd., Richmond Heights MO 63117. (314)862-2643. **Website:** www.boulevardmagazine.org. **Contact:** Jessica Rogen, Editor. Offered annually for unpublished short fiction to a writer who has not yet published a book of fiction, poetry, or creative nonfiction with a nationally distributed press. Holds first North American rights on anything not previously published. Open to any writer with no previous publication by a nationally known press. Guidelines for SASE on website. Accepts works up to 8,000 words. Simultaneous submissions are allowed, but previously accepted or published work is ineligible. Entries will be judged by the editors of *Boulevard Magazine*. Submit online or via postal mail. Deadline: December 31. Prize: $1,500, and publication in one of the next year's issues.

JOHN W. CAMPBELL MEMORIAL AWARD FOR BEST SCIENCE FICTION NOVEL OF THE YEAR

1445 Jayhawk Blvd, Suite 3001, University of Kansas, Lawrence KS 66045. (785)864-2518. **E-mail:** Gunn.SF.Center@gmail.com. **Website:** www.sfcenter.ku.edu/campbell.htm. **Contact:** Chris McKitterick. Honors the best science fiction novel of the year. Entries must be previously published. Open to any writer. Accepts inquiries by e-mail. "Ordinarily publishers should submit work, but authors have done so when publishers would not. Send for list of jurors." Results announced in July. For contest results, see website. Deadline: Check website. Prize: Campbell Award trophy. Winners receive an expense-paid trip to the Campbell Conference to receive their award. Their names are also engraved on a permanent trophy. Judged by a jury.

CANADIAN AUTHORS ASSOCIATION AWARD FOR POETRY

192 Spadina Avenue, Suite 107, Toronto ON M5T 2C2 Canada. (416)975 1756. **E-mail:** admin@canadianauthors.org. **Website:** www.canadianauthors.org. **Contact:** Anita Purcell, Executive Director. Offered annually for a full-length English-language book of poems for adults, by a Canadian writer. Deadline: January 31. Prize: $1,000 and a silver medal. Judging: Each year a trustee for each award appointed by the Canadian Authors Association selects up to 3 judges. Identities of the trustee and judges are confidential.

CANADIAN AUTHORS ASSOCIATION EMERGING WRITER AWARD

192 Spadina Avenue, Suite 107, Toronto ON M5T 2C2 Canada. **Website:** www.canadianauthors.org. **Contact:** Anita Purcell, Executive Director. Annual award for a writer under 30 years of age deemed to show exceptional promise in the field of literary creation. Deadline: January 15. Prize: $500. Judging: Each year

a trustee for each award appointed by the Canadian Authors Association selects up to 3 judges. Identities of the trustee and judges are confidential.

KAY CATTARULLA AWARD FOR BEST SHORT STORY

Texas Institute of Letters, P.O. Box 609, Round Rock TX 78680. **E-mail:** tilsecretary@yahoo.com. **Website:** www.texasinstituteofletters.org. Offered annually for work published January 1-December 31 of previous year to recognize the best short story. The story submitted must have appeared in print for the first time to be eligible. Writers must have been born in Texas, must have lived in Texas for at least 2 consecutive years, or the subject matter of the work must be associated with Texas. See website for guidelines. See website for details and instructions on entering the competition. Deadline: January 10. Prize: $1,000.

PEGGY CHAPMAN-ANDREWS FIRST NOVEL AWARD

The Bridport Prize, The Bridport Prize, P.O. Box 6910, Dorset DT6 9QB United Kingdom. **E-mail:** info@bridportprize.org.uk. **Website:** www.bridportprize.org.uk. **Contact:** Kate Wilson, Programme Manager. Award to promote literary excellence and new writers. Enter first chapters of novel, up to 8,000 words (minimum 5,000 words) plus 300 word synopsis. Send SSAE for entry form or enter online. Deadline: May 31. Prize: 1st Place: £1,000 plus mentoring & possible publication; Runner-Up: £500. Judged in 2019 by Naomi Wood with The Literary Consultancy & A.M. Heath Literary Agents.

THE ARTHUR C. CLARKE AWARD

55 Burtt House, Fanshaw Street, London N1 6LE U.K. **E-mail:** clarkeaward@gmail.com. **Website:** www.clarkeaward.com. **Contact:** Tom Hunter, Award Director. Annual award presented to the best science fiction novel published between January 1 and December 31 of the year in question, receiving its first British publication during the calendar year. Deadline: 2nd week in December. Prize: £2,016 (rising by £1 each year), and an engraved bookend. Judged by representatives of the British Science Fiction Association, the Science Fiction Foundation, and Sci-Fi-London Film Festival

THE DANAHY FICTION PRIZE

Tampa Review, University of Tampa, Tampa Review, 401 W. Kennedy Blvd., Tampa FL 33606-1490. (813)253-6266. **E-mail:** utpress@ut.edu. **Website:** www.ut.edu/TampaReview. Annual award for the best previously unpublished short fiction. Prefers mss between 500-5,000 words. Deadline: December 31. Prize: $1,000, plus publication in *Tampa Review* and 1-year subscription to *Tampa Review*. Judging is by the editors of Tampa Review.

DEBUT DAGGER

Crime Writers' Association, Debut Dagger, Dea Parkin, CWA Secretary, The Writing House, 3 Dale View, Chorley Lancashire PR7 3QJ United Kingdom. **E-mail:** secretary@thecwa.co.uk. **Website:** https://thecwa.co.uk/the-debuts/. **Contact:** Dea Parkin. Annual competition for unpublished crime writers. Submit the opening 3,000 words of a crime novel, plus a 1,000-1,500 word synopsis. Open to any writer without agent representation who has not had a full-length novel traditionally published. (Self-published only is acceptable, including the novel entry itself.) Accepts entries in Word doc or doc, txt, rtf or pdf. Submissions should not include entrant's name anywhere on the document. See website for full rules and guidelines on how to submit. To bring new writers to the attention of publishers and create opportunities for crime novelists of the future. Deadline: February 28. Submission period begins November 1. Prize: £500. All shortlisted entrants will, with their permission, have their entry sent to interested UK literary agents and publishers, and receive brief feedback on their entries. Any changes to the above will be posted to the website. Judged by a panel of top crime editors and agents as well as the CWA's head of Criminal Critiques. The shortlisted entries are sent to agents. Any changes to the above will be posted to the website.

WILLIAM F. DEECK MALICE DOMESTIC GRANTS FOR UNPUBLISHED WRITERS

Malice Domestic, P.O. Box 8007, Gaithersburg MD 20898-8007. **E-mail:** malicegrants@comcast.net. **Website:** www.malicedomestic.org. **Contact:** Harriette Sackler, Malice Domestic Grants Chair. Offered annually for unpublished work in the mystery field. Malice awards 1 grant to unpublished writers in the Malice Domestic genre at its annual convention in May. The competition is designed to help the next generation of Malice authors get their first work published and to foster quality Malice literature. Malice Domestic literature is loosely described as mystery stories of the Agatha Christie type; i.e., traditional mysteries. These works usually feature no excessive gore, gratuitous violence, or explicit sex. Writers who have been published previously in the mystery field,including publication of a mystery novel, short story, or dramatic work, are ineligible to apply. Members of the Malice Domestic Board of Directors and their families are ineligible to apply. Malice encourages applications from minority candidates. Guidelines online. Deadline: November 1. Prize: $2,500, plus a comprehensive registration to the following year's convention and 2 nights' lodging at the convention hotel.

THE FAR HORIZONS AWARD FOR SHORT FICTION

The Malahat Review, University of Victoria, P.O. Box 1800, Stn CSC, Victoria BC V8W 3H5 Canada. (250)721-8524. **E-mail:** malahat@uvic.ca. **E-mail:** horizons@uvic.ca. **Website:** www.malahatreview.ca. **Contact:** L'Amour Lisik, Marketing and Circulation Manager. Submissions must be unpublished. No simultaneous submissions. Submit 1 piece of short fiction, 3,500 words maximum; no restrictions on subject matter or aesthetic approach. Include separate page with author's name, address, e-mail, and title; no identifying information on mss pages. E-mail submissions are accepted. Do not include SASE for results; mss will not be returned. Guidelines available on website. Winner and finalists contacted by e-mail. Open to "emerging short fiction writers from Canada, the US, and elsewhere" who have not yet published their fiction in a full-length book (48 pages or more). Deadline: May 1 of odd-numbered years. Prize: $1,000 CAD, publication in fall issue of *The Malahat Review*. Announced in fall on website, Facebook page, and in quarterly e-newsletter *Malahat Lite*.

THE GHOST STORY SUPERNATURAL FICTION AWARD

The Ghost Story, P.O. Box 601, Union ME 04862. **E-mail:** editor@theghoststory.com. **Website:** www.theghoststory.com. **Contact:** Paul Guernsey. Biannual contest for unpublished fiction. "Ghost stories are welcome, of course—but submissions may involve *any* paranormal or supernatural theme, as well as magic realism. What we're looking for is fine writing, fresh perspectives, and maybe a few surprises in the field of supernatural fiction." Guidelines available online. Length: 1,500-10,000 words. Deadline: April 30 and September 30. Winner receives $1,000 and publication. Two Honorable Mentions each win $250 plus publication. Judged by the editors of *The Ghost Story*.

GIVAL PRESS NOVEL AWARD

Gival Press, LLC, P.O. Box 3812, Arlington VA 22203. (703)351-0079. **E-mail:** givalpress@yahoo.com. **Website:** www.givalpress.submittable.com. **Contact:** Robert L. Giron. Offered every other year, with the next deadline being May 30, 2020 and book publication in 2021, for a previously original unpublished novel (not a translation). Guidelines by phone, on website, via e-mail, or by mail with SASE. Results announced late fall of same year. Winners notified by phone. Results made available to entrants with SASE, by e-mail, on website. Enter via portal: www.givalpress.submittable.com. Open to any author who writes original unpublished ms/work in English. Length: 30,000-100,000 words. Cover letter should include name, address, phone, e-mail, word count, novel title; include a short bio and short synopsis. Only the title and word count should appear on the actual ms. Writers may submit own work. Purpose is to award the best literary novel. Deadline: May 30, 2020. Prize: $3,000, plus publication of book with a standard contract and author's copies. Final judge is announced after winner is chosen. Entries read anonymously.

GIVAL PRESS SHORT STORY AWARD

Gival Press, Gival Press Short Story Award; Gival Press, LLC; Att'n: Robert L. Giron, Editor, P.O. Box 3812, Arlington VA 22203. (703)351-0079. **E-mail:** givalpress@yahoo.com. **Website:** www.givalpress.submittable.com. **Contact:** Robert L. Giron, Editor-in-Chief. Annual literary, short-story contest. Entries must be unpublished. Open to anyone who writes original short stories, which are not a chapter of a novel, in English. Receives about 100-150 entries per category. Guidelines available online, via e-mail, or by mail. Results announced in the fall of the same year. Winners notified by phone. Results available with SASE, by e-mail, and on website. Enter via portal: www.givalpress.submittable.com. Length: 5,000-15,000 words. Include name, address, phone, e-mail, word count, title on cover letter; include short bio. Only the title and word count should be found on ms. Writers may submit their own fiction.

Recognizes the best literary short story. Deadline: August 8. Prize: $1,000 and publication on website. Judged anonymously.

MARJORIE GRABER-MCINNIS SHORT STORY AWARD

ACT Writers Centre, ACT Writers Centre, Gorman Arts Centre, Ainslie Ave., Braddon ACT 2612 Australia. (02)6262 9191. **Fax:** (02)6262 9191. **E-mail:** admin@actwriters.org.au. **Website:** www.actwriters.org.au. Open theme for a short story with 1,500-3,000 words. Guidelines available on website. Open only to unpublished emerging writers residing within the ACT or region. Deadline: October 26. Submissions period begins in early September. Prize: $600 and publication. 5 runners-up receive book prizes. All winners may be published in the ACT Writers Centre newsletter and on the ACT Writers Centre website.

HADOW STUART SHORT STORY COMPETITION

Fellowship of Australian Writers (WA), FAWWA, PO Box 6180, Swanbourne WA 6910, P.O. Box 6180, Swanbourne WA 6910 Australia. (61)(08)9384-4771. **Fax:** (61)(08)9384-4854. **E-mail:** fellowshipaustralianwriterswa@gmail.com. **Website:** www.fawwa.org. Annual contest for unpublished short stories (maximum 3,000 words). Reserves the right to publish entries in a FAWWA publication or on website. Guidelines online or for SASE. Deadline: June 1. Submissions period begins April 1. Prize: 1st Place: $1,000; 2nd Place: $300; 3rd Place: $100.

HAMMETT PRIZE

International Association of Crime Writers, North American Branch, 243 Fifth Avenue, #537, New York NY 10016. **E-mail:** crimewritersna@gmail.com. **Website:** www.crimewritersna.org. **Contact:** J. Madison Davis. Award for crime novels, story collections, or nonfiction by 1 author. "Our reading committee seeks suggestions from publishers, and they also ask the membership for recommendations." Nominations announced in January; winners announced in fall. Winners notified by e-mail or mail and recognized at awards ceremony. For contest results, send SASE or e-mail. For guidelines, send SASE or e-mail. Accepts inquiries by e-mail. Entries must be previously published. To be eligible, the book must have been published in the US or Canada during the calendar year. The author must be a US or Canadian citizen or permanent resident. Award established to honor a work of literary excellence in the field of crime writing by a US or Canadian author. Deadline: December 15. Prize: Trophy. Judged by a committee of members of the organization. The committee chooses 5 nominated books, which are then sent to 3 outside judges for a final selection. Judges are outside the crime-writing field.

WILDA HEARNE FLASH FICTION CONTEST

Big Muddy: A Journal of the Mississippi River Valley, WHFF Contest, Southeast Missouri State University Press, One University Plaza, MS 2650, Cape Girardeau MO 63701. (573)651-2044. **E-mail:** upress@semo.edu. **Website:** www.semopress.com. **Contact:** James Brubaker, publisher. Annual competition for flash fiction, held by Southeast Missouri State University Press. Work must not be previously published. Send maximum of 500 words, double-spaced, with no identifying name on the pages. Submit via Submittable. Deadline: October 1. Prize: $500 and publication in *Big Muddy: A Journal of the Mississippi River Valley*. The Editors

DRUE HEINZ LITERATURE PRIZE

University of Pittsburgh Press, Drue Heinz Literature Prize, University of Pittsburgh Press, 7500 Thomas Blvd., 4th Floor, Pittsburgh PA 15260. **Fax:** (412)383-2466. **E-mail:** info@upress.pitt.edu. **Website:** www.upress.pitt.edu. Offered annually to writers who have published a book-length collection of fiction or a minimum of 3 short stories or novellas in commercial magazines or literary journals of national distribution. Does not return mss. Manuscripts must be received during May and June 2019. That is, they must be postmarked on or after May 1 and on or before June 30th. Prize: $15,000. Judged by anonymous nationally known writers such as Robert Penn Warren, Joyce Carol Oates, and Margaret Atwood.

LORIAN HEMINGWAY SHORT STORY COMPETITION

P.O. Box 2011 c/o Cynthia. D. Higgs: Key West Editorial, Key West FL 33045. **E-mail:** shortstorykeywest@hushmail.com. **Website:** www.shortstorycompetition.com. **Contact:** Eva Eliot, editorial assistant. Offered annually for unpublished short stories up to 3,500 words. Guidelines available via e-mail, or online. Accepts inquiries by e-mail, or visit website. Entries must be unpublished. Open to all writers whose work has not appeared in a nationally distributed publication with a circulation of 5,000 or more. Looking for excellence, pure and simple—no genre restrictions, no theme restrictions. We seek a writer's voice that cannot be ignored. All entrants will receive a letter from Lorian Hemingway on the competition's Facebook fan page and a list of winners, via the FB fan page or as requested by e-mail.Results announced the first week of August on the competition's FB fan page, and shortly after on the competition website. Only the first-place winner will be notified by phone prior to announcement. Award to encourage literary excellence and the efforts of writers whose voices have yet to be heard. Deadline: May 15. Prizes: 1st Place: $1,500, plus publication of his or her winning story in *Cutthroat: A Journal of the Arts*; 2nd-3rd Place: $500; honorable mentions will also be awarded. Judged by a panel of writers, editors, and literary scholars selected by author Lorian Hemingway. Lorian Hemingway is the competition's final judge.

TONY HILLERMAN PRIZE

Wordharvest, St. Martin's Press, 175 Fifth Avenue, New York NY 10010. (505)471-1565. **E-mail:** tonyhillermanprize@stmartins.com. **Website:** www.wordharvest.com. **Contact:** Anne Hillerman and Jean Schaumberg, Co-organizers. Awarded annually, and sponsored by St. Martin's Press, for the best first mystery set in the Southwest. Murder or another serious crime or crimes must be at the heart of the story, with the emphasis on the solution rather than the details of the crime. Multiple entries accepted. Accepts inquiries by e-mail, phone. Entries should be unpublished; self-published work is generally accepted. Length: no less than 220 type written pages, or approximately 60,000 words. Cover letter should include name, address, phone, e-mail, list of publishing credits. Please include SASE for response. Writers may submit their own work. Entries should be mailed to St. Martin's Press: St. Martin's Minotaur/THWC Competition, St. Martin's Minotaur, 175 Fifth Ave., New York, NY 10010. Honors the contributions made by Tony Hillerman to the art and craft of the mystery. Deadline: January 2. Prize: $10,000 advance and publication by St. Martin's Press. Nominees will be selected by judges chosen by the editorial staff of St. Martin's Press, with the assistance of independent judges selected by organizers of the Tony Hillerman Writers Conference (Wordharvest), and the winner will be chosen by St. Martin's editors.

L. RON HUBBARD'S WRITERS OF THE FUTURE CONTEST

Author Services, Inc., L. Ron Hubbard's Writers of the Future Contest, 7051 Hollywood Blvd., Los Angeles CA 90028. (323)466-3310. **Fax:** (323)466-6474. **E-mail:** contests@authorservicesinc.com. **Website:** www.writersofthefuture.com. **Contact:** Joni Labaqui, Contest Director. Foremost competition for new and amateur writers of unpublished science fiction or fantasy short stories or novelettes. Offered to find, reward and publicize new speculative fiction writers so they may more easily attain professional writing careers. Open to writers who have not professionally published a novel or short novel, more than 2 novelettes, or more than 3 short stories. Entry stories must be unpublished. Limit 1 entry per quarter. This is an international contest. Results announced quarterly in e-newsletter. Winners notified by phone. Contest has 4 quarters. There shall be 3 cash prizes in each quarter. In addition, at the end of the year, the 4 first-place, quarterly winners will have their entries rejudged, and a grand prize winner shall be determined. Eligible entries are previously unpublished short stories or novelettes (under 17,000 words) of science fiction or fantasy. Guidelines for SASE or on website. Accepts inquiries by fax, e-mail, phone. Mss: White paper, black ink; double-spaced; typed; each page appropriately numbered with title, no author name. Include cover page with author's name, address, phone number, e-mail address (if available), as well as estimated word count and the title of the work. Online submissions are accepted. Hard copy submissions will not be returned. Deadline: December 31, March 31, June 30, September 30. Prize (awards quarterly): 1st Place: $1,000; 2nd Place: $750; and 3rd Place: $500. Annual grand prize: $5,000. Judged by David Farland (initial judge), then by a panel of 4 professional authors.

INK & INSIGHTS WRITING CONTEST

Critique My Novel, 1802 S Lincoln, Amarillo TX 79102. **E-mail:** contest@inkandinsights.com. **Website:** https://inkandinsights.com. **Contact:** Catherine York, contest administrator. Ink & Insights is a writing contest geared toward strengthening the skills of independent writers by focusing on feedback. Each entry is assigned four judges who specialize in the genre of the manuscript. They read, score, and comment on specific aspects of the segment. The top three mss in the Master and Nonfiction categories move on to the Agent Round and receive a guaranteed read and feedback from a panel of agents. Send the first 10,000 words of your manuscript (unpublished, self-published, or published through a vanity/independent press). Include a cover sheet that contains the following information: novel title, genre, word count of full ms, e-mail address. Do not put name on submission. See website for full details and formatting guidelines. Deadline: May 30 (regular entry), June 30 (late entry). Prize: Prizes vary depending on category. Every novel receives personal feedback from four judges. Judges listed on website, including the agents who will be helping choose the top winners of the Master category.

THE IOWA SHORT FICTION AWARD & JOHN SIMMONS SHORT FICTION AWARD

Iowa Writers' Workshop, Iowa Writers' Workshop, 507 N. Clinton St., 102 Dey House, Iowa City IA 52242-1000. **Website:** www.uiowapress.org. **Contact:** James McCoy, Director. Annual award to give exposure to promising writers who have not yet published a book of prose. Open to any writer. Current University of Iowa students are not eligible. No application forms are necessary. Announcement of winners made early in year following competition. Winners notified by phone. No application forms are necessary. Do not send original ms. Include SASE for return of ms. Entries must be unpublished, but stories previously published in periodicals are eligible for inclusion. The ms must be a collection of short stories of at least 150 word-processed, double-spaced pages. Deadline: September 30. Submission period begins August 1. Prize: Publication by University of Iowa Press. Judged by senior Iowa Writers' Workshop members who screen mss; published fiction author of note makes final selections.

JESSE H. JONES AWARD FOR BEST WORK OF FICTION

P.O. Box 609, Round Rock TX 78680. **E-mail:** tilsecretary@yahoo.com. **Website:** http://texasinstituteofletters.org. Offered annually by Texas Institute of Letters for work published January 1-December 31 of year before award is given to recognize the writer of the best book of fiction entered in the competition. Writers must have been born in Texas, have lived in the state for at least 2 consecutive years at some time, or the subject matter of the work should be associated with the state. See website for details and information on submitting. Deadline: January 10. Prize: $6,000.

JAMES JONES FIRST NOVEL FELLOWSHIP

Wilkes University, James Jones First Novel Fellowship, c/o M.A./M.F.A. in CreativeWriting, Wilkes University, 84 West South Street, Wilkes-Barre PA 18766. (570)408-4547. **Fax:** (570)408-3333. **E-mail:** jamesjonesfirstnovel@wilkes.edu. **Website:** www.wilkes.edu/. Offered annually for unpublished novels (must be works-in-progress). This competition is open to all U.S. citizens who have not previously published novels. Submit a 2-page (maximum) outline or synopsis of the entire novel and the first 50 pages of the novel-in-progress are to be submitted. The ms must be typed and double-spaced; outline may be single-spaced. Entrants submitting via snail mail should include their name, address, telephone number, and e-mail address (if available) on the title page, but nowhere else on the manuscript. For those entrants submitting online, name, address, telephone number, and e-mail address should appear only on your cover letter. Cover letter should be dropped in the cover letter box and outline and ms should be attached as one document. The award is intended to honor the spirit of unblinking honesty, determination, and insight into modern culture exemplified by the late James Jones. Deadline: March 15. Submission period begins October 1. Prize: $10,000; 2 runners-up awards of $1000 each may be given.

THE LAWRENCE FOUNDATION AWARD

Prairie Schooner, 110 Andrews Hall, University of Nebraska-Lincoln, Lincoln NE 68588-0334. (402)472-0911. **Fax:** (402)472-9771. **E-mail:** prairieschooner@unl.edu. **Website:** www.prairieschooner.unl.edu. Offered annually for the best short story published in Prairie Schooner in the previous year. Only work published in *Prairie Schooner* in the previous year is considered. Work is nominated by editorial staff. Results announced in the Spring issue. Winners notified by mail in February or March. Prize: $1,000. Judged by editorial staff of *Praire Schooner*.

LAWRENCE FOUNDATION PRIZE

Michigan Quarterly Review, 0576 Rackham Bldg., 915 E. Washington St., Ann Arbor MI 48109-1070. (734)764-9265. **E-mail:** mqr@umich.edu. **Website:** www.michiganquarterlyreview.com. **Contact:** H.R. Webster, managing editor. This annual prize is awarded by the *Michigan Quarterly Review* editorial board to the author of the best short story published in *MQR* that year. The prize is sponsored by

University of Michigan alumnus and fiction writer Leonard S. Bernstein, a trustee of the Lawrence Foundation of New York. Approximately 20 short stories are published in *MQR* each year. Guidelines available under submission guidelines on website. Prize: $1,000. Judged by editorial board.

LITERAL LATTÉ FICTION AWARD

Literal Latté, 200 E. 10th St., Suite 240, New York NY 10003. **E-mail:** litlatte@aol.com. **Website:** www.literal-latte.com. **Contact:** Edward Estlin, contributing editor. Award to provide talented writers with 3 essential tools for continued success: money, publication, and recognition. Offered annually for unpublished fiction (maximum 20,000 words). Guidelines online. Open to any writer. Deadline: January 30. Prize: 1st Place: $1,000 and publication in *Literal Latté*; 2nd Place: $300; 3rd Place: $200; also up to 7 honorable mentions. All winners published in *Literal Latté*. The Editors

LITERAL LATTE SHORT SHORTS CONTEST

Literal Latté, Literal Latté Awards, 200 E. 10th St., Suite 240, New York NY 10003. **E-mail:** litlatte@aol.com. **Website:** www.literal-latte.com. **Contact:** Jenine Gordon Bockman, Editor. Keeping free thought free since 1994. Deadline: June 30. Prize: $500. Judged by the editors.

LITERARY FICTION CONTEST

The Writers' Workshop of Asheville, NC, Literary Fiction Contest, 387 Beaucatcher Rd., Asheville NC 28805. **E-mail:** writersw@gmail.com. **Website:** www.twwoa.org. Submit a short story or chapter of a novel of 5,000 words or less. Multiple entries are accepted. All work must be unpublished. Pages should be paper clipped, with your name, address, phone and title of work on a cover sheet. Double-space and use 12-point font. Deadline (postmarked or emailed): September 30. Prize: 1st Place: Your choice of a 2 night stay at the Mountain Muse B&B in Asheville, 3 free online workshops, or 50 pages line-edited and revised by editorial staff; 2nd Place: 2 free workshops or 35 pages line-edited; 3rd Place: 1 free workshop or 25 pages line-edited; 10 Honorable Mentions. Judged by published writing instructors.

THE MARY MACKEY SHORT STORY PRIZE CATEGORY

Soul-Making Keats Literary Competition, The Webhallow House, 1544 Sweetwood Dr., Broadmoor Village CA 94015-2029. **E-mail:** soulkeats@mail.com. **Website:** www.soulmakingcontest.us. **Contact:** Eileen Malone. Open annually to any writer. One story/entry, up to 5,000 words. All prose works must be typed, page numbered, and double-spaced. Identify only with 3x5 card. Deadline: November 30. Prize: Cash prizes.

THE MALAHAT REVIEW NOVELLA PRIZE

The Malahat Review, University of Victoria, P.O. Box 1800 STN CSC, Victoria BC V8W 3H5 Canada. (250)721-8524. **E-mail:** malahat@uvic.ca. **E-mail:** novella@uvic.ca. **Website:** malahatreview.ca. **Contact:** L'Amour Lisik, Marketing and Circulation Manager. Held in alternate (even-numbered) years with the Long Poem Prize. Submit novellas between 10,000 and 20,000 words in length. Include separate page with author's name, address, e-mail, and novella title; no identifying information on mss pages. E-mail submissions are now accepted. Do not include SASE for results; mss will not be returned. Guidelines available on website. 2010 winner was Tony Tulathimutte, 2012 winner was Naben Ruthnum, and the 2014 winner was Dora Dueck. Winner and finalists contacted by e-mail. Offered to promote unpublished novellas. Obtains first world rights. After publication, rights revert to the author. Open to any writer. Deadline: February 1 (even years). Prize: $1,500 CAD and one year's subscription. Winner published in summer issue of *The Malahat Review* and announced on website, Facebook page, and in quarterly e-newsletter *Malahat Lite*. Three recognized literary figures are assigned to judge the contest each year.

THE MAN BOOKER PRIZE

Four Colman Getty PR, Marion Fraser, Four Culture, 20 St Thomas Street, London SE1 9BF United Kingdom. (44)020 3697 4256. **Website:** www.themanbookerprize.com. **Contact:** Marion Fraser. Books are only accepted through UK publishers. However, publication outside the UK does not disqualify a book once it is published in the UK. Open to any full-length novel (published October 1-September 30). No novellas, collections of short stories, translations, or self-published books. Open to citizens of the Commonwealth or Republic of Ireland. Deadline: June 14. Prize: £50,000; Each shortlisted author receives £2,500. Judges appointed by the Booker Prize Management Committee.

MARY MCCARTHY PRIZE IN SHORT FICTION

Sarabande Books, 822 E. Market St., Louisville KY 40206. (502)458-4028. **Fax:** (502)458-4065. **E-mail:** info@sarabandebooks.org. **Website:** www.sarabandebooks.org. **Contact:** Sarah Gorham, editor-in-chief. Annual competition to honor a collection of short stories, novellas, or a short novel. All mss should be between 150 and 250 pages. All finalists considered for publication. Guidelines available online. Prize: $2,000 and publication (standard royalty contract).

MEMPHIS MAGAZINE FICTION CONTEST

Memphis Magazine, Fiction Contest, c/o *Memphis* magazine, P.O. Box 1738, Memphis TN 38101. (901)521-9000, ext. 451. **Fax:** (901)521-0129. **E-mail:** fiction@memphismagazine.com. **Website:** www.memphismagazine.com. The Very Short Story Contest will recognize ten winning entries annually, every month except February and August. Authors are strongly encouraged to bring Memphis or the Mid-South into their stories. The Very Short Story Contest welcomes entries of up to 750 words, maximum. See website for guidelines and rules. Entries accepted throughout the year. $200 gift certificate at Novel, a Memphis independent bookstore.

DAVID NATHAN MEYERSON PRIZE FOR FICTION

Southwest Review, Southern Methodist University, P.O. Box 750374, Dallas TX 75275-0374. (214)768-1037. **Fax:** (214)768-1408. **E-mail:** swr@smu.edu. **Website:** www.smu.edu/southwestreview. **Contact:** Greg Brownderville, editor-in-chief. Annual award given to a writer who has not published a first book of fiction, either a novel or collection of stories. Submissions must be no longer than 8,000 words. Work should be printed without the author's name. Name and address should appear only on the cover letter. Submissions will not be returned. Deadline: May 1 (postmarked). Prize: $1,000 and publication in the *Southwest Review*.

MILKWEED NATIONAL FICTION PRIZE

1011 Washington Ave. South, Open Book, Suite 300, Minneapolis MN 55415. (612)332-3192. **Fax:** (612)215-2550. **E-mail:** editor@milkweed.org. **Website:** www.milkweed.org. **Contact:** Patrick Thomas, Editor and Program Manager. Annual award for unpublished works. Mss should be one of the following: a novel, a collection of short stories, one or more novellas, or a combination of short stories and one or more novellas. Mss should be of high literary quality and between 150-400 pages in length. Work previously published as a book in the US is not eligible, but individual stories or novellas previously published in magazines or anthologies are eligible. Guidelines available online. Deadline: Rolling submissions. Check website for details. Prize: Publication by Milkweed Editions and a cash advance of $5,000 against royalties, agreed upon in the contractual arrangement negotiated at the time of acceptance. Judged by the editors.

MONTANA PRIZE IN FICTION

Cutbank Literary Magazine, *CutBank*, University of Montana, English Dept., LA 133, Missoula MT 59812. **E-mail:** editor.cutbank@gmail.com. **Website:** www.cutbankonline.org. **Contact:** Allison Linville, Editor-in-Chief. The Montana Prize in Fiction seeks to highlight work that showcases an authentic voice, a boldness of form, and a rejection of functional fixedness. Accepts online submissions only. Send a single work, no more than 35 pages. Guidelines available online. Deadline: January 15. Submissions period begins November 9. Prize: $500 and featured in the magazine. Judged by a guest judge each year.

THE HOWARD FRANK MOSHER SHORT FICTION PRIZE

Vermont College of Fine Arts, 36 College St., Montpelier VT 05602. (802)828-8517. **E-mail:** hungermtn@vcfa.edu. **Website:** www.hungermtn.org. **Contact:** Cameron Finch, managing editor. The Howard Frank Mosher Short Fiction Prize is an annual contest for short fiction. Enter one original, unpublished story under 10,000 words. Do not put name or address on the story; entries are judged blind. Accepts submissions online. Deadline: March 1. Prize: One first place winner receives $1,000 and online publication. One runner-up receives $100 and online publication. Other finalists are considered for print publication.

NATIONAL READERS' CHOICE AWARDS

Oklahoma Romance Writers of America (OKRWA), **E-mail:** nrca@okrwa.com. **Website:** www.okrwa.com. **Contact:** Kathy L Wheeler, NRCA Chair. To provide writers of romance fiction with a competition where their published novels are judged by readers. See the website for categories and descriptions. Additional award for best first book. All entries must have an original copyright date during the current contest year. Entries will be accepted from authors, editors, publishers, agents, readers, or whoever wants to fill out the entry form, pay the fee, and supply the books. No limit to the number of entries, but each title may be entered only in one category. Open to any writer published by an RWA approved non-vanity/non-subsidy press. For guidelines, send e-mail or visit website. Deadline: October 1st. Prize: Plaques and finalist certificates awarded at the awards banquet hosted at the Annual National Romance Writers Convention. Judged by readers.

NATIONAL WRITERS ASSOCIATION NOVEL CONTEST

The National Writers Association, NWA Novel Contest, 10940 S. Parker Rd. #508, Parker CO 80134. **E-mail:** natlwritersassn@hotmail.com. **Website:** www.nationalwriters.com. **Contact:** Sandy Whelchel, Director. Open to any genre or category. Open to any writer. Contest begins December 1. Entries must be unpublished. Length: 20,000-100,000 words. Contest forms are available on the NWA website or an attachment will be sent upon request via e-mail or with an SASE. Annual contest to help develop creative skills, recognize and reward outstanding ability, and increase the opportunity for the marketing and subsequent publication of novel mss. Deadline: April 1. Prize: 1st Place: $500; 2nd Place: $250; 3rd Place: $150. Judged by editors and agents.

NATIONAL WRITERS ASSOCIATION SHORT STORY CONTEST

NWA Short Story Contest, 10940 S. Parker Rd., #508, Parker CO 80134. **E-mail:** natlwritersassn@hotmail.com. **Website:** www.nationalwriters.com. Any genre of short story manuscript may be entered. All entries must be postmarked by July 1. Contest opens April 1. Only unpublished works may be submitted. All manuscripts must be typed, double-spaced, in the English language. Maximum length is 5,000 words. Those unsure of proper manuscript format should request Research Report #35. The entry must be accompanied by an entry form (photocopies are acceptable) and return SASE if you wish the material and rating sheets returned. Submissions will be destroyed, otherwise. Receipt of entry will not be acknowledged without a return postcard. Author's name and address must appear on the first page. Entries remain the property of the author and may be submitted during the contest as long as they are not published before the final notification of winners. Final prizes will be awarded in June. The purpose of the National Writers Assn. Short Story Contest is to encourage the development of creative skills, recognize and reward outstanding ability in the area of short story writing. July 1 (postmarked). Prize: 1st Prize: $250; 2nd Prize: $100; 3rd Prize: $50; 4th-10th places will receive a book. 1st-3rd place winners may be asked to grant one-time rights for publication in *Authorship* magazine. Honorable Mentions receive a certificate. Judging will be based on originality, marketability, research, and reader interest. Copies of the judges' evaluation sheets will be sent to entrants furnishing an SASE with their entry.

THE NELLIGAN PRIZE FOR SHORT FICTION

Colorado Review/Center for Literary Publishing, Colorado State University, 9105 Campus Delivery, Dept. of English, Colorado State University, Ft. Collins CO 80523-9105. (970)491-5449. **E-mail:** creview@colostate.edu. **Website:** https://nelliganprize.colostate.edu. **Contact:** Stephanie G'Schwind, editor. Annual competition/award for short stories. Receives approximately 1,000 stories. All entries are read blind by Colorado Review's editorial staff. Ten to fifteen entries are selected to be sent on to a final, outside judge. Stories must be unpublished and between 10 and 50 pages. "The Nelligan Prize for Short Fiction was established in memory of Liza Nelligan, a writer, editor, and friend of many in Colorado State University's English Department, where she received her master's degree in literature in 1992. By giving an award to the author of an outstanding short story each year, we hope to honor Liza Nelligan's life, her passion for writing, and her love of fiction." Deadline: March 14. Prize: $2,000 and publication of story in *Colorado Review*. Judged by a different writer each year. 2019 judge is Joan Silber.

NEW LETTERS PRIZE FOR FICTION

New Letters, University of Missouri-Kansas City, *New Letters* Awards for Writers, UMKC, University House, 5101 Rockhill Rd., Kansas City MO 64110-2499. (816)235-1168. **E-mail:** newletters@umkc.edu. **Website:** www.newletters.org/writers-wanted/writing-contests. **Contact:** Ashley Wann. Offered annually for the best short story to discover and reward new and upcoming writers. Buys first North American serial rights. Open to any writer. Short story should not exceed 8,000 words. Deadline: May 18. 1st Place: $1,500 and publication in a volume of *New Letters*.

SEAN O'FAOLAIN SHORT STORY COMPETITION

The Munster Literature Centre, Frank O'Connor House, 84 Douglas Street, Cork Ireland. +353-0214319255. **E-mail:** munsterlit@eircom.net. **Website:** www.munsterlit.ie. **Contact:** Patrick Cotter, artistic director. Entries should be unpublished. Anyone may enter contest. Length: 3,000 words max. Cover letter should include name, address, phone, e-mail, word count, novel/story title. Purpose is to reward writers of outstanding short stories. Deadline: July 31. Prize: 1st prize €2,000; 2nd prize €500. Four runners-up prizes of €100 (approx $146). All six stories to be published in *Southword Literary Journal*. First-Prize Winner offered week's residency in Anam Cara Artist's Retreat in Ireland.

FRANK O'CONNOR AWARD FOR SHORT FICTION

descant, Texas Christian University's literary journal, descant, c/o TCU Department of English, Box 298300, Fort Worth TX 76129. **E-mail:** descant@tcu.edu. **Website:** www.descant.tcu.edu. **Contact:** Matthew Pitt, Editor. Offered annually for an outstanding story accepted for publication in the current edition of the journal. Publication retains copyright but will transfer it to the author upon request. Deadline: April 1. Open to submissions September 1. Prize: $500.

ON THE PREMISES CONTEST

On The Premises, LLC, 4323 Gingham Court, Alexandria VA 22310. **E-mail:** questions@onthepremises.com. **Website:** www.onthepremises.com. **Contact:** Tarl Kudrick or Bethany Granger, co-publishers. *On the Premises* aims to promote newer and/or relatively unknown writers who can write creative, compelling stories told in effective, uncluttered, and evocative prose. Each contest challenges writers to produce a great story based on a broad premise that the editors supply as part of the contest. Submissions are accepted only through web-based submissions system. Entries should be unpublished. Length: minimum 1,000 words; maximum 5,000. No name or contact info should be in ms. Writers may submit own work. Check website for details on the specific premise that writers should incorporate into their story. Results announced within 2 weeks of contest deadline. Winners notified via e-mail and with publication of *On the Premises*. Results made available to entrants on website and in publication. Deadline: Short story contests held twice a year; smaller mini-contests held four times a year; check website for exact dates. Prize: 1st Prize: $220; 2nd Prize: $160; 3rd Prize: $120; Honorable Mentions receive $60. All prize winners are published in *On the Premises* magazine in HTML and PDF format. Judged by a panel of judges with professional editing and writing experience.

KENNETH PATCHEN AWARD FOR THE INNOVATIVE NOVEL

Eckhard Gerdes Publishing, 1110 Varsity Blvd., Apt. 221, DeKalb IL 60115. **E-mail:** egerdes@experimentalfiction.com. **Website:** www.experimentalfiction.com. **Contact:** Eckhard Gerdes. This award will honor the most innovative novel submitted during the previous calendar year. Kenneth Patchen is celebrated for being among the greatest innovators of American fiction, incorporating strategies of concretism, asemic writing, digression, and verbal juxtaposition into his writing long before such strategies were popularized during the height of American postmodernist experimentation in the 1970s. See guidelines and application form online at website. Deadline: All submissions must be postmarked between January 1 and July 31. Prize: $1,000 and 20 complimentary copies. Judged by novelist Dominic Ward.

THE PATERSON FICTION PRIZE

The Poetry Center at Passaic Community College, One College Blvd., Paterson NJ 07505. (973)684-6555. **Fax:** (973)523-6085. **E-mail:** mgillan@pccc.edu. **Website:** www.pccc.edu/poetry. **Contact:** Maria Mazziotti Gillan, executive director. Offered annually for a novel or collection of short fiction published the previous calendar year. For more information, visit the website or send SASE. Deadline: February 1. Prize: $1,000.

WILLIAM PEDEN PRIZE IN FICTION

The Missouri Review, 357 McReynolds Hall, Columbia MO 65211. (573)882-4474. **Fax:** (573)884-4671. **E-mail:** mutmrcontestquestion@moreview.com. **Website:** www.missourireview.com. **Contact:** Michael Nye, managing editor. Offered annually for the best story published in the past volume year of the magazine. All stories published in *The Missouri Review* are automatically considered. Guidelines online or for SASE. Prize: $1,000 and a reading/reception.

PEN/FAULKNER AWARD FOR FICTION

PEN/Faulkner Foundation, 641 S Street NW, Third Floor, Washington DC 20001. (202)898-9063. **E-mail:** shahenda@penfaulkner.org. **Website:** www.penfaulkner.org. **Contact:** Shahenda Helmy, Programs & Logistics Director. Offered annually for best book-length work of fiction by an American citizen published in a calendar year. Deadline: October 31. Prize: $15,000 (one Winner); $5,000 (4 Finalists).

EDGAR ALLAN POE AWARD

1140 Broadway, Suite 1507, New York NY 10001. (212)888-8171. **E-mail:** mwa@mysterywriters.org. **Website:** www.mysterywriters.org. Mystery Writers of America is the leading association for professional crime writers in the United States. Members of MWA include most major writers of crime fiction and nonfiction, as well as screenwriters, dramatists, editors, publishers, and other professionals in the field. Categories include: Best Novel, Best First Novel by an American Author, Best Paperback/E-Book Original, Best Fact Crime, Best Critical/Biographical, Best Short Story, Best Juvenile Mystery, Best Young Adult Mystery, Best Television Series Episode Teleplay, and Mary Higgins Clark Award. Purpose of the award: Honor authors of distinguished works in the mystery field. Previously published submissions only. Submissions should be made by the publisher. Work must be published/produced the year of the contest. Deadline: November 30. Prize: Awards ceramic bust of "Edgar" for winner; certificates for all nominees. Judged by active status members of Mystery Writers of America (writers).

THE KATHERINE ANNE PORTER PRIZE FOR FICTION

Nimrod International Journal, The University of Tulsa, 800 S. Tucker Dr., Tulsa OK 74104. (918)631-3080. **Fax:** (918)631-3033. **E-mail:** nimrod@utulsa.edu. **Website:** www.utulsa.edu/nimrod. **Contact:** Eilis O'Neal. Submissions must be unpublished. Work must be in English or translated by original author. Author's name must not appear on ms. Include cover sheet with title, author's name, address, phone number, and e-mail address (author must have a US address by October of contest year to enter). Mark "Contest Entry" on submission envelope and cover sheet if submitting by mail. Include SASE for results only; mss will not be returned. 7,500-word maximum for short stories. Postmark Deadline: April 30. 1st Place: $2,000 and publication; 2nd Place: $1,000 and publication. Judged by the *Nimrod* editors, who select the finalists, and a recognized author, who selects the winners.

PRESS 53 AWARD FOR SHORT FICTION

Press 53, 560 N. Trade St., Suite 103, Winston-Salem NC 27101. (336)770-5353. **E-mail:** kevin@press53.com. **Website:** www.press53.com. **Contact:** Kevin Morgan Watson, Publisher. Awarded to an outstanding, unpublished collection of short stories. Details and guidelines available online. Deadline: December 31. Submission period begins September 1. Finalists and winner announced no later than May 1. Publication in October. Prize: Publication of winning short story collection, $1,000 cash advance and 50 copies of the book. Judged by Press 53 publisher Kevin Morgan Watson.

PRISM INTERNATIONAL ANNUAL SHORT FICTION CONTEST

Creative Writing Program, UBC, Buch. E462 - 1866 Main Mall, Vancouver BC V6T 1Z1 Canada. (604)822-2514. **Fax:** (604)822-3616. **Website:** prismmagazine.ca/contests. **Contact:** Jessica Johns, executive editor, promotions. Maximum word count: 6,000 words. Offered annually for unpublished work to award the best in contemporary fiction. Works of translation are eligible. Guidelines by SASE, by e-mail, or on website. Acquires first North American serial rights upon publication, and rights to publish online for promotional or archival purposes. Open to any writer except students and faculty in the Creative Writing Department at UBC, or people who have taken a creative writing course at UBC with the 2 years prior to the contest deadline. Deadline: January 31. Prize: 1st Place: $1,500; 1st Runner-up: $600; 2nd Runner-up: $400; winner is published.

THOMAS H. RADDALL ATLANTIC FICTION AWARD

Writers' Federation of Nova Scotia, 1113 Marginal Rd., Halifax NS B3H 4P7 Canada. (902)423-8116. **Fax:** (902)422-0881. **E-mail:** director@writers.ns.ca. **Website:** www.writers.ns.ca. **Contact:** Marilyn Smulders, executive director. The Thomas Head Raddall Atlantic Fiction Award is awarded for a novel or a book of short fiction by a full-time resident of Atlantic Canada. Detailed guidelines and eligibility criteria available online. Deadline: First Friday in December. Prize: Valued at $25,000 for winning title.

HAROLD U. RIBALOW PRIZE

Hadassah Magazine, Hadassah WZOA, 40 Wall St., 8th Floor, New York NY 10005. (212)451-6286. **Fax:** (212)451-6257. **E-mail:** magtemp3@hadassah.org. **Website:** www.hadassahmagazine.org. **Contact:** Deb Meisels, coordinator. Offered annually for English-language (no translation) books of fiction (novel or short stories) on a Jewish theme published the previous year. Books should be submitted by the publisher. Administered annually by *Hadassah Magazine*. Deadline: April 15. The official announcement of the winner will be made in the fall.

✪ THE ROGERS WRITERS' TRUST FICTION PRIZE

The Writers' Trust of Canada, 460 Richmond St. W., Suite 600, Toronto ON M5V 1Y1 Canada. (416)504-8222. **Fax:** (416)504-9090. **E-mail:** djackson@writerstrust.com. **Website:** www.writerstrust.com. **Contact:** Devon Jackson. Awarded annually to the best novel or short story collection published within the previous year. Presented at the Writers' Trust Awards event held in Toronto each fall. Open to Canadian citizens and permanent residents only. Deadline: July 18. Prize: $50,000 and $5,000 to 4 finalists.

ETHEL ROHAN NOVEL EXCERPT PRIZE CATEGORY

Soul-Making Keats Literary Competition Category, The Webhallow House, 1544 Sweetwood Dr., Broadmoor Vlg. CA 94015-2029. **E-mail:** soulkeats@mail.com. **Website:** www.soulmakingcontest.us. **Contact:** Eileen Malone. Open annually to any writer. Send maximum of 25 pages. Include a 1-page synopsis indicating category at top of page. Identify with 3x5 card only. Ongoing Deadline: November 30. Prize: 1st Place: $100; 2nd Place: $50; 3rd Place: $25.

THE SATURDAY EVENING POST GREAT AMERICAN FICTION CONTEST

The Saturday Evening Post Society, 1100 Waterway Blvd., Indianapolis IN 46202. **E-mail:** fictioncontest@saturdayeveningpost.com. **Website:** www.saturdayeveningpost.com/fiction-contest. "In its nearly 3 centuries of publication, *The Saturday Evening Post* has included fiction by a who's who of American authors, including F. Scott Fitzgerald, William Faulkner, Kurt Vonnegut, Ray Bradbury, Louis L'Amour, Sinclair Lewis, Jack London, and Edgar Allan Poe. The *Post*'s fiction has not just entertained us; it has played a vital role in defining who we are as Americans. In launching this contest, we are seeking America's next great, unpublished voices." Entries must be character- or plot-driven stories in any genre of fiction that falls within the *Post*'s broad range of interest. "We are looking for stories with universal appeal touching on shared experiences and themes that will resonate with readers from diverse backgrounds and experience." Stories must be submitted by the author and previously unpublished (excluding personal websites and blogs), and 1,500-5,000 words in length. No extreme profanity or graphic sex scenes. Submit story via the online at www.saturdayeveningpost.com/fiction-contest. All submissions must be made electronically in Microsoft Word format with the author's name, address, telephone number, and e-mail address on the first page. Do not submit hard copies via the mail; physical mss will not be read. "Due to staff limitations, we will not be able to update entrants on the status of their stories. We will inform winners or runners-up within 30 days of publication. We regret we will not be able to notify non-winning entrants." Deadline: July 1. The winning story will receive $500 and publication in the magazine and online. Five runners-up will be published online and receive $100 each.

SCREAMINMAMAS MAGICAL FICTION CONTEST

1911 Cleveland St., Hollywood FL 33020. **E-mail:** screaminmamas@gmail.com. **Website:** www.screaminmamas.com/contests. **Contact:** Darlene Pistocchi, editor/managing director. This contest celebrates moms and the magical spirit of the holidays. If you had an opportunity to be anything you wanted to be, what would you be? Transport yourself! Become that character and write a short story around that character. Can be any genre. Length: 800-3,000 words. Open only to moms. Deadline: June 30. Prize: Publication.

SCREAMINMAMAS VALENTINE'S DAY CONTEST

1911 Cleveland St., Hollywood FL 33020. **E-mail:** screaminmamas@gmail.com. **Website:** www.screaminmamas.com/contests. **Contact:** Darlene Pistocchi, editor/managing director. "Looking for light romantic comedy. Can be historical or contemporary—something to lift the spirits and celebrate the gift of innocent romance that might be found in the everyday life of a busy mom." Length:

600-1,200 words. Open only to moms. Deadline: June 30. Prize: Publication.

SHEEHAN YA BOOK PRIZE

Elephant Rock Books, P.O. Box 119, Ashford CT 06278. **E-mail:** elephantrockbooksya@gmail.com. **Website:** elephantrockbooks.com/ya.html. **Contact:** Jotham Burrello and Amanda Hurley. Elephant Rock is a small independent publisher. Their first YA book, *The Carnival at Bray* by Jessie Ann Foley was a Morris Award Finalist, and Printz Honor Book. Runs contest every other year. Check website for details. Guidelines are available on the website: http://www.elephantrockbooks.com./about.html#submissions. "Elephant Rock Books' teen imprint is looking for a great story to follow our critically acclaimed novel, *The Carnival at Bray*. We're after quality stories with heart, guts, and a clear voice. We're especially interested in the quirky, the hopeful, and the real. We are not particularly interested in genre fiction and prefer standalone novels, unless you've got the next *Hunger Games*. We seek writers who believe in the transformative power of a great story, so show us what you've got." Deadline: July 1. Prize: $1,000 as an advance. Judges vary year-to-year.

STONY BROOK SHORT FICTION PRIZE

Stony Brook Southampton, 239 Montauk Highway, Southampton NY 11968. **Website:** www.stonybrook.edu/fictionprize. "Only undergraduates enrolled full time in United States and Canadian universities and colleges for the current academic year are eligible. This prize has traditionally encouraged submissions from students with an Asian background, but we urge all students to enter." Submissions of no more than 7,500 words. All entries must be accompanied by proof of current undergraduate enrollment, such as a photocopy of a grade transcript, a class schedule or payment receipt showing your full time status. See website for full details. Deadline: March 15. Prize: $1,000.

STORYSOUTH MILLION WRITERS AWARD

E-mail: terry@storysouth.com. **Website:** www.storysouth.com. **Contact:** Terry Kennedy, editor. Annual award to honor and promote the best fiction published in online literary journals and magazines during the previous year. Anyone may nominate one story for the award. To be eligible for nomination, a story must be longer than 1,000 words. See website for details on how to nominate someone. Most literary prizes for short fiction have traditionally ignored web-published fiction. This award aims to show that world-class fiction is being published online and to promote to the larger reading and literary community. Deadline: August 15. Nominations of stories begins on March 15. Prize: Prize amounts subject to donation. Check website for details.

THEODORE STURGEON MEMORIAL AWARD FOR BEST SHORT SF OF THE YEAR

Center for the Study of SF, 1445 Jayhawk Blvd, Room 3001, University of Kansas, Lawrence KS 66045. (785)864-2518. **Fax:** (785)864-1159. **E-mail:** cssf@ku.edu. **Website:** sfcenter.ku.edu/sturgeon.htm. **Contact:** Kij Johnson, professor and associate director. Entries must be previously published. Guidelines available in December by phone, e-mail or on website. Accepts inquiries by e-mail and fax. Entrants for the Sturgeon Award are by nomination only. Results announced in July. For contest results, send SASE. Award to "honor the best science fiction short story of the year." Prize: Trophy. Winners receive expense-paid trip to the University and have their names engraved on the pernmanent trophy.

THREE CHEERS AND A TIGER

E-mail: editors@toasted-cheese.com. **Website:** tclj.toasted-cheese.com. **Contact:** Stephanie Lenz, editor. Contestants are to write a short story (following a specific theme) within 48 hours. Contests are held first weekend in Spring (mystery) and first weekend in Fall (science fiction/fantasy). Word limit announced at the start of the contest, 5 pm ET. Contest-specific information is announced 48 hours before the contest submission deadline. Results announced in April and October. Winners notified by e-mail. List of winners on website. Entries must be unpublished. Open to any writer. Accepts inquiries by e-mail. Cover letter should include name, address, e-mail, word count and title. Information should be in the body of the e-mail. It will be removed before the judging begins. Prize: Amazon gift certificates and publication. Blind-judged by *Toasted Cheese* editors. Each judge uses his or her own criteria to choose entries.

THE THURBER PRIZE FOR AMERICAN HUMOR

77 Jefferson Ave., Columbus OH 43215. **Website:** www.thurberhouse.org. Entry fee: $65 per title. Published submissions or accepted for publication in U.S. for the first time. Primarily pictorial works such as

cartoon collections are not considered. Word length: no requirement. See website for application form and guidelines. Results announced in September. Winners notified in person in New York City. For contest results, visit website. This award recognizes the art of humor writing. Deadline: March 31. Prize: $5,000 for the finalist, non-cash prizes awarded to two runners-up. Judged by well-known members of the national arts community.

STEVEN TURNER AWARD FOR BEST FIRST WORK OF FICTION

6335 W. Northwest Hwy., #618, Dallas TX 75225. **Website:** www.texasinstituteofletters.org. Offered annually for work published January 1-December 31 for the best first book of fiction. Writers must have been born in Texas, have lived in the state for at least 2 consecutive years at some time, or the subject matter of the work should be associated with the state. Guidelines online. Deadline: normally first week in January; see website for specific date. Prize: $1,000.

ANNUAL VENTURA COUNTY WRITERS CLUB SHORT STORY CONTEST

Ventura County Writers Club Short Story Contest, P.O. Box 3373, Thousand Oaks CA 91362. **E-mail:** vcwc.contestchair@gmail.com. **Website:** www.venturacountywriters.com. **Contact:** Contest Chair. Annual short story contest for youth and adult writers. High school division for writers still in school. Adult division for those 18 and older. Club membership not required to enter and entries accepted worldwide as long as fees are paid, story is unpublished and in English. Enter through website. 2,500 word limit. See formatting on website. Winners get cash prizes and are published in club anthology. Deadline: November 15. Adult Prizes: 1st Place: $500; 2nd Place: $250; 3rd Place: $125. High School Prizes: 1st Place: $100; 2nd Place: $75; 3rd Place: $50.

WAASNODE SHORT FICTION PRIZE

Passages North, Department of English, Northern Michigan University, 1401 Presque Isle Ave., Marquette MI 49855. (906)227-1203. **Fax:** (906)227-1096. **E-mail:** passages@nmu.edu. **Website:** www.passagesnorth.com. **Contact:** Jennifer Howard. Offered every 2 years to publish new voices in literary fiction (maximum 10,000 words). Guidelines for SASE or online. Submissions accepted online. Deadline: April 15. Submission period begins February 15. Prize: $1,000 and publication for winner; 2 honorable mentions are also published; all entrants receive a copy of *Passages North*. Judged by Anne Valente in 2018.

WABASH PRIZE FOR FICTION

Sycamore Review, Department of English, 500 Oval Dr., Purdue University, West Lafayette IN 47907. **E-mail:** sycamore@purdue.edu; sycamorefiction@purdue.edu. **Website:** www.sycamorereview.com/contest/. **Contact:** Kara Krewer, editor-in-chief. Annual contest for unpublished fiction. For each submission, send one story (limit 7,500 words). Ms pages should be numbered and should include the title of the piece. All stories must be previously unpublished. See website for more guidelines. Submit via online submissions manager. Deadline: November 15. Prize: $1,000 and publication.

THE WASHINGTON WRITERS' PUBLISHING HOUSE FICTION PRIZE

Washington Writers' Publishing House, P.O. Box 15271, Washington DC 20003. **E-mail:** wwphpress@gmail.com. **Website:** www.washingtonwriters.org. Fiction writers living within 75 miles of the Capitol are invited to submit a ms of either a novel or a collection of short stories (no more than 350 pages, double-spaced). Author's name should not appear on the manuscript. The title page of each copy should contain the title only. Provide name, address, telephone number, e-mail address, and title on a separate cover sheet accompanying the submission. A separate page for acknowledgments may be included for stories or excerpts previously published in journals and anthologies. Send electronic copies to wwphpress@gmail.com or mail paper copies and/or reading fee (check to WWPH) with SASE to: Washington Writers' Publishing House Fiction Prize, c/o Elisavietta Ritchie, P.O. Box 298, Broomes Island, MD 20615. Deadline: November 15. Submission period begins July 1. Prize: $1,000 and 50 copies of the book.

THOMAS WOLFE PRIZE AND LECTURE

North Carolina Writers' Network, Thomas Wolfe Fiction Prize, Great Smokies Writing Program, Attn: Nancy Williams, CPO #1860, UNC, Asheville NC 28805. **Website:** englishcomplit.unc.edu/wolfe. The Thomas Wolfe Fiction Prize honors internationally celebrated North Carolina novelist Thomas Wolfe. The prize is administered by Tommy Hays and the Great Smokies Writing Program at the University of North Carolina at Asheville. Competition is open to all writers, regardless of geographical location or prior publication. Submit 2 copies of an unpublished fiction ms (short story or self-contained novel excerpt) not to exceed 12 double-spaced, single-sided pages. Deadline: January 30. Submissions period begins December 1. Prize: $1,000 and potential publication in *The Thomas Wolfe Review*.

TOBIAS WOLFF AWARD FOR FICTION

Bellingham Review, Mail Stop 9053, Western Washington University, Bellingham WA 98225. (360)650-4863. **E-mail:** bellingham.review@wwu.edu. **Website:** www.bhreview.org. **Contact:** Susanne Paola Antonetta, editor-in-chief; Bailey Cunningham, managing editor. Offered annually for unpublished work. Guidelines available on website; online submissions only. Categories: novel exceprts and short stories. Entries must be unpublished. Length: 6,000 words or less per story or chapter. Open to any writer. Electronic submissions only. Enter submissions through Submittable, a link to which is available on the website. Winner announced in August and notified by e-mail. Deadline: March 15. Submissions period begins December 1. Prize: $1,000, plus publication and subscription.

WORLD FANTASY AWARDS

P.O. Box 43, Mukilteo WA 98275. **E-mail:** sfexecsec@gmail.com. **Website:** www.worldfantasy.org. **Contact:** Peter Dennis Pautz, president. Offered annually for previously published work in several categories, including life achievement, novel, novella, short story, anthology, collection, artist, special award-pro and special award-nonpro. Works are recommended by attendees of current and previous 2 years' conventions and a panel of judges. Entries must be previously published. Published submissions from previous calendar year. Word length: 10,000-40,000 for novella, 10,000 for short story. All fantasy is eligible, from supernatural horror to Tolkien-esque to sword and sorcery to the occult, and beyond. Cover letter should include name, address, phone, e-mail, word count, title, and publications where submission was previously published, submitted to the address above and the panel of judges when they appear on the website. Results announced November 1 at annual convention. For contest results, visit website. Guidelines available in December for SASE or on website. Awards to recognize excellence in fantasy literature worldwide. Deadline: June 1. Prize: Trophy. Judged by panel.

WOW! WOMEN ON WRITING QUARTERLY FLASH FICTION CONTEST

WOW! Women on Writing, P.O. Box 2832, Winnetka CA 91396. **E-mail:** contestinfo@wow-womenonwriting.com. **Website:** www.wow-womenonwriting.com/contest.php. **Contact:** Angela Mackintosh, editor. Contest offered quarterly. Entries must be 250-750 words. "We are open to all themes and genres, although we do encourage writers to take a close look at our literary agent guest judge for the season if you are serious about winning." Deadline: August 31, November 30, February 28, May 31. Prize: 1st place: $400 cash prize, $25 Amazon gift certificate, story published on WOW! Women On Writing, interview on blog; 2nd place: $300 cash prize, $25 Amazon gift certificate, story published on WOW! Women On Writing, interview on blog; 3rd place: $200 cash prize, $25 Amazon gift certificate, story published on WOW! Women On Writing, interview on blog; 7 runners up: $25 Amazon gift certificate, story published on WOW! Women on Writing, interview on blog; 10 honorable mentions: $20 gift certificate from Amazon, story title and name published on WOW!Women On Writing. Judged by a different guest every season, who is either a literary agent, acquiring editor or publisher.

WRITER'S DIGEST SHORT SHORT STORY COMPETITION

Writer's Digest, 5720 Flatiron Pkwy., Boulder CO 80301. (715)445-4612; ext. 13430. **E-mail:** WritersDigestWritingCompetition@aimmedia.com. **Website:** www.writersdigest.com. **Contact:** Nicole Howard. Looking for fiction that's bold, brilliant, and brief. Send your best in 1,500 words or fewer. All entries must be original, unpublished, and not submitted elsewhere at the time of submission. *Writer's Digest* reserves one-time publication rights to the 1st-25th winning entries. Winners will be notified by Feb. 28. Early bird deadline: November 15. Final deadline: December 15. Prize: 1st Place: $3,000 and a trip to the Writer's Digest Conference; 2nd Place: $1,500; 3rd Place: $500; 4th-10th Place: $100; 11th-25th Place: $50 gift certificate for writersdigestshop.com.

WRITERSWEEKLY.COM'S QUARTERLY 24-HOUR SHORT STORY CONTEST

WritersWeekly.com, BookLocker.com, Inc., 200 2nd Ave. S., #526, St. Petersburg FL 33701. **E-mail:** writersweekly@writersweekly.com. **Website:** https://www.24HourShortStoryContest.com/. **Contact:** Angela Hoy, Publisher. A popular and fun quarterly contest in which registered entrants receive an assigned topic at start time (usually noon Central Time on a Saturday), and have 24 hours to write and submit a story on that topic. All submissions must be returned via e-mail. Each contest is limited to 500 people. Upon registration, entrant will receive guidelines and details on competition, including submission process. All past topics and winners are listed on the website, as well as the contest rules and hints for winning. Deadline: Quarterly—see website for dates. Prize: 1st Place: $300 + a publishing contract; 2nd Place: $250; 3rd Place: $200. There are also 20 honorable mentions and 60 door prizes (randomly drawn from all participants). The top 3 winners' entries are posted on WritersWeekly.com (non-exclusive electronic rights only). Writers retain all rights to their work. See website for full details on prizes. Judged by Angela Hoy (publisher of WritersWeekly.com and Booklocker.com).

ZOETROPE: ALL-STORY SHORT FICTION COMPETITION

Zoetrope: All-Story, Zoetrope: All-Story, Attn: Fiction Editor, 916 Kearny St., San Francisco CA 94133. (415)788-7500. **E-mail:** contests@all-story.com. **Website:** www.all-story.com/contests.cgi. Acclaimed annual short fiction competition. Considers submissions of short stories no longer than 5,000 words. For details, please visit the website this summer. Deadline: October 1. Submission period begins July 1. Prizes: 1st place: $1,000 and publication on website; 2nd place: $500; 3rd place: $250.

ZONE 3 FICTION AWARD

Zone 3, Austin Peay State University, P.O. Box 4565, Clarksville TN 37044. (931)221-7031. **Fax:** (931)221-7149. **E-mail:** wallacess@apsu.edu. **Website:** www.apsu.edu/zone3/contests. **Contact:** Susan Wallace, Managing Editor. Annual contest for unpublished fiction. Open to any fiction writer. Accepts entries online and via postal mail. Deadline: April 1. Prize: $250 and publication.

NONFICTION

AMERICA & ME ESSAY CONTEST

Farm Bureau Insurance, P.O. Box 30400, Lansing MI 48909. **E-mail:** lfedewa@fbinsmi.com. **Website:** FarmBureauInsurance.com. **Contact:** Lisa Fedewa. Focuses on encouraging students to write about their personal Michigan heroes: someone who lives in the state and who has encouraged them, taught them important lessons, and helped them pursue their dreams. Open to Michigan eighth graders. Contest rules and entry form available on website. Encourages Michigan youth to recognize the heroes in their communities and their state. Deadline: November 18. Prize: $1,000, plaque, and medallion for top 10 winners. Home office volunteers.

ANTHEM ESSAY CONTEST

Ayn Rand Institute, P.O. Box 57044, Irvine CA 92619-7044. (949)222-6550. **E-mail:** essays@aynrand.org. **Website:** https://www.aynrand.org/students/essay-contests#anthem-1. **Contact:** Anthony Loy. Offered annually to encourage analytical thinking and excellence in writing (600-1,200 word essay), and to expose students to the philosophic ideas of Ayn Rand. For information contact essays@aynrand.org or visit our website. Open to 8th, 9th and 10th graders. See website for topics. Deadline: April 25. 1st Place: $2,000; 2nd Place (3): $250; 3rd Place (5): $100; Finalist (50): $25.

THE ASCAP FOUNDATION DEEMS TAYLOR/VIRGIL THOMSON AWARDS

American Society of Composers, Authors & Publishers, One Lincoln Plaza, New York NY 10023. (212)621-6318. **E-mail:** jlapore@ascap.com. **Website:** www.ascap.com/music-career/support/deems-taylor-guidelines.aspx. **Contact:** Julie Lapore. The ASCAP Foundation Deems/Taylor Awards program recognizes books, articles, broadcasts, and websites on the subject of music selected for their excellence. Written works must be published in the U.S. in English, during the calendar year of the awards. The subject matter may be biographical or critical, reportorial or historical—almost any form of nonfiction prose about music and/or its creators. However, instructional textbooks, how-to-guides, or works of fiction will not be accepted. Honors the memory of composer/critic/commentator Deems Taylor. Deadline: May 31. Submission period begins February 1. Prize: Several categories of cash prizes are presented to writers of award-winning books and newspaper, journal, or magazine articles (includes program notes, liner notes, and online publications). Awards are also presented to the authors and journalists, as well as to their respective publishers.

ATLAS SHRUGGED ESSAY CONTEST

Ayn Rand Institute, P.O. Box 57044, Irvine CA 92619-7044. (949)222-6550, ext. 269. **Fax:** (949)222-6558. **E-mail:** essays@aynrand.org. **Website:** https://www.aynrand.org/students/essay-contests#atlasshrugged-1. **Contact:** Anthony Loy. Offered annually to encourage analytical thinking and excellence in writing, and to expose students to the philosophic ideas of Ayn Rand. Open to 12th graders, college undergraduates, and graduate students. Essay length: 800-1,600 words. Essays are judged both on style and content. Guidelines and topics available on the website. The winning applicant will be judged on both style and content. Judges will look for writing that is clear, articulate and logically organized. Winning essays must demonstrate an outstanding grasp of the philosophic meaning of *Atlas Shrugged*. Essay submissions are evaluated in a fair and unbiased four-round judging process. Judges are individually selected by the Ayn Rand Institute based on a demonstrated knowledge and understanding of Ayn Rand's works. Deadline: September 19. 1st Place: $25,000; 2nd Place (3 awards): $2,500; 3rd Place (5 awards): $500; Finalists (50 awards): $100.

THE CONGER BEASLEY JR. AWARD FOR NONFICTION

New Letters, University of Missouri-Kansas City, *New Letters* Awards for Writers, UMKC, University House, 5101 Rockhill Rd., Kansas City MO 64110-2499. (816)235-1168. **Fax:** (816)235-2611. **E-mail:** newletters@umkc.edu. **Website:** www.newletters.org. **Contact:** Ashley Wann. Contest is offered annually for unpublished work to discover and reward emerging writers and to give experienced writers a place to try new genres. Acquires first North American serial rights. Open to any writer. Guidelines by SASE or online. Entries should not exceed 8,000 words. Deadline: May 20. 1st Place: $2,500 and publication in a volume of *New Letters*.

THE CANADIAN AUTHORS AWARD FOR CANADIAN HISTORY

192 Spadina Avenue, Suite 107, Toronto ON M5T 2C2 Canada. (416) 975 1756. **E-mail:** admin@canadianauthors.org. **Website:** www.canadianauthors.org. **Contact:** Anita Purcell, Executive Director. Offered annually for a work of historical nonfiction on a Canadian topic by a Canadian author. Entry form required. Obtain entry form from contact name or download from website. Deadline: January 15. Prize: $2,000. The CAA Awards Chair appoints a trustee for this award. That trustee selects 2 judges. The identities of the trustee and judges are confidential throughout the judging process. Decisions of the trustee and judges are final, and they may choose not to award a prize. A shortlist of the best 3 entries in each category is announced in June. The winners are announced at the gala awards banquet during the annual CanWrite! conference in June.

MORTON N. COHEN AWARD

Modern Language Association of America, Morton N. Cohen Award, Modern Language Association, 85 Broad Street, Suite 500, New York NY 10004-2434. (646)576-5141. **Fax:** (646)458-0030. **E-mail:** awards@mla.org. **Website:** www.mla.org. **Contact:** Coordinator of Book Prizes. Awarded in odd-numbered years for a distinguished collection of letters. At least 1 volume of the edition must have been published during the previous 2 years. Editors need not be members of the MLA. Under the terms of the award, the winning collection will be one that provides readers with a clear, accurate, and readable text; necessary background information; and succinct and eloquent introductory material and annotations. The edited collection should be in itself a work of literature. Deadline: May 1. Prize: A cash award and a certificate to be presented at the Modern Language Association's annual convention in January.

CARR P. COLLINS AWARD FOR NONFICTION

The Texas Institute of Letters, The Texas Institute of Letters, P.O. Box 609, Round Rock TX 78680. **E-mail:** tilsecretary@yahoo.com. **Website:** http://texasinstituteofletters.org/. Offered annually for work published January 1-December 31 of the previous year to recognize the best nonfiction book by a writer who was born in Texas, who has lived in the state for at least 2 consecutive years at one point, or a writer whose work has some notable connection with Texas. See website for guidelines and instructions on submitting. Deadline: January 10. Prize: $5,000.

CREATIVE NONFICTION BOOK AWARD

Zone 3, Austin Peay State University, Austin Peay State University, P.O. Box 4565, Clarksville TN 37044. (931)221-7031. **Fax:** (931)221-7149. **E-mail:** wrighta@apsu.edu; collinsa@apsu.edu. **Website:** www.apsu.edu/zone3/contests. **Contact:** Amy Wright, acquisitions editor; Aubrey Collins, managing editor. This competition is open to all authors writing original works in English. Manuscripts that embrace creative nonfiction's potential by combining lyric exposition, researched reflection, travel dialogues, or creative criticism are encouraged. Memoir, personal narrative, essay collections, and literary nonfiction are also invited. Submit one copy of your ms, 120-300 pages. Accepts entries via postal mail or online. Separate instructions for both, see website for guidelines and details. Submissions Accepted: January 1-April 1 (in odd years). Prize: $1,000 and publication.

CREATIVE NONFICTION CONTEST

PRISM International, Creative Writing Program, UBC, Buch. E462—1866 Main Mall, Vancouver BC V6T 1Z1 Canada. **E-mail:** promotions@prismmagazine.ca. **Website:** www.prismmagazine.ca. Maximum word count: 5,000. Offered annually for published and unpublished writers to promote and reward excellence in literary creative nonfiction. *PRISM* buys first North American serial rights upon publication. Also buys limited web rights for pieces selected for the website. Open to anyone except students and faculty of the Creative Writing Program at UBC or people who have taken a creative writing course at UBC in the 2 years prior to contest deadline. All entrants receive a 1-year subscription to *PRISM*. Entries are accepted via Submittable at http://prisminternational.submittable.com/submit or by mail. Deadline: July 15. Prize: $1,500 grand prize, $600 runner-up, and $400 second runner-up.

ANNIE DILLARD AWARD FOR CREATIVE NONFICTION

Bellingham Review, Mail Stop 9053, 516 High St., Western Washington University, Bellingham WA 98225. (360)650-4863. **E-mail:** bellingham.review@wwu.edu. **Website:** www.bhreview.org. **Contact:** Susanne Paola Antonetta, editor-in-chief; Bailey Cunningham, managing editor. Offered annually for unpublished essays on any subject and in any style. Guidelines available online. Deadline: March 15. Submission period begins December 1. Prize: $1,000, plus publication and copies. All finalists considered for publication. All entrants receive subscription.

THE DONNER PRIZE

The Award for Best Book on Public Policy by a Canadian, The Donner Canadian Foundation, 23 Empire Ave., Toronto ON M4M 2L3 Canada. **E-mail:** sherry@naylorandassociates.com. **Website:** www.donnerbookprize.com. **Contact:** Sherry Naylor. Annual award that rewards excellence and innovation in public policy writing by Canadians. Deadline: November 30. Prize: Winning book receives $50,000; shortlisted titles get $7,500 each.

EVANS BIOGRAPHY & HANDCART AWARDS

Mountain West Center for Regional Studies, Room 339, Old Main, 0735 Old Main Hill, Utah State University, Logan UT 84322-0735. (435)797-0299. **Fax:** (435)797-1092. **E-mail:** mwc@usu.edu. **Website:** http://mountainwest.usu.edu. **Contact:** Evelyn Funda, Director. The Evans Biography and Evans Handcart Awards are biennial awards. Biographies and autobiographies for the Evans Awards must focus on the stories of people who have shaped or reflect the character of the Interior West or what's been described as "Mormon Country"—that region historically influenced by Mormon institutions and social practices. Neither the book's subject nor author need to belong to the Mormon faith. It was important to the founders of the awards that the works have both literary and historical merit and that the Evans Biography Award be judged on a national level. The Evans Handcart Award reflects a personal perspective, including family histories and, if possible, recognizes work by new authors or authors new to the genre. Send 6 copies of the book and one copy of the author's resume. See website for details. Deadline: February 1 in even calendar years for books published the previous two calendar years. Prize: $10,000 for the Evans Biography Award; and $2,500 for the Evans Handcart Award. Judged by a local and national jury of five scholars and book experts.

ILA DINA FEITELSON RESEARCH AWARD

International Literacy Association, Awards and Grants, P.O. Box 8139, Newark DE 19714-8139. (302)731-1600, ext. 227. **Fax:** (302)368-2449. **E-mail:** ilaawards@reading.org. **Website:** www.literacyworldwide.org/about-us/awards-grants. **Contact:** Wendy Logan, executive programs manager. This is an award for an exemplary work published in English in a refereed journal that reports on an empirical study investigating aspects of literacy acquisition, such as phonemic awareness, the alphabetic principle, bilingualism, or cross-cultural studies of beginning reading. Articles may be submitted for consideration by researchers, authors, et al. Copies of the applications and guidelines can be downloaded in PDF format from the website. Deadline: January 15. Prize: $500 award and recognition at the International Literacy Association's annual conference. Judged by ILA Dina Feitelson Research Award Committee.

HENDRICKS AWARD

The New Netherland Institute, The Annual Hendricks Award Committee; New Netherland Institute Cultural Education Center, Room 10D45, 222 Madison Ave., Albany NY 12230-0001. **Fax:** (518)473-0472. **E-mail:** awards@newnetherlandinstitute.org (please use 'Hendricks Award' in the subject line). **Website:** www.newnetherlandinstitute.org. Given annually to the best book or book-length ms relating to any aspect of New Netherland and its legacy. 2 categories of submissions will be considered in alternate years: (1) recently completed dissertations and unpublished book-length manuscripts, and (2) recently published books. If there is no suitable winner in the designated category in any particular year, submissions from the alternate category will be considered. In addition, submissions from previous years will be reconsidered for the Award. Entries must be based on research completed or published within 3 years prior to the deadline for submission. Entries may deal with any aspect of New Netherland and its legacy. Biographies of individuals whose careers illuminate aspects of the history of New Netherland and its legacy are eligible, as are manuscripts dealing with literature and the arts, provided that the methodology is historical. Deadline: February 1. Prize: $5,000 and a framed print of a painting by L.F. Tantillo. Judged by a 5-member panel of scholars.

THE HUNGER MOUNTAIN CREATIVE NONFICTION PRIZE

Vermont College of Fine Arts, 36 College St., Montpelier VT 05602. (802)828-8517. **E-mail:** hungermtn@vcfa.edu. **Website:** www.hungermtn.org. **Contact:** Cameron Finch, managing editor. Annual contest for the best writing in creative nonfiction. Submit essays under 10,000 words. Guidelines available on website. Accepts entries online. Deadline: March 1. Prize: $1,000 and publication. Two honorable mentions receive $100 each. TBA.

ILA TIMOTHY AND CYNTHIA SHANAHAN OUTSTANDING DISSERTATION AWARD

International Literacy Association, Awards and Grants, P.O. Box 8139, Newark DE 19714-8139. (302)731-1600, ext. 227. **Fax:** (302)731-1057. **E-mail:** ILAAwards@reading.org. **Website:** www.literacyworldwide.org/about-us/awards-grants. **Contact:** Wendy Logan, Executive Programs Manager. Dissertations in reading or related fields are eligible for the competition. Studies using any research approach (ethnographic, experimental, historical, survey, etc.) are encouraged. Each study is assessed in the light of this approach, the scholarly qualification of its report, and its significant contributions to knowledge within the reading field. The application process is open to those who have completed dissertations in any aspect of the field of reading or literacy of the calendar year. A routine check is made with the home university of the applicant to protect all applicants, their universities, and the International Reading Association from false claims. Studies may use any research approach (ethnographic, experimental, historical, survey, etc.). Each study will be assessed in light of its approach, its scholarship, and its significant contributions to knowledge within the reading/literacy field. Deadline: March 15.

TILIA KLEBENOV JACOBS RELIGIOUS ESSAY PRIZE CATEGORY

Soul-Making Keats Literary Competition, The Webhallow House, 1544 Sweetwood Dr., Broadmoor Vlg. CA 94015-2029. **E-mail:** soulkeats@mail.com. **Website:** www.soulmakingcontest.us. **Contact:** Eileen Malone. Call for thoughtful writings of up to 3,000 words. "No preaching, no proselytizing." Open annually to any writer. Previously published material is accepted. Indicate category on cover page and on identifying 3x5 card. Up to 3,000 words, double-spaced. See website for more details. Ongoing Deadline: November 30. Prize: 1st Place: $100; 2nd Place: $50; 3rd Place: $25.

GAIL ANN KENNA CREATIVE NONFICTION PRIZE CATEGORY

Soul-Making Keats Literary Competition, The Webhallow House, 1544 Sweetwood Dr., Broadmoor Vlg. CA 94015-2029. **E-mail:** soulkeats@mail.com. **Website:** www.soulmakingcontest.us. **Contact:** Eileen Malone. Creative nonfiction is the child of fiction and journalism. Unlike fiction, the characters and events are real, not imagined. Unlike journalism, the writer is part of the story she tells, if not as a participant then as a thoughtful observer. Must be typed, page numbered, and double-spaced. Each entry up to 3,000 words. Identify only with 3x5 card. Open annually to any writer. Deadline: November 30. Prizes: First Place: $100; Second Place: $50; Third Place: $25.

KATHERINE SINGER KOVACS PRIZE

Modern Language Association of America, Katherine Singer Kovacs Prize, Modern Language Association, 85 Broad Street, Suite 500, New York NY 10004-2434. (646)576-5141. **Fax:** (646)458-0030. **E-mail:** awards@mla.org. **Website:** www.mla.org. **Contact:** Annie Reiser, Coordinator of Book Prizes. Offered annually for an outstanding book published in English or Spanish in the field of Latin American and Spanish literatures and cultures. Competing books should be broadly interpretive works that enhance understanding of the interrelations among literature, the other arts, and society. Books must have been published in the previous year. Authors need not be members of the MLA. Must send 6 copies of book. Deadline: May 1. Prize: A cash award and a certificate to be presented at the Modern Language Association's annual convention in January.

THE GILDER LEHRMAN LINCOLN PRIZE

Gettysburg College and Gilder Lehrman Institute of American History, The Gilder Lehrman Lincoln Prize, 300 N. Washington St., Campus Box 413, Gettysburg PA 17325. (717)337-8255. **Fax:** (717)337-6597. **E-mail:** lincolnprize@gettysburg.edu. **Website:** www.gettysburg.edu/lincolnprize. **Contact:** Diane Brennan. The Gilder Lehrman Lincoln Prize, sponsored by the Gilder Lehrman Institute and Gettysburg College, is awarded annually for the finest scholarly work in English on Abraham Lincoln, the American Civil War soldier, or a subject relating to their era. Send 6 copies of the nominated work. Deadline: November 1. Prize: $50,000.

LITERAL LATTÉ ESSAY AWARD

Literal Latté, 200 E. 10th St., Suite 240, New York NY 10003. **E-mail:** litlatte@aol.com. **E-mail:** www.literal-latte.com/submissions/. **Website:** www.literal-latte.com. **Contact:** Jenine Gordon Bockman. Mind-stimulating entertainment caffeinating writers careers. Since 1994. Acquires first rights. Visit website for guidelines and tastes. Deadline: September 30. Prize: 1st Place: $1,000; 2nd Place: $300; 3rd Place: $200. Judged by the editors.

TONY LOTHIAN PRIZE

Under the auspices of the Biographers' Club, E6 Albany, Piccadilly, London W1J 0AR United Kingdom. (44)7985920341. **E-mail:** ariane.bankes@gmail.com. **Website:** www.biographersclub.co.uk. **Contact:** Ariane Bankes, prize administrator. Entries should consist of a synopsis and 10 pages of a sample chapter for a proposed biography, plus CV, sources and a note on the market for the book: 20 pages maximum in all, unstapled. Open to any writer who has not previously published or been commissioned to write a biography. Deadline: July 27. Prize: £2,000. Judges have included Michael Holroyd, Victoria Glendinning, Selina Hastings, Frances Spalding, Lyndall Gordon, Anne de Courcy, Nigel Hamilton, Anthony Sampson, and Mary Lovell.

JAMES RUSSELL LOWELL PRIZE

Modern Language Association of America, James Russell Lowell Prize, Modern Language Association, 85 Broad Street, Suite 500, New York NY 10004-2434. (646)576-5141. **Fax:** (646)458-0030. **E-mail:** awards@mla.org. **Website:** www.mla.org. **Contact:** Coordinator of Book Prizes. Open only to members of the Modern Language Association. To qualify for the prize, a book must be an outstanding literary or linguistic study, a critical edition of an important work, or a critical biography. Open to studies dealing with literary theory, media, cultural history, or interdisciplinary topics. Books must be published in the previous year. Authors must be current members of the MLA. Send 6 copies of the book. Deadline: March 1. Prize: A cash award and a certificate to be presented at the Modern Language Association's annual convention in January.

RICHARD J. MARGOLIS AWARD

c/o Margolis & Bloom, LLP, Richard J. Margolis Award of Blue Mountain Center, 667 Boylston St., 5th Floor, Boston MA 02116. (617)294-5951. **Fax:** (617)267-3166. **E-mail:** hsm@margolis.com. **E-mail:** award@margolis.com. **Website:** www.margolisaward.org. **Contact:** Harry S. Margolis. Sponsored by the Blue Mountain Center, this annual award is given to a promising new journalist or essayist whose work combines warmth, humor, wisdom, and concern with social justice. Applicants should be aware that this award is for nonfiction reporting and commentary, not for creative nonfiction, fiction, or poetry. Applications should include at least 2 examples of your work (published or unpublished, 30 pages maximum) and a short biographical note including a description of your current and anticipated work. Also please indicate what you will work on while attending the Blue Mountain residency. Please send to award@margolis.com. Deadline: July 1. Prize: $5,000, plus a 1-month residency at the Blue Mountain Center.

HOWARD R. MARRARO PRIZE

Modern Language Association of America, Howard R. Marraro Prize, Modern Language Association, 85 Broad Street, Suite 500, New York NY 10004-2434. (646)576-5141. **Fax:** (646)458-0030. **E-mail:** awards@mla.org. **Website:** www.mla.org. **Contact:** Coordinator of Book Prizes. Offered in even-numbered years for an outstanding scholarly work on any phase of Italian literature or comparative literature involving Italian. Books must have been published in the previous year. Authors must be members of the MLA. Requires 4 copies of the book. Deadline: May 1. Prize: A cash award and a certificate to be presented at the Modern Language Association's annual convention in January.

KENNETH W. MILDENBERGER PRIZE

Modern Language Association of America, Kenneth W. Mildenberger Prize, Modern Language Association, 85 Broad Street, Suite 500, New York NY 10004-2434. (646)576-5141. **Fax:** (646)458-0030. **E-mail:** awards@mla.org. **Website:** www.mla.org. **Contact:** Annie Rieser, Coordinator of Book Prizes. Offered in odd-numbered years for a publication from the previous year in the field of language, culture, literacy, or literature with a strong application to the teaching of languages other than English. Author need not be a member of the MLA. Books must have been published in the previous 2 years. Requires 4 copies of the book. Deadline: May 1. Prize: A cash award and a certificate, to be presented at the Modern Language Association's annual convention in January.

C. WRIGHT MILLS AWARD

The Society for the Study of Social Problems, 901 McClung Tower, University of Tennessee, Knoxville TN 37996-0490. (865)689-1531. **Fax:** (865)689-1534. **E-mail:** mkoontz3@utk.edu. **Website:** www.sssp1.org. **Contact:** Michele Smith Koontz, Administrative Officer and Meeting Manager. Offered annually for a book published the previous year that most effectively critically addresses an issue of contemporary public importance; brings to the topic a fresh, imaginative perspective; advances social scientific understanding of the topic; displays a theoretically informed view and empirical orientation; evinces quality in style of writing; and explicitly or implicitly contains implications for courses of action. Self-nominations are acceptable. Edited volumes, textbooks, fiction, and self-published works are not eligible. Eligible books must be first edition (not a reprint or later edition) and bear a 2018 copyright date. Exceptions may be made for a book bearing a 2017 copyright, but that was not released until 2018 for the first time. Deadline: December 15. Prize: $1,000 stipend. C. Wright Mills Award Committee

MLA PRIZE FOR A BIBLIOGRAPHY, ARCHIVE, OR DIGITAL PROJECT

Modern Language Association of America, MLA Prize for a Bibliography, Archive, or Digital Project, 85 Broad Street, Suite 500, New York NY 10004-2434. (646)576-5141. **Fax:** (646)458-0030. **E-mail:** awards@mla.org. **Website:** www.mla.org. **Contact:** Coordinator of Book Prizes. Offered in even-numbered years for an outstanding enumerative or descriptive bibliography, archive, or digital project. Open to any writer or publisher. At least 1 volume must have been published in the previous 2 years. Editors need not be members of the MLA. Criteria for determining excellence include evidence of analytical rigor, meticulous scholarship, intellectual creativity, and subject range and depth. Deadline: May 1. Prize: A cash prize and a certificate to be presented at the Modern Language Association's annual convention in January.

MLA PRIZE FOR A FIRST BOOK

Modern Language Association of America, MLA Prize for a First Book, 85 Broad Street, Suite 500, New York NY 10004-2434. (646)576-5141. **Fax:** (646)458-0030. **E-mail:** awards@mla.org. **Website:** www.mla.org. **Contact:** Annie Reiser, Coordinator of Book Prizes. Offered annually for the first book-length scholarly publication by a current member of the association. To qualify, a book must be a literary or linguistic study, a critical edition of an important work, or a critical biography. Studies dealing with literary theory, media, cultural history, and interdisciplinary topics are eligible; books that are primarily translations will not be considered. See listing for James Russell Lowe Prize—prize offered for same criteria. Deadline: March 1. Prize: A cash award and a certificate to be presented at the Modern Language Association's annual convention in January.

MLA PRIZE FOR A SCHOLARLY EDITION

Modern Language Association of America, MLA Prize for a Scholarly Edition, 85 Broad Street, Suite 500, New York NY 10004-2434. (646)576-5141. **Fax:** (646)458-0030. **E-mail:** awards@mla.org. **Website:** www.mla.org. **Contact:** Annie Reiser, Coordinator of Book Prizes. Offered in odd-numbered years for an outstanding scholarly edition. Editions may be in single or multiple volumes. At least 1 volume must have been published in the 2 years prior to the award deadline. Editors need not be members of the MLA. To qualify for the award, an edition should be based on an examination of all available relevant textual sources; the source texts and the edited text's deviations from them should be fully described; the edition should employ editorial principles appropriate to the materials edited, and those principles should be clearly articulated in the volume; the text should be accompanied by appropriate textual and other historical contextual information; the edition should exhibit the highest standards of accuracy in the presentation of its text and apparatus; and the text and apparatus should be presented as accessibly and elegantly as possible. Deadline: May 1. Prize: A cash award and a certificate to be presented at the Modern Language Association's annual convention in January.

MLA PRIZE FOR INDEPENDENT SCHOLARS

Modern Language Association of America, MLA Prize for Independent Scholars, 85 Broad Street, Suite 500, New York NY 10004-2434. (646)576-5141. **Fax:** (646)458-0030. **E-mail:** awards@mla.org. **Website:** www.mla.org. **Contact:** Annie Reiser, Coordinator of Book Prizes. Offered in even-numbered years for a scholarly book in the field of English or other modern languages and literatures. Book must have been published within the 2 years prior to prize deadline. At the time of publication of the book, author must not be enrolled in a program leading to an academic degree or hold a tenured, tenure-accruing, or tenure-track position in post-secondary education. Authors need not be members of the MLA. Requires 6 copies of the book and a completed application. Deadline: May 1. Prize: A cash award, a certificate, and a year's membership in the MLA.

MONTANA PRIZE IN CREATIVE NONFICTION

CutBank Literary Magazine, *CutBank*, University of Montana, English Dept., LA 133, Missoula MT 59812. **E-mail:** editor.cutbank@gmail.com. **Website:** www.cutbankonline.org. **Contact:** Allison Linville, Editor-in-Chief. The Montana Prize in Creative Nonfiction seeks to highlight work that showcases an authentic voice, a boldness of form, and a rejection of functional fixedness. Accepts online submissions only. Send a single work, no more than 35 pages. Guidelines available online. Deadline: January 15. Submissions period begins November 9. Prize: $500 and featured in the magazine. Judged by a guest judge each year.

LINDA JOY MYERS MEMOIR VIGNETTE PRIZE CATEGORY

Soul-Making Keats Literary Competition, Webhallow House, 1544 Sweetwood Dr., Broadmoor Village CA 94015-2029. **E-mail:** soulkeats@mail.com. **Website:** www.soulmakingcontest.us. **Contact:** Eileen Malone. Open annually to any writer. One memoir/entry, up to 1,500 words, double spaced. Previously published material is acceptable. Indicate category on first page. Identify only with 3x5 card. Ongoing Deadline: November 30. Prize: 1st Place: $100; 2nd Place: $50; 3rd Place: $25.

NATIONAL BUSINESS BOOK AWARD

BMO Financial Group, The National Business Book Award, 10 Delisle Ave., Suite 214, Toronto ON M4V 3C6 Canada. (416)868-1500. **Website:** www.nbbaward.com. Offered annually for books published January 1-December 31 to recognize excellence in business writing in Canada. Publishers nominate books. TBD. Prize: $30,000 (CAN).

NONFICTION AWARD

Saskatchewan Book Awards, Inc., Saskatchewan Book Awards, P.O. Box 20025, Regina SK S4P 4J7 Canada. (306)569-1585. **E-mail:** director@bookawards.sk.ca. **Website:** www.bookawards.sk.ca. Offered annually. This award is presented to a Saskatchewan author for the best book of nonfiction, judged on the quality of writing. Deadline: November 1. Prize: $2,000 (CAD).

FRANK LAWRENCE AND HARRIET CHAPPELL OWSLEY AWARD

Southern Historical Association, Room 111 A, LeConte Hall, Athens GA 30602-1602. (706)542-8848. **Fax:** (706)542-2455. **E-mail:** sdendy@uga.edu. **Website:** thesha.org. **Contact:** Dr. John B. Boles, Editor. Awarded for a distinguished book in Southern history published in even-numbered years. The decision of the Award Committee will be announced at the annual meeting in odd-numbered years. The award carries a cash payment to be fixed by the Council, a certificate for the author(s), and a certificate for the publisher. Deadline: March 1.

THE PHI BETA KAPPA AWARD IN SCIENCE

The Phi Beta Kappa Society, 1606 New Hampshire Ave. NW, Washington DC 20009. (202)265-3808. **Fax:** (202)986-1601. **E-mail:** awards@pbk.org. **Website:** www.pbk.org/bookawards. **Contact:** Awards Coordinator. Offered annually for outstanding contributions by scientists to the literature of science. To be eligible, biographies of scientists must have a substantial critical emphasis on their scientific research. Entries must have been published in the previous calendar year. Entries must be submitted by the publisher. Entries must be preceded by a letter certifying that the book(s) conforms to all the conditions of eligibility and stating the publication date of each entry. Two copies of the book must be sent with the nomination form. Books will not be entered officially in the competition until all copies and the letter of certification have been received. Open only to original works in English and authors of US residency and publication. The intent of the award is to encourage literate and scholarly interpretations of the physical and biological sciences and mathematics; monographs and compendiums are not eligible. Deadline: January 15. Prize: $10,000.

PRESERVATION FOUNDATION CONTESTS

The Preservation Foundation, Inc, 2313 Pennington Bend, Nashville TN 37214. (615)889-2968. **E-mail:** preserve@storyhouse.org. **E-mail:** preserve@storyhouse.org. **Website:** www.storyhouse.org. **Contact:** Richard Loller, Publisher. 4 contests offered annually for unpublished nonfiction: (1) Biography/Autobiography (1,000-10,000 words)—A true story of an individual personally known to the author or a true story from the author's life (the whole or an episode). (2) Animal Nonfiction (1,000-10,000 words)—Stories should be true accounts of personal encounters with wild birds, fish, butterflies, snails, lions, bears, turtles, etc.; not pets. (3) General Nonfiction (1,000-10,000 words)—Any appropriate nonfiction topic. (4) Travel Nonfiction (1,000-10,000 words)—Must be the true story of trip by author or someone personally known by author. Contests are open to any previously "unpublished writer," defined as those not earning a living by their writing and having earned no more than $750 by creative writing in any previous year. Stories must be submitted by e-mail. No paper mss can be considered. No story may be entered in more than one contest. See website for contest details. Our purpose is to "Preserve the extraordinary stories of 'ordinary' people." Deadline: Biographical and Animal, April 30. General and Travel, August 31. Prizes: In each category: First Place $200, Runner-up $100. Judged by a jury of three outside judges.

EVELYN RICHARDSON MEMORIAL NONFICTION AWARD

Writers' Federation of Nova Scotia, 1113 Marginal Rd., Halifax NS B3H 4P7 Canada. (902)423-8116. **Fax:** (902)422-0881. **E-mail:** director@writers.ns.ca. **Website:** www.writers.ns.ca. The Evelyn Richardson Memorial Nonfiction Award is awarded for a book of creative nonfiction by a resident of Nova Scotia. Detailed guidelines and eligibility criteria available online. Deadline: First Friday in December. Prize: Valued at $2,000 for the winning title.

ALDO AND JEANNE SCAGLIONE PRIZE FOR COMPARATIVE LITERARY STUDIES

Modern Language Association of America, 85 Broad Street, Suite 500, New York NY 10004-2434. (646)576-5141. **Fax:** (646)458-0030. **E-mail:** awards@mla.org. **Website:** www.mla.org. **Contact:** Coordinator of Book Prizes. Offered annually for outstanding scholarly work in comparative literary studies involving at least 2 literatures. Works of literary history, literary criticism, philology, and literary theory are eligible, as are works dealing with literature and other arts and disciplines, including cinema; books that are primarily translations will not be considered. Books must have been published in the past calendar year. Authors must be current members of the MLA. Requires 4 copies of the book. Deadline: May 1. Prize: A cash award and a certificate to be presented at the Modern Language Association's annual convention in January.

ALDO AND JEANNE SCAGLIONE PRIZE FOR FRENCH AND FRANCOPHONE STUDIES

Modern Language Association of America, 85 Broad Street, Suite 500, New York NY 10004-2434. (646)576-5141. **Fax:** (646)458-0030. **E-mail:** awards@mla.org. **Website:** www.mla.org. Offered annually for an outstanding scholarly work in French or francophone linguistics or literary studies. Works of literary history, literary criticism, philology, and literary theory are eligible for consideration; books that are primarily translations will not be considered. Books must have been published in the previous year. Authors must be current members of the MLA. Requires 4 copies of the book. Deadline: May 1. Prize: A cash award and a certificate to be presented at the Modern Language Association's annual convention in January.

ALDO AND JEANNE SCAGLIONE PRIZE FOR ITALIAN STUDIES

Modern Language Association of America, 85 Broad Street, Suite 500, New York NY 10004-2434. (646)576-5141. **Fax:** (646)458-0030. **E-mail:** awards@mla.org. **Website:** www.mla.org. **Contact:** Coordinator of Book Prizes. Offered in odd-number years for an outstanding scholarly work on any phase of Italian literature or culture, or comparative literature involving Italian. This shall include works that study literary or cultural theory, science, history, art, music, society, politics, cinema, and linguistics, preferably but not necessarily relating other disciplines to literature. Books must have been published in the previous year. Authors must be members of the MLA. Requires 4 copies of the book. Deadline: May 1. Prize: A cash award and a certificate to be presented at the Modern Language Association's annual convention in January.

ALDO AND JEANNE SCAGLIONE PRIZE FOR STUDIES IN GERMANIC LANGUAGES & LITERATURE

Modern Language Association of America, 85 Broad Street, Suite 500, New York NY 10004-2434. (646)576-5141. **Fax:** (646)458-0030. **E-mail:** awards@mla.org. **Website:** www.mla.org. Offered in even-numbered years for an outstanding scholarly work on the linguistics or literatures of any of the Germanic languages (Danish, Dutch, German, Norwegian, Swedish, Yiddish). Works of literary history, literary criticism, philology, and literary theory are eligible for consideration; books that are primarily translations will not be considered. Books must have been published in the previous 2 years. Authors must be members of the MLA. Requires 4 copies of the book. Deadline: May 1. Prize: A cash award, and a certificate to be presented at the Modern Language Association's annual convention in January.

ALDO AND JEANNE SCAGLIONE PUBLICATION AWARD FOR A MANUSCRIPT IN ITALIAN LITERARY STUDIES

Modern Language Association, 85 Broad Street, Suite 500, New York NY 10004-2434. (646)576-5141. **Fax:** (646)458-0030. **E-mail:** awards@mla.org. **Website:** www.mla.org. **Contact:** Coordinator of Book Prizes. Offered annually for an outstanding ms dealing with any aspect of the languages and literatures of Italy, including medieval Latin and comparative studies or intellectual history if the work's main thrust is clearly related to the humanities. Materials from ancient Rome are eligible if related to postclassical developments. Also eligible are translations of classical works of prose and poetry produced in Italy prior to 1900 in any language (e.g., neo-Latin, Greek) or in a dialect of Italian (e.g., Neapolitan, Roman, Sicilian). Eligible are book manuscripts in English or Italian that are ready for submission or already submitted to a press. Mss must be approved or ready for publication before award deadline. Authors must be current members of the MLA, residing in the United States or Canada. Requires 4 copies, plus contact and biographical information. Deadline: June 1. Prize: A cash award and a certificate to be presented at the Modern Language Association's annual convention in January.

WILLIAM SANDERS SCARBOROUGH PRIZE

Modern Language Association of America, 85 Broad Street, Suite 500, New York NY 10004-2434. (646)576-5141. **Fax:** (646)458-0030. **E-mail:** awards@mla.org. **Website:** www.mla.org. **Contact:** Coordinator of book prizes. Offered annually for an outstanding study of black American literature or culture. Books must have been published in the previous year. Authors need not be members of the MLA. Requires 4 copies of the book. Deadline: May 1. Prize: A cash award, and a certificate to be presented at the Modern Language Association's annual convention in January.

SCHOLARLY WRITING AWARD

Saskatchewan Book Awards, Inc., P.O. Box 20025, Regina SK S4P 4J7 Canada. (306)569-1585. **E-mail:** director@bookawards.sk.ca. **Website:** www.bookawards.sk.ca. **Contact:** Courtney Bates-Hardy, Executive Director. Offered annually. This award is presented to a Saskatchewan author for the best contribution to scholarship. The work must recognize or draw on specific theoretical work within a community of scholars, and participate in the creation and transmission of scholarly knowledge. Prize: $2,000 (CAD).

SCREAMINMAMAS CREATIVE NONFICTION CONTEST

1911 Cleveland St., Hollywood FL 33020. **E-mail:** screaminmamas@gmail.com. **Website:** www.screaminmamas.com/contests. **Contact:** Darlene Pistocchi, editor/managing director. "Looking for stories that revolve around the kids and/or pets. Must be true! Take an incident or scene that is embedded in your brain and share it with us. Story can be dramatic or humorous, happy or sad. Looking for the real deal." Stories should be 600-1,000 words. Open only to moms. Deadline: March 31. Prize: Publication.

THE SHAUGHNESSY COHEN PRIZE FOR POLITICAL WRITING

The Writers' Trust of Canada, 460 Richmond St. W., Suite 600, Toronto ON M5V 1Y1 Canada. (416)504-8222. **Fax:** (416)504-9090. **E-mail:** djackson@writerstrust.com. **Website:** www.writerstrust.com. **Contact:** Devon Jackson. Awarded annually for a nonfiction book of outstanding literary merit that enlarges understanding of contemporary Canadian political and social issues. Presented at Politics and the Pen each spring in Ottawa. Open to Canadian citizens and permanent residents only. Prize: $25,000 and $2,500 to 4 finalists.

MINA P. SHAUGHNESSY PRIZE

Modern Language Association of America, 85 Broad Street, Suite 500, New York NY 10004-2434. (646)576-5141. **Fax:** (646)458-0030. **E-mail:** awards@mla.org. **Website:** www.mla.org. **Contact:** Coordinator of Book Prizes. Offered in even-numbered years for a work in the fields of language, culture, literacy, or literature with strong application to the teaching of English. Books must have been published in the previous 2 years. Authors need not be members of the MLA. Requires 4 copies of the book. Deadline: May 1. Prize: A cash prize, a certificate, to be presented at the Modern Language Association's annual convention in January, and a 1-year membership in the MLA.

CHARLES S. SYDNOR AWARD

Southern Historical Association, Rm. 111 A LeConte Hall, Athens GA 30602-1602. (706)542-8848. **Fax:** (706)542-2455. **E-mail:** sdendy@uga.edu. **Website:** sha.uga.edu/awards/syndor.htm. **Contact:** Southern Historical Association. Offered in even-numbered years for recognition of a distinguished book in Southern history published in odd-numbered years. Publishers usually submit books. Deadline: March 1.

WABASH PRIZE FOR NONFICTION

Sycamore Review, Department of English, 500 Oval Dr., Purdue University, West Lafayette IN 47907. **E-mail:** sycamore@purdue.edu; sycamorenf@purdue.edu. **Website:** www.sycamorereview.com/contest/. **Contact:** Kara Krewer, editor-in-chief. Annual contest for unpublished nonfiction. For each submission, send one nonfiction piece (limit 7,500 words). Ms pages should be numbered and should include the title of the piece. All stories must be previously unpublished. See website for more guidelines. Submit via online submissions manager. Deadline: April 15. Prize: $1,000 and publication.

THE HILARY WESTON WRITERS' TRUST PRIZE FOR NONFICTION

460 Richmond St. W., Suite 600, Toronto ON M5V 1Y1 Canada. (416)504-8222. **Fax:** (416)504-9090. **E-mail:** djackson@writerstrust.com. **Website:** www.writerstrust.com. **Contact:** Devon Jackson. Offered annually for a work of nonfiction published in the previous year. Presented at the Writers' Trust Awards event held in Toronto each fall. Open to Canadian citizens and permanent residents only. Deadline: July 18. Prize: $60,000; $5,000 to 4 finalists.

THE ELIE WIESEL PRIZE IN ETHICS ESSAY CONTEST

The Elie Wiesel Foundation for Humanity, 555 Madison Ave., 20th Floor, New York NY 10022. **Fax:** (212)490-6006. **Website:** www.eliewieselfoundation.org. **Contact:** Leslie Meyers. This annual competition is intended to challenge undergraduate juniors and seniors in colleges and universities throughout the US to analyze ethical questions and concerns facing them in today's complex society. All students are encouraged to write thought-provoking, personal essays. Deadline: December 14. Prize: 1st Prize: $5,000; 2nd Prize: $2,500; 3rd Prize: $1,500; Honorable Mentions (2): $500. Judged by a distinguished panel of readers who evaluate all contest entries. A jury chooses the winners.

WRITING CONFERENCE WRITING CONTESTS

P.O. Box 664, Ottawa KS 66067-0664. (785)242-2947. **Fax:** (785)242-2473. **E-mail:** jbushman@writingconference.com. **E-mail:** support@studentq.com. **Website:** www.writingconference.com. **Contact:** John H. Bushman, contest director. Unpublished submissions only. Submissions made by the author or teacher. Purpose of contest: To further writing by students with awards for narration, exposition and poetry at the elementary, middle school, and high school levels. Deadline: January 8. Prize: Awards plaque and publication of winning entry in The Writers' Slate online, April issue. Judged by a panel of teachers.

YEARBOOK EXCELLENCE CONTEST

100 Adler Journalism Building, Iowa City IA 52242-2004. (319)335-3457. **Fax:** (319)335-3989. **E-mail:** quill-scroll@uiowa.edu. **Website:** www.quillandscroll.org. **Contact:** Jeff Browne, executive director. High school students who are contributors to or staff members of a student yearbook at any public or private high school are invited to enter the competition. Awards will be made in each of the 18 divisions. There are two enrollment categories: Class A: more than 750 students; Class B: 749 or less. Winners will receive Quill and Scroll's National Award Gold Key and, if seniors, are eligible to apply for one of the Edward J. Nell Memorial or George and Ophelia Gallup scholarships. Open to students whose schools have Quill and Scroll charters. Previously published submissions only. Submissions made by the author or school yearbook adviser. Must be published in the 12-month span prior to contest deadline. Visit website for list of current and previous winners. Purpose is to recognize and reward student journalists for their work in yearbooks and to provide student winners an opportunity to apply for a scholarship to be used freshman year in college for students planning to major in journalism. Deadline: October 10.

ZONE 3 CREATIVE NONFICTION BOOK AWARD

Zone 3, Austin Peay State University, P.O. Box 4565, Clarksville TN 37044. (931)221-7031. **Fax:** (931)221-7149. **E-mail:** wallacess@apsu.edu. **Website:** www.apsu.edu/zone3/contests. **Contact:** Susan Wallace, Managing Editor. This competition is open to all authors writing original works in English. Looking for manuscripts that embrace creative nonfiction's potential by combining lyric exposition, researched reflection, travel dialogues, or creative criticism. Memoir, personal narrative, essay collections, and literary nonfiction are also invited. Submit one copy of ms of 150-300 pages. Accepts entries online and via postal mail. Deadline: April 1. Prize: $1,000 and publication.

WRITING FOR CHILDREN & YOUNG ADULTS

JANE ADDAMS CHILDREN'S BOOK AWARD

Jane Addams Peace Association, 777 United Nations Plaza, 6th Floor, New York NY 10017. (212)682-8830. **E-mail:** info@janeaddamspeace.org. **Website:** www.janeaddamspeace.org. **Contact:** Heather Palmer, Co-Chair. The Jane Addams Children's Book Award annually recognizes children's books, published the preceding year, that effectively promote the cause of peace, social justice, world community, and the equality of the sexes and all races, as well as meeting conventional standards for excellence. Books eligible for this award may be fiction, poetry, or nonfiction. Books may be any length. Entries should be suitable for ages 2-12. See website for specific details on guidelines and required book themes. Deadline: December 31. Judged by a national committee of WILPF members concerned with children's books and their social values is responsible for making the choices each year.

AMERICAN ASSOCIATION OF UNIVERSITY WOMEN YOUNG PEOPLE'S LITERATURE AWARD

4610 Mail Service Center, Raleigh NC 27699-4610. (919)807-7290. **E-mail:** michael.hill@ncdcr.gov. **Website:** www.ncdcr.gov. **Contact:** Michael Hill, Awards Coordinator. Annual award. Book must be published during the year ending June 30. Submissions made by author, author's agent. or publisher. SASE for contest rules. Author must have maintained either legal residence or actual physical residence, or a combination of both, in the state of North Carolina for 3 years immediately preceding the close of the contest period. Only published work (books) eligible. Recognizes the year's best work of juvenile literature by a North Carolina resident. Deadline: July 15. Prize: Awards a cup to the winner and winner's name inscribed on a plaque displayed within the North Carolina Office of Archives and History. Judged by 3-judge panel.

HANS CHRISTIAN ANDERSEN AWARD

Nonnenweg 12, Postfach Basel CH-4009 Switzerland. **E-mail:** liz.page@ibby.org. **E-mail:** ibby@ibby.org. **Website:** www.ibby.org. **Contact:** Liz Page, Director. The Hans Christian Andersen Award, awarded every two years by the International Board on Books for Young People (IBBY), is the highest international recognition given to an author and an illustrator of children's books. The Author's Award has been given since 1956, the Illustrator's Award since 1966. Her Majesty Queen Margrethe II of Denmark is the Patron of the Hans Christian Andersen Awards. The awards are presented at the biennial congresses of IBBY. Awarded to an author and to an illustrator, living at the time of the nomination, who by the outstanding value of their work are judged to have made a lasting contribution to literature for children and young people. The complete works of the author and of the illustrator will be taken into consideration in awarding the medal, which will be accompanied by a diploma. Candidates are nominated by National Sections of IBBY in good standing. Prize: Awards medals according to literary and artistic criteria. Judged by the Hans Christian Andersen International Jury.

MARILYN BAILLIE PICTURE BOOK AWARD

The Canadian Children's Book Centre, 40 Orchard View Blvd., Suite 217, Toronto ON M4R 1B9 Canada. (416)975-0010, ext. 222. **Fax:** (416)975-8970. **E-mail:** meghan@bookcentre.ca. **Website:** www.bookcentre.ca. **Contact:** Meghan Howe. The Marilyn Baillie Picture Book Award honors excellence in the illustrated picture book format. To be eligible, the book must be an original work in English, aimed at children ages 3-8, written and illustrated by Canadians. Books published in Canada or abroad are eligible. Eligible genres include fiction, non-fiction and poetry. Books must be published between Jan. 1 and Dec. 31 of the previous calendar year. New editions or re-issues of previously published books are not eligible for submission. Send 5 copies of title along with a completed submission form. Deadline: mid-December annually. Prize: $20,000.

MILDRED L. BATCHELDER AWARD

Association for Library Service to Children, Division of the American Library Association, 50 E. Huron St., Chicago IL 60611-2795. (800)545-2433. **Fax:** (312)280-5271. **Website:** www.ala.org/alsc/awardsgrants/bookmedia/batchelderaward. The Batchelder Award is given to the most outstanding children's book originally published in a language other than English in a country other than the United States, and subsequently translated into English for publication in the US. Visit website for terms and criteria of award. The purpose of the award, a citation to an American publisher, is to encourage international exchange of quality children's books by recognizing US publishers of such books in translation. Deadline: December 31.

THE GEOFFREY BILSON AWARD FOR HISTORICAL FICTION FOR YOUNG PEOPLE

The Canadian Children's Book Centre, 40 Orchard View Blvd., Suite 217, Toronto ON M4R 1B9 Canada. (416)975-0010, ext. 222. **Fax:** (416)975-8970. **Website:** www.bookcentre.ca. **Contact:** Meghan Howe. Awarded annually to reward excellence in the writing of an outstanding work of historical fiction for young readers, by a Canadian author, published between Jan 1 and Dec 31 of the previous calendar year. Open to Canadian citizens and/or permanent residents of Canada. Books must be published between January 1 and December 31 of the previous year. Books must be first foreign or first Canadian editions. Autobiographies are not eligible. Jury members will consider the following: historical setting and accuracy; strong character and plot development; well-told, original story; and stability of book for its intended age group. Send 5 copies of the title along with a completed submission form. Deadline: January 15th, annually. Prize: $5,000.

THE IRMA S. AND JAMES H. BLACK AWARD

Bank Street College of Education, 610 W. 112th St., New York NY 10025-1898. (212)875-4458. **Fax:** (212)875-4558. **E-mail:** kfreda@bankstreet.edu. **Website:** http://bankstreet.edu/center-childrens-literature/irma-black-award/. **Contact:** Kristin Freda. Award give to an outstanding book for young children—a book in which text and illustrations are inseparable, each enhancing and enlarging on the other to produce a singular whole. Entries must have been published during the previous calendar year. Publishers submit books. Submit only 1 copy of each book. Does not accept unpublished mss. Deadline: December 6. A scroll with the recipient's name, and a gold seal designed by Maurice Sendak. Judged by a committee of older children and children's literature professionals. Final judges are first-, second-, and third-grade classes at a number of cooperating schools.

BOSTON GLOBE-HORN BOOK AWARDS

The Boston Globe, Horn Book, Inc., 300 The Fenway, Palace Road Building, Suite P-311, Boston MA 02115. (617)278-0225. **Fax:** (617)278-6062. **E-mail:** bghb@hbook.com; info@hbook.com. **Website:** www.hbook.com/bghb/. Offered annually for excellence in literature for children and young adults (published June 1-May 31). Categories: picture book, fiction and poetry, nonfiction. Judges may also name up to 2 honor books in each category. Books must be published in the US, but may be written or illustrated by citizens of any country. The Horn Book Magazine publishes speeches given at awards ceremonies. Guidelines for submitting books online. Submit a book directly to each of the judges. See www.hbook.com/bghb-submissions for details on submitting, as well as contest guidelines. Deadline: May 15. Prize: $500 and an engraved silver bowl; honor-book recipients receive an engraved silver plate. Judged by a panel of 3 judges selected each year.

ANN CONNOR BRIMER BOOK AWARD

Eric Drew, c/o Tantallon Public Library Halifax Public Libraries, 60 Alderney Drive, Dartmouth Dartmouth NS B2Y 4P8 Canada. (902)490-2742. **Website:** www.atlanticbookawards.ca/. **Contact:** Laura Carter, Atlantic Book Awards Festival Coordinator. In 1990, the Nova Scotia Library Association established the Ann Connor Brimer Award for writers residing in Atlantic Canada who have made an outstanding contribution to writing for Atlantic Candian young people. Author must be alive and residing in Atlantic Canada at time of nomination. Book intended for youth up to the age of 15. Book in print and readily available. Fiction or nonfiction (except textbooks). Book must have been published within the previous year. November 1. Prize: $2,000. Two shortlisted titles: $250 each.

CHILDREN'S AFRICANA BOOK AWARD

Outreach Council of the African Studies Association, c/o Rutgers University-Livingston campus, 54 Joyce Kilmer Ave., Piscataway NJ 08854 USA. (703)549-8208; (301)585-9136. **E-mail:** africaaccess@aol.com. **E-mail:** Harriet@AfricaAccessReview.org. **Website:** www.africaaccessreview.org. **Contact:** Brenda Randolph, Chairperson. The Children's Africana Book Awards are presented annually to the authors and illustrators of the best books on Africa for children and young people published or distributed in the U.S. The awards were created by the Outreach Council of the African Studies Association (ASA) to dispel stereotypes and encourage the publication and use of accurate, balanced children's materials about Africa. The awards are presented in 2 categories: Young Children and Older Readers. Entries must have been published in the calendar year previous to the award. Work submitted for awards must be suitable for children ages 4-18; a significant portion of book's content must be about Africa; must by copyrighted in the calendar year prior to award year; and must be published or distributed in the US. Books should be suitable for children and young adults, ages 4-18. A significant portion of the book's content should be about Africa. Deadline: December 31 of the year book is published. Judged by African Studies and Children's Literature scholars. Nominated titles are read by committee members and reviewed by external African Studies scholars with specialized academic training.

CHILDREN'S BOOK GUILD AWARD FOR NONFICTION

E-mail: theguild@childrensbookguild.org. **Website:** www.childrensbookguild.org. Annual award. "One doesn't enter. One is selected. Our jury annually selects one author for the award." Honors an author or illustrator whose total work has contributed significantly to the quality of nonfiction for children. Prize: Cash and an engraved crystal paperweight. Judged by a jury of Children's Book Guild specialists, authors, and illustrators.

CHILDREN'S LITERATURE LEGACY AWARD

50 E. Huron, Chicago IL 60611. (800)545-2433. **Fax:** (312)280-5271. **E-mail:** alscawards@ala.org. **Website:** http://www.ala.org/alsc/awardsgrants/bookmedia/clla. The Children's Literature Legacy Award honors an author or illustrator whose books, published in the United States, have made, over a period of years, a significant and lasting contribution to children's literature through books that demonstrate integrity and respect for all children's lives and experiences. The candidates must be nominated by ALSC members. Medal presented at Newbery/Caldecott/Legacy banquet during annual conference. Judging by Legacy Award Selection Committee.

MARGARET A. EDWARDS AWARD

50 East Huron St., Chicago IL 60611-2795. (312)280-4390 or (800)545-2433. **Fax:** (312)280-5276. **E-mail:** yalsa@ala.org. **Website:** www.ala.org/yalsa/edwards. **Contact:** Nichole O'Connor. Annual award administered by the Young Adult Library Services Association (YALSA) of the American Library Association (ALA) and sponsored by *School Library Journal* magazine. Awarded to an author whose book or books, over a period of time, have been accepted by young adults as an authentic voice that continues to illuminate their experiences and emotions, giving insight into their lives. The book or books should enable them to understand themselves, the world in which they live, and their relationship with others and with society. The book or books must be in print at the time of the nomination. Submissions must be previously published no less than 5 years prior to the first meeting of the current Margaret A. Edwards Award Committee at Midwinter Meeting. Nomination form is available on the YALSA website. Deadline: December 1. Prize: $2,000. Judged by members of the Young Adult Library Services Association.

DOROTHY CANFIELD FISHER CHILDREN'S BOOK AWARD

Midstate Library Service Center, Dorothy Canfield Fisher Book Award Committee

Vermont Department of Libraries, c/o Vermont Department of Libraries, 60 Washington Street St., Suite 2, Barre VT 05641. (802)828-6954. **E-mail:** grace.greene@state.vt.us. **Website:** https://libraries.vermont.gov/services/children_and_teens/book_awards/dcf. **Contact:** Grace W. Greene. Annual award to encourage Vermont children to become enthusiastic and discriminating readers by providing them with books of good quality by living American or Canadian authors published in the current year. E-mail for entry rules. Titles must be original work, published in the U.S., and be appropriate to children in grades 4-8. The book must be copyrighted in the current year. It must be written by an American author living in the U.S. or Canada, or a Canadian author living in Canada or the U.S. Deadline: December of year book was published. Prize: Awards a scroll presented to the winning author at an award ceremony. Judged by children, grades 4-8, who vote for their favorite book.

THE NORMA FLECK AWARD FOR CANADIAN CHILDREN'S NON-FICTION

The Canadian Children's Book Centre, Norma Fleck Award for Canadian Children's Non-Fiction, c/o The Canadian Children's Book Centre, Suite 217, 40 Orchard View Blvd., Toronto ON M4R 1B9 Canada. (416)975-0010 ext. 222. **Fax:** (416)975-8970. **E-mail:** meghan@bookcentre.ca. **Website:** www.bookcentre.ca. **Contact:** Meghan Howe. The Norma Fleck Award was established by the Fleck Family Foundation to recognize and raise the profile of exceptional nonfiction books for children. Offered annually for books published between January 1 and December 31 of the previous calendar year. Open to Canadian citizens and/or permanent residents. Books must be first foreign or first Canadian editions. Nonfiction books in the following categories are eligible: culture and the arts, science, biography, history, geography, reference, sports, activities, and pastimes. Deadline: January 15. Prize: $10,000. The award will go to the author unless 40% or more of the text area is composed of original illustrations, in which case the award will be divided equally between author and illustrator.

FLICKER TALE CHILDREN'S BOOK AWARD

Fargo Public Library, 102 3rd Street North, Fargo ND 58102. **E-mail:** aemery@fargolibrary.org. **Website:** www.ndla.info/flickertale. **Contact:** Amber Emery. Award gives children across the state of North Dakota a chance to vote for their book of choice from a nominated list of 20: 4 in the picture book category, 4 in the intermediate category, 4 in the juvenile category (for more advanced readers), and 4 in the upper-grade-level nonfiction category. Also promotes awareness of quality literature for children. Previously published submissions only. Submissions nominated by librarians and teachers across the state of North Dakota. Deadline: April 1. Prize: A plaque from North Dakota Library Association and banquet dinner. Judged by children in North Dakota.

THEODOR SEUSS GEISEL AWARD

Association for Library Service to Children, Division of the American Library Association, 50 E. Huron, Chicago IL 60611. (800)545-2433. **Fax:** (312)280-5271. **E-mail:** alscawards@ala.org. **Website:** http://www.ala.org/alsc/awardsgrants/bookmedia/geiselaward. The Theodor Seuss Geisel Award is given annually to the author(s) and illustrator(s) of the most distinguished American book for beginning readers published in English in the United States during the preceding year. The award is to recognize the author(s) and illustrator(s) who demonstrate great creativity and imagination in his/her/their literary and artistic achievements to engage children in reading. Terms and criteria for the award are listed on the website. Entry will not be returned. Deadline: December 31. Prize: Medal, given at awards ceremony during the ALA Annual Conference.

GOLDEN KITE AWARDS

Society of Children's Book Writers and Illustrators (SCBWI), SCBWI Golden Kite Awards, 8271 Beverly Blvd., Los Angeles CA 90048-4515. (323)782-1010. **Fax:** (323)782-1892. **E-mail:** bonniebader@sbcwi.org. **Website:** www.scbwi.org. **Contact:** Bonnie Bader, Golden Kite Coordinator. Given annually to recognize excellence in children's literature in 4 categories: fiction, nonfiction, picture-book text, and picture-book illustration. Books submitted must be published in the previous calendar year. Both individuals and publishers may submit. Submit 4 copies of book. Submit to one category only, except in the case of picture books. Must be a current member of the SCBWI. SUBMISSIONS FOR THE 2020 AWARDS WILL OPEN IN TWO WAVES: May 1 – June 30, 2019 (for books published between January-June 2019); July 1 – November 15, 2019 (for books published between July-December 2019). Prize: One

Golden Kite Award Winner and at least one Honor Book will be chosen per category. Winners and Honorees will receive a commemorative poster, also sent to publishers, bookstores, libraries, and schools; a press release; and an announcement on the SCBWI website and on SCBWI Social Networks.

CAROL OTIS HURST CHILDREN'S BOOK PRIZE

Westfield Athenaeum, 6 Elm St., Westfield MA 01085. (413)562-6158, Ext. 5. **Website:** www.westath.org. **Contact:** Sarah Scott, Youth Services Librarian. The Carol Otis Hurst Children's Book Prize honors outstanding works of fiction and nonfiction, including biography and memoir, written for children and young adults through the age of 18, which exemplify the highest standards of research, analysis, and authorship in their portrayal of the New England Experience. The prize will be presented annually to an author whose book treats the region's history as broadly conceived to encompass one or more of the following elements: political experience, social development, fine and performing artistic expression, domestic life and arts, transportation and communication, changing technology, military experience at home and abroad, schooling, business and manufacturing, workers and the labor movement, agriculture and its transformation, racial and ethnic diversity, religious life and institutions, immigration and adjustment, sports at all levels, and the evolution of popular entertainment. The public presentation of the prize will be accompanied by a reading and/or talk by the recipient at a mutually agreed upon time during the spring immediately following the publication year. Books must have been copyrighted in their original format during the calendar year, January 1 to December 31, of the year preceding the year in which the prize is awarded. Any individual, publisher, or organization may nominate a book. See website for details and guidelines. Deadline: December 31. Prize: $500.

INTERNATIONAL LITERACY ASSOCIATION CHILDREN'S AND YOUNG ADULT'S BOOK AWARDS

P.O. Box 8139, 800 Barksdale Rd., Newark DE 19714-8139. (302)731-1600, ext. 221. **E-mail:** kbaughman@reading.org. **E-mail:** committees@reading.org. **Website:** www.literacyworldwide.org. **Contact:** Kathy Baughman. The ILA Children's and Young Adults Book Awards are intended for newly published authors who show unusual promise in the children's and young adult's book field. Awards are given for fiction and nonfiction in each of 3categories: primary, intermediate, and young adult. Books from all countries and published in English for the first time during the previous calendar year will be considered. See website for eligibility and criteria information. Entry should be the author's first or second book. Deadline: March 15. Prize: $1,000.

THE IODE ONTARIO JEAN THROOP BOOK AWARD

IODE Ontario, c/o Linda Dennis, 45 Frid Street, Suite 9, Hamilton ON L8P 4M3 Canada. (905)522-9537. **E-mail:** iodeontario@gmail.com. **Website:** www.iode-ontario.ca. **Contact:** Linda Dennis. Each year, IODE Ontario presents an award intended to encourage the publication of books for children between the ages of 6-12 years. The award winner must be a Canadian citizen, resident in Toronto or the surrounding area, and the book must be published in Canada. Deadline: December 31. Prize: Award and cash prize of $2,000. The Selection Committee for the Award is comprised of members from the Toronto IODE Primary Chapters and members from the IODE Ontario Executive.

JEFFERSON CUP AWARD

P.O. Box 56312, Virginia Beach VA 23456. (757)689-0594. **Website:** www.vla.org. **Contact:** Salena Sullivan, Jefferson Cup Award Chairperson. The Jefferson Cup honors a distinguished biography, historical fiction, or American history book for young people. The Jefferson Cup Committee's goal is to promote reading about America's past; to encourage the quality writing of United States history, biography, and historical fiction for young people; and to recognize authors in these disciplines. Deadline: January 31.

THE EZRA JACK KEATS BOOK AWARD FOR NEW WRITER AND NEW ILLUSTRATOR

University of Southern Mississippi, de Grummond Children's Literature Collection, 118 College Dr., #5148, Hattiesburg MS 39406-0001. **E-mail:** ellen.ruffin@usm.edu or claire.thompson@usm.edu. **Website:** https://www.degrummond.org/. **Contact:** Ellen Ruffin, Curator of the de Grummond Children's Literature Collection and Claire Thompson, Ezra Jack Keats Book Award Coordinator. Annual award to an outstanding new author and new illustrator of children's books that portray universal qualities of childhood in our multicultural world. Many past winners have gone on to distinguished careers, creating books beloved by parents, children, librarians, and teachers around the world. Writers and illustrators must have had no more than 3 books previously published. Prize: The winning author and illustrator will each receive a cash award of $3,000. Judged by a distinguished selection committee of early childhood education specialists, librarians, illustrators, and experts in children's literature.

EZRA JACK KEATS/KERLAN MEMORIAL FELLOWSHIP

University of Minnesota Libraries, 113 Elmer L. Andersen Library, 222 21st Ave. S, Minneapolis MN 55455. **E-mail:** asc-clrc@umn.edu. **Website:** https://www.lib.umn.edu/clrc/awards-grants-and-fellowships. This fellowship from the Ezra Jack Keats Foundation will provide $3,000 to a talented writer and/or illustrator of children's books who wishes to use the Kerlan Collection for the furtherance of his or her artistic development. Special consideration will be given to someone who would find it difficult to finance a visit to the Kerlan Collection. The Ezra Jack Keats Fellowship recipient will receive transportation costs and a per diem allotment. See website for application deadline and for digital application materials. Winner will be notified in February. Study and written report must be completed within the calendar year. Deadline: January 30. $3,000 to fund a trip to visit the Kerlan Collection.

KENTUCKY BLUEGRASS AWARD

Website: www.kasl.us. The Kentucky Bluegrass Award is a student-choice program. The KBA promotes and encourages Pre-K through 12th-grade students to read a variety of quality literature. Each year, a KBA committee for each grade category chooses the books for the 4 Master Lists (K-2, 3-5, 6-8, and 9-12). All Kentucky public and private schools, as well as public libraries, are welcome to participate in the program. To nominate a book, see the website for form and details. Deadline: March 1. Judged by students who read books and choose their favorite.

CORETTA SCOTT KING BOOK AWARDS

ALA American Library Association, 50 E. Huron St., Chicago IL 60611-2795. (800)545-2433. **E-mail:** olos@ala.org. **Website:** www.ala.org/csk. **Contact:** Office for Diversity, Literacy and Outreach Services. The Coretta Scott King Book Awards are given annually to outstanding African American authors and illustrators of books for children and young adults that demonstrate an appreciation of African American culture and universal human values. The award commemorates the life and work of Dr. Martin Luther King, Jr., and honors his wife, Mrs. Coretta Scott King, for her courage and determination to continue the work for peace and world brotherhood. Must be written for a youth audience in 1 of 3 categories: preschool-4th grade; 5th-8th grade; or 9th-12th grade. Book must be published in the year preceding the year the award is given, evidenced by the copyright date in the book. See website for full details, criteria, and eligibility concerns. Purpose is to encourage the artistic expression of the African American experience via literature and the graphic arts; including biographical, historical, and social history treatments by African American authors and illustrators. Deadline: December 2nd at 4pm CST. Judged by the Coretta Scott King Book Awards Committee.

THE VICKY METCALF AWARD FOR LITERATURE FOR YOUNG PEOPLE

The Writers' Trust of Canada, 460 Richmond St. W., Suite 600, Toronto ON M5V 1Y1 Canada. (416)504-8222. **E-mail:** djackson@writerstrust.com. **Website:** www.writerstrust.com. **Contact:** Devon Jackson. The Vicky Metcalf Award is presented to a Canadian writer for a body of work in children's literature at The Writers' Trust Awards event held in Toronto each fall. Open to Canadian citizens and permanent residents only. Prize: $25,000.

MILKWEED PRIZE FOR CHILDREN'S LITERATURE

Milkweed Editions, 1011 Washington Ave. S., Suite 300, Minneapolis MN 55415. (612)332-3192. **Fax:** (612)215-2550. **E-mail:** editor@milkweed.org. **Website:** www.milkweed.org. Milkweed Editions will award the Milkweed Prize for Children's Literature to the best mss for young readers that Milkweed accepts for publication during the calendar year by a writer not previously published by Milkweed. All mss for young readers submitted for publication by Milkweed are automatically entered into the competition. Seeking full-length fiction between 90-200 pages. Does not consider picture books or poetry collections for young readers. Recognizes an outstanding literary novel for readers ages 8-13, and encourage writers to turn their attention to readers in this age group. Prize: $10,000 cash, in addition to a publishing contract negotiated at the time of acceptance. Judged by the editors of Milkweed Editions.

NATIONAL YOUNGARTS FOUNDATION

National YoungArts Foundation, 2100 Biscayne Blvd., Miami FL 33137. (305)377-1140. **Fax:** (305)377-1149. **E-mail:** info@youngarts.org; apply@youngarts.org. **Website:** www.youngarts.org. The National YoungArts Foundation (formerly known as the National Foundation for Advancement in the Arts) was established in 1981 by Lin and Ted Arison to identify and support the next generation of artists and to contribute to the cultural vitality of the nation by investing in the artistic development of talented young artists in the visual, literary, design, and performing arts. Each year, there are approximately 11,000 applications submitted to YoungArts from 15-18 year old (grades 10-12) artists. From these, approximately 700 winners are selected who are eligible to participate in programs in Miami, New York, Los Angeles, and Washington D.C. (with Chicago and other regions in the works). YoungArts provides these emerging artists with life-changing experiences and validation by renowned mentors, access to significant scholarships, national recognition, and other opportunities throughout their careers to help ensure that the nation's most outstanding emerging artists are encouraged to pursue careers in the arts. See website for details about applying. Prize: Cash awards up to $10,000.

JOHN NEWBERY MEDAL

Association for Library Service to Children, Division of the American Library Association, 50 E. Huron, Chicago IL 60611. (800)545-2433. **Fax:** (312)280-5271. **E-mail:** alscawards@ala.org. **Website:** http://www.ala.org/alsc/awardsgrants/bookmedia/newberymedal/newberymedal. The Newbery Medal is awarded annually by the American Library Association for the most distinguished contribution to American literature for children. Previously published submissions only; must be published prior to year award is given. SASE for award rules. Entries not returned. Medal awarded at Caldecott/Newbery/Legacy banquet during ALA annual conference. Deadline: December 31. Judged by Newbery Award Selection Committee.

NEW VOICES AWARD

LEE & LOW BOOKS, Att'n: New Voices Award, 95 Madison Ave., Suite 1205, New York NY 10016. **Website:** www.leeandlow.com. Open to students. Annual award. Lee & Low Books is one of the few minority-owned publishing companies in the country, and has published more than 100 first-time writers and illustrators. Winning titles include *The Blue Roses*, winner of a Patterson Prize for Books for Young People; *Janna and the Kings*, an IRA Children's Book Award Notable; and *Sixteen Years in Sixteen Seconds*, selected for the Texas Bluebonnet Award Masterlist. Submissions made by author. SASE for contest rules or visit website. Restrictions of media for illustrators: The author must be a writer of color who is a resident of the U.S. and who has not previously published a children's picture book. For additional information, send SASE or visit Lee & Low's website. Encourages writers of color to enter the world of children's books. Deadline: August 31. Prize: $2,000, standard publication contract (regardless of whether or not writer has an agent), and an advance against royalties; New Voices Honor Award: $1,000 prize. Judged by Lee & Low editors.

THE ORIGINAL ART

128 E. 63rd St., New York NY 10065. (212)838-2560. **Fax:** (212)838-2561. **E-mail:** kim@societyillustrators.org; info@societyillustrators.org. **Website:** www.societyillustrators.org. **Contact:** Kate Feirtag, exhibition director. The Original Art is an annual exhibit created to showcase illustrations from the year's best children's books published in the US. For editors and art directors, it's an inspiration and a treasure trove of talent to draw upon. Previously published submissions only. Request "call for entries" to receive contest rules and entry forms. Works will be displayed at the Society of Illustrators Museum of American Illustration in New York City October-November annually. Deadline: July 18. Judged by 7 professional artists and editors.

HELEN KEATING OTT AWARD FOR OUTSTANDING CONTRIBUTION TO CHILDREN'S LITERATURE

CSLA, 10157 SW Barbur Blvd. #102C, Portland OR 97219. (503)244-6919. **Fax:** (503)977-3734. **E-mail:** sharper1@kent.edu. **Website:** www.cslainfo.org. **Contact:** S. Meghan Harper, awards chair. Annual award given to a person or organization that has made a significant contribution to promoting high moral and ethical values through children's literature. Recipient is honored in July during the conference. Awards certificate of recognition, the awards banquet, and one-night's stay in the hotel. A nomination for an award may be made by anyone. An application form is available online. Elements of creativity and innovation will be given high priority by the judges.

PATERSON PRIZE FOR BOOKS FOR YOUNG PEOPLE

The Poetry Center at Passaic County Community College, One College Blvd., Paterson NJ 07505. (973)684-6555. **Fax:** (973)523-6085. **E-mail:** mgillan@pccc.edu. **Website:** www.pccc.edu/poetry. **Contact:** Maria Mazziotti Gillan, executive director. Award for a book published in the previous year in each age category (Pre-K-Grade 3, Grades 4-6, Grades 7-12). Deadline: February 1. Prize: $500.

THE KATHERINE PATERSON PRIZE FOR YOUNG ADULT AND CHILDREN'S WRITING

Hunger Mountain, Vermont College of Fine Arts, 36 College St., Montpelier VT 05602. (802)828-8517. **E-mail:** hungermtn@vcfa.edu. **Website:** www.hungermtn.org. **Contact:** Cameron Finch, managing editor. The annual Katherine Paterson Prize for Young Adult and Children's Writing honors the best in young adult and children's literature. Submit young adult or middle grade mss, and writing for younger children, short stories, picture books, poetry, or novel excerpts, under 10,000 words. Guidelines available on website. Deadline: March 1. Prize: $1,000 and publication for the first place winner; $100 each and publication for the three category winners. Judged by a guest judge every year.

PENNSYLVANIA YOUNG READERS' CHOICE AWARDS PROGRAM

Pennsylvania School Librarians Association, 134 Bisbing Road, Henryville PA 18332. **E-mail:** pyrca.psla@gmail.com. **Website:** www.psla.org. **Contact:** Alice L. Cyphers, co-coordinator. Submissions nominated by a person or group. Must be published within 5 years of the award—for example, books published in 2013 to present are eligible for the 2018-2019 award. Check the Program wiki at pyrca.wikispaces.com for submission information. View information at the Pennsylvania School Librarians' website or the Program wiki. Must be currently living in North America. The purpose of the Pennsylvania Young Reader's Choice Awards Program is to promote the reading of quality books by young people in the Commonwealth of Pennsylvania, to encourage teacher and librarian collaboration and involvement in children's literature, and to honor authors whose works have been recognized by the students of Pennsylvania. Deadline: September 15. Prize: Framed certificate to winning authors. Four awards are given, one for each of the following grade level divisions: K-3, 3-6, 6-8, YA. Judged by children of Pennsylvania (they vote).

PEN/PHYLLIS NAYLOR WORKING WRITER FELLOWSHIP

PEN America, PEN American Center, 588 Broadway, Suite 303, New York NY 10012. **E-mail:** awards@pen.org. **Website:** www.pen.org/awards. **Contact:** Arielle Anema, Literary Awards Coordinator. Offered annually to an author of children's or young-adult fiction. The Fellowship has been developed to help writers whose work is of high literary caliber but who have not yet attracted a broad readership. The Fellowship is designed to assist a writer at a crucial moment in his or her career to complete a book-length work-in-progress. Candidates have published at least one novel for children or young adults which have been received warmly by literary critics, but have not generated sufficient income to support the author. Writers must be nominated by an editor or fellow author. See website for eligibility and nomination guidelines. Deadline: Submissions open during the summer of each year. Visit PEN.org/awards for up-to-date information on deadlines. Prize: $5,000.

PLEASE TOUCH MUSEUM BOOK AWARD

Memorial Hall in Fairmount Park, 4231 Avenue of the Republic, Philadelphia PA 19131. (215)578-5153. **Fax:** (215)578-5171. **E-mail:** hboyd@pleasetouchmuseum.org. **Website:** www.pleasetouchmuseum.org. **Contact:** Heather Boyd. This prestigious award has recognized and encouraged the publication of high quality books. The award was exclusively created to recognize and encourage the writing of publications that help young children enjoy the process of learning through books, while reflecting PTM's philosophy of learning through play. The awards to to books that are imaginative, exceptionally illustrated, and help foster a child's life-long love of reading. To be eligible for consideration, a book must be distinguished in text, illustration, and ability to explore and clarify an idea for young children (ages 7 and under). Deadline: October 1. Books for each cycle must be published within previous calendar year (September-August). Judged by a panel of volunteer educators, artists, booksellers, children's authors, and librarians in conjunction with museum staff.

POCKETS FICTION-WRITING CONTEST

P.O. Box 340004, Nashville TN 37203-0004. (615)340-7333. **Fax:** (615)340-7267. **E-mail:** pockets@upperroom.org. **Website:** www.pockets.upperroom.org. **Contact:** Lynn W. Gilliam, senior editor. Designed for 6- to 12-year-olds, *Pockets* magazine offers wholesome devotional readings that teach about God's love and presence in life. The content includes fiction, scripture stories, puzzles and games, poems, recipes, colorful pictures, activities, and scripture readings. Freelance submissions of stories, poems, recipes, puzzles and games, and activities are welcome. Stories should be 750-1,000 words. Multiple submissions are permitted. Past winners are ineligible. The primary purpose of *Pockets* is to help children grow in their relationship with God and to claim the good news of the gospel of Jesus Christ by applying it to their daily lives. *Pockets* espouses respect for all human beings and for God's creation. It regards a child's faith journey as an integral part of all of life and sees prayer as undergirding that journey. Deadline: August 15. Submission period begins March 15. Prize: $500 and publication in magazine.

MICHAEL L. PRINTZ AWARD

Young Adult Library Services Association, Division of the American Library Association, 50 E. Huron, Chicago IL 60611. (800)545-2433. **Fax:** (312)280-5276. **E-mail:** yalsa@ala.org. **Website:** www.ala.org/yalsa/printz. **Contact:** Nichole O'Connor, program officer for events and conferences. The Michael L. Printz Award annually honors the best book written for teens, based entirely on its literary merit, each year. In addition, the Printz Committee names up to 4 honor books, which also represent the best writing in young adult literature. The award-winning book can be fiction, nonfiction, poetry or an anthology, and can be a work of joint authorship or editorship. The books must be published between January 1 and December 31 of the preceding year and be designated by its publisher as being either a young adult book or one published for the age range that YALSA defines as young adult, e.g. ages 12 through 18. Deadline: December 1. Judged by an award committee.

PURPLE DRAGONFLY BOOK AWARDS

Story Monsters LLC, 4696 W Tyson St, Chandler AZ 85226-2903. (480)940-8182. **Fax:** (480)940-8787. **E-mail:** linda@storymonsters.com. **Website:** www.dragonflybookawards.com. **Contact:** Cristy Bertini, contest coordinator. The Purple Dragonfly Book Awards were conceived with children in mind. Not only do we want to recognize and honor accomplished authors in the field of children's literature, but we also want to highlight up-and-coming, newly published authors, and younger published writers. Divided into 55 distinct subject categories ranging from books on the environment and cooking to sports and family issues, and even marketing collateral that complements a book, the Purple Dragonfly Book Awards are geared toward stories that appeal to children of all ages. We are looking for books that are original, innovative and creative in both content and design. A Purple Dragonfly Book Awards seal on your book's cover, marketing materials, or website tells parents, grandparents, educators, and caregivers that they are giving children the very best in reading excellence. Our judges are industry experts with specific knowledge about the categories over which they preside. Being honored with a Purple Dragonfly Book Award confers credibility upon the winner and gives published authors the recognition they deserve and provide a helping hand to further their careers. The awards are open to books published in any calendar year and in any country that are available for purchase. Books entered must be printed in English. Traditionally published, partnership published and self-published books are permitted, as long as they fit the above criteria. Submit materials to: Cristy Bertini, Attn: Dragonfly Book Awards, 1271 Turkey St., Ware, MA 01082. Deadline: May 1. The grand prize winner will receive a $500 cash prize, a certificate commemorating their accomplishment, 100 Grand Prize seals, a one-hour marketing consulting session with Linda F. Radke, a news release announcing the winners sent to a comprehensive list of media outlets, and a listing on the Dragonfly Book Awards website. All first-place winners of categories will be put into a drawing for a $100 prize. In addition, each first-place winner in each category receives a certificate commemorating their accomplishment, 25 foil award seals, and mention on Dragonfly Book Awards website. All winners receive certificates and are listed in Story Monsters Ink magazine. Judged by industry experts with specific knowledge about the categories over which they preside.

QUILL AND SCROLL WRITING, PHOTO AND MULTIMEDIA CONTEST AND BLOGGING COMPETITION

School of Journalism, Univ. of Iowa, 100 Adler Journalism Bldg., Iowa City IA 52242-2004. (319)335-3457. **E-mail:** quill-scroll@uiowa.edu. **E-mail:** quill-scroll@uiowa.edu. **Website:** quillandscroll.org. **Contact:** Jeffrey Browne, Contest Director. Entries must have been published in a high school or professional newspaper or website during the previous year, and be the work of a currently enrolled high school student when published. Open to students. Annual contest. Previously published submissions only. Submissions made by the author or school media adviser. Deadline: February 5. Prize: Winners will receive *Quill and Scroll*'s National Award Gold Key and, if seniors, are eligible to apply for one of the scholarships offered by *Quill and Scroll*. All winning entries are automatically eligible for the International Writing and Photo Sweepstakes Awards. Engraved plaque awarded to sweepstakes winners.

THE RED HOUSE CHILDREN'S BOOK AWARD

Red House Children's Book Award, 123 Frederick Road, Cheam, Sutton, Surrey SM1 2HT United Kingdom. **E-mail:** info@rhcba.co.uk. **Website:** www.redhousechildrensbookaward.co.uk. **Contact:** Sinead Kromer, national coordinator. The Red House Children's Book Award is the only national book award that is entirely voted for by children. A shortlist is drawn up from children's nominations and any child can then vote for the winner of the three categories: Books for Younger Children, Books for Younger Readers and Books for Older Readers. The book with the most votes is then crowned the winner of the Red House Children's Book Award. Deadline: December 31.

TOMÁS RIVERA MEXICAN AMERICAN CHILDREN'S BOOK AWARD

Dr. Jesse Gainer, Texas State University, 601 University Drive, San Marcos TX 78666-4613. (512)245-2357. **E-mail:** riverabookaward@txstate.edu. **Website:** www.riverabookaward.org. **Contact:** Dr. Jesse Gainer, award director. Texas State University College of Education developed the Tomas Rivera Mexican American Children's Book Award to honor authors and illustrators who create literature that depicts the Mexican American experience. The award was established in 1995 and was named in honor of Dr. Tomas Rivera, a distinguished alumnus of Texas State University. The book will be written for younger children, ages pre-K to 5th grade (awarded in even years), or older children, ages 6th grade to 12 grade (awarded in odd years). The text and illustrations will be of highest quality. The portrayal/representations of Mexican Americans will be accurate and engaging, avoid stereotypes, and reflect rich characterization. The book may be fiction or non- fiction. See website for more details and directions. Deadline: November 1.

✪ ROCKY MOUNTAIN BOOK AWARD: ALBERTA CHILDREN'S CHOICE BOOK AWARD

Box 42, Lethbridge AB T1J 3Y3 Canada. **E-mail:** rockymountainbookaward@shaw.ca. **Website:** www.rmba.info. **Contact:** Michelle Dimnik, contest director. Annual contest. No entry fee. Awards: Gold medal and author tour of selected Alberta schools. Judging by students. Canadian authors and/or illustrators only. Submit entries to Richard Chase. Previously unpublished submissions only. Submissions made by author's agent or nominated by a person or group. Must be published within the 3 years prior to that year's award. Register before January 20th to take part in the Rocky Mountain Book Award. SASE for contest rules and entry forms. Purpose of contest: "Reading motivation for students, promotion of Canadian authors, illustrators and publishers." Gold Medal and sponsored visit to several Alberta Schools or Public Libraries. Judged by students.

SCBWI MAGAZINE MERIT AWARDS

4727 Wilshire Blvd., Suite 301, Los Angeles CA 90010. (323)782-1010. **Fax:** (323)782-1892. **E-mail:** grants@scbwi.org. **Website:** www.scbwi.org. **Contact:** Stephanie Gordon, award coordinator. The SCBWI is a professional organization of writers and illustrators and others interested in children's literature. Membership is open to the general public at large. All magazine work for young people by an SCBWI member—writer, artist or photographer—is eligible during the year of original publication. In the case of co-authored work, both authors must be SCBWI members. Members must submit their own work. Requirements for entrants: 4 copies each of the published work and proof of publication (may be contents page) showing the name of the magazine and the date of issue. Previously published submissions only. For rules and procedures see website. Must be a SCBWI member. Recognizes outstanding original magazine work for young people published during that year, and having been written or illustrated by members of SCBWI. Deadline: December 15 of the year of publication. Submission period begins January 1. Prize: Awards plaques and honor certificates for each of 4 categories (fiction, nonfiction, illustration and poetry). Judged by a magazine editor and two "full" SCBWI members.

SKIPPING STONES BOOK AWARDS

Skipping Stones, P.O. Box 3939, Eugene OR 97403-0939. **E-mail:** editor@skippingstones.org. **Website:** www.skippingstones.org/wp. **Contact:** Arun N. Toke', Exec. Editor. Open to published books, publications/magazines, educational videos, and DVDs. Annual awards. Submissions made by the author or publishers and/or producers. Send request for contest rules and entry forms or visit website. Many educational publications announce the winners of our book awards. The winning books and educational videos/DVDs are announced in the July-September issue of *Skipping Stones* and also on the website. In addition to announcements on social media pages, the reviews of winning titles are posted on website. For several years now, Multicultural Education, a quarterly journal has been republishing all the book award winners' reviews. *Skipping Stones* multicultural magazine has been published for over 28 years. Recognizes exceptional, literary and artistic contributions to juvenile/children's literature, as well as teaching resources and educational audio/video resources in the areas of multicultural awareness, nature and ecology, social issues, peace, and nonviolence. Deadline: February 28.

Prize: Winners receive gold honor award seals, attractive honor certificates, and publicity via multiple outlets. Judged by a multicultural selection committee of editors, students, parents, teachers, and librarians.

SKIPPING STONES YOUTH HONOR AWARDS

P. O. Box 3939, Eugene OR 97403-0939. (541)342-4956. **E-mail:** editor@skippingstones.org. **Website:** www.SkippingStones.org/wp. **Contact:** Arun N. Toké, editor. Now celebrating its 30th year, *Skipping Stones* is a winner of N.A.M.E., EDPRESS, Newsstand Resources, Writer and Parent's Choice Awards. Open to students ages 7 to 17. Annual awards. Submissions made by the author. The winners are published in the October-December issue of *Skipping Stones*. Everyone who enters the contest receives the Autumn issue featuring Youth Awards. SASE for contest rules or download from website. Entries must include certificate of originality by a parent and/or teacher and a cover letter that included cultural background information on the author. Submissions can either be mailed or e-mailed. Up to ten awards are given in three categories: (1) Compositions (essays, poems, short stories, songs, travelogues, etc.): Entries should be typed (double-spaced) or neatly handwritten. Fiction or nonfiction should be limited to 1,000 words; poems to 30 lines. Non-English writings are also welcome. (2) Artwork (drawings, cartoons, paintings or photo essays with captions): Entries should have the artist's name, age and address on the back of each page. Send the originals with SASE. Black & white photos are especially welcome. Limit: 8 pieces. (3) Youth Organizations: Describe how your club or group works to: (a) preserve the nature and ecology in your area, (b) enhance the quality of life for low-income, minority or disabled or (c) improve racial or cultural harmony in your school or community. Use the same format as for compositions. Recognizes youth, 7 to 17, for their contributions to multicultural awareness, nature and ecology, social issues, peace and nonviolence. Also promotes creativity, self-esteem and writing skills and to recognize important work being done by youth organizations. Deadline: June 25. Judged by *Skipping Stones* staff.

SYDNEY TAYLOR BOOK AWARD

Association of Jewish Libraries, **E-mail:** chair@sydneytaylorbookaward.org. **Website:** www.sydneytaylorbookaward.org. **Contact:** Ellen Tilman, chair. The Sydney Taylor Book Award is presented annually to outstanding books for children and teens that authentically portray the Jewish experience. Deadline: November 30. Cannot guarantee that books received after November 30 will be considered. Prize: Gold medals are presented in 3 categories: younger readers, older readers, and teen readers. Honor books are awarded in silver medals, and notable books are named in each category. Winners are selected by a committee of the Association of Jewish Libraries. Each committee member must receive an individual copy of each book that is to be considered.

SYDNEY TAYLOR MANUSCRIPT COMPETITION

Association of Jewish Libraries, Sydney Taylor Manuscript Award Competition, 204 Park St., Montclair NJ 07042-2903. **E-mail:** stmacajl@aol.com. **Website:** www.jewishlibraries.org/main/Awards/SydneyTaylorManuscriptAward.aspx. **Contact:** Aileen Grossberg. This competition is for unpublished writers of juvenile fiction. Material should be for readers ages 8-13. The manuscript should have universal appeal and reveal positive aspects of Jewish life that will serve to deepen the understanding of Judaism for all children. Download rules and forms from website. Must be an unpublished fiction writer or a student; also, books must range from 64-200 pages in length. "AJL assumes no responsibility for publication, but hopes this cash incentive will serve to encourage new writers of children's stories with Jewish themes for all children." To encourage new fiction of Jewish interest for readers ages 8-13. Deadline: September 30. Prize: $1,000. Judging by qualified judges from within the Association of Jewish Libraries.

✪ TD CANADIAN CHILDREN'S LITERATURE AWARD

The Canadian Children's Book Centre, 40 Orchard View Blvd., Suite 217, Toronto ON M4R 1B9 Canada. (416)975-0010, ext. 222. **Fax:** (416)975-8970. **E-mail:** meghan@bookcentre.ca. **Website:** www.bookcentre.ca. **Contact:** Meghan Howe. The TD Canadian Children's Literature Award is for the most distinguished book of the year. All books, in any genre, written and illustrated by Canadians and for children ages 1-12 are eligible. Only books published in Canada are eligible for submission. Books must be published between January 1 and December 31 of the previous calendar year. Open to Canadian citizens and/or permanent residents of Canada. Deadline: mid-December. Prizes: Two prizes of $50,000, 1 for English, 1 for French. $20,000 will be divided among the Honour Book English titles and Honour Book French titles, to a maximum of 4; $2,500 shall go to each of the publishers of the English and French grand-prize winning books for promotion and publicity.

VEGETARIAN ESSAY CONTEST

The Vegetarian Resource Group, P.O. Box 1463, Baltimore MD 21203. (410)366-VEGE. **Fax:** (410)366-8804. **E-mail:** vrg@vrg.org. **Website:** www.vrg.org. Write a 2-3 page essay on any aspect of veganism/vegetarianism. Entrants should base their paper on interviewing, research, and/or personal opinion. You need not be a vegetarian to enter. Three different entry categories: age 14-18; age 9-13; and age 8 and under. Prize: $50.

VFW VOICE OF DEMOCRACY

Veterans of Foreign Wars of the U.S., National Headquarters, 406 W. 34th St., Kansas City MO 64111. (816)968-1117. **E-mail:** kharmer@vfw.org. **Website:** https://www.vfw.org/VOD/. The Voice of Democracy Program is open to students in grades 9-12 (on the Nov. 1 deadline), who are enrolled in a public, private or parochial high school or home study program in the United States and its territories. Contact your local VFW Post to enter (entry must not be mailed to the VFW National Headquarters, only to a local, participating VFW Post). Purpose is to give high school students the opportunity to voice their opinions about their responsibility to our country and to convey those opinions via the broadcast media to all of America. Deadline: November 1. Prize: Winners receive awards ranging from $1,000-30,000.

RITA WILLIAMS YOUNG ADULT PROSE PRIZE CATEGORY

Soul-Making Keats Literary Competition, The Webhallow House, 1544 Sweetwood Dr., Broadmoor Vlg. CA 94015-2029. (650)756-5279. **Fax:** (650)756-5279. **E-mail:** soulkeats@mail.com. **Website:** www.soulmakingcontest.us. **Contact:** Eileen Malone. For writers in grades 9-12 or equivalent age. Up to 3,000 words in prose form of choice. Complete rules and guidelines available online. Deadline: November 30 (postmarked). Prize: $100 for first place; $50 for second place; $25 for third place. Judged (and sponsored) by Rita Wiliams, an Emmy-award winning investigative reporter with KTVU-TV in Oakland, California.

PAUL A. WITTY OUTSTANDING LITERATURE AWARD

P.O. Box 8139, Newark DE 19714-8139. (800)336-7323. **Fax:** (302)731-1057. **Website:** www.reading.org. **Contact:** Marcie Craig Post, executive director. This award recognizes excellence in original poetry or prose written by students. Elementary and secondary students whose work is selected will receive an award. Deadline: February 2. Prize: Not less than $25 and a citation of merit.

WORK-IN-PROGRESS GRANT

Society of Children's Book Writers and Illustrators (SCBWI), 8271 Beverly Blvd., Los Angeles CA 90048. (323)782-1010. **E-mail:** grants@scbwi.org; wipgrant@scbwi.org. **Website:** www.scbwi.org. Six grants—one designated specifically for picture book text, chapter book/early readers, middle grade, young adult fiction, nonfiction, and multicultural fiction or nonfiction—to assist SCBWI members in the completion of a specific project. Open to SCBWI members only. Deadline: March 31. Open to submissions on March 1.

THE YOUNG ADULT FICTION PRIZE

Victorian Premier's Literary Awards, State Government of Victoria, The Wheeler Centre, 176 Little Lonsdale Street, Melbourne VIC 3000 Australia. (61)(3)90947800. **E-mail:** vpla@wheelercentre.com. **Website:** http://www.wheelercentre.com/projects/victorian-premier-s-literary-awards-2016/about-the-awards. **Contact:** Project Officer. Visit website for guidelines and nomination forms. Prize: $25,000.

YOUNG READER'S CHOICE AWARD

Paxson Elementary School, 101 Evans, Missoula MT 59801. **E-mail:** hbray@missoula.lib.mt.us. **Website:** www.pnla.org. **Contact:** Honore Bray, president. The Pacific Northwest Library Association's Young Reader's Choice Award is the oldest children's choice award in the U.S. and Canada. Nominations are taken only from children, teachers, parents and librarians in the Pacific Northwest: Alaska, Alberta, British Columbia, Idaho, Montana and Washington. Nominations will not be accepted from publishers. Nominations may include fiction, nonfiction, graphic novels, anime, and manga. Nominated titles are those published 3 years prior to the award year. Deadline: February 1. Books will be judged on popularity with readers. Age appropriateness will be considered when choosing which of the three divisions a book is placed. Other considerations may include reading enjoyment; reading level; interest level; genre representation; gender representation; racial diversity; diversity of social, political, economic, or religions viewpoints; regional consideration; effectiveness of expression; and imagination. The Pacific Northwest Library Association is committed to intellectual freedom and diversity of ideas. No title will be excluded because of race, nationality, religion, gender, sexual orientation, political or social view of either the author or the material.

GENERAL

AUSTRALIAN CHRISTIAN BOOK OF THE YEAR AWARD

SparkLit, P.O. Box 198, Forest Hill VIC 3131 Australia. **E-mail:** admin@sparklit.org. **Website:** www.sparklit.org. **Contact:** The Awards Coordinator. SparkLit empowers and encourages Christian writers and publishers. (The Society for Promoting Christian Knowledge Australia and the Australian Christian Literature Society.) The Australian Christian Book of the Year Award is given annually to an original book written by an Australian citizen normally resident in Australia. A short list is released in July. The results are announced and prizes are presented in August. The award recognizes and encourages excellence in Australian Christian writing. Deadline: March 31. Prize: $3,000 (AUD), a framed certificate, and extensive promotion.

CDS DOCUMENTARY ESSAY PRIZE

1317 West Pettigrew St., Duke University, Durham NC 27705. (919)660-3685. **E-mail:** samantha.bechtold@duke.edu. **Website:** https://documentarystudies.duke.edu/awards/documentary-essay-prize. **Contact:** Samantha Bechtold. The Documentary Essay Prize from the Center for Documentary Studies at Duke University is given biennially for the best in short-form documentary writing. The 15 to 20 page essay should demonstrate a reliance on documentary methods, specifically immersive fieldwork, research, and interviewing conducted over periods of time. More information available at documentarystudies.duke.edu/awards. February 15 deadline. Submissions accepted now. The winner receives $3,000, features in Center for Documentary Studies' print and digital publications, and inclusion in the Archive of Documentary Arts at Rubenstein Library at Duke University.

THE FOUNTAINHEAD ESSAY CONTEST

Ayn Rand Institute, P.O. Box 57044, Irvine CA 92619-7044. **E-mail:** essays@aynrand.org. **Website:** https://www.aynrand.org/students/essay-contests#thefountainhead-. Competition for 11th and 12th grade students. Essays will be judged on whether the student is able to argue for and justify his or her view—not on whether the Institute agrees with the view the student expresses. Judges will look for writing that is clear, articulate and logically organized. Winning essays must demonstrate an outstanding grasp of the philosophic meaning of *The Fountainhead*. Length: 800-1,600 words. Open to 11th and 12th graders. Deadline: April 25. 1st Place: $10,000; 2nd Place: $2,500 (3 Winners); 3rd Place: $500 (5 Winners); Finalists: $50 (50 Winners).

THE GLENNA LUSCHEI PRAIRIE SCHOONER AWARDS

Prairie Schooner, 110 Andrews Hall, P.O. Box 880334, Lincoln NE 68588-0334. (402)472-0911. **Fax:** (402)472-1817. **E-mail:** prairieschooner@unl.edu; psbookprize@unl.edu. **Website:** http://prairieschooner.unl.edu/. **Contact:** Kwame Dawes. Annual awards for work published in *Prairie Schooner* in the previous year. Offers one large prize and 10 smaller awards. See website for more details. Contact *Prairie Schooner* for further information. Prize: One award of $1,500 and 10 awards of $250 each.

SUE GRANZELLA HUMOR PRIZE

Category in the Soul-Making Keats Literary Competition, The Webhallow House, 1544 Sweetwood Dr., Broadmoor Vlg. CA 94015-2029. **E-mail:** soulkeats@mail.com. **Website:** www.soulmakingcontest.us. **Contact:** Eileen Malone. Any form, 3,000 words or less. One piece per entry. Previously published material is accepted. Open annually to any writer. Deadline: November 30. Prize: First Place: $100; Second Place: $50; Third Place: $25. Judged by Sue Granzella.

INSCRIBE CONTESTS

InScribe Christian Writers' Fellowship, PO Box 99509, Edmonton AB T5B 0E1 Canada. **E-mail:** fellowscripteditor@gmail.com. **Website:** www.inscribe.org. **Contact:** Contest Director. Check Website www.inscribe.org for updated details. Contest details are included in *Fellowscipt* magazine. Deadline: Contests offered twice per year. See website for details. Prize: 1st Place: $100; 2nd Place: $50; 3rd Place: $30. InScribe reserves the right to publish winning entries in its magazine, *FellowScript*, and/or on its website Judged by a different judge for each category. All judging is blind.

MLA PRIZE IN UNITED STATES LATINA & LATINO AND CHICANA & CHICANO LITERARY AND CULTURAL STUDIES

Modern Language Association of America, MLA Prize in United States Latina & Latino and Chicana & Chicano Literary and Cultural Studies, MLA Prize in United States Latina and Latino and Chicana and Chicano Literary and Cultural Studies, Modern Language Association, 85 Broad Street, Suite 500, New York NY 10004-2434. (646)576-5141. **Fax:** (646)458-0030. **E-mail:** awards@mla.org. **Website:** www.mla.org. **Contact:** Annie Reiser, Coordinator of Book

Prizes. Offered in odd-numbered years for an outstanding scholarly study in any language of United States Latina and Latino or Chicana and Chicano literature or culture. Books must have been published in the two previous years before the award. Authors must be current members of the MLA. Requires 4 copies of the book. Deadline: May 1. Prize: A cash award, and a certificate to be presented at the Modern Language Association's annual convention in January.

NACUSA YOUNG COMPOSERS' COMPETITION

Box 49256 Barrington Station, Los Angeles CA 90049. **E-mail:** rentows@aol.com. **Website:** nacusa.us. **Contact:** Dr. Wieslaw Rentowski. Applications online. Must be a paid member of NACUSA. The competition is open to all NACUSA members who are American citizens or residents, who have reached their 18th birthday but have not yet reached their 32nd birthday by the submission deadline. Encourages the composition of new American concert hall music. Deadline: December 15. Prize: All prizes come with a possible performance on a NACUSA National concert. 1st Prize is $400; 2nd Prize is $300; 3rd Prize is $200. Judged by a committee of experienced NACUSA composer members.

OHIOANA WALTER RUMSEY MARVIN GRANT

Ohioana Library Association, 274 E. First Ave., Suite 300, Columbus OH 43201. (614)466-3831. **Fax:** (614)728-6974. **E-mail:** ohioana@ohioana.org. **Website:** www.ohioana.org. **Contact:** David Weaver, executive director. Open to unpublished authors born in Ohio or who have lived in Ohio for a minimum of 5 years. Must be 30 years of age or younger. Guidelines for SASE or on website. Winner notified in early summer. Up to 6 pieces of prose may be submitted; maximum 60 pages, minimum 10 pages double-spaced, 12-point type. Entries must be unpublished. Award to encourage young, unpublished writers 30 years of age or younger. Competition for short stories or novels in progress. Deadline: January 31. Prize: $1,000.

DAVID RAFFELOCK AWARD FOR PUBLISHING EXCELLENCE

National Writers Association, 10940 S. Parker Rd., #508, Parker CO 80134. **E-mail:** natlwritersassn@hotmail.com. **Website:** www.nationalwriters.com. **Contact:** Sandy Whelchel. Contest is offered annually for books published the previous year. Published works only. Open to any writer. Guidelines for SASE, by e-mail, or on website. Winners will be notified by mail or phone. List of winners available for SASE or visit website. Purpose is to assist published authors in marketing their works and to reward outstanding published works. Deadline: May 15. Prize: Publicity tour, including airfare, valued at $5,000.

RAMIREZ FAMILY AWARD FOR MOST SIGNIFICANT SCHOLARLY BOOK

The Texas Institute of Letters, P.O. Box 609, Round Rock TX 78680. **E-mail:** tilsecretary@yahoo.com. **Website:** http://texasinstituteofletters.org. Offered annually for submissions published January 1-December 31 of previous year to recognize the writer of the book making the most important contribution to knowledge. Writer must have been born in Texas, have lived in the state at least 2 consecutive years at some time, or the subject matter of the book should be associated with the state. See website for guidelines. Deadline: Visit website for exact date. Prize: $2,500.

BYRON CALDWELL SMITH BOOK AWARD

The University of Kansas, Hall Center for the Humanities, 900 Sunnyside Ave., Lawrence KS 66045. (785)864-4798. **E-mail:** vbailey@ku.edu. **Website:** www.hallcenter.ku.edu. **Contact:** Victor Bailey, director. Offered in odd years. To qualify, applicants must live or be employed in Kansas and have written an outstanding book published within the previous 2 calendar years. Translations are eligible. Guidelines for SASE or online. Deadline: March 1. Prize: $1,500.

FRED WHITEHEAD AWARD FOR DESIGN OF A TRADE BOOK

Texas Institute of Letters, P.O. Box 609, Round Rock TX 78680. **E-mail:** tilsecretary@yahoo.com. **Website:** www.texasinstituteofletters.org. Offered annually for the best design for a trade book. Open to Texas residents or those who have lived in Texas for 2 consecutive years. See website for guidelines. Deadline: early January; see website for exact date. Prize: $750.

THE WRITERS' TRUST ENGEL/FINDLEY AWARD

The Writers' Trust of Canada, 460 Richmond St. W., Suite 600, Toronto ON M5V 1Y1 Canada. (416)504-8222. **Fax:** (416)504-9090. **E-mail:** djackson@writerstrust.com. **Website:** www.writerstrust.com. **Contact:** Devon Jackson. The Writers' Trust Engel/Findley Award is presented annually at The Writers' Trust Awards Event, held in Toronto each fall, to a Canadian writer for a body of work in hope of continued contribution to the richness of Canadian literature. Open to Canadian citizens and permanent residents only. Prize: $25,000.

JOURNALISM

AAAS KAVLI SCIENCE JOURNALISM AWARDS

American Association for the Advancement of Science, AAAS Office of Public Programs, 1200 New York Ave. NW, Washington DC 20005. **E-mail:** sja@aaas.org. **Website:** sjawards.aaas.org/. **Contact:** Awards Coordinator. The AAAS Kavli Science Journalism Awards represent the pinnacle of achievement for professional journalists in the science writing field. The awards recognize outstanding reporting worldwide for a general audience and honor individuals (rather than institutions, publishers or employers) for their coverage of the sciences, engineering, and mathematics. Entries are submitted online only at http://sjawards.aaas.org. See website for guidelines and details. Deadline: August 1. Prize: $5,000 and $3,500 awards in each category; award includes travel expenses to AAAS Annual Meeting for awards ceremony. Judged by committees of reporters and editors.

THE AMERICAN LEGION FOURTH ESTATE AWARD

The American Legion, The American Legion, 700 N. Pennsylvania St., Indianapolis IN 46204. (317)630-1298. **E-mail:** pr@legion.org. **Website:** www.legion.org/presscenter/fourthestate. **Contact:** Julie Campbell. Offered annually for journalistic works published the previous calendar year. Subject matter must deal with a topic or issue of national interest or concern. Entry must include cover letter explaining entry, and any documentation or evidence of the entry's impact on the community, state, or nation. No printed entry form. Guidelines available by SASE or online. Deadline: March 1. Prize: $2,000 stipend to defray expenses of recipient accepting the award at The American Legion National Convention in August/September. Judged by members of the Media & Communications Commission of The American Legion.

AMY WRITING AWARDS

The Amy Foundation, P.O. Box 16091, Lansing MI 48901. (517)323-6233. **Fax:** (517)321-2572. **E-mail:** amyawards@wng.org. **Website:** www.amyfound.org. The Amy Foundation Writing Awards program is designed to recognize creative, skillful writing that applies in a sensitive, thought-provoking manner the biblical principles to issues affecting the world today, with an emphasis on discipling. Submitted articles must be published in a secular, non-religious publication (either printed or online) and must be reinforced with at least one passage of scripture. The article must have been published between January 1 and December 31 of the current calendar year. Deadline: January 31. Prize: 1st Prize: $10,000; 2nd Prize: $5,000; 3rd Prize: $4,000; 4th Prize: $3,000; 5th Prize: $2,000; and 10 prizes of $1,000.

INVESTIGATIVE JOURNALISM GRANT

Fund for Investigative Journalism, 529 14th St. NW, 13th Floor, Washington DC 20045. (202)662-7564. **E-mail:** sbergo@fij.org. **Website:** www.fij.org. **Contact:** Sandy Bergo, Executive Director. Offered 3 times/year for original investigative print, online, radio, and TV stories and books. Guidelines online. See website for details on applying for a grant. Deadlines: Vary. Check website. Grants of $500-10,000. (Typical grant: $5,000.)

ANSON JONES, MD, AWARDS

Texas Medical Association, Texas Medical Association, 401 W. 15th St., Austin TX 78701-1680. (800)880-7955. **Fax:** (512)370-1693. **E-mail:** knowledge@texmed.org. **Website:** www.texmed.org. **Contact:** Tammy Wishard, Outreach Coordinator. Offered annually to Texas news media for excellence in communicating health information to the public. Open only to Texas general-interest media for work published or aired in Texas during the previous calendar year. Guidelines posted online. Deadline: January 10. $500 for winner in each category; $1,000 for Texas Health Journalist of the Year.

FRANK LUTHER MOTT-KAPPA TAU ALPHA RESEARCH AWARD IN JOURNALISM

Kappa Tau Alpha, Dr. Beverly Horvit,, KTA Executive Director,, School of Journalism, 76 Gannett Hall, University of Missouri, Columbia MO 65211-1200. (573)882-7685. **E-mail:** umcjourkta@missouri.edu. **Website:** www.kappataualpha.org. **Contact:** Dr. Beverly Horvit, KTA Executive Director. Offered annually for best researched book in mass communication or journalism. Submit 6 copies; no forms required. Deadline: December 9. Prize: $1,000. Judged by a panel of university professors of journalism and mass communication and national officers of Kappa Tau Alpha.

NATIONAL MAGAZINE AWARDS

National Magazine Awards Foundation, 2300 Yonge St, Suite 1600, Toronto ON M4P 1E4 Canada. (416) 939-6200. **E-mail:** staff@magazine-awards.com. **E-mail:**

staff@magazine-awards.com. **Website:** www.magazine-awards.com. **Contact:** Barbara Gould. The National Magazine Awards Foundation is a bilingual, not-for-profit institution whose mission is to recognize and promote excellence in the content and creation of Canadian print and digital publications through an annual program of awards and national publicity efforts. Deadline: January 20. Cash prizes for winners. Certificates and seals for all finalists and winners. Judged by 200+ peer judges from the Canadian magazine industry.

SCIENCE IN SOCIETY AWARDS

National Association of Science Writers, Inc., P.O. Box 7905, Berkeley CA 94707. (510)647-9500. **E-mail:** director@nasw.org. **Website:** www.nasw.org. **Contact:** Tinsley Davis. Offered annually for investigative or interpretive reporting about the sciences and their impact on society. Categories vary by year and generally include: books, commentary and opinions, science reporting, long form science reporting, and science reporting for a local or regional market. Material may be a single article or broadcast, or a series. Works must have been first published or broadcast in North America between January 1 and December 31 of the previous year. NASW established the Science in Society awards to provide recognition — without subsidy from any professional or commercial interest — for investigative or interpretive reporting about the sciences and their impact on modern society. NASW especially encourages entries of critical, probing pieces that would not receive an award from a special interest group. Beginning with the first award in 1972, winners have demonstrated innovative reporting that goes well beyond the science itself and into ethical problems and social implications. A committee of accomplished peers judges the entries each year. Deadline: February 1. Prize: $2,000, and a certificate of recognition in each category.

SOVEREIGN AWARD

The Jockey Club of Canada, P.O. Box 66, Station B, Etobicoke ON M9W 5K9 Canada. (416)675-7756. **Fax:** (416)675-6378. **E-mail:** jockeyclub@bellnet.ca. **Website:** www.jockeyclubcanada.com. **Contact:** Stacie Roberts, exec. dir. The Jockey Club of Canada was founded in 1973 by E.P. Taylor to serve as the international representative of the Canadian Thoroughbred industry and to promote improvements to Thoroughbred racing and breeding, both in Canada and internationally. Submissions for these media awards must be of Canadian Thoroughbred racing or breeding content. They must have appeared in a media outlet recognized by The Jockey Club of Canada. See website for eligibility details and guidelines. Deadline: December 31.

TRANSLATION

AMERICAN-SCANDINAVIAN FOUNDATION TRANSLATION PRIZE

The American-Scandinavian Foundation, 58 Park Ave., New York NY 10016. (212)779-3587. **E-mail:** grants@amscan.org; info@amscan.org. **Website:** www.amscan.org. **Contact:** Carl Fritscher, Fellowships & Grants Officer. The annual ASF translation competition is awarded for the most outstanding translations of poetry, fiction, drama, or literary prose written by a Scandinavian author born after 1900. Accepts inquiries by e-mail or through online application. Instructions and application available online. Entries must be unpublished. Length: No more than 50 pages for drama and fiction; no more than 25 pages for poetry. Open to any writer. Results announced in November. Winners notified by e-mail. Results available on the ASF website. Guidelines available online. Deadline: June 15. Prize: The Nadia Christensen Prize includes a $2,500 award, publication of an excerpt in *Scandinavian Review*, and a commemorative bronze medallion. The Leif and Inger Sjöberg Award, given to an individual whose literature translations have not previously been published, includes a $2,000 award, publication of an excerpt in *Scandinavian Review*, and a commemorative bronze medallion.

THE WILLIS BARNSTONE TRANSLATION PRIZE

The Evansville Review, Dept. of Creative Writing, University of Evansville, 1800 Lincoln Ave., Evansville IN 47722. (812)488-1042. **E-mail:** evansvillereview@evansville.edu. **Website:** https://www.evansville.edu/majors/creativewriting/evansvilleReview-Barnstone.cfm. The competition welcomes submissions of unpublished poetry translations from any language and time period (ancient to contemporary). The length limit for each translation is 200 lines. Deadline: December 1. Prize: $1000 for a translated poem. In the event that the judge selects multiple winners, the prize money will be divided equally among the winners. Final Judge: Willis Barnstone.

DER-HOVANESSIAN PRIZE

New England Poetry Club, 376 School St., Watertown MA 02472. **E-mail:** contests@nepoetryclub.org. **Web-**

site: www.nepoetryclub.org. **Contact:** Audrey Kalajin. For a translation from any language into English. Send a copy of the original. Funded by John Mahtesian. Contest open to members and nonmembers. Poems should be typed and submitted in duplicate with author's name, address, phone, and e-mail address of writer on only 1 copy. Label poems with contest name. Entries should be sent by regular mail only. Entries should be original, unpublished poems in English. No poem should be entered in more than 1 contest, nor have won a previous contest. Deadline: May 31. Prize: $200. Judges are well-known poets and sometimes winners of previous NEPC contests.

SOEURETTE DIEHL FRASER AWARD FOR BEST TRANSLATION OF A BOOK

P.O. Box 609, Round Rock TX 78680. **E-mail:** tilsecretary@yahoo.com. **Website:** http://texasinstituteofletters.org. Offered every 2 years to recognize the best translation of a literary book into English. Translator must have been born in Texas or have lived in the state for at least 2 consecutive years at some time. Check website for guidelines and instructions on submitting. Deadline: January 10. Prize: $1,000.

JOHN GLASSCO TRANSLATION PRIZE

Literary Translators' Association of Canada, ATTLC | LTAC; Concordia University, LB-601, 1455 de Maisonneuve Boulevard West, Montréal QC H3G 1M8 Canada. (514)848-2424, ext. 8702. **E-mail:** info@attlc-ltac.org. **Website:** attlc-ltac.org/john-glassco-translation-prize. **Contact:** Glassco Prize Committee. Offered annually for a translator's first book-length literary translation into French or English, published in Canada during the previous calendar year. The translator must be a Canadian citizen or permanent resident. Eligible genres include fiction, creative nonfiction, poetry, and children's books. Deadline: July 9. Prize: $1,000 and a 1-year membership to LTAC.

THE HAROLD MORTON LANDON TRANSLATION AWARD

Academy of American Poets, 75 Maiden Lane, Suite 901, New York NY 10038. (212)274-0343. **Fax:** (212)274-9427. **E-mail:** awards@poets.org. **Website:** www.poets.org. **Contact:** Programs Coordinator. This annual award recognizes a poetry collection translated from any language into English and published in the previous calendar year. A noted translator chooses the winning book. Deadline: February 15. Prize: $1,000.

FENIA AND YAAKOV LEVIANT MEMORIAL PRIZE IN YIDDISH STUDIES

Modern Language Association of America, Leviant Memorial Prize, Modern Language Association, 85 Broad Street, Suite 500, New York NY 10004-2434. (646)576-5141. **Fax:** (646)458-0030. **E-mail:** awards@mla.org. **Website:** www.mla.org. **Contact:** Coordinator of book prizes. Offered in even-numbered years for an outstanding English translation of a Yiddish literary work or the publication of a scholarly work. Cultural studies, critical biographies, or edited works in the field of Yiddish folklore or linguistic studies are eligible to compete. See website for details on which they are accepting. Books must have been published within the past 4 years. Authors need not be members of the MLA. Requires 4 copies of the book. Deadline: May 1. Prize: A cash prize and a certificate, to be presented at the Modern Language Association's annual convention in January.

PEN AWARD FOR POETRY IN TRANSLATION

PEN America, 588 Broadway, Suite 303, New York NY 10012. **E-mail:** awards@pen.org. **Website:** www.pen.org/awards. **Contact:** Arielle Anema. This award recognizes book-length translations of poetry from any language into English, published during the current calendar year. All books must have been published in the US. Translators may be of any nationality. US residency/citizenship not required. Submissions must be made publishers or literary agents. Self-published books are not eligible. Books with more than 2 translators are not eligible. Re-translations are ineligible, unless the work can be said to provide a significant revision of the original translation. Deadline: Submissions are accepted during the summer of each year. Visit PEN.org/awards for updated on deadline dates. Prize: $3,000. Judged by a single translator of poetry appointed by the PEN Translation Committee.

PEN TRANSLATION PRIZE

PEN America, 588 Broadway, Suite 303, New York NY 10012. **E-mail:** awards@pen.org. **Contact:** Arielle Anema, Literary Awards Coordinator. *PEN will only accept submissions from publishers or literary agents.* This award is offered for book-length translations from any language into English, published during the current calendar year. No technical, scientific, or bibliographic translations. Self-published books are not eligible. Although all eligible books must have been published in the United States, translators may be of any nationality; US residency or citizenship is not required. PEN will only accept submissions from publishers or literary agents. Deadline: Submissions will be accepted during the summer of each year. Visit PEN.org/awards for up-to-date information on deadlines. Prize: $3,000. Judged by three to five translators and/or writers selected by the PEN Translation Committee.

LOIS ROTH AWARD

Modern Language Association, 85 Broad Street, suite 500, New York NY 10004-2434. (646)576-5141. **Fax:** (646)458-0030. **E-mail:** awards@mla.org. **Website:** www.mla.org. Offered in odd-numbered years for an outstanding translation into English of a book-length literary work. Translators need not be members of the MLA. Translations must have been published in the previous calendar year. Requires 6 copies, plus 12-15 pages of text in the original language. Deadline: April 1. Prize: A cash award and a certificate to be presented at the Modern Language Association's annual convention in January.

ALDO AND JEANNE SCAGLIONE PRIZE FOR A TRANSLATION OF A LITERARY WORK

Modern Language Association, 85 Broad Street, suite 500, New York NY 10004-2434. (646)576-5141. **Fax:** (646)458-0030. **E-mail:** awards@mla.org. **Website:** www.mla.org. **Contact:** Coordinator of Book Prizes. Offered in even-numbered years for an outstanding translation into English of a book-length literary work. Translations must have been published in the previous calendar year. Translators need not be members of the MLA. Requires 6 copies of the book, plus 12-15 pages of text in the original language. Deadline: April 1. Prize: A cash award and a certificate to be presented at the Modern Language Association's annual convention in January.

ALDO AND JEANNE SCAGLIONE PRIZE FOR A TRANSLATION OF A SCHOLARLY STUDY OF LITERATURE

Modern Language Association of America, 85 Broad Street, Suite 500, New York NY 10004-2434. (646)576-5141. **Fax:** (646)458-0030. **E-mail:** awards@mla.org. **Website:** www.mla.org. **Contact:** Coordinator of Book Prizes. Offered in odd-numbered years for an outstanding translation into English of a book-length work of literary history, literary criticism, philology, or literary theory. Translators need not be members of the MLA. Books must have been published in the previous 2 years. Requires 4 copies of the book. Deadline: May 1. Prize: A cash award and a certificate to be presented at the Modern Language Association's annual convention in January.

ALDO AND JEANNE SCAGLIONE PRIZE FOR STUDIES IN SLAVIC LANGUAGES AND LITERATURES

Modern Language Association of America, 85 Broad Street, Suite 500, New York NY 10004-2434. (646)576-5141. **Fax:** (646)458-0030. **E-mail:** awards@mla.org. **Website:** www.mla.org. **Contact:** Coordinator of Book Prizes. Offered in odd-numbered years for an outstanding work on the linguistics or literatures of the Slavic languages. Books must have been published in the previous 2 years. Requires 4 copies of the book. Authors need not be members of the MLA. Deadline: May 1. Prize: A cash award and a certificate to be presented at the Modern Language Association's annual convention in January.

POETRY

49TH PARALLEL AWARD FOR POETRY

Western Washington University, Mail Stop 9053, Bellingham WA 98225. (360)650-4863. **E-mail:** bellingham.review@wwu.edu. **Website:** www.bhreview.org. **Contact:** Susanne Paola Antonetta, Editor-in-Chief; Bailey Cunningham, Managing Editor. Annual poetry contest, supported by the *Bellingham Review*, given for a poem of any style or length. Upload entries via Submittable online. Up to 3 poems per entry. Deadline: March 15. Submissions period begins December 1. Prize: $1,000. Nickole Brown.

J.M. ABRAHAM POETRY AWARD

Writers' Federation of Nova Scotia, 1113 Marginal Rd., Halifax NS B3H 4P7 Canada. (902)423-8116. **Fax:** (902)422-0881. **E-mail:** director@writers.ns.ca. **Website:** www.writers.ns.ca. **Contact:** Marilyn Smulders, Executive Director. The J.M. Abraham Poetry Award is an annual award designed to honor the best book of poetry by a resident of Atlantic Canada. Formerly known as the Atlantic Poetry Prize. Detailed guidelines and eligibility criteria available online. Deadline: First Friday in December. Prize: Valued at $2,000 for the winning title.

AKRON POETRY PRIZE

The University of Akron Press, 120 E. Mill St., Suite 415, Akron OH 44308. **E-mail:** uapress@uakron.edu. **Website:** www.uakron.edu/uapress/akron-poetry-prize/. **Contact:** Mary Biddinger, Editor/Award Director. Submissions must be unpublished. Considers simultaneous submissions (with notification of acceptance elsewhere). Submit at least 48 pages and no longer than 90 pages. See website for complete guidelines. Manuscripts will be accepted via Submittable.com between April 15 and June 15 each year. Competition receives 500+ entries. 2018 winner was Kimberly Quiogue Andrews for *A Brief History of Fruit*. Winner posted on website by September 30. Intimate friends, relatives, current and former students of the final judge (students in an academic, degree-conferring program or its equivalent), and current faculty, staff, students, and alumni of the University of Akron or the Northeast Ohio MFA Program (NEOMFA) are not eligible to enter the Akron Poetry Prize competition. Deadline: June 15. Open to submissions on April 15. Prize: $1,500, plus publication of a book-length ms.

THE AMERICAN POETRY REVIEW/ HONICKMAN FIRST BOOK PRIZE

320 S. Broad St., Hamilton 313, Philadelphia PA 19102. (215)717-6800. **E-mail:** escanlon@aprweb.org. **Website:** www.aprweb.org. **Contact:** Elizabeth Scanlon, editor. The prize is open to poets who have not published a book-length collection of poems with a registered ISBN. Translations are not eligible nor are works written by multiple authors. 2018 guest judge is Sharon Olds. Reading period: August 1-October 31. Prize: $3,000, plus publication

THE ANHINGA-ROBERT DANA PRIZE FOR POETRY

Anhinga Press, P.O. Box 3665, Tallahassee FL 32315. **E-mail:** info@anhinga.org. **Website:** www.anhinga.org. **Contact:** Kristine Snodgrass, Co-director, Publisher. Offered annually for a book-length collection of poetry by an author writing in English. Guidelines on website. Past winners include Robin Beth Schaer, Hauntie. Mss must be 48-80 pages, excluding front matter. Deadline: Submissions will be accepted from February 15-May 31. Prize: $2,000, a reading tour of selected Florida colleges and universities, and the winning ms will be published. Past judges include Evie Shockley, Eduardo C. Corral, Jan Beatty, Richard Blanco, Denise Duhamel, Donald Hall, Joy Harjo.

THE MURIEL CRAFT BAILEY MEMORIAL AWARD

4956 St. John Dr., Syracuse NY 13215. (315)488-8077. **E-mail:** poetry@comstockreview.org. **Website:** www.comstockreview.org. **Contact:** Peggy Flanders, Associate Managing Editor (poetry@comstockreview.org); Betsy Anderson, Managing Editor (elanders2@yahoo.com). Annual contest for best previously unpublished poem. Submit unpublished poems, 40 lines or less. Deadline: July 15. Prize: 1st place: $1,000; 2nd place: $250; 3rd place: $100; honorable mentions receive 1-year subscription to *Comstock Review*. Judged by David Kirby in 2019.

BARROW STREET PRESS BOOK CONTEST

P.O. Box 1558, Kingston RI 02881. **Website:** www.barrowstreet.org or wilde@my.uri.edu. The Barrow Street Press Book Contest award will be given for the best previously unpublished ms of poetry in English. Submit a 50-80 page unpublished ms of original poetry in English. Please number the pages of your ms and include a table of contents and an acknowledgments page for any previously published poems. Include two title pages. The author's name, address, and telephone number should appear on the first title page only and should not appear anywhere else in the ms. The second title page should contain only the ms title. Deadline: June 30. Prize: $1,000. 2019 Judge: Jericho Brown.

ELINOR BENEDICT POETRY PRIZE

Passages North, Northern Michigan University, 1401 Presque Isle Ave., Marquette MI 49855. **E-mail:** passages@nmu.edu. **Website:** passagesnorth.com/contests/. **Contact:** Jennifer A. Howard, Editor-in-Chief. Prize given biennially for a poem or a group of poems. Check website to see if award is currently being offered this year. Deadline: April 15. Submission period begins February 15. Prize: $1,000 and publication for winner; 2 honorable mentions are also published; all entrants receive a copy of *Passages North*. Tarfia Faizullah.

BERMUDA TRIANGLE PRIZE

The Poet's Billow, 6135 Avon St., Portage MI 49024. **E-mail:** thepoetsbillow@gmail.com. **Website:** http://thepoetsbillow.org. **Contact:** Robert Evory. Annual award open to any writer to recognize 3 poems that address a theme set by the editors. Finalists with strong work will also be published. Submissions must be previously unpublished. Please submit online. Deadline: April 30. Submission period begins November 15. Prize: $50 each to 3 poems. The winning poems will be published and displayed in The Poet's Billow Literary Art Gallery and nominated for a Pushcart Prize. If the poet qualifies, the poem will also be submitted to The Best New Poets anthology. Judge TBD.

THE PATRICIA BIBBY FIRST BOOK AWARD

Patricia Bibby Award, Tebot Bach, P.O. Box 7887, Huntington Beach CA 92615-7887. **E-mail:** mifanwy@tebotbach.org; info@tebotbach.org. **Website:** www.tebotbach.org. **Contact:** Mifanwy Kaiser. Annual competition open to all poets writing in English who have not committed to publishing collections of poetry of 36 poems or more in editions of over 400 copies. Offers award and publication of a book-length poetry ms by Tebot Bach. Complete guidelines available by e-mail or on website. Deadline: November 1. Prize: $500 and book publication. Judges for each year's competition announced online.

BINGHAMTON UNIVERSITY MILT KESSLER POETRY BOOK AWARD

Binghamton University Creative Writing Program, Department of English, General Literature, and Rhetoric, Library North Room 1149, Vestal Parkway East, P.O. Box 6000, Binghamton NY 13902-6000. (607)777-2713. **Fax:** (607)777-2408. **E-mail:** cwpro@binghamton.edu. **Website:** www2.binghamton.edu/english/creative-writing/binghamton-center-for-writers. **Contact:** Maria Mazziotti Gillan, Creative Writing Program Director. Annual award for a book of poems written in English, 48 pages or more in length, selected by judges as the strongest collection of poems published in that year. Print on demand is acceptable, but no self-published or vanity press work will be considered. Each book submitted must be accompanied by an application form available online. Poet or publisher may submit more than 1 book for prize consideration. Send 2 copies of each book. Deadline: February 1. Prize: $1,000.

THE BITTER OLEANDER PRESS LIBRARY OF POETRY AWARD

BOPLOPA, The Bitter Oleander Press, 4983 Tall Oaks Dr., Fayetteville NY 13066-9776. (315)637-3047. **E-mail:** info@bitteroleander.com. **Website:** www.bitteroleander.com. **Contact:** Paul B. Roth. The Bitter Oleander Press Library of Poetry Award (BOPLOPA) is now in its 7th year after replacing the 15-year long run of the Frances Locke Memorial Poetry Award. Guidelines available on website. Entrants may not be friends, previous winners or employees of The Bitter Oleander Press. Deadline: June 15 (postmarked). Open to submissions on May 1. Early or late entries will be disqualified. Prize: $1,000, plus book publication of the winning ms. the following spring.

BLUE LIGHT POETRY PRIZE AND CHAPBOOK CONTEST

P.O. Box 150300, San Rafael CA 94915. **E-mail:** bluelightpress@aol.com. **Website:** www.bluelightpress.com. **Contact:** Diane Frank, chief editor. The Blue Light Poetry Prize and Chapbook Contest offers publication of your chapbook by Blue Light Press, 10 free copies of your book, and a 50% discount for additional books. (See separate listing in Book/Chapbook Publishers). Deadline: June 30. The winner will be published by Blue Light Press, with 10 free copies of the author's book. We offer a a 50% discount for additional books. We have a group of poets who read manuscripts. Some years, we publish more than one winner.

TIPS "Our new anthology, *River of Earth and Sky: Poems for the Twenty-First Century,* has more than 100 poets whose work we deeply admire. It will show you the kind of poetry we love to publish."

BLUE MOUNTAIN ARTS

SPS Studios, Inc., Blue Mountain Arts, Inc., P.O. Box 1007, Boulder CO 80306. (303)449-0536. **Fax:** (303)447-0939. **E-mail:** editorial@sps.com. **Website:** www.sps.com. **Contact:** Ingrid Heffner. Family owned and operated independent greeting card company thriving since its founding in 1971. Specializes in expressing feelings that may be difficult for buyer to express. With its own fine art department creating watercolor paintings and multimedia cards, handlettered, Blue Mountain Arts is sold worldwide and is unique with our poetry, artwork, handmade papers that make lifelong buyers. Familiarize yourself with the Blue Mountain Arts writing style, either at a greeting card store or online at our Blue Mountain Arts Amazon store. To put your best writing out there! No deadlines for every day poetry. Write editorial@sps.com for seasonal deadlines. If your poetry is accepted and tests well, you will get $300 and 24 copies of your card. Judged by the Blue Mountain Arts editorial staff.

THE BOSTON REVIEW ANNUAL POETRY CONTEST

Poetry Contest, Boston Review, P.O. Box 425786, Cambridge MA 02142. (617)324-1360. **Fax:** (617)452-3356. **E-mail:** review@bostonreview.net. **Website:** www.bostonreview.net. Offers $1,500 and publication in *Boston Review* (see separate listing in Magazines/Journals). Any poet writing in English is eligible, unless he or she is a current student, former student, or close personal friend of the judge. Submissions must be unpublished. Submit up to 5 poems, no more than 10 pages total, via online contest entry manager. Include cover sheet with poet's name, address, and phone number; no identifying information on the poems themselves. No cover note is necessary for online submissions. No mss will be returned. Guidelines available for SASE on website. Deadline: June 1. Winner announced in early November on website. Prize: $1,500 and publication.

BOULEVARD POETRY CONTEST FOR EMERGING POETS

Boulevard, 4125 Juniata Street, #B, St. Louis MO 63116. **E-mail:** editors@boulevardmagazine.org. **Website:** www.boulevardmagazine.org. **Contact:** Jessica Rogen, Editor. Annual Emerging Poets Contest offers $1,000 and publication in *Boulevard* (see separate listing in Magazines/Journals) for the best group of 3 poems by a poet who has not yet published a book of poetry with a nationally distributed press. All entries will be considered for publication and payment at regular rates. Submissions must be unpublished. Considers simultaneous submissions. Submit 3 poems, typed; may be a sequence or unrelated. On page one of first poem type poet's name, address, phone number, and titles of the 3 poems. Deadline: June 1. Prize: $1,000 and publication.

BARBARA BRADLEY PRIZE

New England Poetry Club, 376 School St., Watertown MA 02472. **E-mail:** contests@nepoetryclub.org. **Website:** www.nepoetryclub.org. **Contact:** Audrey Kalajin. For a lyric poem under 20 lines, written by a woman. Contest open to members and nonmembers. Poems should be typed and submitted in duplicate with author's name, address, phone, and e-mail address of writer on only 1 copy. (Judges receive copies without names.) Copy only. Label poems with contest name. Entries should be sent by regular mail only. Special delivery or signature required mail will be returned by the post office. Entries should be original, unpublished poems in English. No poem should be entered in more than 1 contest, nor have won a previous contest. No entries will be returned. NEPC will not engage in correspondence regarding poems or contest decisions. Deadline: May 31. $200. Judged by well-known poets and sometimes winners of previous NEPC contests.

BRICK ROAD POETRY BOOK CONTEST

Brick Road Poetry Press, Inc., 513 Broadway, Columbus GA 31901-3117. (706)649-3080. **Fax:** (706)649-3094. **E-mail:** kbadowski@brickroadpoetrypress.com. **Website:** www.brickroadpoetrypress.com. **Contact:** Ron Self and Keith Badowski, Co-Editors/Founders. Annual competition for an original collection of 50-100 pages of poetery. Book-length poetry mss only. Simultaneous submissions accepted. Single-sided, single-spaced only. Electronic submissions are preferred, see website for details. No cover letter. Deadline: November 1st (Submission period begins August 1st). $1,000, publication in both print and e-book formats, and 25 copies of the book. May also offer publication contracts to the top finalists. Judged by Keith Badowski and Ron Self, Brick Road Poetry Editors.

BRIGHT HILL PRESS ANNUAL FULL-LENGTH POETRY BOOK COMPETITION AND BRIGHT HILL PRESS ANNUAL POETRY CHAPBOOK COMPETITION

Bright Hill Press, Bright Hill Press Inc., 94 Church St., Treadwell NY 13846. Phone/**Fax:** (607)829-5055. **Fax:** (607)829-5054. **E-mail:** wordthur@stny.rr.com. **Website:** www.brighthillpress.org. **Contact:** Bertha Rogers, Editor; Beatrice Georgalidis, Executive Director. Bright Hill Press Annual Full-length Poetry Book Competition: Send 48-64 pages, bio, TOC, acknowledgments page, and 2 title pages (1 with name, address, etc.; 1 with title only). Poems can be published in journals or anthologies, but ms must not be published elsewhere, including self-published. Guidelines online for SASE or via e-mail. Simultaneous submissions welcome, but BHP must be notified if ms taken elsewhere. See website for deadline and other guidelines. Bright Hill Press Annual Poetry Chapbook Competition: Send 16-24 pages, bio, TOC, acknowledgments page, and 2 title pages (1 with name, address, etc.; 1 with title only). Poems can be published in journals or anthologies, but ms must not be published elsewhere, including self-published. Guidelines online for SASE, or via e-mail. Simultaneous submissions welcome, but BHP must be notified if ms taken elsewhere. See website for deadline and other guidelines. Bright Hill's purpose is to publish superior poetry. Deadline: December 31 (full-length poetry book competition); November 30 (chapbook competition). Book competition: $1,000, publication, and 30 copies of the winning book. Chapbook competition: $350, publication, and 30 copies of the winning chapbook.

BRIGHT HILL PRESS POETRY CHAPBOOK COMPETITION

Bright Press Hill & Literary Center, 94 Church St., Treadwell NY 13846. (607)829-5055. **E-mail:** brighthillpress@stny.rr.com; wordthur@stny.rr.com. **Website:** www.brighthillpress.org. The annual Bright Hill Press Chapbook Award recognizes an outstanding collection of poetry. Guidelines available for SASE, by e-mail, or on website. Collection of original poetry, 48-64 pages, single spaced, one poem to a page (no name) with table of contents. Ms must be submitted in Times New Roman, 12 pt. type only. No illustrations, no cover suggestions. Bio and acknowledgments of poems that have been previously published should be included in a separate document or in comments box if submitting online. See website for more details, and information on submitting a hard copy. Deadline: December 31. Prize: A publication contract with Bright Hill Press, $350, publication in print format, and 30 copies of the printed book. Judged by a nationally known poet.

BRITTINGHAM PRIZE IN POETRY

University of Wisconsin Press, 1930 Monroe St., 3rd Floor, Madison WI 5311-2059. (608)263-1110. **Fax:** (608)263 1132. **E-mail:** rwallace@wisc.edu. **E-mail:** uwiscpress@uwpress.wisc.edu. **Website:** www.wisc.edu/wisconsinpress/poetryguide.html. **Contact:** Ronald Wallace and Sean Bishop, Series Co-Editors. The annual Brittingham Prize in Poetry is 1 of 2 prizes awarded by The University of Wisconsin Press (see separate listing for the Felix Pollak Prize in Poetry in this section). The Press also publishes two or three additional books annually, drawn from the contest submissions. Submissions must be unpublished as a collection, but individual poems may have been published elsewhere (publication must be acknowledged). Considers simultaneous submissions if notified of selection elsewhere. Submit 60-90 unbound ms pages, typed single-spaced (with double spaces between stanzas). Clean photocopies are acceptable. Include 1 title page with poet's name, address, and telephone number and 1 with title only. No translations. Strongly encourages electronic submissions via web page. SASE required for postal submissions. Will return results only; mss will not be returned. Guidelines available on website. The Brittingham Prize in Poetry is awarded annually to the best book-length manuscript of original poetry submitted in an open competition. The award is administered by the University of Wisconsin–Madison English Department, and the winner is chosen by a nationally recognized poet. The resulting book is published by the University of Wisconsin Press. Deadline: Submit August 15-September 15. Prize: Offers $1,000, plus publication. Judged by a distinguished poet who changes annually.

BURNING BUSH POETRY PRIZE

P.O. Box 4658, Santa Rosa CA 95402. **Website:** www.bbbooks.com. Purpose of contest is to reward a poet whose writing inspires others to value human life and the natural world instead of values based on short-term economic advantage; speaks for community-centered values and democratic processes, and especially for those whose voices are seldom heard; demonstrates poetic excellence; and educates readers of the relevance of the past to the present and future. Deadline: June 1.

BOB BUSH MEMORIAL AWARD FOR FIRST BOOK OF POETRY

Texas Institute of Letters, P.O. Box 609, Round Rock TX 78680. **E-mail:** tilsecretary@yahoo.com. **Website:** www.texasinstituteofletters.org. Offered annually for best first book of poetry published in previous year. Writer must have been born in Texas, have lived in the state at least 2 consecutive years at some time, or the subject matter should be associated with the state. Deadline: See website for exact date. Prize: $1,000.

CAA POETRY AWARD

Canadian Authors Association, 192 Spadina Avenue, Suite 107, Toronto ON M5T 2C2 Canada. **Website:** canadianauthors.org/national. Contest for full-length English-language book of poems for adults by a Canadian writer. Deadline: January.

CAROLINA WREN PRESS POETRY SERIES CONTEST

120 Morris St., Durham NC 27701. (919)560-2738. **Fax:** (919)560-2759. **E-mail:** carolinawrenpress@earthlink.net. **Website:** www.carolinawrenpress.org. **Contact:** Andrea Selch, Poetry Editor. Carolina Wren Press is a nonprofit organization whose mission is to publish quality writing, especially by writers historically neglected by mainstream publishing, and to develop diverse and vital audiences through publishing, outreach, and educational programs. Submit a copy of a 48-72 page manuscript. Manuscript should be single-spaced and paginated. Please

include a table of contents. Title page should not include author information--no name, address, etc. Within the manuscript, do include a page acknowledging individual poems that have been previously published. Open only to poets who have had no more than 1 full-length book published. Deadline: June 15 of odd-numbered years. Prize: $1,000 and publication.

CAVE CANEM POETRY PRIZE

Cave Canem Foundation, Inc., 20 Jay St., Suite 310-A, Brooklyn NY 11201-8301. (718)858-0000. **Website:** www.cavecanempoets.org. This 1st book award is dedicated to the discovery of exceptional mss by black poets of African descent. Deadline: March 31. 1st place: $1,000, plus publication by University of Georgia Press, 15 copies of the book, and a featured reading. Evie Shockley.

CIDER PRESS REVIEW BOOK AWARD

P.O. Box 33384, San Diego CA 92163. **E-mail:** editor@ciderpressreview.com. **Website:** http://ciderpressreview.com/. Annual award from *Cider Press Review*. Submissions must be unpublished as a collection, but individual poems may have been previously published elsewhere. Submit book-length ms of 48-80 pages. Submissions can be made online using the submission form on the website or by mail. If sending by mail, include 2 cover sheets—1 with title, author's name, and complete contact information; and 1 with title only, all bound with a spring clip. Does not require SASE; notification via e-mail and on the website, only. Mss cannot be returned. Online submissions must be in Word for PC or PDF format, and should not include title page with author's name. The editors strongly urge contestants to use online delivery if possible. Review the complete submission guidelines and learn more online at website. Deadline: November 30. Open to submissions on September 1. Prize: $1,500, publication, and 25 author's copies of a book-length collection of poetry. Author receives a standard publishing contract. Initial print run is not less than 1,000 copies. CPR acquires first publication rights. Editors of Cider Press Review.

CLEVELAND STATE UNIVERSITY POETRY CENTER BOOK COMPETITIONS

Cleveland State University Poetry Center, Cleveland State University Poetry Center, 2121 Euclid Avenue, Rhodes Tower, Room 1841, Cleveland OH 44115. (216)687-3986. **E-mail:** poetrycenter@csuohio.edu. **Website:** www.csupoetrycenter.com. **Contact:** Caryl Pagel. The Cleveland State University Poetry Center was established in 1962 at the former Fenn College of Engineering to promote poetry through readings and community outreach. In 1971, it expanded its mission to become a national non-profit independent press under the auspices of the Cleveland State University Department of English, and has since published nearly 200 rangy, joyful, profound, astonishing, complicated, surprising, and aesthetically diverse collections of contemporary poetry and prose by established and emerging authors. The Cleveland State University Poetry Center publishes between 3 and 5 collections of contemporary poetry and prose a year, with a national distribution and reach. The Poetry Center currently acquires manuscripts through 3 annual contests (1 dedicated to publishing and promoting first books of poetry, 1 to supporting an established poet's career, and 1 to publishing collections of literary essays). In addition to publishing, the Poetry Center actively promotes contemporary poetry and prose through an annual reading series, collaborative art events, participation in national writing conferences, and as an educational resource for Cleveland State University's undergraduate, M.A., and N.E.O.M.F.A. students by providing assistantship and internship opportunities, as well as involving students in the editorial and production aspects of literary publishing. See website for specific details and rules. Deadline: April 5. Prize: First Book and Open Book Competitions Awards: Publication and a $1,000 prize for an original manuscript of poetry in each category. 2018 Judges: CAConrad (First Book); Samuel Amadon, Leora Fridman, and Jane Lewty (Open Book); Brian Blanchfield (Essay).

CLOCKWISE CHAPBOOK COMPETITION

Tebot Bach, Tebot Bach, Clockwise, P.O. Box 7887, Huntington Beach CA 92615-7887. (714)968-0905. **Fax:** (714)968-4677. **E-mail:** mifanwy@tebotbach.org. **Website:** www.tebotbach.org/clockwise.html. Annual competition for a collection of poetry. Submit 24-32 pages of original poetry in English. Must be previously unpublished poetry for the full collection; individual poems may have been published. Full guidelines, including submission info, available online. Deadline: August 31. Prize: $500 and a book publication in Perfect Bound Editions. Winner announced in November with publication in May. Judged by Gail Wronsky.

TOM COLLINS POETRY PRIZE

Fellowship of Australian Writers (WA), Fellowship of Australian Writers (WA), P.O. Box 6180, Swanbourne WA 6910 Australia. (61)(08)9384-4771. **Fax:** (61)(8)9384-4854 or. **E-mail:** fellowshipaustralianwriterswa@gmail.com. **Website:** www.fawwa.org. Annual contest for unpublished poems, maximum 60 lines. Reserves the right to publish entries in a FAWWA publication or on its website. Guidelines online or for SASE. See website for details, guidelines, and entry form. Deadline: 15th December. Prize: 1st Place: $1,000; 2nd Place: $200; 3rd Place: $100.

THE COLORADO PRIZE FOR POETRY

Colorado Review,/ Center for Literary Publishing, Department of English, Colorado State University, 9105 Campus Delivery, Ft. Collins CO 80523. (970)491-5449. **E-mail:** creview@colostate.edu. **Website:** coloradoprize.colostate.edu. **Contact:** Stephanie G'Schwind, editor. Submission must be unpublished as a collection, but individual poems may have been published elsewhere. Submit mss of 48-100 pages of poetry on any subject, in any form, double- or single-spaced. Include 2 titles pages: 1 with ms title only, the other with ms title and poet's name, address, and phone number. Enclose SASE for notification of receipt and SASE for results; mss will not be returned. Guidelines available by SASE, e-mail, or online at website. Poets can also submit online via online submission manager through website. January 14. $2,000 and publication of a book-length ms. Judged by Kazim Ali.

CONCRETE WOLF POETRY CHAPBOOK/ LOUIS AWARD CONTEST

P.O. Box 445, Tillamook OR 97141. **E-mail:** concretewolfpress@gmail.com. **Website:** http://concretewolf.com. Prefers collections that have a theme, either obvious (i.e., chapbook about a divorce) or understated (i.e., all the poems mention the color blue). Likes a collection that feels more like a whole than a sampling of work. No preference as to formal or free verse. Slightly favors lyric and narrative poetry to language and concrete, but excellent examples of any style will grab their attention. Considers simultaneous submissions if notified of acceptance elsewhere. See website for details. Deadline: November 30 and March 31. Prize: Publication and 100 author copies of a perfectly-bound collection distributed by the Ingram catalog and available on Amazon.

THE CONNECTICUT RIVER REVIEW POETRY CONTEST

P.O. Box 270554, W. Hartford CT 06127. **E-mail:** connpoetry@comcast.net. **Website:** ctpoetry.net. Send up to 3 unpublished poems, any form, 80-line limit. Include 2 copies of each poem: 1 with complete contact information and 1 with no contact information. Include a SASE. Deadline: September 30. Open to submissions on August 1. 1st Place: $400; 2nd Place: $100; 3rd Place: $50. Leslie McGarth

CRAB ORCHARD SERIES IN POETRY FIRST BOOK AWARD

First Book Award, Dept. of English, Mail Code 4503, Southern Illinois University Carbondale, 1000 Faner Dr., Carbondale IL 62901. (618)453-6833. **Fax:** (618)453-8224. **E-mail:** jtribble@siu.edu. **Website:** www.craborchardreview.siu.edu. **Contact:** Jon Tribble, series editor. Annual award that selects a first book of poems for publication from an open competition of manuscripts, in English, by a U.S. citizen, permanent resident, or person who has DACA/TPS status who has neither published, who has neither published, nor committed to publish, a volume of poetry 48 pages or more in length in an edition of over 500 copies (individual poems may have been previously published; for the purposes of the Crab Orchard Series in Poetry, a ms which was in whole or in part submitted as a thesis or dissertation as a requirement for the completion of a degree is considered unpublished and is eligible). Current or former students, colleagues, and close friends of the final judge, and current and former students and employees of Southern Illinois University Carbondale and authors who have published a book with Southern Illinois University Press or have a book under contract with Southern Illinois University Press are not eligible. See website for complete formatting instructions and guidelines. Accepts submissions only through Submittable, online. Mss are recommended to be a minimum of 50 pages to a recommended maximum of 100 pages of original poetry, but no manuscript will be rejected solely because of length. Considers simultaneous submissions, but series editor must be informed immediately upon acceptance. Author's name should appear nowhere in manuscript. Do not include acknowledgments page. Deadline: July 8. Submission period begins May 15. Prize: $2,500 and publication. Judged by a published poet. Check website for current judge.

CRAB ORCHARD SERIES IN POETRY OPEN COMPETITION AWARDS

Department of English, Mail Code 4503, Faner Hall 2380, Southern Illinois University Carbondale, Carbondale IL 62901. (618)453-6833. **Fax:** (618)453-8224. **E-mail:** jtribble@siu.edu. **Website:** www.craborchardreview.siu.edu. **Contact:** Jon Tribble, series editor. Annual competition to award unpublished, original collections of poems written in English by United States citizens, permanent residents, or persons who have DACA/TPS status (individual poems may have been previously published; for the purposes of the Crab Orchard Series in Poetry, a ms which was in whole or in part submitted as a thesis or dissertation as a requirement for the completion of a degree is considered unpublished and is eligible). Two volumes of poems will be selected from the open competition of mss. Current or former students, colleagues, and close friends of the final judge, and current and former students and employees of Southern Illinois University Carbondale and authors who have published a book with Southern Illinois University Press or have a book under contract with Southern Illinois University Press are not eligible. See website for complete formatting instructions and guidelines. Accepts submissions only through Submittable, online. Mss are recommended to be a minimum of 50 pages to a recommended maximum of 80 pages of original poetry, but no manuscript will be rejected solely because of length. Considers simultaneous submissions, but series editor must be informed immediately upon acceptance. Deadline: November 19. Submission period begins October 1. Prize: Both winners will be awarded a publication contract with Southern Illinois University Press, a $1,000 prize, and a $1,500 as an honorarium for a reading at Southern Illinois University Carbondale. Both readings will follow the publication of the poets' collections. Judged by a published poet. Check website for current judge.

THE CRAZYHORSE PRIZE IN POETRY

Crazyhorse, Department of English, College of Charleston, 66 George St., Charleston SC 29424. (843)953-4470. **E-mail:** crazyhorse@cofc.edu. **Website:** http://crazyhorse.cofc.edu. **Contact:** Prize Director. The *Crazyhorse* Prize in Poetry is for a single poem. All entries will be considered for publication. Submissions must be unpublished. Submit online or by mail up to 3 original poems (no more than 10 pages). Include cover page (placed on top of ms) with poet's name, address, e-mail, and telephone number; no identifying information on mss (blind judging). Accepts multiple submissions with separate fee for each. Include SASP for notification of receipt of ms and SASE for results only; mss will not be returned. Guidelines available for SASE or on website. Deadline: Crazyhorse welcomes general submissions of fiction, nonfiction, and poetry from September 1st through May 31st, with the exception of the month of January, during which we only accept entries for the Crazyhorse Prizes. Prize: $2,000 and publication in *Crazyhorse*. Judged by genre judges for first round, guest judge for second round. Judges change on a yearly basis.

DANCING POETRY CONTEST

Artists Embassy International, AEI Contest Chair, Judy Cheung, 704 Brigham Ave., Santa Rosa CA 95404-5245 USA. (707)528-0912. **E-mail:** jhcheung@comcast.net. **Website:** www.dancingpoetry.com. Any subject, any form or free verse, suitable for a general audience. **Contact:** Judy Cheung, contest chair. Line Limit: 40 lines maximum each poem. No limit on number of entries. Send 2 typed, clear copies of each entry. Show name, address, telephone number, e-mail, and how you heard about the contest on one copy only. Poems must be in English or include English translation. Deadline: April 15. Prizes: Three Grand Prizes will receive $100 each, plus the poems will be danced and videotaped at this year's Dancing Poetry Festival; 6 First Prizes will receive $50 each; 12 Second Prizes will receive $25 each; and 30 Third Prizes will receive $10 each. Judged by members and associates of Artists Embassy International and the Poetic Dance Theater Company.

JAMES DICKEY PRIZE FOR POETRY

Georgia State University, James Dickey Prize for Poetry, P.O. Box 3999, Atlanta GA 30302-3999. **Website:** fivepoints.gsu.edu. The James Dickey Prize for Poetry is for the best previously unpublished poem. Deadline: December 1. Open to submissions on September 1. Winner receives $1000 and publication in the Volume 16, number 1 issue.

FAR HORIZONS AWARD FOR POETRY

The Malahat Review, University of Victoria, P.O. Box 1800, Stn CSC, Victoria BC V8W 3H5 Canada. (250)721-8524. **E-mail:** malahat@uvic.ca. **Website:** www.malahatreview.ca. **Contact:** L'Amour Lisik,

Marketing and Circulation Manager. The biennial Far Horizons Award for Poetry offers $1,000 CAD and publication in *The Malahat Review* (see separate listing in Magazines/Journals). Winner and finalists contacted by e-mail. Winner published in fall in *The Malahat Review* and announced on website, Facebook page, and in quarterly e-newsletter *Malahat lite*. Submissions must be unpublished. No simultaneous submissions. Submit up to 3 poems per entry, each poem not to exceed 60 lines; no restrictions on subject matter or aesthetic approach. Include separate page with poet's name, address, e-mail, and poem title(s); no identifying information on mss pages. E-mail submissions are acceptable: please send to horizons@uvic.ca. Do not include SASE for results; mss will not be returned. Full guidelines available on website. Open to "emerging poets from Canada, the United States, and elsewhere" who have not yet published a full-length book (48 pages or more). Deadline: May 1 (even-numbered years). Prize: $1,000.

JANICE FARRELL POETRY PRIZE CATEGORY

Soul-Making Keats Literary Competition, The Webhallow House, 1544 Sweetwood Dr., Broadmoor Vlg. CA 94015. **E-mail:** soulkeats@mail.com. **Website:** www.soulmakingcontest.us. **Contact:** Eileen Malone. Previously published okay. Poetry may be double- or single-spaced. One-page poems only, and only 1 poem/page. All poems must be titled. Three poems/entry. Identify with 3x5 card only. Open to all writers. Deadline: November 30. Prizes: First: $100, Second: $50, Third: $25. Judged by a local San Francisco Bay Area successfully published poet.

THE JEAN FELDMAN POETRY PRIZE

Washington Writers' Publishing House, 4640 23rd Rd. N., Arlington VA 22207. **E-mail:** wwphpress@gmail.com. **Website:** www.washingtonwriters.org. **Contact:** Holly Karapetkova. Poets living within 75 miles of the Capitol are invited to submit a ms of either a novel or a collection of short stories. Ms should be 50-70 pages, single spaced. Author's name should not appear on the manuscript. The title page of each copy should contain the title only. Provide name, address, telephone number, e-mail address, and title on a separate cover sheet accompanying the submission. A separate page for acknowledgments may be included for stories or excerpts previously published in journals and anthologies. E-mail electronic copies to wwphpress@gmail.com or mail paper copies and/or reading fee (check to WWPH) with SASE to: The Jean Feldman Poetry Prize, WWPH, c/o Holly Karapetkova, 4640 23rd Rd. N., Arlington, VA 22207. Deadline: November 15. Submission period begins July 1. Prize: $1,000 and 50 copies of the book.

FIELD POETRY PRIZE

Oberlin College Press/FIELD, 50 N. Professor St., Oberlin OH 44074-1095. (440)775-8408. **Fax:** (440)775-8124. **E-mail:** oc.press@oberlin.edu. **Website:** www.oberlin.edu/ocpress/prize.htm. **Contact:** Marco Wilkinson, Managing Editor. Offered annually for an unpublished book-length collection of poetry (mss of 50-80 pages). Contest seeks to encourage the finest in contemporary poetry writing. Open to any writer. Deadline: May 31. Opens to submissions on May 1. Prize: $1,000 and a standard royalty contract.

THE FINISHING LINE PRESS OPEN CHAPBOOK COMPETITION

Finishing Line Press, P.O. Box 1626, Georgetown KY 40324. **E-mail:** finishingbooks@aol.com. **Website:** www.finishinglinepress.com. **Contact:** Christen Kincaid, Director. Annual competition for poetry chapbook. $1,000

FIRST BOOK AWARD FOR POETRY

Zone 3, Austin Peay State University, Austin Peay State University, PO Box 4565, Clarksville TN 37044. (931)221-7031. **E-mail:** zone3@apsu.edu. **Website:** zone3press.com. **Contact:** Andrea Spofford, Poetry Editor; Aubrey Collins, Managing Editor. Biennial poetry award for anyone who has not published a full-length collection of poems (48 pages or more). A biennial award (i.e., 2020, 2022). Accepts entries via postal mail or online. Separate instructions for both; see website for guidelines and details. Jan.1-May 1, 2020. Prize: $1,000 and publication.

FISH POETRY PRIZE

Fish Poetry Contest, Fish Publishing, Dunbeacon, Durrus, Bantry Co. Cork P75 VK72 Ireland. **E-mail:** info@fishpublishing.com. **Website:** www.fishpublishing.com. **Contact:** Clem Cairns. For poems up to 300 words. Age Range: Adult. The best 10 will be published in the Fish Anthology, launched in July at the West Cork Literary Festival. Entries must not have been published before. Enter online or by post. See website for full details of competitions, and for information on the Fish Editorial and Critique Services and the Fish Online Writing Courses. Do not put your name or address or any other details on the poem; use a separate sheet. Receipt of entry will be acknowleged by e-mail. Poems will not be returned. Word count: 300 max for each poem. You may enter as many as you wish, provided there is an entry fee for each one. Full details and rules are online. Entry is deemed to be acceptance of these rules. Publishing rights of the 10 winning poems are held by Fish Publishing for one year after the publication of the Anthology. The aim of the competition is to discover and publish new poets. Deadline: March 31. 1st Prize: $1,000. 2nd Prize: A week at Anam Cara Writers" Retreat in West Cork. Results announced May 15. Judged by Billy Collins in 2019.

FOLEY POETRY CONTEST

Foley Poetry Contest, America Magazine, 1212 Avenue of the Americas, New York NY 10019. (212)581-4640. **Fax:** (212)399-3596. **Website:** www.americamagazine.org. *America*, the national Catholic weekly by the Jesuits of North America, sponsors the annual Foley Poetry Contest. Offers $1,000 and 2 contributor's copies for the winning poem. Winner will be announced in the mid-June issue of America and on the website. Runners-up will have their poems printed in subsequent issues of *America*. Submissions must be unpublished and may not be entered in other contests. "Submit 1 poem per person, not to exceed 30 lines of verse, in any form. Name, address, telephone number, and e-mail address (if applicable) should be appended to the bottom of the page. Poems will not be returned, and e-mailed submissions are not accepted." Guidelines available in magazine, for SASE, or on website. Competition receives more than 1,000 entries/year. Submissions must be unpublished and may not be entered in other contests. "Submit 1 poem per person, not to exceed 30 lines of verse, in any form. Name, address, telephone number, and e-mail address (if applicable) should be appended to the bottom of the page. Poems will not be returned, and e-mailed submissions are not accepted." Guidelines available in magazine, for SASE, or on website. Deadline: March 31. Open to submissions on January 1. $1,000

THE FOUR WAY BOOKS LEVIS PRIZE IN POETRY

Four Way Books, POB 535, Village Station, New York NY 10014. (212)334-5430. **Fax:** (212)334-5435. **E-mail:** editors@fourwaybooks.com. **Website:** www.fourwaybooks.com. **Contact:** Ryan Murphy, Associate Director. The Four Way Books Levis Prize in Poetry offers publication by Four Way Books (see separate listing in Book Publishers), honorarium, and a reading at one or more participating series in New York City. Open to any poet writing in English who has not published a book-length collection of poetry. Entry form and guidelines available on website at www.fourwaybooks.com. Submission Dates: January 1 - April 7 (postmark) or online via our submission manager by April 8 at 3 AM EST. Winner announced by e-mail and on website. Prize: Publication and $1,000. Copies of winning books available through Four Way Books online and at bookstores (to the trade through University Press of New England). 2019 Judge: Gregory Pardlo

GERTRUDE PRESS POETRY CHAPBOOK CONTEST

P.O. Box 28281, Portland OR 97228. **E-mail:** editor@gertrudepress.org; poetry@gertrudepress.org. **Website:** www.gertrudepress.org. Annual chapbook contest for 25-30 pages of poetry. Individual poems may have been previously published; unpublished poems are welcome. Poetry may be of any subject matter, and writers from all backgrounds are encouraged to submit. Include list of acknowledgments and cover letter indicating how poet learned of the contest. Include 1 title page with identifying information and 1 without. Guidelines available in *Gertrude* (see separate listing in Magazines/Journals), for SASE, by e-mail, or on website. Deadline: May 15. Submission period begins September 15. Prize: $200, publication, and 25 complimentary copies of the chapbook.

ALLEN GINSBERG POETRY AWARDS

The Poetry Center at Passaic County Community College, One College Blvd., Paterson NJ 07505-1179. (973)684-6555. **Fax:** (973)523-6085. **E-mail:** mgillan@pccc.edu. **Website:** www.poetrycenterpccc.com. **Contact:** Maria Mazziotti Gillan, Executive Director. All winning poems, honorable mentions, and editor's choice poems will be published in *The Paterson Literary Review*. Winners will be asked to participate in a reading that will be held in the Paterson Historic District. Submissions must be unpublished. Submit up to 5 poems (no poem more than 2 pages long). Send 4 copies of each poem entered. Include cover sheet with poet's name, address, phone number, e-mail address and poem titles. Poet's name should not appear on poems. Include SASE for results only; poems will not be returned. Guidelines available for SASE or on website. February 1st, 2020. Prize: 1st Prize: $1,000; 2nd Prize: $200; 3rd Prize: $100.

GIVAL PRESS POETRY AWARD

Gival Press, LLC, P.O. Box 3812, Arlington VA 22203. (703)351-0079. **E-mail:** givalpress@yahoo.com. **Website:** www.givalpress.submittable.com. **Contact:** Robert L. Giron, editor. Offered every other year, with the next deadline of December 15, 2019, with book publication in 2020, for a previously unpublished poetry collection as a complete ms, which may include previously published poems; previously published poems must be acknowledged, and poet must hold rights. Guidelines for SASE, by e-mail, or online. Open to any writer, as long as the work is original, not a translation, and is written in English. The copyright remains in the author's name; certain rights fall to the publisher per the contract. Enter via portal: www.givalpress.submittable.com. Must be at least 45 typed pages of poetry, on one side only. Entrants are asked to submit their poems without any kind of identification (with the exception of the titles) and with a separate cover page with the following information: Name, address (street, city, state, and zip code), telephone number, e-mail address (if available), short bio, and a list of the poems by title. Checks drawn on American banks should be made out to Gival Press, LLC. The competition seeks to award well-written, origional poetry in English on any topic, in any style. Deadline: December 15 (postmarked). Prize: $1,000, publication, and 20 copies of the publication. The editor narrows entries to the top 10; previous winner selects top 5 and chooses the winner—all done anonymously.

PATRICIA GOEDICKE PRIZE IN POETRY

CutBank Literary Magazine, *CutBank*, University of Montana, English Dept., LA 133, Missoula MT 59812. **E-mail:** editor.cutbank@gmail.com. **Website:** www.cutbankonline.org. **Contact:** Billy Wallace, Editor-in-Chief. The Patricia Goedicke Prize in Poetry seeks to highlight work that showcases an authentic voice, a boldness of form, and a rejection of functional fixedness. Accepts online submissions only. Submit up to 5 poems. Guidelines available online. Deadline: January 15. Submissions period begins November 9. Prize: $500 and featured in the magazine. Judged by a guest judge each year.

GOLDEN ROSE AWARD

New England Poetry Club, 654 Green St., No. 2, Cambridge MA 02139. **E-mail:** contests@nepoetryclub.org; info@nepoetryclub.org. **Website:** www.nepoetryclub.org. **Contact:** NEPC contest coordinator. Given annually to the poet, who by their poetry, and inspiration to and encouragement of other writers, has made a significant mark on American poetry. Traditionally given to a poet with some ties to New England so that a public reading may take place. Contest open to members and nonmembers. Poems should be typed and submitted in duplicate with author's name, address, phone, and e-mail address of writer on only 1 copy. (Judges receive copies without names.) Copy only. Label poems with contest name. Entries should be sent by regular mail only. Special-delivery or signature-required mail will be returned by the post office. Entries should be original, unpublished poems in English. No poem should be entered in more than 1 contest, nor have won a previous contest. No entries will be returned. NEPC will not engage in correspondence regarding poems or contest decisions. Judged by well-known poets and sometimes winners of previous NEPC contests.

THE GREEN ROSE PRIZE IN POETRY

New Issues Poetry & Prose, Deptartment of English, Western Michigan University, 1903 W. Michigan Ave., Kalamazoo MI 49008-5463. **E-mail:** new-issues@wmich.edu. **Website:** www.newissuespress.com. Offered annually for unpublished poetry. The university will publish a book of poems by a poet writing in English who has published 1 or more full-length collections of poetry. *New Issues* may publish as many as 2 additional mss from this competition. Guidelines for SASE or online. *New Issues Poetry & Prose* obtains rights for first publication. Book is copyrighted in the author's name. Considers simultaneous submissions, but *New Issues* must be notified of acceptance elsewhere. Submit a ms of at least 40 pages, typed; single-spaced preferred. Clean photocopies acceptable. Do not bind; use manila folder or metal clasp. Include cover page with poet's name, address, phone number, and title of the ms. Also include brief bio, table of contents, and acknowledgments page. Submissions are also welcome through the online submission manager: www.newissuespoetryprose.submittable.com. For hardcopy manuscripts only, you may include SASP for notification of receipt of ms and SASE for results only; mss will be recycled. Guidelines available for SASE, by fax, e-mail, or on website. Winner is announced in January or February on website. The winning manuscript will be published in spring of following year. 2016 winner was Nadine Sabra Meyer (*Chrysanthemum, Chrysanthemum*). Deadline: Submit May 1-September 30. Winner is announced in January or February on website. Prize: $1,000, publication of a book of poems, and reading w/ $500 stipend + travel costs.

THE GRIFFIN POETRY PRIZE

The Griffin Trust for Excellence in Poetry, The Griffin Trust For Excellence In Poetry, 363 Parkridge Crescent, Oakville ON L6M 1A8 Canada. (905)618-0420. **E-mail:** info@griffinpoetryprize.com. **Website:** www.griffinpoetryprize.com. **Contact:** Ruth Smith, Executive Director. The Griffin Poetry Prize is one of the world's most generous poetry awards. The awards go to one Canadian and one international poet for a first collection written in, or translated into, English. Submissions must come from publishers. A book of poetry must be a first-edition collection. Books should have been published in the previous calendar year. June 30, 201 for books published between January 1, 2019 and June 30, 2019; December 31, 2019 for books published between July 1, 2019 and December 31, 2019. Prize: Two $65,000 (CAD) prizes. An additional $10,000 (CAD) goes to each shortlisted poet for their participation in the Shortlist Readings. Judges are chosen annually by the Trustees of The Griffin Trust For Excellence in Poetry.

THE DONALD HALL PRIZE IN POETRY

Association of Writers & Writing Programs, 5700 Rivertech Ct., Suite 225, Riverdale Park MD 20737-1250. **E-mail:** chronicle@awpwriter.org. **Website:** www.awpwriter.org. The Donald Hall Prize for Poetry offers an award of $5,500, supported by Amazon.com, and publication by the University of Pittsburgh Press. Deadline: March 3. Opens to submissions January 1.

JAMES HEARST POETRY PRIZE

North American Review, University of Northern Iowa, 1222 W. 27th St., Cedar Falls IA 50614-0516. (319)273-3026. **Fax:** (319)273-4326. **E-mail:** nar@uni.edu. **Website:** www.northamericanreview.org. Contest to find the best previously unpublished poem. Deadline: October 31. Prize: 1st place: $1,000; 2nd place: $100; 3rd place: $50.

THE HILARY THAM CAPITAL COLLECTION

The Word Works, Nancy White, c/o SUNY Adiorndack, 640 Bay Rd., Queensbury NY 12804. **E-mail:** editor@wordworksbooks.org. **Website:** www.wordworksbooks.org. **Contact:** Nancy White, Editor. The Hilary Tham Capital Collection publishes only poets who volunteer for literary nonprofits. Every nominated poet is invited to submit; authors have until May 1 to send their ms via online submissions at website, or to Nancy White. Details available online. Deadline: May 1. $25 reading fee Past judges include Denise Duhamel, Kimiko Hahn, Michael Klein, and Eduardo Corral.

THE BESS HOKIN PRIZE

Poetry, 61 W. Superior St., Chicago IL 60654. (312)787-7070. **Fax:** (312)787-6650. **E-mail:** editors@poetrymagazine.org. **Website:** www.poetrymagazine.org. Offered annually for poems published in *Poetry* during the preceding year (October-September). Upon acceptance, *Poetry* licenses exclusive worldwide first-serial rights, including electronic rights, for publication, as well as non-exclusive rights to reprint, reuse, and archive the work, in any format, in perpetuity. Copyright reverts to author upon first publication. "Established in 1948 through the generosity of our late friend and guarantor, Mrs. David Hokin, and is given annually in her memory." Prize: $1,000.

FIRMAN HOUGHTON PRIZE

New England Poetry Club, 53 Regent St., Cambridge MA 02140. **E-mail:** info@nepoetryclug.org. **Website:** www.nepoetryclub.org. **Contact:** Mary Buchinger, Co-President NEPC. For a lyric poem in honor of the former president of NEPC. Contest guidelines available on website. Deadline: May 31. Prize: $200. Judged by well-known poets and sometimes winners of previous NEPC contests.

TOM HOWARD/MARGARET REID POETRY CONTEST

Winning Writers, 351 Pleasant St., PMB 222, Northampton MA 01060-3961. (866)946-9748. **Fax:** (413)280-0539. **E-mail:** adam@winningwriters.com. **Website:** www.winningwriters.com. **Contact:** Adam Cohen. Winning Writers provides expert literary contest information to the public. It is one of the "101 Best Websites for Writers" (*Writer's Digest*). Offers annual awards of Tom Howard Prize, for a poem in any style or genre, and Margaret Reid Prize, for a poem that rhymes or has a traditional style. See website for guidelines and to submit your poem. If you win a prize, requests nonexclusive rights to publish your submission online, in e-mail newsletters, in e-books, and in press releases. Submissions maybe published or unpublished, may have won prizes elsewhere, and may be entered in other contests. Length limit: 250 lines per poem. Deadline: September 30. Submission period begins April 15. Prizes: Two top awards of $1,500 each, with 10 Honorable Mentions of $100 each (any style). All entries that win cash prizes will be published on the Winning Writers website. The top two winners will also receive one-year gift certificates from the contest co-sponsor, Duotrope (a $50 value). Judged by Soma Mei Sheng Frazier, assisted by Jim DuBois.

ILLINOIS STATE POETRY SOCIETY ANNUAL CONTEST

Illinois State Poetry Society, Alan Harris, 543 E. Squirrel Tail Dr., Tucson AZ 85704. **E-mail:** oasis@alharris.com. **Website:** www.illinoispoets.org. **Contact:** Alan Harris. Annual contest to encourage the crafting of excellent poetry. Guidelines and entry forms available for SASE. Deadline: September 30. Cash prizes of $50, $30, and $10. 3 Honorable Mentions. Poet retains all rights. Judged by out-of-state professionals.

INDIANA REVIEW POETRY CONTEST

Ballantine Hall 465, Indiana University, 1020 E. Kirkwood Ave., Bloomington IN 47405-7103. **E-mail:** inreview@indiana.edu. **Website:** indianareview.org. **Contact:** Tessa Yang, Editor. Contest for poetry in any style and on any subject. Open to any writer. Mss will not be returned. No works forthcoming elsewhere are eligible. Simultaneous submissions accepted, but in the event of entrant withdrawal, contest fee will not be refunded. Deadline: March 31. Submission period begins February 1. Prize: $1,000, plus publication in the *Indiana Review* and contributor's copies. Judged by Gabrielle Calvocoressi.

INDIANA REVIEW POETRY PRIZE

Indiana Review, Poetry Prize, Indiana Review, Ballantine Hall 529, 1020 E. Kirkwood Ave., Bloomington IN 47405-7103. **E-mail:** inreview@indiana.edu. **Website:** www.indianareview.org. Offered annually for unpublished work. Open to any writer. Guidelines available on website. All entries are considered for publication. Send no more than 3 poems per entry, 8 pages maximum. Each fee entitles entrant to a 1-year subscription. No longer accepts hardcopy submissions. Deadline: March 31. Submission period begins February 1. Prize: $1,000 and publication. Judged by Gabrielle Calvocoressi in 2018. Different judge every year.

IOWA POETRY PRIZE

University of Iowa Press, University of Iowa Press, 119 West Park Rd.,100 Kuhl House, Iowa City IA 52242-1000. (319)335-2000. **Fax:** (319)335-2055. **E-mail:** uipress@uiowa.edu. **Website:** www.uiowapress.org. Offered annually to encourage poets and their work. Submissions must be postmarked during the month of April; put name on title page only. This page will be removed before ms is judged. Open to writers of English (US citizens or not). Mss will not be returned. Previous winners are not eligible. Mss should be 50-150 pages in length. Poems included in the collection may have appeared in journals or anthologies; poems from a poet's previous collections may be included only in manuscripts of new and selected poems. Deadline: April 30. Prize: Publication under standard royalty agreement.

ALICE JAMES AWARD

Alice James Books, University of Maine at Farmington, 114 Prescott St., Farmington ME 04938. (207)778-7071. **Fax:** (207)778-7766. **E-mail:** ajb@alicejamesbooks.org; info@alice jamesbooks.org. **Website:** www.alicejamesbooks.org. **Contact:** Alyssa Neptune, managing editor. Offered annually for unpublished, full-length poetry collections. Emerging and established poets are welcome. Submit 48-100 pages of poetry. Guidelines for submissions available online. Deadline: November 1. Prize: $2,000, publication, and distribution through Consortium.

ALICE JAMES AWARD

Alice James Books, Alice James Award, 114 Prescott St., Farmington ME 04938. (207)778-7071. **Fax:** (207)778-7766. **E-mail:** ajb@alicejamesbooks.org. **Website:** www.alicejamesbooks.org. **Contact:** Alyssa Neptune, Managing Editor. For complete contest guidelines, visit website or send a SASE. Open to anyone residing in the United States. Offered annually for unpublished, full-length, poetry collection. Deadline: November 1. Prize: $2,000 , book publication, and distribution through Consortium. Editorial Board.

RANDALL JARRELL POETRY COMPETITION

North Carolina Writers' Network, Terry L. Kennedy, MFA Writing Program, 3302 MHRA Building, UNC Greensboro, Greensboro NC 27402-6170. **E-mail:** tlkenned@uncg.edu. **Website:** www.ncwriters.org. **Contact:** Terry L. Kennedy, director. Offered annually for unpublished work to honor Randall Jarrell and his life at UNC Greensboro, by recognizing the best poetry submitted. The competition is open to any writer who is a legal resident of North Carolina or a member of the North Carolina Writers' Network. Submissions should be one poem only (40-line limit). Poem must be typed (single-spaced) and stapled in the left-hand corner. Author's name should not appear on the poem. Instead, include a separate cover sheet with author's name, address, e-mail address, phone number, and poem title. Poem will not be returned. Include a self-addressed stamped envelope for a list of winner and finalists. The winner and finalists will be announced in May. Deadline: March 1. Prize: $200 and publication at *storySouth* (www.storysouth.com). Judged by Lauren Moseley in 2018.

JUNIPER PRIZE FOR FICTION

University of Massachusetts Press, 180 Infirmary Way, 4th Fl., Amherst MA 01003. (413)545-2217. **Fax:** (413)545-1226. **E-mail:** info@umpress.umass.edu; cjandree@umpress.umass.edu. **E-mail:** juniperprize@umpress.umass.edu. **Website:** www.umass.edu/umpress. **Contact:** Courtney Andree. The Juniper Prize for Fiction is awarded annually to two original manuscripts of fiction: one short story collection and one novel. The University of Massachusetts Press publishes the winning manuscripts and the authors receive a $1,000 award upon publication. Competition open to all writers in English. Novels, novellas, and collections of stories are all eligible. Work that has previously appeared in magazines, in whole or in part, may be included, but should be so identified on the cover sheet. Mss must be at least 150 pages and no longer than 350 pages. Guidelines available on website. Deadline: September 30. Submissions period begins August 1. Winners announced online in April on the press website. Prize: $1,000 cash and publication.

JUNIPER PRIZE FOR POETRY

University of Massachusetts Press, 180 Infirmary Way, 4th Fl., Amherst MA 01003. (413)545-2217. **Fax:** (413)545-1226. **E-mail:** info@umpress.umass.edu; cjandree@umpress.umass.edu. **E-mail:** juniperprize@umpress.umass.edu. **Website:** www.umass.edu/umpress. **Contact:** Courtney Andree. The University of Massachusetts Press offers the annual Juniper Prize for Poetry, awarded in alternate years for the first and subsequent books. Considers simultaneous submissions, but if accepted for publication elsewhere, please notify immediately. Mss by more than 1 author, entries of more than 1 mss simultaneously or within the same year, and translations are not eligible. Submit paginated ms of 50-70 pages of poetry, with paginated contents page, credits page, and information on previously published books. Include 2 cover sheets: 1 with contract information, 1 without. Mss will not be returned. Guidelilnes available for SASE or on website. Deadline: September 30. Submission period begins August 1. Winners announced online in April on the press website. Prize: Publication and $1,000 in addition to royalties.

BARBARA MANDIGO KELLY PEACE POETRY AWARDS

Nuclear Age Peace Foundation, Nuclear Age Peace Foundation, PMB 121, 1187 Coast Village Rd., Suite 1, Santa Barbara CA 93108-2794. (805)965-3443. **Fax:** (805)568-0466. **E-mail:** cwarner@napf.org. **Website:** www.wagingpeace.org; www.peacecontests.org. **Contact:** Carol Warner, Poetry Award Coordinator. The Barbara Mandigo Kelly Peace Poetry Contest was created to encourage poets to explore and illuminate positive visions of peace and the human spirit. The annual contest honors the late Barbara Kelly, a Santa Barbara poet and longtime supporter of peace issues. Awards are given in 3 categories: adult (over 18 years), youth (between 12 and 18 years), and youth under 12. All submitted poems should be unpublished. Deadline: July 1 (postmarked or e-mailed). Prize: Adult: $1,000; Youth (13-18): $200; Youth (12 and under): $200. Honorable Mentions may also be awarded. Judged by a committee of poets selected by the Nuclear Age Peace Foundation. The foundation reserves the right to publish and distribute the award-winning poems, including honorable mentions.

MILTON KESSLER MEMORIAL PRIZE FOR POETRY

Creative Writing Program, Binghamton University, Department of English, General Literature, and Rhetoric, Library North Room 1149, Vestal Parkway East, P.O. Box 6000, Binghamton NY 13902-6000. **Website:** www.binghamton.edu/english/creative-writing/binghamton-center-for-writers/binghamton-book-awards/kessler-poetry-awards.html. **Contact:** Maria

Mazziotti Gillan, Director. Annual award for best previously published book (previous year). Deadline: March 1. 1st place: $1,000.

THE JAMES LAUGHLIN AWARD

The James Laughlin Award, The Academy of American Poets, 75 Maiden Lane, Suite 901, New York NY 10038. **Website:** www.poets.org. Offered since 1954, the James Laughlin Award is given to recognize and support a second book of poetry forthcoming in the next calendar year. It is named for the poet and publisher James Laughlin, who founded New Directions in 1936. Deadline: May 15. $5,000; an all-expenses-paid weeklong residency at The Betsy Hotel in Miami Beach, Florida; and distribution of the winning book to approximately 1,000 Academy of American Poets members.

LEVIS READING PRIZE

Virginia Commonwealth University, Department of English, Levis Reading Prize, VCU Department of English, 900 Park Avenue, Hibbs Hall, Room 306, Box 842005, Richmond VA 23284-2005. (804)828-1331. **Fax:** (804)828-8684. **E-mail:** bloomquistjmp@mymail.vcu.edu. **Website:** www.english.vcu.edu/mfa/levis. **Contact:** John-Michael Bloomquist. Offered annually for books of poetry published in the previous year to encourage poets early in their careers. The entry must be the writer's first or second published book of poetry. Previously published books in other genres, or previously published chapbooks or self-published material, do not count as books for this purpose. Entries may be submitted by either author or publisher, and must include 3 copies of the book (48 pages or more), a cover letter, and a brief biography of the author including previous publications. (Entries from vanity presses are not eligible.) The book must have been published in the previous calendar year. Entrants wishing acknowledgment of receipt must include a self-addressed, stamped postcard. Deadline: February 1. Prize: $5,000 and an expense-paid trip to Richmond to present a public reading. Judges come from faculty of the VCU Department of English and MFA Program in Creative Writing.

THE RUTH LILLY POETRY PRIZE

Poetry, 61 W. Superior St., Chicago IL 60654. (312)787-7070. **Fax:** (312)787-6650. **E-mail:** editors@poetrymagazine.org; info@poetryfoundation.org. **Website:** www.poetrymagazine.org. Awarded annually, the $100,000 Ruth Lilly Poetry Prize honors a living U.S. poet whose lifetime accomplishments warrant extraordinary recognition. Established in 1986 by Ruth Lilly, the Prize is one of the most prestigious awards given to American poets and is one of the largest literary honors for work in the English language. Deadline: No submissions or nominations considered. Prize: $100,000.

LITERAL LATTÉ POETRY AWARD

Literal Latté, Literal Latté Awards, 200 E. 10th St., Suite 240, New York NY 10003. **E-mail:** LitLatte@aol.com. **Website:** www.literal-latte.com. **Contact:** Jenine Gordon Bockman, Editor. Offered annually to any writer for unpublished poetry (maximum 2,000 words per poem). All styles welcome. Winners published in *Literal Latté*. Acquires first rights. Deadline: Postmark by July 15. Prizes: 1st Place: $1,000; 2nd Place: $300; 3rd Place: $200. Judged by the editors.

LITERAL LATTE FOOD VERSE CONTEST

Literal Latte, 200 E. 10th St., Suite 240, New York NY 10003. **E-mail:** litlatte@aol.com. **Website:** www.literal-latte.com. Any topic with Food as an ingredient. **Contact:** Jenine Gordon Bockman, editor. 25 years of stimulating the careers of writers and the minds of readers. Open to any writer. Poems should have food as an ingredient. Submissions required to be unpublished. Guidelines online at website. Submit poems, up to 10,000 words each. Literal Latté acquires first rights. Annual contest to give support and exposure to great writing. Deadline: March 15. Prize: $500. Judged by the editors.

LUMINA POETRY CONTEST

Sarah Lawrence College, Sarah Lawrence College, Slonim House, 1 Mead Way, Bronxville NY 10708. **Website:** www.luminajournal.com. Poetry competition held once every 3 years by the Sarah Lawrence College's graduate literary journal. Rotates with a fiction and nonfiction contest. Submit online. Include a 100-word bio at the bottom of cover letter. Submit up to 3 poems, 60 lines maximum per poem. Does not accept previously published material or simultaneous submissions. Deadline: October 15. Prize: 1st Place: $500 and publication; 2nd Place: $250 and publication; 3rd Place: $100 and online publication.

THE MACGUFFIN'S NATIONAL POET HUNT CONTEST

The MacGuffin, Poet Hunt Contest, Schoolcraft College, 18600 Haggerty Rd., Livonia MI 48152. (734)462-5327. **Fax:** (734)462-4679. **E-mail:** macguffin@

schoolcraft.edu. **E-mail:** macguffin@schoolcraft.edu. **Website:** https://www.schoolcraft.edu/macguffin/contest-rules. **Contact:** Gordon Krupsky, Managing Editor. *The MacGuffin* is a national literary magazine from Schoolcraft College in Livonia, Michigan. An entry consists of 3 poems. Poems must not be previously published, and must be the original work of the contestant. See website for additional details. The mission of *The MacGuffin* is to encourage, support, and enhance the literary arts in the Schoolcraft College community, the region, the state, and the nation. Deadline: June 15. Submissions period begins April 1. Prize: $500. Featuring guest judge Richard Tillinghast.

NAOMI LONG MADGETT POETRY AWARD

Broadside Lotus Press, Inc., Broadside Lotus Press, c/o Dr. Gloria House, 8300 East Jefferson Ave., Apt. #504, Detroit MI 48214. (313)736-5338. **E-mail:** broadsidelotus@gmail.com. **Website:** www.broadsidelotuspress.org. **Contact:** Gloria House. Offered annually to recognize an unpublished book-length poetry ms by an African American. Guidelines available online. Poems in the ms should total *approximately* 60-90 pages, exclusive of a table of contents or other optional introductory material. Poems that have been published individually in periodicals or anthologies are acceptable. Will not consider an entire collection that has been previously published. Deadline: March 1. Submission period begins January 2. Prize: $500 and publication by Lotus Press.

MAIN STREET RAG'S ANNUAL POETRY BOOK AWARD

Main Street Rag Publishing Company, P.O. Box 690100, Charlotte NC 28227-7001. (704)573-2516. **E-mail:** editor@mainstreetrag.com. **Website:** www.mainstreetrag.com. **Contact:** M. Scott Douglass, publisher/managing editor. Submit 48-84 pages of poetry, no more than 1 poem/page (individual poems may be longer than 1 page). Guidelines available on website. The purpose of this contest is to select manuscripts for publication and offer prize money to the manuscript we feel best represents our label. Deadline: February 2. Prize: 1st Place: $1,200 and 50 copies of book; runners-up are also be offered publication. Judged by 1 panel that consists of *MSR* editors, associated editors and college-level instructors, and previous contest winners.

THE MALAHAT REVIEW LONG POEM PRIZE

The Malahat Review, Box 1800 STN CSC, Victoria BC V8W 3H5 Canada. **E-mail:** malahat@uvic.ca. **Website:** www.malahatreview.ca. **Contact:** L'Amour Lisik, Publicity Manager. Long Poem Prize is offered in alternate years with the Novella Contest. Open to any writer. Offers 2 awards of $1,000 CAD each for a long poem or cycle (10-20 printed pages). Includes publication in *The Malahat Review* and a 1-year subscription. Open to entries from Canadian, American, and overseas authors. Obtains first world rights. Publication rights after revert to the author. Submissions must be unpublished. No simultaneous submissions. Submit a single poem or cycle of poems, 10-20 published pages (a published page equals 32 lines or less, including breaks between stanzas); no restrictions on subject matter or aesthetic approach. Include separate page with poet's name, address, e-mail, and title; no identifying information on mss pages. Do not include SASE for results; mss will not be returned. Guidelines available n website. Deadline: February 1 (odd-numbered years). Prize: Two $1,000 prizes. Winners published in the summer issue of *The Malahat Review*, announced in summer on website, Facebook page, and in quarterly e-newsletter *Malahat lite*. Judged by 3 recognized poets. Preliminary readings by editorial board.

THE MORTON MARR POETRY PRIZE

Southwest Review, Southern Methodist University, P.O. Box 750374, Dallas TX 75275-0374. (214)768-1037. **Fax:** (214)768-1408. **E-mail:** swr@mail.smu.edu. **Website:** www.smu.edu/southwestreview. **Contact:** Greg Brownderville, editor-in-chief. Annual award for poem(s) by a writer who has not yet published a book of poetry. Submit no more than 6 poems in a "traditional" form (e.g., sonnet, sestine, villanelle, rhymed stanzas, blank verse, et al.). Submissions will not be returned. Deadline: September 30. Prizes: $1,000 for 1st place; $500 for 2nd place; plus publication in the *Southwest Review*.

LENORE MARSHALL POETRY PRIZE

The Lenore Marshall Poetry Prize, The Academy of American Poets, 75 Maiden Lane, Suite 901, New York NY 10038. (212)274-0343, Ext. 13. **Fax:** (212)274-9427. **E-mail:** awards@poets.org. **Website:** www.poets.org. **Contact:** Programs Coordinator. Established in 1975, this $25,000 award recognizes the most outstanding book of poetry published in the United States in the previous calendar year. The prize includes distribution of the winning book to hundreds of Academy of

American Poets members. Deadline: May 15. Prize: $25,000.

MARSH HAWK PRESS POETRY PRIZE

Marsh Hawk Press, Marsh Hawk Press, Inc., P.O. Box 206, East Rockaway NY 11518-0206. **E-mail:** marshhawkpress1@aol.com. **Website:** www.MarshHawkPress.org. **Contact:** Prize Director. The Marsh Hawk Press Poetry Prize offers $1,000, plus publication of a book-length ms. Additionally, The Robert Creeley Poetry Prize and The Rochelle Ratner Poetry Award, both cash prizes, go to the runners-up. Submissions must be unpublished as a collection, but individual poems may have been previously published elsewhere. Submit 48-84 pages of original poetry in any style in English, typed single-spaced, and paginated. (Longer mss will be considered if the press is queried before submission.) Contest mss may be submitted by electronic upload. See website for more information. If submitting via Post Office mail, the ms must be bound with a spring clip. Include 2 title pages: 1 with ms title, poet's name, and contact information only; 1 with ms title only (poet's name must not appear anywhere in the ms). Also include table of contents and acknowledgments page. Include SASE for results only; ms will not be returned. Guidelines available on website. Deadline: 11:59 PM EST on April 30. $1,000; book publication; and promotion, including a book launch in New York City. To be announced

KATHLEEN MCCLUNG SONNET PRIZE CATEGORY

Soul-Making Keats Literary Competition, The Webhallow House, 1544 Sweetwood Dr., Broadmoor Village CA 94015-2029. **E-mail:** soulkeats@mail.com. **Website:** www.soulmakingcontest.us. **Contact:** Eileen Malone. Call for Shakespearean and Petrarchan sonnets on the theme of the "beloved." Previously published material is accepted. Indicate category on cover page and on identifying 3x5 card. Open annually to any writer. Ongoing Deadline: November 30. Prize:1st Place: $100; 2nd Place: $50; 3rd Place: $25.

THE KATHRYN A. MORTON PRIZE IN POETRY

Sarabande Books, Inc., Sarabande Books, Inc., 822 E. Market St., Louisville KY 40206. (502)458-4028. **E-mail:** info@sarabandebooks.org. **Website:** www.sarabandebooks.org. **Contact:** Sarah Gorham, Editor-in-Chief. The Kathryn A. Morton Prize in Poetry is awarded annually to a book-length ms (at least 48 pages). All finalists are considered for publication. Competition receives approximately 1,400 entries. Guidelines available online. Mss can be submitted online or via postal mail. Deadline: February 15. Submissions period begins January 1. Prize: $2,000, publication, and a standard royalty contract.

SHEILA MARGARET MOTTON PRIZE

New England Poetry Club, Mary Buchinger, NEPC President, 53 Regent Street, Cambridge MA 02140. (617)744-6034. **E-mail:** info@nepoetryclub.org. **Website:** www.nepoetryclub.org. **Contact:** Mary Buchinger, NEPC President. Awarded for a book of poems published in the last 2 years. Send 2 copies of book. Deadline: May 31. Prize: $250. Judged by well-known poets and sometimes winners of previous NEPC contests.

NATIONAL POETRY COMPETITION

The Poetry Society, 22 Betterton St., London WC2H 9BX United Kingdom. 020 7420 9880. **E-mail:** info@poetrysociety.org.uk. **Website:** www.poetrysociety.org.uk. **Contact:** Competition Organizer. The Poetry Society was founded in 1909 to promote "a more general recognition and appreciation of poetry." Since then, it has grown into one of Britain's most dynamic arts organizations, representing British poetry both nationally and internationally. Today it has nearly 4,000 members worldwide and publishes *The Poetry Review*. With innovative education and commissioning programs, and a packed calendar of performances, readings and competitions, The Poetry Society champions poetry for all ages. Open to anyone aged 17 or over. Submissions must be unpublished (poems posted on websites are considered published). Submit original poems in English, on any subject, no more than 40 lines/poem, typed on 1 side only of A4 paper, double- or single-spaced. Each poem must be titled. No identifying information on poems. Do not staple pages. Accepts online submissions; full details available on the National Poetry Competition pages on the Poetry Society website. Entry form (required) available for A5 SAE (1 entry form covers multiple entries, may be photocopied). Include stamped SAE for notification of receipt of postal entries (confirmation of online entries will be e-mailed at time of submission); poems will not be returned. Guidelines available on website. Deadline: October 31. 1st Prize: £5,000; 2nd Prize: £2,000; 3rd Prize: £1,000; plus 7 commendations of £200 each. Winners will be published in *The Poetry Review*, and on the Poetry Society website; the top 3 winners will receive a year's free membership of The Poetry Society. Mona Arshi, Helen Mort, and Maurice Riordan

NATIONAL WRITERS ASSOCIATION POETRY CONTEST

The National Writers Association, NWA Poetry Contest, 10940 S. Parker Rd. #508, Parker CO 80134. **E-mail:** natlwritersassn@hotmail.com. **Website:** www.nationalwriters.com. **Contact:** Sandy Whelchel, Director. Annual contest to encourage the writing of poetry, an important form of individual expression but with a limited commercial market. Deadline: October 1. Prize: 1st Place: $100; 2nd Place: $50; 3rd Place: $25.

THE PABLO NERUDA PRIZE FOR POETRY

Nimrod International Journal, 800 S. Tucker Dr., Tulsa OK 74104. (918)631-3080. **Fax:** (918)631-3033. **E-mail:** nimrod@utulsa.edu. **Website:** www.utulsa.edu/nimrod. **Contact:** Eilis O'Neal. Annual award to discover new writers of vigor and talent. Open to US residents only. Submissions must be unpublished. Work must be in English or translated by original author. Submit 3-10 pages of poetry (1 long poem or several short poems). Poet's name must not appear on manuscript. Include cover sheet with poem title(s), poet's name, address, phone, and email address (poet must have a US address by October of contest year to enter). Mark "Contest Entry" on submission envelope and cover sheet if submitting by mail. Include SASE for results only; manuscripts will not be returned. Deadline: April 30. Prizes: 1st Place: $2,000 and publication; 2nd Place: $1,000 and publication. Judged by the *Nimrod* editors (finalists). A recognized author selects the winners.

THE NEW ISSUES POETRY PRIZE

New Issues Poetry & Prose, New Issues Poetry & Prose, Department of English, Western Michigan University, 1903 W. Michigan Ave., Kalamazoo MI 49008-5463. **E-mail:** new-issues@wmich.edu. **Website:** www.newissuespress.com. Offered annually for publication of a first book of poems by a poet writing in English who has not previously published a full-length collection of poems in an edition of 500 or more copies. *New Issues Poetry & Prose* obtains rights for first publication. Book is copyrighted in author's name. Guidelines for SASE or online. Additional mss will be considered from those submitted to the competition for publication. Considers simultaneous submissions, but *New Issues* must be notified of acceptance elsewhere. Submit ms of at least 40 pages, typed, single-spaced preferred. Clean photocopies acceptable. Do not bind. Include cover page with poet's name, address, phone number, and title of the ms. Also include brief bio and acknowledgments page. Submissions are also welcome through the online submission manager: www.newissuespoetryprose.submittable.com. For hardcopy submissions only, you may include a SASE for results only; no mss will be returned. Winning manuscript will be named in May and published the following fall. Deadline: December 30. Prize: $1,000, publication of a book of poems, reading w/ $500 stipend + travel costs. A national judge selects the prize winner and recommends other mss. The editors decide on the other books considering the judge's recommendation, but are not bound by it. 2018 judge: Cathy Park Hong.

NEW LETTERS PRIZE FOR POETRY

New Letters Awards for Writers, UMKC, University House, 5101 Rockhill Rd., Kansas City MO 64110-2499. (816)235-1168. **E-mail:** newletters@umkc.edu. **Website:** www.newletters.org. **Contact:** Ashley Wann. The annual *New Letters* Poetry Prize awards $1,500 and publication in *New Letters* (see separate listing in Magazines/Journals) to the best group of 3-6 poems. All entries will be considered for publication in *New Letters*. Submissions must be unpublished. Considers simultaneous submissions with notification upon acceptance elsewhere. Accepts multiple entries with separate fee for each. Submit up to 6 poems (need not be related). Include 2 cover sheets: 1 with poet's name, address, e-mail, phone number, prize category (poetry), and poem title(s); the second with category and poem title(s) only. No identifying information on ms pages. Accepts electronic submissions. Include SASE for notification of receipt of ms and entry number, and SASE for results only (send only 1 envelope if submitting multiple entries); mss will not be returned. Guidelines available by SASE or on website. Current students and employees of the University of Missouri-Kansas City, and current volunteer members of the *New Letters* and BkMk Press staffs, are not eligible. Deadline: May 20 (postmarked). $1,500 and publication.

NFSPS POETRY CONVENTION MADNESS CONTEST

Peter Stein, PO Box 17344, Minneapolis MN 55417. **E-mail:** pwilliamstein@yahoo.com; schambersmediator@yahoo.com. **Website:** www.mnpoets.com. **Contact:** Peter Stein; Sue Chambers. Enter to win your way to the NFSPS National Poetry Convention in Chaska, MN, June 9th-13th. For more details about the event, visit www.nfspsconvention.com. Must be original work of the contestant. Deadline: January 31. Prizes: 1st Place: Hotel Lodging at Oak Ridge Convention Center for 4 nights, June 9th-12th. 2nd Place: Meals payed for during the course of the convention. 3rd Place: Registration to the Convention. 1st-3rd Honorable Mentions: Subscription to Poem by Post for one year.

THE NIGHTBOAT POETRY PRIZE

Nightboat Books, 310 Nassau Avenue, Brooklyn NY 11222. **E-mail:** info@nightboat.org. **Website:** www.nightboat.org. **Contact:** Stephen Motika. Annual contest for previously unpublished collection of poetry (48-90 pages). Deadline: November 15. 1st place: $1,000, plus publication and 25 copies of published book.

OHIO POETRY DAY CONTESTS

Dept. of English, Heidelberg College, 310 East Market, Tiffin OH 44883. **Website:** ohiopoetryday.blogspot.com. **Contact:** Bill Reyer, Contest Chair. Several poetry categories open to poets from Ohio and out-of-state. Deadline: May 15. Prizes range $5-100.

GUY OWEN AWARD

Southern Poetry Review, Department of Languages, Literature, and Philosophy, Armstrong Atlantic State University, 11935 Abercorn St., Savannah GA 31419-1997. (912)344-3196. **E-mail:** editor@southernpoetryreview.org. **Website:** www.southernpoetryreview.org. **Contact:** Tony Morris, associate editor. The annual Guy Owen Prize offers $1,000 and publication in *Southern Poetry Review* to the winning poem selected by a distinguished poet. All entries will be considered for publication. Submissions must be unpublished. "We consider work published online or posted there as previously published." Considers simultaneous submissions if indicated as such. Submit 3-5 poems (10 pages maximum). Include cover sheet with poet's name and contact information; no identifying information on ms pages. No e-mail or disk submissions. Include SASE for results only; mss will not be returned. Guidelines available in magazine, for SASE, by e-mail, or on website. Deadline: May 31 (postmarked). Open to submissions March 1.

PANGAEA PRIZE

The Poet's Billow, 6135 Avon St, Portage MI 49024. **E-mail:** thepoetsbillow@gmail.com. **Website:** http://thepoetsbillow.org. **Contact:** Robert Evory. Annual award open to any writer to recognize the best series of poems, ranging between two and up to seven poems in a group. Finalists with strong work will also be published. Submissions must be previously unpublished. Please submit online. Deadline: May 1. Prize: $100. The winning poem will be published and displayed in The Poet's Billow Literary Art Gallery and nominated for a Pushcart Prize. If the poet qualifies, the poem will also be submitted to The Best New Poets anthology. Judged by the editors, and, occasionally, a guest judge.

THE PATERSON POETRY PRIZE

The Poetry Center at Passaic County Community College, One College Blvd., Paterson NJ 07505. (973)684-6555. **Fax:** (973)523-6085. **E-mail:** mgillan@pccc.edu. **Website:** www.pccc.edu/poetry. **Contact:** Maria Mazziotti Gillan, executive director. The Paterson Poetry Prize offers an annual award for the strongest book of poems (48 or more pages) published in the previous year. The winner will be asked to participate in an awards ceremony and to give a reading at The Poetry Center. Minimum press run: 500 copies. Publishers may submit more than 1 title for prize consideration; 3 copies of each book must be submitted. Include SASE for results; books will not be returned (all entries will be donated to The Poetry Center Library). Guidelines and application form (required) available for SASE or on website. Deadline: February 1. Prize: $1,000.

PAVEMENT SAW PRESS CHAPBOOK AWARD

321 Empire St., Montpelier OH 43543-1301. **E-mail:** info@pavementsaw.org. **E-mail:** editor@pavementsaw.org. **Website:** www.pavementsaw.org. **Contact:** David Baratier, editor. Pavement Saw Press has been publishing steadily since the fall of 1993. Each year since 1999, they have published at least 4 full-length paperback poetry collections, with some printed in library edition hard covers, 1 chapbook, and a yearly literary journal anthology. They specialize in finding authors who have been widely published in literary journals but have not published a chapbook or full-length book. Submit up to 32 pages of poetry. Include signed cover letter with poet's name, address, phone

number, e-mail, publication credits, a brief biography, and ms title. Also include 2 cover sheets: 1 with poet's contact information and ms title, 1 with the ms title only. Do not put name on mss pages except for first title page. No mss will be returned. Deadline: December 31 (postmark). Prize: Chapbook Award offers $500, publication, and 40 author copies.

JEAN PEDRICK PRIZE

New England Poetry Club, 2 Farrar St., Cambridge MA 02138. **E-mail:** contests@nepoetryclub.org. **Website:** www.nepoetryclub.org. **Contact:** Audrey Kalajin. Prize for a chapbook of poems published in the last two years. Send 2 copies of the chapbook. Deadline: May 31. Prize: $100. Judged by well-known poets and sometimes winners of previous NEPC contests.

PEN/JOYCE OSTERWEIL AWARD FOR POETRY

PEN America, 588 Broadway, Suite 303, New York NY 10012. **E-mail:** awards@pen.org. **Website:** www.pen.org/awards. **Contact:** Arielle Anema, Literary Awards Coordinator. *Candidates may only be nominated by members of PEN.* This award recognizes the high literary character of the published work to date of a new and emerging American poet of any age, and the promise of further literary achievement. Nominated writer may not have published more than 1 book of poetry. Offered in odd-numbered years and alternates with the PEN/Voelcker Award for Poetry. Electronic letters of nomination will be requested during open submissions season. Submissions will be accepted during the summer of even-numbered year. Visit PEN.org/awards for up-to-date information on deadlines. Prize: $5,000. Judged by a panel of 3 judges selected by the PEN Awards Committee.

PENNSYLVANIA POETRY SOCIETY ANNUAL CONTESTS

5 Coachmans Court, Norwalk CT 06850. **Website:** nfsps.com/pa. **Contact:** Colleen Yarusavage. Pennsylvania Poetry Society offers several categories of poetry contests with a range of prizes from $10-100. Deadline: January 15.

PEN/VOELCKER AWARD FOR POETRY

PEN America, 588 Broadway, Suite 303, New York NY 10012. **E-mail:** awards@pen.org. **Website:** www.pen.org/awards. **Contact:** Arielle Anema, Literary Awards Coordinator. The PEN/Voelcker Award for Poetry, established by a bequest from Hunce Voelcker, this award is given to a poet whose distinguished and growing body of work to date represents a notable and accomplished presence in American literature. The poet honored by the award is one for whom the exceptional promise seen in earlier work has been fulfilled, and who continues to mature with each successive volume of poetry. The award is given in even-numbered years and carries a stipend of $5,000. Please note that submissions will only be accepted from Professional Members of PEN and that it is understood that all nominations made for the PEN/Voelcker Award supplement internal nominations made by the panel of judges. PEN Members are asked to submit a letter of nomination through an online submissions form. Deadline: Nominations from PEN Members will be accepted during the summer of each odd-numbered year. Visit PEN.org/awards for up-to-date information on deadlines. Prize: $5,000. Judged by a panel of 3 poets or other writers chosen by the PEN Literary Awards Committee.

PERUGIA PRESS PRIZE

Perugia Press, P.O. Box 60364, Florence MA 01062. **Website:** www.perugiapress.com. **Contact:** Susan Kan. Submissions must be unpublished as a collection, but individual poems may have been previously published in journals, chapbooks, and anthologies. Considers simultaneous submissions if notified of acceptance elsewhere. Follow online guidelines carefully. Electronic submissions available through website. No translations or self-published books. Multiple submissions accepted if accompanied by separate entry fee for each. Use USPS or electronic submission, not FedEx or UPS. Winner announced by April 1 by e-mail or SASE (if included with entry). The Perugia Press Prize is for a first or second poetry book by a woman. Poet must have no more than 1 previously published book of poems (chapbooks don't count). Deadline: November 15. Open to submissions on August 1. Prize: $1,000 and publication. Judged by panel of Perugia authors, booksellers, scholars, etc.

THE PLEIADES PRESS EDITORS PRIZE FOR POETRY

Pleiades Press, Pleiades Press, Dept of English, Martin 336, University of Central Missouri, Warrensburg MO 64093. (660)543-8106. **E-mail:** pleiades@ucmo.edu. **Website:** www.ucmo.edu/pleiades/. The annual Pleiades Press Editors Prize for Poetry is open to all American writers, regardless of previous publication. Submission must be unpublished as a collection, but individual poems may have been previously published elsewhere. Submit at least 48 pages of poetry (one copy). Include 2 cover sheets: one with ms title, poet's name, address, and phone number; the second with ms title only. Also include acknowledgments page for previously published poems. Guidelines online. Deadline: May 11. Prize: $2,000 and the winning collection will be published in paperback and nationally distributed.

THE POETRY CENTER BOOK AWARD

The Poetry Center, San Francisco State University, 1600 Holloway Ave., San Francisco CA 94132. (415)338-2227. **Fax:** (415)338-0966. **E-mail:** poetry@sfsu.edu. **Website:** www.sfsu.edu/~poetry. Offered annually for books of poetry and chapbooks, published in year of the prize. "Prize given for an extraordinary book of American poetry written in English." Please include a cover letter noting author name, book title(s), name of person issuing check, and check number. Will not consider anthologies or translations. Deadline: January 31 for books published and copywrited in the previous year. 1st place: $500 and an invitation to read in the Poetry Center Reading Series.

POETRY SOCIETY OF AMERICA AWARDS

15 Gramercy Park, New York NY 10003. **E-mail:** psa@poetrysociety.org. **Website:** www.poetrysociety.org. Offers 7 categories of poetry prizes between $250-2,500. 5 categories are open to PSA members only. Free entry for members; $15 for non-members. Submit between October 1-December 22.

POETS & PATRONS ANNUAL CHICAGOLAND POETRY CONTEST

Sponsored by Poets & Patrons of Chicago, 416 Gierz St., Downers Grove IL 60515. **E-mail:** eatonb1016@aol.com. **Website:** www.poetsandpatrons.net. **Contact:** Barbara Eaton, director. Annual contest for unpublished poetry. Guidelines available for self-addressed, stamped envelope. The purpose of the contest is to encourage the crafting of poetry. Deadline: September 1. Prize: 1st Place: $45; 2nd Place: $20; 3rd Place: $10 cash. Poet retains rights. Judged by out-of-state professionals.

POETS OUT LOUD PRIZE

Poets Out Loud, Fordham University at Lincoln Center, 113 W. 60th St., Room 924-I, New York NY 10023. (212)636-6792. **Fax:** (212)636-7153. **E-mail:** pol@fordham.edu. **Website:** www.fordham.edu/pol. Annual competition for an unpublished, full-length poetry ms (50-80 pages). Deadline: November 1. Prize: $1,000, book publication, and book launch in POL reading series.

FELIX POLLAK PRIZE IN POETRY

University of Wisconsin Press, 1930 Monroe St., 3rd Floor, Madison WI 53711. (608)263-1110. **Fax:** (608)263-1120. **E-mail:** uwiscpress@wisc.edu. **Website:** uwpress.wisc.edu. The Felix Pollak Prize in Poetry is awarded annually to the best book-length ms of original poetry submitted in an open competition. The award is administered by the University of Wisconsin–Madison English department, and the winner is chosen by a nationally recognized poet. The resulting book is published by the University of Wisconsin Press. Submissions must be unpublished as a collection, but individual poems may have been published elsewhere (publication must be acknowledged). Considers simultaneous submissions if notified of selection elsewhere. Submit 50-80 unbound ms pages, typed single-spaced (with double spaces between stanzas). Clean photocopies are acceptable. Include 1 title page with poet's name, address, and telephone number; 1 title page with title only. No translations. Complete guidelines available online. Deadline: September 15. Prize: $1,000 cash prize, plus publication.

A. POULIN, JR. POETRY PRIZE

BOA Editions, Ltd., 250 Goodman St. N., Suite 306, Rochester NY 14607. **E-mail:** contact@boaeditions.org. **Website:** www.boaeditions.org. The A. Poulin, Jr. Poetry Prize is awarded to honor a poet's first book, while also honoring the late founder of BOA Editions, Ltd., a not-for-profit publishing house of poetry, poetry in translation, and short fiction. Published books in other genres do not disqualify contestants from entering this contest. Entrants must be a citizen or legal resident of the US. Poets who are at least 18 years of age, and who have yet to publish a full-length book collection of poetry, are eligible. Translations are not eligible. Individual poems may have been previously published in magazines, journals, anthologies, chapbooks of 32 pages or less, or self-published books of 46 pages or less, but must be submitted in ms form. Submit 48-100 pages of poetry, paginated consecutively, typed or computer-generated in 11 point font. Bind physical manuscripts with spring clip (no paperclips) and postmark by November 30. Include cover/title page with poet's name, address, telephone number, and e-mail address. Also include the table of contents, list of acknowledgments, and entry form (available for download on website). Multiple entries accepted with separate entry fee for each. Electronic submissions accepted via Submittable. Deadline: November 30. Open to submissions on August 1. Prize: Awards $1,000 honorarium and book publication in the A. Poulin, Jr. New Poets of America Series.

PRESS 53 AWARD FOR POETRY

Press 53, 560 N. Trade St., Suite 103, Winston-Salem NC 27101. (336)770-5353. **E-mail:** kevin@press53.com. **Website:** www.press53.com. **Contact:** Kevin Morgan Watson, publisher. Awarded to an outstanding, unpublished collection of poetry. Details and guidelines available online. Deadline: July 31. Submission period begins April 1. Winner and finalists announced on by November 1. Publication in April. Prize: Publication of winning poetry collection as a Tom Lombardo Poetry Selection, $1,000 cash advance and 50 copies of the book. Judged by Press 53 poetry series editor Tom Lombardo.

THE PSA NATIONAL CHAPBOOK FELLOWSHIPS

Poetry Society of America, 15 Gramercy Park, New York NY 10003. (212)254-9628. **Fax:** (212)673-2352. **Website:** www.poetrysociety.org. Open to any US citizen or anyone currently living within the US who has not published a full-length poetry collection. Charges $12 entry fee. Winner receives $1,000 and welcomed as guest for a month-long artist's residency at PLAYA and invited to teach a single class at Purchase College for $1,000 under the sponsorshp of the Royal and Shirley Durst Chair in Literature. Deadline: December 22.

RATTLE POETRY PRIZE

Rattle, 12411 Ventura Blvd., Studio City CA 91604. (818)505-6777. **E-mail:** tim@rattle.com. **Website:** www.rattle.com. **Contact:** Timothy Green, Editor. *Rattle*'s mission is to promote the practice of poetry. To enter, purchase a one-year subscription to *Rattle* at the regular $25 rate. Open to writers, worldwide; poems must be written in English. No previously published works or works accepted for publication elsewhere. No simultaneous submissions are allowed. Send up to 4 poems per entry. "More than anything, our goal is to promote a community of active poets." Deadline: July 15. Prize: One $10,000 winner and ten $200 finalists will be selected in a blind review by the editors of *Rattle* and printed in the Winter issue; one $1,000 Readers' Choice Award will then be chosen from among the finalists by subscriber and entrant vote. Judged by the editors of *Rattle*.

RHINO FOUNDERS' PRIZE

RHINO, The Poetry Forum, P.O. Box 591, Evanston IL 60204. **E-mail:** editors@rhinopoetry.org. **Website:** rhinopoetry.org. **Contact:** Editors. Send best unpublished poetry (3-5 pages). Visit website for previous winners and more information. Submit online or by mail. Include a cover letter listing your name, address, e-mail, and/or telephone number, titles of poems, how you learned about RHINO, and fee. Mss will not be returned. Deadline: October 31. Open to submissions on September 1. Prize: $500, publication, featured on website, and nominated for a Pushcart Prize. Two runners-ups will receive $50, publication, and will be featured on website. Occasionally nominates runner-up for a Pushcart Prize.

ROANOKE-CHOWAN POETRY AWARD

The North Carolina Literary & Historical Assoc., 4610 Mail Service Center, Raleigh NC 27699-4610. (919)807-7290. **Fax:** (919)733-8807. **E-mail:** michael.hill@ncdcr.gov. **Website:** litandhist.ncdcr.gov. **Contact:** Michael Hill, awards coordinator. Offers annual award for an original volume of poetry published during the 12 months ending June 30 of the year for which the award is given. Open to authors who have maintained legal or physical residence, or a combination of both, in North Carolina for the 3 years preceding the close of the contest period. Submit 3 copies of each entry. Guidelines available for SASE or by fax or e-mail. Winner announced October 15. Deadline: July 15.

LORI RUDNITSKY FIRST BOOK PRIZE

Persea Books, P.O. Box 1388, Columbia MO 65205. **Website:** www.perseabooks.com. "This annual competition sponsors the publication of a poetry collection (at least 40 pages) by an American woman poet who has yet to publish a full-length book of poems." Deadline: October 31. Prize: $1,000, plus publication of book. In addition, the winner receives the option of an all-expenses-paid residency at the Civitella Ranieri Center, a renowned artists retreat housed in a 15th-century castle in Umbertide, Italy.

BENJAMIN SALTMAN POETRY AWARD

Red Hen Press, P.O. Box 40820, Pasadena CA 91114. (818)831-0649. **Fax:** (818)831-6659. **E-mail:** productioncoordinator@redhen.org. **Website:** www.redhen.org. Offered annually for unpublished work to publish a winning book of poetry. Open to any writer. Name on cover sheet only, 48 page minimum. Send SASE for notification. Deadline: August 31. 1st place: $3,000 and publication.

MAY SARTON AWARD

New England Poetry Club, 654 Green St., No. 2, Cambridge MA 02139. (617)744-6034. **E-mail:** contests@nepoetryclub.org. **Website:** www.nepoetryclub.org. **Contact:** NEPC contest coordinator. "Given intermittently to a poet whose work is an inspiration to other poets. Recipients are chosen by the board." "Contest open to members and nonmembers. Poems should be typed and submitted in duplicate with author's name, address, phone, and e-mail address of writer on only 1 copy. (Judges receive copies without names.) Copy only. Label poems with contest name. Entries should be sent by regular mail only. Special delivery or signature required mail will be returned by the post office. Entries should be original, unpublished poems in English. No poem should be entered in more than 1 contest, nor have won a previous contest. No entries will be returned. NEPC will not engage in correspondence regarding poems or contest decisions." To recognize emerging poets of exceptional promise and distinguished achievement. Established to honor the memory of longtime Academy Fellow May Sarton, a poet, novelist, and teacher who during her career encouraged the work of young poets. Deadline: May 31. Prize: $250. Judges are well-known poets and sometimes winners of previous NEPC contests.

SCREAMINMAMAS MOTHER'S DAY POETRY CONTEST

1911 Cleveland St., Hollywood FL 33020. **E-mail:** screaminmamas@gmail.com. **Website:** www.screaminmamas.com/contests. **Contact:** Darlene Pistocchi, editor/managing director. "What does it mean to be a mom? There is so much to being a mom—get deep, get creative! We challenge you to explore different types of poetry: descriptive, reflective, narrative, lyric, sonnet, ballad, limerick. you can even go epic!" Open only to moms. Deadline: December 31. Prize: Publication.

SLAPERING HOL PRESS CHAPBOOK COMPETITION

The Hudson Valley Writers' Center, 300 Riverside Dr., Sleepy Hollow NY 10591. (914)332-5953. **E-mail:** info@writerscenter.org. **Website:** www.writerscenter.org. **Contact:** Margo Stever, editor. The annual competition is open to poets who have not published a book or chapbook, though individual poems may have already appeared. Manuscripts may be either a collection of poems or one long poem and should be a minimum of 16 pages and a maximum of 20 pages (not including the title page or table of contents). Purpose is to provide publishing opportunities for emerging poets. Deadline: June 15. The winner receives a $500 cash award, publication, ten copies, a reading at the Hudson Valley Writers Center, plus travel expenses up to $500 if needed. Winning poets are also offered editorial and marketing advice.

SLIPSTREAM ANNUAL POETRY CHAPBOOK CONTEST

Slipstream, Slipstream Poetry Contest, Dept. W-1, P.O. Box 2071, Niagara Falls NY 14301. **E-mail:** editors@slipstreampress.org. **Website:** www.slipstreampress.org. **Contact:** Dan Sicoli, co-editor. *Slipstream Magazine* is a yearly anthology of some of the best poetry you'll find today in the American small press. Send up to 40 pages of poetry: any style, format, or theme (or no theme). Send only copies of your poems, not originals. Manuscripts will no longer be returned. See website for specific details. Offered annually to help promote a poet whose work is often overlooked or ignored. Open to any writer. Deadline: December 1. Prize: $1,000, plus 50 professionally-printed copies of your book.

HELEN C. SMITH MEMORIAL AWARD FOR BEST BOOK OF POETRY

The Texas Institute of Letters, P.O. Box 609, Round Rock TX 78680. **E-mail:** tilsecretary@yahoo.com. **Website:** http://texasinstituteofletters.org/. Offered annually for the best book of poems published January 1-December 31 of previous year. Poet must have been born in Texas, have lived in the state at some time for at least 2 consecutive years, or the subject matter must be associated with the state. See website for submission details and information. Deadline: January 10. Prize: $1,200.

THE RICHARD SNYDER MEMORIAL PUBLICATION PRIZE

Ashland Poetry Press, 401 College Ave., Ashland University, Ashland OH 44805. **E-mail:** app@ashland.edu. **Website:** www.ashlandpoetrypress.com. **Contact:** Cassandra Brown, managing editor. Submissions must be unpublished in book form. Considers simultaneous submissions. Submit 50-96 pages of poetry. Competition receives 400+ entries/year. Winners will be announced in *Writer's Chronicle* and *Poets & Writers*. Copies of winning books available from Small Press Distribution and directly from the Ashland University Bookstore online. The Ashland Poetry Press publishes 2-4 books of poetry/year. Deadline: April 1. Prize: $1,000 plus book publication. Judged by Elizabeth Spires in 2016.

SOCIETY OF CLASSICAL POETS POETRY COMPETITION

The Society of Classical Poets, 11 Heather Ln., Mount Hope NY 10940. **E-mail:** submissions@classicalpoets.org. **Website:** www.classicalpoets.org. **Contact:** Evan Mantyk, president. Annual competition for a group of poems that address one or more of the following themes: exposing the negative effects of socialism and communism on the West, raising awareness about human rights abuses in China, or celebrating the beauty of classical arts. Poems must incorporate meter and rhyme. All entries are considered for publication. Submit 1-3 poems. The poems should not total more than 50 lines. Deadline: December 31. Prize: $1,000. Judged by Evan Mantyk, the society's president.

THE SOW'S EAR CHAPBOOK COMPETITION

The Sow's Ear Review, 1748 Cave Ridge Rd., Mount Jackson VA 22842. **E-mail:** sepoetryreview@gmail.com. **Website:** www.sowsearpoetry.org. **Contact:** Sarah Kohrs, managing editor. *The Sow's Ear Poetry Review* sponsors an annual chapbook competition. Open to adults. Open to adults. Send 22-26 pages of poetry plus a title page and a table of contents, all without your name. On a separate sheet list chapbook title, your name, address, phone number, e-mail address if available, and publication credits for submitted poems, if any. No length limit on poems, but no more than one poem on a page. Simultaneous submission is allowed, but if your chapbook is accepted elsewhere, you must withdraw promptly from our competition. Poems previously published are acceptable if you hold publication rights. Send SASE or e-mail address for notification. Entries will not be returned. To submit online, visit our website. Deadline: May 1 (postmark). Prize: Offers $1,000, publication as the spring issue of the magazine, 25 author's copies, and distribution to subscribers.

THE SOW'S EAR POETRY COMPETITION

The Sow's Ear Poetry Review, 1748 Cave Ridge Rd., Mount Jackson VA 22842. **E-mail:** sepoetryreview@gmail.com. **Website:** www.sowsearpoetry.org. **Contact:** Sarah Kohrs, managing editor. Open to adults. Send unpublished poems to the address above. Please do not put your name on poems. Include a separate sheet with poem titles, name, address, phone, and e-mail address if available, or a SASE for notification of results. No length limit on poems. Simultaneous submission acceptable (checks with finalists before sending to final judge). Send poems in September or October. Deadline: November 1. Prize: $1,000, publication, and the option of publication for approximately 20 finalists.

THE EDWARD STANLEY AWARD

Prairie Schooner, 110 Andrews Hall, P.O. Box 880334, Lincoln NE 68588-0334. (402)472-0911. **Fax:** (402)472-9771. **E-mail:** prairieschooner@unl.edu. **Website:** www.prairieschooner.unl.edu. **Contact:** Ashley Strosnider. Offered annually for poetry published in *Prairie Schooner* in the previous year. Prize: $1,000. Editorial staff

STEVENS POETRY MANUSCRIPT CONTEST

NFSPS Stevens Poetry Manuscript Competition, 4 Bowie Pt, Sherwood AR 72120. **E-mail:** stevens.nfsps@gmail.com. **Website:** www.nfsps.org. **Contact:** Amanda Partridge, chair. National Federation of State Poetry Societies (NFSPS) offers annual award of $1,000, publication of ms, and 50 author's copies for the winning poetry manuscript by a single author. Submit 48-70 pages of poetry by a single author, typewritten, or computer printed. No illustrations. No author identification in the manuscript. No more than one poem per page. May include previously published poems (acknowledgements on separate sheet). Simultaneous and multiple submissions permitted. Deadline: Fall, varies from year to year. For 2018, probably September 15; Submissions open August 15. Prize: $1,000, publication and 50 copies of the book.

THE RUTH STONE POETRY PRIZE

Vermont College of Fine Arts, 36 College St., Montpelier VT 05602. (802)828-8517. **E-mail:** hungermtn@vcfa.edu. **Website:** www.hungermtn.org. **Contact:** Cameron Finch, managing editor. The Ruth Stone Poetry Prize is an annual poetry contest. Enter up to 3 original, unpublished poems. Do not include name or address on submissions; entries are read blind.

Accepts submissions online. Deadline: March 1. Prize: One first place winner receives $1,000 and publication on Hunger Mountain online. One runner-up receives $100 and online publication. Other finalists considered for print publication.

THE ELIZABETH MATCHETT STOVER MEMORIAL AWARD

Southwest Review, Southern Methodist University, P.O. Box 750374, Dallas TX 75275-0374. (214)768-1037. **Fax:** (214)768-1408. **E-mail:** swr@mail.smu.edu. **Website:** www.smu.edu/southwestreview. **Contact:** Greg Brownderville, editor-in-chief. Offered annually to the best works of poetry that have appeared in the magazine in the previous year. Please note that mss are submitted for publication, not for the prizes themselves. Guidelines for SASE and online. Prize: $300. Judged by Greg Brownderville.

STROKESTOWN INTERNATIONAL POETRY COMPETITION

Strokestown International Poetry Festival, Strokestown Poetry Festival Office, Strokestown, County Roscommon Ireland. (+353) 71 9633759. **E-mail:** director@strokestownpoetry.org. **Website:** www.strokestownpoetry.org. **Contact:** Martin Dyar, Director. Poem cannot exceed 70 lines. Ten short-listed poets will be invited to Strokestown for the festival. This annual competition was established to promote excellence in poetry and participation in the reading and writing of it. Acquires first publication rights. Deadline: January. Prize: 1st Place: €1,500; 2nd Place: €500; 3rd Place: €300; 3 shortlisted prizes of €100 each.

THE TAMPA REVIEW PRIZE FOR POETRY

University of Tampa, 401 W. Kennedy Blvd., Tampa FL 33606. 813-253-6266. **E-mail:** utpress@ut.edu. **Website:** www.ut.edu/tampareview. Annual award for the best previously unpublished collection of poetry (at least 48 pages, though preferably 60-100). Deadline: December 31. Prize: $2,000, plus publication.

THE TENTH GATE PRIZE

The Word Works, P. O. Box 42164, Washington D.C. 20015 USA. **E-mail:** editor@wordworksbooks.org. **Website:** www.wordworksbooks.org. **Contact:** Leslie McGrath, Series Editor; Nancy White, Editor. Publication and $1000 cash prize awarded annually by The Word Works to a full-length ms by a poet who has already published at least 2 full-length poetry collections. Submit 48-80 pages. Include acknowledgments and past book publications in the "NOTES" section of the online submissions manager. Submit via online submissions manager: wordworksbooks.org/submissions. Founded in honor of Jane Hirshfield, The Tenth Gate Prize supports the work of mid-career poets. Deadline: July 15. Open to submissions on June 1. Prize: $1,000 and publication. Judged by the editors.

TOR HOUSE PRIZE FOR POETRY

Robinson Jeffers Tor House Foundation, Poetry Prize Coordinator, Tor House Foundation, Box 223240, Carmel CA 93922. (831)624-1813. **Fax:** (831)624-3696. **E-mail:** thf@torhouse.org. **Website:** www.torhouse.org. **Contact:** Eliot Ruchowitz-Roberts, Poetry Prize Coordinator. The annual Prize for Poetry is a living memorial to American poet Robinson Jeffers (1887-1962). Open to well-crafted poetry in all styles, ranging from experimental work to traditional forms, including short narrative poems. Poems must be original and unpublished. Each poem should be typed on 8 1/2" by 11" paper, and no longer than three pages. On a cover sheet only, include: name, mailing address, telephone number and email; titles of poems; bio optional. Multiple and simultaneous submissions welcome. Deadline: March 15. Prize: $1,000 honorarium for award-winning poem; $200 Honorable Mention.

KINGSLEY & KATE TUFTS POETRY AWARDS

Claremont Graduate University, Claremont Graduate University, 160 E. Tenth St., Harper East B7, Claremont CA 91711-6165. (909)621-8974. **E-mail:** tufts@cgu.edu. **Website:** https://arts.cgu.edu/tufts-poetry-awards/. The annual $100,000 Kingsley Tufts Poetry Award is presented for book published by a mid-career poet; the Award was created to honor the poet and provide the resources to allow the writer to continue working towards the pinnacle of their craft. The $10,000 Kate Tufts Award is presented annually for a first book by a poet of genuine promise. "Any poet will tell you that the only thing more rare than meaningful recognition is a meaningful payday. For two outstanding poets each year, the Kingsley and Kate Tufts awards represent both." Deadline: July 1, for books published in the preceding year. Prize: $100,000 for the Kingsley Tufts Poetry Award and $10,000 for the Kate Tufts Discovery Award. Please see website for current judges.

UTMOST CHRISTIAN POETRY CONTEST

Utmost Christian Writers Foundation, 121 Morin Maze NW, Edmonton AB T6K 1V1 Canada. (780)265-

4650. **E-mail:** nnharms@telusplanet.net. **Website:** www.utmostchristianwriters.com. **Contact:** Nathan Harms, executive director. Utmost is founded on—and supported by—the dreams, interests and aspirations of individual people. Contest is only open to Christians. Poems may be rhymed or free verse, up to 60 lines, but must not have been published previously or have won any prize in any previous competition of any kind. Submit up to 5 poems. Deadline: February 28. Prizes: 1st Place: $1,000; 2nd Place: $500; 10 prizes of $100 are offered for honorable mention; $300 for best rhyming poem; and $200 for an honorable mention rhyming poem. Judged by a committee of the Directors of Utmost Christian Writers Foundation (who work under the direction of Barbara Mitchell, chief judge).

DANIEL VAROUJAN AWARD

New England Poetry Club, 376 School St., Watertown MA 02472. **E-mail:** contests@nepoetryclub.org. **Website:** www.nepoetryclub.org. **Contact:** Audrey Kalajin. For an unpublished poem (not a translation) worthy of Daniel Varoujan, a poet killed by the Turks in the genocide which destroyed three-fourths of the Armenian population. Previous winners may not enter again. Send entry in duplicate, one without name and address of writer. Deadline: May 31. Prize: $1,000. Judged by well-known poets and sometimes winners of previous NEPC contests.

VASSAR MILLER PRIZE IN POETRY

University of North Texas Press, 1155 Union Circle, #311336, Denton TX 76203. (940)565-2142. **Fax:** (940)565-4590. **Website:** http://untpress.unt.edu. **Contact:** John Poch. Annual prize awarded to a collection of poetry. Submit 50-80 pages. In years when the judge is announced, it is asked that students of the judge not enter to avoid a perceived conflict. All entries should contain identifying material only on the one cover sheet. Entries are read anonymously. Deadline: Mss may be submitted between 9 A.M. on September 1 and 5 P.M. on October 31, through online submissions manager only. Prize: $1,000 and publication by University of North Texas Press. Judged by a different eminent writer selected each year. Some prefer to remain anonymous until the end of the contest.

MARICA AND JAN VILCEK PRIZE FOR POETRY

Bellevue Literary Review, New York University School of Medicine, OBV-A612, 550 First Ave., New York NY 10016. (212)263-3973. **E-mail:** info@blreview.org. **Website:** www.blreview.org. **Contact:** Stacy Bodziak. The annual Marica and Jan Vilcek Prize for Poetry recognizes outstanding writing related to themes of health, healing, illness, the mind, and the body. All entries will be considered for publication. No previously published poems (including Internet publication). Submit up to 3 poems (5 pages maximum). Electronic (online) submissions only; combine all poems into 1 document and use first poem as document title. See guidelines for additional submission details. Guidelines available for SASE or on website. Deadline: July 1. Prize: $1,000 for best poem and publication in *Bellevue Literary Review*. Previous judges include Mark Doty, Cornelius Eady, Naomi Shihab Nye, Tony Hoagland, Kazim Ali, and Ada Limon.

WABASH PRIZE FOR POETRY

Sycamore Review, Department of English, 500 Oval Dr., Purdue University, West Lafayette IN 47907. **E-mail:** sycamore@purdue.edu; sycamorepoetry@purdue.edu. **Website:** www.sycamorereview.com/contest/. **Contact:** Anthony Sutton, editor-in-chief. Annual contest for unpublished poetry. For each submission, send up to 3 poems (no more than 6 total pages). Ms pages should be numbered and should include the title of each poem. See website for more guidelines. Submit online via Submittable. Deadline: December 1. Prize: $1,000 and publication.

THE WASHINGTON PRIZE

The Word Works, Dearlove Hall, SUNY Adirondack, 640 Bay Rd., Queensbury NY 12804. **E-mail:** editor@wordworksbooks.org. **Website:** www.wordworksbooks.org. **Contact:** Rebecca Kutzer-Rice, Washington Prize administrator. In addition to its general poetry book publications, The Word Works runs four imprints: The Washington Prize, The Tenth Gate Prize, International Editions, and the Hilary Tham Capital Collection. Selections announced in late summer. Book publication planned for spring of the following year. Submit a poetry ms of 48-80 pages. Submit online with no identifying information appearing within the manuscript; or, if on paper, include 2 title pages, 1 with and 1 without author information, including an acknowledgments page, a table of contents and a brief bio. Electronic submissions are accepted at www.wordworksbooks.org/submissions. The Washington Prize allows poets from all stages of their careers to compete on a level playing field for publication and national recognition. Deadline: Submit January 15-March 15 (postmark). Prize: $1,500 and publication of a book-length ms of original poetry in English by a living US or Canadian citizen. Judged by two tiers of readers, followed by five final judges working as a panel.

WERGLE FLOMP HUMOR POETRY CONTEST

Winning Writers, 351 Pleasant St., PMB 222, Northampton MA 01060. (866)946-9748. **Fax:** (413)280-0539. **E-mail:** adam@winningwriters.com. **Website:** www.winningwriters.com. **Contact:** Adam Cohen. Winning Writers provides expert literary contest information to the public. It is one of the "101 Best Websites for Writers" (*Writer's Digest*). Submit one humor poem online. Length limit: 250 lines. The poem should be in English. Inspired gibberish is also accepted. Submissions may be previously published and may be entered in other contests. Deadline: April 1. Prize: 1st prize of $1,000; 2nd prize of $250; 10 honorable mentions of $100 each. All winners of cash prizes published on website. The winner will also receive a one-year gift certificate from the contest co-sponsor, Duotrope (a $50 value). Judged by Jendi Reiter, assisted by Lauren Singer Ledoux.

WHITE PINE PRESS POETRY PRIZE

White Pine Press, P.O. Box 236, Buffalo NY 14201. **E-mail:** wpine@whitepine.org. **Website:** www.whitepine.org. **Contact:** Dennis Maloney, editor. Offered annually for previously published or unpublished poets. Manuscript: 60-80 pages of original work; translations are not eligible. Poems may have appeared in magazines or limited-edition chapbooks. Open to any US citizen. Deadline: November 30 (postmarked). Prize: $1,000 and publication. Final judge is a poet of national reputation. All entries are screened by the editorial staff of White Pine Press.

STAN AND TOM WICK POETRY PRIZE

Wick Poetry Center, P.O. Box 5190, Kent OH 44240. (330)672-2067. **E-mail:** wickpoetry@kent.edu. **Website:** www.kent.edu/wick/stan-and-tom-wick-poetry-prize. **Contact:** David Hassler, director. Offered annually to a poet who has not previously published a full-length collection of poetry (a volume of 50 or more pages published in an edition of 500 or more copies). Submissions must consist of 50-70 pages of poetry, typed on one side only, with no more than one poem included on a single page. Also accepts submissions online through Submittable. See website for details and guidelines. Deadline: May 1. Submissions period begins February 1. Prize: $2,500 and publication of full-length book of poetry by Kent State University Press.

MILLER WILLIAMS POETRY PRIZE

University of Arkansas Press, McIlroy House, 105 N. McIlroy Ave., Fayetteville AR 72701. (479)575-7258. **E-mail:** cmoss@uark.edu, mbieker@uark.edu. **Website:** https://www.uapress.com/millerwilliamspoetryseries/. **Contact:** Billy Collins, judge and series editor; Mike Bieker, director. Each year, the University of Arkansas Press accepts submissions for the Miller Williams Poetry Series and from the books selected awards the Miller Williams Poetry Prize in the following summer. Mss should be between 60-90 pages. Individual poems may have been published in chapbooks, journals, and anthologies. Guidelines available online. Submit online. Deadline: September 30. Accepts submissions all year long. Prize: $5,000 and publication. One finalist will also receive publication. Judged by Billy Collins, series editor.

THE J. HOWARD AND BARBARA M.J. WOOD PRIZE

Poetry, 61 W. Superior St., Chicago IL 60654. (312)787-7070. **Fax:** (312)787-6650. **E-mail:** editors@poetrymagazine.org. **Website:** www.poetrymagazine.org. Offered annually for poems published in *Poetry* during the preceding year (October-September). Upon acceptance, *Poetry* licenses exclusive worldwide first serial rights, including electronic rights, for publication, as well as non-exclusive rights to reprint, reuse, and archive the work, in any format, in perpetuity. Copyright reverts to author upon first publication. Prize: $5,000.

WORKING PEOPLE'S POETRY COMPETITION

Partisan Press, Blue Collar Review, P.O. Box 11417, Norfolk VA 23517. **E-mail:** red-ink@earthlink.net. **Website:** www.partisanpress.org. Poetry should be typed as you would like to see it published, with your name and address on each page. Include cover letter with entry. Guidelines online. Deadline: May 15. Prize: $100, 1-year subscription to *Blue Collar Review* and 1-year posting of winning poem to website. Judged by editorial committee.

JAMES WRIGHT POETRY AWARD

Mid-American Review, Dept. of English, Bowling Green State University, Bowling Green OH

43403. (419)372-2725. **Fax:** (419)372-4642. **E-mail:** clouda@bgsu.edu. **Website:** www.bgsu.edu/midamericanreview. **Contact:** Abigail Cloud, poetry editor. Offered annually for unpublished poetry. Open to all writers not associated with *Mid-American Review* or judge. Guidelines available online or for SASE. Deadline: November 1. Prize: $1,000 and publication in spring issue of *Mid-American Review.* Judged by editors and a well known poet, i.e., Kathy Fagan, Bob Hicok, Michelle Boisseau. Judged by Maggie Smith in 2016.

THE YALE SERIES OF YOUNGER POETS

Yale University Press, P.O. Box 209040, New Haven CT 06520-9040. **Website:** youngerpoets.yupnet.org. The Yale Series of Younger Poets champions the most promising new American poets. The Yale Younger Poets prize is the oldest annual literary award in the United States. Open to U.S. citizens under age 40 at the time of entry who have not published a volume of poetry; poets may have published a limited edition chapbook of 300 copies or less. Poems may have been previously published in newspapers and periodicals and used in the book ms if so identified. No translations. Submit 48-64 pages of poetry, paginated, with each new poem starting on a new page. Accepts hard copy and electronic submissions. Deadline: November 15. Submissions period begins October 1.

ZONE 3 FIRST BOOK AWARD FOR POETRY

Zone 3, Austin Peay State University, Austin Peay State University, PO Box 4565, Clarksville TN 37044. (931)221-7031. **Fax:** (931)221-7149. **E-mail:** spofforda@aspu.edu; wallacess@apsu.edu. **Website:** www.apsu.edu/zone3/. **Contact:** Andrea Spofford, poetry editor; Susan Wallace, managing editor. Offered annually for anyone who has not published a full-length collection of poems (48 pages or more). Submit a ms of 48-80 pages. Deadline: May 1. Prize: $1,000 and publication.

GIVAL PRESS OSCAR WILDE AWARD

Gival Press, LLC, Gival Press Oscar Wilde Award, Gival Press LLC, P.O. Box 3812, Arlington VA 22203. (703)351-0079. **E-mail:** givalpress@yahoo.com. **Website:** www.givalpress.com. **Contact:** Robert L. Giron, Editor. Award given to the best previously unpublished original poem—written in English, of any length, in any style, typed, double-spaced on 1 side only—that best relates gay/lesbian/bisexual/transgendered (GLBTQ) life, by a poet who is 18 years or older. Enter via portal: www.givalpress.submittable.com. Entrants are asked to submit their poems without any kind of identification (with the exception of titles) and with a separate cover page with the following information: name, address (street, city, and state with zip code), telephone number, e-mail address (if available), and a list of poems by title. Checks drawn on American banks should be made out to Gival Press, LLC. May submit via portal: www.givalpress.submittable.com. Deadline: June 27 (postmarked). Prize: $100; the poem, along with information about the poet, will be published on the Gival Press website. Judged by the previous winner, who reads the poems anonymously.

MULTIPLE WRITING AREAS

AESTHETICA ART PRIZE

Aesthetica Magazine, P.O. Box 371, York YO23 1WL United Kingdom. (+44)1904 629 137. **E-mail:** info@aestheticamagazine.com; artprize@aestheticamagazine.com. **Website:** www.aestheticamagazine.com. The Aesthetica Art Prize is a celebration of excellence in art from across the world and offers artists the opportunity to showcase their work to wider audiences and further their involvement in the international art world. There are 4 categories: Photograpic & Digital Art, Three Dimensional Design & Sculpture, Painting & Drawing, Video Installation & Performance. See guidelines at Artwork & Photography, Fiction, and Poetry. See guidelines at www.aestheticamagazine.com. The Aesthetica Art Prize is a celebration of excellence in art from across the world, and offers artists the opportunity to showcase their work to wider audiences and further their involvement in the international art world. Deadline: August 31. Prizes include: £5,000 main prize courtesy of Hiscox; £1,000 Student Prize courtesy of Hiscox; group exhibition and publication in the Aesthetica Art Prize Anthology. Entry fee is £24 and permits submission of 2 works in one category. The panel comprises influential art figures; including curators, academics and artists whose expertise spans all media.

ALCUIN SOCIETY AWARDS FOR EXCELLENCE IN BOOK DESIGN IN CANADA

The Alcuin Society, P.O. Box 3216, Stn. Terminal, Vancouver BC V6B 3X8 Canada. **E-mail:** awards@alcuinsociety.com; info@alcuinsociety.com. **Website:**

www.alcuinsociety.com. **Contact:** Leah Gordon. The Alcuin Society Awards for Excellence in Book Design in Canada is the only national competition for book design in Canada. Winners are selected from books designed and published in Canada. Awards are presented annually at appropriate ceremonies held each year. Winning books are exhibited nationally and internationally at the Tokyo, Frankfurt, and Leipzig Book Fairs, and are Canada's entries in the international competition in Leipzig, "Book Design from all over the World", in the following spring. Submit previously published material from the year before the award's call for entries. Submissions made by the publisher (Canadian), author (any), or designer (Canadian). Deadline: varies annually. Prizes: 1st, 2nd, 3rd, and Honourable Mention in each category (at the discretion of the judges). Judged by professionals and those experienced in the field of book design.

MARIE ALEXANDER POETRY SERIES

English Department, 2801 S. University Ave., Little Rock AR 72204. **E-mail:** mariealexandereditor@gmail.com. **Website:** mariealexanderseries.com. **Contact:** Nickole Brown. Annual contest for a collection of previously unpublished prose poems or flash fiction by a U.S. writer. Deadline: July 31. Open to submissions on July 1. Prize: $1,000, plus publication.

ALLIGATOR JUNIPER AWARD

Alligator Juniper/Prescott College, 220 Grove Ave., Prescott AZ 86301. (928)350-2012. **Fax:** (928)776-5102. **E-mail:** alligatorjuniper@prescott.edu. **Website:** www.prescott.edu/alligatorjuniper/national-contest/index.html. **Contact:** Skye Anicca, Managing Editor. Annual contest for unpublished fiction, creative nonfiction, and poetry. Open to all age levels. Each entrant receives a personal letter from staff regarding the status of their submission, as well as minor feedback on the piece. Accepts simultaneous submissions, but inform on cover letter and contact immediately should work be selected elsewhere. Maximum length: 30 pages or 5 poems. Deadline: October 1. Prize: $1,000 plus publication in all three categories. Finalists in each genre are recognized as such, published, and paid in copies. Judged by distinguished writers in each genre and Prescott College writing students enrolled in the Literary Journal Practicum course.

AMERICAN LITERARY REVIEW CONTESTS

American Literary Review, P.O. Box 311307, University of North Texas, Denton TX 76203-1307. (940)565-2755. **E-mail:** americanliteraryreview@gmail.com. **Website:** www.americanliteraryreview.com. Contest to award excellence in short fiction, creative nonfiction, and poetry. Multiple entries are acceptable, but each entry must be accompanied with a reading fee. Do not put any identifying information in the file itself; include the author's name, title(s), address, e-mail address, and phone number in the boxes provided in the online submissions manager. Short fiction: Limit 8,000 words per work. Creative Nonfiction: Limit 6,500 words per work. Deadline: October 1. Submission period begins June 1. Prize: $1,000 prize for each category, along with publication in the Spring online issue of the *American Literary Review*.

ANNUAL WRITING CONTEST

Lumina, the literary journal of Sarah Lawrence College., Sarah Lawrence College Slonim House, One Mead Way, Bronxville NY 10708. **E-mail:** lumina@gm.slc.edu. **Website:** www.luminajournal.com/contest. Annual writing contest in poetry, fiction, or creative nonfiction (varies by year). Please visit website in August/September for complete and updated contest rules. Typical reading period: September 1 - November 15. Electronic submissions only. Deadline varies by year. Usually in the early fall. Prize: Cash.

ARTIST TRUST FELLOWSHIP AWARD

1835 12th Ave., Seattle WA 98122. (209)467-8734, ext. 11. **Fax:** (866)218-7878. **E-mail:** info@artisttrust.org. **Website:** www.artisttrust.org. **Contact:** Miguel Guillen, Program Manager. Fellowships award $7,500 to practicing professional artists of exceptional talent and demonstrated ability. The Fellowship is a merit-based, not a project-based, award. Recipients present a Meet the Artist Event to a community in Washington state that has little or no access to the artist and their work. Awards 14 fellowships of $7,500 and 2 residencies with $1,000 stipends at the Millay Colony. Artist Trust Fellowships are awarded in 2-year cycles. Applicants must be 18 years of age or older, Washington State residents at the time of application and payment, and generative artists. Deadline: January 17. Applications available December 3. Prize: $7,500.

ARTS & LETTERS PRIZES

Arts & Letters Journal of Contemporary Culture, Campus Box 89, GC&SU, Milledgeville GA 31061. (478)445-1289. **E-mail:** al.journal@gcsu.edu. **Website:** al.gcsu.edu. **Contact:** The Editors. Offered annually for unpublished work. Deadline: March 31. Prize:

$1,000 prize for each of the four major genres. Fiction, poetry, and creative nonfiction winners are published in Fall or Spring issue. The prize-winning, one-act play is produced at the Georgia College campus (usually in March). Judged by the editors (initial screening); see website for final judges and further details about submitting work.

AUTUMN HOUSE POETRY, FICTION, AND NONFICTION PRIZES

5530 Penn Ave., Pittsburgh PA 15206. (412)362-2665. **E-mail:** info@autumnhouse.org. **Website:** autumnhouse.org. **Contact:** Christine Stroud, Editor-in-Chief. Offers annual prize and publication of book-length ms with national promotion. Submission must be unpublished as a collection, but individual poems, stories, and essays may have been previously published elsewhere. Considers simultaneous submissions. "Autumn House is a nonprofit corporation with the mission of publishing and promoting poetry and other fine literature. We have published books by Sherrie Flick, Ed Ochester, Gerald Stern, Sharma Shields, Clifford Thompson, Danusha Lameris, Cameron Barnett, Dickson Lamb, Harrison Candelaria Fletcher, Ada Limon, and many others." Submit 50-80 pages of poetry or 200-300 pages of prose (include 2 cover sheets requested). Guidelines available for SASE, by e-mail, or on website. Competition receives 1,500 entries/year. Winners announced through mailings, website, and ads in *Poets & Writers, American Poetry Review*, and *Writer's Chronicle* (extensive publicity for winner). Copies of winning books available from Amazon.com, Barnes & Noble, and other retailers. Deadline: June 30. Prize: The winner (in each of 3 categories) will receive book publication, $1,000 advance against royalties, and a $1,500 travel/publicity grant to promote his or her book. Judged by Cornelius Eady (poetry), Aimee Bender (fiction), and Paul Lisicky (nonfiction).

AWP AWARD SERIES

Association of Writers & Writing Programs
5700 Rivertech Ct, Suite 225, 20737-1250, 5700 Rivertech Ct, Suite 225, Riverdale Park MD 22030. **E-mail:** supriya@awpwriter.org. **Website:** www.awpwriter.org. **Contact:** Supriya Bhatnagar, Director of Publications. AWP sponsors the Award Series, an annual competition for the publication of excellent new book-length works. The competition is open to all authors writing in English, regardless of nationality or residence, and is available to published and unpublished authors alike. Guidelines on website. Entries must be unpublished. Open to any writer. Entries are not accepted via postal mail. Offered annually to foster new literary talent. Deadline: Postmarked between January 1 and February 28. Prize: AWP Prize for the Novel: $2,500 and publication by New Issues Press; Donald Hall Prize for Poetry: $5,500 and publication by the University of Pittsburgh Press; Grace Paley Prize in Short Fiction: $5,500 and publication by the University of Massachusetts Press; and AWP Prize for Creative Nonfiction: $2,500 and publication by the University of Georgia Press. Creative Nonficton: Debra Monroe; Novel:Bonnie Jo Campbell; Poetry: Natasha D. Trethewey; Short Fiction: Dan Chaon.

THE BLACK RIVER CHAPBOOK COMPETITION

Black Lawrence Press, 279 Claremont Ave, Mount Vernon NY 10552. **E-mail:** editors@blacklawrencepress.com. **Website:** www.blacklawrence.com. **Contact:** Kit Frick, senior editor. Twice each year Black Lawrence Press will run the Black River Chapbook Competition for an unpublished chapbook of poems or short fiction between 16-36 pages in length. Submit through Submittable. Spring deadline: May 31. Fall deadline: October 31. Prize: $500, publication, and 10 copies. Judged by a revolving panel of judges, in addition to the Chapbook Editor and other members of the BLP editorial staff.

THE BOARDMAN TASKER PRIZE FOR MOUNTAIN LITERATURE

The Boardman Tasker Charitable Trust, 8 Bank View Rd., Darley Abbey Derby DE22 1EJ UK. 01332 342246. **E-mail:** steve@people-matter.co.uk. **Website:** www.boardmantasker.com. **Contact:** Steve Dean. Offered annually to reward a work with a mountain theme, whether fiction, nonfiction, drama, or poetry, written in the English language (initially or in translation). Subject must be concerned with a mountain environment. Previous winners have been books on expeditions, climbing experiences, a biography of a mountaineer, and novels. Guidelines available in January by e-mail or on website. Entries must be previously published. Open to any writer. Writers may obtain information, but entry is by publishers only (includes self-publishing). Awarded for a work published or distributed for the first time in the United Kingdom during the previous year. Not an anthology. The award is to honor Peter Boardman and Joe Tasker, who disappeared on Everest in 1982. Deadline: August 1. £3,000 Judged by a panel of 3 judges elected by trustees.

BOROONDARA LITERARY AWARDS

City of Boroondara, 340 Camberwell Rd., Camberwell VIC 3124 Australia. **E-mail:** bla@boroondara.vic.gov.au. **Website:** www.boroondara.vic.gov.au/literary-awards. Contest for unpublished work in 2 categories: Open Short Story from residents of Australia (1,500-3,000 words); and Young Writers who live, go to school or work in the City of Boroondara: 5th-6th grade (Junior), 7th-9th grade (Middle), and 10th-12th grade (Senior), prose and poetry on any theme. Deadline: 5pm on the last Friday of August. Prizes: Young Writers, Junior: 1st Place: $300; 2nd Place: $200; 3rd Place: $100. Young Writers, Middle: 1st Place: $450; 2nd Place: $300; 3rd Place: $150 and Senior: 1st Place: $600; 2nd Place: $400; 3rd Place: $200. Open Short Story: 1st Place: $1,500; 2nd Place: $1000; 3rd Place $500.

THE BRIDPORT PRIZE

P.O. Box 6910, Bridport, Dorset DT6 9QB United Kingdom. **E-mail:** info@bridportprize.org.uk; kate@bridportprize.org.uk. **Website:** www.bridportprize.org.uk. **Contact:** Kate Wilson, Bridport Prize Programme Manager. Award to promote literary excellence, discover new talent. Categories: Short stories, poetry, flash fiction, first novel. Entries must be unpublished. Length: 5,000 maximum for short stories; 42 lines for poetry, 250 words for flash fiction and 8,000 words max for opening chapters of a novel. Deadline: May 31 each year. Prize: £5,000; £1,000; £500; various runners-up prizes and publication of approximately 13 best stories and 13 best poems in anthology; plus 6 best flash fiction stories. 1st Prize of £1,000 for the best short, short story of under 250 words. £1,000 plus up to a year's mentoring for winner of Peggy Chapman-Andrews Award for a first novel. A second anthology containing extracts of the twenty long-listed novels will be published for the first time in 2019. Judged by 1 judge for short stories (in 2019, Kirtsty Logan), 1 judge for poetry (in 2019, Holly McNish) and 1 judge for flash fiction (in 2019 Kirsty Logan). The Novel award is judged by a group comprising representatives from The Literary Consultancy, A.M. Heath Literary Agents, and (in 2019) judge Naomi Wood.

BRITISH CZECH AND SLOVAK ASSOCIATION WRITING COMPETITION

24 Ferndale, Tunbridge Wells Kent TN2 3NS England. **E-mail:** prize@bcsa.co.uk. **Website:** www.bcsa.co.uk/competitions. Annual contest for original writing (entries should be 1,500-2,000 words) in English on the links between Britain and the Czech/Slovak Republics, or describing society in transition in the Republics since 1989. Entries can be fact or fiction. Topics can include history, politics, the sciences, economics, the arts, or literature. Deadline: End of July. Winners announced in November. Prize: 1st Place: £400; 2nd Place: £150.

CALIFORNIA BOOK AWARDS

Commonwealth Club of California, 110 The Embarcadero, San Francisco CA 94105. (415)597-6700. **Fax:** (415)597-6729. **E-mail:** bookawards@commonwealthclub.org. **Website:** https://www.commonwealthclub.org/events/california-book-awards. **Contact:** Priscilla Vivio, bookawards@commonwealthclub.org, pvivio@commonwealthclub.org. Offered annually to recognize California's best writers and illuminate the wealth and diversity of California-based literature. Award is for published submissions appearing in print during the previous calendar year. Can be nominated by publisher or author. Open to California residents (or residents at time of publication). Submit at least 6 copies of each book entered with an official entry form. Open to books, published during the year prior to the contest, whose author must have been a legal resident of California at the time the manuscript was submitted for publication. Entry form and guidelines available for SASE or on website. Deadline: December 22. Prize: Medals and cash prizes to be awarded at publicized event, annually in June for previous year submissions. Judged by 12-15 California professionals with a diverse range of views, backgrounds, and literary experience.

CBC LITERARY PRIZES/PRIX DE LA CRÉATION RADIO-CANADA

CBC/Radio-Canada, Canada Council for the Arts, Banff Centre for Arts and Creativity, P.O. Box 6000, Montreal QC H3C 3A8 Canada. (877)888-6788. **E-mail:** canadawrites@cbc.ca. **Website:** www.cbcbooks.ca. **Contact:** Daphné Santos-Vieira, coordinator. The CBC Literary Prizes competitions are the only literary competitions that celebrate original, unpublished works in Canada's two official languages. There are 3 categories: short story, nonfiction and poetry. Submissions to the short story category must be up to 2,500 words maximum and for the nonfiction category they must be up to 2,000 words; poetry submissions must be up to 600 words (there are no minimum word counts for the CBC Literary Prizes). Poetry submissions can take the form of a long narrative poem, a sequence of connected poems, or a group of unconnected poems. Canadian citizens, living in Canada or abroad, and permanent residents of Canada are eligible to enter. Deadline: October 31 for short story; February 28 for nonfiction; May 31 for poetry. See website for when each competition is accepting entries. Prize: For each category, in both English and French: 1st Prize: $6,000; 4 finalists each receive $1,000. In addition, winning entries are published on CBCbooks.ca and broadcast on CBC radio. Winning authors also get a two-week writing residency at the Banff Centre for Arts and Creativity. First publications rights are granted to CBC/Radio-Canada. Submissions are judged blind by a jury of qualified writers and editors from around the country. Each category has 3 jurors.

CHRISTIAN BOOK AWARD® PROGRAM

ECPA/Christian Book Award®, 5801 S. McClintock Dr, Suite 104, Tempe AZ 85283. (480)966-3998. **Fax:** (480)966-1944. **E-mail:** info@ecpa.org. **Website:** www.ecpa.org. **Contact:** Stan Jantz, ED. The Evangelical Christian Publishers Association (ECPA) recognizes quality and encourages excellence by presenting the ECPA Christian Book Awards® (formerly known as Gold Medallion) each year. Categories include Christian Living, Biography & Memoir, Faith & Culture, Children, Young People's Literature, Devotion & Gift, Bibles, Bible Reference Works, Bible Study, Ministry Resources and New Author. All entries must be evangelical in nature and submitted through an ECPA member publisher. Books must have been published in the calendar year prior to the award. Publishing companies submitting entries must be ECPA members in good standing. See website for details. The Christian Book Award® recognizes the highest quality in Christian books and is among the oldest and most prestigious awards program in Christian publishing. Submission period runs September 1-30. Judged by experts, authors, and retailers with years of experience in their field.

THE CITY OF VANCOUVER BOOK AWARD

Cultural Services Dept., Woodward's Heritage Building, 111 W. Hastings St., Suite 501, Vancouver BC V6B 1H4 Canada. (604)871-6634. **Fax:** (604)871-6005. **E-mail:** marnie.rice@vancouver.ca; culture@vancouver.ca. **Website:** https://vancouver.ca/people-programs/city-of-vancouver-book-award.aspx. The annual City of Vancouver Book Award recognizes authors of excellence of any genre that reflect Vancouver's unique character, rich diversity and culture, history and residents. The book must exhibit excellence in one or more of the following areas: content, illustration, design, format. The book must not be copyrighted prior to the previous year. Submit four copies of book. See website for details and guidelines. Deadline: May 22. Prize: $3,000. Judged by an independent jury.

CLOUDBANK BOOKS

Vern Rutsala Book Contest, Cloudbank Books, P.O. Box 610, Corvallis OR 97339. (541) 752-0075. **E-mail:** michael@cloudbankbooks.com. **Website:** www.cloudbankbooks.com. **Contact:** Michael Malan. *Cloudbank* is a 96-to-112 page print journal published annually. Included are poems, flash fiction, and book reviews. Regular submissions and contest submissions are accepted. The annual Vern Rutsala Book Contest results in a published book of poetry and/or flash fiction, plus monetary prize. For Cloudbank Contest and regular submissions the writer's name, address, email, and the titles of the poems/flash fiction pieces being submitted should be typed on a cover sheet only, not on the pages of poems or flash fiction. Submit no more than 5 poems or flash fiction pieces (500 words or less) for the Contest or regular submissions. For the Vern Rutsala Book Contest submit an unpublished manuscript of 60 to 90 pages with two cover pages, one with contact information and one without. Deadlines: Submissions for the journal's annual Cloudbank Contest are accepted from Nov. 1 through the last day in February. Non-contest submissions for the journal are accepted through April 30. Submissions for the Vern Rutsala Book Contest are accepted from July 1 through Oct. 31. The Cloudbank Contest prize is $200 and publication. Two contributors' copies are sent to all writers whose work appears in the magazine. The Vern Rutsala Book Contest winner receives $1,000 and publication of the manuscript. The Cloudbank Contest is judged by Editor Michael Malan and editorial staff. The Vern Rutsala Book Contest has an outside judge.

DIAGRAM/NEW MICHIGAN PRESS CHAPBOOK CONTEST

New Michigan Press, P.O. Box 210067, English, ML 445, University of Arizona, Tucson AZ 85721. **E-mail:** nmp@thediagram.com. **Website:** www.thediagram.com. **Contact:** Ander Monson, editor. The annual *DIAGRAM*/New Michigan Press Chapbook Contest offers $1,000, plus publication and author's copies, with discount on additional copies. Submit 18-44 pages of poetry, fiction, nonfiction, mixed-genre, or genre-bending work. Do not send originals of anything. Include SASE. Guidelines available on website. Deadline: April 26. Prize: $1,000, plus publication. Finalist chapbooks also considered for publication. Judged by editor Ander Monson.

DIAGRAM/NEW MICHIGAN PRESS CHAPBOOK CONTEST

Department of English, University of Arizona, New Michigan Press, P.O. Box 210067, Tucson AZ 85721-0067. **E-mail:** nmp@thediagram.com; editor@thediagram.com. **Website:** www.thediagram.com/contest.html. **Contact:** Ander Monson, editor. Contest for prose, poetry, or hybrid manuscript (images ok) between 18-44 pages. Deadline: April 28. Check website for more details. Prize: $1,000 and publication. Typically we also published 3-5 finalist chapbooks. Judged by editor Ander Monson.

THE VIRGINIA FAULKNER AWARD FOR EXCELLENCE IN WRITING

Prairie Schooner, 110 Andrews Hall, University of Nebraska-Lincoln, Lincoln NE 68588-0334. (402)472-0911. **Fax:** (402)472-1817. **E-mail:** PrairieSchooner@unl.edu. **Website:** www.prairieschooner.unl.edu. **Contact:** Kwame Dawes. Offered annually for work published in *Prairie Schooner* in the previous year. Categories: short stories, essays, novel excerpts, and translations. Reads unsolicited mss between May 1 and September 1. Winning entry must have been published in *Prairie Schooner* in the year preceding the award. Results announced in the Spring issue. Winners notified by mail in February or March. Prize: $1,000. Judged by editorial board.

THE WILLIAM FAULKNER-WILLIAM WISDOM CREATIVE WRITING COMPETITION

Faulkner - Wisdom Competition, Pirate's Alley Faulkner Society, Inc., Faulkner – Wisdom Competition, 624 Pirate's Alley, New Orleans LA 70116. (504)586-1609. **E-mail:** faulkhouse@aol.com. **Website:** https://faulknersociety.org. general craft **Contact:** Rosemary James, Award Director. See guidelines posted at www.wordsandmusic.org. Deadline: May 31. Prizes: $750-7,500 depending on category. Judged by established authors, literary agents, and acquiring editors.

FINELINE COMPETITION FOR PROSE POEMS, SHORT SHORTS, AND ANYTHING IN BETWEEN

Mid-American Review, Dept. of English, Bowling Green State University, Bowling Green OH 43403. (419)372-2725. **E-mail:** mar@bgsu.edu. **Website:** www.bgsu.edu/midamericanreview. **Contact:** Abigail Cloud, Editor-in-Chief. Offered annually for previously unpublished submissions. Contest open to all writers not associated with current judge or *Mid-American Review*. Deadline: June 1. Prize: $1,000, plus publication in fall issue of *Mid-American Review*; 10 finalists receive notation plus possible publication. Judge will be a contemporary writer of note.

FISH SHORT MEMOIR PRIZE

Fish Publishing, Durrus, Bantry Co. Cork P75 VK72 Ireland. **E-mail:** info@fishpublishing.com. **Website:** www.fishpublishing.com. **Contact:** Clem Cairns. Annual worldwide contest to recognize the best memoirs submitted to Fish Publishing. Submissions must not have been previously published. Enter online or via postal mail. See website for full details. Word limit: 4,000. Deadline: January 31. Prize: 1st Prize: $1,000. 2nd prize is a week at Casa Ana Writers Retreat in Andalusia, Spain, with $300 traveling expenses. The 10 best memoirs will be published in the Fish Anthology, launched in July at the West Cork Literary Festival. Judge for 2019 is Chrissie Gittens.

THE FLORIDA REVIEW EDITOR'S PRIZE

Dept. of English, P.O. Box 161346, University of Central Florida, P.O. Box 161346, Orlando FL 32816. **E-mail:** flreview@mail.ucf.edu. **Website:** http://floridareview.cah.ucf.edu/. Annual awards for the best unpublished fiction, poetry, and creative nonfiction. Deadline: March 17. Prize: $1,000 (in each genre) and publication in *The Florida Review*. Judged by the editors in each genre. Judging is blind, so names should not appear on mss.

FOREWORD'S INDIES BOOK OF THE YEAR AWARDS

Foreword Magazine, Attn Foreword INDIES, Foreword Reviews, 413 E 8th St, Traverse City MI 49686. (231)933-3699. **Website:** www.forewordreviews.com. **Contact:** Michele Lonoconus. Awards offered annually. In order to be eligible, books must have a current-year copyright and be independently published, which includes university presses, privately held presses, and self-published authors. International submissions are welcome. New editions of previously published books are eligible if significant content has been changed and the book has a new ISBN. Reissued editions in new formats are not eligible. *Foreword's*INDIES Book of the Year Awards were established to bring increased attention from librarians, booksellers, and avid readers to the literary achievements of independent publishers and their authors. Deadline: January 15th. Prize: $1,500 cash will be awarded to a Best Fiction and Best Nonfiction choice. Our awards process is unique and well-respected because we assemble a jury of volunteer booksellers and librarians to make the final judgment on the books and who select winners based on their experience with readers. Their decisions also take into consideration editorial excellence, professional production, originality of the narrative, author credentials relative to the subject matter, and the value the title adds to its genre.

FREEFALL SHORT PROSE AND POETRY CONTEST

Freefall Literary Society of Calgary, 922 9th Ave. SE, Calgary AB T2G 0S4 Canada. **E-mail:** editors@freefallmagazine.ca. **Website:** www.freefallmagazine.ca. **Contact:** Ryan Stromquist, Managing Editor. Offered annually for unpublished work in the categories of poetry (5 poems/entry) and prose (3,000 words or less). Recognizes writers and offers publication credits in a literary magazine format. Contest rules and entry form online. Acquires first Canadian serial rights; ownership reverts to author after one-time publication. Deadline: December 31. Prize: 1st Place: $500 (CAD); 2nd Place: $250 (CAD); 3rd Place: $75; Honorable Mention: $25. All prizes include publication in the spring edition of *FreeFall Magazine*. Winners will also be invited to read at the launch of that issue, if such a launch takes place. Honorable mentions in each category will be published and may be asked to read. Travel expenses not included. Judged by current guest editor for issue (who are also published authors in Canada).

GOVERNOR GENERAL'S LITERARY AWARDS

Canada Council for the Arts, 150 Elgin St., P.O. Box 1047, Ottawa ON K1P 5V8 Canada. (800)263-5588, ext. 5573 or (613)566-4414, ext. 5573. **Website:** ggbooks.ca. The Canada Council for the Arts provides a wide range of grants and services to professional Canadian artists and art organizations in dance, media arts, music, theatre, writing, publishing, and the visual arts. Books must be first-edition literary trade books written, translated, or illustrated by Canadian citizens or permanent residents of Canada and published in Canada or abroad in the previous year. In the case of translation, the original work must also be a Canadian-authored title. For complete eligibility criteria, deadlines, and submission procedures, please visit the website at www.canadacouncil.ca. The Governor General's Literary Awards are given annually for the best English-language and French-language work in each of 7 categories, including fiction, non-fiction, poetry, drama, young people's literature (text), young people's literature (illustrated books), and translation. Deadline: Depends on the book's publication date. See website for details. Prize: Each GG winner receives $25,000. Non-winning finalists receive $1,000. Publishers of the winning titles receive a $3,000 grant for promotional purposes. Evaluated by fellow authors, translators, and illustrators. For each category, a jury makes the final selection.

GREAT LAKES COLLEGES ASSOCIATION NEW WRITERS AWARD

The Great Lakes Colleges Association, 535 W. William St., Suite 301, Ann Arbor MI 48103. (734)661-2350. **Fax:** (734)661-2349. **E-mail:** wegner@glca.org. **Website:** https://glca.org/glcaprograms/new-writers-award. **Contact:** Gregory R. Wegner, Director of Program Development: wegner@glca.org. The Great Lakes Colleges Association (GLCA) is a consortium of 13 independent liberal arts colleges in Ohio, Michigan, Indiana, and Pennsylvania. Nominations should be made by the publisher and should emphasize literary excellence. A publisher can nominate only one author per year for any given category. A publisher can nominate one author in each of the three categories (poetry, fiction, creative nonfiction) in a single year if desired. The Award's purpose is to celebrate literary achievement in a writer's first-published volume of fiction, poetry, or nonfiction. Deadline: June 25, 2019. Any work received with a postmark after this date will not be accepted. Prize: Honorarium of at least $500 from each member college that invites a winning to give a reading on its campus. Each award winner receives invitations from several of the 13 colleges of the GLCA to visit campus. At these campus events an author will give readings, meet students and faculty, and occasionally visit college classes. In addition to the $500 honorarium for each campus visit, travel costs to colleges are paid by the GLCA's member colleges. Judged by professors of literature and writers in residence at GLCA colleges.

GREEN PIECES PRESS ARIZONA LITERARY CONTEST BOOK AWARDS

Green Pieces Press, 6939 East Chaparral Rd., Paradise Valley AZ 85253-7000. (480)219-4559. **E-mail:** Director@AzLiteraryContest.com. **Website:** www.AzLiteraryContest.com. **Contact:** Lisa Aquilina, publisher. Green Pieces Press is honored to receive the baton from its contest predecessor and sponsor a refreshed, retooled 2019 annual literary competition for published books, unpublished novels, and Arizona Book of the Year. Cash prizes awarded ($1,000 Book of the Year) from Green Pieces Press. First Place in each of the nine categories ($200). Second Place $100, Third Place $50. All category finalists in 2019 have their literary works published in the *Arizona Literary Magazine 2020*. NEW PRIZE in 2019 for Unpublished Novel category. All Finalists have their completed manuscript submitted to Ingram Elliot Book Publishers for consideration and potential award of a standard, traditional publishing contract. All published work must have 2018 or 2019 copyright date at time of submission. Poetry, short story, essay, and new drama writing submissions must be unpublished. Work must have been published in the current or immediate past calendar year. Considers simultaneous submissions. Entry form and guidelines available on website or upon request. Deadline: September 1, 2019. Begins accepting submissions January 1, 2019. Finalists notified by Labor Day weekend. Prizes: Grand Prize, Arizona Book of the Year Award: $1,000. All categories: 1st Prize: $200; 2nd Prize: $100; 3rd Prize: $50. Unpublished Novel finallists also have their manuscripts submitted to IngramElliott Book Publishers for consideration to be awarded traditional publishing contract. Features in *Arizona Literary Magazine 2020*. Judged by nationwide published authors, editors, literary agents, and reviewers. Winners announced prior to Thanksgiving 2019. International entries encouraged; only caveat, all entries must be written in English.

HACKNEY LITERARY AWARDS

Hackney Literary Awards, 4650 Old Looney Mill Rd., Birmingham AL 35243. **E-mail:** info@hackneyliteraryawards.org. **Website:** www.hackneyliteraryawards.org. **Contact:** Myra Crawford, PhD, Executive Director. Offered annually for unpublished novels, short stories (maximum 5,000 words), and poetry (50 line limit). Guidelines on website. Deadline: September 30 (novels), November 30 (short stories and poetry). Prize: $5,000 in annual prizes for poetry and short fiction ($2,500 national and $2,500 state level). 1st Place: $600; 2nd Place: $400; 3rd Place: $250; plus $5,000 for an unpublished novel. Competition winners will be announced on the website each March.

ERIC HOFFER AWARD

Hopewell Publications, LLC, P.O. Box 11, Titusville NJ 08560-0011. **Fax:** (609)964-1718. **E-mail:** info@hopepubs.com. **Website:** www.hofferaward.com. **Contact:** Dawn Shows, EHA Coordinator. Annual contest for previously published books. Recognizes excellence in independent publishing in many unique categories: Art (titles capture the experience, execution, or demonstration of the arts); Poetry (all styles); Chapbook (40 pages or less, artistic assembly); General Fiction (nongenre-specific fiction); Commercial Fiction (genre-specific fiction); Science Fiction/Fantasy; Historical Fiction; Short Story/Anthology; Mystery/Crime; Children (titles for young children); Middle Reader; Young Adult (titles aimed at the juvenile and teen markets); Culture (titles demonstrating the human or world experience); Memoir (titles relating to personal experience); Business (titles with application to today's business environment and emerging trends); Reference (titles from traditional and emerging reference areas); Home (titles with practical applications to home or home-related issues, including family); Health (titles promoting physical, mental, and emotional well-being); Self-help (titles involving new and emerging topics in self-help); Spiritual (titles involving the mind and spirit, including relgion); Legacy Fiction and Nonfiction (titles over 2 years of age that hold particular relevance to any subject matter or form); E-book Fiction; E-book Nonfiction. Open to any writer of published work within the last 2 years, including categories for older books. This contest recognizes excellence in independent publishing in many unique categories. Also awards the Montaigne Medal for most though-provoking book, the Da Vinci Eye for best cover, and the First Horizon Award for best new authors. Results published in the US Review of Books. Deadline: January 21. Grand Prize: $2,500; honors (winner, runner-up, honorable mentions) in each category, including the Montaigne Medal (most thought-provoking), da Vinci Art (cover art), First Horizon (first book), and Best in Press (small, academic, micro, self-published).

TOM HOWARD/JOHN H. REID FICTION & ESSAY CONTEST

Winning Writers, 351 Pleasant St., PMB 222, Northampton MA 01060-3961. (866)946-9748. **Fax:** (413)280-0539. **E-mail:** adam@winningwriters.com. **Website:** www.winningwriters.com. **Contact:** Adam Cohen, president. Since 2001, Winning Writers has provided expert literary contest information to the public. Sponsors four contests. One of the "101 Best Websites for Writers" (*Writer's Digest*). Open to all writers. Submit any type of short story or essay. Both published and unpublished works are welcome. If you win a prize, requests nonexclusive rights to publish your submission online, in e-mail newsletters, in e-books, and in press releases. See website for guidelines and to submit your entry. Prefers inquiries by e-mail. Length: 6,000 words max per entry. Writers may submit own work. Winners notified by e-mail. Results made available to entrants on website. Deadline: April 30. Prizes: Two 1st prizes of $2,000 will be awarded, plus 10 honorable mentions of $100 each. Top 12 entries published online. The top two winners will also receive one-year gift certificates from the contest co-sponsor, Duotrope (a $50 value). Judged by Dennis Norris II, assisted by Lauren Singer Ledoux.

THE JULIA WARD HOWE/BOSTON AUTHORS AWARD

The Boston Authors Club, The Boston Authors Club, Boston Authors Club, Attn. Mary Cronin, 2400 Beacon Street, Unit 208, Chestnut Hill MA 02467. **E-mail:** bostonauthors@aol.com. **Website:** www.bostonauthorsclub.org. **Contact:** Alan Lawson. This annual award honors Julia Ward Howe and her literary friends who founded the Boston Authors Club in 1900. It also honors the membership over 110 years; consisting of novelists, biographers, historians, governors, senators, philosophers, poets, playwrights, and other luminaries. Boston Authors Club has been awarding the Julia Ward Howe Prizes (named after the Club's first President) to outstanding adult and young-reader books for over 20 years. These awards recognize exceptional books by Boston-area authors in four separate categories: Fiction, Nonfiction, Poetry, and the Young Reader category. Authors must live or have lived (college counts) within a hundred 100-mile radius of Boston within the last 5 years. Subsidized books, cook books and picture books are not eligible. Deadline: January 31. Prize: $1,000. Judged by the members.

INSIGHT WRITING CONTEST

Insight Magazine, Insight Writing Contest, 55 W. Oak Ridge Dr., Hagerstown MD 21740-7390. **Fax:** (301)393-4055. **E-mail:** insight@rhpa.org. **Website:** www.insightmagazine.org. **Contact:** Omar Miranda, Editor. Annual contest for writers in the categories of student short story, general short story, and student poetry. Unpublished submissions only. General category is open to all writers; student categories must be age 22 and younger. Deadline: July 31. Prizes: Student Short and General Short Story: 1st Prize: $250; 2nd Prize: $200; 3rd Prize: $150. Student Poetry: 1st Prize: $100; 2nd Prize: $75; 3rd Prize: $50.

THE IOWA REVIEW AWARD IN POETRY, FICTION, AND NONFICTION

The Iowa Review, University of Iowa, 308 English-Philosophy Building, Iowa City IA 52242. **E-mail:** iowa-review@uiowa.edu. **Website:** www.iowareview.org. *The Iowa Review* Award in Poetry, Fiction, and Nonfiction presents $1,500 to each winner in each genre and $750 to runners-up. Winners and runners-up published in *The Iowa Review*. Submissions must be unpublished. Considers simultaneous submissions (with notification of acceptance elsewhere). Submit up to 25 pages of prose, (double-spaced) or 10 pages of poetry (1 poem or several, but no more than 1 poem per page). Submit online. Include cover page with writer's name, address, e-mail and/or phone number, and title of each work submitted. Personal identification must not appear on ms pages. Guidelines available on website. Deadline: January 31. Submission period begins January 1. Judges for the 2019 Awards are Kiki Petrosino (poetry), Rebecca Makkai (fiction), and Roxane Gay (nonfiction).

JAPAN-U.S. FRIENDSHIP COMMISSION PRIZE FIR THE TRANSLATION OF JAPANESE LITERATURE

Japanese Literary Translation Prize, Columbia University, Donald Keene Center, c/o Department of East Asian Languages and Cultures, 407 Kent Hall MC 3907, 1140 Amsterdam Ave., New York NY 10027 USA. **Website:** http://www.keenecenter.org/. **Contact:** Yoshiko Niiya, Program Coordinator. The Donald Keene Center of Japanese Culture at Columbia

University annually awards Japan-U.S. Friendship Commission Prizes for the Translation of Japanese Literature. A prize is given for the best translation of a modern work or a classical work, or the prize is divided between equally distinguished translations. Translators must be citizens or permanent residents of the United States. Deadline: June 3. Prize: $6,000.

THE STEPHEN LEACOCK MEMORIAL MEDAL FOR HUMOUR

Bette Walker, 149 Peter St. N., Orillia ON L3V 4Z4 Canada. (705)326-9286. **E-mail:** awardschair@leacock.ca. **Website:** www.leacock.ca. **Contact:** Bette Walker, Award Committee, Stephen Leacock Associates. The Leacock Associates awards the prestigious Leacock Medal for the best book of literary humor written by a Canadian and published in the current year. The winning author also receives a cash prize of $15,000, thanks to the generous support of the TD Financial Group. 2 runners-up are each awarded a cash prize of $3,000. Deadline: Postmarked before December 31. Prize: $15,000.

LEAGUE OF UTAH WRITERS WRITING CONTEST

The League of Utah Writers, The League of Utah Writers, P.O. Box 64, Lewiston UT 84320. (435)755-7609. **E-mail:** luwcontest@gmail.com; luwriters@gmail.com. **Website:** www.luwriters.org. Open to any writer, the LUW Contest provides authors an opportunity to get their work read and critiqued. Multiple categories are offered; see website for details. Entries must be the original and unpublished work of the author. Winners are announced at the Annual Writers Round-Up in September. Those not present will be notified by e-mail. Deadline: May 31. Submissions period begins March 1. Prize: Cash prizes are awarded. Judged by professional authors and editors from outside the League.

LES FIGUES PRESS NOS BOOK CONTEST

Les Figues Press, c/o Los Angeles Review of Books, 6671 Sunset Blvd., Suite 1521, Los Angeles CA 90028. (323)734-4732. **E-mail:** info@lesfigues.com. **Website:** www.lesfigues.com. **Contact:** Teresa Carmody, Founding Editor. Les Figues Press creates aesthetic conversations between writers/artists and readers, especially those interested in innovative/experimental/avant-garde work. The Press intends in the most premeditated fashion to champion the trinity of Beauty, Belief, and Bawdry. Submit a 64-250 page unpublished manuscript through electronic submissions manager. Eligible submissions include: poetry, novellas, innovative novels, anti-novels, short story collections, lyric essays, hybrids, and all forms *not otherwise specified*. Guidelines available online. Deadline: March 20 (submissions open until midnight PST). Prize: $1,000, plus publication by Les Figues Press.

THE HUGH J. LUKE AWARD

Prairie Schooner, 110 Andrews Hall, University of Nebraska-Lincoln, Lincoln NE 68588-0334. (402)472-0911. **Fax:** (402)472-1817. **E-mail:** prairieschooner@unl.edu. **Website:** www.prairieschooner.unl.edu. **Contact:** Kwame Dawes. Offered annually for work published in *Prairie Schooner* in the previous year. Results announced in the Spring issue. Winners notified by mail in February or March. Prize: $250. Judged by editorial staff of *Prairie Schooner*.

MANITOBA BOOK AWARDS

Manitoba Writers' Guild, c/o Manitoba Writers' Guild, 218-100 Arthur St., Winnipeg MB R3B 1H3 Canada. (204)944-8013. **E-mail:** info@manitobabookawards.com. **Website:** www.manitobabookawards.com. **Contact:** Ellen MacDonald. The awards honor books written by Manitobans, published in Manitoba or about Manitoba. More than $30,000 in prizes is awarded each year to Manitoba writers. The Manitoba Book Awards celebrates literary excellence, originality and diverse talent. Some of Canada's best writers have springboarded to national and international acclaim after winning the Manitoba Book Awards. Previous winners include: Carol Shields (1993), David Bergen (1993,1996, 2009), Miriam Toews (1998, 2000), Margaret Sweatman (1991, 2001), Sandra Birdsell (1992), Jake MacDonald (2002), Allan Levine (2010), Barbara Huck (2014) and Wab Kinew (2016). The 18 awards to be presented at the 29th annual Manitoba Book Awards include Alexander Kennedy Isbister Award for Non-Fiction/Prix Alexander-Kennedy-Isbister pour les études et les essais, Beatrice Mosionier Aboriginal Writer of the Year Award /Prix Beatrice-Mosionier pour l'écrivain.e autochtone de l'année (English/Français/Indigenous Languages), Carol Shields Winnipeg Book Award/Prix littéraire Carol-Shields de la ville de Winnipeg, The Chris Johnson Award for Best Play by a Manitoba Playwright /Prix Chris-Johnson pour la meilleure pièce par un dramaturge manitobain, Eileen McTavish Sykes Award for Best First Book, John Hirsch Award for Most Promising Manitoba Writer/Prix John-Hirsch pour l'écrivain manitobain le plus prometteur, Lansdowne Prize for Poetry / Prix Lansdowne de poésie, Le Prix Littéraire Rue-Deschambault, Manuela Dias Book Design and Illustration Awards/Prix Manuela—Dias de conception graphique et d'illustration en édition—4 categories, Margaret Laurence Award for Fiction, Mary Scorer Award for Best Book by a Manitoba Publisher/Prix Mary-Scorer pour le meilleur livre par un éditeur du Manitoba, McNally Robinson Books for Young People Awards—2 categories, McNally Robinson Book of the Year Award, and Lifetime Achievement Award—English/Français. Guidelines and submission forms available online. Open to Manitoba writers only. Publishers are encouraged to send 4 (four) copies per award of any eligible books to the Manitoba Writers' Guild on or before Dec. 1 (postmark date) for books published January 1 and October 31. The deadline for books published between November 1 and December 31, is January 15. Deadline: December 1 and January 15. Prize: Several prizes up to $5,000 (CAD). Jurors selected by the Manitoba Writers' Guild.

THE MCGINNIS-RITCHIE MEMORIAL AWARD

Southwest Review, Southern Methodist University, P.O. Box 750374, Dallas TX 75275-0374. (214)768-1037. **Fax:** (214)768-1408. **E-mail:** swr@mail.smu.edu. **Website:** www.smu.edu/southwestreview. **Contact:** Greg Brownderville, editor-in-chief. The McGinnis-Ritchie Memorial Award is given annually to the best works of fiction and nonfiction that appeared in the magazine in the previous year. Mss are submitted for publication, not for the prizes themselves. Guidelines for SASE or online. Prize: $500. Judged by Greg Brownderville.

A MIDSUMMER TALE

E-mail: editors@toasted-cheese.com. **E-mail:** amtcontest19@toasted-cheese.com. **Website:** www.toasted-cheese.com. **Contact:** Theryn Fleming, Editor. A Midsummer Tale is open to non-genre fiction and creative nonfiction. There is a different theme each year. Entries must be unpublished. Accepts inquiries by e-mail. Cover letter should include name, address, e-mail, word count, and title. Length: 1,000-5,000 words. Open to any writer. Guidelines available in April on website. Deadline: June 21. Results announced on July 31. Winners notified by e-mail. List of winners on website. Prize: Amazon gift certificates and publication in Toasted Cheese. Entries are blind-judged by at least one Toasted Cheese editor

MINNESOTA BOOK AWARDS

The Friends of the Saint Paul Public Library, 1080 Montreal Ave., Suite 2, St. Paul MN 55116. (651)222-3242. **Fax:** (651)222-1988. **E-mail:** mnbookawards@thefriends.org. **Website:** www.mnbookawards.org. **Contact:** Bailey Veesenmeyer: bailey@thefriends.org. A year-round program celebrating and honoring Minnesota's best books, culminating in an annual awards ceremony. Recognizes and honors achievement by members of Minnesota's book and book arts community. All books must be the work of a Minnesota author or primary artistic creator (current Minnesota resident who maintains a year-round residence in Minnesota). All books must be published within the calendar year prior to the Awards presentation. Deadline: Books should be entered by 5 p.m. on the third Friday in November.

MISSISSIPPI REVIEW PRIZE

Mississippi Review, Mississippi Review Prize, 118 College Dr., #5144, Hattiesburg MS 39406-0001. (601)266-4321. **Fax:** (601)266-5757. **E-mail:** msreview@usm.edu. **Website:** www.mississippireview.com. Annual contest starting August 1 and running until January 1. Winners and finalists will make up next spring's print issue of the national literary magazine *Mississippi Review*. Each entrant will receive a copy of the prize issue. Contest is open to all writers in English except current or former students or employees of The University of Southern Mississippi. Fiction entries should be 1,000-8,000 words, poetry entries should be 3-5 poems totaling 10 pages or less. There is no limit on the number of entries you may submit. Online submissions must be submitted through Submittable site: mississippireview.submittable.com/submit. No mss will be returned. Previously published work is ineligible. Winners will be announced in March and publication is scheduled for June of following year. Entries should have "MR Prize," author name, address, phone, e-mai,l and title of work on page 1. Deadline: January 1. Prize: $1,000 in fiction and poetry. Judged by Andrew Malan Milward in fiction, and Angela Ball in poetry.

MOUNTAINS & PLAINS INDEPENDENT BOOKSELLERS ASSOCIATION READING THE WEST BOOK AWARDS

Mountains & Plains Independent Booksellers Association, 2105 Union Dr., Lakewood CO 80215. **E-mail:** Submission is via an online form, posted on the website (www.mountainsplains.org) in the fall of each year. **Website:** http://www.mountainsplains.org/reading-the-west-book-awards/. **Contact:** Kelsey Myers. Mountains & Plains Independent Booksellers Association is a professional trade organization with the primary mission of supporting independent bookseller members in a 12-state region in the West. Also welcomes as members colleagues in the book industry including authors, publishers, sales representatives, and others. The purpose of these annual awards is to honor outstanding books published in the previous calendar year which are set in the region (Arizona, Colorado, Kansas, Montana, Nebraska, Nevada, New Mexico, Oklahoma, South Dakota, Texas, Utah, and Wyoming) or that evoke the spirit of the region. The author's place of residence is immaterial for these awards. Deadline: Nomination period September 1 to December 31 for books published in the previous calendar year. Prize: All nominated titles are listed on the website (www.mountainsplains.org). Shortlist and winning titles are recognized via a press release, e-announcement, and on the website. Winners are recognized at a Reading the West luncheon at the Fall Discovery Show and in promotional materials. Judged by 2 panels of judges, 1 for adult titles and 1 for children's titles. Other categories/panels may be convened at the Association's discretion.

NATIONAL BOOK AWARDS

The National Book Foundation, 90 Broad St., Suite 604, New York NY 10004. (212)685-0261. **E-mail:** nationalbook@nationalbook.org. **Website:** www.nationalbook.org. The National Book Foundation and the National Book Awards celebrate the best of American literature, expand its audience, and enhance the cultural value of great writing in America. The contest offers prizes in 4 categories: fiction, nonfiction, poetry, and young people's literature. Books should be published between December 1 and November 30 of the previous year. Submissions must be previously published and must be entered by the publisher. General guidelines available on website. Interested publishes should phone or e-mail the Foundation. Deadline: Submit entry form, payment, and a copy of the book by May 15. Prize: $10,000 in each category. Finalists will each receive a prize of $1,000. Judged by a category specific panel of 5 judges for each category.

NATIONAL OUTDOOR BOOK AWARDS

921 S. 8th Ave., Stop 8128, Pocatello ID 83209. (208)282-3912. **E-mail:** wattron@isu.edu. **Website:** www.noba-web.org. **Contact:** Ron Watters. Nine categories: History/biography, outdoor literature, instructional texts, outdoor adventure guides, nature guides, children's books, design/artistic merit, natural history literature, and nature and the environment. Additionally, a special award, the Outdoor Classic Award, is given annually to books which, over a period of time, have proven to be exceptionally valuable works in the outdoor field. Application forms and eligibility requirements are available online. Applications for the Awards program become available in early June. Deadline: August 22. Prize: Winning books are promoted nationally and are entitled to display the National Outdoor Book Award (NOBA) medallion.

THE NEUTRINO SHORT-SHORT CONTEST

Passages North, Passages North, Northern Michigan University, 1401 Presque Isle Ave., Marquette MI 49855. (906)227-1203. **Fax:** (906)227-1096. **E-mail:** passages@nmu.edu. **Website:** www.passagesnorth.com. **Contact:** Jennifer Howard. Offered every 2 years to publish new voices in literary fiction, nonfiction, hybrid-essays, and prose poems (maximum 1,000 words). Guidelines available for SASE or online. Deadline: April 15. Submission period begins February 15. Prize: $1,000, and publication for the winner; 2 honorable mentions also published; all entrants receive a copy of *Passages North*. 2019: Tarfia Faizullah

NEW ENGLAND BOOK AWARDS

NEIBA, 1955 Massachusetts Ave., #2, Cambridge MA 02140. (617)547-3642. **Fax:** (617)547-3759. **E-mail:** ali@neba.org. **Website:** www.newenglandbooks.org. **Contact:** Nan Sorensen, Administrative Coordinator. All books must be either written by a New-England-based author or be set in New England. Eligible books must be published between September 1, 2017 and August 31, 2018 in either hardcover or paperback. Submissions made by New England booksellers and publishers. Submit written nominations only; actual books should not be sent. Award is given to a specific title: fiction, non-fiction, children's, or young adult. The titles must be either about New England, set in

New England. or by an author residing in the New England. The titles must be hardcover, paperback original, or reissue that was published between September 1 and August 31. Entries must be still in print and available. Deadline: June 14. Prize: Winners will receive $250 for literacy to a charity of their choice. Judged by NEIBA membership.

NEW LETTERS LITERARY AWARDS

New Letters, University of Missouri-Kansas City, 5101 Rockhill Rd., Kansas City MO 64110-2499. (816)235-1168. **E-mail:** newletters@umkc.edu. **Website:** www.newletters.org/writers-wanted/writing-contests. **Contact:** Ashley Wann. Award has 3 categories (fiction, poetry, and creative nonfiction) with 1 winner in each. Offered annually for previously unpublished work. For guidelines, send an SASE to *New Letters*, or visit http://www.newletters.org/writers-wanted/writing-contests. Deadline: May 18. 1st place: $1,500, plus publication in poetry and fiction category; 1st place: $2,500, plus publication in essay category. Judged by regional writers of prominence and experience. Final judging by someone of national repute. Previous judges include Maxine Kumin, Albert Goldbarth, Charles Simic, and Janet Burroway.

NEW MILLENNIUM AWARDS FOR FICTION, POETRY, AND NONFICTION

New Millennium Writings, New Millennium Writings, 340 S Lemon Ave #6906, Walnut CA 91789. (865)254-4880. **Website:** www.newmillenniumwritings.org. **Contact:** Alexis Williams, Editor and Publisher. No restrictions as to style, content, or number of submissions. Previously published pieces acceptable if online or under 5,000 print circulation. Simultaneous and multiple submissions welcome. Each fiction or nonfiction piece is a separate entry and should total no more than 6,000 words, except for the Short-Short Fiction Award, which should total no more than 1,000 words. (Nonfiction includes essays, profiles, memoirs, interviews, creative nonfiction, travel, humor, etc.) Each poetry entry may include up to 3 poems, not to exceed 5 pages total. All 20 poetry finalists will be published. Include name, phone, address, e-mail, and category on cover page only. Apply online via submissions manager. Send SASE or IRC for list of winners or await your book. Deadline: Postmarked on or before January 31 for the Winter Awards and June 23 for the Summer Awards. Prize: $1,000 for Best Poem; $1,000 for Best Fiction; $1,000 for Best Nonfiction; $1,000 for Best Flash Fiction (Short-Short Fiction).

NEW SOUTH WRITING CONTEST

English Department, Georgia State University, P.O. Box 3970, Atlanta GA 30302-3970. **E-mail:** newsoutheditors@gmail.com. **Website:** newsouthjournal.com/contest. **Contact:** Anna Sandy, editor-in-chief. Offered annually to publish the most promising work of up-and-coming writers of poetry (up to 3 poems) and fiction (9,000-word limit). Rights revert to writer upon publication. Guidelines online. Deadline: April 15. Prize: 1st Place: $1,000 in each category; 2nd Place: $250 Judged by Natalie Eilbert in poetry and SJ Sindu in prose.

NORTHERN CALIFORNIA BOOK AWARDS

Northern California Book Reviewers Association, Northern California Book Awards, c/o Poetry Flash, 1450 Fourth St. #4, Att'n: NCBR, Berkeley CA 94710. (510)525-5476. **E-mail:** ncbr@poetryflash.org; editor@poetryflash.org. **Website:** www.poetryflash.org. **Contact:** Joyce Jenkins, Executive Director. Annual Northern California Book Award for outstanding book in literature; open to books published in the current calendar year by Northern California authors. NCBR presents annual awards to Bay Area (northern California) authors annually in fiction, nonfiction, poetry, and children's literature. Previously published books only. Must be published the calendar year prior to spring awards ceremony. Submissions nominated by publishers; author or agent could also nominate published work. Send 3 copies of the book to attention: NCBR. Encourages writers and stimulates interest in books and reading. Deadline: January 18. Prize: $100 honorarium and award certificate. Judging by voting members of the Northern California Book Reviewers.

NOVA WRITES COMPETITION FOR UNPUBLISHED MANUSCRIPTS

Writers' Federation of Nova Scotia, 1113 Marginal Rd., Halifax NS B3H 4P7. (902)423-8116. **Fax:** (902)422-0881. **E-mail:** programs@writers.ns.ca. **Website:** www.writers.ns.ca. **Contact:** Robin Spittal, Communications and Development Officer. Annual program designed to honor work by unpublished writers in all 4 Atlantic Provinces. Entry is open to writers unpublished in the category of writing they wish to enter. Prizes are presented in the fall of each year. Categories include: short form creative nonfiction, long form creative nonfiction, novel, poetry, short story, and writing for children/young adult novel. Judges return written comments when competition is concluded. Page lengths and rules vary based on categories. See website for details. Anyone resident in the Atlantic Provinces since September 1st immediately prior to the deadline date is eligible to enter. Only 1 entry per category is allowed. Each entry requires its own entry form and registration fee. Deadline: January 3. Prizes vary based on categories. See website for details.

OHIOANA BOOK AWARDS

Ohioana Library Association, 274 E. First Ave., Suite 300, Columbus OH 43201-3673. (614)466-3831. **Fax:** (614)728-6974. **E-mail:** ohioana@ohioana.org. **Website:** www.ohioana.org. **Contact:** David Weaver, executive director. Writers must have been born in Ohio or lived in Ohio for at least 5 years, but books about Ohio or an Ohioan need not be written by an Ohioan. Finalists announced in May and winners in July. Winners notified by mail in early summer. Offered annually to bring national attention to Ohio authors and their books, published in the last year. (Books can only be considered once.) Categories: Fiction, nonfiction, juvenile, poetry, and books about Ohio or an Ohioan. Deadline: December 31. Prize: $1,000 cash prize, certificate, and glass sculpture. Judged by a jury selected by librarians, book reviewers, writers and other knowledgeable people.

OKLAHOMA BOOK AWARDS

200 NE 18th St., Oklahoma City OK 73105. (405)521-2502. **Fax:** (405)525-7804. **E-mail:** connie.armstrong@libraries.ok.gov. **Website:** www.odl.state.ok.us/ocb. **Contact:** Connie Armstrong, executive director. This award honors Oklahoma writers and books about Oklahoma. Awards are presented to best books in fiction, nonfiction, children's, design and illustration, and poetry books about Oklahoma or books written by an author who was born, is living or has lived in Oklahoma. SASE for award rules and entry forms. Winner will be announced at banquet in Oklahoma City. The Arrell Gibson Lifetime Achievement Award is also presented each year for a body of work. Previously published submissions only. Submissions made by the author, author's agent, or entered by a person or group of people, including the publisher. Must be published during the calendar year preceding the award. Deadline: January 10. Prize: Awards a medal. Judging by a panel of 5 people for each category, generally a librarian, a working writer in the genre, booksellers, editors, etc.

OPEN SEASON AWARDS

The Malahat Review, University of Victoria, P.O. Box 1700, Stn CSC, Victoria BC V8V 2Y2 Canada. (250)721-8524. **Fax:** (250)472-5051. **E-mail:** malahat@uvic.ca. **Website:** www.malahatreview.ca. **Contact:** L'Amour Lisik, publicity manager. The Open Season Awards accepts entries of poetry, fiction, and creative nonfiction. Winners published in the spring issue of *The Malahat Review*, announced in the winter on our website, social media pages, and in our monthly e-newsletter, *Malahat lite*. Submissions must be unpublished. No simultaneous submissions. Submit up to 3 poems of 100 lines or less; 1 piece of fiction 2,500 words maximum; or 1 piece of creative nonfiction, 2,500 words maximum. No restrictions on subject matter or aesthetic approach. Include separate page with writer's name, address, e-mail, payment order number, and title(s); no identifying information on mss pages. Submissions accepted via Submittable using the Open Season Awards form (only available when contest is running). Mailed and emailed submissions are no longer accepted. Guidelines available on website. Winners will be contacted by email. Deadline: November 1. Prize: $6,000 over three categories (poetry, fiction, creative nonfiction) and publication in *The Malahat Review*.

OREGON BOOK AWARDS

925 SW Washington St., Portland OR 97205. (503)227-2583. **Fax:** (503)241-4256. **E-mail:** la@literary-arts.org. **Website:** www.literary-arts.org. **Contact:** Susan Denning, director of programs and events. The annual Oregon Book Awards celebrate Oregon authors in the areas of poetry, fiction, nonfiction, drama and young readers' literature published between August 1 and July 31 of the previous calendar year. Awards are available for every category. See website for details. Entry fee determined by initial print run; see website for details. Entries must be previously published. Oregon residents only. Accepts inquiries by phone and e-mail. Finalists announced in January. Winners announced at an awards ceremony in November. List of winners available in April. Deadline: August 26. Prize: Grant of $2,500. (Grant money could vary.) Judged by writers who are selected from outside Oregon for their expertise in a genre. Past judges include Mark Doty, Colson Whitehead and Kim Barnes.

JUDITH SIEGEL PEARSON AWARD

Judith Siegel Pearson Award, c/o Department of English, Wayne State University, Attn: Royanne Smith, 5057 Woodward Ave., Ste. 9408, Detroit MI 48202. **E-mail:** fm8146@wayne.edu. **Website:** https://wsu-writingawards.submittable.com/submit. **Contact:** Donovan Hohn. Offers an annual award for the best creative or scholarly work on a subject concerning women. The type of work accepted rotates each year: nonfiction in 2018; fiction in 2019; drama in 2020, poetry in 2021. Open to all interested writers and scholars. Only submit the appropriate genre in each year. Submit electronically on the web site listed here. Deadline: February 22. Prize: $500. Judged by members of the writing faculty of the Wayne State University English Department.

PEN CENTER USA LITERARY AWARDS

PEN Center USA, P.O. Box 6037, Beverly Hills CA 90212. (323)424-4939. **E-mail:** awards@penusa.org. **E-mail:** awards@penusa.org. **Website:** www.penusa.org. Offered for work published or produced in the previous calendar year. Open to writers living west of the Mississippi River. Award categories: fiction, poetry, research nonfiction, creative nonfiction, translation, young adult, graphic literature, drama, screenplay, teleplay, journalism. Guidelines and submission form available on website. No anthologies or self-pubished work. Deadline: See website for details. Prize: $1,000.

PENGUIN RANDOM HOUSE CREATIVE WRITING AWARDS

One Scholarship Way, P.O. Box 297, St. Peter MN 56082. (212)782-9348. **Fax:** (212) 782-5157. **E-mail:** creativewriting@penguinrandomhouse.com. **Website:** www.penguinrandomhouse.com/creative-writing. **Contact:** Melanie Fallon Hauska, director. Offered annually for unpublished work to NYC public high school seniors. 72 awards given in literary and nonliterary categories. Four categories: poetry, fiction/drama, personal essay, and graphic novel. Applicants must be seniors (under age 21) at a New York high school. No college essays or class assignments will be accepted. Word length: 2,500 words or less. Applicants must be seniors (under age 21) at a New York high school. Results announced mid-May. Winners notified by mail and phone. For contest results, send SASE, fax, e-mail or visit website. Deadline: February 3 for all categories. Graphic Novel extended deadline: March 1st. Prize: Awards range from $500-10,000. The program usually awards just under $100,000 in scholarships.

THE PINCH LITERARY AWARDS

Literary Awards, The Pinch, Department of English, The University of Memphis, Memphis TN 38152-6176. (901)678-4591. **Website:** www.pinchjournal.com. Offered annually for unpublished short stories of 5,000 words maximum or up to three poems. Guidelines on website. Cost: $20, which is put toward one issue of *The Pinch*. Deadline: March 15. Prize: 1st place Fiction: $1,500 and publication; 1st place Poetry: $1,000 and publication. Offered annually for unpublished short stories and prose of up to 5,000 words and 1-3 poems. Deadline: March 15. Open to submissions on December 15. Prizes: $1,000 for 1st place in each category.

PNWA LITERARY CONTEST

Pacifc Northwest Writers Association, PMB 2717, 1420 NW Gilman Blvd., Suite 2, Issaquah WA 98027. (452)673-2665. **Fax:** (452)961-0768. **E-mail:** pnwa@pnwa.org. **Website:** www.pnwa.org. Annual literary contest with 12 different categories. See website for details and specific guidelines. Each entry receives 2 critiques. Winners announced at the PNWA Summer Conference, held annually in mid-July. Deadline: February 20. Prize: 1st Place: $600; 2nd Place: $300; 3rd Place: $100. Judged by an agent or editor attending the conference.

PRAIRIE SCHOONER BOOK PRIZE

Prairie Schooner and the University of Nebraska Press, Prairie Schooner Prize Series, 123 Andrews Hall, Lincoln NE 68588-0334. (402)472-0911. **E-mail:** PSBookPrize@unl.edu. **Website:** prairieschooner.unl.edu. **Contact:** Kwame Dawes, editor. Annual competition/award for poetry and short story collections. The Prairie Schooner Book Prize Series welcomes manuscripts from all living writers, including non-US citizens, writing in English. Both unpublished and published writers are welcome to submit manuscripts. Writers may enter both contests. Simultaneous submissions are accepted, but we ask that you notify us immediately if your manuscript is accepted for publication somewhere else. No past or present paid employee of Prairie Schooner or the University of Nebraska Press or current faculty or student at the University of Nebraska will be eligible for the prizes. Deadline: March 15. Prize: $3,000 and publication through the University of Nebraska Press.

THE PRESIDIO LA BAHIA AWARD

Sons of the Republic of Texas, 1717 Eighth St., Bay City TX 77414-5033. (979)245-6644. **Fax:** (979)244-3819. **E-mail:** srttexas@srttexas.org. **Website:** www.srttexas.org. **Contact:** Scott Dunbar, chairman. "Material may be submitted concerning the influence on Texas culture of our Spanish Colonial heritage in laws, customs, language, religion, architecture, art, and other related fields." Offered annually to promote suitable preservation of relics, appropriate dissemination of data, and research into Texas heritage, with particular attention to the Spanish Colonial period. Deadline: September 30. Prizes: $2,000 available annually for winning participants; 1st Place: Minimum of $1,200; 2nd and 3rd prizes at the discretion of the judges. Judged by members of the Sons of the Republic of Texas on the Presidio La Bahia Award Committee.

PRIME NUMBER MAGAZINE AWARDS

Press 53, 560 N. Trade St., Suite 103, Winston-Salem NC 27101. (336)770-5353. **E-mail:** kevin@press53.com. **Website:** www.press53.com. **Contact:** Kevin Morgan Watson, publisher. Awards $1,000 each for poetry and short fiction. Details and guidelines available online. Deadline: April 15. Submission period begins January 1. Finalists and winners announced by August 1. Winners published in Prime Number Magazine in October. Prize: $1,000 cash. All winners receive publication in Prime Number Magazine online. Judged by industry professionals to be named when the contest begins.

PRISM INTERNATIONAL ANNUAL SHORT FICTION, POETRY, AND CREATIVE NONFICTION CONTESTS

PRISM International, Creative Writing Program, UBC, Buch. E462, 1866 Main Mall, Vancouver BC V6T 1Z1 Canada. **E-mail:** promotions@prismmagazine.ca. **Website:** www.prismmagazine.ca. **Contact:** Claire Matthews. Offered annually for unpublished work to award the best in contemporary fiction, poetry, drama, translation, and nonfiction. Works of translation are eligible. Guidelines are available on website. Acquires first North American serial rights upon publication, and limited web rights for pieces selected for website. Open to any writer except students and faculty in the Creative Writing Department at UBC, or people who have taken a creative writing course at UBC within 2 years of the contest deadline. Entry includes subscription. Deadlines: Creative Nonfiction: July 15; Fiction: January 15; Poetry: October 15. Prize: All grand prizes are $1,500, $600 for first runner up, and $400 for second runner up. Winners are published.

PUSHCART PRIZE

Pushcart Press, P.O. Box 380, Wainscott NY 11975. (631)324-9300. **Website:** www.pushcartprize.com. **Contact:** Bill Henderson. Published every year since 1976, The Pushcart Prize - Best of the Small Presses series "is the most honored literary project in America. Hundreds of presses and thousands of writers of short stories, poetry and essays have been represented in the pages of our annual collections." Little magazine and small book press editors (print or online) may make up to six nominations from their year's publicatoins by the deadline. The nominations may be any combination of poetry, short fiction, essays or literary whatnot. Editors may nominate self-contained portions of books — for instance, a chapter from a novel. Deadline: December 1.

THE RBC BRONWEN WALLACE AWARD FOR EMERGING WRITERS

The Writers' Trust of Canada, 460 Richmond St. W., Suite 600, Toronto ON M5C 1P1 Canada. (416)504-8222. **Fax:** (416)504-9090. **E-mail:** djackson@writerstrust.com. **Website:** www.writerstrust.com. **Contact:** Devon Jackson. Presented annually to a Canadian writer under the age of 35 who is not yet published in book form. The award, which alternates each year between poetry and short fiction, was established in memory of Bronwen Wallace and honours her wish to help more writers achieve success at a young age. Prize: $10,000. Two finalists receive $2,500 each.

SUMMERFIELD G. ROBERTS AWARD

Sons of the Republic of Texas, 1717 Eighth St., Suite 12, Bay City TX 77414-5033. (979)245-6644. **Fax:** (979)244-3819. **E-mail:** aa-srt@son-rep-texas.net. **Website:** www.srttexas.org. **Contact:** Kenneth Pfeiffer, chairman. The mss must be written or published during the calendar year for which the award is given. No entry may be submitted more than one time. There is no word limit on the material submitted for the award. The manuscripts may be fiction, nonfiction, poems, essays, plays, short stories, novels, or biographies. The competition is open to all writers everywhere; they need not reside in Texas nor must the publishers be in Texas. Judges each year are winners of the award in the last 3 years. The purpose of this award is to encourage literary effort and research about historical events and personalities during the days of the Republic of Texas,1836-1846, and to stimulate interest in this period. Deadline: January 15. Prize: $2,500.

ERNEST SANDEEN PRIZE IN POETRY AND THE RICHARD SULLIVAN PRIZE IN SHORT FICTION

University of Notre Dame, Dept. of English, 356 O'Shaughnessy Hall, Notre Dame IN 46556-5639. (574)631-7526. **Fax:** (574)631-4795. **E-mail:** creative-writing@nd.edu. **Website:** http://english.nd.edu/creative-writing/publications/sandeen-sullivan-prizes. **Contact:** Director of Creative Writing. The Sandeen & Sullivan Prizes in Poetry and Short Fiction is awarded to the author who has published at least one volume of short fiction or one volume of poetry. Awarded biannually, but judged quadrennially. Though the Sandeen Prize is open to any author, with the exception of graduates of the University of Notre Dame, who has published at least one volume of short stories (Sullivan) or one collection of poetry (Sandeen), judges pay special attention to second volumes. Please include a vita and/or a biographical statement which includes your publishing history. Will also see a selection of reviews of the earlier collection. Please submit two copies of mss and inform if the mss is available on computer disk. Include an SASE for acknowledgment of receipt of your submission. If you would like your manuscript returned, please send an SASE. Manuscripts will not otherwise be returned. Submissions Period: May 1 - September 1. Prize: $1,000, a $500 award and a $500 advance against royalties from the Notre Dame Press.

SANTA FE WRITERS PROJECT LITERARY AWARDS PROGRAM

Santa Fe Writers Project, 369 Montezuma Ave., #350, Santa Fe NM 87501. **E-mail:** info@sfwp.com. **Website:** www.sfwp.com. **Contact:** Andrew Gifford. Annual contest seeking fiction and nonfiction of any genre. The Literary Awards Program was founded by a group of authors to offer recognition for excellence in writing in a time of declining support for writers and the craft of literature. Past judges have included Benjamin Percy, Jayne Anne Phillips, Robert Olen Butler, Emily St. John Mandel, and David Morrell. Deadline: July 15th. Prize: $2500 and publication. Judged by Carmen Maria Machado in 2019.

SASKATCHEWAN BOOK AWARDS

315-1102 8th Ave., Regina SK S4R 1C9 Canada. (306)569-1585. **E-mail:** director@bookawards.sk.ca. **Website:** www.bookawards.sk.ca. **Contact:** Courtney Bates-Hardy, executive director. Saskatchewan Book Awards celebrates, promotes, and rewards Saskatchewan authors and publishers worthy of recognition through 14 awards, granted on an annual or semiannual basis. Awards: Fiction, Nonfiction, Poetry, Scholarly, First Book, Prix du Livre Français, Regina, Saskatoon, Indigenous Peoples' Writing, Indigenous Peoples' Publishing, Publishing in Education, Publishing, Children's Literature/Young Adult Literature, Book of the Year. November 1. Prize: $2,000 (CAD) for all awards except Book of the Year, which is $3,000 (CAD). Juries are made up of writing and publishing professionals from outside of Saskatchewan.

THE MONA SCHREIBER PRIZE FOR HUMOROUS FICTION AND NONFICTION

3940 Laurel Canyon Blvd., #566, Studio City CA 91604 USA. **E-mail:** brad.schreiber@att.net. **Website:** www.bradschreiber.com. **Contact:** Brad Schreiber. Established in 2000 to honor Mona Schreiber, a writer and teacher. Entry fees are the same as in 2000 and money from entries helps pay for prizes. No SASEs. Non-US entries should enclose US currency or checks written in US dollars. Include e-mail address. No previously published work. The purpose of the contest is to award the most creative humor writing, in any form, under than 750 words, in either fiction or nonfiction, including but not limited to stories, articles, essays, speeches, shopping lists, diary entries, or anything else writers dream up. Complete rules and previous winning entries on website. Deadline: December 1. Prize: 1st Place: $500; 2nd Place: $250; 3rd Place: $100. Judged by Brad Schreiber, journalist, consultant, instructor, author of, among other books, the humor-writing, how-to *What Are You Laughing At?*

SHORT GRAIN CONTEST

P.O. Box 3986, Regina SK S4P 3R9 Canada. (306)791-7749. **E-mail:** grainmag@skwriter.com. **Website:** www.grainmagazine.ca/short-grain-contest. **Contact:** Jordan Morris, business administrator (inquiries only). The annual Short Grain Contest includes a category for poetry of any style up to 100 lines and fiction of any style up to 2,500 words, offering 3 prizes. Each entry must be original, unpublished, not submitted elsewhere for publication or broadcast, nor accepted elsewhere for publication or broadcast, nor entered simultaneously in any other contest or competition for which it is also eligible to win a prize. Entries must be typed on 8½x11 paper. It must be legible. No simultaneous submissions. A separate covering page must be attached to the text of your entry, and must provide the following information: Author's name, complete mailing address, telephone number, e-mail address, entry title, category name, and line count. Online submissions are accepted, see website for details. An absolutely accurate word or line count is required. No identifying information on the text pages. Entries will not be returned. Names of the winners and titles of the winning entries will be posted on the *Grain Magazine* website in August; only the winners will be notified. Deadline: April 1. Prize: $1,000, plus publication in *Grain Magazine*; 2nd Place: $750; 3rd Place: $500.

SKIPPING STONES HONOR (BOOK) AWARDS

P.O. Box 3939, Eugene OR 97403 USA. (541)342-4956. **Fax:** (541)342-4956. **E-mail:** editor@skippingstones.org. **Website:** www.skippingstones.org. **Contact:** Arun N. Toké. *Skipping Stones* is a well respected, multicultural literary magazine now in its 29th year. For multicultural and nature books and teaching resources. Entries must be previously published. Open to published books and teaching resources that appeared in print during a 2-year period prior to the deadline date. Guidelines for SASE or e-mail and on website. Accepts inquiries by e-mail or phone. The Annual Honors list includes approximately 25 books and teaching resources in three categories. Annual award to promote multicultural and/or nature awareness through creative writings for children and teens and their educators. Seeks authentic, exceptional, child/youth friendly books that promote intercultural, international, intergenerational harmony, or understanding through creative ways. Deadline: February 29. Prize: Honor certificates; gold seals; reviews; press release/publicity. Judged by a multicultural committee of teachers, librarians, parents, students and editors.

THE BERNICE SLOTE AWARD

Prairie Schooner, 110 Andrews Hall, PO Box 880334, Lincoln NE 68588-0334. (402)472-0911. **Fax:** (402)472-1817. **E-mail:** PrairieSchooner@unl.edu. **Website:** www.prairieschooner.unl.edu. **Contact:** Kwame Dawes. Categories: short stories, essays, and poetry. For guidelines, send SASE or visit website. Only work published in the journal during the previous year will be considered. Work is nominated by the editorial staff. Offered annually for the best work by a beginning writer published in *Prairie Schooner* in the previous year. Celebrates the best and finest writing that they have published for the year. Prize: $500. Judged by editorial staff of *Prairie Schooner*.

JEFFREY E. SMITH EDITORS' PRIZE IN FICTION, NONFICTION AND POETRY

The Missouri Review, 357 McReynolds Hall, UMC, Columbia MO 65201. (573)882-4474. **Fax:** (573)884-4671. **E-mail:** contest_question@moreview.com. **Website:** www.missourireview.com. **Contact:** Editor. Offered annually for unpublished work in 3 categories: fiction, essay, and poetry. Guidelines online or for SASE. Deadline: October 16. Prize: $5,000 and publication for each category winner.

KAY SNOW WRITING CONTEST

Willamette Writers, Willamette Writers, 2108 Buck St., West Linn OR 97068. (503)305-6729. **Fax:** (503)344-6174. **E-mail:** reg@willamettewriters.com. **Website:** www.willamettewriters.org. Willamette Writers is the largest writers' organization in Oregon and one of the largest writers' organizations in the United States. It is a non-profit, tax-exempt Oregon corporation led by volunteers. Elected officials and directors administer an active program of monthly meetings, special seminars, workshops, and an annual writing conference. Continuing with established programs and starting new ones is only made possible by strong volunteer support. See website for specific details and rules. There are six different categories writers can enter: Adult Fiction, Adult Nonfiction, Poetry, Juvenile Short Story, Screenwriting, and Student Writer. The purpose of this annual writing contest, named in honor of Willamette Writer's founder, Kay Snow, is to help writers reach professional goals in writing in a broad array of categories and to encourage student writers. Deadline: April 23. Submission deadline begins January 15. Prize: One first prize of $300, one second place prize of $150, and a third place prize of $50 per winning entry in each of the six categories. Student first prize is $50, $20 for second place, $10 for third.

SOCIETY OF MIDLAND AUTHORS AWARD

Society of Midland Authors, P.O. Box 10419, Chicago IL 60610-0419. **E-mail:** marlenetbrill@comcast.net.

Website: www.midlandauthors.com. **Contact:** Marlene Targ Brill, awards chair. Since 1957, the Society has presented annual awards for the best books written by Midwestern authors. The Society began in 1915. The contest is open to any title published within the year prior to the contest year. Open to adult and children's authors/poets who reside in, were born in, or have strong ties to a Midland state, which includes Illinois, Indiana, Iowa, Kansas, Michigan, Minnesota, Missouri, Nebraska, North Dakota, South Dakota, Ohio, and Wisconsin. The Society of Midland Authors (SMA) Award is presented to one title in each of 6 categories: adult nonfiction, adult fiction, adult biography and memoir, children's nonfiction, children's fiction, and poetry. There may be honor book winners as well. Books and entry forms must be mailed to the 3 judges in each category; for a list of judges and the entry and payment forms, visit the SMA website. Do not mail books to the society's P.O. box. The fee can be sent to the SMA P.O. box or paid via Paypal. Deadline: The first Saturday in January for books from the previous year. Prize: $500 and a plaque that is awarded at the SMA banquet in May in Chicago. Honorary winners receive a plaque. Check the SMA website for each year's judges at the end of October.

SOUL-MAKING KEATS LITERARY COMPETITION

The Webhallow House, 1544 Sweetwood Dr., Broadmoor Vlg. CA 94015-2029. **E-mail:** soulkeats@mail.com. **Website:** www.soulmakingcontest.us. **Contact:** Eileen Malone, contest founder/director. Annual open contest offers cash prizes in each of 12 literary categories. Competition receives 600 entries/year. Names of winners and judges are posted on website. Winners announced in January by SASE and on website. Winners are invited to read at the Koret Auditorium, San Francisco. Event is televised. Submissions in some categories may be previously published. No names or other identifying information on mss; include 3x5 card with poet's name, address, phone, fax, e-mail, title(s) of work, and category entered. Include SASE for results only; mss will not be returned. Guidelines available on website. Ongoing Deadline: November 30. Prizes: 1st Prize: $100; 2nd Prize: $50; 3rd Prize: $25.

STORY MONSTER APPROVED BOOK AWARDS

Story Monsters LLC, 4696 W. Tyson St., Chandler AZ 85226. (480)940-8182. **Fax:** (480)940-8787. **E-mail:** linda@storymonsters.com. **E-mail:** cristy@storymonsters.com. **Website:** www.dragonflybookawards.com. **Contact:** Cristy Bertini. The Story Monsters Approved! book designation program was developed to recognize and honor accomplished authors in the field of children's literature that inspire, inform, teach, or entertain. A Story Monsters seal of approval on your book tells teachers, librarians, and parents they are giving children the very best. Kids know when they see the Story Monsters Approved! seal, it means children their own age enjoyed the book and are recommending they read it, too. How do they know that? Because after books pass a first round of rigorous judging by industry experts, the books are then judged by a panel of youth judges who must also endorse the books before they can receive the official seal of approval. Guidelines available online. Send submissions to Cristy Bertini, Attn.: Dragonfly Book Awards, 1271 Turkey St., Ware, MA 01082. There is no deadline to enter. Books are sent for judging as they are received. The Book of the Year winner will receive a feature interview and a full-page ad in Story Monsters Ink® magazine, a certificate commemorating their accomplishment, and 50 Story Monsters Approved! seals. All authors earning a Story Monsters Approved! designation receive a certificate commemorating their accomplishment; 50 award seals, a news release sent to a comprehensive list of media outlets, and listings on our website and in Story Monsters Ink® magazine. Our judging panel includes industry experts in the fields of education and publishing, and student judges.

✪ SUBTERRAIN MAGAZINE'S LUSH TRIUMPHANT LITERARY AWARDS COMPETITION

P.O. Box 3008 MPO, Vancouver BC V6B 3X5 Canada. (604)876-8710. **Fax:** (604)879-2667. **E-mail:** subter@portal.ca. **Website:** www.subterrain.ca. Entrants may submit as many entries in as many categories as they like. Fiction: Max of 3,000 words. Poetry: A suite of 5 related poems (max of 15 pages). Creative Nonfiction (based on fact, adorned with fiction): Max of 4,000 words. All entries must be previously unpublished material and not currently under consideration in any other contest or competition. Deadline: May 15. Prize: Winners in each category will receive $1,000 cash (plus payment for publication) and publication in the Winter issue. First runner-up in each category will be published in the Spring issue of *subTerrain*.

THE TEXAS INSTITUTE OF LETTERS LITERARY AWARDS

E-mail: Betwx@aol.com. **Website:** www.texasinstituteofletters.org. The Texas Institute of Letters gives annual awards for books by Texas authors and writers who have produced books about Texas, including Best Books of Poetry, Fiction, and Nonfiction. Awards are also given for best Short Story, Magazine or Newspaper Article, Essay, and best Books for Children and Young Adults. Work submitted must have been published in the year stipulated, and entries may be made by authors or by their publishers. Complete guidelines and award information is available on the Texas Institute of Letters website.

TORONTO BOOK AWARDS

City of Toronto c/o Toronto Arts & Culture, Cultural Partnerships, City Hall, 9E, 100 Queen St. W., Toronto ON M5H 2N2 Canada. **E-mail:** shan@toronto.ca. **Website:** www.toronto.ca/book_awards. The Toronto Book Awards honor authors of books of literary or artistic merit that are evocative of Toronto. There are no separate categories; all books are judged together. Any fiction or nonfiction book published in English for adults and/or children that are evocative of Toronto are eligible. To be eligible, books must be published between January 1 and December 31 of previous year. Deadline: April 30. Prize: Each finalist receives $1,000 and the winning author receives$10,000 ($15,000 total in prize money available).

THE JULIA WARD HOWE AWARD

The Boston Authors Club, 33 Brayton Road, Brighton MA 02135. (617)783-1357. **E-mail:** alan.lawson@bc.edu. **Website:** www.bostonauthorsclub.org. **Contact:** Alan Lawson, president. Julia Ward Howe Prize offered annually in the spring for books published the previous year. Two awards are given: one for adult books of fiction, nonfiction, or poetry, and one for children's books, middle grade and young adult novels, nonfiction, or poetry. No picture books or subsidized publishers. There must be two copies of each book submitted. Authors must live within 100 miles of Boston the year their book is published. Deadline: January 15. Prize: $1,000 in each category. Several books will also be cited with no cash awards as Finalists or Highly Recommended.

THE ROBERT WATSON LITERARY PRIZE IN FICTION AND POETRY

The Robert Watson Literary Prizes, *The Greensboro Review*, MFA Writing Program, 3302 MHRA Building, Greensboro NC 27402-6170. (336)334-5459. **E-mail:** tgr@uncg.edu. **Website:** www.greensbororeview.org. **Contact:** Terry Kennedy, editor. Offered annually for fiction (up to 25 double-spaced pages) and poetry (up to 10 pages). Entries must be unpublished. Open to any writer. Guidelines available online. Submit online: https://greensbororeview.submittable.com/submit. Deadline: September 15. Prize: $1,000 each for best short story and poem. Judged by editors of *The Greensboro Review*.

WESTERN AUSTRALIAN PREMIER'S BOOK AWARDS

State Library of Western Australia, Perth Cultural Centre, 25 Francis St., Perth WA 6000 Australia. (61) (8)9427-3151. **E-mail:** premiersbookawards@slwa.wa.gov.au. **Website:** pba.slwa.wa.gov.au. **Contact:** Karen de San Miguel. Annual competition for Australian citizens or permanent residents of Australia, or writers whose work has Australia as its primary focus. Categories: children's books, digital narrative, fiction, nonfiction, poetry, scripts, writing for young adults, West Australian history, and Western Australian emerging writers. Submit 5 original copies of the work to be considered for the awards. All works must have been published between January 1 and December 31 of the prior year. See website for details and rules of entry. Deadline: January 31. Prize: Awards $25,000 for Premier's Prize; awards $15,000 each for the Children's Books, Digital Narrative, Fiction, and Nonfiction categories; awards $10,000 each for the Poetry, Scripts, Western Australian History, Western Australian Emerging Writers, and Writing for Young Adults; awards $5,000 for People's Choice Award.

WESTERN HERITAGE AWARDS

National Cowboy & Western Heritage Museum, 1700 NE 63rd St., Oklahoma City OK 73111-7997. (405)478-2250. **Fax:** (405)478-4714. **Website:** www.nationalcowboymuseum.org. **Contact:** Jessica Limestall. The National Cowboy & Western Heritage Museum Western Heritage Awards were established to honor and encourage the legacy of those whose works in literature, music, film, and television reflect the significant stories of the American West. Accepted categories for literary entries: western novel, nonfiction book, art book, photography book, juvenile book, magazine article, or poetry book. Previously published submissions only; must be published the calendar year before the awards are presented. Requirements for entrants: The material must pertain to the development or preservation of the West, either from a historical or contemporary viewpoint. Literary entries must have been published between December 1 and November 30 of calendar year. Five copies of each published work must be furnished for judging with each entry, along with the completed entry form. Works recognized during special awards ceremonies held annually at the museum. There is an autograph party preceding the awards. Awards ceremonies are sometimes broadcast. The WHA are presented annually to encourage the accurate and artistic telling of great stories of the West through 16 categories of western literature, television, film and music; including fiction, nonfiction, children's books and poetry. See website for details and category definitions. Deadline: November 30. Prize: Awards a Wrangler bronze sculpture designed by famed western artist, John Free. Judged by a panel of judges selected each year with distinction in various fields of western art and heritage.

WESTERN WRITERS OF AMERICA

271 CR 219, Encampment WY 82325. (307)329-8942. **E-mail:** wwa.moulton@gmail.com. **Website:** www.westernwriters.org. **Contact:** Candy Moulton, executive director. Eighteen Spur Award categories in various aspects of the American West. Send entry form with your published work. Accepts multiple submissions, each with its own entry form, available on our website. The nonprofit Western Writers of America has promoted and honored the best in Western literature with the annual Spur Awards, selected by panels of judges. Awards, for material published last year, are given for works whose inspirations, image and literary excellence best represent the reality and spirit of the American West. Deadline: January 4. Judged by independent Judges.

WESTMORELAND POETRY & SHORT STORY CONTEST

Westmoreland Arts & Heritage Festival, 252 Twin Lakes Road, Latrobe PA 15650-9415. (724)834-7474. **Fax:** (724)850-7474. **E-mail:** info@artsandheritage.com. **Website:** www.artsandheritage.com. **Contact:** Diane Shrader. Offered annually for unpublished work. Two categories: Poem and Short Story. Short story entries no longer than 4,000 words. Family-oriented festival and contest. Deadline: February 17. Prizes: Award: $200; 1st Place: $125; 2nd Place: $100; 3rd Place: $75.

WILLA LITERARY AWARD

Women Writing the West, 8547 East Arapaho Rd., #J-541, Greenwood Village CO 80112-1436. **E-mail:** 2019willachair@gmail.com. **Website:** www.womenwritingthewest.org. **Contact:** Carmen Peone. The WILLA Literary Award honors the year's best in published literature featuring women's or girls' stories set in the West. Women Writing the West (WWW), a nonprofit association of writers and other professionals writing and promoting the Women's West, underwrites and presents the nationally recognized award annually (for work published between January 1 and December 31). The award is named in honor of Pulitzer Prize winner Willa Cather, one of the country's foremost novelists. The award is given in 8 categories: historical fiction, contemporary fiction, original softcover fiction, creative nonfiction, scholarly nonfiction, poetry, children's fiction and nonfiction and young adult fiction/nonfiction. Entry forms available on the website. Deadline: November 1–February 1. Prize: $150 and a trophy. Finalist receives a plaque. Both receive digital and sticker award emblems for book covers. Notice of Winning and Finalist titles mailed to more than 4,000 booksellers, libraries, and others. Award announcement is in early August, and awards are presented to the winners and finalists at the annual WWW Fall Conference. Also, the eight winners will participate in a drawing for 2 two week all expenses paid residencies donated by Playa at Summer Lake in Oregon. Judged by professional librarians not affiliated with WWW.

TENNESSEE WILLIAMS/NEW ORLEANS LITERARY FESTIVAL CONTESTS

Tennessee Williams/New Orleans Literary Festival, 938 Lafayette St., Suite 514, New Orleans LA 70113. (504)581-1144. **E-mail:** info@tennesseewilliams.net. **Website:** www.tennesseewilliams.net/contests. **Contact:** Paul J. Willis. Annual contests for: Unpublished One Act, Unpublished Short Fiction, Unpublished Flash Fiction, and Unpublished Poem. Plays should run no more than one hour in length. Unlimited entries per person. Production criteria include scripts requiring minimal technical support for a 100-seat theater. Cast of characters must be small. See website for additional guidelines and entry form. Fiction must not exceed 7,000 words. Poetry submissions should be 2-4 poems not exceeding 400 lines total. "Our competitions provide writers a large audience during one of the largest literary festivals in the nation." Deadline: October 1 (One Act, Fiction); October 15 (Poetry, Very Short Fiction). Prize: One Act: $1,500, staged read at the next festival, VIP All-Access Festival pass, and publication in Bayou. Poetry: $1,000, public reading at next festival, VIP all-access pass, publication in Louisiana Cultural Vistas Magazine. Fiction: $1,500, public reading at next festival, publication in Louisiana Literature, VIP all-access pass. Very Short Fiction: $500, publication in the New Orleans Review, VIP all-access past. Judged by special guest judges, who change every year.

THE WORD AWARDS

The Word Guild, The Word Guild, Suite # 226, 245 King George Rd, Brantford ON N3R 7N7 Canada. 800-969-9010 x 1. **E-mail:** info@thewordguild.com. **E-mail:** info@thewordguild.com. **Website:** www.thewordguild.com. **Contact:** Karen deBlieck. The Word Guild is an organization of Canadian writers and editors who are Christian, and who are committed to encouraging one another and to fostering standards of excellence in the art, craft, practice and ministry of writing. Memberships available for various experience levels. Yearly conference Write Canada (please see website for information) and features keynote speakers, continuing classes and workshops. Editors and agents on site. The Word Awards is for work published in the past year, in almost 30 categories including books, articles, essays, fiction, nonfiction, novels, short stories, songs, and poetry. Please see website for more information. Deadline: January 15. Prize $50 CAD for article and short pieces; $100 CAD for book entries. Finalists book entries are eligible for the $5,000 Grace Irwin prize. Judged by industry leaders and professionals.

WORLD'S BEST SHORT-SHORT STORY CONTEST, NARRATIVE NONFICTION CONTEST & SOUTHEAST REVIEW POETRY CONTEST

The Southeast Review, Florida State University, English Department, Tallahassee FL 32306. **E-mail:** southeastreview@gmail.com. **Website:** www.southeastreview.org. **Contact:** Erin Hoover, editor. Annual award for unpublished short-short stories (500 words or less), poetry, and narrative nonfiction (6,000 words or less). Visit website for details. Deadline: March 15. Prize: $500 per category. Winners and finalists will be published in *The Southeast Review*.

WRITER'S DIGEST ANNUAL WRITING COMPETITION

Writer's Digest, 5720 Flatiron Pwky., Boulder CO 80301. (715)445-4612, ext. 13430. **E-mail:** WritersDigestWritingCompetition@aimmedia.com. **Website:** www.writersdigest.com. Writing contest with 9 categories: Inspirational Writing (spiritual/religious, maximum 2,500 words); Memoir/Personal Essay (maximum 2,000 words); Magazine Feature Article (maximum 2,000 words);Children's/Young Adult Fiction (maximum 2,000 words) Short Story (genre, maximum 4,000 words); Short Story (mainstream/literary, maximum 4,000 words); Rhyming Poetry (maximum 32 lines); Nonrhyming Poetry (maximum 32 lines); Stage Play/TV/Movie Script (first 15 pages and 1-page synopsis). Entries must be original, in English, unpublished/unproduced (except for Magazine Feature Articles), and not accepted by another publisher/producer at the time of submission. Writer's Digest retains one-time publication rights to the winning entries in each category. Deadline: May (early bird); June. Grand Prize: $5,000 and a trip to the Writer's Digest Conference to meet with editors and agents; 1st Place: $1,000 and $100 of Writer's Digest Books; 2nd Place: $500 and $100 of Writer's Digest Books; 3rd Place: $250 and $100 of Writer's Digest Books; 4th Place: $100 and $50 of Writer's Digest Books; 5th Place:$50 and $50 of Writer's Digest Books; Sixth through Tenth place winners in each category:$25; and more.

WRITER'S DIGEST SELF-PUBLISHED BOOK AWARDS

Writer's Digest, 5720 Flatiron Pwky., Boulder CO 80301. (715)445-4612, ext. 13430. **E-mail:** writersdigestselfpublishingcompetition@aimmedia.com. **Website:** www.writersdigest.com. **Contact:** Nicole Howard. Contest open to all English-language, self-published books for which the authors have paid the full cost of publication, or the cost of printing has been paid for by a grant or as part of a prize. Categories include: Mainstream/Literary Fiction, Genre Fiction, Nonfiction, Inspirational (spiritual/new age), Life Stories (biographies/autobiographies/family histories/memoirs), Children's Books, Reference Books (directories/encyclopedias/guide books), Poetry, and Middle-Grade/Young Adult Books. Judges reserve the right to re-categorize entries. Judges reserve the right to withhold prizes in any category. All winners will be notified in October. Entrants must send a printed and bound book. Entries will be evaluated on content, writing quality, and overall quality of production and appearance. No handwritten books are accepted. Books must have been published within the past 5 years from the competition deadline. Books which have previously won awards from *Writer's Digest* are not eligible. Early bird deadline: April 2. Prizes: Grand Prize: $8,000, a trip to the Writer's Digest Conference, promotion in *Writer's Digest*, 10 copies of the book will be sent to major review houses, and a guaranteed review in *Midwest Book Review*; 1st Place (9 winners): $1,000 and promotion in *Writer's Digest*; Honorable Mentions: $50 worth of Writer's Digest Books and promotion on writersdigest.com. All entrants will receive a brief commentary from one of the judges.

WRITER'S DIGEST SELF-PUBLISHED E-BOOK AWARDS

Writer's Digest, 5720 Flatiron Pkwy., Boulder CO 80301 (715)445-4612, ext. 13430. **E-mail:** writersdigestselfpublishingcompetition@aimmedia.com. **Website:** www.writersdigest.com. **Contact:** Nicole Howard. Contest open to all English-language, self-published e-books for which the authors have paid the full cost of publication, or the cost of publication has been paid for by a grant or as part of a prize. Categories include: Mainstream/Literary Fiction, Genre Fiction, Nonfiction (includes reference books), Inspirational (spiritual/new age), Life Stories (biographies/autobiographies/family histories/memoirs), Children's Books, Poetry, and Middle-Grade/Young Adult Books. Judges reserve the right to re-categorize entries. Judges reserve the right to withhold prizes in any category. All winners will be notified by December 31. Entrants must enter online. Entrants may provide a file of the book or submit entry by the Amazon gifting process. Acceptable file types include: .epub, .mobi, .ipa. Word processing documents will not be accepted. Entries will be evaluated on content, writing quality, and overall quality of production and appearance. Books must have been published within the past 5 years from the competition deadline. Books which have previously won awards from *Writer's Digest* are not eligible. Early bird deadline: August 1; Deadline: September 4. Prizes: Grand Prize: $5,000, promotion in *Writer's Digest*, $200 worth of Writer's Digest Books, and more; 1st Place (9 winners): $1,000 and promotion in *Writer's Digest*; Honorable Mentions: $50 worth of Writer's Digest Books and promotion on writersdigest.com. All entrants will receive a brief commentary from one of the judges.

WRITERS-EDITORS NETWORK INTERNATIONAL WRITING COMPETITION

CNW Publishing, P.O. Box A, North Stratford NH 03590-0167. **E-mail:** contestentry@writers-editors.com. **E-mail:** info@writers-editors.com. **Website:** www.writers-editors.com. **Contact:** Dana K. Cassell, executive director. Annual award to recognize publishable talent. New categories and awards for 2018: Nonfiction (unpublished or self-published; may be an article, blog post, essay/opinion piece, column, nonfiction book chapter, children's article or book chapter); fiction (unpublished or self-published; may be a short story, novel chapter, Young Adult [YA] or children's story or book chapter); poetry (unpublished or self-published; may be traditional or free verse poetry or children's verse). Guidelines available online. Open to any writer. Maximum length: 4,000 words. Accepts inquiries by e-mail, phone and mail. Entry form online. Results announced May 31. Winners notified by mail and posted on website. Results available for SASE or visit website. Deadline: March 15. Prize: 1st Place: $150 plus one year Writers-Editors membership; 2nd Place: $100; 3rd Place: $75. All winners and Honorable Mentions will receive certificates as warranted. Most Promising entry in each category will receive a free critique by a contest judge. Judged by editors, librarians, and writers.

WRITERS' GUILD OF ALBERTA AWARDS

Writers' Guild of Alberta, Percy Page Centre, 11759 Groat Rd., Edmonton AB T5M 3K6 Canada. (780)422-8174. **Fax:** (780)422-2663. **E-mail:** mail@writersguild.ca. **Website:** writersguild.ca. **Contact:** Executive Director. Offers the following awards: Wilfrid Eggleston Award for Nonfiction; Georges Bugnet Award for Fiction; Howard O'Hagan Award for Short Story; Stephan G. Stephansson Award for Poetry; R. Ross Annett Award for Children's Literature; Gwen Pharis Ringwood Award for Drama; Jon Whyte Memorial Essay Award; James H. Gray Award for Short Nonfiction. Eligible entries will have been published anywhere in the world between January 1 and December 31 of the current year. The authors must have been residents of Alberta for at least 12 of the 18 months prior to December 31. Unpublished mss, except in the drama and essay categories, are not eligible. Anthologies are not eligible. Works may be submitted by authors, publishers, or any interested parties. Deadline: December 31. Prize: Winning authors receive $1,500; short piece prize winners receive $700.

WRITERS' LEAGUE OF TEXAS BOOK AWARDS

Writers' League of Texas, 611 S. Congress Ave., Suite 200A-3, Austin TX 78704. (512)499-8914. **Fax:** (512)499-0441. **E-mail:** sara@writersleague.org. **Website:** www.writersleague.org. **Contact:** Sara Kocek. Open to Texas authors of books published the previous year. To enter this contest, you must be a Texas author. "Texas author" is defined as anyone who (whether currently a resident or not) has lived in Texas for a period of 3 or more years. This contest is open to indie or self-published authors as well as traditionally-published authors. Deadline: February 28. Open to submissions October 7. Prize: $1,000 and a commemorative award.

LAMAR YORK PRIZE FOR FICTION AND NONFICTION CONTEST

The Chattahoochee Review, Georgia Perimeter College, 2101 Womack Rd., Dunwoody GA 30338-4497. (770)274-5479. **E-mail:** gpccr@gpc.edu. **Website:** thechattahoocheereview.gpc.edu. **Contact:** Anna Schachner, Editor. Offered annually for unpublished creative nonfiction and nonscholarly essays and fiction up to 5,000 words. *The Chattahoochee Review* buys first rights only for winning essay/ms for the purpose of publication in the summer issue. Entries should be submitted via Submittable. See website for details and guidelines. Deadline: January 31. Submission period begins October 1. Prize: 2 prizes of $1,000 each, plus publication. Judged by the editorial staff of *The Chattahoochee Review.*

THE YOUTH HONOR AWARDS

Skipping Stones Youth Honor Awards, Skipping Stones Magazine, Skipping Stones Magazine, P.O. Box 3939, Eugene OR 97403. (541)342-4956. **E-mail:** info@skippingstones.org. **E-mail:** editor@skippingstones.org. **Website:** www.skippingstones.org/wp. **Contact:** Arun N. Toke, Editor and Publisher. *Skipping Stones* is an international, literary, and multicultural, children's magazine that encourages cooperation, creativity, and celebration of cultural and linguistic diversity. It explores stewardship of the ecological and social webs that nurture us. It offers a forum for communication among children from different lands and backgrounds. *Skipping Stones* expands horizons in a playful, creative way. This is a non-commercial, nonprofit magazine with no advertisements. In its 31st year. Original writing and art from youth, ages 7 to 17, should be typed or neatly handwritten. The entries should be appropriate for ages 7 to 17. Prose under 1,000 words; poems under 30 lines. Word limit: 1,000. Poetry: 30 lines. Non-English and bilingual writings are welcome. To promote multicultural, international and nature awareness. Deadline: June 25. Prize: An Honor Award Certificate, issues of Skipping Stones magazine and five nature and/or multicultural books. They are also invited to join the Student Review Board. Everyone who enters the contest receives the autumn issue featuring the ten winners and other noteworthy entries. Editors and interns at the *Skipping Stones* magazine.

PROFESSIONAL ORGANIZATIONS

AGENTS' ORGANIZATIONS

ASSOCIATION OF AUTHORS' AGENTS (AAA), 5-8 Lower John St., Golden Square, London W1F 9HA. E-mail: anthonygoff@davidhigham.co.uk. Website: www.agentsassoc.co.uk.

ASSOCIATION OF AUTHORS' REPRESENTATIVES (AAR). E-mail: info@aar-online.org. Website: www.aar-online.org.

ASSOCIATION OF TALENT AGENTS (ATA), 9255 Sunset Blvd., Suite 930, Los Angeles CA 90069. (310)274-0628. E-mail: shellie@agentassociation.com. Website: www.agentassociation.com.

WRITERS' ORGANIZATIONS

ACADEMY OF AMERICAN POETS 584 Broadway, Suite 604, New York NY 10012. E-mail: academy@poets.org. Website: www.poets.org.

AMERICAN CRIME WRITERS LEAGUE (ACWL), 17367 Hilltop Ridge Dr., Eureka MO 63205. Website: www.acwl.org.

AMERICAN INDEPENDENT WRITERS (AIW), 1001 Connecticut Ave. NW, Suite 701, Washington DC 20036. E-mail: info@aiwriters.org. Website: americanindependentwriters.org.

AMERICAN MEDICAL WRITERS ASSOCIATION (AMWA), 30 West Gude Dr., Suite 525, Rockville MD 20850-4347. E-mail: amwa@amwa.org. Website: www.amwa.org.

AMERICAN SCREENWRITERS ASSOCIATION (ASA), 269 S. Beverly Dr., Suite 2600, Beverly Hills CA 90212. (866)265-9091. E-mail: asa@goasa.com. Website: www.asascreenwriters.com.

AMERICAN TRANSLATORS ASSOCIATION (ATA), 225 Reinekers Ln., Suite 590, Alexandria VA 22314. (703)683-6100. E-mail: ata@atanet.org. Website: www.atanet.org.

EDUCATION WRITERS ASSOCIATION (EWA), 2122 P St., NW Suite 201, Washington DC 20037. E-mail: ewa@ewa.org. Website: ewa.org.

HORROR WRITERS ASSOCIATION (HWA), 244 5th Ave., Suite 2767, New York NY 10001. E-mail: hwa@horror.org. Website: www.horror.org.

THE INTERNATIONAL WOMEN'S WRITING GUILD (IWWG), P.O. Box 810, Gracie Station, New York NY 10028. Website: www.iwwg.com.

MYSTERY WRITERS OF AMERICA (MWA), 1140 Broadway, Suite 1507, New York NY 10001. (212)888-8171. E-mail: mwa@mysterywriters.org. Website: www.mysterywriters.org.

NATIONAL ASSOCIATION OF SCIENCE WRITERS (NASW), P.O. Box 7905, Berkeley, CA 94707. (510)647-9500. E-mail: lfriedmann@nasw.org. Website: www.nasw.org.

NATIONAL ASSOCIATION OF WOMEN WRITERS (NAWW), 24165 IH-10 W., Suite 217-637, San Antonio TX 78257. Phone/Fax: (866)821-5829. Website: www.naww.org.

ORGANIZATION OF BLACK SCREENWRITERS (OBS). 1999 W. Adams Blvd., Mezzanine, Los Angeles CA 90018. Website: www.obswriter.com.

OUTDOOR WRITERS ASSOCIATION OF AMERICA (OWAA), 121 Hickory St., Suite 1, Missoula MT 59801. E-mail: krhoades@owaa.org. Website: www.owaa.org.

POETRY SOCIETY OF AMERICA (PSA), 15 Gramercy Park, New York NY 10003. Website: www.poetrysociety.org.

POETS & WRITERS, 90 Broad St., Suite 2100, New York NY 10004. (212)226-3586. Fax: (212)226-3963. Website: www.pw.org.

ROMANCE WRITERS OF AMERICA (RWA), 114615 Benfer Rd., Houston TX 77069. (832)717-5200. Fax: (832)717-5201. E-mail: info@rwanational.org. Website: www.rwanational.org.

SCIENCE FICTION AND FANTASY WRITERS OF AMERICA (SFWA), P.O. Box 877, Chestertown MD 21620. E-mail: execdir@sfwa.org. Website: www.sfwa.org.

SOCIETY OF AMERICAN BUSINESS EDITORS & WRITERS (SABEW), University of Missouri, School of Journalism, 30 Neff Annex, Columbia MO 65211. (602) 496-7862. E-mail: sabew@sabew.org. Website: www.sabew.org.

SOCIETY OF AMERICAN TRAVEL WRITERS (SATW), 7044 S. 13 St., Oak Creek WI 53154. E-mail: satw@satw.org. Website: www.satw.org.

SOCIETY OF CHILDREN'S BOOK WRITERS & ILLUSTRATORS (SCBWI), 8271 Beverly Blvd., Los Angeles CA 90048. E-mail: scbwi@scbwi.org. Website: www.scbwi.org.

WESTERN WRITERS OF AMERICA (WWA). E-mail: spiritfire@kc.rr.com. Website: www.westernwriters.org.

INDUSTRY ORGANIZATIONS

AMERICAN BOOKSELLERS ASSOCIATION (ABA), 200 White Plains Rd., Suite 600, Tarrytown NY 10591. (914)591-2665. E-mail: info@bookweb.org. Website: www.bookweb.org.

AMERICAN SOCIETY OF JOURNALISTS & AUTHORS (ASJA), 1501 Broadway, Suite 302, New York NY 10036. (212)997-0947. E-mail: director@asja.org. Website: www.asja.org.

ASSOCIATION FOR WOMEN IN COMMUNICATIONS (AWC), 3337 Duke St., Alexandria VA 22314. (703)370-7436. E-mail: info@womcom.org. Website: www.womcom.org.

ASSOCIATION OF AMERICAN PUBLISHERS (AAP), 71 5th Ave., 2nd Floor, New York NY 10003. Website: www.publishers.org.

THE ASSOCIATION OF WRITERS & WRITING PROGRAMS (AWP), Mail Stop 1E3, George Mason University, Fairfax VA 22030. Website: www.awpwriter.org.

THE AUTHORS GUILD, INC., 31 E. 32nd St., 7th Floor, New York NY 10016. E-mail: staff@authorsguild.org. Website: authorsguild.org.

CANADIAN AUTHORS ASSOCIATION (CAA), P.O. Box 581, Stn. Main Orilla ON L3V 6K5 Canada. Website: www.canauthors.org.

CHRISTIAN BOOKSELLERS ASSOCIATION (CBA), P.O. Box 62000, Colorado Springs CO 80962. Website: www.cbaonline.org.

THE DRAMATISTS GUILD OF AMERICA, 1501 Broadway, Suite 701, New York NY 10036. Website: www.dramatistsguild.com.

NATIONAL LEAGUE OF AMERICAN PEN WOMEN (NLAPW), 1300 17th St. NW, Washington DC 20036-1973. Website: www.americanpenwomen.org.

NATIONAL WRITERS ASSOCIATION (NWA), 10940 S. Parker Rd., #508, Parker CO 80134. Website: www.nationalwriters.com

NATIONAL WRITERS UNION (NWU), 256 West 38th St., Suite 703, New York, NY 10018. E-mail: nwu@nwu.org. Website: www.nwu.org.

PEN AMERICAN CENTER, 588 Broadway, Suite 303, New York NY 10012-3225. E-mail: pen@pen.org. Website: www.pen.org.

THE PLAYWRIGHTS GUILD OF CANADA (PGC), 215 Spadina Ave., Suite #210, Toronto ON M5T 2C7 Canada. E-mail: info@playwrightsguild.ca. Website: www.playwrightsguild.com.

VOLUNTEER LAWYERS FOR THE ARTS (VLA), One E. 53rd St., 6th Floor, New York NY 10022. (212)319-2787. Website: www.vlany.org.

WOMEN IN FILM (WIF), 6100 Wilshire Blvd., Suite 710, Los Angeles CA 90048. E-mail: info@wif.org. Website: www.wif.org.

WOMEN'S NATIONAL BOOK ASSOCIATION (WNBA), P.O. Box 237, FDR Station, New York NY 10150. E-mail: publicity@bookbuzz.com. Website: www.wnba-books.org.

WRITERS GUILD OF ALBERTA (WGA), 11759 Groat Rd., Edmonton AB T5M 3K6 Canada. E-mail: mail@writersguild.ab.ca. Website: writersguild.ab.ca.

WRITERS GUILD OF AMERICA-EAST (WGA), 555 W. 57th St., Suite 1230, New York NY 10019. E-mail: info@wgaeast.org. Website: www.wgaeast.org.

WRITERS GUILD OF AMERICA-WEST (WGA), 7000 W. Third St., Los Angeles CA 90048. Website: www.wga.org.

WRITERS UNION OF CANADA (TWUC), 90 Richmond St. E., Suite 200, Toronto ON M5C 1P1 Canada. E-mail: info@writersunion.ca. Website: www.writersunion.ca.

GLOSSARY

#10 ENVELOPE. A standard, business-size envelope.

ADVANCE. A sum of money a publisher pays a writer prior to the publication of a book. It is usually paid in installments, such as one-half on signing contract; one-half on delivery of complete and satisfactory manuscript.

AGENT. A liaison between a writer and editor or publisher. An agent shops a manuscript around, receiving a commission when the manuscript is accepted. Agents usually take a 10-15% fee from the advance and royalties.

ARC. Advance reader copy.

ASSIGNMENT. Editor asks a writer to produce a specific article for an agreed-upon fee.

AUCTION. Publishers sometimes bid for the acquisition of a book manuscript that has excellent sales prospects. The bids are for the amount of the author's advance, advertising and promotional expenses, royalty percentage, etc. Auctions are conducted by agents.

AVANT-GARDE. Writing that is innovative in form, style, or subject.

BACKLIST. A publisher's list of its books that were not published during the current season, but that are still in print.

BIMONTHLY. Every two months.

BIO. A sentence or brief paragraph about the writer; can include education and work experience.

BIWEEKLY. Every two weeks.

BLOG. Short for weblog. Used by writers to build platform by posting regular commentary, observations, poems, tips, etc.

BLURB. The copy on paperback book covers or hard cover book dust jackets, either promoting the book and the author or featuring testimonials from book reviewers or well-known people in the book's field. Also called flap copy or jacket copy.

BOILERPLATE. A standardized contract.

BOUND GALLEYS. Prepublication edition of book, usually photocopies of final galley proofs; also known as "bound proofs."

BYLINE. Name of the author appearing with the published piece.

CATEGORY FICTION. A term used to include all types of fiction.

CHAPBOOK. A small booklet usually paperback of poetry, ballads, or tales.

CIRCULATION. The number of subscribers to a magazine.

CLIPS. Samples, usually from newspapers or magazines, of a writer's published work.

COFFEE-TABLE BOOK. A heavily illustrated oversize book.

COMMERCIAL NOVELS. Novels designed to appeal to a broad audience. These are often broken down into categories such as western, mystery and romance. See also genre.

CONTRIBUTOR'S COPIES. Copies of the issues of magazines sent to the author in which the author's work appears.

CO-PUBLISHING. Arrangement where author and publisher share publications costs and profits of a book. Also known as cooperative publishing.

COPYEDITING. Editing a manuscript for grammar, punctuation, printing style, and factual accuracy.

COPYRIGHT. A means to protect an author's work.

COVER LETTER. A brief letter that accompanies the manuscript being sent to an agent or editor.

CREATIVE NONFICTION. Nonfictional writing that uses an innovative approach to the subject and creative language.

CRITIQUING SERVICE. An editing service in which writers pay a fee for comments on the salability or other qualities of their manuscript. Fees vary, as do the quality of the critiques.

CV. Curriculum vita. A brief listing of qualifications and career accomplishments.

ELECTRONIC RIGHTS. Secondary or subsidiary rights dealing with electronic/multimedia formats (i.e., the Internet, CD-ROMs, electronic magazines).

ELECTRONIC SUBMISSION. A submission made by modem or on computer disk.

EROTICA. Fiction that is sexually oriented.

EVALUATION FEES. Fees an agent may charge to evaluate material. The extent and quality of this evaluation varies, but comments usually concern salability of the manuscript.

FAIR USE. A provision of the copyright law

that says short passages from copyrighted material may be used without infringing on the owner's rights.

FEATURE. An article giving the reader information of human interest rather than news.

FILLER. A short item used by an editor to "fill" out a newspaper column or magazine page. It could be a joke, an anecdote, etc.

FILM RIGHTS. Rights sold or optioned by the agent/author to a person in the film industry, enabling the book to be made into a movie.

FOREIGN RIGHTS. Translation or reprint rights to be sold abroad.

FRONTLIST. A publisher's list of books that are new to the current season.

GALLEYS. First typeset version of manuscript that has not yet been divided into pages.

GENRE. Refers either to a general classification of writing, such as the novel or the poem, or to the categories within those classifications, such as the problem novel or the sonnet.

GHOSTWRITER. Writer who puts into literary form an article, speech, story, or book based on another person's ideas or knowledge.

GRAPHIC NOVEL. A story in graphic form, long comic strip, or heavily illustrated story; of 40 pages or more.

HI-LO. A type of fiction that offers a high level of interest for readers at a low reading level.

HIGH CONCEPT. A story idea easily expressed in a quick, one-line description.

HONORARIUM. Token payment.

HOOK. Aspect of the work that sets it apart from others and draws in the reader/viewer.

HOW-TO. Books and magazine articles offering a combination of information and advice in describing how something can be accomplished.

IMPRINT. Name applied to a publisher's specific line of books.

JOINT CONTRACT. A legal agreement between a publisher and two or more authors, establishing provisions for the division of royalties the book generates.

KILL FEE. Fee for a complete article that was assigned and then cancelled.

LEAD TIME. The time between the acquisition of a manuscript by an editor and its actual publication.

LITERARY FICTION. The general category of serious, non-formulaic, intelligent fiction.

MAINSTREAM FICTION. Fiction that transcends popular novel categories such as mystery, romance and science fiction.

MARKETING FEE. Fee charged by some agents to cover marketing expenses. It may be used to cover postage, telephone calls, faxes, photocopying or any other expense incurred in marketing a manuscript.

MASS MARKET. Non-specialized books of wide appeal directed toward a large audience.

MEMOIR. A narrative recounting a writer's

(or fictional narrator's) personal or family history; specifics may be altered, though essentially considered nonfiction.

MIDDLE GRADE OR MID-GRADE. The general classification of books written for readers approximately ages 9-11. Also called middle readers.

MIDLIST. Those titles on a publisher's list that are not expected to be big sellers, but are expected to have limited/modest sales.

MODEL RELEASE. A paper signed by the subject of a photograph giving the photographer permission to use the photograph.

MULTIPLE CONTRACT. Book contract with an agreement for a future book(s).

MULTIPLE SUBMISSIONS. Sending more than one book or article idea to a publisher at the same time.

NARRATIVE NONFICTION. A narrative presentation of actual events.

NET ROYALTY. A royalty payment based on the amount of money a book publisher receives on the sale of a book after booksellers' discounts, special sales discounts and returns.

NOVELLA. A short novel, or a long short story; approximately 7,000 to 15,000 words.

ON SPEC. An editor expresses an interest in a proposed article idea and agrees to consider the finished piece for publication "on speculation." The editor is under no obligation to buy the finished manuscript.

ONE-TIME RIGHTS. Rights allowing a manuscript to be published one time. The work can be sold again by the writer without violating the contract.

OPTION CLAUSE. A contract clause giving a publisher the right to publish an author's next book.

PAYMENT ON ACCEPTANCE. The editor sends you a check for your article, story or poem as soon as he decides to publish it.

PAYMENT ON PUBLICATION. The editor doesn't send you a check for your material until it is published.

PEN NAME. The use of a name other than your legal name on articles, stories or books. Also called a pseudonym.

PHOTO FEATURE. Feature in which the emphasis is on the photographs rather than on accompanying written material.

PICTURE BOOK. A type of book aimed at preschoolers to 8-year-olds that tells a story using a combination of text and artwork, or artwork only.

PLATFORM. A writer's speaking experience, interview skills, website and other abilities which help form a following of potential buyers for that author's book.

POD. Print on demand.

PROOFREADING. Close reading and correction of a manuscript's typographical errors.

PROPOSAL. A summary of a proposed book

submitted to a publisher, particularly used for nonfiction manuscripts. A proposal often contains an individualized cover letter, one-page overview of the book, marketing information, competitive books, author information, chapter-by-chapter outline, and two to three sample chapters.

QUERY. A letter that sells an idea to an editor or agent. Usually a query is brief (no more than one page) and uses attention-getting prose.

REMAINDERS. Copies of a book that are slow to sell and can be purchased from the publisher at a reduced price.

REPORTING TIME. The time it takes for an editor to report to the author on his/her query or manuscript.

REPRINT RIGHTS. The rights to republish a book after its initial printing.

ROYALTIES, STANDARD HARDCOVER BOOK. 10 percent of the retail price on the first 5,000 copies sold; 12 percent on the next 5,000; 15 percent thereafter.

ROYALTIES, STANDARD MASS PAPERBACK BOOK. 4-8 percent of the retail price on the first 150,000 copies sold.

ROYALTIES, STANDARD TRADE PAPERBACK BOOK. No less than 6 percent of list price on the first 20,000 copies; 7½ percent thereafter.

SASE. Self-addressed, stamped envelope; should be included with all correspondence.

SELF-PUBLISHING. In this arrangement the author pays for manufacturing, production and marketing of his book and keeps all income derived from the book sales.

SEMIMONTHLY. Twice per month.

SEMIWEEKLY. Twice per week.

SERIAL. Published periodically, such as a newspaper or magazine.

SERIAL FICTION. Fiction published in a magazine in installments, often broken off at a suspenseful spot.

SERIAL RIGHTS. The right for a newspaper or magazine to publish sections of a manuscript.

SHORT-SHORT. A complete short story of 1,500 words.

SIDEBAR. A feature presented as a companion to a straight news report (or main magazine article) giving sidelights on human-interest aspects or sometimes elucidating just one aspect of the story.

SIMULTANEOUS SUBMISSIONS. Sending the same article, story or poem to several publishers at the same time. Some publishers refuse to consider such submissions.

SLANT. The approach or style of a story or article that will appeal to readers of a specific magazine.

SLICE-OF-LIFE VIGNETTE. A short fiction piece intended to realistically depict an interesting moment of everyday living.

SLUSH PILE. The stack of unsolicited or misdirected manuscripts received by an editor or book publisher.

SOCIAL NETWORKS. Websites that connect users: sometimes generally, other times around specific interests. Four popular ones at the moment are Facebook, Twitter, Instagram and LinkedIn.

SUBAGENT. An agent handling certain subsidiary rights, usually working in conjuction with the agent who handled the book rights. The percentage paid the book agent is increased to pay the subagent.

SUBSIDIARY RIGHTS. All rights other than book publishing rights included in a book publishing contract, such as paperback rights, book club rights and movie rights. Part of an agent's job is to negotiate those rights and advise you on which to sell and which to keep.

SUBSIDY PUBLISHER. A book publisher who charges the author for the cost to typeset and print his book, the jacket, etc., as opposed to a royalty publisher who pays the author.

SYNOPSIS. A brief summary of a story, novel or play. As part of a book proposal, it is a comprehensive summary condensed in a page or page and a half, single-spaced.

TABLOID. Newspaper format publication on about half the size of the regular newspaper page.

TEARSHEET. Page from a magazine or newspaper containing your printed story, article, poem or ad.

TOC. Table of Contents.

TRADE BOOK. Either a hardcover or softcover book; subject matter frequently concerns a special interest for a general audience; sold mainly in bookstores.

TRADE PAPERBACK. A soft-bound volume published and designed for the general public; available mainly in bookstores.

TRANSLATION RIGHTS. Sold to a foreign agent or foreign publisher.

UNSOLICITED MANUSCRIPT. A story, article, poem or book that an editor did not specifically ask to see.

YA. Young adult books.

BOOK PUBLISHERS SUBJECT INDEX

FICTION

Adventure

Comic Books

Confession

Contemporary

Erotica

Ethnic

Experimental

Fantasy

Feminist

Gay

Gothic

Hi-Lo

Historical

Horror

Humor

Juvenile

Lesbian

Literary

Mainstream

Military

Multicultural

Multimedia

Mystery

Occult

Picture Books

Plays

Poetry

Poetry in translation

Regional

Religious

Romance

Science Fiction

Short Story Collections

Spiritual

Sports

Suspense

Translation

War

Western

Young Adult

NONFICTION

Agriculture

Alternative Lifestyles

Americana

Animals

Anthropology

Archeology

Architecture

Electronics

Entertainment

Environment

Ethnic

Fashion

Film

Finance

Foods

Games

Gardening

Gay

Government

Health

History

Hobbies

Horticulture

House and Home

Humanities

Labor

Language

Law

Lesbian

Literary Criticism

Literature

Marine Subjects

Medicine

Memoirs

Military

Money

Multicultural

Music

Nature

New Age

Nutrition

Parenting

Philosophy

Photography

Politics

Pop Culture

Psychic

Psychology

Public Affairs

Real Estate

Recreation

Regional

Religion

Science

Sex

Social Sciences

Sociology

Software

Spirituality

Sports

Stage

Translation

Transportation

Travel

True Crime

War

Womens Issues

Womens Studies

World Affairs

Young Adult

GENERAL INDEX

Q

R

S